2001

University of St. Francis Library
3 0301 00210107 5

W9-DDD-247

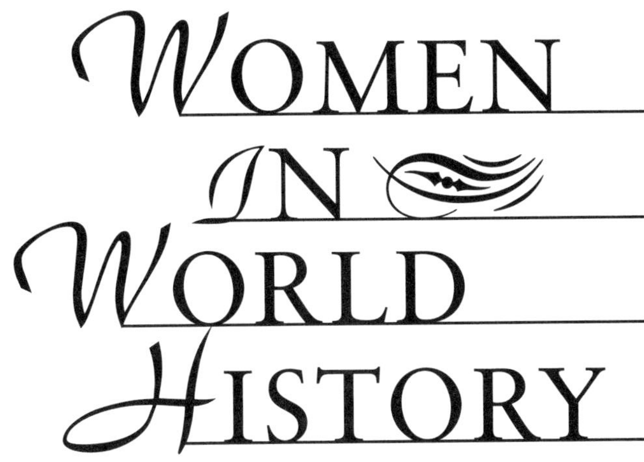

Women in World History

A Biographical Encyclopedia

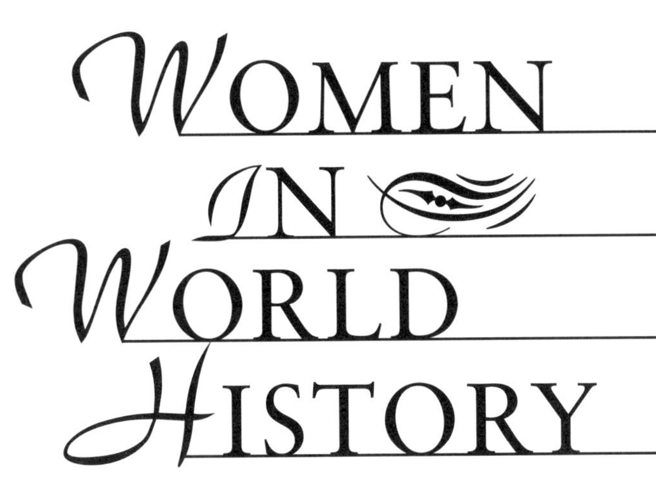

Women in World History

A Biographical Encyclopedia

VOLUME
12
O-Q

Anne Commire, Editor
Deborah Klezmer, Associate Editor

YORKIN PUBLICATIONS

GALE GROUP
Detroit
New York
San Francisco
London
Boston
Woodbridge, CT

Yorkin Publications

Anne Commire, *Editor*
Deborah Klezmer, *Associate Editor*
Barbara Morgan, *Assistant Editor*

Eileen O'Pasek, Gail Schermer, Patricia Coombs, James Fox,
Catherine Cappelli, Karen Rikkers, *Editorial Assistants*
Karen Walker, *Assistant for Genealogical Charts*

Special acknowledgment is due to Peg Yorkin who made this project possible.

Thanks also to Karin and John Haag, Bob Schermer, and to
the Gale Group staff, in particular Dedria Bryfonski, Linda Hubbard, John Schmittroth, Cynthia Baldwin,
Tracey Rowens, Randy Bassett, Christine O'Bryan, Rebecca Parks, and especially Sharon Malinowski.

The Gale Group

Sharon Malinowski, *Senior Editor*
Rebecca Parks, *Editor*
Laura Brandau, *Assistant Editor*
Linda S. Hubbard, *Managing Editor*

Margaret A. Chamberlain, *Permissions Specialist*
Mary K. Grimes, *Image Cataloger*

Mary Beth Trimper, *Production Director*
Evi Seoud, *Assistant Production Manager*

Cynthia Baldwin, *Product Design Manager*
Tracey Rowens, *Cover and Page Designer*
Michael Logusz, *Graphic Artist*

Barbara Yarrow, *Graphic Services Manager*
Randy Bassett, *Image Database Supervisor*
Dan Newell, *Imaging Specialist*
Christine O'Bryan, *Graphics Desktop Publisher*
Dan Bono, *Technical Support*

Gale Group, Inc.
27500 Drake Road
Farmington Hills, MI 48331-3535

Library of Congress Catalog Card Number 99-24692
A CIP record is available from the British Library

ISBN 0-7876-4071-9
Printed in the United States of America.

Library of Congress Cataloging-in-Publication Data

Women in world history : a biographical encyclopedia / Anne Commire, editor, Deborah Klezmer, associate editor.
p. cm.
Includes bibliographical references and index.
ISBN 0-7876-3736-X (set). — ISBN 0-7876-4069-7 (v. 10). —
ISBN 0-7876-4070-0 (v. 11) — ISBN 0-7876-4071-9 (v. 12) — ISBN 0-7876-4072-7 (v. 13) — ISBN 0-7876-4073-5 (v. 14)
1. Women—History Encyclopedias.2. Women—Biography Encyclopedias.
I. Commire, Anne. II. Klezmer, Deborah.
HQ1115.W6 1999
920.72'03—DC21 99-24692

10 9 8 7 6 5 4 3 2 1

O., Anna (1859–1936).

See Pappenheim, Bertha.

Oakar, Mary Rose (1940—)

Eight-term Democratic U.S. congressional representative from Ohio. *Born on March 5, 1940, in Cleveland, Ohio; daughter of Joseph Oakar and Margaret Oakar; attended Catholic schools in Cleveland; graduated from Lourdes Academy (1958); Ursuline College, Cleveland, B.A. (1962); John Carroll University, Cleveland, M.A. (1966); graduate studies at Royal Academy of Dramatic Arts, London, England (1964), Westham Adult College in Warwickshire, England (1968), and Columbia University, New York City (1963).*

Born on March 5, 1940, in Cleveland, Ohio, Mary Rose Oakar attended Catholic schools and graduated from Lourdes Academy in 1958. She obtained a bachelor's degree from Ursuline College in 1962 and earned a master's at John Carroll University in 1966. She also studied at the Royal Academy of Dramatic Arts in London, at Westham Adult College, also in England, and at Columbia University in New York City. In her late teens, she worked as a sales clerk. From 1963 to 1975, Oakar taught English, drama and speech at a high school and a community college, both in Cleveland. From 1973 to 1976, she was a member of the Cleveland City Council. Politically active, she served as Democratic State Central committeewoman from 1973 to 1975 and as an alternate delegate to the Democratic National Convention in 1976.

In 1976, Oakar won the Democratic primary for an open House seat in Ohio's 20th Congressional District, defeating 11 other candidates, and went on to win the general election to the 95th and 7 succeeding Congresses (January 3, 1977–January 3, 1993). In Congress, she worked her way up the ladder to the position of vice chair of the Democratic Caucus in the 99th and 100th Congresses. She also chaired the Subcommittee on Personnel and Police and the Subcommittee on Economic Stabilization of the Committee on Banking, Finance and Urban Affairs, and worked on the Committee on Post Office and Civil Service and the Select Committee on Aging. These positions afforded Oakar the opportunity to pursue issues such as the economic redevelopment of older industrial areas, equal and comparable pay for working women, and benefits for congressional employees.

Mary Rose Oakar

Oakar was unsuccessful in her reelection bid to the 103rd Congress in 1992 because of her association with the House banking scandal. For her role in this, she pleaded guilty to an election law misdemeanor and was fined $32,000. Oakar returned to Cleveland, where she has since resided, and is president and CEO of a public relations and consulting firm, Mary Rose Oakar and Associates, Inc.

In 1999, Oakar announced plans to return to public life and reportedly was considering a run for the Ohio General Assembly's 13th district, which includes Oakar's traditional political base as well as several other areas. That same year, Oakar was recognized for her lifelong commitment to public service and efforts to increase voter participation with the Spirit of Democracy Award, presented by Ohio's secretary of state. In addition, she has served on the advisory board for the White House Conference on Aging and on the board of "Builders for Peace," an organization dedicated to bringing about peace in the Middle East.

SOURCES:

Office of the Historian. *Women in Congress, 1917–1990.* Commission on the Bicentenary of the U.S. House of Representatives, 1991.

Jo Anne Meginnes, freelance writer, Brookfield, Vermont

Oakley, Annie (1860–1926)

Sharpshooter and equestrian who helped create the image of the self-reliant frontierswoman in late 19th-century America. *Name variations: Annie Oakley (stage name from 1882); Annie Butler in private life after her marriage. Born Phoebe Anne Mosey (also sometimes given in records as Moses and Mozee) on August 13, 1860, on a farm near Woodland (now Willowdell), in Darke County, Ohio; died in Greenville, Ohio, on November 3, 1926; sixth daughter of Jacob Mosey and Susan Mosey (both farmers of Darke County, Ohio); had basic schooling in orphanage; mainly self-taught; married Frank Butler (a professional marksman), on June 20, 1876 or 1882 (died November 21, 1926); children: two stepdaughters.*

Annie Oakley was one of the most celebrated entertainers in America in the late 19th and early 20th centuries. A crack shot and a skilled rider, she starred in Buffalo Bill's Wild West Show, but she was also a skillful competitor in shooting contests and a good businesswoman. Escaping from humble origins, she was always careful to show that she was a "true lady" in the Victorian manner, and not just a rough-and-tumble "showgirl." Ironically, she came from Ohio and spent very little of her life in the "wild west" even though she did more than anyone else to create the popular image of the American frontierswoman.

She was born Phoebe Anne Mosey in 1860, the sixth daughter of Jacob and **Susan Mosey**, Quakers and poor farmers in Darke County, Ohio, who lived precariously. Her only brother and another sister soon followed. When Oakley was five, her father Jacob was caught in a blinding snowstorm as he rode his wagon home with much-needed supplies. He arrived barely alive and, contracting pneumonia, died before the end of the winter (February 11, 1866). Her mother then married Daniel Brumbaugh in August 1867. Two years later, Annie was sent by her overtaxed mother to a nearby state orphanage, run by a family friend. The friend contracted Oakley out to a family nearby who quickly reneged on their promise to send her to school in return for farm work. Instead, they kept her working at home, beat her without mercy, and gave her no education. Some of Oakley's recent biographers believe that the father of this family, whom she always referred to as the "he-wolf," sexually abused her as well. Finally in 1872, Oakley ran away and returned to the orphanage, where she helped out by hunting for food in the woods, and reestablished contact with her mother and siblings. By then, her stepfather had died as the result of a fall, and her mother was once more a widow, with a new baby. In 1874, Susan would marry a mailman and old friend, Joseph Shaw.

Oakley quickly learned to be a good hunter and an extremely accurate shot, bringing home small game and birds for the family. Right-handed by preference, she soon became equally adept with her left. She learned how to shoot ducks in the head so that pieces of shot would not be embedded in the meat when it was brought to the table. At the same time, she tried hard to make up for lost time in education, and practiced reading, writing, and the more delicate female arts, such as fancy needlework. In her writing and domestic work, as in her hunting, she was almost excessively attentive to order and detail, but her methodical ways paid off. The earnings from her hunting enabled her mother, whose new husband Joseph was going blind, to pay off a mortgage on a family farm started 13 months previously.

Her first opportunity to move into a wider world came when, as a teenager, she entered a Cincinnati shooting contest against Frank Butler, a well-known marksman, and defeated him. Butler, who was about ten years her senior and already well known as a theatrical gunman, accepted this defeat in a good spirit and began to woo Oakley. Within a year, they had married, though whether the year was 1876 or 1882 remains unclear because publicity agents later knocked six years off her real age and re-dated the events of her early life accordingly. Butler was divorced and had two daughters, whom Oakley adopted, but the couple had no children of their own.

Under the tutelage of Butler, who was a sensible businessman as well as a crack shot, Phoebe Mosey, who had now taken the name Annie Oakley, became a celebrity in traveling variety shows and circuses. She made her own costumes—ankle-length dresses with buckskin fringes and, often, a cowboy hat, and performed lively shooting acts, skipping around the arena, bringing down fast-moving targets, and kicking up her heels as she left the ring. She had never been farther west than Kansas but she came to epitomize in appearance and manner the women of the West, or at least the popular idea of such women. Her big break came when she was accepted into the Buffalo Bill Wild West Exposition, run by William ("Buffalo Bill") Cody. Cody had rejected her on her first application but when his partner Nate Salsbury saw her shooting at clay pigeons he was sufficiently impressed to hire her on the spot. Among the acts she perfected as part of the show were shooting clay pigeons in rapid succession, shooting down

Annie Oakley

clusters of glass balls thrown through the air, and riding a galloping horse sidesaddle while untying a ribbon from one of its legs.

Most women working the burlesque, vaudeville, and show circuit in the late 19th century had reputations for fast living and slatternly behavior. Oakley did everything she could to distance herself from this image. Wrote **Glenda Riley**, "She believed that a quintessential Victorian woman must embody five major qualities. A genuine lady should be modest, married, domestic, benevolent, and a civilizing force." Her dresses were modestly buttoned up to the neck, she always rode horses sidesaddle, even for stunt shooting, and she was ostentatious about having a husband and a settled domestic life, never drinking or gambling, and fulfilling her family's Quaker principles. Being on the road nearly all the time made it difficult for her to have a settled Victorian home of the approved sort, but she compensated by decorating her boarding house rooms and her circus tent with elaborate draperies and knick-knacks, and by inviting women to tea like a good society matron. She positioned herself at the doorway of her tent between acts, embroidery in hand, to indicate that she was living up to the delicate, domestic ideal. In many ways she was, of course, a convention-breaker, taking on the kind of challenges previously reserved almost entirely to men. But she did not think of herself as a feminist and was not a votes-for-women advocate. She managed instead to blend a stage presence of Western daring with an offstage manner of unviolated femininity.

Annie was a natural for Buffalo Bill's Wild West. She embodied everything that he and his growing public held dear: humble beginnings, hard work, persistence, and lively personality. She had no apparent foibles or flaws. She was petite and pretty. She could shoot and ride. What more could the owners of the fledgling Wild West Exposition ask?

—Glenda Riley

The Wild West show became an enormous popular hit during her first season, the summer and fall of 1885, and it ran throughout the next summer at Staten Island, New York, attracting 360,000 visitors. Cody was one of the first showmen to romanticize the Western frontier just as it was closing, and he helped create the larger-than-life, storybook image of cowboys, Indians, settlers, prospectors, and soldiers which has been a staple of American popular culture ever since. He also aimed to be an educator, and collected testimonials from generals and presidents who declared that his shows enabled men and women who had never been out West to get a real taste of it. Cody, an excellent equestrian and marksman, came from North Platte, Nebraska. He had previously worked as a hunter providing transcontinental railroad building crews with buffalo meat (hence his nickname) and, like most white Americans of his era, he was excited by the rapid expansion of Euro-American civilization. But he could also see the tragic aspect of the story, especially from the Native Americans' point of view. His colorful troupe of Western "types" delighted audiences in the rising industrial towns east of the Mississippi and were sufficiently famous by 1887 to be invited to England as part of the celebrations of Queen ***Victoria**'s 50th year on the throne, her Golden Jubilee. The queen herself came to see the show, as did her son Prince Edward (Edward VII), daughter-in-law ***Alexandra of Denmark**, and ex-Prime Minister William Gladstone. All were introduced to Annie Oakley and found her an enchanting mix of feminine delicacy and Western flair.

While the show was in England, however, Oakley and Buffalo Bill began to fall out. Both were reticent about the causes of the rift, though they certainly involved his decision to add another woman sharpshooter to his entourage, an ill-mannered, boastful, but talented teenager named **Lillian Frances Smith**. British journalists wrote admiringly of both women but usually gave the greater accolades to Oakley, who more nearly fit their ideal of a good woman. (Smith later raised eyebrows by running away with one of the show's cowboys.) At the end of the British season, Oakley and her husband left the Wild West show, toured alone in Europe for the rest of that summer, and then returned as independents to America. Working for another Wild West show the next summer, she won a challenge for her new boss, "Pawnee Bill," by killing 49 out of a group of 50 live pigeons in mid-air before an audience of 12,000.

Oakley rejoined Buffalo Bill's Wild West the next year, now that Lillian Smith had left under a cloud of scandal. Annie became its star attraction during a Paris exhibition on the 100th anniversary of the French Revolution, in the shadow of the newly built Eiffel Tower. Her show was becoming steadily more elaborate. She introduced such tricks as shooting the ash off a cigarette in her husband's mouth, shooting a dime from between his finger and thumb, and shooting an apple off her pet dog's head. In addition, she and Cody perfected a set of melodramatic theatrical scenes in which settlers showed their mettle and Western soldiers their bravery in rescuing helpless women and children from bandits or Indians.

The king of Senegal, a French colony in Africa, offered Cody 100,000 francs for her, declaring that he could use her to hunt the man-eating tigers which afflicted his people. A French noble also wrote her a love letter and proposed taking her away from the show, enclosing his photograph. She replied by shooting the man's

Annie Oakley

picture through the head and sending it back, with the words "Respectfully declined" across the top. Her stage name, "Miss Oakley," and her girlish appearance, led male fans to assume that she was unmarried and in need of a protector. They did not realize that this image was carefully contrived by her husband, so she was bombarded with love letters and marriage proposals wherever she went.

The Wild West show was a central feature at the great Chicago Exposition in 1893, and Oakley again proved a great draw to shooting enthusiasts and her personal fans. The 1890s also witnessed a craze for bicycles, which were then being mass produced for the first time. Oakley bought one in England and claimed later that she was the first lady cyclist in London. She took it back to America, learned how to ride without using her hands, and to shoot down moving targets as she went along. She also designed a modest yet practical cycling outfit for women which did not involve Bloomers, which she regarded as unladylike. But her conformity to feminine ideals did not prevent her from offering to raise a regiment of armed fighting women when America went to war against Spain in 1898.

Frank Butler remained an effective manager for Oakley. He cultivated good relations with journalists to help ensure that she had favorable press everywhere and arranged lucrative publicity deals with the gun and ammunition makers whose equipment she used. Throughout her years with the Wild West show, Oakley entered shooting contests and usually proved the equal or superior of the men she encountered, including a succession of American champions. She soundly defeated the crown prince of Russia on one visit to England and made a distinguished showing at the Grand American Handicap in Kansas City in 1902, the last big shooting contest to use live pigeons. The sports magazines and associations honored her with medals, trophies, and regular stories, so that by the turn of the century she had a huge collection of honors. Her renown opened up sport shooting to other women. These were the years in which for the first time women became participants in such sports as croquet, tennis, and archery, and many of them cited Annie Oakley as an inspirational example. She believed that women would benefit from taking up shooting, both as a form of exercise and for self-defense. In interviews, she defended the idea that women on the city streets should have revolvers hidden in their umbrellas, ready to repulse assailants.

By 1900, when Oakley was 40, the couple had decided to leave the traveling show and settle down for a while. Since 1893 they had owned a house, built to their own specifications, in Nutley, New Jersey, and had spent there whatever months' break from the traveling routine they could manage. In 1901, they were involved in a train crash when the second section of the Wild West train in which they were sleeping collided head on with a freight train in North Carolina. Oakley's back was injured, and she had a succession of spine operations in the ensuing months. She cited this crisis to her fans to explain her decision to leave the show, adding that the shock of the accident had turned her hair white overnight (though in fact it had turned soon after she was accidentally left too long in a scalding spa bath) and forced her to don a wig. But Oakley found it difficult to settle down to domestic life in New Jersey, fell out regularly with her servants, and finally sold the house in 1904, to resume her wandering life in hotels, boarding houses, and tents.

That same year, she sued more than 30 newspapers around the United States for carrying a story which said that Annie Oakley was a cocaine addict who had been stealing to finance her habit, and that she was now in prison. In fact a Chicago woman had pretended to be Oakley, and the press had not checked its facts. The real Oakley, eager to defend her unsullied reputation, won several cases, which prompted most of the other newspapers to settle out of court. She took particular pleasure in winning damages of $27,500 from the Chicago news baron William Randolph Hearst, who had added insult to injury by sending a private detective to Greenville, Ohio, trying to dig up scandals against her.

Over the next few years, much of the couple's income came from Frank Butler's work as a salesman for an ammunition company in Connecticut and from Oakley's winnings in competitive shooting matches, though she also played heroines in several stage melodramas. She enjoyed a brief comeback in the arena between 1911 and 1913 with the Vernon Seavers Young Buffalo Show, and even had the pleasure of giving free tickets to children from the orphanage where she had lived as a child. In this show, she developed a new trick of firing behind her back, using a mirror to aim, and was still able to hit targets with unerring accuracy. Another stunt was to split playing cards held lengthwise with a single shot.

Through the teens of the new century, she moved frequently between Florida, Ohio, Maryland, and New Jersey, still shooting competitively, hunting, and teaching other women how to shoot. When America became involved in the First World War, she wrote to President Woodrow Wilson offering to raise a regiment of women sharpshooters for home defense in the event of a German invasion. He declined but was glad to learn that Oakley, at her own expense, was giving shooting exhibitions to young army recruits in hastily constructed military camps. By 1922, now 62, she was contemplating another comeback, and considering movie offers, but was involved in a serious car accident near Daytona, Florida, which landed her in hospital for more than a month. From then on, she was forced to wear a leg brace and could walk only with difficulty.

Annie Oakley died in Greenville, Ohio, on November 3, 1926, near her family and friends, after trying to write an autobiography which was left unfinished. Frank Butler died less than three weeks later. Oakley was reintroduced to later generations of young Americans in 1946 in the musical *Annie Get Your Gun,* starring ***Ethel Merman** on Broadway and ***Betty Hutton** on film. In 1953, ABC television created a popular Annie Oakley television show starring **Gail Davis**, which ran for four seasons (1953–56).

SOURCES AND SUGGESTED READING:

Havighurst, Walter. *Annie Oakley of the Wild West.* NY: Macmillan, 1954.

Kasper, Shirl. *Annie Oakley.* Norman, OK: University of Oklahoma Press, 1992.

Riley, Glenda. *The Life and Legacy of Annie Oakley.* Norman, OK: University of Oklahoma Press, 1994.

COLLECTIONS:

Annie Oakley Foundation, Greenville, Ohio; Nutley Historical Society, Nutley, New Jersey.

Patrick Allitt,
Professor of History, Emory University,
Atlanta, Georgia

Oakley, Violet (1874–1961)

American artist, specialist in murals, mosaics, stained glass, and portraits, who is known particularly for her murals at the Pennsylvania state capitol in Harrisburg. *Born in Bergen Heights, New Jersey (some sources cite New York City), in 1874; died in 1961; daughter of Arthur Edmund Oakley and Cornelia (Swain) Oakley; studied art at the Art Students League in New York; attended Académie Montparnasse in Paris; attended the Pennsylvania Academy; attended Drexel Institute; never married; no children.*

Born in 1874 in Bergen Heights, New Jersey, Violet Oakley was descended from a long line of artists, prompting her to remark that her urge to draw was "hereditary and chronic." Beset by severe asthma as a child, she was not sent to college because her family felt she was too frail for the rigors of advanced study. She later credited the restoration of her health to her conversion from Episcopalian to Christian Science. Oakley began her art training at New York's Art Students League at the age of 19, studying with Carroll Beckwith and Irving R. Wiles. She next studied in Paris, with E. Amanlean and Raphael Colin at the Académie Montparnasse, and in England with Charles Lazar. Returning to her family, now relocated in Philadelphia, Oakley enrolled briefly at the Pennsylvania Academy, then in 1897 transferred to Drexel Institute to study with Howard Pyle, the famous illustrator who was then attracting many students. In Pyle's class, she met and befriended ***Jessie Wilcox Smith** and ***Elizabeth Shippen Green.** The women formed a triumvirate of sorts, taking a studio together in Philadelphia and committing to each other as "sympathetic companions." Later, they shared a country home, the Red Rose Inn, in Villanova, Pennsylvania, where another companion, **Henrietta Cozens**, joined the household as "wife."

Oakley received many of her early commissions through Pyle, who teamed her up with Smith to illustrate an 1897 edition of Longfellow's poem *Evangeline.* He also encouraged her interest in the art of stained glass, which brought additional commissions her way, including one from All Angels Church in New York City. In 1902, Oakley received her most extensive commission—to produce 18 murals for the governor's room at the new Pennsylvania state capitol which was to be built in Harrisburg. Although the commission for the main body of artwork was awarded to Edwin Austin Abbey, Oakley was the first woman to ever receive such a large mural assignment, and she prepared with a period of intense study and meditation.

Choosing as her theme the founding of the colony of Pennsylvania by William Penn, Oakley immersed herself in Penn's Quaker philosophy of brotherhood, religious freedom, and world peace. Her identification with the visionary was so complete that she began to view her mural assignment as a "sacred mission." Whatever her process, the results were extraordinary indeed. The unveiling in 1906 was greeted with much acclaim, and Oakley was awarded a gold medal of honor from the Pennsylvania Academy. She later summarized her research for the murals in *The Holy Experiment* (1922), a book in which she also set forth many of her own philosophical beliefs.

In 1911, when Abbey died, Oakley was called upon to complete the murals for the capitol, an enormous undertaking for the artist who was also busy with a flood of other work. The assignment occupied the better part of the next 16 years, during which she completed the *Unity Panel* (9' high x 46' wide) and a 9-mural series called *The Creation and Preservation of the Union,* both for the Senate chamber. Ten years of the project were spent on 16 murals for the Supreme Court room which comprise *The Opening of the Book of the Law.* Between 1913 and 1917, while working on the capitol murals as well as her other commissions, Oakley also taught a mural class at the Pennsylvania Academy. One of her students, **Edith Emerson**, became her assistant.

Following the completion of the murals in 1927, Oakley devoted the remainder of her life to the cause of world peace. Traveling to Geneva, Switzerland, she recorded in drawings and paintings the deliberations for the founding of the League of Nations, then displayed them around the world to promote the League. These pictures, along with images of her Supreme Court murals, were later reproduced in the book *The Law Triumphant* (1933).

SOURCES:

Carter, Alice A. *The Red Rose Girls: An Uncommon Story of Art and Love*. NY: Abrams, 2000.

Rubinstein, Charlotte Streifer. *American Women Artists*. Boston, MA: G.K. Hall, 1982.

Barbara Morgan,
Melrose, Massachusetts

Oberheuser, Herta (1911—)

German physician whose complicity in the medical experiments at the Ravensbrück concentration camp for women led to her sentence of 20 years' imprisonment at the Nuremberg Medical Trial of 1946–1947.

Name variations: Hertha Oberheuser. Born in Cologne on May 15, 1911; University of Bonn, M.D., 1937.

Since antiquity, the Hippocratic Oath has called on physicians to heal humanity and to show tenderness and mercy to those afflicted with illness. In Nazi Germany, the medical profession not only ignored its own ideals but became an active accomplice in the murderous racial agenda of Adolf Hitler's regime. The Third Reich's physicians could boast of having the highest percentage of Nazi Party members of any profession—an astonishing 45%. Their ratio of membership in the brown-shirted SA (*Sturmabteilung* or Storm Troopers) and the elite black-shirted SS (*Schutzstaffel*) was, respectively, two and seven times that of teachers. Even before the Third Reich, with few exceptions, German physicians had for decades been sympathetic to authoritarian, nationalist, and racist beliefs and ideologies. The German medical community, generally comprised of conservative males determined to preserve their professional and gender privileges, was ill-equipped to resist the seductions of Adolf Hitler's movement which promised the restoration of traditional social and cultural hierarchies.

In the case of Herta Oberheuser, the only woman physician to be indicted by the Nuremberg Military Tribunal in the Medical Case of 1946–1947, the motives underlying her actions were complex but hardly unfathomable. Born in Cologne in 1911, Oberheuser grew up in a Germany in chaos. Her father, an engineer, had survived World War I physically, but found it difficult to adapt to a postwar world in which Germany was a humiliated nation. Like millions of other German families, the Oberheusers found themselves economically devastated by inflation and permanently embittered by their loss in status. Growing up in Düsseldorf, Herta absorbed the prejudices of her milieu, particularly the festering resentments of her ultra-nationalistic family. In the 1932 elections in which Adolf Hitler ran for the presidency, Oberheuser and her parents voted for the Nazi Party. Like millions of others in the impoverished German middle class, they believed that only Hitler's movement would be able to rescue the nation from the economic misery of the world depression, by creating jobs for millions of the unemployed. Only Hitler's movement could restore Germany's honor by tearing up the humiliating Versailles Treaty.

Encouraged by her family and despite economic sacrifices, Oberheuser enrolled in a gymnasium to qualify for a professional career in medicine. The Oberheusers felt that a medical career would enable Herta to live free of the privations and low social status that the family had long endured. The intelligent, ambitious young woman studied medicine at the University of Bonn, but commuted to Düsseldorf where she worked part-time. As she began her studies in 1933, the Nazi Party seized control of Germany. A reign of terror and a propaganda campaign quickly swept aside all organized opposition, so that by July 1933 the German Reich had become a one-party totalitarian state. Although she gave little thought to the details of the political revolution that had swept through Germany, Oberheuser supported the Nazis, even though one of the new regime's policies called for eliminating women from virtually all of the nation's professional positions.

In 1935, Oberheuser volunteered to serve as an unpaid medical assistant in the Düsseldorf branch of the *Bund Deutscher Mädel* (BDM or League of German Girls), the female counterpart organization of the Hitler Youth. Although at this time only 0.5% of the Nazi Party's members were female, about one-fifth of these were medical students or practicing physicians. In 1937, Oberheuser earned her M.D. degree from the University of Bonn. Specializing in dermatology, she quickly found a post at the municipal pediatric clinic (*Kinderstation*) in Düsseldorf.

In August 1937, Oberheuser joined the Nazi Party and became a member of the Nazi professional organization *Nationalsozialistischer Ärzt-*

ebund (National Socialist Physicians' League). Despite her political loyalty and willingness to devote long hours at the pediatric clinic, Oberheuser soon realized that as a woman in Nazi Germany her chances of receiving equal treatment in relation to her male colleagues in medicine were virtually nil. Indeed, the discrimination at the Düsseldorf clinic was blatant and hurtful, particularly financially. At a time when specialized medical textbooks could cost as much as 70 reichsmarks, Oberheuser's monthly salary was 100 reichsmarks. Her male counterparts in Düsseldorf earned fully four times that amount.

In 1940, she saw an advertisement in a Nazi medical journal about a job as medical officer for the "medical care of female criminals" at the Ravensbrück concentration camp. Since it paid a significantly higher salary than the one she was earning in Düsseldorf, Oberheuser applied for the position and was accepted. Situated 90 kilometers north of Berlin on the Havel River and near a village of the same name, the Ravensbrück concentration camp for women had begun operations in May 1939 when 867 female prisoners were transferred there from the Lichtenburg concentration camp in East Prussia. Ravensbrück was part of the vast SS empire of terror, repression, surveillance and economic exploitation, the heart of which was the nationwide system of concentration camps that had begun at Dachau and other KZs (*Konzentrationslager* or concentration camp) in March 1933.

Soon after Germany conquered Poland in September 1939, women members of the Polish resistance movement began to be sent to Ravensbrück. While the camp contained only about 2,000 prisoners at the end of 1939, most of them German citizens, by the end of 1942 the facility's prisoner population had grown to 10,800. Many of these women were Polish, and along with other citizens of Slavic countries they were regarded by a Nazi state based on a racist ideology of Aryan supremacy as mere *Untermenschen*—"sub-humans" fit only for menial labor, or worse. It was because of these ideological assumptions, and the abandonment of medical ethics that customarily protect humans from dangerous or potentially fatal experimentation being performed on their bodies, that a group of Ravensbrück prisoners were forced to undergo tests that maimed all and killed some.

Starting in July 1942, experiments to investigate the effectiveness of the antibiotic sulfanilamide against infections sustained by soldiers in battle took place at Ravensbrück. The doctor in overall charge of these experiments was Karl Gebhardt, chief surgeon of the SS and German Police and SS Führer Heinrich Himmler's personal physician. Gebhardt had been attending physician at the bedside of SS functionary Reinhard Heydrich after he was the victim of an assassination plot in Prague in May 1942. When Heydrich died of his wounds Gehhardt's medical skills were questioned. Some in the SS hinted that Heydrich might have lived had Gebhardt chosen to treat his patient with massive doses of sulfanilamide, arguing that such intervention would have reversed the severe infection that resulted in fatal gangrene and putrefaction. At this point Himmler requested Gebhardt to prove experimentally that sulfanilamide was effective against gangrene and putrefaction in wounded soldiers. Because these experiments, if successful, would save the lives of severely wounded German soldiers, it was argued that the purpose of the experimentation was in fact humane, and that it was not only justifiable in terms of urgent military necessity but could, in the final analysis, be regarded as being profoundly humanitarian in nature. The exact opposite was to be the case.

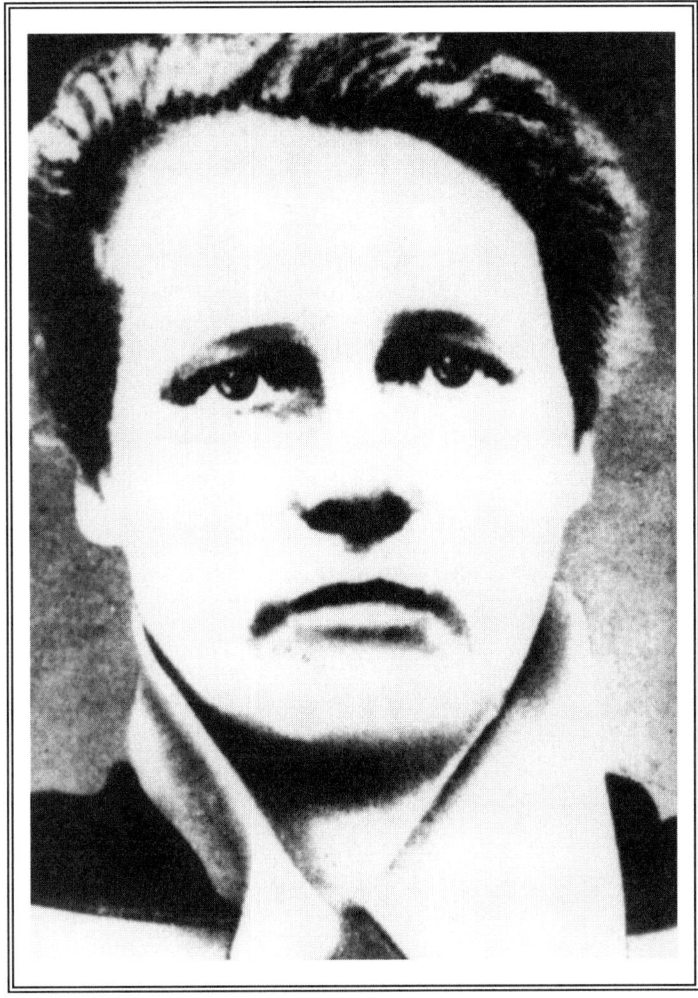

Herta Oberheuser

The experiments to determine the most effective treatment of war wounds began at Ravensbrück on July 20, 1942. Unlike the French physician ***Adelaide Hautval**, who refused to participate in Nazi medical atrocities during her incarceration at Auschwitz, Oberheuser used them to advance her career. Until shortly before the experiments were finally terminated in September 1943, she determined who would be chosen for the tests—a total of 74 Polish women political prisoners. Almost all of them were young (their ages ranged from 16 to 45, with most in their early 20s), and the great majority were members of the intelligentsia, being either students or teachers. Resistance activists, they had been sentenced to death in typical SS fashion, without benefit of trial or jury.

After preliminary experimentation had taken place on 15 male inmates from another concentration camp, the first series of experiments began on 60 of the 74 Polish women. They were experimented on in 5 groups of 12 subjects each. In addition to simulations of simple injuries, Oberheuser and her colleagues Gebhardt and Fritz Ernst Fischer created the severe condition known as gas gangrene in the women, who came collectively to be known as "the Ravensbrück Lapins" (rabbits or guinea pigs). Working as a junior member of the team, Oberheuser assisted her colleagues in cutting into the limbs of the Polish women and then stuffing their open wounds with staphylococci and streptococci bacteria, gas gangrene cultures, and tetanus. Circulation of the women's normal blood supply was interrupted by tying off blood vessels at both ends of wounds so as to create a condition similar to that of a battlefield wound. These infections were then aggravated by filling the open wounds with dirt, wood shavings, and ground glass. Once the procedure was completed, the wounds were sewn up. At this point, the now-raging infections would be treated with sulfanilamide and other drugs to determine effectiveness.

When it became known at SS medical headquarters in Berlin that of the experimental subjects none had yet died, chief medical officer of the SS Dr. Ernst Robert Grawitz demanded that the virulence of the infections created in the women's wounds be increased. When this was done on a group of 24 Polish prisoners by Oberheuser and her colleagues (after an earlier group of 36 had been experimented on), five women died as a result not only of the severity of their infections (brought on by introduction into their wounds of highly infectious staphylococci, and other bacteria), but also because the "experimenters" were interested only in the properties of sulfanilamide, and thus would use no other drug or procedure on the women they had infected.

These infections resulted in excruciating agony for all of the Polish women who had been operated on. Of the five who died, **Weronica Kraska** succumbed to tetanus and **Kazimiera Kurowska** died at age 23 after being artificially infected with gangrene bacillus that caused her leg to swell and turn black. Kurowska, forced to endure "unbelievable pain," was provided with medical care for only a few days, even though amputation of her gangrenous leg might have saved her life. **Zofia Kiecol** and **Aniela Lefanowicz**, both of whom had been intentionally infected with oedema malignum, suffered agonizing pain from their swollen, infected legs, but were medically ignored after two or three days; eventually both died from severe bleeding. **Alfreda Prus**, a university student before her arrest, was also infected with oedema malignum. Her good health kept her alive a few days longer than Kiecol and Lefanowicz, but eventually she too succumbed to infection, suffering terrible pain and finally dying of a massive hemorrhage. Miraculously, another member of the infected group, **Maria (Marysha) Kusmierczuk**, not only survived the experiment but survived Ravensbrück itself, living to testify against Oberheuser and several of her colleagues at the Nuremberg Medical Trial in 1946–1947. One prisoner, **Barbara Pietrzyk**, survived five different operations, a fact that would be documented after the war by a commission of Polish physicians who in 1946 examined survivors at the Gdansk Medical Academy.

Additional experiments on the surviving Ravensbrück Lapins, who included one German and one Ukrainian woman, resulted in eight more deaths, bringing the total to 13. Although the women had been promised that their participation in the experiments, which was involuntary, would result in a commutation of their death sentences, this promise was never kept. Six of the women were executed after the experiments on them had been terminated—obviously to silence them. In 1943, **Apolonia Rakowska** was shot while her wounds were still festering.

Oberheuser was an indispensable member of the German team. To many of the women, the well-groomed young doctor in the SS uniform was "*der Teufel mit dem Engelsgesicht*" (the devil with the face of an angel). Besides her participation in the sulfanilamide studies, she was an active member of the team that carried out a series of pseudo-scientific investigations to study bone, muscle, and nerve regeneration, as well as bone transplantation from one person to another. These experiments, which began at Ravensbrück in September 1942 and lasted until the end of 1943, included the smashing of bones with hammers as well as the removal of sections of bones, muscles, and nerves from the test subjects. In one "experiment" performed by SS physicians Fischer and Gebhardt, muscles and shoulder bones were transplanted from one patient to another, with predictable consequences. Three kinds of bone operations were performed: artificially induced fractures, bone transplantations, and bone splints. On the operating table, the bones of the lower part of both legs of a number of women were broken or shattered with a hammer. Later, the bones were joined with or without special clips and the legs placed in a plaster cast. Post-operative care, for which Oberheuser was responsible, was minimal. As a result, the women suffered intense agony, mutilation, and permanent disability. Some of the young women were operated on more than once. On one occasion, when a prisoner asked for painkillers, Oberheuser told her that the healing process would take even longer if painkilling drugs were applied to wounds.

After the war, a number of ex-prisoners commented on Oberheuser's cruelty. Besides her inhuman "treatments," she also killed a number of them. In her Nuremberg trial deposition of November 1, 1946, she admitted that she had given lethal injections to five or six woman who "were close to death." During the trial, she defended her actions under cross-examination as having been "mercy killings" (*Gnadentod*), no more than "medical assistance for suffering patients who were in agony." On other occasions during the war, Oberheuser had revealed a remarkably callous nature. When **Anna Heil**, a German woman, received news that her sister had died in Ravensbrück, she contacted Oberheuser hoping to discover more details on her sister's final days. Oberheuser hit Heil in the face and stomach, while screaming at her, "She is gone! Because she was only a useless eater [*unnötiger Fresser*], and we really don't need those sort of people around any more!"

On several occasions, the Polish women protested the cruelty of their medical "treatment." When **Jadwiga Kaminska**, who could speak some German, courageously protested to Oberheuser on behalf of all the Polish women, Oberheuser's response was simply to shrug her shoulders without a word. On another occasion, a group of Polish women drew up a written protest, and went to the camp commandant, SS-Hauptsturmführer Max Kögel. The petition declared, "We, the undersigned, Polish political prisoners, ask the Commandant whether he knows that since the year 1942 experimental operations have taken place in the camp hospital. . . . We ask whether we were operated on as a result of sentences passed on us because, as far as we know, international law forbids the performance of operations even on political prisoners."

Not surprisingly, there was no official response. Soon, however, one of the female overseers came to the barrack where **Vladislava Karolewska**, one of the leaders of the protest, was being kept. The names of Karolewska and nine other women were called out. When the overseer asked the women, "Why do you stand in line as if you were to be executed?" Karolewska responded that as far as they were concerned, the operations they had undergone had been worse than executions and that as a group they would prefer to be executed rather than operated on again. Karolewska had already undergone two operations, and endured excruciating pain, and while recovering in the hospital had been abused by Oberheuser. Soon after, two SS men entered her unlit cell, held her down with force, and gave her an injection. When she regained consciousness, Karolewska felt severe pain in her feet and was suffering from a high temperature; she had been operated on a third time.

In June 1943, Oberheuser was assigned a new position, as a pediatrician at the main SS hospital at the Hohenlychen Medical Institute near Berlin. After two and a half years at Ravensbrück, she was moving up in the SS medical hierarchy. Hohenlychen was regarded as a promotion, because its chief surgeon was Karl Gebhardt, one of the most powerful men in the SS and Oberheuser's superior during the time she was part of the experimental team at Ravensbrück. Oberheuser was at Hohenlychen when the war ended in the spring of 1945, and some months after this she was arrested along with most of her colleagues, including Gebhardt and Fischer.

For the "Lapins" at Ravensbrück, the last years of the war brought no improvements in their lives, despite Oberheuser's departure. Their wounds healed slowly, if at all, leaving many of them permanently crippled. In early 1945, when it became obvious that Nazi Germany would lose the war, their lives were further endangered as the various administrators of concentration camps took measures to destroy all evidence of their criminal conduct. An attendant confided to the women that an extermination squad was scheduled to arrive at Ravensbrück within a few days. With the assistance of a few sympathetic attendants, most of the women were able to hide out in other barracks to avoid detection. Those few who were too sick to be moved dug little "foxholes" for themselves in their regular barracks block, hiding under the floorboards. For three days and nights they lay there, without food or water, suffering from fever. On the second day, they heard the stomping and scuffling of heavy boots directly overhead. Years later, survivor **Helena (Helenka) Piasecka** recalled: "We were very sick and we were stained by our own filth. I don't suppose human beings ever had less reason to want to live, yet that was when the will to live was strongest. We knew that if we could survive for just a few more days we might be able to let the world know."

On the night of April 29–30, 1945, Soviet soldiers liberated Ravensbrück. They found 3,500 gravely ill and exhausted female prisoners, with the healthier ones caring for the most enfeebled. The surviving Polish "Lapins" returned home to a nation that was, along with the formerly Nazi-occupied areas of the Soviet Union, the most devastated state in Europe. At least six million Poles had died during the occupation and war. Ninety percent of Poland's Jews had been systematically murdered in the Holocaust. Most of the Ravensbrück women returned to families that had been decimated or virtually annihilated. Yet as a group they refused to give up. While some returned to school or careers as quickly as they could, hoping to forget the past, a few made an effort to tell the world about what had been done to them in Ravensbrück in the name of "science" and "medical progress."

Starting only a few months after the conclusion of the Nuremberg trial of major war criminals, the Nuremberg Medical Trial began in late October 1946. Unlike the main Nuremberg trial, which was constituted as an International Military Tribunal representing the United States, Great Britain, the Soviet Union, and France, the medical trial and others that followed it were solely under American jurisdiction and control. On trial were 23 defendants, many of whom had medical degrees and had held high positions in the SS or the German Armed Forces. All except Oberheuser were male, and most observers agreed that there was more than sufficient evidence that she had been significantly involved in activities of a criminal and inhumane nature, although her position both within the SS and at the Ravensbrück camp while medical experiments took place there was of a secondary and subordinate nature. At the camp, she had assisted Fritz Fischer, who ranked as an SS-Sturmbannführer (equivalent to major), while both she and Fischer carried out their assignments under the authority of Gebhardt, who was an SS-Gruppenführer (major general). Gebhardt's power within the SS and the Nazi Reich was attested to by the fact that he held other high positions including major general in the Waffen-SS, was Himmler's personal physician, served as chief surgeon of the Staff of the Reich Physician SS and Police, and last but not least was president of the German Red Cross.

During the trial, which lasted from October 1946 until August 1947, Oberheuser did not stand out among the 22 other defendants. She tried to evade responsibility for the many atrocities revealed during the trial, either pleading forgetfulness or trying to minimize her culpability, arguing that while she had attempted to administer therapeutic care according to established medical principles, that was impossible in the environment of a concentration camp, one that she "had never cared for." She characterized herself "as a woman in a difficult position" who "did the best" she could. She argued that on the occasions—five or six, according to her—when she gave fatal dosages of intravenous injections, she had released terminally ill prisoners from their "hopeless suffering." Oberheuser gave the standard argument of accused war criminals, namely of merely following orders, adding to this that as a dermatologist she had had little or no knowledge of the precise medical needs of the Polish women prisoners before, during, or after the experiments.

The 23 medical trial defendants were sentenced on August 20, 1947. Seven, including Gebhardt, were sentenced to death and executed in June 1948. Five were given life imprisonment, while four, including Oberheuser, received various terms of incarceration. Oberheuser was found guilty of having committed both war crimes and crimes against humanity, and was sentenced to a term of 20 years. But she would not serve out her sentence. For Washington, the rapidly developing Cold War environment meant that West Germany had to be turned into a dependable partner of the West as quickly as possible. A rearmed Germany would be expected to play a key role resisting Soviet power in the heart of Europe. For the United States, implementing this strategy included the termination of such "anti-German" activities as war crimes trials and long sentences for former officials of the Third Reich suspected of complicity in war crimes and crimes against humanity.

Concrete evidence of a radical change in American policy toward defeated Germany was clearly evident when several defendants in the medical trial with dubious backgrounds were secretly hired by the U.S. military. Under their new masters, they continued their research in such areas as aviation medicine and biological warfare. With few exceptions, several hundred medical personnel who had inflicted pain, suffering and often death on more than 1,200 individuals in facilities other than Ravensbrück went unpunished as alliances shifted due to the Cold War. In 1952, Oberheuser benefited directly from these policy changes, being released from prison for her "good conduct." Not only did Oberheuser regain her freedom, she was legally defined as a *Spätheimkehrerin* (late returnee from foreign captivity) and given a generous financial grant in compensation for her sufferings. She quickly established a medical practice.

Settled in the town of Stocksee bei Plön in the northern province of Holstein, Oberheuser built up a thriving practice as a pediatrician. She had become a respected physician by the time information circulating within the international medical community about her wartime activities began to put pressure on her. For a considerable time she was supported by a West German medical establishment that was hiding many skeletons in its professional closet. Eventually, however, massive publicity from abroad and from such critical journals as *Der Spiegel* in 1960 shamed officials into revoking her medical license. Since that time, nothing has been heard of Herta Oberheuser.

SOURCES:

Anderson, Erica. "These Women Were Nazi Guinea Pigs," in *Look*. Vol. 23, no. 6. March 17, 1959, pp. 110–114.

"Human Laboratory Animals," in *Life*. Vol. 22, no. 8. February 24, 1947, pp. 81–82, 84.

Klier, Freya. *Die Kaninchen von Ravensbrück: Medizinische Versuche an Frauen in der NS-Zeit.* Munich: Knaur Verlag, 1994.

Machlejd, Wanda, ed., *Experimental Operations on Prisoners of Ravensbrück Concentration Camp.* Poznan: Wydawnictwo Zachodnie, 1960.

McKale, Donald M. "Purging Nazis: The Postwar Trials of Female German Doctors and Nurses," in William S. Brockington, Jr., and W. Calvin Smith, eds., *The Proceedings of The South Carolina Historical Association 1981.* Aiken, SC: The South Carolina Historical Association-USC-Aiken, 1981, pp. 156–180.

Taake, Claudia. *Angeklagt: SS-Frauen vor Gericht.* Oldenburg: BIS-Bibliotheks- und Informationssystem der Universität Oldenburg, 1998.

Trials of War Criminals before the Nuernberg Military Tribunals under Control Law No. 10, Nuernberg October 1946–April 1949. 15 vols. Washington, DC: U.S. Government Printing Office, 1949–1952, Vols. 1 and 2.

John Haag,
Associate Professor of History, University of Georgia, Athens, Georgia

Oberon, Merle (1911–1979)

***Indian-born actress, best known for her performance in* Wuthering Heights.** *Name variations: Queenie Thompson; acted briefly as Estelle Thompson. Born Estelle Merle O'Brien Thompson on February 19, 1911, in Bombay, India; died on November 23, 1979, in Los Angeles, California; daughter of Arthur Terrence O'Brien Thompson (a mechanical engineer for the British railways) and Charlotte Constance (Selby) Thompson (a nurse's assistant); attended La Martinière school in Calcutta; married Alexander Korda (a director), in 1939 (divorced 1945); married Lucien Ballard (a cinematographer), in 1945 (divorced 1949); married Bruno Pagliai (an Italian industrialist), in 1957 (divorced 1973); married Robert Wolders (an actor), in 1975; children: Francesca Pagliai and Bruno Pagliai, Jr. (both adopted in 1959).*

Selected filmography in U.S., unless otherwise noted: The Three Passions *(UK, bit, 1929);* Wedding Rehearsal *(UK, 1932);* Men of Tomorrow *(UK, 1932);* The Private Life of Henry VIII *(UK, 1933);* The Battle *(*Hara-Kiri *or* Thunder in the East, *UK, 1934);* The Broken Melody *(UK, 1934);* The Private Life of Don Juan *(UK, 1934);* The Scarlet Pimpernel *(UK, 1935);* Folies-Bergère *(1935);* The Dark Angel *(1935);* These Three *(1936);* Beloved Enemy *(1936);* I Claudius *(UK, unfinished, 1937);* Over the Moon *(UK, 1937);* The Divorce of Lady X *(UK, 1938);* The Cowboy and the Lady *(1938);* Wuthering Heights *(1939);* The Lion Has Wings *(UK, 1939);* 'Til We Meet Again *(1940);* That Uncertain Feeling *(1941);* Affectionately Yours *(1941);* Lydia *(1941);* Forever and a Day *(1943);* Stage Door Canteen *(1943);* First Comes Courage *(1943);* The Lodger *(1944);* Dark Waters *(1944);* A Song to Remember *(1945);* This Love of Ours *(1945);* Night in Paradise *(1946);* Temptation *(1946);* Night Song *(1947);* Berlin Express *(1948);* Pardon My French *(1951);* 24 Hours of a Woman's Life *(*Affair in Monte Carlo, *UK, 1952);* Todo es Posible en Granada *(Sp., 1954);* Desiree *(1954);* Deep in My Heart *(1954);* The Price of Fear *(1956);* Of Love and Desire *(1963);* The Oscar *(1966);* Hotel *(1967); (also prod., co-edit.)* Interval *(1973).*

Merle Oberon, who is best remembered for her striking portrayal of the tormented Cathy in the 1939 film version of ***Emily Brontë**'s *Wuthering Heights*, was a popular movie actress during the 1930s and 1940s. Oberon's beauty alone sustained her career into the 1950s, although her private life attracted as much attention as her films; she was married four times and often involved in romantic affairs. Following her death in 1979, Michael Korda, her nephew by her first marriage to Alexander Korda, said of her: "Her greatest achievement was not in her roles, but herself, as Merle Oberon. She was her own work of art."

Oberon kept the details surrounding her birth a secret throughout her life, insisting that she was born into an aristocratic family in Tasmania. In truth, she was born in 1911 in Bombay's overcrowded St. George's Hospital, the daughter of Arthur Terrence O'Brien Thompson, a mechanical engineer for the British railways, and **Charlotte Selby Thompson**, a Ceylonese nurse's assistant. Fearing she might be ostracized as a half-caste, Merle initiated the lie about her past when she entered show business and by several accounts eventually came to believe her own legend. Oberon was raised in Bombay and Calcutta and was educated until the age of 11 at the strict La Martinière school in Calcutta, an austere place where she was very much a loner. After she left, she was tutored at home by her hard-working mother, then entered business school at the age of 15. Her first job was as a typist in a department store.

At age 17, Oberon made her way to London, where she initially worked as a dance-hall girl under the name Queenie Thompson. By now

Merle Oberon

a regal beauty, she was hired as an extra in a number of British films and eventually caught the eye of Hungarian-born director-producer Alexander Korda who was starting his own film company and offered the actress a five-year contract. Korda cast her in the small role of ***Anne Boleyn** in *The Private Life of Henry VIII* (1933), the first British talkie to attract an international audience. Oberon went on to play leads with Korda's company, including a Japanese woman in *The Battle* (1934) and Lady Blakeney in the film adaptation of ***Emma Orczy**'s *The Scarlet Pimpernel* (1935), opposite Leslie Howard, with whom she also had a love affair. In 1935, Korda sold half her contract to the Goldwyn studios, thus launching Oberon's Hollywood career. Following an inauspicious debut in *Folies Bergère* (1935), she gained credibility in *The Dark Angel* (1935), with Fredric March, for which she was nominated for an Academy Award. In 1937, Oberon returned to England to star in the ambitious *I Claudius* with Charles Laughton, but her involvement in a near-fatal car crash halted the already troubled project in mid-production. Following her recovery, Korda starred her in several comedies, including *Over the Moon* (1937) and *The Divorce of Lady X* (1938), opposite a very young Laurence-Olivier .

Olivier was her co-star again in *Wuthering Heights*, although Oberon's first choice for the role of Heathcliff had been Douglas Fairbanks, Jr., and Olivier had desperately wanted his new love ***Vivien Leigh** for the role of Cathy. Tension on the set was heightened by the dictatorial style of the film's director William Wyler. The finished product, however, bore little evidence of the traumatic shoot, and Oberon's career went into high gear. Frank Nugent, critic for *The New York Times,* was generous in his acclaim, praising the "wild spirit" that marked her performance. Despite other glowing reviews, Oberon was not nominated for an Academy Award that year, an "appalling" oversight according to her biographers, Charles Higham and Roy Moseley.

Oberon's private life fascinated the gossip columnists, beginning with her engagement in 1934 to Joseph Schenck, producer and chair of the board of 20th Century-Fox, whom she abandoned for actor Leslie Howard, whom she subsequently left for actor David Niven. "It was Merle's pattern," write Higham and Moseley. They also suggest that she was ahead of her time in her choice of men, preferring them to be "neither subservient nor dominating, but to be her equal, her partner and friend as well as her physical lover." Oberon was also married four times; her first husband Alexander Korda was in love with her for years before they wed in 1939. The marriage, however, was failing by 1945, when Oberon met and fell in love with 35-year-old cinematographer Lucien Ballard, who also worked to provide special lighting for the star after a reaction to sulfa drugs and subsequent dermabrasion treatments severely damaged her skin. (Ballard developed and patented a new light, the "Obie," named for Oberon, which was widely used in the industry.) Differences began to emerge between the two, however, early in the relationship. "Merle was prone to daydreams, reveries, and romantic abstractions, whereas Ballard was tough and without interest in mysticism, spiritualism, which was beginning to fascinate Merle," write Higham and Moseley. In the wake of Oberon's divorce from Korda in 1945, the two married, although Ballard later said he dreaded being thought of as "Mr. Merle Oberon," and only married the actress because she wore him down. The union lasted just four years, during which time Oberon met her great love, Count Giorgio Cini, a handsome and wealthy Italian aristocrat who was killed in a plane crash in 1949, not long after Oberon's divorce from Ballard was granted.

While Oberon's private life flourished during the 1940s, her career began to decline. Two successive comedies, *That Uncertain Feeling* (1941) and *Affectionately Yours* (1941), failed at the box office, and her performance in Korda's romantic *Lydia* (1941) disappointed the critics, although she herself thought it was one of her best efforts. A turn as ***George Sand**, in *A Song to Remember* (1945), opposite Cornel Wilde as Chopin, drew out-and-out ridicule. "William Bendix being Chopin would have been no less incongruous than Merle Oberon being George Sand in a smart sort of ***Vesta Tilley** outfit," snarled critic Richard Winnington. By 1947, Oberon was relegated to the lower half of double bills, and by the mid-1950s was playing supporting roles, notably in *Desiree* (1954) and *Deep in My Heart* (1954).

In 1957, Oberon married wealthy Italian industrialist Bruno Pagliai, who, though not good-looking, exuded power, money, and charm. They adopted two children, a girl and a boy, and settled into two lavish homes: one in Mexico City and another in Cuernavaca. While her husband was frequently away on business, Oberon doted on her children and ran her two households with a military precision that frequently strained those who worked for her. While she bloomed as an international hostess, she made fewer and fewer films. One of her infrequent appearances was in *Of Love and Desire* (1963), filmed in her own house and at her own expense. She hired then-unknown Richard Rush to direct. "As an actress—and as a human being—she was like a jeweled Swiss clock," he said. "Exquisite perfection. Finely timed. One thinks of her as part of an older Hollywood, an older tradition, but her working style was very like that of a Method-trained actor or actress. Everything she did was totally internalized." The finished product, nonetheless, was leveled by the critics, although it did surprisingly well at the box office. Higham and Moseley believe that although it is not a particularly good film, it is one of Oberon's most interesting because it completely captures her spirit. "With its lush musical score, opulent images and scenes of passion, jealousy, abandon, and reconciliation, it is like a Victorian novel, and it was clearly very close to Merle's soul." Two of Oberon's other films of the '60s, *The Oscar* (1966) and *Hotel* (1967), both enjoyed wide showings as well.

Oberon also produced her last film, *Interval* (1973), which was financed by Pagliai, although their marriage was all but over by then. In the movie, Oberon portrays an aging woman who falls in love with a younger man, played by Robert Wolders, her new paramour. The film received scathing reviews, the critic for *The New York Times* writing that "on a scale of awfulness, it is almost sublime." In 1975, after a difficult split from Pagliai, Oberon and Wolders, who was 25 years her junior, married and settled into a beach house in California.

Following a trip to Australia in the fall of 1978, Oberon was stricken with chest pains, and subsequently underwent heart bypass surgery. The healing process produced thick scars called keloids, which were so painful that she underwent steroid treatments to achieve some relief. Oberon never recovered completely from her ordeal and was even too ill to attend her daughter **Francesca Pagliai**'s wedding. She died of a stroke on Thanksgiving eve in 1979. (Starting in 1981, Wolders would live with ***Audrey Hepburn** until her death.)

Oberon left a million dollars of her estate to the Motion Picture Country House and Hospital, and the auctioning of her extensive jewelry collection raised close to another million for various other cinema charities. Six years after her death, her nephew Michael Korda wrote a novel based on Oberon's life entitled *Queenie* (1985), which was made into a television miniseries in 1987.

SOURCES:

Garraty, John A., and Mark C. Carnes, eds. *American National Biography*. NY: Oxford University Press, 1999.

Higham, Charles, and Roy Moseley. *Princess Merle: The Romantic Life of Merle Oberon.* NY: Coward-McCann, 1983.

Katz, Ephraim. *The Film Encyclopedia.* NY: HarperCollins, 1994.

Shipman, David. *The Great Movie Stars: The Golden Years.* Boston, MA: Little Brown, 1995.

Barbara Morgan,
Melrose, Massachusetts

Oblate Sisters of Providence.

See Lange, Elizabeth Clovis.

O'Brien, Catherine (1881–1963)

***Irish artist.** Name variations: Kitty O'Brien. Born in Ennis, County Clare, Ireland, in 1881; died in 1963; studied at the Metropolitan School of Art, Dublin, and the Tower of Glass.*

Catherine O'Brien studied the art of stained glass at the Metropolitan School of Art in Dublin, where a department on church decoration had been instituted at the behest of artist ***Sarah Purser** at the turn of the 20th century. She joined the Tower of Glass (An Túr Gloine), a Dublin workshop dedicated to creating fine stained glass, a few years after Purser founded it in 1903. The workshop, whose co-operative members also made mosaics and related crafts, went on to achieve recognition as one of the premier creators of stained glass in the world. O'Brien continued running the workshop after Purser's death in 1943. Her windows can be seen throughout Ireland, including the following locations: St. Brendan's Cathedral, Loughrea; Killoughter Church, Ballyhaise, County Cavan; St. Nicholas' Church, Carrickfergus, County Antrim; Downpatrick Church, County Down; and St. John the Baptist's Church, Clontarf, Dublin.

SOURCES:

Newmann, Kate, comp. *Dictionary of Ulster Biography.* The Institute of Irish Studies, the Queen's University of Belfast, 1993.

Howard Gofstein,
freelance writer, Oak Park, Michigan

O'Brien, Edna (1930—)

***Irish writer, best known for her controversial novel* The Country Girls.** *Born Edna O'Brien in Tuamgraney, County Clare, Ireland, on December 15, 1930; daughter of Michael O'Brien and Lena Cleary O'Brien; educated at Scariff National School; attended Convent of Mercy, Loughrea, Galway, and Pharmaceutical College of Ireland; married Ernest Gebler (a novelist), in 1951 (divorced 1964); children: two sons, Carlos and Sasha.*

Awards: Kingsley Amis Award (1962); Yorkshire Post Award (1971).

Born in Tuamgraney, County Clare, Ireland, in 1930, Edna O'Brien wrote from an early age, despite the fact that her mother "had a detestation of literature," said O'Brien, "she'd allow no books in the house." It was her teacher at Scariff National School who encouraged her. After her arrival in Dublin in the late 1940s to study pharmacy, O'Brien bought a cheap, introductory selection of James Joyce edited by T.S. Eliot. It was a turning point. Joyce was to have a powerful influence on O'Brien's work, and the character of Molly Bloom continued to fascinate her. In 1981, O'Brien wrote a book about Joyce's marriage to ***Nora Barnacle Joyce**; as well, her short story "Irish Revel" and her novel *Down by the River* (1996) both pay homage to Joyce's short story "The Dead."

O'Brien was encouraged to write professionally by Peadar O'Donnell, editor of *The Bell*, Ireland's leading literary journal, and by her husband, the novelist Ernest Gebler, whom she married in 1951. They moved to London in 1959 and within weeks of her arrival O'Brien had written her first novel, *The Country Girls* (1960). "To be on an island," O'Brien wrote in 1976, "makes you realise that it is going to be harder to escape and that it will involve another birth, a further breach of waters. Nevertheless, an agitation to go." The move to London gave her the necessary perspective of distance that enabled her to write about Ireland. *The Country Girls* "wrote itself; my arm held the pen," she claimed. In the book, and its two sequels *The Lonely Girl* (1962) and *Girls in Their Married Bliss* (1964), O'Brien gave voice to Irish female sexuality in her exploration of the emotional and erotic experiences of Caithleen Brady and her friend Baba. When O'Brien revised *Girls in Their Married Bliss* in 1967, Caithleen decides to be sterilized as a protest against male betrayal. The books were banned in Ireland (*The Country Girls* was described as a "smear on Irish womanhood") under the stringent censorship legislation that was not relaxed until the late 1960s. Around then, O'Brien wrote five plays for television, as well as screenplays of some of her novels and short stories. She also contributed to Kenneth Tynan's erotic revue *Oh! Calcutta!* In the 1970s, she turned her attention to the theater and wrote three plays which were produced in London, Dublin and New York.

O'Brien says that her writing, which she describes as an "insane impulse," comes from "desperation. . . . Inspiration usually comes from some alarming, visceral experience. Words have to be picked with the point of a sword. . . . A writer is free to tell us what he or she sees. There are lines which express this, 'swift as the lightning in the collied dark', I think they capture what it is to be a writer." Memory was her strongest ally: "The further I went away from the past, the more clearly I returned inwardly." In addition to Joyce, Chekhov, whom she describes as "the truest voice I would ever know," has strongly influenced her work, as has Yeats (she wrote a screenplay about his great muse, ***Maud Gonne**).

Catholicism has also had a major influence on O'Brien's work. Reared in the rigid, puritanical Catholicism of pre-Vatican II Ireland, she has referred to the "inherited mantle of guilt" that is the legacy of the Irish Church. She was brought up as a "fervent Catholic and every ounce of indoctrination was charged with punishment," though she acknowledged that this also encouraged "a furtive desire, a wild and over-fertile fantasy life." Her relationship to Ireland is complex. Her real quarrel with Ireland, she wrote in *Mother Ireland* (1976), began after she left in 1959: "I thought of how it had warped me, and those around me, and their parents before them, all stooped by a variety of fears—fear of church, fear of phantoms, fear of ridicule, fear of hunger . . . and fear of their own deeply ingrained aggression that can only strike a blow at each other, not having the innate authority to strike at those who are higher." But time changes everything, she acknowledged, "including our attitude to a place. Irish? In truth I would not want to be anything else. It is a state of mind as well as an actual country."

Her long absence provoked criticism that she was out of touch with the country and the changes which had taken place since the 1960s. O'Brien has conceded that she is unfamiliar with the new urban Ireland but is emphatic that she knows her Ireland: "I know those roads and fields and tractors, every last bit of them. I know them psychically, physically, geographically, spiritually. They have seeped into my creativity." In the 1990s, there was a shift in her writing from the exploration of female experience to a broader social and political canvas. Her depiction of male characters was also altered. Previously "the men in my books were either Heathcliffs or bishops," said O'Brien. "I see now that men are as capable of fear and need and vulnerability as women." In *The House of Splendid Isolation* (1994), she looks at the troubled politics of Northern Ireland through a protagonist who is an Irish republican terrorist on the run. In *Down by the River* (1996), she explored the troubling subject of child sex abuse and incest (the book was loosely based on two real-life cases in Ireland).

Edna O'Brien

SOURCES:

Eckley, Grace. *Edna O'Brien*. Lewisburg: Bucknell University Press, 1974.

O'Brien, P. "The silly and the serious: An Assessment of Edna O'Brien," in *Massachusetts Review*. Vol. 28. Autumn 1987.

O'Hara, K. "Love Objects: love and obsession in the stories of Edna O'Brien," in *Studies in Short Fiction*. Vol. 30. Summer 1993.

Deirdre McMahon,
lecturer in history at Mary Immaculate College,
University of Limerick, Limerick, Ireland

O'Brien, Kate (1897–1974)

Irish writer. *Born Catherine O'Brien in Limerick, Ireland, on December 3, 1897; died in Canterbury, England, on August 13, 1974; daughter of Thomas O'Brien (a horse dealer) and Catherine (Thornhill) O'Brien; educated at Laurel Hill Convent and University College Dublin; B.A. in modern literature, 1919; married Gustaaf Renier (a Dutch journalist), on May 17, 1923 (divorced 1925).*

Awards: Hawthornden Prize (1932).

Kate O'Brien was born in 1897 into a prosperous, middle-class family in Limerick, Ireland. The family's prosperity was new, and traumatic memories of the Great Famine of the 1840s still lingered among her older relatives. Five of her novels deal with the period from the Famine to the Second World War, from the arrival of her grandparents in Limerick, escaping an impoverished countryside, to the time when her own links with the city were diminishing. Her mother died in 1903, and later that year she went as a boarder to Laurel Hill, a local convent school. Although the school curriculum stressed "ladylike" accomplishments, it also emphasized the new educational opportunities opening up for women. O'Brien's time at the school was happy and this was reflected in the positive portrayals of women religious in her novels. (Two of her maternal aunts were also nuns in another Limerick convent.)

In *My Ireland* (1963), Kate O'Brien wrote that Limerick was where she started "to view the world and to develop the necessary passion by which to judge it. It was there indeed that I learnt the world and I know that wherever I am, it is still from Limerick that I look out and make my surmises." Limerick, fictionally disguised as Mellick, appears in five of her nine novels: *Without My Cloak* (1931), *The Ante-Room* (1933), *Pray for the Wanderer* (1938), *The Land of Spices* (1941), and *The Last of Summer* (1943). The Mellick novels reflect O'Brien's own personal odyssey. In the first two she explores the lives of the Considine and Mulqueen families and particularly their women, who are constrained by the demands of their wealthy, patriarchal families in late Victorian Ireland. *Pray for the Wanderer* had a contemporary setting, and aspects of O'Brien are evident in the leading character Matt Costelloe, a writer paying a rare visit to his family in Ireland, disillusioned with the new Ireland which has banned his books. Two of O'Brien's novels were banned under Irish censorship legislation: *Mary Lavelle* (1936) and *The Land of Spices* (1941), the latter because of a single sentence referring to homosexuality. Her friend and biographer **Lorna Reynolds** has written that O'Brien's heroines "are in search of two absolutes, freedom and love, and . . . the freedom to love, not just to succeed in the marriage market but to be able to offer themselves to another human being in the freedom of choice." In *Mary Lavelle,* the heroine offers herself to her married lover and in doing so takes responsibility for her own life.

O'Brien's father died in 1916, and later that year she won a scholarship to University College Dublin, where she studied modern literature. After obtaining her degree in 1919, she went to England and worked in journalism and teaching. In 1922, she journeyed to the United States on a political mission with her brother-in-law. She married the Dutch journalist Gustaaf Renier in 1923, but the marriage lasted less than a year; they were divorced in 1925. O'Brien went to Spain for ten months, working as a governess for a family in Bilbao. She drew on these experiences for her novel *Mary Lavelle* and wrote about Spain, which she visited frequently in the 1920s and 1930s, with great insight and affection. When the Spanish Civil War broke out in 1936, her Republican sympathies were evident in her book *Farewell Spain* (1937), which Spanish critics praised for its accuracy and which was an elegy for the Spain she loved. Because of her anti-Franco comments, she was banned from Spain for 20 years. Her most financially successful book was *That Lady* (1946), a novel based on the life of the 16th-century princess of Eboli, ***Ana de Mendoza**, an independent woman who refused to let her life be dictated by Philip II of Spain. *That Lady* was made into a Hollywood film in 1955 with ***Olivia de Havilland** in the title role. In 1951, O'Brien published the biography of another remarkable Spanish woman, St. ***Teresa of Avila**, whom she admired for her independence and dynamism.

O'Brien worked in London for the British Ministry of Information during World War II. After the armistice, the success of *That Lady* gave her financial security, and in 1950 she returned to Ireland where she lived in the picturesque village of Roundstone near Galway. She was allowed to return to Spain in 1957 and visited it again two years before her death, when she was the guest of the Irish seminar at the University of Valladolid. However, her books were less successful in the 1950s, and royalties began to dry up. In 1960, O'Brien moved back to England and supported herself by journalism and travel writing. Her last years were dark: she talked of the horrors of growing old and was depressed at the neglect of her books. When she died in 1974, few of her books were in print. Kate O'Brien was dismissed as a romantic novelist, in part because she wrote about a feminine, provincial world. In 1979, the Irish poet **Eavan Boland**, who with others felt that O'Brien was not sufficiently honored in her lifetime, approached O'Brien's executors on behalf of the Irish publishers Arlen House for permission to reprint some of her novels. Over the following decade, most of O'Brien's work was reprinted by Arlen House and by Virago, the London women's press. This prompted major reassessments of her work and her importance as an early Irish feminist writer.

SOURCES:

Logan, John. ed. *With Warmest Love: Lectures for Kate O'Brien 1984–93*. Limerick: Mellick Press, 1994.

Reynolds, Lorna. *Kate O'Brien: A Literary Portrait*. Gerrards Cross: Colin Smythe, 1987.

Walshe, Eibhear, ed. *Ordinary People Dancing: Essays on Kate O'Brien*. Cork: Cork University Press, 1993.

Deirdre McMahon,
lecturer in history at Mary Immaculate College,
University of Limerick, Limerick, Ireland

O'Brien, Kitty (1881–1963).

See O'Brien, Catherine.

O'Brien, Margaret (1937—)

American actress who was a child star of the 1940s.

Born Angela Maxine O'Brien on January 15, 1937, in

Los Angeles, California; daughter of Gladys Flores (a dancer); married Harold Robert Allen, Jr. (a commercial artist), in 1959 (divorced); married a second time (separated); children: daughter.

Selected filmography: Babes on Broadway *(1941);* Journey for Margaret *(1942);* Dr. Gillespie's Criminal Case *(1943);* Thousands Cheer *(1943);* Madame Curie *(1943);* Lost Angel *(1944);* Jane Eyre *(1944);* The Canterville Ghost *(1944);* Meet Me in St. Louis *(1944);* Music for Millions *(1944);* Our Vines Have Tender Grapes *(1945);* Bad Bascomb *(1946);* Three Wise Fools *(1946);* The Unfinished Dance *(1947);* Tenth Avenue Angel *(1947);* Big City *(1948);* Little Women *(1949);* The Secret Garden *(1949);* Her First Romance *(1951);* Glory *(1956);* Heller in Pink Tights *(1960);* Diabolic Wedding *(Peru, 1971);* Annabelle Lee *(Peru, 1972);* Amy *(1981).*

Margaret O'Brien

The winner of a special 1944 Academy Award as Outstanding Child Actress, Margaret O'Brien is considered by many to have been one of the most talented child stars ever to appear in film. Although never quite as popular as ***Shirley Temple (Black)**, she was one of MGM's moneymakers during the 1940s, but like most young actors her career took a nosedive with the onset of puberty. Fortunately, the large salary she drew in her heyday was tucked away for her in a trust fund because of California's Coogan Law.

She was born Angela Maxine O'Brien in 1937 in Los Angeles, California, to dancer **Gladys Flores**. (Her Irish father died a few months before her birth, and her mother later married band leader Don Sylvio.) O'Brien began modeling at three and made her movie debut at age four in *Babes on Broadway* (1941). She subsequently appeared in a variety of roles in both musicals and dramas, exuding a heart-felt conviction unusual in one so young. "This grave little girl, who can give the screen a morning glow by simply stumping into camera range . . . is something out of the ordinary in performing children," wrote ***C.A. Lejeune** of O'Brien's performance in *Music for Millions* (1944). "She belongs more with the Menuhins and Mozarts than with the Shirley Temples." Critic James Agee was equally enthralled after viewing the dark-eyed, pig-tailed moppet in the role of younger sister Tootie in *Meet Me in St. Louis* (1945). "Many of her possibilities and glints of her achievement hypnotize me as thoroughly as anything since Garbo," he wrote. That same year, O'Brien turned in one of her most sensitive performances in *Our Vines Have Tender Grapes*, the story of a Norwegian farming community in Wisconsin, with Edward G. Robinson.

O'Brien was precocious off-screen as well. She became a charming radio personality, guesting on popular variety shows, and trading barbs with such seasoned comedians as Edgar Bergen and Bob Hope. At the height of her popularity, she also gave numerous public readings. O'Brien continued turning in impeccable performances, but MGM used her to enhance second-rate movies with diminishing results. The best of her later films, the second screen version of ***Louisa May Alcott**'s *Little Women* (1949), was an exception, although the adaptation of ***Frances Hodgson Burnett**'s *The Secret Garden*, released the same year, fell flat. In 1951, MGM suspended O'Brien when she refused to appear in *Alice in Wonderland*. (The picture was never made.) When she resurfaced at Columbia in an unsuccessful debut as an adolescent in *Her First Romance* (1951), it marked the beginning of the end of her movie career. She went on to appear in a few foreign films, in stock, and on television, where a reprise of her role as Beth in a musical version of "Little Women" and a role in a "Studio One" production were notable. In the late 1970s, she worked as a civilian aide to Secretary of the Army Clifford Alexander. In the 1990s, she was an active fund raiser for AIDS charities. As for O'Brien's Oscar, a departing maid took it as a souvenir in 1954. It turned up at a flea market in 1995 and was re-presented to the actress. "The poor thing has been through a lot," she said.

SOURCES:

Katz, Ephraim. *The Film Encyclopedia.* NY: HarperCollins, 1994.

Lamparski, Richard. *Whatever Became Of . . . ?* 2nd series. NY: Crown, 1968.

People Weekly. April 10, 2000, p. 128.

Shipman, David. *The Great Movie Stars: The Golden Years.* Boston, MA: Little, Brown, 1995.

SUGGESTED READING:

Ellenberger, Allan R. *Margaret O'Brien: A Career Chronicle and Biography,* 2000.

Barbara Morgan,
Melrose, Massachusetts

O'Brien, Miriam (1898–1976)

American mountaineer. *Name variations: Miriam Underhill. Born in Forest Glen, Maryland, in 1898; died in Lancaster, New Hampshire, on January 7, 1976; daughter of a Boston newspaperman; met and married Robert Underhill, in 1932; children: two sons.*

Traversed the Wellenkuppe and Obergabelhorn (1924); climbed the Dolomites and Aiguilles of Chamonix (1926); climbed the Via Miriam (named after her) on the Torre Grande in the Dolomites with her friend Margaret Helburn (1927); made first complete ascent of Les Aiguilles du Diable and was first female lead of the Grépon (1928); made first all-women's ascent of the Mer de Glace face of the Grépon (1929); made first all-women's ascent of the Matterhorn with Alice Damesme (1932).

Once considered the greatest woman climber in America, Miriam O'Brien started her climbing career on a summer foray in the foothills of the White Mountains of New Hampshire when she was six, accompanied by parental tourguides.

Following years of easy climbs in Chamonix and Switzerland, she traversed the Wellenkuppe and Obergabelhorn in 1924. On July 7, 1927, O'Brien, along with **Margaret Helburn**, Angelo and Antonio Dimai and **Angela Dibona**, climbed the Via Miriam in the Dolomites. That same year, she and Helburn made the first female ascent of the Grépon by way of the Mer de Glace face. Once again, however, O'Brien had climbed with a guide at the front, and she was becoming aware that the greatest thrill was enjoyed by the one who had the authority, made the decisions, decided the tactics, and was cognizant of the approaching weather, avalanches, stone falls, and crevasses. "I saw no reason why women, ipso facto, should be incapable of leading a good climb." But some men disagreed, and one of them did so in print:

> There is more to leading than first meets the eye, a lot that must be learned, and this is best learned by watching competent leaders attentively and coming to understand their decisions. Women, however, never bother to do this. Since they know that they will never be allowed to lead anyway, they just come walking along behind, looking at the scenery. Therefore, even if they were given an opportunity to lead, they would be completely unprepared.

In 1928, after O'Brien led the attack on the Grépon with her guide as second, "The Alpine Journal wavered between incredulity and stern disapproval," wrote ***Dorothy Pilley**, "announcing the first woman's lead of the Grépon with a hesitating 'it is reported' and declaring that 'Few ladies, even in these days, are capable of mountaineering unaccompanied.'" O'Brien then determined that if a woman were to truly lead, there should be no men in the party. The following year, on August 17, 1929, she and French climber **Alice Damesme** climbed, guideless and manless, the face of the Mer de Glace to the Summit of the Grépon, at one time regarded as the hardest route in the Alps. Etienne Bruhl was disconsolate: "The Grépon has disappeared," he mourned. "Of course there are still some rocks standing there, but as a climb it no longer exists. Now that it has been done by two women alone no self respecting man can undertake it. A pity, too, because it used to be a very good climb." In 1930, **Marjorie Hurd** made a manless ascent of the Torre Grande at Cortina.

In 1931 and 1932, O'Brien, along with Damesme and **Jessie Whitehead**, made repeated attempts to make the first all-women's ascent of the Matterhorn by the Hörnli route, but the weather prevailed. Finally, on August 13, 1932, they completed their task. Following that, O'Brien married, had children, and reserved most of her climbs for family outings.

SOURCES:

Birkett, Bill, and Bill Peascod. *Women Climbing: 200 Years of Achievement.* London: A&C Black, 1989.

SUGGESTED READING:

Underhill, Miriam. *Give Me the Hills.* Methuen, 1956.

Ocampo, Silvina (1903–1993)

Argentinean poet and short-story writer. *Born in 1903 (some sources cite 1906) in Buenos Aires, Argentina; died in Buenos Aires in 1993; daughter of Manuel Ocampo (an architectural engineer) and Ramona Máxima Aguirre; sister of writer Victoria*

Ocampo (1890–1979); studied painting in Paris; married Adolfo Bioy Casares (a writer), in 1934 or 1940; children: daughter Marta.

Selected writings: Viaje olvidado *(Forgotten Journey, 1937); (co-editor)* Antología de la literatura fantástica *(Anthology of Fantastic Literature, 1940, published with an introduction by Ursula Le Guin as* The Book of Fantasy, *1988);* Enumeración de la patria y otros poemas *(Enumeration of the Mother Country and Other Poems, 1942);* Autobiografia de Irene *(Autobiography of Irene, 1948);* Poemas de amor deseperado *(Poems of Desperate Love, 1949);* Los nombres *(The Names, 1953);* La furia y otros cuentros *(The Storm and Other Stories, 1959);* Lo amargo por dulce *(Bitterness Through Sweetness, 1962);* El pecado mortal *(The Mortal Sin, 1966);* Informe del cielo y del infierno *(Report on Heaven and Hell, 1970);* La naranja maravillosa: cuentos juveniles *(The Marvelous Orange: Juvenile Stories, 1977, reissued 1998);* Cornelia frente al espejo *(Cornelia in Front of the Mirror, 1988);* Leopoldina's Dream *(translated by Daniel Balderston, 1988).*

Argentinean writer Silvina Ocampo, who was once proclaimed "one of the best poets in Spanish" by her friend Jorge Luis Borges, is little known outside of her native country, and her works have only rarely been translated into English. Born into a wealthy family in Buenos Aires in 1903, Ocampo established a solid reputation as a poet and short-story writer and was a member of Buenos Aires' lively literary community from the 1930s. She and her husband, the writer Adolfo Bioy Casares, hosted a weekly open house attended by Borges, poet Ezequiel Martínez Estrada and Chilean novelist ***María Luisa Bombal**, among others. Ocampo's sister ***Victoria Ocampo** was a respected writer and founder of *Sur* magazine, and Bioy Casares, a frequent collaborator with Borges, also became an important figure in Argentinean letters.

Ocampo's first book of prose was *Viaje olvidado* (Forgotten Journey), published in 1937. Her first book of poetry, which has been described as an exploration of "the opposing ideas of the infinite and the apparent," *Enumeracíon de la patria y otros poemas* (Enumeration of the Mother Country and Other Poems), was published in 1942. Later volumes of poetry such as *Poemas de amor deseperado* (Poems of Desperate Love, 1949) and *Lo amargo por dulce* (Bitterness Through Sweetness, 1962) became more introspective. The latter, which was admittedly autobiographical, won the National Poetry Award. Her short stories, most of which focus on everyday life, were published in several collections, including *La furia y otros cuentos* (The Storm and Other Stories, 1959) and *El pecado mortal* (The Mortal Sin, 1966). In her later years, she also wrote a number of books for children.

Ocampo is probably best known to English-language readers for her collaboration with Bioy Casares and Borges as an editor of the *Antología de la literatura fantástica* (Anthology of Fantastic Literature). Originally published in 1940, it was released in English in 1988 as *The Book of Fantasy*, to huge acclaim from a select group of readers. In her introduction, **Ursula K. Le Guin** relates Bioy Casares' version of the book's genesis, which occurred one night in Buenos Aires in 1937 when the three friends were discussing "fantastic literature . . . the stories which seemed best to us. One of us suggested that if we put together the fragments of the same type, we would have a good book. As a result we drew up this book . . . simply a compilation of stories from fantastic literature which seemed to us to be the best." The book includes works by writers as varied as the three editors, Thomas Carlyle, Rabelais, Tsao Hsueh-Chin, ***Mary Shelley**, and Petronius. Its impact on the many English-language writers who read it was described by Alberto Manguel, himself a first-rate anthologist, in the *Ottawa Citizen*: "It provided readers with a guide to realms that had until then belonged to either campfire tales or to the psychological novel, and it showed to writers vast areas of fiction that demanded neither the journalistic constraints of a Sinclair Lewis nor the fancies of children's fairy tales."

SOURCES:

Borges, Jorge Luis, Silvina Ocampo, and A. Bioy Casares, eds. *The Book of Fantasy.* NY: Viking, 1988.

Buck, Claire, ed. *The Bloomsbury Guide to Women's Literature.* NY: Prentice Hall, 1992.

Contemporary Authors. Vol 131. Detroit, MI: Gale Research, 1991.

SUGGESTED READING:

Klingenberg, Patricia Nisbet. *Fantasies of the Feminine: The Short Stories of Silvina Ocampo.* Lewisburg, PA: Bucknell University Press, 1999.

Jacqueline Mitchell,
freelance writer, Detroit, Michigan

Ocampo, Victoria (1890–1979)

Well-known and respected essayist, editor, publisher, and patron of the arts, who also advanced the cause of women's rights in Argentina. *Pronunciation: Vik-TOH-reah O-CAM-po. Born Ramona Victoria Epifanía Rufina Ocampo on April 7, 1890, in Buenos Aires, Argentina; died on January 27, 1979, at Villa Ocampo, San Isidro, Argentina; daughter of Manuel Ocampo (an architectural engineer) and Ramona Máx-*

*ima Aguirre; sister of writer *Silvina Ocampo (1903–1993); taught by private tutors at home; married Luis Bernardo de ("Monaco") Estrada; no children.*

Pursued self-definition and mildly rebelled (1900s–29); cultivated great literary figures such as Ortega y Gasset and Tagore; established literary magazine Sur *(1931) and Editorial SUR, a publishing house (1933); helped found the Union of Argentine Women (1936); arrested by the Perón regime (1953); was the first woman named to the Argentine Academy of Letters (1977).*

Major works: Testimonios *(Testimony, 10 vols., 1935–77);* Autobiografía *(Autobiography, 4 vols., 1979–82);* De Francesca a Beatriz *(From Francesca to Beatrice, 1924);* 338171 T.E. *(a biography of T.E. Lawrence, 1942, 1963).*

Our small individual lives count for little, but all our lives united will carry such force that history will change its course.

—**Victoria Ocampo**

In the early 1920s, the fleeting image of the beautiful young woman in short sleeves and unchaperoned, speeding through the streets of Buenos Aires behind the wheel of a Packard, attracted a flurry of cat-calls from those offended by such unwomanly behavior. Rebellion against patriarchal orthodoxy and a struggle to strike out in directions independent of traditional expectations would highlight the life of that driver, Victoria Ocampo. In popular mythology, the persistent image of Ocampo was and is that of "a flamboyant, widely traveled collector of famous figures, both Argentine and international," writes **Janet Greenberg**. She was a femme fatale, Count Hermann Keyserling's "Amazon of the Pampas" who "flaunted her fortune and sexuality." There is no question that she polarized opinion; she was the *bête noire* of the Catholic Church and hated by the followers of dictator Juan Domingo Perón. But she was also known affectionately as *Señora Cultura* ("Mother Culture"), the first lady of Argentine culture and letters and a vigorous proponent of women's rights.

Ocampo's early years are well documented in large part because she felt that everyone had a particular destiny, a role to play in life. Consequently, she wrote voluminously about her childhood in a search for signs of the course of her life. Ocampo was born in 1890 into a wealthy family that on both sides had a distinguished lineage that could be traced to Argentina's origins as a Spanish outpost in the 16th century. A great-aunt Victoria, whom Ocampo called "Vitola," was her favorite relative and became a second mother. "There is no doubt," wrotes **Doris Meyer**, "that Vitola was the first to inspire her to dream of doing great things with her life."

Opposite page

Victoria Ocampo

In 1896, the Ocampo family embarked on its first trip to Europe, a customary practice for Argentina's wealthiest families. During the family's extended sojourn in Paris, Victoria's first schooling was in French. Indeed, in later years her written work reflected her love of French which she preferred to Spanish and for which she was criticized by Argentine nationalists in the 1930s and 1940s. Victoria's schooling continued upon the Ocampos' return to Argentina in 1897. She and her sisters were taught at home by tutors who were expected to groom them to be good wives and mothers. Subjects were concentrated in the humanities, history, religion and basic math. Languages were stressed and Ocampo became fluent in French, English, and Italian as well as her native Spanish. Piano and voice training were also considered positive attributes of a woman. Ocampo was something of a nightmare for her tutors. Her intensity and desire to learn were reflected in her aggressive independence and rebellious nature; she learned but was a difficult student. Victoria's independence, if wholly unleashed, would have certainly clashed with the conservatism of her parents—but she held back out of love and respect and channeled her energies into books. Ocampo became a voracious reader.

The 30 years between 1900 and 1929—i.e., from puberty through the loss of the great but illicit love in her life, Julián Martínez—"are characterized," writes Greenberg, "by a seemingly endless series of rites of passage." Ocampo saw herself as a "timid rebel victimized by a complex system of double standards that held her prisoner." In 1905, after viewing a performance of the great French actress **Marguerite Moreno**, Victoria seemed intent on a career in the theater. This was not possible in Argentine society without creating a scandal, however, and Victoria again placed the well-being of her parents ahead of her inclinations. Her frustrations are most evident in the remarkable letters she wrote to **Delfina Bunge**. "I'm weary of feeling misunderstood. I wish to be known for what I am," she complained to Bunge in 1907, "a person 'who thinks,' a person who unceasingly analyzes herself."

Travel to Europe occupied the Ocampo family in 1908, and Victoria took classes at the Sorbonne with French philosopher Henri Bergson and discovered the work of Saint Augustine, Friedrich Nietzsche, and Arthur Schopenhauer from whom she learned respectively about dualism, hero-worship, and the inadequacy of reason as a guide. As a prescient 18-year-old, Ocampo looked for a way to escape from not only the parents who constrained her but from what she saw as the materialistic, shallow culture that prevailed in Buenos Aires; she began to search for "true culture." Escape took the form of marriage in 1912 to a scion of the Argentine oligarchy, Luis Bernardo de Estrada, also known as "Monaco."

The marriage was a disaster and within a year they led separate lives; divorce was not possible. Appearances were maintained for the family's sake, though Victoria engaged in a passionate adulterous affair with Julián Martínez, a cousin of her husband. According to John King, "She found a way through these dilemmas caused by social control through writing." Ocampo's first two published pieces concerned Dante's *Divine Comedy* and masked her own search for, in Meyer's phrase, "direction and wholeness." *De Francesca a Beatriz,* published in 1924, marks "the beginnings," writes King, "of Victoria's break with her class and with society's network of moral and social prejudices." Her "pilgrimage towards self-confidence and self-sufficiency in a man's world was punctuated by a series of love-hate relationships with certain male writers" of the 1920s whom she worshipped as heroes. Most prominent were philosophers José Ortega y Gasset, Rabindranath Tagore, and Count Hermann Keyserling. Meyer observes that each of these men had a "profound influence on her personal and literary development" and her perception of the dialectic between the sexes.

In 1929, Ocampo finally identified her proper course in life after a decade of false starts. In 1931, she founded the cultural journal *Sur,* destined to become Latin America's longest-lived, best known, and highest quality publication of this genre. The review was intended as a cultural bridge between South America, North America and Europe. Its international focus ran against the strong and growing current of narrow nationalism in the 1930s. To help defray the review's publication costs, Ocampo opened a publishing house, Editorial Sur, in 1933.

In 1935, the first volume of her *Testimonios* was published and laid bare her view of life and literature. "What moves me most in man is the human being who suffers, struggles, and seeks his expression," wrote Ocampo (translated by Meyer). "What interests me is the way in which this being is resolving his human problem, the way in which he is accepting, enduring, and carrying out his human destiny." Through her writ-

ing, she would be a witness to the drama of her times. And she would capture those times from the perspective of a woman. Indeed, early in the *Testimonios,* Ocampo "insisted," writes **Francine Masiello**, "on the right to be received as a female author." "My only ambition," wrote Ocampo, "is to write one day, no matter how well or poorly, but as a woman."

After 1935, Victoria and ***Alicia Moreau de Justo** were the acknowledged leaders of the Argentine women's movement, although each approached their task from different perspectives. Moreau sought a leveling of society along the lines of democratic socialism; Ocampo, the practitioner of aristocratic liberalism, felt that a leveling was neither possible nor desirable. While Victoria for the most part avoided the world of politics, in 1936 she was one of the creators of the Argentine Women's Union, which fought hard against attempts by a conservative government to annul civil rights for women gained in legislation in 1926. Newly back from a European trip during which she witnessed firsthand the anti-feminism of Benito Mussolini and the policies of fascist governments that urged women to produce soldiers for the state, Victoria was particularly attuned to issues of women's rights. Furthermore, she had made the acquaintance of English author ***Virginia Woolf** who encouraged Victoria to strike a blow for women. In a radio speech delivered in 1936, Ocampo, as reported by **Nancy Caro Hollander**, argued that the feminist movement in Argentina "should begin to speak of 'women's liberation' instead of 'women's emancipation,' because the term referred better to the reality of the master-slave relationship between men and women." The Union's campaign generated a good deal of support, and the offensive legislation was not passed. Two years later, when several members of the Union attempted to transform the organization into a mouthpiece for leftist political ideas, Ocampo withdrew. Her retirement was not because of ideology per se or because of her upper-class credentials, but because of the politicization of the movement. Her positions were always apolitical, but they were positions that could generate a good deal of controversy. King notes that her "support of 'personalist' Catholic philosophers in *Sur* . . . incurred the wrath of the traditional, reactionary Argentine church." Indeed, she "was a threat to the stable moral codes in several respects: she lived openly as a separated woman, flaunting the sacred vows of matrimony; . . . she published dangerously progressive Catholic ideas," and she had given up Catholicism in favor of Eastern philosophers.

During 1942, Ocampo undertook to write a biography of T.E. Lawrence (Lawrence of Arabia) entitled *338171 T.E.*, which was his number in the Royal Air Force. Although Lawrence was different in almost every respect from Victoria, it is clear why he became the subject of her interest. Lawrence's affinity for the desert was not unlike an Argentine's relationship with the pampa. Lawrence, like Ocampo, wrestled with a crisis of the spirit and was forced to confront an essential dualism in his personality. He was a man playing a role set by destiny; he acted to achieve self-realization. Victoria Ocampo also played a role, and her written work was certainly an act of self-realization and self-identification.

While war raged in Europe, Ocampo welcomed the voluntary and involuntary exiles from Spain and France. Buenos Aires seemed to be an oasis in a sea of fascism. But times were changing in Argentina, and in 1943 a military coup set the stage for the emergence of the dictatorial regime of Juan Domingo Perón. Not surprisingly, Ocampo was officially branded both as a dissenting intellectual and persona non grata. *Sur* continued to publish, however, for the government did not deem it a threat. As Perón's government began to lose its grip on power after the death of ***Eva Perón** in 1952, there were more open manifestations of discontent. In 1953, several bombs detonated in the Plaza de Mayo during one of Perón's speeches, and Ocampo was one of about a thousand intellectuals and dissidents arrested and imprisoned. She was released after nearly a month of captivity, following an international furor. The intervention of Nobel Prize-winning Chilean poet ***Gabriela Mistral** was instrumental in securing Ocampo's freedom.

Ocampo had begun to write her *Autobiografía* in 1952, although the first volume would not be published until after her death. Greenberg sees the six-volume work as a "classic case of feminist consciousness-raising. The story outlines the conflict between who she is and who others want her to be, and offers a justification of who she became." When set against all her written work, the *Autobiografía* is "the boldest possible affirmation of self-narration: it represents an attempt to lay down the shield of the mirrored reflections of her self through others."

Beginning in the late 1950s and continuing until her death two decades later, Ocampo was the recipient of numerous awards. In 1965, she won the Maria Moors-Cabot prize and was made a Commander of the British Empire (CBE). Two years later, when Harvard University gave her an honorary degree, she was described as a "dauntless lady; bright burning spirit; exemplar and defender of the unfettered mind." Ocampo's relationship with Tagore and her admiration of Mohandas Gandhi were recognized in 1968 when *Indira Gandhi, on the occasion of a state visit to Argentina, gave her a Doctorate Honora Causas of the University of Visva Barathi. When Ocampo died in 1979, at age 89, she was memorialized by many. Noted critic Emir Rodríguez Monegal wrote that her *Testimonios* needed the passage of time to be read for what they really were, "the chronicle of a woman who, in a country of condescending machos, dared to think and to feel and love just as she pleased."

SOURCES:

Greenberg, Janet. "A Question of Blood: The Conflict of Sex and Class in the *Autobiografía* of Victoria Ocampo," in Seminar on Feminism and Culture in Latin America, in *Women, Culture, and Politics in Latin America.* Berkeley, CA: University of California Press, 1990.

Hollander, Nancy Caro. "Women in the Political Economy of Argentina," unpublished PhD. dissertation, UCLA, 1974.

King, John. "Victoria Ocampo (1890–1979): Precursor," in Susan Bassnett, ed., *Knives & Angels: Women Writers in Latin America.* London: Zed Books, 1990.

Masiello, Francine. *Between Civilization & Barbarism: Women, Nation, and Literary Culture in Modern Argentina.* Lincoln, NE: University of Nebraska Press, 1992.

Meyer, Doris. *Victoria Ocampo: Against the Wind and the Tide.* Austin, TX: University of Texas Press, 1990.

Vazquez, Maria Esther. *Victoria Ocampo.* Buenos Aires: Planeta, 1991.

SUGGESTED READING:

Carlson, Marifran. *¡Feminismo!: The Woman's Movement in Argentina From Its Beginning to Eva Peron.* Chicago, IL: Academy Chicago, 1988.

Paul B. Goodwin, Jr.,
Professor of History, University of Connecticut, Storrs, Connecticut

O'Casey, Eileen (1900–1995)

Irish actress and author. *Born Eileen Carey in 1900; died at a London home for retired actors at age 95 in April 1995; married Sean O'Casey (the Irish playwright), in 1927; children.*

Actress Eileen Carey, age 27, met playwright Sean O'Casey, age 47, in Dublin in 1926; she was auditioning for his controversial play, *The Plough and the Stars.* They were married the following year. Because of the riot at the play's premiere and the ensuing turmoil, the couple moved to England where he could write and she could continue her acting career. After her husband's death in 1964, Eileen O'Casey published three books about their life together: *Sean*, *Cheerio, Titan*, and *Eileen.*

Ochoa, Blanca Fernández (c. 1964—)

Spanish skier. *Born around 1964; sister of Francisco Ochoa (who won a gold medal in slalom at Sapporo).*

Blanca Fernández, who had been a regular on the World Cup tour for 11 years, came away from three Olympics without a medal. In 1992, in Albertville, Ochoa won the bronze in the slalom. "I can forget the failures that have haunted me," she told a reporter that day. "You cannot imagine the enormous work of an entire life that went into this."

SOURCES:

Time. March 2, 1992.

Ochoa, Ellen (c. 1958—).

See Astronauts: Women in Space.

Ochowicz, Sheila Young (b. 1950).

See Young, Sheila.

Ochs, Iphigene (1892–1990).

See Sulzberger, I.O.

Ocllo-Mama.

See Mama-Ocllo.

O'Connell, Sister Anthony (1814–1897).

See O'Connell, Mary.

O'Connell, Helen (1920–1993)

American big-band singer of the early 1940s. *Name variations: Helen DeVol. Born in Lima, Ohio, on May 23, 1920; died of cancer on September 9, 1993, in San Juan Capistrano, California; dropped out of school after her sophomore year; later received diploma from Hollywood High School; married Clifford Smith, Jr. (a Navy aviator and heir to a Boston investment fortune), in 1941 (divorced 1951); married Thomas T. Chamales (an author), in 1957 (died 1960); married Bob Paris (a musician), in 1964 (annulled 1965); married Frank DeVol (a composer and conductor), in 1991; children: four daughters.*

Noted as the sunniest of the big-band era singers, Helen O'Connell made a name for herself with the Jimmy Dorsey band in the early 1940s, particularly teamed with Bob Eberly on such hits as "Green Eyes" and "Tangerine."

O'Connell's perky good looks and infectious smile were a large part of her appeal; one journalist likened her charming dimples to "two quote marks around a happy phrase."

O'Connell, who was born in 1920 in Lima, Ohio, and grew up in Toledo, was not the first singer in her Irish-American family. Her older sister Alice sang with dance bands around Ohio to help support the family after the death of their father. When Alice eloped, Helen inherited her evening gowns and her place behind the microphone. She sang for band after band until 1939, when orchestra leader Jimmy Dorsey heard her one night in a Greenwich Village club and hired her the next day. O'Connell's strength was in novelty tunes rather than ballads ("Amapola," "Six Lessons from Madame La Zonga," "The Jumpin' Jive"), and when teamed with Eberly, she most often followed his romantic interpretation of the song with an upbeat, bouncy second chorus. "As soon as you heard four bars of her singing you knew it was Helen O'Connell," said singer Don Cornell. O'Connell and Eberly became the most popular male-female singing duo on the big-band circuit; they were also linked romantically until both married others. During the height of her popularity, O'Connell also appeared in two movies: *The Fleet's In* (1942) and *I Dood It* (1943).

Helen O'Connell

O'Connell wed a Navy aviator in 1941, but remained with the band until 1943. She was at the height of her career when she left to care for her children while her husband was in the service. "I got tired of all the traveling around by bus and train, and all the one-nighters," she told a reporter for *The New York Times*. "I love music and show business, and it's done a lot for me. But when you have children to raise, it's not a healthy life." O'Connell also later admitted that she had issues with Dorsey over her salary and the lack of royalties on her recordings. The singer settled in Los Angeles, and was pretty much out of show business during the late 1940s except for an appearance in the movie *The Fabulous Dorseys* (1947). O'Connell used the down time to complete her high school education, enrolling at Hollywood High School under her married name.

Following her divorce in 1950, O'Connell took up singing again, cutting several records and appearing on television with Bob Eberly and later with the Russ Morgan orchestra. In 1957, she joined Dave Garroway on the early morning "Today Show," where she covered the weather and features but sang very little. She also appeared on the twice-weekly, 15-minute "The Helen O'Connell Show" for NBC. On one of the "Today Show" telecasts, O'Connell met author Thomas T. Chamales who was promoting his new book *Never So Few*. The couple married two weeks later, but Chamales turned out to be an abuser, and they were separated at the time of his death in a house fire in 1960. A subsequent marriage to musician Bob Paris ended in an annulment after only ten months. In 1991, she married composer-conductor Frank DeVol.

O'Connell reignited her career a third time in the late 1970s and 1980s, when a nostalgia craze swept the country. She toured in the show *4 Girls 4* for several years, with singers ***Rosemary Clooney**, ***Margaret Whiting**, **Rose Marie**, and sometimes ***Kay Starr**, and appeared at Manhattan's Rainbow Grill and the Drake Hotel in Chicago. O'Connell was still performing at the time of her final illness.

SOURCES:

Carr, Ian, Digby Fairweather, and Brian Priestley. *Jazz, The Rough Guide*. London: Rough Guides, 1995.

"Helen O'Connell" (obituary), in *The Day* [New London, CT]. September 10, 1993.

Hemming, Roy, and David Hajdu. *Discovering Great Singers of Classic Pop*. NY: Newmarket Press, 1991.

Kinkle, Roger D. *The Complete Encyclopedia of Popular Music and Jazz: 1900–1950*. New Rochelle, NY: Arlington House, 1974.

Lamparski, Richard. *Whatever Became of . . . ?* 3rd series. NY: Crown, 1970.

Barbara Morgan,
Melrose, Massachusetts

O'Connell, Mary (1814–1897)

Irish-born American nun, nurse, and administrator. *Name variations: Sister Anthony; Sister Anthony O'-Connell. Born in County Limerick, Ireland, on August 15, 1814; died in Cincinnati, Ohio, on December 8, 1897; daughter of William O'Connell and Catherine (Murphy) O'Connell; educated at the Ursuline Academy in Charlestown, Massachusetts.*

Mary O'Connell devoted her life to helping the sick, the injured, and the orphaned, and was a key figure in the establishment and operation of hospitals and orphanages in and around Cincinnati, Ohio. She was born the elder of two daughters in County Limerick, Ireland, and her mother died when she was twelve; little else is known about her early life in Ireland. At some point she emigrated to the United States, after which she attended the Ursuline Academy in Charlestown, Massachusetts. In June 1835, under the guidance of the Reverend William Tyler of Boston, she became a member of the community of the American Sisters of Charity in Emmitsburg, Maryland. Not quite two years later, she took her final vows, becoming Sister Anthony. The order then sent her to work at St. Peter's Orphanage in Cincinnati, which was then a young and rapidly growing city on the western frontier.

Over a decade later, organizational changes in the Sisters of Charity led O'Connell and her six associates to request that they be severed from their order, and in 1852 they obtained permission from Archbishop John Purcell to establish themselves as the Sisters of Charity of Cincinnati. O'Connell was elected procuratrix (financial officer), a position she would hold for a number of years. She was also named superior of St. John's Hotel for Invalids (later St. John's Hospital), which the order founded shortly thereafter. The hospital was affiliated with the Miami Medical College, whose faculty included Dr. George Curtis Blackman, the foremost surgeon in the Ohio Valley. In 1854, the order established a visiting nurse service as a hospital outreach project. Due primarily to O'Connell's efforts, in June of that year the Sisters of Charity acquired a new orphanage, St. Joseph's, in the suburb of Cumminsville. She was appointed superior of that institution as well, a responsibility she relinquished a few years later in order to devote herself to running St. John's.

Shortly after the start of the Civil War, O'-Connell and a number of her colleagues traveled to nearby Camp Dennison to nurse the victims of a severe measles epidemic. St. John's grew crowded with sick soldiers from western Virginia during their absence, and the number of patients grew rapidly after their return. Cincinnati was conveniently located on the Ohio River, and the local branch of the U.S. Sanitary Commission developed new evacuation techniques using the local waterways. In 1862, after the Union capture of Fort Donelson in Dover, Tennessee, hundreds of wounded were transported to Cincinnati, nearly overwhelming the city's hospitals. O'Connell received high praise from the commission for her help in training volunteers in hospital routine at this time.

After the terrible Battle of Shiloh later that year, the commission reversed its procedure and hired boats to transport doctors and nurses to the battlefield. O'Connell gained further renown for her tireless work as a field nurse, which included searching for wounded, assisting in surgery, and caring for patients in the floating hospitals. After the battle of Richmond, Kentucky, Governor O.P. Morton of Indiana asked Archbishop Purcell for nurses to care for the Indiana wounded, and as one of those selected O'Connell was officially attached to the Army on September 1, 1862. She worked first at Stone's River, with the Army of the Cumberland, before receiving an assignment at Base Hospital Number 14 in Nashville, Tennessee. When smallpox broke out in nearby camps for refugee slaves, O'Connell provided the sick with medical care there. On March 23, 1864, the Ohio General Assembly voted a commemoration to the wartime services of the Sisters of Charity.

Upon her return to Cincinnati that year, O'Connell resumed her post as superior of St. John's, which was now structurally ill-equipped to keep pace with the demand for its services. In the summer of 1866, a cholera epidemic swept the city, inspiring two wealthy Cincinnati Protestants who admired O'Connell's work and leadership to purchase the former U.S. Marine Hospital, which was presented to the order on her birthday. The new building was renamed Good Samaritan Hospital and opened in October under O'Connell's supervision. Some years later, when she saw a need for a separate institution to care for unwed mothers and foundling children, O'Connell approached one of those benefactors, Joseph C. Butler, for help. He purchased the order a large home in the suburb of Avondale, which opened in 1873 as St. Joseph's Foundling and Maternity Hospital; O'Connell served as superior, and Dr. William E. DeCourcy, an eminent obstetrician, was chief of the medical staff.

In 1880, Bishop William Henry Elder asked O'Connell to retire from her administrative positions at both Good Samaritan and St. Joseph's. Her sudden removal, which was apparently in response to unfounded assertions of friction between her and the college medical staff over hospital policies, was a shock to an admiring public, and raised unflattering speculation and loud criticism in the secular press. O'Connell continued to live at St. Joseph's until her death in 1897, at age 83. Large crowds came to mourn at her pontifical requiem in the cathedral, after which she was buried in her order's cemetery at Mount St. Joseph in Cincinnati.

SOURCES:

James, Edward T., ed. *Notable American Women, 1607–1950*. Cambridge, MA: The Belknap Press of Harvard University Press, 1971.

Malinda Mayer,
writer and editor, Falmouth, Massachusetts

O'Connor, Flannery (1925–1964)

Major 20th-century American writer whose work is celebrated for its unflinching, grotesquely comic, moral vision. *Name variations: Mary Flannery O'-Connor. Pronunciation: FLAN-er-y. Born Mary Flannery O'Connor on March 25, 1925, in Savannah, Georgia; died of complications of disseminated lupus on August 3, 1964, in Milledgeville, Georgia; daughter of Edward Francis O'Connor and Regina (Cline) O'Connor; attended parochial schools in Savannah, graduated from Peabody High School in Milledgeville, Georgia; A.B. from Georgia State College for Women; M.F.A. from State University of Iowa; never married; no children.*

Lived in Savannah from birth until 1938, when family moved to Milledgeville; father died of lupus (1941); graduated from high school (1942); attended Georgia State College for Women (1942–45); graduated with a major in social science; accepted into Writers' Workshop at the State University of Iowa, where she earned an M.F.A. (1947); published first story, "The Geranium" (1946); was a resident at Yaddo writers' colony near Saratoga Springs, N.Y. (1948–49); lived briefly in New York City before going to live with Robert and Sally Fitzgerald in Connecticut (1949); after first attack of lupus (1950), moved with mother to Andalusia, a farm near Milledgeville where she spent the rest of her life under treatment to control her disease; published first novel, Wise Blood *(1952); published first collection of short stories,* A Good Man Is Hard to Find *(1955); won first prize in the O. Henry awards for short stories for "Greenleaf" (1957); traveled to Lourdes and Rome with mother (1958); published second novel,* The Violent Bear It Away *(1960); lupus reactivated in severe form after hospitalization for abdominal surgery (February 1964).*

Selected writings: Wise Blood *(novel, 1952);* A Good Man Is Hard to Find *(short stories, 1955);* The Violent Bear It Away *(novel, 1960);* Everything That Rises Must Converge *(short stories, 1965);* Mystery and Manners: The Occasional Prose of Flannery O'-Connor *(ed. by Sally and Robert Fitzgerald, 1970);* The Complete Short Stories of Flannery O'Connor *(1971);* The Habit of Being: Letters of Flannery O'-Connor *(ed. by Sally Fitzgerald, 1979);* Flannery O'-Connor: Collected Works *(fiction, criticism, and letters ed. by Sally Fitzgerald, 1988).*

When a friend proposed the idea of a biography to Flannery O'Connor in a letter in 1958, she promptly wrote back, "As for biographies, there won't be any biographies of me because, for only one reason, lives spent between the house and the chicken yard do not make exciting copy." Indeed, O'Connor's career as a fiction writer was shaped by an unlikely combination of conditions that circumscribed her personal experience but at the same time deepened her imaginative vision of the distinctive fictional world she fashioned. Limited by the incurable disease she endured through most of her life as a writer, she drew upon her experience living in the rural, largely fundamentalist Christian South and upon her strong religious faith to develop an aesthetic vision that gives her work its unique perspective and intensely personal style.

Born on March 25, 1925, to Edward Francis O'Connor and **Regina Cline O'Connor**, Mary Flannery O'Connor spent her early years in the progressive, commercial, cosmopolitan culture of the Catholic community in Savannah, living in the O'Connor family home opposite the Cathedral of St. John the Baptist on the city square. Her father was a respected member of the business community, a real estate agent whom O'Connor later remembered as having the desire but not "the time or money or training" to write. She attended parochial elementary school and had begun her first year at Sacred Heart High School in Savannah when her father was diagnosed as terminally ill with disseminated lupus, a degenerative and incurable auto-immune disease that causes the body to produce antibodies that attack its own tissues; the family moved from Savannah to Regina Cline O'Connor's ancestral home in Milledgeville, Georgia.

Flannery O'Connor

A strong contrast to Savannah, Milledgeville, formerly the capital of Georgia, had declined in importance politically, economically, and culturally while Savannah and Atlanta developed as the state's dominant urban centers. Milledgeville remained a rural town, steeped in the traditions of the old South, provincial in its customs, refined in its manners, and largely evangelical Christian in its religious orientation. The Cline family home, built in 1820, had once served as the governor's mansion. It was purchased in 1886 by O'Connor's maternal grandfather, who lived there as the mayor of Milledgeville for 22 years.

Although O'Connor's maternal ancestors were part of a tradition of Catholic leadership in the region that antedates the American Confederacy, Milledgeville had no Catholic high school in 1938, when the O'Connors relocated, and so Flannery enrolled in Peabody High School, where her chief interests were writing, drawing cartoons, and painting. In 1941, at age 45, Edward O'Connor died.

Upon her graduation from Peabody in 1942, O'Connor matriculated at Georgia State College for Women (now Georgia College). Anticipating a career in writing or cartooning, she became involved in student publications, serving as art editor of the newspaper, editor of the literary quarterly, and feature editor of her senior yearbook. She drew a weekly cartoon for the student newspaper and frequently sent cartoons to *The New Yorker,* which encouraged her talent but did not print her work. She graduated in 1945 with a degree in social studies.

One of her teachers at Georgia State was sufficiently impressed with O'Connor's writing to send some of the pieces she had published in the college literary magazine to the Writers' Workshop of the State University of Iowa, and on the basis of the promise they demonstrated, she was awarded a Rinehart Fellowship. By the time she left Milledgeville for Iowa, Mary Flannery O'-Connor had sufficient confidence in her future as a writer to anticipate the effect of her name appearing on a dust jacket. She legally changed her name to Flannery O'Connor in 1945.

At Iowa, she read widely in modern and contemporary authors, especially Southern and Catholic writers. She wrote, absorbed criticism, and learned the value of revision under the direction of Paul Engle at the Writers' Workshop, at which she was often too shy to read her compositions. Her reputation for reticence belied a strong underlying confidence in her abilities that led her to pursue publication aggressively. In 1946, she sold her first story, "The Geranium," which appeared in the summer issue of *Accent.* In 1947, she completed her M.F.A., submitting a thesis consisting of six short stories. She stayed at Iowa for another year, serving as a part-time teaching assistant and continuing her reading and writing.

In 1948, O'Connor was invited to spend the winter at Yaddo, the writers' colony near Saratoga Springs, New York, where she worked on a manuscript that was to become her first novel, *Wise Blood.* While at Yaddo, she made lasting friendships with fellow writers Robert Lowell and ***Elizabeth Hardwick** and established important connections with the New York publishing world. She engaged **Elizabeth McKee** as her literary agent, and during her residence at Yaddo published "The Capture" in *Mademoiselle* and "The Train," the basis of a chapter of *Wise Blood,* in the *Sewanee Review.* Through Lowell, she met Robert Giroux, who would later become her editor and publisher, and Robert and **Sally Fitzgerald**, who remained her close friends throughout her life. Poet and translator Robert Fitzgerald would become her literary executor; Sally Fitzgerald would edit the selection of letters published as *The Habit of Being;* and together, the Fitzgeralds would edit her critical and occasional prose, *Mystery and Manners.*

In 1949, O'Connor lived briefly in an apartment in New York City where she continued work on *Wise Blood.* Two chapters, "The Heart of the Park" and "The Peeler," were published in the *Partisan Review.* Later that year, she went to live with the Fitzgeralds on their farm near Ridgefield, Connecticut. A letter written to Elizabeth McKee at this time reveals a great deal about O'Connor's writing process and her gradual discovery of her subject matter, theme, and aesthetic perspective as she wrote *Wise Blood:* "I don't have my novel outlined and I have to write to discover what I am doing. . . . I don't know so well what I think until I see what I say; then I have to say it over again." As she wrote and rewrote, the novel grew in a variety of directions, to over 1,000 pages. Then, under the discipline of focusing her subject through the double filter of her metaphysical and aesthetic vision, the novel gradually began to take the distinctive stamp of her art.

Wise Blood grows out of the realistic, contemporary, provincial Southern setting that O'-Connor knew intimately, but its realistic backdrop contrasts sharply with characters inflated to cartoon-like grotesquerie and driven to bizarre and violent actions by the disjunction between their psychic and spiritual needs and the secular and material values of the modern world. Having laid claim to the rural fundamentalist South as her literary territory, O'Connor made it distinctively her own through her "Catholic" adaptation of the grotesque tradition, in which characters with names like Hazel Motes, Enoch Emery, Sabbath Hawks, and Hoover Shoats are seen as incomplete human beings spiritually diminished and psychically deformed by a culture that has fallen under the domination of an arid rationalist and materialist philosophy and the opportunistic pursuit of personal gratification. In the fallen Eden of the rural South, Hazel Motes, a young man who has returned from World War I to find his childhood home vacant and abandoned, sets out to become an itinerant preacher of the nihilistic gospel of the Church without Christ, but his obstinate flight from God's grace and redemptive power paradoxically becomes a spiritual quest for faith and meaning, ending in saint-like martyrdom.

As O'Connor's purpose became clearer to her, however, the direction *Wise Blood* was taking became less desirable to the publishing firm that had an option on the novel. When her editor at Rinehart expressed misgivings that eventually led to a release from her contract, Robert Giroux offered to publish the book through Harcourt, Brace. Thus with her first novel, O'-Connor had the good fortune of establishing an enduring relationship with an editor and publisher who understood and sympathized with her literary vision.

Just as she was discovering the central theme and personal style that became the hallmarks of her fiction, the tragic event that would affect the rest of her life and career occurred. O'Connor was stricken, at age 25, with disseminated lupus erythematosus, the disease of which her father had died. Her first attack transpired in December of 1950 when she left the Fitzgeralds to visit home for the Christmas holidays. In *The Habit of Being,* Sally Fitzgerald reports that when she put Flannery on the train for Georgia, "she was smiling, perhaps a little wanly but wearing her beret at a jaunty angle. She looked much as usual, except. . . [for] a kind of stiffness in her gait. . . . By the time she arrived she looked, her uncle later said, 'like a shriveled old woman.'" She was hospitalized in Atlanta, where she was reported near death. Treatment with blood transfusions, massive doses of a new experimental drug called ACTH, and cortisone stabilized her condition, and she was well enough to leave the hospital in the spring of 1951. The lupus went into remission, but the disease or the treatment or a combination of the two had seriously weakened her and had caused such extensive deterioration of her hip bones that she could not climb stairs. It was clear that a return to the North to resume her independent life as a writer was out of the question.

Instead, O'Connor and her mother decided to make their permanent home at Andalusia, the 150-year-old dairy farm outside Milledgeville that her mother had inherited from a brother. At Andalusia, O'Connor lived in an environment that minimized her discomfort and disability: a first-floor suite allowed plenty of room to read, write, and rest, and a large screened-in porch provided easy access to the outdoors and a place where she could enjoy visitors without feeling confined to the atmosphere of a sickroom. Regina assumed the management of the farm and the care of her daughter, and soon Flannery returned to her writing, eager to complete *Wise Blood.*

Living in rural Georgia once again immersed O'Connor in the setting and characters she had already chosen as her essential subject matter. Her imagination found fresh nourishment in observing the genteel provincial society of her mother's friends in Milledgeville, the rural characters she came in contact with while buying livestock with her mother or visiting a doctor's office, the African-American families employed for generations on the farm, and the succession of itinerant white tenants who passed through Andalusia. Their lives, characters, and language were transformed into the comedy, tragedy, humor, satire, and pathos of O'Connor's fiction.

The writer operates at a peculiar crossroads where time and place and eternity somehow meet.

—Flannery O'Connor

At the farm, O'Connor also resumed her childhood hobby of raising fowl by collecting a menagerie of chickens, ducks, pheasants, quail, geese, pea-fowl, and swans that fascinated and amused her. Her favorites were the peacocks, whose brilliant tail feathers she distributed as gifts to friends. Even this hobby found its way into her fiction, most markedly in the symbolic description of the peacock's stunning display as an emblem of the second coming of Christ in "The Displaced Person," one of her most admired stories.

Her life had assumed a pattern of reading, writing, and rest adapted to her illness by the time *Wise Blood* was published in 1952. Critical reaction to the novel was mixed. Most critics placed her work in the tradition of Southern grotesque fiction. Some admired her skillful use of language and imagery, her irony and humor; others criticized a strain of cruelty they found in her depiction of mentally and physically defective characters given to bizarre and violent actions; but few recognized the religious perspective that provided the rationale for her grotesque characters and their behavior. As she later explained in "Some Aspects of the Grotesque in Southern Fiction," "Whenever I am asked why Southern writers particularly have a penchant for writing about freaks, I say it is because we are still able to recognize one. To be able to recognize a freak, you must have some conception of the whole man, and in the South the conception of the whole man is still, in the main, theological." Equally confusing to early critics was a style that developed a serious theme—Hazel Motes' belated and reluctant religious conversion—through comic characterization and incidents culminating in the violent, tragic catastrophe of Hazel's self-blinding, suffering, and death.

Following the publication of *Wise Blood,* which had taken O'Connor several years and great effort to complete, she concentrated on refining her art as a short-story writer. In the next two years, she wrote several of her best-known stories, publishing most of them in magazines and literary reviews. Her talent was recognized in 1953, when she was awarded the *Kenyon Review* Fellowship in Fiction, to which she was reappointed in 1954. Also in 1954, her story "The Life You Save May Be Your Own" received second prize in the O. Henry short-story awards.

In 1955, her first collection of short stories, *A Good Man Is Hard to Find and Other Stories,* established her reputation as a major talent in this genre. The title story, perhaps O'Connor's best-known work, is the piece that she most enjoyed reading to audiences when she was later invited to discuss her work at colleges and universities. In this tale, an escaped convict known as the Misfit, a psychopathic killer troubled by metaphysical questions who murders a vacationing family of six, is the unlikely agent of one of O'Connor's recurrent themes: the necessity of a violent awakening to the possibility of redemptive grace. The Misfit is cast in a dialectical relationship with the complacently moral and respectable grandmother in the story, whose recognition, in the moment before she is shot, that the Misfit is "one of [her] own children" represents her first real understanding of the equal value of all human souls in the eyes of God. And the Misfit's judgment on her—"She would of been a good woman if it had been somebody there to shoot her every minute of her life"—acts as a shocking awakening for the reader to both the Misfit's and O'Connor's moral seriousness in a story that begins as comedy and ends in mass murder. The shock value of the story's gory climax illustrates O'Connor's view of the role of the artist, who is called like an Old Testament prophet to awaken torpid minds and spirits to the reality of the ultimate things: life, death, and judgment. The volume also included such widely admired stories as "The Life You Save May Be Your Own," "A Late Encounter with the Enemy," "The Temple of the Holy Ghost," "A Circle in the Fire," and "The Displaced Person."

By 1955, the continuing deterioration of her bones caused by the steroids she was taking to keep her alive made it impossible for O'Connor to walk without the aid of crutches. Nonetheless, she continued to perfect her art in such stories as "Good Country People," "You Can't Be Any Poorer Than Dead," and "The Artificial Nigger," the story that she called "my favorite and probably the best thing I'll ever write." She was awarded a second O. Henry prize for "A Circle in the Fire." But longer fiction remained a challenge to her, and in 1955 she began a story she felt might "become a novel." She would spend the next five years working intermittently on *The Violent Bear It Away.*

Her fiction was widely known and admired enough by 1956 to bring her a series of invitations to lecture and read her works at various colleges and universities. She undertook these trips as long as her health allowed, enjoying both the opportunity to meet her audiences and the additional income such visits brought. In the next several years, she read or spoke at more than 20 colleges and universities and participated in many local and regional arts festivals, book clubs, and writers' panels. Also in 1956, she began publishing book reviews, many of them on theological or religious works for Catholic magazines. Writing these reviews and the one short story published that year, "Greenleaf," offered a break from the new novel she was finding difficult to shape. As she wrote to a friend, "I have put up the novel for a short spell and am writing a story and it's like a vacation in the mountains." The following year, she published several short stories and reviews, lectured, and received two more O. Henry awards.

In 1958, after much medical consultation to see if she was fit for the trip, she went with her mother on a pilgrimage to Lourdes and Rome at the insistence of an elderly cousin who paid for the trip. She wrote that she expected Lourdes "to be a comic nightmare," and Sally Fitzgerald records that O'Connor "dreaded the possibility of a cure in those circumstances," but once there, she was persuaded to take the baths with other pilgrims seeking relief from illness and affliction. In Rome, she received a special blessing at an audience with the pope. She returned to Milledgeville exhausted and glad to be at home.

She resumed work on her novel with renewed vigor and the help of a Ford Foundation grant. *The Violent Bear It Away,* which some critics have hailed as her masterwork, was published in 1960. Like *Wise Blood,* this novel focuses on a character attempting to escape his destiny as a prophet in a world that has lost all sense of spiritual values. And like Hazel Motes, Marion Tarwater discovers the hopelessness of evading prophetic responsibility, which O'Connor saw as an essential function of art. As she wrote to **Shirley Abbott**, "my 'message' (if you want to call it that) is a highly moral one. Now whether it's 'moralistic' or not I don't know. . . . Let me make no bones about it: I write from the standpoint of Christian orthodoxy. . . . I find this in no way limits my freedom as a writer and that it increases rather than decreases my vision."

With the publication of *The Violent Bear It Away,* O'Connor's literary reputation was secured. Critics recognized Flannery O'Connor as a major voice in 20th-century American fiction. As her stories were reprinted in anthologies and became widely read, taught, and discussed in college classes, her fame grew. She was presented with honorary Doctor of Letters degrees from Saint Mary's College of Notre Dame in 1962 and from Smith College in 1963. With modesty and good humor, she enjoyed both the fame that brought her prizes and invitations to read and lecture and the suspicion with which she was regarded as a famous homegrown writer in a small Southern town. She valued the many friendships based on literary and religious interests that she had developed over the years and had maintained through her lively letters. She began to prepare a second volume of short stories, which she hoped to have ready for publication in fall of 1964.

Toward the end of 1963, O'Connor began to suffer from fainting spells and weakness. She was treated for anemia, and for a while seemed to improve. In February of 1964, however, her doctors discovered that her weakness was caused by a benign fibroid tumor. Surgery, always considered risky for a lupus patient, became necessary because of the alarming growth of the tumor, and after massive doses of cortisone to prepare her, she underwent abdominal surgery on February 25. As feared, the surgery reactivated the lupus in a severe form. Extremely weakened, she was limited to an hour or two of work a day at a typewriter moved next to her bed. Still cheerful and good-humored, she continued collecting, revising, and arranging the volume of short stories she had been working on. On July 7, at her own request, she received the Last Rites of the Catholic Church. Her condition gradually deteriorated until she fell into a coma and died of kidney failure in Milledgeville Hospital on August 3.

Everything That Rises Must Converge, her second collection of short stories, published posthumously in 1965, met with virtually universal praise. Called the "greatest of Flannery O'Connor's books" by **Joyce Carol Oates**, the volume included, in addition to the title story, such well-known works as "The Enduring Chill," "Revelation," and "Parker's Back." In 1971, *The Complete Stories of Flannery O'Connor* won the National Book Award. Her reputation continued to grow with the publication of her occasional prose, *Mystery and Manners* (1969), and her letters, *The Habit of Being* (1979). In the space allotted her "between the house and the chicken yard," Flannery O'Connor had built a fascinating and distinctive imaginative world that has enriched the tradition of American letters.

SOURCES:

Browning, Preston M., Jr. *Flannery O'Connor.* Carbondale, IL: Southern Illinois University Press, 1974.

Fickett, Harold, and Douglas R. Gilbert. *Flannery O'Connor: Images of Grace.* Grand Rapids, MI: 1986.

Getz, Lorine M. *Flannery O'Connor: Her Life, Library and Book Reviews.* NY: Edward Mellen Press, 1980.

Oates, Joyce Carol. "The Visionary Art of Flannery O'Connor," in *Southern Humanities Review.* Vol. 7, no. 3. Summer 1973.

O'Connor, Flannery. *The Habit of Being: Letters of Flannery O'Connor.* Ed. by Sally Fitzgerald. NY: Farrar, Straus & Giroux, 1979.

———. *Mystery and Manners: Occasional Prose.* Ed. by Sally Fitzgerald and Robert Fitzgerald. NY: Farrar, Straus & Giroux, 1969.

Walters, Dorothy. *Flannery O'Connor.* NY: Twayne, 1973.

SUGGESTED READING:

Flannery O'Connor: Collected Works, 1988.

Flannery O'Connor: Modern Critical Views. Ed. by Harold Bloom. NY: Chelsea House, 1986.

Patricia B. Heaman,
Professor of English, Wilkes University,
Wilkes-Barre, Pennsylvania

O'Connor, Sandra Day (1930—)

First woman appointed to the U.S. Supreme Court. *Born Sandra Day on March 26, 1930, in El Paso, Texas; daughter of Harry A. Day (a rancher) and Ada May (Wilkey) Day; attended Radford School, a private institution in El Paso, Texas; graduated from El Paso's Austin High School in 1946; graduated magna cum laude from Stanford University, 1950; Stanford Law School, LL.B., 1952; married John Jay O'Connor III (a lawyer), on December 20, 1952; children: Scott, Brian, and Jay.*

Lived with her maternal grandmother in El Paso, Texas (1935–43); returned to Lazy B. Ranch while at-

tending school in Lordsburg, New Mexico (1943); returned to El Paso to attend Radford School (1944); after leaving Radford School, attended Austin High School in El Paso until graduating (1946); graduated Stanford University (1950); graduated Stanford University Law School (1952); admitted to the California bar (1952); served as deputy county attorney in San Mateo, California (1952–53); moved to Frankfurt, Germany (1953) and served as a civilian lawyer for the Quartermaster Corps; admitted to Arizona bar (1957); practiced law in Maryvale, Arizona (1958–60); served as Arizona's assistant attorney general (1965–69); served as a member of the Arizona state senate (1969–75); elected senate majority leader (1972); elected and served as Maricopa County judge (1975–79); served as Arizona Court of Appeals judge (1979–81); confirmed as U.S. Supreme Court justice (1981).

"She is truly a 'person for all seasons,'" said President Ronald Reagan on July 7, 1981, upon nominating Sandra Day O'Connor to be a Supreme Court justice, "possessing those unique qualities of temperament, fairness, intellectual capacity and devotion to the public good which have characterized the 101 'brethren' who have preceded her." Not since George Washington named the first Supreme Court justice had a "non-brethren" served on America's highest tribunal. Sandra Day O'Connor was to become the 102nd justice, but only the first woman to sit on the Supreme Court (the 107th justice would be ***Ruth Bader Ginsburg**). When she was later confirmed by the U.S. Senate, Senator Edward Kennedy declared, "Americans can be proud this day as we put one more 'men only' sign behind us."

The halls of the Supreme Court seem far removed from Arizona's remote Lazy B. Ranch, where Sandra Day O'Connor spent her early childhood. Living with her parents in a four-room adobe home that had neither running water nor electricity until she was seven, O'Connor readily adapted to life on the range. She learned to drive both a truck and a tractor by the time she was ten. Her father taught her to mend fences, to fire her own .22 rifle, and to ride a horse. "I didn't do all the things boys did," O'Connor remembered, "but I fixed windmills and repaired fences." Reflecting on this part of her life, she later said, "I always loved horses; that was an important part of my childhood. The other thing, I guess, was reading, because there weren't that many people of my age around; none, in fact, unless I brought them to visit. I would read a lot because my parents had many books, many more than most people in that area." After she was sworn in as a Supreme Court justice, she confided to Reagan, "As far as I'm concerned, the best place in the world to be is on a good cutting horse working cattle."

She had been born Sandra Day on March 26, 1930, in El Paso, Texas, the daughter of Harry A. Day and **Ada May Day**. Because they wanted her to be well educated, her parents sent Sandra at the age of five to live with her maternal grandmother back in El Paso, where she enrolled in Radford, a private school for girls. When she was 13, she returned home and for one year attended school in Lordsburg, New Mexico. Except for that year and summers at the Lazy B., she lived with her grandmother, who was very supportive of her from kindergarten through high school. Said O'Connor, "She would always tell me that I could do anything I wanted to do."

After O'Connor graduated from El Paso's Austin High School, she moved to California to attend Stanford University, graduating in 1950 with a major in economics. She then enrolled in Stanford Law School where she became editor of the *Stanford Law Review*. In 1952, O'Connor graduated third highest in a class of 102. William H. Rehnquist, who later became the chief justice of the Supreme Court, was the top student that year. In December 1952, she married John J. O'Connor III, whom she had met at Stanford. It may have been John's sense of humor that attracted her attention. "It just bubbles out of him on an impromptu basis," said O'Connor. "Sometimes the first statement of the day will be some funny little comment that will have us both laughing. He has kept me laughing for thirty years."

Young, ambitious, and intelligent, Sandra O'Connor hoped she would soon find a suitable position in her chosen profession. To her dismay, she discovered that, because of her gender, doors were closed. "I interviewed with law firms in Los Angeles and San Francisco," she noted, "but none had ever hired a woman before as lawyer, and they were not prepared to do so." One firm that offered her a job as a legal secretary had a partner named William French Smith; 29 years later, as attorney general of the United States, he would contact her about an opening on the U.S. Supreme Court. O'Connor finally landed a job in the public sector as deputy county attorney in San Mateo, California. It was a "wonderful job," she said later; the position "influenced the balance of my life because it demonstrated how much I did enjoy public service."

After John O'Connor graduated from Stanford Law School in 1953, he served the U.S. Army as a lawyer in Frankfurt, Germany, for

Sandra Day O'Connor

three years, while O'Connor worked as a civilian lawyer for the Quartermaster Corps in Frankfurt. In 1957, the O'Connors returned to the States where, in Maryvale, Arizona, Sandra established her own law firm with a partner. It was a "diverse, small-town type of practice," she said. "We did whatever business we could get to come out way."

About the same time, the couple's first son, Scott, was born; when, in 1960, a second son, Brian, arrived, O'Connor said that she "stopped work for about five years and stayed home with the children when they were really small." Said John, "You look at her resume and you think 'My God, the woman must be some kind of machine.' But the amazing thing is that she has always retained her priorities. The family has always come first." Two years later, O'Connor gave birth to a third son, Jay. Her sons would later achieve success both in their careers and in their involvement in community affairs.

In 1965, O'Connor assumed another public service position when she became Arizona's assistant attorney general, a post she occupied until 1969. Governor Jack Williams then appointed O'Connor to an unexpired term in Arizona's state senate. She obviously enjoyed the state legislature, and in 1970 and again in 1972 she won reelection to the senate. She so impressed her colleagues that in 1972 she became majority leader, the first woman to hold that office in any state senate.

When a candidate is endorsed by Ted Kennedy and Barry Goldwater, there's got to be something good about her.

—**Senator Barry Goldwater**

After serving in the legislature for five years, O'Connor decided not to return to the legislative branch of government. Said one of her colleagues, "At the end of her term she was at a crossroads. She had to choose between politics and the law." Thus, in the 1974 election, she successfully ran for judge on the Maricopa County Superior Court.

Democratic Governor Bruce Babbitt named O'Connor to the Arizona Court of Appeals in 1979. Although she had proved she was a staunch Republican by attending the 1972 Republican National Convention as an alternate delegate and then later serving as co-chair of the Arizona Committee to Re-elect the President, Babbitt nominated her nonetheless. "I had to find the finest talent available to create confidence in our new merit system," he said. "Her intellectual ability and her judgment are astonishing."

In 1980, when Ronald Reagan ran for president, he promised to nominate "the most qualified woman I can find" to be a Supreme Court justice. On July 7, 1981, Reagan fulfilled this promise when, after Justice Potter Stewart announced his retirement, the president selected Sandra Day O'Connor to fill the vacancy. In naming O'Connor, Reagan said, "That is not to say I would appoint a woman merely to do so. That would not be fair to women, nor to future generations of Americans whose lives are so deeply affected by the decisions of the court. Rather, I pledged to appoint a woman who meets the very high standards I demand of all court appointees." In O'Connor, the president found a woman who met "the very high standards" of which he had spoken.

The appointment of O'Connor met with wide approval. Except for certain conservatives, wrote a reporter for *Time* magazine, "reaction ranged from warm to ecstatic." Keeping in mind that Reagan had been criticized for not choosing more women for high-level positions in the executive department, one of his aides said, "This is worth twenty-five assistant secretaries, maybe more." Although Reagan was considered a political conservative, his appointment was praised by liberals as well as most conservatives. ***Barbara Jordan**, the African-American lawyer who had served with distinction in the House of Representatives, congratulated the president: "The Supreme Court was the last bastion of the male; a stale, dark room that needed to be cracked open." Democratic Senator Edward Kennedy declared that every citizen "can take pride in the President's commitment to select such a woman for this critical office." Republican Senator Barry Goldwater of Arizona, when he heard that the Reverend Jerry Falwell, the leader of the Moral Majority, had said "all good Christians" should be concerned about O'Connor's appointment, irately responded, "Every good Christian ought to kick Falwell right in the ass."

Opposition to O'Connor's nomination sprang from those characterized as the New Right. One critic, **Carolyn Gerster**, a former president of the National Right to Life Committee, charged that the nominee "is unqualified because she's proabortion." Paul Brown, who headed the Antiabortion Life Amendment Political Action Committee, accused Reagan of violating a promise made by the Republicans which stated that only persons who supported "traditional family values and the sanctity of human life" would be named justices. "We have been betrayed," he concluded. Some also opposed O'Connor because she had supported the Equal Rights Amendment.

Following her nomination, O'Connor declared that it was a "momentous day in my life and the life of my family," and she promised that if confirmed she would do her best "to serve the Court and this nation in a manner that will bring credit to the President, to my family and to all the people of this great nation." Beyond that she refused to go, averring that she could not answer "substantive questions" prior to her confirmation hearings before the Senate Judiciary Committee. The U.S. Constitution specifies that a Supreme Court nominee must be approved by the U.S. Senate. Thus, until confirmation hearings began in September, the American public learned more about Sandra Day O'Connor, the person, than about her views on controversial issues that might be considered by the Supreme Court. Therefore, American citizens came to know that O'Connor was a superb cook who specialized in Mexican dishes, was "a popular party giver and—goer," wore such "sensible clothes as suits with silk blouses and matching ascots," and liked to dance, and play golf and tennis. She was also an Episcopalian with a sense of humor and, always "a lady," would not try "to high-hat anyone." If confirmed, she would be the youngest member of the Supreme Court.

O'Connor's confirmation hearings before the Senate Judiciary Committee began on September 9, 1981. In her opening statement, she indicated that her experience as a state court judge and a state legislator had "strengthened my view that the proper role of the judiciary is one of interpreting and applying the law, not making it." She also asserted that as a nominee, she could not tell how she "might vote on a particular issue which might come before the Court." She concluded her opening statement with a personal note as a way of introducing her family. In this manner, Sandra Day O'Connor, a mother of three, asserted that in her view "marriage is more than an exchange of vows." She believed marriage to be "the foundation of the family, mankind's basic unit of society, the hope of the world and the strength of our country. It is the relationship between ourselves and the generations to come."

The nominee then responded to questions from the committee. She made clear that for her, abortion was "simply offensive" and "repugnant," admitting at the same time that she was "over the hill" and would never become pregnant again. "It's easy for me to say now," she acknowledged. To the dismay of some of her opponents, she refused to state her opinion concerning the 1973 Supreme Court decision that declared abortion to be a constitutionally protected right.

She seemed to reflect her conservatism when she indicated that not every bit of evidence illegally obtained necessarily should be barred at a trial. Her response appeared to favor the so-called "good faith" exception under which evidence is admissible if acquired by the police in a mistaken but "good faith" belief that their procedures were correct. When questioned about court-ordered busing, she remembered a 75-mile round trip to school while living on the ranch. Her own experience made her question mandated busing. In answering other questions, O'Connor indicated support for the death penalty and opposition to women fighting on the battlefield. She also stated that she would allow television cameras in courtrooms.

On the last day of the hearing, O'Connor continued to evoke criticism from those opposed to legalized abortion. However, the Judiciary Committee was generally impressed with her performance. Senator Howard M. Metzenbaum said that he felt she was "too conservative" on some issues. Yet he planned to vote for her, saying to those who opposed her, "I find something un-American about any appointee being judged on one issue and one issue alone."

On September 15, 1981, the Senate Judiciary Committee decided to recommend O'Connor's appointment. All members voted in favor except Alabama Senator Jeremiah Denton, who voted "present." He characterized O'Connor as a "distinguished jurist" and a "fine lady," but he declined to say "yes" because O'Connor refused to call into question the 1973 Supreme Court decision legalizing abortion.

Six days later, the Senate confirmed the appointment by a 99–0 count. Senator Max Baucus, an O'Connor supporter, was out of town and did not vote. On September 25, with Reagan present, Sandra Day O'Connor took the oath of office. Chief Justice Warren E. Burger welcomed her to the Court: "I wish you a very long life and a long and happy career in our common calling." On September 28, O'Connor began working with her new colleagues when the Supreme Court met for a week of closed-door sessions preceding the official beginning of its new term on the first Monday of October. Not because it was "woman's work," but because she was the Court's most junior member, it was O'Connor's obligation to send for anything the justices needed, from lawbooks to coffee.

O'Connor soon "became a respected and admired colleague," wrote one observer, who demonstrated "commendable security and poise." She writes well and is "an assiduous worker." A 1984 poll indicated that about a fourth of Americans could think of at least one woman qualified to be vice president. O'Connor was picked more often than any other. According to a *New York Times* report, when Chief Justice Burger retired in September 1986, Reagan considered O'Connor as his replacement. However, because she had been on the Supreme Court for a relatively short time, he named William H. Rehnquist instead.

In a March 1988 article, the *Atlantic Monthly* noted that O'Connor was no dogmatic ideologue. Instead, she "appears to keep one eye on the Constitution, one eye on the real world and an open mind to what she sees." Thus, those who hoped to "discern the future direction of the Supreme Court on abortion and affirmative action should keep both eyes on her." By 1992, *The New York Times* reported that a trio of moderately conservative justices, Sandra O'Connor, Anthony Kennedy, and David Souter were exerting "effective control" over the direction of the Supreme Court.

Especially in cases concerning religion, affirmative action, and abortion, Justice O'Connor has been influential. In decisions relating to religion, she has tended to reject arguments that call for strict separation of church and state. She prefers state neutrality or accommodation. Therefore, in a 1984 five-to-four decision, she sided with the majority in the Court's ruling that when Pawtucket, Rhode Island, included a nativity scene in its annual Christmas display, the city did not violate the Constitution. The Supreme Court ruled that the display, which also included a Santa house, a Christmas tree, and cut-out animal figures, did not promote or endorse Christian beliefs, but only depicted the historical origins of Christmas.

Although O'Connor has stated clearly her negative personal opinion of abortion, she has also indicated that "personal views and philosophies of a Supreme Court justice should be set aside in resolving matters that come before the Court." Thus, she has refused to overturn the 1973 Supreme Court decision that states a woman has the constitutional right to an abortion. The majority opinion on July 1, 1992, written by Justices Souter, Kennedy, and O'Connor, affirming *Roe* v. *Wade*, noted that "the liberty of the woman is at stake in a sense unique to the human condition and so unique to the law."

> The mother who carries a child to full term is subject to anxieties, to physical constraints, to pain that only she must bear. That these sacrifices have from the beginning of the human race been endured by women with a pride that ennobles her in the eyes of others and gives to the infant a bond of love cannot alone be grounds for the state to insist she make the sacrifice.
>
> Her suffering is too intimate and personal for the state to insist, without more, upon its own vision of the woman's role, however dominant that vision has been in the course of our history and our culture. The destiny of the woman must be shaped to a large extent on her own conception of her spiritual imperatives and her place in society.

At the same time, O'Connor has let stand the right of a state to place certain restrictions on abortion as long as they are not "unduly burdensome" to a woman. Therefore, she found constitutional a Pennsylvania law that required a woman to delay an abortion for 24 hours and listen to a presentation designed to persuade her to change her mind; it also required a teenager to gain the consent of one parent or a judge. She also voted to uphold state legislation that prohibited the expenditure of public funds for abortions. Even so, conservative Justice Antonin Scalia has blasted her for her opinions on the subject.

During the time O'Connor has been on the Supreme Court, a number of state laws relating to affirmative action have been challenged. Justice O'Connor has argued that affirmative action legislation is constitutional if it can be proved such laws are necessary to rectify prior discrimination. She seems to have succeeded in convincing a majority of her colleagues that this is the proper course. She was, therefore, in the majority when the Supreme Court upheld the promotion of a California woman by a Santa Clara government agency over a slightly more qualified male competitor. This action had been taken because "not one woman" had been employed previously in some 238 "skilled craft positions," seemingly indicating that in the past there had been discrimination against women. At the same time, she criticized the language used by Justice William J. Brennan as being too expansive and insufficiently well defined, which might lead to unfair discrimination against men.

O'Connor has been forced to confront challenges in her personal life while serving on the Supreme Court. On October 21, 1988, she underwent a mastectomy. In a November 3, 1994, meeting of the National Coalition for Cancer Survivorship she admitted that during and after her surgery "there were a few tears shed along the way." At the same time, this crisis "fostered a desire in me to make each and every day a good day." She found "the best thing about all of this" was the fact "that I had a job to go to." She concluded that her illness and the attention of the media had created enormous stress for her family and, thus, she told herself, "You'd better shape up and make a go of this because you're causing a lot of distress for other people." When her mother died in April 1989, Justice O'Connor presided over a private service at which her mother's ashes were scattered atop a mountain overlooking the family ranch. Said O'Connor's sister-in-law, **Sue Day**, "That's the only time I've seen her shed a tear."

Soon after Reagan nominated Sandra Day O'Connor to the Supreme Court, she was asked how she wanted to be remembered. O'Connor pondered what she called the "tombstone question" and then responded, "Here lies a good judge."

SOURCES:

Abraham, Henry J. *Justices and Presidents: A Political History of Appointments to the Supreme Court.* NY: Oxford University Press, 1992.

Friedelbaum, Stanley H. *The Rehnquist Court.* Westport, CT: Greenwood Press, 1994.

Lacayo, Richard. "The Justice in the Middle," in *Time.* July 9, 1990, p. 27.

Lamb, Charles M., and Stephen C. Halpern, eds. *The Burger Court: Political Profiles.* Urbana, IL: University of Illinois Press, 1991.

Magnuson, Ed. "The Brethren's First Sister," in *Time.* July 20, 1981, pp. 8–10, 17–19.

Marie, Joan W. "Her Honor: The Rancher's Daughter," in *Saturday Evening Post.* September 1985, pp. 42–47, 109.

McLoughlin, Merrill. "Sandra Day O'Connor: Woman in the Middle," in *Ladies' Home Journal.* November 1989, pp. 218–219, 297–299.

Moritz, Charles, ed. *Current Biography Yearbook 1982.* NY: H.W. Wilson, 1983.

O'Brien, David M. *Storm Center: The Supreme Court in American Politics.* NY: W.W. Norton, 1986.

Press, Aric, *et al.* "A Woman for the Court," in *Newsweek.* July 20, 1981, pp. 16–21.

Quindlen, Anna. *Thinking Out Loud.* NY: Random House, 1993.

"Sandra Day O'Connor," in *National Cyclopedia of American Biography*, 1984.

Sperling, Gene. "Justice in the Middle," in *Atlantic Monthly.* March 1988, pp. 26–27, 30–33.

Williams, Marjorie C., and Al Kamen. "America's Most Influential Woman," in *Reader's Digest.* December 1989, pp. 71–76.

SUGGESTED READING:

Rehnquist, William H. *The Supreme Court: How It Was, How It Is.* NY: Morrow, 1987.

Savage, David G. *Turning Right: The Making of the Rehnquist Supreme Court.* NY: Wiley, 1992.

Witt, E. *A Different Justice.* Washington, DC: Congressional Quarterly Press, 1986.

Robert Bolt,
Professor of History, Calvin College,
Grand Rapids, Michigan

Octavia (c. 69–11 BCE)

Link and mediator between two great Roman antagonists—her brother Octavian (Augustus) and her husband Marc Antony—who helped to avert Roman civil war for nearly a decade. *Name variations: sometimes designated "Minor" or "the Younger." Born around 69 BCE; died in 11 BCE, probably in or near Rome; daughter of G. Octavius (a Roman senator and governor of Macedonia) and Atia the Elder (niece of Julius Caesar); sister of Octavius (later designated Octavian and finally Augustus [there is some scholarly difference as to whether the Octavia in question is actually Octavian's older half-sister, also named Octavia, whose mother was* ***Ancharia****]); married Gaius Claudius Marcellus (a Roman consul) sometime before 54 BCE (died 40 BCE); married M. Antonius (Marc Antony), in 40 BCE (divorced 32 BCE); children: (first marriage) Marcus Claudius Marcellus, Marcella the Elder, and Marcella the Younger; (second marriage) Antonia Major (b. 39 BCE) and ****Antonia Minor*** *(36 BCE–37 CE).*

Married Marc Antony to seal the "Treaty of Brundisium," capping an agreement for peace between him and Octavian (40 BCE); mediated between the two men (37 BCE), helping to negotiate the Treaty of Tarentum; received protections of Tribunician office and other legal privileges (35 BCE).

Octavia was born into a family destined, through its connection to Julius Caesar, to become the most prominent and powerful in the Roman Empire. Her ambitious father G. Octavius, first in his branch of the family to become a Roman senator, distinguished himself by governing the province of Macedonia and winning an important battle in Thrace. Her mother ❧ **Atia the Elder**, niece of Julius Caesar, provided the blood link by which Octavia's brother Octavian (later the great emperor Augustus) was eventually able to assert personal control over the empire. Because of Octavia's warm, personal relationship with him, she exerted an indirect but vital influence on the empire in her own right. The ancient historians portray Octavia as a woman who exercised her powers for good in what was then a culturally appropriate way for a woman: by informal mediation.

❧ **Atia the Elder** (c. 80 BCE–?)

Roman noblewoman. *Name variations: Atia Maior or Major; Atia the Elder. Born around 80 BCE; daughter of ****Julia Minor*** *(c. 100–51 BCE, sister of Julius Caesar) and M. Atius Balbus; married G. Octavius (a native of Velitrae to the north of Rome who died in 59 BCE); married L. Marcius Philippus; children: (first marriage) Gaius Julius Caesar Octavianus, also known as Octavian (63 BCE–14 CE, later Augustus Caesar); and ****Octavia*** *(c. 69–11 BCE).*

Little is known about Octavia's early life, apart from the fact that her father died when she was in her early teens, and her mother died a few years later. She was married at a young age to Gaius Claudius Marcellus, who served in 50 BCE as consul, the highest political office in Rome. On one occasion, although she was already married, her great-uncle Julius Caesar offered her in marriage to Pompey in order to stabilize the relationship between the two men. Clearly, she was already considered a possible peacemaking link, but in this case, nothing came of it.

In 44 BCE, the overwhelming control Julius Caesar exercised over virtually every aspect of Roman life led an estimated 60 aristocratic opponents to participate in an assassination plot. On March 15, Caesar entered the senate and was stabbed by the conspirators 23 times. Octavian was completing his education with Apollonia in Epirus when he learned that Julius Caesar's will had made him son and heir.

If only Octavia, who in addition to her beauty possessed great dignity of character and good sense, could become united with M. Antony and win his love, . . . this alliance . . . would restore harmony to the Roman world.

—Plutarch

After the assassination, Marc Antony was all-powerful in Rome until he seized public funds and made for Cisalpine Gaul (northern Italy) with the legions at his disposal. Declaring Antony a public enemy, the senate gave Octavian full command of the Roman Army to protect the city. In 43 BCE, Octavian defeated Antony at Mutina (present-day Modena), but Antony escaped to the south of Gaul (France) and took refuge with the local governor Lepidus. Together, the two raised a new army. Octavian realized that an alliance with Antony would be more beneficial than a civil war and so convinced the senate to reverse its declaration of Antony as public enemy. Granted extraordinary powers by the senate, which feared civil war, Octavian, Antony, and Lepidus formed a triumvirate legally empowered to govern the empire for five years. As the three launched a bloodbath to destroy the "enemies of Rome," 300 senators and over 2,000 knights were slain. In October of 40 BCE, the Roman world was divided between them, with Octavian receiving Europe, Antony the East, and Lepidus the African provinces.

Meanwhile, Octavia had given birth to a son, Marcus Claudius Marcellus, and a daughter *__Marcella the Elder__. Her husband G. Marcellus died in 40 BCE, just before another daughter *__Marcella the Younger__ was born. A Roman widow was expected and required to grieve for ten months before considering remarriage, but Octavia's grief was cut short for political reasons by a special dispensation from the senate in Rome. Octavian and Marc Antony, the two most powerful commanders in the Roman Empire, reached a peace agreement that year, known as the Treaty of Brundisium. Since Marc Antony's wife, *__Fulvia__, had just died, a marriage between him and Octavia was quickly arranged with the intent of cementing the tenuous relationship between the two men. The treaty narrowly averted civil war.

According to Plutarch, an ancient Greek biographer, the populace strongly desired this marriage. It was thought that, if they married, the beautiful and wise Octavia would manage to win Marc Antony's love, and "this alliance would prove the salvation of their own affairs and would restore harmony to the Roman world." After the betrothal, according to Greek historian Appian, Octavian and Marc Antony embraced each other and "shouts went up from the soldiers and congratulations were offered to each of the generals, without intermission, through the entire day and night." By all indications, Octavia willingly accepted this marriage as her duty, and she believed she was a crucial link in maintaining peace between the two men. Her influence was effective in this regard for nearly a decade.

An early illustration of her positive influence on her brother Octavian is recorded by Cassius Dio. In this incident, a man who had been designated for death in the cruel bargains struck among the triumvirs (Octavian, Marc Antony, and Lepidus) was hidden by his wife in a chest. This woman then spread the rumor that her husband had died and solicited Octavia's help, hoping that Octavia's influence would somehow save her husband's life as well as the family's fortunes. Octavia succeeded in arranging for Octavian to enter the theater alone during a popular festival—at which point the woman approached him. She informed him of her deed and then had the chest brought in and produced her husband. Octavian released the family from the sentence of death.

Octavia accompanied Antony to Athens where they spent a pleasant first year of marriage. Antony adopted the Greek mode of dress, and together they attended lectures and festivals. The Athenians demonstrated their love for Octavia by bestowing various honors upon her, and during this period, to celebrate their marriage and to show good faith, Antony minted a coin with Octavia's portrait on the obverse, making Octavia one of the first Roman women ever to be so honored.

But by 37 BCE, Antony and Octavian were again at odds. Octavia now had a daughter, ***Antonia Major**, with Antony, and though she was expecting their second child (***Antonia Minor**) she begged permission to accompany Antony to Italy, hoping to effect a new reconciliation between the two men. Wisely, she first secured the backing of Octavian's influential advisors, and then she approached her brother Octavian personally. When Octavian listed his grievances against Marc Antony, she had a response prepared for each objection. Arguing that—as wife of one and sister of the other—her fate would be unbearable if they should go to war with each other, she prevailed upon Octavian to accept a dinner invitation from Marc Antony. Plutarch dramatically paints the background for this tense dinner: a huge army camped on land and an opposing army in a fleet offshore, poised with the potential for destruction. Yet the Treaty of Tarentum which resulted from this meeting extended the triumvirate, and thereby the peace, for another five years. The men exchanged military resources, and to further cement the agreement arranged a future marriage between Marc Antony's older son and Octavian's young daughter ***Julia** (39 BCE–14 CE). Marc Antony again struck new coins, in one case placing Octavian and himself on one side and Octavia on the other.

Nevertheless, the peace agreements showed early signs of inherent weakness. Octavia returned to the east with Marc Antony, yet when they had only reached Corcyra (Corfu) he sent her back, claiming that he did not want her endangered by his upcoming military campaigns. He entrusted Octavia and his daughters to Octavian, and she returned to Rome. It was widely believed, however, that Antony had sent her home on a pretext so that he could spend the winter with his former lover, the charming and politically powerful ***Cleopatra (VII)**, ruler of Egypt.

Antony's affair with Cleopatra was regarded negatively by the Romans mostly because a mutual political alliance directed against Octavian could place Rome in danger of civil war. That winter, Marc Antony further scandalized Rome by recognizing his paternity of Cleopatra's twins— ❧▸ **Cleopatra V Selene** and Alexander Helios—and by participating in an oriental religious ceremony with the Egyptian queen, implying to the east that they were a divine couple. Although

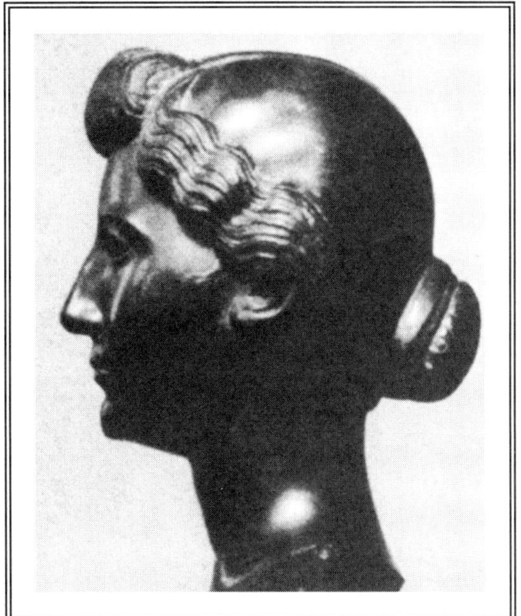

Octavia

Antony was still officially married to Octavia, this was the beginning of his breach with the west.

In 35 BCE, Octavian had a law passed giving both his wife ***Livia Drusilla** and his sister Octavia "the same security and inviolability as the tribunes enjoyed," as Dio puts it. This grant or rights associated with public office to women was novel, and it legally protected them from both physical and verbal injury. At the same time, Octavian gave both women the freedom to manage their own affairs without the permission of a guardian. Honorific statues were erected for them. In 34 BCE, to celebrate his defeat of Dalmatia and to further honor his sister, Octavian named a library for Octavia.

Despite these honors from her brother, and the lack of attention from her husband, Octavia retained a sense of loyalty to Marc Antony and a sense of duty to the empire. In 35 BCE, she sailed to meet her husband, bringing troops and gold which she had begged from Octavian in order to reinforce her husband's military efforts in the east. Antony accepted the gifts and the select troops but refused to let Octavia join him, sending her back to Rome from Athens, sight unseen. Again, he used the pretense of the dangers of war. Plutarch says, however, that Cleopatra had convinced Marc Antony to send Octavia home, fearing that if she ever joined Antony he might indeed return to her. Cleopatra maintained that Antony's marriage to Octavia was merely political while their own relationship was based on true love—and there seems to have been some truth in her argument.

◂❧ ***Cleopatra V Selene.*** *See Cleopatra VII for sidebar.*

Octavia's forced return to Italy placed her in danger of becoming the justification for a declaration of civil war. Plutarch surmises that Octavian gave permission for the gift of troops and gold only to generate an opportunity to declare war based on Antony's treatment of Octavia, now that she held the legal protections of a tribune. Citing the disrespect shown to her by her husband, Octavian suggested that Octavia move back into his own household. For Octavia, however, that move would represent her worst fears and the failure of her life's mission. Still loyal to duty, she exercised her right to act without the approval of a guardian and refused to leave Marc Antony's house. Plutarch says that she begged Octavian, unless he had other reasons for going to war, "to ignore Antony's behaviour toward her, for it would be intolerable, she pleaded, to have it said of the two greatest imperators in the world that they had plunged the Roman people into civil war, the one out of love and the other out of jealousy for the rights of a woman." She continued to raise Antony's children, both her own and those of his former wife Fulvia. She entertained Marc Antony's guests and even asked her brother favors for them, as if the marriage relationship were intact. Plutarch observes that Octavia actually did Antony a disservice by acting so nobly because, by comparison to her, he seemed so unworthy.

In 34 BCE, Marc Antony formally set up an inheritance for his children with Cleopatra in an ornate public ceremony, and, in 32 BCE, he sent orders to turn Octavia out of his house, thereby divorcing her. He broke tradition, however, by allowing her to keep all the children after their divorce (children normally stayed in their father's household), except for his oldest son who served in the army with him.

Octavia cried bitterly. Not only had she failed to keep the peace, but her treatment had become the very point over which her brother Octavian could rally support against his antagonist. This was indeed the opportunity for which Octavian had been waiting. Perhaps in deference to his sister, however, Octavian did not declare war on Antony, but on Cleopatra. Antony was represented as a great Roman general who had been enticed into weak degeneracy by a wicked foreign queen. The outcome of this war was complete victory for Octavian.

This, however, did not represent the end of Octavia's influence. As her brother Octavian (granted the title *augustus* in 27 BCE) becomes master of the Roman world, she continues to enter the narratives of the ancient sources, chiefly being noted as a mother. After her husband's death in 30 BCE, Octavia not only raised her own and Fulvia's children, demonstrating fairness to all (she put forward one of Fulvia's children for extra favor from Octavian), but also raised the children of Cleopatra. Octavia herself arranged the marriage of Cleopatra's daughter with King Juba II in Africa.

Octavia's son M. Marcellus was married in 25 BCE to his cousin, Octavian's young daughter Julia, and was groomed as probable successor to Octavian. Octavia's desires, now that her other endeavors had failed, centered on this son and his prospects for inheriting the rule of the empire. Sadly for Octavia, her hopes were dashed when he died young. Seneca, philosopher and advisor to Emperor Nero, criticizes her for what he considers inordinate grief over her son's death, saying that she never again took off mourning clothes and refused to take joy in life.

Yet Octavia's importance as blood link in maintaining the power of the Julio-Claudian family was to be crucial for years to come. Octavia's daughter Antonia Minor would become the mother of Claudius, future emperor, and Antonia Major would become the grandmother of Nero, the emperor who followed Claudius. When Octavia died in 11 BCE, the entire Roman Empire formally mourned her death. Her sons-in-law carried her body in a procession, honors were voted for her, and two orations were given at her funeral, one by the great Octavian himself.

Octavia had exercised her influence for good to the greatest degree possible without stepping beyond commonly acceptable boundaries for a woman in her time, place, and position. She had accepted seriously the role of informal mediator and link between powerful men through marriage, even to the point of defying their wishes for the sake of meticulous duty and high ideals. That she did not ultimately succeed does not lessen the fact that she staved off a Roman civil war for ten years.

SOURCES:

Appian. *The Civil War.*

Bauman, Richard A. *Women and Politics in Ancient Rome.* NY: Routledge, 1992.

Cassius Dio. *The Roman History.*

Delia, Diana. "Fulvia Reconsidered," in *Women's History and Ancient History.* Ed. by Sarah B. Pomeroy. Chapel Hill, NC: University of North Carolina Press, 1991.

Hewsen, Robert. "Augustus," in *Historic World Leaders.* Ed. by Anne Commire and Deborah Klezmer. Detroit, MI: Gale Research, 1994.

"Octavia," in *Cambridge Ancient History.*

"Octavia," in *Oxford Classical Dictionary.*

Plutarch. "Marc Antony," in *Parallel Lives.*

Singer, Mary White. "Octavia's Mediation at Tarentum," in *Classical Journal.* Vol. 43, pp. 173–177.
Suetonius. "Life of Julius Caesar" and "Life of Augustus," in *Lives of the Twelve Caesars.*
Syme, Ronald. *The Roman Revolution.* NY: Oxford University Press, 1960.

Sylvia Gray Kaplan,
Adjunct Faculty, Humanities,
Marylhurst College, Oregon

Octavia (39–62 CE)

Roman empress. *Name variations: Olympia. Born around 39 CE; executed in 62 CE; daughter of the emperor Claudius, emperor of Rome (r. 10 BCE–54 CE) and his third wife Valeria Messalina (c. 23–48 CE); became first wife of Nero (37–68), emperor of Rome (r. 54–68), in 53 CE (divorced 62 CE).*

To ensure her son Nero's succession, ***Agrippina the Younger**—fourth wife of Claudius—arranged a marriage between the 16-year-old Nero and 11-year-old Octavia, daughter of Claudius and ***Valeria Messalina.** But Nero deserted Octavia for ***Acte**, and then for ***Poppaea Sabina.** Through Poppaea's jealousy, a charge of adultery was brought against Octavia, and she was sent to the island of Pandataria. While there, almost immediatelly following a notice of divorce, she was executed by order of Nero when she was only 22 years old. Shortly after, Nero married Poppaea. Although he seems to have cared for her as much as he cared for anyone, in 65 CE he killed Poppaea by kicking her in the stomach. Octavia is the heroine of *Octavia*, the only extant Roman historical play, or *fabula praetexta.* This tragedy has been attributed, probably wrongly, to Lucius Annaeus Seneca, the noted Stoic rhetorician and philosopher and Nero's tutor.

Oda (806–913)

Countess of Saxony. *Born in 806; died in May 913; daughter of Billung I and* **Aeda**; *married Liudolf (c. 806–866), count of Saxony, around 836; was the great-grandparent of Otto I the Great (912–973), king of Germany (r. 936–973), Holy Roman emperor (r. 962–973); children: Duke Bruno (killed in 880); Otto (c. 836–912), duke of Saxony;* ****Liutgard*** *(d. 885);* ****Hathumoda*** *(d. 874);* ****Gerberga*** *(d. 896);* ****Christine of Gandersheim*** *(d. 919).*

Oda (fl. 1000)

Queen of Poland. *Flourished around 1000; fourth wife of Boleslav Chrobry (967–1025), king of Poland (r. 992–1025).*

Oda of Bavaria (fl. 890s)

Holy Roman empress. *Flourished in the 890s; married Arnulf of Carinthia (b. around 863), king of Germany (r. 887–899), king of the East Franks, Holy Roman emperor (r. 896–899); children: Louis III the Child (b. 893), king of Germany (r. 899–911).*

Oda of Germany and North Marck (fl. 900s)

Duchess of Poland. *Second wife of Mieszko I, prince of the Polanians (d. 992); his first wife was* ****Dobravy of Bohemia.***

Oda of Lorraine (fl. mid-1000)

Countess of Brabant and Lorraine. *Flourished in mid-1000; died on October 23, year unknown; daughter of Gozelo I, duke of Lower Lorraine (r. 1023–1044); married Lambert II, count of Brabant and Louvain (d. after Sept 21, 1062); children: Henry II, count of Brabant and Louvain (d. 1078).*

Odam, Dorothy (b. 1920).

See Coachman, Alice for sidebar on Tyler, Dorothy J.

O'Day, Anita (1919—)

American jazz singer. *Name variations: Anita Colton. Born Anita Belle Colton on October 18, 1919, in Kansas City, Missouri (some sources cite Chicago); married Don Carter (a drummer, divorced); married Carl Hoff (a professional golfer, marriage ended); no children.*

A singer with the big bands of Gene Krupa and Stan Kenton during the 1940s, Anita O'Day established a new trend among female singers with her brilliant jazz improvisations. As a teenager during the Depression, she worked as a contestant in dance marathons and walkathons, in which the winners were the last couple able to remain on their feet. At age 19, she got her first professional singing job with the Max Miller combo at Chicago's Three Deuces club. In 1941, she was hired by Krupa, with whom she recorded her biggest hit, "Let Me Off Uptown." Other successful vocals, often shared with trumpet star Roy Eldridge, included "That's What You Think," "Thanks for the Boogie Ride," and "Boogie Blues." O'Day did a stint with Stan Kenton in 1944, recording the million-selling "And Her Tears Flowed Like Wine," among others, and then returned to Krupa for most of 1945. The following year, she embarked on a successful solo career.

Unlike most female big-band singers, O'Day refused to be pigeonholed into singing only love songs. When performing with Krupa, she frequently wore a jacket and tie, like the rest of the band, instead of a fancy gown. She also preferred to be called a "song stylist" rather than a singer, and often used her voice like an instrument, emphasizing the rhythm in a song and not merely the words. In 1956, she released her first full-length solo album, *Anita*, a success that was followed by 14 more albums on the Verve label. (A number of other albums were released on other labels.) Her performance two years later at the Newport Jazz Festival is included in the highly regarded 1958 documentary *Jazz on a Summer's Day*, which also features performances by Theolonius Monk, ***Mahalia Jackson**, Louis Armstrong and Big Maybelle (***Mabel Smith**). Beginning in 1964, O'Day made several tours of Japan, and later toured in Sweden and England as well. She also appeared at the Berlin festival in 1970. Her autobiography *High Times, Hard Times* (1981) details the harsh life she lived during the 1950s and 1960s (while still managing to perform remarkably well), which included longtime heroin addiction, an arrest for possession, illegal abortions, and bad relationships. She nearly died of a drug overdose in 1966, and finally quit heroin cold turkey in 1969. O'Day reached a career milestone in 1985 with a concert at Carnegie Hall celebrating her 50th year in jazz, and was still giving occasional performances in the late 1990s.

SOURCES:

Clarke, Donald, ed. *The Penguin Encyclopedia of Popular Music*. London & NY: Viking, 1989.

Kinkle, Roger D. *The Complete Encyclopedia of Popular Music and Jazz: 1900–1950*. New Rochelle, NY: Arlington House, 1974.

SUGGESTED READING:

O'Day, Anita, with George Eells. *High Times, Hard Times*, 1981.

Barbara Morgan,
Melrose, Massachusetts

O'Day, Caroline (1869–1943)

American congressional representative (January 3, 1935–January 3, 1943). *Born Caroline Love Goodwin on June 22, 1869, in Perry, Georgia; died on January 4, 1943, in Rye, New York; daughter of Sidney Prior Goodwin (a Confederate veteran and businessman) and Elia (Warren) Goodwin; graduated from Lucy Cobb Institute, Athens, Georgia, in 1886; married Daniel O'Day (an oil contractor), on April 30, 1901 (died 1916); children: Elia Warren (b. 1904); Daniel (b. 1906); Charles (b. 1908).*

Member of the New York State Board of Charities, later the State Board of Social Welfare (1923–35); chair of the women's division of the New York Democratic State Committee (1923–26); first vice-chair of the New York Democratic State Committee (1926–34); congressional representative at large for New York State (January 3, 1935–January 3, 1943).

Caroline O'Day, a four-term congressional representative from New York State and a champion for women's rights and human rights in the Democratic Party, was born on a Georgia plantation in 1869. The third of four daughters of a Confederate veteran, and the great-niece of a member of the Congress which rejected the so-called Crittenden compromise, a last-ditch effort to restrict slavery to a certain portion of the South and thus stave off the Civil War, she grew up in an area of Georgia that still bore the scars of Sherman's devastating "march to the sea" from Atlanta to Savannah, and biographers have speculated that this background was the source of her strongly held belief in pacifism. O'Day attended the Lucy Cobb Institute in Athens, Georgia, where she studied art and music and decided to pursue a career as an artist. After graduating, she studied art briefly in New York City before moving to Europe, where she supported herself by working as a magazine illustrator. In Paris, she studied with James McNeill Whistler, and exhibited work at the Paris Salons of 1899 and 1900. She also painted and studied in the Netherlands and in Munich.

Having apparently stopped painting, O'Day returned to New York City in 1901 and married Daniel O'Day, whom she had met in Paris. The son of an associate of oil tycoon John D. Rockefeller, Daniel served for a time as a vice-president of the Standard Oil Company, and later became an independent oil operator. With three young children by 1908, O'Day concerned herself mostly with her family during this time, although there were hints of the activism that would be a hallmark of her later life. She was active in the struggle for women's suffrage, a cause likewise backed by her husband, and supported American neutrality in World War I, holding peace meetings in her home prior to the country's entry into the war. Her strong stand on the issue of peace later prompted her to join the Women's International League for Peace and Freedom, an offshoot of the National Women's Party. O'Day became more deeply involved in New York politics and social welfare issues after the death of her husband in 1916. She volunteered at *Agnes E. Meyer's Maternity Center in New York City, and became active in the New York Consumers' League, the Women's Trade Union League, and *Lillian Wald's Henry Street Settlement on the Lower East Side, for which she served on the board of directors.

Caroline O'Day

O'Day joined the Democratic Party after women gained the right to vote in 1920, and in 1923 she was appointed by Governor Alfred E. Smith to the State Board of Charities (later the State Board of Social Welfare), a position she would hold until 1935. That year, she was also chosen to succeed **Harriett May Mills** as chair of the women's division of the Democratic State Committee. To organize women in New York, O'Day, her friend ***Eleanor Roosevelt**, **Nancy Cook** (1884–1962), and **Marion Dickerman** (1890–1983) between them (they traveled in pairs) visited each county in the state once a year. They also led groups of women to the legislature in Albany to show, and urge, support for Smith's progressive programs. O'Day was one of the main backers of the push to dissolve the women's division and include its functions within the main organization; after this merger, she served as first vice-chair of the Democratic State Committee. She worked for Smith's unsuccessful presidential campaign in 1928, and for Franklin D. Roosevelt's presidential campaign in 1932. She was later appointed state director of the National Recovery Administration by the newly elected Roosevelt.

O'Day was nominated for New York's at-large seat in the House of Representatives at the 1934 state Democratic Convention. According to *The New York Times*, her platform, in its entirety, was as follows: "higher standards for wage earners, adequate relief at lowest cost to the taxpayer, a power program of benefit to the consumer, a sound fiscal policy, friendly foreign relations and wider opportunity for women in government." First lady Eleanor Roosevelt received some criticism for stumping for her friend, but O'Day nonetheless beat 11 other candidates to win the 1934 election. The wide margin of her victory would be repeated in her re-elections in 1936, 1938, and 1940.

While serving in Congress, O'Day helped attach child labor amendments to the 1936 Walsh-Healy Act, which set employment standards for government contractors, and to the 1938 Fair Labor Standards Act, which fixed minimum ages for employment. She served on the Committee on Insular Affairs and the Committee on Immigration and Naturalization, and from 1937 to 1943 was chair of the Committee on Election of President, Vice President, and Representatives in Congress. She also chaired the committee that sponsored ***Marian Anderson**'s historic concert at the Lincoln Memorial on Easter Sunday, 1939, attended by some 75,000 people and arranged by Secretary of the Interior Harold Ickes after Anderson had been barred from performing at segregated Constitution Hall. O'Day supported all the major New Deal measures but, as a pacifist, voted against the repeal of the arms embargo portion of the 1939 Neutrality Act, which authorized arms sales to nations at war with Nazi Germany. Similar concerns led her to vote against the Selective Training and Service bill in 1940.

A popular representative who earned support with persuasive arguments and careful preparation of facts, and whose genuine concern for people of all stripes was repaid with loyalty and respect, O'Day declined to seek a fifth term due to health problems. She retired from Congress on January 3, 1943, and died of a cerebral hemorrhage the following day.

SOURCES:

James, Edward T., ed. *Notable American Women, 1607–1950.* Cambridge, MA: The Belknap Press of Harvard University Press, 1971.

The New York Times. November 7, 1934.

Office of the Historian. *Women in Congress, 1917–1990.* Commission on the Bicentenary of the U.S. House of Representatives, 1991.

Jacqueline Mitchell,
freelance writer, Detroit, Michigan

O'Day, Dawn (1917–1993).

See Montgomery, L.M. for sidebar on Anne Shirley.

Oddon, Yvonne (1902–1982)

French librarian who was a key member of the Musée de l'Homme network, the first important resistance organization to actively oppose the German occupation of France. *Born in France in 1902; died in 1982.*

When tourists to Paris visit the Eiffel Tower, many spend time at the Place du Trocadéro in order to get a panoramic view. Some will decide to enter the Musée de l'Homme located in the Palais de Chaillot, a museum known throughout the scholarly world. In this imposing building, inaugurated in 1937, exhibits explore all facets of humanity through the sciences of biological anthropology, paleoanthropology and prehistory, and ethnology. Now a division of France's Museum of Natural History, the Musée de l'Homme was intended as an experiment in popular education. Under its curator Paul Rivet, it also found itself enmeshed in the political strife of the troubled 1930s, given the fact that Rivet's scholarly beliefs in a common humanity, despite differences in cultural and external appearances, clashed with the racist ideologies of the day, particularly those embodied in France's increasingly arrogant neighbor, Nazi Germany.

The staff assembled by Rivet shared his commitment, including the museum's librarian, Yvonne Oddon. Diminutive in stature, Oddon came from a French Protestant family in a predominantly Catholic nation, making her particularly sensitive to the plight of those suffering from injustice or persecution. Oddon had embarked on a career in librarianship in the early 1920s, at a time when the field was just starting to open to women. After graduating from the American School in Paris in 1924, she studied under **Margaret Mann** at the Paris Library School, then followed Mann to the United States, when Mann was appointed a faculty member of the newly created University of Michigan Library School. During her two years on the Michigan library staff (1926–28), Oddon gained valuable experience in modern library methods, particularly in the areas of cataloguing and classification. In 1931, a few years after her return to France, she and Charles Henri Bach coauthored *Petit guide du bibliothécaire*, a useful guide which espoused Anglo-American cataloguing rules and advocated a simplified Dewey Decimal classification for small public libraries.

In 1934, a study visit to the Library of Congress in Washington, D.C., provided Oddon with additional information on American library theories and practices. Convinced that what she had learned in the States would be of value to French libraries, Oddon returned to Paris determined to implement significant reforms. Her opportunity came soon enough, when in 1937 she was appointed director of the library in the newly created Musée de l'Homme. Oddon had worked at the museum since 1929, when it was known as the Musée d'Ethnographie du Trocadéro (established in 1878), was housed in the old Trocadéro Palace, and had a collection that was largely old, dusty and mildewed. The reborn museum officially reopened in May 1937, at its new home situated in the gleaming white Palais Chaillot. Despite the skepticism of many of her colleagues, who argued that most libraries in France lacked adequate personnel to properly classify the books and maintain order in American-style open stacks, Oddon believed that on balance the system she had seen was superior; so she embarked on the task of classifying the sizable collection according to the Library of Congress method, the first time this approach was used in France.

In September 1939, the calm world of museum librarianship was shattered for Oddon and her colleagues. For the second time in a generation, France found itself at war with Germany. This time, unlike in 1914, many of the French populace harbored defeatist sentiments. In the final years of an increasingly fragile peace, many feared the domestic Left as much or more than Nazi Germany, bringing forth the slogan often heard on the Right, "Better Hitler than Blum." "Blum" referred to Léon Blum, the premier of the Popular Front government, a man who was anathema to many French conservatives and Fascists because he was both a Jew and a Socialist. At the Musée de l'Homme, Oddon and her colleagues paid close attention to the war news even though for more than eight months the French-German conflict was largely confined to border incursions and soon became known as "the Phony War." This ended dramatically on

May 10, 1940, when Hitler's legions attacked Belgium, the Netherlands, and France in a brilliantly conceived and executed display of *Blitzkrieg* tactics. Within days, French forces were in headlong retreat. When German troops entered Paris on June 18, the nation was in a state of profound shock.

In June 1940, only a small minority of French citizens entertained hope when they heard Charles de Gaulle, a little-known general, broadcast over the BBC: "I tell you that nothing is lost for France. One day—victory." The overwhelming majority decided to go on with their lives as if nothing had changed. For them, physical survival was sufficient. The new government, located in the southern French town of Vichy and headed by Marshal Henri-Philippe Pétain, a hero of World War I, and Pierre Laval, a political chameleon, was supported by most of the population for the simple reason that France had been so utterly defeated by the Germans that any form of resistance seemed futile. A not inconsiderable number of the French were enthusiastic supporters of Pétain and Laval, whose anti-Marxist, anti-Liberal ideology, summed up in the triad "Patrie, Travail, Famille," gave them hope for the restoration of traditional French cultural and moral values.

From the first phase of the German occupation, the staff of the Musée de l'Homme refused to accept France's defeat, and their attitude of defiance only seemed to grow. Even before France and Germany went to war in 1939, the Musée de l'Homme had engaged in a struggle with the spurious Nazi doctrine of Aryan supremacy and "superior" vs. "inferior" races of mankind. The museum's leading staff members were active in an organization founded by Rivet, the Vigilance Committee of Anti-Fascist Intellectuals. This group early discerned the dangers of racism, and tried to halt the spread of its doctrines within French academic circles. Even before war began, Oddon and the committee had used the museum's mimeograph machine to produce anti-Nazi manifestoes.

By then, Oddon was well known to archivists and librarians as a leading proponent of modern library science. She did not always take herself seriously, possessed a good sense of humor, and inspired both affection and respect among her closest colleagues, as well as the museum's hundred or so employees. Similar strength of character could be found in abundance in Oddon's colleagues at the Musee de l'Homme. Director Rivet, an authority on the American Indian, was a celebrity in French intellectual circles as well as an elected city official. His right-hand man was Anatole Lewitzky, a leading authority on Siberian shamanism. Russian-born, Lewitzky had accompanied his family to Switzerland after the Bolshevik revolution, but soon moved to Paris where like many White Russians he earned a living driving a taxi while he completed his university studies. Boris Vildé, a specialist in linguistics, was another Russian-born scholar. Vildé had lived in Germany in the early 1930s but had been disturbed by the rise of Nazism and fled to France after spending time in a German prison as a result of his beliefs. **Jacqueline Bordelet**, though she was only a part-time employee in the museum's typing pool, quickly became another member of the museum's inner circle. Working toward a graduate degree, Bordelet was in awe of Lewitzky, Oddon, Rivet and Vildé. Soon, her life and theirs would become intertwined.

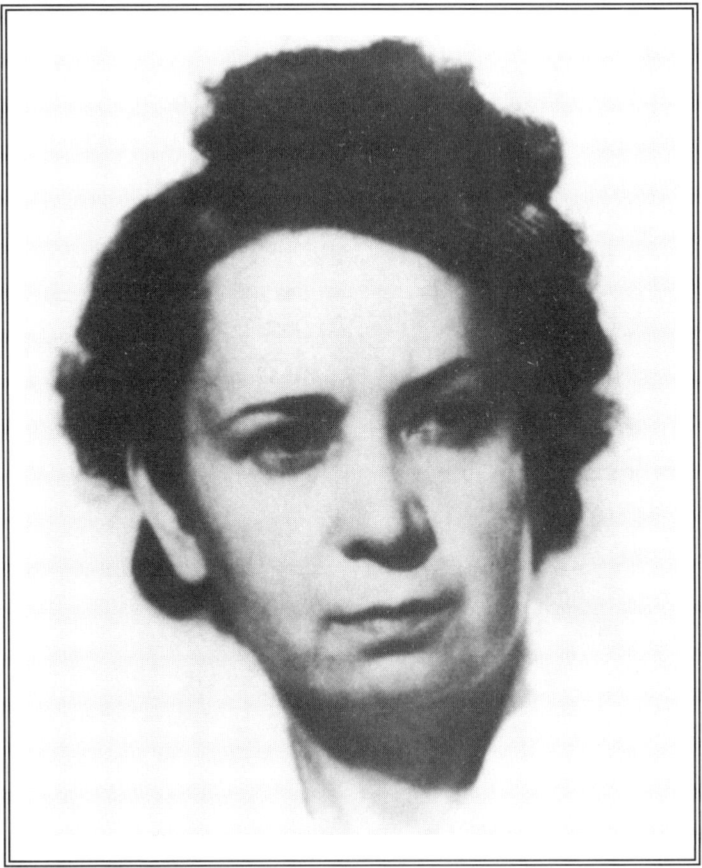

Yvonne Oddon

In the first months of the German occupation, Oddon spent much of her time at her desk in the museum's library on the third floor, sending books and clothing to prisoner-of-war camps. Soon she also found herself involved in harboring fugitives from the Germans, directing them to friends who could assist them in crossing the border to the unoccupied zone of the southern French provinces. Too busy to commute to the museum from her apartment in central Paris, Oddon slept on a couch in the basement office of her colleague Lewitzky, who had returned from his military service. Vildé too had now returned from his unit, and both he and Lewitzky soon noticed that Oddon was unusually busy, not only making telephone calls but receiving visits from people they had never before seen. These included **Josie Meyer** and **Penny Royall**, who were on the staff of the U.S. Embassy in Paris. Before long, Lewitzky and Vildé made it clear to Oddon that they had caught on to her activities and fully shared her sympathies. The trio spent hours devising ways to make contact with the Free French forces in London and collect information of military value for de Gaulle and the British.

As the weeks passed, the Musee de l'Homme network grew, becoming France's first important resistance group. One of its most active members would be the historian **Agnes Humbert**, who had long been a friend of Oddon's. A member of the staff of the Musée des Arts et Traditions Populaires—also situated in the Palais Chaillot—Humbert had been sickened by what was taking place at her museum, which included the purging of its library of books by Jewish authors, and the presence in its offices and corridors of pro-Pétain society women who were enthusiastic about France's "rejuvenation" under the regime of the octogenarian marshal. Humbert was able to recruit two additional intellectuals to the circle, Jean Cassou, director of the Museum of Modern Art, and Claude Aveline, a poet and author of children's books who had been a close friend of Anatole France. All members of the growing resistance circle were fully aware of the risks. For several members of the Musee de l'Homme organization, however, the danger was greatly magnified because they were Jews, including Aveline and Léon-Maurice Nordmann, a lawyer.

By September 1940, Vildé was the organization's leader, with Oddon and Lewitzky as his principal aides. In attempts to find a reliable method of contacting London, another museum staff member, René Creston, made three trips to Brittany. There, he recruited friends in the port city of Saint-Nazaire, which had become the site of a strategically vital German submarine base. Creston and his friends drew up maps and plans of the port and the base itself, particularly its vulnerable system of water locks. He then passed these documents on to the Musée de l'Homme group, who by now were in regular contact with British agents and French citizens who traveled to London. This crucially important intelligence data found its way to London, where it was evaluated and would be of great use to the Royal Air Force when the time came to bomb the German base at Saint-Nazaire (the base would be severely damaged in 1942). Unfortunately, several couriers were intercepted, thus alerting the Germans to the existence of an extensive French resistance circle.

Several other women played important roles in the museum network. Rivet's secretary, **Marie-Louise Joubier**, served as the typist and mimeograph operator for the sub-group led by Creston. She carried out her clandestine assignments in the museum's basement, for German officers and soldiers could be expected to show up unannounced in the Musée de l'Homme at any time, peeking into offices and wandering up and down corridors. There was also the pious **Madame Templier**, who owned a small shop in Auteuil where she sold religious books and articles. She had been discovered when she imprudently displayed General de Gaulle's portrait in her shop window. Alerted by Penny Royall, Oddon visited Templier's shop and persuaded her to be the network's "mailbox," where messages, papers and plans of various sorts could be left and picked up.

Other women whose activities complemented the network's overall strategy, which included strengthening contacts with newly emerging resistance groups, included the anthropologist ***Germaine Tillion**, as well as **Lucie Boutillier du Rétail**, and **Claire Oberge**. Military plans and false identification papers were prepared in the office of **Esperance Blain**, whose support came from a group of elderly women at the Paris City Hall, expert at pilfering ration cards. In the town of Béthune, war widow and garage owner **Sylvette Leleu**, assisted by the nurse Sister Marie Laurence (who had been born in Ireland as **Katherine MacCarthy**) were able to smuggle soldiers from German POW camps to safety, as well as relay military intelligence to Vildé. Other members of the Béthune unit of the network were café owner **Angeles Tardiveau** and the waitress known only as "**Mimi la Blonde.**" These women took great risks in smuggling prisoners out of German internment camps, and if possible facilitating their movement to neutral Spain and Portugal, or even directly to England.

By the fall of 1940, the Musée de l'Homme organization decided to publish a resistance newspaper, and, as a trial run, prepared a mimeographed pamphlet. Several thousand copies, carrying the title "Vichy Makes War!" and castigating the Pétain government, were discreetly dropped in mailboxes, placed near post office counters or on Métro trains, and slipped into goods displayed in department stores. The organization also made a large number of stickers bearing the legend "Vive de Gaulle," and stuck them all over Paris, in telephone booths, subway passageways, and even public urinals. On more than one occasion, members of the group followed a German staff car or truck, waited until it stopped at a traffic light, then affixed a resistance sticker to the vehicle.

Although a number of anti-German publications had already appeared in the summer and fall of 1940, with such titles as *Pantagruel*, *Maintenir*, *L'Homme Libre*, *L'Université Libre*, and *Libération*, the name chosen by the Musée de l'Homme network for its journal, *Résistance*, would take a special place in the history of the French underground movement. A crudely mimeographed news sheet printed on both sides of two pages, *Résistance* was grandly subtitled the "Official Bulletin of the National Committee for Public Safety." Printed by five young men in the town of Aubervilliers, it was produced in the rooms of the local Aeronautics Club. Its first official issue, released on December 15, 1940, called on the French people to:

> Resist! . . . To resist is to keep your heart and your head. But it is above all to act, to do something which yields positive results through useful and reasoned action. . . . Practice an inflexible discipline, a constant prudence, an absolute discretion. Beware of lightweights, those who talk too much, and traitors. . . . We have only one ambition, one passion, one wish: to accomplish the rebirth of a France that is pure and free.

By the time the third issue of the illegal newspaper appeared on January 31, 1941, the resistance circle's fate had been sealed. The arrest earlier that month of Léon-Maurice Nordmann, who had been distributing copies of *Résistance* despite the fact that as a Jew he was at far greater risk, marked the impending collapse of the Vildé organization. When he had attempted to find safety by escaping to England, Nordmann was betrayed by Albert Gaveau, a traitor who had infiltrated the highest reaches of the circle.

Relentlessly pursued by both French authorities and the German occupying forces, the Musée de l'Homme network began to unravel. Charged with having provided shelter for Nordmann, **Elisabeth de la Panouse**, Countess Bourdonnaye, was arrested. Only weeks after Nordmann's arrest, on February 10, 1941, Lewitzky and Oddon were also arrested by an SS officer and Gestapo agents. Vildé remained free for a short time, but he chose to surrender in the hope that he could convince the Germans that the responsibility for the Musée de l'Homme organization's activities was his and his alone.

The trial of Oddon, Vildé, Lewitzky and 16 other defendants began in Fresnes on January 8, 1942. The German presiding judge, Captain Ernst Roskothen, was not a Nazi and clearly sympathized with the defendants. But his powers were greatly circumscribed by the presence on the court of a Nazi, Captain Gottlob, who made clear that harsh verdicts were expected by Berlin. This would indeed be the case. Seven men, including Vildé, Lewitzky, and Nordmann, were condemned to death. Three of the women, Oddon, Leleu, and a student **Alice Simmonet**, were found guilty of espionage and also sentenced to be executed. The three other women on trial received varying sentences. Jacqueline Bordelet was acquitted and released. Sentenced to six months in prison, Countess Bourdonnaye was also released because of the time she had already spent in prison. Found guilty of anti-German crimes, Agnes Humbert was sentenced to five years' imprisonment, to be served in Germany. In her statement to the court after sentence was pronounced, Oddon simply noted that she was certain that she had acted as her father, who had died of wounds in battle during the First World War, would have wished. She had only done her duty to her country, and as far as she was concerned her conscience was clear.

On February 23, 1942, the seven condemned men were executed by firing squad. All refused blindfolds, and four of them went to their deaths singing the "Marseillaise" in unison. Even Gottlob appeared affected, noting, "They all died as heroes, even Nordmann." Fearing a public relations disaster if they were executed, a "compassionate" Nazi regime decided on appeal to commute the death sentences of Oddon, Leleu and Simmonet. The women were deported to Germany, where they spent the next three years in concentration camps. All survived their ordeals. Oddon returned home to Paris in 1945, where she resumed her career as chief librarian at the Musée de l'Homme. She remained self-effacing about her role in the Resistance and never published her memoirs. When the International Council of Museums (ICOM) was created in Paris in November 1946, it was given responsibility for UNESCO's Documentation Centre, designated the UNESCO/ICOM Documentation Centre. Oddon was appointed its first director. Under her leadership, this body went on to become a major resource center for museums, providing research services to museum professionals and researchers in all fields, as well as providing information to UNESCO headquarters in Paris and to member states of that U.S. subsidiary organization. Oddon also continued to head the library of the Musée de l'Homme, keeping up with the latest advances in library science. She retired from her library career in 1964, and died in 1982, one of the most celebrated heroines of the French Resistance.

SOURCES:

Bach, Charles Henri, and Yvonne Oddon. *Petit guide du bibliothécaire.* 3rd rev. ed. Paris: Éditions "Je Sers," 1948.

Blanc, J. "Germaine Tillion and the Musée de l'Homme Network: Early Work of the Resistance in Occupied France," in *Ésprit.* No. 2. February 2000, pp. 89–103.

Blumenson, Martin. *The Vildé Affair: Beginnings of the French Resistance.* Boston, MA: Houghton Mifflin, 1977.

Dank, Milton. *The French Against the French: Collaboration and Resistance.* Philadelphia, PA: J.B. Lippincott, 1974.

Ehrlich, Blake. *Resistance: France 1940–1945.* Boston, MA: Little, Brown, 1965.

Femmes dans la Résistance: Actes du Colloque tenu a l'initiative de l'Union des femmes françaises a la Sorbonne, les 22 et 23 novembre 1975. Paris: Éditions du Rocher, 1977.

Francos, Ania. *Il était des femmes dans la Résistance.* Paris: Stock, 1978.

Ghrenassia, Patrick. "Le Musée de l'Homme dans la Résistance," in *La Quinzaine littéraire.* No. 491. August 1–31, 1987, p. 15.

Guidez, Guilaine. *Femmes dans la guerre (1939–1945).* Paris: Perrin, 1989.

Humbert, Agnes. *Notre guerre: Souvenirs de Résistance, Paris 1940–1941.* Paris: Éditions Emile-Paul Frères, 1946.

Maack, Mary Niles. "Women Librarians in France: The First Generation," in *The Journal of Library History.* Vol. 18, no. 4. Fall 1983, pp. 407–449.

Michel, Henri. *The Shadow War: Resistance in Europe, 1939–1945.* Translated by Richard Barry. London: Deutsch, 1972.

Musée de l'Armée, Paris, General de Gaulle Wing. Permanent exhibit, "The Second World War, the Free French Forces and Fighting France, 1939–1945."

Oddon, Yvonne. "Une bibliotheque universitaire aux États-Unis," in *Revue du Livre et des Bibliotheques.* Vol. 3. June–August 1935.

———. "Une bibliotheque universitaire aux États-Unis: la bibliotheque de l'Université de Michigan," in *Revue des Bibliotheques.* Vol. 38, nos. 4–6, 1928, pp. 129–156.

———. *Elements of Museum Documentation (Elément de documentation muséographique).* Jos, Nigeria: The Jos Museum, 1968.

———. "Rapport sur mon activité de résistance," manuscript in the Musée de l'Homme Collection, Ellen Clarke Bertrand Library, Bucknell University, Lewisburg, Pennsylvania.

Roskothen, Ernst. *Gross-Paris 1941–1944: Ein Wehrmachtsrichter erinnert sich.* Rev. ed. Tübingen: Hohenrain-Verlag, 1989.

Rossiter, Margaret L. *Women in the Resistance.* NY: Frederick A. Praeger, 1986.

Rouquet, François. "Dans la France du Maréchal," in Christine Fauré, ed., *Encyclopédie politique et historique des Femmes: Europe, Amérique du Nord.* Paris: Presses Universitaires de France, 1997, pp. 663–684.

Schoenbrun, David. *Soldiers of the Night: The Story of the French Resistance.* NY: New American Library, 1981.

Tillion, Germaine. "Premiere Résistance en Zone Occupée (Du Côté du Réseau 'Musée de l'Homme-Hauet-Vildé')," in *Revue d'Histoire de la deuxieme Guerre Mondiale.* Vol. 8, no. 30. April 1958, pp. 6–22.

Weitz, Margaret Collins. *Sisters in the Resistance: How Women Fought to Free France, 1940–1945.* NY: John Wiley, 1995.

John Haag,
Associate Professor of History, University of Georgia, Athens, Georgia

Ode of Heristal (b. 586).

See Dode.

Odena, Lina (1911–1936)

Spanish Communist whose suicide when captured by the Nationalists made her a Spanish Republican martyr during the Civil War. *Name variations: Catalina Odena. Born Catalina Odena in Barcelona, Spain, in 1911; died in 1936.*

Born in Barcelona in 1911, Lina Odena joined the Communist Youth and became one of its leaders. She briefly visited the Soviet Union for training and indoctrination and then returned to Spain. Odena served as secretary-general of Catalonia's Communist Youth and later held a position on the national organization's secretariat.

When the Civil War broke out in July 1936, she joined government forces that put down an attempted military rising in Almería on July 20. In the following days, she worked as a reporter for the *Mundo Obrero.* Traveling through the province of Granada, Odena became lost and was seized by a detachment of Falangist troops. Before they completely understood the prize they had captured, Odena took out a pistol and shot herself in the head. Her suicide made Odena a Republican and Communist heroine. The government named a military unit and the center of the Unified Socialist Youths in Barcelona in her name.

SOURCES:

Estivill, Angel. *Lina Odena, la gran heroína de las juventudes revolucionarias de España.* Barcelona: Maucci, 1936.

Kahn, Evelyn. *Lina Odena: heroina del pueblo.* Madrid: Ediciones Europa-América, 1936.

Kendall W. Brown,
Professor of History, Brigham Young University, Provo, Utah

Odetta

Odetta (1930—)

Influential American folk singer. *Born Odetta Holmes on December 31, 1930, in Birmingham, Alabama; daughter of Reuben Holmes and Flora (Sanders) Holmes; graduated from Los Angeles City College; married Don Gordon, in 1959 (divorced); married Iversen Minter, in 1977; no children.*

The career of African-American folk singer and musician Odetta has spanned five decades and won her international fame. Born in 1930 in Birmingham, Alabama, she grew up in Los Angeles, California, with her mother **Flora Sanders Holmes** and her stepfather Zadock Felious. The family listened to the radio broadcast from the Metropolitan Opera on Saturdays because her mother loved opera, while her stepfather, who preferred popular music, frequently took her to hear black bands; they also enjoyed listening to the Grand Old Opry. Odetta sang and played piano from her earliest years, and when she was 13 her mother arranged for her to receive private lessons in classical voice. By the time she graduated from high school in 1947 she had decided to pursue a singing career. Her first professional work was in the chorus of the Broadway musical *Finian's Rainbow* in Los Angeles, when she was 19. She continued to work in summer musicals while completing a degree in music at Los Angeles City College and working as a housekeeper.

Odetta had initially been introduced to folk music by fellow chorus members in *Finian's Rainbow*. Drawn to the genre's political and social reform messages and its celebration of the working class, as well as to its roots in African culture, she taught herself how to play the guitar and began singing at parties and fund raisers. In 1952, she started to perform folk music at clubs in Los Angeles and San Francisco, including the latter city's Hungry i, and by the following year was booked for the first time at New York City's famous Blue Angel nightclub. She returned to New York City frequently throughout the decade, becoming a leader in the rebirth of folk music in Greenwich Village. Her early audiences responded to Odetta's powerful, soulful voice and emotionally charged music. Through the 1950s, her repertoire expanded into a number of genres, including spirituals, blues, jazz, and social protest songs. In 1952, she met folk singers Pete Seeger and Harry Belafonte, who both took an interest in furthering her career. With their help, Odetta released her first album, *The Tin Angel*, in 1954. Other records followed on the RCA, Riverside, and Tradition labels. She also acted in theater productions in the 1950s, as well as in several movies, including 1954's *The Last Time I Saw Paris*, with ***Elizabeth Taylor** and Van Johnson.

The decade of the 1960s was Odetta's most productive. As the "flower children" blossomed, she performed at folk festivals and in solo concerts across the United States, in addition to releasing 16 albums that were played throughout the nation. As her fame increased, Odetta came to influence the musical development of many prominent folk and rock musicians, including Bob Dylan and ***Janis Joplin**. She usually performed solo, accompanied only by her guitar, because she wanted the freedom to choose her material according to the responses of her audience rather than having to stick to a prearranged set.

The popularity of folk music as a whole decreased in the 1970s, although Odetta remained in demand by major folk festival promoters. She performed in England and toured in the Soviet Union and Eastern Europe. She also continued to act on occasion, appearing in "The Autobiography of Miss Jane Pittman" in 1974 and on other television shows. While Odetta released albums through the mid-1980s, the emergence of new musical genres and a trend away from acoustical music cost her much of her former popularity. She recorded no new albums between 1985 and 1999, although she continued to perform occasionally. Then, at age 69, Odetta began a comeback on the folk and blues music scene with a new studio album, *Blues Everywhere I Go*, on the Vanguard label. The record, which included several ***Bessie Smith** songs as well as what she happily called the "devilish" "You Gotta Know How," was nominated for a Grammy Award and a pair of W.C. Handy Awards. Along with a compilation of earlier songs, *Odetta: Best of the Vanguard Years*, also released in 1999, the album and her subsequent tour both introduced her music to younger audiences and renewed interest in her older work. That September, President Bill Clinton awarded Odetta the National Endowment for the Arts' Medal, in recognition of her central role in the folk-music revival and of her enormous impact on the development of several generations of musicians.

SOURCES:

Greenburg, Mark. "Power and Beauty: The Legend of Odetta," in *Sing Out!* Vol. 36, no. 2, Aug.–Sept.–Oct. 1991, pp. 2–8.

"Odetta Kicks Back" in *The Boston Globe.* March 17, 2000, pp. C15–C16.

Smith, Jessie Carney, ed. *Notable Black American Women.* Book II. Detroit, MI: Gale Research, 1996.

Southern, Eileen. *Biographical Dictionary of Afro-American and African Musicians.* Westport, CT: Greenwood Press, 1982.

Laura York,
Riverside, California

Odette de Pougy (fl. 1266)

Abbess of France at the convent of Notre-Dame-aux-Nonnains. *Flourished around 1266 in France; never married; no children.*

Odette de Pougy, whose origins are obscure, became a bold and ambitious French abbess. She entered the convent of Notre-Dame-aux-Nonnains as a young woman, and her force of character and leadership abilities led to her being chosen abbess there. In 1266, Odette became involved in a conflict with Pope Urban IV which would last until her death. The abbey was built on extensive grounds of which Odette, as abbess and thus principal manager of the abbey's property, was fiercely protective. The pope planned to build a church on a part of the abbey lands which had been the site of his father's shoe shop. He even went so far as to send a work crew to the site to begin construction.

Odette was strongly opposed to any infringement of the abbey's rights, and took decisive action. She led an armed party down to the construction site, frightened off Urban's crew, and tore down all they had erected. The pope did not give up on his plans to honor his father, and some time later another crew was set to work. Again Odette led a group against the workmen. This time Urban retaliated against the disobedient abbess by excommunicating her and every nun under her authority. But even this was not enough to frighten Odette into submission; she remained at the abbey, continuing her duties in blatant disregard of the excommunication, until her death about 15 years later. Urban had to wait until Odette had been buried before he could finally build his church.

SOURCES:

Gies, Frances, and Joseph Gies. *Women in the Middle Ages.* NY: Harper and Row, 1978.

Laura York,
Riverside, California

Odgive d'Angleterre (902–951).

See Edgifu.

Odilia (fl. 620)

Frankish abbess. *Flourished around 620 in Alsace; daughter of Adalric, a noble of Alsace; never married; no children.*

Odilia was the daughter of Adalric, a Frankish noble who encouraged her religious calling. She was either born blind or became blind as a child but, despite her disability, founded a nunnery on her father's lands in the Vosges Mountains above Hohenburg in Alsace and became its abbess. It was at the nunnery, where she lived with numerous other women in seclusion, that Odilia regained her sight, a miracle she felt was a reward from God for her deep devotion. The Alsatian convent soon became a destination for many pilgrims who were blind or afflicted with eye diseases, for it was believed that Odilia's sanctity could cure them. Little else is known about her.

Laura York,
Riverside, California

Odle, Mrs. Alan (1873–1957).

See Richardson, Dorothy M.

Odoevtseva, Irina (c. 1895–1990)

Russian novelist and poet. *Name variations: Iraida Gustavovna Heinecke (also seen as Geinike); Iraida Gustavovna Ivanova; Irina Odóevtseva or Irina Vladimorovna Odoyevtseva. Born Iraida Gustavovna Heinecke (also seen as Geinike) in 1895 (some sources cite 1901, but 1895 is generally considered more likely) in Riga, Latvia; died in October 1990; father was a lawyer and landlord; married Georgii Vladimirovich Ivanov (a poet), in September 1921 (died 1958); married Iakov Nikolaevich Gorbov (a novelist), in March 1978 (died 1982).*

Selected writings—novels: Angel smerti *(Angel of Death, 1927),* Izolda *(1931),* Zerkalo *(Mirror, 1939),* Naslediye *(Heritage, n.d.),* Ostav nadezhdu navsegda *(All Hope Abandon, 1954); poetry:* Dvor chudes *(Court of Wonders, 1922),* Kontrapunkt *(1951),* Stikhi napisannye vo vremya bolezni *(Verses Written While Ill, 1952),* Stikhi *(1960),* Desyat let *(Ten Years, 1961),* Odinochestvo *(Solitude, 1965),* Zlataya tsep *(The Golden Chain, 1975); memoirs:* Na beregakh Nevy *(On the Banks of the Neva, 1967),* Na beregakh Seny *(On the Banks of the Seine, 1983).*

Born Iraida Gustavovna Heinecke in Riga, Latvia, probably in 1895, Irina Odoevtseva (a pseudonym) was the youngest member of the St. Petersburg Poets Guild. Other members of the Guild included Georgii Ivanov, whom she married in September 1921, and Georgii Adamovich. She published her first volume of poetry, *Dvor chudes* (Court of Wonders), in St. Petersburg in 1922, after which she left Russia with her husband. They settled in Paris, where they were active in émigré literary circles, including ***Zinaida Gippius**' Green Lamp society, and by the 1930s her husband had become one of the most prominent émigré poets. During this period, Odoevtseva concentrated on writing prose, and published several novels, including *Angel smerti* (Angel of Death, 1927), *Izolda* (1931), and *Zerkalo* (Mirror, 1939). The public enjoyed these stories, which are usually classified as light reading rather than serious literature, and they were translated into several languages.

Odoevtseva and her husband lived comfortably on money provided by her father, and later by his estate, until the start of World War II. After the Nazis occupied France, and their home was bombed, lack of money for necessities forced them to sell many of their personal possessions. In the postwar years, both suffered from health problems, and sales of their literary works provided their sole, and erratic, income. Odoevtseva again began writing poetry during this time, although it was the money she obtained for her novel *Ostav nadezhdu navsegda* (All Hope Abandon, 1954) which enabled her and her husband to move to a retirement home in the south of France. Among her later collections of poetry were *Kontrapunkt* (1951), *Stikhi napisannye vo vremya bolezni* (1952), *Stikhi* (1960), *Desyat'et* (1961), and *Odinochestvo* (1965). This mature poetry was noted for its formal discipline, which contrasted sharply with its irony and combination of real and surreal images. After her husband's death in 1958, Odoevtseva moved to Gagny, near Paris, and joined the staff of the journal *Russkaia mysl'*. In 1967, she published a volume of literary memoirs, *Na beregakh Nevy* (On the Banks of the Neva). She married for a second time in March 1978, to novelist Iakov Gorbov, who died in September 1982. The following year, she published a second volume of memoirs, *Na beregakh Seny* (On the Banks of the Seine). She returned in 1987 to St. Petersburg (then called Leningrad), where a new interest in and appreciation of the cultural achievement of Russian émigrés was taking place; a selection of her poems was published in a Russian journal the following year. Irina Odoevtseva died in October 1990.

SOURCES:

Bede, Jean-Albert, and William B. Edgerton, general eds. *Columbia Dictionary of Modern European Literature*. NY: Columbia University Press, 1980.

Buck, Claire, ed. *The Bloomsbury Guide to Women's Literature*. NY: Prentice Hall, 1992.

SUGGESTED READING:

Foster, L.A. *Bibliografiia russkoi zarubezhnoi literatury, 1918–1968*. Boston: G.K. Hall, 1970.

Handbook of Russian Literature. New Haven, CT: Yale University Press, 1985.

Markov, V., and M. Sparks, eds. *Modern Russian Poetry*.

Odoevtseva, I.V. *Na beregakh Seny*. Paris: La Presse libre, 1983.

Sabova, A. "Snova na beregakh Nevy," afterword to I.V. Odoevtseva, *Na beregakh Nevy*. Moskva: Khudozhestvennaia literatura, 1988.

Struve, Gleb. *Russkaia literatura v izgnanii*. Paris: YMCA-Press, 1984.

COLLECTIONS:

The Irina Odoevtseva Papers are held in the general collection of the Beinecke Rare Book and Manuscript Library, Yale University, New Haven, Connecticut.

Jo Anne Meginnes,
freelance writer, Brookfield, Vermont

O'Doherty, Eileen (b. 1891).

See Shiubhlaigh, Maire Nic for sidebar.

O'Doherty, Eva (1826–1910).

See O'Doherty, Mary Anne.

O'Doherty, Mary Anne (1826–1910)

Irish poet. *Name variations: Eva O'Doherty; Eva Mary Kelly; Mary Anne Kelly; Mrs. Kevin Izod O'Doherty of Ireland. Born Mary Eva Kelly in Ireland in 1826; died in Brisbane, Australia, in 1910: married Kevin Izod O'Doherty (a medical practitioner and political activist), in 1854.*

Although popular during her time, Mary Anne O'Doherty is read today mainly for her historical significance. As Eva Kelly, she began her writing career in Ireland as a contributor of patriotic verse to the *Nation*, becoming known as "Eva of the *Nation*." Her engagement to medical practitioner and political activist Kevin O'Doherty was marked by his sentencing and transportation to Australia in 1848, so the marriage was postponed until he was freed in 1854. The couple lived in Paris and Dublin before finally settling in Brisbane, Australia, where O'-Doherty continued to write poetry while her husband practiced medicine and dabbled in politics. Two collections of O'Doherty's verse (both entitled simply *Poems*) were published during this time, the first in San Francisco in 1877 and the second in 1880. In 1886, the couple returned to Ireland, where Kevin served briefly as a member of the House of Commons. They subsequently returned to Queensland. O'Doherty's last volume of verse, *Selections*, was published in 1908, two years before her death.

SOURCES:

The Concise Dictionary of National Biography. Oxford: Oxford University Press, 1992.

Wilde, William H., Joy Hooten, and Barry Andrews. *The Oxford Companion to Australian Literature*. Melbourne, Australia: Oxford University Press, 1985.

Howard Gofstein,
freelance writer, Oak Park, Michigan

O'Donnell, Finula (fl. 1569–1592).

See Macdonald, Finula.

O'Donnell, Mary Stuart (fl. early 1600s)

Irish aristocrat and adventurer. *Born in England in the early 17th century; daughter of Rory also known* *as Ruaidhrí O'Donnell (1575–1608), 1st earl of Tirconnell (Tyrconnel or Tir Chonaill), and Brigid Fitzgerald; granddaughter of* ***Finula MacDonald;** married Dudley O'Gallagher (killed 1635); remarried, 1639.*

In the late years of the 16th century, Irish dissent against Queen ***Elizabeth I** was spearheaded by Ruaidhrí O'Donnell, a son of the chief of the O'Donnell clan, his brother Hugh Roe O'Donnell (known as Red Hugh), and Hugh O'Neill, the 3rd earl of Tyrone. After the rebels' disastrous loss at the battle of Kinsale in 1601, Roe fled the country, while O'Donnell and O'Neill accepted Elizabeth's sovereignty. In 1603, after Elizabeth's death and the accession of King James I, Ruaidhrí O'Donnell was created the 1st earl of Tirconnell. Five years later, a further plan hatched by the two earls for rebellion against British rule was betrayed, and they, along with numerous family members and supporters, hastily left Ireland for Rome, in what is known as the Flight of the Earls.

Sometime shortly thereafter was born Mary Stuart O'Donnell, the daughter of Ruaidhrí O'Donnell and **Brigid Fitzgerald.** When she was 12 years old, she was placed in the care of her grandmother in England. In 1626, when she was probably in her late teens, she rebelled against her grandmother's matchmaking plans by leaving her household. Dressed as a man, O'Donnell traveled with friends to the port of Bristol, and sailed for Brussels while still in disguise. In an era when women only rarely traveled alone, and then at risk because they lacked the protection of a man, she apparently enjoyed the benefits conferred by men's clothing, for she continued to dress as and present herself as a man for some time in Europe, much to the embarrassment of her brother Hugh. Little is known of her life after this time, although she was engaged for a time to an O'Neill, and married a man named Dudley O'Gallagher. He was killed in 1635, and four years later she married another Irishman, name unknown, with whom she lived impoverished in Rome.

SOURCES:

Cannon, John, ed. *The Oxford Companion to British History.* Oxford: Oxford University Press, 1997.

Newmann, Kate, comp. *Dictionary of Ulster Biography.* The Institute of Irish Studies, the Queen's University of Belfast, 1993.

Howard Gofstein,
freelance writer, Oak Park, Michigan

O'Donnell, Phyllis (1937—)

Australian surfer. *Born in New South Wales, in 1937.*

Phyllis O'Donnell took up the sport of surfing as a weekend activity while living in Sydney, then became serious about it after a move to the Gold Coast. At the time, she was one of only a handful of women surfers of note. O'Donnell won her first women's title at the Australian invitational held at Bondi in 1963. The following year, she won both the Australian championship and the first Women's World championship, held at Manly Beach. She won the Australian women's title again in 1965. Between 1964 and 1973, O'Donnell was Queensland's women's champion eight times, and during that period also represented Australia and defended her title in California and Hawaii.

Odoyevtseva, Irina Vladimirovna

(c. 1895–1990).

See Odoevtseva, Irina.

Odozi Obodo, Madam

(1909–1995)

Igbo woman who founded one of the leading indigenous independent churches in Igboland, the Christ Holy Church of Nigeria. *Name variations: Ngozi Okoh; Madam Okoh; Prophetess Odozi Obodo. Born Ngozi Ozoemena in 1909 in Onitsha, Igboland, Nigeria; died in Ndoni, Rivers state, Nigeria, in November 1995; only child of parents who were petty traders from Onitsha; married D.C. Okoh (a civil servant), in 1925; children: D.C. Okoh, Sr. (1935–1980, who ran the affairs of the church with his mother until his death); grandchildren: D.C. Okoh, Jr. (who took over the affairs of the church after his father's and grandmother's deaths).*

Was an illiterate housewife and petty trader; believed she was called by God to carry out God's ministerial work (1948); became a church minister, a preacher, a prophet, a spiritual healer, and head of a famous church in Nigeria; recognized for her spiritual powers by many, including the government of Rivers state of Nigeria which honored her twice (1988, 1992).

Women in Nigeria, especially in Igboland, have long played significant roles in both traditional religions, in which some serve as priestesses and diviners, and in Christian religions. Christianity first was brought to Igboland, in eastern Nigeria, by Simon Jonas, who visited Aboh in 1841. In 1957, a mission was established at Onitsha by Reverend John C. Taylor of the Church Missionary Society, who was followed to the area on December 8, 1885, by two

Roman Catholic missionaries. Finally, the Presbyterian Church established its first mission in Igboland at Uwana in 1888. From these centers, various denominations of Christianity spread throughout Igboland. Common to each branch were activities of Christian missionaries which tended to perpetuate the status of Igbo (Ibo) women as second-class citizens. As they did throughout the world, the churches emphasized women's wifely duties and attempted to lessen their roles outside the home. N. Mbanefo writes:

> The place of women within Christianity throughout its history has important similarities to Islam in its stress on the domestic role of women and their public subordination. Christianity provided women with a large but a subordinate public role in religion but stressed their domestic duties as against the independent occupations which they had been expected to pursue in many pre-colonial Nigerian societies.

Women were rarely allowed to take part in the decision-making of the various churches, and even those who had acquired a Western education were denied administrative positions. They were not made priests or clerics, and the most active role they were permitted (which many took advantage of) was participation in women's associations. Possibly in response to this exclusion, women played a major role in the establishment of indigenous independent churches in Igboland. Among these churches or religious sects founded by women, there is none as widespread and famous as the Christ Holy Church of Nigeria founded by Madam Odozi Obodo.

She was born Ngozi Ozoemena in 1909 in Onitsha, Igboland, Nigeria, and married D.C. Okoh, a civil servant, in 1925. In 1943 at Enugu, she heard a "divine call," a voice repeatedly referring her to "Matthew, 10." Because she was newly converted and illiterate, it was only through a friend that she learned that the phrase referred to a passage in the Bible. In the King James version, Matthew 10:1 reads:

> And when he had called unto *him* his twelve disciples, he gave them power *against* unclean spirit, to cast them out, and to heal all manner of sickness and all manner of disease.

Believing this to be her mission, Ngozi Okoh became Madam Odozi Obodo—*Odozi Obodo* means reconstructor of community—and began a prayer ministry that would grow to become the Christ Holy Church of Nigeria.

Odozi Obodo's ministry initially had no name. During the Nigerian Civil War (1967–70), it became known as the Odozi Obodo Church. After the war, prevailing hardship caused many people to seek solace in *Aladura* or spiritual churches (in which prophetesses and prophets, through visions, offer solutions for people's earthly problems). Odozi Obodo's church expanded to embrace non-Igbo-speakers, and in recognition of these new members its name was changed to Christ Holy Church of Nigeria. Madam Odozi Obodo, who became known as Prophetess, was believed by her followers to be endowed with great spiritual power and the ability to bring to the people messages from God and angels. Through prayers, fasting, and intercession, she is said to have solved problems afflicting followers ranging from disease to poverty to barrenness to troubled relationships, and these results won further converts to her ministry. Church members credited her with the power of prophecy and with having prophesied about individuals, the church community, and even national issues. Her preaching was usually conducted in the Igbo language, and her ability, as an illiterate, to read the Igbo-language Bible baffled her followers, and thus was interpreted as a miracle. Her essential message was that with "faith in God" all things are possible.

There are seven levels in the hierarchy of Christ Holy Church. At the apex of the pyramid is Odozi Obodo as the church founder, followed by the Most Reverend (a position which has been occupied only by her son and grandson). Beneath these, in descending order, are General Superintendent, Superintendent, Missionaries (Reverends, Evangelists and Elders), Prophetesses, and members. Despite the fact that the church was founded by a woman, the only rank above member available to women is that of prophetess, which they occupy by virtue of being endowed with spiritual and prophetic powers. Male members ascend the hierarchy either through spiritual membership (which begins with the position of Evangelist-Catechist and culminates in Most Reverend) or regular membership, the highest rank of which is Elder of the church. Membership is obtained either through conversion or by birth; in both cases it is authenticated by the sacrament of baptism, which is usually administered only when the follower has reached adulthood.

Odozi Obodo retired from active ministerial work in 1976, although she reportedly continued to perform miracles, healing sick people who visited her at Ndoni. It is said that in 1988 she helped a man who had been blind since childhood regain his sight. That same year, and again in 1992, she was honored by the Rivers state government of Nigeria. She also has been credited for uplifting the religious, educational, and economic status of a number of Igbo and Nigerians. By 1995, the year Madam Odozi Obodo died, the church could claim a following in the hundreds of thousands; it is headquartered at Onitsha, and some 300 branches are scattered throughout Nigeria, in cities including Lagos, Ibadan, Benin, Calabar, Enugu, Aba, Owerri, and Port-Harcourt, and even in the Muslim-dominated cities of Jos, Kano, and Kaduna, Kano. Odozi Obodo's grandson, the Most Reverend D.C. Okoh, Jr., who became head of Christ Holy Church after her death, once explained the church's rapid expansion thus:

> People have seen what God is using mama [Odozi Obodo] to do, performing all sorts of miracles, ranging from child delivery, barrenness, marriage problems, illnesses, diseases to hardship. And, therefore, they are attracted to the church for they have seen and believed that mama is worshiping a Living God. They know that their benefit from their membership of the church does not end with solving their worldly problems, but also includes having salvation and eternal life. Even now that mama has retired, God is still using the ministers to do the same work.

SOURCES:

Chuku, G.I. "Sex Roles in an Indigenous African Church: A Historical Sketch of Christ Holy Church of Nigeria," paper presented at the 3rd Annual Conference of the Center for Igbo Studies, on "Religion and Development in Igboland," at Abia State University, Uturu, Nigeria, July 7–9, 1994.

Crumbley, D.H., "Even a woman: Sex Roles and Mobility in an Aladura Hierarchy," in *West African Journal of Archaeology.* Vol. 15. 1985, pp. 130–137.

Ilogu, E. *Christianity and Igbo Culture: A Study of the Interaction of Christianity and Igbo Culture.* Enugu, Nigeria: Nok Publishers, 1974.

Mbanefo, N. "Colonialism and Urban Participation in the Labour Force," paper presented at the conference on the "Impact of Colonialism on Nigerian Women," Institute of African Studies, University of Ibadan, Nigeria, October 16–19, 1989.

SUGGESTED READING:

Ayandele, E.A. *The Missionary Impact on Modern Nigeria, 1842–1914.* London: Longman, 1966.

Ekechi, F.K. *Missionary Enterprise and Rivalry in Igboland, 1857–1914.* London: Frank Cass, 1971.

Osinulu, C. "Religion and the status of Nigerian women," in F.A. Ogunsheye *et al.*, eds., *Nigerian Women and Development.* Ibadan, Nigeria: Ibadan University Press, 1988, pp. 423–432.

Gloria Ifeoma Chuku, Ph.D.,
Lecturer in History, School of Humanities,
Imo State University, Owerri, Nigeria

Oelrichs, Blanche (1890–1950).

See Strange, Michael.

Offaley, Baroness (c. 1588–1658).

See Digby, Lettice.

Ogier, Bulle (1939—)

French actress. *Born in Boulogne-sur-Seine, France, in 1939; married; children: one daughter, Pascale Ogier (1960–1984), also an actress.*

Selected filmography: L'Amour fou *(1968);* Pauline s'en va *(1969);* Pierre et Paul *(1969);* Piège *(1969);* Les Stances à Sophie *(*Sophie's Ways, *1970);* La Salamandre *(*The Salamander, *1971);* Rendez-vous à Bray *(1971);* La Vallée *(*The Valley, *1972);* La Charme discret de la Bourgeoisie *(*The Discreet Charm of the Bourgeoisie, *1972);* Le Gang des Otages *(*The Hostages, *1973);* Io e lui *(It., 1973);* Projection privée *(1973);* Céline et Julie vont en Bateau *(*Celine and Julie Go Boating, *1974);* La Paloma *(1974);* Mariage *(*Marriage, *1975);* Un Divorce Heureux *(1975);* Maîtresse *(*Mistress, *1975);* Jamais plus toujours *(1976);* Duelle *(1976);* Serail des Journées entières dans les Arbres *(*Days in the Trees, *1976);* Le Navire Night *(1979);* La Mémoire courte *(Bel.-Fr., 1979);* Die dritte Generation *(*The Third Generation, *Ger., 1979);* Agatha et les Lectures limitées *(1981);* Le Pont du Nord *(also co-sc., 1982);* La Derelitta *(1983);* Tricheurs *(1984);* O Meu Case *(*Mon cas, *Port.-Fr., 1986);* Das weite Land *(Ger., 1987);* Candy Mountain *(Can.-Switz.-Fr., 1987);* La Bande des Quatre *(1989);* North *(1991);* Personne ne M'Aime *(*No One Loves Me, *1994);* Regarde les Hommes Tomber *(1994);* Irma Vep *(1996).*

A French stage star and a pioneer of the café-theatre movement, Bulle Ogier made her film debut in *L'Amour fou* (1968) and subsequently found a niche interpreting unconventional roles in the films of the French New Wave. She appeared in Luis Buñuel's surreal fable *The Discreet Charm of the Bourgeoisie* (1972) and was notable as the compassionate dominatrix in Barbet Schroeder's *Mistress* (1976). Ogier's daughter, **Pascale Ogier**, also an actress, died at age 24, shortly after winning the Best Actress award at Cannes for her role in *Les Nuits de la Pleine Lune* (*Full Moon in Paris,* 1984).

Ogiva.

Variant of Ogive.

Ogive (902–951).

See Edgifu.

Ogive of Luxemburg (d. 1030)

Countess of Flanders. *Name variations: Ogiva; possibly Orgina. Died in 1030; daughter of Frederick (c. 965–1019), count of Luxemburg; sister of* ****Imagi of Luxemburg*** *(c. 1000–1057); was first wife of Baldwin*

IV (c. 980–1035), count of Flanders (r. 988–1035); children: Baldwin V the Pious (b. around 1012), count of Flanders.

Ogot, Grace (1930—)

Kenyan author and politician who is considered an outstanding member of Kenya's (and East Africa's) first generation of writers. *Born Grace Emily Akinyi on May 15, 1930, at Butere, near Kisumu, Central Nyanza, Kenya; married Bethwell Allan Ogot (a noted Kenyan historian), in 1959; children: daughter, Wasonga Grace; sons, Odera-Akongo, Otieno Mudhune, Onyuna.*

Selected works: The Graduate *(Nairobi: Uzima, 1980);* The Island of Tears *(Nairobi: Uzima, 1980);* Land Without Thunder *(Nairobi: East African Publishing, 1968);* The Other Woman: Selected Short Stories *(Nairobi: Transafrica, 1976);* The Promised Land: A True Fantasy *(Nairobi: East African Publishing, 1966);* The Strange Bride *(Nairobi: Heinemann Kenya, 1989).*

One of Kenya's most distinguished artists, Grace Ogot creates worlds that blend magic and reality. In her life as well, she achieved success in contexts that are both African and Western. She was born Grace Akinyi in 1930 into a Luo-speaking family. While being lulled to sleep as a child, she would listen to traditional folktales told by her paternal grandmother, who was a renowned storyteller in the area. An influence at least as powerful as these ancient African stories were the Bible stories read to her by her father, a teacher of religion. At school, she said, she "extremely enjoyed" the compulsory storytelling lessons, and after reading whatever "little booklets I could lay a hand on," she discovered that some of the stories she had written herself compared favorably to what she had just read. In 1949, she began instruction as a nurse at the training hospital at Mengo, near Kampala, in Uganda, where she received her degree in 1953. In 1955, she went to London where she completed a three years' course of additional training at the British Hospital for Mothers and Babies.

Grace had definite opinions as to what constituted good writing, but never considered writing anything for publication until after her 1959 marriage to noted Kenyan historian Bethwell Allan Ogot. Although both she and Bethwell were highly educated, Grace's bride price was traditionally East African: 25 head of cattle. Ogot would give birth to four children over the next years, but from the start of her marriage she nonetheless was determined to have a career, initially working as a broadcaster, scriptwriter, and editor for the BBC Africa Service in London. Even before she mustered the courage to submit her writing to a publisher, Ogot was encouraged by her husband, who was convinced of her literary talent. But the decisive moment for Ogot's future writing career came in 1962, when she was about to start as a nursing sister in charge of student health services at Makerere University College in Uganda. Attending a campus conference on African writers, she was both disappointed and challenged when it became clear that book exhibits from East Africa were lacking. Obviously, something needed to be done to create a viable literary tradition in East Africa, particularly in her home nation of Kenya, which had just received its independence. Along with other East Africans present, including **Ngugi wa Thiong'o**, Ogot was determined to change the situation. Having read her short story "A Year of Sacrifice" at the Makerere conference, Ogot did another draft and submitted it to the journal *Black Orpheus*, which published it in 1963. (The story would be included in the 1968 book *Land Without Thunder* under the title "The Rain Came.")

Ogot initially wrote short stories in her first language, Luo; she would also write in Kiswahili and English, the two official national languages of Kenya. In 1966, her book *The Promised Land*, the first novel by a Kenyan woman writer and a work of lasting substance, was issued by Nairobi's East African Publishing House. In the novel, Nyapol, a young Luo woman, reveals an independent streak after her marriage to Ochola, her sympathetic but impractical husband. They attempt to escape poverty by migrating to Tanzania where farming will bring them prosperity. For a while, Tanzania's "promised land" lives up to its name, but jealous neighbors, led by a witch doctor who casts a spell, appear to bring on troubles for the couple when the husband comes down with a terrible skin affliction. Only when he decides to return to Kenya is Ochola cured of his mysterious disease. Throughout *The Promised Land*, Ogot characterizes Nyapol's conduct as an example of traditional Kenyan cultural values; she is a dutiful wife who protects and follows her husband. Similar characters appear in *The Other Woman*, a collection of short stories published in 1976. Above all else, preservation of the family is more important than the achievement of personal happiness, autonomy, or self-fulfillment.

Despite the positive responses she received from critics and a small but enthusiastic Kenyan reading public, from the start of her career

Grace Ogot had to budget her writing time carefully; customarily, she set weekends aside for that purpose. An assured source of income came from her column in the *East African Standard.* During the week, she raised her children and carried out community work, such as serving as a member of the Nairobi Rent Tribunal. For years, she also owned and managed "Lindy's," a downtown Nairobi specialty shop for babies and girls. As well, she worked for a period for the "Voice of Kenya," broadcasting a weekly radio magazine in both Luo and Kaswahili. She was a public relations officer for the Air India Corporation of East Africa, and served as founding chair of the Writer's Association of Kenya.

In 1975, Ogot served as a Kenyan delegate to the United Nations General Assembly. In October 1983, Kenyan President Daniel arap Moi appointed her a member of the nation's Parliament. Ogot displayed considerable independence in July 1985, when she resigned her presumably safe seat as a nominated M.P. to successfully contest the Gem constituency in a by-election. This was the first time in Kenyan history that a nominated M.P. had resigned from Parliament in order to seek an electoral mandate. Since then, Ogot has published little, but she has remained active in the intellectual life of Nairobi. While she had emerged by the 1980s as the doyenne of progressive society in the nation's capital, Ogot's position in a nation that remains profoundly traditional is complex at best. Although her writings present strong women who at the same time remain embedded in a traditional tribal social order, she has taken pains to avoid a feminist label.

The dilemma of Kenyan feminists surfaced in 1987 in a court struggle waged by a Kenyan widow, **Wambui Otieno**. Wambui, wife of prominent criminal lawyer S.M. Otieno, caused a national storm over customary law, women's rights, and intertribal marriages. After the death of her husband, a Luo, in December 1986, she planned to bury him in Nairobi, where the couple had lived and raised 15 children, and where he had had a successful career. Even though S.M. Otieno had requested that he be buried in Nairobi, his clan took the matter to court to challenge his widow and heirs. After a series of court cases involving 12 separate actions, including appeals, the authorities awarded custody of S.M. Otieno's remains to his clan to be taken to his birthplace in Western Kenya for burial according to Luo custom.

Soon after the court decision, Ogot publicly complained about the exclusion of widows from

Grace Ogot

Luo decision-making regarding funerals, arguing that Kenyan women desired changes in the traditions and that widows should be respected. At this time, the National Council of Women of Kenya (NCWK), an umbrella organization of women's groups, was mounting a campaign to reform the flaws in the nation's statutes pertaining to the rights of women. Ogot's public statement was just what the NCWK needed in order to legitimate its campaign. As Kenya's most eminent Luo woman in public life, and one of only two women members of Parliament at the time, as well as an internationally respected author, Ogot, it seemed clear, would be a key ally in the struggle. This hope was illusory. When posters with her picture were displayed in the booths set up across Nairobi for the NCWK campaign, which aimed to collect a million signatures on a petition to be presented to both the attorney general and the Law Reform Commission on the matter of new legislation for spousal and next-of-kin rights on funerals, Ogot was outraged. She noted with displeasure that she had not been asked for permission to use her picture in the campaign, and in her capacity as an assistant minister in the government she ordered police to remove the posters. Apparently acting on their own initiative, police took matters further and arrested (and briefly jailed) two young volunteers who had been engaged in the solicitation of signatures. **Wangari Maathi**, NCWK chair, apologized to Ogot while at the same time denying that her organization had meant to be disrespectful. With the signature booths gone, and police displeasure at the entire effort at reform evident to one and all, the campaign fizzled out by late February 1987, after having been able to gather only 4,000 signatures.

Ogot took pains to distance herself from the position of the NCWK in the burial controversy. In a letter published in the *Weekly Review*, she qualified the statements she had made earlier, asserting: "I reminded all married women always to remember that the husbands they loved had a mother, father, sisters and brothers and the extended family who also loved him, and all were entitled to share the joys and sorrows of the family." In many ways, Ogot's comments in the Otieno burial controversy revealed the contradictions facing the handful of Kenyan women who, like herself, had chosen a career in public life. She was expected to be a voice for the nation's women, and indeed this had been the basis of her first, appointed, term of parliamentary service. At the same time, however, she was also expected to serve her political constituencies, which in Kenya meant vigorously upholding the interests of the ethnic and tribal voters who made her career possible. Forced to choose between her commitment to women's progress and her loyalty to her Luo constituency, she chose the latter. In political terms, this was doubtless the only rational choice. Notes scholar **Patricia Stamp**: "As [Kenyan] ethnic politics increasingly rely on more stringently controlled and patriarchal gender relations, it appears impossible for a democratically elected woman to espouse feminist causes."

In her writings, however, Ogot has made a strong case for viewing Kenya's women in a new light. Self-assertive women triumph on the pages of her books over the forces of patriarchy and male cruelty, violence, and ineptitude. In "The Middle Door," the heroine Mrs. Muga whips out a toy pistol and by sheer bluff disarms a couple of policemen intent on raping her. In the story "The Empty Basket," men are confused and indeed panic-stricken when a huge snake is discovered in Aloo's room. Aloo, however, is able to retain her presence of mind and thus rescue her baby from danger. Sometimes the heroic protagonists created by Ogot represent an emerging myth of new Kenyan womanhood that is part of a spirit of national self-assertion. Along with other women Kenyan writers, such as Ngugi wa Thiong'o and **Micere Wa Mugo**, Ogot has written about female heroism during the Kenyan War of Independence (customarily called the Mau Mau Insurrection by the British). These women depicted not only in "The Middle Door" but also in *The Graduate* are based on real-life personalities, but they also fill the need for a unifying national mythology. Kenya's Jomo Kenyatta also worked to create the tradition of a nationwide struggle for freedom based on his slogan, "*Tulipigania kama simba*" ("We fought like lions"). Although only a minority of Kenyans had taken up arms against the British, Kenyatta's sense of national pride was shared by Ogot and other Kenyan intellectuals who were determined in the years after the achievement of independence in 1963 to create unifying national traditions.

In this effort to mold a strong national spirit, Ogot has played a significant and lasting role. In her novels and short stories, she has attempted to relate the rich traditions of Luo history and folklore to the younger generation of Kenyans. Strongly influenced by the oral traditions, she has blended experiences and events into freshly conceived stories. Although Ogot is aware of how powerful—and sometimes destructive—the forces of change are in today's Africa, she remains convinced of the enduring values embodied in her own Luo beliefs and traditions. Whatever judgments history will one day render on Grace Ogot's political career, there can be little doubt that as a writer, and as her nation's first woman novelist, she has left a mark on her nation's spiritual evolution and will very likely be seen by posterity as a major figure in the intellectual life of contemporary Kenya.

SOURCES:

Achufusi, Grace Ify. "Conceptions of Ideal Womanhood: The Example of *Bessie Head and Grace Ogot," in *Neohelicon*. Vol. 19, no. 2, 1992, pp. 87–101.

Achufusi, Ify. "Problems of Nationhood in Grace Ogot's Fiction," in *Journal of Commonwealth Literature*. Vol. 26, no. 1, 1991, pp. 179–187.

Berrian, Brenda F. "Grace Ogot (15 May 1930—)," in Bernth Lindfors and Reinhard Sander, eds., *Dictionary of Literary Biography*, Vol. 125: *Twentieth-Century Caribbean and Black African Writers*. 2nd Series. Detroit, MI: Gale Research, 1993, pp. 184–187.

———, ed. *Bibliography of African Women Writers and Journalists: Ancient Egypt–1984*. Boulder, CO: L. Rienner, 1985.

Brown, Lloyd Wellesley. *Women Writers in Black Africa*. Westport, CT: Greenwood Press, 1981.

Bruner, Charlotte H., ed. *Unwinding Threads: Writing by Women in Africa*. 2nd ed. Oxford, UK: Heinemann, 1994.

Burness, Donald. "Grace Ogot," in *Wanasema: Conversations with African Writers.* Athens, OH: Ohio University Monographs in International Studies, Africa Series, 1985, pp. 59–66.

Condé, Maryse. "Three Female Writers in Modern Africa: ***Flora Nwapa, Ama Ata Aidoo** and Grace Ogot," in *Présence Africaine.* No. 82, 1972, pp. 132–143.

Flanagan, Kathleen. "African Folk Tales as Disruptions of Narrative in the Works of Grace Ogot and ***Elspeth Huxley**," in *Women's Studies.* Vol. 25, no. 4, 1996, pp. 371–384.

Ganguly, Shailaja. "An Afternoon with Grace Ogot," in *Femina.* September 8–22, 1979, p. 39.

Lindfors, Bernth. *Mazungumzo: Interviews with East African Writers, Publishers, Editors, and Scholars.* Athens, OH: Ohio University Monographs in International Studies, Africa Series, 1981.

Matzke, Christine. "Ogot, Grace Emily Akinyi," in Ute Hechtfischer *et al.*, eds., *Metzler Autorinnen Lexikon.* Stuttgart and Weimar: Verlag J.B. Metzler, 1998, pp. 397–398.

Mohr, Norma. "The Many Windows of Grace Ogot," in *Africa Report.* Vol. 17, no. 7. July–August 1972, pp. 21–22.

Moore, Gerald. "The Language of Literature in East Africa," in *The Dalhousie Review.* Vol. 53, no. 4. Winter 1973–74, pp. 688–700.

Mwanzi, Helen. *Notes on Grace Ogot's* Land Without Thunder. Nairobi: Heinemann, 1982.

Nichols, Lee. *African Writers at the Microphone.* Washington, DC: Three Continents, 1984.

Nnaemeka, Obioma. "From Orality to Writing: African Women Writers and the (Re)Inscription of Womanhood," in *Research in African Literatures.* Vol. 25, no. 4. Winter 1994, pp. 137–157.

Ogot, B.A., and W.R. Ochieng, eds. *Decolonization and Independence in Kenya, 1940–93.* Athens, OH: Ohio University Press, 1995.

Ogot, Grace. "The African Writer," in *East Africa Journal.* Vol. 5. November 1968, pp. 35–37.

Ogunyemi, Chikwenye Okonjo. "Womanism: The Dynamics of the Contemporary Black Female Novel in English," in *Signs: Journal of Women in Culture and Society.* Vol. 11, no. 1, 1985, pp. 63–80.

Oladele, Taiwo. *Female Novelists of Modern Africa.* NY: St. Martin's Press, 1985.

Reid, Margaret A. "Conflict or Compromise: The Changing Roles of Women in the Writings of Rebekah Njau and Grace Ogot," in *MAWA Review.* Vol. 5, no. 2, 1990, pp. 51–55.

Stamp, Patricia. "Burying Otieno: The Politics of Gender and Ethnicity in Kenya," in *Signs: Journal of Women in Culture and Society.* Vol. 16, no. 4, 1991, pp. 808–845.

Stratton, Florence. *Contemporary African Literature and the Politics of Gender.* London: Routledge, 1994.

Tsuchiya, Satoru. "Modern East African Literature: From *Uhuru* to *Harambee*," in *World Literature Today.* Vol. 52, no. 4, 1978, pp. 569–574.

Zell, Hans, Carol Bundy, and Virginia Coulon, eds. *A New Reader's Guide to African Literature.* 2nd rev. ed. London: Heinemann, 1983.

John Haag,
Associate Professor of History, University of Georgia, Athens, Georgia

O'Hagan, Mary (1823–1876)

Religious leader who founded the Convent of Poor Clares, Kenmare, Ireland. *Born in Belfast, Ireland, in 1823; died in Kenmare, Ireland, in 1876.*

Born in 1823 in Belfast, Ireland, and devoting her life to the Sisters of Poor Clares, Mary O'Hagan entered the convent in Newry in 1844, when she was 21, becoming abbess there in 1853. In 1861, she established another convent of Poor Clares in Kenmare, where she also served as abbess until her death in 1876.

O'Hair, Madalyn Murray (1919–1995)

American lawyer, atheist philosopher, and social activist. *Born Madalyn Mays on April 13, 1919, in Pittsburgh, Pennsylvania; murdered in 1995; daughter of John Irvin Mays (a civil engineer) and Lena C. (Scholle) Mays; attended University of Toledo, 1936–37, University of Pittsburgh, 1938–39; Ashland College, B.A., 1948; graduate study at Western Reserve University (now Case Western Reserve University), 1948–49, and Ohio Northern University, 1949–51; awarded LL.B, South Texas College of Law, 1953; J.D., South Texas College of Law, 1954; M.P.S.W., Howard University, 1954–55; Ph.D., Minnesota Institute of Philosophy, 1971; married J. Roths, in 1941 (divorced); married William J. Murray (divorced 1950s); married Richard Franklin O'Hair (an intelligence agent), on October 18, 1965 (divorced 1976); children: (second marriage) William J. Murray III; Jon Garth Murray; (third marriage) legally adopted her granddaughter Robin Murray-O'Hair.*

Served in the Women's Army Corps during World War II, achieving rank of second lieutenant; worked as psychiatric social worker (1948–64); was an attorney for the Department of Health, Education and Welfare (HEW), Washington, D.C. (1956–59); with son, successfully sued the Baltimore Public Schools in protest of mandatory school prayer and Bible reading; served as director of the American Atheist Center (1965–77); served as director, American Atheist Radio Series (1968–77); became editor-in-chief, American Atheist Magazine *(1965); co-founded, with Richard O'Hair, American Atheists, Inc. (formerly Society of Separatists) and served as secretary (1965–75) and president (1975–86).*

Selected works: Why I Am an Atheist *(1965);* The American Atheist *(1967);* What on Earth is an Atheist! *(1969);* Let Us Prey; an Atheist Looks at Church Wealth *(1970); (ed.)* The Atheist Viewpoint *(1972).*

Belligerent, bad-tempered and unashamedly foul-mouthed, Madalyn Murray O'Hair wore with pride her mid-1960s label of "the most hated woman in America." She earned this enmity through her self-appointed role as the country's most visible and outspoken atheist, and through her participation in one of the major Supreme Court cases of the second half of the 20th century.

America at the dawn of the 21st century routinely is cited as one of the most religious of developed countries, with poll respondents overwhelmingly affirming a belief in God and (to a somewhat lesser extent) in God's place in national and local affairs, and with politicians increasingly proffering their spiritual beliefs as a sign of their trustworthiness and electability. While the Constitution enshrines the separation of church and state, on a practical level religion pervades much of America's politics: major religious institutions lobby for or against both federal and state legislation, and groups like the Moral Majority and the Christian Coalition back political representatives with the explicit intention of affecting the tone of the country. United States currency carries the phrase "In God We Trust"; in 1954, during the Cold War, words in the Pledge of Allegiance were altered from the original "one nation, under my flag" to "one nation, under God"; presidents taking office and participants in court trials swear oaths on the Bible (though the latter may decline if they so choose). In 1963, lawsuits brought by O'Hair and her son in Baltimore and Ed Schempp and his children in Philadelphia, claiming that mandatory prayer and Bible reading in public schools violated the establishment clause of the First Amendment, went to the Supreme Court. In *Abington School District* v. *Schempp*, the Court ruled that schools were not allowed to elevate Christianity over other religions, and that forced prayer was unconstitutional; Justice Tom Clark wrote: "In the relationship between man and religion, the state is firmly committed to a position of neutrality." Battles over school prayer nonetheless continue to this day, but in the furor that ensued after the Supreme Court's decision, O'Hair grabbed firm hold of the spotlight and waged war against religion in public life.

O'Hair, who claimed to have been an atheist since the age of 12, served in the armed forces during World War II and received an extensive education at prestigious American universities. She became a lawyer and worked for a time at the Department of Health, Education and Welfare before capitalizing on her sudden notoriety to found, and loudly promote, American Atheists, Inc., to support the separation of church and state. American Atheists was the first national organization for atheists (she would later found some seven others), and as its head she pressed her case in television talk shows, college campuses, interviews, a weekly radio show and a staggering number of lawsuits. After encountering repeated resistance to her writing from publishers, in 1969 O'Hair founded the Atheist Press to publish *What on Earth is an Atheist!* (based on her "American Atheist Radio Series"), and through sheer persistence went on to publish over 25 works with major publishers. She stressed the irrational nature of religion and its negative effect on believers as well as the negative position of women in Christianity, and, among many other battles, she fought without success against tax exemption for religious organizations, prayer before NASA flights, and "In God We Trust" on U.S. currency. O'Hair made her views known without compromise and without a shred of tact ("the Old Testament is about a vicious, ugly, hate-ridden God, and the New Testament is about an incompetent one"), and even those who shared her views frequently ended up alienated from O'Hair herself. Some left American Atheists to found separate atheist associations, a few of which O'Hair also sued, and in later years some of these ex-associates accused her of the same egotistical excesses that had ruined a number of American evangelists. Working closely with O'Hair were her granddaughter **Robin Murray-O'Hair**, whom she had adopted and whom friends described as "inseparable" from her, and her second son, Jon Garth Murray. (She and her eldest son William Murray, with whom she had brought the Supreme Court suit, became bitterly estranged after he publicly announced his discovery of God and became a fundamentalist preacher.) The three lived and worked together, though not without loud disagreements, and enjoyed a fairly luxurious lifestyle as a result of income from their positions within atheist organizations. While both her celebrity and her success in lawsuits dimmed markedly over the years, O'Hair remained publicity-hungry and litigation-prone in the cause of atheism. She reportedly was planning to travel to New York City to picket a visit from Pope John Paul II when she disappeared, along with her son and granddaughter, in September 1995.

The circumstances surrounding their disappearance remained murky for years; local police were apparently reluctant to investigate, and for over a year no missing persons report was filed by anyone in American Atheists or by William Murray. At the time, the IRS was investigating

American Atheists for probable tax problems, and just prior to their disappearance Jon Murray had illicitly used organization funds to purchase half a million dollars in gold coins; thus, among the theories floated was that they used the stolen funds to make a quick getaway to a new life. Others suggested that O'Hair, whose health was somewhat shaky, had gone away to die secretly in order to prevent Christians from praying for her. In 1999, a three-time felon was tried on charges of kidnapping, extortion and robbery of the O'Hairs, with prosecutors theorizing that he and two cronies, one a former office manager for American Atheists serving a prison term at the time of the trial, the other himself murdered by the time of the trial, had kidnapped the O'Hairs, killed them for the gold coins, and buried them somewhere in Texas. He was found guilty only of extortion, but this theory was finally proved correct. In March 2001, bones dug up on a west Texas ranch were identified as the remains of O'Hair and her relatives. Somewhat lost in the speculation that followed her disappearance was recognition of O'Hair's contribution to the ongoing, often rancorous, discourse among Americans that is vital to the country's democratic principles. Before she barged her way onto the national scene and refused to go away, merely to question the presence of Christian rhetoric or beliefs in secular life was, often, to invite suspicion and distrust. While she championed atheism, she also helped to usher in the atmosphere most Americans now take for granted, in which schoolchildren are not expected to mouth prayers of a religion that may not be their own, and Judaism and, increasingly, Islam are also accorded the basic respect of publicly acknowledged holidays long granted only to Christianity.

SOURCES:

The Day [New London, CT]. September 29, 1995; December 8, 1995; December 16, 1995; October 4, 1996.

Irons, Peter, and Stephanie Guitton, eds. *May It Please the Court*. NY: The New Press, 1993.

Kersey, Ethel M. *Women Philosophers: a Bio-critical Source Book*. NY: Greenwood Press, 1989.

The New York Times. May 5, 2000; June 3, 2000; March 16, 2001.

"Whatever Happened to the World's Most Famous Atheist?" in *The Progressive*. February 1999.

"Where's Madalyn?" in *Time*. February 10, 1997.

O'Hara, Anne (1875–1951).

See Martin, Anne Henrietta.

O'Hara, Mary (1885–1980)

***American author of the bestselling* My Friend Flicka.**

Name variations: Mary O'Hara Alsop; Mary Sture-Vasa; Mary O'Hara Alsop Sture-Vasa. Born Mary Alsop on July 10, 1885, in Cape May Point, New Jersey; died of arteriosclerosis on October 14, 1980, in Chevy Chase, Maryland; daughter of Reese Fell Alsop (an Episcopal cleric) and Mary Lee (Spring) Alsop; educated at Ingleside in New Milford, Connecticut, and at the Packer Institute in Brooklyn; studied music and languages in Europe; married Kent Parrot, in 1905 (divorced); married Helge Sture-Vasa, in 1922 (divorced 1947); children (first marriage): Mary O'Hara; Kent, Jr.

Selected works: Let Us Say Grace *(1930);* My Friend Flicka *(1941);* Thunderhead *(1943);* Green Grass of Wyoming *(1946);* The Son of Adam Wyngate *(1952, reissued as* The Devil Enters by a North Window, *1990);* Novel-in-the-Making *(1954);* Wyoming Summer *(1963);* The Catch Colt *(play, 1964);* A Musical in the Making *(1966);* The Catch Colt *(novella, 1979);* Flicka's Friend: The Autobiography of Mary O'Hara *(1982).*

Mary O'Hara, the future author of the beloved *My Friend Flicka* and *Thunderhead*, was born at Cape May Point, New Jersey, in

Mary O'Hara

1885, and grew up in non-rural Brooklyn Heights, New York, dreaming of owning a horse. The daughter of an Episcopal minister and a descendant of William Penn and of Gardiner Spring, after whom Spring Street in New York City was named, she was writing before she turned ten. O'Hara attended Ingleside, a finishing school in Connecticut, and the Packer Institute in Brooklyn. She also spent two years in Europe studying music and languages, and would later compose music as well as write.

With her husband Kent Parrot, whom she married in 1905, O'Hara moved to California, where she chanced into a job as a screenwriter's assistant. After ascending the ranks in short order she became, at his request, a staff writer for acclaimed director Rex Ingram (who had risen to prominence directing ***June Mathis**' *The Four Horsemen of the Apocalypse*, released in 1921). In that capacity, O'Hara wrote the adaptations and continuities of such films as *Toilers of the Sea* (1923), *Black Oxen* (1924), and *Turn to the Right* (1927).

After her first marriage ended in divorce, in 1922 O'Hara married her second husband Helge Sture-Vasa. In 1930, they moved from Hollywood to Wyoming, where they lived on a dairy ranch that O'Hara also ran. This became the setting for her most enduring novel, *My Friend Flicka* (1941), which lovingly details the relationship between a young boy named Ken and his wild colt, Flicka. The story was widely praised and hugely popular upon its publication, and has since gone on to be ranked as a children's classic and translated into numerous languages. Although some reviewers criticized the book for its sentimental tone and melodrama, most lauded its emotional power and simplicity. One reviewer compared it to other classic "boy-and-his-horse" stories, writing, "[It] has the quality of *The Yearling*, but it is tougher and wilder. . . . It has the intensity of Lincoln Steffens' memorable little tale of his own Christmas pony, and has the strength of John Steinbeck's stories of Joady and his red pony." The movie version of the book, released in color in 1943 with child star Roddy McDowall as Ken, was also well received and has remained a popular children's movie. (A television series based on the book aired on ABC-TV in the 1957 season.)

O'Hara's sequel to *My Friend Flicka* was so highly anticipated that the publisher received 50,000 orders before its publication in 1943. The story of *Thunderhead*, the name of Flicka's first foal, chronicles Ken's relationship with that fierce, independent horse, and the book proved as successful as its predecessor. Writing in *The New York Times*, Orville Prescott commented, "It is that rare achievement, a sequel to a great and richly deserved success that in no way disappoints or falls short of its distinguished predecessor. . . . In Miss O'Hara, I believe, we have one of the most important and most enduring novelists now writing in America." Roddy McDowall again starred in the movie adaptation, 1945's *Thunderhead—Son of Flicka*.

O'Hara, who moved back to the East Coast after her second divorce in 1947, continued to write stories of ranch life, although they did not achieve the stunning success of her first two novels. Her later works include *Green Grass of Wyoming* (1946), which was also made into a movie, *The Son of Adam Wyngate* (1952), and *Wyoming Summer* (1963), based on a diary she had kept while living in the state. A number of her musical compositions were also published, and in the early 1960s she wrote *The Catch Colt*, a "folk musical" that was produced in Cheyenne, Wyoming, and at The Catholic University in Washington, D.C. *Flicka's Friend: The Autobiography of Mary O'Hara* was published in 1982, two years after her death from arteriosclerosis in Chevy Chase, Maryland.

SOURCES:

Commire, Anne. *Something About the Author.* Vols. 2 & 34. Detroit, MI: Gale Research.

Contemporary Authors. Vol. 9–12R. Detroit, MI: Gale Research.

Current Biography 1944. NY: H.W. Wilson, 1944.

RELATED MEDIA:

Green Grass of Wyoming (89-min. film), starring **Peggy Cummins**, Robert Arthur, and Charles Coburn, released in 1948.

My Friend Flicka (89-min. film), starring Roddy McDowall, Preston Foster and **Rita Johnson**, released in 1943.

Thunderhead—Son of Flicka (78-min. film), starring Roddy McDowall, Preston Foster and Rita Johnson, released in 1945.

Jacqueline Mitchell,
freelance writer, Detroit, Michigan

O'Hara, Maureen (1920—)

Irish-born actress, best known for her portrayals of feisty women. *Born Maureen FitzSimons on August 17, 1920, at Milltown (also seen as Millwall), near Dublin, Ireland; one of the six children of Charles FitzSimons (a clothing manufacturer) and Marguerite (Lilburn) FitzSimons (an erstwhile actress and singer); graduate of the Guildhall School of Music, Trinity College; received a degree and an associateship from the London College of Music; graduate of the Abbey Theatre School; married George Hanley Brown (a*

Maureen O'Hara

film director), in 1939 (divorced 1941); married Will Price (a film director), on December 29, 1941 (divorced 1953); married Charles Blair (a retired brigadier general), in 1968 (died in a plane crash, 1978); children: one daughter, ***Bronwyn Bridget Price*** *(b. 1944).*

Selected filmography: (bit part) Kicking the Moon Around *(*The Playboy *or* Millionaire Merry-Go-Round, *UK, 1938):* My Irish Molly *(*Little Miss Molly, *UK, 1939);* Jamaica Inn *(UK, 1939);* The Hunchback of Notre Dame *(1939);* A Bill of Divorcement *(1940);* Dance Girl Dance *(1940);* They Met in

Argentina *(1941);* How Green Was My Valley *(1941);* To the Shores of Tripoli *(1942);* Ten Gentlemen from West Point *(1942);* The Black Swan *(1942);* The Immortal Sergeant *(1943);* This Land Is Mine *(1943);* The Fallen Sparrow *(1943);* Buffalo Bill *(1944);* The Spanish Main *(1945);* Sentimental Journey *(1946);* Do You Love Me? *(1946);* Sinbad the Sailor *(1947);* The Homestretch *(1947);* Miracle on 34th Street *(1947);* The Foxes of Harrow *(1947);* Sitting Pretty *(1948);* The Forbidden Street *(*Britannia Mews, *US-UK, 1949);* A Woman's Secret *(1949);* Father Was a Fullback *(1949);* Bagdad *(1949);* Comanche Territory *(1950);* Tripoli *(1950);* Rio Grande *(1950);* Flame of Araby *(1951);* At Sword's Point *(1952);* Kangaroo *(1952);* The Quiet Man *(1952);* Against All Flags *(1952);* The Redhead from Wyoming *(1953);* War Arrow *(1954);* Malaga *(*Fire Over Africa, *UK-US, 1954);* The Long Gray Line *(1955);* The Magnificent Matador *(1955);* Lady Godiva *(1955);* Lisbon *(1956);* Everything but the Truth *(1956);* The Wings of Eagles *(1957);* Our Man in Havana *(UK, 1959);* The Parent Trap *(1961);* The Deadly Companions *(*Trigger Happy, *1961);* Mr. Hobbs Takes a Vacation *(1962);* Spencer's Mountain *(1963);* McLintock! *(1963);* The Battle of the Villa Fiorita *(US-UK, 1965);* The Rare Breed *(1966);* How Do I Love Thee? *(1970);* Big Jake *(1971);* Only the Lonely *(1991).*

Often described as strong-willed or "fiery," Irish-born actress Maureen O'Hara was one of the brightest, most beautiful film stars of the 1940s and 1950s, and was particularly notable as the action heroine of a series of technicolor swashbucklers and westerns. Although she made few movies after her third marriage in 1968 to retired Brigadier General Charles F. Blair (the first pilot to make a solo flight over the Arctic Ocean and the North Pole), she is still seen every Christmas in television airings of the film *Miracle on 34th Street* (1947), playing the bemused mother of moppet ***Natalie Wood**. O'Hara made one of her few forays out of retirement in 1991, to play opposite John Candy in the romantic comedy *Only the Lonely*, and again in 1995, to appear in the CBS special "The Christmas Box," based on the bestselling book by Richard Paul Evans.

O'Hara was born near Dublin in 1920, the daughter of Charles FitzSimons, a clothing manufacturer, and **Marguerite Lilburn FitzSimons**, a former actress who had worked at the Abbey Theatre. Of her three sisters and two brothers, all would appear on the British or American screen with the exception of her oldest sister, who would become a nun. O'Hara began acting in little backyard dramas when very young and made her stage debut at age five, reciting a poem between the acts of a school play. That same year, she entered the Burke School of Elocution, where she continued as a student until she left Dublin 12 years later.

By the time she was 14, O'Hara had won numerous dramatic awards and was already enrolled in Dublin's prestigious Abbey Theatre School. Following her graduation, she accepted an invitation to go to London for a screen test. She qualified for a small part in a movie that was never produced, but a cut of her scene came to the attention of Charles Laughton and Erich Pommer (partners in Mayflower Pictures), who suggested her for the leading role in the screen version of ***Daphne de Maurier**'s *Jamaica Inn* (1939), opposite Laughton and Robert Newton. The success of her debut in that British-made film, directed by Alfred Hitchcock, led to a trip to Hollywood, where she was cast as Esmeralda in *The Hunchback of Notre Dame* (1939), again co-starring with Laughton, who played Quasimodo. Under contract to Mayflower, O'Hara made several subsequent films, then came to the attention of director John Ford, who cast her as Angharad in *How Green Was My Valley* (1941), a film that won six Academy Awards and gave O'Hara's career a boost. She went on to play the leads in several other films directed by Ford, who considered her one of Hollywood's finest actresses.

O'Hara's shimmering red hair, hazel eyes, and creamy complexion won her the title of "Queen of Technicolor," and her 5'8" frame and athletic prowess lent credibility to the adventurous heroines she was frequently called upon to play. She performed her own stunts, whether it be riding horseback over rough terrain, jumping off embankments, crossing swords with Errol Flynn in *Against All Flags* (1952), or jousting with John Wayne, her co-star in *The Quiet Man* (1952) and four other films. O'Hara's pluck and tenacity off the set was also legendary. Early in her career, when studio executives suggested she bob her nose, she simply told them, "Goodbye."

O'Hara was married three times. Her first two husbands were film directors George Hanley Brown (from 1939 to 1941), and Will Price (from 1941 to 1952), with whom she had a daughter, Bronwyn Bridget, named after her older sister. In 1968, when the actress married Charles Blair, she left Hollywood to live in St. Croix, where she assisted her husband in managing Antilles Airboats, an airline which sent seaplanes around the world. When Blair died in a plane crash in 1978, O'Hara took over his job, becoming the first woman president of a commercial airline. For many years, she also maintained homes in Los Angeles and New York, as well as in East Cork, Ireland, where she participated in a number of civic activities. There was never much to entice her out of retirement. "None of the scripts sent to me intrigued me that much," O'Hara said in 1995, just before the airing of "The Music Box." "It's much more fun to go fishing and play golf in Ireland and do the same thing in St. Croix than making something you don't believe in."

SOURCES:

Current Biography 1953. NY: H.W. Wilson, 1953.

Katz, Ephraim. *The Film Encyclopedia*. NY: HarperCollins, 1994.

"Maureen O'Hara," in *People Weekly*. September 20, 1999.

Parker-Beck, June. "Where Are They Now?," in *Remember*. April–May, 1995.

Thomas, Bob. "Maureen O'Hara shines in a new Christmas story," in *The Day* [New London, CT]. December 17, 1995.

Barbara Morgan,
Melrose, Massachusetts

O'Hare, Anne (1880–1954).

See McCormick, Anne O'Hare.

O'Hare, Kate Richards

(1876–1948)

Prominent leader of the Socialist Party of America, working on behalf of social democratic reforms, workers' rights, women's issues, and prisoners' rights, who was imprisoned for her opposition to World War I. *Name variations: Kate Cunningham. Born Carrie Kathleen Richards on March 26, 1876, in Ottawa County, Kansas; died in Benicia, California, on January 10, 1948, of a heart attack; daughter of Andrew Richards and Lucy (Sullivan) Richards, both homesteaders; attended Ottawa County public schools, Central High School, Kansas City, Missouri; Pawnee City (Nebraska) Academy, teaching certificate, 1893; married Francis P. O'Hare, on January 1, 1902 (divorced 1928); married Charles C. Cunningham, in November 1928; children: (first marriage) Richard (b. 1903);* ***Kathleen O'Hare****; twins Victor and Eugene.*

Moved with family to Kansas City, Missouri (1887); taught for one year at a rural school; worked for the Florence Crittenton Mission (1896); undertook clerical work and then became a machinist in her father's shop and joined the International Order of Machinists; became interested in labor issues and joined the Socialist Party of America; trained at a school for socialist organizers (1901), where she met and married fellow student Frank P. O'Hare; traveled cross country speaking on behalf of the Socialist Party; had children while family lived in Kansas City, Kansas, and homesteaded in Oklahoma (1904–08); became a columnist for various socialist newspapers and toured constantly as a socialist lecturer; held national offices in the Socialist Party, including its representative to the international socialist movement in London (1913); ran for the U.S. House of Representatives in Kansas (1910); moved to St. Louis (1911) as columnist and associate editor of the National Rip-Saw; *ran for the U.S. Senate from Missouri (1916); opposed U.S. intervention in World War I; indicted in Bowman, North Dakota, and convicted under the Espionage Act for antiwar speeches; served 14 months of a 5-year sentence in the Missouri State Penitentiary (1919–20); toured on behalf of amnesty for political prisoners and the abolition of prison contract labor; founded Commonwealth College of New Llano, Louisiana (1923), and, later, of Mena, Arizona; served on the staff of Upton Sinclair's End Poverty in California movement (1934–35); appointed to the staff of Progressive Congressman Thomas R. Amlie of Wisconsin (1937); worked on the staff of the California Director of Penology (1939–40).*

Selected works: What Happened to Dan, The Sorrows of Cupid, *and* Kate O'Hare's Prison Letters.

In 1914 when World War I erupted, Kate O'Hare published numerous columns condemning the war as an imperialist adventure and, earlier than most social critics, warned against the possibility of U.S. intervention. In April 1917, she chaired the key policy-making committee at the Emergency Convention of the Socialist Party which met during the same week that the U.S. Congress declared war on Germany. Her committee condemned the war as unjust, and encouraged workers of all belligerent countries to refuse to support their governments' war policies, and she supported a resolution demanding that any conscription program require a national referendum. In one of her columns, O'Hare wrote,

> I am a Socialist, a labor unionist and a follower of the Prince of Peace FIRST; and an American, second. I will serve my class, before I will serve the country that is owned by my industrial masters. . . . The world is my country, the workers are my countrymen, peace and social justice are my creeds, and to these and these alone I owe loyalty and allegiance.

O'Hare toured the country, delivering essentially the same basic antiwar speech wherever she went. After presenting her remarks on July 17,

1917, in Bowman, North Dakota, she was arrested, tried, convicted and sentenced to five years under the Espionage Act.

Born in 1876 in Ottawa County in central Kansas during its boom years, Kate Richards was one of five children in a homesteading family. Her ancestors on both sides had immigrated to the American colonies, and had gradually moved west from Virginia, her father having been born in Ohio and her mother in Illinois. Her father fought for the Union during the Civil War, and her parents married the year after the war ended in 1866. Her early childhood was happy as she thrived on the farm chores as well as hunting and fishing with her siblings and father, and visiting relatives of their extended kinship network on nearby farms. She was an adventurous and curious child who idolized her father. Andrew Richards imparted to her his religious and civic concerns, and taught his children, as O'Hare later remembered, that "the only religion acceptable to God was to serve the people with all our heart and soul." He also imparted to her his political and social interests, and she listened avidly to his discussions of current events with other farmers. **Lucy Richards**, as a full-time homemaker, was not taken as a role model by her daughter who did not have as close a relationship to her mother as to her father.

By 1887, the Kansas economic boom had collapsed, and many homesteaders lost their land. Andrew Richards, facing economic ruin, sold his stock and moved to Kansas City, Missouri, sending for his family when he found work. The move from a rural life of self-sufficiency to urban dependency in a slum area scarred 11-year-old Kate, who later wrote, "Of that long, wretched winter . . . the memory can never be erased, never grow less bitter." She was upset not only by the decline in her family's fortunes but also by the plight of other dislocated families and homeless tramps.

Kate continued her education and graduated from Central High School in 1892. She developed some interest in missionary work, but the next year earned a teaching certificate at Pawnee City Academy in Nebraska and became a teacher in a one-room schoolhouse. She taught for one year, during which she started to submit columns for a Populist newspaper. However, suffering from exhaustion, she abandoned her teaching career in 1895 and was attracted to uplift work with the downtrodden of Kansas City. Her concern over existing social conditions led her, as with so many other young women of the era, to focus on the issues of public drunkenness and prostitution, and she undertook volunteer activities on behalf of the Kansas City branch of the Florence Crittenton Mission located in the city's red-light district. After months of escorting district inhabitants to the mission's programs, Richards lost confidence in such pursuits.

She went to work in the machine shop which Andrew Richards now operated. She handled correspondence and billing, and then managed to push her way into the shop as an apprentice machinist. Despite the taunts of her shopmates, she continued her work as a machinist and became one of the first women to join the International Association of Machinists. Drawn to the economic and political debates around her, she attended union meetings, and one day heard the legendary "Mother" Jones (***Mary Harris Jones**), a rabble-rousing 70-year-old labor organizer. This encounter introduced her to the emerging socialist movement, to which she then devoted her life.

In October 1901, Kate enrolled in the International School of Socialist Economy in Girard, Kansas, which offered a training program for socialist organizers. There she solidified her commitment to socialism, and at the conclusion of the course married a fellow student, Francis Patrick O'Hare of St. Louis, on January 1, 1902. The newlyweds spent their honeymoon barnstorming through Kansas and Missouri as socialist organizers.

They established a home in Kansas City, Kansas, while nevertheless traveling extensively on behalf of the Socialist Party of America. They organized among Pennsylvania coalminers and immigrants in New York City. By then, Kate O'Hare's writing career began to blossom as she published features in various newspapers and magazines, and produced a series of investigative reports on working conditions in various industries. O'Hare wrote her own column for the socialist *Coming Nation* and started to develop a following within the movement. A son, Richard, was born in 1903, but his birth did not diminish O'Hare's activism, nor did the arrival of three more children over the next five years.

The O'Hares moved to Oklahoma Territory in 1904 where they homesteaded in tandem with Frank O'Hare's organizational activities for the party and Kate O'Hare's writings for socialist newspapers. Kate O'Hare in these years became a well-known public lecturer, especially popular at socialist encampments in the Southwest, week-long tent meetings where she and other speakers such as Eugene V. Debs, the Socialist

Kate Richards O'Hare

Party's perennial presidential candidate, drew crowds of thousands. She eclipsed her husband's influence in the socialist movement and undertook extensive speaking tours across the country. From this time through 1919, she spent much of her time on the road, juggling child-care and other family responsibilities with her public commitments as best she could.

Kate Richards O'Hare became one of the most popular Socialist Party figures, the leading woman socialist from the west and one of the most sought-after public speakers. She lectured about the need for a social democratic system to replace capitalism so that workers would enjoy the full fruits of their labor. Promoting a variety of reforms while looking toward the transformation of the economic system, she discussed dangerous working conditions, inadequate wages, and the plight of women and children in the work force. She focused attention on the exploitation of white working farmers and black sharecroppers, although she displayed the prejudices against African-Americans so rampant in her era. She also championed a number of reforms on behalf of women, including women's suffrage, enhanced educational opportunity, the elimination of prostitution, and the legalization of divorce and birth control and abortion information. Placing all of these views within a social democratic frame of reference, O'Hare was aligned to the reformist wing of the growing Socialist Party which emphasized—rather than violent revolution—piecemeal reforms to modify the free enterprise system toward collective control.

I am dangerous to the special privileges of the United States; I am dangerous to the white slaver and to the saloonkeeper; and I thank God that at this hour I am dangerous to the war profiteers of this country who rob the people.

—Kate Richards O'Hare

O'Hare served in virtually all offices of the Socialist Party between 1908 and 1917 as its following grew nationally. She was elected as a delegate to its various conventions, and she served on its National Executive Committee, its Woman's National Committee, and the International Socialist Bureau, the executive body of the international socialist movement, only the second woman to serve in that capacity, having been preceded by the renowned ***Rosa Luxemburg**. She campaigned on the Socialist ticket for the U.S. House of Representatives in 1910 from Kansas and for the U.S. Senate in Missouri in 1916. As a woman, she was nevertheless denied entry to the party's inner circle, but her popularity with the party's rank-and-file was enormous.

Kate O'Hare and her family lived in Kansas City, Kansas, from 1909 to 1911 after they left Oklahoma. In 1911, however, they moved to what would be their most permanent home, St. Louis, when both O'Hares were invited to join the staff of a socialist monthly called the *National Rip-Saw*. Kate O'Hare became an assistant editor and Frank the circulation manager while she continued her speaking tours. She at once became a star attraction of the St. Louis branch of the Socialist Party and participated in various civic activities as well. She was appointed by the mayor to a municipal committee on unemployment, investigated cost-of-living issues for presentation to the Missouri State Senate Minimum Wage Commission, and was active in the local women's suffrage movement and the National Women's Trade Union League.

When World War I began in Europe in 1914, O'Hare used her columns to emphasize her socialist commitment to internationalism rather than nationalism. She scolded European socialists who supported their nations in the war, and she warned against the possibility of the United States becoming ensnared in that war. She argued that America should prohibit food and weapon exports to the belligerents, and she co-authored a play entitled "World Peace" which celebrated international brotherhood and was performed before enthusiastic audiences on the socialist lecture circuit. As the preparedness movement grew, O'Hare and many of her comrades continued to oppose it. By spring 1917, when war against Germany was imminent, O'Hare was a delegate to the Emergency Convention of the Socialist Party which was meeting at the time war was declared. She was elected to head the committee formulating party policy, and supported its endorsement of international solidarity and its condemnation of conscription and war taxes. For the next three months following the convention, she crisscrossed the country advising her audiences that capitalism was responsible for the war and that only socialism could insure international peace and harmony. She stated that perhaps support for the war could be somewhat justified "for democracy in Germany, if we had a little [more] of it at home." O'Hare also spoke of how the war was affecting women in Europe, and said that they had been reduced to "the status of breeding animals on a stock farm."

O'Hare delivered that same lecture more than 75 times, and agents of the Justice Department—who routinely monitored her talks as well as those of other critics of the war—did not believe that she was in violation of any law. Nevertheless, she was arrested in North Dakota on July 29, 1917, under the Espionage Act for her speech at Bowman on July 17, charged with a statement which she denied making that American women were now "nothing more nor less than brood sows to raise children to get into the army and be made into fertilizer." Her arrest was not so much due to the incendiary atmosphere caused by the war as a result of political infighting in Bowman unrelated to her.

Over the next four months, O'Hare raised money for her defense while witnessing the indictment of other socialist comrades and the disruption of socialist publications, including her own periodical, *Social-Revolution*, formerly the *National Rip-Saw.* She was tried in December 1917 under a clause of the Espionage Act, before a clearly unsympathetic jury and a judge who had published anti-socialist tracts and had publicly scorned career women. The jury quickly found her guilty. In her impassioned statement before being sentenced, O'Hare spoke of what she said was the essence of the case against her: "This crime . . . was the same charge that was brought . . . against George Washington and Patrick Henry , . . . The crime is this: 'She stirs up the people.' . . . I plead guilty of that crime. . . . For twenty years, I have done nothing but stir up the people."

She was sentenced to five years in prison and, because no federal penitentiary existed for women at that time, entered the Missouri State Penitentiary at Jefferson City on April 15, 1919, after losing an appeal of her case before the U.S. Supreme Court. She served her time in one of the oldest prisons in the country which still followed outmoded penal practices, such as the silence system during meals and the housing of contagious prisoners among the healthy. The Jefferson City facility required its inmates to perform contract labor six days a week for private manufacturers under onerous conditions. O'Hare, who was not opposed to prison work itself, denounced the existing system as scab labor. The impact of her incarceration on her was somewhat alleviated in the first months by the fact that anarchist ***Emma Goldman** lived in the adjacent cell. These two prominent representatives of antagonistic radical movements became fast friends, as together they attempted to minister to the needs of less advantaged inmates. O'Hare also tried to research case studies of her fellow inmates for later publication, although the prison officials did not cooperate with her efforts and eventually confiscated her notes for what might have been a study of some importance to penologists. O'Hare was also prevented from teaching classes for the inmates, but she did succeed in using her influence to improve some of the prison conditions. The experience of incarceration enhanced her sense of identity with other women which she had never before really embraced, and gave her a greater appreciation of the burdens of black prisoners.

O'Hare's prison term was commuted by President Woodrow Wilson in 1920 after 14 months, and her political and civil rights were restored by presidential action soon thereafter. O'Hare quickly returned to her travels as a public speaker. The Socialist Party had fragmented during the war so, while she still considered herself a socialist, she focused on a campaign for amnesty for remaining World War I political prisoners, including her idol, Debs, who languished in the Atlanta Federal Penitentiary. In 1922, she led a so-called "children's crusade" to Washington to dramatize the plight of political prisoners; it reaped wide publicity and most of the prisoners were released in the next 18 months. Her other goal was to abolish contract labor by prisoners, an aim largely achieved in 1929 through the passage of the Hawes-Cooper Bill. In addition, she supported various progressive political activities in the 1920s.

Meanwhile, Kate O'Hare turned to a topic that had intrigued her for years, educational opportunities for workers. Labor education had been of interest to her ever since she had enrolled in a training course for organizers, and during the war she and Frank had briefly been involved in labor education in a colony in Ruskin, Florida, near Tampa. In 1922, the O'Hares joined the Llano Co-operative Colony in rural Louisiana, to which they moved their revived newspaper, the *National Rip-Saw,* and established a college for workers, called Commonwealth College. When factionalism soon destroyed the periodical and split the colony, the college relocated to Mena, Arkansas, where Kate O'Hare served as professor of sociology, trustee, fund raiser and field director, among other positions. The various strains, however, took their toll. Stress which dated back to the war era culminated in Kate and Frank O'Hare separating in 1924. They divorced in 1928, and that same year Kate Richards O'Hare married Charles C. Cunningham, a Southern attorney and businessman, and they settled in California.

Kate O'Hare, the name she still used as a public personality, attempted to retire to private life. However, in 1934 she re-entered the public arena when she joined the staff of Upton Sinclair's End Poverty in California (EPIC) movement during the Depression. After two years of work for EPIC, she retired briefly again but in 1937 worked on the staff of a Progressive Party congressional representative from Wisconsin, Thomas R. Amlie. In that capacity, she attempted to nudge Franklin D. Roosevelt's New Deal toward a more egalitarian and planned economy. The next year, with Amlie's defeat, she once more left public life. But in 1939 she accepted an appointment to assist California's Penology Department in an effort to reform and modernize the state's prison system, especially San Quentin. Many of the reforms implemented represented ideas which O'Hare had long expounded.

In 1940, at the age of 64, she finally eased out of such formal responsibilities. She continued to speak before civic groups in Benicia, California, where she and her husband lived, and she occasionally met with the State Crime Commission at the invitation of Governor Earl Warren. She was clearly a well-respected public figure. Kate Richards O'Hare Cunningham died in her home on January 10, 1948, of a heart attack at the age of 71.

SOURCES:

Foner, Philip S., and Sally M. Miller, eds. *Kate Richards O'Hare: Selected Writings and Speeches.* Baton Rouge, LA: Louisiana State University Press, 1982.

Miller, Sally M. *From Prairie to Prison: The Life of Social Activist Kate Richards O'Hare.* Columbia, MO: University of Missouri Press, 1993.

O'Hare, Kate Richards. *Kate O'Hare's Prison Letters.* Girard, KS: Appeal to Reason, 1919.

SUGGESTED READING:

Basen, Neil K. "Kate Richards O'Hare: The 'First Lady' of American Socialism, 1901–1917," in *Labor History.* Vol. XXI, no. 2. Spring 1980, pp. 165–199.

Sannes, Erling N. "'Queen of the Lecture Platform': Kate Richards O'Hare and North Dakota Politics, 1917–1921," in *North Dakota History.* Vol. LVIII, no. 4. Fall 1991, pp. 2–19.

COLLECTIONS:

Some correspondence of Kate O'Hare's is found in the Frank P. O'Hare Papers, Missouri Historical Society, St. Louis; and some of her printed works may be found in the Socialist Party of America Collection at Perkins Library, Duke University, Durham, North Carolina.

Sally M. Miller,
Professor of History, University of the Pacific,
Stockton, California

Oignies, Marie d' (1177–1213).

See Mary of Oignies.

Oignt, Marguerite d' (d. 1310)

Mystic and writer of Poletins. *Name variations: Marguerite de Duyn. Died in 1310 at priory of Poletins, near Lyons, France; never married; no children.*

Marguerite d'Oignt was a holy woman of France in the Middle Ages. Although the details of her early life are unclear, she probably came from a wealthy family, for she was made a prioress, a position usually held by a noblewoman. She joined the new Carthusian order of nuns as a young woman, and was highly educated at the priory of Poletins near Lyons where she gained renown for her piety and mystical visions. In a few years, she was elected prioress of the house. Her fame spread as she began publishing her revelations and meditations, in which she revealed her visions and stressed the need for total self-abnegation in order to find God.

In the biography written of her by a contemporary, it is reported that Marguerite wrote and published to enlighten others, but more important she wrote for her own health. After a mystical experience, Marguerite would become so ill it seemed to others she was near death; but when she forced herself to write down what she had seen and heard, she would be completely cured. Marguerite wrote both in Latin and in French, so that academics and clerics as well as less educated people could benefit from her words. Among her works were a *Life of St. Beatrice*, a book of meditations, and several revelations of her visions.

SOURCES:

Klapisch-Zuber, Christiane, ed. *A History of Women in the West: Silences of the Middle Ages.* Vol. II. Cambridge, MA: Belknap, 1992.

Laura York,
Riverside, California

O'Keeffe, Adelaide (1776–c. 1855)

Irish poet and novelist. *Name variations: Adelaide O'Keefe. Born on November 5, 1776, in Dublin, Ireland; died probably in 1855; daughter of John O'Keeffe (an actor turned playwright); never married; no children.*

Selected works: Original Poems Calculated to Improve the Mind of Youth *(1808);* National Characters Exhibited in 40 Geographical Poems *(1808);* Patriarchal Times; or the Land of Canaan *(1811);* Zenobia, Queen of Palmyra *(1814);* Poems *(1819);* Dudley *(1819);* Poems for Young Children *(1849);* The Broken Sword: A Tale *(1854).*

Born in Ireland in 1776, Adelaide O'Keeffe was the daughter of John O'Keeffe, who in 1780 moved his family to London, where he wrote popular comic plays for the Haymarket, Covent Garden, and Drury Lane theaters. While somewhat overshadowed by her famous father, as an adult O'Keeffe emerged as a poet and author in her own right. In 1804, she contributed 34 poems to *Original Poems for Infant Minds*, compiled by ***Ann** and ***Jane Taylor**. Signed simply "Adelaide," these poems remain perhaps her most well-known work. O'Keeffe continued to write poetry for children, including *Original Poems Calculated to Improve the Mind of Youth* (1808), *National Characters Exhibited in 40 Geographical Poems* (1808), and *Poems for Young Children* (1849), and also wrote a number of books for adult readers, including *Patriarchal Times; or The Land of Canaan* (1811), **Zenobia, Queen of Palmyra* (1814), and the three-volume novel *Dudley* (1819). O'Keeffe never married, and before her father died in 1833 she spent much of her time caring for him. Her last novel, *The Broken Sword: A Tale*, was published in 1854, and she is thought to have died the following year.

Jacqueline Mitchell,
freelance writer, Detroit, Michigan

O'Keeffe, Georgia (1887–1986)

American abstract artist, one of the foremost artists of the 20th century, whose long, stormy relationship with photographer Alfred Stieglitz was one of the principal art legends of the century. *Name variations: Georgia O'Keeffe before and after marriage; "Pat" to her art school friends. Born Georgia Totto O'Keeffe in Sun Prairie, Wisconsin, on November 15, 1887; died in a Santa Fe (New Mexico) hospital on March 6, 1986; daughter of Francis Calixtus O'Keeffe and Ida Wyckoff (Totto) O'Keeffe; married Alfred Stieglitz, in December 1924 (died 1946); no children.*

Moved to Williamsburg, Virginia, with family (1902); attended the Art Institute of Chicago, for formal studies (1905); attended Art Students League in New York (1907); went to work as a commercial artist in Chicago (1910); enjoyed summer study with Alon Bement at the University of Virginia (1912); first visited the American west (August 1912), taking a temporary job supervising drawing teachers in Amarillo, Texas (1912–14); met avant-garde photographer Alfred Stieglitz (1914); taught art in a small South Carolina Methodist junior college (1915); returned to Texas (1916) to teach at West Texas Normal College in Canyon; taught at University of Virginia (1916); began affair with Stieglitz who was married (1918); married (1924); had career as independent artist (1919–86); bought a house in the village of Abiquiu, New Mexico (early 1930s); death of Stieglitz (1946); made first visit to Europe (1953); visited Peruvian Andes (1956); spent three months traveling around the world (1959).

Selected works among the over 2,300 she created: Tent Door at Night *(1913);* Black Lines *(1916);* Pink and Green Mountains III *(1917);* The Flag *(1918);* Trees and Picket Fence *(1918);* From the Plains *(1919);* Blue and Green Music *(1919);* Red and Blue Plums *(1920);* Lake George *(1923);* Red Canna *(c. 1923);* Dark Abstraction *(1924);* Pattern of Leaves *(1924);* Large Dark Red Leaves on White *(1925);* East River No. 1 *(1926);* Morning Glory with Black *(1926);* Shelton Hotel, New York, No. 1 *(1926);* Black Iris *(1926);* Red Hills and Sun, Lake George *(1927);* Poppy *(1927);* Shell 1 *(1927);* White Flower *(1929);* Black Hollyhock with Blue Larkspur *(1929, sold for $1.98 million in 1987);* Ranchos Church Taos, New Mexico *(1930);* Jawbone and Fungus *(1930);* Dark Mesa and Pink Sky *(1930);* White Trumpet Flower *(1932);* Stables *(1932);* Barn with Snow *(1933);* Jimson Weed *(c. 1934);* Pink Roses *(1934);* Sunflower #2 *(1935);* Purple Hills near Abiquiu *(1935);* Three Shells *(1937);* Pink Sweet Peas *(1937);* From the Faraway Nearby *(1937);* Pink Shell with Seaweed *(c. 1938);* White Camelia *(1938);* Beauford Delaney *(c. 1940);* From the White Place *(1940);* Pelvis with Moon *(1943);* Black Place No. 1 *(1944); the Pelvis series (1944);* Poppies *(1950);* Grey Tree by the Road *(1952);* Winter Trees III *(1953);* Patio with Cloud *(1956);* Only One *(1959);* Blue B *(1959);* White Patio with Red Door I *(1960);* Sky Above Clouds IV *(1965); the Black Rock series (1970).*

Georgia O'Keeffe was the foremost American woman artist of the 20th century. Her distinctive paintings of flowers, skulls, and abstracted Western landscapes are instantly recognizable, and she was so exhaustively photographed by her patron and lover Alfred Stieglitz that her severe, unsmiling face and slim figure are familiar to everyone at all interested in 20th-century American art. She lived to the age of 98 and, after falling briefly out of fashion in the 1950s, regained her early renown and became an icon to women artists and feminists in the 1970s and since.

Georgia Totto O'Keeffe was born on November 15, 1887, on a prairie farm in Sun Prairie, Wisconsin, where her father raised dairy cattle. She was the second of seven children, including sisters **Claudia**, **Ida**, and **Anita**, and was schooled, in early childhood, at the local one-room schoolhouse, walking to school each day, observing nature. She showed an early aptitude for drawing and for music, playing piano and violin. Her maternal Grandmother Totto was tall, dignified, and spoke with precision. When she reprimanded her grandchild for touching one of the ornaments in a collection in the parlor, "I was so fascinated by her precise way of speaking," recalled O'Keeffe, "that I would do it again just to hear her say, 'You must not do that a-gain.'" **Mary Catherine O'Keeffe**, her paternal grandmother, was also elegant, with braided hair, who always wore blue at home or black when she came to visit. O'Keeffe's later habit of "wearing black with white collars or other one-toned suits, keeping her silver hair plaited or pinned at the nape of her neck, having ramrod posture, speaking precisely, and assembling collections of 'untouchable' ornaments from nature, all may stem from the conscious and subconscious influence of her two grandmothers," writes **Jan Garden Castro**.

The O'Keeffes moved to Williamsburg, Virginia, when Georgia was 15 in the hope that their children would get a better education on the East Coast—her mother **Ida Totto O'Keeffe** felt she had married "down" and was eager to give her daughters as much "finish" as possible. In any event, Georgia's father Francis O'Keeffe endured a succession of business failures, and the family, tense and argumentative, was often unhappy. Georgia went to a succession of church-run boarding schools where she proved intellectually and artistically precocious.

Family poverty was not yet too acute, and from school she moved to the Art Institute of Chicago, for formal studies. Her first prize in the life class there, says biographer **Benita Eisler**, was "a triumph of discipline over distaste." Next she spent a year at the Art Students League in New York. Further training there was in the style of William Merritt Chase, a dominant figure in the New York art world who had become very rich as a portraitist. Chase made his students work on a new still life painting every day. "There was something fresh and energetic and fierce and exacting about him that made him fun," she wrote of him later. One of her still lifes, of a dead rabbit beside a metal pot, won a prize—a funded summer of work at the Art Students League's school by Lake George, in upstate New York. By 1910, however, the deterioration of the family's fortunes obliged O'Keeffe to earn her own living, and she went to work as a commercial artist in Chicago, drawing lace and embroidery for advertisements, and fearing that she might never be able to enjoy the life of a fine artist. Subsequent summer study with Alon Bement at the University of Virginia in 1912, however, introduced her to the methods of Arthur Wesley Dow, a pioneer teacher of abstract art in America, and her ambition revived.

O'Keeffe first visited the arid American west in August 1912, when she took a temporary job supervising drawing teachers in Amarillo, Texas. She was amazed by the dusty flatness of the Texas panhandle country, and by the immensity of the sky. Unlike many of her contemporaries, however, she was delighted rather than intimidated by this near-desert landscape, which was to become a central theme in her life's work. Although she was well read in aesthetic theory she began to trust her own style, rather than relying on what she had learned in classes, and she found a way to convey the beauty of a landscape that many contemporaries saw as forbidding and alien. She also fought successfully at the school board level to change the method of school art teaching; she abandoned textbooks and encouraged the children to draw in their own way from things around them. "Self-expression," now common in art teaching, was revolutionary then.

Back East after her two years in Texas, and now teaching in a small South Carolina college, O'Keeffe sent some of her black-and-white charcoal drawings to a New York friend, ***Anita Pollitzer**. Impressed, Pollitzer took them to the avant-garde photographer Alfred Stieglitz, whose gallery, known by its Fifth Avenue address simply as "291," was the home of the "Photo-Secession" group and a venue of modern artists and photographers. Stieglitz was a larger-than-life figure, passionate, argumentative, intensely partisan in favor of the daring young artists of the age, and the subject of fierce loves and hatreds. He was delighted with O'Keeffe's works too, saying they were the best art work he had seen by a woman and that they, almost alone among contemporary American works, were not influenced by French models. He hung them in his gallery, without even asking for O'Keeffe's consent. It was a great honor and opportunity for her, and after an initial protest she was soon reconciled to his having taken the liberty.

Still poor and in need of work, she completed her formal training as an art teacher at Columbia Teachers College, finally studying under Arthur Wesley Dow himself, and gaining from him a new appreciation for the principles of composition in oriental art. She then returned to Texas in 1916 to teach at West Texas Normal College in Canyon, about 20 miles south of Amarillo. She wrote Stieglitz and Pollitzer frequent enthusiastic letters about the setting, in which she took regular marathon walks. Just after arriving, she told Pollitzer: "The whole sky—and there is so much of it out here—was just blazing—and gray-blue clouds were rioting all through the hotness of it—and the ugly little buildings and windmills looked great against it." Although she continued to trust her own artistic vision, she was also reading Wassily Kandinsky's *Concerning the Spiritual in Art,* with its influential theory of colors. Kandinsky and the vitalist philosopher Henri Bergson both believed that

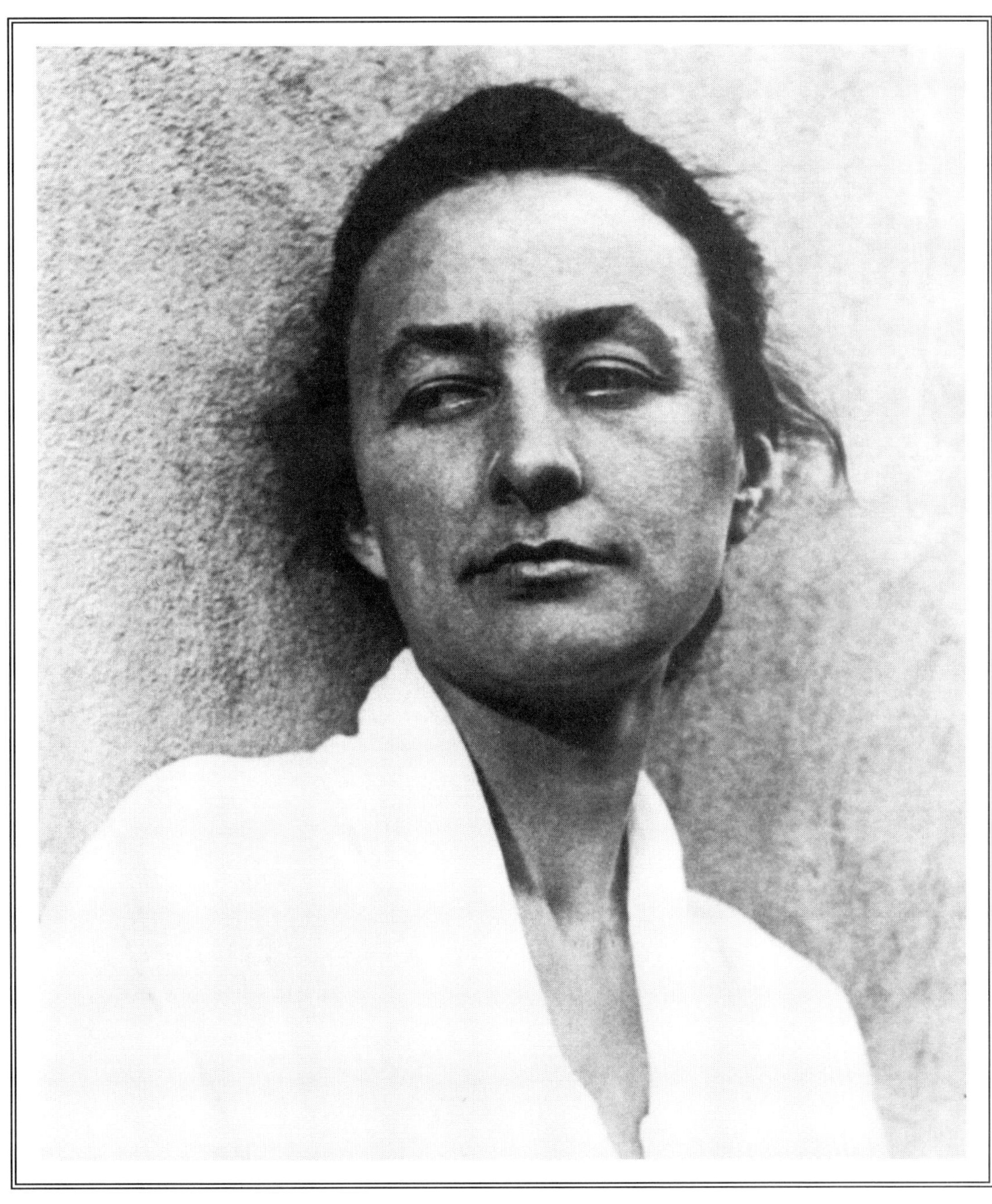

Georgia O'Keeffe

particular colors had social, psychological, and even political implications and influences. O'Keeffe also followed them by believing in the possibility of painting musical effects. Her painting *Blue and Green Music* (1919) is one of her best-known attempts to make this connection.

Her correspondence and friendship with Stieglitz (who was separated from his wife, **Emmeline Obermeyer Stieglitz**) turned into a romance, and after another year they became lovers even though he was 23 years her senior. Changing conditions, personal and political (the First World War) had led to the closing of his gallery, 291, and the termination of his journal, *Camera Work,* which had been about to run a major article on O'Keeffe's work. Even so, he had enough money to support her and give her much-needed time to paint, so she was able to give up her teaching job. He took hundreds of photographs of her, including numerous now-famous nude studies, which intensified New York art circles' gossip about the couple.

They married in December 1924, after his divorce, though O'Keeffe continued to use her own surname throughout life. Stieglitz staged a major show of her work in 1923 at the Anderson Galleries, New York, which drew a lot of press coverage. Some of it, written in the idiom of Freudian psychology, which was just then becoming popular, claimed that the abstract paintings, and the close-up flower paintings in which she had more recently specialized, were really graphic expressions of female sexuality. Critic Paul Rosenfeld, for example, said that the paint in some of her works "appears licked on with the point of the tongue, so vibrant and lyrical are they," and that "the essence of very womanhood permeates her pictures." A satirical squib in *The New Yorker* claimed of her next exhibition (1926) that "psychiatrists have been sending their patients up to see O'Keeffe's canvases. . . . If we are to believe the evidence the gallery is littered with mental crutches, eye bandages, and slings for souls. They limp to the shrine of Saint Georgia and they fly away on the wings of the libido." O'Keeffe denied claims like these but acknowledged that some customers probably heard the titillating theories about her work and "bought the paintings with their ears rather than their eyes." Annual shows and critical admiration led to rapid increases in the prices she could ask, and in 1928 six of her flower paintings sold for what was then the massive price, for works by a living artist, of $25,000. Success, critical and commercial, meant that she could now devote herself entirely to painting.

My pleasant disposition likes the world with nobody in it.

—**Georgia O'Keeffe**

With Stieglitz, she spent winters in New York City and summers at his family home by Lake George in upstate New York—near the Art Students League school where she had spent the summer of 1908. Single-minded and dedicated, she concentrated on painting during all the daylight hours, dressed plainly, was usually quiet and reserved, and made a marked contrast to his gregarious, argumentative art-world friends and family. She did, however, have an explosive temper if disturbed at work, and her tolerance for children—she had none of her own—was low. To escape the noise and company, she began to work in an old shed, the "shanty," on the estate, and did numerous pictures of it and other vernacular American buildings in the following years. She enjoyed the solitude and silence of night-time trips on the lake in a rowboat with Stieglitz, which also prompted several paintings. O'Keeffe rarely theorized about her own work: she was matter-of-fact and down to earth in her remarks about it, and far more meaning has been read into it by other observers than from her own claims. A grateful artist and friend, Marsden Hartley, wrote that "she has no preachment to offer and utters no rubbish on the subject of life and its problems."

Her paintings of Lake George and the surrounding hills, meanwhile, influenced Stieglitz's own work. Hitherto, he had not devoted much energy to photographing nature, but under O'Keeffe's tutelage he began a now-famous series of photographs of clouds, the "Equivalent" series, whose abstract blacks and whites are reminiscent of her sky paintings. Similarly her flower paintings drew his attention to the abstract possibilities inherent in nature photography. Conversely, many of his cityscapes inspired her own skyscraper paintings of the mid-1920s, with the same strong geometric lines but a higher level of abstraction and simplification.

O'Keeffe loved the desert country of the southwest and was eager to return, but Stieglitz had a heart condition which made him reluctant to travel. He was afraid that the 6,000-foot elevation of her favorite New Mexico places would bring on breathing difficulties or even a heart attack. O'Keeffe, annoyed by his reluctance to come with her (he never did visit New Mexico) but undeterred, began taking annual trips without him, driving out west in a Ford Model A. In the years after 1930, she settled into paintings which mixed recognizable objects, such as the mesas and rock outcrops of the Western landscape, or the skulls of sheep and cattle, with abstract color field backgrounds.

For a while, she was a frequent visitor to the artistic colony at Taos run by ***Mabel Dodge Luhan**, an eccentric patron of the arts whose fourth husband, Tony Luhan, was a local Pueblo Indian. D.H. and ***Frieda Lawrence** were among the distinguished artists and writers who spent time at Taos, which developed a reputation for both homosexual and heterosexual promiscuity. O'Keeffe had numerous affairs with both men and women in the 1920s, with Mabel Luhan herself, and with the artist Paul Strand and the African-American poet Jean Toomer. When Mabel Luhan was back East in a hospital, O'Keeffe even had a fling with Tony Luhan and wrote about it in detail to Mabel. As biographer Benita Eisler remarks of this episode: "That she was frequently and gratuitously cruel is documented by all those who knew her."

O'Keeffe's fame and fortune were secure by the late 1920s. In 1927, when she was only 40, she was given the unusual honor of a major ret-

Georgia O'Keeffe

rospective exhibition by the Brooklyn Museum. Even after the Wall Street Crash, when the Great Depression was making life difficult for many artists, O'Keeffe prospered. She was among the very few artists whose works continued to command good sales and high prices. She was given a $10,000 commission for decorating ***Elizabeth Arden**'s beauty salon in New York in 1934, one of the worst years of the Depression, a job she undertook over Stieglitz's protest against murals as an art form. Her numerous affairs and her knowledge that Stieglitz also had many lovers led to a growing estrangement between them, and in the early 1930s O'Keeffe had a succession of nervous breakdowns.

After recuperating at the Ghost Ranch, a remote New Mexico getaway for the rich 70 miles northwest of Santa Fe, O'Keeffe decided to settle there for the whole of every summer and bought a house in the village of Abiquiu. Extensively remodeled by O'Keeffe, it was a beautiful, low-profile design in adobe with projecting log beams, and became a central motif in many of her later paintings. Its flat roof and the simple ladders she used to climb there recur in dozens of them, as do New Mexico's roadside crosses, adobe buildings, and animal bones. The finely painted bones, notably cow skulls and deer antlers, became one of her trademark images, and in 1938 *Life* magazine ran an article about them, "Georgia O'Keeffe Turns Dead Bones to Live Art," which included Ansel Adams' photographs of her dragging a half-decayed cow's head and ribs to her studio.

Adams was one of the great Western photographers of the century—the two of them were mutual admirers, and one of their camping trips to Arizona together gave rise to another of her most famous works, *From the Faraway Nearby,* in which a deer skull with elaborate antlers hovers over a desert and mountain landscape. Numerous other artists, including her friend Marsden Hartley, had enjoyed visiting and painting New Mexico, but the landscape made a profounder impression on O'Keeffe than on any other. She became quite proprietorial about it, and gave her own names to many of the distinctive landforms she encountered, such as "Black Place" and "White Place," each of which she painted repeatedly over the following years. She continued to spend each winter in New York, and despite their storms she and Stieglitz still lived together.

The Museum of Modern Art devoted a show to her works in 1946, the first time since its creation 17 years before that it had given an entire exhibition to one woman. Later that year, however, Stieglitz's death finally ended their long and immensely productive relationship. O'Keeffe began to travel widely, driving 5,600 miles through Mexico on one excursion, and making her first visit to Europe in 1953, as adventurous as ever though she was now in her mid-60s. A visit to the Peruvian Andes in 1956 led to a new series of paintings and appears to have been more influential on her continued development than her belated visit to Paris, the old center of Western art. In 1959, she spent three months wandering around the world, traveling westwards through the Far East, Middle East, and southern Europe. Visiting Italy for the first time at the age of 72, she declared the great Roman monuments, classical and Catholic, "extraordinarily vulgar," especially by comparison with the more manageable scale of palaces and temples in the Middle East.

Her status, meanwhile, continued to grow. Further recognition came in 1950 when the Metropolitan Museum of Art used one of her cow skull paintings as the cover for its exhibition of "One Hundred American Painters of the 20th Century." By then she was also the recipient of numerous awards and honorary degrees, and rich enough to be able to buy a second spectacular New Mexico house. During the 1950s, the vogue for Abstract Expressionism, and the rapid succession of art fads in the 1960s, temporarily eclipsed O'Keeffe's reputation. However, a massive retrospective of her work at the Whitney Museum in 1970, supervised by O'Keeffe herself, revitalized her reputation for a new generation, and enabled her to enjoy a long, golden twilight in her old age.

O'Keeffe continued to work hard and because she often completed a painting in one or two days (and lived to the age of 98) her total output was immense. She experimented with paintings based on views from the air in the 1960s, when she flew often, some of which, reduced to planes of white cloud and blue sky, were reminiscent of the contemporaneous "color field" Abstract Expressionists. The biggest of them, *Sky Above Clouds IV,* was 24-feet long. She began it in 1962 and, returning periodically, finished it in 1965, which was quite different from her usual practice of working constantly on one canvas until it was done. It was the biggest painting of her career, and now hangs in the Art Institute of Chicago, one of the few museums big enough to accommodate it. It became, in effect, the signature piece from the last phase of her career. As critic and biographer Charles Eldredge remarks of her old age: "The long and sustained applause for O'Keeffe and her work was fueled by forces in the world around her," including "a resurgent feminist movement's search for Founding Mothers; and an aging population's fascination with geriatric productivity." In her last years, she suffered from deteriorating eyesight. Ever resourceful, she switched to throwing pots, relying more on her sense of touch. She also gathered up drawings, letters, and fragmentary writings and compiled them as an unconventional autobiography, *Georgia O'Keeffe* (1976). Her companion in these last years was a young sculptor and ceramic artist, Juan Hamilton, who was strikingly similar in appearance to the way Stieglitz had looked 60 or 70 years earlier. He helped her with practical and artistic tasks, and tried to keep at bay the growing number of artistic pilgrims coming uninvited to visit her in Abiquiu. They became close friends and, after her death in March 1986, he scattered her ashes from one of her favorite New Mexico mountain tops.

In 1987, 438,000 visited her retrospective at the National Gallery of Art in Washington. In the summer of 1997, the Georgia O'Keeffe Museum, dedicated to her art, opened in Santa Fe, New Mexico. The museum was the result of the efforts of **Anne Marion**, a Texas cattle baron, and her husband John. The opening exhibit served as a "walk-through of O'Keeffe's career," reported *Time*. "Through it all runs a whiff of pure Americana, a longing for an untroubled world sprung from native soil. 'It is breathtaking as one rises up over the world one has been living in,' O'Keeffe once wrote, 'and looks down at it stretching away and away.'"

SOURCES AND SUGGESTED READING:

Castro, Jan Garden. *The Art & Life of Georgia O'Keeffe*. NY: Crown, 1985.

Cowart, J., and J. Hamilton. *Georgia O'Keeffe: Art and Letters*. Washington, DC: National Gallery of Art, 1981.

Eisler, Benita. *O'Keeffe and Stieglitz*. NY: Doubleday, 1991.

Eldredge, Charles C. *Georgia O'Keeffe*. NY: Harry N. Abrams, 1991.

Hoffman, Katherine. *An Enduring Spirit: The Art of Georgia O'Keeffe*. Metuchen, NJ: Scarecrow Press, 1984.

Hogrefe, Jeffrey. *O'Keeffe: The Life of an American Legend*. NY: Bantam, 1992.

Lisle, Lauri. *Portrait of an Artist: A Biography of Georgia O'Keeffe*. Seaview, 1980.

Madoff, Steven Henry. "O'Keeffe Enshrined," in *Time*. July 28, 1997.

Peters, Sarah W. *Becoming O'Keeffe*. NY: Abbeville Press, 1991.

Pollitzer, Anita. *A Woman on Paper*. NY: Simon and Schuster-Touchstone, 1988.

Robinson, Roxana. *Georgia O'Keeffe: A Life*. NY: Harper and Row, 1989.

COLLECTIONS:

Stieglitz-O'Keeffe Archive, Yale University; Newberry Library, Chicago; Archives of American Art, Washington D.C.; Georgia O'Keeffe Museum, Santa Fe, New Mexico.

RELATED MEDIA:

"Georgia O'Keeffe" (60-min.), documentary by ➤ **Perry Miller Adato** which includes an interview with O'Keeffe, aired on Public Broadcasting System (PBS), 1977, and won the Red Ribbon from the American Film Festival.

Patrick Allitt,
Professor of History, Emory University,
Atlanta, Georgia

➤ Adato, Perry Miller

American film director. *Born in Yonkers, New York; studied at the Marshalov School of Drama and the New School for Social Research, both in New York.*

Perry Miller Adato was the first woman to win an award from the Directors Guild of America (DGA) with her 1977 documentary on ***Georgia O'Keeffe**. Aired on Public Broadcasting System (PBS), it was also exhibited at a London film festival. Adato's documentaries on Carl Sandburg (1982) and Eugene O'Neill (1986) were also honored by the DGA. Other documentaries feature ***Gertrude Stein**, ***Mary Cassatt**, ***Louise Nevelson**, Pablo Picasso, and Dylan Thomas. Perry Adato began her career working as director of the Film Advertising Center in New York through the 1950s and 1960s. She was then a film consultant and researcher for CBS in New York before becoming an associate producer, then producer, of cultural documentary films for WNET, the Public Broadcasting System in New York City. In 1984, Adato received an honorary doctorate (LHD) from Illinois Wesleyan University.

O'Kelley, Mattie Lou (c. 1908–1997)

American folk artist. *Born in Georgia, around 1908; died in Decatur, Georgia, in July 1997.*

A self-taught folk artist who was said to have possessed "a unique vision," Mattie Lou O'Kelley took up her paint brush at the age of 60 and created a memoir of canvases depicting rural Southern life in the early part of the 20th century. Her autobiographical paintings, with such titles as *Papa Feeding the Stock at 4 a.m.*, *Bringing in the Night Water*, and her self-portrait, *Mattie in the Morning Glories*, document the hard work and simple pleasures of her youthful days in the Georgia countryside. Initially, O'Kelley also served as her own agent, once traveling by bus to show her paintings to Gudmund Vigtel, the director of the High Museum of Art in Atlanta. Vigtel purchased a still life for the museum, which later came to the attention of Robert Bishop, who is now credited with discovering O'Kelley. Bishop, an art dealer and later the director of the American Museum of Folk Art in New York City, was delivering a lecture on quilts at the High Museum in 1975, when he first viewed the still life and was told about the "painting lady" who delivered it to the museum. Bishop was so impressed with that he embarked on a mission to bring O'Kelley to the attention of the American public. Her work is now included in a number of museum collections, including the American Museum of Folk

Art. Bishop also wrote an introduction to O'Kelley's art book *Mattie Lou O'Kelley: Folk Artist.* The artist died in 1997, age 89.

SOURCES AND SUGGESTED READING:

"Milestones," in *Time.* August 11, 1997, p. 25.
"Obituary," in *The Day* [New London, CT]. July 31, 1997.
O'Kelley, Mattie Lou. *Mattie Lou O'Kelley: Folk Artist.* Intro. by Robert Bishop. Bulfinch, 1989.

Barbara Morgan,
Melrose, Massachusetts

Okoh, Ngozi (1909–1995).

See Odozi Obodo, Madam.

Okwei of Osomari (1872–1943)

Nigerian trader who created an extensive business network throughout Nigeria and was crowned* omu *or queen of Osomari in 1935, a tribute to her leadership and success. *Name variations: Omu Okwei, queen of Osomari or Ossomari; Felicia Ifeoma Ekejiuba or Ekejuba. Pronunciation: Oak-way. Born Felicia Ifeoma Ekejiuba in 1872; died in Onitsha, Nigeria, in 1943; daughter of Prince Osuna Afubeho, of the Ibo tribe, and one of his several wives; never formally educated, but began to learn about trade at age nine; married Joseph Allagoa, in 1889 (divorced 1890); married Opene of Abo, in 1895; children: (first marriage) Joseph; (second marriage) Peter.*

By age 15, began building a trading network; went into partnership with mother-in-law, Okwenu Ezewene (1896–1904); became an agent of the Royal Niger Company (1904); was one of Nigeria's wealthiest women (1920s); crowned Omu (Queen) Okwei of Osomari (1935), a title bestowed on no one else after her death.

Felicia Ifeoma Ekejiuba, who would be known as Omu Okwei, was born in 1872, the daughter of Prince Osuna Afubeho of the Ibo (Igbo) tribe. Her father was a celebrated warrior and a wealthy man, the owner of many trading and war canoes as well as several hundred slaves who fought and traded for him throughout Nigeria. Her grandfather was King (Atamanya) Nzedegwu of Osomari, who had reigned in the mid-19th century, establishing trading relations with the British and also inviting Roman Catholic missionaries into his kingdom. Okwei's mother, one of the prince's several wives, was from a family of equal prominence; her father Obi Aje was the son of Obi Ossai, an important king of Abo who had signed agreements with British traders in 1830.

Okwei's mother had no male child who survived to adulthood, which limited her claims to her husband's property. It was in the Nigerian tradition for women to support themselves, however, usually through farming and trading, and Okwei's mother was an astute and successful trader, selling vegetables, palm oil, cloth, and a wide variety of goods throughout the country. Recognizing that her daughter's future prosperity might well depend on her ability to trade, Okwei's mother sent her, at age nine, to live with one of her aunts among the Igala. Nigeria was a country of many tribes and languages, and success in trade depended on mastering the system of extensive trade networks and the languages spoken in trade, one of which was Igala. While living with her aunt, Okwei learned Igala and basic business practices. She traded first in fruits and vegetables, then moved into yams and poultry.

Okwei rejoined her mother when she was 15, after her father had died, and they lived at Atani, a port on the River Niger. In 1889, when she was 17, she chose to marry a trader named Joseph Allagoa, whose family's importance was not equal to hers. Upon marriage, a daughter traditionally received a dowry from her family which she would use as capital in her trading ventures, but Okwei's family, disapproving of Allagoa, refused to provide her with one. Headstrong and independent, Okwei nonetheless married the man of her choice. Through him and his friends she met and cultivated many important traders and agents. True to her family's expectations, her husband left her the following year, shortly after the birth of her son Joseph, but the valuable business relationships she had forged survived the breakup. With her line of merchandise expanded to include pots, pans, lamps, and clothes, she traveled along the River Niger, exchanging the manufactured goods for foodstuffs from Nigerians which she then sold to the Europeans at a profit. Friendly, hardworking, and honest, Okwei was popular with Africans and Europeans alike.

In 1895, Okwei once again married the man of her choice. Opene of Abo was the son of **Okwenu Ezewene**, a wealthy woman trader, but Okwei's family opposed this marriage as well, and again refused to give her a dowry. With her son, Okwei relocated to Onitsha, where her new husband and mother-in-law lived, and began working in partnership with Okwenu. Through Okwenu's contacts, she expanded her products to include tobacco and cotton goods, while also taking care of her family, which grew to include a second son, Peter.

One great obstacle to trade was the lack of a universal Nigerian currency; Nigerians in Onitsha used cowrie shells as money, refusing to trade in the British currency used by the Europeans. To bridge this divide, trade was frequently conducted through the use of tickets, which could be converted into either British currency or Nigerian cowrie shells. In 1904, Okwei dissolved her partnership with her mother-in-law and set up an independent trading unit, becoming an agent of the Royal Niger Company. She exchanged liquor, tobacco, pots, plates, lamps and matches, which were in great demand among Nigerians, for palm oil, which was in great demand among Europeans. As an agent of the Royal Niger Company, Okwei accumulated 400 tickets, which she used to procure yet more palm oil. This she sold to the Europeans at an enormous profit, which she used to enlarge her business.

By 1915, Okwei had built a financial empire and the backbone of her enterprises shifted. Always flexible and resourceful, she built up trading links with powerful men—Chief Quaker Bob Manuel, an important trader; Jack Cooper, the Niger Company manager; and John Windfall, the bank manager at Onitsha—who were especially useful at reserving goods for her and extending credit. As her profits grew, Okwei began lending money to a network of smaller traders in exchange for a commission on their sales. As well, domestic services became important to her enterprise. Okwei made use of her excellent relationships with both business associates and employees when she arranged for some of her more beautiful maids to become the wives or mistresses of bank managers, interpreters, shopkeepers, clerks, and influential businessmen whom she knew well. Her business associates appreciated the introductions she facilitated, and the maids reportedly were grateful for an opportunity to enhance their status; through the marriages that resulted from these introductions, she established valuable, lifelong ties in the competitive environment of business.

During World War I, Okwei showed her adaptability to new conditions when the market for palm oil in Europe collapsed and she shifted instead to ivory and coral beads, which were in greater demand there. She then began importing goods directly from England, a feat which required a great deal of money and organization but reaped enormous profits. After 1918, the British decided to end the ticket system and introduce a new standard currency. Nigerians had by this time accepted the old currency, but they wanted nothing to do with the new money; Okwei made the old currency available at an exchange rate of two old shillings to five new shillings, and reaped yet another prodigious profit. Over the years she had invested in a great deal of ivory, gold, and silver jewelry, far more than she could ever wear, and she now began to rent pieces of it out for ceremonial occasions, putting more of her capital to work. By the 1920s, Okwei was a tremendously wealthy woman, with a multitude of servants working in her businesses and many homes. She was an influential member of several social clubs, and became one of the first people in Onitsha to own a car. She also bought a fleet of trucks to supplement the canoes that conveyed her goods far and wide. A great landholder, she owned more than a third of the land along the banks of the River Niger at Onitsha, and rented or leased it for more income.

The powerful entrepreneur was also a devoted wife and mother, and a great believer in Nigeria's traditional way of life, putting family first and foremost. Her second marriage had proved quite happy despite the objections of her relatives, who had regarded Opene as not particularly hardworking. This assessment proved correct, but his lackadaisical attitude suited Okwei, who preferred to make the decisions; in their amicable relationship, she was the breadwinner and he the supporter of her business efforts. She saw to it that both her sons were educated, and as adults they attained important positions in Nigeria; Joseph Allagoa became a district interpreter and court registrar in the British Civil Service, and Peter Opene was employed by the Royal Niger Company. Both of her sons' careers further increased Okwei's ties with business and government circles.

In August 1935, Nigerians of Osomari recognized Okwei's achievements by crowning her *omu,* or queen, of Osomari. This was one of the highest political titles among the Osomari, and her election, a rare honor, was not due solely to her royal birth, for Nigerians crowned only those they deemed worthy. As queen, Okwei became part of a traditional "dual-sex" government, in which the positions of queen and king were occupied by unrelated but co-equal individuals. The queen oversaw the needs of women, and the king oversaw the needs of men; each conferred with their own council of the same sex before making important decisions. Omu Okwei was called upon to settle disputes, initiate community development programs, and oversee the market women who were still the backbone of Nigerian small business. She conferred regularly with the Obi chiefs as well as with the district officer who represented the British colonial government. Throughout her career, she remained adept at moving between Nigerian and colonial culture, and in her new position she applied this skill to the benefit of her people.

In this period of late British colonialism, Omu Okwei was an important transitional figure in Nigeria. She understood the emerging business system better than most Nigerians, and indeed better than most colonialists. At a time when Nigeria had few roads or railways, she built up a trading empire using river transport. She fully understood the British system of currency, using it to accumulate capital, and her organizational and business skills allowed her to trade directly with British manufacturers. Her vast business network was not unlike the great industrial empires founded in America by men like Cornelius Vanderbilt, John D. Rockefeller, and Andrew Carnegie. As a figure of prominence and royalty, Omu Okwei maintained many Nigerian traditions, but she was not rigidly bound by social practices or conventions, as is illustrated by her two marriages to men of her own choosing. She related to British colonials as equals, and won their respect for her business acumen. Her shrewd understanding of the intricacies of credit, banking, currency systems, and relationships with suppliers made her a wealthy woman. Throughout her career, she was also known for her honesty and fairness; shoddy business practices were not a part of her enterprise. She became the epitome of a successful entrepreneur, a role which, while new for Nigerian women, was built on the country's long tradition of female entrepreneurship, and she maintained the best of her own culture while borrowing from the best of Europe's.

Many *omu* had reigned before Omu Okwei, but when she died, in 1943, Nigerians agreed that she was the greatest and most powerful of them all. A marble statue was erected in her memory, and one of the main streets in Onitsha was named for her. Since her death, no other woman has held the title of *omu*.

SOURCES:

Boahen, A. *Topics in West African History*. London: Longmans, 1966.

Coleman, J.S. *Nigeria: Background to Nationalism*. Berkeley, CA: University of California Press, 1971.

Ekejiuba, Felicia. "Omu Okwei of Osomari," in *Nigerian Women in Historical Perspective*. Edited by Bolanle Awe. Lagos, Nigeria: Sankore Publishers, 1992, pp. 89–104.

———. "Omu Okwei, the Merchant Queen of Osomari: A Biographical Sketch," in *Journal of the Historical Society of Nigeria*. Vol. III, no. 4, 1967.

Hatch, John Charles. *Nigeria. A History*. London: Secker & Warburg, 1971.

Okonjo, Kamene. "Nigerian Women's Participation in National Politics: Legitimacy and Stability in an Era of Transition," in *Working Paper #221*. East Lansing, MI: Women and International Development Program, Michigan State University, July 1991.

Karin Loewen Haag,
writer, Athens, Georgia

Olberg, Oda (1872–1955)

German-born journalist and political activist whose successful European career was terminated with the rise of Fascism in Italy, Germany, and Austria. *Name variations: Oda Olberg-Lerda; Gracchus. Born Oda Olberg in Lehe bei Bremerhaven, Germany, on October 2, 1872; died in Buenos Aires, Argentina, on April 11, 1955; married Giovanni Lerda; children: Marcella, Renata, Edgardo, and one other son.*

Like many committed Socialists, Oda Olberg was not born into the working class. Rather, she was born in 1872 in Lehe bei Bremerhaven, Germany, the daughter of a distinguished officer of the new German Navy, and grew up in comfortable middle-class circumstances in the early years of Otto von Bismarck's German Reich. As a nurse, Olberg became familiar with misery on a vast scale, including working and living conditions that she believed were caused by capitalism, and she soon began writing for the Social Democratic press. Over the next decades, her articles would appear in most of the important newspapers and journals of the German and Austrian Social Democratic movements. Despite her youth, Olberg was respected for her intellect and dedicated Socialism, and earned a reputation as one of the most talented writers in the German Social Democratic movement. Among others, she impressed and became acquainted with the movement's leader, August Bebel.

In 1896, in fragile health, Olberg moved to Italy. Almost immediately she met, fell in love, and in 1897 married Giovanni Lerda, an up-and-coming Italian Socialist. But anti-government riots during May 1898, in which many lives were lost when martial law was proclaimed in most large Italian cities, made life so precarious for the couple as Socialists that they sought refuge for some months in nearby Switzerland. Having quickly learned and mastered the Italian language, Olberg made a successful career for herself in the world of Italian Socialist journalism. In a short time, she became the foreign affairs editor of the Italian Socialist Party's main organ, the newspaper *Avanti!* Her articles began to appear regularly in German and Austrian Social Democratic newspapers, including Vienna's *Arbeiter-Zeitung* and Berlin's *Vorwärts*, as well as the highly influential ideological journals, *Der Kampf*, *Die Neue Zeit*, and the *Sozialistische Monatshefte*. Starting in 1899, she became the official foreign correspondent of the *Arbeiter-Zeitung*.

Olberg was one of the first professional female journalists in German-speaking Central

Europe. As late as 1927, only about 3% of the full-time journalists in Vienna were women. Even among those few women who had been able to create careers for themselves in journalism, the overwhelming majority specialized in ostensible women's areas such as fashion, society, or home economics. As a highly respected journalist who wrote about politics and world affairs, Olberg was very much the exception. As well, she was able to balance the demands of being a wife and mother of four children with the pressures of a career. Her friends, including Karl and *Luise Kautsky, would often express their astonishment at the breadth and depth of her knowledge.

A feminist as well as a Socialist, Olberg argued persuasively in favor of complete social, economic and personal emancipation for women. Her polemics on behalf of this cause within the Social Democratic movement, which was ideologically committed to women's rights but in reality remained deeply patriarchal, gave courage to women and also served to alert receptive men that significant inequities had not been addressed. In 1902, Olberg reacted to a contemporary polemic by Paul Julius Möbius, *Über den physiologischen Schwachsinn des Weibes* (On the Physiological Imbecility of the Female Sex), by publishing the rejoinder *Das Weib und der Intellectualismus* (The Female Sex and Intellectualism). Olberg's book was widely read and became an indispensable source for Social Democratic women activists, who, writes Luise Kautsky, came to regard it as "one of the most effective weapons in their struggles."

Living as they did in Rome in the early 1920s, Olberg and Lerda witnessed the increasingly violent atmosphere that culminated in the seizure of power by Benito Mussolini and his Fascist Party. Fascist blackshirts took over the streets through brute force, and Olberg and Lerda lived in fear. Scores of Communists, Socialists, Catholics and liberals were murdered by Fascist thugs while the police remained indifferent, indeed often sympathizing with Mussolini's followers. Olberg reported the deteriorating situation in the Austrian and German Social Democratic press. In 1923, she also published a comprehensive study on the new phenomenon of Italian Fascism, a book that remains of interest to historians of the movement. By the mid-1920s, as the Mussolini dictatorship was tightening its grip on Italy, Olberg was forced to think of going into exile. Terror directed against her and her husband hastened his death in 1927. That same year, she went to Argentina, where her son Edgardo had settled. But she yearned for Europe and in 1928 returned, settling in Vienna. In Austria, Olberg resumed her journalism, becoming a full-time correspondent for Vienna's flagship Social Democratic newspaper, the *Arbeiter-Zeitung*.

As an expert on Fascism, Olberg wrote many articles on the topic over the next years. The onset of the world economic depression in 1929 sparked the growth of fascistic movements throughout the world, particularly in Germany where Adolf Hitler's National Socialists (Nazis) menaced an increasingly fragile democratic system. Not only Social Democrats, but liberals and democrats as well, read Olberg's articles for insights into the alarming growth of totalitarian sympathies among the masses of Central Europe. Her short but trenchant study of Nazism, published in 1932, was one of the best analyses of the Hitler movement on the eve of its seizure of power.

Olberg also wrote about the human cost of the economic depression. In an April 1931 article for the *Arbeiter-Zeitung*, she described conditions at the Simmeringer Obdachlosenheim, a homeless shelter near Vienna. In 1933, she explored the misery of Vienna's beggars ("Das Bettlerelend in Wien"). As well, on many occasions her Vienna apartment, which she shared with her oldest daughter **Marcella**, became a temporary refuge for politicals who had escaped Fascist Italy.

In 1933, the National Socialists came to power in Germany, creating a reign of terror for liberals, democrats, Marxists and Jews. In February 1934, after the forces of Fascism destroyed the parliamentary government, the Austrian Social Democrats staged a bloody uprising that was doomed from the start. Along with many other Social Democrats, Olberg was forced to flee. After a brief stay in Switzerland, she rejoined Edgardo in Buenos Aires, Argentina. Soon, she welcomed her daughters Marcella and **Renata**.

Olberg attempted to improve the family's finances by resuming her journalistic career in exile. Writing articles in Spanish, she was able to publish in a number of Argentinean journals, including the respected *Critica*. She also published in the German-language *Argentinisches Tageblatt*. Despite these successes, Olberg's life in exile was difficult. Since few Central European political exiles had fled there, she was cut off from events back home. While journals and newspapers had been founded in Czechoslovakia, France, Great Britain and the United States by anti-Fascist and anti-Nazi political exiles, in the 1930s Argentina was essentially a backwater in the war against Hitler and Mussolini. By participating in the activities of local Social Democratic organizations founded by Argentineans of Austrian, German, and Italian background, in time Olberg was able to overcome at least some of her feelings of isolation. She also began publishing her articles in influential exile journals abroad, including the *Neuer Vorwärts* and the *Pariser Tageszeitung*, both published in Paris, the *Neue Volks-Zeitung* of New York, as well as *Das Andere Deutschland*, *Deutsche Blätter* (Chile), *Deutsche Freiheit*, and the scholarly *Zeitschrift für Sozialforschung*.

In 1937, Olberg was a founding member of the exile organization "Das Andere Deutschland" (The Other Germany), which quickly became one of the most effective anti-Nazi groups in Latin America. Soon after, her health declined precipitously due to a cardiac condition. Even so, Olberg did not stop writing. From 1944 through 1948, she published articles in the journal *Das Andere Deutschland*. She also wrote a book that was both autobiographical and philosophical, *Der Mensch, sein eigener Feind: Betrachtungen über Gerechtigkeit* (Humanity Its Own Worst Enemy: Reflections on Justice). Published in Spanish in 1946 by a small Argentine publishing house, the book attracted little attention in a country convulsed by a social revolution led by Juan Domingo Peron and ***Eva Perón**.

As Olberg's health continued to decline, it became clear that she would never again set foot on European soil. Occasionally, she contributed an article to the revived *Arbeiter-Zeitung*, but the Peronista regime's press and mail censorship complicated her situation considerably. Olberg died in Buenos Aires on April 11, 1955.

SOURCES:

Archiv der Sozialen Demokratie, Bonn. Nachlass Friedrich Stampfer.

Botz, Gerhard. "Austro-Marxist Interpretation of Fascism," in *Journal of Contemporary History.* Vol. 11, no. 4. October 1976, pp. 129–156.

Byer, Doris. "Sexualität—Macht—Wohlfahrt: Zeitgemässe Erinnerungen an das 'Rote Wien,'" in *Zeitgeschichte.* Vol. 14, no. 11–12. August–September 1987, pp. 442–463.

Friedrich, Birgit. "Publizist/inn/en und Journalist/inn/en aus Österreich im argentinischen Exil (1934 bis 1949): Biographien, Publizistik und Lebensbedingungen." Diplomarbeit, Grund- und Integrativwissenschaftliche Fakultät, University of Vienna, July 1990.

Kammer für Arbeiter und Angestellte, Vienna: Tagblatt-Archiv, folder "Oda Olberg."

Laureiro, Eusebio A., ed. *Crítica del fascismo.* Montevideo: Centro d estudios Ariel, 1935.

Mocek, Reinhard. "The Program of Proletarian *Rassenhygiene*," in *Science in Context.* Vol. 11, nos. 3–4. Fall-Winter 1998, pp. 609–617.

Olberg, Oda. *Das Elend in der Hausindustrie der Konfektion.* Leipzig: F.W. Grunow Verlag, 1896.

———. *Der Fascismus in Italien.* Jena: Thüringer Verlagsanstalt, 1923.

———. "Im Obdachlosenheim," in *Arbeiter-Zeitung* [Vienna]. April 8, 1931.

———. "Ist der Faschismus eine Klassenbewegung?," in *Karl Kautsky, der Denker und Kämpfer: Festgabe zu seinem siebzigsten Geburtstag.* Vienna: Verlag der Wiener Volksbuchhandlung, 1924.

———. "Marsch ohne Ziel," in *Arbeiter-Zeitung* [Vienna]. December 25, 1932.

———. *Der Mensch, sein eigener Feind: Betrachtungen über Gerechtigkeit.* Nuremberg: Nest-Verlag, 1948.

———. *Nationalsozialismus.* Vienna: Hess Verlag, 1932.

———. "Nordamerikas Erbsünde," in *Arbeiter-Zeitung* [Vienna]. May 15, 1932.

———. "Polemisches über Frauenfrage und Sozialismus," in Wally Zepler, ed., *Sozialismus und Frauenfrage.* Berlin: Verlag von P. Cassirer, 1919.

———. "Theorie des Faschismus," in *Vorwärts* [Berlin]. June 21, 1929.

———. *Das Weib und der Intellectualismus.* Berlin: Akademischer Verlag für sociale Wissenschaften/J. Edelheim, 1902.

———. "Wirklichkeitsmut," in *Vorwärts* [Berlin]. December 25, 1932.

Petersen, Jens. "Der italienische Faschismus aus der Sicht der Weimarer Republik: Einige deutsche Interpretationen," in *Quellen und Forschungen aus italienischen Archiven und Bibliotheken.* Vols. 55–56, 1976, pp. 315–360.

Schieder, Wolfgang. "Das italienische Experiment: Der Faschismus als Vorbild in der Krise der Weimarer Republik," in *Historische Zeitschrift.* Vol. 262, no. 1. February 1996, pp. 73–125.

Schwartz, Michael. "'Euthanasie'-Debatten in Deutschland (1895–1945)," in *Vierteljahrshefte für Zeitgeschichte.* Vol. 46, no. 4. October 1998, pp. 617–665.

———. *Sozialistische Eugenik: Eugenische Sozialtechnologien in Debatten und Politik der Deutschen Sozialdemokratie 1890–1933.* Bonn: Verlag von J.H.W. Dietz, 1996.

John Haag,
Associate Professor of History,
University of Georgia, Athens, Georgia

Oldenburg, Alexandra (1844–1925).

See Alexandra of Denmark.

Oldenburg, Alexandra (1870–1891).

See Alexandra Oldenburg.

Oldenburg, Alexandra (1921–1993).

See Alexandra, Queen of Yugoslavia.

Oldenburg, Astrid (1932—)

Norwegian princess. *Name variations: Astrid Ferner. Born on February 12, 1932, in Oslo, Norway; daughter of Olav V, king of Norway (r. 1957–1991), and* ****Martha of Sweden*** *(1901–1954); sister of Harold or Harald V, king of Norway (r. 1991—); married John*

Ferner, on January 12, 1961; children: Katherine Ferner; Benedikte Ferner; Alexander Ferner; Elizabeth Ferner; Charles Ferner.

Oldenburg, Cecily (1911–1937)

Sister of England's Prince Philip. *Born on June 22, 1911, in Tatoi, near Athens, Greece; died in an airplane crash on November 16, 1937, in Steene, Belgium; daughter of ****Alice of Battenberg*** *and Prince Andrew of Greece; sister of Prince Philip, duke of Edinburgh (who married Elizabeth II, queen of England); married George Donatus of Hesse (1906–1937), on February 2, 1931; children: Louis of Hesse-Darmstadt (1931–1937); Alexander of Hesse (1933–1937); Joanna of Hesse-Darmstadt (1936–1939).*

On November 16, 1937, Cecily Oldenburg was killed in an airplane crash near Steene, Belgium, while on a flight to England to attend the wedding of her brother, Prince Philip, to Princess Elizabeth (the future ***Elizabeth II**). Her husband, mother-in-law (***Eleanor of Solms-Hohensolms-Lich**), and two sons were also killed. Cecily's daughter, one year old at the time, died two years later.

Oldenburg, countess of.

See Hedvig (d. 1436).

Oldenburg, duchess of.

See Friederike of Hesse-Cassel (1722–1787).
See Elisabeth of Saxe-Altenburg (1826–1896).
See Sophie Charlotte of Oldenburg (1879–1964).
See Olga Alexandrovna (1882–1960).

Oldenburg, Ingeborg (1878–1958).

See Ingeborg of Denmark.

Oldenburg, Margaret (b. 1895)

Princess of Bourbon-Parma. *Born Margrethe Françoise on September 17, 1895; daughter of Valdemar Oldenburg (b. 1858) and ****Mary Oldenburg*** *(1865–1909); married René Charles Marie, prince of Bourbon-Parma, on June 9, 1921; children: Jacques (b. 1922); ****Anne of Bourbon-Parma*** *(b. 1923); Michel Marie (b. 1926); Andre (b. 1928).*

Oldenburg, Margaret (1905–1981)

Sister-in-law of Queen Elizabeth II. *Name variations: Princess of Hohenlohe-Langenburg. Born on April 18, 1905, in Athens, Greece; died on April 24, 1981, in Bad Wiesse, Germany; daughter of Prince Andrew of Greece and ****Alice of Battenberg*** *(1885–1969); sister of ****Cicely Oldenburg*** *(1911–1937) and Prince Philip, duke of Edinburgh (who married ****Elizabeth II****, queen of England); married Godfrey, 8th prince of Hohenlohe-Langenburg, on April 20, 1931; children: Kraft, 9th prince of Hohenlohe-Langenburg;* ***Beatrice von Hohenlohe-Langenburg*** *(b. 1936); and four others.*

Oldenburg, Marina (1906–1968).

See Marina of Greece.

Oldenburg, Martha (1971—)

Norwegian princess. *Born Martha Louise on September 22, 1971, in Oslo, Norway; daughter of Harold V, king of Norway (r. 1991—), and ****Sonja*** *(b. 1937), queen of Norway.*

Oldenburg, Mary (1847–1928).

See Marie Feodorovna.

Oldenburg, Mary (1865–1909)

Danish princess. *Name variations: Mary d'Orleans; Princess Marie d'Orleans. Born on January 13, 1865; died on December 4, 1909; daughter of Robert (1840–1910), duke of Chartres, and ****Françoise d'Orleans*** *(1844–1925); married Waldemar (son of Christian IX of Denmark), on October 22, 1885; children: Aage Christian Alexander (b. 1887), count of Rosenborg; Axel Christian George (b. 1888); Erik Frederick (b. 1890), duke of Rosenborg; Viggo Christian (b. 1893); ****Margaret Oldenburg*** *(b. 1895).*

Oldenburg, Mary (1876–1940).

See Marie.

Oldenburg, princess of.

See Amalie (1818–1875).

Oldenburg, Olga (1851–1926).

See Olga Constantinovna.

Oldenburg, Ragnhild (1930—)

Norwegian princess. *Name variations: Princess Ragnhild; Ragnhild Lorentzen. Born Ragnhild Alexandra Oldenburg on June 9, 1930, in Oslo, Norway; daughter of Olav V, king of Norway (r. 1957–1991), and ****Martha of Sweden*** *(1901–1954); sister of Harold or Harald V, king of Norway (r. 1991—); married Erling Lorentzen, on May 15, 1953; children: Haakon (b. 1954); Ingeborg Lorentzen (b. 1959, who married Paolo Ribeiro); ****Ragnhild Lorentzen*** *(b. 1968).*

Oldenburg, Sophia (b. 1914).

See Sophia of Greece.

Oldenburg, Theodora (1906–1969).

See Theodora Oldenburg.

Oldenburg, Thyra (1853–1933).

See Thyra Oldenburg.

Oldfield, Anne (1683–1730)

One of the most celebrated actresses of the English stage. *Name variations: Mrs. Oldfield; Ann Oldfield. Pronunciation: OLD-feld. Born in London, England, in 1683; died at age 47 on October 23, 1730; daughter of a soldier; married Arthur Mainwaring (1668–1712); married Charles Churchill, a lieutenant general (died 1745); children: (first marriage) one son; (second marriage) one son.*

An English actress, Anne Oldfield appeared at the Drury Lane for several years before she was finally recognized for her talent rather than her beauty and elegance alone. But following her creation of Lady Betty Modish in Colley Cibber's *Careless Husband* in 1704, Oldfield was generally acknowledged as the best actress of her time, the "acknowledged successor of the great Mrs. Mountfort (***Susanna Verbruggen**)." Even the usually grudging Cibber, who had reluctantly given her the part because Verbruggen was ill, admitted that she had as much to do with the play's success as he. She was also lauded for her Lady Townley in Cibber's *Provoked Husband.*

In genteel comedy, Oldfield was unrivaled, and she later won laurels for her work in tragedy. Her list of parts was long and varied; she excelled as ***Cleopatra (VII)**, and also played Calista in Nicholas Rowe's *Fair Penitent* and created the title role in his *Tragedy of* ***Jane Shore*** (1714). Her acting was the delight of her contemporaries, while her beauty and generosity produced a spate of eulogists.

Sought out by people of fashion, Oldfield generally frequented the theater in a chair, attended by two footmen, while wearing a dress she had just worn to some aristocratic dinner. She kept her powers to the end; a few months before her death in 1730, she played the tragic role of James Thomson's *Sophonisba,* acting this last part, it was said, superbly.

Anne Oldfield was buried beneath the monument of William Congreve in Westminster Abbey. According to her maid **Margaret (Betty) Saunders,** Oldfield was interred in a shawl of fine Brussels lace, a holland shift with double ruffles of the same lace, and a pair of new kid gloves, while her body was wrapped in a winding sheet. This elicited from Alexander Pope the well-known lines from his "Moral Essays," Epistle I:

> Odious! in woolen! 'twould a saint provoke,
> Were the last words that poor Narcissa spoke;
> No, let a charming chintz and Brussels lace
> Wrap my cold limbs and shade my lifeless face;
> One would not, sure, be frightful when one's dead,
> And—Betty—give this cheek a little red.

SUGGESTED READING:

Authentick memoirs of the life of that celebrated actress Mrs. Ann Oldfield, containing a genuine account of her transactions from her infancy to the time of her decease. 2nd ed., London: 1730.

The Lovers Miscellany, a collection of amorous tales and poems, with memoirs of the life and amours of Mrs Ann Oldfield. London: 1731.

Memoirs of Mrs. Anne Oldfield. London: 1741.

Oldfield, Pearl Peden (1876–1962)

U.S. congressional representative from Arkansas (January 9, 1929–March 3, 1931). *Born on December 2, 1876, in Cotton Plant, Arkansas; died on April 12, 1962, in Washington, D.C.; interred in Oaklawn Cemetery in Batesville, Arkansas; educated in public schools and at Arkansas College in Batesville, Arkansas; married William Allan Oldfield (a congressional representative, died 1928).*

Pearl Peden Oldfield was born in Cotton Plant, Arkansas, on December 2, 1876, and received her education in public schools there and at Arkansas College in Batesville, Arkansas. She was married to William A. Oldfield, a ten-term congressional representative, who died while in office on November 19, 1928. Since her husband had won reelection shortly before his death, Pearl Oldfield was elected as a Democrat to the 70th and 71st Congresses on January 9, 1929, to fill the vacancy. She was sworn in on January 11, 1929.

Oldfield represented Arkansas during a period of natural disaster and economic depression, caused in part by the flooding of the Mississippi River in 1927. She was responsible for sponsoring legislation that maintained federal aid for the rehabilitation of farmlands damaged by the floods and, in January 1931, she worked for the approval of a $15 million food appropriation to help reduce malnutrition in drought-stricken areas. She also sponsored legislation that authorized the Arkansas Highway Commission to construct free bridges over the Black and White rivers in her district. Oldfield also served on the Committee on Coinage, Weights and Measures, the

Committee on Expenditures in the Executive Departments, and the Committee on Public Buildings and Grounds. She served in the House from January 9, 1929, to March 3, 1931, and chose not to run for reelection to the 72nd Congress.

SOURCES:

Office of the Historian. *Women in Congress, 1917–1990.* Commission on the Bicentenary of the U.S. House of Representatives, 1991.

Jo Anne Meginnes, freelance writer, Brookfield, Vermont

Olds, Elizabeth (1896–1991)

American artist, known for her Depression-era lithographs and silk-screen prints. *Born in Minneapolis, Minnesota, in December 1896; died on March 4, 1991; studied at the Minneapolis School of Art (1918–20), and the Art Students League, in New York (1920–23); never married; no children.*

Born in 1896 in Minneapolis, Minnesota, Elizabeth Olds attended that city's School of Art and then won a scholarship to New York's Art Students League, where she studied under George Luks of the Ash Can School. She often accompanied Luks on sketching expeditions into the poor neighborhoods of New York, and was strongly influenced by his grim renderings. After three years of training, Olds embarked on a journey to discover her own form of expression, a quest that first took her to Paris. In 1926, she was awarded a Guggenheim fellowship to study painting in Europe, the first woman to receive that prestigious award.

Finally convinced that her path lay in her American roots, Olds returned to the United States in 1929, at the onset of the Depression. She settled in Omaha, Nebraska, where she began producing the socially conscious works for which she would become known. Her early "Stockyard Series" of lithographs, depicting the workers and the grim activities of the city's stockyards, won critical acclaim and a silver medal from the Kansas City Art Institute. Art critic **Emily Genauer** commented on the abstract quality in these early works. "She attacks [the slaughterhouse scenes] as problems in design, seeking to achieve something of the violence and grossness and at the same time, matter-of-factness of the whole procedure through sheer pattern carried out in black and white."

In 1935, Olds returned to New York, where she went to work for the graphics division of the Federal Art Project. She continued to create lithographs extolling laborers. Her work *1939 A.D.*, in which capitalists are being driven from the Stock Exchange by a group of workers, sent a strong political message, as did *Scrap Steel* (1935–39), in which the workers toiling to erect a building are dwarfed by enormous cast-off shapes that dominate the foreground of the print. In 1937, Olds had her first of many solo exhibitions at the American Contemporary Artists Gallery in New York. It was comprised of her drawings of life in the steel mills, which later became a series of lithographs.

Olds believed deeply that art belonged to the people, and she wanted to produce her prints and silk screens in large quantities to reach the widest possible audience. In 1938, she became a founding member of the Silk Screen Unit of the Federal Art Project, a group of artists who helped transform the silk-screen process so that it could produce large editions to be sold at reasonable prices. Like many artists of the day, Olds created political illustration for the left-wing magazine *The New Masses*, and beginning in 1940, she became a frequent contributor to *The New Republic* and *Fortune* magazines. She

Pearl Peden Oldfield

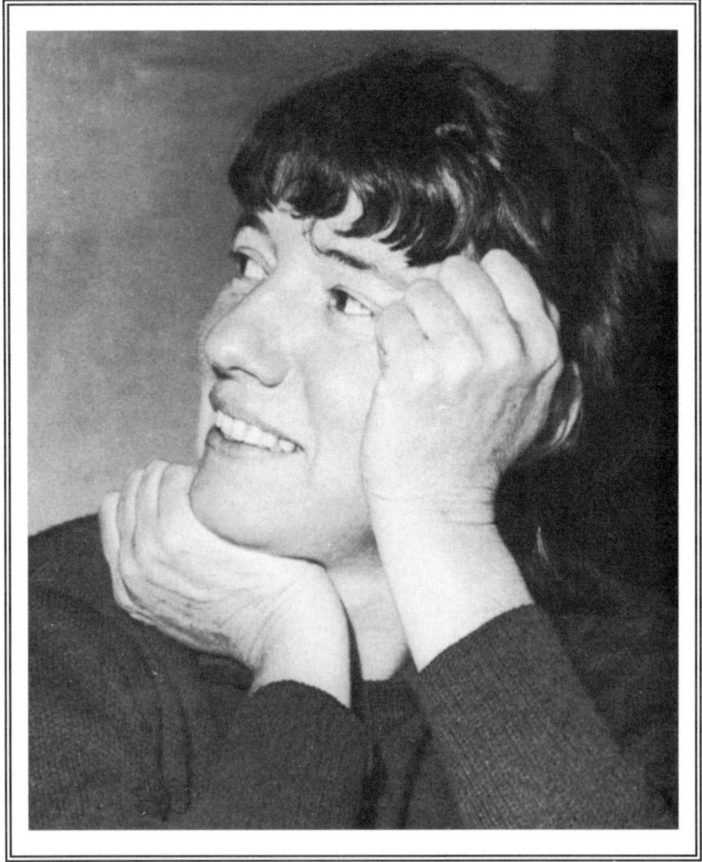

Elizabeth Olds

also wrote and illustrated six children's books, three of which were chosen as Literary Guild selections. Olds died in 1991, at age 95.

SOURCES:

Bailey, Brooke. *The Remarkable Lives of 100 Women Artists.* Holbrook, MA: Bob Adams, 1994.

Rubinstein, Charlotte Streifer. *American Women Artists.* Boston, MA: G.K. Hall, 1982.

Barbara Morgan,
Melrose, Massachusetts

Olga (c. 890–969)

Earliest female ruler of Russia who became the first Russian canonized by the Orthodox Christian Church. *Name variations: Saint Olga, Ol'ga, or Olha; Helga (Scandinavian); Helen or Helena (baptismal name); Vesheii (wise). Born to a Slavic family around 890 in Pskov, Russia; died in Kiev, Russia, in 969; traditionally believed to be the daughter of a prince from Pskov; married Igor, grand prince of Kiev (r. 912–945); children: Svyatoslav also known as Sviatoslav I, grand prince of Kiev (r. 962–972); grandchildren: Vladimir, grand prince of Kiev (r. 980–1015).*

In 945, Olga, widow of Grand Prince Igor of Kiev, was elevated to the regency in the name of their son Sviatoslav (I), then a minor. Her assumption of authority was based on old Slavonic customs that provided widows with equal rights and civic independence. The liberality of this custom accorded women a position considerably better than those in other European lands in the same period. Olga, much wiser than her husband, would use the regency to exact vengeance on her husband's murderers, improve revenue collections, strengthen law, convert to Christianity and prepare her son for his eventual inheritance. This remarkable woman would later be canonized by the Orthodox Christian Church and was given a prominent historical place as the first famous woman in Russian history.

Olga was born, according to legends, around 890 to a princely Slavic family in Pskov, Russia. Although her name is derived from the Scandinavian "Helga," anthropological studies of her direct descendants strongly suggests that she was of Slavic ancestry. There is some speculation that she received the Scandinavian name at the time of her marriage to Grand Prince Igor of Kiev, whom she met by chance when his hunting party visited Pskov. Olga became very wealthy and held landed estates in various parts of the kingdom. The *Primary Chronicle,* the earliest written source for Russian history, mentions that in her own right she owned Vyshgorod, Olzhichi, and several other villages, as well as hunting grounds and game preserves in the regions of Novgorod and Kiev.

Igor is described in the *Primary Chronicle* as a greedy, violent, and unsuccessful ruler who was a descendant of the legendary Varangian, Rurik. During his reign, Igor continued the policies of his predecessor Oleg (c. 879–912), who had been a great warrior and diplomat. Igor led a disastrous campaign into Transcaucasia in 913–14, though he did gradually bring the Slavic tribes between the Dneister and Danube rivers under his control. He also led an unsuccessful expedition against the Byzantine Empire in 941. Three years later, Igor's second campaign against the Byzantines resulted in a commercial treaty that had limited advantages for Kiev. Igor had to pacify the Pecheneg and Derevlian tribes living in the steppes north of the Black Sea. In 945, Igor was killed by the Derevlians while attempting to extract more than the customary tribute from the tribe.

Because Sviatoslav was a mere boy at the time of his father's death, his mother Olga assumed power as regent of the Kievan state. Olga had not been Igor's only wife but she apparently encountered no opposition from his other wives' families. Tradition says that Igor admired her more than his

Olga being baptized in Constantinople, 957.

other wives for her exceptional wisdom. Indeed, the Russian people called her *vesheii* (wise) out of admiration for her skillful and shrewd policies. The *Primary Chronicle* describes Olga as both clever and ruthless in her use of power. She was as strong-willed and energetic as Igor and certainly ruled more perceptively. With her accession to the regency, this extraordinary woman became the most powerful ruler over the most extensive lands in 10th-century Russia.

Olga's first action as regent was to avenge her husband's death. During this era of Russian history, family members were virtually required to avenge the murder of a relative. Olga's vengeance is one of the more dramatic episodes recorded in the *Primary Chronicle*. Following the murder of Igor, the Derevlians sent 20 men to Kiev to propose that Olga marry their leader, Prince Mal. Olga gave the Derevlians a gracious welcome, listened to their marriage proposal, pretended that their overtures pleased her, and requested the delegation return in a more formal manner the following day; her subjects would carry them in one of their boats. She then commanded her subjects to dig a large trench near the castle. Displaying arrogant pride, the Derevlians were carried to the castle but suddenly their boat was dropped into the trench, and they were buried alive by Olga's soldiers. Olga bent over and inquired whether they found so much honor to their taste.

Olga then sent emissaries to Prince Mal to announce her intentions to come to him, but her people insisted, she told him, that the noblest Derevlian lords should escort her. Mal, who intended to marry Olga, dominate the youthful Sviatoslav, and seize the Kievan throne, dispatched his nobles to Kiev. When the Derevlians arrived, they were offered baths before entering her presence. After they entered the bathhouse, Olga's men locked the doors and set it on fire. The Derevlians were burned to death.

She returned to her city of Kiev and dwelt at peace in it . . . the wisest of women.

—**Russian Primary Chronicle**

Olga then arrived at the court of Prince Mal with a small escort, saying her entourage would follow, and requested large amounts of mead and food to be provided for a funeral banquet at Igor's grave. After she mourned at the grave, she invited the Derevlians to share in the banquet. When they inquired about the Derevlian retinue which was sent to accompany her, Olga replied that they were with the rest of her train. With that, the Derevlians accepted the mead and became joyously drunk. Olga and her reinforced soldiers fell upon the Derevlians and killed 5,000 of them.

The *Primary Chronicle* reports that Olga returned to Kiev where she and her son Sviatoslav raised a larger army for the final conquest of the Derevlians. In 946, after ravaging the smaller towns, they besieged Mal's capital, Izkorosten. After a lengthy siege, she offered them peace if each house would pay a simple tribute of three pigeons and three sparrows. After the naive Derevlians paid the tribute, Olga ordered her men to attach sulphur and cloth firebrands to the birds' tails. The birds then flew to their roosts in the eaves and gables of the highly combustible thatched-roof houses in Izkorosten. As the people fled the burning city, they fell into Olga's ambushes. Thousands were killed, enslaved, or forced to become tribute-paying subjects of Kiev. Prince Mal was captured and executed on Olga's order. She also imposed a heavy tribute on the Derevlians, two parts of which went to Kiev, and the third part to her capital of Vyshegorod.

This account from the *Primary Chronicle* is based on mythology and legend, and the story of the incendiary birds is common in Scandinavian folklore. Portions of the narrative are probably true, and there are known historical facts in the account. Igor did try to extort additional revenues from the Derevlians, and they did murder him in 945. Olga did lead a successful and brutal retaliation against her husband's murderers in 946. The Derevlian towns were burned down, many nobles killed, and Prince Mal did not survive Olga's vengeance. The lands of the Derevlians did become revenue sources for Olga's treasury in 946. Whether the chronicler told events as they happened or embroidered his narrative with folklore, he described Olga's actions with undisguised admiration for her shrewdness and ingenuity.

One of Olga's greatest domestic accomplishments was the establishment of the first internal revenue system in Russia. Her principal objective was to prevent circumstances like the incident leading to Igor's death. She abolished the *poliudie* which was the customary and dangerous winter trip by the Kievan prince to collect the annual tribute. Olga instead divided the Kievan lands into districts called *pogosts,* each under the authority of an agent or board empowered to collect taxes. This reform established a system of uniform taxes paid by the entire population rather than tribute collected from individual tribes. It eliminated the autonomy of local princes while centralizing financial administration in the newly conquered lands of the Derevlians and Novgorodians. The lands previously owned by the Kievan princes had been under a similar, but less efficient, administration prior to Olga's regency. She personally traveled to collect taxes as far as Novgorod and Pskov by sleigh while wrapped in fur clothing and covers. Olga made it very clear, to all of her subordinate princes, who wielded the power in Kiev.

Her most notable claim to fame was her conversion to Christianity and her visit to Constantinople in 957. Olga became the first of the royal Kievans to adopt Orthodox Christianity, although the date of her acceptance is not totally certain. According to Russian sources, she was baptized in Constantinople in 957 in a ceremony attended by the Byzantine emperor and the patriarch of Constantinople. However, documents in Constantinople indicate that she was a Christian prior to her 957 visit. It seems likely that she was baptized in Kiev around 955 and, following a second christening in Constantinople, took the Christian name Helen. Olga was certainly not the first Russian baptized (there were Christians in Igor's court who had taken oaths at the St. Elias Church in Kiev for the Russo-Byzantine

Treaty in 945), but she was the most important at the time of her christening.

In the midsummer of 957, when Olga left Kiev for Constantinople, she took with her a retinue of more than 100, including nobles, ladies, serving maids, 43 merchants, and her priest, Gregory. They arrived in the late summer but had to wait for several days in a palace outside the city of Constantinople. The chronicles report that Olga was beautiful and that she wore her best jewelry and clothes. On September 9, 957, she and her retinue were ceremoniously received by Emperor Constantine VII Porphyrogenitus in one of his palaces which was embellished with silk curtains, marble columns, sculptured fountains, and gilded domes. Olga was escorted forward by two courtiers as her name was announced. She presented the emperor with gifts of sable, ermine and Derevlian slaves. Without a single word, she was dismissed and led from the chamber, while organ music filled the air.

Olga and her ladies were led through a maze of courts and corridors to a pavilion. After waiting for a maddening amount of time, they were summoned for a second audience with Empress ***Helena Lekapena.** Olga had to then wait until several Byzantine women were presented to the empress before she and then her ladies were escorted to the throne. Later, a third reception was hosted by the imperial couple in a more informal way. After being seated, Olga was given a lengthy audience to discuss her business with them through interpreters. That same evening, Olga and her ladies attended an elegant banquet hosted by the imperial family while a second banquet was simultaneously held in an adjacent hall for the male nobles and merchants in her entourage. The guests did not sit at the same table as the hosts, but at a distance on a lower level. After the dinner, Olga was invited to join the imperial couple in another room for dessert, and she was informally seated with the emperor and empress.

Olga remained in Constantinople for more than a month. Twice during her visit, she and members of her retinue were presented with monetary gifts. Constantine also gave Olga gifts of gold, silver, clothing and ceramic vessels. On October 18, the imperial couple held a final meeting with Olga before her departure. Afterwards, the empress and the royal princesses—including Agatha and ***Theodora**—held a banquet for Olga while the emperor presided over a separate banquet with the male members of her retinue. Olga left Constantinople with many rich gifts. Although she was probably impressed with the splendor of the emperor's court, she was apparently not humbled by her visit. The following year, Constantine sent her a message asking when he would receive the gifts she had promised him. Olga replied that he would receive the gifts after he came to Kiev and stood around her palace as long as she stood waiting in his.

Olga's visit to Constantinople to seek a metropolitan bishop for Kiev did not succeed. She was willing to recognize the authority of the patriarch of Constantinople as head of the church but demanded autonomy for the Russian Church. Olga and the Russian princes were afraid the Byzantine emperor would insist that they not only submit to the patriarch's authority but also acknowledge the authority of the emperor. This was a real consideration for Olga, given the closeness of church-state relations in Byzantium. When her efforts failed, she turned to the West and asked Holy Roman Emperor Otto I (r. 962–973) to appoint an archbishop to Kiev and send priests to Russia. When Otto sent Adalbert of Trier, an ordinary bishop with limited authority, Olga realized that the Russian Church would be subordinate to the German clergy. Upon Adalbert's arrival in Kiev, he met with such an unfriendly reception that he abandoned his mission and returned to Trier in 962.

Olga had accepted Christianity but failed to obtain an international recognition for the Russian Church. She also failed in her efforts to get her son Sviatoslav to accept Christianity. He once told her that his companions would laugh at him if he embraced her religion. Though he attained his majority in 964, he continued to let Olga dominate his government because he, like his father, was constantly involved in military campaigns. She could never persuade him to remain peacefully in Kiev and govern his people.

Olga died after a long illness on July 11, 969. Although he disapproved, Sviatoslav respected his mother's request that her priest, Gregory, conduct a Christian funeral without the ritual pagan burial feast. Her conversion and dedication to Christianity had certainly strengthened the Christian party in Kievan Russia but it did not result in the conversion of the entire kingdom. Sviatoslav I (r. 962–972) remained a pagan until his death while campaigning against the Pechnegs in 972. His son and successor, Vladimir (r. 980–1015), officially adopted Orthodox Christianity for the Russians in 988. Realizing that Olga and Vladimir marked the transition between pagan and Christian Russia, the Russian Orthodox Church canonized both of them. Olga's feast day is July 11. Her tomb remained for over two centuries in

Kiev but was destroyed in 1240 by the Mongolian-Tatar armies of Batu Khan.

SOURCES:

Cross, S.H., and O.P. Sherbowitz-Wetzor. *The Russian Primary Chronicle.* Cambridge, MA: Medieval Academy of America, 1953.

Dvornik, Francis. *The Slavs: Their Early History and Civilization.* Boston, MA: American Academy of Arts and Sciences, 1956.

Sokol, Edward D. "Ol'ga (?–969) Saint," in *Modern Encyclopedia of Russian and Soviet History.* Vol. 26, 1982, pp. 14–19.

Toynbee, Arnold J. *Constantine Porphyrogenitus and His World.* London: Oxford University Press, 1973.

Vernadsky, George. *Kievan Russia.* New Haven, CT: Yale University Press, 1959.

Volkoff, Vladimir. *Vladimir: The Russian Viking.* Woodstock, NY: Overlook Press, 1985.

SUGGESTED READING:

Dmytryshyn, Basil, ed. *Medieval Russia: A Source Book 900–1700.* Hinsdale, IL: Dryden Press, 1973.

Grekov, Boris. *Kiev Rus.* Moscow: Foreign Languages Publishing House, 1959.

Paszkiewicz, Henry K. *The Origin of Russia.* London: Allen & Unwin, 1954.

Riha, Thomas. *Readings in Russian Civilization.* 3 vols. Chicago, IL: University of Chicago Press, 1964.

Tikhomirov, M. *The Origins of Christianity in Russia.* Moscow: Foreign Language Publishing House, 1959.

Zenkovsky, Serge A., ed. *Medieval Russia's Epics, Chronicles, and Tales.* NY: E.P. Dutton, 1963.

Phillip E. Koerper,
Professor of History, Jacksonville State University,
Jacksonville, Alabama

Olga (1884–1958)

Danish royal. *Name variations: Olga Guelph. Born Olga Adelaide Louise Mary Alexandrina Agnes on July 11, 1884, in Gmunden, Austria; died on September 21, 1958, in Gmunden; daughter of Ernest Augustus, 3rd duke of Cumberland and Teviotdale, and ****Thyra Oldenburg*** *(1853–1933, daughter of ****Louise of Hesse-Cassel*** *and Christian IX, king of Denmark).*

Olga (1895–1918).

See Alexandra Feodorovna for sidebar.

Olga, Princess Paley (1865–1929)

Russian princess. *Name variations: Olga Karnovicova or Karnovich; Princess Paleij. Born on December 2, 1865; died on September 2, 1929; daughter of Valerian Karnovich and Olga Meszaros; became morganatic wife of Paul (son of Alexander III, tsar of Russia), on September 27, 1902; children: Vladimir Pavlovitch (1897–1918);* ***Natalie Pavlovna*** *(1905–1981), princess Paley;* ***Irene Pavlovna*** *(1908–1990, who married Theodore Romanov and Hubert de Monbrison), countess Paley. Paul's first wife was ****Alexandra Oldenburg*** *(1870–1891).*

Olga Alexandrovna (1882–1960)

Russian princess and grand duchess. *Name variations: Grand Duchess Olga; Olga Romanov or Romanof; duchess of Oldenburg; Olga Koulikovsky. Born on June 13, 1882; died on November 24, 1960; interred in York Cemetery, Toronto, Ontario, Canada; daughter of ****Marie Feodorovna*** *(1847–1928) and Alexander III (1845–1894), tsar of Russia (r. 1881–1894); sister of Nicholas II, tsar of Russia (r. 1894–1917); married Peter, duke of Oldenburg, on July 27, 1901 (divorced 1916); married Major Nicholas Alexandrovitch Koulikovsky, on November 1, 1916; children: (second marriage) Tikhon Koulikovsky (b. 1917); Goury Koulikvosky (b. 1919).*

SUGGESTED READING:

Vorres, Ian. *The Last Grand Duchess: Her Imperial Highness Grand Duchess Olga Alexandrovna.* NY: Scribner, 1965.

Olga Constantinovna (1851–1926)

Queen and regent of Greece. *Name variations: Konstantinovna; Olga Romanov; Olga of Russia. Born on September 3, 1851; died on June 18, 1926, in Florence, Italy; buried in Tatoi, near Athens, Greece; daughter of Constantine Nicholaevitch (son of Nicholas I, tsar of Russia) and ****Alexandra of Saxe-Altenburg*** *(1830–1911); married William of Denmark also known as George I (1845–1913), king of the Hellenes (r. 1863–1913), on October 27, 1867; children: Constantine I (1868–1923), king of the Hellenes (r. 1913–1917, 1920–1922); George (1869–1957, who married ****Marie Bonaparte****); ****Alexandra Oldenburg*** *(1870–1891); Nicholas (1872–1938); ****Marie*** *(1876–1940); Olga (1880–1880); Andrew (1882–1944); Christopher (1888–1940).*

Olga Feodorovna (1839–1891).

See Cecilia of Baden.

Olga Iurevskaya (1873–1925)

Countess of Merenberg. *Name variations: Olga Yourievsky. Born in 1873 (some sources cite 1874); died on August 15, 1925; daughter of ****Ekaterina Dolgorukova*** *(1847–1922) and Alexander II (1818–1881), tsar of Russia (r. 1885–1881); married George, count of Merenberg, on May 12, 1895; children: George (b. 1897), count of Merenberg;* ***Olga***

von Merenberg *(b. 1898, who married Michael Tarielovitch, count Loris-Melikoff).*

Olga of Russia (1822–1892)

Queen of Wurttemberg. *Name variations: Grand duchess Olga; Olga Romanov. Born on August 30, 1822; died on October 30, 1892; daughter of Nicholas I (1796–1855), tsar of Russia (r. 1825–1855), and* ****Charlotte of Prussia*** *(1798–1860); married Charles I (1823–1891), king of Wurttemberg (r. 1864–1891), on July 13, 1846.*

Olga of Russia (1851–1926).

See Olga Constantinovna.

Olga Oldenburg (1903–1981)

Greek princess. *Name variations: Princess Olga; Olga of Greece. Born on June 11, 1903; daughter of Nicholas of Greece and* ****Helena of Russia*** *(1882–1957); married Paul Karadjordjevic (Prince Paul, regent of Yugoslavia), on October 22, 1923: children: Alexander, crown prince (b. 1924); Nicholas (b. 1928); Elizabeth Karadjordjevic (b. 1936).*

Oliphant, Carolina (1766–1845).

See Nairne, Carolina.

Oliphant, Margaret (1828–1897)

British novelist and biographer. *Name variations: Mrs. Oliphant; Margaret Oliphant Wilson. Born Margaret Oliphant Wilson on April 4, 1828, in Wallyford, Scotland; died on June 25, 1897, in Windsor, Berkshire, England; daughter of Francis Wilson (a minor customs official) and Margaret (Oliphant) Wilson; married her cousin Francis Oliphant (an artist), in 1852 (died 1859); children: Maggie (died 1864); Cyril; Frank; two who died in infancy.*

Selected writings: Passages in the Life of Mrs. Margaret Maitland *(1849);* Caleb Field: A Tale of the Puritans *(1851);* Katie Stewart *(1852);* Memoirs and Resolutions of Adam Graeme of Mossgray *(1852);* The Quiet Heart: A Story *(1854);* The Athelings *(1857);* The Days of My Life: An Autobiography *(1857);* Orphans: A Chapter in Life *(1858);* Life of Edward Irving *(1862);* Salem Chapel *(1863);* The Perpetual Curate *(1864);* Miss Marjoribanks *(1866);* The Minister's Wife *(1869);* Squire Arden *(1871);* May *(1873);* Whiteladies *(1874);* Phoebe Junior: A Last Chronicle of Carlingford *(1876);* The Greatest Heiress in England *(1879);* The Fugitives: A Story *(1879);* He That Will Not when He May *(1880);* Literary History of England *(1882);* Hester *(1883);* The Ladies Lindores *(1883);* Stories of the Seen and Unseen *(1885);* A House Divided Against Itself *(1886);* Kirsteen *(1890);* Jerusalem: Its History and Hope *(1891);* The Marriage of Elinor *(1892);* The Victorian Age of English Literature *(1892);* The Cuckoo in the Nest *(1892);* A House in Bloomsbury *(1894);* Sir Robert's Fortune *(1895);* The Ways of Life: Two Stories *(1897);* Annals of a Publishing House *(1897–98);* Autobiography and Letters *(1899);* Queen Victoria: A Personal Sketch *(1901).*

Margaret Oliphant was a prolific writer who over the span of some 50 years authored more than 100 novels, numerous travel books, histories, and biographies, over 50 short stories, and at least 400 periodical essays. While she enjoyed the distinction of being Queen ***Victoria**'s favorite novelist, Oliphant struggled to maintain a writing pace that would generate the income needed to support a number of dependent relatives. The necessity of speed and the whims of her audience kept her work from maintaining the quality needed for an enduring literary reputation, and by the end of the 19th century she was all but forgotten. Although her industry ultimately led to her obscurity, as one critic noted, "The really surprising thing is not that she produced a great deal of hack-work, but that so much is so good."

The last child of Francis and **Margaret Oliphant Wilson**, Margaret Oliphant was born in Scotland on April 4, 1828. Though there is no record of a formal education, the young girl inherited a love of learning from her mother. She began writing in her teens (efforts which she claimed her family treated with gentle mockery rather than with support), and at age 21 published her first novel, *Passages in the Life of Mrs. Margaret Maitland* (1849).

With the serial publication of her novel *Katie Stewart* in 1852, Oliphant began a long association with *Blackwood's Edinburgh Magazine*. Perhaps the single most influential literary and political journal in the British Empire in the 1820s and 1830s, *Blackwood's* was known for "tales of terror," and remained an important publication throughout the Victorian Age. Oliphant would go on to publish numerous travel pieces, historical evaluations, literary reviews and short fiction in the magazine. Also in 1852 she married Francis Wilson Oliphant, an artist who was her cousin, and moved to London with him. There he established a stained glass studio, and she gave birth to four children, two of whom died in infancy. Her husband's tuberculosis caused the family to move to Rome in 1859, but the warmer Italian climate failed to halt the progress of the disease, and he died later that year. Pregnant, heavily in debt, and alone with her children in a foreign country, Oliphant was in dire straits, and a bout of writer's block exacerbated her financial and emotional strain. She returned to Britain with her children, eventually settling in Ealing.

Out of her sorrow came Oliphant's most successful series, *The Chronicles of Carlingford.* Published in *Blackwood's* between 1861 and 1876, and subsequently in novel form as *Salem Chapel* (1863), *The Perpetual Curate* (1864), *Miss Marjoribanks* (1866), and *Phoebe Junior: A Last Chronicle of Carlingford* (1876), the series focused on the intertwined relationships of English Dissenters in a small town. Narrower in scope than Anthony Trollope's 'Barsetshire' novels, after which the books were modeled, Oliphant's work focused an ironic but not unkind gaze on church politics and questions of doctrine and vocation. At the time of their anonymous publication, the novels were thought by many to have come from the pen of George Eliot (***Mary Anne Evans**). In addition to establishing her reputation, the *Chronicles* set a precedent that would be repeated throughout Oliphant's life, in which she produced her best work during her times of greatest sadness.

Tragedy continued to haunt her. While on a tour of Italy in 1864, her 11-year-old daughter Maggie died of gastric fever in Rome. Oliphant wrote feverishly to provide money for a sound education for her two sons, and settled in Windsor, England, so that they could attend Eton. However, her ever-growing household hindered her attempts to earn enough money to support her surviving children. When her brother Frank's business collapsed in 1868, his son joined her household. Two years later Frank's wife died, and he and his two daughters also moved in. A distant cousin, **Annie Walker**, likewise took refuge with the family as a penniless orphan. In addition to all these people, Oliphant supported her alcoholic brother Willie, who had lost his position as a Presbyterian minister and was living in Rome.

With so many people dependent on her, Oliphant turned out books at an astonishing rate. She wrote full-length novels while also producing a regular stream of articles for *Blackwood's*, as well as a number of biographies. Her *Life of Edward Irving* (1862) was particularly praised, and was followed by biographies of John Tulloch (1888), Laurence Oliphant (who was no relation, 1891), and Thomas Chalmers (1893). In 1882, she wrote a *Literary History of England*, and ten years later, with her son Frank, wrote *The Victorian Age of English Literature*.

Oliphant's novels largely consisted of popular romances involving unhappy marriages. *The Athelings* (1857), a huge success, was considered the best of her domestic romances. Other noted titles were *The Greatest Heiress in England* (1879), *Hester* (1883), *The Ladies Lindores* (1883), *Kirsteen* (1890), and *Sir Robert's Fortune* (1895). Victorian novels routinely were published in three volumes, however, and as Oliphant's plots often petered out before she adequately filled the requisite three volumes, many of her longer works suffer from extraneous padding. The contrast between her novels and the tighter writing of her short fiction heightens critical appreciation of her short stories, many of which focus on individual relationships rather than a large social panorama. She also made important contributions to the supernatural genre, which were among *Blackwood's* stock-in-trade. Unlike the typical Victorian thrillers, Oliphant's "tales of the seen and unseen" (which was also the title of one of her story collections) were generally explorations of the unknown as it relates to the living, rather than attempts to terrorize the reader. Several of her stories portray the spirit realm with genuine sympathy, and in an era when disease and childbirth regularly claimed victims from all classes, her audience appreciated the comforting thought that departed loved ones might be close by. Her story "The Open Door" is claimed by some as one of the best ghost stories ever written, and remains frequently anthologized, as do her "The Library Window" and "The Secret Chamber." The last important writing she did in the final years of her life was also a short story, published in *The Cornhill Magazine* in 1893. An exploration of contemporary assumptions that young widows who did not, as expected, withdraw from society must in consequence be sexually permissive, "The Widow's Tale" concerns a woman who enters into a loveless second marriage. Her new husband spends her small inheritance and does not permit her children to live with them. Some have speculated that the story explains why the author never married a second time.

Although some of Oliphant's essays indicate that she did not support the notion of women's rights, the female characters she wrote were often far from the Victorian ideal of submissive and nurturing wife and mother. Many, like Oliphant herself, were strong women forced to support weak men, in some cases by taking employment outside the home; biographers have traced this recurring theme to her disappointment with the men in her own life. In addition to her economically crippled brothers, Oliphant's sons failed to make a way for themselves, despite her sacrificial arrangements for their first-rate education. Oliphant blamed her indulgence of them for their failures. She was equally hard on herself in regards to her writing, noting in her autobiography (despite the earlier speculation about *The Chronicles of Carlingford*) that she would never be mentioned in the same breath with George Eliot. She stated flatly that "to bring up the boys for the service of God was better than to write a fine novel, supposing even that it was in me to do so."

The death of her son Cyril in 1890 began the "ebb tide," as she called it, of Oliphant's life. Her health began to decline, and the death of Frank, her last surviving child, in 1894 was a further blow. Her final project was a history of the Blackwood publishing house, which remained unfinished at the time of her death in 1897 at her home in Windsor, England. It was published posthumously, as was her *Autobiography and Letters*, in 1899.

SOURCES:

Buck, Claire, ed. *The Bloomsbury Guide to Women's Literature.* NY: Prentice Hall, 1992.

Fisk, Mary Lou, in *Dictionary of Literary Biography,* Vol. 159. *British Short-Fiction Writers, 1800–1880.* Edited by John R. Greenfield. Detroit, MI: Gale Research, 1996.

Kunitz, Stanley J., and Howard Haycraft, eds. *British Authors of the Nineteenth Century.* NY: H.W. Wilson, 1936.

Shattock, Joanne. *The Oxford Guide to British Women Writers.* Oxford and NY: Oxford University Press, 1993.

Uglow, Jennifer S., comp. and ed. *The International Dictionary of Women's Biography.* NY: Continuum, 1985.

Winnifrith, Tom. *Dictionary of Literary Biography,* Vol. 18. *Victorian Novelists After 1885.* Edited by Ira B. Nadel and William E. Fredeman. Detroit, MI: Gale Research, 1983.

Jacqueline Mitchell,
freelance writer, Detroit, Michigan

Oliveira Campos, Narcisa Amalia de (1852–1924).

See Amália, Narcisa.

Oliver, Edith (1913–1998)

***American drama critic for* The New Yorker.** *Born in New York, New York, on August 11, 1913; died at her home in Manhattan on February 23, 1998; daughter of Samuel Goldsmith and Maude (Biow) Goldsmith; graduated from Horace Mann School in New York City, 1931; attended Smith College, 1931–33; never married.*

Edith Oliver was an influential drama critic at *The New Yorker* for over 30 years. She began her career as a radio actress, working on such shows as "Philip Morris Playhouse" and "Gangbusters." She also wrote the radio quiz show "True or False" and, from 1940 to 1952, wrote and produced "Take It or Leave It: The $64 Question." Oliver began contributing to *The New Yorker* in 1947 and joined its staff in 1961 as a movie and off-Broadway theater critic. For many years, Oliver spent her summers serving as a dramaturg of fledgling plays at the Eugene O'Neill Theater Center in Waterford, Connecticut. Said its chair George White: "[Edith] was packaged like the quintessential elderly lady that a Boy Scout would help across the street, except that she drank martinis, smoked cigarettes and could, on occasion, have a mouth like a sailor." Oliver retired from *The New Yorker* in 1992.

Oliver, Edna May (1883–1942)

American actress. *Born Edna May Nutter in September 1883, in Malden, Massachusetts; died on November 9, 1942; educated in Boston; married D.W. Pratt (divorced).*

Selected theater: debuted in Boston (1911); debuted in New York at the Fulton Theater as Juliet in The Master *(1916); appeared as Penelope Budd in* Oh, Boy *(1917), as Hannah in* Icebound *(1923), as Ethel Drake in* The Cradle Snatchers *(1925); first appeared as Parthy Ann in* Showboat *(1927).*

Selected filmography: Wife in Name Only *(1923);* Three O'clock in the Morning *(1923);* Icebound *(1934);* Manhattan *(1924);* The Lucky Devil *(1925);* Lovers in Quarantine *(1925);* The American Venus *(1926);* Let's Get Married *(1926);* The Saturday Night Kid *(1929);* Cimarron *(1931);* Laugh and Get Rich *(1931);* Cracked Nuts *(1931);* Newly Rich *(1931);* Fanny Foley Herself *(1931);* Ladies of the Jury *(1932);* The Penguin Pool Murder *(1932);* The Conquerors *(1932);* It's Great to Be Alive *(1933);* Ann Vickers *(1933);* Only Yesterday *(1933);* Little Women *(1933);* Alice in Wonderland *(1933);* The Poor Rich *(1934);* Murder on the Blackboard *(1934);* We're Rich Again *(1934);* The Last Gentleman *(1934);* David Copperfield *(1935);* Murder on a Honeymoon *(1935);* No More Ladies *(1935);* A Tale of Two Cities *(1935);* Romeo and Juliet *(1936);* Parnell *(1937);* Rosalie *(1937);* Paradise for Three *(1938);* Little Miss Broadway *(1938);* The Story of Vernon and ***Irene Castle**

Edna May Oliver

(1939); Second Fiddle (1939); Nurse *Edith Cavell (1939); Drums Along the Mohawk (1939); Pride and Prejudice (1940); Lydia (1941).

Massachusetts-born actress Edna May Oliver made a career out of supporting character roles, on stage and in silent films and talkies, although she did snag the lead in an occasional low-budget comedy or mystery. She was particularly adroit with droll and acerbic spinster roles, such as Aunt March in *Little Women* (1933), Aunt Betsey in *David Copperfield* (1935), the Nurse in *Romeo and Juliet*, and the Widow McKlennar in *Drums Along the Mohawk* (1939), for which she received a Best Supporting Actress Academy Award nomination. Her last film *Lydia* (1941) was made just a year before her death at the age of 59.

Olivero, Magda (1914—)

Italian soprano. *Born on March 14, 1914, in Saluzzo, Italy; studied with Luigi Gerussi, Simonetto and Ghedini.*

Made debut in Turin (1933), in London at Stoll Theater (1952), in U.S. (Dallas) as Medea (1967), at Metropolitan Opera (1975).

Magda Olivero was over 60 years old when she made her Metropolitan Opera debut in 1975. Despite 40 years on international opera stages, she had never been invited to sing there. When Olivero began performing in 1933, the verismo style was at its height, and she would continue to be a formidable advocate of the style, though it had all but vanished by the end of her career. Said Dalla Rizza, "God has helped Magda to keep going so people can still know what it was like when singing was art." Many recordings document her great abilities.

John Haag,
Associate Professor of History, University of Georgia, Athens, Georgia

Oliveros, Pauline (1932—)

American composer who established her reputation in avant-garde, electronic, theatrical, and meditation music. *Born in Houston, Texas, on May 30, 1932; daughter of Edith Gutierrez; studied with Paul Koepke, Robert Erickson and William Palmer.*

Received grants to develop a voltage-controlled audio mixer for use in electronic music composition and performance as well as an electronic environment which also included design sound and light control devices; received a Guggenheim fellowship (1973–74), resulting in the composition of Crow Two: A Ceremonial Opera*; received the prestigious Beethoven Prize (1977) for her piece* Bonn Feier.

Known mainly for her contributions to electronic music and mixed media as well as for being a pioneer in the exploration in meditative states as they relate to music, Pauline Oliveros was born in Houston, Texas, in 1932. From childhood, she was receptive to sounds from electrical systems and remembered listening to her grandfather's crystal radio and wind-up Victrola. Her interest in composition was the result of a high school English class that was devoted to creative projects. From this, *Variations* was composed, a mixed instrumental sextet, which was later featured in the San Francisco Modern Music Festival. When her mother gave her a tape recorder in the late 1950s, Oliveros recorded hundreds of sounds, then transformed them with changes in speed. She felt musicians must expand their sound vocabulary into the new field of electronic music.

In 1962, she received a prize for Best Foreign Work from the Foundation Gaudeamus in

Bilthoven, Holland, for *Sound Patterns*, which was composed for mixed chorus. Oliveros founded the San Francisco Tape Music Center which concentrated on electronic music in the early 1960s. In 1967, she received an appointment as a faculty member at the University of California at San Diego where she eventually became a full professor. A prodigious composer, Oliveros was extremely creative. She once used an array of garden hoses and lawn sprinklers as part of a musical ensemble that was accompanied by alarm clocks and various domestic utensils. Jugglers, fortune-tellers, piano movers, and floor sweepers were sometimes part of her performances. As her talent developed, Oliveros moved into mixed media, combining electronic music with theater. Pauline Oliveros received many national and international prizes for her work in recognition of her status as one of the 20th century's most innovative composers.

SOURCES:

Cohen, Aaron I. *International Encyclopedia of Women Composers*. 2 vols. NY: Books & Music (USA), 1987.

John Haag,
Athens, Georgia

Olivia (1830–1910).

See Briggs, Emily Edson.

Olivier, Edith (c. 1879–1948)

English novelist and biographer. *Born Edith Maud Olivier around 1879 in the rectory at Wilton, Wiltshire, England; died on May 10, 1948, at home on the earl of Pembroke's estate in Wilton, England; daughter of Dacres Olivier (rector of Wilton and chaplain to the earls of Pembroke) and Emma (Eden) Olivier; sister of Henry Eden Olivier (b. 1866, an Anglican priest and writer); taught by mother in early years, had first governess at age 12, and attended St. Hugh's Hall, Oxford University, during four nonconsecutive terms; never married.*

Selected works: (novels) The Love Child *(1927),* As Far as Jane's Grandmother's *(1928),* Underground River *(1929),* The Triumphant Footman *(1930),* Dwarf's Blood *(1931),* The Seraphim Room *(published in U.S. as* Mrs. Chilvester's Daughters, *1932); (short stories)* Moonrakings *(1930); (biographies)* The Eccentric Life of Alexander Cruden *(published in U.S. as* Alexander the Corrector, *1934),* Mary Magdalen *(1935); (autobiography)* Without Knowing Mr. Walkley: Personal Memories *(1938); also author of* Country Moods and Tenses *(1941).*

Edith Olivier, who was born in the rectory at Wilton, Wiltshire, England, had originally hoped for a career in the theater, but her upbringing in a strict Victorian household precluded this. Instead, she devoted herself to writing. Her novels, for the most part, are imaginative and concentrate on the portrayal of human emotions.

As one of the ten children of the Reverend Canon Dacres Olivier, Edith grew up in a rigid, clerical household, which was dominated by her kind but stern father. The year of her birth, estimated as 1879, is unclear because Olivier refused to reveal it, saying she was "horrified to discover how much older I am than most writers. I seem to be completely out of date." Her mother **Emma Eden Olivier**, daughter of a bishop, oversaw Edith's early education, but by the age of 12, governesses had assumed this responsibility. Though she won a scholarship to study at St. Hugh's Hall, Oxford University, she was able to attend only sporadically because of poor health, and completed four nonconsecutive terms there. Due to her strict upbringing, suitors were discouraged as was her interest in a career in the theater. Instead, Olivier stayed at home and trained the church choir, conducted the choral society, managed the girls' club, and acted in private theatrical activities. The title of her autobiography, *Without Knowing Mr. Walkley* (1938), was a reflection of her unfulfilled theatrical ambitions. Olivier had once declared that she "would have lived in vain" if she died without ever having met Arthur Walkley, then a drama critic of *The London Times*. Walkley, however, predeceased her, without the longed-for meeting.

While at Oxford, Olivier occasionally dined with Charles Lutwidge Dodgson, who wrote *Alice's Adventures in Wonderland* under the pseudonym Lewis Carroll. She was also close friends with writers ***Sylvia Townsend Warner**, David Garnett, and ***Elinor Wylie**, and artist Rex Whistler, who provided the decorations for several of her books. During World War I, Olivier was an officer in the Women's Land Army in Wiltshire; she also served as mayor of Wilton for several terms.

Her first novel *The Love Child* (1927) concerned a lonely girl and her imaginary companion. *As Far as Jane's Grandmother's* (1928) was "a symbolic picture of life in my father's house." *The Triumphant Footman* (1930) was an amusing fantasy based on an actual family footman who masqueraded as a noble. *Dwarf's Blood* (1931) became a selection of the New York Literary Guild. *Moonrakings* (1930) was a collection of short stories set in Wiltshire. Olivier also wrote two biographies: ***Mary Magdalen*** (1935) and *The Eccentric Life of Alexander Cruden* (1934);

Cruden was the compiler of an 18th-century Biblical concordance. Edith Olivier died at her home on the earl of Pembroke's estate in 1948.

SOURCES:

Kunitz, Stanley J., and Howard Haycraft, eds. *British Authors of the Nineteenth Century.* NY: H.W. Wilson, 1936.

Shattock, Joanne. *The Oxford Guide to British Women Writers.* Oxford and NY: Oxford University Press, 1993.

Jo Anne Meginnes,
freelance writer, Brookfield, Vermont

Olivier, Fernande (1884–1966)

French artist's model who was also the mistress of Pablo Picasso. *Name variations: Madame de la Baume. Born Amélie Lang out of wedlock in 1884; died in 1966; raised by her mother's half-sister; married Paul Percheron, around 1899.*

A tall, provocative redhead, Fernande Olivier was Pablo Picasso's first mistress of note, living with the artist between 1905 and 1912. The two initially met in the summer of 1904, but after a brief passionate interlude parted ways; almost a year later, they took up residence at Picasso's studio in Paris' Bateau Lavoir. Their seven-year relationship spanned one of Picasso's most creative periods, culminating with his experimentation in Cubism which, according to Norman Mailer, in his interpretive biography *Portrait of Picasso as a Young Man*, ultimately drove the lovers apart. In the latter of two memoirs about her years with the artist, *Picasso and His Friends* (1933) and *Souvenirs Intimes* (1955), Olivier expresses the concern she had as early as 1906, over Picasso's refusal to conform: "A great ambition excites him. He has always refused to show in exhibitions, to become part of the artistic movement of his time. He wants to create a new form, be an innovator rather than a follower of great traditions. . . . [H]e wishes to subject his art to new laws. So, he struggled against all his human sentiments." While she was eventually repelled by Picasso's darker visions, Olivier, in retrospect, called her years with the artist the happiest of her life.

Fernande Olivier herself was no stranger to darkness. Born out of wedlock in 1884, she was raised in the middle-class household of her aunt and uncle who had a daughter of their own whom they favored. "There were never caresses for me and that induced me to live very much within myself," she recalled. At an early age, she married Paul Percheron, an older man (the brother of the housemaid's fiancé); during the marriage, he alternately doted on her and beat her. After about a year of this and a miscarriage that left her barren, Olivier abandoned her husband and moved to Paris. (She would remain so terrified of Percheron, however, that she never made the effort to divorce him.) She was in dire straits when she met Laurent Debienne, a young sculptor for whom she agreed to pose and grant sexual favors in return for room and board. Debienne introduced her to other artists for whom she also posed, and she soon began earning a respectable living as a model, calling herself Madame de la Baume. Coming home from work one day in the rain, she encountered the 22-year-old Picasso, who lived nearby. Obviously smitten, he was holding a tiny kitten out to her and blocking her path.

Olivier accompanied him to his studio, where she was impressed with his work, but somewhat put off with the squalid conditions of his living space and his lack of personal hygiene. She thought him a gentle, caring lover, however, the first she had encountered, and so returned on several occasions over the next ten days. Even so, she remained ambivalent about Picasso's growing obsession with her. "His eyes implore me. He watches, religiously, whatever I do. . . . [W]hen I awake, I find him at the head of the bed, his eyes full of anguish, fixed on me." Concluding that she was not yet ready for a serious commitment, Olivier returned to Debienne, then after a short time left him again and moved in with Ricard Canals and his wife **Benedetta Canals**, finally returning to Picasso in September 1905. Her awakening passion for the artist may have been related to their discovery of opium, which they smoked two or three times a week. "We can wonder if they would ever have begun to live together without the opium," writes Mailer. "Once the bridge was crossed, however, once she knew she could have extraordinary experiences in bed with him, then many a need and many a mutual social advantage would keep them together for years."

During those early days, Olivier, who once described herself as indolent, spent a good deal of time in bed, while Picasso waited on her by day and worked throughout the night. For a while, she dabbled in painting herself, asking for Picasso's advice, which he refused. "Amuse yourself," he told her. "What you do is more interesting than what you would do under the instruction of another." Olivier soon resorted to passing her time reading. Their first years together coincided with Picasso's burgeoning friendships with Max Jacob and Guillaume Apollinaire, and his obsession with ***Gertrude**

Stein, whom he had met in 1905, and who sat for him on as many as 90 occasions (culminating in the classic portrait of her in 1906). The couple often attended Stein's lively Saturday night salons and also partook of the night life in Montmartre, although Picasso was possessive and never let Olivier out of his sight. In 1906, after selling some of his works, Picasso had enough money to take Olivier to Spain, her first extended journey. In Barcelona, they visited his friends and family and then traveled to Gósol, a small village in the Pyrenees where Picasso, unusually calm and relaxed, was able to focus on his work. It was perhaps their happiest time together.

When they returned to Paris, Picasso began the experimentation that would result in his early Cubist masterpiece, *Les Demoiselles d'Avignon*. Coinciding with the new direction of Picasso's work was Olivier's impulsive decision to adopt a child, an event that probably took place in the spring of 1907. John Richardson suggests that Picasso, despite his ambivalence toward children, may have agreed to the adoption out of guilt, having persuaded an earlier mistress to have an abortion. Whatever the case, Olivier visited a Montmartre orphanage and was attracted to an adolescent girl named Raymonde, the daughter of a French prostitute. Raymonde had been rescued by a Dutch couple, Apollinaire writes. The couple had tried to teach Raymonde to play the violin; when she displayed no musical talent, they abandoned her once more. Accounts differ as to the amount of time the child remained with Olivier and Picasso, although there is agreement that she was quite spoiled by her adoptive parents as well as by their friends. Olivier was particularly indulgent, writes Richardson, "forever brushing Raymonde's hair, tying it up in ribbons, and seeing that she went off to school prettily dressed." Richardson maintains that Raymonde was at the studio for four months, during which time Picasso amused her with drawings of his dog Frika and her puppies, and of *castellers*, tumblers that had performed at the folk festivals of his youth. Mailer suggests that Olivier grew tired of Raymonde after only a week, theorizing that the bitterness and lack of compassion in her own childhood made it impossible for her to raise someone else's child. Richardson, however, believes that Olivier may have had different concerns, suggesting that some of Picasso's sketches of the child in the *Demoiselles* sketchbooks depict her sitting naked with her legs wide apart, washing her feet. "Young girls excited Picasso," he writes. "They also disturbed him; they put him in mind of his dead sister, **Conchita**. Fernande would have had cause for alarm. The decision in late July to return Raymonde to the orphanage would have gone against her warmth of heart but not her better judgment. The girl was *de trop*—in the way." Whatever the time frame, the child was given to Max Jacob with instructions to return her to the orphanage, but Jacob was unable to do so and in the end left her with a local concierge instead. Mailer speculates that the unfortunate outcome of the whole affair may have caused Picasso and Olivier to separate temporarily a few months later.

Fernande Olivier with Picasso.

Although the details go unrecorded, Olivier and Picasso reunited in November 1907, taking up residence again in Picasso's studio. In the spring of 1908, a young drug-addicted German painter of their acquaintance committed suicide in the Bateau Lavoir, an event that had great impact upon the couple. They were, first of all, put off by opium. "Sick in spirit," recorded Olivier, "our own nerves deranged, we decided to no longer touch the drug." The tragedy also spurred a move out of Paris, to a farm in Rue-des-Bois, near Griel, although this turned out to be a mistake. Uninspired by country living, Picasso was depressed and unable to work ("Everything smells like mushrooms," he complained), and they soon returned to Paris.

In the summer of 1909, Picasso once again took Olivier to Barcelona, then up to Horta de Ebro, where he began a particularly productive period, although Olivier was hardly pleased with his new Cubist renditions of her. "It may seem trifling to speak of a somewhat vain young woman's reaction to Cubism, but [her] face was her fortune, and she could scarcely watch with philosophic detachment while it was carved into ridges," writes Patrick O'Brian in *Pablo Ruiz Picasso*, "especially as the ridges and the corresponding hollows . . . belonged to a woman of sixty or more." The relationship was further strained by their recent separation, and by the fact that Olivier was ill, either with a kidney ailment or a venereal disease. "Life is sad. Pablo is in a bad mood, and I have received nothing from him in the way of moral or physical comfort," she wrote to Gertrude Stein. She recovered her health, but as Mailer remarks, "something had hardened in the relationship." In a photograph from Horta de Ebro, Olivier is curiously holding the hand of a disgruntled child. "One more buried anger between Picasso and herself," writes Mailer, "the children she will never give birth to, and the recollection of the sad fiasco of the child they adopted for a week."

Upon their return to Paris, the couple moved out of Bateau Lavoir and into an apartment on the boulevard de Clichy, an upgrade that Olivier had probably wanted for years. Although she adored Picasso's energy and talent, she remained, as Mailer points out, a product of her middle-class upbringing, and therefore was frequently embarrassed by her lover's crudeness. Picasso was also ambivalent about their new middle-class amenities and became moody and given to bouts of hypochondria. Despite their problems, the couple made an effort to improve their social standing, seeing friends, and entertaining at home, although life had little of the spirit and excitement of their earlier days together.

A new woman, ***Eva Gouel**, entered Picasso's life as early as November 1911, although his affair with her was kept secret for six months. Actually, Gouel, who was the mistress of a sculptor named Marcoussis, was introduced to Picasso by Olivier, who at the time may have also been ready for a new lover. In May 1912, she ran off with an Italian painter named Ubaldo Oppi. "Fernande ditched me for a Futurist," Picasso wrote to his friend and collaborator Georges Braque. "What am I going to do with the dog?" The relationship did not end quite so neatly, however. Olivier soon tired of Oppi and went looking for Picasso, who was hiding in Céret with his new love. There were several confrontations there, and upon their return to Paris, before they went their separate ways.

On her own once again, Olivier eked out a small sum of money by selling the few drawings Picasso had given her, then began the scramble to earn a living. She was employed by a friend of Max Jacob's, then went to work for an antique dealer. For three years after that, she appeared at the Lapin Agile, where, displaying a deep, resonant voice, she recited Baudelaire and Duvigny. She then resorted to anything that came her way: she was a tutor, a secretary, a cashier, and even read horoscopes for a time. From 1918 to 1938, she lived with Roger Karl, an actor who had worked with ***Sarah Bernhardt**, but in 20 years he apparently never really made her happy. Perhaps, as Mailer contends, she always remained in love with Picasso.

SOURCES:

Mailer, Norman. *Portrait of Picasso as a Young Man*. Boston, MA: Atlantic Monthly Press, 1955.

O'Brian, Patrick. *Pablo Ruiz Picasso*. NY: Putnam, 1976.

Richardson, John. "The Doomed Adoption," in *At Random*. Fall 1996, pp. 46–47.

Barbara Morgan,
Melrose, Massachusetts

Olivier, Lady (1913–1967).

See Leigh, Vivien.

Olivier, Lady (b. 1929).

See Plowright, Joan.

Olkyrn, Iris (1866–1953).

See Milligan, Alice.

Olsen, Tillie (c. 1912—)

American writer whose fiction and nonfiction speaks for those who are least represented in Western literature and who has, through her writing and life, brought to the reading public hundreds of writers who would otherwise have remained silent or unknown. *Name variations: Tillie Lerner. Born Tillie Lerner in 1912 or 1913 in Nebraska (neither the date nor the town is documented); daughter of Samuel Lerner (a laborer and political activist) and Ida (Beber) Lerner; attended Omaha public schools through 11th grade; studied creative writing at San Francisco State College, 1953–54, and Stanford, 1955–56; married Jack Olsen, in 1943 (died 1989);*

children: Karla (b. 1932); Julie (b. 1938); Katherine Jo (b. 1943); Laurie (b. 1948).

Honorary degrees: Hobart and William Smith Colleges, Geneva, New York (1984), Clark University, Worchester, Massachusetts (1985), Albright College, Reading, Pennsylvania (1986); Litt. D. from University of Nebraska (1979) and Knox College, Galesburg, Illinois (1982).

Fellowships: Stegner fellowship in creative writing (1955–56), Radcliffe fellowship (1962–64), National Endowment for the Arts award (1967), American Academy and National Institute of Arts and Letters award (1975), Guggenheim fellowship (1975–76), Ministry to Women Award of Unitarian Universalist Federation (1980), Senior Fellowship of the National Endowment for the Humanities (1983–84), Bunting Fellowship at Radcliffe (1985–86), Mari Sandoz Award (1991), Rea Award for the Short Story (1994).

Visiting professorships: Stanford (1971), Massachusetts Institute of Technology (1973–74), Amherst College (1969–70), University of Massachusetts, Boston (1974), University of California, San Diego (1978), Radcliffe (1980), University of Minnesota (1986), University of California, Los Angeles (1987).

Family settled in Omaha, Nebraska (c. 1917); left Omaha Central High School (1929); worked at odd jobs to help support family; joined Young Communist League and was jailed in Kansas City, Kansas, for organizing packinghouse workers (1932); moved to Faribault, Minnesota, to recover from first stages of tuberculosis; began Yonnondio *and gave birth to Karla (1932); settled permanently in San Francisco (1933); arrested for taking part in San Francisco Maritime Strike, wrote poetry and reportage for YCL (1934); attended American Writers Congress in New York (1935); spent next 20 years raising her four daughters, working at a succession of low-paying jobs to help support family, participating in community, union, and political activity, and writing; enrolled in creative writing course at San Francisco State University (1953–54); received Stegner fellowship in creative writing to attend Stanford University (1955–56); received Ford Foundation grant in literature (1959); won O. Henry award for year's best American short story for "Tell Me a Riddle" (1961); worked on recovered manuscript of* Yonnondio *and biographical interpretation of* Life in the Iron Mills *by Rebecca Harding Davis (1972); was international visiting scholar, Norway; film version of "Tell Me a Riddle" produced (1980); May 18 declared Tillie Olsen Day in San Francisco (1981); visited Soviet Union and China (1984).*

*Selected writings: (fiction) "Requa" (*Iowa Review, *Vol. 1, Summer 1970, reprinted as "Requa-I" in* Best American Short Stories, *edited by* ***Martha Foley** *and David Burnett, Boston: Houghton Mifflin, 1971),* Tell Me a Riddle *(Philadelphia: Lippincott, 1961, includes "I Stand Here Ironing," "Hey Sailor, What Ship?," "O Yes," "Tell Me a Riddle"),* Yonnondio: From the Thirties *(NY: Delacorte, 1974); (poetry) "I Want You Women Up North to Know" (under name Tillie Lerner,* Partisan, *Vol. 1, March 1934, reprinted in* Writing Red: An Anthology of American Women Writers, 1930–1940, *edited by Charlotte Nekola and Paula Rabinowitz, NY: The Feminist Press, 1987); (nonfiction prose)* Mother to Daughter, Daughter to Mother: A Daybook and Reader *(Old Westbury, NY: Feminist Press, 1984),* Silences *(NY: Delacorte, 1978), "The Strike" (under name Tillie Lerner,* Partisan Review, *Vol. 1, September–October 1934).*

The circumstances and choices of Tillie Olsen's life—political involvement, the struggle to survive the Depression, wide reading, marriage, motherhood, and work—convinced her that she could and must make literature "out of the lives of despised people," as she writes in *Silences*, her 1978 nonfiction work. In the 1930s, she described in her diary the people she wanted to write about:

> [T]hat whole generation of exiled revolutionaries, the kurelians and croatians, the bundists and poles; and the women, the mothers of six and seven; . . . the housewives whose Zetkin and Curie and Bronte hearts went into kitchens and laundries and the patching of old socks; and those who did not speak the language of their children, who had no bridge . . . to make themselves understood.

This steady vision has guided every phase of Olsen's writing career, leading her to work that moves powerfully against the literary and critical currents of the mainstream, and even partially against the countercurrents created by the literary Left and the feminist movement of the 1970s, both of which shaped and supported her as a writer. She believes strongly that circumstances, rather than lack of skill or courage, silenced her for 20 years and almost completely stopped her from writing, as she believes they silence many potentially fine writers. In turn, it was, in her opinion, a combination of social, political, and economic circumstances, supportive communities, and "special, freaky luck" that allowed her to envision herself as a writer and, finally, to carve out the territory of her stories. Her fiction—the four short stories in *Tell Me a Riddle,* her novel *Yonnondio: From the Thirties,* and the novella "Requa"—rescues from oblivion the lives and communal histories of people still outside the visual field of most American readers, writers, and scholars. Through her example and her urging, she has inspired many people usually marginalized by society to begin to imagine themselves as writers; since the publication of *Silences*, "breaking silence" has become readily understood as a shorthand description of the event in which an individual or group tells a long-suppressed story. Finally, and just as important, Olsen has been responsible for restoring forgotten writers to new generations of readers. In the 1970s, she gleaned and published in *Women's Studies Newsletter* long lists of writers, almost all of them women, whom most readers had never heard of, let alone read; and at her urging the Feminist Press reprinted ◂ **Rebecca Harding Davis**' *Life in the Iron Mills,* the first of many forgotten classics to be recovered in the last decades of the 20th century.

In the question session after a reading and lecture Olsen gave during her residency at the University of Minnesota in 1986, a member of the audience asked her where she got her serenity. Her answer was vehement: "I have no serenity." Yet, a few days earlier a newspaper interviewer had asked her what she thought of critics who characterize her works as grim and pessimistic. Her answer then was also vehement: "What the world has given to us doesn't have to stay as it is because we are capable and have changed it. . . . It's not unremittingly grim to know that we haven't changed enough things yet. . . . I have a lot of belief in us." These are the oppositions Olsen's writing holds in balance: urgency and anger, but never despair; hope, but never a serene or cynical acceptance of the contradictions that fragment the lives of the people she identifies with and portrays—mothers, the old, working men and women, members of ethnic and cultural minorities, struggling artists. Olsen has, in **Annie Gottlieb**'s words, "taken an oath, with a character in *Yonnondio,* 'to rebel against what will not let life be.'"

▸ Davis, Rebecca Harding (1831–1910)

American novelist. *Born Rebecca Blaine Harding on June 24, 1831, in Washington, Pennsylvania; died in Mt. Kisco, New York, September 29, 1910; grew up in Huntsville, Alabama, and Wheeling, West Virginia; graduated from the Washington (Pennsylvania) Female Seminary, 1848; married L. Clarke Davis (editor of the* Philadelphia Inquirer *and the* Philadelphia Public Ledger*), in March 1863; children: Richard Harding Davis (1864–1916, a journalist); and others.*

Rebecca Harding Davis was the first novelist in the country to introduce the labor question into fiction. A regional writer, she began gaining her reputation for grim reality with *Life in the Iron Mills,* which was first published in the *Atlantic Monthly* in April 1861. The following year, the *Atlantic* serialized her "A Story of Today," which became *Margaret Howth* in book form. Davis contributed many short stories and sketches to periodicals, was contributing editor for the *New York Tribune,* and wrote a number of novels, including *A Law Unto Herself* (1878) and *Waiting for the Verdict* (1868), about racism in America. Her later works include *Dallas Galbraith, Berrytown, Natasqua, Silhouettes of American Life, Kent Hampden,* and *Doctor Warrick's Daughters.* Davis' eldest son, Richard Harding Davis, followed his mother's path, becoming a war correspondent, novelist, and one of the most influential journalists of his day.

Tillie Olsen was born in 1912 or 1913 (her birth certificate is lost) to committed Jewish socialist parents. She was the second of six children of Samuel and **Ida Beber Lerner**, Russian Jews who had taken part in the 1905 Revolution to overthrow the tsar. When the revolution failed, they fled to the United States to avoid imprisonment, eventually settling in Omaha, Nebraska. Like many revolutionary Jews of their generation, they had rejected their religion but not the strong sense of communal responsibility that is part of the Eastern European Jewish tradition. Their socialist and communal convictions were reinforced in the United States, where Olsen's father was active in the burgeoning labor movement and the Nebraska Socialist Party, of which he served as secretary. As well, both her mother and father were active in the Omaha Workmen's Circle, a socialist organization that took the place of the synagogue for Jews who no longer held traditional religious beliefs. The young Tillie Lerner, therefore, spent her childhood in a home that was a center of political activity; she remembers that she and her brothers and sisters slept on chairs placed next to each other when guests stayed at their house. Part of her early education certainly came from the conversation and oratory of socialist leaders like Eugene V. Debs and from political pamphlets.

When she was very young, Olsen began working to help support her family, but even so she was able to stay in school through the 11th grade, several years longer than most children of working-class parents at the time. Her college-prep high school made her painfully aware of the economic and class differences between her own family and the families of her wealthier

Tillie Olsen

classmates; it also introduced her to the wonders of literature, and books quickly became a refuge. In high school, she set out to read her way through the Omaha public library's collection of fiction, poetry, and biography. The reading list gleaned from her journals by **Deborah Rosenfelt** is amazingly broad and deep, but it shows that Olsen, even at that young age, was especially drawn to those writers who shared her commitment to social justice. One of the most influential events of her life was reading Rebecca Harding Davis' *Life in the Iron Mills* "in one of three water-stained, coverless, bound volumes of the *Atlantic Monthly,* bought for ten cents each in an Omaha junkshop" when Olsen was 15. Although she did not discover the author's name until many years later, this anonymously published work told her "literature can be made out of the lives of despised people," and "you, too, must write." *Life in the Iron Mills,* along with the rest of her wide reading, provided an impetus to her own writing: she discovered that the lives of the people she knew well and the language they spoke were a part of literature. What she could say had not yet been said.

Olsen began writing for publication in the 1930s, the decade of the Great Depression. Young political activists like Olsen were concerned not only about unjust economic structures in the United States, but also about revolutionary movements around the world and the struggle against fascism in Europe. In her study of the socialist roots of Olsen's fiction, Rosenfelt writes: "Olsen felt herself to be part of a valid, necessary, and global movement to remake the world on a more just and humane model."

Because Olsen, even at age 18, was involved in the labor movement and was a member of the Young Communist League (YCL), while at the same time eager to write, this climate was invigorating for her. This double dedication also created problems, because her time, energy, and talent were divided. She worked at a wide variety of jobs (from tie presser to model to packing house worker) simply to stay alive; she was a grassroots labor organizer in a movement that demanded action as well as words; and she was a writer torn between her desire to write fiction and the movement's need for pamphlets and articles.

By an odd twist, these conflicting demands came together to produce the early chapters of *Yonnondio: From the Thirties,* Olsen's first piece of fiction. She was jailed in 1932 for helping organize packing-house workers in Kansas City, Kansas. As she describes the experience: "I spent some time in KC in the Argentine jail, where I developed first pleurisy, then incipient T.B. It meant I had to be taken care of, was given thinking-writing time." She spent that time in Faribault, Minnesota, where she began working on *Yonnondio.* She also became pregnant, and was 19 when her daughter Karla was born.

That same year, Olsen moved to California, where she continued both her writing and her political activities. She helped organize maritime and agricultural workers, and again was jailed for her efforts. She wrote two accounts of the 1934 San Francisco General Strike, both of which were published—"Thousand Dollar Vagrant" in *New Republic* and "The Strike" in *Partisan Review.* The latter magazine also published the first chapter of *Yonnondio,* then called "The Iron Throat," and two poems. Based on the promise they saw in that first chapter, Bennett Cerf and Donald Klapfer of Random House offered her a contract for the novel. However, in addition to her political activities, Olsen was holding down a job, sometimes two, and caring for her daughter. She gave up the contract and didn't finish the book until 38 years later.

Olsen says of the early years of the Depression:

> In 1931 and '32 and '33, when a third of the nation was ill-housed, ill-clothed, ill-nourished, there were a million people riding the boxcars, most of them young, the homeless youth. . . . The family behind us cooked . . . their dog to eat. Those were the Hoover years of no welfare, no-nothingism, and denial, when there were long, long lines and apples, everything that people know about now in that shadowy mythical way.

Yet it is surely part of Olsen's good luck that she began to write in an atmosphere of heightened social consciousness surrounded by people who valued writing and saw it as revolutionary political work. She found in the Left, and particularly in socialist-feminist writers, a two-stranded tradition that did not consider either her perceptions or the world in which she lived to be subjects unsuited for literature.

Important as the influence of the political Left was on Olsen's writing, it would be a mistake to emphasize it to the exclusion of other shaping circumstances, the most important being her life as a wife, mother, and worker. This combination of circumstances both modified and deepened her vision and almost silenced her as a writer. Sometime before the end of the '30s, Olsen stopped writing. In 1936, she began living with Jack Olsen, a longshoreman, union organizer, and companion in the YCL, and had two more daughters, Julie in 1938 and Katherine Jo in 1943. She and Jack were married that same year, before he left for the Army. In 1948, daughter Laurie was born. During most of those years, Olsen continued to work at a long succession of jobs to help support her family. She notes that her "hands were maybe two, three years of my life in water washing clothes, before the automatic washer, instead of writing on my pad"; she did not begin writing again until the mid-50s.

When Olsen describes herself as a writer, she says that she has been extraordinarily lucky for a person from her circumstances, but also that she has suffered irreparable harm. She documents both the luck and the harm in *Silences,* in which she describes her triple life of mother, worker, and writer:

> A full extended family life; the world of my job; . . . and the writing, which I was somehow able to carry around within me through work, through home. Time on the bus even when I had to stand, was enough; the stolen moments at work, enough; the deep night hours for as long as I could stay awake, after the kids were in bed, after the household tasks were done, sometimes during. It is no accident that the first work I considered publishable began: "I stand here ironing, and what you asked me moves tormented back and forth with the iron."

In 1954, at the urging of her daughter Karla, Olsen took a creative-writing class at San Francisco State University. The story she began for that class, "Help Her to Believe," earned her a Stegner fellowship in creative writing at Stanford. In the eight months of relative freedom that followed, she finished "Help Her to Believe" (which became "I Stand Here Ironing") and "Hey Sailor, What Ship?," and began "Tell Me a Riddle." These three stories plus "O Yes" were published in periodicals between 1956 and 1960; in 1961, "Tell Me a Riddle" was awarded the O. Henry first prize for the best American short story of the year. That year also saw publication of a collection of these four stories, titled *Tell Me a Riddle.*

While the stories in *Tell Me a Riddle* are deceptively simple, Olsen's compressed, poetic style, broken by gaps and silences, suggests ever-widening social, historical, and political contexts. In "I Stand Here Ironing," a mother ponders the life of her 19-year-old daughter Emily, a child she gave birth to when she herself was 19 and a single mother. In an internal monologue, the nameless mother traces the life of this child of the Depression, of poverty, of "anxious, not proud, love," of a world shadowed by the Cold War and the atomic bomb. The story ends with a plea: "Only help her to know—help make it so there is cause for her to know—that she is more than this dress on the ironing board, helpless before the iron."

"O Yes," another story of mothers and daughters, evokes the racial climate of the early 1950s, before the civil-rights movement. Carole, a white girl, and Parialee, a black girl, are close friends, as are their mothers, until junior high inexorably sorts them by race and class. At a black Baptist church service, Carole realizes the depth of her betrayal of her friend, and the depth of her identification with people she has been told are not like her.

"Tell Me a Riddle" details the story of Eva and David, Eastern European Jews, who, like Olsen's parents, fled Russia after the 1905 revolution. After 47 years of marriage and the hard work of raising seven children through war and depression, their differing needs now threaten to tear them apart. David wants to settle into a retirement home established by his Workmen's Circle; Eva, after living the traditional role of wife and mother, wants "to move to no one's rhythms but her own," in a solitude that will permit her to reclaim her early revolutionary self. David has given up his early dreams and wants to enjoy the relative affluence of the '50s; Eva, now dying of cancer, has never given up those dreams of universal peace and freedom from oppression, not only for their children but for all children. As she speaks of their youthful dreams on her deathbed, David says in wonder, "Eva! Still you believed?"

> [Tillie Olson is] a writer of such generosity and honesty, she literally saves our lives.
>
> **—Alice Walker**

In view of the political climate of the '50s, these stories seem even more remarkable. Olsen has described 1955–56, the time of her Stegner fellowship at Stanford and one of her most fruitful as a writer, as "a presage year for our country." It was the year "of ***Rosa Parks**, Birmingham, Little Rock. Year of the first happenings of freedom movements, movements against wrong, which were to convulse and mark our nation and involve numberless individual lives." But is was also, she writes, a "year that began still in the McCarthyite shadow of fear; of pervasive cynical belief that actions with others against wrong were personally suspect, would only end in more grievous wrong, year of proclamation that the young were a 'silent generation,' future 'organization men.'" Tillie and Jack Olsen had already fallen under the McCarthyite shadow of fear. In 1953, Jack was subpoenaed to testify before the House Un-American Activities Committee on charges that he was a Communist. He was blacklisted, which meant that he could no longer work in the warehouses on the San Francisco docks. Though Olsen was not called before the Committee, she has said in an interview with **Abby Werlock** that she was fired from several jobs when FBI agents arrived at her workplace to reveal her affiliations. However, despite the conformity of the 1950s and the McCarthy-induced fear of communal action, all of Olsen's stories from this period call readers into kinesthetic and emotional identification with "thwarted lives." Her stories gather around themselves a community whose members are called to acknowledge responsibility and work for social change.

In 1970, Olsen published "Requa," her least known but most experimental work. In both "Requa" and "Hey Sailor, What Ship?" the protagonists are working men and boys, to whom Olsen accords the same respect she gives her women characters. In "Requa," Stevie is orphaned and left traumatized when his mother dies. He has no one but his uncle Wes, a salvager in a Depression-era junkyard who is battling his own poverty, loneliness, and exhaustion. Wes discovers a depth of patience in himself as he performs the ordinary tasks of child-rearing, and, despite his own need for love, offers love to this "ghostboy." In this story of loss, Olsen delineates the strength and courage that explain, to borrow **Blanche Gelfant**'s description, "the mystery of survival in a wasteland."

Under the impetus of the feminist movement of the 1970s, Olsen's stories began to be read and taught, sometimes from mimeographed copies passed from hand to hand, and she began to receive fellowships, honorary degrees, and requests to speak and teach. In 1971, she participated in the Modern Language Association (MLA) forum, "Women Writers in the Twentieth Century," where she gave a speech that has since become famous under its published title, "Women Who are Writers in Our Century: One Out of Twelve." In this talk, she urges her listeners to count the number of women writers included in anthologies, class lists, critical overviews, etc., and then account for the small numbers. She writes that the ratio of women writers to men who are published, anthologized, and awarded prizes can be understood "only in the context of this punitive difference in circumstance, in history, between the sexes; this past, hidden or evident, that . . . continues so terribly, so determiningly to live on."

In 1978, Olsen published *Silences,* a compilation of two addresses ("Silences in Literature" and "One Out of Twelve"), her biographical interpretation of *Life in the Iron Mills,* and an after-section called "Acerbs, Asides, Amulets, Exhumations, Sources, Deepenings, Roundings, Expansions," in which she liberally documents the ideas presented in the two talks that begin the book. Olsen writes that silence should be the natural environment for the word, "that necessary time for renewal, lying fallow, gestation, in the natural cycle of creation." But for most of humanity throughout most of history, silence has not been that fertile environment. "The silences I speak of here are unnatural," she writes, "the unnatural thwarting of what struggles to come into being, but cannot." Olsen concentrates most on the societal circumstances that stifle creativity, and in particular the creation of literature.

The 1970s also brought *Yonnondio: From the Thirties* to readers. Olsen had thought the manuscript was lost until, some 38 years after she published the first chapter, scattered pages were discovered. Working at ***Marian MacDowell**'s MacDowall Colony, the older Tillie Olsen entered into "an arduous partnership" with that "long ago young writer," ordering the manuscript pages and choosing among the drafts, as she says in her foreword to the book. But the vision and the words of the *Yonnondio* that was finally published in 1974 are those of her 19-year-old self.

Although it is less artistic and more overtly political than "Requa" and the stories in *Tell Me a Riddle, Yonnondio* heralds the themes that have preoccupied Olsen all her life. The novel traces the Holbrook family's desperate migration, from a mining town in Wyoming, to a tenant farm in South Dakota, to a packing-house city much like the Omaha where Olsen grew up. Jim and Anna Holbrook use all their strength to create a better life for their five children, but in one powerful scene after another, Olsen shows the loneliness and fragility of working-class families in an uncaring society. While the story evokes great sympathy for men like Jim, Anna Holbrook and her oldest daughter Mazie are the story's center. As Deborah Rosenfelt says, *Yonnondio,* like all of Olsen's work, "testifies to her concern for women, her vision of their double oppression if they are poor or women of color, her affirmation of their creative potential. . . . Indeed, her writings about . . . the complex, painful, and redemptive interactions between mother and child have helped a new generation of women writers to treat that subject with a fullness and honesty never before possible in American literature." In 1984, Olsen collected in the daybook *Mother to Daughter, Daughter to Mother* the writings of many women about the sometimes joyful, sometimes painful subject of mothering. She introduces the collection with her regret that mothers still have not told their stories in their own words; the book's blank pages, arranged like a calendar, are an invitation for busy mothers to do just that.

Jack Olsen, her husband of 46 years, died in 1989. Olsen remains in the third-floor San Francisco apartment that she has lived in for over 30 years. Her works continue to be read, reprinted, anthologized, and translated into many languages, and the body of critical responses to her life and work is growing. Writers around the world, especially women and writers of color, name her as an inspiration, and readers find in her fiction a revolutionary power that makes it both useful and beautiful.

SOURCES:

Burkom, Selma, and Margaret Williams. "De-Riddling Tillie Olsen's Writings," in *San Jose Studies.* Vol. 2, no. 1. February 1976, pp. 65–83.

Faulkner, Mara. *Protest and Possibility in the Writing of Tillie Olsen.* Charlottesville, VA: University Press of Virginia, 1993.

Gelfant, Blanche H. "After Long Silence: Tillie Olsen's 'Requa,'" in *Studies in American Fiction.* Vol. 12, no. 1. Spring 1984, pp. 61–69.

Gottlieb, Annie. "Feminists Look at Motherhood," in *Mother Jones.* November 1976, pp. 51–53.

Pearlman, Mickey, and Abby H.P. Werlock. *Tillie Olsen.* Boston, MA: Twayne, 1991.

Rosenfelt, Deborah Silverton, ed. "From the Thirties: Tillie Olsen and the Radical Tradition," in *Tell Me a Riddle: Women Writers, Texts and Contexts.* New Brunswick, NJ: Rutgers, 1995, pp. 133–176.

Van Horn, Christina. "Writer Tillie Olsen: Upbeat on Women's Future," in *The Boston Globe.* Vol. 31. May 1981, p. 6A.

Walker, Alice. "Saving the Life That Is Your Own: The Importance of Models in the Artist's Life," in *In Search of Our Mother's Gardens: Womanist Prose.* San Diego, CA: Harcourt, 1983.

Yalom, Marilyn. "Tillie Olsen," in *Women Writers of the West Coast: Speaking of Their Lives and Careers.* Edited by Marilyn Yalom. Santa Barbara, CA: Capra, 1983, pp. 57–66.

SUGGESTED READING:

Coiner, Constance. *Better Red: The Writing and Resistance of Tillie Olsen and* ***Meridel Le Sueur.* NY: Oxford University Press, 1995.

Hedges, Elaine, and Shelley Fisher Fishkin, eds. *Listening to Silences: New Feminist Essays.* NY: Oxford University Press, 1994.

Nelson, Kay Hoyle, and Nancy Huse, eds. *The Critical Response to Tillie Olsen.* NY: Greenwood Press, 1994.

Orr, Elaine Neil. *Tillie Olsen and a Feminist Spiritual Vision.* Jackson, MI: University Press of Mississippi, 1987.

COLLECTIONS:

Some of Olsen's manuscripts housed in the Berg Collection of English and American Literature at the New York Public Library.

RELATED MEDIA:

Tell Me a Riddle, film starring Melvyn Douglas, ***Lila Kedrova**, and **Brooke Adams**; directed by **Lee Grant**, Filmways, 1980.

Stories recorded by WBAI-radio in New York City and the Lamont Poetry Room at Harvard University.

Mara Faulkner, O.S.B.,
assistant professor of English,
College of St. Benedict, St. Joseph, Minnesota,
and author of *Protest and Possibility in the Writing of Tillie Olsen*
(University Press of Virginia)

Olympia (39–62 CE).

See Octavia.

Olympias (c. 371–316 BCE)

Wife of Philip II of Macedon and mother of Alexander the Great, who pursued dynastic interests through her son and grandson until the struggle to establish the latter as the sole king of an enormous empire prompted enemies to orchestrate her execution. *Name variations: Myrtale; Polyxena; Stratonike. Pronunciation: Oh-LIM-pee-as. Born Polyxena in (or about) 371 BCE, probably at Dodona in Epirus; died at Pydna in Macedonia in 316 BCE; daughter of King Neoptolemus of Epirus, who died when she was young; raised by his brother, Arybbas; educated as befit a princess: she was literate, versed in politics and economic management, and devoted to esoteric religious rites; married Philip II, king of Macedon, in 357 BCE; children: Alexander III the Great (356–323 BCE), king of Macedon; Cleopatra (b. 354 BCE).*

Honored with the name "Olympias" by her husband after the twin good fortunes of Alexander's birth and Philip's chariot victory in the Olympic Games (356 BCE); relationship with Philip had cooled (late 330s); suspected of complicity when Philip was assassinated (336 BCE); during son's Asian sojourn (334–323 BCE), helped look after his interests in Europe (where she feuded with Antipater, also appointed by Alexander); after Alexander's death (June 323 BCE), and the posthumous birth of his son, Alexander IV (autumn 323 BCE), championed her grandson's dynastic interests against the rival claims of Philip III (Philip II's son by a different wife); resulting conflict led her to murder of Philip III and his wife, Eurydice (317 BCE); captured by Cassander, son of Antipater and a supporter of Philip III, was judicially executed (316 BCE).

Epirus, the land of Olympias' birth, was a backward state on the northwestern frontier of the Greek world—in many ways akin to its northeastern counterpart, the realm of Macedon. Epirus' very existence helped to shield the more advanced Greek city-states in the south from the devastation threatened by various "barbarian" peoples (chief among them the Illyrians) whose homelands lay between modern Greece and the Danube River. The Epirotes were a Greek people, but one whose isolation on the frontier of the Hellenic world retarded their political and social development. Although most Greeks in the south had abandoned or severely restricted kingship long before the 4th century BCE, at the time of Olympias' birth (c. 371), Epirus was still ruled by a powerful monarch. In addition, its people were spread over the countryside—not concentrated into cities with more advanced economies, as was the case in the south.

Olympias' name at birth was Polyxena. Her father, King Neoptolemus of Epirus, died when she was very young, leaving her to be reared (and her future to be arranged) by his brother and royal successor, Arybbas. At the time of Neoptolemus' death, the Illyrians who lived to the north of Epirus constituted a potent military threat, for leaders possessing both military and political skill had begun to consolidate the various Illyrian tribes into a coalition, which, if unchecked, could develop the institutions of a permanent and imperialistic state. Shortly after the accession of Arybbas, Macedon's old king (Amyntas III) died, bringing his son, Alexander II, to the throne of that land. Like Arybbas, Alexander II dreaded Illyrian ambitions on his realm, and their common fear drove both to a defensive alliance.

In their part of the world such pacts were usually reinforced by marriage ties, and this association was no different. Although probably no more than two or three years of age at the time (369 BCE), Olympias traveled with Arybbas eastward to the sacred island of Samothrace off the Thracian coast, where they met with a Macedonian contingent led by Philip (II), himself at most 14 years old, the youngest brother of King Alexander II. There, under the cover of religious initiation into the Samothracian mysteries, with the collaboration of at least some Thracians, and far from watchful Illyrian eyes, the marriage of Philip and Olympias was arranged. While she was obviously too young to be a bride in 369 BCE, her betrothal to Philip nevertheless constituted a formal contract which would in the future be consummated. In the meantime, it sufficed to bind the two kingdoms together in common opposition to the Illyrians.

The visit to Samothrace and the Samothracian rites perhaps left a lasting impression upon the young girl, for later in life Olympias devoted much of her time to esoteric religious worship (her penchant for ritual snakes apparently left Philip cold). Regardless, although the exact nature of these mysteries is unknown, they appear to have represented initiations of some sort, with the devotee "transformed" by the secrets therein revealed. As such, it was probably at Samothrace where Polyxena (as Olympia was then called) experienced her first name change (in baptismal fashion), becoming "Myrtale."

The 360s were a tumultuous decade in the north, especially in Macedon. Under the shadow of an Illyrian peril, Alexander II not only sought foreign allies, but also attempted domestic reforms, including the creation of an effective infantry force to complement the already existing, and well respected, national cavalry. Since infantries throughout the Greek world were traditionally drafted from a state's sedentary farming population, and since Macedon had too few such farmers to compose a viable unit (most of its population was still supported by herding), Alexander's reform demanded social and economic changes as well as military innovation. However, since the development of a farming population required some redistribution of land, vested interests were bound to be adversely affected. The perhaps predictable result of this reform was domestic unrest, culminating in Alexander's assassination (367 BCE). The rival responsible for the murder (a Ptolemy) dominated Macedonian affairs for about two and a half years (although a pretender named Pausanias challenged him) before himself succumbing to assassination—this time organized by Alexander II's next younger brother, Perdiccas III. Perdiccas ruled for about five years, building on his older brother's policies. By 360 BCE, he had at his command a sizable infantry force, which in that year he mustered to repel an Illyrian invasion of his realm. However, Perdiccas failed: when his battle against the Illyrians was over, he and several thousand of his troops lay dead.

This disaster propelled Perdiccas III's younger brother, Philip II, to the forefront. With Illyrians plundering the land, and with several other foreign enemies (including such Greek states as Athens) exploiting the opportunity to both pillage and seize Macedonian territory, Philip's realm initially was no larger than the small army he had at his personal command. Nevertheless, displaying strategic competence, military expertise, boundless energy, and diplomatic tact, within a handful of years Philip not only expelled all invaders and re-established the security of his kingdom, he also led a reconstituted army to major victories against many of his enemies, including the Illyrians whose military power he crippled.

A large part of Philip's success resulted from his marriage diplomacy: to secure long-term advantage he would draw upon his dynasty's polygamous heritage and in the course of his reign acquire seven wives—**Audata**, Olympias, **Meda**, ***Nicesipolis**, ***Philinna**, **Roxana**, and **Cleopatra of Macedon**—without divorcing any previously wed. Philip's polygamy was politically motivated, for his wives would not be mere spouses—they would also be vital liaisons between Macedon and the states which their original families represented (six of Philip's wives were foreign; only the last was from Macedon).

Although Olympias was Philip's first betrothed, she did not become his first wife. Nonetheless because of the importance of Epirus, as soon as Olympias was old enough (357 BCE), she took her place by Philip's side.

When Olympias came to Philip's court (at Pella) she was not his most important spouse; however, the birth of Alexander (III the Great) in 356 BCE (and ⚘▸ **Cleopatra** two years later) raised her status considerably. Despite Philip's multiple wives, he did not have many children. In fact, besides Alexander, Philip had only one other son, Arrhidaeus (the future Philip III), with Philinna, who was from the Thessalian city of Larissa. Alexander seems to have been the older of these two, for when Philip (who was campaigning at the time) almost simultaneously learned of his chariot's victory in the Olympic Games and of the birth of Alexander, in honor of both propitious events, he renamed Polyxena "Olympias"—the name that she would be known by thereafter, although military activity late in life would earn her the nickname "Stratonike" (Victorious in Battle). Primogeniture was not a Macedonian custom, but as the years passed it became evident that Arrhidaeus was not mentally competent. As a result, Alexander faced no sibling rivalry and most gladly accepted a gifted youth as Philip's uncontested heir. With this status came an even greater elevation in Olympias' importance, and she became established as Philip's chief wife.

As such, Olympias had many responsibilities in the palace, including the management of its women's quarters and the palace's staff, as well as some authority over its domestic arrangements and finances. Since the royal household was at once both a private and a public institution, her duties brought her authority which few women in her time knew. In addition to her palace duties, her proximity to Philip and Philip's heir made her a figure to be reckoned with at court. She took every opportunity to supplement her political influence. In fact, her ambition to rule as a "queen" alongside Philip eventually provoked him, as he found her too willing to meddle in affairs which he considered exclusively his. As the years passed, whatever affection the two had ever felt diminished and a kind of rivalry grew over their son. In fact, because of her intimate emotional relationship with Alexander, until the boy reached puberty Philip was forced to concede her more influence than he otherwise wished her to wield.

Growing up, Alexander saw little of his father, whose expanding interests and foreign conquests frequently meant that he was not at home. In traditional fashion, Alexander was left in the care of his mother, who both nourished the growing prince and arranged for his primary education. Fully realizing that her power at court largely depended on her control of Alexander, Olympias guarded her maternal prerogatives. Thanks to Olympias' influence, her relative, Leonidas, became Alexander's chief-of-tutors. In addition to maintaining tight control over Alexander's associates, Olympias personally supervised the young boy as frequently as she could. In the process, she both demonstrated her love for Alexander (which he always reciprocated) and worked to drive an emotional wedge between him and his father. How successful she might have been in this endeavor is uncertain. Certainly, Philip took pleasure in his maturing heir, and (despite later misunderstandings) Alexander openly respected his father's achievements. Whether love accompanied respect, however, is information lost to us, for the highly charged political climate of the court made normal family relationships difficult at best.

When Alexander was 13, Philip thought the time had come to separate the boy from his mother and to immerse him fully in the world of men. As a result, in 343 BCE Philip summoned Aristotle—not to Pella, where Alexander would remain under his mother's influence, but to Mieza (a garden spot about a day's journey west of Pella)—to establish a school for Alexander and other boys from the court of about the same age. There the prince remained for three years, distanced from Olympias. When Alexander was recalled to Pella (340 BCE), he immediately began to assume a variety of public responsibilities under the tutelage of his father and his father's most trusted friends. As a result, although Alexander and Olympias were not incommunicado, their time spent together was diminished.

Though Philip clearly acknowledged Alexander as his heir, several incidents during the final years of Philip's life indicate that Alexander remained emotionally closer to Olympias than to his father, and that he was prone to misread his fa-

⚘▸ Cleopatra (b. 354 BCE)

Princess of Macedon. *Born around 354 BCE; daughter of* ****Olympias*** *(c. 371–316 BCE) and Philip II, king of Macedon; sister of Alexander III the Great (356–323 BCE), king of Macedon; married her uncle Alexander (brother of her mother Olympias), king of Epirus.*

ther's actions. Chief among these was Philip's last (but first Macedonian) marriage. At the wedding feast, the uncle of the bride, Cleopatra of Macedon, toasted the union with the wish that it would produce a "legitimate" heir for Philip. Alexander, who was present, naturally took offense, and when Philip would not avenge the insult (almost certainly because he was fettered by the well-established bonds of hospitality), Alexander first removed Olympias to Epirus and then fled himself to Illyria, seeking support for his claim. Not all of the nuances of the situation are understood, but the swift reconciliation of father and son proves that Philip had no intention of disinheriting Alexander, although he seems to have been angling to establish the newly wed Cleopatra of Macedon as his chief wife in place of Olympias.

Duris reports that the first war between two women pit Olympias against Eurydice; in it Olympias advanced in the manner of a Bacchant, accompanied by tambourines.

—**Athenaeus**

This and other differences of opinion between Philip and Alexander were apparently overcome by the fall of 336 BCE, at which time a marriage was celebrated between Olympias' and Philip's daughter Cleopatra and her uncle (Olympias' brother, another Alexander), who was now the king of Epirus. Where Olympias resided between her flight to Epirus and the marriage of her daughter is unknown, although it is quite likely that she may have remained in Epirus, unsuccessfully attempting to aggravate her brother against her husband. If so, then her brother's marriage to Cleopatra may be considered Philip's counter-move, for, clearly, the marriage established her brother as a close ally of Philip. Regardless of where Olympias might have been before, her presence at the wedding validated Cleopatra's nuptials. Thus, it should come as no surprise that when a private vendetta led a Macedonian noble to assassinate Philip at the celebration's culminating event, Olympias was suspected of having abetted the executioner. Despite suspicions, Olympias' intimacy with Alexander III, now king, placed her above formal accusation.

However important Cleopatra's marriage was to Philip's Epirote strategy, it was also staged as a rally to kick off Philip's next major foreign-policy initiative—the invasion of the Persian Empire (had he not been assassinated, he intended to immediately join troops already campaigning in northwestern Turkey). As luck had it, his death delayed Alexander's invasion of Asia for almost two years, for the new king first had to prove that he was every bit as talented as his father, whose constant campaigning for over 20 years had established Macedon's ascendancy throughout the Balkans. By the spring of 334 BCE, however, Alexander was ready to pursue his father's dream. Needing reliable allies to look after things in Europe while he was in Asia, Alexander chose three whom he considered beyond reproach: Antipater (one of Philip's most trusted companions), Olympias, and his sister, Cleopatra. The first two shared duties in Macedonia, while Cleopatra operated from Epirus. In typical fashion, the precise responsibilities of each were left undefined—a fact which would soon lead Antipater to resent what he considered to be the interference of Olympias in the administration of Macedonian affairs.

After 334 BCE, both Olympias and Cleopatra assumed their right to govern in the Balkans—an attitude which would grow when Olympias' brother, the Epirote Alexander, invaded Italy (333 BCE) in a pale reflection of his nephew's campaign. The Epirote's death abroad (330 BCE) would only stimulate the ambitions of both thereafter. With the Alexanders away, Olympias and Cleopatra maintained high profiles. Acting as heads of state, they received ambassadors, oversaw administration (including the organization of famine relief in a year of bad harvests), presided over religious business, and kept the Alexanders abreast of Balkan affairs. The undefined limits of their power, however, embroiled them in an increasingly bitter series of disputes with Antipater, with both sides inundating the great Alexander with letters of complaint. Busy with more pressing affairs, he did little but return reassuring responses while endorsing the status quo. Eventually, however, Olympias' rivalry with Antipater became so intense that she fled Macedon for Epirus a second time (331 BCE). There, she remained, viciously attacking Antipater until after the death of her son eight years later. Alexander died before acting on his mother's protests, but it appears that her constant assault had an effect, for although the order was nullified by Alexander's death (June 323 BCE), shortly before that event, using ominous words, Alexander commanded Antipater to "join" him in Babylon.

Alexander the Great's death precipitated a dynastic crisis. He had married officially at least twice while in Asia, but neither spouse had given birth before his demise. One wife (the Bactrian **Roxane**), however, was several months pregnant when he died. The choice facing Alexander's

Roxane. See full entry under Roxane.

army at Babylon was not an enviable one, for only two candidates remained as potential kings: the first was Alexander's incompetent half-brother Arrhidaeus, and the other was Roxane's child, although no one knew if it would be a boy. As events violently unfolded, it was decided to elevate Arrhidaeus (under the throne name Philip III) at once since much royal business (especially that which was religious) was only ceremonial (although it was believed that a descendant of the royal family had to preside over such affairs). A proviso, however, was added: if Roxane's child were a boy, he would share the throne of an unprecedented "joint kingship." When Roxane gave birth to Alexander IV, this eventuality came to pass. Unfortunately, the inability of either king to assert himself led to the formation of conniving factions, more interested in social advancement than in the well-being of either monarch.

The resulting intrigues split the Macedonian world and forever shattered Alexander's empire. The chief partisan supporting the claims of Alexander IV was Olympias, both because she wished her grandson to reign as Macedon's sole king, and because she realized that he would require a lengthy regency before he could rule for himself. Who better as regent, thought Olympias, than she? Arrhidaeus' faction came to be led by his 15-year-old second cousin and niece, ***Eurydice** (c. 337–317 BCE, a granddaughter of both Perdiccas III and Philip II), who, in 322 BCE, became Arrhidaeus' wife in the knowledge that she could manipulate him as a puppet. Both Olympias and Eurydice realized the stakes, as both attempted to foster their mutually exclusive visions of the future.

This rivalry was complicated by the ambitions of Alexander's generals, all of whom were used to serving dynamic kings, and many of whom began to envision the subdivision of the expansive Macedonian Empire. A sweeping civil war followed, with the first casualty being Alexander's dynasty. During the fray, the two kings became valuable pawns. First, they fell under the control of a general named Perdiccas (whose loyalty Olympias and Cleopatra attempted in vain to win [thanks to counter-moves by Antipater] through an offer of the latter in marriage). Upon Perdiccas' death, the kings fell into the hands of Antipater who returned them (along with Eurydice) to Macedon (321 BCE). There, Antipater, one of the few who hoped to reunify the Macedonian world under the old monarchy, jealously guarded both kings from harm. To accomplish this feat, he both cowed would-be secessionists and protected each king from his foremost feminine adversary: Arrhidaeus rested safely only because Olympias remained in Epirus, and Alexander IV (along with Roxane) continued to live only because Antipater closely guarded the actions of Eurydice.

Antipater, however, died in 319 BCE, and his hand-picked successor—surprisingly, not his son Cassander, but rather an old associate in arms, Polyperchon)—lacked both the prestige and talent to keep Antipater's dream alive. When it became clear to Polyperchon that virtually none of his military peers in Asia or Africa recognized his authority, and that he was even losing control of southern Greece, he attempted to restore his flagging fortunes through a closer association with Olympias—now, as the mother of Alexander the Great (who was posthumously metamorphosed into a god), revered by most common Macedonians. As a result, Polyperchon invited Olympias to return to Macedon to care for her grandson, but, even though Olympias hesitated (fearing a trap?), in issuing his invitation when he did Polyperchon seriously erred. Subsequently forced to campaign in the Peloponnesus, Polyperchon neglected to take the kings with him to the south. As a result, Eurydice was at least temporarily free of her "guardian" and threatened by the imminent return of Olympias to Macedon. Seizing the moment, she issued a proclamation in Arrhidaeus' name, decommissioning Polyperchon as royal guardian and elevating Cassander to that position. This move upset Olympias greatly because of her deep hatred of Cassander's father Antipater.

Before Cassander could respond, Olympias raised an army among the Epirotes and invaded Macedonia. Having no immediate champion, the then 20-year-old Eurydice organized and commanded an army. The two met in western Macedonia, but, before blows were struck, Eurydice's men—awestruck by the sight of the religiously attired mother of Alexander the Great—deserted. Having thus fallen into Olympias' hands, Arrhidaeus and Eurydice were summarily executed (317 BCE). Then, venting bile stored up by years of "exile" in Epirus and countless slights to her ambitions, Olympias allowed her army to ravage portions of Macedon. Of particular savagery was her vindictive desecration of the cemetery of Antipater's family.

Her overreaction cost Olympias public support throughout Macedon, with the result that when Cassander finally made an appearance, the populace accepted as legitimate the commission given him by the dead Eurydice. Olympias, Alexander IV, Roxane and another member of the royal house, one ***Thessalonike**, the youngest daughter of Philip II whom Cassander would eventually marry, were besieged by Cassander in Pydna, with no allies in a position to help them. In 316 BCE, after a long siege, and with starvation figuring in her capitulation, Olympias surrendered. Cassander spirited Alexander IV and Roxane away to Amphipolis where they were kept under house arrest (officially, "under close protection to insure their safety") until both were quietly murdered (officially they died "natural deaths") in 310 BCE.

Olympias met with a swifter fate. Though she was an unredeemable enemy, Cassander nevertheless wished to avoid the odium of being known as the murderer of Olympias. As a result, he attempted to bribe others to commit the act, and the ghost of Alexander momentarily saved her. Yet, knowing that public opinion could turn again in favor of the now powerless Olympias, Cassander decided to effect her destruction quickly. This time, after a hasty trial, Olympias was turned over to the relatives of some of those she had been responsible for killing during her recent Macedonian rampage. These relatives, driven by a sense of responsibility to their dead kin, were able to disregard Olympias' majesty and see to her demise. Not wishing to create a martyr whose death might someday hamper his growing desire to rule Macedon as his own, Cassander ordered that Olympias be given but a humble burial. Nevertheless, unknown supporters gained control of her body, and, whether during the ascendancy of Cassander's house (316–294 BCE) or later, an appropriate tomb was constructed near Pydna which drew visitors for hundreds of years.

SOURCES:

Arrian. *The Campaigns of Alexander.* Trans. by A. de Selincourt. Harmondsworth: Penguin, 1976.

Curtius Rufus. *The History of Alexander.* Trans. by J. Yardley. Harmondsworth: Penguin, 1981.

Diodorus Siculus. *The Library of History.* Vols. 7–9. Trans. by C.L. Sherman, C.B. Welles, and R.M. Geer. Cambridge: Harvard University Press, 1952, 1963, 1974.

Justin. *The History of the World.* Trans. by J.S. Watson. London: Bohn, 1875.

Plutarch. "Life of Alexander," in *The Age of Alexander.* Trans. by I. Scott-Kilvert. Harmondsworth: Penguin, 1973.

SUGGESTED READING:

Carney, E.D. "Olympias," in *Ancient Society.* Vol. 18, 1987, pp. 35–62.

Greenwalt, W.S. "Polygamy and Succession in Argead Macedonia," in *Arethusa.* Vol. 22, 1989, pp. 19–45.

Macurdy, G.H. *Hellenistic Queens.* Baltimore, MD: Johns Hopkins, 1932.

RELATED MEDIA:

Alexander the Great (141-min. film), starring Richard Burton and ***Danielle Darrieux** as Olympias, 1956.

W.S. Greenwalt,
Associate Professor of Classical History, Santa Clara University, Santa Clara, California

Olympias (c. 365–408)

Deaconess in Constantinople. *Born around 365; died in 408 in Nicomedia; buried at a monastery on the shore of the Bosporus; in the early 7th century, remains removed from the original site to the convent she had founded; married Nebridius (prefect of Constantinople), in 386 (died 386).*

Of aristocratic birth, Olympias was born in Constantinople and was briefly married (386) to Nebridius, the prefect of the city before he died. In order to maintain their political prominence, Olympias' family thereafter betrothed her to a relative of Theodosius I, the reigning emperor of the Roman Empire. Olympias refused the offer of a second husband, a slight which infuriated Theodosius, who as a consequence confiscated for a time her extensive estates in Thrace, Galacia, Cappadocia, and Bithynia, as well as her property in Constantinople itself. Political clout matters, however, and after some delicate negotiating, Olympias' connections won back her properties in 391. Thereafter, preferring a religious life to a worldly one, Olympias used her wealth to underwrite a host of Christian causes. One of her closest friends and advisors was John Chrysostom, then the bishop of Constantinople. John was especially dedicated to issues of social justice and the plight of the poor, and as a result Olympias spent a fortune trying to address these concerns. John, despite his charitable work, was also a controversial political player (at a time when religion *was* politics), with the result that Olympias often found herself an unpopular figure at court.

Court life, however, did not dominate Olympias' interests: after her wealth had been restored, she was ordained a deaconess and founded a convent (situated near Hagia Sophia) to promote the religiosity of others. Nevertheless, politics always overshadowed her world. When John Chrysostom was exiled from Constantinople for opposing the imperial will, Olympias refused to recognize the religious authority of his appointed successor. As a result of her second, public confrontation with the emperor, she was exiled from the capital to Nicomedia. There, Olympias received letters of consolation, most notably from John. She was never recalled to her native city. She died in 408 in Nicomedia and was buried at a monastery on the Asiatic shore of the Bosporus.

Olympias was eventually officially recognized as a saint and her convent in Constantinople continued to flourish until it was physically destroyed during the famous "Nika" riots of 532. Justinian, however, restored in 537 what Olympias had originally endowed. In the early 7th century, when a Persian invasion threatened the Byzantine control of all of Anatolia, Olympias' remains were removed from the original site of their burial to the convent she had founded.

William S. Greenwalt,
Associate Professor of Classical History, Santa Clara University, Santa Clara, California

Olympias

Ancient Greek painter. *Would have flourished long before the birth of Pliny the Elder in 23* CE.

Olympias is mentioned at the end of Pliny the Elder's list of women painters in his *Natural History*. His notice can be quoted in full: "A certain Olympias also painted; the only fact recorded about her is that Autobulus was her pupil." Neither Olympias nor Autobulus are mentioned in other Classical sources, so it is impossible to add to Pliny's scant information. It is worth comment, however, that Olympias is the only woman on the list who is said to have taught her art, and the fact that her student was a man contrasts interestingly with the training that *__Aristarete__, *__Irene__, and perhaps *__Timarete__ are said to have received from their fathers.

Peter H. O'Brien,
Boston University

Olympic Ice Hockey.

See Team USA: Women's Ice Hockey at Nagano.

O'Malley, Grace (c. 1530–1603)

Shipowner, sea captain and pirate, who alternately resisted and negotiated with representatives of the crown in Ireland, and with Elizabeth I, in order to safeguard her own position and that of her dependents. *Name variations: Grainne Ui Mhaille or Mhaol; Grany Imallye; Grana O'Malley; Grany O'Maly; Granuaile or Grania Uaile or Grana Wale; queen of Connaught. Born Grace O'Malley around 1530; died, probably at Rockfleet Castle, County Mayo, around 1603; daughter of Owen O'Malley (chieftain of Umhall Uachtarach) and Margaret (daughter of Conchobhar Og Mac Conchobhair mic Maoilseachloinn); married Donal O'Flaherty, around 1546 (died around 1565); married Richard Burke, around 1566 (died 1583); children: (first marriage) Owen, Murrough, Margaret; (second marriage) Tibbot.*

As wife of Donal O'Flaherty, was involved in the government of the O'Flaherty territories and commanded the clan's vessels on missions of trade and piracy (c. 1546–65); on O'Flaherty's death, established her headquarters on Clare Island, from which she continued her activities; repulsed an attack on her fortress of Rockfleet (or Carrickahowley) by government forces (1574); met the viceroy, Sir Henry Sidney, to offer her services (1577); captured during a raid on the earl of Desmond's lands, and imprisoned in Limerick and Dublin (c. 1577–78); with her second husband, Richard Burke, attended a meeting between Gaelic chiefs and the president of Connaught in Galway (1582); on Burke's death, took possession of Rockfleet, from where she continued her operations (1583); implicated in rebellion on a number of occasions (1586–90); reported to have been involved in piracy off the west coast (1590–91); traveled to London, where she had an audience with, and obtained a pardon from, Queen Elizabeth I (1593); involved in rebellion, but subsequently came to terms with the government (1596–97); her ships intercepted on a raiding mission off the Mayo coast (1601).

In the late summer of 1593, a meeting took place at the palace of Greenwich, near London, between two equally remarkable women. On the one hand was *__Elizabeth I__, then 60 years old and at the height of her power and splendor. The French ambassador, writing not long afterwards, reported that, despite her age, her appearance was as magnificent as ever and her intelligence as acute: "she is," he concluded, "a very great Princess who knows everything." Yet on this occasion it was her visitor who cut the more exotic figure. Wrapped in her great chieftain's cloak, her hair held with a silver bodkin, Grace O'Malley was the first Gaelic woman to visit the Elizabethan court, and as such was the object of considerable curiosity. Moreover, she was preceded by a formidable reputation. Hailing from the most far-flung of the queen's dominions, from the western coast of the troublesome neighboring island of Ireland, O'Malley was herself a ruler and commander, a woman, according to Elizabeth's officials, "famous for her stoutness of courage and person, and for sundry exploits done by her at sea," the "chief commander and director of thieves and murderers," a "terror to all merchantmen that sailed the Atlantic," and a significant threat to English authority in Ireland.

Undaunted by the unfamiliarity and brilliance of her surroundings and by the fact that she came as a supplicant, O'Malley apparently approached the encounter as one, not between sovereign and subject, but between equals. Certainly, this was the account favored by Irish sources, such as this, much later, description of the scene, reproduced in **Anne Chambers**' biography *Granuaile*:

> And courteous greeting Elizabeth then pays,
> And bids her welcome to her English land
> And humble hall. Each looked with curious gaze
> Upon the other's face, and felt they stand
> Before a spirit like their own. Her hand
> The stranger raised—and pointing where all pale,
> Thro' the high casement, came the sunlight
> bland,
> Gilding the scene and group with rich avail;
> Thus, to the English Sov'reign, spoke proud
> "Grana Wale."

More important, the outcome of this confrontation between the queen and the erstwhile rebel and pirate was to prove Grace O'Malley as impressive an opponent in debate as she had shown herself to be in action, a woman capable of responding pragmatically to circumstances and of defending her own interests in conditions of unprecedented danger and flux.

Like her contemporary Elizabeth, O'Malley came of a family accustomed to government and to political and military struggle. Born in about 1530, she was the daughter of **Margaret O'Malley** and a Gaelic chieftain Owen O'Malley. The O'-Malleys were hereditary lords of an area known as the Umhalls (or Owels) in present-day County Mayo; situated on the rocky and dangerous northwest coast of Ireland, their domain included a large number of offshore islands as well as territory on the mainland, and the O'Malleys were known for their prowess as seafarers, having traditionally practiced as fishermen and traders. On occasion, too, their ships and sailors were hired to various warring tribes on a mercenary basis, while piracy was another, not uncommon, source of income for the clan. Thus, in 1513, not long before Grace's birth, three O'Malley vessels attacked the coastal settlement of Killybegs, burned the town and took many prisoners before being overcome by a local force. As the powerful and prosperous lords of a remote region, the O'Malleys' independence and way of life had been little affected by the Norman invasion of the 12th century, and the native Irish Brehon laws and customs continued to apply in their territories for another four centuries. During that period, English rule was largely confined to an area around Dublin; by the mid-16th century, however, efforts were underway to extend Crown authority throughout the country, thus placing unprecedented pressure on the old Gaelic order over which the O'Malleys and their fellow chieftains presided.

The young Grace O'Malley was brought up in her father's territory of the Umhalls, possibly on Clare Island, just off the Mayo coast. While little is known of her youth, it is likely, given the evidence of her later career, that she had an early training both in the business of government and in seafaring: according to legend, she acquired her nickname "Granuaile" when, in an effort to obtain permission to sail on one of her father's ships, she cut her hair short like a boy's, thus becoming known as Grainne Mhaol (Grace the bald). More probably, however, the name was a corruption of the Gaelic Grainne Ui Mhaille (O'Malley) or Grainne Umhaill (of the Umhalls).

When she was about 16 years old, Grace married for the first time. As the daughter of a chieftain, her marriage was a matter of some dynastic and political importance, and her husband Donal O'Flaherty was the tanaist, or designated successor, to the head of the O'Flaherty clan, which controlled the neighboring territory of Iar Connacht. There is evidence to indicate that women in Gaelic Ireland may have enjoyed a certain degree of autonomy within marriage and, in accordance with this tradition, Grace, in addition to her duties as wife and mother, apparently took an active part in local political affairs and in the seafaring enterprises in which the O'Flaherties, like the O'Malleys, had a traditional involvement. Thus, the mayor and corporation of the Galway, reporting at about this time to the English Council, deplored:

> The continuing roads used by the O'Malleys and Flaherties with their galleys along our coasts, where there have been taken sundry ships and barks bound for this poor town, which they have not only rifled to the utter overthrow of the owners and merchants, but also have most wickedly murdered divers of young men to the great terror of such as would willingly traffic.

As the letter pointed out, activities of this kind also challenged the interests of the government, at a time when it was attempting, in a more forceful and systematic way than hitherto, to enforce its writ throughout the kingdom of Ireland. During the 1560s, this policy impacted directly on Grace's own position, when the authorities, in an effort to pacify a troublesome local chief and ensure his loyalty, named him ruler of Iar Connacht in place of the current chieftain, in the process disinheriting her husband as the acknowledged heir apparent. However, Grace's part in this particular dispute ended shortly afterwards, when Donal was killed in a tribal skirmish, leaving her free to return, with an entourage of about 200 followers, to her father's kingdom. Basing herself on Clare Island at the mouth of Clew Bay, she sent out her galleys to trade, to levy tolls on passing ships, and to plunder those which refused her demands. Not long afterwards she took as her second husband Richard Burke, whose territory included the northeastern coast of the Bay, a man described by the Gaelic annalists as "plundering, warlike, unquiet and rebellious." The marriage was almost certainly one of convenience on O'Malley's part: tradition has it that, in accordance with Brehon law, she married him for "one year certain," and at the end of that time dismissed him, while retaining possession of his fortress of Rockfleet or Carrickahowley. In fact, her association with Burke continued for a longer period, but Rockfleet was to be her main stronghold for the rest of her life, and, in 1574, she successfully defended it against an attack by government forces intent on putting an end to her piratical activities. Nevertheless, Grace was realistic enough to recognize the necessity of coming to terms with the queen's representatives, and, in 1577, she had a meeting in Galway with Sir Henry Sidney, in the course of which she offered the services of her "three galleys and 200 fighting men, either in Scotland or Ireland" to the lord deputy. Writing to the queen's secretary, Walsingham, of the encounter, Sidney described O'Malley as "a most famous feminine sea captain . . . a notorious woman in all the coasts of Ireland." Although O'Malley was accompanied on this occasion by her husband, Sidney had no doubt of her dominance over Burke: as he remarked, "she was as well by sea as by land more than Mrs Mate with him."

O'Malley's formal submission to English authority apparently brought about little alteration in her activities. Numerous legends record her presence in many different parts of the country, and describe her personal involvement in various battles and expeditions. During one of these, she was captured by the powerful southern magnate, the earl of Desmond, whose lands she had pillaged, and who, in a letter to the lord deputy, described her as "a woman that hath impudently passed the part of womanhood and been a great spoiler, and chief commander and director of thieves and murderers at sea to spoil this province." Imprisoned first for 18 months in Limerick jail and later in Dublin, Grace finally managed to secure her freedom on the promise of good behavior. Her release, however, coincided with the outbreak of a rising in which her husband was one of the insurgents. Whether O'Malley knew beforehand of Burke's intentions or sympathized with his actions is unknown; however, regarding the rebels' defeat as inevitable, she now intervened to urge his voluntary submission to the crown. Having made peace with the government, Burke won its support for his claim to assume the Gaelic title of the MacWilliam Burke, and was knighted in September 1581. In October of that year, he and other Gaelic and Anglo-Irish lords attended a conference in Galway with Malby, the current president of Connaught. Many of the nobles brought their wives with them, and Malby in his report gave a special mention to Grace as one of those present, and "thinketh herself," according to the governor, "to be no small lady."

> This was a notorious woman in all the coasts of Ireland.
>
> —Sir Henry Sidney

In April 1583, however, Richard Burke died, and Grace, entitled, according to Gaelic custom, to one-third of her dead husband's property, took immediate action to safeguard her inheritance. According to her own account, she "gathered together all her own followers, and with 1,000 head of cows and mares departed and became a dweller in Carrikahowley," from where she continued her operations, both on land and sea. In 1586, when her son-in-law, another Richard Burke, and other leading Gaelic families rose in a short-lived revolt against the crown forces in Connaught, she joined them, and took part in the successful defense of the island fortress of Castle Hag against the forces of the new governor of Connaught, Sir Richard Bingham. The rebellion, however, was finally crushed, and O'Malley was arrested, and deprived of much of her livestock. According to her own account (in the third person):

> She was apprehended and tied with a rope, both she and her followers at that instant were spoiled of their said cattle and of all that ever they had besides the same, and brought to Sir Richard [Bingham] who caused a new pair of gallows to be made for her last funeral where she thought to end her days.

While Grace was released after a short period, her son, Owen O'Flaherty, who had not been involved in the rebellion, was murdered by the governor's forces, and her own freedom of action was hampered by close government scrutiny. When her son-in-law took up arms again, "fear compelled her to fly by sea into Ulster," where she found refuge with the two leading northern clans, the O'Neill and the O'Donnell, until after three months, with the rebellion under control and Bingham temporarily absent abroad, she felt able to return to her own territory. Aware of continuing government distrust, she took the precaution of traveling to Dublin to seek and obtain a royal pardon for herself and her family. Nevertheless, when further unrest broke out in Connaught following the defeat and shipwreck of the Spanish Armada in 1588, Grace and a number of her Burke relatives, including her son, Tibbot, were again implicated. Though the Gaelic forces enjoyed a number of successes, they were eventually forced to sue for peace in January 1590. Grace, however, was either unaware of or determined to disregard the truce, and continued her own operations; on April 21, Bingham reported to London that:

> Immediately after the peace was concluded, Grana O'Malley, with two or three baggage boats full of knaves, not knowing that the peace was made, committed some spoil in the Island of Arran upon two or three of Sir Thomas le Strange's men.

According to Bingham, Grace's son-in-law, Richard Burke, himself deeply involved in the recent rebellion and now anxious to protect his own position, "hath Grana O'Malley in hand till she restore the spoils and repair the harms." However, O'Malley continued to give the government cause for concern: a few months later, in June 1591, Bingham, following a skirmish between some Scottish mercenaries and the Burkes, reported that "Grany O'Maly is preparing herself with some twenty boats in her company to repair after [the Scots] in revenge of her countrymen, and for the spoil they committed in those parts." Two years later, she launched an attack on her own son, Murrough O'Flaherty, who had allied himself with Bingham against Grace and the Burkes. According to the governor's report of the incident, O'Malley "manned out her navy of galleys and landed in Ballinehinchie where [Murrough] dwelleth, burned his town and spoiled his people of their cattle and goods and murdered 3 or 4 of his men which offered to make resistance."

It was scarcely surprising, given such activities, that Bingham, writing to his masters in London, should have described Grace as "a notable traitoress and nurse to all rebellions in the Province for 40 years." But at over 60 years old, with the English government slowly but surely extending its control over even the remotest areas of the country, including her own domain and, most significantly, undermining her domination of Clew Bay, Grace was prompted to seek her own accommodation with her longtime opponents. The course which she chose to take was typically bold: in mid-1593, she wrote directly, and as a "loyal and faithful subject," to Queen Elizabeth. Her object was to ensure her own survival and prosperity, and she began, therefore, by offering a justification of her past career, which implied that, as a result of the policies pursued by the queen's representatives in the west, she had been "constrained . . . to take arms and by force to maintain herself and her people by sea and land the space of forty years past." Describing her own history, pleading the "little time she has to live" and her current destitution, she listed her requests: firstly, "in regard of her great age, she most humbly beseeches your majesty of your princely bounty and liberality to grant her some reasonable maintenance for the little time she has to live," secondly, that her sons and other relations should be allowed to surrender and to retain their lands. Thirdly, and most audaciously, she requested that she should be permitted to continue her activities without interference from Bingham and under the command of the queen herself, "to invade with sword and fire all your highness' enemies, wheresoever they are or shall be, without any interruption of any person or persons whatsoever."

As a result of this appeal, Grace was asked to complete a questionnaire, which sought information on her family, her marriages, and her status as a widow. Meanwhile, however, Bingham had arrested both her son, Tibbot, and her brother, Donal, convincing Grace of the need for prompt and decisive action: in late July, therefore, she set sail from Connaught for London in one of her own ships, with the intention of obtaining an audience with the queen. Bingham, wary of the allegations which Grace might make against his own administration, felt it necessary to notify his superiors at court of O'Malley's coming, to urge that he be given a chance to defend himself against any accusations which she might make, and to warn them of the consequences of receiving her. As he reminded Lord Burghley, the queen's private secretary, she had been a "rebel from . . . childhood and continually in action," and for the queen to hear her complaints or to reward her in any way would be to encourage further treasons. Despite his protests, however, in early September 1593, Grace O'Malley was summoned to appear before Elizabeth at her summer palace at Greenwich.

Despite the legends which have grown up about the meeting between the two women, little is, in fact, known of their conversation, which was conducted in their common language of Latin, but the outcome makes it clear that Grace scored a notable success in securing the queen's goodwill and in achieving the goals which she had set herself. Shortly after the meeting, Elizabeth wrote to Bingham to order the release of Tibbot and of Grace's brother, Donal:

> So as the old woman may understand we yield thereto in regard of her humble suit.... And further, for the pity to be had of this aged woman ... we require you to deal with her sons in our name to yield to her some maintenance for her living the rest of her old years.... Although she hath in former times lived out of order ... she hath confessed the same with assured promises by oath to continue most dutiful, with offer ... that she will fight in our quarrel with all the world.

O'Malley, having returned to Mayo, immediately brought pressure to bear on Bingham to carry out the queen's wishes, and the governor, despite his own disapproval of the concessions granted to Grace and his continuing distrust of her, had little choice but to comply. In November, he reported to Burghley that he had gone some way to meet her demands, "the woman ... swearing that she would else repair presently to England" to lodge further complaints against him. However, alarmed by Grace's potential to continue her seafaring career under the queen's protection, Bingham retaliated by quartering troops on her land and by ordering that all her voyages be placed under military surveillance. The limitation which this placed on her freedom, and the financial hardship which it entailed, prompted Grace to flee south. Taking refuge in Munster, she wrote to Burghley to declare her loyalty and seek fulfillment of the queen's promise of the "quiet possession of the third parts of the lands of her late husbands ... and to live secure of her life."

The Council, however, faced with the possibility of further insurrection in Ulster and Connaught, had little time or inclination to attend to O'Malley's complaints and she had, once more, to rely on her own efforts to maintain her position. Thus, when the Burkes again rebelled and murdered Bingham's brother, Grace and her son, Tibbot, allied themselves with their kinsmen and joined the northern army of Red Hugh O'Donnell, which had invaded Connaught. Riven by internal differences, with the countryside devastated by warfare, and harried by government troops, the rebel forces soon fell into disarray; in April 1596, Tibbot, almost certainly with his mother's approval, deserted them and joined forces with the English. By now, Bingham had been removed from office, and Tibbot's alliance with the government and his usefulness to them secured not only his own safety and prosperity, but also that of Grace who, from her fortress of Rockfleet, was able once more to direct the operations, both legal and illegal, of her galleys. Reported to have taken part in raids on the lands of other chieftains, she was also engaged in trade and apparently provided support to the queen's forces in their continuing struggle against the rebels: in 1597, the new governor of Connaught, Clifford, recorded a payment of £200 to Tibbot, his brother and his mother "for their valuable services by sea."

Little further is known of the career of Grace O'Malley, although she was certainly still alive in July 1601, when an English warship, on patrol off the northwest coast, encountered and intercepted an Irish galley. This vessel, with 30 oars and a crew of 100, put up a spirited resistance before being overcome; it came, the captain discovered, "out of Connaught, and belongs to Grany O'Malley ... and, as I learned since, this with one other galley, was set out and ... was purposed to do some spoils upon the countries and islands" off Donegal. It is clear, therefore, that neither old age nor government supervision had been sufficient to diminish Grace's will or her capacity for survival. Her death, probably at Rockfleet in about 1603, coincided with the final defeat of the rebellion and the irretrievable breakdown of the old Gaelic order, but long before that she herself had shown an acute awareness of political realities and of the necessity to accommodate herself to them, in order to protect her own and her family's interests. The forcefulness of her personality and the uniqueness of her career are commemorated in folklore, in place names and, most remarkably, given the absence of such ideology in her own calculations, in her emergence as an embodiment of the nationalist Ireland of later centuries.

However distorted the version of events, O'Malley's hold on the popular imagination is evidence of the extent of her achievement: at a time when women, in both English and Gaelic society, were assigned a subordinate position, she maintained her personal independence in the management of her own affairs, in relations with her fellow nobles, and in negotiations with the crown and its representatives. In her struggle for survival, she made use of whatever weapons were available to her, at one moment exploiting her weakness as an "aged woman" and a widow in order to achieve concessions, at another, as "terror to all merchantmen that sailed the Atlantic," or as "notable traitoress," defending her rights against all, both Gaelic and English, who sought to restrict them.

SOURCES:

Appleby, J.C. "Women and Piracy in Ireland: From Grainne O'Malley to Anne Bonny," in Margaret MacCurtain and Mary O'Dowd, eds. *Women in Early Modern Ireland*. Dublin: Wolfhound Press, 1991, pp. 53–68.

Chambers, Anne. *Granuaile: The Life and Times of Grace O'Malley*. Dublin: Wolfhound Press, 1979.

Schwind, Mona L. "Nurse to all rebellions: Grace O'Malley and sixteenth-century Connacht," in *Eire-Ireland*. Vol. 13, 1978, pp. 40–61.

SUGGESTED READING:

Canny, Nicholas P. *The Elizabethan Conquest of Ireland: A Pattern Established, 1565–76*. Sussex: Harvester Press, 1976.

Ellis, Steven G. *Tudor Ireland: Crown, Community and the Conflict of Cultures, 1470–1603*. London: Longman, 1985.

Rosemary Raughter,
freelance writer in women's history,
Dublin, Ireland

Omlie, Phoebe Fairgrave (1902–1975)

American aviation pioneer. *Born Phoebe Jane Fairgrave on November 21, 1902, in Des Moines, Iowa; died of lung cancer on July 17, 1975, in Indianapolis, Indiana; daughter of Andrew Fairgrave (a saloon keeper) and Madge (Traister) Fairgrave; attended Madison School, Mechanic Arts High School and Guy Durrel Dramatic School (St. Paul, Minnesota); married Vernon Omlie (a pilot and flight instructor), on January 22, 1922 (died 1936).*

Phoebe Fairgrave Omlie

Set 15,200-foot parachute-jumping record (1922); with husband, opened airport in Memphis, Tennessee (c. 1923); was the first woman to be issued a federal pilot's license and first woman to receive aircraft and mechanic's licenses (1920s); was the first woman to be granted a transport pilot's license by the U.S. Department of Commerce (1927); was the first woman to complete a Ford National Air Reliability Tour (1928); appointed first woman government official in aviation (1933); worked for the Civil Aeronautics Administration (1941–52).

The only daughter and second child of Andrew Fairgrave and **Madge Traister Fairgrave** of Des Moines, Iowa, Phoebe Fairgrave Omlie was born on November 21, 1902, and as a young girl fell in love with aviation after seeing an air show. Unhappy with secretarial work following her schooling in St. Paul, Minnesota, she took four plane rides at Curtiss Field and used a $3,500 inheritance left to her by her grandfather to purchase her own plane. To justify the venture to her parents, the 17-year-old found work as a stunt performer for the Fox Moving Picture Company's popular serial starring ***Pearl White**, *The Perils of Pauline*. The job required her to wing-walk. Her pilot during filming was Vernon Omlie, a World War I veteran and flying instructor at Curtiss Field. He also taught her how to fly, although his fellow instructors thought her too young and diminutive (and possibly just too female) to become a pilot. She made her first parachute jump at this time, and in 1921, after she joined the Glenn Messer Flying Circus, set a 15,200-foot parachute-jumping record.

As a member of Messer's troupe, she developed and performed the "double parachute jump." The feat involved jumping from a plane, deploying a chute, cutting it loose and then, after free falling, deploying a second chute. She later noted that these stunts were performed to satisfy a public that saw flying as a mere novelty; she preferred to put aviation, and her bravery, to work in practical ways. The same year she joined the flying circus, she and Vernon acted as spotters during a forest fire in the northwest, and six years later, when Mississippi River flooding ravaged Little Rock, Arkansas, they airlifted supplies, rescued stranded residents and ferried the mail.

In 1923, Phoebe and Vernon (whom she had married the previous year) opened the first airport in Memphis, Tennessee. There they also opened one of the country's first flying schools, which she ran while working as an instructor and competing in airplane races. She became the first woman in America to be granted a transport pilot's license by the Department of Commerce in 1927, and the following year was appointed assistant to the president of the Mono Aircraft Corporation, under whose sponsorship she toured until 1931 to promote both the company and aviation throughout the United States and South America. Also in 1928, with a monthlong tour of 13 states in 5,000 miles, she became the first woman to complete a Ford National Air Reliability Tour. On August 18, 1929, flying a Monocoupe, Omlie completed the 2,350-mile Women's Air Derby, traveling from Santa Monica, California, to Cleveland, Ohio, in 24 hours and 12 minutes. She set an altitude record of 24,500 feet and went on to set more records at the 1929 and 1930 National Air Races in Cleveland. In the 1931 National Air Races, women and men competed together for the first time; with the highest number of overall points of all competitors, Omlie won an automobile and $2,500. She also won the Transcontinental Handicap Air Derby that year.

During the campaigns for the 1932 presidential election, she became a confidante of Franklin Roosevelt when she suggested the use of aircraft to facilitate his campaign. Roosevelt took her advice, and Omlie would eventually log 5,000 hours in the air delivering speakers to that year's Democratic National Convention. Her successful counsel to the president-to-be resulted in her appointment by Roosevelt to a liaison position between the National Advisory Committee for Aeronautics and the Bureau of Air Commerce, making her the first woman to hold a federal aviation post.

Omlie retired from that position in 1936, after her husband died in a commercial airline crash. She returned to Memphis, determined to enact reforms she and her husband had formulated for the aviation industry, including the establishment of state-sponsored schools dedicated to the training of civilian pilots. The proposal was successful, and later Omlie's flying school became the model for the national Civilian Pilot Training program. She was also successful in introducing a preparatory aviation course into Tennessee's high schools, which later was copied by other states.

Omlie returned to Washington in 1941, during World War II, to work as a senior flying specialist for the Civil Aeronautics Administration (CAA). She also helped to train 5,000 airport ground personnel as part of a joint Works Progress Administration and Office of Education initiative. When women were forced from Civilian Pilot Training programs, an irate Omlie received permission to return to Tennessee to set up a school to train women flight instructors. The school was so successful it became a model for other states, and many of its students became instructors at Civilian Pilot Training schools; she was awarded a citation by the National Education Association in 1942 for this work.

Omlie rejoined the Civilian Aeronautics Administration in Washington the following year and remained there until 1952, when she quit in distress at what she considered the "socialization" of the aviation industry. She lost her life savings in a cattle ranch venture and then crusaded to stop federal involvement in citizens' private lives, lobbying Washington for state control of school systems and other initiatives in 1967. Despite shrinking assets, she worked to bring various conservative groups together until just before her death from lung cancer in Indianapolis on July 17, 1975.

SOURCES:

Olsen, Kirstin. *Remember the Ladies: A Woman's Book of Days.* Pittstown, NJ: Main Street Press, 1988.

Read, Phyllis J., and Bernard L. Witlieb. *The Book of Women's Firsts.* NY: Random House, 1992.

Sicherman, Barbara, and Carol Hurd Green, eds. *Notable American Women: The Modern Period.* Cambridge, MA: The Belknap Press of Harvard University Press, 1980.

SUGGESTED READING:

Planck, Charles. *Women With Wings,* 1942.

Howard Gofstein,
freelance writer, Oak Park, Michigan

Omm Seti or Omm Sety (1904–1981).

See Eady, Dorothy Louise.

O'Morphi, Louise (1737–1814).

See Pompadour, Jeanne-Antoinette for sidebar on Marie-Louise O'Murphy.

Omu Okwei (1872–1943).

See Okwei of Osomari.

O'Murphy, Marie-Louise (1737–1814).

See Pompadour, Jeanne-Antoinette for sidebar on Marie-Louise O'Murphy.

Onassis, Christina (1950–1988)

Greek heiress. *Name variations: Cristina Onassis. Born on December 11, 1950, in New York City; died of an apparent heart attack on November 19, 1988, in Buenos Aires, Argentina; daughter of Aristotle Onassis (a billionaire shipping tycoon) and Athina (Livanos) Onassis; attended the Hewitt School in New York City, St. George's College, Lausanne, Switzer-*

land, and Queen's College in London; married Joseph Bolker (a realtor), on July 26, 1971 (divorced 1972); married Alexander Andreadis (a mechanical engineer), on July 22, 1975 (divorced 1976); married Sergei Kauzov, on August 1, 1978 (divorced c. 1980); married Thierry Roussell (a businessman), on March 17, 1984 (divorced c. 1987); children: (fourth marriage) Athina Roussell (b. January 29, 1985).

Although she became "the richest woman in the world" at the age of 24, Christina Onassis lived a sad life marred by failed marriages, family deaths, and problems with her self-image. As the only surviving child of Greek shipping tycoon Aristotle Onassis, upon the death of her father in 1975 she inherited a large share of the vast Onassis fortune, which at the time was estimated to be between $400 million and $1 billion.

Onassis was born on December 11, 1950, in New York City. Her father's lucrative shipping business allowed the family, which included Christina's older brother Alexander, to live in incredible luxury with homes and investments all over the world. Christian Dior designed the clothes worn by the doll she played with, and the ponies she rode had been gifts from the king of Saudi Arabia. The family also spent time on their 325-foot yacht, named the *Christina* by her father, who called her "My Golden One." However, the same wealth which provided Onassis with such stupendous material comforts also deprived her of a secure home life, as her father was frequently away on business and her mother Athina (called **Tina Onassis**) lived the peripatetic life of a high-society jet-setter. Her family relationships were further shaken when her parents divorced in 1960, amidst rumors of (and much worldwide press speculation about) Aristotle's affair with acclaimed opera star ***Maria Callas**. These early disruptions may have been the cause of Onassis' lifelong battles with depression and with her weight; as an adult, she dieted extensively, which may well have undermined her health, and was also said to have relied heavily on barbiturates and amphetamines.

As a child, Onassis, who by the time she reached adulthood would be able to speak Greek, English, French, Spanish, and Italian, was educated mainly by foreign governesses. She then was sent to expensive private schools, including the Hewitt School in New York City and the fashionable Swiss finishing school St. George's College in Lausanne (she later spent a few months studying at Queen's College in London). Her parents remained hot topics in the press during this time, as they went on to other sensational relationships which included Aristotle's marriage in 1968 to ***Jacqueline Kennedy**, the widow of President John F. Kennedy. Both Onassis and her brother reportedly had pleaded with their father not to marry Kennedy, whom they distrusted, and despite public disavowals to the contrary the relationship between Christina and the former first lady is believed to have been a cold one. The intense public scrutiny which followed Kennedy after her second marriage inevitably heightened Onassis' own profile, and it was much remarked upon when in 1971, at the age of 20, she married Joseph Bolker, a middle-aged, divorced Los Angeles realtor with four daughters. The marriage, which had been opposed by her parents from the beginning, lasted only nine months, becoming the first in what would be a series of failed marriages. Misfortune continued to follow Onassis when her brother Alexander was killed in a plane crash in 1973 and her mother died suddenly of pulmonary edema the following year.

Upon the death of Alexander—who had been designated heir of the Onassis shipping empire—Aristotle turned to his daughter as his successor. She went with him on business trips, undertook an extensive tutorial in shipping with one of his closest advisors, and was encouraged to participate in negotiations with business associates. While she maintained the life of an international jet-setter, she also worked regularly at the company's headquarters in Monaco, though this did not silence those who questioned her capacities when her father died in 1975. He left 47.5% of his business to Onassis and the remaining majority to a foundation that was to be established in memory of his son, and she quickly showed a good understanding of finance by minimizing estate taxes through adroit use of legal loopholes and shelters. She remained involved in the business for the rest of her life, although the extent to which she actually directed its activities has been debated. Jacqueline Kennedy contested Aristotle's will, leading to a bitter court battle which was finally ended by Christina's settlement of $26 million on her stepmother.

Some three months after her father's death, Onassis married Alexander Andreadis, who also came from a Greek shipping family, but this lasted only a little more than a year. Two more husbands, Sergei Kauzov (married in 1978) and Thierry Roussell (married in 1984), came and left her troubled life. In 1985 she gave birth to her only child, a daughter whom she named **Athina (Roussell)**, after her mother. She kept custody of her daughter after her divorce from Roussell and set about raising her personally, as she herself had not been raised. While visiting a friend in Buenos Aires, Argentina, Christina Onassis died unexpectedly on November 19, 1988, apparently of a heart attack. (There has been speculation that the heart attack was brought on by years of constant dieting and drug use.) It was a sad end to a life surrounded by luxury and lived in unhappiness. As her sole heir, her three-year-old daughter became, like her mother before her, one of the wealthiest people in the world.

SOURCES:

Current Biography Yearbook, 1976. NY: H.W. Wilson, 1976.

Dempster, Nigel. *Heiress: The Story of Christina Onassis.* Charnwood Publications, 1990.

Jacqueline Mitchell,
freelance writer, Detroit, Michigan

Onassis, Jacqueline (1929–1994).

See Kennedy, Jacqueline.

Ondra, Anny (1903–1987)

Polish-born film actress. *Born Anna Sophie Ondrakowa on May 15, 1903, in Tarnow, Poland; died in 1987; married director Karel Lamac (divorced 1933); married Max Schmeling (a boxer), in 1933.*

Selected filmography: Woman with Small Feet *(Czech, 1919);* Song of Gold *(Czech, 1920);* Dratenicek *(Czech, 1920);* Gilly in Prague *(Czech, 1921);* Zigeunerliebe *(Aus-Ger., 1922);* Der Mann ohne Herz *(Aus-Ger., 1923);* Ich liebe Dich *(Aus-Ger., 1925);* Der erste Kuss *(Aus-Ger., 1928);* God's Clay *(UK, 1928);* Blackmail *(UK, 1929);* Glorious Youth *(UK, 1929);* The Manxman *(UK, 1929);* Das Mädel aus USA *(Ger., 1930);* Die grosse Sehnsucht *(Ger., 1930);* Eine Freundin so goldig wie Du *(Ger., 1930);* Mamsell Nitouche *(Ger., 1931);* Die Fledermaus *(Ger., 1931);* Baby *(Ger., 1932);* Kiki *(Ger., 1932);* Eine Nacht im Paradies *(Ger., 1932);* Die Tochter des Regiments *(Ger., 1933);* Klein Dorrit *(Ger., 1934);* Polenblut *(Ger.-Czech., 1934);* Knock-Out *(Ger., 1935);* Der Junge Graf *(Ger., 1935);* Ein Màdel vom Ballett *(Ger., 1936);* Donogoo Tonka *(Ger., 1936);* Der unwiderst Ehliche *(*The Irresistible Man, *Ger., 1937);* Narren im Schnee *(Ger., 1938);* Der Gasmann *(Ger., 1941);* Himmel wir erben ein Schloss *(Ger., 1943);* Schön muss man sein *(Ger., 1951);* Zürcher Velobung *(Ger., 1957).*

Trained as a dancer, Polish-born actress Anny Ondra began her career in 1919, in the Czechoslovakian film *Woman with Small Feet,* and quickly gained popularity in both comic and serious roles. During the 1920s, she formed a production company with director-producer Karel Lamac, whom she also married. Ondra made a number of films under Lamac's direction, and also gave a memorable performance in Alfred Hitchcock's early talkie *Blackmail* (1929), although her heavily accented voice had to be dubbed. Ondra divorced Lumac in 1933, to marry boxer Max Schmeling.

O'Neal.

Variant of O'Neill.

O'Neal, Peggy (c. 1799–1879).

See Eaton, Peggy.

O'Neal, Rose (c. 1817–1864).

See Greenhow, Rose O'Neal.

O'Neale.

Variant of O'Neill.

O'Neale, Margaret (c. 1799–1879).

See Eaton, Peggy.

O'Neale, Peggy (c. 1799–1879).

See Eaton, Peggy.

O'Neil.

Variant of O'Neill.

O'Neil, Kitty (1947—)

American athlete and stunt performer. *Born in 1947 in Corpus Christi, Texas; married Duffy Hambleton (a stunt performer).*

Held the official waterskiing speed record at 104.85 miles per hour (1970); held the women's world land speed record (1976); was the only woman in the world deemed qualified for international motorcycle competition (1977); was the first woman accepted into Stunts Unlimited, an assemblage of Hollywood's top stunt performers; set records for the longest fall and the highest fall accomplished by a woman while set ablaze (1977); was the only woman to perform the "cannon car rollover" stunt.

Athlete and stunt performer Kitty O'Neil rose above personal hardship to set stunt records during her appearances on such 1970's television shows as "Policewoman," "The Bionic Woman," and "Baretta." Born in 1947 in Corpus Christi, Texas, she was rendered deaf at four months old following simultaneous attacks of measles, mumps and chicken pox. Her mother, a full-blooded Cherokee, attended classes at the University of Texas at Austin to learn how to help her daughter read lips and communicate, and was so successful that O'Neil went on to become an outstanding music student who won awards as both a piano and a cello player.

O'Neil had a concurrent interest in sports. She won the Junior Olympic Southwest District Diving title, and caught the attention of two-time Olympic diving champion Sammy Lee. After moving to Anaheim, California, she trained with Lee and won over 30 blue ribbons and numerous first-place trophies and gold medals. She also placed 12th in the U.S. team trials for the 1964 Tokyo Olympics and took a first-place finish in the women's 10-meter diving championship. In 1970, she captured the official waterskiing speed record at 104.85 miles per hour. Six years later, she held the women's world land speed record, traveling 322 miles per hour in a 38-foot, three-wheeled rocket-powered land missile. O'Neil raced boats, drag cars, production sports cars, dune buggies and motorcycles. In 1977, she was the only woman in the world deemed qualified for international motorcycle competition when the Féderation Internationale Motorcycliste granted her a professional license.

O'Neil became a stunt performer under the tutelage of her husband Duffy Hambleton. On a television special in 1977, she set records for both the longest fall by a woman and the highest fall attempted by a woman while afire, completing a 112-foot drop in a protective fire suit that had been set ablaze. She was the first woman accepted into Stunts Unlimited, an elite company of Hollywood's top stunt performers, and as of 1992 she was the only woman to perform a stunt in which a moving car is flipped over by an explosive device—the "cannon car rollover." In 1979, O'Neil's life story was dramatized in a CBS made-for-TV movie, "Silent Victory: The Kitty O'Neil Story."

SOURCES:

Read, Phyllis J., and Bernard L. Witlieb. *The Book of Women's Firsts*. NY: Random House, 1992.

Howard Gofstein,
freelance writer, Oak Park, Michigan

O'Neill, Agnes Boulton (1893–1968).

See Boulton, Agnes.

O'Neill, Carlotta (1888–1970)

American actress and third wife of playwright Eugene O'Neill. *Name variations: acted under Carlotta Monterey. Born Hazel Neilson Tharsing in Oakland, California, in December 1888; died in New Jersey in 1970; daughter of Christian Neilson Tharsing (a fruit farmer) and Nellie (Gotchett) Tharsing; attended St. Gertrude's Academy, Rio Vista, California; studied abroad, 1906–11; studied at the Academy of Dramatic Arts under Sir Herbert Beerbohm Tree; married John Moffat (a lawyer), in 1911 (divorced); married Melvin C. Chapman, Jr. (a law student), in 1916 (divorced 1923); married Ralph Barton (a caricaturist), in 1923 (divorced 1926); married Eugene O'Neill (1885–1953, a playwright), on July 22, 1929; children: (second marriage) Cynthia Jane Chapman.*

When summarizing her 24-year marriage to eminent American playwright Eugene O'Neill following his death in 1953, Carlotta O'Neill laid to rest any romantic notions surrounding their life together. "I worked like a dog," she said. "I was his secretary. I was his nurse. I built and ran his houses. He wrote the plays, I did everything else. Gene loved me as much as he could love anyone, but the only real love he had was for writing plays. He lived completely within himself." Carlotta did preface her assessment by noting that living with O'Neill was "mentally stimulating," and thus a privilege. "My God, how many women have husbands who are very stimulating?"

Carlotta was O'Neill's third wife and a veteran of her own three failed marriages when she wed the playwright in 1929. It is a wonder she chose to marry at all, given her mother's example. Born in Oakland, California, in 1888, and christened Hazel Neilson Tharsing, she was the sole offspring of the union between Christian Neilson Tharsing, a 40-year-old fruit farmer and widower, and 18-year-old **Nellie Gotchett**, who, at her own mother's urging, had married Tharsing strictly for security. Nellie, who was apparently quite fertile, avoided the burden of having children by horseback riding during her early pregnancies to induce miscarriages, but Carlotta resisted her efforts. When the child was four, Nellie walked out of the marriage, leaving Carlotta with Nellie's sister Mrs. John Shay of Oakland.

Carlotta spent nine years with the Shays, although Nellie visited frequently. A thin, shy child, she also had an eye problem that was corrected with surgery and with glasses, which she abandoned after a few years. To help her vision, she adopted her doctor's suggestion of carrying her head high and thrown back, which gave her the haughty look that eventually came to define her personality. At 13, Carlotta was sent to St. Gertrude's, a Catholic academy in Rio Vista, California, where she spent three years. Her classmates recalled her as overly dramatic and mysterious, but very much a loner. After toying with the idea of becoming a nun, she settled on the theater, to which she had first been drawn during her childhood elocution lessons, which the Shays provided to help overcome her shyness. (Her commanding voice turned out to be one of her most appealing features.) To further prepare for the theater, she spent five years abroad between 1906 and 1911, taking ballet and singing lessons, and studying acting at Sir Herbert Beerbohm Tree's Academy of Dramatic Arts. She made her first and final appearance on the London stage in a revival of *The Geisha*.

Carlotta's career, barely off the ground, was temporarily halted in 1911 by her first marriage, to John Moffat, a Scottish lawyer who dabbled in the stock market. The marriage ended when he threatened to shoot her, although the couple apparently remained friends following their divorce. Carlotta picked up her career and a new surname (Monterey, from the town in California) and made her Broadway debut in a little sex farce called *Taking Chances*. A tour as Luana in *The Bird of Paradise* followed, during which she discovered that she hated touring. "I would rather not work at all," she said, "than go on the road."

In 1916, she married Melvin C. Chapman, Jr., a law student seven years her junior. (Her mother Nellie was at the time the mistress and housekeeper of Chapman's widowed father, making for complicated family interactions.) Carlotta wed Chapman in order to have a child, having been told that motherhood would improve her acting. But less than a year after giving birth to a girl named **Cynthia Jane Chapman**, in a replay of her own abandonment, she left the baby with her mother and returned to the stage. Carlotta did not divorce Chapman, however, until 1923, when she was preparing to marry Ralph Barton, a caricaturist. Their union was described as stormy and passionate, and they divorced in 1926, after Carlotta returned from an out-of-town tour to find him in bed with another woman. Shortly after leaving Chapman, and before marrying Barton, Carlotta became the mistress of James Speyer, a wealthy older banker who made the actress one of his main philanthropies by establishing a trust fund in her name which provided her a lifetime annual income of around $14,000. (Carlotta spent much of the money satisfying her passion for clothes and for shoes, of which at one point she supposedly had 300 pair.) She split with Speyer when she married O'Neill, but only after obtaining his blessing on the union.

Carlotta first met Eugene O'Neill in 1922, when she agreed to take over a role in his play *The Hairy Ape*, as a favor to director Arthur Hopkins. They met again in 1926, shortly after the end of her marriage to Barton, while she was summering in Maine with ◆ **Elisabeth Marbury**, who served as an agent to both of them. At that time, O'Neill, who had seemingly licked the alcoholism that dominated his early years, was married to ***Agnes Boulton**, his second wife and the mother of two of his three children, Shane (b. 1919) and ***Oona O'Neill Chaplin** (b. 1925). O'Neill's earlier marriage to **Kathleen Jenkins**, whom he had divorced in 1912, had produced his first son and namesake Eugene (b. 1910). One day, when Eugene and Agnes were guests for tea at Marbury's, Carlotta was dispatched to take the playwright to the boathouse so he could swim. A romance between the two seemed unlikely at the time, as Carlotta was harboring a bit of a grudge. On the way to the water, she scolded the playwright, calling him rude for not thanking her for going into his play "with hardly a rehearsal." Her attitude changed a short time later, however, when O'Neill emerged from the boathouse wearing a woman's swimsuit, the only one he could find to put on. "It was much too large for him, but that didn't seem to bother him—he wanted his swim. I thought to myself, He can't be so stuck on himself if he'd do something like that."

◆ **Marbury, Elisabeth.** *See de Wolfe, Elsie for sidebar.*

There is some controversy over who pursued whom as the courtship between Carlotta and Eugene continued during the fall when O'Neill was in New York overseeing rehearsals of *Marco Millions*. Louis Sheaffer, in the second of his two biographies of the playwright, *O'Neill: Son and Lover*, gives Carlotta the edge. At first O'Neill was flattered by the actress' attentions, but did not want to end his marriage. Increasingly, however, he was drawn to Carlotta's declarations of love and her interest in his work. Most important, he was attracted by her strength. "Agnes was uncertain of herself," said O'Neill's friend **Elizabeth Shepley Sergeant**, "so she couldn't help Gene any, while Carlotta always appeared perfectly at ease. She was reassuring to him."

Though O'Neill would not be free to marry Carlotta until 1929, in February 1928 he left Agnes and his family in Bermuda and sailed off to "honeymoon" with Carlotta in Europe. "To say that Carlotta and I are in love in the sense of any love I have ever experienced before is weak and inadequate," he said at the time. But O'Neill, an introspective and nervous man under the best of conditions, was under strain from the unraveling of his marriage and the separation from his children. While he and Carlotta were visiting Shanghai, he disappeared for two weeks on a prolonged drunk and ended up in a hospital where he reportedly had a mild nervous breakdown. Carlotta, devastated at what she viewed as a betrayal, left him briefly, but ultimately could not dissolve the relationship. Following a reconciliation, they rented a 45-room château, "Le Plessis," near Tours. The playwright began work on *Mourning Becomes Electra*, a trilogy based on the Greek legend of the House of Atreus, while Carlotta tended to upgrading his lifestyle. On July 22, 1929, shortly after Agnes had obtained a divorce, the couple married in a small ceremony in Paris. Carlotta said it seemed "the first time I'd ever really been married. The others were just legalized affairs."

During his early years with Carlotta, O'Neill produced three important plays: *Strange Interlude*, *Mourning Becomes Electra*, and *Ah! Wilderness*, although his greatest works would come later in his life. The playwright was always lavish in praising Carlotta's contribution to his work, crediting her with keeping the house running efficiently, so that "nary an outside worry has touched me or bogged my stride even for a moment." Indeed, Carlotta went to great lengths to insure her husband's well-being, even to the point of having the household help wear bedroom slippers so that their moving about would not generate any sounds that might interrupt his concentration. She also had a special chair made for him in England, something resembling a padded dentist's chair which had movable arm and leg supports to insure his optimum comfort. "All her thoughts were of him; she looked after him like a mother," said ***Lillian Gish** who, with George Jean Nathan, was one of the first visitors to Le Plessis. "I've been around many couples in my time but I've never known any others so close, so devoted, as Carlotta and Gene." Sergeant, however, worried about the rather grand style in which the O'Neills were now living. "I'm not sure that handmade shoes and a château, with menus written on and placed in silver holders, were the best sort of environment for the artist in Gene," she said.

The O'Neills returned to the United States in 1931, staying in New York for a time, but eventually building an oceanside home, "Casa Genotta," in Sea Island, Georgia, where they lived for four years. Early in 1932, Carlotta had a rather strained reunion with her mother and daughter, the first in five years. According to Sheaffer, Carlotta had less feeling for Cynthia than she did for the O'Neill pet Dalmatian "Blemie," whom she once characterized as "the only one of our children who never disappointed us." Cynthia, who also saw little of her father and was now being rejected by her grandmother, felt that she did not belong to anyone. The visit ended with the O'Neills driving the girl to boarding school in Connecticut. She stayed there only a term, then returned to Nellie in California. (Mother and daughter would continue to see each other at intervals. Cynthia would marry at 17, then divorce to marry Roy Stram, with whom she had a son, Gerald Eugene. He was named partly after O'Neill, who was the closest thing to a father she ever had. For several years, beginning in 1942, Cynthia worked for O'Neill, typing his scripts and some of his correspondence, but Carlotta shut her out of their lives again in 1944.)

A decline in O'Neill's health, combined with the area's extreme living conditions, compelled the couple to leave Sea Island. They spent some time in Seattle where they thought of settling, but the dreary weather there drove them south to the San Francisco Bay area. There they eventually built yet another home, "Tao House," located in Danville. The couple resided there from 1937 to 1944, during which time O'Neill enjoyed a period of great creativity, but also one of personal hardship. His health further declined with emergency surgery for appendicitis in 1936, and the onset of increasingly intense tremors (diagnosed in 1942 as Parkinson's disease), that often made writing impossible. He also encountered problems with his younger children, who had been left with their mother and only occasionally visited him. Shane did poorly in school and seemed to lack direction, while Oona, a budding actress, eloped with 54-year-old actor-director Charlie Chaplin in 1943, at age 18, devastating her father to such a degree that he never spoke to her again. Carlotta was also ill during this period, plagued by an arthritic spine. Nonetheless, she continued to serve as mistress of the house, leaving her husband free to write his greatest plays: *A Touch of the Poet* (the first and only completed drama of what had been conceived as a cycle of plays about the failure of the American dream); *The Iceman Cometh*, *Hughie*, *Long Day's Journey into Night*, and *A Moon for the Misbegotten*.

As O'Neill's physical condition worsened, Carlotta began to feel isolated and to resent her role as caregiver and overseer of the house. "I feel imprisoned—and want to scream my way out," she wrote to **Eline Winther** in October 1943. "I want to go back where I belong. The East. I want to see my friends. People who are doing things." At Carlotta's urging, the O'Neills sold the house in February 1944 and briefly took an apartment at the Fairmont Hotel in San Francisco, before moving into a six-room penthouse in New York, which Carlotta decorated to the hilt. But her joyous return to New York was short-lived. She began to object to O'Neill's reunions with his old bohemian friends, and to his contact with a string of young actresses who were eager just to be in his company. Years after his death, Carlotta described O'Neill's behavior during this period as that of "a wayward child, a delinquent." She grew jealous and certain that he no longer loved her. "He was impotent the last ten years of his life, and he hated me for it. If he'd known anything about love, this wouldn't have bothered him. . . . Things would be going along all right between us when out of the blue he would say, 'I don't know whether I hate myself more or you.'"

In January 1948, after a particularly heated battle during which O'Neill slapped her, Carlotta packed her bags and left, taking refuge in a hotel. O'Neill, after several futile attempts to fetch her back, got drunk one evening with a friend, then fell and fractured his left shoulder. Hospitalized, he conducted desperate negotiations for a reconciliation from his hospital room, while Carlotta ranted to her friends about how her husband had humiliated her and worried her into the madhouse. After weeks of back-and-forth pleas and accusations, the couple reconciled in O'Neill's hospital room. "He needs me, he can't live without me!" Carlotta declared to one of the doctors. Indeed, she was probably right. "She made herself into a necessity for Gene," said playwright Marc Connelly. "O'Neill was always a sort of submerged fellow, and the progression of his illness did not help any against this tendency. . . . Carlotta completed the job by practically wrapping Gene up in swaddling clothes."

Following O'Neill's recovery, the couple moved yet again to a refurbished cottage at Marblehead Neck in Massachusetts. By this time, O'Neill was both physically and financially dependent on Carlotta, who had sold her nest egg of stocks and bonds to buy the place. "Out of great sorrow, and pain, and misunderstanding, comes a new vision of deeper love and security and above all, serenity, to bind us ever closer in our old age," O'Neill wrote to his wife in a copy of *The Iceman Cometh*.

The suicide in 1950 of O'Neill's eldest son Eugene, Jr., a brilliant but unsettled scholar who turned to alcohol, was the next blow to the playwright. "Wracked with guilt feelings, he sealed his lips on his agony," wrote Sheaffer. With her husband now consumed by unspoken grief, as well as debilitating palsy, life in the Marblehead cottage became more and more confining and difficult for Carlotta, who out of fatigue and frustration began to deliberately provoke disputes. To relieve her growing stress, she also relied more and more upon sedatives, and, as a result of a growing sensitivity to the bromides, began to experience periods of impaired judgment and disorientation. This led to another separation, in February 1951, during which O'Neill, who was also suffering from bromide intoxication, refused to be reunited with Carlotta and, at the prodding of one of his psychiatrists, signed a petition alleging that she was insane and should be placed under guardianship. At the same time, he changed his will to eliminate her as executor. Carlotta retaliated with her own petition, accusing her husband of cruel and abusive treatment and requesting separation support. Amid much speculation concerning the future of the relationship, the O'Neills came close to a permanent separation, but were reconciled one last time, although only after the playwright agreed to change back his will and rename Carlotta as his executor and sole heir.

The O'Neills' last home together was a suite in Boston's Shelton Hotel, where they would reside for the next two years. During this time, Carlotta employed a nurse to help care for Eugene, who was now confined to the apartment. Hotel employees, familiar with Carlotta from a previous stay, found her generous if demanding. "She dressed old-fashioned," said **Joan Orlando**, the dining-room hostess, "mostly in black—black stockings, high-neck dresses, black hat, long black coat, and always wore sunglasses. Her cane fascinated me, a black one with a black marble head. She used it in talking, for emphasis, and whenever she approached the door would raise it imperiously."

Until the end, O'Neill continued his habit of presenting his wife with birthday, anniversary, and Christmas messages, as well as dedications, which she later published under the title *Inscriptions: Eugene O'Neill to Carlotta Monterey O'Neill*. Shortly after their final reconciliation, he had his attorneys draw up a document that gave Carlotta full ownership and command of all his work, evidence, according to Sheaffer, "not only of his attachment to her but of his fading interest in life and the things of this world." O'Neill died of a massive infection on November 27, 1953, about a month after his 65th birthday, with his wife at his bedside. Carlotta, according to his instructions, kept the funeral very private. "I carried out every wish of Gene's to the letter," she said, "and it was very difficult. He wished no publicity . . . nobody to be at the funeral . . . no religious representative of any creed or kind."

Following her husband's death, Carlotta faded from public scrutiny until her controversial release of the play *Long Day's Journey into Night*, O'Neill's intensely autobiographical work tracing his own tragic family life through the story of the dysfunctional Tyrone family. Sixteen years earlier, when the play was written, O'Neill's son, Eugene, Jr., had asked his father to withhold it for 25 years because he felt that the strongly personal nature of the work might impact his social position at Yale, where he was teaching. At the time, O'Neill agreed. Shortly after her husband's death and despite the earlier death of Eugene, Jr., Carlotta told **Anne Crouse** that she fully intended to keep the play locked up for the 25-year period. In 1955, Carlotta obviously had a change of heart, for she gave the publication rights to Yale University Press, which printed the text, opening a floodgate of offers to produce the work. The play, which had its world premiere at the Royal Theater in Stockholm, Sweden, in February 1956, was first performed in America on November 6, 1956. Directed by Jose Quintero, it starred Fredric March and ***Florence Eldridge** as the elder Tyrones, and Jason Robards, Jr., and Bradford Dillman as the Tyrone sons Jamie and Edmund. The play was the dramatic sensation of the 1956–57 Broadway season, garnering O'Neill a posthumous Pulitzer Prize, his fourth. Although many close to the playwright felt that Carlotta had erred in releasing the work, Sheaffer was not so sure. "The matter can be viewed from more than one angle," he wrote: "legally, as the playwright's executrix and sole heir, she had the authority to do as she pleased; morally, her act is something else again; yet at the same time all interested in the American drama can be grateful that she released at an early date what many consider the finest American play ever written."

In 1956, **Barbara Gelb**, who with her husband, editor Arthur Gelb, was in the process of writing the biography *O'Neill* (1962), conducted several interviews with Carlotta, whom she called "very, very much the grande dame." Years later, at the request of actress ***Colleen Dewhurst**, who was looking for a vehicle that she could tour to college campuses, Gelb wrote a one-woman melodrama about Carlotta called *My Gene,* which was produced in 1987. "Barbara gave Carlotta, who has always been known as a bitch, a life with another side to her," said Dewhurst, explaining that audiences would come away with a new understanding of Carlotta's strong influence over the playwright. The critics were harsh on the two-hour production, complaining that it contained more fact than drama, although Gelb said she removed 50 pages of factual material from the script during rehearsals. It is difficult to imagine what Carlotta would have said about Gelb's interpretation of her life, but she would have rejoiced at having her story told.

SOURCES:

Garraty, John A., and Mark C. Carnes, eds. *American National Biography*. Oxford: Oxford University Press, 1999.

Rosen, Leah. "At Last Carlotta O'Neill, Eugene's Feisty Widow Takes Stage Center in a Play by Barbara Gelb," in *People Weekly.* March 23, 1987.

Sheaffer, Louis. *O'Neill: Son and Artist.* Boston, MA: Little, Brown, 1973.

Wilmeth, Don B., and Tice L. Miller, eds. *Cambridge Guide to American Theater*. Cambridge: Cambridge University Press, 1993.

Barbara Morgan,
Melrose, Massachusetts

O'Neill, Eliza (1791–1872)

Irish actress. *Name variations: Lady Eliza Becher. Born in 1791; died on October 29, 1872; daughter of an actor in Drogheda, Ireland; married an Irish member of Parliament, William Wrixon (afterwards Baron Becher), in 1819.*

A beautiful young Irish actress, Eliza O'Neill enjoyed one of the shortest and most brilliant careers on the English stage. She was the daughter of an impoverished actor in Drogheda, Ireland, where she made her first appearance as a child. Later, she played in the theaters of Belfast and Dublin, and her reputation led to a London engagement. On October 6, 1814, she made her debut at Covent Garden as Juliet to William Conway's Romeo. Though the management had modest expectations for the production, the houses were crowded nightly, and O'Neill was praised lavishly. William Macready, speaking of her debut, wrote: "Her beauty, grace, simplicity, and tenderness were the theme of every tongue. The noble pathos of [***Sarah**] **Siddons**' genius no longer served as the grand commentary and living exponent of Shakespeare's text, but in the native elegance, the feminine sweetness, the unaffected earnestness and gushing passion of Miss O'Neill the stage had received a worthy successor of her."

For five years, she was a reigning favorite, delighting audiences with her comedic portrayals, including Lady Teazle, and causing a sensation when she took on the tragic roles of Belvidera, Mrs. Haller, Mrs. Beverley, and Monimia.

Throughout her theatrical career, O'Neill retained a flawless reputation, and in 1819 she married an Irish member of Parliament, William Wrixon, afterwards Baron Becher, and retired from the stage. Lady Becher, who lived to be 81, was usually referred to as "the great Miss O'Neill."

SUGGESTED READING:

Jones, Charles Inigo. *Memoirs of Miss O'Neill; containing her public character, private life and dramatic progress.* London, 1816.

O'Neill, Jan (b. 1941).

See Court, Margaret for sidebar on Jan Lehane.

O'Neill, Maire (1885–1952)

***Irish actress.** Name variations: Mary Allgood; Molly Allgood or Molly O'Neill. Born Mary Allgood in Dublin, Ireland, on January 12, 1885 (some sources cite 1887); died in Basingstoke, Hampshire, England, on November 2, 1952; daughter of George Allgood and Margaret Harold Allgood; sister of actress Sara Allgood (1883–1950); married G.H. Mair (a journalist), in 1911 (died January 1926); married Arthur Sinclair (an actor), in June 1926 (divorced); children: (first marriage) Pegeen and John.*

Maire O'Neill was born Mary Allgood, though she would always be known as Molly, in Dublin in 1885, the product of a mixed marriage. Her father George Allgood, a printing compositor of English stock and a member of his local Orange lodge, insisted his eight children be raised Protestant while her mother **Margaret Allgood** smuggled them to Catholic services. Not surprisingly, the marriage was unhappy. Apart from religious differences, there were marked differences of temperament, and the children had to indulge their love of singing, dancing and acting when their father was out of the house. However, George died in 1894 when his children were still young, and when Margaret went back to work, Molly was sent to a Protestant orphanage from which she eventually ran away. This appears to have been her only period of formal education.

After leaving the orphanage, Molly was apprenticed to a dressmaker and then worked in a shop. Her sister ***Sara Allgood** had joined ***Maud Gonne**'s Inghinidhe na hEireann (Daughters of Ireland), which took a particular interest in drama. Sara joined William Fay's Irish National Theatre Society and in 1904 became a full-fledged professional actress in the first Abbey Theatre company. Molly was equally determined to be an actress, but wanted a separate identity from her famous sister. As Maire O'Neill, she first appeared on stage in February 1905 in a walk-on part in J.M. Synge's *The Well of the Saints.* Synge, the Abbey's most gifted dramatist, was soon attracted to O'Neill and gave her roles in two of his plays: Cathleen in *Riders to the Sea* and the more important Nora in *The Shadow of the Glen.* The relationship between them was looked on with disfavor by Sara, who had expected to be cast in the leads, and by Lady ***Augusta Gregory**, one of the Abbey's three directors (with Synge and Yeats), who thought that O'Neill, poor, uneducated and 14 years younger, was no match for Synge.

Physically, she was more beautiful than her sister. O'Neill had, as **Elizabeth Coxhead** observed, "the heartbreaking prettiness which can be so much more dangerous than classical beauty. . . . She had the combination of virginal Irish innocence and strong come-hither so well calculated to drive men mad." Her relationship with Synge, though known at the time, was ignored in the early biographies and memoirs about the Abbey. Yeats and Lady Gregory disapproved, as did Synge's family from whom Synge was estranged when he became secretly engaged to O'Neill. It was not until 1959 and the publication of the biography of Synge by David Greene and Edward Stephens that O'Neill's personal and artistic importance to Synge was made widely known. They became engaged in 1906 but quarrels were frequent as **Ann Saddlemyer**, editor of their correspondence, has noted. Both had violent tempers, and Synge's tendency to play Pygmalion to O'Neill's Galatea exasperated her with his scrutinizing of her friends, her clothes, her reading, in fact her entire lifestyle. O'Neill was by temperament a rebel and was often impatient and careless with Synge. But their love endured, and in January 1907 there were the first performances of Synge's *The Playboy of the Western World,* in which O'Neill created the role of Pegeen Mike with which she became indelibly associated. However, even before they met Synge was suffering from Hodgkin's disease which gradually worsened. He died in March 1909 and left the draft of a final play for O'Neill, *Deirdre of the Sorrows,* which was performed in January 1910. He also left her a small income which helped her in later years when she was in straitened circumstances.

O'Neill remained at the Abbey until 1911. She performed the role of the Woman in Shaw's *The Shewing-Up of Blanco Posnet* and, according to Lennox Robinson, brought unaccustomed tears to the dramatist's eyes because of the power of her portrayal. In 1911, she married G.H.

Mair, a distinguished journalist on the *Manchester Guardian*, and moved to England. She joined the Liverpool Repertory and appeared in *The Shadow of the Glen*, Hauptmann's *Hannele*, and Shaw's *Candida*. In 1913, Sir Herbert Beerbohm Tree engaged her as Nerissa in his production of *The Merchant of Venice*. The following year, she was invited to appear in America in George Birmingham's comedy *General John Regan*. She returned to the Abbey in 1916 to play in Lennox Robinson's *Whiteheaded Boy*, and also appeared in the London production. Whereas Sara Allgood's tragedy was "grandiose, Molly's was intimate and personal," wrote Robinson. "She could be deliciously impish."

O'Neill's husband died in January 1926. It had been a happy marriage and so her children were shocked when just six months later she married Arthur Sinclair, with whom she acted in a London production of *Juno and the Paycock*. After their marriage, they and Sara toured Britain and America regularly in O'Casey's plays, although the two sisters were often not on speaking terms. The marriage to Sinclair proved unhappy and eventually ended in divorce. O'Neill's only son was killed in 1942 and she had increasing problems with alcohol. Her last 20 years were, as Coxhead writes, a formidable rake's progress but it was not a completely tragic story: "she was a naturally gay soul, and contrived to get a large amount of fun out of her predicaments." She continued to act until the end, and died of burns received in an accident just before she was due to broadcast a radio production of O'Casey's *The Silver Tassie*.

SOURCES:

Coxhead, Elizabeth. "Sally and Molly" in *Daughters of Erin: Five Women of the Irish Renascence*. London: Secker & Warburg, 1965.

"Maire O'Neill," in *Irish Times* (obituary). November 3–4, 1952.

Saddlemyer, Ann, ed. *Letters to Molly: John Millington Synge to Maire O'Neill*. Cambridge, MA: Harvard University Press, 1971.

Deirdre McMahon,
lecturer in history at Mary Immaculate College,
University of Limerick, Limerick, Ireland

O'Neill, Margaret (c. 1799–1879).

See Eaton, Peggy.

O'Neill, Moira (c. 1865–1955).

See Skrine, Agnes.

O'Neill, Oona (1925–1991).

See Chaplin, Oona O'Neill.

O'Neill, Peggy (c. 1799–1879).

See Eaton, Peggy.

O'Neill, Rose Cecil (1874–1944)

American artist, illustrator, poet, and novelist, noted for her "Kewpies," sentimental cupid figures that sparked an international craze. *Name variations: Rose O'Neill Latham; Rose O'Neill Wilson; Rosie O'Neill. Born Rose Cecil O'Neill on June 25, 1874, in Wilkes-Barre, Pennsylvania; died of heart failure on April 6, 1944, in Springfield, Missouri; oldest of three daughters and second of six surviving children of Alice Asenath Cecelia (Smith) O'Neill and William Patrick O'Neill (a book merchant); attended Convent School of the Sacred Heart, Omaha, Nebraska; enrolled at the Convent of the Sisters of St. Regis, New York (1889–96), but followed no formal curriculum; married Gray Latham, in 1892 (divorced, though some accounts say she was widowed, 1901); married Harry Leon Wilson, in 1902 (divorced 1907); children: none.*

Awards: elected to Société des Beaux Artes, Paris (1921). Exhibits: Galerie Devambez, Paris (spring, 1921); Wildenstein Galleries, New York (1922).

Selected works as author-illustrator: The Loves of Edwy *(MA: Lothrop, 1904),* The Lady in the White Veil *(NY: Harper and Brothers, 1909),* Kewpies and Dottie Darling *(NY: George H. Doran, 1912),* Kewpies: Their Book, Verse and Poetry *(NY: Frederick A. Stokes, 1913),* Kewpie Cutouts *(1914);* The Kewpie Primer *(1916),* The Master-Mistress *(NY: Knopf, 1922),* Kewpies and the Runaway Baby *(NY: Doubleday, Doran, 1928),* Garda *(NY: Doubleday, Doran, 1929),* The Goblin Woman *(NY: Doubleday, Doran, 1930); as illustrator: Harry Leon Wilson's* The Lions of the Lord *(Boston: Lothrop, 1903) and* The Boss of Little Arcady *(Boston: Lothrop, 1905) and others, her brother George O'Neill's* Tomorrow's House; or the Tiny Angel *(NY: E.P. Dutton, 1930), and the works of several other authors. Illustrations published in* Omaha World Herald, Great Divide, Truth, Cosmopolitan, Puck, Life, Harper's, Good Housekeeping, Collier's, Woman's Home Companion, Ladies' Home Journal, *among others.*

Rose O'Neill, artist, novelist and poet, a true Renaissance woman, was perhaps best known for her Kewpie dolls, whose popularity earned her an honored place in the popular culture of 20th-century America. She drew her famed Kewpies as a comic strip for over a quarter of a century, and the dolls she created were a marketing phenomenon that circled the globe.

Born in Wilkes-Barre, Pennsylvania, in 1874, Rose was the daughter of William Patrick O'Neill, a book merchant, and **Alice Smith O'Neill**. Shortly after her birth, the family

Rose O'Neill (left) with her sister Callista. Photo by Jessie Tarbox Beals.

moved to Omaha, Nebraska, where O'Neill attended the Sacred Heart Convent School. At 13, she won an art competition sponsored by the *Omaha Herald*, with a drawing so remarkable for her age it was suspected of being done by an adult. She began drawing a series of weekly cartoons as a result of this award, continuing until the family moved to New York to further her art career. By age 15, O'Neill was publishing her drawings in such major magazines as *Puck, Life* and *Harper's*. After a brief and unsuccessful acting stint with a Shakespearean touring company,

O'Neill put her creative talents to work as a writer and illustrator. At this time, her family moved to Missouri, where they settled in a remote area in the Ozark Mountains. This home, Bonniebrook, was to have an important influence on O'Neill, and she returned there often for the emotional sustenance it provided.

O'Neill's brief first marriage, at 18, was to Gray Latham, who died about five years later. (According to some accounts they were divorced before his death.) Around the turn of the century, she married Harry Leon Wilson, the editor of *Puck* magazine. Wilson's first novel, *The Spenders*, was illustrated by O'Neill, as were his subsequent novels written over the next three years. During this period, O'Neill, who by now had a secure reputation as an illustrator, wrote her first novel, *The Loves of Edwy* (1904). She and her husband traveled to Europe with their friends Booth Tarkington and his first wife **Laurel Fletcher Tarkington** shortly thereafter. While Wilson and Booth collaborated on a play, *The Man from Home* (1908), the couples stayed in Capri and then in Paris. Wilson was given to mood swings which O'Neill found hard to cope with, however, and shortly after their return to America in 1907 they were divorced. She moved to Bonniebrook in Missouri, where she continued to contribute illustrations, poems and short stories to leading magazines of the day.

O'Neill created the first Kewpies (which she claimed to have seen in a dream) in 1909, with encouragement from an editor of the *Ladies' Home Journal*. These plump childish figures with small wings and huge foreheads were an instant hit with Americans just emerging from the Victorian Age, who also loved the sentimental verse tales—filled with babies, birds and flowers—that Kewpies initially illustrated. Soon Kewpies were decorating everything from greeting cards to kitchen utensils, but their popularity only increased after 1912, when the first Kewpie dolls were made in Germany. With assistance from her sister **Callista O'Neill**, who worked as her secretary and business manager, O'Neill obtained a patent on Kewpies in 1913 and oversaw the manufacturing of nine different sizes of the bisque dolls in Germany. (In later years, she and her sister briefly would run a Kewpie store on Madison Avenue in New York City.) When World War I intervened, production of the dolls shifted to the U.S., where they were made from celluloid, chalk, wood and later fabric. O'Neill spent most of the 1910s living in Europe, becoming a familiar figure among expatriates in Paris, and returned to America in 1918.

Thanks to her Kewpies, royalties from which brought her an estimated $1.5 million, she was now a rich woman, and she used her money to indulge her love of the romantic and the dramatic. She updated her family's beloved Bonniebrook, maintained a studio on New York City's Washington Square, and frequently went barefoot while dressed in Grecian-style robes. She also kept a villa in Capri which had been partially willed to her by American painter Charles Caryl Coleman. In 1921 she bought a 10-acre estate near Westport, Connecticut, which she named Carabas Castle after the putative marquis who is assisted by the cat in "Puss in Boots." A large, flamboyant blonde, O'Neill threw open her castle to her artist friends, who included ***Charlotte Perkins Gilman**, Witter Bynner, and **Lillian Fiske**, and often treated her guests to marathon readings from the works of poet Francis Thompson. (A 1934 "Profiles" article in *The New Yorker* notes that O'Neill's weekend guests were known to stay for as long as two years.) Active within the artistic community of New York, O'Neill also worked avidly in the women's suffrage movement, producing posters and drawings for the cause.

During the 1920s, she also wrote and created non-Kewpie art. In the spring of 1921, O'Neill exhibited a group of drawings at the Galerie Devambez in Paris, and based on the strength of this collection was elected to the Société des Beaux Arts. This phase of her work, which she referred to as her "Sweet Monsters," has been noted for its resemblance to the visionary work of William Blake and of Kahlil Gibran (a friend), as well as to Rodin, at whose studio she studied after his death. The collection was exhibited at a solo show at the Wildenstein Galleries in New York the following year, and O'Neill sculpted several large-size pieces based on these drawings. Her writing is usually noted for its affinity for Celtic Romanticism, as in the collection of poetry *The Master-Mistress* (1922), which includes such motifs as noble stags, untrustworthy lovers, and fairies, and in the Gothic romances *Garda* (1929) and *The Goblin Woman* (1930).

During the 1930s, when the Kewpie rage had lessened, O'Neill created "Scootles, the Baby Tourist" as a companion to the Kewpies. Her money squandered after some two decades of an exuberant social life, she retired to Bonniebrook, where she lived with her sister Callista and continued to paint, draw, and involve herself in a number of commercial projects. A Kewpie movie project faltered in negotiations with a Hollywood studio, during which time O'Neill designed "Ho-Ho," a laughing Buddha doll that caused an outcry from Buddhists worldwide when it was later mass produced. She died of heart failure due to stroke-induced paralysis at the home of a nephew in Springfield, Missouri, in her 70th year, and was buried at Bonniebrook. After her death, national and international collectors' organizations were formed to preserve and inform the public of the memory and work of Rose O'Neill. Original Kewpie dolls, even those once won for a few cents at traveling carnivals, are now highly prized collectibles.

SOURCES:

Axe, John. *Kewpies—Dolls & Art.* Cumberland, MD: Hobby House Press, 1987.

Charmonte, Paula, ed. *Women Artists in the United States: A Selective Bibliography and Resource Guide on the Fine and Decorative Arts, 1750–1986.* Boston, MA: G.K. Hall, 1990.

James, Edward T., ed. *Notable American Women, 1607–1950.* Cambridge, MA: The Belknap Press of Harvard University Press, 1971.

Kunitz, Stanley J., and Howard Haycraft, eds. *Twentieth Century Authors.* NY: H.W. Wilson, 1942.

Liberty's Women. Springfield, MA: G&C Merriam, 1980.

The New York Times (obituary). April 7, 1944.

"Profiles (Kewpie Doll)," in *The New Yorker.* November 24, 1934.

Weiss, Deborah, ed. *The World Encyclopedia of Comics.* NY: Chelsea House, 1976.

SUGGESTED READING:

Formanek-Brunell, Miriam. *The Story of Rosie O'Neill: An Autobiography.* MO: University of Missouri, 1997.

COLLECTIONS:

Branson, Missouri, art and artifacts pertaining to Rose O'Neill in the collection of Dr. and Mrs. Bruce Trimble, Shepherd of the Hills Farm (Rose O'Neill Room).

Point Lookout, Missouri, collection of Kewpie dolls, original artwork and copies of books, Museum of The School of the Ozarks.

St. Louis, Missouri, 200 items located in the Missouri Historical Society, Jefferson Memorial Building, Forest Park.

Laurie Twist Binder,
Library Media Specialist, Buffalo Public Schools, Buffalo, New York, and freelance graphic artist and illustrator

Onians, Edith (1866–1955)

Australian social reformer who devoted herself to saving teenage boys from poverty and delinquency.

Born Edith Charlotte Onians on February 2, 1866, in Lancefield, Victoria, Australia; died on August 16, 1955, in Highbury, Australia; daughter of Richard Onians and Charlotte Onians; educated as boarding student at Fontainebleau Ladies' College in St. Kilda, Australia; never married.

Began the City Newsboys' Club (1897); studied boys' clubs and children's courts overseas (1901–02, 1911–12); participated in the Imperial Health Conference held in London (1914); wrote a memoir of her work with the Newsboys' Club (1914); appointed to board which enforced the Street Trading Act (1926).

In 1897 in Melbourne, Edith Onians, whose only previous employment had been as a Sunday school teacher, began what she called the City Newsboys' Club. At the time, many poor children and teenagers hawked newspapers on the streets for a pittance, and while most of them also attended school, some did not, and some did not have homes. It was these latter children to whom she wanted to extend a "friendly hand"; Onians believed strongly in every child's potential, whether they were poor or rich. She thus began inviting newsboys to come off the street to attend a class she taught, and was so successful in this that within six years the club had expanded to include recreational activities and workshops held in an old factory. Onians' father encouraged her work until his death in 1906, after which she used some of the income she inherited to help finance the club.

Interested in theories of child development and the implications to society of juvenile delinquency, Onians traveled to Europe and the United States in 1901–02 and 1911–12 to study boys' clubs and children's courts—she preferred the term "juvenile courts"—and wrote about her observations in her 1914 book *Men of Tomorrow.* Her efforts won the support of **Janet Clarke**, Keith Murdoch and other well-known figures, and the club moved into a two-story building with a pool, gymnasium, library, and workshops. In 1914, she explained her methods to the Imperial Health Conference in London; she first caught the interest of boys, generally about 15 or 16 years old, with games, she said, and those who returned on a regular basis were approached to enroll in trade or educational classes. Of the 400-some boys who arrived each year, not all of them newsboys, about half stayed, and any students who showed particular aptitude were sent to the Working Men's College. Among the skills taught at the club were metalwork, cabinet-making, woodwork and boot repair; in later years, classes in radio and electrical engineering were added. Former "old boys," who included engineers, master builders, journalists and craftsmen, often returned to help "Miss" as instructors. At least one erstwhile newsboy went on to become a member of the Australian Parliament. In 1923, a third story was added to the club's building, and a camp in the country was later started as well.

Although fewer young children sold newspapers after school attendance began to be more rigorously enforced and small stipends were allowed to widows with young children, Onians sought to regulate their employment through the issuing of licenses. After passage of the Street Trading Act of 1926, she was appointed to its licensing board; boys under 12, and all girls, were prohibited from street selling, and boys between 12 and 14 were required to be licensed. She also later became a justice of the peace and vice-president of both the Victorian Council for Mental Hygiene and the Vocational Guidance Center. Onians wrote a memoir about her life with the Newsboys' Club, *Read All About It*, and worked there until her death on August 16, 1955.

SOURCES:

Radi, Heather, ed. *200 Australian Women*. NSW, Australia: Women's Redress Press, 1988.

Jo Anne Meginnes,
freelance writer, Brookfield, Vermont

Onions, Mrs. Oliver (1878–1978).

See Ruck, Berta.

Ono no Komachi (c. 830–?)

Japanese poet, one of her nation's most celebrated, who wrote passionately about the sorrows associated with love. *Pronunciation: Owe-noh noh Koe-machee. Born probably between 830 and 835; location not known.*

In ancient Japan, where poetry was esteemed, Ono no Komachi was thought to be its most accomplished practitioner. Virtually nothing, however, is known of her life. Some of her poems indicate that she was a lady-in-waiting in the imperial capital between 850 and 859. During this time, she and the most outstanding literary lights in Japan exchanged poems they had written.

Ono no Komachi wrote love poems, more than 100 of which were preserved in imperial anthologies. She expressed the sentiment, common in her aristocratic circles, that men were unfaithful and romantic love brought unhappiness. It was said that the poet, who often wrote about unrequited love, was in love with an emperor.

In the Japanese popular imagination, Ono no Komachi is a romantic figure around whom legends have grown, and the greatest of the nation's dramatists have written about her. In their plays, Ono no Komachi is known for her beauty, wit, and elegance, and has many lovers. (To this day, a Japanese beauty is dubbed a "Komachi.") While in her poems men were the source of unhappiness, in these tragedies written by men Ono no Komachi is a hard-hearted woman and ultimately the cause of her own suffering. In the most famous of these dramas, one of her many suitors, a Captain Fukakusa, travels a great distance to court her. Komachi advises him that she will not meet with him until he has proven his faithfulness by making the long journey from his house to hers for 100 nights. He complies with her wishes for 99 nights, traveling through rain, hail, and snow; but on the last night, he is caught in a snowstorm and perishes. In her dotage, so the drama goes, Komachi is possessed by the vengeful spirit of Fukakusa and driven to madness. Alone, destitute, she wanders in search of salvation by the grace of Buddha. The woman presented in the drama, however, has little in common with the woman presented in Komachi's poems.

SOURCES:

Weber-Schafer, Peter. *Kodansha Encyclopedia of Japan*. Itasaka Gen, ed. Tokyo: Kodansha, 1983.

SUGGESTED READING:

Hirshfield, Jane, with Mariko Aratani, trans. *The Ink Dark Moon: Love Poems by Ono no Komachi and *Izumi Shikibu*. NY: Scribner, 1988.

Linda L. Johnson,
Professor of History, Concordia College,
Moorhead, Minnesota

Onshi (872–907)

Empress of Japan. *Born in 872; died in 907; consort of Emperor Uda (867–945); sister of Fujiwara no Nakahira (875–945).*

Oosterwyck, Maria van (1630–1693)

Dutch painter of flower pieces and still lifes. *Name variations: Oosterwijk. Born on August 20, 1630, in Nootdorp, near Delft, Holland, the Netherlands; died in December 1693, near Uitdam; never married; no children.*

Although there are only two dozen extant works credited to the Dutch flower painter Maria van Oosterwyck, it is quite possible that some of her work has been attributed to Jan Davidsz de Heem (1606–1683), who may have been an early teacher, and to Willem van Aelst (1625–c. 1683), who for years sought her hand in marriage. According to Arnold Houbraken, Oosterwyck worked slowly, which would also account for such a limited output.

Writing in 1718, Houbraken also provides what little biographical information is available on the artist: the daughter of a Dutch Protestant minister, she displayed an artistic gift early in life and was sent by her father to study with de Heem. Modern scholars question this assumption, as de Heem lived most of his life in Antwerp and only returned to Utrecht, his birthplace, briefly from 1669 to 1672, by which time Oosterwyck was well into her career. **Germaine Greer**, in *The Obstacle Race*, claims that Oosterwyck simply went to Antwerp to study with de Heem, which may indeed have been the case. Houbraken also tells us that van Aelst failed in his romantic pursuit of the artist because of her devotion to her career. Her single-mindedness was rewarded with an international reputation, including the patronage of Louis XIV, king of France, Holy Roman Emperor Leopold I, Stadholder William III (later king of England), and the king of Poland.

All but one of Oosterwyck's paintings are flower pictures, and they are considered some of the best of the period. "She liked to set her vases on marble table tops and nearly always included grasses with green and white striped leaves," writes **Ann Sutherland Harris** and **Linda Nochlin**. "Another favorite motif is a red emperor butterfly perched in the lower foreground with its wings spread." All of her works are reminiscent of de Heem and van Aelst in feeling, although, according to Greer, her later paintings reveal more open compositions, with bolder contrasts. Greer also points out that her later asymmetrical forms might reflect van Aelst's influence, "unless his reflects her influence upon him."

Oosterwyck's one foray outside of flower painting may have produced her greatest masterpiece. Called *Vanitas*, the work was painted when the artist was 38, and was possibly commissioned for Emperor Leopold. The "Vanitas" of the title refers to a genre of still life developed in Leyden in the 1620s, probably because of the concentration of Calvinist scholars in that city at the time. Harris and Nochlin describe it as the most intellectual and literary form of still life, and the only one with a moral message. Three classes of objects are regularly included in the genre: symbols of a professional and personal life, objects that represent the passage of time, and objects that refer to life after death, such as a strand of ivy or a laurel branch. Oosterwyck's work is characteristic. Four objects figure prominently in the painting: a large vase of flowers; a globe with signs of the zodiac; a skull wreathed in ivy; and an account book. Countless smaller objects are strewn about a marble table in purposeful disorder, each having particular symbolic relevance. Harris and Nochlin suggest that the artist may have been drawn to this genre through Jan de Heem, and that it may have had particular significance for her because she was known to be quite religious.

Vase of Tulips, Roses and Other Flowers with Insects, *1669, by Maria van Oosterwyck.*

One of the most beautiful examples of Oosterwyck's flower paintings is a work titled *Vase of Tulips, Roses, and Other Flowers with Insects* (1669). On a small panel, the artist meticulously replicated a vase of flowers dominated by two large striped tulips, with a dragonfly perched on a strand of grass hanging over the edge of the vase, the transparency of its wings captured against a white peony. The motif butterfly is perched above the artist's name. Although the painting recalls earlier Dutch flower paintings, it is a strongly personalized work. "Clearly she was aware of prevailing fashion," write Harris and Nochlin, "but she perfected a personal variant that stressed an exquisitely detailed finish, much play with reflections and varied textures, and more symbolism than was usual for flower pictures at that time. In this work, the fly in the foreground can represent sin and the destruction of worldly possessions, the glass vase and the grass the fragility of human life, and the butterfly resurrection." The artist died in the home of her sister's son in Uitdam in December 1693.

SOURCES:

Greer, Germaine. *The Obstacle Race.* NY: Farrar, Straus and Giroux, 1979.

Harris, Ann Sutherland, and Linda Nochlin. *Women Artists: 1550–1950.* NY: Alfred A. Knopf, 1976.

Houbraken, Arnold. *De groote schouburgh der Nederlantsche konstschilders en schilderessen* (a compilation of artists' biographies), 1718–20.

Barbara Morgan, Melrose, Massachusetts

Opie, Amelia (1769–1853)

English writer. *Born Amelia Alderson on November 12, 1769, in Norwich, England; died on December 2, 1853, in Norwich; daughter of James Alderson (a physician) and Amelia (Briggs) Alderson; married John Opie (a painter), on May 8, 1798 (died 1807); no children.*

Selected works: Dangers of Coquetry *(1790);* The Father and Daughter *(1801);* Poems *(1802);* Adeline Mowbray; or, The Mother and Daughter *(1805);* Simple Tales *(1806);* Temper *(1812);* Tales of Real Life *(1813);* Valentine's Eve *(1816);* New Tales *(1818);* Tales of the Heart *(1820);* Madeline *(1822);* Illustrations of Lying, in All Its Branches *(1825);* The Black Man's Lament; or, How to Make Sugar *(1826);* Detraction Displayed *(1828);* Lays for the Dead *(1834).*

While she is now little known, Amelia Opie was a popular and prolific writer in the first quarter of the 19th century, and numbered among her friends and acquaintances some of the major figures of her day. An only child whose informal education consisted mostly of learning to dance, play music, and speak French, she was taught early about the horrors of slavery (of which she would later write) by her mother, who died when Opie was 15. Opie then assumed charge of her father's household in her hometown of Norwich and entered society life. She was well liked in local society and received a similar reception on a trip to London in 1794, where she mixed with progressive intellectuals including politician John Horne Tooke, the painter Thomas Holcroft, William Godwin, and *__Mary Wollstonecraft__. She also met artist John Opie, whom she married on May 8, 1798.

Opie had published her first novel, *The Dangers of Coquetry,* anonymously in 1790, and her new husband urged her to pursue her writing further—mostly to prevent her from attending the parties he himself disliked. In 1801, she established her reputation as a writer with *The Father and Daughter*, which achieved significant popularity despite some critics' disparagement of its static characterization and tired seduction plot. The story of a father driven insane by his daughter's flight into the arms of a libertine, and their subsequent reconciliation, *The Father and Daughter* eventually went through ten editions and supposedly caused Walter Scott to cry. She released a volume of poetry, titled simply *Poems*, the following year, and in 1805 published the immensely successful *Adeline Mowbray; or, The Mother and Daughter*. Opie got the idea for her story from incidents in the life of her friend Wollstonecraft, who while unmarried had had a daughter (*__Mary Shelley__) with her lover Gilbert Imlay, and died in 1797 of complications of childbirth shortly after her marriage to William Godwin. While the novel presents Adeline Mowbray and her unconventional beliefs sympathetically, later critics have noted that her death at the end of the novel serves to reinforce justification for society's rigid conventions.

Opie's next book, a collection of short stories entitled *Simple Tales*, received less-than-favorable reviews upon its release in 1806, with critics complaining of conventional plots and unoriginal characters. After her husband's death the following year, she returned to Norwich, where she lived with her sickly father while maintaining her friendships with important literary and artistic figures; among these were *__Germaine de Staël__, William Wordsworth, Walter Scott, playwright and novelist *__Elizabeth Inchbald__, Richard Brinsley Sheridan, and *__Sarah Siddons__. She also wrote some of what is considered her best work, including her second collection of short stories, *Tales of Real Life* (1813). Opie began to show an increasing interest in Quakerism from 1814, and it is from about this point that critics trace a general decline in the quality of her work, including the short-story collections *New Tales* (1818) and *Tales of the Heart* (1820), although her final novel, *Madeline* (1822), still receives generally good notices.

In 1825, Opie formally joined the Society of Friends, and gave up writing fiction as contrary to her religious views. (She still mingled in society, however, and contrived to wear her Quaker gray clothes fashionably.) She abandoned the completion of a novel for which she had already received a publishing contract, and focused her energies on philanthropy and on morally uplifting or instructive tracts. These included *Illustrations of Lying, in All Its Branches* (1825) and *Detraction Displayed* (1828), as well as pamphlets and essays decrying the evils of slavery. British critics found these works too moralistic to be palatable, although *Illustrations* reportedly enjoyed some success in America. Somewhat of a puzzle among her friends and reading public, an established writer who had chosen to end her career apparently in mid-stream, Opie remained active and healthy until only a few months before the end of her long life, and was working on her memoirs at the time of her death in Norwich in 1853. A street in her hometown is named in her honor.

SOURCES:

Buck, Claire, ed. *The Bloomsbury Guide to Women's Literature.* NY: Prentice Hall, 1992.

Howard, Susan K. "Amelia Opie" in *Dictionary of Literary Biography,* Vol. 116: *British Romantic Novelists, 1789–1832.* Edited by Bradford K. Mudge. Detroit, MI: Gale Research, 1992.

Kunitz, Stanley J., and Howard Haycraft, eds. *British Authors of the Nineteenth Century.* NY: H.W. Wilson, 1936.

Shattock, Joanne. *The Oxford Guide to British Women Writers.* Oxford and NY: Oxford University Press, 1993.

Simmons, James R. "Amelia Opie" in *Dictionary of Literary Biography,* Vol. 159: *British Short-Fiction Writers, 1800–1880.* Edited by John R. Greenfield. Detroit, MI: Gale Research, 1996.

Jacqueline Mitchell,
freelance writer, Detroit, Michigan

Opie, Iona (1923—)

British author and authority on children's literature and lore. *Born Iona Archibald on October 13, 1923, in Colchester, England; daughter of Sir Robert George Archibald (a pathologist) and Olive (Cant) Archibald; educated in English schools; married Peter Opie (an author and folklorist), on September 2, 1943 (died February 5, 1982); children: James Opie; Robert Opie;* ***Letitia Opie****.*

Selected writings—all with husband, Peter Opie, except as noted: (compiler) I Saw Esau *(1947); (ed.)* The Oxford Dictionary of Nursery Rhymes *(1951); (compiler)* The Oxford Nursery Rhyme Book *(1955);* The Lore and Language of Schoolchildren *(1959);* Children's Games in Street and Playground *(1969);* Children's Games *(1969); (ed.)* Three Centuries of Nursery Rhymes and Poetry for Children *(1973, rev. ed., 1977); (ed.)* The Oxford Book of Children's Verse *(1973); (ed.)* The Classic Fairy Tales *(1974); (ed.)* The Oxford Book of Narrative Verse *(1983);* Children's Games in Street and Playground: Chasing, Catching, Seeking, Hunting, Racing, Dueling, Exerting, Daring, Guessing, Acting, Pretending *(1984);* Tail Feathers from Mother Goose: The Opie Rhyme Book *(1988); (with son, Robert Opie, and Brian Alderson)* The Treasures of Childhood: Books, Toys, and Games from the Opie Collection *(1989); (with Moira Tatem)* A Dictionary of Superstitions *(1989);* The People in the Playground *(1993).*

Awards: joint winner with husband of the Coote Lake Research Medal (1960); M.A., Oxford University (1962); joint winner of European Prize of the City of Caorle (Italy, 1964); joint winner with husband, Chicago Folklore Prize (1970); D.Litt., Southampton University (1987); May Hill Arbuthnot Lecturer, 1991.

Born Iona Archibald in Colchester, England, on October 13, 1923, Iona Opie was the daughter of Sir Robert George Archibald and **Olive Cant Archibald**. She was raised primarily by her mother because her father, a pathologist who studied tropical diseases, spent most of his time in Khartoum, Africa, where he was the director of the Wellcome Research Laboratories. As a child, Iona hoped to follow in his footsteps as a plant pathologist. An obedient daughter who was diligently cared for by her mother, Iona looked forward to her father's infrequent visits for the casualness and freedom he brought with him. She loved her pets, teddy bears, and reading books and, by age 14, began buying antiquarian books. Although she preferred not to participate in most sports or activities, her mother made sure she received some instruction and had some knowledge of many of them.

In 1941, Iona joined the Women's Auxiliary Air Force Meteorological Section and remained there until 1943, rising to the rank of sergeant. While in the service, she read *I Want to Be a Success*, a book written by Peter Opie. Impressed, she wrote to him. He replied; they met, fell in love, and were married. Upon learning that she was pregnant, Iona left the service, and the Opies were forced to relocate to a remote town, Waresley. It was there, while at loose ends, that they would begin a collaborative project that would occupy their time for the next 40 years. During a walk, they had encountered a ladybird and were reminded of an old children's rhyme featuring such a bird. Curious as to where the verse came from, they went to the Kensington Public Library in London, but the only information they could find was in a book that had been published in 1842. The Opies decided that a new book on the origins of nursery rhymes was needed and, for the next seven years, worked on the *Oxford Dictionary of Nursery Rhymes*. Published in 1951, the book was followed by *The Oxford Nursery Rhyme Book* (1955) and *The Lore and Language of Schoolchildren* (1959), which was based on the responses of 5,000 schoolchildren. In 1960, Iona served as the author and host of a series based on the latter book, also entitled *The*

Lore and Language of Schoolchildren, which was on the British Broadcasting Corporation (BBC) network. In 1969, *Children's Games in Street and Playground* was published, and this time Iona surveyed 10,000 children. For a later project, she researched children's games by going to a playground weekly for 12 years. Both the *Dictionary* and the Opies' later book, *The Classic Fairy Tales* (1974), are structured the same way—the earliest versions of each verse or story are given, a discussion of its origins ensues, and comparisons to similar verses and stories from other countries follows. During this period, Iona divided her time between conducting research for their books and taking care of her own three children, while her husband devoted himself to earning a living as a writer.

Shortly after they had married, the Opies began collecting all types of children's books, always with an eye to future research and projects. In addition to their books, which included numerous first editions and association copies, they collected comics, toys, games and educational aids. Their goal was to collect on the physical side what they were compiling on the oral side in books. "As with the games," Peter explained, "we're interested in classifying both the attraction and what makes the thing work. Toys have been looked at as sentimental objects, but we want to look at them 'scientifically.'" Following Peter Opie's death in 1982, at age 63, more than 20,000 volumes of the couple's children's book collection went to the Bodleian Library, Oxford. Though the collection was appraised at £1 million, Iona had determined that if the Bodleian could raise half of that amount, she would give them the other half. With the patronage of Charles, the prince of Wales, the money was raised within 18 months.

Since the death of Peter, Iona Opie has continued collecting children's literature, researching and recording. She served as editor for *Tail Feathers from Mother Goose: The Opie Rhyme Book* (1988), and with her son Robert Opie and author Brian Alderson, she has published *The Treasures of Childhood: Books, Toys and Games from the Opie Collection* (1989), and with **Moira Tatem**, *A Dictionary of Supersti-*

tions (1989). In addition, she has been a contributor to the *Encyclopedia Britannica*, *New Cambridge Bibliography of English Literature*, and other reference works.

SOURCES:

Commire, Anne. *Something About the Author.* Vol. 3 and Vol. 63. Detroit, MI: Gale Research.

Jo Anne Meginnes,
freelance writer, Brookfield, Vermont

Oporto, duchess of.

See Hayes, Nevada (1885–1941).

Oppenheim, Méret (1913–1985)

Swiss-German painter and sculptor. *Name variations: Meret Oppenheim. Born in Berlin-Charlottenburg in 1913; died in Switzerland in 1985 (some sources cite 1986); studied briefly at the Académie de la Grande Chaumière.*

Works include Quick, Quick, the Most Beautiful Vowel Is Voiding *(1934);* Fur-Covered Cup, Saucer and Spoon *(*Breakfast in Fur, *1936);* My Nurse *(1936);* The Couple *(1956);* Primeval Venus *(1962);* Octavia *(1969);* Word Wrapped in Poisonous Letters *(1970);* Pair of Gloves *(1985).*

Born in Berlin at the onset of World War I, Méret Oppenheim was taken by her family to her mother's native Switzerland, where she grew up. At age 19, she moved to Paris and enrolled briefly at the Académie de la Grande Chaumière. There she became friends with ***Sophie Tauber-Arp** and Surrealists Hans Arp and Alberto Giacometti, who introduced her to the Surrealist movement. Oppenheim participated in Surrealist meetings and group exhibitions, knew Pablo Picasso, and for a time was romantically linked to Max Ernst. Throughout her stay in Paris, she also modeled nude for many photographs for her friend Man Ray, including *Méret Oppenheim—Erotique Violée*. In 1933, a series of Oppenheim woodcuts and paintings were shown at the Surrealist Exhibition. That same year, her first solo show was held in Basle at the Galerie Schulthess.

Oppenheim was best known for creating household objects out of unexpected materials. Her *Fur-Covered Cup, Saucer, and Spoon* caused a sensation at the 1936 International Surrealist Exhibit in London, and is still considered a quintessential symbol of Surrealism; it is now at the Museum of Modern Art in New York City. Thrown by the celebrity suddenly thrust upon her, Oppenheim returned to Basle four years later, marking what **Whitney Chadwick** has called "the beginning of an eighteen-year period of artistic crisis and redirection." She produced very little art during World War II. Beginning in the late 1950s, she again created and exhibited sculptures, paintings, and artworks incorporating such ordinary objects as tools or shoes, as well as Surrealist furniture. (In 1939, she had taken part in an exhibition of fantastic furniture with ***Léonor Fini**, Max Ernst and others at the Galerie René Druin and Leo Castelli in Paris.) Oppenheim resisted the Surrealist label, however, noting that "every idea is born with its form." A major retrospective of her work was held at the Moderna Museet in Stockholm in 1967, by which time her reputation in Europe was again secure, and she remained active as an artist until her death in 1985. In 1996, the first major museum exhibition of Oppenheim's work in the United States was held at the Guggenheim Museum in New York City.

SOURCES AND SUGGESTED READING:

Carley, Michal Ann. "Meret Oppenheim & Hannah Höch: Laying Groundwork for Art in a New Century," in *Fiberarts: The Magazine of Textiles.* Vol. 24, no. 4. January–February, 1998, pp. 46–51.

Chadwick, Whitney. *Women Artists and the Surrealist Movement.* Boston, MA: Little Brown, 1985.

Glueck, Grace. "After a Furry Teacup, What Then?," in *The New York Times.* June 28, 1996.

Oppenheimer, Jane Marion (1911–1996)

American biologist and educator. *Surname pronounced OPP-en-HIGH-mer. Born Jane Marion Oppenheimer on September 19, 1911, in Philadelphia, Pennsylvania; died on March 19, 1996, in Philadelphia; daughter of James Harry Oppenheimer and Sylvia (Stern) Oppenheimer; Bryn Mawr, B.A., 1932; Yale University, Ph.D. in zoology, 1936.*

Jane Oppenheimer was best known for her experiments studying the effects of weightlessness on fish embryos. She also had a keen interest in the historical aspects of biology and wrote several articles and books on the subject. A member of several scientific organizations, including the American Society of Zoologists and the American Association for the Advancement of Science, she won several awards for her research, including, among others, the Wilbur Cross Medal from the Yale Graduate Alumni Association.

Oppenheimer was born in Philadelphia in 1911. She received a B.A. from Bryn Mawr in 1932 and a Ph.D. in zoology from Yale University in 1936, and then held fellowships at Yale (1935–36), the American Association of University Women's Berliner (1936–37), and the University of Rochester (1937–38). Oppenheimer returned to Bryn Mawr in 1942 as professor and researcher; she would remain there for her entire career, retiring in 1980 as the Kenan Professor Emeritus of Biology and History of Science. Oppenheimer then continued to write, teach, and conduct experiments for many more years.

Most of her experiments had focused on embryological development. In one major survey, she studied the growth of the central nervous system in fish, the results of which were applied by scientists to human embryological development. Perhaps Oppenheimer's most notable test was carried out on board a Soviet spacecraft, one of four American studies that was conducted on the first American-Soviet joint space venture. Her experiment, studying the effects of weightlessness on the physiology of killifish eggs at five stages of development, earned her the National Aeronautics and Space Administration's Achievement Award and the Soviet Kosmos Award, both in 1975.

Oppenheimer was also interested in the history of science, the process by which scientific thought developed. In particular, she turned her attention to 18th-century British medicine and in 1986 edited the English version of *The Autobiography of Karl Ernst von Baer* (1792–1876). An Estonian-born biologist, von Baer suggested that all mammalian embryos are similar, and that during the earliest stages of development, they form several layers of tissue that eventually differentiate into specific structures. Oppenheimer's other books include *Essays in the History of Embryology and Biology* (1976) and *Foundations of Experimental Embryology* (2nd ed., 1974). In 1992, age 80, Oppenheimer was elected to the American Academy of Arts and Sciences. She died four years later, after a brief illness, on March 19, 1996, at her home in Philadelphia.

SOURCES:

Bowman, John S. *The Cambridge Dictionary of American Biography.* Cambridge: Cambridge University Press, 1995.

The Day [New London, CT]. March 23, 1996, p. B3.

Christine Miner Minderovic,
freelance writer, Ann Arbor, Michigan

Oppens, Ursula (1944—)

Renowned American pianist and advocate of new music. *Born in 1944 in New York City; daughter of Kurt Oppens (a writer) and Edith Oppens (a classical pianist); received undergraduate degree from Radcliffe College and graduate degree from the Juilliard School of Music; studied under Rosina Lhévinne, Leonard Shure and Guido Agosti; lived with Julius Hemphill (a jazz musician and composer, d. 1995).*

A champion of modern composers whose work on their behalf has earned her the honorific "Saint Ursula," Ursula Oppens is also an accomplished classical pianist who believes that exposure to contemporary music only heightens appreciation of the classical canon. Composer Charles Wuorinen described her as "a wonderful musical citizen . . . devoted to the cause of living music by living composers." A founder, with cellist Fred Sherry and percussionist Richard Fitz, of the pioneering new-music group Speculum Musicae in the early 1970s, she has spent over 30 years helping modern composers find a wider audience by commissioning, playing, and recording their works.

Oppens was born in 1944 to Jewish parents who had fled the Nazi occupation of Prague. **Edith Oppens**, a classical pianist, and Kurt Oppens, a writer who focused on music, were both music teachers in New York and Aspen, Colorado, and she grew up surrounded by music. While she was still quite young, her piano lessons with her mother had given way to lessons with Victor Babin and Leonard Shure, but as a young adult she still had no definite plans to make a career of music. After studying economics and literature at Radcliffe, she entered graduate school at the Juilliard School of Music, where she studied with ***Rosina Lhévinne**. In 1969, Oppens won the Busoni International Piano Competition, launching her professional career. She was awarded an Avery Fisher Career Grant seven years later.

Over the years, Oppens has performed with orchestras and symphonies in most major American cities, including New York, Chicago, San Francisco, Los Angeles, Houston and Atlanta, as well as at Tanglewood and at Aspen. Her international appearances include performances in Paris, London, Geneva, Edinburgh, Bonn, Japan, Bergama, Brussels, Vienna, Stockholm and other cities, and she has made numerous recordings. Among the composers whose works she has premiered or commissioned are Elliott Carter (a joint commission for *Night Fantasies*), Tobias Picker (*Old and Lost Rivers*), Frederic Rzewski (the premiere of his huge set of variations, *The People United Will Never Be Defeated*, which she also recorded), **Joan Tower**, Julius Hemphill, Wuorinen (*The Blue Bamboula*), Anthony Davis (*Middle Passage*), Conlon Nancarrow (*Two Canons for Ursula*), **Lois Vierk**, and John Harbison (Piano Sonata No. 1). In

1998–99, with the Arditti String Quartet, Oppens premiered Elliott Carter's Piano Quintet, commissioned in honor of his 90th birthday by the Library of Congress.

SOURCES:

Time. March 8, 1993.

Ullman, Michael. "Saint Ursula" in *The Atlantic Monthly.* May 1998, pp. 112–116.

Oraib (797–890)

Arabian singer of Arab classical music who was one of the most famous and wealthy of her era. *Name variations: Oreib; Uraib; Arib. Born in Baghdad (present-day Iraq) in 797; died in July or August of 890; illegitimate daughter of Garaf ibn Yahya al-Barmaki also seen as Jafar ibn Yahya al-Barmaki (husband of ****Abassa****).*

Although many in the West believe that all Arabian women were confined to the harem, this is not true. The legendary Oraib, and many like her, refused to be confined, even though for a time she was a slave. Oraib was the illegitimate daughter of Jafar al-Barmaki. The Barmak family was of Persian origin; many of its members held high administrative positions in the government and they were also known as patrons of the arts. When Oraib was six, her mother died and her father was executed; consequently she was sold into slavery. Eventually, she came into the hands of Abdallah ibn Ismail al-Marakibi, an overseer of Caliph Harun al-Rashid's horses, who took her to Basra (now Iraq) to be educated. Arabian songstresses were highly educated, and so Oraib learned calligraphy, grammar, poetry, singing, and playing the lute. Exceptionally beautiful and talented, she was also headstrong, but al-Marakibi refused to sell her when approached by al-Amin, then a crown prince. When al-Amin became caliph, he had al-Marakibi imprisoned, fined him 500,000 dinars, and took Oraib. She remained in his court until he was murdered in 812.

Though al-Marakibi forcefully reclaimed Oraib when the caliph was murdered, she escaped from him. The new caliph, al-Mamun (r. 813–833), considered the singer to be part of his inheritance and confined her to the royal harem. Despite this, she continued to meet with her lover, Mohammed bin Hamid, until al-Mamun had her thrown into the dungeon, whipped, and fed on bread and water. When she was unrepentant, he admired her stance and released her to marry her lover. Even so, the caliph loved her, gave her the surname al-Mamuniya, and asked her to accompany him on his expedition against Byzantium. When al-Mamun died, his brother inherited Oraib but freed her.

When al-Mutawakki succeeded to the throne in 847, Oraib had great influence over him, and the court of Samarra became her domain. By this time, she had established her own singing school and had become a very wealthy woman. There was a great rivalry between two schools of music during this period. Oraib was the foremost singer of classical music, a school of Arabian music led by Ibrahim al-Mausuli (d. 804) and his son Ishaq (d. 850) which dominated. However, the romantic school led by Ibrahim al-Mahdi was making inroads with the help of songstress ***Shariyya**. The public was divided in its loyalty to both singers. Oraib and Shariyya often appeared in public together, with one half of the audience applauding its favorite, and the other half booing her. At age 70, said to know 21,000 melodies, Oraib continued to sing at the court of al-Mutazz, and on his orders music theoretician Yahya Ibn Ali made a collection of her songs. Oraib lived into her 90s, surviving ten caliphs. Her songs were performed for centuries after her death, and she is remembered as one of the Arab world's greatest singers.

SOURCES:

Cohen, Aaron I. *International Encyclopedia of Women Composers.* 2 vols. NY: Books & Music (USA), 1987.

John Haag,
Athens, Georgia

O'Rane, Patricia (1901–1985).

See Dark, Eleanor.

Orange, princess of.

See Catherine of Brittany (1428–c. 1476).
See Jeanne of Bourbon (d. 1493).
See Anna of Saxony (1544–1577).
See Coligny, Louise de (1555–1620).
See Amelia of Solms (1602–1675).
See Mary of Orange (1631–1660).
See Albertina Agnes (d. 1696).
See Caroline of Ansbach for sidebar on Anne (1709–1759).
See Wilhelmina of Prussia (1751–1820).

Orantes, Ana (c. 1937–1997)

Spanish woman whose violent death changed attitudes on domestic abuse in her nation. *Born around 1937; died in Granada, Spain, in December 1997; married Jose Parejo (divorced).*

On December 4, 1997, 60-year-old Spanish housewife Ana Orantes discussed on a television talk show the physical abuse she had suffered for 20 years at the hands of her then ex-husband, Jose Parejo. He watched the show, and swore to friends he would kill her. This he did on December 17, by beating her, showering her with gasoline, and setting her on fire. Mistreatment of wives had not been made a punishable offense in Spain until the late 1960s, and domestic-violence laws favored abusers by allowing each case to be reviewed as a first-time offense, therefore often permitting abusers to walk away with nothing more than a small fine. The huge public outcry after Orantes' murder, however, led to review and revision of these laws. Women across the country began demonstrating for tougher penalties, and women's groups called for reform of both the legal system and the society that saw fit to let *terrorismo familiar* (domestic violence) off lightly. Prime Minister Jose Maria Aznar introduced legislation calling for a stricter penal code, specially-trained police units, and sensitivity-training courses for judges. By the following year, murders in Spain of women by their partners or ex-partners, the rate of which had held steady for several years, had dropped by nearly half, and the campaign against domestic violence was continuing.

SOURCES:

The Christian Science Monitor. January 19, 1999.

"Less Abuse?" in *Newsweek.* April 27, 1998.

Orcutt, Maureen (1907—)

Golfer and writer. *Name variations: Mrs. J.D. Crews. Born on April 1, 1907, in New York City; sister of William and Sinclair Orcutt, both golfers; married J.D. Crews.*

The daughter of a journalist, golfer Maureen Orcutt won over 65 championships during her long career, although the National Golf championship continually eluded her. Her winning streak began with the Metropolitan Junior, which she won in 1922 and 1924, when she was just a teenager. She went on the win ten Women's Metropolitans between 1926 and 1968, including three North and South championships, seven Women's Easterns, ten New Jersey Women's 54-Hole Medal titles, and six New Jersey State championships. One of her most outstanding performances was in the 1934 Florida East Coast championship, when she beat **Helen Hicks** on the 19th hole to win permanent possession of the Flagler gold trophy. She also won the Canadian Women's Amateur in 1930 and 1921, and came in second in the USGA Women's Amateur in 1927. The golfer occasionally teamed up with her two brothers Bill and Sinclair, and she won the Metropolitan Brother-Sister eight times, four with Bill and four with Sinclair. Orcutt was a member of the Curtis Cup team in '22, '34, '36, and '38, and as a senior won two USGA Women's Senior championships, in 1962 and 1966. She also won three North and South Seniors, and six Metropolitan Women's Seniors.

Hicks, Helen. *See Berg, Patty for sidebar.*

From her earliest days as a player, Orcutt also wrote about the sport for various New York newspapers and golf magazines. In 1927, she joined the sports department of *The New York Times*, working there until 1972, when she retired to Durham, North Carolina. Orcutt was elected to the Ladies' PGA Hall of Fame in 1966 and was the recipient of the 1969 Tanqueray Award, honoring her 50 years in golf.

Orczy, Emma (1865–1947)

Hungarian-born English author. *Name variations: Emmuska Orczy; Baroness Orczy. Born Emmuska Magdalena Rosalia Maria Josefa Barbara Orczy on September 23, 1865, in Tarna-Örs, Hungary; died on November 12, 1947, in London, England; daughter of Baron Felix Orczy (a gifted amateur composer) and Countess Emmuska Wass; married Montagu Barstow, in 1894 (died 1943); children: John Montagu Orczy Barstow (b. 1899).*

Selected writings: The Emperor's Candlesticks *(1899);* By the Gods Beloved *(1905);* The Scarlet Pimpernel *(1905);* The Tangled Skein *(1907);* The Old Man in the Corner *(1908);* Lady Molly of Scotland Yard *(1910);* Meadowsweet *(1912);* Unto Caesar *(1914);* The Old Scarecrow *(1916);* Silver-leg *(1918);* Castles in the Air *(1921);* The Honorable Jim *(1924);* The Celestial City *(1926);* Blue Eyes and Grey *(1928);* Skin o' My Tooth *(1928);* The Divine Folly *(1937);* Pride of Race *(1942);* Links in the Chain of Life *(1947).*

Born on September 23, 1865, in Tarna-Örs, Hungary, Emma Orczy, daughter of Countess **Emmuska Wass** and Baron Felix Orczy, was raised on the vast estates of her father. As a gifted amateur composer, Baron Orczy moved in a social circle that included the noted composers Franz Liszt, Richard Wagner, Charles Gounod, and Jules Massenet. Orczy had fond memories of her childhood as part of Hungary's landed aristocracy, but the family left the country in 1868 after the baron's agricultural innovations caused an outburst of peasant violence against him. The family moved to Budapest, where Baron Orczy became Supreme Administrator of the National Theatre, and endeavored to create the finest operatic productions in Europe. During this time, Emma and her sister went to convent schools in Brussels and Paris. Emma first whetted her literary appetite for adventure and romance by writing and acting in plays which focused heavily on those two genres.

The Orczy family settled in London in the 1880s, when Emma was in her mid-teens. She spoke only Hungarian, French, and German, and devoted her first six months in London to learning English. Unlike many aristocratic women, Orczy wanted to pursue higher education, but her father rejected her plea to go to Cambridge. She initially studied music at schools in Brussels and Paris, but found greater success in her study of painting at the West London School of Art and at Heatherley's.

At Heatherley's, Orczy met Montagu Barstow, an illustrator, whom she later married. In collaboration with her husband, she began to translate and illustrate fairy tales, and wrote romance and adventure stories for the popular press. Her first novel, *The Emperor's Candlesticks* (1899), was a failure. However, her next venture, *The Scarlet Pimpernel*, was widely successful. Even though the book initially was rejected by 12 publishers, Orczy sparked interest in it through an adaptation produced in the autumn of 1903 at the Nottingham Theatre Royal, with Fred Terry in the leading role. The novel was finally published to coincide with the 1905 London production. *The Scarlet Pimpernel* (and its 12 sequels) tells the story of Sir Percy Blakeney, an English rescuer of French aristocrats during the French Revolution's Reign of Terror (1793–94). His rescues depend on a double identity: at home, he is known as a foppish, languid man of society, but as the daring Scarlet Pimpernel, he repeatedly risks death while saving those unjustly condemned in France. Readers and theater patrons alike adored the Blakeney character as the perfect figure of English manhood, and *The Scarlet Pimpernel* came to be known as a quintessentially English novel—an impressive accomplishment for an author who did not even speak English until her mid-teens. The book inspired five movies, including a 1934 version starring acclaimed actor Leslie Howard, and by the 1940s it had been translated into 20 languages.

From that point on, Orczy wrote prolifically, including the sequels to her most famous book, as well as other adventures and romances. She also wrote detective stories—some of which predated her *Pimpernel*—known as the Old Man in the Corner series. Deliberately avoiding the style of Sir Arthur Conan Doyle's famous Sherlock Holmes stories, Orczy made a special contribution to the new armchair detective genre by starting her stories with the denouement and then working backward through the plot. Her hero was the brilliant and disagreeable Bill Owen who solves crimes, solely through the application of rigorous logic, from the corner of the ABC Teashop to the amazement of his audience, Polly Burton, a young journalist. The first of seven collections of the stories appeared in 1908.

From the CBS movie The Scarlet Pimpernel, *starring Anthony Andrews and Jane Seymour.*

Orczy also created the first fictional woman detective in her *Lady Molly of Scotland Yard* (1910), a series of 12 tales told by Lady Molly's devoted maid. While Molly is described as an intelligent, risk-taking woman of the world, most critics agree that she does not function either as an entirely believable character or a fully convincing detective. All of Lady Molly's cases involve only women and her sole motivation for crime-solving is to clear the falsely tarnished name of her lover. Once she accomplishes her mission, she gives up detective work forever. Orczy also created Irish lawyer Patrick Mulligan for another collection of detective stories, *Skin o' My Tooth* (1928).

In 1908, Orczy and her husband bought an estate away from London, where they cultivated an impressive garden. After World War I, they moved to Monte Carlo, although Orczy returned to her adopted homeland after Montagu's death and the end of World War II. She died in London on November 12, 1947.

SOURCES:

Contemporary Authors. Vol. 104. Detroit, MI: Gale Research, 1982.

Staples, Katherine. "Emma Orczy" in *Dictionary of Literary Biography*. Vol. 70: *British Mystery Writers, 1860–1919*. Edited by Bernard Benstock. Detroit, MI: Gale Research, 1988.

This England. Spring 1998, pp. 48–50.

Jacqueline Mitchell,
freelance writer, Detroit, Michigan

Ordonówna, Hanka (1904–1950)

Polish actress and singer who was the star performer at Warsaw's leading cabaret of the interwar decades, Qui pro Quo, and also appeared successfully on stage and in films. *Name variations: Hanka Ordonka; Hanka Ordonowna; Maria Anna Tyszkiewiczowa; Marysia Pietruszynska; Maria Anna Pietruszyskich. Born Maria Anna Pietruszynska in Warsaw, Russian Poland, on August 11, 1904; died in Beirut, Lebanon, on September 2, 1950; married Count Michael Tyszkiewicz.*

A melancholy hit song of the 1930s, "Milosc ci Wszystko Wybaczy" ("Love Forgives Everything"), was the signature tune of Hanka Ordonówna, a wildly popular cabaret and film star of interwar Poland. Warsaw was then one of Europe's liveliest cities. The defeat of Germany during World War I, as well as the political chaos in Russia precipitated by two revolutions in 1917, enabled Poland to be reborn as a nation in November 1918. Under foreign rule since the end of the 18th century, the Poles struggled to create a society that was both stable and prosperous in the 1920s and 1930s. In both instances, success was minimal. Much of the country remained mired in rural poverty, and by 1926, when war hero Marshal Józef Pilsudski overthrew the democratic parliamentary regime, which had disillusioned the populace with its inability to initiate reforms, many Poles turned away from the frustrations of politics. By the mid-1920s, most of Warsaw's artists and intellectuals chose to ignore the seemingly intractable woes of their young nation, concentrating instead on their creative endeavors.

Soon after World War I, with newly independent Poland still struggling, a 16-year-old student at the Warsaw Opera and Ballet School was offered a job at the Sphinx, one of the capital's better-known cabarets. Her director decided that her name, Marysia Pietruszynska, was too ordinary, so he settled on Hanka Ordonówna, thus launching a stellar career. Soon, Hanka moved to a cabaret named Mirage. After a fire shut its doors, she danced for a while in a second-class theater in Lwów, then toured Wilno and other Polish cities. Though she began her career as a dancer, Ordonówna soon switched to singing. Her voice, low-pitched, throaty, and highly evocative, would bring her great success over the next two decades.

Ordonówna returned to her native city of Warsaw to continue her career. While talented and ambitious, she had no serious training, but she was fortunate enough to become acquainted with one of Warsaw's best-known cabaret lyricists of the day, **Zofia Bajkowska**. A talented writer, Bajkowska had also achieved a celebrity of sorts, often shouting obscene phrases at those who had given her offense. Bajkowska noted that Hanka had picked up "some bad habits": she waved her hand under her nose and rolled her eyes, both "provincial" mannerisms. Even Ordonówna's hat was dismissed as old-fashioned and "definitely not Warsaw." After several weeks of intensive coaching, Hanka auditioned for a job at Warsaw's Qui Pro Quo. Since its opening on April 4, 1919, in a former roller-skating rink, this 500-seat cabaret had showcased the nation's most talented performers. Though the manager Jerzy Boczkowski saw considerable talent in Ordonówna, he did not feel she was ready; she did a spell at another the Stanczyk (The Jester) before he hired her.

At the time, the Qui Pro Quo boasted several female star performers, including **Zula Pogorzelska** and **Mira Ziminska.** Equally talented as a singer and dancer, Pogorzelska was often compared to the French cabaret star ***Mistinguett**, while Ziminska, who had a long career in cabaret, films, and stage productions, specialized in portraying young wives who betrayed their husbands. Hanka soon became an indispensable member of the ensemble, which numbered about 16 artists. The leading personalities of Warsaw attended the cabaret. On one such occasion, shortly before he seized power in the bloody coup d'etat of May 1926, Pilsudski heard Ordonówna sing a pretty song entitled "Mimosa"; he was pleased.

In 1926, now the toast of Warsaw's cabaret crowd, Ordonówna made her film debut in *Orle* (*The Eaglet*), directed by Viktor Bieganski. A pioneering docudrama, the movie was based on a successful Warsaw to Tokyo flight by a Polish aviator. Its premiere at the Apollo Lejman Cinema on Marszalkowska, Warsaw's equivalent of Broadway, was one of the social events of the year. In attendance were such political luminaries as Polish president Ignacy Moscicki and the deputy foreign minister, Józef Beck.

For five years (1926–31), Ordonówna was the star at Qui Pro Quo while living with Hungarian-born Fryderyk (Fritz) Járosy, the cabaret's master of ceremonies. With his faulty Polish grammar and syntax, Járosy delighted audiences; indeed, his manglings became part of everyday speech. In a city with many problems, all but the poorest citizens could scrape together a few zlotys to buy a ticket to the cabaret. **Zofia Chadzynska** recalled, "It was an antidote for sadness."

Newly established cabarets began to offer stiff competition, however, and there may have been a decline in the quality of Qui Pro Quo's acts when a number of its talented writers, including Andrzej Wlast, moved on. In March 1930, the cabaret celebrated its 11th anniversary with "Qui Pro Quo's Jubilee," for which Ordonówna's most memorable contribution was a song, "Trudno" ("It's Difficult"), about trying to retain the love of her man. The show was a smash hit, Qui Pro Quo's finest hour, said Tadeusz Boy-Zelenski in Warsaw's influential *Morning Courier*. It was also near its final hour. By 1931, the world depression had made terrible inroads into the Polish economy, and the cabaret closed its doors for good that April.

Shortly before, Ordonówna had discovered that Járosy was having an affair with a young dancer, **Stefania Górska**. Outraged, she ended the relationship and married Count Michael Tyszkiewicz in a quiet ceremony at Warsaw's Holy Cross Church. But her in-laws regarded her as a permanent outsider, a woman known to "have a past"; when the newlyweds arrived at Michael's family estate near Wilno, they learned that his relatives had vacated the estate, leaving only the servants behind. She would always be regarded as an alien by certain members of the Polish *szlachta*, the landed gentry that traditionally dominated the nation's intellectual, social and political life.

Soon after, Ordonówna made her first solo tour of Europe, giving critically acclaimed performances in Berlin, Vienna, and Paris. Despite her family situation and Poland's perennial problems, Ordonówna's career flourished throughout the troubled 1930s. In 1933, she starred in the film *Szpieg w Masce* (The Masked Spy), playing opposite two of Poland's best-known actors of the period, Boguslaw Samborski and Jerzy Pichelski. One of the film's songs, which she later recorded, quickly became her trademark tune. Written by the famous poet Julian Tuwim, "Love Forgives Everything" was a sensation from the moment the film opened in Warsaw at the Adria Theater on Theatter Square.

Polish stamp honoring Hanka Ordonówna, issued in 1996.

By the mid-1930s, Ordonówna wanted to branch out into other artistic areas, particularly as a dramatic actress. Her opportunity arrived in the person of Juliusz Osterwa, then one of the most important Polish stage directors, who while living in Russia during World War I had come under the influence of the great director Constantin Stanislavski and the innovative Moscow Art Theater. Back in Poland after the war, he was appointed director of Warsaw's National Theater, assumed control of Cracow's prestigious Slowacki Theater, and directed the Reduta Theater on Copernicus Square, where new Polish plays were staged. During the Depression, he hit on the idea of engaging Ordonówna in order to rescue his theaters from financial ruin. She first appeared in a play directed by Osterwa, *Wieczór Trzech Króli* (Night of the Three Kings), and then played opposite him in a comedy entitled *Teoria Einsteina* (Einstein's Theory). They also became romantically involved. After the affair was broken off, apparently by Hanka, Osterwa showed some of her letters to her husband. The count's reaction is not known, but the marriage survived.

Ordonówna continued to delight Warsaw audiences over the next several years. In 1936, she starred in *Frontem do Radosci* (A Smiling Face), a revue directed by Járosy. Less successful was a show she produced herself called *Widowiska Nr. 1* (Spectacle No. 1). All in all, however, she was regarded as Poland's equivalent of a Hollywood superstar. Her performances played to full houses, and her records sold extremely well, particularly "Love Forgives Everything." Some performers tried to emulate her, while others caricatured her; none of it bothered her in the least.

In 1938, Ordonówna made a month-long tour of the United States, appearing in shows in New York and other cities with large Polish-speaking populations. In 1939, her glamorous world came to a sudden, violent end. In the early morning hours of September 1, 1939, German units attacked Poland with overwhelming force, destroying the nation's armed forces within days. Late in August, when war with Nazi Germany appeared inevitable, Hanka had met with Tadeusz Wittlin to prepare a song program she could take to the front lines to entertain Polish troops. The program never went beyond the planning stage; the only entertaining Ordonówna did during these tragic days was to sing for wounded soldiers at Warsaw's train station.

The next years would be difficult for Poland and for its artists, including Ordonówna. Along with other entertainers, she was arrested by the Gestapo, allegedly on a tip from the director Tymoteusz Ortym. After being released, she was observed in the Europejski Hotel bar, looking frightened and disheveled. With conditions in Warsaw deteriorating from day to day, Hanka and Michael went to his family estate outside Wilno, where she and other former Warsaw stars were somehow able to recreate their own small cabaret. Eventually, however, Michael was arrested by the Soviet NKVD and taken to Moscow. After the "liberation" of Lithuania by the Red Army in the summer of 1940, Hanka was invited to perform in Moscow, where she attempted to establish contact with her husband; she also entered into friendships with Soviet officers that some Poles have described as being "scandalous" in nature. After giving a few performances in Moscow, Hanka too was arrested and sent to a labor camp in Uzbekistan.

In the harsh conditions of the labor camp, Ordonówna's health broke down, and she contracted tuberculosis. She did not die, however, and when the Stalin regime allowed the formation of a Polish Army under General Wladyslaw Anders, in 1942 she became part of an epic exodus of Poles from the Soviet Union to the Middle East. Here she was reunited with her husband, who had also survived a Soviet prison camp. Hanka's health remained fragile, and she was hospitalized in several sanatoriums, including one in Jerusalem. There, a Jewish physician fell in love with her. His affection was not reciprocated, and one night while Hanka was absent from her apartment, the doctor entered it and hanged himself. After the war, Ordonówna and her husband settled in Beirut, at that time a beautiful city in a prosperous and peaceful Lebanon. There, in the summer of 1950, far from her beloved city of Warsaw, she contracted typhus and died on September 2, 1950. On April 30, 1996, Poland's postal service honored Hanka Ordonówna by depicting her on a 40 Groszy commemorative postage stamp.

SOURCES:

Gasiorowski, Professor Zygmunt J. Personal communication.

Gronski, Ryszard Marek. *Jak w Przedwojennym Kabaracie.* Warsaw: Wydawnictwo Artystyczne i Filmowe, 1987.

Meyer, Stanislaw. *My City: Reminiscences.* Newton, UK: Montgomeryshire, 1947.

Nowicki, Ron. *Warsaw: The Cabaret Years.* San Francisco, CA: Mercury House, 1992.

"Ordonowna[,] Hanka," in Bogdan Suchodolski, ed., *Wielka encyklopedia powszechna PWN.* 13 vols. Warsaw: Panstwowe Wydawnictwo Naukowe, 1962–1970, Vol. 8, 1966, p. 280.

Sokol, Stanley S., and Sharon F. Mrotek Kissane. *Polish Biographical Dictionary.* Wauconda, IL: Bolchazy-Carducci, 1992.

Wittlin, Tadeusz. *Piesnarka Warszawy: Hanka Ordonówna i Jej Swiat.* London: Polska Fundacja Kulturalna, 1985.

Wynot, Edward, Jr. *Warsaw between the Wars: Profile of the Capital City in a Developing Land, 1918–1939.* Boulder, CO: East European Monographs, 1983.

John Haag,
Associate Professor of History, University of Georgia, Athens, Georgia

Oreib (797–890).

See Oraib.

O'Reilly, Leonora (1870–1927)

Labor leader, suffragist, advocate of vocational training for women and an early leader of the Women's Trade Union League, who struggled for many years, seeking a balance between feminism and labor politics. *Name variations: Nora. Born on February 16, 1870, in New York City; died at home in Brooklyn,*

New York, on April 3, 1927, of heart disease; daughter of John O'Reilly (a printer and grocer) and Winifred (Rooney) O'Reilly (a garment worker); attended public school until age 11; graduated from the Pratt Institute, 1900; never married; children: Alice (adopted in 1907 and died in 1911).

Started work at 11 in a collar factory (1881); inducted into the Knights of Labor (1886); formed the Working Women's Society (1886); joined the Synthetic Circle (1888) and the Social Reform Club (1894); organized a women's local for the United Garment Workers Union (1897); was a founder of the National Women's Trade Union League (1903) and a member of its executive committee (1903–15); was a founding member of the New York Women's Trade Union League (1904); was a founder of the group that became the National Association for the Advancement of Colored People (1909); joined the Socialist Party (1910); appointed chair of the industrial committee of the New York City Woman Suffrage party (1912); served as a trade union delegate to the International Congress of Women (1915); was a trade union delegate to the International Congress of Working Women (1919).

Leonora O'Reilly published little in her lifetime, leaving behind only a handful of articles. Yet, in the early years of the 20th century, at the height of her career as a labor organizer and reformer, O'Reilly made on the average of one speech a day. She was a powerful orator who could move an audience with plain talk about the conditions women faced as industrial workers. And she spoke from her own experience.

In 1912, Leonora O'Reilly appeared before a Joint Senate Committee then hearing testimony regarding women's suffrage. This woman who went to work in a garment factory at age 11 was not afraid to speak her mind before the political leaders of her day. Representing working-class women, she told the U.S. Senators there assembled: "You can not or will not make laws for us; we must make laws for ourselves. We working women need the ballot for self-protection; that is all there is to it."

Such determined candor came from a lifetime of hard work and a childhood spent in poverty. O'Reilly was born in New York City, the daughter of Irish immigrants. Her father John O'Reilly had worked as a union printer before opening up his own small grocery store shortly before his daughter's birth in 1870. Her mother **Winifred Rooney O'Reilly** had come to America in the 1840s, escaping the devastation of the Irish potato famine only to live on the edge of poverty in her new homeland. Winifred worked as a garment worker before marriage, a trade she returned to when the grocery store failed and her husband and young son died in 1871. Leonora was not yet two years old.

Leonora and her mother were always close; the older woman had a strong influence on her daughter. It was Winifred who taught Leonora to sew, and the two worked into the night finishing garments Winifred brought home from the factory. It was also Winifred who instilled in Leonora an interest in trade unionism as a remedy to the harsh conditions industrial workers then faced. As a young child, Leonora had attended union meetings with her mother. Not surprisingly, only a few years after leaving school and starting work in a collar factory, O'Reilly became a union member herself when she joined the Knights of Labor in 1886. She was then 16 years old.

> I suffer torture dividing the woman's movement into the Industrial Group and all the other groups. Women, real women anywhere and everywhere, are what we must nourish and cherish.
>
> —Leonora O'Reilly

Her induction into the Knights of Labor was sponsored by a family friend, Jean Baptiste Hubert. Known as Uncle B, Hubert encouraged the young Leonora to learn French and to stay true to the trade unionist sentiments espoused by her mother. After joining the Knights, O'Reilly also met the Italian socialist Victor Drury; he would be her lifelong mentor. Before coming to America, he had been involved in radical politics in Europe, including the Paris Commune of 1870. This radicalism, and the need to sacrifice for a greater cause, was passed on to Drury's young protégé. With his encouragement, O'Reilly established the Working Women's Society in 1886. Years later, she would repay the older man's support by caring for him during the last few years of his life, until his death in 1918.

Although she worked long hours in the collar factory, O'Reilly devoted her evenings to organizing this group which sought to educate workers and the public in general regarding the exploitation of labor. Led by O'Reilly, the Society's activities came to the attention of the wealthy and reform-minded ***Josephine Shaw Lowell** who helped generate more publicity and went on to establish the National Consumers' League in 1890. With the assistance of the League, the data collected by the Working Women's Society would help persuade the New

York State Assembly to pass the Mercantile Inspection Act of 1896.

Winifred O'Reilly also inspired her daughter to continue her education, even though the young girl had left school at age 11. This Leonora did as part of a circle of self-taught workers interested in philosophical and social issues of the day. In 1888, she joined the Synthetic Club, a study group devoted to the philosophy of Positivism. Through the club, and her later membership in the Ethical Culture Society's Social Reform Club which she joined in 1894, O'Reilly became part of a lively, intellectual working-class environment, where she developed a philosophical basis for her lifelong activism on behalf of working-class women.

By the mid-1890s, O'Reilly was working ten hours a day in a shirtwaist factory and taking classes at night. She learned shorthand and went to the YWCA gym. She was still a leader of the Working Women's Society, and her activities there brought her to the attention of another well-to-do reformer, **Louise Perkins**. Perkins, then associated with the Henry Street Settlement House, came to see something quite special in the younger woman and encouraged her to become involved with the various programs offered at Henry Street. Using the settlement house as her base of operations, O'Reilly organized a women's local of the United Garment Workers.

However, it soon became clear to Perkins that O'Reilly's special talents as a labor organizer and public speaker had to play a secondary role as long as she was obliged to support herself. Therefore, in 1897 Perkins enlisted the aid of several other wealthy women and raised enough money to give O'Reilly a year off from the factory, enabling her to work full-time at Henry Street. During her year in residence, O'Reilly was in charge of a boys' club, investigated conditions in local sweatshops, and ran an experimental cooperative garment factory. Unfortunately, the cooperative soon proved to be unsuccessful as the goods produced were of too fine a quality to be sold on the regular market. Nonetheless, O'Reilly learned a valuable lesson as manager and instructor of the cooperative's employees. Not only did she discover in herself a particular talent for teaching, she also became increasingly aware of the importance of vocational training for women workers. O'Reilly saw in such training a way to instill pride in one's work and a greater self-appreciation of the worker's part in production. Quite possibly, such training might even "act as an incentive to unionization."

With that in mind, O'Reilly enrolled in the domestics arts program at the Pratt Institute, again relying on the financial support of her middle- and upper-class friends. She graduated in 1900, trained now as a sewing teacher. However, because she had not taken the necessary academic courses, she could not be certified to teach in the New York public schools. Instead, O'Reilly worked briefly as head resident at yet another settlement house, the Asacog Settlement in Brooklyn, and taught sewing through the privately funded Alliance Employment Bureau. In 1902, she began work at the Manhattan Trade School for Girls.

While she would remain at the school for seven years, for most of which as head of the sewing machine operating department, O'Reilly was frustrated by her experiences as a faculty member. The school's head, **Mary Schenck Woolman**, was much more conservative than O'Reilly regarding trade unions and discouraged her from engaging in any organizational activity. At the same time, O'Reilly was deeply disappointed that she, or any other working-class woman, was not made a member of the school's board of directors.

In this omission, she saw a genuine lack of concern for the viewpoints of the people the school had been established to serve. Although O'Reilly had been associating with women from outside her class for years, she still harbored doubts about the motivations of middle- and upper-class reformers. While she had been involved with them in organizations such as the Working Women's Society, worked alongside them in various settlement houses, had even benefited from their generosity, O'Reilly frequently felt that many reformers were condescending and lacked a true appreciation of working-class life. Her experiences as a teacher at the Manhattan Trade School for Girls only reinforced her fears.

Yet, her nascent feminism encouraged O'Reilly to continually seek out like-minded women of whatever class, working together to address the concerns of working-class women. O'Reilly's attempts in 1897 to organize female garment workers into their own local had been frustrated from the start by the ambivalence of a male-dominated trade union movement. She frequently found much more support for her activities among those women of moderate, even great wealth, many of whom had attended college but soon realized that few if any careers were open to them despite their education.

At the same time, many of these educated women of means were sincerely troubled by the

Leonora O'Reilly (right) with her mother Winifred Rooney O'Reilly.

harsh conditions under which industrial workers labored and lived. They felt a particular bond with women of the working class because the gender ideology of the day made all women, regardless of status, second-class citizens. In this spirit of sisterhood and in recognition of the apparent inability or lack of interest on the part of male trade unions in organizing women workers, the Women's Trade Union League (WTUL) was formed in 1903. The WTUL was to be a cross-class alliance of both working-class women and their middle- and upper-class allies, dedicated to organizing women workers into viable unions. Ambiguously affiliated with the American Federation of Labor (AFL) from its inception, the WTUL also sought to educate women workers as well as agitate for protective labor legislation.

Historian **Meredith Tax** has written that Leonora O'Reilly "was in many ways the soul of the WTUL." Her abilities as an organizer and speaker and her passion carried the WTUL through its early years. O'Reilly was at the initial meeting, along with settlement house workers William English Walling and ***Jane Addams** and veteran labor organizer ***Mary Kenney O'-Sullivan**, which gave birth to the WTUL. She was for the next dozen years a member of the national executive board as well as a founder of the New York branch of the WTUL in 1904.

O'Reilly's correspondence and diary entries from this period testify to her concerns that the WTUL was fated to be yet another organization of "Lady Bountifuls" condescending to the needs of working-class women. Her concerns were realized when the New York branch supported the publication of a supposed autobiography of **Dorothy Richardson** (not to be confused with British author ***Dorothy M. Richardson**), *The Long Day: The Story of a New York Working Girl, as Told by Herself*. For O'Reilly, this book written by a middle-class ally was not only untrue, it was a "rank exploitation of the working women of New York." In response, O'Reilly briefly resigned from the WTUL in 1905. She soon rejoined the WTUL and for the next few years continually sought to balance feminist politics with the interests of the working class. Such a balance was precariously maintained, fraught with tension. O'Reilly's personal struggle was mirrored in the WTUL itself until its demise in 1950.

Upon her return to the WTUL, O'Reilly devoted herself to that organization with her usual fervor despite lingering misgivings. She also encouraged the involvement of other women who would be of vital service to the WTUL in the years ahead. **Mary Dreier**, a middle-class woman from Brooklyn, was an old friend who had worked with O'Reilly at Asacog House. Dreier would soon become president of the New York WTUL. Her sister, **Margaret Dreier Robins**, also joined and went on to be a leader of the Chicago branch and president of the WTUL on the national level. Both Dreier sisters were greatly impressed by O'Reilly's speaking talents and her tireless devotion to the cause of working women. Concerned that O'Reilly's health was suffering from overwork, Dreier gave her a lifetime annuity in 1909, enabling O'Reilly to quit her teaching job and become a full-time organizer for the WTUL. In that same year, O'Reilly was elected vice president of the New York branch.

***Dreier, Mary** and **Margaret Dreier Robins.** See Dreier sisters.*

For the working women of New York, the next few years were volatile ones. Given her organizing experience and her position within the WTUL, O'Reilly was constantly on call. As one of the leaders of the 1909 strike of women garment workers, known as the "Uprising of the Thirty Thousand," she demonstrated, picketed and made daily speeches. As chair of the New York WTUL's fire-protection committee, O'Reilly spearheaded an investigation into workplace safety after the tragic fire at the Triangle Shirtwaist Company where 146 women died in 1911. In that effort, she was assisted by her friend and fellow working-class organizer, ***Rose Schneiderman**. Upon release of their official report, both women received the thanks of the International Ladies' Garment Workers Union at the 1912 ILGWU annual convention.

The security provided through the lifetime annuity from Mary Dreier also allowed O'Reilly to become involved with a variety of activities, some not directly related to working-class women. In 1909, she was among those, including ***Ida Wells-Barnett**, ***Mary White Ovington**, and W.E.B. Du Bois, who signed the call for the National Negro Conference, out of which would be formed the National Association for the Advancement of Colored People (NAACP); she would also serve on the first NAACP General Committee. A year later, O'Reilly joined the Socialist Party and was active in the New York faction. Long interested in women's suffrage as a partial remedy to the harsh conditions of industrial labor, she became chair of the New York City Woman Suffrage Party's industrial committee. She made numerous speeches on the need for women's suffrage, including her April 1912 appearance before the U.S. Senate.

The annuity from Dreier also made possible a change in O'Reilly's personal life. In 1909, she bought a home in Brooklyn. Her mother, who lived with her, was now in failing health. In their Brooklyn home, O'Reilly also cared for her daughter Alice, whom she had adopted in 1907. The child's death in 1911 was an event from which O'Reilly never fully recovered. Her grief, along with the stress of caring for her mother while engaged in her varied reform activities, caused her already fragile health to further decline.

At the same time, circumstances within the WTUL once again caused O'Reilly to break ties with the organization she had helped form. She was opposed to the minimum wage for women legislation which the WTUL started campaigning for in 1909. While O'Reilly supported legislation regarding maximum hours, she and several other WTUL members agreed with the official AFL stance against the minimum wage, fearing that "the floor would become the ceiling." While the minimum-wage issue split the New York WTUL chapter, that branch was further threatened by a divisive 1914 election for local president after the resignation of Mary Dreier.

Despite the fact that both candidates, Rose Schneiderman and **Melinda Scott**, were working class, their support fell along class and ethnic lines. Scott had the support of the allies while Schneiderman's support came from the primarily Jewish working-class members. The nasty politicking surrounding this election, which eventually went to Scott, was the last straw for O'Reilly. She had always been quick to condemn the middle- and upper-class allies for what O'Reilly perceived to be their inherent class prejudices. After the 1914 election, she told Mary Dreier that the WTUL "ought to die, the sooner, the better."

While the organization did not soon die, one of its primary leaders did resign from office. Citing health problems, O'Reilly ended her daily association with the WTUL in 1915. Indeed, she was suffering from heart disease, yet her frustrations from working for change within a cross-class alliance were as much responsible for her resignation as her declining health. She spent her last active years focused on international causes.

In 1915, as a trade union delegate to the International Congress of Women, held at The Hague, O'Reilly made a stirring speech regarding women workers. As a pacifist, she was against American involvement in World War I. As a socialist, she enthusiastically supported the Russian Revolution of 1917. Two years later, with the end of World War I, the WTUL appointed O'Reilly to their committee on social and industrial reconstruction. That same year, 1919, O'Reilly went to Washington as a delegate to the WTUL-sponsored International Congress of Working Women. There, she met a Hindu woman, **Parvatbai Athavale**, who eventually lived with her a year or so and sparked O'Reilly's interest in the education of Indian women. O'Reilly also became involved with the cause of Irish independence.

Her participation in the 1919 Congress was to be O'Reilly's last major effort on behalf of working women. Her final years were consumed by her own poor health and the care of her increasingly senile mother. O'Reilly managed to rally briefly in 1925, when she presented a year-long course on labor movement theory at the New School for Social Research. The woman who had been an activist for 40 years could now only address the theoretical aspects of the cause of labor. She died at age 57 in her Brooklyn home of the heart disease which had plagued her for years.

In her accomplishments as a woman of the working class, O'Reilly was certainly exceptional. Yet, her worldview never allowed her to forget her origins. It was the source of her strength as an organizer and as an orator. It was also the source of much tension as she sought to balance her class loyalties with the feminism espoused by her middle- and upper-class allies and friends. This tension was never resolved, and it frustrated her efforts on behalf of her primary goal. Leonora O'Reilly dedicated her life to improving conditions for those countless millions who, as she had in her early years, labored merely to survive. She did so with some success and much dignity.

SOURCES:

Bularzik, Mary J. "The Bonds of Belonging: Leonora O'Reilly and Social Reform," in *Labor History.* Vol. 24, 1983, pp. 60–83.

Lagemann, Ellen Condliffe. "Leonora O'Reilly, 1870–1927," in *A Generation of Women: Education in the Lives of Progressive Reformers.* Cambridge, MA: Harvard University Press, 1979.

Tax, Meredith. "Leonora O'Reilly and the Women's Trade Union League," in *The Rising of the Women: Feminist Solidarity and Class Conflict, 1880–1917.* NY: Monthly Review Press, 1980.

SUGGESTED READING:

Dye, Nancy Schrom. *As Equals and As Sisters: Feminism, the Labor Movement, and the Women's Trade Union League of New York.* Columbia, MO: University of Missouri Press, 1980.

COLLECTIONS:

Correspondence, papers, and memorabilia located in the Schlesinger Library, Radcliffe College.

Kathleen Banks Nutter,
Manuscripts Processor at the Sophia Smith Collection,
Smith College, Northampton, Massachusetts

Orelli, Susanna (1845–1939)

Swiss social reformer, founder-leader of the Frauenverein für Mässigkeit und Volkswohl (Women's Union for Temperance and Social Advancement), who emphasized the creation of alternatives to taverns and restaurants that served alcoholic beverages. *Name variations: Susanna Orelli-Rinderknecht. Born Susanna Rinderknecht on December 27, 1845, in Oberstrass, Canton Zurich, Switzerland; died in Zurich on January 12, 1939; had four sisters; married Johannes Orelli; no children.*

Consumption of massive amounts of alcohol was a destructive fact of life in pre-industrial Western societies. Immoderate drinking seemed to many, particularly men, the only way to cope with society's demands. Overindulging with

Swiss stamp honoring Susanna Orelli, issued in 1945.

beer, wine, and distilled spirits not only enabled them to drown their sorrows, but also was regarded as a mark of their masculinity. Murder and mayhem, including spousal and child abuse, was often the result.

Born Susanna Rinderknecht in 1845, she grew up in a peasant family in the Swiss town of Oberstrass. There, she witnessed several incidents caused by drunkenness. On one occasion, her parents woke her in the middle of the night, when it appeared that a raging fire might leap from their burning barn to their home. Soon the cause became clear: an alcoholic, recently released from an asylum, had set the barn on fire. As well, the son of Susanna's neighbor, a young man who had become increasingly addicted to alcohol, shot himself fatally while in a state of drunken depression. Her dependable, hard-working stepbrother, whom she loved dearly, counted among his farm duties the occasional delivery of a load of barley scraps to the local brewery. While there, he would be given a large mug of beer. One day, inebriated, he fell off his coach seat while on the way home and was killed.

Then illness struck her sister. After becoming infected with typhus, **Caroline Rinderknecht** became mentally disturbed because of side effects in her brain. While visiting her sister at the Burghölzli mental institution, Susanna witnessed the effects of chronic alcoholism on some of the patients. Caroline recovered, and Susanna vowed to dedicate her life to helping people in need. Her impulses extended to risking her own safety; she once nursed back to health a neighbor's family who had become gravely ill during a cholera epidemic.

Ironically, it was the liberalization of Swiss economic life that exacerbated the already significant problem of alcohol. In 1874, a revision of the Swiss constitution removed the restraints on trade and commerce that had been enforced by the guilds since the Middle Ages. Like mushrooms, new breweries and taverns appeared everywhere, so that by 1882 in Zurich alone there was one tavern for every 130 of the city's citizens, children included. During this period, Swiss national alcohol consumption statistics were alarming. Since most families were accustomed to drinking alcoholic beverages at every meal, even children became accustomed to imbibing intoxicants from their earliest years. In Swiss hospitals, the medieval tradition of providing a daily wine ration to patients in order to protect them from plagues remained a time-honored custom that few questioned.

By the 1880s, rampant public drunkenness had become a major problem in Zurich. With countless taverns, many Zurich men spent most of their free hours drinking to excess. Streets were filled with drunken men, some of whom acted aggressively not only toward each other but toward women as well. Even so, Zurich citizens voted down an 1893 referendum to create a nightly closing time for the public dispensing of drink. Both Susanna and Caroline were determined to help change this situation, and they spent hours as volunteers at the Burghölzli institution, where its progressive director, Professor Auguste Forel, tried to make the public aware of the sufferings brought on by the problem.

Susanna's efforts would be somewhat reduced in the early 1880s when she met and fell in love with Johannes Orelli, a widowed mathematics professor. Despite their age difference—she was 36, he almost 60—the couple married on Christmas Day, 1881, in Zurich's Predigerkirche. Their union ended suddenly four years later, when Johannes died of a stroke. Following the death of their parents, Susanna Orelli asked Caroline to move in with her. Financially secure and living in a large house in the Zeltweg district of Zurich, the sisters would become increasingly involved over the next few years in the pressing social issue of alcoholism.

Through a chance meeting with the noted Swiss poet Conrad Ferdinand Meyer, Orelli reestablished her relationship with Forel and became an active member of the Verein des Blauen Kreuzes (Union of the Blue Cross), as well as the Alkoholgegnerbund (Alliance of Opponents of Alcohol). She also formed friendships and alliances with like-minded individuals, including the physician who had succeeded Auguste Forel as Burghölzli director, Professor Eugen Bleuler, and his wife, Dr. **Hedwig Bleuler-Waser**, an activist who founded and became leader of another reform group, the Bund abstinenter Frauen (Union of Abstinent Women).

Although she was one of the most active members of the Alkoholgegnerbund, Orelli soon came to feel that its program, which attempted to change deep-rooted habits through lectures and pamphlets, was fated to achieve only modest results. A more realistic alternative to alcohol consumption than mere moralizing would have to be offered to the citizens of Zurich. Orelli disagreed strongly with those in the reform community who longed for an outright ban on the sale of alcohol. She believed that only more attractive alternatives to public places that featured alcohol (including inns, restaurants, and taverns) would be able to turn the tide. A model for such reforms already existed in the Swiss cities of Basel and Bern, where non-alcoholic restaurants were flourishing. From this point on, Orelli advocated the founding of alcohol-free restaurants in Zurich. She was convinced that the people of Zurich would see the advantages of patronizing restaurants that enabled them to eat better and more cheaply.

From her home, Orelli worked as the key member of an "Initiative Committee for the Creation of a New Tavern." When it appeared that formidable financial and organizational hurdles stood in the way, Orelli suggested a more realistic approach. As an interim step, she and her fellow reformers opened a modest coffeehouse, the Kafeestube zum kleinen Martahof. On Zurich's Stadelhoferstrasse, the café was located in an old painter's atelier that had been renovated by Orelli and her friends. Here, Zurich citizens could drink coffee and cocoa, as well as eat simple yet nourishing meals at budget prices. The café's success did not dampen Orelli's wish to open a larger, full-scale non-alcoholic restaurant. To raise funds, she and her group organized a bazaar held on June 19–20, 1894. Their efforts raised the impressive sum of 17,000 Swiss Francs.

Encouraged, Orelli's group—which consisted of 15 public-spirited and well-connected women—constituted itself officially as the city's Frauenverein für Mässigkeit und Volkswohl (Women's Union for Temperance and Social Advancement). Despite its aims, the organization avoided use of the terms "abstinence" and "alcohol-free" in its public pronouncements. Only many years later, in 1910, when her efforts had long been deemed successful by Zurich burghers, did the organization change its name to the more candid Zürcher Frauenverein für alkoholfreie Wirtschaften (Zurich Women's Union for Non-Alcoholic Restaurants). For several years, Orelli's group successfully managed their café-restaurant on the Martahof. But this site, which could accommodate no more than 55 customers at a time, was clearly too small for the Frauenverein's goals.

On April 1, 1898, their group inaugurated a non-alcoholic establishment in the Karl der Grosse (Charlemagne) building. Despite some disparagement from the press, this restaurant, universally called "der Karli" by the locals, was a success from the first day. With a seating capacity of 250, Karl der Grosse was designed to appeal to Zurich's middle class. And come they did: the large assembly room, with impressive rococo paintings, was filled night after night as diners enjoyed good food washed down with mineral water and fruit juice. The venture was a huge success; after only a few years, the organization was able to end its leasing arrangement, purchasing the building outright.

Orelli's group then opened a spa hotel on the unspoiled Zürichberg, which when completed would enable hikers to spend a few hours or even a night, providing them with a spectacular view of the city below. Modestly priced rooms, as well as nourishing meals with fruit juices (or hot chocolate in the winter months), also brought droves of Zurich citizens. Inaugurated in the chilly month of November 1900, the Frauenverein spa hotel (Kurhaus) on the mountain was another resounding success. Although some of the local newspapers poked fun at the fruit juices served there as "insipid beverages," the spa's full cash register was impressive.

Orelli ran a tight ship at the Frauenverein hotel. The waitresses were professional and lived, carefully supervised, on the premises. Tips were discouraged and only young women from "better families" were employed. Orelli successfully attracted members of the nascent industrial working class to her establishments. Even though her religious beliefs clashed with the Marxism of the workers, she threw out a welcome mat to a social strata that often suffered the most from the ravages of alcohol abuse. In 1910, the workers' Volkshaus was inaugurated on Zurich's Helvetiaplatz in festivities that eschewed the consumption of alcohol. Beyond the borders of Zurich, Orelli became active in efforts to build alcohol-free community centers (Gemeindestuben and Gemeindehäuser) throughout Switzerland. In 1918, at age 73, she accepted the first presidential post of the Zürcher Frauenverein. Despite her advancing years, she remained a shrewd negotiator on behalf of her organization. By the time of her retirement from the administration of the Frauenverein in 1921, Orelli could point with pride to the 13 successful restaurants that the organization ran in that year in the city of Zurich.

In the final decades of her long life, Susanna Orelli was regarded by most Swiss as a national institution. In 1919, the medical faculty of the University of Zurich awarded her—a woman whose formal education had been modest indeed—an honorary doctorate "in recognition of her great accomplishments in the field of public health and welfare." Despite the encroaching ailments of old age, including weakening eyesight, she remained intellectually active. Susanna Orelli died in Zurich on January 12, 1939. She has been honored by Switzerland in many ways, including a street named in her honor on the

Zürichberg, as well as a fountain named for her at the intersection of Orelliweg and Schattengasse. On December 1, 1945, a Swiss postage stamp, with a surcharge for charitable purposes and bearing her portrait, was issued in her honor. In 1994, Zurich celebrated her centenary. Remarkably, a number of the non-alcoholic restaurants established so long ago by Susanna Orelli and her fellow crusaders are still in existence in Zurich, including the Rütli on the Zähringerstrasse, the venerable Karl der Grosse (still affectionately called "der Karli"), the Seidenhof and Olivenbaum, and the Kurhaus Zürichberg overlooking the city.

SOURCES:

Hildebrandt, Irma. *Die Frauenzimmer kommen: 16 Zürcher Portraits*. 2nd rev. ed. Munich: Eugen Diederichs Verlag, 1997.

"Savoir-vivre," in *Tages-Anzeiger*. May 6, 2000, p. 65.

Schaer, Sigi. "Ein Festakt 'und ein Lächeln dazu': 100 Jahre Zürcher Frauenverein für alkoholfreie Wirtschaften," in *Neue Zürcher Zeitung*. June 16, 1994, p. 53.

———. "Zürcher Strassennamen erläutert und dargestellt: Eine Ausstellung im Haus zum Rech am Neumarkt 4," in *Neue Zürcher Zeitung*. December 9, 1999, p. 47.

Schnyder, Moia. *Zwei Pionierinnen der Volksgesundheit: Susanna Orelli-Rinderknecht, 1845–1939—Else Züblin-Spiller, 1881–1948*. Wetzikon: AG Buchdruckerei Wetzikon, 1973.

Siegel, Monique R. *Weibliches Unternehmertum: Zürcherinnen schreiben Wirtschaftsgeschichte*. Zurich: Verlag Neue Zürcher Zeitung, 1994.

John Haag,
Associate Professor of History, University of Georgia,
Athens, Georgia

Orinda (1631–1664).

See Philips, Katherine.

Orkin, Ruth (1921–1985)

Twentieth-century American photojournalist and filmmaker. *Born Ruth Orkin in Boston, Massachusetts, on September 3, 1921; died of cancer in New York, New York, on January 18, 1985; daughter of Sam Orkin (a businessman) and Mary Ruby Orkin (a former actress); attended Beverly Hills and Eagle Rock high schools, 1935–39; married Morris Engel, in 1945; children: Andy Engel (b. 1959);* ***Mary Engel*** *(b. 1961).*

Awards: third-prize winner in Life *magazine's Young Photographers Contest (1951); Silver Lion Award at the Venice Film Festival (1953); Academy Award nominee for Best Motion Picture Story (1953); voted one of the Top Ten Women Photographers in the U.S. by the Professional Photographers of America (1959); Manhattan Cultural Award for Photography (1980).*

Family moved to California (1924); received her first camera, a 39c Univex (1931); had first photo exhibit, at Eagle Rock camera store (1939); undertook a solo 2,000-mile bicycle trip to the World's Fair, New York City (1939); was first female messenger hired by MGM Studios (1941); joined the Women's Army Auxiliary Corps (1941); moved to New York City (1943); purchased her first 35mm camera (1943); photographed classical musicians at Tanglewood Music Festival (1946–50); photographed her famous six-picture sequence "The Cardplayers" (1947); traveled with the Israeli Philharmonic during its first American tour (1951); collaborated with husband on the award-winning feature film Little Fugitive *(1953); collaborated with husband on a second feature,* Lovers and Lollipops *(1955); "The Cardplayers" included in Edward Steichen's "Family of Man" exhibition at the Museum of Modern Art (1955); photographs included in the Photography in the Fine Arts exhibition at the Metropolitan Museum of Art (1965); had first retrospective exhibit, Nikon House (1974); was an instructor, School of Visual Arts (1976–78); was an instructor, International Center for Photography (1980); posthumous retrospective exhibit at the International Center of Photography, New York City (1995).*

Selected works: A World Through My Window *(1978);* A Photo Journal *(1981);* More Pictures from My Window *(1983).*

America was a golden age of photojournalism from around 1930 to 1960. In this 30-year period, before television's domination, advances in printing methods led to a deluge of illustrated magazines. It was through the photographs and accompanying text in such magazines as *Life*, *This Week*, and *Look*, that most middle-class Americans learned about business, culture, politics, and other nations. Among the most successful photojournalists of the time was Ruth Orkin. Throughout her extensive career, which began around 1942, Orkin's photographs were regularly reprinted in national family magazines and exhibited in galleries and museums across the country. She photographed a wide variety of subjects—from Hollywood starlets to classical musicians to people on the street. Orkin's special gift was her ability to artfully render the most complicated human drama in a single image. "Intelligent, precise, often human dramas," said Gordon Parks, "her work always seemed to find a human story to tell by looking more closely than the rest of us."

Ruth Orkin was born on September 3, 1921, in Boston, Massachusetts, the only child of Sam and **Mary Ruby Orkin.** In 1924, the family moved to Los Angeles where Ruth grew up under the spell of Hollywood and the motion-picture industry. Before her marriage, Mary Orkin had toured the country as part of a vaudeville act, "The Lillian Sisters," and had worked briefly as a silent-movie actress. Though she settled down to a life of domesticity with her husband and daughter, Mary remained passionately interested in show business. She regularly attended film premieres and celebrity funerals, usually in the company of her daughter. Ruth herself was stage-struck. As an adolescent, she had a reputation for being one of the most aggressive and successful autograph hounds in Los Angeles and was once interviewed about her autographing exploits on a popular local radio show. In 1935, at age 13, she started a movie diary and for the next seven years faithfully recorded and rated every film she saw.

Her father Sam Orkin was a businessman who possessed a mechanical wizardry. He owned and operated a successful company, The Orkin Fleet, where he designed and built toy boats that are now collectibles. The Orkins nurtured their only child's budding interests while enjoying a comfortable lifestyle. At age ten, Ruth got her first camera, a 39c Univex. Two years later, she received a darkroom set. At 14, she acquired a one-dollar Baby Brownie Camera and began taking snapshots of her classmates and teachers for a nickel apiece. At 16, she started to photograph with a Pilot 6 camera and shortly thereafter held her first photographic exhibit at a local camera store. The following year, she read Richard Halliburton's *The Royal Road* which inspired her to travel. After her high school graduation in 1939, Orkin undertook a grueling 2,000-mile solo bicycle trip, staying in youth hostels along the way, to attend the World's Fair in New York City. Later, she put together a scrapbook of the cross-country adventure, which had generated a good deal of publicity, with some 300 contact prints and a diary.

Upon her return to California, she enrolled in the Los Angeles Community College but left after one year. "My main ambition was to make movies," she later wrote. The following year, in 1940, 21-year-old Orkin became the first "messenger girl" at MGM studio, a job she hoped would lead to a career in the movie business. The position allowed her to observe the technical side of filmmaking, an area which greatly interested her. She learned how to operate a moviola and the sound-mixing boards, and watched editing and dubbing sessions. Orkin aspired to become a camera operator, but she soon learned that the cinematographers' union did not admit women. Undaunted, she joined the Women's Army Auxiliary Corps (WAACS) later that year under the mistaken notion that she was to be sent to the Signal Corps in Astoria, New York, where she would be trained to make films. As it turned out, she was posted to Arkansas where her ambitions to be a filmmaker were thwarted once again.

In 1943, Orkin moved to New York City with the idea of becoming a professional photographer, a vocation that seemed friendlier to women. She worked at a series of odd jobs, including a stint as a nightclub photographer, to save money to buy her first 35mm camera. "The minute I had that 35mm camera, a whole new world of seeing opened to me. I went wild shooting in public places, looking for the best light and for subjects who wouldn't be aware of my presence." She set up a makeshift darkroom in her tiny apartment and began perfecting her technique. Though she was primarily self-taught, Orkin socialized with other photographers, including Weegee and Arnold Newman.

Her first professional assignments were for small publications, including *Publishers Weekly, Musical Courier,* and *Chess Review*. Her reputation as a talented and original photographer was quickly established, however, and throughout the 1940s and early 1950s Orkin's black-and-white photographs of celebrities and street scenes appeared regularly in *Look, Life, Ladies' Home Journal, Coronot, Collier's, Cosmopolitan,* and *This Week*. What distinguished an Orkin photograph was the extraordinary drama that was revealed in the most seemingly ordinary face, action, or scene. Critics praised her uncanny ability to create a story out of a single image. Her subjects were often celebrities and well-known figures, and the efforts she took with each assignment paid off in surprising ways: a triumphant and regal Artur Rubinstein strolling down a Manhattan street greeting admirers; a laughing, playful Albert Einstein (1953); a brooding, reflective Marlon Brando dressed as Brutus (1952); and a straight-faced Woody Allen posing before a painting at the Metropolitan Museum of Art (1963). One of her most intimate portraits was the 1949 photograph of ***Carson McCullers** cradled in the arms of ***Ethel Waters** after an opening night performance of McCullers' play *The Member of the Wedding*. The photograph was taken as part of an assignment for *Life,* though the magazine initially refused to run the picture: the image of a white woman nestled in the arms of a black woman was deemed too controversial.

Although Orkin remained smitten with Hollywood, she recognized the darker side of the motion-picture business. With the viewpoint of an erstwhile messenger girl and the skill of a professional photographer, Orkin returned to MGM in 1948, intent on capturing the seamier side of the business. Many of these photographs were later published in *This Week,* a Sunday supplement with a circulation of 12 million.

Orkin was also fascinated by street scenes, and some of her best-known photographs, including the 1946 "Jimmy the Storyteller" sequence which appeared in *Look* magazine, were shot in the West Village neighborhood where she took up residence in 1945. In 1947, Orkin photographed her famous six-picture sequence, "The Cardplayers," which depicts three young children sitting around a wagon playing cards. The sequence was later included in Edward Steichen's groundbreaking 1955 "Family of Man" exhibit at the Museum of Modern Art.

In the finest tradition of photojournalism, her photographs tell extended stories.

—Miles Barth

In 1945, Orkin inaugurated one of her most important photographic projects when she photographed a shirtless Leonard Bernstein for *The New York Times.* Orkin was a great fan of classical music, and the assignment sparked an extended study of classical musicians. She preferred shooting them in rehearsal, she said, because "you get to listen to all that great music and the subjects are ideal; they're moving constantly and are too engrossed in their work to be aware of the camera." From 1947 though 1953, she photographed most of the top conductors and soloists performing in the United States, including Bernstein, Isaac Stern, Arturo Toscanini, Vladimir Horowitz, and Dimitri Mitropoulos. During the summers, she regularly attended and photographed rehearsals at Lewisohn Stadium in New York and at the Tanglewood Music Festival in Massachusetts. Orkin published her own illustrated guidebook to Tanglewood in 1947 and 1948, and in 1947 seven of the prints were included in an exhibition of music photographs at the Museum of Modern Art.

In 1951, she photographed the Israeli Philharmonic's first American tour and then accompanied the symphony back to Israel. While there, she lived for a few months on a kibbutz, then traveled and photographed Florence, Venice, Paris, Rome, and London. While abroad that year, she took what is arguably her best-known image, "American Girl in Italy," which depicts a young woman clutching the shawl around her neck, nervously hurrying past a group of openly admiring Italian men. As with many of her well-known photographs, this single-image drama was artfully posed by Orkin.

In 1952, she married Morris Engel, a photographer and filmmaker whom she had met at the Photo League, and over the next four years she concentrated on filmmaking. Their first collaboration, *Little Fugitive,* about a young boy who mistakenly believes he has killed his brother and runs away to Coney Island, was released in 1953 to great critical acclaim. The film received the Silver Lion award at that year's Venice Film Festival, was nominated for an Academy Award for Best Screenplay, and was credited by the filmmaker François Truffaut for influencing the French New Wave. In 1955, Orkin and Engel collaborated on another acclaimed film, *Lovers and Lollipops.*

In 1959, Orkin was voted one of the Top Ten Women Photographers in the U.S. by the Professional Photographers of America. Following the birth of her son Andy that same year (a daughter Mary was born in 1961), Orkin ceased working professionally and concentrated instead on raising and photographing her children. "I was fascinated by every stage of [their] development, and I felt compelled to record in both words and pictures each momentous occasion." By this time, the family had moved to a 15th-floor apartment overlooking Central Park, and Orkin began taking color photographs of the panoramic view from the window. The photographs, taken without filters, were shot in every season and at all hours. From the skyline to park concerts, celebrations, demonstrations, parades, and riots, her images captured the magic and complexity of the city. In 1978, 81 of these photographs were published as *A World Through My Window.* A sequel, *More Pictures from My Window,* followed in 1983. The collections, said Parks, were "classics of American photography."

In the 1960s and 1970s, Orkin's photographs began appearing in museum exhibitions and galleries. In 1965, her pictures were included in a photography exhibition at the Metropolitan Museum of Art, and in 1974 her first retrospective exhibit was held at the Nikon House in New York City. That same year, Orkin published her autobiography, *A Photo Journal.* In 1980, she received the First Annual Manhattan Cultural Award in Photography. Throughout the early 1980s, despite being diagnosed with cancer, Orkin continued to work. She died on January 18, 1985, age 63.

SOURCES AND SUGGESTED READING:

Chicago Sun-Times. December 16, 1979.

The New York Times. October 5, 1979, September 17, 1985.

Orkin, Ruth. *More Pictures from My Window.* NY: Rizzoli, 1983.

———. *A Photo Journal.* NY: Viking Press, 1981.

———. *Ruth Orkin.* NY: M. Engel, The Estate of Ruth Orkin, 1995.

———, and Arno Karlen. *A World Through My Window.* NY: Harper and Row, 1978.

Suzanne Smith,
freelance writer, Decatur, Georgia

Orkney, countess of.

See Douglas, Elizabeth (d. before 1451).
See Villiers, Elizabeth (c. 1657–1733).

Orkney, Elizabeth Hamilton, countess of.

See Villiers, Elizabeth (c. 1657–1733).

Orleans, duchess of.

See Blanche of France (1328–1392).
See Visconti, Valentina (1366–1408).
See Bonne of Armagnac (d. 1415).
See Marie of Cleves (1426–1486).
See Anne of Beaujeu for sidebar on Jeanne de France (c. 1464–1505).
See Marguerite of Lorraine (fl. 1632).
See Henrietta Anne (1644–1670).
See Charlotte Elizabeth of Bavaria (1652–1722).
See Montespan, Françoise for sidebar on Françoise-Marie de Bourbon (1677–1749).
See Augusta Maria of Baden-Baden (1704–1726).
See Louisa Henrietta de Conti (1726–1759).
See Montesson, Charlotte Jeanne Béraud de la Haye de Riou, marquise de (1737–1805).
See Louise Marie of Bourbon (1753–1821).
See Maria Dorothea of Austria (1867–1932).

Orleans, Maid of.

See Joan of Arc (c. 1412–1431).

Orlova, Liubov (1902–1975)

Russian actress and singer, the most popular Soviet film star of her time, who achieved a status equivalent to that of her contemporaries in Hollywood. *Name variations: Liubov'; Lyubov or Lubov Orlova; Luba Orlova. Born Liubov Petrovna Orlova on February 11, 1902, in Zvenigorod (now part of Greater Moscow); died in Moscow on January 26, 1975; interred at Moscow's Novodevichye Cemetery; professionally trained in music and dance; married Grigorii or Gregori Alexandrov.*

Awards: Order of Lenin (1939); two USSR State Prizes (1941, 1950); honored as a People's Artist of the USSR (1950).

Liubov Orlova, the beloved Russian actress of the Soviet era who reigned for more than four decades as a superstar of the world's first "worker's state," was born in 1902 in Zvenigorod (now part of Greater Moscow) into a family that was anything but proletarian. Her father's family, the Orlovs, was one of the oldest and most distinguished of the Russian Empire, distantly related to the counts Tolstoy. A photograph of Count Leo Tolstoy taken around 1908 at his estate Yasnaya Polyana shows Tolstoy with a pretty little girl on his knee, a girl who would be celebrated as the first star of the Soviet silver screen. Beautiful and talented, Orlova studied music at the Moscow Conservatory (1919–22), and perfected her dancing skills at the choreographic section of Moscow's Theatrical Technicum (1922–25). Starting in 1926, she delighted audiences at Moscow's V.I. Nemirovich-Danchenko Musical Theater with her singing. Over the next years, she would star in many of this theater's productions, including such audience favorites as the operettas *La Périchole* (Offenbach) and *Les Cloches de Corneville* (Planquette).

Starting in the early 1930s, Orlova began to appear in Soviet motion pictures. In her first film *Petersburg Nights* (1933), directed by Gregori Roshal, she made an immediate impact, with her high cheekbones and large, slanting eyes, despite being cast only in a supporting role. In *Jazz Comedy* (1933), Orlova took a Cinderella role, depicting a housewife who became a stage star. In 1934, she appeared in a film that would change the course of her life when the gifted director Gregori Alexandrov (1903–1983) chose her to star as Aniuta in his *Veselye Rebiata* (The Happy Guys), released in the United States as *Moscow Laughs*. Unlike most Soviet films of the period, which were drenched with Marxist propaganda, *The Happy Guys* was a quick-moving and lighthearted musical comedy that was immensely successful at the box office. Orlova, by then a seasoned singer-actress but still largely unknown, became an overnight national sensation.

By 1936, the dictatorship of Joseph Stalin had turned brutal, as purge trials uncovered "enemies of the people." A knock on the door in the middle of the night meant the dreaded secret police. Yet that same year, Stalin proclaimed that Socialism had been achieved, that the ideal Communist society was on the horizon. A slogan attributed to Stalin, "Life has become better, life has become happier," could be read in the press, heard on the radio, and seen on billboards. It was in this surrealistic atmosphere that Alexandrov began directing another musical comedy, *Tsirk* (The Circus). The story line was simple but unconventional: Marion Dixon, Orlova's role, was a circus artiste, who had been hounded out of America by a lynch mob because she had given birth to an illegitimate baby whose father was African-American. In flight from her racist tormentors, though still in the U.S., Dixon meets a man named Franz von Kneischitz on a train. This German entrepreneur, who soon becomes Marion's Svengali, is the villain of *The Circus*. He speaks Russian with a clipped German accent, has a moustache, and parts his hair (like Adolf Hitler) on the right side. Clearly an evil genius, he makes Dixon the star of a circus act called "The Flight to the Moon," in which she is fired from a cannon through a hoop that is turned into a crescent moon.

Soon, Dixon and von Kneischitz are performing in the Soviet Union. The plot is energized when Dixon meets the hero Ivan Martynov, a superb-looking blonde with the sterling character traits to be found among Stalin's New Soviet Man. After many vicissitudes which Soviet film audiences found highly entertaining, love blossoms between Martynov and Dixon. Alexandrov's direction was indebted to Hollywood techniques, and in the film's "Flight to the Moon" sequence, there are echoes of such American films as *Gold Diggers* as well as the elaborate dance routines of Busby Berkeley. *The Circus* became an immense hit, not only because of Alexandrov's imaginative directing and Orlova's talents, but also because it featured catchy music by the talented Soviet composer Isaak O. Dunaevskii. Dunaevskii composed an impressive number of hit tunes for the musical comedy films of Alexandrov and Ivan Pyrev, the two unchallenged masters of the genre. *The Circus* went on to become the greatest box-office success in the history of the Soviet cinema.

The final minutes of *The Circus* delighted millions of Soviet moviegoers. Von Kneischitz becomes desperate and seizes Marion's precious baby. Shouting "Halt!" in German, in a thick Russian accent he announces to the world her "secret," namely that "she was a Negro's mistress! She has a black child. . . . This is a racial crime. She has no place in civilized society!" In protest, the circus workers seize the child and begin to sing a lullaby in a variety of languages, first by a Russian woman, then by a Ukrainian man, then by a Tatar, a Georgian, a Jew, and finally by a black. This sequence is meant to sum up, in contrast to racist America and anti-Semitic Nazi Germany, the tolerant, multinational Soviet Union, where racism and national hatreds have been banished. As Marion and her perfect man Martynov begin to sing a popular tune extolling the Soviet Union, the scene changes, transplanting them to Red Square and the annual Soviet May Day parade. Marion marches proudly—an equal among equals in the socialist commonwealth—with her circus colleagues, all of them dressed in spotless white. A nudge and a glance toward the Lenin Mausoleum, and implicitly towards the figure of Stalin, whose iconic image has just been displayed. Dixon's eyes light up with the devotion of a True Believer when she sees Stalin off-screen on the podium.

With the immense success of *The Circus*, Orlova became a star. Frequently dubbed the "prima donna of Soviet cinema," she was a glamorous figure in a society that continued to glorify proletarian muscle and industrial productivity. Yet, Stalinism was creating a new class of bureaucrats whose privileges allowed them to at least fantasize about the material goods known to exist in the capitalist West. Although her roles were those of "women of the people," Orlova nevertheless reflected a certain amount of elegance and even hinted at sexuality. Film critic Sergei Nikolaevich has written (*Ogonek*, 1992) that Orlova's film image was one of "the ideal woman of the 1930s, the *femina sovietica*, a contemporary Valkyrie in a white sweater with a severe perm," a politically pure woman who nonetheless embodied the essences of both ***Marlene Dietrich** and ***Greta Garbo**.

That the Stalinist Soviet Union had nurtured such a talent was a clear indication that the Soviet system had scored another victory over the decadent West. Stalin remarked to her new husband, director Alexandrov, at a Kremlin reception: "Remember, comrade Aleksandrov! Orlova is our national property." Behind the aura of their professional success, there remained the system of terror created and maintained by Lenin and Stalin. This grim reality impacted even on artists who had created *The Circus*. Vladimir S. Nil'sen (1906–1942), its chief cinematographer, was arrested at the height of the Great Purge in September 1937 and shot in January 1942. The film's production manager, Zahak Darvetsky, was also arrested. At a time of escalated state terrorism, *The Circus* would be the first in a trilogy of musical comedy films immensely popular with audiences, along with *Volga-Volga* and *Bright Path*. Stalin and his henchmen, writes one critic, "raised the volume on propaganda by recruiting all mass media to the task of maintaining the mythical illusion that life had indeed become brighter and happier."

Despite the appearance of a cultural thaw in the mid-1930s, Stalin never loosened his grip over Soviet cinema and was often referred to as "the Kremlin censor." Reality and illusion blurred in Soviet films, which were philosophically grounded in a theory of "revolutionary Romanticism." Stalin was as much the victim as the perpetrator of these illusions, for his view of the Soviet countryside appears to have been gleaned not from objective data but from the Soviet films he saw.

In 1938, Orlova starred in another Alexandrov-directed musical comedy, *Volga-Volga*, which became Stalin's favorite film. In it, she is Strelka, a gifted village letter carrier whose simple and melodious songs propel her into the position of a highly popular state-sponsored singer. In 1939, Orlova's character in *The Mistake of Kochin the Engineer* not only enjoys moments of happiness but also finds death, as the victim of the dark forces still lurking in the Soviet Union. In the 1940 film *Bright Path* (also known as *The Radiant Road* but released in the United States in 1942 under the title *Tanya*), she plays another Cinderella role. In an industrial textile town near Moscow, she is Tanya Morozova, a peasant weaver responsible for 240 looms. Thanks to the quality of her productive labor, Tanya is invited to the Kremlin, where she is given the highest Soviet award, the Order of Lenin. She goes on to study engineering and is one day elected a Deputy to the nation's highest representative assembly, the Supreme Soviet.

After World War II, which brought on staggering Soviet losses (between 20 and 30 million were killed), Orlova appeared in an unusual 1947 film entitled *Spring*. In her virtuoso performance in a modernized "twins" plot, Orlova plays both the scientist Nikitina and the actress Shatrova, who in turn plays Nikitina. The action of this Alexandrov film, partly filmed in Prague, was built on numerous amusing substitutions. In typical Alexandrov style, the background was thoroughly unrepresentative of the harsh realities of postwar Soviet life, which earned *Spring* harsh words from some critics who noted in print, "Do Soviet scientists live in such sumptuous mansions and villas?"

Although she was now well into her 40s, Orlova remained very much a star and played the leading role of Janet Sherwood in the film *Meeting on the Elbe* (1949), a glorification of Stalin to honor the aging dictator's 70th birthday. During this period, Orlova's acting took on a new depth. Critical responses were also positive when she appeared as Tatiana in *Mussorgsky* (1950), directed by Gregori Roshal. In 1952, she starred as Ludmilla Glinka, wife of the 19th-century Russian musical pioneer Mikhail Glinka, in the cinematic biography *Glinka: Man of Music*, a film that—despite Cold War tensions—was praised by *The New York Times'* critic as one "with a few faults and some virtues of solid gold." Orlova's last important role was in 1960, when she appeared as Varvara Komarova in *Russian Memory*, a performance that did not disappoint her many millions of fans.

Liubov Orlova in Volga-Volga.

Starting in 1955, Orlova became a permanent member of Moscow's Mossovet Theater, where she appeared in a broad range of roles, including Jessie in Konstantin Simonov's *The Russian Question* and ***Mrs. Patrick Campbell** in Jerome Kilty's *Dear Liar*. By now, she had been handed all the major honors that the Soviet Union could bestow on a performing artist. These included the Order of Lenin (awarded to both her and her husband in February 1939), as well state Prizes of the USSR in 1941 and 1950. In 1950, she was proclaimed a People's Artist of the USSR. Orlova died in Moscow on January 26, 1975, and was buried in Moscow's Novodevichye Cemetery. Even now, a generation after her death, her gravesite still draws visitors.

SOURCES:

Anderson, Trudy. "Why Stalinist Musicals?," in *Discourse*. Vol. 17, no. 3. Spring 1995, pp. 38–48.

Attwood, Lynne. *Red Women on the Silver Screen*. London: Pandora, 1993.

Bezelianskii, Iurii. *Vera, Nadezhda, Liubov'—: Zhenskie Portrety.* Moscow: OAO Izd-vo "Raduga," 1998.

Birkos, Alexander S. *Soviet Cinema: Directors and Films*. Hamden, CT: Archon Books, 1976.

Dickinson, Thorold, and Catherine De La Roche. *Soviet Cinema*. Reprint. NY: Arno Press, 1972.

Frolov, Ivan. *Liubov' Orlova: V Grime i Bez Grima*. Moscow: Panorama, 1997.

Horton, Andrew, ed. *Inside Soviet Film Satire: Laughter With a Lash*. Cambridge, UK: Cambridge University Press, 1993.

Leyda, Jay. *Kino: A History of the Russian and Soviet Film*. 3rd ed. Princeton, NJ: Princeton University Press, 1983.

Nowell-Smith, Geoffrey, ed. *The Oxford History of World Cinema*. Oxford, UK: Oxford University Press, 1996.

Romanov, Aleksei Vladimirovich. *Liubov' Orlova v iskusstve i v zhizhni*. Moscow: "Iskusstvo," 1986.

"Russians Suggest Hollywood 'Rebel,'" in *The New York Times*. December 9, 1947.

Shlapentokh, Dmitry, and Vladimir Shlapentokh. *Soviet Cinematography, 1918–1991: Ideological Conflict and Social Reality.* NY: A. de Gruyter, 1993.

Solov'eva, I. and V. Shitova. "Liubov' Orlova," in *Aktëry sovetskogo kino*. Vyp. 2. Moscow: Iskusstvo, 1966.

Stites, Richard. *Russian Popular Culture: Entertainment and Society since 1900*. Cambridge, UK: Cambridge University Press, 1992.

Taylor, Richard. "The Illusion of Happiness and the Happiness of Illusion: Grigorii Aleksandrov's '*The Circus*,'" in *The Slavonic and East European Review.* Vol. 74, no. 4. October 1996, pp. 601–619.

———. "Singing on the Steppes for Stalin: Ivan Pyrev and the Kolkhoz Musical in Soviet Cinema," in *The Slavic Review.* Vol. 58, no. 1. Spring 1999, pp. 143–159.

———, and Derek Spring, eds. *Stalinism and Soviet Cinema*. London and NY: Routledge, 1993.

———, and Ian Christie, eds. *The Film Factory: Russian and Soviet Cinema in Documents*. Cambridge, MA: Harvard University Press, 1988.

Youngblood, Denise J. *Movies for the Masses: Popular Cinema and Soviet Society in the 1920s*. Cambridge, UK: Cambridge University Press, 1992.

Zorkaia, Neia Markovna. *The Illustrated History of the Soviet Cinema*. NY: Hippocrene Books, 1989.

RELATED MEDIA:

Liubov' Orlova (video of Soviet motion picture biography of Orlova), directed by Gregori Alexandrov, San Francisco, CA: Ark's Intervideo.

"*Liubov Orlova, Tvorcheskii' Portret: Fragmenty Kinofil'mov* (stsenyu iz spektaklei teatra im. Mossoveta)," Melodiia (LP recording issued in 1983).

Tsirk (The Circus, video of 1936 *Mosfilm* release), Sarasota, FL: Polart, distributed by Chicago, IL: Facets Multi-Media.

Veselye Rebiata (The Happy Guys, video of 1934 Moskovskogo Kinokombinata release), Sarasota, FL: Polart, distributed by Chicago, IL: Facets Multi-Media.

Volga-Volga (video of 1938 *Mosfilm* release), San Francisco, CA: Ark's Intervideo.

John Haag,
Associate Professor of History, University of Georgia, Athens, Georgia

Ormani, Maria (fl. 1453)

Manuscript artist of Florence. *Flourished in 1453 in Florence, Italy; never married; no children.*

Maria Ormani was an Italian nun and artist. Though her origins are obscure, it is known that she was born in Florence and entered a convent there as a young woman. Ormani showed a great inclination towards the arts, and besides her classical learning she also studied painting. Eventually she became a prominent illustrator of manuscripts at her convent's scriptorium. She was apparently quite proud of her accomplishments, for she signed her work, an unusual occurrence in medieval artwork.

Her name is discovered in a breviary (a collection of hymns and prayers) she illuminated in 1453. Ormani included in the breviary a self-portrait in a nun's habit with a statement proclaiming herself the artist of the work—the image shows an attractive young woman, hands folded in front of her, with her head cocked to one side, gazing out of a decorated border. Little else is known about Ormani's life.

SOURCES:

Chadwick, Whitney. *Women, Art, and Society*. London: Thames & Hudson, 1990.

Laura York,
Riverside, California

Orme, Mary (1810–1884).

See Nichols, Mary Gove.

Ormerod, Eleanor A. (1828–1901)

English entomologist. *Born at Sedbury Park, Gloucestershire, England, on May 11, 1828; died at St. Albans on July 19, 1901; daughter of George Ormerod, F.R.S. (author of* The History of Cheshire*).*

Eleanor A. Ormerod was born at Sedbury Park, Gloucestershire, England, in 1828. She was raised on a large estate in the countryside, and even as a very young child was fascinated by the numerous insects found there, which she continued to study as she grew up. As an adult, she enjoyed a local reputation as an expert on insects and agriculture. When, in 1868, the Royal Horticultural Society began collecting insect pests for practical purposes, Ormerod contributed largely to it and was awarded the Flora medal of the society. In 1877, she distributed a pamphlet, *Notes for Observations on Injurious Insects,* to those interested in this field. When the recipients readily sent her the results of their researches, the well-known *Annual Series of Reports on Injurious Insects and Farm Pests* was launched. In 1881, Ormerod published a special report on the "turnip-fly." The following year, she was appointed consulting entomologist to the Royal Agricultural Society, a post she held until 1892, and for several years she was also a lecturer on scientific entomology at the Royal Agricultural College, Cirencester. Her renown was not limited to England. Her treatise on *The Injurious Insects of South Africa* was respected worldwide, and she received silver and gold medals from the University of Moscow for her models of insects harmful to plants, as well as the large silver medal from the Société Nationale d'Acclimatation de France (1899). She also wrote the *Cobden Journals, Manual of Injurious Insects,* and *Handbook of Insects Injurious to Orchard and Bush Fruits.* Just before her death in 1901, Ormerod was granted an honorary LL.D. from Edinburgh University, the first woman upon whom the university had conferred this degree. In making the presentation, the dean of the legal faculty said: "The preeminent position which Miss Ormerod holds in the world of science is the reward of patient study and unwearying observation. Her investigations have been chiefly directed towards the discovery of methods for the prevention of the ravages of those insects which are injurious to orchard, field and forest. Her labours have been crowned with such success that she is entitled to be hailed the protectress of agriculture and the fruits of the earth—a beneficent Demeter of the 19th century."

Ormonde, countess of.

See Bohun, Eleanor (fl. 1327–1340).
See Fitzalan, Amy (fl. 1440).
See Hankford, Anne (1431–1485).
See Beaufort, Eleanor (d. 1501).

Orpah (fl. 1100 BCE)

Biblical woman. *Born a Moabite; flourished around 1100 BCE; married Chilion (younger son of Elimelech and Naomi).*

Following the death of her husband Chilion, Orpah set out for Bethlehem with her mother-in-law ❧▸ **Naomi** and her sister-in-law ***Ruth**, both of whom had also lost their husbands. Unlike Ruth, however, Orpah made only part of the journey, then decided to return to Moab to be with her people and her gods.

◂❧ **Naomi.** See Ruth for sidebar.

Orr, Alice Greenough (1902–1995)

American rodeo champion. *Name variations: Alice Greenough. Born Alice Greenough in Montana in 1902; died on August 31, 1995, at her home in Tucson, Arizona; grew up on a ranch near Red Lodge, Montana; dropped out of school at age 14; married Ray Cahill; married Joe Orr; children: (first marriage) two, including Jay Cahill.*

Alice Greenough Orr grew up on a ranch near Red Lodge, Montana, and spent her childhood breaking wild horses; as a teenager, she delivered mail on horseback on her 35-mile route, often through snow drifts. Her goal was to become a forest ranger, one of the many opportunities newly opened to women when men marched off to World War I. When the men returned, however, the door was again closed, so Orr went to work in a rooming house. In 1929, she and her sister read an ad for bronc riders for a Wild West show.

For 20 years, under her maiden name Alice Greenough, Orr was the reigning queen of the rodeo bronc riders. Named to both the Cowboy and Cowgirl halls of fame, she won four world saddle bronc championships and was a star attraction on rodeo tours of the U.S., Australia, and Europe. (She once had tea with the queen of England, Queen ***Mary of Teck**.) Fearless, Orr rode fighting bulls into Spanish arenas, sans sword; she would then dismount and turn the bull over to a matador. She also did occasional stunt work for motion pictures and was a member of the Riding Greenoughs, a team which included her sister **Marge Henderson** and her brothers Bill and Turk. The Greenoughs could execute most rodeo events from trick riding to bull riding.

During the 1930s, competitors in rodeos were often stiffed by tour operators. To combat this, in 1936 Orr, along with others, founded what is now known as the Professional Rodeo Cowboys Association. In 1946, she began to run her own rodeo with her second husband Joe Orr. She frequently did exhibitions of saddle bronc riding, an event requiring so much more skill than bareback riding that it is no longer a competitive event on the women's circuit. After retiring in 1954, Orr continued with occasional movie assignments until she turned 80. Her last public appearance was in 1992, at a parade in Red Lodge. She died in 1995 at age 93.

Orrery, countess of.

See Monckton, Mary (1746–1840).

Orris (1820–1897).

See Ingelow, Jean.

Orsini, Adriana (fl. 1469–1502).

See Borgia, Lucrezia for sidebar on Adriana Mila.

Orsini, Alfonsina (d. 1520).

See Medici, Alfonsina de.

Orsini, Belleza (d. 1528)

Italian condemned to death for sorcery. *Died in 1528.*

The meager information about Belleza Orsini's life comes from the trial documents of the court in Fiano, where she was called to defend herself, with no success, against the charge of sorcery. A semi-educated 60-year-old, widowed at a young age, she practiced general medicine and phytotherapy and perhaps procured abortions, reaping the mistrust and hate of the little rural community of Collevecchio. Like thousands of women charged with sorcery and condemned to the stake, a proud Orsini committed suicide instead in 1528, after having confessed to never-done infamies in the vain attempt to save her life.

SOURCES:

Craveri, M. *Sante e streghe: Biografie e documentidal XIV al XVII secolo.* Milano: Feltrinelli, 1981.

Processo per stregoneria di Bellezza Orsini da Collevecchio, c. 1528, Archives in Fiano Romano, registered by A. Bertolotti in "Rivista Europea." Vol. XXXII, no. VI, 1883.

SUGGESTED READING:

Tozzi, Ileana. *Bellezza Orsini, cronaca di un processo per stregonieria.* Pescara: Nova Italica, 1990.

Ileana Tozzi, D. Litt.,
and member of Società Italiana delle Storiche
and Deputazione di Storia Patria, Rieti, Italy

Orsini, Clarice (c. 1453–1487).

See Medici, Clarice de.

Orsini, Isabella (1542–1576).

See Medici, Isabella de.

Orsini, Marie-Anne de la Tremouille (c. 1642–1722).

See Marie-Anne de la Trémouille, princess of the Ursins.

Orthryth of Mercia (fl. 7th c.)

Queen of Mercia. *Name variations: she is possibly *Ostrith. Born in the late 7th century in Northumbria, England; died in Mercia.*

Orthryth was a Saxon princess of Northumbria, England. Her marriage to the king of Mercia was arranged as part of a political liaison between the two small kingdoms, at a time when all of the British isle was divided into competing, warlike tribal kingdoms. But the peace between Northumbria and Mercia did not last long, and soon Queen Orthryth found herself warring, unwillingly, for Mercia against her native people. Orthryth believed in peace, however, and after her husband died she worked unceasingly to effect a truce. She was an intelligent, clever woman; unfortunately, this eventually worked against her, for she was killed by nobles opposed to her peaceful goals.

Laura York,
Riverside, California

Ortiz, Cristina (1950—)

Brazilian pianist who is highly acclaimed for her recordings of Heitor Villa-Lobos and other Brazilian composers. *Born in Bahia, Brazil, on April 17, 1950.*

Cristina Ortiz studied first in Brazil and then in Paris with ***Magda Tagliaferro**; advanced studies took place later with Rudolf Serkin. In 1969, she was the winner of the Van Cliburn Competition. Her successful New York recital debut took place in 1971, and by the mid-1970s she had launched an international touring career. Specializing in the works of French composers, Ortiz also made highly acclaimed recordings of the compositions of Heitor Villa-Lobos and other Brazilian composers.

John Haag,
Athens, Georgia

Ortíz de Dominguez, Josefa (c. 1768–1829)

Known as "the mother of Mexico's nationhood" and one of a handful of women of the elite class to support actively Mexico's independence from Spain between 1810 and 1821. *Name variations: Josefa Ortiz de Dominguez; La Corregidora. Born María Josefa Ortíz Girón in 1768 (some historians cite 1775), in either Valladolid or Mexico City; died at home in Mexico City on May 3, 1829; daughter of Captain Juan José Ortíz and Manuela Girón, about whom nothing is known; probably educated at home by an older sis-*

ter and other relatives; could read and write with fluency when she entered the prestigious school and asylum for women, the Colegio de las Vizcaínas in Mexico City on May 30, 1789; married the distinguished government official, Miguel Dominguez, regularized in 1793; children: María Ignacia (b. 1792); J.M. Florencio (b. 1793); Mariano (b. 1794); M. Dolores (b. 1796); Miguel (b. 1797); M. Juana (b. 1799); M. Micaela (b. 1800); Remigio (b. 1801); M. Teresa (b. 1803); M. Manuela (b. 1804); M. Ana (b. 1806); J.M. Hilarion (b. 1807); M. Magdalena (b. 1811); M. del Carmen (b. 1812).

Despite their numerous children and her husband's high position in the royalist bureaucracy, both participated in a conspiracy in Querétaro to overthrow Spanish rule (1810); warned co-conspirators in neighboring Guanajuato, Father Miguel Hidalgo and militia Captain Ignacio Allende, that their plans to overthrow the viceregal government had been betrayed (September 14, 1810); arrested and imprisoned the day Hidalgo commenced the revolt against Spanish rule (September 16, 1810); released for lack of evidence of sedition (October 22, 1810); secretly continued to support the independence movement until arrested and taken to Mexico City under heavy guard (December 29, 1813); imprisoned in the Convent of St. Teresa (January 6, 1814); released due to serious illness (April 1814); resumed contacts with insurgents and rearrested (December 22, 1815); imprisoned in the Convent of St. Catherine of Siena until her release (June 17, 1817); after Mexico gained independence, deplored the seizure of power by ex-royalist Agustín Iturbide, who was crowned emperor (1822); refused to serve as "dame of honor" in the empress' court; vindicated after Iturbide's overthrow (1823); lived to see her husband's elevation to the highest ranks of the executive and the judiciary in the early Republic of Mexico.

Josefa Ortíz de Dominguez, the brave, decisive, and legendary heroine of Mexico's independence movement, has been admired, extolled and praised by Mexicans for over eight generations. Without her timely warning in mid-September 1810 to the priest-turned-revolutionary Miguel Hidalgo and his associates, the independence movement might have been postponed for years. Yet despite Josefa's enduring fame we know little about her parents, the year of her birth, or her first 20 years. What we do know for certain about Josefa from several authentic paintings and drawings is that she was a *criolla,* which automatically placed her in the elite ranks of the 10% of the Mexican population that could boast of primarily Spanish ancestry.

Orphaned at an early age and reportedly raised by an elder sister, in May 1789 Josefa entered one of the most notable schools for women in Mexico City, the Colegio de las Vizcaínas. Established earlier in the 18th century by enlightened and wealthy Vizcayans (Basques), the school was run by educated women and was a haven for genteel orphans, young women without dowries, and needy widows. At Las Vizcaínas, younger residents were given a rigorous religious education and were also taught the domestic arts, to prepare them for either a religious life or marriage.

In 1790, approximately a year after Josefa entered Las Vizcaínas, the school was inspected by members of the city council and Miguel Dominguez, a court attorney in the viceregal government. Miguel was one of the relatively few *criollos* to attain a high position in the Spanish-run bureaucracy in Mexico City and later in the provincial capital of Querétaro. He was a distinguished lawyer whose intelligence and integrity were, beginning in 1784, recognized and rewarded by three successive viceroys. When Miguel met Josefa, he was 34, and had been a lonely widower for four years. In need of a suitable wife to help him raise four children from a first marriage, Miguel soon asked the rectora (director) of Las Vizcaínas for permission to visit Josefa regularly. He was enchanted by her great beauty, high spirits, intelligence, and lively conversation. Within months, Miguel made known his desire to marry Josefa, and, early in 1791, she left the school with her intended.

Three years after leaving Las Vizcaínas, and at age 25, Josefa was raising her own two children as well as her four stepchildren. She was endowed with an exceptionally strong constitution, for between 1794 and 1812, she went on to give birth to 12 more children. Raised as an orphan, she delighted in her large family, lavishing all the love and nurturing she had missed as a child on her devoted husband and their children.

At the end of 1800 and after the birth of their seventh child, Miguel, who had for 15 years served several viceroys with distinction and probity, was named by Viceroy Marquina to the prestigious and remunerative post of *corregidor de letras* (chief legal and financial administrator) of the prosperous city and province of Querétaro. The provincial capital was the center of wool weaving in the Viceroyalty of New Spain, while agriculture, commerce, and artisanry also flourished in the province. As *corregidor,* Miguel was not only the chief legal and financial representative of the Viceroyalty, but was also president of the municipal council, protector of the Indians, inspector general of the province, and inspector of the many wool-weaving mills in the city of Querétaro.

After a long and arduous journey that took over a month, Miguel and Josefa arrived in Querétaro with their seven children and the youngest of Josefa's stepchildren. They occupied the second story of the splendid government mansion known as the "Casas Reales" or Royal Houses. While Josefa, known from this time forward as La Corregidora, managed a large residence and supervised their children's upbringing, the corregidor embarked on a new phase of his bureaucratic career.

So many soldiers to guard one poor woman! But I with my blood shall fashion a patrimony for my children.

—Josefa Ortíz de Dominguez

Miguel, who always took his duties very seriously, immediately began inspecting the *obrajes* and *trapiches,* or wool-weaving mills, that employed up to 4,000 workers in Querétaro alone. He soon discovered that the workers, who were lured to the mills by monetary advances, were miserably exploited by the mill owners and overseers, whom the workers characterized as "tyrants rotted by greed." The mill owners were primarily *gachupines,* a derisive term for peninsular-born Spaniards. While Spaniards in Mexico numbered only about 70,000 out of a total population of over 6 million, they were deeply resented by most Mexicans because they monopolized the highest positions in church and state and were vastly over-represented in commerce, banking, manufacturing, and mining in New Spain. In one of the most memorable reports to a Viceroy penned by a Mexican public official and dated November 17, 1801, Miguel detailed the horrible conditions in the woolen mills, contrasting them with the decent treatment accorded the debt-free workers in the tobacco factory, the treasury, and the artisans' shop in the city.

The corregidor's concern for the poor and oppressed won him the eternal enmity of the Spaniards in Querétaro, but the gratitude and love of the poor and those *criollos* who were as enlightened and compassionate as he. Josefa, despite her many concerns as wife, homemaker, and mother, devoted considerable time and attention to charitable acts. It is reported that no one in need was turned away from her door empty-handed. While the mill owners and other Spaniards did all they could to undermine the corregidor's position, Miguel and Josefa were looked upon as saintly by the needy, the oppressed, and the enlightened of Querétaro.

A series of dramatic events after the arrival of a new viceroy, Iturrigaray, in 1803 and lasting until independence was achieved in 1821, had a profound and mostly negative impact on Miguel and Josefa. In 1805, the viceroy, incensed at Miguel's eloquent protest against Iturrigaray's ill-conceived attempt to aid Spain by expropriating Mexican church funds that provided low-interest loans to many landowners and entrepreneurs, suspended Miguel from office. With the help of supportive and influential friends, the couple managed to survive until 1807, when Madrid ordered that Miguel be reinstated as corregidor. On the other hand, after Napoleon's troops occupied all of Spain by May 1808, a call by Viceroy Iturrigaray for the establishment of a national congress won the instant and enthusiastic approval of both Miguel and Josefa and many other *criollos* in the realm.

Iturrigaray's plan to include Mexicans in his government during the emergency was overruled by Spaniards in Mexico City who, in mid-September 1808, arrested him and illegally removed him from office. Many educated Mexicans, who by now wanted a total break with Spain, began holding secret meetings, first in the city of Valladolid (now Morelia) in western Mexico and, once the conspirators there were betrayed, in Querétaro.

In that city in early 1810, Miguel and Josefa and a number of *criollo* priests, lawyers, small landowners, civil servants and members of the colonial militia formed a "literary society" to cloak their true purpose. They met regularly at the Dominguez residence and then at other locations. The Querétaro conspirators corresponded and met with like-minded patriots in neighboring Guanajuato and accumulated caches of arms and ammunition in various safe houses in both provinces. By late August, and assured of the support of a number of militia units, the conspirators planned to begin an uprising in mid-October 1810. As happened in the 1809 Valladolid conspiracy, in Querétaro the plot was revealed by insiders who had a change of heart.

On September 14, 1810, the corregidores learned of the betrayal and took action immediately. That night, Miguel, in order to avoid further suspicion and to insure that his co-conspirators were unharmed by royalists, found himself in the anomalous position of having to round up and jail his fellow conspirators. Meanwhile, Josefa warned a loyal bailiff, Ignacio Pérez, who occupied quarters below her, of their danger. She begged him to warn four fellow conspirators in neighboring Guanajuato—the priest Miguel Hidalgo, and the militia officers Allende, Abasola, and Aldama—that their plans for the October uprising had been discovered.

As soon as the corregidora's message reached them, on the night of September 16, 1810, the resolute Father Hidalgo raised the banner of revolt in his parish at Dolores. Bearing the popularly revered image of the Virgin of Guadalupe, within days Hidalgo was joined by thousands of poor Mexicans who responded to his call by shouting "Long live the Virgin of Guadalupe" and, without any encouragement from Hidalgo and his associates, the ominous "Death to the *gachupines.*"

The corregidores and most *criollos* who wanted independence had envisioned a purely military revolt between Mexican militia units and the royalist army. Instead, the Hidalgo revolt soon degenerated into a ghastly civil war in which civilians were the chief victims. Miguel and Josefa were especially appalled when 300 Spanish men, women, and children in Guanajuato were all slaughtered by hordes who, unlike their leaders, were bent more on revenge than independence. While many *criollos* shifted their allegiance back to the royalists after the massacres, Josefa, and to a lesser extent her husband, never wavered in support for independence.

On the night of September 16, when Hidalgo began the independence movement in Guanajuato, a minor official in Querétaro arrested and imprisoned both Miguel and Josefa. The next day a higher official intervened and released Miguel, who was returned to his post as corregidor. However, Josefa, no doubt because of her emphatic support for independence, was not released until October 22, 1810. At the time, she was pregnant with her 13th child, born on March 14, 1811, only months before Hidalgo and his associates were captured, interrogated, and then executed in late July 1811.

Totally dependent on his salary to support his family and convinced that independence was unattainable, Miguel had no alternative but to fulfill his duties until his term ended in 1813. Josefa, on the other hand, was unwavering in her support of Hidalgo's successors, the lawyer Ignacio Rayón in western Mexico and the priest-turned-general José María Morelos in the south. She wrote secretly to both from 1811 to late 1813, despite the high risk to herself, her children, and her husband.

On December 14, 1813, a viceregal political agent and visitor general wrote from Querétaro that "La Corregidora is the most effective agent [of the insurgency] in spreading hatred against the King, Spain and the [royalist] cause." On December 29, 1813, Viceroy Calleja, who was responsible for the military defeat of Hidalgo and his successors, ordered that Josefa be arrested and brought to Mexico City. That same day, Calleja wrote to Miguel that the "scandalous conduct" of his wife in support of the revolution had led to her arrest. Calleja warned Miguel that he was to do nothing to impede his wife's arrest for sedition. Miguel was forced to turn his wife over to a military officer and the many soldiers who accompanied him. On the way to Mexico City and as fearless as ever, Josefa tried to win over the soldiers who were guarding her. She was told to be silent by the officer in charge. Her famous response was, "You were ordered to take me prisoner but not to silence me. Carry out your orders and I will fulfill my obligations."

Josefa, ailing and in her last pregnancy, was imprisoned in the severe Convent of Saint Teresa. After appeals to Viceroy Calleja by her husband and herself, she was released to Miguel's custody by April 1814. Shortly after, she suffered a miscarriage. To increase their woe, Miguel was beginning to suffer from cataracts. In Mexico City, their eldest children supported them and paid the rent for the modest house they occupied on the aptly named "Street of the Sad Indian."

Despite their desperate situation, Josefa resumed her pro-independence activities by writing and meeting with other insurgents. On December 22, 1815, an incensed Viceroy Calleja had her arrested again, and she languished in the Convent of Saint Catherine of Siena until Calleja's more humane successor, Viceroy Apodaca, released her on June 17, 1817.

When Spain finally lost control of Mexico in August 1821, Miguel and Josefa, republicans to the core, were appalled when an ex-royalist army officer Agustín Iturbide seized power and had himself declared emperor of Mexico in 1822. Before his coronation, Josefa and Miguel met with old insurgents and anti-Iturbidistas in their modest residence. Detected by Iturbide's minions, they were placed under house arrest. After Iturbide's coronation, his consort **Ana Maria Huarte Iturbide** was in need of respected women to form part of her court. When her envoys offered Josefa the post of "dame of honor" to the empress, Josefa is reported to have responded that "she who is sovereign in her own home cannot be servant of an Empress."

Vindication for the long-suffering Dominguez family came after Iturbide was overthrown on March 30, 1823. Immediately after, a Supreme Executive Power was established to guide the emerging nation in its transition to a constitutional republic. Two days later, Miguel, despite his failing vision, was appointed to that body. After the promulgation of a new constitution on October 10, 1824, Miguel was appointed to serve as chief justice of the newly formed Supreme Court.

Despite these honors, the couple remained at the old house on the Street of the Sad Indian. Josefa, unlike another heroine of Mexican independence, *Leona Vicario**, refused any compensation for her enormous suffering and sacrifices in the cause of independence. Her health began to fail by 1827 and when she died on May 2, 1829, her distraught husband and children led an enormous procession to her "beloved prison," the Convent of St. Catherine of Siena, where she was interred. Her grief-stricken husband survived Josefa by a little more than a year.

While the memory of the exemplary corregidor is revered in all of Mexico, it is Josefa who has received the most attention in history books and in public monuments. After her death and into the 20th century, La Corregidora was memorialized by numerous plaques in churches, convents, government buildings, schools and private residences in Mexico City and Querétaro. An imposing statue of a seated Josefa Ortíz de Dominguez graces the beautiful colonial Plaza of Santo Domingo in the capital. A copy is also found in Querétaro; both stand as a fitting tribute to one of the most remarkable women in Mexico's history.

SOURCES:

Leduc, Alberto, *et al. Diccionario de Geografía, Historia y Biografía.* 3 vols. Mexico: Librería de la Vda. de C. Bouret, 1910.

Ramírez lvarez, José Guadalupe. *Doña María Josefa Ortíz de Dominguez: Corregidora de Querétaro.* Querétaro, Qro: Ediciones, Culturales del Gobierno del Estado, 1975.

Rosa Pérez, Jesús. *Heroínas de México: Doña Josefa Ortíz de Dominguez: La Corregidora de Querétaro.* México: Imprenta Manuel Leon Sanchez, 1964.

Sosa, Francisco. *Biografías de Mexicanos Distinguidos.* México: Oficina Tipográfica de la Secretaría de Fomento, 1884.

Vara de González, Armida. *Doña Josefa Ortíz de Dominguez.* México: Departamento Editorial de la Presidencia, 1976.

SUGGESTED READING:

Zárate Toscano, Verónica. *Josefa Ortíz de Dominguez.* México: Comisión Nacional para las Celebraciones del 175 Aniversario de la Independencia Nacional y 75 Aniversario de la Revolución Mexicana, 1985.

Anna Macías,
Professor Emerita of History, Ohio Wesleyan University, Delaware, Ohio

Ortrud of Schleswig-Holstein-Sonderburg-Glucksburg (1925—)

Princess of Schleswig-Holstein-Sonderburg-Glucksburg. *Born in 1925; daughter of Albert, prince of Schleswig-Holstein-Sonderburg-Glucksburg, and* ****Hertha of Ysenburg and Budingen*** *(1883–1972); married Ernest Augustus Guelph, in 1951; children: six, including Ernest Augustus and Alexandra.*

Orzeszkowa, Eliza (1841–1910)

Polish advocate for women's rights and novelist. *Name variations: Eliza Orzeszko or Orszeszko. Born Eliza Pawlowska in 1841 in Milkowszczyzna, Lithuania; died 1910 in Grodno, Poland; married Pietr Orzeszko (a Polish noble), in 1857; no children.*

Eliza Orzeszkowa is one of the best-known Polish writers of the 19th century. Born into a rural gentry family in Lithuania in 1841, she was well educated in Warsaw. She married a fellow student, Pietr Orzeszko, when she was 16. They were forced to flee their home during the Polish revolt against Russian rule in 1863. When the revolt failed, many of its supporters, including Eliza's husband, were sent into exile in Siberia by the Russian government. Orzeszkowa never saw him again, and undertook a long struggle to have her marriage annulled. His estates were confiscated, while she lost her own inherited lands due to high taxation, thus losing her only sources of income.

Orzeszkowa settled in Grodno (in present-day Byelorussia) in 1866 and turned to writing as a means of supporting herself. Her experiences during the rebellion against Russia combined with her intellectual upbringing to lead her to write novels and short stories that are at once patriotic, feminist, and humanitarian. Perhaps her most powerful novel was her second, *Marta*, published in 1872. In it, Orzeszkowa drew on her own story to depict the life of a young Polish widow struggling to survive in a society which denied women basic legal rights. Writing with the pragmatism and realism characteristic of the period's Positivist literary movement, Orzeszkowa addressed the need to free women from the tradition of arranged marriages and for increased employment opportunities. She viewed education as fundamental to the emancipation of women, especially poor women, and advocated a free public education system for all Polish children. By the 1870s, Orzeszkowa had become a well-known and outspoken proponent of women's rights, a role she maintained both in her fiction and politically throughout her life. A leader of the emerging feminist movement in Poland, Orzeszkowa wanted to expand women's roles in Polish society beyond the conventional roles of wife and mother.

Her works are often openly anti-Russian and strongly Polish nationalist. Orzeszkowa was also moved by the desperate situation of the Polish peasantry and wrote with sensitivity about their struggles against oppressive landowners, for example in *Cham*, published in 1889. Several novels, most notably *Eli Makower* (1874) and *Meir Ezofowicz* (1878), addressed the widespread religious and racial intolerance faced by Polish Jews.

Her realistic characters and frank, sympathetic depictions of the hardships endured by the Polish underclasses brought Orzeszkowa a surprisingly wide readership. Her popularity marked an increasing recognition of women writers in her native country, although she was one of only a handful of Polish women able to support themselves as authors. It also marked the emergence of progressive ideology in a society whose literature had previously been characterized by conservative secular and religious themes. Orzeszkowa achieved a considerable foreign audience as well.

Her novels of the 1890s coincided with and helped shape the period of Polish literature called "Young Poland." Like other works of the period, they addressed the disillusionment of Polish intellectuals with the economic and cultural impact of industrialization being felt across Europe, which had brought little prosperity to Eastern Europe. As more and more Polish women began to work outside the home in the newly industrialized towns, activists like Orzeszkowa fought for protections in the workplace and for higher wages. In 1896, she converted her own home into a sort of underground school for young women, to provide the learning she believed was necessary for them to become truly equal members of Polish society.

Orzeszkowa died at age 69 at her home in Grodno. As the leading advocate in the 19th century for women's equality in a period of economic and social transition, Orzeszkowa was perhaps the major influence on the later development of the Polish women's movement.

SOURCES:

Jaworski, Rudolf, and Bianka Pietrow-Ennker, eds. *Women in Polish Society.* Boulder, CO: East European Monographs, 1992.

Morska, Irena. *Polish Authors of Today and Yesterday.* NY: S.F. Vanni, 1947.

Laura York,
Riverside, California

Osborn, Emily Mary (1834–c. 1885)

British artist who specialized in portraits as well as genre and narrative paintings. *Born in Essex, England, in 1834; died around 1885; attended art classes at Mr. Dickinson's Academy, London; never married; no children.*

Although she earned the bulk of her living from her genre paintings and portraits, British artist Emily Mary Osborn is best known for her narrative paintings, particularly those dealing with the plight of women. She was born in Essex in 1834, the eldest child of a cleric. In 1848, her father was transferred to a church in London, where Osborn began art classes at Mr. Dickinson's Academy. She continued her studies with John Mogford, a minor landscape painter, and with James Matthew Leigh, a portrait and history painter who exercised great influence over her developing style. In 1851, at age 17, Osborn had some of her genre and landscape paintings accepted at the Royal Academy. She continue to exhibit there through 1884, and later also had exhibitions at the British Institution and the Society of British Artists, as well as in such commercial establishments as Grosvenor Gallery and the New Gallery, in London. Early in her career, Osborn was honored by the eminent patronage of Queen *__Victoria__ who purchased two of her paintings: *My Cottage Door* (1855) and *The Governess*, the latter of which won acclaim at the Royal Academy show of 1860.

The narrative mode, in which Osborn painted some of her best-known works, was originally made popular by William Hogarth (1697–1764) in the 18th century and was still in vogue well into the 19th century. (Modern-day art historians tend to dismiss the narrative and domestic paintings of this period as trivial and sentimental when compared to other art of its day.) A narrative painting was intended to be "read," rather than simply viewed, and to be appreciated for its message as well as its visual appeal. Many of Osborn's paintings of this type deal with themes of victimized women, often those who are social outcasts or the target of prejudice. A work called *Nameless and Friendless* (1857) is particularly rare in that it depicts the plight of a woman artist attempting to sell her work. In the center foreground of the painting, a poorly dressed young woman just in from the rain is displaying her artwork to an elderly dealer. In the background several gentlemen in top hats ogle the young woman, as they look up from a print of a dancing girl. Also in the background stands an anonymous woman who is obviously better dressed than the main figure. Every detail of the painting, notes *Ms.* magazine, from composition to the costume of the central figure, serves the drama which it relates. "That she is an unmarried orphan is indicated by her black dress and ringless left hand; that she is poor, by her worn clothes, unfashionable shawl, and shabby, dripping umbrella; that her social status is low is emphasized by the eloquent emptiness of the chair against which the umbrella is propped. Had she been a wealthy 'lady' client . . . she would naturally have been sitting down rather than standing up."

Osborn's other narrative works include *For the Last Time* (1864), *God's Acre* (1868), and the prize-winning *Half the World Knows Not How the Other Half Lives* (1864), and all deal with the dark themes of poverty and death in the lives of young women. More cheerful were Osborn's portraits, among them *Philip Gosse, Jr.*, *Madame Bodichon*, and a more ambitious work, *Mrs Sturgis and Children*, a life-sized portrait which appeared in the Royal Academy Exhibition of 1855. **Ann Sutherland Harris** and **Linda Nochlin** explain that a portrait of this type, of an upper-class woman and her children in an outdoor setting, is reminiscent of the works of Thomas Gainsborough (1727–1788), Joshua Reynolds (1723–1792), and Thomas Lawrence (1769–1830). Osborn's work is unique in that the background setting is a beach rather than a landscape. They attribute this to the possible influence of William Powell Frith's work *Life at the Seaside*.

SOURCES:

"Emily Mary Osborn (1834–c. 1885)," in *Ms.* July 1974.

Harris, Ann Sutherland, and Linda Nochlin. *Women Artists: 1550–1950.* NY: Alfred A. Knopf, 1976.

Barbara Morgan,
Melrose, Massachusetts

Osborne, Dorothy (1627–1695)

English letter writer. *Born in 1627 in Chicksands Priory, Bedfordshire, England; died in 1695 in Moor Park, near Farnham, Surrey, England; daughter of Sir Peter Osborne (an eminent Royalist) and Lady Dorothy Danvers; married William Temple, in 1654 or 1655; children: Diana Temple; John Temple; several who died in infancy.*

Dorothy Osborne was born in 1627 in Chicksands Priory, England, the youngest of 11 children of Sir Peter Osborne and Lady **Dorothy Danvers**. Osborne met Sir William Temple when she was 21; for the next seven years, they courted, mostly through correspondence, because their families disapproved. Despite this and an attack of smallpox which left Dorothy scarred, the two married in 1654 or 1655. Her husband, a Royalist like her father, would become a diplomat, statesman, and writer.

During their 40 years of marriage, Osborne was William's advisor, and support. She was a diplomat and hostess during his service as ambassador in Brussels, The Hague, Ireland, and London. Charles II even commended her for her bravery during a sea battle against the Dutch in 1671, and her friendship with the future Queen ***Mary II** aided her husband's negotiations concerning Mary's royal marriage to William III. They lost several children in infancy, and daughter Diana died at age 14. Their son John became secretary-at-war before jumping to his death from a boat near London Bridge. Osborne herself died in 1695 in Surrey, England.

Osborne's letters were known for their wit and acerbic tone, and were extremely useful to historians for the detail they provide about the lives of young English women of the time. The letters written to her future husband before their marriage, from 1652 to 1654, were published by T.P. Courtenay in his 1836 *Memoirs of the Life, Works and Correspondence of Sir William Temple.* E.A. Parry published the complete series of 70 letters from Osborne to Temple in 1888; another edition, praised by ***Virginia Woolf**, was published in 1928.

SOURCES:

Buck, Claire, ed. *The Bloomsbury Guide to Women's Literature.* NY: Prentice Hall, 1992.

Shattock, Joanne. *The Oxford Guide to British Women Writers.* Oxford: Oxford University Press, 1993.

Jacqueline Mitchell,
freelance writer, Detroit, Michigan

Osborne, Margaret (1918—)

American tennis player. *Name variations: Margaret Osborne duPont; Mrs. W. duPont. Born Margaret Osborne on March 4, 1918, in Joseph, Oregon; married William duPont, in 1947 (divorced 1964); children: one son.*

Won first national title (1936); won French Open singles titles (1946, 1949); won Wimbledon singles title (1947); won U.S. championship singles titles (1948, 1949, 1950); with Louise Brough, won French Open doubles titles three times, Wimbledon doubles titles five times, the U.S. doubles championship twelve times; won U.S. mixed doubles championship nine times; inducted into the Tennis Hall of Fame (1967).

Born in 1918, Margaret Osborne spent her earliest years on a farm in Oregon before her family moved to Spokane, Washington, when she was ten. In Spokane, she frequently passed by some old tennis courts, and her mother, seeing Margaret's interest, gave her a tennis racket. When the family moved to San Francisco shortly thereafter, she began playing on the public tennis courts at Golden Gate Park. Soon she was competing in junior club tournaments, though she did not receive her first formal tennis lesson (from an ex-Davis Cup contender) until she was 17. The following year, in 1936, Osborne won the national girl's 18-and-under title. She was ranked 7th in the nation by the time she turned 20, and while winning 37 major tournaments over the next two decades would be ranked in the national Top 10 a total of 14 times, reaching #1 in 1948 and remaining there until 1950.

In 1942, Osborne joined with *****Louise Brough** in a doubles partnership that would go down in tennis history. Their games were very similar: they both drove the ball hard from the baseline and attacked the net so frequently that critics said they played like men. With Osborne in the leadership role, the duo went on to win five Wimbledon doubles and 12 U.S. doubles championships. Until Osborne's temporary retirement in 1951 to give birth to her son, the two women were an unbeatable force on the court, and they competed together at select events until the mid-1950s. Though they were best friends off the court, they were fierce competitors when matched against each other in singles competition—an event that occurred so often that sportswriters began to refer to them as "the inevitable Osborne and Brough." Between them, they won every Wimbledon and U.S. singles title between 1947 and 1951. Their rivalry produced some exciting tennis, including the 1949 Wimbledon final, which Brough won, and the 1948 Forest Hills final, which ended with Osborne triumphant. Playing solo, Osborne also won the French championship in 1946 and 1949, Wimbledon in 1947, the U.S. championship in 1948, 1949, and 1950, and the Wightman Cup 10 times.

There were other doubles partners, including **Sarah Palfrey**, Bill Talbert, Ken McGregor, Ken Rosewall, and Neale Fraser. In fact, Osborne was playing mostly doubles when she turned 40 in 1958; that same year, she ranked 5th in the nation. In 1960, playing with Fraser at the U.S. mixed doubles championships, she won her last major title. Osborne was a nine-time captain of the U.S. Wightman Cup team, leading them to victory in eight competitions; one of these was the last game of her career, in 1962.

Osborne and her husband divorced in 1964, and she later shared a home and a successful thoroughbred breeding and racing business in El Paso, Texas, with **Margaret Varner Bloss**, a former doubles partner. With her 37 victories at major tournaments, Osborne was once ranked 4th in the list of all-time women's tennis champions, following *****Margaret Smith Court** (62 wins), *****Martina Navratilova** (54 wins), and *****Billie Jean King** (39 wins). Considered one of the finest all-around American tennis players, she was inducted into the Tennis Hall of Fame in 1967.

SOURCES:

Johnson, Anne Janette. *Great Women In Sports*. Detroit, MI: Visible Ink, 1998.

King, Billie Jean. *We Have Come a Long Way: The Story of Women's Tennis*. NY: McGraw-Hill, 1988.

Jacqueline Mitchell,
freelance writer, Detroit, Michigan

Osborne, Mary (1921–1992)

American jazz guitarist. *Born on July 17, 1921, in Minot, North Dakota; died in Bakersfield, California, on March 4, 1992; married Ralph Scaffidi (a trumpet player).*

When singer-guitarist Mary Osborne was 17 and listening to musicians playing in her hometown of Bismarck, North Dakota, she heard a new instrument—an electric guitar. "The only electric guitar I knew of was the Hawaiian guitar," she said. "I'd listen to all the jazz guitarists of the time, but they all played acoustic. But here was Charlie Christian playing Django Reinhardt's 'St. Louis Blues' note for note but with an electric guitar. It was the most startling thing I'd ever heard." The next day, she found a guitar for $85. A friend built an amplifier for $45 and her career was launched. She soon went on the road with a female trio, was a guitarist for Dick Stabile, and then joined Buddy Rogers' band. When Osborne arrived in New York, Rogers' group broke up, but she quickly got jobs at radio stations, recording studios, and clubs on West 52nd. Eventually, she formed her own trio. She and her husband, trumpeter Ralph Scaffidi, moved to Bakersfield, California, where they formed the Osborne Guitar Company (later Osborne Sound Laboratories), which manufactured amplifiers for guitars, then branched out into public-address systems. Well known in the jazz world, Mary Osborne recorded nine albums, backed recordings for *****Mary Lou Williams**, Coleman Hawkins, and *****Ethel Waters**, and continued to give concerts before her death in 1992.

SOURCES:

Kinkle, Roger D. *The Complete Encyclopedia of Popular Music and Jazz: 1900–1950*. Vol. 3. New Rochelle, NY: Arlington House, 1974.

"Mary Osborne, Electric Guitarist, Lauded in Jazz World, Dies at 70," in *The New York Times Biographical Service.* March 1992, p. 271.

John Haag,
Associate Professor of History, University of Georgia, Athens, Georgia

Osborne, Sarah.

See Witchcraft Trials in Salem Village.

Osborne, Susan M. (1858–1918)

American philanthropist. *Born in 1858; died in 1918.*

At age 19, Susan Osborne founded the Home for Friendless Women and Girls in New York City, and later established a refuge shelter there. For 41 years, she continued as the active head of these institutions, which were supported by voluntary subscriptions, and it was one of her rules that no one was to be turned away. Besides caring for homeless girls and women, Osborne also fed, clothed, and partly supported many homeless men.

Osburga (?–c. 855)

Queen of Wessex and the English. *Name variations: Osburh; Osburgha; she is often confused with a St. Osburga who founded Coventry Abbey. Date of birth unknown; died around 855; daughter of Oslac the Thane of the Isle of Wight, grand butler of England; became first wife of Æthelwulf also known as Ethelwolf or Ethelwulf (c. 800–858), king of Wessex and the English (r. 839–856, abdicated), about 835 (divorced 853); children: Ethelstan, king of Kent; Ethelbald (c. 834–860), king of Wessex and the English (r. 855–860); Ethelbert (c. 836–865), king of Kent and the English (r. 860–865); Ethelred I (c. 840–871), king of the English (r. 865–871); Alfred the Great (c. 848–c. 900), king of the English (r. 871–899);* ****Ethelswyth*** *(c. 843–889). Ethelwulf's second wife was* ****Judith Martel.***

Osburga was queen to Ethelwulf, son of Egbert, a great king of Wessex who had come out of exile in France around 800 to take back his territory from the king of Mercia. She had at least six children, including Alfred the Great. It is commonly assumed that Osburga, thought to be noble by birth and nature, could also read, a rare accomplishment for a woman of her day. The Welsh monk Asser relates in his *Life of King Alfred:* "Now it chanced a certain day that his Mother showed to him and to his brothers a book of Saxon poetry, which she held in her hand, and said, 'I will give this book to that one among you who shall the most quickly learn it.' . . . [Alfred] took the book from her hand and went to his master, and read it: and when he had read it he brought it back to his Mother and repeated it to her."

Osburn, Lucy (1835–1891)

British nurse universally admired as "Australia's Florence Nightingale." *Born in Leeds, England, on May 10, 1835; died of diabetes in Harrogate, England, on December 22, 1891; daughter of William Osburn and Ann (Rimington) Osburn; had a sister Ann; studied at the Nightingale Training School of Nursing attached to London's St. Thomas' Hospital, graduating in September 1867; studied midwifery at King's College Hospital; never married; no children.*

Against family's wishes, studied nursing in London; chosen by Florence Nightingale to introduce her nursing principles to Australia (1868); despite her own poor health, transformed the Sydney Infirmary and Dispensary into a model institution; resigned her position (1884) because of declining health, returning to England where she continued to minister to the indigent sick.

Lucy Osburn was an enthusiastic traveler in an age when most women rarely left their hometowns; she accompanied her father William Osburn, a respected Egyptologist, on several of his research trips to the land of the Nile. From childhood on, Lucy suffered from chest infections and bronchitis during the foul British winter months, and spent many winters in milder climes working as an unpaid secretary for her father. Unmarried and in her mid-20s, Osburn surprised her family when she announced that she wished to take up nursing as a career. Unaware of the changes that ***Florence Nightingale** had succeeded in bringing about in British hospitals, William opposed her plans as completely unsuitable for his intelligent, cultivated daughter. Prior to Nightingale's reforms, the lowly and low-paying task of nursing in filthy and overcrowded public hospitals had often fallen by default to women who were—by reason of ignorance, incapacity or alcohol—unable to find other work.

The inheritance of a small legacy gave Osburn a degree of independence that made it possible for her to defy her father. In 1866, she enrolled in the Nightingale Training School of Nursing attached to London's prestigious St. Thomas' Hospital. Here she gained valuable experience working in both men's and women's surgical, medical, and accident wards. Impressed by Nightingale's insistence on "hygienic principles" which saw hospitals not as filthy places where the poor went only to suffer and die, but as institutions where skill and compassion could restore many to health and allow the moribund to die in dignity, Osburn quickly developed into a skilled, no-nonsense medical professional. Determined to become a nurse, she remained steadfast despite the fact that her father had turned her portrait to the wall. Fortunately, Osburn could rely on the emotional support of her sister **Ann**, a teacher who dreamed of leaving the oppressive Osburn home and founding a school based on modern, progressive principles.

After graduating from her training course in September 1867, Osburn had earned the title of Sister Osburn, one of "Miss Nightingale's nurses." She promptly continued her education by studying midwifery at another major teaching hospital in London, King's College Hospital. In 1867, the government of the Australian state of New South Wales appealed to Nightingale for trained nurses to staff the Sydney Infirmary and Dispensary. Osburn was invited to apply for the job of Lady Superintendent at this hospital, known locally as either the Old Sydney Hospital or the Rum Hospital, so-called because it had been built decades earlier with a levy raised on the sale of rum. Osburn was expected to establish a training school in New South Wales based on Nightingale's principles.

Along with five other nursing sisters, Osburn arrived in Sydney Cove on March 1868, after a long and typically uncomfortable voyage. Wearing their white starched caps and nurse's uniforms, they were greeted by cheering crowds lining the Circular Quay and Macquarie Street. Lucy, slim, pretty, and well educated, quickly enchanted the New South Wales colonial secretary Sir Henry Parkes, who had requested the nurses and through whose efforts an Act requiring hospitals to be inspected had recently been passed by the provincial legislature. Within a week of their arrival, however, ceremonial pleasantries would be replaced by a full-blown medical emergency. After the visiting duke of Edinburgh had been shot and wounded by a mentally unbalanced man named Henry James O'Farrell, Lucy Osburn was called on to supervise the successful nursing back to health of the convalescent duke.

Sydney Hospital on Macquarie Street dated back to 1816, and Osburn soon realized the immensity of the work she faced. Shown around the long building with wide verandas, she and the other nurses were horrified to learn that there was no running water, that the hospital's wards were swarming with vermin, and that the kitchens were "thick with grease." Roaches could be seen in the patients' bandages. The stench in the wards was overpowering, the result of filth, neglect and poor ventilation. The terrible odor of the facility was a combination of makeshift latrines, open sewers, and the putrefying flesh of patients who, covered with bedsores, lay neglected by the staff on mattresses that were rotting from urine and fecal matter. At night, huge black rats roamed at will, running across patients' beds, even invading the mortuary and gnawing on corpses. Osburn was appalled, and several of her nurses were physically ill after their initial exposure to the conditions.

Lucy Osburn

Although she and her nurses had been promised quarters in a new nurses' residence, this facility was not yet finished. Consequently, they had to live in damp, dirty rooms in the already overcrowded hospital. Despite Osburn's weak constitution and an attack of dysentery which laid her low for two months, bringing on frequent vomiting attacks in April and May 1868 (but which, typically, she made light of in her letters to Nightingale), she was determined to reform the hospital and acted swiftly to impose discipline on the staff. The hospital's "nurses" were underpaid and had few if any qualifications for their various jobs. Some had been cleaners, unimpressive to behold, with unwashed hair and bawdy vocabularies. Some, Osburn suspected, supplemented their incomes as prostitutes while others picked up a few shillings by smuggling alcohol to patients. Often, the "nurses" became drunk alongside their patients, even having sex with them. Despite this, by December 1868, Osburn had been able to train 16 nurses.

The obstacles she faced were at times so huge that she felt total isolation. She was opposed by the hospital's visiting surgeon, Sir Alfred Roberts, although he had been instrumental in prodding Parkes to contact Nightingale. On a visit to London, Roberts discovered that Nightingale had received unfavorable letters about Osburn from two of her nurses, **Bessie Chant** and **Annie Miller**. The reason for Miller's displeasure was clear: she had been disciplined by Osburn for allowing a married house surgeon to visit her bedroom at night, and she feared reprisals from his wife if the incident should become known. On his return to Sydney, Roberts spread rumors that Nightingale was disappointed with Osburn's work. Fortunately, Osburn had found a champion in Parkes, who wrote her that Roberts was "a respectable professional man . . . but he is . . . a fusy [sic], officious diletente [sic] in all matters of sanitary reform, who spoils his own efforts to be useful by his desire to be the authority on all occasions." Roberts believed in the necessity of medical reforms, but he found it hard to believe that these changes might come from a "mere nurse" like Lucy Osburn.

Further opposition to Osburn's reform efforts came from one of her own nurses, Sister **Haldane Colquhoun Turriff**. Capable and talented as well as caustic and controlling, Turriff saw herself as Osburn's successor and wrote negative letters to Nightingale in the hope that Osburn would be dismissed and she would replace her. When the nurses' three-year contracts came up for renewal in 1870, Turriff was not recommended for a new contract by Osburn who, with Nightingale, had been alienated by her actions. Turriff continued her career as first matron at Melbourne's Alfred Hospital, where she was successful enough that even her critics had to concede that her nurses were the best in that city.

Even with Turriff's departure, many difficulties remained. Medicine at this time was an exclusively male profession; there were no female physicians in the wards who could support Osburn. Thus, she had to depend on male doctors for help in her reform efforts, and many of them supported Roberts, whose main goal appeared to be one of sabotaging the Osburn agenda. This included refusing to write essential information about a patient's condition on the chart that hung at the end of each bed. When Osburn tried to hold lectures for trainee nurses, Roberts or one of his medical colleagues would arrive unexpectedly and demand that the nurses return to their ward duties or prepare patients for surgery.

Even the most innocent incidents could turn into nasty confrontations. When Osburn ordered a staff member to burn a roach-infested box of moldy books that included some pages torn from an old Bible, the event was, as she recounted, "magnified into a systematic and determined burning of Bibles on my part." In this instance, the deliberate distortion was spread by Sister Annie Miller. Once the garbled Bible-burning story appeared in print in the *Protestant Standard*, a legislative subcommittee was hastily convened to judge Osburn's actions. After six weeks of deliberations and political posturing, she was cleared of all charges. Despite these incidents, Osburn refused to bow to pressure. Indeed, Sir Henry Parkes and others in public life became increasingly impressed by her.

Growing discontent with the slow pace of change at the hospital, which many now laid at the door of Osburn's corrupt and incompetent superiors, led in 1873 to the New South Wales Legislative Assembly appointing a Royal Commission of Inquiry. Much information was gathered during the commission's life, which examined 59 witnesses, including Osburn. Further inquiries took place that same year when the Royal Commission on Public Charities was convened under the chair of Judge Sir William Charles Windeyer. Although Roberts presented evidence that Osburn had failed in her duties, Judge Windeyer, a strong advocate of social reforms, was not convinced. He was likely strengthened in his determination to back Osburn because of the resolve of his remarkable wife, Lady ***Mary Windeyer**. One of Australia's women's rights pioneers, in 1895 Mary Windeyer founded the Women's Hospital of Sydney. She was also president of the Womanhood Suffrage League of New South Wales and played leadership roles in the Women's Industrial Exhibition of 1888, and in the Woman's Christian Temperance Union of New South Wales. In the Royal Commission's final report, written by Judge Windeyer, Osburn was strongly vindicated. The report presented the public with incontrovertible evidence of Sydney Hospital's "horrible" conditions. The Commission accused the politicians of the House Committee of "utter neglect" of the situation, and accused those in charge of the institution of having made every major managerial error Nightingale warned against. Beside praising Osburn for the "vast improvement in the nursing services," the commisson also gave her a raise.

In the public indignation that followed the release of the report, Superintendent John Blackstone was fired. With his departure, it became easier for Osburn's reforms to be implemented from the ground up. Slowly, the Sydney Hospital under Osburn's leadership became a model institution. Osburn was now officially in charge of wards and patients, as well as cooking and domestic staffs. With each passing year, higher levels of professionalism were attained. Personally, Osburn forged strong bonds of friendship with Lady Windeyer and her daughter, Osburn's namesake **Lucy Windeyer**, as well as with **Emily Macarthur** and her daughter ***Elizabeth Macarthur Onslow**. However, despite her professional achievements in Australia, which had laid the strong foundations of one of the best nursing systems in the world, Osburn increasingly longed to return to England, particularly in order to see her sister Ann again. In 1884, with reforms firmly in place, she resigned her post. By this time, Osburn had been diagnosed with diabetes, a life-threatening illness in this time before the discovery of insulin.

Arriving in London, she sought the best medical advice, hoping she could one day return to Australia. By 1886, her iron will had enabled her to bring her illness under control, and in that year she began working as an underpaid district nurse among the sick poor of London's Bloomsbury district. Once again displaying remarkable powers of concentration despite fragile health, she remained the workaholic she had always been and so advanced to the position of Superintendent of the Southwark, Newington and Walworth District Nursing Association. Although she still spoke of returning to far-off Australia, Osburn's diabetic condition grew worse with each passing year, and her physicians advised her not to undertake such strenuous travel. She became frailer, and increasingly suffered from fainting attacks. On December 1891, while visiting her sister Ann's boarding school, Dunorlan, in Harrogate, Lucy Osburn died of complications of diabetes. She was 56 years old. From the funds she had left behind in New South Wales, Osburn bequeathed £100 to young Lucy Windeyer. Australians continue to honor the determined woman who brought the ideals of modern nursing, the reforms of Florence Nightingale, to what was then a remote outpost of the British Empire.

SOURCES:

Bessant, Bob. "Milestones in Australian Nursing," in *The Collegian: Journal of the Royal College of Nursing, Australia.* Vol. 6, no. 4. October 1999, insert section, pp. 1–3.

Conway, Jill. "Gender in Australia," in *Daedalus: Journal of the American Academy of Arts and Sciences.* Vol. 114, no. 1, 1985, pp. 343–368.

Cope, Sir Zachary. *Six Disciples of Florence Nightingale.* London: Pitman, 1961.

De Vries, Susanna. *Strength of Spirit: Pioneering Women of Achievement from First Fleet to Federation.* Alexandria, NSW: Millenium Books, 1995.

Evans, E.P. "Nursing in Australia," in *International Nursing Review.* Vol. 12, 1936.

Griffith, John. "Osburn, Lucy (1835–1891)," in Douglas Pike *et al.*, eds., *Australian Dictionary of Biography.* 15 vols. Melbourne: Melbourne University Press, 1966–2000, Vol. 5., 1974, pp. 377–378.

Horne, Donald. *The Australian People: Biography of a Nation.* Sydney: Angus & Robertson, 1972.

MacDonnell, Freda. *Miss Nightingale's Young Ladies: The Story of Lucy Osburn and Sydney Hospital.* Sydney: Angus & Robertson, 1970.

Mitchell, Anne M. *The Sydney Hospital Archive: History and the Bicentenary.* Sydney: Sydney Hospital, 1984.

Sussman, M.P. "Lucy Osburn and Her Five Nightingale Nurses," in *Medical Journal of Australia.* May 1, 1965.

Watson, J. Frederick. *The History of the Sydney Hospital from 1811 to 1911.* Sydney: W.A. Gullick, Government Printer, 1911.

Ziegeler, Stephan. *Ärzte und ihre Wirkungsstätten in Australien (1788–1928).* Lohmar: Josef Eul Verlag, 1997.

COLLECTIONS:

Florence Nightingale Papers, British Library, London.

John Haag,
Associate Professor of History, University of Georgia, Athens, Georgia

Osburn, Sarah.

See Witchcraft Trials in Salem Village.

Osceola.

See Dinesen, Isak.

Osgood, Frances (1811–1850)

American writer rumored to have had an affair with Edgar Allan Poe. *Name variations: Fanny Osgood; (pseudonyms) Florence, Ellen, Kate Carol. Born Frances Sargent Locke on June 18, 1811, in Boston, Massachusetts; died on May 12, 1850, in New York City; daughter of Joseph Locke (a merchant) and Mary (Ingersoll) Foster Locke; sister of writer Andrew Aitchison Locke, and half-sister of writer Anna Maria Wells; educated at home; married Samuel Stillman Osgood (a portrait painter), on October 7, 1835; children: Ellen Frances Osgood (b. 1836); May Vincent Osgood (b. 1839); Fanny Fay Osgood (1846–1847).*

Selected works: The Casket of Fate *(1838);* A Wreath of Wild Flowers *(1838);* The Poetry of Flowers and the Flowers of Poetry *(1841);* The Snowdrop: A New Year's Gift for Children *(1842);* A Letter about the Lions *(1849);* Poems *(1850).*

Frances Osgood was born Frances Sargent Locke in 1811, the second daughter among seven children of **Mary Ingersoll Locke** and Boston merchant Joseph Locke. She was educated at home during a childhood spent mostly in Hingham, Massachusetts, and by age 14 was publishing in the *Juvenile Miscellany* under the pseudonym Florence. (Her brother Andrew Aitchison Locke and half-sister **Anna Maria Wells** would also become writers of some renown.) When she was 25, Frances married Samuel Stillman Osgood, a young Boston portrait painter whom she had met when he asked to paint her portrait. The couple moved to London, where their daughter **Ellen Frances Osgood** was born in 1836. Osgood moved in London literary circles, contributed to reputable periodicals, and published two collections of verse while in England. Her poetry, which could be humorous but often was romantic and sentimental, employing flowers or birds to expound on themes of love, was generally well reviewed.

Osgood returned to America with her family after the death of her father, and moved to New York City in 1839, the same year her daughter **May Osgood** was born. Frances' poems and stories began appearing frequently in many of the prominent journals and newspapers of the day, and she became a member of good standing in the city's literary community. She also published several collections of poetry and prose. By the mid-1840s, she and her husband were estranged and living in separate residences. Osgood invariably seems to be described as "childlike," "wraithlike," "ethereal," and even as embodying a sort of "primal innocence," and she reportedly evoked a protective urge in most of her admirers, both male and female. It was apparently this urge to protect her that caused the ugly aftermath of what may have been her love affair with Edgar Allan Poe.

Frances Osgood

Osgood met Poe early in 1845, shortly after he had lauded her talent as a poet (or, rather, as a woman poet) at a public lecture. Poe was then basking in renown as a result of the first publication of "The Raven," which drew perhaps more attention than had any single poem in some hundred years. While many Poe biographers consider their relationship innocent and fairly inconsequential in and of itself (most believe that it was entirely platonic, and carried out primarily through correspondence), rumors of a physical affair have persisted since the 1840s. According to John Evangelist Walsh, Osgood and Poe had not only an affair but a child, Osgood's last daughter Fanny Fay, who died before she was two years old. Walsh bases this conclusion on a number of letters and circumstances, as well as the fact that Osgood was still living apart from her husband at the time of her last pregnancy, and had told none of her friends that she and her husband had been reconciled. Her friendship, or affair, with Poe quickly became intimate after their first meeting, and their conversations at literary salons were noted among their acquaintances. Osgood would later write of Poe, "For hours I have listened to him, . . . entranced by the strains of such pure and almost celestial eloquence as I have never read or heard elsewhere." Walsh states that Poe's invalid wife **Virginia Poe** was pleased by the friendship, which she believed was having a calming effect on her husband and helping to prevent him from falling into ruinous alcoholic binges, until early in 1846, when she discovered a letter Osgood had written.

The letter, which informed Poe that Osgood was three months' pregnant, requested him to visit her to help with choosing a name for the baby before she went into confinement. Virginia, we are told, recalled that Poe had visited Osgood in Rhode Island three months previously, and began to wonder. She told her mother **Maria Clemm**, who lived with and cared for them, of her vague suspicions, and Clemm made what she no doubt thought were discreet inquiries to ***Elizabeth Ellet**, another literati and a friend of both Osgood's and Poe's, as to whether Osgood had reconciled with her husband. She also happened to mention that Osgood was pregnant. Thus was set in motion a chain of events that all but ruined Poe in New York literary society, and quite probably contributed to the many dark stories and stains on his character that have come down through the years.

Soon, *****Margaret Fuller** and *****Anne C.L. Botta**, friends of Osgood's and acquaintances of Poe's, appeared at his door and requested the return of all letters Osgood had sent him. Poe was offended, and became even more so when, in explanation, they told him that Ellet had seen and described one of those letters. He made an injudicious remark which made Fuller and Botta think that Ellet herself had written him compromising letters, and with that phrase earned Ellet's undying enmity. Her brother threatened him; she published unflattering remarks about him in newspapers and spoke against him to all her friends; and as quiet rumor spread about Osgood's pregnancy and the possible circumstances behind it, the New York literary community blamed Poe for taking advantage of an innocent and closed ranks against him. (Many remembered a story Osgood had published the previous summer, "Ida Grey," which at the time had raised speculation about its main characters' close resemblance to Osgood and Poe.) Those who had already disliked or genuinely loathed him particularly sharpened their knives, and a wildly popular serial story featuring a thinly disguised, mocking portrayal of Poe was published in a local paper.

Osgood did not speak to or correspond with Poe during these incidents. She reconciled with her husband, and gave birth to her sickly baby girl in June 1846. In January 1847, Virginia Poe died. Poe visited Osgood during the following autumn, apparently meeting the baby that may have been his, and legend has it that during this visit he begged Osgood to elope with him. If he did, she refused him, and they never saw each other again. Her baby daughter died shortly thereafter, and by 1849 Osgood was suffering obvious symptoms of tuberculosis and was frequently restricted to her bed. That October, Poe died five days after having been found lying insensible in a Baltimore gutter. A poem Osgood wrote in tribute after learning of his death, "The Hand that Swept the Sounding Lyre," was published in her *Poems* in 1850, the year she died. This book was dedicated to Rufus Griswold, a journalist, anthologist, and erstwhile colleague of Poe's, who admired Osgood enormously. On the day of Poe's funeral, Griswold had published an anonymous "tribute" that praised him as a writer but vilified him as a person. Maria Clemm then engaged him to edit Poe's collected works, which he published in 1850 with a 35-page so-called memoir of the writer filled with slander and lies and accusations of perversion, insanity and drug use. This memoir was used as the basis for all biographical writing on Poe for nearly 40 years, and remains the source for much of the dark swirl of decadence still surrounding his name. Walsh suggests that the vicious memoir was Griswold's way of avenging Frances Osgood.

SOURCES:

James, Edward T., ed. *Notable American Women, 1607–1950.* Cambridge, MA: The Belknap Press of Harvard University Press, 1971.

Walsh, John Evangelist. *Plumes in the Dust: The Love Affair of Edgar Allan Poe and Fanny Osgood.* Chicago, IL: Nelson-Hall, 1980.

Jacqueline Mitchell,
freelance writer, Detroit, Michigan

O'Shay, Constance (1891–1959).

See Lupino, Ida for sidebar on Connie Emerald.

O'Shea, Katherine (1845–1921)

English woman whose love for Charles Stewart Parnell ended in scandal and disgrace. *Name variations: Kitty O'Shea; Katherine O'Shea Parnell. Born Katherine Wood on January 30, 1845, at Bradwell, Essex, England; died on February 5, 1921, at 39 East Ham Road, Littlehampton, Sussex, England; daughter of Sir John Page Wood; married Captain William H. O'Shea (1840–1905, a politician and adventurer), on January 24, 1867 (divorced 1891); married Charles Stewart Parnell (1846–1891), in June 1891; sister-in-law of* ****Anna Parnell*** *(1852–1911); children: (with Parnell) three, including daughters, Clare and Katie (both born between 1882 and 1884).*

The effervescent Kitty O'Shea was born in 1845 in Bradwell, Essex, England, daughter of Sir John Page Wood. In 1867, age 22, she married the extravagant Captain William O'Shea of the 18th Hussars. When his father would no longer pay his bills, William sold his commission in the Hussars and bought a partnership in an uncle's bank in Madrid, where he and Kitty settled. William soon quarreled with his uncle, however, and the couple picked up stakes and moved to Hertfordshire, England, where William started a stud farm. It was soon bankrupt. He then managed a sulphur mine in Spain for 18 months until it failed. It was Kitty's wealthy Aunt Ben, Mrs. Benjamin Wood, who had kept them going. In 1875, when her aunt, then 83, was newly widowed, Kitty became her companion. Aunt Ben installed her in a house near her own in Eltham, Kent, and provided her with a handsome allowance. William, who had lodgings in London, saw Kitty on his rare visits to Eltham. In 1880, he joined the Irish Party and was elected member of Parliament for Clare.

In 1880, Kitty O'Shea met Charles Stewart Parnell, the Irish Protestant who had fought for land reform and Irish Home Rule and was the beloved and respected leader of his predominantly Catholic country. By then, Kitty had been living apart from her husband for almost five years. The illicit liaison between Parnell and O'Shea, a poorly kept secret from the start, eventually would destroy Parnell's career. Most political insiders knew of the affair, and Captain O'Shea—although claiming later that he had not known—almost certainly knew and expected to benefit from it politically. Parnell's and O'Shea's relationship was nothing if not domestic; Parnell established a study and lab for himself at her home in Kent by 1882, and he and O'Shea would eventually have three children, including two daughters, **Clare** and **Katie Parnell**.

Despite this new-found (and short-lived) domestic tranquility, Parnell's political life in the 1880s became quite tumultuous. The agitation by the Land League, of which Parnell was president, seriously unnerved the ruling British authorities, and Parliament passed the Protection of Person and Property (Ireland) Act in early 1881 as a coercive measure. Becoming desperate, the British government had Parnell and other leaders of the League arrested in October 1881 on suspicion of treasonable activities. The Kilmainham treaty, under whose terms Parnell and the others were released, was not agreed to until the following May. On May 6, 1882, Lord Frederick Cavendish, England's chief secretary for Irish Affairs, along with his under secretary, was stabbed to death while walking in Phoenix Park, Dublin. The public outrage in England over these assassinations was immense, and Parliament promptly passed an extremely harsh crimes bill for Ireland.

As the decade wore on, the question of land reform and tenant rights became increasingly subordinated to the issue of Home Rule, for which a bill was defeated in 1886. Parnell's popularity soared in Ireland throughout this time. One interesting measure of how well he was beloved came through the public disclosure of Parnell's finances: once the people of Ireland realized how indebted their leader was, they promptly set up a subscription fund for him and raised over £37,000.

A hero in Ireland, Parnell was seen as a villain in England. In 1887, the London *Times* published a series of articles on "Parnellism and Crime," featuring several forged but damaging letters supposedly written by Parnell. The troubles caused by these articles did not abate for over two years—at which point Captain O'Shea filed for divorce. O'Shea named Parnell as a co-respondent in the suit and portrayed him as the most sordid of adulterers. The fact that Parnell considered himself, for all intents and purposes, married to the woman whom Captain O'Shea had abandoned years ago was lost amid patently false stories of Parnell beating hasty retreats from the O'Shea home by slipping down fire escapes.

The divorce created an enormous scandal, but Parnell's countrymen did not immediately abandon him. The outcry in England, however, was so great that other Irish leaders were privately informed that they could expect no cooperation in Parliament—and no hope of Home Rule—as long as Parnell was one of them. Perhaps reluctantly—no one is sure—Parnell was condemned by the country that had once hailed him as its uncrowned king. In late 1890 and early 1891, candidates for Parliament supported by Parnell were defeated, and Parnell began to recede from the Irish political scene. He married Kitty O'Shea at Steyning, near Brighton, on June 25, 1891, and only a little over three months later, on October 6, he died in her arms.

The reaction to the divorce was certainly what cost Parnell his political leadership, but it should be remembered that at the time there was deep-rooted opposition in England to both Parnell and Home Rule. It is quite possible to see the moral outrage directed at Parnell's personal life as, for the most part, a convenient way to eliminate his political threat to the order of the British Empire. Nevertheless, his long-standing relationship with Kitty O'Shea was in direct contradiction to the morality of his day. His death so soon after the scandal makes his political fall appear particularly tragic; in his passing, Ireland lost one of its great leaders. Though from that time on Kitty O'Shea experienced chronic emotional breakdowns, she lived to be 76, dying on February 5, 1921, at 39 East Ham Road, Littlehampton, Sussex.

SUGGESTED READING:

Foster, R.F. *Charles Stewart Parnell: The Man and his Family.* Humanities Press, 1976.

Larkin, Emmet. *The Roman Catholic Church and the Fall of Parnell.* Liverpool, 1979.

O'Shea, Katherine. *Charles Stewart Parnell: His Love Story and Political Life.* London, 1914.

O'Shea, Kitty (1845–1921).

See O'Shea, Katherine.

O'Shea, Tessie (c. 1913–1995)

British-born singer and actress. *Born in Cardiff, Wales, around 1913; died in a nursing home on April 21, 1995, in Leesburg, Florida.*

Selected theater: headlined British revues On With the Show *and* High Time*; made American debut in* The Girl Who Came to Supper *(1963); appeared in* A Time for Singing *(1966),* Something's Afoot *(1976), and* Broadway Follies *(1981).*

Selected filmography: The Russians Are Coming, the Russians Are Coming *(1966);* Bedknobs and Broomsticks *(1971).*

An old-fashioned music-hall performer who cheerfully capitalized on her wide girth, Tessie O'Shea was born around 1913 in Cardiff, Wales, and made her first tour at the age of seven. At 15, already the veteran headliner of the Bristol Hippodrome and other variety theaters throughout Britain, she appeared in a Blackpool revue singing "Two-Ton Tessie from Tennessee," the song that ultimately became her anthem. During her heyday in England, O'Shea sang for the royal princesses ***Elizabeth (II)** and ***Margaret Rose**.

O'Shea's American debut in 1963, as a fish-and-chip peddler in *The Girl Who Came to Supper*, turned into a Tony-winning performance for the actress. During a brief 12-minute turn on stage, she sang and danced her way through a medley of four Noel Coward songs, stopping the show. Her success led to a stint on the CBS variety series "The Entertainers" in 1964. O'Shea's later Broadway shows included *A Time for Singing* (1966), *Something's Afoot* (1976), and *Broadway Follies* (1981). She also played bit parts in the movies *The Russians Are Coming, the Russians are Coming* (1966) and *Bedknobs and Broomsticks* (1971). O'Shea, who never married, spent her later years in East Lake Weir, Florida.

SOURCES:

"Obituary," in *The Day* [New London, CT]. April 22, 1995.

Osiier, Ellen (1890–1962).

See Mayer, Helene for sidebar.

Osipenko, Polina (1907–1939).

See group entry under Grizodubova, Valentina, Polina Osipenko, and Marina Raskova.

Osmanoglu, Gevheri (1904—)

Turkish composer and player of the oud, tanbur, and lavta. *Born in Constantinople (now Istanbul) in 1904.*

Born into a musical family in Constantinople (now Istanbul) in 1904, Gevheri Osmanoglu learned to play several instruments from her father. Among these were the oud (a lyre), the tanbur (a guitar-like instrument), and the lavta (an ancient lute). When Turkey was declared a republic, Osmanoglu's family moved to Paris, where she remained for the next 32 years. Though she did not continue her studies of Turkish music until her return to her country, she became very skilled on the tanbur in later life. Osmanoglu wrote a number of compositions, many of them folksongs, and her work is preserved in recordings made by Turkish radio and television.

John Haag,
Athens, Georgia

Osomari, queen of.

See Okwei of Osomari (1872–1943).

Ossoli, Margaret Fuller (1810–1850).

See Fuller, Margaret.

Osten, Maria (1908–1942)

German frontline reporter for Moscow's **Deutsche Zentral-Zeitung** ***during the Spanish Civil War who was later executed by the Soviets.*** *Name variations: Maria Gresshöner or Gresshoener. Born Maria Emilie Alwine Gresshöner in Muckum bei Bünde, Westphalia, Germany, on March 20, 1908 (some sources cite 1909); executed in Moscow on August 8, 1942; daughter of Heinrich Gresshöner and Anna Maria (Pohlmann) Gresshöner; had sisters Änne and Hanna; married Yevgenii Cherbiakov, a Russian director (divorced around 1931); companion of Mikhail Yefimovich Koltsov (1898–1940, Russian writer and an editor of* Pravda*); children: (adopted) Hubert L'Hoste; José.*

Among the many tragedies of the turbulent 20th century, one of the most chilling was the massive loss of life among Germans who fled Nazi Germany in the 1930s by moving to the Soviet Union, a land they were convinced would provide them with a secure refuge. But it was here, in a nation that proclaimed its desire to build a socialist society based on principles of justice, that they would discover that the dictatorship of Joseph Stalin was no less inhuman than that of Adolf Hitler. Among the countless German idealists who lost their lives in the USSR was Maria Osten.

Born Maria Gresshöner in 1908 in Westphalia, she grew up in a privileged environment, her parents being prosperous landowners. As a child, her life at the family estate, Jägerborn, was one filled with servants and status. When Maria was four, her family acquired another estate near Neugolz, in West Prussia, where traces of rural feudalism remained. Early aware of the injustices of German life during and after World War I, Maria rebelled against her family's conservatism. She dropped out of her Lyceum studies at age 15 and two years later (1925) moved to Berlin, supporting herself by working in a tuberculosis sanatorium. In her spare time, she took art lessons with noted artists Ludwig Meidner and Willy Jaeckel.

Later in 1925, Maria began working for Malik-Verlag, one of Weimar Germany's most innovative left-wing publishing houses. Although her duties there demanded much of her time, she also wrote two short stories of high quality. Instilled with the spirit of the *Neue Sachlichkeit* (New Objectivity) literary movement, her stories appeared in two well-received anthologies, *24 neue deutsche Erzähler* (1929) and *30 Erzähler des neuen Deutschland* (1932), and she was encouraged to continue writing by Malik-Verlag's publisher, Wieland Herzfelde. In 1930, he also incorporated a photographic portrait of Maria into the graphic design for the dust jacket of Ilya Ehrenburg's novel, *The Loves of Jeanne Ney.*

Given the fact that most of the authors associated with Malik-Verlag were either members of, or highly sympathetic toward, the Communist Party of Germany (*Kommunistische Partei Deutschlands*, KPD), Maria became increasingly attracted by the idea that Communism was the only solution for the unemployment and social injustice becoming ever more prevalent during the worldwide economic depression. She moved in intellectual circles that were almost exclusively Communist-oriented. Among the most important influences on her at this time was the playwright Bertolt Brecht, who was briefly her lover.

At the end of a brief marriage to Soviet director Yevgenii Cherbiakov, in 1932 she moved to the Soviet Union to work as a journalist and author, changing her name to Maria Osten (Osten means "the East" in German). She then met and fell in love with Soviet journalist Mikhail Koltsov. A dedicated Communist, Koltsov had joined the Bolshevik Party in 1918, becoming one of the editors of the party newspaper *Pravda* in 1922. In Koltsov, Osten found the love of her life, and she became profoundly loyal to the Soviet cause. When the Nazis seized power in Germany in 1933, Osten could no longer go home. In Moscow, she busied herself with various literary and journalistic projects, while also maintaining contacts with leaders of anti-Nazi literary circles both within the USSR and in other countries, including Brecht, ***Helene Weigel**, Johannes Robert Becher, Ernst Busch, and Egon Erwin Kisch.

Osten threw herself into anti-fascist journalistic activities. In 1934–35, she and Koltsov reported from the Saar region, an industrial area that had been under French administration since 1920 and was scheduled for a January 1935 plebiscite to decide whether it should be returned to (a now Nazi) Germany. Though Osten was disappointed when the plebiscite was overwhelmingly decided in favor of the Reich, she and Koltsov had adopted a young working-class Saar boy named Hubert L'Hoste. After returning to Moscow, she wrote a book for children entitled *Hubert im Wunderland* (Hubert in the Land of Wonders), with a foreword by Georgi Dimitrov, hero of the Reichstag Fire Trial in Nazi Germany and now president of the Comintern (Communist International). Appearing in print in Moscow in 1935 in both German and Russian-language editions, *Hubert im Wunderland* compared the quality of life in the Western world, which was portrayed as one of capitalist exploitation and feverish preparation for war, with Osten's highly idealized "socialist realist" picture of the Soviet Union. Here, she was convinced, was a nation that did not advance at the expense of social injustice, unemployment, or ethnic hatred. For a time, because of his adoptive mother's book, Hubert was a Soviet celebrity of sorts; he was even received in the Kremlin by the leading military commanders, Tukhachevsky and Budennyi.

In 1936, the proclamation of a new Soviet Constitution by Stalin appeared to give added weight to the belief that a new and better social order had been created. Ominously, in that same year the first of a series of purge trials—resulting in death sentences for many former political allies of both Vladimir Lenin and Stalin—began to mar the landscape. Inspired by the revered author Maxim Gorky's call for a new Soviet literature, Osten ignored the gathering political storm, instead concentrating on her own writings, and on collaborating with both Soviet and German-exile authors to help publish such influential anti-Nazi publications as the journal *Das Wort* and the international anthology *Ein Tag der Welt* (One Day the World), which appeared in print in 1937.

Whatever doubts Osten and Koltsov may have had about Soviet realities, they appeared insignificant in relation to the growing aggressiveness of the forces of European Fascism. In July 1936, supported militarily and politically by Hitler and Mussolini, a clique of Spanish generals led by Francisco Franco raised the banner of revolt against a democratically elected republican government. Almost immediately the antifascist forces of the world, ranging from anarchists and liberal democrats to Socialists and Communists, rallied to the cause of the endangered Spanish Republic. Soon after the outbreak of the civil war in Spain, Osten was sent there as a war correspondent for Moscow's *Deutsche Zentral-Zeitung* (*DZZ*). Bravely, she sought stories at the front lines, reporting on the soldiers of the Spanish Republic, both Spaniards and the men and women who came from many nations to serve in the International Brigades. The Spanish Republicans were almost always at a disadvantage when it came to weapons. Not only Franco's forces but "volunteers" from Nazi Germany and Fascist Italy brought death and destruction with their superior military technology. The Republicans most feared the fascists' airpower, which was merciless in seeking civilian targets, including the Basque town of Guernica that would be immortalized in Pablo Picasso's mural of the same name.

By the end of 1937, only months after they had appeared in the *DZZ*, Osten's articles were collected in book form in the Russian-language *Reportages from Spain*. Koltsov, who had also been in Spain, collected notes for a book on the Spanish conflict as well. While they were there, Osten and Koltsov had adopted another child, a Spanish boy named José. In 1938, Osten left a doomed Spain to accept a new assignment, that of editor of the Paris office of the Moscow-based German-language journal *Das Wort* (The Word). Published since 1936, *Das Wort* had secured the support of many important German literary exiles, including Brecht and Lion Feuchtwanger. Osten had become acquainted with Feuchtwanger during his December 1936 visit to the Soviet Union, when she served as his host and guide. She was also involved in organizing the creation of a new firm, the Verlag 10. Mai, in order to publish a series of books on themes of current interest.

As well, she contributed articles to the German exile newspaper *Deutsche Volkszeitung*, which was published in Paris but read in anti-Nazi circles throughout the world. In her spare moments, she also worked on the manuscript of a novel, *Kartoffelschnaps* (Vodka). Despite the political terror that dominated life in Moscow, both Osten and Koltsov—loyal Stalinists—appeared to have weathered the storm. For a long time, many of Osten's journalistic colleagues in Russia had been decimated by the Stalinist terror, vanishing into the night as "wreckers" and "enemies of the people." In June 1937, *DZZ* editor *Julia Annenkova had been arrested, never to return. Over a period of three days in February 1938, virtually the entire editorial staff of the paper was liquidated. Very likely because she was in Spain (and later in Paris), Osten escaped the dreaded knock on the door.

Maria Osten

Koltsov's career also gave all appearances of flourishing as never before. His newly published book *Ispanskii Dnevnik* (Spanish Diary) was immensely successful, and in the summer of 1938 he was elected a deputy to the Supreme Soviet. Besides continuing to work as a *Pravda* editor, Koltsov was involved with the Zhurgaz publishing firm, headed the foreign relations branch of the Soviet Writers' Union, and edited the periodicals *Krokodil*, *Ogonek*, and *Za rubezhom* (Beyond the Borders). Quickly, however, everything changed. Despite the fact that Koltsov was an uncritical supporter of Stalin, he fell out of favor. During a private talk with "the boss," Stalin asked Koltsov if he owned a gun and if he ever entertained the thought of killing himself. Koltsov told his brother, political cartoonist Boris Yefimov, that he could sense "an ominous, hostile breeze blowing from somewhere." The downfall of the feared head of the NKVD (Soviet Secret Police), Nikolai Yezhov, on December

8, 1938, seemed to signal the end of the terror, but not for Koltsov. Late in the night of December 12, while working in the Pravda editorial offices, he was arrested.

Osten heard of Koltsov's arrest while in Paris and made plans to clear him from what she knew were false charges. Arriving in Moscow in May 1939, along with her adopted son José, she was unable to undo the "misunderstanding" that had led to Koltsov's arrest and imprisonment. At this point, because of her connections to the doomed Koltsov, Osten lost whatever protection she had enjoyed from the leadership of the exiled German Communists in Moscow. On July 3, 1939, a so-called Small Commission of KPD leaders declared her party membership to be "at rest," presumably with further investigations to follow. A further ominous development took place on October 14, 1939, when Osten was expelled from the KPD.

From then on, Osten was filled with fear and frustration. When she arrived at the door of her adopted son Hubert's apartment, she was told by both Hubert and his new wife that they could not let her enter; she had become much too dangerous to be associated with. As a member in good standing of the Komsomol (Young Communist League), he did not intend to "besmirch" his own name. For some inexplicable reason, Osten was not arrested at this point. Instead, she and José moved into a room in a cheap Moscow hotel. Through the Soviet Writers' Union, she was able to find a job at one of Moscow's film studios, Lenfilm. Still at liberty when Brecht and his family stopped in Moscow in May 1941, on their way to California, Osten displayed once again her capacity for generosity. A member of the Brecht group, **Margarete Steffin**, one of Brecht's major collaborators, had to be hospitalized in Moscow with end-stage tuberculosis, and Osten spent hours in the hospital with her as she slowly died. The Brecht group, which consisted of the playwright and his wife Helene Weigel, their children, as well as **Ruth Berlau**, had already left Moscow when Steffin died in early June 1941. Osten's telegram dated June 5, 1941, informing Brecht of Steffin's death is the last document she wrote that has survived.

Probably seeking to make her situation more secure, Osten had become a Soviet citizen around the time of Brecht's visit. This decision may have been fatal, making her only more visible to the ever-suspicious NKVD. The immediate triggering event for her arrest was the unexpected attack on the Soviet Union by Nazi Germany and its allies on June 22, 1941. Despite their anti-Nazi credentials, German exiles in the USSR were now viewed as potential allies of Hitler, and on June 24, 1941, Osten was arrested in Moscow by the NKVD. Both of her adopted sons would apparently vanish into the vast interior of the Soviet Union, José without a trace, and Hubert to Kazakhstan as a deportee. Hubert L'Hoste survived the deportation, married a second time, but wound up in the Gulag for several years. After his release, he would die in August 1959, at age 36, of a ruptured appendix.

Osten was shot in Moscow on August 8, 1942. Koltsov had already suffered the same fate, on February 2, 1940. At the time of her arrest, the manuscript of Osten's novel *Kartoffelschnaps*, on which she had been working for a number of years, vanished. The death of Stalin in 1953 made it possible to look with candor at the toll taken by his dictatorship, particularly during its purges. In 1957, Osten was posthumously rehabilitated by the Military Tribunal of the Moscow Military District, the wartime sentence against her being declared unjust and without foundation. In the German Democratic Republic (GDR), where de-Stalinization never went beyond timid first steps, Maria Osten's name was mentioned only occasionally and with considerable caution despite her former fame. Her fate in many ways remained an embarrassment to an East German leadership compromised by its close ties to the harshest aspects of Sovietism.

The life of Maria Osten was never investigated by scholars in either of the two post-1945 Germanies, and only on rare occasions did excerpts from her writings appear in print in the GDR. During the 1980s, the final years of the GDR, the regime's half-hearted attempts at openness resulted in feeble attempts to confront the Stalinist past. One such occasion was the celebration of Maria Osten's 80th birthday on March 20, 1988, which took place in a remote cemetery in the GDR; there, a memorial plaque in her honor was unveiled next to her parents' gravesite in the village of Loitz-Kreis Demmin. Present that day was an informer for the GDR Ministry of State Security (*Ministerium für Staatssicherheit* or *Stasi*) who dutifully informed Stasi headquarters in East Berlin that an unauthorized ceremony to honor a victim of Stalinism had just taken place.

SOURCES:

Barck, Simone, ed. "Osten, Maria (d.i. Maria Gresshöner)," in *Lexikon sozialistischer Literatur: Ihre Geschichte in Deutschland bis 1945*. Stuttgart: Metzler, 1994, pp. 364–365.

Conquest, Robert. *The Great Terror: Stalin's Purge of the Thirties*. Rev. ed. Harmondsworth: Penguin, 1971.

El-Akramy, Ursula. *Transit Moskau: Margarete Steffin und Maria Osten.* Hamburg: Europäische Verlagsanstalt, 1998.

Gelfand, Natalija V. *Deutsche revolutionäre Schriftsteller und ihre Bundesgenossen 1918–1945.* Berlin: Aufbau-Verlag, 1987.

Gresshöner, Maria. "Mehlgast," in Hermann Kesten, ed., *24 neue deutsche Erzähler: Frühwerke der neuen Sachlichkeit.* Reprint. Munich: Kurt Desch Verlag, 1973.

———. "Zigelski hatte Glück," in Wieland Herzfelde, ed., *Dreissig neue Erzähler des neuen Deutschland.* Frankfurt am Main: Röderberg-Verlag G.m.b.H., 1983.

Hermann, Frank. *Malik: Zur Geschichte eines Verlages, 1916–1947.* Düsseldorf: Droste Verlag, 1989.

Hermsdorf, Klaus, Hugo Fetting, and Silvia Schlenstedt. *Exil in den Niederlanden und in Spanien.* Frankfurt am Main: Röderberg-Verlag, 1981.

Huss-Michel, Angela. *Die Moskauer Zeitschriften "Internationale Literatur" und "Das Wort" während der Exil-Volksfront (1936–1939).* Frankfurt am Main: Peter Lang, 1987.

Jarmatz, Klaus, Simone Barck, and Peter Diezel. *Exil in der UdSSR.* Frankfurt am Main: Röderberg-Verlag, 1979.

Koltsov, Mikhail. *Ispanskii Dnevnik* (Spanish Diary). Moscow: "Khodozhestvennaia literatura," 1938.

Kreuzer, Helmut. "Zum Spanienkrieg: Prosa deutscher Exilautoren," in *LiLi: Zeitschrift für Literaturwissenschaft und Linguistik.* Vol. 15, no. 60, 1985, pp. 10–43.

Krispyn, Egbert. *Anti-Nazi Writers in Exile.* Athens: University of Georgia Press, 1978.

Krüger, Dirk. "Maria Osten," in Renate Wall, ed., *Lexikon deutschsprachiger Schriftstellerinnen im Exil, 1933–1945.* Freiburg im Breisgau: Kore Verlag, 1995, Vol. 2, pp. 53–56.

———. "Maria Osten: Spanienkämpferin und Stalinopfer," in *unsere zeit.* Vol. 21, no. 207. September 8, 1989.

Melzwig, Brigitte. *Deutsche sozialistische Literatur, 1918–1945.* Berlin: Aufbau-Verlag, 1975.

Mühlen, Patrik von zur. "Säuberungen unter deutschen Spanienkämpfern," in *Exilforschung: Ein internationales Jahrbuch.* Vol. 1, 1983, pp. 165–176.

Müller, Reinhard, ed. *Die Säuberung. Moskau 1936: Stenogramm einer geschlossenen Parteiversammlung.* Reinbek bei Hamburg: Rowohlt Taschenbuch, 1991.

Osten, Maria. "Frühling in Madrid," in *Deutsche Zentral-Zeitung* [Moscow]. May 1, 1937, p. 2.

———. *Hubert im Wunderland.* Moscow: Verlagsgenossenschaft ausländischer Arbeiter in der UdSSR, 1935.

———. "Ich such ein spanisches Kind," in *Deutsche Zentral-Zeitung* [Moscow]. October 29, 1936, p. 2.

———. "Madrid," in *Deutsche Volks-Zeitung* [Paris]. July 10, 1938, p. 5.

———. "Ostelbien," in *Das Wort: Literarische Monatsschrift.* Vol. 2, no. 4–5. April–May 1937, pp. 107–111.

———. "Spanische Frontzeitungen," in *Deutsche Zentral-Zeitung* [Moscow]. May 5, 1937, p. 3.

———. "Spanische Jugend," in *Deutsche Zentral-Zeitung* [Moscow]. October 14, 1936, p. 2.

———. "Spanische Kinder," in *Deutsche Zentral-Zeitung* [Moscow]. October 18, 1936, p. 2.

———. "Spanische Reportagen," in *Neue deutsche Literatur: Monatsschrift für Literatur und Kritik.* Vol. 34, no. 7. July 1986, pp. 10–22 (translated excerpts from her 1937 Russian-language book *Spanish Reportages*).

———. "Das Vieh rückt ein," in *Deutsch für Deutsche.* Leipzig: Verlag für Kunst und Wissenschaft Albert Otto Paul, 1935.

Pike, David. *German Writers in Soviet Exile, 1933–1945.* Chapel Hill: University of North Carolina Press, 1982.

Plener, Ulla, ed. *Leben mit Hoffnung in Pein.* Frankfurt an der Oder: Frankfurt Oder Edition, 1997.

Regler, Gustav. *Der grosse Kreuzzug: Tagebuch 1937 aus dem Spanischen Bürgerkrieg.* Basel: Stroemfeld-Roter Stern, 1996.

Schwarz, Helga W. "Maria Osten—Reporterin in den Schützengräben vor Madrid," in *Neue Deutsche Presse.* No. 9. September 1989.

Shentalinsky, Vitaly. *Arrested Voices: Resurrecting the Disappeared Writers of the Soviet Regime.* NY: Martin Kessler, 1996.

Thornberry, Robert S. "Writers Take Sides, Stalinists Take Control: The Second International Congress for the Defense of Culture (Spain 1937)," in *The Historian.* Vol. 62, no. 3. Spring 2000, pp. 589–605.

Walter, Hans-Albert. "No pasarán! Deutsche Exilschriftsteller im Spanischen Bürgerkrieg," in *Kürbiskern: Literatur und Kritik.* No. 1, 1967, pp. 5–27.

Weber, Hermann. *"Weisse Flecken" in der Geschichte: Die KPD-Opfer der Stalinschen Säuberungen und ihre Rehabilitierung.* 2nd rev. ed. Frankfurt am Main: ISP, 1990.

Yefimov, Boris. "Mikhail Koltsov," in *Soviet Literature.* No. 7, 1968, pp. 159–163.

Zenker, Edith, ed. *Veröffentlichungen deutscher sozialistischer Schriftsteller in der revolutionären und demokratischen Presse 1918–1945: Bibliographie.* 2nd rev. ed. Berlin: Aufbau-Verlag, 1969.

John Haag,
Associate Professor of History, University of Georgia,
Athens, Georgia

Ostenso, Martha (1900–1963)

Canadian-American writer. *Born on September 17, 1900, in Bergen, Norway; reared in Minnesota, South Dakota, and Canada; died on November 24, 1963, in Seattle (one source cites Tacoma), Washington; daughter of Sigurd Brigt Ostenso and Lena (Tungleland) Ostenso; married Douglas Leader Durkin (a writer), on December 16, 1944 (or 1945); attended University of Manitoba, beginning in 1918; attended Columbia University, 1921–22; received honorary M.E., Wittenberg University.*

Emigrated to the United States at age two to live in small towns in Minnesota and South Dakota (1902); contributed to the junior page of the Minneapolis Journal *as a child; emigrated to Canada to live in Manitoba (1915); taught one semester of school in Manitoba (1918); worked as a social worker with the Bureau of Charities in Brooklyn, New York*

(1920–23); studied novel-writing techniques at Columbia University (1921–22); published first book, A Far Land: Poems by Martha Ostenso *(1924); won first prize in a competition for best first novel by a North American writer for* Wild Geese *(1925).*

Selected writings: A Far Land: Poems by Martha Ostenso *(1924);* Wild Geese *(1925);* The Dark Dawn *(1927);* The Young May Moon *(1929);* The Waters under the Earth *(1930);* The Mandrake Root *(1938);* And They Shall Walk: The Life Story of Sister Elizabeth *(1943);* O River, Remember *(1945).*

Born in Norway in 1900, Martha Ostenso was the daughter of an ambitious man who moved his family to America in 1902 and to Canada in 1915. Ostenso, whose last name means "eastern sea," spent her childhood growing up in prairies and small towns in Minnesota and South Dakota, and near the Interlake district in Manitoba, Canada. From these surroundings, she observed the lives and problems of farmers of Scandinavian ancestry. She also acquired writing experience by contributing to the junior page of the *Minneapolis Journal*.

Ostenso attended the University of Manitoba beginning in 1918, while also teaching school and working as a reporter for the *Winnipeg Free Press*. She traveled to Brooklyn, New York, to work as a secretary for the Bureau of Charities from 1920 to 1923. Ostenso later noted that her negative experiences in New York's Lower East Side gave her an appreciation for the true value of farm country. In New York, she attended Columbia University from 1921 to 1922 to study techniques of novel writing.

By this time, Ostenso was already living with her future husband, writer Douglas Leader Durkin; they may have met at the University of Manitoba. (Because his wife refused to give him a divorce, Durkin and Ostenso would not marry until 1944.) They would collaborate on most of Ostenso's published novels, with Durkin often creating the outline of a plot from Ostenso's ideas and then editing the book she wrote from that outline. While the collaboration was successful, and their income eventually allowed them to live well, a number of critics have blamed weaknesses in her later novels on Durkin's influence. Ostenso's first book, a collection of poems, was published in 1924 under the title *A Far Land: Poems by Martha Ostenso*.

In a major competition the following year, her novel *Wild Geese* (1925) was chosen over 1,300 manuscripts to win the $13,500 top prize for best first novel by a North American writer. Ostenso claimed that she first heard the story told in the book while vacationing during a university summer break in Oeland, in the Interlake district of Manitoba, where *Wild Geese* is set. The title, and dominant motif, of the book refers to the endless quest of wild geese as they fly over Oeland during each spring and fall migration. Judith Gare is locked in a psychological struggle with her farmer father Caleb, whose burning desire to increase his landholdings also includes the plan to keep his four children on the farm permanently, as cheap labor. While she is torn with love for her vulnerable mother, whom Caleb uses to keep his children in line, Judith also passionately wishes for spiritual, sexual, and romantic fulfillment, and this, along with the encouragement of a female friend, finally enables her to break away from her family and leave the farm for the city. Throughout the novel, Judith also functions as a kind of symbol of nature, her deeply felt and unpossessive love of the land contrasting with her father's need to control and shape it.

While *Wild Geese* is now acknowledged as a classic depiction of life in the inhospitable environment of the Canadian west, the book was little known for nearly 20 years, and only with its glowing mention in **Clara Thomas**' *Canadian Novelists, 1920–1945* was the book presented to a wide audience. Among Ostenso's other novels set in Canada are *The Young May Moon* (1929) and *Prologue to Love* (1932), although in 1929 she settled in the United States, living first in New Jersey and finally in Brainerd, in northern Minnesota. In 1943, Ostenso published *And They Shall Walk: The Life Story of Sister Elizabeth*, detailing the experiences of Australian nurse Sister ***Elizabeth Kenny**, who worked with victims of polio. The book was written in collaboration with Kenny, and was filmed as *Sister Kenny* in 1946 with ***Rosalind Russell** in the title role. While Ostenso's later novels did not receive the lasting acclaim of *Wild Geese*, a number of them were translated into German, Norwegian, Polish, and other European languages. She also acquired some renown as a painter in Scandinavia. Ostenso died unexpectedly while visiting Seattle on November 22, 1963.

SOURCES:

Buck, Claire, ed. *The Bloomsbury Guide to Women's Literature.* NY: Prentice Hall, 1992.

Harding, Anthony John. "Martha Otenso" in *Dictionary of Literary Biography,* Vol. 92: *Canadian Writers, 1890–1920.* Edited by W.H. New. Detroit, MI: Gale Research, 1990.

Kunitz, Stanley J., and Howard Haycraft, eds. *Twentieth Century Authors.* NY: H.W. Wilson, 1942.

Daniel E. Brannen, Jr.,
freelance writer, York, Pennsylvania

Ostermeyer, Micheline (1922—)

French discus thrower and concert musician. *Born on December 23, 1922, in Rang-du-Fliers, France; married in 1952.*

Moved to Tunisia with her family (1929); at age 14, moved back to France to study music at the Paris Conservatory (1936); returned to Tunisia with the advent of World War II (1940) and joined the French Athletic Association, competing in several track and field events; at end of war, returned to France and music studies (1945); won Olympic gold medals in the discus and the shot put, as well as the bronze in the high jump (1948); retired from track and field competition (1951); married and moved to Lebanon with husband (1952); following the death of her husband over a decade later, returned to France to teach music at a conservatory just outside Paris.

Micheline Ostermeyer was born in France in 1922, but raised primarily in Tunisia. By age 13, she was studying piano at the Paris Conservatory. When her music studies were interrupted by World War II, Ostermeyer returned to Tunisia where she made her broadcast debut over Radio Tunisia in 1941. For the next 16 years, she would have a distinguished career on the concert stage, touring Europe, North Africa, and the Middle East, playing in recital and with orchestras. Just months before competing in the London Olympics in 1948, she graduated with honors from the Paris Conservatory.

Ostermeyer was also a competitive athlete, becoming a champion in several track-and-field events. Throughout her sports career, she won 30 major titles and set more than 50 records, always using methods that protected her hands. At the Olympics, she was a multiple-medal winner, taking gold medals in the shot put (13.75), a new event, and in the discus (41.92), as well as a bronze in the high jump behind ***Alice Coachman** of the U.S. and ***Dorothy Odam Tyler** of Great Britain, who tied. Before the Games, Ostermeyer had thrown the discus in only one other competition.

A severe muscle strain effectively ended her track-and-field career in 1951. In 1952, she married and moved to Lebanon. Following her husband's death, she moved back to Paris with her children and became a professor at the École Nationale de Musique; some of her students went on to prominent and critically acclaimed careers.

Micheline Ostermeyer

Ostrith (d. 697)

Queen of Mercia. *Name variations: Osthryth; she is possibly* ***Orthryth.** *Died in 697; daughter of* ***Eanfleda** *(626–?) and Oswy (Oswin, Oswio), king of Northumbria; married Ethelred, king of Mercia.*

O'Sullivan, Mary Kenney (1864–1943)

American labor organizer. *Name variations: Mary Kenney. Born Mary Kenney in Hannibal, Missouri, on January 8, 1864; died in West Medford, Massachusetts, on January 18, 1943; one of four children of Michael Kenney and Mary (Kelly) Kenney; married John (Jack) F. O'Sullivan, on October 10, 1894; children: four, one of whom died in infancy.*

Founded Chicago Women's Bindery Union No. 1 (1891); appointed first woman organizer for the American Federation of Labor (AFL, 1892); co-founded Union for Industrial Progress, part of the Women's Educational and Industrial Union of Boston (1894); was executive secretary, Union for Industrial Progress (1894–1903); co-founded National Women's Trade Union League (WTUL, 1903); served as WTUL national secretary (1903–06), treasurer (1907), and vice-president (1909–11); served as factory inspector, Massachusetts State Board of Labor and Industries (1914–34).

Mary Kenney O'Sullivan was born in 1864 in Hannibal, Missouri, the daughter of Irish immigrants. She went to work at the age of fourteen after only five years of schooling. As the only child still at home when her father died, O'Sullivan would support her invalid mother for the next 20 years. She started out as an apprentice dressmaker but soon went to work in a bookbindery. There, she rose to forewoman in four years and went to Keokuk, Iowa, when her firm closed its plant in Hannibal. By the late 1880s, O'Sullivan was in Chicago, working in a large bookbindery.

After her years as a bookbinder, a trade famous for limiting women's access to the higher-paid and more skilled facets of production, O'Sullivan felt that only through organization could women hope to advance in the craft. She soon became a leader of the Chicago labor movement and in 1891 organized her fellow women binders into their first union. O'Sullivan lived at Hull House for a time and became friends with its founder, ***Jane Addams**. In 1892, AFL president Samuel Gompers appointed O'Sullivan the first women's organizer. She spent several months organizing women in various trades in New York and Massachusetts but had limited success, due in part to the ambivalence of the AFL regarding the unionization of women. Returning to Chicago, O'Sullivan joined with ***Florence Kelley** and other Hull House activists in agitating for a factory inspection law. In 1893, the Illinois legislation passed such a law, and O'Sullivan was appointed a deputy inspector.

Mary Kenney O'Sullivan

In 1894, Mary Kenney married John O'Sullivan, a Boston labor leader. In Boston, she gave birth to four children (one of whom died in infancy), and continued to organize workers and develop contacts with middle- and upper-class women who were interested in labor issues. In 1894, along with ***Mary Morton Kehew**, president of the Women's Educational and Industrial Union of Boston, O'Sullivan organized the Union for Industrial Progress, which sought to investigate the conditions of labor for women in Boston. During the 1890s, both O'Sullivans were leaders of the Boston trade union movement and part of the labor reform community based in Denison House, a Boston settlement. Mary Kenney O'Sullivan, with the encouragement of her husband and the support of elite women reformers, organized women laundry workers, garment makers, and rubber workers. As Denison House co-founder and Wellesley College professor ***Vida Dutton Scudder** later remembered, O'Sullivan was "a noble young woman on fire for her cause."

In 1902, John O'Sullivan died, and Mary Kenney O'Sullivan, with three children to support, took a job managing a model tenement. Along with William English Walling, a New York settlement house worker, O'Sullivan founded the Women's Trade Union League in 1903. The League, which sought to organize women workers and agitated for protective labor legislation, included working-class, middle- and upper-class women in its membership. O'Sullivan, the original secretary and an early vice-president, left the League in 1912 in protest over its lack of support for the striking textile workers in Lawrence, Massachusetts. In 1914, she became one of five women factory inspectors appointed to the newly created Massachusetts State Board of Labor and Industries. O'Sullivan was also an advocate of women's suffrage and an active pacifist. In 1926, she traveled to Dublin, Ireland, as a delegate to the annual conference of the Women's International League for Peace and Freedom. She retired at the age of 70 and died of heart disease nine years later, in 1943, at her West Medford home.

SOURCES:

Carson, Mina. *Settlement Folk: Social Thought and the American Settlement Movement, 1885–1930.* Chicago, IL: University of Chicago Press, 1990.

Tax, Meredith. *The Rising of the Women: Feminist Solidarity and Class Conflict, 1880–1917.* NY: Monthly Review Press, 1980.

COLLECTIONS:

Mary Kenney O'Sullivan papers and the Papers of the National Women's Trade Union League, both at the Schlesinger Library, Radcliffe College.

Kathleen Banks Nutter,
Manuscripts Processor at the Sophia Smith Collection,
Smith College, Northampton, Massachusetts

O'Sullivan, Maureen (1911–1998)

Irish-born actress. *Born on May 17, 1911, in Boyle, County Roscommon, Ireland; died on June 22, 1998, in Phoenix, Arizona; married John Farrow (a screenwriter), in 1936 (died 1963); married James E. Cushing (a real-estate contractor), in 1983; children: (first marriage) seven, including Michael Farrow (1940–1958) and actress Mia Farrow (b. 1945).*

Selected filmography: Song O' My Heart *(1930);* So This Is London *(1930);* Just Imagine *(1930);* The Princess and the Plumber *(1930);* A Connecticut Yankee *(1931);* Skyline *(1931);* The Big Shot *(1931);* Tarzan the Ape Man *(1932);* The Silver Lining *(1932);* Fast Companions *(1932);* Skyscraper Souls *(1932);* Information Kid *(1932);* Strange Interlude *(1932);* Okay America *(1932);* Payment Deferred *(1932);* Robber's Roost *(1933);* The Cohens and Kellys in Trouble *(1933);* Tugboat Annie *(1933);* Stage Mother *(1933);* Tarzan and His Mate *(1934);* The Thin Man *(1934);* Hide-Out *(1934);* The Barretts of Wimpole Street *(1934);* David Copperfield *(1935);* West Point of the Air *(1935);* Cardinal Richelieu *(1935);* The Flame Within *(1935);* Woman Wanted *(1935);* Anna Karenina *(1935);* The Bishop Misbehaves *(1935);* The Voice of Bugle Ann *(1936);* The Devil Doll *(1936);* Tarzan Escapes *(1936);* A Day at the Races *(1937);* The Emperor's Candlesticks *(1937);* Between Two Women *(1937);* My Dear Miss Aldrich *(1937);* A Yank at Oxford *(1938);* Hold That Kiss *(1938);* Port of Seven Seas *(1938);* The Crowd Roars *(1938);* Spring Madness *(1938);* Let Us Live *(1939);* Tarzan Finds a Son *(1939);* Sporting Blood *(1940);* Pride and Prejudice *(1940);* Maisie Was a Lady *(1941);* Tarzan's Secret Treasure *(1941);* Tarzan's New York Adventure *(1942);* The Big Clock *(1948);* Where Danger Lives *(1950);* Bonzo Goes to College *(1952);* All I Desire *(1953);* Mission Over Korea *(1953);* Duffy of San Quentin *(1954);* The Steel Cage *(1954);* The Tall T *(1957);* Wild Heritage *(1958);* Never Too Late *(1965);* The Phynx *(cameo, 1970);* Too Scared to Scream *(1985);* Hannah and Her Sisters *(1986);* Peggy Sue Got Married *(1986);* Stranded *(1987).*

A delicate Irish beauty, actress Maureen O'Sullivan made her mark in film history as Jane, the scantily clad mate of Tarzan in a series of six movies she made with Johnny Weissmuller during the 1930s and and early 1940s. (She was replaced by **Brenda Joyce** in 1945.) O'Sullivan deserves equal recognition, however, for her more serious roles in such films as *The Barretts of Wimpole Street* (1934), *Cardinal Richelieu* (1935), *Anna Karenina* (1935), and *Pride and Prejudice* (1940).

The daughter of a British army major, O'Sullivan was born in 1911 in County Roscommon, Ireland, and educated in a convent outside London and at a Paris finishing school. At age 18, with no acting experience, she was discovered by American director Frank Borzage who negotiated her film debut in *Song O' My Heart* (1930), with the great Irish tenor John McCormack. O'Sullivan subsequently signed a contract with Fox, but eventually transferred to MGM, which produced the popular Tarzan series. The actress, who had never read Edgar Rice Burroughs' Tarzan books, had no idea what she was getting into. When she first met Johnny Weissmuller, "he was standing with just that loin cloth, and he was holding a spear in his hand," she told interviewer Ray Nielsen in 1997, "and he had his foot on a lion that was supposedly dead. It was probably a prop. . . . Anyway, he was supposed to spear this lion. It was very effective, and he raised his arm, and had the golden makeup on, and I thought he looked absolutely . . . terrific." The Tarzan movies were immensely popular, although some theatergoers objected to O'Sullivan's minimal costuming. "It started such a furor," she recalled. "Letters started coming in. It added up to thousands of women objecting to my costume. . . . It's funny. We were unreal people, and yet we were real."

O'Sullivan married director-screenwriter John Farrow in 1936, and had her first child Michael four years later. (Michael would die in an airplane collision in 1958.) Her children eventually numbered seven, including well-known actress **Mia Farrow**, and O'Sullivan put her career on hold to raise them. As her children

Maureen O'Sullivan

grew more independent, she gradually returned to the screen. "They like to have me come home and tell them what Bob Hope said, and so forth," she said. "It makes their mother seem more exciting." In the 1950s, she hosted the television series "Irish Heritage"; in the 1960s, she appeared in several Broadway and touring theater productions and was briefly a regular on the "Today" show. In 1962, she played opposite Paul Ford in the Broadway production of *Never Too Late* (1962), a role she reprised in the 1965 film version. O'Sullivan appeared with her daughter Mia in Woody Allen's *Hannah and Her Sisters,* playing Mia's mother, in 1985. Her last movies were *Peggy Sue Got Married* (1986) and *Stranded* (1987).

John Farrow died in 1963. Twenty years later, O'Sullivan married real-estate contractor James Cushing, and spent her later years commuting between homes in New Hampshire, New York, and Arizona, with frequent visits to her 30 grandchildren. When the actress died in 1998, she was eulogized as much for her spirit as her career. Said her long-time agent John Springer, "She was warm, generous, kind, and loving."

SOURCES:

Katz, Ephraim. *The Film Encyclopedia.* NY: HarperCollins, 1994.

"Mia's Mama," in *People Weekly.* July 6, 1998.

Nielsen, Ray. "A Final Interview with Maureen O'Sullivan (1911–1998)," in *Classic Images.* August 1998, pp. C10–C13.

"Obituary," in *The Day* (New London, CT). June 23, 1998.

"Obituary," in *Newsday.* June 24, 1998.

Barbara Morgan,
Melrose, Massachusetts

Oswald, Marina (1941—)

Russian-born wife of presidential assassin Lee Harvey Oswald. *Name variations: Marina Alexandrovna Medvedeva; (erroneously) Marina Pruskova; Marina Oswald Porter. Born Marina Nikolayevna Prusakova on July 17, 1941, in Molotovsk, Russia; daughter of Klavdia Prusakova (a laboratory worker); received diploma from the Pharmacy Institute, 1959; married Lee Harvey Oswald, on April 30, 1961 (died November 24, 1963); married Kenneth Porter, in 1965 (divorced 1974); children: (first marriage) June Lee Oswald (b. February 1962); Audrey Marina Rachel Oswald (b. October 1963); (second marriage) Mark Porter (b. 1966).*

Marina Nikolayevna Prusakova, who would later become the wife of Lee Harvey Oswald, was born to an unmarried laboratory worker in Molotovsk, USSR, in 1941. In earliest childhood, she was raised largely by her grandmother, who hated Stalin and showered Marina with love. She later lived with her mother, stepfather and younger siblings in a village in Moldovia (where she witnessed the dispossession of local *kulaks*) and then in Leningrad (now St. Petersburg), where the family shared a small room with her stepfather's unkind mother. Even while young, Marina had an uneasy sense that she was "different" from other people and unwanted, feelings that only increased after she learned of her illegitimacy. She never discovered the full name of her real father or the circumstances surrounding her conception, although she heard vague whispers that he had been branded an enemy of the people and punished accordingly. Marina's stepfather became increasingly cold to her as she grew older, and she deeply resented her mother's unwillingness to stand up for her, or even to kiss her while he was present. They were almost completely estranged by the time her mother died of cancer when Marina was 15. Her stepfather then began hinting, and finally demanding, that she should find somewhere else to live. After graduating from the Pharmacy Institute in Leningrad in 1959, she moved in with relatives in Minsk.

At a dance in March 1961, Marina met Lee Harvey Oswald, who had been sent to Minsk to live as a "stateless person" after arriving in Moscow in October 1959. He had left America planning to become a citizen of the USSR, but Soviet authorities, unsure of his real motivations and believing him to have mental problems, had no intention of granting him citizenship. As the only American in Minsk, however, he was an object of much curiosity and fascination. Marina, who had many boyfriends at the time, began dating him. While initially she was not sure whether she even particularly liked him, he soon proposed, and they were married on April 30, 1961, less than two months after they had met. Lee had become disillusioned with the Soviet Union, and was already planning on returning to the United States at the time of the marriage, although he had not told Marina this. They left for America in June 1962 and settled in Texas, where Marina, who spoke no English, hoped to live a cosmopolitan lifestyle. Within a year of their arrival, Lee had bought two rifles.

Marina and Lee had a daughter, June, in February 1962, but their marriage was tense. Lee was moody and secretive, wildly ambitious despite having no particular achievements to build on, and frequently beat Marina and forced her to have sex with him. He was an erratic worker at each of the number of low-level jobs he briefly held. Early in 1963, he concocted a plan to assassinate Edwin A. Walker, a prominent member of the John Birch Society, and came home late one night to tell Marina "I shot Walker." As it turned out, he had missed. He was not caught, and Marina kept her silence. Later, when she found him, as she believed, leaving the house with a gun on a spur-of-the-moment mission to shoot Richard Nixon, she locked him in the bathroom. After that, they moved to New Orleans, and then later to Dallas, where Lee got a job at the Texas School Book Depository.

Like most of the nation, Marina and Lee avidly followed all news of President John F. Kennedy and his wife ***Jacqueline Kennedy**, and they had cried when the Kennedys' baby son Patrick died in August 1963. Marina was pregnant at the time, and in October, while living with a friend, she gave birth to her second daughter, Audrey. Relations with Lee were strained. Less than five weeks later, on November 22, she watched on television as the Kennedys arrived in Dallas. That day Lee Harvey Oswald assassinated the president and murdered J.D. Tippit, a police officer, while unsuccessfully trying to escape. According to **Priscilla Johnson McMillan**, when officers searched the Oswalds' garage soon after and discovered that Lee's rifle was missing, Marina knew her husband was responsible for the killings. She saw him briefly in custody the next morning, and the following day, while he was being transferred from the city jail, Lee was shot and killed by nightclub owner Jack Ruby.

Marina and her children were under Secret Service protection for a time, and she was interviewed for months by the Secret Service, the FBI and the Warren Commission. Financial assistance and marriage proposals from strangers poured in, magazines wanted interviews and photographs, and hustlers tried to interest her in schemes (such as her touring the country with her husband's body) to profit from her notoriety. In 1965, after some of the spotlight had dimmed, she remarried and moved to a ranch. In later years, she worked in a department store, and became a U.S. citizen in 1990. Initially convinced that Lee had acted alone, Marina gradually came to believe some variety of the many conspiracy theories that continue to swirl around Kennedy's assassination, and to proclaim that her husband had been an innocent patsy in a political plot and subsequent cover-up.

SOURCES:

At Random. Summer 1995, pp. 12–19.

Ladies' Home Journal. May 1993.

McMillan, Priscilla Johnson. *Marina and Lee.* NY: Harper & Row, 1977.

Newsweek. August 11, 1975, September 26, 1977.

Time. October 24, 1977.

Daniel E. Brannen, Jr.,
freelance writer, York, Pennsylvania

Oswalda, Ossi (1897–1948)

German silent-film star. *Born Oswalda Stäglich in Berlin, Germany, in 1897; died in 1948.*

Selected filmography: Nacht des Grauens *(1916);* Schupalast Pinkus *(1916);* Der Gmb-H Tenor *(1916);* Ossis Tagebuch *(1917);* Wenn Vier dasselbe machen *(1917);* Ein fideles Gefängnis *(1917);* Prinz Sami *(1918);* Der Rodelkavalier *(1918);* Der Fall Rosentopf *(1918);* Das Mädel vom Ballet *(1918);* Meier aus Berlin *(1919);* Meine Frau die Filmschauspielerin *(1919);* Schwabenmädle *(1919);* Die Austerprinzessin *(*The Oyster Princess, *1919);* Die Puppe *(*The Doll, *1919);* Der blinde Passagier *(1922);* Das Mädel mit der maske *(1922);* Colibri *(also prod., 1924);* Blitzzug der Liebe *(*Express Train of Love, *1925);* Das Mädchen mit Protektion *(1925);* Die Kleine vom Varieté *(1926);* Ein tolle Nacht *(1926);* Wochenendbraut *(1928);* Eddy Polo mit Pferd und Lasso *(1928);* Das Haus ohne Männer *(1928);* Ossi hat die Hosen an *(1928);* Der Keusche Joseph *(1930);* Der Stern von Valencia *(1933).*

One of Germany's most popular silent stars during the 1920s, Ossi Oswalda was a protégé of the great German director Ernst Lubitsch, who is also credited with discovering ***Pola Negri**. Oswalda was a model and chorus dancer before making her film debut in *Nacht des Grauens* (1916). Particularly memorable among her Lubitsch collaborations are *The Oyster Princess* and *The Doll* (both 1919). Like many silent-screen performers, Oswalda did not survive the advent of sound and retired in 1933.

Otero, Caroline (1868–1965)

***Spanish-born dancer and courtesan who flourished in Paris' Golden Age, known as the* Belle Époque.** *Name variations: La Belle Otero; Augustina Otero; billed in New York as Countess Carolina de Otero; (nickname) Lina. Born Augustina Iglesias Otero (but took the name Caroline Otero after her older sister Carolina died as a child) in the village of Valga or Balga, in the Spanish province of Galicia, Spain, on November 4 (or 24), 1868; died in Nice, France, on April 10, 1965; daughter of a Spanish Gypsy (Roma) prostitute and an unknown father, possibly a Greek noble; did not attend school, but spoke French and English; married at 15 (divorced).*

Toured in cabarets in eastern Spain and southern France (1882–89); made debut on the legitimate stage at the Eden Musée in New York City (October 1, 1890); went on first European tour (1891–92); appeared in Paris at the Cirque d'Été (1892); went on world tour (1894); appeared in Paris, including the Folies Bergère (1894–95); went on Italian tour (1896–97); returned to New York (1897); gave last performance in London in the revue Come Over Here *(November 1913); retired from the stage (June 1914).*

Referred to as one of 19th-century Paris' "grand horizontals," La Belle Otero ostensibly made her living as a Spanish dancer, although it appears that she had a lucrative side business in the boudoir. Born Augustina Otero in Galicia in 1868, one of seven illegitimate children of a Cadiz Gypsy (Roma), she took the name Caroline Otero after her older sister Carolina died as a child. Her father was possibly a Greek noble. At 11, Otero was raped and rendered infertile; at 12, she ran away from home; by age 15, she had wandered through Spain and southern France, acquiring a trio of lovers and an Italian husband whom she claimed in her memoirs was "as handsome as Bizet's Toreador," but whom she abandoned to pursue a dancing career in Marseilles.

She eventually found her way to Paris, where she performed at the Cirque d'Été and other music halls, then joined the Folies Bergère where she became renowned for her wild Spanish fandango as well as for the real jewels adorning her famed bosom. (Reportedly, her breasts inspired the twin cupolas of the Hotel Carlton in Cannes.) Otero by no means limited her dancing to the stage, but performed in restaurants and cafes as the spirit moved her, arousing the male patrons in attendance to near frenzy. After viewing her after-hours show at Maxim's one evening, the cartoonist Sem remarked, "I feel that my thighs are blushing."

Caroline Otero

During Otero's music-hall days, the writer *Colette, who was then performing as a pantomimist and sometimes shared the bill, was occasionally invited back to Otero's house for supper. In her memoirs *Mes Apprentissages*, Colette writes of Otero's boundless energy and huge appetite. ("When finally she pushed her plate aside, it would be after it had been emptied four, even five times.") After dinner ended at ten, Otero would frequently dance until two in the morning for her own pleasure. "Throwing her robe aside, she danced in her chemise and swirling silk petticoat," wrote Colette. "The sweat ran down to her thighs. She'd grab a sauce-spotted napkin from the table and wipe her face, her neck, her armpits. Then she'd dance again and again."

Otero's reputation in the boudoir was as formidable as her fandango. Numbered among her lovers were the crowned heads of England, Spain, and Serbia, the kaiser, the Russian grand dukes Peter and Nicholas, the duke of Westminster, the French premier Aristide Briand, and the Italian writer Gabriele d'Annunzio, most of whom she met during her many dancing tours. While she was performing at New York's Eden Musée, she lived with the manager, a man named Jurgens, who at the end of her engagement stole the box-office receipts so he could follow her back to Paris. In her somewhat overblown autobiography, Otero modestly suggested that all men fell dead over her. In fact, several did, noted ***Cornelia Otis Skinner**: "Comte Chevedolé, a prominent member of the Jockey Club, blew his brains out after he had squandered his fortune on her. An explorer named Payen offered her ten thousand gold francs for one night of her lavishments and when she turned him down, put on a similar brain-blowing performance in the Bois outside the Chinese Pavilion where they'd first met."

During her heyday, Otero lived on what was then the rue Georges Bizet in a magnificent house run by 15 servants and a private secretary. She dressed garishly, flaunted her vast array of jewelry, and drove around town in an oversized blue satin upholstered carriage pulled by four black horses. It was not unusual for the dancer to show up at a party wearing a daringly décolleté evening gown with her entire collection of jewelry adorning body parts from head to ankle. On one gala evening, she was decked out in three pearl necklaces (one a former possession of the Empress ***Eugénie**), eight bracelets, ten ruby clips, a pearl and diamond tiara, and her famous diamond bolero, a piece valued at 2,275,000 gold francs which she kept in the vaults of the Crédit Lyonnais. (She often performed in the bolero, at which times two armed gendarmes were stationed in the wings.)

Although she amassed great wealth, Otero had a lust for the gambling table and lost money as fast as she made it. When she abandoned her career at 45, claiming she wanted to retire "in full beauty," she had already squandered most of her fortune. Gradually, she sold off her elegant furniture and jewelry piece by piece, after which she took a one-room apartment in Nice, where she lived for the rest of her life. Although she grew somewhat fat with age, she retained a touch of flair, reminiscent of the age in which she lived. "When Otero departs," wrote **Anne Manson** in Guilleminault's *La Belle Epoque*, "there will depart with her the last symbol of an epoch, superficial, light and at the same time virtuous, covetous toward others yet madly extravagant in its pleasures, full of faults but not without its splendor." Caroline Otero died in 1965, at age 97.

SOURCES:

Guilleminault, Gilbert. *La Belle Epoque*.

Lewis, Arthur H. *La Belle Otero*. Trident, 1967.

Otero, Caroline. *Le Roman de la Belle Otero*. Paris, 1919.

Richardson, Joanna. *The Courtesans: The Demi-monde in 19th Century France*. World, 1967.

Skinner, Cornelia Otis. *Elegant Wits and Grand Horizontals*. NY: Houghton Mifflin, 1962.

RELATED MEDIA:

La Belle Otéro (Fr. film), starring ***Maria Felix**, 1954.

Barbara Morgan,
Melrose, Massachusetts

Otero, Katherine Stinson (1891–1977).

See Stinson, Katherine.

Ottenberg, Nettie Podell
(1887–1982)

American social worker, one the first formally trained in the U.S., who worked for more than 60 years to improve laws and social policies affecting women and children. *Pronunciation: OT-in-berg. Born Nettie Podell in Ukraine, Russia, on April 5, 1887; died in Washington, D.C., on May 11, 1982; daughter of Mordecai "Max" Podell (a bookkeeper) and Mannie Podell; attended New York School of Philanthropy and graduated in first class, 1905; married Louis Ottenberg, on April 10, 1912 (died May 10, 1960); children: Regina Ottenberg; Miriam Ottenberg; Louis Ottenberg, Jr.*

Immigrated to America (1893); spent childhood in New York, NY; moved to Washington, D.C. (1912); worked as juvenile probation officer, Philadelphia (1906–09); examined newly arrived immigrant girls, Brooklyn Council of Jewish Women (1909–11); organized and ran first political settlement house for suffrage workers, Harlem, New York (1909–11); was state organizer and speaker, New York State Suffrage Association (1912); helped manage suffrage parade down Pennsylvania Avenue (March 1913); was a founding member of a Voteless D.C. chapter of the League of Women Voters (1920), and served as president (1937–39); served as president for Washington, D.C. Section, National Council of Jewish Women (1937–39) and representative to its Women's Joint Congressional Committee (1928–77); appointed to Public Welfare Advisory Committee on day care (1963); won first federal funding for day care (1964); was a board member, National Child Day Care Association, Washington, D.C. (1964–70s); advocated use of federal Medicaid money for early and periodic screening, diagnosis and treatment for underprivileged children (1971); given Official Commendation for Meritorious Public Service from the District of Columbia (1971).

On July 17, 1962, 75-year-old Nettie Podell Ottenberg testified before Senator Robert Byrd and his District Appropriations Subcommittee. Given just five minutes, she wasted no time in asking for $100,000 to establish a day-care center for the children of welfare mothers. Representing 23 organizations, she argued that providing day care would enable poor women to get off relief rolls and into the work force. Ottenberg was grateful when Byrd gave her five more minutes. "Finally, he looked over my head and asked those who were supporting me to stand," she later recalled. "My heart was in my mouth. I turned around. The whole room was standing up." The committee eventually allocated $50,000; Nettie Ottenberg had won the first federal money for day care in Washington, D.C.

Ottenberg was no stranger to poverty. She was born in the Ukraine, in Russia, in 1887, the daughter of Mordecai Max Podell and **Mannie Podell**. Her father had gone to America in 1893, where, working as a bookkeeper, he saved enough money in six months to send for his family. Mannie and the children had to bribe officials and cross the Russian border quickly. In 1893, the family moved into a tenement in New York's Lower East Side Jewish neighborhood; Nettie was then five. As a young teenager, she often took neighborhood children to Central Park to get them off the streets. At 16, she stumbled over a starving woman in a tenement stairwell. She asked a Jewish social service organization for assistance, but was disappointed when they sent investigators instead of food and clothing.

Only an eighth-grade graduate but determined to help fix the system, Ottenberg passed a high-school equivalency exam and entered the first class of the New York School of Philanthropy to study social work. She supplemented classroom seminars with field work, studying working conditions for women firsthand. She took a job in a feather and flower factory, steaming feathers in a basement, receiving one dollar for her 54-hour work week.

After graduating in 1905, Ottenberg went to work organizing a settlement house on New York's Upper East Side. She dealt with hostility between Irish and Jewish residents and convinced rival gangs to use the playroom and other settlement house services. The experience led to an interest in juvenile justice, and she left New York to work as a probation officer in Philadelphia's juvenile courts in 1906.

In 1908, she began reading about women's efforts to win the right to vote. Her experience with poor families in New York and Philadelphia convinced her that suffrage could empower poor women to improve conditions for themselves and their children. She returned to New York and convinced Mrs. O.H.P. Belmont (***Alva Smith Belmont**) to rent a house in Harlem as the United States' first political settlement house. Ottenberg ran the settlement as a home base for suffragists organizing nearby from 1909 to 1911. From February to July 1912, she traveled for the New York State Suffrage Association, organizing statewide support. She had married Louis Ottenberg that April and finally joined him in Washington, D.C., at the end of the summer. In Washington, she helped organize the pivotal 1913 suffrage parade down Pennsylvania Avenue. The parade marked suffragists' first public demand for a constitutional amendment and gave birth to ***Alice Paul**'s radical National Woman's Party.

After women won the right to vote in 1920, Ottenberg still had a battle to wage for the citizens of Washington, D.C. Legislative control of the city rested with Congress, and residents had no congressional representative, no local elections, and no vote for the president. The city government was run by a three-man commission appointed by the president. Ottenberg helped found a "Voteless D.C." chapter of the League of Women Voters. Most local chapters worked toward a national platform, but Ottenberg and other members of the D.C. chapter met with League leaders ***Maud Wood Park** and ***Belle Sherwin** in 1925 and obtained permission to work toward independent goals.

The Voteless D.C. chapter fought only for federal voting rights until 1938, when they saw the Lewis-Randolf Joint Congressional Resolution as a possible route to local as well as federal representation. Ottenberg had taken over as president of the chapter in 1937, and she rallied support for the resolution, convincing the National League of Women Voters to accept this broader platform for District suffrage. "I'd hate to think women were working just for women," she said. "We feel that our work is for the good of the country as a whole. When we worked for the ballot we urged that we could become good citizens. I think we have proved that we can and that we can work in a nonpartisan way for legislation that will benefit the group as a whole." District citizens finally won the right to vote for the president in 1962 and for a city council in 1964.

Ottenberg led the Voteless D.C. chapter of the League of Women Voters to other victories. As chair of the Social Hygiene Committee, she saw the abolition of taxi dance halls in 1934. Her committee also won congressional sponsorship for a new adoption law, doing away with the practice of baby brokers. On behalf of the chapter, Ottenberg fought to establish a Police Department Women's Bureau and better facilities for women prisoners. During her presidency in 1938, the chapter succeeded in its efforts to improve the juvenile court system.

Well into her 60s, she was still searching for new solutions to improve conditions for poor families. In 1957, she visited tax-supported daycare facilities in Copenhagen, Denmark. Impressed, after her return home she called together representatives from 23 local organizations and began the fight for federally funded day-care facilities in Washington, D.C. In 1962, her dramatic testimony before Robert Byrd's Senate District Appropriations Subcommittee won federal funding for a day-care center in the Arthur Capper Public Housing Unit. Responding to criticism of federally funded day care, Ottenberg said, "If mothers are expected to work and be independent and self-supporting, we've got to provide day care for children. The alternatives are to keep the family on relief, or let them go to work and then pick up the tab for the cost of delinquency." In 1963, the D.C. Board of Commissioners appointed her to the Public Welfare Advocacy Committee on Day Care, and she helped establish the Office of Economic Opportunity's National Capital Area Day Care Association.

When the OEO was abolished, the National Child Day Care Association began running daycare centers across the city. In 1971, Ottenberg discovered a rarely used clause in the Medicaid Bill which provided comprehensive medical treatment for poor children. As a board member of the National Child Day Care Association, she helped win a foundation grant to study the use of the city's day-care centers for screening children. That success led, in 1973, to a three-year grant from the Department of Health, Education and Welfare to implement Early Periodic Screening, Diagnosis and Treatment programs for poor children.

Ottenberg's activities resulted in numerous articles, commendations and awards. On the occasion of her 90th birthday, she received letters from vice-president Walter Mondale, Secretary of Health, Education and Welfare Caspar Weinberger and others. D.C. mayor Walter Washington wrote, "Your lifetime work as a volunteer lobbyist for a wide range of social welfare legislation has been an invaluable contribution to our community and has made you one of Washington's most remarkable and valued citizens." Nettie Ottenberg died in Washington, D.C., in 1982, at age 95.

SOURCES:

Dickson, Harold D., Sandra Balfour, and James Ballard. *The National Child Day Care Association EPSDT Demonstration Project, October 1, 1973 through June 30, 1977*. San Antonio, TX: Health Services Research Institute, 1978.

Jenkins, Sara, ed. "Nettie Ottenberg interviewed by Rebecca Wardell," in *Past Present: Recording Life Stories of Older People*. Washington, DC: St. Alban's Parish, 1978.

Kernan, Michael. "The Mother of Day Care: Granny Patrols at 90," in *The Washington Post*. August 10, 1977, p. B1.

Meringolo, Denise D. Interviews with Louis Ottenberg, Jr. 1995–1996.

Sadler, Christine. "League President Also Interested in Obtaining Autonomy School Board Once Enjoyed," in *The Washington Post*. July 8, 1938.

SUGGESTED READING:

Baum, Charlotte, Paula Hyman, and Sonya Michel. *The Jewish Woman in America*. NY: Dial Press, 1976.

Fishman, Sylvia Barack. *A Breath of Life: Feminism in the American Jewish Community*. Hanover, NH: Brandeis University Press, 1995.

COLLECTIONS:

The League of Women Voters Collection, Manuscripts Division, Library of Congress, Washington, D.C.; Women's Joint Congressional Committee Collection, Manuscripts Division, Library of Congress, Washington, D.C.

Denise D. Meringolo,
Curator, Jewish Historical Society of Greater Washington, Washington, D.C.

Ottendorfer, Anna Uhl (1815–1884)

German-born American newspaper publisher and philanthropist. *Born Anna Sartorius on February 13, 1815, in Wurzburg, Bavaria (now part of Germany); died on April 1, 1884, in New York City; daughter of Eduard Sartorius (by some accounts Eduard Behr, a small shopkeeper); received very little education; married Jacob Uhl (a printer, died 1852); married Oswald Ottendorfer (an editor), on July 23, 1859; children: (first marriage) six, including Edward Uhl; Mathilde Uhl von Riedl; Emma Uhl Schalk; and Anna Uhl Woerishoffer.*

Emigrated to New York City from Bavaria (c. 1836); with first husband, bought a print shop and began printing German weekly (1844); bought newspaper outright and with husband shared all responsibilities of printing and publishing it (1845); managed entire newspaper business after Jacob Uhl's death (1852); married Oswald Ottendorfer, who had become editor of her newspaper (1859); contributed $100,000 to build home for elderly women of German ancestry (1875); contributed another $100,000 to establish fund in her son's memory to support the study of German in American schools (1881); gave funds for women's pavilion and a German dispensary and reading room to hospital (1882 and 1884, respectively).

Born Anna Sartorius in Bavaria in 1815, Anna Uhl Ottendorfer was the daughter of Eduard Sartorius (some sources give her surname as Behr). Her father was a small shopkeeper of modest means, and she received a very limited education prior to her marriage to Jacob Uhl, a printer. It is not clear whether she married Uhl before or after she came to America and settled in New York City in 1836. In 1844, the couple purchased a print shop and along with it the contract for printing the German weekly *New-Yorker Staats-Zeitung*. By 1845, they had purchased the paper from its founder and editor, Gustav Neumann. Anna played an important part in the success of the paper, sharing all duties with her husband, while also raising six children. Through their hard work, the paper became a daily in 1849 and was distributed to other cities with large German communities as well. When Jacob Uhl died suddenly in 1852, Anna took over the paper's leadership. In July 1859, she married Oswald Ottendorfer, who had joined the paper in 1851 and become editor in 1858. Under his guidance, the paper increasingly represented the liberal German viewpoint, not only in New York City, but also in Milwaukee and other areas of German settlement. The paper strongly supported the Union in the Civil War and later opposed the political machine of Tammany Hall. Following her marriage to Ottendorfer, Anna assumed the general managership of the paper, and devoted more time to philanthropic causes.

Anna Ottendorfer's monetary gifts to organizations most often reflected her strong social consciousness and her desire to maintain and encourage German traditions in America. With a $100,000 gift, in 1875, she founded the Isabella Home for aged German-American women in Astoria, New York. The home was named for a daughter who had died two years before. After a son died in 1881, she established the Hermann Uhl Memorial Fund with contributions totaling almost $100,000. This fund promoted the study of German in American schools, and its chief beneficiary was the German-American Teachers' College of Milwaukee. She also donated $225,000 toward the building and furnishing of a women's pavilion at New York's German Hospital, and a German dispensary and reading room. Ottendorfer was awarded a gold medal by *__Augusta of Saxe-Weimar__, empress of Germany, in recognition of her efforts on behalf of German culture in America. She also was active in the Children's Aid Society and the State Charities Aid Association.

Anna Ottendorfer suffered from chronic heart disease, and in February 1883, she had a disabling heart attack. She died the next year at her New York home on April 1, survived by her second husband and four of her six children: Edward Uhl, who was the business manager of the *Staats-Zeitung*; **Mathilde von Riedl** of Bavaria; **Emma Schalk**; and **Anna Uhl Woerishoffer**, wife of a New York banker and mother of the social worker *__Carola Woerishoffer__. Ottendorfer left $250,000 to various German-American institutions, as well as $25,000 to be divided among the employees of the newspaper. At her death, City Hall flags were lowered to half-staff and her funeral cortege proceeded along black-draped streets to Greenwood Cemetery in Brooklyn, New York.

SOURCES:

McHenry, Robert, ed. *Famous American Women*. NY: Dover, 1980.

Uglow, Jennifer S., comp. and ed. *The International Dictionary of Women's Biography*. NY: Continuum, 1985.

SUGGESTED READING:

Wittke, Carl. *The German-Language Press in America*, 1957.

Jo Anne Meginnes,
freelance writer, Brookfield, Vermont

Ottesen-Jensen, Elise (1886–1973)

Norwegian-born feminist and author who was the leading advocate of sex education and sex law reform in Sweden (1920s–1950s) and a leader in the international family planning movement. *Name variations: (pseudonym) Ottar. Born in Jaaren [Jaeren], Hojland, Sweden (now Norway), on January 2, 1886; died in Stockholm, Sweden, on September 4, 1973; daughter of Immanuel Ottesen and Karen Ursula (Essendrop) Ottesen; had 17 siblings; married Albert Jensen, in 1931; children: one son (died two days after birth in 1917).*

Elise Ottesen-Jensen, one of the major personalities in European family planning and sex education, was born in 1886 as the 17th of 18 children, only 11 of whom survived infancy. The daughter of **Karen Essendrop Ottesen** and Immanuel Ottesen, a Lutheran cleric, Elise Ottesen grew up in the Hojland area, on the west coast of Norway. Later in life, she would recall the "incredibly beautiful" coastal region, and the experience of walking through moors covered with purple heather. After a happy childhood, Elise entered adolescence and began to question her father's views. Although both her parents were relatively liberal for their day, even allowing their children to dance, Norwegians then tended to be pietistic and guilt-ridden, regarding even innocent pleasures as potentially sinful. When Elise's youngest, unmarried sister **Magnhild Ottesen** became pregnant, Immanuel, hoping to ward off family disgrace, sent her to Denmark to await the birth. Back home, having borne a child out of wedlock, Magnhild was barred from enrolling in a nurse's training program; thus, she could never advance beyond working as a nurse's aide. A few years later, after her child died, Magnhild's mental state deteriorated, and she was institutionalized in an asylum for the mentally disturbed. There, fixated by the loss of her child, she spent her time sewing baby clothes, and died in 1934, only 44 years old.

Ottesen-Jensen had wanted to become a physician, but family finances made this impossible, so she settled on becoming a dentist. While studying, however, she lost three fingers in a laboratory explosion, forever ruling out dentistry as a career. After working for a short time as a stenographer at the national Parliament, she decided to take up journalism.

Convinced that her nation was much in need of social and economic reforms, Ottesen found herself increasingly drawn to the labor movement. Unlike the Scandinavia of a generation later, which embodied model welfare-state programs designed to serve social needs from cradle to grave, early in the 20th century these nations were gripped by poverty and backwardness. Between 1815 and 1939, 1,250,000 Swedes and 850,000 Norwegians emigrated to the United States. Women, particularly if they were poor, lived in terror of unwanted pregnancies, and a 1910 Swedish law decreed severe penalties for those who had an abortion. During this period, Ottesen-Jensen quickly became a respected journalist. Using the pen name "Ottar," she covered the 1912 Olympic summer games, which took place in Stockholm. Her articles on the need for reform of Sweden's abortion laws, as well as her spirited advocacy of women's rights, including suffrage, made her well known in working-class circles. In 1913, she met Albert Jensen. A well-known Swedish syndicalist, Jensen espoused views that were progressive and often radical. Through him, Elise met and was influenced by Hinke Bergegren, a male radical who was unusually sensitive to the women's agenda of the day. Ottesen-Jensen was particularly struck by Bergegren's slogan "Love Without Babies," which advocated smaller families for workers, as opposed to the often grim reality of babies without love.

In October 1917, while living in Copenhagen, where she and Albert had found refuge after being expelled from Norway because of their opposition to World War I, Elise gave birth to a son who died two days later. She was gravely ill with puerperal fever for a time, after which she could no longer bear children. Soon after, she and Jensen moved to Stockholm, which was to be Elise's home for the rest of her life. Many of her friends in Stockholm were physicians, nurses and social workers, who often spoke of the need for limiting family size, as well as the need for sex education in the schools. In 1923, Elise Ottesen-Jensen published her first article on the need for parents to answer, in an honest fashion, questions about sex that were posed to them by their children. She also began to lecture and to write on the importance of every woman being educated in the details of contraception, so that only wanted children would be born.

Ottesen-Jensen was a charismatic public speaker who made a powerful impact on her audiences. Indefatigable, she traveled up, down, and across the nation in her Ford automobile, sooner or later making an appearance in virtually every town and village. Many of these areas, remote and impoverished, resembled what in the post-1945 world has been designated as "underdeveloped." She often shared the crowded dwellings and simple food of her working-class hosts. She would fit women for diaphragms in outhouses and even in her Ford, which served as "a traveling clinic." Despite censure, resistance, and lingering taboos about discussing sexuality in public, she continued her work. The state-supported Lutheran and Dissenter churches were critical of her activities, regarding public discussion of birth control as "immoral," something that served to encourage "sinful" behavior. At times, criticism went beyond verbal attacks, as when she was spat on while riding in a streetcar in Bergen, Norway. She spread the message through clearly written pamphlets, including *Unwanted Children* (1926) and *Tell Your Child the Truth* (1945). She also published a periodical devoted to these social problems, which she believed was essential in an environment in which both "society and the state had defaulted" and in which many Swedes, men and women alike, continued to regard sexuality as an area of life that was unclean and must be kept hidden at all costs.

Elise Ottesen-Jensen's idea of sex education was all-inclusive, and she often would discuss subjects that were then even more taboo, including masturbation and homosexuality. Her view was that masturbation in a healthy adolescent was a normal activity that did no harm. On homosexuality, she stressed that it was a biological phenomenon and should not be stigmatized as a criminal offense. In speeches and writings, she argued passionately that the existing statutes against homosexuality should be scrapped. She also refused to condemn premarital sex, noting that it was simply a fact already taking place, and to continue to do so—as the clergy and social conservatives did—only served to add a psychological burden on young people, as well as stigmatize those children who had been born out of wedlock.

By the end of the 1920s, Ottesen-Jensen was broadening her horizons beyond Scandinavia. In 1928, she met many of the world's leading advocates of birth control when she attended the international congress, held that year in Copenhagen, of the World League for Sexual Reform. In 1929 and 1930, at birth-control conferences held in London and Zurich, Elise met fellow pioneers *__Margaret Sanger__, and Abraham and **Hannah Stone**. These personal contacts would deepen over the next years. During the 1930s,

Ottesen-Jensen was busier than ever. Personally, however, all was not well. Although she and Albert were finally married in 1931, after living together for almost two decades, their relationship showed signs of tension. In the spring of 1935, returning home from a lecture tour, Elise found her husband in bed with a young woman who had been staying with them. Although they did not permanently separate until September 1937, their marriage was doomed from that point on.

Despite the travails of her private life, intense work kept Ottesen-Jensen on track as a reformer. Her most important tasks during this decade were her many activities on behalf of Sweden's National League for Sexual Education (RFSU), an organization she played a key role in founding in 1932. A decade later, in 1942, she could point to many victories achieved and others clearly within sight. Elementary school curriculums began to incorporate sex education into their lesson plans. In that year, "Ottar House," named in honor of Ottesen-Jensen, opened its doors as a home for unwed mothers and their children. Wrote a journalist at the time: "Elise is one of Sweden's greatest sex educators" and a woman with a powerful personality "who never swerves from doing what she views as right." During World War II, Ottesen-Jensen provided assistance to Jewish refugees who had fled Nazi-occupied Norway and Denmark. In several instances, she lobbied for official permission to authorize the employment of Jewish physicians in birth-control activities. In later decades when she visited Israel, Ottesen-Jensen was warmly greeted by those she had helped during the difficult war years.

In 1945, sex education became obligatory in Sweden's school system. The following year, Ottesen-Jensen convened an international conference in Stockholm that resulted in the founding of the International Committee on Planned Parenthood. America's Margaret Sanger was chosen as first president of this organization, which was to become the International Planned Parenthood Federation (IPPF) at a conference held in India in 1952. At this meeting, **Dorothy Brush** identified "the five outstanding women" of the international birth-control movement as being Margaret Sanger, Elise Ottesen-Jensen, **Dhanvanthi Rama Rau**, **Shidzue Kato**, and **Constance Goh Kok Kee**. Few birth control activists were surprised when Ottesen-Jensen was elected as the organization's second president in 1959. In 1963, certain that the IPPF had been able to define its goals clearly and was in good hands, Elise resigned as founder-president, retaining the title of president emeritus. In 1972, she was nominated for the Nobel Peace Prize. She had already received an impressive number of awards, including the Lasker Award in 1945, the Illis Quorum gold medal from the Swedish Medical Board in 1951, and an honorary doctorate (in medicine) from the University of Uppsala in 1958. In Israel in 1966, both a street and a child-care center called Ottar House was named in her honor.

After being ill with uterine cancer for several years, Ottesen-Jensen died in Stockholm on September 4, 1973. In a newspaper tribute, her friend **Greta Bolin** recalled how as long ago as 1933 Elise had said: "I dream of the day when every child that is born is welcome, when men and women are equal, and sexuality is an expression of intimacy, pleasure and tenderness."

SOURCES:

"Elise Ottesen-Jensen 1886–1973," in *People* [London]. Vol. 19, no. 1, 1992, p. 24.

Huston, Perdita. *Motherhood by Choice: Pioneers in Women's Health and Family Planning.* NY: Feminist Press, 1992.

Israel, Sarah. "'Ottar': Fearless Pioneer," in *Economic and Political Weekly* [Mumbai, India]. Vol. 33, no. 11. March 14–20, 1998, pp. 583–584.

Linder, Doris H. *Crusader for Sex Education: Elise Ottesen-Jensen (1886–1973) in Scandinavia and on the International Scene.* Lanham, MD: University Press of America, 1996.

———. "Ottesen-Jensen, Elise," in Warren F. Kuehl, ed., *Biographical Dictionary of Internationalists.* Westport, CT: Greenwood Press, 1983, pp. 557–559.

Mankell, Henning. *Älskade Syster: Ett Drömspel om Elise Ottesen-Jensen, svensk Agitator och Kvinna.* Stockholm: Ordfront, 1983.

Ottesen-Jensen, Elise. *Livet Skrev: Memoarer 1886–1966.* Stockholm: Ordfronts Förlag Riksförbundet för Sexuell Upplysning, 1986.

———, and Ingrid Primander. *Arbetarrörelsen—Männens eller Mänsklighetens Rörelse?* Stockholm: Federativ, 1980.

Riksförbundet för Sexuell Upplysning. *40 År med RFSU: Sexualupplysning i Sverige fran 30-Talet till Idag.* Edited by Carl Adam Nycop, Greta Sörlin and Lena Swanberg. Stockholm: RFSU, 1973.

Suitters, Beryl. *Be Brave and Angry: Chronicles of the International Planned Parenthood Federation.* London: International Planned Parenthood Federation, 1973.

COLLECTIONS:

Elise Ottesen-Jensen Papers, Labor Movement Archives, Stockholm, Sweden; International Planned Parenthood Federation Archives, University of Cardiff.

John Haag,
Associate Professor of History, University of Georgia, Athens, Georgia

Ottey-Page, Merlene (1960—)

Jamaican sprinter. *Name variations: Merlene Ottey. Born Merlene Ottey on May 10, 1960, in Jamaica; attended the University of Nebraska; married Nat Page (an American high jumper-hurdler), in 1984.*

As of 1999, Jamaican sprinter Merlene Ottey-Page had won more World championship medals (14) than any other athlete, male or female. She also won 34 medals in major championships. Her victories include the 1982 NCAA championship in the 100-meter sprint, and the 1982 Commonwealth Games gold medal in the 200-meter. Ottey won the bronze medal in the 200-meter run at both the Moscow Olympics in 1980 and the Los Angeles Olympics in 1984, where she also won the bronze in the 100-meter run. At age 39, Ottey continued to compete against championship-caliber sprinters 15 years younger.

Daniel E. Brannen, Jr.,
freelance writer, York, Pennsylvania

Otto, Kristin (1966—)

East German swimmer. *Born in 1966 in East Germany.*

Won Olympic gold medals at Seoul in the 50-meter freestyle, 100-meter freestyle, 100-meter backstroke, 100-meter butterfly, 4x100-meter freestyle relay and 4x100-meter medley relay (1988); set the world record in the 100-meter with a time of 54.73 (1986), which stood for years.

Kristin Otto won six gold medals from one venue: Seoul, Korea. Women swimmers tend to peak between 15 and 17. When Kristin Otto arrived at the 1988 Summer Olympics at Seoul, she was 22, dubbed by *Time* magazine the "Golden Oldie." But Otto disagreed. "I know I haven't reached my limits," she said. The 6'1" Otto won gold medals in the 50-meter freestyle (25.49), the first time the event was in Olympic contention. She followed that with a gold in the 100-meter freestyle with a time of 54.93, outdistancing **Yong Zhuang** of China. She then won the 100-meter backstroke with a time of 1:00.89, besting ***Krisztina Egerszegi** of Hungary (who would take the gold in the 200-meter backstroke). Otto also won the 100-meter butterfly with a time of 59.00 for an Olympic record, beating teammate **Birte Weigang**. Otto, **Katrin Meissner**, **Daniela Hunger**, and **Manuela Stellmach** then took the 4x100-meter freestyle relay with a time of 3:40.63, an Olympic record. (America was awarded the bronze.) In the 4x100-meter medley relay, Otto, **Silke Hörner**, Weigang, and Meissner won gold with a time of 4:03.74, another Olympic record.

Otto-Peters, Luise (1819–1895)

Co-founder of the General German Women's Association and editor of the first German women's political newspaper, the* Frauen-Zeitung, *who was the most important figure in the early German women's movement. *Name variations: Louise Otto; Louise Otto-Peters; Luise Otto; Luise Peters; Louise Peters; Luise Otto Peters; (pseudonym) Otto Stern. Pronunciation: AH-toh PEE-ters. Born Luise Otto on March 26, 1819, in Meissen, Germany; died on March 13, 1895, at Leipzig; fourth daughter of Wilhelm Otto (a court assessor) and Charlotte Matthäi Otto (daughter of a porcelain painter); had three sisters; educated at home; married August Peters (a poet and revolutionary), on July 8, 1858 (died July 4, 1864); no children.*

Published first poem (1842); published first book, Songs of a Young German Woman *(*Lieder eines deutschen Mädchens, *1847); published the social novel* Schloss und Fabrik *(*Castle and Factory, *1845); edited the* Women's Newspaper *(*Frauen-Zeitung, *1849–52); was a co-founder of the General German Women's Association and was elected its first president (1865); co-edited the association's journal,* New Paths *(*Neue Bahnen, *1866–95); co-founded the Leipzig Women's Educational Association (1865); co-founded the Leipzig Women's Writers Association (1890).*

Selected works: Ludwig the Waiter *(*Ludwig der Kellner, *1843);* Schloss und Fabrik *(*Castle and Factory, *1845);* Songs of a Young German Woman *(*Lieder eines deutschen Mädchens, *1847);* The Spirit of Nature: The Harmonies of Nature in Contemporary Women's Lives *(*Der Genius der Natur: Harmonien der Natur zu dem Frauenleben der Gegenwart, *1869);* The Right of Women to Employment *(*Das Recht der Frauen auf Erwerb, *1866);* The Life of Women in the German Empire *(*Frauenleben im deutschen Reich, *1876);* Private Stories of World History *(*Privatgeschichten der Weltgeschichte, *1868–72);* The Path of My Life *(*Mein Lebensgang, *1893).*

Among the earliest feminists in Germany, Luise Otto-Peters was the most active and the most significant. Primarily a writer—who produced poems, novels, novellas, short stories, historical works, and even two opera librettos—she spent much of her time working as a journalist, publishing the first newspaper in Germany specifically devoted to women's issues. The co-founder of the first major women's organization in Germany, Otto-Peters came to believe that such organizations, by providing education and vocational training for women, would achieve the equality of men and women in everyday life and thus "emancipate" the German middle class.

Meissen, the city of Otto-Peters' birth in 1819, a quiet town with a population of about 8,000, was far removed from the more bustling, nearby city of Dresden. Otto-Peters' mother **Charlotte Matthäi Otto**, who tried to imbue her children with an artistic sensibility, was the daughter of a painter for Meissen's famous porcelain industry. Her father Wilhelm Otto, a court assessor, wanted to keep his four daughters acquainted with the most up-to-date political and social issues. Otto-Peters proudly recalled his excitement when the state of Saxony passed legislation which would allow women to be executors over estates; it would, he told his daughters, end some of the helplessness of women.

Otto-Peters' home-based education consisted of reading and discussing the writings of classical German writers such as Wolfgang Goethe and Friedrich Schiller, as well as more popular writers such as the American novelist James Fenimore Cooper and the English novelist Sir Walter Scott. The French novelist ***George Sand**, a woman who assumed a male nom de plum in order to be taken more "seriously" by readers, was a special favorite.

By the time Otto-Peters reached the age of 22, a series of family misfortunes had forced her to make difficult choices. Her oldest sister, **Clementine**, died in 1832; both of her parents died in the years 1835 and 1836; and her fiancé died in 1841. Although she had a small inheritance, Otto-Peters was placed in a difficult financial situation. In similar circumstances, many middle-class German women chose to eke out a living by working as companions to wealthy older women or as governesses to the children of wealthy families. Instead, Otto-Peters chose to try to make a living as a writer and to maintain a male-free household with her sisters. For the rest of her life, she would essentially support herself through her writings. Her first poem was published in 1842. She wanted to publish a volume of her poetry, but Ernst Keil, a Leipzig publisher with liberal views, suggested that women published too much poetry. He convinced her to write a prose book, which appeared as the two-volume novel *Ludwig the Waiter* (*Ludwig der Kellner*) in 1843. Her first volume of poetry appeared in 1847 under the title *Songs of a Young German Woman* (*Lieder eines deutschen Mädchens*).

Short stories or articles by Otto-Peters appeared in some of Keil's magazines and journals, such as *Unser Planet* (*Our Planet*) and *Lighthouse* (*Leuchtturm*). During the 1840s, she also published articles in a newspaper in Saxony owned by Robert Blum, a German liberal who would be executed by the Austrian government for his activities during the revolutions of 1848. Since many of Otto-Peters' articles during the 1840s contained political comments—*Ludwig der Kellner* was temporarily banned by the government of Saxony, until she agreed to eliminate some passages—she occasionally published under the pseudonym Otto Stern; all of her other publications appeared under her own name, and generally under her married name, Luise Peters.

Otto-Peters' commitment to German liberalism was apparent in her 1845 *Schloss und Fabrik* (*Castle and Factory*), a social novel of the type that was also popular in Britain and France during the first half of the 19th century. Although the novel has been criticized for a reliance on stereotyped characters or plot lines—such as an impoverished but benevolent noble family—it was notable for its presentation of independent, committed women characters who lived fulfilling lives despite a lack of love or marriage. The novel, sections of which had to be omitted because of the demands of a government censor, portrayed the managerial class as the cause of much social conflict in Germany. *Schloss und Fabrik* also reflected Otto-Peters' belief that middle-class Germans, such as herself, should be greatly concerned over the treatment of both male and female workers in the new factories arising in Germany.

Otto-Peters argued that most women in her time were "puppets of men" and lived their lives through their children, through parenthood, and through their husbands. Her goals were "to build courage and insight into women through education, independence, and integrity." Marriage was not to be a welfare institution; if working conditions for women were improved, women would be able freely to decide if they wanted to marry or not. During the decade of the 1840s, she appealed to a labor commission in Saxony to investigate working conditions for women, and she also sent a letter to a Berlin committee of male workers, demanding that they include the "working rights" of women in their platform.

In 1843, an essay by Otto-Peters argued that women had a responsibility to be involved in "public" areas of life. By the time that she moved to Leipzig in 1848, where she would remain for most of the rest of her life, Otto-Peters had become a women's rights advocate and organizer, an educator, a publicist, and, to some degree, a political writer.

The revolution of 1848 brought Otto-Peters into contact with August Peters, a political agitator and a leading figure in revolutionary circles of Dresden. Peters was from a working-class family, with ties to the political figure and eventual German Marxist leader August Bebel, who called him the "foremost of the men fighting for women's rights" in Germany. Not long after they met in 1849, August Peters was imprisoned for his revolutionary activity, in May 1850. When they were married in 1858 after his release from prison, Otto-Peters was 39 years old. In the six years they had together before his death, the couple published the *People's Newspaper for Central Germany* (*Mitteldeutsche Volkszeitung*).

In 1849, Otto-Peters founded the *Frauen-Zeitung*, which published its first issue in April of that year. The appearance of a newspaper specifically devoted to women's concerns was an event of special significance, because although German newspapers of the time sometimes touched on women's issues, the newspapers themselves were circulated in clubs which had male-only policies. The *Frauen-Zeitung*'s stated purpose was to disseminate information of a political and social nature that was related to women, on the theory that discussions "among sisters" would "bind women together" and make them stronger. It was to be a forum for discussions, opinion pieces, and debates related to the duties and rights of women in German society. Its masthead bore the proclamation, "I am recruiting women citizens for the realm of Liberty."

Participation by women in the workings of the state is not just a right, but also a duty.

—Luise Otto-Peters

Although it often reflected the liberal ideas and spirit of the revolutions of 1848 in Germany, the *Frauen-Zeitung* sometimes focused on the new social questions raised by the Industrial Revolution, publishing articles about the working hours, wages, and health problems of women factory workers, lace-makers, knitters, and seamstresses. When a new umbrella organization of male workers (entitled the German Workingmen's Brotherhood) was created in 1848, Otto-Peters contributed to the journal of the Brotherhood, reminding its male founders not to forget women workers.

The *Frauen-Zeitung* insisted that the liberation of males had to be accompanied, in any revolution, by the liberation of women. Otto-Peters noted that of all of humanity, "we are half." She argued that freedom cannot be divided, meaning that political freedom had to accompany freedom of conscience, and that Germany could not have a true republic without concern for workers. Women had the right to become responsible and self-determining citizens of the state. But Otto-Peters insisted that women should not try to be men, and she did not want to be seen as a "liberated woman," which she regarded as being a grotesque copy of men.

Believing that education was particularly important for unmarried women, Otto-Peters argued that they could live independent lives only if they had educational and vocational qualifications, so that they were not a burden on their families and did not feel forced to "sell" themselves to men. Women were under a "double exploitation"; paid less than men, they also labored in working conditions that led them to prostitution. If more women were allowed into teaching and commercial jobs, marriage could regain its "natural rights" and would no longer be a "welfare institution." The *Frauen-Zeitung* suggested at one point that women should buy only goods that had been made and sold by women, at least until women had been given a wider variety of jobs than handwork or domestic help.

During the period of reaction that followed the unsuccessful revolutions of 1848, the newspaper generally avoided political commentary. Otto-Peters' reluctance to challenge government censors, plus her belief that it was "too early" to campaign for the right to vote for German women, has led some writers to view her as too compliant—as, in one writer's words, too easily accepting "the roles which the official ideology had assigned to women." Otto-Peters' tactics, however, kept the *Frauen-Zeitung* publishing for four years—much longer than other "revolutionary" publications—until 1852, when it succumbed to government bans on political activity by women. For a time, the newspaper was saved by transferring "control" to a male publisher. But although the newspaper had published articles by men, Otto-Peters chose to close the newspaper rather than accept a male editor.

In 1865, Otto-Peters, together with **Auguste Schmidt**, **Henriette Goldschmidt**, and **Ottilie von Steyber**, founded the General German Women's Association. The Leipzig meeting that established the organization was the first general meeting in Germany presided over by a woman. Otto-Peters was elected the association's president. While most German women's groups of the time functioned basically as philanthropic organizations, Otto-Peters intended that the association embrace social and political issues which affected women. At its founding, the association had 32 members, most of them living in the metropolitan areas of Hamburg, Zwickau, Lissa, and Krems. Within a decade, it grew to encompass some 20 regional clubs, and its membership grew to some 10,000, including a scattering of men. The journal of the new association, entitled *New Paths* (*Neue Bahnen*), was co-edited by Otto-Peters.

The same year that the association was founded, Otto-Peters was a co-founder of a women's club in Leipzig that was directed at helping women workers reach their highest level of "intellectual perfection." The major goal of the Leipzig Women's Education Association was to win paid work for women and to raise their intellectual qualifications. Since a particular concern was the "unfortunate sisters" in the working class, the association sponsored evening activities for working women which combined entertainment with cultural and educational talks, as well as child care.

What the two associations had in common was the conviction that education was the path through which women might help themselves and overcome social and political barriers to equality with men. The General German Women's Association petitioned the government to allow women to work in the post office and telegraph offices, and petitioned local and national governments asking that education for women be improved. Believing that it could help proletarian women move "up the ladder" through education, the association described itself as "working to remove all obstacles against the expansion of female labor."

The next year, Otto-Peters provided a platform for both associations with her book *The Right of Women to Employment* (*Das Recht der Frauen auf Erwerb*), which argued that while women might continue as wives and mothers, they should have access to occupational training and the professions. "It is an absolute necessity," she wrote, "to free women's work from the bounds of prejudices. . . . We can do this through agitation in women's organizations and through the press, through productivity associations . . . and through the creation of schools and shelters for women." Otto-Peters insisted that women could continue to work as wives and mothers but must also be able to support themselves, a goal that might be reached only when they had access to working in "teaching and the professions."

Throughout her career, Otto-Peters acknowledged that the right to vote was a logical goal of the women's movement: "Women demand the right to vote, because any group, which is not allowed to participate in the political process, is oppressed; the principle of equality before the law must lead, inevitability, to women's participation in our political life." Still, Otto-Peters rejected the idea that the new journal, *New Paths*, should pursue political discussions, citing German laws which forbade women's participation in politics. She reinforced that view in 1876, when she resisted placing demands for the right to vote in the association's platform, arguing that it was too soon to press for such a change.

In her 50-year career, Otto-Peters produced a wide variety of writings. Reflecting her mother's influence, she produced books insisting that there were close connections between art and politics, such as her *The Spirit of Nature: The Harmonies of Nature in Women's Lives* (*Der Genius der Natur: Harmonien der Natur zu dem Frauenleben*, 1871). Also among the more than 50 books she published were historical novels, such as *Rome in Germany* (*Rom in Deutschland*, 1873), as well as the librettos for two operas (*Niebelungen*, 1852 and *Theodor Körner*, 1872).

Two works stood out. Her *Private Stories of World History* (*Privatgeschichten der Weltgeschichte*, 1868–72) was a series of 12 historical sketches of women which underlined the general neglect of women in world history, at a time when women's names were missing from biographical books or reference works. For Otto-Peters, it was important not only to recount the lives of notable women, but also for women to be the storytellers. Even in her novels, many of her women characters thought it important to influence the environment around them, rather than be controlled by it.

Her *A Woman's Life in the German Empire* (*Frauenleben im deutschen Reich*, 1876), a semi-autobiographical book, documented everyday life for women in her time, particularly for preindustrial families, and included comments about their reading habits. It said that when women were preparing food, it was not unusual to hear someone reciting from Walter Scott or Ernst Wagner (a German novelist). Similar recitations occurred when women sewed together, and they "lost none of their dignity" in the process. It observed that earlier women who were considered "cultured" generally could not read or write; a woman who wrote under her own name was considered daring. Yet technology, the book argued, would transform the labor process in ways that would benefit women. Technology would "free much of the work of women in the house," taking care of "menial work" so that women would have more time for "creative achievement." "The more that handwork is replaced by the machine," she wrote, "the more time that women will have to solve their problems."

In 1890, Otto-Peters and another writer, **Mathilde Clasen-Schmid**, founded a writers' club in Leipzig, which they intended as a cultural and artistic club for women. Otto-Peters and Clasen-Schmid expressed the hope that such clubs would help women "accomplish extraordinary things in areas of life, intellectual or otherwise, entirely on their own." They also hoped that women writers would provide more accurate prose writings about women, since they believed that when men wrote about women, they were often incorrect in the motivations that they attributed to women.

One of Otto-Peters' last books, *The Course of My Life* (*Mein Lebensgang*, 1893), was especially revealing. Despite its title, it was not a true autobiography but a collection of her writings, particularly unpublished poems. Although Otto-Peters began her career as a poet, and although she often avoided political topics in her writings after the failed revolutions of 1848, *The Course of My Life* revealed that she had continued to write poetry on political topics. Fittingly, when she died in 1895, she was buried in Leipzig, next to the grave of her revolutionary-minded husband, who had shared her hopes that the revolutions of 1848 would "emancipate" both men and women.

SOURCES:

Boetcher, Joerges, Ruth-Ellen. "1848 from a Distance: German Women Writers on the Revolution," in *Modern Language Notes*. Vol. 97, no. 1, 1982, pp. 590–614.

Evans, Robert J. *The Feminist Movement in Germany, 1894–1933*. London and Beverly Hills: SAGE, 1976.

Frevert, Ute. *Women in German History*. Trans. by Stuart McKinnon-Evans. Hamburg: Berg, 1989.

Koepcke, Cordula. *Louise Otto-Peters: Die rote Demokratin*. Freiburg: Herderbücherei, 1981.

Ludwig, Johanna, and Rita Jorek, eds. *Luise Otto-Peters: Ihr Literarisches und publizistisches Werk*. Leipzig: Leizpig University Press, 1995.

SUGGESTED READING:

Fout, John C., ed. *German Women in the Nineteenth Century: A Social History*. London: Holmes & Meier, 1984.

Riemer, Eleanor, and John Fout. *European Women: A Documentary History*. NY: Schocken: 1980.

COLLECTIONS:

Materials on the General German Women's Association are housed in the Staatsarchiv Hamburg, Hamburg, Germany.

Otto-Peters' published works have been cataloged by the Luise Otto-Peters Society in Leipzig.

Some papers of Otto-Peters' are held in the Deutscher Staatsbürgerinnen-Verband (the Union of German Women Citizens) in Berlin, Germany; some materials are held in the University Library of the University of Leipzig, Germany.

Some sources for this early period of the German women's movement are published in Margrit Twellmann, *Die deutsche Frauenbewegung im Spiegel repräsentativer Frauenzeitschriften: Ihre Anfänge und erste Entwicklung, 1843–1889* (Meisenheim am Glan: Kronberg, 1976).

Niles R. Holt,
Professor of History, Illinois State University,
Normal, Illinois

Otway-Ruthven, Jocelyn
(1909–1989)

Irish historian. *Name variations: J.A. Otway-Ruthven. Born Jocelyn Annette Otway-Ruthven in Dublin, Ireland, on November 7, 1909; died in Dublin on March 18, 1989; second of four children of Captain Robert Mervyn Birmingham Otway-Ruthven and Margaret Casement Otway-Ruthven; Trinity College, Dublin, B.A., 1931; Girton College, Cambridge, Ph.D., 1937.*

Awards: Fellow of the Royal Historical Society; Member of the Royal Irish Academy.

Was a lecturer, Trinity College, Dublin (1938–51); appointed Lecky Professor of History (1951); named a fellow of Trinity College (1968); served as dean of Faculty of Humanities (1969–73); was a member of the Irish Manuscripts Commission; was a member of International Commission for the History of Representative and Parliamentary Institutions. Selected publications: A History of Medieval Ireland *(Benn, 1968).*

Jocelyn Otway-Ruthven, who would be named one of the first women fellows at Trinity College, was born in Dublin in 1909. Her youth was marred by family tragedy; two of her sisters died young, and her father died in 1919 when she was only ten years old. In 1916, one of her mother's relations, Roger Casement, was hanged for treason in the aftermath of the failed Easter rebellion in Dublin. (Otway-Ruthven never tried to hide the family connection with Casement and would occasionally mention it in conversation, to the pained surprise of some of her more conservative colleagues in Trinity.) Otway-Ruthven belonged to the second generation of women who entered Trinity, following the example of such predecessors as ***Constantia Maxwell** (whom she succeeded as Lecky Professor of History in 1951).

Writing in 1977, Otway-Ruthven recalled what Trinity was like for the 200 women students who were carefully segregated from the men when she first entered the college 50 years earlier. "We must wear coats and hats or gowns. . . . [W]e might not speak to a man, even if he were our brother (it was explained that the citizens of Dublin, looking through the Front Gate, would be scandalized); any parties must be chaperoned; we must be out of College by 6 p.m. In lectures and the library we sat apart. . . . No provision whatever was made for meals for women members of staff." Academically, her time at Trinity was more rewarding, and she later paid warm tribute to her first teacher there, Edmund Curtis. Following graduation, Otway-Ruthven went to Cambridge to study for a doctorate. In 1937, she won the Thirlwall prize and her prize-winning essay on the "King's Secretary and the Signet Office" in the 15th century was published by Cambridge University Press in 1939. (However irksome as the restrictions at Trinity had been, Cambridge was even more difficult; women were not admitted to degrees there until 1948.)

When Otway-Ruthven returned to Trinity as a lecturer in history in 1938, the position of women academics had scarcely improved since the first appointment of Constantia Maxwell in 1909. They were excluded from the Fellowship and from the Common Room. Otway-Ruthven deeply resented this discrimination: "We were paid less than men doing the equivalent work, and I have been told that this was right since, not being available for consultation in the Common Room, we were less useful to the College." "Can you imagine it, Mr Provost," laughed A.A. Luce, professor of theology, at the thought of a woman fellow. "Mrs Quiverful, FTCD" (Fellow of Trinity College Dublin). Ancient institutions change slowly, as Otway-Ruthven was only too aware, and the struggle for equality was a long one. Women were eventually admitted to the Common Room in 1958, and in 1968 Otway-Ruthven was named one of the first women fellows.

Otway-Ruthven built up the Medieval History Department into one of the finest departments in the college. One of her most distinguished students, F.S.L. Lyons, who later became provost of Trinity, recalled that "the first and most valuable lesson she taught us was that history was not a soft option. . . . However little we made of it at the time, [it] did give us the most valuable of all experiences—a sense of the past, a realization that the past has its own immediacy, its own contemporaneity." Another former student, James Lydon, who later became a colleague of Otway-Ruthven at Trinity, has left a vivid view of her. "She gave the impression of being very cold and aloof. She was a very tall woman and spoke in a terrifying deep voice. But once you got to know her, there was a very different person altogether. As a historian, working through record evidence she was just unbeatable. Her contribution to Irish history at that level will never be surpassed." Lydon also noted her kindness to students who were in difficulties. In her later years, she was active in the affairs of the Irish Federation of University Teachers.

The main focus of Otway-Ruthven's historical research was the exploration of the impact of the 12th-century Norman conquest of Ireland. However, with the eradication of so many priceless medieval records following the destruction of the Four Courts in the Irish civil war in 1922, the task was often daunting. Otway-Ruthven was determined to fill the gap and to reconstruct as much as possible of Ireland's medieval sources. She published extensively in a number of scholarly journals. In the foreword to her *History of Medieval History* (1968), which was the culmination of decades of research, Otway-Ruthven averred that it was "no more than an interim report" and that "there is still an infinity of work to be done." By the time she retired in 1980, she had become one of the legendary figures in Trinity and, indeed, Dublin. Her retirement gave her more time to devote to her interest in alpine plants. She died in March 1989, just a few months short of her 90th birthday.

SOURCES:

Lydon, James. "Professor J.A. Otway-Ruthven," in *Trinity Trust News*. Vol. 5, no. 2, Dublin, 1980.

———. "Interview" in *History Ireland*. Vol. 3, no. 1, Dublin, 1995.

Lyons, F.S.L. Foreword to *England and Ireland in the Later Middle Ages: Essays in Honor of Jocelyn Otway-Ruthven*. Ed. by James Lydon. Dublin: Irish Academic Press, 1981.

Otway-Ruthven, J.A. "Women in College 1927–77" in *Trinity Trust News*. Vol. 2, no 2, Dublin, 1977.

Deirdre McMahon,
lecturer in history at Mary Immaculate College, University of Limerick, Limerick, Ireland

Ouden, Willemijntje den (b. 1918).

See Fraser, Dawn for sidebar.

Oudh, begum of (c. 1820–1879).

See Hazrat Mahal.

Ouida (1839–1908).

See Ramée, Louise de la.

Oumansoff or Oumansov, Raïssa (1883–1960).

See Maritain, Raïssa.

Oury, Anna Caroline de Belleville (1808–1880).

See Belleville-Oury, Anna Caroline de.

Ouspenskaya, Maria (1876–1949)

Legendary Russian stage and screen actress who was nominated for Academy Awards for* Dodsworth *(1936) and* Love Affair *(1939). *Name variations: Marie Ouspenskaya. Born in Tula, Russia, on July 29, 1876; died in a fire that also destroyed her home in Hollywood, California, on December 3, 1949.*

Select filmography in U.S., unless otherwise noted: The Cricket on the Hearth *(Russian, 1915);* Worthless *(Russian, 1916);* Dr. Torpokov *(Russian, 1917);* Buried Alive *(Russian, 1918);* Khveska *(*Hospital Guard, *Russian, 1923);* Tanka–Traktirshista Protiv Otsa *(Russian, 1929);* Dodsworth *(1936);* Conquest *(1937);* Love Affair *(1939);* The Rains Came *(1939);* Judge Hardy and Son *(1939);* Dr. Ehrlich's Magic Bullet *(1940);* Waterloo Bridge *(1940);* The Mortal Storm *(1940);* The Man I Married *(1940);* Dance Girl Dance *(1940);* Beyond Tomorrow *(1940);* The Wolf Man *(1941);* The Shanghai Gesture *(1942);* Kings Row *(1942);* The Mystery of Marie Roget *(1942);* Frankenstein Meets the Wolf Man *(1943);* Destiny *(1944);* Tarzan and the Amazons *(1945);* I've Always Loved You *(1946);* Wyoming *(1947);* A Kiss in the Dark *(1949).*

The tiny but eminently memorable Maria Ouspenskaya was born in Tula, Russia, in 1876 and gained early fame with the Moscow Art Theater. In 1923, she made her American stage debut with *Tsar Fyodor Ivanovitch*. She appeared on Broadway in *The Saint, The Witch, Dodsworth, Abide with Me, Daughters of Atreus, Outrageous Fortune,* a revival of *The Jest,* and an updated *Taming of the Shrew.* For a number of years, she also ran a New York acting school.

Ouspenskaya became a dominant Hollywood character actress from 1936 through the 1940s. Unfortunately, the distinguished actress is best remembered for her performance as the fortuneteller Maleva, mother of a werewolf, in *The Wolf Man* (1941), which starred Claude Rains, Lon Chaney, and ***Evelyn Ankers**. In the film, Ouspenskaya warns Chaney, and the audience, in her ominous heavy accent by reciting the ersatz Gypsy (Roma) folk rhyme: "Even the man who is pure in heart/ And says his prayers by night/ May become a wolf when the wolf-bane blooms/ And the autumn moon is bright." Note Jay Nash and Stanley Ross in their *Motion Picture Guide:* "Ouspenskaya is marvelous in her restrained portrayal as the wise old gypsy who foretells the tragedy that is to befall the innocent Chaney." Earlier, Ouspenskaya had been nominated for Best Supporting Actress for her portrayal of Baroness von Obersdorf in 1936's *Dodsworth,* starring Walter Huston and ***Mary Astor**, as well as for her performance in *Love Affair* in 1939.

Ousset, Cécile (1936—)

French pianist, known for championing lesser-known piano scores. *Name variations: Cecile Ousset. Born in Tarbes, France, on March 3, 1936.*

Cécile Ousset was born in Tarbes, France, in 1936 and made her debut at a pianist at age five. She studied with Marcel Ciampi at the Paris Conservatoire, where she won a first prize and graduated at age 14 in 1950. From 1953 through 1962, she won many of the major piano competitions, including the Pagés, the ***Marguerite Long**-Jacques Thibaud, the Geneva, the Queen Elisabeth of Belgium (in honor of ***Elizabeth of Bavaria**), the Busoni, and the Van Cliburn prizes. Since the 1960s, she has enjoyed a world virtuoso career, performing almost all of the great concertos throughout the world. In some of the solo pieces of Saint-Saëns, she is virtually unchallenged, and critics have praised her recordings. Acclaimed for her Chopin and Schumann interpretations, Ousset is also well known for championing such lesser-known scores as Camille Saint-Saëns' *Allegro appassionato.*

John Haag,
Athens, Georgia

Outhwaite, Ida Rentoul (1888–1960)

Highly popular Australian children's fantasy illustrator who assisted in raising the status of illustration in her country and the quality of publishing for children. *Signed work: I.S. Rentoul, I.S.R. Pronunciation: OOTH-wait. Born Ida Sherbourne Rentoul on June 9, 1888, in Melbourne, Victoria, Australia; died in Melbourne on June 25, 1960; daughter of John Laurence Rentoul (a Presbyterian moderator-general and professor of theology) and Annie Isobel (Rattray) Rentoul (an amateur watercolorist); sister of Annie Rattray Rentoul (1882–1978); attended Presbyterian Ladies' College; married (Arthur) Grenbry Outhwaite, on December 9, 1909; children: Robert Rentoul (1910–1941); Anne Isobel Rentoul (b. 1911); Wendy Laurence Rentoul (b. 1914); William Grenbry Rentoul (1919–1945).*

Published first illustrated stories (1903); began illustrating for magazines (1903); illustrated first book, Mollie's Bunyip, *by A.R. and I.S. Rentoul (Melbourne 1904); began exhibiting in Australia (1907); published* Elves and Fairies *in Melbourne (1916); exhibited in Paris and London (1920); wrote and illustrated four*

Ida
Rentoul
Outhwaite

books (1928–35); earned last substantial commission for Legends From the Outback *by P.M. Power (London, 1958).*

Major works illustrated: Tarella Quin's Gum Tree Brownie and Other Faerie Folk of the Never Never *(Melbourne: G. Robertson, 1907); Annie R. Rentoul's* The Lady of the Blue Beads *(Melbourne: G. Robertson, 1908); Quin's* Before the Lamps are Lit *(Melbourne: G. Robertson, 1911); Annie R. Rentoul and Grenbry Outhwaite's* Elves and Fairies *(Melbourne: Lothian, 1916); Ida Rentoul Outhwaite and Grenbry Outhwaite's* The Enchanted Forest *(London:*

A&C Black, 1921); A.R. Rentoul's The Little Green Road to Fairyland *(London: A&C Black, 1922); I.R. Outhwaite and Grenbry Outhwaite's* The Little Fairy Sister *(London: A&C Black, 1923); A.R. Rentoul, I.R. Outhwaite, and Grenbry Outhwaite's* The Fairyland of Ida Rentoul Outhwaite *(Melbourne: Ramsay, 1926); I.R. Outhwaite's* Blossom: a Fairy Story *(London: A&C Black, 1928); I.R. Outhwaite's* Bunny and Brownie *(London: A&C Black, 1930); I.R. Outhwaite's* A Bunch of Wildflowers *(Sydney: Angus & Robertson, 1933); "Benjamin Bear" comic strip,* Weekly Times *(Sydney, 1933–39); Tarella Quin Daskein's* Chimney Town *(London: A&C Black, 1934); I.R. Outhwaite's* Sixpence to Spend *(Sydney: Angus & Robertson, 1935).*

In September 1916, Ida Rentoul Outhwaite, a 28-year-old illustrator, witnessed the publication of her most ambitious project: *Elves and Fairies*. The book had been promoted, edited, and largely financed by her husband, the verse written by her sister and—the real draw—the full-page pictures, in watercolor and pen and ink, had been created by Ida. The originals of these pictures were exhibited at a Melbourne gallery and almost all sold in a matter of hours. Separate reproductions were produced and decorated the walls of kindergartens, schools and homes for decades afterwards. The four-color process used for *Elves and Fairies* had required the largest outlay known in Australian publishing history, but despite the consequently high price for a children's book, all 1,500 copies were quickly purchased. It was, in short, the most successful Australian art publication to date, much of its success due to timing. Ida Outhwaite's work tapped into a vogue for fairies; her illustrations, comprised of delicate forms and gracefully flowing lines, were influenced by *art nouveau*, a style then much admired, and employed by such well-known English illustrators as Arthur Rackham and Aubrey Beardsley; and, most important to the local audience, the pictures and verse depicted an Australian landscape and the book was an entirely Australian production.

Elves and Fairies can be seen as the pinnacle of Ida Outhwaite's long and highly productive career. She possessed abundant energy and an enthusiasm for drawing that lasted from her infancy to her final years. The history of her waxing and waning popularity is the history of changing tastes in children's literature and in art, and indicates the tenor of each new decade.

Ida Sherbourne Rentoul was born in 1888 into a well-educated, artistic family in Melbourne, in the colony of Victoria, Australia. She had a sister, ❧▸ **Annie Rattray Rentoul**, six years her elder, and two younger brothers. Her parents were prominent figures in Melbourne society. Her father, the Reverend John Laurence Rentoul, had immigrated from Ireland in 1879 with his English wife, ❧▸ **Annie Isobel Rentoul**, to take up a Presbyterian ministry and later to become the Presbyterian Church's moderator-general. He was also a professor of theology, a supporter of Australian Aboriginal rights, and the author of various books of verse. Ida's mother was a skilled watercolorist and reportedly helped Ida learn to draw. Both parents, creative and intellectually active, encouraged their children, and the family bustled with drawn, written, and play-acted productions. They lived at Ormond College at the University of Melbourne and annual holidays were taken by the beach or in the country. Outhwaite remembered that as a child she spent hours looking intently into the grass, watching the "tiny things that grew and crept there and tried to draw them afterwards." She had begun drawing birds and her toy animals and dolls from the age of two; she continued to draw throughout her early childhood.

When she went to school, at Presbyterian Ladies' College in Melbourne, she did reasonably well in her studies, particularly modern languages. She might have been a better student if she hadn't drawn figures in the margins of her school books and practiced making long, smooth dashes in ink during the dull moments of her lessons. She later maintained she was hardly ever caught. In a 1947 article for the Melbourne Art Training Institute, Outhwaite recalled: "It was when I was eleven that someone gave me a bottle of indian ink and some Gillot nibs and I discovered the bliss of working in black and white, which has always been and always will be my favourite medium."

Ida's pictures were tending towards fantasy figures; large-headed, thin-limbed goblins with simple, grinning faces and fairies with fluted gowns and butterfly wings. These were unmistakably creatures of the European (including the British) folkloric and illustrative tradition. Outhwaite enjoyed the drawings of British and continental illustrators—she said that as a child she "pored over" the works of Beardsley and Daniel Vierge. Elements of her drawing style were, even at this early stage, identifiably influenced by such artists—her use of decorative detail was Beardsley-like, for instance, and the idealized prettiness and stillness of her child and fairy figures was reminiscent of the work of the popular English children's illustrator ***Kate Greenaway**.

Rentoul, Annie Rattray (1882–1978)

Australian educator and writer. *Born Annie Rattray Rentoul on September 22, 1882; died in 1978; daughter of John Laurence Rentoul (a Presbyterian moderator-general and professor of theology) and* ****Annie Isobel Rentoul*** *(an amateur watercolorist).*

***Ida Rentoul Outhwaite**'s elder sister Annie Rattray Rentoul found a particular interest in classics and ancient languages. In 1902, she became the first student at Presbyterian Ladies' College (PLC) to take the classics exhibition. She went on to earn a first-class honors degree at the University of Melbourne in 1905 as well as winning the Wyselaskie Scholarship in Classics and Logic and sharing the Higgins prize for poetry. From 1913, Annie was a well-liked and inspiring teacher of classics, ancient history and English literature at PLC. In addition to teaching classes, she also organized the PLC library and spent much time with her students, arranging clubs and excursions, writing limericks for them, providing afternoon teas and a sympathetic ear for their problems.

Annie's many published fairy stories proved lastingly popular. The verses she wrote for *Elves and Fairies* and *Fairy Land* were not as well received—largely because, as reviewers recognized, she had written them not from her own inspiration, but in order to accompany her sister's pictures.

It was Annie that members of the Outhwaite family turned to in times of grief. She nursed her brother for years after his nervous breakdown and both her mother and her sister came to live with her when their husbands died. After retiring from PLC, she taught at Melbourne Grammar School between 1942 and 1945. She died, after living a generous life, at age 96 in 1978.

Rentoul, Annie Isobel (c. 1855–1928)

Australian artist. *Born Anne Isoble Rattray in South America around 1855; died in Hawthorne, Melbourne, in 1928; married John Laurence Rentoul (a Presbyterian moderator-general and professor of theology); children: six, including Ida Rentoul Outhwaite (1888–1960) and Annie Rattray Rentoul (1882–1978).*

Although little is known about ***Ida Rentoul Outhwaite**'s mother, she was an artist in her own right. Born in England around 1855, she moved to Australia with her husband, the Reverend John Laurence Rentoul, in 1879. She was an amateur watercolorist and her interests lay in literature, art, and music rather than in the parish duties which at that time were the more usual occupation of a minister's wife. She and John had six children, two of whom died at an early age. Annie Isobel encouraged her daughters and sons in their artistic exploits. She and Ida collaborated in creating *Mollie's Staircase* in 1906. A writer for the *Sydney Morning Herald* said in 1917, Ida Rentoul's "mother is English; with an eye that can see the beautiful in art and a hand that can hold a pencil to illustrate it." When her husband died suddenly in 1926, Annie Isobel bought a house in Hawthorn, Melbourne, with her unmarried daughter, ***Annie Rattray Rentoul.**

This kind of influence was to be expected. While Outhwaite was growing up in Australia during the 19th century, the books available were, on the whole, European, and primarily British. There were few Australian publishing firms producing stories and picture books for children—they could not compete with the volume of high quality imports. A large proportion of these imports were fairy stories, then in fashion. The interest had gained its initial impetus from the translation of the Grimm brothers' stories in 1823 and those of Hans Christian Andersen in the 1840s. As the century progressed, more stories involving magic and legend were translated from various cultures. Writers in Britain began to investigate their local folklore and create their own stories. Illustrators of these fantastic tales added to the popular enthusiasm for fairies and their kin. Outhwaite had been told fairy stories when she was a child: "I think it was through Hans Andersen," she said, "that I first fell in love with Fairyland."

There was another influence. Alongside her fantasy figures, Outhwaite drew eucalyptus trees, kookaburras, kangaroos, and teddy-bearish koalas. Although she had first fallen in love with fairyland through Andersen's stories, "it was in the bush that I really met the fairies."

At about the age of 11, Ida received firm encouragement when a friend arranged to have a scene of hers reproduced in an English magazine. Over the next few years, she and various members of her family produced Christmas cards and illustrated serial stories for magazines. In 1904, when Ida was 16 and her sister Annie was 22, they published their first book, *Mollie's Bunyip*, a story about a small girl beckoned by the wind to explore the wilderness near her home. She becomes lost and only finds her way home the next day with the "gentle guiding," from a spirit of the bush, the Bunyip. Another story, *Mollie's Staircase,* followed in 1906, produced by Ida and her mother.

The Australian audience found these productions charming and whimsical, despite their clumsiness, and they sold well. Their popularity can be attributed partly to their being the creations of a well-known family, but the point most often commented upon by reviewers was their Australian content. Here were some works for Australian youngsters that portrayed the environment in which they were growing up.

There had been a gradual shift in the priorities of the expanding colonial community in the mid-19th century, from solely serving the empire to identifying local interests as well. A growing nationalism encouraged local artists. Painters such as Tom Roberts and others of the Heidelberg School of impressionists flourished, along with such writers as Henry Lawson, "Banjo" Paterson, and ***Miles Franklin**, who contributed to defining national images and a national ethos. When Australia was federated in 1901, the enthusiasm for Australian symbols and a pride in local productions grew. It was not surprising that Outhwaite's work found a ready audience and that, encouraged by nationalistic praise, she continued to use Australian subject matter.

The striking thing about Mrs Outhwaite's pictures and her sister's verses is that they are Australian . . . and yet the fairies are fairies still.

—*Times Literary Supplement* (1916)

During 1906 and 1907, Outhwaite was a regular illustrator for *The Western Mail* and *The Native Companion*. Her decorative vignettes showed a growing grasp of composition and a knack for drawing humorously as well as seriously. Some work by her and her sister was exhibited in the First Australian International Women's Exhibition, held in Melbourne in 1907. The sisters were commissioned to write and illustrate the stories of the pantomimes *Humpty Dumpty* in 1907 and then *Peter Pan* when it came to Melbourne in 1908. Outhwaite also had the pleasure of seeing her work come to life when she designed the costumes for *Humpty Dumpty* and several other children's plays and ballets.

The characters Outhwaite drew for the pantomime booklets were full of personality, and each scene filled the picture space solidly. Similar strengths were evident in her illustrations for *Gum Tree Brownie and Other Faerie Folk* by Tarella Quin, published in 1907. This was the first of many books that Ida and Quin completed together, within which Outhwaite did some of her most imaginative work. She felt that Quin's "ideas of weird beings were just what she had wanted to stimulate her imagination."

Outhwaite was a member of the Victorian Artists' Society in 1908 and 1909. It was one of the few prolonged contacts with other professional artists she made, for one of the main characteristics of her artistic career was the lack of formal training. It was this factor that reviewers most frequently blamed for the stiffness of Ida's figures and her overuse of formulas instead of obtaining variety and verve by drawing from life. Outhwaite appears later to have regretted the lack. "I just had to plod along without having any teaching, which was a pity. I should have been a much better artist if I could have studied more and amused myself less." At the same time, however, she had her own approach. She felt that imagination was highly important and this was best cultivated by "watching, always watching, and putting down impressions afterwards." Indeed, in her *Who's Who in Australia* entry she described her recreations as drawing, reading and "standing and staring."

When Ida was 21, she married Grenbry Outhwaite, a 34-year-old barrister and solicitor, on December 9, 1909. Many found the match improbable. One man recalled "wondering how such a great bullock of a man as A.G.O. could possibly have anything to say about fairies. He had a voice like a foghorn." Nevertheless, Grenbry was a patron of the arts and an experienced businessman who took the job of managing the promotion of Outhwaite's work, an aspect she preferred not to deal with. The couple had a son in 1910, and a daughter a year later. (Another daughter, Wendy, was born in 1914, and their last child, William, in 1919.) Despite these changes, Ida maintained her illustrating, though at a slower pace. "One's work must suffer," she told an interviewer for *Women's World* in 1923. "How can one remain really inspired when 'leg-of-mutton' matters constantly intervene." She was able, however, "to spend seven of her precious twenty-four hours in her tiny studio, nestled away in the quietest spot of a very beautiful garden." Having hired help eased the domestic workload. Over the next few years, Outhwaite painted a mural for a children's hospital ward, illustrated song books, drew for *The Lone Hand* from 1909, and illustrated another Quin story, *When the Lamps are Lit*, in 1911.

Outhwaite's style was now well defined and fairly fixed. Historian H.M. Saxby has said that *art nouveau*, strong in art and design in Europe, influenced most Australian artists from 1895 to 1905, and that some of them continued to use the style through the first decades of the new century. The emphasis on decorative, sinuous lines and typical and symbolic natural forms common to *art nouveau* was a strong part of Ida's work. Her reviewers often remarked on the influence of particular artists, particularly Beardsley, Rackham, and Edmund Dulac, but also recognized that her style was her own. One of the unique characteristics of her work was fastidious detail. She would create intricate silhouettes of trees and hills against a finely streaked night sky. One could see the roughness of bark, the delicate fronds of ferns, waves of countless tiny stars carrying a crescent-moon boat, and large portions of her landscapes were often filled with the leaves and flowers of minute vines. In a piece she wrote for young artists in 1947, Outhwaite noted: "There is something magical in seeing what you can do, what texture and tone and color you can produce merely with a pen point and a bottle of ink; to find out that wind can be suggested with a few long sweeping lines, and a quiet moony sky by a few straight ones round the outline of a halfpenny."

Some, including a reviewer for the *Bulletin* in 1923, felt that her "darkling backgrounds" were too ominous for children's stories, being "more suggestive of demon kings" than fairies and bluebirds. It was more generally agreed, however, that her pictures were far more gentle than the frequently grotesque distortions and alarming creatures rendered by Beardsley or Rackham.

The First World War curbed Ida's plans to exhibit in England, so she and Grenbry concentrated on launching her in Australia instead. Despite the shortages and preoccupations that attended a world war, Grenbry pushed through the triumphant publication of *Elves and Fairies* and, with the 1916 edition and 1919 reprint, found it welcomed by a British and American audience as well as an Australian one. Ida had found time to complete the 15 watercolors and 30 black-and-white illustrations in between contributing to group exhibitions to raise funds for the Red Cross. The proceeds from *Elves and Fairies* were also donated to the Red Cross.

The 1920s were Outhwaite's most productive years. She accepted a great many advertising commissions and contributed to exhibitions throughout Australia while also holding many solo exhibitions and illustrating more children's books, several of which she wrote herself. Despite the long hours, she and Grenbry enjoyed an active social life. Journalists were keen to obtain news and interviews from the famous illustrator many Australians considered "their own." Consequently, this period provides most of the rare glimpses of Outhwaite's personality and voice, for she left no personal papers.

One interviewer for *Woman's World* described her as unassuming, being "infinitely happier discoursing on her sister's talent." Another, for Melbourne *Punch* in 1921, said "she admits to loving a risk," and reported a placidity of demeanor that would be "struck aside for a moment by a flash of romanticism" when she spoke of her love for poetry or flying by airplane. "She is little and dark," reported the *Sun* in March 1917, "with bright, quick eyes and a manner that makes you understand why the fairies have stayed with her."

Several interviewers in the early '20s commented resentfully that Outhwaite's family responsibilities were keeping her from illustrating and exhibiting more. Indeed, Ida seems never to have met with anything but encouragement to pursue an intense, personal career that kept her in the public eye. Feminism had long been a strong force in Australia, and a career in art—even in a commercial art such as illustration—had become an acceptable occupation for women by the time Ida was born. Fantasy illustration in Australia was, in the 1920s, actually dominated by women. One of these was ***May Gibbs**, creator of the *Snugglepot and Cuddlepie* children's stories and, consequently, of some of Australia's most loved national symbols. Gibbs distilled—more completely than Outhwaite had—the essence of the Australian bush into unique fantasy characters. Other fantasy illustrators such as Christian Yandell, **Pixie O'Harris** and Harold Gaze relied, as Ida did, more on the European fantasy tradition. Some artists were inspired by Outhwaite's style and drew in the same vein, as did **Edith Alsop** and **Ethel Spowers**, for instance. **Ethel Jackson Morris** was likewise inspired, but her designs were clearer, simpler, and free from the ornamentation of Ida's work.

In 1920, the Outhwaites were able to travel to Europe for a year. Ida's exhibitions in Paris and London drew crowds, much praise and even royal commendation, for Queen ***Mary of Teck** of Britain and Prince George of Greece both purchased pictures. While in London, the Outhwaites had arranged a publishing contract with A&C Black, a firm with a reputation for high-quality children's books. On returning to Australia, Grenbry (possibly with Ida) wrote *The Enchanted Forest,* a story about a girl's explorations of a magical forest full of frightening goblins and witches, friendly fairies, and bumbling koalas.

Reviewers found Ida's illustrations charming, entertaining, and the stronger part of the book. Her next book, *The Little Green Road to Fairyland,* written by Annie, was of a similar size and skill (1922). This, according to Muir and Holden, was one of the best loved of all Australian children's stories from the 1920s to the 1950s. In 1923, the sisters produced *The Little Fairy Sister*, also published by the London firm.

All these books were popular; fairies were still a cherished subject. They were viewed with fondness and the possibility of their existence was occasionally entertained by adults as well as children. When an English man claimed to have photographed some fairies and a gnome playing with his daughters, the photographs were reproduced in newspapers and their authenticity hotly debated for some time. Sir Arthur Conan Doyle wrote, seriously, it seems, supporting the possible authenticity of the photos. Outhwaite told an interviewer that she did not agree with Doyle. "To her," said the Melbourne *Punch* in February 1921, "these elf children merely represent a world of beautiful nonsense."

Her next production, in 1926, was *The Fairyland of Ida Rentoul Outhwaite,* a lavish volume similar to *Elves and Fairies.* However, *Fairyland* was not greeted as the earlier book had been. It received brief, non-committal reviews and did not sell well, being more a collector's piece, because the subject matter was too similar to all of Ida's other works to entice her more general public to pay the five guineas required. Her A&C Black storybooks could be bought for much less and were more entertaining.

As the 1920s drew to a close, Outhwaite's audience dwindled. The decade of over-abundance brought the Depression of the 1930s in its wake. It was an adverse period for the publishing industry worldwide and the quality of production plummeted. In addition to being less able to afford the lavish Outhwaite books, the public was no longer much interested in fairies and frivolities. Outhwaite's work—both new offerings and reprints—were not purchased as often as before. Her style and subject matter had not changed over two and a half decades, and there were complaints of a feeling of sameness.

Yet, now in her 40s, Outhwaite had not lost her energy or interest in illustration. She turned her hand to the new trend in children's books: animal stories. She had illustrated a series of animal stories back in 1918, the "Wee Willie Winkie Zoo Books" written by **Annie Osbourne**, but these new works were completely her own creation. Outhwaite wrote with fluidity, and with an understanding of what interested a child. *Blossom; a Fairy Story* (1928) and *Bunny and Brownie* (1930) were substantial stories with exciting, magical journeys that involved animals as major characters who could talk to the child characters. In 1935, she wrote *Sixpence to Spend,* a story for young children about Albert the koala and his difficulties in finding a present for his mother's birthday. The pictures are simple and clear, the characters are drawn close to the viewer and fill the picture frame with an intimacy not seen in her earlier works. Her koala character was based on the comic strip she had been drawing for the *Weekly Times* between 1933 and 1938. He was similar to the koala in **Dorothy Wall**'s *Blinky Bill* stories, but Albert lacked the freshness of the more popular Blinky. Despite Outhwaite's adoption of a clearer, looser style and the change to animal stories, there was the difficulty, as Holden and Muir have suggested, that the public identified Ida so closely with fairies that when she turned to other subject matter they lost interest.

On June 16, 1938, Grenbry died at age 63, and Ida soon moved into an apartment with her sister in central Melbourne. During the Second World War, Outhwaite worked in the censor's office, translating the letters of prisoners of war. It was a tragic time. She lost both her sons to the war: 32-year-old Robert in 1941 and her youngest, William, in 1945.

In her last decades, Outhwaite illustrated several more story books and some crudely printed nursery rhyme and song books. She had enjoyed a successful career, but it had clearly possessed difficulties; she concluded her 1947 article for budding artists: "Cultivate a rhinoceros hide. You will need it." Ida Rentoul Outhwaite died on June 25, 1960, age 72.

Although Outhwaite's popularity ebbed in the later part of her life, during the height of her career, writes Saxby, she "recognised and catered for the imaginative needs of childhood." Through her work, her frequent exhibitions, and wide acclaim, Outhwaite helped to raise the status of illustration as an occupation and encouraged many younger artists. Her popularity was rekindled in the last few decades of the 20th century, and the antics of her koalas, fairies and elves are delighting children and adults once again.

SOURCES:

Bulletin. November 8, 1923, p. 28.

"A Creator of Fairies," in *Punch* (Melbourne). February 10, 1921, p. 11.

"Elves and Fairies: The Art of Ida Rentoul," in Sydney *Sun.* March 15, 1917, p. 5.

"Elves and Fairies," in *The New York Times*. January 19, 1919, Section 8, p. 24.

Holden, Robert. *Koalas, Kangaroos and Kookaburras: 200 Australian Children's Books and Illustrators 1857–1988*. Exhibition catalogue. NSW: James Hardie Industries, 1988.

"Ida Rentoul Outhwaite: the Peter Pan Artist," in *Woman's World*. December 1, 1923, pp. 19, 47.

"Illustrated Books," in *Times Literary Supplement*. December 13, 1917, p. 613.

Langmore, Diane. "Ida Rentoul Outhwaite," in Ritchie, J. (gen. ed.), *Australian Dictionary of Biography*. Vol. 11. Melbourne: Melbourne University Press, 1988, pp. 109–110.

Muir, Marcie. *A History of Children's Book Illustration*. Melbourne: Oxford University Press, 1982.

———, and Robert Holden. *The Fairy World of Ida Rentoul Outhwaite*. Sydney: Craftsman House, 1985.

Saxby, H.M. *A History of Australian Children's Literature 1841–1941*. Sydney, 1969.

Smith, Spartacus. "Catching Fairies in the Camera," in *Sydney Mail*. January 19, 1921, pp. 10–11.

SUGGESTED READING:

McVitty, Walter. *Authors and Illustrators of Australian Children's Books*. Sydney: Hodder & Stoughton, 1989.

Outhwaite, Ida Rentoul, and Annie Rentoul. *Elves and Fairies*. Melbourne: Lothian, 1992.

COLLECTIONS:

Correspondence of Outhwaite's and Annie R. Rentoul with Lothian Publishers, Lothian Papers, La Trobe Library, Melbourne.

Original works, art galleries of New South Wales (Sydney), Victoria (Melbourne), Hobart and Launceston.

Original works, illustrated books and ephemera, James Hardie Library of Australian Fine Arts.

Postcards produced by A&C Black, from *The Enchanted Forest*, Terry O'Neill Papers, National Library of Australia, Canberra.

Jenny Newell,
researcher, *Australian Dictionary of Biography*,
Australian National University, Canberra, Australia

Overbeck, Carla.

See Soccer: Women's World Cup, 1999.

Overlach, Helene (1894–1983)

German Communist leader who led the Roter Frauen- und Mädchenbund (Red Girls' and Women's League) during the Weimar Republic. *Name variations: Lene Overlach; (underground names) Frieda, Klara, Frau Teschmer. Born in Greiz, Thuringia, Germany, on July 7, 1894; died in East Berlin on August 7, 1983; daughter of Martin Overlach; mother's name unknown; never married; children: daughter, Hanna.*

Long before the German Communist movement was drowned in a sea of blood by Adolf Hitler, it had been betrayed by Joseph Stalin. By the late 1920s, Stalin had been able to seize control of the Communist Party of Germany (Kommunistische Partei Deutschlands or KPD), making its leaders loyal to him and Soviet national interests. This included decreeing rapid switches of the party line to suit the shifting needs of the USSR, and precluded creating a working alliance between Communist and Social Democratic workers which might have halted Hitler's rising Nazi Party. Stalin was afraid that a Marxist Germany would destabilize the European power balance and endanger his own regime, so consequently he sabotaged any possibility of the emergence of an anti-Hitler coalition in that nation. Stalin's maneuvers do not negate the lives of many Germans who chose Communism as their political base in the years after 1918. Many were sincere in their desire to create a society based on social justice and free of the conditions that had in the past made Germany a reactionary and militaristic state that trampled on the rights both of its own citizens and of its neighbors. Helene Overlach was one of these Germans. A major figure in the German Communist movement, she was willing to risk her life in the struggle against the evils of Nazism.

Overlach was born in Greiz in 1894, the third of four children of Dr. Martin Overlach, a well-respected, liberal physician in that small Thuringian town. Greiz was the capital of the Principality of Reuss, whose sovereign prince, Henry XXII, resided there. Overlach's father medically treated both the bluebloods of the Reuss family and the local poor, and from an early age Helene became aware of the contrast between the rich who never seemed to work, and the poor who seemed to labor for long hours. She also noted the arrogance of the aristocratic elite, and even of members of the middle class, toward the poor. After her family moved to Berlin in 1904, Overlach became increasingly aware of the class tensions and economic exploitation that underlay all aspects of the German social order.

The death of her father in 1912 was a psychological and financial blow to the family. To support herself, Overlach worked 12-to-14-hour days, six days a week, in an office. By that time she had been able to complete her secondary schooling, including the local Realgymnasium and an advanced Commercial School, but her dreams of studying medicine had to be abandoned. At the start of World War I in 1914, she volunteered to work as an auxiliary nurse in one of Berlin's emergency military hospitals (*Militärlazarett*). Before too many months had passed, Overlach began to notice the discrepancies between the patriotic rhetoric of the state and the sufferings the war had unleashed, particularly on the working class and poorest sectors of the German population—the old, the women, and the children. In 1915, one of her brothers died soon after being severely wounded at the front. By 1917, like many other Germans, Overlach had come to reject the official justifications for continuing the war. As she saw it, the conflict was one between equally guilty imperialist states, and the working classes would only continue to suffer if hostilities continued.

In 1917, Overlach chanced upon a pamphlet by a still-obscure Russian Marxist revolutionary, Vladimir Lenin. His analysis of the nature of the war, as far as she could see, was quite convincing. Overlach was in Berlin in November 1918, when the armistice was announced and Kaiser Wilhelm I abdicated and fled the country. On November 9, 1918, she joined thousands of other Berliners in the mass demonstration that marked the end of the Hohenzollern monarchy and the beginning of the improvised German Republic. She volunteered her services to the Workers' and Soldiers' Council of Berlin, assisting soldiers recently repatriated from the front. Above all else, she witnessed the rapidly deteriorating relationship between radical Social Democrats, soon to call themselves Communists, and the majority Social Democrats. The Communist Party of Germany (KPD) was led by Karl Liebknecht and ***Rosa Luxemburg**, who would within weeks fall victim to the murderous rage of private armies known as the Freikorps. After working as a teacher in a business school, Overlach left Berlin in October 1919, to move to Munich.

At the time of her arrival there, the Bavarian capital was still reeling from the events of recent months. In 1919, Munich lived through two short-lived revolutionary uprisings by the extreme Left, as well as bloody military reprisals from the forces of the Right. (Although she was unaware of it, Overlach arrived in Munich precisely at the time of the birth of Adolf Hitler's Nazi movement.) While working as a secretary in a lawyer's office, she joined a Leftist youth movement, the Freie Sozialistische Jugend (Free Socialist Youth). Here, she came in contact with **Franziska Bergmann-Rubens**, who would by December 1920 become a leading member of Germany's Communist Youth Movement. By the end of 1920, Overlach had officially become a Communist. From 1921 to 1925, she was active in several places, including Berlin where she worked at party headquarters as secretary to Wilhelm Pieck, one of the top KPD leaders. She also worked in Düsseldorf in the Rheinland-Westphalen section of the party. In 1923, she met ***Clara Zetkin** for the first time, and under unusual circumstances. Delegated to meet Zetkin at the Hamm train station, both she and Zetkin were arrested there by a French military officer. After several hours, both were released.

Overlach sharpened her skills as a journalist and agitator throughout the 1920s. From 1923 to 1925, she worked as a member of the editorial staff of Essen's KPD newspaper, the *Ruhr-Echo*. She also worked briefly in Breslau (now Wroclaw, Poland) as chief editor of that city's KPD journal, the *Schlesische Arbeiter-Zeitung*. Overlach became closely identified with the KPD faction led by the party's later supreme leader, the former dock worker Ernst Thälmann. She took the side of the Thälmannites in their battles with ***Ruth Fischer** and others who were hostile to the increasing domination of the KPD by the Soviet forces led by Stalin.

By the end of 1925, Overlach had proven herself to be a reliable member of the Thälmann faction. This, along with the favorable impression she had made on Zetkin, led to Overlach being chosen the de facto leader of the KPD women's organization, the Roter Frauen- und Mädchenbund (Red Girls' and Women's League, RFMB), founded in Berlin on November 29, 1925. Although Zetkin was the nominal RFMB leader, the actual day-to-day work of heading the organization fell to Overlach. Aged and infirm, Zetkin actually lived in Moscow much of the time during these years, even though she was universally regarded as the Grand Old Lady of German Communism and was a member of the Reichstag (Parliament). Through agitation and propaganda, RFMB membership grew significantly from around 9,000 in May 1926 to around 20,000 that November. These numbers, however, may have been manipulated, and while the KPD leadership in Berlin may have looked upon these women as potential militant Communist stalwarts, between 70% and 80% of them were listed as "*parteilos*"—not belonging to a political party.

During the years of the Weimar Republic (1919–33), women made up between 7% and 17% of the membership of the KPD. The party had great difficulty in recruiting working-class women, and a high percentage of women in the KPD were housewives, unemployed, or from the urban intelligentsia. Many were indifferent to politics, while others were essentially conservative in their ideals. Some union members were strongly committed to the moderate Social Democratic Party. Overlach believed that the majority of Germany's women, being oppressed in various ways, could in fact be made sympathetic to the message of German Communism. From the mid-1920s, she worked to spread the word, both to the population at large, and within the male-dominated KPD leadership. As her influence within a now increasingly Stalinized KPD grew, Overlach worked to recruit more women into the orbit of German Communism. In March 1927, at the 11th Party Congress of the KPD, held in Essen, she was elected a member of the national Central Committee and was put in charge of women's affairs. In May 1928, Overlach was elected to the Reichstag, representing a working-class district in Düsseldorf. Her influence within the KPD leadership, now totally Stalinized, was confirmed in 1929 when she was re-elected to the Central Committee. More important, she now became a candidate member of the policy-making KPD Politburo.

By 1930, Germany was in the throes of a rapidly worsening economic crisis. The misery brought on by growing unemployment brought recruits and votes for the KPD, but benefited Hitler's Nazi movement even more. The KPD spent much of its energy demonizing the sluggish Social Democrats, attacking them as "Social Fascists" who were little better than Hitlerites. Overlach was concerned with these developments but had become a cog in the machinery of the KPD. In 1930, the RFMB was absorbed by an organization that existed as much on paper as in reality, the Kampfbund gegen den Faschismus (Fighting League Against Fascism). More to the point, in March 1930, Overlach was seriously injured at a political demonstration. As if to symbolize her—and the KPD's—growing loss of control over the situation in Germany, starting in 1930 Overlach became increasingly involved in Soviet and international Communist activities. In March 1931, the women's division of the Communist International in Moscow asked her to collect data on women's work carried out by the French and British Communist parties. In 1931 and 1932, Overlach traveled to France and the United Kingdom to collect this data. While there, she met with local Communist leaders, including Jacques Duclos and Maurice Thorez in France and Harry Pollitt in England.

Although she had largely retired from heading the women's affairs division of the KPD by 1931, relinquishing these tasks to **Roberta Gropper** and **Lisa Ullrich**, Overlach remained active in this area in a less formal way. On October 24, 1931, she addressed 1,500 women in Berlin at a Congress of Working Women. At this assembly, powerful appeals for working-class solidarity were mixed with descriptions of Nazi violence in the streets of German cities, towns, and villages. Although this was by far the largest working-class meeting of German women before 1945, the reality of the situation was that it was too little and too late to stop Nazism. At a mass rally of 10,000 women on October 22 in Berlin's *Sportpalast*, Overlach appealed to her audience: "We are a power to be reckoned with, if we chose to unite."

Hitler formed a "legal" cabinet on January 30, 1933. Within a month's time, the Reichstag building was in flames under mysterious circumstances and the Communist Party was banned. As a KPD leader, Overlach was included on an arrest list dated February 28, 1933. She now went underground, using aliases: "Frieda," "Klara" and "Frau Teschmer." Unlike top leaders like Thälmann who were arrested in March, Overlach remained free until a few days before Christmas 1933, when she was arrested in Essen. In August 1934, she was sentenced to three years' penal servitude on the standard Nazi-concocted charge of "preparation for high treason." For the next several years, Overlach was imprisoned with other women political prisoners—almost all of them either Communists or Social Democrats—at the Ziegenhain and Gotteszell penitentiaries, as well as at the Aichach women's prison. On December 30, 1936, she was told she would continue to be incarcerated under the legal category of "protective custody" (*Schutzhaft*) despite the fact that her term of confinement had been served. Overlach was taken to the Moringen concentration camp for women, and later to the Lichtenburg concentration camp. There, her health deteriorated dramatically, and manifestations of serious cardiac problems became evident.

Convinced that she was no longer a threat to the Third Reich, officials released the seriously ill Overlach in May 1938. In Berlin, she began earning her living as a typist in an office. Some time later, she was able to find work teaching in a business school. Every third day, she had to go to the local police office to sign papers. She was also regularly spied on by the Gestapo. Most painful to Overlach was the fact that she could not see her daughter Hanna, who had been living for years in Switzerland. A bittersweet reunion between mother and daughter took place in 1942, when Hanna, then aged 11, was expelled from Switzerland. In August 1944, a few weeks after the failed July 20 assassination attempt on Hitler, Overlach was again arrested. Her name was on a list of the Reichssicherheitshauptamt (Reich Security Main Office) designated "*Rückkehr unerwünscht*" (return not to be desired), meaning that she was designated to be killed. She was sent to the notorious Ravensbrück concentration camp for women, where her already fragile health declined rapidly. Several of her friends at Ravensbrück were able to find a way to get the seriously ill Overlach (under a false identity) on a list of Polish women prisoners who were going to be sent to Sweden. On April 22, 1945, while the war still raged, the transport of women prisoners left Ravensbrück, arriving in Malmö, Sweden, on May 1.

With her health largely restored, Overlach returned to Berlin in late April 1946. Happily, she was again able to find her daughter, then almost 15 years old. Overlach joined the newly formed Socialist Unity Party—the old KPD in all but name. Despite her impressive credentials from pre-Nazi days, Overlach was not chosen to serve in a leadership position. As a woman, and as a Communist who had survived in the heart of Nazi Germany rather than in exile in the West or in Moscow, she was perhaps not considered a reliable Stalinist, even though she had never given any indications of a lack of resolve in this sector. Instead, Overlach was chosen to be director of East Berlin's Institute for Vocational School Teacher Training. In September 1950, she became a professor at the Pedagogical Academy in East Berlin.

At the end of 1954, Overlach retired from her professional duties. By now a venerable party veteran, she was awarded a number of high distinctions by the SED leadership of the German Democratic Republic. These included the Clara Zetkin Medal in 1955, and the Bar of Honor of the Fatherland's Order of Achievement in Gold (Ehrenspange zum Vaterländischen Verdienstorden in Gold) in 1969. On the occasion of her 75th birthday in July 1969, she was awarded the prestigious Karl Marx Order. On many occasions during her long retirement years, Overlach could be seen as an honorary delegate at SED party conferences. She spent her final years, in declining health, at East Berlin's Clara Zetkin Old Age Home, where she died at the age of 89 on August 7, 1983. In a public statement on the occasion of her passing, the SED Central Committee noted that with the death of Helene Overlach, "our Party has lost a revolutionary fighter who had been a member of the organized working class since the days of her youth, and who dedicated her entire life to the cause of peace and Socialism." Going beyond the mechanical official rhetoric, her friends and family could recall a woman who had attempted to change the world for the better, only to find that to do so was an extremely difficult task.

SOURCES:

Arendt, Hans-Jürgen. "Das Schutzprogramm der KPD für die arbeitende Frau vom 15. Oktober 1931," in *Beiträge zur Geschichte der Deutschen Arbeiterbewegung*. Vol. 11, no. 2, 1969, pp. 291–311.

———. "Der Erste Reichskongress werktätiger Frauen Deutschlands 1929," in *Zeitschrift für Geschichtswissenschaft*. Vol. 20, no. 4, 1972, pp. 467–479.

———. "Die kommunistische Frauenpresse in Deutschland 1917 bis 1933," in *Beiträge zur Geschichte der Arbeiterbewegung*. Vol. 29, no. 1, 1987, pp. 78–88.

———. "Sie stritt mit Herz und Verstand für den Sozialismus: Helene Overlach," in *Beiträge zur Geschichte der Arbeiterbewegung*. Vol. 30, no. 6, 1988, pp. 803–812.

———. "Weibliche Mitglieder der KPD in der Weimarer Republik—Zahlenmässige Stärke und soziale Stellung," in *Beiträge zur Geschichte der Arbeiterbewegung*. Vol. 19, no. 4, 1977, pp. 652–660.

"1500 Delegierte auf dem Kongress werkttätiger Frauen," in *Die Rote Fahne* [Berlin]. No. 191. October 27, 1931, 1. Beilage, p. 1.

Fischer, Ruth. *Stalin and German Communism: A Study in the Origins of the State Party.* Cambridge, MA: Harvard University Press, 1948.

Koonz, Claudia. *Mothers in the Fatherland: Women, the Family, and Nazi Politics.* NY: St. Martin's Press, 1987.

Overlach, Helene. *Frauen im Kampf um Brot und Freiheit! II. Reichskongress werktätiger Frauen in Berlin.* Berlin: "Peuvag," 1931.

"Richtlinien für die Arbeit der Frauen- und Mädchenstaffeln des Kampfbunds gegen den Faschismus," document in Staatsarchiv Bremen, Bestand 4,65-II.H.4.a.32 (Polizeidirektion Bremen).

Rosenhaft, Eve. *Beating the Fascists?: The German Communists and Political Violence, 1929–1933.* Cambridge: Cambridge University Press, 1983.

Schumacher, Martin, Katharina Lübbe, and Wilhelm Heinz Schröder. *M.d.R.: Die Reichstagsabgeordneten der Weimarer Republik in der Zeit des Nationalsozialismus—Politische Verfolgung, Emigration und Ausbürgerung, 1933–1945. Eine biographische Dokumentation.* 3rd revised ed. Düsseldorf: Droste Verlag, 1994.

Schuster, Kurt G.P. *Der Rote Frontkämpferbund, 1924–1929.* Düsseldorf: Droste Verlag, 1975.

Ullrich, Lisa. "Die proletarischen Frauen gehören in die Wehrorganisationen des Proletariats," in *Die Internationale.* Vol. 12, no. 17. September 1, 1929, pp. 558–560.

Waters, Elizabeth. "In the Shadow of the Comintern: The Communist Women's Movement, 1920–43," in Sonia Kruks, Rayna Rapp and Marilyn B. Young, eds., *Promissory Notes: Women in the Transition to Socialism.* NY: Monthly Review Press, 1989, pp. 29–56.

Weber, Hermann. *Die Wandlung des deutschen Kommunismus: Die Stalinisierung der KPD in der Weimarer Republik.* 2 vols. Frankfurt am Main: Europäische Verlagsanstalt, 1969.

John Haag,
Associate Professor of History, University of Georgia,
Athens, Georgia

Ovington, Mary White (1865–1951)

American civil-rights reformer who was a founder of the NAACP. *Born Mary White Ovington on April 11, 1865, in Brooklyn, New York; died on July 15, 1951,* *in Newton Highlands, Massachusetts; daughter of Theodore Tweedy Ovington (a china and glass importer) and Ann Louise (Ketcham) Ovington; attended Packer Collegiate Institute, 1888–91; attended Radcliffe College, 1891–93.*

Worked as registrar of Pratt Institute in Brooklyn; was head worker at Greenpoint Settlement (1895–1903); served as vice-president of the Brooklyn Consumers' League; was assistant secretary of the Social Reform Club; joined the Socialist Party of America (c. 1905); was a social worker at Greenwich House; helped to found the National Negro Committee, later to become the National Association for the Advancement of Colored People (c. 1909); published Half a Man: The Status of the Negro in New York *(1911); served as chair of the board of the NAACP (1919–32).*

Mary White Ovington was a white feminist and civil-rights activist who was one of the founders of the National Association for the Advancement of Colored People (NAACP). Born the third of four children in Brooklyn, New York, in 1865, Ovington received an abolitionist, Unitarian upbringing from parents who erroneously taught her that the Reconstructionist amendments following the Civil War had ended the problem of racial discrimination in America. During Ovington's youth, the Reverend John White Chadwick of the Second Unitarian Church in Brooklyn Heights educated her about social reform and women's rights. At Radcliffe College from 1891 to 1893, economic historian William J. Ashley taught Ovington to see the connection between economic class and social problems.

After the depression of 1893 forced her to drop out of college, Ovington embarked on a career of social work in various New York housing projects. There she came to believe that African-Americans' economic class caused as many problems as the treatment they received because of their race. During this time, she worked for the Pratt Institute in Brooklyn and then at Greenpoint Settlement, a Pratt housing project that Ovington helped to found. She also served as vice-president of the Brooklyn Consumers' League and assistant secretary of the Social Reform Club, where a speech by Booker T. Washington in 1903 made Ovington aware of the problem of racial discrimination in the North. Ovington joined the Socialist Party of America around 1905 and dedicated the remainder of her life's work to fighting for racial equality.

In 1904, Ovington began research for *Half a Man: The Status of the Negro in New York,* about the housing and employment problems of African-Americans in Manhattan, which would be published in 1911. During her research, she met and began to correspond with W.E.B. Du Bois, the African-American social critic and educator. In the following years, Ovington worked primarily with the National League for the Protection of Colored People and the Committee for Improving the Industrial Condition of Negroes in New York (both forerunners of the National Urban League).

Following a race riot in Springfield, Illinois, in August 1908, Ovington and others, including Du Bois and ***Ida Wells-Barnett,** formed the National Negro Committee in 1909, which several years later would become the NAACP. Their goal was to end racial discrimination and segregation and to fight for civil and legal rights. Their activist stance conflicted with Booker T. Washington's support of more gradual reform, and challenged his leadership of the African-American community. For 40 years, Ovington served the NAACP in many important positions, including chair of the board (1919–32) and treasurer (1932–47). Whatever her title, Ovington was an active policymaker, fund raiser, and lobbyist. She also had a flair for personal relations, which she used early in the NAACP's history to mediate disputes between Du Bois, the publicity director and only African-American in the NAACP's national leadership, and Oswald Garrison Villard, chair of the board.

One of Ovington's most important contributions came in 1923 when, as chair of the board, she convinced the NAACP to direct its energies away from anti-lynching legislation (which efforts were being resolutely ignored by Congress) in favor of attaining equal federal aid for black and white public-school systems. The NAACP's efforts in this regard over the next decade were a precursor to the public school desegregation movement that began in the late 1940s. When Du Bois supported "voluntary segregation" in 1934, Ovington maintained the NAACP's goal of integration.

Over the years Ovington wrote a number of books and articles, including a profile of black leaders, *Portraits in Color* (1927). Her autobiography, *The Walls Came Tumbling Down,* which includes much of the history of the NAACP, was published in 1947, the year of her retirement from the organization. Ovington suffered from hypertension and depression in her later years, and died in July 1951 in a nursing home in Newton Highlands, Massachusetts.

SOURCES:

James, Edward T., ed. *Notable American Women, 1607–1950.* Cambridge, MA: The Belknap Press of Harvard University Press, 1971.

Ovington, Mary White. *Black and White Sat Down Together: The Reminiscences of an NAACP Founder.* Edited by Ralph E. Luker. Feminist Press, 1995.

Wedin, Carolyn. *Inheritors of the Spirit: Mary White Ovington and the Founding of the NAACP.* NY: Wiley, 1997.

Women's Review of Books. June 1995.

Daniel E. Brannen, Jr., freelance writer, York, Pennsylvania

Owen, Laurence (1945–1961)

American figure skater. *Born in Massachusetts in 1945; died in a plane crash on February 15, 1961; daughter of Maribel Vinson Owen (1911–1961, a skater and coach) and Guy Owen (a top-ranked skater who died in 1952); sister of Maribel Owen (1941–1961, a figure skater).*

Laurence Owen

Placed 3rd in the U.S. Nationals and 6th at the Winter Olympics in Squaw Valley (1960); placed 1st in the U.S. Nationals senior singles and 1st in the North American championship (1961).

Sixteen-year-old Laurence Owen was at the beginning of a more-than-promising career in figure skating when she boarded a Boeing 707 in New York on a Sabena Airlines flight to Prague, Czechoslovakia, by way of Brussels, to compete in the World championship. Three days earlier, she had won the North American singles championship in Philadelphia, preceded by the January 27th singles title at the 1961 U.S. National figure skating singles competition held in Colorado Springs. She had topped her main competition **Stephanie Westerfeld**. "Her free-skating has an air, a style," wrote **Barbara Heilman** for the cover story in *Sports Illustrated,* "an individuality which sets it apart from all the work done in free skating in recent years." Owen also had, said one photographer, "the greatest natural smile I've ever seen." With her bronze-medalist mother ***Maribel Vinson Owen** as team coach, Laurence Owen was America's hope for the 1964 Olympics in Innsbruck. (The door had been opened when ***Carol Heiss-Jenkins** retired to teach.)

After the jet had circled for a landing over Brussels airport, it veered north, away from the airport toward the small community of Berg. Workers in the field reported that they heard a noise, and the jet began to lose altitude; suddenly it rose in the air and then fell. When it slammed into the countryside and burst into flames, all 72 passengers were killed, including Laurence Owen, her mother, her sister ***Maribel Owen**, 16 members of the U.S. figure-skating team, and four other coaches; one farmer on the ground also died.

At the time of her death, Owen was living with her mother, sister, and grandmother in Winchester, Massachusetts; her father had died when she was seven. Dreaming of a career as a writer, she was a senior and honor roll student at Winchester High School and had just been accepted to her mother's alma mater, Radcliffe. Steffi Westerfeld was also killed in the crash.

SOURCES:

Boston Globe. February 15, 1961.

Heilman, Barbara. "Mother Set the Style," in *Sports Illustrated.* February 13, 1961.

Owen, Margaret (d. 1941).

See Lloyd George, Margaret.

Owen, Maribel (1941–1961)

American figure skater. *Born Maribel Owen, Jr., in Massachusetts in 1941; died in a plane crash on Feb-*

*ruary 15, 1961; daughter of *Maribel Vinson Owen (1911–1961, a skater and coach) and Guy Owen (a top-ranked skater who died in 1952); sister of Laurence Owen (1945–1961, a figure skater).*

Participated in the Winter Olympics at Squaw Valley; placed 1st in the U.S. National senior pairs competition and 2nd at the North American championships (1961).

Maribel Owen was on her way to Prague to compete in the figure skating pairs competition with her partner, 28-year-old Dudley Richards, when their plane crashed over Belgium. Three days earlier, she and Richards had placed second in the North American championships in Philadelphia, preceded by a first at the January 27th U.S. National figure skating championships at Colorado Springs. Along with her sister ***Laurence Owen**, Maribel executed "programs far removed in kind and execution from the usual tedious but to-be-respected arrangements of jumps and spins," wrote **Barbara Heilman** in *Sports Illustrated.* Maribel Owen was a senior at Boston University, preparing for a career in teaching.

SOURCES:

Boston Globe. February 15, 1961.

Heilman, Barbara. "Mother Set the Style," in *Sports Illustrated.* February 13, 1961.

Owen, Maribel Vinson (1911–1961)

American figure skater and coach. *Name variations: Maribel Y. Vinson; Maribel Vinson-Owen. Born Maribel Y. Vinson in Winchester, Massachusetts, in 1911; died in a plane crash on February 15, 1961; daughter of Thomas Vinson (a renowned skater) and Gertrude Vinson; graduated from Radcliffe College; married Guy Owen (a top-ranked skater who died in 1952); children: Maribel Owen (1941–1961, a figure skater); Laurence Owen (1945–1961, a figure skater).*

Finished 4th at the Olympics (1928); won the bronze medal in figure skating (1932); won the U.S. National figure skating championships nine times (1928–33 and 1936–37); won the U.S. pairs title six times.

Born in Winchester, Massachusetts, in 1911, Maribel Vinson Owen was the daughter of **Gertrude Vinson** and Thomas Vinson, an accomplished skater; she was three when she donned her first skates—double runners. In 1928, she beat out ***Theresa Weld (Blanchard)** for the U.S. National figure skating championship. A bold and daring competitor and a master of school figures, Owen placed fourth at the Olympics in St. Moritz. (Fifteen-year-old ***Sonja Henie** took the gold, **Fritzie Burger** of Austria placed second, while **Beatrix Loughran** of the United States came in third.) "The American champion Vinson was competing for the first time. She was one of the new guard skaters," wrote Henie in her autobiography. "There was a new approach, new life, and a stiffer challenge in the field than there had been at Chamonix in my dismal 1924." In the 1932 Winter Olympics at Lake Placid, New York, Owen carried home a bronze medal, once more behind silver-medalist Burger and gold-medalist Henie. In 1936, Owen teamed up with George Hill for the Olympic pairs competition in Garmisch-Partenkirchen, placing 5th.

Upon her amateur retirement, Owen kept her hand heavily into the sport. She not only wrote of women's sports for *The New York Times,* but she continued as a coach; her pupils included ***Tenley Albright**, as well as her two daughters ***Laurence** and ***Maribel Owen**. After her husband died in 1952, Owen became father, mother, coach and breadwinner to her eleven- and seven-year-old daughters while also supporting her own mother. In those 18-hour days, Owen would train her children in the early morning then leap "from class to class at rinks all over and around Boston," wrote **Barbara Heilman**. She also wrote the book *Figure Skating is Fun* (1961). In February 1961, Maribel Vinson Owen was killed with her two daughters and the rest of the U.S. figure skating team when their plane went down over Berg, Belgium.

SOURCES:

Boston Globe. February 15, 1961.

Heilman, Barbara. "Mother Set the Style," in *Sports Illustrated.* February 13, 1961.

Owen, Ruth Bryan (1885–1954).

See Rohde, Ruth Bryan Owen.

Owens, Claire Myers (1896–1983)

American writer. *Name variations: (pseudonym) Claire Myers Spotswood. Born Clairene Lenora Allen Myers in Denton, Texas, in 1896; died in Rochester, New York, in 1983; only daughter and one of two children of Coren Lee Myers (a schoolteacher and principal) and Susan (Allen) Myers; graduated from Temple High School, 1913; B.S. in Domestic Science, College of Industrial Arts (now Texas Woman's University), Denton, Texas, 1916; married first husband reporter George Wanders (divorced); married third husband H. Thurston Owens III, in 1937 (died 1969).*

Selected writings: The Unpredictable Adventure *(1935);* Love is Not Enough; Awakening to the Good

(1958); Discovery of Self *(autobiography, 1963);* Zen and the Lady *(1979).*

Claire Myers Owens, born in 1896 and raised in Denton, Texas, as a proper Southern belle, shook loose her strict upbringing, after graduating from college with a degree in domestic science, to take up more liberal pursuits. Her early years away from home, dramatized in her later fiction, were venturesome and varied, including social work in Chicago and an Alabama mining camp and residence in a commune in the Blue Ridge Mountains. When she reached New York, she worked at several well-known bookshops and wrote reviews for *Publishers Weekly*, all the while keeping up an active social life with a variety of "beaux" selected from New York's literati. (It has been rumored that she had an affair with Thomas Wolfe, but there is nothing in her autobiography to substantiate the story.)

Claire Myers Owens

Her first book, *The Unpredictable Adventure*, was published in 1935. Labeled a fantasy novel and subtitled "A Comedy of Woman's Independence," it parallels Owens' life and explores the double standard by which she felt women were judged. Considered bold and ahead of its time, it was banned by the New York Public Library because of its explicit treatment of female sexuality. The *Los Angeles Times* described it as "more instructive than most manuals about what a young girl ought to know." Owens published the book under the name Claire Myers Spotswood, supposedly to exploit her connection to Alexander Spotswood, the 18th-century governor of Virginia. Although she was commissioned to write seven more fantasy adventure books, none were forthcoming. Instead, she concentrated on magazine articles, book reviews, short stories, and novels. Most of her work dealt with women's quest for self-fulfillment through a balance of love and work. In the manuscript notes Owens submitted to the publishers of her novel *Love is Not Enough*, set in the Depression year 1932, she wrote: "When democracy fails to work in people's personal lives, intense suffering ensues, no less than in national life. . . . [E]quality of the classes in America like equality of the sexes, however difficult, is nevertheless desirable."

In 1949, in the midst of her third marriage to wealthy businessman Thurston Owens III, Owens experienced a spiritual enlightenment that changed the direction of her life and writing. In *Awakening to the Good: Psychological Or Religious?* (1958), one of three autobiographical studies, she describes it as the day her "Reason united with [her] Intuition and Feeling and [she] was made whole." In an effort to share her epiphany with the world, Owens undertook the study of the humanistic and transpersonal psychology of Abraham Maslow and Anthony Sutich, as well as the philosophy of Aldous Huxley, who became a close friend. In 1954, she met and interviewed psychologist Carl Jung and later wrote a prize-winning article about their encounter. At age 70, Owens took up Zen, eventually selling her mansion to join the Zen Center in Rochester, New York. Her last publication, *Zen and the Lady* (1979), traces the journey to her spiritual enlightenment through the Zen practice of meditation. At age 83, Owens said in an interview on a Rochester television show, "I am the happiest person I know." She died by her own hand in the Zen colony at Rochester, at age 87.

SOURCES:

Harris, Miriam Kalman. "Claire Myers Spotswood Owens: From Southern Belle to Grand Amoureuse," in *Southern Quarterly*. Fall 1992.

Barbara Morgan,
Melrose, Massachusetts

Owens-Adair, Bethenia

(1840–1926)

American physician and eugenics advocate. *Born Bethenia Angelina Owens on February 7, 1840, in Van Buren County, Missouri; died of inflammation of the lining of the heart on September 11, 1926, in Portland, Oregon; daughter of Thomas Owens (a farmer) and Sarah Damron Owens; Eclectic Medical College, M.D., 1874; University of Michigan, M.D., 1880; married Legrand Hall, on May 4, 1854 (divorced 1859); married Colonel John Adair, in 1884 (died 1915); children: (first marriage) George (b. April 17, 1856); Mattie Belle Palmer (adopted 1875); (second marriage) daughter (b. 1887, died with three days of birth); (adopted) Victor Adair Hill and John Adair, Jr.*

Bethenia Owens-Adair was three years old in 1843, when her parents picked up stakes and moved their family from Missouri to Oregon. These were the early years of western migration, and the enterprise was an enormous one. The family, which grew to include nine children, settled finally in 1853 in the Umpqua Valley, across the river from Roseburg, Oregon. Owens-Adair received scant education and was married at age 14 to Legrand Hill, who had been a hired hand on the family farm. Not quite two years later she gave birth to a son, George, and three years after that, in 1859, she divorced her neglectful husband and stopped using his last name. In order to better support her son, she struggled for five years to obtain a basic education, and in 1867 opened a dressmaking and millinery shop in Roseburg.

Owens-Adair supported the suffrage movement, and in 1871 she arranged for ***Susan B. Anthony** to visit Roseburg. She also read the *New Northwest*, a local women's rights publication, where she learned about women who had become doctors. Her interest in medicine had already been encouraged by a Roseburg physician who, aware of her local reputation for nursing skills, had given her a copy of *Gray's Anatomy*. In 1873, over the protests of her family, Owens-Adair left Oregon and her successful dressmaking shop to study medicine at the Eclectic Medical College in Philadelphia, Pennsylvania. Her son George, who was then 17 (and who would also later become a doctor), moved into the house of ***Abigail Scott Duniway**, editor of the *New Northwest*. She returned to Oregon in 1874 with her M.D. degree and set up practice in Portland, but was regarded with a measure of suspicion by the local medical community because the Eclectic Medical College was considered somewhat disreputable (the dean was convicted of selling false degrees), and because the medicine she had been taught there, including "Medicated vapor baths," was unorthodox. Thus, in 1878, at age 38, she enrolled at the University of Michigan medical school, intent on obtaining trustworthy credentials. She received her M.D. degree in 1880, and did postgraduate work at the university as well as in Chicago and at some hospitals in Europe. When she returned to Portland in 1881 and set up a successful, traditional medical practice, she became one of the first women doctors in Oregon. She also became active in the Oregon State Medical Society. Although she specialized in diseases of the eyes and ears, the majority of her patients were women and children.

While continuing to support suffrage, Owens-Adair was also active in the local branch of the Women's Christian Temperance Union, and was an officer of the Roseburg lodge of Good Templars. She put both her son George and a daughter she had adopted in 1875, **Mattie Belle Parker**, through the Willamette Medical College. In 1884, she married Colonel John Adair, a farmer and land developer whom she had known since her youth. Three years later, at age 47, she gave birth to a daughter who died within three days. Over the next several years, while she continued to practice medicine, she and her husband adopted two more children, one of whom was Owens-Adair's grandson. In 1899, seeking relief for her rheumatoid arthritis, the family moved to the drier climate of North Yakima, Washington, where her son George practiced medicine. There Owens-Adair again set up a medical practice.

Around this time she began to take an interest in eugenics, which from the late years of the 19th century was being widely and enthusiastically discussed. Virtuously touted as improvement of the human race, eugenics advocated the selective breeding of humans for intelligence and other praiseworthy qualities. The flip side of this—which many in the movement considered more important—was the discouragement of breeding by "inferior" individuals, specifically by sterilization. In the first quarter of the 20th century, many right-minded, educated, and influential people convinced of their own good intentions believed that eugenic sterilization offered a solution to at least part of society's ills (or to those pesky poor people who behaved contrary to upper-class norms). By the time of her retirement from active practice in 1905, Owens-Adair had become a champion of sterilization for, among others, the mentally retarded, epileptics, and those who were "feebleminded" or "insane." A strong believer in heredity, she felt that preventing such individuals from passing on their genes was a social necessity. (Not so many years later, the Nazis would wholeheartedly agree.) Soon the preeminent advocate for eugenic sterilization in the Pacific Northwest, Owens-Adair joined with several other physicians in 1907 to lobby the legislatures in both Washington State and Oregon for passage of a bill mandating sterilization of people committed to state mental institutions. Washington passed a version of this bill two years later; Oregon followed suit in 1925, one year before her death. In 1927, the U.S. Supreme Court affirmed the validity of a sterilization law in Virginia (*see entry on Carrie Buck*). Among the books Owens-Adair published on the subject were *Human Sterilization* (1910), *Human Sterilization: Its Social and Legislative Aspects* (1922), and *The Eugenic Marriage Law and Human Sterilization* (1922).

SOURCES:

Edgerly, Lois Stiles, ed. *Give Her This Day: A Daybook of Women's Words.* Gardiner, ME: Tilbury House, 1990.

Kaufman, Martin, *et al.*, eds. *Dictionary of American Medical Biography.* Vol. 1. Westport, CT: Greenwood Press, 1984.

Uglow, Jennifer S., comp. and ed. *The International Dictionary of Women's Biography.* NY: Continuum, 1985.

SUGGESTED READING:

Evans, Elwood. *History of the Pacific Northwest II*, 1889.

Gaston, Joseph. *The Centennial History of Oregon*, 1912.

Miller, Helen Markely. *Woman Doctor of the West: Bethenia Owens-Adair*, 1960.

Owens-Adair, Bethenia. *Dr. Owens-Adair: Some of Her Life Experiences,* 1906.

Ross, Nancy Wilson. *Westward the Women,* 1944.

Christine Miner Minderovic,
freelance writer, Ann Arbor, Michigan

Owenson, Miss Sydney (1780–1859).

See Morgan, Sydney.

Oxford, countess of.

See Mortimer, Margaret (d. around 1296).
See Vere, Maud de (fl. 1360s).
See Badlesmere, Maud (d. 1366).
See Howard, Elizabeth (c. 1410–1475).
See Trussel, Elizabeth (1496–1527).
See Howard, Anne (d. 1559).

Oxford and Asquith, countess of.

See Asquith, Margot (1864–1945).

P., Kaare (1873–1942).

See Anker, Nini Roll.

Paalen, Alice (1904–1987).

See Rahon, Alice.

Paasche, Maria (1909–2000)

Anti-Nazi activist in the 1930s. *Name variations: Maria Therese von Hammerstein. Born Maria Therese von Hammerstein in 1909 in Magdeburg, Germany; died on January 21, 2000, in San Francisco, California; daughter of General Kurt von Hammerstein (commander-in-chief of the German army, 1930–34, and anti-Hitler conspirator); granddaughter of General Walther von Lüttwitz; sister of anti-Hitler conspirators Ludwig von Hammerstein and Kunrat von Hammerstein; studied agriculture at public schools in Berlin; attended University of Berlin; married John H. Paasche, in 1935 (died 1994); children: Gottfried Paasche; Joan Briegleb; Michaela Grudin; Virginia Dakin.*

Transported Jews to Prague (1930s); smuggled information to anti-Nazi community; exiled in Japan during World War II; emigrated to United States (1948); worked as literary researcher; subject of documentary Silent Courage: Maria Therese von Hammerstein and Her Battle Against Nazism *(1999).*

One of seven children born to General Kurt von Hammerstein, commander-in-chief of the German army from 1930 to 1934, Maria Paasche began life as Maria Therese von Hammerstein in Magdeburg, near Berlin, in 1909. Growing up in an important army family—her grandfather General Walther von Lüttwitz was involved in the 1920 putsch against the Weimar Republic—Paasche and her siblings enjoyed a childhood less constrained and conservative than their environment would suggest.

Encouraged to explore intellectually and politically outside their immediate circle and inspired by her many Jewish friends, Paasche began to nurture plans to move to Palestine. She left the convent she was attending and took up agricultural studies at a public school, preparing for life in the Middle East; she went on to study at the University of Berlin.

Committed to political activism, like most of her siblings, Paasche soon realized the implications of Adolf Hitler's rise to power. In the early 1930s, she began helping Jews escape from Nazi Germany, transporting them to Prague—still a free city—on her motorcycle. She also took newspapers to the anti-Nazi community there, warning the Jewish community in Prague about Hitler's plans, based on intelligence information received from her father.

As Hitler's fortunes rose, Paasche's family lived in military accommodations under close surveillance. Her father did not attend her wedding in 1935 to John H. Paasche, although he gave his blessing. John's background made him a target in Nazi Germany. Not only was he part Jewish, but his father Hans Paasche was a former navy captain, discharged after becoming a pacifist and known to the authorities for serving as a pallbearer at the funeral of assassinated socialist leader ***Rosa Luxemburg**.

Maria and John Paasche moved to Palestine to join their Zionist friends, but a typhoid epidemic drove them back to Germany. As a Jew, John was prohibited from studying law there, so he took up oriental languages instead. Persistently interrogated by the Gestapo about the activities of friends and relatives, the couple decided to emigrate to Japan.

In 1939, Maria's father plotted to lure Hitler to his headquarters on the Western front and kill him. Chancellor Heinrich Brening called von Hammerstein "the only man who could remove Hitler—a man without nerves." The attempt was unsuccessful, however, and the general died of cancer in 1943. A year later, two of her brothers, Ludwig and Kunrat, joined another conspiracy to kill Hitler. They both escaped with their lives and became fugitives. Maria Paasche's mother and two youngest siblings were sent to concentration camps because of their refusal to reveal the conspirators' whereabouts. They remained imprisoned until freed by the Allies at the end of the war.

In Japan, as Maria and John Paasche raised their family, they were spied on by the Japanese police. They lived in fear that their political background would be revealed to the German exile community, which was comprised predominantly of Nazi sympathizers. John Paasche worked after the war as a translator for the American occupiers and, in 1948, the family emigrated to San Francisco. While her husband worked in a tomato-canning factory, Maria cleaned houses. She eventually became a literary researcher, fluent in German, Russian, English and French. Her husband, who earned a master's degree from Berkeley and worked in the Chinese section of the Library of Congress, died in 1994.

The heroism of Maria Paasche remained largely unknown until, as an old woman, she went to live in the Jewish Home for the Aged in San Francisco. Her son Gottfried began researching her political activities despite his mother's long silence on the subject. "She never lost her fear of naming names," he said. The information he gathered on her wartime work became a 1999 documentary, *Silent Courage: Maria Therese von Hammerstein and Her Battle Against Nazism*, a film sponsored by B'nai B'rith and the German government. Maria Paasche died in San Francisco in January 2000, at age 90.

SOURCES:

Obituary. *The New York Times*. February 13, 2000.

Paula Morris, D.Phil.,
Brooklyn, New York

Paca (1825–1860).

See Eugénie for sidebar.

Pachler-Koschak, Marie (1792–1855)

Austrian pianist who was one of Beethoven's favorite performers. *Born in Graz, capital of the Austrian province of Styria, on October 2, 1792; died in Graz on April 10, 1855.*

Marie Pachler-Koschak had a distinguished career. In 1817, in one of the rare letters in which he praises a performing musician, Ludwig van Beethoven wrote Pachler-Koschak: "I have not found anybody who performs my compositions as you do, and I am not excluding the great pianists, who often have merely mechanical ability or affectation. You are the true fosterer of my spiritual children."

John Haag,
Athens, Georgia

Pack, Elizabeth (1910–1963).

See Brousse, Amy.

Packard, Clarissa (1794–1888).

See Gilman, Caroline.

Packard, Elizabeth (1816–1897)

American mental health and legal reformer. *Born Elizabeth Parsons Ware on December 28, 1816, in Ware, Massachusetts; died of paralysis on July 25, 1897, in Chicago, Illinois; daughter of Samuel Ware (a Congregational minister) and Lucy (Parsons) Ware; married Theophilus Packard, Jr. (a Calvinist minister), in 1839; children: Theophilus (b. 1842); Isaac Ware (b. 1844); Samuel (b. 1847); Elizabeth Ware (b. 1850); George Hastings (b. 1853); Arthur Dwight (b. 1858).*

Taught as the principal teacher in a girls' school at the age of 19 (c. 1835); spent five weeks in the state hospital for mental illness (1836); married Theophilus Packard and moved to Illinois (1839); committed to an insane asylum by her husband (1860); released (1863); acquitted of insanity in a jury trial in Kankakee, Illinois (1864); published books supporting the rights of married women and mental health patients, and lobbied for legislative reform in both areas (1860s–70s).

Elizabeth Packard, forced by her husband into an insane asylum in 1860 for voicing her religious beliefs, witnessed and experienced abuse by institution doctors and attendants. After she was acquitted of insanity by a jury in 1864, she began a crusade for the rights of married women and mental health patients. According to **Phyllis Chesler**, "Elizabeth Packard understood that women needed more, not less, legal speech; that insecure people, both men and women, conspired to silence women within the family, the church, and the state."

The well-educated daughter of a Congregational minister and a mother who had a history of mental illness, Packard (named Elizabeth Parsons Ware upon her birth in Massachusetts in 1816) grew up into an intelligent, strong-minded, charming, and well-spoken woman with a deep spiritual commitment to Christianity. Shortly before her 20th birthday, she was treated for five weeks in the state hospital at Worcester, Massachusetts, for mental illness, and released back into her father's care upon her recovery. At age 23, she married Theophilus Packard, a strict Calvinist cleric 14 years her senior. They moved several times, finally settling in Illinois. From 1842, Packard gave birth to six children in 16 years, during which time she was an impeccable homemaker who grew her family's vegetables, sewed their clothes, tutored the children, and helped Theophilus write his sermons.

However, Packard's Christianity did not always agree with doctrine. She privately believed that the female embodiment of the Holy Ghost dwelled within her, and at Sunday school she taught that human beings were born good, not evil. Her family frequently had to relocate within Illinois because of trouble caused in Theophilus' church by these beliefs. Theophilus himself believed that his wife's duty was to remain silent about her convictions and support his own by her example. Their conflicts reached a climax in 1860, when Packard openly opposed him on religious matters among his congregation. His retaliation, in her own words, took this form:

> Early on the morning of the 18th of June, 1860, as I arose from my bed, . . . I saw my husband approaching my door with two physicians, both members of his church and of our Bible-class,—and . . . [with the] sheriff. . . . Fearing exposure I hastily locked my door. . . . [M]y husband forced an entrance into my room through the window with an axe! . . . [E]ach doctor felt my pulse, and without asking a single question both pronounced me insane. . . . This was the only medical examination I had. This was the only trial of *any kind* that I was allowed to have, to prove the charge of insanity brought against me by my husband. I had no chance of *self defense* whatever. My husband then informed me that the "forms of law" were all complied with, and he therefore requested me to dress myself for a ride to Jacksonville to enter the Insane Asylum as an inmate.

All the forms of law had, in fact, been met, for under Illinois law a man could have his wife committed to an insane asylum with the asylum superintendent's agreement. At the time, many states had laws permitting the forced committal of women to insane asylums at the request of their husband or other family members. It is impossible to know how many of these women were genuinely mentally ill, particularly given the discrepancy between the meaning of that term in the mid-19th century and in contemporary times, but it is certain that many women who spent time in asylums were simply bothersome or upsetting to their families, whether because of their personalities, opinions, or behavior. (In some cases women were committed so that their husbands could more easily spend their money and sell their property.) In Elizabeth Packard's case, a difference of religious opinion was enough to label her insane.

Packard spent 42 months in the Jacksonville asylum. Some four months after her arrival, she argued for her release in a 21-page brief to the superintendent, a physician named Andrew McFarland, who ignored her request. She then sent him letters documenting the abuse of patients she saw all around her. He ultimately transferred her to the Eighth Ward, reserved for the most deeply disturbed patients, and denied her requests for a private room, protection from violent inmates, exercise, and paper on which to write. Packard described the asylum as a prison rather than a hospital. In the midst of this, she compassionately attempted to take care of other inmates.

In the autumn of 1863, Packard's eldest son came of age, and by offering to take responsibility for her persuaded his father to permit her to leave the asylum. After convincing doctors that she was both God-fearing and sane, Packard was released. Life at home, however, was another prison, for Theophilus forbade the children to speak to her, intercepted her mail, locked her in her room, and made plans to have her committed for life in Massachusetts. After six weeks, she managed to send a note to friends who convinced a judge to order Theophilus to prove Packard's insanity in court. The trial caused much local excitement, and received mention in national newspapers. A jury acquitted her of insanity in 1864, and she returned home to find that Theophilus had mortgaged her house and returned to Massachusetts with their children.

The public notice she had gained from the trial enabled Packard to sell subscriptions for books she had not yet written, and she was thus able to support herself while she wrote, among numerous others, *The Exposure on Board the Atlantic & Pacific Car of the Emancipation for the Slaves of Old Columbia, . . . or, Christianity and Calvinism Compared: With an Appeal to the Government to Emancipate the Slaves of the Marriage Union* (1864); *Marital Power Exemplified in Mrs. Packard's Trial, . . . or, Three Years' Imprisonment for Religious Belief* (1866); and her two-volume autobiography *Modern Persecution: Insane Asylums Unveiled* (Vol. I, 1873) and *Married Women's Liabilities* (Vol. II). With her earnings, Packard bought a house in Chicago in 1869, and she convinced Theophilus to return their minor children to her custody.

In addition to writing, Packard lobbied numerous state legislatures for laws protecting the rights of married women and mental patients. She was especially anxious to change the laws in Massachusetts, under which Theophilus had potential legal power over her, and her lobbying resulted in laws protecting the rights of mental patients in Massachusetts, Illinois (where the state legislature passed "Mrs. Packard's Personal Liberty Bill"), Iowa, and Maine. In 1869, she lobbied for an Illinois law to give married women the right to control their property, which was approved in the legislature as framed by Illinois reformer ***Myra Bradwell.** In 1874, seeking to provide asylum inmates with mail access, Packard was rebuffed by the postmaster general. With her charm and intelligence, she then went, uninvited, to the White House to introduce herself to the first lady, ***Julia Grant.** While surprised, Grant took a liking to Packard and arranged for her to meet President Ulysses S. Grant. The following year, Congress passed a bill granting asylum inmates access to on-site federal post offices. After the 1870s, Packard retired from public life, although she continued publishing through the early 1880s. She died in Chicago in 1897, and was buried in Rose Hill Cemetery.

SOURCES:

Chesler, Phyllis. "Rebel with a Cause" in *On the Issues.* Fall 1995, pp. 11–12, 58–59.

Geller, Jeffrey L., and Maxine Harris. *Women of the Asylum: Voices from Behind the Walls, 1840–1945.* NY: Doubleday, 1994 (includes a chapter of Packard's writings).

James, Edward T., ed. *Notable American Women, 1607–1950.* Cambridge, MA: The Belknap Press of Harvard University Press, 1971.

SUGGESTED READING:

Sapinsley, Barbara. *The Private War of Mrs. Packard.* Paragon House, 1995.

Daniel E. Brannen, Jr., freelance writer, York, Pennsylvania

Packard, Sophia B. (1824–1891)

American educator and founder of Spelman College. *Born on January 3, 1824, in New Salem, Massachusetts; died on June 21, 1891, in Washington, D.C.; daughter of Winslow Packard (a farmer) and Rachel (Freeman) Packard; attended the local district school; attended New Salem Academy in 1845 for at least a term; received a diploma from the Charlestown (Massachusetts) Female Seminary, 1850; never married; lifelong companion of Harriet E. Giles; no children.*

Taught for several years in Massachusetts schools; became preceptress and a teacher in the New Salem (Massachusetts) Academy (1855); with her lifelong companion, Harriet E. Giles, taught at the Connecticut Literary Institution, Suffield, Connecticut (1859–64); was co-principal of the Oread Collegiate Institute in Worcester, Massachusetts (1864–67); became pastor's assistant under the Rev. George C. Lorimer (1870); presided over organizing meeting of the Woman's American Baptist Home Mission Society, and played active role in organization (1877); toured South to determine what type of aid should be given to African-American population (1880); moved to Atlanta, Georgia, and with Giles opened the Atlanta Baptist Female Seminary (1881); Atlanta Baptist Female Seminary relocated and was renamed Spelman Seminary, with a hall erected and named after Packard (1888); became treasurer of the board of trustees and president of Spelman Seminary (1888).

Sophia B. Packard was born on January 3, 1824, in New Salem, Massachusetts, the fifth child of Winslow Packard, a farmer, and **Rachel Freeman Packard.** She attended district school and at the age of 14 began teaching in rural schools. Thereafter, she alternated years between teaching and studying. In 1845, she attended New Salem Academy for a brief time, and in 1850 received a diploma from the Charlestown (Massachusetts) Female Seminary, where she was an assistant teacher for one year. She went on to teach in Cape Cod schools for four years, and in 1855 became preceptress and a teacher in the New Salem Academy. It was there that she met **Harriet E. Giles**, who became her lifelong friend and companion. She remained at the Academy for one year and then moved to Orange, Massachusetts, where both she and Giles taught for three years.

Packard and Giles ran a school of their own in Fitchburg, Massachusetts, for a brief time, and then in 1859 accepted positions at the Connecticut Literary Institution in Suffield, Connecticut. They remained there until Packard became co-principal of the Oread Collegiate Institute in Worcester, Massachusetts, in 1864. While there, she carried out administrative duties in addition to teaching classes in metaphysics and literature. In 1866, Dr. John Shepardson, her co-principal, resigned. Packard had a tense relationship with Shepardson's successor, and the next year both she and Giles left the school and moved to Boston. After being employed at an insurance company for a time, in 1870 Packard became a pastor's assistant. She held this position, which was usually granted only to men and involved visiting the sick, conducting women's prayer meetings, and teaching Sunday school, under Reverend George C. Lorimer at the Shawmut Avenue Baptist Church and later at the Tremont Temple.

In 1877, Packard presided over the organizing meeting of the Woman's American Baptist Home Mission Society (WABHMS, a subsidiary of the American Baptist Home Mission Society), which was concerned with the plight of freed slaves in the South. She served as treasurer and corresponding secretary and sat on virtually every committee the group had. In February 1880, she traveled in the South to determine what form of assistance the African-American population most needed, and decided to open a school for African-American girls and women in Georgia. The WABHMS was not keen on the idea, but she persuaded them to lend support and moved to Atlanta with Giles in April 1881. They opened the Atlanta Baptist Female Seminary in a church basement; soon the school's enrollment increased from 11 to 80, and by the next year, despite several months during which the WABHMS withdrew all financial support, it had reached 150. In 1882, the American Baptist Home Mission Society made a down payment on a permanent site for the school, and in 1883 the school moved to its new home. Wealthy oil magnate John D. Rockefeller, who heard Packard speak on the school's behalf in Cleveland, Ohio, was so impressed by her and her cause that in 1884 he paid the balance owing on the new property. The school's name was changed to Spelman Seminary, in honor of his wife *__Laura Spelman Rockefeller__ and her parents, who had strongly supported abolition. Rockefeller Hall was built in 1886, and Packard Hall was erected in 1888. That year a state charter was granted to the school, and Packard became the school's president and treasurer of the board of trustees. She continued to hold these posts until her death on June 21, 1891, at which time 464 students were attending Spelman Seminary; Harriet E. Giles succeeded Packard as president. In 1924, Spelman Seminary became Spelman College, and five years later it was affiliated with Atlanta University. At the beginning of the 21st century, it remains one of the top historically black liberal arts colleges for women in America.

SOURCES:

James, Edward T., ed. *Notable American Women, 1607–1950*. Cambridge, MA: The Belknap Press of Harvard University Press, 1971.

McHenry, Robert, ed. *Famous American Women*. NY: Dover, 1980.

Jo Anne Meginnes,
freelance writer, Brookfield, Vermont

Packer, Ann E. (1942—)

English runner. *Name variations: (married name) Ann Brightwell. Born Ann E. Packer in Moulsford, Berkshire, England, on March 8, 1942.*

Won English Schools 100 yards (1959); won WAAA long jump (1960); finalist in the 200 meters in the European Championship (1962); was a finalist in the 80-meter hurdles in the Commonwealth Games; won the silver medal in the 400 meters, setting a European record of 52.2, and the gold medal in the 800 meters at 2:01.1, a new world record, both in the Tokyo Olympic games (1964).

England's versatile Ann Packer retired at age 22, after winning two Olympic medals. In the 1964 Tokyo Olympics, on six consecutive days, she ran in the heats and in the semifinal and final of the 400 meters and the 800 meters. Having won the silver in the 400 meters, a race she expected to win, Packer won a gold medal in the 800 meters, a race she had run only twice in her life. The psychological stress was daunting. "If I'd gone out in the first round of the 800 meters," she said," nobody would have been surprised."

Paddleford, Clementine (1900–1967)

American food editor and columnist. *Born Clementine Haskin Paddleford in Stockdale, Kansas, on September 27, 1900; died on November 13, 1967; daughter of Solon Marian Paddleford (a prosperous farmer) and Jennie (Romick) Paddleford; Kansas State College School of Journalism, B.A., 1921; graduate work at New York University; married Lloyd D. Zimmerman (an engineer), on July 10, 1923 (separated within the year and divorced in 1932); children: (ward) Clare Duffe.*

Once referred to by *Time* magazine as "the best-known food editor in the United States," Clementine Paddleford wrote for the New York *Herald Tribune*, the monthly magazine *Gourmet*, and *This Week,* the syndicated Sunday magazine. Paddleford, who grew up in her mother's kitchen in Kansas, became women's editor of *Farm and Fireside* (1924–29), before turning to freelance writing. In 1932, doctors removed a malignant growth from her larynx and vocal cords. It took her six months to relearn speech and far longer to deal with the self-consciousness imposed by her now husky voice and the tube that would remain in her throat to aid her breathing. She joined the *Herald Tribune* in 1936.

Padilla, Juana Azurduy de (1781–1862).

See Azurduy de Padilla, Juana.

Paetina (fl. 30 CE)

Roman noblewoman. *Name variations: Aelia Paetina. Flourished around 30 CE; became second wife of Claudius (10 BCE–54 CE), Roman emperor (r. 41–54 CE), before 27 CE (divorced 38 CE); children:* ****Claudia***

*Antonia (27–66 CE). Claudius' first wife was *Plautia Urgulanilla; after his divorce from Paetina, he married *Valeria Messalina, then *Agrippina the Younger.*

Page, Dorothy G. (d. 1989).

See Butcher, Susan for sidebar.

Page, Estelle Lawson (b. 1907).

See Berg, Patty for sidebar.

Page, Geraldine (1924–1987)

***American actress who won an Academy Award for her performance in* The Trip to Bountiful.** *Born on November 22, 1924, in Kirksville, Missouri; died on June 13, 1987, in New York City; only daughter and eldest of two children of Leon Page (a osteopathic doctor) and Pearl (Maize) Page; attended the University of Chicago and the Herbert Berghof School, New York; graduated from the Goodman Theater Dramatic School, Chicago, 1945; married Alexander Schneider (a violinist), in 1954 (divorced 1957); married Rip Torn (an actor and director), in 1958; children: (second marriage)* **Angelica Torn**; *(twins) Anthony and Jonathan Torn.*

Selected theater: made New York debut as the Sophomore in Seven Mirrors *(Blackfriars Guild, 1945); appeared as Pagan Crone in* Yerma *(Circle in the Square, 1951), Alma in* Summer and Smoke *(Circle in the Square, 1952), Lily Barton in* Midsummer *(Vanderbilt, January 1953), Marcelline in* The Immoralist *(Royale, February 1954), Lizzie Curry in* The Rainmaker *(Cort, October 1954, and on tour), Amy McGregor in* The Innkeepers *(John Golden, February 1956); made London debut as Lizzie Curry in* The Rainmaker *(St. Martin's, May 1956); appeared as Abbie Putnam in* Desire Under the Elms *and Natalia Islaev in* A Month in The Country *(Studebaker, Chicago, 1956), Mrs. Shankland and Miss Railton-Bell in* Separate Tables *(Music Box, July 1957), Alexandra del Lago in* Sweet Bird of Youth *(Martin Beck, March 1959), Sister Bonaventure in* The Umbrella *(Locust, Philadelphia, January 1962), Nina Leeds in a revival of* Strange Interlude *(Hudson, March 1963), Olga in* The Three Sisters *(Morosco, June 1964), Julie Cunningham in* P.S. I Love You *(Henry Miller, November 1964), Oriane Brice in* The Great Indoors *(Eugene O'Neill, February 1966), Baroness Lemberg in* White Lies *and Clea in* Black Comedy *(Ethel Barrymore, February 1967), Angela Palmer in* Angela *(The Music Box, October 1969); toured in* Marriage and Money *(1971); appeared in* The Marriage Proposal *and* The Boor *(Playhouse in the Park, Philadelphia, July 1971); appeared as *Mary Todd Lincoln in* Look Away *(Playhouse, January 1973), and Regina Giddons in* The Little Foxes *(Academy Festival in Lake Forest, Illinois); appeared in* Absurd Person Singular *(Music Box, October 1974); appeared as Madame Arcati in* Blithe Spirit *(1987).*

Selected filmography: Out of the Night *(1947);* Taxi *(1953);* Hondo *(1953);* Summer and Smoke *(1961);* Sweet Bird of Youth *(1962);* Toys in the Attic *(1963);* Dear Heart *(1965);* The Three Sisters *(videotape of Actors Studio presentation, 1966);* Monday's Child *(filmed theater production, 1967);* You're a Big Boy Now *(1967);* The Happiest Millionaire *(1967);* What Ever Happened to Aunt Alice? *(1969);* Trilogy *(including "A Christmas Memory" and "The Thanksgiving Visitor" episodes, which originally aired on television);* The Beguiled *(1971);* J.W. Coop *(1972);* Pete 'n' Tillie *(1972);* Happy as the Grass Was Green *(*Hazel's People*, 1973);* The Day of the Locust *(1975);* Nasty Habits *(UK, 1976);* The Rescuers *(voice only, 1977);* The Three Sisters *(1977);* Interiors *(1978);* Harry's War *(1981);* Honky Tonk Freeway *(1981);* I'm Dancing as Fast as I Can *(1982);* The Pope of Greenwich Village *(1984);* The Bride *(1985);* Flanagan *(1985);* White Night *(1985);* The Trip to Bountiful *(1985);* My Little Girl *(1986);* Native Son *(1986).*

Geraldine Page achieved instant stardom for her portrayal of the lovelorn spinster Alma Winemiller in the 1953 off-Broadway production of Tennessee Williams' *Summer and Smoke*. She went on to become one of the icons of stage, screen, and television, winning particular acclaim for her performances in several subsequent Williams plays. Despite her star power, Page remained a student of her craft throughout her career, and was one of the leading proponents of the Method. "Acting isn't simply a matter of going to the theater from 8 to 11," she said in an 1985 interview. "It's a day-to-day process of collecting details . . . choosing from experience. . . . I have a passionate curiosity about people and . . . things. I guess you could say I'm nosy."

Page was born in Kirksville, Missouri, in 1924, the daughter of an osteopathic physician who had once dreamed of being a writer. She had first wanted to become a pianist, and then a painter, but zeroed in on acting as a teenager. "It was after seeing ***Laurette Taylor** doing nothing and making it everything that I decided to be an actress," she recalled. "Father wanted me to be a writer instead." She studied for the stage at the Goodman Theater School in Chicago and then formed an acting group which played for four summer seasons at Lake Zurich, 35 miles outside

From the movie The Trip to Bountiful, *starring Rebecca DeMornay and Geraldine Page (right).*

the city. During the winters, Page made the rounds in New York, supporting herself with every manner of work, from selling books to wrapping thread cones at the International Thread Company. After working intermittently with the Blackfriars and with a group at the Hotel Des Artistes, she was recognized by director Jose Quintero, who cast her in *Summer and Smoke*. The critics heaped praise on the newcomer, calling her "great," "astounding," and "sheer magic," and audiences flocked to the small Circle-in-the-Square theater in Greenwich Village to see the production. For her performance, Page won her first New York Drama Critics award.

The role led to a seven-year contract with independent film producer Charles K. Feldman, as well as to her Broadway debut as the idealistic but uneducated heroine Lily in **Vina Delmar**'s *Mid-Summer* (January 1953). Writing for *The New Yorker*, Wolcott Gibbs called Lily possibly "the noblest woman put on the stage in my generation . . . who might be completely insufferable if the role were in any other hands than those of Geraldine Page, an actress of great charm and pathos and almost matchless technique." Page next played Marcelline, the wife of a homosexual, in *The Immoralist* (1954), then had a successful run as another lonely spinster, Lizzie Curry, in *The Rainmaker* (1954), a role in which she had an opportunity to display her comedic talent. "As a comedienne, Miss Page has some unexpected qualities," wrote Brooks Atkinson. "She is fresher than the play and equally funny." Page subsequently toured with the production and made her London debut as Lizzie in May 1956.

Page's next American triumph was as the aging movie queen in Tennessee Williams' *Sweet Bird of Youth* (1959), a role for which she received her second New York Drama Critics Award for Best Actress. "Loose-jointed, gangling, raucous of voice, crumpled, shrewd, abandoned yet sensitive about some things that live in the heart, Miss Page is at the peak of form in the raffish characterization," reported Atkinson. Kenneth Tynan concurred, calling the performance "a display of knockdown flamboyance and drag-out authority that triumphantly quells all doubts about this actress' ability to transcend her mannerisms."

Once established in her career, Page was selective about her roles, turning down as many parts as she accepted. Among her Broadway roles were Nina Leeds in a revival of Eugene O'Neill's *Strange Interlude* (1963) and Olga in *The Three Sisters* (1964). Although best known for her stage work, she also made several widely acclaimed movies, some of which were film versions of her stage hits. She was nominated for Academy Awards as Best Actress for *Summer and Smoke* (1961), *Sweet Bird of Youth* (1962), and *Interiors* (1978), and as Best Supporting Actress for *Hondo* (1953), *You're a Big Boy Now* (1967), *Pete 'n' Tillie* (1972), and *The Pope of Greenwich Village* (1984). She finally won the coveted statue for Best Actress for her performance in *The Trip to Bountiful* (1985). Page also won Emmy Awards for her performances in the teleplays of Truman Capote's "A Christmas Memory" (1967) and "The Thanksgiving Visitor" (1969). The actress was appearing as Madame Arcadi in *Blithe Spirit* when she died in 1987, following a heart attack.

SOURCES:

Current Biography. NY: H.W. Wilson, 1953.

Gareffa, Peter M., ed. *Contemporary Newsmakers, 1987.* Detroit, MI: Gale Research, 1987.

Katz, Ephraim. *The Film Encyclopedia.* NY: HarperCollins, 1994.

Morley, Sheridan. *The Great Stage Stars.* Australia: Angus & Robertson, 1986.

Barbara Morgan,
Melrose, Massachusetts

Page, Merlene Ottey- (b. 1960).

See Ottey-Page, Merlene.

Page, Patti (1927—)

American popular singer of the late 1940s and 1950s. *Born Clara Ann Fowler on November 8, 1927, in Claremore, Oklahoma; one of 11 children of Benjamin A. Fowler (a railroad worker) and Margaret (Wright) Fowler; briefly attended Tulsa University; married Charles O'Curran, on December 28, 1956 (divorced); married Jerry Filiciotto (a retired aerospace executive), in May 1990; no children.*

Gold record hits include: "With My Eyes Wide Open I'm Dreaming" (1949); "All My Love" (1950); "Tennessee Waltz" (1950); "Would I Love You (Love You, Love You)" (1951); "Mockin' Bird Hill" (1951); "Mr. and Mississippi" (1951); "Detour" (1951); "I Went to Your Wedding" (1952); "You Belong to Me" (1952); "That Doggie in the Window" (1953); "Changing Partners" (1953); "Cross Over the Bridge" (1954); "Allegheny Moon" (1956); "Old Cape Cod" (1957); "Left Right Out of Your Heart" (1958); The Waltz Queen *(album, 1958);* Golden Hits *(album, 1960);* Greatest Hits *(album, 1967).*

One of only five singers (and the only woman) whose hits spanned five decades on the Billboard country charts, singer Patti Page sold more than 100-million records during her career, among them 13 gold singles, including "Tennessee Waltz" (the largest selling single by a female artist), "Old Cape Cod," "Allegheny Moon," and the legendary "Doggie in the Window."

Born Clara Ann Fowler in Muskogee, Oklahoma, in 1927, Page was the second youngest of 11 children. Her father Benjamin Fowler, a railroad foreman, barely made enough money to put food on the table, and her mother **Margaret Wright Fowler** picked cotton to supplement the family's income. Page remembers walking barefoot to school so she could save her one pair of shoes for Sunday. As a young girl, she sang in church with her sisters and also did some professional singing around Tulsa, but her real ambition was to become a commercial artist. She briefly attended Tulsa University on an art scholarship, but left to take a job on the radio. Before long, she was starring on several programs, including a country-western show. In 1949, Page signed with Jack Rael, who, after hearing her sing on the radio, quit his job as musician-manager for the Jimmy Joy band to become her manager. Their relationship would be one of the most enduring in entertainment history. "In a business that too often works on the basis of 'don't tell me what you did for me yesterday, tell me what you're doing for me today,'" writes Bernie Woods, "Patti's conduct re Rael over the years was completely contrary to most artist-manager relationships."

Rael's first important booking for the young singer was on ABC Radio's "Breakfast Club," hosted by Don McNeil. Several appearances on the popular morning program led to a show of her own on CBS and a contract with Mercury Records, an independent company that had just been launched in Chicago. After a slow start with the fledgling enterprise, Page's 11th release, "Confess," a song originally intended for Vic Damone, put her on the charts. Due to budget constraints, Page sang all the back-up parts on the recording, creating an overdubbing effect that revolutionized the industry. On her next record, "With My Eyes Wide Open I'm Dreaming," Page sang four-part harmony with herself, creating an even more unusual multiple-voice effect and earning her the first of many gold records. Her third hit, "Tennessee Waltz," a blockbuster for Mercury, was actually the flip side of a Christmas song that the company had thought would be a major seller. "Tennessee Waltz" made Page the first popular singer to cross-over to country, and earned her the sobriquet, "The Singing Rage."

Hit followed hit, including "Mockin' Bird Hill," "Would I Love You," "All My Love," "Detour," "I Went to Your Wedding," "Doggie in the Window," and "Cross Over the Bridge," among others. In 1961, Page switched to Columbia Records and, even with Beatlemania sweeping the country, managed to make the Top 10 in 1965 with the title song from the film *Hush, Hush, Sweet Charlotte*. From the 1960s on, the singer based herself in Nashville, and perfected her "country" sound.

Along with her successful recording career, Page made regular appearances on television, becoming the only musical performer in the history of the medium to have her own weekly series on all three networks. The singer also appeared in the 1960 movie *Elmer Gantry* with Burt Lancaster, and in a much-acclaimed stage production of *Annie Get Your Gun*.

In 1980, Page was given the Pioneer Award by the Academy of Country Music (ACM), which recognized her groundbreaking, multiple-voice technique and her successful cross-over into country music. She was later elected to the board of ACM and was inducted into the Oklahoma Hall of Fame. Since 1990, Page has been married to Jerry Filiciotto, a retired aerospace executive, and divides her time between homes in California and New Hampshire.

SOURCES:

Kinkle, Roger D. *The Complete Encyclopedia of Popular Music and Jazz, 1900–1950*. New Rochelle, NY: Arlington House.

Woods, Bernie. *When the Music Stopped: The Big Band Era Remembered*. NY: Barricade, 1994.

SUGGESTED READING:

Page, Patti. *Once Upon a Dream*, 1966.

Barbara Morgan,
Melrose, Massachusetts

Page, Ruth (1899–1991)

American dancer and choreographer. *Name variations: Ruth Fisher. Born on March 22, 1899, in Indianapolis, Indiana; died in Chicago, Illinois, on August 15, 1991; daughter of Lafayette Page (a brain surgeon) and Marian (Heinly) Page (a professional pianist); attended Tudor Hall School, a private school in Indianapolis, and the French School in New York City; studied ballet with Anna Pavlova, Adolph Bolm, and Enrico Cecchetti; married Thomas Hart Fisher (a Chicago lawyer), in 1925.*

Patti Page

Ruth Page grew up in a distinguished household. Her father Lafayette Page, a brain surgeon, helped establish the children's wing of the James Whitcomb Riley Hospital; her mother **Marian Page**, a pianist, helped found the Indianapolis Symphony Orchestra. Their house was often the meeting place for composers, writers, dancers, and artists. One such was ***Anna Pavlova**, who, impressed with the talents of 15-year-old Ruth, urged Marian to let the girl accompany her group on a one-year South American tour.

Ruth made her Chicago debut in 1919, creating the lead role in *The Birthday of the Infanta*. With her teacher and partner Adolph Bolm, she went on several tours with his American ballet company, Ballet Intime. From 1921 to 1923, she was *première danseuse* in Irving Berlin's Broadway hit *Music Box Revue*. The following year, she joined the experimental Chicago Allied Arts, as prima ballerina, where she was allowed to choreograph; her first efforts were *The Flapper and the Quarterback* and *Oak Street Beach.* From 1926 to 1928, she was guest soloist with the Metropolitan Opera Company in New York City before forming her own company, with a partner and two other female dancers, to tour Japan and Russia. In 1933, Page created *La Guiablesse* for the Chicago Symphony Orchestra, which featured ***Katherine Dunham**.

During the years 1934–37, 1942–43, and 1945, Ruth Page was *première danseuse* and ballet director of the Chicago Opera Company, where she choreographed *Hear Ye! Hear Ye!,* with music by Aaron Copland, *An American Pattern,* with music by Jerome Moross, and a revival of her ballet of Ravel's *Bolero,* which she toured. In 1938, she founded the Page-Stone Ballet company with Bentley Stone. Their production of *Frankie and Johnny* ran longer than any other ballet in Chicago's history. She was the first choreographer to turn a full-length opera into a full-length ballet, remaking *Carmen* into *Guns and Castanets* in 1939. Though the Page-Stone partnership disbanded in 1941, she restaged three of their works for the Ballet Russe de Monte Carlo: *Frankie and Johnny* (1945), *The Bells* (1946), and *Billy Sunday* (1948). In 1956, in connection with the Chicago Lyric Opera, Page organized the Chicago Opera ballet, subsequently renamed Ruth Page's International Ballet in 1966, and remained its director for a number of years. In 1970, she founded the Ruth Page School of Dance, which, as of the year 2000, had over 300 students.

SUGGESTED READING:

Martin, John. *Ruth Page: An Intimate Biography.* NY: Marcel Dekker, 1977.

Page, Ruth. *Page by Page.* Brooklyn, NY: Dance Horizons, 1978.

Paget, Lady Arthur (1865–1919).

See Paget, Mary.

Paget, Mary (1865–1919)

English-American social leader, philanthropist and war nurse. *Name variations: Minnie Paget; Minnie Stevens; Mrs. Arthur Paget; Lady Arthur Paget. Born Mary Stevens in 1865; died in 1919; daughter of Paran Stevens of Boston, Massachusetts; married Sir Arthur H. Paget (British envoy to Belgrade).*

American-born Mary "Minnie" Paget, the daughter of a wealthy Boston socialite, was one of the foremost leaders of London society during the reign of Edward VII (r. 1901–1910). Her home was frequented by the celebrated in society, literature, and art, as well as by Edward and his queen, ***Alexandra of Denmark**. During the Boer War, Paget equipped a hospital ship and named it the *Maine*. She also made a collection of furniture of the period of James I for the Jamestown Exposition.

When her husband Sir Arthur Paget was minister at Belgrade, Lady Paget became well known for her services in relieving distress and suffering during the first and second Balkan wars. She worked in the hospitals day and night, nursing the sick and wounded with courage and self-sacrifice. During World War I, Paget rendered valuable service in Serbia, where she maintained a hospital and worked in cooperation with the American Red Cross. The Serbians, from the monarch downward, revered her, and her services there won the praise of the Austro-Hungarian government, one of the rare occasions in which a warring nation honored the subject of an enemy nation.

Paget, Muriel (1876–1938)

British philanthropist. *Name variations: Lady Muriel Paget; Muriel Evelyn Vernon Paget. Born in 1876; died in 1938; daughter of the 12th earl of Winchilsea; married Sir Richard Arthur Surtees Paget (1869–1955), 2nd baronet, of Cranmore (a barrister and physicist), in 1897.*

A noted British philanthropist, Lady Muriel Paget supported a number of local and worldwide efforts to aid the sick and underprivileged. In 1905, she founded the Invalid Kitchens of London, of which she served as honorary secretary until her death in 1938. Her work abroad included the organization of the Anglo-Russian Hospital in Russia (1915–17), as well as the inauguration and administration of hospital and child-welfare organizations in Czechoslovakia, Latvia, Estonia, Lithuania, and Rumania. From 1924 until her death, she also conducted relief work for British subjects in Russia. Paget received the OBE in 1918 and the CBE in 1938.

Paget, Rosalind (1855–1948)

English social reformer, nurse, and midwife. *Name variations: Dame Rosalind Paget. Born Mary Rosalind Paget in 1855; died in 1948; daughter of John Paget (1811–1898, a police magistrate and author); cousin of* ****Eleanor Rathbone*** *(1872–1946).*

A nurse at London Hospital, Rosalind Paget helped found the Midwives' Institute (Royal College of Midwives) in 1881, and also worked to obtain the registration of midwives, which was granted in 1902. Paget was awarded a DBE in 1935.

Paget, Violet (1856–1935)

Prolific and wide-ranging English writer. *Name variations: (pseudonym) Vernon Lee. Born on October 14, 1856, in Boulogne-sur-Mer, France; died on February 13, 1935, in San Gervasio, Italy; daughter of Henry Ferguson Paget and Matilda (Abadam) Lee-Hamilton; never married; no children.*

At 13, published first essay (1869); published first and best-known book, Studies of the Eighteenth Century in Italy *(1880); also won wide acclaim for another travel guide,* Genius Loci *(1890).*

Selected writings: Studies in the Eighteenth Century in Italy *(1880);* The Countess of Albany *(1884);* Miss Brown: A Novel *(1884);* Euphorian: Being Studies of the Antique and Mediaeval in the Renaissance *(1884);* Hauntings: Fantastic Stories *(1890);* Vanitas: Polite Stories *(1892);* Genius Loci: Notes on Places *(1899);* Ariadne in Mantua: A Drama in Five Acts *(1903);* Penelope Brandling: A Tale of the Welsh Coast in the Eighteenth Century *(1903);* Pope Jacynth *(1904);* Horus Vitae *(1904);* The Enchanted Woods *(1905);* The Spirit of Rome: Leaves from a Diary *(1906);* Gospels of Anarchy *(1908);* The Sentimental Traveller: Notes on Places *(1908);* Vital Lies *(1912);* The Beautiful *(1913);* The Tower of Mirrors *(1914);* The Ballet of Nations: A Present-day Morality *(1915);* Satan, the Waster *(1920);* The Handling of Words *(1923);* For Maurice *(1927);* Music and Its Lovers: An Empirical Study of Emotional and Imaginative Responses to Music *(1932);* Supernatural Tales *(2 vols., 1955–56).*

Violet Paget, who used the pseudonym Vernon Lee, was a prolific writer whose 40-plus publications included travel books, short stories, novels, historical fiction, satire, international politics, women's rights, psychology, and aesthetic critiques of the arts. While her formidable intelligence, critical powers, and strong personality were widely noted, Paget's contemporary reputation and popularity peaked early, then steadily declined, in part due to what was perceived as arrogance as well as a certain lack of social tact.

Paget's English father, Henry Ferguson Paget, was involved in the Warsaw insurrection of 1848. Forced to flee Poland, Henry went to France, where he met a Welsh widow, **Matilda Lee-Hamilton**, and tutored her invalid son Eugene Lee-Hamilton, who later became a poet. Henry and Matilda soon married, and Violet, who would be their only child, was born in 1856 near Boulogne, France. The family moved frequently during her youth, mostly within Germany. Her parents and older half-brother, as well as a series of German governesses, were Paget's principal educational influences, and with her parents' tutoring she grew up evaluating the intellectual and aesthetic developments of the period. Matilda has been described as a highly intellectual but strongly anti-social woman, and Paget would later trace some of her difficulties in dealing with other people to having grown up with what she called her "acutely neuropathic and hysterical" family members.

During the winter of 1866–67, while in Nice, France, the Pagets met and became close friends with the Sargent family, whose young son John Singer Sargent was the same age as Paget. (Years later he would paint her portrait.) The following year, when Paget was 11 years old, the family began wintering in Rome, often with the Sargents. **Mary Singer Sargent**, who led Paget and her own two children on enthusiastic sightseeing excursions around Rome and its vicinity while vividly describing many other places, became a major influence on Paget, and in emulation of Mary Sargent's keen interest in Italian history she began collecting ancient Italian coins. She also wrote a short essay on the adventures of a coin, "Les Aventures d'une piece de monnaie," beginning with its coinage out of a Macedonian helmet and moving onwards as it passed through Italy's history. The piece was published in 1870, shortly before her 14th birthday.

The Paget family finally settled in Florence in 1873. Already a student of 18th-century Italy, Paget published four essays on Italian music and literature in an 1877 edition of *Fraser's Magazine*. Believing that the writing of a woman would not be taken seriously in those Victorian times, she published three of the essays under the pseudonym Vernon Lee. She would continue to employ this name in her professional life, and soon began calling herself Vernon Lee in her personal life as well. In 1880, using various collected bits of information from her trips around Italy, Paget published her initial major work, *Studies of the Eighteenth Century in Italy*. An examination of Italian art (the first by an English scholar) via the culture in which the artists lived, the book earned great respect for its research and "conspicuous ability," and secured Paget's literary reputation.

Paget, who never married, had a series of female companions throughout her life. Perhaps due to the lack of warmth she experienced in her upbringing, she avoided physical contact in public. (And, possibly, in private: according to her literary executor and friend **Irene Cooper Willis**, while Paget indeed loved women, "she never faced up to sexual facts. . . . [Her love affairs with women] were all perfectly correct. Physical contact she shunned.") After a brief early relationship with **Annie Meyer**, Paget met poet Mary Robinson (***Agnes Mary F. Duclaux**) in 1880, and began a relationship that would last seven years. With Robinson, Paget began making annual trips to England in 1881 to promote her work and meet with publishers and with England's artistic society, including Robert Browning, Oscar Wilde, William Morris, and Henry James, whom she had become friends with in Italy. She found further success with a puppet show, a set of aesthetic essays, and, early in 1884, *The Countess of Albany*, a biography of ***Louise of Stolberg-Gedern**, the incompatible wife of Bonnie Prince Charlie. Pressed to produce a novel, that year Paget also published *Miss Brown: A Novel*, which met immediate and intense criticism. Essentially a satirical attack on the London art scene, the book featured many characters who were thinly disguised representations of actual people (including Wilde, Dante Gabriel Rossetti, Morris, and his wife **May Morris**). Paget's reputation suffered, and a number of her friends and acquaintances "cut" her completely. Paget herself was astonished at the book's reception—she claimed she had never intended it as a *roman à clef*—and pondered with dismay her own motivations for writing it. While scandal raged that year, she published other works which were largely overlooked, including *Euphorian: Being Studies of the Antique and Mediaeval in the Renaissance*.

When Robinson left her suddenly in 1887 to marry a severely crippled man, Paget suffered a serious nervous breakdown. A previous acquaintance, **Clementina (Kit) Anstruther-Thomson**, aided her recovery, and they established a close relationship that would continue through the next decade. During her convalescence, Paget wrote her first major fiction, a series of short ghost stories published in 1890 as the well-received *Hauntings: Fantastic Stories*. Many later critics would consider her stories of the supernatural, including "Oke of Okehurst," "A Wicked Voice," and "Winthrop's Adventure," her best works of fiction, and Montague Summers himself claimed that "even Le Fanu and M.R. James cannot be ranked above the genius of this lady." Two years later, however, she published another collection of short fiction, *Vanitas: Polite Stories* (1892), which included the story "Lady Tal." The narrative, which contained an obvious and unflattering portrait of Henry James and, it has been presumed, Paget as the title character, caused much scandal among the cognoscenti. James ended their friendship without speaking to her again, and a number of her other friends abruptly dropped her as well. ("Lady Tal" remains one of Paget's most frequently anthologized stories.)

Returning to travel essays in the later 1890s, Paget contributed weekly travel pieces to the *Westminster Gazette* and described her philosophical approach to travel writing in *Limbo and Other Essays* (1897). Influenced by her ongoing relationship with Anstruther-Thomson, she wrote four more volumes, including the widely acclaimed *Genius Loci: Notes on Places* (1899), based on her extensive European travels. In that year, Anstruther-Thomson, her health failing and her equanimity perhaps tested by Paget's constant restless travel, moved away. Though missing her good friend, Paget continued her prodigious writing, including a play, *Ariadne in Mantua: A Romance in Five Acts* (1903), the short-story collection *Pope Jacynth* (1904), and the essay collections *Hortus Vitae* (1904), *The Enchanted Woods* (1905) and *The Sentimental Traveller* (1908).

As anticipation of war began brewing in the 1910s, Paget incorporated a strong and highly unpopular pacifist position into her works. Her acceptance and popularity waned once again while she preached against growing nationalism, although her efforts were appreciated by such fellow-thinkers as Bertrand Russell, ***Olive Schreiner**, and Lady ***Ottoline Morrell**. She published *The Ballet of Nations: A Present-day Morality* in 1915, followed by *Satan, the Waster: A Philosophic War Trilogy* in 1920, as well as several political pamphlets for the Union of Democratic Control. Damage wrought by World War I to society and the European landscape devastated Paget, and while her 1923 study of fiction, *The Handling of Words*, was respectfully received (and lauded in the later part of the century), her general reputation as a writer declined considerably during the '20s. New, younger writers had claimed the scene, and Paget belonged to the older generation; sadly, however, she spent most of her last years doubting her literary worth. In 1924, she received an honorary doctor of letters degree from the University of Durham, but she became increasingly reclusive as gradually she lost her hearing and began suffering from heart problems. Her last book, *Music and Its Lovers: An Empirical Study of Emotional and Imaginative Responses to Music* (1932), was considered too technical for the public but not sufficiently scientific for academia, and was poorly received. Violet Paget died in February 1935 in San Gervasio and was buried in Florence's Allori Cemetery.

SOURCES:

Buck, Claire, ed. *The Bloomsbury Guide to Women's Literature.* NY: Prentice Hall, 1992.

Edelstein, Debra, in *Dictionary of Literary Biography,* Vol. 57: *Victorian Prose Writers After 1867.* Ed. by William B. Thesing. Detroit, MI: Gale Research, 1987.

Kunitz, Stanley J., and Howard Haycraft, eds. *Twentieth Century Authors.* NY: H.W. Wilson, 1942.

O'Neill, Patricia, in *Dictionary of Literary Biography,* Vol. 174: *British Travel Writers, 1876–1909.* Ed. by Barbara Brothers and Julia Gergits. Detroit, MI: Gale Research, 1997.

Rutledge, Amelia A., in *Dictionary of Literary Biography,* Vol. 178: *British Fantasy and Science-Fiction Writers Before World War I.* Ed. by Darren Harris-Fain. Detroit, MI: Gale Research, 1997.

Shattock, Joanne. *The Oxford Guide to Women Writers.* Oxford: Oxford University Press, 1993.

Smith, Jane Bowman, in *Dictionary of Literary Biography,* Vol. 156: *British Short-Fiction Writers, 1880–1914: The Romantic Tradition.* Ed. by William F. Nafftus. Detroit, MI: Gale Research, 1996.

Srebrnik, Patricia Thomas, in *Dictionary of Literary Biography,* Vol. 153: *Late-Victorian and Edwardian Novelists.* Ed. by George M. Johnson. Detroit, MI: Gale Research, 1995.

SUGGESTED READING:

Gunn, Peter. *Vernon Lee: Violet Paget, 1856–1935.* London: Oxford University Press, 1964.

Richard C. Hanes,
freelance writer, Eugene, Oregon

Pagliughi, Lina (1907–1980)

American soprano. *Born on May 27, 1907, in Brooklyn, New York; died on October 2, 1980, in Ruicone, Italy; studied with Manlio Bavagnoli; married tenor Primo Montanari.*

Debuted in Milan (1927); sang at Teatro alla Scala (1930–47); debuted in Monte Carlo (1931) and Covent Garden (1938); sang with Italian radio until her retirement (1956).

Born in Brooklyn in 1907 to Italian parents, Lina Pagliughi returned to Italy for her singing career. At age eight, she began giving public recitals, and it soon became clear that hers would be an operatic career. She was taken to Milan for study with Manlio Bavagnoli and debuted there at the Teatro Nazionale in 1927. After her marriage to tenor Primo Montanari, she appeared at many Italian theaters, including Teatro all Scala where she performed for 17 years. But Pagliughi's short, stocky stature limited her roles. In 1948, she gave up the stage and began singing on radio until her retirement in 1956. Pagliughi became a popular recording and radio star.

John Haag,
Athens, Georgia

Pahlavi, Ashraf (1919—)

Princess of Persia, twin sister of the shah of Iran, and Iranian advocate for women's and human rights. *Name variations: Princess Ashraf Pahlevi. Born on October 26, 1919, in Tehran, Iran; daughter of Tajolmolouk and Reza Shah Pahlavi, shah of Iran (r. 1925–1941 abdicated); sister of* ***Shams Pahlavi*** *(1917–1996); twin sister of Muhammad Reza Pahlavi also known as Riza I Pahlavi, shah of Iran (r. 1941–1979, deposed); married Ali Ghavam (a prime minister), in 1936 or 1937 (divorced 1941); married Ahmed Chafik or Shafiq Bey (b. 1911, director general of civil aviation), in 1944 (divorced 1960); married Dr. Mehdi Boushehri (b. 1916); children: (first marriage) Prince Shahram Ghavam (b. 1939); (second marriage) Prince Chahriar Chafik also seen as Shahriar or Shahryar Chafik (b. 1945 and killed in Paris on December 7, 1979); Princess* ***Azadeh Chafik*** *(b. 1951, who married Farshad Vahid).*

Selected writings: Faces in a Mirror *(1980);* Time for Truth.

The twin sister of Muhammad Reza Pahlavi, the shah of Iran from 1941 to 1979, Princess Ashraf Pahlavi was born on October 26, 1919, the daughter of Reza Shah Pahlavi and **Tajolmolouk**. In a country that had traditionally granted women few rights or freedoms, Princess Ashraf Pahlavi's father and her twin brother broke new ground when they became instrumental in establishing equal rights for Iranian women. During his reign, Reza Shah granted women equal educational opportunities, established the girl-guide movement, abolished the veil, and urged women to work outside their homes. Under Muhammad Reza Pahlavi's rule, the Pahlavi family continued the further emancipation of women, granting them the right to vote and to run for elected office in 1963. Princess Ashraf Pahlavi shared her family's determination to better the situation of women, and she played an active role serving as president of the Women's Organization of Iran (WOI). WOI was very active and participated in many international gatherings. Of particular note was the UN Conference on Women's Rights in Mexico in 1975, where Princess Ashraf proposed the formation of a permanent research and training institute for women's affairs, which was established in Tehran, Iran. The WOI provided Iranian women with family welfare centers where childcare, vocational training, family planning and legal issues were addressed. The organization also emphasized the importance of literacy and of teaching women marketable skills. The WOI carried out studies of the problems facing women and offered possible solutions. Iranian laws and textbooks were reviewed to ensure that women were not unfairly discriminated against.

Princess Ashraf also served as chair of the Iranian Human Rights Committee and presided over several important international conferences, including the UN Commission of the Status of Women, the UN Commission on Human Rights, and the International Human Rights Conference held in Tehran in 1988. On December 10, 1974, Human Rights Day, she presented UN Secretary-General Kurt Waldheim with a declaration upholding the need for greater efforts to be made to ensure real equality between women and men throughout the world.

In her publication *The Plot Against the Pahlavis*, Princess Ashraf covers the campaign against her brother, Muhammad Reza Pahlavi, a campaign that she feels was amplified in the media and the Western press. *Faces in the Mirror* (1980) concerns the family's abdication and exile, including the events that surrounded the removal of her brother, and the takeover by the Khomeini regime, and addresses accusations that were made against her and her family.

Jo Anne Meginnes,
freelance writer, Brookfield, Vermont

Pahlavi, Farah (1938—)

Empress of Iran. *Name variations: Farah Diba. Crowned empress on October 26, 1967. Born in Tehran, Iran, on October 14, 1938; daughter of Sohrab Diba (a captain in the imperial Iranian army) and Farideh Ghotbi; attended Tehran's Jeanne d'Arc and Razi schools; attended the École d'Architecture in Paris; became third wife of Muhammad Reza Pahlavi also known as Riza I Pahlavi, shah of Iran (r. 1941–1979, deposed), on December 20, 1959; children: Prince Reza (crown prince) also known as Reza II Pahlavi (b. 1960); Princess* ***Farahnaz*** *(b. 1963); Prince Ali Reza (b. 1966); Princess* ***Leila*** *(b. 1970).*

The last crowned empress of Iran, Farah Pahlavi was born in Teheran in October 1938. Her father, an army officer, died when she was nine years old, after which her mother ensured that she received an excellent education first in Teheran and later in Paris. She was 21 when she became the third wife of Muhammah Reza Shah Pahlavi, the shah of Iran, in 1959. The 40-year-old shah had previously divorced two wives, the Egyptian princess **Fawzia** (sister of King Farouk) and the Iranian commoner ***Soraya Pahlavi**, for incompatibility and for not providing him with a male heir; this Farah Pahlavi accomplished the year after her marriage with the birth of their son Prince Reza.

The shah was dedicated to social and economic reform (although not to dissent from his political opponents), and granted Iranian women the right to vote and to hold elected office in 1963. Empress Farah became both a symbol and a champion of women's broader roles in Iranian society, and was a highly visible patron of numerous charitable, cultural, medical and educational organizations. She also made it a point to travel throughout the country to meet with ordinary citizens. A strong proponent of the arts, she supported the creation of museums and the preservation of ancient art as well as the efforts of young artists. Farah also had three more children, princesses **Farahnaz** (b. 1963) and **Leila** (b. 1970) and prince Ali Reza (b. 1966). In 1967, she became the first woman in 2,500 years to be crowned empress of Iran.

Meanwhile, however, the deteriorating economy, growing discontent with secularization, repression, and perceived U.S. influence, as well as the calls of exiled Islamic fundamentalists like the Ayatollah Khomeini, were roiling the Iranian landscape. In 1978 martial law was imposed in response to riots, and the following year the shah was deposed. He traveled to the United States for medical treatment, prompting the newly established revolutionary government to seize the U.S. embassy in Teheran and hold 66 Americans hostage for over a year, demanding his return to Iran. After the shah's death in Egypt in 1980, Farah became empress regent, although this was largely a symbolic title. In the years since, she has traveled widely, living mostly in Paris but frequently visiting her four children in the United States. She remains a supporter of the arts, and maintains hope that she will one day return to Iran.

Pahlavi, Soraya (1932—)

Empress of Iran. *Name variations: Princess Soraya Esfandiari Bakhtiari; Princess Soraya; HM Empress Soraya; Queen of Persia. Born Soraya Esfandiari*

*Bakhtiari on June 22, 1932, in Isfahan, Iran; daughter of Khalil Esfandiari Bakhtiari and Eva Karl; educated in Isfahan, England and Switzerland; became second wife of Muhammad Reza Pahlavi also known as Riza I Pahlavi, shah of Iran (r. 1941–1979, deposed), on February 12, 1951 (divorced on March 14, 1958); no children. Muhammad Reza Pahlavi was also married to Fawzia and to *Farah Pahlavi.*

Born in 1932 in Isfahan, central Iran, to a German mother and a father who belonged to a powerful but non-royal Iranian family, Soraya Pahlavi was educated first in Isfahan and then in England and Switzerland. This foreign background caused some grumblings among the Iranian citizenry when in 1951 she was married to the shah of Iran, Muhammad Reza Shah Pahlavi, who had divorced his first wife **Fawzia** three years earlier. Soraya spent seven years at the royal court in Iran, where she reportedly kept a pet seal in the palace fountain. However, she failed to give birth to any children (specifically, a male heir), and in 1958 the shah divorced her. She later wrote *Soraya: The Autobiography of Her Imperial Highness Princess Soraya.*

Susan J. Walton,
freelance writer, Berea, Ohio

Pakhmutova, Alexandra (1929—)

Russian composer whose work was enormously popular. *Name variations: Alexandra Nikolaievna Pakhmutova. Born in Beketovka, near Stalingrad, USSR (now Volgograd, Russia), on November 9, 1929; studied at the Moscow Conservatory, graduating in 1953; continued to do post-graduate work at the Moscow Conservatory, concentrating on composition studies with Vladimir Shebalin.*

Named "Artist of the USSR" (1977).

In the post-Stalinist Soviet Union, there were periods when optimists felt that, with luck and effort, the system could be made to work, and that in time it would evolve into an essentially humane society free of oppression. This spirit was sometimes reflected, if only imperfectly, in music. One of the most optimistic composers of the late Soviet period was Alexandra Pakhmutova. Born into modest circumstances in 1929, just as the Stalinist regime was tightening its grip on Soviet life, she survived the privations of World War II, graduating from the Moscow Conservatory in 1953, the year of dictator Joseph Stalin's death. Pakhmutova discovered her artistic metier in 1955, when her bouncy Trumpet Concerto was given its premiere in Moscow on June 11 of that year. This work became immensely popular in the USSR and a recording of it was even available in the West. Equally favored throughout the 1960s and 1970s were Pakhmutova's urban ballads, songs meant to mirror Soviet reality by alluding to pressing problems but within an essentially positive framework. Using simple texts, these songs praised Soviet achievements in space, reminded Soviet citizens of their duty to believe in a better future, or simply reminded listeners, as she did in a 1974 song, there was always "Hope." The composer's more orthodox side could be seen in her 1957 suite for narrator, children's chorus and orchestra, *Lenin is in Our Hearts.* Pakhmutova never claimed to be a profound artist; her compositions were simple, optimistic and joyful, and while her music may not have accurately reflected Soviet life, it echoed the hopes of those who believed that their society was still capable of being reformed by people of good will.

John Haag,
Athens, Georgia

Pakington, Dorothy (d. 1679)

English author and moralist. *Died on May 10, 1679; daughter of Thomas Coventry, 1st baron of Coventry; married Sir John Pakington (1620–1680).*

The daughter of a baron, and well educated as a woman of rank, Dorothy Pakington was recognized for her intellect as well as her piety. She was reputedly the author of a series of theological volumes, including *The Gentlemen's Calling, The Ladies' Calling, The Government of the Tongue, The Christian's Birthright,* and *The Causes of the Decay of Christian Piety.* At the time of her death, she was working on a book entitled *The Government of the Thoughts,* which, although unfinished, was highly praised by a Dr. Fell, who characterized her as "wise, humble, temperate, chaste, patient, charitable, and devout." He added that she lived a life of austerity, throughout which she maintained "an undisturbed serenity."

In 1697, years after her death, another volume, *The Whole Duty of Man,* was also attributed to her, although internal evidence determined that the author was probably Richard Allestree, a practicing divine, who indeed may have also authored some of the other works ascribed to Lady Pakington.

SOURCES:

The Concise Dictionary of National Biography (Vol. III). Oxford: Oxford University Press, 1992.

King, William C., ed. *Woman.* Springfield, MA: King-Richardson, c. 1900.

Palatinate, electress of.

See Marie of Brandenburg-Kulmbach (1519–1567).
See Anna Constancia (1619–1651).
See Elizabeth Amalia of Hesse (1635–1709).
See Medici, Anna Maria Luisa de (1667–1743).

Palatine, Charlotte-Elisabeth, princess (1652–1722).

See Charlotte Elizabeth of Bavaria (1652–1722).

Palatine, countess.

See Matilda of Saxony (978–1025).
See Richesa of Lorraine (d. 1067).
See Gertrude of Swabia (c. 1104–1191).
See Agnes of Saxony (fl. 1200s).
See Matilda of Nassau (fl. 1285–1310).
See Irmengard of Oettingen.
See Magdalena (fl. late 1500s).
See Christina of Sweden for sidebar on Catherine (1584–1638).
See Gonzaga, Anne de (1616–1684).
See Charlotte (1896–1985).

Palatine, electress.

See Dorothea of Denmark (1520–1580).
See Louisa Juliana (1576–1644).
See Elizabeth of Bohemia (1596–1662).
See Maria Leopoldina (1776–1848).

Palatine, Madame.

See Charlotte Elizabeth of Bavaria (1652–1722).

Palatine, Princess.

See Elizabeth of Bohemia (1618–1680).
See Louisa (1622–1709).
See Charlotte Elizabeth of Bavaria (1652–1722).

Paleij, princess (1865–1929).

See Olga, Princess Paley.

Palencia, Isabel de (1878–c. 1950)

Twentieth-century Spanish author and diplomat.

Name variations: Isabel Oyarzábal de Palencia. Born Isabel Oyarzábal on June 12, 1878 (some sources cite 1881) in Málaga, Spain; died around 1950; daughter of Juan Oyarzábal and Anne Guthrie (a Scot); married Ceferino Palencia Tubau (an artist), on July 8, 1909; children: Ceferino; Marissa.

The first Spanish woman to hold an ambassadorial post, Isabel de Palencia was born on June 12, 1878, in Málaga, Spain, the daughter of Juan Oyarzábal and **Anne Guthrie**, a Scot. Her well-to-do family had links to important Spanish political figures. Perhaps because her mother was Protestant (she eventually converted to Catholicism) and a foreigner, Isabel never accepted the cultural and religious conservatism of Spain. She found her education at the Convent of the Assumption restricting, and, to the dismay of her family's conservative friends, decided to become a stage actress. Isabel also wanted to earn a living, because of the independence it would give her. Eventually forsaking the stage, she turned to journalism. She was employed as a foreign correspondent for several English-language publications and for two years published Spain's first woman's magazine, *La Dama*.

By the time she married artist Ceferino Palencia Tubau on July 8, 1909, Isabel had also become concerned about social conditions in Spain. She worked with Spanish women's organizations to fight for female suffrage and education and began associating with Spanish socialists. In the 1920s, Palencia traveled to the U.S. under the auspices of the Institute of International Education, lecturing on gender conditions in Spain. In 1926, she published *The Regional Costumes of Spain.* Proclamation of the Second Spanish Republic in 1931 drew her more and more into politics.

When the Spanish Civil War began in July 1936, Palencia proved a useful spokesperson for the Republic fighting against Francisco Franco, who was backed by Hitler and Mussolini. In October 1936, she went to Scotland to speak to a Labour Party gathering, where she called for repeal of the International Non-Intervention Agreement that prevented the Republic from obtaining armaments. Later that month, she toured Canada and the United States, raising humanitarian funds for the Republic and seeking to dispel anti-Communist propaganda. U.S. Catholics criticized her, pointing to Spanish leftists' attacks on churches and clergy. At the end of 1936, the Republican government named Palencia its ambassador to Sweden, the first time a Spanish woman had served in such a position. It later extended her authority to include Finland.

Palencia remained in her diplomatic post until the war ended with the Republic's defeat in early 1939. Unable to return to Spain, she and her family emigrated to Mexico. There she continued to write, including an autobiography, *I Must Have Liberty* (1940), fiction, and a biography of ***Alexandra Kollontai**, a Soviet diplomat and friend. Palencia also lectured in the U.S. against the fascist powers during World War II and remained a vocal critic of the Franco regime in Spain.

SOURCES:

Palencia, Isabel de. *I Must Have Liberty.* NY: Longmans, Green, 1940.

Kendall W. Brown,
Professor of History, Brigham Young University,
Provo, Utah

Paletzi, Juliane (d. 1569)

***Princess of Uglitsch.** Died in 1569; daughter of Dimitri Paletski; married Yuri (1533–1563), prince of Uglitsch, on November 3, 1548; children: Vassili of Uglitsch (b. 1559).*

Paley, Babe (1915–1978).

See Cushing Sisters.

Paley, Grace (1922—)

***Distinguished American short-story writer, poet, professor, and prominent peace activist, who established herself as a major voice in 20th-century American literature.** Pronunciation: Pay-lee. Born Grace Goodside on December 11, 1922, in New York City; daughter of Isaac Goodside (a physician) and Manya (Ridnyik) Goodside (a photographer and medical assistant); attended Hunter College (1938–39); married Jess Paley, on June 20, 1942 (divorced 1972); married Bob Nichols, in 1972; children: (first marriage) Nora Paley (b. 1949); Danny Paley (b. 1951).*

Studied poetry with W.H. Auden (early 1940s); published first collection of short stories, The Little Disturbances of Man *(Doubleday, 1959), to critical acclaim; received a Guggenheim fellowship (1961); participated in the first demonstration by the War Resister's League (1963); taught at Sarah Lawrence College (1966–88); traveled to Vietnam (1969), Chile (1972), Moscow (1973), China (1974); elected to the American Academy of Letters (1980); granted National Endowment for the Arts fellowship (1987); recipient of the Edith Wharton Citation of Merit, naming Paley first official state writer of New York (1989); received REA Award for Short Stories (1992); given Vermont Award for Excellence in the Arts (1993).*

Selected writings: The Little Disturbances of Man *(Doubleday, 1959);* Enormous Changes at the Last Minute *(Farrar, Straus and Giroux, 1975);* Later the Same Day *(Farrar, Straus, 1985);* Leaning Forward *(Granite Press, 1985);* Long Walks and Intimate Talks *(Feminist Press at the City of New York, 1991);* New and Collected Poems *(Tilbury House, 1992);* Grace Paley: The Collected Stories *(Farrar, Straus, 1994);* Just As I Thought *(Farrar, Straus, 1998).*

"Few other fiction writers in late twentieth-century American letters have had so great an influence as Grace Paley on the basis of so few books in a lifetime of work," notes **Charlotte Zoë Walker**. A self-described "somewhat combative pacifist and cooperative anarchist," Paley was born the youngest of three children to Russian-Jewish immigrant parents in 1922. At the time of her birth, her sister Jeanne was 16 and her brother Victor was 14, making Paley the cherished infant in a family of adults. Her father Isaac and mother Manya had immigrated to the United States from the Ukraine in 1906, after which they anglicized their last name from Gutseit to Goodside. In America, they lived with Isaac's mother Natasha and his sisters Luba and Mira. By the time of Paley's birth, the hard times of newly arrived immigrants were behind them. Her father had a successful medical practice in the Bronx and was the center of attention in a family of women. His lively personality, more extroverted than his wife's, and his significance as the main breadwinner, contributed to Paley's youthful assessments of where the "interest in life" resided: "When I was a little girl I was a boy—like a lot of little girls who like to get into things and want to be where the action is, which is up the corner someplace, where the boys are." Although she grew up finding men's talk alluring, she would eventually conclude that it was the talk of women which was directly linked to life.

The household offered a haven to newly arrived Russian-Jewish immigrants. Paley's biographer **Judith Arcana** noted that the Goodsides' friends were "immigrant families in the Jewish Bronx neighborhood—no longer 'socialist' but certainly 'social democrats'—[who] were almost always egalitarian in their ideas, but rarely in their daily lives." Paley was surrounded by lively cultural and political discussions as she absorbed both old and new world flavors. Her parents had been political dissidents in Russia and were sensitive to the repercussions of political involvement. "My family was political," she told **Joann Gardner**. "It was just their way of thinking about the world." The Russian language, which Paley acquired, was spoken at home, as was Yiddish.

As a bright, energetic teenager in the 1930s, Paley posed a great hope scholastically for her parents, and they were dismayed when her life did not follow the expected course. She was a good student until her studies stopped being easy, later noting, "I thought if I had to do any work it meant I was stupid." Her growing unrest at school and parental expectations combined to steer her away from academic excellence. At 15, she entered Hunter College as a freshman only to drop out after a year. Remarked Paley of her horrified parents to *New York Times* journalist **Nina Darnton**: "They didn't know that 25 years later everyone would be doing it." She took a typing course at her father's insistence. Paley's developing sexuality also alarmed the Goodsides, who had a typical European reluctance to deal with such matters openly.

With a love of literature, Paley read voraciously and wrote poems. "I didn't know I was going to *Be* anything. I knew I was going to write. I think of it more as a verb than a noun," she told Gardner. At age 17, she took a class with W.H. Auden at the New School for Social Research in New York. She would later recall his influence on her work at the time, telling **Wendy Lesser** in an interview for the Internet magazine *Salon,* "When I was very young, I wrote a lot like Auden. It's kind of comical, because after all, I didn't have a British accent. . . . I didn't yet realize that you have two ears. One ear is that literary ear, and it's a good old ear. . . . But there was also something else that I had but I didn't know it. I only knew it in my own speech, and that is the ear of the language of home, and the language of your street and your own people."

Responding to an environment of open discussion, Paley had become independent-minded which brought her into greater conflict with her parents. While her family, tied to the past, replayed the Russian Revolution, she was intellectually stimulated by leftist thinking as well as by current affairs in Europe, Africa and the United States.

In 1942, she married Jess Paley, who came from a German Jewish background. Although neither family was especially religious, the Goodsides, unlike the Paleys, were immersed in Jewish culture. Perceiving Grace as opting for the traditional role of wife and mother, her parents thought that she would at least find safety in marriage. The same year they were married, Paley traveled with her husband when he joined the Signal Corps. Her exposure to army camp life during World War II was to influence her views of the military mentality. During their travels in Florida, North Carolina, Texas, and New York, she wrote and published poetry in magazines. When Jess was shipped overseas, Grace stayed with friends, finally returning to New York to live in Greenwich Village. She briefly attended New York University in the early 1940s only to find herself once again not responding to studies in an academic setting. Her mother died in 1944, when Paley was 22. Selling his medical practice, Paley's father painted and wrote, living until 1973.

Returning from service, Paley's husband was disoriented and under great stress, common difficulties for veterans. Grace worked at clerical jobs in political organizations such as the Southern Conference for Human Welfare, earning little money but being exposed to politics. Jess eventually developed a career as a motion-picture cinematographer, which often took him away from home. Their daughter **Nora Paley** was born in 1949, followed by their son Danny Paley in 1951.

Money was scarce for the family, and Paley was busy with her children and working odd jobs. In 1952, she began writing stories as an extension of her poetry. She told Lesser: "When I started writing stories, I had a kind of a breakthrough. . . . I suddenly broke into the language that I then continued to write with. That was an important hour in my life. It was a sudden thing. I was sick and had a few weeks off, so I had the time to listen. I was able to use both ears suddenly." In a *Ms.* article during 1992, Paley remarked, "I love the short story form, because it's as tough as a poem, but also embraces life easily."

In the late 1950s, her early story "A Woman Young and Old" was published by the men's magazine *Nugent* which changed the title to "Rough Little Customer." Without consulting Paley, the editors also changed the text to suit their readers, infuriating the young author. "Goodbye and Goodluck" and "The Contest" were published in *Accent* magazine in 1956.

Living in Greenwich Village, Paley made friends in Washington Square Park with other mothers and their children, and she joined the PTA. "For me, going to the park with my children turned out to be one of the luckiest things I ever did," she told Gardner. "That daily experience among other women was the source or drive for a lot of my stories." Initially through neighborhood issues, Paley experienced the difficulties and rewards of challenging governing officials. She and her community PTA won a battle with the city when a fence was put up to reroute traffic around Washington Square Park, making it safe for children to play. Political activism was to take an important role in her life during the following years as she lent her voice to the antiwar, antinuclear, and environmental movements. Her daughter Nora remarked that Paley became politically active as an "outgrowth of motherhood," and Judith Arcana termed her activism "radical compassion."

Through a friend, Paley's stories were given to Ken McCormick at Doubleday, and she was told that if she wrote seven more Doubleday would publish a volume. *The Little Disturbances of Man: Women and Men at Love* ap-

Grace Paley, courtesy of Farrar, Straus and Giroux, publisher of Collected Stories.

peared in 1959 and was highly regarded. Notes Walker: "The jaunty, warm, honest, and ironic voice of the stories in *The Little Disturbances of Man: Women and Men at Love* speaks truths that women immediately recognized, in a manner that men found amusing rather than threatening. This unusual combination has its roots in her immigrant Jewish background and the neighborhood life of the city." Paley received a Guggenheim fellowship in 1961, the same year that she was a founder of the Greenwich Village Peace Center.

Gaining eloquence as a speaker, and acting as an incisive force in defining the Peace Center's activities, Paley engaged in demonstrations and civil disobedience focused on protesting the Vietnam War, handed out leaflets, and counseled draftees. She was arrested on numerous occasions. In 1966, Paley served a six-day stay in the Woman's House of Detention in New York for participating in a sit-down blocking of the Armed Forces Day Parade. Arcana remarks that Paley, "conscious of the mutual impact of citizen and state," had "developed an analysis of the complicated relationships among capitalism, racism, and imperialism." Paley often took her children with her to demonstrations, and both Nora and Danny have commented on their mother's fearlessness during these events. Jess Paley, however, was not an activist.

Everyone, real or invented, deserves the open destiny of life.

—Grace Paley

In the 1960s, Paley taught at Columbia and Syracuse universities before taking a post at Sarah Lawrence College, where she would teach creative writing and literature for 18 years. In 1966, she received a grant from the National Endowment for the Arts. *The Little Disturbances of Man* was reissued in hardcover by Viking Press (1968) and in paperback by American Library's Plume Books (1973).

In 1967, Paley left her husband. Although she knew Bob Nichols, the man who would become her second husband, as a friend and fellow activist beginning in the days of the Peace Center, they did not become involved with each other until both their marriages had dissolved. She divorced Jess in 1972, marrying Nichols the same year.

Beginning with her trip to Vietnam in 1969, representing the antiwar movement which had played a role in the return of political prisoners, Paley traveled throughout the world "accumulating knowledge and understanding born of going outside the neighborhood and bringing it all back home," notes Arcana. The year they were married, Grace and Bob went to Chile in time to experience the hope for democracy in that country, which was shattered with Salvador Allende's death and the subsequent military takeover. In 1973, Paley went to Russia as a delegate from the War Resister's league to the World Peace Conference. Here, in the country of her parents, she found a sense of familiarity in the language and the people.

Paley's second collection of short stories, *Enormous Changes at the Last Minute,* was published in 1974. Fifteen years had passed since her first collection, and the volume reflected her increased social and political awareness. This work also was well received. The same year, she and her husband visited China.

Paley made news in 1978 as a prominent member of what came to be called the Washington Eleven. On Labor Day, the War Resister's League representatives, including Paley, left a White House tour and walked onto the lawn. They distributed leaflets and displayed a banner which read: "No Nuclear Weapon—No Nuclear Power—U.S. or U.S.S.R." Arrested for illegal entry ("stepping on the grass," said Paley), the 11 representatives (including three other writers: **Karen Malpede**, Glen Pontier, and Van Zwisohn) were put on probation for three years. Much publicity and outcry surrounded the arrests which brought attention to the government's heavy-handed approach to pacifists, particularly in contrast to the manner in which American protesters were dealt with for demonstrating in Russia's Red Square. Wrote Donald Barthelme in *The New York Times* on February 2, 1979:

> Our Government seems to be proceeding in a somewhat ham-handed fashion here. The demonstrators offered no threat whatsoever to the President, to the White House, to America as an idea, or even to the grass—they walked on it, says Grace Paley, "softly and carefully, armed only with paper." . . . At the same time that the Washington group was making its protest, seven other Americans opened a similar banner, written in Russian, in Moscow's Red Square. This group also distributed leaflets. They were arrested by the Soviet authorities, yelled at for a while, then let go.

Paley's third collection of stories, *Later the Same Day,* and a poetry collection, *Leaning Forward,* appeared in 1985. The following year, she became the first recipient of the ***Edith Wharton** Citation of Merit and was named the first state author of New York. She was selected for the award, which was created by the legislature to promote creative writing, by William Kennedy, Raymond Carver, **Mary Gordon**, and Robert Towers. Said Kennedy of Paley's work: "Her stories dramatize the heady, bittersweet moments of change in our lives and the deep continuity that gives us the gritty strength to survive these social and sexual upheavals."

In 1994, Farrar, Straus and Giroux brought out a volume of Paley's called *The Collected Stories*, consisting of selected stories from her other books. In his *New York Times* book review, Robert Pinsky remarked:

> "Her distinctive, sure-footed command of the short-story form brings to fictional material a quality that must be called poetry. By this I mean not mere verbal sauce of some rich or creamy kind but the ability of language to dance with playful, lordly authority about the contours of reality, intimate yet somehow aloof."

In the same review, Pinsky also noted that her stories "crystallize brief moments in which whole lives reveal their inner truth."

Restoring "something to the scales," Paley employs women narrators in her stories. She uses dialogue to move her tales forward and to reveal characters who speak with various dialects of New York speech. Her tone is often described as seriocomic. Ivan Gold in *Commonweal* noted Paley's "quirky, anguished, funny, loving, deep and antic glimpses" into her characters "in a prose as resilient and unpredictable as one imagines the fate of her characters to be."

Paley continues to travel, accepting speaking engagements, conducting workshops and maintaining homes in New York and Vermont. Once asked why she had never written a novel, she replied: "Art is too long and life is too short." On a life dedicated to art, family, teaching, and actively championing the principles she believes in, she remarked in 1997: "I never tried to keep a balance. I just got dragged every which way, pulled and pushed. It's not a bad way to live." She noted to **Harriet Shapiro** in 1974: "It may be my political feelings, but I think . . . literature . . . makes justice in the world."

SOURCES:

Arcana, Judith. *Grace Paley's Life Stories.* Chicago, IL: University of Illinois Press, 1993.

Barthelme, Donald. "Grace Paley Faces Jail with 3 Other Writers," in *The New York Times.* February 2, 1979.

Baumbach, Jonathan. *Partisan Review,* 1975.

Darnton, Nina. "Taking Risks: The Writer as Effective Teacher," in *The New York Times.* April 13, 1986.

Gardner, Joann. *American Poetry Review.* March–April 1994.

Gold, Ivan. *Commonweal,* 1968.

"Grace Paley Honored As State Author," in *The New York Times.* November 14, 1986.

Harris, Robert. *The New York Times Book Review,* 1985.

Paley, Grace. *Enormous Changes at the Last Minute.* NY: Farrar, Straus, and Giroux, 1974.

———. *Later the Same Day.* NY: Farrar, Straus, and Giroux, 1985.

———. *The Little Disturbances of Man.* NY: Doubleday, 1959.

———. *Ms.,* 1992.

Pinsky, Robert. *The New York Times Book Review,* 1994.

Rogovoy, Seth. "Amazing Grace: From Diapers to Demonstrations," in *Berkshire Eagle.* June 19, 1997.

Shapiro, Harriet. *Ms.* May 1974, p. 43.

Walker, Charlotte Zoë. "Grace Paley," in *Dictionary of Literary Biography,* Volume 218: *American Short-Story Writers Since World War II.* 2nd series. Ed. by Patrick Meanor and Gwen Crane. Detroit, MI: Gale Group, 1999.

SUGGESTED READING:

Mickelson, Anne Z. *Reaching Out: Sensitivity and Order in Recent American Fiction by Women.* Scarecrow Press, 1979.

Paley, Grace. *The Collected Stories.* NY: Farrar, Straus, and Giroux, 1994.

———. *Leaning Forward.* Granite Press, 1985.

———, and Vera B. Williams. "Three Hundred Sixty-Five Reasons Not to Have Another War: 1989 Peace Calendar," in *New Society,* 1988.

Penelope Ann Kines,
freelance writer, New York City

Paley, princess (1865–1929).

See Olga, Princess Paley.

Palfi, Marion (1907–1978)

German-born photographer who specialized in portraits and social documentary. *Name variations: Marion Magner. Born in Berlin, Germany, on October 21, 1907; died in Los Angeles, California, in November 1978; daughter of Victor Palfi (a theater producer); married Erich Abraham, in mid-1930s (divorced); married Benjamin Weiss, in 1940 (divorced 1944); married Martin Magner (a Danish-born producer-director), in 1955.*

Born in 1907 in Berlin, Germany, to Hungarian parents, photographer Marion Palfi was the daughter of Victor Palfi, a theater producer of note. She acted in several German films before taking up the study of photography in 1932. From 1934 to 1936, she operated her own portrait studio in Berlin, during which time she also freelanced for industry and magazines. In 1936, she moved her operation to Amsterdam, a change of locale that may have been prompted by the failure of her marriage to Erich Abraham.

Palfi's second marriage was to American Benjamin Weiss, with whom she came to New York in 1940. Following a divorce from Weiss in 1944, she received a Rosenwald Fellowship which she used to travel around the United States photographing examples of racial discrimination. This led to a photo-essay, "There Is No More Time," which documented segregation in the South. During the 1950s, Palfi produced a book on child neglect and juvenile delinquency, *Suffer Little Children,* and also documented conditions among the elderly. She married her third husband, Martin Magner, a Danish-born producer-director, in 1955.

During the 1940s and 1950s, Palfi's work was represented in a number of major museum exhibitions, including Edward Steichen's *Family of Man*, at the Museum of Modern Art in New York in 1955. Palfi was also a member of the Photo League, but resigned in 1949, fearing that she might lose her U.S. citizenship because of the group's political orientation.

Palm, Etta Aelders (1743–1799)

Secret agent of the Dutch, Prussian, and French governments who was also a prominent advocate of women's rights during the French Revolution. *Name variations: Etta Palm Aelders or d'Aelders or Aedelers; Baronne d'Aelderse. Pronunciation: ET-tah EL-ders PAHM. Born Etta Lubina Johanna Derista Aelders in Groningen, Netherlands, in April 1743; died of a breast infection in The Hague, March 28, 1799, and was buried in an unmarked grave in a cemetery in Rijswijk; daughter of Johan Aelders van Nieuwenhuys (d. 1749) and his second wife, Agatha Pierteronella de Sitten; well educated at home by her mother; married Christiaan Ferdinand Loderwijk Palm (a humanities student), in 1762 (divorced or separated in 1763); children: Agatha (b. 1763, who died in infancy).*

Became an adventurer after her husband's disappearance (1763); moved to Paris and set up a salon (1773); became an agent for France (1778), and possibly for Prussia (1780s); opposed the Patriot movement in the Dutch Republic (1784–87); became an agent for the stadholder (1788); joined the Social Circle during the French Revolution and spoke out on women's rights (1790–91); founded and directed the Patriotic and Charitable Society of the Women Friends of Truth (1791–92); was briefly arrested on suspicion of spying (1791); presented a radical petition on women's rights (1792); went to the Dutch Republic and served as a diplomatic intermediary (1792–93); was imprisoned by the Batavian Republic (1795–98).

The Paris *Gazette universelle* in its July 25, 1791, issue characterized the recently arrested Etta Palm as "an adventuress, an intriguer, calling herself a baroness although having known no other barons save those who had honored her with their visits." The description was apt but incomplete. For one thing, she was suspected, rightly, of being a spy. For another, she was, with ***Olympe de Gouges** and ***Anne-Josèph Théroigne de Méricourt**, one of the three most prominent advocates of women's rights during the early years of the French Revolution.

Etta Lubina Johanna Derista Aelders was born in Groningen, Netherlands, in April 1743, the child of Johan Aelders van Nieuwenhuys, owner of a papermill and a pawnshop, and his second wife, **Agatha Pierteronella de Sitten**, daughter of a silk cloth merchant. After Johan's death in 1749, Agatha, a strong, independent woman who had married beneath her social rank, continued to operate the pawnshop in partnership with a Jew. Eventually she went bankrupt because the authorities withdrew her license, alleging irregular operations; possibly anti-Semitism also influenced their decision. From her mother, Etta received a fine education, learning German, French, English, and perhaps a little Italian. Also, her mother indoctrinated her with strongly Orangist (i.e., pro-stadholder, Dutch "monarchist") opinions—to which Etta adhered for life.

Etta was a gadabout teenager, popular with the university students and receiving several marriage proposals, including one from a married man. In 1762, she wed a humanities student, Christiaan Ferdinand Loderwijk Palm, son of Haarlem's prosecutor. Palm's parents opposed the marriage but relented after they eloped. The next year she gave birth to a daughter, Agatha, who soon died. Because she had continued her premarital ways, Etta's husband probably raised questions about the baby's paternity; he divorced her, left for the Dutch East Indies, and disappeared. Despite the divorce—if divorce there actually was—Etta considered herself a widow, and legal documents referred to her as Madame Palm. Moreover, she pretended Christiaan was a baron and henceforth styled herself "Baroness Palm d'Aelders."

Etta became an adventurer, a bourgeois woman "wandering through social stratification with relative ease," writes **Judith Vega**. In due course she took up with Jan Minniks, a young Groningen lawyer, weak and irresponsible, whose wife had divorced him after he had run through her money. On April 13, 1768, he was, nevertheless, named consul in Messina, Sicily, and Etta accompanied him as his "wife." Some sources say he left her in Provence when she became ill, others that she arrived in Messina with him. He became instantly unhappy with his post and unsuccessfully applied for one at Tripoli. They returned together to Holland, where at Breda she met a 50ish lieutenant general of cavalry named Grovestina who had court connections. He took her to Brussels, where a friend, the Dutch ambassador there, introduced her to diplomatic high society. In 1773, she left Grovestina and moved to Paris bearing letters of introduction to the eminent philosophes Jean d'Alembert and Denis Diderot.

Palm furnished an apartment near the Palais-Royal in a "rather coquettish" style, a contemporary reported, her bedroom featuring four large mirrors, one at the foot of the bed. The "baroness" attracted a considerable number of visitors and spent recklessly from profits on shares provided by powerful friends supplying the army with gunpowder and saltpeter. Little precise information exists as to who her visitors were, although it is known that shortly before and during the early years of the Revolution they included the philosopher Condorcet and politicians Pierre Choudieu, Claude Basire, François Buzot, François Chabot, Jean-François de Menou, Théodore de Lameth, Emmanuel Fréteau, Jérôme Pétion, Jean-Louis Carra, and even Maximilien de Robespierre.

Palm's complicated and quite murky career as a secret diplomatic agent—in effect, a spy—began much earlier, in February 1778, when a frequenter of her salon, the Comte de Maurepas, Louis XVI's chief minister, asked her to go to the Netherlands to find out if the Dutch would remain true to their defensive alliance with England if France entered the American Revolutionary War. (While on mission she met up with Minniks, who is said to have become a spy for England.) She returned in March to report that the Dutch were uninterested in supporting England in this war. This mission put her into contact with the Dutch ambassador to France, with whom she henceforth maintained close relations. At some point in the 1780s, she also became a close friend of Count Bernhard von der Goltz, the Prussian envoy to Paris, and as a result (according to a lover, Choudieu) became an informant for Prussia. For how long she was engaged is not known. She is said to have been in direct contact with Princess ***Wilhelmina of Prussia** (1751–1820), sister of the king of Prussia and wife of Stadholder William V (r. 1766–1795). In 1791, however, Palm denounced the charge that she was a Prussian agent as "an odious calumny."

Palm's strong Orangist sympathies put her in the stadholder's camp during the political upheavals in the Dutch Republic in the 1780s that culminated in the Patriots' Revolt (1785–87). Despite her receptiveness to the Enlightenment and the idea of government resting upon the consent of the people, as became evident in her favorable reaction to the French Revolution, she regarded the stadholderate as a guarantor of order and (she hoped) peaceful reform as opposed to the claims of the discordant, proto-democratic Patriot movement, which was resorting to civil war. She may have played some role in thwarting a plot in 1784 against the stadholder's chief adviser, the duke of Brunswick-Wolfenbüttel. The claim, however, that she helped persuade the French government not to come to the Patriots' aid in 1787, thus opening the way for Prussia to intervene to crush them, seems at best highly questionable; for France, racked by a major financial and political crisis, intervention simply was not an option.

In 1788, Apollonius Lampsins, sent to France to propagandize in favor of the Orangists, recommended Palm to William's chief minister, Grand Pensionary Laurens van de Spiegel. The latter hired her to send him information not found in the press about the changing leadership in France and to spread in Paris information from The Hague. Until late 1792, she engaged in a lengthy correspondence with van de Spiegel, doing good work and being well paid for it. Perhaps with Lampsins' help, she published in 1788 a 36-page pamphlet, *Réflexions sur l'ouvrage intitulé Aux Bataves sur le Stadhoudérat par le Comte de Mirabeau*, attacking Mirabeau's pro-Patriot pamphlet. She became an outspoken opponent of the approximately 6,000 Patriot exiles in France and in the press hotly defended the stadholderate against their attacks, sometimes on her own, sometimes at van de Spiegel's request.

Thus, Etta Palm, "la belle hollandaise"—slender, buxom, but said to lack "highly refined" features—was no stranger to political circles when the Revolution began in 1789. In 1791, she admitted that it had taken her a while to become as staunch a supporter of the Revolution as she was by then. And for understandable reasons. She was, after all, in the pay of the stadholder's government and probably also of the Prussians. In conventional terms, she was a monarchist because she supported the stadholder and opposed the Patriot exiles. Yet, as noted, from the start she sympathized with the French revolutionaries, who were opposing Louis XVI's regime and proclaiming the sovereignty of the people in the Declaration of the Rights of Man (August 1789). Hence, Palm has often been portrayed as a political schizophrenic.

The charge loses most of its force, however, when one views her in the context of Dutch politics, which were highly unconventional by prevailing European norms. For good, if not altogether justifiable, reasons, she regarded the Patriot exiles as mostly aristocrats masquerading as democrats in order to preserve and extend their old political privileges. At the same time, she, and many others of the Dutch, saw no contradiction between preserving the stadholderate and introducing more democratic structures and practices into the endlessly complicated Dutch regime. Indeed, in December 1789 she is found urging a moderately receptive van de Spiegel to institute reforms giving the common people more influence. And in early 1790, she also was assuring the French government (which was giving subsidies to the Patriots) that the Dutch government, contrary to press reports, was not involved in a counter-revolutionary plot hatched by the Marquis de Maillebois.

Nature has formed us to be your equals, your companions and your friends.

—Etta Palm, 1791

Palm's personal involvement with the Revolution and women's issues included membership in a Fraternal Society of Patriots of One and the Other Sex but centered on the Social Circle (founded in early 1790) and its club (founded on October 13), the Confederation of the Friends of Truth. Meeting at the Palais-Royal, this large and important club became the only one involved seriously in women's issues up to 1793. In 18th-century France, the mass of women were not yet interested in women's rights. Only from 1787 did pamphlets appear in any number, and during the Revolution feminism was never a concern even of a majority of women's clubs, which mostly were auxiliaries of the men's clubs. For her part, Palm did all she could to fight the undertow, becoming the leading female feminist in the Confederation, complemented on the male side by Condorcet.

She made her first public statement on November 26, 1790, when at a Confederation meeting she came to the aid of one Charles-Louis Rousseau, who was being jeered for raising questions about the rights of women. Could it be, she asked, that the "holy Revolution, which gave men their rights, has rendered Frenchmen unjust and dishonest toward women?" Her success brought her an invitation to make a formal speech, which she did on December 30. It was applauded by many, warmly opposed by some, and distributed to provincial societies, where it inspired the Revolution's first recorded discussions of the rights of women. (One society, at Creil-sur-Oise, even awarded her a medal.) Apart from a call for equal education for females, she offered no program of action but instead concentrated on depicting the sad status of women as a "slavery" which mocked the ideals of the Revolution: "Our life, our liberty, our fortune is not ours at all." She celebrated the particular virtues of women and evoked the example of the women of ancient Rome as she had in November. "Justice must be the first virtue of free men," she cried, "and justice demands that the laws be the same for all beings, like the air and the sun." She closed by calling for a "second revolution, in our customs."

Through the winter and spring of 1791, Palm was very active speaking and writing for the women's cause. Evidently she wrote a pamphlet which has not been discovered or was not printed. In July, however, because of accusations against her by a journalist, **Louise Robert-Keralio**, and others that she was a disloyal, dishonest foreigner, she published a 46-page collection of speeches, letters, and a petition entitled *Appel aux françoises sur la régénération des moeurs et nécessité de l'influence des femmes dans un gouvernement libre, Par Etta-Palm, née d'Aelders* (Appeal to Frenchwomen on the Regeneration of Customs and Necessity of the Influence of Women in a Free Government). Of special importance was a speech given on March 18 and published in the *Bouche de fer* (the Social Circle's newspaper) on the 23rd which called for establishment of an all-female society in Paris (following the lead of Bordeaux, Creil, Limoges, Alais, and Tulle), said to be the city's first.

The Patriotic and Charitable Society of the Women Friends of Truth, launched on March 25 with the aid of the Social Circle, was an ambitious project. Palm proposed founding a society in each ward (section) of Paris, with a general directory comprised of the officers of these societies meeting weekly to coordinate them; moreover, similar societies would be started in all 83 departments of France and would correspond with the Paris confederation. (The similarity to the Social Circle and Jacobin networks is obvious.) Following Palm's outline, the tasks of the societies came to include 1) lobbying for women's rights; 2) surveillance of the "enemies of liberty"; 3) inquiries to distinguish dishonest indigents from those deserving public assistance; 4) committees to visit and succor poverty-stricken families; 5) founding of schools and workshops for needy girls aged 7 to 16; and 6) providing shelters and wet-nurse services for poor young women drifting into Paris from the provinces.

The society never came close to becoming a Paris-wide, much less nationwide, association, despite Palm's hard work. Nary a school was founded. On April 7, 1792, she publicly complained of the "general indifference" that had plagued her creation, and by the fall of 1792 it had faded away. Why had it failed? The high fee of three *livres* per month kept all but fairly wealthy women away, nor was inviting ***Marie Louise d'Orleans** (1750–1822), princesse de Bourbon, to be a patron a wise political move. While the society did lobby for a fair divorce law and against Article XIII of the Criminal Code, which gave only men the right to prosecute for adultery and imprison the errant spouse for up to two years, it was Palm's belief that the customs of France were not yet ripe for women to compete with men politically. The society consequently lacked focus, becoming, wrotes **Joan Landes**, "something between a charitable association of the wealthy for indigent women and a political club on behalf of female rights." Moreover, the need for a women's society in Paris seemed less pressing than in the provinces because the central government was close by and women already could participate in the mixed clubs and sit in the galleries of the National Assembly. And, not least of all, the bourgeois women involved doubtless were put off by Palm's marginal social status, as was also the case with Olympe de Gouges and Anne Théroigne de Méricourt, engaged in similar efforts. Only when ❧▸ **Pauline Léon** and ***Claire Lacombe** founded the Club of Revolutionary Republican Citizenesses in 1793, with the simple goals of "foiling the projects of the enemies of the Republic" and lowering the price of bread, might any headway be made among the masses of working-class women.

Meanwhile, back in the spring of 1791, the Social Circle and the Confederation were edging leftward toward republicanism when "the flight to Varennes" (June 20–21), the king's attempt to escape abroad to lead a counter-revolutionary offensive, persuaded them to come out for dethronement. A republican demonstration at the Champ de Mars on July 17—in which Palm probably took part—resulted in a "massacre" of 12 demonstrators. In the ensuing crackdown, Palm, who was taking up a collection for victims, was arrested on the night of July 18–19 as a suspicious foreigner, as was a Jewish banker, Ephraïm, thought to be an agent of Prussia. Both were released after three days for lack of evidence. The Social Circle, intimidated, announced the end of the Confederation and on July 28 of the *Bouche de fer* as well. As noted, however, Palm's society continued for another year.

The society's work and her correspondence with van de Spiegel kept her occupied during 1791–92. Van de Spiegel, concerned about her political activity and radicalism, cautioned her (Sept. 1791) to moderate her zeal. A former lover, François Chabot, introduced her to Claude Basire, a rising young deputy in the new Legislative Assembly (Oct. 1791–Aug. 1792) and in the following Convention (Sept. 1792), with whom she carried on a yearlong affair. He obtained a seat on the powerful Committee of General Security, which made him a likely source of inside information.

Palm's last notable political initiative came on April 1, 1792, when she led a small delegation from her society to the Legislative Assembly and spoke in favor of a petition on women's rights. This petition was a truly radical document for that time. It called for 1) equal civil and political rights for both sexes; 2) admission of women to all civil and military posts (she had long supported the companies of women soldiers, "amazons," sprouting in a few places); 3) a "moral and national" education for all girls; 4) the same age, 21, for majority for men and women; and 5) the right of divorce (a divorce law on the agenda was passed on August 30). The assembly's president thanked her unctuously and sent the petition to a committee, where it expired unread. It did arouse some comment in the press for a few days, but the outbreak of war with Austria (and soon Prussia) on April 20 presently occupied all minds.

◂❧ ***Léon, Pauline.*** *See Lacombe, Claire for sidebar.*

Palm probably participated, along with Léon and Théroigne de Méricourt, in the "visit to the king" (June 20, 1792), a quasi-insurrection presaging the fall of the throne which came in the rising of August 10. Her role, if any, in the latter event is unclear. By then, most of the leading politicians were those members of the Social Circle who had revived the Jacobin Club in the fall of 1791. They were moderate republicans nicknamed "Girondins" and in effect ran the government until they were overthrown in June 1793 by more radical Jacobins, the "Mountaineers" (Montagnards), who began the Reign of Terror (to July 1794). By then, Palm was long off the scene and living in Holland. Perhaps she had sensed that events were running into more dangerous waters—certainly for her, given her suspicious past and connections. Whatever the case, in October 1792 she informed the French foreign minister, Pierre-Henri Lebrun, that she was on her way to the Dutch Republic (she arrived by November 4 at the latest) and asked if he would pay her for information. Lebrun, who privately called her "an intriguer," accepted (Nov. 26). He hoped, among other things, to use her contacts with Princess Wilhelmina to help detach Prussia from Austria.

The French victory over the Austrians at Jemappes (Nov. 6) led to immediate occupation of the Austrian Netherlands (Belgium) and raised the question of an invasion of Holland. Lebrun, however, told Palm to assure van de Spiegel of France's pacific intentions toward all neutrals. Simon Schama, a leading authority on Dutch affairs in these years, affirms that Palm, "a double agent of consummate craft," tried with some success to resolve the major differences between France and the still-neutral Dutch and British. But France decided (Nov. 27) to open the Scheldt River to free navigation—a violation of the Peace of Westphalia, which gave the Dutch a trade monopoly on this vital Belgian river. Opening the Scheldt, called "that cursed river" by Palm, gravely threatened Dutch shipping and related English interests, and it doomed the peace. The execution of Louis XVI (Jan. 21, 1793) was only the last straw. Palm tried to persuade Lebrun that the French warmongers were either royalists or Montagnards intent on destroying the Girondin leadership, but in vain. France declared war on the Dutch and British on February 1.

It seems unlikely, although it is often asserted, that Palm had returned to France before January 1793, by which time she was in the Netherlands for good. With the war, her role as intermediary and spy disintegrated. Lebrun complained that her information was of little value, and his successor, François Defourges, finally cut her loose on October 5, 1793, without having paid her for many months despite her despairing appeals. Meanwhile, probably the cruelest blow was delivered by van de Spiegel. On May 9, he curtly ended their relations now that the war was on. He enclosed a paltry 20 ducats. Reduced to misery, she appealed to William V on June 30, 1794, to no avail, and a week later to van de Spiegel, suggesting she could be useful in negotiating with the French. He sent no reply except 600 florins for past services.

The French conquest of the Dutch Republic early in 1795 put her between two fires. William fled to England, while the Dutch Patriots, under French control, established the Batavian Republic (1795–1806). Desperate, Palm claimed to be a French citizen and thus entitled to return. The French told her to await the peace treaty. She then tried to contact Orangist elements but failed. On May 18, the inevitable occurred when the Patriot regime, after checking with the French, arrested her for suspected plotting against the Batavian Republic. She was detained at The Castle in The Hague. There she gave her interrogators confused or misleading answers while flatly denying having served either the Dutch or French governments. The Patriots, however, knew her too well from her years as their chief denouncer in Paris. On February 14, 1796, they imprisoned her at a castle in Woerden. Van de Spiegel was there in a comfortable political confinement, but she was put among the common criminals, assigned a one-room cell, and allowed one hour's daily exercise.

Palm was released on December 20, 1798, under a general amnesty for political prisoners, and took shelter with a friend. The French meanwhile, pronouncing her an émigré, had confiscated her papers and property in Paris on June 25, 1794, and sold all but her political correspondence on September 8–9. Penniless, the "Baroness" Palm d'Aelders died of a breast infection on March 28, 1799. She was buried the next day in an unmarked grave in the cemetery at Rijswijk, a suburb of The Hague.

Etta Palm's historical importance rests upon her role as a pioneer feminist during the French Revolution, not as a courtesan or secret agent. Was she a devotee of the Revolution because it served her purpose as an agent? To some degree, no doubt. She took care not to let the Patriot émigrés, patronized by the French government, outflank her. Zeal for the Revolution and France's role as a torchbearer served to keep her *persona grata* with the changing governments until her association with the Girondin faction finally discredited her in the eyes of the victorious Montagnards.

While her political stance appears—inevitably—self-serving to a degree, it also has a convincing ring of sincerity. She, with Théroigne, de Gouges, Lacombe, and Léon, for a long time believed—naïvely, it turned out—that women's rights were in the mainstream of revolutionary thought. To this extent they were "revolutionaries first and women second," writes **Candice Proctor**. Palm's approach ran counter to the current which in the 19th century would confine women to a separate, special domestic role "defined," in itself, writes Vega, "as a positive contribution to public and social life." Palm believed that the only reason women lacked full rights was because of social custom (*moeurs*) and male power, not nature. She applied her radical interpretation of the Enlightenment's natural rights theory to marriage and government, private and domestic spheres without differentiation. She refused to accept, notes Vega, "the difference in [current] liberal thought between the citizen and the natural man"; if it were accepted, women inevitably would be confined to women's roles, to domesticity. Interestingly, she, a courtesan, denounced the frivolity and idleness of the lives of most upper-class women. Changing the *moeurs* of men and women of such a society would be a long, arduous task.

By the time she left France permanently, she had become discouraged by the unreceptiveness of both men and women to any idea of altering traditional female roles in a fundamental way. Indeed, the whole issue of women's rights during the French Revolution remained clouded. And what improvements were enacted—e.g., divorce legislation, 21 as the majority age, equal inheritance rights, a voice in property administration and decisions affecting children—were mostly sponged away a decade later by the Napoleonic Code. Palm's ideas would not make much headway for more than a century after her sad end in an unmarked grave.

SOURCES:

Abray, Jane. "Feminism in the French Revolution," in *American Historical Review.* Vol. 80, 1975, pp. 43–62.

Cerati, Marie. *Le Club des citoyennes républicaines révolutionnaires.* Paris: Éditions sociales, 1966.

Decaux, Alain. *Histoire des françaises.* Vol. 2: *La Révolte.* Librairie Académique Perrin, 1972.

Dreyfous, Maurice. *Les Femmes de la Révolution française (1789–1795).* Paris: Société française d'éditions d'art, n.d.

Duhet, Paule-Marie, ed. *Les Femmes et la Révolution, 1789–1794.* Paris: Julliard, 1971.

Les Femmes dans la Révolution française, Vol. 2. Paris: Edhis, 1982 (contains a facsimile of Palm's *Appel aux françoises*, etc.) Paris: l'Imprimerie du Cercle Social, 1791.

Hastier, Louis. "Une aventurière batave sous la révolution," in *La Revue des deux-mondes.* No. 5, 1964, pp. 65–86 (a précis of H. Hardenberg's biography [see below]).

Hufton, Olwen. *Women and the Limits of Citizenship in the French Revolution.* Toronto: University of Toronto Press, 1992.

Kates, Gary. *The Cercle Social, the Girondins, and the French Revolution.* Princeton, NJ: Princeton University Press, 1985.

Kennedy, Michael. *The Jacobin Clubs in the French Revolution: The First Years.* Princeton, NJ: Princeton University Press, 1982.

Landes, Joan B. *Women and the Public Sphere in the Age of the French Revolution.* Ithaca, NY: Cornell University Press, 1988.

Levy, Darlene, Harriet B. Applewhite, and Mary D. Johnson, eds. *Women in Revolutionary Paris, 1789–1795: Selected Documents.* Urbana, IL: University of Illinois Press, 1979.

Proctor, Candice E. *Women, Equality, and the French Revolution.* Westport, CT: Greenwood Press, 1990.

Rendall, Jane. *The Origins of Modern Feminism: Women in Britain, France, and the United States, 1780–1860.* NY: Schocken, 1984.

Schama, Simon. *Patriots and Liberators: Revolution in the Netherlands 1780–1813.* NY: Alfred Knopf, 1977.

Vega, Judith. "Feminist Republicanism: Etta Palm-Aelders on Justice, Virtue and Men," in *History of European Ideas.* Vol. 10, no. 3, 1989, pp. 333–351.

———. "Luxury, Necessity, or the Morality of Men: The Republican Discourse of Etta Palm-Aelders," in *Les Femmes de la Révolution: Actes du colloque international, 12–13–14 avril 1989, Université de Toulouse-La Mirail.* Toulouse: Presses universitaires du Mirail, 1989, pp. 363–370.

SUGGESTED READING:

Bosher, J.F. *The French Revolution.* NY: W.W. Norton, 1988.

Furet, François, and Denis Richet. *French Revolution.* Trans. by Stephen Hardman. NY: Macmillan, 1970.

Gutwerth, Madelyn. *The Twilight of the Goddesses: Women and Representation in the Age of the French Revolutionary Era.* New Brunswick, NJ: Rutgers University Press, 1992.

Hardenberg, H. *Etta Palm, een Hollandse Parisienne 1743–1799.* Assen (Neth.): Van Gorcum, 1962.

Hunt, Lynn, ed. *The French Revolution and Human Rights: A Brief Documentary History.* Boston, MA: Bedford Books of St. Martin's Press, 1996.

Koppins, W.J. *Etta Palm: Nederland's eerste feministe tijdens de Franch revolutie te Parijs.* Zeist (Neth.): Ploegsma, 1929.

Melzer, Sara E., and Leslie W. Rabine, eds. *Rebel Daughters: Women and the French Revolution.* NY: Oxford University Press, 1992.

Rabaut, Jean. *Histoire des féminismes français.* Paris: Éditions Stock, 1978.

Schama, Simon. *Citizens: A Chronicle of the French Revolution.* NY: Alfred Knopf, 1989.

Spencer, Samia, ed. *French Women and the Age of Enlightenment.* Bloomington, IN: Indiana University Press, 1984.

COLLECTIONS:

Paris: Archives nationales, T. 1601, fol. 8383 (papers of Etta Palm-Aelders); AF III, 426, 2501. Bibliothèque nationale: Lb40 2610. *Bouche de fer*, 1790–91.

David S. Newhall,
Professor Emeritus of History, Centre College,
Danville, Kentucky

Palmer, Alice Freeman (1855–1902)

American educator who, at age 26, was named president of the fledgling Wellesley College. *Name variations: Alice E. Freeman. Born on February 21, 1855, in Colesville, New York; died on December 6, 1902, in Paris, France; daughter of James Freeman (a farmer and physician) and Elizabeth (Higley) Freeman (a teacher); University of Michigan, B.A., 1876; married George Palmer, on December 23, 1887; no children.*

Served as president of Wellesley College (1881–87); awarded doctorate by the University of Michigan (1881); went on annual speaking tours (1889–92); served as dean of the women's college of the University of Chicago (1892–94); published Why Go to College? *(1897).*

In the course of her short life, Alice Freeman Palmer became the most celebrated woman educator of her time, nationally and internationally known for her success in integrating women into the American system of higher education. She was born in 1855, the eldest of four children of James Freeman, a prosperous farmer of upstate New York, and **Elizabeth Higley Freeman**, a teacher and social reformer active in the temperance movement. When Alice was six, her father moved to Albany to pursue a degree in medicine; although Elizabeth Freeman supported his goal, she was left to manage the farm and care for four small children with virtually no assistance from James for three years. This experience influenced Alice's later determination to remain an independent woman.

In 1864, Palmer's father moved the family to Windsor and opened a medical practice. There Alice enrolled at the Windsor Academy, a private coeducational secondary school. An intelligent and curious girl, she excelled in school, following a classical curriculum which emphasized Greek, Latin, and mathematics. She remained at the academy for seven years. As a senior, she was briefly engaged to one of her professors, but Palmer had decided to go to college, and her new educational ambitions led her to break off the engagement. She graduated at the head of her class in 1872. In that year, she also underwent a religious conversion to Presbyterianism. Her religious upbringing had been conventional, not marked by deep piety, but after 1872 she became a leader in her church. This period of intense religious feeling and activity lasted only a few years; although she would remain devoted to the principles of Christian service all her life, education and not religious service would become her calling.

Alice Freeman Palmer

Her parents did not encourage her to pursue a college education. The Freemans had little money to spare, and they wanted to save money for college for their son. In addition, although by the 1870s there were numerous state colleges open to women in the United States, there were still few careers open to women besides teaching, which did not necessarily require a four-year college degree. Alice persisted, however. Her desire for higher education stemmed not only from her intense intellectual curiosity and desire for broader life experiences, but also from her pragmatism. She recognized that she might have to support herself financially even if she married, and she wanted the skills to do so. Her mother had been forced to support a family while her father went to school, and Palmer was determined to be prepared for such a situation.

After months of argument, she finally won her parents' approval by offering to pay for the education of her younger siblings once she graduated and was working as a teacher. In June 1872, at age 17, she and her father visited the University of Michigan at Ann Arbor, where Palmer took the entrance examinations. She did not pass in Greek or mathematics but the college president chose to admit her anyway. She began coursework in the fall, again following a classical curriculum based on ancient languages but adding English, the sciences, and history in later semesters.

Judging from her diary and correspondence from these years, her college experience was particularly enjoyable despite her hard work; the administration was generally encouraging of women's higher education, and she was one of several dozen female students. She emerged as a student leader and a top student, and enjoyed an active social life. Palmer also found time to be active in her church, teaching Sunday school and leading the Student Christian Association on campus.

Yet her years at Ann Arbor were not carefree. She had little money, and in her junior year she had to leave the university in the middle of the academic year to teach in order to help her parents meet expenses. Her father's medical practice was failing due to his poor health and the economic depression of the early 1870s, and Palmer often could not pay her bills. The Freemans continued to support her as best they could, allowing her to return to college for her senior year. Alice was chosen to give one of the commencement addresses when she graduated in June 1876 at age 21.

A few months later she and her younger sister **Ella Freeman** moved to Wisconsin, where Palmer took a teaching job at a women's academy in Lake Geneva. The school had promised her a salary in addition to free education for Ella. However, the school was unable to pay, and Alice fell into debt. In June 1877, she left Lake Geneva and returned to Ann Arbor, where she hoped to pursue graduate study in history. In Ann Arbor, she lived with **Lucy Andrews**, her closest friend and roommate from her college days with whom she shared a deep friendship.

Such intimate relationships between women, referred to as romantic friendships or Boston marriages, were not uncommon among middle-class women in the late Victorian era, when male-female relationships were usually kept distant and circumscribed by social convention. Although they would eventually grow apart, this friendship was Palmer's most important relationship as a young woman, and she continued to keep in touch with Andrews for years after they ceased to live together.

Palmer spent the summer of 1877 studying history, but in the fall she became principal at a high school in nearby Saginaw; her sister Ella also accepted a teaching position there. Together their incomes allowed them to support their virtually bankrupt parents. Both James Freeman and Alice's sister **Estelle Freeman** were ill with tuberculosis, increasing the financial and emotional burden Alice faced in providing for her family. Even at her young age, she felt her family obligations strongly and, to conserve costs, arranged to move the Freemans to Saginaw. Her parents and siblings appear to have accepted her leadership position in the family with little question, and allowed her to make decisions about their finances and housing arrangements. Her father also allowed her to assume his personal debts as her own.

The next two years were a trying period for Palmer, as she struggled to bring order to the poorly run high school of which she was principal while taking care of her family's many needs. Although her organizational skills and persistence served Palmer well during these years, the strain of her work combined with the death of her sister Estelle in 1879 to leave her exhausted and in poor health. Yet by late 1879 her father had improved somewhat and was able to resume his medical practice; her brother had entered medical school, and her remaining sister, Ella, had married. Although her family continued to ask for financial help from her for the rest of her life, finally Palmer could consider her own needs. She eagerly accepted a faculty position in history offered by Henry F. Durant, founder and treasurer of the newly established Wellesley College in Massachusetts, and left her family in Saginaw for New England.

At Wellesley, Palmer joined a small campus community where students and the all-female faculty lived and worked together in a shared residence. She had a challenging teaching load of history courses, and was obligated by the evangelical Durant to give a daily Bible class, in addition to public lectures and domestic duties. In February 1881, overwork took a toll on her health, and she suffered a lung hemorrhage which her doctors feared would be fatal. Yet she returned to teaching after only a few months' rest, displaying the dedication to her job and her students that made her popular with students and faculty.

In 1881, her loyalty and administrative abilities led a dying Henry Durant to overlook her youth—she was 26—and name her to succeed ***Ada Lydia Howard** as president of Wellesley. (Howard's job had been limited to executing the policies set by Durant. After his death, she herself became ill and was forced to retire before having the opportunity to run the college on her own.) Palmer remained president for six years, overseeing Wellesley's progress from a fledgling institution to a leader among American women's colleges. Soft-spoken but authoritative, she created a less hierarchical administration by integrating the faculty into policy decisions and keeping close relationships with the students, who affectionately nicknamed her "the Princess." Facing head-on the college's academic and financial problems, Palmer expanded Wellesley's faculty and curriculum and raised academic standards. Although she was unable to solve permanently its funding problem, she did keep Wellesley solvent during its difficult first years.

In addition to her daily administrative responsibilities, Palmer took on a public role in an era when college presidents were consulted by political leaders on diplomatic issues and public policy questions. She was a vocal member of numerous local and national educational associations, including the American Association of University Women. She usually spoke on the need to expand educational opportunities for women, yet she also addressed the need for higher standards for admission and faculty training, and for the modernization of curricula to include more focus on the sciences. Palmer believed that college was crucial to ennobling the mind and to fostering in young people the desire and ability to devote themselves to service, whether as doctors, teachers, or parents. Although she was most closely associated with a women's college, she strongly advocated the benefits of coeducation for both men and women. Her eloquence and public visibility made her a national figure, attracting media attention to the problems of the American education system. Although she completed a doctorate at Michigan in 1881, her contributions to the improvement of higher education would lead to numerous honorary degrees as well, including a doctorate from Columbia University in 1887.

Palmer also led Wellesley's religious life, conducting chapel services and organizing the Christian student association. Although Wellesley remained a Christian school, Palmer was not evangelical and the college was open to women of all religious beliefs. By the end of her years as president she had begun to secularize the curriculum, transforming the daily Bible study into a Biblical studies department. Palmer's other accomplishments at Wellesley include the implementation of systems for tenure and seniority for the faculty, two principles which would later become the norm among American colleges.

In 1886, Alice met a widowed Harvard philosophy professor, George Herbert Palmer. They fell in love, but for months they debated whether to marry. The conflict centered on Alice's career; she was in high demand at Wellesley and as a public speaker and authority on higher education. Although both supported a woman's right to work and earn her own income, neither could abandon the social convention that married women did not work, because a woman's first duty was always to her husband. It was an agonizing decision for Palmer; the correspondence between them from this period shows two intellectuals trying to reconcile their love with their belief in a woman's right to a career. In the end Alice decided to marry George and resigned from Wellesley following their wedding in December 1887. Yet her emotional and intellectual need for meaningful work would lead her back to Wellesley only a few weeks later, and correspondence from her later years shows that she always felt ambivalent about her decision to marry.

Learning alone is not enough for women.

—Alice Freeman Palmer

At Wellesley, although she was officially only on the board of trustees, she became in essence a co-president with her successor ***Helen Shafer** (1839–1894), whom she herself had picked, and used her experience and expertise to guide Wellesley's development in its faculty recruitment, curricula, and budget. She also became an important supporter of the fledgling Harvard Annex, the women's adjunct to Harvard later to become Radcliffe College. But in June 1888, George Palmer persuaded his wife to take a year-long European tour, both as a honeymoon and to give Alice the rest her health required after years of exhausting work.

She returned to her work refreshed and determined to maintain her place as a leading educator. Taking up her unofficial role at Wellesley again, she continued to participate in educational associations, and did a yearly lecture tour. In 1889, she was named to the Massachusetts Board of Education, of which she remained an active member until her death. After finally deciding to give up her career to marry, Palmer was busier professionally than ever. In constant demand by schools, colleges, and associations, she traveled across the East and Midwest on a paid speaking tour for several months a year, earning a considerable supplemental income. She continued to lead in the struggle to make the Harvard Annex into its own permanent, funded women's college, in particular heading the effort to raise an endowment for the college. Yet she was clearly divided between her desire to be George Palmer's wife and her desire to be a leader of higher education. Even while she was on the road, she reassured George in her letters that her first commitment was to him.

In 1892, the uneasy agreement between Palmer and her husband about her professional activities became a conflict. William Rainey Harper, founder of the University of Chicago, offered the couple important positions at the new college: Alice to be dean of the women's college, and George to be head of the philosophy department. While Alice was eager to accept the joint appointments, her husband did not want to leave his position at Harvard and wrote to Harper declining the offer for both of them. Yet Palmer refused to give up her chance to guide the development of a major coeducational institution. After months of debate, they compromised; Alice would accept a temporary dean position starting in fall 1892, and would spend no more than three months a year in Chicago. George would remain at Harvard.

From the start, Palmer recognized the importance of Chicago's admission of women students to its programs as a model for other coeducational schools to follow. Hoping to make Chicago a leader in equality for women in higher education, as dean she fought for fair treatment for female faculty and students. She counseled Harper on issues beyond her official duties as the dean of the women's college, advising him on budgets, facilities, residences, faculty appointments, admissions, and student life. In all Palmer had a major impact on the early growth of the university. Yet by the end of her second year, growing policy disagreements with Harper, who was trying to narrow her administrative role, led Alice to resign her post in December 1894. Never robust in health, she also had wearied of frequent travel between Chicago and her home in Cambridge.

In August 1895, the Palmers sailed again for Europe on a year-long sabbatical, staying in France, Italy, and Germany. On their return in 1896, Palmer took up her neglected work as a trustee of Wellesley College once again. She led the other trustees in improving Wellesley's academic standards, hiring a better-educated faculty, and making student and faculty life more secular. Despite her long absence from Wellesley's affairs, she quickly re-emerged at the center of the college's administration, testifying to the respect in which the Wellesley community held her. For the next several years, she combined this work with extensive and frequent speaking tours across the eastern United States, as well as consultant work with the administrations of other colleges, such as Barnard and John Hopkins. While the issue of women's education remained her primary concern as always, Palmer was recognized and consulted as an expert in coeducational curriculum development, faculty hiring, and the provision of a nurturing and stimulating campus life. In 1897, her most popular speech, "Why Go To College?," was published to promote her message of full equality for women and the importance of higher education for both sexes in creating happier, more prosperous citizens.

In addition to their professional duties, the Palmers maintained a full social and family life. They frequently entertained friends and relatives at their home in Cambridge and their farm outside Boston. They also took into their home numerous children during the 1890s, helping impoverished relatives and friends by taking care of their children or providing a home for young adults attending Harvard and Radcliffe. The Palmers were dedicated foster parents who took much pleasure in caring for young people, and their correspondence shows that they sometimes regretted their choice not to have children of their own. Overall the turn of the century was a prosperous, active, and contented period for Alice Freeman Palmer; she was at the pinnacle of her profession and enjoyed a rich family life as well.

In September 1902, Palmer and her husband took a break from their demanding schedules for another European vacation. Two months later in Paris, she underwent emergency surgery for an intestinal disorder, and died at the hospital three days later, on December 6. George Palmer had her body cremated and brought her ashes back to Massachusetts. Alice Freeman Palmer was 47 years old.

She was remembered nationwide as a dedicated teacher and a leading voice in American educational reform. Ceremonies at all of the colleges with which she had been associated honored her memory. Wellesley's trustees set up scholarships in her name, while the University of Michigan established the Alice Freeman Palmer chair. The University of Chicago paid tribute to her with a campanile erected in her honor in 1908. George Palmer memorialized Alice Freeman Palmer by publishing some of the poems she had written for him in *A Marriage Cycle* and the few essays on education she had written in his book *The Teacher: Essays and Addresses on Education*. George also composed a full-length biography on his late wife, published in 1915.

SOURCES:

Bordin, Ruth. *Alice Freeman Palmer: The Evolution of the New Woman.* Ann Arbor, MI: University of Michigan Press, 1993.

Palmer, George H. *The Life of Alice Freeman Palmer.* Boston, MA: Houghton Mifflin, 1915.

———, and Alice Freeman Palmer. *The Teacher: Essays and Addresses on Education.* Boston, MA: Houghton Mifflin, 1908.

SUGGESTED READING:

Glasscock, Jean, ed. *Wellesley College 1875–1975: A Century of Women.* Wellesley, MA: Wellesley College, 1975.

Hazard, Caroline, ed. *An Academic Courtship: Letters of Alice Freeman Palmer and George Herbert Palmer.* Cambridge, MA: Harvard University Press, 1940.

Solomon, Barbara M. *In the Company of Educated Women: A History of Women and Higher Education in America.* New Haven, CT: Yale University Press, 1985.

COLLECTIONS:

Alice Freeman Palmer Papers, Bentley Historical Library, University of Michigan, Ann Arbor, Michigan.

Alice Freeman Palmer Papers, Wellesley College Archives, Wellesley College, Wellesley, Massachusetts.

Laura York, M.A. in History,
University of California, Riverside, California

Palmer, Anne (1661–1722).

See Villiers, Barbara for sidebar.

Palmer, Barbara (c. 1641–1709).

See Villiers, Barbara.

Palmer, Barbara (1672–1737).

See Villiers, Barbara for sidebar.

Palmer, Bertha Honoré

(1849–1918)

Chicago socialite and philanthropist who was the main organizer of the Woman's Building at the Columbian Exposition of 1893. *Name variations: Mrs. Potter Palmer; Bertha Honore Palmer. Born Bertha Honoré in Louisville, Kentucky, on May 22, 1849; died of breast cancer in Chicago, Illinois, on May 5, 1918; daughter of Henry H. Honoré (a busi-*

nessman in hardware and cutlery) and Eliza J. (Carr) Honoré; graduated from the Convent of the Visitation in Georgetown, Washington, D.C., 1867; married Potter Palmer (an entrepreneur), on July 28, 1870; children: sons Honoré (b. February 1, 1874) and Potter II (b. October 8, 1875).

As a leading figure in Chicago society, Bertha Honoré Palmer was at the center of social events and causes in that city throughout her life. She organized benefits, held receptions, and hosted dinners to fete scions of American business and government, European nobility, labor leaders, and welfare reformers; she was also a supporter of ***Jane Addams**' welfare work at Hull House, and was concerned with the issues of women in the workplace. But no activity engaged her more or better encompassed her vision and her skills than her role as chair of the board of "Lady Managers" at the Columbian Exposition held in Chicago in 1893. Four months after the closing of the extended "world's fair," Governor John Altgeld of Illinois wrote to Palmer from the state capital at Springfield, praising her for the job she had done and assuring her that the cause of women's rights had been advanced a century by her work. Posterity, he wrote, would view "the delicate hand that directed this work [as] the hand of a genius." More than a century later, if such language seems a bit flowery, and the attitude condescending, evidence would indicate that the governor's sentiments were in fact not far wrong.

Bertha Honoré Palmer was born in Louisville, Kentucky, on May 22, 1849, the daughter of Henry H. Honoré, who was descended from a Louisville mercantile family, and **Eliza J. Carr Honoré**, who was related to the Edward D'Arcy family who settled 17th-century Maryland. As members of old aristocratic Southern families, both parents also took particular pride in the French portions of their lineage. Bertha Honoré had a younger sister, **Ida**, and four brothers, Adrian, Henry, Nathaniel, and Lockwood. Heir to a mercantile business in hardware and cutlery, in 1855 Henry Honoré moved his family to the frontier city of Chicago, where his enterprises in business and land development eventually expanded to include philanthropies involving the "planned parks and developments along with the boulevard system that girdles Chicago today."

Opposite page
Bertha Honoré Palmer

Bertha attended St. Xavier's Academy in Chicago, and following the end of the Civil War traveled to Washington, D.C., to attend the Convent of the Visitation in Georgetown. Distinguished for her academic achievements in botany, logic, philosophy, astronomy, literature, algebra, and chemistry, she was one of six students in the senior circle who received highest honors at her graduation in June 1867. She was also chosen to be one of the harpists who performed the Grand March at the graduation ceremony. After her return to Chicago she became a popular debutante there, and soon was being courted by Potter Palmer, a wealthy young entrepreneur whom she had first met when she was 12. They were married at her family's home by the Rev. J.S. Sweeney on July 28, 1870. The ceremony, which was attended by 40 close friends, was followed by an elaborate reception and dinner for 500 guests. After a honeymoon tour of Europe, the newlyweds returned to Chicago. The following year, they were among the many who lost most of their property in the disastrous Chicago fire of October 8, 1871, but the couple and their parents were able to regroup and reestablish themselves with the same prosperity they had known before. After the reconstruction of the Palmer House Hotel, the Palmers briefly took up residence there while awaiting the completion of their new "castle" on Chicago's Lakeside Drive. Palmer and her husband had two sons, Honoré, born on February 1, 1874, and Potter II, born on October 8, 1875, the fourth anniversary of the Chicago fire.

The ostentatious new home of the Potter Palmers included an elevator and a barbican and turret in the European style, and its numerous rooms were decorated with tapestries, furniture, art and mosaics from Europe. (After the 1890s, the art would include a magnificent collection of French Impressionist paintings.) Reportedly, there were no outside locks on the mansion's doors. Benefit galas, dinners, and receptions were a way of life for the couple, and Palmer, entertaining in her diamond tiara and "rope of pearls," was Chicago's social queen. ***Ishbel Ross** suggested the grandeur of Palmer's life with the title of her 1960 biography, *Silhouette in Diamonds: The Life of Mrs. Potter Palmer.*

The grandeur was not without substance, however, as the World's Columbian Exposition would prove. In April 1890, President Benjamin Harrison signed into law a bill establishing the World's Columbian Exposition, intended to celebrate the 400th anniversary of the arrival of Christopher Columbus on the American continent. Chicago was chosen as the site for this event, which was to be dedicated on October 20–21, 1892, and to open for visitors in May 1893. Prior to its passage, Representative William Springer of Illinois had amended the World's Fair bill to include a "Board of Lady Managers," consisting of two delegates from each state and eight at-large members from Chicago. These new positions were intended to enrich the event with the input of women, a concept that was expanded to encompass the inclusion in the fair of a Woman's Building. When the Board of Lady Managers convened on November 20, 1890, Bertha Honoré Palmer was elected "president" and assumed the title of chair. For the next three years, this office was to engage her time and energy while providing a forum for her excellent management abilities and leadership skills.

Early on, the board decided that the Woman's Building would serve as a sort of museum exhibit illustrating the progress of women through the previous 400 years. At Palmer's direction, it was also decided that the building itself would be designed by a woman. The architect chosen was ***Sophia Hayden**, the first woman to graduate from the four-year architecture program at the Massachusetts Institute of Technology, and her building was the first constructed on the fair grounds. Also under the management of the Board of Lady Managers—more specifically, Palmer—were two other installations, a Children's Building and a dormitory for women visitors. All were run "in the black."

The Palmers made a trip to Europe, working up a general enthusiasm for the exposition as they appealed to governments and to women in various countries to participate in the exhibits for the Woman's Building. A contemporary source said of Palmer, "few women and not many men have become so widely known and universally admired as Mrs. Palmer—all nations have received her and delighted to honor her, giving aid in securing exhibits for the success of this project." Royal dignitaries lent their influence in obtaining the contributions from their countries. Queen ***Margaret of Savoy** (1851–1925) of Italy sent a treasure of historic laces, and Lady **Ishbel Aberdeen** of Scotland oversaw the establishment of the Irish Village, augmented with the handiwork of Irish women, on the exposition's popular Midway. The aristocracy of other countries—Austria, Belgium, Spain, Turkey, Japan, Siam (now Thailand), Egypt, Mexico, and nations of South America—all made substantial contributions, assembling what grew into a magnificent exhibit of women's art and handicrafts from around the world. In August 1892, well before the opening of the exposition, the Woman's Building was proclaimed "Woman's Triumph" by *Harper's Bazaar*.

Displays were also provided by most states, notable among them Utah, which offered a silk

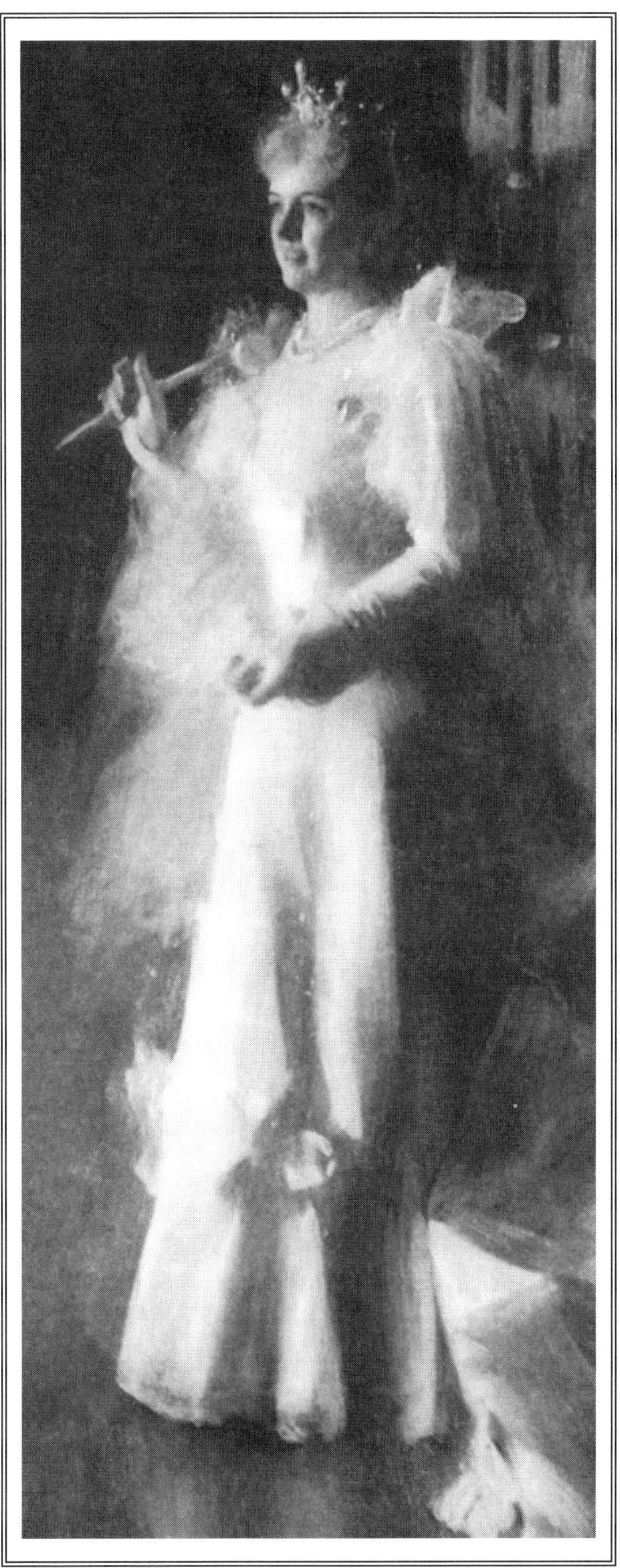

exhibit, and Ohio, which contributed a pottery exhibit. Among the larger works of art were two great murals, one signifying "modern woman" by *Mary Cassatt, *The Modern Woman as Glorified by Worth* and one of "primitive woman" by *Mary Fairchild (MacMonnies) Low, *Young Women Pursuing Fame*. Cassatt, an American working in Paris who was associated with the French Impressionists, greatly admired Palmer's organizing powers and her determination that women should be seen as "someone" and not "something." Demonstrating this very point, the exhibits within the Woman's Building also included an extensive library of women's publications, scientific and mechanical inventions made by women, a model kitchen, and statistics of women's contributions to business and labor as well as examples of their contributions to the arts, industry, sciences, and reform.

Nearby was the Children's Building, which served both as a day-care facility and as an exhibit of the latest methods in child-raising and in medical and educational practices related to children, including the new kindergarten techniques. Children's art was exhibited as well as new methods of lip-reading for deaf children. The Woman's Dormitory provided clean, safe accommodations at reasonable prices for women attending the exposition without male companions.

> It was the proudest moment of my life when I was told last Saturday, with a heartfelt handshake . . . by one of our visitors, that seeing me had given her more pleasure than anything at the Fair, except the Ferris wheel.
>
> **—Bertha Honoré Palmer**

Reputed to be one of the most popular buildings of the Fair, the Woman's Building offered daily addresses by noted women speakers from America and other countries, as well as musicals, banquets, and teas. The building's roof garden was a favorite dining facility, notable also for featuring a dishwashing machine, which had been designed by a woman. Models of this same machine were used at a number of food establishments throughout the fair. In May 1893, the month the exposition opened, Palmer and her Lady Managers also sponsored the World's Congress of Representative Women, a week of intensive meetings featuring delegates from women's organizations around the world. The World's Congress Auxiliary of the World's Columbian Exposition, also under the auspices of the Lady Managers, offered a daily program of lectures, addresses and musical programs featuring women artists. The talks were later compiled in *The Congress of Women Held in the Woman's Building*.

More than 27 million people attended the Columbian Exposition during the six months it was open, from May 1, 1893, to October 30, 1893. By consolidating and displaying the achievements and interests of women in an unprecedented manner to such a wide audience, Palmer and her board created what turned out to be a catalyst for the entire woman's movement. *Susan B. Anthony declared that the fair had done more for the cause of woman suffrage than had 25 years of agitation, giving the suffrage movement "unprecedented prestige in the world of thought." Speaking at the International Women's Congress in Berlin in 1904, a decade after the exposition's end, renowned sculptor *Adelaide Johnson referred back to the event when she declared that the days were over when women artists were "looked upon with curiosity, classed, and perhaps indulged as freaks." She noted that "the great impetus in the United States of America that ushered so many women into this active work as professionals in the plastic forms of art, came with the Columbian Exposition in Chicago in 1893."

At the closing meeting of the Board of Lady Managers, Palmer conveyed her satisfaction with the Woman's Building with considerable pride and a touch of humor, referring to the amusement ride that had been proclaimed the fair's symbol of American ingenuity:

> Here we have welcomed and listened to the great thinkers of our own and other countries, and to musicians from every clime; we have welcomed guests both distinguished and humble, among the most pleasant gatherings being the popular Saturday afternoon receptions, when all were made welcome and we were overwhelmed by discovering the number of our friends, and the warmth of their kindly feeling. It was the proudest moment of my life when I was told last Saturday, with a heartfelt handshake, and with accents of deepest sincerity, by one of our visitors, that seeing me had given her more pleasure than anything at the Fair, except the Ferris wheel.

The particular focus on women's achievements was not repeated at the national and international expositions that followed, although in 1900 President William McKinley appointed Palmer the only woman member of the national commission representing the U.S. at the Paris Exposition. With her husband, she lived in Paris for two years while working on the commission, and for her contributions to the exposition Palmer was presented with France's Legion of Honor. She was only the third women in history so honored, after *Rosa Bonheur and *Florence Nightingale.

The Palmers' successful marriage was ended with Potter Palmer's death in May 1902. Palmer continued her social and philanthropic activities, serving as a trustee of the Woman's College of Chicago's Northwestern University and expanding her fortune and interests with land holdings and business ventures in Florida. Demonstrating her father's zest for development, after 1910 she invested in 80,000 acres in Florida, building up an industry of orange groves and a Brahma cattle ranch in Hillsborough and Sarasota counties that increased her $8 million inheritance from her husband to more than $20 million. Palmer also encouraged and sponsored the region as a recreation and retirement center. She remained close to her siblings throughout their lives, and eventually enjoyed the company of six grandchildren. Bertha Palmer died of breast cancer in Chicago on May 5, 1918, just short of her 69th birthday. The city's flag was lowered to half mast on order of Mayor G.W. Franklin. At her funeral at St. James' Episcopal Church, the Imperial Quartet sang two of her favorite hymns, "Lead Kindly Light" and "One Sweetly Solemn Thought," in a service that brought an epoch in Chicago history to a close.

SOURCES:

Eagle, Mary Kavanaugh Oldham, ed. *The Congress of Women: Held in the Woman's Building, World's Columbian Exposition, Chicago, U.S.A., 1893.* Chicago, IL: International, 1895.

Harper's Bazaar, issues published in 1892 and 1893.

Hinding, Andrea, ed. *Woman's History Sources: A Guide to Archives and Manuscript Collections in the United States.* Vol. 1. NY: R.R. Bowker, 1979.

Ross, Ishbel. *Silhouette in Diamonds: The Life of Mrs. Potter Palmer.* NY: Harper and Brothers, 1960.

Weimann, Jeanne Madeline. *The Fair Women: The Story of the Woman's Building World's Columbian Exposition.* Chicago, IL: Academy, 1981.

COLLECTIONS:

Sarasota Historical Commission has correspondence, Palmer's will, and clippings; Library Manuscripts Division of the Chicago Historical Society has letters and other documents relating to the business of the Board of Lady Managers which were kept by Bertha Palmer.

Harriet Horne Arrington,
women's biographer, Salt Lake City, Utah

Palmer, Elizabeth (1778–1853).

See Peabody, Elizabeth Palmer (1804–1894) for sidebar.

Palmer, Frances Flora (1812–1876)

English-born American lithographer. *Name variations: Fanny Palmer; Frances Flora Bond Palmer; occasionally signed work "F.F. Palmer." Born Frances Flora Bond on June 26, 1812, in Leicester, England; died of tuberculosis on August 20, 1876, in Brooklyn, New York; daughter of Robert Bond (an attorney) and Elizabeth Bond; married Edmund Seymour Palmer, in early 1830s (died 1859); children: Flora E. and Edmund Seymour (possibly twins, b. about 1834).*

Immigrated to United States (early 1840s); drew great praise for two lithographic views of Manhattan (1849); later lithographs captured the American public's imagination regarding western expansion and manifest destiny (late 1860s).

Selected works: The High Bridge at Harlem New York *(1849);* American Farm Scenes *(1853);* American Winter Scenes *(1854);* American Country Life *(1855);* A Midnight Race on the Mississippi *(1860);* The 'Lighting Express' Train, Leaving the Junction *(1863);* American Express Train *(1864);* Season of Blossoms *(1865);* The Rocky Mountains, Emigrants Crossing the Plains *(1866);* Across the Continent, Westward the Course of Empire Takes Its Way *(1868).*

Frances Palmer, benefiting from a well-bred English education, became a noted American artist. Pressed by the need to be the chief provider for her family and committed to her art, she proved herself capable of capturing America's imagination. She masterfully portrayed scenes and events that embodied the widespread belief in the nation's limitless potential during the rapid U.S. expansion of the mid-19th century.

Frances Palmer, called Fanny, was born in England on June 26, 1812, the first of three children of Robert and **Elizabeth Bond**. A well-to-do London lawyer, her father provided for her education at private schools, including Miss Linwood's, where she studied music, art and lithography. Her brother and sister were also educated in the arts. In the early 1830s, she married Edmund Seymour Palmer, a gentlemanly type who soon proved to be financially unreliable, and gave birth to their children Flora and Edmund Seymour, Jr. (assumed to be twins) around 1834. Financial burdens mounted. In the early 1840s, accompanied by Frances' brother, sister, and brother-in-law, the family sailed to New York City. There Palmer used her earlier training in drafting to start a lithographic printing and publishing business, F. & S. Palmer, with her husband, producing prints of landscapes and of flowers as well as music cover sheets. Soon she added architectural elevations on stone. Though she exhibited exceptional skills in lithography, the business faltered, and in 1848 the family moved to Brooklyn.

In 1849, Palmer joined the prestigious Nathaniel Currier lithograph firm as a staff artist. She attained instant success with the publication of two lithographic views of Manhattan. A watercolor painting that many later would consider her most significant original artwork, *The High Bridge at Harlem New York*, also was published as a lithograph by Currier that year. Over the next decade, Palmer produced numerous mid- to large-sized country landscapes and farm scenes directly on the stone medium. She also developed the process for printing a background tint from stone. Her better works during this time included *American Farm Scenes* (1853), *American Winter Scenes* (1854), and *American Country Life* (1855). Palmer also collaborated with Charles Currier in improving the lithographic crayon. In 1857, James M. Ives joined the firm, which became known as Currier & Ives. Through Ives' artistic influence, Palmer's work became more varied and dramatic, as exhibited by *A Midnight Race on the Mississippi* (1860), *The 'Lightning Express' Train, Leaving the Junction* (1863), and *American Express Train* (1864). In the later 1860s, she adopted an epic art style along U.S. western expansion themes. Among the most notable examples of these lithographs are the wagon train in *The Rocky Mountains, Emigrants Crossing the Plains* (1866) and *Across the Continent, Westward the Course of Empire Takes Its Way* (1868). Unfortunately, Ives also exerted a negative influence on Palmer's work, as he drew human figures in her lithographs which meshed poorly with her artistic style. Palmer became recognized as one of Currier & Ives' most prolific artists, producing around 200 known lithographs for the firm (many other works likely appeared anonymously) before her retirement in 1868. Her artwork was reproduced hundreds of times on calendars and greeting cards throughout the 20th century, uncredited except for the name of Currier & Ives.

Well known as a personable, cheerful, yet intense individual, Palmer had a habit of working while bent closely over her projects which eventually left her with a permanent stoop. As one of the top American lithographers of her time, as well as the only woman then working in the medium, she enjoyed broad success with the public. Her reproductions hung in many homes, both capturing and propelling the romanticized vision of the new American West for the many who had never seen it. (Palmer herself never traveled beyond New Jersey.) Her husband, who had worked in a tavern, died in 1859 from a possibly drunken tumble down the stairway of a Brooklyn hotel. Her son died in 1867 from tuberculosis, the same disease that killed Palmer herself, at age 64, in 1876. She was buried in Brooklyn's Greenwood Cemetery.

SOURCES:

James, Edward T., ed. *Notable American Women, 1607–1950*. Cambridge, MA: The Belknap Press of Harvard University Press, 1971.

Read, Phyllis J., and Bernard L. Witlieb. *The Book of Women's Firsts*. NY: Random House, 1992.

Rubinstein, Charlotte Streifer. *American Women Artists*. Boston, MA: G.K. Hall, 1982.

SUGGESTED READING:

Currier and Ives' America (1952) and *A Currier & Ives Treasury* (1955), both edited by Colin Simkin, contain many of Palmer's lithographs.

Richard C. Hanes,
freelance writer, Eugene, Oregon

Palmer, Helen (1917–1979)

Australian writer and teacher. *Born Helen Gwynneth Palmer on May 9, 1917, in Emerald, Victoria, Australia; died on May 6, 1979, in Australia; daughter of Vance Palmer (a writer) and Nettie Palmer (1885–1964, a writer and literary critic); attended Presbyterian Ladies' College in Melbourne, 1934; Melbourne University, B.A., Dip.Ed., 1939.*

Began career as a teacher (1939); joined the Women's Australian Auxiliary Air Force as director of educational services (1942); traveled to China (1952); founded (1957) and edited Outlook, *a journal dedicated to progressive socialist issues (1957–70).*

Selected writings: An Australian Teacher in China *(1953);* Beneath the Southern Cross *(1954);* Australia: The First Hundred Years *(with Jessie MacLeod, 1956);* After the First Hundred Years *(with MacLeod, 1961);* Fencing Australia *(1961);* 'Banjo' Paterson *(1966).*

Helen Palmer was born in 1917 in Emerald, Victoria, Australia, the daughter of ***Nettie Palmer** and Vance Palmer, both writers and social activists. Helen continued the tradition by espousing progressive causes, particularly in education and in humanist socialism. After graduating from Melbourne University in 1939, she began teaching in Victoria, Australia. During World War II, she served as educational services director of the Women's Australian Auxiliary Air Force, and then was employed at the Commonwealth Office of Education in Sydney. In 1948, she returned to Melbourne and resumed teaching.

Palmer was a member of the Communist Party of Australia, and traveled against the Australian government's wishes: while the Korean War raged, she attended the 1952 Asian and Pacific Peace Congress in Beijing, China, and published her experiences on this journey the following year in *An Australian Teacher in China*. (That year, she also contributed a poem about a famous shearers' strike, "The Ballad of 1891," to the musical *Reedy River*.) In 1957, around the time she was expelled from the Communist Party, Palmer founded and began editing *Outlook*, a bimonthly journal focused on discussions of various progressive socialist issues. The range of issues included political developments in the Soviet Union, Australian policy issues, apartheid in South Africa, civil liberties for Aborigines, and the Vietnam War. She served as editor of the journal until it ceased publication in 1970.

Throughout her life, Palmer's spirited debates about the educational process influenced the quality and philosophy of the Australian education system. On a practical level, she made a case for teaching social history and authored several Australian historical texts for schools in the 1950s and 1960s. As a member of the New South Wales Teachers' Federation, she also strove to improve teachers' working conditions. Years later, her analyses concerning the central role of education in the lives of Australians would be at the forefront of educational policy discussions. Witty and quiet spoken, Palmer exerted a profound influence on progressive Australian thinking, and remained an important figure on the Australian left for decades.

SOURCES:

Radi, Heather, ed. *200 Australian Women: A Redress Anthology.* NSW, Australia: Women's Redress Press, 1988.

Wilde, William, Joy Hooten, and Barry Andrews. *The Oxford Companion to Australian Literature.* Melbourne, Australia: Oxford University Press, 1985.

SUGGESTED READING:

Bridges, Doreen, ed. *Helen Palmer's Outlook*, 1982.

Richard C. Hanes,
freelance writer, Eugene, Oregon

Palmer, Henrietta (1856–1911).

See Winter, John Strange.

Palmer, Janet Gertrude (1885–1964).

See Palmer, Nettie.

Palmer, Lilli (1914–1986)

A refugee from Nazi Germany who became a noted film and stage actress, writer, and painter. *Name variations: Lilli Peiser; Maria Lilli Peiser. Born Maria Lilli Peiser on May 24, 1914, in the German city of Posen (now Poznan, Poland); died of cancer on January 27, 1986, in Los Angeles; daughter of Dr. Alfred Peiser (a surgeon) and Rose (Lissman) Peiser; attended Ilka Gruning School of Acting, Berlin, 1930–32; married Rex Harrison (an actor), in January 1943 (divorced 1957); married Carlos Thompson (an actor), in 1957; children (first marriage) Carey.*

Made first stage appearance (1932); exiled in France (1933); exiled in Britain (1934); made first film appearance (1935); met Rex Harrison (1939); emigrated to U.S. (1945); made first American film (1946); endured Carole Landis affair (1948); made first appearance on Broadway (1949); started New York television program, "Lilli Palmer Presents" (1951); made first German film (1954); met Carlos Thompson (1955); divorced Harrison and married Thompson (1957); held first art exhibit, London (1965); published autobiography (1975); wrote first novel, The Red Raven *(1978).*

Selected filmography: Crime Unlimited *(UK, 1935);* Secret Agent *(UK, 1936);* The Gentle Sex *(UK, 1943);* English Without Tears *(UK, 1944);* The Rake's Progress *(UK, 1945);* Cloak and Dagger *(US, 1946);* Body and Soul *(US, 1947);* The Four-Poster *(US, 1952);* Feuerwerk *(Ger., 1954);* Anastasia—Die letzte Zarentochter *(Ger., 1956);* Madchen in Uniform *(Ger., 1958);* But Not For Me *(US, 1959);* Conspiracy of Hearts *(UK, 1960);* The Pleasure of His Company *(US, 1961);* Le Rendezvous de Minuit *(Fr., 1961);* The Counterfeit Traitor *(US, 1962);* Miracle of the Wild Stallions *(US, 1963);* Operation Crossbow *(UK, 1965);* Amorous Adventures of Moll Flanders *(UK, 1965);* Oedipus the King *(UK, 1968);* Lotte in Weimar *(E. Ger., 1968);* The Boys from Brazil *(US, 1978);* The Holcroft Covenant *(UK, 1985).*

Plays: No Time for Comedy *(1940);* My Name is Aquilon *(1949);* Caesar and Cleopatra *(1950);* Bell, Book and Candle *(1951);* Suite in Three Keys *(1966).*

Writings: (autobiography) Change Lobsters—and Dance *(1975); (novel)* The Red Raven *(1978); (novel)* A Time to Embrace *(1980); (novel)* Night Music *(1982).*

A woman of broad interests, Lilli Palmer was an important film and stage actress in the United States and Europe in the three decades following World War II; she was also an accomplished novelist and painter. As both a successful performer in her own right as well as the wife of renowned actor Rex Harrison, she was an acquaintance, and sometimes friend and confidante, to many leading figures in the arts and international society of her time, including *****Helen Keller**, Noel Coward, and George Bernard Shaw. Despite her later achievements, as a young German woman and aspiring actress of

Jewish extraction, Lilli Palmer found her life entangled with some of the most tragic and painful events of the 20th century. Her years as a refugee and her subsequent return to Germany loomed large in her own assessment of her life.

The year of her birth, 1914, saw Europe plunged into the prolonged trauma of World War I, in which her father, a noted physician, served with distinction in the German army. The close of the war brought territorial losses to Germany, including the family's home city of Posen which became a part of Poland. During the mid-1920s, after a period of agonizing postwar unrest marked by failed attempts at revolution by forces on both the extreme right and the extreme left, Germany enjoyed a brief era of renewed stability and prosperity. Her family prospered once again in their new home in Berlin.

The onset of the great global economic crisis in 1929 shattered Germany's recovery and discredited the recently established parliamentary government of the Weimar Republic. German life witnessed the growing strength of Adolf Hitler's Nazi party with its message of open hatred against the Jewish population of Germany. For a time, a privileged schoolgirl like Lilli was able to concern herself with crushes on her teachers, relations with her playmates, and early ventures on the school stage. When Hitler came to power in the first months of 1933, however, individuals like Palmer and her family were among the first to be affected.

Lilli Palmer was born Lilli Peiser in the city of Posen, then in the eastern portion of the province of Prussia, on May 24, 1914. Her mother Rose was an aspiring actress who had given up her stage career to marry Alfred Peiser, the young doctor with whom she would live in middle-class contentment for a quarter of a century. The second of three daughters, Lilli grew up in Berlin in the 1920s where her father was by then chief of surgery at a major hospital.

As she recalled in her autobiography, "There was never any doubt in my mind that I would become an actress." She fought off her father's urging that she follow in his footsteps to become a physician. Instead, she reveled in putting on informal plays with her friends at grammar school, such as their version of Fritz Lang's film *The Nibelungs*. At the age of 16, she prevailed upon her father to let her start attending high school in the mornings while she spent her afternoons at a drama school. She graduated in the spring of 1932 with a contract to perform at the Darmstadt State Theater.

The young Jewish actress was blissfully unaware of the political changes about to sweep away her family's position and her own ambitions for a career on the German stage. The operetta in which she landed her first good role opened shortly after Hitler became the head of Germany's government in early 1933. "Now that Hitler was actually in power," she later recalled thinking, "he would surely realize how complicated everything was and stop screaming." In short order, however, her new contract with the Frankfurt Opera was canceled. Her final appearance at Darmstadt took place in a poisonous atmosphere: the local Nazi Storm Troop leader threatened to disrupt the performance. Only word that her father was a decorated veteran of World War I persuaded him to allow the play to go on without interruption.

With no future in prospect on the German stage, Lilli left to join her sister **Irene Peiser** in Paris. The two young refugees survived by singing in small-time cabarets, improvising costumes from raincoats. With Germans unwelcome in France, they presented themselves as "The Viennese Sisters." In early 1934, they returned briefly to Germany on the occasion of their father's death. The growing isolation of families like theirs was evident in the fact that the Peisers' youngest daughter had been forced to leave the school that each of her older sisters had attended. In a more profound tragedy five years later, Palmer's Aunt Cilly committed suicide just before Nazi police agents of the Gestapo could arrest her.

Back in Paris, Palmer's luck changed. During one of her nightclub appearances, she attracted the attention of executives from the Disney film company. A series of crucial introductions followed: to United Artists executives, to film star Douglas Fairbanks, and to the British film producer Alexander Korda. Fluent in English—her father had insisted that she learn it as a child—she crossed the Channel with high hopes. In 1934, she began work on a cluster of films in Britain. She soon acquired one of the most precious possessions for a refugee in Europe in the 1930s: the right to live and work permanently in Britain.

Two individuals helped to shape her life and career over the next decades. Drama coach **Elsa Schreiber** took the young novice in hand and taught Palmer the techniques of acting. In 1939, at the start of World War II, she met the English actor Rex Harrison. She had recently ended a long-standing relationship with Rolf Gerard, a painter and medical student. Married with a young son, Harrison was separated from his first wife **Marjorie Thomas**.

Lilli Palmer

The courtship of Lilli Palmer and Rex Harrison coincided with the early portion of World War II, and both were witnesses to the Battle of Britain. Driving around the countryside near London, they looked up to see British and German fighter planes battling for control of the sky. With his help, she obtained desirable roles in the English theater. The two appeared together in plays given in morning and afternoon performances designed to take place when German bombers were least likely to attack.

In January 1943, Harrison and Palmer were married, and, shortly thereafter, Lilli discovered she was pregnant. She continued as a film actress during her pregnancy, but the war was a constant factor in her life. As an enemy alien in wartime Britain, the young actress was refused permission to drive an ambulance. She was restricted in the distance she could travel from home without police permission, and she had to be at home by midnight.

There was personal danger as well. In 1943, a bomb landed in her garden, leveling her home and causing her a minor injury in the form of a cut wrist, but leaving her pregnancy unaffected. A few months later, her baby, a son named Rex

Carey Alfred and known as Carey, was born in the midst of the great incendiary bombing raid of February 19, 1944. Less than four months later, a German V-2 bomb landed outside the Harrisons' home in Buckinghamshire. Carey, who was in a baby carriage on the house's terrace, survived the blast only because he was sheltered by a mass of shrubbery.

Did I ever imagine then how things were going to turn out? No, Thank God. . . . Just as well one doesn't know in advance.

—Lilli Palmer

Harrison was released from service in the RAF in 1944, and the two of them began touring to entertain Allied troops. Immediately after World War II, Palmer accompanied her husband to the United States where he was to star in an adaptation of ***Margaret Landon**'s book *Anna and the King of Siam*. Palmer was cast to star opposite Gary Cooper in the film *Cloak and Dagger,* a story of World War II espionage in which she played an Italian resistance fighter. Her career was overshadowed by her husband's, however; *Anna and the King of Siam* became a notable hit, while *Cloak and Dagger* was a critical and box-office failure.

The two foreigners soon found their initial encounter with the American movie community, as well as the surrounding curiosity of American journalism, personally unsettling. It began when Rex Harrison became involved with an American movie actress, ***Carole Landis**. A veteran of four marriages and an affair with producer Daryl Zanuck, Landis had no promising future in films, was in financial difficulties, and apparently expected Harrison to leave his wife in order to marry her.

When Harrison finally apprised Palmer of the situation, she "withdrew from the battlefield" and departed temporarily for New York and her sister **Hilde Peiser** in the summer of 1948; upon her return, she found her husband entangled in a major scandal and around 50 photographers waiting in front of their house. Carole Landis had committed suicide on the night of July 4 after dinner with Harrison. He discovered her body when he came to see her the following day. Local newspapers pointed to Rex Harrison as the villain of the event, casting him as a haughty Englishman who had led a troubled young American woman into a fatal relationship. In an effort to stop the vicious rumors, Palmer and Harrison granted an interview with local journalists only to see themselves portrayed as callous foreigners. They left Hollywood under a cloud: one gossip columnist claimed the Harrisons were evading their creditors; anonymous hate mail followed them to New York; ***Hedda Hopper**, one of the most influential of the Hollywood columnists, proclaimed, "Rex Harrison's career is dead as a mackerel."

The couple began a new stage in their artistic careers in the New York theater. With the help of her old coach Elsa Schreiber, Palmer achieved critical acclaim in *My Name is Aquilon,* a play that ran briefly. But at first it was Rex Harrison who was rewarded with a hit, *Anne of a Thousand Days,* and a Tony for his performance. Tapping the dramatic technique she had learned from Schreiber, Palmer saw her American stage career come alive with her performance as Cleopatra in George Bernard Shaw's *Caesar and Cleopatra.* The drama critic of *The New York Times* noted that "her Cleopatra is nothing short of ideal."

The two actors had been close to poverty during the wartime years in London, and their stage successes brought them a welcome prosperity. In 1949, they built a house on the Italian Riviera at Portofino. Their circle of guests ranged from ***Greta Garbo** to the Duke (Edward VIII) and ***Duchess of Windsor**. The former English king, whose mother ***Mary of Teck** (1867–1953) had been a German princess, liked to recite German poetry to Palmer and to chat with her in her native language.

Along with her husband, Palmer starred in the Broadway hit *Bell, Book and Candle* in 1950. It was the first time they had done a stage play together since 1941. One critic commented on the realism of their love scenes together, noting that "it is reassuring to know they are married in real life." She took on the added responsibility of her own program, "Lilli Palmer Presents," in the new medium of television. It was a weekly 15-minute talk show in which she let her own European background dictate the telecast's contents. "I told Americans about everything under the sun that interested me," she said; the topics ranged from Finnish saunas to the love life of George Bernard Shaw.

Success in New York led to new movie offers. The prospect of returning to the scene of so much painful publicity back in 1948 was alarming. Nonetheless, Palmer and Harrison decided to risk it. "Armed to the teeth" with advice from American friends who were conversant with Hollywood, they returned to the West Coast in 1952. They discovered that yesterday's scandal had been largely forgotten. For the press, as she later wrote, "we simply didn't exist" until Rex Harrison's smash success in *My Fair Lady* in 1956.

In 1954, Palmer returned to Germany to make her first film in her native language. The offer had come from Erik Charell, an old friend who had produced the operetta in which she had made her stage debut in the early 1930s. Shocked and uncertain at the opportunity to return to her native country, she put her hesitations aside when her brother-in-law, the British prosecutor at the Nuremberg war crimes trials, told her it was her obligation to go. "Bridges have to be built," he insisted.

The returning refugee found her stay both intriguing and unsettling. Among the film crew, she encountered former Nazis as well as innocent victims of the war's violence. She wondered how she would have behaved if her family had been acceptable Aryans and welcome members of Hitler's society. When a director from the same Frankfurt theater that had ousted her 20 years before asked her to appear on his stage, she concluded simply, "I'd come full circle." From this point onward, she accepted a number of roles in German films, although none gave her the scope for a memorable or distinguished performance.

While Palmer was in Germany, Harrison stayed in London making a film. There he fell in love with the English actress ***Kay Kendall**. In short order, Palmer's marriage with Rex Harrison collapsed. She later recalled that the wartime years of their marriage and the period immediately afterward had been deeply satisfying: "We had seven years of true happiness together." Nonetheless, Palmer had faced and accepted Harrison's romantic entanglements without open protest since their days in Hollywood. This affair was different, and Harrison's tie with Kendall in the years from 1954 through 1956 signaled his apparent abandonment of the marriage. Palmer's despair was so evident that in 1956 a sympathetic friend played matchmaker and put Palmer in contact with the Argentine movie actor Carlos Thompson. Thompson had piqued her interest in a casual meeting at a Hollywood party the previous year.

Palmer's future with the man who was to become her second husband was complicated by the remnants of her first marriage. At the close of 1956, Harrison learned that Kendall was dying of leukemia. The doctor supervising the case met with the Harrisons and urged them to make provisions to care for the stricken young actress. As Palmer described it in her autobiography, she urged Harrison to marry Kendall. "You've got to consider it like a war mission. You've got to do it." He himself concluded it would be best not to inform Kay of her fatal illness. The situation took a complicated turn when Palmer received an impulsive plea from Harrison. Desperate for emotional support, he asked her to promise she would leave Thompson and return to him after Kendall's death. As she wrote, she was unable to say no and to let him "cope alone, unaided, and in total secrecy." Instead, she said, "I lied and pledged myself to return to him when all was over." In short order, she filed for divorce to end her marriage of 14 years, Harrison married Kendall, and Palmer married Thompson. Three years later, after Kendall's death in September 1959, she wrote a final letter to Harrison, ending their relationship permanently.

In the following two decades, Palmer continued her career as a film actress. She returned to Hollywood for a number of undistinguished parts opposite stars like Clark Gable and Fred Astaire. In 1962, however, she gave one of her most memorable performances as the doomed German resistance figure Marianne von Mollendorf in *The Counterfeit Traitor* with William Holden. Meanwhile, she exhibited her artistic versatility with showings of her paintings. Her interest in the visual arts dated back to the close of World War II, but it was only in the mid-1960s that she got up the courage to display her work in London. Starting with a one-woman exhibition at Tooth's Gallery in 1965, she found a favorable response from both art critics and buyers; each group declared in its own way, "She's a painter."

In the following decade, she became a writer as well. Her autobiography, originally published in German, was released in English as *Change Lobsters—and Dance*. The book became a best-seller and was praised as a thoughtful outsider's view of Hollywood when it appeared in 1975. She followed it up with three novels over the next eight years.

From the late 1960s onward, Palmer and her second husband lived and worked primarily in Europe, with Carlos Thompson achieving notable success as a writer and historian. Her last U.S. movie appearance came in 1978 in *The Boys from Brazil*. This time the distinguished leading man with whom she appeared was Laurence Olivier.

Palmer's relatively quiet career, in which she combined film, television, and occasional stage appearances with her writing and painting, was disrupted once by a bitter public squabble with Harrison. In 1974, he published an autobiography entitled *Rex*. The former couple had had only meager contact over the years, coming together on a rare occasion in 1971 when their son Carey was married. Nonetheless, she found herself outraged at the way in which he had virtually left her out of his account of 14 years of his life.

Palmer decided she had to respond. The German version of her own autobiography had already appeared. Her book told of Harrison's affair with Landis but it omitted the story of Kendall's role in the breakup of their marriage. Now she included the Kendall episode in the English version of her book. Harrison publicly criticized her for doing so and denied he had planned to return to Palmer after Kay Kendall's death. She answered by announcing that she had kept his letters from the years of Harrison's marriage to Kendall, and she threatened him with legal action if he continued to defame her.

Film historian David Shipman characterized Palmer's movie career in 1970 by noting that she "never quite got the right breaks in Hollywood and she usually had to make much out of little." Nonetheless, she made film appearances in four languages and her acting career stretched for nearly 50 years, from her first appearance in an obscure British film to her role as *****Natalya Narishkina**, the mother of Tsar Peter I of Russia, in a 1986 television mini-series entitled "Peter the Great." Lilli Palmer died of cancer in Los Angeles on January 27, 1986.

SOURCES:

Burgess, Patricia, ed. *The Annual Obituary: 1986*. Chicago, IL: St. James Press, 1986.

Moseley, Roy, with Philip and Martin Masheter. *Rex Harrison: The First Biography*. London: New English Library, 1987.

Palmer, Lilli. *Change Lobsters—and Dance: An Autobiography*. NY: Warner Books, 1976.

Shipman, David. *The Great Movie Stars: The Golden Years*. NY: Bonanza, 1970.

SUGGESTED READING:

Eyles, Allen. *Rex Harrison*. London: W.H. Allen, 1985.

Harrison, Rex. *A Damned Serious Business*. NY: Bantam Books, 1991.

——. *Rex: An Autobiography*. NY: William Morrow, 1975.

Neil Heyman,
Professor of History, San Diego State University,
San Diego, California

Palmer, Lizzie Merrill (1838–1916)

American philanthropist whose bequest founded the Palmer Motherhood and Home Training School in Detroit, later known as the Merrill-Palmer Institute.

Born Lizzie Pitts Merrill in Portland, Maine, on October 8, 1838; died at Great Neck, Long Island, New York, on July 28, 1916; only child of Charles Merrill (a lumber baron) and Frances (Pitts) Merrill; married Thomas Witherell Palmer (a businessman), on October 16, 1855 (died 1913); no children, but raised and educated several homeless children.

The only child of a lumber baron, Lizzie Palmer was born in Portland, Maine, and was raised there and in central Michigan, where the family moved in the 1850s. At age 17, she married Thomas Palmer, a young Detroit businessman who later became a partner in her father's business. The couple settled outside of Detroit, where they were active politically (supporting woman suffrage and prohibition), and also initiated their lifelong involvement in philanthropy. They supported the Detroit Institute of Art, the YMCA, The University of Michigan, and a number of hospitals in the area. They also founded the Michigan branch of the Society for the Prevention of Cruelty to Animals.

In 1883, Thomas was elected to the U.S. Senate, and the couple went to Washington. Despite her delicate health, a holdover from her youth, Palmer became an active and popular hostess. In 1899, she accompanied her husband to Spain, where he served for a year as a U.S. minister. When he resigned his position, they returned to Detroit, bringing with them the young son of a Spanish military officer, who subsequently became their ward. He was the first of several children that the couple, who had no children of their own, took in over the years and educated. Once out of public life, the Palmers lived at their country estate, a 600-acre farm outside of the city that Thomas had inherited from his mother. (In 1887, they had built a four-room log cabin on the property, and outfitted it with authentic pioneer heirlooms from their own family. In 1893, the cabin became part of Palmer Park, a parcel of land the Palmers gave to the city of Detroit for public use.)

Due to a further decline in her health, Palmer spent more and more time in her later years at a second family residence, Larchmont Manor, on Long Island Sound, New York. Following her husband's death in 1913, she devoted her remaining years to plans for the disposition of her now sizable fortune. She died of pneumonia in 1916, leaving the bulk of her estate—estimated at $3 million—for the founding and maintenance of Palmer Motherhood and Home Training School, an institution for girls. The school, which opened in 1922 under the directorship of **Edna Noble White**, the head of the home economics department at Ohio State University and the president of the American Home Economics Association, educated young women of college age in the principles of homemaking and motherhood. Implementing a course of study based on observation and experience, the school's focal points were its self-contained nursery school, where children were observed and studied, and its residence halls, where students provided all of their own meals and homemaking needs. The school, which evolved into the Merrill-Palmer Institute of Human Development and Family Life, also served as a vital resource to the Detroit community through its nursery school, summer camp, and guidance programs, and through its research and teacher-training.

SOURCES:

James, Edward T., ed. *Notable American Women, 1607–1950.* Cambridge, MA: The Belknap Press of Harvard University Press, 1971.

Barbara Morgan, Melrose, Massachusetts

Palmer, Mary (1716–1794)

English author. *Born Mary Reynolds in 1716; died in 1794; sister of painter Sir Joshua Reynolds (1723–1792); married John Palmer, in 1740.*

The older sister of Sir Joshua Reynolds, a leading figure in 18th century British art, Mary Palmer was the author of *Devonshire Dialogue* (first complete edition, 1839), which is frequently reprinted.

Palmer, Mignon (1885–1970).

See Nevada, Emma for sidebar on Mignon Nevada.

Palmer, Nettie (1885–1964)

Australian critic, poet, and journalist. *Name variations: Janet Gertrude Palmer. Born Janet Gertrude Higgins on August 18, 1885, in Bendigo, Victoria, Australia; died on October 19, 1964; daughter of John Higgins (an accountant) and Catherine (MacDonald) Higgins; University of Melbourne, B.A., 1909, M.A., 1912; married Vance Palmer (a writer), on May 23, 1914; children: Aileen Palmer (b. 1915); Helen Palmer (1917–1979, a writer).*

Selected writings: The South Wind *(1914);* Australian Story-Book *(1928);* Talking It Over *(1932);* Fourteen Years: Extracts from a Private Journal 1925–1939 *(1948);* Henry Handel Richardson *(1950);* Bernard O'Dowd *(1954).*

Assisted by a strong interest in comparative world literature, writer Nettie Palmer dedicated much of her career to gaining a wider readership for the works of Australian authors. In turn, the respect she attained in literary circles provided her with a forum for promoting socialist ideals and combating the spread of fascism in the 1930s.

She was born in Bendigo, Victoria, Australia, in 1885, and was educated by her mother before attending Miss Rudd's seminary in Malvern and the Presbyterian Ladies' College. In 1909, she received an undergraduate degree from the University of Melbourne with a major in classical and comparative literature, and the following year traveled to Europe to study languages in London, Marburg, and Paris. (By mid-life she would speak a number of languages, including French, German, Greek and Spanish.) In London, she met writer Vance Palmer and through him became involved in guild socialism. Upon her return to Australia in 1911, she pursued a graduate degree at the University of Melbourne, where she met Bernard O'Dowd, further forging her commitment to socialism and cultural nationalism. She taught modern languages and began making contributions to the local socialist press. After receiving a masters of arts degree in 1912, she returned to London, where she married Vance Palmer two years later.

Palmer gave birth to her first daughter **Aileen** and published two volumes of poetry, *The South Wind* (1914) and *Shadowy Paths* (1915), while living in London. The family then moved to Emerald, Victoria, where her second daughter ***Helen Palmer** was born in 1917. In partnership, both Palmer and her husband became important contributors to Australia's literary circles. An outspoken foe of mandatory military enlistment during World War I, Palmer wrote a regular column for *Argus*. Her commitment to promoting Australian literature and authors meanwhile began to take shape, and her favored means of promotion became literary critiques. In 1924, she published her own *Modern Australian Literature 1900–1923*. The book was widely praised and immediately opened greater opportunities for her career.

After suffering a miscarriage in 1926, Palmer plunged into her literary career with increased energy. Her *Australian Story-Book* (1928), a highly received collection highlighting both well-known and lesser-known Australian writers, was considered to have set new standards for the short-story form. From 1928 to 1938, Palmer wrote a personal column, "A Reader's Notebook," for *All About Books*, and from 1927 to 1933 regularly contributed longer pieces to the *Illustrated Tasmanian Mail*. In

1929, she moved with her family to Melbourne, where she published *Henry Bourne Higgins* (1931) and *Talking It Over* (1932), a collection of her own essays, as well as co-edited a collection of women's writings in *The Centenary Gift Book* (1934). She was the first to recognize the importance of novelist ***Henry Handel Richardson**, and wrote critical studies of the works of several others, including **Barbara Baynton** and ***Katharine Susannah Prichard**, bringing them greater visibility. She also became active in various organizations, including the Australian Literary Society, the Verse-Speaking Association, and the Fellowship of Australian Writers. She found time to assist her husband with some of his literary efforts as well.

In the 1930s, Palmer again became involved in international political issues as she opposed the rise of fascism and promoted world peace. Continuing to travel widely, she attended the Writers' Congress in Paris in 1935 and was in Spain in 1936 when the Civil War broke out. She became a member of the Spanish Relief Committee, for which she wrote several booklets, and also joined the Joint Spanish Aid Council and Refugee Emergency Committee, dedicated to helping Spanish Civil War refugees and emigrants.

By the 1940s, she was maintaining a full schedule with writing, lecturing, and editing the memoirs, poem collections, and short stories of others. What many regarded as her best work, *Fourteen Years: Extracts from a Private Journal 1925–1939*, was published in the journal *Meanjin* in 1948. In the 1950s, Palmer published three books, *Henry Handel Richardson* (1950), the first major study of that writer, *The Dandemongs* (1952), a history of an area near Melbourne, and *Bernard O'Dowd* (1954), which underscored his influence in Australia. Both she and her husband also became frequent broadcasters over ABC radio through the 1940s and 1950s. After her husband's death in 1959, Palmer worked on her autobiography, but it remained unfinished due to her failing health. Credited with raising the prestige of Australian literature in general, and Australian women's literature in particular, Palmer died on October 19, 1964.

SOURCES:

Buck, Claire, ed. *The Bloomsbury Guide to Women's Literature.* NY: Prentice Hall, 1992.

Radi, Heather, ed. *200 Australian Women: A Redress Anthology.* NSW, Australia: Women's Redress Press, 1988.

Wilde, William H., Joy Hooten, and Barry Andrews. *The Oxford Companion to Australian Literature.* Melbourne, Australia: Oxford University Press, 1985.

SUGGESTED READING:

Modjeska, Drusilla. *Exiles at Home*, 1981.

Richard C. Hanes,
freelance writer, Eugene, Oregon

Palmer, Phoebe Worrall

(1807–1874)

American evangelist and author. *Born on December 18, 1807, in New York City; died on November 2, 1874, in New York City; daughter of Henry Worrall (an owner of a machine shop and iron foundry) and Dorothea Wade; married Walter Clark Palmer (a physician), on September 28, 1827; children: Alexander and Samuel (both died in infancy).*

Began conducting popular Methodist revival meetings in New York City (c. 1835); published the first of eight books promoting the perfectionist movement (1845); edited the movement's principal journal, Guide to Holiness *(1862–74).*

Selected writings: The Way of Holiness *(1845);* Entire Devotion *(1845);* Faith and Its Effects *(1846);* Incidental Illustrations of the Economy of Salvation *(1852);* Promises of the Father *(1859);* Four Years in the Old World *(1867);* Pioneer Experiences *(1868).*

Born in New York City into a strict Methodist family with nine other children, at age 19 Phoebe Worrall Palmer married Walter Palmer, a young homeopathic physician. She planned to raise her own family in the Methodist tradition, but tragedy struck early when both of her sons died shortly after birth. Palmer and her husband reached back to their religious roots, and interpreted the deaths as a sign from God that they were meant to dedicate their lives to religious service. In 1832, at a revival meeting at New York City's Allen Street Methodist Episcopal Church, the Palmers publicly committed themselves to a lifetime of support of the growing revivalist movement in American Methodism.

Palmer had honed her literary skills early, writing poems by age ten and participating daily in family worship. She soon realized her ability to reach others when preaching the gospel, and assumed leadership of a weekly afternoon prayer group for women shortly after it was founded in 1835 by her sister **Sarah Lankford**. The Tuesday Meeting for the Promotion of Holiness routinely included scripture reading, singing, prayers, and personal testimony. Palmer and the group embraced the search for complete sanctification in conformance with the doctrine of Christian perfection. While it had been a tenet of Methodism since the religion's founding by

John Wesley in the mid-16th century, perfection had been more or less ignored by American Methodists in the first years of the 1800s. By the 1830s, the notion (that God could free a believer of both inward and outward sin, and thus grant the believer some share of holiness, or perfection) was gaining broad popularity, and what would come to be known as the Holiness movement was underway. Palmer's residence, the site of prayer meetings for 37 years, became the inspirational center of the perfectionist movement's growth, directly influencing prominent Methodist leaders. This influence continued blossoming as attendance steadily increased, and by 1856 had become evangelical, attracting followers from other denominations. During this period, Palmer began writing a series of books championing the perfectionist movement. The first, 1845's *The Way of Holiness*, apparently sold 24,000 copies over six years. In 1862, after her husband purchased the movement's principal journal, *Guide to Holiness*, to which Palmer had been a frequent contributor, she became its editor. She would hold the post for the rest of her life, during which time the journal's circulation rose to 30,000.

Active in tending to the poor and imprisoned, Palmer served as secretary of the New York Female Assistance Society for the Relief and Religious Instruction of the Sick Poor from 1847 to 1858. In 1850, through the Methodist Ladies' Home Missionary Society, she founded the Five Points Mission to care for the indigent in a seedy inner-city section of New York. Also around 1850, the Palmers began traveling to promote the perfectionist doctrine, first leading holiness revivals in the eastern United States and Canada, and then throughout the rest of the country. In 1859, they traveled to England, where they influenced thousands during a four-year stay. Her 1867 book *Four Years in the Old World* relates their experiences. After returning to New York City, Palmer and her husband continued their revivalist work, primarily under the auspices of the National Association for the Promotion of Holiness, until her death in 1874.

SOURCES:

James, Edward T., ed. *Notable American Women, 1607–1950.* Cambridge, MA: The Belknap Press of Harvard University Press, 1971.

McHenry, Robert, ed. *Famous American Women.* NY: Dover, 1980.

Richard C. Hanes,
freelance writer, Eugene, Oregon

Palmer, Mrs. Potter (1849–1918).

See Palmer, Bertha Honoré.

Palmer, Sandra Jean (1941—)

American golfer. *Born on March 10, 1941, in Fort Worth, Texas; awarded a degree in physical education from North Texas State University.*

Had 21 professional career wins, including U.S. Women's Open (1975); was named LPGA Player of the Year (1975).

Small of frame (5'1½", 117 pounds) and seldom driving a ball more than 220 yards, Sandra Jean Palmer won 14 LPGA events between 1971 and 1975, becoming one the most formidable competitors in modern women's golf. Born in 1941 in Fort Worth, Texas, Palmer began caddying at age 13 and was hooked on the game from that time on. A graduate of North Texas State University where she was a cheerleader and homecoming queen, Palmer joined the LPGA tour in 1964, but did not win a major competition until 1971, when she eagled out of the sand on the final hole in the Sealy Classic to beat **Donna Caponi Young**. Thus began a winning streak that lasted through 1975, and included the 1971 Heritage Classic, the 1972 Four-Ball and Title-holders, the 1973 Pompano Beach, Angelo's Four-Ball, St. Paul, and National Jewish Hospital Opens, the 1974 Cameron Park Open, the 1974 Burdine's and Cubic Classics, the 1975 ***Dinah Shore** Colgate Winners Circle, and the 1975 USGA Women's Open. Known for her intensity, Palmer made up for her lack of driving ability with a brilliant short game. Her career winnings through 1975, when she was named LPGA Player of the Year, were over $300,000. In 1986, she became the 13th pro in the LPGA to pass the million-dollar mark.

Palmer, Sophia French (1853–1920)

***Nurse and administrator who was the first editor-in-chief of the* American Journal of Nursing.** *Born on May 26, 1853, in Milton, Massachusetts; died on April 27, 1920, at Forest Lawn, New York; fifth daughter and seventh among ten children of Simeon Palmer (a physician) and Maria Burdell (Spencer) Palmer; graduated from the Boston Training School for Nurses (now the Massachusetts General Hospital School of Nursing), on July 15, 1878; never married; children: adopted an eight-year-old daughter in 1906.*

Born in Milton, Massachusetts, in 1853, one of ten children of **Maria Spencer Palmer** and Simeon Palmer, a New England physician, Sophia Palmer may have inherited her interest in nursing from her father, although it is recorded that Simeon practiced medicine only "as occasion required," preferring to devote the majority of his time to literary pursuits. Little is known about Palmer's early education, but at age 22 she entered the Boston Training School for Nurses (now the Massachusetts General Hospital School of Nursing), then under the superintendentship of *__Linda Richards__. Upon graduating two years later (July 1878), she went to Philadelphia, where she served for several years as the private nurse for a doctor specializing in nervous and mental illnesses.

In 1884, Palmer returned to New England, becoming superintendent of the new St. Luke's Hospital in New Bedford, Massachusetts. She resigned after a year, when the fledgling enterprise ran into hard economic times and was forced to pare down its nursing staff. She returned to private practice, and also spent nine months pursuing graduate study at the Massachusetts General Hospital (1888). In 1889, she moved to Washington, D.C., where she founded and then served as the administrator of the training school for nurses at the Garfield Memorial Hospital. Despite some initial hostility from the medical staff for her new training program, Palmer remained at Garfield for seven years. In 1896, she took over as superintendent of the Rochester (New York) City Hospital and Training school, remaining there for four years.

In addition to her administrative duties, Palmer was instrumental in the development of professional nursing organizations, and she also had a hand in establishing and editing several professional nursing journals. From 1893 to 1895, she helped edit the *Trained Nurse and Hospital Review* (published by the training school of the Buffalo General Hospital.). She was a founding member of the American Society of Superintendents of Training Schools for Nurses (1893) and served as its representative in organizing the national Nurses' Associated Alumnae of the United States and Canada (later the American Nurses' Association). Most significantly, Palmer was the first editor-in-chief of the *American Journal of Nursing*, which published its introductory issue in October 1900. She served as editor until her death in 1920, using her home as an office, and also assumed full responsibility for the business management of the publication. Known for her outspoken editorials, Palmer promoted reforms in nursing education and wrote about vital social issues of the day. She also used the pages of the journal to advocate legislation requiring state supervision of nursing schools and the registration of trained nurses. When the New York law regulating the nursing profession was passed in 1903, Palmer was appointed a member of the Board of Nurse Examiners, and was elected its first chair.

Sophia Palmer, who never married, was described by friends as sympathetic and caring, although she could be militant and impatient when it came to nursing reform. Having a particular interest in young people, in 1906 she adopted an eight-year-old girl, who died at the age of 20. Palmer remained active in the nursing profession until her death in 1920, following a cerebral hemorrhage. Two libraries were established in her memory: the Sophia F. Palmer Library of the *American Journal of Nursing*, and the Palmer-Davis Library of the Massachusetts General Hospital School of Nursing.

SOURCES:

James, Edward T., ed. *Notable American Women, 1607–1950*. Cambridge, MA: The Belknap Press of Harvard University Press, 1971.

Read, Phyllis J., and Bernard L. Witlieb. *The Book of Women's Firsts*. NY: Random House, 1992.

Barbara Morgan,
Melrose, Massachusetts

Palmerston, Viscountess (d. 1869).

See Lamb, Emily.

Palmyra, queen of.

See Zenobia (r. 267–272).

Palucca, Gret (1902–1993)

German dancer and dance teacher who was ranked among the most influential figures in Germany's world of modern dance. *Born in Munich, Germany, on January 8, 1902; died in Dresden on March 22, 1993.*

Managed her own school of dance in Dresden (1925–39 and 1945–93).

Gret Palucca was for almost seven decades one of Germany's most famous and influential modern dancers and dance teachers. Born in Munich in 1902, she studied from 1920 to 1925 with the innovative dancer *__Mary Wigman__. The encounter with Wigman was crucial for the artistic evolution of Palucca, who until then had been frustrated by what she felt to be the artistic rigidity of ballet technique. Once under Wigman's tutelage, she dedicated herself to creating forms of dance expression that reflected her own inner spirit. Described by Wigman as "a narrow-hipped, boyish-looking girl with a pert face framed by reddish-blond hair," Palucca was in many ways an unlikely student. But, as Wigman soon discovered, she possessed both the psychological elements needed to succeed as a dancer and physical abilities that appeared only rarely in an artist, particularly the capacity for powerful leaps. Palucca's approach to dance was different than that of Wigman whose style might be characterized as one of melancholy, complexity, and solemnity. Emphasizing the bonds between dance and music, Palucca's style was invariably more carefree and optimistic. Jack Anderson has noted that her choreographic approach was one that concerned itself with "movement qualities, rather than emotional states."

In 1925, Palucca founded her own school in Dresden, the Privatschule des Neuen Künstlerischen Tanzes (Private School for the New Artistic Dance). By the late 1920s, in her repertory was the highly popular *Technical Improvisations* (1927), which was compared by some writers on dance to a Chopin étude. Her choreography, inspired by music and linked to German expressionist culture, was rooted in improvisation, and improvisation became a key element in her pedagogy. The visual arts too provided inspiration for the dances of "*die Palucca*" (early in her performing career she omitted her given name on programs). Among those who greatly influenced her (and vice versa) were Wassily Kandinsky, who admired "the unusually precise structure" of her dances, and Laszlo Moholy-Nagy, who praised her as "the most lucid of today's dancers." Said Moholy-Nagy: "She is for us the newly found law of motion." Visual artists of the Weimar period often detected in her style an almost architectural quality. Palucca appears to have been inspired by a Mondrian work which was hung on the wall above her studio piano. Other artists who responded to her dance recitals included Lyonel Feininger, Walter Gropius, Ernst Ludwig Kirchner, and Paul Klee.

Highly successful with German audiences as a leading exponent of contemporary *Ausdruckstanz* (expressionist dancing), by the late 1920s she was giving as many as 100 performances in a season. Her audiences were delighted by the ongoing explorations of her dancing, which even included a dance based on her morning warmup exercises. Rudolf Arnheim, a lifelong admirer of her work, has written of the abstract purity and objectivity of Palucca's art, which he likened to "a systematic exploration of the anatomy." Even contemporary skeptics of Palucca's work—like the American dance critic John Martin, who detected mannerisms as well as compositions that were to him "utterly unimaginative"—also had to concede that Palucca was doubtless an artist of substance. Palucca offered a perceptive insight into her style with the remark: "Ich will nicht hübsch und niedlich tanzen" (I do not wish to dance in a manner that is either pretty or dainty).

German postage stamp issued in honor of Gret Palucca.

Palucca's life was her dancing, and she paid little attention to political developments in the artistically brilliant but crisis-plagued Weimar Republic. While many dancers fled Germany in 1933 after the creation of Adolf Hitler's dictatorship because they were Jewish or politically radical, Palucca remained in Dresden where she continued to train students and enjoy a reputation as one of Germany's most talented dancers. Although the National Socialists were violently opposed to most modern trends in the arts, their attitude toward modern dance was ambivalent. Indeed, during the first years of the Third Reich, modern dance was held in high esteem, a circumstance which provided the regime with effective propaganda about the continuing quality of the arts in Hitler's New Germany. With their emphasis on assuring the physical supremacy of the German *Volk*, the Nazis looked to support an area of artistic creativity that cultivated bodily strength, physical beauty, and vitality. The Nazi state was proud and even boastful of the disciplined and perfectly trained bodies, and the established international reputations, of those expressionist dancers like Palucca who had chosen to remain in Germany.

Palucca's dances, which carried no direct political message, were not necessarily linked to the National Socialist Weltanschauung, but neither did they offer any unequivocal rejection of its values. For Palucca, the ability to perform held the highest priority in her life. Thus, she performed at the Berlin Dance Festival in 1934 and played a role in the pageantry that accompanied the staging of the Olympic Games in Berlin in 1936. Largely ignoring politics, she continued to teach, emphasizing that her students find their own individual styles. "Ich will gewiss keine Nachahmer erziehen" (I definitely have no desire to create imitations of myself), she said.

I do not wish to dance in a manner that is either pretty or dainty.

—Gret Palucca

After several years of increasing uncertainty, in 1939 Nazi officialdom declared Palucca's Dresden dance school to be *artfremd* (alien and foreign), and shut it down. She spent the war years informally instructing a few private pupils and maintaining her own dancing skills. Palucca survived the Dresden firestorm that destroyed virtually all of the city in February 1945.

After Germany's defeat, Dresden was in the Soviet Occupation Zone of Germany. Despite the fact that she had remained in Germany during the Nazi years, Palucca was not regarded as having been tainted by the fascist dictatorship. Consequently, she soon began to benefit from official support of both the new, anti-Nazi municipal administration of Dresden and Soviet cultural officers. In July 1945, with Dresden still in ruins, Palucca presented her first postwar solo dance recital. Soon after, she once again began to instruct students in her own dance school. In 1950, she performed her last Tanzabend (dance evening). In 1952—three years after the Soviet Occupation Zone had metamorphosed into the German Democratic Republic (GDR) in 1949—her school was nationalized as the Tanzhochschule Dresden (Dresden Academy of Dance). She remained its unchallenged director, enjoying not only immense prestige but also guarantees of generous state subsidies. Starting in 1948, she also taught summer classes on the Baltic island of Hiddensee, where her students used the beach, the lighthouse, and the dunes for performances. In 1950, she was a founding member of the GDR's prestigious German Academy of the Arts; in 1955, she moved her school into a newly restored building on Dresden's venerable Basteiplatz; and in 1962, she was awarded the prestigious title of Professorin.

Although some Western dance critics believed that the GDR's restrictive artistic atmosphere had led to a "freezing in time" of Palucca's pedagogy of dance, others were impressed by her continued vitality as a teacher. Her school was highly regarded not only in the GDR but throughout the eastern bloc as an institution dedicated to the preservation of the traditions of German interpretive and expressionist dance. Advancing age forced Palucca to cut down on her hours of teaching, but she insisted on giving regular children's classes until she was well into her 80s. Her students included such important figures in the arts in Germany as ***Ruth Berghaus**, **Hannelore Bey**, **Arila Siegert**, and **Hanne Wandtke**.

Palucca was the recipient of many honors in the final decades of her long life. These included the GDR National Prize (which she was awarded on several occasions) and the German Dance Prize of the national organization of professional dance instructors. In 1972, she received the city of Dresden's Martin Andersen Nexö Prize and in 1979 was given the key to the city in which she lived virtually all of her artistic life. Some years later, a Dresden street was also named after her.

Gret Palucca lived to see Germany's reunification take place in 1989–1990. In 1992, she was awarded the Grosses Bundesverdienstkreuz (Large Federal Cross of Achievement) of the German Federal Republic. Soon after, she died in Dresden on March 22, 1993. By her own request, she was buried in the picturesque cemetery on the island of Hiddensee. On October 8, 1998, Palucca was honored by the German postal system when she was depicted on a 440 pfennig stamp which became part of the definitive "Women in German History" series.

SOURCES:

Anderson, Jack. *Art Without Boundaries: The World of Modern Dance.* Iowa City, IA: University of Iowa Press, 1997.

Arnheim, Rudolf. "Visiting Palucca: Portrait of the Dancer," in *Dance Scope.* Vol. 13, no. 1. Fall 1978, pp. 6–11.

"Gret Palucca zum Fünfundachzigsten," in *Sinn und Form.* Vol. 39, no. 1. January–February 1987, pp. 55–12.

Jarchow, Peter, and Ralf Stabel. *Palucca: Aus Ihrem Leben, über ihre Kunst.* Berlin: Henschel Verlag, 1997.

Kant, Marion. "Palucca: 'Ich bin ganz gut durchgekommen': Eine tanzpolitische Chronik des Jahres 1951," in *Tanzforschung Jahrbuch.* Vol. 5, 1994, pp. 39–52.

Knight, Judson. "Palucca, Gret," in Taryn Benbow-Pfaltzgraf and Glynis Benbow-Niemier, eds., *International Dictionary of Modern Dance.* Detroit, MI: St. James Press, 1998, pp. 606–608.

Krull, Edith, and Werner Gommlich. *Palucca.* 3rd ed. Berlin: Henschelverlag Kunst und Gesellschaft, 1967.
Künstler um Palucca: Ausstellung zu Ehren des 85. Geburtstages, 27. Mai bis 14. August 1987–Staatliche Kunstsammlung Dresden Kupferstich-Kabinett. Dresden: Staatliche Kunstsammlung, 1987.
Lohberg, Gabriele, ed. *Ernst Ludwig Kirchner—der Tanz: Gret Palucca zum Gedenken.* Davos: Kirchner Verein, 1993.
Moss, Suzan F. "Spinning Through the Weltanschauung: The Effects of the Nazi Regime on the German Modern Dance," Ph.D. dissertation, New York University, 1988.
Müller, Hedwig. "Palucca, Gret," in Selma Jeanne Cohen, *et al.*, eds., *International Encyclopedia of Dance.* 6 vols. NY: Oxford University Press, 1998, Vol. 5, pp. 65–66.
Olivier, Antje, and Sevgi Braun. *Anpassung oder Verbot: Künstlerinnen und die 30er Jahre.* Düsseldorf: Droste Verlag, 1998.
Rydberg, Olaf. *Die Tänzerin Palucca.* Dresden: C. Reissner Verlag, 1935.
Schumann, Gerhard, ed. *Palucca: Porträt einer Künstlerin.* Berlin: Henschelverlag Kunst und Gesellschaft, 1972.

RELATED MEDIA:

Wagner-Régeny, Rudolf. *Zwei Tänze für Palucca.* Vienna: Universal Edition, 1951 (composition for piano solo).

John Haag,
Associate Professor of History, University of Georgia, Athens, Georgia

Panagiotatou, Angeliki (1878–1954)

Greek scientist, specializing in tropical diseases, who was the first woman to become physician, microbiologist, and professor of hygiene at the National University of Athens. *Name variations: Angeliki Panajiotatou. Born in 1878 (some sources cite 1875); died in 1954; attended the Medical School of the National University of Athens; advanced studies in Germany.*

A highly respected microbiologist whose research into tropical diseases halted the spread of a number of lethal epidemics of cholera and typhus, Angeliki Panagiotatou overcame the prevailing prejudices of her time to achieve world recognition in her field. Born in Greece in 1878, she received her early medical training at the National University of Athens, where she and her sister were the first women to be accepted at the medical school. Following further studies in Germany, Panagiotatou accepted a position as a lecturer at Athens, but her appointment was surrounded by controversy and students refused to attend a class taught by a woman. Forced to resign, she spent some time teaching at Cairo University in Egypt, then took up the directorship of the general hospital in Alexandria. During her tenure there, her experiments dealing with the identification of lethal epidemics were presented at numerous international conventions. In addition to her scientific work, Panagiotatou enjoyed many cultural and literary pursuits, and her home in Alexandria became a meeting place for Greek and other foreign artists and intellectuals. She returned to Greece in 1938 and was appointed a professor at the National University of Athens, where she now commanded the respect and admiration of both her students and her fellow academics.

Pan Chao (c. 45–c. 120).

See Ban Zhao.

Pandit, Vijaya Lakshmi (1900–1990)

Indian diplomat and politician, often called the "Lamp of India," who was a leading figure in one of Asia's most important political dynasties and became the first Asian, and the first woman, to preside over the UN General Assembly. *Name variations: Nan; Vijayalaxmi Pandit; Vijay Laksmi Pandit; Mrs. Ranjit Pandit; Swarup Kumari Nehru. Pronunciation: Pundit. Born Swarup Kumari Nehru on August 18, 1900, at Anan Bhavan, Allahabad, India; died on December 1, 1990, in India; daughter of Motilal Nehru (1861–1931, a prominent lawyer dedicated to Mohandas Gandhi's nonviolent campaign to free India from colonial rule) and a mother, full name unknown, who was a Swarup from the Punjab; sister of Jawaharlal Nehru (1889–1964, prime minister of India); tutored at home by a governess; married Ranjit Sitaram Pandit (a lawyer and activist for independence), on May 10, 1921; children: three daughters, Chandralekha Mehta (a journalist), Nayantara Sahgal (a novelist), Rita Dar (a director of public relations).*

Was a member of Indian National Congress Party; imprisoned by the British (1932–33); elected to Allahabad Municipal Board (1934); elected to Assembly of the United Provinces (Uttar Pradesh, 1936); first Indian woman to become a Cabinet minister as minister of Local Self-Government and Public Health (1937); imprisoned by the British (1940); imprisoned again (1942–43); elected to India's Constituent Assembly (1946); was leader of Indian Delegation to the United Nations (1946–48, 1952–53, and 1963); was India's first ambassador to the Soviet Union (1947–49); served as ambassador to the United States (1949–52) and concurrently to Mexico (1949–51); was the first woman and first Asian to serve as president of the UN General Assembly (1953–54); served as Indian high commissioner (ambassador) to the United Kingdom (1954–61); served as governor of the state of Maharashtra (1962–63); defied Indira Gandhi's takeover of the Indian government and the imprisonment of thousands of opposition members (1975–77).

In June 1975, during one of the turbulent periods in the long struggle for independence and democracy on the subcontinent of India, Prime Minister ***Indira Gandhi** cited a "deep and widespread conspiracy" as reason for declaring a state of emergency throughout the land. In the months that followed, thousands who opposed her government were arrested, total censorship was imposed on all organs of the press, and even the writings of Mohandas K. Gandhi and Jawaharlal Nehru, whose lives had been dedicated to the achievement of Indian independence, were proscribed by law. In the blink of an eye, the largest democracy in Asia had been transformed into a dictatorship.

Then, in an extraordinary move encapsulating a half-century of India's complex political history, an elderly woman, retired after decades of diplomatic and government service, stepped forward to lead an opposition movement determined to defeat the prime minister. Already in her late 70s, an internationally recognized stateswoman as well as a survivor of several years in prison, Vijaya Lakshmi Pandit rallied most of India behind her, and led a movement that resulted in a call for new elections, the defeat of Indira Gandhi, and the preservation of democracy on the Indian subcontinent. For Pandit, this political play was to some degree the extension of a family dispute, involving both the limits of social and political privilege and the necessity of personal sacrifice for the sake of nationalistic ideals, because the prime minister was her niece, and these adversaries had shared the same social and family background, and even the same household, for the better part of their lives.

The girl who became Vijaya Lakshmi Pandit was the child of prominent Hindus, Saraswt Brahmans who originally came from India's Kashmir valley. A number of her kin had served as functionaries in the British Raj. Her father Motilal Nehru had studied at Allahabad University for a bachelor's degree which he did not complete, but became a serious student of law and built an extremely successful law practice from which the family's fortune was derived. His wife was a Swarup, from the Punjab, who had been wed to him when she was 14 in a traditional arranged marriage, and their large household was typical of many aristocratic homes of the time, incorporating two entirely different lifestyles side-by-side. On Pandit's father's side, the house boasted Western furniture, Sèvres china, and crystal, while her mother occupied rooms furnished in a traditional Indian manner, in which only vegetarian foods were served.

The Nehru household was typically Indian, in that many aunts, uncles, and cousins lived there together, but it was unconventional in other ways. Because Motilal Nehru was opposed to traditional caste distinctions and orthodox prejudices, many of the family's servants were from the untouchable caste, forbidden by orthodox Hindu tradition from fraternizing with Brahman families. Because he had equally strong views about the status of women, he saw to it that his daughter received the same education in their home as her brothers Jawaharlal and Krishna, under the tutelage of an English governess, Miss Hooper. Once, while Vijaya Lakshmi was in the room, a friend chastised him about the way he was raising his daughter, asking, "Is it necessary to let an Indian girl behave in the uncouth manner of the English? Why is she being educated according to foreign standards and being given so much freedom? Do you intend to make her into a lawyer like yourself?" Her father responded by asking her directly if she would like to read law, leaving her with the abiding impression that the option was open to her, although it was not one she chose to pursue.

When it came to finding their daughter a husband, however, her parents followed the Indian tradition of obtaining the services of a matchmaker. Given the task was Mahadev Desai, then secretary to Mohandas Gandhi. Desai suggested that she read an article in the journal *Modern Review*, "At the Feet of the Guru," written by Ranjit Sitaram Pandit, a talented young barrister. After she read the article and showed interest, Pandit was invited to the Nehru home, where, after a visit of three days, he proposed.

Marriage meant many changes for the young woman known up to this time as Swarup Kumari. According to Hindu custom, she was now adopted into the clan of her in-laws, and received a new name that combined her husband's name with the name of the province from which he came. Thus, henceforth, she would be known as Vijaya Lakshmi Pandit, but before the wedding Ranjit wrote to his bride, "I have come many miles and crossed many bridges to come to you—but in the future you and I must cross our bridges hand in hand." Indeed, their life together would be shared on an equal footing, whether in raising their family, striving for their country's freedom, or going to prison.

At the time of the Pandits' marriage in 1921, the national movement to obtain India's freedom from British rule by nonviolent methods had made considerable headway, and both Pandit's father and her brother Jawaharlal Nehru were becoming deeply involved. The great leader of the movement was Mohandas Gandhi, respectfully called the Mahatma, who gave his blessing to the young couple. Describing Gandhi's influence, Jawaharlal Nehru once said that he "seemed to cast a spell on all classes and groups of people and drew them into one motley crowd struggling in one direction." In the early years of her marriage, Pandit's husband and her father both gave up lucrative law practices in order to devote their energies to the political arm of the movement, the Indian National Congress. Pandit herself joined the Non-Cooperation movement as a soldier of non-violence. By 1929, when her beloved brother Jawaharlal presided over the Congress session, the Pandits had three daughters, **Rita** (**Dar**), **Chandralekha** (**Mehta**), and **Nayantara** (**Sahgal**). Pandit's political activities by this time included organizing and leading processions as well as delivering fiery speeches. On January 27, 1932, she was arrested, along with one of her sisters, for defying the Crown by publicly observing Indian Independence Day. Her youngest daughter was three when she was fined and sentenced to one year in prison.

At the end of her imprisonment, Pandit continued her political activities. Ranjit Pandit supported his wife's work and sacrifice; the couple were partners in their determination to bring democratic rule to India by nonviolent means. In 1936, the Congress Party swept the polls in many provinces and Pandit won a seat in Uttar Pradesh. In July 1937, she accepted the post of minister for Local Self-Government and Education. As Pandit said of her new job, "This was the first time a woman had been given the position of Minister and had to work with men as her subordinates and colleagues." While forging her way through this new territory, she had the solid support of her family, once noting, "I had a husband who was always at my side when needed—critical and understanding."

One of her first acts as minister was to auction off a beautiful silver tray that had been given as a gift and donate the proceeds to a local hospital. Finding that the Public Health Department in her charge was poorly organized, she described it as the "untouchable" among the ministries. Pandit was disturbed by the inadequacy of hospital care, commenting, "The poor, especially the women, were terrified at the idea of going to a hospital, and they had a point. Once admitted they were more or less left to their fate." She became dedicated to improving health care for women, and visited provincial hospitals and clinics in an effort to change the notion that the poor, and especially poor women, were expendable. Among the many modern social programs she instituted were those to provide clean drinking water for villages, milk for children, and playgrounds throughout India.

Vijaya Lakshmi Pandit

As minister of health, Pandit dealt at times with India's complex religious and ethnic tensions. Once she attended a festival in Hardwar, a city of hereditary Hindu priests, where she was visited by a deputation of priests requesting that the government forbid the slaughter of cows in the city. At first glance, the request appeared legitimate, since the cow is sacred to Hindus, but a close reading of the petition revealed that the ban was not intended for Hardwar, but for nearby Jawalapur, which was Muslim. Since a number of Muslim butchers made their living in Jawalapur, the request was revealed to be not religious so much as an attempt by Hindu priests to cause economic destruction among the Muslims. When Pandit denied the request, the house where she was staying was surrounded by a rowdy crowd which shouted and broke windows. Pandit flung open a door, stood on a chair and took off her watch, indicating a countdown that allowed the crowd ten minutes to calm down. The crowd shortly dispersed, and she later received an apology for the incident.

In the late 1930s, although the British had made concessions to the Indian National Congress, India remained under colonial rule. With the onset of World War II, there were many, including Pandit, who objected to Great Britain's decision that India should take part in the war. Protests led Pandit to another imprisonment in 1940, and in August 1942 she was imprisoned a third time, along with Ranjit and other Congress leaders, for issuing a "Quit India" resolution. After nine months, she was released on grounds of ill health, and during 1943, although still not well, she organized the Bengal Famine Relief. Ranjit remained in prison, where his health continued to deteriorate. Released too late to be saved, he died on January 14, 1944. Grief-stricken and under threat of re-imprisonment, Pandit continued her work for independence; in 1945, with one of her daughters, she left for America to avoid another sentence.

When India finally gained independence in August 1947, Pandit's diplomatic career was already under way. She served as India's Ambassador to the United Nations in 1946 and 1947 (a position she would also fill in 1963). From 1947 to 1949, she was her country's first ambassador to the Soviet Union, where she was touched by the warmth of the people living under the drastic conditions that followed World War II there. Pandit next served concurrently as ambassador to the United States from 1949 to 1952, and as ambassador to Mexico from 1949 to 1951. In September 1953, she achieved the signal honor of becoming the first woman and the first Asian elected president of the UN General Assembly. She served in this capacity until the following year, when she became India's ambassador to Great Britain, Ireland, and Spain, concurrent postings she would hold until 1961. Despite her repeated imprisonments and the circumstances of her husband's death, Pandit liked the British people and regarded England as her second home. This breadth of perspective, which allowed her to recognize that no other colonial power had done as much for democracy as had the British, led others to call her the "Lamp of India."

Devotion to family was a lifelong characteristic of Pandit's. She was always deeply fond of her brother Jawaharlal Nehru, and of his daughter Indira, whom she described as an older daughter to her own children. The egalitarian attitudes instilled by her father prevailed into the next generation, as Pandit saw that her daughters were well educated. The oldest, Rita, later became a director of public relations as well as a diplomat's wife; Chandralekha became a journalist, wife and mother, and the marriage of her own daughter to a Muslim extended the long tradition of toleration in the Nehru-Pandit household; Nayantara became a novelist. Pandit's daughters had sacrificed much for their parents' political involvement, but all remained devoted to the high ideals that had necessitated the hardships.

The death on May 27, 1964, of her brother Jawaharlal Nehru, prime minister of India since 1950, came as a great shock to Pandit. She soon was elected to serve in the seat he had held for 17 years in the National Congress, but resigned on July 8, 1968, to devote herself to social service and international work. Two years earlier, Nehru's daughter Indira Nehru Gandhi had decided to follow in her father's political footsteps, and within a few years her government began to demonstrate certain disturbing trends. Posters of Gandhi, with exhortations for unity under "The Leader," were plastered around the country, and members of the government were encouraged to be "committed" to her leadership. Worse, Gandhi began to groom her son, Sanjay, as a kind of crown prince, an action having no place in a true democracy. Pandit was in England when the state of emergency was declared by Indira Gandhi in June 1975, and she immediately returned home. There she found many of her friends imprisoned, and conditions in her own home all too reminiscent of the days before India's independence, with her phone tapped, her letters censored, and her movements under constant surveillance. Believing that political conditions were even worse than they had been under British rule, Pandit decided that she must oppose her niece, no matter what the cost.

For the next two years she was vocal in her opposition to the government, knowing that even as a woman in her late 70s she might be thrown into jail. Because India was still under censorship, most of her outcries were heard only in the international press, but on January 18, 1977, the state of emergency was suddenly lifted. Pandit remained determined that elections must be held and her niece defeated. Shortly after her friends in the opposition were released from prison, a coalition was formed for the express purpose of changing the Indian leadership. Soon there were calls for elections, the opposition found overwhelming support, the campaign began to build, and in 1977 Indira Gandhi was defeated.

Gandhi never forgave her aunt for her prominent role in her ouster. While Pandit regretted the loss of her niece's affection, she believed the familial relationship had been a necessary sacrifice to ensure that Indian democracy would thrive. Indira Gandhi was reelected as prime minister in 1980. Her family did, in fact, become a kind of dynasty in Indian politics: after her assassination in 1984, she was succeeded by her son Rajiv Gandhi, who served as prime minister until he, too, was assassinated in 1991, and in the following years his wife **Sonia Gandhi** became prominent in the Congress Party. Nevertheless, Pandit's timely opposition played an important role in preventing the development of a dictatorship in India. Throughout her long and distinguished career, Vijaya Lakshmi Pandit never allowed new roles, new obligations, or even imprisonment to intimidate her. The nonviolent teachings of Mahatma Gandhi were the hallmark of her career, and she always believed enlightened leadership to be more important than political power. Indeed, her most important quality, perhaps, was forgiveness. After the defeat of her niece, Pandit wept for them both.

SOURCES:

Mishra, Akhilesh. "Vijayalaxmi Pandit" in *Dictionary of National Biography.* Ed. by S.P. Sen. Calcutta: Institute of Historical Studies, 1974, pp. 297–300.

Pandit, Vijaya Lakshmi. "The Family Bond" in *A Study of Nehru.* Ed. by Rafiq Zakaria. Bombay: Times of India, 1960, pp. 125–127.

———. *The Scope of Happiness.* NY: Crown, 1979.

"Vijay Lakshmi Pandit, Politician and Nehru's Sister, Is Dead at 90," in *The New York Times.* December 2, 1990.

Karin Haag,
freelance writer, Athens, Georgia

Pandita Ramabai (1858–1922).

See Ramabai, Pandita.

Pankhurst, Adela (1885–1961)

Participant with her mother and sisters in the prewar militant British women's suffrage movement, who emigrated to Australia in 1914 where she helped found, at different times, two ideologically opposed organizations, the Australian Communist Party and the Australian Women's Guild of Empire. *Name variations: Adela Walsh. Born Adela Constantia Mary Pankhurst in Manchester, England, on June 19, 1885; died on May 23, 1961, in Australia; youngest daughter of Richard Marsden Pankhurst and Emmeline Goulden Pankhurst (1858–1928); sister of Christabel (1880–1958), Sylvia (1882–1960), Frank, and Harry Pankhurst; married Tom Walsh (a socialist labor leader), in 1919; children: Richard Walsh (b. 1919), and daughters Sylvia Walsh (b. 1920), Christian Walsh (b. 1921), and Ursula Walsh (b. 1923).*

Death of her brother Frank (1888); death of her father (1898); death of her brother Harry (1910); emigrated to Australia (1914); published influential pacifist booklet, Put up the Sword! *(1915); joined the Victoria Socialist Party (1917); death of her mother (1928); founded the Australian Women's Guild of Empire (1929); interned (1942); widowed (1943).*

Selected writings: Put up the Sword! *(1915);* Betrayed: A Play in Five Acts *(1917);* The Dawn *(1917); (editor)* The Empire Gazette *(c. 1930–39).*

Historical scholarship traditionally has depicted ***Emmeline Pankhurst** and ***Christabel Pankhurst** as sharing the political spotlight, with ***Sylvia Pankhurst** standing in their shadow. Adela is nowhere to be seen. Ironically, Adela, the Pankhurst whom history has forgotten, was in many ways the most memorable—she was the most politically radical, ideologically inconsistent, and personally humane of the three sisters.

Adela Pankhurst was born in Choriton upon Medlock, Manchester, Lancashire, England, on June 19, 1885, the fourth child of Richard and Emmeline Pankhurst. As a child, she was quite small for her age and suffered from an almost paralytic weakness of the legs which prevented her from walking until the age of three. Educated at home and at Manchester High School for Girls, she also attended the Disley Road School as a trainee teacher, though she did not complete her pedagogical training. Following the family tradition, she became deeply involved in socialist politics and gravitated toward the pacifist movement.

After leaving school, Adela worked as a primary school teacher until she decided to join her mother and elder sisters in the Women's Social and Political Union (WSPU) where she served as a lecturer and a paid organizer. Although small in stature (she was slightly under five feet tall), she was a tireless worker for the WSPU. She was probably the most likeable of the Pankhurst women, as well as a brilliant speaker and a diligent organizer. She made friends easily and never asked WSPU volunteers to take any risk she was not personally prepared to share with them. For that reason, she was one of the first militants to be arrested, go to prison and be forcibly fed. Described by historian David Mitchell as being "recklessly dedicated" to the cause, she once traveled to Scotland to campaign for women's suffrage in a mid-winter election with a serious case of pleurisy. Nonetheless, according to some sources, her contributions to the movement seldom were recognized by her mother or Christabel, and she faced much sharper criticism from them than did her colleagues.

The major reason for this discriminatory treatment is that Adela, to the great disappointment of her mother, sided with Sylvia Pankhurst against Emmeline and Christabel concerning the proper goals and tactics for the militant suffragists to pursue. Although they welcomed any woman from any socio-economic class who wished to join the WSPU, the senior Pankhursts were determined to build a membership comprised primarily of upper- and middle-class women dedicated to the single goal of women's suffrage even if, initially, it meant that only women who owned property would be enfranchised. Adela, like Sylvia, believed that the WSPU should concentrate its recruitment efforts on working-class women, pledge itself never to accept any form of limited women's suffrage, and include proletarian women's socio-economic concerns on its agenda. Nonetheless, as socialists, Adela and Sylvia Pankhurst accepted the principle of organizational discipline and, when they could not prevail in family counsels, carried out official WSPU policies, grafting on their own touches where possible.

In 1912, Sylvia Pankhurst, with Adela's assistance, got an opportunity to put her socialist principles into operation when some of the wealthier branches of the WSPU underwrote the opening of a branch office in London's East End, a working-class district. The East London Federation of Suffragettes of the WSPU (ELFS) differed from WSPU standard policy in that it encouraged the participation of working-class men in its demonstrations and work projects, maintained at least unofficial ties with the Labour Party, and sometimes, in addition to pursuing the vote, dealt with other problems faced by working-class women. Sylvia's ELFS organized huge working-class demonstrations in favor of women's suffrage and endorsed the militancy which the WSPU advocated, but the ELFS' quasi-independent policies rankled Emmeline and Christabel.

By 1913, Adela's socio-political views had become almost as exasperating for her mother as were Sylvia's. Her outspoken deviationist opinions concerning proletarian women's socio-economic needs were particularly vexing for Emmeline and Christabel, perhaps because she presented them so eloquently. In 1913, Adela (who, like Sylvia, suffered all of her life from a host of annoying minor physical ailments) was afflicted with a serious case of pleurisy which caused her to collapse and resulted in the loss of her voice. Her doctors warned her that her condition would be aggravated by almost everything she did as a WSPU organizer, especially public speaking, going to prison and being forcibly fed. Therefore, in 1913, she took a hiatus from WSPU work and looked for an alternative career, at least on a temporary basis. Adela decided that she would like to be a gardener (although she had never shown the least aptitude for work of that sort), and her mother offered to pay for her to attend Studley Horticultural College, Warwickshire, if she agreed that she never would speak in public in England again.

Although Adela successfully completed her course, she never learned to enjoy gardening. She wanted to return to the political fray, and grew increasingly despondent because she was hamstrung by her vow to her mother. The solution to this dilemma came when ***Vida Goldstein**, head of an Australian socialist-feminist organization, was visiting England and invited Adela to come "down under" and work as an organizer with the militant separatist Women's Political Association. Therefore, on February 22, 1914, Adela Pankhurst boarded the *Geelong* with her personal possessions and £20 in cash and emigrated to Victoria, Australia, so that she might continue the work she longed to do without dishonoring her promise to her mother.

In the same year, she worked to form an Australian Women's organization to concentrate on political issues. With the outbreak of the Great War (1914–18), Adela Pankhurst worked assiduously in the Women's Political Association and the Women's Peace Army to organize opposition to both conscription and the war itself. She wrote a number of pacifist tracts, including the influential *Put up the Sword!* which she published in 1915. Nonetheless, in 1917 she resigned from the Women's Political Association when the majority of its membership refused to endorse a plan which she and Vida Goldstein proposed to broaden its party platform to include more openly Marxist goals. In a letter to **Cecilia John**, she explained: "I am getting more near to Anarchism and I.W.W. [International Workers of the World] everyday. . . . I hate the idea of government[,] . . . and socialist politicians . . . would abuse power just as liberal and labour."

After breaking with the Women's Political Association, Adela Pankhurst joined the Victoria Socialist Party (VSP) where she took a job as a political organizer and lecturer. She quickly adapted militant suffragist tactics to Australian politics. Especially effective was the technique of unrelenting and strident questioning of opponents' political leaders at public meetings in order to disrupt their activities.

Considered by many to be the VSP's best speaker, she toured Western Australia, wrote for a variety of VSP publications and quickly made a name for herself in radical political circles. Her articles were very well received by the general public as well as by socialists because she avoided traditional left-wing jargon and wrote in a distinctly un-Marxist style.

After the inauguration of military conscription in Australia, she wrote *Betrayed: A Play in Five Acts* which depicted Australia as a militaristic penal state, and edited *The Dawn,* a monthly socialist newsletter for children. She became so popular so quickly that by June 1917 the *Socialist* was advertising a "plaster bust of Miss Pankhurst for sale at 3s 6d."

During this time, Adela was fined and sent to prison several times for her political activities, and she met and fell in love with Tom Walsh, a militant socialist and union organizer who was 18 years older than she. She also was arrested for leading a large demonstration of women from the Socialist Women's League to demand wartime rationing of food, clothing, and other essential items and for inciting a delegation of unemployed workers to smash the windows of (capitalist) department stores in Melbourne in order to obtain the clothes and blankets they needed. After her release on remand (bail), the Reverend Frederick Sinclaire married Adela Pankhurst and Tom Walsh at the Free Religious Fellowship hall in Melbourne on September 30, 1917, and she became a stepmother to his three daughters. Despite later rumors that she had married Walsh only to avoid deportation, there is no evidence that their union was anything but a loving marriage—a partnership based upon mutual affection which lasted until Walsh's death in 1943. Adela's new domestic responsibilities did not, however, dilute her radicalism, and she was arrested again in late 1917—this time for offensive behavior—and sentenced to nine months in prison. After refusing to accept the government's offer of release if she agreed not to speak in public, she began serving her sentence in Pentridge jail. Despite a petition to obtain her immediate freedom signed by thousands, she was not released until January 1918 when her physicians recommended early release on medical grounds. Adela attempted to resume her strenuous schedule of feminist, socialist, and pacifist activism, but she became mentally and physically exhausted, and had to resign as an organizer from the Victoria Socialist Party in May 1918. That did not stop Emmeline and Christabel Pankhurst from printing a "tart" condemnation of both Sylvia and Adela in the pages of their jingoistic newspaper, *Britannia.*

Put up the sword!

—**Adela Pankhurst**

In May 1919, soon after the birth of her first baby, Richard, named for Adela's father, the new family moved to Sydney where Tom took over the Australian Seamen's Union which made him first its secretary, then its general secretary, and finally its president (1921–25). During this time, Adela helped with her husband's attempt to mobilize and expand his union. In addition, the couple took an active role in the early meetings which led to the formation of the Australian Communist Party. After its founding, they both were asked to serve on the provisional Executive Committee but, although they professed their belief in Marxism, it was of the utopian, humanistic sort—a vision of the universe which did not blend well with the more hard-line Marxism practiced by the Australian Communist Party. Predictably, they soon turned against the Communist Party's sabotage tactics which involved political obstructionism and industrial disruption.

In October 1920, Adela gave birth to her first daughter, Sylvia, whom she named for her sister. She soon became pregnant again with her second daughter, Christian, in 1921. A third daughter, Ursula, was born two years later. Adela was a poor cook and an indifferent laundress and cleaner, but she insisted on keeping house for her husband and family. Nonetheless, raising four children and three stepchildren did not keep her from raising political Cain. Friends reported that she often could be found grinding out radical political articles with one child on her lap and another at her shoulder. A good example of the work she did is a landmark article in feminist Marxism called "Communism and Social Purity" which traced the evils of prostitution to the economic pressures and emotional blackmail put on young women by capitalism. It was printed in *The Worker's Dreadnought* by her sister Sylvia in February 1921.

As the Australian Communist Party became increasingly more strident and doctrinaire, Adela and Tom broke with both it and communism in general. They reembraced socialism by rejoining the Victoria Socialist Party in 1923 and remained active and influential in labor politics on both the local and national levels. In fact, during the early 1920s, Tom Walsh was one of the most important left-wing politicians on the continent and, for a while at least, Adela may have been the most influential woman in Australia.

In the mid-1920s, Tom Walsh clashed with a left-wing faction of his union over strategy and politics, a battle which resulted in his losing control of his union in 1928 and retiring from active political life. To the relief of his family, Tom took over most of the cooking and housekeeping for them. This allowed Adela to invest more time in her political work and writing. She began moving increasingly further to the political right and by 1928 former communist Adela Pankhurst had become so conservative that she had begun speaking out in favor of industrial peace, national unity, the British Empire, and the traditional family. By June 1928, she was busily engaged in plans to start an Australian branch of the Industrial Peace Union of Great Britain. By the early 1930s, she had come to believe that the worldwide depression had been caused by economic stagnation which could be alleviated by industrial co-operation which would increase the efficiency and raise the economic productivity of the Imperial economy. In the course of her work, Adela Pankhurst, erstwhile Marxist and union official, routinely crossed picket lines to speak out against strikes—actions which usually brought about a predictably hostile reception from the pickets and crowds.

Veering even further to the political right, she grew increasingly dogmatic and chauvinistic and, in 1928, founded the Australian branch of the extremely successful Women's Guild of Empire, a conservative imperial organization which had been founded in the mid-'20s by a former suffragist, ***Flora Drummond**. The Australian branch of the Guild actively raised money to relieve suffering among working-class women and children. In addition to administrative work, Adela took on the task of editing the Guild's publication, *The Empire Gazette*, and did a good deal of writing for it until she resigned as editor on October 1, 1939.

To reward her for this Marxist apostasy, in 1937, Adela was awarded a King George VI Coronation Medal for her work in the Women's Guild of Empire. By this time, she had moved so far to the political right that she was afraid Britain might abandon its commitment to Australia. As a part of her newly launched anti-Bolshevik campaign, she flirted with fascism, joined W.J. Miles' and P.R. Stephensen's isolationist "Australia First" movement, and visited Japan in January 1940 as a guest of the Japanese government. Upon her return, she actually recommended that Australia sign a trade agreement and a treaty of friendship with the Japanese empire, a political position which made her very unpopular in the fall of 1940. Nonetheless, she decided to stand as a candidate for the Australian Federal Senate on a pro-Japanese, semi-fascist platform. Her campaign was a miserable failure, but she continued, unrepentantly, to dress in Japanese gowns as late as the fall of 1941. Although she recanted after the Japanese attack on Pearl Harbor and resigned her membership in the isolationist Australia First movement, in March 1942 she was interned. When she learned that her husband was dying, she was prepared to sacrifice her principles in order to be with him during his final days and petitioned the government for her release on humanitarian grounds. Adela's appeal failed and her release was delayed until October 13, 1942—two days after she had begun a suffragist-style hunger strike in internment.

Upon her release, she studied nursing, a profession which she practiced after the death of her favorite daughter, Sylvia, and that of her husband in 1943. She devoted her long nursing career primarily to caring for developmentally challenged children. Just before her death on May 23, 1961, at the Home of Peace Hospital in Wahroonga, Sydney, she received religious instruction and was accepted into the Roman Catholic Church. Adela Pankhurst was buried with Catholic rites and laid beside her husband in the Unitarian section of Northern Suburbs cemetery—a maverick even in death.

SOURCES:

*Castle, Barbara. *Sylvia and Christabel Pankhurst.* NY: Penguin, 1987.

Damousi, Joy. "Socialist Women in Australia: 1890–1920," in *Melbourne Historical Journal.* Vol. XVII, 1985, pp. 59–68.

Liddington, Jill, and Jill Norris. *One Hand Tied Behind Us: The Rise of the Women's Suffrage Movement.* London: Virago, 1984.

Mitchell, David. *The Fighting Pankhursts.* NY: Macmillan, 1967.

——. *Women on the Warpath.* London: Jonathan Cape, 1966.

Pankhurst, Christabel. *Unshackled: The Story of How We Won the Vote.* Ed. by Lord Frederick W. Pethick-Lawrence. London: Hutchinson, 1959.

Pankhurst, Estelle Sylvia. *Life of Emmeline Pankhurst: The Suffragette Struggle for Women's Citizenship.* London: T.W. Laurie, 1935.

———. *The Suffragette Movement: An Intimate Account of Persons and Ideals.* London: Longmans, Green, 1932.

Pankhurst, Richard. *Sylvia Pankhurst: Artist and Crusader.* NY: Paddington Press, 1979.

Romero, Patricia. *E. Sylvia Pankhurst: Portrait of a Radical.* London: University Press, 1987.

SUGGESTED READING:

Dangerfield, George. *The Strange Death of Liberal England 1910–1914,* c. 1935 (NY: Capricorn Books, reprint, 1961).

Rosen, Andrew. *Rise Up, Women! The Militant Campaign of the Women's Social and Political Union 1903–1914.* London: Routledge & Kegan Paul, 1974.

RELATED MEDIA:

"Shoulder to Shoulder," produced by the British Broadcasting Company (BBC), based on the documentary book of the same name compiled and edited by **Midge MacKenzie**, was shown in the U.S. as a 6-part series on "Masterpiece Theater," 1988. Adela Pankhurst appears in Episode 1 but very little attention is devoted to her.

Nancy Ellen Rupprecht,
Associate Professor of History and Director of Women's Studies, Middle Tennessee State University, Murfreesboro, Tennessee

Pankhurst, Christabel (1880–1958)

English co-founder of the Women's Social and Political Union and the strategist behind its increasingly militant policy and violent tactics. *Name variations: Dame Christabel Pankhurst. Born Christabel Harriette Pankhurst in Manchester, England, on September 22, 1880; died in Los Angeles, California, on February 13, 1958; eldest of four children of Richard Marsden Pankhurst, LL.D., and Emmeline Goulden Pankhurst (1858–1928); sister of Sylvia (1882–1960), Adela (1885–1961), Henry Francis (Frank), and Francis Henry (Harry) Pankhurst; children: adopted daughter Betty, in 1930.*

Death of brother Frank (1888); death of father (1898); attended Victoria University in Manchester and received a first class degree in law, LL.B. (1906); co-founded the Women's Social and Political Union (1903); death of brother Harry (1910); unsuccessfully stood for Parliament (1918); death of her mother (1928); adopted a daughter (1930); was made a Dame Commander of the British Empire (DBE, 1936); moved to the United States (1940).

Selected writings: The Parliamentary Vote for Women *(Manchester: A. Haywood & Son, 189?);* The Commons Debate on Woman Suffrage with a reply by Christabel Pankhurst *(London: The Woman's Press, 1908);* The Militant Methods of the NWSPU *(London: The Woman's Press, 1908);* The Great Scourge and How to End It *(London, 1913, reprinted in Jane Marcus, ed.,* Suffrage and the Pankhursts. *London and NY: Routledge & Kegan Paul, 1987, pp. 187–241);* The War *(NY: Suffrage Pub., 1914);* International Militancy *(London: WSPU, 1915);* No Peace without Victory *(Knightsbridge: WSPU, 1917);* Industrial Salvation *(London: The Woman's Party, 1918);* The Lord Cometh! *(1922);* Pressing Problems of the Closing Age *(1922);* Some Modern Problems in the Light of Biblical Prophecy *(1922);* The World Unrest or Visions of the Dawn *(1926);* Seeing the Future *(London: Harper & Brothers, 1929);* The Uncurtained Future *(London: Hodder & Stoughton, 1940);* Unshackled: The Story of How We Won the Vote *(ed. by Lord Frederick W. Pethick-Lawrence, London: Hutchinson, 1959); editor of* The Suffragette *(1908–15).*

Christabel Pankhurst was born in Manchester, England, in 1880, the daughter of Richard Marsden Pankhurst and ***Emmeline Pankhurst**. Because Richard believed that little girls needed beautiful names he chose Christabel from one of Coleridge's poems:

The lovely lady, Christabel,
Whom her father loves so well.

Adored by both her parents, she was almost a textbook illustration of the first child born to a middle-class family. In childhood as well as adulthood, she was beautiful, intelligent, graceful, confident, charming, and charismatic. Throughout their lives, a special bond of love and respect existed between Emmeline and Christabel Pankhurst which never developed between any of the other Pankhurst children and their mother.

She was educated at home where she learned to read at a remarkably early age. Christabel later attended Manchester High School for Girls until 1896 when she moved to Geneva to learn French in the home of her mother's schoolfriend, **Noemie de Rochefort Dufaux**. With her father's death in 1898, she returned to Manchester where she helped her mother rear her younger siblings and took a position as her mother's assistant when she was appointed Registrar of Births and Deaths.

Following in the family tradition of radical politics, Christabel joined the Manchester Women's Trade Union Council and began working actively behind the scenes on behalf of women's causes. In 1901, she joined and was made a member of the executive committee of the North of England Society for Women's Suffrage. Through these organizations, she met **Esther Roper** and ***Eva Gore-Booth** who had come north to organize female mill workers for both suffrage and socio-economic causes. They encouraged her to devote her oratorical skills to the women's movement because Christabel's dramatic speaking style, beguiling voice, and intelligent repartee made her a speaker in great demand on the topic of women's suffrage. As she later described her commitment to women's emancipation, "Here, then, was an aim in life for me—the liberation of politically fettered womanhood."

In 1903, Christabel joined with her mother in breaking with the Labour Party to form a more radical independent women's suffrage organization, the Women's Social and Political Union (WSPU). From its inception, the WSPU was committed to activism and political independence, but no one who studied its organization carefully could doubt that it was tightly controlled by the Pankhurst women despite the existence of a titular executive board.

> Do not beg, do not grovel!
>
> **—Christabel Pankhurst**

After searching for a metier for some time, Christabel decided to follow in her father's footsteps by reading law at Victoria University in Manchester. In 1904, she applied for admission to Lincoln's Inn where her father had been a member but was refused because of her gender. In 1905, she won a prize for International Law and she took joint first class honors in the LL.B. exam in 1906 despite her heavy speaking schedule and her deep personal commitment to the new WSPU. Soon thereafter, she moved to London to join her family and establish the headquarters of WSPU in Clement's Inn.

During the same year, Christabel and ***Annie Kenney** were sent to prison after inaugurating the WSPU policy of militancy by resisting arrest after haranguing a Liberal Party meeting when Sir Edward Grey refused to explain his stand on women's suffrage. They were manhandled and, when a policeman treated Christabel roughly, she spat at him, because her arms were restrained and she had no other way to commit an assault. This incident is significant because, for the first time, it was covered by a newspaper, thus breaking the unofficial boycott against women's suffrage press coverage. As Christabel explained, "Where peaceful means had failed, one act of militancy succeeded and never again was the cause ignored by that or any other newspaper."

When the WSPU was re-formed in the autumn of 1907 after a split in its ranks, Christabel was appointed its chief organizer. From this point on, she followed an almost unwavering course of increasingly militant political action to obtain votes for women, and she managed to convince the majority of WSPU followers that if women observed a course of defiant action, they would prevail in the end. She used her legal training to justify the use of force and violence in the quest for votes for British women. As she explained:

> According to a recognized legal principle force may be used in order to preserve property, to save life or to vindicate a right. . . . On this same principle, those who are claiming the vote are clearly entitled to use such force as is necessary to vindicate this supreme right of citizenship. . . . The Women's Social and Political Union, believing that "rebellion against tyrants is obedience to God," intend to continue their campaign of protest, using just so much force, and no more, as is necessitated by the action of the Government.

Emmeline Pankhurst provided the moral authority within the WSPU, but it was Christabel's organizing ability, strategy, and policies which charted the increasingly violent direction which radical women's suffrage politics took in Britain.

"Queen Christabel," as the press dubbed her because of her extraordinary charisma and imperious manner, eventually became almost as famous as her mother and, like her mother, became one of the first non-royal, non-theatrical celebrities in Britain. However, some suffrage workers complained that when the press focused its attention on her personality it detracted from the cause of votes for women. They interpreted her legendary "flair" as arrogant egotism. Nonetheless, it was Christabel Pankhurst's undoubted ability to inspire courage and determination in the genteelly brought up middle- and upper-class women who formed the bulk of the WSPU's membership that enabled the suffragists—dubbed by the *London Daily Mail*, the Suffragettes—to carry out so many spectacular and dangerous acts of political sabotage. Her ability to inspire devotion in her followers was legendary in suffrage circles. As WSPU stalwart Annie Kenney explained, "If the world were on one side and Christabel Pankhurst on the other, I would walk straight over to Christabel Pankhurst." Similarly, suffragist **Grace Roe** declared, "I would follow her anywhere."

The most crucial decisions Christabel made were the intersecting policies of limiting WSPU efforts solely to the issue of women's suffrage (no matter how worthy other women's causes were) and her determination to direct recruitment propaganda primarily toward middle- and upper-class women. Christabel's sister ***Sylvia Pankhurst** vehemently opposed these policies because she believed they were taking the Pankhursts further away from their socialist

Christabel Pankhurst

roots and turning the WSPU into an elitist organization which ignored the dire socio-economic issues which faced working-class women. Christabel, however, successfully maintained that by diluting the suffrage issue with others, no material progress would be made for any women. She also contended that upper-class women were much more newsworthy than their proletarian sisters and that most working-class women had neither the time nor the energy to devote their lives to the suffrage cause. Moreover, she argued that the vote gave women of all classes the tool they needed most to fight subsequent battles.

The only other issue which was included on the WSPU agenda was a frontal attack on the sexual oppression of women which Christabel believed was the reverse side of their political oppression. These mirror-image issues had to be fought simultaneously because the misogynistic theory of separate male and female spheres of competence on which both were based was rooted deeply in British life, custom, law, and culture. It provided the justification for male oppression of women and served to camouflage "the doctrine that women is sex and beyond that nothing." Therefore, Christabel Pankhurst argued that the vote:

> is the symbol of freedom and equality. . . . Women's disenfranchisement is to them a perpetual lesson in servility. . . . The inferiority of women is a hideous lie which has been enforced by law and woven into the British constitution, and it is quite hopeless to expect to reform . . . the relationship [between] the sexes until women are politically enfranchised.

Christabel was not exaggerating the depth of misogyny imbedded in the anti-women's suffrage position or the sexual nature of it. The attack against women's suffrage was led by Sir Almoth Wright, a pioneering physician in vaccine therapy, who claimed to speak in the name of science when he argued:

> The question of suffrage, and with it the larger question as to the proper sphere of woman, finally turns upon the question to what imprint women's sexual system leaves upon her physical frame, character and intellect. . . . [Women's character defects] as irremediable as "racial characters" delineated her proper sphere and settled once and for all any nonsense as to women's suffrage.

Although Christabel Pankhurst believed that the separate-spheres ideology which oppressed women was so imbedded in British culture that it pervaded and limited many aspects of women's lives, she chose to focus on the two issues which she believed were the most vital. The vote for women was of primary importance because "through the vote women will gain a new confidence in themselves and a real power to help themselves." The vote, she believed, would enable them to look inward to develop a sense of personal worth rather than to allow themselves to be defined and valued in terms of their relationship to men. The second prong of her attack was directed against prostitution and venereal disease which she believed were a natural result of patriarchal control of society. The double standard which made sex outside of marriage an indelible stain for women but a mere peccadillo for men led the men to seek out the services of prostitutes, many of whom were infected with social diseases. The husbands contracted venereal disease from them and transmitted it to their unsuspecting wives. This led not only to misery for the women involved, but to birth defects and a variety of socio-sexual problems in respectable families. Using extremely separatist language, Christabel urged abstention for men and women alike and argued vehemently against lowering high standards of sexual morality. She insisted that the suffragist's political militancy must be coupled with a lifestyle which was both sexually and morally above reproach. In her book on prostitution and VD, *The Great Scourge,* she summarized the behavioral mandates inherent in her theories in the slogan, "Votes for women, chastity for men!"

By this time, a trace of racism had crept into Christabel's theories and policies. She began to argue that because male lust would lead to the degeneration of racial strength and the production of half-caste children, this eventually would weaken the British Empire. Therefore, women needed the vote for racial reasons as well as for personal ones because they had "a service to render to the state as well as the home, to the race as well as the family."

After Black Friday (November 18, 1910), when demonstrators were beaten and sexually groped by police officers and rioters for nearly six hours, resulting in broken bones, ripped flesh, and the death of at least two of the demonstrators from injuries suffered during the beatings, WSPU political violence escalated. This attests to the WSPU's unconditional rejection of both women's second-class political status and the "angel in the house" role that Victorian society prescribed for middle-class women. The drastic nature of the measures they were prepared to take to achieve the goals of political, economic, and legal equality lends credence to the suffragists' contention that they considered themselves not merely protestors but guerrilla warriors on the front lines of a civil war undertaken to destroy the patriarchal foundation upon which the British government rested.

Women's increased militancy led to the arrest of so many WSPU leaders that it became imperative that either Emmeline or Christabel Pankhurst find a place of safety from which to direct policy. Because Christabel was the acknowledged theoretician, strategist, and tactician of the WSPU while Emmeline was its anchor and role model, it was Christabel who fled to Paris in disguise in 1912. However, from her continental vantage point she lost touch with the day-to-day realities of the British political arena and her policies became increasingly ephemeral, visionary, and dogmatic. Eventually, she became almost indifferent to the suffrage bills which were introduced into Parliament and to significant changes which were taking place in British politics. While in Paris, Christabel also joined the lesbian feminist circle led by Princess Edmond de Polignac (***Winnaretta Singer**), but there is no indication that she ever adopted a gay lifestyle.

After 1912, under Christabel's direction from Paris, a pattern of rapidly increasing violence characterized WSPU political policy. Even when Prime Minister Herbert Asquith appeared to be holding out an olive branch to British women in 1914, because of his government's record of duplicity when dealing with the WSPU, Christabel rejected her sister Sylvia's corresponding call for a universal political truce for all women's suffrage organizations. However, when the Great War broke out in 1914, Christabel was so convinced that the suffrage cause was all but won that she returned to England to transform the WSPU into a patriotic organization. She argued that it was Britain's duty to rescue France and British women's duty to aid in the campaign. On October 15, 1915, she changed the name of the WSPU's official journal *The Suffragette* to *Britannia* and offered her services to the government to help in recruiting and organizing women's war work. She believed that by sharing in the war effort the WSPU would put the government in a position in which it would have to extend the right to vote to British women because, if it did not, she wrote, "Mrs. Pankhurst and her Suffragettes would resume militancy as soon as the war was ended, and no government could arrest and imprison women who, in the country's danger, had set aside their campaign to help the national cause." For whatever reason, the Representation of the People Act of 1918 gave the vote to women of 30 and men of 25, an inequity which was removed by the so-called "Flapper Law" of 1928.

The enfranchisement of women and the end of the war in 1918 enabled Christabel to run for Parliament as a coalition candidate for the industrial constituency of Smethwick. She was narrowly defeated, primarily because she insisted on running on a rather unpopular platform which advocated a visionary future of industrial salvation which would make Britain happy and prosperous through the use of automation tightly controlled by a collective economy. Nonetheless, Christabel polled a vote of 8,614, the most of any woman who ran for office in the first election in which women could participate. It must have been maddening for her to see ***Nancy Astor**, a woman who had not participated in the suffrage campaign and whose wealth and connections eased her political career path, become the first woman to be take a seat in Parliament even though she had polled fewer votes than Christabel had amassed. (Countess ***Constance Markievicz** had won a seat in 1916 but, as a member of the Irish delegation, she did not enter Parliament.) In 1919, Christabel disbanded both the Women's Party and *Britannia*. She stood once more for Parliament, this time for the Abbey division of Westminster, but did not contest the election and retired from political life soon thereafter.

When the British Parliament passed the Sex Disqualification [Removal] Act in 1919, Christabel's law degree would have permitted her to begin practicing law in British courts, but she showed no interest in a career before the bar. Instead, she accepted an invitation from her friend Lord Northcliffe to write a series of substantive articles on the WSPU suffrage and war campaigns for his *Weekly Dispatch* under the title "The Confessions of Christabel." In Confession #1, "Why I never Married," she explained that she had remained single in order to demonstrate "my own personal unending unyieldingness as a leader." Another article attacked writers and politicians who argued that it was women's war effort rather than WSPU militancy that secured the vote for women. Christabel countered that women's suffrage would never have been granted if British politicians had not feared a resumption of WSPU guerrilla warfare. Although these articles were well received, she chose not to develop a career in journalism.

In January 1921, she advertised in several newspapers for "lucrative, non-political employment." Although she received many offers, including several from film companies, none of them interested her. (One music-hall entertainer, a Mr. Selbit, offered her the job of "sawing through a woman," an indication that despite women's winning the vote, misogynism had not been exorcised in Britain.)

When Christabel Pankhurst visited her mother in Canada and the United States in 1921, she became increasingly interested in Second Adventism, a movement which proclaimed the Second Coming of Christ. In 1922, she published her first Second Adventist books (*The Lord Commeth!* and *Pressing Problems of the Closing Age*) and, in 1926, her monograph *The World's Unrest or Visions of the Dawn* demonstrated both her increasing political conservatism and her avid millenialism. All three books were so well received in the British and North American evangelical religious communities that she was selected to give a series of prestigious lectures at Knox Presbyterian Church in Toronto, Ontario, which attracted audiences so large that the overflow crowd had to be shut out of the church. In *The Fighting Pankhursts,* David Mitchell argues that "in the U.S. and Canada, Christabel Pankhurst raised Second Adventism almost single-handedly from its backstreet fundamentalist rut, lending it a dull gleam of intellectual prestige."

In 1926, Emmeline Pankhurst convinced Christabel, against her better judgment, to go the French Riviera where they opened the English

Teashop of Good Hope, a British-style tea room in Jean-les-Pins. Like Emmeline's other commercial enterprises, it was a financial failure. The Pankhurst women returned to England in 1926. Two years later, Emmeline died, leaving Christabel to face the largest personal loss of her life.

By 1930, Christabel had recovered enough from her grief to put her life back on track. First she adopted a daughter (Betty); then she re-emerged on the British political scene preaching the gospel of Second Adventism and supporting Conservative Party political candidates and ideas. As in North America, she was in great demand as an orator and she wrote a series of best-selling polemical tracts on the Second Advent. Those who heard her speak attested to her commanding and captivating presence on stage. Although her voice was shriller than her mother's had been, she had the same ability to project it to the back of any auditorium without a microphone. Her immense popularity as a public speaker is documented by the fact that several times she was able to fill the Royal Albert Hall (seating capacity, 10,000) to overflowing when discussing the Second Coming.

In 1936, as part of His Majesty's New Year's Honors, Christabel Pankhurst was proclaimed a Dame Commander of the British Empire (DBE), an honor which she prized for the remainder of her life. Nonetheless, in 1940 she moved permanently to the United States where her adopted daughter had emigrated. She finally settled in Santa Monica, California, where she was considered something of a personality, a strange combination of former suffragist revolutionary, evangelical Christian and almost stereotypically proper "English lady" who always was in demand as a lecturer. During World War II, she was one of the keynote speakers selected to address an important Christian Fellowship Bible Conference in Los Angeles. This appearance made her an even more popular orator on the religious circuit, a career choice which also enabled her to speak on political and women's issues when she wished to do so. With the advent of regular television broadcasting in the post-World War II era, Christabel Pankhurst became a frequent panelist on California public affairs telecasts.

One of the strangest episodes of her later life helped to alleviate her economic difficulties and allowed her to pick and choose only those public lectures she wished to deliver. This was the substantial legacy that she received under quasi-ghoulish circumstances. **Olivia Durand-Deacon,** an aged but wealthy British widow, was brutally murdered by her companion John George Haigh who then carefully dissolved her corpse in a bath of acid. For reasons which she apparently did not disclose, Durand-Deacon bequeathed an annuity of £250 to Christabel.

Not long after she received this bizarre legacy, Christabel was involved in an automobile accident in which her friend, the driver, was killed. Although she was seriously injured, she recovered completely and resumed her active life. It was, therefore, quite unexpected when Christabel Pankhurst died suddenly. On February 13, 1958, her housekeeper found her dead, sitting bolt upright in a straight-backed chair in her Santa Monica living room. Unlike her mother, her body had not been seriously weakened through forcible feeding and, unlike Sylvia and Adela, she had not been plagued with headaches, neuralgia, and a host of minor physical complaints. Indeed, except for a few minor colds and an occasional bout of influenza, Christabel had not known sickness and had not been ill before her death.

At her crowded memorial service at the Church of St. Martin-in-the-Fields (Trafalgar Square, London), her former WSPU comrade Lord Frederick Pethick-Lawrence (husband of ***Emmeline Pethick-Lawrence**) praised Christabel Pankhurst as the most brilliant political tactician of her time and a woman who had "changed the course of human history and changed it for the better."

In 1959, a bronze medallion honoring Christabel struck by Peter Hills was added to the memorial statue of her mother in Victoria Tower Gardens. An excellent oil painting of her by **Ethel Wright** is in the possession of Mrs. Victor Duval, and the National Gallery owns a chalk drawing of her by **Jessie Holliday**.

SOURCES:

***Castle, Barbara.** *Sylvia and Christabel Pankhurst.* NY: Penguin, 1987.

Garner, Les. *Stepping Stones to Women's Liberty: Feminist Ideas in the Women's Suffrage Movement, 1900–1918.* Rutherford, NJ: Fairleigh Dickinson University Press, 1984.

Kent, Susan Kingsley. *Sex and Suffrage in Britain, 1860–1914.* Princeton, NJ: Princeton University Press, 1987.

Liddington, Jill, and Jill Norris. *One Hand Tied Behind Us: The Rise of the Women's Suffrage Movement.* London: Virago, 1984.

Marcus, Jane, ed. *Suffrage and the Pankhursts.* London: Routledge & Kegan Paul, 1987.

Mitchell, David. *The Fighting Pankhursts.* NY: Macmillan, 1967.

——. *Queen Christabel: A Biography of Christabel Pankhurst.* London: Macdonald and Jane's, 1977.

——. *Women on the Warpath.* London: Jonathan Cape, 1966.

Pankhurst, Christabel. *Unshackled: The Story of How We Won the Vote.* Ed. by Frederick W. Pethick-Lawrence. London: Hutchinson, 1959.

Pankhurst, Emmeline. *My Own Story.* NY: Hearst's International, 1914 (London: Virago, reprint, 1979).

Pankhurst, Estelle Sylvia. *The Suffragette: The History of the Women's Militant Suffrage Movement 1905–1910.* London: Gay and Hancock, 1911.

———. *The Suffragette Movement: An Intimate Account of Persons and Ideals.* London: Longmans, Green, 1932.

SUGGESTED READING:

Dangerfield, George. *The Strange Death of Liberal England 1910–1914,* c. 1935 (NY: Capricorn Books, reprint, 1961 [Dangerfield's interpretation of the British Women's Suffrage movement, based upon Sylvia's interpretation of it, became the standard source on the movement for at least a generation]).

Rosen, Andrew. *Rise Up, Women! The Militant Campaign of the Women's Social and Political Union 1903–1914.* London: Routledge & Kegan Paul, 1974.

Strachey, Ray. *"The Cause": A Short History of the Women's Movement in Great Britain.* Port Washington, NY: Kennikat Press, 1969.

RELATED MEDIA:

"Shoulder to Shoulder," produced by the British Broadcasting Company (BBC), based on the documentary book of the same name compiled and edited by **Midge MacKenzie**, was shown in the U.S. as a 6-part series on "Masterpiece Theater," 1988; the episodes are titled, "The Pankhurst Family," "Annie Kenney," "Lady Constance Lytton," "Christabel Pankhurst," "Outrage," and "Sylvia Pankhurst." While Christabel Pankhurst is included in all 6 parts, and is featured in Episodes 1 and 4, the series is based on Sylvia Pankhurst's interpretation of the WSPU suffrage campaign and, therefore, is slanted against Christabel's interpretation of it.

Nancy Ellen Rupprecht,
Associate Professor of History and Director of Women's Studies, Middle Tennessee State University, Murfreesboro, Tennessee

Pankhurst, E. Sylvia (1882–1960).

See Pankhurst, Sylvia.

Pankhurst, Emmeline (1858–1928)

Matriarch of radical feminism in Britain who, along with her daughter Christabel, founded the Women's Social and Political Union, the organization which represented the most militant wing of the British women's suffrage movement. *Born Emmeline Goulden in Manchester, England, on July 14, 1858; died on June 14, 1928, in London, England; eldest of 11 children (including five daughters) of Robert Goulden (owner of a calico-printing and bleach works) and Sophia Jane Craine (Crane) Goulden; married Richard Marsden Pankhurst, LL.D., in 1879; children: Christabel Harriet Pankhurst (1880–1958); Estelle Sylvia Pankhurst (1882–1960); Francis Henry (Frank) Pankhurst (1884–1888); Adela Constantia Mary Pankhurst (1885–1961); Henry Francis (Harry) Pankhurst (1889–1910).*

Death of son Frank (1888); widowed (1898); founded Women's Social and Political Union (1903); death of son Harry (1910); co-founded the British Women's Party (1917); moved to Canada (1918); returned to England (1926).

Selected writings: The Trial of the Suffragette Leaders *(London: The Woman's Press, 190?);* The Importance of the Vote *(London: The Woman's Press, 1908);* Verbatim report of Mrs. Pankhurst's speech, delivered 13 November 1913 at Parson's Theater, Hartford, Conn. *(Hartford: Connecticut Woman Suffrage Association, 1913);* My Own Story *(London: G. Nash, 1914).*

The lives of Emmeline Pankhurst and her daughters challenge several significant gender stereotypes which are prevalent in Western patriarchal culture: among them are the assumption that the British, especially British women, are mild-mannered and reserved; the notion that political violence is foreign to women's nature; and finally, the belief that each generation of women in the 20th century has been more articulate and assertive in demanding its legal and political rights. Those who think that we have "come a long way, baby" need only to study the lives of the remarkable Pankhurst women to discover how dangerous it is to base historical generalizations on journalists' assumptions and cigarette slogans.

Unlike the case of most political rebels, Emmeline Goulden Pankhurst's radicalism was home grown. The third generation of female social activists in her family, she was born in 1858 in Manchester, England, the daughter of Robert Goulden and **Sophia Jane Goulden**. Her grandmother, **Mary Goulden**, had been a member of the Anti-Corn Law League while both her parents were actively involved in a variety of radical political causes in Manchester. In 1865, her father helped found the original Women's Suffrage Committee, and her mother also worked actively for women's emancipation. Indeed, Emmeline was only 14 years old when her mother first took her to a women's suffrage meeting.

Although she shared her parents' deep personal commitment to social causes, Emmeline also loved beautiful things and always wore feminine clothing because she believed it enhanced her personal style. Throughout her life, she paid careful attention to both her appearance and her voice. She never shouted, but her diction was so pure and her voice was so powerful and resonant that she never needed to use a microphone, regardless of the size of the auditorium in which she was speaking. There is little doubt that her striking, frail beauty, confident demeanor, dignified carriage, sonorous voice, and photogenic face were assets in her political endeavors.

She attended a private school in Manchester until the age of 15 when she was sent to Paris to the École Normale in the Avenue de Neuilly where she became close friends with **Noemie de Rochefort (Dufaux)**, daughter of Marquis Henri de Rochefort-Lucay, the dashing hero of the abortive revolutionary Paris Commune of 1871. The Rochefort family introduced Emmeline to the literary and political circles of Paris, an experience which dazzled her, and to French couturiers who helped her to develop a personal style of fashion. During this sojourn, the love of all things French became imbedded in her personality as did her distaste for most things German.

Upon returning to her parents' home in Manchester at age 18, Emmeline settled into their radical socio-political circle. Dr. Richard Marsden Pankhurst, a barrister who had made a reputation both as a political thinker and an activist, was a frequent guest in the Goulden home. When 20-year-old Emmeline met and married 40-year-old Richard it was a genuine love match based on mutual respect.

After their wedding in 1879, Pankhurst became deeply involved with her husband's career as well as with the causes they both championed. Despite the difference in their ages, their marriage was an almost unqualified success, and their home, "Old Trafford" at One Dayton Terrace, Manchester, was a happy one. Emmeline's commitment to women's legal and political emancipation was matched or surpassed by her husband who had helped to draft the Women's Disabilities Removal Act, the first Women's Suffrage bill submitted to Parliament (1870), and served as counsel for the claimants in the groundbreaking *Chorlton* v. *Lings* case of 1868 in which 5,346 women householders of Manchester unsuccessfully demanded the right to vote under the existing law. With his wife's support, he also drafted the Married Women's Property Act of 1882, argued many women's rights cases before the bar, and unsuccessfully stood for election as a Liberal parliamentary candidate from Rotherhithe in 1884. Emmeline Pankhurst's active participation in her husband's campaign taught her to speak with ease in public, to deal successfully with hecklers, and even how to dodge the mice (alive and dead), tomatoes, flour and stones sometimes hurled at British political speakers, especially those speaking in favor of women's suffrage. In the same year, the Pankhursts broke with the Liberal Party because its leader, William Gladstone, refused to put women's suffrage into the Reform Bill of 1884; and, soon thereafter, they joined the Fabian Society.

In 1895, they moved to London where Emmeline Pankhurst attempted to help with the faltering family finances by opening Emerson and Co., a small "fancy goods" shop selling silks, pottery, lampshades, and bric-a-brac in the West End of the city—an enterprise which soon was awash in red ink. At first, they lived above the shop at 165 Hampsted Rd., Bloomsbury, but with the failure of Emerson's, the family moved to 8 Russell Square at the corner of Barnard Street where Emmeline immersed herself in running a political salon which included prominent socialist and progressive thinkers such as Kier Hardie, ***Annie Besant**, ***Elizabeth Cady Stanton**, Sir Charles Dilke and ***Emily Dilke**, and William Morris. In addition, in 1889, Emmeline and Richard Pankhurst co-founded the Women's Franchise League to obtain the right for women to vote in local elections.

Between 1880 and 1889, despite this whirlwind of political activity, Emmeline Pankhurst gave birth to five children—***Christabel** (b. September 22, 1880), ***Sylvia** (b. May 5, 1882), Frank Henry (b. February 1884 and died in childhood of diphtheria in 1888), ***Adela** (b. June 19, 1885), and Henry Frank, known as Harry (b. July 1889 and died of poliomyelitis in 1910). Her mothering was, at best, erratic. She personally raised her eldest daughter, Christabel, with whom she formed an intensely close lifelong bond, and was somewhat involved in the upbringing of her second daughter, Sylvia. Although she managed to instill a sense of love and security in the rest of her brood through spurts of maternal solicitude, for the most part she allowed governesses to supervise the upbringing of the younger children. This scattergun approach to parenting did not seem to lessen the love and loyalty that the Pankhurst children felt for both parents.

Financial reverses forced the Pankhursts to return to Manchester in 1893 where they took up residence at 4 Buckingham Crescent, Victoria Park. Richard Pankhurst resumed his legal career, and the couple soon became involved with the work of the Manchester Suffrage Society. In 1894, they joined the new Independent Labour Party for which Richard stood twice, unsuccessfully, as a candidate for Parliament. Emmeline not only worked actively in her husband's election campaigns, she also organized free canteen

Emmeline Pankhurst

restaurants for the poor and in 1895 was elected to an unpaid post on the Board of Poor Law Guardians of a workhouse.

In 1898, she crossed the Channel to visit Christabel who was perfecting her French by living in Geneva with her mother's old schoolfriend Noemie de Rochefort Dufaux, and her husband Swiss painter Frédéric Dufaux. During the visit, a telegram from Sylvia, reading "Father ill. Come.," called her back to England. On the return train, she learned of the death of her husband from a perforated ulcer when she spotted its announcement in bold newspaper headlines. Because her husband's death left her in dire financial straits, Pankhurst accepted paid employment as a Registrar of Births and Deaths in Rusholme, Manchester, and, in 1898, reopened Emerson's, her "fancy goods" shop. Despite the need to make a living sufficient to support a four-child household, she found time to work on behalf of women's emancipation and sit on the Manchester School Board.

In 1903, as a tribute to his work on behalf of feminist and social causes, the Labour Party in Manchester named a new meeting facility in Salford, Pankhurst Hall, in Richard Pankhurst's memory. They commissioned Sylvia Pankhurst to decorate it and paint murals on the walls but, paradoxically, when the work was complete, the Labour Party refused to permit women to enter it because they wanted it as a social club open only to male party members. It was this incident which precipitated Emmeline Pankhurst's decision to break with the Labour Party.

And my last word is to the Government: I incite this meeting to rebellion!

—Emmeline Pankhurst (speech delivered at Royal Albert Hall, London, October 17, 1912)

On October 10, 1903, along with Christabel, she invited a few trusted Labour women to her home at 62 Nelson Street where she founded the Women's Social and Political Union (WSPU), an organization which was from its inception independent of all political parties and committed to direct and immediate radical political action to achieve its only goal—women's suffrage. As Pankhurst later explained, "There is no department of life in which the possession of the Parliamentary Vote will not make things easier for women today." Indeed, she believed that because the vote for women was so crucial, the WSPU had to vigorously oppose whatever party was in power until it committed itself irrevocably to women's suffrage as a party measure.

WSPU political activism at first entailed only tactical militancy in harassing Liberal politicians and disrupting their meetings. When arrested for such disruptions, WSPU members were sentenced to prison terms because, taking their cue from the Pankhursts, they invariably refused on principle to pay the fines assessed by courts which did not consider them full citizens. In the early years, this militancy on the part of the WSPU distinguished it from all other suffrage organizations and in 1906 led Emmeline Pankhurst to sever all ties with the moderate National Union of Women's Suffrage Societies (NUWSS) led by ***Millicent Garrett Fawcett.**

Emmeline Pankhurst's concept of political strategy and tactics was influenced by two main sources: her late husband and her eldest daughter. Christabel had a logical, trained legal mind which was supported by the uncompromising sureness which often characterizes youthful political theoreticians. Even though Emmeline Pankhurst always asserted that violence was a temporary expedient made necessary by circumstances, the WSPU's commitment to increasingly militant political action forced her to resign her post as Registrar of Births and Deaths in Manchester (which entailed the loss of her government pension) in 1907. During the same year, she moved the offices of the WSPU to Clement's Inn in London where she believed militancy would be more effective.

Because the WSPU was controlled by the Pankhursts and run autocratically, any dissent within the ranks resulted in splits within the WSPU and the subsequent formation of splinter groups, all of which were more moderate than the WSPU but much more radical than the NUWSS. One such organization was the Women's Freedom League which was founded in 1907 by ***Charlotte Despard** following her dismissal from the WSPU board by Emmeline Pankhurst after unsuccessfully attempting to alter the WSPU by turning it into a more democratic organization. It was, perhaps, prophetic that in 1907 Sylvia and Adela Pankhurst would have welcomed a more democratic WSPU, but they supported the autocratic administrative policy dictated by Emmeline and Christabel Pankhurst out of family loyalty. Nonetheless, since the younger Pankhurst daughters retained their father's democratic and socialist principles, the increasingly conservative political outlook which began to permeate WSPU policy after 1907 would become the source of a family rift and a second ideologically dictated split within the WSPU in 1914.

Suffragette (the name given to the WSPU radicals by the *London Daily Mail* in 1906) disputations and demonstrations were an unremarkable constant on the British political scene until serious violence first broke out in 1908 at Caxton Hall. Here, in response to a large suffrage demonstration, members of the crowd (who the demonstrators charged were plainclothes policemen) attacked the women with truncheons (billy clubs) and seriously wounded several of the demonstrators. This, the Pankhursts believed, was a red flag waved in their faces by the government.

Emmeline Pankhurst being carted off after an attempt to enter the gates of Buckingham Palace to see the king.

Therefore, Christabel and Emmeline Pankhurst argued, since patriarchal Britain respected the rights of property more than those of women, the only way to attack government was to strike blows at the thing it most respected, private property. They responded by massive rounds of stone throwing and property destruction designed to force the government to deal seriously with the cause of women's suffrage. British insurance companies, which had to pay large claims for much of the damage, were particular targets of the WSPU. "The argument of the broken window pane," as Emmeline Pankhurst described this violence against property, began with a relatively mild campaign of window smashing which eventually escalated into what she called "guerrilla warfare" by British women against their government.

Increased property violence led to the arrests of large numbers of suffragists and the increasingly hostile treatment of these prisoners by the authorities. To counter this, women suffrage prisoners began hunger striking—a tactic adopted by several later political protest movements. This led to severe retaliation when the government instituted the practice of forcible feeding in Strangeways Jail in September 1909. It was a cruel and brutal procedure which often left healthy victims severely debilitated and led to the death or permanent invalidism of several prominent suffrage workers who were not in robust health, such as Lady *Constance Lytton. Emmeline Pankhurst endured many episodes of forcible feeding which left her weak, bruised, and battered but still defiant. Hundreds of dedicated hunger strikers were prepared to equal her show of dedication. As Pankhurst described the valor of women's suffrage hunger-strikers in 1913:

> At the present time there are women lying at death's door recovering enough strength to undergo operations . . . [who] have not given in and won't give in, and who will be prepared, as soon as they get up from their sick-beds to go on as before. There are women who are being carried from their sick-beds on stretchers into [WSPU] meetings.

Outrage at the government's cruelty in continuing forcible feeding, despite pleas from the British medical and religious communities, attracted more women to the suffrage cause and more contributions to the WSPU. On November 18, 1910, known unaffectionately as "Black Friday," an incident similar to that at Caxton Hall took place except that in this instance the beatings administered to women suffragists were accompanied by humiliating sexual groping. This went on for nearly six hours and resulted in broken bones, ripped flesh, torn clothes, and the death of at least two of the demonstrators from injuries suffered during the beatings.

The year 1910 also brought great personal sorrow to Emmeline Pankhurst with the premature deaths of her only surviving son Harry in January, and her sister, suffragist ➡ **Mary Goulden Clarke**, in December, from a stroke brought on by the sapping effects of brutal forcible feeding after a hunger strike. Pankhurst wrote that her sister was simply "too frail to weather this rude tide of militant struggle."

The year 1910 also was the coronation year for the new monarch, George V. In order for the coronation to proceed without embarrassing demonstrations, Prime Minister Herbert Asquith negotiated a "truce" with the WSPU and the other suffrage leagues: government support for some form of women's suffrage in exchange for a domestic armistice. Christabel was skeptical about the good faith with which this offer was made, but her mother persuaded her to accept the truce. All activist women's suffrage protest ceased. Although the general framework of the settlement which eventually resulted in votes for women was worked out during this time, Christabel had correctly assessed the government's motives. Almost a year to the day since Black Friday, Asquith announced that the government would sponsor a new suffrage bill which would apply only to men and added insult to injury when he noted "democracy has no quarrel with the distinctions made by nature."

This was a signal for open revolt by the WSPU which escalated its violence during the next two and a half years into what the Pankhursts termed "civil war" against the government, using such tactics as organized arson and bombing. The Pankhursts made it clear that the only quarter to be given was that, however violent, suffragists would never under any circumstances take a human life. As Emmeline Pankhurst explained, "If we wish to succeed, we must take to guerrilla warfare. We have to fight by our woman's wit. One thing we regard as sacred and that is human life." The remarkable intelligence network put together by the Pankhursts allowed them to keep this pledge despite their unshakable commitment to domestic terrorism after 1912. Paradoxically, some historians have argued that the Pankhursts' reluctance to take human lives or to destroy hard economic targets, such as producing factories, or targets that could jeopardize British national security made them less dangerous and, therefore, less effective. The Pankhursts' stance, nonetheless, provides a concrete historical example disproving the theory that, no matter how much effort is expended in its execution, a terrorist organization cannot conduct an effective campaign of domestic violence which is limited by a respect for human life.

During this period of escalating violence, the four Pankhurst women were arrested so frequently that they realized that at least one of them had to be invulnerable to the government. Therefore, with the blessing of her mother, Christabel donned a flimsy disguise and escaped from England to Paris in 1912. From her safe haven in France, she could continue to direct WSPU policy and edit the union's journal, *The Suffragette,* while her mother took charge of the tactical direction of the movement.

After 1912, the WSPU was more violent and disrupted public life in Britain more consistently than any other dissident political group. Although some WSPU members defected to less radical suffrage organizations during this time, those who remained were prepared to go to extraordinary lengths to support the Pankhursts' call for guerrilla warfare. Emmeline Pankhurst explained that radically violent actions undertaken by women were warranted because, "we, being voteless, have no constitutional means whatever for the redress of our grievance." From her first arrest in 1908 to the end of the suffrage terrorist campaign in 1914, Pankhurst considered herself to be a soldier in the front lines of battle. When arrested for militant acts, she declared, "I look upon myself as a prisoner of war."

Although many WSPU terrorists were young, women of all ages participated in the struggle. Even very old women startled the police by applying for gun licenses while wearing the women's suffrage colors of purple, green, and white or smashing plate-glass windows in stores and offices by shooting stones through them with catapults (slingshots) fired from the open upper-decks of London's buses. (Judo-trained female body guards often protected "shooters" from civilians who might disarm them.) However, the women not only organized massive campaigns of window breaking and defacing private and public property, they burned so many letters in mailboxes that the number of private delivery services in central London escalated rapidly. Paintings were slashed and priceless sculpture was smashed; the organ was flooded at the Albert Hall; the tea pavilion at Kew Gardens was burned and its Orchid House was destroyed; race courses were burned; concession stands were blown up as were abandoned castles, unused railroad cars, and non-producing factories; "votes for women" was burned with acid into the "sacred cricket fields" of Oxford, Cambridge, and many elite prep schools such as Eton and Harrow; boats and boat houses were destroyed, as were bowling greens and sports arenas; and "no votes, no golf" was burned into the putting greens of golf links. Even the king was not spared: he must have been horrified on the day he discovered that the purple, green, and white flags of the women's suffrage movement had been substituted for the Royal Crests on his private golf course. Telephone wires all over Britain were cut; envelopes containing snuff and red paper were sent to Cabinet ministers; women's suffrage graffiti was chalked or painted on walls and pavements; and false fire alarms were set off in Britain's major cities. Communications were disrupted all over the British Isles; in fact, on three different occasions all communication between London and Glasgow was cut completely, at least once for a full day. Seats in theaters and sporting arenas often were slashed or stencilled with "votes for women" signs; kiosks at Regents Park were destroyed; bombs were placed in insurance company offices, government buildings and Liberal Party property; Cabinet minister David Lloyd George's new house was set ablaze; stained-glass windows in churches were shattered; women's suffrage leaflets were dropped from hot-air balloons floating over London's parks; and telegrams were sent by WSPU militants bogusly calling up the Army Reserves and the Territorial Guards.

Clarke, Mary Goulden (d. 1910)

English suffragist. *Died in December 25, 1910, in Manchester, England; daughter of Robert Goulden (owner of a calico-printing and bleach works) and Sophia Jane Craine (Crane) Goulden; sister of Emmeline Pankhurst (1858–1928); married.*

Mary Goulden Clarke was the daughter of Robert Goulden and **Sophia Jane Goulden** and the sister of ***Emmeline Pankhurst.** Mired in an unhappy marriage, Clarke became an organizer for the WSPU in Brighton where, frail and sensitive, she often faced down the seaside rowdies with courage. Arrested for window-breaking on Black Friday, treated roughly by police and bands of toughs, and force-fed in jail for one month, she died two days after her release while attending Christmas dinner with Emmeline and other members of the Pankhurst family. After Mary had quietly left the table, Emmeline found her unconscious; Clarke died of a burst blood vessel in her brain.

In 1913, the government countered with a new tactic by passing the so-called "Cat and Mouse" bill (The Prisoners' Temporary Discharge Act) which allowed the release of hunger-striking suffrage prisoners and their re-arrest on the same charge without the formality of any type of court procedure when they had recovered their health. Despite the fact that the "Cat and Mouse" act ran counter to the established principles of English law, the government used it extensively. For example, between January and June 1914, Emmeline Pankhurst was arrested and released 12 times, the final time in such a debilitated condition that she was not recognized by some of her colleagues.

In 1914, Pankhurst had to deal with what she considered to be the aberrant behavior of two of her daughters—Sylvia, who had organized a working-class suffrage organization within the WSPU called the East London Federation of Suffragettes (ELFS), and Adela who supported her. Sylvia's vocal disapproval of her mother and sister's elitist strategy and autocratic methods embarrassed Christabel who believed that, despite the huge demonstrations of working-class men and women in support of women's suffrage organized by her sister, Sylvia's efforts were counter-productive. So long as Sylvia and Adela espoused socialism, they could not embrace the principle that only women of property would first be enfranchised—a compromise Emmeline and Christabel were prepared to make in order to get the principle of votes for women recognized. Adela emigrated to Australia to work with a socialist-feminist organization run by ***Vida Goldstein.** Sylvia crossed the Channel to what proved to be a family showdown in Paris. Emmeline Pankhurst agreed with Christabel that Sylvia's independence from WSPU policy was intolerable and expelled her and the ELFS from the WSPU. Sylvia then garnered alternative funding to continue her work in London's East End while the WSPU escalated its campaign of violence against property, but Pankhurst family unity was shattered.

What ultimately would have happened to women's suffrage had the Great War (1914–18) not intervened is difficult to predict with certainty. It is possible that if a Labour-Liberal coalition government had been Asquith's only possibility of remaining in power, he would have accepted a form of women's suffrage since Labour was almost irrevocably committed to the full democratization of British society as a condition for a coalition partnership. Despite what seemed to be a peace offering by Asquith when he agreed to receive a deputation of working-class women affiliated with the ELFS, Christabel and Emmeline refused to believe that he was acting in good faith and ordered yet another escalation of suffrage terrorism despite Sylvia's call for a truce. Indeed, between January and July 1914 over 100 buildings were set on fire by "suffragette" guerrillas who now proudly called themselves "Outragettes." Pankhurst pointed out to the government that if it received no cooperation from the WSPU it had only itself to blame.

> A new kind of woman has been created by the present Government, . . . the Outragette. She began simply as one asking that women should have votes. Later she became a Suffragette and then a Militant, and finally, . . . an Outragette, a window-smasher, a rioter, wrecker and incendiary.

The outbreak of World War I in Europe in 1914 delayed what many believed would be a showdown between the government and the WSPU. Emmeline Pankhurst certainly believed that the vote for women was nearly won when war was declared in 1914. Not only were scores of dedicated women prepared to escalate the violence even further, they also were prepared to add thirst to their hunger strikes, a tactic which they understood would lead inevitably to their deaths. As Emmeline explained on a visit to America in December 1913, "Now, I want to say to you who think women cannot succeed, we have brought the government of England to this position, that it has to face this alternative: either women are to be killed or women are to have the vote. . . . Now that is the outcome of our civil war." The London *Times* shared this opinion when it stated in 1914 that "the only alternative to votes for women was death for the advocates of votes for women." Emmeline, Christabel, and Sylvia Pankhurst also shared the belief that no British government could survive the deaths of a substantial number of prominent British women. Whether or not they were correct, they certainly believed that victory was the inevitable outcome of their struggle. Therefore, once war on Germany was declared, ardent WSPU suffrage guerrillas transformed themselves into super-patriots almost overnight on orders from Emmeline and Christabel Pankhurst.

Christabel soon returned from France under a political amnesty, and *The Suffragette,* proclaiming itself to be "Second to none in Patriotism," transformed itself into a war paper. To emphasize that women's suffrage was officially on the back burner for the duration of the war, on October 15, 1915, Emmeline and Christabel Pankhurst changed the name of *The Suffragette* to *Britannia,* and WSPU members undertook a variety of war work such as organizing a spectacular march in 1916 to support women's right to work in war industries. In 1915, Emmeline took on a very different type of war work when she adopted four war orphans who were, by and large, to be cared for by professional governesses. Only Sylvia and Adela remained true to their father's socialist and pacifist principles and violently opposed the war. Emmeline Pankhurst was so disgusted by Sylvia's behavior that she telegraphed WSPU headquarters, "Strongly repudiate Sylvia's foolish and unpatriotic conduct; I regret I cannot prevent use of [Pankhurst] name."

Although Emmeline and Christabel Pankhurst co-founded the Women's Party in 1917, a party which supposedly combined conservative politics with feminist and suffrage activity, suffrage demonstrations were suspended for the duration of hostilities. Nonetheless, it is undoubtedly true that the war itself was instrumental in securing votes for women. The massive participation of women in the war economy and in auxiliary military services either convinced many politicians that women deserved full citizenship or it provided a convenient justification for politicians to change their position on women's suffrage without appearing to back down to pressure. Moreover, the government could have no doubt that if votes for women were not granted, guerrilla activity would resume but this time it would be carried out by women who had unselfishly suspended working for their own cause to serve their country. And the Pankhursts probably were correct in assuming that no government which allowed a substantial number of prominent women patriots to die in prison from starvation, water deprivation, or forcible feeding would be able to govern. For whatever reason, women were enfranchised in January 1918, the last year of the war. Although women were given the right to vote at age 30 while men could vote at 25, this was less of a patriarchal conspiracy than an attempt to even out the gender balance in the British electorate, a result of the large number of men killed during the Great War. (This inequity was rectified in 1928 in the so-called "Flapper Law" which made the voting age the same for both sexes.)

While Emmeline Pankhurst seldom was actively involved in feminist organizations championing women's causes in the postwar era, she often spoke out on a variety of women's issues. In particular, she demanded that all barriers against women's employment in industry be removed, and she vocally condemned protective legislation for women in industry on the grounds that it was punitive, discriminatory, and paternalistic.

In 1918, after the war, Pankhurst aided in her daughter Christabel's unsuccessful attempt to win a parliamentary seat, spoke out in favor of a strict embargo on almost all non-Anglo-Saxon immigration to Britain, and then moved to Canada. She made a living there and in the United States by lecturing on behalf of social hygiene. In 1922, she joined the National Council for Combatting Venereal Disease (renamed the Canadian Social Hygiene Council in 1923) as its chief lecturer and even began the process of adopting Canadian citizenship. Although she thought she would be happier in North America than in England, in 1924 she sailed to Bermuda where she spent a year before returning to Europe.

Financial considerations precluded her caring for all four of her adopted "war babies," so she found wealthy families for two of them and took the others to the French Riviera where, along with Christabel, she opened the English Teashop of Good Hope, a British-style tea room in Jean-les-Pins. It was no more successful than her earlier business enterprises, and, in 1926, she returned to England where she joined the Conservative Party, and agreed to stand for Parliament in the 1928 election as a candidate from the Whitechapel district of London. However, in the midst of the campaign her health deteriorated rapidly and she died of jaundice on June 14, 1928, in London. Some historians believe that the weakening of her constitution through repeated episodes of forcible feeding over several years hastened her death. During her last weeks of life, Pankhurst was overjoyed to get a letter from her estranged daughter Adela, seeking reconciliation and announcing she had renounced Marxism and embraced the British Empire. Nonetheless, she emphatically refused to forgive her estranged daughter Sylvia and neither corresponded with her nor lifted her familial excommunication long enough to grant Sylvia's request to visit her deathbed. Ironically, Emmeline Pankhurst's funeral was the only time after the suffrage campaign ended that Sylvia and Christabel Pankhurst met in person.

A portrait of Emmeline Pankhurst by artist **Georgina Brackenbury**, a former suffragist, hangs in the British National Gallery. In 1930, a bronze statue of her created by sculptor A.G. Walker (which looks very much like the Brackenbury portrait) was erected in her memory in Victoria Tower Gardens overlooking the houses of Parliament that she helped open to women. A replica of the Walker statue later was erected in Toronto, Ontario.

SOURCES:

Garner, Les. *Stepping Stones to Women's Liberty: Feminist Ideas in the Women's Suffrage Movement, 1900–1918.* Rutherford, NJ: Fairleigh Dickinson University Press, 1984.

Kamm, Josephine. *The Story of Emmeline Pankhurst.* NY: Meredith, 1968.

Liddington, Jill, and Jill Norris. *One Hand Tied Behind Us: The Rise of the Women's Suffrage Movement.* London: Virago, 1984.

Mitchell, David. *The Fighting Pankhursts.* NY: Macmillan, 1967.

———. *Women on the Warpath.* London: Jonathan Cape, 1966.

Pankhurst, Christabel. *Unshackled: The Story of How We Won the Vote.* Ed. by Frederick W. Pethick-Lawrence. London: Hutchinson, 1959.

Pankhurst, Emmeline. *My Own Story.* NY: Hearst's International, 1914 (London: Virago, reprint, 1979).

Pankhurst, Estelle Sylvia. *Life of Emmeline Pankhurst: The Suffragette Struggle for Women's Citizenship.* London: T.W. Laurie, 1935.

———. *The Suffragette: The History of the Women's Militant Suffrage Movement 1905–1910.* London: Gay and Hancock, 1911.

———. *The Suffragette Movement: An Intimate Account of Persons and Ideals.* London: Longmans, Green, 1932.

Rosen, Andrew. *Rise Up, Women! The Militant Campaign of the Women's Social and Political Union 1903–1914.* London: Routledge & Kegan Paul, 1974.

Schneir, Miriam. *Feminism: The Essential Historical Writings.* NY: Vintage Books, 1972.

SUGGESTED READING:

Barker, Dudley. "Emmeline Pankhurst," in *Prominent Edwardians.* NY: Atheneum, 1969.

Dangerfield, George. *The Strange Death of Liberal England 1910–1914,* c. 1935 (NY: Capricorn Books, reprint, 1961 [Dangerfield's interpretation of the British Women's Suffrage movement, based upon Sylvia's interpretation of it, became the standard source on the movement for at least a generation]).

Kent, Susan Kingsley. *Sex and Suffrage in Britain, 1860–1914.* Princeton, NJ: Princeton University Press, 1987.

Tickner, Lisa. *The Spectacle of Women: Imagery of the Suffrage Campaign 1907–1914.* Chicago, IL: University of Chicago Press, 1988.

RELATED MEDIA:

"Shoulder to Shoulder," produced by the British Broadcasting Company (BBC), based on the documentary book of the same name compiled and edited by **Midge MacKenzie**, was shown in the United States as a 6-part series on "Masterpiece Theater," 1988. The episodes are titled, "The Pankhurst Family," "Annie Kenney," "Lady Constance Lytton," "Christabel Pankhurst," "Outrage," and "Sylvia Pankhurst." While Emmeline Pankhurst is featured in all 6 parts, she dominates Episodes 1 and 5. Like the book, the documentary accepts Sylvia Pankhurst's interpretation of suffrage history rather than that of her mother and sister Christabel.

COLLECTIONS:

The British Library in London has copies of the pamphlets and speeches of the Pankhursts and copies of WSPU journals including long runs of *The Suffragette* and *Votes for Women.*

Correspondence relating to the years before the WSPU moved to London in 1906 can be found in the Manchester Central Library in Manchester, England.

The Museum of London holds many WSPU papers and records. Concerning the Pankhursts, it holds a good deal of their correspondence with one another and with other women's suffrage leaders in the collection "The Suffragette Fellowship."

COLLECTIONS OF PUBLISHED DOCUMENTS RELATING TO THE PANKHURSTS:

Available on microfiche are collections from the "Fawcett Society Archives on Women's Studies" at the City of London Polytechnic (these contain letter collections which include Pankhurst contributions and periodicals connected with a variety of women's suffrage organizations; they also may be ordered through Norman Ross Publishing).

The bulk of Sylvia Pankhurst's papers, including correspondence with her family, is deposited in the International Institute of Social History in Amsterdam. However, most of it is available on microfilm under the title "Women, Suffrage and Politics: The Papers of Sylvia Pankhurst, 1882–1960." The 37-reel collection is available from Adam Matthew Publications through Norman Ross Publishing in New York.

Marcus, Jane, ed. *Suffrage and the Pankhursts.* London and NY: Routledge & Kegan Paul, 1987 (except for one selection by WSPU leader Frederick W. Pethick-Lawrence written in 1908, "The Trial of the Suffragette Leaders," this book is composed entirely of the text of articles and speeches by Emmeline, Christabel and Sylvia Pankhurst concerning various aspects of the women's suffrage campaign).

Pankhurst, E. Sylvia. *A Sylvia Pankhurst Reader.* Ed. by Kathryn Dodd. Manchester, England: Manchester University Press, 1993 (this collection of Sylvia Pankhurst's speeches, articles, and excerpts from her longer works, contains a section on the suffrage era but concentrates on the post-1914 period).

Two excellent collections of women's suffrage documents are available on microfilm from Research Publications International. The first, titled "Fighting for the Vote: the Suffrage Fellowship" is available in 14 reels. It contains papers of both the WSPU and the WFL as well as personal papers of several key suffragist leaders. The second, titled "Struggle and Triumph: Women's Suffrage in Britain 1895–1920" is available in 31 reels and contains the papers of the International Women's Suffrage Alliance, the National Union of Women's Suffrage Societies, the Parliamentary Committee for Women's Suffrage and the Manchester League for Woman's Suffrage as well as an extensive newspaper-clipping file. A third document collection from Research Publications contains 91 reels of sources on women's participation in the Great War under the title "A Change in Attitude: Women, War and Society 1914–1918."

Nancy Ellen Rupprecht,
Associate Professor of History and Director of Women's Studies,
Middle Tennessee State University, Murfreesboro, Tennessee

Pankhurst, Estelle Sylvia (1882–1960).

See Pankhurst, Sylvia.

Pankhurst, Sylvia (1882–1960)

British artist, writer and political activist, primarily for socialist, anti-fascist and feminist causes. *Name variations: E. Sylvia Pankhurst; Estelle Sylvia Pankhurst. Born Estelle Sylvia Pankhurst in Manchester, England, on May 5, 1882; died in Addis Ababa on September 27, 1960; second daughter of Richard Marsden Pankhurst and Emmeline Goulden Pankhurst (1858–1928); sister of Christabel (1880–1958), Adela (1885–1961), Frank, and Harry Pankhurst; educated at the Manchester High School for Girls, the Municipal School of Art, Manchester; the Accademia, Venice, and the Royal Academy of Art in London; lived with Italian radical socialist Silvio Corio; children: (with Corio) son, Richard Kier Pethick Pankhurst (b. 1928).*

Death of brother Frank (1888); death of father (1898); was one of the original members who began the WSPU (1903); joined the Labour Party (1904); death of brother Harry (1910); founded the East London Federation of Suffragettes (ELFS, 1912); joined the pacifist movement during the Great War

(1914–18) and the British Communist Party in the postwar era; continued to work on art sporadically, but was dedicated primarily to socialist-feminist causes; her mother died and she gave birth to a son, Richard Kier Pethick Pankhurst (1928); thereafter, became more deeply involved in anti-fascist politics; in later life, adopted the cause of Abyssinian independence and helped found Abyssinian Association; moved to Ethiopia (1956), where she died (1960).

Selected art: the Holloway Brooch and the Suffragette Tea Service. Well known for her paintings and drawings of working-class women, she designed many of the logos, posters, murals, and journal covers for the women's suffrage, socialist, feminist, anti-fascist, and pacifist causes which she championed.

Selected writings: The Suffragette: The History of the Women's Militant Suffrage Movement 1905–1910 *(Boston: Woman's Journal, 1911);* Rebel Ireland: Thoughts on Easter Week 1916 *(London: Worker's Socialist Federation, 1920);* Lloyd George takes the Mask Off *(London: Worker's Socialist Federation, 1920);* Soviet Russia as I Saw It *(London: Worker's Dreadnought Federation, 1921);* Writ on a Cold Slate *(London: Dreadnought, 1922);* Education of the Masses *(London: Dreadnought, 1924);* India and the Earthly Paradise *(Bombay: Sunshine, 1926);* Delphos: The Future of International Language *(London: K. Paul, 1927);* Save the Mothers: A Plea for Measures to Prevent the Annual Loss of about 3,000 Child-Bearing Mothers and 20,000 Infant Lives in England and Wales and a Similar Grievous Wastage in Other Countries *(London: A.A. Knopf, 1930);* The Suffragette Movement: An Intimate Account of Persons and Ideals *(London: Longmans, Green, 1932);* The Home Front: A Mirror to Life in England During the World War *(London: Hutchinson, 1932);* The Life of Emmeline Pankhurst: The Suffragette Struggle for Women's Citizenship *(London: T.W. Laurie, 1936);* The Ethiopian People *(Essex: New Times and Ethiopia News Book Dept., 1946);* Ethiopia: A Cultural History *(Essex: Lalibela House, 1955). Founded and edited* The Women's Dreadnought, The Worker's Dreadnought, *and* New Times; *edited* Ethiopian News *(1936–56) and* Ethiopian Observer.

From the time she was old enough to understand such things, it must have been painfully obvious to Sylvia Pankhurst that her elder sister Christabel was her mother's favorite. Beautiful, intelligent, graceful, gregarious and talented, *__Christabel Pankhurst__ was able to charm and captivate almost everyone around her, including her younger sisters. While Sylvia was intelligent, she also was plain, awkward, serious, determined and contentious, qualities which turn-of-the-century England considered to be more admirable than loveable, especially in young girls. Nonetheless, her considerable artistic talent helped Sylvia to garner a modicum of personal attention and gave her an outlet to express her ideas and emotions. Her art kept her from being totally obscured by her mother's flair and her sister's sparkle.

Sylvia Pankhurst was born on May 5, 1882, in Manchester, England, the daughter of Richard Marsden Pankhurst and *__Emmeline Pankhurst__. Her father doted on her (as he did each of his children) and fondly called her "Miss Woody Way," a play on words from the Latin term for woods, *sylvan.* Her early school years were unhappy, primarily because she had no friends. She hated school because her schoolmates made fun of her agnosticism and radical political beliefs.

Richard Pankhurst realized that the unorthodox and unpopular social and religious teachings he had instilled in his family were a greater burden for Sylvia than his other children because she took them so seriously and attempted to explain them so earnestly. Whereas Christabel used her charm to disarm those who taunted her, Sylvia attempted to convert them or at least convince them of the legitimacy of her position. Earnest young children seldom are popular with their peers, and Sylvia Pankhurst was no exception. Her father attempted to compensate for Sylvia's unpopularity by paying special attention to her in a number of small ways, such as taking her on long walks where he would sing to her Shakespeare's lyric "Who is Sylvia, What is She?" from *Two Gentlemen of Verona.*

Her attitude toward formal education changed when she entered the Manchester High School for Girls, an institution which recognized her artistic talent and encouraged her to pursue it at the Municipal School of Art, Manchester. Here she won a variety of medals and awards for art as well as a traveling scholarship which allowed her to study at the Accademia, Venice, before she continued her British artistic education by means of a scholarship to the Royal Academy of Art in London. In 1901, she won the Lady Whitworth scholarship of £30 and tuition fees awarded to the best woman student of the year.

In 1898, her beloved father died of a perforated ulcer. It was an especially traumatic time for Sylvia because at age 16 she was the eldest member of the family at home during his final crisis and was, therefore, the one responsible for the decisions made about his care. Although her mother and sisters never blamed her, she always felt guilty about not replacing their old-fashioned family doctor with a more modern and scientifically trained physician and for waiting too long to summon her mother home from Geneva. The death of her only brother, Harry, from poliomyelitis in 1910 added to this psychological burden because once again she believed she somehow should have been able to help.

In 1903, Sylvia joined with her mother and sister in founding the Women's Social and Political Union (WSPU). The next year, she joined the Fulham branch of the International Labour Party, making a commitment to socialism which she would honor in various forms throughout her life.

The name of our paper, *The Women's Dreadnought*, is symbolic of the fact that the women who are fighting for freedom must fear nothing.

—Sylvia Pankhurst

While Sylvia was studying at the Royal Academy of Art, her mother came to London to live with her. In 1906, they founded the London Committee of the WSPU which became the movement's national headquarters. Sylvia supported herself by working as a speaker and organizer for the WSPU, activities which supplemented the income she earned as a freelance artist. Her undeniable artistic talent helped compensate for her mother's undisguised preference for Christabel, a bias which may help to explain why Sylvia's later writings on the suffrage movement are subtly critical of her mother and blatantly critical of her sister's policies and actions.

Although this dual career was exhausting, Sylvia was happy, because she was able to combine art with activism by painting murals for WSPU branch office walls, designing posters and banners for suffrage demonstrations, and creating women's suffrage artifacts such as the "Suffragette Tea Service" and the "Holloway Brooch," a pin bestowed on suffragists who had been imprisoned and forcibly fed for the movement. In addition to this political and artistic activity, in 1910 she began writing articles for *The Suffragette* (the WSPU's official journal) and then launched a career as an international lecturer on women's suffrage topics, speaking in the United States in 1911, Scandinavia in 1913, and Central Europe in 1914. During this period, she bore her full share of privation for the cause. She was imprisoned 13 times and was forcibly fed on several of those occasions when she undertook hunger strikes.

Partly because she was upset with the autocratic structure of the WSPU and the imperious demeanor of Christabel and their mother, in 1912 Sylvia founded the East London Federation of Suffragettes of the WSPU (ELFS) with the help of ***Flora Drummond** and the financial backing of three wealthy WSPU branches, the Kensington, Chelsea, and Paddington offices. This satisfied Sylvia's longtime desire to combine her feminist, pacifist, and socialist objectives so that she could work toward accomplishing all of them within a single organization. From its inception, the ELFS was committed to work for women's suffrage, pacifism, broader women's social issues, and a variety of feminist economic and political goals. As she explained the need for working women's participation in the political process, "'One Woman, One Vote.'. . . We must get out among the people and make them realize that women need votes, and that men, and the nation, need the equal comradeship of men and women."

The ELFS was successful, but each of its successes further irritated Christabel who believed that the fortunes of women's suffrage were linked to upper-class "ladies" whose mistreatment by the government would outrage the majority of the British public and bring important financial support to the suffrage movement.

The first major clash between Sylvia and her mother and sister arose over a difference in interpretation of the WSPU's mandate when the elder Pankhursts decided to close the East London branch of the WSPU. Therefore, in 1914, after Sylvia had repeatedly ignored her sister's decrees, she was summoned to a meeting in France with her mother and Christabel. There, she was given orders to end non-suffrage activities, close the office, disband the ELFS, return to the general WSPU and toe its middle-class party line. Sylvia obstreperously refused; this defiance led to her expulsion from the WSPU by her mother and sister. Christabel justified their actions by reminding her sister, "You have your own ideas. We do not want that. We want our women to take their orders and march in step like an army." Clearly, in the estimation of Emmeline and Christabel Pankhurst, there was room in the WSPU for neither secondary issues nor individualism.

Sylvia accepted her sister and mother's decision with regret but she refused to back down. Instead, she removed the words "of the WSPU" from the title of the ELFS, re-established it as an independent organization, found alternate funding, increased her organizing and political efforts, and continued to battle both capitalism and sexism as she worked for the total democratization of British society. After separating from

Sylvia Pankhurst speaking in London's East End.

the WSPU, the ELFS resumed its political activism and began planning a massive rent strike in support of women's suffrage.

Thereafter, however, Emmeline and Christabel simply ignored Sylvia's presence on the suffrage scene. For example, when Sylvia was speaking at Bethnal Green, rotten fish heads and rags soaked in the public urinals were thrown at her by a hostile crowd. Despite the event's obvious propaganda value, *The Suffragette,* controlled by Christabel, ignored the incident. The Pankhurst family confrontation in 1914 was the beginning of what would become a permanent estrangement between Emmeline and Sylvia.

Sylvia Pankhurst's *Memoirs* argue that the efforts made by the thousand upon thousands of working-class women and men in the East London Federation were more important in the long run in getting the vote for women than the flagrant violence practiced by the WSPU. Her evidence for this opinion is based on the immediate prewar era. In June 1914, desperately weak after enduring a hunger-and-thirst strike in prison, Sylvia had herself carried to and laid upon the steps of the Strangers Entrance to Parliament where she pledged to eschew food and water until her death if the Asquith government did not make some gesture of commitment to women's suffrage. At that point, Herbert Henry Asquith agreed to receive a deputation of working-class women to discuss suffrage and immediately thereafter seemed to soften his stance on the issue when, after deploring the "criminal methods" of the WSPU, he told Sylvia's East End delegation on June 20 that "if women were to have the vote it would have to be on a wide basis." Sylvia took this as an indication that they had been successful. Since the Great War broke out almost immediately thereafter, and women's heroic war work was to change many minds about women's right to vote, it is difficult to know how serious Asquith was about committing the Liberal government to supporting women's suffrage.

The final straw which severed the familial bond between mother and daughter was Sylvia's unalterable opposition to Britain's participation in World War I (1914–18). The ELFS became an important part of the British pacifist opposition to the war by expanding the limits of Federation concerns beyond women's suffrage and thereby making the group much more politically revolutionary than it had been under the WSPU. It adopted standard Marxist rhetoric which argued that the war was simply a battle between international capitalists for the control of world markets using the working classes as expendable cannon fodder to fight their battles for them. The Federation began organizing public lectures on pacifism and Marxism which portrayed the war as detrimental to the interests of the working class. This attitude was bound to inflame Emmeline's national chauvinism. Indeed, her British jingoism was so all-encompassing that she considered Sylvia's vocal pacifism an indelible disgrace to the family, and she bitterly regretted the fact that she did not have the power to prevent her daughter from using the Pankhurst name. Emmeline would never relent or modify her estrangement from Sylvia, even when her daughter asked for permission to visit her during her final illness in 1928.

During the war, while her mother and sister became bombastic patriots, Sylvia and her younger sister ***Adela Pankhurst** (who had emigrated to Australia) were actively involved with both pacifist agitation and war-relief work. Within the East London Federation, Sylvia founded a pacifist and socialist paper, *The Worker's Dreadnought* (1914–24), set up medical and maternity welfare clinics, a Montessori school, a co-operative toy factory, a garment factory for unemployed women workers, a day-care center, inexpensive restaurants where the poor could eat at or below the cost of the food, and founded the League of Rights for Soldiers' and Sailors' Wives and Relatives to attempt to improve military pensions and allowances. She also was actively involved in the antiwar movement through the Women's International League for Peace and Freedom and continued to agitate for women's right to vote through the Labour Council for Adult Suffrage.

By war's end, in November 1918, votes had been granted to British women over age 30, but Sylvia remained in the thick of activist radical politics. She had steered the ELFS further to the Marxist left after Lenin had usurped power in Russia during the Russian Revolution of 1917. When the war ended, she was able to convert the Federation into an organization ready to take its place in the vanguard of organizations struggling to achieve the world revolution which both Marx and Lenin had prophesied. As usual, Sylvia was prepared to lead her troops into the political fray.

As a result of her Marxist activism, in November 1920 a seriously ill Sylvia Pankhurst was fined and sentenced to a six-month Second Division prison term for incitement to sedition and antiwar propaganda. In that same year, the East London Federation of Suffragettes formed the organizational basis for the Communist Party of Great Britain (CPGB).

During the next year, she traveled to Moscow to attend the Second Congress of the Third International and to meet Lenin. Upon her return, she founded a People's Russian Information Bureau and published *Soviet Russia as I Saw It* in 1921. She remained a prominent member of the CPGB until her fierce individualism overcame her Marxist discipline and she began attacking a number of Lenin's policies in print in *The Worker's Dreadnought.* Her refusal to turn the paper over to the party leadership when ordered to do so in 1921 led to her expulsion from the party. Ironically, in 1924 *The Worker's Dreadnought* went bankrupt, and she was forced to close it. During this time, she also worked on and published four books, *Writ on a Cold Slate,* a volume of poems which first appeared in print in 1922; *Education of the Masses* (1924); an academic study of India called *India and the Earthly Paradise* (1926); and *Delphos: The Future of International Language* (1927).

Although Sylvia continued to work avidly for a variety of feminist and socialist concerns, for a short time she stepped out of the political limelight in order to retire to a cottage outside London where she lived openly with her lover, the Italian radical socialist Silvio Corio whose views had forced him into exile at the turn of the century. After migrating from Rome to Paris to Holland, he finally settled in London. Corio was a brilliant political journalist who continued to write in exile for the rest of his life. In him, a man eight years her senior, Sylvia found not only a lover and companion, but an equal revolutionary partnership much like that of her parents. In 1924, they opened a workers' cafe called The Red Cottage at Woodford. Although Sylvia contributed her share to the enterprise, the bulk of the work was done by Corio, especially after December 3, 1927, when, at the age of 45, Sylvia Pankhurst gave birth to her first and only child, Richard Kier Pethick Pankhurst. She named her son for the three men most dear to her—Richard, her father; Kier Hardie, her political mentor who also may have been her lover; and her closest male friend, Frederick Pethick-Lawrence, the erstwhile "Prince Consort" of the WSPU and husband of *__Emmeline Pethick-Lawrence__. Although her relationship with Corio was common knowledge, she always refused to name the father of her child officially in order to protest against what she considered the social oppression of unmarried mothers.

In addition to raising Richard, Sylvia worked steadily on her writing and in 1930 published *Save the Mothers: A Plea for Measures to Prevent the Annual Loss of about 3,000 Child-Bearing Mothers and 20,000 Infant Lives in England and Wales and a Similar Grievous Wastage in Other Countries,* a fierce argument demanding better obstetric care for pregnant women.

The death of her mother and the birth of her son within a year of each other apparently put Sylvia in a reflective mood. In 1931, she began to come to terms with her past by writing a richly detailed, if obviously biased, history of the WSPU, *The Suffragette Movement,* presenting her side of the family political controversy. In 1932, she wrote *The Home Front,* a study of women's participation in the Great War, and in 1936 she published a biography of her late estranged mother, *The Life of Emmeline Pankhurst,* probably as much for personal reasons as for posterity. In the first two books, she criticized both her mother's and sister's policies, an editorial decision which did little to endear her to Christabel.

Although she never abandoned her crusades for feminist and socialist concerns, after Adolf Hitler was elected chancellor of Germany in 1933 she became deeply involved with the anti-fascist movement in Britain. At the urging of Corio, she decided to concentrate on the cause of Abyssinia (Ethiopia) which Benito Mussolini had invaded in 1935.

On May 5, 1936, Sylvia returned to active political work by founding a paper called *New Times and Ethiopia News* which she intended as a voice for the underprivileged and oppressed throughout the world. In fact, during World War II she briefly changed the title of the *New Times* to the *National Anti-Fascist Weekly* in order to underscore this commitment. Nonetheless, her heart was with the cause of Abyssinia, and she played an active role in the worldwide effort to restore its independence. In particular, she edited the *Ethiopian News* from 1936 to 1956, helped to establish the Abyssinian Association, actively led the crusade to raise funds for an orthopaedic unit and a rehabilitation wing for a hospital in Addis Ababa, and wrote several books and pamphlets on the Ethiopian situation. The most important of these works were *The Ethiopian People* (1946) and *A Cultural History of Ethiopia* (1955).

Sylvia did not visit Ethiopia until 1944, but once there she became deeply committed not only to the plight of Abyssinia but to Ethiopia itself. Two years after the death of Corio in 1954, she emigrated to Ethiopia with her son Richard. He became an instructor at the University in Addis Ababa where she edited the *Ethiopian Observer* until her death. During the five years of his exile, Ethiopian Emperor Haile Selassie had counted on Sylvia as one of his most trusted advisers, and when he returned to Ethiopia he kept up their connection.

In the midst of her fund-raising and editorial activities in Addis Ababa, death took Sylvia Pankhurst unexpectedly. She had been busily making plans to go camping with her son and daughter-in-law when a coronary thrombosis forced her to postpone the trip. She died from heart failure on September 27, 1960. Emperor Haile Selassie broke precedent by attending her funeral as a tribute to her quarter-decade of dedication to Abyssinia and her lifetime dedication to humanity.

SOURCES:

*__Castle, Barbara.__ *Sylvia and Christabel Pankhurst.* NY: Penguin, 1987.

Dangerfield, George. *The Strange Death of Liberal England 1910–1914,* c. 1935 (NY: Capricorn Books, reprint, 1961 [Dangerfield's interpretation of the British Women's Suffrage movement, based upon Sylvia's interpretation of it, became the standard source on the movement for at least a generation of both historians and the general public]).

Liddington, Jill, and Jill Norris. *One Hand Tied Behind Us: The Rise of the Women's Suffrage Movement.* London: Virago, 1984.

Marcus, Jane, ed. *The Fighting Pankhursts.* NY: Macmillan, 1967.

———. *Suffrage and the Pankhursts.* London: Routledge & Kegan Paul, 1987.

———. *Women on the Warpath.* London: Jonathan Cape, 1966.

Pankhurst, Christabel. *Unshackled: The Story of How We Won the Vote.* Ed. by Lord Frederick W. Pethick-Lawrence. London: Hutchinson, 1959.

Pankhurst, Emmeline. *My Own Story.* NY: Hearst's International, 1914 (London: Virago, reprint, 1979).

Pankhurst, Estelle Sylvia. *The Suffragette: The History of the Women's Militant Suffrage Movement 1905–1910.* London: Gay and Hancock, 1911.

———. *The Suffragette Movement: An Intimate Account of Persons and Ideals.* London: Longmans, Green, 1932.

———. *A Sylvia Pankhurst Reader.* Ed. by Kathryn Dodd. Manchester, England: Manchester University Press, 1993.

Pankhurst, Richard. *Sylvia Pankhurst: Artist and Crusader.* NY: Paddington Press, 1979.

Romero, Patricia. *E. Sylvia Pankhurst: Portrait of a Radical.* London: University Press, 1987.

SUGGESTED READING:

Blease, W. Lyon. *The Emancipation of English Women.* NY: Arno Press, 1977.

Garner, Les. *Stepping Stones to Women's Liberty: Feminist Ideas in the Women's Suffrage Movement, 1900–1918.* Rutherford, NJ: Fairleigh Dickinson University Press, 1984.

Raeburn, Antonia. *The Suffragette View.* NY: St. Martin's Press, 1976.

Rosen, Andrew. *Rise Up, Women! The Militant Campaign of the Women's Social and Political Union 1903–1914.* London: Routledge & Kegan Paul, 1974.

Tickner, Lisa. *The Spectacle of Women: Imagery of the Suffrage Campaign 1907–1914.* Chicago, IL: University of Chicago Press, 1988.

RELATED MEDIA:

"Shoulder to Shoulder," produced by the British Broadcasting Company (BBC), based on the documentary book of the same name compiled and edited by **Midge MacKenzie**, was shown in the U.S. as a 6-part series on "Masterpiece Theater," 1988. The episodes are titled, "The Pankhurst Family," "Annie Kenney," "Lady Constance Lytton," "Christabel Pankhurst," "Outrage," and "Sylvia Pankhurst." While Sylvia Pankhurst is included in all 6 parts, she is emphasized in the first and last episodes which portray her as the "hero" of the women's suffrage movement.

COLLECTIONS:

Of particular interest is the collection of Sylvia Pankhurst's papers on deposit in Amsterdam and available in the U.S. through microfilm.

Nancy Ellen Rupprecht,
Associate Professor of History and Director of Women's Studies, Middle Tennessee State University, Murfreesboro, Tennessee

Panova, Vera (1905–1973)

Soviet Russian novelist, short-story writer and dramatist who was one of the most beloved writers in the USSR starting in the mid-1940s. *Name variations: Vera Fyodorovna (or Feodorovna or Fëdorovna) Panova; (pseudonyms) Vera Veltman; V. V-an; V.V.; V. Starosel'skaiia; V.S. Born Vera Fedorovna Panova on March 20, 1905, in Rostov-on-Don, Russia; died in Leningrad on March 3, 1973; daughter of a bank clerk; married Arseny Staroselsky, in 1925 (divorced); married Boris Vakhtin (died); married David Yakovlevich Rivkin (a writer under the pseudonym David Dar); children: one daughter, two sons.*

Selected writings: Ilya Kosgor *(play, 1939);* V staroi Moskve *(In Old Moscow, 1940);* Sputniki *(The Train or The Travelling Companions, 1946);* Kruzhilikha *(The Factory, 1947);* Iasnyi bereg *(The Clear Shore, 1949);* Vremena goda *(Seasons of the Year, 1953, translated by Vera Traill as* Span of the Year*);* Serezha *(1955);* Seryozha *(1955);* Metelitsa *(play, The Blizzard, 1957);* Sentimental'nyi roman *(A Sentimental Novel, 1958);* Evdokia *(1959).*

The life of Russian writer Vera Panova, like that of millions of her Soviet compatriots, was one filled with struggle and tragedy. Living and working through the Stalinest era, she won the Stalin Prize three times but nevertheless maintained her artistic integrity in writings that did not bend to the dictates of political expediency. Despite her travails, she was able to survive and prevail, mostly by creating books that presented honest portrayals of ordinary, flawed humans, books that became bestsellers. Particularly beloved were the novels *Sputniki*, set in World War II, and *Seryozha*, which has become a world classic in the literature about children.

Panova was born in 1905 in Rostov-on-Don, a colorful city with an ethnically mixed population and streets crammed with bazaars and shops. Her father was a poorly paid bank employee who was nevertheless highly cultured. Proficient in three languages, he loved books. Vera was only five when he accidently drowned in the Don River in 1910 and the family was left destitute. Her mother had to take work in an office, and Vera attended to all of the household chores, including cooking and laundering. Largely relying on her father's excellent library, she educated herself and had a particular fascination with history. Panova also began to write, both in verse and prose. Still a child, she made up her mind to one day become a famous, successful author. By the time she was ten, her first poem appeared in print after a relative submitted it without her knowledge to a magazine. After only two years of high school, she had to drop out because of the family's financial predicament, and she began to support herself by the age of 14.

By 1917, a year of two revolutions in Russia, the young Panova had become an oft-published writer, with a number of her pieces appearing in Rostov's student journal *Iunaia mysl'* (Young Ideas). Over the next few years, she continued to publish in various journals. In 1922, she took a job as a journalist with a Rostov newspaper, *Trudovoi Don* (The Working Don). By the late 1920s, Panova had made considerable advances in her career and was employed by the newspaper *Sovetskii iug* (The Soviet South). Here she was in charge of the feuilleton section (devoted to literature and light writing on various topics), and over the next years her sketches and stories appeared under the pseudonym "Vera Veltman." Although she was interested in many aspects of contemporary intellectual and political life, Panova did not commit herself to any of the literary groups that dotted the Soviet literary landscape during the 1920s and early 1930s. Instead, she concentrated on perfecting her craft as a journalist and making a name for herself in local children's magazines and newspapers. By 1933, she had found enough confidence to begin writing plays. Many years later, in 1958, she would publish an evocative and largely autobiographical work, *Sentimental'nyi Roman* (A Sentimental Novel), based on these years.

In 1925, she married Arseny Staroselsky. They divorced after only two years, and soon after Panova married Boris Vakhtin. This union was more successful, but in 1937, during the height of Stalin's Great Purge, Vakhtin was falsely denounced and arrested. He would perish in the Gulag. Alone and forced to support herself and her three children, Panova worked harder than ever, both as a journalist and as a creative writer. Two of her plays from this period—*Ilya Kosgor* (1939) and *V staroi Moskve* (In Old Moscow, 1940)—won prizes. The latter was staged successfully in Moscow in 1941 and was being prepared for its Leningrad premiere when Nazi Germany attacked the Soviet Union in June 1941.

At the time, Panova and her daughter, who lived near Leningrad in the town of Pushkin, were unable to escape from the rapidly advancing German forces. For a period of months, they lived under Nazi occupation. Neither would be molested, but Panova became a virtual slave laborer, helping the local peasants when they were ordered by the Germans to work in the fields. One of Panova's jobs for the hated occupiers was to type records on an ancient typewriter. Despite the obvious risks, she used that same typewriter to secretly write the first chapters of a play which would later be staged as *Metelitsa* (The Blizzard). She hid the typescript in a stack of firewood, where she had also secreted notes for a projected work to be called *Ostland*. Unfortunately, the *Ostland* materials would later be lost.

Determined to be free from the nightmare of living under the Nazi New Order, in late 1943 Panova and her daughter escaped from Pushkin by trekking on foot for several hundred miles in order to join her sons and aged mother in Shishaki. Here, Panova continued to write, using a thick accountant's ledger because of the severe paper shortage during the war. In 1944, she settled in the city of Perm, supporting herself, her three children, her mother, and an orphan child by working long hours writing scripts for the local radio station and newspapers. In her little spare time, she continued to write and that same year published her first long story, *Sem'ja Pirozhkovykh* (The Pirozhkov Family); this would later be reworked and reprinted in 1959 under the title *Evdokia*. Panova also began to collect materials for a study of people's lives in a factory in the Urals, which would eventually emerge as the novel *Kruzhilikha* (The Factory, 1947).

In late 1944, Panova accepted an unusual journalistic assignment from the Perm branch of the Soviet Writers' Union: to write a brochure about the work carried out on a military hospital train. She spent several months on Hospital Train No. 312 and published the pamphlet. Panova then greatly expanded on her impressions of life on the train in *Sputniki* (The Train also seen as The Travelling Companions, 1946), a novel that turned her into a major star in the Soviet literary firmament. *Sputniki* was an innovative work for Soviet literature, which had been confined for more than a decade in the intellectual straitjacket of Socialist Realism. The doctrine of Socialist Realism, which reflected Stalin's political and intellectual agenda, centered around the dogma that art and literature were duty-bound to present only a positive picture of Soviet life and in a style that was accessible to even the most unsophisticated citizen.

While *Sputniki* did not criticize the Soviet system, neither did it create false heroes. In fact, it depicted the staff of the hospital train as decent sorts who were not exceptional. In their imperfections, none of these workers resembled the stereotypical "New Soviet Man or Woman." Their strengths and weaknesses were average and their lives little more than run-of-the-mill. With sympathy, Panova chronicled the staff's basic humanity which enabled them to contribute to the final Soviet victory simply because they did their duty as best they could, almost always under difficult conditions. They contributed not by fighting in battles—there are no battle scenes in *Sputniki*—but by laboring day in and day out in quite ordinary and even seemingly trivial situations. The book quickly became a bestseller, won the author a coveted Stalin Prize (the first of three she would receive during the dictator's lifetime), and was to retain its reputation as one of the best Soviet works on what is known in Russia as the Great Patriotic War. As a result of *Sputniki*'s success, Panova won a coveted membership in the Soviet Writers' Union.

Nothing that compromises artistic truth can be tolerated in art.

—Vera Panova

Despite Cold War tensions, *Sputniki* even received a favorable response from critics in the West. Writing in *The Saturday Review of Literature* in 1949, John Woodburn called the novel:

> almost unique in that it presents neither the highly moralistic tone which pervaded the [pre-revolutionary] Russian novel . . . nor the intense . . . chauvinism and propagandism which has characterized so much of Soviet literature. . . . [Panova's book] is simply a warm, humanistic, occasionally sentimental montage of the lives of a group of ordinary people which could, without a great deal of transposition, have been set in almost any other country during a time of war.

Panova's next novel *Kruzhilikha* (The Factory, 1947) was based on her wartime observations of life and labor in a Urals factory. Although it was equally successful with the Soviet reading public, this work failed to please a number of literary critics because of its deviations from the party line of Socialist Realism. The book's main character—the factory director Listopad who displays many less-than-ideal character traits—was declared by the critics to be a "negative hero," and the book received additional criticism for not sufficiently contrasting "good" with "bad" personality traits. In a series of character sketches, Panova shows how the stresses of work in the factory erode the lives of its director and workers (or is used by them to escape their own personal problems). Somewhat puzzlingly, this book too won the author a Stalin Prize.

By this time in her career, Panova had more to lose. In 1945, she had married David Rivkin, a fellow writer who appeared in print under the pseudonym David Dar. The marriage would last until Panova's death. Panova and her family resettled with David and his two children (from a previous marriage) in Leningrad. In 1949, she published her third novel, *Iasnyi bereg* (The Clear Shore), about life on a Soviet collective farm in the period immediately after the war. Here, Panova took no risks, instead praising Stalin on many occasions and generally writing obediently within the confines of the Socialist Realist doctrine. Although she won her third Stalin Prize for this book, Panova was frank in later years in acknowledging that it was in fact a very weak work of art. Among its propagandistic pages there are nonetheless some sensitively written fragments, particularly those devoted to the five-year-old boy Seryozha. In 1955, after Stalin's death, Panova would return to Seryozha to write a novella of that name, a work that is generally acknowledged to be of high artistic quality.

Within weeks of Stalin's death in March 1953, a "thaw" began to be observed in many facets of Soviet life. In the intellectual sphere, writers and other artists opened their desk drawers to bring long-hidden works to the public's attention. Panova sent to her publisher a book manuscript that would first appear in print starting in November 1953, in the journal *Novyi mir*, as *Vremena goda* (Seasons of the Year, translated by **Vera Traill** as *Span of the Year*). In this daring novel that would never have seen the light of day under Stalin's regime, Panova took an unblinking look at the realities of Soviet life.

Set in "a typical Russian town which we shall call Ensk," *Vremena goda* looks at two families, the Bortasheviches and the Kuprianovs. The book's most vivid character, Stepan Bortashevich, has achieved a position of power and responsibility. He is essentially a weak man who, led astray in part because of his wife Nadezhda, becomes involved in financial corruption. As the militia arrives to arrest him, Stepan commits suicide. The novel's major female character, Dorofeya Kuprianova, is an exemplary Communist who is active in party affairs and successful in her own career in industry. Whereas her daughter, a student, is also an exemplary Soviet citizen, Dorofeya's son Gennadi is very much a black sheep, and he is deeply enmeshed in the rackets run by Stepan Bortashevich.

Vremena goda became a storm-center of controversy. Panova had presented to the reading public characters who were not only far from perfect but also unheroic to the point of being largely obsessed with obtaining ever more creature comforts, particularly better housing. A number of critics—and her ever-loyal reading audience—rapturously praised the book. Articles in *Izvestia*, the *Literary Gazette*, and other journals welcomed the novel as a change from the unconvincing Socialist Realist works of the last years of Stalin's rule, and some hailed it as possibly even marking a genuine turning point in the history of Soviet literature. Conservative forces mounted a counterattack in the Soviet Communist Party newspaper *Pravda* (May 27, 1954). Entitled "What Sort of Seasons are These?," the article took Panova to task and admonished the highest bureaucrats for their laxity in allowing such unwelcome tendencies in Soviet cultural life to remain unchallenged.

Despite her powerful critics, Panova seemed to have mastered the art of survival in a totalitarian state. After 1953, she was able to maintain a secure place in the top ranks of Soviet writers. By this time, she was well known not only in the USSR, but also in many foreign countries where her novels had appeared in translation. In 1954 and again in 1959, she was a major personality at the Writers' Congresses that elected her a member of the Presidium of the Union of Soviet Writers. In 1955, she was awarded the Order of the Red Banner of Labor, an honor that would be repeated in 1965. Because of her national and international reputation, she received permission to travel to the West, including Italy and the United Kingdom. In 1960, Panova made a five-week trip to the United States along with a group of other Soviet writers. Although most of her published observations on American life are well within the range of Soviet orthodoxy, she was clearly an observant tourist, noting above all else the extraordinary material abundance to be found in the United States. Her travels in America resulted in an increased awareness of new literary trends in the West which is clearly reflected in the epilogue she wrote for the Russian edition of J.D. Salinger's *The Catcher in the Rye*. Here, she praised Salinger's work as "this novel about a loafer, a petty liar, a swaggering dandy, a strange, unlucky young creature, a novel outwardly so simple, but so complex in its inner structure, [that it] creates a whirlwind of feelings and thoughts. . . . This is the hallmark of a really important book."

One of the most courageous aspects of Panova's career was her uncompromising attitude toward Soviet anti-Semitism. Living in a society that boasted of having abolished anti-Semitism from the tsarist past, but still kept it alive in virtually all aspects of its public life, Panova often grappled with this issue in her works. In her play *Metelitsa* (The Blizzard), she presents characters of Russian and Estonian nationality

Vera Panova

who are no less inhuman in their hatred of Jews than are the invading Nazis. Panova makes clear that it was the Jews, along with Soviet *politruks* (the political commissars attached to Red Army units), who topped the lists as targets for the Wehrmacht and SS Einsatzgruppen to round up and annihilate. Jews are treated with great sympathy in *Metelitsa*, in which the rabbi's wife represents the voice of conscience. Jakub Blum has noted that the philosophy of Panova's drama derives directly from Dostoevsky's idea that once God, the supreme moral authority in the universe, has ceased to exist everything is permissible. As a play with "an almost prophetic eloquence," *Metelitsa* views both the Jews' fate and the hatred toward them as part of the modern world's headlong rush toward the self-destruction of humanity. For Panova, anti-Semitism was more than a socially and politically undesirable phenomenon. It was a major component of the contemporary world's degradation of human dignity. Panova suggested to the play's audience that Hitler's mass murder of Jews was facilitated in the occupied Soviet Union by Jew-haters who were part of an anti-Semitic way of life that flourished both before and during the Soviet era.

In July 1967, Panova suffered a stroke which paralyzed the left side of her body. She responded only slowly to medical treatment, and in time it became clear that there was no hope of a complete recovery. Now confined to her bed, chair, and desk, this woman who served as family head, breadwinner, and nationally revered literary figure had to depend on others, including her husband and nurses. With her limited physical energies, deteriorating eyesight, and a life regulated by physicians, she concentrated virtually all of her will power on writing. Encouragement came not only from those closest to her, but from grandchildren, her great-grandson Mitya, and countless readers who had been informed of her situation. **Diana Tevekelyan** wrote that, during her final years, the ill, frail author remained:

> Proud, independent and self-reliant . . . [and was] . . . disgusted with her weakness and was unsparing of herself. She spent the whole day propped in a wheelchair at her desk in a large room with a tall window, but with all the lights on. Opposite the desk stood a huge bookcase stuffed with manuscripts and books she needed for her work. Near the window stood another large table covered with a dark checkered woolen cloth. On it were magazines, a stack of writing paper on cardboard, files, books with markers—all that she needed during the day's work. . . . Panova could never reconcile herself to her illness and resign herself to passivity. . . . She was a great worker and on the day she died, March 3, 1973, the desk she worked at showed it: a finished text for a radio broadcast, a contract for a new book, the proofs of *Of My Life, Books and Readers* for *Neva* magazine, various sheets of paper and notes written in her own hand, and the first pages of a new novel.

By this time, Panova was greatly respected, even revered. Her books were read by millions, and her plays had been seen by millions more on stage, screen, and the new medium of Soviet television.

Because she had requested a church burial, the Soviet press and media failed to announce the death of Vera Panova. In line with this official hostility, Leningrad morgue workers even refused to transport her body to a church for religious services. This harsh response, however, failed to dim the luster of a writer who had risked much to remain true to her ideals, once declaring, "Nothing that compromises artistic truth can be tolerated in art." Even in her own lifetime, discerning critics recognized that her work would be of lasting significance despite its creation under the conditions of a totalitarian state. In 1969, London's *Times Literary Supplement* noted: "Her great strength [is] a sense of the poetry and glamour of quite ordinary lives at certain moments." In analyzing the memorable female characters she had created (Lena in *Sputniki*, Dorofeya in *Vremena goda*, and Valya in a short story of that name), the noted literary historian **Xenia Gasiorowska** called these and Panova's other female heroes "living, proud, suffering soul[s]."

SOURCES:

Alexandrova, Vera. *A History of Soviet Literature, 1917–1964: From Gorky to Solzhenitsyn.* Garden City, NY: Doubleday, 1964.

Amalrik, Andrei. *Notes of a Revolutionary.* Translated by Guy Daniels. NY: Alfred A. Knopf, 1982.

Berelowitch, Alexis. "De Listopad a Onisimov: Deux Visions du responsable Stalinien," in *Cahiers du Monde russe et soviétique.* Vol. 32, no. 4. October–December 1991, pp. 627–638.

Blum, Jakub, and Vera Rich. *The Image of the Jew in Soviet Literature: The Post-Stalin Period.* London: Institute of Jewish Affairs, London-Ktav Publishing House, 1984.

Brown, Deming. *Soviet Attitudes toward American Writing.* Princeton, NJ: Princeton University Press, 1962.

Brown, Edward James. *Russian Literature Since the Revolution.* Cambridge, MA: Harvard University Press, 1982.

Clark, Katerina. *The Soviet Novel: History as Ritual.* 3rd ed. Bloomington, IN: Indiana University Press, 2000.

Dunham, Vera S. *In Stalin's Time: Middleclass Values in Soviet Fiction.* Durham, NC: Duke University Press, 1990.

Gasiorowska, Xenia. *Women in Soviet Fiction 1917–1964.* Madison, WI: University of Wisconsin Press, 1968.

H., E. "Towards a Soviet Bourgeoisie? Implications of 'The Thaw' and 'The Seasons,'" in *The World Today.* Vol. 11, no. 7. July 1955, pp. 300–308.

Harris, Claudia. "Cultural Impediments to Economic Reform in the Former Soviet States," in *Journal of Management Inquiry.* Vol. 4, no. 2. June 1995, pp. 140–155.

Hartmann, Anne, and Wolfram Eggeling. *Sowjetische Präsenz im kulturellen Leben der SBZ und frühen DDR 1945–1953.* Berlin: Akademie Verlag, 1998.

Horvath, Gladys. "A Critical Analysis of Three Short Stories by Vera Panova," M.A. thesis, Kutztown State College, Pennsylvania, 1972.

Kreuzer, Ruth L. Hinkle. "A New Bright Shore for Sereza," in *Slavic and East European Journal.* Vol. 27, no. 3. Fall 1983, pp. 339–353.

Kuzmichyov, Igor. "New Books," in *Soviet Literature.* No. 7 (340), 1976, pp. 182–185.

Marsh, Rosalind, ed. *Women and Russian Culture: Projections and Self-Perceptions.* Oxford, UK: Berghahn Books, 1998.

Ninov, Aleksandr Alekseevich. "Return to the Theater (On the Fate of Vera Panova's Plays)," in *Soviet Studies in Literature.* Vol. 16, no. 1. Winter 1979–80, pp. 47–87.

Panova, Vera. "Evdokia," in Helena Goscilo, ed., *Russian and Polish Women's Fiction.* Translated by Helena

Goscilo. Knoxville, TN: University of Tennessee Press, 1985, pp. 108–179.

———. *The Factory.* Translated by *Moura Budberg. London: Putnam, 1949.

———. "Insomnia: A Play in Three Acts," in *Soviet Literature.* No. 10 (463), 1986, pp. 66–116.

———. *Looking Ahead.* Translated by David Skvirsky. Moscow: Foreign Languages Publishing House, 1950.

———. *On Faraway Street.* Translated by Rya Gabel. Adapted by Anne Terry White. NY: George Braziller, 1968.

———. "Panova on Salinger," in Carl R. Proffer, ed., *Soviet Criticism of American Literature in the Sixties: An Anthology.* Ann Arbor, MI: Ardis, 1972, pp. 3–10.

———. *Selected Works.* Translated by Olga Shartse and Eve Manning. Moscow: Progress Publishers, 1976.

———. "Seryozha," in Krystyna Pomorska, ed., *Fifty Years of Russian Prose: From Pasternak to Solzhenitsyn.* 2 vols. Cambridge, MA: MIT Press, 1973, Vol. 2, pp. 245–326.

———. *Seryozha: Several Stories from the Life of a Very Small Boy.* Translated by Nicholas Berkoff and Ann Baxandall Krooth. Berkeley, CA: Harvest, 1996.

———. *Span of the Year.* Translated by Vera Traill. Reprint ed. Westport, CT: Hyperion Press, 1977.

———. *Sputniki—The Travelling Companions.* NY: Blaisdell, 1965.

———. *Time Walked.* London: Harvill Press, 1957 (reprinted as *A Summer to Remember*, NY: Thomas Yoseloff, 1962).

———. *The Train.* Translated by Moura Budberg. NY: Alfred A. Knopf, 1949.

Rogers, Thomas F. "Ethical Idealism in Post-Stalin Fiction," in *The Rocky Mountain Social Science Journal.* Vol. 12, no. 2. April 1975, pp. 29–40.

Shalapentokh, Vladimir. "The Justification of Political Conformism: The Mythology of Soviet Intellectuals," in *Studies in Soviet Thought.* Vol. 39, no. 2. March 1990, pp. 111–135.

Smith, Melissa T. "Women in the Wings: Russian Women Playwrights in the Twentieth Century," in Toby W. Clyman and Diana Greene, eds., *Women Writers in Russian Literature.* Westport, CT: Greenwood, 1994, pp. 189–203.

Svirski, Grigori. *A History of Post-War Soviet Writing: The Literature of Moral Opposition.* Translated and edited by Robert Dessaix and Michael Ulman. Ann Arbor, MI: Ardis, 1981.

Tevekelyan, Diana. "'Everything Said Must Be True,'" in *Soviet Literature.* No. 3 (396), 1981, pp. 141–152.

———. "'You Describe Life As It Is' (On the Work of Vera Panova)," in *Soviet Literature.* No. 10 (463), 1986, pp. 141–146.

Werth, Alexander. "The Seasons," in *The New Statesman and Nation* [London]. Vol. 48, no. 1221. July 31, 1954, pp. 126–127.

Woodburn, John. "Stalin Prize, First Class," in *The Saturday Review of Literature.* Vol. 32, no. 18. April 30, 1949, p. 14.

Yureva, Serafima Mikhailovna. *Vera Panova: Stranitsy zhizni.* Tenafly, NJ: Hermitage, 1993.

John Haag,
Associate Professor of History, University of Georgia, Athens, Georgia

Pansy (1841–1930).

See Alden, Isabella.

Panthea (?–c. 545 BCE)

Noblewoman of Susa whose virtue and loyalty, as recorded by Xenophon, won the respect of Cyrus II the Great. *Died around 545 BCE; married Abradatas or Abradatus.*

Panthea is a character in the *Cyropaedia*, Xenophon's historical romance written during the first half of the 4th century BCE, although it is quite possible that Xenophon based his portrayal on an actual woman and her tragic fate. Panthea is said to have been captured by Cyrus II the Great, founder of the Persian Empire, when he overran the camp of the recently slain king of Assyria, whose realm Cyrus was in the process of conquering. Panthea was in the entourage of the Assyrian king because her husband, Abradatas, was the lord of Susa, an ally of the Assyrian king, and at the time on his way to Bactria in a diplomatic effort to raise an alliance against Cyrus. Hearing from Araspas (the Mede who actually took Panthea into custody) that Panthea was the most beautiful woman in Asia, Cyrus refused even to gaze upon her (even though, since she was extraordinarily comely, she had been set aside for him by right of conquest) lest passion override his sense of propriety and lead him to force himself upon her. As a result, Panthea remained in the care of Araspas, who, upon learning that Cyrus refused her out of a fear that he might wish to possess her illicitly, scoffed at Cyrus' admitted weakness. Although he initially believed himself to be above such infatuation, Araspas fell so deeply in love with Panthea that he threatened to take her against her will (throughout, Panthea remained true to her husband, whom she truly loved). Fearing rape, Panthea notified Cyrus of her plight by means of her attendant eunuch. Amused at Araspas' inability to control his passion (especially after his censure of Cyrus), but nevertheless worried that Araspas might demean himself by dishonoring Panthea, Cyrus separated the two by sending Araspas to spy on Croesus, king of Lydia, whose land Cyrus was about to invade.

Panthea was thereafter treated with so much respect at the command of Cyrus that she is said to have come to an appreciation of his true worth. As a consequence, she asked Cyrus to allow her to contact Abradatas, so as to win him over to Cyrus' cause. Abradatas, freed from his association with Assyria by the death of his one-time ally and convinced by Panthea of

Cyrus' nobility, agreed to serve Cyrus. Thus, Panthea and Abradatas were lovingly reunited in the service of the Persian king.

When it came time for Cyrus' final battle against Croesus, Abradatas is reported to have volunteered to command that portion of Cyrus' army which would be in the most peril. Cyrus, gracious as always, accepted this offer. Just before the battle was engaged, Panthea, proud of her husband's bravery, made a gift to him of a new breastplate and magnificent robe. Both then publicly acknowledged their love for the other and Abradatas was off, never to return, for while fighting heroically in the midst of a chariot melee, he was killed. Before Cyrus could even reclaim Abradatas' body, Panthea was on the scene and making preparations for her husband's appropriate burial. Appreciating her piety, Cyrus left the affairs of burial in Panthea's hands, but promised to underwrite the expense of the appropriate ceremonies. What Cyrus did not expect, however, then occurred. Unable to face life without her beloved, Panthea committed suicide so that she could be interred with Abradatas. Following her example, all of her personal train did likewise, a testimony to her worth. Too late Cyrus learned of Panthea's plans, but after the fact he is said to have appropriately honored the caliber of both Panthea and Abradatas.

William S. Greenwalt,
Associate Professor of Classical History, Santa Clara University,
Santa Clara, California

Paola (1937—)

Queen of the Belgians. *Name variations: Paola Ruffo de Calabria or di Calabria; Paolo Ruffo of Calabria. Born Paola Ruffo di Calabria in Italy on September 11, 1937; married Albert (b. 1934), prince of Liège, later Albert II, king of the Belgians (r. 1993—); children: Crown Prince Philippe (b. 1960); Princess* ***Astrid*** *(b. 1962, who married Archduke Lorenz of Austria); Prince Laurent (b. 1963).*

Paoli, Betty (1814–1894)

Austrian poet, essayist, and fiction writer who was the first woman journalist in Austria. *Name variations: Barbara Grund; Barbara Elisabeth Glück; (pseudonym) Branitz. Born Babette Barbara Elisabeth Glück in Vienna on December 30, 1814, out of wedlock; died in Baden bei Wien on July 5, 1894; daughter of a Hungarian noble and Theresia Glück; never married.*

The circumstances of Betty Paoli's birth and early years—she was born in Vienna, the illegitimate child of a Hungarian noble and Belgian-born **Theresia Glück**—did not give much cause for optimism. Nonetheless, her intellectual gifts would help her become a highly respected poet, a master of several other literary genres, and Austria's first female journalist. Extremely popular during her lifetime, her poetry was declared by contemporaries to be equal to that of ***Annette von Droste-Hülshoff** and ***Letitia Elizabeth Landon**. Paoli enjoyed a large circle of friends including such leading writers as ***Marie Ebner-Eschenbach**, Franz Grillparzer, and Adalbert Stifter. Her biography of Grillparzer was the first monograph to be written about this major literary personality.

In Paoli's youth, her mother took her on many trips, moving from place to place and thus giving life a look of instability. Paoli did, however, receive a good education. She became acquainted with a wide range of literary classics and mastered several languages. When her stepfather, a military physician, died and her mother lost her fortune, the teenage Paoli faced a life of poverty and had little choice but to make her own way. Starting in 1830, she began supporting herself by working as a governess for a number of families. For two years, from 1833 to 1835, she worked for a Russian family living on a rural estate in a remote region of Galicia near the Russo-Polish frontier. She was accompanied by her mother who could not cope with the cultural and physical demands of the situation. While returning to Vienna during the winter, Theresia died of the harsh conditions.

Not yet 20 years old, Paoli went back to Vienna in the spring of 1835 and began to support herself as a language tutor and translator. She also began contributing poetry and prose to various newspapers and periodicals in Vienna and Prague. Pleasantly surprised when her work began appearing in print, she adopted the nom de plume Betty Paoli with the publication of her short story "Clary" in the *Wiener Zeitschrift*. Her choice of "Paoli" was derived from the Corsican freedom fighter Pasquale de Paoli. For an almost penniless single woman to select as her pen name a foreign, male, revolutionary identity was a bold step in the reactionary climate of 1830s Vienna. Of the many intellectual influences she was exposed to during these years, writings from a Russia rapidly rising to the heights of world literature were significant. Impressed by the powerful messages of Russian writers, she translated into German a number of works by Alexander Pushkin and Ivan Turgenev.

With the publication in 1841 of her first book of poems, a small volume simply titled

Gedichte (Poems), Paoli went from being an unknown writer without the support of a patron to being the author of a volume which caused a sensation in Austrian literary circles. Revealing the inner life of a female poet, *Gedichte* was for its day an unusually frank unveiling of passion, melancholy, anger (toward the man who betrays her), and renunciation. While many of the poems in the book address an unnamed beloved, the collection is primarily the story of a woman whose unhappy past has led her to regard poetic expression as her one source of personal consolation.

The remarkable success of *Gedichte* brought Paoli fame, countless readers, and access to the salon of **Henriette Wertheimer**, wife of the Viennese philanthropist Joseph Wertheimer. Betty became Henriette's companion, and—in addition to being relieved of financial worries—she now found herself at the heart of Viennese literary and artistic life. Soon after the publication in 1843 of her second collection of poems, *Nach dem Gewitter* (After the Storm), she took on a new role, that of reader and companion to Princess **Marie Anna von Schwarzenberg**. As part of the princess' household, Paoli developed a close literary friendship with another of Princess Schwarzenberg's readers, the gifted writer Adalbert Stifter. The warmth of their friendship was reflected by Stifter when he portrayed both Paoli and the princess in his book *Nachsommer* (Indian Summer). During this period, Paoli also became acquainted with and was influenced by such noted writers as Franz Grillparzer and Nikolaus Lenau.

The travels that were part of the yearly routine of being connected to the Schwarzenberg family also provided inspiration for Paoli. During an 1844 trip to Berlin, she became acquainted with the circle around ***Rahel Varnhagen**, which included ***Bettine von Arnim**. The brief stay in Berlin left its mark on Paoli's book *Romancero* (1845), a work she dedicated to von Arnim. Most critics regard *Romancero* as containing Paoli's most artistically viable epic poems, including several which touched on a politically sensitive issue for the unstable Habsburg multinational state: the unfulfilled Italian yearning for freedom.

In early 1848, when a revolution broke out in Vienna which toppled Prince Metternich's reactionary regime, Paoli at first praised the political and intellectual freedom resulting from the upheaval. Within a few months, however, she distanced herself from the reforms, describing the situation in letters to close friends as one of anarchy and bloodshed brought on by an unsavory alliance of industrial workers and idealistic students no better than a "radical mob." The year was a disquieting one for the writer, not only because of its violence. In April 1848, her patron Princess von Schwarzenberg died, ending Paoli's employment. Furthermore, the revolution threatened the social order that made the *Taschenbuch* (pocket book) a popular literary genre with bourgeois women. A quintessential expression of the pre-1848 conservatism of Austrian and German Biedermeier culture, the *Taschenbuch* now went into a period of decline. With it went much of Paoli's economic security, as her primary source of income for over a decade had been derived from this genre. Added to her insecurities were political squabbles with friends and acquaintances, to the extent that she became known to her detractors as the "schwarzgelbe Hyäne" (black and yellow hyena), a reference to a club comprising individuals who remained loyal to the cause of the Habsburg throne.

Fortunately for Paoli, in 1849 she found employment as a companion to **Countess Bünau**, who lived in Dahlen near Dresden, in Germany. Temporarily disillusioned by the bitterness of political and literary controversies, she expanded her knowledge in various fields, particularly art history. At this time, while remaining associated with Countess Bünau until 1854, Paoli worked in Paris for a few months as a freelance correspondent for the Viennese newspaper *Neue Freie Presse*. In Paris, she met such luminaries as Heinrich Heine and ***George Sand**.

Paoli quickly felt herself comfortable in the world of journalism. By 1852, she had returned to Vienna and was publishing in the newspaper *Wiener Lloyd*. For the next several years, Paoli published regularly in the Viennese press, but despite her intense efforts she remained financially impoverished. For a time, at least part of her income was derived from her role as companion to a Russian expatriate, **Madame Bagréef-Speranski.** By 1855, however, Paoli had become a successful theater and art critic, publishing first in the newly founded *Österreichische Zeitung*. She then appeared in print in a number of other respected Viennese newspapers including the *Wiener Allgemeine Zeitung* and, most important, in the highly influential mouthpiece of the upper middle class, the *Neue Freie Presse*. As an art critic covering both museums and galleries, she wielded considerable influence. She was equally powerful in her role as a theater critic, as her opinions could determine the success or failure of a play at the famous Burgtheater or other Viennese playhouses. Paoli also maintained a literary relationship to the Burgtheater, for which she translated French plays under the pseudonym "Branitz." Her reviews were both perceptive and finely written. By now, she enjoyed the reputation of being Austria's first woman journalist.

The last four decades of Paoli's life were dominated by relationships she maintained with her intimate circle of female friends. Of these, **Ida von Fleischl-Marxow**, whose Jewish family was one of the most wealthy and influential in Vienna, was by far the most important. In the late spring of 1855, Paoli entered into the final phase of a long, creative life, moving in with Ida and her family. In a remarkable arrangement that remained viable for many years (she would live with them until her death in 1894), Paoli lived harmoniously with Ida, her husband, and her sons. Sharing intense sisterly love with Ida, Paoli flourished personally and professionally. Among her own and Ida's closest friends was Marie Ebner-Eschenbach.

In declining health during the last two decades of her life, Paoli published less than she had previously. In the works she did publish, the aging author revealed an increasing social compassion, particularly for the sufferings of the industrial working classes. In her poem "Der Minotaurus," she pleads for society to provide them with the material necessities of life in order to prevent class warfare which would likely result in the destruction of ordered society.

Betty Paoli died in Baden bei Wien on July 5, 1894. On January 24, 1895, a memorial ceremony to honor her was held in Vienna by that city's prestigious Verein der Schriftstellerinnen und Künstlerinnen (Association of Female Authors and Artists). In a moving address, the Burgtheater's star actor Joseph Lewinsky paid tribute to a woman who had risen from a difficult early life to become Austria's first female journalist and one of the most respected literary personalities of imperial Vienna's golden age.

SOURCES:

Adamec, Friedrich. "Betty Paoli und ihr Freundeskreis," Ph.D. dissertation, University of Vienna, 1951.

Bettelheim-Gabillon, Helene. "Betty Paoli," in *Neue Österreichische Biographie*. Vol. 5, 1928, pp. 48–65.

Brinker-Gabler, Gisela, Karola Ludwig, and Angela Wöffen, eds., *Lexikon deutschsprachiger Schriftstellerinnen, 1800–1945*. Munich: Deutscher Taschenbuch, 1986.

Garland, Mary. *The Oxford Companion to German Literature*. 3rd ed. NY: Oxford University Press, 1997.

Gluck, Jolan. "Betty Paoli: Die Dichterin im Spiegel Ihres Jahrhunderts," Ph.D. dissertation, City University of New York, 1989.

Gürtler, Christa, and Sigrid Schmid-Bortenschlager. *Eigensinn und Widerstand: Schriftstellerinnen der Habsburgermonarchie*. Vienna: Verlag Carl Ueberreuter, 1998.

Hacken, Richard D., ed. *Into the Sunset: Anthology of Nineteenth-Century Austrian Prose*. Riverside, CA: Ariadne Press, 1999.

Kernmayer, Hildegard. *Judentum im Wiener Feuilleton (1848–1903): Exemplarische Untersuchungen zum literarästhetischen und politischen Diskurs der Moderne*. Tübingen: Max Niemeyer, 1998.

Lewinsky, Joseph. *Gedenkrede auf Betty Paoli*. Vienna: Verlag des Vereines der Schriftstellerinnen und Künstlerinnen in Wien, 1895.

Paoli, Betty. *Die schwarzgelbe Hyäne*. Ed. by Joseph Halper. Graz: Stiasny Verlag, 1957.

———. "To a Man of the World," in Susan L. Cocalis, ed., *The Defiant Muse: German Feminist Poems from the Middle Ages to the Present*. NY: Feminist Press, 1986, p. 51.

Rose, Ferrel. "Betty Paoli," in Donald G. Daviau, ed., *Major Figures of Nineteenth-Century Austrian Literature*. Riverside, CA: Ariadne Press, 1998, pp. 387–415.

Scott, Annie A. *Betty Paoli: An Austrian Poetess of the Nineteenth Century*. London: George Routledge, 1926.

Wozonig, Karin S. *Die Literatin Betty Paoli: Weibliche Mobilität im 19. Jahrhundert*. Vienna: Löcker Verlag, 1999.

Zechner, Rosa. "'In unwandelbarer Zuneigung ergeben': Betty Paoli (1814–1894) und ihr Freundinnenkreis," in *Homme*. Vol. 4, no. 1, 1993, pp. 18–39.

Zinck, Karl Hugo. "Betty Paoli (1814–1894) und Dr. Joseph Breuer (1842–1925) in ihrer Zeit," in *Vierteljahrsschrift des Adalbert Stifter Insituts des Landes Oberösterreich*. Vol. 25, 1976, pp. 143–159.

John Haag,
Associate Professor of History, University of Georgia, Athens, Georgia

Paolini Massimi, Petronilla (1663–1726).

See Massimi, Petronilla Paolini.

Paparriga, Alexandra (1945—)

Greek archaeologist, accountant, and politician who was the first woman to be elected secretary general of the Communist Party of Greece. *Name variations: Aleka Papariga. Born in Athens, Greece, in 1945; studied history and archaeology at the University of Athens; married; children: one daughter.*

Trained as an archaeologist but active in the Communist Party of Greece (KKE) since 1968, Alexandra Papariga was barred from pursuing a teaching post in archaeology during the right-wing military dictatorship (1967–74). Unable to work, she became more active politically, founding the Women's Federation of Greece (OGE) and participating in various international women's fora, including the United Nations. She was also elected a member of the Central Committee of the Communist Party in 1978 and advanced to the executive branch of the party as a member of the KKE Political Bureau in 1986. In 1991, with the support of the orthodox wing, she was elected secretary general, the first woman ever to lead the party. In 1993, she was elected to Parliament for the second electoral district of Athens; she was reelected in 1996.

Papas, Irene (1926—)

Greek actress. *Born Irene Lelekou on March 9, 1926, in Chiliomodion, Greece.*

Selected filmography: Lost Angels *(Gr., 1950);* Necropolitia *(*Dead City, *Gr., 1951);* Le Infedeli *(It., 1953);* Dramma nella Casbah *(*The Man from Cairo, *It.-US, 1953);* Theodora Imperatrice di Bisanzio *(*Theodora Slave Empress, *It., 1954);* Attila *(It., 1954);* Tribute to a Bad Man *(US, 1956);* Antigone *(Gr., 1960);* The Guns of Navarone *(UK-US, 1961);* Electra *(Gr., 1962);* The Moon-Spinners *(UK-US, 1964);* Zorba the Greek *(Gr.-US, 1964);* Mas alla de las Montanas *(*The Desperate Ones, *Sp.-US, 1967);* A ciascuno il suo *(*We Still Kill the Old Way, *It., 1967);* The Brotherhood *(US, 1968);* Z *(Fr.-Alg., 1969);* Anne of the Thousand Days *(UK-US, 1969);* A Dream of Kings *(US, 1969);* The Trojan Women *(Fr.-US, 1971);* Roma Bene *(It.-Fr., 1971);* Le Faro da Padre *(*Bambina, *It., 1974);* Moses *(UK-It., 1976);* The Message *(*Mohammad Messenger of God, *UK, 1976);* Iphigenia *(Gr., 1977);* Bloodline *(US, 1979);* Cristo si e fermato a Eboli *(It.-Fr., 1979);* Lion of the Desert *(Libya-UK, 1980);* Erendira *(Pan.-Fr., 1983);* Into the Night *(US, 1985);* The Assisi Underground *(It.-UK, 1985);* Sweet Country *(Pan.-Gr., 1986);* High Season *(UK, 1987);* Cronica de una Muerte anunciada *(*Chronicle of a Death Foretold, *It.-Fr., 1987);* Island *(Austral., 1989);* Drums of Fire *(UK, 1991);* Zoe *(UK, 1992);* Up Down and Sideways *(US, 1993).*

An international actress acclaimed for her portrayals of some the most famous heroines of classical Greek drama, Irene Papas began her career as a teenager, singing and dancing in variety shows and only playing an occasional straight role. She made her first film, *Lost Angels* (1950), in Greece, and also appeared in several Italian films before signing a contract with Metro-Goldwyn-Mayer. Americans first viewed the actress in

Irene Papas in Gabriel Garcia Marquez's Erendira.

Tribute to a Bad Man (1956) and *The Guns of Navarone* (1961), but it was her appearance in *Electra* (1962) and *Zorba the Greek* (1964), both of which were directed by Michael Cacoyannis, that established her as an international star. Papas, a striking woman whose intensity is frequently compared to that of ***Anna Magnani**, went on to play leading roles in international productions and on the American stage and screen. As well, in 1979 she collaborated with Vangelis on *Odes*, a collection of songs dealing in part with the Greek resistance to the Ottoman Empire in the early 19th century and before. In 1986, she collaborated a second time with Vangelis for the album *Rhapsodies*, on which she sings Greek lyrics based on Greek Orthodox Christian hymns. On April 10, 2000, the European Cinema Panorama honored Papas for her lifetime achievement and contribution to cinema.

Papia of Envermeu (fl. 1020)

Duchess of Normandy. *Name variations: Popa. Flourished around 1020; became second wife of Richard II the Good (d. 1027), duke of Normandy (r. 996–1027); children: William, count of Arques and Toulouse; Mauger, archbishop of Rouen (d. 1055);* ***Popa of Normandy.*** *Richard II's first wife was* ****Judith of Rennes*** *(c. 982–1018).*

Pappenheim Bertha (1859–1936)

German feminist and social worker, founder of the Federation of Jewish Women's Associations and several pioneering Jewish social organizations in Germany and Austria, who was later revealed to be "Anna O.," the subject of a famous case in the early history of psychoanalysis. *Name variations: "Anna O."; (pseudonym) Paul Berthold. Pronunciation: BEAR-tah PAH-pen-highm. Born on February 27, 1859, in Vienna, Austria; died at Isenburg, Germany, on May 18, 1936; daughter of Sigmund Pappenheim (a grain dealer) and Recha (Goldschmidt) Pappenheim; had two sisters and one brother; educated by governesses and at a Catholic school in Vienna; never married.*

Treated by Dr. Josef Breuer in Vienna (1880–82); moved to Frankfurt with family (1889); was described as patient "Anna O." in Studies in Hysteria, *by Breuer and Sigmund Freud (1895); became director of the Jewish Orphanage for Girls (1895); translated into German and published the English feminist Mary Wollstonecraft's* A Vindication of the Rights of Women *(1899); wrote a play entitled* Women's Rights *(1899); raised the issue of the "white slavery" of young Jewish women in Eastern Europe (1900); traveled to Eastern Europe and the Middle East (1903–05); spoke at the International Congress to Fight White Slave Traffic in London (1910); founded home for Wayward Girls and Illegitimate Children in Neu-Isenburg, Germany (1907); founded Care by Women, an organization seeking to apply the goals of feminism to Jewish social work (1902); founded the Federation of Jewish Women's Associations (1904), and served on the organization's board of directors (1914–24); translated into German and published the* Memoirs of Glückel von Hameln *(1910); wrote a newspaper article advocating a national Jewish welfare association for Germany (1916); participated in the founding of the Central Welfare Office of German Jews (1917); honored with a stamp by West Germany as a pioneer in German social work (1954).*

Selected works: (under pseudonym Paul Berthold) In the Rummage Shop *(1894);* The Work of Sisyphus: Letters from Travels in the Years 1911 and 1912 *(1924);* The Work of Siysphus 2: Continuation *(1929); German translation of Mary Wollstonecraft's* A Vindication of the Rights of Women *(1899); (play)* Women's Rights *(1899); (under pseudonym Paul Berthold)* The Jewish Problem in Galicia *(1900);* On the Condition of the Jewish Population in Galicia *(1904); (translated into German)* Memoirs of Glückel von Hameln *(1910);* Tragic Moments *(1913).*

Although she might have remained at home, as was generally expected of unmarried daughters of wealthy European families in the late 19th century, Bertha Pappenheim selected a different path, forging a career as a feminist and a pioneer in Jewish social work in Germany and her native Austria. To do so, she had to overcome a serious psychological crisis while in her early 20s, a crisis documented in an early book on psychoanalysis, in which she was named only "Anna O." Pappenheim's true identity was not revealed until 1953, some 20 years after her death, when Freud's biographer Ernest Jones linked "Anna O." to Pappenheim and claimed that she was the real author of some of Freud's methods.

Bertha Pappenheim was born in 1859 and grew to adulthood in Leopoldstadt, the Jewish section of Vienna. Her father Sigmund Pappenheim, the son of an Hungarian Orthodox Jewish family, was a grain dealer who had inherited most of his wealth and the co-founder of an Orthodox school in Vienna. Her mother **Recha Goldschmidt Pappenheim** was from a well-to-do German family. Pappenheim's maternal lineage could be traced to a number of wealthy or prominent Austrian-German Jewish families and included the poet Heinrich Heine.

Pappenheim was the third of three daughters, although only she and a brother, Wilhelm, would live to adulthood. Educated by a governess, she was also sent to a Catholic school which the family believed offered a better education than other Viennese schools. By her early adult years, she could speak fluent French, Italian, and English. She later wrote that she did not get along with her mother but felt favored by her father. She also came to resent her brother, who was given a university education—at a time when most German-speaking universities in Europe did not offer degrees to women. Even as a young woman, she noted that the birth of a baby girl was greeted with a more muted reaction than the birth of a baby boy—sometimes with the words, "Only a girl." Although she planned to remain in the family home as a young woman, doing charity work or other volunteer work, her strong sibling rivalry with her brother became a motivation for her to achieve more.

In 1880, the family moved to the Liechtensteinerstrasse neighborhood of Vienna, which was located next to the street where Sigmund Freud lived and worked from 1881 through 1938. At the time of the family's move, Pappenheim's father, a tuberculosis patient, was in declining health. As Pappenheim assumed the job of being his nurse and staying near his bed most of the time, she began to exhibit psychological difficulties which disturbed her family. She was said to experience problems with her hearing and speech, and she often would not respond to her family. She at times lost the ability to speak German, her native language, choosing to speak English instead. One of her arms and both of her legs were paralyzed, and at times she exhibited a paralyzed neck. She refused to eat and apparently could not read or write.

After a succession of doctors failed to change Pappenheim's behavior, the family decided to consult Josef Breuer, who was considered one of the most talented doctors in the city and whose clinical staff included the young physician Sigmund Freud, the founder of psychoanalysis. Of all the doctors whom the family consulted, Pappenheim would respond only to Breuer who described her as bubbling over "with vitality." She was, he wrote, petite and frail-looking but had had an active life and was an avid horseback rider. He thought her highly intelligent, with a "great grasp" of things. She also struck him as energetic, tenacious, and persistent, and he added that sometimes she was obstinate but that this quality usually gave way to a regard for others, or "basic kindness."

In the early 1880s, Breuer was among a number of Viennese physicians who treated his patients with hypnosis. Since Pappenheim easily could be placed into a trance, he was able to motivate her to tell of her life, and she often spoke of seeing a girl in her mind's eye sitting next to a patient's bed. During such trances, Pappenheim would also complain of "black snakes" and criticize both her mother and her nurse. Breuer also noticed that, under hypnosis, Pappenheim's arm was not paralyzed. His treatment of her, and his conversations about her with Freud in November 1881, became the basis for a book both men published, *Studies in Hysteria*. In the book, Pappenheim was identified only as "Anna O."

> There are people of spirit and there are people of passion, both less common than one might think. Rarer still are people of spirit and passion. Rarest of all is a passionate spirit. Bertha Pappenheim was a woman with just such a spirit.
>
> **—Martin Buber**

The more that Pappenheim talked about her troubles while under a hypnotic trance, the more she seemed to improve. While her symptoms worsened after the death of her father in 1881, and a similar regression seemed to occur when Pappenheim left Breuer's hospital for a brief time to live with her mother, Breuer continued to induce her to talk under hypnosis, terming his treatment the "talking cure." He reported that he even talked her through a "mock pregnancy." Of all the doctors, only Breuer could place her into a trance, and she would respond only to his questions. Pappenheim reached a point where she could rise from her bed and walk around her bedroom. The paralysis of her arm was the last symptom to disappear.

As "Anna O.," Pappenheim played a role in the development of psychoanalysis, since Freud believed that she demonstrated that patients who talked about their cases seemed to undergo at least some improvement. He commented to Breuer that Pappenheim's symptoms seemed to disappear in proportion to her resurrection of buried memories.

Released for a time to visit her family's summer home, she began to place herself into trances. She reported that she missed Breuer, a situation described by Freud as the first case of "transference"—of a patient transferring to a therapist the affection usually felt for a family member or spouse. Breuer's wife was said to be upset with the amount of time her husband was spending with one patient, however, and that, plus the phantom pregnancy, reportedly caused Breuer to break off the treatment in 1882. He told Freud that "Anna O." was suffering so much that death would be merciful for her. Fellow psychoanalyst Carl Jung later said that Freud told him that Pappenheim was "not cured" when Breuer's treatment ceased.

After Breuer broke off treatment, Pappenheim was sent for care to a Swiss hospital. Little is known about her life during the 1880s, but she apparently overcame her difficulties by 1889, the year that her family moved to Frankfurt. She would live there the rest of her life. In 1890, Pappenheim began a career as a writer, publishing a book of stories which resembled children's fairy tales, *In the Rummage Store*. The book, which described various kinds of unhappiness in families, appeared under the pseudonym Paul Berthold.

Pappenheim also began to show an interest in the publications and writings of the German feminist ***Helene Lange**, who headed a national association of German schoolteachers. She translated into German and published *A Vindication of the Rights of Women*, the 1792 book by the early English feminist ***Mary Wollstonecraft** which asserted that women should be companions of men rather than their playthings and that women should have equal educational opportunities with men. In 1899, Pappenheim wrote a play entitled *Women's Rights*, in which women were portrayed as the victims of cynical manipulation by men.

Pappenheim insisted that unmarried women from well-to-do families should reject the traditional role of remaining at home and search for vocational training and education. Young Jewish girls, she complained, were in some ways more sheltered and less educated than their Christian counterparts; she wrote in 1902 that she feared the "Christian girls" knew more about topics such as art and politics. If women were kept in ignorance of what went on "beyond the home," she believed, they would fail to see the "human tragedies" of sickness, poverty, and crime.

In 1895, she became interested in welfare work; her first position as a social worker was as director of the Jewish Orphanage for Girls in Frankfurt. Pappenheim accepted the position as a temporary measure but remained there for 12 years. Since she saw female emancipation as a path out of poverty for many young women, she also organized a girls' club for young women who had left the orphanage. It encompassed a lecture room, dining facilities, and a library.

When Pappenheim published *The Jewish Problem in Galicia* in 1900, she involved herself in controversy. The book described alarming conditions experienced in Poland by young women, particularly women living in ghettos. She wrote of small communities in Eastern Europe where "outside" men would visit and pretend to be searching for a wife, whom they would then force into "white slavery." She argued that wealthy Turkish Jews were financing activities to involve some of these young women in prostitution or the "white slavery" trade. Pappenheim refused to place blame on the prostitutes, but she accused other women of letting innocent girls suffer.

In 1902, Pappenheim attended her first conference on "white slavery." As well, arguing that men always follow their own private interests, Pappenheim founded that year Care by Women, an organization which sought to apply the ideas of German feminists to Jewish social work. It also sought to implement the latest social work techniques and included an employment service and counseling center for women.

After 1905, when her mother died and her brother remarried, she was freed of family responsibilities and could travel outside of Europe. She chose to travel to parts of Eastern Europe, including Poland and Russia, as well as to Greece, Turkey, Egypt, and Jerusalem. She used the trip to gather information on the forcing of Jewish women into prostitution. Many of her findings and experiences on trips were summarized in two volumes she wrote under the title *The Work of Sisyphus*. She also described her trips when she spoke in London in 1910 at the International Congress to Fight White Slave Traffic.

In 1907, she founded a home for Wayward Girls and Illegitimate Children in Neu-Isenburg, intended to help young women who had been "emotionally, physically, and intellectually damaged." This project was so close to her heart that she remained the head of the home for 29 years and kept it operating despite the shortages of World War I and the inflation of the 1920s in Germany.

Although Pappenheim never married and was not a mother, her feminism became centered around marriage and motherhood. She became convinced that women who worked to help children and adolescents became "spiritual mothers," even if they did not experience "real" motherhood. She came to consider one particular orphan she worked with as her daughter, and she spoke proudly of her "loyalty as a mother."

When the International Council of Women met in Berlin in 1904, Pappenheim had used the occasion to found the Federation of Jewish Women's Associations. She was the Federation's first president and remained on the organization's board of directors from 1914 to 1924. The Federation, which attained a membership of 50,000, established its own homes, clubs, and schools for girls, as ways to prepare young Jewish women for careers. The Federation also worked to replace many volunteer social workers with trained professionals.

The organization reflected Pappenheim's conviction that the family was sacred and that women were fulfilling a sacred role as wives and mothers. She was the major contributor to the Federation's newsletter, particularly on the subjects of social work and "white slavery." The Federation was also part of the abolitionist movement in German feminism, the movement to abolish the German tradition of municipally regulated (and in many cases, municipally sponsored) bordellos in major German cities. At Pappenheim's urging, the Federation also campaigned for some reform of Jewish wedding traditions: she argued that the Ketubah, a Jewish wedding certificate, facilitated "white slavery" since it required only the signature of the groom and two witnesses (who could be accomplices).

In 1916, Pappenheim advanced the idea of a national Jewish welfare association in Germany; the association was created the next year, under the name of the Central Welfare Office of German Jews. Despite the demands of her organizations, Pappenheim continued to publish. In 1910, she translated from medieval German Yiddish into German the memoirs of a distant relative, ***Glückel of Hameln**, who described what it meant to be a wife, mother, and Jew in Germany in the late 17th and early 18th centuries. In 1913, Pappenheim published a play, *Tragic Moments*, which voiced concerns over white slavery and continuing anti-Semitism in Germany, while portraying Zionism in favorable terms.

By the 1920s, Pappenheim also had involved herself in further controversies. In 1920, she told a meeting of the Federation that having children was a "woman's privilege" and that abortion was a "crime against the human race." She also found herself a somewhat controversial figure within German Judaism. While Pappenheim believed that her social work was strengthening the Jewish people, Orthodox Jews, who tended to like her religious ideas, were often lukewarm to her feminism and reform plans. More "progressive" Jewish groups liked the latter but found themselves criticized by her for lacking religious devotion. She believed that in a crisis, "too many Jews reach for their Goethe rather than their Bible." When B'nai B'rith asked Pappenheim to help form a women's auxiliary, she refused, commenting that she did not want to create a "tail end" for a male-dominated group. She also thought that many Zionist men did not hold women in sufficiently high regard and believed that many Zionists were not religious enough.

Bertha Pappenheim

Although ill health in 1924 forced Pappenheim to relinquish the presidency of the Federation, she continued to work on other projects. She created a social-work curriculum for the *Lehrhaus*, an adult learning project headed by her friend, the theologian and philosopher Martin Buber. In 1924, she translated into German and published a collection of medieval folk, Talmudic, and Bible stories entitled *Mayse Bukh*. She also translated into German the *Ze'enah U'Ree'nah*, a women's Bible which was a popular version of the books of Moses and Talmudic stories.

With the Nazi accession to power in 1933, Pappenheim's relationship with the Zionist movement worsened for a time. She initially thought that Nazism was a transient phenomenon and opposed Zionist plans to send Jewish children to Palestine, calling them "population politics." She had changed her opinion by the time the Nuremberg racial laws were proclaimed by the Nazi government in 1935. The next year, at age 77, she was summoned to Gestapo headquarters for questioning because one of the girls in her orphanage had been heard to comment that Hitler looked like a criminal.

During a vacation in 1934, Pappenheim had been hospitalized in Munich and diagnosed with cancer. When she died of the disease in 1936, she left behind a request that each person visiting her grave honor her with one small stone. She had planned to visit a Jewish girls' seminary in Poland, but her death prevented that. It was a small mercy, since the students would be forced into a brothel by Nazis three years later and her orphanage would be burned. Her death also came before the Nazi government began to use her writings on Jewish involvement in "white slavery" as part of its anti-Semitic propaganda.

In 1954, Bertha Pappenheim was recognized as a pioneer in social work when the West German government—at the suggestion of the welfare department of Freiburg and of Dr. Leo Baeck, a concentration camp survivor and a former president of the Organization of German Jews—issued a stamp in her honor.

SOURCES:

Edinger, Dora. *Bertha Pappenheim: Leben und Schriften.* Frankfurt: Ner Tamid Verlag, 1963.

Kaplan, Marion A. *The Jewish Feminist Movement in Germany: The Campaigns of the Jüdischer Frauenbund, 1904–1938.* Westport, CT: Greenwood Press, 1979.

Rosenbaum, Max, and Melvin Muroff, eds. *Anna O.: Fourteen Contemporary Interpretations.* NY: The Free Press, 1984.

SUGGESTED READING:

Edinger, Dora. *Bertha Pappenheim: Freud's Anna O.* Highland Park, IL: Congregation Solel, 1968.

Evans, Richard J. *The Feminist Movement in Germany, 1894–1933.* Beverly Hills, CA: Sage, 1976.

Freeman, Lucy. *Anna O.* NY: Walker, 1972.

Jones, Ernest. *The Life and Work of Sigmund Freud.* NY: Basic Books, 1953.

Whyte, L.L. *The Unconscious Before Freud.* NY: Basic Books, 1960.

COLLECTIONS:

Materials relating to Bertha Pappenheim are contained in the archives of the Leo Baeck Institute in New York City.

Niles R. Holt,
Professor of History, Illinois State University,
Normal, Illinois

Paradis, Maria Theresia von (1759–1824)

Austrian composer who wrote numerous works for the piano and founded an institute for musical education. *Born in Vienna on May 15, 1759; died in Vienna on February 1, 1824; daughter of the imperial secretary in the court of Empress Maria Theresa of Austria (1719–1780); studied with Leopold Kuzeluch and Vincenzo Righini.*

At age two or three, Maria Theresia von Paradis became completely blind. Her godmother, Empress ***Maria Theresa of Austria**, was determined that this handicap would not deter the talented child, so Maria studied piano with Leopold Kuzeluch and singing with Vincenzo Righini. In 1779, von Paradis sang the soprano part in Giovanni Battista Pergolesi's *Stabat Mater* while accompanying herself on the organ at a concert before the empress. Von Paradis became friendly with Mozart and Salieri, two rival composers at the court who dedicated works to her. A virtuoso pianist, she began touring Europe as well as composing pieces for her own concerts. Her librettist, Johan Riedlinger, devised a wooden pegboard which used different shaped pegs for different note values which allowed von Paradis to write down her music. Demand for original music was growing rapidly during this period, as more and more people were able to afford instruments. Von Paradis composed several piano sonatas, three cantatas, two operas and many songs as well as other works. She also founded and headed a music school in Vienna, where she taught singing and piano, whose express purpose was improving women's musical education.

John Haag,
Athens, Georgia

Paradis, Marie (fl. 1808).

See d'Angeville, Henriette for sidebar.

Parain-Vial, Jeanne (1912—)

French philosopher. *Born in 1912; agrégée in philosophy, University of Lyon, 1938; Ph.D., Sorbonne, 1951; teacher at Aix-en-Provence; teacher at University of Dijon.*

Selected works: Le sens du Présent: Essai sur la rupture de l'unité originelle *(1952);* De l'être musical *(1952);* Gabriel Marcel ou les niveau de l'éxperience *(1966);* La nature du fait dans les sciences humaines *(1967);* Analyses structurales et idéologies structuralistes *(1969);* Tendances nouvelles de la philosophie *(1978).*

Jeanne Parain-Vial has been known particularly for her philosophy of time and her philosophy of science and aesthetics. Although her early interest in time was sparked by reading the philosopher Gabriel Marcel, she considers herself a follower of Plato because of her belief that some ways of understanding, especially those of certain historical periods, are superior to others. According to her, the sciences of different times approximate an order which is divinely given; these approximations succeed to various degrees, each being partly but never wholly correct. For Parain-Vial, while science is objective because results can be reproduced, it is also subjective because it cannot escape the limitations of human experience and intelligence. The humanities are even more subjective than science, because they involve a reality that is beyond individual experience and replication, and which depends upon interpretation.

SOURCES:

Kersey, Ethel M. *Women Philosophers: a Bio-critical Source Book*. NY: Greenwood Press, 1989.

Catherine Hundleby, M.A. Philosophy, University of Guelph, Guelph, Ontario, Canada

Pardo Bazán, Emilia (1852–1921)

Leading Spanish writer of the 19th century, known for her novels, essays, and short stories. *Name variations: Emilia Pardo-Bazán or Pardo-Bazan. Born on September 16, 1852, in La Coruña, Spain; died in Madrid on May 12, 1921, from complications of diabetes; only child of the count and countess of Pardo Bazán; married José Quiroga (a lawyer), on July 10, 1868; children: Jaime, Carmen, Blanca.*

Born on September 16, 1852, in La Coruña, Spain, Emilia Pardo Bazán was the only child of the count and countess of Pardo Bazán. Her parents considered her intellectually precocious and took great pains with her education. To some extent, they used Rousseau's Emile as a model for her upbringing and apparently encouraged her to read everything, except modern French novels. Her marriage to José Quiroga, a lawyer, in 1868, and her father's election in 1869 to the Constitutent Cortes of Spain's First Republic, took Emilia to the fringes of aristocratic circles of Madrid. She also traveled widely in Western Europe, compiling diaries that served her later literary efforts, and read contemporary science, history, and philosophy but for a while ignored novels as too frivolous.

Although she had written poetry for years, Pardo Bazán turned seriously to other literary endeavors in the mid-1870s. Her first triumph, albeit a local one, was winning first prize in a provincial contest for an essay about an 18th-century Spanish intellectual (*Ensayo crítico de las obras del Padre Feijóo*). Reading contemporary French and then Spanish novels, however, turned her to that literary genre, which earned Pardo Bazán her greatest renown. Her first novel, *Pascual López*, appeared in 1879, followed by *Un viaje de novios* two years later. Meanwhile, she wrote a series of essays explaining Naturalism to Spanish readers (published as *La cuestión palpitante*), which progressives extolled and conservatives condemned. Yet she also wrote a religious study of St. Francis of Assisi that was warmly received by many Spanish readers. Although Pardo Bazán rejected Naturalism's atheism, her novels of the 1880s pioneered the movement's entry into Spain. In 1886, she met leading French advocates of Naturalism, including Edmond de Goncourt and Emile Zola, and published *Los pazos de Ulloa*, one of her most important novels.

Emilia Pardo Bazán

As her fame grew, Pardo Bazán delighted in the attention she received. Controversy often enveloped her, in part because of her own contradictions. She supported the religiously conservative Carlist cause, and her Catholicism prevented Pardo Bazán from fully adhering to Naturalism. Nonetheless, she championed feminism in Spain and published a number of important essays advocating equal rights and better education for women. Her views on literature and feminism offended her husband, and they separated. In some ways she was politically progressive, but she also yearned to be a full-fledged aristocrat. Although Pardo Bazán inherited her father's title in 1890, it was a papal rather than a hereditary Spanish one. In 1891, she campaigned for membership in the Spanish Royal Academy. Had her gender not been an issue, her achievements undoubtedly would have secured her election. Pardo Bazán's novels of the 1890s did not match the quality of her earlier works, but she remained a leading cultural figure in Spain.

Celebrity and frustration characterized her later years. Spain's defeat in the Spanish-American War dismayed her, and she became increasingly critical of what she perceived to be the degenerate culture of her homeland. In 1906, two of her plays received indifferent critical and popular responses, yet she was chosen to head the Literary Section of the Atheneum, Madrid's most prestigious intellectual club. The next year Alphonso XIII acknowledged her achievements by conferring the hereditary title of countess upon her. In 1916, her hometown of La Coruña erected a statue in her honor and the Central University of Madrid named her a professor. Nearly all her students were men, however, and most rejected her as an unconventional woman. Pardo Bazán died in Madrid on May 12, 1921, from complications of diabetes.

SOURCES:

González-Arias, Francisca. *Portrait of a Woman as Artist: Emilia Pardo Bazán and the Modern Novel in France and Spain.* NY: Garland, 1992.

Hemingway, Maurice. *Emilia Pardo Bazán: The Making of a Novelist.* NY: Cambridge University Press, 1983.

Pattison, Walter T. *Emilia Pardo Bazán.* NY: Twayne, 1971.

Kendall W. Brown,
Professor of History, Brigham Young University, Provo, Utah

Pardoe, Julia (1804–1862)

British novelist and historical writer. *Born in 1804 (some sources cite 1806) in Beverley, Yorkshire, England; died on November 26, 1862, in London, England; daughter of Major Thomas Pardoe and Elizabeth Pardoe; never married; no children.*

Although she is not well known today, Julia Pardoe was a popular writer of travel literature and historical works in the 19th century. Raised in an affluent family, she showed early signs of writing ability and composed a book of poetry which her parents arranged to have published in 1818, when Pardoe was only 13. The work went into several printings, and a second book of poetry followed in 1824. Her first novel, a historical romance titled *Lord Morcar of Hereward*, was published in 1829.

In the early 1830s, she produced two more romances, but began to suffer from ill health. Advised to vacation in a warmer climate as a cure, Pardoe and her father, a British army officer, traveled to Portugal in 1835. Pardoe had a keen eye for descriptive detail and kept careful notes on her visit in her journal, which became the basis of her first travelogue, *Traits and Traditions of Portugal*. The book included a dedicatory preface thanking Princess ***Augusta Guelph** (1768–1840) for her support. Pardoe and her father then undertook extended stays in Turkey, France, and Hungary between 1836 and 1837. On her return to England, she settled in London, where she wrote two travelogues on Turkey, published in 1837 and 1838, and one book each on the people and customs of southern France and Hungary.

Pardoe's travel writing, flowery in style and vivid in description, was more commercially successful and critically praised than were her poetry or romances. However, she turned back to novels and short stories in the late 1830s, often using the foreign cities she had lived in as her settings. In 1842, again suffering from ill health, Pardoe moved back to her parents' home, though in her final years she would return to London.

Over the next 15 years, she published six more romances. Her wide readership in Britain and the United States brought her a considerable income from book sales and from the serialization of some of her novels in British periodicals prior to their release in book form. Although her work was in general favorably reviewed, Pardoe's ornate, wordy writing style and the lack of strong themes in her books brought her numerous critics as well. In the mid-1840s, Pardoe began writing historical works on European royalty. Though the books are not scholarly by today's standards, she brought a dynamic narrative style and dramatic flair to her subjects' lives; *Louis XIV and the Court of France in the Seventeenth Century* (1846) was especially popular among her readers. At age 56, she was honored by the British government with a pension in recognition of her literary achievements. In November 1862, Julia Pardoe died at her London home.

SOURCES:

Pardoe, Julia. *The Court and Reign of Francis the First.* NY: J. Pott, 1901.

Schlueter, Paul, and June Schlueter, eds. *Encyclopedia of British Women Writers.* New Brunswick, NJ: Rutgers University Press, 1998.

Laura York,
Riverside, California

Parek, Lagle (1941—)

Estonian architect and politician. *Born in 1941.*

Employed by the Estonian Architectural Memorials Institute for 11 years (1972–83), Lagle Parek was charged with "anti-Soviet agitation" in 1983 and imprisoned for four years. Following her release, she pursued her political ideals, becoming the leader of the center-right Estonian National Independence Party (ERSP) from 1989 to 1993. She ran for president of Estonia in the 1992 elections, finishing fourth with 4.3% of the vote. Appointed interior minister in October 1992, Parek remained in office until

November 1993, at which time she resigned amid allegations of friction between the police and the army.

Parepa-Rosa, Euphrosyne (1836–1874)

English soprano. *Name variations: Euphrosyne Parepa Rosa. Born Euphrosyne Parepa de Boyesku on May 7, 1836 (one source cites 1839), in Edinburgh, Scotland; died on January 21, 1874, in London, England; daughter of Baron Georgiades de Boyesku of Bucharest (a noble) and a mother whose last name was Seguin (a lyric stage actress); niece of Arthur Edward Sheldon Seguin; married Captain Henry de Wolfe Carvell, in 1864 (died 1865); married Carl August Nicholas Rosa (a violinist), in 1867; no children.*

Made debut in Malta, and performed throughout Europe (1850s); debuted in London (1857); toured America for the first time (1866); performed in Egypt (1872–73).

Selected major roles: Amina in La Sonnambula *(Malta, 1855); appearance in* Il Puritani *(London, 1857); Rosina in* The Barber of Seville *(U.S., 1860s).*

The daughter of a Bucharest noble who died when she was an infant and a mother who then went on the stage as a lyric actress to earn a living, Euphrosyne Parepa-Rosa made her singing debut at age 16, in Malta. Able to speak English, Italian, French, German, and Spanish with ease, she subsequently toured Naples, Genoa, Rome, Florence, Madrid, and Lisbon. Her powerful soprano and energetic delivery made her a great favorite of European audiences, and during the two years she performed on the Continent she won accolades from both music critics and the public. Parepa-Rosa made her London debut in 1857, receiving high praise for her performance in *Il Puritani*. She continued performing in England for nine years. During this time she married a British East India officer, Henry de Wolfe Carvell, who died only 16 months later. In 1866, Parepa-Rosa traveled to America, on tour with cornetist Levy and violinist Carl Rosa, and debuted in New York City. She married Carl Rosa in 1867, and together they established an English opera company which toured cities throughout the United States from 1869 to 1872. Parepa-Rosa routinely performed concerts, oratorio, and opera as often as 20 times in as many days, and became well loved by the public; one of her greatest successes in the United States was as Rosina in *The Barber of Seville*. Possessed of a voice with great reach and thorough balance, Parepa-Rosa also demonstrated flawless intonation and enunciation. Music critics considered her unequaled in both oratorio and concert. During the winter of 1872–73, she performed in Egypt at the court of the khedive, and died a year later, in London, at the age of 38.

SOURCES:

Concise Dictionary of National Biography. Oxford and NY: Oxford University Press, 1992.

King, William C. *Woman: Her Position, Influence, and Achievement Throughout the Civilized World: From the Garden of Eden to the Twentieth Century.* Springfield, MA: King-Richardson, 1900.

Parton, James, *et al. Eminent Women of the Age.* Hartford, CT: S.M. Betts, 1868.

Richard C. Hanes,
freelance writer, Eugene, Oregon

Pargeter, Edith (c. 1913–1995)

British author. *Name variations: (pseudonym) Ellis Peters. Born around 1913; died in Madeley, England, on October 14, 1995.*

Although she wrote some 60 books, including historical novels and a wartime trilogy, Edith Pargeter, who wrote under the name Ellis Peters, is remembered primarily as the creator of the popular Cadfael Chronicles, a series of murder mysteries about a crime-solving 12th-century monk. The stories, some of which were filmed for PBS television starring Sir Derek Jacobi, were bestsellers and translated into 20 languages.

Pargeter began writing crime stories in 1959, turning out a series of Inspector Felse novels. She published her first book featuring the Benedictine monk Brother Cadfael in 1977. In addition to his intellect and powers of observation, Cadfael's skill as an herbalist also aided him in his detective work. The author's other books include *The Heaven Tree Trilogy* and *Brothers of Gwynedd Quartet*, as well as a set of historical novels, and *The Eighth Champion of Christendom*, a wartime trilogy. She also won an award for several Czech translations. Pargeter resided for most of her life in the Shropshire area of western England, which was also the setting of her Cadfael stories. She died there on October 14, 1995, following a stroke.

SOURCES:

"Obituary," in *Boston Globe.* October 16, 1995.

"Passages," in *People Weekly.* October 30, 1995.

Paris, countess of.

See Hedwig (c. 915–965).

See Maria Isabella (1848–1919).

See Isabella of Orleans (b. 1911).

Paris, queen of.

See Ingoberge (519–589).
See Vultrogotha (fl. 558).
See Maria Isabella (1848–1919).

Pariseau, Esther (1823–1902).

See Joseph, Mother.

Parish, Mrs. Henry II (1910–1994).

See Parish, Sister.

Parish, Sister (1910–1994)

American interior designer and entrepreneur. *Name variations: Mrs. Henry Parish II. Born Dorothy May Kinnicutt in 1910; died in Dark Harbor, Maine, in September 1994; daughter of Gustav Hermann Kinnicutt (a financier) and May Appleton (Tuckerman) Kinnicutt; married Harry Parish, on February 14, 1930 (died 1977); children: two daughters, including Apple Parish Bartlett, and a son.*

Paley, Babe *and* ***Betsey Whitney.*** *See Cushing Sisters.*

An untrained socialite who took up interior design during the Depression in order to preserve her lifestyle, Sister Parish was the driving force behind the renowned Parish-Hadley firm and the creator of the "American Country" look, which graced the homes of the nation's socially elite for six decades. Parish gained notoriety during the late 1950s, when First Lady ***Jacqueline Kennedy** hired her to assist with various White House renovations, although the two women had a falling out before the work was finished. (Parish once shrugged off a question concerning the rift, remarking, "Jackie got along much better with men than with women.") Behind her patrician facade, Parish was a "crusty old gal" who loved to tell jokes, toted her Pekingese "Yummy" to client meetings, and gave cocktail parties to mix her old guard cronies with her younger New York friends.

Dorothy May Kinnicutt (dubbed "Sister" by her three-year-old brother) was to the manor born in 1910, the daughter of Gustav Hermann Kinnicutt, a wealthy New York financier, and **May Tuckerman Kinnicutt**, who was known for her "instinctive good taste" and an "innate sense of a well-ordered, properly regulated life." As a child, Parish was dressed in ermine coats to ward off the winter chill, and was shuttled between the family residences in Far Hills, New Jersey (Mayfields), and Dark Harbor, Maine. Following her coming out in 1927, she spent a year in the family's apartment on the Quai d'Orsay in Paris. She married Henry Parish in 1930 and briefly lived in Manhattan, before moving to Far Hills, New York, where she raised the couple's three children. The country look Parish created for her own house—inspired by the homes of her childhood—was the envy of her neighbors, who soon began calling her for advice. One neighbor, Senator Joseph S. Frelinghuysen, enlisted her help in decorating a new restaurant in the area. "The place was called Howard Johnson's," Parish said. "I did what I could. I dressed the waitresses in aqua, did the walls in aqua, made the place mats in aqua. I guess I must have thought it was quite chic, but I haven't done a thing in aqua since."

In the midst of the Depression, when her husband's salary was cut in half, Parish went into the decorating business officially. "She had been accustomed to living a certain way, and she was going to do everything in her power to maintain it for herself and her children," said her granddaughter. Using the intuitive aesthetic sense that had always guided her, she began designing interiors for an exclusive clientele that included Charles and **Jane Engelhard**, Bill and **Babe Paley**, Jock and **Betsey Whitney**, Gordon and **Ann Getty**, and, of course, Jacqueline Kennedy. (When Kennedy first hired Sister Parish, one newspaper headline announced, "Kennedys Pick Nun to Decorate White House.") In 1962, Parish acquired a partner, Albert Hadley, and founded the design firm Parish-Hadley.

Continuity, comfort, and character were the hallmarks of Parish's country-house designs. "As a child," she wrote, "I discovered the happy feelings that familiar things can bring—an old apple tree, a favorite garden, the smell of a fresh-clipped hedge, simply knowing that when you round the corner, nothing will be changed, nothing will be gone. . . . Some think a decorator should change a house. I try to give permanence to a house, to bring out the experiences, the memories, the feelings that make it a home." Parish's style encompassed vibrant colors (red walls, for example, with a different shade of red for the floor) and a savvy mix of heirlooms, custom-made furnishing, and inexpensive accessories.

While Parish was outwardly confident about her work, she was often overcome with self-doubt. "I have ached all my life, thinking I have done wrong or could have done better," she once confided. She frequently sought comfort in the restorative powers of her own houses, particularly the Parish place in Maine. She also found peace within her family, to whom she was fiercely devoted. During her husband's last summer in Maine, before his death in 1977, she nursed him by sprinkling sea water on his forehead and hands, which she fetched from the ocean in a watering can she had brought back from France.

Parish survived her husband by 17 years, dying in 1994 at her beloved retreat in Dark Harbor. In late summer 2000, her daughter **Apple Parish Bartlett** and granddaughter **Susan Bartlett Crater** published a lively, loving tribute to the designer, *Sister: The Life of Legendary American Decorator, Mrs. Henry Parish II.*

SOURCES:

"Forecasts," in *Publishers Weekly.* July 3, 2000.
"Milestones," in *Time.* September 19, 1994.
Norwich, William. "Interiors," in *The New York Times Book Review.* August 20, 2000.

SUGGESTED READING:

Bartlett, Apple Parish, and Susan Bartlett Crater. *Sister: The Life of Legendary American Decorator, Mrs. Henry Parish II.* St. Martin's, 2000.

Barbara Morgan,
Melrose, Massachusetts

Park, Ida May (d. 1954)

Film director who worked at Universal Studios in the early 1900s. *Date of birth unknown; died in 1954; married Joseph De Grasse (an actor).*

Selected filmography: Bondage *(director, scenario, 1917);* Fires of Rebellion *(director, scenario, 1917);* The Flashlight *(director, scenario, 1917);* Bread *(1918);* Broadway Love *(1918);* The Model's Confession *(1918);* Risky Road *(director, adaptation, 1918);* Vanity Pool *(1918);* Boss of Powderville *(1918?);* Amazing Wife *(director, scenario, 1919);* The Butterfly Man *(director, scenario, 1920);* Bonnie May *(scenario, 1921);* The Midlanders *(scenario, 1921).*

Lost to history along with her films, Ida May Park was one of only a handful of women directors at Universal Studios during the early 1900s. Unlike some women in film during the period, however, who acted and only occasionally directed a film or two, Park concentrated solely on directing, making a series of movies between 1917 and 1920. Since no directing credits for her appear after 1920, she might have returned to writing vehicles for her husband, actor Joseph De Grasse.

Park got her start as a stage actress, then branched out into writing. She began directing on her husband's projects, and made 12 features with him in as many months before going solo in 1917. Unlike ***Lois Weber**, Park was not a revolutionary or an idealist, but, as suggested by Richard Koszarski, a pragmatist who "subordinated all else to getting the product out on time and under budget." "I want my people to do good work because of their regard for me and not because I browbeat them into it," she said in a 1918 interview for *Photoplay.* "I believe in choosing distinct types and then seeing that the actor puts his own personality into his parts, instead of making every part in a picture reflect my personality."

Park, who turned down her first opportunity to direct because she thought it was work unsuited to a woman, later changed her mind, writing that women's "emotional and imaginative faculties gives them a great advantage." Notes Koszarski, by 1934 ***Dorothy Arzner** was the only woman director working in Hollywood.

SOURCES:

Acker, Ally. *Reel Women: Pioneers of the Cinema 1896 to the Present.* NY: Continuum, 1991.

Barbara Morgan,
Melrose, Massachusetts

Park, Maud Wood (1871–1955)

American suffragist. *Born Maud May Wood in Boston, Massachusetts, on January 25, 1871; died in Reading, Massachusetts, on May 8, 1955; eldest of three children of James Rodney Wood and Mary Russell (Collins) Wood; graduated summa cum laude from Radcliffe, 1898; married Charles Edward Park (d. 1904), in 1898; married Robert Hunter, in 1908 (died 1928); children: none.*

In 1900, Maud Wood Park was the youngest delegate to the National American Woman Suffrage Association (NAWSA). One year later, she had replaced ◈ **Alice Stone Blackwell** as chair of the Massachusetts Woman Suffrage Association. Park would remain at that post for seven years. Adept at lobbying, she was also a member of the Congressional Committee of the National American Woman Suffrage Association and, from 1919 to 1924, was the first president of the League of Women Voters. With ***Alice McLellan Birney**, Park helped organize the first Parent-Teacher Association in Boston. When not stumping for reform, Maud Park was writing. She authored the play **Lucy Stone* (1936) and co-authored *Victory, How Women Won It: A Centennial Symposium, 1840–1940.* Her chronicle of the passing of the 19th amendment, *Front Door Lobbying,* was published posthumously in 1960.

◈ ***Blackwell, Alice Stone.*** *See Stone, Lucy for sidebar.*

Park, Ruth (c. 1923—)

New Zealand-born Australian author. *Born around 1923 in Auckland, New Zealand; attended St. Benedict's College, Auckland University, and New Zealand University; married D'Arcy Niland (a writer), in 1942 (died 1967); children: Anne, Rory, Patrick, Deborah, Kilmeny.*

Won The Sydney Morning Herald *prize for* The Harp in the South *(1948); created "The Muddle-Headed Wombat" series for ABC Children's Session (beginning 1960s).*

Selected writings—for adults: The Harp in the South *(1948),* Poor Man's Orange *(1949, published in the United States as* 12½ Plymouth Street, *1951),* The Witch's Thorn *(1951),* A Power of Roses *(1953),* Pink Flannel *(1955),* Der Goldene Bumerang *(The Golden Boomerang, German, 1955),* The Drums Go Bang! *(autobiography, written with D'Arcy Niland, 1956),* One-a-Pecker, Two-a-Pecker *(1957, published in England as* The Frost and the Fire, *1958),* The Good-Looking Women *(1961, also published as* Serpent's Delight, *1962),* Swords and Crowns and Rings *(1977),* A Fence around the Cuckoo *(autobiography, 1992),* Fishing in the Styx *(autobiography, 1993); for children:* The Hole in the Hill *(1961),* The Ship's Cat *(1961),* The Road Under the Sea *(1962), "The Muddle-Headed Wombat" (series of 14 books, 1962–81),* The Sixpenny Island *(1968),* Callie's Castle *(1974),* Come Danger, Come Darkness *(1978),* Playing Beatie Bow *(1980),* When the Wind Changed *(1980),* The Big Brass Key *(1983)* My Sister Sif *(1986),* Callie's Family *(1988).*

Ruth Park

One of the most prolific writers of Australian literature in the 20th century, Ruth Park spent her early years in isolated areas of New Zealand amid a storytelling family. After attending the University of Auckland and the University of New Zealand, she worked as a proofreader and editor of the children's page for the *Auckland Star*, followed by a position as editor of the children's page for *Zealandia*, in Auckland. During this time she received a letter from a young man in Sydney, Australia, D'Arcy Niland, who was seeking advice about making writing his profession. Shortly after the start of World War II Park took a vacation in Australia, where she met Niland. They were married in Sydney in 1942. For a year they traveled around the Australian outback as Niland was sent by the wartime government to various jobs. Pregnant, Park then moved to Sydney, where the only housing she could find was in the slums of Surry Hills. This community would provide the environment for *The Harp in the South,* one of her most beloved books.

By 1944, Niland had joined Park in Surry Hills, and the couple began working as full-time writers. Writing successfully made the difference as to whether the family ate or not, so they wrote everything, including copy, jingles, advertisements, paragraphs, short stories, and articles. (Park later noted that the mail carrier, bearing first rejections and then paychecks, became the most important person in their lives.) *The Harp in the South* was published in 1948 and won *The Sydney Morning Herald* prize in novel competition. Based on the people Park met in Surry Hills and the lives they led, the book depicts grinding poverty and its attendants child abuse, prostitution, despair and untimely death, but celebrates the tenacity and love of life of the people who manage to survive while beset with such problems. Initially excoriated by many residents of Sydney for denigrating their city, *The Harp in the South* has since gone on to a secure place in Australian culture, and has never gone out of print. It has been translated into some 37 languages, used as a standard text in Australian schools, and adapted into a successful television series, a play, and a children's story. A sequel, *Poor Man's Orange* (1949), was also successful, as was a prequel, *Missus* (1985).

Both Park and her husband believed passionately in the writers' craft, and pursued it systematically as a business. While occasionally this has meant that her work is treated by critics as somewhat inferior to "serious" literature, her popularity and success at making a living for herself and her family, which included five children, solely through writing would seem to make that point moot. (Niland also published several bestselling novels, including *The Shiralee.*) In the 1950s Park wrote two novels that drew on her early memories of New Zealand, *The Witch's Thorn* (1951), another bestseller, and *Pink Flannel* (1955). Her 1977 novel *Swords and Crowns and Rings*, set in Australia in the early years of the 20th century, won the *Miles Franklin Award and also became a bestseller. *Der Goldene Bumerang* (The Golden Boomerang, 1955) was a factual book about Australia published in German for German readers (it has also been translated into Inuit). Park's love of her adopted country has been demonstrated in a number of books about Australia, including *The Companion Guide to Sydney* (1973) and *Ruth Park's Sydney* (1999). With her husband, she also wrote several plays for radio and television, including *No Decision*, which won a £1,000 British award in 1961.

By the early 1960s Park had begun writing children's books, aiming only to create books that would get "worn out in the library." Having little interest in book awards, her only criterion was whether children liked to read her books or not, and she frequently tried her stories out on kindergartners. Park wrote for the ABC Children's Session for decades, creating "The Muddle-Headed Wombat" series, which resulted in 14 books published between 1962 and 1981. Of her numerous children's books, two particularly notable works were *Playing Beatie Bow* (1980), which won the Children's Book of the Year Award for 1981, and *When the Wind Changed* (1980), winner of the 1981 New South Wales Premier's Award.

Among the honors Park has received are the Order of Australia (1987), the Australian Book Industry's Lloyd O'Neill Magpie Award (1993), and an honorary doctorate from the University of New South Wales (1994). She has also written several autobiographies, including *The Drums Go Bang!* (1956, with her husband), *A Fence around the Cuckoo* (1992), and *Fishing in the Styx* (1993), in which she noted that "a storyteller . . . is all I have ever wanted to be."

SOURCES:

Buck, Claire, ed. *The Bloomsbury Guide to Women's Literature.* NY: Prentice Hall, 1992.

Hetherington, John. *Forty-Two Faces.* London: Angus & Robertson, 1963.

Wilde, William, Joy Hooten, and Barry Andrews. *The Oxford Companion to Australian Literature.* Melbourne, Australia: Oxford University Press, 1985.

Richard C. Hanes,
freelance writer, Eugene, Oregon

Parker, Bonnie (1910–1934)

American bankrobber and folk legend who became Public Enemy Number One as one of the Barrow gang during the hard times of the Great Depression.

Born on October 1, 1910, in Rowena, Texas; shot to death on May 23, 1934; daughter of Emma Parker; married Roy Thornton, but was known for her long relationship with Clyde Barrow; no children.

The memory of Bonnie Parker will forever be linked with Clyde Barrow and the legend they created with their violent deeds in the early 1930s. Audiences who thrilled to the 1967 movie *Bonnie and Clyde*, starring the beautiful **Faye Dunaway** as Bonnie and the handsome Warren Beatty as Clyde, may have difficulty reaching behind this cinematic spectacular to come to grips with the more sordid reality. Although the question of whether Bonnie and Clyde were appreciated as folk heroes in their day is controversial, nevertheless, they became folk legends.

Popular history has relegated the notorious pair onto the same pages as Jesse and Frank James and even Robin Hood. Sympathetic press began only four months after their deaths when Bonnie's mother **Emma Parker** and Clyde's sister **Nell Barrow Cowan** published their book *Fugitives: The Story of Clyde Barrow and Bonnie Parker.* Actually written by professional journalist **Jan Fortune**, the book conveys the impression "that Bonnie and Clyde were both physically attractive and charming young people driven to a life of crime by unfair police harassment."

This theme was nothing new; those living outside the law from William Tell to John Dillinger often appealed to the lower class as larger-than-life figures freed from the shackles of poverty and the humdrum existence of everyday life. Further, these folk heroes, also from the lower class, ostensibly struck back against injustice and dared to right wrongs by taking on, through action, established societal order. Such considerations were still at the root of the success of the 1967 film *Bonnie and Clyde.* Wrote John Treherne: "For many Americans in the latter years of the 1960s, *Bonnie and Clyde* became symbols of defiance against materialist capitalism and their nation's conflict in Vietnam." Further, Treherne asserts:

> It was Bonnie Parker who supplied the unique ingredient: the image of the tiny feminine figure with a machine-gun, who chose to die with the man she loved. It was as though *Annie Oakley had teamed up with Billy the Kid, or as if Maid Marian had fought with bow and arrow beside her Hood.

Bonnie Parker was born on October 1, 1910, in Rowena, Texas. The blonde-haired, blue-eyed Bonnie was the second of three children of Emma Parker and a bricklayer father who was able to support his family in a moderately comfortable style in their small agricultural town, population 600. Ironically, the Parkers regularly attended the Rowena Baptist Church, and there was little to suggest from her early childhood that this delicate youth would grow into Public Enemy Number One. In fact, Bonnie was terrified of guns and was intensely devoted to her mother, a devotion that would last a lifetime.

Hardship began at the age of four when Parker's father died and the family had to move to the home of her maternal grandmother in Cement City, in the suburbs of Dallas. There, everyday existence was tough and criminal elements lurked: the family's quality of life rapidly deteriorated.

Parker, who began school at age six, excelled in her studies, especially in spelling, writing, and acting, the latter revealing a streak of exhibitionism which would carry into her adult career in crime. While living and playing in a poor, rough community, she became involved in her share of fighting.

At 15, she became interested in boys, and married her first flame, Roy Thornton, the following year. The two moved into a house two blocks from her mother for a period of several months, but Parker missed Emma to such an extent that she coaxed Roy into moving with her back home. Then, in 1926, the Parkers, with Thornton, moved to a house on Olive Street in Dallas. However, after a few months, Thornton, who had already embarked on an odyssey of crime, began the first of a series of abandonments which would eventually lead to the failure of the marriage. The entries in Parker's diary written during this period are filled with despair, while passage after passage complains of intense boredom.

At 18, she began working at Marco's Café in downtown Dallas, where she annoyed the management by offering free meals to the clientele and may have paid for food for the down-and-outs from her own meager wages. While her family insisted these actions were examples of her essential good heart, others have suggested the acts were due to a showy exhibitionism or rebellion. She realized she no longer loved her husband, and refused to let him return after his last abandonment. Shortly after, Thornton was arrested for robbery and sentenced to five years in prison.

For several months in 1929, Bonnie worked at another café in Houston Street, Dallas, where she confided to patrons that she would like a career in acting, singing, or writing poetry. As she left this job, however, the Great Depression hit, and unable to find work Parker returned home. Then, in January 1930, while staying at a girlfriend's house in West Dallas, she met Clyde Barrow, a man who would lead her desires and career in an entirely different direction.

Clyde Barrow had been born on March 24, 1909, the sixth of eight children, into an extremely poor family in Telico, Texas. Barrow had a childhood of neglect and he hated school. His happiest moments were spent watching silent movies of famous cowboy outlaws, and while playing he usually imagined himself to be Jesse James. Neighbors reported his preoccupation with guns and with tormenting pet and farmyard animals. At 12, his family moved into the tough neighborhood of West Dallas known as the "Bog." Barrow quit high school at age 16, went through a series of jobs, and developed an interest in girls and fast cars. Soon after, he embarked on a life of petty, then more serious, crime, following in the footsteps of his brother Buck Barrow, who was sitting in a Texas jail.

The meeting between Bonnie and Clyde at her friend's house was instant magic. Emma Parker thought Clyde was "a likeable boy, very handsome, with his dark wavy hair, dancing brown eyes. . . . [H]e had what they call charm." Clyde's sister, Nell, described Bonnie:

> [She was] an adorable little thing, more like a doll than a girl. She had yellow hair that kinked all over her head like a baby's, the loveliest skin I've ever seen without a blemish on it, a regular cupid's bow of a mouth, and blue, blue eyes. . . . [S]he had dimples that showed constantly when she talked, and she was so tiny, she was only four feet ten inches tall, and weighed between eighty-five and ninety pounds. Her hands took a number five glove, and her feet a number three shoe.

For Bonnie, Clyde would prove a fatal attraction. Soon after she took him home to stay with her mother, the police came and arrested him for committing several robberies and burglaries. Distraught, Bonnie moved to a cousin's house in Waco where Clyde was being detained in jail while waiting trial. On March 11, 1930,

Bonnie Parker

at Clyde's prompting, she smuggled a .32 Colt revolver into jail, enabling her lover to escape the following day. Unfortunately for young love, Clyde was apprehended after one week on the lam and was sent to the Texas State Penitentiary in Huntsville to serve a 14-year sentence.

However, Clyde Barrow was released in February 1932, under a general parole offered by Texas Governor Ross Sterling. Clyde, having cut off two of his toes in prison in order to avoid arduous work details, recuperated with Bonnie's assistance, made a two-week attempt to go straight, then persuaded Parker to join him in a life of crime. This new life would soon become costly; within weeks, Bonnie was arrested for stealing a car, and she was held for three months in jail. In the meantime, Clyde and associated gang-members killed for the first time in April, murdering John Bucher, a jeweler in Hillsboro, Texas, and making off with a mere $40.

The Barrow gang would never be known for taking large sums of money; rather, they would go down in history for their indiscriminate taking of lives. During July and early August, the gang conducted at least three robberies; then on August 5 they mortally wounded Sheriff C.G. Maxwell and killed Deputy Sheriff E.C. Moore at a roadside dance hall near Atoka, Oklahoma.

> You have heard the story of Jesse James,
> Of how he lived and died.
> If you are still in need of something to read,
> Here's the story of Bonnie and Clyde.
>
> **—Bonnie Parker**

The gang fled in a series of stolen cars and holed up at the house of Bonnie's aunt, **Millie Stamps**, near Carlsbad, New Mexico. There, they kidnapped a deputy sheriff who was making inquiries about their car, but released him unhurt. On August 30, they ran a police road block and wounded another officer. At least two more robberies occurred in October, and Howard Hall was killed defending his store in Sherman, Texas. On December 5, the gang killed Doyle Johnson in Temple, Texas, and stole his car. Another mortal shooting and kidnapping occurred in January 1933, as the gang continued to avoid traps laid by the law.

Then in March, the new governor of Texas, ***Miriam "Ma" Ferguson**, pardoned Clyde's brother Buck. On April 13, as Bonnie and Clyde and their teen-aged accomplice W.E. Jones rested in a bungalow in Joplin, Missouri, they were joined by Buck and his wife **Blanche Barrow**, who had convinced Buck to go straight. He never got the chance. Responding to a local tip-off, police had surrounded the house in an attempt to capture Bonnie and Clyde. In a blaze of fire, the Barrow gang shot its way free, killing a constable and a detective in the process.

The gang would be hard to catch. Clyde was not only a crack shot; he was also a highly skilled driver able to cover phenomenal distances, and he was often aided by an uncanny "sixth sense" which alerted him to danger. Parker herself was reportedly an excellent relief driver and soon became expert in the handling of guns. Periodically, the gang would raid an armory to replenish supplies, which included machine-guns and several varieties of pistols and rifles. Additionally, the forces of the law were stretched thin, and the fact that the gang deliberately and frequently crossed state lines, especially between Texas, Oklahoma, Missouri and Louisiana, complicated questions of legal jurisdiction.

Bonnie and Clyde, in fact, were not the only problems facing law enforcement in 1933, for America was experiencing a virtual crime wave. During that year, 12,000 murders, 50,000 robberies, 3,000 kidnappings and 100,000 assaults were estimated to have taken place. This was the era of John Dillinger, ***Ma Barker**, "Pretty Boy" Floyd, Al Capone, and "Machine Gun" Kelly, who was expertly guided by his wife ***Kathryn Kelly**. For every gangster who was executed under due process, six lawmen died in the line of duty. Over 20 killings were attributed to Bonnie and Clyde, although only a dozen could be substantiated: nine of these were law enforcers.

Despite initial successes, however, beginning in June 1933 the gang began to suffer a series of reverses. Bonnie experienced serious burns when Clyde overturned their car near Wellington, Texas, on June 10, and was in great pain for several weeks. Then, on July 19, the gang fought a gun battle with police at Platte City, Missouri, in which Buck and Blanche were severely wounded. Four days later, a large posse ambushed the gang near Dexter, Iowa. Bonnie, Clyde, Buck and Blanche were all wounded. Blanche and Buck, who would later die of his wounds, were taken prisoner, while Bonnie and Clyde escaped with W.D. Jones. After laying low, the gang was back in action in November, but Jones was captured.

A new gang was assembled in January 1934, when Bonnie and Clyde in conjunction with other gangsters arranged a break of several prisoners from Eastham Prison Farm in Texas. After shooting a prison guard, Bonnie and Clyde hit the road again with Joe Palmer, Ray Hamilton and his girlfriend **Mary O'Dare**, and Henry Methven. After robbing another bank as well as a National Guard Armory in Texas in February, the gang quarreled and split up the following month.

In March, Bonnie and Clyde visited their respective mothers in south Dallas and narrowly avoided capture. On April 1, they shot E.B. Wheeler and H.D. Murphy, two motorcycle patrolmen in Grapevine, Texas, who had dared to approach them. Five days later, they killed Constable Cal Campbell in Miami, Oklahoma.

Meanwhile, their exploits had become front-page news: Clyde was nicknamed "The Texas Rattlesnake," while Bonnie was known as "Suicide Sal" because of a poem she had written and sent to the press:

> Some day they will go down together,
> And they will bury them side by side.
> To a few it means grief.
> To the law it's relief.
> But it's death to Bonnie and Clyde.

Life was now too dangerous for the couple and the various members of their outlaw gang to stay in hotels or even in campgrounds or tourist cabins. They lived and slept in cars; they would drive one until it broke down, then steal another. Periodic robberies, mostly with a spur-of-the-moment, amateurish flair, kept them in pocket money but little else.

The law, meanwhile, had determined to bring them in. The shoot-out at Platte City had involved a posse of 100 peace officers, while the ambush at Dexter had been made by 400. Then, in February 1934, a posse of nearly 1,000 men had been dispatched into the Cookson Hills of Oklahoma to find the gang with orders to "shoot-to-kill." Officers of the Federal Bureau of Investigation (FBI) had begun to support local police.

The state of Texas was equally determined and ordered Frank Hamer, a tough and experienced Texas Ranger, known as the fastest draw in the state, to track down and destroy the gang. Hamer, who had killed 65 outlaws, studied their haunts and patterns of movement and took to the road as they did. On May 23, 1934, he and a veteran posse of six laid a deadly ambush near Gibsland, Louisiana. Hamer had worked a deal with Ivan Methvin, father of Henry Methvin, the last gang member who had been loyal to Bonnie and Clyde. There would be clemency for Henry, if Ivan helped set up the notorious outlaw pair who had been living with the Methvins at their home and in various backwoods cabins. Henry, informed of the arrangement, slipped away from Bonnie and Clyde to safety. Suspecting nothing, and believing Henry merely had gotten lost, the pair informed Ivan of the route they would take the next day while looking for Henry, intent on arranging a rendezvous.

At nine o'clock on the morning of May 23, Bonnie and Clyde pulled up alongside Ivan Methvin's truck, which appeared to have a flat tire, at the designated meeting place. Bonnie, in a new red dress and red shoes, was eating a sandwich. Clyde asked about Henry, and Ivan asked the pair for a drink of water. Bonnie's last word was "Sure." As she reached for a thermos, Ivan scrambled under his truck and one of the posse, lying concealed by the side of the road, yelled for the gang to put their hands up. The pair went for their guns while Clyde attempted to drive away. For four minutes, the posse sprayed the car with bullets: Bonnie and Clyde were each hit about 50 times. The last stanza of Bonnie's poem had been prophetic: it was "death to Bonnie and Clyde."

But though they went "down together," they were not buried "side by side." Clyde was buried in West Dallas Cemetery while Bonnie was laid first to rest several miles away in Fish Trap Cemetery. While few attended Clyde's funeral, crowds mobbed Bonnie's burial, and a quartet sang "Beautiful Isle of Somewhere." Parker was later moved to Crown Hill Memorial Park Cemetery near Love Airfield in Dallas. Her mother had the following inscription carved on the headstone:

> As the flowers are all made sweeter
> By the sunshine and the dew,
> So this old world is made brighter
> By the lives of folks like you.

Even if the families of the victims Bonnie helped murder would disagree, there were those who would sympathize with the woman who often had told her mother of her love for Clyde, and her determination to die with him when that inevitable time came. Bonnie and Clyde had started their notorious legend long before their deaths by taking a large number of photographs of themselves posing before the camera, gun in hand, and by writing messages and testimonies to the press for publication. Wrote Jay Robert Nash:

> To themselves they were American frontier heroes, pathfinders of a new and violent age to be admired. Bonnie, especially, . . . made sure that a photographic record would be left behind to mark her distinctive contribution to American crime.

After their deaths, wax effigies of the couple would be fashioned for museums, movies would portray them as glamorous, and rock and country-western songs would extol their struggles with the law.

SOURCES:

Hinton, Ted. *Ambush: The Real Story of Bonnie and Clyde*. Bryan, TX: Shoal Creek, 1979.

Hyde, H. Montgomery, *et al.*, eds. *Crimes and Punishment*. NY: Marshall Cavendish, 1986.

Jenkins, John H., and H. Gordon Frost. *"I'm Frank Hamer": The Life of a Texas Peace Officer*. Austin, TX: Pemberton Press, 1980.

Nash, Jay Robert. *Encyclopedia of World Crime: Criminal Justice, Criminology, and Law Enforcement*. Vol. 1. Wilmette, IL: Crime Books, 1989.

Treherne, John. *The Strange History of Bonnie and Clyde*. NY: Stein & Day, 1985.

SUGGESTED READING:

Deford, Miriam. *The Real Bonnie and Clyde.* NY: Ace Books, 1968.

Fortune, Jan I. *Fugitives: The Story of Clyde Barrow and Bonnie Parker.* Dallas, TX: Ranger Press, 1934.

Philips, John Neal, and André L. Gorzell. "Tell Them I Don't Smoke Cigars: The Story of Bonnie Parker," in *Legendary Ladies of Texas.* Ed. by Francis Edward Abernathy. Dallas, TX: E-Heart Press, 1981.

RELATED MEDIA:

Bonnie and Clyde, starring Faye Dunaway, Warren Beatty, and **Estelle Parsons**, directed by Arthur Penn, edited by ***Dede Allen**, produced by Warner Bros., 1967.

The Bonnie Parker Story, starring **Dorothy Provine** and Jack Hogan, produced by AIP, 1958.

David L. Bullock, Ph.D.,
author of *Allenby's War: The Palestine-Arabian Campaigns, 1916–1918* (London: the Blandford Press, 1988)

Parker, Catherine Langloh

(c. 1856–1940)

Australian writer who published the first serious studies on Aboriginal culture. *Name variations: Katie Langloh Parker or K. Langloh Parker; Catherine Stow. Born Catherine Field on May 1, 1856 (some sources cite 1855), in Encounter Bay, South Australia; died on March 27, 1940, in Adelaide, South Australia; daughter of Henry Field (an overlander and pastoralist) and Sophia Field; married Langloh Parker (a pastoralist), on January 12, 1875 (died 1903); married Percy Randolph Stow (a lawyer), on November 7, 1905; no children.*

Published the first systematic description of Aborigine legends and indigenous folkways (1896); posthumously awarded a Children's Book of the Year Award for published collection of her studies (1954).

Selected writings: Australian Legendary Tales: Folklore of the Noongahburrahs *(1896);* More Australian Legendary Tales *(1898);* The Euhlayi Tribe: A Study of Aboriginal Life in Australia *(1905);* The Walkabouts of the Wur-Run-Nah *(1918);* Woggheeguy: Australian Aboriginal Legends *(1930).*

Living in rural South Australia in the 1860s as the fourth of eight children, Catherine Parker befriended indigenous Aborigines who became her childhood companions. In a tragic moment, Parker was rescued from drowning by an Aborigine girl in an incident in which two of Parker's sisters died. The trauma of that experience helped forge her later dedication to learning more about Aborigine culture and preserving information about their vanishing traditions.

Parker, known to her family and friends as Katie, initially grew up the rural Darling Downs region of Queensland, where she was educated at home by her mother **Sophia Field.** Sophia herself had been well schooled in world literature and passed this interest along to her daughter, who became an avid reader. The family moved to Adelaide, South Australia, and soon thereafter Sophia died in childbirth. Parker was 16 when their father sent her and her younger sister to a small private school. A few years later, in January 1875, she married Langloh Parker, a pastoralist like her father. The Parkers moved to Bangate in the northwestern region of New South Wales in 1879. While there, Parker began to involve herself with local Aborigine groups, learning their language and carefully recording their traditional myths through an interpreter. Accumulating a good deal of information, she first published the material in *Australian Legendary Tales: Folklore of the Noongahburrahs* in 1896. This book represented the first systematic treatment of Aborigine culture in print. She soon followed with another volume, *More Australian Legendary Tales*, in 1898.

By the late 1890s drought had taken its toll, and the Parkers moved to another location in New South Wales, where Langloh died in 1903. Journeying to England shortly afterwards, Parker met Westminster lawyer Percy Randolph Stow. They married in November 1905 and returned to Adelaide, where they became involved in local intellectual circles and she continued to write. Among her later books were *The Euhlayi Tribe: A Study of Aboriginal Life in Australia* (1905), *The Walkabouts of the Wur-Run-Nah* (1918), and *Woggheeguy: Australian Aboriginal Legends* (1930), the latter two of which were published under the name Catherine Stow. The first person to objectively and systematically record at length and publish traditional legends of the Aborigines, Parker died in 1940. *Australian Legendary Tales*, a volume of her studies edited by **Henrietta Drake-Brockman** and published in 1953, won a Children's Book of the Year award in 1954, and her first two books were republished in 1978 in their original form. A previously unpublished manuscript, *My Bush Book: K. Langloh Parker's 1890s Story of Outback Station Life*, was published in 1982 with a background and biography of Parker by **Marcie Muir**.

SOURCES:

Buck, Claire, ed. *The Bloomsbury Guide to Women's Literature.* NY: Prentice Hall, 1992.

Radi, Heather, ed. *200 Australian Women: A Redress Anthology.* NSW, Australia: Women's Redress Press, 1988.

Wilde, William H., Joy Hooten, and Barry Andrews. *The Oxford Companion to Australian Literature.* Melbourne, Australia: Oxford University Press, 1985.

Richard C. Hanes,
freelance writer, Eugene, Oregon

Parker, Claire (1906–1981)

American pioneer film animator who, with husband Alexander Alexeieff, co-invented the "pin screen" method, involving the illumination of thousands of pinheads to produce a printlike effect in animated films. *Born in Boston, Massachusetts, in 1906 (some sources cite 1907); died in 1981; attended Bryn Mawr College, Bryn Mawr, Pennsylvania; also studied in Austria and France; married Alexander Alexeieff (an animator), in 1941.*

Selected filmography: Night on Bald Mountain *(1933);* Étude sur L'Harmonie des Lignes *(1934);* Rubens *(1935);* En Passant *(1942);* The Nose *(1963);* Pictures at an Exhibition *(1972);* Three Moods *(*Trois Thèmes, *1980).*

Born in Boston, Massachusetts, in 1906, Claire Parker studied art at Bryn Mawr College and in Europe, where she met and fell in love with Russian-born animator Alexander Alexeieff in 1931. They immediately became collaborators and in 1932 began work on an animated interpretation of composer Modest Mussorgsky''s *Night on Bald Mountain* (1933). One of Parker's major contributions to the film was the coordination of music and image, a difficult task at the time, since the music track could not be transferred to tape. The film, now considered a classic, is included in nearly every film library in the Western world. In 1935, Parker produced *Rubens*, based on an exhibition at Paris' Orangerie and one of the first films of its kind. During the '30s and '50s, the couple also made a number of innovative advertising films, including *Étude Sur L'Harmonie des Lignes* (Exercise in Line Harmony), which Parker directed in 1934.

The "pin screen" technique that the couple co-invented has been likened to the pointillism technique used by painter Georges Seurat (1859–1891). Parker detailed the procedure in a 1961 article:

> The pinboard is a black-and-white technique somewhat analogous to the half-tone process: the picture is made up of a very large number of very small black elements on a white ground. The darkness of a tone corresponds to the individual size of each black element on a given portion of the white ground. . . . The further forward a pin is pushed, the longer its shadow becomes. As there are a million pins on a board, we never consider the pins individually, but always as a group, like paint on a brush.

Parker and Alexeieff married in 1941, and moved to the United States that same year, but they returned to France in 1947. They continued to make animated films until 1980, including the interpretation of another Mussorgsky composition, *Pictures at an Exhibition* (1972). Alexeieff, who had the more prominent name in animation at the time, was always generous in acknowledging Parker's contribution to their collaboration. "If there had been no Claire Parker," he once said, "I would have never done animation. I would never have been capable of doing it alone."

SOURCES:

Acker, Ally. *Reel Women.* NY: Continuum, 1991.
Katz, Ephraim. *The Film Encyclopedia.* NY: HarperCollins, 1994.

Barbara Morgan,
Melrose, Massachusetts

Parker, Cynthia Ann (c. 1827–c. 1864)

Indian captive who married a Comanche chief and became the mother of Chief Quanah Parker. *Born around 1827 in either Clark County or Crawford County, Illinois; died of self-inflicted starvation following the deaths of two of her children around 1864 (some sources cite 1870); daughter of Silas M. Parker (a farmer) and Lucy (Duty) Parker; married Peta Nocoma (a Quahadi Comanche chief), in 1845; children: sons Quanah and Pecos; daughter Topsannah.*

Taken captive by Native Americans after attack on Texas settlement where she lived (1836); refused attempt to ransom her (1840s); captured with her daughter during attack on Nocoma's camp by Texas Rangers and reunited with her white family (1860); died of self-inflicted starvation after learning of her son's death and after her daughter's death (1864 or 1870).

Cynthia Ann Parker was born in Illinois, probably in 1827, the eldest child of Silas and **Lucy Parker**. Accounts vary as to whether Baptist Elder John Parker was her paternal grandfather or her uncle, but either way he was responsible for leading his extended family to Texas, where Cynthia Ann and her parents and siblings settled in 1834, in what is now the town of Groesbeck. The group built a settlement called Fort Parker and created a company of Texas Rangers. On May 19, 1836, hundreds of Caddo, Comanche, and Kiowa Indians attacked their settlement. Five settlers were killed and five were taken captive, among them nine-year-old Cynthia Ann. Within months, all the captives were located except Cynthia Ann, who had been sent to Chatua and **Tabbi-nocca**, a Tenowish Comanche couple who raised her as a daughter. She adapted to Native American culture and ways, and in the 1840s, when attempts were made to ransom her, she chose to stay with her tribe. In 1845, she married

Peta Nocoma, a fierce Comanche chief who was famous for leading raids (including the Fort Parker attack at which she had been taken captive). They had three children, two sons, Quanah and Pecos, and a daughter, **Topsannah**, and Peta Nocoma refrained from taking another wife as was accepted for prominent warriors. Gradually, Parker became a legend among local white settlers, who called her the "White Comanche."

On December 18, 1860, a band of Texas Rangers and local volunteers led by Captain Lawrence Sullivan Ross attacked Nocoma's camp on the Pease River, possibly mistaking it for a hostile village. Women were shot down as they fled, and Nocoma was wounded in the battle. Quanah and Pecos managed to escape, but Parker and Topsannah were captured and taken to Camp Cooper. Parker was identified by her uncle Isaac Parker in January 1861 and sent to live with her white relatives. She relearned English but showed no desire to remain in white society, unsuccessfully attempting to escape several times and continuing to mourn for her absent husband and sons. While she never recounted her experiences among the Comanche, many whites took advantage of her name and published fictional memoirs, letters, and articles aimed at inflaming anger at Native Americans. In the fall of 1864, Parker learned that her son Pecos had died of smallpox, and a few months later Topsannah died of influenza. Heartbroken, Parker starved herself to death in either in 1864 or 1870. She was buried in the Fosterville Cemetery in Henderson County, Texas. Peta Nocoma never remarried, and continued to raid settlements until his death from a wound that became infected. Their surviving son Quanah Parker grew up to be a famous Comanche war chief, the last to surrender in 1875. Years later, when he learned of his mother's death, he questioned everyone he could find who had known her after she had returned to white society. He hung a painting of her in his parlor, and adopted her name as the surname of his family. In 1910, Congress granted him $1,000 to have her body brought from Texas and reinterred in a cemetery near his home in Oklahoma. He was buried next to her after he died the following year. In 1957, their burial site was acquired as part of a government missile range, and the two bodies were removed to a post cemetery. Eight years later, Topsannah's grave in Texas was located, and her remains were reburied beside her mother.

SOURCES:

Bataille, Gretchen M., ed. *Native American Women.* NY: Garland, 1993.

James, Edward T., ed. *Notable American Women, 1607–1950.* Cambridge, MA: The Belknap Press of Harvard University Press, 1971.

SUGGESTED READING:

Becker, Daniel A. "Comanche Civilization with History of Quanah Parker," in *Chronicles of Oklahoma.* June 1923.

Hacker, Margaret Schmidt. *Cynthia Ann Parker: The Life and the Legend.* El Paso, TX: Texas Western Press, 1990.

Haley, J. Evetts. *Charles Goodnight: Cowman & Plainsman*, 1936.

Jackson, Grace. *Cynthia Ann Parker.* San Antonio: 1959.

Jones, William Moses. *Texas History Carved in Stone*, 1958.

Peckham, Howard H. *Captured by Indians*, 1954.

Waldraven-Johnson, Margaret. *White Comanche: The Story of Cynthia Ann Parker and Her Son, Quanah.* NY: Comet Press, 1956.

Waltrip, Lela, and Rufus Waltrip. *Indian Women.* NY: David McKay, 1964.

Wellman, Paul I. "Cynthia Ann Parker," in *Chronicles of Oklahoma.* June 1934.

Wood, Norman B. *Lives of Famous Indian Chiefs*, 1906.

COLLECTIONS:

Parker family documents at the Eugene C. Barker History Center, University of Texas, Austin; Quanah Parker files at the Fort Sill archives, Lawton, Oklahoma.

Jo Anne Meginnes,
freelance writer, Brookfield, Vermont

Parker, Dorothy (1893–1967)

American writer and critic whose collections of short stories and verse, along with her well-publicized acerbic wit, made her one of America's most famous and widely quoted women of the 20th century. *Born Dorothy Rothschild on August 22, 1893, in West End, New Jersey; died on June 7, 1967, in New York City; one of four children of Eliza Rothschild and Henry Rothschild; attended private and parochial schools in New York City; married Edward Parker, in 1917 (divorced 1928); married Alan Campbell, in 1933 (divorced 1942, remarried 1950); no children.*

Began literary career at age 24 as caption writer for Vogue *(1916); transferred to* Vogue's *sister publication,* Vanity Fair *(1917); eventually promoted to literary and dramatic criticism and began publishing short stories; joined the staff of Harold Ross' new humor magazine,* The New Yorker *(1926); became a fixture of New York's literary smart set and a member of the Algonquin Round Table; plagued throughout her life by depression and alcoholism, exacerbated by ruinous love affairs and two ultimately unhappy marriages.*

A curious parcel arrived at the office of New York attorney Oscar Bernstien one sultry afternoon in mid-July 1973. The package had been mailed from the Ferncliff Crematory on Long Island, where its contents had been stored for six years. Now, Bernstien learned, the mortal remains of his former client Dorothy Parker were his responsibility, although there were no instructions indicating what he was to do with the small wooden box. For the next 15 years, the ashes of one of America's brightest literary wits would lie forgotten in a filing cabinet of an anonymous Wall Street law firm before finding a permanent resting place, a fate that made one of the epitaphs Dorothy had written for herself, "Excuse My Dust," seem peculiarly apt.

She had not often been of so meek a nature during her lifetime. She had, after all, held her own as one of the few female members of the Algonquin Round Table, that garrulous and acerbic luncheon crowd of literary egotists who gathered each week during the 1920s at the famed hotel on West 44th Street. Between the two World Wars, in fact, Parker was labeled the wittiest woman in America. Her theater reviews in national magazines, her volumes of light verse and her *bon mots* were endlessly quoted and endlessly misquoted. She wrote serious fiction in the form of short stories, although she described writing as "holy hell"—so much so that friends claimed Parker had to lie down for three hours after composing a telegram. In her private life, she put away alcohol in any number of speakeasies during Prohibition and took lovers when she pleased, entertaining many of them in her rooms at the Algonquin—someplace, she said, where she could "lay my hat and a few friends." She covered her frequent depressions with a layer of wry humor, and the slashed wrists left from the first of several suicide attempts with pale blue ribbons and bows. She seemed at times to enjoy her notoriety, and in one of her early poems had written:

They say of me, and so they should,
It's doubtful if I come to good.

Even her birth had been at least a little notorious, for she had arrived unexpectedly a month early in West End, New Jersey, rather than in the bustling city she would later claim as her own. Henry Rothschild ("No, dear, not *those* Rothschilds," Dorothy was always quick to point out) had packed his wife **Eliza Rothschild** and his three children off to the shore for the summer, as he did every year, remaining in New York during the week to look after his prosperous ready-to-wear cloak business on lower Broadway. Since their marriage in 1880, Eliza had given birth to two sons, Harold and Bertram, and a daughter, **Helen**. In January 1893, six years after Helen's birth, Eliza announced she was expecting a fourth child the following autumn, but went into labor in late August as a hurricane threatened the New Jersey shore. Dorothy was born on August 22, just before the storm pounded West End with torrential rains. Rainswept weather would become a recurring motif in her writings. Her earliest memory, Parker once said, was of the sight of rain falling outside a long-forgotten window, and she would later write that she loved New York best on a rainy day, when its streets were "black and shining as ripe olives."

The Rothschild household was rarely quiet, full of Henry's many sisters and brothers who came visiting and filled the air with their raucous jokes and wisecracks; while the Irish servants came and went with alarming frequency, disappearing under various perceived derelictions of duty loudly argued throughout the house. It was all perfectly normal to young Dorothy, fussed over by aunts and uncles who cooed about her delicate, pale skin and her luxurious brown hair. In June 1898, as usual, the family left sweltering New York for West End. But the next month, Eliza was stricken by coughing fits that left her gasping for breath, and by intestinal disorders that left her weak and nauseated. On July 20, as another storm raged overhead, five-year-old Dorothy learned that her mother had died of "colic," as the doctor wrote on Eliza's death certificate. "My mother," Parker tersely said many years later, "promptly went and died on me." Her mother's passing marked the end of a blissfully normal childhood and the beginning of Parker's lifelong suspicion of domestic tranquillity.

Only weeks after Eliza's death, Henry sold the townhouse and moved his children twice in six months before announcing his marriage to **Eleanor Lewis**, a retired schoolteacher and the second Christian woman the Jewish Henry had taken to the altar. To make matters worse, Henry did not object when the strictly Catholic Eleanor enrolled Dorothy in the nearby Blessed Sacrament Academy where, Parker complained to her father, the sisters were ill-tempered and her classmates taunted her for having a Jewish father. When Eleanor collapsed and died of a cerebral hemorrhage three years after marrying Henry, Parker was convinced her undisguised hatred for the woman had brought about her demise.

The remainder of Dorothy's adolescence was relatively uneventful, Henry remaining a bachelor for the rest of his life while doting on his youngest daughter, smoothing over her occasional rebellions at Blessed Sacrament and sending her and Helen off to Bellport on Long Island for the summer. By 1907, both Helen and Bert had married and Parker's eldest brother Harold, the black sheep of the family, had disappeared and was never heard from again. Parker herself enrolled at a private girls' school in Morristown, New Jersey. Discovering there were no Jews at the school, and that none were likely to be allowed, Henry placidly wrote on Parker's application that he was Episcopalian. Dorothy lasted precisely six months. She did not return for the fall term in 1908, and at 15, declined to attend any school at all. It was the end of her formal education. She would admit only once in public, many years later, that she had never finished high school. "But, by God, I *read*," was all she could offer as a defense.

It's not the tragedies that kill us. It's the messes. I can't stand messes.

—Dorothy Parker

For the next five years, Dorothy and her father shared a small apartment on New York's West Side, not far from the old family home. Henry had retired from the clothing business by now, and spent his days looking after his investments, taking long walks with his daughter, and trading the doggerel verse he and his youngest daughter liked to compose for each other. "If to your Papa you are good," Henry wrote from New York to Parker in Bellport:

> You shall have both clothes and food
> You shall live on milk and honey
> And never know the need of money.

Parker wrote back:

> This morning I received your "pome"
> How did you do it all alone?
> When you come down on Sunday, Pa. . . .
> No, nothing rhymes, except cigar.

Life for Dorothy was ordered, if dull, during these five years. But her father never seemed to recover from the death of one of his brothers on the *Titanic* in 1912, his health spiraling downward until, just after Christmas 1913, Henry died of a heart attack. Never able to resist dramatic embellishments to her early life, Parker would later portray herself as an abandoned, destitute waif after her father's death. Although it was true that Henry had squandered a good deal of his fortune on questionable investments, there was enough left for Parker to live comfortably in either Helen's or Bert's household, both of which were buffeted by marital difficulties. By now Dorothy's mistrust of placid domesticity had grown to outright loathing, and she longed to set herself free from family ties.

Accordingly, she took a job at a dance school to earn money, playing piano at the height of the dance craze that was sweeping the country. At the same time, she began submitting some of her light verse to New York newspapers and magazines. Such short poems on topics or personalities of the day were then an immensely popular form of social commentary. In late 1914, as war rumbled through Europe, Dorothy submitted a poem to *Vanity Fair,* edited by Frank Crowninshield. The piece was a sharp bit of social satire on the sort of leisured women who spent long summer afternoons on each other's front porches, leaving the details of making money to their husbands on Wall Street. Parker's deft use of colloquial phrases and clever rhymes attracted Crowninshield's attention. He accepted the poem for publication and sent her a check for $25, all that Parker needed to wheedle her way into a job interview with "Crownie," as his associates called him. The result was the offer of a position as a caption writer for *Vanity Fair*'s sister publication, the fashion magazine *Vogue*, at $10 a week. Moving into a small room in a boarding house on upper Broadway, Parker eagerly looked forward to her brilliant literary debut. "I thought I was ***Edith Sitwell**," she later said.

The reality proved somewhat different. As soon as the excitement of having her own room and her own job wore off, the endless procession of fashion illustrations needing descriptive captions had all the makings of a literary dead-end. Parker's growing irritation began to bubble out through her pen. "There was a little girl who had a little curl right in the middle of her forehead," Parker scribbled when a photograph of a model wearing a frilly nightgown crossed her desk. "When she was good she was very, *very* good, and when she was bad she wore this divine nightdress of rose-colored mousseline de soie, trimmed with frothy Valenciennes lace." *Vogue*'s editor, the strait-laced ***Edna Woolman Chase**, was not amused at the sexual innuendo and decided to keep a closer eye on the young woman she described as "treacle-sweet of tongue but vinegar witted."

Crowninshield accepted a few more of her poems for *Vanity Fair*, notably a diatribe against happy, homemaking women that was so cleverly vitriolic that he forced her to use a pseudonym before he would print it. Soon, prose pieces began to arrive on his desk in the style of writing Crowninshield most favored, a bemused, detached, wry tone once described as the "Elevated Eyebrow School of Journalism." Dorothy became such a master at it that Crowninshield finally began to take her writing, and the idea of a position at his magazine, seriously. "Her perceptions were so sure," he later said, "her judgment

Dorothy Parker

so unerring, that she always seemed to hit the center of the mark."

Meanwhile, Parker was exploring new ground in her personal life. During a vacation at a Connecticut hotel in the summer of 1916, she met the handsome scion of a wealthy Hartford family with a New England lineage so ancient that they truly came over on the *Mayflower*. This was of no consequence, however, to Edwin Pond Parker II, who delighted Dorothy with his scandalous family stories and his complete indifference to the fact that she was Jewish. Since he was employed at the time as a stockbroker for the family's Wall Street firm, she found herself dining at expensive restaurants after work, while Eddie, as she now called him, consumed the considerable amounts of alcohol that only seemed to make him funnier. Dorothy disliked the taste of alcohol and abstained.

Eddie, Dorothy discovered with some nervousness, was the first man with whom she was actually in love. By the time the United States entered World War I in 1917, he announced his intention of enlisting and asked her to marry him. On June 30 of that year, Dorothy Rothschild became Dorothy Parker in a civil ceremony in Yonkers, New York; a few days later, Eddie enlisted as an ambulance driver and left for his basic training. Alone as soon as she was married, Dorothy was once again betrayed by her visions of domestic bliss. She rarely saw Eddie, except for the few days he was on leave, while the dullness of Army routine rapidly transformed him into a hopeless alcoholic, his skin so pallid that his platoon mates took to calling him "Spook." Many years later, in her short story *The Lovely Leave* published in the 1940s during another World War, she described the tense hopes with which a young wife waits for her husband's approaching one-day leave:

> When they were together again, when they could see and hear and touch each other, there would be no stiltedness. They would talk and laugh together. They would have tenderness and excitement. It would be as if they had never been separated. . . . "Oh, please let it be all right," she whispered. "Please keep me from doing wrong things. Please let it be lovely."

But with Eddie paying more attention to his bottle than to her during their brief times together, arguments were frequent and mutual accusations bitter. It was almost with relief that Eddie left for the European front late in 1917.

Frank Crowninshield provided the antidote to Parker's bleak domestic situation by offering his young discovery the position of *Vanity Fair*'s drama critic. P.G. Wodehouse had been doing the honors for the past several years, but had announced an indefinite leave of absence to supervise the production of a musical comedy he had co-written. Parker jumped at the opportunity. Her reviews were just as unusual as her position as New York's only female drama critic, entirely different from the sober musings of her newfound peers. In one of her first reviews in June 1918, of a production of *Hedda Gabler,* she chattily told her readers that the only flaw in the evening for her had been the gunshot with which Hedda dispatches herself at the end of the play. "I do wish that [Mr. Ibsen] had occasionally let the ladies take bichloride of mercury, or turn on the gas, or do something quiet and neat around the house," she complained. "I invariably miss most of the lines in the last act of an Ibsen play; I always have my fingers in my ears, waiting for the loud report that means the heroine has just Passed On." As the months passed, however, Dorothy's subversive wit became more evident. In one review, she declined to print the names of the cast because, she said, she refused "to tell on them"; in another, she advised anyone about to attend a performance, "If you don't knit, bring a book"; and she once was so bored with a show that she chose to ignore it entirely and wrote instead about the efforts of a woman sitting nearby to retrieve a glove that had fallen to the floor. By January 1919, after barely a year as a critic, Parker was precociously lamenting the passing of "the happy days—the days when people rushed gladly to the theater, enjoyed every minute of it, applauded enthusiastically, wished there were more." She might have been describing the enthusiasm of her own readership, for she had become to her intense gratification one of the most popular and widely quoted of *Vanity Fair*'s columnists.

Five months later, Parker arrived at work one morning to discover a sandy-haired, blue-eyed, slender young man sharing her office. He was Robert Benchley, a freelance writer who had been contributing humorous pieces to *Vanity Fair* for some time, and who had now been hired by Crowninshield as the magazine's new managing editor. The off-beat sense of humor that characterized his writing had been described by one admirer as a "little skid off the hard road and right up to the edge of the swamp," but Benchley's prim behavior gave no such intriguing impressions. He came from a modest, blue-collar Massachusetts background, had attended Harvard thanks to the generosity of a family friend, and now lived in a plain two-bedroom cottage in placidly suburban Larchmont with his wife **Gertrude Benchley** and two sons. He commuted to work every morning on the train, entering his daily newspaper purchase in a meticulously kept pocket ledger; carefully addressed Dorothy as "Mrs. Parker"; and expressed great shock when Dorothy admitted she had once attended a cocktail party. "Mark my words," he warned her severely, "alcohol will coarsen you."

Several days later, a third cipher took up residence in the office. He was Robert Sherwood, a lanky Canadian journalist afflicted with respiratory problems who had been hired by Crowninshield with no particular position or duties in mind. It was rumored that Sherwood had impressed Crowninshield by showing up for his job interview in a kilt, the military uniform of his wartime regiment, the Canadian Black Watch. Parker and Benchley were at first suspicious of the future Pulitzer Prize-winning playwright, who spoke in short bursts because of his difficulties breathing and was so shy that he often turned his back on the stenographer sent to take dictation from him. Parker told Benchley that talking to Sherwood was "like riding the Long Island Railroad—it gets you nowhere in particular," but in a few weeks, this odd little trio could often be seen walking down West 44th Street to lunch; and in the coming months, it would evolve into a rebellious clique within *Vanity Fair* that would cause Crowninshield to regret his hiring decisions.

In August 1919, Eddie Parker returned from Europe, where he had been stationed in Germany after the war's end a year earlier. Parker had not seen him for nearly two years and was not prepared for the extent of his deterioration. Eddie, Dorothy learned, had become addicted to morphine during treatment for injuries received in a bombing attack, to say nothing of the alcoholism exacerbated by the stress of life on the front lines. Over the coming years, the marriage was buffeted by increasingly violent arguments over Dorothy's social life and plagued by Eddie's jealousy of Parker's success as a writer. Dorothy, on her part, was horrified by Eddie's pleas to return to Hartford with him for a life of housework and dull days at the country club, and by the mid-1920s wrote, in her poem "Day Dreams":

> If you and I were one, my dear,
> A model life we'd lead.
> We'd travel on, from year to year,
> At no increase in speed.
> Ah, clear to me the vision of
> The things that we should do!
> And so I think it best, my love,
> To string along as two.

Dorothy and Eddie would finally separate in 1924. Four years later, Eddie would not contest Parker's petition for a divorce on grounds of "intolerable cruelty."

Amid the turmoil of her personal life, Parker's relationship with Benchley and Sherwood assumed greater importance. Crowninshield's patrician leadership at *Vanity Fair* acted as a catalyst for the threesome's more rebellious instincts, and the stream of admonitory notes from Crowninshield about arriving late for work, taking unusually long lunch hours, and Benchley's fondness for pasting photographs of corpses on the office walls was studiously ignored. Parker, meanwhile, began complaining none too subtly about her low wages, and soon had formed a mock labor union with Benchley and Sherwood which peppered the desks of fellow workers with its manifesto. In January 1920, Crowninshield invited Parker to tea to inform her that Wodehouse was returning to the magazine as drama critic and that no new position would be found for her. Dorothy suspected that her scathing reviews of a series of plays produced by some of the magazine's biggest advertisers had something to do with her firing. Crowninshield let Sherwood go that same day, apparently regarding the two of them as bad influences on Benchley. But Benchley surprised everyone, especially Parker, by resigning in protest, even though Gertrude had just given birth to a third son and he had just purchased a new home in Scarsdale. "It was the greatest act of friendship I'd ever known," said Parker.

By the time of her *Vanity Fair* demise, Dorothy Parker had become a member in good standing of a group of journalists and literary hangers-on that gathered each week for lunch at the Algonquin Hotel, on West 44th Street. It had begun as a publicity stunt for *The New York Times*' theater critic, Alexander Woollcott, just back from the war in June 1919. The *Times*' press agents sent out invitations to a number of columnists throughout the city to hear Woollcott's tales of life on the front as a medical intern. Among Parker's fellow diners that first day were, of course, Benchley and Sherwood, and Harold Ross, a tall Midwesterner who had edited the military newspaper *Stars and Stripes* in Paris during the war and would soon have an idea for a weekly humor magazine he would call *The New Yorker*. The war stories, jokes and gossip were of such high quality at that first meeting that it was decided to try it again the following week, and thus was born the Algonquin Round Table, the fluctuating membership of which would include over the next decade such luminaries of the stage and page as playwrights George S. Kaufman and Marc Connelly, novelists ***Edna Ferber** and Ring Lardner, and even actors Harpo Marx and ***Tallulah Bankhead**. The Algonquin's manager at the time, Frank Case, hurriedly moved his raucous customers into a separate room after their first meeting, and sat them around a huge round table; and it was Case who noticed "the young girl" who would "simply sit, now and then saying something at which the others would laugh, and that was the end of it." Woollcott called Parker "a blend of Little Nell and Lady Macbeth."

Dorothy chose to launch her verbal weapons carefully and concisely, delivered with a deadpan expression that associates soon learned was a sign of a pending assault; for while writing was torture to her, Parker's facility with the spoken word was unmatched. She spared no one, especially females of her acquaintance. When told that one such friend had injured her leg while visiting London, Parker suspected it had happened while the woman was "sliding down a barrister"; and when protests against Parker's merciless treatment of another of her victims included the statement that the lady in question wouldn't hurt a fly, Parker shot back, "As long as it was buttoned up." Such was her quick-wittedness that without a moment's hesitation, Parker met the challenge of defining the word "horticulture" with "You can lead a horticulture, but you can't make her think."

But wordplay at parties could not pay bills. For some weeks after their departure from *Vanity Fair,* Parker and Benchley set up shop as freelance journalists, renting an office on Broadway so tiny that Parker claimed "it would have been adultery" if it was any smaller. They weren't quite sure what they were supposed be doing, and spent much of the time talking about themselves or chatting with friends who dropped in. After a month, Parker found a job as drama critic with a literary magazine called *Ainslee's,* and supplemented her income by contributing pieces on a variety of topics to *Ladies' Home Journal* and *The Saturday Evening Post.* Benchley, too, eventually found a paying position as drama critic for *Life,* where Sherwood had become assistant editor, and often stayed at Dorothy and Eddie's apartment when he had a close deadline after a show's opening night.

By the early 1920s, Parker's relationship with Benchley was attracting considerable attention. At a gathering at the Round Table, where the two always sat together, a guest turned to Woollcott and asked if Dorothy was Mrs. Benchley. "So I have always understood, but it *is* Mrs. Parker," was Woollcott's catty reply. If Woollcott's implied sexual affair did exist, it must have been extraordinarily discreet; but since discretion would not have been the first characteristic to come to mind for any of the Round Table's regulars, it must be assumed that the relationship between Parker and Benchley was more in the nature of the affectionate camaraderie of two people who thought uncannily alike. Robert Sherwood described their relationship as an intellectual one; and when Marc Connelly, the last surviving member of the Round Table, told biographer **Marion Meade** in the early 1980s that all of them "just hated being apart," he could just as well have been describing the state of affairs between Parker and Benchley.

Parker was certainly attractive enough to encourage the opposite sex. A portrait of her painted by Greenwich Village artist ***Neysa McMein** in 1923 hints at the combination of girlish charm and formidable intellect that may have intimidated some men, but irresistibly attracted others. Among her potential suitors was Edmund Wilson, who later wrote that Parker's liberal use of scent, which made him ill, was the only thing that prevented his courting. Screenwriter Donald Ogden Stewart, a friend of Robert Sherwood, thought that Parker's delicate figure and large, soulful eyes were "absolutely devastating." Still married at this point, Parker primly avoided romantic entanglements, dealt as best she could with Eddie's alcoholism and abusive behavior, and turned out light pieces for *Life* and *The Saturday Evening Post* to keep debtors at bay.

But the pressures were mounting. In her best-known short story, "Big Blonde," published in 1929, Parker depicted a woman who turns to alcohol in the midst of an ill-conceived and hasty marriage to an abusive husband. "She could not recall the definite day that she started drinking," Parker wrote of her alter-ego. "There was nothing separate about her days. Like drops upon a window-pane, they ran together and trickled away." And like "Big Blonde"'s Hazel Morse, Dorothy had found that Scotch, taken neat, eased things considerably. That same year, the previously teetotaling Benchley made much the same discovery, starting with an orange blossom pressed on him by friends while celebrating Jack Dempsey's 1922 championship victory over Georges Carpentier at Tony Soma's on West 49th Street, one of Prohibition's better-known speakeasies. Benchley eventually settled on rye as his drink of choice, and from then on, neither he nor Parker would abandon alcohol's solace for more than a few, hung-over hours.

Parker described in clinical detail for her readers her morning-after ailments, which she called "the Rams." They were, she wrote, "much like the heebie-jeebies, except that they last longer, strike deeper, and are, in general, fancier." Less severe cases she classified as "the German Rams," but both could surely be traced to suspicious food eaten the previous evening, especially celery sticks. Despite these occasional penalties, Parker found alcohol liberating, even stimulating, and it is no coincidence that her first published short story was written at this time. "Such a Pretty Little Picture" was published in H.L. Mencken's *Smart Set* in 1922. It was a sly, ironic jab at the type of suburban domesticity back in Scarsdale which was driving Benchley to drink, and at the kind of hopeless marriage of which Parker had direct experience. She cast Benchley as her Mr. Wheelock, who clips his hedges on a peaceful suburban street on a peaceful summer evening while dreaming of escaping, "when Adelaide was sewing on buttons, up on the porch, and Sister was playing somewhere about. He would time it so that he'd just make the 6:03 for the city comfortably."

"Such a Pretty Little Picture" appeared in print just as Eddie disappeared for the first of many long absences, and just as Dorothy embarked on the first of her many notorious affairs. One of the newer Round Tablers was a handsome young newspaper reporter from Chicago, Charles MacArthur, who had left a wife behind in the Midwest to seek his fortune in New York as a playwright. Parker's interest in MacArthur was immediate and intensely passionate. She ignored the usual warnings about affairs between two already married people and about MacArthur's roving eye, apparent to everyone but her. Late in 1922, Parker discovered she was pregnant and had an abortion, bitterly characterizing MacArthur's reported $30 contribution to the cost of the procedure as being like Judas giving a refund. MacArthur soon left her to return to Chicago. (He went on to write, with Ben Hecht, *The Front Page* and eventually married actress ***Helen Hayes**.)

Soon after, on a quiet Sunday afternoon in mid-January, Parker as usual called out to a local restaurant to ask for her dinner to be delivered. Then she went into the bathroom and slit her wrists with one of Eddie's rusty razor blades, thoughtfully leaving the apartment door unlocked and thus allowing the delivery boy to find her unconscious from blood loss when he arrived with her dinner. On her release from the hospital a week later, Eddie returned and tried to patch things up. Parker, for her part, quit her magazine job and settled down to serious writing, producing her second short story, "It's Too Bad," about an estranged couple who try to keep up appearances but ultimately divorce—another bit of quasi-autobiography. It was in her poetry, meanwhile, that she probed the pained aftermath of her affair with MacArthur. Nevertheless, the number of her affairs only seemed to multiply, especially after Parker was adopted by the wealthy social set whose glittering parties on sumptuous Long Island estates kept Prohibition at bay. During these long, alcohol-soaked weekends, Parker consorted with fellow writers like F. Scott Fitzgerald, Ring Lardner, and James Thurber, all adopted as amusing guests by hosts whose prosperity came and went as quickly as the canapés.

Among Parker's paramours during this period was playwright Elmer Rice, whose anti-machine-age play *The Adding Machine* had taken Broadway by storm. The affair may have been short-lived, but it begat Dorothy's first effort for the stage. Rice agreed to help Parker adapt her story of a hen-pecked suburban husband who nearly runs off with a chorus girl, with Parker supplying the dialogue and Rice the dramatic framework. *Close Harmony* (originally called *Soft Music*) opened on Broadway early in 1924, receiving respectful reviews but failing to attract full houses and closing after three weeks. Parker had been expecting the worst, despite the good reviews. She later called the play "insipid and dull," and would not write for the stage again for many years.

As with her first short story, Parker had drawn the inspiration for her initial play from Benchley, who actually *was* having an affair with a former chorus girl. Benchley was by now spending most of his time in New York. He had become somewhat of a stage celebrity after delivering a comic monologue called "The Treasurer's Report" at a Round Table theatrical evening to such good effect that he was appearing nightly with it on Broadway in *The Music Box Revue*. Later, Benchley would travel to Hollywood to take small roles in comedy pictures and star in a series of short filmed lectures he had written with names like *The Sex Life of the Polyp*.

As their careers began to diverge, Parker took up residence in the Algonquin Hotel, which Mencken considered the most comfortable hotel in America. "The distance from the front door to the elevator is only forty feet," he wrote, "an important consideration to a man whose friends all drink too much, and sometimes press the stuff on him." With the Round Table just a short elevator ride away, Parker became even more entrenched there and often invited everyone back upstairs for another round of drinking. During one of these extended sessions, Harold Ross and his wife **Jane Grant** announced that they were raising money for a new humor magazine, a sophisticated weekly for the smart set and not, as Ross famously pointed out, "for the old lady in Dubuque." He solicited ideas from the Round Tablers for the first issue of *The New Yorker*, which was published in February 1925, Parker contributing a theater review and appearing on the masthead as an advisor. Six months later, circulation had dropped to less than 3,000 and the magazine's financial condition was so perilous that when Ross asked Parker why she was late turning in an article, she replied, "Somebody was using the pencil." No one expected the magazine to survive.

By 1926, after a lengthy affair with journalist-playwright Deems Taylor ended badly and another attempt to patch things up with Eddie failed, Parker tried to kill herself a second time by taking an overdose of Veronal, a barbiturate used as a sleeping medication. "Big Blonde"'s Hazel Morse tries the same method of self-annihilation. Through Hazel, Parker recounted buying the pills in New Jersey, where they were available without a prescription, and how the large white pills were difficult to swallow—so difficult that, like Hazel, she failed to take enough of them and woke up two days later in a hospital. Ironically, the attempt had come while Parker was undergoing treatment and psychological counseling to cut down on her drinking. She gave up both the treatment and the counseling, continued her drinking, and decided that travel might pull her out of her slump.

Benchley had recently returned from a trip to Europe and had told her about the lively expatriate colony of writers and artists living in Paris, including Ernest Hemingway, whose work Dorothy much admired. Parker, who sailed in February 1926, remained in Paris for nearly a year, although it was hardly the cure she had been expecting. She was lonely most of the time and found the close-knit circle of Americans there more inbred than the Round Table. Her efforts to begin a novel she had been contemplating were fruitless, although she began collecting her poetry into a volume she called *Enough Rope,* published on her return at the end of 1926. "The rope is caked with salty humor . . . and tarred with a bright black authenticity," *The Nation* said; while the *New York Herald Tribune* more succinctly and appropriately described her verse as "whiskey straight." Her fame had grown to such proportions that her outspoken involvement in the infamous Sacco-Vanzetti case of 1927 attracted nationwide attention.

Most of the politically cynical Round Tablers were caught off-guard by Parker's newfound social conscience and her attraction to socialist causes. She had traveled to Boston to join the protest against the guilty verdict and ensuing death penalty visited on two Italian immigrants whose murder trial had turned into a nationwide focus of ethnic bigotry. America's young Communist Party saw the court ruling as a reactionary attack on socialism and organized street protests and press campaigns in support of winning an appeal to prevent the executions. Parker marched down Beacon Street behind writer John Dos Passos, who was covering the event for the Communist Party's newspaper *The Daily Worker,* as both sang the Party's anthem "The Internationale." Parker told friends in New York that she expected to be arrested, and she was not disappointed, spending a few hours in a Boston jail before friends bailed her out. Her growing fame was evidenced by the gaggle of reporters waiting for her as she left the prison. The next day she paid a $5 fine for loitering and for a mysterious misdemeanor called "sauntering." Upon learning that an appeals court had refused to overturn the death penalty and that Sacco and Vanzetti would be electrocuted that night, she declared, "My heart and soul are with the cause of socialism." Parker offered no public explanation for her activism, but many years later she would remember visiting the sweatshops her father operated to produce his capes and gloves, full of immigrants working 12- and 14-hour days, six days a week, for absurdly low wages.

At *The New Yorker,* meanwhile, things were looking brighter. Ross had somehow managed to keep the magazine afloat and circulation was actually increasing. In October 1927, Parker took on a weekly book-review column for the magazine, for which she signed herself "Constant Reader." Like her earlier theater reviews, these new efforts were unusual. An autobiography by British socialite ***Margot Asquith**, Constant Reader thought, had "all the depth and glitter of a worn dime." But she saved her most potent venom for A.A. Milne's *The House at Pooh Corner,* and Milne's invention of the word "hummy." At her first experience of it, she wrote, "Tonstant Weader fwowed up." Milne was a favorite target and had the misfortune of opening his melodrama *Give Me Yesterday* on Broadway when Parker had temporarily taken over Benchley's play reviewing column in *The New Yorker.* "If *Give Me Yesterday* is a fine play," she groused, "I am Richard Brinsley Sheridan."

In 1928, with her divorce from Eddie finalized, Parker published her second poetry collection, *Sunset Gun,* to great acclaim. It was dedicated to John Garret, a wealthy banker with whom she had been carrying on a tempestuous affair, even though Garret had left her for a "show girl" by the time the book appeared on the shelves. "Big Blonde" appeared six months later in the literary magazine *The Bookman,* also to much praise, and was named the best short story of 1929 in the prestigious O. Henry Competition. But with her literary star rising, Parker perversely decamped for Hollywood.

It was the money that attracted her, a ludicrously high $300 a week for three months' work offered to her by MGM which, like all the big studios, was trying to polish up its image by hiring respected writers. Parker found the experience at first mystifying, later exasperating. MGM's head of production, Irving Thalberg, had never heard of her and at their first meeting did not seem sure why she had been hired; and she had difficulty on her first writing assignment because no one seemed to know what the film was about. When she finally produced a few pages of script for another film, Thalberg complained that her dialogue wasn't suitable for "the little totties." At the end of her three months, Parker had written only the lyrics for a song included in a Cecil B. De Mille film called *Dynamite.* At least she had spent time with Benchley, who was then shooting three films, and with her favorite wealthy couple, Gerald and **Sara Murphy**, who were in town while Gerald served as an advisor on a film featuring African-American spirituals, on which he was inexplicably an expert. Parker declined to renew her contract and fled back to New York. Perhaps to purge herself of the bad taste of the movie business, she rashly agreed to write a novel for the newly formed Viking Press and decided Europe would be the perfect place to write it.

She traveled to London, Paris, and to Antibes on France's Côte d'Azur, where she stayed with the Murphys at their fabled Villa America and hobnobbed with Scott and ***Zelda Fitzgerald**, who had taken a house nearby. None of it proved inspirational, and she wrote little of the promised novel which, she had decided, would be called "Sonnets in Suicide." When one of the Murphys' sons fell ill with tuberculosis, Parker tagged along with the family to Switzerland and to a sanitarium where the young Murphy began a slow, painful recovery. In telegrams to Benchley, she confessed she found the environment sterile and depressing, the sanitarium full of the air of death. She finally left for home early in 1930, but still her novel refused to take shape. While she could stand the autobiographical pain of a short story, the torments of a full-length work were too much. Profoundly depressed, Parker drank a bottle of shoe polish and ended up in a hospital while Viking hurriedly compiled a collection of her short stories, published as *Laments for the Living* and including "Big Blonde." Although it went through four editions in its first month, and received good reviews, Parker swore she'd never write again. After another stay with the Murphys in Switzerland in the spring and summer of 1931 which failed to relieve her low spirits, and another disastrous affair, this one with a handsome young newspaper reporter, Parker took another overdose of barbiturates—not enough to kill her, as she found when she came to in another hospital bed.

Slowly, she recovered. She also drew strength from her new friendship with ***Lillian Hellman**, who in four years would take Broadway by storm with her play *The Children's Hour,* and who was in the midst of a long-running relationship with Dashiell Hammett, one of Parker's favorite writers. Parker was awed by Hellman's shrewd, eminently practical approach to the business of writing, while Hellman was equally impressed by, and a little afraid of, Parker's quick intelligence and verbal agility. The friendship would last the rest of Parker's life.

By 1933, Parker was in sufficiently good spirits to be attracted to a good-looking young actor named Alan Campbell. Besides his acting, Campbell had written a few short pieces for *The New Yorker.* Alan seemed to understand her moods, was a respectable, but not sloppy, drinker, and combined a mischievous sense of humor with a good deal of common sense. He was 29; Parker, 40. The two of them were soon sharing an apartment, Parker discovering that Campbell had the added advantage of being a good cook and housekeeper—two talents that had eluded her, as anyone who had visited Parker's several apartments could testify. When Campbell was offered a job in summer stock in Denver, Parker was so infatuated that she went with him. But Denver was less tolerant than New York, especially of sharp-tongued literary wits living in sin with handsome young actors. Campbell and Parker tried to concoct a story of a secret marriage, but failed to check with each other first and gave different versions of the supposed event, much to the merriment of the press. With Alan's job in danger and Parker's reputation as a loose woman about to become national news, the only solution was to actually get married. The ceremony before a justice of the peace took place just over the border in New Mexico on the night of June 18, 1933.

Parker now entered, much to her surprise, "a sort of coma of happiness," she enthused to Woollcott, in which she found that being Alan's wife was "lovelier than anything I ever knew could be." Back in New York, the new marrieds were approached by a theatrical producer with Hollywood connections, who suggested they could make a comfortable living as a screenwriting team. It was another testament to her attachment to Campbell, who was eager to travel west, that she signed a contract with Paramount for the impressive salary of $1,000 a week. Campbell, for his part, would be paid $250. The Hollywood press adopted them as the town's favorite new creative team while they settled down to write their first script together, *One Hour Late,* for ***Sylvia Sidney**, although a later version finally ended up on screen. Within a few months, their combined salaries allowed them to rent a house in Beverly Hills. Parker's euphoria continued while her drinking abated considerably. "Aside from the work, which I hate like holy water," she wrote to Woollcott, "I love it here. I love having a house. I love its being pretty wherever you look."

While she and Campbell turned out the screenplay for David Selznick's *A Star Is Born* (starring ***Janet Gaynor**, for which Parker and Campbell were nominated for an Academy Award) and contributed dialogue to such films as Alfred Hitchcock's *Saboteur* (in which Parker appears briefly riding in a car with Hitchcock), Parker's leftist politics again came to the fore. While she had often expressed support for both Stalin's Russia and for the Communist Party, later scrutiny during the McCarthy hearings of the 1950s failed to prove that Parker had done anything more than lend her name to a variety of charitable causes that turned out to be Party fronts. Conservative suspicion about her deepened, however, when she began actively recruiting new members for the recently formed Screen Writers' Guild at a time when many unions had been infiltrated by the American Communist Party. The studios had countered the Guild by forming The Screen Playwrights which, they claimed, was adequate protection for film writers. It was, Parker later scoffed, "like trying to get laid in your mother's house. Somebody was always in the parlor, watching." When Parker and Campbell traveled to Spain during that country's civil war in 1937, Dorothy became a passionate supporter of the doomed Loyalist cause. The suffering and devastation she saw affected her deeply, especially in the Loyalist stronghold of Valencia, which was bombed four times during her visit. "These people who pulled themselves up from centuries of oppression and exploitation cannot go on to a decent living, to peace and progress and civilization without the murder of their children," she wrote, "because [Hitler and Franco] want more power. It is incredible, it is fantastic, it is absolutely beyond belief . . . except that it is true." She warned that the Loyalist defeat in Spain would be the spark for something worse, and was proved right two years later when Hitler invaded Poland.

While the world rushed to war, Parker's domestic situation, despite her activist pronouncements, was decidedly bourgeois. With the proceeds from their work in Hollywood, Parker and Campbell purchased a farm house in rural Bucks County, Pennsylvania, where their deep-rooted urban sensibility provoked much discussion among the locals, who failed to see the charm in Alan's choice of ten shades of red to decorate the living room. But two pregnancies which ended in miscarriages, social ostracism in Hollywood by many of their friends over Parker's politics, and disputes with studios over pictures which never got made began to have their effect on what had seemed to be an ideal marriage. Friends noticed that Parker, always petite and slight of build, had now ballooned to 150 pounds. Her spirits soured to such a degree that she even accused Campbell, whose bisexuality had been widely rumored, of cheating on her with other men—almost certainly untrue. Her mood was not improved when the studio kept Campbell on a writing project and replaced her with another female writing partner; while Harold Ross, for the first time in their relationship, rejected one of her short stories for publication in *The New Yorker*. By 1942, her excessive drinking returned to such a degree that a stay in a sanitarium was called for while Campbell announced that he was enlisting and went off to basic training in Florida. Things only seemed to grow worse after Campbell's departure. Woollcott died in 1943, collapsing of a heart attack during a radio broadcast. Even worse, Robert Benchley died in New York of a cerebral hemorrhage just two years after the death of Woollcott. He was 56. Parker was in California when she heard the news, and exclaimed bitterly "That's dandy!," a remark Gertrude Benchley misinterpreted as a cruel joke.

Campbell had already left for Europe when Benchley died, leaving Parker to find what comfort she could in alcohol, cigarettes and sympathetic friends. After these wartime shocks, she received almost calmly Campbell's news that he had fallen in love with an English woman. Although the affair had cooled by the time of his return in 1946, the farm in Pennsylvania was sold and Parker traveled to Las Vegas for a divorce on grounds of mental cruelty, ignoring the fact that she herself had often disparaged Campbell. He was more charitable. "I'm sorry it's over," he said. "We had a wonderful time."

Parker wasted no time in finding another writing partner, lover and drinking companion. He was Ross Evans, whom Campbell had met in the Army and introduced to her. Evans was working in New York at the time as a radio announcer but had literary pretensions. The pair's output paled beside what Parker had accomplished with Campbell, although Evans helped Parker complete her second play, *The Coast of Illyria,* based on the life of the tragic English writer ***Mary Lamb**. It premiered in Dallas in April 1949 to mediocre reviews, ran for three weeks, and was never heard from again. Evans also traveled with her back to Hollywood, claiming co-author credit for an adaptation of *Lady Windermere's Fan* for Fox and a comedy, *Come Back to the Stable,* starring ***Loretta Young** and ***Celeste Holm** as nuns. But it was Parker's collaboration with another writer, Frank Cavett, that brought her her second Academy Award nomination, for Universal's *Smash-Up: The Story of a Woman*, in which the main character (played by ***Susan Hayward**) was an alcoholic housewife. Her boozy affair with Evans ended in Mexico, where Parker objected to his attentions to another woman and Evans promptly dumped her.

Just as promptly, Parker returned to Los Angeles and remarried Alan Campbell, on August 17, 1950. "Who in life gets a second chance?," she rhetorically queried friends. Campbell seemed less confident, but admitted he had been the one to float the idea. Given this lack of enthusiasm from both partners, it was hardly surprising when the arguments resumed and, little more than a year later, Campbell walked out on her. Jilted twice in as many years, Parker retreated to the only safe haven she knew: New York.

"I get up every morning and want to kiss the pavement," she said after moving into the Volney, a residential hotel on East 74th. It was, and is, a genteel sort of place, occupied in Parker's time mainly by meticulously preserved widows who filled the halls with wafts of their perfume as they came and went in their rounds of teas, lunches, and evenings at the theater. No doubt these delicate gentlewoman observed Parker with as much interest as she watched them, for she was considerably younger than any of them and was from a world they only read about in newspapers and magazines. Inspired, Parker was soon at work on a new play, *Ladies of the Corridor*, again with a collaborator. He was Arnaud d'Usseau, whom she had met in California but whose main success had come with two Broadway hits written with another partner who had died. The relationship this time was strictly business, with d'Usseau's wife keeping a careful eye on Parker's alcohol consumption as work progressed. The play had its debut in October 1953, but as with her two previous works for the stage, reviews were only respectful and hardly enthusiastic. It closed in six weeks, but Parker to the end of her life maintained it was the best thing she had ever written. The subject matter of her second effort with d'Usseau, which detailed the seduction of a divorced man by a gay lover, failed to attract a producer willing to stage it. It was the last play Parker would write.

With the McCarthy hearings in full swing and a nervous Hollywood unwilling to hire anyone with a Communist taint, Parker returned to fiction for her living. (Although never formally accused of being a Communist, Parker's name temporarily appeared on the blacklist.) With Harold Ross' death in 1951, the magazine he had founded nearly 30 years before ceased to have a personal meaning for her, and it was to *Esquire* that she transferred her allegiance when that magazine offered her a regular book-review column—her first since "Constant Reader" days. She doggedly read her assignments for five years, producing 46 columns in that time and complaining loudly that the magazine's editor was a worse taskmaster than Ross ever was. By 1958, after having such difficulty meeting deadlines that *Esquire*'s editorial staff began referring to the traumatic experience of getting an overdue piece from her as a "high forceps delivery," Parker found herself again out of a regular job. She was 65.

Friends attempted to help. One persuaded a publisher to offer Parker an advance to write her autobiography, but she eventually returned it. "Rather than write my life story, I would cut my throat with a dull knife," she said. Lillian Hellman, working with Leonard Bernstein on a musical based on Voltaire's *Candide*, persuaded her to contribute lyrics to the show. Parker produced the lyrics for only one number, "Gavotte," although Bernstein later said she was a delight to work with, "very sweet, very drunk, very forthcoming." Everyone hoped that Parker's induction into the National Institute of Arts and Letters would bring her some work, even after Dorothy arrived at the awards ceremony decidedly tipsy, delivered an acceptance speech that consisted solely of "I never thought I'd make it!," and chose to stumble to her feet and deliver it again in the middle of another speaker's remarks. When her old friend Edmund Wilson later paid her a visit at the Volney, he reported that she "had somewhat deteriorated [and] had big pouches under her eyes." Entering the apartment, he said, was like stepping back in time to the '20s, when he had once thought of courting America's wittiest woman.

Her savior turned out to be none other than Alan Campbell, to whom she was still legally married despite their ten-year separation. Campbell was still in California and had been offered a job at Fox adapting a French play for the screen—but only if Parker would work with him. Dorothy soon boarded a plane for Los Angeles hoping for a comeback of both her marriage and her career. But the script they produced for Fox, an intended vehicle for ***Marilyn Monroe** called *The Good Soup*, was never produced and further offers of work were not forthcoming. There were a few dollars to be had from the sale of television rights to some of her short stories, from speaking fees for lectures on various literary subjects, and from a disastrous decision to teach a writing course at California State, where she found her students ignorant of not only her own former status but of the major writers she presented to them, many of whom she had known personally.

Meanwhile, Alan Campbell failed to find any work at all and sunk deeper into idle drinking. Parker returned home one afternoon in 1963 expecting to find him, as usual, passed out in a small room he had built for himself off the main bedroom. Instead, she found his lifeless body. Campbell had apparently taken an overdose of Seconal and then placed a plastic bag over his head. He was 59. Just as it had when she learned of Benchley's death, Parker's shock spilled out in bitter remarks others interpreted as callous. One female friend, for example, ventured to ask if there was anything she could do. "Get me a new husband," Parker snapped. She refused to attend Campbell's funeral or to talk about their marriage, except to vapidly tell the Associated Press that she and Campbell had had "29 great years together."

But Campbell's death affected her more deeply than she would admit, and after her health began declining precipitously and a broken shoulder from a fall refused to heal properly, Parker finally turned her back on California once and for all and returned to New York in March 1963. Her new apartment at the Volney was smaller than her previous one and a bit cramped for both Dorothy and the live-in nurse her precarious health required. She wrote little, piled the review copies of current books sent to her by a hopeful *Esquire* in a corner, and lamented to the few visitors she received that hardly any of the friends from the old days remained to cheer her. She was especially distraught over the death of Gerald Murphy, sending Sara Murphy a mournful telegram that merely read: "Dearest Sara, Dearest Sara." In her last published work in a magazine, a brief accompanying text to a series of paintings of Manhattan life at the turn of the century for *Esquire*, she admitted to "nostalgia for those rooms of lovely lights and lovelier shadows and loveliest people. . . . It is the sort of nostalgia that is only a dreamy longing for some places where you never were."

Her health seemed to improve somewhat during 1964, and by 1965 there were plans for a stage play based on her writings, invitations to society dinners at which Parker imbibed with her old abandon and managed to shoot quips and barbs across the table with her former aplomb, as well as a series of taped radio interviews about her life. This last project survived through three sessions before Parker's leg-pulling and tale-spinning destroyed any credibility the series might have had. Lillian Hellman, one of the few survivors from old times, wrote in her diary that Parker had become "too strange for safety or comfort," a frail, 80-pound old woman who greeted her visitors in pastel house dresses and chain-smoked her Chesterfields while wheedling guests into pouring her the Scotch doctors had forbidden her.

On the afternoon of Wednesday, June 7, one of the Volney's maids came to Parker's apartment, as usual, with a fresh supply of towels and bed linens. She found Dorothy dead, apparently of a heart attack which had struck while Parker was sitting in bed, reading. Many Americans were surprised to read of her passing, for they had assumed she had died long ago. She had committed, wrote the late Brendan Gill, "an inexcusable social and aesthetic blunder: she was . . . the guest who is aware that he has outstayed his welcome and who yet makes no attempt to pack his things and go."

In accordance with the will Parker had prepared two years earlier, her body was sent to the Long Island crematory, where her ashes would remain until arriving at Oscar Bernstien's office. She appointed Hellman as her executor, but even Hellman was surprised to find that Parker had left her entire estate, amounting to some $20,000, to Martin Luther King, Jr. "She must have been drunk when she did it," Hellman grumbled. With King's assassination the following year, the assets of the estate passed to the National Association for the Advancement of Colored People (NAACP) which, in 1988, finally laid Parker's ashes to rest in a specially constructed memorial garden at its headquarters in Baltimore. The

NAACP continues to control the rights to Parker's work, all of which remains in print. The Viking Press' *The Portable Dorothy Parker*, in fact, remains among the top ten bestsellers in its "Portable" series, even though Parker once claimed she never much thought about her public. "There must be a magnificent disregard for your reader," she once said, "for if he cannot follow you, there is nothing you can do about it." Given that disregard, her literary immortality would have surprised her; but then Parker never expected things to happen the way she imagined. In her earlier days of death wishes and suicide attempts, Parker had dictated the conditions under which she wanted to meet her end:

> Oh, let it be a night of lyric rain
> And singing breezes, when my bell is tolled.
> I have so loved the rain that I would hold
> Last in my ears its friendly, dim refrain.

But she died during the afternoon of a pleasant, sunny day, with temperatures in the 80s. There was no rain in the forecast.

SOURCES:

Kurth, Peter. "One Man's Love Affair With Two Dorothys," in *Forbes*. Vol. 156, no. 7. September 25, 1995.

Meade, Marion. *Dorothy Parker: What Fresh Hell Is This?* NY: Villard, 1988.

Parker, Dorothy. *The Portable Dorothy Parker.* 2nd ed. NY: Viking, 1976.

Rosmond, Babette. *Robert Benchley: His Life And Good Times*. NY: Doubleday, 1970.

RELATED MEDIA:

Mrs. Parker and the Vicious Circle (film), directed by Alan Rudolph, starring **Jennifer Jason Leigh** as Dorothy Parker, 1994.

Norman Powers,
writer-producer, Chelsea Lane Productions,
New York, New York

Parker, Eleanor (1922—)

American actress. *Born in Cedarville, Ohio, on June 26, 1922; married four times; children: four.*

Selected filmography: They Died with Their Boots On *(bit, 1941);* Busses Roar *(1942);* Mission to Moscow *(1943);* The Mysterious Doctor *(1943);* Between Two Worlds *(1944);* Come By Night *(1944);* The Last Ride *(1944);* The Very Thought of You *(1944);* Hollywood Canteen *(1944);* Pride of the Marines *(1945);* Of Human Bondage *(1946);* Never Say Goodbye *(1946);* Escape Me Never *(1947);* Always Together *(1947);* The Voice of the Turtle *(1948);* The Woman in White *(1948);* It's a Great Feeling *(1949);* Chain Lightning *(1950);* Caged *(1950);* Three Secrets *(1950);* Valentino *(1951);* A Millionaire for Christy *(1951);* Detective Story *(1951);* Scaramouche *(1952);* Above and Beyond *(1953);* Escape from Fort Bravo *(1953);* The Naked Jungle *(1954);* Valley of the Kings *(1954);* Many Rivers to Cross *(1955);* Interrupted Melody *(1955);* The Man with the Golden Arm *(1955);* The King and Four Queens *(1956);* Lizzie *(1957);* The Seventh Sin *(1957);* A Hole in the Head *(1959);* Home from the Hill *(1960);* Return to Peyton Place *(1961);* Madison Avenue *(1962);* Panic Button *(1964);* The Sound of Music *(1965);* The Oscar *(1966);* An American Dream *(1966);* Warning Shot *(1967);* The Tiger and the Pussycat *(1967);* Eye of the Cat *(1969);* Sunburn *(1979).*

A talented, stunning redhead who graced the screen during the 1940s and 1950s, Eleanor Parker was born in 1922 in Cedarville, Ohio, and received her early acting experience at the Cleveland Playhouse, as well as in stock and at the Pasadena Playhouse. Making her film debut under contract to Warner Bros., she worked her way up through the studio ranks during the 1940s, then transferred to MGM in the 1950s. She played a variety of roles, from vixens to long-suffering wives, and won Academy Award nominations as Best Actress for her performances in *Caged* (1950), *Detective Story* (1951), and *Interrupted Melody* (1955), in which she portrayed Australian opera singer ***Marjorie Lawrence**. After 1960, Parker made few films, among them *The Sound of Music* (1965).

Parker, Jane (d. 1542?)

English royal and sister-in-law of Anne Boleyn. *Name variations: Jane Boleyn. Executed around 1542; daughter of Henry, Lord Morley; married George Boleyn, 2nd viscount Rochford and brother of* ****Anne Boleyn** *(George was beheaded and burned at Tyburn in 1536); children: George Boleyn, dean of Lichfield. Jane Parker was portrayed by* **Judy Kelley** *in the 1933 movie* The Private Life of Henry VIII.

Parker, K. Langloh (c. 1856–1940).

See Parker, Catherine Langloh.

Parker, Minerva (1861–1949).

See Nichols, Minerva.

Parker, Suzy (1932—)

American model and actress. *Born Cecilia Parker on October 29, 1932, in San Antonio, Texas; sister of Dorian Leigh (a model); married Bradford Dillman (an actor).*

Selected filmography: Funny Face *(1957);* Kiss Them for Me *(1957);* Ten North Frederick *(1958);*

The Best of Everything *(1959);* Circle of Deception *(1961);* The Interns *(1962);* Flight from Ashiya *(1964);* Chamber of Horrors *(1966).*

A statuesque beauty, Suzy Parker was a highly successful fashion model, known as one of the "Revlon girls," along with **Lauren Hutton**, **Barbara Britton**, and Parker's older sister **Dorian Leigh**. *Life* magazine devoted a cover to her in 1957, the year Parker made her film debut in *Funny Face*. Despite starring roles opposite such leading men as Cary Grant (*North by Northwest*) and Gary Cooper (*Ten North Frederick*), she never clicked with movie audiences. Her last film appearance was in *Chamber of Horrors* (1966). Parker married actor Bradford Dillman and retired to raise a family.

Parker-Bowles, Camilla (1947—)

English woman romantically linked to the prince of Wales. *Name variations: Camilla Parker Bowles. Born Camilla Shand on July 17, 1947, at King's College Hospital in London, England; eldest of three children of Bruce Shand (an army officer turned educational film representative) and Rosalind (Cubitt) Shand; attended Queen's Gate, London; married Andrew Parker-Bowles (a cavalry officer), in July 1973 (divorced 1995); children: Thomas Parker-Bowles;* ***Laura Parker-Bowles.***

The 30-year love affair between Camilla Parker-Bowles and Charles, prince of Wales, is often compared to that of Camilla's notorious great-grandmother ***Alice Keppel**, the famous society beauty who was the mistress of King Edward VII from 1898 until his death in 1910. (Although evidence is circumstantial, it is widely believed that their union brought forth the writer ***Violet Keppel Trefusis** and Camilla's maternal grandmother, **Sonia Keppel** Cubitt.) But unlike Alice's royal liaison at the turn of the century, Camilla's affair with Charles, played out in the tabloid-driven information age, has very nearly destroyed the reputation of the royal family.

Camilla, the eldest of three children (her sister **Annabel Elliott** is an antique dealer; her brother Mark Shand is an explorer), had an upper-class English upbringing which included a Sussex country home, private schools, and horses. Her father, Major Bruce Shand, a war hero, spent 16 years in the Queen's service as Clerk of the Cheque and Adjutant of the Yeoman of the Guard, and her late mother, **Rosalind Shand**, was a member of the Cubitt family; the Cubitts amassed a fortune building London's Belgravia district. "Milla," as Camilla is called by her friends, was not a distinguished student, preferring to be outdoors, hunting and shooting. Blonde and flirtatious, she was part of a cadre of young debutantes who frequented the polo matches at Windsor Park Green in the early '70s, and it was there that she met the unsophisticated, shy Charles. They had a great deal in common, and Camilla was a particularly good listener, something the young Charles needed at the time. There was also what one friend described as an "electric magnetism" between the two from the beginning. "It was like watching two steam trains heading towards each other at full pelt." Charles was so smitten that he considered marrying Camilla, but the Palace nixed any such idea, citing her torrid on-again, off-again affair with Andrew Parker-Bowles, a dashing cavalry officer. In 1972, Charles left for a Royal Navy tour in the Caribbean; by the time he returned, Camilla had married Andrew and was settling into the life of a country gentlewoman. It was a union that allowed both partners their independence. While Andrew pursued his military career and his friendships with other women, Camilla embarked on her own extramarital affair with Charles.

The prince's "fairy tale" marriage to Lady ***Diana** Spencer was obviously doomed from the start. Purportedly, Charles went to bed with Camilla just days before the nuptials, telling her that it would be the last time they made love. Diana was said to have intercepted a gold bracelet engraved with the letters GF ("Girl Friday," Charles' nickname for Camilla) that Charles had purchased. For a long time, the powerful forces within Buckingham Palace kept the truth about the royal marriage hidden from the public, and Diana's enormous popularity took much of the spotlight off her frequently absent husband. With Andrew Morton's tell-all book, *Diana: Her True Story,* however, and the 1993 publication of the embarrassing so-called Camillagate tapes, revealing an intimate phone conversation between Charles and Camilla, the deception was over. Hounded by the press and vilified as the "other woman," Camilla hit bottom. Concerned for her husband and her children, as well as for herself, she lost 30 pounds in two months and was forced to flee her house. "For a time she thought she was the most hated woman in the country," said a friend. "She had the hate mail, she had crank calls, and though Andrew did his best to support her, his patience was wearing thin."

By 1996, both Camilla and Charles had divorced their respective mates, and Camilla had moved to Ray Mill house near Highgrove. Tensions had eased to the degree that the couple spent several evenings a week together, and enjoyed occasional afternoons puttering in Charles' extensive gardens. With the passage of another year, they felt confident enough to be seen together in public, and there was speculation about marriage. (The couple could not be married in the Church of England, nor could Camilla ever be queen, but they could be wed in a civil ceremony.) In July, Charles threw a 50th birthday party for Camilla at his country home, even inviting photographers to record her arrival, as well as her departure the next morning. Earlier in the month, *The Daily Mail* had asked, "Isn't it time we stopped hating this dignified woman?," although another tabloid accused the pair of "orchestrating a campaign to get public acceptance."

Following Diana's tragic death, Camilla once again took to hiding from public view, but slowly the couple emerged once again. In November 1998, Camilla hosted a gala birthday party for Charles at Highgrove, attended by a host of dignitaries as well as princes William and Harry, Charles and Diana's sons. Then in January 1999, the pair made their debut as an official couple, staging a long-awaited photo opportunity outside London's Ritz Hotel where they had celebrated Camilla's sister's 50th birthday. But the fate of the lovers is still very much in the hands of Charles' mother, Queen ***Elizabeth II**, who ended her three-decades-long avoidance of Camilla when they were formally introduced on June 3, 2000.

SOURCES:

Benson, Ross. *Charles: The Untold Story*. NY: St. Martin's Press, 1993.

Kantrowitz, Barbara, and Jean Seligmann. "A Royal Kodak Moment," in *Newsweek*. Vol. 133, no. 6. February 8, 1999, p. 57.

McGuire, Stryker. "The Lady in Waiting," in *Newsweek*. Vol. 132, no. 10. September 7, 1998, pp. 48–50.

"Nifty at Fifty," in *People Weekly*. Vol. 50, no. 20. November 30, 1998, pp. 130–138.

"Prince Charles and Camilla Parker Bowles," in *People Weekly*. February 12, 1996, p. 171.

Seward, Ingrid. "Camilla Revealed," in *Maclean's*. Vol. 110, no. 34, August 25, 1997, pp. 48–50.

Wilson, Christopher. *A Greater Love*. NY: William Morrow, 1994.

SUGGESTED READING:

Graham, Caroline. *Camilla: The King's Mistress*. Contemporary, 1997.

Parkes, Bessie Rayner (1829–1925).

See Evans, Mary Anne for sidebar.

Parkhouse, Hannah (1743–1809).

See Cowley, Hannah.

Parkhurst, Charlotte (d. 1879)

California stagecoach driver who lived as a man and became the first American woman to vote in a presidential election. *Name variations: Charley (also seen as Charlie) Parkhurst; "One-Eyed" Charley; Charley Darkey Parkhurst. Born probably in New Hampshire; died near Watsonville, California, on December 29, 1879; children: may have had at least one child.*

Among the thousands upon thousands of people who flocked to California during the gold rush that began in the late 1840s was one who dressed in men's clothes, did not speak much, and never grew a beard. Calling herself Charley Parkhurst, she became a stagecoach driver, sometimes controlling a six-horse team pulling a 20-passenger coach, and from the mid-1850s drove the mountain route between Santa Cruz and San Jose. This was a dangerous job on rugged roads where one misstep could plunge horses, coach and occupants over the side of the mountain, and armed robbers were not uncommon; legend has it that on being ambushed on the job a second time Parkhurst killed the would-be robber with a shotgun. She wore a black patch to cover a missing eye that had been kicked out by a horse, and, while not voluble, she drank, smoked, and played cards and rolled dice with other drivers, familiarly called "whips," and with miners. In 1868, Parkhurst voted in the presidential election between Civil War hero Ulysses S. Grant and former governor of New York Horatio Seymour, giving her age as 55 when registering. Around that time she quit driving a stagecoach and ran a saloon and way station on the road between Santa Cruz and Watsonville. She next raised cattle and then chickens, and after suffering from poor health died in a cabin near Watsonville on December 29, 1879. Those preparing Parkhurst's body for burial in the Watsonville Cemetery were stunned to discover that "One-Eyed" Charley was, in fact, a woman, and the ordinary, self-contained ex-stagecoach driver became famous throughout California.

Little is known for sure about Parkhurst's early years, although sources suggest (or speculate) that she was born Charlotte Parkhurst in New Hampshire around 1812 and consigned to an orphanage in Massachusetts at a young age. At some point, she apparently fled the orphanage dressed as a boy, and found work as a stable hand. (Obviously preferring to work outdoors, she probably found this more congenial than the domestic service that was one of the better options available to girls from orphanages at the time.) She learned how to drive a team of horses, and by 1850 or 1851 had arrived in California. A doctor who examined her dead body is said to have claimed that she had borne at least one child. While much was made after her death of her "deception," it has also been suggested that many who knew Parkhurst were aware that she was a woman, and apparently saw no reason to challenge her. In 1955, the Pajaro Valley Historical Association placed a stone above her grave in the Watsonville Cemetery (now the Pioneer Cemetery). Its inscription, which includes note of the fact that she was the first woman to vote in a United States presidential election—American women did not gain suffrage until 52 years after she cast her vote—memorializes her as a "Noted whip of the gold rush days."

SUGGESTED READING:

Ryan, Pam Munoz. *Riding Freedom.* NY: Scholastic Press, 1998 (a fictionalized account of Parkhurst's life for grades 3 to 6, includes factual information in author's note).

Howard Gofstein,
freelance writer, Oak Park, Michigan

Parks, Rosa (1913—)

Veteran African-American activist whose arrest for refusing to give up her seat to a white man on a segregated bus in Montgomery, Alabama, triggered a black boycott of the bus line and helped launch the civil-rights movement in the United States. *Born Rosa Louise McCauley on February 4, 1913, in Tuskegee, Alabama; daughter of James McCauley (a carpenter) and Leona (Edwards) McCauley (a schoolteacher); attended segregated schools in Pine Level and Montgomery, Alabama; received high school diploma, 1933; married Raymond Parks, in 1932 (died 1977); no children.*

*Awards: Spingarn Medal from National Association for the Advancement of Colored People (1979); Martin Luther King, Jr., Nonviolent Peace Prize (1980); ****Eleanor Roosevelt*** *Woman of Courage Award from Wonder Woman Foundation (1984); received the Presidential Medal of Freedom (1996); awarded the Congressional gold medal (1999); awarded at least ten honorary degrees.*

Sent to Montgomery to live with relatives and attend Montgomery Industrial School for Girls (1924); became secretary of the local NAACP, forced from city bus for using "white" door (December 1943); after repeated efforts, was registered to vote (1945); became adviser to NAACP Youth Council (1949); arrested and convicted of refusing, in violation of Alabama law, to surrender a bus seat to a white man (December 1955); participated in the Montgomery Bus Boycott (1955–56); U.S. Supreme Court affirms lower court decision declaring bus segregation to be unconstitutional (November 13, 1956); moved to Detroit (1957); participated in March on Washington (1963); participated in Selma-to-Montgomery march for voting rights (March 1965); worked in Detroit office of Congressman John Conyers (1965–88); beaten and robbed by a burglar (1994); bust of Rosa Parks unveiled at the Smithsonian Institution (February 28, 1991); awarded the Congressional gold medal (1999); awarded first Governor's Medal of Honor for Extraordinary Courage from state of Alabama (December 1, 2000); Rosa Parks Library and Museum at Troy State University opened (December 1, 2000).

Publications: Rosa Parks: My Story *(Dial, 1992);* Quiet Strength *(Zondervan, 1994).*

Shortly after 5:00 PM, on Thursday, December 1, 1955, Rosa Parks, a seamstress at the Montgomery Fair department store, caught the Cleveland Avenue bus on her way home from work. By city ordinance, Montgomery buses were racially segregated. The first ten seats on the Cleveland Avenue bus were reserved for whites; the remaining 26 seats were for blacks. Parks took a seat in the 11th row, along with two other black women and a black man.

Two blocks later, after the bus stopped at the Empire Theater, white passengers filled the front of the bus. The white driver, James F. Blake, ordered the four black passengers in the 11th row to stand and make room for one white man. Strictly speaking, under the Montgomery ordinance, Blake lacked the authority to extend the white section of the bus, but Alabama state law seemed to give drivers broad discretion to maintain segregation on their vehicles. At first, none of the blacks moved. Blake repeated his order. "Y'all better make it light on yourselves and let me have those seats." Everyone but Parks moved to the back of the bus. When Blake told her, "I'm going to have you arrested," Parks replied, "You may go on and do so." As hurried and nervous passengers began to scramble off the bus, Blake called the police, and within minutes Rosa Parks was under arrest. That arrest produced a yearlong black boycott of Montgomery's buses, catapulted Martin Luther King, Jr., to national prominence as a civil-rights leader, and marked the beginning of a grassroots movement for racial equality in the United States. It also earned Parks a reputation as "the first lady of civil rights" and "the mother of the civil rights movement." "To this day," writes **Rita Dove**, she "remains a symbol of dignity in the face of brute authority. . . . It is the modesty of Rosa Parks' example that sustains us. It is no

less than the belief in the power of the individual, that cornerstone of the American Dream, that she inspires, along with the hope that all of us—even the least of us—could be that brave, that serenely human, when crunch time comes."

Rosa Parks grew up in a segregated society. Her mother **Leona Edwards McCauley** was a rural schoolteacher. Her father James McCauley was an itinerant carpenter and stone mason. They met in Pine Level, Alabama, where Leona taught school and James' brother pastored a black church. The couple married in April 1912 and moved to Tuskegee, where Rosa was born on February 4, 1913. The family soon moved again, to Abbeville, Alabama, James' hometown, and then returned to Pine Level. Shortly after leaving Abbeville, Leona gave birth to a son, Sylvester McCauley, and at about the same time, James left Pine Level to look for work in the North. Rosa, not quite three years old, had little contact with her father as she grew older.

At Pine Level, Leona and the children lived with her parents, Sylvester and **Rose Edwards**. Since Sylvester was the son of a white plantation owner and a slave housekeeper, Rosa was of mixed African and Scotch-Irish descent. Influenced by her mother and grandfather, Rosa became a studious, well-mannered child who understood and resented the dangers and indignities faced by blacks living in the Deep South. In later years, Parks said she never saw a member of the Ku Klux Klan as a child, but she recalled her grandfather keeping a gun in the house for protection. "If people said the Klan was going to come," she remembered, "you'd stay inside." A small, light-complected girl, Parks also remembered Grandfather Edwards attending a rally of the Universal Negro Improvement Association, the black nationalist organization founded by Marcus Garvey, that was active in the 1920s. The UNIA rejected her grandfather because, ironically, he was too light-skinned. Parks said years later, "that ended our talk about going back to Africa."

I did not get on the bus to get arrested. I got on the bus to go home.

—Rosa Parks

In 1924, Parks' mother sent her to the Montgomery Industrial School for Girls, a private school operated by **Alice L. White**. Miss White's School, as it was commonly known, enjoyed an excellent academic reputation, but the headmistress, a white liberal from Melrose, Massachusetts, was generally ostracized by Montgomery's white community, and the school closed before Rosa could graduate. She later attended Montgomery's Booker T. Washington Junior High School and then took classes under student-teachers at Alabama State Teachers College for Negroes (now Alabama State University). Montgomery did not have a regular public high school for blacks until 1938. Parks' mother hoped her daughter could become a teacher herself, and Rosa apparently considered a nursing career, but at age 16, as Leona's health began to fail, Rosa quit school to look after her mother and her younger brother.

In 1931, Rosa met Raymond Parks, a black barber from Randolph County, Alabama. Raymond, who had endured an even more difficult childhood than Rosa, had little formal education, but he stimulated her interest in civil rights. "Parks," she said (she always referred to him by his last name), "was . . . the first real activist I ever met." A member of the National Association for the Advancement of Colored People (NAACP), Raymond helped with the legal defense (apparently by raising money) of the "Scottsboro boys," a group of very young black men convicted, on all but nonexistent evidence, of raping two white women, ***Ruby Bates** and **Victoria Price**. Meanwhile, Rosa returned to school and finally earned a high school degree, although few good jobs were open to educated black women in Montgomery in the 1930s. Rosa Parks worked as a housekeeper, an insurance agent, an office clerk, and eventually as an assistant tailor at Montgomery Fair. Soft spoken, dignified, and a faithful member of the African Methodist Episcopal Church, Parks came to be considered a part of Montgomery's black middle class, but her inability to find a suitable job, along with a general pattern of racial discrimination, fueled in her what historian J. Mills Thornton has described as "a certain bitterness."

In 1943, Parks joined the NAACP after she saw a picture of Johnnie Carr, a classmate from Miss White's School, in the local black newspaper. Carr was serving as the organization's secretary. Though Raymond was no longer an active member, Rosa replaced her old friend as secretary, and held the post until 1956. She ran the Montgomery office for E.D. Nixon, the state president of the NAACP and an official in the Brotherhood of Sleeping Car Porters, an important black trade union. As secretary, Parks reported acts of violence against Alabama blacks to the national headquarters, and she encouraged Montgomery blacks to register to vote. She tried to register too, first in 1943 and again in 1944, before finally becoming, in 1945, one of the few registered black voters in Alabama. Parks also served as an adviser to the NAACP's local Youth Council and tried, unsuccessfully, to win African-American teenagers access to Montgomery's main public library.

A major grievance of Montgomery blacks was the city's segregated bus system, the primary means of transportation for 50,000 African-Americans. Besides being physically separated from whites, blacks experienced other forms of discrimination on buses as well. They were required, for example, to pay their fare at the front of the vehicle and then leave the bus to re-enter through a back door. The drivers, many blacks said, would sometimes pull away before black passengers could get back on the bus. In December 1943, Parks herself had been ordered off a bus for using the "white-only" front door. The bus driver "wanted me to get off the bus and go around and get back on," she said. "I wouldn't do it." Livid, he grabbed her coat sleeve and forced her off the bus. "I was afraid he would attack me physically," she said. For the next 12 years, Parks remembered the face of that driver. "I saw him occasionally when I was waiting for the bus, but I didn't ride the bus if he was driving."

Rosa Parks under arrest in Montgomery.

Even before Parks' arrest in 1955, ***Jo Ann Robinson**, an English professor at Alabama State and a member of the Women's Political Council (WPC), a black civic group, had been contemplating a bus boycott, as had other African-American leaders. The NAACP was also looking for a test case to challenge bus segregation in court. Other black women, in particular **Claudette Colvin**, had run afoul of the system by refusing to surrender seats to white passengers. In the spring of 1955, Montgomery police physically removed the 15-year-old Colvin from a bus. But NAACP officials decided not to pursue her case when they learned she was pregnant and unmarried. They needed a representative who would be above reproach, and Rosa Parks was perfect for the role. As civil-rights leader Ralph David Abernathy, then pastor of Montgomery's black First Baptist Church, explained, "She had an air of gentility about her that usually evoked respect among whites as well as blacks, and I doubt that anybody who knew her could have imagined that she would ever end up in jail." Yet Parks said later that she had not intended to become a test case. "I wasn't planning to be arrested at all," she said. "I had a full weekend planned. It was December, Christmastime. It was the busy time of year, and I was preparing for the weekend workshop for the Youth Council." On the other hand, she did not, as legend has it, refuse to move simply because she was too tired. "The only tired I was," she has written, "was tired of giving in." In a hurry to get home that night, and with her mind on other things, Parks had not noticed as she boarded the bus that it was being driven by the same man with whom she had tangled 12 years earlier. "He was still mean looking," she said.

By the weekend following her arrest, the WPC, local NAACP officials, and a group of black ministers had organized a bus boycott to begin on Monday, December 5, the day Parks was to be tried in the City Recorder's Court. After a brief hearing, a white judge fined Parks ten dollars, plus four dollars in court costs. Her lawyers immediately announced that they would appeal. On the same day, the Montgomery Improvement Association (MIA) was organized to direct the boycott. Under the leadership of Martin Luther King, Jr., at the time the young minister of the Dexter Avenue Baptist Church, the MIA created an efficient network of taxis, private cars, and church station wagons to provide an alternative to the city buses. Parks served on the MIA board of directors. For the next year, few blacks rode the city system. But Montgomery officials refused to desegregate the buses until the Supreme Court, in November 1956, upheld a lower court decision declaring segregation on Alabama's city buses to be unconstitutional. The boycott itself had not ended discrimination on the buses, but it set a precedent for the kind of peaceful mass protest that would characterize the civil-rights movement for the next decade and help produce such landmark legislation as the Civil Rights Act of 1964 and the Voting Rights Act of 1965.

Parks meanwhile lost her job at Montgomery Fair, and Raymond quit his job as a barber at the nearby Maxwell Air Force Base. Alabama authorities indicted her, and dozens of other black leaders, for violating an anti-boycott law, but her case never came to trial. In 1957, to escape harassment, Parks, her mother, and Raymond moved to Detroit, where her brother Sylvester had lived since the end of World War II. She spent 1958 at the Hampton Institute in Virginia, where she served as hostess for visitors to the historic black college, but she soon returned to Detroit to be with her family. In Detroit, she worked as a seamstress, became active in the Southern Christian Leadership Conference, and served as a deaconess at St. Matthew AME Church. She attended the civil-rights rally climaxing the 1963 March on Washington and heard Martin Luther King deliver his famous "I Have a Dream" speech. In March 1965, she participated in King's march from Selma, Alabama, to Montgomery in support of black voting rights. From 1965 to 1988, she worked in the Detroit office of U.S. congressional representative John Conyers, a black Democrat. Parks has remained active in recent years, although her husband Raymond died in 1977, and her mother died in 1978. In 1987, Parks founded the Rosa and Raymond Parks Institute for Self-Development to promote the education of disadvantaged young people.

Parks made headlines once more in September 1994 when a burglar entered her home, stole $50 in cash, and beat her in the face and chest. The Detroit community was outraged, as were people around the world. A suspect was arrested within hours.

In recent years, Parks has received many honors. In 1996, she received the Presidential Medal of Freedom from Bill Clinton. In 1999, she was given the Congressional gold medal, the highest civilian award given by Congress. Her portrait hangs in Detroit's Museum of African-American History and a Rosa Parks bust is on display at the Smithsonian Institution. "I have more honorary degrees and plaques and awards than I can count," she wrote in 1992, "and I appreciate and cherish every single one of them." On December 1, 2000, 45 years to the day after she refused to give up her seat on the bus, Parks attended the dedication of Troy State University's Rosa Parks Library and Museum, which stands on the streetcorner where she was arrested. Prior to the ceremony, Parks was awarded Alabama's first Governor's Medal of Honor for Extraordinary Courage. Montgomery's old Cleveland Avenue, where Parks was arrested in December 1955, is today Rosa Parks Boulevard.

SOURCES:

Abernathy, Ralph David. *And the Walls Came Tumbling Down: An Autobiography*. NY: Harper & Row, 1989.

Dove, Rita. "The Torchbearer," in *Time*. June 14, 1999.

Garrow, David J., ed. *The Walking City: The Montgomery Bus Boycott, 1955–1956*. Brooklyn, NY: Carlson, 1989.

Hill, Ruth Edmonds. "Rosa Parks" in Jessie Carney Smith, ed., *Notable Black American Women*. Detroit, MI: Gale Research, 1992.

The New York Times. December 2, 2000, p. A16.

Parks, Rosa, with Jim Haskins. *Rosa Parks: My Story*. NY: Dial Books, 1992.

Ragghianti, Marie. "I Wanted to Be Treated Like a Human Being," in *Parade*. January 19, 1992.

Robinson, Jo Ann. *The Montgomery Bus Boycott and the Women Who Started It.* Knoxville, TN: University of Tennessee Press, 1987.

SUGGESTED READING:

Branch, Taylor. *Parting the Waters: America in the King Years, 1954–63.* NY: Simon & Schuster, 1988.

Brinkley, Douglas. *Rosa Parks.* "Penguin Lives" series. Lipper-Viking Books, 2000.

Parks, Rosa, and Gregory Reed. *Quiet Strength.* Zondervan, 1995.

Sitkoff, Harvard. *The Struggle for Black Equality, 1954–1992.* Rev. ed. NY: Hill and Wang, 1993.

COLLECTIONS:

Black Women Oral History Project Interview with Rosa Parks, Schlesinger Library, Radcliffe College, Cambridge, MA.

The Rosa L. Parks Collection, Archives of Labor and Urban Affairs, Wayne State University, Detroit, Michigan.

Rosa Parks Library and Museum at Troy State University, Montgomery, Alabama, includes an interactive exhibit reenacting Parks' arrest as well as a statue of Parks and documentation of the bus boycott.

Jeff Broadwater,
Assistant Professor of History, Barton College,
Wilson, North Carolina

Parlby, Irene (1868–1965)

Canadian politician, feminist and advocate of social reform. *Pronunciation: I-reen-ee Parl-bee. Born Mary Irene Marryat on January 9, 1868, in London, England; died on July 12, 1965, in Red Deer, Alberta; first child of Colonel Ernest Lindsay Marryat (an engineer) and Elizabeth Lynch Marryat; had no formal education; married Walter Parlby, in 1897; children: Humphrey Parlby (b. 1899).*

Irene Parlby was born Mary Irene Marryat on January 9, 1868, into a comfortable, middle-class family in London, England. Her father Ernest Lindsay Marryat had formerly enjoyed a distinguished career in the British army, rising to the rank of colonel in the Royal Engineers. Following his resignation from the army, he had become a civil engineer working for railroad companies in India. Her mother **Elizabeth Lynch Marryat** had returned from India to London for the birth of her daughter but, immediately following this event, rejoined her husband. The family was closely related to the famous author Captain Frederick Marryat.

The Marryats spent the next 16 years alternating homes in India (1868–71, 1881–84) and England. In India, Ernest was attached to the military base at Rawalpindi in the Punjab but, during the hot season, the family retired to Murree in the Himalayan foothills. During these years, Parlby's education (along with that of her seven siblings) was entirely in the hands of a series of governesses. The quality of her tutors varied considerably, but she did manage to establish an adequate grounding in such subjects as history, music, drawing, French, and arithmetic. Irene's father finally retired from India in 1888. He returned to England and bought a house at Lympsfield in Surrey but continued to serve as an official in the London offices of the Bengal North-Western Railroad and the Delta Light Railway.

Parlby greatly enjoyed the years she spent in India and left with much regret. Her new life in England, however, had its own attractions. The family's social position allowed her the opportunity to engage in a variety of sporting activities, such as tennis and field hockey, and she was also an enthusiastic equestrian. Meanwhile, in the evenings, there were many parties and dances to attend. Parlby occasionally traveled abroad to Europe and, when she was 17, spent six months in Germany with some family friends. During these months, she studied music and became fluent in the German language.

Despite her rich and varied social whirl, Parlby was dissatisfied and began to seek a vocation in life. In this, she was encouraged by her father who, singularly for a man in this era, approved of women attending college and entering the professions. Ernest suggested to his daughter a variety of careers but strongly recommended that she study medicine. He was disappointed when she declined this option but allowed her to make up her own mind. When, however, Irene suggested that she was considering becoming an actor or a writer, Ernest drew the line and politely, but firmly, said no.

In 1894, Parlby was taken seriously ill, and it was recommended that she spend some time in Switzerland until her health improved. After several months, she was able to return to England but her enforced convalescence had left her more dissatisfied than ever with her status in life. Not long after, however, she was introduced to an old family friend, Mrs. Westhead, who, with her husband, had just returned from Canada for a holiday in England. The Westheads, who owned a small ranch at Buffalo Lake, approximately 30 miles east of Edmonton in present-day Alberta, Canada, invited Irene to return to Canada with them and live on their ranch. With her father's approval, she left England in May 1896.

Once settled at the ranch at Buffalo Lake, Parlby thoroughly began to enjoy her life in a pioneer community. She helped Mrs. Westhead in various tasks around the house but had plenty of time to engage in her favorite hobby, horseback riding. As Parlby later recounted, she was "never homesick" for she felt "the exhilarating feeling of living where the world was really young . . . the freshness, the spaciousness, the extraordinary quietness of an unpeopled land."

Among the few neighbors at Buffalo Lake were two brothers, Edward and Walter Parlby. The former had arrived from England in 1886 to establish his own small ranch. His brother Walter had attended Oxford University where he had been noted as both an outstanding scholar and athlete. Originally, Walter had wished to enter the church but, when his father did not approve, had traveled instead to Assam in India to work on a tea plantation. Walter had come from Assam in 1890 in what was intended to be only a short visit to his brother, but he had been so impressed with life in the Canadian west that he had never left.

She has set a high standard in every way for Canadian women engaging in political careers.

—The Edmonton Journal

Shortly after Irene's arrival at Buffalo Lake, she and Walter were introduced. She was impressed by this tall, quiet-spoken and witty man who combined a love of ranching with a love of scholarly investigation. They took to each other immediately and were married in March 1897. Following the ceremony, the couple moved into their own nearby ranch (located by what is now called Parlby Lake) and settled down to raising cattle and breeding horses. Despite the severe winters and the constant threat of an onset of stock diseases, the couple enjoyed their new life together. In late 1899, however, they left their ranch and traveled to England, where Irene gave birth to their son, Humphrey.

The family returned home the following spring accompanied by **Gladys Marryat** one of Irene's sisters. Shortly afterwards, their father Ernest paid them a visit, and he was so impressed by the country that he decided to move the rest of his family to the same location. For the next few years, the Parlbys and the Marryats settled down to expand their ranching interests. They were so successful that they quickly became among the most prominent families in the area.

The province of Alberta (along with the province of Saskatchewan) was created only in 1905, out of what was then the Northwest Territories. At that time, it lacked any provincial farmers' organization. This situation was only remedied four years later with the formation of the United Farmers of Alberta (UFA), to represent the economic and political interests of farmers to both the provincial and federal governments. Its main demands were for tariff reductions on the sale of agricultural products, financial aid for livestock marketing, an insurance program guarding farmers against the effects of bad weather, rural credit aid, and the creation of a cooperative distribution system for farm products.

At its convention in 1912, UFA delegates outlined a series of education programs that were designed to propagate their views more widely and to increase the organization's membership. More significantly, the delegates passed a strongly worded resolution supporting the principle of women's suffrage and urged women to organize themselves for their own betterment in particular and for the betterment of the farming industry in general. In the following years, the UFA made good on its previous resolutions by allowing women farmers to enroll on equal terms in the organization. So many women did so that it quickly became necessary to organize them in a special women's auxiliary.

Irene Parlby had always been impressed by how, in rural areas, women and men were able to act cooperatively on terms of relative equality. She was enthusiastically supported in these views by both her husband and father, who urged her to stand as secretary of the women's auxiliary club in their area. In this capacity, she was elected as a delegate to the 1916 UFA convention in Calgary, at which she read a paper entitled "A Woman's Place in the Nation." This performance so impressed her colleagues that they elected her the provincial president of the auxiliary movement. One of Parlby's first tasks was to increase the independence of the movement, and this was recognized by a change of name to the United Farm Women of Alberta (UFWA).

In June of the same year, Parlby conducted her first organizational tour throughout Alberta. She believed that increasing the number of UFWA branches would broaden the amount of social contact between farm women, who were still largely isolated. In addition, she began a program of close cooperation with leaders of the UFA in order to coordinate their approach on all matters of welfare affecting farm people. She also assumed a leading role in pressuring the provincial government to enact improvements in the standards of child welfare. Finally, Irene argued for the provision of a system of public health nurses in rural areas where the lack of doctors often put the lives of pregnant women and their babies in jeopardy.

Irene Parlby

Her reputation as an articulate advocate of the rights of farm women quickly gained Parlby a national reputation. In February 1918, she was invited by the Canadian government to attend the Dominion conference in the nation's capital, Ottawa. There, she was asked to advise on a variety of issues, including the role of women in war industries and the question of women's immigration. She was also asked to recommend appointees to sit on the Board of Governors at the University of Alberta (a position she herself held from 1919 to 1921) as well as on the executive committee of the Alberta Red Cross society. Two years later, in 1920, Parlby stepped down as president of the UFWA.

Since its inception, the UFA had enjoyed a tacit political alliance with the Liberal Party administration which then dominated Alberta politics. For many years, this alliance led to the implementation of several progressive pieces of legislation, including suffrage for women (granted in 1916), measures to extend rural credit, and the formation of cooperative ventures. The UFA had less success, however, when it came to influencing the policies of the federal Canadian government. Things came to a head at the end of World War I, when an increasingly weak provincial Liberal administration was unable to do anything to persuade Prime Minister Robert Borden to address the issues of rural poverty. At its convention in 1919, the UFA called for a more active policy of intervention in the political process.

Their chance came with the provincial election that was called in early July 1921. Much to their own surprise, the UFA won a majority of seats in the Alberta legislature with Parlby easily winning in the riding (district) of Lacombe. The new premier of Alberta, Herbert Greenfield, was an old friend of the Parlbys and one of his first acts was to appoint Irene a minister without portfolio in the new government. According to the official statement, she was chosen "primarily as representing the women of the province and to bring the woman's viewpoint to the discussion of governmental affairs." With this appointment, Parlby became only the second woman in Canadian politics to be nominated to a Cabinet post.

As a minister without portfolio, Parlby had no special area of responsibility under her jurisdiction. Rather, she was assigned the job of ambassador-at-large and charged with promoting government policy, particularly in the fields of welfare, education, and health. In addition, she was assigned a number of special duties by her Cabinet colleagues. For instance, in 1924, she was the official government observer to the first conference of the International Council of Women held in Washington, D.C. Four years later, the Alberta government sent her on a tour of Denmark and Sweden in order to study the organization and impact of rural cooperatives. Her subsequent report did much to promote the growth of similar enterprises in Alberta.

One of Parlby's most important contributions to the women's movement in Canada began in 1927. In that year, ***Emily Murphy**, a police magistrate in Edmonton, invited Parlby, along with ***Louise McKinney**, ***Nellie McClung**, and ***Henrietta Muir Edwards**, to petition the Judicial Committee of the Imperial Privy Council in London (the supreme legal authority of the British Empire). At that time, women were not allowed to be appointed to the Senate, the upper house of the Canadian legislature. This was because Section 24 of the British North America Act stated that only "qualified persons" were eligible to sit in the Senate and, according to the Supreme Court of Canada, women could not be considered as qualified persons. After a long legal challenge (which was strongly supported throughout by Parlby and her other Cabinet colleagues), the Privy Council overruled the Supreme Court's decision. It was this ruling, the culmination of what is now known as the "Persons" case, which led to the appointment of the first female senator in Canadian history, ***Cairine Wilson**.

In 1930, the federal prime minister R.B. Bennett, asked Parlby to represent Canada as a delegate to the Assembly of the League of Nations in Geneva, Switzerland. She later described this assignment as one of the "highlights of her life" for it gave her the opportunity to meet some of the most distinguished international leaders of the day. Unfortunately, on her trip home she became seriously ill, and this precluded her active involvement in politics for a considerable time. In 1934, she announced her intention to not seek re-election in the provincial election due the following year. This turned out to be a fortuitous decision. The economic circumstances of the Great Depression had taken a heavy toll on the popularity of the UFA; so much so that, in the election, every one of their members of Parliament lost his or her seat.

This event marked the effective end of Irene Parlby's public career. She retired to the family ranch, where she spent most of her time in what was now her favorite hobby, gardening. Nevertheless, Parlby did continue to take an active interest in farm women's organizations and rural affairs. She wrote occasionally for magazines (such as *The Grain Growers Guide, The Canadian Magazine* and *The Country Guide*) on such topics as gardening, current affairs, and the value of cooperation. In the 1940s, she participated in a number of radio broadcasts for the nationally based Canadian Broadcast Corporation.

Her husband died in 1952, and in the years that followed Parlby suffered increasingly from recurring bouts of ill health. She lived in quiet seclusion before passing away in her sleep in July 1965, only three years short of her 100th birthday.

SOURCES:

Kaplan, Fred. "Irene Parlby," in *Alberta Historical Review.* Spring 1962.

MacLean, Una. "The Honorable Irene Parlby," in *Alberta Historical Review.* Spring 1959.

McKinlay, Claire Mary. *The Honorable Irene Parlby.* Edmonton: West Canada Graphic Industries, 1978.

Roe, Amy J. "Then and Now," in *The Country Guide.* January 1939.

SUGGESTED READING:

Aubrey, Louis. *A History of the Farmers' Movements in Canada.* Toronto: Ryerson Press, 1924.

Cleverdon, Catherine Lyle. *The Women Suffrage Movement in Canada.* Toronto: University of Toronto Press, 1950.

Morton, W.L. *The Progressive Party in Canada.* Toronto: University of Toronto Press, 1950.

COLLECTIONS:

Private papers and letters held by the Parlby family.

Dave Baxter,
Department of Philosophy, Wilfrid Laurier University,
Waterloo, Ontario, Canada

Parlo, Dita (1906–1971)

German-born actress. *Born Grethe Gerda Kornstadt (or Kornwald), on September 4, 1906, in Stettin, Germany; died in 1971.*

Selected filmography—in Germany: Die Dame mit der Maske *(*The Lady with the Mask, *1928),* Geheimnisse des Orients *(*Secrets of the Orient, *1928),* Heimkehr *(*Homecoming, *1928),* Ungarische Rhapsodie *(*Hungarian Rhapsody, *1928),* Manolescu *(1929),* Melodie des Herzens *(*Melody of the Heart, *1929); in the US:* The Hollywood Revue of 1929 *(German-language version, 1930),* Menschen hinter Gittern *(German-language version of* The Big House, *1930),* Kismet *(German-language version, 1931),* Honor of the Family *(1931),* Mr. Broadway *(1933); in France:* Rapt *(*The Mystic Mountain, *Fr.-Switz., 1934),* L'Atalante *(1934),* Mademoiselle Docteur *(*Street of Shadows, *1937),* L'Affaire du Courrier de Lyon *(*The Courier of Lyons, *1937),* La Grande Illusion *(*Grand Illusion, *1937),* Ultimatum *(1938),* Paix sur le Rhin *(1938),* L'Inconnue de Monte-Carlo *(1939),* Justice est faite *(*Justice Is Done, *1959),* Quand le Soleil montera *(1956),* La Dame de Pique *(1965).*

Dita Parlo was born Grethe Gerda Kornstadt in 1906 in Stettin, Germany. From her first appearance in the film *The Lady with the Mask* (1928), she was marked for stardom in her native country, although her delicate, romantic persona never quite won over Hollywood audiences. After a few unsuccessful American projects in the early 1930s, she made her way to France, where she enjoyed another resurgence of popularity. Shortly after the outbreak of World War II, however, she was arrested as an alien by the French authorities and deported back to Germany. She reemerged in the 1950s, appearing in three more films before her death in 1971.

Parloa, Maria (1843–1909)

American domestic economist and author. *Born Maria Parloa on September 25, 1843, in Massachusetts; died of acute nephritis on August 21, 1909, in Bethel, Connecticut; nothing is known of her parents or early years; attended the Maine Central Institute, in Pittsfield.*

Maria Parloa, an authority on the proper preparation of food and household management, lectured and wrote on these subjects extensively. In 1877, she was special instructor at various seminaries, and gave courses of lessons in sickroom cookery to Harvard medical students. After visiting Paris for study, she opened a cooking school in New York City. Her publications include *Miss Parloa's New Cook Book and Marketing Guide, The Young Housekeeper,* and *Home Economics.*

Parlow, Kathleen (1890–1963)

Canadian violinist. *Born Kathleen Mary Parlow in Calgary, Canada, in 1890; died in 1963.*

Born in Calgary, Canada, in 1890, Kathleen Parlow received her first musical instruction in San Francisco, California, from Henry Holmes, an English violinist. Her progress was so rapid that in 1905 he took her to London and exhibited her in concert as a prodigy; it brought her a command performance before England's queen, ***Alexandra of Denmark**. Later, Parlow studied with Leopold Auer in St. Petersburg, and made her debut as an artist in the Russian capital in 1908. Her success was overwhelming. After touring extensively until 1941, she retired in Toronto to teach and lead her own string quartet.

Parma, duchess of.

See Guzman, Leonora de for sidebar on Maria of Portugal (1313–1357).
See Margaret of Parma (1522–1586).
See Maria of Portugal (1538–1577).
See Margaret of Parma (1612–?).
See Farnese, Elizabeth (1692–1766).
See Louise Elizabeth (1727–1759).
See Maria Amalia (1746–1804).
See Marie Louise of Austria (1791–1847).
See Theresa of Savoy (1803–1879).
See Louise of Bourbon-Berry (1819–1864).

Parnell, Anna (1852–1911)

Co-founder and leader of the Ladies' Land League, the first women's political organization in Ireland, which was suppressed by her brother, Charles Stewart Parnell, in 1882. *Born Catherine Maria Anna Mercer Parnell on May 13, 1852, at Avondale, near Rathdrum, County Wicklow; drowned off Ilfracombe, Devon, in 1911; daughter of John Henry Parnell (a landowner) and Delia (Stewart) Parnell; sister of Charles Stewart Parnell (1846–1891, Irish reformer and politician); sister-in-law of* ****Katherine O'Shea*** *(1845–1921); educated at home, at the Royal Dublin Society Art School and the South Kensington School of Design; never married; no children.*

Following her father's death (1859), the family left Avondale, living in Dublin, Paris and London; while studying in London, attended parliamentary sittings and wrote accounts of them for an Irish-American journal; helped to organize an American fund for the relief of famine in Ireland (1879–80); established the Central Land League of the Ladies of Ireland (LLL), of which she became organizing secretary and effective leader (January 1881); co-ordinated and took part in the League's activities throughout Ireland (1881–82); LLL dissolved by her brother, Charles Stewart Parnell (August 1882), after which she retired from public life; moved to England, where she lived for the remainder of her life (1886); Charles Stewart Parnell died, having lost the support of the majority of his own Irish Party (1891); with publication of Michael Davitt's The Fall of Feudalism in Ireland, *which contained criticism of the LLL (1904), was prompted to produce her own account,* The Tale of a Great Sham; *unable to find a publisher; lost manuscript of* Tale *discovered (1959) and published (1986).*

The summer of 1882 saw Ireland in a state of acute political tension: the recently released leaders of the Land League were engaged in delicate negotiations with the government; the country had recently been shocked by the murder of the chief secretary and under-secretary by members of a nationalist secret society; and agrarian violence, evictions and distress were widespread in the countryside. On a morning in June, Anna Parnell arrived as usual at the headquarters of the Ladies' Land League, which under her leadership had been in the forefront of the struggle for tenant rights. Among the volunteer workers already in the office was the young ***Katharine Tynan**, who in her autobiography, *Twenty-five Years,* described Parnell's entrance that day, with "her curiously gentle, gliding pace . . . the very embodiment . . . of a delicate austere lady, just verging on spinsterhood." Speaking as softly as ever, but with "a subdued excitement in her face and manner," Parnell told Tynan and the others that she had just encountered the viceroy and his armed escort in the street outside. Said Parnell:

> I went out into the roadway and stopped his horse. "What do you mean, Lord Spencer," I said, "by interfering with the houses I am building for evicted tenants?" He only stared at me and muttered something, lifting his hat. I held his horse by the head-piece till he heard me. Then I went back to the pavement.

Horrified, her listeners protested that her action was insane, that she might have been killed, but Parnell was unrepentant. "I had to tell him," she said, "that he ought not to interfere with the housing of the evicted tenants."

This incident epitomizes the passion, courage and disregard for convention which characterized so much of Anna Parnell's history. Born at the family home of Avondale in 1852, she was the tenth child and fifth daughter of John Parnell, a substantial landowner, and his American wife, **Delia Parnell**. As Roy Foster points out in his biography of Anna's brother, Charles Stewart Parnell, the children of the family divided into two distinct groups, the first generally quiet and retiring, while the second—to which Anna, her older sister **Fanny Parnell**, and Charles Stewart belonged—was "strong-minded, individualistic . . . intellectually oriented and politically minded." In this, Foster suggests, they resembled their mother, whose romantic nationalism has often been suggested as a strong childhood influence. In fact, this influence has probably been exaggerated, and Delia was in any case frequently absent during these years. The Parnells' marriage was apparently unhappy, and Delia, a strong-minded but erratic woman, disliked Irish country life, preferring instead to spend long periods in London and Paris; she and most of her children, including the seven-year-old Anna, were in Paris when her husband died suddenly in 1859.

John Parnell's death left his family poorly provided for; his widow and daughters were to have an income of only £100 a year, and Anna was later to write bitterly of Irish landlords' treatment of their own womenfolk, whose allowances were the first economies at times of distress, and who were, she considered, "little less the victims of the landlords than the tenants themselves." Thus, Anna's political views were shaped from the beginning by a strong sense of injustice, both on her own account and on behalf of her gender; though the Ladies' Land League was ostensibly a nationalist and not a feminist movement, it did nonetheless represent an assertion of the right of women to a political voice. Even as girls, Anna and Fanny were passionately interested in politics, both American and Irish, and in the current debate on the role of women; according to one account quoted by Foster, as a young woman Anna was "a regular reader . . . of New York and Boston journals, and . . . dipped into the lectures of American oratoresses who stood on the equal rights platform."

Parnell's formal education, like that of most girls of her class, was scanty, but she showed an early talent for art, and went on to take classes first in Dublin and later in London. By now, her brother Charles had begun his political career as a member of Parliament for the Irish Party at Westminster, and Anna frequently attended parliamentary sessions, sitting in the section of the public gallery set aside for women. These debates were often stormy: the Irish Party, in pursuit of its goal of home rule, had adopted a strategy of obstructing parliamentary business, and Charles Parnell himself was rapidly assuming a position of leadership within the party. From her seat in the "ladies' cage," Anna observed these developments, and noted her impressions in a series of well-informed and humorous articles, published in 1880 in an Irish-American paper, *The Celtic Monthly.*

By the end of the 1870s, however, political unrest in Ireland had given way to agricultural depression, to shortage and even famine, and ultimately to a tenant movement, culminating in the founding, in autumn 1879, of a National Land League, with Charles Parnell as its president. Anna, on a visit to her mother and Fanny, who were now living in America, threw herself into the direction of a Famine Relief Fund, displaying in the process the organizational skill, the self-confidence and the will to command which she shared with Charles, and which marked her later political career.

By mid-1880, with the land agitation intensifying in Ireland, contributions from Irish-Americans were showing a decline. It was at this point that Fanny Parnell conceived the idea of an organization which would, she hoped, bring "women's attributes of compassion and enthusiasm" to the ongoing struggle; as a result of her efforts, the first meeting of the New York Ladies' Land League was held on October 15, 1880. Within a short time, further branches were established throughout America, the success of the movement prompting the Land League in Ireland to consider the possibility of

Anna Parnell

setting up a similar organization there. The incentive to do so became greater with the increasing likelihood that the government would introduce a Coercion Act, under which the existing League leaders could be arrested: as one of them, Michael Davitt, pointed out, female supporters could be particularly useful in the event of repression, since the government might well be reluctant to move against them. Moreover, he said, his bias notwithstanding:

> No better allies than women could be found for such a task. They are, in certain emergencies, more dangerous to despotism than men. They have more courage, through having less scruples, when and where their better instincts are appealed to by a militant and just cause in a fight against a mean foe.

By now, Parnell was back in Ireland, and early in 1881 she received a letter from her brother, as president of the Land League, informing her of the decision to establish a Ladies' Land League (LLL), and asking her to take charge of the new body's Dublin office. This possibility had already been suggested to her by

Fanny; initially, however, Anna was unenthusiastic about the proposal, doubting both her own ability to do the job and the willingness of Irish women to join such an organization. She may, too, have been aware that, with the exception of Davitt, the members of the executive were dubious about the idea of a sister movement, which they regarded as a "most dangerous experiment," which might expose the whole cause to "public ridicule." However, she agreed to take on the task, becoming organizing secretary and effective leader of the Central Land League of the Ladies of Ireland, formally established in Dublin on January 31, 1881.

In a declaration issued shortly after its formation, the executive of the LLL appealed to all Irishwomen to take part in its campaign, and outlined its expectations of what that would involve.

> You cannot prevent the evictions, but you can and must prevent them from becoming massacres. Form yourselves into branches. . . . Be ready to give information of evictions in your districts, to give advice and encouragement to the unhappy victims, to collect funds, and to apply those which may be entrusted to you as emergencies arise.

Despite, or perhaps because of, the challenge which it presented to its members, the LLL expanded rapidly. By May 1881, it had 321 branches throughout Ireland, together with others in Britain, the U.S., Canada, Australia, and New Zealand. Public meetings were held throughout the country, at many of which Parnell herself was the main speaker: according to the *Nation* newspaper in April 1881, "the energy of Miss Anna Parnell is something extraordinary. Her desire to serve the cause of the Irish tenant is so great that she hardly gives herself a moment's rest."

During these first months of its existence, the LLL acted, officially at least, in full co-operation with the Land League; thus, finding its records in disarray, its members took on the compilation of a detailed register of estates, described admiringly by Davitt as "the most perfect system that can be imagined," while also organizing propaganda, sending representatives to monitor evictions and to urge support for the campaign, and offering practical assistance to those expelled for non-payment of rent. However, while some of the male leaders saw the LLL as primarily a charitable organization, Anna "strongly objected" to such a view. It was, she stressed, "a relief movement" rather than a charity, and on one occasion, praised for her ability to "work as well as weep," she retorted that she would leave the weeping to the men. Other differences also became apparent: the Ladies received little in the way of advice or material assistance from the parent body, and, as their confidence and capabilities grew, were more inclined to criticize its policy and management. As Anna declared, albeit lightly, in April, "I observe that we have succeeded today in getting rid of the men nearly entirely—and I am sure that we all feel much more comfortable in consequence." More serious were emerging political disagreements, with the LLL interpreting the ultimate aim of the movement in a more radical light than the male leadership. Thus, while Anna believed that "the programme of a permanent resistance until the aim of the League shall be attained, was the only logical one," her brother and his colleagues favored a more pragmatic approach. For Charles Parnell, the land war was part of a wider movement for Irish political independence; he was, therefore, anxious not to alienate more prosperous farmers who sought, not land redistribution, but simply secure possession and a reduction in rent, and were unlikely to subscribe to any policy, such as a comprehensive rent strike, which would leave them liable to eviction. While official rhetoric advocated payment of rent only "at the point of a bayonet," in practice, as Anna found, "the Land League had by no means the same objection to rent being paid as we had." Increasingly, she and the other Ladies became aware that, in encouraging the tenants' resistance, they were acting in opposition to League policy, and succeeding only in "raising forlorn hopes in the people."

As women operating in the political domain, the Ladies also faced criticism from other quarters, including members of the Catholic clergy. In March, for instance, Archbishop McCabe of Dublin issued a pastoral letter in which he denounced the organization as "degrading" to Irishwomen, who "are asked to forget the modesty of their sex, and the high dignity of their womanhood by leaders who seem utterly reckless of consequences." Supporters of the Land League, both lay and clerical, were quick to rush to the Ladies' defense, but there were many, even among these, whose attitude was distinctly ambivalent. Thus, the editor of the *Irish Canadian* newspaper regretted not so much the archbishop's condemnation, as the extreme language used; he himself, he acknowledged, regarded this organization of females as "bordering on the questionable." The hostile *Times* took a loftier line, dismissing the women's capacity for action with the remark that "when treason is reduced to fighting behind petticoats and pinafores, it is not likely to do much mischief."

In October 1881, however, the LLL acquired a new importance with the banning of the Land League and the arrest of those leaders not already in prison. The women's organization now assumed the task for which it originally had been intended, taking control of all the functions of the League to such effect that Cowper, the current viceroy, demanded "new measures" to deal with the continued agitation which, he alleged, "has been taken up by women [who] go about the country conveying messages and encouraging disaffection." In December, the LLL itself was suppressed, and in defiance of the ban, mass meetings were held all over the country on January 1, 1882. As one observer remarked, "five thousand ladies of Ireland were calling on the government to arrest them, and were preaching Land League doctrines as they were never preached before." Over the following months, LLL meetings were broken up by the police and a number of its members arrested, with 13 members serving jail sentences on a variety of charges. The women's willingness to face the indignities of imprisonment—and without the privileges which the male prisoners enjoyed—was an embarrassment to many Land League supporters: an editorial in the League paper *United Ireland* contrasted the courage of the Ladies with the apparent tameness of their male colleagues. "Shall it be said," it asked:

> That, while the Ladies' Land League met persecution by extending their organisation and doubling their activity and triumphing, the National Land League to which millions of men swore allegiance melted away and vanished the moment Mr Forster's policemen shook their batons at it?

Such comparisons of the performance of the female and male Land Leaguers were hardly calculated to calm the leadership's distrust of the women's role. Moreover, in its efforts to carry out League policy, the LLL was faced with the difficulty, as Anna expressed it, of trying to "make ropes of sea sand." Charles Parnell, without consulting the Ladies, who would, after all, have the responsibility of trying to persuade tenants to observe it, had finally issued a "No-Rent Manifesto." However, the declaration was more a cover for compromise with the government than a realistic policy, and Charles, because of his enforced absence, could evade responsibility for its almost inevitable failure. Increasingly, with the implementation of William Gladstone's 1881 Land Act, which granted tenants the right of free sale and introduced a method of arbitration in rent disputes, the more prosperous farmers came to terms with their landlords, leaving only the rural poor and the landless still defiant; violence and intimidation intensified, and this new crime wave was attributed to the policies pursued by the Ladies. In fact, agrarian violence was an established feature of Irish rural life, and Parnell himself was said to have predicted that if he were imprisoned, "Captain Moonlight" would take his place. Moreover, such activity was fostered not only by the government's refusal to make concessions, but also by the policies of the Land League itself, which throughout its campaign had employed a rhetoric which it had no intention of putting into practice, creating confusion and frustration among the most disadvantaged sectors of the rural population.

> I consider the actions of particular individuals are unimportant in history, while the actions of groups, classes, etc. of persons are most important, because the former are not met with again, and the latter are.
>
> **—Anna Parnell**

The worsening conditions, together with a vastly increased work load, added to the difficulties of Anna and the Ladies, as they faced the likelihood of a defeat for which they, rather than the male leaders, would take the blame. When, in early 1882, Charles and his lieutenants ordered the abandonment of the "no-rent" call, the Ladies refused to comply, despite their own realization that the policy had now little chance of success; their intransigence intensified Charles' distrust, and his determination to reach an agreement with Prime Minister Gladstone. The worsening situation also presented the LLL with serious financial difficulties. With the escalation in the number of arrests, requests for financial assistance multiplied, and Anna calculated that the Ladies had spent almost £70,000 over a period of 12 months, most of it on relief for evicted tenants and on assistance for prisoners and their families.

With the signing of the "Kilmainham Treaty" with Gladstone, and the release of the prisoners in May 1882, Charles entered a new phase in his political life, in which the Ladies were an embarrassing irrelevance. While thanking them for the "noble manner" in which they had contributed to the campaign, he believed, in reality, that they had done considerable damage. The murders of the new chief secretary and under-secretary, occurring only a few days after his release, intensified his determination to destroy an organization which he had always detested, and which, under the control of his sister, "as like him as a woman can be like a man," according to Tynan, "had taken a course of its own, and one in many ways opposed to his wishes and policy."

Anna and the Ladies, for their part, fully reciprocated his hostility, distrusting the "fictitious triumph" of the deal which he had made with the government; far from wishing to continue their activities, they expressed their desire to disband without "unnecessary delay," looking forward to their release, in Anna's words, from a "long and uncongenial bondage." However, they agreed to continue in existence pending a decision by the leadership on their future role. One proposal was that, while the LLL itself should be dissolved, the women should continue to perform a purely benevolent function within the movement. This option was scornfully rejected, partly because the Ladies had strong political objections to offering relief without resistance, partly because they refused to act as "a perpetual petticoat screen behind which [the men] could shelter, not from the government, but from the people." In addition, there was friction over financial affairs, with the male leadership accusing the Ladies of extravagance. While Anna argued that the LLL should dissolve unilaterally on the grounds of insolvency, a majority of her colleagues on the executive opposed this, believing that to make the quarrel public would undermine the credibility of the movement as a whole. In August, however, with the Ladies' overdraft standing at £5,000, the men declared that they would discharge the debt only if the Ladies disbanded on their terms, that is, with the women continuing to provide clerical assistance. Evading this condition by a subterfuge, the LLL dissolved itself. "Thus," as Anna wrote in *The Tale of a Great Sham,* "the Israelites made good their escape, and . . . at length the ghost of the Ladies' Land League rested in peace."

In fact, Anna herself had already effectively withdrawn from leadership of the League, following the sudden death in July of her sister, Fanny, which, combined with the effects of strain and overwork, precipitated a complete physical and nervous collapse. However, it is clear from her own account that she had no intention of continuing her association with a movement within which women had no status and with whose aims and methods she so deeply disagreed. Embittered by her brother's attitude towards the LLL, she broke off all relations with him, creating an estrangement which lasted until his death almost ten years later. No less disillusioned with Irish politics in general, she cut herself off almost entirely from public and political life, and after her recovery moved to England, where she was to live, in obscurity and often in poverty, for most of the rest of her days. She did, however, retain some links with Ireland: in 1900, for instance, she sent a donation to ***Maud Gonne**'s Patriotic Children's Treat, and in 1907 she was invited by a new nationalist party, Sinn Fein, to speak on behalf of their candidate in a by-election, although the experience apparently gave her little reason to revise her unfavorable view of Irish political life.

By the summer of 1911, 59-year-old Anna Parnell was staying in lodgings at Ilfracombe in Devon. An enthusiastic swimmer since childhood, she bathed every day, and on September 20, disregarding a warning of dangerous seas, she went swimming as usual. She was seen to be in difficulties and the alarm was raised, but by the time rescuers reached her, she was dead. She had been living under a false name, and it was only on the following day that she was identified as Anna Parnell, "one of the two splendid sisters who did so much to make Parnell what he was," as the local paper reported. Unlike her brother, however, whose funeral in Dublin had been the occasion for a massive outpouring of grief and remorse, Anna Parnell was buried quietly in Ilfracombe, in the presence of just seven strangers, and far away from the scenes of her greatest efforts and notoriety.

For Parnell, history was about movements and not personalities; characteristically, therefore, her concern in her final years was not to justify her own actions, but to offer a true account of the struggle of which she had been a part. In 1904, Michael Davitt published his *Fall of Feudalism in Ireland,* in which he accused the Ladies' Land League of abetting agrarian violence. "Everything recommended, attempted, or done in the way of defeating the ordinary law . . . ," he claimed, "was more systematically carried out under the direction of the ladies' executive than by its predecessor." Deeply hurt and angered by Davitt's interpretation, Parnell set out to write her own version of the land war, *The Tale of a Great Sham.* Described by its editor, Dana Hearne, as "a searing attack on the male leadership of the Land League and a penetrating critique of its major political strategy," the *Tale* also demonstrated clearly the subordination of female interests and concerns within a male-dominated nationalist body. Unable to find a publisher for her work, in 1909 Anna handed it over to the republican activist ***Helena Molony** (1884–1967), then editor of the paper *Bean na hEireann.* Shortly afterwards, during a police raid on the journal's offices, the parcel containing the manuscript disappeared. Only rediscovered in 1959, it was finally published in 1986, so that at last, almost a century after the events which it described, Anna Parnell's personal account of the work, the achievements, and the fate of the Ladies' Land League could be known.

SOURCES:

Cote, Jane McL. *Fanny and Anna Parnell: Ireland's Patriot Sisters*. London: Macmillan, 1991.

Foster, R.F. *Charles Stewart Parnell: The Man and His Family.* Sussex: Harvester Press, 1976.

Parnell, Anna. *The Tale of a Great Sham*. Ed. with an introduction by Dana Hearne. Dublin: Arlen House, 1986.

Tynan, Katharine. *Twenty-five Years: Reminiscences*. London: Smith, Elder, 1913.

Ward, Margaret. "The Ladies' Land League," in *Irish History Workshop*. Vol. 1, 1981, pp. 27–35.

SUGGESTED READING:

Bew, P. *Land and the National Question in Ireland, 1858–82*. Dublin: 1980.

Foster, R.F. *Modern Ireland, 1600–1972*. London: Allen Lane, 1988.

Rosemary Raughter,
freelance writer in women's history,
Dublin, Ireland

Parnell, Katherine O'Shea (1845–1921).

See O'Shea, Katherine.

Parnis, Mollie (1905–1992)

American fashion designer, philanthropist, and socialite. *Name variations: Mollie Parnis Livingston. Born on March 18, 1905, in New York City; died on July 18, 1992, in New York City; one of the three daughters of Abraham Parnis and Sara (Rosen) Parnis; graduated from Wadleigh High School, 1923; married Leon Livingston (a textile specialist), on June 26, 1930; children: one son, Robert.*

Although she could neither draw nor sew, Mollie Parnis was one of New York's leading couturiéres for five decades, creating dresses that were understated, comfortable, and versatile. Away from her Seventh Avenue fashion house, which she started with her businessman husband Leon Livingston in 1933, Parnis presided over a Park Avenue residence that became a salon for actors, journalists, and Democratic politicians. After closing her design enterprise in 1984, the designer formed the Mollie Parnis Livingston Foundation, through which she channeled a number of philanthropic ventures.

Parnis, who was born in 1905 in New York City and raised on the Lower East Side, completed her academic education at Wadleigh High School, graduating in 1923. Although she thought about studying law, she went to work instead as an assistant saleswoman in the showroom of a blouse manufacturer, and it was there that she recognized her innate ability to design. "What happened to me could happen to any young person with something to contribute in the field of fashion," she recalled. "I got into the habit of stepping into the designing rooms and making a suggestion . . . adding a jabot to a blouse or changing a sleeve. Before long I was asked if I'd like to try my hand at designing." Parnis subsequently joined the dress firm of David Westheim, remaining there for 18 months. After her marriage to Leon Livingston in 1930, she retired from business for three years.

In July 1933, against the advice of friends, the Livingstons established their own firm, Parnis-Livingston, Inc. From the beginning, Livingston handled the business end of the enterprise, while Parnis tended to the designs. Since she did not draw or sew, a staff of professional designers translated her conceptions into the finished product. Limiting production to dresses alone, and manufacturing a line of wearable clothes ranging in price from $90 to $150, the venture was immediately successful. "Good fashion doesn't mean a dress is supposed to knock people backward at first glance," Parnis once said, explaining her philosophy of design. "We are not in favor of the idea that to be daring is to be fashionable. We believe that good fashion is understated, and that a woman can be unselfconscious in it." Her line included "trim little suits" and dresses with fitted waistlines and soft, full skirts. In 1955, Parnis departed from her usual design by introducing the sheath dress, which hugged the figure in a narrow silhouette.

Parnis' clientele included such notables as ***Mamie Eisenhower**, ***Margaret Truman**, and ***Sarah Churchill**, as well as a number of stage and screen stars. In 1955, the designer made international headlines when Mamie and another guest appeared at a Washington party wearing the same dress. Parnis explained that she did not sell directly to any wearer and that she seldom made a one-of-a-kind dress. "That is what makes this country a great democracy," she added, in an early example of political spin.

Following her retirement in 1984 and the formation of her foundation, Parnis was involved in several philanthropic projects, among them a series of financial grants to worthy young journalists. She also provided for a series of "vest-pocket" parks in Manhattan and in Jerusalem, Israel.

SOURCES:

Candee, Marjorie Dent, ed. *Current Biography 1956*. NY: H.W. Wilson, 1956.

Graham, Judith, ed. *Current Biography 1992*. NY: H.W. Wilson, 1992.

Barbara Morgan,
Melrose, Massachusetts

Parnok, Sophia (1885–1933)

Russian poet. *Name variations: Sonya Parnokh; (pseudonym) Andrey Polyanin. Born on July 30, 1885, in Taganrog, Russia; died in August 1933, in Kirinsky, USSR; daughter of Yakov Solomonovich Parnokh (a pharmacist and apothecary owner) and Alexandra Parnokh (a doctor); married briefly to Vladimir Volkenshtein, in 1907; no children.*

Published first book of poetry (1916); wrote successful libretto for an opera staged at Moscow's Bolshoi Theater (1930).

Selected writings: Poems *(1916);* Roses of Pieria *(1922);* The Vine *(1923);* Music *(1926);* In a Hushed Voice *(1928);* Almast *(libretto, 1930).*

Sophia Parnok, named Sonya Parnokh at birth, was born in 1885 into an affluent Jewish professional home in Taganrog, Russia. A southern port town on the inland Azov Sea, Taganrog was outside the immediate influence of Russian politics at a time when religious minorities, including Jews, were pervasively persecuted; while most Jewish settlers were forced to live within the Pale of Settlement, Parnok and her siblings were raised to think of themselves first and foremost as Russians. Their father, the local apothecary, was indifferent to religion and highly assimilated into Russian culture, and the family was materially comfortable and lived among the intellectual elite. While she was still quite young, however, her mother **Alexandra Parnokh**, a doctor, died while giving birth to twins.

Sophia Parnok

Parnok attended the Empress Marie Gymnasium for Girls for ten years, studying a wide range of topics, including several languages, music, and math. She was also educated by a governess who became her stepmother, and she "carried away from her childhood the strong feeling that she had had no childhood, that she had emerged into adulthood at too young an age," wrote her biographer **Diana Burgin**. Already beginning to write poetry in her youth, Parnok was rebellious against her family's settled existence, believing it restrained her creativity. When she was about 20, she left to study music in Geneva, Switzerland. Before completing a degree there, she moved back to Russia, this time to St. Petersburg, where she studied history, philosophy, and law.

Beginning to write seriously, Parnok was first published in a literary journal in 1906. Several of her literary reviews at this time were published under the male name Andrey Polyanin, as she believed that her work thus would be more seriously accepted within the male-dominated literary circles. In 1907, Parnok married Vladimir Volkenshtein, but the marriage was brief in large part due to her lesbianism, of which she had become aware very early in her youth. She accepted and celebrated this facet of her self, frequently invoking mythological goddesses and the poet ***Sappho** in her work: in one poem, using the voice of Aphrodite, Parnok writes, "There's talk, Sappho: / They want to know to whom you write your eternal love songs, / Nectar of the gods! To young men or to maids?"

As the strictures of the Victorian era faded and then were swept away in the sea change brought by World War I, women's contributions to and acceptance in Russian poetry increased. Using her own name, Parnok published her first book of poetry in 1916, simply titled *Poems*. During this time she maintained intimate relationships with several women, including **Nadezhda Polyakova**, and began writing freely about her experiences. Her love affairs directly influenced her work, leading to surges of creativity that linked artistry and eroticism. An intense two-year relationship with poet ***Marina Tsvetayeva**, who was married and the mother of a child, coincided with a particularly creative period.

Following the 1917 Russian Revolution, Parnok moved to Sudak, in the Crimea, where she continued writing poetry and also wrote a libretto for an opera. She returned to Moscow in 1922, the same year she published her second book of poetry, *Roses of Pieria*. This was followed in 1923 by *The Vine* and in 1926 by *Music*. In an effort to avoid Soviet censorship, with some others she established a small press called Uzel (meaning "knot" or "group"). The government soon learned of the operation and shut it down. Her final book of poetry, 1928's *In a Hushed Voice*, was published after it had been edited by censors. Later considered by critics a major work, the book went essentially unnoticed at the time. In 1930, Parnok completed a libretto for an opera, *Almast*, which was successfully staged at the Bolshoi Theater in Moscow; it was the last of her work made public in her lifetime. In 1931, she met her last love and companion, physicist **Nina Vedneyeva**, who greatly influenced her work during the following years. Parnok's health grew steadily worse until she died of heart problems in August 1935, in the village of Kirinsky, near Moscow. Her death barely received mention in the Moscow papers.

Much of Parnok's literary career corresponded to a time of increasingly severe repression in Russia, as the group became idealized and prized far above the individual; Joseph Stalin denounced lyric poetry in particular for being out of step with his political goals for the country. Despite the very limited printings of her work and her small audience, Parnok persisted in writing in a bold style, publishing five volumes of poetry, a significant quantity of literary critiques, and the libretti to several operas. (It is believed that much of her unpublished work has been lost.) She was the only openly lesbian voice in Russian poetry at a time when homosexuality was considered psychologically abnormal and a sign of moral degradation in Russian society. Beginning in the 1970s, interest in Parnok's work grew significantly. A collection of Parnok's poetry, *Sophia Parnok: Collected Works*, was published in the United States in 1979 by **Sophia Polyakova** of Leningrad University (it was not published in the USSR), and her life and work have become the subject of several books, including 1994's *Sophia Parnok: The Life and Works of Russia's Sappho* by Diana Lewis Burgin.

SOURCES:

Burgin, Diana Lewis. *Sophia Parnok: The Life and Work of Russia's Sappho*. NY: New York University Press, 1994.

Contemporary Authors. Vol. 148. Detroit, MI: Gale Research.

SUGGESTED READING:

Polyakova, Sophia. *The Sunset Days of Yore: Tsvetayeta and Parnok*. Ardis Press, 1983.

Richard C. Hanes,
freelance writer, Eugene, Oregon

Parr, Anne (d. 1552)

Countess of Pembroke. *Died on February 20, 1552; sister of* **Catherine Parr** *(1512–1548, last queen of Henry VIII); daughter of Thomas Parr and* ***Maud Greene Parr****; married William Herbert, 1st earl of Pembroke, before 1534; children: Henry Herbert, 2nd earl of Pembroke (d. 1601, who married* ***Mary Herbert*** *[1561–1621]). Anne Parr was appointed a lady-in-waiting by her sister Catherine.*

Parr, Catherine. *See Six Wives of Henry VIII.*

Parr, Catherine (1512–1548).

See Six Wives of Henry VIII.

Parr, Harriet (1828–1900)

British writer. *Name variations: (pseudonym) Holme Lee. Born on January 31, 1828, in York, England; died on February 18, 1900, in Shanklin, Isle of Wight; daughter of William Parr (a salesman of luxury goods) and Mary (Grandage) Parr; educated in York; never married; no children.*

Selected works: Maude Talbot *(1854);* Gilbert Massinger *(1855);* Thorney Hall *(1855);* Kathie Brand *(1856);* Against Wind and Tide *(1859);* Annie Warleigh's Fortunes *(1863);* Her Title of Honour *(1871);* Straightforward *(1878);* A Poor Squire *(1882);* Legends from Fairyland *(1860).*

The author of over 30 novels as well as a substantial work on the life of ***Joan of Arc** (1866), British writer Harriet Parr was born and educated in York, England, and set her sights on the literary profession at an early age. Her career was significantly helped along by the patronage of Charles Edward Mudie, the proprietor of the famous circulating library. Parr's novels, published under the pseudonym Holme Lee, were sentimental and moralistic in tone, very much in keeping with the times. Her second novel, *Gilbert Massinger* (1855), was sent to Charles Dickens, who praised it but pronounced it too long for publication in his journal *Household Words*. Parr also wrote a number of children's stories and published a collection called *Legends from Fairyland* (1860). The writer, who never married, died on the Isle of Wight in 1900.

SOURCES:

Shattock, Joanne. *The Oxford Guide to British Women Writers.* Oxford: Oxford University Press, 1993.

Parr, Katharine (1512–1548).

See Six Wives of Henry VIII.

Parr, Maud Greene (1495–1529)

English noblewoman. *Name variations: Maud Greene or Green. Born Maud Green or Greene in 1495; died in 1529; daughter of Sir Thomas Green or Greene of Northamptonshire; married Sir Thomas Parr of Kendal; children:* ◂ ***Catherine Parr*** *(1512–1548, last queen of Henry VIII): William Parr, marquess of Northampton; *****Anne Parr*** *(d. 1552).*

▸ ***Parr, Catherine.*** *See Six Wives of Henry VIII.*

Parra, Teresa de la (1889–1936)

Venezuelan novelist and short-story writer. *Name variations: Ana Teresa Parr Sanojo; (pseudonym) Frufru. Born in 1889 (some sources cite 1891 or 1895) in Paris, France; died of tuberculosis in 1936; longtime companion of* ***Lydia Cabrera*** *(1900–1991, Cuban-born American scholar of Afro-Cuban culture, particularly santeria); no children.*

Selected writings: Diario de una señorita que se fastidiaba *(Diary of a Lady Who Was Bored, 1922, published as* Ifigenía, *1924);* Las memórias de Mamá Blanca *(1929, published in English as* Mama Blanca's Souvenirs, *1959);* Cartas *(Letters, 1951);* Epistolario íntimo *(Private Letters, 1953);* Obras completas *(Complete Works, 1965).*

One of Venezuela's best-known writers, Teresa de la Parra was born to wealthy parents in Paris at the end of the 19th century, and as a child lived on her family's plantation in Tazón, near Cúa, Venezuela. According to some sources, she attended Catholic school in Valencia, Spain, where her family moved in 1906 after her father's death; other sources relate that she was educated in Paris. Sources agree, however, that Parra returned to Caracas, Venezuela's capital, as an adolescent. Her first book, *Diario de una señorita que se fastidiaba* (Diary of a Lady Who Was Bored, 1922), uses the format of a young woman's letter and journal to explore the limited options available to women in Caracas in the early 1900s. In the novel, 18-year-old María Eugenia struggles with the social conventions of the patriarchal society around her, much in the same manner as some of the female characters of ***Edith Wharton**, Parra's contemporary. A *succès de scandale* upon its publication, the novel caused some outraged conservatives to accuse Parra of "undermining the morals of young women." It was republished two years later as *Ifigenía*, with the title serving as an ironic comment on the main character's sense of self (she compares herself to Iphigenia, the daughter of Agamemnon and Clytemnestra of Greek myth).

While Parra's first novel received much praise, her second novel, *Las memórias de Mamá Blanca* (1929), is considered her masterpiece. The memoir of an elderly woman who recounts her childhood on a sugarcane plantation, the book also paints a portrait of the now-vanished world of Venezuelan plantation society at the end of the 19th century. It was published in English for the first time in 1959 as *Mama Blanca's Souvenirs*, and again in 1993 as *Mama Blanca's Memoirs.* Like much of her work, the novel is fictionalized autobiography, drawing on her childhood memories of living on her family's plantation.

Teresa de la Parra's work remains highly acclaimed in South America and in Europe, where she lived for many years. She formed a group of French and South American writers in 1926, and the following year began lecturing on the role of women in South America, which she continued doing throughout her life. A frequent traveler, in her final years Parra returned to Europe to seek a cure for the tuberculosis which ultimately claimed her life in 1936, when she was only 47. Her remains were moved to Caracas 11 years later.

SOURCES:

Buck, Claire, ed. *The Bloomsbury Guide to Women's Literature.* NY: Prentice Hall, 1992.

Hampton, Janet Jones. Review of *Iphigenia* in *Belles Lettres.* Fall 1994, p. 79.

Uglow, Jennifer S., ed. and comp. *The International Dictionary of Women's Biography.* NY: Continuum, 1989.

SUGGESTED READING:

Parra, Teresa de la. *Iphigenia (the diary of a young lady who wrote because she was bored).* Translated by Bertie Acker. Austin, TX: University of Texas Press, 1994.

——. *Mama Blanca's Memoirs.* Translated by Harriet de Onis and Frederick H. Fornoff. Pittsburgh, PA: University of Pittsburgh Press, 1993.

Maria Sheler Edwards, M.A.,
Ypsilanti, Michigan

Parren, Kalliroe (1861–1940)

Greek feminist, journalist, novelist, and educator. *Name variations: Kallirroi Parren. Born in 1861 in Crete; died in 1940; married a French journalist.*

Was founding editor of The Ladies' Newspaper *(1887); founded the Union for the Emancipation of*

Women (1894), the Union of Greek Women (1896), and the Lyceum of Greek Women (1911).

Kalliroe Parren, a Greek journalist and educator who devoted her life to women's causes, spent the first ten years of her career as a headmistress of girls' schools in Russia and the Balkan nations, where her fluency in French, English, Italian, and Russian as well as her native Greek was useful. When she married a French journalist who worked in Athens, she left teaching and joined him in that city. In 1887, she founded *The Ladies' Newspaper* (also seen as *The Women's Newspaper*), the first weekly publication exclusively run by and directed to women. It would publish for 30 years. In addition to the standard news stories of the day, *The Ladies' Newspaper* also featured reports on social customs, family life, and education, as well as the problems women faced in legal matters, prison conditions, and other areas.

While her newspaper raised awareness on and provided information about women's issues, Parren rallied support for those causes by founding the Union for the Emancipation of Women in 1894, and the Union of Greek Women in 1896. She combined her earlier experiences in education with her passion for women's causes by founding schools for orphans and widows, where educated women provided basic instruction in reading and writing. Parren also founded a hospital for the terminally ill, and influenced government policies. Her efforts led to laws concerning the protection of working women and children, the admission of women to the University and the Polytechnic of Athens (despite public opposition), and the appointment of female doctors to women's prisons.

In 1911, Parren founded the Lyceum of Greek Women, an organization which provided support for women in the areas of education, employment, home economics, and child care. She also wrote novels with feminist themes, a feminist play (which was never staged), and two studies: *The History of Women* and *The History of Greek Women from 1650–1860*. In 1936, her achievements in advancing the status of women were recognized by the Greek Academy, which awarded her the Golden Cross of the Saviour. Parren's accomplishments laid the groundwork for an organized Greek women's movement which 12 years after her death would achieve the vote for women, a right Parren had called for during her lifetime.

SOURCES:

Buck, Claire, ed. *The Bloomsbury Guide to Women's Literature*. NY: Prentice Hall, 1992.

Uglow, Jennifer S., comp. and ed. *The International Dictionary of Women's Biography*. NY: Continuum, 1985.

Maria Sheler Edwards, M.A.,
Ypsilanti, Michigan

Parris, Elizabeth.

See Witchcraft Trials in Salem Village.

Parrish, Anne (1760–1800)

American philanthropist. *Born on October 17, 1760, in Philadelphia, Pennsylvania; died on December 26, 1800, in Philadelphia.*

Anne Parrish's life of philanthropy began as a plea and a promise. In 1793, when she was 33 years old, a yellow fever epidemic swept her hometown of Philadelphia. Because her Quaker parents were among those stricken, she vowed to devote her life to charitable works if they recovered. Her parents did survive the epidemic, and Parrish fulfilled her vow by founding the first charitable organization for women in the country. Established in 1795 as the House of Industry, the organization would provide employment opportunities to poor women in Philadelphia for over 125 years. The following year, Parrish established a school for needy girls that would later be known as the Aimwell School. Offering a curriculum of basic studies supplemented by training in domestic skills, the school grew quickly to some 50 pupils. Teachers were added, and the school moved to larger quarters several times to keep up with the growing number of students. The Aimwell School remained in operation until 1923, over a century after Parrish's death in 1800.

SOURCES:

McHenry, Robert, ed. *Famous American Women*. NY: Dover, 1980.

Maria Sheler Edwards, M.A.,
Ypsilanti, Michigan

Parrish, Anne (1888–1957)

American writer and illustrator. *Born on November 12, 1888, in Colorado Springs, Colorado; died of a cerebral hemorrhage on September 5, 1957, in Danbury, Connecticut; daughter of Maxfield Parrish (the illustrator) and Anne Lodge Parrish (a painter); sister-in-law of* ****M.F.K. Fisher****; educated in private schools in Colorado and Delaware and studied art at the Philadelphia School of Design for Women; married Charles Albert Corliss, in 1915 (died 1936); married Josiah Titzell (a poet who wrote novels as Frederick Lambeck), in 1938.*

Selected writings: Pocketful of Poses *(1923); (for children)* Knee High to a Grasshopper *(with Dillwyn Parrish, 1923); (for children)* The Dream Coach *(with D. Parrish, 1924);* Lustres *(with D. Parrish, 1924);* Semi-Attached *(1924);* The Perennial Bachelor *(1925);* Tomorrow Morning *(1926);* All Kneeling *(1928);* The Methodist Faun *(1929); (for children)* Floating Island *(1930);* Loads of Love *(1932);* Sea Level *(1934);* Golden Wedding *(1936);* Mr. Despondency's Daughter *(1938);* Pray for a Tomorrow *(1941);* Poor Child *(1945);* A Clouded Star *(1948); (for children)* The Story of Appleby Capple *(1950);* And Have Not Love *(1954);* The Lucky One *(1958).*

Anne Parrish was born in Colorado Springs, Colorado, in 1888, the daughter of **Anne Lodge Parrish**, a portrait painter, and famed illustrator Maxfield Parrish. She spent her childhood in Colorado Springs and at the home of her grandmother in Claymont, Delaware, later claiming to have been "slightly educated" in private schools in both those states. She then studied painting at the Philadelphia School of Design for Women, but decided against a career in art and turned instead to writing. Parrish did not completely abandon her art education, however, for she wrote and illustrated two of her early books in collaboration with her brother Dillwyn, who was also an artist and writer. One of these, *The Dream Coach* (1924), was nominated for the prestigious Newbery Medal, as were two more of her books for children, *Floating Island* (1930) and *The Story of Appleby Capple* (1950).

Parrish wrote more than a dozen novels for adults, many of which featured protagonists who have been described as "poseurs" (the title of one of her earliest books was *A Pocketful of Poses*) and a "sharply contrived" style of writing that evinced little sympathy for her characters. *The Perennial Bachelor* (1925) won the Harper Prize, and *All Kneeling* (1928) became a bestseller, but none of her books remain in print. Parrish lived in New York for many years, and traveled frequently; she claimed to have visited every country except Russia and Australia. Later in life she moved to Connecticut with her second husband, writer Josiah Titzell, where she died of a cerebral hemorrhage in 1957.

SOURCES:

Commire, Anne, ed. *Something About the Author.* Vol. 27. Detroit, MI: Gale Research.

Kunitz, Stanley J., and Howard Haycraft, eds. *Twentieth Century Authors.* NY: H.W. Wilson, 1942.

Maria Sheler Edwards, M.A.,
Ypsilanti, Michigan

Parrish, Celestia (1853–1918)

American educator. *Name variations: Celeste Parrish. Born Celestia Susannah Parrish on September 12, 1853, on a plantation near Swansonville, Pittsylvania County, Virginia; died on September 7, 1918, in Clayton, Georgia; daughter of William Perkins Parrish (a plantation owner) and Lucinda Jane Walker; graduated from Roanoke Female Institute (later Averett College), 1876; graduated from Virginia State Normal School (later Longwood College), 1886; studied mathematics and astronomy at the University of Michigan, 1891–92; attended summer sessions at Cornell University, 1893–95, and received Ph.B., 1896; attended summer sessions under John Dewey at the University of Chicago, 1897–99; never married; children: one adopted daughter.*

Taught in Danville Public Schools (1874–83), at the Roanoke Female Institute (1884), Virginia State Normal School (1886–91), and the Randolph-Macon Woman's College (1892–1902); founded an alumnae association at Randolph-Macon; served as professor of pedagogic psychology and head of the department of pedagogy at the Georgia State Normal School (1902–11); served as Virginia state president and national vice-president of Association of Collegiate Alumnae; founded and served as first president of the Southern Association of College Women (1903); served as first president of Georgia's Mothers and Teachers Cooperative Club; worked on behalf of the public schools in the South as the state supervisor of rural schools for the North Georgia District (1911–18).

Celestia Parrish was born in 1853 on a plantation in antebellum Virginia, the first of her parents' three children. She early displayed a strong intellect, which her wealthy father encouraged. The Civil War, however, soon wiped out the schools in her area, and claimed the lives of her parents as well. Parrish and her younger brother and sister were placed under the guardianship of an uncle and two maiden aunts. When she was 15, her uncle died, and her aunts soon made it known that they wished to be relieved of their obligation to their niece. Therefore, with little formal education of her own, the 16-year-old took a job teaching in the rural schools of Pittsylvania County, where she had been born.

She worked for five years in the rural schools, with little success at first. After she was inspired by a book on pedagogy, Parrish vowed to become a better teacher, and eventually became well known locally as an excellent instructor. As a result, she received an invitation to teach in the public schools of Danville, Virginia, where she stayed for nine years. During this period, Parrish supported herself and her sister while they attended the Roanoke Female Institute. She earned her diploma in 1876, and went on to study for a summer at the University of Virginia, which at the time would not admit women to study during regular sessions.

After resigning from the Danville schools in 1883, Parrish taught for a year at the Roanoke Female Institute before enrolling as a student at the Virginia State Normal School. When she graduated in 1886, she accepted on offer to teach mathematics at the school. However, Parrish's desire to become a "cultivated woman," as she described it, soon led her to develop a plan to study at "a great university" in the North. She left for the University of Michigan in 1891, where she studied mathematics and astronomy for a year. Upon her return to Virginia, Parrish accepted a position at the newly founded Randolph-Macon Woman's College in Lynchburg, an institution committed to making higher education accessible to Southern women.

While at Randolph-Macon, Parrish was required to teach psychology, a field in which she had little experience. Not one to let a lack of formal training restrain her, in 1893 she enrolled in a summer session at Cornell University, where she met eminent experimental psychologist Edward Bradford Titchener. She returned to Randolph-Macon in the fall and established what was probably the first psychology lab in the South. Parrish continued her studies at Cornell during the next two years, and published a paper, "The Cutaneous Estimation of Open and Filled Spaces," in the January 1895 issue of the *American Journal of Psychology*. At age 42, she met her longstanding goal of achieving a college degree when she graduated from Cornell in June 1896 with a Ph.B.

During the following three summers, Parrish studied at the University of Chicago under progressive educator John Dewey. After observing his Laboratory School, she was eager to bring Dewey's methods of education to the South. Therefore, she left Randolph-Macon in early 1902 to become the professor of pedagogic psychology and the head of the department of pedagogy at the Georgia State Normal School (now George Peabody College of Education at the University of Georgia). Impressed by her ideas, philanthropist George Foster Peabody granted $10,000 for the establishment of Muscogee Elementary School. This school served as a sort of laboratory for Parrish's work, which included training hundreds of teachers in such progressive educational methods as doing away with traditional divisions between subjects and involving parents in cooperative relationships with the school. It was during this time that Parrish became the first president of the statewide Mothers and Teachers Cooperative Club, and helped establish a parent-teacher association in Georgia.

Parrish's dedication to her own higher education motivated her to make that goal more accessible for other women. She worked to open educational opportunities for women by publishing a series of writings arguing for the admission of women to Southern universities and for more support of existing women's colleges. As the state president and national vice-president of the Association of Collegiate Alumnae (later the American Association of University Women), she worked to improve the quality of education available to women and in 1903 founded the Southern Association of College Women to further that purpose. A Baptist, Parrish was also involved in religious organizations, including missionary societies, the Young Christian Women's Association (YWCA), and the Women's Christian Temperance Union (WCTU).

Parrish resigned her post at Georgia State Normal School in 1911 to accept an appointment as the state supervisor of rural schools for the North Georgia District, a very poor area which encompassed over 2,400 schools in 48 counties. She embraced the challenge of overseeing more than 3,800 teachers in a locale that did not value education and provided very few, if any, tax dollars for that purpose. She continued in this post for the rest of her life, visiting every single county at least once a year, organizing teachers' institutes, and acting as an advocate of schools to public officials.

Celestia Parrish never married, but adopted a daughter, and took over the care of her brother's two sons. She died in 1918, just five days before her 65th birthday, in her home in Clayton, Georgia. The monument on her gravesite at the Clayton Baptist Church honors her as "Georgia's Greatest Woman."

SOURCES:

James, Edward T., ed. *Notable American Women, 1607–1950.* Cambridge, MA: The Belknap Press of Harvard University Press, 1971.

McHenry, Robert, ed. *Famous American Women.* NY: Dover, 1980.

Maria Sheler Edwards, M.A.,
Ypsilanti, Michigan

Parrish, Mrs. Dillwyn (1908–1992).

See Fisher, M.F.K.

Parsons, Betty Pierson (1900–1982)

American artist and art promoter. *Born in New York City on January 31, 1900; died in 1982; daughter of J. Fred Pierson and Suzanne (Miles) Pierson; educated privately; married Schuyler Livingston Parsons, on May 8, 1919 (divorced 1923); no children.*

Dubbed the "midwife of the New York School," Betty Parsons gained renown as a promoter of the New York abstractionists of the 1940s, and was instrumental in the careers of well-known artists such as ***Lee Krasner**, ***Perle Fine**, Jackson Pollock, ***Anne Ryan**, Mark Rothko, and ***Irene Rice Pereira**. Parsons also enjoyed some success as a painter and sculptor in her own right.

Born in 1900 and raised among the New York aristocracy, Parsons turned down a spot on the U.S. Olympic tennis team to pursue an art career. Married in 1919 and divorced in 1923, she spent the next ten years studying sculpture and working in Paris, where she moved in an elite literary and artistic circle that included ***Gertrude Stein**, Man Ray, and Alexander Calder. Her own talent was such that she had a solo show in 1927. In 1933, a victim of the stock-market crash, Parsons was forced to return to the United States. She spent three years teaching in Santa Barbara, California, before returned to New York City.

While continuing to enjoy considerable success with her own watercolors, which she exhibited at the Midtown Gallery, Parsons took a job in the gallery of ***Mary Sullivan**, where she began learning the business side of art. From 1941 to 1945, she held increasingly responsible gallery positions, and in 1946 she opened her own enterprise. The Parsons Gallery soon became popular with the New York abstractionists, who enjoyed the freedom within its walls to design their own exhibitions. Parsons, whose own art was now moving into the abstract, never showed her work at her own gallery, but continued to exhibit at other galleries in New York throughout the '40s, '50s, and '60s. Betty Parsons eventually moved to Long Island, New York, setting up a studio on a cliff overlooking the ocean. She continued to produce abstract paintings and sculptures until late into her 70s.

SOURCES:

Bailey, Brooke. *The Remarkable Lives of 100 Women Artists.* Holbrook, MA: Bob Adams, 1994.

Parsons, Eliza (c. 1748–1811)

British novelist and dramatist. *Born Eliza Phelps around 1748; died in Leytonstone, Essex, England, on February 5, 1811; only daughter of a wine merchant; married a turpentine merchant who died in 1790; children: eight.*

Selected works: The History of Miss Meridith *(1790);* The Errors of Education *(1791);* Woman as She Should Be *(1793);* The Castle of Wolfenbach *(1793);* Lucy *(1794);* The Girl of the Mountains *(1794);* The Mysterious Warning *(1794).*

A popular writer of Gothic fiction, Eliza Parsons produced more than 19 works (one source cites 60 books, "all mediocre"), some of which were read by such notables as Horace Walpole, ***Elizabeth Montagu**, the prince of Wales (future George IV) and his paramour ***Maria Anne Fitzherbert**. Parsons also translated Molière's two-act farce *The Intrigues of a Morning*, which was produced at Covent Garden in 1792, and published six tales of Jean de La Fontaine under the title *Love and Gratitude* (1804).

Little is known about Parsons' early life. The daughter of a Plymouth wine merchant, she married a turpentine dealer by the name of Parsons at an early age and moved with him to London, where he relocated and expanded his business. After the enterprise burned to the ground in 1782, he secured an appointment with the Lord Chamberlain. It was not until her husband's death in 1790 that Parsons took up the pen to support her eight children. One of her popular novels, *The Mysterious Warning* (1796), is described by **Joanne Shattock** as "an adaptation of Hamlet, a moral fable about the destructive effects of the passions on man's hopes for salvation." Despite the novel's dark nature, Parsons wrote a dedication to the prince of Wales, noting: "I have never written a line tending to corrupt the heart, sully the imagination, or mislead the judgment of my young readers."

Although a widely read author, Parsons was barely able to make ends meet, and on at least one occasion narrowly escaped debtors' prison. She died in 1811, at which time only four of her eight children were still alive.

SOURCES:

Shattock, Joanne. *The Oxford Guide to British Women Writers.* Oxford: Oxford University Press, 1992.

Barbara Morgan,
Melrose, Massachusetts

Parsons, Elsie Clews (1875–1941)

American anthropologist and sociologist. *Name variations: Elsie Worthington Parsons; Elsie Worthington Parsons Clews; (pseudonym) John Main. Born on November 27, 1875, in New York City; died on Decem-*

ber 19, 1941, in New York City; daughter of Henry Clews (founder of a New York City banking firm) and Lucy Madison (Worthington) Clews; attended Miss Ruehl's private school, New York City; Barnard College, A.B., 1896; Columbia University, A.M., 1897, Ph.D., 1899; married Herbert Parsons (a lawyer and U.S. congressional representative), on September 1, 1900; children: Elsie (b. 1901); John Edward (b. 1903); Herbert (b. 1909); McIlvaine (b. 1911); two who died in childhood.

Taught history at Columbia's Horace Mann High School (1897); taught graduate courses in sociology and on the family as a lecturer at Columbia University (1902–05); published first book, The Family *(1906); made first visit to the Southwest (1915); studied Native American tribes in a series of annual field trips (1916–36); lectured on anthropology at the New School for Social Research (1919); served as president of the American Folklore Society (1918–20); was associate editor of* Journal of American Folklore *(1918–41); served as president of the American Ethnological Association (1923–25); served as the first female president of the American Anthropological Association (1940–41).*

Selected works: The Family *(1906); (under pseudonym John Main)* Religious Chastity *(1913); (under pseudonym John Main)* The Old-Fashioned Woman *(1913);* Fear and Conventionality *(1914);* Social Freedom *(1915);* Social Rule *(1916);* Folk-Tales of Andros Island, Bahamas *(1918);* Folk-Lore of the Cape Verde Islands *(1923);* Folk-Lore of the Sea Islands, South Carolina *(1923);* The Social Organization of the Tewa of New Mexico *(1929);* Hopi and Zuñi Ceremonialism *(1933);* Folk-Lore of the Antilles, French and English *(3 vols., 1933–43);* Mitla: Town of the Souls *(1936);* Pueblo Indian Religion *(2 vols., 1939);* Peguche, Canton of Otavalo *(1945).*

Born in 1875, the first child and only daughter of a wealthy family, Elsie Clews Parsons spent her childhood in Newport, Rhode Island, and in New York City. While her mother **Lucy Madison Worthington Clews**, a society woman who was a descendant of President James Madison, would have much preferred that her daughter follow her into society life, Parsons opted for intellectual pursuits. She attended the recently established Barnard College for women, and after her graduation in 1896 continued her education at Columbia University. There she studied history and sociology, earning a master's degree in 1897 and a doctoral degree in 1899. The following year, she married Herbert Parsons, a Harvard- and Yale-educated lawyer who would go on to serve three terms as a Republican U.S. congressional representative from New York.

Over the next decade, Parsons gave birth to six children (only four of whom survived to adulthood), but did not eschew her career for motherhood. She lectured at Columbia and wrote her controversial first book, *The Family*, in 1906. In this groundbreaking treatise, Parsons provided sociological arguments against cultural roles for men and women, and asserted that women should have equal professional opportunities. She also advocated "trial marriage," a notion that her husband's political opponents used against him. To protect his career, Parsons published her next two books, in 1913, under the pseudonym "John Main." These were *Religious Chastity*, an examination of sexual practices associated with various religions, and *The Old-Fashioned Woman*, a discussion of ways in which gender-specific behavior is ingrained in children and played out in adulthood. Subsequent books, including *Fear and Conventionality* (1914), *Social Freedom* (1915), and *Social Rule* (1916), were published under her own name and addressed the need for women to be freed from the kinds of social conventions that had so restrained her as a young woman.

Parsons moved in nonconformist circles; she occasionally attended the New York salons of ***Mabel Dodge Luhan**, and her friends included Max Eastman, founder of the *Masses*, and Walter Lippman, who in 1914 was a founder of the liberal *New Republic*. She was a committed pacifist during World War I, and lectured at the New School for Social Research, an institution committed to academic freedom. Among her students there was young anthropologist ***Ruth Benedict**, whom she encouraged to study with Franz Boas.

In 1915, during her first visit to the Southwest, Parsons' attention was captured by Native American culture. She subsequently began the work that would establish her as one of the leading authorities on the Pueblo Indians and other Native tribes in North America, Mexico, and South America. Beginning in 1916, she left her oldest daughter Elsie (called Lissa) in charge of the younger children and lived for extended periods of time among the Zuñi, Hopi, Taos, Tewa, Laguna, and other Native peoples. Her field research, influenced by her friend from Columbia University, Franz Boas, resulted in over 100 scholarly papers and several books, including *The Social Organization of the Tewa of New Mexico* (1929), *Hopi and Zuñi Ceremonialism* (1933), *Mitla: Town of the Souls* (1936), and one of her most highly regarded works, the two-volume *Pueblo Indian Religion* (1939). Her interest in rapidly disappearing cultures also led her to study West Indian and African-American folklore. Parsons studied, among others, inhabitants of the Carolina coastal islands (called Gullahs) and the Portuguese-speaking Cape Verdeans in Massachusetts coastal towns. Her research was published by the American Folklore Society, for which she served as president from 1918 to 1920, and included such works as *Folk-Lore from the Cape Verde Islands* (1923) and *Folk-Lore of the Sea Islands, South Carolina* (1923).

Parsons also served as the president of the American Ethnological Society (1923–25) and was the associate editor of the *Journal of American Folklore* from 1918 until her death. She supported these groups financially, and privately contributed to the research of many young scholars. After her husband died in 1925, Parsons extended her trips and devoted herself even more fully to her work. She remained a pacifist throughout her life, and in 1940 endorsed Norman Thomas, the socialist candidate for president. Elsie Parsons died the following year, only weeks after her 66th birthday, of complications following an appendectomy. At the time, she was serving a term as the first female president of the American Anthropological Society.

SOURCES:

Bailey, Brooke. *The Remarkable Lives of 100 Women Healers and Scientists.* Holbrook, MA: Bob Adams, 1994.

Edgerly, Lois Stiles, ed. *Give Her This Day.* Gardiner, ME: Tilbury House, 1990.

James, Edward T., ed. *Notable American Women, 1607–1950.* Cambridge, MA: The Belknap Press of Harvard University Press, 1971.

McHenry, Robert, ed. *Famous American Women.* NY: Dover, 1980.

Publishers Weekly. March 31, 1997, p. 56.

Weatherford, Doris. *American Women's History.* NY: Prentice Hall, 1994.

SUGGESTED READING:

Deacon, Desley. *Elsie Clews Parsons: Inventing Modern Life.* Chicago, IL: University of Chicago Press, 1997.

Maria Sheler Edwards, M.A.,
Ypsilanti, Michigan

Parsons, Emily Elizabeth

(1824–1880)

Civil War nurse. *Born in Taunton, Massachusetts, on March 8, 1824; died in Cambridge, Massachusetts, on May 19, 1880; eldest of seven children of Theophilus Parsons (a lawyer and later Dane Professor of Law at Harvard University) and Catherine Amory (Chandler) Parsons; graduated from Cambridge (Massachusetts) High School; student and volunteer nurse at the Massachusetts General Hospital; never married; no children.*

Born in Taunton, Massachusetts, in 1824, the eldest of seven children of a lawyer who was also a staunch supporter of Abraham Lincoln, Emily Parsons grew up in Cambridge, where she graduated from Cambridge High School. Her early life was beset with a series of physical problems that made day-to-day activities particularly challenging. At five, a household accident blinded her right eye and impaired her sight in the left, and at seven, a bout with scarlet fever permanently damaged her hearing. In 1843, she suffered a severe ankle injury that made walking difficult and painful. Despite these afflictions, Parsons remained upbeat and active and was described as a particularly compassionate individual. After high school, she remained at home, assisting with the household and serving various charitable activities through her church.

Parsons was 37 years old when the Civil War broke out, and she became determined to volunteer as a nurse, although her father was against it. Following an 18-month course of study at the Massachusetts General Hospital, she was assigned to the Fort Schuyler military hospital on Long Island Sound near New York City, and was placed in charge of 50 patients. Working 16-hour days, with duties that included assisting the surgeon, supervising orderlies, administering medicine and diets, and ordering supplies, Parson flourished in her newfound career. "To have a ward full of sick men under my care is all I ask," she wrote in a letter to her mother. "I should like to live so all the rest of my life."

The rigorous schedule and the damp conditions at Fort Schuyler took a toll on Parson's delicate constitution, and in December she was forced to leave the facility. While recuperating in New York City, she met ***Jessie Benton Frémont**, who was recruiting nurses for a Western Sanitary Commission hospital in St. Louis. Thinking her health would improve in the West, Parson accepted Frémont's offer and in January 1863 began work at Lawson Hospital, St. Louis. A month later, she was appointed head nurse of the *City of Alton*, a hospital transport ship which steamed down the Mississippi carrying sick and wounded soldiers to hospitals in Memphis. "I feel now as if I had really entered into the inner spirit of the times,—the feeling which counts danger as nothing," she wrote at the time. Unfortunately, her enthusiasm was tempered by a bout of malarial fever which she contracted on the river.

It was not until April that Parsons had recovered sufficiently to begin an assignment as supervisor of nurses at the newly established Benton Barracks Hospital in St. Louis, a 2,500-bed facility and the largest military hospital in the West. It was one of the most important appointments given to a woman during the Civil War, and Parsons proved more than adequate for the job. An outstanding administrator as well as a capable and compassionate nurse, she was popular with both patients ("her boys," she called them) and staff. "I wonder what I shall do with myself when the war is over," she queried in another letter home. "I never can sit down and do nothing."

Following the war, Parsons continued hospital work, opening a general hospital in a rented house in Cambridge where she lived and treated destitute women and children who could not pay. Chartered in 1871 as Cambridge Hospital (later named the Mount Auburn Hospital), it is still in operation, although serving a broader patient base. Parsons died in her parents' home in Cambridge in 1880, at the age of 56. That same year, her father edited and published her war-time letters under the title *Memoir of Emily Elizabeth Parsons*, for the benefit of Mount Auburn Hospital.

SOURCES:

Edgerly, Lois Stiles, ed. *Give Her This Day*. Gardiner, ME: Tilbury House, 1990.

James, Edward T., ed. *Notable American Women, 1607–1950*. Cambridge, MA: The Belknap Press of Harvard University Press, 1971.

Barbara Morgan,
Melrose, Massachusetts

Parsons, Harriet (1906–1983)

American producer. *Born in Burlington, Iowa, on August 23, 1906; only child of Louella Parsons (a Hollywood gossip columnist) and John Dement Parsons (a real-estate salesman); graduated from Horace Mann School for Girls, New York, 1924; Wellesley College, B.A., 1928; married King Kennedy (a writer and publicist), on September 28, 1939 (divorced April 1946).*

Harriet Parsons was born in Burlington, Iowa, in 1906, the daughter of John Dement Parsons and the powerful Hollywood columnist ***Louella Parsons**. At age six, Harriet appeared as "Baby Parsons" in two Essanay movies, *Margaret's Awakening* and *The Magic Wand*. Following graduation from Wellesley College, she wrote for *Modern Screen, Movie Mirror, Silver Screen*, and *Photoplay*, became a radio commentator ("Harriet Parsons' Hollywood Highlights" on NBC), and a columnist for *Liberty* and the Hearst Syndicate. In 1928, taking a job offered to her mother, Parsons produced a series of short subjects called *Screen Snapshots* for Columbia. From 1933 to 1940, she produced over 100 of them. She then produced another series, *Meet the Stars*, for Republic.

Harriet Parsons' first full-length film was *Joan of the Ozarks* (1942), starring ***Judy Canova** and Joe E. Brown. She also produced many highly successful films, including *The Enchanted Cottage* (1945), starring ***Dorothy McGuire** and Robert Young, *Night Song* (1947), with ***Merle Oberon**, ***Ethel Barrymore**, and Dana Andrews, *I Remember Mama* (1947), starring ***Irene Dunne**, *Never a Dull Moment* (1950), starring Dunne and Fred MacMurray, *Clash by Night* (1951), with ***Barbara Stanwyck**, and *Susan Slept Here* (1954), starring **Debbie Reynolds**. In 1953, Parsons was the only card-carrying woman member of the Screen Producers' Guild.

Parsons, Louella (1881–1972).

See joint entry under Hopper, Hedda and Louella Parsons.

Partenide, Fidalma (1663–1726).

See Massimi, Petronilla Paolini.

Parthia, queen of.

See Laodice (fl. 129 BCE).
See Rhodogune (fl. 2nd c. BCE).

Parton, Sara Willis (1811–1872).

See Fern, Fanny.

Partridge, Dora (1893–1932).

See Carrington, Dora.

Parturier, Françoise (1919—)

French novelist, journalist, and playwright. *Name variations: (pseudonym) Nicole. Born in Paris, France, in 1919; attended Paris University; married Jean Gatichon, in 1947.*

Selected works: (with Josette Raoul-Duval) Albertine in the Lion's Den *(novel, 1958);* The Five-day Lover *(novel, 1961);* An Open Letter to Men *(essay, 1968);* An Open Letter to Women *(essay, 1974);* This Crazy Life *(play, 1977);* Letter from Ireland *(essay, 1979);* Romatuelle's Heights *(novel, 1983).*

A French feminist whose popular writings challenge sexual and racial inequality, Françoise Parturier attended Paris University, then taught briefly in the United States (1950–51), before becoming a professional journalist and writer.

From 1956 on, her work appeared in a number of popular French journals, including *Literary News* and *Le Figaro*. She collaborated with **Josette Raoul-Duval** on three novels (published under the pseudonym Nicole), before beginning to write under her own name in 1959. Her subsequent work includes novels, feminist essays, and a three-act play, *This Crazy Life* (1977).

Parun, Vesna (1922—)

Croatian poet. *Born on the island of Zlarin in 1922.*

One of her country's most controversial and influential poets, Vesna Parun was born in 1922 and enjoyed an idyllic childhood in Dalmatia until the outbreak of World War II. Her first collection of poems, *Zore i vihori* (Dawns and Gales), published in 1947, extols her youth, and is considered by some to be her best work, although it was attacked by the Left as too metaphysical in tone and out of step with the prevailing school of Socialist Realism. With this condemnation, Parun became an inspiration to a whole new generation of post-war poets.

Silenced for a time, Parun did not publish another collection until 1955, when she issued *Crna maslina* (The Black Olive Tree). Over the course of the next decade, she published several more volumes, focusing on personal rather than political issues and detailing a number of blissful but short-lived romantic relationships. Considered the best of these poems are "Konjanik" ("The Horseman," 1962) and "Bila sam djecak" ("I Was a Boy," 1963). In 1971, Parun was once again condemned as reactionary by some Yugoslav literary critics for a series of articles in the Catholic periodical *Glas koncila,* in which she described and defended her return to Catholicism.

SOURCES:

Bédé, Jean-Albert, and William B. Edgerton, eds. *Columbia Dictionary of Modern European Literature.* NY: Columbia University Press, 1980.

Buck, Claire, ed. *The Bloomsbury Guide to Women's Literature.* NY: Prentice Hall, 1992.

Barbara Morgan,
Melrose, Massachusetts

Parviainen, Katri (1914—)

Finnish javelin champion. *Name variations: Kaisa Parviainen; K.V. Parviainen. Born on December 3, 1914.*

Katri Parviainen, the first Finnish woman to win an Olympic medal, placed second in the 1948 Olympic Games in London with a javelin throw of 43.79 meters (143'8"). **Herma Bauma** of Austria won the gold with a throw of 45.57; **Lily Carlstedt** of Denmark placed third.

Parysatis I (fl. 440–385 BCE)

Queen of Persia. *Flourished from 440 to 385 BCE; daughter of Artaxerxes I, king of Persia, and Andia, a Babylonian; married half-brother Darius II Ochus, king of Persia (r. 424–404 BCE), in 424 BCE (died 404 BCE); children: daughter, Amestris; two sons, Arsaces also known as Artaxerxes II, king of Persia (r. 404–358 BCE), and Cyrus (d. 401 BCE).*

Parysatis I was the daughter of Artaxerxes I, king of Persia, and **Andia**, a Babylonian, and the half-sister and wife of Darius II, king of Persia from 424 to 404 BCE. Darius and Parysatis shared the same father. Darius' mother **Cosmartidene** was another Babylonian, but not one of Artaxerxes' legitimate wives (polygamy and concubinage abounded at the Persian court), for Darius is commonly referred to in sources as "the Bastard." Therefore, of royal paternity but of illegitimate birth, Darius originally had no hope of ascending his father's throne. He had some station, however, for before Artaxerxes' death he was appointed as the satrap of Hyrcania and was married to Parysatis.

Artaxerxes I's only legitimate male son, Xerxes, died shortly after Artaxerxes himself. There followed a scramble to seize the throne among Artaxerxes' illegitimate sons. One such, Sogdianus, briefly held royal authority before being deposed and succeeded by Darius. Abetting Darius' unexpected coup was Parysatis' political savvy. She remained influential during her husband's entire reign: one source reports that whenever Darius felt his throne in jeopardy—which was not infrequent given his birth and contested accession—the first party he consulted was Parysatis. She apparently maintained a kind of intelligence network both at court and throughout the empire for the purpose of uncovering any whiff of disloyalty. As a result of the information she fed to Darius, more than one royal relative, noble, and even humble eunuch was executed for treason. It is also significant that in a society accustomed to royal polygamy, Parysatis was Darius' only official wife. The couple had two sons, Arsaces and Cyrus, and a daughter, **Amestris**.

An episode which occurred near the end of Darius' reign reveals much about Parysatis' influence and character. To secure ties with the Persian aristocracy, Darius arranged two marriages: that of Arsaces to ***Statira I**, and that of Amestris to Statira's half-brother, Teritouchones. Amestris' marriage to Teritouchones never took place, however, since the would-be groom was willful enough to reject the royal union in favor of a marriage with another of his half-sisters. Outraged by this insult to the imperial dignity, Parysatis had all of Teritouchones' siblings and half-siblings put to death, except for Statira herself, who was saved only because Arsaces intervened on her behalf; he then married her.

Darius II's reign was troubled, and not only because of his birth. Coming to power in 424, he ruled through most of the Peloponnesian War (431–424), the great conflict which pitted the Athenian Empire against the Spartan alliance. Although the principals in this conflict were Greeks and independent of Persian authority, their war was largely conducted along Persia's western frontier and definitely affected Persia's interests. A large portion of the Athenian Empire—that is, the one-time autonomous Greek poleis situated along the Anatolian coastline and comprising many of the islands of the Aegean—had once belonged to Persia. As such, when Sparta and Athens warred against each other, opportunity knocked for the Persians who hoped to reclaim what had been lost to Athens by supporting the Spartan cause. They did so primarily by providing the financial wherewithal Sparta needed to build and maintain a fleet capable of competing with Athens for maritime supremacy. For this support, Persia expected Sparta to cede back to Persia what had been Persia's. The whole issue, however, was a delicate one, for Sparta officially fought the Peloponnesian War to liberate the Greeks under Athenian control, and it just would not have done to let it be known that Sparta had agreed to turn many of the states thus freed directly over to the control of Persia. Making this situation even more complex was Darius' sometimes shaky status and the political rivalries of the satraps of western Anatolia (especially Pharnabazus and Tissaphernes), who acted as Persia's primary agents for Greek affairs. In an effort to bring Persia's Greek policy under more centralized control, Darius posted his younger son, Cyrus, to the west in 408 with orders to aid and abet the Spartan cause. There Cyrus remained until the death of Darius in 404. When Cyrus' friend and ally Lysander finally toppled Athens later that year, Cyrus was at the Persian court attending the coronation of his older brother Arsaces, who took the throne name Artaxerxes II (r. 404–358).

Cyrus, however, was ambitious and sought the throne for himself. For unknown reasons, he was abetted in his ambitions by Parysatis. When Cyrus returned to the west, with his mother's blessing he launched a coup. In order to do so he cut a deal with the Spartans, agreeing to allow Sparta to consolidate all of what Athens had ruled into a new Spartan Empire (a move definitely not popular in Greece). In return, Cyrus gained an alliance and the right to recruit Greek mercenaries into his rebellious army. Nevertheless, Cyrus failed in his attempted coup, primarily because his brother retained the support of the Persian nobility. In 401, at Cunaxa in Babylonia, Cyrus died in battle. Artaxerxes II thus retained his throne and, among other initiatives, turned his attention to the recovery of those states which Cyrus had bartered away to the Spartans for their support of his revolt. By 386, success had arrived, for in that year Artaxerxes II imposed the so-called "King's Peace," which saw the Greeks of Asia and the island of Cyprus returned to the Persian fold.

As for Parysatis, it is not known why Artaxerxes II did not avenge himself on his mother for her open support of Cyrus. Although at some later date, she was temporarily exiled by her son to her estates in Babylonia, immediately after Cyrus' unsuccessful rebellion Parysatis seems to have suffered nothing at all. In fact, Artaxerxes II allowed her to journey to Babylon to recover the body of Cyrus and to supervise its proper return to Persia. Perhaps Artaxerxes II found Parysatis' network of connections and her willingness to warn him against the political disloyalty of others too valuable to challenge, or perhaps he merely lived in awe of his mother's powerful personality. Whatever the truth, Artaxerxes II heeded Parysatis' advice time and time again, even when the benefits to his authority of doing so were mixed at best. For example, Parysatis secured the deaths of many who had supported Artaxerxes II over Cyrus, mostly because she resented their opposition to Cyrus. In one instance, Parysatis turned Artaxerxes II against a noble named Mithradates, who had fought for Artaxerxes at Cunaxa, not for any act of disloyalty but because Mithradates contradicted the official version of Cyrus' death, which had it that Artaxerxes II personally had struck his brother down (which he manifestly had not done). Thus, in an extreme act of face saving, Artaxerxes II, at his mother's urging, murdered a political loyalist. Parysatis also caused the death of a court eunuch named Masabates who had the audacity to attempt to mutilate the corpse of Cyrus before its royal burial, even though it was a Persian custom to treat traitors in such fashion. Artaxerxes II went along with Parysatis even though by doing so he honored a rebellious sibling and besmirched his own royal dignity. Yet again, even figures as powerful as Tissaphernes the satrap eventually suffered because of Parysatis' hatred. He, too, had played a role in Cyrus' downfall, and although other personalities and issues were involved in his execution in 395, Parysatis' motives for urging Artaxerxes II to demand his death went back to the role Tissaphernes had played in Cyrus' failed revolt.

The one time Artaxerxes II stood up to his mother concerned his wife Statira I. Like Darius II, Artaxerxes only had one legitimate wife. As a result, Statira alone at court held the status of the "King's Wife." This sparked Statira's ambitions to replace Parysatis, who as the "King's Mother" had retained her status as Artaxerxes' primary advisor. When, however, it looked as if Statira was gaining too much influence over Artaxerxes II, Parysatis simply had her poisoned. Artaxerxes II reacted by temporarily exiling his mother from court, but for some unknown reason eventually reconciled with Parysatis and recalled her to court. There, to prevent another challenge to her hold over Artaxerxes II, Parysatis is reported to have urged her son to marry his daughters by Statira, **Atossa** and **Amestris**. This was incest in Persia and broke with social custom. Parysatis almost certainly advised Artaxerxes II as she did for two reasons: because the unpopularity of the marriages would have put Artaxerxes even more under her influence than ever before, and because the youth, inexperience, and social vulnerability of his new wives would have prevented them from challenging Parysatis' status at court.

Official records prove that Parysatis owned property in Syria, Babylonia and Media (in fact, Parysatis' estates in Syria supplied troops for Cyrus' rebellion), at the least, and she probably possessed many estates which are not historically attested. We even know the name of the steward (Ea bullissu) who ran one of her properties, and the revenues she collected from some of her enterprises. Clearly, Parysatis was very wealthy in her own right—a wealth which gave her great leeway during the reigns of her husband and son to travel privately and to finance her personal and political agenda from her own purse.

William Greenwalt,
Associate Professor of Classical History, Santa Clara University, Santa Clara, California

Parysatis II (c. 350–323 BCE)

Persian princess and wife of Alexander the Great. *Born around 350 BCE; died in 323 BCE; youngest daughter of Artaxerxes III Ochos, king of Persia (r. 359/8–338 BCE) and sister of Artaxerxes IV, king of Persia (r. 338–336 BCE); married Alexander III the Great (356–323 BCE), king of Macedonia (r. 335–323 BCE).*

Parysatis II was the youngest daughter of the Persian king Artaxerxes III Ochos (r. 359/8–338), and the sister of his successor Artaxerxes IV (r. 338–336). When the latter was assassinated in 336, Darius III, an Achaemenid (but from a collateral arm of Persia's royal house), seized the Persian throne. After the murder of her brother, Parysatis, her mother, and her sisters remained at the court of their relative.

Darius III was the king of Persia when Alexander III the Great invaded Asia in 334. However, since Persia proper lay hundreds of miles from the Mediterranean Sea, and since Darius had to mobilize an army worthy of facing his adversary, the two kings did not meet in battle until November of 333. When Persian kings went on campaign, they did so with elaborate entourages, including many of their relatives and much of their court. Darius maintained this tradition, and among the many women of his family who traveled west with him to meet Alexander was Parysatis II. As he closed on Alexander, Darius took the precaution of establishing his family and court in the fortified city of Damascus before moving north to engage the invader, which he did unsuccessfully at Issus. After his defeat, Darius fled east, leaving his court and Parysatis to be captured by Parmenion, Alexander's second-in-command. Among the Persian hostages whom Alexander held (and treated very well) were women from collateral branches of the Achaemenid royal house: those, like Parysatis, who were of the line of Artaxerxes III, and those directly related to Darius III himself, including his daughter, ***Statira III**.

These hostages remained with Alexander as he made his way through Syria, Israel, Egypt, Israel and Syria again, and then into Iraq, where he met and defeated Darius a second time at Gaugamela in October 331. (Darius would be assassinated in 330 because of his losses to Alexander.) When Alexander campaigned through the heartland of the Persian Empire and then its easternmost appendages, his Persian hostages were probably installed in Susa (in western Iran). We know that when Alexander continued eastward through what is now Iran, Afghanistan, Turkmenistan, Uzbekistan, Tajikistan, Pakistan and India, they did not accompany him, and since they were at Susa when Alexander returned to that city from his eastern conquests, they had probably remained at Susa all along.

At Susa in 324, Alexander celebrated his conquests with the mass marriage of some 90 of his officers to the daughters of Persian nobles. At that time, Alexander married both Parysatis and Darius III's daughter Statira III (he was already married to *Roxane), in order to lay claim to the lines of the last two Achaemenid kings. Thereafter, Parysatis lived as one of Alexander's three wives, receiving all of the honor such an exalted status endowed. And being a wife of Alexander *was* exalted; about the time of his last two marriages, Alexander requested—and was given—divine honors, that is, he was worshiped as a living god. This idyll did not last long, however. When Alexander died in June of 323, Roxane struck with a ruthlessness which Alexander himself would have understood. To protect the political future of Alexander's unborn child whom she gave birth to after he died, Roxane murdered both Parysatis and Statira III.

William Greenwalt,
Associate Professor of Classical History,
Santa Clara University, Santa Clara, California

Pascal, Jacqueline (1625–1661).

See Port Royal des Champs, Abbesses of.

Pascalina, Sister (1894–1983)

German nun who was a powerful confidante of Pope Pius XII. *Name variations: Josefine Lehnert; La Popessa. Born on August 25, 1894, in Ebersberg, Bavaria, Germany; died of a brain hemorrhage in 1983 in Vienna, Austria; seventh of twelve children of farmers George and Maria Lehnert.*

Joined the Teaching Sisters of the Holy Cross (a Catholic convent) at age 15 (1910); took her final vows at age 19 and adopted the name Sister Pascalina (1914); met Eugenio Pacelli, the future Pope Pius XII (1917); moved to Munich to head Pacelli's household (1917); moved to Berlin with Pacelli (1925); moved to the Vatican and worked in the press relations office (1930); transferred to the secretariat of the Vatican (1932); traveled with Pacelli to the U.S. (1936); served Pacelli during his term as Pope Pius XII (1939–58); exiled to Switzerland (1958); built retirement home in Italy (1960s).

Sister Pascalina, who would be instrumental to Eugenio Pacelli during a rise through the ranks of Catholic diplomacy that culminated in his becoming Pope Pius XII, was born into a poor German family of farmers in 1894. Josefine Lehnert, as she was christened, was a carefree child until the age of seven, when she took her first communion and became very serious in her

Sister Pascalina

commitment to her faith. Because of her authoritarian nature, religious devotion, and self-discipline, her siblings gave her the nickname "Mother Superior." By the time Josefine was 15, her devotion to God led her to leave home and join a convent, against her parents' wishes. In 1914, when she was 19, she took her final vows of poverty, chastity and humility and adopted the name Sister Pascalina, taken from the word "Paschal," which is synonymous with Easter.

Part of Pascalina's duties as a young nun at the convent included caring for traveling or ill clergy members. In 1917, she cared for a middle-aged archbishop named Eugenio Pacelli, completely devoting herself to nursing him back to health. While the powerful Vatican diplomat never thanked Pascalina for her work, he requested her transfer from the convent to his residence in Munich, to act as his head of staff. Pascalina moved to Munich in 1917, residing there with Pacelli through the years of World War I. In 1925, Pacelli brought Pascalina with him when he was transferred to Berlin, where he served as the first Apostolic Nuncio to the German Reich. During the same year, Mussolini was declared dictator of Italy, and Pacelli was called upon to negotiate between the Vatican and the dictator. His efforts resulted in the 1929 Lateran Treaty, and earned him an appointment in Rome as a cardinal. Two months later, in February 1930, Pacelli was made Vatican secretary of state, a post second only to the pope.

Although Pascalina's relationship to Pacelli was one of chaste service and godly devotion, she was left behind in Berlin due partly to the rumors that had developed about them. It was a painful separation for Pascalina. However, an American priest who had befriended her, Monsignor Francis Spellman (later the archbishop of the diocese of New York), facilitated her move to Italy and eventually made her his assistant in the Vatican office of press relations. It was not long before Pope Pius XI himself recognized Pascalina's abilities, and assigned her to work with Pacelli once again.

Pascalina served as a caregiver and confidante to Pacelli, who came to rely heavily on her advice. Even while rumors about their relationship continued to spread, she accompanied him on his first trip to the United States in 1936, which was also the first in history by any Vatican secretary of state. The trip, during the early unrest that would erupt into World War II, was meant to nurture already strong diplomatic relations between the Vatican and President Franklin Roosevelt's administration. Three years later, in 1939, Pius XI died suddenly of a heart attack, and Pacelli was elected to replace him as Pope Pius XII.

Pascalina defied the misogynistic atmosphere of the Vatican by remaining close to the pope during his reign. This lasted through World War II (his behavior during the war was increasingly criticized throughout the end of the 20th century, particularly as efforts towards his canonization were made by the Vatican) and into the 1950s. Pius XII was strongly conservative in both religion and politics, on several occasions threatening communists with excommunication. Pascalina held more influence over him than anyone else in the Vatican, earning her the irreverent nickname "La Popessa." She was also referred to as his "Guardian Angel," for she stood between the pope and those who wanted an audience with him. While the cardinals of the Vatican were jealous of her influence and power, even her enemies admitted that had Pascalina been a man, she would have been Pius XII's successor.

Instead, however, after his death on October 9, 1958, Pascalina was forced out of the Vatican, and went into exile in Switzerland. She came out of exile in the early 1960s to discuss with Pope John XXIII the harm that she predicted the reforms of the Second Vatican Council would visit upon Catholicism, disagreeing with what she viewed as a relaxation of the authority of the Holy See. In her later years, Pascalina secured funding from an old friend of Pius' to build Casa Pastor Angelicus, a retirement home for herself and other retired nuns, on a hill overlooking Rome. She died of a brain hemorrhage in Vienna in 1983.

SOURCES:

Murphy, Paul I. *La Popessa: Biography of Sister Pascalina, the Most Powerful Woman in Vatican History.* NY: Warner Books, 1983.

Time. November 28, 1983.

Maria Sheler Edwards, M.A.,
Ypsilanti, Michigan

Pasionaria, La (1895–1989).

See Ibárruri, Dolores.

Pasta, Giuditta (1797–1865)

Italian soprano. *Born Giuditta Maria Costanza Negri in Saronno near Milan, Italy, on October 26, 1797; died in Blevio, Lake Como, Italy, on April 1, 1865; studied at the Conservatory of Milan with Bartolomeo Lotto and Giuseppe Scappa.*

Debuted (1815); debuted in Paris (1816), London (1817), Vienna (1829), St. Petersburg (1840); created title roles in Pacini's Niobe *(1826), Donizetti's* Anna Bolena *(1830), Bellini's* Norma *and Amina in* La sonnambula *(1831).*

One of 19th-century Europe's greatest sopranos, Giuditta Pasta influenced Italy's finest romantic composers, Gaetano Donizetti (1797–1848), Vincenzo Bellini (1801–1835), and Gioacchino Rossini (1792–1868), all of whom wrote operas for her. Pasta was one of three sopranos who helped mould the first years of the romantic period of opera. She was a superstar along with ***Henriette Sontag** and ***Maria Malibran**.

An Italian of Jewish origin, Pasta was born in Milan, Italy, in 1797. She received her early training from Giuseppe Scappa and Davide Banderali, and made her debut in the première of Scappa's opera *Le tre Eleonore*, in 1816. This was followed by performances at the Théâtre Italien in Paris in Paer's *Il principe di Taranto* (1816), and at the King's Theater in London, where she appeared as Telemachus in Cimarosa's *Penelope* (1817). Pasta then embarked on another year of study, returning to the stage in Pacini's *Adelaide Comingo* in 1819, in Venice. A subsequent tour of all the major opera centers in Italy culminated in her performance as Desdemona in Rossini's *Otello,* at the Théâtre Italien in 1821, a triumphant appearance that established her as a major talent.

Pasta's career hit its zenith between 1821 and 1831. She returned to London as Desdemona in 1824, and also performed Zerlina and Semiramide. Highly acclaimed were her portrayals of Amina in Bellini's *La sonnambula* (1831), and the title role in his *Norma* (1831), which she sang for her debut at Milan's La Scala, in 1831. Pasta's repertoire also included the title roles in Donizetti's *Anna Bolena* (1830), Pacini's *Niobe* (1826), and Bellini's *Beatrice di Tenda,* and she excelled as Strauss' Electra, Salome, and the Dyer's Wife as well as Marie in *Wozzek,* all intense roles.

Pasta's brilliance apparently had as much to do with her acting as it did with her vocal quality, which was criticized as uneven toward the end of her career. "Pasta's greatness lay in her naturalness, truth of expression and individual timbre, which enabled her within a phrase, to achieve soul-stirring emotion," writes Kenneth Stern. "She could execute intricate *fioritura* but channelled her bravura to illuminate the drama, though she was often criticized for faulty intonation. An accomplished actress, her department and portrayal of dignity were without peer."

Pasta formally retired from the stage in 1835, although she continued to make occasional appearances, performing in London in 1837, and in Berlin and Russia in 1840–41. Eventually, it is said, she tired of competing with her own legend. Her last engagement, for which she received $40,000, was with the opera in St. Petersburg, after which she retired to her villa near Lake Como. She died in 1865.

SOURCES:

Sadie, Stanley, ed. *The New Grove Dictionary of Opera,* Vol 3. London: Macmillan Press, 1992.

Uglow, Jennifer S., ed. *The International Dictionary of Women's Biography.* NY: Continuum, 1985.

SUGGESTED READING:

Ferranti-Giulini, M. *Giuditta Pasta e i suoi tempi,* 1935.

Pasternak, Josephine (1900–1993)

Russian-born British philosopher, poet, and intellectual, and sister of novelist Boris Pasternak. *Name variations: Anna Ney or Anna Nei; Josephina Pasternak; Josephine Leonidovna Pasternak; Zhosefina Pasternak; Zozefina Pasternak; Zhozefina Leonidovna Pasternak. Born Zhosefina Leonidovna Pasternak in Moscow, Russia, on February 19, 1900; died in Oxford, England, on February 16, 1993; daughter of Leonid Osipovich Pasternak (1862–1945) and Rosalia (Rozalia) Isidorovna Kaufman Pasternak (1867–1939); sister of Aleksandr Pasternak (1893–1982), Boris Pasternak (1890–1960), and Lydia Leonidovna Pasternak-Slater (1902–1989); married Fyodor Pasternak.*

Long overshadowed by the fame of both her father Leonid Pasternak and brother Boris Pasternak, Josephine Pasternak is finally reaping some of the respect her life and work deserves. The Pasternak family, a highly assimilated Russian-Jewish clan, was unusually gifted. Notes Ronald Hingley, three of the Pasternaks were "superlatively endowed" with talents within, or at least bordering on, genius. The family consisted of "three suns or stars, and three minor bodies, related to them," wrote Josephine. "The minor bodies were: Aleksandr, **Lydia** and myself. The suns were: father, mother and Boris." Her father Leonid was one of Russia's best-known Impressionist painters. Her mother **Rosalia Pasternak** was a brilliant pianist whose career was placed on hold when her children were born; later, her musical ambitions would be largely frustrated by war, revolution, and poor health.

Josephine Pasternak was born in Moscow in 1900. By the time she was 11, her brother Boris, 10 years her senior, was reading his poetry to her for critiques. A child of unusual sensibility, she dwelled in a home filled with music, art, and some of Russia's most original thinkers, who came to visit her father's studio. It was Josephine who entertained Albert Einstein when he sat for his portrait. Boris would remember Josephine as a little girl whose concern for the downtrodden extended even to the steps of their dacha, which she kissed out of sympathy for their suffering when people walked on them. With her thoughtful, melancholy face and dark plaits of hair, young Josephine served as a model for her father, whose sketches of her are among his finest. In a 1934 letter to Leonid, Boris would write: "I think your best subjects were Tolstoy and Josephine. How you drew them! Your drawings of Josephine were such that she grew up according to them, followed them in her life."

Living in a Russia that found itself in the grips of a devastating world war, a revolution, and then a merciless period of civil war created ever greater difficulties for the Pasternaks. In St. Petersburg, Lenin's Bolsheviks seized power in an almost bloodless takeover, but in Moscow, where the Pasternaks lived, the situation was considerably different. Here, bloody street fighting would take place before the Bolsheviks triumphed. Both Josephine and her younger sister were trapped with a cousin by the gun battles, and they were profoundly relieved to hear that the rest of their family was safe. Later, the Pasternaks discovered a dozen bullets embedded in the inside walls of their flat, and the outer plaster of the building was permanently pockmarked. Life in Moscow became increasingly difficult over the next several years. Although Leonid sympathized with the aims of the revolution, both he and Rosalia suffered from impaired health. Urgently needing proper medical care, Leonid and Rosalia, along with their daughters Josephine and Lydia, emigrated to Germany in June 1921.

There, the Pasternaks maintained close ties with Boris, who had remained in revolutionary Russia, which began calling itself the Soviet Union in December 1922. In 1924, Josephine married Fyodor Pasternak, her second cousin; the couple lived in Munich, where Fyodor prospered as a banker. Josephine's interest in philosophy intensified and in 1931 she was awarded a doctorate in philosophy by the University of Munich. Throughout these years, she wrote, publishing a small but growing number of poetry under the pseudonym Anna Ney. Many of her poems from the 1930s are powerful commentaries on the times. "The Murder of Dollfuss" concerns the Austrian leader who was murdered in a botched Nazi coup in 1934. "Chamberlain at Munich" declares that "the world will burn up in shame." Still another is a memorial to a German-Jewish woman in Munich who took her life by poison during the *Kristallnacht* pogrom of November 1938.

In 1938, Josephine's first volume of collected poems, *Koordinaty* (Coordinates), was published. That same year, she and her husband, along with her aged parents, fled Nazi Germany for the safety and academic serenity of Oxford, England. In August 1939, on the eve of the outbreak of World War II, Rosalia succumbed to the heart disease that had long impaired her health. Having survived the war, Leonid died in May 1945, only weeks after the end of hostilities in Europe. Josephine would later note: "When Mother died it was as if harmony had abandoned the world. When father died it seemed as if truth had left it."

After 1945, Josephine remained at Oxford, where her sister Lydia also lived. Widely known and loved there, Josephine was described as "a deeply self-abnegating, nervous and charming woman of great beauty and intellectual spirit." Devoted to advancing her father's artistic legacy and reputation, she edited and published his memoirs, which appeared in a full edition in Moscow in 1975 as well as in abridged form in England in 1982. She also organized exhibitions of his work in the United Kingdom, Germany, the Soviet Union, and the United States. Assisted by Lydia, in 1958 Josephine worked in cooperation with Oxford's Ashmolean Museum to create the Leonid Pasternak Memorial Exhibition of Paintings and Drawings, the first major retrospective of the great Russian artist's work in the West. Despite advancing years, she also managed to work on a substantial philosophical manuscript, an informal study in epistemology entitled *Indefinability*, which would appear in print in 1999, six years after her death.

As Josephine Pasternak grew older and physically more frail, she lived her life more and more in her writing. Often during these years, as in her 1958–64 correspondence with the venerable theater director Gordon Craig, she never personally met her correspondent. In 1981, she saw her second and last collection of verse, *Pamyati Pedro* (Memories of Pedro), appear in print. Most of the poems in the collection, which was published by the Russian-language YMCA Press in Paris, were written between 1934 and 1939. Major reviews in *The Times Literary Supplement* of London and *World Literature Today* were enthusiastic. The former spoke of "poems [that] belong to a living tradition, and . . . can be read with respect," whereas the latter ended by noting, "These poems reach into our conscience; they instruct us and transform us." The two opening pieces of *Pamyati Pedro* were dedicated to the dog Pedro, "whose suffering, when he is given away of necessity by his master, comes to typify that of all tormented beings."

As one of the last survivors of the pre-revolutionary Russian intelligentsia, Josephine Pasternak embodied a rich, marvelous tradition. Destined to be less well known than her brilliant parents and older brother Boris, she nevertheless left behind considerable achievements when her long life ended. She had lived most of her years in a world of exile that in the final analysis always remained an alien environment for her. But as her tender obituary in *The Times* of London noted, after her death on February 16, 1993 (only three days short of her 93rd birthday), she would be remembered by her friends and family as "a woman of unfailing kindness and refinement, a gifted mimic and a raconteuse of genius. Her life was dominated by the ever-present past. On her deathbed she was abrim with memories of her childhood 90 years before: her *nyanya* pounding mustard, answering Josephine's perpetual 'What's that?' with wry peasant wit: 'Russian honey.' Her first kiss was bestowed by a drunken beggar, under her *nyanya*'s horrified

eyes, after Josephine had given him her only lucky kopek for pity's sake. She remembered, too, a transcendental experience in a Russian meadow—long grass, silver birches, a scrap of paper in the sunlight, many years ago."

The family Pasternak with Boris standing second from left and Josephine on right in white blouse.

SOURCES:

Dyck, J.W. "Boris Pasternak: The Caprice of Beauty," in *Canadian Slavonic Papers-Revue Canadienne des Slavistes.* Vol. 16, no. 4. Winter 1974, pp. 612–626.

Fleishman, Lazar. *Boris Pasternak: The Poet and His Politics.* Cambridge, MA: Harvard University Press, 1990.

Gifford, Henry. "Times of Dislocation," in *TLS: The Times* [London] *Literary Supplement.* No. 4082, June 26, 1981, p. 736.

Hingley, Ronald. *Pasternak: A Biography.* NY: Alfred A. Knopf, 1983.

"Josephine Pasternak," in *The Times* [London]. February 18, 1993, p. 19.

Lamont, Rosette C. "Verse," in *World Literature Today.* Vol. 56, no. 2. Spring 1982, pp. 361–362.

Levi, Peter. *Boris Pasternak.* London: Hutchinson, 1990.

Ney, Anna. "Anti-Semitism," in Jenny Hartley, ed. *Hearts Undefeated: Women's Writing of the Second World War.* London: Virago, 1995, pp. 243–244.

——. *Koordinaty: Stikhi* (Coordinates: Verses). Reprint of 1938 ed. Berlin: Petropolis, [1979?].

Pasternak, Josephine. *Indefinability: An Essay in the Philosophy of Cognition.* Copenhagen: Museum Tusculanum, 1999.

——. "Patior," in *The London Magazine.* Vol. 4, no. 6. September 1964, pp. 42–57.

——. *Pamyati Pedro* (Memories of Pedro). Paris: YMCA Press, 1981.

Pasternak, Leonid. *Zapisi raznykh let* (Notes from Various Years). Ed. by Zhosefina Leonidovna Pasternak. Moscow: Sovetsky khudozhnik, 1975.

Pasternak, Leonid Osipovich. *The Memoirs of Leonid Pasternak.* London: Quartet, 1982.

Salys, Rimgaila. "'Ever EGC': Gordon Craig's Letters to Josephine Pasternak," in *Elementa: Journal of Slavic Studies and Comparative Cultural Semiotics.* Vol. 3, no. 3, 1997, pp. 225–269.

——. *Leonid Pasternak, the Russian Years, 1875–1921: A Critical Study and Catalogue.* 2 vols. Oxford: Oxford University Press, 1999.

——. "A Tale of Two Artists: Valentin Serov and Leonid Pasternak," in *Oxford Slavonic Papers.* Vol. 26, 1993, pp. 75–86.

Zaltsberg, Ernst. "In the Shadows: Rosalia Pasternak, 1867–1939," in *East European Jewish Affairs.* Vol. 28, no. 1. Summer 1998, pp. 29–36.

John Haag,
Associate Professor of History, University of Georgia, Athens, Georgia

Paston, Agnes (c. 1405–1479)

English aristocrat. *Name variations: Agnes Berry. Born around 1405 in Norfolk, England; died on August 17, 1479, in London; daughter of Edmund Berry, lord of Hertfordshire; married William Paston (a lawyer and judge), in 1420 (died 1444); mother-in-law of Margaret Paston (1423–1484); children: John Paston (b. 1421); Edmund Paston (b. 1425);* ***Elizabeth Paston*** *(b. 1429); William Paston (b. 1436); Clement Paston (b. 1442).*

Agnes Paston, a wealthy English woman of the gentry class, was the daughter of Sir Edmund Berry, lord of Hertfordshire. In 1420, she married William Paston, a highly respected justice of the local court systems. Though his family belonged to the upper peasantry, William had managed to acquire substantial properties and bring himself up into the landed gentry.

As well, financial considerations led him to marry Agnes. She was her father's only heir, and in 1433 the couple were greatly enriched by Agnes' inheritance of lands in Norfolk and Hertfordshire. The Pastons found themselves to be of like mind in terms of maintaining a high social and financial status. Like most landowners, they were concerned mostly with preserving their properties. Their eldest son John became a lawyer and married the woman his parents carefully chose for him, a wealthy though not noble heiress named Margaret Mauteby (***Margaret Paston**). When Agnes' husband died in 1444, she gained control of over half of William's estates, since he willed her a considerable amount of property, and her own dower lands were returned to her control. Most of the remaining portion of William's lands went to John, with provisions made for their other sons as well.

Agnes moved in with John and Margaret, a relationship that proved difficult at times for her daughter-in-law, for both women had forceful, domineering personalities. Agnes was a skilled administrator of her own property, but often conflicted with Margaret over the marriages of Margaret's children—she felt that Margaret was too sentimental, letting her children marry for love (with the notable exception of a daughter **Margery Paston Calle**). Eventually Agnes moved to London to live with her third son, William. She remained an active participant in her family's affairs until her death in 1479. Details of her life are preserved in the voluminous collection of Paston family letters.

SOURCES:

Anderson, Bonnie S., and Judith P. Zinsser. *A History of Their Own.* Vol. I. NY: Harper & Row, 1988.

Virgoe, Roger, ed. *Private Life in the Fifteenth Century: Illustrated Letters of the Paston Family.* NY: Weidenfeld and Nicolson, 1989.

Laura York,
Riverside, California

Paston, Margaret (1423–1484)

English gentlewoman who withstood a number of sieges. *Name variations: Margaret Mauteby. Born in 1423; died in 1484; daughter of* ***Margery Berney*** *and John Mauteby; daughter-in-law of Agnes Paston (c. 1405–1479); married John Paston, around 1440; children: eight, including* ***Margery Paston Calle.***

Margaret Paston is just one example of how upper-middle-class women in mid-15th century England routinely functioned in quasi-military roles. She married John Paston, son of ***Agnes Paston**, around 1440. Over the years, her husband was frequently absent on business, leaving her to defend hearth and home. For example, in January 1450, the Paston estates at Gresham were besieged by a Lord Molynes and a thousand-strong armed force. To prepare for the siege, Margaret had written to her husband asking him to send crossbows, winches, and bolts. With only 12 other defenders, Margaret made a stand, but the walls were destroyed around her; she was evicted and the house was sacked. On two other occasions, Margaret Paston was forcibly attacked. She protected the manor of Drayton, even conducting forays in 1465 to seize property claimed both by her husband and the duke of Suffolk. After her husband's death in 1466, Margaret continued to oversee the family properties for her oldest son, who never married.

SOURCES:

Bennett, H.S. *The Pastons and their England.* Cambridge: Cambridge University Press, 1932.

Haskell, Ann S. "The Paston Women on Marriage in Fifteenth-Century England," in *Viator.* Vol. 4, 1973, pp. 459–471.

Pasture, Elizabeth M. de la (1890–1943).

See Dashwood, Elizabeth Monica.

Patch, Edith (1876–1954)

American entomologist. *Born Edith Marion Patch in 1876 in Worcester, Massachusetts; died in 1954; University of Minnesota, B.S., 1901; University of Maine, M.S., 1910; Cornell University, Ph.D., 1911; honorary degree from University of Maine, 1937; never married; no children.*

Served as head of the department of entomology, University of Maine Agricultural Experiment Station

(1904–37); served as head of the University of Maine Agricultural Experiment Station (1924–37); appointed president of the Entomological Society of America (1930).

A leading entomologist who had a genus and several species of insects named in her honor, Edith Patch was also the first woman to be elected president of the Entomological Society of America. Her most important research was on aphids, flying insects that attack nearly every species of plant. One of Patch's most significant findings was that the melon aphid lived in wintertime as an egg in the "live-for-ever" weed. Consequently, by removing the weed the damage caused by aphids to crops the following spring was markedly reduced.

Patch was born in Worcester, Massachusetts, in 1876, the youngest of six children. When she was eight, she moved with her family to prairie land near Minneapolis, Minnesota, which was fertile ground for insects. As a student, Patch won a $25 prize for her essay on the monarch butterfly; she used the money to buy *A Manual for the Study of Insects*, written by the eminent entomologist John Henry Comstock and illustrated by ***Anna Botsford Comstock**. Patch attended college at the University of Minnesota, majoring in English and winning prizes for some of her sonnets. Despite her talent for writing, after she received her bachelor's degree in 1901 she looked for jobs in entomology. She found none, however, for at the time there were no women entomologists and no jobs for women in the field.

Patch spent the next two years supporting herself by teaching English, until she received a letter from Charles D. Woods at the University of Maine. Seeking someone to head the entomology department he was organizing, Woods offered her the post on condition that she work for one year without pay, giving him time to assess her abilities. Patch jumped at the offer; before long, Woods granted her a salary and a teaching position in recognition of her skills while ignoring criticism from his colleagues for hiring a woman. (In response to one man's outraged protest, "A woman can't catch grasshoppers!," Woods supposedly replied, "It would take a lively grasshopper to escape Miss Patch.") In 1904, he appointed her head of the Department of Entomology at the Maine Agricultural Experiment Station.

While at the University of Maine, she also earned her M.S. in 1910. The following year, she earned a Ph.D. from Cornell University, where she had the opportunity to study under John Henry Comstock, author of her cherished book. Comstock considered her an exceptional student, and used part of her doctoral thesis in his towering achievement, *Introduction to Entomology* (also illustrated by Anna Botsford Comstock). After receiving her doctorate, Patch began her ongoing research on aphids, focusing on economic and ecological entomology and the life histories and ecology of migratory aphids. Now well known and in great demand, she received aphid specimens from other researchers throughout the world. While retaining her position as head of the department of entomology, in 1924 she was appointed head of the Maine Agricultural Experiment Station itself. In 1930, she was named president of the Entomological Society of America, the first woman so honored. (After her appointment, she received a congratulatory letter from one male colleague who felt that the tardiness of the recognition was due only to the fact that she was not a man.)

Edith Patch wrote extensively during her career, publishing 15 technical books, including an extensive tome about aphids, *Food Plant Catalogue of the Aphids*, and approximately 100 papers. She also published several popular children's books about insects and nature, most of which were written after her retirement from the University of Maine in 1937. An internationally respected scientist, who due to her tenacity and ability broke into the traditional male-dominated academic environment, she was a member of several scientific organizations, including the American Association for the Advancement of Science, the American Society of Naturalists, and the American Association of Economic Entomologists. She never married or had children and in her retirement years apparently led a rather lonely life, particularly after a sister to whom she was extremely attached died. Upon her death in 1954, Patch left all of her belongings to her physician and his wife.

SOURCES:

Bailey, Brooke. *The Remarkable Lives of 100 Women Healers and Scientists.* Holbrook, MA: Bob Adams, 1994.

Bailey, Martha J. *American Women in Science: A Biographical Dictionary.* Santa Barbara, CA: ABC-CLIO, 1994.

SUGGESTED READING:

Banta, Margaret Myers. *Women in the Field: America's Pioneering Naturalists.* College Station, TX: Texas A&M University Press, 1991.

Herzenberg, Caroline L. *Women Scientists from Antiquity to the Present.* West Cornwall, CT: Locust Hill Press, 1986.

Mozans, H.J. *Women in Science.* Notre Dame, IN: University of Notre Dame Press, 1991.

Ogilvie, Marilyn Bailey. *Women in Science.* Cambridge, MA: MIT Press, 1986.

Rossiter, Margaret W. *Women Scientists in America.* Baltimore, MD: Johns Hopkins University Press, 1982.

COLLECTIONS:

Edith Patch's papers are located at the Raymond H. Folger Library at the University of Maine in Orono, Maine.

Christine Miner Minderovic,
freelance writer, Ann Arbor, Michigan

Paterson, Emma (1848–1886)

English labor organizer. *Born Emma Ann Smith on April 5, 1848, in London, England; died of diabetes on December 1, 1886, in Westminster; only child of Henry Smith (a schoolmaster) and Emma Dockerill Smith; privately educated by her father; married Thomas Paterson, on July 24, 1873.*

Founded the Women's Protective and Provident League, known as the Women's Trade Union League after 1891 (1874); was the first woman to attend the annual Trades Union Congress (1875); edited The Women's Union Journal *(1876–86); founded the Women's Printing Society (1876). Published several articles.*

Emma Paterson, who lived less than 39 years, founded an organization which would long outlast her. Well into the 20th century, her league would organize working women, advocate vocational training, and seek protective labor legislation in both Great Britain and the United States. When Paterson organized the Women's Protective and Provident League (WPPL), later known as the Women's Trade Union League (WTUL), she relied on the help of middle- and upper-class allies and trade unionists. That spirit of attempting to cross class lines, while not always successfully done, would be the hallmark of the League.

Emma Paterson was born in 1848 in London, the only child of Henry Smith, a National Society schoolmaster, and **Emma Dockerill Smith**. Young Emma was particularly close to her father, who encouraged her to learn the classics as well as perfect her whistling. When Henry died, his 16-year-old daughter was devastated, and she and her mother were left in poverty. Both mother and daughter tried running their own school but it soon failed. Young Emma, after working as a governess and a private secretary, eventually found her calling. In 1867, at age 19, she became the assistant secretary for the Working Men's Club and Institute Union. Emma worked for the Club for five years, coming to understand the importance of trade unionism for workers. After a brief period as secretary for the Women's Suffrage Association, she married one of the original members of the Working Men's Club, Thomas Paterson. Thomas, a cabinetmaker by trade, was interested in trade unionism, so the newlyweds took an extended honeymoon to the United States with the intent of investigating union activity there. Emma came into contact with women workers as exploited as those in England and was impressed by the women typographers and umbrella makers who had formed unions. After several months of travel, the Patersons returned to England and Emma went into action. In 1874, she founded the Women's Protective and Provident League.

Paterson did not support protective legislation aimed only at women and children (although the league in later years did), seeing that combination as degrading to women workers. While she wanted women workers to be able to organize into trade unions just as men did, Paterson felt strongly that separate unions for women would give them greater representation. It was her hope that the WPPL would provide "the feeling of strength and mutual sympathy and helpfulness afforded by close association with others." Having briefly apprenticed to a bookbinder in her youth, Paterson first sought out women bookbinders. Within a few months of its formation, the WPPL assisted in the organization of 300 women bookbinders, the longest lasting of the WPPL-affiliated unions. However, until her death in 1886 at age 38, Paterson also organized women milliners, garment makers, and upholsters. In addition, she established the WPPL as a member of the male-dominated Trade Unions Congress. When Lady ***Emily Dilke** assumed control of the WPPL in 1887, she took charge of a vital organization dedicated to women workers, thanks to the determination and skill of Emma Paterson.

SOURCES:

Goldman, Harold. *Emma Paterson: She Led Woman Into a Man's World.* London: Lawrence & Wishart, 1974.

Kathleen Banks Nutter,
Manuscripts Processor at the Sophia Smith Collection, Smith College, Northampton, Massachusetts

Paterson, Isabel (c. 1886–1961)

Canadian-born literary critic and novelist. *Born Isabel Bowler on Manitoulon Island, Lake Huron, Canada, around 1886; died in 1961; daughter of Francis Bowler and Margaret (Batty) Bowler; attended public schools in Mountain View and Cardston, Alberta, Canada; married Kenneth Birrell Paterson.*

Selected works: The Shadow Riders *(1916);* The Magpie's Nest *(1917);* The Singing Season *(1924);* The Fourth Queen *(1926);* The Road of the Gods

(1930); Never Ask the End *(1932);* The Golden Vanity *(1934);* If It Prove Fair Weather *(1940).*

Described as fiercely opinionated, decidedly Tory, and disarmingly humorous, Isabel Paterson was a literary critic for the New York *Herald Tribune* for many years, writing the popular column, "Turns With a Bookworm."

Of Irish heritage, she was born Isabel Bowler around 1886 on Manitoulon Island, Lake Huron, Canada, and educated in public schools. She worked briefly as a secretary with the Canadian Pacific Railroad before immigrating to the United States, where she worked for newspapers in Spokane and Vancouver, Washington. She then went to New York, writing for the *American* and for *Hearst's Magazine*, taking up her post at the *Herald Tribune* in 1922. Paterson, who had married Kenneth Birrell Paterson (sources hint that it was not an enduring union), wrote under her married name.

In addition to literary criticism, Paterson wrote a number of novels, which, by her own admission, were brought forth with great agony. "Anyone writing a novel is inclined to feel that it would be better never to have been born," she wrote while in the throes of producing *If It Prove Fair Weather* (1940). "I've had a number of novels published already. One of them is good, and two others what I'd call fair. The one now being written is of course superlative. An outstanding feature . . . is that it has no social significance whatever." When not at work, Paterson, who made her home in the country, was a passionate gardener.

SOURCES:

Kunitz, Stanley J., and Howard Haycraft, eds. *Twentieth Century Authors.* NY: H.W. Wilson, 1942.

Barbara Morgan,
Melrose, Massachusetts

Patey, Janet Monach (1842–1894)

English vocalist. *Name variations: Janet Whytock. Born Janet Whytock in London, England, on May 1, 1842; died in Sheffield on February 28, 1894; studied singing under J. Wass, Pinsuti and Mrs. Sims Reeves; married John Patey (a bass singer), in 1866.*

Janet Monach Patey had a fine alto voice, which developed into a contralto. Her first appearance, as a child, was made at Birmingham; her first regular engagement was in 1865, in the provinces. From 1866, the year she sang at the Worcester festival, she was recognized as one of the leading contraltos, and, on the retirement of **Charlotte Helen Sainton-Dolby** in 1870, Patey was without rival both in oratorio and in ballad music. She toured in America in 1871, and sang in Paris in 1875 and in Australia in 1890.

Patiniere, Agnes (fl. 1286)

Flemish artisan. *Flourished in 1286 in Douai, Flanders; married Jehanne Dou Hoc.*

Agnes Patiniere, an artisan, lived in the Flemish town of Douai. Her life and involvement in a civil lawsuit provides clues about the realities of labor in a medieval town for a woman, of the inequities she faced and the resources she had for redress. All of Patiniere's family worked as laborers in the wool industry, and she also entered that field. Probably around age 30, Patiniere married Jehanne Dou Hoc, also a laborer of Douai. Both were trained in wool-dying, particularly in extracting and dying with woad, a plant which yields a bright blue color. Patiniere is recorded as a participant in a lawsuit brought in 1286 against her employer, wool merchant Jehanne Boinebroke. Patiniere and 44 other employees (about half female) filed a suit complaining of wages not paid, underpayment for services, unfair property seizures, and evictions without cause.

Boinebroke, one of the wealthier merchants of Douai, owned extensive lands as well as his wool business. Like most textile merchants at that time, he operated his business under the "putting-out" system, similar to modern piecework: he supplied his laborers with materials for a fee, then paid them when they finished weaving or dying the cloth. Laborers like Patiniere were forbidden from working for a second employer, making them economically dependent on one merchant. In addition, like many successful entrepreneurs, Boinebroke owned the houses in which most of his employees lived, for which they paid him rent.

Patiniere's allegation against Boinebroke was that he had seized from her mother a quantity of dye in payment of a debt; Patiniere claimed the value of the dye to be in excess of the debt owed, and asked for £20 in losses. When it was her turn to testify, Patiniere brought in numerous witnesses who corroborated her story. In the end, the court found Boinebroke guilty of some infractions, though not all, and forced him to pay back wages and reparations. This was probably the best the plaintiffs could have received, given the defendant's powerful position in the town; still, it shows that as dependent as they were, urban laborers were not completely powerless. Patiniere received £5 for her claim. After the settlement of the suit, Agnes Patiniere disappears from the town's records.

SOURCES:

Gies, Frances, and Joseph Gies. *Women in the Middle Ages*. NY: Harper and Row, 1978.

Laura York,
Riverside, California

Patrick, Mary Mills (1850–1940)

American educator and missionary. *Born on March 10, 1850, in Canterbury, New Hampshire; died on February 25, 1940, in Palo Alto, California; oldest of six children of John Patrick (a farmer) and Harriet (White) Patrick; graduated from Lyons Collegiate Institute, 1869; University of Iowa, M.A., 1890; University of Bern, Ph.D., 1897; honorary LL.D. from Smith College, 1914; honorary Litt.D. from Columbia University, 1922.*

Appointed as a teacher at a mission school in Erzurum (1871); transferred to American High School for Girls in Constantinople (1875); became co-principal (1883) and then sole principal of the American High School (1889); converted the school into the American College for Girls and served as its first president until her retirement (1890–1924).

Born in 1850, Mary Mills Patrick grew up on a farm in North Boscawen, New Hampshire, before her family moved to a farm in Iowa when she was 15. Her mother was descended from members of the Plymouth Colony, and her father, a farmer whose own father had been a longtime Congregationalist minister, encouraged an atmosphere of learning in their home; Patrick's brother George would become a professor of philosophy and psychology, and Patrick herself would become an educator.

Patrick graduated from Lyons Collegiate Institute in 1869, and two years later accepted a teaching appointment from the American Board of Commissioners for Foreign Missions in Erzurum, in what is now eastern Turkey. During the four years she taught there, she traveled on horseback some 3,000 miles through the countryside and learned both ancient and modern Armenian. In 1875, she transferred to the American High School for Girls in Constantinople (now Istanbul), where she would spend the rest of her teaching career. In 1883, Patrick became co-principal of the school, which mostly enrolled students from the Ottoman Empire's minority Christian populations, and was named sole principal six years later. During this time, she learned Turkish and also Greek, through spending her summers in nearby Greek villages.

In the late 1880s, with plans to convert the high school into a college, Patrick returned to the United States to study at the University of Iowa, from which she received a master's degree in 1890. She secured a college charter from the Commonwealth of Massachusetts, and upon her return to Constantinople used it to transform the American High School for Girls into the American College for Girls, of which she was appointed president. The school was more commonly known as Constantinople Women's College, and enrolled more than 250 students each year.

During summer breaks, Patrick studied in Heidelberg, Zürich, Berlin, Leipzig, and Paris, eventually earning a Ph.D. from the University of Bern in 1897. Her thesis, *Sexus Empiricus and Greek Scepticism*, was published in 1899. A continuing interest in Greek culture and philosophy would lead her to write another book on Greek thought, *Sappho and the Island of Lesbos*, in 1912, and *The Greek Skeptics* in 1929.

When a fire destroyed the college in 1905, a new site was purchased in Arnavutköyü, on the European shore of the Bosporus. The college cut all ties to the mission board in 1908, when a new charter was granted, and moved onto its new campus in 1914. The American College for Girls survived the Balkan Wars and World War I, and after the secular Turkish republic rose from the ashes of the Ottoman Empire the school played an important role in the education of young Turkish women. The international student body numbered over 400 in 1924, when Patrick retired. She returned to America and lived in New York City, where she devoted her time to writing. Her last books were *Under Five Sultans*, a history and memoir published in 1929, and *A Bosporus Adventure*, a history of the college published in 1934. Two years later she moved to Palo Alto, California, where she lived until her death of coronary occlusion, at age 90, in 1940. Her ashes were buried in her hometown of Canterbury, New Hampshire.

SOURCES:

James, Edward T., ed. *Notable American Women, 1607–1950*. Cambridge, MA: The Belknap Press of Harvard University Press, 1971.

McHenry, Robert, ed. *Famous American Women*. NY: Dover, 1980.

Maria Sheler Edwards, M.A.,
Ypsilanti, Michigan

Patterson, Alicia (1906–1963)

***American newspaper editor and publisher who founded* Newsday.** *Born Alicia Patterson in Chicago,*

Illinois, on October 15, 1906; died at age 56 of bleeding ulcers on July 2, 1963; second of three daughters of Joseph Medill Patterson (founder of the New York Daily News*) and Alice (Higinbotham) Patterson; sister of* ***Josephine Patterson Albright*** *(who wrote a column for* Newsday*) and* ***Elinor Patterson Baker****; niece of Eleanor Medill Patterson (1881–1948); educated at Foxcroft in Middleburg, Virginia, and in Europe; married James Simpson, Jr. (director of Marshall Field & Company), in 1920s (divorced one year later); married Joseph W. Brooks, in 1931 (divorced 1939); married Harry F. Guggenheim, in 1939.*

Alicia Patterson was born in Chicago, Illinois, in 1906, the second of three daughters of Joseph Medill Patterson and **Alice Higinbotham Patterson**; her paternal aunt was ***Eleanor Medill Patterson**. Alicia came to prominence as founder, editor, and publisher of Long Island's successful tabloid *Newsday.* As a pilot, she also set the women's New York to Philadelphia air record.

Patterson grew up on a farm in Libertyville, Illinois, preferring athletic activities for recreation, such as riding and swimming. In 1927–28, she worked as a cub reporter on her father's newspaper, the *New York Daily News;* she then joined the staff of the family-owned *Liberty* magazine. In 1931, Patterson became a transport pilot, setting records and writing several articles about her experiences. She returned to the *Daily News* as literary critic in 1932, where she reviewed books until 1943.

In 1939, she married her third husband, the mining magnate Harry F. Guggenheim. When the two learned that the *Nassau County Journal* in Hempstead, Long Island, was for sale, they snatched it up, turned it into a tabloid against the advice of her father, and renamed it *Newsday.* In six years, it began to show a profit; four years later, it was moved to nearby Garden City. By 1955, *Time* magazine considered it "the fastest-growing and most profitable big daily paper started in the United States in the last twenty years," and it has remained in operation through the start of the 21st century. Unlike her isolationist relatives, Alicia Patterson was an internationalist. She also successfully campaigned to purchase Walt Whitman's birthplace in Huntington, Long Island, as a memorial to the poet.

Patterson, Audrey (b. 1926).

See Faggs, Mae for sidebar.

Patterson, Cissy (1881–1948).

See Patterson, Eleanor Medill.

Patterson, Eleanor Medill (1881–1948)

Editor and publisher of the **Washington Times-Herald** ***who was one of America's leading press magnates, the first woman to possess such status.*** *Name variations: Cissy Patterson; Eleanor M. Gizycka. Born Elinor Josephine Patterson on November 7, 1881, in Chicago, Illinois; changed name early in life to Eleanor Medill Patterson; died on July 24, 1948, in Washington, D.C.; daughter of Robert Wilson Patterson, Jr. (a newspaper editor) and Elinor Medill (an heiress and socialite); aunt of* ****Alicia Patterson*** *(1906–1963, founder of* Newsday*); married Count Josef Gizycki (a cavalry officer and playboy), on April 14, 1904 (divorced June 1917); married Elmer Schlesinger (a corporation lawyer), on April 11, 1925 (died February 1929); children: (first marriage) Leonora Felicia Gizycka (b. 1905).*

One of the most controversial individuals in the field of journalism, in 1940 Cissy Patterson was the only woman editor and publisher of an American metropolitan daily. Moreover, she made her *Washington Times-Herald* the first multiple-edition daily newspaper in the United States. Some obituaries referred to her as "the greatest editor in America" and "the most powerful woman in the country."

Patterson's many-sided personality always aroused controversy. Arthur Brisbane, her journalistic father-confessor, called her "The Bird of Paradise." *Times-Herald* staffer ***Adela Rogers St. Johns** thought of her as the reincarnation of Queen ***Elizabeth I.** Gossip columnist Walter Winchell found her "the craziest woman in Washington, D.C." To *Time* magazine, she was "the most hated woman in America." An erratic, lonely person, whose impulsive cruelties could match her admitted kindness and talent, Patterson once referred to herself as "just a plain old vindictive shanty Irish bitch."

Cissy Patterson was born Elinor Josephine Patterson in Chicago on November 7, 1881. While still a youth she adopted the name Eleanor Medill Patterson. Her brother gave her the nickname Cissy, an appellation later adopted by the press but personally only by close friends. Patterson's family was among Chicago's bluebloods. Her father Robert Wilson Patterson, Jr., advanced from a night telegraph operator to managing editor of the *Chicago Tribune,* and was later its publisher. Unhappy in marriage, he was a heavy drinker and spent long sessions in a sanitorium. Her mother **Elinor (Nellie) Medill**

Patterson was a prominent socialite and the daughter of Joseph Medill, owner of the *Chicago Tribune,* a founder of the Republican Party, and an early backer of Abraham Lincoln. Cissy's brother, Joseph (Joe) Medill Patterson, founded the *New York Daily News.* Also later receiving prominence were her cousins, Medill McCormick and Robert (Bertie) Rutherford McCormick, the sons of her mother's sister ***Katherine Medill McCormick** and Robert Sanderson McCormick, heir to the McCormick farm-equipment company; Medill and Bertie respectively became U.S. senator and publisher of the *Tribune.*

Cissy found her father indulgent, her mother a cold social climber. She loved Grandfather Joseph Medill most of all. Her youth centered on the family's 91-room mansion in Chicago, summers in Newport, and frequent trips to Europe. At age 15, she enrolled as a student at Miss (**Heloise**) **Hersey**'s School in Boston, after which she attended Miss (***Sarah**) **Porter**'s school in Farmington, Connecticut.

As a young woman, the tall, slender Cissy Patterson was striking, and throughout her life she was the center of attention. Notes **Lynne Cheney**, "Her nose was a little too upturned, her forehead a little too broad for classic beauty, but her red hair, elegant figure, and proud bearing helped her dominate whatever room she entered."

Patterson's entry into European court society came at age 21, when she joined her uncle, Robert Sanderson McCormick, in Vienna, where he was American minister, then ambassador, to Austria-Hungary in 1901–02. At age 22, she fell in love with the 35-year old Count Josef (Gizy) Gizycki. Tall, thin, and arrogant, Gizycki was a Polish noble whose urbanity, charm, and good looks matched his passion for gambling, horses, and women. Although his title was Austrian, his family owned estates in eastern Poland, a territory then belonging to Russia. After a whirlwind courtship, in which Gizycki followed her from one continent to another, Patterson finally won the consent of her reluctant parents. On April 14, 1904, they were married in Washington, D.C.

After the initial burst of passion had worn off, it became clear that the debt-ridden Gizycki had married Patterson for her $30,000-a-year income. Blansko, his "castle," lay in Nowosilica, a muddy village inside the Russian border lying halfway between Warsaw and Odessa. The first thing to strike her on arrival was the number of village children who looked like her husband. The "castle" resembled nothing so much as a huge dilapidated barn; even the windows lacked curtains and shutters. Suddenly Patterson found herself extremely lonely, a stranger in her own house. Soon Gizy was saying to Cissy:

> You have no money, you have no children, you have no sense. You are no good as a wife. You bore me to death. And when your papa returns, I'll ask him to do me the favor of taking you back to America with him.

For several years, Patterson endured Gizycki's philandering. "He was a sensualist," she later recalled. "He simply lived for the senses, exercising and wine and women, that's all he cared for." Yet on September 3, 1905, she had a daughter, **Felicia Gizycka** (her last name was a feminine form of Gizycki). In January 1908, at the French resort of Pau, Gizycki beat Patterson during a quarrel about his women, and she fled to London with baby Felicia. She once wrote, "I had a longing to get away from this man, whom I hated, and whom I wished dead—or myself dead—anyway to be free of this man who had become my master from the first day I saw him."

A few months later, the count and some accomplices, disguised in fur and goggles, took the tiny Felicia from her nursery in Hampton and hid her in a convent in Austria. Headlines all over the world read COUNT KIDNAPS BABY, and Patterson suddenly became a celebrity. Several months later, she persuaded president-elect William Howard Taft to appeal directly to Tsar Nicholas II. Upon revisiting his Russian castle, Gizycki was briefly jailed by the tsar's police. In August 1909, Patterson returned to the United States with her daughter, and in June 1917, after an eight-year legal tangle, she was granted a divorce. Throughout her life, Cissy could never get close to Felicia. When Felicia married journalist Drew Pearson in 1925, Cissy herself found Pearson attractive, and remained friendly with him even when, in 1928, the marriage ended in divorce. Felicia would bitterly attack her mother in the novel *Flame of Smoke,* a damning account of a New York sophisticate who serves as guardian of her bewildered niece.

After Patterson returned to the U.S., she lived the life of a socialite, dividing her time between Chicago, New York, and Washington. Over the years, her name was linked with a number of prominent men, often married. Among these were the German ambassador, Count von Bernstorff; Senator William E. Borah (Rep.-Idaho); Nicholas Longworth, Speaker of the House of Representatives and husband of ***Alice Roosevelt Longworth**; diplomat William E. Bullitt; newspaper editor Walter Howey; and Thomas Justin White, general manager for the Hearst chain.

In August 1916, experiencing severe emotional strain, Patterson traveled to Jackson Hole, Wyoming, where she took up big-game hunting, mixed with the community, and even adopted the garb of a typical Westerner—man's shirt, boots, britches, and a five-gallon hat. She bought a ranch at Flat Creek from a new lover, cowboy and former rustler Cal Carrington, who had been illiterate until age 21. In 1921, Patterson was the first woman to shoot the Salmon River rapids, called "The River of No Return."

In 1926, Patterson's first novel, *Glass Houses,* was published in America. Three years earlier it had been published in French under the title *André en Amérique* and serialized in the *Revue de Paris.* Using the name Gizycka, she offered a witty if cruel satire on Washington society. Readers familiar with her private life easily identified Senator Borah, Alice Longworth, Cal Carrington, and Cissy herself. After Gizycki's death in Vienna in 1926, she wrote *Fall Flight* (1928), a fictionalized account of her youth and marriage.

Meanwhile, on April 11, 1925, she married Elmer Schlesinger, heir to a Chicago department-store fortune. A Harvard-educated corporation lawyer whose clients included the *Chicago Tribune,* Schlesinger was counsel for the U.S. Shipping Board. As both Patterson and Schlesinger possessed abundant means, they leased an apartment on Fifth Avenue, bought Vincent Astor's 47-acre estate at Sands Point, Long Island, and traveled in a luxuriously fitted private railroad car. In 1927, while the executive mansion was receiving a new roof, Calvin and *__Grace Coolidge__ stayed at Patterson's Washington mansion, 15 Dupont Circle, which Coolidge found larger than the White House. The Patterson-Schlesinger marriage too became shaky, for both husband and wife possessed more than their share of narcissism. Elmer soon lost himself in high-pressure business deals, while Cissy was swept up in Washington's social whirl. In February 1929, Schlesinger died of a heart attack on a golf course in Aiken, South Carolina.

Eleanor Medill Patterson

Again adrift, Mrs. Eleanor Medill Patterson—the name she assumed again after 1929—

considered a career in journalism. Writes biographer Ralph G. Martin, "Her life had largely been a world of self-indulged impulses: another trip, another house, another lover." Yet she approached her friend Arthur Brisbane, the most widely read columnist in America, the richest newspaper employee, and the right-hand man of William Randolph Hearst. Brisbane persuaded Hearst to hire Cissy as editor of his *Washington Herald.* Fourth in circulation among the capital's five dailies, the *Herald* had long been operating at a loss. Forgoing his usual drive for profit, Hearst wanted a morning paper that could, he hoped, influence one of the most important readerships in the world.

On August 1, 1930, Patterson assumed the post, in the process declaring that she shared her publisher's opposition to Prohibition, the League of Nations, the World Court, and naval disarmament. Though Hearst was her hero, she often disregarded his orders, refusing to run some of his syndicated editorials and features and designing her own format.

Entering the newspaper business as a novice, Patterson seemed at first merely to be seeking attention, as for example in her personal attacks on Alice Longworth. Other erstwhile friends also became subject to her public wrath, including son-in-law Drew Pearson, who was one of her columnists; Walter Winchell, also a columnist for her paper; and Cabinet member Harold Ickes, once a frequent dinner companion.

She was an American duchess, a product of her times, personifying in her many lives a whole succession of romanticized heroines . . . innocent heiress abroad, western sportswoman, feuding editor and swashbuckling boss.

—Paul F. Healy

But Patterson learned the trade quickly. Ruling with an iron hand, she revamped the entire operation. Notes biographer Martin, "Within a year, she had made it the most provocative paper in the nation's capital. She had converted Hearst's sickest paper into one of his most successful." She encouraged her reporters at every turn, fought hard for circulation and advertising, used the best paper and the best ink, and showed a genuine instinct for style, photography, and typography. She created a prototypical gossip-and-scandal section called Page 3, was the first person to cable fashion news out of Paris, and sponsored a column, "The Male Animal," that carried the first letter on homosexual problems to ever appear in an American newspaper. Seeking to attract a female readership, she invented the modern woman's page, in the process recruiting so many women reporters that *Time* referred to the paper as "Cissy's Henhouse."

Patterson often wrote copy herself, going over draft after draft to make her writing terse yet lively. In 1931, she interviewed gangster Al Capone; in 1932, she circulated among Washington's Bonus Marchers; in 1936, she toured the impoverished areas of eastern Tennessee in a rented Model-A Ford. Once she disguised herself as a destitute woman ("Maude Martin") to report on the plight of the jobless in the Depression, spending three nights in Salvation Army headquarters. Over the years, her contributions to the Salvation Army would tally over half a million dollars.

Often favoring local stories over international ones, Patterson focused many crusades on the nation's capital. She sought hot lunches for District of Columbia schoolchildren, anonymously underwriting the program herself until Congress acted. Other Patterson causes included home rule for the District of Columbia, slum clearance, the cleaning of the Potomac River, efficiency in the police department, decent facilities for tuberculosis victims, and adequate schooling for crippled children. The former hunter-turned-animal-lover supplied oxygen for a dying gorilla in the Washington zoo and hired a helicopter to drop food on starving ducks in Rock Creek Park. (The packages failed to hit their target, killing a number of ducks.)

Yet Patterson was by no means easy to work for. True, she could be impulsively generous, as when she invited women employees to help themselves from her tremendous wardrobe. Yet she fired seven editors in sequence, and many other staff members as well, and if some were rehired, their future was not always assured. In 1935, she lost a two-year battle with the rival *Washington Post* over such popular comic strips as "Dick Tracy," "Andy Gump," and "Gasoline Alley." She immediately had her chauffeur deliver one pound of raw meat, her pound of flesh, to the *Post*'s publisher Eugene Meyer, attaching the note, "So as not to disappoint you." Meyer, who was Jewish, was not amused by the Shylock analogy, and even Patterson later admitted, "I guess I made a mistake that time."

In 1937, when Hearst faced major financial difficulties, Patterson heeded the prompting of Hearst's mistress and confidante ***Marion Davies** and lent the California publisher $1 million. On August 7 of that year, she leased

Hearst's morning *Washington Herald*, which she was already editing, and the evening *Washington Times,* taking an option to purchase. On January 28, 1939, she became their full-fledged owner, and three days later she combined the papers into the round-the-clock *Washington Times-Herald*. The new paper published ten editions within 24 hours: five from dusk until dawn and five others through the day. By 1943, Patterson had made the *Times-Herald* the most widely read paper in the city and put it in the black as well. By now she owned six residences, including establishments in Marlboro, Maryland, Siesta Key, Florida, Port Washington, Long Island, and Nassau. Her personal and business employees totalled 1,300.

Like her brother Joe, publisher of the *New York Daily News,* Patterson retained an early admiration for Franklin D. Roosevelt, whom she called "a real American of the finest type." To Patterson, ***Eleanor Roosevelt**, with whom she never broke, was "the noblest woman I have ever known." From the beginning, both Cissy and Joe were strong New Dealers, in 1940 supporting FDR for a third term.

The break came in December 1940, when Roosevelt proposed the lend-lease bill. The president, both publishers believed, sought full-scale U.S. entry into World War II. By the middle of 1941, Cissy was referring to Roosevelt as a dictator. Her isolationism stemmed back to the First World War, when the entire family opposed intervention. It was strengthened by Joe's postwar disillusionment and his belief that FDR had acted deceitfully. Three days before Pearl Harbor, Cissy's *Washington Times-Herald* and her cousin Bertie's *Chicago Tribune* published War Department plans that included the drafting of ten million men, a joint U.S.-British invasion by July 1, 1943, and a five-million-man American Expeditionary Force in 215 divisions. In the summer of 1942, both papers published an account of the battle of Midway, detailed enough to indicate that the U.S. had broken the Japanese code. The government attempted to prosecute both newspapers for betraying war secrets but ended up dropping the charge.

The feud between Roosevelt and the Patterson siblings was the fiercest one of all. The president questioned their patriotism, making slurs about what he called the "McCormick-Patterson axis." The Luce publications called Cissy, Bertie, and Joe "The Three Furies of Isolationism." In August 1942, Representative Elmer Holland (Dem.-Pa.) demanded that the Federal Bureau of Investigation investigate "America's No. 1 and No. 2 exponents of the Nazi propaganda line—Cissy and Joe Patterson." Once a bomb was thrown into the *Times-Herald* building.

Cissy retaliated quickly. She attacked the "Yellow Potomac set," civil servants whom she claimed were avoiding combat with soft Washington berths. At one point, she collected a page of gruesome wartime scenes, juxtaposing them with Roosevelt's 1940 campaign pledge not to enter "any foreign war." She called interventionist author ***Clare Boothe Luce** "a lovely asp," and Vice President Henry Wallace "a crystal-gazing crackpot."

Soon after the war ended, Patterson's world began to come apart. Lonely and overweight, she suffered from alcoholism and heart disease. She fought bitterly with her daughter, quarreled with old friends over trivial matters, and no longer appeared daily in the press room. Patterson suffered a crushing blow in 1946 when her brother Joe died, and she threatened to form a combination against Bertie over control of the *New York Daily News*. Suspicious even of her servants, whom she thought were spying on her, she kept guns by her bedside and in her car and purse. In July 1948, her step-daughter **Halle Schlesinger** found her dead in the bedroom of her Dower House estate near Marlboro, Maryland, evidently of a heart attack. Patterson left the *Times-Herald* to seven of its executives, but as they lacked the operating capital to sustain it, they sold it to Colonel Robert R. McCormick.

The highly quotable Alice Roosevelt Longworth, daughter of Theodore Roosevelt, experienced both the best and worst sides of Patterson's personality. "Cissy's life was so much richer than mine," she said. "I said a lot of things, but Cissy did them."

SOURCES:

Gizycka, Eleanor M. [Eleanor Medill Patterson]. *Glass Houses*. Minton, Balch, 1926.

———. *Fall Flight*. Minton, Balch, 1928.

Gizycka, Felicia. *Flower of Smoke*. NY: Scribner, 1939.

Healy, Paul F. *Cissy: The Biography of Eleanor M. "Cissy" Patterson*. NY: Doubleday, 1966.

Hoge, Alice Albright. *Cissy Patterson*. NY: Random House, 1966.

Martin, Ralph G. *Cissy*. NY: Simon & Schuster, 1979.

SUGGESTED READING:

John Tebbel. *An American Dynasty*. NY: Doubleday, 1947.

Justus D. Doenecke,
Professor of History, New College of the University of South Florida, Sarasota, Florida

Patterson, Elizabeth (1785–1879).

See Bonaparte, Elizabeth Patterson.

Patterson, Elizabeth J. (1939—)

U.S. congressional representative, Democrat of South Carolina, 100th–102nd Congresses, January 3, 1987–January 3, 1993. Born Elizabeth Johnston on November 18, 1939, in Columbia, South Carolina; daughter of Olin D. Johnston (1896–1965, former governor of South Carolina as well as U.S. senator, 1945–65) and Gladys Atkinson Johnston; attended public schools in Kensington, Maryland, and Spartanburg, South Carolina; Columbia College, Columbia, South Carolina, B.A. in political science, 1961; graduate study at University of South Carolina, 1961–62; married Dwight Fleming Patterson, Jr., in 1967; children: Dwight Fleming DeWitt Patterson; ***Catherine Leigh Patterson.***

Served as recruiting officer for the Peace Corps (1962–64); served as recruiting officer for VISTA (1965–67); was director of a Head Start program (1967–68); was staff assistant for Representative James R. Mann (1969–70); served on Spartanburg County Council (1975–76); was a member of South Carolina senate (1979–86); elected as a Democrat to the 100th and to the two succeeding Congresses (January 3, 1987–January 3, 1993).

Elizabeth J. Patterson

Born Elizabeth Johnston in Columbia, South Carolina, in 1939, Elizabeth J. Patterson began her political life in childhood. Even as a young girl, Patterson was permitted by her mother **Gladys Atkinson Johnston** and her father Olin D. Johnston to work on his Senate campaigns. Johnston, a former governor of South Carolina, served as a U.S. senator from 1945 to 1965.

Patterson attended public schools in Kensington, Maryland, and Spartanburg, South Carolina, later taking a B.A. in political science at Columbia College, where she graduated in 1961. After a stint at graduate school at the University of South Carolina, Patterson started on her own path towards public service. In the 1960s, she worked as a recruiting officer for the Peace Corps and VISTA, eventually becoming coordinator for the Head Start program for the South Carolina Office of Economic Opportunity.

In 1967, she had married Dwight Fleming Patterson, Jr., and they had two children, Dwight and Catherine. After two years working as staff assistant for South Carolina Representative James R. Mann, beginning in 1969, Patterson took a break from professional life. In 1975, ten years after her father's death, Patterson was elected to her first political office, serving on the Spartanburg County Council until 1976.

She became a member of the South Carolina senate in 1979, serving until 1986. That year, when four-term Republican Representative Carroll Campbell, Jr., decided not to seek reelection, Patterson declared her candidacy for the House seat in South Carolina's Fourth Congressional District. She was elected as a Democrat to the 100th Congress, taking her seat in 1987. In the 1988 election, Patterson managed to win reelection in a district that voted overwhelmingly for the Republican presidential candidate. Serving in three successive Congresses, Patterson sat on the Committee on Veterans' Affairs, the Committee on Banking, Finance and Urban Affairs, and the Select Committee on Hunger. In 1992, Patterson was an unsuccessful candidate for reelection to the 103rd Congress.

SOURCES:

Office of the Historian. *Women in Congress, 1917–1990.* Commission on the Bicentenary of the U.S. House of Representatives, 1991.

Paula Morris, D.Phil.,
Brooklyn, New York

Patterson, Louise (1901–1999).

See Thompson, Louise.

Patterson, Martha (1828–1901).

See Johnson, Eliza McCardle for sidebar.

Patterson, Mary Jane (1840–1894)

African-American educator. *Born in 1840 near Raleigh, North Carolina; died in 1894; second of five children of Henry Patterson (a mason and former slave) and Emeline Patterson; graduated from Oberlin College, 1862.*

Taught in Philadelphia (1862–69); appointed to Washington, D.C., school system (1869); served as principal of Washington Colored High School (1871–72, 1873–84).

Mary Jane Patterson was born in pre-Civil War North Carolina in 1840, the daughter of Henry Patterson, an escaped slave, and **Emeline Patterson**. When the Fugitive Slave Act was passed in 1850, virtually encouraging the kidnapping and selling of free blacks into slavery, the family moved north and settled in Oberlin, Ohio, where her father prospered as a mason. While her older brother also became a mason, Patterson and her three younger siblings attended Oberlin College, the first co-educational college in America and the first (in 1835) to admit African-Americans as students. There she and two of her sisters, **Channie** and **Emma**, studied to become teachers. When Patterson received her degree from Oberlin in 1862, she became the first African-American woman to graduate from college in the United States.

Patterson taught in Philadelphia until 1869, when she and her sister Channie were appointed to teach in the black school system in Washington, D.C., which was renowned for the excellence of the education it offered. (Their parents and their sister Emma later joined them in the city.) Two years after she arrived, Patterson was appointed principal of Washington Colored High School, the city's only high school for African-Americans and one of the premier schools for African-Americans in the country. She served one year as principal, after which she was replaced by Richard T. Greener, who was Harvard University's first black graduate and the father of ***Belle da Costa Greene**. He stayed only one year, however, and in 1873 Patterson was reinstated as principal, a post she would hold for 11 more years.

The school flourished under her leadership. Because its enrollment grew, however, in 1884 the school board again decided to replace Patterson as principal with a man. Patterson remained at the school as a teacher for the rest of her life, never marrying and continuing to dedicate herself to educating the descendants of ex-slaves. Months before her death at the age of 54, Patterson was working with colleague ***Mary Church Terrell** to incorporate the Colored Women's League of Washington, D.C., which later became the National Association of Colored Women.

SOURCES:

Weatherford, Doris. *American Women's History.* NY: Prentice Hall, 1994.

Maria Sheler Edwards, M.A.,
Ypsilanti, Michigan

Patterson-Tyler, Audrey (1926–1996)

African-American runner. *Name variations: Audrey Patterson. Born on September 27, 1926; died at age 69 after a heart attack in San Diego, California, in September 1996.*

Audrey Patterson-Tyler was the first African-American woman to win an Olympic medal, taking the bronze in the 200 meters in the 1948 London Olympics. Following her retirement from competition, Patterson-Tyler coached more than 5,000 youths in track and field.

Patti, Adelina (1843–1919)

Spanish-born soprano who was one of the greatest of her century. *Pronunciation: pa-TEE. Name variations: Marchioness de Caux; Baroness Cederström or Cederstrom. Born Adelina Juana Maria Patti on February 19, 1843, in Madrid, Spain; died on September 27, 1919, at Craig-y-Nos Castle, Brecknockshire, Wales; daughter of Salvatore Patti (an Italian singer) and Caterina Chiesa Barili-Patti (a Spanish singer known before her marriage as Signora Barili); younger sister of* ***Carlotta Patti*** *(1835–1889), a singer, and Amelia Patti, who married Maurice Strakosch; raised and educated in New York City; married Louis de Cahuzac, marquis de Caux, in 1868 (divorced 1885); married Ernesto Nicolini (a tenor), in 1885 (died 1898); married Baron Rolf Cederström, in 1899; no children.*

Debuted at Covent Garden (1861), Berlin (1861), Brussels (1862), Paris (1862), Vienna (1863), Paris Opéra (1867), Teatro alla Scala (1877), Metropolitan (1887); retired (1906); appeared in recitals 1906–14).

The Spanish-born soprano Adelina Patti was the most renowned singer in Europe and the United States for over 30 years. She was born in

1843, the youngest of three children, into a family of opera singers and musicians. Her parents were opera performers well known in Europe by the time of Patti's birth in Madrid, where they were on tour. Her Italian father was Salvatore Patti; her Spanish mother was **Caterina Chiesa Barili-Patti**, known before her marriage as Signora Barili. Caterina also had four children from an earlier marriage, and all seven of her children would enjoy successful careers as singers.

When Adelina Patti was four the family moved to New York, where her father became an opera house manager. Her half-brother Ettore Barili gave Patti voice lessons starting at age five; by the age of seven Adelina was recognized as a child prodigy and the next year she gave her debut concert at New York City's Tripler Hall. Audiences and critics at subsequent concerts were stunned by the maturity, range, and purity of her voice. Her success in New York led to a three-year tour of American cities, unprecedented for such a young child, from 1851 to 1854. A second concert tour followed in 1857. Patti's sister **Amelia Patti** was married to the renowned pianist Maurice Strakosch; he took care of Adelina while on tour and served as her manager, instructor, and accompanist. She received only a minimal education, although her family background and musical training made her fluent in Spanish, French, Italian, and English. Her parents and Strakosch continued training Patti in the demands of operatic singing until they felt she was prepared to sing opera professionally. They arranged for her critically praised debut in the title role of *Lucia di Lammermoor* at the New York Academy of Music in 1859; she was 16, and would perform in opera continually for the next half-century, enjoying a career that was decades longer than that of most opera singers. Soon after her debut Patti faced serious family crises, as her father's struggling opera house failed and her mother left the family in 1860 to return to Rome. Patti then began to provide much of the family's income through her performances.

She toured the eastern United States and the West Indies from 1859 to 1861. In 1861, she went abroad, under the care of her father and Strakosch, to perform in *La sonnambula* at the Covent Garden opera house in London. She was enthusiastically received in London, where she was to perform every autumn for 25 years.

Patti remained on tour in Europe virtually continuously for 20 years, not returning to New York until 1881. She played to crowded houses in Berlin, Brussels, Amsterdam, Vienna, Paris, and across Italy. The operatic roles she chose ranged from light comedy, which she preferred, to tragedy, but whatever role she appeared in, critics were universal in their praise of her acting ability and the emotive power of her voice.

While in Paris in 1866, through her friendship with Empress ***Eugénie**, Patti met the aristocrat Louis de Cahuzac, marquis de Caux, who served as a personal servant to the French emperor Napoleon III. They wished to marry but the marquis was not allowed to retain his privileged position at the French court if he married a working woman. Since Patti would not consider giving up her career, de Caux eventually resigned his post. This freed the couple to marry in 1868, when the new marchioness was 25 years old and her husband 42; however, the marriage lasted less than a decade, and they obtained a legal separation in 1877. As Patti was by then a celebrity throughout Europe and the United States, her marital problems brought scandal to the opera world and were the subject of often sensationalistic newspaper articles in many of the countries she had performed in. In the divorce suit, de Caux charged Patti with an adulterous affair with her co-star, Italian tenor Ernesto Nicolini. She admitted to the affair, but maintained in her defense that de Caux was jealous, controlling, and violent, and that he allowed her no access to her substantial income. The divorce would be finalized in 1885, when de Caux was awarded a settlement of $300,000 from Patti. Freed at last from her unhappy marriage, Patti married Nicolini a few months later.

Despite her personal problems during the separation and divorce, Patti continued to travel widely. She did a concert tour on her return to New York in 1881, followed by two operatic tours of the United States. Throughout the 1880s and 1890s, she was the most highly paid and most visible singer in Europe and the United States, receiving press coverage for her appearances as well as for her shocking personal life, legendary jewel collection, enormous wealth, and for her demanding, often capricious personality. She maintained homes across Europe, where she was friends with and frequently host to Europe's royalty and aristocracy. Her fame even led to mentions in contemporary literature and drama, such as Tolstoy's *Anna Karenina* and Oscar Wilde's *The Picture of Dorian Gray*.

Patti gave a farewell performance at the New York Metropolitan Opera House in 1887. She and Nicolini then left for another extended tour abroad, performing in Spain and Argentina. In 1895, at age 52, Patti gave six farewell appearances at Covent Garden. She and Nicolini

Adelina Patti

then went into semi-retirement on an estate in Wales called Craig-y-Nos Castle which Patti had purchased some years before, and where she lived with Nicolini prior to their marriage. Patti adopted Wales as the native land she had never truly had, and was respected by the Welsh for her generosity to charitable causes and to her poor neighbors.

Ernesto Nicolini died in 1898. Patti, age 56, remarried a year later. Her third husband, a Swedish aristocrat named Baron Rolf Cederström, was a former military officer who, at the time Patti met him in 1897, was director of the Health Gymnastic Institute in London. At the time of their marriage, Cederström was only 28; their age difference and his occupation made the renowned opera star once again the subject of a flood of news articles and gossip columns.

The urgings of Patti's American fans called her back to the stage in 1903, when she began her last operatic tour at New York's Carnegie Hall. Although Patti was by then considerably older than most opera singers were at retirement, audiences were still moved by her powerful performances. In 1906, at age 63, she made her formal farewell appearance at Albert Hall in London. She also made numerous recordings which have preserved her work and demonstrate the remarkable purity and range which captivated her admirers and which had once led the composer Giuseppe Verdi to call Patti the greatest voice he had ever heard.

Adelina Patti was called out of retirement to perform occasionally at charity events in Wales and England through 1914, when she left the stage for good at age 71. She spent the remaining five years of her life at Craig-y-Nos Castle, where she died in 1919, at age 76. At her wish, her husband buried her in the celebrity cemetery Père Lachaise in Paris. He eventually remarried, selling Craig-y-Nos Castle to the Welsh National Memorial Association which converted it into the Adelina Patti Hospital. The hospital remained in operation until 1986, when the castle and its grounds were turned into a national park and cultural center.

SOURCES:

Cone, John F. *Adelina Patti: Queen of Hearts*. Portland, OR: Amadeus Press, 1993.

Klein, Herman. *The Reign of Patti*. NY: Century Press, 1920.

Lauw, L. *Fourteen Years with Adelina Patti*. New York and London, 1884.

Laura York,
Riverside, California

Pattison, Dorothy W. (1832–1878)

English surgical nurse. *Name variations: Sister Dora. Born Dorothy Wyndlow Pattison in 1832; died in 1878; sister of Mark Pattison, a scholar, writer, and follower of Cardinal Newman who was once married to* ****Emily Dilke*** *(1840–1904).*

In 1864, Dorothy Pattison entered a Church of England Sisterhood of the Good Samaritan, adopting the name Sister Dora. From 1867 to 1877, she was a surgical nurse and had sole charge of a new hospital in Walsall. Pattison had great skill in surgery and was tireless in her philanthropy. She was beloved among the poorer classes among whom she labored. A window was placed in her memory in the parish church, and a statue of her was erected in Walsall.

Patton, Frances Gray (1906–2000)

American writer. *Born Frances Gray Lilly on March 19, 1906, in Raleigh, North Carolina; died on March 28, 2000, in Durham, North Carolina; daughter of Robert Lilly (a newspaper editor) and Mary S. MacRae (Gray) Lilly; attended Trinity College (now Duke University); graduated from the University of North Carolina, Chapel Hill; married Lewis Patton (an English professor), in 1927; children: Robert, Mary, and Susannah.*

Selected works: The Finer Things in Life *(1951);* Good Morning, Miss Dove *(1954);* A Piece of Luck *(1955);* Twenty-Eight Stories *(1969).*

Frances Gray Patton earned a place in American letters through her single novel, *Good Morning, Miss Dove* (1954), and her numerous short stories, which appeared in *The New Yorker* and other major magazines during the 1940s and 1950s and were collected in several volumes. The novel, which was dubbed a minor classic, was developed from an earlier short story "The Terrible Miss Dove" and chronicles the life of a strict but beloved geography teacher in a small American town, whose sudden illness impacts the entire community. *Good Morning, Miss Dove* enjoyed enormous popularity in both the United States and London, although *The New York Times*' reviewer Charles Poore thought it "ruthlessly sentimental." The formidable Dove, described as "the public conscience of Liberty Hill," is a dedicated teacher who deems herself responsible for the character of each child in her classroom, a task which encompasses preparing the children for the "inescapable perils of independent thinking" and driving home the fact that "life demanded all the disciplined courage and more, that one could bring to it." It was a Book-of-the-Month Club selection and in 1955 was made into a movie starring ***Jennifer Jones**.

A fourth-generation North Carolinian, Patton may have been influenced by her literary family. Her father Robert Lilly was the editor of *The Raleigh Times*, her brothers were journalists, and her mother **Mary S. Gray Lilly** also published occasional pieces. Patton began writing for her high-school newspaper, then attended the University of North Carolina on a playwriting fellowship. In 1927, she married Lewis Patton, a University of North Carolina English professor. The couple settled in Durham, where they raised three children, two daughters and a son.

The first of Patton's short stories, "A Piece of Bread," concerning a young Southern girl's encounter with a chain gang, won a Kenyon Review prize in 1945, and was included in that year's *O. Henry Memorial Award Prize Stories.* Henceforth, her stories appeared regularly in *Collier's*, *Harper's*, and *McCall's*, as well as *The New Yorker*, and were collected in *The Finer Things in Life* (1951) and *A Piece of Luck* (1955). Patton published a third volume of stories, *Twenty-Eight Stories*, in 1969. A life-long resident of Durham, Patton also taught creative writing at Duke University and the University of North Carolina. She died in March 2000, at age 94.

SOURCES:

Mainiero, Lina, ed. *American Women Writers: From Colonial Times to the Present.* NY: Frederick Ungar, 1982.

"Obituary," in *The New York Times.* April 2, 2000.

Barbara Morgan,
Melrose, Massachusetts

Pauahi, Princess (1831–1884).

See Bishop, Bernice Pauahi.

Pauker, Ana (c. 1893–1960)

Foreign minister of Rumania, one of the leading Communist officials in Eastern Europe in the period after World War II, who was the first woman to serve as Cabinet minister in charge of a European country's international relations. *Pronunciation: POW-ker. Born Ana Rabinovici in Moldavia in northern Rumania sometime in 1893 or 1894; died in Bucharest in June 1960; daughter of a Jewish butcher who held the status of rabbi in his community; attended medical school in Switzerland for a period beginning in 1915; married Marcel Pauker, a fellow Rumanian student (died, probably in 1937); children: three.*

Studied for a period in Switzerland (1915–21); joined Communist Party (1921); elected to Central Committee (1922); imprisoned (late 1920s); in exile in Moscow (1931–34); imprisoned in Rumania (1935); husband executed in the Soviet Union (c. 1937); released from prison at request of Soviet Union (1940); reentered Rumania with the Red Army (1944); led Communist demonstrations in Bucharest (1944–45); appointed foreign minister of Rumania, helped to organize the Warsaw Pact (1947); attacked the heretical leadership of the Yugoslav Communist Party (1948); named vice-premier (1949); treated in the Soviet Union for breast cancer (1950); purged from Communist Party (1952).

A leading Communist for many years, Rumanian Ana Pauker played a crucial role in Eastern Europe following World War II. She returned to her native country in 1944 from exile in the Soviet Union and led the way in establishing a Communist government in Rumania. Rising to the position of foreign minister, the first woman in modern European history to reach this high office, she became a key figure in her country's government. A cold and forbidding figure with a reputation as the most loyal follower of Joseph Stalin in Rumania, she was known as "the Iron Lady." Stalin himself described her as "the cleverest woman Communist outside Russia."

Nonetheless, her position was precarious. The Rumanian Communist Party was the setting for intense internal rivalries, and Pauker soon found herself confronted by such enemies as Gheorghe Gheorghiu-Dej. Another source of danger came from relations, marked by distrust, between the Soviet dictator Stalin and the leadership of the Soviet satellite states in Eastern Europe. When Communist dictator Joseph Tito of Yugoslavia broke with Stalin in 1948, the Soviet leader's suspicions of all Eastern European Communists reached a new peak. Within this dangerous political environment, even a veteran party member like Pauker found her position, and perhaps her life, in danger. She fell from her post in 1952.

In subsequent years, Pauker's successful rivals continued to blacken her reputation in the interest of bolstering their own political position. High points in her career such as the expansion of the Rumanian Communist Party, agricultural collectivization, and her leadership in the Central Committee Secretariat were reinterpreted. The scattershot assault on her reputation painted her as a figure of unbridled ambition who was also, paradoxically, a tool of the Soviet leaders.

The country to which Pauker returned in the closing months of World War II had undergone a difficult and complex experience between 1940 and 1944. Under pressure from the victorious Germans in the fall of 1940, King Carol II consented to having important areas of Rumania torn away to be given to the Soviet Union and Hungary. With his unpopularity at a new high, Carol was forced to leave the country, and General Ion Antonescu took over as the military ruler. German pressure on Rumania continued, and, when Hitler attacked the Soviet Union in the summer of 1941, the Rumanians joined in the war.

Initially, Rumania's stand on the German side had popular support. Many Rumanians, including the country's political leaders, thought that the Soviet Union was Rumania's natural enemy. Moreover, Rumania's military cooperation with Hitler let Antonescu's government retake territory lost to the Russians in 1940. It also allowed Rumania to go further, bringing large adjacent areas of Soviet territory, including the major port city of Odessa on the Black Sea, under Rumanian control.

As the war began to turn against Germany, Rumanian enthusiasm for the alliance with Berlin faded. In late August 1944, as Soviet troops began to occupy Rumanian territory, young King Michael, Carol II's son and successor, took a number of dramatic steps. He forced Antonescu out of power, replacing him with a coalition cabinet representing most of the political spectrum. Rumania then left the war, and, within a few days, reentered it on the Allied side.

In these dramatic times, there was little evidence of an active Communist Party. Writes Robert King: "From its founding in 1921 until the arrival of Soviet troops in Rumania in 1944, the RCP [Rumanian Communist Party] played a peripheral role in Rumania's political life." The party was dominated by intellectuals and lacked ties to the peasants who made up a majority of the Rumanian population. Many of its leading constituents were Jews or members of the country's Hungarian or Bulgarian minorities; thus they were not accepted as true Rumanians by most of the country's population. The party had been declared an illegal organization and driven underground in April 1924. It was under firm Soviet control in the 1930s, a period in which it was also the target of effective police suppression. At the party's peak around 1936, it probably had only 5,000 members. In 1944, on the eve of its taking power, its membership may have numbered only 1,000.

Ana Pauker

Despite later claims by Gheorghiu-Dej, Communists played no role in wartime Rumania. Thus, the party lacked the prestige of its counterpart in Yugoslavia. There, Joseph Tito could claim that Communism had become a legitimate and significant force due to its leadership of the anti-Nazi resistance movement. Some of the party's main figures like Gheorghiu-Dej had been imprisoned since the mid-1930s. Most Rumanian Communist leaders, including Ana Pauker, had been in exile in the Soviet Union. They now returned with the victorious Soviet army and made their bid for power. From the close of the war, Ana Pauker was one of the members of the party's inner circle.

The future foreign minister and vice-premier was born in Moldavia, in the northern part of the pre-World War I Kingdom of Rumania, in 1893 or 1894. The details of her life up to 1944 are sketchy, with various sources presenting divergent accounts. All agree that she was the daughter of a Jewish butcher whom his community had named as its rabbi. She attended medical school for a time in Switzerland, married a fellow student, Marcel Pauker, and returned home sometime around the end of World War I. She joined the newly founded Communist Party in 1921 and served time in prison for illegal political activities. Sometime around the close of the 1920s or the start of the 1930s, she began a prolonged stay in the Soviet Union.

Returning to Rumania in the mid-1930s, Pauker was rearrested and sentenced to prison for ten years. By then, she had apparently become a staunch supporter of the Soviet Union and its dictator Joseph Stalin. Marcel Pauker, like many foreign Communists, was caught up in the purges that shook Soviet society in the late 1930s and was reportedly put to death by the Soviet police sometime around the height of the purges in 1937. According to some sources, Pauker denounced her husband as a follower of Leon Trotsky and thus hastened his death.

Events took a temporarily favorable turn for her after she had spent a prolonged period behind bars. Due to the Hitler-Stalin Pact of

1939, Nazi Germany and the Soviet Union were temporarily allies. With Rumania under German domination, the Soviet Union in 1940 successfully requested that Pauker and other Communists be released. Only a year later, Hitler and Stalin were at war; the situation that had favored her release now disappeared.

The next several years found her in Moscow where she played the role of propagandist to her native country. Her broadcasts in Rumanian over Radio Moscow were directed to her countrymen at home. She also helped to organize a Rumanian division to serve in the Soviet army, drawn from Rumanians serving with the Germans whom the Soviets had captured.

Less than three years after the close of the war, Rumania had a Communist government. The presence of the Soviet army and firm pressure from Stalin's government in Moscow dominated the scene. Pauker played an active role in Rumania's evolution from monarchy to Soviet satellite. She led a street demonstration in late 1944 in which the Communists claimed several workers were killed when police fired on the crowd. In the ensuing political uproar, the coalition government, headed by peasant party leader Nicolae Penescu, was forced from office. In 1945, following a trip to Moscow with Gheorghiu-Dej in which the two probably received instructions from the Soviet government, Pauker helped undermine the government of General Nicolae Radescu. In late February, the Soviet leader Andrei Vyshinsky visited Bucharest, forcing a politically weakened Radescu out of office.

The combination of domestic turmoil, to which Pauker contributed, and Soviet pressure, moved the political balance steadily to the left. Stephen Fischer-Galati has suggested that Pauker and others with her Moscow background unsuccessfully urged Soviet leaders to move quickly to set up a thoroughly Communist government after Radescu's fall in 1945. This did not occur, but a series of coalition governments, each with the Communists in an increasingly prominent role, led gradually to a complete victory despite the party's weak popular support. Political opposition was crushed, and, in November 1947, a government dominated by Communists took office. Three members of the party who had spent the war years in the Soviet Union took important positions, with Pauker becoming foreign minister.

Pauker played a key role in forcing King Michael, the hero of the coup in August 1944, into exile. The young monarch traveled to Britain for a royal wedding in late 1947, and he returned to Rumania after announcing his own forthcoming marriage to Princess **Anne of Bourbon-Parma.** The Rumanian foreign minister took the lead in opposing the marriage. The excuse she gave was the financial strain it would place on Rumania. According to Robert Wolff, the real objection was the fear it would rally popular enthusiasm behind the king.

By early 1948, Michael had been forced to abdicate. In February 1948, Rumania signed a treaty tying its interests to those of the Soviet Union. In March, a new constitution turned the country into the Rumanian People's Republic. The government began to collectivize agriculture on the Russian model in March 1949. Pauker played a leading part in the process of revolutionizing Rumanian agriculture, and her activities here became a weapon for her political opponents to use against her in future years.

In a recent article with a new perspective on her career, Robert Levy has argued that Pauker was a moderate on the question of the peasantry. He sees this as an early example of her conflict with Gheorghiu-Dej, dating back to 1947. In Levy's view, Pauker's years in the Soviet Union as a witness to forced collectivization had made her reluctant to endorse such a radical, painful change for Rumania. Thus, she was neither "the classic Muscovite" nor "an abject and dogmatic Stalinist."

A major effort in which Pauker took the lead was the expansion of the party in the period starting in late 1944. By February 1948, the party had grown to 800,000 members. Meanwhile, the process of making decisions for the party, and thus for the country as a whole, became increasingly centralized. The four-person Central Committee Secretariat, to which Pauker belonged, played the key role in Rumanian life during these years. Included in the Secretariat was Gheorghiu-Dej. This small body was probably the place where the rivalry between the factions in the party's leadership became most evident.

Anne of Bourbon-Parma (1923—)

Princess of Bourbon-Parma. *Born Anne Antoinette Francoise Charlotte on September 18, 1923, in Paris, France; daughter of Rene, prince of Bourbon-Parma, and* ****Margaret Oldenburg*** *(b. 1895, granddaughter of Christian IX of Denmark); married Michael I (b. 1921), king of Rumania (r. 1927–1930, 1940–1947), on June 10, 1948; children:* ****Margaret*** *(b. 1949);* ****Helen*** *(b. 1950);* ****Irene*** *(b. 1953);* ****Sophia*** *(b. 1957);* ****Mary*** *(b. 1964).*

Nonetheless, Pauker's credentials as a loyal Stalinist remained strong. In August 1948, for example, she took the lead in condemning the leadership of the Communist Party of Yugoslavia. The action of Tito in breaking with Stalin shook the façade of Communist solidarity throughout Eastern Europe and heightened tensions between Moscow and each of the satellite capitals. But Pauker's firm support for the Russians seemed unquestionable.

Ana Pauker was the trail-blazer for all women who have entered politics in the last 30 years.

—Greta Fink

Later that same year she presented another example of staunch loyalty to Communist ideals. The Rumanian government cracked down on the nation's Jewish Union in November in a campaign designed to weaken Zionist feeling among the country's Jewish population. Zionism came under direct government attack. Pauker's father and brother were in Israel at this time, and Israeli Prime Minister David Ben-Gurion attacked her in burning words. "Ana Pauker—the daughter of a rabbi," he said, "is preventing her own brethren from returning to the Promised Land." Over the next several years, while she continued to serve as foreign minster, the Rumanian authorities became more brutal in their treatment of the country's Jewish population and in their verbal assaults on the Israeli government. In 1952, Jewish emigration to Israel was forbidden.

Pauker's political ascendancy reached its peak in April 1949, when she became one of Rumania's vice-premiers. Soon afterward, the conflicts within the leadership of the country's Communist Party began to cause her major difficulty. A crucial development in the Rumanian Party during the postwar period had been the development of two factions. One, led by Gheorghiu-Dej, played up its role in the coup of August 1944 as the basis to its claim to power. The other, with Pauker in a prominent role, found itself tagged as "the Muscovites" or "Moscow Stalinists" as opposed to Gheorghiu-Dej's "Rumanian Stalinists." The group led by Pauker and Vasile Luca had spent the war years in the Soviet Union. They were also Jewish or members of other ethnic minorities.

Rivalry between the two factions went on below the surface of Rumanian political life until Pauker and a number of her colleagues with similar backgrounds were purged in 1952. The precise course of events and the motives of the participants in the intra-party conflict remain uncertain. An initial split took place in June 1950, when Gheorghiu-Dej criticized Pauker for her mistakes in recruiting new party members after World War II. Pauker may have found her position at home weakened by a prolonged absence in 1950; ill with breast cancer, she spent much of the year receiving medical treatment in the Soviet Union.

In the spring of 1952, Pauker lost her position in the Politburo, the top-ranking body of the Communist Party. She remained the country's foreign minister for a time, but she lost that post as well in July. In September, she lost her last official position, that of vice-premier. Wolff discounts the possibility that Pauker's career went downhill because of a desire by Rumanian leaders to match the growing anti-Semitism evident in the Soviet Union. One of her colleagues whose career also went into eclipse was a known anti-Semite; moreover, figures rising to replace Pauker and her coterie were themselves Jewish. Fischer-Galati suggests, however, that the success of "the Rumanian Stalinists in June 1952 was carefully planned from the formal inception of the offensive in 1950."

For King, a plausible explanation for Pauker's political demise was the fact that several veteran Communist leaders, including Pauker, were now consulting together regularly within the Secretariat of the Central Committee. In this era of Stalinist paranoia due to Tito's defection, their joint thinking may have made them seem a dangerous center of opposition to Stalin, one that the Soviet leader needed to have brought under control.

Pauker's career retained its significance long after her fall from power. Rumania became one of the most independently minded of the Soviet satellite states in Eastern Europe by the early 1960s. Its leaders found it increasingly useful to resurrect Pauker as a symbol of the Soviet domination they now challenged. Thus, she was the target of intense criticism by the victorious Gheorghiu-Dej at the party's gathering in late November and early December 1961. He resurrected the issue of Pauker's alleged errors in the summer of 1944. The successful Rumanian leader claimed that Pauker had neglected to play a role in the coup that overthrew Antonescu's dictatorship whereas he, Gheorghiu-Dej, and other Communists in Rumania had stood at the center of this important event. Meanwhile, Pauker and other Communists located in the Soviet Union had allegedly looked to the Soviet army to bring Communism to power. After Gheorghiu-Dej's death in 1965, his successor Nicolae Ceausescu continued the campaign. Thus,

Pauker was identified with Soviet interests at a time when later Rumanian leaders wanted to claim a closer link with non-Communist elements and to downplay the Russian role in bringing Communism to power in Rumania.

Pauker's success in increasing the ranks of the party also became a tool for her enemies in 1961. She was accused of bringing in unreliable elements, including former members of the Iron Guard fascist movement that had played a large role in Rumanian life in the 1930s. She was also accused by Gheorghiu-Dej of forming a three-person faction that dominated the Central Committee Secretariat and using it to serve their personal interests. Here, too, Pauker's political success in the period after 1945 was turned against her.

Pauker and her colleagues did not suffer the customary penalty for fallen Communist leaders in Eastern Europe during the Stalinist era. They were not subjected to a "show trial," although some sources indicate that Pauker spent some time in prison, in a Soviet mental institution, and in Bucharest under house arrest. When Stalin died in March 1953, rumors flew that the factions of the Rumanian Communist Party would be reunited. That summer, Gheorghiu-Dej replied to a question from a foreign correspondent at a news conference about Pauker's whereabouts by stating that she was still in Bucharest. But there was no reunification. Pauker vanished from the spotlight for the remainder of her life. Some sources indicate the former national leader held a series of minor government positions starting in 1954. She died in Bucharest, probably of a heart attack, sometime in early June 1960.

SOURCES:

Current Biography. NY: H.W. Wilson, 1948.

Fink, Greta. *Great Jewish Women: Profiles of Courageous Women from the Maccabean Period to the Present.* NY: Menorah, 1978.

Fischer-Galati, Stephen. *Twentieth Century Rumania.* NY: Columbia University Press, 1970.

Ionescu, Ghita. *Communism in Rumania, 1944–1962.* London: Oxford University Press, 1964.

King, Robert R. *A History of the Romanian Communist Party.* Stanford, CA: Hoover Institution Press, 1980.

Levy, Robert. "The 'Right Deviation' of Ana Pauker," in *Communist and Post-Communist Studies.* Vol. 28, no. 2, 1995, pp. 239–254.

"Pauker Reported Dead," in *The New York Times.* June 15, 1960.

Wolff, Robert. *The Balkans in Our Time.* Rev. ed. Cambridge, MA: Harvard University Press, 1974.

SUGGESTED READING:

Fischer-Galati, Stephen, ed. *Romania.* NY: Frederick A. Praeger, 1957.

Palmer, Alan. *The Lands Between: A History of East-Central Europe since the Congress of Vienna.* NY: Macmillan, 1970.

Roberts, Henry L. *Rumania: Political Problems of an Agrarian State.* New Haven, CT: Yale University Press, 1951.

Neil M. Heyman,
Professor of History, San Diego State University,
San Diego, California

Paul, Alice (1885–1977)

Relentless women's rights activist who led the final push for suffrage and wrote the Equal Rights Amendment. *Born Alice Paul on January 11, 1885, in Moorestown, New Jersey; died of heart failure at home in Moorestown on July 9, 1977; daughter of William Mickle Paul (a banker and businessman) and Tacie Parry Paul; attended Quaker schools in Moorestown; Swarthmore College, B.S. in biology, 1905; University of Pennsylvania, M.A. in sociology, 1907; University of Pennsylvania, Ph.D. in sociology, 1912; Washington College, LL.B., 1922; American University, LL.M., 1927; American University, D.C.L., 1928; never married.*

Studied and served as a social worker in England (1906–10), where she joined the Women's Social and Political Union; returned to U.S. to found the Congressional Union and National Woman's Party which utilized militant, flamboyant civil disobedience tactics to dramatize the suffrage cause; wrote the Equal Rights Amendment (1923) and worked the rest of her life to remove all legal restrictions on women's rights.

On October 20, 1917, Alice Paul was arrested at the west gate of the White House for picketing. She carried a banner that read: "The time has come to conquer or submit. For us there can be but one choice. We have made it." Taken from the District Police Court to the D.C. jail, having received a seven-month sentence for obstructing traffic, Paul was placed in solitary confinement. Immediately, she initiated a hunger strike that lasted over three weeks. Since Paul served as the National Woman's Party's undisputed leader, prison authorities tried to discredit her by characterizing the zealous suffragist as insane, even moving her to a "psychopathic" ward and depriving her of sleep. Moreover, Paul was brutally force-fed. Ultimately, however, the psychologists brought in to testify to her "persecution complex" could not help the government. As one physician reported, Alice Paul has "a spirit like *__Joan of Arc__, and it is useless to try to change it. She will die but she will never give up."

Born on January 11, 1885, in Moorestown, New Jersey, Alice Paul grew up in an affluent Quaker household. Both parents were descended from principal founders of English American colonies. Her father William M. Paul was a descendant of William Penn, Jr., while her mother **Tacie Parry Paul** could trace her bloodline back to John Winthrop. Alice would be the first of four children; she had two brothers, William, Jr., and Parry, and a sister, **Helen**.

The Paul siblings grew up in a pleasant family environment where an unwavering dedication to scholarship and service prevailed. President of the Burlington County Trust Company, William also invested in a number of successful business ventures and owned a farm. Tacie served as clerk of the Friends Meeting House in Moorestown, a small community nine miles east of Philadelphia. Alice attended the Quaker school there. She loved to read, especially the classics, and particularly the novels of Charles Dickens. Shy and modest, Paul was a serious student and cared little for frivolous pursuits of any sort.

Like a number of other women's rights leaders, such as ***Susan B. Anthony**, ***Lucretia Mott**, and ***Abby Kelley**, Alice Paul was prepared by her Quaker education and religious training for a life of service and a firm commitment to progressive ideas. Within the Society of Friends, women served in various leadership positions and enjoyed equality, in theory and often in practice, with men. But Quakers also accepted notions of gender separatism, such as the tradition of separate business meetings for women, which fostered independent thinking and action free of male influence. When asked by Robert S. Gallagher in 1972 about her interest in women's suffrage, Paul replied, "It wasn't something I had to think about" as a member of the Society of Friends. Since equality of the sexes was always "one of their principles," Paul "never had any other idea."

Alice Paul's maternal grandfather had been one of the founders of Swarthmore College and Tacie attended this institution before marrying William, though she did not graduate. Alice, too, would enroll at Swarthmore when she was 16. Shortly afterward, while she was away at school, her father contracted pneumonia and died suddenly. Paul dealt with her tragic loss, it seems, by devoting all her energies to Swarthmore. Not only did she succeed as a student, but as an athlete. Though slender and gentle, she joined the girls' basketball team and class field hockey team. She took third in the women's tennis tournament. She chose to major in biology, though she had limited interest and less background in the field. She simply wanted to face the challenge of studying something new. As it turned out, she found herself drawn to political science, sociology, and economics, and following graduation in 1905, accepted a College Settlement Association fellowship at the New York School of Philanthropy. In 1907, she earned her master's degree in sociology at the University of Pennsylvania, with minor fields in political science and economics.

Having earned a scholarship to study social work, in the fall of 1907 Paul traveled to England to train at the Woodbrooke Settlement for Social Work. She attended the University of Birmingham as part of this arrangement, and while there went to hear ***Christabel Pankhurst** speak. As other students shouted down the radical suffragist, Paul was intrigued by Pankhurst's message. Christabel's father Richard Marsden Pankhurst, one of the founders of the British Labour Party, had advocated women's suffrage. After his death, his widow, ***Emmeline Pankhurst**, and daughters, Christabel and ***Sylvia Pankhurst**, broke with the Labour Party to form the Women's Social and Political Union (WSPU) in 1903. Influenced by labor unions and Irish revolutionaries, the WSPU turned toward militant tactics designed to generate publicity for the cause. The "suffragettes" (the term used by the *London Daily Mail* to differentiate the WSPU from other suffragists) disrupted political meetings to provoke violent reprisals from police and jailings. Targeting the party in power, the Liberals, they resorted to hunger strikes in prison. These widely publicized strikes prompted the government to forcibly feed the activist women.

In 1908, Alice Paul moved to London to study sociology and economics at the London School of Economics. She also accepted a position as the assistant secretary to the Dalston branch of the Charity Organization Society in London, then worked for the Peel Institute of Social Work at Clerkenwell and the Christian Social Union Settlement of Hoxton. She began attending WSPU meetings in London, though she also prepared to return home. Just before her scheduled departure, Paul agreed to accompany about 100 women on a march to Parliament. She did not anticipate any problem, since the deputation was led by Emmeline Pankhurst, but the group was arrested at the entrance to Parliament and taken to the Cannon Row Police Station where Alice faced charges.

She received no jail time for this first offense, but the incident was one of the most important in her life. While at the police station, she saw a protester with an American flag pin on her coat and struck up a conversation. ***Lucy Burns** would become her closest associate and

Alice Paul

friend for many years. Like Alice, Lucy was bright, well educated, and committed strongly to social justice issues. She graduated from Vassar in 1902, then studied at Yale University, the University of Berlin, and the University of Bonn. She was in London on vacation from school when she first became involved in the Social and Political Union. The arrest was also her first.

After the government dropped the case, WSPU leaders asked Paul to go to Norwich to "rouse the town" in preparation for a planned visit and speech by Winston Churchill. She organized nightly meetings in the marketplace where she called on the citizens to demand that Churchill provide his views on wome. Then, while he spoke, she participated in an anti-government meeting outside the hall, and police arrested her. As in the first demonstration, she experienced no jail time. However, her next assignment reunited Alice with Lucy Burns, and earned the two women their first trip to prison. They protested at Limehouse in London during a David Lloyd George meeting and received two-week sentences. After conducting a five-day hunger strike, they were released.

Blatch, Harriet Stanton. See Stanton, Elizabeth Cady for sidebar.

Paul continued her efforts on behalf of the WSPU until the end of 1909. She traveled to Scotland, where she received a ten-day jail sentence for holding a street meeting in Dundee while Churchill spoke. She was released after a four-day hunger strike. Then in December, Paul and Burns were asked to disrupt the Lord Mayor's banquet at Guildhall. Alice went into the hall early in the morning and waited secretly in the gallery all day. Lucy entered the hall below with the guests. After disturbing the meeting, they were arrested and sentenced to 30 days in Holloway Jail and immediately initiated hunger strikes. This time, prison authorities force-fed the two suffragists. This would be Paul's last experience with British jails, as she sailed for America in January 1910. Lucy Burns remained abroad for two more years.

Paul's health suffered considerably from her prison experiences, especially the hunger strikes. Always thin and frail looking, she appeared emaciated upon her return to the United States. However, she immediately resumed her studies at the University of Pennsylvania. Having written her Ph.D. dissertation on women's legal status in Pennsylvania, she received her doctorate in sociology in 1912. While completing her studies, Alice organized street meetings in Philadelphia promoting women's suffrage, patterned after British protests. She spoke to various suffrage groups about the radical British tactics she knew firsthand and looked forward to devoting more time and energy to the cause.

Eastman, Crystal. See Balch, Emily Greene for sidebar.

When Lucy Burns returned to her home in Brooklyn in the summer of 1912, Alice visited her there. The two discussed how they could best use their abilities and experiences to further the suffrage cause in the United States and decided to join forces to work toward the passage of a constitutional amendment by direct lobbying in Washington, D.C. They then approached National American Woman Suffrage Association (NAWSA) leaders with this idea, including president ***Anna Howard Shaw**, who ultimately gave the idea her blessing. Also present during the first meetings with NAWSA were ◂ **Harriet Stanton Blatch** and ***Mary Ware Dennett**. Blatch, the daughter of ***Elizabeth Cady Stanton**, had lived in England for 20 years and appreciated the direct-action techniques of the WSPU. She had founded the Women's Political Union in New York in 1907, which modeled some of its activities after British efforts, and she liked what Paul had to say. Dennett, the organization's corresponding secretary, also saw the value of generating more publicity. The matter was referred to the National Board of NAWSA through ***Jane Addams**, and Lucy Burns and Alice Paul were allowed to take over the moribund Congressional Committee in Washington, which for years had existed merely on paper.

Burns and Paul moved to Washington in December 1912 to bring life to the Congressional Committee. It would not be an easy task. There was no office, no budget, and few supporters. As Paul noted in an interview that appeared in *American Heritage* in 1974, NAWSA leaders "didn't take [our] work seriously; or they wouldn't have entrusted it to us, two young girls." They rented a basement room at 1420 F Street and began asking local suffragists to volunteer time to the effort, and to provide funds, if possible. Paul usually did the asking herself, in a direct manner devoid of any emotion or small talk. It seems few people could say no to the sincere, selfless activist. By the end of 1913, the office had grown to ten rooms and often bustled with the activities of volunteers. Alice herself devoted all her energy—literally every waking hour—to the suffrage movement.

Three women joined Paul and Burns on the Congressional Committee and would provide essential leadership. They included ◂ **Crystal Eastman**, the talented social betterment lawyer from New York; ***Mary Ritter Beard**, the historian and women's rights activist who also enjoyed some first-hand experience in the British suffrage campaign; and **Dora Lewis** of Philadelphia, a woman of some wealth. The leaders of the Congressional Committee decided to begin their work by planning a demonstration for March 3, 1913, the day before Woodrow Wilson's inauguration. The procession of about 8,000 women started at the Capitol and began its march up Pennsylvania Avenue past the White House to gather at the Daughters of the American Revolution's Constitution Hall. Huge crowds in Washington for the inauguration witnessed the parade, and some chose to verbally harass the marchers while police stood by and watched. The crowd was so large—some newspapers estimated it at half a million—that the marchers could barely make their way down Pennsylvania Avenue. Secretary of War Henry Stimson ultimately summoned troops from Fort Myer to restore order and get the suffragists to their destination, which took six hours.

Woodrow Wilson arrived in Washington during the suffrage procession, and as he made his way to his hotel, he asked his driver, "Where are all the people?" The man replied, "Over on the Avenue watching the Suffrage Parade." Alice Paul had achieved more than she expected with this first planned event. It remained in the news for weeks as politicians demanded an investigation of police practices in Washington. The district chief of police lost his job while the Senate conducted a lengthy investigation. Though there were no significant acts of physical violence against the women, the rude comments of many bystanders received a great deal of attention.

The publicity generated by the parade opened the door for the Congressional Committee to demand quick action on a federal suffrage amendment. Paul liked the public exposure, but her major concern was lobbying members of Congress, and pressuring Wilson himself. The very first deputation of suffragists to meet with the president visited the White House on March 17 and was led by Alice Paul. Two more deputations talked with Wilson before the end of the month. The president proved cordial and acted mildly interested in the cause, but feigned ignorance on the subject and talked about the time not being right to address the issue.

Many members of Congress were equally evasive or apathetic. Thus, the Congressional Committee planned another demonstration to coincide with the opening day of the new Congress, April 7. Representatives of all 435 congressional districts brought petitions favoring the suffrage amendment to Washington, and then a procession marched to the Capitol. Welcomed by pro-suffrage congressmen, the suffragists were escorted to the gallery, where they witnessed the introduction of the Mondell-Chamberlain Amendment. This really represented the reintroduction of the Anthony Amendment of 1878 under the name of new congressional sponsors. It asked that "the right of citizens of the United States to vote shall nor be denied or abridged by any State on account of sex."

Following the two organized demonstrations, Alice Paul recognized the need to extend the lobbying activities of the Congressional Committee, to expand the work beyond the five women who constituted the committee. The result was the formation of the Congressional Union (CU), an organization sanctioned by NAWSA committed to securing the federal amendment. As it quickly grew, it was accepted as an auxiliary to NAWSA, and the Congressional Committee came to serve as its executive board. Pressure on members of Congress continued with greater force, and by June 1913, the Senate Committee on Women's Suffrage reported favorably on the amendment. As the CU and NAWSA organized petition drives, hearings, and other events, the Senate prepared for the first debate on the suffrage issue since 1887.

> [Alice Paul has] a spirit like Joan of Arc, and it is useless to try to change it. She will die, but she will never give up.
>
> —**Physician's report to prison officials, 1917**

In 1914, the Congressional Union broke away from the National American Woman Suffrage Association. Some of the differences between NAWSA and the CU were simply financial, having to do with the status of the CU as a NAWSA auxiliary. However, the conflict ran deeper than this. At the annual NAWSA convention in 1913, Alice Paul and her colleagues in the Congressional Union called for an immediate, all-out campaign to pass the federal amendment. NAWSA leaders such as Shaw and *__Carrie Chapman Catt__ wished to focus on state referendums, and they won the argument at the convention. Faced with making a choice between heading the Congressional Committee or the new Congressional Union, which NAWSA leaders demanded of Paul, she chose the latter. Paul, Burns, and those working with them drifted away from NAWSA, a shift that became more pronounced as 1914 progressed.

First, Paul and Burns, drawing upon their experiences in England, decided that holding the "party in power" responsible for failure to pass the amendment would add a new dynamic to partisan politics. The Congressional Union began to campaign against Democrats, who held the presidency and enjoyed a congressional majority, regardless of individual stands on the suffrage issue. NAWSA leaders condemned the policy as inappropriate for the American political system, since there were pro-suffrage politicians on both sides of the aisle in Congress. Second, on March 2 a new suffrage amendment was introduced in Congress, the Shafroth-Palmer amendment. Endorsed by NAWSA, this measure would require that every state hold a referendum on women's suffrage if 8% of voters signed an initiative petition. The CU, however, stood opposed to this focus on state-by-state action.

During the election campaign of 1914, the Congressional Union targeted Democratic candidates for Congress from the nine western states where women enjoyed the right to vote. Only 19 of 45 Democrats won, and some that did prevailed by slim majorities. The clout of the CU was on the rise, while NAWSA foundered. Dramatic activities garnered headlines for Alice Paul and her small group, but no one seemed to be paying attention to the National American Woman Suffrage Association. The CU also continued its lobbying efforts among congressmen as they looked forward to a House vote on the suffrage amendment, which took place in early 1915 (the Senate had voted 35 to 34 against the amendment in early 1914). The measure lost 204 to 174, but the event commanded a great deal of attention, thanks in great measure to the CU.

As the Congressional Union continued its pressure on politicians in 1916, much of the organization's attention was directed to the presidential campaign. When it met in June, the CU created the National Woman's Party (NWP) for the states where women voted. From this point until March of 1917, Paul's group used the Congressional Union name for members who lacked the vote, while the "Women's Party" referred to Western states' branches. After March 2, 1917, they simply called themselves the Woman's Party. The group opposed Wilson as the Democratic leader and because he refused to endorse the suffrage amendment. Other issues swept Wilson into office in 1916, and as the nation moved toward war in early 1917 the president announced that he would receive no further suffrage deputations. At this point, Alice Paul made a controversial decision—the Congressional Union would picket the White House every day.

On January 10, 1917, at ten in the morning, twelve members of the CU took up positions in front of the east and west gates of the White House. They carried purple, white, and gold banners, bearing the colors of the CU and Woman's Party, including one that asked, "Mr. President, what will you do for suffrage?" The women marched in a slow, square movement, holding the banners for passers-by to see. For the next 18 months, over 1,000 women from all over the country participated. They picketed day and night, in summer and winter, on every day of the week except Sundays. Though president of the Woman's Party, Alice Paul took her turn picketing like everyone else.

After the declaration of war against Germany, confrontations with bystanders at the site of the picketing became frequent. On June 20, when a Russian mission representing the Kerensky government arrived at the White House, banners were ripped from the hands of WP members and destroyed. A crowd rushed the pickets, forcing the police to intervene to protect the marchers. The next day, the Washington chief of police informed Alice Paul that picketing must stop or the suffragists would be arrested. On the morning of June 22, dozens of policemen took up positions outside Woman's Party headquarters. However, Lucy Burns and two other women slipped out and made their way to the east gate of the White House. After a few minutes, they were arrested and taken to the police station. As more and more women faced arrest in subsequent days, no one was actually charged. But then six Woman's Party members went to trial in police court on June 27. Found guilty of "obstructing the highway," they received three-day sentences. They would be the first of 97 suffragists to go to jail, as the CU continued to employ non-violent civil disobedience tactics.

Alice Paul battled ill health in the summer of 1917 and did not picket. But on October 20, she was arrested for obstructing traffic and sentenced to seven months in the District of Columbia prison. Placed in solitary confinement, she went on a hunger strike immediately, which lasted 22 days. During the last week, authorities forcibly fed the Woman's Party president using tubing placed into her nose. She was moved to the hospital and ultimately to a "psychopathic ward." Her lawyer, whom she was not allowed to see, got her removed back to the hospital, where the force-feeding continued. Undaunted by the force-feeding, the isolation, the attempts to paint her as insane, and other horrors of life as a prisoner, Alice Paul stood firm. Fearful that Paul or others of the suffragists would fall gravely ill or die, and under great pressure from mounting public sentiment, the government released all the women from jail on November 27 and 28. Later, the D.C. Court of Appeals overturned all the convictions.

The picketers were released from jail a week before Congress convened. The House quickly set a date, January 10, to vote on the Anthony Amendment. Woodrow Wilson spoke favorably of women's suffrage in his message to Congress, then came out in favor of the amendment on January 9. The next day, the House voted for it, 274–136, which achieved the necessary two-thirds vote. The Senate delayed until October, however, when the measure failed by two votes to win passage. During the months between the votes in Congress, Alice Paul, the architect of Woman's Party tactics, employed some new stunts designed to pressure political leaders by keeping the issue of suffrage on the front page of newspapers. They burned the speeches of Wilson at public monuments, because they believed he made too little effort to secure passage of the Anthony amendment. They burned "watchfires" in front of the White House, Senate, and other federal sites. Hundreds more picketers faced arrest, and most conducted hunger strikes during their brief incarcerations. Alice Paul was arrested a few times for her involvement in protests, often enduring very rough handling by police. After the two-vote loss, the NWP worked to defeat anti-suffrage senators up for election in the fall.

The National Woman's Party, and the revitalized National American Woman Suffrage Association under the leadership of Carrie Chapman Catt, played a major role in the election of 1918, and most new members of Congress were pro-suffrage. The House reaffirmed its vote of 1918 with a resounding 304 to 89 vote, then on June 4, 1919, the Senate acted. Though the vote was close, Alice Paul watched from the gallery as the amendment prevailed with the necessary 66 "ayes." The NWP knew they had won even before the roll call, and there was little excitement. They immediately turned their attention to the ratification vote in the states, which was secured when the Tennessee House voted in favor on August 18.

When asked later, Alice Paul did not recall celebrating the final victory of women's suffrage; rather, she set to work closing up the headquarters and paying off debts. But the Woman's Party did not disband, instead turning its attention to the broader question of women's rights. A large NWP convention met in February 1921 whose agenda was controlled rather firmly by Paul. The delegates endorsed her program to "remove all remaining forms of the subjection of women" through the passage of an amendment ending gender discrimination. After two years full of debate and legal consultations, Alice Paul penned the simple line that became the Equal Rights Amendment. Announced publicly at the site of the first great women's convention of 1848, Seneca Falls, the ERA stated simply: "Men and women shall have equal rights throughout the United States and every place subject to its jurisdiction."

When Paul and the WP first proposed the ERA in the 1920s, they had few allies. The Women's Trade Union League, League of Women Voters (the successor of NAWSA), General Federation of Women's Clubs, U.S. Women's Bureau, and the two major political parties opposed it. Moreover, the NWP made little headway before World War II.

Alice Paul believed that she would be better equipped to champion the cause of women's rights if she were trained thoroughly in law. Thus, she earned three law degrees during the 1920s: an LL.B. from Washington College of Law (1922) and an LL.M. (1927) and D.C.L. (1928) from American University. She returned to Europe as chair of the Woman's Research Federation (1927–37), where she founded the World Women's Party. In Geneva in the 1930s, she lobbied the League of Nations on women's rights issues. Paul served on the Women's Consultative Committee on Nationality of the League and as a board member of the Equal Rights International. She returned to the United States in 1941 to work for the Equal Rights Amendment, which both major parties endorsed in 1944. Paul chaired the NWP beginning in 1942.

Upon Paul's return to the U.S., she moved in with her sister Helen, and, later, with activist **Elsie Hill**, her closest friend. Totally committed to various causes, Paul never married. After the late 1960s, and Hill's death, she lived alone in Ridgefield, Connecticut. Paul protested at rallies for women's rights and against the Vietnam War while in her 80s. She would witness the passage of the ERA by Congress in 1972 and subsequently worked for its ratification. In 1972, she met with historian Robert S. Gallagher, and the interview appeared in the February 1974 issue of *American Heritage*. She responded to dozens of questions frankly and intelligently. But what stands out the most about her answers are two personal qualities: absolute modesty and a tendency to care little about the past. When asked how she assessed her own contributions to women's rights, she consistently minimized her role. "Each of us puts in a little stone," she remarked about activists, "and then you get a great mosaic at the end."

Alice Paul suffered a stroke in 1974 which left her permanently disabled. She died on July 9, 1977. Unique among American political activists in her single-minded devotion to women's rights, Paul lived her long life in the best Quaker tradition, zealously devoted to service.

SOURCES:

Gallagher, Robert S., "'I Was Arrested Of Course . . .': An Interview With Miss Alice Paul," in *American Heritage*. Vol. 25. February 1974, pp. 16–24, 92–94.

Irwin, Inez Haynes. *Up Hill With Banners Flying*. Washington, DC: The National Woman's Party, 1964.

Lunardini, Christine A. *From Equal Suffrage to Equal Rights: Alice Paul and the National Woman's Party, 1910–1928*. NY: New York University Press, 1986.

SUGGESTED READING:

Flexner, Eleanor. *Century of Struggle: The Woman's Rights Movement in the United States.* NY: Atheneum, 1968.

Scott, Anne Firor, and Andrew MacKay Scott. *One Half the People: The Fight for Woman Suffrage.* Philadelphia, PA: Lippincott, 1975.

COLLECTIONS:

The Arthur and Elizabeth Schlesinger Library, Radcliffe College, has a small collection of Paul papers. The National Woman's Party in Washington holds many papers on Paul, which have been duplicated by the Microfilm Corporation of America.

John M. Craig,
Professor of History,
Slippery Rock University, Slippery Rock, Pennsylvania,
and author of *Lucia Ames Mead and the American Peace Movement*

Paul, Josephine Bay (1900–1962).

See Bay, Josephine Perfect.

Paula (347–404)

Roman widow and associate of Jerome who founded two influential religious communities in Bethlehem. *Born in 347; died in 404; daughter of Rogatus and Blesilla; married Toxotius; children: four daughters, Blesilla (d. 384), Paula the Younger, Eustochium, and Rufina; one son, Toxotius.*

Paula was born in 347, the daughter of patricians, Rogatus and **Blesilla**. Her ancestry was among the loftiest to be found within the Roman aristocracy of the 4th century, for through her Hellenic (by descent) father, Paula traced her roots back to Agamemnon, while through her mother, she was related to the great Scipios and Gracchi of Republican fame. Paula's parents were Christian, and she was so raised, although near relatives on both sides of her family remained pagan throughout her life. Her parents were also extremely wealthy, owning extensive estates in both Italy and Greece. Paula had at least one brother about whom nothing is known. Well educated in both the secular and religious fields as befit one of her status and faith, Paula was early introduced to the intra-Christian doctrinal conflicts of her time, for in her youth the Arian Emperor Constantius II roughly handled the bishops of Rome and their orthodox followers. Perhaps the memory of these assaults upon orthodoxy influenced Paula's subsequent distaste for theological deviancy.

Married at age 15 to Toxotius, a man of her own elevated social standing (for he bore the blood of the Julian house in his veins) but a pagan, Paula nevertheless knew a happy marriage. The couple had four daughters (eldest to youngest: **Blesilla, Paula the Younger, Eustochium**, and **Rufina**) and one son (Toxotius) before the elder Toxotius died when Paula was 31, a loss which grieved her much. Little is known about Paula during the time of her marriage, except that her friends constituted a virtual "who's who" within the Christian and pagan elite of Rome. The most influential of these was ***Marcella** (325–410), a Christian who, spurred by reports from the East about the development of the monastic movement, had established a chaste community of Christian women in her palace on the Aventine Hill. Marcella's "convent" engaged in prayer, scriptural study, and good works, and was so successful at encouraging others to do the same that her example was enthusiastically endorsed both by the reigning pope, Damasus, and by the up-and-coming Biblical exegete, Jerome.

Paula began to live in the manner of Marcella. Although she did not join the latter's community in a formal sense, as a widow Paula embraced a life of chastity, kept in close contact with Marcella's establishment, and allowed her daughter, Eustochium, to take up residence with that community. Inspired by notions of Christian charity, Paula also began to distribute largesse amongst the poor, and she personally began to eschew outward manifestations of wealth, coming to prefer to dress in sackcloth rather than in the silk she had once known. Of particular importance for the future, through Marcella, Paula met Jerome, whose devout disciple she became. Thus living a life of alms-giving, prayer, and scriptural study, Paula began her withdrawal from the secular world—a process which was accelerated by the visit to Rome of the eastern bishops, Paulinus and Epiphanius, who came to the city (382) in order to participate in a synod devoted to the problem of Arianism. Paula acted as host for Epiphanius, providing housing for that influential cleric from Cyprus during his stay. Although intrigued by the encouragement of her guest to visit the East, Paula nevertheless delayed abandoning Rome primarily because of her concern and affection for her children, one of whom, Toxotius, long flirted with paganism (although he eventually became a devout Christian).

Eventually, however, several influences converged to induce Paula to follow her growing desire to take up residence in the Holy Land. First, her daughter Blesilla, once briefly married but thereafter (with Paula and Eustochium) a spiritual intimate of Marcella and Jerome, died in 384, leaving Paula as emotionally distraught as she had been after the death of her husband. Second, the example of ***Melania the Elder** (one of

Paula's Roman Christian friends), who had left Rome first to tour the Holy Land and then to become an abbess in Jerusalem, enticed Paula to follow suit. And third, Pope Damasus also died (again in 384). This loss hit Paula very personally, for after Damasus' demise the orthodox Christian community in Rome split into increasingly acrimonious factions. Before long, petty jealousies came to the fore, with the result that Jerome, who had been Damasus' good friend, came under attack by some who would assume Damasus' mantle. Among the charges raised against Jerome was his intimacy with so many Roman matrons, including especially Paula. In fact, it was suggested that there was more than a spiritual bond between Jerome and Paula—a charge which both vehemently denied. Nevertheless, the time had come (385) for Paula to become a religious pilgrim. After splitting most of her wealth among her three children who would remain in Italy, Paula, with Jerome and Eustochium as companions, left Italy for the attractions of the Christian East.

Journeying to Jerusalem by way of Cyprus (where she was briefly reunited with Epiphanius) and Antioch (where she visited with Paulinus), Paula's group reached Jerusalem in the winter of 385–86. There the trio visited the major religious sites before beginning a tour of the Holy Land, beginning with Bethlehem. This visit moved Paula deeply, but her passion to follow in the footsteps of Jesus stirred her on. After a circuit through Palestine, Paula, Jerome and Eustochium returned to Jerusalem, where they visited the new monastic foundations of Melania the Elder and Rufinus, before setting off to Egypt, there to acquaint themselves with the religious community in Alexandria and the monastic foundations of the hostile countryside.

Returning to Bethlehem by late 386, Paula decided to establish two religious communities of her own near the site of Jesus' nativity—undoubtedly influenced by the example of Melania the Elder, and by what she had seen in Egypt. Building began immediately on twin foundations—one for Paula and her growing troop of feminine companions, and one for Jerome and his smaller group of comrades (the buildings of these religious communities were completed in 389). The rules which governed the lives of those who lived in these houses were, by Paula's choice, based upon those of Pachomius: poverty and mortification of the flesh were embraced, as was a life divided among physical labor, study and prayer. Isolation, however, was neither attempted nor realized, for Paula and her associates maintained correspondences with friends and family throughout the empire, and they welcomed many guests to their religious refuge.

Thus established, Paula's foundations flourished, and her fame grew in association with that of Jerome. The most lasting work produced under Paula's patronage at Bethlehem focused upon Jerome's religious writing. Spurred on by Paula, who wished to associate with her religious foundations a noteworthy library revolving around his work, Jerome wrote a string of Biblical commentaries while resident at Bethlehem. Also, it was there that he produced his famous edition of the Bible, a work destined to have profound impact upon the medieval church.

Unfortunately, all was not to remain tranquil for Paula and Jerome. In the year 394, a doctrinal argument focused upon the dubious orthodoxy of Originism against which Jerome, with Paula in alliance, raged. The debate put Jerome and Paula at odds with their one-time friends, Melania the Elder and Rufinus. In addition, their strong stand against Origin's influence undermined their relationship with John, bishop of Jerusalem. Intensifying the religious issues involved were petty jealousies, as the reputation of the foundations at Bethlehem began to eclipse anything being produced in Jerusalem. Although several attempts over the years were made to mediate this dispute (including one mounted by Theophilus, bishop of Alexandria) and to reunite in friendship the primary disputants, the damage was never really repaired, and Paula's erstwhile respect for her Roman counterpart was never completely restored. Indeed, Melania's orthodoxy came under suspicion, and hostilities between Paula and her continued, especially after the allies of Jerome and Paula attempted to enlist in their cause ***Melania the Younger**, the granddaughter namesake of Paula's religious rival.

A second infringement upon the peace of Paula's foundations was of less lasting significance. In 395, the threat of an invasion of Huns forced the temporary evacuation of Bethlehem, with the result that Paula, Jerome and their associates took up temporary residence in the city of Joppa. However, the potential attack upon Bethlehem never materialized, and all returned to what had become their home in the following year. There, Paula was met by both good and bad news. The bad news was that Paula's daughter, Paula the Younger (who had been married to the Roman Senator Pammachius) had died, a fact which wounded Paula deeply. The good news was that Paula now had a granddaughter—also named Paula—the child of Toxotius and his wife **Laeta**. (This Paula would later care for Jerome in his old age.) Regardless of the vicissitudes of family life, religion—both that connected with the daily running of her communities, and that which continued to wage war against the evils of creeping Originism—continued to demand most of Paula's attention over the last decade of her life.

By the late 390s, a third problem, however, had begun to concern Paula, for by that time her personal fortune had run out. On a private level this did not bother Paula at all, for she had long since renounced the comforts of wealth. Nevertheless, she became concerned that without enough money, the continuing work of her communities would be threatened. Eustochium, of course, remained at her mother's side and helped financially as much as she could. But even with that assistance, funds became tight. As a result, Paula was forced to borrow heavily upon the reputation of her family's wealth and status, so that when she died at age 57 in 404, she was deeply in debt. Despite this obvious problem, Jerome (with Eustochium at his side) continued with his work as Paula hoped he would. Jerome also continued to stir up considerable controversy, as he never ceased to attack theological deviancy where he saw it. In fact, Jerome's attacks affected Paula's communities after her death. For instance, angered by Jerome's theological positions, a band of Pelagians destroyed the buildings which had been erected with Paula's money and at her command. Fortunately, Eustochium—as steadfast in her piety as had been Paula—rebuilt what had been destroyed.

The passing of Paula moved Jerome greatly, for he saw in her the epitome of feminine Christian piety. His words, thus, serve as an appropriate epithet for Paula's impact on those around her: "Even if all of the parts of my body were transformed into tongues and were capable of speech, I could never find words to recount the virtues of the holy and venerable Paula."

William S. Greenwalt,
Associate Professor of Classical History, Santa Clara University,
Santa Clara, California

Pauli, Hertha (1909–1973)

Austrian-born writer, actress, literary agent, and screenwriter. *Born Hertha Ernestine Pauli in Vienna, Austria, on September 4, 1909; died in Bay Shore, Long Island, New York, on February 9, 1973; daughter of Wolfgang Pauli and Bertha Schütz Pauli; sister of Wolfgang Pauli, who won the Nobel Prize in physics; married Ernest B. Ashton (Ernst Basch), in 1951.*

In 1909, Hertha Pauli was born in Vienna into an assimilated Jewish family of great talents. Her father Wolfgang Pauli was both a successful physician and a pioneering investigator of the emerging science of biochemistry, while her mother **Bertha Schütz Pauli**, a descendant of the dramatist Friedrich Schütz, was a regular contributor to Vienna's leading bourgeois newspaper, the *Neue Freie Presse*. Hertha's brother Wolfgang Pauli would be awarded the 1945 Nobel Prize in physics.

Hertha studied drama and acting at Vienna's Academy of Arts and after graduation became a member of the Lobetheater in Breslau, Germany (today Wroclaw, Poland). Noticed by the leading German theatrical producer Max Reinhardt, she performed successfully in the early 1930s in Berlin at his Deutsches Theater. In 1933, the anti-Semitism of the new Third Reich ended Pauli's German career, and she was forced to return to Austria. In Vienna, she struggled to support herself, working as a freelance writer and establishing a literary agency, the "Österreichische Korrespondenz." Among the literary mediums Pauli mastered during this stage were poetry, short stories, radio scripts, and Feuilletons (literary essays for the Viennese press).

In 1936, Pauli published *Toni: Ein Frauenleben für Ferdinand Raimund* (Toni: A Woman's Life for Ferdinand Raimund), a historical novel set in the 19th century. The following year, she published a biography of the great Austrian pacifist *__Bertha von Suttner__, entitled *Nur eine Frau* (Only a Woman). Not surprisingly, a book that denounced all wars was banned in a Nazi Germany feverishly preparing for one.

In March 1938, on the day German troops marched into Austria, Pauli fled to Paris, where she earned a precarious living as a publisher's representative and shared the uncertainties of other refugees from Nazism. Friendships with a number of gifted fellow writers—including the brilliant but alcoholic Austrian novelist Joseph Roth, with whom she spent hours at his Stammtisch at the Café Tournon—helped ease the misery of exile. Pauli also developed strong friendships with **Lois Sevareid** and her American journalist husband Eric Sevareid.

In June 1940, with German troops marching into the French capital, Pauli made her escape on foot to the south of France, finally arriving in Marseilles. Now with little money, she lived in a room in a cheap hotel. She made a small income and wrote anti-Nazi messages that she hoped would be smuggled into Germany. After several months in Marseilles, it became clear to Pauli and most of the other refugees that sooner or later they would wind up in the hands of the Germans unless they could escape from Europe.

The arrival in the south of France of the American Varian Fry, representative of the Emergency Rescue Committee, proved providential for Pauli and many hundreds of others whose lives were in danger because they were Jews or anti-Nazis, or both. Supported by Thomas Mann and ***Eleanor Roosevelt** in his efforts to rescue as many of Europe's endangered intellectuals as possible, Fry set up an escape route over the Pyrenees for refugees to flee southern France, which was controlled by the pro-Nazi Vichy regime. Accompanied by another refugee, Carl Frucht, Pauli was able to cross the frontier into Spain in seven hours of climbing via an old smugglers' path. On the night of September 3–4, 1940, she sailed for New York from Lisbon on a Greek vessel, the *Nea Hellas*.

Unlike some immigrants who remained psychologically torn between their old and new homes, Pauli set out to Americanize herself once she arrived in New York. She quickly mastered American English which she was soon able to write in clear, idiomatic prose. Determined to succeed as an author in her new homeland, in 1942 she published a biography of the founder of the Nobel Prize, *Alfred Nobel: Dynamite King, Architect of Peace*. The following year, she published a book for young readers, *Silent Night: The Story of a Song*. This book's success convinced Pauli that she had found her métier, namely writing books for a juvenile audience. For the rest of her life, Pauli would produce a large number of books for this market, including *The Most Beautiful House and Other Stories* (1949), *The Golden Door* (1949), *Lincoln's Little Correspondent* (1952), *Three Is a Family* (1955), *Bernadette and the Lady* (1956), *The First Easter Rabbit* (1961), *The Two Trumpeters of Vienna* (1961), *Handel and the Messiah Story* (1968), and *Pietro and Brother Francis* (1971). The success of *Silent Night* also encouraged her to write more books for the Christmas market, including *The Story of the Christmas Tree* (1944), *St. Nicholas' Travels* (1945), *Christmas and the Saints* (1956), *The First Christmas Tree* (1961), *America's First Christmas* (1962), *Little Town of Bethlehem* (1963), and *The First Christmas Gifts* (1965).

In 1948, Pauli published a history of the Statue of Liberty, *I Lift My Lamp: The Way of a Symbol*, a subject that was likely of particular interest to her as a refugee. Written in collaboration with her husband Ernest B. Ashton (originally Ernst Basch), this book would be reprinted in 1969. The same subject matter appeared in a 1965 version for young readers, *Gateway to America: Miss Liberty's First Hundred Years*.

Hertha Pauli

Writing full-scale novels remained a challenge for Pauli, and in 1957 she published one entitled *Cry of the Heart*. This was followed in 1959 by *Jugend nachher* (Youth Afterwards), written in German and published in Vienna. The idea for *Jugend nachher* had been sparked by children in Nazi concentration camps and the emergence of alienated, violent youth in the presumably contented, prosperous European world of the late 1950s. In 1965, she published *The Secret of Sarajevo* (1965), an accurate, detailed account of the assassination that started World War I.

Despite her painful memories, Pauli found it possible to occasionally visit Austria after World War II. In 1967, the Republic of Austria awarded her its Silver Medal of Honor. In 1970, she published her autobiography in Vienna, *Der Riss der Zeit geht durch mein Herz* (The Fissure of Our Age Tears Through My Heart), which appeared in 1972 in the United States as *Break of Time*. An active member of PEN, Hertha Pauli listed her avocational interests as "dogs, cats, and swimming." She died in Bay Shore, Long Island, New York, on February 9, 1973.

SOURCES:

Patsch, Sylvia M. "'Nur eine Frau': Hertha Pauli zum 80. Geburtstage," *Illustrierte Neue Welt* [Vienna]. August–September 1989, pp. 33–34.

Pauli, Hertha. *Alfred Nobel: Dynamite King, Architect of Peace*. NY: L.B. Fischer, 1942.

Spalek, John, Konrad Feilchenfeldt, and Sandra H. Hawrylchak, eds. *Deutschsprachige Exilliteratur seit 1933*, Vol. 4: *Bibliographien: Schriftsteller, Publizisten, und Literaturwissenschaftler in den USA*, Part 3: N–Z. Bern: K.G. Saur Verlag, 1994.

Stern, Guy. "Hertha Pauli," in Dokumentationsarchiv des österreichischen Widerstandes und Dokumentationsstelle für neuere österreichische Literatur, eds., *Österreicher im Exil 1934 bis 1945: Protokoll des internationalen Symposiums zur Erforschung des österreichischen Exils von 1934 bis 1945*. Vienna: Österreichischer Bundesverlag, 1977, pp. 495–508.

Wall, Renate. *Lexikon deutschsprachiger Schriftstellerinnen im Exil, 1933–1945*. 2 vols. Freiburg im Breisgau: Kore Verlag, 1995.

John Haag,
Associate Professor of History, University of Georgia,
Athens, Georgia

Paulina.

Variant of Paula.

Pauline of Saxe-Weimar (1852–1904)

Grand duchess of Saxe-Weimar. *Born on July 25, 1852; died on May 17, 1904; daughter of ****Augusta of Wurttemberg*** *(1826–1898) and Hermann Henry, prince of Saxe-Weimar; married Charles Augustus, grand duke of Saxe-Weimar, on August 26, 1873; children: William Ernest (b. 1876), grand duke of Saxe-Weimar; Bernard Charles (b. 1878).*

Pauline of Wurttemberg (1800–1873)

Queen of Wurttemberg. *Born on September 4, 1800; died on March 10, 1873; daughter of Louis Frederick Alexander, duke of Wurttemberg, and ****Henrietta of Nassau-Weilburg*** *(1780–1857); became third wife of William I (1781–1864), king of Wurttemberg (r. 1816–1864), on April 15, 1820; children: ****Catherine Frederica of Wurttemberg*** *(1821–1898, who married her cousin Frederick); Charles I (1823–1891), king of Wurttemberg (r. 1864–1891); ****Augusta of Wurttemberg*** *(1826–1898, who married Hermann of Saxe-Weimar).*

Pauline of Wurttemberg (1810–1856)

Duchess of Nassau. *Born Pauline Frederica Marie on February 25, 1810; died on July 7, 1856; daughter of ****Catherine Charlotte of Hildburghausen*** *(1787–1847) and Paul of Wurttemberg; married William George (1792–1839), duke of Nassau, on April 23, 1829; children: ****Helen of Nassau*** *(1831–1888); Nicholas of Nassau (1832–1905, who married Natalia Alexandrovna Pushkin, countess Merenberg); ****Sophia of Nassau*** *(1836–1913).*

Pauline of Wurttemberg (1877–1965)

Princess of Wied. *Born Pauline Olga Helene Emma on December 19, 1877; died in 1965; daughter of ****Maria of Waldeck*** *(1857–1882) and William II (1848–1921), king of Wurttemberg (r. 1891–1918, abdicated); married Frederick William, 6th prince of Wied, on October 29, 1898; children: Herman William (b. 1899); Dietrich William (b. 1901).*

Paulze, Marie Anne Pierrette (1758–1836).

See Lavoisier, Marie.

Pavlova, Anna (1881–1931)

One of the greatest classical Russian ballerinas of the 20th century who was responsible for popularizing ballet throughout the world. *Pronunciation: PAV-lov-a. Born Anna Matveevna Pavlova on January 31, 1881 (o.s.), in St. Petersburg; died of pneumonia in The Hague, the Netherlands, on January 23, 1931; illegitimate daughter of Lazar Jacovlevich Poliakov (an aristocratic banker) and Liubov Fedorovna Pavlova (a laundress); attended Imperial Ballet School, 1891–99; reputedly married Victor Dandré, in 1914; no children.*

Was a member of the Maryinsky Theater company (1899–1913), second soloist (1902), first soloist (1903), ballerina (1905), prima ballerina (1906); danced with Diaghilev's Ballets Russes in Paris (1909) and London (1911); formed her own company, Les Ballets d'Anna Pavlova (1912) which toured throughout the world until her death; lived in London (1912–31).

Ballet: best known for her roles in La Bayadère, Giselle, Bacchanale, *and* The Dying Swan. *Film:* The Dumb Girl of Portici *(1915). Publication:* Pages from My Life *(1912).*

The snow was lightly falling in St. Petersburg as the sleigh carrying **Liubov Pavlova** and her daughter Anna arrived at the Maryinsky Theater. To celebrate the Russian Orthodox Christmas in January 1890, Liubov was taking her eight-year-old to see *The Sleeping Beauty.* It was the first time the young girl had been to any theater, much less the legendary Maryinsky, and she was understandably excited as they climbed the steep stairs to the upper balcony. For the next three hours Anna, like many girls of her age before and since, was enthralled by the fairy-tale scenery, Tchaikovsky's enchanting music, and the marvelous dancing of the ballerinas. When it was over, Liubov asked her daughter if she would like to dance one of the waltzes sometime. "I should rather dance the part of the Princess," Anna replied. "One day I shall be the Princess and shall dance upon the stage of this theater." This was an unlikely dream for the frail daughter of an impoverished single mother. At Anna's insistence, she was taken for an interview with the director of the Imperial Ballet School who told her without great enthusiasm to come back when she was ten years old for an audition. Much to his surprise, since only one in three applicants was traditionally accepted, Anna returned, passed, and in 1891 entered the prestigious school. After eight years of rigorous training, she graduated with flying colors and was accepted into the Maryinsky Theater company. Seven years later, she was a prima ballerina and acclaimed as one of Russia's greatest dancers. Triumphant tours of Europe followed, culminating in two seasons with Serge Diaghilev's Ballets Russes in Paris and London. In 1912, she formed her own company and for the next 19 years toured the world popularizing ballet and building her reputation as "the greatest dancer of the century." She died a rich and famous woman shortly before her 50th birthday.

Few would have predicted such an illustrious career when Anna Pavlova was born two months prematurely on January 31, 1881. Her father of record was a Russian peasant soldier, Matvei Pavlovich Pavlov, who either died or deserted his family when she was two years old. Anna never knew him and in later life refused to speak about him. Unlike most Russians, she disliked being addressed by her patronymic, Anna Matveevna. According to Oleg Kerensky, her biological father was Lazar Jacovlevich Poliakov, a wealthy and respected Jewish banker who was a patron of the arts. Anna's physical characteristics as well as some of her later comments seem to confirm this parentage.

Anna's mother Liubov was 22 years old when her only child was born. She was uneducated, very religious and poor. She is described in most accounts as being a laundress though there is some evidence that she worked in the Imperial Ballet School as keeper of the linens and later may have run her own laundry. There is speculation that she met Poliakov at the Ballet School or at one time had been employed as a servant in his household. Her continued need for full-time employment made it difficult for her to raise Anna in St. Petersburg. As a result, her undernourished child was sent off to the more healthy environs of Ligovo, a summer community 50 miles from the Russian capital, to live in her grandmother's dacha or cottage. Given the poverty of the Pavlova household, it is possible that Poliakov arranged for this retreat and that he also provided the Christmas ballet tickets which proved so instrumental in his illegitimate daughter's subsequent life. The only memory Anna has left us of these early years concerns her growing love of nature which came from spending hours wondering alone through the fields and forests surrounding Ligovo.

Her dream of becoming a ballet student became a reality in 1891, perhaps because the director on second glance liked her delicate physique and her determination, perhaps because Poliakov said a good word on her behalf. The Imperial Ballet School was one of the few places in tsarist Russia where birth and wealth meant little. Once accepted, a student paid no tuition and received accommodation, meals and clothing at no cost for eight years. Accommodation, to be sure, was in a dormitory room shared with 20 other girls and uniforms which changed only in color as a student passed through the grades. For some, it was like a "silken prison" where discipline was strict and casual contact with boys forbidden. Anna's day started at 8 AM with the ringing of a bell, dressing under the "stern eye of a governess," saying prayers, then having breakfast of tea, bread, and butter. The rest of the morning was devoted to ballet lessons. The afternoons were given over to academic training though here too emphasis was placed on subjects relating to the theater—French, dramatic art, and music. Breaks in this routine were few: occasionally the tsar or a member of his entourage dropped by to have tea with the young dancers who were considered part of his extended family; on Sundays, Anna's mother could visit; on holidays, she could go home or more likely to Ligovo.

In 1899, at age 18, Pavlova graduated from the Imperial Ballet School and was immediately accepted into the Maryinsky Theater company, not as a member of the corps de ballet, but as a *coryphée* who danced with two or three other promising graduates. One contemporary described her at the time as:

> a very thin girl, slightly above average height. A charming smile, and beautiful eyes that were a little sad. Her legs were long, slim and very beautiful, with extraordinarily arched instep. Her whole body was graceful, delicate, and ethereal, as if she were trying to leave the earth.

For the next decade Anna Pavlova perfected her skills and continued to grow as a dancer. Five or six hours a day rehearsing at the Maryinsky were supplemented by private lessons in St. Petersburg or Italy. As Keith Money has noted, "her natural talent, the curious poetry of her body, was so outstanding that nobody could ignore it." One of those who noticed it was Marius Petipa, the ballet master and choreographer of the company. In 1902, the year in which she became a second soloist, he chose her over many more senior dancers for the female lead in *La Bayadère*. A year later, he gave her the prized title role in *Giselle* in which she was an instantaneous success. One reviewer wrote, "*Giselle* is certainly Pavlova's most finished creation, giving promise that in her there is an unfolding of exceptional talent." A growing group of admirers, known as "the Pavlovtzi," showed up at every performance to enthusiastically applaud their favorite. In 1906, she reached the pinnacle of her profession when she was given the title of prima ballerina and with it an annual salary of 3,000 rubles. The critic Arnold Haskell notes that by this time she excelled "in the portrayal of the pathetic, of some ephemeral being that came to life and then withered and died all on a summer's day." These qualities were used to full advantage in *The Dying Swan* specially choreographed for her in 1907 by Petipa's successor, Michel Fokine, which became her signature dance for the next 23 years.

Ballet flourished in Russia during the decade and a half before the First World War. The music of Tchaikovsky and Glazunov, the choreography of Petipa and Fokine, and the dancing of ***Matilda Kshesinskaia**, Vaslav Nijinsky, and Pavlova made Russian ballet the finest in Europe. Unlike elsewhere, ballet in St. Petersburg and Moscow was high culture, rivalling symphonic music and certainly surpassing the legitimate theater as the art form of the intelligentsia and the aristocracy. The ballet season coincided with the winter social season and leading ballerinas such as Anna Pavlova were much sought-after celebrities. It was not uncommon for male members of the royal family or respected entrepreneurs to escort ballerinas to social events and to further their careers in whatever way they could. Rarely, however, did these liaisons lead to marriage. In 1900, Pavlova met Victor Dandré, a well-to-do man 11 years her senior who loved ballet and was active in the St. Petersburg City Council. In time, Dandré became her "protector." He helped finance her private lessons, her trips abroad, and her acquisition of a large apartment with its own dance studio in an artistic neighborhood of St. Petersburg. He was to become her lifelong companion.

Russian society was in ferment, both politically and artistically, during this period. Politically, the grievances of the lower classes spilled over in an abortive revolution in 1905. Many of the ballerinas, despite their upper-class friends and admirers, came from less privileged backgrounds and often sympathized with the demonstrators. Anna Pavlova was not alone in speaking out against the shooting of factory workers in January 1905. Ten months later, she and some of her colleagues addressed a petition to the director of the Maryinsky Theater demanding more freedom and less dictation inside the ballet company. When these demands were not met, they followed the lead of the St. Petersburg workers by holding a one-day strike. Underlying their demands was a desire for more artistic freedom. Russian ballet had become very conventional, very traditional. Some of the younger dancers, Pavlova among them, wanted more innovative choreography, more comfortable costumes, less stylized performances, and less of a caste system within the company. Neither the Russian government nor the Maryinsky management was interested in meaningful reform. Some of the dancers were fired, others no longer got prized roles, and still others, such as Anna Pavlova, were sent abroad on foreign tours. In May 1908, she and 20 of her colleagues visited the capitals of Scandinavia and then Prague and Berlin. The next year, she made another tour of the major cities of Germany and Austria. She found she enjoyed life outside of her native country and getting away from the restrictions of her employers. In turn, the Russian dancers and Pavlova in particular were enthusiastically received, and did much to spread the fame of Russian ballet and to popularize it as a legitimate art form in Europe.

But this was still classical Russian ballet in the Maryinsky tradition. Others of the 1905 strikers wanted to push the boundaries of ballet further than the Maryinsky directors would allow either in St. Petersburg or on officially sanctioned tours of Europe. In 1909, Serge Diaghilev convinced Fokine, Nijinsky, Pavlova and several other leading Russian dancers to join a

Anna Pavlova

new company—Ballets Russes—and to try out their ideas in Paris, the cultural capital of Europe. Ballets Russes took Paris by storm. During a period of six weeks in May and June 1909, Diaghilev alternated a night of Russian opera with one of Russian ballet. Fokine's innovative choreography, Léon Bakst's spectacular sets and costumes, and the virtuoso dancing of Nijinsky and *Tamara Karsavina brought ballet into the 20th century and won over the Parisian audiences. Because of previous engagements in Vienna, Pavlova did not arrive until early June, in time to dance only six performances of *Les Sylphides* and *Cléopâtre*. This was enough for *Le Figaro*'s reviewer: "This one is a glory," he wrote of Pavlova. "A sacred flame burns in her. Mere technique and accuracy in her art do not constitute her aim; when she dances, the result is that undefinable thing, a masterpiece."

Pavlova was at the height of her powers in the summer of 1909 and also at the turning point in her career. One option open to her was to continue dancing with Ballets Russes in Western Europe as Diaghilev fervently wished. This would have been remunerative, and it would have allowed her to participate in the revolutionary change Ballets Russes brought to the field of dance over the next two decades. While Pavlova joined Diaghilev for the 1911 season in London, where she partnered Nijinsky in several memorable performances at Covent Garden, she declined to become a permanent member of his company. Some have suggested that she did not wish to share the limelight with younger and more dynamic stars such as Nijinsky and Karsavina or to accept the dictates of Diaghilev himself. Others, perhaps with more cause, have noted her dislike of the harshly dissonant music Diaghilev was commissioning Igor Stravinsky to write for his company.

Is it some creature from fairyland, some spirit of ethereal grace freed from the terrestrial trammels of the flesh? . . . No. Merely Pavlova, the incomparable Pavlova.

—*Manchester Evening News*

Another option was to return to St. Petersburg to resume her privileged life as an acclaimed prima ballerina at the Maryinsky Theater. In 1909, she remarked: "I have no wish to break completely with Russia. The memory of my childhood, my first steps on the stage and my first success is associated with St. Petersburg. I would never leave Russia forever." She did indeed dance the 1909–10 season with the Maryinsky, and she agreed to go on an extended company-arranged tour of the United States in the winter of 1910–11. Despite a signed contract, which she acknowledged promised her the "highest salary a ballerina had ever received," her visits to St. Petersburg during the next two seasons were notably shorter, and she resigned her position altogether in 1913. This move might be explained by the lack of interesting roles offered even to prima ballerinas or by the fact that she was subject to mandatory retirement at the rapidly approaching age of 35 in 1916. Her stated justification in the year of her resignation was that "the same old ballets are being staged at the Maryinsky, with the same antiquated scenery and costumes that we Russians abroad have left far behind." Unstated but undoubtedly paramount in her decision was the predicament of Victor Dandré—her patron, "protector," and sometime lover. In February 1911, Dandré had been arrested on a charge of embezzlement. Pavlova, who learned about this while in the United States, asked that her earnings be used to satisfy his 35,000 ruble bail. Shortly before his scheduled trial in the fall, however, Dandré forfeited her bail and any possible career for himself in Russia by fleeing the country and joining Pavlova in London.

This, plus their strained financial position, dictated that Pavlova's subsequent career should follow a third and more risky option of dancing on her own or at the head of her own company. This alternative was not entirely new to her. She had been approached after her success with Ballets Russes in Paris by promoters wishing to arrange performances for her at the Metropolitan Opera in New York and the Palace Theater in London. In February 1910, she sailed for New York where for two months she performed late at night after the conclusion of the opera at the Met or to audiences in Boston and Baltimore where ballet was a novelty of the first order. That summer, she shared the Palace stage in London with violinists, singers, and other music-hall entertainers. Since her audiences were enthusiastic and the pay good, she had no hesitation about returning to the Palace during the next three summers. In the winter of 1911–12 and the fall of 1912, she experimented with touring the British countryside with her own small troupe, presenting excerpts from Russian ballets to music-hall audiences.

After Dandré arrived in London, he took over as business manager for her growing ballet enterprise. Together they acquired a large house in Golders Green near Hampstead Heath in London. "Ivy House" became their home and headquarters for the next two decades. Anna liked spending her free time in the large garden or spoiling the white swans in the estate's pool. She turned one of the rooms in Ivy House into a ballet studio where she trained a half-dozen English girls each year in the art of Russian ballet. The best of them were given Russian names (Hilda Boot, for example, became **Hilda Butsova**) and hired as supporting dancers for her small touring company. The precise nature of Pavlova's relationship with Dandré was a source of considerable gossip inside the company and of controversy among her biographers. On frequent occasions, she said she would not marry, "that a true female artist must be consumed in her art." In 1924, perhaps to satisfy public opinion in the United States, she contradicted herself when she told reporters that she had been married to Dandré for many years. Some of her associates later claimed that the ceremony took place in New York in 1914. A marriage certificate, however, has never been found and, after Pavlova's death, an English judge rejected Dandré's claim that he was her legal husband.

In June 1914, as war clouds gathered over Europe, Anna and a few soloists visited Russia once again. After dancing in St. Petersburg and Moscow, they caught one of the last trans-continental trains back to London. While Pavlova, unlike most of her colleagues, sympathized with many of the aims of the Russian Revolution three years later, she never again returned to the land of her birth. She spent the war years in the West plying her trade and popularizing classical ballet. Her stamina and ingenuity were remarkable. Shortly after arriving in New York in October 1914, she set out on a 16-month tour of 197 American, Canadian, and Cuban cities. Traveling mostly by train, she and her small company performed almost every night before audiences who rarely had seen an "ocular opera," as ballet was often called. Promotional work in the form of interviews, informal auditions, and receptions consumed whatever time that was not spent traveling, rehearsing, and performing. When the rest of her company took a short vacation in the summer of 1915, Pavlova went off to Hollywood to make a full-length silent film, *The Dumb Girl of Portici*. For four months in 1916, she even tried her hand at vaudeville, dancing nightly in "The Big Show" before audiences of 5,000 at the Hippodrome in New York. Next came South America. Departing by tramp steamer in February 1917, Pavlova and company spent over two and a half years crisscrossing the Caribbean, Central America and South America, coping with revolutions, strikes, makeshift stages, third-rate orchestras, and the influenza pandemic.

One might have thought that she would have welcomed the end of the war and the chance to return to a more normal life in Western Europe. In October 1920, however, after less than a year of performing in London and on the Continent, her missionary zeal and Dandré's financial ambitions brought "Les Ballets d'Anna Pavlova" and its 400 pieces of luggage back to the United States for another tour. This gruelling, coast-to-coast junket was repeated in 1921–22 and again in 1923–24 with excursions into Mexico and Canada. When the novelty of Russian ballet began to wear off in North America, Pavlova and 24 of her dancers set sail for a half-year tour of the Far East in September 1922. Conditions for dancing were even more primitive there and knowledge of ballet was virtually non-existent, but everywhere except in China the company was enthusiastically received. In Rangoon, Pavlova was advertised as "The Sensation of All the Civilized World," and from Japan and India she borrowed national music and dance styles to incorporate into future performances in Europe. A tour of South Africa, Australia, and New Zealand was arranged for 1926 and return visits to South America, Australia, and India took up most of 1928 and 1929. In all, Pavlova traveled 350,000 miles by boat and train and gave over 4,000 performances popularizing the art of ballet.

Anna Pavlova, Vienna, 1913.

Almost every fall during the 1920s, Pavlova managed to stay in Ivy House for a month while fulfilling her commitments at London's Covent Garden. If travel schedules permitted, Dandré fitted in shorter tours of the British Isles as well as to most countries of Europe outside of the Soviet Union. Time and again, at least in Europe, her path crossed that of Diaghilev's Ballets Russes. Curiously, the two companies complemented rather than competed with one another, and together they brought ballet to the same level of public acceptance in Europe that it had once enjoyed in Imperial Russia. Diaghilev concentrated on developing new styles of dance set to unconventional music for an increasingly sophisticated urban audience. Pavlova remained committed to her classical Russian training and offered shorter works which were accessible, undemanding, and agreeable to a less knowledgeable mass audience. She has been criticized by balletomanes for contributing little to the evolution of modern choreography, for avoiding ambitious full-length works after 1911, for developing few new dancers of note, and for her sometimes questionable technique. No one, however, has ever questioned her stage presence, the emotional impact of her graceful dancing, or her dedication and success in winning thousands of converts to ballet throughout the world.

By the end of 1930, Pavlova was beginning to tire of her hectic pace and was increasingly bothered by a sore knee. After a short Christmas vacation in Cannes, she went to Paris where she caught a cold while rehearsing for a forthcoming tour of the Netherlands. Over the objections of her doctor, she insisted on making the trip. Upon her arrival in The Hague, a mounting fever confined her to her bed in the Hôtel des Indes and forced a rare postponement of a scheduled performance. Six days later, on January 23, 1931, after more than 30 years of dancing and a week short of her 50th birthday, the "incomparable Pavlova" died of pneumonia.

SOURCES:

*Fonteyn, Margot. *Pavlova: Portrait of a Dancer.* NY: Viking, 1984.

Kerensky, Oleg. *Anna Pavlova.* London: Hamish Hamilton, 1973.

Money, Keith. *Anna Pavlova: Her Life and Art.* NY: Alfred Knopf, 1982.

SUGGESTED READING:

Lazzarini, John, and Roberta Lazzarini. *Pavlova: Repertoire of a Legend.* NY: Schirmer, 1980.

"Pavlova (1881–1931)," in *Dance Magazine.* Vol. XLV, no. 1. January 1976, pp. 43–75.

RELATED MEDIA:

"Homage to Pavlova," London Records, 1973.

The Immortal Swan (film), edited by Victor Dandré, 1936.

"The Legend of Anna Pavlova," National Educational Television, 1967.

R.C. Elwood,
Professor of History, Carleton University, Ottawa, Canada

Pavlova, Karolina (1807–1893)

Russian poet, translator, and 19th-century belletrist who composed verse in Russian, French, and German and translated freely between these languages, and whose influential literary translations generally move from Russian into French or German. *Born Karolina Karlovna Jaenisch in the Russian city of Yaroslavl in 1807; died in Dresden in 1893; daughter of Karl Jaenisch (served at the School of Medicine and Surgery in Moscow); married Nikolai Pavlov (a writer), in December 1836.*

Karolina Pavlova was a talented poet and translator of 19th-century Russia. Although generally categorized as a "Russian" literary figure, Pavlova became a literary polyglot because of her particular biography and interests, and thus she belongs to that class of 19th-century belletrists who transcended national categorization. The apogee of her career occurred in Russia during the 1840s, but she would live the latter half of her life in her second native land, Germany. Throughout both periods, she composed verse in Russian, French, and German and translated freely between these languages. Her most poignant original creations appear generally in Russian, and her greatly influential literary translations generally move from Russian into French or German.

Karolina Karlovna Jaenisch was born in 1807 in the Russian city of Yaroslavl. The principal portion of her childhood and the first portion of her adulthood were spent in Moscow. Her father, the transplanted German national Karl Jaenisch, served at the School of Medicine and Surgery in Moscow. He cared deeply for Karolina and was committed to providing his daughter with a comprehensive education. Since young women could not enter the formal education system, Karolina received extensive home tutoring. Her education, coupled with her literate upbringing in German culture, provided the young Karolina with the foundation of erudition which would mark her adult years.

A German by familial bonds and a Russian by geographical and social situation, Karolina readily assimilated the three languages of her surroundings: German, French (the language of international discourse and of educated Russian society), and Russian; by all indications, she operated equally comfortably in all three. She also had a certain knowledge of Spanish, Italian, Swedish, and Polish. This "multi-lingualism" would become yet another trademark of her future oeuvre.

In the 1820s, Karolina entered Moscow's literary *beau monde*, and two important events mark this decade in her life. First, she began to translate verse between the various languages which were native to her. The translation of verse comprised a standard component of language and literature education during this period, and presumably Karolina first engaged in such activities in the course of her philological education. However, because of her marked talents, such exercises naturally evolved into independent, creative endeavors. The second notable event was her association with the preeminent Polish poet of the day, Adam Mickiewicz. Mickiewicz was uniformly recognized as the leading voice of Polish Romanticism and as a poet of unimpeachable talents. Although a committed Polish patriot living during a period when the Russian Empire controlled Poland, Mickiewicz remained a sociable literary figure, esteemed by Russian literary society, and he was a recognized face in the Russian literary salons of the day. Karolina and Adam entertained notions of marriage during the late 1820s, but the potential union was rejected, most likely on national and/or religious grounds. Although Karolina would have been recognized as a Russian at this time, she remained a Lutheran throughout her life, a fact which links her again with her German ancestry, and whether Russian or German, Orthodox or Lutheran, Karolina's background would have conflicted with that of the Polish Catholic Adam. Certain accounts suggest that Karolina's family pressed refusal. Others suggest that, while reluctant, the family and her father ultimately would have allowed the marriage, but Karolina herself decided against it on practical grounds.

The relationship with Adam nonetheless exhibited a marked influence on Karolina's life because of her exposure to yet another literary tradition (her initial knowledge of the Polish language would have come through Mickiewicz) and because of her first exposure to a poet of great talent and significance. Her association with Adam appears to have increased her commitment to her experiments in verse and to her translations, and in this respect the relationship assumes a certain mentor-protégé quality from a professional perspective.

Karolina's first publication appeared in 1833. She issued a collection under the title *Nordlicht,* containing the translations of numerous Russian poets into German. Her most historically significant translations moved from Russian into French and German, and thus *Nordlicht* marks the beginning of a large portion of her intellectual efforts.

In the mid-1830s, Karolina developed an acquaintance and later a romance with the prose writer, Nikolai Pavlov. The two married in December of 1836, and Karolina Pavlova acquired the family name by which she is known ever after (in Russian, feminine forms of family names have the grammatical marker of a final "a"). The circumstances and motivations behind Pavlov's courtship remain unclear. Certain accounts point to Nikolai's predilection for gambling and his attraction to Karolina's sizable inheritance. Contemporaries and mutual acquaintances of the two, however, record a heartfelt romance and an initial love shared by both. Whatever the case, the marriage soon transformed into something quite unpleasant for both; the reasons seem to be relatively clear. Whether or not he concealed mercantile intentions initially, Nikolai eventually coveted his wife's wealth and later indeed gambled away the Jaenisch estate into which he had married. Moreover, Nikolai engaged in infidelities which naturally eroded the substance of the marriage. Finally, he is almost uniformly considered an inferior literary talent, and envy regarding his wife's literary abilities almost certainly soured his disposition toward her. Whereas Karolina Jaenisch Pavlova often earns the rubric "underappreciated," Nikolai Pavlov is generally considered a writer with unrealized potential.

The difficulties of their marriage notwithstanding, the Pavlovs held a literary salon which would become one of Pavlova's major contributions to the literary history of the period. The salon received virtually all of the luminaries of the day—poets, scholars, artists, musicians—and indeed members of all political and aesthetic inclinations were welcomed. The salon was, by all accounts, a place of rich social life and a fecund ground for intellectual and artistic exchanges. It first opened its doors in 1839 and lasted until the mid 1840s, at which time the growing rancor between the two vying political-intellectual trends of the day, Slavophilism and "Westernism," necessitated its closing. The Pavlovs tried to renew their salon later in the 1840s, but by this point, the death of certain prominent figures and the emigration of one of the salon's established visitors, the prominent thinker and Westernizer Aleksandr Herzen, left the salon bereft of its former glory. Pavlova's own politics were unique; on the one hand, she tended to be more sympathetic to the Slavophile and socially conservative elements, but on the other, she was regarded as something of an outsider because of her ancestry. Above all, she valued art and her beloved craft of poetry, and this sensibility led her away from the politicized literature promulgated by the liberals and later the socialists. The program of viewing literature as social commentary and the valuation of literature for its ability to influence social attitudes were anathema to this woman who devoted herself to beauty and her "holy craft" above all else. It is not surprising, therefore, that she would become close to the young Fet, a person of similarly mixed heritage, who fiercely defended the musicality and pure beauty of poetry in a time when social commentary dominated literary criticism.

The 1840s were a productive period for Pavlova's literature. From 1844 to 1848, she composed the largest of her works, the multigenre piece *A Double Life.* The work appears ostensibly as a novel but nonetheless differs from the conventional, 20th-century understanding of the novel due to its peculiar form which combines both a prose narrative and abundant lyric verse. The novel genre was experiencing its formative evolution in the 1830s and 1840s, and *A Double Life* belongs to a group of works during this period which press the questions of longer narrative genres. Concurrently, Pavlova was also actively engaged in her lyric poetry, and she composed some of her most memorable and valued pieces. She often shared her verse with her salon visitors, and one can assume that the intellectual ferment provided by her guests prompted the special productivity of these years.

In the early 1850s, Pavlova's life would take its most painful and significant turn. By this time, her husband had squandered virtually all her wealth, and Karolina was not fully aware of her husband's activity until the estate was essentially lost. In 1852, she instigated civil action against her husband. The proceedings, the circumstances of which are not clear, led to Nikolai Pavlov's arrest and internal exile. Despite Nikolai's conduct, the intellectual community blamed Karolina for her husband's detention, and she was effectively ostracized. She departed for Dorpat in 1853, moved to Dresden in 1858, and lived there for the remainder of her life.

Pavlova's *de facto* exile injured her profoundly but by no means ended her literary career. She continued her composition of poetry, with her most productive period crossing the point of exile and lasting from the 1840s to her release of the collection *Poems* in 1863. Also during this period she formed the most significant collaboration of her life. The esteemed and talented Alexei K. Tolstoy, a poet, essayist, and humorist, whose best-known novel is *Prince Serebryany,* visited Pavlova in Germany, and the two began a long, productive professional relationship which lasted until Tolstoy's death. Pavlova translated large portions of Tolstoy's work into French and German, and thanks to her, Tolstoy became one of the few Russian poets to successfully cross into the international scene and to garner international acclaim. Pavlova also became an active reader and collaborator in the composition of Tolstoy's work, and he praised her for her insight and literary gifts.

After Tolstoy's death in 1875, Pavlova faded into obscurity from which she would not emerge again. She died in 1893 in Dresden, and Russian literature had completely forgotten her. Valerii Briusov, the prominent figure of Russian Symbolism, praised Pavlova's verse and restored her memory with the publication of a collection of her works in 1915. Although certainly not occupying a prominent place in the Russian literary mindset, Pavlova's memory has been preserved by several subsequent figures of the 20th century, including the more prominent poets ***Marina Tsvetaeva** and ***Anna Akhmatova**. Tsvetaeva's lyric collection *Craft* owes its title to an utterance proffered by her predecessor Pavlova who pronounced her poetry her "holy craft."

Pavlova's literary activity can be divided into three areas: original works, translations, and the maintenance of her literary salon. The last two areas should not be discounted as insignificant for two reasons. First, as Pavlova was a woman, opportunities for publishing original works would not have been widely available. Thus, her translations and salon offered venues for participation in the literary community and for expression of her literary sensibilities. Secondly, regarding the salon specifically, the literary salon constituted a vital portion of the literary culture of the day. The salons represented the stage for new work and an "editorial" conference for work in progress, and they, along with the so-called "fat journals," were the principal stage for the exchange and evolution of literary and aesthetic ideas. Pavlova's salon therefore positioned her as a literary force and significant influence in Russia of the 1840s.

Nevertheless, her original works are of course her most important, lasting legacy, and her poetry places her as the preeminent Russian woman poet until the emergence of Symbolism in the 1890s. Pavlova's works do not exhibit uniform genius, and she is generally at her best when engaged with the internal questions of the heart and soul and when she avoids the clichés of the Sentimentalist and Romantic styles. Certain consistent questions, all of them interconnected, regularly recur in Pavlova's lyrics: alienation, the inner self, the divide between the internal and external worlds, and the nature of poetry itself.

The question of alienation emerges from Pavlova's particular position; that which endows Pavlova with her particularly variegated biography also perpetually confers upon her the label of outsider. She was never fully accepted as a Russian because of her German heritage, but Germany would not necessarily offer her a national home either. Ironically, her political inclinations were more sympathetic to the Russian Slavophiles, but this group would never truly accept her and indeed excoriated her after her husband's arrest. She was a woman who aspired to participate in the male-dominated literary sphere, but she also rejected the "George Sandism" and "emancipation" promulgated by the emergent feminine voices of Russia. These various influences led Pavlova to compose her contemplative verse, which has a sad undercurrent to its feelings of alienation. At its best and most poignant, this undercurrent is often understated and coupled with a sense of resignation. She conveys this resignation through frequent references to hopes and passions "in vain" and to the "poor in spirit," denoting those who have hoped and been disappointed. In "About the past, about the perished," she writes:

The heart is oppressed by the wordless thought
Of what's past, of what's perished, what's old;
I have met with much evil in life,
I have spent much emotion in vain,
I have sacrificed much to no point.

Such sentiments do not dominate all of Pavlova's verse, and what at times appears as alienation may also appear as a willful and celebratory withdrawal into the inner self. This inner life is indeed linked to Pavlova's vision of poetry, another frequent theme, because the moment of introspection and meditation can lead to a sense of true beauty (poetry) and a vision of higher truth. Thus, she opens "Life calls us" with a declaration of the individual's purpose—the apperception of distant paradise:

Life calls us, and we go, massing our courage;
But in the short hour when grief's thunder stints,
And passions sleep, when the heart's strife is mute,
The soul takes breath awhile from the world's troubles,
And suddenly the far-off Edens shine,
And meditations come to power again.

The full impact of Pavlova's largest work, *A Double Life,* is achieved only when seen within the context of her poetic vision. The dual-genre aspect of the work reflects this aesthetic perspective, and the "real world" portions of the work appear in prose, whereas the "inner world" portions appear in poetry. The poetic segments themselves comprise a poetic cycle much as the prose chapters comprise a "novel." Not coincidentally, the poems are situated as dreams, and as such they reflect the deeper symbolism occurring as Pavlova moves into her genre of meditation and vision. The plot of *A Double Life* prepares these dreams, which arguably contain the greater substance of the whole work.

The plot follows the young woman protagonist who is of the age of emergence into society. The prose sections of the work reveal her absorption into conventional society with its pretenses, hypocrisy, and gossip. In this regard, *A Double Life* can serve as a social statement, a sort of "society tale," satirizing and debunking the conventional life of the period. It resembles Pavlova's other work of substantial length, the narrative poem *Quadrille.* In that work, Pavlova is even more direct in questioning the dames' and debutantes' roles in society, lampooning those who fall into the pattern of balls and gossip and lamenting those who would aspire to something more substantive—something more poetic in Pavlova's discourse. Although eschewing the politics of "emancipation," she clearly observes that society deprives a woman of the search for substantive intellectual and spiritual pursuits, relegating her instead to the niceties of good society and drawing-room talents.

What Pavlova seeks manifests itself in the poetic segments of *A Double Life* and in her lyric poetry. The "second" life referred to in the title is that which is beyond the conventional, expected existence of a Russian woman. As she expresses it, Pavlova wishes her protagonist and any individual generally to "live the soul's life fully":

You will understand inspiration's secret,
You will live the soul's life fully.
What the genius learns in waking
You will learn, my child, in sleep.

Because of this perspective, Pavlova writes a great deal of poetry about poets and poetic creation which, for her, are tantamount to holiness, and this juncture represents the subject of Pavlova's most famous piece "You have stayed whole within my beggared heart." The opening stanza reads:

You have stayed whole within my beggared heart,
I salute you, my sorrowing verse!
My bright light above the ashes
Of my blessings and my joys!
The one thing in this shrine
That even sacrilege could not touch;
My misfortune! my enrichment!
My holy craft!

Here all of Pavlova's particular personality comes together: the alienation, the duality of the external and internal worlds, the introspection, the celebration in the beautiful, and the spirituality of aesthetic creation. This poem presages much of the 20th-century poetic spirit from Tsvetaeva and Akhmatova because of its view of the internal poetic spirit which endures through a profane external world. The religious language is particularly emphatic, and Pavlova demonstratively asserts her ability to persevere in her "second" world and in her inner shrine, despite all external efforts to deprive her of a true home. Her home of course was neither Russian society nor Dresden; rather, she persistently dwelt in her holy craft.

SOURCES:

Greene, Diana. "Nineteenth-Century Women Poets: Critical Reception vs. Self-Definition," in *Women Writers in Russian Literature.* Ed. by Toby W. Clyman and Diana Greene. Westport, CT: Greenwood, 1994.

Heldt, Barbara. *Terrible Perfection: Women and Russian Literature.* Bloomington, IN: Indiana University Press, 1987.

Kelly, Catriona, ed. *An Anthology of Russian Women's Writing, 1777–1992.* Oxford: Oxford University Press, 1994.

———. *A History of Russian Women's Writing: 1820–1992.* Oxford: Clarendon, 1994.

Pavlova, Karolina. *A Double Life.* Trans. by Barbara Heldt Monter. Ann Arbor, MI: Ardis, 1978.

Perkins, Pamela and Albert Cook, eds. *The Burden of Sufferance: Women Poets of Russia.* NY: Garland, 1993.

Andrew Swensen,
Western Michigan University, Kalamazoo, Michigan

Pawlikowska, Maria (1891–1945)

Poet and playwright who in the years since her death has been recognized as one of Poland's most original modern poets. *Name variations: Maria Kossak; Maria Pawlikowska-Jasnorzewska; Marii Pawlikowskiej-Jasnorzewskiej; Maria Jasnorzewska Pawlikowska. Born Maria Kossak in Cracow, Austrian Poland, on November 24, 1891; died in exile in Manchester, England, on July 9, 1945; daughter of Wojciech Kossak; cousin of Zofia Kossak (1890–1968); married three times, her last husband was the aviator Stefan Jasnorzewski.*

Now universally regarded as one of Poland's most original modern poets, in her own lifetime Maria Pawlikowska was a highly controversial artist, whose verse was considered little better than infantile scribblings by some critics while she was hailed as a major voice with a talent approximating that of genius by others. She was born into an aristocratic family in 1891. Both her father Wojciech Kossak and her paternal grandfather Juliusz Kossak were celebrated painters, and her cousin was the writer ***Zofia Kossak**. A stimulating home environment during her childhood and adolescence encouraged intellectual independence. Pawlikowska was educated at home by private tutors until she enrolled at Cracow's Academy of Fine Arts, intending to become a painter like her father. Although she displayed considerable talent at painting, Maria was eventually more drawn to writing.

She had written poetry since childhood, but her literary debut did not take place until 1922, when she published her first volume of verse, *Niebieskie migdaly* (Blue Haze). In this work, the young author's style—based on an economy of words along with a disregard for most of the traditional rules of versifying—was already in evidence. From 1922 until the German attack on Poland in September 1939, she would publish 11 more books of poetry, as well as one volume of lyrical prose.

Pawlikowska's major themes remained the same throughout her career: her personal preoccupation with youth, aging and the onset of old age, as well as her fears in the realms of love, death, and nature. Even before the poet had reached her mid-30s, she was considering the effects of old age. In her 1924 poem "Starosc" (Old Age), she reflected:

> I am alone.
> My name is Grandmother—
> I feel like a black stain
> On the world's rainbow-colored tapestry.

In many of her poems, Pawlikowska viewed the passage of time much like a personal tragedy, seeing it as synonymous with the fading of her own looks and desirability. Such feelings are strongly reflected in her poems "Przekwitla tancerka" (The Faded Dancer) and "Stara kobieta" (The Old Woman). By 1926, when she published *Pocalunki* (Kisses), Pawlikowska had established a reputation, scandalous in conservative circles, for both her unconventional personal life (she was married three times) and innovative poetry steeped in erotic themes. By the early 1930s, she would be known in literary circles as "the flower" or "the Polish ***Sappho.**"

During the crisis-ridden decade of the 1930s, Pawlikowska wrote a number of controversial plays in addition to publishing more poetry. Although several of these plays were successfully staged, often becoming storm centers of dispute, various factors prevented most of them from being published until 1985, four decades after her death. First performed in Cracow in December 1938, her *Baba Dziwo* (The Amazing Woman) was an antitotalitarian and antifascist "tragic farce" whose female protagonist was a thinly veiled dictator of Hitlerite proportions. In Warsaw, the German Embassy lodged a protest against the play, regarding it as an insult directed against the Third Reich and its führer. Only weeks before war broke out in September 1939, Pawlikowska published *Szkicownik poetycki* (Poetic Sketchbook), containing allusions to the conflict on the horizon. As early as 1937, in her poem "Krystalizacja" (Crystallization), she had pointed an accusing finger at herself for having been politically indifferent until so late a date:

> How did you dare to write about roses
> When history was burning like a forest in the summer heat?

Maria and her third husband, the pilot Stefan Jasnorzewski, fled Poland in September 1939 to escape the German invaders. After a brief period in Rumania, they moved to Paris, but here too they were forced to flee Nazi forces in the summer of 1940. They settled in Blackpool, England, where Polish aviators had their headquarters. Two volumes of verse published under the difficult circumstances of exile in 1940 and 1941 reflect the poet's despair. She described the war's destructive fury as a form of "helpless insanity of the insane." Adding to her grief were the deaths of her parents and her own rapidly declining health due to cancer. Two major surgeries and radiation therapy slowed but could not stop her illness. Stoically, she recorded her own process of dying in *Ostatnic notatniki* (Final Notes), a work that would not be published until 1993.

Maria Pawlikowska died in Manchester, England, on July 9, 1945. Held in low esteem by Marxist literary critics because of the subjective and pessimistic nature of the verse, her work was relatively little known in People's Poland for decades. Starting in the late 1960s, however, she began to be reevaluated, and since that time, her powerful literary legacy has enjoyed a renaissance among Polish readers.

Polish postage stamp issued in honor of Maria Pawlikowska, 1983.

SOURCES:

Ariadne's Thread: Polish Women Poets. Trans. and ed. by Susan Bassnett and Piotr Kuhiwczak. London: Forest Books-UNESCO, 1988.

Faas, Marta. "Das janusköpfige Denken der polnischen Dichterin Maria Pawlikowska-Jasnorzewska," in Heinrich Riggenbach and Felix Keller, eds., *Colloquium Slavicum Basiliense.* Berne: Peter Lang, 1981, pp. 103–123.

Gasiorowski, Professor Zygmunt J. Personal communication.

Hurnikowska, Elzbieta. *Natura w Salonie Mody: O Miedzywojennej liryce Marii Pawlikowskiej-Jasnorzewskiej.* Warsaw: Panstwowy Instytut Wydawnictwo, 1995.

Milanowski, Anna. "Pawlikowska-Jasnorzewska, Maria (geb. Kossak)," in Ute Hechtfischer, *et al.*, eds., *Metzler Autorinnen Lexikon.* Stuttgart: Verlag J.B. Metzler, 1998, pp. 419–420.

——. *Über die Poesie von Maria Pawlikowska-Jasnorzewska-anders.* Vienna: VWGÖ, 1991.

Milosz, Czeslaw. *The History of Polish Literature.* 2nd ed. Berkeley, CA: University of California Press, 1983.

Pawlikowska-Jasnorzewska, Maria. *Wybór poezji.* Ed. by Jerzy Kwiatkowski. 3rd ed. Wroclaw: Zaklad Narodowy im. Ossolinskich, 1972.

Peterkiewicz, Jerzy, Burns Singer, and Jon Stallworthy, eds. *Five Centuries of Polish Poetry, 1450–1970.* 2nd ed. London: Oxford University Press, 1970.

Pruska-Carroll, Malgorzata. "Poetry of Maria Pawlikowska-Jasnorzewska: Femininity and Feminism," in *The Polish Review.* Vol. 26, no. 2, 1981, pp. 35–50.

Zacharska, Jadwiga. "Renesans Pawlikowskiej," in *Poezja.* Vol. 4, no. 6, 1968, pp. 71–73.

John Haag,
Associate Professor of History, University of Georgia,
Athens, Georgia

Paxinou, Katina (1900–1973)

***Greek stage and film actress who won an Academy Award for her performance in* For Whom the Bell Tolls.** *Born Katina Konstantopoulou (also seen as Constantopoulos) in Piraeus, Greece, in 1900; died of cancer on February 22, 1973, in Athens; daughter of Basil Konstantopoulou; studied voice at the Geneva*

Conservatoire; married Ivannis Paxinou (divorced); married Alexis Minotis (an actor and director), in 1940; children: a daughter.

Selected theater: originally appeared in opera in Athens; first dramatic appearance was in La Femme Nue *in Athens (1924); made New York debut as Clytemnestra in* Electra *(1930); appeared as Clytemnestra in* Agamemnon *(Greek National Theatre, 1932), in title role in* Anna Christie *(Greek National Theatre, 1932), as Mrs. Alving in* Ghosts *(Greek National Theatre, 1934), as Phaedra in* Hippolytus *(Greek National Theatre, 1937), as Lady Windermere in* Lady Windermere's Fan *(Greek National Theatre, 1937), as Goneril in* King Lear *(Greek National Theatre, 1938), as Mrs. Chevely in* An Ideal Husband *(Greek National Theatre, 1938), in title role in* Electra *(London, 1939), as Gertrude in* Hamlet *(London, 1939), in title role in* Hedda Gabler *(New York, 1942), as Bernarda in* The House of Bernarda Alba *(New York, 1951, Greece, 1954), as Jocasta in* Oedipus Rex *(London, 1966), in title role in* Hecuba *(London, 1966).*

Selected filmography: For Whom the Bell Tolls *(1943);* Hostages *(1943);* Confidential Agent *(1945);* Mourning Becomes Electra *(1947);* Uncle Silas *(*The Inheritance, *UK, 1947);* Prince of Foxes *(1949);* Mr. Arkadin *(*Confidential Report, *Sp.-Fr., 1935);* The Miracle *(1959);* Rocco e i suoi Fratelli *(*Rocco and His Brothers, *It.-Fr., 1960);* Tante Zita *(*Zita, *Fr., 1968);* Un Eté sauvage *(Fr., 1972).*

From the movie For Whom the Bell Tolls, *starring Katina Paxinou (left), Ingrid Bergman, and Gary Cooper.*

A formidable actress whose career encompassed stage and screen, Katina Paxinou was born in 1900 in Piraeus, Greece, and studied voice at the Geneva Conservatoire, intent on a career as an opera singer. She switched to acting in 1924, and shortly thereafter joined the Greek National Theatre, becoming the company's leading actress. Paxinou excelled in the classical Greek roles, but she also translated and directed a number of English-language plays, among them Eugene O'Neill's *Anna Christie*, in which she also played the title role. One of her most famous roles was Mrs. Alving in Henrik Ibsen's *Ghosts,* a part she first portrayed in 1934, and thereafter reprised annually for six years.

Paxinou made her London debut in 1939 in Sophocles' *Electra,* and she was still performing there when World War II broke out. Unable to return to Greece, she sailed for the United States, making her Broadway debut in the title role of *Hedda Gabler* (1942). Hollywood soon beckoned, and the very next year she won an Academy Award for Best Supporting Actress for her portrayal of Pilar in *For Whom the Bell Tolls*, a film adaptation of the Ernest Hemingway novel, starring ***Ingrid Bergman** and Gary Cooper. Paxinou made several additional Hollywood films before returning to Greece with her second husband, actor-director Alexis Minotis, with whom she frequently acted. She returned to New York in 1951, portraying Bernarda in Garcia Lorca's *The House of Bernarda Alba*, a role she repeated in Greece in 1954. Throughout the 1960s, the actress continued to perform on stage in London and Greece, and also appeared in an occasional European film. She and her husband later established the Royal Theatre in Athens.

COLLECTIONS:

Katina Paxinou Museum, 13 Thoukididou, Plaka.

Barbara Morgan,
Melrose, Massachusetts

Payne, Ethel (1911–1991)

African-American journalist. *Name variations: Ethel Lois Payne. Born on August 14, 1911, in Chicago, Illinois; died on May 4, 1991; daughter of William Payne (a Pullman porter) and Bessie (Austin) Payne (a high school Latin teacher); educated at Lindblom High School, Crane Junior College in Chicago, the Garrett Institute, and the Medill School of Journalism at Northwestern University.*

Awards, honors: received first prize, Illinois Press Association, for series on adoptions (1952); honorable mention, Heywood Broun Memorial Award, for series on "Industry, USA" (1953); Third Annual World Understanding Award, Chicago Council for Outstanding Reporting (1956); Citation for Outstanding Reporting, Windy City Press Club, Chicago (1957); award for Vietnam report, Capital Press Club, Washington, D.C.; Excellence in Journalism Award, African Methodist Episcopal Church; 100 Outstanding Black Women citation, Operation PUSH, Chicago (1967); citations from National Urban Coalition, National Association of Business & Professional Women, Delta Sigma Theta Sorority, and National Association of Black Journalists; Roosevelt University, Chicago, Freedom Award (1970–80); testimonial dinner establishing professorship at Fisk University, Washington, D.C. (1982); Distinguished Service Award, Africare, Washington, D.C. (1983); Award for International Reporting, Capital Press Club (1985); chosen as one of the Top 100 Black Business & Professional Women of 1985, Dollars & Sense *magazine; Transafrica African Freedom Award (1987).*

Ethel Payne was one of the few African-American women journalists covering Washington, D.C., in her era. An investigative reporter for some 40 years whom many of her peers called "The First Lady of the Black Press," she was also the first African-American woman radio and television commentator employed by a national network and a passionate advocate of civil rights.

Payne got her start in journalism while working as an Army service club director in Tokyo, Japan, from 1948 to 1951. She was visited by two correspondents from the *Chicago Defender*, which throughout much of the 20th century was the most influential black newspaper in America. Payne had been recording in her diary observations on discrimination within the American forces stationed in Japan, and the correspondents persuaded her to send these to the *Defender*. What the paper published revealed illegal segregation within the military, and news of the hundreds of babies that American soldiers fathered with Japanese women and then abandoned. Returning to Chicago, Payne enrolled in the Medill School of Journalism at Northwestern University. After receiving her degree, she joined the staff of the *Chicago Defender*, for which she would write for 27 years.

The paper soon transferred her to Washington, D.C., where she became a White House correspondent. Race issues were rarely mentioned in much of the American press, which sought either to avoid or to ignore such stories at that time, but Payne sought to create public awareness of racial injustice. At a press conference, she asked President Dwight D. Eisenhower to explain why the Howard University choir, which had been invited to perform alongside choirs from Emory and Duke universities at a Republican celebration on Lincoln Day, had been prevented from performing. Expressing surprise, Eisenhower responded he would apologize if indeed a racial snub had been intended. This story received extensive coverage, and while it brought attention to a legitimate problem, it also brought Payne accusations from some African-American journalists of simply trying to get her name known. In another confrontation with Eisenhower over bringing an end to segregated practices in interstate travel, he bristled and, in her own words, "chewed [her] out," saying that he did not intend to do any "special favors for any special interest group." After this incident, she was banned from White House press conferences. She nonetheless remained intent upon exposing and attacking segregation and the treatment of minorities.

Civil rights were a top priority for Payne, who often quoted activist Frederick Douglass' admonition to "agitate, agitate, agitate." She covered the civil-rights movement continuously from the mid-1950s, including the 1955–56 Montgomery bus boycott inspired by *Rosa Parks**, the 1963 church bombing that killed **Addie Mae Collins**, **Denise McNair**, **Carol Robertson**, and **Cynthia Wesley** (all children and known as the **Birmingham Four**), and the March on Washington the same year. Among the many other stories she reported were those on wars and revolutionary movements in Africa, the experiences of African-American soldiers in the war in Vietnam (where she spent three months), the Apollo 17 Moon Launch, and the International Women's Year Conference in Mexico City in 1975. Throughout the next decade, she continued to travel and report widely, in the U.S., Africa, Asia, Europe, and South America. Payne was a commentator on CBS radio and television for ten years, and, after she left the *Defender* in her late 60s, wrote a nationally syndicated newspaper column. The recipient of numerous awards and honors, including a professorship in journalism established in her name at Fisk University, she continued freelance reporting and traveling until her death in 1991.

Birmingham Four. *See Davis, Angela for sidebar.*

SOURCES:

Smith, Jessie Carney, ed. *Notable Black American Women.* Detroit, MI: Gale Research, 1992.

SUGGESTED READING:

Dunnigan, Alice. *A Black Woman's Experience—From Schoolhouse to White House.*

Washington Press Club Foundation. Transcripts from oral history project on prominent women journalists.

Jo Anne Meginnes,
freelance writer, Brookfield, Vermont

Payne, Sylvia (1880–1974)

English psychoanalyst. *Born Sylvia Moore in 1880; died in 1974; graduated from the London Hospital School of Medicine in 1906; married J.E. Payne (a surgeon); children: three.*

A pioneer in the use of psychoanalysis, Sylvia Payne was the daughter of a cleric, and qualified for her medical degree at the London Hospital School of Medicine (now the Royal Free Hospital School of Medicine). During World War I, she served as commandant and medical officer at the Torquay Red Cross Hospital, for which she was created CBE in 1918. Payne subsequently became a psychiatrist at the London Clinic of Psychoanalysis. At the time, psychoanalysis was a new and controversial discipline, and Payne helped establish it as a legitimate and valuable form of therapy. She later served variously as chair of the board of directors of the Institute of Psychoanalysis, president of the British Psychoanalytical Society, and a fellow of the British Psychological Society. Payne was married to J.E. Payne, a surgeon; they had three children.

Payne, Virginia (1908–1977)

American actress who portrayed the title role on the popular radio soap opera "Ma Perkins" for 27 years. *Name variations: Ma Perkins. Born on June 19, 1908, probably in Cincinnati, Ohio; died on February 10, 1977, in Cincinnati.*

Vance, Nina. *See Women of the Regional Theater Movement in America.*

Known for decades as the kindly old woman from "Rushville Center," Virginia Payne portrayed the title role on the popular daytime radio serial "Ma Perkins" for 27 years (7,065 consecutive broadcasts), from its debut on December 4, 1933, to its demise in 1960. The show, which previewed for 16 weeks out of Cincinnati station WLW, then moved to Chicago, sponsored by Proctor and Gamble. It was P&G's first foray into network radio, and the show's success sent sales of Oxydol laundry detergent soaring; it also helped make "soap opera" part of the American lexicon. Aired in 15-minute segments, five days a week, the serial centered on the everyday problems of a widowed grandmother (Ma Perkins), who ran a lumberyard in a small town with the help of her old friend Shuffle Shober, played by Charles Egleston. Plots included Ma's ongoing family problems, with particular focus on married daughter Evey, president of the gossipy women's club The Jolly Seventeen, and a "heartache" to her mother. Actor Murray Forbes, who played Evey's long-suffering husband Willie Fitz, was also with the soap opera from the onset, but other characters had as many as three different interpreters during the run of the show.

Purportedly, Ma Perkins' character was originally conceived as a raucous old woman, much like ***Marie Dressler**'s character in the popular *Min and Bill* movies. Payne, who was 23 when she originated the role, softened the character into a tolerant, warm-hearted woman who was constantly at odds with the town's small-minded residents. So successful was her portrayal that listeners frequently wrote to her for advice on personal problems.

After 13 successful years in Chicago, the show moved to New York, where it enjoyed continued popularity for another 13 years. When it went off the air in 1960, loyal listeners wrote thousands of letters of protest to the station. During the show's final broadcast, a re-creation of Thanksgiving dinner at Ma's house, the station was flooded with calls from angry, disappointed fans, some of them in tears.

For Payne, however, the end of the show was liberating. She went on to appear on other radio and television shows as well as on stage; one of her later roles was that as "Apple Granny" on a commercial for apple juice. In 1963, she portrayed Mary Tyrone in Eugene O'Neill's *Long Day's Journey into Night* at the Alley Theater in Houston, under the direction of **Nina Vance**. During her career, Payne was also an active member of the American Federation of Television and Radio Artists (AFTRA) and served a term as its national president.

SOURCES:

Johnson, Greg. "New Owners Hope Oxydol Brand Isn't All Washed Up," in *Los Angeles Times.* July 2, 2000.

Lamparski, Richard. *Whatever Became of . . . ?* 3rd series. NY: Crown, 1970.

Barbara Morgan,
Melrose, Massachusetts

Payne-Gaposchkin, Cecilia (1900–1979)

American astrophysicist, an authority on variable stars and galactic structure, who was the first to receive a Ph.D. in astronomy from Radcliffe (1925) and

the first woman to achieve the rank of professor at Harvard University (1956). *Name variations: Cecelia Gaposhkin; Cecilia Gaposchkin. Born Cecilia Helena Payne on March 10, 1900, in Wendover, England; died on December 7, 1978, in Cambridge, Massachusetts; daughter of Edward John Payne (a lawyer and historian) and Emma (Pertz) Payne (an artist); attended private schools; Newnham College, Cambridge University, B.A., 1923; Radcliffe College, Ph.D. in astronomy, 1925; married Sergei I. Gaposchkin (an astronomer), on March 6, 1934; children: Edward Michael Gaposchkin; Katherine Leonora Gaposchkin; Peter John Arthur Gaposchkin.*

One of the 20th century's most renowned women scientists, astrophysicist Cecilia Payne-Gaposchkin conducted pioneering research into the composition and classification of stars, contributing greatly to our knowledge of the structure of the Galaxy. She also successfully raised a family while pursuing a career in a profession not widely open to women. Her love of science was clear in her poem "Research," which appears at the end of her autobiography. "O Universe, O Lover/ I gave myself to thee/ Not for gold/ Not for glory/ But for love."

Cecilia Helena Payne was born on May 10, 1900, in Wendover, England, into a family of intellectuals. Although her father died when she was four, along with her brother and sister, she received a private school education and attended college. After graduating from Newnham College, Cambridge, where her interest in astronomy surfaced, Cecilia won a National Research Fellowship which allowed her to pursue graduate study at Radcliffe College and the Harvard College Observatory in the United States. In 1925, she received the first Ph.D. ever awarded in astronomy from Radcliffe, submitting a brilliant doctoral thesis in which she determined temperature scale for stellar atmospheres and also concluded that stars are made up primarily of hydrogen and helium, with traces of other elements, a theory still held. After receiving her advanced degree, knowing she would not find work in her chosen field if she returned to England, Payne-Gaposchkin remained at the observatory, although in doing so she was forced to limit her research to those guidelines set by the faculty. In 1927, after serving her apprenticeship as a research fellow, she became a permanent member of the Harvard College observatory staff, serving in a somewhat ill-defined position. During that time, in addition to advising graduate students and teaching an occasional class, she published a second book, *Stars of High Luminosity* (1930).

In 1933, in conjunction with a book on novae and other variable stars she was planning with Russian astronomer Boris Gerasimovich, Cecilia traveled to Europe, where she met astronomer Sergei Gaposchkin, a Russian émigré who had just finished his doctorate at Berlin University. Unable to return to the USSR because of his political views, he appealed to her to find him a job a Harvard, which she managed to do even in the midst of an economic depression that resulted in layoffs among the observatory staff. In March 1934, Cecilia and Sergei surprised their colleagues by "eloping" to New York City, where they were married by a justice of the peace. At the time, Cecilia adopted the hyphenated name Payne-Gaposchkin; she wanted to keep her own name for professional continuity. While she continued to pursue her career, however, she faced the additional challenges of managing a home and raising a family. She continued to work through her three pregnancies (while curtailing her public appearances), but found that child care became her greatest obstacle.

Cecilia Payne-Gaposchkin

When nannies failed to meet her needs, she resorted to bringing her children to the observatory, much to the consternation of her fellow workers. Still, her career flourished at Harvard. In 1938, she was appointed Phillips Astronomer and a lecturer at the observatory, and in 1956, she became the first woman to receive tenure and the first to be appointed chair of the astronomy department.

While Payne-Gaposchkin's early work focused on the spectra of the stars and presented the first convincing evidence that the stars are similar to the sun in their chemical make-up, her later work, much of it conducted with her husband, concentrated on the study of variable stars. The couple's research included the exhaustive study of 1,500 specimens located over the entire sky, from which they made several million observations and documented them in numerous publications. In addition to projects with her husband, Payne-Gaposchkin collaborated with other members of the observatory staff, and also worked independently, studying unusual stars, such as those that pulsate violently or that explode (*Astrophysical Journal*, May 1946). Some of her research involved the analysis of astronomical photographs and spectrum studies (*Astrophysical Journal*, July and November 1946). She also wrote *Stars in the Making* (1952), *Introduction to Astronomy* (1954), *Variable Stars and Galactic Structure* (1954), and *Galactic Novae* (1957).

In the course of her career, Payne-Gaposchkin received numerous awards for her scientific accomplishments, including the first ***Annie Jump Cannon** Medal of the American Astronomical Society (1934), and the Henry Norris Russell Prize for a lifetime of distinguished scientific research from the American Astronomical Society (1976). She was awarded honorary degrees from Wilson College, Smith College, Cambridge University, and the Western College for Women, and in 1952 was the recipient of an Award of Merit for outstanding scientific achievements from her alma mater, Radcliffe College. The only honor that apparently eluded her was election to the National Academy of Sciences.

Payne-Gaposchkin retired from the Harvard faculty in 1966, but retained her association with the observatory. In retirement, she wrote about some of her 19th-century ancestors and also prepared her autobiography, which was published posthumously in 1984.

In her acceptance speech and memorial lecture for the Henry Norris Russell Prize, delivered in 1977, two years before her death, Payne-Gaposchkin touched upon the high points of a scientific career, from the exuberant discoveries of youth to the deeper understandings that come with maturity:

> The reward of the young scientist is the emotional thrill of being the first person in the history of the world to see something or to understand something. Nothing can compare with the experience; it engenders what Thomas Huxley called the Divine Dipsomania. The reward of the old scientist is the sense of having seen a vague sketch grow into a masterly landscape. Not a finished picture, of course; a picture that is still growing in scope and detail with the application of new techniques and new skills. The old scientist cannot claim that the masterpiece is his own work. He may have roughed out part of the design, laid on a few strokes, but he has learned to accept the discoveries of others with the same delight that he experienced his own when he was young.

SOURCES:

Bailey, Brooke. *The Remarkable Lives of 100 Women Healers and Scientists.* Holbrook, MA: Bob Adams, 1994.

Current Biography 1957. NY: H.W. Wilson, 1957.

Garraty, John A., and Mark C. Carnes, eds. *American National Biography.* Vol. 17. NY: Oxford University Press, 1999.

Gilbert, Lynn, and Gaylen Moore. *Particular Passions.* NY: Clarkson N. Potter, 1981.

SUGGESTED READING:

Haramundanis, Katherine, ed. *Cecilia Payne-Gaposchkin: An Autobiography and Other Recollections* (1984).

Barbara Morgan,
Melrose, Massachusetts

Payson, Joan Whitney (1903–1975)

American philanthropist. *Born Joan Whitney on February 5, 1903, in New York City; died on October 4, 1975, in New York City; only daughter and one of two children of Payne Whitney (an investor) and Helen (Hay) Whitney; graduated from Miss Chapin's School, New York City; attended Barnard College for a year; married Charles Shipman Payson (an industrialist and Wall Street investor), on July 5, 1924; children: three daughters and two sons (one of whom was killed in World War II).*

Unpretentious, generous, and one of the world's wealthiest women, Joan Whitney Payson was the granddaughter of W.C. Whitney, a New York streetcar magnate who served as secretary of the navy under President Grover Cleveland. Her father Payne Whitney enlarged the family fortune with astute investments in lumber, banking, and real estate; her mother **Helen Hay Whitney** was the daughter of John Hay, an assistant private secretary to President Abraham Lincoln who later served as U.S.

secretary of state. The Whitney family bred horses on a 1,000-acre farm near Lexington, Kentucky, and raced them at Saratoga Race Track in Saratoga Springs, New York, an enterprise which W.C. had a hand in developing. Joan's mother founded the Greentree Stable which produced the 1931 Kentucky Derby winner Twenty Grand, as well as other thoroughbreds. (When Helen died in 1944, Joan and her brother Jock Whitney inherited Greentree, which they continued to operate.) Joan was riding as soon as she could walk, and later recalled being taken as a child to Saratoga where she was allowed to bet a quarter on each race. Her mother was also a great baseball fan and often took her daughter with her to watch the New York Giants play at the Polo Grounds

Following her graduation from New York's exclusive Chapin School, and a year at Barnard College, Joan met and married Charles Shipman Payson, the son of a wealthy Portland (Maine) family who was attending Yale in preparation for a career as an industrialist and Wall Street banker. The wedding at Manhasset, New York, on July 5, 1924, was a society event of note, as were most of the Payson celebrations that followed. (Lindsay Van Gelder of the *New York Post* once likened the Paysons' lifestyle to an F. Scott Fitzgerald novel.)

Social events not withstanding, Joan Payson was enterprising and energetic and in 1929 founded Young Books, a children's book store. It gradually expanded to include a wider range of books and in 1942 merged with the Wakefield Book Store, which remained under Payson's ownership. During the 1930s and 1940s, Payson, along with her brother Jock, gave financial backing to a number of successful plays and movies, including *A Streetcar Named Desire*, *Rebecca*, and *Gone With the Wind*.

Maturity did not diminish Payson's childhood enthusiasm for baseball and during the 17 years that the Giants were in New York, she not only attended their home games but purchased close to 10% of the team's stock. In 1960, when team owner Horace Stoneham decided to move the team to San Francisco, Payson offered to buy the club to keep it in New York, but Stoneham would not sell. In 1962, she put up 85% of the funds to establish the New York Mets, and then played a crucial role in urging Casey Stengel to come out of retirement to manage the team. For the first five years, the Mets never finished higher than ninth place in a ten-team league, but New Yorkers staunchly supported them. "To Joan Payson . . . making money was never the primary object to owning the Mets," wrote David Dempsey. "[I]ndeed, the object may well have been getting rid of money, and it is highly ironic that what might have been a fine tax loss has proved to be such a good investment." In 1969, under the new management of Gil Hodges, the Mets won the National League's Eastern Division title, went on to defeat Atlanta in the playoffs, and then beat the Baltimore Orioles to win the World Series.

Through the years, Payson's philanthropic projects widened to encompass medical, art, and civic institutions, among them New York Hospital, St. Mary's Hospital in Palm Beach, Florida, The United Hospital Fund, the Lighthouse in Manhattan, and the North Shore Hospital in Manhasset, Long Island, which she also founded. She served as president of the Helen Hay Whitney Foundation, which financed research in rheumatic fever, rheumatic heart disease, and diseases of the connective tissues. She supported the New York Metropolitan Museum of Art and the Museum of Modern Art, in New York City, and established the Country Art Gallery in Westbury, Long Island. (Payson's private art collection contained paintings by Goya, El Greco, Van Gogh, Cezanne, Gauguin, Matisse, Renoir, Corot, and Toulouse-Lautrec.) Payson was also active politically, holding membership in the Women's National Republican Club of New York City, and donating regularly to the Republican Party.

The Paysons had five children, three daughters and two sons, one of whom was killed in World War II. They maintained numerous residences around the country, most of which were accessed by the family's private Pullman car, the "Adios II." Despite her wealth and society connections, Payson was described as "completely unaffected, warm, and innately gracious." While interviewing her for *The New York Times Magazine*, Dempsey noted her "childlike directness" and "feeling of gratitude that anyone would think her life worth prying into." Joan Payson died in New York on October 4, 1975.

SOURCES:

Dempsey, David. *The New York Times Magazine*. June 23, 1968.

Moritz, Charles, ed. *Current Biography 1973*. NY: H.W. Wilson, 1973.

———. *Current Biography 1975*. NY: H.W. Wilson, 1975.

Barbara Morgan,
Melrose, Massachusetts

Peabody, Elizabeth Palmer (1778–1853).

See Peabody, Elizabeth Palmer (1804–1894) for sidebar.

Peabody, Elizabeth Palmer
(1804–1894)

American author, educator and social reformer who played a central role in the Transcendentalist movement and pioneered the idea of kindergarten education in the United States. *Born Elizabeth Palmer Peabody in Billerica, Massachusetts, on May 16, 1804; died in Boston on January 3, 1894; daughter of Nathaniel Peabody (a doctor and dentist) and Elizabeth Palmer Peabody (1778–1853, an author and teacher); sister of Mary Peabody Mann (1806–1887) and Sophia Peabody Hawthorne (1809–1871); aunt of* ****Rose Hawthorne Lathrop*** *(1851–1926); never married.*

Author of numerous books and articles on philosophy, theology and education; was the first female publisher in the U.S.; was active in abolitionist, Native American rights and women's suffrage movements; founded first kindergarten in America (1860).

Selected works: First Steps to the Study of History *(1832);* A Record of a School *(1835);* Moral Culture of Infancy, and Kindergarten Guide *(1863);* Reminiscences of the Rev. William E. Channing *(1880).*

In the early 1840s, Boston was a city in intellectual turmoil. Inspired by democratic hopes, young people challenged inherited conventions and institutions. They were sure they could do better, and many drafted blueprints for a new society that would have no greed, no slavery, no inequality between the sexes, no injustice of any kind. Some proposed new religious faiths, others championed free love or vegetarianism, socialism or mesmerism. "What a fertility of projects for the salvation of the world!" marvelled Ralph Waldo Emerson, the man whose writings had inspired so many of these utopian dreams.

For those who wanted to join in on what Emerson called this "din of opinion and debate," there was one place to be, a bookshop on West Street run by Elizabeth Palmer Peabody. The very fact that the store was owned and run by a woman was proof enough that here was a place devoted to radical new ideas. Inside the shop, walls were lined floor to ceiling with exciting books—the latest Romantic philosophy imported from Europe, the first, still obscure masterpieces of a new American literature, pamphlets promoting every radical cause. As exciting as the books were the patrons. William Ellery Channing, mentor to abolitionists and religious radicals, dropped by each day to read the papers. Emerson, Bronson Alcott and other Transcendentalists were regular customers. On Wednesday evening, Boston's best-educated women gathered to discuss feminism and philosophy with the great ***Margaret Fuller.**

Elizabeth Peabody's West Street bookshop was a breeding ground for new ideas, an incubator for the literary movement we now honor with the name "the American Renaissance." To this movement, Peabody was not just a bookseller, but a guiding spirit. She had a keen eye for new talent, introduced people of like minds, and inspired the intellectual curiosity of all who crossed her path. As biographer **Louise Hall Tharp** put it, she always made it her business to know "what each customer had read and what each customer ought to read next." Long after closing time, Peabody stayed in the shop, discussing theology and literature with customers who were usually short on money, but long on enthusiasm. Though the bookshop on West Street lasted only a decade, it was just one example of Elizabeth Peabody's lifetime of devotion to learning. For over 70 years, she championed new, and sometimes controversial, reforms in the education of women and young children.

Though she cared little about such things, Elizabeth could trace her ancestry back to some of the earliest and most respectable families of colonial Boston. Her mother, also named Elizabeth, *did* care about her lineage. She was proud to be a Palmer, granddaughter of a wealthy man who had been a member of the Continental Congress and one of the city's greatest revolutionary patriots. At a time when higher education was denied to most girls, ➤ **Elizabeth Palmer (Peabody)** had educated herself, enjoying access to her grandfather's extensive library. She developed a passion for learning that she would one day pass on to her daughter, and was known by her friends as "the walking dictionary." But the Palmer family fortune had been unwisely invested, her parents died young, and she came of age with only memories of her family's past glories. To support herself, she became a teacher.

Elizabeth Palmer pinned her hopes of recovering her social status on her husband Nathaniel Peabody, a thoughtful and unassuming young man who aspired to become a doctor. While he attended classes at Harvard Medical School, she ran a girl's boarding school in their home in Billerica. There, in 1804, her daughter Elizabeth Palmer Peabody was born, the first of six children. Nathaniel proved a disappointment to his wife, however. He had little social ambition, and decided to pursue the less lucrative and less prestigious field of dentistry. At a time when most dentists simply pulled teeth, Nathaniel experimented with the novel idea of filling cavities. But customers were skeptical, and his practice in the family's new home in Salem always provided a rather marginal living for his growing family.

Perhaps frustrated by her husband's financial failures, Mrs. Peabody channeled her ambitions into her children. She began Elizabeth's education at a very young age, and perhaps most important, she taught her daughter to ignore her society's conventional view that the male-dominated fields of theology, philosophy, and politics were too difficult for delicate female minds. Mrs. Peabody was "a rock of strength and stability," writes historian Bruce Ronda, "a model for her daughter of both strength of character and maternal, self-sacrificial spirit."

In her teenage years, Elizabeth taught in her mother's school. At 19, she left home, briefly establishing her own school in Boston, and then working as a governess for a wealthy family in Maine. While there, she was courted by a young man who, when she rejected him, apparently committed suicide. The incident seemed to haunt her in later years. Coupled with her mother's less than enthusiastic endorsement of a married woman's lot in life, this may explain why Elizabeth never married. In 1825, she returned to Boston, and recruited her younger sister ***Mary Peabody (Mann)** to help start a new school. By economizing, Elizabeth was able to support herself on very little, and still sent money home to support her parents. She also took a maternal interest in her youngest sister, ***Sophia Peabody Hawthorne**, paying for painting lessons which enabled her to become an accomplished artist.

While teaching in Boston, Elizabeth became an ardent admirer of the Rev. William Ellery Channing, the leader of Boston's "Liberal" Christians. His preaching confirmed her own conclusion that human nature was essentially good, and that God wanted people to use this divine spark within as a guide to improve themselves and to reform the world's evils. Like many other young and idealistic Bostonians at the time, Elizabeth decided to answer his call to live a life fully devoted to spreading "Christian benevolence."

Channing and Elizabeth became lifelong friends. He was her most important mentor, guiding her studies while treating her as an intellectual equal. Channing's friendship gave Elizabeth confidence, and provided her with an introduction to the highest circles of Boston's intellectual elite. In 1827, she gave a series of history lectures to women audiences, making her the nation's first female lecturer. Ignoring criticisms that she was being "unfeminine," she offered the joys of higher learning to women who had always been denied that opportunity. Her vast knowledge of literature and philosophy, her infectious enthusiasm and her gift for conversation soon made her a fixture in Boston's intellectual life.

> **Peabody, Elizabeth Palmer** (1778–1853)
> ***American author and teacher.*** *Name variations: Elizabeth Palmer. Born Elizabeth Palmer in 1778; died in 1853; married Nathaniel Peabody; children:* ****Elizabeth Palmer Peabody*** *(1804–1894);* ****Sophia Peabody Hawthorne*** *(1809–1871);* ****Mary Peabody Mann.***

Peabody gave back to Channing as much as he had given her. At the time, he had not published his sermons, delivered from cryptic, hastily written notes. Though he was reluctant, Peabody insisted that she should be allowed to transcribe and edit his sermons for publication. Thanks to her painstaking efforts, Channing's ideas soon reached a much wider audience, advancing his own prestige and accelerating the growth of religious liberalism in New England.

In 1834, Elizabeth began to gather students for a new school. Again ignoring gender taboos, she planned to teach boys as well as girls. Then she met Bronson Alcott, a mystical philosopher and schoolteacher who had just arrived in Boston, searching for a new position as a teacher. (His daughter ***Louisa May Alcott** had been born two years earlier.) To Peabody, he seemed "like an embodiment of light and yet calm, solemn and simple." Alcott believed that, before children were born, their souls already existed. When they came into this world, he said, children brought with them the insights and intuitions which they had carried over from this spiritual realm. His mission as an educator, he told Peabody, was to help students recover this innate religious and moral knowledge. To do this, he guided them through Socratic "conversations," teaching them to probe the inner recesses of their souls for these divine intuitions.

Always excited by new ideas and happiest, as Tharp put it, "when giving more than she could afford," Peabody turned over her new school to Alcott. Since he was more interested in soul-searching than "book learning," she agreed to help him at his "Temple School" for a few hours a day, teaching the conventional academic subjects for a modest salary. On the first day of class, Alcott searched 20 eager young faces, and solemnly asked, "Which of you have gone inward and viewed yourselves?" None had, and so he began to lead them through daily sessions of journal writing and self-analysis. Peabody was so impressed by Alcott's method that she soon began to stay all day, in order to make a written record of the daily "conversations." The following year, she published the results as *A Record of a School* (1835). To the Transcendentalists who shared Alcott's decidedly unorthodox views about human nature, the book established him as an important figure. To others, it proved him a dangerous crackpot.

Peabody was beginning to have her own doubts about Alcott's method. She decided that he worked too hard on his students' spiritual development, while ignoring their physical and mental training. And she felt that his constant demand that children search their souls was making them too self-centered. "I think you are liable to injure the modesty and unconsciousness of good children," she told him, "by making them reflect too much upon their actual superiority." Making matters worse, Alcott never paid her a cent of her salary. She left the school in 1836, just as Alcott was preparing to publish a new collection of the transcripts which she had recorded.

While most mortals instinctively take care of number one, she alone totally neglected that important numeral, and spent all her life, all her strength . . . in the cause of others.

—Sarah Clarke

Peabody warned Alcott not to publish the book, or at least to edit out the "questionable parts." She was particularly worried about a conversation about Christ's miraculous birth which strayed into talk about biological birth. She advised Alcott that, to many readers, this would sound like sex education for young children, scandalous in Victorian Boston. He ignored her appeal and published *Conversations With Children on the Gospels* in 1836. Just as Peabody had predicted, the book provoked a storm of controversy. Parents withdrew their children, and Alcott was forced to close the Temple School. At her request, Peabody's name appeared nowhere in the book, but everyone knew that she was the anonymous "recorder." As a result, she was condemned as well, and found that she could no longer find a teaching position in Boston. Though badly used by Alcott, and full of her own doubts about his ideas, Elizabeth was one of the few who defended him against the public's vicious attack.

Driven from her profession, Peabody was characteristically undaunted. "I am . . . exceedingly trustful of the future," she wrote, and sought new avenues for her intellectual energies. She wrote articles for religious journals, calling for a radical Christian reform of society. "Why not begin to move the mountain of custom and convention?" she asked her readers. She continued to preside over "reading parties" for women, wrote books about history, and stayed abreast of the revolutionary ideas being developed by Europe's romantic philosophers. Because of her remarkable depth of learning, she was one of two women, along with Margaret Fuller, who were invited to join the Transcendentalists in their philosophical gatherings. In 1840, she opened her famous bookstore on West Street, making that spot the movement's Boston headquarters until the shop closed in 1850.

For a female to sell books was unprecedented. But Peabody decided to go further, publishing them as well. Her first venture was one of her friend Channing's abolitionist pamphlets. Though the book sold well, Peabody once again put her ideals ahead of her profits, and gave away most of the proceeds to the anti-slavery cause. A judicious critic, always anxious to encourage new talent, she also discovered the mystical poet Jones Very and published some of Nathaniel Hawthorne's earliest works. She became not only his publisher but also his sister-in-law when he married her youngest sister, Sophia. In 1841, Peabody became publisher of the *Dial*, the Transcendentalists' journal. Though carefully managing the magazine's small assets, she could not make it pay, and had to sell out to another publisher, who soon abandoned the project entirely. Thought short-lived, the *Dial* is now considered a major landmark in American literary history.

Like many New England intellectuals, Elizabeth became increasingly absorbed in the anti-slavery cause in the decade before the Civil War. Risking mob violence, she attended abolitionist meetings and wrote articles denouncing slavery. In 1859, after John Brown's failed attempt to start a slave revolt at Harper's Ferry, she traveled to Virginia to plead with the governor, in a vain attempt to save one of Brown's accomplices from the gallows.

When war broke out in 1861, and the Union army faltered, Peabody made another journey South, this time to report to Abraham Lincoln the dissatisfaction that many of his New England supporters were feeling about his execution of the war. Both parties left that meeting impressed by the other. While in Washington, Peabody became concerned about the plight of the many slave children who had been orphaned by the war, after she saw hundreds of them wandering, hungry and

Elizabeth Palmer Peabody

scared, on the city's streets. She organized an orphanage and school for these children, found volunteer teachers, and raised over $1,000 for construction.

After the war, Peabody found new causes to champion. Working with ***Julia Ward Howe**, she organized women's suffrage meetings. And, moved by tales of injustice against the Piute Indians, she raised money to help the tribe build schools. But her real passion in the postwar years was kindergartening, a new approach to early childhood education developed in the 1850s by a German named Friedrich Froebel. Froebel criticized schools for placing too much emphasis on discipline and academic achievement, especially with young children. Play, Froebel wrote, was a more natural and enjoyable way for children to learn, and he developed ways to teach young ones by using games, physical activities such as gardening, and songs and stories.

In 40 years of teaching and writing about education, Peabody had arrived at many of Froebel's conclusions on her own. Her own mother had been a firm believer in the importance of early childhood education. And, as a Transcendentalist educator, Peabody shared Froebel's view that the natural instincts of children are healthy and sound, that they respond better to love and nurture than to stern discipline, and that true education should develop not only the mind and body but, most important, the spirit. Excited by the way Froebel had put these ideas into practice, she started the first kindergarten class in America in 1860, in partnership with her sister Mary Peabody Mann, the widow of another famous New England educator, Horace Mann.

For the next three decades, Elizabeth devoted much of her time to spreading the kindergarten gospel. She published a journal called the *Kindergarten Messenger,* toured the country recruiting talented young women for teachers, traveled to Germany to learn more about Froebel's schools, gave countless lectures and wrote many articles and books about the value of kindergartens. Through her efforts, kindergarten schools and teacher-training programs were established all around the country. Though a new generation of kindergarten leaders had less interest in the spiritual idealism of the movement's 19th-century founders, Froebel's method was eventually adopted by most public schools in the nation.

All through her 80s, Elizabeth remained active, still writing, promoting kindergartens and, now reconciled with Alcott, lecturing about literature and education at his Concord School of Philosophy. In the eyes of some Gilded Age Bostonians, including the young novelist Henry James, Peabody was a comical and eccentric figure, a caricature of the city's faded golden age of starry-eyed do-gooders. She was oblivious to matters of fashion and propriety, her large frame usually draped in a simple and rumpled old black dress, long out of style. She charged around Boston, raising funds and recruiting her friends for new causes, always overflowing with ideas and ready to talk about Chinese grammar or Milton's poetry or Froebel's philosophy.

Though some laughed, many more honored her as the "grandmother of Boston." To them, she was a symbol of all that was noble and courageous about the New England conscience. For 70 years, she had remained true to her convictions, even when society had criticized her as "unfeminine" or denounced her as a dangerous radical. Still more, she had never been embittered by her setbacks, never stopped serving others and believing that, through education, society itself could be transformed. In 1894, at the age of 90, she went to her grave still sure that people were essentially good, still hoping for the day when men and women would work together to fulfill what she called "Christ's Idea of Society."

SOURCES:

Roberts, Josephine E. "Elizabeth Peabody and the Temple School," in *New England Quarterly.* September 1942.

Ronda, Bruce A., ed. *Letters of Elizabeth Palmer Peabody: American Renaissance Woman.* Middletown, CT: Wesleyan University Press, 1984.

Snyder, Agnes. *Dauntless Women in Childhood Education, 1856–1931.* Washington, DC: Association for Childhood Education International, 1972.

Tharp, Louise Hall. *The Peabody Sisters of Salem.* Boston, MA: Little, Brown, 1950.

SUGGESTED READING:

Rose, Anne C. *Transcendentalism as a Social Movement, 1830–1850.* New Haven, CT: Yale University Press, 1981.

Ernest Freeberg, Ph.D. in American History, Emory University, Atlanta, Georgia

Peabody, Josephine Preston (1874–1922)

American poet and dramatist. *Name variations: Josephine Marks. Born in Brooklyn, New York, on May 30, 1874; died in Cambridge, Massachusetts, on December 4, 1922; second of the three daughters of Charles Kilham Peabody (a merchant) and Susan Josephine (Morrill) Peabody; attended Radcliffe College as a special student, 1894–96; married Lionel Simeon Marks (a professor of mechanical engineering at Harvard University), on June 21, 1906; children: Alison Marks (b. 1908); Lionel Marks (b. 1910).*

Born in Brooklyn in 1874 and raised in a home where intellectual and cultural activities were valued and encouraged, Josephine Peabody was immersed in literature and the arts from an early age. However, her idyllic environment was shattered with the death of her younger sister in 1882, and the death of her father two years later, events that left her mother **Susan Morrill Peabody** financially and spiritually bereft. Susan took Josephine and her older sister to live with their maternal grandmother in Dorchester, Massachusetts, where Josephine finished her elementary education. She enrolled in Girls' Latin School in Boston in 1889 but was forced by ill health to leave in her junior year. Meanwhile, from an early age, she had spent her spare time reading, and writing verses, short stories, and plays. In 1894, she had a poem published by Horace Scudder, the editor of the *Atlantic Monthly*, who also became her mentor. With his help, and that of another local philanthropist, Peabody was able to enroll at Radcliffe College for two years of study as a special student.

She began writing in earnest in 1896, and had her first volume of poetry, *The Wayfarers*, published in 1898. It was followed by *Fortune and Men's Eyes*, a one-act play built around Shakespeare's sonnets, and *Marlowe*, a play in verse about Christopher Marlowe. All of Peabody's early work reflected her intense interest in Shakespeare, Browning, and the Pre-Raphaelites and was marked by a delicate beauty, refinement, and otherworldliness.

To help support her blossoming literary career, Peabody held a lectureship in poetry and literature at Wellesley College from 1901 to 1903. During the summer of 1902, with help from a friend, she was able to travel in Europe, after which she published another collection of poems, *The Singing Leaves* (1903), and a choric idyl entitled *Pan,* which was performed in Ottawa in 1904.

In 1906, Peabody married Lionel S. Marks, an engineering professor at Harvard; after a year's tour of Europe, they settled in Cambridge, Massachusetts. The coupled celebrated the arrival of a daughter, **Alison Marks**, in 1908, a year which also saw the publication of Peabody's *The Book of Little Past*, a volume for children. It was followed a year later by *The Piper*, a poetic play on the Pied Piper legend, which won the Stratford Prize Competition and was produced in the summer of 1910 at the Memorial Theatre in Stratford-upon-Avon. (The year 1910 also marked the arrival of her second child, a son, Lionel.) Peabody's play was subsequently produced in London that same year, and at the New Theater, New York, in 1911.

During her later years, Peabody embraced a number of liberal and radical reform movements, a change of course which was reflected in her writing. In 1909, she joined the Fabian Society and in 1911 published *The Singing Man*, a collection of poems dealing with human rights. Her later works included another volume of poems, *Harvest Moon* (1916), and three more plays: *The Wolf of Gubbio* (1913), a drama about St. Francis of Assisi, *The Chameleon* (1917), a comedy, and *Portrait of Mrs. W.* (1922), a prose play about British feminist ***Mary Wollstonecraft**. During the last ten years of her life, Peabody struggled with hardening of the arteries, enduring surgery in 1912 and 1915, and lapsing into a two-week coma in January 1922. She died the following December, age 48.

SOURCES:

James, Edward T., ed. *Notable American Women, 1607–1950*. Cambridge, MA: The Belknap Press of Harvard University Press, 1971.

McHenry, Robert, ed. *Famous American Women*. NY: Dover, 1983.

Barbara Morgan,
Melrose, Massachusetts

Peabody, Kate Nichols Trask (1853–1922).

See Trask, Kate Nichols.

Peabody, Lucy (1861–1949)

American missionary. *Name variations: Lucy McGill Waterbury. Born Lucy Whitehead McGill in Belmont, Kansas, on March 2, 1861; died in Danvers, Massachusetts, on February 26, 1949; second child and first daughter of John McGill (a merchant) and Sarah Jane (Hart) McGill; graduated from the Rochester Academy, 1878; attended the University of Rochester: married Norman Mather Waterbury (a Baptist minister), on August 18, 1881 (died 1886); married Henry W. Peabody (a businessman), on June 16, 1906 (died 1908); children: (first marriage) three, of whom two survived to adulthood.*

Born Lucy McGill in 1861 in Belmont, Kansas, Baptist lay leader Lucy Peabody spent most of her childhood in Pittsford, New York, and in nearby Rochester, where the McGill family relocated in 1873. Following her graduation from Rochester Academy, she taught for three years at the local State School for the Deaf. In 1881, at age 20, she married Norman Waterbury, a Baptist minister, and two months later sailed with him to India under missionary appointment. There, they worked among the Telugus people of Madras until Waterbury's death in 1886. Left with three small children, Peabody returned to Rochester. (One of her children died on the journey home.)

In 1890, after a brief period of teaching, Peabody took a position as corresponding secretary of the Woman's Baptist Foreign Missionary Society and moved to its Boston headquarters. Simultaneously, she established the Farther Lights Society, a girls' auxiliary of the mission society. With her friend ***Helen Barrett Montgomery**, she also promoted an annual day for united prayer for missions, an observance which today is known as the World Day of Prayer. In 1902, she was appointed chair of the Central Committee on the United Study of Foreign Missions (an outgrowth of the New York Ecumenical Missionary Conference of 1900), a post she would hold until 1929. In this capacity, she helped produce a series of textbooks which were used by women's study groups, and by a network of 30 summer schools for mission study.

In June 1906, Lucy resigned from her Missionary Society post to marry Henry Wayland Peabody, the wealthy founder of a Boston importing and exporting firm (Henry W. Peabody & Company). Henry died in 1908, leaving Lucy financially secure and free to pursue her religious and philanthropic work. In the year of her husband's death, she founded *Everyland*, a missionary journal for children which she funded herself and edited until 1920.

In 1912, Peabody became a founding member of the Committee on Christian Literature for Women and Children (formed under the aegis of the Interdenominational Conference of Woman's Boards of Foreign Missions in the United States and Canada), whose objective involved collecting, translating, and publishing magazines for distribution around the world. A year later, she became vice-president for the foreign department of the newly unified Woman's American Baptist Foreign Mission Society, an organization through which she transformed the Interdenominational Conference into the more effective Federation of Women's Board of Foreign Missions (1916). In conjunction with the Board of Foreign Missions, she made two world tours (1913 and 1919), inspecting various missions and mission schools. From 1920 to 1923, she led an extensive fund-raising drive to raise $2 million (upon which a $1 million pledge by John D. Rockefeller was contingent) to finance the establishment of seven women's colleges in the Far East. Successful in her efforts, she later served on the board of three of the colleges: the Woman's Christian College in Madras, India; the Women's Christian Medical College in Vellore, India; and Shanghai Medical College.

In 1921, in a dispute over ecumenism, which she favored, Peabody resigned as vice-president of the Woman's American Baptist Foreign Mission Society. By 1927, disagreements concerning missionary qualification and modernist theology, which she opposed, caused Peabody to resign from the remainder of her denominational offices. Aided by a group of sympathetic Baptist missionaries in the Philippines led by her son-in-law, Peabody formed the Association of Baptists for World Evangelism, serving as president of the new organization until 1934. From 1928, she also edited the association's periodical, *Message*.

During the 1920s, Peabody devoted considerable time in defense of prohibition, helping to form the Woman's National Committee for Law Enforcement, of which she was president for ten years. Lucy Peabody died of heart disease in 1949.

SOURCES:

James, Edward T., ed. *Notable American Women, 1607–1950.* Cambridge, MA: The Belknap Press of Harvard University Press, 1971.

McHenry, Robert, ed. *Famous American Women.* NY: Dover, 1983.

Barbara Morgan,
Melrose, Massachusetts

Peabody, Mary (1806–1887).

See Mann, Mary Peabody.

Peabody, Sophia (1809–1871).

See Hawthorne, Sophia Peabody.

Peacock, Lucy (fl. 1785–1816)

English bookseller and author. *Flourished between 1785 and 1816.*

Lucy Peacock, about whom little is known, was the keeper of a book shop on Oxford Street, in London, and also wrote children's stories anonymously.

Peacock, Miriam (1836–1914).

See Leslie, Miriam Folline Squier.

Peake, Mary S. (1823–1862)

African-American educator who was the first teacher in the American Missionary Association schools. *Born in Norfolk, Virginia, in 1823; died in Hampton, Virginia, on February 22, 1862; from age six, attended private school in Alexandria, Virginia, for several years; married Thomas D. Peake, in 1851; children: one daughter, Hattie ("Daisy") Peake.*

Born in Norfolk, Virginia, in 1823, Mary Peake was the daughter of a free mulatto woman and a prominent Englishman. At age six, she was sent to live with relatives in Alexandria, Virginia, so she could attend a private school for free blacks. When a law was passed closing all "colored" schools in the area, Peake returned to Norfolk, where she made a living as a seamstress. At this time, she also became a devout Christian, joining the First Baptist Church in Norfolk. Following her mother's marriage in 1847, the family moved to Hampton, Virginia, where Peake began teaching both children and adults in her home. In 1851, she married Thomas D. Peake, with whom she had a daughter, **Hattie Peake**.

During the Civil War, the Confederate forces burned many of the homes in Hampton, hoping to discourage the black villagers from siding with the Union cause. The Peakes lost their home to the fires and took refuge at Fort Monroe. Peake was soon enlisted by the American Missionary Association to begin a school for the children at the facility. Using the first floor of her cottage as a classroom, she opened the doors to the school in September 1861 and had 50 students within a few days. In addition to teaching her students to read and write, she also taught them to pray and sing hymns. Peake, whose health was on the decline from the time of her marriage, was dedicated to the cause of education and soon began teaching adults in the evenings. Even as her health steadily worsened, she continued to conduct classes from her bed. Mary Peake died of tuberculosis on February 22, 1862.

SOURCES:

Smith, Jessie Carney, ed. *Notable Black American Women*. Detroit, MI: Gale Research, 1992.

Barbara Morgan,
Melrose, Massachusetts

Peale, Anna Claypoole (1791–1878).

See Peale Sisters.

Peale, Margaretta Angelica (1795–1882).

See Peale Sisters.

Peale, Sarah Miriam (1800–1885).

See Peale Sisters.

Peale Sisters

Portrait and still-life painters who widened the opportunities for American women as professional artists.

Peale, Anna Claypoole (1791–1878). *Name variations: Anna Peale; Anna Staughton; Anna Duncan. Pronunciation: Peel. Born Anna Claypoole Peale on March 6, 1791, in Philadelphia, Pennsylvania; died in Philadelphia on December 25, 1878; first daughter of James Peale (1749–1831, a painter) and Mary Claypoole Peale (1753–1829); learned painting from father and encouraged by her famous uncle, Charles Willson Peale; married Reverend Dr. William Staughton, in 1829; married General William Duncan, in 1841 (died 1864); no children.*

Painted miniature portraits and still lifes; exhibited at the Pennsylvania Academy of the Fine Arts (PAFA, 1811–42); elected to membership (Academician) in the PAFA (1842); was a popular miniature painter (1820–41); did work in Baltimore, Boston, Washington, D.C., but primarily in Philadelphia.

Paintings: Self-Portrait *(Art Institute of Chicago, 1818);* Marianne Beckett *(Historical Society of Pennsylvania, 1829);* Gen. Andrew Jackson *(Yale University Art Gallery, 1819);* James Peale, Mrs. James Peale, Rembrandt Peale, *and* Nathaniel Kinsman *(1820–24, R.W. Norton Art Gallery, Shreveport);* Rosalba Peale *(Detroit Institute of Arts, 1820);* Mrs. Andrew Jackson *(Ladies Hermitage Association, Nashville, 1819);* Edgar Allan Poe *(Walters Art Gallery, Baltimore, 1834);* Miss Susannah Williams *(Maryland Historical Society, Baltimore, 1825).*

Peale, Margaretta Angelica (1795–1882). *Born Margaretta Angelica Peale on October 1, 1795, in Philadelphia, Pennsylvania; died in Philadelphia on January 17, 1882; second daughter of James Peale (1749–1831, a painter) and Mary Claypoole Peale (1753–1829); never married; no children.*

Still life and portrait painter; exhibited Artists' Fund Society and the Pennsylvania Academy of the Fine Arts (1828–31).

Paintings: Catalog Deception *(owned by James Ogelsby Peale, 1813);* Still Life: Grapes and Pomegranates *(Maryland Historical Society);* Still Life: Strawberries and Cherries *(Pennsylvania Academy of the Fine Arts);* Still Life *(Smith College Museum of Art, Northampton, Massachusetts, 1828).*

Peale, Sarah Miriam (1800–1885). *Name variations: known as Sally. Born Sarah Miriam Peale on May 19, 1800, in Philadelphia, Pennsylvania; died in Philadelphia on February 4, 1885; third daughter of James Peale (1749–1831, a painter) and Mary Claypoole Peale (1753–1829); never married; no children.*

Painter of canvas portraits and still lifes (ranging in size from 8x10 to 17x22, both in rectangles and ovals); painted portraits of statesmen in Washington; exhibited annually at the Pennsylvania Academy of the Fine Arts (1824–31); elected a member of that institution (1824); moved to Baltimore as a painter of portraits (1825); lived in St. Louis as a painter of portraits and still lifes (1847–78); returned to Philadelphia (1877).

Paintings: earliest known portrait, Self Portrait *(collection of Mr. and Mrs. Charles Coleman Sellers, 1818); other portraits include* Mrs. Theodore Denny, Sarah Jane Armstrong, John Montgomery, *and* Mrs. George Henry Keerl *(Peale Museum, Baltimore, 1826–35),* Edward Johnson Cole, Anthony Thompson, Mrs. George Michael Krebs, Children of Commodore John Daniel Danels *and* William Hollingsworth *(Maryland Historical Society, 1824–36),* Henry A. Wise *(Virginia Museum of Fine Arts, 1842),* Thomas Hart Benton *(Missouri Historical Society, 1842); still life paintings include* Still Life: Watermelon and Grapes *(Maryland Historical Society, 1820),* Peaches, Plums & Grapes *(Peale Museum, Baltimore),* A Slice of Watermelon *(Wadsworth Atheneum, Hartford, 1825),* Still Life *(Reading Public Museum and Art Gallery, 1880); a number of portraits are privately owned (see Wilbur H. Hunter and John Mahey,* Miss Sarah Miriam Peale, 1800–1885: Portraits and Still Life, *1967).*

The three artist daughters of James Peale and **Mary Claypoole Peale** grew up among the cultural elite of Philadelphia and were members of that remarkable extended family of Peales, many of whom were artists. James and his brother Charles Willson Peale (1741–1827), the doyen of the group, believed that women had as much right as men to realize their creative potential. James, himself a moderately accomplished painter, learned his craft by assisting Charles. The sisters' maternal grandfather, James Claypoole, Sr. (1720–1784) had been the first professional painter in Philadelphia, and their maternal uncle, James Claypoole, Jr. (died c. 1796) was also a painter. The sisters were close to their painter cousins, the children of Charles Willson Peale. The actual schooling of Anna, Margaretta, and Sarah is unknown, but all three were given art instruction by their father. Soon they were allowed to paint backgrounds and such delicacies as drapes and lace for the portraits of James Peale, who suffered from diminishing eyesight. Encouraged by their father and uncle, the sisters created paintings of their own, at first imitating or copying works of Peale family members, and then developing their own subjects and styles. Anna and Sarah discovered they could earn a livelihood at art.

The Peale sisters were pioneers in establishing a niche in professional life for American women. As artists, they had to overcome obstacles. In the early 19th century, women were expected to dabble in the arts but not to do so seriously as professionals. It was the time of the cult of pure womanhood, and women's place was to promote a felicitous domesticity. Paramount was the attendance to household duties. Women artists, not being allowed to study nude models, were not prepared to paint subjects that made up a leading art genre of the time—large-scale historical, Biblical, and allegorical themes.

Anna Claypoole Peale learned how to paint miniatures of watercolor on ivory from cousin Raphaelle Peale and from her father, who thought that this kind of artistic employment was "most suitable for a lady." Anna also studied oil painting with her father. The pictures produced by father and daughter separately under each one's names bear a close resemblance, showing that Anna not only adopted much of the style of her parent, particularly in the handling of skin tones, short and long strokes in painting hair, and dark marks at the end of a mouth to show a slight smile, but also that she probably did much of the work on James Peale's paintings.

After the exhibition of two of her miniatures at the Pennsylvania Academy of the Fine Arts, Anna's work was in much demand. A visit to Washington, D.C., lasting from November 1818 through January 1819, as a companion of her father and her uncle and aunt, Charles Willson Peale and **Hannah Peale**, led to commissions from prominent persons. The lively and carefully detailed countenances on her miniature portraits attracted further clients. Before leaving for the Washington journey, Charles Willson Peale wrote: "my Niece Anna Peale will accompany us, her merrit in mineature-painting brings her into high estimation, and so many Ladies and Gentlemen desire to sett to her that she frequently is obleged to raise in her prices." In Washington, Anna painted portraits of Andrew Jackson and his wife ***Rachel Donelson Jackson**, President James Monroe, and other important political leaders, including Richard M. Johnson and John Randolph of Roanoke.

Back in Philadelphia, in spring 1819 Anna and sister Sarah, to gain an artistic mastery of the human form, attended a 15-lecture course in anatomy for sculptors and artists offered by Dr. Calhoun, physician at the Pennsylvania Hospital. "We were much interested in a lecture on the human Scull," wrote Sarah. Besides Philadelphia and Washington, Anna also painted for brief periods in Boston and Baltimore. Her miniatures on ivory were exhibited at the Boston Atheneum and the Pennsylvania Academy of the Fine Arts. In 1824, along with Sarah, she was elected an Academician (member) of the latter institution.

The only one of the three sisters to marry, Anna wed Rev. Dr. William Staughton (1770–1829) on August 27, 1829. Staughton, a popular Baptist cleric, had just been appointed president of the Georgetown (Kentucky) Theological College. En route to assume his new position, Staughton died, only three months after the marriage. Anna resumed her painting and continued to exhibit at the Pennsylvania Academy of the Fine Arts. Occasionally, she did portraits slightly larger than miniature size. She also produced a few still-life paintings that conveyed a stark reality that beckoned for the attention of the viewer.

On June 10, 1841, Anna married General William Duncan (1772–1864), "a gentleman highly esteemed in social life." She gave up painting for marital bliss, but upon her husband's death resumed her work. Throughout her career, Anna executed a number of miniatures of young women, who were usually depicted, as **Elsa H. Fine** writes, with "widely placed and fully opened eyes . . . rather long noses," and "pursed lips that turn up at the edges." Anna's *Miss Susannah Williams* (1825) "varies from her typical production in that the subject was over sixty when she sat for Anna, and the artist captured some of the weariness of old age."

Anna Claypoole Peale with younger sister Margaretta.

Margaretta Angelica, the least accomplished or prolific of the three artist sisters, gained a fair reputation for the quality of her portraits and still lifes. She also exhibited regularly at the Pennsylvania Academy of the Fine Arts, although she did not progress beyond her original talent. Lacking technical ability, she compensated by employing an easy gracefulness and a blunt impression of naiveté. Her still-lifes usually had an emphasis on geometric balance that reflected the Federalist style then predominant in architecture. One of Margaretta's earliest paintings (1813), executed in photographic detail, was *Catalog Deception,* a copy of a similar work by cousin Raphaelle Peale. An obituary in a Philadelphia newspaper observed that Margaretta had a "superior talent in painting fruit" and that she "possessed a remarkable memory, and was noted for the simplicity and loveliness of her character."

Sarah Miriam Peale was the most successful artist of the women Peales. As did her sisters, she learned to paint from her father. In 1816, she began painting still lifes, exhibiting *Flowers* the following year at the Pennsylvania Academy of the Fine Arts. Her showing of a self-portrait,

Portrait of a Lady (1818), brought recognition from the Philadelphia art community. This work set a style for her later portraits, with faces frontal, but with torso in three-quarters profile; the subjects smiled as if ready to break out laughing. Charles Willson Peale said of his niece's self-portrait that it was "wonderfully like." Two years later, he commented, "Sarah has shewn great talents for painting in oil, but she must be spurred on to work by a view of profit, by it she becomes very industrous."

Sarah spent long visits in Baltimore, and in 1825 settled there. During the 1820s, she worked out of a studio in the Peale Museum, established by Charles' son Rembrandt Peale. The younger Peale gave Sarah instruction, which refined her skills. From Rembrandt, Sarah improved her draftsmanship and adopted techniques for skin tone in her portraits, chiefly through diffusing light and producing glossy surfaces. She also honed her talents for depicting lace and other intricate patterns from her study with Rembrandt Peale.

Sarah Miriam Peale, Self–Portrait, *c. 1830.*

Late in 1818, Sarah joined her father, sister Anna, and Charles and Hannah Peale in Washington. Sarah won some portrait commissions, and "bright of eye and cheek, dressed in the very latest," writes Charles Coleman Sellers, "made a conquering progress that her venerable uncle could only watch with pride." It seems that Sarah, or Sally, as she was called by family and friends, was somewhat of a flirt. Charles Willson Peale observed in 1821 that she "as usual" was "breaking all the beaux' hearts, and won't have any of them." Like Margaretta, Sarah never married.

Sarah stayed in Baltimore until 1847, holding her own in garnering portrait commissions from among the city's substantial middle to upper class. In competition with more noted artists such as Thomas Sully, she executed some 100 portraits during the Baltimore years, including that of Marquis de Lafayette, who gave her four sittings during his 1824–25 tour. During 1841–43, she made portraits of prominent statesmen in Washington, D.C., many of them closely associated with President John Tyler's administration, including Daniel Webster and other Cabinet members and various senators and congressional representatives. Before the Baltimore years, one of the handsomest portraits that she executed was that of John Neal (1793–1876), who for a while had seriously courted her. Neal was an appealing figure for young Sarah's heart, a flamboyant writer of romances and poetry and a staunch woman's rights advocate.

Besides portraits of individuals, Sarah did paintings of family groups—children, mother and child, and husband and wife. Notable in this category is *Children of Commodore John Daniel Danels* (1826). The five Danels children have happy, playful countenances, while from the shadows two young black slaves peer upon the scene. Unlike her single portraits, which depicted the decorative elegance of clothing but left mostly a void as to accessories and background, the Danels' group portrait shows a full room and its furnishings, including an oriental rug, flowers, and a mantle piece.

In her portraits, Sarah generally gave much attention to costume decoration, which, as Wilbur H. Hunter and John Mahey write, compensated "for a relative lack of genius both as a draftsman and as a colorist." One comes away from a Sarah Peale portrait impressed with "the delight taken in rendering fabrics, fur, bits of jewelry, eye glasses, books and pamphlets . . . for they give the pictures life and vitality, and a visual interest essential to the success of the compositions."

Sarah painted only a few still lifes during the first part of her career; these paintings sold for one-third less than her portraits. Her favorite motif for the still lifes was fruit, and especially watermelon seeds. Such still lifes, extolling abundance, appealed to the middle class. Sarah's *Still-Life: Watermelon and Grapes* (1820) is her most famous rendition in this genre. As were the other Peales, Sarah was influenced by Dutch, Flemish, and Spanish still lifes. The translucent watermelon slice and seeds complement the lacy grape leaves, which as a "baroque" protruding element hang over the front side of the table. **Mary Lucas Cassell** notes that the painting "is a rare example of one early nineteenth-century woman artist's realization of her potential. It appeals to the senses, the intellect, and the imagination, but most important it is Sarah Miriam Peale's triumph—a delightful and uplifting work."

At the invitation of Trusten Polk, a future governor and Democratic senator, and other residents of St. Louis, Sarah, in 1847, went to live in St. Louis, where she resided for the next 31 years. Her portraits were in much demand, but few made their way to Eastern exhibitions; today, most of these paintings are either unlocated or in private collections. A St. Louis newspaper in 1849 said of Sarah's portraits of the local elite that "she has transferred their features to the canvas with an accuracy and life like expression, that cheats the beholder into the belief that he is looking at the original." In the 1860s, Sarah began to concentrate on still-life painting of fruit pieces. In 1859 and 1861, in the category of "Fruit Painting, in Oil," she won first prize at the St. Louis Fair, and a second-place award in 1662.

Sarah rejoined her sisters in Philadelphia in the summer of 1878. Soon afterwards, Anna died, followed by Margaretta in 1882. With the passing of Sarah and Titian Ramsay Peale in 1885, the dynasty of the "painting Peales" ceased.

Anna Claypoole Peale and Sarah Miriam Peale, if not among the first rank, were major artists, and were as prodigious in output during their early careers as any of their peers. Both gained an independence beyond the conventional role of women. Anna was the accomplished miniaturist, and Sarah excelled, using oil and canvas, at portraiture and still life. Margaretta mastered the basics of the Peale style of realism. Anna and Sarah matured in their art, creating portraits conveying the distinctive personalities of their subjects. Their still lifes had vigor and freshness. Like those of other Peales, the works of the sisters had a sharp focus, enhanced by painting upon drawings of their subjects. Sarah Miriam Peale was the most important woman artist in America until the end of the 19th century.

SOURCES:

Born, Wolfgang. "The Female Peales: Their Art and Its Tradition," in *American Collector.* August 1946, pp. 12–14.

Cassell, Mary Lucas. "Sarah Miriam Peale (1800–1885): *Still-Life of Watermelon and Grapes.*" Unpublished M.A. thesis, Department of Art History, University of Virginia, 1993.

Elam, Charles H. *The Peale Family: Three Generations of American Artists.* Detroit, MI: Wayne State University Press, 1967.

Gordon, Jean. "Early American Women Artists and the Social Context in Which They Worked," in *American Quarterly.* Vol. 30, 1978, pp. 54–69.

Hunter, Wilbur H., and John Mahey. *Miss Sarah Miriam Peale, 1800–1885: Portraits and Still Life.* Exhibition, February 5, 1967, through March 26, 1967. Baltimore, MD: The Peale Museum, 1967.

Sellers, Charles Coleman. *Charles Willson Peale.* Vol. 2 (Later Life). Philadelphia, PA: American Philosophical Society, 1947.

———. *Charles Willson Peale.* NY: Scribner, 1969.

SUGGESTED READING:

Fine, Elsa H. *Women & Art: A History of Women Painters and Sculptors from the Renaissance to the 20th Century.* Montclair, NJ: Allanheld & Schram-Prior, 1978.

King, Joan. *Sarah M. Peale: America's First Woman Artist.* Boston, MA: Branden, 1987 (historical fiction).

Miller, Lillian B., ed. *The Selected Papers of Charles Willson Peale and His Family.* 3 vols. New Haven, CT: Yale University Press, 1988–1991.

COLLECTIONS:

Exhibit collections of the Pennsylvania Academy of the Fine Arts, Philadelphia, and the Baltimore Museum of Art.

Harry M. Ward,
Professor of History, University of Richmond,
and author of *Colonial America, 1607–1763* (Prentice Hall, 1991)
and *The American Revolution: Nationhood Achieved, 1763–1788*
(St. Martin's Press, 1995)

Pearce, Caroline (1925—).

See Pearce Sisters.

Pearce, Jean (1921—).

See Pearce Sisters.

Pearce, Louise (1885–1959)

American physician and pathologist who was part of the team that developed the drug tryparsamide to treat sleeping sickness. *Born Louise Pearce in Winchester, Massachusetts, on March 5, 1885; died in New York, New York, on August 10, 1959; daughter of Susan Elizabeth Hoyt and Charles Ellis Pearce; graduated from Girl's Collegiate School, Los Angeles, California, 1903; Stanford University, A.B., 1907; attended Boston University; Johns Hopkins University,*

M.D., 1912; lived with Ida A.R. Wylie (1885–1959, a novelist); never married; no children.

*Awards: Order of the Belgian Crown (1921); honorary Doctor of Science, Wilson College (1947); honorary Doctor of Medical Science, Beaver College (1948); ****Elizabeth Blackwell*** *Award (1951); Women's Medical College of Philadelphia citation (1952); honorary Doctor of Medical Science, Women's Medical College of Philadelphia (1952); King Leopold II Prize (1953); officer of the Royal Order of the Lion (1953).*

Moved to California (c. 1890); Paul Ehrlich discovered salvarsan (1910); interned at Johns Hopkins Hospital (1912); named fellow of the Rockefeller Institute (1913); worked with Wade Hampton Brown on arsenic-based compounds (1913–19); tested tryparsamide, Belgian Congo (1920); investigated syphilis in rabbits (1920–28); appointed trustee, New York Infirmary for Women and Children (1921); appointed associate member of the Rockefeller Institute (1923); discovered the Brown-Pearce Carcinoma (1924); appointed to the General Advisory Council of the American Social Hygiene Association (1925); appointed visiting professor of syphilology at Peiping Union Medical College, China (1931); appointed to the National Research Council (1931); isolated the rabbit pox virus (1932); named member of the board of the Corporation of the Philadelphia Women's Medical College (1941); death of Wade Hampton Brown (1942); director of the Association of University Women (1945); became president of the Corporation of the Philadelphia Women's Medical College (1946); retired (1951).

Selected publications: (with W.H. Brown) "Chemotherapy of trypanosoma and spirochaete infections. Biological series. I. The toxic action of N-phenylglycineamide-p-arsonic acid," in Journal of Experimental Medicine *(Vol. 30, 1919); (with C.M. Van Allen) "Effects of operative interference with the endocrines on the growth and malignancy of a transplanted tumor of the rabbits," in* Transactions of the Association of American Physicians *(Vol. 38, 1923); (with A.E. Casey) "Studies in the blood cytology of the rabbit. I. Blood counts in normal rabbits," in* Journal of Experimental Medicine *(Vol. 51, 1930); "The treatment of human trypanosomiasis with tryparsamide: A Critical Review" (Rockefeller Institute for Medical Research, Monograph no. 23, 1930); "Experimental Syphilis of Oriental Origin: Clinical Reaction in the Rabbit," in* Journal of Experimental Medicine *(Vol. 67, 1938); "Hereditary osteopetrosis of the rabbit. II. X-ray, haematologic, and chemical observations," in* Journal of Experimental Medicine *(Vol. 88, 1948); "Hereditary distal foreleg curvature in the rabbit. II. Genetic and pathological aspects," in* Journal of Experimental Medicine *(Vol. 111, 1960).*

Louise Pearce, one of the central participants in the development and testing of tryparsamide to treat sleeping sickness, was born in Winchester, Massachusetts, on March 5, 1885, the only daughter of **Susan Elizabeth Hoyt** and Charles Ellis Pearce, who ran a tobacco and cigar business. Soon after 1889, the family moved to Los Angeles, California, where Pearce attended the Girl's Collegiate School for three years.

In 1907, Pearce was awarded a bachelor's degree from Stanford University in Palo Alto, where she had studied histology and physiology. She spent two years as a medical student at Boston University, before transferring to the Johns Hopkins School of Medicine in 1909. In 1912, Pearce became a doctor of medicine and interned at the Johns Hopkins Hospital, where she was the first woman to be on the staff of the psychiatry department. Notes **Marion Fay**: "Many of her teachers and her classmates were, or were to be, outstanding figures in American medicine, and they greatly influenced her scientific career."

In 1913, Pearce was the first woman to be appointed as an assistant to Dr. Simon Flexner, the Rockefeller Institute's original director. Initially, her efforts were to go towards isolating the bacillus of scarlet fever, whooping cough, and measles. Instead, she was asked to do chemotherapeutic research with pathologist Wade Hampton Brown, testing arsenic-based compounds on the parasite which causes African trypanosomiasis or sleeping sickness.

During his explorations of Africa, Dr. David Livingstone was the first to report on the effects of the tsetse fly on European livestock. But it was Thomas Winterbottom, a Scottish physician who practiced in Sierra Leone during the late 18th century, who provided one of the earliest descriptions of the effects of the sleeping sickness on humans:

> At the commencement of the disease, the patient has commonly a ravenous appetite, eating twice the quantity of food he was accustomed to take when in health, and becoming very fat. When the disease has continued some time, the appetite declines, and the patient gradually wastes away. . . . The disposition to sleep is so strong, scarcely to leave a sufficient respite for the taking of food; even the repeated application of a whip, a remedy which has been frequently used, is hardly sufficient to keep the poor wretch awake. . . . The disease, under every

mode of treatment, usually proves fatal within three or four months.

In 1910, German chemist Paul Ehrlich discovered salvarsan arsphenamine, a natural compound containing arsenic. Ehrlich was known as the father of chemotherapy—the science of treating diseases with poisons which act against the infecting agent, but not against the patient. He used salvarsan to treat syphilis, but it had no effect on sleeping sickness.

Simon Flexner was determined to find an arsenic-based drug for the treatment of sleeping sickness, a disease all too common in equatorial Africa. The First World War interrupted supplies of salvarsan from Germany, therefore threatening a syphilis epidemic in the United States. Flexner assigned two biochemists employed by the Rockefeller Institute, W.A. Jacobs and Michael Heidelberger, to produce salvarsan. He also assigned Louise Pearce and Wade Hampton Brown to test the various arsenic-based compounds which might have an effect on sleeping sickness. The team investigated the effects of more than 243 arsenicals upon rabbits, mice, rats, and guinea pigs.

As John J. McKelvey noted, "the trouble with arsenic . . . was that it was devastating and nondiscriminating. It attacked the host and the parasite with equal vigor." Jacobs and Heidelberger adapted one of Ehrlich's arsenicals, and replaced its carboxyl group with amide, thus reducing its toxicity to tissue. After six years of extensive testing, Pearce and Brown discovered that the substance was successful in the treatment of rabbits with syphilis. The new drug was named tryparsamide, short for TRYPanosome-ARSenic-AMIDE. It also appeared to have a beneficial effects on animals with the trypanosoma parasitic protozoa transmitted by the tsetse fly, which causes sleeping sickness.

In May 1920, Louise Pearce was asked by the Rockefeller Institute to travel alone to the Belgian Congo (Republic of Congo), where thousands died each year from sleeping sickness. She was, as J.D. Fulton described, "of resolute character and endowed besides with great physical strength and vigor." In the Congo, she undertook field trials of the new drug on victims suffering from the disease. Pearce worked in Léopoldville, in a hospital laboratory put at her disposal by the Belgian colonial administration.

During the next several months, Pearce initiated a carefully planned treatment program for 77 patients in various phases of the illness. She employed graded doses of tryparsamide, which were administered intravenously, and closely monitored the results. Pearce found that the parasites were purged from the bloodstream within weeks, and that mental functions in the more serious cases returned to normal. The health of the majority of patients was restored, even those with advanced cases of sleeping sickness.

Tryparsamide owes its effectiveness to the fact that it reaches the cerebro-spinal fluid in concentrated form, and affects the trypanosomes in the central nervous system. Pearce's test results were spectacular, and the new experimental drug proved to be a tremendous improvement over atoxyl, also known as Bayer 205, a drug previously used on sleeping sickness victims. Atoxyl possessed trypanocidal action, but the drug proved useless in later stages of the disease.

In 1923, Dr. Eugène Jamot, who received 250 grams of tryparsamide from Pearce in New York, treated 14 patients in French Cameroon with single injections. As with earlier compounds such as atoxyl, which Albert Schweitzer described as "frightfully dangerous," Jamot anticipated that an overdose might cause blindness in his patients. It did not. Jamot's work confirmed Pearce's results. Several years later, however, one of Jamot's overzealous colleagues overdosed 700 patients, who all went blind. As well, it was discovered that over time certain strains of sleeping sickness developed a resistance to the drug.

Pearce's monograph, "The Treatment of Human Trypanosomiasis with Tryparsamide," became a formative work in the field. It reviewed ten years of clinical trials in the Congo, and delineated research done by other European scientists in Equatorial Africa and Cameroon. In another article published in 1925, Pearce reported on later clinical results in the Belgian Congo:

> Van den Branden and Van Hoof, who have continued the observations and treatments in Léopoldville, reported in October, 1923, on the condition of 55 patients first treated three years previously. . . . Twenty of these patients were early cases . . . all were alive and in good health when last seen. . . . Thirty-five patients were advanced cases of various types with pronounced lethargy. Three very advanced patients had died. Thirty-two patients were alive and well.

Writes Peyton Rous, Pearce "brought about one of the most shining and spectacular of the early purposeful achievements of the Institute, the conquest of sleeping sickness." The pathological, chemical, and clinical aspects of Pearce's work deeply impressed the Belgian government, which began widely employing tryparsamide in the Congo. In recognition of Pearce's work, the Belgian government rewarded her with the

Order of the Crown of Belgium in 1921. In a commencement address at Bryn Mawr College in the same year, Dr. Simon Flexner held Pearce up as an example of the contributions which women were capable of making to science.

In 1923, Pearce was appointed an associate member of the Rockefeller Institute. She subsequently concentrated her research efforts on the biology and inheritance of disease, related in particular to syphilis and cancer. She continued to work in close association with Wade Hampton Brown. From 1920 to 1928, the pair investigated syphilis in rabbits, which closely mimics the syphilis found in humans. Their research proved of great value to immunologists, and in the development of treatments for human diseases. With Brown, she also discovered the Brown-Pearce Carcinoma, which is found in rabbits, and successfully transplanted the tissue from the carcinoma into other rabbits. For decades, the Brown-Pearce Carcinoma was the only available laboratory cancer tumor in the study of human disease and was employed by medical researchers around the globe.

In 1929, Pearce and Brown began a selective breeding program of rabbits. Together they studied birth defects and the rabbit's genetic susceptibility to infection. Their research project was threatened when the rabbit colony suffered three epidemics of rabbit pox. Eventually, Pearce isolated the virus which causes rabbit pox, a disease similar to human smallpox. In time, the rabbit colony outgrew its quarters at the Rockefeller Institute. In 1935, it was transferred to Princeton University.

By 1940, Pearce had isolated more than two dozen inherited diseases and deformities in rabbits, which had implications for the treatment of human disease. After Wade Brown's death in 1942, she continued this research alone. Eventually, Pearce terminated the breeding program and edited their results on osteopetrosis and achondroplasia for publication. Though she published several more papers after her retirement in 1951, the bulk of the remaining research would be destroyed upon her death. Several articles were also published posthumously.

Pearce was keenly interested in the medical education of women. She was an active and enthusiastic member of the American Association of University Women, as well as of its international counterpart. She became director of the Association of University Women in 1945, a position she held until 1951. She also served on the board of the Women's Medical College of Philadelphia beginning in 1941, and in 1946 she became president of the college.

Pearce's interests were many and varied, running the gamut from tropical medicine to bacteriology to cancer. She was a member of numerous professional bodies, including the American Society of Exploratory Pathology, the American Association of Cancer Research, the Pathology Society of Great Britain and Ireland, the Peiping Society of Natural History, and the Société belge de Médicine tropicale.

Pearce spent her entire career at the Rockefeller Institute, from 1913 to 1951. She maintained an active interest, however, in many areas of medicine, and served various other organizations. She was appointed a trustee of the New York Infirmary for Women and Children in 1921, and worked for the institution until 1928. In 1925, Pearce joined the General Advisory Council of the American Social Hygiene Association, remaining on the council until 1944. She was also appointed to the National Research Council in 1931. As well, Pearce maintained a six-year association with Princeton Hospital, beginning in 1940.

Little is known of Pearce's personal life. As George W. Corner noted:

> Preeminently the professional physician-scientist, Dr. Pearce left few traces of her personality in the official record. Surviving friends recall her as a cordial and hospitable woman, who appreciated social amenities, and had a fondness for fine clothes, jewelry, books, and art. A vigorous individual, possessed of an incisive mind, Louise Pearce not only held her own in conservation with male colleagues, but also enlivened the rather sedate atmosphere of the Rockefeller Institute.

In 1951, Louise Pearce retired from the Rockefeller Institute. She spent the remaining years of her life at Trevenna Farm, in Skillman, New Jersey, where she shared a home with novelist ***Ida A.R. Wylie**. Pearce loved to travel and spent considerable time in France and England. It was on a return voyage from Europe in 1959 that she fell ill aboard ship; she died shortly after her arrival in the United States, in a New York hospital, on August 10, 1959. She was 74. Ida Wylie died two months later.

Louise Pearce was the recipient of many honors and awards. In 1931, she served as a visiting professor with the Peiping (Beijing) Union Medical College in China. She was awarded numerous honorary degrees, from institutions such as Wilson College, Beaver College, and the Women's Medical College of Philadelphia. In 1953, the Belgian government awarded Pearce the King Leopold II Prize, and a check worth $10,000, in recognition of her contribution to finding a treatment for sleeping sickness 34 years earlier. As well, she and her colleagues were awarded the Royal Order of the Lion and their work chronicled in the ironically titled *Man Against Tsetse*. The two medals awarded by the Belgian government now hang along with Pearce's portrait in the president's office of the Women's Medical College of Philadelphia. Over the years, Pearce accumulated an incomparable collection of works on syphilis, from early manuscripts to the latest books. She bequeathed this extensive collection to Johns Hopkins University upon her death.

Louise Pearce conducted extensive studies on experimental syphilis. The discovery of the Brown-Pearce Carcinoma proved to be a significant contribution to our understanding of cancer. Her early work on the treatment of sleeping sickness is perhaps her best known, and the most clinically influential, of her research. But she was also deeply concerned about the education of women in medicine, and generously volunteered her time to many organizations. In sum, as J.D. Fulton put it: "She proved a good citizen of the world."

SOURCES:

Fay, Marion. "Louise Pearce," in *The Journal of Pathology and Bacteriology*. Vol. 82. London: Oliver & Boyd, 1961.

Flexner, Simon. "The Scientific Career for Women," in *The Scientific Monthly*. Vol. 13. NY: Scientific Press, 1921.

Fulton, J.D. "Dr. Louise Pearce," in *Nature*. Vol. 184. London: Macmillan, 1959.

McGrew, Roderick E. *Encyclopedia of Medical History*. NY: McGraw-Hill, 1985.

McKelvey, John J. *Man Against Tsetse*. Ithaca, NY: Cornell University Press, 1973.

Peitzman, S.J. "Pearce, Louise," in *Dictionary of American Medical Biography*. Vol. 2. Westport, CT: Greenwood Press, 1984.

Who Was Who in America. Vol. 3. Chicago, IL: A.N. Marquis, 1966.

SUGGESTED READING:

Corner, George W. "Pearce, Louise," in *Notable American Women: The Modern Period*. Edited by Barbara Sicherman and Carol Hurd Green. Cambridge, MA: The Belknap Press, 1980.

Hugh A. Stewart, M.A., Guelph, Ontario, Canada

Pearce, May (1915–1981).

See Pearce Sisters.

Pearce, Morna (1932—)

See Pearce Sisters.

Pearce Sisters (fl. 1936–1956)

Australian field hockey players.

Pearce, Caroline (1925—). *Name variations: Caroline Ash. Born in 1925, in Moulyinning, Australia; married.*

Pearce, Jean (1921—). *Name variations: Jean Wynne. Born in 1921, in Moulyinning, Australia; married.*

Pearce, May (1915–1981). *Name variations: May Campbell. Born in 1915, in Moulyinning, Australia; died in 1981; married.*

Pearce, Morna (1932—). *Name variations: Morna Hyde. Born in 1932, in Moulyinning, Australia; married.*

Born and raised in the tiny farming community of Moulyinning, Australia, the legendary Pearce sisters (no relation to the famous hockey-playing Pearce brothers) dominated Australian women's field hockey from 1936 to 1956. The eldest sister May, who played left-inner and captained for both state and national teams, was regarded as a scoring phenomenon, making 100 goals in 1936 alone. After 1948, she left the field of play to become a coach and administrator. Second sister Jean, a center half-back and also a captain, was the master of the assisted play, coming from out of nowhere with great loping strides to support a teammate in making a goal. After leading Australia to its first victory over England in 1953, Jean retired from the game. Caroline Pearce, known as "Tib," played only from 1946 to 1950, and joined May and Jean on the 1948 unbeaten Australian team which toured New Zealand. Morna, the youngest Pearce, was known for her stick work, and played for Australia when Jean was captain in 1953. Morna herself captained in the international tournament at Sydney in 1956, and that same year won the WA's first Sportsman (*sic*) of the Year award.

Pearl, Cora (c. 1837–1886)

English-born courtesan. *Name variations: Eliza Crouch. Born Eliza Emma Crouch near Plymouth, England, around 1837; died in Paris, France, in 1886; daughter of a musician father and a singer mother.*

On holiday in Paris around 1858, English prostitute Eliza Crouch fell in love with the city and decided to stay. Although not a great beauty, known as Cora Pearl, she became one of the most notorious courtesans of the Second Empire, amassing seemingly inexhaustible wealth and earning a spot in the *Dictionary of National Biography*. At the height of her legendary career, she was said to have received her clientele (which at one time included Prince Jérome Bonaparte, cousin of Emperor Napoleon III) in a reception salon carpeted in violet petals, upon which she danced a cancan before plunging into a bathtub filled with champagne. From time to time, she reputedly gave extravagant dinners for upwards of 20 men, sometimes offering herself naked on a silver platter as the *plat du jour*. Her gorgeous figure was said to have elicited gasps from the appreciative spectators. Sadly, Pearl's decline paralleled that of the Second Empire, and she is said to have died penniless in a Paris garret at age 50. Her once lavish residence became the Travellers Club, one of the most exclusive residential clubs in Europe.

Cora Pearl

SUGGESTED READING:

Binder, Pearl. *The Truth about Cora Pearl.*

Pearl, Cora. *Grand Horizontal: The Erotic Memoirs of a Passionate Lady.* NY: Stein & Day, 1983.

Barbara Morgan,
Melrose, Massachusetts

Pearl, Minnie (1912–1996)

American entertainer who was the first humorist in country music to achieve worldwide recognition. *Name variations: Ophelia Colley Cannon; Sarah Ophelia Colley. Born Sarah Ophelia Colley in Centerville, Tennessee, in 1912; died in Nashville on March 4, 1996; youngest of five daughters of Thomas K. Colley (a lumber merchant) and Fannie Tate (House) Colley; attended Ward-Belmont College; married Henry Cannon (her manager), in 1947.*

Joined the Grand Ole Opry (1940); inducted into the Country Music Association's Hall of Fame (October 13, 1975); received Brotherhood Award from National Conference of Christians and Jews (1975).

With her trademark price tag dangling from a dime-store hat and her greeting of "Howdyyyyy! I'm just so proud to be here," Minnie Pearl worked at the Grand Ole Opry for 56 years. She had arrived at a time of transition, when hillbilly music crossed over to the more respectable country and western. Pearl was the first country music humorist to gain worldwide recognition.

Minnie Pearl was born Sarah Ophelia Colley in Centerville, Tennessee, in 1912. "I was a mistake from the start," she wrote in her autobiography. Her mother, a finishing school graduate, was 37 and had four girls in school when she learned she was pregnant once more. She was also one of the social leaders of Centerville, population 500. The epitome of genteel Southern womanhood, **Fannie House Colley** was an accomplished pianist who supplied the background music for recitals, plays, and musicals at the local opera house.

As baby Sarah, Pearl served as a doll-in-residence; her older sisters dressed and undressed her and paraded her up the street in a layette. Pearl claims she was so spoiled by all the love and attention that her father called her G.M. (general manager). The soft-spoken and dignified Thomas Colley owned a lumberyard and sawmill that was located near Grinder's Switch, which was hardly a town, more of a spur track for loading freight trains that Pearl would later claim as her home. Thomas, who had given up waiting for a son, took her with him when he was surveying lumber camps. To her mother's chagrin, Pearl was turning into a rough-and-tumble type. Thomas also taught her to "never let the truth interfere with a good story."

By age four, she was plunking out tunes on the piano. By age six, she was playing the piano at World War I bond rallies and belting out such songs as "If He Can Fight Like He Can Love, It's Good-bye Germany." In exchange for free admission, she began to supply background music for the silent movies at the local cinema, until her mother found out. Stagestruck, Pearl would appear in front of anything that smacked of an audience, convinced she was going to be the most celebrated actress of all time, despite advance reports, overhead in passing, that she was a trifle plain. Following high school, she planned to attend a first-rate college, as her sisters had done, then move on to the American Academy of Dramatic Art or the Pasadena Playhouse.

The stock-market crash of 1929 changed all that. Pearl was offered two years at Ward-Belmont in Tennessee, or four years at the University of Tennessee. She chose Ward-Belmont for its drama department and its director **Pauline Sherwood Thompson**, who was highly respected throughout the South. But Ward-Belmont, untouched by the Depression, was also an elite finishing school, where Southern girls from prestigious backgrounds and old money matriculated. Pearl knew she was out of her element within the first 24 hours. "I felt like I'd been dropped into a funeral home," she wrote. Dinner conversation revolved around shopping in Paris, London, and Rome; Pearl's travels had taken her to Nashville. It did not help when Townsend told

Minnie Pearl

her that she had ruined her voice while cheerleading in high school, but Pearl's piano playing and talent eventually ingratiated her.

Upon graduation, she opened a studio to teach drama in Centerville, aware that she would not be allowed to leave home to seek her fortune until she reached a respectable age, at least 21. When that time came, she joined The Sewell Company, a theatrical production enterprise that booked shows in schools, churches, and civic organizations in rural communities.

While the company supplied the director, sets, and script, locals were used in the cast. "Like the Music Man coming to River City," wrote Pearl, she traveled as a director from town to town during the winters for the next six years. She was also the summer director of the Wayne P. Sewell Training School in Roscoe, Georgia.

In her travels, a character named Minnie Pearl began to evolve, based partially on the matriarch of a mountain family she had lived with for ten days. She would pull out Minnie Pearl whenever she arrived in towns, speaking to groups, telling them how glad she was to be there. "It was a lot easier than standing up there as Ophelia Colley," she wrote. Pearl told her father about the mountain woman she had met and mimicked her. "You'll make a fortune off that some day," he said, "if you keep it kind."

In 1939, a friend asked her to do Minnie Pearl for a Pilots Club Convention. Up until then, she had not worn a costume. "I dressed her as I thought a young country girl would dress to go to meetin' on Sunday or to come to town on Saturday afternoon to do a little trading and a little flirting." She wore a pale yellow dress of cheap organdy with a round collar, white cotton stockings, and a straw hat. (The price tag would come later, the beneficiary of a genuine mistake.) The night of the convention, "as I passed among the tables in my costume, speaking to people, smiling and saying Howdy, an incredible thing happened to me. I felt myself moving out of Sarah Ophelia Colley into Minnie Pearl. . . . It gave me a wonderful sense of freedom I hadn't had before."

In the spring of 1940, bookings for Sewell slowed to a crawl. The 28-year-old Pearl found herself back home in Centerville, out of work, careerless, unmarried, and extraordinarily depressed. She took a job with the local branch of the Works Progress Administration (WPA), running a recreation center for children. Still pulling out Minnie Pearl on occasion, she was asked to trot her out for a bankers' convention. It was the turning point. Someone of influence saw the show, and she was offered an audition for the Opry.

Despite the fact that she had never been a fan of country music, Pearl seized the chance. She longed for a job in show business and longed to be out of Centerville. In November 1940, Minnie Pearl made her three-minute Opry debut. Her mother's review: "Several people woke up." Asked to return the following week, she was greeted with 300 pieces of mail and was signed on as a regular at $10 a week. She also joined Roy Acuff's show on the road, but her lack of experience revealed itself quickly and Acuff had to let her go. She reworked her routines, wrote more material with her sister **Virginia Colley**, loosened up even more, and went back out on the road with Pee Wee King.

Pearl would become a mainstay of the Opry and would also appear for 20 years on the syndicated television show "Hee Haw." In 1966, she was voted Country Music Woman of the Year by the Country Music Association; in 1975, she was named to the Country Music Hall of Fame. Diagnosed with cancer in 1985, Pearl had a double mastectomy. Two years later, President Ronald Reagan presented her with the Courage Award from the American Cancer Society for her volunteer work. Pearl also suffered a mild stroke in 1991; forced to retire, she could not attend that year's White House ceremony to receive her National Medal of Art. Minnie Pearl died in Nashville of a brain seizure or stroke on March 4, 1996.

SOURCES:

Pearl, Minnie, with Joan Dew. *Minnie Pearl: An Autobiography.* NY: Simon and Schuster, 1980.

Pearsall, Phyllis (1906–1996)

English artist, writer and mapmaker. *Born Phyllis Gross in London, England, in 1906; died in Shoreham, England, on August 28, 1996; daughter of Alexander Gross (1880–1958, a Hungarian-born map publisher of Jewish descent) and Isabelle Crowley (1886–1938, a playwright and suffragist); sister of Anthony Gross (1905–1995, a painter); married Richard Pearsall, in 1928.*

Phyllis Pearsall was born in London in 1906. Her father Alexander Gross, of Jewish descent, was a Hungarian-born map publisher. Her mother **Isabelle Crowley**, part Irish, part Anglo-Italian Catholic, was a playwright and suffragist whose feminist play *Break the Walls Down* opened at the Savoy in 1913. Phyllis's brother was Anthony Gross, an artist. Pearsall was 16 in 1922 when her parents separated. Bankrupt, her father emigrated to America where he continued to make maps in New York. Her mother, meanwhile, lived with Alfred Everett Orr, an American portrait painter.

Pearsall, who wrote, painted and traveled, took on the task of map making after getting lost in London in 1935 while consulting the most recent street map available—which was 20 years old. From her father, she borrowed a draughtsman, James Duncan, who assisted her in cataloguing 23,000 streets for the first edition of her *Geographer's A–Z Street Atlas.* Pearsall worked 18 hours a day; by the time the atlas was completed in 1936, she had walked 3,000 miles to compile it. When the book-buying establishment greeted the work with no more than apathy, the Geographer's A–Z Map Company was formed by Pearsall, who had 10,000 copies of her work printed, 250 of which she delivered in a wheelbarrow to W.H. Smith on a sale-or-return basis. Highly successful, the book served as Pearsall's model for additional maps of other British cities which followed. The company's prosperity allowed her to continue her writing and painting, endeavors at which she also reaped rewards. Pearsall was philanthropic with her shares in the lucrative Map Company, passing them in the 1960s to a trust which benefited her employees. She died on August 28, 1996. Her famous atlas, considered indispensable, can be found in homes, cars, and newsagents throughout London.

SUGGESTED READING:

Pearsall, Phyllis. *From Bedsitter to Household Name: The Personal Story of A–Z Maps.* Seven Oaks, England: Geographer's A–Z Map Co., 1990.

Peary, Josephine (1863–1955)

American author and Arctic explorer who accompanied her husband Robert E. Peary on two hazardous expeditions to the far North (1891 and 1893). *Name variations: Jo Peary; Josephine Diebitsch Peary. Born Josephine Diebitsch in Washington, D.C., on May 22, 1863; died in Portland, Maine, on December 19, 1955; daughter of Herman Henry Diebitsch and Magdalena Augusta (Schmid) Diebitsch; married Robert Edwin Peary (an Arctic explorer), in 1888; children:* ***Marie Ahnighito Peary Stafford*** *(b. 1893); Francine (d. 1899 in infancy); Robert Peary, Jr. (b. 1903).*

Arctic explorer Josephine Peary was born in Washington, D.C., in 1863 to parents who had emigrated from Germany; her long life began when Abraham Lincoln was president and ended in the first decade of the Atomic Age. The first Caucasian woman to live in the world's high Arctic regions, Josephine played a significant role in advancing the career of her husband, Arctic explorer Robert E. Peary, whom she accompanied on exhibitions and for whom she would raise funds to effect his rescue in 1895. In total, Josephine would spend three winters and eight summers in the high Arctic region.

In 1882, Josephine, known as Jo, met Robert Edwin Peary, a civil engineer in the U.S. Navy, at a Washington dance. Their courtship was slowed by his long trips to Greenland and Nicaragua in the next years. Married in Washington in 1888, the couple lived first in New York City and then in Philadelphia, where Robert was assigned to the naval shipyard.

Josephine Peary

With a longstanding, overpowering desire to discover the North Pole, by 1891 Robert had obtained financial support from Philadelphia's Academy of Natural Sciences to organize an expedition to North Greenland. He then stunned the nation by announcing that Jo Peary would accompany him. The harsh Arctic region was considered totally inappropriate for a Caucasian woman, making the plans for Jo's participation the subject of much discussion and controversy. Other members of the expedition included Robert's African-American servant Matthew Henson, Frederick Cook, and Louisville's John McKee Verhoeff, who was the trip's most generous cash contributor. The journey began on a less than perfect note when Robert broke his leg during the voyage north; he had to be carried ashore upon their arrival in July 1891 at McCormick Bay, North Greenland.

The explorers quickly built their new home, Red Cliff House. The work of unpacking supplies and nursing her injured husband so exhausted Jo that she slept through the departure of the ship that had brought them to their bleak new home. Soon, however, as one of the group of seven explorers, she set fox traps, investigated nearby cliffs, and carried her Colt .38 revolver while traveling as a member of hunting parties in search of deer, seal, and walrus meat. Inside Red Cliff House, the Pearys' room measured 7.5'x12', with the remaining room shared by the other five explorers. The seven Americans had as neighbors a local Inuit family, and in December 1891 they shared Christmas dinner with them. Jo paid the Inuit women to make Arctic clothing for the group, work which she supervised. She also cooked and often took short exploratory trips in the area. By mid-January 1892, the light had started to return, and she noted in her journal: "I take advantage of it by indulging in long snow-shoe tramps. I can now walk for hours without tiring . . . and feel more comfortable than I have felt while shopping in Philadelphia or New York on a winter's day." In April 1892, she and Robert made a sledge journey in Inglefield Gulf to visit some Inuit settlements and discovered several new glaciers and mountain peaks on their way. Jo's prim Victorian upbringing had not prepared her for the alien odors and standards of hygiene customary for the Inuit, and she could not follow the Inuit custom of stripping naked while indoors.

In May 1892, Robert and three others began a journey across the Greenland ice cap. Remaining behind at Red Cliff House were Jo, Henson and Verhoeff. While Robert was confident about the undertaking, Jo had been told by the Inuit that her husband was fated to die on the ice cap, and she had grave misgivings about the journey. As days went by, she grew despondent, and both she and Henson had frequent personality clashes with Verhoeff. In excellent physical condition, and as the expedition's most generous financial donor, Verhoeff was bitter about having been excluded from the trek. Later, after Jo and Robert were reunited, they mapped Inglefield Gulf together. In their absence, Verhoeff mysteriously vanished on a lone trek to McCormick Bay. The Pearys sent out extensive search parties, but only a cache of mineral specimens and footprints leading along a glacier face were ever discovered. Verhoeff's body was never found. His family, aware of the tensions between him and the Pearys, became convinced that he had met with foul play or lost his life as a result of Robert Peary's neglect. His disappearance remains an unsolved mystery.

Having written a book about her adventures entitled *My Arctic Journal* (1893), in July 1893 Jo was pregnant when she returned to Greenland on her second expedition to the far North. Many newspaper editorials were highly critical of Peary's decision to deliver her child in the high Arctic. Arriving in Greenland, the Peary expedition discovered that Red Cliff House had been destroyed by fire, but they quickly built a new home, Anniversary Lodge, on the old site. In September 1893, Jo gave birth to a healthy daughter, Marie Ahnighito, who would soon be known throughout the world as the "Snow Baby" (Ahnighito was the name of an Eskimo woman who made Marie's first suit of fur). The infant had been born farther north than had any white child previously.

In 1894, the Peary expedition ran into danger. Robert failed to cross the ice cap, and rapidly diminishing food supplies forced most of the expedition members to abandon the expedition. With neither a physician nor a nurse available, Jo reluctantly returned home with her infant daughter, convinced that Robert would soon be able to follow them. As it turned out, this was not the case. There had been no plan to send a ship in 1895 to retrieve Robert. In fact, the expedition's sponsors had decided that it would be reasonable for him to sail his small cutter 700 miles down the Greenland coast to the safety of permanent Danish settlements.

Convinced that her husband's life would be at risk if he did this, Jo made clear her opposition to such a dangerous journey and set about raising the $10,000 needed to charter a relief vessel. She quickly amassed a fund of about $7,000 but became alarmed when contributions began to dwindle. The remaining funding, however, was supplied by the National Geographic Society and Morris Jesup, the wealthy president of the Peary Arctic Club. Robert arrived on the relief ship with two meteorites which he had discovered in Greenland.

Both Pearys returned in 1897 to bring back another meteorite Robert had found earlier. Weighing 100 tons, it was the largest known meteorite in the world, and there were considerable difficulties getting it on board ship. Years later, the American Museum of Natural History would purchase it from Jo Peary for the then handsome sum of $40,000, and it still impresses visitors to that Manhattan museum.

In 1898, Robert was granted a five-year leave of absence from the Navy in order to carry out an expedition to the North Pole. Once again pregnant, Jo chose to remain at home with daughter Marie. To contribute to the expedition, she sewed a large American flag for him to use in marking new discoveries (it is now on display at the headquarters of the National Geographic Society in Washington, D.C.). While he was gone, she gave birth to a daughter, Francine, who died in 1899 at the age of six months. Meanwhile, on expedition Robert lost most of his toes to frostbite. Nonetheless, he remained in the Arctic, determined to be the first person to reach the North Pole. In March 1900, Jo returned to Greenland with Marie. Soon after arriving, she made three disquieting discoveries. One was that he had not returned to Greenland but was rather in northernmost Canada, more than 200 miles away. Another, even more upsetting to Jo, was that her husband had a second family; a young Inuit woman, **Alaqasina**, had become his lover and given birth to two sons. Lastly, the ice had now entrapped Jo's ship for the winter.

Throughout these difficult months, little Marie relished the opportunity to play in the land of her birth. (She would later write two books concerning her childhood: *The Red Caboose with Peary in the Arctic* [1932] and *The Snowbaby's Own Story* [1934].) When Robert returned to the ship, he and Jo were reconciled. Despite his physical impairments, he refused to return to the United States for medical treatment. Jo and Marie made the journey home but returned again to Greenland in 1902. This time, Jo was able to persuade Robert to come home to recuperate. In 1903, she gave birth to their third and last child, Robert, Jr.

Jo Peary was at the family home on Eagle Island, Maine, when she received word from her husband that he had finally reached his lifelong goal, the North Pole. In 1910, she and their children accompanied him on a triumphal tour of Europe. In 1911, he was awarded a medal by the U.S. Congress as well as a retirement pension. The Pearys divided their time between their homes in Maine and Washington, D.C., raising their two children. Robert Peary died in 1920 and was buried in Arlington National Cemetery.

Even before his death, Robert's claims of reaching the North Pole and discovering various other Arctic regions were being critically examined. With the passage of time, most polar scholars have come to doubt his claims. For all his flaws, he was in many ways the embodiment of a traditional, stubbornly heroic figure, and Jo helped him in the pursuit of his goals by working to secure vitally needed public support for his expeditions. It is quite possible that without her vigorous intervention on his behalf in 1895, Robert might have lost his life. As his widow, she remained loyal to her husband's memory, choosing to avoid comment on the many bitter controversies that swirled around his legacy as an explorer.

After her husband's death, she never returned to Greenland. Jo Peary lived in Maine to an advanced age and, on May 6, 1955, was awarded a special gold medal by the National Geographic Society in recognition of her contributions to Robert E. Peary's expeditions to North Greenland and the Arctic regions of Canada. She died soon after, in Portland, Maine, on December 19, 1955.

SOURCES:

Bergmann, Linda S. "Women Against a Background of White: The Representation of Self and Nature in Women's Arctic Narratives," in *American Studies*. Vol. 34, no. 2. Fall 1993, pp. 53–68.

Heckathorn, Ted. "Peary, Josephine Diebitsch," in John A. Garraty *et al.*, eds., *American National Biography*. Vol. 17. NY: Oxford University Press, 1999, pp. 215–217.

Herbert, Wally. *The Noose of Laurels: Robert E. Peary and the Race to the North Pole*. NY: Doubleday, 1989.

Keeney, Arthur H. and Virginia T. Keeney. "From Louisville to the North Pole: Did Peary Leave Verhoeff to Die?," in *Filson Club History Quarterly*. Vol. 70, no. 2, 1996, pp. 130–142.

Peary, Josephine Diebitsch. *Children of the Arctic*. NY: F.A. Stokes, 1903.

———. *My Arctic Journal*. NY: Contemporary, 1893.

———. *The Snow Baby: A True Story with True Pictures*. 5th ed. NY: F.A. Stokes, 1901.

Peary, Robert E. *Northward over the Great Ice*. 2 vols. NY: F.A. Stokes, 1898.

Stafford, Marie Ahnighito Peary. *The Red Caboose with Peary in the Arctic*. NY: William Morrow, 1932.

———. *The Snowbaby's Own Story*. Philadelphia, PA: Lippincott, 1934.

Stafford, Marie Peary. "The Peary Flag Comes to Rest," in *National Geographic Magazine*. Vol. 106, no. 4. October 1954, pp. 519–532.

Tamplin, Ronald, ed. *Famous Love Letters: Messages of Intimacy and Passion*. Pleasantville, NY: Reader's Digest, 1995.

Weems, John Edward. *Peary: The Explorer and the Man*. Los Angeles, CA: Jeremy P. Tarcher, 1988.

John Haag,
Associate Professor of History, University of Georgia, Athens, Georgia

Pechey-Phipson, Edith (1845–1908)

British physician who as senior medical officer of the Cama Hospital in Bombay, India (1886–94), was in charge of the first hospital in the world to be entirely staffed by women. *Born Mary Edith Pechey in Langham, Essex, England, on October 7, 1845; died in Folkestone, England, on April 14, 1908; daughter of William Pechey and Sarah Rotton Pechey; married Herbert Phipson; no children.*

Edith Pechey was born in England in 1845 to William Pechey, a Baptist minister, and **Sarah Rotton Pechey**, a woman who was unusually well educated for her day. After teaching school for a few years, Edith decided that she wanted to become a physician, a goal which represented a very high form of optimism for a woman in the 1860s, given that all British medical schools excluded women. Still, the world was changing rapidly, and in 1869, after a vigorous campaign by ***Sophia Jex-Blake**, the University of Edinburgh admitted Pechey and three other women as its first female medical students. The victory, however, was by no means perfect. Edith, Jex-Blake, and, by start of term, five other women (**Mary Anderson, Isabel Thorne, Matilda Chaplin, Helen Evans**, and **Emily Bovell**), now referred to as the "Edinburgh Seven," were segregated from the male students, attending separate lectures for which they had to pay their professors four times the regular tuition required from the male students. In order to afford her classes, Edith gave lectures on physiology to women in Leeds. The indignities endured by Pechey and the other women reached a new level in 1874, when the University of Edinburgh expelled them on the grounds that their admission had violated the institution's by-laws. Although the women sued, they lost the case and were thus forced to continue their medical educations elsewhere.

Pechey went to Switzerland, then the most progressive country in terms of providing women access to a medical education, and completed her studies at the University of Berne. After the English College of Physicians remained adamant in its refusal to license women, in the summer of 1877 the Royal College of Physicians of Ireland decided to admit Pechey, Jex-Blake, and several other women to their final examinations. Upon receiving her license, Pechey established a successful private practice at Leeds and Birmingham. She also took time off to study surgery at the University of Vienna. While her medical career flourished, she became an eloquent, passionate advocate of women's suffrage. In 1883, she would accept a position as senior medical officer in Bombay (modern-day Mumbai), India, at the first hospital not only specifically built for women but also staffed entirely by women.

Because India's religious traditions did not permit women to be treated, or even seen, by male physicians, there were no properly trained medical personnel in the Indian subcontinent to meet the medical needs of many millions of girls and women, other than a few missionaries with medical training. Pechey felt strongly that Christian missionary work and professional medicine of the highest caliber should be maintained as strictly separate realms. In an inaugural address she gave in 1878 at the London School of Medicine for Women, she exhorted her audience, mincing no words: "Christian England is renowned in every land for adulterated goods. Let it not be said that under the very guise of Christianity the medical help she sends out is also an inferior article."

By the 1880s, some limited medical training was beginning to be offered to women at the Medical College of Madras, and across India a few schools had been set up to train local midwives. India's elite, both Hindus and Parsees, sought to improve the situation, and in Bombay a wealthy Parsee philanthropist, Pestonji H. Cama, made a generous offer to endow a women's hospital, with the proviso that it would then be maintained by the government. An American businessman living in Bombay, George A. Kittredge, initiated the Medical Women for India Fund in order to gain the support of British and Indian philanthropists for the women's hospital project. The fund was successful, attracting such influential subscribers as Randolph Churchill, Winston Churchill's father.

Kittredge offered Pechey the top post at Bombay's proposed Cama Hospital, at a guaranteed monthly salary of 500 rupees. She arrived in December 1883. Quickly revealing the decisiveness that would mark her entire tenure in India, Pechey insisted that she and her entire staff be paid on exactly the same scale as male physicians. Her argument, as compelling today as it was in 1883, was that lesser—and discriminatory—compensation could serve only to undermine the professional status of women while strengthening the ancient and lingering prejudice that women in medicine were not as well qualified as their male colleagues. Although promised, the salaries would be long delayed, as the hospital committee, the British government, and Pechey's supporters argued the merits of equal pay. In the end, Pechey and her staff won the battle.

Until the completion of the Cama Hospital in 1886, Pechey had a private practice and also administered a temporary medical dispensary for poor Indian women. Interested in the culture and civilization of India, she studied the Hindustani language. Indefatigable, Pechey became the moving force in a drive to set up a nurses' training school closely associated with the Cama Hospital. Soon, her efforts began to yield positive results, evidenced both by British women physicians who chose to have careers in India, and by growing numbers of Hindu women who began to study medicine in the United Kingdom and the United States. Despite strong local opposition, Pechey was a tireless advocate of expanded educational opportunities for Indian girls and young women. She also campaigned against what she saw as the social evils of child marriage and the proscribed remarriage of widows. In essence, she believed that India's women were ready for emancipation from the benighted and restrictive aspects of Hindu religious and social traditions.

In March 1889, Edith Pechey married Herbert Phipson, a like-minded social reformer. A wine merchant by profession, Herbert was also an enthusiastic naturalist. From this point on, Edith would be known as Edith Pechey-Phipson. As senior medical officer of the Cama Hospital, Pechey-Phipson successfully oversaw the administration of the complex institution. She also continued to study various aspects of Indian history and culture. Her scholarly interests were reflected in her selection to the Senate of the University of Bombay, making her the first woman to be so appointed. She was also elected a member of the Royal Asiatic Society.

Pechey-Phipson resigned from her Cama Hospital position in 1894 when diabetes began to seriously affect her health. She refused to abandon her career, however, and continued to maintain a private medical practice. When bubonic plague erupted in Bombay in 1896, she was a leader in the struggle to bring the pestilence under control. This outbreak was followed by a cholera epidemic and a widespread famine, and Pechey-Phipson remained active in the forefront of the medical response to the human suffering.

In 1905, after 22 years of medical work in India, she returned with her husband to England. Despite her fragile health, she remained committed to social change and invested much of her time in campaigning for women's suffrage. Edith Pechey-Phipson died after cancer surgery in Folkestone on April 14, 1908.

SOURCES:

Blake, Catriona. *The Charge of the Parasols: Women's Entry to the Medical Profession.* London: Women's Press, 1990.

Bonner, Thomas N. *To the Ends of the Earth: Women's Search for Education in Medicine.* Cambridge, MA: Harvard University Press, 1992.

Burton, Antoinette. *Burdens of History: British Feminists, Indian Women and Imperial Culture, 1865–1915.* Chapel Hill, NC: University of North Carolina Press, 1994.

———. "Contesting the Zenana: The Mission to Make 'Lady Doctors for India,' 1874–1885," in *Journal of British Studies.* Vol. 35, no. 3. July 1996, pp. 368–397.

Lutzker, Edythe. *Edith Pechey-Phipson, M.D.: The Story of England's Foremost Pioneering Woman Doctor.* NY: Exposition Press, 1973.

———. "Edith Pechey-Phipson, M.D.: The Untold Story," in *Medical History.* Vol. 11, no. 1. January 1967, pp. 41–45.

———. *Women Gain a Place in Medicine.* London: McGraw-Hill, 1969.

Martel, Carol M. "Pechey-Phipson, Mary Edith," in James Stuart Olson and Robert Shadle, eds., *Historical Dictionary of the British Empire.* 2 vols., Westport, CT: Greenwood Press, 1996, Vol. 2, pp. 874–875.

Pechey-Phipson, Edith. *Inaugural Address . . . London School of Medicine for Women.* London: McGowan's Steam Printing, 1878 (History of Women Microfilm Collection, Reel 404, No. 2903).

Riddick, John F. *Who Was Who in British India.* Westport, CT: Greenwood Press, 1998.

John Haag,
Associate Professor of History, University of Georgia, Athens, Georgia

Pechstein, Claudia (c. 1973—)

German speedskater. *Born around 1973.*

Claudia Pechstein won the silver medal in the 1998 Olympic Games at Nagano in the 3,000 meters. In the 5,000, though her "legs felt heavy" at the start, she became the second woman to skate under seven minutes with a time of 6:59.61 (the first being ***Gunda Niemann** a few minutes earlier with a time of 6:59.65); Pechstein snatched the gold from Niemann's grasp by 4/100ths of a second. Her previous best time in the 5,000 had been 7:14.37. The bronze went to **Lyudmila Prokasheva** of Kazakstan.

Peck, Annie Smith (1850–1935)

American mountaineer and explorer who gained international celebrity (1908) by becoming the first person to reach the top of Peru's highest mountain, Huascaràn. *Born on October 19, 1850, in Providence, Rhode Island; died on July 18, 1935, in New York City; youngest of five children of George Peck (a lawyer and state legislator) and Anna Smith Peck; graduated from the Rhode Island State Normal School, 1872; graduated from the University of Michigan with a degree in Greek, 1878, M.A., 1881; never married; no children.*

Captivated by her first sight of the Swiss Alps during a Continental tour (1885); climbed her first major mountain, California's Mount Shasta (1888) and went on to lead expeditions up important European heights before discovering the Andes of South America; gained international fame (1908) after six attempts by becoming the first to reach the top of Peru's highest mountain, Huascaràn; when not climbing mountains, explored the headwaters of the Amazon River, traversed Peru's vast inland desert on horseback, and lectured widely on her experiences; at age 80, embarked on a seven-month air tour of South America encompassing 20,000 miles (1930), after which she became an enthusiastic proponent of air travel.

The residents of the tiny Peruvian village of Yungay were astonished one September day in 1904 when a wiry, gray-haired American woman arrived in their midst, having traveled overland by horseback from the country's Pacific coast to its northern wilderness, sandwiched between the two major ranges of the mighty Peruvian Andes. Annie Peck Smith was the first North American many of the villagers had seen, and the fact that she was traveling in the company of a brawny ex-seafarer, without proper chaperons, provoked even more gossip. Still more astounding was Peck's announced intention to scale Peru's highest mountain, Huascaràn, towering over Yungay at a height that had only been estimated at some 28,000 feet, since no one had ever attempted the climb to take accurate measurements. It was an impossible task, the villagers said, but Peck was used to insurmountable obstacles, having tackled them with aplomb during the preceding 54 years.

The first and in many ways the most difficult obstacle was her gender, for Peck had been born into in a mid-19th century world in which women's opportunities were severely circumscribed. Born in Providence, Rhode Island, on October 19, 1850, she was the youngest of George and Anna Smith Peck's five children, and the only daughter. Peck would later suggest that competing with four older brothers made her more willing in later life to take on challenges considered unsuitable for women. Her childhood was comfortable; George Peck was a lawyer and state legislator, and Annie was fortunate to be sent to the state's best schools for young women, graduating from the Rhode Island State Normal School in 1872. But the college education given as a matter of course to her brothers was denied her, and Peck was obliged to take up teaching as one of the few career opportunities open to her. After a brief period teaching at Providence High School, she accepted a position as headmistress of a girls' high school in Saginaw, Michigan. With her heart set on college, she soon had saved enough money to enroll in 1875 at the University of Michigan, which had begun accepting women just four years earlier. She was 24 at the time and determined to receive her degree in Greek before reaching 27—a goal she achieved by adopting a rigorous study schedule that led to her graduation in just three years. A master's degree followed in 1881. Peck established yet another beachhead that same year when she was named a Latin and elocution professor at Purdue University, becoming one of the first women to be given a professorship at an American university. While at Purdue, she attended a lecture by one of the school's professors describing his recent travels in Europe, the highlight being a climb up Switzerland's Matterhorn. The professor's offhand comment that women would be forever barred from such lofty adventures because of their weaker constitutions lodged in Peck's mind, although at the time she had no inkling of its future effect.

By 1892, after a sabbatical spent studying in Europe (during which she became the first woman admitted to the American School of Classical Studies in Athens), Peck had become so famous for her lectures on classical Greek archaeology and architecture that she was able to support herself entirely on lecture fees and was listed in 1893's *Leading American Women from All Walks of Life* as "educator, musician, profound classical scholar, and distinguished archaeologist." But the encyclopedia's entry failed to mention a new talent, for it was during her European tour that Peck was captivated by the towering peaks that would become her obsession in later life. "My allegiance . . . was transferred for all time to the mountains," she later wrote of her first glimpse of the Matterhorn in 1885. "On beholding this majestic, awe-inspiring peak, I felt that I should never be happy until I, too, should scale those frowning walls which have beckoned so many upwards, a few to their own destruction." In short order, she was climbing minor peaks in Switzerland and in Greece; by 1888, she had ascended California's Mount Shasta—at some 14,000 feet, her first important climb—and reported that "the exercise was delightful and invigorating," as if she had merely taken a stroll. In 1895, she achieved her dream of ten years earlier by climbing the Matterhorn, which had first been conquered only 30 years earlier with the loss of four lives. She was not the first to disprove the Purdue professor's opinion of women and mountains, for two women had already ascended the 14,690 feet to the summit by the time Peck attempted it, the first being ***Lucy Walker** in 1871. Her own contribution was to abandon the cumbersome full skirts worn by proper Victorian women for all occasions, even mountain climbing, in favor of knee-length pantaloons and a tunic. (On the very day Peck climbed the Matterhorn in such an outfit, a woman in Arkansas was prosecuted for wearing bloomers in public.) Americans were so fascinated with Peck's feat that the Singer Sewing Machine Company began including picture cards of her in full climbing gear with its machines, and she was dubbed "Queen of the Climbers" in the press. It was all, Peck said, "unmerited notoriety," but her success on one of the world's most famous peaks led her to consider more difficult climbs.

Her attention turned to Mexico which, unlike Europe and America, still contained unexplored stretches punctuated by equally unexplored mountains. Mexico's Orizaba and Popocatépetl beckoned as North America's third- and fifth-highest peaks, respectively. Orizaba, some 4,000 feet higher than the Matterhorn, proved no more difficult in 1897 and brought Peck another first, since no woman up to that time had reached such a high altitude. It

Annie Smith Peck

was also Peck's first attempt to use her skill for scientific purposes, as she employed a mercurial barometer given to her by the U.S. Weather Bureau to measure Orizaba's height at 18,660 feet—close to the present accepted measurement of 18,700 feet. Her ascent of Popocatépetl (not much of a challenge, actually, the mountain having first been scaled in 1519) was her first climb to be funded by the press, with the *New York Sunday World* paying her expenses in exchange for exclusive rights to the story she would write. Her account was less than the hair-raising adventure the paper was expecting. Peck truthfully reported that she had been accompanied by guests from the hotel at the mountain's base, that she had enjoyed a festive lunch with them just short of the peak, and that the son of one of the guests scrambled up ahead of her and had actually reached the peak before she did, much to everyone's amusement. As the paper frantically cobbled together a phony tale of hardship and determination, Peck began to consider her next challenge, "a little genuine exploration to conquer a virgin peak," she said, "to attain some height where no *man* had previously stood."

Her stated condition could have been applied to most of the peaks of South America, for few of them had ever been tackled by the Eurocentric male aristocracy from which most of the West's mountaineering adventurers came. Peck's choice was Bolivia's Mount Sorata, said to be the highest peak in the Western Hemisphere (a claim later disproved) and one which no man or woman had yet attempted. But despite the publicity surrounding her ascents of Orizaba and Popocatépetl, Peck struggled for the next four years to raise sufficient funds for the expedition. The decidedly undramatic climb up Popocatépetl had made the rounds of the newspapers, none of which chose to invest in Peck's next adventure; and manufacturing companies Annie felt might be willing to lend their names to the expedition still had difficulties with a single, middle-aged woman obsessed with mountains. It was not until June 1903 that Peck had raised what she felt was enough money to sail for South America. In the first of a series of unfortunate judgments of male character, she traveled in the company of a professor of geology she had met only once before and two mountain guides from Switzerland she had hired after learning that one of them had been a member of an earlier, unsuccessful ascent of Mount Sorata. She also brought along two barometers for measuring Sorata's altitude, one to take measurements at the base and one at the summit; two contraptions called hypsometers, which measured the temperature at which water boiled at various heights to determine altitude above sea level; and in the event all else failed, surveying equipment that would allow her to determine Sorata's height by triangulation. For further experimentation, medical devices were taken along to record the human body's reaction to height and thin air. Finally, Peck packed oxygen cylinders fitted with rubber bags and mouthpieces in the first recorded use of oxygen on a mountaineering expedition, although the cumbersome cylinders were later abandoned.

Thus provisioned, the little party arrived at a Peruvian coastal city in July and embarked by train on an almost vertical climb up the Andes' western range for the Peruvian-Bolivian border. Their destination was Lake Titicaca, the world's highest lake. Within 60 hours of travel, Peck later reported, they had ascended by train to nearly 15,000 feet above sea level, "sufficient to disturb the interior economy of all save the soundest constitution." Annie suggested that the party rest and acclimate to the higher altitudes, but the professor insisted they go on, despite his complaints of a severe headache, and continue across Lake Titicaca by steamer. Mount Sorata loomed up over the far southern shore, but another train journey was needed to bring them to La Paz, Bolivia's capital city, followed by an arduous journey of several days by mule to finally arrive at the foot of Sorata.

The first phase of the climb passed uneventfully as the group made camp at 15,000 feet; but then the male treachery that would plague Peck during her entire climbing career struck. First, the professor refused to leave camp for the next segment of the ascent, pleading severe nausea and headaches, while the porters complained that the snow line was much lower than in previous years and, lacking proper footwear, obstinately declined to continue further. Worse, they grew threatening enough that one of the Swiss guides proposed calling in the military. In the face of growing disorganization and with the South American winter coming on, Peck felt she had no choice but to give up and return to La Paz. "To manage . . . men seemed beyond my power," she later wrote. "Perhaps some of my more experienced married sisters would have done better." The professor and the Swiss guides abandoned her in La Paz while Peck found some consolation in reaching the coast by crossing Peru's daunting "Pampa of Islay," a 100-mile stretch of desert which she traversed by mule in the company of a native mule driver and an American man she had met. "In strange lands, far from home . . . one is apt to feel that all men from the United States are brothers," she wrote in a decidedly more charitable mood toward the opposite sex. "Most men under such circumstances are disposed to be polite." She arrived back in New York in the early winter of 1903, but left for Peru again in June 1904, still determined to climb Mount Sorata.

This time, her traveling companion was an Austrian who claimed Alpine experience, but once again Peck failed to make the summit of Sorata because of what she believed was male incompetence, including a near-fatal plummet into a deep crevasse when two of her porters untied themselves from her support rope as she teetered on the edge before pulling herself back. Then, within two hours of the summit and with night coming on, the Austrian and the porters refused to entertain her suggestion of making an overnight cave camp and insisted they descend. Again, Peck had no choice. It was her last attempt at Sorata, even though later measurements based on her diary suggest she may have been within 400 feet of Sorata's 20,867-foot summit, making her the first person to reach such an altitude on the mountain's slopes. "Oh, how I longed for a man with the pluck and determination to stand by me to the finish!," she later complained.

Despite these laments, Peck resolved not to leave South America until she had scaled a major peak. She abandoned Sorata in favor of the far more formidable Huascaràn, another "virgin peak" rising from Peru's remote northern wilderness. She found the brawny ex-seafarer who accompanied her to Yungay in a hotel in Lima, where she heard him speaking fluent Spanish to the hotel clerk and, again arriving at one of her spontaneous and unfortunate character judgments, decided to ask for his help in climbing Huascaràn. Her first sight of Huascaràn from Yungay filled both of them with a sense of foreboding. "Many thousand feet rise the rocky slopes," Peck later wrote after her first glimpse of the twin-peaked behemoth. "The immense glacier below the peaks was so visibly and terribly cut with a multitude of crevasses that it seemed impossible for the most skillful, much less for men wholly inexperienced, to find their way through such a maze." All went reasonably well during the first three days of climbing, as Peck's party made its tortuous way toward the mountain's north peak with avalanches thundering around them, but the final assault across a crevasse-riven glacier and up a treacherous rock cliff stalled when Annie's brawny ex-seafarer proved so inept with the guide rope that she was obliged to abandon it. Then the other male members of the party—porters and a newspaper editor from the Peruvian press—refused to go any farther. Peck struggled on alone, and without a guide rope, for a few more feet to plant a cross made by the natives in Yungay at the edge of the glacier. "This courageous American woman, notwithstanding that below her feet was a precipice reaching down to the glacier, took the cross and resolutely traversed this dangerous place where at every step she was liable to go down to certain death," the newspaper editor later reported to his readers. The ex-seafarer, whom Annie quickly paid off and dismissed as soon as they were off the mountain, confessed to having been so frightened that he intended never to climb another mountain again.

Just five days later, Peck attempted Huascaràn again, this time only in the company of native porters from Yungay. Again, the mountain defeated her, blasting the party with a major storm on the second day of the climb and stranding them some 2,000 feet below the saddle connecting Huascaràn's two peaks. Slogging their way through another two days of arduous climbing, Peck's party reached an altitude of some 18,000 feet—the highest point on Huascaràn anyone had ever reached—before they finally retreated because of continued bad weather. But Peck remained convinced that, with better equipment and more careful planning, she could reach the summit. Accordingly, she spent much of the remainder of 1905 and the first half of 1906 seeking funding in New York for a third attempt, although she had to settle for $700 offered to her by *Harper's Magazine*—hardly enough to buy her the Swiss guides and modern equipment she wanted, but sufficient to find her once again in Peru by early June 1906. She recruited Indian porters, ignored warnings that the American gentleman she met in Lima who asked to accompany her was emotionally unstable, equipped the party with the heavy woolen socks, ice picks, climbing irons and Alpenstocks that had been lacking from previous expeditions, and began her third assault of Huascaràn in late July. The usual trouble started only two days into the climb, as the party camped on a glacier in bitter cold wind for the night. The Indians declared they would go no farther; the "loco," as they called Peck's American companion, claimed he had developed colic from eating rice only half-cooked in air so thin it took two hours to boil water; and everyone declared they were reluctant to tie themselves to the guide rope for fear of being dragged down by another's fall. Annie struggled on with just one of the Indians and the ailing loco, but got no closer to the north peak than on her previous attempt when she decided to once again retreat. Within a week, she was at it again, and again in the company of the loco, whose idea it was to try once more; but this fourth attempt fared even worse than the others when the American did, indeed, seem to lose his emotional balance and disappeared for an entire night, narrowly avoiding freezing to death when Annie found him lying on a ridge and dragged him back to camp. Equipment was lost down crevasses; an amateur climber the American had brought along abandoned the party with Peck's climbing irons; and the guides demanded more money before they would climb beyond the

17,500 feet the party had reached by the second day. Again, Peck called a retreat, at which point the American broke away from the party, reached Yungay on his own, and disappeared. Annie later heard that he had been institutionalized by his family.

At this point, Peck finally admitted that Huascaràn had defeated her, at least for the moment; but instead of returning to New York, she indulged her deepening fascination with South America by visiting the world's highest copper mine, located near Lima and some 14,000 feet above sea level. Even a fall from a mule that resulted in several fractured ribs failed to keep her from attempting to find the source of the Amazon in the Raura Range, then a pristine wilderness where few had ever set foot. Her identification of two glacier-fed lakes in the Range as possible sources still stands, for even today the exact source of the world's longest river remains in dispute. But Huascaràn still gripped her imagination as she returned to New York in 1906. *Harper's*, thrilled with the exciting story Peck gave them about her last failed attempt, quickly offered another $3,000 to fund another expedition, but Peck was determined not to tackle Huascaràn again until she had enough money for proper equipment and her favored Swiss guides. Consequently, it was not until 1908 and a generous donation from a wealthy New York doyenne that she felt ready. Peck was now 58 years old.

Before sailing for Peru, she stopped off in Washington to meet with President Theodore Roosevelt, a fellow adventurer if a less enthusiastic supporter of Peck's vigorous calls for women's suffrage. Although "not quite committed to Woman Suffrage," she later wrote in her diary, "he was not the sort to decry women's ability or, when it had been proved, to throw stumbling blocks in her way." Peck was also pleased to note that Teddy Roosevelt had become an honorary member of the American Alpine Club, of which she had been a founding member. Dashing on to her ship at the last moment, she arrived back in Yungay by early August. On the morning of August 6, she began a new assault on Huascaràn, but again was forced to turn back after a record eight days trying to reach the summit. The litany of disasters was by now familiar—one of the two recalcitrant native porters forgot to pack the film for the camera Peck intended to use to document the climb; a Swiss guide complained of altitude sickness and left the party; and backpacks containing food rations and even their portable stove disappeared down bottomless crevasses. When the party finally straggled back into Yungay on August 15, everyone expected Peck to give up once and for all despite the fact that she had come closer to Huascaràn's north peak than in any of her other four attempts, reaching an estimated 22,000 feet. Further surprise ensued when Annie announced that once she re-provisioned, she would immediately undertake a sixth climb. Ten days later, she was off again.

Peck felt sure of victory on her sixth try, for she had assembled the most complete set of equipment in her climbing history, even though a modern-day rank amateur would find the gear laughably inadequate. Peck reported that she wore "three suits of lightweight woolen underwear, two pairs of tights, canvas knickerbockers, two flannel waists [i.e., vests], a little cardigan jacket, two sweaters, and four pairs of woolen stockings." For the first time, she wore a woolen ski mask, having worn no face protection of any sort on her previous climbs and suffering badly from sunburn and blistered skin. The expedition departed on August 28. The new stove Annie had purchased was nearly lost on the second day, when one of the guides carrying it slipped into a glacial crevasse but was pulled out as the stove clattered deeper into the chasm. With the stove retrieved after a treacherous descent on a rope by Peck's one remaining Swiss guide, the party soldiered on until they had climbed to within a few hundred feet of the north peak by the third day. Stopping to take measurements and gather her energy for the final attempt, Peck was outraged to find that one of the guides had slipped away and climbed alone to the summit, stealing the distinction from her. Still, after six tries, she finally stepped onto the 40-foot-wide summit of Peru's highest mountain and accomplished the goal she had set for herself so long before.

"My recollection of the descent is as of a horrible nightmare," Peck wrote some months later in a book about her accomplishment, for the party did not reach the mountain's summit until late afternoon and was forced to make their descent to the nearest camp on the ridge between Huascaràn's two peaks by weak moonlight. She slipped at least six times, sliding perilously close to the edge of the glacier and oblivion before being checked by her guide rope and hauled back; and for the first time in her climbing career, Peck said, she felt terror. "Several times I declared that we should never get down alive," she recalled. A bitterly cold 48 hours huddled in a flapping tent followed, for the party was too tired to continue and the alcohol to light their stove could not be found. Worse, the guide who had sneaked to the peak ahead of Annie was now severely frostbitten after refusing to wear the extra layers of socks and shirts she had provided and was barely able to walk. After five days on the mountain, nearly two days of which had been without fire or water, the party finally reached Yungay and the news was telegraphed to the world that Annie Smith Peck had become the first person (the rebellious guide notwithstanding) to reach the summit of Peru's mighty Mount Huascaràn.

Peck's triumph was soon tarnished by a challenge to the estimate of Huascaràn's height on which her claims of having reached the highest altitude of any human being were based. (Mount Everest would not be conquered by Sir Edmund Hillary for another four decades.) Huascaràn, she had estimated based on readings she had taken the day before she had attained the summit, stood at some 24,000 feet; but her claim was immediately challenged by ***Fanny Bullock Workman**, a wealthy socialite who, with her husband, had been climbing peaks in the Himalayas while Peck was exploring the Andes. So incensed were the Workmans that they spent $13,000 to send a team of surveyors to Yungay to determine the exact height of Huascaràn's north peak, which they set at 21,812 feet. "She has not the honor of breaking the world's record," groused Workman in an article published in *Scientific American*, "for my two ascents of respectively 22,568 and 23,300 debar her from that honor in the case of women, while a number of men have made ascents exceeding her highest." Peck retorted that she had never meant her estimate to be taken as an accurate measurement and pointed out that while the Workmans could afford to spend $13,000 to send a surveying team to South America, she had been forced to make do with less than half that sum to actually climb the mountain. Besides, she pointed out, even if the Workmans' figure were correct (and it was close to the figure accepted today), she was still the first person, man or woman, to climb to the summit of Peru's highest and most formidable peak.

Peck published in 1911 her description of her feat, although the Workmans' continued gibes about her claims meant it took Annie two years to find a publisher. Her financial situation grew so precarious that she was obliged to write to her friend Robert E. Peary, who had led his famous expedition to the North Pole, for a loan. "I thought when I had climbed my mountain my troubles would be over," she wrote to him, "never dreaming that fate could pay you such a shabby trick." Still, Peck was now a world celebrity as she entered her sixth decade. She continued her love affair with South America by lecturing extensively there on her experiences, and took advantage of a climb up Peru's second-highest peak, Nevado Coropuna, to plant a "Votes For Women" flag on its summit and have a photograph of it distributed throughout the United States. She delivered her lectures in Spanish in Lima, Buenos Aires, Montevideo and other South American cities; and by 1911 she had traveled so extensively on the continent that she was able to publish her own guide book, illustrated with her own photographs, of a tour from Panama to Tierra del Fuego. In 1922, her intimate knowledge of Latin America was put to good use in producing an economic survey which became required reading for the Pan-American Union, formed to foster economic ties between North and South America.

She went where a chipmunk wouldn't go!

—A mountaineering guide

In the late 1920s, as she approached 80 years of age, Peck discovered a new passion in the nascent aviation industry. She met in New York with Wilbur Wright who, with his brother Orville, had achieved the first free flight at Kitty Hawk, North Carolina, in 1903, just as Peck was preparing for her first climb of Huascaràn; and she hoped that her success in Peru might even tempt Charles Lindbergh to offer her a ride aloft. "Had he been aware I had climbed higher on my two feet than he in his airplane, perhaps he would have asked me," Peck said after no such invitation was forthcoming. But when air service from Panama to several South American cities was inaugurated in early 1929, she finally took to the air. Peck determined to tour South America by air and did so during 1930, visiting every country except Venezuela and covering some 20,000 miles in seven months.

But even Annie Smith Peck had to admit that her age was beginning to tell. The air tour would have been exhausting for anyone, but when she collapsed just before attending a dinner in her honor in New York in November 1930, she admitted that it was due to "ten years' overwork." She recovered quickly enough, and felt well enough to continue climbing small mountains in New Hampshire during her early 80s. In 1934, after celebrating her 84th birthday, she embarked on what was to have been a 75-city lecture tour through Europe, but she returned to New York after fainting while attempting to climb the Acropolis in Athens, the tour's first stop. Again, she seemed to revive; but after a short illness in the early summer of 1935, Annie Smith Peck died peacefully in her Manhattan apartment.

Opinions of Peck's actual expertise as a mountain climber vary, some pointing to a penchant for under-provisioning and poor choices for guides that sometimes led to lamentable results, while others stress that the fact a woman of her time even dared to set foot on a mountain mostly under her own power is credit enough. But there is no dispute over Peck's remarkable accomplishment in setting herself a formidable goal and reaching it, no matter how long or difficult the journey. Another single-minded woman, ***Amelia Earhart**, recognized a kindred spirit when the two met in the early 1930s. "Miss Peck," observed Earhart, "would make almost anyone appear soft."

SOURCES:

Olds, Elizabeth Fagg. *Women of the Four Winds.* NY: Houghton Mifflin, 1985.

Peck, Annie Smith. *A Search for the Apex of America.* NY: Dodd Mead, 1911.

Norman Powers,
writer-producer, Chelsea Lane Productions, New York, New York

Peck, Ellen (1829–1915)

American con artist. *Born Ellen Crosby, and known as Nellie, in 1829 in Woodville, New Hampshire; died in 1915.*

A con artist who used her wiles to swindle a series of lovers out of at least one million dollars in the late 19th and early 20th centuries, Ellen Peck earned a reputation as the "Queen of Confidence Women," an accolade all the more astonishing in light of her late start in criminal activities. Born in 1829 in Woodville, New Hampshire, Peck left her family and moved to New York City at the age of 51. There she ingratiated herself to elderly soap tycoon B.T. Babbit. After becoming his mistress, she robbed him of $10,000 in negotiable bonds, selling them and pocketing the proceeds. When her lover thought that he might have misplaced the bonds, Peck offered her assistance in locating them; he paid her a fee of $5,000, and she disappeared.

Babbit realized that he had been taken and summoned the authorities, who located Peck and arrested her four years later. At age 55, she was sentenced to four years' imprisonment. Upon her release from custody in 1888, Peck went back to her old ways, and after promising to marry a doctor named Marks she conned him out of $20,000 and left him at the altar. Police later caught up with Peck for this swindle, but not before she managed to steal an unknown but substantial sum from robber baron Jay Gould, who was then in his 50s.

In 1894, posing as the wife of Swedish Navy Admiral Johann Carll Hansen, Peck took out fraudulent bank loans totaling more than $50,000. She then began a sexual relationship with Dr. Christopher Lott, a Brooklyn physician for whom she had started working. She stole $10,000 from Lott and physically debilitated him: the physician, who was in his 80s, was so badly hobbled by their sexual activities that he found it necessary to hire a nurse to take care of him. An apparently equal-opportunity thief, Peck then formed a romantic attachment with the nurse and stole the woman's life savings of $4,000.

Peck was arrested for the last time in 1913, after she swindled a married Latin-American businessman. At age 84, she had seduced the man in her cabin aboard a luxury cruise ship bound for Veracruz, and in exchange for her silence she demanded and received ownership of several coffee plantations in his possession. When she died two years later, she was said to be worth more than one million dollars, which she had hidden in banks throughout the United States.

SOURCES:

Nash, Robert Jay. *Look for the Woman.* NY: M. Evans, 1981.

Howard Gofstein,
freelance writer, Oak Park, Michigan

Pedersen, Helga (1911—)

Danish lawyer and politician. *Born in 1911.*

Appointed the first woman judge at the European Court of Human Rights in 1971, Helga Pedersen was formerly a member of the Danish Parliament from 1950 to 1971, during which she distinguished herself as an advocate of prison and penal reform and the advancement of women's legal status. Pedersen also served as a supreme court justice and was a delegate to UNESCO from 1949 to 1974. She is the recipient of the gold medal from the Association of World Peace Through Law.

Peebles, Florence (1874–1956)

American biologist and teacher. *Born in Pewee Valley, Kentucky, in 1874; died in Pasadena, California, in 1956; daughter of Thomas Peebles and Elizabeth (Cummins) Peebles; graduated from Girls' Latin School, Baltimore, Maryland; Woman's College of Baltimore (later Goucher College), B.A., 1895; Bryn Mawr College, Bryn Mawr, Pennsylvania, Ph.D., 1900; never married; no children.*

A creative research biologist and an influential teacher, Florence Peebles was born in 1874 in Pewee Valley, Kentucky, but received her secondary education at Girls' Latin School in Baltimore. After earning a B.A. from Woman's College of Baltimore (later Goucher College), she attended Bryn Mawr, studying biology under Thomas Hunt Morgan, with whom she shared an interest in regeneration. Between 1894 and 1924, she conducted research on marine specimens, working much of the time out of the Marine Biological Laboratory at Woods Hole, Massachusetts. She was awarded a Ph.D. from Bryn Mawr in 1900.

Peebles taught biology for 30 years, beginning in 1897 as a demonstrator in biology at Bryn Mawr, where she later became an associate professor. She also held teaching and administrative posts at Goucher College, Miss Wright's School (in Bryn Mawr, Pennsylvania), and the Sophie Newcomb College at Tulane University. Following her "retirement" from teaching in 1928, she established a bacteriology department at Chapman College in California, where she also served as professor of biology until 1942. Another retirement attempt was thwarted when she founded the biology laboratory at Lewis and Clark College in Portland, Oregon.

At the age of 80, after finally leaving teaching, Peebles established herself as an authority on gerontology ("Grandma and grandpa should be rehabilitated—not scrapped," she said). In 1946, she moved to Pasadena, California, where she was involved in many community activities, particularly as a counselor for the aged. Peebles suffered a stroke in August 1956, and, although confined to a convalescent home, she remained active and involved to the end of her life. She died in December 1956, leaving behind an unpublished autobiography.

SOURCES:

Ogilvie, Marilyn Bailey. *Women in Science.* Cambridge, MA: MIT Press, 1993.

Peel, Lady (1894–1989).

See Lillie, Beatrice.

Peeters, Clara (1594–after 1657)

Flemish painter of still lifes. *Baptized on May 15, 1594, in Antwerp, Belgium; died after 1657; daughter of Jan Peeters; married Hendrick Joossen, on May 31, 1639.*

Although art scholars have credited some 26 still lifes to Flemish painter Clara Peeters, only a few sketchy details about her life have come to light. The artist was baptized in Antwerp on May 15, 1594, and her father's name was Jan Peeters, although his occupation is not known. At age 45, she married Hendrick Joossen on May 31, 1639, and apparently had no children. Although a death certificate has not yet been located, Peeters died sometime after 1657, which is the latest date to appear on one of her paintings.

During her early career, Peeters specialized in breakfast or banquet pieces—tabletop arrangements of luxurious objects such as goblets, coins, flowers, and shells, and expensive food and drink. Her earliest signed work was painted in 1608, when she was just 14 or 15 years of age, and predates all known dated examples of Flemish still-life painting of its type. (According to **Ann Sutherland Harris** and **Linda Nochlin**, "fewer than ten pictures of flowers and fewer than five of food produced in the Netherlands can be securely dated before 1608, when Peeters painted her first recorded work. Thus she would appear to be one of the originators of the genre.") The technical skill and sophisticated composition of the four still-lifes that Peeters painted before age 17 have given rise to speculation concerning how she attained her skills. Many believe that she must have received some instruction, although there is no evidence that her father was a painter, or that she apprenticed through the Antwerp painters' guild. Harris and Nochlin suggest that Peeters may have been influenced by Osias Beert, who was painting in Antwerp as early as 1602, and whose signed works are close in type to hers, but there is no solid proof of a relationship between the two artists.

Peeters' paintings are a sensual feast for the eyes, attracting the viewer with a "virtuosic *trompe-l'oeil* illusionism," notes **Nancy Heller**. A particular characteristic of the artist's work is her use of reflected miniature self-portraits, which she painted, often many times over, on the surface of a wine glass or on the shiny metal shell of a vase or cup. This technique first appeared in her *Still Life* (1612), which is described in detail by **Germaine Greer** in *The Obstacle Race*:

> It shows three tall vessels, a pottery vase of anemones, hyacinths, tulips and a snakeshead lily, and two gilt cups with covers standing about a Chinese celadon bowl out of which hangs a golden chain. The natural beauty of the flowers is counterbalanced by a group of exotic shells. The composition is deceptively simple, for cunning asymmetries weave among the elegant verticals, creating a nervous vortex in their stillness. On the shiny bosses of the furthermost cup, Clara Peeters has carefully painted her

own reflection in miniature, six times, in the flare of light from a window.

Although flower painting was popular in Flanders and Holland during the 17th century, attracting both male and female artists, Peeters seldom painted flowers on their own, although she included arrangements of them in her still-lifes. One exception is *Flowers in a Glass Vase* (1615), which depicts a single small bouquet in a glass vase decorated with a strange mask and a small mouse nibbling at petals beside the vase. When compared to the more formal paintings of its type, Peeters' work is notable in its simplicity and natural effect.

Peeters seems to have changed her style after 1620, producing a group of paintings featuring everyday items such as large cheeses stacked one upon another, bowls holding bread and rolls, and stoneware jugs of wine and beer. These simpler works may have been intended to appeal to changing artistic tastes, as her earlier pictures had gone out of style. A work entitled *Still Life with Cheese, Bread, and Pretzels* (c. 1630), representative of this later style, is almost austere when compared to earlier paintings. "Her later works reject every obvious means of appeal to the spectator," write Harris and Nochlin. "The objects shown are intrinsically humble and relatively simple to paint. There are fewer of them than in the earlier works and the color scheme is even more restricted that in the works of Dutch contemporaries such as Claesz and Heda." However, despite the less spectacular quality of these later efforts, Harris and Nochlin contend that they are quite impressive enough to uphold the artist's overall reputation.

SOURCES:

Greer, Germaine. *The Obstacle Race*. NY: Farrar, Straus & Giroux, 1979.

Harris, Ann Sutherland, and Linda Nochlin. *Women Artists, 1550–1950*. CA: Los Angeles County Museum of Art, 1976.

Heller, Nancy G. *Women Artists*. NY: Abbeville Press, 1987.

Barbara Morgan,
Melrose, Massachusetts

Pegge, Catherine (fl. 1657).

See Gwynn, Nell for sidebar.

Peggy.

Variant of Margaret.

Pejacevic, Dora (1885–1923)

Croatian composer and violinist who is credited with founding modern Croatian chamber and orchestral music. *Name variations: Countess Dora Pejacevic or Pejacsevich. Born in Bucharest, Rumania, on September 10, 1885; died in Munich, Germany, on March 5, 1923.*

Dora Pejacevic's musical training was classical. In Zagreb, she studied violin with V. Huml, theory with C. Junek, and instrumentation with D. Kaiser. Later, she went to Dresden to study composition and violin with P. Sherwood and H. Petri and then to Munich where W. Courvoisier was her teacher. Most of her compositions, 49 of 58 completed works, are for the piano and were strongly influenced by Schumann, Brahms, Grieg, and Tchaikovsky. These include two Piano Sonatas, two Piano Quintets (the first one published in Dresden in 1909), two String Quartets, and Sonatas for both violin and cello. Pejacevic's orchestral works include an Overture, a Piano Concerto, a Concert Fantasy for Piano and Orchestra, and a Symphony (1916). Her compositions were performed more often abroad than in her own country, but she is now credited with founding modern Croatian chamber and concert music. Several of her compositions were recorded by the Jugoton recording company in Zagreb.

John Haag,
Athens, Georgia

Pelagia

Saint. Born in Antioch.

Like St. John Chrysostom, who delivered two sermons about her, St. Pelagia was from Antioch. Determined to remain a virgin, at age 15 she turned away the many who admired her beauty. When she was seized by the soldiers of a magistrate intent upon claiming her, she jumped off the roof of a house so as not to allow dishonor. Wrote Chrysostom:

> Behold this tender virgin, she knew only her own maiden bedchamber; suddenly soldiers burst into it and summoned her to the tribunal. . . . [I]t was a miracle that she could have answered them, found strength to look at them, to have open her mouth, to have breathed. There must have been something there stronger than human strength, something which came from God, for her to have kept so free and tranquil. . . . Pelagia thought of a ruse so unexpected and so wise that the soldiers were stunned. Calmly and gaily, feigning a change of mind, she asked them to let her withdraw a moment, just for long enough to put on the finery suited to a new bride. Not only had they no objection, but they declared they were pleased to be able to bring a girl nicely turned out to the judge. And she, walking with composure out of the room, ran up to the roof of the house and flung herself into space. . . . And

so it was that St. Pelagia removed her body from impure attack; thus she delivered her soul for its ascent to heaven; thus she rendered innocuous her mortal remains and abandoned them to an enemy.

St. Pelagia's festival was celebrated on October 8, a day also assigned in the Greek *synaxaria* to two other saints named Pelagia. One of these is the Cilician **Pelagia of Tarsus.** The other, from Antioch like the Pelagia of Chrysostom, was also known as Margarito. Her story has become legendary, and it was argued by Herman Usener in his *Legenden der heiligen Pelagia* that she was not a true personage but rather a Christian travesty of Aphrodite. A celebrated dancer and courtesan, she was converted by the bishop Nonnus. This Pelagia was baptized and disguised herself in the dress of a male penitent. She entered a grotto on the Mount of Olives. Following three years of penance, she died there.

Pelham, Mary Singleton Copley (c. 1710–1789)

Colonial shopkeeper who was the mother of artist John Singleton Copley. *Name variations: Mary Singleton Copley. Born Mary Singleton in Ireland, around 1710; died in Boston, Massachusetts, on April 29, 1789; one of three children of John Singleton and Jane (Bruffe) Singleton; married tobacconist Richard Copley (died c. 1741); married Peter Pelham (an engraver, portrait painter, and schoolmaster), on May 22, 1748 (died December 1751); children: (first marriage) John Singleton Copley (1738–1815, the artist); (second marriage) Henry Pelham.*

A Boston shopkeeper and mother of the celebrated American portrait painter John Singleton Copley, Mary Pelham was born in Ireland and immigrated to Boston with her first husband Richard Copley around 1738, just before or immediately following John's birth. In Boston, Copley opened a tobacco shop which Pelham took over after his death around 1741. In May 1748, she became the third wife of Peter Pelham, a mezzotint engraver, portrait painter, and schoolmaster who brought to the marriage five children from his previous marriages. The couple added another son of their own, Henry, in 1749. Pelham continued to work, moving her shop from Long Wharf to Lindel's Row, and, according to the *Boston News-Letter*, selling "the best Virginia Tobacco, cut, Pigtail and spun, of all sorts, by Wholesale, or Retail, at the cheapest Rates." In December 1751, Peter died, and Mary was once again a widow.

John Singleton Copley, who showed early signs of artistic talent, had benefited greatly from his mother's second marriage, having had at his disposal both Peter's expertise and his materials and books. In 1753, Copley exhibited his first paintings, as well as an unusual mezzotint. He went on to become an acclaimed colonial portraitist. In 1774, married and with a family of his own, Copley left Boston to study abroad. Mary would not see him again, although she rejoiced in his ensuing success: "Your fame, my dear son, is sounded by all who are lovers of the art you bid fair to excel in," she wrote to him in February 1788. "May God prosper and cause you to succeed in all your undertakings, and enroll your name among the first in your profession." Mary Pelham died in Boston the following year, age 79.

SOURCES:

James, Edward T., ed. *Notable American Women, 1607–1950.* Cambridge, MA: The Belknap Press of Harvard University Press, 1971.

Barbara Morgan,
Melrose, Massachusetts

Pelikan, Lillian (1892–1931).

See Leitzel, Lillian.

Pell, Anna Johnson (1883–1966).

See Wheeler, Anna Johnson Pell.

Pelletier, Madeleine (1874–1939)

French physician and the first woman in her nation admitted to an internship in psychiatry who became a highly controversial socialist journalist and "integral" feminist, a precursor of 1960s' feminists. *Pronunciation: MAD-LEH PELL-eh-tee-ay. Born Anne Pelletier (later adopted name Madeleine) in Paris, France, on May 18, 1874; died in the Perray-Vaucluse asylum near Paris on December 29, 1939, and was buried in the asylum's cemetery; daughter of Louis Pelletier (b. 1831) and Anne de Passavy (b. 1836); educated in a convent school, then by herself, and at the University of Paris Faculty of Medicine; never married; no children.*

Left school (1886); passed the baccalaureate examinations after intensive self-study (1896–97); studied and published in anthropology and medicine (1898–1906); admitted as a psychiatric intern (1903); failed examination to enter the state psychiatric service (1906); was active in freemasonry (1904–46); led Women's Solidarity (1906–12); founded and directed La Suffragiste *(1907–14); fined for breaking a window at a polling place (1908); wrote seven books on feminist and political topics (1908–14); was a member of the Socialist Party's Permanent Administrative Council (1909–11); ran for public offices (1910, 1912); was a member of the Communist Party (1920–26); went to Moscow to view the Russian Communist regime (1921); was a leading advocate of birth control (1920s–1930s); published two autobiographical novels (1932–33); was investigated as a possible abortionist (1933); published* La Rationalisation sexuelle *and participated in the Poldës pornography trial (1935); suffered a stroke (1937); arrested for directing an abortion and committed to an asylum (1939).*

Principal writings—all published in Paris unless otherwise noted: (medical thesis) L'Association des idées dans la manie aiguë et dans la débilité mentale *(J. Rousset, 1903);* La Femme en lutte pour ses droits *(Giard et Brière, 1908);* Ideologie d'hier: Dieu, la morale, la patrie *(Giard et Brière, 1910);* L'Emancipation sexuelle de la Femme *(Giard et Brière, 1911);* Philosophie sociale: les opinions, les partis, les classes *(Giard et Brière, 1912);* Justice sociale? *(Giard et Brière, 1913);* Le Droit à l'avortement *(Librairie internationale d'édition scientifique, 1913);* L'Éducation féministe des filles *(Giard et Brière, 1914);* In anima vila, ou un crime scientifique: Pièce en trois actes *(Conflans-Ste.-Honorine: A. Lorulot, 1920);* Mon voyage aventureux en Russie communiste *(Giard, 1922);* Supérieur! Drame des classes sociales en cinq actes *(Conflans-Ste.-Honorine: A. Lorulot, 1923);* L'Amour et la maternité *(La Brochure mensuelle, 1923);* Trois Contes *(L. Beresniak, n.d.);* Capitalisme et communisme *(Nice: Imprimerie de Rosenstiel, 1926);* Une Vie nouvelle: roman *(Figuière, 1932);* La Femme vierge: roman *(Bresle, 1933);* La Rationalisation sexuelle *(Éditions du Sphinx, 1935).*

When Madeleine Pelletier died alone in an asylum in 1939, she was well on her way to total obscurity. In the decades before and after World War I, she had been one of the most visible and by all odds most controversial advocates of women's rights. But beginning in the 1970s, when the women's movement underwent skyrocketing growth, she was rediscovered because, well before ***Simone de Beauvoir**, Pelletier had proclaimed that, in Beauvoir's words, "women are not born but made," i.e., that gender roles are mostly determined not by biology but by society. Unlike Beauvoir, however, Pelletier had been marginalized during her life because of her origins and highly unconventional behavior and was never admitted to the French intellectual establishment.

Madeleine (baptized Anne) Pelletier was born on May 18, 1874, in Paris and lived in a squalid two-room dwelling; her parents sold fruit and vegetables from the front room. Her father Louis Pelletier had emigrated from Champeaux (Deux-Sèvres) to Paris and become a cabdriver. When Madeleine was four, he was paralyzed by a stroke and ceased to work; he would die when she was in her teens. Her mother **Anne de Passavy**, born out of wedlock in Clermont-Ferrand (Puy-de-Dôme), was raised by peasants in Auvergne and then became a domestic in Paris, where she met and married Louis. They had a son, who left home when Madeleine was young, and possibly another daughter, who died in infancy. Madeleine later said her mother had suffered 11 miscarriages—an example (not lost on her daughter) of problems caused women by sex.

Madeleine's mother was much the dominant character, her father being a quiet, sensible, beleaguered man. Anne de Passavy, more intelligent than he, was a fanatical, outspoken Catholic and royalist, hence not a popular figure in an anticlerical, working-class neighborhood. She was also dirty and slovenly; the single room they shared stank of unemptied chamber pots, rotting garbage, and sweat. Unlike so many (mostly bourgeois-born) socialists with whom she later associated, Madeleine found nothing romantic about life in the slums, nor did she harbor any illusions about the character or intelligence of the working class. As for herself, from an early age she had ambitions. But when she once said in all innocence she'd like to be a great general some day, her mother tartly replied, "Women are not soldiers; they are nothing at all; they marry, cook, and raise their children." Tensions between mother and daughter mounted.

From ages six to twelve, Madeleine attended a convent school. She was unhappy there. She felt ashamed because her clothes were shabby and dirty, and the discipline only incited her to rebel. She left school and through her teens was at loose ends while living at home.

Her school leaving likely was connected with probably the most defining event of her life, namely, her first menstruation. Totally ignorant about such matters, she thought she was dying and received no help from her mother. Her father, in his dry, down-to-earth manner, explained the "facts of life." She found the whole business of menstruation, intercourse, and childbirth repulsive and was sickened to realize that she and her mother shared with all women what she considered a stern physical subjection to nature—one, moreover, not experienced by men. As **Felicia Gordon** has written, "To some extent her career can be interpreted as unraveling the consequences of her rejection of the female experience as she saw it played out in her mother's life."

While a teen, Pelletier changed her name from Anne (her mother's) to Madeleine and began to wear some male attire; the previous example of *George Sand notwithstanding, this was regarded as shocking. Still, she resembled her mother in believing strongly in justice and the coming of a better world, if from human effort and not from heaven, and she had her mother's stubbornness in the face of criticism and unpopularity. Pelletier later gave few details regarding her teenage years beyond saying that she often attended meetings of feminist and anarchist groups. Chief among the former was one led by **Astié de Valsayre**, who had once fought a duel with an Englishwoman. As for the anarchists, she would associate with them all her life but never adopted their view that a stateless society was a practical possibility. What attracted her was their passion for liberty. She met and admired the aging anarchist icon ***Louise Michel** ("The Red Virgin of Revolution"), though she distrusted her revolutionary mysticism. Michel advised Pelletier that feminism was too confining, that she must get into (socialist) politics. Pelletier began to realize that she needed to find means to support herself if she were to have any chance to further the causes of liberty and women's rights. She decided to resume her education.

She did so not by returning to school but by teaching herself, a daunting enterprise given the challenges of the baccalaureate examinations required for admission to a university. Women were allowed to take the "bacs" but were offered no formal preparation and thus needed tutors. Penniless (and a burden to her mother), Pelletier studied on her own. She passed the exams in July 1896 and July 1897, and, after a year gaining a required certificate in physics, chemistry, and natural science, she enrolled in 1898 at the Faculty of Medicine of the University of Paris. (As of 1900, the Faculty had 3,746 men and 179 women students, of whom 380 and 98 respectively were foreigners.) Meanwhile, at some point her mother died. Charles Letourneau (1831–1902), a distinguished anthropologist whom Pelletier had met while auditing his lectures, supplied the critical help she needed to win scholarships. In December 1902, she applied for an internship in psychiatry, a specialty closed to women because they lacked political rights—a transparent excuse protecting a male enclave. She showed up for the entrance exam anyway and, of course, was denied. At Pelletier's instigation, ***Marguerite Durand**'s all-female *La Fronde* and other papers launched a campaign. The embarrassed authorities finally relented, and on December 3, 1903, she (and one **Constance Pascal**) sat for the exam and was admitted.

Until 1906, Pelletier served at various asylums. Harassment from doctors and patients made it a trying passage. Again she faced a roadblock when she was (as a woman) denied admission to the final examination required to obtain a permanent post in the state system. A month before the March 19 exam, however, she was suddenly granted permission. Very active now in freemasonry, socialism, and feminism, and lacking sufficient time to prepare, she narrowly failed the exam. It was probably the cruelest blow of her life. (For unknown reasons she was denied a second chance, assuming she applied for one.) She was thus excluded from the scientific elite and the research opportunities she craved. Lacking the necessary connections, she was now on her own as a general practitioner in poor neighborhoods. Her only anchor was certification as a physician for the postal department, which had many female employees.

As noted, Pelletier had led a crowded life while studying medicine. In truth, anthropology, not medicine, was her greatest love. Since the medical and anthropology faculties had close ties, she attended anthropology lectures and even co-authored four notable articles in anthropology. Her chosen field, psychiatry, in which she wrote four articles and her thesis (1903), was then a testing ground for sociological, anthropological, and evolutionary theories. Though Pelletier wanted to become a professional anthropologist, the Société d'Anthropologie had only 10 women among its 550 members. What chance did she have for a post in such a milieu? Virtually none, she was frankly told. So she stayed with medicine.

Her studies in anthropology nevertheless profoundly influenced her thought on social and feminist issues. Letourneau, in particular, led her to view society, like nature itself, as evolving toward liberty. To Pelletier, this all but proved that the emancipation of women was inevitable. Evolutionary theory permeated her writings. Influenced, too, by the theory of Jean-Baptiste Lamarck (1744–1829) that acquired characteristics can be inherited, she viewed much of behavior as a product of social influences acting over long periods of time. Her articles in craniometrics (currently involved in a soon-to-be discredited theory that skull and other body measurements are indicators of intelligence) led her toward a view that women, despite their smaller brains, might be more "evolved" than men. Yet it is striking that, unlike some feminists, she never claimed a superiority for women over men, nor did she idealize them; the two sexes simply were equal, no more, no less.

On the other hand, she wrote in 1904, "There is no need to conceal the fact that our civilization . . . is the achievement of a restricted elite." This idea remained with her for life. She craved recognition as a member of that elite, and, due to her success against huge odds in the demanding French educational system, she believed she had earned it. Freemasonry attracted her precisely because it comprised a powerful elite dedicated to her fundamental ideals of "republicanism, progressivism, materialism, anticlericalism, and social justice." She wanted to open the order fully to women; mixed lodges were at best merely tolerated. In April 1904, she joined a mixed lodge of the Human Rights branch of the Grand Symbolic Scottish Rite, founded by ***Maria Deraismes** and Georges Martin, and proudly brought Louise Michel in with her. Pelletier was intensely active, spoke frequently in lodge meetings on feminist and socialist themes, and surprisingly soon was named assistant secretary-treasurer of the board of freemasonry's weekly *Bulletin.* In her zeal to make mixed lodges the rule, however, she changed lodges, alienated male and female supporters, quarreled with powerful members, and once threatened one with a revolver she had begun to carry. Rather disillusioned after 1906, she poured her energies into feminist and socialist activities, but for the rest of her life she attended freemason meetings and encouraged women to join in order to open previously closed venues and to gain experience in public debate.

From 1904 to 1914, Pelletier worked ceaselessly promoting feminism and socialism. She was much in the public eye as a radical and eccentric figure in these movements, and her meager medical practice left her plenty of time for them. From early 1906 until it faded out around 1911–12, she headed Women's Solidarity (La Solidarité des Femmes), a "radical" feminist organization with socialist leanings. ***Eugénie Potonié-Pierre** (1844–1898) and **Marie Martin** had founded it in 1891, and from 1898 to 1906 **Caroline Kauffmann** (d. 1926) ran it until she asked Pelletier to take over. Bored, isolated, and depressed, she accepted. She later described it as composed of "30-odd women all talking at once." Pelletier wanted to start a mass women's movement such as the ***Pankhursts** had built in England. But she and the members of Women's Solidarity never fully understood each other. Her working-class expressions and gestures, her male attire, and her coolly analytical approach ("masculine" rather than emotional, sensitive, "feminine") put off these bourgeois women, almost none of whom wanted anything truly radical in ends or means. In Pelletier's opinion, "What they wanted above all was to pass their time pleasantly." The divisions in the women's movement (some two dozen major groups) and internal quarrels—"Every feminist has her own private feminism," she moaned—frustrated her intention, as did the Catholic-grounded conservatism of the masses of French women.

In the political realm, Pelletier put primary emphasis on obtaining the vote, with emancipation coming ultimately via legislation; without the ballot, women had neither political power nor status as full adults. Pelletier led or joined in a number of public actions designed to draw attention to the suffrage issue. Briefly, on March 18, 1906, she and ***Hubertine Auclert** led a march and rally at the Musée Social, and Solidarity put up posters in that election year despite some physical intimidation. On June 3, Pelletier and Kauffmann caused a stir when they showered the Chamber of Deputies with leaflets from the visitors' gallery, but the government prudently declined to prosecute them. And on December 24, they led a delegation to the Chamber to ask the Socialist leader Jean Jaurès for support. They marched again on June 17, 1907, and revisited Jaurès, who had done little. Then, on May 3 during the municipal elections of 1908, Auclert overturned a ballot box. Pelletier had gone home, but the press portrayed her as having been present. A week later (May 10), Pelletier led around ten Solidarity members who promised to break windows at a poll if they were not admitted. When they were refused, Pelletier threw a stone and shattered a window. She was fined 16 francs, but the real damage was done among her fellow feminists, who regarded such behavior as outrageous.

In fact, Auclert's and Pelletier's were the only violent acts of the whole French suffragist movement—in sharp contrast to events in England. One understands the envy Pelletier felt when on June 21 she watched hundreds of thousands of "suffragettes" rally at Hyde Park. The French rallies in 1906–07 had attracted fewer than a hundred marchers. After the summer of 1908, Pelletier's suffragist influence faded. In March 1914, while the English movement was climaxing in violence and excited rallies, she helped organize a demonstration. It was a fiasco, with around 50 demonstrators and 200 "Sunday strollers" attending. Pelletier had totally failed to gain a large following: "My adherents and I are like day and night," she admitted. Order and prudence, the watchwords of the French feminists, had prevailed—that and male prejudice, plus fears that votes for women would revive the Catholic-conservative threat to the republic.

Despite her setbacks in the suffragist cause, Pelletier pressed her feminist views on a host of subjects in pamphlets, brochures, books, and her monthly magazine, *La Suffragiste,* which appeared irregularly from December 1907 until 1914. It was heavily subsidized by Madame Remember (**Louise Beverley Dupont**, 1845–1925), who fiercely loathed all men (which Pelletier did not), and whom Pelletier had to humor by publishing her diatribes. In her writings, Pelletier proposed a radical agenda of "integral feminism." Its goals included suppression of all laws subordinating one sex to another; admission of women to all schools, occupations, and political positions; and—going beyond nearly all feminists anywhere—a total emancipation of women's private lives, i.e., full control over their own bodies, and the same right as men to sexual pleasure. As she wrote in 1912, "Feminism can never go too far" in its demand for equality.

Fundamentally, writes **Christine Bard**, Pelletier wanted to create "a world free of the bipolarity of the genders," because only in such a world would true equality be possible. The masculine should be the norm since it is men who have the power: "As long as . . . women continue to remain women, feminism will only be a vain word." A woman "should not be a woman in the way the world expects." Pelletier was struck by the paradox that women wanted men to shelter them yet also wanted equality with them. A woman must learn to make her own way and be economically independent, otherwise she becomes sexually enslaved by using her talent, youth, and beauty trying to catch a man. She must "virilize" herself, for "it is necessary to be men socially." To this end, because femininity is mostly the result of social conditioning, not biology, and because women, mother to daughter, tend to collaborate in their own oppression, girls' education should emphasize such things as assertiveness training (as it would later be called), tolerance of pain, and the use of weapons. Girls should be clothed like boys and given feminized forms of men's names (e.g., Renée for René). In short, she would not feminize girls' education but masculinize girls—not as an end, however, but as a means to achieve sexual equality.

Pelletier's behavior and her views on various women's issues confirmed her adherence to these basic tenets. She drew much attention because she sometimes dressed partly or entirely in men's clothing. Dress reform was needed, she believed, to change women's attitudes. She noted the power of uniforms as reflections of mentalities. Conventional women's clothing advertized women's powerlessness and their enslavement to male sexual desires. Dressed as a man, she said she was proclaiming "I am your equal." She despised "feminine" feminists, like Marguerite Durand, and hated décolletage; she would "show off mine when men adopt a special kind of trouser showing off their ——." In practical terms, she found that male attire gained her liberty and security in the street, although she also admitted, "I am short and fat, I have to disguise my voice and walk quickly in order not to be discovered."

> I remain a feminist. I will remain one until my death even though I don't like women as they are now any more than I like the working class as it is. Slave mentalities revolt me.
>
> **—Madeleine Pelletier**

Naturally, questions arose as to her sexuality. Was she a lesbian? She denied it, writing to her feminist friend Arria Ly (**Josephine Gondon**, 1881–1934) that the "voyage to Lesbos tempts me no more than the voyage to Cythera" (Aphrodite's birthplace). If she had been a lesbian, she surely would have defended it—which she did not. She said she regarded lesbianism as an abnormality which ought to be tolerated but which would disappear when total sexual equality is achieved. Nor was she heterosexual. Men neither attracted nor repelled her sexually. Her personal disgust for sexuality, doubtless stemming from her childhood, alienated her from all forms of it. Objectively, she regarded sexual intercourse as "a physiological function like nutrition or breathing." For herself, she adopted virginity: "I have not wished to educate my genital senses." This choice was a political statement, she maintained. Unlike Ly, she did not advocate virginity as the norm for all women. It was only that in society as it is, sexual relations are exploitive, so she was refusing to take part in the oppression.

As regards motherhood and the family, Pelletier's views were "scarred," writes Gordon, by her own family life. Going beyond almost every feminist of her time, she would abolish the "patriarchal" family altogether and replace it with free unions, with children to be cared for by the state. She was not hostile to motherhood but wanted it to be a free choice, an "episode" in a woman's life, not its raison d'être. She deplored the prejudice against unwed mothers. Unlike most feminists, she would deal with the double standard not by repressing males but by giving females the same liberty in sex as in all other matters. Like other feminists, however, she also believed feminists had to be careful about violating society's sexual mores lest they harm the cause. She was very critical of *Marie Curie, for example, when the widowed Curie's love affair with an unhappily married colleague Paul Langevin became fodder for the newspapers (1910–11).

Two other issues bear special mention: prostitution and abortion. Pelletier was nearly alone in discussing prostitution without raising moral questions. She remarked wryly that it marked a progress in civilization when men got the idea of paying a woman instead of simply forcing her. Anyhow, until they received full rights and equality, married women were in effect prostitutes. She opposed prostitution per se, although she excused it in the case of poor women; for "enlightened" women it was unacceptable. The answer lay not in state regulation (as in France) but in economic independence for women.

Her views on abortion—which, like providing contraceptive information, was illegal (if loosely enforced) in France—drew more attention than almost anything else she said or did and (as will be seen) led to her ultimate tragedy. She never admitted performing abortions, but the presumption is strong that she did. Physicians and mainstream feminists opposed abortion; she was the first female physician in France to call for a right to abortion: "Our right to control over our bodies is absolute." She admitted abortion rights would increase "dissoluteness," but she regarded that as preferable to infanticide (a real crime in her eyes) and the enslavement of women to pregnancy. Despite sweeping statements, however, she believed abortions should be limited to the first trimester; if a woman can't make up her mind by then, she deserves no consideration.

Pelletier was very ambitious to play a role, and what better stage than politics? From 1906 to 1912, she became the most prominent woman in the Unified Socialist Party (SFIO), the only one serving (1909–11) on its Permanent Administrative Council. She chose the Socialist Party because it alone was formally opened to women and because of her beliefs. Even though disillusioned (as with the masons) and ceasing regular party activity after 1912, she remained a socialist by conviction: "If I am a socialist it is because I passionately love justice." Marxism per se held no special appeal for her: "All I know is that I am in favor of social justice . . . the abolition of inheritance, free education at every stage, generous subsidies for children, old people and the ill, no more class distinctions, no more worship of money. Intelligence and work should be the only means to success."

Her rise was remarkably swift. She made her mark in debates at the annual party congresses and the international congress at Stuttgart (1907), mainly trying to win a support for women's suffrage going beyond fine words. She first joined the Guesdiste (orthodox Marxist) faction but, finding it too stodgy, in July 1907 she joined Gustave Hervé's revolutionary, anti-militarist faction and became in effect its second-in-command. Her provocative behavior (including slapping a critic) aroused dissention, however, and in June 1911 she denounced Hervé as a false revolutionary. (She was perceptive: he went over to rabid nationalism during the war.) Pelletier drifted even further leftward, to the anarchists, although she still rejected their belief in a stateless society and found them no more friendly to women's issues than the Socialists had been. The Socialists would be "the last to take our ideas seriously," she wrote in disgust, and the working class "will be the last to come to feminism. It is in the nature of things, the ignorant respect only force."

Pelletier's foray into politics proved a failure. Yet some of her analyses remain valuable for an understanding of revolutionaries and women in politics. Ignoring simplistic explanations like "betrayal," she framed a psycho-social analysis of the operation of co-optation (as it would be termed now), why the revolutionary fervor of socialist politicians fades the higher they advance. And she was especially cogent in describing why women felt intimidated in the political parties and why at the grassroots level parties ignored women's issues. She concluded that parties needed to form women's sections. Yet, while she took the initiative in getting such organizations approved at the international and national levels, she did nothing to implement the resolutions. Why? Because she was jealous of other female leaders? Because she suspected the women's sections would become "kindergartens," as she put it? Because she raised her self-esteem by participating in the (powerful) male environment? There is no clear answer.

Twice she ran for office—symbolically, of course: for the Chamber in 1910 and for the Paris municipal council in 1912. She obtained 340 of 8,698 votes in 1910 and 306 of 3,610 in 1912, very creditable showings under the circumstances. These races, however, underscored a basic conflict between her socialist and feminist activities. Revolutionary socialism—she sometimes even advocated terrorist deeds—held that only revolution would bring a just society by abolishing classes, and hence elections and parliaments were irrelevant. As a feminist, however, she believed "equality between the sexes can well be realized in present society," that by granting the vote the state would pave the way for creation of a feminine elite "which will in turn bring about a transformation of mentalities." Obtaining the suffrage, while "perhaps an illusory goal," was "a stage women must pass through to free themselves." She never satisfactorily resolved this conflict.

By the eve of the First World War (1914–18), Pelletier was depressed by personal and financial woes. She had written seven books (1908–14) and frequent articles for *L'Humanité, La Guerre sociale, Équité, Le Libertaire* (1914, 1919–21), *L'Idée libre* (1912–24), and her own *La Suffragiste* (to 1914), but success had eluded her. She adopted two small girls, probably for company; the police (who kept her under surveillance) suspected a morals case in the making. She became a full-time temporary doctor for the postal service in 1912; run-ins with the administration (e.g., absences without leave) resulted in her relegation to part-time status in 1916. (She was fired in 1928.) To her credit, she battled her depression by earning a *license ès sciences* in chemistry during the war.

When the war came, she tried to become the first female army doctor but was denied. She worked briefly with the Red Cross in 1914—and was rescued from a mob in Nancy which, from her appearance, thought she was a spy. She also advocated drafting women to prove there was no difference in bravery between males and females; she herself visited the Marne fields alone only days after the battle. The war appalled her. Although she attended socialist and pacifist meetings and contributed to a feminist pacifist weekly, *La Voix des Femmes* (1917–23), she prudently avoided open war resistance. She kept a remarkable war diary (Aug. 25, 1914–Sept. 27, 1918) in which she recorded her alarm at the growth of irrationality and non-scientific belief systems and her disgust over the chauvinism of many feminists and socialists and the willingness of the workers to fight their brothers: "At bottom these people have got what they deserve; humanity is stupid."

The war over, she ardently defended the Russian Revolution in her revived *La Suffragiste* (1919), which printers' costs soon forced her to close. Back in politics, as a delegate to the Socialist Party congress at Tours in 1920, she joined the Communist schismatics. Frustrated because the Communist Party leaders distrusted her enough not to name her a delegate to a congress in Moscow, in May 1921 she set off for Moscow alone, intending to settle there. It took her six weeks, traveling alone *sans* passport and relying on the left-wing underground to get through. She returned in late autumn after realizing she missed the comforts and freedoms of Paris too much. Unlike many other pilgrims from the West, she kept her critical senses intact. The appalling degradation and fatalism of the masses, the suffocating bureaucracy, and especially the police terror cooled her ardor for this revolution. As for feminism, women had equality on paper but not much in reality. She asserted the revolution had brought "enlightenment" to thousands, and she expressed confidence that things would work out. Communism was still better than capitalism in the long run. A revolutionary elite would clean up ("degrease") the people, whom she dubbed "the amorphous dough good only to take the shape that a small number of intelligent and daring people wish to give it." All in all, the experience was sobering. A decade later, she admitted, "In theory I am a revolutionary, in practice I only kill the lice that my patients make me a present of from time to time."

Pelletier stayed in the Communist Party until 1926. Only with the Communists, for example, could fascism be defeated. But her libertarian anarchist side won out over her belief in authoritarian revolutionary government. Party discipline was not for her. Besides, the Communists were proving no more likely to get votes for women than were any others. The Senate's defeat of a suffrage bill in 1922 was a bitter blow. After the mid-1920s, Pelletier mostly worked outside the parties. In 1932, she joined Paul Louis' tiny Party of Proletarian Unity (PUP) and, surprisingly, accepted election as secretary of the women's commission—perhaps because it included some men. She also was on the executive committee of an organization of left-wing pacifists founded by the Communist Party, and in 1933 she joined the "integral" pacifist organization Mundia. But none of her political posts preoccupied her. Nor did her place on the executive committee of the sizeable antifascist-pacifist Movement Against Imperialist War (Amsterdam-Pleyel), animated by Henri Barbusse and Romain Rolland. She attended its congresses in 1932 and 1933, where she defended the Soviet Union's cause, but she found them too dominated by Communists, especially Germans. After

Hitler came to power (1933), her pacifism faded and her antifascism became more pronounced.

Dearest to her heart was the feminist cause. As a leading light among the proponents of birth control ("neo-Malthusians"), she was a target of the strong "neo-natalist" movement in the 1920s and 1930s to raise France's population following the huge losses of the war. In 1929, she defended abortion at the London congress of the World League for Sexual Reform and continued her advocacy of it and other feminist concerns in books, articles, and meetings of the Club du Fourbourg, a well-attended public debate society. Her frank discussion of sexual topics there helped bring on the widely discussed prosecution in 1935 of Léo Poldës, the club's founder, for pornography. She defended him and her views at the trial. (He paid a small fine.) Two years before, the abortion issue had singed her personally when the police investigated her after a complaint that she was performing abortions, but she was not formally charged. The affair had frightened her into contemplating moving to Zagreb, Yugoslavia, where her friend Arria Ly lived.

Pelletier's medical practice bloomed enough that she was able to buy a car and a weekend retreat in the country at Gif-sur-Yvette, ten miles southwest of Paris. It was another place to write. In addition to her usual articles for left-wing and feminist publications like *La Voix des Femmes* (where she was especially important), *La Nouvelle Revue socialiste, L'Insurgé, Plus Loin, Le Semeur contre tous les Tyrans, L'Intransigeant, Les Vagabonds, Anarchie, Lueurs, La Rumeur,* and *L'Éveil de la Femme*, plus 15 articles for *L'Encyclopédie anarchiste,* she wrote *La Rationalisation sexuelle* (1935), a recasting of her *L'Emancepation sexuelle de la Femme* (1911) and *Le Droit à l'Avortement* (1913). Under Freud's influence, she became less concerned with legal reform and more with women's psychology, notably the role of masochism in explanations of why women resist liberation.

Perhaps because her views on contraception and sexual emancipation were in effect censored in the 1920s and 1930s, Pelletier turned to fiction, writing three short stories, two plays (unproduced), and two novels. Besides an unpublished autobiography, "Doctoresse Pelletier: Mémoires d'une féministe" (early 1930s) and a memoir dictated in her last months, "Anne dite Madeleine Pelletier," these writings contain extensive autobiographical details. Their leitmotif, writes Gordon, is that of a solitary, working-class intellectual frustrated by contemporary society and family alienation. *Une Vie nouvelle* (A New Life, 1932), even though the protagonist is a man, climaxes in a feminist-communist utopia following a revolution. The masses are governed by an authoritarian elite and pursue self-improving education; people live in hotels, preserving individuality and communal life but not the family; complete sexual freedom prevails, with children cared for by the state if the mother wishes; even the pope becomes a communist, and he has an organ transplant to live longer. The book illustrates her continuing attempt, unsuccessful, to reconcile individualism and collectivism. In *La Femme vierge* (The Virgin Woman, 1933), she imagines—at last—a truly powerful woman. She becomes a successful politician in Germany, where she is accidentally killed in a crossfire between revolutionaries and government forces.

Pelletier suffered a tragic end. Partly paralyzed by a stroke in late 1937, she, with her nurse and maid, was arrested for supervising an abortion on April 25, 1939. The case resulted from incest between a teenaged sister and brother. Suspiciously, the timing of the arrest coincided with a neo-natalist anti-abortion campaign. The judge ordered a mental examination; the psychiatrist reported she was "totally irresponsible." Accordingly, Pelletier—the first woman psychiatric intern in France—was committed on June 2 (May 27?) to the Perray-Vaucluse asylum at Épinay-sur-l'Orge, near Paris. Doubtless she was in bad health (stroke, arteriosclerosis, lung and eye problems) and exhibiting signs of failing judgment. But ill enough to warrant committal without the charge of abortion? There is strong reason to suspect the judge responded to political pressure to "put away" this scandalous woman to avoid a potentially messy trial.

"You can't imagine," she wrote to ***Hélène Brion**, "how terrible it is to be in an asylum when one has all one's mental faculties." A pacifist socialist friend, Brion was her only visitor, five times. Pelletier dictated to her some memoirs of her childhood, "Anne dite Madeleine Pelletier," which exhibit no mental impairment, but her health deteriorated. She died in the asylum, alone, on December 29, 1939, and was buried without ceremony in the asylum's cemetery.

Madeleine Pelletier was an anomaly: a feminist who identified with men and thought her sex was "the worst misfortune of my life." She sought to free women and the working class but identified with neither. If she failed to build a massive women's movement, she had in some measure herself to blame. ***Angelica Balabanoff**, a fellow revolutionary, remarked that it was too bad nature—she might have added a traumatic childhood—seemed to have deprived her of "a little kindness, of sympathy for those around her, a little trust [*confiance*]." Pelletier's misanthropy, superior airs, and acid tongue sooner or later alienated everyone around her; even Brion was more disciple than friend.

Despite—more likely because of—her peculiarities, Pelletier was an independent, original, unclassifiable thinker. In her own fashion, she became what she fought to make all women become: an independent creature not enslaved by her biology. She was probably the first to put an equal right to sexual pleasure into the context of political rights, as witnesses, for example, her stand on contraception and abortion. But beyond legal considerations, she helped mightily to shift the focus of debate from the political to the social and sexual origins of women's oppression. As one of the earliest inventors of the concept of social gender (or possibly *the* earliest), she argued convincingly that psychological sex is almost wholly a social, not biological, construct.

Virtually everything she attempted failed somehow. "Evidently I was born several centuries too early," she wrote. Well, a good 50 years, anyhow. Time brought reparation, for she has come to be ranked as one of the earliest and most important theorists of the 20th century's feminist movement.

SOURCES:

Bard, Christine. *Les Filles de Marianne: Histoire des féminismes 1914–1940.* Paris: Fayard, 1995.

———, dir. *Madeleine Pelletier: Logique et infortunes d'une combat pour l'égalité.* Paris: Côté-Femmes Éditions, 1992.

Biographical Dictionary of French Political Leaders since 1870. David S. Bell, Douglas Johnson, and Peter Morris, eds. NY: Simon & Schuster, 1990.

Dictionnaire biographique du mouvement ouvrier français. Jean Maitron, ed. Paris: Éditions ouvrières, 1964—.

Gordon, Felicia. *The Integral Feminist: Madeleine Pelletier, 1874–1939. Feminism, Socialism, and Medicine.* Minneapolis, MN: University of Minnesota Press, 1990.

Hause, Steven, with Anne Kenney. *Women's Suffrage and Social Politics in the French Third Republic.* Princeton, NJ: Princeton University Press, 1984.

Maignien, Claude, and Charles Sowerwine. *Madeleine Pelletier, une féministe dans l'arène politique.* Paris: Les Éditions ouvrières, 1992.

McMillan, James F. *Housewife or Harlot: The Place of Women in French Society, 1870–1940.* NY: St. Martin's Press, 1981.

Rabaut, Jean. *Histoire des feminismes français.* Paris: Éditions Stock, 1978.

Robertson, Priscilla Smith. *An Experience of Women: Pattern and Change in Nineteenth-Century Europe.* Philadelphia, PA: Temple University Press, 1982.

Scott, Joan Wallach. *Only Paradoxes to Offer: French Feminists and the Rights of Man.* Cambridge, MA: Harvard University Press, 1996.

Sowerwine, Charles. *Sisters or Citizens? Women and Socialism in France since 1876.* Cambridge: Cambridge University Press, 1982.

SUGGESTED READING:

Bock, Gisela, and Pat Thane, eds. *Maternity and Gender Policies: Women and the Rise of the European Welfare States, 1880–1950.* London: Routledge, 1991.

Boxer, Marilyn. "Socialism Faces Feminism in France: The Failure of Synthesis in France," in Marilyn J. Boxer and Jean H. Quataert, eds., *Socialist Women.* Boston, MA: Houghton Mifflin, 1978, pp. 75–111.

———. "When Radical and Socialist Feminism Were Joined: The Extraordinary Failure of Madeleine Pelletier," in Jane Slaughter and Peter Kern, eds., *European Women of the Left: Socialism, Feminism, and the Problem Faced by Political Women, 1880 to the Present.* Westport, CT: Greenwood Press, 1981, pp. 51–74.

Boyau, Rémy. *Histoire de la Fédération Française de l'Ordre Maçonnique Mixte International: Le Droit Humaine.* Paris: Fédération, 1976.

Hause, Steven, C. *Hubertine Auclert: The French Suffragette.* New Haven, CT: Yale University Press, 1987.

Klejman, Laurence, and Florence Rochefort. *L'Égalité en marche: Le Féminisme sous la Troisième République.* Paris: Presses de la Fondation nationale des sciences politiques/ Éditions des femmes, 1989.

Maitron, Jean. *Le Mouvement anarchiste en France.* 2 vols. 2nd ed. Paris: Maspero, 1975.

Mitchell, Claudine. "Madeleine Pelletier (1874–1939): The Politics of Sexual Oppression," in *Feminist Review.* No. 33, 1989, pp. 72–91.

Reynolds, Sian. *Alternative Politics: Women and Public Life in France between the Wars.* Stirling French Publications, no. 1. University of Stirling, 1993.

Roberts, Mary Louise. *Civilization without Sexes: Reconstructing Gender in Postwar France, 1917–1927.* Chicago, IL: University of Chicago Press, 1994.

Smith, Paul. *Feminism and the Third Republic.* Oxford: Clarendon Press, 1996.

Sonn, Richard D. *Anarchism and Cultural Politics in Fin-de-Siècle France.* Lincoln, NE: University of Nebraska Press, 1989.

Weisz, George. "Reform and Conflict in French Medical Education, 1870–1914," in Robert Fox and George Weisz, eds., *The Organization of Science and Technology in France, 1808–1914.* Cambridge: Cambridge University Press, 1984, pp. 61–94.

Wheelwright, Julie. *Amazons and Military Maids: Women Who Dressed as Men in the Pursuit of Life, Liberty, and Happiness.* London: Pandora Press, 1989.

Wright, Gordon. *France in Modern Times.* 5th ed. NY: W.W. Norton, 1995.

COLLECTIONS:

Paris: Archives nationales (Académie de Paris, Faculté de Medicine, Faculté des Sciences); Archives de Paris (Internat des asiles de l'Assistance publique); Bibliothèque historique de la Ville de Paris (Fonds Bouglé, Caroline Kauffmann, F. Buisson); Bibliothèque Marguerite Durand (Dossier Pelletier); Institut Français d'Histoire Sociale (Fonds Sowerwine).

David S. Newhall,
Pottinger Distinguished Professor of History Emeritus,
Centre College,
author of *Clemenceau: A Life at War* (1991)

Pels, Auguste van (1900–1945).

See Frank, Anne for sidebar.

Pember, Phoebe Yates (1823–1913)

Confederate hospital administrator. *Born Phoebe Yates Levy on August 18, 1823, in Charleston, South Carolina; died on March 4, 1913, in Pittsburgh, Pennsylvania; fourth of seven children of Jacob Clavius Levy (a businessman) and Fanny (Yates) Levy; married Thomas Pember (died July 1861); no children.*

Phoebe Pember was born in 1823 and grew up in Charleston, South Carolina, the fourth of seven children, all but one of them girls. Her father, whose family had immigrated to Charleston from Poland, was a successful businessman and an early advocate of Reformed Judaism. Her mother was English. Little is known about Pember's early life, although her letters and reminiscences indicate that she was well educated. Sometime during the late 1850s she married Thomas Pember of Boston, who died of tuberculosis in 1861. Pember returned to her parents' home and with the advent of the Civil War moved with them to Marietta, Georgia, where they resided with relatives.

Pember felt confined in the small house in Marietta, and when in 1882 she was offered the position of matron at Chimborazo, a large Confederate Army hospital near Richmond, she immediately accepted. In her new post, Pember was in charge of housekeeping and food service for 31 wards, and it is estimated that she and her staff cared for 15,000 soldiers during the course of the war. As the first woman administrator appointed at the military hospital, she encountered her share of opposition, although she refused to let it deter her. The doctors and stewards particularly objected to her control as matron over the dispensing of whiskey, and they did their best to undermine her authority when possible. Pember remained firmly in charge, however, often aided by a pistol, which she kept at the ready.

Even without detractors, Pember's job was overwhelming, and she was often short of staff. Her salary of $40 a month was so inadequate that she was forced to moonlight, writing articles for magazines and copy writing for the War Department after a full day in the wards. Stress and overwork began to take its toll, and in the summer of 1863 she fell ill. At the suggestion of the surgeon general, upon her recovery she took a room in the city, commuting to the hospital each morning in the ambulance dispatched for daily marketing. The change of residence afforded Pember the opportunity for some socialization, and her wit and charm, coupled with a "pretty, almost Creole accent," made her a welcome guest in Richmond society. She gradually lost her taste for the social whirl, however, finding it frivolous in light of the relentless war.

Pember remained at Chimborazo through its occupation by Union forces in April 1865, then returned to Georgia. In 1879, she published a wartime remembrance, *A Southern Woman's Story*, which, although lacking immediacy, provides a valuable account of the inner workings of a major Confederate hospital. A second edition of the book, edited by **Bell I. Wiley**, was published in 1959, and includes a biographical sketch of Pember and nine of her wartime letters. Phoebe Pember died in 1913, at age 90.

SOURCES:

Edgerly, Lois Stiles, ed. *Give Her This Day*. Gardiner, ME: Tilbury House, 1990.

James, Edward T., ed. *Notable American Women, 1607–1950*. Cambridge, MA: The Belknap Press of Harvard University Press, 1971.

Barbara Morgan,
Melrose, Massachusetts

Pembroke, countess of.

See Clare, Isabel de (c. 1174–1220).
See Bohun, Maud (fl. 1240s).
See Marjory (d. 1244).
See Marie de St. Pol (1304–1377).
See Mortimer, Agnes (fl. 1347).
See Manny, Anne (b. 1355).
See Herbert, Katherine (c. 1471–?).
See Grey, Catherine (c. 1540–1568).
See Parr, Anne (d. 1552).
See Herbert, Mary (1561–1621).
See Clifford, Anne (1590–1676).

Peña, Tonita (1893–1949)

First Pueblo woman watercolorist. *Name variations: Tonita Pena; Quah Ah (Little Bead or Pink Shell). Born Quah Ah on May 10, 1893, in the Tewa pueblo called San Ildefonso in what is now the state of New Mexico; baptized in the Catholic Church as Maria Antonia Peña; died in September 1949; third child and second daughter of Ascencion Vigil Peña and her husband Natividad Peña; attended San Ildefonso Day School and St. Catherine's, Santa Fe; married Juan Rosario Chavez, on March 2, 1908 (died May 17, 1912); married Felipe Herrera, on July 14, 1913 (died July 16, 1920); married Epitacio Arquero, on June 12, 1922; children: (first marriage) Helia Chavez (b. April 4, 1909); Richard Chavez (b. February 12, 1912); (second marriage): Hilario J. (b. May 17, 1920, be-*

came the noted artist Joseph H. Herrara); (third marriage) Maria Cyrella Arquero (b. February 22, 1923); Virginia Arquero (December 15, 1924–May 8, 1926); Margaretta Arquero (b. August 21, 1927); Sam Arquero (b. July 26, 1929); Victoria Arquero (b. March 4, 1935).

Using traditional Tewan motifs as the source of her paintings, Tonita Peña (born Quah Ah) was the only woman in a group of painters known as the "San Ildefonso Self-taught group." Though the assemblage included such significant artists as Julian Martinez (husband and collaborator of ***Maria Montoya Martinez**) and Alfonso Roybal, Peña was the first Pueblo woman easel painter and the first Puebloan to work in watercolor.

Born into a family of artists in 1893, in the Tewa pueblo called San Ildefonso in what is now the state of New Mexico, Peña began painting at an early age. Encouraged by her teachers, in particular, **Esther B. Hoyt** at the San Ildefonso Day School, Peña began to experiment with watercolors while still a child and may have sold her earliest works when she was as young as 16.

Anthropologist Edgar L. Hewett took an interest in Peña early on. It was Hewett who bought most of what she produced for the Art Museum in Santa Fe, where Peña's work was seen by another noted anthropologist, Dr. Kenneth Chapman. Aware that her style was developing in a unique way, Hewett supplied her with watercolors imported from England as well as quality art paper. These men would support and encourage Peña throughout her often tragic life.

Influenza had always been a particularly ferocious enemy of native tribes. In 1905, Peña had suffered the first of several losses to the disease when her mother and younger sister died. Unable to care for Peña, her father sent her to live in Cochiti, 50 miles away. Because in Cochiti the Puebloans speak Keres, a different dialect than the one she grew up speaking, Tonita had to learn a new language, new dances, and new songs. For the first few months, she stayed close to her aunt's side, taking comfort in her painting.

Peña first married just before her 15th birthday, but influenza would strike again, taking the life of her young husband. By age 19, she was a widow with two small children and an incomplete education. Leaving the children with her aunt, she returned to finish school while continuing to work as an artist.

In 1913, Peña married Felipe Herrera, a worker in the iron oxide mines. Herrera was extremely supportive of Tonita's painting and enabled her to finally complete her schooling. The couple had one son, Hilario J. (the noted artist Joseph H. Herrara), before Felipe was killed in a mining accident. When Peña was 29, she married Epitacio Arquero, a former mine worker turned farmer. The couple settled in Cochiti, where Arquero was eventually elected governor of the Pueblo. Peña and Arquero had six children, and they enjoyed a long, productive life together. As well, Peña's artistic life continued to flourish. Her watercolors were shown widely in museums and commercial art galleries. In 1931, at the American Indian Tribal Arts exhibition, her watercolor *Spring Dances* was labeled "best in show." When Tonita Peña died in 1949, she had probably influenced and advanced Pueblo painting more than any other artist, male or female, leading her to be nicknamed the Grand Old Lady of Pueblo Art.

SOURCES:

Dockstader, Frederick J. *Great North American Indians: Profiles in Life and Leadership.* NY: Van Nostrand Reinhold, 1977.

Gray, Samuel, ed. *Tonita Peña.* Albuquerque, NM: Avanyu Press, 1990.

Deborah Jones,
Studio City, California

Pendarves, Mary (1700–1788).

See Delany, Mary Granville.

Pendleton, Ellen Fitz (1864–1936)

American educator who was president of Wellesley College (1911–36). *Born Ellen Fitz Pendleton in Westerly, Rhode Island, on August 7, 1864; died in Newton, Massachusetts, on July 26, 1936; youngest of nine children of Enoch Burrows Pendleton (a merchant and postmaster) and Mary Ette (Chapman) Pendleton; graduated from Westerly High School; Wellesley College, Wellesley, Massachusetts, B.A., 1886, M.A., 1891; attended Newnham College, Cambridge, England, in 1889–90; never married; no children.*

The youngest of nine children of progressive, well-to-do parents, Ellen Pendleton was valedictorian of her high school graduating class in Westerly, Rhode Island, and graduated from Wellesley College in 1886. After receiving her undergraduate degree, she remained at the college as a temporary tutor, and in 1888 was appointed an instructor in mathematics. She spent the next year pursuing graduate study at Newnham College, in Cambridge, England, then returned to Wellesley where she was awarded an M.A. in 1891. Pendleton served variously as secretary of the college, head of College Hall, dean, and associate professor of mathematics before becoming acting president in 1910, during the illness of President *Caroline Hazard. After Hazard's resignation in 1911, Pendleton was elected president of the college, becoming the first alumna ever appointed to the post.

During her 25-year tenure at Wellesley, Pendleton oversaw a remarkable increase in the college's endowment, to nearly $10 million, as well as a complete rebuilding of the physical plant, most of which was destroyed by a fire in March 1914. Within three weeks of the blaze, Pendleton had temporary structures constructed to accommodate classes, and embarked on a $3 million capital campaign to rebuild. Within a decade, seven new brick structures had been constructed, and another eight were added before her retirement in 1936, in all comprising six dormitories, four apartment buildings for faculty, three academic buildings, an alumnae building, and an administration building.

In addressing academic issues, Pendleton called for the relaxation of the college's entrance requirements and instituted a broader curriculum, offering students honors courses, independent research, and a wider choice of electives, but she rejected vocational training or narrowly specialized courses. Although not an academic theorist, Pendleton was praised by colleagues for her practical approach. "No one knew better than she how things really worked," said Smith College President William Allan Neilson, "and this practical experience in the actual operation of the curriculum must have saved the College many mistakes and much futile experiment." Pendleton was also a strong believer in academic freedom; she unsuccessfully appealed the dismissal by the trustees of pacifist *Emily Greene Balch in 1918, and took an active role in opposing the 1935 Massachusetts legislation requiring all teachers to sign a loyalty oath.

Pendleton's educational interests reached far beyond her own institution. In 1917, she was elected president of the New England Association of Colleges and Secondary Schools. She also served as president of the College Entrance Examination Board, vice-president of Phi Beta Kappa, and vice-president of the Associated Boards for Christian Colleges in China. When the American Peace Prize was founded by Edward Bok in 1923, Pendleton was the single woman named as a juror.

Ellen Pendleton, or "Pres. Pen," as she was respectfully dubbed by students, retired in 1936, and died just a month later of a cerebral hemorrhage. She left her entire estate to Wellesley, the institution which had dominated her life for over 50 years.

SOURCES:

James, Edward T., ed. *Notable American Women, 1607–1950.* Cambridge, MA: The Belknap Press of Harvard University Press, 1971.

McHenry, Robert, ed. *Famous American Women.* NY: Dover, 1983.

Barbara Morgan,
Melrose, Massachusetts

Peninnah

Biblical woman. *Name variations: Penina. Pronunciation: pih-NIN-uh. One of two wives of Elkanah of Ephraim, a Levite.*

One of the wives of Elkanah of Ephraim, a Levite and a man of wealth and position, Peninnah taunted *Hannah, Elkanah's other wife, because she remained barren; Peninnah had given birth to many children. Hannah's continual prayers for a child were finally answered with the birth of the prophet Samuel.

Penn, Gulielma Springett
(1644–1694)

English Quaker, first wife of William Penn, who was a leading figure of early Quaker women's meetings in England. *Name variations: Guli or Guly. Pronunciation: Goo-lee-EL-ma. Born Gulielma Maria Springett in February 1644, probably in London (the exact date and place are undocumented); died in Warminghurst, Sussex, on February 23, 1694; daughter of Sir William Springett (a lawyer) and Mary (Proude) Springett Penington; stepdaughter of Sir Isaac Penington, son of the mayor of London; married William Penn, on April 4, 1672; children: Gulielma Maria (b. 1673); William and Mary (twins, b. 1674); Springett (b. 1676); Laetitia (b. 1678); William (b. 1681); Gulielma Maria (b. 1685); and an unnamed infant (b. 1683).*

Joined Quakers at age 15 with her mother and stepfather; was active in Quaker women's meetings in London, Buckinghamshire, and Sussex.

In the 1943 English film *Courageous Mr. Penn,* William Penn falls madly in love with the beautiful Quakeress Gulielma Springett, marries her, is nearly devastated by her early death, and dies while reading her love letters. As her final letter floats from his limp hand to the ground, a middle-aged servant named Hannah looks sadly on. This film fantasy is, of course, far from reality, for William Penn married a second time

(*Hannah Penn), but historians, like filmmakers, have focused on his first marriage as the romance of his life, even though the documentary evidence for Gulielma's relationship with him is sparse.

Born in 1644, Gulielma Maria Springett was the posthumous daughter of Sir William Springett, a lawyer and a knight who died while fighting on Oliver Cromwell's side during the English Civil War. Gulielma was born a few weeks after her father's death; about ten years later, her mother Mary married Isaac Penington, Jr., the eldest son of Isaac Sr., the Puritan lord mayor of London. Both Isaac and **Mary Penington** thought of themselves as Seekers, searching for religious truth, and they were part of the in-gathering of like-minded people who constituted the early Quaker movement when it took hold in London in the 1650s. The family estate in Buckinghamshire served as a gathering place for Friends, overseen by Mary and Gulielma during Isaac Penington's several imprisonments, and Gulielma became a leading figure in Quaker women's meetings.

Gulielma probably met William Penn soon after he became a Quaker, in 1667; they were married five years later in proper Quaker fashion and settled at Rickmansworth, outside London. In 1677, they moved to a larger house at Warminghurst Manor in Sussex. The couple had eight children, but only three lived past infancy: Springett, William, Jr., and **Laetitia Penn**. Except for making one journey with her husband immediately following their marriage, Gulielma seems to have remained at Warminghurst while William Penn traveled to Germany and Holland, throughout England, and to Pennsylvania in 1682–84. After his return and a brief period of prominence as a friend of King James II, William was forced into hiding when the Glorious Revolution sent the king into exile and the government of Pennsylvania was taken over by the crown. In February 1694, just as her husband was being cleared of charges and regaining control of the colony, Gulielma died of a lengthy illness at the age of 49.

The mythologizing of Gulielma Penn began with her husband's publication of the account of her death. "I never did, to my knowledge, a wicked thing in all my life," she said on her deathbed, according to William. In the succeeding centuries, her image has remained that of a Quaker saint.

SOURCES:

Dunn, Mary Maples, *et al.*, eds. *The Papers of William Penn.* 5 vols. Philadelphia, PA: University of Pennsylvania Press, 1981–87.

Hirsch, Alison Duncan. "A Tale of Two Wives: Mythmaking and the Lives of Gulielma and Hannah Penn," in *Pennsylvania History.* Vol. 61. 1994, pp. 429–456.

Hodgkin, L.V. *Gulielma: Wife of William Penn.* London: Longmans, Green, 1947.

COLLECTIONS:

Majority of papers located at the Historical Society of Pennsylvania, Philadelphia; Library of the Society of Friends and Public Record Office, London.

Alison Duncan Hirsch,
Assistant Professor of American Studies and History,
Pennsylvania State University, Harrisburg, Pennsylvania

Penn, Hannah (1671–1726)

Acting proprietor of Pennsylvania (1713–26) who successfully balanced competing interests of creditors, colonists, and crown to insure that her sons would inherit the proprietorship and that Quaker interests would be preserved in the colony. *Name variations: HP. Born Hannah Callowhill in 1671 in Bristol, England; died in London in December 1726; daughter of Quakers Thomas Callowhill (a linendraper) and Hannah (Hollister) Callowhill; married William Penn (Quaker and founder of Pennsylvania), in 1696; children: John (b. 1700), Thomas (b. 1702), Hannah Margarita (b. 1703), Margaret (b. 1704), Richard (b. 1706), Dennis (b. 1707), Hannah (b. 1708).*

Traveled to Pennsylvania with her husband (1699–1701); was active in Quaker women's meetings in Bristol, Berkshire, Sussex, and London; managed Pennsylvania proprietary affairs in secret for nearly six years after her husband suffered a stroke (1712), and openly for eight more years following his death (1718).

In December 1712, at the age of 41, Hannah Penn became the virtual proprietor of Pennsylvania, a position she maintained until her death in December 1726. For the first five and a half years, she managed the colony's affairs discreetly, using the proprietor's name as if she were merely conveying his instructions. William Penn, her husband of 16 years, had suffered a series of apoplectic strokes, which left him severely incapacitated, unable to speak or write clearly. After his death in July 1718, Hannah Penn was openly in charge as the guardian for her minor sons, the heirs to the proprietorship.

Born on February 11, 1671, Hannah Callowhill, Jr., was the sixth of nine children and the only one to survive to adulthood. She was named after her mother and in memory of her parents' third child, an earlier Hannah, who had died in infancy. Her father Thomas Callowhill was a buttonmaker and linendraper, or cloth merchant. Her mother **Hannah Hollister Callowhill** was the eldest daughter of a wealthy

Bristol grocer and property-owner; the grocer and his wife, among the first Quakers in the city, had donated the land for the Quaker meeting-house. From her parents and grandparents, Hannah Penn had a rich spiritual as well as material inheritance.

During Hannah's childhood, Bristol authorities persecuted Quakers (or Friends, as they called themselves) and sent hundreds to jail, including her father and other relatives. In 1682, so many Quakers were imprisoned that only the children were left to conduct meetings for worship, until even they were arrested. Bristol's Quaker schools were forcibly closed and the schoolmaster imprisoned when Hannah was 11, probably cutting short her formal education and leaving her with lifelong doubts about her writing competence. She was past school age when the school reopened in 1690 with Patrick Logan, and later his son James, as schoolmaster; in years to come, her friend James Logan would instruct her in Pennsylvania's proprietary affairs. Quakers believed in "instructing girls and young maidens in whatsoever things were civil and useful," and, in spite of the lack of formal education, Hannah did receive the necessary knowledge for a merchant's daughter. Her handwriting was clear and her spelling only slightly more inconsistent than that of the Oxford-educated William Penn. She also learned basic arithmetic and perhaps some simple accounting skills.

By 1689, the English government established religious toleration, and the period of Hannah's young adulthood was relatively peaceful for Quakers. The women's meeting, in which Hannah's mother was a leading member, was active in instituting poor relief, particularly for widows and children. Most of the early Bristol women's meeting records have been lost, but Hannah was probably active with her mother. (She was involved in women's meetings in Berkshire and Sussex later in life.) Quaker women's meetings were intended to give women a degree of authority separate from, but in conjunction with, the men's meeting. They were an embodiment of the Quaker heritage that upheld women's spiritual equality, the idea that, as William Penn wrote, "Sexes make no difference, since in souls there is none." Quakerism called on women and men alike to bring forth the Inner Light, the divine spark that could direct both public and private life.

Perhaps the most famous Quaker of the day was William Penn, the sole aristocrat among early Friends. A curiosity as well as a charismatic speaker, Penn drew thousands to hear him speak in town squares and open fields. When he came to Bristol on a ministering tour of the West Country in fall 1694, he was still recovering from the death of his first wife, ***Gulielma Penn**, a few months earlier. Some Friends were scandalized when he began to court Hannah, who was less than half his age. He wrote several letters reassuring her that he loved her; she was "amiable in my eye, above many" and "my heart, from the very first, has cleaved to thee." In spite of his protestations of love, Hannah was unsure of his motivations in marrying her. She sensed some disjunction between his behavior and Quaker ideology about marriage, which held that marriage should be by mutual consent, based on "leadings" and "openings" from the Lord. Hannah had heard the gossip that William was only after her money; she feared that he believed his stature among Friends made him irresistible, and that he was forcing her into a relationship that she was not sure she wanted. She herself had planned on not marrying at all, she told him, but to dedicate herself to Quaker work. He reassured her that she could serve the Lord by marrying him: "since thou wert for liveing to the Lord, as thy Husband, thou thus maryest him in me."

After a year of such persuasion, she married him in Bristol in March 1696, and rumor had it that her parents paid a dowry of £10,000 on the condition that the couple make their married home in Bristol; if so, the money was quickly gone, for within a few years William was borrowing large sums of money. But at first he kept his part of the bargain, and for the next few years, they lived alternately at Bristol and at Warminghurst, his country estate in Sussex, with his two surviving children from his first marriage (a third, his eldest son, died a few weeks after William married Hannah, casting a pall over their early married life).

By late 1699, William had persuaded the Callowhills to allow him to take their daughter to Pennsylvania, and Hannah accompanied her husband on his second and final trip to the colony. This trip gave her firsthand knowledge of the colony and many friends there, both of which would stand her in good stead later. She gave birth to her first child, John, a month after a harrowing three-month voyage across the Atlantic. During her stay in the colony, she managed two households, a rented city house and the family estate at Pennsbury, north of Philadelphia on the Delaware River. The Penns had both European servants and African slaves (only later did Quakers oppose slavery), but managing her household was a challenge for this new mother separated from family and friends during her sojourn in what she called "this desolate land" of Pennsylvania. In addition to the usual tasks as mistress of a large household—supervising laundry, cooking, gardening, and sewing—she entertained visitors, including the governors of neighboring colonies and the chiefs of local Native American bands. When her husband became ill at Pennsbury, she conveyed his instructions to officials in Philadelphia. This pattern of alternating household tasks and affairs of state—a sort of 18th-century double shift—would continue through the rest of her life.

Although William Penn had promised colonists that he would remain in Pennsylvania, he had told the Callowhills and English Quakers that he would come back to England, and within two years the family was making the return voyage. When the Penns left Pennsylvania in 1701, colonial leaders regretted Hannah's departure as much as their proprietor's. Isaac Norris wrote: "His excellent wife as she is beloved by all . . . so is leaving us heavy and of real sorrow to her friends. She has . . . a wonderful evenness humility and freedom. Her sweetness and goodness is become her character and I believe it is extraordinary. In short we love her and she deserves it."

On their return, William resumed his lobbying activities on behalf of his colony and Quakers in England, spending most of his time in London while Hannah and their children stayed with her parents in Bristol. During his long absences, his second wife was more demanding than "sweetly consenting" Gulielma had been. In 1703, when William was in London, Hannah wrote that he was trying her "great patience," so that "I cannot with any Satisfaction endure thy absence much Longer." Throughout their courtship and marriage, William felt constrained to come to Hannah or to meet her halfway. Given William Penn's constant travels, this was an important issue. If Hannah had been intimidated at first by his self-confidence, she overcame it. Before they were married, he had a good deal of pedantic, paternalistic advice for her, about how to manage servants, about what kind of coach to drive, about what medicine to take. But she and her family had the final word about servants and the house the couple rented. Increasingly in their marriage, he came to rely on her for emotional support. The need to be together was not only on her side; he too expressed regret at his separation from "my ould & beloved bedfellow."

In addition to being an affectionate husband, William Penn was a talented politician and determined advocate, but he was not a very astute businessman. Throughout his life, he lived far beyond his means, borrowed money indiscriminately, and signed loan documents without reading them carefully. These weaknesses came to the fore in 1708 when he was imprisoned in the Fleet jail for failure to pay his debts to the heirs of his former steward, to whom he had mortgaged Pennsylvania. (He had kept the mortgage a secret from Pennsylvanians as well as from English Friends, including perhaps his own wife.) Hannah moved to London to be near her husband during his imprisonment, and her father was the largest contributor among the English Quakers who bought up the mortgage and secured William's release. When Friends in the colony, disgusted with their proprietor, refused to contribute, William Penn became so exasperated that he began to negotiate the sale of the Pennsylvania government to the crown.

Hannah returned to her parents' home in Bristol while her husband searched for a new one, and in 1709 they moved with their five surviving children—John, Thomas, Richard, Dennis, and **Margaret Penn**—to Ruscombe House in Berkshire, a convenient location on the road from London to Bristol. The family settled down happily in the first real home they had known together since the visit to Pennsylvania. Three years later, while still in the middle of negotiations to sell Pennsylvania's government to the crown, William suffered a series of strokes and was severely incapacitated. He eventually recovered some of his ability to walk and to speak, but continued to be unable to do any business or even to write, except for signing his name with great difficulty.

During the final years of William Penn's life, most of Hannah's time was spent caring for her invalid husband and her children. She dispatched her two eldest sons to apprenticeships, John in Bristol and Thomas in London, where they could also serve as her business agents in those two cities. With their assistance, and the help of a few selected advisors, she took on the responsibility of managing all the family affairs, including the Pennsylvania proprietorship. Initially, she expressed reservations in her own ability; she hesitated to act "for fear of mismanagement," she said, because she was "but a woman." James Logan expressed his confidence in her: "As she is blest with a strong judgement and excellent good sense to a degree uncommon to her sex, I doubt not but she will endeavour for the best and surest methods to bring all to a perfect settlement."

She learned quickly, mastering the various skills needed and demonstrating that, whatever the inadequacies in her formal education, she possessed a lively intellect. After her husband became incapacitated, she quickly absorbed the knowledge she needed to protect not only her own family's legal interests but also those of Pennsylvania Quakers. She learned enough about geography to understand the Pennsylvania-Maryland boundary dispute. She learned the rudiments of double-entry bookkeeping and used it in keeping her accounts from 1715 to 1719, when her son John took over the family books. (She dropped the double-entry method quickly, perhaps because she only needed one column: her accounts consist almost entirely of money going out, with almost nothing coming in.) She even found time to make observations of a solar eclipse, demonstrating an interest in natural science shared with her husband and with her friend James Logan.

She is blest with a strong judgement and excellent good sense.

—James Logan, proprietary secretary of Pennsylvania

Hannah continued to manage family affairs after her husband's death, as executor of William Penn's will and guardian of their children, all minors. Her initial reaction to his death was one of grief and anxiety: "Wo is me," she wrote a friend, "that I have lived to see this day of striping, this most desolate day." But as Logan commented, she now had the advantage of being able to act openly as executor and guardian. Until her own death in 1726, Hannah Penn remained involved in proprietary affairs. Although she had been afraid she might mismanage things, she came to manage quite well. During her tenure as acting proprietor, she presided over two changes of deputy governors; handled negotiations over the longstanding Pennsylvania-Maryland border controversy; resolved conflicts with the English government over laws passed in Pennsylvania; and battled in the courts with her stepson, William Penn, Jr., over the terms of William, Sr.'s will. The will was settled in her favor just weeks before she died, and her sons and grandsons remained proprietors of Pennsylvania down to the American Revolution.

Although she was never a Quaker minister or elder, as her husband had been, Hannah's letters speak of participation in Quaker activities such as collecting clothing or money for poor relief and preparing food and lodging for visiting Yearly Meeting representatives. Caring for a large household and managing a colonial proprietorship left little time for the usual Quaker activities. But Quaker values were all-important. Hannah spoke to her children of "the hapiness of silence in meetings" and of the need to keep to plain dress. She feared that her children were succumbing to the temptation of fashion instead of following her plain example. In 1717, she urged 15-year-old Thomas to make sure his hat was "tack[e]d up in a very fr[ien]d like way, for the fantasticall cocks in thine, & thy brother Johns hats, has burthened my spiritt much." Simple dress symbolized an entire way of life to her. "I have a multitude of toyls and cares," she told Thomas, "but they would be greatly middigated if I may but behold thee & thy brother, persuing hard after virtue, and leaveing as behind your backs the toyish allurements & snares of this uncertain world." (Quaker simplicity did not mean buying inexpensive goods, however; as did other well-to-do Friends, Hannah often purchased expensive fabrics in simple shades of tan or gray.)

As it had for her husband, Pennsylvania represented a merging of family interest and Quaker values. Legal documents show that Hannah personally held to the Quaker testimony against oaths, and her letters to Pennsylvanians show a concern that the colony's laws continue to be in accord with Quaker principles.

Hannah Penn may have reached the upper limits of political power for women in early 18th-century Anglo-America, with her special status as "proprietress." A product of a society that unquestioningly assumed that men were the heads of households, and therefore a family's only direct political participants, Hannah Penn never sought the position of proprietor for herself. Yet once she became the acting proprietor, she quietly but consistently asserted her authority in order to balance the competing interests involved in the colony's management. Her management preserved the family's economic and political power and insured the continuation of Quaker authority in Pennsylvania for the next three decades. What was still most important to her, in the end, was living "to the Lord." Her marriage changed the way in which she did so, but the purpose of her life remained the same.

SOURCES:

Drinker, Sophie. *Hannah Penn and the Proprietorship of Pennsylvania.* Philadelphia, PA: Society of Colonial Dames, 1958.

Dunn, Mary Maples, *et al.*, eds. *The Papers of William Penn.* 5 vols. Philadelphia, PA: University of Pennsylvania Press, 1981–87.

Hirsch, Alison Duncan. "A Tale of Two Wives: Mythmaking and the Lives of Gulielma and Hannah Penn," in *Pennsylvania History.* Vol. 61. 1994, pp. 429–456.

Hodgkin, L.V. *Gulielma: Wife of William Penn.* London: Longmans, Green, 1947.

SUGGESTED READING:

Bacon, Margaret Hope. *Mothers of Feminism: The Story of Quaker Women in America.* San Francisco, CA: Harper & Row, 1986.

Mack, Phyllis. *Visionary Women: Ecstatic Prophecy in Seventeenth-Century England.* Berkeley, CA: University of California Press, 1992.

COLLECTIONS:

Majority of papers located at the Historical Society of Pennsylvania, Philadelphia; Library of the Society of Friends and Public Record Office, London.

Alison Duncan Hirsch,
Assistant Professor of American Studies and History, Pennsylvania State University, Harrisburg, Pennsylvania

Pennell, Elizabeth Robins

(1855–1936)

American writer. *Name variations: Elizabeth Robins. Born on February 21, 1855, in Philadelphia, Pennsylvania; died of chronic myocarditis on February 7, 1936, in New York City; daughter of Edward Robins (a bank president) and Margaret (Holmes) Robins; educated at Sacred Hearts convents near Paris and in Torresdale, Pennsylvania; married Joseph Pennell (an artist), in June 1884; no children.*

First published in the Atlantic Monthly *(1881); published "A Ramble in Old Philadelphia," the first of many collaborations with Joseph Pennell (1882); served as art critic for American and English newspapers; traveled through and wrote about Europe with her husband (1884–1917); with husband, wrote biography of James McNeill Whistler (1908).*

Selected writings: Life of Mary Wollstonecraft *(1884); (with Joseph Pennell)* A Canterbury Pilgrimage *(1885); (with J. Pennell)* Our Sentimental Journey through France and Italy *(1888); (with J. Pennell)* The Stream of Pleasure *(1891); (with J. Pennell)* To Gipsyland *(1893);* Feasts of Autolycus, the Diary of a Greedy Woman *(1896);* Delights of Delicate Eating *(1900); (with J. Pennell)* The Life of James McNeill Whistler *(1908);* Our House and London Out of Our Windows *(1912);* The Lovers *(1917);* A Guide for the Greedy *(1923);* Our Philadelphia *(1914);* Life and Letters of Joseph Pennell *(1929).*

Elizabeth Robins Pennell was born in Philadelphia on February 21, 1855, the daughter of Edward Robins, a bank president, and **Margaret Holmes Robins**, who died while Pennell was quite young. Elizabeth was raised Catholic and attended Sacred Heart convents, primarily Eden Hall in Torresdale, Pennsylvania, although she spent a year at the convent in Conflans, near Paris, when she was six. She and her sister also spent many of their school breaks and holidays at the convent in Torresdale. Not an especially good student and sometimes troublesome, Pennell nevertheless graduated from school in 1872 and then returned to Philadelphia to live with her father and new stepmother. She made her debut into Philadelphia society, but afterwards found the life of a young society woman unsatisfying.

Thus when Pennell's uncle Charles Godfrey Leland, a prominent essayist and humorist, returned from a trip abroad in 1880 and engaged her as his assistant, she welcomed the chance to do something different. Leland was working on a project to integrate the arts into the public school curriculum, and he had hoped to use Pennell's artistic talent, but found that she had very little. Instead, he encouraged her to begin writing, and in 1881 her first article, "Mischief in the Middle Ages," was published in the *Atlantic Monthly*. Pennell continued to write for the magazine, mostly articles on history and mythology, and, with the help of Leland's influence, also published in Philadelphia newspapers and a weekly magazine, the *American*. When Leland was asked in 1881 by the editor of *Scribner's Magazine* to write text to accompany eight etchings by a young Philadelphia artist named Joseph Pennell, he instead proposed Elizabeth for the job. The March 1882 publication of "A Ramble in Old Philadelphia" marked the first collaboration in what would prove to be a long series between Elizabeth and Joseph, who were married in June 1884. In the same year, she published her first book, *Life of* ****Mary Wollstonecraft***. By then she had also become an art critic for the Philadelphia *Press* and the *American*.

After their marriage, the Pennells sailed for Europe, where Joseph created the illustrations for William Dean Howells' *Tuscan Cities*. The newlyweds took a summer bicycling trip through England, which resulted in their first book together, *A Canterbury Pilgrimage* (1885). For the next 33 years, they worked in London during the winters and toured Europe, by cycle or sometimes by foot, during the summers. Their tales of these trips were published in many American and English magazines between 1884 and 1898, and also resulted in nine books written by Elizabeth and illustrated by her husband. These included *An Italian Pilgrimage* (1886), *Our Sentimental Journey through France and Italy* (1888), *Our Journey to the Hebrides* (1889), *The Stream of Pleasure* (1891), *To Gipsyland* (1893), and *Over the Alps on a Bicycle* (1898). Their friend Edward Tinker later wrote, "She with her books and he with his drawings have done more than any other two people I know to spread in America a popular knowledge of the art of the old world, of the everyday life of its people, of the beauty of its countryside, and of the architectural loveliness of its cities."

During this time Pennell also filled in for her husband as art critic for the London *Star* on a regular basis, and eventually took over the column herself. As her prominence as an art critic grew, she was published in other newspapers and journals as well, including the London *Chronicle* and the New York *Nation*. For five years, she also wrote a column on cooking for the *Pall Mall Gazette*. These columns were published in three collections, *Feasts of Autolycus, the Diary of a Greedy Woman* (1896), *Delights of Delicate Eating* (1900) and *A Guide for the Greedy* (1923).

The Pennells had a wide circle of friends in the artistic world, including George Bernard Shaw, Aubrey Beardsley, and Phil May. In 1892, they also began a friendship with James McNeill Whistler and in 1900 agreed to write his biography. Published in 1908, *The Life of James McNeill Whistler* proved very successful, running to three printings; the texts of the fifth and sixth editions (published in 1911 and 1919, respectively) were completely revised by the Pennells.

In 1906, Elizabeth published a biography of her mentor and uncle, Charles Godfrey Leland, after which she and her husband made a trip to northern France and subsequently collaborated on *French Cathedrals, Monasteries, and Abbeys, and Sacred Sites of France* (1909). Other writings by Pennell during the early years of the century included *Our House and the People In It* (1910), *Our House and London Out of Our Windows* (1912), *Our Philadelphia* (1914), and *Nights: Rome, Venice in the Aesthetic Eighties; London, Paris in the Fighting Nineties* (1916). She also wrote a novel, *The Lovers* (1917). That same year, the outbreak of World War I caused the Pennells to move back to the United States. They lived initially in Philadelphia before settling in Brooklyn, New York, in June 1921. Joseph died in 1926, after which Elizabeth collected his pictures of New York and Philadelphia and oversaw the creation of descriptive lists of his work. She also wrote the two-volume *Life and Letters of Joseph Pennell* (1929) before her death from chronic myocarditis on February 7, 1936, in New York City.

SOURCES:

James, Edward T., ed. *Notable American Women, 1607–1950*. Cambridge, MA: The Belknap Press of Harvard University Press, 1971.

McHenry, Robert, ed. *Famous American Women*. NY: Dover, 1980.

Kari Bethel, freelance writer, Columbia, Missouri

Pennington, Mary Engle (1872–1952)

American chemist who developed refrigeration techniques to preserve perishable foods. *Name variations: M.E. Pennington; Polly. Born Mary Engle Pennington on October 8, 1872, in Nashville, Tennessee; died of a heart attack in New York, New York, on December 27, 1952; daughter of Henry Pennington (a businessman) and Sarah B. Molony Pennington; University of Pennsylvania, certificate of proficiency, 1892, Ph.D., 1895.*

Was a fellow in botany, University of Pennsylvania (1895–97); was a fellow in physiological chemistry, Yale University (1897–98); was a research worker, department of hygiene, University of Pennsylvania (1898–1901); worked as consultant, Philadelphia Clinical Laboratory (1898–1907); was a lecturer, Woman's Medical College of Pennsylvania (1898–1906); was director, Philadelphia Department of Health and Charities' bacteriological laboratory (1901–07); was first chief and bacteriological chemist, United States Department of Agriculture's Food Research Laboratory, Philadelphia, Pennsylvania (1905–19); developed refrigeration techniques to prevent food spoilage and devised standards for refrigerated railroad cars (1907–17); earned the Food Administration's Notable Service Medal (1918); was director of research and development, American Balsa Company, New York City (1919–23); was first female member of the American Society of Refrigerating Engineers (1920); was a private chemical consultant to food industry and developed techniques to freeze food and design commercial and household refrigerators (1922–52); co-authored Eggs *(1933); won the Francis P. Garvan Medal for women in chemistry presented by the American Chemical Society (1940); made fellow, American Society of Refrigerating Engineers (1947); was first female member of Poultry Historical Society's Hall of Fame; was vice-president American Institute of Refrigeration at time of death (1952).*

Selected publications: (with Georgiana Walter) "A Bacterial Study of Commercial Ice Cream," in New York Medical Journal *(November 1907); "Changes Taking Place in Chickens in Cold Storage," in* USDA Yearbook *(1907, pp. 197–206); (with Howard C. Pierce) "The Effect of the Present Method of Handling Eggs on the Industry and the Product," in* USDA Yearbook *(1910, pp. 461–476); (with Helen M.P. Betts and Pierce) "How to Kill and Bleed Market Poultry," in* USDA Bureau of Chemistry *(circular no. 61, 1910); "Studies of Poultry From the Farm to the Consumer," in* USDA Bureau of Chemistry *(circular no. 64, 1910); (with Evelyn Witmer and Pierce) "The Comparative Rate of Decomposition in Drawn and*

Undrawn Market Poultry," in USDA Bureau of Chemistry *(circular no. 70, 1911); "The Handling of Dressed Poultry a Thousand Miles from the Market,"* in USDA Yearbook *(1912, pp. 285–292); "Practical Suggestions for the Preparation of Frozen and Dried Eggs,"* in USDA Bureau of Chemistry *(circular no. 98, 1912); (with Pierce) "An All-Metal Poultry-Cooling Rack,"* in U.S. Bureau of Chemistry *(circular no. 115, 1913); "Supplementing Our Meat Supply With Fish,"* in USDA Yearbook *(1913, pp. 191–206); (with Arden D. Greenlee) "The Refrigeration of Dressed Poultry in Transit,"* in USDA Bulletin *(no. 17, 1913); (with Minnie K. Jenkins, E.Q. St. John, and William B. Hicks) "A Bacteriological and Chemical Study of Commercial Eggs in the Producing Districts of the Central West,"* in USDA Bulletin *(no. 51, 1914); (with Pierce and Harlan L. Shrader) "The Egg and Poultry Demonstration Car Work in Reducing our $50,000,000 Waste in Eggs,"* in USDA Yearbook *(1914, pp. 363–380); (with Jenkins and Betts) "How to Handle Eggs,"* in USDA Bulletin *(no. 565, 1918);* Why We Refrigerate Foods *(Chicago: National Association of Ice Industries, 1926); (with Frank L. Platt and Clara Gebhard Snyder)* Eggs *(Chicago: Institute of American Poultry Industries, 1933);* The Care of Perishable Food Aboard Ship *(NY: G. Ehlenberger, 1942);* The Freezing of Eggs *(NY: American Society of Refrigerating Engineers, 1948).*

Chickens played a major role in Mary Engle Pennington's scientific achievements. Considered the greatest refrigeration authority in the early 20th century, she focused on preserving poultry products, and her methods to refrigerate perishable foods drastically changed consumer behavior. Before refrigeration, people bought food fresh from the market and risked being poisoned. Foods such as dairy and poultry products, if improperly stored, often transmitted deadly bacteria. As America urbanized and cities swelled with foreign and rural immigrants, large supplies of safe food became necessary. Pennington provided means to bring food from the farm to the consumer, minimizing food-related illnesses and deaths and farmers' losses from spoiled and wasted foods. She designed refrigerated storage and transportation methods and developed frozen-food research. Her work revolutionized the way Americans eat: fresh foods are now available every day of the year.

Mary Engle Pennington, called Polly, was born in Nashville, Tennessee, on October 8, 1872, the daughter of Henry and **Sarah Molony Pennington**, but lived in the South only briefly. Maps of Nashville reveal her paternal family's influence; the Cumberland River curves around Pennington Bend northeast of the state capitol. Young Mary moved with her family to Pennsylvania, living in a large three-story, red-brick house. Sarah Pennington's Quaker family, the Engles, lived in West Philadelphia, and Mary's great-grandfather, Joseph Engle, a Pennsylvania judge, had been an escort for General Lafayette when he visited America in 1825. Pennington always considered Philadelphia, not Nashville, to be her hometown, declaring, "I'd never have been born anywhere but Philadelphia if I'd had anything to do with it." Her younger sister, Helen, was born in that city in 1878.

Henry Pennington, an entrepreneur, founded a label manufacturing business in Philadelphia. He was also fond of gardening. Encouraged to assist him, Mary became familiar with vegetables and plants and especially enjoyed examining flowers. In addition to learning about flora, Pennington discovered local fauna, in particular chickens, at Philadelphia markets. Every Saturday morning, she accompanied her mother to market, and occasionally they ventured to farms outside the city to place orders. Stalls that were full of produce in summer stood empty in winter. Pennington became aware that when hens laid fewer eggs and scarcities occurred out of season, prices soared too high for many people to afford fresh eggs. She pondered whether there was any means to store eggs year round.

When she was 12, she discovered a *Rand's Medical Chemistry* text in the Philadelphia Mercantile Library, and the librarian agreed to let her borrow it. An avid reader, Pennington devoured the tome while sitting on the family porch. She realized that elements, invisible to the naked eye, built everything that surrounded her and were necessary to sustain life. Oxygen was in air, nitrogen was in soil, and hydrogen was in water. "Suddenly, one day, I realized, lickity hoop, that although I couldn't touch, taste, or smell them, they really existed. It was a milestone," Pennington declared. "Like a flash of light in a dark place, I got the idea of the realness of the invisible world."

Intrigued, Pennington asked the headmistress at her private girls' school if she would offer chemistry lectures. Since science was not a proper subject for young ladies, the headmistress was scandalized and refused. Though somewhat surprised by Mary's sudden enthusiasm, Pennington's family supported her new-found interests. In 1890, she approached the dean and asked to enroll in the Towne Scientific School at the University of Pennsylvania, which was near the Pennington home. Both Dean Horace Jayne and chemistry professor Dr. Edgar F. Smith supported coeducation and allowed her admittance. Pennington completed the required courses, including chemistry, biology, bacteriology, and zoology, in two years. The only woman in her class, Pennington received a certificate of proficiency, not a B.S. like her male peers, because the university refused to grant degrees to women.

Deemed eligible by faculty to continue her studies according to a university statute regarding "extraordinary cases," Pennington ignored the discrimination that she had encountered and pursued postgraduate work in chemistry. Her scholarship as a graduate student and her thesis on "Derivatives of Columbium and Tantalum" earned her a doctorate in 1895. Pennington's feat was a rarity: she was honored with a Ph.D. without having a bachelor's degree. She soon discovered that the chemistry profession had the same bias as academia when it came to female practitioners. Though Pennington was the third woman to join the American Chemical Society, it remained staunchly masculine. At that time, most women chemists applied their knowledge and skills to what was then considered the more "feminine" field of home economics, which welcomed them.

But Mary Pennington elected to stick with the pure sciences. Continuing her interest in plants, she was a research fellow in chemical botany at the University of Pennsylvania for two years, teaching graduate students plant physiology. Then she devoted a year to postgraduate study of physiological chemistry at Yale University. Working with Dr. Russell Chittenden, she conducted pioneering research on the effect of color on plant growth, bathing *Spirogyra nitida* (mermaid's hair) with varicolored lights. Pennington then returned to Philadelphia. Continually aware that well-educated women scientists were not highly in demand or approved of, she contemplated ways to promote her scientific work and unearth opportunities for her imagination. Enterprisingly, she founded the Philadelphia Clinical Laboratory to offer doctors better laboratory resources. She performed accurate bacteriological analyses for approximately 400 physicians who paid an annual minimum of $50 each. At the same time, she was a research worker in the University of Pennsylvania's department of hygiene.

Pennington's expertise won her an appointment at the Woman's Medical College of Pennsylvania, where she lectured and directed the chemistry laboratory until 1906. Teaching physiological chemistry, she co-authored an article with her student and cousin, **Georgiana Walter**, for the *New York Medical Journal*.

Pennington's successful independent research resulted in her being named director of the newly created Philadelphia Department of Health and Charities' bacteriological laboratory. At that time, reform was a popular platform for progressives, and Pennington revised her goals, choosing to apply science to improve society instead of focusing on pure science in the laboratory. She quickly became an expert in food chemistry. Her initial work concerned eradicating impure milk that might transmit deadly diseases, including tuberculosis. Without laws to protect food products, Pennington faced an unusual challenge; she wanted to insure that the source of milk was healthy. Since retail milk sellers could not verify whether the milk they bought from dairies was uncontaminated, Pennington established the first systematic dairy and milk inspection standards, including a scientific examination of cattle herds, which were adopted by municipal health boards nationwide. She then urged retailers to handle milk safely, mainly to preserve it at low temperatures. She devised profitable means for dairy producers and dealers who cooperated with her.

Pennington then tackled "hokey-pokey" vendors, whose pushcart ice cream had caused outbreaks of sickness, and even a few fatalities, among city schoolchildren. When she analyzed a slide sample of the ice cream, she discovered millions of bacteria. Inviting the vendors to her laboratory to see the slides, she also showed them slides of ice cream prepared in a sanitary environment and explained that, by simply sterilizing their kettles and ladles in boiling water, they could prevent illness. Upset at the microscopic dangers, many of the ice-cream sellers agreed to adopt preventative steps. Once personnel in dairies and ice-cream factories understood the invisible dangers, most managers agreed to cooperate and adopt her suggestions for food handling. As a result, Pennington improved the quality of life for consumers and formed the basis for her refrigeration research.

In 1907, family friend Dr. Harvey W. Wiley, chief of the Bureau of Chemistry in the U.S. Department of Agriculture (USDA), urged her to research refrigeration as a method of food preservation for the federal government. Previously, she had investigated for Wiley rumors that turkeys had been frozen for a decade and then served at a banquet. By examining the history of slaughtered poultry in warehouses, Pennington determined that birds could be stored for one year at freezing temperatures. Impressed with her findings, Wiley asked Pennington to take a civil service examination. At first, the uninformed Pennington "was mad as wrath," then agreed to be tested. Concerned, however, that government bureaucrats would not approve the appointment of a female bacteriological chemist, Wiley advised her to sign her exam "M.E. Pennington." After that, Pennington published many of her articles the same way, and often her clients did not realize that she was a woman. She humorously recalled how one executive asked his secretary "to get rid of the woman" when Pennington appeared in his office.

At the turn of the 20th century, female government employees, like many women in academia, encountered discrimination. Generally assigned stereotypical female work, they were underpaid and seldom promoted. Women scientists worked in isolated positions or were clustered in areas, such as the Bureau of Plant Industry, where they performed work that male employees refused to do. For the most part, the only women achieving managerial positions accomplished this in the aforementioned field of home economics. Pennington managed to overcome these obstacles and was a pioneering female federal scientist. Officials hired her as a bacteriological chemist, believing she was a man because of her initials; she performed so admirably and indispensably that when they realized she was a woman, they had no grounds to dismiss or demote her.

By 1908, Wiley appointed Pennington as the first chief of the newly established U.S. Food Research Laboratory, a division of the Bureau of Chemistry. At her insistence, Pennington's laboratory was created in Philadelphia so that she could be near her family and professional colleagues and continue her consulting work. Although Wiley wanted her to work in Washington, D.C., the strong-willed Pennington refused, fearing that her work might become entangled in administrative red-tape. She agreed to appear annually in the capitol to ask for appropriations.

Pennington conducted experiments in the laboratory and negotiated on behalf of the government with food agents. The laboratory became a nucleus for research concerning food handling and storage, especially in preventing spoilage of eggs, poultry, and fish. Supervising a staff ranging from four to fifty researchers, she devised techniques that various facets of the food industry, such as warehousing, packaging, and distributing, adopted.

Her goal was to insure enforcement of the first Pure Food and Drug Act, passed in 1906, which fomented bitter legal controversies with food producers. Pennington conducted laboratory analyses for Wiley to use in court to serve as proof that the law had been violated. During this time, she managed to devise successful refrigeration techniques and gain respect for her professional expertise. Many food dealers sought her advice to develop hygienic procedures and avoid prosecution.

Acting as the official American delegate, Pennington attended the First International Congress of Refrigeration in Paris in 1908 (she would participate in these congresses throughout her life). The only female delegate, she delivered an address for Wiley. Refrigeration became her primary research focus. Although she did not invent refrigeration, Pennington developed procedures to insure that refrigerated foods remained fresh and edible, and helped establish the refrigeration industry.

Considered America's foremost authority on the refrigeration of perishable foods, Pennington enabled wide geographical access to healthy fresh foods year round. At that time, the law did not permit government inspectors to enter packing houses and wholesale food buildings. Seeking cooperation between government and dealers, Pennington convinced owners to permit her access to these businesses and explore food handling problems firsthand. Chickens were her primary concern. Along with her laboratory assistants, Pennington focused on problems encountered in killing and storing chickens. They had already examined chickens in retail stores, but only by obtaining access to the poultry processing industry were they able to suggest solutions. Wrapping her brown hair in a towel and wearing gloves and an apron, she assisted in the killing process in the abattoirs and quickly dismissed wringing and axing necks as sanitary killing methods.

Instead of immersing chickens in boiling water to pluck off feathers, which caused deterioration during storage and transportation, she invented a sharp knife to pierce the brains and cut the jugular veins from inside. This method of slaughter resulted in the feathers being easily removed without immersion, while the bodies remained intact during shipping. She also discovered suitable temperatures to remove body heat and freeze-dry the birds for storage, avoiding packing on ice which melted en route and often waterlogged carcasses. During this work, Pennington developed guidelines for poultry storage limits and patented an all-metal poultry-cooling rack in 1912.

Pennington's ideas were also used in the design of refrigerator cars. Concentrating her efforts on the transportation of food, she researched and determined the necessary temperature during cold storage processes to refrigerate foods safely in rail cars (and later in trucks). She focused on humidity control in freezing rooms, because as freezing temperatures occurred, the air in the freight car lost its ability to retain moisture and food became dry. Once the food was thawed, it regained water and became moldy. "At temperatures above freezing," she commented, "one is between the Scylla of excessive drying and the Charybdis of mold." Riding in a caboose outfitted as a laboratory and living quarters, Pennington studied the chickens as they traveled cross-country, monitoring electrical thermometers to record temperatures. Following foodstuffs thousands of miles from producer to market, often working all day in a warehouse and sleeping on the train, Pennington enthused, "That's the way to travel, leisurely jogging along, talking over the crops with the farmers at the crossings, switched into a train yard at night instead of speeding through space and being hustled out of a berth at daybreak."

She gained national publicity for this feat (much of it inaccurately stating that she rode in the refrigerated cars) and ultimately improved transportation conditions with the standardized refrigeration car. Through her work, Pennington enabled poultry producers to kill chickens in prime condition, dry-pluck and freeze-dry them, and sell them to consumers in as edible a state as they were when fresh killed. Next, she decided to achieve similar results with eggs.

Because hens laid the bulk of their eggs in the spring, poultry producers sought improved egg storage in order to supply eggs to consumers at consistently affordable prices throughout the year. Farmers disliked the low prices they received when eggs were plentiful, and consumers often eliminated eggs from their diets during the winter months. Pennington began to explore means to cold-store eggs safely.

The problem required several considerations. First, farmers delivering eggs to warehouses had to make sure that eggs were fresh, especially in the summer; eggs in warehouses would be only as fresh as they were when stored. Then Pennington had to determine the best temperatures and methods to store eggs. Aware that farmers were motivated by financial rewards, she helped create the first egg quality charts which graded eggs scientifically, deciding which eggs were suitable for storage and would retain the nutritious qualities of fresh-laid eggs.

Pennington focused on egg-breaking factories, where cracked and blemished eggs were broken and dried or frozen. The residue was sold to bakers and confectioners who used the powdered product for cooking. However, egg-breaking factories tended to be unsanitary, and USDA Secretary James Wilson threatened to close them. Fearing that farmers would suffer heavy financial losses, Pennington sought a compromise. She convinced egg-breaking plants to refrigerate their products and follow her methods "of near-surgical asepsis," in which buildings were sterilized with steam and workers trained to follow sanitary handling measures. Pennington's work saved millions of dollars worth of eggs from wastage.

Next, she turned her attention to egg transportation problems. Utilizing a branch food research laboratory in Indianapolis, Pennington continued her analyses of temperatures. Her investigations enabled eggs from the Midwest, America's "Egg Basket," to be delivered safely throughout the United States. She also helped design cushioning packaging to eliminate broken eggshells and reduced profits. She wrote about her experiences in the book *Eggs*.

Simultaneously, Pennington contributed to America's World War I efforts. Women scientists found that the war provided new professional opportunities, though their role was often minimized. President Woodrow Wilson established the U.S. Food Administration in August 1917. Scientists concentrated on increasing domestic food production while decreasing American consumption of food in order to alleviate European food shortages.

Pennington acted as a consultant to the Food Administration's perishable products division. She and her staff, dubbing themselves "the imperishables," secured safe means to export agricultural produce. As demand for transporting perishable foods greatly increased with the need to feed troops, Pennington solidified refrigerator car standards. American railroads contributed 40,000 refrigerator cars to the war effort. After evaluating them in 1917, Pennington declared that only 3,000 cars were suitably insulated and ventilated to transport meat; she assisted the government in establishing official standards for ice-cooled refrigerator cars, which remained current through World War II (mechanically refrigerated cars were introduced in the 1950s). Herbert Hoover, chair of the (U.S.) Commission for Relief in Belgium and a fellow

Quaker, presented her with a Notable Service Medal for her wartime work with perishable foods, and Pennington received public accolades. Through her war efforts, food producers, shippers, warehouses, and government agencies were united toward the common goal of preserving food. Calling her "Auntie Sam," the railway and poultry workers considered her "the voice of conscience in the refrigerating world." Both the food industry and consumers accepted the use of refrigerated food, expediting the creation of such facilities.

After the armistice in 1919, Pennington resigned from the USDA to become director of the research and development department of the American Balsa Company in New York City. A manufacturer of insulating materials, the company was willing to double her government salary. After three years, she, like many women scientists, chose to create her own independent consulting office, in the city's Woolworth Building. She devoted her energy to developing effective means to handle, ship, and store perishable foods for packing houses, shipping firms, and warehouses. Pennington traveled frequently, as much as 50,000 miles per year in America and abroad, to investigate industries, steamers, refrigerator cars, and egg-breaking factories.

She also directed the Household Refrigeration Bureau of the National Association of Ice Industries from 1923 to 1931. Acting as a publicist, she convinced three universities—Columbia, Purdue, and Chicago—to add household refrigeration courses to their curricula. Because no textbooks existed, she wrote pamphlets, which were more popular than scholarly in context, entitled "The Romance of Ice," "Desserts Frozen with Ice and Salt," and "Journeys with Refrigerated Food." Millions of these booklets were circulated; she also dispensed information on radio programs.

Refining her food preservation techniques, Pennington attacked a new problem, that of frozen foods. She realized that canning and smoking were viable preservation methods but insisted that freezing was better because foods remained fresh. She designed and built refrigerated warehouses and coolers as well as refrigerators for both industry and homes. Pennington also conducted original research concerning frozen-food processing, again concentrating on poultry. Writing and editing numerous articles for scholarly journals, popular magazines, and government bulletins, she discussed quality control in the refrigeration industry. She co-authored several works with her sister, **Helen M.P. Betts**. Having first experimented with freezing sweet corn in Minnesota in 1913, Pennington preceded Clarence Birdseye, who is usually credited with initiating industrial food freezing. Evaluating the best freezing processes for each variety of food, she especially enjoyed telling how she located strawberries in a Pacific Coast cold-storage plant and transported them by rail to Philadelphia. The berries were used to make the first out-of-season, fresh-fruit strawberry ice cream available in America.

Mary Pennington also helped the fish industry develop a standardized process to scale, skin, freeze, and dry-pack fish fillets as soon as the catch was delivered to the factory. Utilizing a government experimental freezer, she studied frozen fish samples to determine chemical changes over several months. She decided that fish which were glazed (frozen into a block of ice, thus sealing the fish from fungus and mold) did not lose nutritional qualities.

During World War II, the Office of the Quartermaster General requested that Pennington serve as a consultant to the Research and Development Branch of the Military Planning Division of the War Shipping Administration. Recognizing the vital role food played in military efforts, she sought new ways to cushion foods because insulating materials were being diverted to wartime usage. Pennington wrote a handbook for troops, *The Care of Perishable Food Aboard Ship*, and advanced her designs of refrigerated spaces for storing and transporting food.

Throughout her career, Pennington accrued many honors. In 1920, she became the first female member of the American Society of Refrigerating Engineers (also a fellow in 1947 and director). She actively participated on the organization's program, educational, and publications committees and was associate editor of *Refrigerating Engineering*'s application data sections from 1944 through 1948. She was a member of the organization's council for two years beginning in 1946 and in 1952 was associate editor of the *Refrigeration Data Book—Applications*, having contributed to previous volumes. She was the first woman elected to the Poultry Historical Society's Hall of Fame. In 1910, she was the only woman starred in the second edition of *American Men and Women of Science*, indicating that she was among the top 1,000 researchers. She won the American Chemical Society's Francis P. Garvan Medal in 1940. Awarded to distinguished female chemists, this golden medallion and its monetary prize were considered, at the time, the most prestigious honor for women scientists. Although the American

Chemical Society had gained more female members and established a women's service committee, women were rarely included on programs until the 1940s. Society awards went to men, not women, and the Garvan medal was the primary means through which women chemists received any recognition or publicity.

Frustrated that journalists mistakenly described her as "the woman who knows more than anyone else about iceboxes," Pennington summarized her career for *The New Yorker* reporter **Barbara Heggie** by noting, "Ye gods and little fishes, I'm an expert in the handling, transportation, and storage of perishables and the application of refrigeration." She worked so hard that her physician ordered her to visit the Caribbean to relax from her busy schedule. Pennington wrote her sister that, in fact, she spent most of her time trying to convince local businessmen of the socioeconomic benefits of refrigeration. Until shortly before her death, she continued to seek solutions and perfect methods concerning perishable foods.

Mary Pennington lived with her Persian cat Bonny in a New York penthouse apartment, overlooking the Hudson River, at 100 Riverside Drive; it was filled with Early American furniture, Quaker samplers, and family mementoes. A dark-eyed, quiet, confident woman, she enjoyed tending her terrace garden, growing the flowers that she loved as a girl. True to her professional achievements, she savored hosting dinner parties, serving primarily frozen foods to her guests. They enjoyed a smorgasbord of produce from a diversity of states—celery from Florida, salmon from Washington, and eggs from Ohio—and such dessert treats as raspberries on ice cream in December. To explain her vision of refrigeration and frozen foods, Pennington quoted poet Alexander Pope: "To take to the poles the products of the sun, And knit the unsocial climates into one."

Pennington promoted science education for women and influenced her niece and namesake, **Polly Betts Elderfield**, to become a chemist. Devoutly religious, Mary was a lifelong member of the Society of Friends. After falling in her apartment, the 80-year-old Pennington died of a heart attack in New York's St. Luke's Hospital on Saturday, December 27, 1952.

Mary Engle Pennington insured access to safe, nutritious diets. She also abetted the American economy and the modern commercialization of food, ensuring food producers steady prices and reliable markets while reducing losses due to spoiled produce. Grocery stores became a convenient means for farmers to sell their produce and for people to purchase healthy food. Cities swelled, absorbing the farmland that had been used to supply local markets, as long-distance hauling of frozen foods to urban areas altered consumer and demographic patterns. Assuring stability of food sources, despite season, weather, or region, Pennington alleviated scarcity of crucial dietary essentials. She almost singlehandedly guaranteed Americans a way to eat nutritiously and expeditiously as technology revolutionized most lifestyles. Every day, millions of Americans heat frozen food in microwave ovens. Pennington altered the way that food is perceived and handled in our society. Remarking that "food is like a newspaper. Good today, no good tomorrow," she recognized her contribution. "There is a thrill when a scientific idea suddenly strikes home in the form of a practical solution to an industrial problem."

SOURCES:

Goff, Alice C. *Women CAN Be Engineers.* Youngstown, OH: self-published, 1946.

Hartwell, Anne. "Mary E. Pennington, Who Keeps Cold Storage Cold," in *Woman's Journal.* November 1930, pp. 11, 42–43.

Heggie, Barbara. "Profiles: Ice Woman," in *The New Yorker.* September 6, 1941, pp. 23–26, 29–30.

"Mary Engle Pennington: October 8, 1872–December 27, 1952," in *Refrigerating Engineering.* February 1953, p. 184.

Yost, Edna. *American Women of Science.* Philadelphia, PA: J.B. Lippincott, 1955.

SUGGESTED READING:

Miles, Wyndham D. *American Chemists and Chemical Engineers.* Washington, DC: American Chemical Society, 1976.

Mullendore, William C. *History of the United States Food Administration, 1917–1919.* Stanford, CA: Stanford University Press, 1941.

Rossiter, Margaret W. *Women Scientists in America: Struggles and Strategies to 1940.* Baltimore, MD: The Johns Hopkins University Press, 1982.

Skolnik, Herman, and Kenneth M. Reese, eds. *A Century of Chemistry: The Role of Chemists and the American Chemical Society.* Washington, DC: American Chemical Society, 1976.

COLLECTIONS:

Correspondence resides in the Bureau of Chemistry files in the USDA Records, National Archives, Washington, D.C.; as well as with the Charles H. Herty Papers, Emory University, Atlanta, Georgia.

Elizabeth D. Schafer, Ph.D.,
freelance writer in history of technology and science,
Loachapoka, Alabama

Pennington, Patience (1845–1921).

See Pringle, Elizabeth Allston.

Penson, Lillian Margery (1896–1963)

British historian and educator. *Name variations: Dame Lillian Penson. Born in 1896; died in 1963; at-*

tended Birkbeck and University Colleges, London; awarded Ph.D. in 1921; named Dame of the British Empire (DBE) in 1951.

After earning a Ph.D. in history in 1921, Lillian Penson began her teaching career at Birkbeck College, where she had received her undergraduate degree. In 1930, she became a professor of modern history at Bedford College, then gradually worked her way up through the ranks. She served as dean of the faculty of arts (1938–44), chair of the Academic Council (1945), and, finally, vice chancellor (1948–51), the first woman to hold such a position. After retiring from Bedford, Penson served as acting chair of the U.S. Educational Commission in the United Kingdom (1953–54). Her writings include *The Colonial Agents of the British West Indies* (1924) and *British Documents on the Origins of the War, 1898–1914* (11 volumes, 1926–38), which she produced with G.P. Gooch and H.W.V. Temperley. She also collaborated with Temperley on *A Century of Diplomatic Blue Books* (1938). Penson was awarded honorary degrees from Cambridge and Oxford universities and was an honorary fellow of the Royal College of Surgeons. She served as honorary vice-president of the Royal Historical Society from 1959 until her death in 1963.

Penthièrre, Jeanne de (c. 1320–1384).
See Jeanne de Penthièrre.

Penthievre, countess of.
See Hawise (d. after 1135).

Penthièvre, Jeanne de (c. 1320–1384).
See Jeanne de Penthièrre.

Pentland, Barbara (1912—)

Canadian composer. *Name variations: Lally Pentland. Born in Winnipeg, Manitoba, Canada, on January 2, 1912.*

Barbara Pentland struggled against parental disapproval and a serious heart ailment to become a musician and composer. After taking piano lessons at a Montreal boarding school, she studied at the Juilliard School of Music with Frederick Jacobi and Bernard Wagenaar, and in the early 1940s with Aaron Copland. Several women composers also were important mentors, including **Cécile Gauthier** in Paris, **Eva Clare** in Winnipeg, and ***Dika Newlin**. In 1955, Pentland studied in Darmstadt, where Anton Webern's music was a strong influence. During the 1970s, the Vietnam War became one of her great concerns and inspired some of her compositions, including *Disasters in the Sun*. Using dissonant linear counterpoint and dodecaphonic melodic structures within a classical structure, Pentland composed over 60 works.

John Haag,
Athens, Georgia

Pentreath, Dolly (1685–1777)

English fishmonger. *Name variations: Dorothy Pentreath; Dorothy Jeffery. Born in Mousehole, on Mounti Bay, Cornwall, England, in 1685; died in Mousehole in 1777; married to a man named Jeffery.*

Reputed to have been the last person to speak native Cornish, Dolly Pentreath was an itinerant fishmonger and fortuneteller by trade. A monument in her honor was erected in 1860 by Prince Louis Lucien Bonaparte, although her place in history was later called into question when it was claimed that Bernard Victor (d. 1875) also spoke native Cornish.

Pepper, Beverly (1924—)

American sculptor and painter. *Born Beverly Stoll on December 20, 1924, in Brooklyn, New York; Pratt Institute, Brooklyn, B.A. in industrial and advertising design, 1941; attended the Art Students League, New York, 1946, Atelier André Lhote, Paris, 1948, and Atelier Fernand Léger, Paris, 1949; married Lawrence Gussin, in 1941 (divorced 1948); married Bill Pepper (an author and journalist), in 1949; children: (first marriage) son; (second marriage) daughter.*

Known for her monumental abstract sculptures and sprawling environmental forms, Beverly Pepper evolved as a sculptor when she was in her late 30s, following a successful career in advertising and several years as a painter. Her sculptures are now part of numerous collections and can be viewed in public installations throughout the world. "Pepper's sculpture has the power to retain its integrity as sculpture but the graciousness to understand its location in a place," writes **Katherine Smith**, who cites the work *Thel* (1977) at Dartmouth College, New Hampshire, and *Amphisculpture* (1974–75) at the AT&T Long Line Center in Bedminister, New Jersey, as examples. "Both works are monumental in their proportions yet literally become part of the landscape," says Smith. "Scale for Pepper is a human quality and one she tempers with a consciousness of geography and place."

Pepper was born Beverly Stoll in 1924 and was raised in a middle-class Jewish family in Brooklyn, New York. A precocious child, she earned a degree in industrial and advertising design from Pratt Institute at the age of 17, then married a fellow student, had a son, and launched a successful career in advertising, all before the age of 21. "She handled big accounts, made lots of money, was very inventive, attractive, flamboyant, and stunningly dressed," writes **Charlotte Rubinstein**, referring to Pepper's early years. In 1948, however, she found herself unhappy with her work and left her job and her husband to study painting in Europe. In Paris, she studied with André Lhote and Fernand Léger, and also met and married her second husband, author-journalist Bill Pepper. The couple traveled extensively for several years, living in Haut du Cagnes, France, and Positano, Italy, before settling in Rome in 1952. Pepper's paintings of this period were social in theme, described in *Art News* as "romantic realism shading into expressionist distortion."

In 1960, influenced by a trip to the Far East, Pepper took up wood sculpture, carving her works from the olive, elm, and mimosa trees that fell in her garden. She took up welded sculpture in 1962, spurred by an invitation to submit a work to an outdoor sculpture exhibition in Spoleto, Italy. Having never welded before, she apprenticed herself to an ironmonger for a crash course, then began creating her own pieces in the new medium. Pepper exhibited her early welded sculptures in the "Sculpture in Metallo" show in Turin in 1965, and was selected for the Venice Biennale in 1972. In 1975, she exhibited in Houston's "Monumental Sculpture of the Seventies," and at the André Emmerich Gallery in New York, in a show that prompted Robert Hughes of *Time* magazine to recognize her as "one of the most serious and disciplined American artists of her generation."

Commenting on the polished stainless steel structures she produced in the late 1960s, Pepper notes that she attempted to create "an object that has a powerful physical presence, but is at the same time inwardly turned, seeming capable of intense self absorption." She achieved this dualism by using highly polished mirrored surfaces of steel which reflect the environment (sky, grass, earth), causing the physical bulk of the sculpture to withdraw. "Surfaces reflecting into one another caused complex illusions," writes Rubinstein. "The insides of these forms, contrasting with the silvery exterior, were in brilliant color—blue, orange, black, or white baked enamel. Many of the pieces were constructed of box-like forms, as shiny as mirrors, falling like shuffled cards, teetering in precarious vertical stacks or cantilevering out into space."

During the 1970s, Pepper began to work with triangular forms, suggesting "tents, architecture and pyramids," and again creating contradictions. "Hollows seen from one side, when viewed from another appear to go in contradictory directions," writes Rubinstein. The massive work *Alpha* (1975), constructed of four orange triangular sheaths, appears solid and heavy from the side, but is quite light and open when viewed from the front, creating what Pepper calls a "precarious balance between the physically self evident and the sense of an elusive inner logic."

Some of Pepper's environmental forms defy classification as sculpture. Her first large environmental project, *Land Canal Hillside* (1971–74), was built along the center-strip divider of a highway in Dallas, Texas. Rubinstein describes it as a series of "rust-colored, corten-steel triangular forms tilted at different angles, set into grass that grows over some of it in angular patterns." Pepper conceived *Amphisculpture* (1974–75), an outdoor concrete amphitheater set in grass on the grounds of the AT&T Long Lines Headquarters, to be an interactive environment, "created to bring people out of their offices and into an involvement with the site. It allows them to enter into it, to sit down or to walk, to be alone or in groups. . . to withdraw in silence." On a site at New Smyrna Beach, Florida, Pepper created *Sand Dunes* (1985), a mylar over wood structure which stretches 100 feet along the beach.

During the late 1980s, Pepper began to create monumental steel columns, which like her earlier works alter the environment in which they are placed. "There has always been a sense of mystery in the massive forms she constructs," writes Smith, "but the columns of recent vintage are perhaps the richest in a sense of history and time." Pepper first exhibited her columns at the piazza at Todi, Italy, a superb location for them, says Smith, "but their intrinsic power is such that even in other less historically rich locations there is a quality of self absorption and mystery about the work to suggest a new form for the term 'monument.'"

Pepper has had countless individual exhibitions in both the United States and Europe, and is the recipient of numerous awards, including the Gold Medal and Sculpture purchase award from the Mostra Internazionale Florino, Italy (1966), the Best Art in Steel award from the Iron and Steel Industry, New York (1970), and the National Endowment for the Arts award (1975).

In 1972, Pepper and her husband purchased a 14th-century castle in Todi, Perugia, overlooking the northern Italian countryside, where she worked out of a nearby industrial workshop equipped with all the heavy equipment she used to create her oversized pieces. The house served as an ideal backdrop for entertaining, which Pepper continued to do with the flair she has had from childhood. The artist's personality, however, is perhaps best expressed in her sculpture. "In my work the image comes from within me—an 'emotion' that is released," she says. "I then apply whatever critical abilities I possess to allow the intermingling of the intellect and emotion. Even if there is a conflict and contradiction between these two, I allow them to feed into one another and eventually merge into one being."

SOURCES:

Heller, Nancy G. *Women Artists: An Illustrated History.* NY: Abbeville Press, 1987.

Hillstrom, Laurie Collier, and Kevin Hillstrom. *Contemporary Women Artists.* Farmington, MI: St. James Press, 1999.

Rubinstein, Charlotte Streifer. *American Women Artists.* Boston, MA: G.K. Hall, 1982.

Barbara Morgan,
Melrose, Massachusetts

Pepys, Elizabeth (1640–1669)

English gentlewoman. *Name variations: Elizabeth de St. Michel; Elizabeth Saint-Michel; Mrs. Pepys. Born Elizabeth de St. Michel in 1640 in Devon, England; died on November 10, 1669, in London; daughter of Alexandre le Marchant, sire of St. Michel, and Dorothea Kingsmill; married Samuel Pepys (a diarist and naval secretary), in December 1655; no children.*

The life of Elizabeth Pepys, which has survived in the famous diary of her husband Samuel Pepys, demonstrates the constraints and possibilities available to a 17th-century European woman. She was born Elizabeth de St. Michel in 1640 in Devon, England, the daughter of **Dorothea Kingsmill** and a French knight, Alexandre le Marchant, sire of St. Michel, who served in the French military and in the retinue of Queen ***Henrietta Maria.** While seeking his fortune, he moved his Irish-born wife and two children from England to Paris. There Elizabeth received a modest education in a convent (despite her Protestantism), excelling particularly in languages. Eventually her family settled in St. Martin-in-the-Fields in England, where Alexandre eked out a living as an inventor. In 1655, Elizabeth met Samuel Pepys, seven years her senior, a tailor's son who had managed to gain a university education. Pepys' family and friends discouraged him from pursuing a penniless, Catholic-educated foreign girl, but it was a love match. Certainly the St. Michels had no money or connections which might help Pepys launch his civil-service career. They married in December 1655, but their mutual poverty and Elizabeth's youth (she was 15 at the time) led the couple to put off setting up their household for another year.

The marriage did not begin well. Pepys was rarely home and Elizabeth had little to occupy her time. His neglect and his numerous affairs with other women led Elizabeth to leave Pepys in 1657. They reconciled some months later, and their remaining 12 years together were spent in relative marital contentment. In Pepys' remarkably candid diary, which he began in 1659, Elizabeth is mentioned in almost every entry, often with affection. As Pepys rose slowly from clerk to an important naval post, their fortunes improved, and the couple began to enjoy a leisured life. They attended the theater and opera together and shared an interest in fashion. They also read together, especially as Samuel's vision failed, and studied music, geography, and arithmetic. Samuel encouraged Elizabeth's education and hired tutors for her in dancing, drawing, and singing. Around 1665, she began to study painting seriously, developing friendships with London's professional artists.

Yet Elizabeth's life should not be romanticized, as some historians have done. She suffered throughout from poor health and was deeply saddened by her failure, despite several pregnancies, to bear any living children. Her marriage was not without its serious problems. In the 17th-century model of marriage, the husband was the authoritarian head of the household, the wife his submissive companion, and Samuel shared this belief. Along with his professions of love and passion for Elizabeth, his diary shows that theirs was not a marriage between equals. Samuel Pepys was a jealous and suspicious husband, not above resorting to violence against Elizabeth or their servants to preserve his authority. He sometimes accused her of adultery, poor housekeeping, and excessive friendliness with servants. He also spent his fortune freely on himself while accusing her of mismanaging her small household allowance. Elizabeth was too strong minded to accept his treatment quietly, which led to long, bitter arguments. She was also angered and embarrassed by Samuel's adultery, especially his affairs with her companion ladies and maids.

During the summer of 1669, Samuel, Elizabeth, and her brother enjoyed an extended trip to the Low Countries and France. A few days after their return to London in November, Elizabeth died of a fever contracted in Flanders. She was 29 years old.

SOURCES:

Delaforce, Patrick. *Pepys in Love: Elizabeth's Story.* London: Bishopsgate Press, 1985.

Ollard, Richard. *Pepys: A Biography.* NY: Holt, Rinehart & Winston, 1974.

Laura York,
Riverside, California

Peratrovich, Elizabeth Wanamaker (1911–1958)

Grand Camp President of the Alaska Native Sisterhood who was in the forefront of the fight to end discrimination against the indigenous peoples in Alaska. *Born Kaaxgal.aat in Petersburg, Alaska, on July 4, 1911; died after a long battle with cancer on December 1, 1958; interred in Juneau's Evergreen Cemetery; a Tlingit, she was born into the Lukaax.adi clan of the Raven moiety; attended Ketchikan High School; continued studies at Western College of Education in Bellingham, Washington; married Roy Peratrovich, on December 15, 1931; children.*

Elizabeth Wanamaker Peratrovich

A Tlingit and Grand Camp President of the Alaska Native Sisterhood (ANS), Elizabeth Peratrovich led the battle to outlaw discrimination against Alaska's indigenous peoples. Born with the Tlingit name of Kaaxgal.aat in Petersburg, Alaska, in 1911, she was adopted after the deaths of her parents while she was still young. Following her graduation from Ketchikan High School, she went on to study in Bellingham, Washington, at Western College of Education. In 1931, she married Roy Peratrovich, of Klawock, in Washington. To raise their family, they returned to Alaska a decade later, in 1941.

From Klawock they moved to Juneau, where they were amazed to see businesses displaying signs which were blatantly discriminatory against Alaska's indigenous peoples. In addition to shop-window signs which read, "No Dogs or Indians Allowed," the discriminatory practices in Juneau during the 1940s included segregated areas in movie theaters and some restaurants (others banned Natives entirely), housing inequalities, and the prohibition of Indian children from public schools.

For years, the Peratrovichs, diligent champions of human rights in Alaska, lobbied for an Anti-Discrimination Bill. Their influence, along with that of the ANS and Alaska Native Brotherhood (ANB), was instrumental in the eventual passing of this legislation in 1945. In that year, the bill was ratified in the state house with relative ease by a 19-to-5 vote, but it met violent opposition when it reached the state senate. Among those opposed was Allen Shattuck who declared: "Far from being brought closer together, which will result from this bill, the races should be kept further apart. Who are these people, barely out of savagery, who want to associate with us whites with 5,000 years of recorded civilization behind us?"

When Senate President Joe Green asked if there was "anyone in the gallery who would like to testify," Elizabeth Peratrovich rose:

> I would not have expected that I, who am barely out of savagery, would have to remind gentlemen with 5,000 years recorded civilization behind them of our Bill of Rights. When my husband and I came to Juneau and sought a home in a nice neighborhood where our children could play happily with our neighbors' children, we found such a house and had arranged to lease it. When the owners learned we were Indians, they said "no." Would we be compelled to live in slums?

When a dubious Shattuck challenged Peratrovich, "Will this law eliminate discrimination?," her response drew applause not only from the gallery but also from the senate floor:

Do your laws against larceny and even murder prevent these crimes? No law will eliminate crimes, but at least you legislators can assert to the world that you recognize the evil of the present situation and speak of your intent to help us overcome discrimination.

Largely thanks to her plea, the senate did just that, passing the bill 11 to 5. Wrote the *Daily Alaska Empire* of Peratrovich's speech, "It was the neatest performance of any witness yet to appear before this session and there were a few red senatorial ears as she regally left the chambers." In 1989, Alaska formally recognized her contribution to the battle for human rights by setting aside February 16 as "Elizabeth Peratrovich Day."

SOURCES:

A Recollection of Civil Rights Leader Elizabeth Peratrovich 1911–1958. Compiled by Central Council of Tlingit and Haida Indian Tribes of Alaska. August 1991.

Percy, Agnes (fl. 1120s)

Sister-in-law of King Henry I. *Flourished around the 1120s; daughter of William Percy, 3rd baron Percy, and* ***Alice Tunbridge*** *(daughter of Richard Tunbridge, earl of Clare); married Josceline Louvain (brother of *****Adelicia of Louvain*** *and brother-in-law of King Henry I); children: Henry Percy; Richard Percy (died around 1244).*

Percy, Anne (fl. 1470s)

Countess of Arundel. *Name variations: Anne Fitzalan. Flourished in the 1470s; married William Fitzalan, 15th earl of Arundel; children: Henry Fitzalan (c. 1476–1544), 16th earl of Arundel, and *****Katherine Fitzalan*** *(fl. 1530s).*

Percy, Eleanor (c. 1250–?).

See Eleanor de Warrenne.

Percy, Eleanor (c. 1413–1472).

See Beaufort, Joan (c. 1379–1440) for sidebar on Eleanor Neville.

Percy, Eleanor (d. 1530)

Duchess of Buckingham. *Name variations: Eleanor Stafford; Alianore Percy. Died in 1530; daughter of Henry Percy (1421–1461), earl of Northumberland (r. 1455–1461), and *****Eleanor Poynings*** *(d. 1483); married Edward Stafford (1478–1521), 3rd duke of Buckingham (executed on May 17, 1521); children: Henry Stafford (b. 1501), Lord Stafford; *****Elizabeth Stafford*** *(1494–1558); Lady* ***Mary Stafford*** *(who married George Nevill, 5th Lord Abergavenny); *****Catherine Stafford*** *(who married Ralph Neville, 4th earl of Westmoreland).*

Percy, Elizabeth (1371–1417)

English noblewoman. *Name variations: Elizabeth Mortimer. Born on February 12, 1371, in Usk, Gwent, Wales; died in April 1417 at Trotton, West Sussex, England; buried in Trotton; daughter of Edmund Mortimer (1352–1381), 3rd earl of March, and Philippa Mortimer (1355–1382); sister of Edmund Mortimer (1376–1438); married Henry Percy (1364–1403), also known as Harry Percy or Hotspur (son of the 1st earl of Northumberland); married Thomas, 1st baron Camoys; children: (first marriage) Henry Percy (1392–1455), 2nd earl of Northumberland (r. 1415–1455); *****Elizabeth Percy*** *(d. 1437).*

A noblewoman and rebel, Elizabeth Percy was immortalized by William Shakespeare as "Kate Percy" in *Henry IV*. Little historical information has survived about the real Elizabeth. Born into an aristocratic English family, she was the daughter of Edmund Mortimer, earl of March, and ***Philippa Mortimer**, and the great-granddaughter of King Edward III. She thus claimed royal descent on her mother's side and was of Welsh descent on her father's side. Her parents arranged a marriage for her with Sir Henry Percy, the eldest son of the earl of Northumberland. Henry Percy, called Harry "Hotspur" because of his boldness in battle, was an important military leader who aided Henry Bolingbroke's (Henry IV) successful rebellion against King Richard II in 1399.

But by 1402, Harry had turned against his former ally. With Elizabeth's support, Harry led a massive rebellion against Henry IV which almost toppled him. This rebellion sought to put Elizabeth's brother Edmund Mortimer on the throne as the rightful heir to England. In 1403, Harry was killed at the Battle of Shrewsbury; his death effectively ended the organized opposition to Henry IV's rule. Trying to recover his authority, Henry IV sought to imprison or kill the remaining leaders of the rebels. One of those whom Henry punished was Hotspur's widow Elizabeth, who was arrested shortly after the Battle of Shrewsbury as a traitor to the king. She was eventually released, although she and her two children were stripped of all rights to Hotspur's properties. But Elizabeth, a resilient woman, remained loyal to Hotspur's memory, and managed to have his remains buried in the tomb of the Northumberland family in York

Minster. She did remarry, however, probably compelled by need to provide for her own and her children's future. Her second husband was a minor noble, Thomas Lord Camoys, who had served in her first husband's army. Thomas was eventually reconciled to the crown, and was in the English army under Henry V at the Battle of Agincourt in 1413. Lady Elizabeth died four years later at age 46 and is buried next to her second husband in the Church of Saint George in Trotton, West Sussex.

SOURCES:

Bevan, Brian. *Henry IV*. NY: St. Martin's Press, 1994.

Laura York,
Riverside, California

Percy, Elizabeth (d. 1437)

Countess of Westmoreland. *Name variations: Elizabeth Neville; Elizabeth Clifford. Died on October 26, 1437, at Staindrop Church; daughter of Henry Percy (1364–1403), also known as Harry Percy or Hotspur (son of the 1st earl of Northumberland), and *__Elizabeth Percy__ (1371–1417); married John Clifford, 7th Lord Clifford, in May 1404; married Ralph Neville, 2nd earl of Westmoreland, in 1426; children: (first marriage) Thomas Clifford, 8th Lord Clifford (b. 1414); (second marriage) John Neville.*

Percy, Elizabeth (1667–1722)

Duchess of Somerset. *Name variations: Lady Elizabeth Percy; countess of Ogle. Born on January 26, 1667, in Petworth, Sussex; died of breast cancer on November 23, 1722, at Northumberland House; interred at Salisbury Cathedral; only surviving daughter and sole heir of Josceline also known as Jocelyn Percy (1644–1670), 11th and last earl of Northumberland, and *__Elizabeth Wriothesly__; married Henry Cavendish, earl of Ogle, on March 27, 1679; married Thomas Thynne (1648–1682), on November 15, 1681 (marriage never consummated because he was murdered by Königsmark, one of her suitors); married Sir Charles Seymour, 6th duke of Somerset, on May 30, 1682; children: Charles Seymour, earl of Herford; __Elizabeth Seymour__ (1685–1734, who married Henry O'Brien, 8th earl of Thomond); Lady __Catherine Seymour__ (d. 1731, who married Sir William Wyndham); Algernon Seymour (b. 1684), 7th duke of Somerset; __Anne Seymour__ (d. 1722, who married Peregrine Hyde Osborne, 3rd duke of Leeds).*

Elizabeth Percy, duchess of Somerset, was mistress of the robes to Queen ***Anne**.

Percy, Elizabeth (d. 1704)

Countess of Northumberland. *Name variations: Elizabeth Howard. Died on March 11, 1704; daughter of Theophilus Howard (1584–1640), 2nd earl of Suffolk (r. 1584–1640), and *__Elizabeth Hume__ (c. 1599–1633); married Algernon Percy (1602–1668), 10th earl of Northumberland (r. 1632–1668), on October 1, 1642; children: Josceline also known as Jocelyn Percy (1644–1670), 11th and last earl of Northumberland. Algernon Percy's first wife was __Anne Cecil__.*

Elizabeth Percy and her admiral-husband Algernon Percy, 10th earl of Northumberland, became guardians of the youngest children of King Charles I, ***Elizabeth Stuart** (1635–1650) and Henry, duke of Gloucester, in 1645.

Percy, Elizabeth (d. 1776)

Duchess of Northumberland. *Name variations: Lady Elizabeth Seymour; Baroness Percy. Died on December 5, 1776; daughter of *__Frances Thynne__ (1699–1754) and Algernon Seymour (b. 1684), Baron Percy, 7th duke of Somerset; married Sir Hugh Smithson (1714–1786, a wealthy Yorkshire baronet who assumed the name Percy), 1st duke of Northumberland (r. 1766–1786), on July 16, 1740; children: Hugh Percy (b. 1742), 2nd duke of Northumberland; Algernon Percy (b. 1750), 1st earl of Beverley.*

Percy, Katherine (b. 1423)

Countess of Kent. *Born on May 28, 1423, in Leconfield, Yorkshire; daughter of Henry Percy (1392–1455), 2nd earl of Northumberland (r. 1415–1455), and *__Eleanor Neville__ (c. 1413–1472); married Edmund Grey (b. 1416), 1st earl of Kent, before 1440; children: Anthony Grey, Baron de Ruthin; George Grey, 2nd earl of Kent; John Grey, Lord Grey of Ruthin; Edmund Grey; __Elizabeth Grey__ (who married Sir Robert Greystoke); __Anne Grey__ (who married John Grey, Lord Grey of Wilton).*

Percy, Mary (1320–1362)

Baroness Percy. *Name variations: Mary Plantagenet. Born in 1320 (some sources cite 1321); died on September 2, 1362; interred at Alnwick, Northumberland; daughter of Henry (b. 1281), 3rd earl of Lancaster, and *__Maud Chaworth__ (1282–c. 1322); married Henry Percy, 3rd baron Percy, in September 1341 (some sources cite 1334); children: Henry Percy (1341–1408), 1st earl of Northumberland (r. 1377–1408); Maud Percy, also seen as Mary Percy (1360–1395, who married John, Lord Ros).*

Perdita (1758–1800).

See Robinson, Mary.

Perec, Marie-Jose (1968—)

French runner. *Born on May 9, 1968.*

Hugely popular in France, Marie-Jose Perec won an Olympic gold medal in the 400 meters in Barcelona in 1992. She also won an Olympic gold medal in the 400 meters in Atlanta in 1996 with a time of 48.25, setting an Olympic record.

Peregrina, La (1814–1873).

See Gómez de Avellaneda, Gertrudis.

Pereira, Irene Rice (1902–1971)

Twentieth-century American modernist painter, poet, and essayist. *Name variations: I. Rice Pereira. Born Irene Rice in Chelsea, Massachusetts, on August 5, 1902; died in Marbella, Spain, on January 11, 1971; daughter of Emanuel (known as Emery) Rice (a baker and businessman) and Hilda Vanderbilt Rice; married Humberto Pereira, in 1929 (divorced 1938); married George Wellington Brown, in 1942 (divorced 1950); married George Reavey, in 1950 (divorced 1959).*

Enrolled in art classes at the Art Students League, New York (1929); traveled through Europe (1931); traveled in North Africa (1932); gave first solo art show, American Contemporary Arts Gallery, New York (1933); was a member of the fine arts faculty, the Federal Arts Project Design Laboratory (1936); painted on glass (1939–52); diagnosed with breast cancer and underwent mastectomy (1943); was a sponsor of the Cultural and Scientific Conference for World Peace held at the Waldorf-Astoria Hotel, New York City (1949); published philosophy, "Light and the New Reality," in Palette *(1952); was the subject of a Whitney Museum retrospective exhibit (1953); converted to Roman Catholicism (1963); received an honorary doctorate from the Free University of Asia, Karachi, Pakistan (1969).*

Selected writings—all self-published: The Transformation of "Nothing" and the Paradox of Space *(1953);* The Nature of Space, a Metaphysical and Aesthetic Inquiry *(1956, reprinted by the Corcoran Gallery of Art, Washington, D.C., 1968);* The Lapis *(1957, reprinted by the Corcoran Gallery of Art, 1970);* Crystal of the Rose *(1959);* The Transcendental Formal Logic of the Infinite: Evolution of Cultural Forms *(1966);* The Finite versus the Infinite *(1969);* The Poetics of the Form of Space, Light and the Infinite *(1969).*

Until recently, modernist painter Irene Rice Pereira was one of the forgotten women of 20th-century American art. For a 20-year period from 1933 to 1953, Pereira was a cutting-edge figure in abstract art whose work was widely praised and regularly exhibited in major galleries, including a 1953 retrospective exhibit at the prestigious Whitney Museum of Art in New York City. Yet in the years that followed, her formal and impersonal style of abstract painting fell out of critical favor, displaced by the abstract expressionist movement to which Pereira objected. By the time of her death in 1971, she had become a marginal figure whose work no longer received critical attention.

The details of Pereira's early life are poorly known, due in part to her reticence and in part to her habit of fabricating her past. She was not, for example, born in 1907 as she always claimed, but on August 5, 1902, in Chelsea, Massachusetts, the eldest of four children of Emery Rice and **Hilda Vanderbilt Rice**. Emery was a Polish emigrant who had arrived in America as a child. Hilda was a native Bostonian of Dutch and German descent. During Irene's childhood, the family moved from the Boston area to Pittsfield and then to Great Barrington, Massachusetts, where her father owned a bakery and raised horses. Irene appears to have received her artistic bent from her father's family, which included musicians, composers, and one sculptor. Emery himself collected fine porcelain, had a taste for fine clothes, and associated with a bohemian crowd he called "gypsies." That he bestowed the sobriquet "gypsy" on Irene may indicate a recognition of their temperamental similarities. By contrast, Pereira described her mother as "very, very formal." The children of the Rice household, she later recalled, played little but dedicated themselves to horses and reading. Pereira devoured Alcott, Austen, and Thackeray, and even tried her hand at writing a biography of ***Joan of Arc**.

When Pereira was seven or eight, her father's business failed, and after returning briefly to Boston the family finally settled in Brooklyn, New York. Their fortunes took a further downhill turn in 1918 with the death of Emery. Though Irene was just 16, the family's desperate financial position required that she switch from an academic to a vocational curriculum in high school, which she completed in the space of six months. She then found employment as a stenographer in an accountant's office.

The dream of a creative life, however, did not die. Pereira immersed herself in the bohemian culture of Greenwich Village and began to take night courses in fashion design and literature. In 1927, she followed her sister **Dorothy Rice**'s lead by enrolling in classes at the Art Students League. Here she was exposed to George Santayana's aesthetic philosophy, which explored the role of art in industrial society—a subject that would inform Pereira's artistic sensibility throughout her career. Around this time, she met Humberto Pereira, a commercial artist rather unsuccessfully pursuing a career as a painter and photographer. The two wed in January 1929. While they unquestionably shared artistic interests, Irene later confessed that she married Humberto primarily to gain independence from her family. The relationship does not appear to have been particularly close, and they divorced in 1938.

The year 1929 marked a watershed in Irene's artistic development as well. In October, she entered a class at the Art Students League taught by Jan Matulka, her first great artistic influence, who exposed her to the art and aesthetic theories of the European avant-garde. With Matulka and a dedicated cadre of other students dubbed "the Communists" for their fierce devotion to the revolutionary canons of modernism, Pereira studied Dada, Surrealism, German Expressionism, Cubism, Bauhaus, and, perhaps most significantly, Constructivism, a Russian-born style of non-representational art employing modern industrial materials in highly formalized organizations of mass, volume, and space. In her two years of study with Matulka, Pereira was encouraged to experiment with the Cubist style, and her compositions from the early 1930s exhibit a severe geometrical composition and frequent use of parallel lines and triangles, exemplified in her *Portrait of Negro* (1932).

In the summer of 1931, Matulka's protégés began to disband. Several went abroad, including Pereira who in September embarked for Paris, the home of the artistic avant-garde. Arriving there in October, she made her way to the prestigious Academie Moderne. What exactly she did at the Academie Moderne is a matter of some confusion. In the years following her return from Europe, Pereira would claim that she studied there, and at one point even asserted that she received instruction from the famous Fernand Léger—a point clearly contradicted by the fact that during her entire stay in Paris Léger was residing in the United States. Late in life, Pereira reversed herself and insisted that she only visited the Academie Moderne, where she found the quality of its instruction disappointing. Whatever the case, Pereira remained in Paris about a month, before moving on to Geneva, Milan, Florence, Venice, and Rome, where she drank in Renaissance art and architecture, all the while composing preparatory studies for paintings she would execute upon her return to the United States. In December, she sailed from Palermo to Tunis and traveled through North Africa. Pereira later attributed her fascination with light and infinite space to a transcendent experience in the Sahara, although her biographer notes that if so, the experience had no discernable effect on her work upon her reappearance in New York in January 1933.

While on the return voyage, Pereira had executed a number of drawings of the ship's machinery and tackle. These served as the basis for a series of semi-abstract oil paintings that she exhibited at her first solo show, held at the American Contemporary Arts Gallery in January 1933. *The New York Times*' art critic, Thomas C. Linn, favorably reviewed the show, commenting: "Here is a young artist who paints boldly and effectively in her large canvases, and with interesting color and whimsical humor in her smaller pictures. Although the marine subjects that Miss Pereira chooses for her abstractions may not interest all, many will recognize her skill." In fact, the subjects Pereira selected, and her treatment of them, were emblematic of the social and aesthetic preoccupations of the 1930s, with the rise of technology and humanity's questionable prospects in a world dominated by machines. Pereira's paintings of this period express a deep ambivalence about the promise of the Machine Age. If on the one hand her commitment to a modernist aesthetic inclined her to incorporate the geometric order and functionalism of industrial society into her art, her canvases betray a growing unease about the degrading implications of living in a world run by machines. In *The Presses* (1933), a small, marginalized human figure pays obeisance to the awesome technological power he supposedly controls; while in *Man and Machine I* and *Man and Machine II* (both 1936), machines actually seem to be dismembering the men who operate them.

In January 1936, Pereira joined the fine arts faculty at the Federal Art Project Design Laboratory, an affiliation she maintained until her resignation in October 1939. During these years, as the shadow of fascism lengthened, Pereira joined ranks with left/liberal artists who pressed their art into the service of the anti-fascist cause. Pereira began painting canvases in a social realist style—among them *Struggling* and *Against War and Fascism* (both 1937)—that conveyed an unambiguous, often heavy-handed political message. By 1939, she was clearly establishing herself among New York artists. In March of that year, she made the first major sale of her work. She also lectured at Columbia University on "New Materials and the Artist," beginning what would be many years of guest lectureships and appointments at colleges and universities around the country. And towards the end of 1939 Pereira began to paint on glass, a medium in which she would accomplish her most acclaimed works of art.

In October 1940, with her government-funded job at the Art Project Easel Division about to be terminated, she applied for and received a position as museum assistant at the new Museum of Non-Objective Painting. Pereira worked there until her resignation in September 1942 following a quarrel with the museum's curator, Baroness ***Hilla Rebay**. In the same month, Pereira married George Wellington Brown, a naval engineer whom she may have met on her travels in Europe ten years before, and began teaching at the Pratt Institute. However, she was forced to resign from Pratt just four months later after being diagnosed with breast cancer, a disease from which her younger sister Dorothy had died a year and a half before. Pereira immediately underwent a radical mastectomy which successfully removed the cancer.

Despite these personal calamities, Pereira's creative energy hardly slackened, and her career continued to soar. Her abstract compositions integrated ever more of her intellectual interests in psychology, physics, alchemy, and occult philosophy. Her paintings, like *Self-Portrait* (1943), increasingly plumbed the depths of the human unconscious by deploying a universal symbolic language drawn from Jungian psychology. In 1948, Pereira herself began to undergo Jungian psychotherapy, a transformative experience she creatively joined with the alchemical idea of the transmutation of substances. Her abstract studies of light and infinite space, especially, played off modern physical and cosmological theories of four-dimensional space-time. Some of Pereira's best-known works created a sense of indefinitely deep space and of pervasive light by superimposing panels of corrugated glass painted with an intricate web of intersecting lines, exemplified by *Undulating Arrangement* (1947).

Pereira's preoccupation with the theoretical ideas underlying her abstract compositions intensified after she met the Irish Surrealist poet George Reavey in August 1949. Pereira and husband George Brown had separated earlier that summer, and upon her return from a trip to Paris in November she and Reavey became lovers. The following summer, Pereira received a divorce from Brown, and in September 1950 she and Reavey were married in London. The couple took up residence in Salford, near the University of Manchester where Reavey held a professorship. Evidently Pereira found the long and gloomy northern English winter dismal, and life in postwar Britain, with its continued rationing of consumer goods and grim reminders of war, depressing. She longed for the sun and the creature comforts of America, and so returned to the U.S. in May 1951, taking a position at Ball State Teachers' College.

My work, as I see it, is a search to apply the concepts of our time to esthetics.

—I. Rice Pereira

To judge by their correspondence when apart, Reavey and Pereira excited each other's interests in occult philosophies and mystic wisdom. Reavey introduced Pereira to Neoplatonism, whose stress on light resonated with her own aesthetic predilections and seemed to prefigure its central role in the 20th-century physical theories to which she understood her work as giving artistic expression. He also encouraged her to draft and publish her philosophy of light, art, and modern experience, which eventually appeared under the title "Light and the New Reality" in *Palette* (1952). This essay, and the writings that followed, which she had to self-publish, represented a bid for an intellectual preeminence in the academic world of arts and letters to which Pereira was not remotely equal, as was painfully clear even to her friends and supporters who urged her to stick to painting. Her prose style was pretentious, her thinking unsystematic, her ideas ultimately incoherent. One of her younger friends remarked how strange it was that when she described her work verbally "[h]er explanations were concise and simple" whereas in print "her words [were] so strangely elaborate; they seemed to have no relation to the conversations I remembered." A critic complained less generously that the philosophical explanations Pereira provided for her paintings "seek to inflate a very little into a whole lot."

The retrospective exhibit of Pereira's work that the Whitney Museum of American Art mounted in the winter of 1953 marked the crowning moment of her career. Thereafter, her star steadily declined. She abruptly stopped producing the painted-glass studies of light and space that had brought her such prominence, and returned to explorations of depth on a flat canvas using "Z" figures, a motif that was not well received critically. Her "philosophy" was derided and then ignored. Moreover, Pereira's style of formal, impersonal abstraction, inspired by European movements of the '20s and '30s, was under challenge by the new American style of Abstract Expressionism. Pereira found herself under political suspicion for having communist affiliations and under artistic threat for having stylistic and intellectual allegiances to foreign masters. She intensified her isolation, however, by distancing herself from the Abstract Expressionists and condemning them. In a letter to *The New York Times* published in 1955, she declared: "In my opinion, it is futile to try to define this style of painting in terms of art. When painters eliminate values, space and dimensions from experience there is no aesthetic." Her attack, however, was of no import; she was first ignored by the artistic world and then quickly forgotten by the avant-garde.

Pereira continued to lecture, exhibit, and write throughout the 1950s and 1960s, though she never regained her former prominence. At the end of 1955, she left Reavey; they divorced four years later. In 1963, she converted to Roman Catholicism. In her final years, she developed a highly inflated self-image, denying the influence of previous artists on her work and claiming, in her private notes at least, that she stood "alongside of Descartes, Copernicus, Newton, Plato." By 1970, when the Whitney devoted an exhibition to women artists, a canvas by Pereira was greeted by *The New York Times*' critic with pleasant surprise, "after not seeing her work for a long time." Pereira did not see the occasion, however, as a chance to celebrate the contributions of women to American art: "My work stood on its own. Whatever trouble I had came from other women." This was to be her last public statement; she died of emphysema on January 11, 1971, in Marbella, Spain.

SOURCES AND SUGGESTED READING:

Bearor, Karen A. *Irene Rice Pereira: Her Paintings and Philosophy.* Austin, TX: University of Texas Press, 1993.

Golemba, Beverly E. *Lesser Known Women.* Boulder, CO: Lynne Rienner, 1992.

Lawter, Estella. *Women as Mythmaker: Poetry and Visual Art By Twentieth Century Women.* Bloomington, IN: Indiana University Press, 1984.

The New York Times. January 22, 1933; May 1, 1955; December 27, 1970.

Rubinstein, Charlotte Streifer. *American Women Artists.* Boston, MA: G.K. Hall, 1982.

Schwartz, Therese. "Demystifying Pereira," in *Art in America.* October 1979, pp. 114–119.

Suzanne Smith,
freelance writer, Decatur, Georgia

Perestrello-Moniz, Filippa

(d. 1483)

Portuguese wife of Christopher Columbus. *Name variations: Filippa Columbus or Columbo; Filippa Colón; Felipa Perestrello e Moniz. Died in 1483; daughter of a Portuguese officer (governor of an island near Madeira); married Christopher Columbus (1451–1506, the explorer), also seen as Cristóbal Colón (Spanish) and Cristoforo Columbo (Italian); children: Diego. Christopher Columbus also had an illegitimate son Ferdinand.*

When Christopher Columbus was born in Genoa, Italy, in 1451, there was no exact knowledge as to the size of the earth and the width of the ocean off the Continent of Europe. Trade for spices and jewels with Asia (called the Indies) had been carried on by land extending over thousands of miles. But such trade was stopped at about this time by the Mohammedan Turks who took control of Asia Minor and the Balkans.

Columbus first went to sea when he was nine or ten years old, making several Mediterranean voyages. Years later, while on a voyage in 1476, he was wounded in a battle at sea off the coast of Portugal. Though his Genoese ship was sunk, he eventually swam to shore and remained in Portugal for about ten years. He and his brother Bartholomew engaged in chart making. Columbus married Filippa Perestrello-Moniz, the daughter of a Portuguese officer, governor of an island near Madeira. Filippa's father had been successfully engaged in the sea trade, and he passed on much of his knowledge and experience. The marriage was brief, with Filippa dying in 1483.

Two reasons traditionally put forth by historians for Columbus's sudden departure from Lisbon around that year were that he was either out of funds or that he feared that John II, king of Portugal, would steal his plan of finding a new passage to Asia. Research by former CIA intelligence analyst Peter Dickson has led Dickson to challenge these explanations, asserting that it is more likely that Columbus fled because there were close family ties between Filippa Perestrello-Moniz and conspirators seeking to kill or dethrone John. Dickson argues for the possibility that, once the plot was discovered, the king's wrath over the conspirators' connection to Filippa drove Columbus to Castile. Filippa left Columbus with one son, Diego Colón, who assumed the title of Admiral when Columbus died on May 20, 1506. In 1509, Diego was appointed governor of Hispaniola.

Perevozchikova, Maria.

See Stanislavski, Maria.

Perey, Marguerite (1909–1975)

French nuclear chemist and physicist who discovered Francium, the 87th element in the periodic table, in 1938. *Born Marguerite Catherine Perey on October 19, 1909, in Villemomble, France; died in Louveciennes, France, on May 14, 1975; youngest of five children of an industrialist; never married.*

Marguerite Perey began her scientific career as the personal assistant and confidante of ***Marie Curie**. A meticulous, determined researcher, in 1938 Perey discovered the last element to be found in nature (i.e., without atomic bombardment) and the first to be discovered in two decades, the long-sought 87th element. In 1962, Perey would become the first woman to be admitted to the French Academy of Sciences.

She was born in 1909 into a financially affluent family in Villemomble, a small suburb northeast of Paris. The outbreak of World War I in 1914 revealed the world's fragile nature to the young Marguerite, who lost her father at the outset of the conflict. She was educated at the École d'Enseignement Technique Féminine, a private but state-recognized school for technicians. After being awarded her Diplôme d'Etat de Chimiste in 1929, she immediately joined the world-famous Paris Institut du Radium, whose director was the illustrious Marie Curie. Madame Curie quickly became aware of the intelligence, skill, and eagerness of her young laboratory assistant, and she chose Perey to be her *préparateur* (personal assistant) and confidante.

When Perey began working at the Institut du Radium, her first assigned task was the purification of actinium, a radioactive element discovered in 1899 by André Louis Debierne (1874–1949). The actinide series had not been investigated as thoroughly as had the other two naturally radioactive families, the radium and thorium series. In the 1930s, little was known about actinium, and even its half-life was uncertain, with estimates ranging from 7 to 22 years. Laboratory investigations of actinium represented a daunting challenge, because it is much rarer than the accompanying rare earth elements, from which it is separated with great difficulty. Determined to overcome the challenges, Perey spent countless hours in the laboratory. Within a few years, most other scientists in the field of radiochemistry joined in recognizing her unusual talents.

By the mid-1930s, Perey had succeeded in preparing the most intense source of actinium ever available. Even then—at only ten millicuries concentrated in a few milligrams of lanthanum oxide—it was minuscule compared to most other laboratory samples. The work she did was not only demanding, but over the decades would expose Perey to dangerous dosages of radioactivity.

The death of Madame Curie in 1934 was a severe blow to Perey, who lost both a patron and a revered scientific mentor. Perey would later recall with considerable emotion the five formative years she had spent in close, nearly daily, contact with Madame Curie. Following Curie's death, André Debierne became the Institut's director. Both he and Curie's daughter, ***Irène Joliot-Curie**, asked Perey to continue her research on the still little-understood properties of actinium, hoping that she would be able to determine its precise half-life.

During the autumn of 1938, Perey observed an anomaly in the beta rays emitted by an actinium sample that had been separated from all of its descendants. With her customary thoroughness, she was able at this time to observe an emission phenomenon that had remained undetected for four decades by a number of earlier and less skillful radiochemists. After numerous painstaking tests, in January 1939 Perey concluded that she had discovered the long-sought element theorized as part of the periodic table, the vacant number 87, eka-caesium. Amazingly, this discovery had not been made by an eminent professor but rather by a modest 29-year-old technician lacking a university degree.

Perey's findings caused considerable disquiet in the Curie laboratory. Even though both Debierne and Joliot-Curie had been kept informed separately of the progress of Perey's investigations, when Joliot-Curie told Debierne of Perey's success at discovering eka-caesium, he flew into a jealous rage over her breakthrough, because he felt he had been equally involved in the work. Possibly as a result of this tension, neither he nor Joliot-Curie were listed as a coauthor in the published note in which Perey reported her discovery. Initially called Actinium K, this element—the most unstable of elements numbered 102 or below in the periodic table as well as the heaviest alkali metal—was renamed Francium in 1945 in honor of Perey's native country. She had briefly considered naming the new element catium (from cation, the term describing positively charged ions) but changed her mind when some of her scientific colleagues suggested that this sounded too much like "cat."

Perey next devoted her energy to the considerable challenge of investigating the chemical and nuclear properties of the newly discovered, highly elusive element. Encouraged by both Debierne and Joliot-Curie, she also began her university studies during the troubled years of World War II, simultaneously attending the Sorbonne and receiving her secondary school *licence* diploma. With this, she became qualified to defend a thesis at the Sorbonne for a Docteur ès Sciences Physiques degree, which she successfully accomplished on March 2, 1946.

Over the next decades, Perey accepted many professional responsibilities and was the recipient of many honors. She worked closely with France's National Center of Scientific Research (CNRS), as well as with the International Union of Pure and Applied Chemistry. Among her awards were the Grand Prix de la Ville de Paris, the Lavoisier Prize of the Académie des Sciences, the Silver Medal of the Société Chimique de France, Officier of the Légion d'Honneur, and Commandeur of the Ordre Nationale du Mérite and of the Order of Palmes Académiques. After being twice awarded the lauréat of France's Académie des Sciences (1950 and 1960), she was elected on March 12, 1962, as the first woman to be a corresponding member of that prestigious body, which had been founded in 1666 during the reign of Louis XIV.

In 1949, Perey was called to occupy a newly created professorial chair of nuclear chemistry at the University of Strasbourg, the only such chair outside of Paris. Here she organized an ambitious program of instruction and research in radiochemistry and nuclear chemistry. Her own research interests included the fixation of Francium on healthy and cancerous organs. In 1958, Perey became director of a significant research facility located at Strasbourg-Cronenbourg which had grown out of a small laboratory she established in the early 1950s. There, various areas within the field of nuclear chemistry were investigated. Very likely as a result of a lifetime of exposure to radiation, she was diagnosed with cancer in the early 1960s. After a long, valiant fight against the illness, Perey died at Louveciennes, France, on May 14, 1975.

SOURCES:

Kauffman, George B., and Jean-Pierre Adloff. "Marguerite Perey and the Discovery of Francium," in *Education in Chemistry.* Vol. 26, no. 5. September 1989, pp. 135–137.

Keller, Cornelius. "Francium," in *Chemiker-Zeitung*. Vol. 101, no. 11. November 1977, pp. 482–486.

McGrayne, Sharon Bertsch. *Nobel Prize Women in Science.* Revised ed. Secaucus, NJ: Citadel, 1998.

Milite, George A. "Marguerite Perey 1909–1975," in Emily J. McMurray, *et al.*, eds., *Notable Twentieth-Century Scientists.* Vol. 3. Detroit, MI: Gale Research, 1995–98, p. 1567.

Rayner-Canham, M.F., and G.W. Rayner-Canham. "Pioneer Women in Nuclear Science," in *American Journal of Physics.* Vol. 58, no. 11. November 1990, pp. 1036–1043.

Venetskii, S. "Francium," in *The Metallurgist.* Vol. 22, no. 1–2, 1978, pp. 61–65.

Yount, Lisa. *A to Z of Women in Science and Math.* NY: Facts on File, 1999.

John Haag,
Associate Professor of History, University of Georgia, Athens, Georgia

Pérez, Eulalia Arrila de

(c. 1773–c. 1878)

Chicana oral historian. *Name variations: Eulalia Arrila de Perez. Born Eulalia Arrila de Pérez in Loreto, California, around 1773; died in California around 1878 (some sources cite 1880, others 1885); daughter of Diego Pérez (a U.S. Navy employee) and Antonia Rosalía Cota; no schooling; married Miguel Antonio Guillér, around 1788 (died around 1818); married Juan Marín, in 1833; children: at least six, daughters Petra, Rita, and María, son Indoro, and two sons who died in infancy.*

Born in Loreto, California, around 1773, Eulalia Arrila de Pérez was nearly 100 years old when she participated in one of the first oral histories of the settlement of California. Dictating her life story, she detailed the growth of what was in the late 18th century a Spanish-held territory. California was first settled in 1769 with a mission at San Diego. Explorers from the Spanish colony of Mexico controlled the region from 21 Franciscan missions, which divided territory and maintained huge cattle ranches, and formally attached the land to Mexico. By the time of Pérez's childhood, the U.S. Navy had established a garrison at Loreto, called Loreto Presidio, where her father was employed though not as an enlisted man. Pérez remarked that both of her parents were Caucasian, but her own deeply burnished skin made it likely that she meant they were native to the area.

Pérez received no formal education. She worked with her mother around the home and at age 15 was married to Miguel Antonio Guillér, a soldier at Loreto Presidio. The couple had several children, including two sons who died in fancy. When the family later moved to San Diego, Pérez maintained the home and worked as a midwife (*partera*).

Eulalia Arrila de Pérez

Her husband died around 1818. Now in her mid- to late 40s, Pérez sought work to support her family. To win a position as housekeeper at the Mission San Gabriel, she had to enter a cooking competition with two other women. On three different days, and with only 24 hours notice, the women were required to prepare a full meal, the merits of which would determine who would be awarded the position. With the help of her traditional Spanish-style food, Pérez won the competition. Her work at Mission San Gabriel was that of *la llavera* (keeper of keys) and included managing all supplies, running the kitchen, and allocating rations. She prepared meals ranging from dinner for a handful to dinner for dozens, while her daughters assisted her with the cooking and housework. Pérez was also known at the mission and through the region for her skills as a *curandera* (healer) and midwife.

In 1833, at the urging of San Gabriel's director whom she held in high regard, Pérez consented to marry Juan Marín, a widower from Spain, although she did not love him. She continued to work at the mission until 1835. Pérez appears to have lived for at least another 40 years. In thanks for her work and that of her family, she was given a house and two small ranches, one of which she was living on at the time of her death around 1878.

SOURCES:

Rebolledo, Tey Diana, and Eliana S. Rivero. *Infinite Divisions: An Anthology of Chicana Literature*. Tucson, AZ: University of Arizona Press, 1993.

Crista Martin,
Boston, Massachusetts

Perez, Gontrada (fl. 1100s)

Mistress of Alphonso VII. *Name variations: Pérez. Flourished in the 1100s; had liaison with Alphonso VII (1105–1157), king of León and Castile (r. 1126–1157); children:* ****Urraca of Castile*** *(d. 1179). Alphonso VII was married to* ****Berengaria of Provence*** *and* ****Ryksa of Poland.***

Perez, Inez (fl. 1400)

Mistress of John I of Portugal. *Name variations: Pérez. Flourished around 1400; daughter of Pedro Esteves and Maria Annes; had liaison with João I also known as John I (1385–1433), king of Portugal (r. 1385–1433); children: (with John I) Alfonso, duke of Braganza (b. around 1377);* ****Beatrice of Portugal*** *(d. 1439, who married Thomas Fitzalan and John Holland). John I was married to* ****Philippa of Lancaster.***

Perez, Maria (fl. 13th c.)

Medieval Spanish composer and singer who wrote sacred plainsong and performed in the courts of Europe. *Name variations: Maria Perez Balteira; La Balteira. Flourished in the 13th century.*

Maria Perez, also known as La Balteira, lived a long, lusty life which might have come from the pages of Chaucer's *Canterbury Tales*. A medieval Spanish composer and singer, she wrote sacred plainsong and performed in the courts of Europe; she was also reckless and profane and loved to gamble. Men were greatly attracted to her, including Alphonso X the Wise (1221–1284) at whose court she sang for a time. Alphonso used Perez as a spy against his Moorish enemies who could not resist her charms. But Perez often wavered between Moors and Spaniards in her loyalties, and at one interval consorted with a Moorish chief. Another time, she fleeced the king's archers and made off with the spoils. Perez often vowed to make a pilgrimage to the Holy Land, but she never got farther than Montpellier, a circumstance which prompted satirical poems and songs to be written about her. Despite her eccentricities, Perez remained much loved by Moors and Spaniards alike. In old age, she renounced her past, took up good works, and bequeathed an estate to the Cistercian monks at Sobrado.

John Haag,
Athens, Georgia

Perham, Margery (1895–1982)

British scholar, writer and lecturer on African affairs. *Name variations: Dame Margery Freda Perham. Born in 1895; died in 1982; educated at St. Anne's School, Abbots Bromley, and St. Hugh's College, Oxford.*

Selected writings: African Apprenticeship *(1929);* Native Administration in Nigeria *(1937);* Africans and British Rule *(1941);* The Life of Lord Lugard *(2 vols., 1956, 1960);* The Colonial Reckoning *(1963);* The Colonial Sequence *(2 vols., 1967, 1970).*

Educated at St. Anne's School, Abbots Bromley, Margery Perham gained an Open Scholarship to St. Hugh's College, Oxford University, in 1914, and left with a first class honors degree in modern history in 1917. She was appointed assistant lecturer at Sheffield University the same year, but later returned to her old college as Tutor and Fellow. Here she was promoted to Reader in colonial administration and was made Fellow of Nuffield College in 1939. She was also associated with the Institute of Colonial (now Commonwealth) Affairs at Oxford. In 1961, Perham became the first woman invited to give the prestigious BBC annual Reith lecture.

In 1922, Perham had suffered a nervous breakdown and stayed with her sister in Somaliland to recover. There she became intrigued with African affairs. A champion of "indirect rule" as proposed by Lord Lugard, she established her authority on the subject with her book *Native Administration in Nigeria* (1937).

SOURCES:

The Europa Biographical Dictionary of British Women. Europa, 1983.

Elizabeth Rokkan,
retired Associate Professor of the Department of English
University of Bergen, Norway

Périchole, La (1748–1819).

See Villegas, Micaela.

Périer, Marguerite (c. 1645–?)

French writer, niece and biographer of Blaise Pascal, whose miraculous cure inspired his religious conversion. *Name variations: Margot Perier. Born in 1645 or 1646; death date unknown; daughter of Florin Périer and* ***Gilberte Pascal Périer*** *(sister of Blaise Pascal);*

had at least two sisters and one brother; educated at Port Royal; had miraculous recovery from an ulcerated eye on March 24, 1656.

Works: Life of Pascal.

Marguerite Périer was the niece and goddaughter of the great French mathematician and physicist Blaise Pascal (1623–1662). Her miraculous cure from a serious illness at the age of ten greatly inspired him. Périer had had an ulcerated eye for two years, causing the area from her eye to her throat to be swollen and sensitive. On March 24, 1656, during a communion service involving a relic believed to be from Christ's crown of thorns (a fragment of a thorn encased in a gold enamel sun), Périer touched the relic to her face at the bidding of one of the nuns at the Abbey of Port Royal. During that day the ulcer disappeared, and the surgery (a cauterization) which the family had been considering was canceled. As well, the severe migraines from which the little girl had suffered never recurred.

The miracle was disputed, particularly by the Roman Catholic Jesuits, as it supported the views of their rivals the Jansenists, but it was officially recognized on October 22. (It now might be explained in terms of natural causes.) Marguerite's cure drew more visitors to Port Royal, which already attracted religious pilgrims, and the relic is said to have continued to provide miraculous cures, although it was ineffective outside of the town.

According to Périer's biography of her uncle Blaise, *A Life of Pascal*, he was converted to Christianity two years earlier, from listening to a sermon by M. Singlin on December 8, 1654. It was the cure of Marguerite, however, which confirmed him in the Jansenist approach. (*See also Port Royal des Champs, Abbesses of.*)

SOURCES:

Mortimer, Ernest. *Blaise Pascal*. London: Methuen, 1959.

St. Cyres, Viscount. *Pascal*. London: John Murray, 1909.

Steinmann, Jean. *Pascal*. Trans. by Martin Turnell. London: Burns & Oates, 1965.

Catherine Hundleby, M.A. Philosophy, University of Guelph, Guelph, Ontario, Canada

Perkins, Betty Williams (b. 1943).

See joint entry under Williams, Betty and Mairead Corrigan.

Perkins, Charlotte (1860–1935).

See Gilman, Charlotte Perkins.

Perkins, Frances (1880–1965)

First American woman to hold a Cabinet office in the federal government, as President Franklin Roosevelt's secretary of labor. *Born Fannie Coralie Perkins in Boston, Massachusetts, on April 10, 1880; died on May 14, 1965, in New York City; daughter of Frederick W. Perkins and Susan E. (Bean) Perkins; attended Worcester Classical High School; graduated, with a major in chemistry and physics, from Mt. Holyoke College, 1902; married Paul C. Wilson, in 1913; children: one daughter, Susanna Winslow Perkins (b. 1916).*

Moved to Chicago as a teacher at Ferry Hall School (1904); became secretary of the Philadelphia Research and Protective Association (1907); worked for the New York Consumers' League (1910); witnessed the Triangle Shirtwaist fire (1911); appointed to Industrial Commission by New York governor Al Smith (1918), reappointed (1922, 1924, 1926); promoted to New York Labor Commissioner with election of Franklin Delano Roosevelt as New York governor (1928); appointed secretary of labor with election of FDR as U.S. president (1932); impeachment proceedings against Perkins thrown out (1935); resigned as secretary of labor (1945); appointed by President Truman to Civil Service Commission (1947).

Frances Perkins was a skillful administrator and politician, deeply loyal to the Democratic Party, patient as a negotiator and conciliator, and tirelessly hard-working. From her early life as a social worker and progressive reformer, she rapidly gained political and practical experience in New York state politics. After a long apprenticeship under Governor Al Smith, she moved onto the national stage with President Franklin Roosevelt and became one of the longest-serving and most trusted members of the New Deal government as well as the first woman to hold a Cabinet seat. Deeply serious and conscientious, she was a pillar of New England rectitude, but one with shrewd practical skills.

Perkins was born in 1880 in Boston to an old Yankee family with Maine connections, but moved while still a child to nearby Worcester, Massachusetts. After amassing a relatively undistinguished school record, she persuaded her father, a wholesale stationery merchant, to let her go to college at Mt. Holyoke. In college, she began to discover a more engaging intellectual world. She majored in chemistry and minored in the other hard sciences, but still found time for acting, sports, and election as class president in her senior year. An influential class on sociology that year also led her, for the first time, to visit factories and the homes of working-class people, and to discover the suffering of the industrial working class and the unemployed poor. Eager to carry on studying, she ran into parental opposition after graduation and for two years lived restlessly at home, acting as a substitute teacher and volunteering at the YWCA. In 1904, against her parents' objections (they had expected her to marry and settle down), she set off for a teaching job in Chicago.

Chicago was then a center of progressive activism, under the theoretical guidance of the philosopher John Dewey and the practical lead of settlement house founder ***Jane Addams**. Perkins got to know both of them along with other city activists. Impressed by the work of the Episcopal Church in aiding the poor, she converted to it from her original Congregationalism. After two years as a teacher, Perkins took the momentous step—again in the face of severe paternal disapproval—of giving up her job and going to live and work full time (without pay) at Jane Addams' Hull House in one of Chicago's worst slum areas. Addams had a lasting influence on Perkins, teaching her how to respond to the constant crises arising in the daily lives of the poor immigrant community, and also how to gain leverage over the city authorities. Recalled Perkins:

> It was [Addams] who taught us to take all the elements of the community into conference for the solution of any human problem—the grasping landlord, the corner saloonkeeper, the policeman on the beat, the president of the university, the head of the railroad, the labor leader—all cooperating through that latent desire for association which is characteristic of the American genius.

From there, she moved in 1907 to Philadelphia, becoming secretary of the Philadelphia Research and Protective Association, whose aim was to protect young women new to the city from falling into destitution, crime, or prostitution. When she threatened to prosecute corrupt employment agency men, two of them followed one night and attacked her. Luckily her cries for help as she beat at them with her umbrella brought local residents into the streets. The attackers fled but she was able to identify and prosecute them. After that, the police and local politicians cooperated with her more actively.

Next Perkins went to New York, with a scholarship to Columbia University where she studied for a master's degree in sociology. Remaining active in social work in the city's worst areas, she found on several occasions that a Tammany Hall boss could be more useful than the city's progressive charity organizations, though Tammany was a by-word for corruption and civic abuse among most of her liberal circle. This experience warned her against thinking that everyone involved on the urban scene could be categorized simply as good or bad, and showed her that it was possible to negotiate with the established urban powers. In 1910, she met ***Florence Kelley**, another alumna of Hull House and now head of the New York Consumers' League, with whom she signed on to work. Living in Greenwich Village, home of a new circle of socialists and bohemians, she was wooed by Sinclair Lewis, then an aspiring novelist (later a Nobel Prize winner), but rejected his proposal of marriage. Also in this period, she met many of the men who were to be her comrades during the New Deal, including Franklin Roosevelt, Robert Wagner, and Al Smith.

Frances Perkins' early efforts to lobby the New York state government in favor of a 54-hour work week were unavailing. In 1911, she witnessed the dreadful fire at the Triangle Shirtwaist Building near where she lived, which killed 146 young workers, most of them Jewish immigrant women, due to overcrowding and lack of fire escape facilities. Perkins had been investigating fire hazards in her work for the Consumers' League and now became an influential witness to the New York Committee of Safety, which was formed in response to the public outcry about the fire. In consequence of her good work on the issue, she was asked to become executive secretary of the committee. Even though she was only 29, her scientific background, her administrative skills, and her obvious competence enabled her to become an expert on fire-related issues in industry, winning the confidence of engineers, architects, and firefighters.

Through her lobbying efforts and the aid of friendly politicians (she was becoming well known in Albany), the state of New York set up a Factory Commission with sweeping powers of supervision and regulation, and before long this commission in turn had taken over her services. With its members, including Al Smith and Robert Wagner, she drove around the state, investigating factories where dangerous machinery, child labor, and lack of fire safety precautions abounded. Under her incitement and guidance, the commission proposed legislation on all these issues and had the gratification of seeing nearly all its recommendations enforced by law over the next decade. No legislative enactment gave her more pleasure than the 54-hour act, passed in 1912, even though seasonal cannery workers were exempted from its provisions. It was characteristic of Perkins, always a political realist, to settle for this unwelcome exemption rather than get no bill at all.

In 1913, Frances Perkins married an economist named Paul Wilson. He was a reforming

Frances Perkins

Republican, whereas she had strong ties to the Tammany Hall Democrats. They agreed to keep political differences out of their marriage, which was difficult at first since he became the reform mayor's executive secretary and budget advisor. But in the city elections of 1917, her husband's party was ousted, and Perkins campaigned for Al Smith as governor the following year without a sense of divided loyalties. She gave birth to her only child, Susanna, in 1916 but was soon back in the political fray, delighted by New York's referendum decision in 1917 to give women the vote.

Smith was elected governor in 1918 and appointed Perkins as one of the five members of the New York State Industrial Commission. After a stormy session in the state senate—where some Republicans vocally opposed her as a dangerous radical, while others found it suspicious that she still called herself Frances Perkins rather than Mrs. Paul Wilson—she was confirmed. Despite frequent criticism, she stuck with her maiden name throughout her public life.

Perkins gained notoriety in 1919 by settling an ugly strike at Rome, New York, between the copper companies and their 4,000 workers. Frayed tempers on both sides had led Governor Smith to send in the state militia, but Perkins was able to bring both sides to negotiations (which the owners had previously refused). Her investigation soon showed that the employers had acted in bad faith, intimidating workers, cutting pay, and increasing hours, but now, in the face of aroused public opinion, they were forced to make concessions to the workforce. The newspapers treated the outcome as a personal victory for Perkins, as did her boss, Governor Smith. In the election of 1920, which saw a Republican landslide all across America, Smith lost his office, but he was back again with a large majority two years later, and Perkins resumed her job. She spent the following years running her department efficiently and fairly, exposing unfair practices, and lobbying hard for a women's eight-hour day. In 1924, she was an ardent supporter of Smith for president, but when the Democratic Convention—held that year in New York City—deadlocked between Smith and William McAdoo, a compromise candidate named John W. Davis got the nod, and went down to defeat in his November contest against Calvin Coolidge. Smith was consoled by retaining his position as New York governor.

In these days when women have far better conditions than they used to have, when modern inventions reduce work, housekeeping can no longer take up all their thoughts and time. . . . I do not see why, because a woman works either in politics or in any other field, her home life must suffer.

—Frances Perkins, 1929

When Smith managed to get the Democratic presidential nomination in 1928, he faced strong opposition from rural southern and midwestern states because he was Catholic, the son of immigrants, and favored a repeal of prohibition. Perkins, being an old-stock Yankee with Puritan ancestors, was the ideal campaigner for Smith, and she spent the summer and fall of 1928 traveling to areas of the country where Smith faced an uphill battle, electioneering on his behalf. She was pelted with eggs and tomatoes at a rally in Independence, Missouri, but calmly endured the barrage and made her speech anyway. In any event, Smith was unable to prevail—probably no Democrat could have won in that year of widespread boom and optimism. Although Smith lost, his nominee for New York governor, Franklin Roosevelt, scraped together a narrow victory margin, and from now on Frances Perkins' star would ascend with Roosevelt's. He at once promoted her from the Industrial Board to the position of labor commissioner.

In the following four years, she witnessed the onset of the Great Depression, and won press notice for frequently challenging President Herbert Hoover's claims that the depression was not very serious. She and Roosevelt also began to work together on schemes to provide unemployment insurance to cushion families suddenly made vulnerable by economic conditions, and she made a study tour of England where an unemployment insurance scheme was already operating. Roosevelt held her work in high esteem, and when he was elected president in November 1932 he decided to appoint her secretary of labor (though she wrote candidly advising him not to appoint her). This was a precedent-breaking decision, first because no woman had previously served as a Cabinet member, and second because every other secretary of labor since the post was founded in 1914 had been a trade union member. But none had yet been as experienced in politics and labor matters as Perkins, who was warmly welcomed by women's organizations and by progressive reformers who recognized that she already had 25 years of honorable experience and accomplishments. The American Federation of Labor (AFL) was furious at losing the position, and conservative congressmen treated her with the same kind of suspicion she had suffered previously in New York.

The first 100 days of the New Deal have become legendary for the administration's hard work and rapid innovations. The Labor Department was caught up in the general excitement, and under Perkins' lead it underwent a complete transformation. She created the Bureau of Immigration and Naturalization, the Bureau of Labor Statistics, a new U.S. Employment Service and, the following year, the Division of Labor Standards. She also played a key role in the planning stages of new agencies, the Civilian Conservation Corps and the Federal Emergency Relief Act, giving testimony to congressional committees and enlisting the aid of longtime New York friends and allies like Harry Hopkins. She swept away a mass of sinecures, jobs held by political cronies of former secretaries, and set new standards for hard work and long hours in a previously slow-moving department. She found it difficult to relax with the press, however, and one journalist wrote that her "social welfare patter" sounded "as if she had swallowed one of her own press releases." She also resented press intrusions into her private life. Her husband was now an invalid, still living partly in New York and partly in Maine, and Perkins tried to keep his name, and that of their 16-year-old daughter, out of the press. She spent weekends with her family as often as possible and hated to have eager journalists track her to them.

The single most important part of the early New Deal was the National Industrial Recovery Act, which created the National Recovery Administration (NRA) with its famous blue eagle symbol. Again Perkins was at the center of the discussions which led to its adoption and drafted the sections of the act referring to labor—section 7A of the act was the first occasion on which the federal government lent its weight to the trade union movement by recognizing the right to collective bargaining between managers and workers in every industry. In 1935, the NRA was found unconstitutional in the famous Schechter "sick chicken" case before the Supreme Court, but by then Perkins and her old New York ally Robert Wagner were ready with an alternative, the National Labor Relations Act.

Perkins also devoted a lot of time in the first years of the New Deal to speaking on behalf of a national unemployment insurance scheme. She made 200 speeches on the issue between 1933 and 1935, traveling widely and on one occasion surviving a nasty car accident en route to a speech in Boston. To the League of Women Voters, she said, with her usual blend of conciliation and determination:

> In two years the United States has worked out a system of job insurance that took Europe years to accomplish. The bill is subject to change, for it is a human instrument, with human imperfections, representing compromises among various factions. But I know that once it is in the laws of this land we shall not abandon it, but improve upon it, from year to year.

She was again able to convince the president and Congress to take action on the idea by gathering up necessary experts to draft the legislation and calm the fears of conservative resisters. She pointed out that every other advanced industrial nation already had a workable scheme of this kind, and that the prophets of doom in the business community who feared the worst from such a scheme had no evidence from these countries to support their gloomy prognosis. As finally passed by a huge majority of Congress (371–33 in the House and 76–6 in the Senate), the Social Security Act of 1935 instituted a federal-based old age pension for all Americans, and a joint federal and state-run unemployment insurance system.

The legislation protecting trade unions, which she had helped create, inspired intense unionization drives throughout the country in the mid-1930s. In the steel and auto industries, management fought ferociously to prevent unions from getting a foothold, and a series of sitdown strikes and confrontations, some of them bloody, punctuated the second half of the decade. Perkins was steadfast in favoring the unions' right to exist, though she did not always win union members' gratitude, because she tried to stay neutral in each particular dispute and to conciliate management and workers. She also declined to take sides when the Congress of Industrial Organizations (CIO) split off from the American Federation of Labor (AFL), leading to a bitter period of intralabor disputes. But if union men were sometimes lukewarm towards the secretary of labor, conservatives and industrialists were often enraged by her. When she declined to use her powers to deport Harry Bridges, a West Coast strike leader and CIO organizer who had migrated to America from Australia in 1920, the House Committee on Un-American Activities alleged that she was a Communist sympathizer, and one of its members, J. Parnell Thomas, instituted impeachment proceedings against her in early 1939. President Roosevelt told her the impeachment was frivolous and that he would protect her if necessary. Sure enough, the judiciary committee found no grounds for proceeding, but the incident demonstrated the fierce feelings Perkins had aroused after six years of active administration.

The next year, she played an active role in the movement to nominate Roosevelt for a third term of office, and was reappointed to her Cabinet position for a third term, making her one of the longest-serving members of the Roosevelt team. By now many of the original New Dealers had been fired or else resigned because of philosophical or practical disagreements with the president, whereas Perkins, who had known him since 1910, remained by his side. After Pearl Harbor, she had the vital task of ensuring smooth relations between management and labor as the economy moved onto a war footing, and she extracted from them a no strikes-no lockouts pledge for the duration of the war, then built up the National War Labor Board. She was careful to protect gains which labor had made in the foregoing years, and not to let businesses profit at workers' expense from the wartime emergency, and she encouraged the large-scale movement of women into the work force when men of military age went into the service. Most of the war years she devoted to coordinating the massive array of organizations involved in labor management.

When Roosevelt won his fourth term of office, she was determined to resign; but Roosevelt, gravely ill, pleaded with her to stay on a little longer and overrode her determination to leave the administration. In consequence, she was still there when Roosevelt died and Harry Truman took his place the following spring. Perkins stayed long enough for Truman to get his bearings, then retired on May 23, 1945. She made a visit to newly liberated Europe later in the same year on behalf of the International Labor Organization, wrote her memoirs and a book about her former boss, *The Roosevelt I Knew,* but was soon back at work inside the government, when President Truman appointed her to the Civil Service Commission. She served as one of the three commissioners until 1953 when she resigned following the death of her husband and the election of the first Republican president in 20 years, Dwight D. Eisenhower.

Frances Perkins remained active through her 70s and into her 80s, teaching classes at the University of Illinois, at Cornell, and at Princeton. She wrote extensively for journals and drafted a biography of her old friend and boss Al Smith, who had died in 1944. She lived long enough to witness the election of President John F. Kennedy and, following his assassination, the succession of Lyndon Johnson. She died in 1965, aged 85, after a lifetime of conscientious public service, having opened up the highest reaches of public life to women for the first time.

SOURCES AND SUGGESTED READING:

Martin, George. *Madam Secretary: Frances Perkins.* Boston, MA: Houghton Mifflin, 1976.

Mohr, Lillian Holmen. *Frances Perkins: "That Woman in FDR's Cabinet!"* North River Press, 1979.

Myers, Elisabeth. *Madam Secretary: Frances Perkins.* NY: Julian Messner, 1972.

Perkins, Frances. *The Roosevelt I Knew.* NY: Viking, 1946.

Severn, Bill. *Frances Perkins; A Member of the Cabinet.* NY: Hawthorn, 1976.

Patrick Allitt,
Professor of History, Emory University,
Atlanta, Georgia

Perkins, Lucy Fitch (1865–1937)

American author of children's books. *Born on July 12, 1865, in Maples, Indiana; died on March 18, 1937, in Pasadena, California; daughter of Appleton Howe Fitch (a factory owner) and Elizabeth (Bennett) Fitch (a teacher); graduated from Museum of Fine Arts School, Boston, 1886; married Dwight Heald Perkins (an architect), on August 18, 1891; children:* ***Eleanor Ellis Perkins*** *(b. 1893, a writer); Lawrence Bradford Perkins (b. 1908).*

Illustrated and wrote first book, The Goose Girl *(1906); began popular and profitable 26-volume "Twins of the World" series with publication of* The Dutch Twins *(1911).*

Selected writings: The Goose Girl *(1906);* A Book of Joys: The Story of a New England Summer *(1907); (series)* The Dutch Twins *(1911),* The Japanese Twins *(1912),* The Irish Twins *(1913),* The Eskimo Twins *(1914),* The Mexican Twins *(1915),* The Cave Twins *(1916),* The Belgian Twins *(1917),* The French Twins *(1918),* The Spartan Twins *(1918),* The Scotch Twins *(1919),* The Italian Twins *(1920),* The Puritan Twins *(1921),* The Swiss Twins *(1922),* The Filipino Twins *(1923),* The Colonial Twins of Virginia *(1924),* The American Twins of 1812 *(1925),* The American Twins of the Revolution *(1926),* The Pioneer Twins *(1927),* The Farm Twins *(1928),* Kit and Kat: More Adventures of the Dutch Twins *(1929),* The Indian Twins *(1930),* The Pickaninny Twins *(1931),* The Norwegian Twins *(1933),* The Spanish Twins *(1934),* The Chinese Twins *(1935),* The Dutch Twins and Little Brother *(completed by her children, 1938).*

Lucy Fitch Perkins was born in 1865, in the rural community of Maples, Indiana, to parents who instilled in their five daughters the New England values of hard work and thrift. She attended school in Hopkinton, Massachusetts, and in Kalamazoo, Michigan, where the family moved in 1879. Perkins early showed an interest in drawing, and at age 16 had some of her cartoons published in the *Kalamazoo Gazette*. She graduated from high school at the head of her class in 1883 and then attended the Museum of Fine Arts School in Boston for three years, where she had many male admirers despite her devout Congregationalism and strong disapproval of dancing and drinking. She met her future husband, Dwight Heald Perkins, during her last year in the Boston school, but the fact that he was a Unitarian kept them from committing to each other at the time.

Having been employed on a freelance basis for *Young Folks Magazine* while still in school, after her graduation Perkins worked for a year as an illustrator at Prang Educational Company in Boston. She then taught for four years at the newly established Pratt Institute in Brooklyn, New York, a manual arts and engineering college. In 1891, she left her teaching position to marry Dwight Perkins, who had become an architect, and settled in Chicago. The couple would have two children, Eleanor Ellis (born 1893) and Lawrence Bradford (born 1908). Although Perkins believed that a woman should depend economically on her husband, Dwight supported her talents and built a studio for her in their home. He became seriously ill in 1893 and she went back to work, first with the Chicago office of the Prang Educational Company. For the next ten years, she illustrated children's books, taught art, lectured, and created murals in schoolrooms. In 1904, the Perkins family moved to the Chicago suburb of Evanston, where Dwight continued his career as an architect. Perkins consequently stopped working outside the home, and in 1906 she published her first book, a collection of children's rhymes entitled *The Goose Girl.* The following year, she wrote a book for adults, *A Book of Joys: The Story of a New England Summer.*

Having seen some drawings Perkins had made of Dutch children, her friend Edwin O. Grover, a publisher, encouraged her to write a series of geographical readers. With the publication of *The Dutch Twins* in 1911, Perkins' writing career took off. Over the next 25 years, she wrote and illustrated 25 more books in the "Twins of the World" series, engaging her young readers with whimsical drawings, humor, simple language, and glimpses into the lives of children from various nations. Several books in the series were historical (including *The Cave Twins* and *The Puritan Twins*). "Twins of the World" proved hugely popular, selling over 2 million copies and being translated into several languages. Perkins preferred learning about a country from someone who had grown up there over strict dependence on library research, and tried out her works in progress on a group of local children whom she called "the poison squad." She kept in mind her original inspirations for the series, a trip to Ellis Island during which she had seen the arrival of immigrants, and a visit to a school in Chicago where a single classroom included children from 27 countries. The books frequently included depictions of the social and economic reasons behind immigration, as well as examples of immigrants' contributions to America. As she noted in *The Junior Book of Authors*, Perkins believed in "the necessity for mutual respect and understanding between people of different nationalities if we are ever to live in peace" and thought that "a really big theme can be comprehended by children if it is presented in a way that holds their interest and engages their sympathies."

Although Perkins is most famous for her Twins books, she also served as editor and illustrator of *Robin Hood: His Deeds and Adventures as Recounted in the Old English Ballads* (1906), *The Twenty Best Fairy Tales by Hans Andersen, Grimm, and Miss Mulock* (***Dinah Maria Mulock Craik** [1907]), and *A Midsummer-Night's Dream for Young People* (1907), and illustrated *A Wonder Book* by Nathaniel Hawthorne (1908), *Stories of the Pilgrims* by **Margaret Blanche Pumphrey** (1910), and *News from Notown* by her daughter E.E. Perkins (1919), among others. Lucy Perkins' children finished her 26th "Twins" book after her death from a coronary thrombosis on March 18, 1937, in Pasadena, California.

SOURCES:

Contemporary Authors. Vol. 137. Detroit, MI: Gale Research.

James, Edward T., ed. *Notable American Women, 1607–1950.* Cambridge, MA: The Belknap Press of Harvard University Press, 1971.

Kunitz, Stanley J., and Howard Haycraft, eds. *The Junior Book of Authors.* 2nd ed. NY: H.W. Wilson, 1951.

McHenry, Robert, ed. *Famous American Women.* NY: Dover, 1980.

SUGGESTED READING:

Perkins, Eleanor Ellis. *Eve among the Puritans: A Biography of Lucy Fitch Perkins*, 1956.

Kari Bethel,
freelance writer, Columbia, Missouri

Perkins, Ma.

See Payne, Virginia.

Perkins, Millie (1938—)

American actress. *Born on May 12, 1938, in Passaic, New Jersey; daughter of a sea captain; married Dean Stockwell (an actor), in 1960 (divorced 1964); married Robert Thom (a writer-director).*

Selected filmography: The Diary of Anne Frank *(1959);* Wild in the Country *(1961);* Ensign Pulver *(1964);* Wild in the Streets *(1968);* Cockfighter *(1974);* Lady Cocoa *(1975);* The Witch Who Came from the Sea *(1976);* Table for Five *(1983);* At Close Range *(1986);* Jake Speed *(1986);* Slamdance *(1987);* Wall Street *(1987);* Two Moon Junction *(1988);* Pistol *(1991);* The Birth of a Legend *(1991);* Sharkskin *(1991).*

A petite brunette with haunting eyes, Millie Perkins had just launched a successful modeling career when she was chosen over numerous other hopefuls for the coveted role of ***Anne Frank** in the film version of *The Diary of Anne Frank* (1959), based on the famous diaries of the young Jewish girl who died in Auschwitz. Despite the enormous hype surrounding the film, and her credible debut performance, Perkins failed to become an established star. She made sporadic appearances over the years in some 15 films, the last of which was *Sharkskin* (1991). The actress has been married twice: to actor-director Dean Stockwell and to writer-director Robert Thom.

Permon, Laure (1784–1838).

See Abrantès, Laure d'.

Perón, Eva (1919–1952)

Argentine social activist and wife of Juan Domingo Perón who represented the revolutionary potential of Peronism and pushed the involvement of women in the nation's politics. *Name variations: Eva María Ibarguren; Eva María Duarte de Perón; Evita. Pronunciation: A-vah Pay-RONE. Born Eva María Ibarguren on May 7, 1919, in Los Toldos, a village in the Province of Buenos Aires, Argentina; died on July 26, 1952, of cancer in Buenos Aires; illegitimate daughter of Juan Duarte (a landowner) and Juana Ibarguren, his mistress; attended elementary school; married Juan Domingo Perón, on October 22, 1945; no children.*

Left her family in Junin and made her way to the capital of Buenos Aires intent on a career in the theater (1934); became a radio personality and actress; married Juan Domingo Perón (1945); went on European "Rainbow Tour" (1947); pushed a social agenda for Argentine workers and the disadvantaged; failed in bid to run for office of vice-president (1951).

In the middle of October 1945, Eva Duarte's dreams appeared to be in shambles. The man to whom she had tied her star, Juan Domingo Perón, was in prison, his political eclipse an accomplished fact. But, according to Peronist accounts of the 17th of October, it was Eva, also known as Evita, who then went to work, rallied the forces of labor and made possible the triumphal return of Perón, to the utter discomfort of his enemies. In the words of her biographers Nicholas Fraser and **Marysa Navarro**:

> For those who have loved her, there has been a faithful, suffering Evita who by her example inspired people to rise up on Perón's behalf; and for those who have hated her, a liar, a scheming woman who drags Perón back to fulfil her desires for power and revenge. But Perón in either case has been considered of little importance; it is Evita who has saved him in the hour of defeat.

Neither perception is accurate. But such were the lives of Evita and Juan Perón, encapsulated in multiple myths that reflect a fanatical love or equally fanatical hate. Indeed, so entrenched are the myths about the Peróns that they have come to assume a separate reality. In Evita's case, they inspired **J.M. Taylor** to entitle her book *Eva Perón: The Myths of a Woman.*

One myth noted that Eva Perón was born on October 17, 1945, the day she "rescued" Juan; an anonymous account assured readers that Eva Perón, like Venus, "who emerged from the sea," combined in "immortal synthesis" art and beauty at the moment of her birth. She did not emerge from the sea, but from the Province of Buenos Aires; and she was not born on October 17, 1945, or even on May 7, 1922, as is noted on her marriage contract, but on May 7, 1919.

Eva's unwed mother, **Juana Ibarguren**, lived in the small village of Los Toldos and was the mistress of Juan Duarte, an estate manager with some political connections, from Chivilcoy, 20 miles distant. Early in the morning of May 7, assisted by an Indian midwife, she gave birth to a fifth illegitimate child by Duarte, a girl named Eva María. For reasons of "propriety," the baby was denied the surname of the father even though she was called Eva María Duarte.

When Duarte died in an automobile accident in 1926, the two mothers of his children, only one of whom was his legal wife, mourned him. Writes Taylor:

> Six-year old Eva arrived at her father's wake accompanied by her mother and her four older siblings, all illegitimate children of Duarte. The society of Chivilcoy had also turned out to pay respects to the brother-in-law of their mayor. This gathering of upright citizens suddenly found itself in the arena of violent confrontation between the family of the deceased wife and that of his concubine. . . . A quarrel broke out and continued . . . until the mayor himself finally intervened, allowing the outcasts a last glimpse of lover and father and the privilege of accompanying the coffin to the cemetery.

Gossip, shame and scandal dogged the young Eva; before his death, her father had abandoned his informal family in 1920, which reduced them to poverty and rendered them the objects of scorn. Eva began attending school at age eight and was remembered as an average student. At age 12, her family moved to the larger city of Junin with perhaps 20,000 inhabitants. Eva's eldest sister, Elisa, had been given a good job there and the family followed. In Junin, Eva attended school and dreamed about the better life she saw on screen in the local movie houses. By 1935, at age 15, she was convinced that she wanted a career as an actress and caught a train for the glamour of Buenos Aires, the capital city of Argentina. The story, repeated in film biographies of Evita's life and in the musical *Evita,* that she seduced tango singer Agustin Magaldi into taking her to Buenos Aires is probably untrue.

In Buenos Aires, in the words of biographers Fraser and Navarro, "she tried the stage

Eva Perón

but only managed to obtain walk-on parts or minuscule roles in second-rate plays, and her attempts to break into films gave her minor parts in three forgettable movies." She had better luck with radio parts, however, enjoying a modestly successful career after 1938; by 1943, she was a recognized soap opera star with her own company. It was also in 1943 that the Argentine military seized power and Eva Duarte, according to historian Joseph Page, "ever mindful of the need to cultivate useful contacts, turned her attention to the men in the braided uniforms." Soon she would come to the attention of Colonel Juan Domingo Perón.

They met at a benefit for the earthquake victims of San Juan, and it was likely Eva who nurtured her relationship with the smiling Colonel Perón. They moved into adjoining apartments and, perhaps because of Perón's influence, her artistic career prospered. She starred in the radio production of a series called "Heroines of History" and in 1944 was given a role in the movie *Circus Cavalcade* at which time she bleached her brunette hair and would forever remain a blonde.

Juan Perón's vision of political power would intimately involve Eva Duarte and Argentina's workers. In 1944, he held two posts, undersecretary of war and secretary of labor, in the government of General Pedro Pablo Ramírez. Perón met daily with labor leaders and increasingly identified with the aspirations of the rank-and-file workers; he delivered on his promises and gave labor a status it had never before enjoyed. Perón began to gather a host of supporters—and enemies.

[L]ife has its real value . . . when one surrenders oneself, completely and fanatically, to an ideal that has more value than life itself. I say yes, I am fanatically for Perón and the *descamisados* [disadvantaged] of the nation.

—Eva Perón

Evita was 24 when she became Perón's mistress. But he did not keep her closeted away. On the contrary, according to Fraser and Navarro, "Perón did not isolate her from his public life; he introduced her to his fellow officers, went to visit her in Radio Belgrano when she was at work, and in fact treated her as if she were his wife." The relationship produced volumes of gossip. When some follow officers questioned the propriety of keeping company with an "actress," a very low-prestige occupation, Perón quipped: "Would you rather I keep the company of an actor?"

Over the course of the next year, Perón maneuvered himself into a position of power in the military government but in the process made many more enemies. They struck in October 1945 and removed him from his three offices—vice-president, minister of war, and secretary of labor and welfare. While Perón appeared to have been neutralized in his bid for complete power and languished in a prison on an island in the middle of the Rio de la Plata, Peronist myth insists that it was Evita who mobilized the workers on Perón's behalf and engineered his return to power. Such was not the case, for at the time her influence was minimal. But the events of the 17th, and especially the outpouring of labor support, refocused her life in a decidedly radical direction. Four days later, on October 22, she married Juan Perón; in November, he announced his candidacy for the forthcoming presidential elections and Evita, the actress of obscure origins, was catapulted into the forefront of Argentine politics.

Perón won the presidential election of 1946 with support from across the political spectrum. Eva, as Argentina's new first lady, would have many roles to play. In 1946, she campaigned over the radio for women's suffrage and began to make her first appearances before labor groups. Her interest in social welfare issues soon earned her the title "Lady of Hope." And in June 1947, she was given the opportunity to represent Argentina to Europe's heads of state.

The visit was apparently suggested to President Perón by Spain's fascist leader Francisco Franco. Following the defeat of Germany and Italy, Franco's Spain was considered a pariah, although its relations with Argentina were excellent. But a visit by President Perón was out of the question. Argentina, itself isolated because of its wartime neutrality, needed to mend its international fences and a state visit to Spain was perceived by the Argentine foreign minister as an unwarranted risk. Eva Perón, however, informed her husband that she would travel to Europe. The trip, which came to be known as the "Rainbow Tour," offers insights into what lay behind her decision.

Page notes that "it is necessary to keep in mind the duality of her roles as first lady and political figure." Certainly one of her goals in traveling to Europe was vindication "in the form of proving to her social superiors that she could beat them at their own game." But vindication of her childhood rejection as well as the cold hostility of the Argentine elite "overlooks the political Evita." She would contribute both to the emerging Peronist Revolution and to her own sense of history. "As a radio actress she had played a number of great women. Now she would join their ranks."

For political reasons, Evita's itinerary was expanded to include Italy, Portugal and France. Even British officials noted that she would be welcome. Her tour through Spain was a personal success, and she made a generally favorable impression in Italy, Portugal and France. The visit to Great Britain never occurred, however, which Evita took as a personal slight. Because the timing of her visit had changed, it would no longer be possible to meet Queen ***Elizabeth**

From the movie Evita, *starring Jonathan Pryce and Madonna.*

Bowes-Lyon, wife of George VI. Evita reportedly told the Argentine ambassador: "Tell the Queen that if she isn't capable of inviting me officially, I don't want to see her."

Upon her return to Argentina, Evita became ever more closely involved with Perón's efforts to create a "New Argentina." In that he purported to be the leader of all Argentines, it made sense for him to entrust his special relationship with labor to Evita, who developed her own charisma with the *descamisados* (literally, "the shirtless ones," implying "those without suitcoats"). Evita, through the new Ministry of Labor, became labor's liaison with President Perón. According to Fraser and Navarro:

> Evita's incorporation into the political structure, albeit in an informal way, allowed Perón to maintain close contact with the rank and file, to strengthen his control of the labor movement, and to continue to be responsible for its gains. It also permitted him to retain his leadership with the *descamisados* by avoiding sharing with another man. As a woman and his wife, Evita represented no danger to him.

Under the heading of social justice, strikes were settled in favor of workers, who won significant increases in their hourly wages. Taken together, the social welfare measures that assisted the disadvantaged were subsumed under the doctrine of *Justicialismo* (justice) which proclaimed the emergence of a "New Argentina." Evita aided the cause with the creation in 1948 of the María Eva Duarte de Perón Foundation, which dispensed money and largesse to the poor. Despite charges of wholesale corruption, in part because no books were kept, the record of the Foundation was impressive. Page writes that it "built homes for orphans, unwed mothers and the elderly; shelters for working women; lunch facilities for schoolchildren; children's hospitals; vacation colonies for workers; low-cost housing; schools for nurses." Often-seen banners carried by workers proclaimed that while *Perón Cumple* (Perón Delivers the Goods), *Evita Dignificá* (Evita Dignifies).

By 1950, Eva commanded an extraordinary presence in the Peronist movement. Officials of whom she disapproved were removed, while those who maintained her favor prospered. In July 1949, she was named president of the women's branch of the Peronist Party which initiated a widespread membership drive and asserted its demand that women appear on Peronist slates for office. At the end of 1950, there were rumors that Juan Perón was prepared to name her as his vice-presidential candidate for the next presidential election. He had already amended the Constitution of 1853 to allow him to run for another six-year term and reaffirmed the right, granted in 1947, of women to vote in national elections. Perón won the 1951 election handily, although he failed in the attempt to have Evita as his running mate. Powerful elements in the military resisted the further elevation of "that woman," who would become commander-in-chief in the event of Perón's incapacitation or death. But it was Evita who was dying. The cancer that would kill her made its presence felt in 1950.

The disease in no way slowed the ever-accelerating pace of Evita's contribution to the Peronist Revolution and her largesse to friends and the poor. During 1950 and 1951, in the opinion of Fraser and Navarro, she became progressively idealized which came not only "from her beauty and her power but also from this habit of giving." The revolutionary in Evita also emerged in full armor at this time. When it was still widely believed that she would be Perón's vice-presidential candidate, she gave a speech that Page describes as:

> a classic in its rhythmic cadences, violent imagery and naked passion. . . . The fires within her invested her voice with a chilling power. . . . Her hyperbole reached its zenith in the peroration, when she invoked her "spiritual authority" to proclaim Perón the victor in the coming elections.

As death approached, Evita grew progressively weaker but still worked beyond what seemed possible. On September 24, 1951, Perón was told that his wife was suffering from an advanced case of cancer of the uterus. Just four days later, while she was receiving a blood transfusion, an abortive coup signaled a growing and dangerous opposition within the armed forces. On her own authority, Evita decided to arm the workers and had money diverted from her Foundation to purchase automatic weapons. President Perón, however, was not willing to go to this extreme and did not allow the creation of a workers' militia.

On October 17, a frail Evita addressed the masses assembled in the Plaza de Mayo in Buenos Aires and urged their vigilance on Perón's behalf. "I ask one thing, comrades. We must all now swear in public to defend Perón and fight to the death on his behalf." In the same month, Evita's ghostwritten autobiography, *La Razón de mi Vida,* translated in English as *My Mission in Life,* appeared. A combination of unabashed adulation for Juan Perón, autobiography and emotion, the book became required reading for Argentine schoolchildren. Her identification with Perón and Peronism was complete. As death neared, her speeches grew more impassioned, violent, and apocalyptic. Public appearances by Evita became less frequent and at 8:25 PM on July 26, 1952, a cancer-ravaged Eva Perón died.

What followed was an outpouring of genuine grief accompanied by, in one critic's words, a "bacchanal of necrophilia." The body lay in state for days while the faithful filed past her bier and was finally taken from public display only after it began to decompose. Millions silently and tearfully watched the funeral procession and some hoped and prayed for Evita's canonization. Doubtless, her death dealt a crushing blow to Perón and to his movement and represented a loss, in Page's words, akin to "amputation."

With Perón's ouster in 1955, Evita's body, which had been lying in a tomb in CGT (the national union) headquarters while a gigantic mausoleum was being constructed, vanished. It had been spirited away by the military so as not to become a rallying point for Peronism and was eventually interred in Milan, Italy. The remains were returned to Argentina by order of ***Isabel Perón** in 1974 and laid to rest next to Juan's in the Olivos chapel.

SOURCES:

Fraser, Nicholas, and Marysa Navarro. *Eva Peron.* NY: W.W. Norton, 1987.

Page, Joseph A. *Peron: A Biography.* NY: Random House, 1983.

Perón, Eva. *My Mission in Life.* NY: Vantage Press, 1952.

Taylor, J.M. *Eva Perón: The Myths of a Woman.* Chicago, IL: The University of Chicago Press, 1979.

Turner, Frederick C., and José Enrique Miguens, eds. *Juan Peron and the Reshaping of Argentina.* Pittsburgh, PA: The University of Pittsburgh Press, 1983.

SUGGESTED READING:

Ortiz, Alicia Dujovne. *Eva Péron: A Biography.* Trans. by Shawn Fields. St. Martin's, 1996.

Rock, David, ed. *Argentina in the Twentieth Century.* Pittsburgh, PA: The University of Pittsburgh Press, 1975.

RELATED MEDIA:

Eva Peron (film), starring **Esther Goris**, nominated by the National Cinema Institute for Best Foreign Film, 1997.

Evita (musical) by Andrew Lloyd Webber and Tim Rice, opened in London on June 21, 1979, starring **Elaine Page**, David Essex, and Joss Ackland, directed by

Hal Prince; opened on Broadway on September 25, 1979, starring **Patti LuPone** and Mandy Patinkin, directed by Hal Prince.

Evita (film), starring **Madonna**, Jonathan Pryce, and Antonio Banderas, directed by Alan Parker, Hollywood Pictures, 1996.

Paul B. Goodwin, Jr.,
Professor of History, University of Connecticut,
Storrs, Connecticut

Perón, Evita (1919–1952).

See Perón, Eva.

Perón, Isabel (1931—)

President of Argentina (1974–76) and head of Argentina's largest political party, the Peronist Party (1974–85), who was the first woman chief executive of a Latin American nation. *Name variations: María Estela Martínez de Perón; Isabelita. Pronunciation: Pay-rone. Born María Estela Martínez Cartas on February 4, 1931, in the province of La Rioja, Argentina; third of five siblings, two older sisters, two younger brothers, of Marcelo Martínez Rosales (a branch manager of the National Mortgage Bank) and María Josefa Cartas; left school after the sixth grade to study ballet, Spanish dancing, French and piano; became third wife of Juan Domingo Perón (president of Argentina, 1946–55, 1973–74), in Madrid, Spain, on November 15, 1961; no children.*

Joined the Cervantes dance troupe (1955); while dancing with Joe Herald's ballet in Panama City, met Juan Perón during his exile from Argentina (1956); became Perón's private secretary; followed him in exile to Venezuela, Dominican Republic, and finally Spain; married him (1961); assumed role as Perón's political representative (after 1961); traveled to Argentina to promote Peronist candidates in provincial elections (1964); spent nine months in Argentina promoting Perón's cause (1965); returned to Argentina (December 1971–March 1972) when the military called for new elections; traveled to Argentina with Perón for four weeks (November 1972); visited Communist China and met with Zhou Enlai and Mao Zedong; was back in Argentina (June 1973); nominated vice-president at Peronist Party convention (August 1973); with Peronists' victory, became vice-president; appeared at state functions when Perón became ill (late 1973); spoke to the International Labor Organization and met with Pope Paul (June 1974); called home to Argentina to assume the presidency after Perón's death (July 1, 1974); declared state of siege to combat economic and political chaos (November 1974); took leave from presidency for health reasons (September 1975); despite increasing opposition, determined to complete her term; succumbed to a military coup and placed under house arrest (March 1976); returned to Spain (1981); was official head of Peronist Party (until 1985); lives in Madrid, Spain, but makes frequent visits to Argentina.

The world of women in Latin America, and in other parts of the globe, is generally circumscribed by family, home, and church. By tradition and practice, women are excluded from the public sphere. It is said that respectable women appear in public only three times: to be baptized, married, and buried. The defining terms for this system of gender relations in Latin America are *machismo* and *marianismo*. *Machismo* reinforces a system of male dominance over women. Women in this system adopt ***Mary the Virgin** as their behavioral ideal. They are devout and self-sacrificing for the sake of their male relatives and children: *marianismo*. Public business such as politics is men's business. One consequence of these values is that Latin American women acquired the vote much later than their North American counterparts; in Argentina, women did not receive the franchise until 1947. Although this restrictive system of gender relations has been challenged in recent decades, its roots run deep in Latin American culture. Societies that embrace such a system would be hard pressed to tolerate a woman in their most public and powerful position—its chief executive. And yet, in Argentina (and since in Nicaragua), before the United States and other Western countries, a woman has worn the presidential sash. Ultimately, Isabel Perón's career reveals both the possibilities and limits of women's roles in Latin American culture.

How did María Estela Martínez de Perón become in 1974 the first woman to assume the presidency of a Latin American nation? At the turn of the century, Argentina was one of the richest trading nations of the world. It produced and marketed wheat and beef from the vast grasslands surrounding Buenos Aires, the capital. Buenos Aires rivaled European cities for its sophisticated society and elegant buildings, expansive parks, and broad avenues. Italians and Spaniards immigrated to Argentina by the thousands to find a better life. The pace of economic development, however, disrupted the traditional political structure. New groups, especially from the working class, demanded access to the halls of power. The ruling class, composed of large landowners, forestalled working-class ambitions by allying with the middle class.

Turmoil created by the Great Depression and World War II further disrupted the political structure. In 1943, the military intervened and deposed the civilian president. The military *junta* quickly fell under the influence of a group of officers committed to nationalism. One of them, Colonel Juan Domingo Perón, used his position as secretary of labor to organize support first for the military government, and then for himself. An ambitious radio and film star named Eva Duarte (***Eva Péron**, known popularly as Evita) assisted him after 1943. Eva showed Perón radio's effectiveness as a means to reach and organize workers. Perón's increasing popularity allowed him to assume the portfolios of minister of war and vice-president and to cultivate influence in the officer corps. By 1945, he was the center of a powerful coalition of workers and the military. Perón's enthusiasm for fascism and his consolidation of power worried democratic forces. The Allied victory over Germany and Japan gave the political parties hope that Argentina would soon return to civilian rule. They saw Perón as an obstacle. In October 1945, opposition to Perón peaked; the president dismissed Perón from his posts and imprisoned him. Perón's supporters in the labor movement and Eva immediately organized a protest on October 17, 1945, in front of the presidential palace and successfully demanded his release. Perón regained his freedom and ministry portfolios. He and Evita married; the next year he won the presidency.

I have not renounced nor have I thought of renouncing. I have not asked for leave nor will I do so; I exercise the full power of the presidency.

—**Isabel Perón (1975)**

In his first term, Perón, with the help of Evita, achieved fundamental changes in Argentina's economy and society. He shifted resources from agriculture to industry and raised workers' standards of living. Eva served as the unofficial minister of welfare, personally dispensing checks and cash, and sponsoring construction of hospitals and summer camps for needy families. In 1948, she organized the women's branch of the Peronist Party to prepare women to exercise the franchise nationally. As labor organized and grew more militant, apprehension among the economic and military elites over Peronism mounted.

While preparing for re-election in 1952, Perón capitalized on Evita's popularity. Her name was placed in nomination for the vice-presidency at the party convention. Strong opposition from military leaders, who refused to consider a woman vice-president, caused Eva to decline, falsely claiming her age constitutionally disqualified her. Shortly after the convention, doctors discovered her cancer. Gravely ill and disappointed at the denial of national office, she nevertheless campaigned for Perón. Her last public appearance came at his inauguration in June 1952. The following month she died.

The Peronist coalition dissolved after Evita's death. The party fractured along traditional lines. Perón remained the only unifying factor. His inability to control inflation, growing resistance to his government by large landowners, disputes with the Catholic Church, and, finally, the disaffection of the military undermined his regime. In September 1955, the military moved against Perón and he fled into exile.

María Estela Martínez came to her majority in the Perón years. The middle daughter of **María Josefa Cartas** and Marcelo Martínez Rosales, a successful banker, María Estela was born in 1931 in La Rioja in the interior of Argentina. The family moved to Buenos Aires when she was two. As a child, she was known as Estelita, but she adopted the name Isabel at confirmation. Her father died when she was six and, to reduce the burden on her widowed mother, Isabel moved in with family friends. She left school after the sixth grade to study ballet and dance. During the Perón years, she joined the Cervantes Dance troupe and then the Avenida Theater. In 1955, the same year as the coup, she joined Joe Herald and his dance troupe which was popularly known as "Joe and his Ballets." It was partially funded by the Eva Perón Foundation. They toured Central America but became stranded by lack of funds in Panama City. Juan Perón, in exile in Panama, frequented the Happyland Club where they performed. He invited the dancers to a party just before Christmas. There Isabel, then 24, met Juan. She moved into the Perón household in January, assuming the tasks of personal secretary and domestic manager. She accompanied Perón as his exile moved from Panama to Venezuela to the Dominican Republic and eventually Spain.

Social pressures in Spain persuaded Juan Perón to formalize his relationship with Isabel, but the intended marriage ran into problems as a result of the Vatican's threat to excommunicate Perón in 1955. To protect Isabel's reputation, the local bishop authorized a marriage of convenience until the excommunication problem was resolved. The couple married in a private ceremony in Madrid on November 15, 1961, and soon built a home there. They settled into a peaceful life of reading, gardening, and fencing.

Argentina's political situation made it impossible for Juan Perón to return before 1972; Isabel traveled there in his stead. On her first visit in 1964, she carried messages to Perón's lieutenant, Jorge Antonio, in Paraguay. She also urged General Stroessner, the Paraguayan dictator, to shelter Jorge Antonio. When Peronist supporters gathered in Paraguay to meet with her, she delivered Perón's message, bolstering the morale of the party faithful and her own leadership abilities. The trip established her place in the Peronist movement and revealed personal political ambitions. Returning to Argentina in 1965 for a nine-month stay, she supervised provincial election campaigns that the Peronists swept. The nine-month visit further enhanced her political experience and visibility.

On her second trip, Isabel acquired a controversial political advisor, José López Rega, who worked as her personal secretary but eventually served her husband as well. López Rega is best known for his affinity for the occult and his difficulties with other leaders of the movement, particularly Jorge Antonio. Even Juan Perón occasionally expressed displeasure with his wife's secretary, but she staunchly protected his position and eventually brought him into their Madrid home. Together, López Rega and Isabel monopolized access to Juan Perón.

Accompanied by López Rega, she traveled to Argentina in 1971 to prepare for national elections and head off challenges to Perón's leadership. Thousands of Peronists awaited her at the airport. By 1971, right- and left-wing factions were clearly defined within the party. Isabel aligned with the former during her three-month stay. She also purchased a home on the outskirts of Buenos Aires, anticipating the restoration of civilian government and her husband's return. The military government resisted, but pledged not to interfere with Perón's visit. After 17 years in exile, the 77-year-old leader landed on November 17, 1972, with his wife and López Rega by his side.

After a brief detention at the airport hotel, the Peróns settled into their new home. Crowds gathered daily to catch a glimpse of Juan Perón at his window. Occasionally, holding a photo enlargement of Evita, Isabel would accompany or replace Juan at the window. They worked to build an electoral coalition to support Perón's choice for president, Héctor Cámpora. Once the Cámpora campaign was underway, the Peróns again left the country, stopping in Paraguay and Peru where Juan Perón met with both heads of state before returning to Madrid. Although he had promised to return to Argentina for the presidential campaign, his age and a strategy of distancing himself from Cámpora prevented it.

Isabel Perón

Juan Perón's resumption of the presidency involved several steps. First, the Perón name was reestablished internationally. Isabel traveled to China for meetings with Mao Zedong and Zhou Enlai. Second, after using Cámpora to reestablish civilian rule, Juan Perón planned to run in early national elections. In the meantime, he selected some of Cámpora's Cabinet members, including López Rega as minister of social welfare (a post Evita had held during Perón's first administration). The Eva Perón Beneficent Foundation was revived under Isabel's leadership.

The Peróns' June 1973 arrival in Buenos Aires signaled real trouble for the party. As thousands gathered along the route to the airport to welcome them, violence erupted between left- and right-wing party members. The fighting caused the Peróns' plane to be diverted and spoiled Juan's triumphant return, while a mild heart attack left him bedridden for several days. Despite these unfavorable omens, most Peronists depended on him to heal the party.

In August, the Peronists met to select a ticket for the September elections. The presidency belonged to Juan Perón; political speculation focused on the vice-presidency. The names bandied about included Isabel's. As the convention celebrated Juan's nomination, a delegate placed her name in nomination, and Peronists approved her by acclamation. Although Juan Perón avoided the convention, Isabel personally assured delegates of her willingness to serve and bestowed her husband's blessing on the slate.

Juan Perón's time in office was short but eventful. He increasingly relied on his wife to fulfill political obligations, and struggled unsuccessfully to control the Peronist youth and political violence. But deteriorating health weakened his efforts. Isabel assumed the presidency briefly in November when Juan suffered a pulmonary edema. His attempts to resume a normal schedule failed, and by 1974 Isabel was making all state appearances. She supervised construction of 10,000 homes in Ciudad Isabel—a project of the ministry of social welfare and reminiscent of Evita Perón's work. In June, she assumed the presidency during Juan's visit to Uruguay and Paraguay. Despite her husband's continuing poor health, Isabel and López Rega left for Europe where she addressed the International Labor Organization in Geneva and planned visits to Rome and Madrid. On June 19th, Juan Perón's doctors advised Isabel and López Rega to cut short their travels. On June 29, Juan transferred all presidential authority to Isabel. Two days later, he died.

The new president first convened a meeting of Cabinet ministers, military commanders, and political leaders at the presidential residence to address attacks on López Rega and doubts about her intentions. She reaffirmed his position as her personal advisor and as minister of social welfare, and her own plans to continue as president and party leader.

Isabel Perón faced enormous political and economic challenges. Terrorist activity from the left and the right accelerated. Inflation ate into workers' salaries and caused unrest in the party. Her association with López Rega became a focus for critics. His fondness for the occult and his presence at Isabel's side convinced many that he was the real power behind the presidency. His ties with the Triple A—a notorious right-wing assassination group that operated with impunity during her presidency—further tarnished her reputation.

The increase in political violence pushed Isabel Perón toward harsher measures, including nationalization and tight control of the three major television stations. In early September, the Montoneros, an armed wing of the Peronist Party, moved into open opposition. Perón responded by sending an anti-terrorist measure to Congress. When the action failed to staunch the bloodshed, she declared a state of siege. It remained in effect for a decade. As assassinations and kidnappings by right- and left-wing extremists continued, her government moved toward conservative Peronists and the military, who promised to deliver peace and stability.

Economic disorder accelerated with the political violence; inflationary pressures defeated wage and price controls established earlier by Juan Perón. Responding to workers' demands, Isabel increased wages, approved new labor legislation, and appealed to the memory of her husband to mobilize support. A September rally attracted 50,000 labor unionists. She also ordered the return of Evita's body to Argentina and led an emotional service laying Eva's body to rest next to Juan's in the Olivos chapel.

Her efforts to restore order and financial stability failed. The following spring, she took the first of several leaves from the presidency to recover from stress. A crisis in June 1975 caused her to lash out at labor leaders protesting austerity measures. Under pressure from a general strike and the urging of military leaders, she reorganized her Cabinet, eliminating the focal point of much criticism, López Rega. She raised the limit on workers' salaries to quiet union opposition, but inflation continued to erode workers' buying power.

The crisis and burdens of office took their toll on her health. In July, she retreated full-time to the official residence; reports spread that she was in a state of extreme fatigue and nervousness. Congressmen called for an official report on her health. Her physician prescribed rest and circulated photographs of a convalescent Isabel.

The economic and political crises gave her little respite. By late summer, as the government neared default on its foreign debt, she returned to her office. Reshuffling her Cabinet once more, she included a member of the armed forces for the first time. The national party convention in late August reconfirmed her leadership but could not protect her health. In early September, she asked Congress for another leave, traveling to Córdoba province with the wives of the leaders (and members of the future *junta*) of Argentina's Armed Forces. Many speculated that she would not return when she transferred power to an old-time Peronist and president of the Senate, Italo Luder. He reorganized the Cabinet again and smoothed relations with the left wing of the party, but failed to persuade her to extend her leave beyond October 17, Peronist Loyalty Day.

Despite increasing calls for her resignation from party leaders and the military, Isabel Perón resumed power as scheduled. At a Loyalty Day rally, she pledged to complete her term of office, also urging Argentines to support the military in its campaign against the subversives.

The professions of loyalty from party members that greeted her return did not stem attacks from her opponents. At the end of October, the Radical Party proposed a congressional investigation of her deposit of $700,000 in public charity funds into her personal bank account. Support from the Peronist majority in Congress wavered and an investigation started. Charges of corruption and malfeasance targeted people around Isabel, forcing her private physician to resign from the National Sports and Tourism office.

On November 3, 1975, she entered the hospital, but refused to relinquish power. The Radical Party pressed the attack with encouragement from some members of the military. While a congressional commission investigated the charges against her, one of the opposition parties brought a motion in the Chamber of Deputies for impeachment.

Isabel rallied one more time, calling on labor, the party, and the Roman Catholic Church to support her presidency. She denounced the investigation of the charitable funds as an unconstitutional infringement of her presidential power. She then rescheduled presidential elections from 1976 to 1977 to reduce pressures for her resignation and investigation into charges of corruption, but the strategy failed. Unwilling to wait another year, a party faction defected in early December, depriving the Peronists of their majority in the lower house where corruption hearings were proceeding. Military leaders warned Perón to resign and transfer power to a constitutional successor or face a military coup. Party loyalists in the Chamber of Deputies averted one more impeachment motion, but could not stem the rising tide of opposition.

Perón stubbornly, but futilely, resisted. On March 24, 1976, military officers commandeered her helicopter and arrested her. The military *junta* that assumed power held her under house arrest in the interior of the country. The coup, which ended Argentina's latest experiment in democracy, marked the beginning of seven years of military rule, and of what became known as the "Dirty War" against Argentine dissenters.

Despite her fall from power, Isabel Perón continued to represent Juan Perón for millions of loyalists. They blocked an attempt to indict her for malfeasance and secured her release from house arrest in 1981. She promptly left for Spain. In the succeeding years, she attempted to retire from the Argentine political scene, but could not reject its appeals. She retained her official title as head of the party until 1985 when Carlos Saúl Menem, a former governor of her home province, replaced her. Still in Spain, she remained an important player in national politics. When Menem secured the party's presidential nomination in 1989, he turned to Isabel for support, and when he won the presidency she returned to Argentina for his inauguration. With this victory, the Peronist Party reasserted its power in Argentine politics; the party continues to revere Isabel as its last link to Juan Perón. She still makes occasional appearances in Argentina, visiting family and commemorating important Peronist events.

While she is still active on the periphery of her nation's politics, Isabel Perón's position in history is firmly established. She will always be both the first woman president of a Latin American nation and the first female head of state in the Western Hemisphere. Although she clearly had political ambitions, she never openly challenged Argentina's gender structure nor articulated a feminist position. Her career embodies the contradictions of women's place in modern Latin American society and politics, demonstrating both the possibilities and the constraints of existing gender roles.

SOURCES:

Cerruti, Gabriela. *El jefe, vida y obra de Carlos Saul Menem.* Buenos Aires: Planeta, 1993.

Crasweller, Robert. *Perón and the Enigmas of Argentina.* NY: W.W. Norton, 1987.

Deheza, José A. *Isabel Perón: ¿Innocente o cupable?* Buenos Aires: Ediciones Cuenca del Plata, 1983.

de Onís, Juan. "Isabelita's Terrible Legacy," in *The New York Times Magazine.* March 21, 1976.

Hodges, Donald, *Argentina 1943–1976: The National Revolution and Resistance.* Albuquerque, NM: University of New Mexico Press, 1976.

Luca de Tena, Torcuato, Luis Calvo, and Esteban Piocovich, eds. *Yo, Juan Domingo Perón Relato autobiográfico.* Barcelona: Editorial Planeta, 1976.

Merkx, Gilbert. "Argentina: Peronism and Power," in *Monthly Review.* Vol. 27, no. 8, 1976, pp. 38–51.

Moneta, Carlos Juan. "Política Exterior del Peronismo," in *Foro Internacional XX:2.* October–December 1979, pp. 220–276.

Page, Joseph A. *Perón: A Biography.* NY: Random House, 1983.

Rock, David. *Argentina 1516–1982.* Berkeley, CA: University of California Press, 1985.

Sobel, Lester A., ed. *Argentina and Perón 1970–1975.* NY: Facts on File, 1975.

Waidatt Herrera, Domingo. *El perfil auténtico e histórico de una mujer predestinada: documental histórico.* Buenos Aires: Talleres Gráficos Lucania, 1974.

Weir, Sara J. "Peronisma: Isabel Perón and the Politics of Argentina," in *Women As National Leaders*. Newbery Park, CA: Sage, 1993, pp. 161–176.

Joan E. Supplee,
Associate Professor of Latin American History,
Baylor University, Waco, Texas

Perovskaya, Sonia (1853–1881)

Member of the Russian aristocracy who turned to terrorism, was executed for engineering the assassination of Tsar Alexander II, and became a national martyr. *Name variations: Sofya or Sofia Perovskaia. Pronunciation: Sown-ya Pair-ov-SKY-ya. Born Sophia Lvovna Perovskaya on September 13, 1853; executed on April 3, 1881; daughter of a general who served briefly as governor-general of St. Petersburg, and a mother who was a member of the nobility; since university education was not open to women, studied to be a teacher; never married; no children.*

Joined the Chaikovski Circle and took part in the Going to the People movement (1870s); arrested for political activities (1874); met Andrei Ivanovich Zhelyabov during the Trial of 193 and acquitted (1878); went underground to avoid political exile; joined Land and Liberty, the first full-fledged political opposition party in Russian history; joined the extremist group Will of the People and made several attempts on the life of Alexander II; led group in the assassination of Alexander II (1881); following execution for murder of the tsar, recognized as a martyr to the cause of revolution in Russia and the Soviet Union.

Sonia Perovskaya

March 1, 1881, was a dreary early spring day in the Russian imperial capital of St. Petersburg. A sprinkling of young men and women, members of the extremist group Will of the People, lingered along the Malaya Sodovaya, near the Ekaterinski Canal, waiting for the horse-drawn carriage of Tsar Alexander II to appear. Under the snow-piled, dirty street ran a tunnel which had been tediously hollowed out in anticipation of this day. If Alexander's carriage passed over the tunnel, a bomb would be detonated to kill the monarch. But if the convoy took another route, members of the group would move in with grenades. Although Alexander had once raised the hopes of a better future for many Russians like themselves, the plotters were convinced there was no room under his autocratic rule for true political reform.

Along the Malaya Sodovaya, Sonia Perovskaya was positioned to observe the course the tsar's convoy would take. As it moved toward the Ekaterinski Canal, she took out a large white handkerchief and blew her nose, signaling the change of direction. When the tsar's carriage passed by, a man stepped out and threw a bomb. The explosion broke the back axle of the carriage, but Tsar Alexander, unharmed, got out to examine the damage. "I am safe, thank God," he said, just as a second man stepped forward and detonated a grenade that killed them both.

Perovskaya, who had planned the operation, came from one of Russia's most ancient and distinguished families, an unusual background for a social revolutionary. On her father's side, she was descended from Empress ***Elizabeth Petrovna** by a morganatic marriage, and her grandfather had been minister of the interior. Her father had served as governor-general of St. Petersburg for three years, during which he enjoyed unlimited credit and ran up huge debts. His dismissal brought a crisis in the family fortunes. For a time, Sonia and her mother went to live on the family estate in the Crimea, then rejoined her father when the estate was sold in 1869. That summer, Sonia's father fell ill, and her mother and sister traveled with him on a round of European resorts to help him recover. In her father's absence, the teenaged Sonia got a taste of freedom she had never known. When the family returned, she declared that she wanted to study and live on her own. Such a request was unusual indeed in aristocratic circles, where it was taken for granted that a woman would live under her father's control until she married and was placed under her husband's authority.

In imperial Russia, there were few avenues of independence open to men, and fewer still for women. In Western Europe, women had only begun to win access to a university education, which was still denied women in Russia. In Perovskaya's case, this repressive system was made no easier by her home life. While she loved her mother, a great beauty who was known for her kindness, she loathed her father, a bully who was cruel and rigidly militaristic.

Under a regime in which all liberties were granted by the state, paperwork was essential to accomplish even simple tasks. Stubborn and determined, Perovskaya persuaded her father to acquire the internal passport necessary for her to live on her own. Once she left home, there is no record that she ever saw her father again. Whenever she returned to see her mother, she used the back stairs so her visits went undetected. Too proud to take money from her mother, she did copying and translation work, while sometimes living alone and at other times with friends. She passed an examination to teach school but never got a diploma, probably because she was considered politically suspicious.

The repressive Russian system, in which the tsars were ruthless in quashing opposition, was a breeding ground for extremists. Although noble families were supposed to be pillars of this autocratic structure, many members of the highly educated noble class were among its staunchest opponents. Their opposition began with the Decembrists, a group of army officers, largely from the aristocracy, who revolted against Tsar Nicholas I on December 14, 1825. Sent into harsh Siberian exile, along with some of their wives, including ***Maria Volkonskaya**, the Decembrists inspired generations of revolutionaries by their willingness to suffer for a more liberal government. In Russia's huge bureaucracy—which carried out the dictates of the tsar and supported a Byzantine system of spies and secret police that ensured all attempts at reform were nipped in the bud—moderate reform was out of the question, and the opposition came to regard extreme solutions as viable alternatives.

Perovskaya joined the Chaikovski Circle, the first and most famous of the secret cultural and philanthropic societies of the 1870s. It began as a group of young people who met to read books and hold discussions, without politics being a part of its original agenda. Gradually, however, its members began to hold classes for illiterate and impoverished factory workers. In 1861, Alexander II had freed the serfs, forcing many off the land and into the cities in search of work. Because the tsar then issued an imperial edict in 1862 forbidding educational activities among the poor as "likely to undermine faith in the Christian religion and in the institution of private property, and to incite the working class to revolt," the Chaikovski Circle had to hold their classes in secret.

By 1873, there was considerable discussion in intellectual circles about whether young people should finish their studies or start a revolutionary mission among the peasants. The imperial government, fearing radical activities among women who had left Russia to obtain education at the university level, especially in Zurich, Switzerland, ordered the students to come home. The returning women were accompanied by many men, and their combined efforts instigated a movement called Going to the People. Hundreds, possibly thousands, of young people acquired the necessary false papers to travel into the countryside, bringing with them a call to revolution.

As in many such movements in Russia, the revolutionaries, with their idealistic vision, were unprepared for the obstacles inherent in a rigid class system that had allowed little if any interaction between the upper and lower classes. Aristocrats like Perovskaya idealized those who worked on the land without any notion of how the average Russian peasant thought or felt, while the peasants, often suspicious of strangers and their doctrines, sometimes turned over members of Going to the People to the police. The hostility encountered by the intellectuals, along with blistered feet, poor food, and fatigue, proved to be disillusioning.

During the mass arrests that followed between 1873 and 1877, hundreds of young people, some altogether innocent of radical activities, were picked up, and many would sit in jail for years awaiting trial. In 1874, Perovskaya was arrested but remained free on bail until her trial in 1878. At the Trial of the 193, as her case was called, she was acquitted, but under a clause which allowed the police to prescribe "administrative exile" she was soon picked up again. She acquired false papers and escaped. Once an idealist, Perovskaya now trod the path to extremism. She joined Land and Liberty, the first full-fledged political opposition party in Russian history, which recruited its early supporters first among the peasantry and then factory workers. In December 1876, Land and Liberty sponsored a gathering of 200 workers outside the Kazan Cathedral which accomplished little, prompting Perovskaya to conclude that propaganda and education were not enough to accomplish their goals. She believed that, if the system were to be changed, assassinations, prison rescues, infiltration of official organizations, and counter-intelligence against police spies were necessary tactics. Soon, she became part of the organization's Section Five which masterminded the terror campaign. Although members of Land and Liberty did not consider terror as a primary weapon (most in fact opposed its use), terror was thought to be justifiable as a means of vengeance against judges who mandated brutal floggings, police spies who turned in reformers, or corrupt officials who cheated people.

As an illegal, Perovskaya acquired a great deal of experience, and her cool head served her well in difficult situations. For example, after a visit to her mother in the Crimea, she was arrested as a suspicious character and taken by police escort to St. Petersburg. She made no attempt to escape her first captors whom she found kind. A second set, however, proved less genial. The three stopped for the night near the train station, one sleeping by the door and the other by the bed. Perovskaya waited until she heard the train for St. Petersburg coming, escaped out a window, and boarded the train without a ticket.

During the Trial of 193, Perovskaya had fallen in love with Andrei Ivanovich Zhelyabov, who was married but had been separated from his wife for some time. A large dashing man with a long black beard who provided great contrast to the diminutive, blue-eyed, blonde Perovskaya, Zhelyabov was the son of a house serf, but he had been allowed to be educated and shared Perovskaya's passion for reform. Wrote a friend of Perovskaya: "She had always been a strong feminist and maintained that men were the inferior sex. She had real respect for very few of them. But Zhelyabov was up to her caliber. She was utterly in love with him, in a way I never thought could happen to her with any man."

They had not started off by being terrorists. . . . They were turned into killers only by the obdurate and unyielding response of the autocracy to all efforts to change the nature of society.

—Edward Crankshaw

When the Land and Liberty party underwent an ideological split, Perovskaya and Zhelyabov joined the splinter group of extremists, Will of the People (Narodnaya Volya). This band of about 20 people, dedicated to the assassination of the tsar, made three attempts to blow up his railway carriage, often employing elaborate means. For one such attack, a member named Stepan Nikolaevic Khalturin accumulated over 100 pounds of dynamite which he secreted under his bunk in the basement of the Winter Palace where he posed as a workman. Tsar Alexander was delayed on his way to dinner in the room where the explosives went off. Although he escaped unharmed, ten members of the palace guard were killed and many others wounded. The bombing spread such fear among the autocracy that it led to greater repression than ever.

The final plot against the tsar's life began with the rental of a building on the Malaya Sodovaya, where the conspirators set up a cheese shop. Although people in the neighborhood found the merchandise scanty, it did not arouse suspicion. The digging of the tunnel began as did the difficult job of hauling away the dirt. Authorities visited the shop, but nothing was suspected. The tunnel was nearing completion when a series of raids by the police swept up many members of Will of the People, including Zhelyabov. Realizing their own arrests were imminent, the remaining members rushed to complete their task.

The arrest of her lover hardened Perovskaya's determination. She finalized the group's plan, supervised the manufacture of the necessary explosives, and held practice sessions, all while urging the group, some of whom had grown reluctant, forward. On that cold afternoon in March, when Perovskaya signaled that the convoy was changing course, she knew that the tunnel had been dug in vain and that they must rely on grenades, comparatively feeble explosives that had to be thrown at close range. One of the group lost his nerve and moved back without making the first throw. Another then threw his grenade, breaking the carriage axle. The completion of the assassination was carried out by Ignatei Grinevitski, who detonated the grenade that killed himself along with the tsar.

The assassins scattered, escaping that day, but were soon rounded up, tried, and found guilty. On April 3, 1881, five members of Will of the People, including Sonia Perovskaya and Andrei Zhelyabov, were hanged in a public execution witnessed by 80,000 people, as 12,000 troops lined the streets. The assassination had not sparked the general revolt the terrorists had hoped for, and, when Alexander III took the throne, he institutionalized a centralized police apparatus that would survive beyond the tsarist empire, becoming a tool equally effective in the hands of the Communists.

When imperial Russia finally disintegrated, terrorists played little role in its demise. The empire simply rotted from within until only a hollow shell was left which collapsed during World War I. A terrorist in tsarist Russia, Sonia Perovskaya became a martyr in the Communist regime that followed.

SOURCES:

Crankshaw, Edward. *The Shadow of the Winter Palace: Russia's Drift to Revolution 1825–1917.* NY: Viking, 1976.

Engel, Barbara Alpern, and Clifford N. Rosenthal, eds. *Five Sisters: Women Against the Tsar.* NY: Alfred A. Knopf, 1975.

Footman, David. *Red Prelude: A Life of A.I. Zhelyabov.* London: Cresset Press, 1944.

Knight, Amy. "The Fritischi: A Study of Female Radicals in the Russian Populist Movement," in *Canadian-American Slavic Studies*. Vol. IX, no. 1. Spring 1975, pp. 1–17.

Sack, A.J. *The Birth of Russian Democracy*. NYC: Russian Information Bureau, 1918.

Venturi, Franco. *Roots of Revolution. A History of the Populist and Socialist Movements in Nineteenth Century Russia*. NY: Grosset and Dunlap, 1960.

Karin Loewen Haag,
freelance writer, Athens, Georgia

Perpetua and Felicitas

Saints and Christian martyrs.

Perpetua (181–203). *Name variations: Vibia Perpetua. Born in Thuburbo, a small town in northern Africa, in 181; executed on March 7, 203, in the amphitheater at Carthage, an ancient city-state on the northern coast of Africa; probably married; children: at least one.*

Felicitas (d. 203). *Name variations: Felicita; Felicitas of Carthage. Executed on March 7, 203, in the amphitheater at Carthage; children: at least one.*

Perpetua was born in Thuburbo, a small town in northern Africa, to a respectable, if not lofty, family. She was probably married, but perhaps not, for no husband is mentioned in the detailed account of the days leading up to her martyrdom. Regardless, she had an infant child when she was executed on March 7, 203, in the arena at Carthage, having several times publicly professed her Christianity. During Perpetua's lifetime, Christianity was technically illegal throughout the Roman Empire (although few then actually bothered to enforce the law) since it refused to acknowledge the official gods of the state whose worship was regarded as a demonstration of political loyalty. Thus, Perpetua's crime was a political one—she was guilty of treason. Unfortunately for Perpetua, Hilarianus (then governor of Africa) was not as tolerant as most of Christianity. Thus when it came to his attention that a group of Christian novitiates (of which Perpetua was one) had been unearthed, he saw to their arrest on capital charges. He gave those arrested several chances to prove their loyalty to the state by sacrificing to the traditional gods, but they did not do so. He therefore arranged to have them put to death during the games which he held to honor the birthday of the ruling emperor's (Septimius Severus) younger son, Geta. Probably, he meant thereby to attract the attention of the emperor. Septimius, however, was not known to be especially virulent in his treatment of Christians, and there is no evidence that Perpetua's death ever attracted his attention.

What has made the death of Perpetua so important over the ages is that she wrote a diary of her last days, now known as "The Martyrdom of Saints Perpetua and Felicitas," which has come down to us (apparently) little altered by subsequent Christian editors. Thus, her account remains a vivid recollection of a tragic encounter between two very different religious perspectives. By her own account, Perpetua was arrested along with four others: Saturninus, Secundulus, Revocatus, and Felicitas. Saturninus and Secundulus were free males, while (the male) Revocatus and (the female) Felicitas were slaves whose masters are unknown. The mere fact that the free and the enslaved found some equality at the time within a Christian context is of some note, although Christianity was not the only salvation cult to disregard legal status when it came to religiosity. Perpetua and her friends had been religiously converted by one Saturus, who, although he was not with his recruits at the time of their arrest, freely gave himself up to the authorities when his disciples' incarceration became known.

Most of what follows is known from Perpetua's own hand. After she was arrested, her father tried to convince her before authorities to denounce her new faith. Far from being a callous pagan, her father felt genuine concern for her, although he clearly did not sympathize with her Christian inclinations as much as did her mother and one of her brothers. Perpetua's father made manifest his feelings for Perpetua in several visits before her execution, and he even made it known to her that she was his favorite child. What clearly emerges from Perpetua's account is that her father loved her, but that he was angered by what he thought was the brainwashing she had received from a dangerous and radical religious cult. (He even was subjected to physical abuse on her account when his advocacy on her behalf became too strident.) Perpetua's mother and a brother visited her regularly in jail; her father did less so, always in an attempt to get her to change her mind. Perpetua attributed these latter visits, however, to the work of the devil, and she never wavered in her devotion to Christianity, even when, on the day of her death, her father held up her baby to her gaze.

In prison, Perpetua was initially distraught by the separation from her baby, but eventually the two were reunited after some free Christian friends bribed her guards both to provide better accommodations for the incarcerated Christians and to allow Perpetua to see her infant regularly. (Why these friends were not also in jail on religious charges is unknown.) Perpetua was not the only mother in the group to face death, for Felicitas gave birth while in prison.

Perpetua recorded four dreams fraught with religious meaning while she was in prison. The first of these produced a vision of a narrow ladder which was fashioned out of bronze and studded with various impediments to upward progress. At the foot of this ladder lay a dragon. With Saturus leading the way, however, and in the name of Jesus Christ, Perpetua made her upward progress, finally to reach a garden occupied by thousands dressed in white to welcome her. Her second dream recalled a long-dead brother, whose current suffering (he not having embraced Christ) was made manifest to her. Her third vision recounted the same brother's cleansing and healing, both effected through her prayers. Finally, Perpetua anticipated her ordeal in the arena: after having been led into the coliseum by a deacon and before a huge crowd, Perpetua was transformed into a man and, with a Christ-like trainer at her side, proceeded to wrestle with an "Egyptian" over whom she was victorious.

Victorious she might have been in her dreams and/or in the next world, but Perpetua, along with Felicitas and their friends, died in the arena. A report of Perpetua's death had her first mauled by a cow (chosen especially because of its gender), although we are not told what was done to the animal to cause it to savage Perpetua. Death itself, apparently yearned for, was finally dealt by an armed gladiator.

SUGGESTED READING:

Salisbury, Joyce E. *Perpetua's Passion: The Death and Memory of a Young Roman Woman.* Routledge, 1997.

William Greenwalt,
Associate Professor of Classical History,
Santa Clara University, Santa Clara, California

Perrault-Harry, Mme (1869–1958).

See Harry, Myriam.

Perrers, Alice (d. 1400)

Mistress of the English king Edward III. *Name variations: Alice de Windsor; Lady of the Sun. Died in 1400; married Sir William de Windsor, deputy of Ireland (died 1384).*

Alice Perrers, who was the mistress of the English king Edward III, probably belonged to the Hertfordshire family of Perrerses, though there was some talk that she was of more humble origins, possibly the daughter of a tiler from Essex. She entered royal service as a woman of the bedchamber to Queen ***Philippa of Hainault** sometime before 1366. Perrers' intimacy with the king began around that time, and during the next few years she received several grants of land and gifts of jewels from him. After Philippa's death in 1369, Perrers became more powerful. Not content with the great influence which she had over Edward, Alice interfered in the proceedings of the courts of law to secure sentences in favor of friends, or of those who paid for her help, actions which induced the Parliament of 1376 to forbid all women from practicing in the law courts. Though Alice was banished, John of Gaunt, duke of Lancaster, allowed her to return to court, and the Parliament of 1377 reversed the sentence against her.

But Perrers once again attempted to influence the courts. Tried by the peers, she was banished after the death of Edward III in June 1377 (it is said that, following her bedside vigil, she tried to pry the rings off his fingers before rigor mortis set in). This sentence was annulled two years later, and Alice regained some influence at court. Her time, however, was mainly spent in lawsuits, one being with William of Wykeham, bishop of Winchester, and another with her dead husband's nephew and heir, John de Windsor.

Perriand, Charlotte (1903–1999)

French furniture and interior designer. *Born on October 24, 1903, in Paris, France; died on October 27, 1999, in Paris, France; attended the École de l'Union Central des Arts Décoratifs; married in 1926 (divorced); married Jacques Martin (a government official), in 1943 (died 1986); children: (second marriage) daughter Pernette Perriand.*

In a career that spanned eight decades, French furniture and interior designer Charlotte Perriand became a legend of the modernist movement. She designed tubular "equipment for living" with Le Corbusier and Pierre Jeanneret, furniture in Japan, lobbies for Air France, workers' housing in the Sahara desert, and the interiors of ski resorts in the French Alps. Calling herself an "interior architect," Perriand subscribed to the modernist notion that furnishings and architecture should be considered a single entity. She also favored flexible space, free-form shapes, natural materials, and functional design with a humanistic touch. Her dining tables, for example, had splayed legs, so that people sitting on either end could stretch out their legs.

Perriand was born in 1903 in Paris, France, and lived there her entire life. An early talent for drawing led her to enroll at the École de l'Union Central des Arts Décoratifs, where she was trained in decorative design. At age 23, she was invited to exhibit at the Exposition Internationale des Arts Décoratifs (from which the term Art Deco originated), and in 1927 she raised eyebrows at the Salon d'Automme with her "bar under the roof" installation, a built-in chrome-walled bar counter and card table with pool-pocket drink holders.

Having distinguished herself as an avant-garde talent on the rise, Perriand applied for work at Le Corbusier's studio, where the famed designer initially dismissed her with the pronouncement, "We don't embroider cushions here." However, after seeing her bar installation, Le Corbusier relented and hired her. She worked with him, and his collaborator Jeanneret, from 1927 to 1937 and was instrumental in the design of the Le Corbusier classic chaise longue and the cube-shaped Grand Confort chair.

In 1940, Perriand was invited to Japan, where she produced modern designs using traditional materials such as bamboo, pine, and woven straw. With the outbreak of the war, the designer moved to Vietnam, where, unable to obtain a return visa to France, she worked for the colonial government. While there, she met her future husband Jacques Martin, a local official. They were married in 1943, and their daughter Pernette was born one year later.

Returning to France in 1946, Perriand was involved in projects ranging from ski resorts to student housing, Fiercely independent, she was selective about her collaborations, although she worked with ***Sonia Delaunay** on some primary-colored bookcases with cupboards for the Cité Universitaire in Paris, and with Jean Prouvé on a table with a built-in overhead fluorescent light, as well as some other designs. She also teamed again with Le Corbusier on a housing project in Marseilles. Much of her time from 1967 to 1982 was spent on the Arcs, a vast compound of ski resorts in the Alps.

The first of a number of retrospectives of Perriand's work was mounted at the Musée des Arts Décoratifs in 1985, followed by shows at the Pompidou Center in Paris and the Design Museum in London, both in 1996, and another at the Architectural League in Manhattan in 1997. Perriand, however, was not given to reminiscing, but remained a forward-thinker until the end of her life. At the time of her death in 1999, at age 96, she was exploring new materials for the 21st century.

SOURCES:

Iovine, Julie V. "Obituaries," in *The New York Times*. November 7, 1999.

Pile, John. *Dictionary of 20th-Century Design*. NY: Roundtable Press, 1990.

Barbara Morgan,
Melrose, Massachusetts

Perricholi, La (1748–1819).

See Villegas, Micaela.

Perry, Agnes (1843–1910).

See Booth, Agnes.

Perry, Antoinette (1888–1946)

American actress, producer, director, and activist who was honored by the American Theater Wing when the Antoinette Perry Awards, known as the "Tonys," were introduced in 1947 in her name. *Born Antoinette Mary Perry on June 27, 1888, in Denver, Colorado; died on June 28, 1946, in New York City; only child of William Russell Perry (an attorney) and Minnie Betsy (Hall) Perry; educated through high school at Miss Wolcott's School, Denver; married Frank Wheatcroft Frueauff (a businessman), on November 30, 1909 (died July 1922); children: Margaret (b. 1913); Virginia (b. 1917, died in infancy); Elaine (b. 1921).*

One of the most enduring figures in the American theater, Antoinette Perry is called to mind each spring with the awarding of the "Tonys," presented in her name to actors, directors, producers, writers, composers, and designers who have made significant contributions to the previous year's New York theatrical season by the American Theater Wing (which she helped establish during World War II). Perry was an actress and a director, but it was her interest in all aspects of the theater, as well as her selfless support of young talent, that truly set her apart.

Antoinette Perry was born in 1888 in Denver, Colorado, the only child of William Perry, an attorney, and **Minnie Hall Perry**, who with Antoinette's maternal grandmother **Mary Hill Hall** brought the Christian Science faith to Colorado in 1886. (Perry would remain a devoted Christian Scientist her entire life.) It was Perry's aunt, **Mildred Hall**, an actress, who influenced her career in the theater. During summers and school holidays, Perry would travel with Hall and her husband, actor George Wessells, as they toured throughout the East and West. After graduating from the exclusive Miss Wolcott's School in Denver, Perry embarked on her own acting career, making her debut in Chicago in *Mrs. Temple's Telegram* and repeating the role for her New York debut later that year. After a supporting role in *Lady Jim* (1906), she co-starred with David Warfield in *The Music Master* (1906), appearing with him again in *A Grand Army Man* (1907). She also toured with *The Music Master* in 1906 and 1908.

In November 1909, Perry left the stage to marry Frank Wheatcroft Frueauff, a Denver businessman with whom she settled in New York. While raising three daughters (the middle of whom died in infancy), Perry became a patron of several young talents, notably composer Deems Taylor, for whom she sponsored the single performance of his experimental musical *What Next!*

Following the sudden death of her husband in 1922, Perry returned to acting, appearing in ***Zona Gale**'s *Mr. Pitt* (1924) with Walter Huston. She subsequently performed in a string of plays, including *Minick* (1924), *The Dunce Boy* (1925), *Engaged* (1925), *Caught* (1925), *The Masque of Venice* (1926), *The Ladder* (1926), and *Electra* (1927). In 1928, Perry took up directing, and it was in this capacity that she made her most significant contribution to the stage. After a moderate success with Ransom Rideout's *Goin' Home*, she directed *Strictly Dishonorable* (1928), a comedy by Preston Sturges, which ran for 557 performances. Over the course of the next 18 years, Perry directed some 30 plays, many of them in collaboration with producer Brock Pemberton, who was also a lifelong friend. Among her most memorable productions were *Christopher Comes Across* (1932), *Personal Appearance* (1934), *Ceiling Zero* (1935), *Red Harvest* (1937), *Kiss the Boys Goodbye* (1938), *Lady in Waiting* (1940), *Cuckoos on the Hearth* (1941), *Janie* (1942), and ***Mary Coyle Chase**'s Pulitzer Prize-winning comedy *Harvey* (1944). Perry, a small woman with a beautiful speaking voice and a wicked sense of humor, viewed directing as all-encompassing, requiring one "to think in terms of architecture—which is movement—of ballet, of music, of emphasis." Her advice to her actors was to "think clearly, feel deeply, and know the strength of spiritual understanding."

Antoinette Perry was also extremely active in numerous professional theater organizations. From 1937 to 1939, she was chair of the committee of the Apprentice Theater of the American Theater Council, and as such conducted 5,000 auditions to encourage new talent. In 1941, she served as president of the Experimental Theater of the Actors' Equity Association, another early showcase of new talent. She also supported the Actors' Fund of America and the Musicians Emergency Fund. With the advent of World War II, Perry helped establish the American Theater Wing, which provided entertainment for military personnel on leave at Stage Door Canteens in various cities, as well as hospital entertainment for the wounded. Through the American Theater Wing, Perry staged a full-scale production of *The Barretts of Wimpole Street*, starring ***Katharine Cornell**, for Allied military audiences in Europe in 1944–45. Perry died suddenly of a heart attack in June 1946, age 58. Soon after, the Antoinette Perry Awards were established in her memory.

Opposite page Eleanor Perry

SOURCES:

James, Edward T., ed. *Notable American Women, 1607–1950*. Cambridge, MA: The Belknap Press of Harvard University Press, 1971.

McHenry, Robert, ed. *Famous American Women*. NY: Dover, 1983.

Wilmeth, Don B., and Tice L. Miller, eds. *Cambridge Guide to American Theatre*. NY: Cambridge University Press, 1993.

Barbara Morgan,
Melrose, Massachusetts

Perry, Eleanor (1915–1981)

American screenwriter and feminist. *Name variations: Eleanor Bayer; (joint pseudonym with first husband) Oliver Weld Bayer. Born Eleanor Rosenfeld in Cleveland, Ohio, in 1915; died of cancer on March 14, 1981; briefly attended Sarah Lawrence College; Case Western Reserve, M.A.; married Leo G. Bayer (a lawyer and writer, divorced); married Frank Perry (a director and producer), around 1960 (separated 1970, divorced 1971); children: (first marriage) William Bayer; Anne Bayer.*

Screenplays: David and Lisa *(1962);* Ladybug, Ladybug *(1963);* The Swimmer *(1968);* Last Summer *(1969);* Trilogy *(1969);* Diary of a Mad Housewife *(1970);* Lady in the Car with Glasses and a Gun *(1970);* The Deadly Trap *(1971);* The Man Who Loved Cat Dancing *(1973).*

Eleanor Perry entered the movie business when she was well into her 40s and within a decade had written the screenplays for nine remarkable films, six of which were directed by her husband Frank Perry. Divorced from Frank in 1971, she subsequently wrote three more screenplays, including *The Man Who Loved Cat Dancing* (1973), which she also co-produced. During production of the film, she encountered and contested so many sexist issues, however, that when it was over Perry was pretty much blacklisted from any future Hollywood projects. From that time on, she focused on changing the movie industry, crusading for better representation of women on screen and more job equity for them off screen, as writers, directors, and producers. Sadly, her campaign was cut short by her death from cancer in 1981.

Eleanor Perry was born Eleanor Rosenfeld in 1915 in Cleveland, Ohio, and received a master's degree in psychiatric social work from Case Western Reserve. She then went to work as a psychiatric case worker, also writing plays on the subject which were produced by the Cleveland Mental Hygiene Association. With her first husband, Leo G. Bayer, a lawyer, she co-authored additional plays and mystery novels. On a trip to New York in 1958, she met and fell in love with Frank Perry, who was then directing for the stage. She subsequently divorced her husband and married Frank, thus embarking on the second phase of her life.

Disheartened with the state of contemporary drama, the Perrys decided to take advantage of the French New Wave way of filming that was just reaching American shores. Their first movie, inspired by Eleanor's interest in mental health issues, was *David and Lisa* (1962), a dramatized case-history about two troubled adolescents. Since no studio would touch the project, the Perrys raised the money and financed the production themselves. The film, produced on a shoestring budget and using then-inexperienced actors, Keir Dullea and **Janet Margolin**, was named Best Picture of the Year by *Time* magazine and won an Academy Award nomination. "Tact, taste, insight and forthrightness make this one of the most incisive and original films treating mental problems," wrote a reviewer for the trade paper *Variety*.

The couple's next film, also independently produced, was *Ladybug, Ladybug* (1963), which explored children's fears of the nuclear age. (Eleanor based her screenplay on a news article about a nuclear alarm that went off in a school during the Cuban missile crisis.) The film's antiwar bias provoked strong feelings, both pro and con, from critics and audiences alike. "It's as if we have put our fingers on a sore spot, made people face things they would rather not think about," Eleanor said at the time. Despite the controversy, however, the film failed at the box office.

The couple would not attempt another film until their 1968 adaptation of John Cheever's short story "The Swimmer," an offbeat tale about a middle-aged Connecticut suburbanite (played by Burt Lancaster) who, finding himself stranded, swims home via the swimming pools of his friends. Although not a commercial success, the movie was produced by Sam Spiegel, giving the Perrys entrée into the Hollywood mainstream. It was followed in 1969 by an adaptation of Evan Hunter's novel *Last Summer*, starring **Barbara Hershey**, Richard Thomas, **Cathy Burns**, and Bruce Davison, and by *Trilogy*, an adaptation of three of Truman Capote's short

stories ("A Christmas Memory," "Miriam," and "Among the Paths to Eden"), all of which were produced separately for television, then edited for distribution as a feature-length film entitled *Truman Capote's Trilogy*. The television airing of "A Christmas Memory" received 18 major awards, including the Peabody as Best Television Show of the Year, the International Television Critics prize, and Emmys for Truman Capote, Eleanor Perry, and the drama's lead actress, ***Geraldine Page**.

The Perrys' last picture together, *Diary of a Mad Housewife* (1970), was Eleanor's adaptation of the **Sue Kaufmann** novel depicting the breakdown of a marriage, and was memorable for the performances of Richard Benjamin and **Carrie Snodgress** as the doomed couple. The movie both revisited the split-up of Perry's first marriage and signaled the end of her second. "Now, I would write the ending differently," she said three years after her separation from Frank, who had initiated divorce proceedings while the film was in production. "I would carry it one step further. I'd show Tina liberating herself, but not through a man. She'd get a job, or go back to school or whatever."

Following the breakup of her marriage, Perry wrote the screenplays for two thrillers, *The Lady in the Car with Glasses and a Gun* (1970) and *The Deadly Trap* (1972). During this time, she joined a consciousness-raising group led by **Susan Brownmiller** and began to speak out against the shabby treatment of women by the movie industry. On a discussion panel at the 1971 New York Film Festival, she said she was "tired of seeing women portrayed as prostitutes or merely love objects" and "that women can be prolific in the field of literature because it is a monastic effort, but the collaborative nature of film-making allows for exclusion of women as undesirable members of the team, or relegation to assignment dealing only with female subjects." At the 1972 Cannes Film Festival, she led a group of women protesting the Federico Fellini movie *Roma*, and also in 1972, she scripted *The Man Who Loved Cat Dancing*, the "first feminist Western," as she called it, based on the novel by **Marilyn Durham**. She then signed to co-produce the film with Martin Poll, who had arranged a deal with MGM for filming and had promised her equal control and input on the project.

From the onset, Perry realized that Poll had no intention of sharing authority. Relegated to a tiny office at MGM, "full of cracks, with a broken air-conditioner and a tiny desk," next to a bathroom, said Perry, she soon found that she had not been consulted about the casting of Burt Reynolds and **Sarah Miles** in the leading roles, or about changes in the script, which had been rewritten by a committee of male writers. In the new version, Miles' character was softened and a violent rape scene was added, Perry said, "Poll thought it 'turned men on.'" The final product bore little resemblance to what Perry had envisioned. "I saw the film as the *African Queen* in the West, a relationship between a man and a woman but an unlikely combination about a liberated woman in the 1880s who had the guts to run away from her husband. I never wanted to show her cooking, making biscuits, heating coffee, getting raped. Well, all those things are indeed in the film."

Although she objected to the final cut, Perry demanded and won solo credit on the popular film that critics hated. As it turned out, the project sullied her reputation, and she had difficulty interesting producers in her new projects: *Clout*, in which **Cicely Tyson**, as a congresswoman, was to star opposite George C. Scott, and a screen adaptation of the **Joyce Carol Oates** novel *Expensive People*.

Disenchanted and angry, Perry helped other women in the industry achieve producer or director status. She set up workshops at the American Film Institute and testified before a Senate educational committee. In 1977, she made headlines when in an interview with former actress ***Grace Kelly**, princess of Monaco, Perry abandoned the preplanned questions about flower collages to elicit instead comments about the princess' thoughts on the image of women in Hollywood. As it turned out, Kelly's opinions were straight out of the 1950s, which dismayed Perry but did not surprise her.

Perry's efforts to bring strong, independent female characters to the screen did not produce results in her lifetime, although, as **Lizzie Francke** posits, she may have sabotaged her own career. "She might have been better off sticking with the New York 'independent' mentality and continuing to write scripts for low-budget films over which she had control," she writes. "But that culture was also very director-oriented; this worked for Perry when she was in partnership with Frank, but she lost her foothold when she went solo." It may also be true, however, that in choosing to challenge the male-dominated movie industry, Perry sacrificed her career to the greater cause.

SOURCES:

Acker, Ally. *Reel Women: Pioneers of the Cinema*. NY: Continuum, 1991.

Capote, Truman, Eleanor Perry, and Frank Perry. *Trilogy: An Experiment in Multimedia*. Toronto, Canada: Macmillan, 1969.

Francke, Lizzie. *Script Girls: Women Screenwriters in Hollywood*. London: British Film Institute, 1994.

Barbara Morgan,
Melrose, Massachusetts

Perry, Julia (1924–1979)

African-American composer who wrote 12 symphonies and several operas. *Born Julia Amanda Perry in Lexington, Kentucky, on March 25, 1924; died in Akron, Ohio, on April 29, 1979; studied with Nadia Boulanger in Paris and Luigi Dallapiccola in Italy.*

Julia Perry studied at the Westminster Choir College in Princeton and then took courses in composition at Tanglewood. She was also a student of ***Nadia Boulanger**, the foremost teacher of composition of the 20th century. In 1957, Perry organized and gave a series of concerts in Europe sponsored by the U.S. Information Service. She was awarded an American Academy and National Institute of Arts and Letters fellowship, the Fontainebleau award, and the Boulanger Grand Prix for her *Violin Sonata* in 1952. At the beginning of the 20th century, percussion and rhythm did not play a large role in Western European music. During the past few decades, however, their roles have been expanded thanks to composers like Perry. In her *Homunculus C.F.*, she wrote a composition for harp, celesta-piano and an ensemble of eight percussionists. Her work creates a "precarious balance between pitch (melodic and harmonic) and rhythm." Perry also wrote two operas and an opera ballet as well as 12 symphonies. She meshed the neoclassic white European tradition with music from her African-American heritage. In 1973, Perry suffered a series of strokes which left her right side paralyzed. She taught herself how to write with her left hand so she could continue to compose.

SUGGESTED READING:

Smith, Jessie Carney, ed. *Notable Black American Women*. Detroit, MI: Gale Research, 1992.

John Haag,
Athens, Georgia

Perry, Lilla Cabot (c. 1848–1933)

American poet and painter who promoted French Impressionism in the U.S. *Born in Boston, Massachusetts, around 1848; died in Hancock, New Hampshire, in February 1933; studied art at Cowles School, Boston; attended the Julian and Colarossi academies in Paris, France; married Thomas Sargeant Perry (a scholar and professor of 18th-century English literature), in 1874; children: three daughters.*

Poet and artist Lilla Cabot Perry is remembered primarily for her association with artist Claude Monet (1840–1926), and for her efforts in promoting French Impressionism in the United States during the early years of the 20th century. She was also a respected artist in her own right, however, as a retrospective of her work at the Hirschl and Adler Galleries in New York in 1969 helped reestablish.

Perry was born around 1848, into the prominent Cabot and Lowell families of Boston, and was raised and educated in the elite social circles of that city. Married in 1874 to Professor Thomas Sargeant Perry, a professor of 18th-century English literature and grandnephew of the renowned Commodore Matthew C. Perry, she hosted one of the city's most celebrated salons for artists and intellectuals. During the 1880s, Perry began to study art at Boston's Cowles School where she was a student of Robert Vonnoh and Dennis Bunker. She also studied at the popular Julian and Colarossi academies in Paris, and with Alfred Stevens. As well, she wrote poetry, publishing the first of her four volumes of works, *Heart of Weed,* in 1886.

A turning point in Perry's personal and professional life was her meeting with French Impressionist Claude Monet in the summer of 1889. For ten summers thereafter, the Perry family lived in a house next door to Monet's at Giverny, the site of his famous water-lily garden. Although Monet did not accept pupils, Perry had frequent discussions with the painter, and with Camille Pissarro (1830–1903), who lived nearby. Inspired by Monet's style and technique, and encouraged by him to paint directly from nature, Perry created such works as *Haystacks, Giverny* (c. 1895), called by **Ann Sutherland Harris** and **Linda Nochlin** "an homage to the master." They go on to explain, however, that Perry did not adhere slavishly to the guidelines of Impressionism: "[A]lthough her subjects are almost always casually arranged in space and involved in commonplace activities, thus reflecting the Impressionistic style, she retained a clearer draftsmanship and a relatively greater concern for detail and volume than appear in French Impressionist work." Linear clarity was a feature of her portraits particularly after 1912, when she stopped spending extended periods in France.

When Perry returned home after that first summer visit in 1889, she brought with her Monet's painting *Étretat,* the first of his work ever seen in Boston. She was surprised and dismayed, however, when few in her circle seemed to like the painting. Along with ***Mary Cassatt**, another Monet proponent, Perry immediately embarked on a campaign to publicize the new art, lecturing and writing articles on Impressionism, and encouraging her wealthy friends to buy Monets. She also promoted Impressionism through her own work, which was always well received by the critics and the public. As Harris and Nochlin point out, "it is no accident that her third volume of poetry, published in 1898, was entitled *Impressions*."

From 1893 to 1901, the Perrys lived in Tokyo, Japan, where Thomas taught English literature at Keiogijiku College. While there, Perry completed more than 80 pictures of Japanese life and scenery. Upon returning to America, she worked mostly in Boston and at her summer home in Hancock, New Hampshire. The light-filled countryside of New Hampshire became the subject of her later landscapes which are fully Impressionistic in character.

In 1914, Perry founded the Guild of Boston Artists, of which she also served as the first secretary. She frequently exhibited with the Guild, as well as with museums and art societies along the East Coast. In 1927, she published *Reminiscences of Claude Monet from 1889 to 1909*. Lilla Cabot Perry died at her New Hampshire home in February 1933.

SOURCES:

Harris, Ann Sutherland, and Linda Nochlin. *Women Artists: 1550–1950*. LA: Los Angeles County Museum of Art, 1976.

Heller, Nancy G. *Women Artists*. NY: Abbeville Press, 1987.

Rubinstein, Charlotte Streifer. *American Women Artists*. Boston, MA: G.K. Hall, 1982.

Barbara Morgan,
Melrose, Massachusetts

Perry, Ruth (1939—)

Liberian politician, the first female head of state in modern Africa, who served as interim president of her war-torn West African nation from August 1996 through July 1997. *Name variations: Ruth Sando Perry. Born in Grand Cape Mount, Liberia, on July 16, 1939; daughter of Marjon and Al-Haji Semila Fahnbulleh; married McDonald Perry; children: four sons and three daughters.*

Ruth Perry was born in 1939 in the rural area of Grand Cape Mount into a family of Vai Muslims, one of Liberia's several indigenous ethnic groups. Thus, she grew up as a member of the majority in a nation where a small minority, the Americo-Liberians, held the reins of power. The oligarchy of the Americo-Liberians (descendants of former American slaves who had been repatriated to Africa from the 1820s through the 1850s) neglected the needs of the indigenous majority, at times even benefiting from their de facto enslavement.

As a child, Perry learned about the traditions of her Vai Muslim family and culture by attending classes at a traditional school, the Sande Society. Her parents, keen on their daughter obtaining a modern as well as a traditional education, also enrolled her in a Roman Catholic school run by missionary nuns in Liberia's capital, Monrovia. Trained as a teacher at the Teachers College of the University of Liberia, for a time Perry taught elementary classes in her hometown of Grand Cape Mount. Soon she married McDonald Perry, who went on to a successful career as a circuit court judge and senator. During these years, Perry gave birth to three daughters and four sons. In 1971, when the last of her children reached school age, she began to work at the Monrovia offices of the Chase Manhattan Bank, advancing through the ranks over the next years. Her husband's death led her into the world of politics when she decided to finish his term as senator.

In 1980, Americo-Liberian rule ended in a bloody revolution which brought a young military officer, Samuel K. Doe, to power. Soon, ordered society in Liberia began to disintegrate, and civil war loomed. In 1985, Doe "won" the Liberian presidency in an election widely seen as rigged. In this same election, Perry won a Senate seat representing the United Party. To protest the fraudulent election, most United Party office-holders and other opposition members boycotted the Senate, asserting that the Doe regime was illegitimate. With the argument that "one cannot resolve problems by staying away," Perry did not join in the protest, thus becoming the lone member of the opposition in the chamber. She also gained considerable publicity at the time by publicly opposing President Doe's efforts to legalize polygamy. The growing chaos in Liberia had an impact on Perry and her family in 1985, when the Chase Manhattan Bank closed its Monrovia offices and she lost her bank job. To support her children, she founded a retail business in Monrovia.

When full-scale civil war broke out in Liberia in 1989, Perry left Monrovia, returning to her home in Grand Cape Mount. Here she helped shelter some of the refugees from the conflict. Over the next seven years, a series of governments came and went in Monrovia, but none of them wielded significant power and the country experienced seemingly endless bloodshed.

Several warlords terrorized the populace, with each one falsely claiming to be in charge of the country. The suffering of the Liberian people appeared to grow worse with each passing year until 1996, when the Economic Community of West African States (ECOWAS) met at Abuja, Nigeria, to bring together the leaders of the four major warring factions. By that time, the civil war and anarchy had cost Liberia 150,000 lives. At least 2.6 million were homeless.

On August 17, 1996, ECOWAS representatives announced that they had drafted a cease-fire agreement between Liberia's warring factions. Also announced on that day was the replacement of Council of State chair Wilton Sankawulo by Ruth Perry. "I didn't lobby for the job," she said in response, "but the good Lord has made his choice and I will continue to pray for guidance." At her swearing-in ceremony in September, to which Perry wore traditional African dress, she became the first woman in contemporary Africa to become a head of state. In her acceptance speech, Perry said that she owed "this pledge to God and to the Liberian people. We have no illusions and shall endeavor to have no other loyalties to any group or faction." She warned the warlords that she would "treat them like a mother and, if necessary, that means discipline" and would not hesitate to flex her executive muscles.

In reality, Perry wielded little in the way of real power, having neither an armed force nor a treasury at her disposal. Nonetheless, within these profound limitations she handled her symbolic, moral role well. She displayed dignity and calm in a devastated nation's demoralizing environment, and helped nudge Liberians toward national elections, which occurred in July 1997. Perry then relinquished her position to the winner, Charles Taylor. At the start of the new millennium, Liberia remained a shattered society. In what is hoped will be a brighter future, Liberians may remember Ruth Perry for her constructive role in their nation's rebirth.

SOURCES:

Brennan, Carol. "Ruth Perry 1939—," in Shirelle Phelps, ed., *Contemporary Black Biography: Profiles from the International Black Community.* Vol. 15. Detroit, MI: Gale Research, 1997, pp. 164–166.

Burke, Jason. "Where Monkey is Best Dish of the Day," in *Guardian Weekly.* July 27–August 3, 2000, p. 3.

French, Howard W. "In Liberia, Life Returns to a Grim Normality," in *The New York Times.* August 21, 1996, p. A6.

"New Interim Leader Is Chosen for Liberia," in *The New York Times.* August 19, 1996, p. A5.

Tuttle, Kate. "Perry, Ruth," in Kwame Anthony Appiah and Henry Louis Gates, Jr., eds., *Africana: The Encyclopedia of the African and African American Experience.* NY: Basic Civitas Books, 1999, pp. 1509–1510.

John Haag,
Associate Professor of History, University of Georgia, Athens, Georgia

Persia, princess of.

See Pahlavi, Ashraf (b. 1919).

Persia, queen of.

Atossa (c. 545–470s BCE).

See Atossa for sidebar on Cassandane (fl. 500s BCE).
See Statira I (c. 425–? BCE).
See Parysatis I (fl. 440–385 BCE).
See Statira II (c. 360–331 BCE).
See Sati Beg (c. 1300–after 1342).
See Soraya, Princess (b. 1932).

Persida.

See Nenadovich, Persida (1813–1873).

Persis

Biblical woman. *Pronunciation: PUR-sis. A Christian woman of Rome.*

Persis, a Christian of Rome, was acknowledged by the apostle Paul, who spoke of her as "beloved" and as having "labored much in the Lord."

Pery, Angela Olivia (1897–1981)

Countess of Limerick and leader of the British and International Red Cross movements. *Born Angela Olivia Trotter in 1897; died in 1981; daughter of Lieutenant-Colonel Sir Henry Trotter; attended North Foreland Lodge, Broadstairs; awarded diploma in social science and administration from London School of Economics; married Edmund Colquhoun Pery ("Mark"), 5th earl of Limerick, in 1926.*

Angela Olivia Pery began her long career with the Red Cross during the First World War, serving as an ambulance driver from 1914 to 1918. In 1928, married and having completed her education, she began serving in the London branch of the British Red Cross Society, working her way up its president in 1939. She was deputy chair of the Joint War Organization, Red Cross, and St. John from 1941 to 1947, and vice-chair of the executive committee of the British Red Cross Society from 1946 to 1963. She also served variously as vice chair of the League of Red Cross Societies (1957– 73) and chair of the supreme coordinating committee of the International Red

Cross (1965–73). Pery was active in a number of other welfare organizations. In addition to honorary degrees from Manchester and Leeds universities, she was awarded a CBE (1942), DBE (1946), GBE (1954), and CH (1974).

Pescara, marchioness of.

See Colonna, Vittoria (c. 1490–1547).

Pesotta, Rose (1896–1965)

Russian-born American labor organizer and union official, who rose from working in a New York City garment factory to become a vice president of the International Ladies' Garment Workers' Union (ILGWU). *Name variations: Rose Peisoty. Born Rose Peisotaya in Derazhnya, Russia (now Ukraine), on November 20, 1896; died in Miami, Florida, on December 7, 1965; daughter of Itsaak Peisoty and Masya Peisotaya; had one sister, Esther; possibly married twice (one source claims she lived with three men, but the relationships were never formalized); no children.*

Rose Pesotta, a lifelong anarchist, was one of the most remarkable women in the American labor movement in the first half of the 20th century. Born Rose Peisotaya in 1896 in Derazhnya, Russia (now Ukraine), she enjoyed a happy Jewish childhood as the daughter of a successful grain merchant. Her formal education included two years in a local girls' school and private tutoring. As a member of some of Derazhnya's radical circles, she read and was greatly influenced by the theories of such anarchist thinkers as Bakunin, Kropotkin, and Proudhon. In 1913, at age 17, she emigrated to America, the Goldene Mdeeni (Land of Gold), not to find wealth but to escape tsarist oppression and rigid parental authority. Her sister **Esther** had already arrived in New York City. On her first day in the new world, Rose's name was changed from Peisotaya to Pesotta during her processing at Ellis Island.

To support herself, Pesotta began working as a waistmaker in one of Manhattan's garment factories. Soon, she joined the International Ladies' Garment Workers' Union (ILGWU), becoming active in Local 25, one of that union's most dynamic locals. She also became involved in anarchist politics among New York's Jewish workers, particularly after being inspired by a speech given in 1914 by anarchist icon ***Emma Goldman**. Her sister Esther characterized Goldman's influence on Rose succinctly: "Emma helped Rose to believe in anarchism like a rabbi believes in God." After Goldman was deported from the United States, Pesotta maintained an active correspondence with her. Throughout her life, Pesotta was a passionate advocate of anarchist ideals, which included a faith in the free association of workers as an alternative to centralized authority, and an abiding distrust of distant, bureaucratic governance.

By the early 1920s, she was serving as a member of the Local 25 executive board. Pesotta had a formative experience in 1922, when she attended summer-school courses for working women at Bryn Mawr College. A year later, she enrolled at Brookwood Labor College at Katonah, New York, a pioneering institution which provided liberal arts courses to young activists from urban factories and shops to encourage them to seek leadership positions within their own unions. Committed to organizing the unorganized as the best method of advancing the ideals of anarchism, in the 1920s Pesotta was drawn to the dramatic political confrontations of the day. She was actively involved in the case of Nicola Sacco and Bartolomeo Vanzetti, two Italian-born anarchists accused of a murder committed during a robbery, whom many believed were sentenced to death more for their politics and ethnicity (and the open biases of the presiding judge) than for the flimsy evidence presented at their trial. From 1922 until Sacco and Vanzetti were executed in 1927, Pesotta was a passionate participant in protests and demonstrations on their behalf, and she was arrested during a demonstration at the time of their executions (along with ***Dorothy Parker** and many others). Despite the fact that few American workers ever took a serious interest in anarchist ideas, Pesotta was very active in New York anarchist circles throughout the 1920s. From 1925 through 1929, she served as general secretary of the anarchist publication *The Road to Freedom*, to which she also contributed articles until its demise in 1932. She echoed Emma Goldman in her denunciation not only of capitalism, but also of the Communist dictatorship in the Soviet Union.

With the coming of Franklin D. Roosevelt's New Deal in 1933, the American labor movement began to enjoy significant support and encouragement from a friendly Washington administration. In 1934, soon after joining the ILGWU staff, Pesotta became the only woman member on the union's General Executive Board. She also became an ILGWU vice president. Unlike the other members of the ILGWU leadership, men who had been socialists in their youth and now supported the Washington-directed liberalism of the New Deal, Pesotta had a different perspective from which she viewed the new situation for American labor. Because of her anarchist values, she retained an abiding faith in working-class mobilization from below, as opposed to state intervention from above on behalf of essentially passive and grateful workers.

As a professed anarchist, Pesotta pleased few in the labor movement in the 1930s. She was seen by anarchist ideological purists as having betrayed their ideals by accepting a paid job with the ILGWU. Socialists, on the other hand, were skeptical that an anarchist could accomplish anything of value either in trade-union work or in the political arena. In a letter to Hippolyte Havel, an ally of Emma Goldman and editor of the anarchist journal *Freedom*, Pesotta granted that American unions were essentially capitalist institutions. But, she asked, "Should we then grow lettuce and cabbages on some deserted farm pending the millennium?"

A highly effective labor organizer, Pesotta spent the 1930s conducting organizing campaigns in Atlantic City, Buffalo, Milwaukee, San Francisco, and Seattle. In both Puerto Rico and Los Angeles, she conducted effective campaigns among female Latino workers, displaying a remarkable ability to communicate effectively with different ethnic groups. Her ability to bridge what at first often appeared to be great cultural, educational and linguistic gaps came from her genuine respect for working people and their labor, a respect derived from her personal experience as a needleworker who regarded her own work as a craft rather than as merely an unskilled trade.

During a period of sit-down strikes, Pesotta was dispatched in February 1936 by the fledgling Congress of Industrial Organizations (CIO) to assist striking rubber workers in Akron, Ohio. A victory was achieved in this first test of the CIO's philosophy of industrial unionism. Pesotta was also to play a leading role in the United Auto Workers' organizing campaign in Flint, Michigan, from December 1936 through January 1937. While in Akron, she fell in love with Powers Hapgood, a Harvard-educated radical and an experienced labor organizer. Despite their attraction to each other, Hapgood had no intention of leaving his wife and children, and their affair was doomed from the start. Nonetheless, the two shared a belief that the industrial union movement offered the best hope for American workers to create a system of popular economic, as well as political, governance. Concerned over the drift towards centralized and bureaucratic rule, along with paternalistic and authoritarian methods of control, which were taking over all aspects of American life, both Pesotta and Hapgood believed that the time to halt these tendencies was running out.

By the end of the 1930s, it seemed apparent to grassroots labor organizers like Pesotta and Hapgood that labor-based democracy was losing the opportunity to hold its own in a society that defined success in terms of large and ever more powerful institutions. Hapgood could only watch as his own union's leader, the mine workers' John L. Lewis, enjoyed vast and virtually unchallenged power. Pesotta was increasingly disturbed by the almost total authority wielded by the autocratic ILGWU leader David Dubinsky. She was upset by the contrast between the egalitarian rhetoric of the ILGWU leadership and its often shabby and disrespectful treatment of the women who comprised at least 85% of the union's membership of 300,000. In a November 1939 letter to Dubinsky, Pesotta informed him in the bluntest terms possible of an unacceptable "state of affairs in our organization and the present moral disintegration within our ranks." She condemned ILGWU policies that had become "complacent, self-righteous, [and] powerful in our own might," but which had virtually abandoned any sense of obligation or connection to the union's overwhelmingly female rank and file. She found that under Dubinsky and the other male ILGWU leaders women had been kept in a subordinate role, the union leaders expected deference to their bureaucratic structure and personalistic control, and the entire system was based on clear limits of internal discussion and debate.

Realizing that the ILGWU leadership's sexism was not likely to change, in February 1942 Pesotta quit her staff position with the union and returned to a job sewing in a Manhattan clothing factory. She had insisted that she be given power to help in the management of the union, only to discover that she was still regarded as a token whose power was symbolic rather than genuine. In 1944, she resigned from her seat on the union's General Executive Board.

Ann Schofield has written that Pesotta "was an intense and charismatic woman, beloved by the thousands of women workers she organized, but her life was largely tragic." In *Notable American Women*, **Alice Kessler-Harris** characterized Pesotta as a "vital and volatile woman," who could "rise from depression and despair to periods of inspired activity." While she may have married twice, she also lived with men, writes Kessler-Harris "[t]wice in the 1920s and again in the 1950s" in informal relationships "preferring the freedom of long and deeply rooted friendships to the ties of marriage." In a letter to the wife of a man with whom she was having an affair, she once explained her choice not to have children by asserting, "Personally, I would not use an innocent babe as an alibi, for nothing is more erroneous than this, and because of this I did not have any children to tie [a man] for life to myself."

Pesotta's awareness of her Jewish heritage and identity deepened as a result of the Holocaust. In 1945, she accepted a position as a fund raiser for the Anti-Defamation League of B'nai B'rith. In 1950, she worked briefly for the American Trade Union Council for Histadrut, the national union of the newly created State of Israel. Soon, however, she returned to a Manhattan garment shop, where she worked until shortly before her death in Miami, Florida, on December 7, 1965. Despite her many considerable achievements as a trade unionist, it seems reasonable to suggest that in a better world Pesotta would likely have been able to achieve even more. In this regard, Schofield places blame on the male leadership of the ILGWU, "whose faults she could see so clearly [and which] turned a deaf ear to her pleas to become more inclusive of its female and multiethnic membership. By doing this, [the union] lost the services of one of its most talented leaders."

SOURCES:

Bourque, Monique C-E. "'Toward a More Humane and Abundant Life': The Work of Anarchist Rose Pesotta in the ILGWU," M.A. thesis, University of Delaware, 1988.

Buhle, Mari Jo. "Pesotta, Rose (1896–1965)," in Mari Jo Buhle, Paul Buhle and Dan Georgakas, eds. *Encyclopedia of the American Left*. 2nd ed. NY: Oxford University Press, 1998, pp. 600–601.

Bussel, Robert. "'A Love of Unionism and Democracy': Rose Pesotta, Powers Hapgood, and the Industrial Union Movement, 1933–1949," in *Labor History*. Vol. 38, no. 2–3, 1997, pp. 202–228.

Fink, Gary M., ed. *Biographical Dictionary of American Labor*. 2nd ed. Westport, CT: Greenwood Press, 1984.

Kessler-Harris, Alice. "Organizing the Unorganizable: Three Jewish Women and their Union," in *Labor History*. Vol. 17, no. 1. Winter 1976, pp. 5–23.

———. "Rose Pesotta," in Barbara Sicherman and Carol Hurd Green, eds., *Notable American Women: The Modern Period*. Cambridge, MA: The Belknap Press of Harvard University Press, 1980.

Laslett, John H.M. "Gender, Class, or Ethno-Cultural Struggle? The Problematic Relationship Between Rose Pesotta and the Los Angeles ILGWU," in *California History*. Vol. 72, no. 1. Spring 1993, pp. 20–39, 95–96.

Leeder, Elaine. *The Gentle General: Rose Pesotta, Anarchist and Labor Organizer*. Albany, NY: State University of New York Press, 1993.

New York Public Library. Rose Pesotta Papers.

Pesotta, Rose. *Bread Upon the Waters*. Edited by John Nicholas Beffel. Reprint ed. Ithaca, NY: ILR Press, 1987.

———. *Days of Our Lives*. Boston, MA: Excelsior, 1958.

Schofield, Ann. "Pesotta, Rose," in John A. Garraty and Mark C. Carnes, eds., *American National Biography*. Vol. 17. NY: Oxford University Press, 1999, pp. 382–383.

Seller, Maxine S. "Beyond the Stereotype: A New Look at the Immigrant Woman," in *Journal of Ethnic Studies*. Vol. 3, no. 1, 1975, pp. 59–70.

Shepherd, Naomi. *A Price Below Rubies: Jewish Women as Rebels and Radicals*. Cambridge, MA: Harvard University Press, 1993.

Sorin, Gerald. "Rose Pesotta in the Far West: The Triumphs and Travails of a Jewish Woman Labor Organizer," in *Western States Jewish History*. Vol. 28, no. 2, 1996, pp. 133–143.

John Haag,
Associate Professor of History, University of Georgia,
Athens, Georgia

Petacci, Clara (c. 1915–1945).

See Sarfatti, Margherita for sidebar.

Peter, Sarah Worthington (1800–1877)

American charity worker and philanthropist. *Born Sarah Anne Worthington on May 10, 1800, near Chillicothe, Ohio; died of a coronary thrombosis on February 6, 1877, in Cincinnati, Ohio; daughter of Thomas Worthington (a farmer, later a governor and then a senator) and Eleanor (Van Swearingen) Worthington; educated at private girls' schools in Frankfort, Kentucky, and Baltimore, Maryland; married Edward King, on May 15, 1816 (died February 1836); married William Peter, on October 21, 1844 (died 1853); children: (first marriage) Rufus (b. 1817); Thomas Worthington (b. 1820); Mary Alsop (b. 1821, died young); Edward (b. 1822, died young); James (b. 1828, died young).*

Helped to found the Cincinnati Protestant Orphan Asylum (1833); established the Philadelphia School of Design (1848); founded and was the first president of the Ladies' Gallery of Fine Arts (now the Cincinnati Academy of Fine Arts); raised funds for and established several convents and charitable organizations.

Born near Chillicothe, Ohio, on May 10, 1800, as the second of ten children in a wealthy family, Sarah Worthington was the daughter of Thomas and **Eleanor Van Swearingen Worthington.** Her father had freed his slaves and moved his family from Virginia in 1797, and he subsequently served as governor of Ohio and then as a senator. Among the public figures Sarah met during her childhood at Adena, the Worthington family mansion, were Aaron Burr and Henry Clay. She was sent at age eight to Mrs. Louise Keats' school, a private girls' institution near Frankfort, Kentucky, and later attended Mrs. Hayward's Academy, a prestigious finishing school in Baltimore, Maryland, from which she graduated in 1815. While her formal studies focused on French, art, and music, subjects then considered appropriate to women, on her own Sarah also studied history and literature.

In 1816, Sarah married Edward King, with whom she would have five children, although only the two oldest sons survived to adulthood. After her marriage, she continued her studies in French language and literature and also began studying medieval history and the natural and physical sciences. She and her family moved to Cincinnati in 1831. Interested in assisting the less fortunate since she was a young woman, Sarah helped found the Cincinnati Protestant Orphan Asylum (now the Children's Convalescent Home) in 1833. Her husband died three years later, and to be nearer her two sons, who were attending Harvard, she moved to Cambridge, Massachusetts. She took advantage of the opportunities offered in the academic community and reportedly studied German under poet Henry Wadsworth Longfellow.

Sarah remained in Cambridge after her sons graduated from college, and on a visit to her son Thomas in Philadelphia met William Peter, the British consul of the city. They were married on October 21, 1844, in Chillicothe, and made their home in Philadelphia, where Sarah Peter again became involved in various charitable enterprises. Among these were an association she organized to provide assistance to seamstresses and fund raising for a shelter for reformed prostitutes, the Rosine House for Magdalens (prostitutes were popularly called Magdalens in reference to *__Mary Magdalene__). Peter was concerned about the plight of women left on their own without means of support, and it occurred to her that they could be taught to produce commercial designs for such items as carpet, wallpaper, and household items that American manufacturers generally imported from Europe. This led her to establish, in 1848, the Philadelphia School of Design, where women learned commercial design as well as wood engraving and lithography. The school provided the first opportunity for American women to learn a financially solvent trade, and while it began in just one room of her home, with a single paid teacher, it was highly publicized by Peter's friend ***Sarah Josepha Hale**, editor of *Godey's Lady's Book*. In 1850, it became affiliated with the Franklin Institute, the first school of industrial arts in America. (The school was still flourishing in 1932, when it became part of the Moore Institute of Art, Science, and Industry.)

In 1851 and 1852, Peter visited Rome and Palestine, and her interests began to turn toward religion. This change may have been accentuated by the death of her son Thomas in 1851, a loss that was followed in 1853 by the death of her second husband. She then joined her only remaining child, Rufus, in Cincinnati, where she again became involved in the artistic world and was the benefactor of several young artists. In 1853, she founded and became the first president of the Ladies' Academy of Fine Arts (now the Cincinnati Academy of Fine Arts). That same year, she left on a two-year visit to Rome, where she converted to Catholicism in 1855. Peter thereafter channeled her efforts toward the church, particularly in the Cincinnati area. She traveled to Europe to raise money for her endeavors and ultimately was responsible for the founding of several local charitable organizations and convents belonging to various orders, including the Sisters of the Good Shepherd (1857), which helped female prisoners, the Sisters of Mercy (1858), which participated in social work and educational efforts, the Order of the Poor of St. Francis (1858), and the Little Sisters of the Poor (1868); she also helped to establish the Cincinnati convent and school of the Order of the Sacred Heart (1869).

Peter visited military prisons during the Civil War, and after the Battle of Shiloh assisted nursing sisters from the Order of the Poor of St. Francis in caring for the wounded. For several years after the war's end she supported an asylum for children orphaned by the conflict. In the late 1860s, she translated *De l'Education des Méres de Famille* by Louis Aimé-Martin and part of *Histoire Générale de l'Eglise* by Joseph Épiphane Darras from the French. Having turned her home in Cincinnati, and much of the proceeds from sales of her possessions, over to the sisters of St. Francis, she lived her last years among them and died of a coronary thrombosis on February 6, 1877.

SOURCES:

James, Edward T., ed. *Notable American Women, 1607–1950*. Cambridge, MA: The Belknap Press of Harvard University Press, 1971.

McHenry, Robert, ed. *Famous American Women*. NY: Dover, 1980.

Read, Phyllis J., and Bernard L. Witlieb. *The Book of Women's Firsts*. NY: Random House, 1992.

SUGGESTED READING:

King, Margaret R. *Memoirs of the Life of Mrs. Sarah Peter*, 1889.

McAllister, Anna Shannon. *In Winter We Flourish: Life and Letters of Sarah Worthington King Peter*, 1939.

COLLECTIONS:

Letters from Peter to members of her family are in the Rufus King Papers at the Cincinnati Historical Society, Cincinnati, Ohio.

Kari Bethel,
freelance writer, Columbia, Missouri

Peterborough, countess of.

See Robinson, Anastasia (c. 1692–1755).

Peterkin, Julia (1880–1961)

Pulitzer Prize-winning American novelist. *Born Julia Mood on October 31, 1880, in Laurence County, South Carolina; died on August 10, 1961; daughter of Julius Andrew Mood (a physician) and Alma (Archer) Mood; Converse College, Spartanburg, South Carolina, B.A., 1896, M.A., 1897; married William George Peterkin, on June 3, 1903; children: William George.*

Published first novel, Black April *(1927); awarded honorary D.Litt. from Converse College (1927); won Pulitzer Prize for* Scarlet Sister Mary *(1929).*

Selected writings: Green Thursday *(1924);* Black April *(1927);* Scarlet Sister Mary *(1928);* Bright Skin *(1932);* Roll, Jordan, Roll *(1933);* A Plantation Christmas *(1934);* Collected Short Stories of Julia Peterkin *(Frank Durham, ed., 1970).*

Born in Laurence County, South Carolina, in 1880, Julia Peterkin was the daughter of Julius Andrew Mood, a country doctor, and **Alma Archer Mood**, who died while giving birth to her. Peterkin was raised largely by a Gullah nurse, her first experience with the people about whom she would later write. Her father encouraged Peterkin's love of literature and writing, and she graduated from Converse College in Spartanburg, South Carolina, with a bachelor of arts degree in 1896, earning a master's degree the following year. She then taught in the small town of Fort Motte, where she met William Peterkin; they married on June 3, 1903, and would have one son. When Julia assumed managerial duties on William's large estate, Lang Syne Plantation, one of her tasks was to supervise approximately 450 Gullah employees. Gullahs (also called Geechee) are descendants of slaves, many from the area of Sierre Leone, who were brought to the coastal areas of South Carolina, Georgia, and northeast Florida in the 18th and 19th centuries to work on rice plantations. Living for generations in isolated communities, often on coastal islands, they have managed to maintain an African-based culture and a distinct dialect containing many African words. Gullah life and culture became the subject matter of Peterkin's fiction.

Her first work appeared in the *Reviewer*, a little magazine edited by **Emily Clark**, and in H.L. Mencken's *The Smart Set*. In 1924, Peterkin published her first book, *Green Thursday*, a collection of *Reviewer* sketches about the struggles of an African-American plantation family; it sold 5,000 copies. *Black April*, a novel about the downfall of a larger-than-life plantation overseer, was published in 1927. *Scarlet Sister Mary*, published the following year, gained her critical acclaim and a Pulitzer Prize for best novel of the year in 1929, eventually selling more than one million copies. Set in a Gullah community, the novel follows Mary Pinesett, who marries at 15, shocks her community, and is ostracized from her church because of her sexual behavior. After the death of her firstborn son, she disavows her earlier lifestyle and is readmitted into the church and the community. The book contains much information about Gullah culture, and Peterkin was praised for her realistic and sympathetic presentation of black characters. (Nonetheless, in part because of this sympathy, *Scarlet Sister Mary* was barred from several Southern public libraries.)

Peterkin's work fits within the framework of "Southern grotesque," with no shortage of violence, murder and illicit liaisons. She intentionally avoided the issue of race relations, preferring, she said, "to present these people in a patient struggle with fate, and not in any race conflict." When taken in the context of their time, her portrayals of plantation life are notable for their lack of what was then nearly standard condescension and stereotype from white writers. In the context of the modern-day, post-civil-rights movement world, however, her works have been criticized by some for just that sort of condescension and stereotype.

Bright Skin (1932), Peterkin's third novel, was a disappointment to fans and supporters, and its lack of success essentially ended her career as a fiction writer. (Some of the blame for this is also due to the Great Depression, during which book promotion fell drastically.) She produced a volume of sketches and essays about black culture titled *Roll, Jordan, Roll*, in 1933, and republished an earlier sketch, *A Plantation Christmas*, in 1934, but these were received with politeness at best. Her popularity fell off quickly, and by the time she died in 1961, all of her works were out of print and her audience had disappeared. Her books remain valuable for the wealth of detail they provide about Gullah life, however, and some interest in her fiction was renewed with the publication of her collected short stories by the University of South Carolina Press in 1970.

SOURCES:

Contemporary Authors. Vol. 102. Detroit, MI: Gale Research.

Kunitz, Stanley J., and Howard Haycraft, eds. *Twentieth Century Authors*. NY: H.W. Wilson, 1942.

Landess, Thomas. "Julia Peterkin" in *Dictionary of Literary Biography*, Vol. 9: *American Novelists, 1910–1945*. Edited by James J. Martine. Detroit, MI: Gale Research, 1981.

Weatherford, Doris. *American Women's History*. NY: Prentice Hall, 1994.

SUGGESTED READING:

Landess, Thomas. *Julia Peterkin*. NY: Twayne, 1976.

Kari Bethel,
freelance writer, Columbia, Missouri

Peters, Ellis (c. 1913–1995).

See Pargeter, Edith.

Peters, Luise (1819–1895).

See Otto-Peters, Luise.

Peters, Mary (1939—)

British athlete who won the gold medal in the Pentathlon at the 1972 Olympic Games in Munich. *Born in Northern Ireland in 1939.*

A competitor in the pentathlon, a grueling five-event competition (hurdles, shot-put, high jump, long jump, and 200-meter run) that has been called a mini-decathlon, Mary Peters not only captured a gold medal at the 1972 Olympic Games in Munich, but did so at age 33, when, as she said, "time was running out." Following her win, she was heralded as an "overnight success," despite 17 previous years as a competitor.

Peters began her Olympic career in Tokyo in 1964, finishing fourth in the pentathlon, in which points are earned for each of the five competitions and the athlete with the highest total takes home the gold. Four years later, in Mexico City, Peters captained the British women's team, but finished a disappointing ninth in the competition. As the 1972 Munich Games approached, she knew it would be her last chance to capture the gold.

On the first day of the two-day competition, Peters came in second in the 100-meter hurdles, and won both the shot-put and the high jump, coming away with a substantial lead in points. "I knew that I had to make the most of my first three events," she recalled, "because the long jump and 200-meters on the second day were not my best events." Indeed, on the second day, ***Heidemarie Rosendahl** of West Germany, the world record-holder in the long jump, leapt close to three feet farther than Peters. In the final event, the 200-meters, Peters was again nosed out by Rosendahl and by **Burglinde Pollak** of East Germany. However, when the finishing times were converted into points, Peters had overcome her rivals, beating Rosendahl by 10 points and Pollak by 33.

SOURCES:

Greenspan, Bud. *100 Greatest Moments in Olympic History*. Los Angeles, CA: General Publishing, 1995.

Peters, Phillis (c. 1752–1784).

See Wheatley, Phillis.

Peters, Roberta (1930—)

American soprano. *Born Roberta Peterman in New York City on May 4, 1930; daughter of Sol Peterman (a shoe salesman) and Ruth (Hirsch) Peterman (a milliner); Elmira College, Litt.D., 1967; Ithaca College, Mus.D, 1968; married Robert Merrill (an opera singer), in 1952 (divorced); married Bertram Fields, in 1955; children: (second marriage) Paul Adam; Bruce Eric.*

Studied with William Pierce Hermann; made Metropolitan debut as Zerlina in Don Giovanni *(1950); remained at the Met for 35 seasons; debuted at Salzburg (1963), and Kirov Opera, Leningrad, and Bolshoi Opera, Moscow (1972); also appeared in recital, musical comedy, and film.*

Born in New York City in 1930 of Austrian parents, Roberta Peters was musical at an early age, although no one in the family shared this inclination. Her father was a shoe salesman; her mother a milliner. Her grandfather, who was a head waiter at ***Jennie Grossinger**'s hotel in the Catskill Mountains, came to know Jan Peerce, the tenor. When Peters was very young, her grandfather asked Peerce to assess her voice. Impressed, he arranged for voice lessons with William Pierce Hermann who immediately recognized Roberta's potential. Hermann urged her parents to withdraw her from school at age 13 and during the next six years she learned 20 operatic roles. He also arranged for her to learn ballet, acting, French, German, and Italian. Offered an opportunity to appear on Broadway at age 16, Peters declined because she was interested only in opera.

When Roberta was 19, Peerce took her to see Sol Hurok, the noted concert manager, who signed her to a contract and arranged for auditions at the Metropolitan Opera. Within a week, Rudolf Bing engaged her to sing in performances scheduled nearly a year later. Her opportunity came much earlier, however. When **Nadine Conner**, who was singing Zerlina in Mozart's *Don Giovanni*, became indisposed, Peters was given six hours' notice to fill in for her and had to hurry to her debut via the subway. Though she had never before appeared on the stage, she received rave reviews and became, literally, an overnight sensation. After this triumph, Peters appeared frequently on television (including commercials and some 65 visits to "The Ed Sullivan Show") and in film and musical comedy, as well as on the opera stage. She remained at the Met for 35 seasons, much loved by her audiences; among the operas in which she sang most frequently were *Il Barbiere di Siviglia*, *Don Pasquale*, *Lucia di Lammermoor*, *Die Zauberflöte* (as the Queen of the Night), and *Rigoletto*. Peters performed beside **Marian Anderson* in Anderson's historic debut at the Met in 1954, and created the role of Kitty in the American premiere of Menotti's *The Last Savage*. She also sang at the White House for numerous presidents.

Roberta Peters

Happily married since 1955 to Bertram Fields, Peters retired from the Metropolitan Opera in 1987, but has continued to take small film roles and to give up to two dozen concerts a year. On November 20, 2000, 50 years and a few days after her fairy-tale debut in *Don Giovanni*, Peters was awarded the Handel Medallion, New York City's top arts award.

SUGGESTED READING:

Peters, Roberta, with Louis Biancolli. *Debut at the Met*, 1967.

John Haag,
Athens, Georgia

Petersen, Alicia O'Shea
(1862–1923)

Australian reformer and political candidate. *Born Alicia Teresa Jane McShane on July 2, 1862, in Broadmarsh, Tasmania, Australia; died on January 22, 1923, in Hobart, Australia; daughter of Hugh McShane and Jane (Wood) McShane (both farmers); married Patrick O'Shea, in 1884 (died 1886); married Hjalma Petersen (a mining investor), in 1891 (died 1912); children: (first marriage) stepson Francis Patrick.*

Became first woman political candidate in Tasmania (1913); established the Bush Nurses and Child Health Associations; campaigned for social reform; ran for Tasmanian House of Assembly (1922).

Descended from convicts sent to the penal colony of Australia, Alicia O'Shea Petersen was born to Catholic farmers on July 2, 1862, in rural Broadmarsh, southern Tasmania, Australia. A cousin with whom she grew up, John Earle, may have influenced her interest in politics, for he later became a founder of the Workers' Political League and the first Labor premier of Tasmania. Petersen worked as a machinist in a clothing factory, an industry infamous even then for its poor conditions, before marrying Patrick O'Shea, a widower with one son, in 1884. He died two years later, after which she continued to live in Wilmot Terrace, Hobart, with her stepson Francis and, after 1891, with her second husband Hjalma Petersen, a mining investor from Sweden who died in 1912.

Influenced by her work experiences, Petersen was a prominent speaker for the Citizens' Social and Moral Reform League in 1906 when the group campaigned for a government inquiry into terrible conditions in clothing workshops. (The League's other goals, which she also supported, included temperance, "social purity," and improved housing for the poor.) While she worked with both the League and with the Women's Political Association, Petersen was a determined independent and affiliated herself with no party. She founded and served as life president of the Australian Women's Association, was a strong proponent of free university education and a councillor of the Workers' Educational Association, and held a sanitation certificate from the Royal Sanitary Institute.

Women in Australia had gained the right to vote in federal elections in 1902, and in 1913 Petersen became the first woman political candidate in Tasmania when she ran for the federal seat of Denison. The press trumpeted her advocacy of the interests of women and children while ignoring the rest of her platform, and opposing candidates brought in women from other cities to campaign against her; she received only 261 votes. Petersen went on to help establish the Bush Nurses and Child Health Associations, under the aegis of the Women's Health Association. She also organized the women's antidraft campaign in 1917 and headed a campaign to raise the age of consent, both of which issues were contrary to much of public sentiment. Petersen again became a political candidate in 1922, when women were first allowed to run for the Tasmanian House of Assembly. The press was equally hostile to her second candidacy. When, on principal, she defied a court charge of contempt during a lawsuit she was involved with, newspapers labeled it a publicity stunt. She then became ill with abdominal cancer and was unable to campaign publicly. Petersen lost heavily at the polls, and died at her home in Hobart on January 22, 1923.

SOURCES:

Radi, Heather, ed. *200 Australian Women: A Redress Anthology.* NSW, Australia: Women's Redress Press, 1988.

SUGGESTED READING:

Pearce, V.F. *A Few Viragos on a Stump: The Womanhood Suffrage Campaign in Tasmania, 1880–1920*, 1985.

Kari Bethel,
freelance writer, Columbia, Missouri

Peterson, Esther (1906–1997)

American labor activist and U.S. government official. *Born Esther Eggertsen in Provo, Utah, on December 9, 1906; died on December 21, 1997; daughter of Lars Eggertsen and Annie (Nielsen) Eggertsen; Brigham Young University, B.A., 1927; Columbia University Teachers College, M.A., 1930; married Oliver A. Peterson, in 1932; children: Eric, Iver, Lars, and Karen.*

Esther Peterson was born Esther Eggertsen in 1906 and grew up with her three sisters and two brothers in Provo, Utah; their grandparents were Danish immigrants who had walked from Omaha to Salt Lake City to join the Mormon Church. Following her graduation from Brigham Young University, Peterson taught physical education at Branch Agricultural College in Cedar City, Utah. She then enrolled at Columbia University's Teachers College in New York. While there, the conservative Peterson had a perception shift while attending meetings of the American Federation of Labor with her future husband, Oliver Peterson. She also met Norman Thomas and David Dubinsky.

From 1930 to 1936, she taught at the Winsor School in Back Bay, Boston, a college prep school for girls. She also volunteered to teach in the industrial department of the local YWCA on Thursday evenings. "I came face to face for the first time with strikes and strikers," she told an interviewer for the *Christian Science Monitor.* "These girls were receiving $1.32 for every dozen dresses they turned out, and the work involved the sewing on of a square pocket. When they were suddenly ordered to make the pocket heart-shaped, the girls demanded more money. It took more time to sew on a heart than a square, and they were paid by the piece. It was called the heart-break strike, and I've never forgotten it."

Peterson was an assistant in economics at Bryn Mawr Summer School for Women Workers in industry (1932–39); taught at the Hudson Shore Labor School in Esopus, New York; held temporary positions at the International Ladies' Garment Workers' Union and the American Federation of Teachers; was assistant director of education for the Amalgamated Clothing Workers of America (1939–44) and served as their Washington legislative representative (1945–48). She also worked with the Swedish Confederation of Trade Unions while living with her husband abroad (1948–52). It was there that she became a good friend of Sigrid Ekendahl, a leading Swedish trade unionist.

When her husband was transferred to Brussels (1952–57), Peterson worked with the International Confederation of Free Trade Unions and helped organize their first international school for working women at LaBrevière near Paris. Returning from Europe, the Petersons moved to Washington, D.C., where Esther lobbied for the AFL-CIO (1958–61). In 1961, she was invited to join John F. Kennedy's "little cabinet" as assistant secretary of labor and director of the Women's Bureau in the U.S. Department

Esther Peterson

of Labor. At that time, Esther Peterson was the highest ranking woman in the U.S. government.

SOURCES:

Christian Science Monitor. February 27, 1961.

Petherick, Mary (fl. 1887)

British mountaineer who made the first ascent of the Teufelsgrat (1887). *Flourished in 1887; married A.F. (Fred) Mummery (a mountaineer), in 1883.*

In 1887, Mary Petherick, her husband Fred Mummery, and Alexander Burgener climbed the Jungfrau, Zinal Rothorn, Drieckhorn, and the Taschorn, making the first ascent of the Teufelsgrat (the Devil's Ridge) in the process.

Pethick-Lawrence, Emmeline (1867–1954)

English suffragist and social worker. *Name variations: Emmeline Pethick; Emmeline Pethick Lawrence. Born in 1867 in Bristol, England; died in 1954; educated at private schools in England, France, and Germany; married Frederick Lawrence (a newspaper editor, politician and suffragist) who took the name Frederick Pethick-Lawrence (later Baron Pethick-Lawrence of Peaslake), in 1901; no children.*

Worked for improvement of conditions for women (early 1900s); served as co-leader and treasurer of the Women's Social and Political Union (1906–12); created and edited periodical Votes for Women *with her husband (1907–14); participated in the Women's Peace Congress at The Hague (1915); served as treasurer of the Women's International League for Peace (1915–22); became president of the Women's Freedom League (1918); named president of honor of the Women's Freedom League (1953).*

Emmeline Pethick-Lawrence was born into a middle-class family in Bristol, England, in 1867. During an unhappy childhood, she attended private schools in England, France, and Germany. Her independent-minded father greatly influenced her own passion for justice and her willingness to go to great lengths to fight for it.

(She would make him proud with her first arrest while demonstrating for suffrage.) After reading Walter Besant's *Children of Gibeon*, about the economic struggles of single working women, Emmeline took up social work. From 1890 to 1895, she was employed at the West London Mission. She also organized a dress-making company that featured an eight-hour day, a minimum wage, and annual holidays, all of which were rare in industry in general and in the clothing industry in particular.

In 1901, Emmeline Pethick married Frederick Lawrence, a newspaper editor and Labour politician, and they merged their last names as well as their efforts toward social reform. Although the Pethick-Lawrences both believed in taking extreme measures to see that justice was done in the women's movement, they rejected violence as a means of achieving that end. Emmeline staged many demonstrations for suffrage, and was arrested several times.

In 1906, she accepted the position of treasurer of the Women's Social and Political Union (WSPU) and, over the next six years, raised a significant amount of money for the organization. She and her husband, along with *__Emmeline Pankhurst__ and *__Christabel Pankhurst__, were the key members of the organization. According to some, the Pethick-Lawrences were the driving force behind the rise of the WSPU. The couple also created and edited the union's periodical, *Votes for Women*, beginning in 1907. According to Emmeline Pethick-Lawrence, "The task before us, as we saw it, was to organise a great campaign of popular demonstrations which should outdo anything achieved before."

In 1912, after a major window-breaking demonstration, the Pethick-Lawrences were jailed on conspiracy charges. Going on hunger strikes while jailed was a common tactic among suffragists, and, after refusing to eat to the point that doctors believed their lives were in danger, both Emmeline and Frederick were released. They returned home and were shocked to find that Emmeline and Christabel Pankhurst had produced a new militant policy for the organization that went against the ideas on which the

Pethick-Lawrences had based their activities of the last six years. ("Short of taking human life," espoused Emmeline Pankhurst, "we shall stop at no step we consider necessary to take.") As the Pankhursts had planned, the Pethick-Lawrences therefore left the organization, with all four maintaining a public front of mutual respect so that, according to Emmeline Pethick-Lawrence, "the damage to the women's movement might be reduced to a minimum." She told the *Daily Graphic* on October 18, 1912, "We are as militant at heart as anyone. It was on the question of the expediency of a certain militant policy . . . that we disagreed." More specifically, Pethick-Lawrence had stated earlier that year that Emmeline and Christabel Pankhurst had come up with a new campaign in which both public and private property secretly would be attacked by suffragists who would then try to escape, rather than giving themselves up for arrest. This was a policy the Pethick-Lawrences could not support.

The Pethick-Lawrences continued to edit *Votes for Women* as an independent publication after their split from the WSPU (Christabel Pankhurst introduced a new journal for the union, *The Suffragette*), and joined the United Suffragists, which encouraged collaboration between men and women. Despite the fact that Emmeline and Frederick effectively had been turned out of an organization that they themselves had helped to create and finance, they never spoke out against the Pankhursts. They simply went their separate ways and continued their work without the WSPU.

Pethick-Lawrence's career as a suffragist had slowed considerably by 1914, the year she and Frederick ceased editing *Votes for Women*. However, she participated in a women's peace conference at The Hague in 1915, and until 1922 served as treasurer of the organization that was created at that conference, the Women's International League for Peace. She was also the longtime president of the Women's Freedom League. Women over the age of 30 gained the right to vote in Britain in 1918, and that year Pethick-Lawrence ran (and lost) as a Labour candidate in the first election open to women. In later life she lived without any apparent hankering for public recognition of the part she had played in securing women's suffrage, and grew increasingly deaf. She did admit to some disappointment that women, having secured the vote, had not used it to institute significant positive change. She and her husband, who served as a Labour politician and as secretary of state for India and Burma (now Myanmar) from 1945 to 1947, remained devoted to one another throughout the years. After suffering a heart attack in 1951, Pethick-Lawrence was essentially bedridden until her death in 1954.

SOURCES:

Harrison, Brian. *Prudent Revolutionaries: Portraits of British Feminists between the Wars.* Oxford: Clarendon Press, 1987.

Mackenzie, Midge. *Shoulder to Shoulder: A Documentary.* NY: Alfred A. Knopf, 1975.

Uglow, Jennifer S., ed. and comp. *The International Dictionary of Women's Biography.* NY: Continuum, 1989.

SUGGESTED READING:

Pethick-Lawrence, Emmeline. *My Part in a Changing World*, 1938.

*Brittain, Vera. *Pethick-Lawrence: A Portrait.* Allen & Unwin, 1963 (biography of Frederick Pethick-Lawrence).

Kari Bethel,
freelance writer, Columbia, Missouri

Petit, Zizi (b. 1924).

See Jeanmaire, Zizi.

Petre, Maude (1863–1942)

English Catholic modernist writer and activist who championed the excommunicated Jesuit George Tyrrell. *Born in Coptfold Hall, Essex, England, in 1863; died in London, England, of a respiratory ailment in December 1942; one of ten children of Arthur Petre and Lady Catherine Howard Petre, a Catholic convert; never married; no children of her own.*

Joined the Society of the Daughters of the Heart of Mary, the Filles de Marie (1890); took vow of perpetual celibacy (1901); published book Catholicism and Independence *and left her leadership position in the Filles de Marie (1907); papal condemnations of modernism with encyclical letters* Pascendi *and* Lamentabili *(1907); death of George Tyrrell (1909); published* Autobiography and Life of George Tyrrell *(1912); published* Modernism: Its Failure and its Fruits *(1918); published her spiritual autobiography,* My Way of Truth *(1937).*

From the Reformation to the early 19th century, Roman Catholics were a small and despised minority in England, subject to punitive fines for non-attendance in Anglican churches, barred from voting, office-holding, military service, and other civil privileges, and often suspected by their neighbors of disloyalty to the crown. The old religion was kept alive largely by a group of landed aristocrats and gentry, among whom the Petre family was one of the wealthiest and most distinguished. In 1829, Parliament "emancipated" Catholics by giving them the vote and abolishing other civil disabilities, and in the following decades English Catholicism began to flourish, but now the lead was taken by a group of intellectually powerful converts from Anglicanism, led by John Henry Newman and Henry Manning. The "old" Catholics, despite their religion, were suspicious of Rome, and tried to keep Vatican directives at arm's length whereas many of the converts were eager "Romanizers," who aimed to build up Roman authority as a counterweight to government power. Maude Petre, true to family tradition, spent much of her life opposing the spread of Roman influence in British Catholicism, and in trying to reconcile her faith with modern intellectual life, rather than seeing it become isolated as an intellectual backwater.

She was born in 1863 in Coptfold Hall, Essex, England, the daughter of Arthur Petre and Lady **Catherine Howard Petre**. Maude's father was a younger son of the 13th Lord Petre, and Maude was herself one of ten children. They grew up free of material worries, conscious of being set apart from society because of their religion, and rarely in the company of outsiders. Petre wrote later:

> I did not attract men as a young girl; had I done so my fate might have been different; for I was exceedingly inflammable myself, though I did not kindle the flame in others. Of course I was not beautiful; I was badly dressed whereas I required careful dressing. I was overwhelmingly shy with outsiders, especially with men near my own age. We had not been taught to bring our goods to the market, and I had a crushing sense of propriety. All this was enough to keep me in the shade.

As a teenager she suffered from religious doubts, feared death and damnation, and was told by her confessor that she could settle her conscience once and for all by studying scholastic theology in Rome. Following his advice, she took rooms with a Roman widow for a year and began to study under a priest (with a chaperon sitting in on all lessons), showing exceptional skill. Rome itself was not to her liking: "How well I remember my visits to the different shrines in Rome, and how I endeavoured to find devotion before statues that actually repelled me. What a horror I conceived of that great statue of the Madonna of St. Agostino . . . and yet how I prayed before it in spite of my dislike!" English Catholic devotions tended to be far more sober than the flamboyant baroque style she found there.

For a time, Petre's studies had the desired effect of settling her scruples, and, when she returned to England to become a religious journalist, she delivered some solid blows for orthodoxy against the "fashionable intellectual fog" of her era, wrote Clyde Crews. In 1890, aged 27, she entered a religious community of women, the Society of the Daughters of the Heart of Mary, not planning to enter a convent, but rather to bear witness to her faith while still working in the world. Rising rapidly in the organization, she became its superior in 1896 and dedicated herself to helping new converts to Catholicism, and to social work in settlement houses and orphanages around London. Petre was at the same time a prolific contributor to the English Catholic periodicals and, in 1896, published a biography of Peter Claver.

In the late 19th century, the Catholic Church under popes Pius IX and Leo XIII rejected many recent advances in science and opposed much of the political transformation of Europe. It tried to build for itself a fortress against the outside world. Just as the pope walled himself into the tiny Vatican State rather than join the newly unified nation of Italy, so his coreligionists tried to insulate themselves against evolutionary theory, historical-critical study of the Bible, comparative religion, and modern philosophy and psychology. One symbol of this Catholic effort was the declaration, at the First Vatican Council (1869–70), of papal infallibility on questions of faith and morals. Another was the *Syllabus of Errors* (1864), which aimed to prevent Catholics from reading about the most creative theories of their non-Catholic contemporaries. When a few priests and scholars, unhappy with the fortress mentality, tried to adapt their faith to the changing world, the Vatican reacted by silencing and excommunicating them, placing their works on the index of prohibited books.

The most prominent Catholic modernists in England were George Tyrrell, an Irish-born convert to Catholicism who had trained as a Jesuit priest, and Baron Friedrich von Hugel, an Anglo-German aristocrat and scholar. Maude Petre first met Tyrrell in 1896, and they rapidly developed a firm friendship, with him acting for a time as her confessor. Petre appears to have fallen deeply in love with Tyrrell, and he became the central figure in her life. Under his guidance, she began to write a detailed diary of her spiritual development and her increasing openness to intellectual currents in the wider world. As his biographer Nicholas Sagovsky has shown, Tyrrell was often unkind to Petre; at times, he found her attentions cloying and almost stifling. At other times, however, he was appreciative of her intense concern for him. In a letter of 1900, for example, he explained his current difficulties with his superiors at length to her, adding:

> I tell you all this because your heart is mine, and I want at least one confessor in whom I can trust. You just prevent me turning into stone, and then when I think how inaccessible you must always be, I feel harder than ever and put you out of my mind lest you should weaken my ruthlessness to no purpose.

They were both aware of the barriers between the fulfillment of their love, and no impropriety marred their long and ardent relationship. She admitted to herself that her love for him was so intense that "nothing else mattered on earth or in heaven" and that for his sake she "could accept slavery or ill-treatment."

To add a safeguard to their relationship, she took a vow of perpetual celibacy in 1901 and struggled to sublimate her feelings: "I pray that God may give [Tyrrell] those spiritual embraces, that spiritual closeness, which I desire, not perhaps carnally, but tangibly and sensibly." She longed to be close to him, and when the Jesuits sent Tyrrell from London to Richmond, Yorkshire, Petre went to live in lodgings close by, accompanied by her two nephews. Villagers soon began to gossip about the Tyrrell-Petre relationship, abetted by Petre's sister-in-law, who disliked her. Tyrrell, already in trouble with his superiors for his modernist writings, reluctantly asked Maude to leave Richmond to silence the rumors, but wrote at the time: "I never felt anything more deeply than the pain of telling her . . . nor did I ever realize before how much I really cared for her and depended on her companionship and sympathy. I am almost afraid the separation will kill her."

Through the following years, Petre befriended the other principal modernists, including von Hugel and Henri Bremond, a French Jesuit, and entered into extensive correspondence with them. She was at this period following Tyrrell into "immanentism," the idea that in our everyday lives we find manifestations of the divine; that, for example, the love of two people for one another is an avenue of God's love for mankind. That insight encouraged her to explore widely in the contemporary world for religious insight, rather than confining herself in the much narrower scholastic channels approved by the official church. Two books she wrote in the early 20th century, *Where Saints Have Trod* (1903) and *The Soul's Orbit* (1904), were adventurous and outward looking by the standards of her era, encouraging her readers to question their faith, using it as a springboard to their experience of the outside world rather than just accepting it passively and shying away from the unfamiliar. Petre also took a new look at asceticism, praising it as a form of self-mastery in God's honor, but criticizing the self-destructive forms it sometimes took and the distorted vanity it often contained. She now contributed frequently to the Catholic press in America as well as England, and in 1904–05 was writing about contemporary European philosophers, including a six-part series on Friedrich Nietzsche, for *The Catholic World,* a journal of the American Paulist Fathers. Her diary from this period shows an intense self-education in the major philosophical and religious authors of the day, along with prolific "modernist" responses to them.

The climax of Catholic anti-modernism came with Pope Pius X's encyclical letter *Pascendi* and a new syllabus of condemned propositions, *Lamentabili* (both 1907), which prohibited Catholics from reading, writing, and speculating on a broad range of "modernist" issues, and required of all priests an oath of loyalty. This was also the year in which Petre published *Catholicism and Independence,* urging the priority of the individual conscience over the authority of priests and bishops, and contrasting the "visible Church," with its fallible human material, to the "invisible Church," immortal and unfailing. The archbishop of Westminster, Cardinal Bourne, urged her to withdraw the book, but she refused, and this defiance led to her dismissal from leadership of the Society of the Daughters of the Heart of Mary. She wrote to an Anglican friend that "a reign of terror" had begun in the Catholic community, adding that she felt "downright ashamed that such mean and ignorant men should be able to do such harm."

Despite all her efforts to preserve Tyrrell in his priesthood, he refused to accept the pope's terms; he was dismissed from the Jesuit order in 1906 and excommunicated in 1907. Petre offered him a house on the grounds of the convalescent home she had founded in Storrington, Sussex, and emphatically refused to evict him when her bishop said she should not be harboring a condemned modernist. Only two years later, in 1909, he was dead, of Bright's disease, the affliction which had also killed her father. Petre was with him to the end, and the drama of his deathbed was increased by the presence of **Norah Shelley**, another of Tyrrell's female admirers, whom Petre bitterly resented. As soon as he had breathed his last, Petre wrote to several prominent newspapers to declare publicly that although he had willingly received the sacraments he had not recanted his ideas on his deathbed. She feared that the Jesuits would circulate rumors to the contrary. Certain of

Tyrrell's rightness, Petre did not want his life and death turned into a pious tale of ultimate submission. Bishop Amigo of Southwark, the ordinary for Sussex, retaliated by denying Tyrrell a burial in the Catholic graveyard. Instead, he was laid to rest in the Anglican churchyard nearby.

Church officials punished Petre by denying her access to the sacraments until she signed a declaration of submission to *Pascendi* and *Lamentabili,* which she resolutely refused to do. Instead she published a long open letter, "To my fellow Catholics," in the London *Times,* reasserting her commitment to intellectual openness in the Church, defending the memory of Tyrrell, and accusing the hierarchy of persecution. French and Italian journals translated and reprinted the open letter and made her the hero of the modernist cause, but chief villain in the eyes of the Vatican party. The bishop of Southwark never lifted his ban, though Petre was able to take communion in the neighboring Catholic Archdiocese of Westminster. For the rest of her life, she never ceased trying to have the ban lifted, arguing that it was unreasonable to single out one member of the laity, trying to compel her to swear oaths of allegiance to papal declarations which were not covered in the definition of papal infallibility, and which in her conscience as a Catholic she believed mistaken.

Petre published Tyrrell's history in 1912, using his own autobiographical fragment for the first part of the book and then finishing the biography in her own words. She became the first historian of Catholic modernism with her 1918 book *Modernism, Its Failures and its Fruits.* Modernism, she said, had been the attempt to respond to contemporary Catholics' anxieties and spiritual hunger, by making a "synthesis between the essential truth of . . . religion and the essential truth of modernity." Without such a synthesis, she believed Catholicism was doomed to become an increasingly marginal religion, yet the unfolding political horrors of the 20th century were showing it to be more necessary than ever.

Petre worked as a nurse in the First World War, at the former abbey of Pontigny in France, where she had earlier attended conferences with other modernist intellectuals. Dismayed by the shattering effects of the war, like so many members of her generation, she was nevertheless loyal to her country. She argued in wartime articles that the English and French battle against German autocracy was the political counterpart to the modernists' battle against Vatican autocracy. At war's end, she wrote *Democracy at the Cross Roads,* a book whose title echoed Tyrrell's *Christianity at the Cross Roads,* in which she argued for preserving, in the hoped-for new democratic world, the best virtues of the dying aristocracy, the class from which she sprang. Among these qualities was fearless adherence to one's own convictions, held in good conscience, the quality she continued to show in the face of Church indignation.

> I am not enclosed in the sense of thinking that only the Church can speak to us of eternal truth, for I know that she herself has sat at the feet of teachers that never bowed to her authority.
>
> **—Maude Petre**

In the interwar years, Petre continued to write prolifically, but although she engaged many political questions, she always circled back to the religious underpinnings of society. Her writings were often elliptical, and even those which purported to be descriptive frequently wandered into religious meditations. Many of the famous converts to Catholicism in the previous century had written books about their religious journey; the most famous being John Henry Newman's *Apologia Pro Vita Sua* (1864). When Petre came to write the story of her religious life, *My Way of Faith* (1937), she remarked that, unlike converts' books, "my tale is to be one not of change, but of adherence; not of conversion, but of stability." Its drama, she added, consisted of her efforts to preserve that faith in the face of constant challenges, "an almost unresting process of transformation." In it, she insisted that whatever her critics might say, she was and would remain a member of the Church, and added that the Church itself, however much it tried to insulate itself from the world outside its boundaries, could not avoid constant engagement: "I am not enclosed in the sense of thinking that only the Church can speak to us of eternal truth, for I know that she herself has sat at the feet of teachers that never bowed to her authority."

Petre was in her late 70s when the Second World War began, but stayed in London throughout the Blitz of 1940, working as a fire lookout. She developed a respiratory ailment and died after a short illness in December 1942, defiantly asserting her place in the Catholic Church right to the end. She was buried beside Tyrrell in the Anglican churchyard at Storrington, with no Catholic priest in attendance, making in effect a farewell bid of defiance to the Church to which she had always clung but which, for much of her life, had viewed her as more a menace than a friend.

SOURCES:

Crews, Clyde F. *English Catholicism: Maude Petre's Way of Faith*. Notre Dame University Press, 1984.

Petre, Maude. *Modernism: Its Failure and Its Fruits*. London: J.M. Dent, 1918.

———. *My Way of Faith*. London: J.M. Dent, 1937.

Sagovsky, Nicholas. *On God's Side: A Life of George Tyrrell*. Oxford: Clarendon Press, 1990.

Ward, Maisie. *Insurrection versus Resurrection*. London: Sheed & Ward, 1938.

Patrick Allitt,
Professor of History, Emory University,
Atlanta, Georgia

Petronilla (1135–1174)

Queen of Aragon. *Born in 1135; died on October 17, 1174, in Barcelona, Spain; daughter of Ramiro II, king of Aragon (r. 1134–1137), and* ****Agnes de Poitiers;*** *married Ramon Berenguer also known as Raymond Berengar IV, count of Provence and king of Aragon (r. 1150–1162), on August 11, 1137; children:* ****Douce of Aragon*** *(1160–1198); Pere; Sancho of Provence, count of Provence (r. 1181–1185); Fernando; Alphonso II the Chaste (b. 1152), king of Aragon (r. 1162–1196).*

Petrova, Olga (1886–1977).

See Guy-Blaché, Alice for sidebar.

Petrovna, Anna (1757–1758).

See Catherine II the Great for sidebar.

Petrovna, Anne (1708–1728).

See Elizabeth Petrovna for sidebar.

Petrovna, Elizabeth (1709–1762).

See Elizabeth Petrovna.

Petrovna, Tatiana Nikolayeva (1924–1993).

See Nikolayeva, Tatiana.

Petruseva, Natalia

Russian speedskater. *Name variations: Natalya.*

Won the gold medal in the 1000 meters in the 1980 Winter Olympic Games in Lake Placid, New York.

Amid rumors of illegal drug use, Russian speedskater Natalia Petruseva nosed out second-place American ***Leah Mueller** by 40 feet to win the gold medal in the 1000-meter event during the 1980 Winter Olympics at Lake Placid, New York. The controversy over Petruseva began a few weeks earlier, when, after winning the world sprint championship in Norway, she had taken seven hours to produce a urine sample. Drug use seemed even more of a possibility when she finished only eighth in the 1,500 meters, the opening Olympic event. However, after coming in third in the 500 meters and winning the 1000 meters, she passed the drug test without incident.

Petry, Ann (1908–1997)

African-American writer. *Name variations: Ann Lane Petry. Born Ann Lane on October 12, 1908, in Old Saybrook, Connecticut; died on April 28, 1997, in Old Saybrook; daughter of Peter C. Lane (a pharmacist) and Bertha (James) Lane (a chiropodist); University of Connecticut, Ph.G., 1931; attended Columbia University, 1943–44; married George D. Petry, in 1938; children: Elisabeth Ann "Liz" Petry.*

Selected writings: The Street *(1946, reprint ed., 1992);* Country Place *(1947); (juvenile)* The Drugstore Cat *(1949);* The Narrows *(1953); (juvenile)* Harriet Tubman: Conductor on the Underground Railroad *(1955, published in U.K. as* A Girl Called Moses: The Story of Harriet Tubman, *1960); (juvenile)* Tituba of Salem Village *(1964); (juvenile)* The Common Ground *(1964); (juvenile)* Legends of the Saints *(1970);* Miss Muriel and Other Stories *(1971).*

Ann Petry's first novel, *The Street*, written about a single black woman and her eight-year-old son in Harlem, sold over 1.5 million copies after its publication in 1946, making her one of the few bestselling African-American women of the time. Almost 50 years later, Petry again came to public attention with the re-release of *The Street*, which proved so far from dated as to be still timely.

Petry was born in 1908 in Old Saybrook, Connecticut. Her father was a pharmacist, and they were one of only two African-American families in an otherwise white community. (This family background is reflected in Petry's 1958 short story *Miss Muriel*.) As a young woman, she earned a pharmacy degree and served as a pharmacist in her family's drugstore. Moving to New York City following her 1938 marriage, she worked in the advertising department of the *Amsterdam News* and as a reporter and woman's page editor for the *People's Voice*. In New York, she became familiar with the culture of Harlem and studied creative writing at Columbia University. One of Petry's interests, as would become evident in much of her writing, was the study of abnormal behavior. She read extensively in psychology and psychiatry to understand how people react to anxieties and frustrations.

Petry's adult fiction depicts the effects of bigotry and poverty on people's lives. Her first published story, "On Saturday the Siren Sounds at Noon," tells of a father's reaction to the deaths of his children. Set in Harlem, the narrative unfolds in flashbacks, brought on by the factory siren which rings just as it did before he discovered the children had perished in a fire. Blaming his neglectful wife for the children's deaths and consumed with grief, the protagonist eventually kills his wife and flings himself in front of a train. "Like a Winding Sheet," which after its initial publication in *Crisis* magazine was reprinted in *Best American Stories of 1946*, deals with how prejudice affects a black factory worker. At the beginning of the story, Johnson, the protagonist, is wrapped in a sheet, which Petry identifies with a burial covering. The racial slurs and the discrimination Johnson constantly endures during a single day are indeed like small deaths. At home that night, his frustration explodes in violence against his beloved wife.

The Street, whose deterministic theme echoes that of Theodore Dreiser's *An American Tragedy*, is the story of Lutie Johnson, an ambitious African-American woman whose life goes through many twists and turns and ultimately ends unhappily. Lutie spends some time in Connecticut working for a wealthy white family and observes their decadent lifestyle. Betrayed by her husband when she returns home to Long Island, she then leaves him and moves to Harlem with her son. Her humiliating and dangerous experiences in the inner city (which include her killing a man in self-defense) culminate in the defection of her son Bub into a life of crime: "The street will get them sooner or later, for it sucked the humanity out of people, slowly, inevitably." Demoralized, Lutie realizes Bub will probably be sent to reform school and abandons him, hoping to rebuild her life in Chicago. Most critics praised the novel's artistry and realism, and several noted that *The Street* succeeded without being propagandistic and without sentimentality.

Petry's adult novel *Country Place* (1947) is a story of change and disillusionment in a Connecticut town. Unlike *The Street*, this book portrayed mostly white characters and was not concerned with racial issues. In this narrative, a World War II veteran returns home to find that his wife has been unfaithful; another plotline concerns an aristocratic family's sordid secrets. *The Narrows* (1953), a novel of racial conflict, is also set in a Connecticut town, this time in a small black neighborhood. The story's protagonist, Link Williams, is an academically and athletically talented African-American who falls in love with a white woman from a prominent family, only later discovering that she is married.

When their affair becomes common knowledge, townspeople of both races condemn the relationship, and Link's life ends tragically when he is killed by members of his lover's family.

Petry defended her "problem" novels in her 1950 essay "The Novel as Social Criticism." Though she wrote her fiction well after the "naturalistic" period of Dreiser and Frank Norris had passed, and at a time when novels that "made a point" were somewhat unfashionable, she still believed that a novel written to make a social argument was superior to one written simply for its artistry. She asserted that the world's greatest novelists, like Dickens and Faulkner, all wrote social criticism to show "how society affects the lives of [their] characters."

Prompted by what she saw as a lack of worthwhile literature for African-American children, Petry also wrote books for young people, including **Harriet Tubman: Conductor on the Underground Railroad* (1955). This nonfiction work, dedicated to her daughter **Elisabeth Ann Petry**, told the story of the former slave who brought hundreds of people out of slavery in Maryland. Other well-received works for juveniles included *The Drugstore Cat* (1949), which again drew on her background in pharmacy, *The Common Ground* (1964), *Legends of the Saints* (1970), and *Tituba of Salem Village* (1964), the story of **Tituba**, a slave woman who was involved in the Salem witch trials in 1692. Petry recounted her own childhood fascination with books in a speech published in *Horn Book Magazine*, and noted that she wanted the characters in her own books to remind youngsters of the importance of African-Americans in history. "Look at them, listen to them," she said. "Watch Harriet Tubman in the 19th century. . . . Look at Tituba. . . . Remember for what a long, long time black people . . . have been a part of America . . . woven into its heart and into its soul."

Tituba. See *Witchcraft Trials in Salem Village.*

SOURCES:

Alexander, Sandra Carlton. "Ann Petry" in *Dictionary of Literary Biography,* Vol. 76: *Afro-American Writers, 1940–1955.* Edited by Trudier Harris. Detroit, MI: Gale Research, 1988.

Buck, Claire, ed. *The Bloomsbury Guide to Women's Literature.* NY: Prentice-Hall, 1992.

Contemporary Authors New Revision Series. Vol. 46. Detroit, MI: Gale Research.

The Day [New London, CT]. April 30, 1997.

Smith, Jessie Carney, ed. *Notable Black American Women.* Detroit, MI: Gale, 1992.

Sally A. Myers, Ph.D., freelance writer and editor

Petry, Lucile (1902–1999)

American founding director of the U.S. Cadet Nurse Corps. *Name variations: Lucile Petry Leone. Born on January 23, 1902, in Frog Heaven, Ohio; died on November 25, 1999, in San Francisco, California; graduated from University of Delaware in 1924; received advanced degrees at Johns Hopkins University School of Nursing, 1927, and Columbia Teachers College, 1929; married Nicholas Leone (divorced 1967).*

Initiated U.S. Public Health Service program to attract women into nursing to cope with expected casualties of war (1941); founded and became director of Cadet Nurse Corps, a more formal effort to attract women to nursing field (1943); became first woman to direct a division of the U.S. Public Health Service (1949); retired from government service (1966); retired as teacher and associate dean at Texas Women's University (1971).

The only child of a small-town school principal, Lucile Petry was born in 1902 in Frog Heaven, Preble County, Ohio, but spent most of her childhood in Selbyville, Delaware. She obtained a bachelor's degree in 1924 at the University of Delaware, and received advanced degrees in 1927 and 1929 at Johns Hopkins University School of Nursing and Columbia Teachers College, respectively. She taught at the schools of nursing at both Yale and the University of Minnesota.

While at the University of Minnesota, she was selected to initiate a program to respond to an anticipated need for more nurses should America become involved in World War II. The program, considered a less radical alternative to drafting nurses, was run under the auspices of the U.S. Public Health Service. In 1943, while America was at war in both Europe and Asia, Petry's talents were tapped again for an even more determined effort to fulfill military and civilian nursing needs. She became the founder and director of the Cadet Nurse Corps, which provided funding to cover the costs of nursing students' tuition, fees, room and board, books, stipends and uniforms. In return, candidates promised to participate in essential military or civilian nursing for as long as the war lasted. The Cadet Nurse Corps proved to be immensely successful, meeting its recruitment goals in 1943 and 1944 and surpassing them in 1945, when there were 112,000 cadets in the program. Petry attributed the Corps' success to the fact that women liked the idea of combining war service with professional education that could be utilized later.

In 1949, Petry became the first woman to direct a division of the U.S. Public Health Service when she was made the head of Nurse Education. She also was the first nurse to be appointed assistant surgeon general. Retiring from government service in 1966, Petry then resumed teaching nursing and became an associate dean at Texas Women's University. She retired from these positions in 1971, and died on November 25, 1999, in San Francisco, age 97.

SOURCES:

The New York Times (obituary). December 5, 1999.

Jo Anne Meginnes, freelance writer, Brookfield, Vermont

Pettis, Shirley Neil (1924—)

U.S. Republican congressional representative, 94th–95th Congresses (April 29, 1975–January 3, 1979). *Name variations: Shirley Pettis-Robe; Shirley Neil Pettis-Robe; Shirley McCumber Pettis-Robe. Born Shirley Neil McCumber on July 12, 1924, in Mountain View, Santa Clara County, California; daughter of Harold Oliver McCumber and Dorothy Susan (O'Neil) McCumber; graduated from Andrews University Academy, 1942; attended Andrews University, Berrien Springs, Michigan, 1942–43, and the University of California, Berkeley, 1944–45; married Jerry Lyle Pettis (a politician and congressional representa-*

tive, died 1975); married Ben Robe, in 1988; children: Peter Dwight Pettis; ***Deborah Neil Pettis.***

Co-founded and managed the Audio-Digest Foundation (1950–53); was a newspaper columnist for the Sun-Telegram, *San Bernardino, California (1967–70); served as vice president of Republican Congressional Wives Club (1975); elected as a Republican to the 94th Congress, by special election (April 29, 1975); reelected to the 95th Congress; was vice president, Women's Research and Education Institute, Washington, D.C. (1980–81); was a member of the Arms Control and Disarmament Commission (1981–83), and Commission on Presidential Scholars (1990–92); was a member, board of directors, Kemper National Insurance Companies (1979—).*

Shirley Pettis was born in Mountain View, California, in 1924, the daughter of Harold McCumber and **Dorothy O'Neil McCumber**. She attended public schools in the 1930s in Berkeley, California, and Berrien Springs, Michigan, graduating from Andrews University Academy in 1942. Pettis attended Andrews University in Berrien Springs in 1942 and 1943, returning to Berkeley to spend a further two years studying at the University of California, Berkeley.

In 1950, Pettis co-founded the Audio-Digest Foundation, which she managed until 1953. When her husband, Jerry L. Pettis, was elected to Congress in 1966, she became a columnist for the *Sun-Telegram* in San Bernardino, writing for the newspaper from 1967 until 1970. Pettis' direct involvement in political life began in 1975, when she became vice president of the Republican Congressional Wives Club. After her husband was killed in a private airplane crash, she ran for his seat in the special election held on April 29, 1975. Securing over 60% of the vote against three other candidates, Pettis was elected as a Republican to the 94th Congress and subsequently reelected to the 95th Congress, serving until 1979.

During her time in Congress, Pettis was appointed to the Committee on Interior and Insular Affairs, which she used to gain legislation protecting the deserts in her district. She was able to secure wilderness status for nearly half a million acres in the Joshua Tree National Monument, establishing the California Desert Conservation area. Pettis also served on the Committee on Education and Labor and the Committee on International Relations.

Pettis decided not to stand for reelection to the 96th Congress. She became vice president of the Women's Research and Education Institute in Washington, D.C., in 1980, joining the Arms Control and Disarmament Commission in 1981. A member of the board of directors of Kemper National Insurance Companies from 1979, Pettis also served on the Commission on Presidential Scholars from 1990 to 1992.

Shirley Neil Pettis

SOURCES:

Office of the Historian. *Women in Congress, 1917–1990.* Commission on the Bicentenary of the U.S. House of Representatives, 1991.

Paula Morris, D.Phil., Brooklyn, New York

Pettit, Katherine (1868–1936)

American settlement worker. *Born on February 23, 1868, near Lexington, Kentucky; died on September 3, 1936, in Lexington; daughter of Benjamin F. Pettit (a farmer) and Clara Mason (Barbee) Pettit; educated in Lexington and Louisville, Kentucky, and at the Sayre Female Institute of Lexington; never married; no children.*

Worked to improve the lives of rural residents in Kentucky; was instrumental in founding (1902) and running the Hindman Settlement School in Knott County (1902–13) and the Pine Mountain Settlement School in Harlan County (1913–30).

Katherine Pettit was one of the new generation of female settlement workers who first became active in the 1890s. Many of these women worked with immigrants in large cities, but Pettit, who was born into a well-to-do farming family and raised in Lexington, Kentucky, concentrated on helping impoverished residents in her home state whose families had lived on the land for generations. She first began to notice the deprivation of residents of the backwoods of Kentucky, many of whom lived isolated from towns or even roads, while working with the Woman's Christian Temperance Union (WCTU) and the Kentucky State Federation of Women's Clubs. Pettit started several programs in the area of the Cumberland plateau to help these people and soon found that her efforts became her life's work. In her 20s, she made annual summer pilgrimages to Perry and Harlan counties, bringing local women seeds to plant flowers and pictures to put in their homes. Later, she worked at a camp near Hazard, Kentucky, which gave housewives instruction in such areas as food preparation, gardening, and homemaking. With her friend **May Stone** and others, Pettit also held other camps called "Industrials" at Sassafras and Hindman, Kentucky, where they had been invited by community leader Solomon Everidge.

Pettit and Stone were encouraged by their positive experiences with the camps, where enthusiastic participants frequently invited them to live in the area and continue their work. Taking their inspiration from well-known settlement workers like ***Jane Addams** and ***Ellen Gates Starr**, they assisted in a fund drive to establish a permanent educational institution in the area. After they made a successful tour through the East, and with contributions from individuals and local organizations, the Hindman Settlement School, in Hindman, Kentucky, opened in August 1902, under the auspices of the WCTU. The institution taught academic subjects in addition to crafts and industrial and domestic courses, and by 1911 had enrolled some 200 students. In an effort to share the culture of the region, in 1907 Pettit published several mountain ballads in an issue of the *Journal of American Folk-Lore*.

Pettit left Hindman (which May Stone continued to run) in 1913 to move to Pine Mountain, in Harlan County. There William Creech, a much-respected "patriarch" of the area, contributed 250 acres for the establishment of a settlement school to aid the community. Pettit and Creech supervised the clearing and planting of the land and the construction of the buildings, and within two years the Pine Mountain Settlement School was serving 40 boarding students. In addition to organizing the school and conducting clinics to control diseases that plagued the area, such as hookworm and a contagious eye disease that frequently resulted in blindness, Pettit also encouraged the production of traditional arts and crafts, and arranged for them to be sold to assist the income of Pine Mountain residents. Pettit retired from the Pine Mountain School in 1930, after which she became an itinerant social worker, giving advice on farming and working with artisans throughout Harlan County. In 1932, four years before her death, the University of Kentucky awarded Pettit the Algernon Sidney Sullivan Medal in honor of her contributions to the state. Both the Hindman Settlement School and the Pine Mountain School remain active parts of their communities at the beginning of the 21st century, although their missions have adapted to cultural changes over the course of nearly 100 years; the Hindman School now focuses on education and educational assistance for children with dyslexia, and Pine Mountain concentrates on providing environmental education to local residents and visitors.

SOURCES:

James, Edward T., ed. *Notable American Women, 1607–1950.* Cambridge, MA: The Belknap Press of Harvard University Press, 1971.

McHenry, Robert, ed. *Famous American Women.* NY: Dover, 1980.

Sally A. Myers, Ph.D.,
freelance writer and editor

Petty, Mary (1899–1976)

American illustrator. *Born in Hampton, New Jersey, in 1899; died in Paramus, New Jersey, in 1976; married Alan Dunn (a cartoonist), in 1927.*

Self-taught and encouraged by her husband, cartoonist Alan Dunn, Mary Petty was employed by *The New Yorker* from 1927 to 1966, during which she created 38 cover illustrations, the last appearing on Mother's Day 1966. Much of her work was satirical in nature, often at the expense of wealthy dowagers. Petty's artwork was exhibited at the Cincinnati Art Museum in 1940 and at Syracuse University in 1979, three years after her death.

Pfeiffer, Emily Jane (1827–1890)

British poet and essayist. *Born on November 26, 1827, in Oxfordshire, England; died in January 1890 in Putney, London, England; daughter of R. Davis (an army officer); married Jurgen Edward Pfeiffer (a banker), in 1853.*

Published ten volumes of poetry and many essays on the condition of Victorian women.

Selected writings: Valesneria *(1857);* Gerard's Monument and Other Poems *(1873);* Glan-Alarch: His Silence and Song *(1877);* Sonnets and Songs *(1880);* The Wynnes of Wynhavod *(1881);* Under the Aspens *(1882);* Flying Leaves from East and West *(1885);* Rhyme of the Lady of the Rock and How it Grew *(1884);* Women and Work *(1887);* Flowers of the Night *(1889).*

Emily Jane Pfeiffer lost the chance for a formal education when her father's bank failed and the family faced financial hardship. Still, with her father's encouragement she educated herself and developed an interest in both painting and poetry. Her husband, Jurgen Edward Pfeiffer, a German banker residing in London, also supported her in her initial publishing efforts. In 1857, she produced her first book of poetry, *Valesneria; or A Midsummer's Night's Dream.* The long poem *Margaret; or The Motherless* was published in 1861. She then produced no writing for the next 12 years, instead spending her time reading in an effort to further her education.

Between 1873 and 1884, Pfeiffer published a number of books of poetry, including *Gerard's Monument and Other Poems* (1873), *Glan-Alarch: His Silence and Song* (1877), *Sonnets and Songs* (1880), *The Wynnes of Wynhavod* (1881), *Under the Aspens* (1882), and *The Rhyme of the Lady of the Rock and How It Grew* (1884). After the death of George Eliot (***Mary Anne Evans**) in 1880, she wrote "The Lost Light" in praise of Eliot and her work. Pfeiffer's final book of poems, *Flowers of the Night* (1889), was published just a year before her death. Some critics compared her poetry, which often used the sonnet form, to that of ***Elizabeth Barrett Browning.**

Pfeiffer was also interested in chronicling the lives of women as she saw them. After taking a trip around the world, she wrote a travel book, *Flying Leaves from East and West* (1885), in which she recorded her impressions of how women lived in various countries she had visited. She was sympathetic to women's problems and wrote numerous essays about such subjects as dress reform, rape, education, sexuality, marriage, and women in the workplace. In *Women and Work* (1887), she decried the lack of employment opportunities available to women in Victorian culture. At her death in 1890, she left considerable money to establish an orphanage, a drama school, and a women's hall at University College, Cardiff, Wales.

SOURCES:

Buck, Claire, ed. *The Bloomsbury Guide to Women's Literature.* NY: Prentice Hall, 1992.

Kunitz, Stanley J., and Howard Haycraft, eds. *British Authors of the 19th Century.* NY: H.W. Wilson, 1936.

Shattock, Joanne. *The Oxford Guide to British Women Writers.* Oxford: Oxford University Press, 1993.

Sally A. Myers, Ph.D.,
freelance writer and editor

Pfeiffer, Ida (1797–1858)

Austrian world traveller and bestselling author whose two round-the-world trips were extraordinary achievements for the day. *Born Ida Laura Reyer in Vienna, Austria, on October 14, 1797; died in Vienna in the night of October 27–28, 1858, of an illness she had contracted during her last adventure in Madagascar; daughter of Aloys Reyer (a merchant) and Anna Rosina Reyer; had six brothers and one sister; married Mark Anton Pfeiffer (a lawyer of Lemberg), in 1820; children: two sons, and one daughter who died soon after birth.*

Ida Pfeiffer was one of the most intrepid travelers of the 19th century. From 1842 until her death, she journeyed to far-off continents and dangerous regions, providing entertainment and knowledge to countless readers through her books. She was beloved by the public and respected by scientists and geographers, and became the first woman to be admitted as an honorary member to the geographical societies of Berlin and Paris.

She was born Ida Laura Reyer into a bourgeois Viennese household in 1797. With six brothers and one sister, her early years were lively. Her father Aloys Reyer, a manufacturer, believed that she could only benefit by competing with her brothers, playing their games and being toughened up in roughneck fashion. But her father's death in 1806 brought drastic change, and most middle-class comforts, including sumptuous meals, became a memory. Although the new Spartan lifestyle would one day be of value to Ida in her travels, for the time being she had to endure her mother's plan for her to become *heiratsfähig* (marriageable). She was forced into becoming acceptably feminine by wearing dresses, taking piano lessons, and learning to knit.

Her hatred of the piano and knitting was so great that she cut into her fingertips with a knife. For several years, she fiercely resisted the various efforts at "feminization." Her proper education was to be the work of her tutor Joseph Franz Emil Trimmel. While he did impart conventional knowledge to the 13-year-old, Trimmel also made available to her travel books which revealed a world of exotic locales and Romantic adventure. Ida fell deeply in love with her tutor, who was not suitable because of his poverty. Aware of the situation, Ida's mother fired Trimmel, but Ida would never forget her first love, or the world he had brought to her attention through reading.

In May 1820, Ida entered into an arranged marriage with Mark Anton Pfeiffer, a Lemberg (modern-day Lviv, Ukraine) attorney, 24 years her senior, who was considered to be a suitable partner. After their Vienna nuptials, the couple moved to Lemberg where Pfeiffer gave birth to two sons and to a daughter who died 18 hours after birth. Her husband was an honest but unlucky lawyer. After he discovered a serious case of official corruption, his law practice was boycotted and economically throttled. By secretly giving music and drawing lessons to more affluent members of the bourgeoisie, Ida added to the family's income and kept food on the table. By the late 1820s, the couple was unofficially separated. The death of Ida's mother in 1831 brought her a modest inheritance, which she invested prudently in order to provide tuition for her two sons. Two years later, she left her husband, a man who "only lived in illusions," and returned to her native city of Vienna with her boys. Despite her financial circumstances, she began planning trips. An excursion to the port city of Trieste, then an Austrian-ruled harbor on the Adriatic Sea, excited her imagination as she saw salt water and ships for the first time in her life.

By the early 1840s, Pfeiffer's sons were grown, and she felt free to do things long imagined. Told by a priest that a trip to the Holy Land would require about 600 Austrian gulden, she began a disciplined savings campaign. With the required sum in hand, on March 22, 1842, she left Vienna via the Danube to make the trip—the first of what would turn out to be five major journeys, including two around the world. In her diaries, which became the basis of her many travel books, Pfeiffer displayed unusual frankness, describing herself as being poor, unattractive, and old, without pretensions to either literary talent or learning. She noted, however, that to her advantage were her maturity, courage, and a sense of independence derived from a life that had been filled with difficulties.

In her travels, Pfeiffer took full advantage of the considerable freedom that advanced age gave to a woman in the mid-19th century. In societies based on traditional gender-specific roles, older women were often defined as being of less importance than younger ones and thus were subject to considerably less male control. She did not have to concern herself with her physical appearance, and, now allowing herself more latitude in both behavior and opinions, found it relatively easy to be direct in discussing any number of matters, including sexuality. Although an alert observer during her ten-month trip to the Middle East, Pfeiffer reflected some traditional European stereotypes when she described local women as being ignorant and lazy. She also indicated, however, that they were often friendly and trusting, and suggested that they might be happier on balance than their European counterparts. After she returned to Vienna, Pfeiffer's friends were so impressed with her tales of adventure that they urged her to find a publisher for her extensive diaries. Released in 1844 as *Die Reise einer Wienerin in das Heilige Land* (Travels of a Viennese Lady in the Holy Land), her book became a bestseller, and Pfeiffer was convinced that she had finally found her niche. In 1845, she made a journey to Scandinavia and Iceland, which quickly resulted in the publication of another popular volume.

On May 1, 1846, Pfeiffer embarked on her most ambitious voyage to date—a trip around the world. By June, she was under sail to Brazil on a modest Danish cargo vessel. Always concerned with her budget, she found this an economical and interesting way to travel. With her usual acute observation, she noted the luminescent marine creatures her ship encountered in South Atlantic waters. In Rio de Janeiro, the evils of slavery left their mark on her sense of social justice, but she also compared the situation of slaves favorably to the situation of many European peasants and Egyptian "fellahs." For the rest of her trip, Pfeiffer would often comment on the miserable lives of those individuals—particularly women and children—who suffered at the very bottom of the social pyramid. Her outrage at injustice runs like a thread throughout all of her travelogues, as does her sympathy for women of the lower classes. She believed that in her own part of the world most of the benefits of women's liberation were likely to accrue to women who were already privileged. This viewpoint would only be strengthened during her absences from Europe.

After returning to Vienna from her round-the-world adventure in November 1848, Pfeiffer organized her diaries and in 1850 published a three-volume account of her travels entitled *Eine Frauenfahrt um die Welt* (A Lady's Journey around the World). Her work again proved to be a resounding success with the reading public. By May 1851, the always restless Pfeiffer was traveling once more, now on her second trip circling the globe, going around the Cape of Good Hope through the Indian Ocean. Her venture would result in valuable acquisitions for the Museum of Natural History, Vienna. Among her many adventures was an encounter with the Dyak cannibals of Borneo, whom she was able to persuade that her flesh, being that of a dried-out old white European lady, would really not be palatable. Wherever she went, Pfeiffer often pointed out issues beneath the surface. In India, when describing the Taj Mahal, she reminded her readers of the human cost in labor and wealth of the exquisite edifice. She also made perceptive comments on reasons for Asian hostility and indifference toward Western missionary efforts, which she believed had little hope of success because most missionaries made no attempts to adapt their mode of dress or style of living to local conditions. Most of all, she noted, they avoided contact with the poor masses, preferring instead to live in a segregated fashion among other missionaries in the wealthiest parts of towns.

Pfeiffer would later take issue with her fellow Europeans' horror at the custom of head-hunting, citing an alarming similarity between this custom and the bloody realities of European battles. Later, on a visit to Versailles, she would be appalled by paintings displayed there glorifying battles; she saw these as comparable to the Dyaks' custom of displaying shrunken heads. Pfeiffer, in fact, praised the Dyaks: "I should like to have passed a longer time among the free Dyaks, as I found them, without exception, honest, good-natured, and modest in their behavior. I should be inclined to place them, in these respects, above any of the races I have ever known." While she was in China, it is quite likely that the only reason Pfeiffer was not physically attacked as a hated *Inglesi* was because she was a seemingly frail and elderly white woman. As such, on her travels she was able to deny complicity in European imperialism's lust for conquest and exploitation. Likely because of her status as an older woman, the indigenous peoples Pfeiffer came in contact with did not see her as an aggressor or spy, making it possible for her to survive in situations that might easily have been fatal for a European male.

Ida Pfeiffer

In 1853, Pfeiffer was visiting a California which was still crazed with gold fever. While there, she made a number of observations on the tragic consequences of that state's racial prejudice against its Native American peoples. After observing the rapidly dwindling Indian population of California, she wrote bitterly: "to this desert men voluntarily banish themselves for the chance of finding a lump of gold! What must a place be, if it had but this attraction, to keep off the avaricious whites?" She wrote admiringly of the American Indians: "They understand no work but basket plaiting. In this art, however, they have attained to great perfection; they know how to make their baskets perfectly water-tight, and manage even to boil their fish in them." Pfeiffer further asserted:

> These Indians are represented as treacherous, cowardly, and revengeful, and only attacking the whites when they find one alone. But, after all, what other means of attack have they against well-armed whites—the domineering race from which they have had so much to suffer. Revenge is really natural

> to man; and if the whites had suffered as many wrongs from them as they from the whites, I rather think they too would have felt the desire of revenge.

Pfeiffer returned to Vienna in May 1855 and published her account of the trip the next year. With adventures on every page, the four-volume set, simply entitled *Meine zweite Weltreise* (My Second Voyage around the World), was snapped up by her loyal reading public.

By 1857, Pfeiffer was again off on an adventure. On what would turn out to be her last trip, she chose to visit the then little-known island of Madagascar, off the coast of southeastern Africa. There, she unwittingly became involved in the struggle between Madagascar's fiercely proud ruler Queen ***Ranavalona I** and French adventurers who were plotting to turn the island into a colonial possession of France. Ranavalona, enraged by these attacks on her nation's sovereignty, took drastic measures to expel the hostile foreigners. Through no fault of her own, Pfeiffer was perceived to be part of these plots and imprisoned. Left with no choice, she escaped from danger by traveling through a disease-ridden jungle, which severely affected her health. Having found refuge on the Indian Ocean island of Mauritius, Pfeiffer briefly considered traveling on to Australia. But she was now seriously ill from a tropical fever that was beginning to destroy her liver, and had to abandon these plans.

She returned home, where she hoped medical science might still cure her. Despite her rapidly declining health, Pfeiffer was to enjoy one more triumph. Just before she died, the two undisputed contemporary giants of scientific geography, Alexander von Humboldt and Carl Ritter, honored the frail but tenacious Pfeiffer by spending several hours with her. Earlier, she had been elected an honorary member of the geographical societies of Berlin and Paris. (The British Royal Geographical Society would not admit her because its statutes refused membership to women.) Ida Pfeiffer died in Vienna on the night of October 27–28, 1858. After her death, her son Oscar edited and published her last book, about her ill-fated trip to Madagascar.

Underneath her conventional Biedermeier exterior, Pfeiffer was in many ways an Austrian steel magnolia. Wrote **Helga Schutte Watt**:

> [Pfeiffer] preached the gospel of simplicity and modesty, [but] she [also] demonstrated courage and achievement. Although she supported traditional concepts, she also undermined them. She upheld the narrowly circumscribed image of the selfless mother and devoted housewife, at the same time living and describing the realization of a woman's dream to roam the world. Without threatening the patriarchal order based on gender, she attacked class privilege, social injustice, and the morality of European wars and conquests.

SOURCES:

Adams, William Henry Davenport. *Celebrated Women Travellers of the Nineteenth Century.* 9th ed. London: W.S. Sonnenschein, 1906.

Agosín, Marjorie, and Julie H. Levison. *Magical Sites: Women Travelers in 19th Century Latin America.* Buffalo, NY: White Pine Press, 1999.

Baker, D.B. "Pfeiffer, Wallace, Allen and Smith: The Discovery of the Hymenoptera of the Malay Archipelago," in *Archives of Natural History.* Vol. 23, no. 2, 1996, pp. 153–200.

Dabak, Shubhangi. "Images of the Orient in the Travel Writings of Ida Pfeiffer and ***Ida Hahn-Hahn**," Ph.D. dissertation, Michigan State University, 1999.

Donner, Eka. *Und nirgends eine Karawane: Die Weltreisen der Ida Pfeiffer (1797–1858).* Düsseldorf: Droste Verlag, 1997.

Fürle, Brigitte, ed. *Eine Frau fährt um die Welt.* Vienna: Promedia Verlag, 1989.

Gürtler, Christa, and Sigrid Schmid-Bortenschlager. *Eigensinn und Widerstand: Schriftstellerinnen der Habsburgermonarchie.* Vienna: Verlag Carl Ueberreuter, 1998.

Habinger, Gabriele. *Eine Wiener Biedermeierdame erobert die Welt: Die Lebensgeschichte der Ida Pfeiffer (1797–1858).* Vienna: Promedia Verlag, 1997.

Heindl, Waltraud. "'Reise nach Madagaskar': Zu den Berichten Ida Pfeiffers über Mauritius und Madagaskar," *Österreichische Osthefte.* Vol. 26, no. 2, 1984, pp. 324–336.

Hildebrandt, Irma. *Hab meine Rolle nie gelernt: 15 Wiener Frauenporträts.* Munich: Eugen Diederichs Verlag, 1996.

Jedamski, Doris. *Images, Self-Images and the Perception of the Other: Women Travellers in the Malay Archipelago.* Hull, UK: University of Hull, Centre for South-East Asian Studies, 1995.

Jehle, Hiltgund. *Ida Pfeiffer, Weltreisende im 19. Jahrhundert: Zur Kulturgeschichte reisender Frauen.* Münster and NY: Waxmann Verlag, 1989.

McLoone, Margo. *Women Explorers in Polar Regions: *Louise Arner Boyd, Agnes Deans Cameron, Kate Marsden, Ida Pfeiffer, Helen Thayer.* Mankato, MN: Capstone Press, 1997.

Miller, Florence Fenwick. *In Ladies' Company: Six Interesting Women.* London: Ward and Downey, 1892.

Pfeiffer, Ida. *Abenteuer Inselwelt: Die Reise 1851 durch Borneo, Sumatra und Java.* Ed. by Gabriele Habinger. Vienna: Promedia, 1993.

———. *Eine Frau fährt um die Welt: Die Reise 1846 nach Südamerika, China, Ostindien, Persien und Kleinasien.* Ed. by Gabriele Habinger. Vienna: Promedia, 1992.

———. *A Lady's Second Journey Round the World.* NY: Harper & Brothers, 1856.

———. *A Lady's Visit to California, 1853.* Oakland, CA: Biobooks, 1950.

———. *A Lady's Voyage Round the World: A Selected Translation from the German of Ida Pfeiffer.* Introduction by Maria Aitken. Reprint ed. London: Century, 1988.

———. *The Last Travels of Ida Pfeiffer, inclusive of a Visit to Madagascar, with a Biographical Memoir of the Author.* Translated by Henry William Dulcken. London: Routledge, 1861.
———. *Reise einer Wienerin in das Heilige Land.* Reprint ed. Frankfurt am Main: Societäts-Verlag, 1980.
———. *Reise in die Neue Welt: Amerika im Jahre 1853.* Ed. by Gabriele Habinger. Vienna: Promedia, 1994.
———. *A Woman's Journey Round the World, from Vienna to Brazil, Chili, Tahiti, China, Hindostan, Persia, and Asia Minor.* 4th ed. London: N. Cooke, 1854.
Slung, Michele B. *Living with Cannibals and Other Women's Adventures.* Washington, DC: Adventure Press-National Geographic Society, 2000.
Stefoff, Rebecca. *Women of the World: Women Travelers and Explorers.* NY: Oxford University Press, 1992.
The Story of Ida Pfeiffer and Her Travels in Many Lands. London: T. Nelson, 1879.
Tinling, Marion, ed. *With Women's Eyes: Visitors to the New World, 1775–1918.* Hamden, CT: Archon, 1993.
———. *Women into the Unknown: A Sourcebook on Women Explorers and Travelers.* CT: Greenwood Press, 1989.
Watt, Helga Schutte. "Ida Pfeiffer: A Nineteenth-Century Woman Travel Writer," in *The German Quarterly.* Vol. 64, no. 3. Summer 1991, pp. 339–352.
Weber, Bernerd Clarke. "Ida Reyer Pfeiffer and Malta," in *Journal of the Faculty of Arts, University of Malta.* Vol. 3, no. 4, 1968, pp. 290–295.

RELATED MEDIA:

Schramm, Cornelia. "Mit Ida Pfeiffer nach Jerusalem" (audiocassette), Berlin: Aufbau Verlag, 1999.

John Haag,
Associate Professor of History, University of Georgia, Athens, Georgia

Pfost, Gracie (1906–1965)

U.S. congressional representative (January 3, 1953–January 3, 1963). Pronunciation: Post. Born Grace Bowers on March 12, 1906, in Harrison, Arkansas; died on August 11, 1965, in Baltimore, Maryland; daughter of William Lafayette Bowers and Lily Elizabeth (Wood) Bowers; educated at Links Business University, Boise, Idaho; married John Walter Pfost (a master mechanic), on August 4, 1923.

Served as Democratic congressional representative from Idaho (1953–63); best remembered for support of a federal dam project and her opposition to the private Snake River dam projects in Idaho (1950s).

Gracie Bowers Pfost was born in 1906 in humble circumstances on an Arkansas farm and moved at an early age to another farm near Boise, Idaho. After graduating from business school, she married John Walter Pfost while still a teenager. Pfost, an ambitious young woman, took a job as a chemical analyst for a milk products company, where she quickly became successful, despite a lack of training in chemistry.

At age 23, Pfost began a career in public service by becoming the deputy county clerk, auditor and recorder for Canyon County, Idaho. She remained in that position for ten years, after which she spent another ten years as the county's treasurer. She also became active in Democratic politics, and served as a delegate to every Democratic national convention from 1944 until the mid-1960s. She made an unsuccessful bid for the U.S. House of Representatives in 1950.

After setting up a real-estate business in Nampa, Idaho, in 1952, Pfost decided to run again for the House in Idaho's 1st District. This time she was successful, becoming the state's first female member of Congress despite the strong showing of Republican presidential candidate Dwight D. Eisenhower in Idaho that year. As a member of the House, she supported Fair Deal legislation, the repeal of the Taft-Hartley act (which restricted some union activity), an increase in the minimum wage, better Social Security benefits, and federal aid to education. She was known as a strong proponent of a federal dam project proposed for the Snake River in Hell's Canyon, Idaho, and was often referred to as "Hell's Belle." A vocal opponent of private power concerns, which she felt would cost con-

sumers too much, she asserted, "I do not intend to be bluffed, bullied, or frightened by the private monopolies." Her motion to approve the federal dam project for the river failed to make it out of committee, however, and the Idaho Power Commission was permitted to construct the dams. Pfost was always a powerful advocate of the concerns of her Idaho district. In 1953, she supported a bill to stabilize the prices of domestic lead and zinc and another to promote the free marketing of newly mined gold.

In 1953, Pfost was appointed to a special committee to investigate and study educational and philanthropic foundations. Formed at a time when anti-communist sentiment was raging in the country, the committee was charged with rooting out "un-American" contributions by these foundations. Pfost and chair Wayne Hays of Ohio, however, objected to the committee's use of unreliable witnesses and testimony and walked out of the deliberations, precipitating the early demise of the committee itself. Disagreeing with the report written by the majority of the committee, she complained to the press that the "foundations have been indicted and convicted under procedures which can only be characterized as barbaric."

Some of the issues Pfost supported during her first term included statehood for Hawaii, an increase in airline subsidies, and Eisenhower's housing stimulation program. She handily defeated Republican Erwin Schwiebert for reelection in 1954, making passage of an Equal Rights Amendment part of her platform. In her second term, she backed such issues as the establishment of the U.S. Air Force Academy and the continuing of a reciprocal trade program. During her stint in Congress, Pfost served on the Committee on Public Works, the Committee on Post Office and Civil Service, and the Committee on Interior and Insular Affairs, where she chaired the public lands subcommittee.

Pfost served a total of five terms in Congress, choosing not to run again in 1962 in order to seek a Senate seat. She was defeated in that race by Republican Len B. Jordan, after which she worked as a Special Assistant for Elderly Housing in the Federal Housing Administration until her death in 1965.

SOURCES:

Current Biography 1955. NY: H.W. Wilson, 1955.

Office of the Historian. *Women in Congress, 1917–1990*. Commission on the Bicentenary of the U.S. House of Representatives, 1991.

Sally A. Myers, Ph.D., freelance writer and editor

Pharandzem (c. 320–c. 364)

Queen of Armenia who, after the capture of her husband, assumed the responsibility for the defense of Armenia during a massive Persian invasion. *Name variations: P'arandzem; (maiden name) Pharandzem Siuni; the name Pharandzem is of Iranian origin, the attested Middle Persian form being Khorandzem. Pronunciation: p'ar-an-DZEM, with a slight hesitation between the* p *and the* a. *Born around 320; daughter of Antiochus Siuni; married Arsaces II, king of Armenia, around 338 (marriage repudiated by Arsaces so he could marry Olympias, c. 355); married Prince Gnel: children: (first marriage) Prince Tiridates, possibly eldest son (b. around 340, possibly died young); Prince Pap (b. around 342).*

Gnel executed by King Arsaces (c. 359); Emperor Julian invaded Persia (Arsaces his ally, 362); Julian killed in Mesopotamia (363); Persian invasion of Armenia and Arsaces captured and taken to Persia (363–64); Pharandzem assumed defense of Armenia, fall of fortress of Artagers; Pharandzem captured and executed.

That Armenian historians have anything to tell us about Queen Pharandzem in a Middle Eastern milieu—where they frequently neglect to provide even the name of a ruler's wife—attests to her extraordinary character. The chronology of her life remains uncertain, and even her motivations are obscure, but there is no doubt that she is one of the most remarkable women to appear in Armenian history before the modern era.

Our earliest source for a biography of Queen Pharandzem is the enigmatic historical text known as the *Epic Histories,* an original Armenian work of the late 5th or early 6th century. Pharandzem of Armenia was killed about 364, by which time she had a grown son old enough to lead an army into battle; thus we may assume that she was born sometime between 320 and 330. Her life may then be placed in the first 40 years following the conversion of Armenia to Christianity and in the context of the momentous consequences of that event.

The decision of King Tiridates the Great of Armenia to convert to Christianity was the most important milestone in the history of the country until the 20th century. Although Armenia was certainly the first nation to embrace Christianity as its state religion, the exact date when this took place and the circumstances surrounding it have only recently begun to become clear. After many wars between Rome and Iran for the domination of Greater Armenia, the two powers agreed with the Treaty of Rhandeia (63 CE) that while the country was to be ruled by a member of the Parthian royal house of the Arsacids (rulers of Iran), the king was to reign as a vassal of Rome. Despite this treaty, the struggle for control of Armenia continued, and the single most important event in the two-and-one-half-century-long conflict that followed was the overthrow of the easy-going Parthian Arsacids in 224 and their replacement as rulers of Iran by the militant Persian Sasanids. Where Parthia had been a nuisance to Rome, Persia was a serious threat, consciously attempting to restore the glories of Achaemenid Persia with the concomitant goal of driving the Romans out of Asia.

After 224, this great international conflict was of major significance for Armenia, where a branch of the Arsacid dynasty of Parthia still ruled. The news of the fall of the Parthian Arsacids was received with horror by their relatives in Armenia, for there was now a real direct threat to the Armenian royal house from that of the new dynasty in Iran. The Persian struggle against Rome naturally came first in the Sasanid scheme of things, while the Armenians maneuvered frantically between the two powers, perforce being driven into the arms of Rome. Although, at first, Rome was unable to be of much help to Armenia, in 297 the Roman army trounced the Persians in Armenia, and the Sasanids were forced to sign a humiliating treaty at the city of Nisibis. This set the stage for the conversion of Armenia to Christianity which was to take place a few years later, and which is intricately linked to the unusual social structure that existed in the country.

The formal Christian conversion of King Tiridates and the royal court by St. Gregory the Illuminator took place in the early 4th century. The year 301 is usually given, but scholars increasingly accept 314 as the correct date. The conversion of Armenia to the faith of the Roman emperor was not well received in Persia but for the time being there was not much that the Sasanids could do about it. While the Armenian kings, by and large, remained committed to Christianity, many princely houses, including that of Siunik, were to remain pagan or crypto-pagan for many years to come.

According to the *Epic Histories*, Pharandzem was the daughter of Antiochus, one of the princes of the house of Siunik (though all other sources make him head of the family, i.e. *the* prince of Siunik). Pharandzem was married to Prince Gnel, nephew of King Arsaces II of Armenia. Gnel's brother, Prince Tirit, having heard of Pharandzem's beauty, contrived to see her, fell in love with her, and sought some means of disposing of his brother so that he might marry her. To this end, he concocted the slander that Gnel wished to be king of Armenia and that he was plotting with various princes to murder King Arsaces and seize his throne. So cleverly did Tirit plant these insinuations that the king came to believe them and developed a plot of his own to place Gnel under arrest. The king sent Vardan, head of the great house of Mamikonian and brother of the commander-in-chief of the king's army, to invite Gnel to the royal encampment at the village of Shahapivan, where the new year's festival called *Navasard* was celebrated each August. Finding Gnel, Pharandzem, and their princely entourage in the nearby village of Araviutk, Vardan enticed him to Shahapivan, assuring him that the king had learned the falseness of the accusations and wished to have him present for the celebration of the festival. Believing Vardan's assurances, Gnel, Pharandzem and their entire suite traveled all night to reach the royal encampment, arriving on Sunday morning on the feast of St. John the Baptist. Upon his appearance at the camp, Prince Gnel was immediately pulled from his horse, arrested, bound and taken away to be executed at a nearby racetrack.

Pharandzem, however, borne into the camp in a litter in her husband's retinue, witnessed the arrest and immediately ran to the tent in which Nerses, the chief bishop of Armenia, was celebrating Sunday mass. Interrupting the service, she told him what was happening and begged for his intercession. The chief bishop immediately terminated the ceremony and hurried to the royal tent, where the king was pretending to be asleep, and begged him in the name of Christ's mercy not to execute his own brother's son. As the king continued to feign sleep, Erezmak, the chief executioner, entered the tent and announced that Gnel had been executed according to the king's command and had already been buried. At this, Nerses condemned the king, cursed him, and predicted the sorry fate that awaited him.

Arsaces then ordered that his nephew Gnel be officially mourned as a royal prince, and commanded that all in the camp should attend the funeral services. At the same time, he observed the disconsolate Pharandzem and conceived a passion of his own for her. Only a few hours later, Gnel's brother Tirit unwisely revealed to Pharandzem his love for her and admitted that it was he who had contrived her husband's death. Pharandzem, horrified and grief-stricken, spread the alarm. When the king learned the true circumstances of Gnel's downfall and how he, himself, had been duped by Tirit, he gave the order for him to be executed as well. King Arsaces then married Pharandzem, but she never forgave him for executing her first husband. Their marriage was so unhappy that when Emperor Constantius II (r. 338–361) offered Arsaces a Roman bride, he accepted. The new bride was **Olympias**, daughter of the former Praetorian prefect Ablabius. Olympias must have arrived in Armenia in the year 358 and shortly afterwards was elevated to the rank of queen. Pharandzem, meanwhile, had given birth to the king's son, Prince Pap, who, when he was old enough, was sent to the Roman court as a hostage for his father's good behavior. Unwilling to see another woman seated on the throne and probably fearing for Pap's accession should Olympias bear the king another son, Pharandzem contrived to have Olympias murdered. Since Olympias' ladies in waiting protected her food from all poison, we are told that Pharandzem found a priest at the royal court, Merjiuinik, who was willing to mix poison in the Holy Eucharist so that Olympias was murdered while taking communion. In return for this deed, Merjiuinik received a single village.

All of these events were interconnected with a long war between Armenia and Iran, which the author of the *Epic Histories* says lasted 34 years. It is in the midst of this account of one massive Persian invasion of Armenia after another that the *Epic Histories,* in a chapter obviously out of place in the text, interrupts its narrative to return to Pharandzem and her son Pap. According to this source, at the time of Pap's birth, Pharandzem had dedicated him to demons and, as he grew to manhood, he became a practitioner of every vice, above all that of sodomy. When the queen learned of this and attempted to remonstrate with him, she saw demons appear in the form of serpents winding themselves around him, whereupon she fled the room crying that her son was possessed and that she had known nothing of this.

Since it is extremely unlikely that Pharandzem would have dared dispatch Olympias while Olympias' Roman patron Constantius II was still alive, the murder must have taken place in 361, the year Constantius died, or very shortly thereafter. Pharandzem was sole queen, once again. Then the Persian king Sapor made peace with Arsaces, summoning him to Persia under a promise of safe conduct but, fearing his closeness to the Roman emperor, upon his arrival having him treacherously imprisoned. He then forced Arsaces to write a letter to Pharandzem telling her and the grandees of Armenia to join him in Iran. Pharandzem, realizing what had happened, ignored the order. In 362, the new emperor Julian (r. 361–363) attacked Persia, undertaking a disastrous campaign into Mesopotamia during which he was wounded and died. The new emperor, Jovian (r. 363–364), anxious to terminate the war at any cost, ceded the overlordship of Armenia to Sapor and gave him a free hand to do whatever he wished there. Sapor immediately invaded the country on a punitive expedition and appears to have ravaged it from end to end.

With the king a prisoner in Persia and his son Pap a hostage with the Romans, it was the queen, alone, who undertook to lead the country. Unable to stop the invaders from ravaging Armenia, she took refuge in the great castle of Artagers, where she shut herself up with a vast number of soldiers, retainers and treasure. The Persians, of course, laid siege to the castle, surrounding it and waiting for it to fall. Pharandzem was not totally isolated, however, for the castle had a secret entrance, and it was through this that certain messengers from the Roman authorities were able to reach her from time to time, urging her to hold out until her son could come to her rescue with a contingent of Roman troops.

Unfortunately, neither Pap nor the Roman forces ever arrived, and, after a large number of the garrison of the castle died suddenly (presumably of some sort of epidemic from the words of the *Epic Histories*), the queen finally surrendered after a courageous and resourceful defense of 14 months. It took nine days, we are told, for the Persians to empty the castle of all its treasure, after which Pharandzem and the other captives were led away together with the booty, presumably to Ctesiphon, the Persian capital located near modern Baghdad. There, Pharandzem was thrown to the Persian troops, who were allowed to rape her to death. This event, taking place some 14 months after the peace of 363, would have occurred sometime in late 364, thus closing the 34-year war that had begun with the death of King Tiridates around 330.

We have, however, a considerably different version of these same events from the late 8th–early 9th-century Armenian historian Moses of Khoren. Relying as he does on written records rather than the oral and epic traditions utilized by the author of the *Epic Histories,* Moses merits a hearing as an independent witness. Both the *Epic Histories* and Moses agree that Arsaces II married Pharandzem after the murder of her husband Gnel but disagree on the circumstances of the murder and as to whether or not she was the king's first wife, as stated by the former, or his second, as asserted by the latter. According to Moses, not only Tirit but Vardan had plotted to do away with Gnel by poisoning the king's mind against his nephew, and here no reason is given for the calumny. The king then sent word to Gnel that he would hunt in the latter's lands at the foot of Mt. Tsalik (where Shahapivan was located, although Moses makes no reference to the town in connection with the murder). There, he ordered Vardan to slay Gnel with an arrow, as if he had been killed by accident. Arsaces, we are told, had Gnel buried some distance away in the royal city of Zarishat; no mention is made of a racetrack. Moses agrees that Arsaces made a pretense of mourning for Gnel and that Chief Bishop Nerses, divining the truth, cursed him for his wicked deed, but adds that King Arsaces rifled his nephew's inheritance and other properties before marrying his widow. It is here that Moses not only tells us that Pharandzem bribed a priest to murder Queen Olympias, whom he describes as Arsaces' first wife, in order to acquire her rank as queen, but also accuses her of ordering the king to kill her uncle Vaghinak so that her father Antiochus might become prince of Siunik. During the time of the great Persian invasion after the death of Julian, we are told that Pharandzem indeed shut herself in the great castle of Artagerk [sic] but that the garrison, unwilling to wait for the arrival of Pap, surrendered on its own accord. The garrison, we are then told, was taken to Persia along with the queen and that all of them were executed by being impaled upon wagon poles.

While we have the word of the author of the *Epic Histories* against that of Moses of Khoren, the matter is less equivocal than it at first appears. The author of the *Epic Histories* is given to embellishments common to the epic tradition in general and to the Iranian epic tradition in particular. Moses, on the other hand, while far from completely reliable, lived too late to understand the requirements of this tradition and, basing himself as he usually does upon written sources, may very well have preserved a more accurate account of events than did the earlier epic source. With this as a guide and an increased understanding of the situation in Armenia in the 4th century provided by the monumental work of **Nina G. Garsoian**, we may venture the following reconciliation of the two narratives that have come down to us.

The story that Pharandzem was the daughter of a younger brother of the prince of Siunik seems probable, for there is no need for the *Epic Histories* to lower her status in the family. It seems likely, too, that early on she had been married to Prince Gnel. The elaborate and vivid story of how Gnel was murdered upon his arrival at the king's encampment at Shahapivan makes a good story but for this very reason may be dismissed as unrealistic. The less spectacular version given by Moses, though not without its fictional elements (the locus of the prince's death being "suitably" placed at a royal hunt), is probably nearer to the truth.

> The figure of Pharandzem remains enigmatic in Armenian literature.
>
> —Nina G. Garsoian

Since Garsoian has shown that the murder of Gnel took place most likely in the summer of 359 (specifically on August 29), it would seem impossible for Olympias to have been Arsaces' second wife (as the *Epic Histories* tells us she was; yet, since Arsaces and Pharandzem had a son old enough to bear arms by the mid-360s, it seems equally impossible for Pharandzem to have been married to Arsaces after Olympias [as Moses asserts]). Garsoian suggests that Armenia, having just emerged from paganism and having been under the heaviest Iranian influence for eight centuries, probably still accepted certain norms of Iranian matrimonial law. Thus, given these laws, it would have been possible for King Arsaces to have been married to Pharandzem and to have had a son with her, and then to have set her aside, giving her to Gnel as his wife in order to marry Olympias, while yet retaining the right to take her back from Gnel at any time he so chose. Thus, Pharandzem must have been married to the king while yet a young woman, to have given birth to his son Pap and then to have been handed to Gnel to make way for Olympias, a gift from the emperor that Arsaces felt unable to refuse. This would account for Pharandzem's hostility to the new queen, whose appearance in Armenia might very well jeopardize her own son's right to the throne. It may have been the Roman awareness of this situation in Armenia, moreover, that led them to demand that young Pap be sent to them as a hostage—in this case, possibly for his mother's good behavior or for that of her prominent family. In speaking of Pap, it is worth noting that a late Armenian source, *The Life of St. Nerses* (9th century), attributes two sons to the marriage of Arsaces and Pharandzem, the other being named Tiridates, who, if he indeed existed, was obviously named after his grandfather, according to the Armenian practice and so must have been the first-born son and who must have died young.

As far as the curious tale of Pap and his demons, and Pharandzem's strange response (she had supposedly dedicated him to the demons at birth and then, years later, was astounded to find him at their mercy), it may be explained by the way that the author of the *Epic Histories* chooses to respond to Pharandzem's paganism, or at least her lack of orthodoxy. As for the story of Moses that Pharandzem had her uncle killed so that her father might become head of the house of Siunik, this may simply be an attempt to reconcile two versions of the story that had come down to the author, the first stating that Pharandzem had been the daughter of a prince of Siunik and second that her father had been the prince of Siunik.

In regard to Pharandzem's role in the Persian invasion of 363, we may note that, not being a woman to shy away from murder, she may well have taken the lead in the defense of Armenia after the deportation of Arsaces to Persia. As for the surrender of Artagers to the Persians, there is probably some truth in both versions of the story that have come down to us: the siege of 14 months probably did generate an epidemic among the garrison, whereupon the commanders, unwilling to wait any longer for Pap's arrival with Roman troops, probably realized that any further defense was hopeless.

The ghastly circumstances surrounding Pharandzem's death make it unlikely that the story was invented, and we must see in this crime a manifestation of how seriously the Persians took the conversion of Armenia to the faith practiced by the emperors of Rome. The message sent abroad to all of the subject peoples of Persia was that the Great King would tolerate no such deviation from the norms of the greater Iranian world and that none nor his family, no matter what their race or rank or gender, would be spared the most extreme penalty. When Moses tells us that the queen was impaled, we may take this as a softening of the story out of deference to the readers' sensibilities, he being unable to accept that a queen of Armenia had died such an ignominious death as described in the *Epic Histories*. Here, however, we can only speculate, for Moses' version may perhaps be the true one and the *Epic Histories* may have invented her ignominious death to show how the wicked queen was punished for her sins.

King Arsaces died in Persian captivity, held until his death in the notorious "Castle of Oblivion," so-called because it was forbidden to mention the name of anyone who had been consigned there. As for Pap, his son and heir, he reigned as a sort of regent while his father lived in captivity (c. 364–c. 368), after his death becoming king in his own right (c. 368–c. 374). Running afoul of the Romans, he was executed for disloyalty to them. Here we have the bald Roman account of the event by Ammianus Marcellinus to compare to the once again more "suitable" account received or concocted by the author of the *Epic Histories*. Pap was succeeded by his cousin, Varazdat (c. 374–c. 378), a famed athlete at one of the last Olympic Games, but after his short reign, the throne passed to Pap's sons, so that the descendants of King Arsaces and Queen Pharandzem continued to reign over Armenia until the monarchy was terminated in 428.

SOURCES:

Ammian Marcellinus. *Res Gestae*. Loeb Classical Library edition.

The Epic Histories. Engl. trans. (with extensive commentary) by Nina G. Garsoian. Cambridge, MA: Harvard University, 1989.

Moses Khorenats'i. *History of the Armenians*. Engl. trans. by R.W. Thomson. Cambridge, MA: Harvard University, 1978.

SUGGESTED READING:

Baynes, N.H. "Rome and Armenia in the Fourth Century," in *English Historical Review*. Vol. XXV. London, 1910.

Hewsen, R.H. "The Successors of Tiridates the Great," in *Revue des études arméniennes*. Vol. XIII. Paris, 1978–79.

Robert H. Hewsen,
Professor of History, Rowan University,
Glassboro, New Jersey

Phebe.

Variant of Phoebe.

Phelps, Almira Lincoln (1793–1884)

American educator and textbook writer. *Name variations: Alma Hart; Almira Hart Lincoln. Born Almira Hart on July 15, 1793, in Berlin, Connecticut; died on July 15, 1884, in Baltimore, Maryland; daughter of Samuel Hart and Lydia (Hinsdale) Hart; sister of Emma Hart Willard (1787–1870); educated at home, at Nancy Hinsdale's academy for girls, at an academy in Pittsfield, Massachusetts, and at the Berlin Academy; married Simeon Lincoln (a newspaper editor), on October 4, 1817 (died 1823); married John Phelps (an attorney), on August 17, 1831 (died 1849); children: (first marriage) James (died in infancy);* ***Emma Lincoln****; Jane Lincoln (d. 1856); (second marriage) Charles Phelps; Almira Phelps; and six stepchildren.*

Headed several boarding schools and seminaries for girls, most notably Patapsco Female Institute in Maryland (1841–56); wrote a number of science textbooks which became standard works in the schools of her day.

Selected writings: Familiar Lectures in Botany *(1829);* Dictionary of Chemistry *(1830);* Lectures to Young Ladies *(1833);* Caroline Westerley *(1833);* Botany for Beginners *(1833);* Chemistry for Beginners *(1834);* Geology for Beginners *(1834);* Natural Philosophy for Beginners *(1835);* Lectures on Chemistry *(1837);* Hours with My Pupils *(1859).*

Almira Lincoln Phelps was born in 1793, the daughter of Samuel and **Lydia Hinsdale Hart**. Growing up in a large, politically liberal family on a farm in Connecticut, Phelps was exposed from an early age to the important issues of her day. She absorbed much from family discussions and informal family education, and was also educated in private academies. Phelps taught for a year at the Berlin Academy, and was directing her own academy in Sandy Hill at the time of her marriage in 1817 to Simeon Lincoln, the editor of the *Connecticut Mirror* in Hartford.

Phelps' sister ***Emma Hart Willard** was renowned as an educator who advocated higher education for women. In an era when women's education was generally confined to domestic arts and artistic accomplishments, Willard's Troy Female Seminary was one of the first institutions for women to emphasize academic subjects. After the death of Simeon Lincoln in 1823, which left Phelps with two small children to raise, she joined the staff of her sister's school, serving for a time as principal in her sister's absence, and became interested in natural sciences. With the encouragement of Rensselaer Polytechnic Institute professor Amos Eaton, she published her first science textbook aimed at women, *Familiar Lectures on Botany*, in 1829. The most successful of a series of textbooks she would write, it had sold 275,000 copies in 9 editions by 1872.

In *Familiar Lectures*, Phelps attempted to place the subject of botany within the context of contemporary society, using examples from history and from poetry, as well as folklore and moral observations, alongside scientific study. She tried, for example, to show that botany had Biblical roots and was related to women's roles by discussing how both Adam and ***Eve** had a role in the newly created world. In this Phelps was following the tenets of Johann Heinrich Pestalozzi, who had advocated an alternative to the dry, technical approach taken by most authors of science textbooks of the time. Pestalozzi believed in beginning with a concrete object, like a flower, and observing how that object's parts determined its inclusion in a classification system. By adopting this method, Phelps was defying common beliefs that women were incapable of comprehending such things as scientific methods, ancient languages, and higher mathematics. According to **Vera Norwood**, women educated by such leaders as Phelps and her sister Emma Willard "spread out across the country, carrying with them the seeds of a new way for the educated woman to spend her time—in pursuit of a better knowledge of her natural environment."

Almira married again in 1831, to John Phelps, a widowed attorney with six children, two of whom were still living at home. She had two more children with her husband, bringing the number of children in the household to six, and during the 1830s remained busy caring for her family at their home in Guilford, Vermont. She continued to write, however, producing a novel, *Caroline Westerley* (1833), in addition to her academic works, which included *Botany for Beginners* (1833), *Geology for Beginners* (1834), *Chemistry for Beginners* (1834), and *Natural Philosophy for Beginners* (1836). She also briefly became principal of a seminary for girls in West Chester, Pennsylvania, and of another seminary in Rahway, New Jersey. In 1841, she became principal of Patapsco Female Institute at Ellicott's Mills, Maryland, and her husband became the school's business manager. Phelps worked to improve the curriculum, especially in the sciences, increased the school's academic standards, and advanced its reputation as a teacher training institution.

Despite her belief in women's intellectual abilities, Phelps was actually quite conservative in her social views. She opposed suffrage for women and was active in the Woman's Anti-Suffrage Association, believing (as did many prominent women of the time) that politics was an unsuitable venue for women. Following the tenets of her day, Phelps felt that higher education for women should train them primarily for their expected roles as wives and mothers; yet she emphasized that her brand of education was designed to take "away from females their helplessness." She claimed that the study of botany "seems peculiarly adapted to females; the objects of its investigation are beautiful and delicate"; yet she also encouraged women to improve their physical health through fresh air and exercise.

Phelps' husband died in 1849, and her daughter Jane was killed in a train accident in 1856. After her daughter's death, she retired from Patapsco Female Institute and settled in Baltimore, where she continued to write books and publish articles in periodicals. She encouraged other women to do the same, once writing in *American Ladies Magazine* that "[we] can render mutual benefits by the suggestions of individual experiences, and as it is often that the most humble and unpretending are the most exemplary, such should be encouraged to write for the ladies' periodicals; because everything dictated by nature and good sense is valuable and interesting." Phelps was honored in 1859 by being only the second woman (following astronomer *Maria Mitchell) elected to the American Association for the Advancement of Science. She died in 1884, on her 91st birthday.

SOURCES:

Edgerly, Lois Stiles, ed. *Give Her This Day: A Daybook of Women's Words*. Gardiner, ME: Tilbury House, 1990.

James, Edward T., ed. *Notable American Women, 1607–1950*. Cambridge, MA: The Belknap Press of Harvard University Press, 1971.

McHenry, Robert, ed. *Famous American Women*. NY: Dover, 1980.

Norwood, Vera. *Made from This Earth: American Women and Nature*. Chapel Hill, NC: University of North Carolina Press, 1993.

Ogilvie, Marilyn Bailey. *Women in Science: Antiquity Through the Nineteenth Century*. Cambridge, MA: MIT Press, 1986.

Sally A. Myers, Ph.D.,
freelance writer and editor

Phelps, Caroline (1854–1909).

See joint entry under Stokes, Olivia Phelps and Caroline Phelps Stokes.

Phelps, Elizabeth Stuart (1844–1911).

See Ward, Elizabeth Stuart Phelps.

Phelps, Olivia Egleston (1847–1927).

See joint entry under Stokes, Olivia Phelps and Caroline Phelps Stokes.

Pheretima (fl. 6th c. BCE)

Queen of Cyrene. *Flourished in the 6th century BCE in Cyrene or Cyrenaica (present-day northern Libya); married Battus III the Lame; children: Arcesilaus III.*

Known from the fourth book of Herodotus' *Histories*, Pheretima was a member of the Battid dynasty which ruled over Cyrene, that part of north Africa where Libya thrusts northward towards Greece. About 625 BCE, the Greek island/polis of Thera, under Battus I, colonized Cyrene but failed to secure the region against indigenous enemies until subsequently reinforced by additional colonists from several Hellenic cities. These were attracted to Cyrene because of the land's rich potential. The precarious situation of this Greek colony, under attack as it was by several local enemies, allowed kingship to flourish in Cyrene long after monarchy had disappeared in the relatively more peaceful Greek homeland. In the fourth generation of the Battid dynasty's rule in Cyrene, the insecurity of the colony was compounded by intra-dynastic dissension, which incited the Libyan natives of the region to try to reclaim the land from which they had been expelled by the Greek invaders. This attempt failed, and peace among the Greeks was restored by the accession of Battus III the Lame to whom Pheretima was married.

Notwithstanding Battus III's accession and a temporary calm, the citizens of Cyrene decided to send a delegation to the oracle of Apollo at Delphi in order to inquire what form of government would best promote their prosperity. They were advised to consult a political arbitrator from the Arcadian city of Mantinea. Upon inquiry there, a man named Demonax was produced who came to Cyrene with the intention of reforming the political organization of the Cyrenian state. Among the political reforms proposed, Demonax suggested that Battus III be deprived of those powers of his office which were not religious in nature, and his former political and military duties be distributed among the people. This was done and Battus III was reduced to but a figurehead. However, when Pheretima's and Battus' son, Arcesilaus III, succeeded to his father's station, he attempted to recover all of the authority which had been stripped from Battus the Lame. Initially, Arcesilaus' coup failed, and he was forced to take refuge on the Greek island of Samos, while Pheretima fled to the city of Salamis on the island of Cyrene. There she took refuge with one Evelthon, from whom she requested an army so that she might recapture what she thought was rightfully her son's. Evelthon honored Pheretima with gifts, but would not give her an army, arguing that such a command was inappropriate for a woman.

At the same time, Arcesilaus raised an army from Samos. With it, and armed with an oracle from Delphi promising success if he would only be gentle in his rule once it had been regained, Arcesilaus attacked Cyrene so as to reclaim his heritage. Initially successful, Arcesilaus nevertheless neglected to temper his rule in accordance with the oracle's command and thus brought on another exile, this time to Barca, a city in north Africa not far from Cyrene (and the hometown of his wife). There, partisans sympathizing with Arcesilaus' enemies in Cyrene assassinated him. Meanwhile, Pheretima, having returned with her son to north Africa, remained in Cyrene to manage its government in lieu of a universally accepted alternative.

When she learned of Arcesilaus' murder in Barca, Pheretima fled Cyrene for Egypt, then under the rule of one Aryandes, who governed that ancient kingdom on behalf of the Persian king Cambyses (r. 530–522 BCE), who had only recently conquered it. Pheretima sought help from this source because Arcesilaus had recently agreed to rule Cyrene as an appendage of Persian rule in Egypt. Aryandes acceded to Pheretima's request, and she returned to her native land at the head of a powerful force. With that army, the Persians laid siege to Barca (for nine months) after the Barcans made it clear that they would not surrender the assassins of Arcesilaus. The Barcans defended themselves stoutly, but eventually in vain. The victorious Persians made a gift of the survivors of this siege to Pheretima, who had those guilty of her son's assassination crucified. To make clear her anger at the loss of her son, she then had the breasts of the wives of her son's assassins cut off and nailed about the city's walls. Thereafter, with the exception of only a few lucky Barcans thought innocent of any animosity toward either her or her dead son, Pheretima returned the majority of the survivors to the Persians as slaves.

The city of Cyrene itself escaped attack at this time, since the primary reason for the Persian expedition was to avenge the death of Arcesilaus upon the Barcans. Before it was decided that Cyrene should also be assaulted in the interests of both Pheretima and the Persians, orders were received from Aryandes (who had remained in Egypt) to the effect that the Persians should return as soon as possible. Having made many enemies in and around Cyrene because of the severity of her punishments at Barca, Pheretima left her native land for the last time in the Persian train. As a postscript to these grisly events, Pheretima herself ended badly. Herodotus reports that during the return to Egypt, she contracted a disease which saw her body horribly waste away, consumed by worms before her very eyes.

William S. Greenwalt,
Associate Professor of Classical History,
Santa Clara University, Santa Clara, California

Phila I.

See Stratonice (c. 319–254 BCE) for sidebar.

Phila II (c. 300 BCE–?).

See Stratonice (c. 319–254 BCE) for sidebar.

Philiberta of Savoy (c. 1498–1524)

Duchess of Nemours. *Name variations: Philiberta de Medici; Philiberte of Savoy. Born around 1498; died in 1524; aunt of Francis I, king of France (r. 1515–1547); married Giuliano de Medici (1479–1516), duke of Nemours, in 1515; no children. Giuliano de Medici's son, the cardinal Ippolito (1511–1535), was illegitimate.*

In early 1515, Giuliano de Medici visited the court of France and left with the charming 17-year-old Philiberta of Savoy, aunt of the French king Francis I, as his bride. Francis also conferred the title duke of Nemours on the well-liked Giuliano. But one year later, on March 17, Giuliano died, age 37, sincerely mourned by Philiberta and the Florentines. Philiberta also died young, at age 26, in 1524.

Philinna (c. 380–after c. 356 BCE)

Thessalian noblewoman. *Born around 380 BCE in Larissa in Thessaly; died after 356 BCE; one of seven wives of Philip II, king of Macedon; children: (with an unnamed man) Amphimachus; (with Philip) Arrhidaeus. Philip's six other wives were* ***Audata****, Olympias,* ***Meda****, ****Nicesipolis****, Roxane and* ***Cleopatra of Macedon****.*

Philinna, from Larissa in Thessaly, was one of the seven wives of Philip II, king of Macedon, and the mother of Arrhidaeus and Amphimachus. Several ancient sources refer to her in derogatory terms ("common," "dancing girl," "whore"), but it is more likely that she was a legitimate wife of Philip rather than a brief acquaintance or a concubine. Philip probably married Philinna in order to secure an alliance with the Aleuadae, the family which dominated Larissan politics. (Larissa was strategically located in northern Thessaly, just to the south of Philip's realm). Philinna's reputation probably came to suffer only after the death of Philip (336 BCE) as a result of slander propagated by the enemies of her son, Arrhidaeus, when he was being put forward as the king of Macedon over the son of Alexander III the Great (317 BCE), who was Philip's son with ***Olympias**.

When she married Philip, Philinna was probably a widow, for Arrian (our best source for the life and times of Alexander the Great) reports that Arrhidaeus had the forenamed brother Amphimachus who was manifestly not Philip's son. In 321 BCE, this Amphimachus was given a satrapy (province) by the successors of Alexander the Great, a fact which suggests: 1) that he was old enough and respected enough in 321 to be given an important command, and thus, that Philinna could not have remarried after Philip's death and then given birth to Amphimachus; and 2) that Amphimachus was high enough born to warrant such a command, which he would not have been if Philinna was of low birth or a professional woman (concubine).

Exactly when Philinna and Philip married is unknown, but since Arrhidaeus was old enough for Philip to broker his marriage to the daughter of the Carian satrap (governor) Pixodarus in early 336 BCE, when Philip was seeking a political toehold in Asia Minor as a prelude to his planned invasion of the Persian Empire, Arrhidaeus was probably at least 20 at the time. (Arrhidaeus never married Pixodarus' daughter because his paranoid half-brother, Alexander the Great, diplomatically intervened, much to Philip's anger.) Thus, Philip's marriage to Philinna probably took place no later than 357, or early in his reign.

Although Arrhidaeus was mentally incompetent (a trait not shared by Amphimachus), after Alexander the Great died (323) Arrhidaeus was hailed as Macedon's king, a position he shared for a time with Alexander IV, the posthumously born son of Alexander the Great and ****Roxane**. One tradition has it that Alexander the Great's mother Olympias (c. 371–316 BCE) was somehow to blame for Arrhidaeus' condition. This is doubtful, but Olympias was responsible for his death in 317 BCE after open civil war pitted the faction supporting Arrhidaeus (led by his then wife ****Eurydice** [c. 337–317 BCE]) against that which championed Alexander IV.

What happened to Philinna after the birth of Arrhidaeus is unknown. It is also not known for sure whether Arrhidaeus or Alexander (born in 356 BCE) was Philip's first-born son; the evidence, however, leans in favor of Alexander having been the older.

William S. Greenwalt,
Associate Professor of Classical History,
Santa Clara University, Santa Clara, California

Philippa.

Variant of Philippine.

Philippa (1394–1430)

Queen of Denmark, Norway, and Sweden. *Name variations: Philippa Plantagenet. Born on July 4, 1394, in Peterborough Castle, Cambridgeshire, England; died on January 5, 1430, at the convent of Valdstena also known as Wadstena, Linkoping, Sweden; interred at the convent of Wadstena; daughter of Mary de Bohun (1369–1394) and Henry IV (1366–1413), king of England (r. 1399–1413); married Erik or Eric VII (or XIII) of Pomerania (1382–1459), king of Denmark (r. 1396–1439), Norway (r. 1389–1442), and Sweden, on October 26, 1406.*

***Margaret I of Denmark** arranged the marriage of Philippa, the daughter of ***Mary de Bohun** and Henry IV, king of England, to her adopted son Eric of Pomerania (Eric VII of Denmark), who was crowned king of each of the Scandinavian kingdoms in 1396. Philippa proved a "good and faithful queen," writes Palle Lauring in *The History of the Kingdom of Denmark*. When Eric was away at war and Copenhagen was besieged, Philippa, as the highest authority, saved the city.

Philippa de Coucy (fl. 1300s)

Countess of Oxford. *Name variations: Philippa di Couci; Philippa de Vere. Born Philippa de Coucy in the mid-1300s; daughter of Enguerrand VII, lord of Coucy and earl of Bedford, and ****Isabella*** *(1332–1382, daughter of ****Philippa of Hainault*** *and King Edward III); married Robert de Vere, 9th earl of Oxford, in 1378 (divorced 1387).*

Philippa de Dreux (d. 1240)

Countess of Bar. *Died on March 17, 1240; daughter of Robert II, count of Dreux, and ****Yolande de Coucy*** *(d. 1222); sister of ****Yolande de Dreux*** *(d. 1238); married Henry II, count of Bar, in 1219; children: ****Margaret*** *(d. 1275), countess of Bar.*

Philippa de Rouergue (c. 1074–1118)

Queen of Aragon and duchess of Aquitaine. *Name variations: Philippa of Toulouse. Born around 1074; died on November 28, 1118, in Fontevraud, Anjou, France; daughter of William IV, count of Toulouse; became second wife of Sancho Ramirez, king of Aragon (r. 1063–1094) and Navarre (r. 1076–1094), in 1086; married William IX, duke of Aquitaine, around 1094 following the death of her first husband; children: (second marriage) William X, duke of Aquitaine (1099–1137); ****Agnes de Poitiers*** *(who married Ramiro II); Raymond I of Poitiers (1115–1149), prince of Antioch. Sancho Ramirez was first married to ****Isabel of Urgel.***

Philippa-Elizabeth (1714–1734)

Princess of Orléans. *Name variations: Philippine-Elizabeth d'Orleans. Born on November 18, 1714; died on May 21, 1734; daughter of Philip Bourbon-Orléans (1674–1723), 2nd duke of Orléans (r.*

*1701–1723) and **Françoise-Marie de Bourbon** (1677–1749).*

Philippa Mareria (c. 1190–1236).

See Mareri, Filippa.

Philippa of Antioch (fl. 1100s)

***Princess of Antioch.** Flourished in the 1100s; daughter of **Constance of Antioch** (1128–1164) and Raymond I of Poitiers, prince of Antioch (d. 1149, son of William IX of Aquitaine); sister of Bohemund III and **Marie of Antioch** (d. 1183); half-sister of **Anne of Chatillon-Antioche** (c. 1155–c. 1185, who married Bela III, king of Hungary); married Andronicus I Comnenus, Byzantine emperor (r. 1183–1185); children: one son. Andronicus married his second wife, **Agnes-Anne of France**, in 1183.*

Philippa of Clarence (1355–1382).

See Mortimer, Philippa.

Philippa of Foix (fl. 13th c.)

***Supporter of the heretical Cathar movement of southern France.** Flourished in the 13th century in Foix.*

Philippa of Foix, born into the lower nobility of France, was an active participant in the new religious sect called Catharism which swept southern France in the early 13th century. Also known as Albigensianism, its followers preached rejection of materialism and of the rituals of the Catholic Church. They also believed that women, through study, could become men's equals and could then preach themselves. Understandably, this sect attracted many French noblewomen, including Philippa of Foix. Philippa made her castle a refuge for the *perfecta*, or "perfect ones," who were the priests of Catharism. After some time, Philippa's devotion to the sect led her to become one of the *perfecta* herself. Her fate after the Cathars were condemned as heretics by the pope is unclear, but it is known that many Cathars were burned at the stake for their heretical views.

Laura York,
Riverside, California

Philippa of Guelders (d. 1547)

***Duchess of Lorraine.** Name variations: Philippa of Gelderland; Philippine von Geldern. Died on February 25, 1547; daughter of Adolf (b. 1438), duke of Guelders, and **Catherine of Bourbon** (d. 1469); became second wife of Rene II (1451–1508), duke of Lorraine (r. 1480–1508), on September 1, 1485; children: Anthony or Antoine (1489–1544), duke of Lorraine (r. 1508–1544); Claude (d. 1550), 1st duke of Guise (r. 1527–1550, who married **Antoinette of Bourbon**); John, 1st cardinal of Lorraine; Ferri (killed at Marignano); Louis (killed at Naples); Francis (killed at Pavia); four daughters who never married (names unknown); and two sons who died in infancy; grandmother of **Mary of Guise** (1515–1560). Rene II's first wife was **Johanna Harcourt** (d. 1488).*

Philippa of Hainault (1314–1369)

***Queen of England and founder of the English textile and coal industries.** Name variations: Phillipa. Pronunciation: HAN-olt. Born in 1314 in Valenciennes, Hainault; died of dropsy on August 14, 1369, at Windsor, England; daughter of William III the Good, count of Hainault and Holland, and Countess Jeanne of Valois (c. 1294–1342); married Edward III (1312–1377), king of England (r. 1327–1377), on January 28, 1328; children: Edward "the Black Prince" (1330–1376), prince of Wales; Isabella (1332–1382); Joanna (1333–1348); William (b. 1336 and died in infancy); Lionel of Antwerp (1338–1368), duke of Clarence; John of Gaunt (1340–1399), duke of Lancaster; Edmund of Langley (1341–1402), duke of York; Blanche (b. 1343 and died in infancy); Mary (1344–1362); William (b. 1345); Margaret (1346–1361); Thomas of Woodstock (1355–1397), duke of Gloucester.*

Married King Edward III (1328); crowned queen (1330); gave birth to Edward the Black Prince (1330); on military campaigns with Edward (1333–45); established textile industry at Norwich (1335); appointed regent (1346); repelled invasion of Scottish army and captured King David of Scotland (1346); established coal industry at Tynedale (1348); became ill with dropsy (1367).

Born into the ruling family of Hainault, Philippa of Hainault became one of England's most popular queens. She was in many ways responsible for the establishment of both the coal industry and the textile industry of England, the two primary sources of England's national wealth for many centuries. She also raised twelve children, including five sons who were renowned warriors and three who were also intellectuals, and daughters who were reputedly well educated and beautiful. Philippa provided a necessary contrast to her husband, Edward III, a great king but one whose impulsiveness and tendency toward violence and vengefulness needed her calm, rational influence.

She was the daughter of *Jeanne of Valois and Count William III the Good of Hainault and Holland. A small but highly prosperous county located in what is now the upper north of France, Hainault derived its wealth from its flourishing textile industry, which obtained much of its raw wool from England. This important economic tie between England and Hainault was the primary motivation for the betrothal of England's heir, Prince Edward, and the count's daughter Philippa.

The most courteous, liberal, and noble lady that ever reigned in her time.

—Jean Froissart

In 1326, young Prince Edward and his mother, Queen *Isabella of France (1296–1358), took refuge at the court of Philippa's father. Called the "she-wolf of France" by her numerous detractors, Isabella was the estranged wife and unpopular queen of Edward II. She had left England with her son in an effort to rally support for her planned revolt against her husband. There was considerable backing from the English nobility for Edward II's deposition, for he was widely perceived as an incompetent, weak ruler. Isabella wanted to depose her husband and place her young son on the throne, with herself and her lover Roger Mortimer as his regents. The count of Hainault supported Isabella's plans, probably because he recognized Edward II's vulnerable position and wished to aid his own county's economic situation by keeping ties with the ruling power of England strong. To this end, he promised his own aid, and helped her gain support from other barons. To show her gratitude and seal their alliance, Isabella apparently promised to marry her son to one of the count's four daughters if she were successful.

Isabella's invasion of England was indeed successful; her husband was captured and imprisoned in November 1326. The next January, he was forced to agree to his dethronement, and Prince Edward, about 16 years old, was crowned as Edward III (Edward II was murdered a few months later on Isabella's orders). Unfortunately for Isabella, Parliament, though grateful for her successful removal of the king, did not appoint her regent of England. However, she exerted considerable power over her son, if only in an unofficial capacity. Isabella and her lover did not forget the help Count William had given them, and late in 1327 an agreement, approved by Parliament, was contracted between the two houses for the marriage of the king and the count's second daughter, Philippa. It was unusual for a younger daughter to be married before her older sister (*Joan of Hainault), but it seems Edward had, during his stay at the Hainault court, favored Philippa over her sisters (Joan and *Margaret of Holland) and had insisted that she become his queen. The couple were married by proxy in October 1327. Philippa, about 13 years old, was reported to be slightly plump but quite beautiful; on her arrival in England in December, she was hailed by the Londoners who seem to have immediately conceived a love for the young queen they came to call Good Queen Philippa. Philippa and Edward, whom all chroniclers describe as very tall, strong, with the blue eyes and blond hair which ran in his family, were married again in a ceremony held at York Minster on January 24, 1328.

Philippa spent the first few years of her queenship under the thumb of her mother-in-law. Isabella and Roger Mortimer were constantly struggling for power against the council of regents appointed by Parliament; one of Isabella's strategies was to keep a tight rein on the activities and expenditures of her son and his wife. Isabella apparently spent Philippa's rich dowry very quickly and kept the total amount of the dowry a secret. She also was the force behind the delay of Philippa's coronation; although Edward was already king when he married, Philippa was not crowned queen until two years later, in March 1330. Probably Isabella's reluctance to allow the ceremony stemmed both from her unwillingness to expend the funds necessary for such an important event, and from her unwillingness to put another woman in what had been her place.

The June following the coronation, Philippa gave birth to her first child, a son named Edward after his father. The birth of this heir, a strong, healthy infant who would later be a military hero called the Black Prince, was greeted with grand tournaments and other festivities in London and throughout the realm. This event was a catalyst to the king's virtual coup d'etat against his mother and Mortimer. Edward was now about 18 years old, eager to take over the reins of government for himself. In a sudden move at the end of 1330, he had Mortimer killed and his grieving mother banished from court. He became at once an active, energetic, reform-minded ruler, clearly one of England's greatest monarchs. Queen Philippa was not made a co-ruler with her husband, but she was given responsibilities other than those usual for a queen-consort. In 1332, she gave birth to a daughter, ➧ **Isabella**, who would always remain her father's favorite child.

One of Philippa's most lasting contributions to England was the founding of the textile industry. As one chronicler wrote after her death, "Blessed be the memory of . . . Philippa of Hainault, who first invented English clothes." Until her reign, the English made very little cloth, generally only by families for their own use. Philippa, recognizing that cloth production had created wealth for her homeland, wanted to bring the industry to England as well. In 1331, on Philippa's urging, Edward wrote to a Flemish weaver asking him to come to England with his apprentices to "exercise their mysteries." In 1335, Philippa established a full-blown manufacturing colony at Norwich, to which the Flemish weaver had relocated. She visited the fledgling colony frequently, and took personal responsibility for the welfare of her workers, English and Flemish. Under her guidance, Norwich grew into an important manufacturing center, from which the technology of cloth production spread to other English cities. Textile production would soon become one of England's most important sources of revenue, and lead them early into the proto-industrial age.

Between 1333 and 1345, Philippa spent much of her time following the English army on Edward's military campaigns, first against Scotland and then France. During these years, and often while on campaign, she also gave birth to eight more children, five sons and three daughters. Philippa set up another court at Ghent after Edward turned his attention away from the Scots to the French, with whom the English had long-standing territorial conflicts, and resided at Ghent off and on for several years. Edward's wars cost England enormous sums of money, but he did not spare his own household in raising the necessary funds. Thus it happened that Edward and Philippa were reduced to near poverty, and the crown jewels were pawned for cash on numerous occasions.

After so many years of near-constant travel, it is not surprising that in 1346, when Edward planned a major invasion of France, Philippa did not protest when Edward appointed her regent in his absence. It was unusual for a queen-consort to be given this much authority in England; Edward's decision reveals the faith and trust he placed in Philippa's judgment. With Edward away on campaign, his old enemy King David II of Scotland (now in league with France) invaded England. He apparently assumed that without its warrior king, his success was assured; however, Philippa rose to the occasion and quickly assembled an army which rode north to repel the Scots. The queen did not participate in the battle, but lent her support and encouragement to the fighting men. The defense was successful, and the king of Scotland was taken prisoner.

Isabella (1332–1382)

English princess and countess of Bedford. *Name variations: Isabel Plantagenet; Isabella de Coucy. Born in Woodstock, Oxfordshire, England, on June 16, 1332; died before October 7, 1382; daughter of* ****Philippa of Hainault*** *(1314–1369) and Edward III (1312–1377), king of England (r. 1327–1377); married Enguerrand VII (1340–1397), lord of Coucy and earl of Bedford, on July 27, 1365; children:* ****Mary de Coucy; *Philippa de Coucy.***

Despite Philippa's experience with military matters, she was celebrated by chroniclers for her generosity of spirit and her calm, thoughtful character. On more than one occasion, she intervened on behalf of Edward's victims, guilty or not, pleading forgiveness to her aggressive warrior husband, who usually acted impulsively when his enemies fell into his hands. One such occasion, told by Philippa's secretary Jean Froissart, followed the victory of Calais in 1346, in which the English army captured Calais after a long siege. Edward ordered the six leading men of the town to give themselves up to him, or he would have all Calais' residents killed. When the six burghers surrendered themselves, Edward ordered them to be beheaded. At this point Philippa, witness to the scene, fell on her knees before Edward and begged him to spare the lives of these men, if not for their sakes then out of love for her. Edward reluctantly relented, and gave the prisoners over to Philippa for her to treat as she wished. Although Philippa did free them, she retained custody of their Calais properties for herself.

After the capture of Calais, Philippa and Edward returned to England in 1347 with their fortunes at a peak and a new daughter; Princess ***Margaret** had been born soon after the victory. The king and queen had in their possession both the king of Scotland, from Philippa's battle against the Scots, and the king of France, from Edward's invasion. Settling down to domestic affairs, Philippa turned her attention to expanding the English economy. Toward this end, she founded a new industry, coal mining, at her estates in Tynedale. The coal trade expanded greatly under her care, and enriched the country as a whole, especially London. But the economy was soon shaken by the appearance of the bubonic plague, which first reached England in 1348. Philippa's second daughter, **Joanna**, was among the first victims. Within a year, as much as a third or more of the English population had

See sidebar on the following page

Joanna (1333–1348)
English princess. *Name variations: Joan Plantagenet. Born in 1333 in Woodstock, Oxfordshire, England; died of the plague on her journey to wed Alphonso XI (1311–1350), king of Castile (r. 1312–1350), on September 2, 1348, in Bordeaux, Aquitaine, France; buried in Bayonne Cathedral, Gascony, France; daughter of* ****Philippa of Hainault*** *(1314–1369) and Edward III (1312–1377), king of England (r. 1327–1377).*

Mary (1344–1362)
English princess. *Name variations: Mary Plantagenet. Born on October 10, 1344, in Waltham, Hampshire, England; died of a form of sleeping sickness at age 17 in 1362; buried at Abingdon Abbey, Oxfordshire, England; daughter of* ****Philippa of Hainault*** *(1314–1369) and Edward III (1312–1377), king of England (r. 1327–1377); married John IV, duke of Brittany (r. 1364–1399), in summer 1361, in Woodstock, Oxfordshire, England.*

succumbed to the disease; many of the dead were city dwellers. Although wages rose drastically at first, due to the sudden decline in workers, soon the king issued a statute that laborers had to accept wages no higher than they had been in 1347; this impoverished thousands, since prices had risen dramatically since the Black Death struck, but their wages remained the same.

Despite the ravages of plague, the royal household was not seriously affected and continued about its usual business. During the late 1340s and into the 1350s, the queen became known as a beneficent patron of the arts. Among the beneficiaries was Geoffrey Chaucer, regarded as the "father of English verse"; Chaucer held a variety of minor posts in the royal administration, and his poetry found an eager and generous supporter in Philippa. Her secretary, Jean Froissart, is one of the most important historians of his time and is a major source of information on the life and times of Edward III and Queen Philippa. Besides these two men, Philippa also provided financial support to many other poets, writers, and artists.

She also could be generous to men whom she felt were truly chivalrous knights, who protected women and treated them well. One celebrated example of her charity involves the renowned French knight Bertrand du Guesclin. He had been captured by her son, Edward, the Black Prince, at the battle of Poitiers in 1357. While he and other prisoners were residing at Philippa's court, du Guesclin's ransom was set at 100,000 crowns, an enormous sum. Hearing of this, the queen told her son that she herself would contribute 50,000 crowns of her own money to the grateful knight's ransom; the chronicler records her as explaining that "though an enemy to my husband, a knight who is famed for the courteous protection he has afforded to my sex, deserves the assistance of every woman."

Philippa gave birth to Thomas of Woodstock, her last child, in 1355. In all, the queen had twelve children, five of whom outlived her. Two of her sons died in infancy, and one at age twelve. In 1361 and 1362, the king and queen lost two of their daughters, Margaret and **Mary**. Philippa's large brood may be held responsible for considerable warfare and chaos in later years; it was with Edward's and Philippa's five surviving sons that the Wars of the Roses had their roots. All her children were reputedly handsome, and all of her sons found fame on the battlefield, especially the eldest, Prince Edward. Although by accidents of fate her daughters did not make politically beneficial marriages, most ended up contented with their matches. The king and queen were known to be proud, doting parents, who spoiled all of their children and seemed unable to discipline them.

Around 1367, Queen Philippa began to suffer from dropsy, a fairly common ailment of her times. She became very weak, and her body was so swollen she could not stand up. She endured this condition for almost two years. In August 1369, she sent a message to her husband that she needed to see him, for she felt herself to be dying. Though Edward hurried to her at Windsor Castle, reaching her on August 14, she was saddened by the fact that only one of her many children, the youngest, Thomas, could be with her on her deathbed; her daughters had left England upon marriage and her four sons (Lionel had died in 1368) were all engaged in various military or political activities overseas. To Edward she made three requests: that he pay her legal debts, make sure the items in her will were carried out, and that he be buried beside her at Westminster. Edward promised all these things would be done, and within a few hours the queen died at age 55. In his history, Froissart wrote of her death and referred to her as "the most courteous, liberal, and noble lady that ever reigned in her time."

Edward mourned his wife greatly, as did the rest of England. She was buried with due ceremony at Westminster Cathedral. Philippa's death marked the beginning of a decline for England; Edward, having lost his rational, clement,

Philippa of Hainault begging Edward to spare the lives of Calais' burghers, 1347.

pious companion, seems to have undergone a significant change for the worse. Certainly there were no English military or political victories after her death. The king began to drink heavily, and took a mistress, ***Alice Perrers**, who was ambitious and greedy, and cared very little for the elderly king. Edward eventually became senile, and could not handle the responsibilities of government. As it was said at the time, he was a glorious king who had outlived his glory. England's state was further reduced on the death in 1376 of the Black Prince, the once-powerful warrior, after a long bout of cancer. Edward III died in neglect in 1377, his rings, so it was reported, stolen by his mistress before she abandoned him on his deathbed. He was 65 years old and had reigned for 50 of those years. The Black Prince's young son succeeded as Richard II to a bankrupt throne and a relationship with France worse than at any previous time.

SOURCES:

Costain, Thomas. *The Three Edwards.* NY: Popular Library, 1958.

Strickland, Agnes. *Lives of the Queens of England.* Vol. 11. Philadelphia, PA: Lea and Blanchard, 1850.

SUGGESTED READING:

Cambridge Medieval History. Vol. VII. Cambridge: Cambridge University Press, 1968.

Froissart, Jean. *Chronicles of England, France, Spain, and Adjoining Countries.* Vol I. Edited and translated by Thomas Johnes. NY: Collier, 1901.

***Tuchman, Barbara.** *A Distant Mirror: The Calamitous Fourteenth Century.* NY: Ballantine, 1978.

Laura York,
freelance writer in medieval history and women's history, Riverside, California

Philippa of Lancaster (c. 1359–1415)

Queen of Portugal. *Name variations: Filipa de Lencastre; Philippa Plantagenet. Born on March 31, 1359 or 1360, in Leicester, Leicestershire, England; died of the plague on July 19, 1415, in Odivelas, Lisbon, Portugal; interred in Batalla Abbey, Portugal; reigned from 1387 to 1415; first child of John of Gaunt (son of Edward III of England) and his first wife Blanche of Lancaster (1341–1369); sister of Henry Bolingbroke (1366–1413, later Henry IV, king of England, r. 1399–1413) and ****Elizabeth of Lancaster*** *(1364–1425, who married John Holland, duke of*

Exeter); married João I also known as John I (1385–1433), king of Portugal (r. 1385–1433), on February 2, 1387, at Oporto Cathedral, Portugal; children: Branca (1388–1388); Affonso (1390–1400); Duarte I (1391–1438), king of Portugal (r. 1433–1438); Pedro or Peter, regent of Portugal (b. 1392); Henry the Navigator (Henrique, the Navigator, 1394–1460); ***Isabella of Portugal*** *(1397–1471, who married Philip the Good of Burgundy); João or John (1400–1442), grand master of Santiago; Fernando or Ferdinand the Constant (1402–1443), grand master of Aviz. (John I also had two children with* ***Inez Perez.****)*

Birth of John I of Portugal (1352); death of Blanche of Lancaster (1369); death of Ferdinand I of Portugal; battle of Aljubarrota (1385); opening of Council of Constance (1414); Portuguese expedition against Ceuta (1415); death of John I (1433).

Philippa of Lancaster was born in 1359 or 1360, the first child of John of Gaunt, son of Edward III, king of England, and his first wife, ***Blanche of Lancaster**. Blanche died from the Black Death in 1369, while John of Gaunt was away in Spain, fighting against Henry II Trastamara of Castile and his French allies. Thereafter, Philippa was raised by ◂ **Catherine Swynford**, her father's mistress from 1371 even after he married ◂ **Constance of Castile** (1354–1394), heir of Peter the Cruel, king of Castile. For the time and her gender, Philippa received an exceptional education, with Geoffrey Chaucer among her tutors. Because of it, she valued *noblesse oblige*, courtly love, and Christian charity.

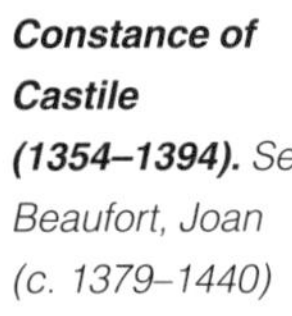

Swynford, Catherine. See Beaufort, Joan (c. 1379–1440) for sidebar.

Constance of Castile (1354–1394). See Beaufort, Joan (c. 1379–1440) for sidebar.

In 1383, events began to unfold in Portugal that determined the direction of Philippa's life. King Ferdinand I died, leaving only his unpopular queen ***Leonora Telles** to govern; their daughter ***Beatrice of Portugal** had married John I, king of Castile and Léon. Leonora Telles threw her support to John of Castile, while Ferdinand's illegitimate half-brother John (later John I, king of Portugal), grand master of Aviz, turned to the English for help. As the daughter of Peter the Cruel, Philippa's stepmother Constance of Castile claimed the Castilian crown because John of Castile's father, Henry II Trastamara, had murdered Peter in 1369 and seized the throne. The English offered help to John of Aviz, in part because the French were allies of the Castilians. To strengthen the alliance further, John of Gaunt offered one his daughters in marriage to a willing John of Aviz. Some anticipated that he would choose Constance, thereby sharing her claim to Castile. But John of Aviz wisely recognized that marriage to Constance would perpetually enmesh him in Castilian politics, whereas he was more concerned about protecting Portuguese independence. Thus, he selected Philippa.

They delayed their marriage until early 1387. As Grand Master of the Order of Aviz, a crusading order, John of Aviz had taken an oath of celibacy. He consequently sought papal permission to marry. Once it had been secured, he and Philippa wed in Oporto on February 2. Chronicler Fernão Lopes described the procession to the cathedral: "The King rode out of the palace, mounted on a white horse, royally dressed in gold cloth. The Queen rode on another, dressed in an equally royal fashion. They wore on their heads gold crowns richly studded with costly gems and mother-of-pearl. Neither of them took precedence but rather they rode in complete equality." Fifteen days of feasts and tournaments celebrated the wedding.

Philippa's predecessor Leonora Telles was lascivious and vengeful, better known for killing her enemies than for behaving with royal dignity. As queen, Philippa conducted herself with the utmost decorum throughout her marriage and helped restore respect for the monarchy. Portugal entered perhaps its most glorious age. The people admired her piety and charitable works. Under her direction the royal palace was remodeled and expanded. She took special care for the education of her children and raised the general cultural level of the Portuguese court. With stability restored to Portugal, she and John returned to visit England on two occasions, and she strengthened the long-lasting alliance between her native and adopted lands. Although publicly deferring to her husband, she wielded great influence through her piety, generosity, and refinement.

Philippa's eight children were an illustrious progeny, the most famous to subsequent generations being Henry the Navigator. Duarte I, who succeeded to the throne, described his mother's influence in his *Leal Conselheiro* (Loyal Counsellor). She encouraged her sons to be crusaders and supported John of Aviz's expedition to Ceuta on 1415. In fact, she ordered the manufacture of three swords, adorned with gold, gems and pearls, with which John was to knight his three eldest sons as they departed for North Africa. To their sorrow, however, Philippa fell ill with the plague just before the army sailed. Summoning the princes to her deathbed, she presented the swords to them. Death claimed her shortly afterward, on July 19, 1415, in Odivelas. Her body was eventually entombed in the great monastery of Batalha, built to commemorate John of Aviz's victory in 1385 over the Castilians and the securing of Portuguese independence.

SOURCES:

Eduarte, King of Portugal. *Leal Conselheiro.* Lisbon: Libraria Bertrand, 1942.

Livermore, H.V. *A New History of Portugal.* Cambridge: Cambridge University Press, 1969.

Lopes, Fernão. *The English in Portugal, 1367–1387.* Trans. by Derek W. Lomax and R.J. Oakley. Warminster: Aris & Phillips, 1988.

Roche, T.W.E. *Philippa: Dona Filipa of Portugal.* London: Phillimore, 1971.

Russell, P.E. *The English Intervention in Spain and Portugal during the Reigns of Edward III and Richard II.* Oxford: Clarendon Press, 1955.

Kendall W. Brown,
Professor of History, Brigham Young University,
Provo, Utah

Philippa of Lesser Armenia (fl. 1200s)

Nicaean empress. *Name variations: Philippa of Little Armenia. Flourished in the 1200s; second wife of Theodore I Lascaris, emperor of Nicaea (r. 1204–1222); briefly married; no children.*

Philippa of Toulouse (c. 1074–1118).

See Philippa de Rouergue.

Philippine.

Variant of Philippa.

Philippine Charlotte (1716–1801)

Duchess of Brunswick-Wolfenbuttel. *Born on March 13, 1716; died on February 17, 1801; daughter of* ****Sophia Dorothea of Brunswick-Lüneburg-Hanover*** *(1687–1757) and Frederick William I (1688–1740), king of Prussia (r. 1713–1740); married Charles, duke of Brunswick-Wolfenbuttel; children: Charles II (1716–1801), duke of Brunswick-Wolfenbuttel; George (b. 1736);* ****Sophie Caroline*** *(1737–1817); Christian Ludwig (b. 1738);* ****Anne Amelia of Saxe-Weimar*** *(1739–1807); Lt. General Frederick Augustus (b. 1740); Albert Henry (b. 1742); Louise (1743–1744);* ****Elizabeth of Brunswick*** *(1746–1840); Friederike (1748–1758);* ***Augusta Dorothea*** *(1749–1803), abbess of Gandersheim; Maximilian (b. 1752).*

Philippine of Luxemburg (d. 1311)

Countess of Hainault and Holland. *Name variations: Phillipine. Died on April 6, 1311; daughter of Henry V the Blond, count of Luxemburg, and* ****Margaret, countess of Bar*** *(d. 1275); married John II, count of Hainault and Holland; children: William II the Good, count of Hainault and Holland;* ****Margaret of Hainault*** *(d. 1342, who married Robert II, count of Artois).*

Philips, Katherine (1631–1664)

Early English poet. *Name variations: Catherine or Katharine; (pseudonym) Orinda. Born Katherine Fowler on January 1, 1631 (some sources cite 1632), in London; died of smallpox on June 22, 1664; daughter of John Fowler (a merchant) and Katherine Oxenbridge (whose father was a fellow of the Royal College of Physicians in London); married James Philips (a Welsh royalist), in 1647; children: a son who died in infancy; daughter Katherine (who married Lewis Wogan of Boulston, Pembrokeshire).*

Katherine Philips was born in London in 1631, the daughter of **Katherine Oxenbridge**, whose father was a fellow of the Royal College of Physicians in London, and John Fowler, a merchant in Bucklersbury, London, who was a devout Presbyterian. Philips is said to have read through the Bible before she was four years old. She would later break with Presbyterian traditions in both religion and politics and become a royalist, an avid supporter of King Charles II and his church policy. At age eight, Philips was sent to a boarding school in Hackney where she began to write verse; she also met **Mary Aubrey**, the first of her close women friends. Aubrey, who influenced Philips' writing, would be referred to as M.A. in several of her poems.

At age 16, Katherine married her stepbrother, 54-year-old James Philips. (Following the death of her husband, Katherine Oxenbridge had married Hector Philips, father of James by a previous marriage.) At her home at the Priory, Cardigan, Katherine Philips instituted a Society of Friendship, a salon where literary companions discussed poetry and religion. Members were known by fanciful names: Philips became "Orinda," dubbed the "matchless Orinda" by her contemporaries; her husband James was "Antenor"; Mary Aubrey was Rosania; **Anne Owen** was Lucasia; Lady ***Margaret Cavendish** was Policrite; and Sir Charles Cotterel, a master of ceremonies at the court of Charles II, was "Poliarchus." Philips was known for her intense female friendships, defined by her as "love refin'd and purg'd from all its dross."

In this milieu, Philips began circulating her poetry, which often celebrated or concerned her friendships and used the same poetic monikers. She had no intention, however, of seeking publication, convinced that it was a violation of feminine modesty. Within cultivated London, she became a literary darling. In 1659, Jeremy Taylor dedicated his "Discourse on the Nature, Offices and Measures of Friendship" to her, while others of importance praised her talent.

In 1662, Philips left for Dublin to oversee her husband's claim to certain Irish estates, and there she was encouraged by Robert Boyle, the earl of Orrery, to translate and adapt Corneille's *Pompey* (*La Mort du Pompée*) for the stage. Following an extremely successful production in 1663 at the Smock Alley Theater, it was published, to her horror, in Dublin and London. When she was warned of an imminent publication of a book of her verse in 1664, she wrote her friend ***Dorothy Osborne**: "I must never show any face among any reasonable people again, for some most dishonest person hath got some collection of my poems as I hear, and hath delivered them to a printer who I hear is [set] upon putting them out and this hath so extremely disturbed me, both to have my private folly so unhandsomely exposed and the belief that I believe the most part of the world are apt enough to believe that I connived at this ugly accident that I have been on the rack ever since I heard it." She managed to have the impending edition suppressed and a retraction of its publishing date printed in the London *Intelligencer.* Returning to London in March 1664 with a nearly completed translation of Corneille's *Horace,* Katherine Philips died abruptly of smallpox on June 22, age 33. Her poems were subsequently released posthumously.

The ambience of her group is finely detailed in *Letters of Orinda to Poliarchus,* published by Bernard Lintot in 1705 and 1709. *Poems, By the Incomparable Mrs K.P.* appeared surreptitiously in 1664, followed by an authentic edition in 1667. *Selected Poems,* edited with an appreciation by ***Louise Imogen Guiney**, appeared in 1904. P.W. Souers' *The Matchless Orinda* was published in 1931.

Philips had two children, one of whom, Katherine, became the wife of Lewis Wogan of Boulston, Pembrokeshire. There is some speculation that the daughter may also have been known as **Joan Philips**, author of *Female Poems on Separate Occasions,* written under the pseudonym Ephelia. The verse is in the style of Katherine Philips.

SOURCES:

Goreau, Angeline. *The Whole Duty of a Woman: Female Writers in Seventeenth-Century England.* NY: Dial, 1985.

Philipse, Margaret Hardenbrook

(d. 1690)

Colonial merchant and shipowner. *Born in Elberfeld, in the Rhine Valley, Prussia; died around 1690; daughter of Adolph Hardenbrook (also seen as Hardenbroeck); married Peter Rudolphus (de Vries), on October 10, 1659 (died 1661); married Frederick Philipse (businessman and later a politician), in October 1662; children: (first marriage) Maria (later adopted by Frederick Philipse and renamed Eve); (second marriage) daughter Annetje; three sons, Philip, Adolph, and Rombout.*

Margaret Philipse, who was quite possibly the first female business agent in the colonies, was born in the Rhine Valley, the daughter of Adolph Hardenbrook (or Hardenbroeck). Few facts about her early life survive, but it is believed that she accompanied her brother Abel to the Dutch colony of New Netherland (now part of New York State), in 1659. That same year, she married Peter Rudolphus (de Vries), a respected merchant trader from New Amsterdam (New York City). The couple had a daughter Maria in 1660.

Philipse began working in 1660, serving as a business agent for Dutch merchants trading with New Netherland. By some accounts, she became a shipowner at this time as well. (Dutch laws were more liberal than most at the time, allowing married women to conduct their own businesses.) Following her husband's death in 1661, Philipse took over his business as a merchant and trader, shipping furs to Holland in exchange for Dutch goods which she sold in New Amsterdam. Records of the time indicate that she was also involved in a number of lawsuits involving her husband's past business pursuits, which may or may not have precipitated her marriage in 1662 to Frederick Philipse, a carpenter turned merchant. Frederick later adopted her daughter, and the couple also had four children of their own: daughter Annetje and sons Philip, Adolph, and Rombout.

Although Frederick grew quite prosperous, Philipse continued to run her own enterprise, frequently traveling between Holland and New Amsterdam in a ship called the *Charles.* Around 1679, two missionaries, Jaspar Danckaerts and Peter Sluyter, made a crossing on the vessel from Amsterdam to New York. They refer in their journal to Philipse's "unblushing avarice" and "excessive covetousness," and record that on one occasion she demanded that the crew search for a mop that had gone overboard; "we, with all the rest, must work fruitlessly for an hour or an hour and a half," they wrote, "and all that merely to satisfy and please the miserable covetousness of Margaret." Philipse seems to have retired soon after that voyage and died about ten years later, around 1690.

SOURCES:
James, Edward T., ed. *Notable American Women, 1607–1950.* Cambridge, MA: The Belknap Press of Harvard University Press, 1971.
Read, Phyllis J., and Bernard L. Witlieb. *The Book of Women's Firsts.* NY: Random House, 1992.

Barbara Morgan,
Melrose, Massachusetts

Phillipa.

Variant of Philippa.

Phillipine of Luxemburg (d. 1311).

See Philippine of Luxemburg (d. 1311).

Phillipot, Alice (1904–1987).

See Rabon, Alice.

Phillipps, Adelaide (1833–1882)

English-born actress and opera singer. *Born in Stratford-on-Avon, England, on October 26, 1833; died at Karlsbad, Germany, on October 3, 1882; interred in Winslow Cemetery, Marshfield, Massachusetts; daughter of Alfred Phillipps (an attorney) and Mary (Rees) Phillipps (a dancing teacher); never married; no children.*

Adelaide Phillipps was born at Stratford-on-Avon, England, in 1833; her family emigrated to America in 1840. Her mother taught dancing, and Adelaide began a career on the Boston stage at age ten. But in 1850 her talent for singing became evident, and through *Jenny Lind and others she was sent to London and to Italy to study. In 1855, she returned to America an accomplished vocalist; for many years she was the leading American contralto, equally successful in oratorio and on the concert platform.

Phillips, Esther (1935–1984)

American rhythm and blues singer who had a number of hits in 1950 with Johnny Otis and his band. *Name variations: Little Esther Phillips. Born Esther Mae Jones in Galveston, Texas, on December 23, 1935; died in Carson, California, on August 7, 1984.*

Born in Texas in 1935, Esther Phillips grew up in California where her family moved after World War II. In 1949, at age 14, she won an amateur talent contest at a club owned by Johnny Otis, the rhythm and blues bandleader. Otis was so impressed with the young girl's mature voice that he invited her to sing and record with his band. Calling herself Little Esther, she recorded "Double Crossing Blues" on the Savoy label with the Otis Orchestra in 1950 and became the youngest female vocalist to land a #1 record on the R&B charts. That same year, she sang a duet with Mel Walker, "Mistrustin' Blues," which went to #1, as did "Cupid's Boogie." Other hits during 1950 included "Misery," "Deceivin' Blues," "Wedding Boogie," and "Faraway Blues." Phillips enjoyed a success that few artists attain in a single year.

At the end of 1950, she left Otis, signed with Federal, and the hits dried up. Of the 30 sides she cut with this label, only one, "Ring-a-Ding-Doo," made the charts, reaching #8 in 1952. One of Phillips' problems was the loss of Johnny Otis; another was drugs. By the time she was 20, she had become addicted to heroin, and her career was over. Ten years later, after a long struggle with her drug habit, she recorded "Release Me," a country tune that went to #1 (1962). Though she had other hits on the Atlantic label, none made the top of the charts. Then Phillips lost her battle with heroin a second time. Once again, she struggled to beat her addiction and in 1972 recorded "Home Is Where the Hatred Is," a haunting account of drug use. Esther Phillips continued to work in the 1970s and 1980s before she died in 1984. She was 49.

SOURCES:
Santelli, Robert. *The Big Book of the Blues: A Biographical Encyclopedia.* NY: Penguin, 1993.

John Haag,
Athens, Georgia

Phillips, Irna (1901–1973)

American radio and television writer who is considered by many to have created the first soap opera. *Born on July 1, 1901, in Chicago, Illinois; died on December 22, 1973, in Chicago; youngest of the ten children of William S. Phillips (a businessman) and Betty (Buxbaum) Phillips; attended public school in Chicago; graduated from Senn High School; University of Illinois, B.A., 1923; University of Wisconsin, M.A.; never married; children: (adopted) Thomas Dirk Phillips and Katherine Louise Phillips.*

Once heralded as the Queen of the Soap Opera, and credited by some with creating the genre, Irna Phillips was born in 1901 and grew up in Chicago, Illinois, the youngest of ten children of German-Jewish immigrants. Her father William S. Phillips, the owner of a dry goods and grocery story over which the family lived, died when she was eight, leaving the children in the care of their mother **Betty Buxbaum Phillips** who managed to keep a roof over their heads and food on the table. Phillips later remembered herself in those days as "a plain, sickly, silent child, with hand-me-down clothes and no friends." Although she had always dreamed of becoming an actress, she was told by a college drama coach that she had "neither the looks nor the stature to achieve professional success," so she went into education instead. She taught speech and drama at a junior college in Fulton, Missouri, then at a normal school in Dayton, Ohio, and picked up a master's degree along the way. While employed as a teacher, Phillips spent vacations working without pay for Chicago radio station WGN. In 1930, she left teaching for good.

That year, responding to a station request, Phillips created the family drama "Painted Dreams," considered by some to have been the first soap opera. A ten-minute daily serial, the show was strongly autobiographical, revolving around a widowed mother from Chicago (played by Phillips), her grown daughter, and their friends. The show ran for two years, and Phillips began to feel as though she had finally found her niche. In 1932, when the station refused to sell the show to the network, Phillips quit WGN and went to work for NBC, collaborating with Walter Wicker on "Today's Children," a new serial that was a rework of the earlier script. It ran until 1938, when Phillips withdrew the show in response to her mother's death. In the meantime, she had also launched two additional soap operas, "The Road of Life," featuring a doctor as the main character, and "The Guiding Light" (created with Emmons Carlson), about a non-sectarian minister. In using professionals as her protagonists, instead of the humbler working "folks" of earlier radio shows, Phillips found a personal trademark that offered her endless possibilities for new stories. She made the most of this pool of new characters, spinning out a series of popular serials, including "Woman in White" (1938), "The Right to Happiness" (1939), "Lonely Women" (1942), and "The Brighter Day" (1948). As early as 1943, Phillips had five serials running concurrently, making it necessary for her to use a chart system to keep from confusing the plots. At the time, she was earning an unheard-of $250,000 a year, making her, according to *Time*, "America's highest-paid serial litterateuse."

Phillips' own life hardly kept pace with the lives of the colorful characters she created. She admitted to several unhappy love affairs, including one with a man who refused to marry her when he discovered that she was unable to have children. Phillips never married, living with her mother until she was 37. At age 42, however, she adopted a son, Thomas, and 18 months later she adopted a daughter, Katherine. Although she made more than enough money, she lived conservatively, socializing with a handful of close friends, and investing most of her capital in annuities.

With the advent of television, Phillips expanded her empire. In the course of 20 years, she created seven shows for the new medium: "The Brighter Day" (1954), "The Road of Life" (1954), "As The World Turns" (1956), "Another World" (1964), "Days of Our Lives" (1965), "Love Is a Many-Splendour'd Thing" (1967), and "The Guiding Light" (which transferred to television in 1952 and went on to become one of the longest-running soap operas in broadcast history).

In addition to introducing "professionals" as main characters, Phillips has also been credited with other innovations, including the "cliff-hanger" ending, the use of organ music to enhance mood and bridge the breaks in narrative, and the "cross over," the migration of major characters from one serial to another. Phillips told *Fortune* magazine in 1938 that her shows were designed to appeal to basic human "instincts" and were intentionally kept at a slow, deliberate pace so that her audience could go on with their chores "without missing a word, tear, or heartbreak."

In her later years, Phillips decried sensationalism in the soaps, although she herself was a pioneer in using subjects like illegitimacy, sex, and murder in her plot lines. As **Evelyn Shaker** points out, "The heroine of 'Right to Happiness' fell in love four times (once with her widowed mother's fiancé), married twice, divorced one husband, accidentally shot the other, was tried for his murder, and bore a child in jail—all in the space of four years." Despite the often steamy entanglements of her plots, marriage and motherhood remained a central theme in Phillips' stories. "Though keenly aware of the ironic distance between this female domesticity she celebrated and her own eager pursuit of a career, Phillips was always an outspoken foe of feminism," writes Shaker, "warning it would weaken women's commitment to home and encourage sexual license."

Perhaps what Phillips really wanted was the life she wrote about, not the life she had. In 1943, about the time she had reached the top of her profession, she told a *Time* reporter that she would give it all up if the right man came along. The writer, who always credited her mother with her success, died of cancer on December 22, 1973.

SOURCES:

Current Biography 1943. NY: H.W. Wilson, 1943.

Shaker, Evelyn. "Irna Phillips," in *Notable American Women: The Modern Period*. Edited by Barbara Sicherman and Carol Hurd Green. Cambridge, MA: The Belknap Press of Harvard University Press, 1980.

Barbara Morgan,
Melrose, Massachusetts

Phillips, Lena Madesin (1881–1955)

American lawyer, women's rights advocate, and writer. *Born Anna Lena Phillips on September 15, 1881, in Nicholasville, Kentucky; died on May 21, 1955, in Marseilles, France; daughter of William Henry Phillips (a judge) and Alice (Shook) Phillips; educated at Jessamine Female Institute, Woman's College of Baltimore (later Goucher College), and Peabody Conservatory of Music; graduated from University of Kentucky Law School in 1917; New York University Law School, LL.M., 1923; lived with Marjory Lacey-Baker (an actress).*

Became one of the first female graduates of the University of Kentucky Law School (1917); founded and presided over both the National and the International Federation of Business and Professional Women's Clubs; practiced law, contributed to publications, and championed women's rights.

Born into a prominent family in Kentucky in 1881, Anna Lena Phillips preferred to use the name Lena Madesin (a version of the French word *médecin*), originally taken to honor her half-brother who at the time was studying medicine in France. Her father was a popular county judge, and her mother was a talented musician who inspired her daughter to pursue a career as a concert pianist. However, while Phillips was at the Peabody Conservatory of Music in 1902, she fell and sustained an arm injury which ended her performing ambitions. After serving as the head of the music department at Jessamine Institute in her hometown of Nicholasville and trying unsuccessfully to sell music she had composed, she took care of her father's household for a time after her mother's death. She remained active in musical activities but in 1915 suffered a nervous breakdown, which ultimately propelled her in new directions.

Phillips entered the University of Kentucky Law School, and in 1917 became one of its first female graduates. She subsequently began to practice law in Nicholasville. As secretary-treasurer of the Kentucky War Fund Committee of the National War Work Council of the YWCA, she was asked by the national organization to take a higher position. She declined, telling the YWCA, "I am not interested in being one of 11 field secretaries," but later took on the position of executive secretary of the YWCA's National Business Women's Committee, which had been formed for businesswomen engaged in war work. In this capacity, she found that there was a definite need for a national organization to promote the interests of business and professional women. In 1919, with the support of the YWCA, she organized a meeting in St. Louis which launched the National Federation of Business and Professional Women's Clubs (NFBPWC). After Phillips was elected executive secretary, she organized the group's first offices and founded its official journal, *Independent Woman*.

Leaving her duties at the NFBPWC in 1923, Phillips received a master's degree in law from New York University Law School and moved in with actress **Marjory Lacey-Baker**, who became her lifelong companion. After a fallow period during which Phillips saw little money coming in, she became a leading female attorney in New York City. She then rejoined the NFBPWC, becoming its membership and program chair and its president from 1926 to 1929. Phillips supported many social and feminist issues, including equal pay for women, the Equal Rights Amendment, and a child labor amendment which opponents denounced as communist. She also backed peace issues such as the World Court and arms limitations.

In 1928, Phillips made several tours through Europe, hoping to establish an international organization of business and professional women. After stepping down as president of the NFBPWC, she became president of the new International Federation of Business and Professional Women's Clubs (IFBPWC), which she led until 1947. In 1933, she was one of the main organizers of the International Congress of Women, held at the Chicago Century of Progress Exposition. Phillips spent a great deal of time in Europe in the 1930s, speaking to women's groups in 22 countries and promoting the rights of women. In 1936, she was a co-speaker with ***Frances Perkins**, U.S. secretary of labor, at the International Federation Congress in Paris. Continuing to speak out against discrimination of all kinds, Phillips renewed her efforts for an equal rights amendment during World War II, saying that "America does not want its women penalized because of laws based upon a feudal tradition." She promoted the election of women to public office at all levels and in 1943 criticized a New York City branch of the NFBPWC which barred two African-American professional women from membership. Though a pacifist for many years, she supported the war effort, in 1945 touring

Sweden and Great Britain on a special mission for the Office of War Information on behalf of European business and professional women. After the war, she helped European women rebuild branches of the IFBPWC, participated in many forums and discussions in the United States about postwar problems, and was a strong supporter of the fledgling United Nations.

Phillips also wrote poetry, short stories, and articles. She contributed often to the *Independent Woman* and other publications, and in 1935 gave up the practice of law to become an associate editor of *Pictorial Review*, for which she wrote a regular column. After moving with Lacey-Baker to Westport, Connecticut, she also made two unsuccessful runs for political office, for the Connecticut legislature in 1942 and for lieutenant governor of Connecticut in 1948. Although a staunch Democrat, she ran for the latter office on the Progressive Party ticket as a supporter of presidential candidate Henry Wallace. This was a controversial move, since Wallace's candidacy was considered suspect by many in an era when, as Phillips put it, "[a] Communist is now being discovered under every bush and I am prepared to be smeared once more."

While she was involved in numerous other activities, Phillips' enthusiasm for the NFBPWC and the IFBPWC never waned, and in May 1955 she undertook a trip to Beirut to explore how professional women were organized in the Middle East. Her journey was cut short by complications from surgery for a perforated ulcer, however, and she died in Marseilles, France, that same month.

Michelle Phillips

SOURCES:

Current Biography 1946. NY: H.W. Wilson, 1946.

Read, Phyllis J., and Bernard L. Witlieb, eds. *The Book of Women's Firsts*. NY: Random House, 1992.

Sicherman, Barbara, and Carol Hurd Green, eds. *Notable American Women: The Modern Period*. Cambridge, MA: The Belknap Press of Harvard University, 1980.

Sally A. Myers, Ph.D., freelance writer and editor

Phillips, Michelle (1944—)

American singer and actress who was a member of The Mamas and the Papas. *Born Holly Michelle Gilliam on June 4, 1944, in Long Beach, California; daughter of Gardner Burnett (a merchant marine) and Joyce Leon (Poole) Gilliam (an accountant); married John Phillips (a singer), on December 31, 1962 (divorced 1968); married Dennis Hopper (an actor), in 1970 (divorced); married Robert Burch (a radio executive; marriage ended); married again, in 2000; children: Gilliam Chynna Phillips (b. 1968, a singer known as Chynna Phillips); Austin Devereux Hines (b. 1982); Aron Wilson (adopted 1988); (stepdaughter)* ***Mackenzie Phillips*** *(an actress).*

Michelle Phillips, who achieved fame as a member of the 1960s folk-rock group The Mamas and the Papas, was born in 1944 in Long Beach, and spent her early childhood in postwar government housing in Los Angeles. She lost her mother to heart disease when she was very young, and as a teenager she experimented with drugs and tried modeling in San Francisco. She also began to frequent the popular folk music clubs that were emerging throughout San Francisco in the early 1960s, among them the famous Hungry i, where she met guitarist and singer John Phillips. In 1962, she followed him to New York, where she modeled and occasionally filled in as a singer with his band, the Journeymen. They were married at the end of that year.

A few years later, as the antiwar and civil-rights movements were in full swing, and hippie "flower children" were creating their own culture, Michelle and John, along with Marshall Brickman, formed the New Journeymen folk group. They lived a freewheeling lifestyle, touring nationwide and performing at the many folk clubs in New York City, where other performers included Peter, Paul, and **Mary (Travers)**, Bob Dylan, and **Joan Baez.** In 1964, Michelle and John took a long vacation in the Virgin Islands with Denny Doherty, a friend and fellow musician. They were joined there by ***Cass Elliot**, a singer who had been in a band with Doherty, and the four spent some five months creating a new band and a new sound.

By 1965, they were back in San Francisco, where the newly formed Dunhill Records label quickly saw the potential in the as-yet-unnamed group's vocal harmonies. The Phillipses, Elliot and Doherty recorded an album even before finalizing their group's name, which became The Mamas and the Papas. Their first single was "California Dreamin'," which would become a sort of theme song for the '60s generation. Written by Michelle and John, the song was an instant hit upon its release in March 1966, landing at #4 on the charts and eventually selling a million copies. In her autobiography, Phillips described "California Dreamin'" as "one of those songs that didn't just reflect what was going on; it gave impetus to change, to turn things around." In May, their second single, "Monday Monday," became the #1 song in the country. The band's album, *If You Can Believe Your Eyes and Ears*, was released the same month and also reached the top of the charts, as did their second album (also released in 1966), *The Mamas and the Papas*. "I Saw Her Again," "Creeque Alley," and "Words of Love," as well as a remake of the **Shirelles**' "Dedicated to the One I Love," all became top hits for the band, and over 30 years later these songs remain staples of radio programming. "Monday Monday" won a Grammy Award in 1967. A particularly significant event for the band took place in June of that year, when they performed at the highly publicized Monterey Pop Festival, along with other folk and rock performers including ***Janis Joplin**, Canned Heat, the Who, Jimi Hendrix, and the Byrds. (The Mamas and the Papas can be seen in the documentary film of the festival, 1969's *Monterey Pop*.)

Phillips enjoyed her newfound success as part of one of the biggest folk-rock bands in the country; as she later wrote, "We had it all: appearance, youth, style, originality, wit, great tunes, and above all, *we could sing*." Ensconced in Bel Air, California, Michelle and John enjoyed a lavish lifestyle, complete with rowdy parties, illicit drugs, conspicuous consumption and fancy cars. She also had a few affairs, including one with Doherty, leading to tensions within her marriage and within the band. Despite their spectacular success, The Mamas and the Papas was gradually divided by drug use, marital infidelities, and infighting. In 1968, the same year the Phillipses' daughter **Chynna Phillips** was born, both the marriage and The Mamas and the Papas were dissolved. (Chynna Phillips would later team up with **Carnie Wilson** and **Wendy Wilson**, daughters of Brian Wilson of the Beach Boys, to form the vocal trio Wilson Phillips.)

After the group's demise, Phillips pursued an acting career and had high-profile romances with actors Dennis Hopper (to whom she was married for eight days), Jack Nicholson and Warren Beatty and with director Roman Polanski (whose wife ***Sharon Tate** had been murdered in 1969). Phillips has appeared in television series and television movies, and her film credits include *Dillinger* (1973), *Shampoo* (1975), *American Anthem* (1986), and *Star Trek: The Next Generation* (1988). The Mamas and the Papas were inducted into the Rock and Roll Hall of Fame in 1998.

SOURCES:

Contemporary Authors. Detroit, MI: Gale Research, 1999.

Phillips, Michelle. *California Dreamin': The True Story of The Mamas and the Papas*. NY: Warner Books, 1986.

Sally A. Myers, Ph.D.,
freelance writer and editor

Phillips, Mrs. Morton (b. 1918).

See joint entry under Friedman, Esther Pauline and Pauline Esther.

Phillips, Zara (1981—)

English royal. *Born Zara Anne Elizabeth Phillips on May 15, 1981, in Paddington, London, England; daughter of* ****Anne*** *(b. 1950), princess royal, and Mark Phillips.*

Phillpotts, Bertha Surtees (1877–1932)

British scholar. *Name variations: Dame Bertha Surtees Newall; Dame Bertha Phillpotts. Born in 1877; died in 1932; graduated from Girton College in Cambridge, 1901; married H.F. Newall (1857–1944, an astrophysicist whose father constructed the Newall telescope), in 1931.*

Dame Bertha Phillpotts studied medieval and modern languages at Girton College, from which she graduated with first class honors in 1901. For the next 12 years, she devoted herself to the study of Scandinavian culture and eventually became the first Lady Carlisle fellow of Somerville College at Oxford. She served as principal of Westfield College from 1919 to 1922, and as mistress of her alma mater from 1922 to 1925. In 1926, she became a university lecturer, a post she would hold until her death. Phillpotts was created a Dame of the British Empire (DBE) in 1929 and two years later published her notable work *Edda and Saga*. She died in 1932.

Lisa Frick,
freelance writer, Columbia, Missouri

Philoclea (1658–1708).

See Masham, Damaris.

Philomena

Saint. *Name variations: Filomena or Filumena.*

In 1802, bones were discovered in the catacomb of ***Priscilla** (fl. 1st c.); near the tomb was a broken tablet with the inscription *Lumena* *paxte cyfi,* which was deciphered to spell *Pax tecum, Filumena*. The occupant of the grave was received as a saint of the Roman Catholic Church, and her renown became universal. Philomena was noted for her miraculous powers of healing the sick through prayer. Henry Wadsworth Longfellow gave the saint's name to ***Florence Nightingale**, partly because of her labors among the sick and dying at Scutari, and partly because the Latin word *philomela* means nightingale. Her feast day is August 10.

Phintys of Sparta (fl. c. 400 BCE)

Greek philosopher. *Flourished around 400 BCE; daughter of Kallikratides (Kallicrates, or Kallikratidas), a Greek admiral.*

Works: On the Moderation of Women.

Little is known about the life of Phintys of Sparta, except that she was the daughter of a Greek admiral, Kallikratides, who died in the 406 BCE battle of Arginusae. The two remaining fragments of her book *On the Moderation of Women* show that her philosophical approach was typical of Pythagorean women in its emphasis on temperance. The Pythagoreans upheld the importance of courage, justice, and moderation in everyday life, and many of them saw women and men as having equal but different roles. Phintys, who argued that philosophy was appropriate for both men and women, regarded moderation as of particular importance for women due to their domestic roles, the demands of which required adaptability to circumstance. She concentrated on the philosophy of domestic life, emphasizing moderation and fidelity. Phintys advocated temperance in everything, including religious practice; recommended modesty in personal appearance (no jewelry); and noted that a woman should be especially discreet when leaving the house. Phintys advises men, on the other hand, to concentrate on the other Pythagorean virtues of courage and justice in their comparatively more-public work.

SOURCES:

Buck, Claire, ed. *Bloomsbury Guide to Women's Literature*. NY: Prentice Hall, 1992.

Kersey, Ethel M. *Women Philosophers: a Bio-critical Source Book*. NY: Greenwood, 1989.

Waithe, Mary Ellen, ed. *A History of Women Philosophers*. Boston, MA: Martinus Nijhoff, 1987–95.

Catherine Hundleby, M.A. Philosophy,
University of Guelph, Guelph, Ontario, Canada

Phipson, Edith Pechey (1845–1908).

See Pechey-Phipson, Edith.

Phlipon, Manon (1754–1793).

See Roland, Madame.

Phoebe of Cenchreae (fl. 1st c.)

Early Christian patron and leader who delivered St. Paul's Epistle to the Romans to the church at Rome c. 57 CE and is increasingly seen by scholars as having played a crucial role in creating the position of deaconess in the early church. *Name variations: Phebe; Phoebe of Cenchrea; Phoebe of Cenchreæ. Flourished in the 1st century; lived in the Greek port city of Cenchreae. Her feast day is September 3.*

Phoebe was a Gentile Christian from the Greek port city of Cenchreae. Derived from Greek mythology, her name means "pure" or "radiant as the moon." In view of the little factual data relating to her, scholars will continue to debate the precise details of Phoebe's life and influence. But in recent decades women in the vanguard of reform within the Christian world have adopted her as the patron founder of the modern-day deaconess movement, which is part of their larger struggle for full gender equality.

St. Paul entrusted Phoebe with delivering his Epistle to the Romans. In this letter, which she carried to Rome, he commends her to the church in Rome, requesting that they treat her as a saint: "I commend to you our sister Phoebe, a deaconess [*diakonos*] of the church at Cenchreae, so that you may welcome her in the Lord as befits the saints, and help her in whatever she may require from you, for she has been a benefactor [*prostasis*] of many and of myself as well" (Romans 16: 1–2).

From this passage, and from Paul's selection of her to carry such an important epistle, we can gather that Phoebe was probably a person of distinction to Paul and the church. The use of the term *diakonos* to describe her position has been controversial, as translations by theologians and historians have been various. *Diakonos* has been translated as "deacon" (in the sense of 1 Timothy 3:8–13), "messenger," "helper," "servant," or even as "minister." In the New Testament, the term is used to describe five people: Paul, Tychicus, Epaphras, Timothy, and Phoebe. Of these, only Phoebe is described as a *diakonos* of a specific congregation, the church at Cenchreae, near Corinth on the Saronic Gulf. Many scholars consider Phoebe to be Paul's spiritual sister, in view of the fact that he calls her both *prostasis* ("benefactor," also translated as "helper," "leader," "champion," "protector," "presider," or even literally as "coach," usually when referring to an Olympic trainer) and *diakonos*. According to Philippians 1, by the early 60s CE some Christian churches had at least one officer called a "deacon." The fact that Phoebe was entrusted with Paul's letter, which concerned how God justifies (frees from the penalty of sin) believers through faith, not works, and how Christ died for both Jews and Gentiles, makes a compelling case for her serving within the church in a position of high status, as a member of the ministry as a deaconess. In Romans 16, Paul is exploiting his network of clients throughout the Roman Empire on her behalf, introducing Phoebe to his web of connections and thereby reciprocating her benefactions. If she did, in fact, serve the early church as a deaconess, her case provides a persuasive argument, reason many, that women should not now be prevented from so serving the church.

In recent decades, a growing number of scholars have produced significant arguments for the case that Phoebe was a woman of wealth and influence within her community. She may have been a wealthy businesswoman, perhaps owning a fleet of ships, which would explain her trip to Rome. Paul likely met her in Corinth on his second missionary trip, and in some way she had been of special help to him. He was probably entertained at her home, and his vow seems to point to a deliverance from severe danger or illness in which she may have attended him (Acts 18:18). Some authors have even suggested that Phoebe may have been a member of the Greek hetaerae, the class of highly cultivated courtesans. It is more than likely that her home was the headquarters of the Christian church at Cenchreae. Her title indicates that she was an important patron of believers in that city and region. As a patron and benefactor who enjoyed the advantages of wealth, education, and influence, she would have had the ability to defend and advance the interests of clients and of individuals lacking civil rights.

The story that Phoebe was Paul's wife has long been discounted, and the idea that she suffered martyrdom at Rome is also considered highly unlikely by most scholars. Her important role in early Christian history has been retained in the traditions of many Orthodox churches of Eastern Europe in a Troparion (a short hymn celebrating a saint or an important event which is used in the daily office and liturgy):

> Enlightened by grace and taught the faith
> by the chosen vessel of Christ
> thou wast found worthy of the diaconate
> and didst bring Paul's words to Rome.
> O Deaconess Phoebe, pray to Christ our God
> that His Spirit
> may enlighten our souls.

SOURCES:

Arichea, Daniel C., Jr. "Who Was Phoebe? Translating Diakonos in Romans 16.1," in *Practical Papers for the Bible Translator.* Vol. 39, no. 4. October 1988, pp. 401–409.

Blasi, A.J. "The Ideology of the Primitive Christian Church in the Epistle of Saint Paul to the Romans and the Letter of Recommendation for Phoebe," in *Social Compass.* Vol. 46, no. 4. December 1999, pp. 507–520.

Ernst, Michael. "Die Funktionen der Phöbe (Röm 16, 1f) in der Gemeinde von Kenchreai," in Friedrich V. Reiterer and Petrus Eder, eds., *Liebe zum Wort: Beiträge zur klassischen und biblischen Philologie, P. Ludger Bernhard OSB zum 80. Geburtstag dargebracht von Kollegen und Schülern.* Salzburg: Otto Müller, 1993, pp. 141–154.

Finger, Reta Halteman. "Phoebe: Role Model for Leaders," in *Daughters of Sarah.* No. 14. March–April 1988, pp. 5–7.

Goodspeed, Edgar J. "Phoebe's Letter of Introduction," in *Harvard Theological Review.* Vol. 44, no. 1. January 1951, pp. 55–57.

Harris, Louise. *Woman in the Christian Church.* Brighton, MI: Green Oak Press, 1988.

Jewett, Robert. "Paul, Phoebe, and the Spanish Mission," in Jacob Neusner, *et al.*, eds., *The Social World of Formative Christianity: Essays in Tribute to Howard Clark Kee.* Philadelphia, PA: Fortress Press, 1988, pp. 142–161.

Kienzle, Beverly Mayne, and Pamela J. Walker, eds. *Women Preachers and Prophets Through Two Millennia of Christianity.* Berkeley, CA: University of California Press, 1998.

Kroeger, Catherine Clark, Mary Evans, and Elaine Storkey, eds. *Study Bible for Women.* Grand Rapids, MI: Baker Books, 1995.

Martimort, Aimé Georges. *Deaconesses: An Historical Study.* Translated by K.D. Whitehead. San Francisco, CA: Ignatius Press, 1986.

Morris, Joan. *The Lady was a Bishop: The Hidden History of Women with Clerical Ordination and the Jurisdiction of Bishops.* NY: Macmillan, 1973.

Ohanneson, Joan. *Woman: Survivor in the Church.* Minneapolis, MN: Winston Press, 1980.

Patterson, Dorothy, general ed. *The Women's Study Bible, New King James Version.* Nashville, TN: Thomas Nelson, 1995.

Ranke-Heinemann, Uta. *Eunuchs for the Kingdom of Heaven: Women, Sexuality, and the Catholic Church.* Translated by Peter Heinegg. NY: Doubleday, 1990.

Ratigan, Virginia Kaib, and Arlene Anderson Swidler, eds. *A New Phoebe: Perspectives on Roman Catholic Women and the Permanent Diaconate.* Kansas City, MO: Sheed & Ward, 1990.

Romaniuk, Kazimierz. "Was Phoebe in Romans 16.1 a Deaconess?," in *Zeitschrift für die Neutestamentliche Wissenschaft und die Kunde der Älteren Kirche.* Vol. 81, no. 1–2, 1990, pp. 132–134.

Schüssler Fiorenza, Elisabeth. *In Memory of Her: A Feminist Theological Reconstruction of Christian Origins.* NY: Crossroad, 1985.

———. "The Quilting of Women's History: Phoebe of Cenchreae," in Paula M. Cooey, Sharon A. Farmer and Mary Ellen Ross, eds., *Embodied Love: Sensuality and Relationship as Feminist Values.* San Francisco, CA: Harper & Row, 1987, pp. 35–49.

———. "Word, Spirit and Power: Women in Early Christian Communities," in Rosemary Ruether and Eleanor McLaughlin, eds., *Women of Spirit: Female Leadership in the Jewish and Christian Traditions.* NY: Simon and Schuster, 1979.

Tucker, Ruth A. *Daughters of the Church.* Grand Rapids, MI: Academie Books, 1987.

Whelan, Caroline F. "Amica Pauli: The Role of Phoebe in the Early Church," in *Journal for the Study of the New Testament.* Issue 49. March 1993, pp. 67–85.

"The Women in Paul's Life," in *Christianity Today.* Vol. 41, no. 12. October 27, 1997, pp. 74–75.

Zagano, Phyllis. *Holy Saturday: An Argument for the Restoration of the Female Diaconate in the Catholic Church.* NY: Crossroad, 2000.

John Haag,
Associate Professor of History, University of Georgia, Athens, Georgia

Phoolan Devi (c. 1956—)

Bandit queen of India. *Born Phoolan Devi (Goddess of Flowers) in the state of Upper Predash, India, around 1956; daughter of Devidin Kewat and Moola; learned to read and write in prison; married Puttilal (a farmer), around 1967; married once more.*

In February 1981, Phoolan Devi and her gang of seven men were charged in absentia with looting, kidnapping, and killing 22 high-caste Hindu men from Behmai, a remote town south of Delhi. Politically, the incident was a firecracker. The Thakurs (landowners) of Uttar Pradesh (UP), who controlled the rural vote, demanded justice so loudly that *__Indira Gandhi__ and the government in Delhi were forced to act. For the following year, police from three states—UP, Madhya Pradesh and Rajastan—pursued Phoolan, one step ahead of the national and international press. Labeled the "Bandit Queen," she became the *__Bonnie Parker__ of India. Sightings made the weekly magazines.

Gandhi was advised that the hunt was costly and that the only recourse was to persuade Phoolan to surrender. *Dacoits* (armed gangs) had been urged to capitulate before, negotiating terms with the government. The Chambral Valley of India has a history of rural banditry dating to the 12th century. For generations, the locals have settled scores their own way in this desolate region. Many revolt against a feudal order in which workers who till the soil reap no rewards. Some are women. In the 1950s, the now-revered ❧▸ **Putli Bai** led one of the most feared gangs in the Valley.

Eventually, Phoolan agreed to a deal, but on her terms: (1) neither she nor members of her gang would be hanged or extradited to UP; (2) with two meals a day, they could share a cell at Gwalior Central Jail (which overlooks the battlefield where *__Lakshmibai__, rani of Jansi, was killed); (3) her family would be moved to Gwalior, Madhya Pradesh, along with her goat and cow; and (4) she and her gang would only serve an eight-year sentence.

The roots of Phoolan Devi's rebellion took hold before she was born. Her illiterate father Devidin was the younger brother of the literate Biharilal. Without Devidin's knowledge, Biharilal bribed the *sarpanch* (chief) of the village, who kept the land records, to transfer all their father's property into his name. As Phoolan told her biographer **Mala Sen:**

> Ignorant of this, my father kept toiling on that land and it was only after he had reached the age of nineteen or twenty that he asked for his share. It was then that the two of them—[Biharilal and his son Maiyadin]—turned him out of the house and my father was forced to build a small hut on the outskirts of the village. They took over the land and my father did not get any share of either the 80 bighas of land we had in the village, or the two-storied family house that my grandfather had built.

At first Devidin appealed to the village council, but Biharilal denied that Devidin was his real brother, claiming he was a servant in his grandfather's house. The villagers urged Devidin to file a suit. Finally in 1949, he took the case to court, but Biharilal, holding all the money, had a distinct financial advantage. Each time Devidin's suit appeared to be progressing, Biharilal and his son would harass him, stealing from his crop, sending thugs to attack.

Phoolan Devi, born around 1956, grew up with this story of injustice. By then, her uncle had four servants and feasted, while Phoolan and her four sisters and one brother lived on a sparse diet. Devidin owned only a small piece of land that provided his family with grain. Said Phoolan:

> My parents were very poor. . . . My father would work the entire day and in the evening come back with food for us and only then could my mother cook to feed all of us. It was out of these meager earnings that they saved up for the court case.

On an afternoon in 1967, when Phoolan was about ten, she talked her reluctant 13-year-old sister **Rukhmini** into entering their uncle's field, now occupied by their cousin Maiyadin, to eat *hora* (chickpeas). After all, Phoolan argued, it was her father's share of the land. Maiyadin discovered them and shooed them home, but Phoolan refused to leave. When Maiyadin signaled his servant to drag the gentle Rukhmini off the land, a furious Phoolan rushed to her sister's defense. Maiyadin informed the village council that Phoolan was stealing hora from his fields, and her parents were beaten. "It was as if they wanted to break every bone in my body," her mother Moola told her later.

Though Indian law forbids girls to wed before age 15, Devidin and Moola made swift marriage arrangements for their daughters. Fortunately, Rukhmini would grow to love her chosen husband and have three children. Phoolan was not so blessed. Puttilal, the man chosen for her, was 20 years her senior. Devidin felt Phoolan could use a firm hand, but Moola, who was against the match, demanded a *gauna* (a period of time before the bride must live with the husband), and three years was agreed upon. Despite this, Phoolan was sent to her husband three months later, when Puttilal threatened to cancel the marriage and the dowry of one milch cow, 100 rupees, and a bike. Said Phoolan:

> I did not understand the meaning of "husband" and when he made passes at me I would scream and shout, not knowing the meaning of these gestures. My fear angered him and he would hit me. He treated me like an animal. He would touch my breasts and say that I was like a baby teetar—a partridge—and asked when I would mature. He was a pervert, in my eyes, and I soon learned that his first wife had died in childbirth at the age of fourteen. The child had also died. When he took me to his home I was eleven.

During the next few years, Phoolan was often sick. In the midst of one illness, her disgusted husband sent for her father to fetch her. Now 13 or 14, Phoolan returned home in disgrace and with little future. Though she was still Puttilal's wife, he had let it be known that he would only take her back for 10,000 rupees. Her parents were terrified that they would be burdened by their daughter for the rest of their lives.

Suresh Chand, son of the *sarpanch* and friend of Maiyadin, began to follow Phoolan around, flirting with her. One evening, while Phoolan was cutting basra in her father's field, he made an advance. She fought him off and ran into the town. Enraged, Suresh caught her, beat her, and told all who would listen that she had attacked him because he had refused her a favor. At home, she was reminded of the rule: they were poor, people like Maiyadin and Suresh Chand were rich; they could not fight them.

Putli Bai (1929–1958)

Indian bandit queen. *Born around 1929 into a Muslim family of prostitutes in Agra, India; daughter of her mother* ***Ashgari*** *(who ran a brothel); died in 1958; children: daughter Tanno.*

One of the most well known and most revered bandit queens in India, Putli Bai reigned in the 1950s. She first came to public attention as a willowy dancer in her mother's traditional *Nauchghar* (brothel of dancing girls) in the town of Agra. Rich landowners and the wealthy throughout the state paid her to dance at festive occasions. At one point, she was asked to dance at a wedding at Dholpur, now in Rajastan. While there, she was kidnapped by the leader of a *dacoit* gang by the name of Sultan who had been smitten with her. Though she attempted two escapes, she eventually chose to stay with Sultan and had a daughter with him who was sent to live with Putli's mother. When Sultan was killed by the police, Putli teamed up with another gang leader, Kalyan Singh, known as Kalla. The Kalla-Putli gang was soon feared throughout the Chambral Valley. Injured in a police gun battle, Putli lost her left arm at the elbow. While she recovered, Kalla had a gang member dress as a woman in a sari during each raid to deflect police boasts that she had been killed. "A few months later," wrote Mala Sen, "Putli was seen in villages again, wielding a rifle, held steady with the stub of her left arm, her aim still accurate." On January 23, 1958, while trying to escape an ambush by crossing the Kunwari River, the 29-year-old Putli was shot and killed. People still pray at the location where her body, along with her rucksack, containing a half bottle of rum and the Koran, was retrieved from the river.

Now Suresh Chand became their nemesis, stirring up the village against them.

To save the family honor, Maiyadin suggested she be returned to her husband. Once more, Phoolan was sent to live with Puttilal, but he had remarried, and his new wife **Vidya** was furious. For the next three years, Vidya treated Phoolan like a field hand, and again the young girl was often ill. At last, Puttilal agreed to accompany her home for a visit with her parents. When they arrived at the banks of the Jamuna River, he went to find a boatman and never returned. At 17, Phoolan was a discarded woman with no future; her mother urged her to commit suicide. Writes Sen:

> Although Phoolan Devi was not aware of it, around this time, about the mid-1970s, women's groups in urban centres up and down the country, groups reflecting various shades of feminism, were highlighting experiences such as hers. Endless cases of "dowry deaths" and sexual assaults against women were being reported, demonstra-

> tions organized and calls made for changes and modifications to the law. All these developments, repeatedly the focus of middle-class attention in the cities, meant little to her. Her isolation and sense of humiliation . . . had become complete.

Phoolan worked the land with her family, determined to stay out of trouble. She also appealed her father's case so eloquently that the hearing was reopened and the claim transferred from the Sessions Court at Kalpi to the Allahabad High Court. This was to be the family's downfall.

> If any woman were to go through my experience, then she too would not be able to think of a normal life. What do I know, except cutting grass and using a rifle?
>
> —Phoolan Devi

In January 1979, Devidin summoned his family. Probably as a result of their court victory, he said, the basra crop had been trampled under by oxen. A few days later, Phoolan's brother came running home with news that Maiyadin was attacking their neem tree with an axe. A neem tree is prized for its shade; its berries heal. When Phoolan raced to the site and caught her uncle and four men in the act, she threw a stone, making a slight cut above her uncle's eye. The men tied her up, called the police, and she was thrown in jail. After a month, she was released on bail, but it was rumored that she had been raped while incarcerated. All Phoolan would later say was, "They had plenty of fun at my expense and beat the hell out of me too." She was now around 22.

Phoolan was then sent to another village to stay with her sister. Upon arrival, she accompanied Rukhmini to a hospital for an operation. On their return, Phoolan's brother-in-law gave them the news: the police were looking for Phoolan; she had purportedly been involved in a *dacoity* (armed raid) at the house of Maiyadin and her parents had been taken to the police station. Immediately, Phoolan set out for home, armed with a paper testifying that she had been with her sister at the hospital at the time of the dacoity. On the way, a mob accosted her and had her arrested. Beaten by the police, she was told to cooperate, to do as Maiyadin and the *sarpanch* told her. Wrote Sen:

> She had arrived at the police station, terrified by the reaction she had provoked in the village. She saw her parents but was not allowed to speak to them. The officer-in-charge made a mockery of the certificate from the hospital, tossing it on the table, saying it was a meaningless piece of paper. Every time she tried to say anything he told her to keep her mouth shut. He also molested her, publicly not surreptitiously, using the end of his cane to lift her sari, examining her all over, while his subordinates watched her "interrogation," adding their own crude and obscene remarks.

The beatings left scars.

Though Moola found a lawyer which led to her daughter's eventual release, Maiyadin was determined. While still out on bail, Phoolan learned that a *dacoit* gang, whose chief lieutenant was a friend of Maiyadin's, intended to kidnap her. She then received a letter from the gang threatening to punish her with the common scarring practice of nose or ear cutting. A second letter followed. Twice the family went to the police with the letters, and friends cautioned Phoolan to leave the village. In July 1979, 25 armed men entered her house at midnight, menaced the family, beat Phoolan, then threatened once more to disfigure her until she agreed to go with them. (Later, when she told this story to the police, they summarized her narrative with, "So you agreed to go with them.")

In bare feet with bound hands, Phoolan was ushered, pleading, through the darkness. She was then forced to accompany them on a long march and river crossing, as each day they moved camp. During the first two days, the leader Babu Singh Gujar raped her often. When Babu Gujar offered her to others, however, his lieutenant Vikram Mullah intervened. Within three days, Vikram had killed Babu Gujar and two others in defense of her honor. Instructed to don one of the dead men's shoes and police uniform, Phoolan became Vikram's mistress. "A piece of property has no choice," she said.

When Moola went to the police to report the kidnapping, they were dismissive. Phoolan, they said, had jumped bail. Besides, Maiyadin claimed that Phoolan had run off with *dacoits,* proving that she had been involved on the raid of his house. He demanded she be registered as a wanted criminal.

Phoolan claims that Vikram treated her well. (Vikram, who was married with a wife and a son, sent them money, but he had left this life behind.) Wrote Sen:

> Stories and legends of [*dacoits*] abound in the area. They are both feared and idolized. Scores of Hindi films have been made about them, enhancing the romantic rebel image they project, songs have been written describing their exploits and endless stories are told about particular bandit leaders. . . . Vikram Mullah . . . was proud to have been integrated into this tradition. . . . Phoolan says he called himself "Vikram Singh *Mas-*

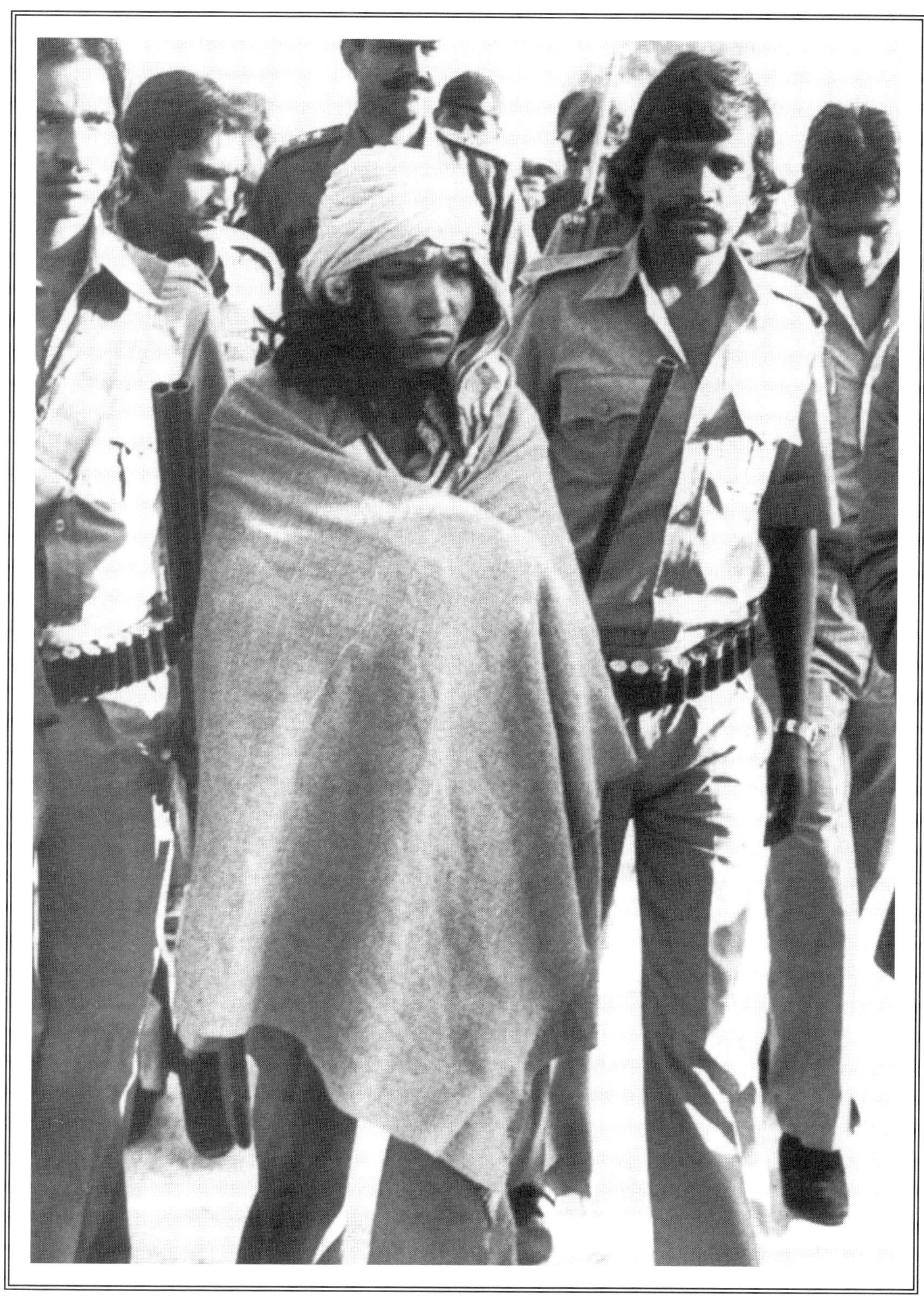

Phoolan Devi

tana," projecting himself as a man already satisfied by all earthly desires and therefore able to give rather than take.

Moola told Sen that Vikram arrived one day at their home to give them news of their daughter and to tell them that he had married her. When Moola asked how, since she was already married, Vikram laughed. In the eyes of God, he said, she was his wife, and, unlike Puttilal, who had come to take a dowry, he had come to leave a dowry. He gave Moola 5,000 rupees and also repaid Phoolan's lost bail.

Phoolan became part of the seven-member gang and learned to fire a gun. *Dacoits*, a pejorative term, prefer to be called *baghis*; they often dress as police, kidnap for ransom or hijack commercial trucks, and see themselves as rebels opposing injustice. Some have a sense of honor; some are just thieves. Vikram, who was also of a lower caste, had a sense of honor; a *dacoit* Robin Hood, he took from the rich and was supported by the poor. He "always considered my needs," said Phoolan. "When we walked through the *behad* (the ravines) hungry and thirsty, he would give me water first. He would insist that I eat even when I said I was not hungry. When he washed his clothes he would wash mine too. He even plaited my hair before I cut it short." The gang looted a convoy of 26 trucks, then left a note on the windshield, claiming this was the work of Vikram Mullah and Phoolan Devi.

Two gang members newly released from jail rejoined the group. One of them, Sri Ram Singh, was revered by Vikram but was rude to Phoolan. When she complained, Vikram told her she had to learn to defend herself: "Hit him and pick up your rifle." Vikram then asked if she wanted to go kidnap her husband Puttilal, so Phoolan led the gang to his house where she beat him up, using her hands, her feet, and her rifle butt. She broke his arms and legs and left him tied to his wife Vidya. Phoolan also left a letter for the police, claiming responsibility.

But Sri Ram Singh's arrival brought nothing but trouble. When Vikram was shot by Sri Ram's accomplice Lala Ram, Phoolan managed to get the wounded Vikram to his brother's house, where a doctor took the bullet out; then the pair rented a room in Kanpur while he recovered for three months. Phoolan noted she felt safer there than she had in years. Though she had become famous in the area, no one knew what she looked like, and the couple wandered freely through town. The peace was shattered when they read in the newspapers that two of their gang had been killed by the police. When the couple returned to the group, Sri Ram set up an ambush. On the night of August 13, 1980, Vikram was shot and killed while he slept next to Phoolan. She had been with him for exactly one year.

For the next three weeks, held captive in a house in the small village of Behmai, Phoolan was raped several times a night. Finally an old priest in the village, who would later be killed by Sri Ram, helped her escape and handed her a 12-bore rifle. Managing to evade a swarm of police, she made her way to the home of her mother's cousin. After resting there, Phoolan joined another gang for the next six months, becoming friends with Man Singh. Though she warned him that she found physical contact with a man now unbearable, in October 1980 the two formed an independent group, the Phoolan Devi-Man Singh gang. Man Singh also treated her as an equal and left her alone. Phoolan, determined to avenge Vikram's death, thought of nothing else. She now carried a .303 Mauser rifle and was a crack shot.

In December 1980, her gang raided 90 homes in Baijamau, the town that housed the upper-caste Thakurs, the caste of her rival Sri Ram. During the raid, she was ruthless, pushing Thakur men and women around, threatening to kill their children, and making herself the most "wanted" of bandits. Lower castes had never before threatened the upper-caste for power. As everyone in Phoolan's gang, now 21 strong, came from lower castes, the people of the village of Sindaus were sympathetic and sheltered them, and they were warmly welcomed in the town.

She convinced another gang to join her on a daring daylight raid in Jangamajpur, a town unknown to them but known for its police force. Fifty gang members entered the town, rounded up wealthy hostages, probably Thakurs, looted the bazaar of gold jewelry, liquor, clothes, and distributed much of it to the poor. After an hour's gun battle with the police, they escaped across the river. By now, the police had increased their numbers, determined to wipe out the *dacoits*; as well, the press had picked up the story of the killing of Vikram Mullah. The government placed a reward of 50,000 rupees on the head of Phoolan Devi, dead or alive.

The gang went on a crime spree: they continued to rob Thakur villages; hijacked lorries by shooting out tires or halting drivers while dressed as police; stopped and robbed the Lucknow Mail express train late one night; and relieved 12 Japanese tourists of their cameras and valuables. Then the gang heard that Sri Ram Singh and Lala Ram would be attending a wedding in the isolated ravine village of Behmai, population 400, a town dominated by Thakurs. The villagers had long sheltered Sri Ram and Lala Ram. Once more, in revenge for Vikram's death, Phoolan called on the services of another gang and entered the village.

The Behmai massacre took place on February 14, 1981. Taken to the banks of the river, 22 Thakur men were shot in the back, as their wives and children listened from their doorways. Only two men survived. The massacre caused a furor in the country and in the national and international press. Thakurs of Uttar Pradesh demanded the head of Phoolan Devi and pressured Indira Gandhi with their large rural vote.

Phoolan has admitted to raiding the village, but she has long claimed that she was not at the massacre site at the banks of the river, though Man Singh admitted being there. Members of her gang back her up. In their book *Devi*, Richard Shears and **Isobelle Gidly** write that the two survivors told them they did not see Phoolan Devi at the river, that the leader of another gang, Ram Avtar, gave the orders to shoot. Said Phoolan:

> It is true that I wanted to avenge Vikram's death. . . . I wanted to kill Sri Ram and Lala Ram but they were not among the dead, as you know. I do not believe in killing people without a positive reason but the situation got out of control and, in the eyes of [the goddess] Durga Mata, I am innocent of these deaths.

Tried and condemned in the press, Phoolan Devi went from heroine to ruthless killer.

She and another woman gang member **Meera Thakur** went into hiding, working as laborers on a building site in a small town, carrying headloads of bricks. No one yet knew what Phoolan looked like. After the women split up, Meera was killed in an encounter with Uttar Pradesh police. Her body was stripped and paraded through a small town, much to the outrage of press and public. "Why naked?," asked an official of Gwalior. "Would they have done that to a man?"

The Uttar Pradesh police became death squads: within six months, more than 700 bandits or suspected bandits had been killed, 5,000 arrested. Meanwhile, the real bandits hit back, killing villagers and police in an orgy of blood. Along with Man Singh, Phoolan was surrounded in the town of Galauli and barely escaped. The couple managed to elude another ambush at Chaurela.

In dealing with the poor, it is a common police practice in India to take a family member hostage. Moola, Phoolan's mother, was jailed for six months as bait; the police also punched and slapped Moola's schoolboy son to force her to remember where her daughter was. Moola was beaten in jail, once hit so hard she needed stitches. As a last resort, they tried to buy her off. "My only crime is that I gave birth to her," Moola told them. They finally released her.

It was the superintendent of police (SP) of Bhind, Rajendra Chaturvedi, who sought Phoolan Devi out and negotiated the terms of capitulation. She was to surrender at a formal ceremony in the market town of Bhind on February 12, 1983. At her insistence, she would only submit to Chaturvedi and asked that pictures of the goddess Durga and Mohandas Gandhi adorn the stage, so that in spirit her surrender would be to them. But overcome with fever the night before, her behavior before the ceremony was erratic. "I was very angry and disturbed and had not eaten for three days," said Phoolan. "I cursed anyone who came before me and I would throw any object within my reach. My extreme anger coloured my vision and I could not see reason."

As Phoolan Devi was now a national legend, thousands turned out to watch her surrender. Her exploits were celebrated in song, statues of her in police uniform were sold in the markets. At the surrender, the woman called Daysu Sundari (beautiful bandit) climbed up onto the 23-foot-high platform built for the occasion, with a red shawl over her khaki uniform and a red bandanna around her head. Man Singh and six others of her gang followed. She turned to the crowd, raised her rifle over her head, then presented it to the portraits of Durga and Gandhi. The crowd's sentiments were mixed: some saw her as a heroine, others as a representation of the incompetence of the law. In the chaos of that day, she enraged journalists with her furious answers in a press conference. She went from "Avtar of Kali" to "Bandit Brat" and "Neurotic Nymphomaniac." Wrote Sen:

> Much of what was printed about Phoolan Devi at the time reflected the nature and prejudice of the men who wrote the articles. For some strange reason, few women covered the story. . . . Some bizarre pieces appeared in various national newspapers.

Many journalists seemed offended by her appearance, disappointed by the physical stature of this "short and dark" woman. They had written that she was six feet tall, and of unsurpassed sexual prowess. Worse, she did not appear thankful to the media for building her into a legend. (Eventually two movies would be released about her. Some claim that a third was near completion when Phoolan sent the producer a note, saying that if she did not like the film she would shoot him. The third was not released.)

Once locked up, authorities would not let anyone in to interview her. Mala Sen asked relatives to visit Phoolan in prison and write down her life story. It took three years for various scribes to painstakingly take down her words, handwritten in Hindi, narrating her side of the events. Phoolan spent 11 years in prison without being convicted. Two years after her release, she was elected to the federal Parliament on a Samajwadi Party ticket in 1996.

SOURCES:

Esquire. October 1985.

Sen, Mala. *India's Bandit Queen: The True Story of Phoolan Devi*. London: Harvill, 1991.

Shears, Richard, and Isobelle Gidly. *Devi: The Bandit Queen*. Hampstead: George Allen & Unwin, 1984.

RELATED MEDIA:

Two movies have been made: *Outlaw, Phoolan Devi* and *The One with Courage*.

Phryne (c. 365–c. 295 BCE)

Greek artist's model who inspired the artists Appeles and Praxiteles. *Pronunciation: FRIN-ih. Born Phryne near Thebes around 365 BCE; died in Athens, at nearly 70 years of age, around 295 BCE; mother was an unknown worker on a Theban chicken farm; father was a passing army officer.*

Modern-day art students look upon the work of Classical Greece and see only the perfection of white marble. In their own time, the statues were vividly painted—the skin tinted in flesh tones, the hair powdered with gold, the eyes inlaid with precious jewels and the toes and lips blushed red. The loss of this color affects the modern viewer, as the statues from antiquity seem cold. There were real models for these statues, however, who contributed not only their face and form but their personalities. One of the most beautiful and most notorious of these was Phryne.

Phryne was born in the mid-4th century BCE, some 40 years after the end of the Peloponnesian War, when Spartan hegemony was threatened by the rebirths of both Athens and Thebes as major Greek powers. In 371, Sparta tried to reclaim Thebes, but the Thebans resisted and the Spartan force was routed. According to tradition, it was a soldier from one such battle who stopped for the night at a chicken farm on the outskirts of the Theban city-state, fathered a baby girl and then left the mother to raise her. Without a father, the baby, whom history knows as Phryne, remained outside the typical Greek family hierarchy. The basis of the *polis* (city-state) was the *oikos* (household), a strictly run patriarchal affair, tied both to clan and to tribal origins. Perhaps her uncle took charge of the girl and noticing her extreme beauty decided to make the most of it. Whether he kidnapped her or simply found a better use for the fatherless girl is unknown, but Phryne was sold as a slave to the hetaerae (courtesans) in Athens by the time she was 15.

Athens in 350 BCE was still the center of Greek culture. Plato's Academy flourished and attracted students like Aristotle who came to study there when he was 17. The Theater of Dionysus witnessed the performance of plays by Sophocles, Euripides and Aeschylus. Art became more realistic as it moved from idealized portraits of gods and men to more natural figures. In addition to its cultural status, Athens was a political leader. In 351 BCE, Athenians like Demosthenes perceived a threat in the ruler of Macedonia, Philip II. Sent to Thebes as a youth to solidify a truce, Philip had absorbed the best of Theban military expertise, an expertise he would adopt and use in his invasion of Greece in 338.

When Phryne reached Athens, however, the city was still enjoying a heyday of wealth and culture; but unlike life in the Golden Age of Pericles, neither the "golden mean" nor the universal man were in vogue. Excess and specialization were the bywords of the day, and those with a gift could find someone to pay their price. In general, women in Athens were outside of this power structure, kept secluded in the gymnaceum, or women's quarters. Most women led very private lives, though the poor, slaves and traders moved freely around the city. In some cases, older, higher status women also had this freedom. Without doubt, however, the hetaerae and intellectuals filled a very special niche in Athenian life. Many hetaerae were considered foreign-born, which meant they came from another city-state besides Athens. Most were classed as courtesans or high-class prostitutes, despite the fact that many evidently fulfilled roles far beyond that of mere sexual partners. Usually unmarried, these women assumed a place in Athenian society not shared by any other group of women. Their independent status was outside the *oikos* and operated in society in their own interest, or sometimes, in the interest of their male companion. Many hetaerae were very well educated, like Pericles' companion ***Aspasia**, the reputed author of his funeral oration, but others played a more typical part as courtesans or entertainers. Phryne's role was that of a model for the most famous artists and sculptors in 4th-century Athens.

At 15, Phryne was only a slave in the ranks of the hetaerae and, therefore, not well placed in either society or in the villas climbing up to the Acropolis. But women slaves and entertainers in Athens who performed well could buy their freedom, and either retire, open a brothel to train other courtesans, or serve as attachés to male business associates. Phryne, intent on earning enough money to buy her freedom, was born

Phryne

with a beautiful body, and it was that body that attracted the most famous painter of the day, Appeles. Stories vary on how he came to notice her. One claims that she chose the day of the Neptune Beach Festival to walk naked into the sea in front of the male population of Athens. Another presents a more subdued version: Phryne was accustomed to bathing twice a day in the public baths; on one such occasion, Appeles spied her and asked her to model for him.

Appeles painted her for his masterpiece, *Aphrodite Emerging*, which has been lost since antiquity. However, contemporary reports lauded both the painting and the beauty of its Aphrodite. The painting was seen by Praxiteles, the foremost Athenian sculptor, who enthused, "If Venus came back to earth she would have the body of Phryne." Praxiteles was then at the forefront of a new type of art, a natural flowing sculpture that emphasized sensuality and beauty. His works invoked a curvilinear voluptuousness that caused its viewers to ponder whether it truly "quivered with life." This immediacy was achieved by working from a live model, and that model was Phryne. He fell in love with her and gazed longingly at her as he tried to "entrap the contours of the love he felt." Desiring her to work exclusively for him, the sculptor formed a relationship with the model that furthered both their careers. Praxiteles became famous, while Phryne became rich. She once woke her lover in the middle of the night to tell him the studio was burning. When he told her to save the statue of Cupid, she surmised that it was the most valuable statue in the studio and later asked for it as a gift. She then sold it for a high price to Caius Caesar.

Commissioned to sculpt an Aphrodite for the city of Cos, Praxiteles naturally used Phryne as the model. The first statue was draped, as was the tradition for representations of the gods, but then Praxiteles became creative. By inventing the nude female statue, he captured Phryne for all antiquity. When both statues were submitted, Cos rejected the nude. Soon, however, the statue was bought by the city of Cnidus and became the famed *Aphrodite of Cnidus.*

If Venus came back to earth she would have the body of Phryne.

—**Praxiteles**

The statue and, by extension, its model were considered the most beautiful in Greece. Mythical Aphrodite herself is supposed to have commented, "Oh! ye Gods! where could Praxiteles have seen me naked?" The king of Bithynia offered to pay the debt of Cnidus in exchange for the statue, but the city refused to sell the prize. "Men . . . speak of [the statue] exactly as if she were a living woman of overwhelming beauty," wrote one contemporary. "One youth, carried away by excitement, leapt up on to the pedestal and threw his arms around the neck." Rapidly, the worship of the goddess and the worship of the model became interwoven. Praxiteles went on to portray Aphrodite arising from the sea many times, while Phryne went on to become a cult figure. Her beauty was viewed as a divine gift, and she would be the only woman ever granted permission to dedicate a golden statue of herself in the Temple of Delphi. The inscription read, "To Phryne who inspired all artists and lovers."

By 335 BCE, Phryne was extremely wealthy. That year, Aristotle opened his school in Athens, and Alexander III the Great destroyed Thebes, killing 6,000 Thebans and selling 20,000 more into slavery. Thebes had dared to lead a rebellion of the Corinthian League against Alexander, who at 20 had just inherited the throne upon the assassination of his father in 336 BCE. Two years before his death, Philip had secured his hold on the Greek city-states and left his son the legacy. The example Alexander made of Thebes was so graphic that no other city dared to revolt. Phryne offered to rebuild the city if a plaque would be inscribed over the gates that read, "Destroyed by Alexander but rebuilt by Phryne."

Though gifts and adulation brought riches, they also aroused jealousy. Phryne ended up on trial for her life, accused of impiety; she was reputed to have made derogatory comments about the Athenian matrons who participated in the Eleusian rites. These mother goddess cults were the only "outside activity" allowed to the average woman in the city-state. The matrons participated in the late-night worship as their one role free from patriarchal control. They took umbrage at Phryne's derision. Others say her problems were caused by male models in Athens who had hoped to become the muse for Praxiteles and found their position usurped by a woman, both publicly and privately. Whatever the case, Phryne found herself facing trial on May 10, 318 BCE, before an all-male jury in the court of the Areopagus.

One of her rejected suitors, Euthais, was the prosecutor for the state, while a young lawyer named Hyperide represented the model. The evidence of the state included a work of art by Praxiteles, *The Weeping Wife and the Laughing Harlot.* Phryne was reputed to be the model for the harlot laughing at the wife and in doing so demonstrating the triumph of lust and extravagance over virtue and steadfastness. The accusations of Euthais were fervent, and the citizenry was antagonistic. At a loss for a rebuttal, Hyperide, who was probably her new companion, put Phryne on the stand, then removed her tunic exclaiming, "You who would worship Aphrodite, take a look at her who the Goddess of Love could claim as sister. Send her to her death if you dare." The stunned jury cried out in amazement and summarily acquitted her.

By this time, Phryne was beyond her prime, though she was still courted and admired. She lived for several more years, a wealthy and successful hetaera. Meanwhile, the *Aphrodite of Cnidus* was considered a synonym for absolute perfection. Later generations can only guess at its beauty by viewing Roman copies that merely hint at the sensuality and "aliveness" of the original. And, by extension, posterity can get only a glimpse of the woman who inspired one of the greatest pieces of art work in history as well as the convention of the female nude. An obscure young woman, born in ignominy, sold into slavery as a young teenager, she used her talent, beauty and brains to climb to the highest rank of the hetaerae, the most educated and "liberated" class of Athenian womanhood.

SOURCES:

Boulding, Elise. *The Underside of History: A View of Women Through Time.* Vol. I. Newbury Park, CA: Sage, 1992.

De La Croix, Horst, Richard G. Tansey, and Diane Kirkpatrick. *Art Through the Ages.* Vol. I. 9th ed. San Diego, CA: Harcourt Brace Jovanovich, 1991.

Janson, Horst Woldemar. *History of Art.* NY: Harry N. Abrams, 1986.

Segal, Muriel. *Painted Ladies.* NY: Stein and Day, 1972.

Uglow, Jennifer S., ed. *The International Dictionary of Women's Biography.* NY: Continuum, 1982.

Michaela Crawford Reaves,
Professor of History, California Lutheran University, Thousand Oaks, California

Phuc, Kim (c. 1963—)

One of the most enduring symbols of the tragedy of the Vietnam War. *Name variations: Phan Thi Kim Phuc. Born around 1963; attended college in Cuba; married in 1992; children: two.*

In 1972, as the Vietnam War raged, nine-year-old Kim Phuc's village near Trang Bang was bombed with napalm. With her clothes burned off her body by the napalm, she ran naked from her village, her arms outstretched, screaming in agony. The Pulitzer Prize-winning photograph of her at that moment, taken by photojournalist Nick Ut before he hurried her to a hospital, is perhaps the best-known image of the Vietnam War, and is considered symbolic of the horrors suffered by innocent bystanders during that lengthy and controversial conflict.

Kim Phuc required extensive surgery for her injuries and continued to receive treatment for the scars and burns covering much of her body well into adulthood. The Communist government of Vietnam used Phuc as a tool of propaganda, though it eventually allowed her to study in Cuba. After marrying a fellow student there, in 1992 she sought political asylum in Canada, where she and her husband settled in Toronto and had two children. In 1996, Phuc appeared at a Veterans Day ceremony at the Vietnam Memorial in Washington, D.C.—her first visit to the site—and laid a wreath at the memorial. She spoke to the 2,000 spectators of hope and forgiveness, but, in keeping with the enduring controversy that surrounds the war, news of her appearance sparked renewed argument in America about whether the United States military or the Vietnam Air Force was responsible for the bombing of her village. In 1997, Phuc founded the Kim Foundation to assist noncombatants victimized by war. That same year, she was named a Goodwill Ambassador for a Culture of Peace by the United Nations Educational, Scientific and Cultural Organization (UNESCO).

SOURCES:

The Baltimore Sun. December 14, 1997.

The Day [New London, CT]. November 12, 1996, pp. A1, A4.

SUGGESTED READING:

Chong, Denise. *The Girl in the Picture: The Story of Kim Phuc, the Photograph, and the Vietnam War.* NY: Viking, 2000.

Howard Gofstein,
freelance writer, Oak Park, Michigan

Pia of Sicily (1849–1882)

Duchess of Bourbon-Parma. *Name variations: Maria Pia of Sicily. Born on August 2, 1849; died on September 29, 1882; daughter of Ferdinand II, king of the Two Sicilies (r. 1830–1859) and* ****Theresa of Austria*** *(1816–1867); married Robert, duke of Bourbon-Parma, on April 5, 1869; children:* ****Marie Louise of Parma*** *(1870–1899); Ferdinand (b. 1871); Louise of Parma (b. 1872); Henry (b. 1873); Maria Imaculata (1874–1914); Joseph (b. 1875); Maria Theresa (b. 1876); Maria Pia (1877–1915); Beatrix of Parma (1879, who married Count Pietro Lucchesi); Elias (b. 1880); Anastasia (1881–1881); Auguste (b. 1882).*

Piaf, Edith (1915–1963)

France's greatest popular singer of the 20th century, whose tragic life made her an interpreter of the lives and loves of ordinary men and women and whose ability to perform despite near-fatal bouts of illness became legendary. *Pronunciation: aye-DEETH pYOFF. Born Edith Giovanna Gassion on December 19, 1915, in Paris, France; died at Plascassier (Alpes-Maritimes) of cirrhosis and hepatitis on October 10, 1963 (some sources erroneously cite the 11th), and was buried at Père Lachaise Cemetery; daughter of Louis-Alphonse Gassion (1881–1944, a contortionist) and Anette Giovanna Maillard (1895–1945, a singer under the name Line Marsa); had a year or two of schooling in Bernay (Eure); married Jacques Pills, in 1952 (divorced 1957); married Théo Sarapo, in 1962; children: (with Louis Dupont) daughter, Marcelle (1933–1935).*

Cured of blindness by a purported miracle (1921); sang in the streets of Paris (1930–35); discovered by Louis Leplée (1935); questioned in Leplée's murder but recovered her career (1936); Raymond Asso got her an appearance at the A.B.C. music hall (1937); had a sensational run at the Bobino (1939); starred in Cocteau's Le Bel Indifférent *(1940); sang for*

French POWs in Germany (1942–43); promoted Yves Montand (1944–46); made New York debut (1947); had affair with Marcel Cerdan (1947–49); began her addiction to morphine and other drugs after two auto accidents (1951); starred at the Olympia (1956, 1958); collapsed in New York, and at Dreux after a "suicide tour" (1959); had a sensational run at the Olympia after long illnesses (1961); made another triumphal return to the Olympia (1962); made last Paris appearance, at the Bobino, and last performance, at Lille (1963).

Selected discography (of some 300): "Chand d'habits" (Alfred-Bourgeat), "L'Étranger" (Monnot, Juel-Malleron), "Les Mômes de la cloche" (Scotto-Decaye), "Mon amant de la Coloniale" (Juel-Asso), all 1936; "Browning" (Villard-Asso), "Mon Légionnaire" (Monnot-Asso), both 1937; "C'est lui que mon coeur a choisi" (d'Yresne-Asso), "Elle fréquentait la rue Pigalle" (Maitrier-Asso), "Le Fanion de la Légion" (Monnot-Asso), "J'entends la sirène" (Monnot-Asso), "Le Mauvais Matelot" (Dreyfus-Asso), all 1938; "Paris-Méditerranée" (Cloërec-Asso), "Je n'en connais pas la fin" (Monnot-Asso), both 1939; "L'Accordéoniste" (Emer), "Le Grand Voyage du pauvre nègre" (Cloërec-Delanoë), "On danse sur ma chanson" (Poll-Asso), all 1940; "C'était un jour de fête" (Monnot-Piaf), "Où sont-ils, mes p'tits copains?" (Monnot-Piaf), both 1941; "C'était une histoire d'amour" (Jal-Contet), "Histoire de coeur" (Monnet-Paif), both 1942; "Le Brun et le blond" (Monnot-Contet), "De l'autre côté de la rue" (Emer), "Y'a pas de printemps" (Monnot-Contet), all 1943; "Regardez-moi toujours comme ça" (Monnot-Contet), 1944; "C'est marveilleux" (Monnot-Contet), "Je m'en fous pas mal" (Emer-French), "Un refrain courait dans la rue" (Chauvigny-Piaf), "Les trois cloches" (Villard-Herrand), "La vie en rose" (Louiguy-Piaf), all 1946; "Un homme comme les autres" (Roche-Piaf), 1947; "Bal dans ma rue" (Emer), "Pour moi tout seule" (Lafarge, Monod-Gérard), "Le Prisonnier de la tour" (Blanche-Calvi), all 1949; "La Fête continue" (Emer), "Hymne à l'amour" (Monnot-Piaf), "Il fait bon t'aimer" (Glanzberg-Plante), all 1950; "Le Noël de la rue" (Heyral-Contet), "Padam . . . Padam" (Glanzberg-Contet), both 1951; "Bravo pour le clown" (Louiguy-Contet); "L'Effet que tu me fais" (Heyral-Piaf), "Johnny, tu n'est pas un ange" (Paul, Stellman-Lemarque, Roberts), all 1953; "La Goualante de pauvre Jean" (Monnot-Rouzaud), "Sous le ciel de Paris" (Giraud-Dréjac), both 1954; "C'est à Hambourg" (Monnot-Delécluse, Senlis), 1955; "Les Amants d'un jour" (Monnot, Delécluse-Senlis), "Autumn Leaves" (Kosma-Prévert, Mercer), "L'Homme à la moto" (Leiber-Stoller, Dréjac), all 1956; "Comme moi" (Monnot, Delécluse-Senlis), "La Foule" (Cabral-Rivgauche), "Les Grognards" (Giraud-Delanoë), "Les Prisons du roy" (Gordon-Rivgauche), "Salle d'attente" (Monnot-Rivgauche), all 1957; "Je sais comment" (Bouquet-Chauvigny, Bouquet), "Mon manège à moi" (Glanzberg-Constantin), both 1958; "Milord" (Monnot-Moustaki), 1959; "Les Amants merveilleux" (Veran-Gall), "Les Blouses blanches" (Monnot-Rivgauche), "Les Flons-Flons du bal" (Dumont-Vaucaire), "Mon Dieu" (Dumont-Vaucaire), "Les Mots d'amour" (Dumont-Rivgauche), "Non, je ne regrette rien" (Dumont-Vaucaire), all 1960; "Les Amants" (Dumont-Piaf), "C'est peut-être ça" (Dumont-Vaucaire), "Exodus" (Gold-Marnay), "Toujours aimer" (Dumont-Rivgauche), all 1961; "A quoi ça sert l'amour" (Emer), "Le Diable à la Bastille" (Dumont-Delanoë), both 1962; "La Chant d'amour" (Dumont-Piaf), "L'Homme de Berlin" (Laï-Vendôme), both 1963.

A tiny figure, barely 4'10", and weighing less than 90 pounds, moonfaced, chalky white, with a broad forehead, wide-set eyes, and auburn hair cut in bangs (later in life a thinning, frizzy mop), garbed always in a short black dress and wearing a small gold cross, her feet firmly planted, her arms and hands at her sides, gesturing only sparingly while belting out a song in a voice which could be heard for a city block—this was Edith Piaf, a giant in the world of popular music whose recordings decades after her death at 48 continued to sell in huge numbers. She was (and doubtless will remain) the greatest exponent of a French specialty, the *chanson réaliste*—songs in the form of minidramas telling of the lives and especially the sad loves of humble folk, the people of the streets. That she herself was a product of those harsh streets and lived a life full of woe and heartbreak added immeasurably to her appeal, which transcended all class boundaries. Hundreds of thousands of people (by some estimates up to two million) lined the streets of Paris to view her cortege on its way to Père Lachaise cemetery. Piaf was in every way a phenomenon, one of the true *monstres sacrés* of the entertainment world in the 20th century.

Legends grew up around her life which she did nothing to dispel. She seems to have believed most of them, in fact, beginning with the tale that she was born on the streets, literally—on a gendarme's cape in front of no. 72, rue de Belleville, in a working-class locale, when her impoverished mother could not get to the hospital in time. There is even a plaque there attesting to the "event," but in truth she was born at the Hôpital Tenon in the grimy faubourg of Ménilmontant.

Edith Piaf

Edith's parents were entertainers. Her mother **Anette Giovanna Maillard** was the daughter of Auguste-Eugène Maillard, a circus worker, and his Algerian Muslim wife, **Emma ("Aïcha") Saïd ben Mohamed**. Edith's father, Louis-Alphonse Gassion, son of a circus performer, was a 5' tall acrobat and contortionist who performed on streets and at fairs. Anette and Louis-Alphonse were married in 1914 when he went off to war. Edith, born on December 19, 1915, owed her un-French name to the heroic British nurse ***Edith Cavell**, who had been executed by the Germans as a spy. Edith's mother soon left her to the slovenly care of Aïcha in order to pursue a life on the streets as a singer. Piaf never really forgave her mother, despite half-hearted attempts on both sides for a reconciliation. Line Marsa, as she called herself, lived on the fringes, singing in cheap clubs and getting jailed time and again for drunkenness and drug abuse. When Edith became famous, her mother would come by now and then for a grudging handout. She died in 1945 of a drug overdose; her frightened boyfriend, a fellow addict, left her on the street rolled up in a blanket.

Although by ordinary standards Edith's father would be termed neglectful, he did see to her care when he was in town; they never lost touch, and Piaf always expressed a sincere love for him. Probably when she was six or seven years old—establishing a firm chronology before she was discovered in 1935 is all but impossible—her Aunt "Zaza" (Zéphoria, Louis' sister) found her living with virtually no care and took her, with Louis' consent, to their mother, who was a cook in a brothel in Bernay in Normandy. Edith lived at the "house" for a year or so, during which time another event occurred surrounded by legend. By some accounts, including her own, she was at Bernay for several years from around the age of two or so, had arrived there blind, and was cured by a miracle following a visit by her and the girls of the brothel (who doted on her) to the shrine of Saint ***Thérèse of Lisieux**. Even if it were only a sudden recovery from a severe case of conjunctivitis, as others have surmised, Piaf always maintained she had indeed been blind and been cured by Saint Thérèse—toward whom she thereafter observed a special devotion. She also noted that whenever she wanted to reach down to bring a song out of her "guts," she would close her eyes to "see" it better.

Sometime around 1922–23, she left Bernay, where she had gotten her only taste of formal schooling, and joined her father on the road through France and Belgium. She did odd jobs for him and, in time, became part of his act by singing a song or two. She learned how to size up an audience, get their attention, and live by her wits on the street. At about age 15, she cut loose to make a living on her own, traveling around Paris and its environs, often with a companion or two, sometimes getting permission to sing for soldiers in barracks. She had a close friend who would come in and out of her life many times thereafter, **Simone ("Momone") Berteaut**, a girl who claimed to be one of Louis' reputed 30 illegitimate children (he was a champion womanizer) and thus Edith's half-sister. After Piaf's death, Berteaut wrote an international bestseller which detailed a tangle of truth and fiction about every phase of Piaf's life and spawned numerous libel suits.

When not singing, Edith and Momone worked at sundry jobs as housemaids, assembling car headlights for Pile Wonder, making funeral wreaths, and varnishing army boots at Topin & Marguet. Once while singing on a corner, Piaf entranced an unemployed construction worker and errand boy, Louis ("P'tit Louis") Dupont. They moved in together, and in February 1933 she gave birth to a daughter, Marcelle. Piaf soon lost any taste for playing mother in a one-room garret and took to the streets again, leaving the baby in the care of Louis or a landlady, although never outright abandoning her. In fact, sometimes she trundled her along on her rounds, wresting a few more *sous* from a pitying public. As she drifted apart from Louis, she had a short, sad affair with a member of the Foreign Legion, which she later claimed, falsely, had inspired Raymond Asso to write her hit *Mon Légionnaire*. Tragedy followed in the summer of 1935 when Louis found her to tell her that Marcelle was ill with meningitis. The child died. To pay for a funeral, Edith got help from some friends, but the money they raised fell ten francs short. In desperation, she prostituted herself for the money, although, according to her other version, the customer, when she described her plight, just gave her the money and walked out, leaving her eternally grateful.

During these years, Edith had become immersed in the Paris underworld. Though promiscuous, she refused to become a prostitute; but she did fall into a relationship with a pimp, Albert, who "protected" her while taking a cut of her singing earnings. She would also spy out nightspots where women with money hung out so he could entice them away and rob them. Eventually she broke with him when one of his henchmen tried to turn a friend of hers, a sweet girl from the provinces, into a prostitute. The girl was found floating in the Seine. In revenge, Albert then tried to shoot Piaf in a bar but only grazed her neck when a man jostled his arm. And so it went—a directionless, sordid existence of singing on corners and in the seediest dives, one-night stands with sailors, brawls, and binges.

Then one day, as if she were the heroine of the most banal melodrama, she was discovered by a passerby while singing on a corner and was set on the road to stardom. The time was October 1935; the place, the corner of the avenue MacMahon and the rue Troyon near the Arc de

Triomphe; the man, Louis Leplée, proprietor of Gerny's, a club just off the Champs-Élysées on the rue Pierre Charron which was currently popular with the smart set. He gave her an audition, said she looked like a *piaf* (Parisian argot for "sparrow"), and a week later, after some quick tutoring, introduced her: "Direct from the street, Kid Sparrow [*la Môme Piaf*]!" She was dressed in a black skirt and a pullover with a scarf hiding a sleeve she hadn't finished knitting. The audience listened in a silence, which lasted for many agonizing seconds after she finished, and then broke into an ovation, Maurice Chevalier himself half-rising to cry, "That kid has what it takes!" She was launched.

Her first year of notoriety was a rollercoaster ride. She made recordings, sang in a film (Jean Lumir's *La Garçonne*), and even sang at a benefit gala, at the Cirque Medrano on February 17. But on April 6, 1936, Leplée was murdered at home, apparently for money by some hoodlums to whom she had probably introduced him. The police grilled her at length, but the crime went unsolved. Leplée's death devastated her personally, and for several months she was ostracized and forced to perform out of town (Brest, Nice, Brussels) or in bistros and between shows at suburban movie theaters. In the autumn, however, the threat of a return to the streets lifted when she got a ten-week radio contract at Radio-Cité and was taken in tow by Raymond Asso (1901–1968), a former shepherd, soldier, and factory manager turned lyricist and currently secretary to the celebrated **Marie Dubas**. In the three years they lived together, Piaf made him famous while he made her a star. He wrote songs for her—often with music by **Marguerite Monnot** (d. 1961), a song composer of genius, classically trained by ***Nadia Boulanger**, who later wrote *Irma la Douce*—but even more important, Asso coached Piaf endlessly, showing her how to behave in polite society, present herself as a professional, and completely master the art of seamlessly welding music to a text, the essence of the *chanson réaliste*. He also made her study other singers—**Damia** (Marie-Louise Damien), **Fréhel**, and above all Marie Dubas, for whose artistry she always expressed the highest admiration. In 1937, Piaf was asked to appear at a gala at the Vélodrome d'Hiver celebrating the Popular Front, but it was when Asso finally persuaded **Mitty Goldin** to put her on in March at the A.B.C., the top music hall in Paris, that she definitively became a star. And she was now Edith–no longer "la Môme"–Piaf.

In 1938, she gave her first formal recital, at the Alhambra, and in 1939 her run at the Bobino music hall caused a sensation. Her recordings sold in bales, composers and lyricists sought her out, and club, music hall, radio, and touring contracts abounded. The war did her career no harm. She recorded and performed in the best venues. Finding she needed more of her own material, she also began to write lyrics. From 1941 to 1943, she lived in relative comfort in an apartment over a fancy bordello much frequented by the Germans. A patriot who enjoyed a special bond with military personnel, she refused to perform in Germany but did receive permission to sing for French POWs held there. She would have her picture taken with them; the photos then would be cropped and used on false identity cards which she would smuggle back to the prisoners for use if they could escape. In 1945, the National Committee of the Theatrical Purge cleared her of any charges of collaboration "with congratulations."

Meanwhile, in 1939 she had left Asso (although she always acknowledged her great debt to him) and taken up with a singer, Paul Meurisse, for two years. Jean Cocteau, with whom she had formed a deep friendship, portrayed their troubled affair in a two-character one-act play, *Le Bel Indifférent,* in which Piaf and Meurisse appeared; she had the only speaking role while Meurisse remained stonily silent. It ran for three months in 1940 to critical applause and launched Meurisse as an actor. The play drew the attention of Georges Lacombe, who cast her in a film, *Montmartre-sur-Seine* (1941). Henri Contet, a publicist on the film and budding lyricist, replaced Meurisse in her life for a year and wrote several of her most successful songs then and later. In the summer of 1944, she met a young "cowboy" singer, Yves Montand, and proceeded to change his style completely. In 1945, they appeared in Marcel Blistène's *Étoile sans lumière,* her favorite film role. Montand, who was starring by 1946, was one of a number of talents she would launch, among them singers Charles Aznavour and Eddie Constantine and the Academy Award-winning composer Francis Laï, once her accordionist.

In 1945, she wrote the words and refrain to her greatest international hit, "La vie en rose." Ironically, one of her few happy songs (a sweetly sentimental piece), she wrote it for another singer, Roland Gerbeau, and recorded it in 1946 only after **Marianne Michel** had done so. Piaf also discovered "Les Compagnons de Chanson" in 1945 and went on tour with these nine young male folksingers. Their 1946 recording of "Les trois cloches" (in English, "Jimmy Brown's Song") was an immense success. It was with them that she first appeared in New York, on October 30, 1947. Audiences liked the group but didn't know what to make of Piaf since her short black dress and repertoire of sad songs did not fit their image of an entertainer from "Gay Paree." Virgil Thomson on the front page of the *Herald-Tribune* educated the public about the tradition she represented, and she finished her stay with triumphant runs at the Club Versailles and the Waldorf-Astoria. She grew to love American audiences, and from then through the 1950s she returned almost yearly, mostly touring the coasts—New York, Washington, Miami, Las Vegas, San Francisco, Hollywood. She also toured in South America. Oddly, she never had much success in England.

A terrifying little sleepwalker who sings her dreams to the air on the edge of a roof.

—Jean Cocteau

It was during her first New York appearance that she became seriously involved with the European middleweight boxing champion Marcel Cerdan, whom she had first met in Paris in 1946. Cerdan was married, and his handlers managed to keep their affair out of the press, though it soon was an open secret. Piaf fell deeply in love with this kind, calm, affectionate man. She was present when he defeated Tony Zale for the world championship on September 21, 1948. When he lost the title to Jake LaMotta the following June, his managers blamed her for "distracting" him. Later that fall, Edith begged Marcel to fly to New York to join her. His Air France plane crashed in the Azores on October 29, 1949. That evening, Piaf went onstage at the Versailles and dedicated her program to his memory. His death devastated her. A superstitious person who believed in the occult, she "communicated" with him for three years through table-tapping seances. Characteristically, too, she met and reconciled with his widow and helped support their three sons.

Cerdan's death and two 1951 automobile accidents, the second of which broke an arm and several ribs, appear to have shoved her strongly down the self-destructive path she had traveled for years. She became addicted to the morphine she received after the accidents, setting off a battle with drug abuse complicated by her longstanding addiction to alcohol. She nevertheless continued to record, appeared in a musical, *La P'tite Lili* (written by Marguerite Monnot and Marcel Achard, 1951), and in five films—*Paris chante toujours* (Pierre Montazel, 1951), *Si Versailles n'était conté* (Sacha Guitry, 1953), *Boum sur Paris* (Pierre Montazel, 1954), *French-Cancan* (Jean Renoir, 1954), and *Les Amants de demain* (Marcel Blistème, 1958).

Opposite page

Edith Piaf

Concert dates and tours, however, became sporadic because of repeated collapses and hospitalizations for cirrhosis, hepatitis, bleeding stomach ulcers, pancreatitis, and detoxification. She also began to suffer from severe arthritis. Her comebacks became legendary. In 1956, she returned to the Paris stage after a two-year absence with a three-month triumph at Bruno Coquatrix's Olympia, now the top venue. On January 13, 1957, she gave a Carnegie Hall recital, and in 1958 she broke all records in another three-month Olympia run. A third auto accident followed on September 6, 1958. (She herself did not drive a car.) From then through 1959, after collapsing at the Waldorf-Astoria in late February, she spent much of the year in hospitals and convalescing—only to collapse again, at Dreux on December 14, 1959, after a "suicide tour" taken in defiance of all advice.

Her endless, chaotic love affairs had continued apace. After liaisons with two professional cyclists, André Pousse and Louis ("Toto") Gérardin, she had married a successful singer, Jacques Pills, in Paris on July 29, 1952, and had a church wedding in New York on September 20, with her close friend ***Marlene Dietrich** as her attendant. Jacques treated her well, but the pressures of their careers and her drug problems led to a divorce (May 16, 1957). After that, there were affairs with a singer, Félix Marten; the art gallery director André Schoeller; lyricist Georges Moustaki, who wrote one of her greatest successes, "Milord" (1959); Douglas Davis, an American painter who did her best portraits; and, in 1960–61, composer and singer Charles Dumont, who wrote a string of hits including her last "signature" song, "Non, je ne regrette rien" (1960).

Piaf's last four years were a kaleidoscope of hospitalizations, recuperations, and miraculous comebacks. A legion of press "ghouls" tracked her everywhere, hoping to be the first to report her death. In 1960, despite a three-month hospitalization for cirrhosis and yet another auto accident that broke some ribs, she made more recordings than in any other year of her life and capped that with a wildly sensational return to the Olympia for a long run, beginning on December 29 with a performance which won 22 curtain calls. In 1961, she underwent operations on May 24 and June 9 for internal ailments but continued recording. On June 15, 1962, she sang in public for the first time in more than a year and again won a great success. In mid-August, she became ill in Besançon while on tour, but on September 27 she tottered onto the Olympia stage, barely able to stand—by now she needed injections before every performance, and periodic transfusions—and received a five-minute ovation before singing a note. She then proceeded to prove that her voice had lost nothing whatever of its impact.

On the September 27 program, she was joined by her latest love, Théo Sarapo, a Greek hairdresser 20 years her junior whom she had made into a decent singer. They were married in an Orthodox ceremony on October 9. She loved "this man who could have been the son I never had," and he repaid her with a touching devotion through her last year. On February 22, 1963, she made her last Paris appearance, at the left-bank Bobino before an audience containing many of the working people who adored her. The ovation went on for 20 minutes. Her last performance was at Lille on March 18, and she made her final recording, "L'Homme de Berlin," in April before being hospitalized again. She spent her last summer on the Riviera in villas and the Cannes hospital, finally succumbing in a rented villa in a hamlet, Plascassier (near Grasse), shortly after 1 PM on October 10, 1963. Her body was secretly rushed by ambulance to her boulevard Lannes apartment so that it could be "officially" announced on October 11 that she had—of course—died in Paris. Learning of her death, Jean Cocteau, who phoned her frequently during her last months, died a few hours later. More than 80,000 people filed by her casket at her home, and on October 14 some 40,000 swarmed into Père Lachaise cemetery, where a disorderly scene ensued. The Catholic Church refused a mass because she had remarried, but permitted a priest to offer graveside prayers. The Foreign Legion, for whom she was a kind of mascot, sent a detachment to present arms. That weekend, her records sold out in Paris—300,000 of them.

In one of her last songs, "Le Droit d'aimer" (F. Laï/R. Neyl, 1962), she sang: "I have the right to love. . . . I have won this right through the fear of losing everything, at the risk of destroying myself to keep love alive. I have paid for this right." Who could deny it? Her well-publicized tribulations were a foundation of her art and touched a universal chord. She said of Marie Dubas that she could make people laugh or cry "while I can only make them cry." But she capitalized on this limitation. Her power owed much to the fact that she was in her person and themes a representative figure of the troubled era (especially in France) of the Great Depres-

sion, the Second World War, and the postwar existentialist wave. And she was able to remain an evocative and even living presence because her career coincided with the explosion of the recording industry, thus bequeathing her voice to posterity.

Piaf's voice was distinctive: warm, throaty, husky, with a rapid vibrato and quite narrow tonal range, but running through it a strand of brass enabling her to be heard in the farthest seats. Her voice and stage presence had the ability to hit audiences "in the gut"—the most common description of the effect. But there were also the words, which to her were more important than the music, words which (as Cocteau put it) "appear to have no source, no author; they seem to spring quite naturally from the very macadam of the streets." She could barely read music but could learn a song in three hearings. That was only the beginning, however, for she worked endless hours with her composers and lyricists to perfect every feature of the notes and words. In practicing and performing, she was guided solely by her instincts. If she sensed that she was beginning to sing mechanically, she would drop the song from her repertoire. "When I am singing I give it everything I have," she said, and in her ability to convey this intense sincerity lay the most obvious source of her success. At the same time, however, she was highly involved in the mechanics of stage presentation—accompaniment, lighting, props, her plain black dress—all of it meticulously designed to further (paradoxically) the image of spontaneity and simplicity. When all elements were in place, she was, as some described her, the most formidable stage presence in France since ***Sarah Bernhardt**.

Piaf's personality—the very wellspring of her artistry—was deeply marked by the trauma inflicted during her first 20 years. She was a cauldron of insecurities and contradictions. She had enormous willpower yet seemed unable to overcome self-destructive passions and addictions. She was a tiny tyrant, jealous and possessive, yet she admired other talented singers and helped a number to get started. She sang sad songs and was subject to severe depression, but she was sociable, loved a good time, and had a wonderful, hearty laugh. She needed people around her—"I'm frightened of solitude"—and had that bottomless need for applause and the love (however transient) of an audience so common among performers. She also knew the loneliness of the great star after the lights go out and the people go home. She was both streetwise and naïve. She made immense sums as one of the highest-paid performers ever, but she spent it heedlessly, or gave it away indiscriminately to people with sob stories, and died millions in debt. She worked hard and played hard, driven to live every day as if it were her last. She was superstitious, a believer in spiritualism, and late in her life joined the Rosicrucians. Although she did not attend mass, she prayed on her knees every night to Saint Thérèse of Lisieux and "sweet little Jesus." A child of the slums, she believed bathing was dangerous, drinking water was bad for you, red wine was good for children, and alcohol killed your "worms." Yet, while she had no formal education, she learned about classical music from Marguerite Monnot and loved Bach, Mozart, Beethoven, and the rest; and she read (on self-education binges) literary classics, history, and philosophy, Teilhard de Chardin being a favorite.

Piaf desperately wanted to be loved. This need doubtless was the source of her many liaisons. She always needed a man near her, remarking once on how comforting it is to hear a man's footfall in a house. She seemed unable to sleep well without a man next to her in bed. Her lovers agreed, however, that it was not sex she really wanted, but security. She always suspected that men did not really love her but only her name and what she could do for them. "I've always searched feverishly for the great love, the true love," she said in an autobiography. She confessed she needed a protective, dominant man, yet she was driven to try to dominate him utterly. She seemed helpless to resolve this contradiction. Sadly, her search for the great love could only fail.

Edith Piaf's passions doomed her—save for one: her passion for singing. That passion was her truest. Through the last tragic decade of her life, it kept her alive. It transformed her before her death from a great performer into a legend.

SOURCES:

Berteaut, Simone. *Piaf*. Paris: Opéra Mundi, 1969 (Eng. trans.) NY: Harper & Row, 1972.

Costaz, Gilles. *Edith Piaf*. Paris: Éditions Seghers, 1988.

Crosland, Margaret. *Piaf*. NY: Putnam, 1985.

Druker, Don. "The Nights of Edith Piaf: A Short Biography of Edith Piaf." Soundprint Media Center, 1995.

Gillen, Henry. "Les ancêtres d'Edith Piaf," in *Heraldique et Généalogie*. Vol. 3, no. 3, 1971, p. 86.

Noli, Jean. *Edith*. Paris: Éditions Stock, 1973.

Piaf, Edith. *The Wheel of Fortune*. Trans. by Peter Trewatha and Andrée Massoin de Virton. Philadelphia: Chilton Books, 1965 (originally published as *Au bal de la chance*. Préface de Jean Cocteau. Paris: Éditions Jeheber, 1958).

———, with Jean Noli. *My Life*. Trans. by Margaret Crosland. London: Peter Owen, 1990 (originally published as *Ma Vie*. Paris: Union Générale d'Éditions, 1964).

SUGGESTED READING:

Blistène, Marcel. *Au revoir, Edith*. Paris: Éditions du Gerfaut, 1963.

Boisonnade, Euloge. *Piaf et Cerdan: L'amour foudroyé*. Paris: Éditions France-Empire, 1983.

Bret, David. *The Piaf Legend*. London: Robson, 1988.

*Flanner, Janet. *Paris Journal, 1956–1964*. NY: Harcourt Brace Jovanovich, 1965.

———. *Paris Was Yesterday, 1925–1939*. Edited by Irving Drutman. NY: Viking Press, 1972.

Gassion, Denise. *Piaf ma soeur*. Paris: Guy Authier, 1977.

Grimault, Dominique, and Patrick Mahé. *Piaf-Cerdan: Un hymne à l'amour, 1946–1949*. Paris: Laffont, 1983.

Hiégel, Pierre. *Edith Piaf*. Paris: Éditions de l'Heure, 1962.

Lange, Monique. *Histoire de Piaf*. Paris: Éditions Ramsay, 1979.

Le Breton, Auguste. *La Môme Piaf*. Paris: Éditions Hachette, 1980.

Monserrat, Joëlle. *Edith Piaf et la chanson*. Paris: Éditions PAC, 1983.

David S. Newhall,
Professor Emeritus of History, Centre College,
author of *Clemenceau: A Life at War* (Edwin Mellen, 1991)

Picasso, Paloma (1949—)

French designer and daughter of Pablo Picasso. *Born in Paris, France, on August 19, 1949; second child and only daughter of Pablo Picasso (1881–1973, an artist) and Françoise Gilot (b. 1922, an artist); studied jewelry design and fabrication at a school in Nanterre, France; married Rafael López-Sanchez (a playwright-director, divorced 1999); married Eric Thevennet (a gynecologist), in February 1999.*

"As a child, I was so shy some people never heard the sound of my voice," said Paloma Picasso, who successfully emerged from her shell to become a top jewelry designer for the prestigious Tiffany and Company as well as an arbiter of fashion among the international set. Indeed, the docile second child of Pablo Picasso and ***Françoise Gilot** was described as a "perfect girl-child" by her famous father, who had little to do with her or her older brother Claude's upbringing, although he sketched and painted them constantly. Paloma, who spent the first four years of her life at Picasso's villa "La Galloise" in Vallauris, has fond memories of her father, despite their limited time together. She recalls occasionally spending the day sketching beside him, although she was not allowed to touch his brushes or paints. "You can touch with your eyes," he would tell her.

After 1953, when Picasso and Gilot separated, Paloma and Claude went to live in Paris with their mother, although they summered with their father at his new villa near Cannes. This arrangement came to an end in 1961, when Picasso married ***Jacqueline Roque** who forbade her husband to see any of his children. After that, Paloma saw her father only twice, literally bumping into him by chance, once in Paris and a second time on the Riviera.

At 18, Paloma began to make her mark with the *beau monde* of Paris. Petite (5'2") and slim, with dark hair, enormous brown eyes, and a profile reminiscent of her father's classical drawings, she had an adventurous flair for clothes, many of which she scavenged from Paris' flea markets. (Her appearance at a dinner party wearing a red turban and black dress with shoulder pads, à la ***Joan Crawford**, supposedly inspired fashion designer Yves St. Laurent to create a collection of 1940s revivals.) Paloma set out to become a jewelry designer after a newspaper erroneously credited her with designing some necklaces for a stage production; in reality, she had borrowed the jewelry from the Folies-Bergères. In 1969, after studying jewelry and fabrication at a school in Nanterre, Paloma was commissioned by St. Laurent to design a line of fashion jewelry. As her career was getting under way, she designed furs for Jacques Kaplan and gold jewelry for Zolotas, a Greek firm. She also dabbled in the cinema, appearing in Walerian Borowczyk's *Immoral Tales* (1974), a film offering four stories concerning sexual obsession. Paloma, as the 17th-century Hungarian countess in the vignette "Erzebet Bathory" (***Elizabeth Bathory**), was cited mainly for her magnificent figure and beautiful face. The film won the Prix de l'Age d'Or and was released in the United States in 1976.

Paloma's association with Tiffany was brokered by her long-time friend John Loring, who invited her to design a table setting for the store in 1979. Her "high-style, all-white end-of-summer-fantasy" was so successful that she was offered a five-year contract almost immediately. Her first collection of jewelry, distinguished by its unusual shapes and sizes, as well as by its bold colored stones, was launched in 1980. Some of the bracelets were called "as massive as buildings," and one reporter for *The New York Times* noted the "billiard-size balls of amethyst, lapis, and tiger eye dotted occasionally with pinhead diamonds." The price tags were also large, ranging from $800 to $43,000. "Nobody else makes jewelry that big that is real jewelry," Paloma said about her innovative use of large stones with gold. Notable among her later creations is the "Love and Kisses" line, consisting of a "XXOO" motif executed in gold or silver, and frequently decorated with diamonds. Fashioned into bracelets, earrings, pendants, and pins, the line has become a classic of modern design.

In 1984, Paloma branched out into perfume, creating a ten-product line bearing her name. "It is a fragrance for a strong woman like myself," she told the *New York Post*'s **Rosemary Kent** (March 26, 1984). Hoping to make a connection between her jewelry and the perfume, Paloma devoted much of her attention to the product's packaging, creating a crystal flask which serves as "a frame" so that the scent becomes "the jewel." The perfume, selling at $160 an ounce, was launched at a swank "coming-out dinner" held on New York's Upper East Side. She would later introduce a new Eau de Parfum, and a line of silk pastel handbags.

When Pablo Picasso died in 1973, leaving no will, Paloma, along with Claude, and **Maya Picasso**, Pablo's other child, filed a lawsuit for a share in the estate, estimated at $250 million, inclusive of some 16,000 works of art. Each of the heirs was awarded their choice from the collection, from which Paloma selected a group of dolls on which her father had painted a likeness of her face. Twenty percent of the estate, including works by Matisse, Renoir, and others from Picasso's private collection, went to the French government in lieu of estate taxes. The artwork became the basis of Paris' Musée Picasso, the world's third Picasso museum (the other two being in Barcelona and Antibes). Having celebrated her 15th year with Tiffany in 1995, Paloma continues to turn out exclusive designs for the venerable jewelry house. "I can't predict the future," she said, "but I do know I don't intend to stop designing."

SOURCES:

Beggy, Carol, and Beth Carney. "Names and Faces," in *The Boston Globe*. May 1, 1999.

"Fresh Fragrance from Paloma Picasso," in *Soap, Perfumery and Cosmetics*. Vol. 69, no. 1. January 1996, p. 7.

Moritz, Charles, ed. *Current Biography*. NY: H.W. Wilson, 1986.

"A Perfect Pair," in *Town & Country*. Vol. 149, no. 5186. November 1995, p. 114.

Pichler, Karoline (1769–1843)

Austrian author whose literary salon was the center of intellectual Vienna for several decades. *Name variations: Caroline Pichler. Born Karoline von Greiner in Vienna, Austria, on September 7, 1769; died in Vienna on July 9, 1843; daughter of Franz Sales von Greiner and Charlotte Hieronymus von Greiner; had one brother; married Andreas Pichler (a government official), in 1796 (died 1837); children:* **Elisabeth Pichler.**

Selected writings: Gleichnisse *(Parables, 1800);* Olivier *(1802);* Leonore *(1803);* Idyllen *(1803);* Ruth *(1805);* Agathokles *(1808);* Stille Liebe *(Quiet Love, 1808);* Frauenwürde *(The Dignity of Woman, 1818);* Die Belagerung Wiens *(1824);* Die Schweden in Prag *(1827);* Die Wiedereroberung Ofens *(1829);* Henriette von England *(1832);* Zeitbilder *(1840);* Sämtliche Werke (1820–1845, *comprises 60 volumes);* Denkwürdigkeiten aus meinem Leben *(Memorable Events of My Life, 4 vols., published posthumously, 1844);* Ausgewählte Erzdhlungen *(4 vols., 1894).*

Although her writings are largely forgotten, for four decades Karoline Pichler was one of the most influential personalities in the intellectual life of pre-1848 Vienna. In her own lifetime, three "complete editions" of her writings appeared in print, and her novels were eagerly read in German-speaking Central Europe and other countries, including France and Great Britain. Her posthumously published memoirs remain an important source of information on the Romantic era in Austria.

She was born in Vienna in 1769 to a family which belonged in social standing to the *Bildungsbürgertum* (educated middle class). The *Bildungsbürgertum* played a vital role in the Habsburg monarchy, providing that state with talented individuals who were not of the aristocracy but served its interests as loyal civil servants. Karoline's father Franz Sales von Greiner was born a commoner but had been knighted by Empress ***Maria Theresa of Austria** in 1771; later, he was named a court advisor and *hofrat* (privy counselor). He married **Charlotte Hieronymus (von Greiner)**, an orphan whom the empress had adopted. Maria Theresa's favorite reader, Charlotte read aloud not only literature but also letters and documents in German and several other languages, including French, Italian, and Latin.

Growing up in this environment, young Karoline was exposed to many cultures and ideas. On numerous occasions, she accompanied her mother on visits with the empress. These memories would still be strong in Pichler's mind in the early 1830s when in her last novel, *Elisabeth von Guttenstein*, she described Maria Theresa with warmth and affection as possessing: "beauty, charm, intellect, modesty, compassion, loyalty to the spouse, tender love for the children, [and] respect for what is right and virtuous."

Despite the excellence of her education (largely conducted by private tutors and informally by her mother), Karoline was expected to become a cultivated wife and loving mother. Reading, writing, and musical performance were acceptable, even fashionable, for women of the educated and propertied classes as long as they remained amateur activities. Following a dissolved engagement after an unhappy love, in 1796 she married Andreas Pichler, an official in the Habsburg court chancellery. The next year, she gave birth to her only child, a daughter Elisabeth. The death of Karoline's father in 1798 changed her life and that of her mother as well. With the loss of Franz's salary, the family, who had been living in their stately home in the heart of Vienna, was forced to move into a modest dwelling in the suburb of Alservorstadt. At this juncture, Pichler decided to submit to a publisher some works she had composed solely for her own pleasure.

From her earliest years, she had written poetry and prose. As early as 1782, she had seen a poem of hers published in the prestigious *Wiener Musenalmanach* (Viennese Almanac of the Muses). Andreas was supportive of her writing activities and persuaded her to revise a work entitled *Gleichnisse* (Parables), which was published in 1800 to considerable critical acclaim. Over the next decades, Pichler would write a number of highly popular novels, including *Leonore* (1803), *Agathokles* (1808), and *Frauenwürde* (The Dignity of Woman, 1818), as well as the novella *Stille Liebe* (Quiet Love, 1808). In *Agathokles*, she presented a vigorous critique of the anti-Christian slant of Edward Gibbon's *Decline and Fall of the Roman Empire*, thus reflecting the Romantic era's embrace of a conservative religiosity. Among the readers impressed by *Agathokles* were some of the literary giants of the day, including Johann Wolfgang von Goethe.

Over a period of almost four decades, Pichler published in many additional literary genres, writing verse, ballads, essays, and historical and patriotic dramas, as well as several Roman Catholic devotional books based on Fénelon's model. A number of her dramas were staged by Vienna's prestigious Burgtheater. In the final years of her life, she published two volumes of *Zeitbilder* (Pictures of the Times, 1839) which examined contemporary history in the form of fiction, at least in part to avoid some of the worst aspects of Habsburg censorship. The work was divided into two sections: one dissected Viennese intellectual and political life in the second half of the 18th century, the other in the first years of the 19th century.

In 1804, the Pichler finances had improved enough for the family, which included Karoline's mother Charlotte, to return to Vienna, and they moved back into her parents' old dwelling. Within a short time, both Pichler and Charlotte were heading one of Vienna's most important cultural and literary salons. Although it could never compete with such elegant houses as that of **Eleonore Fliess**, ***Fanny von Arnstein**, or Arnstein's daughter **Henriette** (Baroness Pereira), the Pichler salon quickly became a meeting place for the most illustrious Viennese intellectuals and artists. As a host, Karoline played an active role in these gatherings, carefully guiding conversations and making certain that a proper mixture of guests was present. Among the illustrious women who frequented the salon were ***Germaine de Staël** and ***Dorothea Mendelssohn** (Schlegel), who became one of Karoline's closest friends. Among the men were Franz Grillparzer, Nikolaus Lenau, Franz Schubert, Adalbert Stifter, and Wilhelm von Humboldt. Schubert set Pichler's poems "Der Unglückliche" (The Unhappy Man) and "Die Nacht" (The Night) to music as Lieder. Von Humboldt left a descriptive portrait of Pichler, calling her: "exceedingly ugly, but stimulating and animated, remaining all the while kindly, genial, and modest."

In addition to its literary and artistic function, the Pichler salon served a political function as well. As Austrian intellectuals redefined their national response to the challenge posed by the French Revolution and Napoleon, a synthesis of new ideas, both dynastic and German-nationalistic, were forged in the pleasant atmosphere provided by Pichler. As it became increasingly apparent that the nation's human resources would need to be more effectively harnessed to throw off the hated French yoke, Pichler made a number of public statements of interest. In her 1810 essay "Über die Bildung des weiblichen Geschlechts" (On the Education of the Female Sex), she argued for new roles for women in society, writing that, in an era of war and social upheaval, women's traditional security, found in the institution of marriage, was being revealed as fragile at best. She pointed to women's "educational ability and capacity for perfection in many areas," which should be developed so as to "make woman a more self-supporting and more useful being to the state than had been the case until now." Pichler concluded her essay with the confident assertion: "The well-educated woman will be—whether she marries or not—a highly valued human being—a complete person."

With the death of her husband in 1837, Pichler realized that she had entered the sunset of her life. As her physical strength waned, she was less able to maintain her salon at its previous level. Meanwhile, a significant change was taking place in Viennese social and intellectual life—a shift from the salon to the coffee house as the center of literary and political discussion. During these years, Pichler wrote her memoirs, which would be published posthumously in 1844 as *Denkwürdigkeiten aus meinem Leben* (Memorable Events of My Life).

In recent decades, Pichler has undergone reevaluation by scholars. Her later novels and historical dramas, which were traditionally seen as being little more than a narrow reflection of anti-Napoleonic Austrian patriotism, are now viewed as containing significant examples of psychological portraiture of the rapidly emerging Central European bourgeoisie of the first half of the 19th century. As a major representative of the essentially conservative Biedermeier Weltanschauung, Pichler can be seen as a significant author, as well as a woman who left her mark on history in a society that attempted to remain rigidly patriarchical. She died in Vienna on July 9, 1843.

SOURCES:

Becker-Cantarino, Barbara, and Gregory Wolf. "Caroline Pichler," in Donald G. Daviau, ed., *Major Figures of Nineteenth-Century Austrian Literature.* Riverside, CA: Ariadne, 1998, pp. 417–434.

Bittrich, Burkhard. "Österreichische Züge am Beispiel der Caroline Pichler," in Karl Konrad Polheim, ed., *Literatur aus Österreich, österreichische Literatur: Ein Bonner Symposion.* Bonn: Bouvier, 1981, pp. 167–189.

Görlich, Ernst Joseph, ed. *Madame Biedermeier.* Graz: Stiasny, 1963.

Hacken, Richard D. *Into the Sunset: Anthology of Nineteenth-Century Austrian Prose.* Riverside, CA: Ariadne, 1999.

Heyden-Rynsch, Verena von der. *Europäische Salons: Höhepunkte einer versunkenen weiblichen Kultur.* Munich: Artemis & Winkler, 1992.

Jansen, Lena [Helena Cornelia Theodora]. *Karoline Pichlers Schaffen und Weltanschauung im Rahmen ihrer Zeit.* Graz: Wächter-Verlag, 1936.

Kord, Susanne. "'Und drinnen waltet die züchtige Hausfrau'? Caroline Pichler's Fictional Auto/Biographies," in *Women in German Yearbook: Feminist Studies in German Literature and Culture.* Vol. 8, 1992, pp. 141–158.

Leuschner, Brigitte, ed. *Schriftstellerinnen und Schwesterseelen: Der Briefwechsel zwischen *Therese Huber (1764–1829) und Karoline Pichler (1769–1843).* Marburg: Tectum, 1995.

Maresch, Maria. "Wiener Geselligkeit im Wandel der Jahre: Karoline Pichlers Salon—Der Treffpunkt des geistigen Biedermeier," in *Wiener Zeitung* [Vienna]. January 3, 1952, p. 3.

Maurach, Bernd. "Karoline Pichler: Unveröffentliches aus dem Nachlass Karl August Böttigers," in *Jahrbuch des Wiener Goethe-Vereins.* Vol. 89–91, 1985–87, pp. 323–325.

Prohaska, Gertrude. "Der literarische Salon der Karoline Pichler." Ph.D. dissertation, University of Vienna, 1946.

Robert, André. *L'idée autrichienne et les guerres de Napoléon: L'apostolat du baron de Hormayr et le salon de Caroline Pichler.* Paris: F. Alcan, 1933.

Stürzl, Erwin A. "Byron and the Poets of the Austrian Vormärz," in *The Byron Journal.* No. 9, 1981, pp. 34–40, 43–46, 49–51.

John Haag,
Associate Professor of History, University of Georgia, Athens, Georgia

Pickell, Ellen Liddy (1861–1889).

See Watson, Ellen.

Pickford, Mary (1893–1979)

Canadian-born film actress and first female studio executive whose ingenue screen persona captivated film audiences in a long series of Cinderella-style stories, many of which she wrote and/or produced. *Born Gladys Louise Smith on April 8, 1893, in Toronto, Canada; died on May 29, 1979, in California, of heart disease; eldest of three children of Charlotte and John Smith; married Owen Moore, in 1911 (divorced 1920); married Douglas Fairbanks (an actor), in 1920 (divorced 1933); married Charles "Buddy" Rogers (an actor), in 1937; children: (second marriage) one stepson.*

Began touring with a vaudeville company at age five, appeared on Broadway by the time she was 14, and in her first film at 16; became the highest-paid film actress up to that time, exercising nearly total control over her career; was among the four partners who formed United Artists Corporation (UA), a film distributor (1919); found her acting career languishing (mid-1920s) when she was no longer able to convincingly play ingenues and turned to more mature dramatic roles which were not well received; retired from the screen (1933) but remained actively involved in the business of film making into the 1950s; received a special Academy Award for her contributions to the industry (1976).

Filmography: various silent shorts (1909–12); The Unwelcome Guest *(1913);* In a Bishop's Carriage *(1913);* Caprice *(1913);* A Good Little Devil *(1914);* Hearts Adrift *(1914);* Tess of the Storm Country *(1914);* The Eagle's Mate *(1914);* Such a Little Queen *(1914);* Behind the Scenes *(1914);* Cinderella *(1914);* Mistress Nell *(1915);* Fanchon the Cricket *(1915);* The Dawn of a Tomorrow *(1915);* Little Pal Rags *(1915);* A Girl of Yesterday *(1915);* Esmeralda *(1915);* Madame Butterfly *(1915);* Poor Little Peppina *(1916);* The Foundling *(1916);* The Eternal Grind *(1916);* Hulda from Holland *(1916);* Less Than the Dust *(1916);* The Pride of the Clan *(1917);* The Poor Little Rich Girl *(1917);* A Romance of the Redwoods

(1917); The Little America *(1917);* Rebecca of Sunnybrook Farm *(1917);* The Little Princess *(1917);* Stella Maris *(1918);* Amarilly of Clothes-Line Alley *(1918);* M'Liss *(1918);* How Could You Jean? *(1918);* Johanna Enlists *(1918);* Captain Kidd Jr. *(1919);* Daddy Long Legs *(1919);* The Hoodlum *(1919);* Heart O' the Hills *(1919);* Pollyanna *(1920);* Suds *(1920);* The Love Light *(1920);* Little Lord Fauntleroy *(1920);* Through the Back Door *(1920);* Tess of the Storm Country *(remake, 1922);* Rosita *(1923);* Dorothy Verdon of Haddon Hall *(1924);* Little Annie Rooney *(1925);* Sparrows *(1926);* My Best Girl *(1927);* The Gaucho *(1927);* Coquette *(first sound film, 1929);* The Taming of the Shrew *(1929);* Secrets *(1933).*

Halfway through the 1976 Academy Award ceremonies, the star-studded proceedings paused for the more subdued presentation of the Academy's annual Lifetime Achievement Award. Its 83-year-old recipient was too ill to accept the award in person and had chosen instead to address the gathering via closed circuit television from her home. The surprise, even shock, was almost audible when the image of an emaciated, pale old woman wearing an ill-fitting wig flickered on the screen, speaking in a voice barely above a whisper. It was difficult to believe that she had at one time been "America's Sweetheart" and the film industry's first female studio executive.

Mary Pickford's career mirrored the explosive growth of "the flickers" during the first 30 years of the century. There was no film industry at all when she was born on April 8, 1893, in Toronto, Canada; and the screen name by which she would be known to millions lay some years in the future. John and **Charlotte Smith** named their first child Gladys Louise, born shortly after they moved into a working-class neighborhood of Toronto where John had found a job as a printer. Charlotte took in sewing to help support the family. By 1897, Pickford's sister Charlotte and brother Jack, Jr., had arrived. John had managed to save enough from his printing job by then to buy and run his own concession stand on a Lake Ontario ferryboat. One winter's day, late for supper and impatiently waiting for the boat to dock, John tried to jump the last few feet ashore, striking his head on a dangling pulley. He died only hours later of a fractured skull. Pickford was six, Lottie just three, and little Jack barely one year old.

For the next year, Charlotte and her three children struggled to survive, often depending on food given to them by neighbors. Pickford looked after the younger ones and kept house, while Charlotte tried to earn as much as she could from her sewing. Even when she began letting out rooms in the house to boarders, it was impossible to make ends meet. One of these boarders, a stage manager at a Toronto theater, suggested that she put the young ones to work on the stage, where there was always a demand for children as extras. By September 1898, Pickford had made her stage debut at Toronto's Princess Theater, playing both a girl and a boy in a long-forgotten melodrama, *The Silver King*. Later, when the same play was presented by another stock company, Charlotte astutely brought Pickford to an audition for the same two parts. She was promptly hired.

Pickford loved the theater from the first—the smells, the excitement, the audience's laughter and applause. For her, she said many years later, it was "an electric impulse, a definite vibration, a palpable bond." It was fortunate she took to the theater so naturally, for it rescued her family from destitution. Charlotte protected her children from the less desirable elements of the business and made life as normal for them as possible. "It was through my mother that I first learned what the term love really means," a very grownup Mary Pickford once recalled. "She diffused love in all directions, as a flower diffused perfume."

For nine years after her first appearance on a stage, Pickford trouped through Eastern Canada, the American Midwest, and the East in a long series of touring productions, many of them written and produced by entrepreneur Harold Reid. Reid took the entire Smith clan under his wing, often casting Charlotte in maid's roles and the two younger children as extras. But it was Pickford as "Baby Gladys" that audiences began to remember, especially in sentimental Reid productions like *The Little Red Schoolhouse* and ***Ellen Price Wood**'s *East Lynne*. By 1901, the program for a production of *East Lynne* announced that "the souvenirs tonight will be of Gladys Smith, the little tot whose work has been so much admired."

Although the family sometimes had to break up to follow different tour routes, they would usually be reunited for the off-season summers in New York, where many of the circuits ended. At the end of the 1907 season, after 10 years on the road, 15-year-old Pickford wanted a permanent home and all that went with one. "When I saw the things that other girls had," she remembered, "I determined to have them. I'd have a fur coat one day, and it would be warmer because I had known what it was like to have insufficient wraps." While Charlotte took the younger children back to Toronto, Pickford stayed with friends in New York, intent on becoming a famous actress. That meant Broadway; and to many starry-eyed actresses in 1907, Broadway meant David Belasco.

Belasco was one of the last Gilded Age theatrical managers and producers, known for lavish melodramatic productions like *The Return of Peter Grimm* and *Tiger Rose*, both of which would eventually be adapted by the upstart film industry. Belasco's style was perfectly suited to Pickford's experience from her road tours, but it took several months of letter-writing and fruitless visits to Belasco's office before the great man agreed to see her. He later admitted to being impressed at the determination shown by the blonde, curly-haired 15-year-old who, when he opened their interview with the rhetorical "So you want to become an actress?," promptly and proudly answered "I *am* an actress! I want to become a *good* one." It was Belasco who came up with a more memorable stage name by asking Gladys Smith to recite the names of her family members, stopping her when she mentioned her maternal grandmother, **Elizabeth Denny Pickford**. When Pickford also mentioned she'd always liked the name Marie, Mary Pickford was born. Mary hastily wired to Charlotte in Toronto: "Gladys Smith now Mary Pickford. Engaged by David Belasco to appear on Broadway this fall."

I have never been a happy woman. It is not my nature.

—**Mary Pickford**

The play was William De Mille's *The Warrens of Virginia*. Belasco was apparently satisfied with her work, especially noting that Pickford was the first to arrive and the last to leave rehearsals, even on days when her scenes were not on the schedule. "She would read and re-read her lines to find out which was the best way to speak them," he later remembered. "She was a very creative and highly intelligent little body." His only advice to her was to "always keep it natural." Since she was required at 15 to play a girl of 8, Pickford chose as her model ***Maude Adams**, who as a grown woman was famous for her portrayal of the youthful Peter Pan. Mary learned from Adams that "the facial muscles of the grownup are controlled, while those of a child only reflect passing moods," and that children hardly ever wrinkle their brows, even when surprised or afraid. It was observations like these that would serve her well under the more demanding eye of the camera. *The Warrens of Virginia* ran for two seasons—the first on Broadway during the winter of 1907–08, and the second on tour starting the following May. Pickford was paid $25 a week on Broadway, and given a $5-a-week raise for the road tour.

After the show closed, however, her career as "a Belasco girl" seemed to stall, there being no parts for her in any of Belasco's upcoming productions. Charlotte dreaded the thought of going back on the road, with its possibility of splitting up the family yet again, and suggested to Mary that a temporary source of income might be found down on 14th Street, where the American Mutascope and Biograph Company had just turned an old brownstone into a studio for producing moving picture shows. On a winter's day late in 1908, Pickford took the trolley downtown and met the man who would do more for her career than David Belasco ever could.

David Wark Griffith was a former actor who would transform what had been a novelty at peep shows and vaudeville halls into a powerful new method of storytelling. Although Biograph was just one of a handful of new companies hastily organized to take advantage of what was thought to be merely a fad, D.W. Griffith was among the first to see its real potential. By the time Mary arrived in the third-floor ballroom that was his makeshift studio, Griffith had been churning out one-reelers for more than a year. Even at this embryonic stage of her film career, Pickford showed a remarkable business sense by demanding, as "a Belasco actress," double the usual $5-a-day salary and a $25-a-week minimum. Griffith agreed. On April 20, 1909, Mary Pickford stepped before the camera for the first time in a one-reel comedy called *Her First Biscuits*.

The work was not much to her liking, particularly the lack of rehearsal time and the demands placed on her to produce an emotion in less than ten feet of hand-cranked film. But it was steady work, from nine in the morning to eight at night, six days a week; and she could add to her income by following the example of many others in Griffith's troupe and writing scenarios—$25 for a one-reel story and $50 for a two-reeler. During her first six months with Biograph, she was able to save $1,200—more money than she had ever had at one time in all her years of trouping on the stage. Over time, she grew to appreciate Griffith's genius for intuitive directing. "We just listened to his voice to get his feeling," she remembered. "[He] devised ways and means of bringing actors out of themselves." Even the informal atmosphere of the studio began to appeal to her, especially the attentions of a fellow actor, Owen Moore, much to Charlotte's disapproval. Within three months, the *New York Dramatic*

Mary Pickford

Mirror specifically mentioned "an ingenue whose work in Biograph pictures is attracting attention" in its review of *They Would Elope*. The anonymity was standard at the time, the film companies fearing that name recognition would inspire their actors to ask for more money. Even fan mail was torn up before it could reach them. Mary was known to the public only as "Little Mary" or "The Girl with the Golden Hair." During the summer of 1909, ***Florence Lawrence** ("The Biograph Girl," as the public knew her) was wooed away by another company. Griffith promptly made Mary the new Biograph Girl and the company's leading lady.

In less than a year, Pickford had appeared in 45 Biograph shorts and could count herself among the first group of motion picture idols, along with *****Mabel Normand**, Harry Carey, and *****Blanche Sweet**. One trade newspaper was sure that the success of Biograph's *A Romance of the Western Hills* "is in great measure due to this actress, and this is a particularly fine example of her art." But Pickford was shrewd enough to realize that her success lay in playing young girls and innocent sweethearts and that she would never be a great dramatic actress. Typically, she accepted her position and made the most of it. "I decided . . . to be a semiprecious stone," she said, "rather than a paste imitation of something more glittering and gorgeous."

In January 1910, Pickford made her first trip with Griffith's troupe to California for two months of work in what was then still a semi-rural backwater not yet called Hollywood. The "studio lot" was just that—a vacant lot at the corner of Grand Avenue and Washington Boulevard in what is now the Culver City section of Los Angeles. The entire cast and crew lived in a boarding house nearby. Owen Moore came west with the troupe after being warned by Griffith, who had caught them necking behind some scenery, to treat Mary gently. A year later, back in New York, she and Moore were married secretly to avoid Charlotte's anger, the two of them continuing to live apart until Pickford finally broke down and confessed. Charlotte and Biograph hid the marriage from the public, fearing it would stain Mary's screen persona as the innocent young virgin. There were also rumors that Pickford had suffered a botched abortion which had left her unable to bear children.

When Owen resigned from Biograph to join Carl Laemmle's Independent Motion Picture Company (IMP), Mary went with him. ("Little Mary's an IMP now!" crowed Laemmle in his advertising.) Pickford's reasons for leaving Griffith were more than romantic, however. Laemmle offered her $175 a week, which Moore jealously noted was more than his own salary. Several months later, Mary broke her contract with IMP, on grounds that she had been a minor when she signed it, and transferred her talents to Majestic Films, this time at an impressive $225 a week. But after only five films, shot in a drafty studio during a particularly cold Chicago winter, Pickford made amends and returned to Biograph in 1911, by which time her asking price had increased several fold. During her absence from Biograph, however, Griffith had discovered *****Lillian Gish**. In 1912, while she was shooting her last film for Biograph, *The New York Hat,* Pickford cabled David Belasco that she wanted to return to the stage. "I've been hiding in the pictures," she told him.

Belasco immediately cast her as the poor blind girl in his 1913 production of Rostand's *The Good Little Devil*, which was seen by a former fur seller from Chicago who had the idea of creating a film company that would bring famous plays starring famous stage actors to movie audiences. Adolph Zukor called his company Famous Players. His first production was *The Good Little Devil,* with Pickford reprising her stage role to such effect that Zukor signed her to a contract for three pictures over fourteen weeks at a salary of $500 per week. For Zukor, Pickford appeared in *The Bishop's Carriage, Caprice,* and *Uncle Tom's Cabin.* By 1914, Zukor had signed her to a full year's contract, at $1,000 a week, and Pickford had announced her formal retirement from the stage. "I'm in the movies for money," she bluntly told *Photoplay.* "In . . . three years and eight months [in motion picture work], I was laid off only four weeks." That same year, she starred in what everyone agreed was her finest picture to date, *Tess of the Storm Country,* although privately Mary disliked the movie. In one-sheets promoting *Tess*, Famous Players billed her by name as "American's foremost film actress."

Over the next six years, Pickford starred in some of the most famous silents of the early cinema, such as *Poor Little Rich Girl, Rebecca of Sunnybrook Farm, Suds,* and *The Little American.* Along the way, Zukor merged his company with Jesse Lasky's Feature Play Company to form Famous Players Lasky, while Pickford's salary went from Zukor's initial $500 per week in 1914 to an astounding $10,000 per week in 1916. The two-year contract she signed that year was a model of shrewd negotiating based on her new-found star power, for it included clauses giving her 50% of the net receipts of each of her films, with a guaranteed minimum of $1 million, and complete creative control over her productions, from writers to directors to casting. The studio was legally obligated to provide her with a secretary and a press agent, along with "parlour class accommodation" on her frequent cross-country train trips between New York and Los Angeles. Like the film industry itself, Mary Pickford was growing up.

Other actors were building star careers, too. Among them was Douglas Fairbanks, the dashing hero of such action films as *The Three Musketeers* and *The Thief of Baghdad*. Pickford and Fairbanks, who was also married, met frequently at social functions and premieres starting in 1914. By 1916, the two had become lovers, often meeting in secret at a house owned by Fairbanks' brother in the Hollywood Hills. But word was bound to leak out. Charlotte, who had tried to prevent Mary's marriage to Owen Moore, was now equally horrified at the possibility of a very public divorce; Moore himself, his career long eclipsed by that of his wife, began drinking to excess. In 1918, with the affair filling the newspapers, Fairbanks' wife **Beth** named Mary in public as her husband's paramour and demanded she step forward and admit it. Pickford called a conference with two friends, scriptwriter ***Frances Marion** and journalist ***Adela Rogers St. Johns**, to decide if her career could survive the scandal. Both of them assured her it would, for Mary's public was as much in love with her, they pointed out, as she was with Fairbanks. "More than anything else I had wanted desperately to be approved of," Pickford wrote many years later, "and that approval Douglas gave me. I had never believed anybody would speak of me, and to me, as he did." In 1919, Pickford began divorce proceedings in Nevada against Owen Moore, giving him $100,000 to hasten the proceedings; while Fairbanks gently persuaded his wife Beth to take similar action against him, citing "an unknown woman" as the cause of the separation. On March 28, 1920, little more than two weeks after her divorce from Moore became final, Pickford married Fairbanks at a private ceremony in Fairbanks' Hollywood home. As a wedding present, Fairbanks bought a rambling, rustic hunters' lodge in Benedict Canyon and remodeled it into a 22-room Tudor mansion he and Mary dubbed "Pickfair," which became a social center for much of Hollywood's artistic elite for the next two decades.

To add to the turmoil of this period, Pickford's long-standing argument with Zukor over "block-booking" of her films reached a critical point. It was Zukor's practice to lure theaters into booking a package of less successful films by using a Mary Pickford picture as bait; without taking the whole package, theaters couldn't have Pickford's film—a practice Mary, and others in similar situations at other studios, felt cheapened the value of their work. In 1918, she refused to renew her contract with Zukor and signed instead with First National Pictures, at a salary of $750,000. In return for the lower salary, First National agreed to book her films separately from any others and, more important, gave Pickford the right to set up her own film company—The Mary Pickford Company—with Mary as its creative head and Charlotte as its business manager. (With her financial acumen, Charlotte had invested most of Mary's earnings safely and wisely, a practice that would see Pickford comfortably through the Depression when other Hollywood stars lost their fortunes.) A year after her signing with First National, however, rumors began spreading that First National and Famous Players would merge to form a virtual monopoly controlling the production and distribution of filmed entertainment. The result of the merger was Paramount Pictures; the answer to it from Pickford and three other key creative Hollywood personalities was United Artists.

The formidable combination of Mary Pickford, Douglas Fairbanks, Charlie Chaplin, and Pickford's old friend D.W. Griffith was in the form of an independent distribution company, the stock of which was not released to each partner until the required number of films, produced at each partner's expense, had been delivered. It was a direct challenge to the near total control the studios held over the choice, production, and distribution of an artist's work. "The satisfaction was in one word: freedom," wrote Pickford. "It's a heady wine, and having tasted it you find it impossible to go back working for someone else." She delivered the first of her required three films a year, via her own company, in the form of her 1920 adaptation of ***Eleanor Porter**'s *Pollyanna,* which grossed well over $1 million worldwide. But there were problems with United Artists from the start. Charlie Chaplin, always meticulous about his films, didn't deliver a movie until 1923's *A Woman of Paris,* which fared badly at the box office and earned him Pickford's deepening displeasure as the years passed. Griffith, who brought the company some $8 million with his pictures in its first three years, was repeatedly rebuffed in his requests for production advances to complete his films, and left the company in 1924 to sign with Paramount. Efforts to increase United Artists' product by contracting films out to independent producers resulted in a string of financially unsuccessful pictures; and all the partners, including Pickford, repeatedly "roadshowed" their own films by renting a theater and opening a picture at their own expense, keeping all the revenue generated for themselves and dulling the market for the picture when it was handed over to UA.

But Pickford's films released during this period are among her best remembered—especially the adaptation of ***Frances Hodgson Burnett**'s *Little Lord Fauntleroy,* in which Mary played both the title role and that of the child's mother, and a remake of her earlier *Tess of the Storm Country.* She stuck to her money-making formula of playing the working-class sweetheart beset by adversity who triumphs in the end, although by 1927's *My Best Girl* critics were hinting that it might be time for a 35-year-old woman to stop playing 18-year-old girls. As if to emphasize the need for a change, the industry's first talking film, *The Jazz Singer,* took the country by storm. *My Best Girl* would prove to be Pickford's last silent picture, as well as her last appearance as a sweet young thing. On June 21, 1928, Pickford walked into a fashionable beauty salon on New York's East 57th Street and walked out two hours later with the short, bobbed, heavily lacquered hair of a Jazz Age flapper. Two months later, she began work on her first "talkie," in her first adult role.

Coquette was little more than a stiffly photographed version of a popular Broadway play of the time, the camera tethered to its new, immobile sound apparatus and separated from the actors by a windowed, soundproof wall. Pickford was convinced the public would never accept the sound of her voice ("That's not me!" she protested on hearing herself for the first time. "It's impossible!"), and she had gone through two directors and two sound technicians before the picture was released to great acclaim in April 1929. It grossed nearly $1.5 million during its run and earned Pickford the Academy's Best Actress award at its second annual ceremony. But *Coquette* would prove to be her last successful picture. Her only screen appearance with her husband, in a 1929 film adaptation of *The Taming of the Shrew,* made only a modest profit, while Pickford herself shut down production on her next effort, *Forever Yours,* commenting later that it was "the most stupid thing I ever saw, including me." She completed and released the film later under a new title, *Secrets,* but it still lost $100,000 at the box office.

Fairbanks' films were faring no better. Friends noted that he seemed to have lost interest in his screen career and was spending long periods of time away from Pickford, traveling around Europe on the pretense of making a travelogue while carrying on an affair with a former "chorus girl" from England. Pickford, too, had indulged in a series of *amours,* the longest running of which was with actor Buddy Rogers, who had played opposite her in *My Best Girl.* Rumors that her marriage was in trouble became so widespread that Mary was forced to answer *Photoplay*'s inquiry in 1931 by saying, "I cannot deny there may be a separation. I can only say there is none now." In June 1933, however, Pickford and Fairbanks were, indeed, legally separated. That same year, Mary officially announced her retirement from the screen and, for nearly a year, rarely left the isolation of Pickfair.

She briefly emerged in 1934 in a stage production of *Alice in Wonderland* (for which journalist Edmund Wilson claimed she had had a facelift) and in a weekly series of radio dramas which were indifferently received, as was a chat show replacement, "Party at Pickfair." Two spiritually inclined books, *Why Not Try God* and *My Rendezvous with Life,* along with the novel *Demi-Widow*—all ghostwritten from Pickford's notes—appeared in 1934 and 1935. But it was the film business that kept beckoning. "Let no one tell you they don't miss their career," she once wrote. "I miss it terribly. It's a constant ache with me." One solution was to form a new film company in partnership with Jesse Lasky, the Pickford Lasky Production Company, which released two unsuccessful pictures through UA in 1935 before being disbanded.

In June 1937, Pickford announced her third marriage, to Buddy Rogers, who had abandoned his sporadic acting career to form a band. Mary accompanied Buddy and his group on their road tours, and it was during a stop in Chicago that she received the news that Douglas Fairbanks had died. "My darling is gone," she was heard to whisper, for she and Fairbanks had remained close even after their separation. Gone with him was Pickford's most enduring link to the old, heady days of a Hollywood just discovering itself.

From now on, the public saw or heard Mary Pickford only in bond drives during the war years or in occasional guest spots on national radio. But Hollywood's business community heard from her often, for she continued to take a direct hand in the increasingly troubled affairs of United Artists. Throughout the 1940s and 1950s, with Pickford and Chaplin the only remaining partners, UA slid precariously closer to bankruptcy. Their continuing rift over business practices which had always been mediated by Fairbanks now grew wider. Pickford accused Chaplin of using United Artists as a private banking account for his infrequent films, while Chaplin complained that she was dictatorial and trying to force him out. A series of disastrous deals with outside producers resulted in ruinously expensive lawsuits and no new product. The ill feeling reached its nadir when Pickford allowed herself to be interviewed by the FBI during the McCarthy era, Chaplin being suspected at the time of Communist sympathies and eventually forced to flee the country. He never forgave her.

Halfway through 1949, UA had already hemorrhaged $400 million and was on the brink of bankruptcy. It was saved by a group of investors to whom Pickford signed over control of the company in 1951 and to whom she sold her remaining shares for around $3 million. She took some satisfaction from the fact that Chaplin had done the same, a year earlier, for little more than $1 million. (United Artists survived and even prospered under its new leadership and became part of MGM/UA Enterprises in 1981.) With the last vestige of her most productive period now gone, Pickford lived quietly and in increasing obscurity at Pickfair. Director Billy Wilder considered her for the part of Norma Desmond in his *Sunset Boulevard,* but after he realized that he could not bear to show "America's Sweetheart" as a faded, delusional movie star, the part went to ***Gloria Swanson**.

A lawyer who visited Pickford in the late 1950s described her as "a lovely person, but sad in some respects. Hollywood had sort of passed her by. She knew it, and didn't like it." Her name was kept alive through her generous donations to the Motion Picture Country Home and Hospital for indigent and retired entertainers, and by the announcement that she had given those of her films which survived, some 50 titles from her Biograph and Famous Players days, to the American Film Institute. Most of her remaining films shot on fragile nitrate stock had deteriorated beyond repair.

In a rare interview given in 1970, Pickford admitted that the film world had changed to such an extent that she knew she could never go back. "Making movies was fun," she said of her early days, "[but] there is not much fun today when one mistake can be fatal. In the old days, a star was loved through good, bad, and indifferent pictures. Today, three bad pictures and a star is finished." She hinted, too, that her memories were too fragile to withstand the brutal business of modern-day film making. "I think illusions are so important," she said. "That's why I haven't gone back to pictures."

Mary did not disclose that she had been diagnosed with advanced heart disease and that her strength was leaving her. Even so, on the night her frail image appeared before the Academy Award audience, she rallied sufficiently to request the camera crew to shoot only her left side so that the slight bump on her nose which had vexed lighting directors in the old days would not be apparent.

Among the last to see her was her stepson, Douglas Fairbanks, Jr., who was a frequent visitor to Pickfair after his father's death. "She would be talking," he once reported, "and I would suddenly realize that she thought I was my father. It was at those times that I realized that she always remained in love with him." On May 29, 1979, Mary Pickford died peacefully at a Santa Monica hospital, after lapsing into a coma at home.

At the Academy tribute held five months after her death, Douglas Fairbanks, Jr., reminded the audience that Pickford's great contribution to the industry had been her guardianship of creative rights. "It was her idea," he said, "that artists who created their own works from the beginning . . . should have the rewards due to them." But for Pickford, there was something even more precious. She recounted in her autobiography a visit to her native Toronto in 1944 during which she appeared before a group of adoring Air Force cadets about to go off to war. "It is good to have lived to know that after so many years off the screen," she wrote, "there were young men who could still pay me the sweetest and most gallant compliment of all—to ask me to be called their collective sweetheart."

SOURCES:

Eyman, Scott. *Mary Pickford: America's Sweetheart.* NY: Donald Fine, 1990.

Katz, Ephraim. *The Film Encyclopedia.* 2nd ed. NY: HarperCollins, 1994.

Pickford, Mary. *Sunshine and Shadow.* NY: Doubleday, 1955.

SUGGESTED READING:

Whitfield, Eileen. *Pickford: The Woman Who Made Hollywood.* KY: University of Kentucky Press, 1997.

Norman Powers,
writer-producer, Chelsea Lane Productions,
New York, New York

Pick-Goslar, Hannah (b. 1928).

See Frank, Anne for sidebar.

Pickthall, Marjorie (1883–1922)

Canadian poet and novelist. *Born Marjorie Lowry Christie Pickthall on September 14, 1883, near Middlesex, England; died on April 19, 1922, in Vancouver, Canada; daughter of Arthur C. Pickthall and Lizzie Helen Mary (Mallard) Pickthall; never married; no children.*

Selected works: (novels) Dick's Desertion: A Boy's Adventures in Canadian Forests *and* A Tale of the Early Settlement of Ontario *(both 1905),* The Straight Road *(1906),* Billy's Hero; or, The Valley of Gold *(1908),* Little Hearts *(1915),* The Bridge *(1922); (poetry)* The Drift of Pinions *(1913),* The Lamp of Poor Souls, and Other Poems *(1916),* The Wood Carver's

Wife *(verse drama, 1922),* The Complete Poems of Marjorie Pickthall *(1927),* Selected Poems *(1957); (short stories)* Angels' Shoes and Other Stories *(1923).*

Marjorie Pickthall, once considered the best Canadian poet of her time, has since slipped into obscurity. Born in Middlesex, England, in 1883, she immigrated to Canada with her family in 1899. Pickthall's talent manifested itself early; she sold her first story at age 15, and while in her early 20s published three juvenile adventure novels. Many of her early poems and stories were seen in *Atlantic Monthly*, *Century*, *Scribner's*, *McClure's*, and *Harper's*, as well as in Canadian newspapers. Pickthall supported her writing by working as a librarian at Victoria College, Toronto, during which she assisted in the compilation of the annual bibliography of Canadian poetry. In 1912, for health reasons, she returned to England, taking a cottage near Salisbury and working as an assistant librarian at the South Kensington Meteorological Offices. During World War I, she assisted the war effort by driving an ambulance. She returned to Canada in 1920, and died two years later of an embolism following surgery.

Pickthall achieved some success as a novelist, although she is best known as a premodernist poet. *The Drift of Pinions* (1913) and *The Lamp of Poor Souls, and Other Poems* (1916) are considered her best collections, containing works of delicate and ethereal quality, although critics found that her mystical references were sometimes difficult to analyze. She also wrote a verse drama, *The Wood Carver's Wife* (1922), which was performed in Montreal and at Hart House, in Toronto. Following Pickthall's death in 1922, her short stories were collected in several volumes, and a complete collection of her poetry, edited by her father, was published in 1927.

SOURCES:

Buck, Claire, ed. *The Bloomsbury Guide to Women's Literature*. NY: Prentice Hall, 1992.

Kunitz, Stanley J., and Howard Haycraft, eds. *Twentieth Century Authors*. NY: H.W. Wilson, 1942.

Barbara Morgan,
Melrose, Massachusetts

Pico, Caterina (d. 1501)

Noblewoman of Mantua. *Name variations: Caterina Gonzaga. Died in 1501; married Rodolfo Gonzaga (1451–1495); children: Luigi Gonzaga of Castelgoffredo and Castiglione della Stiviere.*

Picon, Molly (1898–1992)

Jewish-American actress, comedian, and singer. *Born on June 1, 1898, in New York City; died on April 6, 1992, in Lancaster, Pennsylvania; eldest of two daughters of Lewis Picon (worked in the needle business) and Clara (Ostrow) Picon (a seamstress); attended Northern Liberties School, Philadelphia; attended William Penn High School, Philadelphia, through her junior year; married Jacob Kalich (a theater manager), on July 29, 1919; no children.*

One of the most beloved figures of the Yiddish theater, the diminutive Molly Picon was the featured attraction at New York's Second Avenue Theater during its heyday between the 1920s and the 1950s. Her appeal, however, was not limited to Jewish audiences, and through vaudeville, Broadway, national and world tours, and appearances on radio and television, Picon became an adored performer the world over.

She was born in 1898 in a tenement in New York City, but grew up in Philadelphia, where the family moved when she was three and where her mother Clara worked as a seamstress for a Yiddish stock company. Her father Lewis, a former rabbinical student, was employed in the needle trade, although it was Clara who earned the bulk of the family income. Little Molly launched her career at age five, singing at an amateur night for children at a local theater and winning a $5 gold piece. At six, she was playing juvenile roles for a Yiddish stock company, and by the time she was a teenager, she was earning $15 a week singing between films at the local nickelodeon. Despite her blooming childhood career, Picon somehow managed to slip in an education, completing three years of high school before yielding completely to the lure of the theater.

During 1918–19, Picon perfected her singing and comedic skills on the vaudeville circuit, traveling from coast to coast in an act called "The Four Seasons." She played Winter, she explains in her autobiography *So Laugh a Little,* because she could do a Russian dance, and because she was the only one who owned a Russian costume. In 1919, she was hired by actor-manager Jacob Kalich, who was heading up a Yiddish stock company at the Grand Opera House in Boston. The two fell in love and married before the year was out, after which Kalich set out to make his talented new bride a star. For a European tour in 1921, he wrote the first of 40 vehicles he would create for his wife over the years, the operetta *Yankele,* or "a Yiddish Peter Pan," as she called it, featuring Picon in the role of a small boy. European audiences, accustomed to heavy musical dramas, were captivated by the humorous musical production and by its talented half-pint star. Upon her return to the United States in 1923,

Picon enjoyed another week-long run of *Yankele* at New York's Second Avenue Theater.

As it turned out, Picon's stay at the Second Avenue Theater stretched into seven years and included a string of starring vehicles written or adapted by Kalich, many featuring the juvenile characters that became Picon's trademark. Early productions included *Tzipke* (1924), *Shmendrik* (1924), *Gypsy Girl* (1925), *Rabbi's Melody* (1926), *Little Devil* (1926), *Little Czar* (1927), *Raizele* (1927), *Mazel Broche* (1928), and *Hello Molly* (1929). Although critics declared Picon enchanting, and frequently noted her skill as a mime, they often found her talent difficult to pin down. One noted her "superb use of voice, face, and hands," while another characterized her as having "the daintiness of a lady and the warmth of a street singer." In each production, Picon delighted her Yiddish following with something new, "walking a tightrope, tap dancing, doing a sleight-of-hand act, entering on a horse, playing a new musical instrument."

Picon would return to the Second Avenue Theater throughout her career, and in 1949, 25 years after her debut there, she appeared in *Abi Gezunt* ("So Long as You're Healthy"), which had the largest advance sale in the history of the Yiddish theater. It was followed by *Saidie Is a Lady* (1950) and *Mazel Tov Molly* (1950), a show based on Picon's life that was also written by her husband.

Picon's theater performances were interspersed with vaudeville and singing tours in the United States and abroad. In Europe, she performed in Yiddish, German, English, and French, depending on her audience. (As the guest of a tribe of Zulus in South Africa, Picon overcame the language barrier with an imitation of Charlie Chaplin.) It was not unusual for her to travel 35,000 to 50,000 miles a year; in 1931 alone, she performed in Berlin, Carlsbad, Bucharest, Vienna, and Paris, and in 1933, she was in Palestine, Poland, and Russia. During World War II, Picon toured the Army camps in the South in 1944 and 1945, and was one of the first entertainers to enter postwar Europe in an attempt to help lift the spirits of the surviving Jews. Picon performed in hospitals, orphanages, and displaced persons' camps, calling the experience difficult emotionally, but ultimately gratifying. "We heard people laugh who hadn't laughed in seven years," she said.

Picon appeared in her first English-speaking dramatic role on Broadway in 1940, performing the lead in *Morning Star*, an undistinguished drama in which she appeared to be the only bright note. More successful were her later shows: *For Heaven's Sake Mother*, *How to Be a Jewish Mother*, *The Front Page*, *Paris Is Out*, *Something Old, Something New*, and *Milk and Honey*, which ran for two seasons in the early 1960s. Picon continued to perform well into her 80s; in 1979, she wrote and appeared in the revue *Those Were the Days*. Molly Picon died on April 6, 1992, age 94.

Molly Picon

SOURCES:

Current Biography 1951. NY: H.W. Wilson, 1951.

Current Biography 1992. NY: H.W. Wilson, 1992.

Picon, Molly, as told to Eth Clifford Rosenberg. *So Laugh A Little*. NY: Julian Messner, 1962.

Willis, John, ed. *Theatre World 1991–1992*. Vol. 48. NY: Theatre Book, 1992.

Wilmeth, Don B., and Tice L. Miller, eds. *Cambridge Guide to American Theatre*. NY: Cambridge University Press, 1993.

Barbara Morgan, Melrose, Massachusetts

Picotte, Susan La Flesche (1865–1915).

See La Flesche, Susan.

Pierangeli, Rina Faccio (1876–1960)

Italian novelist, poet, and essayist. *Name variations: Rina Faccio; (pseudonym) Sibilla Aleramo. Born Rina Faccio in Alessandria, Italy, in 1876; died in Rome on January 13, 1960; daughter of Ambrogio Faccio and Ernesta Faccio; attended elementary school; married Ulderico Pierangeli; children: one son (b. 1895).*

Selected works: (novels) Una donna *(1906, published in English as* A Woman at Bay, *1908),* Il passaggio *(The Passage, 1919),* Transfigurazione *(Transfiguration, 1922),* Amo, dunque sono *(I Love, Therefore I Am, 1927),* Il frustino *(The Whip, 1932); (prose collections)* Andando e stando *(Going and Staying, 1921),* Gioie d'occasione *(Joys on Sale, 1930),* Orsa minore *(1938),* Russia alto paese *(Russia, Lofty Country, 1953); (poetry)* Momenti *(Moments, 1920),* Poesie *(Poems, 1929),* Si alla terra *(Yes to the Earth, 1935),* Selva d'amore *(Forest of Love, 1947),* Aiutatemi a dire *(Help Me to Say, 1951),* Luci della mia sera *(Lights of My Evening, 1956).*

Rina Faccio Pierangeli was born in Alessandria, Italy, in 1876, one of four daughters of **Ernesta Faccio** and Ambrogio Faccio, a science teacher. She received her only formal education, elementary school, while growing up in Milan. When Rina was 12, the family moved to Marches, a small town in southern Italy, where Ambrogio managed a glass factory and Rina spent her adolescence. Shortly after their arrival, she was raped by one of her father's employees. Shamed by the rape, she married her attacker Ulderico Pierangeli when she was 16. The following year, her mother was pronounced insane and confined in the Macerata asylum. Rina, who feared taking after her mother, spiralled into depression because of frequent physical assaults from Ulderico. Though Rina's son, born in 1895, was the focal point of her life, she attempted suicide in 1897. She continued to regard suicide as an escape from her husband until she read Guglielmo Ferrero's 1898 book *L'Europa giovane*, which described the typical Latin marriage as a prison sentence. She saw her own marriage reflected in the book and felt liberated by the feminist ideals she had encountered. Rina began to write and publish her opinions, and in 1899 the family moved to Milan so that she could edit the feminist journal *L'Italia Feminile*. In the urban environment, and with a new understanding of herself, Rina flourished. But her husband soon forced her to quit the post and return to Marches. In 1902, she left him and their son.

She went to Rome where she began an affair with Giovanni Cena, the director of the literary journal *La Nuova Antologia*. With Cena, she was to found and direct schools for the Russian countryside's illiterate peasants. Cena encouraged Pierangeli to write her life story, and in 1906 the autobiographical *Una donna* (A Woman) was published under the pseudonym Sibilla Aleramo. A great success, the work was soon translated into a number of European languages (its importance would be reasserted years later with a reprint in 1973).

In 1910, Pierangeli left Cena and began two decades of travel and affairs throughout Europe (including a romance with Tito Zaniboni, whose attempt on Benito Mussolini's life landed Rina in jail for two days in 1925). She published many works—novels, essays, and poetry—during the first half of the 20th century. Her prose collection *Gioie d'occasione* (Joys on Sale, 1930) won the Prix de la Latinité in Paris (1933), and her poetry collection *Selva d'amore* (Forest of Love, 1947) took the Versilia Prize (1948). Pierangeli also wrote two dramas—*Endimione* (1923) and the unpublished "Francesca Diamante"—and translated works by ***Marie-Madeleine de La Fayette** and Charles Vildrac, in addition to her translations of the love letters of ***George Sand** and Alfred de Musset.

Pierangeli was an active member of the Italian Communist Party from 1946 until her death, talking to groups of workers and farmers and giving poetry readings. Her political beliefs alienated most publishers, and she was sustained in a small attic room in Rome by a pension granted to her by Italy (1933). She had a ten-year affair with a student 40 years younger, but was alone when she died at age 83.

SOURCES:

Aleramo, Sibilla. *A Woman.* Berkeley, CA: University of California Press, 1980.

Bédé, Jean-Albert, and William B. Edgerton, general eds. *Columbia Dictionary of Modern European Literature.* NY: Columbia University Press, 1980.

Crista Martin,
fiction and freelance writer,
Boston, Massachusetts

Pierce, Mrs. Franklin (1806–1863).

See Pierce, Jane Means.

Pierce, Jane Means (1806–1863)

American first lady from 1853 to 1857 who never functioned in that capacity due to the loss of her third son in a train accident just weeks before her husband's inauguration. *Name variations: Mrs. Franklin Pierce; Jeanie Pierce. Born Jane Means Appleton on March 12, 1806, in Hampton, New Hampshire; died* *on December 2, 1863, in Andover, Massachusetts; daughter of Elizabeth (Means) Appleton and Rev. Jesse Appleton (president of Bowdoin College); married Franklin Pierce (president of the United States, 1853–1857), on November 19, 1834, in Amherst, New Hampshire; children: Franklin, Jr. (died three days after birth); Frank Robert (1840–1844); Benjamin (1841–1853).*

On January 6, 1853, Jane and Franklin Pierce witnessed the death of their 11-year old son Benjamin, when a train in which the family was traveling suddenly derailed. For Jane Pierce, ill with consumption and anguished by the previous loss of two other sons, this was the final blow. When her husband was inaugurated as president two months later, she was too weak with grief to accompany him to Washington.

Shy and delicate, "Jeanie" Appleton was born in Hampton, New Hampshire, in 1806, the daughter of **Elizabeth Means Appleton** and Jesse Appleton, a Calvinist minister and president of Bowdoin College. Jane grew up in a deeply religious New England environment, under the watchful eye of her father. Well educated but frail, she was deprived of exercise and fresh air because the reverend felt that these were inappropriate for girls. He died when Jane was 13, and the family moved to Elizabeth's family home in Amherst, New Hampshire. It was there, in 1826, that Jane met Franklin Pierce, a young law student. Although his devotion to her was clear, she and her family strongly disapproved of his drinking and his political ambitions. The couple did not marry until 1834, when Jane was 28. Dressed in the traveling clothes and bonnet she had been wed in, she and Franklin left immediately for Washington, where he would be installed as a newly elected U.S. congressional representative.

Franklin soon advanced to the Senate, but Jane hated Washington and spent as little time there as possible. The climate aggravated her fragile health, and the lavish evening parties went against her religious beliefs. Jane's absence and disapproval did not diminish her husband's political aspirations, but the death of their three-day-old son and the arrival of two others, Frank in 1840 and Benjamin in 1841, did. Concerned for his wife, Franklin left the Senate in 1842, at the height of his career, and retired to Concord, New Hampshire. When son Frank died of typhus two years later, Jane's spirit was further shattered. Franklin turned down President James K. Polk's offer of an appointment as attorney general because of Jane's ill health. Despite her protests, however, a restless Franklin enlisted in the Mexican War, returning in 1848, a general and a local hero.

The next four years were possibly the happiest in Jane's life. Her husband was home and their third son, Benjamin, was thriving. When Franklin was chosen as the presidential candidate of the Northern Democrats in 1852, Jane was so distressed that she is said to have fainted at the news. Young Benjamin evidently shared his mother's disdain for politics. He reportedly said to her, "I hope he won't be elected, for I should not like to be at Washington and I know you would not either."

Jane Means Pierce

When Jane was finally able to join her husband in the White House after the death of Benjamin, she spent most of her time in her bedroom, writing letters to her deceased son. Formal entertaining was presided over by her aunt **Abby Kent Means**, or by ***Varina Howell Davis**, second wife of the secretary of war. When Jane did appear, "her woebegone face, with its sunken dark eyes and skin like yellowed ivory, banished all animation in others." She became known as the "shadow in the White House."

While the slavery issue continued to polarize the nation, Franklin ended his political career by signing the Kansas-Nebraska Bill, opening the door for the election of James Buchanan in 1856. Leaving Washington, the Pierces toured Europe, but Jane longed for home. In later years, her depression increased and her health declined further. She died of tuberculosis at age 57, and was buried with her sons at Old North Cemetery in Concord, New Hampshire.

SOURCES:

Healy, Diana Dixon. *America's First Ladies: Private Lives of the Presidential Wives.* NY: Atheneum, 1988.

Klapthor, Margaret Brown. *The First Ladies.* Washington, DC: The White House Historical Association, 1979.

Melick, Arden David. *Wives of the Presidents.* Maplewood, NJ: Hammond, 1977.

Paletta, LuAnn. *The World Almanac of First Ladies.* NY: World Almanac, 1990.

Barbara Morgan,
Melrose, Massachusetts

Pierce, Sarah (1767–1852)

American educator who headed Litchfield Female Academy, a school with a national reputation for excellence. *Born on June 26, 1767, in Litchfield, Connecticut; died on January 19, 1852, in Litchfield; daughter of John Pierce (a potter and farmer) and Mary (Paterson) Pierce; never married; no children.*

Sarah Pierce was an educator in an era when few other occupations were open to women. She was born in Litchfield, Connecticut, in 1767, the youngest of John and **Mary Paterson Pierce**'s seven children. Her brother John, the only son in the family, took over family responsibilities when their father died, and sent 14-year-old Sarah and her sister Nancy to New York City to be trained in setting up a school. She began her teaching career back in Litchfield in 1792 with just a few students in her dining room.

Litchfield, though not a metropolis, was a center for commerce and culture and boasted a law school. The teacher known as Miss Pierce began to attract a following, and in 1798 citizens of the town donated a building. The school, which would be incorporated as the Litchfield Female Academy in 1827, became nationally known for its excellent academics and the training it offered in conduct and manners. Students, ranging in age from seven years to women in their early 20s, came from all over the country and eventually numbered around 130. A few boys also were enrolled in later years. The attendance of children of well-known national figures was proof of her school's reputation; the Reverend Lyman Beecher of Hartford, for example, sent his children ***Catharine Beecher**, Henry Ward Beecher, and ***Harriet Beecher (Stowe)** to Pierce's school, providing religious instruction in exchange for their tuition.

Between 1811 and 1818, Pierce published four volumes entitled *Sketches of Universal History Compiled from Several Authors. For Use of Schools*. These works, organized in question-and-answer form, had been prompted by complaints about boring textbooks from her students, and were designed to make learning more interesting. At the Litchfield Female Academy, students were taught subjects ranging from academic ones like spelling, grammar, arithmetic, and geography to "feminine" pursuits like painting, needlework, and dancing. Young men of the town's law school participated in some of the school's dancing and dramatic events; the plays presented featured wholesome scripts written by Pierce herself. Atypical of the era, in which physical activity was generally thought harmful for growing girls, she also saw to it that her students got sufficient exercise.

Pierce never married, dedicating herself wholeheartedly to her school and its pupils. She was described by a former student as a small, fragile-looking person with a firm disposition. Writing to a niece in 1842, she showed her schoolteacher's resolute mindset: "I hope you will be careful to acquire a good style, and a handsome mode of writing letters and notes, as they show a woman's education on more occasions than almost anything else she is called on to perform." After running the school almost wholly by herself, in 1814 she accepted the help of her nephew, John Pierce Brace, whom she had sent to college. He became principal of the school around 1825, while Pierce continued to teach her favorite course, "universal history." She retired in 1833, one year after her nephew had left to head the Hartford Female Seminary, and without their guidance the school declined and closed about ten years later. Her contributions were remembered, however, and at Litchfield's centennial celebration in 1851, one year before her death, the chief justice of Connecticut praised her for giving "a new tone to female education" in the country.

SOURCES:

Edgerly, Lois Stiles, ed. *Give Her This Day.* Gardiner, ME: Tilbury House, 1990.

James, Edward T., ed. *Notable American Women, 1607–1950.* Cambridge, MA: The Belknap Press of Harvard University Press, 1971.

McHenry, Robert, ed. *Famous American Women.* NY: Dover, 1980.

Sally A. Myers, Ph.D.,
freelance writer and editor

Pieronne of Brittany (d. 1430)

French peasant soldier. *Name variations: Pierrone; Pierronne. Burned at the stake in Paris in 1430.*

Pieronne of Brittany was a contemporary of ***Joan of Arc** and suffered the same fate as the sainted warrior. Pieronne, a young French peasant woman when France was struggling to free its territories from its English enemies, saw visions of God appearing to her and urging her to fight for her nation. Subsequently, she joined the army. Pieronne fought boldly and gained some renown among her fellow soldiers; yet, like Joan of Arc, she was eventually arrested and condemned to die at the pyre for practicing witchcraft. (*See also Women Prophets and Visionaries in France at the End of the Middle Ages.*)

Laura York,
Riverside, California

Pierre, Eugénie Potonié (1844–1898).

See Potonié-Pierre, Eugénie.

Pierrepont, Elizabeth Chudleigh (1720–1788).

See Chudleigh, Elizabeth.

Pigeon, Anna and Ellen (fl. 1860s)

English mountaineers. *Flourished in the 1860s; crossed the Sesia Joch in 1869.*

In September 1869, Anna and Ellen Pigeon, along with a guide and a porter, crossed the Sesia Joch between Zermatt and Alagna, described at the time as a daring exploit, after spending 18 hours on the mountain. The Alpine Club was so dumbfounded by the feat that it demanded to see notes of the expedition. The Pigeon sisters also made the first female traverse of the Matterhorn up the Breuil side and down the Zermatt; eventually, they would ascend the mountain from all four approaches: the North East (or Hörnli Ridge), which drops to Zermatt, Switzerland; the Zmutt Ridge; the West Face (the Italian Ridge); and the Furggengrat.

Pike, Mary (1824–1908)

American author. *Name variations: (pseudonyms) Mary Langdon and Sydney A. Story, Jr. Born Mary Hayden Green on November 30, 1824, in Eastport, Maine; died on January 15, 1908, in Baltimore, Maryland; first of six children of Elijah Dix Green (a bank director and colonel of militia) and Hannah Claflin (Hayden) Green; attended the Female Seminary, Charlestown, Massachusetts; married Frederick Augustus Pike (a lawyer and politician), on September 28, 1845 (died 1886); children: one adopted daughter.*

The eldest of six children, Mary Pike was born in Eastport, Maine, in 1824, but grew up in nearby Calais, where her father was a deacon in the Baptist church, the director of the Washington County Bank, and a colonel of militia. Pike attended local schools and in 1840 entered the Female Seminary of Charlestown, Massachusetts, where she undertook a three-year course. In September 1845, she married Frederick Augustus Pike, a Calais lawyer who would later enter politics. The couple had no children of their own, but adopted a daughter.

In 1854, Pike published the first of her two antislavery novels, *Ida May*, the melodramatic story of a white child kidnapped into slavery, written under the pseudonym Mary Langdon. The book, following closely on the heels of *****Harriet Beecher Stowe**'s popular *Uncle Tom's Cabin* (1852), enjoyed immediate success, selling 60,000 copies in less than two years and generating several British editions. Pike's second novel, *Caste: A Story of Republican Equality*, concerning a quadroon forbidden to marry a white man, was published in 1856, under the pseudonym Sydney A. Story, Jr. While it was not as successful as her first effort, *Caste* was well received by critics and readers. She wrote another novel, *Agnes* (1858), before abandoning writing to take up landscape painting.

From 1861 to 1869, during Frederick's terms in Congress, the Pikes lived in Washington, D.C. They then spent several years in Europe before returning to Calais. Following her husband's death in 1886, Pike lived in Plainfield, New Jersey, devoting her later years to charitable and religious work. She died on January 15, 1908.

SOURCES:

James, Edward T., ed. *Notable American Women, 1607–1950*. Cambridge, MA: The Belknap Press of Harvard University Press, 1971.

Mainiero, Lina, ed. *American Women Writers: From Colonial Times to the Present*. NY: Frederick Ungar, 1981.

McHenry, Robert, ed. *Famous American Women*. NY: Dover, 1980.

Barbara Morgan,
Melrose, Massachusetts

Pilkington, Laetitia (c. 1708–1750)

British writer and memoirist. *Born Laetitia Lewen around 1708 in Dublin, Ireland (some sources cite 1712); died on August 29, 1750 (some sources cite 1759), in Dublin; daughter of John Lewen (a physician); mother's maiden name was Meade; married Matthew Pilkington (a vicar and poet), in 1725 (divorced 1738); children: three, including son John Carteret Pilkington.*

Selected writings: The Statues: or The Trial of Constancy: A Tale for Ladies *(1739);* An Excursory View on the Present State of Men and Things *(1739);* Memoirs *(vol. 1, 1748);* The Turkish Court: or The London 'Prentice *(play, produced 1749);* Memoirs *(vol. 2, 1749);* Memoirs *(vol. 3, finished by son John Carteret Pilkington, 1754);* The Celebrated Mrs. Pilkington's Jests; or The Cabinet of Wit and Humour *(1764).*

Laetitia Pilkington, whom ***Virginia Woolf** called "a very extraordinary cross between Moll Flanders and Lady Ritchie (***Anne Isabella Ritchie** [1837–1919])," was born in the early 18th century in Dublin, Ireland. Her father, an obstetrician and physician of Dutch extraction, encouraged her interest in poetry. In 1725, she married Matthew Pilkington, the vicar of Donabate and Portrahan in the Dublin area. Her husband also wrote poetry, and some time after their marriage the couple were introduced into the literary circle around celebrated Irish writer Jonathan Swift. Swift edited some poetry for Matthew and made sure that he received an appointment as chaplain to the Lord Mayor of London. Matthew, however, was a disappointment, failing to perform his job satisfactorily and apparently engaging in adultery. This seemed to be no secret in London, and, after Pilkington joined him there, relations between them became strained. Rumor in Dublin had it that she, too, was involved in extramarital activity, and her reputation had been damaged by the time she left London, without her husband, and returned home.

Pilkington and her husband were divorced in 1738, and with money scarce she moved back to London with her three children, hoping to live off earnings as a writer. Although she published both *The Statues* and *An Excursory View on the Present State of Men and Things* in 1739, she was not able to support herself at that time. She had a number of "questionable" relationships with men and for a while moved in with James Worsdale, a painter. Her fortunes declined again, and she was imprisoned for debt. Later (perhaps after escaping from debtors' prison), she opened a book shop and a print shop, producing letters and pamphlets to order. She was for a time befriended by writer Samuel Richardson.

Back in Dublin in 1748, Pilkington produced the first volume of her *Memoirs*, the work for which she is best known. Among other things, the book describes the intimate details of the domestic life of Swift during the time she knew him, and thus has become an authoritative source for information on Swift's later life. (Her reputation never quite recovered from her earlier lifestyle, however; even the 1992 edition of the British *Concise Dictionary of National Biography* identifies her as an "adventuress" rather than as a writer.) Pilkington and her ex-husband had a running battle over the unflattering portrait she had painted of him in the *Memoirs*. He issued a pamphlet, *Seasonable Advice to the Publick Concerning a Book of Memoirs Lately Published*, in 1748, and she added her response, *An Answer to Seasonable Advice to the Publick* . . . shortly thereafter. She wrote two additional volumes of memoirs, the last of which was published after her death with additions by her son John Carteret Pilkington. She also is thought to have been the author of a comedy, *The Turkish Court*, produced on the stage in Dublin in 1749, though never published. After her death, her witty sayings were collected in a book, *The Celebrated Mrs. Pilkington's Jests*, and her poems were included in *Poems by Eminent Ladies* in 1755.

SOURCES:

Buck, Claire, ed. *The Bloomsbury Guide to Women's Literature*. NY: Prentice Hall, 1992.

The Concise Dictionary of National Biography. Oxford: Oxford University Press, 1992.

Shattock, Joanne. *The Oxford Guide to British Women Writers*. Oxford: Oxford University Press, 1993.

SUGGESTED READING:

Messenger, Ann, ed. *Gender at Work: Four Women Writers of the Eighteenth Century*, 1990.

Sally A. Myers, Ph.D.,
freelance writer and editor

Pilkington, Mary (1766–1839)

British writer. *Born Mary Hopkins in 1766 in Cambridge, England; died in 1839; daughter of man named Hopkins (a surgeon); married a man named Pilkington (a surgeon), in 1786.*

Selected writings: Obedience Rewarded and Prejudice Conquered *(1797);* Edward Barnard *(1797);* Historical Beauties for Young Ladies *(1798);* Marvellous Adventures *(1802);* The Disgraceful Effects of Falsehood *(1807);* Original Poems *(1811);* Celebrity *(1825).*

Mary Pilkington was the daughter of a surgeon who died when she was only 15 years old. She then made her home with her grandfather, a cleric, until her marriage in 1786 to the surgeon who had succeeded her father. While her husband was assigned to a position in the navy and was gone for long periods, she spent eight years working as a governess.

After beginning her writing career, Pilkington turned out an astonishing number of educational works, moral tracts, and novels, some of which were translated into French, using the proceeds to help meet living expenses. She was particularly interested in improving the moral character of the young. Little is known about her later life except that she suffered a debilitating illness around 1810 and that she died in 1839.

SOURCES:

Concise Dictionary of National Biography, Vol. III. Oxford: Oxford University Press, 1992.

Kunitz, Stanley J., and Howard Haycraft, eds. *British Authors of the Nineteenth Century*. NY: H.W. Wilson, 1936.

Sally A. Myers, Ph.D.,
freelance writer and editor

Pilley, Dorothy (1893–1986)

British mountaineer who made the first ascent of the North Ridge of the Dent Blanche. *Name variations: Dorothy Pilley Richards. Born in 1893; died in 1986; married I(vor) A(rmstrong) Richards (1893–1979, British literary critic and theorist).*

Dorothy Pilley was probably the best-known English woman climber in the 1920s and 1930s. Her husband, literary critic and theorist I.A. Richards, had suffered a bout of tuberculosis and developed an interest in mountain climbing while he recovered in northern Wales. The couple, who lived in Cambridge, would climb together quite often. In 1928, along with her husband and Joseph and Antoine Georges, Pilley ascended the North Ridge of the Dent Blanche. Her autobiography, *Climbing Days*, was published by Secker & Warburg in 1953.

Pimentel, Eleonora (c. 1768–1799)

Italian patriot. *Name variations: Marchesa de Fonseca; Marquesa of Fonseca. Born Eleonora Pimentel in Rome around 1768 or possibly 1758; raised in Naples; executed in Naples on July 20, 1799; married the marquis of Fonseca, in 1784.*

The heroine and martyr of the 1799 Neapolitan uprising, Eleonora Pimentel was born in Rome around 1768 and raised in Naples, where she was a poet and part of the city's literati. She was also an Italian patriot who sympathized with the French republicans (the Jacobins), and was an active follower of the popular party of Naples. After serving time in prison in 1798, she founded and edited the anti-royalist newspaper *Monitore Napoletano*. Upon the restoration of the Neapolitan monarchy, however, she was executed along with other revolutionaries, signaling, in the minds of many historians, the end of liberalism in southern Italy. "The liberal elites came out of the woodwork and were cut down and decimated," said Patrice Higgonet, a professor of French and European history at Harvard University. "It didn't affect the course of European history, but for Italy it was as if Madison and Jefferson had been hung after the Battle of Trenton."

Although Pimentel has long been revered by Italian leftists and feminists, general interest in her was renewed with the release in 1993 of an Italian-language biography by **Maria Macciocchi**, entitled *Cara Eleonora*. The Pimentel legend was also revisited that year by American writer **Susan Sontag**, who quoted Pimentel's final testament in *The Volcano Lover: A Romance*, a novel about Lord Horatio Nelson and Lady ***Emma Hamilton** set in 18th-century Naples. In January 1999, however, mere interest erupted into controversy with the premier of the new opera *Eleonora* at the San Carlo opera house in Naples. Starring **Vanessa Redgrave** in the title role, the opera reopened old political wounds, unleashing heated debates and angry demonstrations. On opening night, local royalists passed out leaflets that read "Jacobin Assassins!"

The opera, written and directed by Italy's Roberto De Simone, was created to commemorate the 200th anniversary of the Neapolitan uprising, and was intended to use the tragic moment in Neapolitan history as a universal protest against the death penalty. "I find the piece tremendously inspiring," said Redgrave, whose readings from Leo Tolstoy, Thomas Mann, and Bertolt Brecht were woven amid the 18th-century religious music of the opera. "It is against the death penalty by any government for any reason."

SOURCES:

Stanley, Alessandra. "Arts Abroad," in *The New York Times*. January 13, 1999.

SUGGESTED READING:

Macciocchi, Maria. *Cara Eleonora*, 1993.

RELATED MEDIA:

Eleonora (opera), starring ***Vanessa Redgrave**, opened at the San Carlo opera house, January 1999.

Pimiko or Pimiku (fl. 3rd c.).

See Himiko.

Pinckney, Eliza Lucas (1722–1793)

South Carolina plantation owner, botanist, and Revolutionary War patriot who introduced commercial-grade indigo as a North American crop. *Name variations: Elizabeth or Eliza Lucas. Pronunciation: Pink-knee. Born Elizabeth Lucas on the island of Antigua in the British West Indies on December 28, 1722; died of cancer in Philadelphia, Pennsylvania, on May 26, 1793; daughter of Major (later Colonel) George Lucas of the British Army and Ann (maiden name unknown) Lucas; studied under tutors in Antigua and at a prestigious girls' school in England; married Charles Pinckney (a neighboring planter), in 1744; children: Charles Cotesworth Pinckney (b. 1746); George Lucas Pinckney (died in infancy, 1747);* ***Harriott Pinckney Horry*** *(b. 1749); Thomas Pinckney (b. 1750).*

Moved with family from Antigua to England (1735); moved to a plantation near Charleston, South Carolina (1738); after father was recalled to active military duty, managed his three plantations and was soon experimenting with indigo and other exotic crops including silk (1739); after marriage to neighboring widower Charles Pinckney, helped to manage a total of five plantations (1744); moved with husband and children to England for five years (1753–58); helped to finance the cause of the colonies during the Revolution (1776–81); entertained President Washington on one of her plantations (1791).

"I love a Garden and a book, and they are all my amusement," wrote Eliza Lucas Pinckney to a friend in 1762 with elegant simplicity. Indeed she did, for she proved to be an almost revolutionary innovator in colonial agriculture and a lifelong reader, ever seeking information, and even gleaning botanical and agricultural inspiration from such disparate writers as the Roman poet Virgil and the 17th-century political theorist John Locke.

An "army brat," Eliza was born in the tropical island colony of Antigua in 1722. Her father George Lucas was a professional soldier in the British garrison there, holding the rank of major. George and **Ann Lucas** were quite wealthy, and their children—Eliza, Mary (known as **Polly Lucas**), and George, Jr.—were educated from their earliest years by learned personal tutors as well as by their mother.

In 1735, the family moved to England, where Major Lucas had been given a new command, and for some three years Eliza's educational horizons were vastly broadened by attendance at a quality girls' school, where she showed a particular fondness for Latin, French, and music that would never fade. She later looked back on this period with great nostalgia.

Three years later, in 1738, at age 16, Eliza accompanied her family to the colony of South Carolina. Her father had taken leave of absence from the army in order to manage three rice plantations bequeathed him on the death of his own father, John. The plantations were all near the bustling, sophisticated port city of Charleston (known then as Charles Town). The family settled on one, situated on the Wappoo Creek, as Eliza later recalled, "from Charles Town 17 mile by land, 6 mile by water."

The family soon was fatherless, for when England went to war with Spain (the War of Jenkin's Ear) in 1739, George was recalled to the army and ordered back to Antigua. Ann by this time was permanently incapacitated by illness, and Eliza, at the tender age of 17, was given by her father the very adult choice of either returning to England to live with relatives, or remaining on the Wappoo. Without hesitation, she decided on the latter, an easy choice for her, because she loved plantation life. But her new responsibilities were to prove far less easy. At Wappoo, Eliza became mistress of the 600-acre plantation, and also had to supervise the family's other two nearby plantations, while seeing to the care of her feeble mother and the education of her younger sister, Polly. George, Jr., had meanwhile been sent back to England to a military school.

It was a full life of 16-hour work days, in which Eliza oversaw scores of slaves (some of whom, in total defiance of local custom, she taught to read and write) as well as a number of white workers, ordered seed and stock and tools, paid bills, and personally tutored Polly, all the while setting aside enough time to read (usually in French) and practice playing the harpsichord for her own cultural development. Eliza thrived on this routine and proved to be extraordinarily efficient, while the plantations flourished under her management. She even found the time, under the guidance of neighboring planter and lawyer Charles Pinckney, for an informal study of law. By the time she was 19, neighbors were seeking her advice on legal matters.

Once in a while, Eliza would leave the plantation on the Wappoo and treat herself to a weekend trip into Charleston, where she stayed with friends, did some personal shopping, and attended parties and the theater. With typical understatement, she wrote to a friend: "Charles Town, the Principal one in this province, is a polite, agreeable place," whose inhabitants lived in a "genteel, English manner."

But it was in the plantation fields and paddies that Eliza was happiest, and her native curiosity drove her beyond management into experimentation. She was the first in South Carolina to successfully plant ginger, and in 1741 she "planted a large fig orchard, with design to dry and export them," which she soon managed to do. Much taken by the Roman poet Virgil, whose writings were loaned to her by Charles Pinckney, she planted a cedar grove to match one of the ancient bard's descriptions, and she also began "making a large plantation of oaks," to beautify one of her properties.

But her most outstanding contribution came through the cultivation of indigo, a very fragile and temperamental plant from which the brilliant blue dye is made. In 1740, her father sent some indigo seeds from Antigua and advice concerning their cultivation. Properly harvested, indigo was much in demand by the huge British textile industry, fetching astronomical prices. Frost caused the failure of Eliza's first crop, but she doggedly kept at it, and in 1744, with help from an experienced dye maker sent by her father, she harvested North America's first high-grade commercial indigo crop at age 22. Eliza earned good money from indigo, and she generously gave away seed and advice to many of her neighbors, including Charles Pinckney. By 1750, South Carolina would dominate the world trade in the blue dyestuff.

Because of her dedication to work on the plantations, Eliza's social life was spotty. George Lucas, who was now kept away by his appointment as governor of Antigua—a signal honor—worried about his daughter from afar, and urged her to marry. He even attempted matchmaking, but to no avail. As she wrote him in Antigua of one proposed suitor, "The riches of Peru and Chili if he had them put together could not purchase a sufficient Esteem for him to make him my husband." She had a mind of her own, and with her father so distant and her mother now deceased, she was literally her own boss.

Her closest friends were the Pinckneys, of Belmont plantation nearby. Mrs. Pinckney was very sickly, and Eliza often visited her, but with Charles she corresponded almost daily, about plantation matters, world events, the writers they both admired, and their very deep religious convictions. When Mrs. Pinckney died of "fevers," Eliza consented to marry Charles a relatively short time after expressing her condolences. The ceremony took place scarcely four months after the burial, an uncouth period of time to allow for mourning by the standards of the day.

Charles Pinckney, South Carolina's first native attorney and a colonel in the militia, served in the colonial legislature, and oversaw two large rice plantations, on which some of Eliza's indigo was also produced. He was, in local terms, "a man of substance." In the first six years of her marriage, Eliza had four children (the second, George Lucas Pinckney, died shortly after birth in 1747). Meanwhile, she was soon managing all five of her family's plantations. Each morning, arising before the sun, she made a list of chores and resolutions for the day, carefully reserving some time for religious contemplation, music and learning. She was nothing if not efficient and organized. Nor did she abandon experimentation. Through the importation of silkworms and mulberry trees, she had modest success after some years in producing a somewhat coarse silk, which she had fashioned into party gowns. Although Charles built two mansions for Eliza in Charleston (one on prestigious East Bay Street), they were rarely used, and the growing family resided increasingly on one of his plantations east of the Cooper River, some ten miles from the town.

In 1753, with their youngest, Thomas, then three years old, the Pinckneys moved to London, where they resided for five very happy years. Charles was honored by appointment as Royal Agent for South Carolina, a position entailing little work but much prestige. Wealthy and lacking for nothing, they enjoyed a flourishing social life, traveled extensively in England, and built a network of influential friends. Before they left England they placed their sons in an exclusive boarding school, and in the spring of 1758, they sailed for home with daughter Harriott.

> I love the Vegitable world extremly. I think it an innocent and useful Amusement.
>
> —**Eliza Lucas Pinckney**

During the couple's long absence, their plantations, which had been run by their various foremen, had deteriorated, at least in Eliza's view, and she was to work in a frenzy for years to restore them to their former state. But she was to work bereaved, for Charles, who was many years her senior, died of malaria in the summer of 1758. As Eliza wrote to many a friend, if she had not had her work, her heart would have broken: "I was for more than 14 year the happiest mortal on Earth! . . . Think what I now suffer." The five plantations, however, took up her time so thoroughly that there was little left to grieve, or even maintain her normally heavy correspondence. Only her sons in England would receive regular letters. Of her full days, she wrote:

> In general then I rise at five o'Clock in the morning, read till seven, then take a walk in the garden or field, see that the servants are at their respective business, then to breakfast. The first hour after breakfast is spent at my musick, the next is constantly employed in recolecting something I have learned lest for want of practise it should be quite lost, such as French and shorthand. After that I devote . . .

and so her schedule progressed efficiently through the day and late into the night, ending with religious devotions.

When Harriott was 19, in 1768, she married a neighboring rice planter, Daniel Horry. Shortly thereafter, Eliza's sons returned to South Carolina and helped her manage the plantations, dabbling also in politics. By 1770, both were considered the brightest rising political stars in the colony. The Revolutionary War validated their stature, and Eliza proudly outfitted her sons in the uniforms of officers in the cause of independence. For eight years both served with great distinction, and both achieved the rank of general by the war's end. Eliza served the colonies' struggle with equal distinction, helping to finance the defense of Charleston, and sending food, cash and equipment to patriot forces throughout the Southern states, until her selfless generosity had left her personal fortune much depleted.

The contributions of Eliza and her sons continued. Charles Cotesworth Pinckney, who served in the legislature following the war, was named to the state delegation sent to Philadelphia in 1787, and helped to write the Constitution of the United States. Thomas, by then serving as governor of South Carolina, was selected to chair the South Carolina committee in charge of the Constitution's ratification. Charles would serve in the U.S. Senate for many years and run for president three times, and both Pinckney men would head the Federalist Party, the party of Washington and John Adams. In 1791, Eliza was personally honored when President Washington, on his only trip to the state, elected to sample her hospitality and stay on the Pinckneys' East Cooper plantation.

Not long after the president's visit, Eliza Pinckney was nearly 70 when she discovered that she had cancer. Finding no relief from local doctors or folk medicines, she traveled to Philadelphia, then still the young nation's capital, in April 1793, to consult a Dr. Tate, who had reputedly cured many cancer patients. She died on May 26, while undergoing treatment, and President Washington, by his own request, served as chief pallbearer at her funeral the following day. She was interred in the churchyard of St. Peter's Episcopal Church. Her surviving children lived unusually long lives for the time, Thomas dying at age 78, Charles Cotesworth and Harriott at 80.

SOURCES:

Bodie, Idella. *South Carolina Women.* 2nd ed. Orangeburg, SC: Sandlapper Publishing, 1990.

Pinckney, Eliza Lucas. *The Letterbook of Eliza Lucas Pinckney, 1739–1762.* Chapel Hill, NC: University of North Carolina Press, 1972.

Rogers, George C. *Charleston in the Age of the Pinckneys.* Norman, OK: University of Oklahoma Press, 1969.

SUGGESTED READING:

Ravenel, Harriet Horry. *Eliza Pinckney.* NY: Adams Press, 1896.

Zahniser, Marvin R. *Charles Cotesworth Pinckney: Founding Father.* Chapel Hill, NC: University of North Carolina Press, 1967.

John Hoyt Williams,
Professor of History, Indiana State University,
Terre Haute, Indiana

Pinkham, Lydia E. (1819–1883)

Founder of the Lydia E. Pinkham Medicine Company, who became the most familiar American woman of her time. *Born on February 9, 1819, in Lynn, Massachusetts; died on May 17, 1883; daughter of William and Rebecca Estes; attended local schools; married Isaac Pinkham; children: five, including Daniel, William, and Aroline Pinkham.*

Born in 1819, Lydia Estes Pinkham was the tenth of twelve children of William and **Rebecca Estes**, who were Quakers active in the anti-slavery cause, and dabbled in mysticism and Swedenborgism. William Estes had several occupations, but made most of his money in real estate. Lydia eagerly joined her parents' crusades and was also an early feminist.

In 1843, Lydia met Isaac Pinkham, a 29-year-old widower with a five-year-old daughter. Isaac was a shoe manufacturer, and at different times was a produce dealer, kerosene distiller, laborer, farmer, and builder. After a short courtship, they married. The following year, Lydia gave birth to her first child, and seemed content to be a housewife. A second child followed in 1847, but this one died, in his first year, of cholera infantum. Other children followed.

As Pinkham raised her children, she often resorted to home remedies. For example, for dyspepsia, she used pleurisy root steeped in boiling water. She kept a notebook, labeled "Medical Directions for Ailments"; one entry read: "A hog's [teat] procured fresh from the slaughter house split in halves, one half to be bound on the sole of each foot and allowed to remain there until perfectly dry, will produce relief and in many cases effect a cure of the complaint called asthma."

Pinkham had been born into a world in which medical knowledge was what it had been a millennium earlier. Typhoid fever and diphtheria were the two leading causes of death. There was no anesthesia. Sterilization was unknown. Life expectancy at birth was around 37 years for men, 40 years for women. More women died in childbirth than of cancer or heart attacks. There were ten medical schools in the nation, but few of those who called themselves doctors had attended any kind of school. There were fewer than 100 institutions recognizable as hospitals, and patients went there to die, not to recover.

Medicines were many but few were efficacious. One patent medicine promised cures for cancer, heart ailments, warts, dysentery, and chilblains; it contained grain alcohol plus a variety of herbs. During Lydia Pinkham's early years the likes of Wright's Vegetable Pills, Oman's Boneset Pills, Vegetine, and Hale's Honey of Horehound and Tar were popular nostrums. They were sold by peddlers, dry goods stores, and groceries, along with pamphlets and books with such titles as "Every Man His Own Physician" and "The People's Common Sense Medical Advisor in Plain English." Coca-Cola, which appeared in 1886, was initially touted as a patent medicine to cure headaches, indigestion, hangovers, and other ailments.

When the Pinkhams suffered financial setbacks during the calamitous panic of 1873, Lydia cast about for ways to supplement the family income. According to family legend, a few years earlier Isaac had endorsed a note for one George Clarkson Todd, who defaulted, obliging Isaac to pay the $25 owed on it. In partial repayment, Todd gave him a formula for a medicine to cure female complaints. The recipe (for 100 pints) was:

8 oz. unicorn root
6 oz. life root
6 oz. black cohosh
6 oz. pleurisy root
12 oz. fenugreek seed

To the resulting mixture was added sufficient alcohol to produce a medicine that was around 20% alcohol, or 40 proof.

At first, the Pinkhams gave away bottles of the medicine, but occasionally they were able to sell them. In 1875, Lydia and two of her sons, Daniel and William, decided to manufacture the medicine on a commercial basis, naming it "Lydia E. Pinkham's Vegetable Compound." They brewed the mixture on the family stove. While Lydia attended to production and wrote advertising copy, the brothers marketed the compound. At first, they printed a brochure, "Guide for Women," which Isaac, now wheelchair-bound, folded and Daniel hand-delivered in Lynn. This resulted in some sales. Encouraged, in 1876 Daniel distributed the circulars in New York, where a leading pharmaceutical dealer, Charles Crittenton, agreed to handle the product. That year, Lydia incorporated the Lydia E. Pinkham Medicine Company. William was named sole proprietor, because he was the only member of the family, besides his sister **Aroline Pinkham**, who was free of debts.

Sales were slow, so to add to the appeal of the Vegetable Compound other ailments were appended to a growing roster of complaints it was supposed to cure. When this did not help, Daniel decided to try his luck in Boston. In desperation, he ran an advertisement in the *Boston Herald,* which did the trick. Sales picked up, and the Pinkhams dedicated more of their revenues to advertising.

Lydia E. Pinkham

In 1879, Daniel, who by then had taken charge of promotion, came up with a jingle: "She is as healthy a woman as can anywhere be found/ Having taken four bottles of Mrs. Pinkham's Compound." He also decided to alter the plain label, and feature a picture of a robustly healthy woman: his mother. Within a few years, Lydia E. Pinkham's Vegetable Compound had become a national medicine, and Lydia Pinkham was one of the nation's most recognizable individuals. In the 1880s, a group of Dartmouth students wrote a song about her:

There's a face that haunts me ever,
There are eyes mine always meet;
As I read the morning paper,
As I walk the crowded street.

Ah! She knows not how I suffer!
Her's is now a worldwide fame,
But till death that face shall greet me.
Lydia Pinkham is her name.

The family turned down an offer of $100,000 for the business and the new trademark.

Within two months of each other, Dan and Will died, and Lydia took on added responsibilities. The company continued to grow. In 1881, sales came to $200,000, and the family prospered. But the now disconsolate Lydia turned once more to spiritualism. A few days before Christmas 1882, Pinkham suffered a paralytic stroke and claimed to have visions of William and Daniel. On May 17, 1883, she died at the age of 64.

Before taking Lydia E. Pinkham's Vegetable Compound I was afflicted with female complaints so that I could hardly walk. My back ached terribly, in fact, I ached all over. Was not able to raise myself up some of the time. I had no appetite and was so nervous that I could hardly sleep. I have taken but two bottles of your Compound and feel like another person; can now eat and sleep to perfection, in fact, am perfectly well.

—Letter to Lydia Pinkham from Mrs. Sue McCullough, Adlai, West Virginia

The company continued to prosper, as progress in gynecological research and practice lagged behind that in other medical fields. By the 1920s, sales of the Vegetable Compound climbed to $3 million annually. Then, in 1938, the American Medical Association cited the Pinkham company for false medical claims, but the company deflected the attack. Nonetheless, the nation's women were turned off by extravagant claims for the Compound. Sales declined as the nation increasingly avoided patent medicines. In 1968, in the face of a shrinking market, the Pinkham family sold the company to Cooper Laboratories for over $1 million.

SOURCES:

Burton, Jean. *Lydia Pinkham Is Her Name.* NY: Farrar, Strauss, 1949.

Stage, Sarah. *Female Complaints: Lydia Pinkham and the Business of Women's Medicine.* NY: W.W. Norton, 1979.

SUGGESTED READING:

Ehrenreich, Barbara, and Dierdre English. *For Her Own Good: 150 Years of Experts' Advice to Women.* Garden City: Doubleday, 1978.

Holbrook, Stewart. *The Golden Age of Quackery.* NY: Macmillan, 1959.

Robert Sobel,
Professor Emeritus of Business History, Hofstra University, Hempstead, New York

Pinkston-Becker, Elizabeth (1903–1989).

See Becker-Pinkston, Elizabeth.

Pinney, Eunice Griswold (1770–1849)

American folk artist. *Born Eunice Griswold in Simsbury, Connecticut, on February 9, 1770; died in Simsbury in 1849; oldest daughter and fourth of eight children of Elisha Griswold (a farmer) and Eunice (Viets) Griswold; educated at home; married Oliver Holcombe, in the late 1700s (drowned); married Butler Pinney, in 1797; children: (first marriage) Hector and Sophia Holcombe; (second marriage) Norman, Viets, and (Minerva) Emeline Pinney.*

Taking up her paintbrush around the age of 40, Eunice Pinney created some of America's earliest primitive watercolors, which, unlike the stereotypical watercolors of the period, are striking in their boldness and vigor. Although Pinney painted only as a hobby, she was amazingly prolific, turning out more than 50 signed works which today are dispersed among her descendants, museums, and private collections.

One of eight children, Pinney was born in 1770 into one of the oldest and wealthiest Episcopalian families of Simsbury, Connecticut. All of the Pinney children were educated at home on the family farm, where, from the age of five, they were expected to participate in chores along with their academic and religious studies. Despite strict discipline, they entertained themselves by putting on family plays, which may account for the sense of drama seen in Pinney's paintings. Sometime in the late 1700s, Eunice married Oliver Holcombe, with whom she had two children. In 1797, following his death in a drowning mishap, she married Butler Pinney of Windsor, Connecticut, and gave birth to three more children. In addition to tending her growing family, Pinney was extremely active in her church.

Pinney's dated watercolors (the earliest being 1809) suggest that she began painting when she was nearly 40, well into her second marriage. "Her style has a robust, solid look, with decisive contours that reveal a mature personality of force and assurance," writes **Charlotte Rubinstein**. Pinney's subject matter was broad in scope, encompassing genre scenes, landscapes, and figure pieces, and frequently reflecting her literary interests, such as in the paintings *Lolotte and Werther* (also seen as *Lolette and Werther*) and *The Cotter's Saturday Night*. Some of her works were apparently inspired from sources at hand. Two paintings, *Mrs. Yorke* and *Children Playing*, are reminiscent of woodcuts from 18th-century children's books. **Mary Black**, in *Notable American*

Women, notes that the figures in Pinney's paintings are "two-dimensional, with form subordinated to composition and bold pattern," an indication of her lack of training. As an example, Black cites the artist's mourning pictures, in which faces are often hidden behind carefully draped handkerchiefs, "a device, one suspects, for getting around the troublesome task of painting features." She points out, however, that Pinney's composition and her use of vibrant color make up for her lack of skill in anatomy, features, and perspective.

Perhaps Pinney's most interesting and characteristic painting is *Two Women* (c. 1815), which portrays two female figures seated across from one another, separated by a table on which rests a candlestick. One woman, apparently older, is holding a child. The painting is filled with various shapes and motifs, all arranged in perfect symmetry, and each contributing to the drama of the work. **Germaine Greer,** in *The Obstacle Race,* points out Pinney's concern with pattern-making, citing the lozenge pattern on the carpet and the meticulous symmetry of the composition around the central spindle of the table and the candlestick. "A tension between the two women, the large complacent mother and the slightly apprehensive other is heightened by the tipped tabletop under the candlestick seen at eye level and the oddness of the candle flame seen between the pale windows."

Pinney's youngest daughter, **Emeline Pinney,** was also interested in art, and taught painting in Virginia before her marriage. Eunice sent her daughter watercolor paintings to use as examples in her classes, "an early instance of a good female role model," notes Rubinstein. Pinney died in 1849.

SOURCES:

Greer, Germaine. *The Obstacle Race.* NY: Farrar, Straus & Giroux, 1979.

James, Edward T., ed. *Notable American Women, 1607–1950.* Cambridge, MA: The Belknap Press of Harvard University Press, 1971.

Rubinstein, Charlotte Streifer. *American Women Artists.* Boston, MA: G.K. Hall, 1982.

Barbara Morgan,
Melrose, Massachusetts

Pintasilgo, Maria de Lurdes

(1930—)

Portuguese politician, social activist, and author who served as prime minister and representative to the United Nations. *Name variations: Pintassilgo. Born on January 18, 1930, in Abrantes, Portugal; first child of Jaime de Matos Pintasilgo (a textile merchant) and Amélia Ruivo da Silva; graduated from Superior Technical Institute, 1953.*

Born on January 18, 1930, in Abrantes, Portugal, Maria de Lurdes Pintasilgo was the first child of **Amélia Ruivo da Silva** and Jaime de Matos Pintasilgo, a textile merchant. When Maria was seven, her family moved to Lisbon. As a secondary student, she twice won the National Prize for her academic achievements. Torn between the arts and sciences, she eventually decided to study chemical and industrial engineering at the Superior Technical Institute, graduating in 1953. As a scientist, she was part of Portugal's Nuclear Energy Commission's first research team. In 1954, Pintasilgo became the first woman employed in research and development for the Companhia União Fabril (CUF). She worked there until 1960.

Despite these demanding positions, she also devoted great energy to Catholic and political activities, passions acquired during her university years. She served as president of the Catholic Feminine University Youth (1952–56) and then headed Pax Romana, the International Movement of Catholic Students (1956–58). From 1964 to 1969, Pintasilgo lived in France, where

Maria de Lurdes Pintasilgo

she was international vice-president of a Catholic organization (Graal) intended to modernize the Church in keeping with Vatican II. Pope Paul VI also named her a member of a group representing Catholicism to the World Council of Churches.

When Pintasilgo returned to Portugal in 1969, the country was entering the final stage of the Salazar dictatorship. Too ill to govern any longer, dictator António de Oliveira Salazar had turned over power to Marcello Caetano, who attempted to reform the regime sufficiently to protect it from liberal and socialist pressure. All Portuguese women were given the right to vote. In 1969, Caetano invited Pintasilgo to stand for election as a deputy to the National Assembly, but she declined. She did, however, accept a position as *procuradora* (attorney) for the Corporative Chamber (1969–74) and produced thoughtful analyses concerning the need for civil freedoms in Portugal and the direction the nation should pursue for economic development. Pintasilgo urged the government to bring an end to Portugal's African colonialism. She also headed a governmental committee that evolved into the Commission of the Feminine Condition, which studied issues related to women in the workplace.

Leaders of the MFA (Armed Forces Movement) that overthrew the reactionary dictatorship on April 25, 1974, brought Pintasilgo into the first provisional government. She held offices in the first three provisional governments after democracy was restored, at one point serving as secretary of state for social security. From 1975 to 1979, she represented Portugal at UNESCO and was elected to its executive council. In 1979, President António Ramalho Eanes named Pintasilgo prime minister of a caretaker government until new elections were held. Following the election, she served as adviser to President Eanes (1981–85). Thereafter, she occupied a post on the University Council of the United Nations and founded the Movement for the Deepening of Democracy in 1983. Pintasilgo continued her activities in Catholic political circles, possessing national and international stature. She was an unsuccessful candidate for the presidency of Portugal. From 1986 to 1989, Pintasilgo represented her country in the European Parliament.

Her published writings include *Sulcos do Nosso Querer Comum* (1980), *Imaginar a Igreja* (1980), *Les Nouveaux Féminismes: Question pour le Chrétiens* (1980), *Dimensões da mudança* (1985), and *As Minhas Respostas* (1985).

SOURCES:

Azevedo, Candido de, ed. *Classe Política Portuguesa: Estes Políticos que Nos Governam*. Lisbon: Pegaso Editores, 1991.

Ferreira, Hugo Gil, and Michael W. Marshall. *Portugal's Revolution: Ten Years On*. NY: Cambridge University Press, 1986.

Kendall W. Brown,
Professor of History, Brigham Young University, Provo, Utah

Pio, Margherita (d. 1452).

See Este, Margherita d'.

Piombino, princess of.

See Bonaparte, Elisa (1777–1820).

Piotrowska, Gabriela (1857–1921).

See Zapolska, Gabriela.

Piozzi, Hester Lynch (1741–1821)

English-Welsh writer and intellectual who was second only to Boswell in fame among writers on Dr. Johnson.

*Name variations: Hester Lynch Thrale; Hester Lynch Thrale Piozzi; Hester Salusbury; Mrs. Thrale; Mrs. Piozzi. Born in January 1741 in Carnarvonshire, Wales; died in May 1821 in Clifton, England; daughter of John Salusbury and Hester Maria Cotton; married Henry Thrale (a brewer), in October 1763 (died 1781); married Gabriel Piozzi (a musician), in July 1784 (died 1809); children: (first marriage) Hester Maria Elphinstone (1764–1857, known as Queeney); Frances (1765–1765); Henry (1767–1776); Anna Maria (b. 1768); Lucy (1769–1773); Susanna (b. 1770); Sophia (b. 1771); Penelope (b. 1772); Ralph (1773–1775); Frances Anna (b. 1775, died at 7 months); Cecilia (b. 1777); Henrietta (b. 1778); grandmother of **Margaret Mercer Elphinstone*** *(1788–1867).*

Hester Lynch Piozzi was born into a genteel but impoverished English household in Carnarvonshire, Wales, in 1741, the only child of John Salusbury and **Hester Maria Cotton**. She was well educated by her parents and showed an early interest in literature and writing. Most of her childhood was spent living with her mother in the homes of various relations as her father tried unsuccessfully to seek his fortune in Wales, England, and Nova Scotia. After his death in 1762, Piozzi's mother and uncle, Sir Thomas Salusbury, arranged a marriage for her with the wealthy landowner and brewer Henry Thrale. Hester herself later recorded that she was not in love and did not want to marry Thrale, but simply obeyed her mother's wishes. They married in October 1763 and moved to Thrale's large estate

Hester Lynch Piozzi

of Streatham Park in Southwark. Of the early years of her marriage, Hester recorded in her diary (published after her death as *Thraliana*) that she and Thrale lived "on terms of great civility and politeness, if not of strong alliance and connection."

In 1764, *Hester Maria (Elphinstone), the first of 12 children, was born and nicknamed Queeney. The next year, a second daughter was born but died a few days later. The year 1765 also saw the first election of Henry Thrale as a Conservative to Parliament, beginning his long political career. Hester enjoyed the excitement of campaigning, followed British politics closely, and worked tirelessly on her husband's behalf. When Queeney was two, her mother began a "family book" to record her daughter's progress and education. Piozzi had always kept personal diaries, but she began the family journal at the encouragement of her good friend, the English writer and lexicographer Dr. Samuel Johnson. This book would expand as more Thrale children were born, detailing births, deaths, illnesses, learning, and other incidents of family life. Her commentaries are remarkably honest and forthright assessments of her family members, and show her to be a rational, caring but strict parent, and a dutiful but not affectionate wife. The Thrale family book stands today as a unique record of daily life in 18th-century England, especially since it was written by a woman.

Their first son, Henry, was born in 1767. Piozzi would continue to give birth to a child every year for the next nine years, which had a severe impact on her health. Her daily life was composed of caring for her many children (who suffered constantly from various childhood diseases), entertaining guests, and writing. She also educated her children herself, tutoring them in reading, grammar, geography, Latin, Greek, and mathematics. After 1772, Piozzi found herself running Thrale's brewery and caring for her sickly husband as well. In that year, the Thrales faced bankruptcy after Henry Thrale risked their prosperous brewery in some poor business ventures. He turned to Piozzi and Samuel Johnson for help; they took over its management and saved the family fortune.

After the crisis had passed, Hester found her husband permanently affected by the narrowly avoided financial disaster. It is possible that Henry Thrale suffered a stroke; previously a cheerful and hardworking man, he became, as the family book shows, withdrawn, irritable, and unwilling to retake control of the brewery. This was not the end of the burdens revealed in the family book, however; Piozzi was also nursing her aging mother, who was dying of cancer. It is remarkable that she found time to keep up entries in no less than five family journals; her writing was probably therapeutic.

In 1773, Piozzi's mother died, a loss followed soon after by the death of four-year-old Lucy Thrale. Of her mother, Hester wrote of having lost her best friend; indeed, her relationship with her mother had been the most intimate and loving of all of her personal relationships. The next year, she campaigned for Henry's second term in Parliament. As he was in poor health, he appeared in public only rarely, while Hester represented him to the voters. Leaving him in Southwark the following year, after the death of their son Ralph, Hester and her five surviving children traveled to France. During the trip her youngest daughter, Frances Anna, died at age seven months. More sadness followed in March 1776 when the Thrales' nine-year-old son Henry died. Piozzi's recording of these deaths shows her both grieved by and resigned to the loss of her children; of her ten children born by 1776, only three lived: Queeney, Susanna, and Sophia.

In 1778, Hester met the man who would become her second husband; Gabriel Piozzi, an Italian singer and musician from Brescia was hired to play at a dinner party she attended. When Henry Thrale's poor health took a turn for the worse, Hester suspected he had contracted a venereal disease from his mistress, the actress **Sophia Streatfeild**. Dutiful as always, however, Piozzi campaigned again for him in the next parliamentary elections, but his bid was unsuccessful. Henry grew steadily weaker; while caring for him during this final illness, Piozzi composed her compelling *Three Dialogues on the Death of Hester Lynch Thrale*, imaginary scenes inspired by the work of Jonathan Swift on how her family and friends would react to the news of her death. Henry Thrale died in April 1781, at age 52.

Piozzi grieved for the loss of the friendship and companionship she had shared with Henry for close to 20 years, and at the same time was deeply worried about her family's financial prospects. She sold the brewery; she had always felt that running such a business was beneath her, and welcomed the chance to be rid of it. As she put her affairs in order, Hester's constant companion was her friend Gabriel Piozzi, whom she had visited with occasionally since their first meeting. Their friendship gradually deepened until in 1783 Hester confessed to her daughters that she was in love and truly happy for the first time in her life.

Her daughters were shocked at what they perceived as Hester's betrayal of their father. They, along with Hester's friends, were more stunned the following year when Hester announced that she was going to marry Gabriel. Family and friends alike advised her not to remarry; they did not like Gabriel, who was not only a foreigner but of humble origins. Hester was most hurt by the opposition of her old friend Samuel Johnson, who wrote stern letters admonishing her for even considering such a match so soon after her widowhood.

Hester was adamant, however, and she and Gabriel were married in July 1784, after which they traveled to Italy for an extended honeymoon. While there, Hester compiled a collection of stories relating to Samuel Johnson, who had died in 1784, and sent them to a publisher friend in London. The collection was published in 1786 as *Anecdotes of the Late Samuel Johnson during the Last Twenty Years of his Life*. The Piozzis returned to London in 1787; Hester records in *Thraliana* that her subsequent visits with her daughters, whom she had left on their own during her trip, were polite but lacked the closeness of earlier years. Hester was also coldly received in London society. She found herself the object of lurid cartoons in literary magazines ridiculing her for marrying so far beneath her, and was also the subject of editorials condemning her for her supposed mistreatment of her children.

Instead of returning to the social life she had known as Thrale's wife, Hester Piozzi turned to literary pursuits. She began work on an edition of the letters of Samuel Johnson; despite their conflict over Gabriel, Hester still admired her friend deeply and wanted to publish his correspondence as a tribute to him. This venture included traveling around England collecting Johnson's letters from his many correspondents, although some, like her own daughter Queeney, refused to give up their letters because of their condemnation of Hester herself. The volumes were published in 1788 to considerable success.

By November 1788, Piozzi had finished another manuscript, *Journey Through France, Italy, and Germany*. Based on her travel journals, this work was published to modest sales in 1789. The Piozzis turned then to building a villa on her farm in Wales and informally adopted Gabriel's young nephew, John Salusbury Piozzi (named in honor of Hester's father), to raise as their own son and heir. This adoption further estranged the couple from Hester's daughters, who feared for their inheritance rights.

Hester continued to produce new written works throughout the 1790s. In addition to her journals, which she never ceased to keep, she published *British Synonymy, or an Attempt at Regulating the Choice of Words in Familiar Conversation* (1794), on polite conversation, and *Three Warnings to John Bull Before He Dies* (1798), on the state of British politics. Her sixth book *Retrospection*, published in 1801, was a multi-volume narrative of world history written in celebration of the new century. Piozzi's prolific writings slowed down after its publication, and she spent the next few years quietly at her Welsh estate. In 1809, Gabriel Piozzi died at age 69 after a long struggle with gout. Hester was devastated, her despondence revealed by her inability to write more than a brief line in her journal for weeks following his death.

Her second widowhood did bring a temporary reconciliation with her daughters. She visited them in London, where she met their husbands and her small grandchildren. But she again caused their estrangement when she arranged her legal adoption of 16-year-old John Salusbury Piozzi in 1810, and wrote a will bequeathing virtually all of her property to him.

Piozzi's triumphant re-entrance into English society as a result of her books was demonstrated on her 80th birthday in January 1820 in Bath. Over 600 guests attended a concert and elaborate banquet in honor of the twice-widowed mother of 12 who had earlier given up acceptance in high society in exchange for love and personal happiness. A year later, Hester Lynch Piozzi summoned her daughters and made peace with them during her final illness in April 1821. She died on May 2, on a trip from Bath to Clifton.

SOURCES:

Hyde, Mary. *The Thrales of Streatham Park*. Cambridge, MA: Harvard University Press, 1977.

Piozzi, Hester Lynch Thrale. *Thraliana: The Diary of Mrs. Hester Lynch Thrale, 1776–1809*. Edited by Katherine Balderston. Oxford: Clarendon Press, 1951.

Laura York, M.A.,
University of California, Riverside, California

Piper, Leonora E. (1859–1950)

Celebrated American medium. *Name variations: Leonore Piper. Born Leonora Evelina Simonds on June 27, 1859, in Nashua, New Hampshire; died on July 3, 1950, in Brookline, Massachusetts; fourth of six children of Stillman Simonds and Hannah (Stevens) Simonds; married William R. Piper (a manufacturer, salesman, and clerk), on October 6, 1881 (died 1904); children: two daughters, Alta Laurette Piper (b. 1884); Minerva Leonora Piper (b. 1885).*

Perhaps the world's most celebrated psychic medium, and certainly one of the most scrutinized, Leonora Piper not only possessed extraordinary gifts, but used them for the good of humanity rather than her own personal gain. Piper, who was by all accounts a paradigm of virtue and integrity, viewed her mission as religious, and regarded herself as a "bringer of glad tidings."

Piper was born Leonora Evelina Simonds in Nashua, New Hampshire, in 1859, and grew up there and in Methuen, Massachusetts, where her family moved when she was still quite young. Her parents, of English descent, were devout Congregationalists, as was Leonora until 1910, when on a visit to England she was baptized and confirmed in the Anglican Church. In 1881, she married William Piper and moved to Boston, where William held various jobs in manufacturing and sales. The couple had two daughters, **Alta Laurette Piper** (b. 1884) and **Minerva Leonora Piper** (b. 1885), and led quiet, unassuming lives.

Leonora had her first experiences with "supernormal" powers in childhood, suffering occasional episodes where she lost consciousness and had visions portending future events. Several years into her marriage, in an attempt to resolve a number of recurring ailments as well as some problems arising from an injury she had sustained, she visited a psychic healer. Although she received little relief from her maladies, she was compelled to return to the clairvoyant a second time. "While seated with the other clients, she suddenly felt herself drawn into a state of suspended animation," writes Robert Somerlott in an article on the psychic for *American Heritage*. "The furniture appeared to whirl around her, her mind reeled, and collapsing on the table, she fell into a deep trance, apparently hypnotic." Subsequently, through the voice of a dead girl named Chlorine, Piper delivered a message to a male member of the circle who believed it to be a communication from his dead son. Word of this incident spread quickly through the Boston spiritualist community, and Piper began holding private consultations, mostly with believers who little doubted her powers. One of her sessions was attended by Harvard philosopher-psychologist William James, who came away so intrigued with Piper that he arranged for a serious investigation of her talent.

In the spring of 1887, through William James and the American Society for Psychical Research, Dr. Richard Hodgson, an English investigator of psychic phenomena, took up the Piper investigation, which he continued to pursue at intervals until his death 18 years later. Having previously exposed a number of psychic frauds, including ***Helena Blavatsky**, Hodgson took extreme care in his study of Piper, diligently monitoring her sittings and testing the validity of her trances by keeping her under constant scrutiny. "Hired detectives often trailed her, volunteers watched her, her utterances were checked and double-checked, and every facet of her private life was scrutinized for evidence of fraud," Somerlott explains. "No fraud was discovered; Mrs. Piper was integrity itself."

Over the first years of the study, Piper, who was now able to invoke her trances at will, delivered to her sitters many personal messages from deceased relatives, receiving her information from a number of controlling figures, including the ghosts of ***Sarah Siddons**, Henry Wadsworth Longfellow, and Johann Sebastian Bach. Eventually a French physician by the name of Phinuit emerged and asserted himself as the controlling spirit, remaining in exclusive command of Piper's pronouncements for some time.

In 1889, Piper visited England under the auspices of the British Society for Psychical Research. Since it was her first trip abroad, testing conditions were thought to be ideal. From the moment she boarded the ship, every precaution was taken to keep Piper's contacts with others to a minimum, and her arrival, according to Somerlott, was more like a kidnapping than a welcome. Piper was greeted on the dock by Oliver Lodge, a professor of physics at University College in Liverpool and head of the committee designated to test her, then she was whisked away by closed carriage to Lodge's home, where she was kept a virtual prisoner until her first seance. The initial test session was conducted before a group of absolute strangers presented to her under assumed names. "As soon as Mrs. Piper was entranced, Dr. Phinuit began to identify them one by one, revealing incidents, details, and occupations," writes Somerlott. "The sitters were astounded. Phinuit made a few mistakes and a few near misses, but the overall impression was amazing as he described homes and rooms, mentioned names of children, and even diagnosed ailments in the light of the subjects' past medical histories—histories that Mrs. Piper could not have known."

One can only imagine what Piper thought of her celebrity and of the constant probing into her private life and affairs. Outwardly, she remained patient, although somewhat bewildered at finding herself the center of attention. Since she was never able to remember her trances, she was hardly impressed with her powers. Her family remained supportive, her daughters only regretting that their mother's "work" took her away from them so often.

Since Piper's controlling spirits were apparently the ghosts of the long-dead, Hodgson first believed that she received her messages through "thought transmission from the minds of distant living persons," but when Phinuit was supplanted by a new control purporting to be George Pelham, a young man who had only recently died, he reversed his view. Basing much of his conclusions on the emergence of Pelham, in February 1898 Hodgson published a report (now considered a milestone in psychic research) in which he affirmed, as Gardner Murphy writes in *Notable American Women*, "the survival of consciousness after death."

Later, Piper's trances came under the control of religious personages known as the "Imperator Group." In addition to expressing their messages through Piper's voice, as was usual with earlier controlling spirits, they also communicated through automatic writing. In 1906, the year after Hodgson's death, Piper again went to England where she participated in several experiments in "cross-correspondence" involving automatists (persons who communicate by automatic writing or another automatic process). "In the most remarkable of the Piper cross-correspondences," writes Murphy, "an investigator, through Mrs. Piper, put to the deceased communicator the question: 'What does the work "Lethe" suggest to you?' Although she had no classical education, Mrs. Piper produced a long series of Latin references well known to the decedent during his lifetime. When the same question was put to a second medium, she also responded with relevant Latin sources, which did not duplicate those communicated by Mrs. Piper."

Piper's powers as a medium were also evaluated by William James in "What Psychical Research Has Accomplished," which appeared in *The Will to Believe and Other Essays* (1897). She was also the subject of some experiments in "trance personalities" conducted by the psychologist G. Stanley Hall, who concluded that some of Piper's "trance personalities" were less knowledgeable about their earthly lives than would have been expected.

By 1909, when Piper visited England again, her powers had significantly diminished, although a later episode involving a warning to Oliver Lodge about the impending death of his son in World War I grabbed some attention. Leonora Piper lived to the age of 91, succumbing to bronchopneumonia in 1950 at her Brookline home. She was buried in Mount Pleasant Cemetery in Arlington, Massachusetts.

SOURCES:

James, Edward T., ed. *Notable American Women, 1607–1950.* Cambridge, MA: The Belknap Press of Harvard University Press, 1971.

"The Medium had The Message: Mrs. Piper and the Professors," in *American Heritage.* Vol. XXII, no. 2. February 1971.

Barbara Morgan,
Melrose, Massachusetts

Pippig, Uta (1965—)

German marathon runner. *Born in Berlin, Germany, in 1965; daughter of two physicians; studied medicine at the University of Berlin.*

On April 15, 1996, Germany's Uta Pippig became the first woman to win three consecutive Boston Marathons, coming from behind in a spectacular finish that only added to the celebratory atmosphere of the 100th anniversary of the event. Battling menstrual cramps, diarrhea, heavy menses, and "palpable embarrassment" that almost caused her to drop out of the race, Pippig pulled ahead of Kenya's **Tegla Loroupe** at the 25-mile mark of the 26-mile course to finish in a time of 2 hours 27 minutes 12 seconds. With a towel wrapped around her bloodied legs, Pippig grinned gallantly and, in a characteristic gesture, threw kisses to the adoring crowd. However, she admitted that it took almost superhuman will to propel herself through the pain. "After four miles, I was thinking several times to drop out because it hurt so much," she said. "But in the end, I won." Later, instead of participating in the usual round of post-race interviews (during which she had in the past charmed the most hardened of journalists), Pippig checked into a Boston hospital, where doctors eventually pronounced her okay.

Uta Pippig was born in 1965 and grew up in East Berlin, the daughter of two physicians. Although she took up running at age 13, she was 17 before she was selected for one of East Germany's elite sports schools. While there, she was given anabolic steroids, which she took for five months until her mother warned her to stop. In 1986, she met her coach, Dieter Hogen, with whom she is also romantically involved. The pair longed to escape to the West, but Pippig held off defecting to protect her parents' medical careers. In 1989, when the Berlin Wall came down, she and Hogen moved to Stuttgart. Pippig entered the University of Berlin medical school in 1994, and then divided her time between Berlin and Boulder, Colorado, where she trained.

After winning the New York Marathon in 1993, Pippig ran the 1994 Boston race in a record time of 2:21:45, the third-fastest marathon ever run by a woman. Even suffering from the lingering effects of a nasty cold, she cut 59 seconds from *__Joan Benoit Samuelson__'s 11-year-old course record. Pippig began training for the 1995 Boston race after four months away from running while taking her medical school entrance exams. (She is pursuing a career in sports medicine.) Working her way back from a re-entry eight-minute mile, she nailed down a second Boston win, although race conditions precluded a personal record. Pippig is ranked third among the all-time fastest women marathon runners, trailing only **Ingrid Kristiansen** and Joan Samuelson.

Although her coach Hogen maintains that it is Pippig's resilience that sets her apart, there are those who believe that her remarkable effort in the 1996 Boston Marathon may have exacted a toll. In the 10,000 meters at the 1996 Atlanta Olympic Games, Pippig took an impressive early lead, but dropped out of the race before the halfway mark due to stress fractures in her right foot. Unable to train for five months, she put the 1997

Boston Marathon out of mind and set her sights on the summer European track circuit. When her training program went better than expected, she decided to try for a fourth win in Boston. It was not to be. Although Pippig kept pace with the leading pack of women during the first half of the race, she fell back at mile 16 and finished fourth in 2:28:51. Top honors went to Ethiopia's **Fatuma Roba**, winner of the gold medal in the 1996 Olympic marathon and the first black African woman to win the Boston Marathon.

SOURCES:

"Boston Marathon." *The Boston Globe.* April 16, 1996.

Huebner, Barbara. "Ethiopian ends Pippig's reign of three years," in *The Boston Globe.* April 22, 1997.

———. "Resourceful Pippig always finds a way," in *The Boston Globe.* April 20, 1997.

Noden, Merrell. "Sports People: Uta Pippig," in *Sports Illustrated.* Vol. 80. April 25, 1994, p. 48.

"Pippig's Progress," in *Runner's World.* September 1995.

Stach, Reiner. "Behind Blue Eyes," in *Runner's World.* June 1995.

Barbara Morgan,
Melrose, Massachusetts

Pirckheimer, Caritas (1467–1532)

German nun and writer. *Born in 1467; died in 1532.*

Descended from a long line of German scholars, Caritas Pirckheimer joined the order of Poor Clares (Convent of St. Klara) at Nuremberg, at age 16, and eventually became abbess. Of superior intelligence, and having received an excellent education, Pirckheimer was able to correspond in Latin with the notables of her day and in doing so became an important voice in the German intelligentsia. In addition to writing a history of her convent, she authored *Denkwürdigkeiten* (1524–28), a documentation of the intellectual, political, and religious arguments of the Reformation in Nuremberg, where her convent became hostage to the unfolding historical events. Like many convent chronicles of the early modern age, it was the result of meticulous and sophisticated research.

Pires, Maria-Joao (1944—)

Portuguese pianist who was especially known for her performances of Mozart. *Born in Lisbon, Portugal, on July 23, 1944.*

Maria-Joao Pires dominated the concert stages in the 1970s and 1980s, and was the most famous Portuguese pianist of that time. She was born in Lisbon in 1944, made her recital debut at age five, and had performed a Mozart concerto in public by age seven. Her musical education took place privately and at the Lisbon Conservatory, while advanced studies were in Munich with Karl Engel. Among the many prizes Pires has won, perhaps the most important was first prize at the 1970 Beethoven Competition in Brussels. A sought-after performer, especially in Europe, Pires performed with the Montreal Symphony in 1986, and finally made her first United States tour in 1988. Her performances of Schumann and Chopin were impressive and revealed an artist on the threshold of greatness. Pires was a superb Mozart performer, particularly of the sonatas, which she has recorded.

John Haag,
Athens, Georgia

Piroska (c. 1085–1133).

See Anna Comnena for sidebar on Priska-Irene of Hungary.

Pirrie, Margaret Montgomery (1857–1935)

First woman justice of the peace in Belfast, Ireland. *Born Margaret Montgomery Carlile in 1857; died in London, England, in 1935; married William Pirrie (partner and later chair of Harland & Wolff's shipbuilding firm), in 1879 (died 1924).*

Born in 1857 and married to William Pirrie in 1879, Margaret Pirrie became Belfast's first woman justice of the peace and the first woman to receive the freedom of the city. Pirrie was also active in charity work, serving as president of the Royal Victoria Hospital. She also served on the Senate of Queen's University, Belfast, and as president of Harland & Wolff's, the Belfast shipbuilding firm of which her husband was chair. (William, who died in 1924, had introduced the innovative designs that led to the building of large ocean liners.)

Pisan, Christine de (c. 1363–c. 1431).

See Christine de Pizan.

Pisano, Nicola (fl. 1278)

Italian sculptor. *Flourished in 1278 in Perugia; married Giovanni Pisano.*

A sculptor of Perugia in Italy, Nicola Pisano worked with her husband Giovanni. One of their projects was a beautifully carved fountain, still in existence, commissioned by the town and finished in 1278. The Pisanos must have been experienced and well-respected artists to be given such an important commission, but nothing else is known about them. It was not unusual in the Middle Ages for urban couples to work together professionally; indeed, the family was the primary unit of labor at the time.

Laura York,
Riverside, California

Piscopia, Elena Lucrezia Cornaro (1646–1684).

See Cornaro Piscopia, Elena Lucrezia.

Pitcher, Molly (1754–1832).

See "Two Mollies."

Pitseolak (c. 1900–1983)

Inuit printmaker. *Name variations: Pitseolak means sea pigeon in Inuit. Born around 1900 on Nottingham Island, Hudson Bay, in Arctic Canada; died on May 28, 1983, in Canada; daughter of Timungiak (mother) and Ottochie (father); married Ashoona; children: 17, most of whom died.*

Elected to Royal Canadian Academy of Arts (1974); awarded the prestigious Order of Canada (1977).

Pitseolak, who was born around 1900 on Nottingham Island, Hudson Bay, in Arctic Canada, married Ashoona and had 17 children (most of whom died young). She and her family lived the traditional nomadic life of the Inuits until Ashoona's death in the late 1950s. While Pitseolak was trying to support her children on the meager salary of a seamstress, her talent as a graphic artist was discovered and encouraged by James A. Houston. Formerly of Steuben Glass, Houston was an administrator for the Department of Northern Affairs and National Resources on Baffin Island. Along with Terence Ryan, art director of the West Baffin Co-op, Houston promoted the works of a group of Inuits who eventually became internationally recognized as Cape Dorset artists.

Pitseolak's graphics, drawn with felt pen or colored pencil, depict the world of her ancestors. The drawings are primitive in style and include mythical figures, animals or birds. Most often they portray Inuit activities, such as the seal hunt. Her designs have been exhibited internationally and several are displayed in Canada's National Gallery. In 1974, Pitseolak was elected to the Royal Canadian Academy of Arts. In 1975, two films were made about her work: *The Way We Live Today* and *Spirits and Monsters.* In 1977, she received Canada's highest civilian honor, the Order of Canada.

Pitseolak continued to draw until her death on May 28, 1983. She left behind perhaps as many as 7,000 original drawings and a wonderful legacy for Inuit artists to follow. Four of her sons, Ottochie, Kumwartok, Kaka and Kiawak, are sculptors, and her daughter **Nawpachee** is a printmaker.

SOURCES:

Eber, Dorothy, ed. *Pitseolak: Pictures Out of My Life.* Toronto: Oxford University Press, 1971.

Wong, Hertha D. *Native American Women: A Biographical Dictionary.* Edited by Gretchen M. Bataille. NY: Garland, 1993.

Deborah Jones,
Studio City, California

Pitter, Ruth (1897–1992)

Major 20th-century British poet who was the first woman to receive the Queen's Gold Medal for Poetry. *Born on November 7, 1897, in Ilford, Essex, England; died on February 29, 1992, in Aylesbury, England; daughter of George Pitter (a teacher) and Louisa (Murrell) Pitter (a teacher); educated at the Coburn School, Bow, London; never married; lived with Kathleen O'Hara; no children.*

Won the prestigious Hawthornden Prize for A Trophy of Arms *(1937); won the William E. Heinemann Award for* The Ermine *(1954); became the first woman to receive the Queen's Gold Medal for Poetry (1955); named a Companion of Literature (1974); named a Commander of the British Empire (1979).*

Selected writings: First Poems *(1920);* First and Second Poems, 1912–1925 *(1927);* Persephone in Hades *(1931);* A Mad Lady's Garland *(1934);* A Trophy of Arms: Poems, 1926–1935 *(1936);* The Spirit Watches *(1939);* The Rude Potato *(1941);* The Bridge: Poems, 1939–1944 *(1945);* On Cats *(1947);* The Ermine: Poems, 1942–1952 *(1953);* Still by Choice *(1966);* Poems, 1926–1966 *(1969, published in U.S. as* Collected Poems*);* The End of Drought *(1975);* A Heaven to Find *(1987);* Collected Poems *(1990).*

One of the most respected English poets of the 20th century, Ruth Pitter was born in 1897 to elementary school teachers George and **Louisa Murrell Pitter**, whom she later described as members "of the superior artisan class, intelligent, idealistic, country-lovers, poetic, altruistic." Money was tight, but her parents, in addition to instilling in Pitter and her younger brother and sister a respect for the value of hard work and frugality, taught them to delight in poetry and the natural world. Through scrimping, the family was able to rent a rundown cottage without running water in the forest in Essex, which they visited whenever they could. Pitter often trekked through the woods there for hours with her father, and the cottage and countryside would appear frequently in her later poetry. She wrote her first poem at the age of five, and attended a local elementary school before moving on to the Coburn School, a Christian charity school in the Bow area of London. At 14, she published a poem for the first time, in the periodical *New Age*. Its editor Alfred R. Orage encouraged her lavishly, and continued to publish her poems for ten years. Nonetheless, Pitter was resolute in her determination not to make a career out of her talent, later writing, "From the very first I realized that there was no money in poetry, and determined not to write for money."

World War I began while she was still attending the Coburn School and undecided about her future plans. The war effectively ended Pitter's formal education (at war's end she would have no money to attend college), and for the next two years she worked as a temporary junior clerk in the War Office, earning 25 shillings a week. Pitter was able to tolerate the mindless clerkship, but by the end of it she was "badly run down," she recalled. "Wishing now to be some sort of artist, however humble," she found a position with an East Coast arts and crafts firm. Pitter worked in eastern Suffolk for a couple named Jennings, who produced furniture and decorated wares marketed by a large pottery company. The job restored her to good health and also provided her with the opportunity to learn the basics of woodwork and painting. She became fairly well known for her products, including inexpensive hand-painted tea trays, signed R.P., which were shipped around the world.

As her skills as an artisan matured and brought her closer toward financial self-sufficiency, in 1920 Pitter published her first collection of poetry. *First Poems*, she later remarked, reflected "almost every possible fault of adolescence." Her assessment was shared by critics; a review in the *Times Literary Supplement* faulted the work for its concentration on technical complexity, suggesting that "in Miss Pitter's poems constructive ability reconciles us to the avoidance of an intellectual effort. She can remodel the secondary elements of life with such skill that we mistake many an affectation for reality." The general consensus of later critics is that within this technically accomplished but unalive collection can be found a glimmer of the art to come.

Building on the strengths in her early work, and studiously endeavoring to avoid some of the weaknesses that had been so apparent in her first book of poems, Pitter began to develop a distinctive poetic voice. Her efforts did not go unnoticed; Hilaire Belloc, the French-born English poet and author, was so impressed by this new work that he urged Pitter to collect her poetry for publication in a volume for which he would write the preface. The resulting collection, *First and Second Poems, 1912–1925* (1927), included selected poems from her first book along with 89 new poems. Hewing rigorously to formal structure and fixed stanzaic patterns such as the sonnet, the poems bore little resemblance to what the vast majority of "modern" poets, such as the Imagists, were writing. In his preface, Belloc hailed Pitter as "an exceptional reappearance of the classical spirit," and said of her work, "Here is beauty and right order, singularly apparent in the midst of such a moral welter."

Despite such praise, reaction to the volume in England was lukewarm, dismaying Belloc. The American literary market was somewhat more receptive when *First and Second Poems* was published in the United States in 1930. Clearly, however, poetry would not generate sufficient funds to pay her living costs. Pitter had moved to London along with the Jennings family after the end of World War I, and there she continued to work on handicrafts in their operation. By 1926, she had set up a household of her own above their workshop. Four years later, however, she was still not making enough to cover her expenses, and so she joined with another employee at the workshop, **Kathleen O'Hara**, to invest £600 to buy out a business similar to the one they worked in. After six months of struggling to learn the basics of business and working long hours decorating furniture and pottery, Pitter and O'Hara were able to turn a profit. They soon moved together into living quarters above their workshop, and became lifelong companions.

August 1931 saw the private circulation of a lengthy, seven-part poem of Pitter's, *Persephone in Hades*, a retelling of the myth which focused not on Demeter but on her daughter. Belloc is believed by many to have financed the publication and distribution of 100 copies of the poem, a work that he said "excels in vision." In a letter to Pitter, Belloc singled out the poem's passage about Persephone's descent into Hell as "not only the finest in the poem but the finest I know." Three years later, Pitter finally captured the interest of British critics with *A Mad Lady's Garland* (1934), a collection of poems which she had contributed, under the heading "Pastiche," over a period of years to her old friend Alfred Orage's *New English Weekly*. With poems detailing, among other things, the unrequited love of an earwig, the piety of a trout, and the laments of a flea, the collection more clearly displayed Pitter's humorous side than had her earlier works. The absurdity of the characters in the poems is accentuated by the formality of style and language ("Armed Earwig I, that erst in prideful plight / Swanked in my mail and only swore by Mars"). In his preface, Belloc praised Pitter's "perfect ear and exact epithet," and *A Mad Lady's Garland* prompted England's poet laureate, John Masefield, to write that "her judgments are merciful and her methods merry." Two years later, even loftier praise greeted the publication of *A Trophy of Arms: Poems 1926–1935* (1936), with its "reticent strength," "sensuous alertness," and unblinking observance of detail. James Stephens, in his preface to the book, said that Pitter was a poet second only to William Butler Yeats. The year after its publication, *A Trophy of Arms* won the prestigious Hawthornden Prize, awarded to the best imaginative work by a British author published in the preceding 12 months. As well, throughout the 1930s Pitter was frequently represented in the annual British anthology of best poems of the year.

Over the next several years, she published *The Spirit Watches* (1939) and *The Rude Potato* (1941), which celebrated such earthy subjects as potatoes and weeds, and her work was often published in literary journals in Britain and the United States. The advent of World War II, however, changed Pitter's life as it did so many others. She and O'Hara were forced to close their workshop-cum-giftshop after their employees were drafted and stocks of imported items could not be replenished, and they both took war jobs with the Morgan Crucible Company in Battersea. Pitter remained at the company until 1945, and somewhere around this time experienced a spiritual crisis and after much thinking and soul-searching converted to Anglicanism. Her wartime poems were released in 1945 in *The Bridge, Poems 1939–1944*. Its title poem relates the tale of Pitter's move from Chelsea, where she made and decorated pottery, to industrial Battersea, where she helped to make containers that were as "simple as doom."

In 1952, Pitter moved with O'Hara to a town near Oxford, where she was able to cultivate the flower and vegetable garden of which she had long dreamed. The following year saw the publication of *The Ermine, Poems 1942–1952*, which won the William A. Heinemann Award in 1954. On October 19, 1955, Pitter became the first woman to receive the Queen's Gold Medal for Poetry. She had been nominated by Masefield and unanimously approved by a full committee whose members included such notables as Walter de la Mare, Charles Morgan, and *__Vita Sackville-West__. In an unusual move, Queen *__Elizabeth II__ herself presented Pitter with the award.

While continuing to write poetry, in the late 1950s Pitter also wrote weekly on country life for the magazine *Woman*, and appeared regularly on the live television show "Brain Trusts," in which viewers tried to stump eminent personalities with questions they had submitted. Her last collections were *Poems 1926–1966* (1968), *The End of Drought* (1975), and *A Heaven to Find* (1987); her *Collected Poems* was published in 1990. Pitter was made a Commander of the British Empire in 1979, and died, after having been blind for several years, at the age of 94 on February 29, 1992.

SOURCES:

Buck, Claire, ed. *The Bloomsbury Guide to Women's Literature*. NY: Prentice Hall General Reference, 1992.

Kunitz, Stanley J., and Howard Haycraft, eds. *Twentieth Century Authors*. NY: H.W. Wilson, 1942.

Landreneau, Francine Muffoletto. "Ruth Pitter" in *Dictionary of Literary Biography*, Vol. 20: *British Poets, 1914–1945*. Edited by Donald E. Stanford. Detroit, MI: Gale Research, 1983.

Shattock, Joanne. *The Oxford Guide to British Women Writers*. Oxford: Oxford University Press, 1993.

Don Amerman,
freelance writer, Saylorsburg, Pennsylvania

Pitts, ZaSu (1898–1963)

American actress. *Born on January 3, 1898, in Parsons, Kansas; died of cancer on June 7, 1963; second daughter and one of four children of Rulandus Pitts and Nellie (Shea) Pitts; graduated from Santa Cruz (California) High School, 1914; married Thomas S. Gallery (a boxing promoter), on July 24, 1920 (divorced 1932); married John Edward Woodall (a tennis champion and real estate broker), on October 8, 1933; children: (first marriage) Ann Gallery; (adopted) Donald Gallery.*

Selected filmography: The Little Princess *(1917);* Rebecca of Sunnybrook Farm *(1917);* A Modern Musketeer *(1917);* A Society Sensation *(1918);* Better Times *(1919);* The Other Half *(1919);* Poor Relations *(1919);* Bright Skies *(1920);* Patsy *(1921);* Is Matrimony a Failure? *(1922);* For the Defense *(1922);* Poor Men's Wives *(1923);* Three Wise Fools *(1923);* Tea—With a Kick *(1923);* Daughters of Today *(1924);* Triumph *(1924);* The Goldfish *(1924);* Changing Husbands *(1924);* The Legend of Hollywood *(1924);* The Fast Set *(1924);* Greed *(1924);* The Great Divide *(1925);* A Woman's Faith *(1925);* Pretty Ladies *(1925);* Thunder Mountain *(1925);* Lazybones *(1925);* Wages for Wives *(1925);* Mannequin *(1926);* Monte Carlo *(1926);* Early to Wed *(1926);* Sunny Side Up *(1926);* Her Big Night *(1926);* Casey at the Bat *(1927);* Wife Savers *(1928);* Buck Privates *(1928);* The Wedding March *(1928);* Sins of the Fathers *(1928);* The Dummy *(1929);* Twin Beds *(1929);* Oh Yeah! *(1929);* Paris *(1929);* This Thing Called Love *(1929);* No No, Nanette *(1930);* Honey *(1930);* All Quiet on the Western Front *(silent version, 1930);* The Devil's Holiday *(1930);* Monte Carlo *(1930);* The Lottery Bride *(1930);* River's End *(1930);* Finn and Hattie *(1931);* Bad Sister *(1931);* Beyond Victory *(1931);* Seed *(1931);* The Guardsman *(1931);* The Unexpected Father *(1932);* Broken Lullaby *(*The Man I Killed, *1932);* Strangers of the Evening *(1932);* Make Me a Star *(1932);* Back Street *(1932);* Blondie of the Follies *(1932);* Once in a Lifetime *(1932);* They Just Had to Get Married *(1933);* Out All Night *(1933);* Professional Sweetheart *(1933);* Her First Mate *(1933);* Meet the Baron *(1933);* Love Honor and Oh Baby! *(1933);* Mr. Skitch *(1933);* The Meanest Gal in Town *(1934);* Love Birds *(1934);* Sing and Like It *(1934);* Private Scandal *(1934);* Dames *(1934);* Their Big Moment *(1934);* Mrs. Wiggs of the Cabbage Patch *(1934);* The Gay Bride *(1934);* Ruggles of Red Gap *(1935);* 13 Hours by Air *(1936);* The Plot Thickens *(1936);* Forty Naughty Girls *(1937);* 52nd Street *(1937);* Nurse ***Edith Cavell** *(1939);* Eternally Yours *(1939);* It All Came True *(1940);* No No, Nanette *(remake, 1940);* Broadway Limited *(1941);* Miss Polly *(1941);* Meet the Mob *(*So's Your Aunt Emma, *1942);* Tish *(1942);* Let's Face It *(1943);* The Perfect Marriage *(1947);* Life with Father *(1947);* Francis *(1950);* The Denver and the Rio Grande *(1952);* This Could Be the Night *(1957);* Teenage Millionaire *(1961);* The Thrill of It All *(1963);* It's a Mad Mad Mad Mad World *(1963).*

ZaSu Pitts

Known as the "Girl with the Ginger Snap Name," ZaSu Pitts played leading and supporting roles in the silents and early talkies, making over 150 movies during a career that spanned close to 50 years. Highly acclaimed for her dramatic roles in the silent films *Greed* (1924) and *The Wedding March* (1928), Pitts was also noted for her scatterbrained comic character roles during the 1930s, notably in films she made with **Thelma Todd** and Slim Summerville.

Pitts, whose unusual first name was pronounced "zay-zoo" and devised in honor of two paternal aunts, Eliza and Susan, was raised in Santa Cruz, California, where her mother ran a boardinghouse after the death of her father in 1908. A mimic from an early age, Pitts went to Hollywood immediately from high school and began her film career as a supporting player in two films starring ***Mary Pickford**, *The Little Princess* (1917) and *Rebecca of Sunnybrook Farm* (1917). ***Frances Marion**, then scenarist for Pickford, had given Pitts her first break. In her early films, Pitts played a series of ugly ducklings, perfecting a woebegone persona that she said was patterned after one of her schoolteachers.

Pitts' most challenging acting roles came from director Erich von Stroheim, who cast her in *Greed* despite objections from the studio that she was "not sexy enough." The movie, adapted from the Frank Norris novel *McTeague*, was a highly realistic drama about avarice and human degradation. It was also long (42 reels finally cut to 10 before its release) and controversial, winning accolades from some critics and condemned by others as "a vile epic of the sewer." Paul Rotha in *The Film Till Now* (1931) wrote that Pitts' portrayal of the hoarding wife was one that "has never been equalled by any other American actress at any time." As well, Pitts turned in a powerful performance as the lame princess in *The Wedding March* (1928), another von Stroheim vehicle, this time exploring the seedy side of imperial Vienna. Pitts' last silent role was opposite the great tragedian Emil Jannings in *The Sins of the Fathers* (1928).

With the advent of talkies, Pitts' career required adjustment. At the suggestion of von Stroheim, Lewis Milestone cast her in the epic talkie *All Quiet on the Western Front* (1930), but when her high, squeaky voice caused preview audiences to laugh, her scenes were reshot with **Beryl Mercer** in the role. Pitts apparently took it in stride, limiting herself from then on to comic characters for which her voice became an asset. During the 1930s, she made a series of 13 highly successful shorts with Thelma Todd and several features with Slim Summerville. She also played memorable characters in *The Guardsman* (1931), with Alfred Lunt and ***Lynn Fontanne**, and *Ruggles of Red Gap* (1935), in which she was a western maid who married an English butler, portrayed by Charles Laughton (said to be her favorite role). During the 1940s, her career began to slow, although during the '50s she was rediscovered on television, appearing in the series "Oh! Susanna," which later became "The Gale Storm Show."

Pitts was married twice; her first husband was boxing promoter Thomas Gallery with whom she had a daughter Ann in 1923. In 1926, when her close friend, actress ***Barbara La Marr**, died, Pitts and Gallery adopted La Marr's son Donald Michael. (Pitts would retain custody of both children after her divorce in 1932.) In October 1933, she married former tennis champion John Edward Woodall, who went on to a career in real estate. Pitts came out of retirement in the 1960s to appear in *Teenage Millionaire* (1961), *The Thrill of It All* (1963), and her last film, *It's a Mad Mad Mad Mad World* (1963). She died in 1963.

SOURCES:

Katz, Ephraim. *The Film Encyclopedia.* NY: HarperCollins, 1994.

Sicherman, Barbara, and Carol Hurd Green, eds. *Notable American Women: The Modern Period.* Cambridge, MA: The Belknap Press of Harvard University Press, 1980.

Barbara Morgan,
Melrose, Massachusetts

Pix, Mary Griffith (1666–1709)

English playwright. *Born Mary Griffith in 1666, in Nettlebed, Oxfordshire, England; died in May 1709 (some sources cite 1720), in London, England; daughter of Roger Griffith (a vicar) and Lucy (Berriman) Griffith; married George Pix (a merchant-tailor), on July 25, 1684; children: at least one (d. 1690).*

Selected writings: Ibrahim, the Thirteenth Emperour of the Turks *(1696);* The Spanish Wives *(1696);* The Innocent Mistress *(1697);* The Deceiver Deceived *(1697);* Queen Catherine; or, The Ruins of Love *(1698);* The False Friend; or, The Fate of Disobedience *(1699);* The Beau Defeated; or, The Lucky Younger Brother *(1700);* The Double Distress *(1701);* The Czar of Muscovy *(1701);* The Different Widows; or, Intrigue à la Mode *(1703);* Zelmane; or, The Corinthian Queen *(1704);* The Conquest of Spain *(1705);* The Adventures in Madrid *(1705).*

Inspired by the work of ***Aphra Behn**, the first professional woman playwright and one of the most prolific dramatists of the Restoration, Mary Griffith Pix was one of three women playwrights—the others being ***Mary de la Rivière Manley** and ***Catherine Trotter Cockburn**—whose works premiered during the London theatrical season of 1695–96. She was the only one of the three to sustain an active career in the theater, and over the course of the next ten years she wrote six comedies and seven tragedies that were produced in London.

Little is known of Pix's early life, though she was born in Nettlebed, Oxfordshire, in 1666, the daughter of **Lucy Berriman Griffith** and local vicar Roger Griffith. She married George Pix, a merchant-tailor, in London on July 25, 1684, when she was 18, and they had at least one child, about whom nothing is known except that she or he was buried at Hawkhurst in 1690. Most of what is known about her personality comes from a play produced at the Drury Lane in 1696, *The Female Wits*, that satirized her, Manley and Trotter. *The Female Wits* presented a caricature of Pix as Mrs. Wellfed, described in the anonymous playwright's stage notes as "a fat Female Author, a good, sociable, well-natur'd Companion, that will not suffer Martyrdom rather than take off three Bumpers in a hand." Pix fares far better than either Manley or Trotter; while the satire mocks their inflated egos, it celebrates Mrs. Wellfed's willingness to poke some fun at herself, much as Pix had done in the dedications of some of her plays. The caricature hints that Mrs. Wellfed may be somewhat ignorant, but this view is disputed by evidence from Pix's own work that points to a fairly comprehensive education for a woman of the day. The satire also indicates that Mrs. Wellfed is friendly and giving, fond of food and drink and her actor companions. If this is an appropriate characterization of Pix as well, her good nature may be part of the reason that she was not the subject of much slander or public opprobrium (as was often the case with women who attempted public careers), although she did not completely escape condescension from mostly male writers.

The first play Pix brought to the London stage was a tragedy, *Ibrahim, the Thirteenth Emperour of the Turks*, which opened in the spring of 1696. Although records are not clear about the length of its original run, it was very popular with the public; revivals were staged in 1702, 1714, and 1715. This was followed by a farce, *The Spanish Wives* (based loosely on *The Pilgrim*, the English translation of a novel by Frenchman Gabriel de Bremond), that debuted in August 1696 and was revived in 1705 and 1711. Pix wrote a novel that attracted little interest, *The Inhumane Cardinal*, before returning to the stage with *The Innocent Mistress*, a comedy first produced in 1697. A year later came a historical tragedy, *Queen Catherine; or, The Ruins of Love*, featuring (without much regard for actual facts) Queen ***Catherine of Valois** and the future King Edward IV at the time of the Battle of Mortimer's Cross in 1461. She next wrote another tragedy, *The False Friend*, produced in 1699, and *The Beau Defeated; or, The Lucky Younger Brother*, a satire that drew on French dramatic influences, including Molière's *Les Precieuses ridicules*, and was first produced in London in 1700. Her 1701 play *The Double Distress*, a blend of tragedy and comedy, was considered her best by some critics. While *The Double Distress* was the last dramatic work to which Pix formally affixed her name, a number of other plays have been attributed to her, including the tragedies *The Czar of Muscovy* (produced in 1701), *Zelmane; or, The Corinthian Queen* (produced in 1704), and *The Conquest of Spain* (1705), as well as the comedies *The Different Widows; or, Intrigue à la Mode* (1703) and *The Adventures in Madrid* (1706). Based on a single mention in a contemporary London paper, Pix is believed to have died in the spring of 1709, although according to some sources she died around 1720.

Mary Pix wrote most of her plays in blank verse, and they were performed by some of the best actors of the day, including ***Anne Bracegirdle**, Thomas Betterton, and ***Elizabeth Barry**. Modern-day critics tend to agree that her tragedies are not very good (*The Concise Dictionary of National Biography* calls them "insufferable"), and that English theater might have been better served if she had confined her writing to comedy, for which she showed a real flair despite some contrived plots. However, both her tragedies and her comedies were popular at a time when there was no shortage of playwrights attempting to cater to an eager theatergoing public that demanded a steady stream of new plays, and her work remains valuable for its reflections on society as the Restoration era drew to a close.

SOURCES:

Buck, Claire, ed. *The Bloomsbury Guide to Women's Literature*. NY: Prentice Hall, 1992.

The Concise Dictionary of National Biography. Oxford: Oxford University Press, 1992.

Goreau, Angeline. *The Whole Duty of a Woman: Female Writers in Seventeenth Century England*. Garden City, NY: The Dial Press, 1985.

Payne, Linda R. "Mary Pix," in *Dictionary of Literary Biography*, Vol. 80: *Restoration and Eighteenth-Century Dramatists*. Edited by Paula Backscheider. Detroit, MI: Gale Research, 1989.

Shattock, Joanne. *The Oxford Guide to British Women Writers*. Oxford: Oxford University Press, 1993.

Don Amerman,
freelance writer, Saylorsburg, Pennsylvania

Pizan, Christine de (c. 1363–c. 1431).

See Christine de Pizan.

Place, Emma (fl. 1896–1905).

See Place, Etta.

Place, Etta (fl. 1896–1905)

American woman who accompanied the outlaws Butch Cassidy and the Sundance Kid to Argentina, where they began a successful ranch and later returned to their outlaw ways. *Name variations: Emma Place; Eva Place. Flourished around 1896–1905; dates and locations for her birth and death are unknown, as are parents' names, marriages, and children; thought to have been educated in the East as a teacher.*

Joined the Wild Bunch, an outlaw gang whose two most notable members were Butch Cassidy and the Sundance Kid; accompanied the two men to Argentina in an attempt to "go straight"; for a time, the trio lived anonymously and ran their own ranch; when their true identities were discovered, they returned to their formerly successful lives as bandits; with Etta as accomplice, they caused a sensation with their daring robberies; evidently, the three later parted paths leaving each to face an unknown fate.

Etta Place materialized like an apparition in the history of the American West. From an unknown past, she joined the scoundrels and bandits who made up the infamous outlaw gang known as the Wild Bunch. While befriending the gang's leader, Butch Cassidy, she developed a romantic relationship with another central gang member, Harry Longabaugh, better known as the Sundance Kid. The three would later travel to South America in a doomed attempt by the two men to "go straight." The loss of their anonymity eventually led them back to the life they knew best: that of the outlaw. With Etta as accomplice, they robbed a number of banks, handily avoiding capture. In much the same way as she appeared, Etta Place suddenly vanished from history with only rumors and myth to explain her fate.

Theories abound regarding Etta's earlier life. Popular locations for her place of birth include Utah, New York City, Pennsylvania, or Wisconsin. Possible identities for her parents range from an Englishman named Ingerfeld to more fanciful alternatives, such as Emily Jane Place and George Capel, alleged son of Arthur Algernon Capel, 6th earl of Essex. (Another contemporary woman named Place, ***Martha Place**, was the first woman to die in the electric chair.) Even the Wild Bunch themselves were rumored to have become her guardians after the death of her father. She is often regarded as a schoolteacher educated in Boston or Buffalo, and sometimes accused of being a prostitute. Whatever her background, circumstances would lead her to become acquainted with the best-known outlaw gang in the American West.

Originally named Robert LeRoy Parker, Butch Cassidy was the celebrated leader of the Wild Bunch, a loosely knit group of outlaws and ne'er-do-wells. Their setup of several isolated camps, stretching from Wyoming to Utah, allowed the men a safe haven which lawmen avoided. After each job, a series of relay horses would quickly deliver the bandits to one of their sanctuaries, most notably Hole-in-the-Wall, Brown's Park, or Robbers' Roost. These tactics netted them much success, especially after railroad or bank robberies.

Etta's first documented appearance was in the winter of 1896–97, when she hooked up with the Wild Bunch as they camped at the Utah hideout Robbers' Roost, preferring the company of Harry Longabaugh (Sundance). Eventually, the two would become involved in a romantic relationship that would span several years and two continents. With the arrival of spring, however, Place again disappears from record, her whereabouts remaining a mystery for nearly four more years.

During the time Etta was unaccounted for, the Wild Bunch successfully lived up to their name. They are credited with a number of major robberies and were increasingly becoming a frustration to the authorities. Efforts by both the law and the Pinkerton Detective Agency, which had been hired to assist in their capture, increased the pressure on their outlaw lifestyle. It is thought that Butch and Sundance finally had had enough, and decided to "go straight" in a land where they were unknown. Etta, Butch, and Sundance decided upon the South American country of Argentina, and arranged an East Coast rendezvous from which to begin their new life.

On February 1, 1901, the trio met as planned in New York City. The men sported new aliases; Butch took the name James (later Santiago) Ryan, while Sundance took Etta's last name, making him Harry (later Enrique) A. Place. Pinkerton flyers describe some of their activities:

> This is to advise all offices that the above named [Harry Longabaugh] was in New York City February 1, 1901, at which time he lived with a woman he called his wife, at the boarding house of Mrs. Taylor, 234 East 12th St. There he used the name of Harry E. Place. . . . The woman with him is said to be his wife and to be from Texas.

Their WANTED posters describe Etta as "about 27 years old, five feet four inches in height, weighing about 110 pounds, medium complexion and wears her brown hair on the top of her head in a roll from forehead. She appears to be a refined type." Their research also discovered "that Longbaugh [sic] under the name of Place was treated in the Pierce Medical Institute, Buffalo, New York, and by a Dr. Weinstein, 174 Second Ave., New York City. We do not know the nature of the ailment he was being treated for." Some sources say that Sundance's condition was an old gunshot wound, while others suggest that he suffered from catarrh, an inflammation of the mucus membranes of the nose and throat.

While not otherwise engaged, the outlaws spent nearly three weeks sightseeing in New York City. Butch purchased a Tiffany lapel watch for Etta, and she and Sundance posed for their now famous photograph at De Young's Studio, 857 Broadway at 17th St. Nearly a year and a half later, the Pinkerton Agency would receive a copy of the photograph. "A great pity we did not get the information regarding the photograph while this party was in New York," wrote one Pinkerton agent. "It shows how daring these men are, and while you are looking for them in the wilderness and mountains they are in the midst of society."

At this point, some accounts insist that Place and Longabaugh departed for South America while Cassidy returned to the American West, following his cohorts south in a year or so later. In support of this is his alleged involvement in the July 3, 1901, holdup of a Great Northern train near Wagner, Montana. The deed is credited to the Wild Bunch, though the identities of the individual members involved have long been disputed. Indeed, with the revolving door of outlaws passing through the ranks of the Wild Bunch over the years, a variety of characters may have been involved. Without further evidence, it is most likely that on February 20, 1901, the three boarded the ship *Herminius,* bound for South America.

She appears to be a refined type.

—Pinkerton Detective Agency

Upon their arrival in Argentina some time in March, Pinkerton records show that Longabaugh went to the London and River Platte Bank and "opened an account with the bank on March 23, 1901, depositing $12,000 in gold notes. He gave his address as the Hotel Europa, Buenos Aires." Apparently, the outlaws spent the next year or so building a ranch in the Andes foothills, in southwest Argentina, as described in the following Pinkerton information:

> On April 2nd, 1902, [Longabaugh using the name Place] and [Cassidy using the name Ryan notified] Argentine Republic Government they had settled on 4 square leagues of Government land within the Province of Chubut, district 16th of 11 October, near Cholila and had 1300 sheep, 500 head of cattle, 35 horses, and asked for the first right to buy some [land] and were settled on land improving it. This petition was signed by Place and Ryan, per Santiago.

Since they obviously occupied the land but the transaction had not been completed, it was noted that the property was "Not Sold Yet, Place and Ryan are squatters."

That same spring, the three again were known to be staying at the Hotel Europa in Buenos Aires, with Cassidy posing as Etta Place's brother. From here, Butch left his companions to return to their ranch, traveling south by water to Rawson, then west by land to Chubut Province. Etta and Sundance boarded a ship to New York, ostensibly to visit Longabaugh's relatives in Pennsylvania and Atlantic City. Their trip included a sojourn to Coney Island, and possible further medical treatment for Longabaugh's unknown condition. Pinkerton records note their return:

> They left New York July 10, 1902, on steamer Honorious. Arrived Buenos Ayres [sic] August 9, 1902, as Harry A. Place, Purser, Mrs. Harry A. Place, Stewardess, which was OK as no passengers were carried, hence put them in the crew's list.

Their classification as service personnel was apparently to allow them to gain passage on what was not a passenger vessel but a freighter.

For the next two-and-one-half years, the trio ran a successful ranching enterprise, with Etta's equestrian skills and knowledge of horses surely contributing to a doubling of their stock. In a letter to his neighbor and close friend Daniel Gibbon, dated February 29, 1904, Cassidy shows genuine immersion in the everyday routine of ranching. "I will want to buy some Rams, so please keep your ears open for we dont know where to look for them. if you hear of any one that want to sell please tell them about us." He concludes with "Kindest Regards to your Wife and Family." A respected dentist and neighbor, George Newbery, stated that the three "were considered respectable citizens."

As had been the case in the United States, many Argentinean crimes were attributed to the trio with little or no reliable evidence. Additionally, sworn sightings occurring simultaneously yet hundreds of miles apart were not uncommon. This may have been the result of their notoriety, or the perception that Cassidy, Longabaugh, and Place were the only *Bandidos Yanqui* (American Bandits) in South America. In fact, there were a number of North American outlaws drifting throughout the Southern Continent, any of whom may have been responsible for the crimes blamed on them. Barring new information, their time ranching was most likely spent lawfully.

March 1903 marked the beginning of the end for the trio in their comfortable exile. Frank Dimaio of the Pinkerton Detective Agency arrived in Buenos Aires and began a three-month investigation. Through his research, he discovered a paper trail and enough eyewitness reports to significantly improve the chance of capturing the outlaws. Curiously, the agency took no action, perhaps because of a reticence on the part of their North American clients to support the operation. When Dimaio departed Buenos Aires empty-handed in May 1903, he assembled and distributed WANTED posters describing Butch, Sundance, and Etta. After returning to the U.S., Pinkerton agents sent a letter to the Buenos Aires police:

> It is our firm belief that it is only a question of time until these men commit some desperate robbery in the Argentine Republic. They are all thorough plainsmen and horsemen, riding from 600 to 1,000 miles after committing a robbery. If there are reported to you any bank or train hold up robberies or any other similar crimes, you will find that they were undoubtedly committed by these men.

Etta Place with the Sundance Kid.

With their identities and whereabouts thus exposed, it became impossible to lead the anonymous, law-abiding life they desired.

Perhaps it was the perception that their situation was hopeless which lured the Wild Bunch back into action. In February 1905, the outlaws heldup the Banco de Tarapaca y Argentino in Rio Gallegos, located in southern Argentina. According to the police report, "two subjects armed with large revolvers, apparently Colts, presented themselves in the establishment." The assistant manager was forced to put "all of the bank's money into a white canvas sack," after which one of the bandits "took under his arm a small tin box that contained approximately 483 pounds sterling." The assistant manager related:

> While one of the thieves covered us, the other went outside and put the sack that contained the money on his horse. About a minute later, I heard the one who was outside say in English something like "all set." The other assailant at once went outside, and they immediately took off in flight on horses that they had already prepared.

A Pinkerton account states that "Etta Place, Harry Long[a]baugh's wife, in male attire, is alleged to have held the horses while Long[a]baugh and Cassidy committed the robbery." After eluding their pursuers, the outlaws eventually returned to their ranch near Cholila. Wenceslao Solis, a Chilean ranch hand employed by Longabaugh, claimed to have assisted in the outlaws' departure from Cholila on May 9, 1905. Evidently, he escorted them north to Lake Nahuel Huapi, where the trio then headed west into Chile. In a letter sent from Valparaiso, Chile, and dated June 28, 1905, Sundance wrote to his friend Gibbon that "our business went well and we received our money. We arrived here today, and the day after tomorrow my wife and I leave for San Francisco."

If Longabaugh and Place did visit San Francisco, they had to return to Argentina in order to meet Cassidy to plan and execute the December 1905 holdup of the Banco de la Nacion in Villa Mercedes. According to the *Buenos Aires Herald*:

> Four well-mounted horsemen rode up to the [bank] and, knife in hand, entered, taking the employees by surprise. The safes were open and two of the brigands emptied them whilst the other two covered the employees. The manager . . . offered resistance [and] was wounded. Before any policemen arrived, the four robbers had re-mounted and disappeared in a cloud of dust.

In a description that obviously referred to Etta, the Argentine newspaper *La Prensa* reported that "one of the bandits was beardless, had small feet and delicate features . . . said woman is a fine rider, to the extent that she is widely admired by the Argentines for her skill and natural ability." Presumably, the fourth bandit was one of several possible fellow outlaws rumored to have been in the region.

With their take from the robbery reported at 12,000 pesos ($137,500 today), an extensive search for the trio was begun. Optimistic rumors of capture soon changed to criticism as no results were forthcoming. In a cynical jab at the powers that be, a *Buenos Aires Herald* editorial on December 23, 1905, touted:

> Those bad, bold, whisky-drinking, hard-riding, round-the-corner-shooting, Anglo-American, gaucho, Bank robbers have not been captured yet. The whole Republic has been astonished by the depravity of those four buccaneers, and all the horses and men of the Province of San Luis have, it would appear, been turned out upon their trail. The authorities of the adjoining provinces have volunteered to co-operate: and yet . . . the robbers are still at large, and their valuable booty unrecovered.

Again, the Wild Bunch fled to Chile, at which point the documentation of their activities gallops off into dozens of conflicting accounts. Popular myth has Etta leaving the men, and Butch and Sundance alternately robbing and working for mining concerns throughout southern and eastern South America. Among the many stories of the two men and their apparent demise, the account by Arthur Chapman published in the April 1930 issue of *Elks Magazine* has been the seed for many accounts, all varying in detail, location, and date. It tells how Cassidy and Longabaugh were looking for food and wandered into the Indian village of San Vicente, Bolivia, in 1909. One of their mules was recognized by a local as having been stolen, and a nearby Bolivian cavalry company was alerted. A bloody stand-off ensued, ending with the injured Butch shooting the mortally wounded Sundance in a mercy killing, and then taking his own life. Other versions have Cassidy and Longabaugh eluding capture, and eventually splitting up to live anonymously throughout North and South America. Regardless of their fate, all accounts seem to lack reasonable evidence and credibility.

As for Etta Place, the remainder of her life is just as unclear. Differing accounts have her traveling to Denver for a medical procedure and settling there, fighting in the Mexican Revolution, living somewhere in South America, residing in Mexico City with Longabaugh, or settling in a number of locations within the United States. This unfortunate lack of facts only adds to the curiosity about one of the most mysterious figures of the American West, the woman who rode with the Wild Bunch.

SOURCES:

Brawer, Moshe. *Atlas of South America.* NY: Simon and Schuster, 1991.

Buck, Daniel, and Anne Meadows. "Leaving Cholila: Butch and Sundance Documents Surface in Argentina," in *True West.* January 1996, p. 21.

Goldman, William (screenplay). *Butch Cassidy and the Sundance Kid.* Beverly Hills, CA: Twentieth Century-Fox Film Corporation, 1969.

Kelly, Charles. *The Outlaw Trail.* NY: Devin-Adair, 1959.
Kirby, Edward M. *The Saga of Butch Cassidy and the Wild Bunch.* Palmer Lake, CO: Filter Press, 1977.
Lamb, F. Bruce. *The Wild Bunch.* Worland, WY: High Plains, 1993.
Meadows, Anne. *Digging Up Butch and Sundance.* NY: St. Martin's Press, 1994.
Parker Betenson, Lula. *Butch Cassidy: My Brother.* Provo, UT: Brigham Young University Press, 1975.
Patterson, Richard. *Historical Atlas of the Outlaw West.* Boulder, CO: Johnson Books, 1985.
Pointer, Larry. *In Search of Butch Cassidy.* Norman, OK: University of Oklahoma Press, 1977.
Redford, Robert. *The Outlaw Trail.* NY: Grosset and Dunlap, 1976.

SUGGESTED READING:

Patterson, Richard. *Butch Cassidy: A Biography.* NE: University of Nebraska, 1998.

RELATED MEDIA:

Butch Cassidy and the Sundance Kid (112 min. film), starring Paul Newman, Robert Redford, and **Katharine Ross** as Etta Place, screenplay by William Goldman, directed by George Roy Hill, produced by 20th Century-Fox, 1969.

Matthew Lee,
freelance writer, Colorado Springs, Colorado

Place, Martha (1848–1899)

American murderer. *Born in 1848; executed at Auburn Prison, New York, on March 20, 1899; married William Place.*

Despite her plea to Theodore Roosevelt, then governor of New York, to commute her death sentence, Martha Place was the first woman to be executed in the electric chair. She had wounded her husband and killed her stepdaughter Ida with an axe on February 7, 1898.

Placencia (fl. 1068)

Queen of Navarre. *Born in France; flourished around 1068; married Sancho IV (1039–1076), king of Navarre (r. 1054–1076), after 1068; children: Garcia, titular king of Navarre; Urraca (a nun). Following the murder of Sancho IV, king of Navarre, Navarre was united with Aragon until 1134.*

Placidia (fl. 440s)

Roman noblewoman. *Flourished in the 440s; daughter of *****Licinia Eudoxia** *(422–before 490) and Valentinian III, West Roman emperor.*

Placidia, Galla (c. 390–450)

Roman empress who, as one of a triumvirate of remarkable women in the waning days of the Roman Empire, reached a position of power and influence.

Name variations: (full name) Aelia Galla Placidia, sometimes called Placidia or Galla Placidia Augusta (though Augusta is only a title accorded to women of the Late Roman imperial family); born around 390 CE; died while on a visit to Rome in 450; daughter of Theodosius I, Roman emperor, and Galla (c. 365–394, daughter of Valentinian I); sister of Emperor Arcadius (r. 395–408) and Emperor Honorius (r. 395–423); married Athaulf (Adolf), chieftain of the Visigoths (West Goths), in 414 (assassinated 415); married Constantius III, in 417 (died 422); children: (first marriage) Theodosius (died in infancy); (second marriage) Valentinian III (b. around 419); Honoria (b. around 420).

Captured by the Goths and taken to Gaul (modern France); married to Athaulf (414); Athaulf assassinated (415); Placidia restored to the Romans (416); married Constantius (417); death of Constantius (422); ascended throne with Valentinian III (423); forced by general Aetius to utilize his services (425); appointed Boniface to be Master of Soldiers to counter growing power of Aetius (430); Boniface defeated Aetius in battle in Italy (432); Aetius fled to Huns, returned with an army; with Boniface dead, Placidia forced to rely upon Aetius once again (433); Honoria, daughter of Placidia, banished to Constantinople for misconduct (434).

At the time of Galla Placidia's birth at the close of the 4th century, the end of the Roman Empire was at hand. The final disasters that would lead to its total collapse in Western Europe would take place while she was still alive. Barely a few years before her birth, however, the Roman world, though badly battered, was still intact. From the lowlands of Scotland to the Syrian desert, from the banks of the Rhine and the Danube to the edge of the Sahara desert, from the Black Sea to the Atlantic Ocean, virtually the entire known civilized world lived under Roman sway. But the last vestiges of republican forms and traditional Roman freedoms had long disappeared. The emperor was no longer the chief magistrate of a government officially representing, at least in theory, the will of the Roman people, but an oriental despot isolated in his palace, surrounded by pomp, ritual, and Asiatic seclusion.

The economy, so fragile in a world with low technology and little control over the forces of nature, had dropped to bare subsistence level for great masses of the people. Sapped by a steady decline in the population, the reasons for which are still not entirely clear, and a concomitant loss of trade and commerce, the cities gradually shrank in size. The middle classes were ruined, and the wealthy more and more took refuge on their rural estates. There, the local country folk, increasingly reduced to serfdom, would shortly, under the pressure of the invasion of the German tribes, give up all they had left for the security and protection offered by the landlords. In the towns, the bishops would become the only remaining figures of authority; in the rural areas, power would revolve upon the local lords. In this way, the society of medieval Europe was beginning to take shape while Rome yet survived.

As wealth decreased, the scramble to obtain more than one's share became increasingly acute. Bribery and corruption became the norm in high places (the government and the bureaucracy); while banditry in low places (the ranks of the common people) now characterized the countryside, adding to the insecurity and contributing to the economic decline. Although the reforms of Diocletian had brought to a close the decades-long crisis of the 3rd century (of the 26 emperors who reigned during a 50-year period, only one died a natural death), the damage that was done to the delicate fabric of the social and economic structure of the Roman world was almost impossible to repair, and, save for the restoration of a sound currency, nothing was ever to be the same again. Yet, for all this, the fundamental strength and resiliency of the Roman world, so rightly regarded with awe by contemporaries and future ages alike, reveals itself in the very fact that the empire, however imperfectly restored by Diocletian and Constantine the Great (r. 307–337), lasted for 173 years in Western Europe after the abdication of the former, and for 11 centuries afterwards in the East. Compared with this tenacious vitality, the career of the Soviet Union is but an episode in Russian history and an ephemeral curiosity in the history of the world.

The history of Ammianus Marcellinus, the last great historian of the Roman Empire, in the late 4th century, ends the series of classical Roman historians whose works illuminate the history of the Roman world until his time. Not until the emergence of Procopius, court historian of Emperor Justinian (r. 527–565), do we have another historian of the first rank. The years from 395 till 527, therefore, the period including the final partition of the Roman Empire in 395, the fall of the Western Empire in 476, and the life of Empress Galla Placidia must be pieced together from a great variety of minor sources, many of them existing only as fragments quoted by later authors, leaving us at the mercy of the chance survival of the snippets passed down to us by such inferior chroniclers as Claudian, Olympiodorus, Zosimus, John of Antioch, John Malalas, Priscus, Cedrenus, Sozomenus, Eunapius, Theophanes, the *Paschale Chronicle,* Orosius and Arian Philostorgus.

Galla Placidia was born at Constantinople around 390, daughter of *Galla and Emperor Theodosius I (r. 379–395), and sister of his successor Arcadius. When Theodosius died in 395, he partitioned the empire into two halves, his son Honorius (r. 395–423) receiving the West and his son Arcadius (r. 395–408) the East, both of them proving to be equally worthless as rulers but both of whom were gifted with highly intelligent advisors. Arcadius' advisor was the general Flavius Stilicho, a partly romanized German of the Vandal tribe, who died in 408. Placidia was raised in Constantinople until the age of six, when, upon the death of her father, she was taken to Rome by Stilicho and his wife, her cousin ➜ **Serena**. There, in the year 410, at the age of scarcely 20, she found herself trapped when the city was suddenly besieged by a horde of Visigoths, i.e. an East Gothic German clan who had crossed into the empire on the frozen waters of the River Rhine on New Year's Eve, 408. Gibbon has described most vividly the Gothic siege of Rome, the first that the imperial capital had had to endure in some eight centuries: the growing famine, the rise of pestilence, the increasing despair, the riots, starvation and cannibalism, and the cowardly execution of Stilicho's widow Serena, an act of despair by a Senate that had to do something and could think of nothing better than to accuse an innocent woman of treason. To give an odor of legality to this affair, the Senate obtained the consent of Galla Placidia. This first official act of the young princess may have been a painful one for her, for she appears to have been raised by Serena, but we know nothing of whatever emotions she may have felt at the time. At length, wearying of death and despairing of any help from Ravenna, the gates of Rome were opened by a slave, and the city was delivered to a three-day sack. Only the great basilicas of St. Peter and St. Paul were spared, together with those fortunate citizens who were able to take refuge there. For the rest, thousands of Romans were slaughtered and thousands more carried off as prisoners while the destruction of priceless works of art robbed the world of countless irreplaceable treasures.

Captured at the fall of the city, Placidia, though treated with the respect appropriate to her rank, was taken from place to place by the Gothic armies as they wended their way on a destructive looting expedition through Italy. Athaulf (Adolf) agreed to leave Italy if Honorius would guarantee the Goths lands in Gaul (modern France) with the status of *foederati* (allies) of Rome, and grant him Galla Placidia as his bride. The emperor—or at least his advisors—flatly refused to consent to such a marriage, but Placidia, who had once refused an offer of marriage from Stilicho, appears to have fallen in love with the young German prince, and she agreed to marry him.

In the beginning of 414, the wedding took place at Narbo where it was celebrated with great splendor by the Goths, rich with the spoils of Italy. For the occasion, Athaulf agreed to wear Roman garb, taking second place to his bride Placidia who was dressed in the clothes of a Roman empress. Fifty youths presented the couple with basins each filled with either golden coins or precious jewels. Athaulf then established himself as king of the Goths under some vague Roman suzerainty, ruling a state stretching from Burdigala (Bordeaux) in the West to the frontiers of Italy and encompassing the whole of southern Gaul and northern Spain.

Settling with her husband in Barcelona, Placidia soon gave birth to a son named Theodosius after his illustrious grandfather, a child whom the Goths intended to be both future emperor of Rome as well as their own king. Unfortunately, however, this child died while still an infant. He was buried in a silver coffin in a church near Barcelona until years later when his still-grieving mother had his remains transferred to the imperial mausoleum next to St. Peter's Basilica in Rome. Soon after his death, in the late summer of 415, Athaulf was assassinated in his palace at Barcelona and was succeeded by Singeric, brother of Athaulf's old enemy, Sarus, whom he had slain. Singeric now slew Athaulf's six children by an earlier marriage and humbled his widow Placidia by making her walk 12 miles, with other far less exalted prisoners, in front of his chariot. One week later, however, Singeric was slain by his own people, who then elected Wallia to be their chieftain on the basis of his anti-Roman policies. Upon trying to reenter Gaul after a failed expedition, the Goths were attacked by Constantius, the Master of Soldiers (*Magister Militum*). The Goths found themselves in a desperate situation and had to accept the status of Roman allies and return Placidia to her brother Honorius in order to receive grain.

Galla Placidia, we are told, would have preferred to remain a widow. But Honorius would not hear of it and had her married to the victorious Constantius, Master of Soldiers. A Roman from Naissus (now Nish) in the Balkan Peninsula, Constantius was the leader of the pro-Roman, anti-Barbarian faction at the Roman court. As Honorius had no children, Constantius, having been made a patrician as a result of his successes in Gaul and having been appointed consul, had ambitions to succeed him. Constantius' marriage to Placidia in January 417, which he had long desired, was a major step towards this goal. Two children were born to this union, a son, the future emperor Valentinian III, and a daughter named ***Honoria** after her uncle.

In 421, Constantius, who had been virtual ruler of the Western Empire since 411, was granted the imperial title of *augustus,* normally borne only by men of the imperial family, probably through the machinations of Placidia. Constantius was now declared co-ruler with Honorius with the title Constantius III, but Theodosius II, emperor of the eastern half of the Roman Empire, refused to recognize this condominium and war may possibly have broken out over the issue had not Constantius died suddenly on September 2, 422. At first, Placidia's position *vis à vis* her brother was high, and for a time she was all-powerful at his court. In short order, however, her relations with Honorius began to deteriorate, possibly as the result of the growing friction between the German entourage she had acquired when she was married to Athaulf, and the clique gathered around Honorius, i.e., the "pro-Barbarian" versus the "pro-Roman" factions at the court. The issue was, most likely, who would inherit the position and authority of Constantius. General Castinus was the probable candidate of Honorius; Count Boniface of Galla Placidia. The emperor's faction naturally won, and Castinus was made Master of Soldiers and immediately set off to lead an expedition against the Vandals in Spain. Boniface, for his part, fled to Africa (Tunisia and Libya), where he officiated as semi-independent governor of the province. Placidia now found herself accused of treason, but fortunately all that she endured was exile to Constantinople with her two children.

En route, via Rome, her ship almost foundered in a storm, during which Placidia

Serena (d. 410)
Roman woman. *Executed in 410; niece of Theodosius I, Roman emperor, and ****Galla*** *(c. 365–394); cousin of ****Galla Placidia*** *(c. 390–450); married Flavius Stilicho (Master of Soldiers), around 384 (died 408); children: daughter who married Honorius.*

vowed to erect a church to St. John the Evangelist if she and her children were saved. Arriving in Constantinople in the spring of 423, she lived as the guest of her nephew Theodosius II and of his sister, ***Pulcheria**, who, less than ten years younger than her aunt, dominated the court. An intelligent woman and a fine scholar, Pulcheria was devoted both to her church and to the welfare of her people. Characterized by extreme piety and chastity, she was instrumental in the calling of the third and fourth ecumenical councils of the church (those of Ephesus in 431 and Chalcedon 20 years later) and was canonized after her death, her feast still celebrated in the Orthodox Church.

Unlike her half brothers Arcadius and Honorius, she was a worthy child of the most Christian and Roman Emperor Theodosius the Great.

—**Stewart Irwin Oost**

Under the protection of her close relatives, Placidia probably lived on the income from lands in the East that she had inherited from her father, Theodosius I, but certainly from a stipend sent to her by Count Boniface. Honorius, however, died of dropsy in the summer of 423, at age 38, shortly after Placidia had settled down in a palace she owned in Constantinople. In 425, having obtained from her a promise of the cession of the disputed province of Illyria and the eastern part of Pannonia to his half of the empire, Theodosius, fearful of seeing the Western Empire fall into unknown and possibly hostile hands, sent his aunt overland to Italy, via Aquileia. An armed force was simultaneously dispatched to establish her six-year-old son on the throne at Ravenna as Valentinian III, with his mother as regent. All opposition in both Rome and Ravenna was speedily crushed. Valentinian was crowned at Ravenna in 425 and his sister Honoria made an *augusta* shortly thereafter.

For the first 12 years of Valentinian's reign, Placidia was the actual ruler of the West. She had given Valentinian, eventually detested for his weakness and treacherousness, a very poor education and had thereby kept him under her thumb. She governed well considering the dire circumstances in which the Western half of the empire now found itself. She stayed on good terms with Pulcheria and her nephew Theodosius II, ruler of the East, and in this way maintained her hold. When her daughter Honoria fell in love with a courtier, Eugenius, in 434, Placidia sent her to Pulcheria who circumvented the romance by clapping Honoria into a convent. In time, Valentinian journeyed to Constantinople where, in 437, he married ***Licinia Eudoxia**, his first cousin once removed, the daughter of Theodosius II and ***Eudocia** (c. 400–460).

As a result of this matrimonial alliance, not only were his ties with the Eastern Empire strengthened, but the Western Empire agreed to relinquish its claims to Dalmatia (western Yugoslavia), a frontier province hitherto disputed by the two empires. The Theodosian Code, a codification of Roman law compiled by a legislative committee under the emperor's name and promulgated in the East on February 15, 438, was accepted by the Senate at Rome on December 23rd of the same year. The Code of Theodosius recognized the independence of the Western Roman Empire. The long reign of Valentinian and his secure position, however, was only partly the result of his close relations with his mother's relatives in the East but rather was largely due to the military prowess of the general Aetius in whose hands real power lay during the second half of his reign, and to the latter's close relations with the Huns, whose hostage he had once been and whose language he had learned. Unfortunately for all concerned, Placidia harbored ill-will toward this able if overly ambitious general, never having forgiven him for supporting the opposition to the accession of her son Valentinian when Honorius died in 423.

The center of Placidia's administration remained at Ravenna on the Adriatic coast at the mouth of the River Padus (Po), rather than at Rome which had proven itself indefensible. Ravenna was walled and was surrounded by a moat created by diverting the Padus, but the city lacked for sufficient drinking water, never having been supplied with an aqueduct. Ravenna was the capital of Italy for some 400 years, during which time many monuments were built there, some of which have survived the centuries although many more have unfortunately been lost, including the cathedral known as the Basilica Ursiana to which Placidia had made rich gifts, and the imperial palace called Laurelwood. Of the surviving monuments, the Oratory of St. Peter, the Baptistry, and the Church of Sts. Nazarius and Celsus (the so-called "tomb of Galla Placidia"), where the imperial tombs were located (those of Honorius, Valentinian III and Placidia's husband, Constantius), all date from her time. Structurally, these buildings are in the Roman tradition; it is the decoration that shows the influence of the East. Ravenna was not only prosperous under the administration of Placidia, but through its close association with Constantinople it became a center for the entry of the slowly evolving "Byzantine" style that was emerging in the Eastern half of the old Roman

Empire. Many artists from Constantinople arrived at the Ravennese court where their influences blended with the arts of Italy. The typical oriental dome, mounted on pendentives over the transept of a cruciform ground plan, first appears in the Church of Sts. Nazarius and Celsus built around 450. Galla Placidia also erected a portico bearing her name at Portus, the port of Rome.

Despite the glitter of the court at Ravenna and the success of Aetius in reconquering most of Gaul, the reign of Valentinian and his mother was marked by irrecoverable losses of territory, with concomitant losses in taxes and military force. The era marked the death knell of the Roman Empire in Western Europe. Fearing the growing power of Aetius, whose victories against the German invaders on the Rhine and Danube came close to saving the empire, Placidia summoned Boniface to Italy in 430, probably planning to use him as a counterpoise. Aetius was now not only commander in chief of the whole Roman army but virtual prime minister of the empire as well. Boniface and Aetius thus found themselves engaged in a civil war with one another, and it was Boniface who appears to have won in the decisive battle that took place at Ariminium (Rimini) in 432. Aetius, having fallen, now took refuge with his old friends among the Huns. Boniface died soon afterwards, and, although Placidia gave his position to his son-in-law Sebastian, Aetius returned with a force of Huns in 433. Aetius forced her to banish Sebastian, to restore him to his former offices, and to grant him the title of patrician. Thereafter, it was Aetius who was virtual ruler of the empire for Valentinian III rather than Placidia.

Devoted to the recovery of Gaul, Aetius ceded all of Northwest Africa—the provinces of Mauritania Tingitana (western Morocco), Mauritania Caesariensis (eastern Morocco), Numidia (Algeria), and Africa (Tunisia and Libya)—to the Vandals, and lost the whole of Spain, Lusitania (Portugal) and Britain. Worse was to follow. In 450, Galla Placidia died on a visit to Rome, and her power over her son passed to her eunuch Heraclius. Heraclius feared the ambitions of Aetius, and it was he, in association with an ambitious senator named Petronius Maximus, who induced the emperor to slay the general with his own hand (September 22, 454) rather than allow him to marry one of Valentinian's two daughters and thus aspire to the throne after the emperor's death. Valentinian III was assassinated together with Heraclius by two of Aetius' aides on March 15, 455. Because the emperor had no son, the throne passed to Petronius Maximus, whose reign, however, was very brief. Twenty-one years later, the Western Roman Empire came to an end.

Like Pulcheria who guided the Eastern Roman Empire during much of the reign of her brother, Placidia had far more character than the emperor whom she served. The Roman world, disastrous as this period was for it, turned out to have been blessed that the women of the imperial family were both willing and able to assert some sort of direction in the affairs of state. The role of Galla Placidia in guiding the Western Roman Empire through so many of its most perilous later years assures her a permanent place as one of the more important women in history.

SOURCES:

The Cambridge Medieval History. Vol. I: *The Christian Roman Empire.* Cambridge, 1967.

Oost, Stewart Irwin. *Galla Placidia Augusta.* Chicago, IL: University of Chicago, 1968.

SUGGESTED READING:

Bury, J.B. *History of the Later Roman Empire from the death of Theodosius I to the death of Justinian.* Volume I. NY: Dover, 1958.

Gorden, C.D. *The Age of Attila.* Ann Arbor, MI, 1960.

Ostrogorsky, G. *The History of the Byzantine State.* New Brunswick, NJ: Rutgers University Press, 1957.

Robert H. Hewsen,
Professor of History, Rowan University of New Jersey, and author of a book and several articles relevant to Late Roman and Byzantine history

Plaisance of Antioch (d. 1261)

Queen and regent of Cyprus and Jerusalem. *Died in 1261; daughter of Bohemund V, prince of Antioch and count of Tripoli (r. 1233–1252), and his second wife* ****Lucienne of Segni*** *(r. around 1252–1258); married Henry I, king of Cyprus (r. 1218–1253); children: Hugh II, king of Cyprus (r. 1253–1267);* ****Isabella of Cyprus*** *(who married Hugh III).*

Planck-Szabó, Herma (1902—)

Austrian figure skater who dominated the international skating world until the rise of Sonja Heine. *Name variations: Herma Szabo; Herma Planck-Szabo or Herma Planck Szabo; also seen as Herma Szabo Planck. Born in Vienna, Austria, on February 22, 1902.*

Won individual World Skating championship (1922, 1923, 1924, 1925, 1926); with Ludwig Wrede, won the national championships in pairs twice and were World champions (1925 and 1927); won the Olympic gold medal in ladies' singles figure skating (1924).

During World War I (1914–19), international sports tournaments were suspended. By the time competition began again at the 1920

Olympics at Antwerp, Herma Planck-Szabó had begun her stellar rise in the world of figure skating. In 1922, she won the first of six National championships. When the World championships were held that same year, she won the first of her five World titles. At the 1924 Olympics at Chamonix, France, she took the gold when seven of nine judges gave her a first place. (**Beatrix Loughran** of the U.S. was awarded the silver; **Ethel Muckelt** of Great Britain won the bronze.) Planck-Szabó was also talented in pairs skating. She and Ludwig Wrede were two-time National champions, as well as World champions in 1925 and 1927. For five years, Herma Planck-Szabó, who was known for her daring jumps and spins, reigned supreme until, at age 25, she lost the World championship to a young Norwegian named ***Sonja Henie**.

Karin Loewen Haag,
Athens, Georgia

Planinc, Milka (1924—)

Yugoslav politician. *Born Milka Malada in Croatia in 1924.*

The first woman ever to serve as prime minister of a Communist country (Croatia), Milka Planinc was born Milka Malada in 1924. In 1943, during World War II, the 19-year-old Planinc joined Marshal Tito's Liberation Army. She began her political career after the war as a member of the League of Yugoslav Communists. Gradually working her way up through the ranks, she eventually became head of the League and a member of the National Parliament, where she earned a reputation as a tough politician. She took over her post as prime minister of Croatia in May 1982, following the inauguration of a new policy to rotate senior government posts to nationals within the various Yugoslavian provinces. She served until May 15, 1986.

Plater, Emilja (1806–1831)

Lithuanian patriot who fought to liberate her country. *Name variations: Emilija Plater; Emily Plater. Born in 1806 in Vilnius, Lithuania; died in Justinava (near Kapčiamiestis) in 1831 of an unspecified illness; daughter of Count Ksawery and Countess* ***Anna Plater****.*

Emilja Plater was born in Vilnius, Lithuania, in 1806, at a time when the country was controlled by the Russian government. From an early age, she desired the forceful liberation of Lithuania, studying military strategy and weaponry, and revering another great female patriot, ***Joan of Arc**. When a number of Lithuanians staged an insurrection, Plater, with her cousin Cezaris, organized an insurgent unit comprising 60 mounted nobles, 280 mounted riflemen, and hundreds of peasants brandishing scythes, planning to overtake the strategically important garrison town of Daugavpils. Russian soldiers thwarted her unit's goal, however, after which Plater participated in the capture of Ukmerge. An attempt to eject the Russians from Vilnius failed, but, following the reorganization of insurgents into military units, Plater received an appointment as commander and was given the rank of captain.

After the battle of Kaunas, during which she barely eluded capture, Plater's regiment retreated towards Šiaulenai. En route it was taken by surprise and defeated, and while many insurgents crossed into Prussia (now Germany) and surrendered, Plater refused to give up. Disguised as a peasant, she was attempting to make her way to nearby Poland, where she hoped to continue fighting against the Russians, when she fell ill and died in 1831.

SOURCES:

Salmonson, Jessica. *The Encyclopedia of Amazons.* NY: Paragon House, 1991.

Uglow, Jennifer S., ed. and comp. *The International Dictionary of Women's Biography.* NY: Continuum, 1985.

Howard Gofstein,
freelance writer, Oak Park, Michigan

Plath, Sylvia (1932–1963)

Pulitzer Prize-winning American poet, novelist, short-story writer, and essayist. *Name variations: (pseudonym) Victoria Lucas. Born in Boston, Massachusetts, on October 27, 1932; committed suicide in London, England, on February 11, 1963; first child of Otto Plath and Aurelia Schober Plath, both professors at Boston University; graduated from Smith College, 1955; married Edward James Hughes known as Ted Hughes (d. 1998, the poet), on June 16, 1956, in London (separated, October 1962); children: Frieda Rebecca Hughes (b. April 1, 1960, a poet who wrote* Wooroloo *and married the Hungarian-born painter Laszlo Lukacs); Nicholas Farrar Hughes (b. January 17, 1962).*

Entered Smith College (1950); attempted suicide (August 1953); graduated summa cum laude (June 1955); received Fulbright fellowship to Cambridge University, England (1955); taught at Smith College (1957–58); returned to England (December 1959); published The Colossus and Other Poems *(autumn 1960); bought house (Green Court) in Devonshire,*

England (1961); moved to London (December 1962); published The Bell Jar *(January 1963);* Collected Poems *awarded the Pulitzer Prize (1982).*

On October 16, 1962, Sylvia Plath wrote to her mother from London, where she was living, "I am a writer. . . . I am a genius of a writer; I have it in me." Four months later, Plath put her head in the open oven in her kitchen and turned on the gas—she was 30 years old. Suicide finally ended her struggle between her "warring selves." The outwardly articulate, energetic, intelligent, and talented young woman "lived an inner hell of her own making." Plath could be charming and affectionate if it served her purpose, but she was also obsessive, jealous, "innately self-righteous," and self-centered. She longed for perfection in her relationships, her writing, and her own life and was disappointed when reality fell short of her expectations. Unable "to re-create the world in her image," she chose to abandon it. In this final desperate act, she snuffed out a great talent that was reaching its acme.

Plath's biographers characterize her as a product of America and of the 1950s; she wanted a career as a writer, but she also felt she must have a husband, children, and a home in order to fulfill her dream, the American dream. With her extraordinary talent, her ambition, drive, and determination, Plath strove to have it all, but when she failed to achieve her "ideal world," she lost hope and her life.

Ironically, Plath's early childhood was near-idyllic. Her father Otto Plath was a professor of etymology at Boston University; he had taught foreign languages at the University of California and at MIT prior to doing graduate work at Harvard and earning a Ph.D. at age 43. Sylvia's mother, **Aurelia Plath**, was his student at Boston University where she was working on her master's degree. After marrying Otto, she gave up teaching languages at a local high school. They encouraged Sylvia to develop her imagination and provided an intellectually stimulating environment for their precocious daughter. However, life in the Plath household revolved around Otto and his scholarship; he wrote at home, and Aurelia worked with him. Sylvia spent much time with her maternal grandparents, the Schobers, who were educated, successful, and cultured Austrian immigrants.

In 1935, Otto and Aurelia had a son, Warren. Sylvia reacted angrily to this unwelcome intruder: "a baby," she wrote later, "I hated babies." She never ceased to crave attention from her father who always maintained a distance from his children, working and taking his meals alone in his study. As **Linda Wagner-Martin** notes, "Otto's approach to raising his children was to involve them in *his* life, rather than becoming a part of their lives." But early on Plath learned how to get her parents' attention; she spoke at an early age, had a large vocabulary, and made up stories and rhymes which she recited to them. In Sylvia's mind, intellectual success was necessary to be loved, a notion subconsciously reinforced by her scholarly parents. Plath's upbringing prepared her to excel in school; a straight "A" student, she treasured praise from teachers and her parents.

From the mid-1930s, Otto's health began to fail, and he became even more withdrawn from his family. He died in October 1940, at age 55. His protracted illness affected Sylvia whose fear of being abandoned was sharpened by his death. When Aurelia told Sylvia that her father had died, the child said calmly, "I'll never speak to God again," and went off to school as usual. Aurelia returned to teaching, and she and the children moved in with her parents to relieve their diminished financial situation. Plath's fear of being abandoned led her to write a note for her mother to sign—Aurelia had to promise not to remarry. She signed the note which only reinforced Sylvia's sense of importance. Insecurity became a constant in Plath's life, and despite having a strong mother and loving grandparents, she became "less sure of her place in the world . . . about her very existence."

When Aurelia was offered a teaching position at Boston University, she and the entire family moved to Wellesley, Massachusetts, an elite, upper-middle-class town where education was highly valued. Sylvia and Warren were surrounded by academics, and classmates who would be admitted to prestigious colleges. Living in Wellesley, Plath would be eligible to attend Wellesley College; still quite young, she "was already creating the ideal 'Wellesley self' who appeared confident, happy, poised, excited by life." Plath's adolescence was culturally stimulating and filled with reading, writing poetry and stories, and winning academic awards. Her first published poem had appeared in *The Boston Sunday Herald* when she was eight and a half years old.

Plath was expected to earn As in high school, and she did. She was not popular, however, which constantly worried her. A "smart loner," with an IQ of nearly 160, she had already received numerous academic and literary awards. She never doubted her scholastic abilities, but she suffered from an irrational fear of being deserted by her family coupled with an increasing self-centeredness. When her mother was approached to become dean of women at Northeastern University in Boston, Plath reacted angrily: "For your self-aggrandizement you would make us complete orphans," she said to Aurelia. Her mother turned down the position.

In her senior year of high school, Plath decided to attend an Ivy League college, but she would need scholarships, since money was always a concern. Plath resented not being able to enjoy the advantages of her wealthier classmates: travel abroad, expensive clothes, friends among the social elite of Wellesley. She would have to earn what others were given. From this time on, Plath wrote not only for critical acclaim but for commercial gain. To her, writing as an artistic expression was associated with earning money. By her final year of high school, she had already published her work in *Seventeen* magazine, *The Christian Science Monitor,* and *The Boston Globe.* However, her intensity and dedication to her academic studies and her writing affected her health. Only perfection was acceptable, anything less brought on "black moods" and bouts of depression. As she noted in her diary, "Never never never will I reach the perfection I long for with all my soul," but she never stopped trying. Plath had set standards which would lead to a lifetime of disappointments.

Plath worked as diligently at being accepted socially as she did at her studies. During the 1950s, girls were expected to marry, and most, including Plath, unquestioningly accepted this social norm. She kept lists of her dates, the prep school or college the young men attended, their families' social status, and their future prospects for success, and she dated a number of "eligible" men who met her criteria. Plath had no intention of being an unmarried career woman—not to marry was considered "unfeminine" in her social circle. But pre-marital sex was strictly avoided by "nice girls." Plath knew, however, that she wanted more than the typical domestic drudgery that marriage implied, and she felt this placed her outside the mainstream of society. She wanted to be a writer. At age 18, Plath wanted it all.

Plath chose to attend Smith College, which meant she would not live at home. In consequence of her excellent academic record, she was awarded two scholarships, one of which came from ***Olive Higgins Prouty** who became one of Sylvia's lifelong mentors and benefactors. Before entering college, Plath's short story "And Summer Will Not Come Again," which had appeared in *Seventeen*, had established her reputation as a writer at Smith. The publication of this story initiated a five-year correspondence with Ed Cohen, a university student in Chicago who was impressed with her work. They openly discussed sex, politics, religion, and the sinister effects of the McCarthy era on America. Plath admitted to Cohen that she was "sarcastic, skeptical and sometimes callous," but had a "vulnerable core"; she was not religious, she admitted—religion was for those "too spineless to think for themselves."

Plath's journals, begun in the summer of 1950, reveal the thoughts, feelings, and dreams she could not vocalize to friends or family: her impatience with people who did not meet her standards, her fear of failure, her need to be worthy of her scholarships and to live up to being a "Smithie." And how could she accept being a subordinate, submissive wife? "Spare me cooking three meals a day," she wrote, "spare me from the relentless cage of routine and rote." Plath wanted freedom to achieve in her chosen field, to be a *famous,* commercially successful writer. That she might have to choose between marriage and a career made her angry and fearful; "What is my life for and what am I going to do with it," she wondered, "I don't know and I'm afraid." In any case, she refused to become "a 'meek' Christian wife." As she expressed it in her journal, "I am I—I am powerful."

Plath was powerful, and she was brilliant and physically attractive. She earned excellent grades, dated men who were her intellectual equals and would be successful, and was active on several councils, boards, and committees on campus. Typically, however, the future was where happiness surely would be found. The present was always just a prelude to a happier future. Writing provided Plath with emotional release, and it would, she hoped, bring her immortality. But her achievements masked an inner turmoil. In a morbidly prescient revelation, Plath wrote in her journal, "I think I will be snuffed out. Black is sleep; black is a fainting spell; and black is death."

In her sophomore and junior years, Plath published poems and short stories in *Seventeen, Mademoiselle,* and *Harper's,* and her essay, "As a Baby-Sitter Sees It," appeared in *The Christian Science Monitor.* She won a prize of $200 for her story "Initiation," from *Seventeen*, a $500 first prize in the Mademoiselle Fiction Contest for "Sunday at the Mintons," and two Smith poetry prizes ($120). To be paid for one's writing would remain a major consideration throughout her life. Her abilities and talents were further recog-

Sylvia Plath

nized at Smith when she was invited to join an arts honorary society and was inducted into Phi Beta Kappa. Despite her impressive accomplishments, Plath was insecure; she had yet to find the "perfect" mate. Dick Norton, the son of family friends, and Myron Lotz, both of whom attended Yale and were entering medical school, were viewed as potential husbands. But Plath's need to control relationships, her jealousy and possessiveness, disturbed her male friends. And when her boyfriends lost interest in her, she reacted angrily to their "betrayal." To marry might require her to "whittle my square edges to fit in a round hole," but, she added, "God, I hope I'm never going to massacre myself that way."

By fall 1952, Plath's self-doubt, irrational sense of failure, and exhausting schedule adversely affected her health; her menstrual cycle was interrupted, and she suffered from insomnia. In November, she wrote her mother: "Everything is empty, meaningless. This is not education. It is hell." And in her journal she noted, "I feel behind my eyes. . . a mimicking nothingness. . . . I want to kill myself. . . . I do not know who I am, where I am going." Her grim outlook hardly matched her cumulative successes; in May 1953, Plath went to New York as one of 20 young women chosen for the Mademoiselle College Board. She worked as a guest managing editor, but comments and criticisms from staff members undermined her confidence and depressed her. On returning home, she was devastated to learn that she had not been accepted for a summer course at Harvard University.

I think I would call myself "The girl who wanted to be God."

—Sylvia Plath

Increasing lethargy and insomnia, worry over her prospective senior thesis and exams, and an ineffectual suicide attempt in July, prompted her mother to seek psychiatric help for Sylvia. As a result, she underwent terrifying electric shock treatments which failed to relieve her problems. On August 24, Plath swallowed almost a full bottle of sleeping pills, leaving a note for her mother saying she "had gone for a long walk," and would return the next day. Two days later, her brother found her under the floor boards of their house. After months of hospitalization, undergoing therapy and further shock treatments, Sylvia was able to return to college in 1954.

Plath continued to be considered an "academic star" on campus with a reputation of being a loner, a beautiful, rather intriguing figure who had tried to take her own life—her disappearance and unsuccessful suicide attempt had made national news. Plath's fragile mental state did not interfere with her achieving excellent grades, writing poems which later won prizes, and for the first time enjoying sexual liaisons with several young men, all of whom measured up to her criteria for a future husband.

After receiving several more prestigious awards at Smith College, Plath graduated in June 1955, summa cum laude. Her academic achievements and her literary talents paid off; she was granted a Fulbright fellowship to study at Newnham College, Cambridge University, in England. All expenses, including books and travel, would be paid for a period of one or two years. Marriage could be deferred, but it was not repudiated. Plath now had two goals, to get the best possible education and to find a husband in England before returning to the States.

At Cambridge, Plath was regarded as a "dramatic, attractive American," ambitious, talented, and self-indulgent. Intending to take advantage of everything Cambridge had to offer, Sylvia was active and involved, writing articles for a local paper, acting in an amateur Dramatic Club, attending classes, and submitting the required weekly essays to her tutors. However, friends in her dormitory residence found Plath difficult at times. She was still prone to angry outbursts and appeared nervous, aggressive, and shrill, especially when she did not get her own way. She dated frequently, still seeking her "true love"—when on February 25, 1956, she bought a copy of a literary magazine and read some poems by Ted Hughes.

Impressed with Hughes' poetry, Plath asked an American friend to introduce her to the poet. They met that same evening at a celebratory party for the magazine, "a collision of two glamorous carnivores." A graduate of Cambridge in anthropology (1954), Hughes was intelligent, cultured, talented, tall (6'6"), and handsome, and became "the greatest living English poet" at the end of the 20th century. Plath recorded their "collision" in her journal; that evening "he kissed me bang smash on the mouth. . . and I bit him long and hard on the cheek and when we came out of the room blood was running down his face." Hughes confirms Plath's description of their encounter in his book of poems *Birthday Letters* (1998). He recalls "the swelling ring of tooth-marks/ That was to brand my face for the next month/ The me beneath it for good." Plath knew that she had found her "true love" though he might be, as she wrote Prouty, "a breaker of things and people." Moreover, Plath wrote that she "suspected that he loved to drink and make conquests of women." Prouty advised her not to rush into marriage, but Plath ignored her mentor's admonishment. To her mother, Sylvia announced that she was in love, a love "which can only lead to great hurt." If Plath had any reservations about Hughes, they could not outweigh her determination. In characteristic fashion, she began to idealize their future life together, setting herself up for the disappointment that reality always had in store.

On June 16, 1956, Edward James Hughes and Sylvia Plath were married in the church of

St. George the Martyr in London; one of the poems in Hughes' *Birthday Letters* poignantly recalls his bride: "In your pink wool knitted dress/ Before anything had smudged anything/ You stood at the altar." The marriage was kept secret from friends and family, except for Aurelia who had attended the wedding. Plath feared she would lose her Fulbright fellowship if she were married.

During their honeymoon in Spain, Sylvia began to realize that wives were expected to do the shopping, cooking, and housework, and she resented it. She loved Ted, but "the consistent bliss she had envisioned" had not materialized. In her journal, in Spain, she noted, "It is very quiet. Perhaps he is asleep. Or dead. How to know how long there is before death." Only a month later, she lamented: "The world has grown crooked and sour as a lemon overnight."

From Spain, the Hugheses went to the village of Heptonstall in Yorkshire to visit Ted's family. They were pleased with the marriage, and Sylvia enjoyed the countryside and seeing Ted in "his home country." On her return to Cambridge, Plath resumed residence at Newnham College; Ted went back to Yorkshire. But they found they could not live apart. After talking to her tutor, **Irene Morris**, Plath was granted permission to complete her year at school and to retain her Fulbright fellowship. In November, she and Ted moved into a small apartment. Plath prepared for her exams and did household chores; she and Ted worked on their own writing each morning for about five hours. He was doing especially well in getting published, and Sylvia served as his agent, sending his poetry to prestigious journals. She appeared to have all she had hoped for; she was married to a marvelously talented man who shared her interests and admired her poetry. Ted was, as Sylvia wrote her brother Warren, "the only man in the world who is my match." Plath worked hard, worried about money, and began behaving "erratically at times." Marriage, she had discovered, interfered with her writing and her scholarship.

Neither she nor Ted wanted to take permanent jobs, but in April 1957, Plath was offered a teaching position at Smith College for the coming academic year. She accepted the position to teach three sections of freshman English, hoping Ted could teach at Amherst or the University of Massachusetts. She did not want him to teach at Smith where he would attract "the predatory Smith students." In the spring, Plath passed her exams and decided not to work on a Ph.D. She wanted to concentrate on her writing. She had recently published in *The Atlantic Monthly*, six poems in *Poetry*, for which she won the Bess Hokin prize, and an essay on life in Spain, which she illustrated, in *The Christian Science Monitor*. Sylvia was anxious to begin a novel about her love for Ted and their first meeting, tentatively titled *Falcon Yard*. They spent the summer writing in a cottage on Cape Cod which Aurelia had obtained for them. Sylvia was not satisfied with what she was writing and became anxious and upset when she thought she was pregnant. If pregnant she could not teach, and she experienced "a black lethal two weeks. . . . The horror . . . of being pregnant [which] would end me, probably Ted, and our writing and our possible impregnable togetherness." Ted tried to be helpful and supportive, but Sylvia seemed to take on the problem of her pregnancy alone. Wagner-Martin notes that Plath assumed the responsibility, the burden that "would unbalance and slant the ledger for the rest of the marriage." Sylvia was not pregnant, but she was angry because she had been unable to concentrate on her writing.

Sylvia and Ted moved to Northampton, less than a mile from the Smith campus, before fall semester began. Plath realized almost at once that she lacked the temperament and patience required to work with students and to correct "eye-socket searing" term papers. Petty bickering among the English faculty also disappointed her. Ted was able to write at home while waiting to begin teaching part-time at the University of Massachusetts in Amherst for the spring term. Sylvia resented that he had time to write and she did not. Teaching and household duties left her exhausted and ill, physically and mentally. Her life, she confided to her journal, was "a grim grind," and "I deserve a year, two years, to live my own self into being." Plath was writing well, but friction over money and over their future plans, coupled with Sylvia's jealous tirades and lack of tact, resulted in violent arguments. Ted was publishing more and was sought after to do readings of his work. But Sylvia was also receiving recognition; she read for a Harvard Library recording of her poetry and also did one for the Library of Congress. Even when she was writing well, Sylvia worried that she was not good enough to earn a living by writing. Ted had no such doubts, and he was less concerned about publishing his work than whether his writing satisfied him.

Plath became depressed, even after she resigned from teaching at the end of the school year, and she and Ted moved to the Beacon Hill area of Boston; here they were able to socialize with literary figures with whom Sylvia was acquainted. And they could devote themselves to writing. Plath was concerned about not having an assured income, but she sold several poems to *The New Yorker,* and Ted insisted they could live off their writings. Sylvia, however, was less confident and took a part-time job at Massachusetts General Hospital for a short time. She did not press Ted to do the same, but she was openly resentful of his ability to turn out excellent work, and she envied his growing reputation. Depressed and angry, Sylvia sought psychiatric help. Some feminists have accused Ted Hughes of causing Plath's depression and of not being sufficiently supportive of her efforts, but their friend, **Dido Merwin**, claims: "Their working symbiosis was a genuine 'marriage of true minds' . . . that [Ted] prized above everything apart from his own writing." Sylvia's self-doubt and depression had plagued her long before she met Ted Hughes. Plath was actually doing some of her best writing at this time, including her story "Johnny Panic and the Bible of Dreams," and several excellent poems. Living in Boston gave her the opportunity each week to attend Robert Lowell's Boston University poetry workshop where she met the talented poet ***Anne Sexton** with whom she became close friends. Plath had found someone with whom she shared "attitudes, knowledge, and experiences." Sexton was not impressed with Plath's poetry at that time, but she liked Sylvia personally. In May 1959, Sylvia's book of poems, *The Bull of Bendylaw*, was chosen as the alternate to the winner of the Yale Younger Poets contest. Plath was furious, for she thought herself a better poet than the winner. She would have to work harder.

Boston was energizing and culturally stimulating, but Sylvia and Ted decided to return to England where Ted would be happier, and they could live more economically. Before departing, they spent the fall at Yaddo, an artists' and writers' colony in upstate New York. Here Sylvia "grew as a poet" and found a "voice" for her writing that was "witty, wry, American, brazen, arrogant," a contrast to what Plath called "drawing room" speech. Her new-found voice is evident in her collection *The Colossus and Other Poems*, which would appear in England in the fall 1960. Colloquial language and subjects based on Plath's own experiences make the collection one of her best and most personal. While on a cross-country trip before sailing for England, Sylvia became pregnant. Obviously motherhood would entail responsibilities that would take precedence over writing. But, as usual, Plath had high expectations that would be dashed by the banal realities of everyday living.

The Hugheses found an apartment in the Primrose Hill area of London near Regent's Park. The next month, Sylvia signed a contract with William Heinemann Ltd. to publish *The Colossus and Other Poems*, scheduled to appear in the fall. *London Magazine* took one of her poems and her story about Massachusetts General Hospital, "The Daughters of Blossom Street." Despite her success, Plath was tired, and the grey, cold winter depressed her. Sylvia became more demanding, insisting she had to have privacy and her own space in their tiny apartment. According to friends, Ted was relegated to working on a borrowed portable table in a dim hallway; Sylvia's needs, they claim, always took precedence over Ted's. Moreover, Plath was becoming more possessive and tactless, resentful of anyone who invaded their lives, even visitors. Their friend Lucas Myers notes that she did not want Ted to talk to anyone but her, that she was "trying to swallow him whole." After the birth of their daughter **Frieda Hughes**, Sylvia's postpartum depression exacerbated her destructive behavior. Domestic duties increasingly consumed Plath's energies while Ted was gaining a national reputation for his poetry and his work for the BBC. Their friends W.S. Merwin and Dido Merwin lent Ted the study in their apartment in which to work quietly. Sylvia convinced Ted to share it with her. She worked in the study in the mornings, Ted in the afternoons. Even though she now had a routine and time to work, Plath was still filled with anger and anxiety over money and her ability to write. She and Ted often quarrelled. Yet Plath loved London and its cultural opportunities, and she loved Ted. In October 1960, she wrote a poem for him ("Love Letter"): "Not easy to state the change you made./ If I'm alive now, then I was dead,/ Though, like a stone, unbothered by it."

By autumn of 1960, Plath was writing well. She produced several good poems and was planning to write a novel. Her poems reveal her deep dissatisfaction with life, as she began to explore her psyche rather than depending on lists of topics Ted had made for her. But Sylvia was restless and depressed. She always needed activity, a change, a "better" future, and began to make plans to find a house and perhaps have a second child. *Colossus* received good reviews which pleased her, and she made the first of many appearances on the BBC. Prouty sent her a congratulatory check of $150. Sylvia, who had always "wanted it all" seemed to have achieved her goal, but debilitating moodiness, frequent ill health, and a miscarriage in February 1961, badly affected her relations with Ted. In a fit of jealousy, she burned Ted's notes and drafts of his new works, an "act of spite," declares Dido Merwin, and adds that Sylvia never felt any regret or showed any remorse for her irrational behavior.

Themes of death and about women and children dominated Plath's poems of the spring 1961, written in a woman's voice. She and Ted appeared together on the BBC, and Sylvia began to write her novel *The Bell Jar*. This book was more than autobiographical; she wanted "to speak for the lives of countless women she had known," women who were forced to make choices; "No woman can have it all," Plath wrote, "but choosing is also difficult." Writing *The Bell Jar* was a liberating experience for Sylvia, as Wagner-Martin notes, and Plath's writing "for the first time ever provided a continuity" for her. The novel is a story of betrayal and of external forces that inhibit and oppress the female heroine. She would initially publish the book under the pseudonym Victoria Lucas.

When Sylvia became pregnant again, she was determined to leave London and live a "simpler" life in the country. She and Ted finally purchased an ancient ten-room house, called Green Court, in Devonshire, in 1961. The property included a stable, a courtyard, gardens, and a large orchard. Typically, Plath threw herself into keeping house and writing. "The Moon and the Yew Tree" is a personal evocation of her Devon yard, located near an old church cemetery. Discomfort, a sense of foreboding, and "images of blackness, fear, and hopelessness" figure large in her poems at this time. In contrast to her dark mood, Plath was increasingly recognized as a major talent; she and Ted continued to win awards and prizes for their work and to maintain their professional contacts in London. Even after the birth of their son, Nicholas, in early 1962, Sylvia tried to care for their large house and property and the two children and to write. A radio play, "Three Women," was taken by the BBC, and she completed *The Bell Jar* which encouraged her to work on her novel about how she and Ted met and her love for him.

But feelings of isolation from London and resentment over not having time for herself, for writing, and for Ted, troubled Sylvia. During the winter and spring of 1962, she was aware that something was wrong; Ted was moody, distant, and his poetry dwelt on "bleak and introspective things" and an "obvious distrust and anger toward the feminine." Plath felt uneasy. Then in May, David and **Assia Wevill** arrived to spend a weekend at Green Court. Sylvia was convinced that Ted was, or would be, involved with Assia who was obviously attracted to him. (Assia Wevill would commit suicide in 1969 by putting her head in a gas oven.) Sylvia's reaction to her suspicions is revealed in her poems "The Rabbit Catcher" and "Event:" "I cannot see your eyes. . . . I walk with an absence," and ending, "I am appalled by the death smell of everything."

As Ted spent more and more time in London, Sylvia, too, began living a more independent life. In her poem "Poppies in July," she realizes: "I am unattached. I am unattached." But she could not calmly accept that her marriage was in trouble, that Ted had severed their "togetherness." When what she referred to as "mysterious" phone calls for Ted occurred, she became agitated, tore out the phone wires, and once again burned Ted's letters, drafts of his work, and her book that described her love for him, "it was, in effect, a funeral pyre." At the same time, Plath's career was taking off; *The Colossus* was published in America, *The Bell Jar* was accepted for publication in England, several of her poems were accepted by prestigious journals, and she was writing a variety of essays and the play for the BBC.

In September 1962, Sylvia decided to seek a legal separation from Ted Hughes. She felt betrayed, her health began to deteriorate, and she could not eat and had trouble sleeping. In letters to her mother, Plath accused Ted of being "immature, selfish, cruel," and a liar who destroyed their happiness. In the midst of uncertainty and despondency, Plath entered one of the most productive periods of her writing career; she wrote most of her "Ariel" poems and her "bee sequence, her survival poetry" (she had taken up bee-keeping in Devon). In her bee poems, the queen bees, i.e., women, survive and endure—"They had got rid of the men/ The blunt, clumsy stumblers, the boors." Plath was aware that she was "writing the best poems of my life; they will make my name."

Despite their separation, Ted helped Sylvia find an apartment in London, again in the Primrose Hill area, in the fall of 1962. She had dreaded spending the winter in Devon and hoped to begin anew in the city where she could have frequent contact with literary friends. Before moving, she continued work on a third novel and put together the poems for *Ariel* which told the story of her life as writer, mother and wife, and of "the dissolution of that life." Exhausted, ill, and incapable of handling even the most routine daily responsibilities, Sylvia, the children, and their nurse moved to London in December 1962. Again, the life in London which she had hoped for and expected did not materialize. Infrequent social invitations from old friends, the rejection of many of her poems by *The New Yorker* and of *The Bell Jar* by Knopf and by Harper & Row in America left her despondent and unable to function. Housekeeping and caring for the children "was all too much trouble, everything was too much trouble," she admitted. She confided in Professor Thomas, a neighbor, that she was angry at her husband and "the other woman" (Assia) and of being "chained to the house and children when she wanted to be free to write and become famous." However, Plath was still able to turn out work of an exceptionally high quality, and she had gained a considerable reputation from publication of *The Bell Jar* in England and from her poetry. Plath's personal life was becoming intolerable. Feeling betrayed, isolated, and tied down by domestic cares, she felt she was "in limbo between her old life and an uncertain grim new one." In the early morning hours of February 11, 1963, Sylvia Plath took her own life.

Not all of Plath's personal, revelatory journals have survived her death. Ted Hughes admitted he destroyed one of the volumes, which created an uproar among scholars and Plath admirers. Hughes has been reviled by some feminists since Plath died; he was picketed during public appearances by women's groups, and angry Plath partisans have obliterated Hughes' name from Plath's tombstone several times.

In one of Plath's last poems, "Edge," she seems to be reflecting on her own situation: "The woman is perfected./ Her dead/ Body wears the smile of accomplishment." This talented, bedeviled woman deserved to wear "the smile of accomplishment" for she had come farther than she could have imagined. She is buried in the village of Heptonstall, in Yorkshire, near the graves of Ted Hughes' family. Ted Hughes died in October 1998.

SOURCES:

Knoll, Jack. "Answering Ariel," in *Newsweek*. February 2, 1998, pp. 58–59.

Stevenson, Anne. *Bitter Fame: A Life of Sylvia Plath*. Boston, MA: Houghton Mifflin, 1989.

Wagner-Martin, Linda. *Sylvia Plath: A Biography.* NY: Simon and Schuster, 1987.

SUGGESTED READING:

Alexander, Paul. *Rough Magic: A Biography of Sylvia Plath*. NY: Viking, 1991.

Kukil, Karen V., ed. *The Unabridged Journals of Sylvia Plath, 1950–1962: Transcripts from the Original Manuscripts at Smith College*. NY: Anchor, 2000.

Plath, Aurelia, ed. *Letters Home by Sylvia Plath, Correspondence, 1950–1963*. NY: Harper & Row, 1975.

Plath, Sylvia. *Ariel*. Edited by Ted Hughes. NY: Harper & Row, 1966.

———. *The Bell Jar*. NY: Harper & Row, 1971.

Rose, Jacqueline. *The Haunting of Sylvia Plath*. Cambridge, MA: Harvard University Press, 1993.

COLLECTIONS:

Manuscripts, work sheets, unpublished poems and fiction, journals and correspondence are located in the Lilly Library, Indiana University, Bloomington, and in the Neilson Library, Rare Book Room, Smith College.

Jeanne A. Ojala,
Professor of History, University of Utah,
Salt Lake City, Utah

Platière, Marie-Jeanne Roland de la (1754–1793).

See Roland, Madame.

Plato, Ann (c. 1820–?)

***African-American writer and poet.** Born around 1820 in Hartford, Connecticut; date of death unknown.*

Ann Plato, who is believed to be only the second African-American woman to publish a book (the first was ***Phillis Wheatley**) as well as the first African-American to publish a book of essays, was born around 1820 and grew up in a small community of mostly free blacks in Hartford, Connecticut. There is scant information about her family, or, indeed, about her. Her poem "I Have No Brother" is about a brother who died when she was young, and it is thought that she had some Native American ancestry, based on her poem "The Natives of America," in which she wrote about the oppression these people faced:

> Tell me a story, father please,
> And then I sat upon his knees.
> Then answer'd he, —"what speech make known,
> Or tell the words of native tone,
> Of how my Indian fathers dwelt,
> And, of sore oppression felt;
> And how they mourned a land serene,
> It was an ever mournful theme."

Plato was greatly influenced by the Congregational Church, which she joined at the age of 13, and she reflected on her church experiences in one of her poems, "Advice to Young Ladies." When she was only about 15, she was teaching at a church school; another poem, "The Infant Class," begins: "This, my youngest class in school, is what I do admire."

Plato self-published her only known book, *Essays; Including Biographies and Miscellaneous Pieces in Prose and Poetry,* in 1841 in Hartford. Although she was probably around the age of 20 then, many of her poems may have been written in her early teens. In the introduction, Rev. W.C. Pennington, pastor of the Colored Congregational Church in Hartford and a well-known abolitionist, wrote: "I am not in the habit of introducing myself or others to notice by the adjective 'colored,' &c., but it seems proper that I should just say here, that my authoress is a colored lady, a member of my church, of pleasing piety and modest worth." He added: "The best way to do justice to young writers, is to weigh their thoughts without so strict a regard to their style as we should pay in the case of elder writers."

Plato's book included 16 essays that addressed such subjects as obedience, nature, religion, and death ("Reflections Upon the Close of Life"), and are strongly Christian in tone. The Puritan theme of her essays also dominated the 20 poems included in the book, written in the typical iambic tetrameter of the period. Most of her poems have death as their theme. "To the First of August," however, is about slavery, her sole poem on the subject. It speaks of the British abolition of slavery in the West Indies in 1838:

Lift ye that country's banner high,
And may it nobly wave,
Until beneath the azure sky,
Man shall be no more a slave.

Plato's work also included four brief biographies of African-American women, **Louisa Sebury**, **Julia Ann Pell**, **Eliza Loomis Sherman**, and **Elizabeth Low**, all of whom suffered illness and died before they reached 30 years of age. Of Eliza Sherman, who died of a lung infection in 1839, Plato wrote that the climate of the South would have been more suitable for reasons of her health, but the laws of slavery, of course, prevented her from going there. It is apparent from these writings that the early death of these women profoundly affected Plato. Even her Author's Farewell spoke of her obsession with the end of life.

Modern critics have been harsh about the overly virtuous tone of Plato's book, which was quite common for literature of the time; **Joan Sherman**, in *Invisible Poets* (1974), said that her essays are "the pious, moralistic effusions of a Puritan girl," and William Robinson called them "routine" and "mercifully brief." Plato's importance, however, lies less in the content of her book than in the mere fact of it. At the time she published, slavery, while roundly condemned in most Northern states, was still the law of the land in some half of the United States (in a number of Southern states it was illegal to teach blacks to read or write), and women of any race were routinely undereducated in comparison to men. Both African-American and a woman, Plato was remarkable for her time because she wrote in a number of mediums and because she decided to publish her work.

SOURCES:

Buck, Claire, ed. *The Bloomsbury Guide to Women's Literature*. NY: Prentice Hall, 1992.

Busby, Margaret, ed. *Daughters of Africa*. NY: Pantheon Books, 1992.

Smith, Jessie Carney, ed. *Notable Black American Women*. Detroit, MI: Gale Research, 1992.

Don Amerman,
freelance writer, Saylorsburg, Pennsylvania

Plautia Urgulanilla (fl. 25 CE)

Roman noblewoman. *Flourished around 25* CE*; first wife of Claudius (10* BCE*–54* CE*), Roman emperor (r. 41–54* CE*), divorced; children: Drusus. Claudius then married* ****Paetina***, ****Valeria Messalina***, *and* ****Agrippina the Younger***.

Pleasant, Mammy (c. 1814–1904).

See Pleasant, Mary Ellen.

Pleasant, Mary Ellen (c. 1814–1904)

African-American civil-rights activist and entrepreneur. *Name variations: Mammy Pleasant; some sources indicate surname as Pleasants or Plaissance. Born on August 19, 1814 (according to her own account), in Philadelphia, Pennsylvania; died on January 11, 1904, in San Francisco, California; married Alexander Smith (a Cuban tobacco planter and abolitionist, died 1848); married John Pleasant (or Pleasants), around 1848 (separated).*

Was involved in civil-rights activities; moved to California (1849), where she owned a boarding house and engaged in legal and illegal business activities (1850s on); was a philanthropist who boasted that she financed John Brown's raid on Harper's Ferry, an account that is unproven.

Historical accounts and the memoirs of Mary Ellen "Mammy" Pleasant paint very conflicting portraits of her early years, while her later years are cloaked in scandalous reports and mystery. Her own most consistent version was that she was born a free person in Philadelphia to a Louisiana-born black mother and Louis Alexander Williams, a Kanaka, or native of Hawaii. Some biographers, however, claim she was born into slavery in Virginia, the child of a black or mulatto slave and a white plantation owner. Still other reports indicate that she was born into slavery in Augusta, Georgia. According to this last account, a visitor to the plantation, impressed with her intelligence, bought her freedom for $600 and sent her to work for a friend, who eventually sent her to work at a store in Nantucket, Massachusetts.

When she ended her work on the island of Nantucket, the family who owned the store helped Pleasant become established in Boston. It was there that she met and married her first husband, Cuban planter and abolitionist Alexander Smith. He died in 1848 and left her with $45,000, a substantial legacy, to be used to support abolitionist causes. Soon after, she married John Pleasant (or Pleasants), who had been an overseer on the Smith plantation. She reportedly was involved in the Underground Railroad, and was so successful in assisting escaping slaves that she had "a price on her head in the South."

Accounts relate that the Pleasants went to California in 1849, during the gold rush, but her husband apparently did not figure very significantly in her life after the journey. Pleasant moved to San Francisco and put her business acumen and entrepreneurial skills, not to mention her reputation as a noteworthy cook, to work. There was much wealth circulating in the heady days of the gold rush, but few luxuries in the area to spend it on. Miners and merchants were clamoring for services, and Pleasant, according to San Francisco newspapers, rejected many offers of employment as a cook from people with means. (One of these included a bid to pay her $500 a month.) Instead, with her name now well known, she opened a boarding house that provided lodging and food, both of which were scarce. Many of Pleasant's boarders rose to prominence in the community and state, and she kept her ties with them. She expanded her business dealings by lending money to businessmen and miners at an interest rate of 10%, while also investing wisely on the advice of her influential boarders and other associates. During this time she gained a reputation as "The Fabulous Negro Madam," acting as a procurer for her male associates. Newspaper reports say she guarded the identities of her clients with absolute devotion, which made her quite popular among those clients. A photograph of Pleasant from around this time reveals a strikingly attractive face with determined features.

Concerned about racial equality, she became increasingly involved in helping others and in civil-rights activities during the 1850s and 1860s. In addition to providing financial assistance for these causes, she sought out and rescued slaves being held illegally in the California countryside. (California had entered the Union as a free state under the Compromise of 1850, but the legal status of slaves brought there by their owners from slave states was vague.) Pleasant also found jobs in wealthy households for runaway slaves and developed an information network. One of the most widely circulated, albeit unsubstantiated, reports on Pleasant concerns her role in abolitionist John Brown's raid on the U.S. arsenal at Harper's Ferry, West Virginia, in 1859. She reportedly sailed to the East in 1858 and in Canada gave Brown $30,000 to finance his battle against slavery. Among Brown's belongings when he was captured was a note that read: "The ax is laid at the foot of the tree. When the first blow is struck there will be more money to help. (signed) W.E.P." Supporters of this theory suggest that the "M" in Pleasant's initials may have been misread as a "W." Skeptics of her account of the Brown connection, however, say that Brown had already left Canada by the time of her visit there, and that she produced no evidence to prove she had given him any money.

Pleasant returned to San Francisco around 1859 and continued both her business activities and her activism. In 1863, she was integral in winning African-Americans the right to testify in court in California (previously, neither African-Americans nor Native Americans were allowed to speak in court in civil or criminal cases, even ones in which they were directly involved). She also fought to win the right of African-Americans to use San Francisco's streetcars. In 1868, she brought two railroads to court and successfully sued them for refusing her passage. Testimony in *Pleasants* v. *North Beach and Mission Railroad Company*, appellant, indicated that a conductor had told her: "We don't take colored people in the cars." The lower court's ruling for Pleasant, awarding her damages of $500, was appealed to the California Supreme Court, where it was upheld. (Legislation forbidding discrimination by race in matters of public accommodations, such as streetcars, would not be passed in California until 1893.)

Pleasant operated a house of ill repute called Geneva's Cottage for a number of years beginning in 1869, and some time later became a housekeeper for wealthy San Francisco banker Thomas Bell and his wife **Teresa Bell** (who may have been an erstwhile employee of Pleasant's). The Bell mansion promptly gained the nickname of "The House of Mystery" for the strange goings-on there, many of which remain murky but evidently provided Pleasant with illicit access to much of the Bell fortune. This association also sparked a major scandal involving one of Bell's business competitors, William

Mary Ellen Pleasant

Sharon, a U.S. senator from Nevada who was also a former resident of Pleasant's boarding house. Pleasant apparently paid several thousand dollars to a woman named **Sarah Hill** to claim she was Sharon's wife and to sue him for a divorce and a property settlement. Hill was successful at the state court level, but that court's decision was later overturned and the marriage contract that she had produced as evidence declared a forgery. While this scam apparently cost Pleasant money (instead of gaining her a share of Sharon's property settlement, as she no doubt intended), she was reported to have wangled a large chunk of Thomas Bell's estate after he died in an unexplained plunge from an upper window of his home.

By mid-1899, however, Pleasant filed for bankruptcy, and requested food and other necessities from acquaintances. (It is thought, nonetheless, that she retained a considerable amount of money even at that time.) She lived her last few months in the San Francisco home of a family named Sherwood who had befriended her, dying on January 11, 1904, and was buried in their burial plot in Napa, California.

SOURCES:

Griffin, Lynne, and Kelly McCann. *The Book of Women: 300 Notable Women History Passed By.* Holbrook, MA: Bob Adams, 1992.

James, Edward T., ed. *Notable American Women, 1607–1950.* Cambridge, MA: The Belknap Press of Harvard University, 1971.

Smith, Jessie Carney, ed. *Notable Black American Women.* Detroit, MI: Gale Research, 1992.

Don Amerman,
freelance writer, Saylorsburg, Pennsylvania

Plectrudis (fl. 665–717)

Queen and regent of Austrasia and Neustria. *Name variations: Plectrud or Plectrude. Flourished between 665 and 717; daughter of Hugobert and* ***Irmina,*** *both founders of Echternach; first and senior wife of Pepin II of Herstol or Heristal, mayor of Austrasia and Neustria (r. 687–714); children: two sons: Grimoald II, mayor of Austrasia and Neustria (d. 714); Drogo, also known as Drogon, duke of Champagne.*

First wife of Pepin II and queen and regent of Austrasia and Neustria, Plectrudis became a factor in the political conflicts of the Frankish kingdoms when Pepin fell ill in 714, the same year that her only surviving son Grimoald II was assassinated in Liège. At the time, Pepin held a tenuous authority over Neustria which he had attempted to unite with Austrasia under his rule. He had accomplished this by defeating the Neustrians at the battle of Tertry (near Saint-Quentin) in 687, but his grip on Neustria remained insecure because the noble Neustrian families still thought of him as an outsider, an Austrasian. Pepin had managed to control Neustria with the help of his and Plectrudis' two sons, but trouble erupted at the first sign of weakness. Upon his illness, and the death of Grimoald (son Drogo had also died), Pepin made Grimoald's six-year-old son Theudoald mayor of the palace of Neustria.

Pepin II, however, had more than one wife. His second wife ***Alphaida** (c. 654–c. 714) had given birth to a son, Charles Martel, around 690. Following Pepin's death, it fell to Plectrudis, his senior wife, to protect the power of her grandson, which was now threatened by Martel. First, she imprisoned Martel and established herself at Cologne, assuming the guardianship of Theudoald. But Martel escaped from her custody and rebelled, with the support of his mother's relatives. At the same time, the Neustrians also revolted, electing their own mayor, Raganfred, and setting up a Merovingian puppet, King Chilperic II. After defeating Theudoald in battle in 715, Raganfred took on Martel, whom he also nearly succeeded in destroying. Martel eventually prevailed, however, and after defeating Raganfred at Vinchy (near Cambrai) in 717, he persuaded Plectrudis to surrender Pepin II's possessions and to accept him as head of the family. Martel went on to defeat the invading Muslims in the famous Battle of Tours (732), while Plectrudis slipped into obscurity. Martel founded the Carolingian dynasty dominant in the Frankish kingdom (today's northern France, Belgium, and parts of western Germany); his grandson Charlemagne would continue the expansion.

Plessis, Alphonsine (1824–1847)

Parisian courtesan whose brief, brilliant, tragic life inspired the novel and play* La Dame aux camélias *("Camille") by Alexandre Dumas* fils *and the opera* La Traviata *by Guiseppe Verdi. *Name variations: "The Lady of the Camellias"; (pseudonym) Marie Duplessis; (fictional names) Margaret Gautier or Gauthier; Marguerite Gautier or Gauthier; Rita Gauthier; Camille; La Dame aux camélias or La Dame aux camelias; Violetta Valéry. Pronunciation: AHL-FON-SEEN play-SEE. Born Rose Alphonsine Plessis in Nonant-le-Pin (Orne) on January 15, 1824; died in Paris on February 3, 1847, and buried at Montmartre Cemetery; daughter of Jean-Martin (called Marin) Plessis (1790–1841) and Marie-Louise-Michelle Deshayes (1794–1834); had about three years of education in a convent school; married Viscount Édouard de Perrégaux, on February 21, 1846; children: (with Count Agénor de Guiche) possibly a son (b. 1841).*

Along with siblings, abandoned by her mother (1832); became a restaurant owner's mistress after her father left her in Paris (1839); was the mistress of Count de Guiche and may have given birth to a child (1840–41); was mistress of Viscount Perrégaux (1842–43); unmistakable symptoms of tuberculosis appeared, became Count Stackelberg's mistress (1844–45); had affair with Dumas fils *(1844–45); had affair with Franz Liszt (1845); married Perrégaux, appeared at the Brussels ball opening the Paris-Brussels railway, and went into seclusion because of illness (1846).*

In 1839, Alphonsine Plessis, aged 15, arrived in Paris from Normandy with her father, Jean-Martin (called Marin) Plessis. He left her with the Vital family, cousins of her deceased mother **Marie-Louise-Michelle Deshayes**, and returned home. A year later, the penniless, barely literate Alphonsine, who spoke with a strong Norman peasant accent, was circulating in high society. Nothing in her background would have predicted such a transformation, for her childhood had been a nightmare of poverty and abuse.

Alphonsine's father was a country peddler, the son of a drunken village prostitute (nicknamed "The Hag") and a seminarian, Louis Descours (d. 1815), who became a government-approved priest during the French Revolution. Marin was fairly handsome, a tall, slender, vigorous man with a bad reputation, for he was sly, impulsive, malicious, violent, and an alcoholic. In time, the peasants called him "Satan" and accused him of sorcery.

Her mother, an exceptionally beautiful, dark-haired woman, was affable, tender, delicate, and intelligent. She had noble ancestry, the Mesnil family, who had fallen on hard times when Alphonsine's great-great-grandfather had squandered the family's resources. His daughter **Anne du Mesnil** (b. 1735) married a servant, Étienne Deshayes. In 1789, their son Louis Deshayes (Alphonsine's grandfather), likewise a servant, married a cousin, **Marie-Madeleine-Louise Marre**. She had two daughters: Alphonsine's mother Marie and **Julie-Françoise Deshayes**. According to a local tale, Marie's real father was Louis' master, a noble who, with Louis' compliance, had exercised his *droit de seigneur*. The story typifies the difficulties confronting Alphonsine's biographers. Some records have been uncovered, but while anecdotal evidence from memoirs and such is abundant and detailed, it is also disputed and seriously lacks chronological precision. Hence, any account becomes strewn with qualifiers.

Marin and Marie married on March 1, 1821, after he promised to reform. They borrowed to start a notions-and-groceries store in Nonant-le-Pin (Orne), a village of some 500 souls about 13 miles by road east of Argentan and 100 miles due west of Paris. Their first born, **Delphine Plessis** (later Mme Paquet), was born in 1822, and Alphonsine followed on January 15, 1824. Marin's "reformation" had ended in a few weeks. His drunken rages only increased when Alphonsine proved not to be the son he had wanted. When the store failed, he returned to peddling, and the family moved from hovel to hovel, finally to a shack in Castelle on the Nonant-Gacé road. The end came when he tried to start a fire on the floor swearing he would burn his family. Marie and the girls fled to the attic and escaped incineration only because a passing messenger heard her cries, burst in, saved them, and beat up Marin.

The children were sent temporarily to an aunt at Trouillière while Marie hid out with friends, including the noblewoman **Mme du Hayes**. When du Hayes heard that an eccentric, wealthy widow, who spent her time in Paris and Switzerland, was seeking a maid-companion without children, du Hayes and others convinced Marie to take the job to save her life. So Marie embraced her daughters, left hidden in a wagon, and never saw them again. She died two years later in Switzerland of "a broken heart" and possibly tuberculosis.

Delphine was put in the care of a Mesnil uncle, trained as a laundress, and at 16 sent to a fine home. Alphonsine, aged 8, was much less fortunate. She was given to an impoverished relative at La Porte, **Agathe Boisard**, who at least saw that she got some schooling at a convent nearby. But after her first communion (at age 11), extreme poverty forced Agathe to make her beg her food from relatives and neighbors, returning home at night. Predictably, Alphonsine fell in with rude farmhands with whom she saw and heard more than a child should. Perhaps before she was 12 and before her first menstruation, she lost her virginity. One story says she seduced a 17-year-old servant named Marcel; that was his version. Hers was that she was 14 and was surprised at a roadside by a passing young noble, Viscount Théodoric de Narbonne-Pelet (1814–1901), who rewarded her with a new gold coin.

Scandalized by talk of her behavior, Agathe finally sent her to Marin, who placed her with a **Mme Toutain**, a laundress employing girls for 10 francs a month. But Alphonsine visited her father monthly, and in August 1836 he took her to Exmes to a 70ish bachelor reprobate, M. Plantier-Devoir, and left her for the weekend. She returned Monday evening with 20 francs for him. These visits became weekly, and she began skipping work. After inquiries, Mme Toutain quietly sent her back to her father, and Marin in turn gave her to Plantier as a servant. The word in the village was that she was being sexually exploited by Marin and Plantier. Marin was called before the mayor, warned, and maybe jailed briefly.

Plessis next became a servant at the inn at Nonant run by the Denis (Denais) family, either placed by her father or fleeing there. After a few months, during which she became ill for a time, Marin suddenly showed up and sent her as an apprentice and servant to an umbrella maker in Gacé (October 1838?). Two months later, he took her home with him. Rumors of incest circulated.

At this point, Marin decided out of fear or calculation to leave her with the Vitals, her maternal relatives in Paris. Partly by boat and by begging rides in wagons, they slowly made their way. Alphonsine later claimed her father had sold her to a band of Gypsies (Roma), a romantic tale but highly suspect. Marin returned to Nonant, fell ill (perhaps from syphilis), and died two years later (February 8, 1841) in utter misery.

The Vitals' little grocery had no need for Plessis, so they sent her to a laundress, **Mme Barget**—or so one version goes. Alphonsine's early years in Paris cannot be reconstructed with precision. She is variously reported to have worked as a laundress, a linen maid (*lingère*), an errand girl for a millinery shop, a hatmaker or dress-sewer, and a clerk in a boutique. Simply put, she was one of the tens of thousands of young working women who lived in garrets and did not always eat regularly. Thousands, among them Plessis, became *grisettes*, fun-loving charmers who thronged to public places and danced in halls and at street fairs. (The waltz, cancan, and soon the polka were veritable crazes in these years.) The girls' hope was somehow to meet an eligible bachelor, preferably monied, and marry. Latin Quarter students were especially sought after, and Plessis soon was noticed there, for she was becoming truly beautiful.

The most absolute incarnation of woman who has ever existed.

—Franz Liszt

Testimonies are unanimous regarding her extraordinary attractiveness. She was tall for that time (5'5¾"), in figure svelte, if possibly too thin, and graceful to the last degree. Her skin was a fashionable translucent white. Her face was a perfect oval; her mouth very small; lips thin but still sensual; teeth regular and brilliantly white; hair velvety, variously described as dark chestnut or black, hanging in long ringlets to her shoulders (*à l'anglais*). Her most striking feature was her eyes: large, deep, very dark, with long lashes and full dark eyebrows, expressive, shining, devouring, sad, mysterious, altogether magnetic. As she matured, her persona joined a graceful restraint with a powerful sexuality, a melding which left men mesmerized.

During the week, Plessis worked long hours. Sundays after Mass, she and her friends would go looking for fun, probably hoping some man might pick up the tab, but she apparently lost one or more jobs for coming to work late on Mondays or skipping altogether. She led a hard existence and often went hungry. Tales later had it that she had been jailed briefly and that she had accepted money from the Russians to spy. A famous anecdote dates from this time. A prominent theater director and *bon vivant*, Nestor Roqueplan (1804–1870), related how he had encountered her at the Pont Neuf one evening standing "entranced" before a fried-potato stand. Young, pretty, delicate, and "dirty as an unkempt snail," she was nibbling on a green apple which she didn't seem to like. "The fried potato was her dream; I offered her a large cone." She blushed in happiness. A year or so later, he was astonished to meet her at the fashionable Ranelaigh dancehall being escorted by Count de Guiche.

In September 1839, a happenstance—a rainstorm—changed her life. She and two girlfriends decided to go to the festival at Saint-Cloud one Sunday. The day turned out rainy, so they hung around the shops at the Palais-Royal and finally sat down in a restaurant. The owner, nameless to history and variously described as a widower in his 40s or 60s and fit or fat, struck up a conversation and finally offered to meet them the following Sunday to take them to Saint-Cloud. The day came and the outing went happily. The man began to see them weekly, but it became clear it really was Alphonsine who interested him. One day in November after another outing, he asked her to go with him to inspect an apartment he had leased on the rue de l'Arcade. She was impressed by the place and then shocked when he said it was hers. A place of one's own was every *grisette*'s dream. To seal the offer, he gave her 3,000 francs for expenses. (This was a huge sum; chambermaids and laborers earned about 350 francs per year.) So she crossed the line and became, when not quite 16, a kept woman, her entryway into a career as a courtesan at the pinnacle of "Tout Paris."

A courtesan has been defined by **Joanna Richardson** as a woman who is "less than a mistress because she sells her love for material benefits [but] more than a prostitute because she chooses her lovers." Unlike even top-grade call girls of later times, courtesans were celebrities. They inhabited a kind of social and moral limbo. Marriage in the middle and upper classes was about property, not love or sex except for the procreation of heirs. So extramarital affairs were viewed with indulgence, albeit much more so for men than for women. Courtesans were respectable in the sense of having an accepted place and role in the monied classes while yet regarded as "fallen" and hence unsuitable for marriage. Even so, many did end up marrying, some into the upper class.

Plessis, by nature an exceptionally fast learner, quickly mastered the ground rules of the profession. Whether sex was a grand passion with her can only be inferred, although it seems likely. Three other passions held sway without question: money, the theater, and gambling. As

Eleonora Duse in La Dame aux camélias.

regards money, she did not love it for its own sake. Once introduced to the world of wealth, she only wanted all the nice things it could buy. She did not, however, forget her origins; freely had she received, so freely did she give, reportedly 20,000 francs per year at her peak. Her lovers never accused her of avarice, only of heedlessness, of letting vast sums run through her fingers like so much sand into a well.

The restaurateur could not keep up the pace for long. He prudently withdrew, it is said. Or perhaps he lost out to a competitor. An oft-repeated story says that while they were at the Prado ballroom one evening, she caught the eye of Count de Guiche and in short order became his mistress. Others say she had one or more lovers before de Guiche took over. In the nature of things, it is all but impossible to reconstruct a secure succession of lovers for a courtesan. It is clear enough, however, that the relationship with de Guiche was by far the most important in establishing her in fashionable society.

Antoine-Agénor, count de Guiche, prince de Bidacher, and future duke de Gramont (1819–1880), was the heir to one of France's grandest titles but to only a relatively modest fortune because of the French Revolution's inroads. He would become a diplomat and finish, as Napoleon III's last foreign minister, by blundering into the catastrophic Franco-Prussian War (1870–1871). He had graduated (1839) from the École Polytéchnique and served briefly as an artillery lieutenant before resigning and becoming an elegant loafer and dandy. A six-foot tall Adonis, he reportedly had brief affairs with the actress ***Rachel** (1821–1858) and the courtesan La Païva (**Thérèse Lachman**, 1819–1884) before meeting Alphonsine. He set her up in a fine apartment at 28, rue de Mont-Thabor, near the Tuilleries, and assumed the role of Pygmalion. Much enamored of her, he had her tutored in reading and writing, manners, dress, conversation, piano playing, and literature, and furnished her with a library of ancient and modern classics which she apparently read with pleasure. It is testimony to her intelligence and perhaps an innate sense of how to act that in a few short months she metamorphosed into a young woman indistinguishable in grace and taste from those to the manner born, at least in public. In private parties at her place, her peasant origins sometimes betrayed themselves in over-drinking and bawdy jokes and songs. She also changed her name to the more distinguished-sounding Duplessis and soon after dropped the plebeian Alphonsine for Marie. (Interestingly, her mother's death certificate reads "Marie Duplessis.") The idyll with de Guiche ended, however, in late 1840 or 1841.

One of the deepest mysteries of Alphonsine's life concerns a stay (July–November) back in Normandy in 1841. Frédéric-Romain Vienne, who was a close acquaintance from Nonant, says in his gossipy biography that it was no mere vacation, as her friends thought, but had been ordered by her doctor after a difficult childbirth at Versailles early in May. Vienne says further that she told him the father had taken charge of the boy's care but that the child had died from an infection a year later. Vienne went on to relate, however, that in 1869 a young man resembling Alphonsine appeared at her sister Delphine's door and asked to see a picture of her. He shed a tear and left after giving Delphine a card saying he was one "Judalet," a commercial employee in Tours. Delphine made inquiries. The local inn had housed no such guest, and the mayor of Tours informed her no Judalet lived there. Vienne is the sole source for this oft-repeated childbirth story. No records at Versailles confirm the birth. As for the alleged father, de Guiche is a strong possibility, but given the nature of her activities, one can only speculate.

Opposite page From the movie Camille, *starring Robert Taylor and Greta Garbo.*

Back in Paris, she led a frenetic existence, a "*ballet des amants*" to support her spending, writes **Micheline Boudet**. She became a favorite of the young lions of the Jockey Club and their witty, dissipated leader, Count Ferdinand de Montguyon; purportedly, seven made a pact reserving a day apiece with her each week. It was through the Club that she met the man often called the "great love" of her life, Viscount Édouard de Perrégaux (1815–1889). Whatever the case with her, he was more smitten than she. Perrégaux was a grandson of a famous financier whom Napoleon I made a senator and first regent of the Bank of France. He had joined the army in 1834, campaigned in North Africa, and resigned on April 6, 1841, as a cavalry lieutenant. His father died in June, so he and his elder brother inherited a huge fortune, although the family's trustees kept watch over it. He was dreamy and melancholic in the current romantic fashion, honest and gentle, but immature still, feckless, susceptible to "all the sentimental weaknesses," notes Johannès Gros. He bought a fine racing stable and plucked a top courtesan, **Alice Ozy** (Julie-Justine Pelloy, 1820–1893), from the duke d'Aumale. In the spring of 1842, however, he met Alphonsine, known to him as Marie Duplessis, and fell helplessly in love.

Perrégaux lavished money and attention on her without stint. He bought a cottage in Bougival, near Versailles, where they spent many enchanted days. In mid-July, they went off on a two-month tour of the German spas capped by Baden-Baden, where she allegedly won 50,000 francs gambling. On their return, they moved into an expensive apartment at 22, rue d'Antin. Quickened by gambling losses in Paris, the pace began to take its toll, allegedly 1,000 francs a day. The figure probably is inflated, but the picture is clear enough. The Bougival cottage had to go, while she pawned silver to pay ballooning debts.

Plessis began to see other men occasionally; she needed money and was tiring of Perrégaux's puppydog devotion. Also, the Perrégaux trustees probably stepped in to tell him to quit, and he reluctantly left town pleading family business. By early 1843, it appears, Alphonsine was on her own again. Men, mostly young, from all sectors—nobility, government, finance, the military—flocked to ask her favor. Not all were rich; but then, no one man could afford to keep her anyway. She tirelessly circulated at society ballrooms, restaurants, race tracks, and above all theaters. Managers gladly reserved her prime boxes on opening nights where she held court between acts for authors, actresses, and Jockey Club swells. She also held soirées at her apartment which attracted the likes of Eugène Sue, Théophile Gautier, Alfred de Musset, and Honoré de Balzac. Perrégaux, back after several months, dropped by occasionally. She granted sexual favors only as she pleased, but even rebuffed suitors still came around to enjoy the scene and be seen. (One not-so-subtle signal: for a few days each month her corsage contained red flowers.) She was captivating, seductive without really trying. As novelist Roger de Beauvoir put it, she was simply wonderful company—high praise from a renowned dandy and wit.

Oral tradition says she sojourned in Italy with an unnamed escort. In early summer 1843, she visited the German spas again. It is also alleged that she sought a respite by returning to Nonant and staying at Narbonne-Pelet's château but that Paris lured her back after a month. These travels may have been connected with concerns about her health. By the winter of 1844–45 at the very latest, she had contracted tuberculosis, "the white death," a plague which cut fearsome swaths through the populace at that time.

Plessis probably had been exhibiting some symptoms in 1842 when Perrégaux first took her to the spas. When or how she had become exposed is impossible to say. It may well, even probably, have occurred during her impoverished childhood. Clearly, her lifestyle per se was not the cause. Certainly it did not aid her fight against the disease, for even when she went to the spas she would soon grow bored with resting and drinking the water and revert to her usual rounds of dancing, partying, and gambling, activities which only intensified when she became convinced she had not long to live. Such behavior spawned a belief that her disease was the result of—and hence even divine punishment for—her sins. In point of fact, given the inability of medicine at that time to do more than alleviate its symptoms, tuberculosis almost certainly

would have killed her even if she had never attended the theater or partied away the nights or bedded any lovers. At the most, death only would have come a little later.

In the summer of 1844, Plessis found her last great patron, Count Gustav Ottonovitch von Stackelberg. He had been the Russian ambassador to Austria during the Congress of Vienna (1814–15) and was now in his 70s and retired in Paris. Extremely rich personally, married to a wealthy woman, and drawing a pension from the tsar, he was physically fit, an aged Don Juan, yet decent, fond, and caring. According to her perhaps-invented story, he approached her while she was visiting, unattended, the spa at Bagnères-de-Luchon (Haut-Goronne) and asked her to accept his support because she bore a striking resemblance to his daughter, who had died of tuberculosis. More than likely he was simply looking for a new love. She agreed, and he set her up in a splendid six-room second-floor apartment at 11 (today 15), boulevard de la Madeleine, a prime location facing the Church of the Madeleine.

Until her malady became acute in the spring of 1846, Plessis was at her zenith. Stackelberg deluged her with jewelry and money. Most courtesans had more money than taste, but not "Marie Duplessis," with her apartment full of art works and fine furnishings; her two coaches and high-stepping English bloodhorses coursing the boulevards and the Bois de Boulogne, where she was driven daily for some repose; her careful daily coiffure and daily new gloves; her wardrobe, smashing yet not showy, featuring many white or pearl-gray gowns which were often set off by lovely shawls and which eliminated muttonchop sleeves, lowered the waist, and introduced a new style, deeply cut in the back; her necklaces ("a river of diamonds"), rings, brooches, pins, bracelets, earrings, watches, and chains (her estate contained 78 such items, which sold for 24,912.50 francs). It remains one of the great mysteries of her time how a dirt-poor, abused, nearly illiterate peasant girl could become in record time a trendsetter of taste and fashion in the world's most sophisticated city, a paragon of grace, modesty, decorum, tact, and, simply stated, unimpeachable elegance. The most famous theater critic of the day, Jules Janin (1804–1874), wrote of Plessis that "unlike ***Lola Montez**," she was never "the heroine of any of the stories of ruin and scandal, of gambling, of debts and duel" to which others owed their vogue, for she never lost a touching sensibility. Wrote Alexandre Dumas *fils*, "She was one of the last of those rare courtesans who had a heart."

Plessis could be frank about herself, although she admitted, "I like to tell lies because they keep the teeth white." The actress **Judith Bernat** (1827–1912) recorded that Alphonsine, who admired her immensely, once confided:

> Why have I sold myself? . . . Because the labor of a working woman would never have procured the luxury for which I have an irresistible need. . . . Despite appearances, I am neither avaricious nor debauched. I wanted to know the refined pleasures of artistic taste, the *joie de vivre* in an elegant and cultivated society. I have always chosen my friends. . . .
>
> And I have loved. Oh yes! Sincerely loved, but nobody has ever returned my love. It is the horror of my life. You are wrong to have a heart when you are a courtesan. You die of it.

She adored flowers but found she was allergic to their odors. So she decked her person and apartment with wild flowers and odorless types, particularly (but by no means exclusively) camellias, a flower as sought after as orchids would become later. Was she known in her lifetime as "The Lady of the Camellias?" An oft-repeated story says she was given the nickname by an old charwoman at the Opéra. Dumas, however, said he invented it for his novel. Since there is no secure evidence of its use before her death, Dumas appears to have the stronger case.

As for Stackelberg, occasionally he was seen with her, but frequently she appeared alone in public. In order to tire her less, he began to host parties at her apartment. Sometimes she was the only woman present, often making a dramatic late appearance; at other times women were invited, among them on several occasions the notorious Lola Montez. Stackelberg remained content providing she honored "his hours," when he "paternally, prudently took his pleasure," writes Maurice Rat. The last man to be naive in such matters, he showed only mild jealousy if she entertained other lovers when he was absent or had left early.

Of these others, the best known are Alexandre Dumas *fils* (1824–1895), and Franz Liszt (1811–1886). Dumas, a fledgling writer, the illegitimate son of the great novelist, saw her at the Variétés theater in September 1844 and was overcome. Of the same age as she (20), handsome, gallant, witty, he was living mostly off handouts from his father. He wrote of her: "This mélange of gaiety, of sadness, of naïveté, of prostitution, this malady even which developed in her an irritability of feelings as well as an irritability of nerves, all that inspired in me an ardent desire to possess her." The affair, more an intense infatuation than a *grand amour*, cooled somewhat after a few months but continued for a year. By that time, he was too deeply in debt to continue. On August 30, 1845, he wrote to her that he must give her up. Two months later they parted for good after a petty quarrel—caused by his failure, it was said, to get tickets from his father for the premiere of *The Three Musketeers*. Obviously, love had died by then. (Forty years later, he reclaimed the August 30 letter at an auction and gave it to ***Sarah Bernhardt**, whose performances as "The Lady of the Camellias" set the standard.) Plessis' affair with Dumas, banal as it may have been (as he later asserted), was to become for both a hugely significant event.

The affair with Liszt, an immense celebrity, the greatest pianist of the century, was mutually passionate but brief. His movements are well documented, so one can establish a quite accurate dating. Plessis likely had attended one of his concerts during his triumphant stay in Paris from mid-April to mid-June 1844. On October 22, 1845, he returned for a brief time before beginning, on November 19, to give concerts in Metz and Luxemburg and at some point in late November and December in Colmar, Nancy, Châlons, Rheims, Nantes, and Angers. After a January 1, 1846, concert at Rennes, he went to the Northeast and Belgium and did not return to Paris. He later wrote to Dr. David-Ferdinand Koreff on February 12, 1847, ten days after her death, affirming that they had been introduced in November. Hence, they must have been together only a week or two that month and then, until January 1, 1846, possibly a few days between his provincial engagements.

Janin's oft-quoted version of their meeting—that she had introduced herself to him and Liszt at a theater intermission and engaged Liszt in a long, animated conversation—is mostly an invention. In old age, Liszt recalled that he and Janin were at the Théâtre-Ambigu. Between acts Janin pointed her out and warned that she had him in her sights. The next day she asked Dr. Koreff, a mutual acquaintance, to invite Liszt to join her circle at her place. Liszt accepted and Koreff introduced them. A fashionable doctor, "half charlatan, half genius," writes André Maurois, Koreff had treated her with some success from winter to June 1845 for severe chest inflammation; he had also treated Liszt's mother **Anna Liszt** and Liszt's former mistress, Countess ➜ **Marie d'Agoult**, who wrote under the pseudonym Daniel Stern.

Liszt, aged 34, attracted women as easily as Plessis did men. She was swept away, and so was he, saying later that while he had no special liking for courtesans, she was an exception: "She had a great deal of heart, a gusto altogether ideal." In a long letter to d'Agoult (May 1, 1847), he called Plessis "the first woman with whom I fell in love"—a puzzling thing to write to one who had been his mistress for ten years and given him three children (including ***Cosima Wagner**). He was also forgetting his first love, **Caroline de Saint-Cricq** (d. 1872).

Plessis knew time was slipping away, and she was becoming desperate to escape to a new life. She told him, "I shall not live; I'm a strange woman, I shall not be able to cling to the life I cannot have and cannot bear. . . . Take me with you wherever you want; I shall not be a burden to you, during the day I shall sleep, in the evening you can let me go to the theater, and at night you can do with me what you want!" Liszt promised he would take her with him to Constantinople. But he could not take her with him to Weimar, where he held a court appointment, or to Vienna. Apparently he promised to meet her in Budapest, where he performed from late April to mid-May. He confessed decades later that the project was "one of the steps of life escaped at great cost, one of those I have most regretted." Realizing she was seriously ill, had he tried to soothe her with a hollow promise? Probably. And probably she knew it. He went on without her to Constantinople and would be at Kiev when he learned of her death. By chance, the night she died his recital would include Carl Maria von Weber's "Invitation to the Dance," her favorite waltz.

On February 3, 1846, a scant month after Liszt's departure for Weimar, she left for London with Perrégaux, and on February 21 they were married at Kensington by the Registrar for the County of Middlesex. Because bans had not been published, the French consul-general in London refused to ratify the marriage, making it null under French law. They separated almost immediately.

This strange episode has no ready explanation, although it is noteworthy that upon her return she immediately had her stationery, linen, and coach doors marked with a coat of arms and called herself the Countess du Plessis (not Perrégaux). Had she begged Perrégaux to lend her a patina of respectability by marrying her? Did he marry her out of pity, or love? Was he in some way deceived and then discarded? Had the affair been a ruse on her part to use a title to help her with Liszt? In a note to him, she confirmed that he could resume his liberty as he had

◄ **Agoult, Marie d'.** *See Wagner, Cosima for sidebar.*

requested. But what were their respective motives? At all events, the "marriage" was known to but a few, she was careful when and where she used a title, and in a trial on April 1 for nonpayment of debt to her lingerie supplier, she finally answered, with obvious discomfort, that she was not married.

Money troubles, never far from her door, had begun to mount. Stackelberg's subsidies had declined. Her clientele thinned as her health slowly ebbed. Doctors and prescriptions began to exact heavy tolls. Bill collectors thronged her antechamber, merchants were having to accept delays, and pawnbrokers began to see her maid frequently—19 times between March 1846 and January 1847.

In May, she rested for three weeks at Nonant but then returned to the whirl, only to leave again, this time for Spa, where, against her doctors' orders, she rode horseback and danced and gambled feverishly. On June 16, having used some pull to obtain a ticket, she made a sensational appearance in Brussels at the grand ball inaugurating the Paris-Brussels railway. She waltzed so beautifully that a great crowd gathered to watch. After this triumph, she sped off to Baden-Baden, Wiesbaden, and Ems. While at Wiesbaden, however, she fell seriously ill. Frightened, and remorseful over something she had done, she wrote a despairing note to Perrégaux from Ems saying she was "alone here and very sick" and begged his forgiveness. Did he reply? For whatever reason, he applied to rejoin the army that summer but was turned down.

In early August, she was back in Paris, quite sick now. Until October, however, she continued to go out to soirées, theaters, the Opéra, restaurants, and the track. The public noticed a weight loss, hollowing cheeks, a slight flush, a reddening of the eyes. And, of course, a worsening cough. From October on, she stayed home except for a daily coach ride. She moved her bed to a small room off the salon overlooking the street. There she could watch the world—her fading world—go by.

The course of her illness—arguably the most famous case of tuberculosis in history—can be measured by surviving prescriptions lists and doctors' bills. She exhibited the full range of symptoms: the cough and bloody sputum; flushing; insomnia; sweating; agitation and lassitude; sudden "recoveries" followed by further declines. She received the best medical care the times could offer. She had dropped Dr. Koreff that spring, saying she thought he was poisoning her; he had, in fact, been giving her a strychnine preparation, thus increasing, not lessening, her agitation. Consultants included Prof. Louis of the Hôtel-Dieu and Dr. Auguste-François Chomel, the king's physician. Her attendants were Dr. Marec of the Salpétrière, who saw her 39 times from mid-September to mid-November, and above all the renowned young Dr. Casimir-Joseph Davaine (1812–1882), who saw her 163 times from October until her death and to whom in gratitude she left a miniature portrait of herself now preserved at the Comédie-Française. She seemed willing to try anything, which makes her case a museum exhibit of pre-Pasteurian medicine. They prescribed a healthy diet fortified with asses' milk, beef gall, frog and snail concoctions, snake bouillon, and such; rest, which she often violated until near the very end; and a catalog of the current remedies, all of which, of course, could only treat symptoms. She was dosed with infusions, fumigations, injections, syrups, decongestants, soporifics, plasters, poultices, salves, blisterings, leeches, and for pain, morphine and opium.

Her visitors dwindled to a pitiful few. Besides her faithful maid, **Clotilde**, and **Clémence Prat**, a fortyish ex-courtesan who was her longtime procuress, there was Stackelberg, occasionally, and young men: an officer and son of a marshal, Count Pierre de Castellane (until he had to leave for Algeria); Édouard Delessert, wealthy son of the prefect of police; and for whole days Count Olympio Aguado, heir to a banking fortune. For some reason, until her last hours she forbade Perrégaux, who, it is said, at times came nevertheless when Clotilde told him she was asleep. She resolved on a last public appearance. It came on December 12, 1846, at the Théâtre du Palais-Royal for the debut of Dumanoir and Clairville's annual vaudeville revue, *La Poudre de coton*. She was borne to her box by a resplendently uniformed valet and his son. They left during the final number. (Another version gives January 15, which seems very late, and the revue as *Les Pommes de terre malades*.) An observer wrote of a woman, "or rather the shadow of a woman, something diaphanous and white, flesh and clothes."

On February 1, Plessis could barely breathe or speak. Davaine bled her and called in a priest from Saint-Roch. She had always been regular at Mass and lately had prayed long at a *prie-dieu* she had bought. She confessed and received the last rites. (Davaine left after a lunch which Clotilde duly noted as "ham for the *praître*, 2 francs.") She allowed Perrégaux to come in, and he remained to the end. Her last words were said to have been, "Despite everything, I loved them all!"

At 3 AM on February 3, she suddenly sat up, wildeyed, gave three cries, then sank back on her pillows and expired. Perrégaux, stricken, performed the last duties. From the street below, the sounds of revelers drifted up, for the pre-Lenten carnival season was in full cry—a detail Verdi was certain not to overlook.

In the jaded City of Light, where the shelf life of most gossip was three days at best, the 23-year-old courtesan's death reverberated for weeks. Her funeral, an expensive Mass at the Madeline on February 5, drew (contrary to Dumas) a respectable crowd. Although her death certificate omitted her title, as luck had it the proper hangings for a countess' funeral earlier in the day were still in place. Not two (according to Dumas) but at least five men followed her casket, crowned with white wreaths, through a cold, misty rain to the Montmartre Cemetery: Perrégaux, Aguado, Delessert, Vienne, and Alfred de Montjoyeux. Some accounts also cite Stackelberg and Alphonsine's sister, Delphine.

The sale of her property on February 24–27 attracted a jostling throng of every social hue. Charles Dickens, visiting in town, sniffed that the spectacle's monopolizing of the news proved that Paris "is corrupt to its marrow." The inventory belies Dumas' picture of creditors stripping even her bed hangings while she lay dying. The record of the sale fills 17 columns in Gros' book—fairly impressive, certainly, but far short of the standards set by, for example, some mistresses of 18th-century grandees. Clothing and linen came to 10,604 francs, including some 76 gowns; silver and jewelry, 30,889, of which 28,861 had been pawned; furnishings, including a clock once belonging to ***Pompadour** and ***Du Barry**, 32,245; books and paintings, 8,893; and stable, 6,386; total, 89,017 francs. The general quality was very high, testifying to her refined tastes. One odd exception was her bed, which the press had portrayed to a titillated public as worthy of ***Cleopatra (VII)**. It turned out to be quite ordinary.

After the pawnbrokers and around 20,000 in debts were paid, Delphine inherited the balance. Delphine's daughter was the residuary, on the interesting condition inserted by Alphonsine that she never come to Paris.

As it happened, the death of Alphonsine Plessis heralded the passing of the Age of Romanticism. It died a year later in the Revolutions of 1848. Notable as "Marie Duplessis" had been, however, her renown soon began to grow, becoming over time one of Romanticism's most enduring remnants. The great engines of this transformation were the novel *La Dame aux camélias* (1848), by Dumas *fils*, and above all his play (1852) by the same name. Verdi's masterpiece *La Traviata* (The Wayward One), based upon the play, sealed her immortality.

Dumas learned of her passing in Marseille while returning from a tour of Spain and North Africa. Deeply moved, he hastened to Paris but arrived only in time for the auction. (Some accounts say he was present at her reburial shortly before.) His novel, written under the sway of youthful passion, contained a preface stating that the story was true, an authorial device dating back at least to Boccaccio. This assertion inevitably set off speculations as to what truly was fact and what was fiction. Was Marguerite Gautier (the name he gave the heroine) really Plessis in all respects? Was the lover-hero de Guiche? Perrégaux? Dumas himself? And so on. The only certainty is that he wrote with Alphonsine in mind. In simplest outline, the play—in the novel Marguerite dies alone and forsaken—tells of a young man (Armand Duval) and a courtesan who fall desperately in love. When his father tells her she must give him up because he can never marry a fallen woman, she nobly does so. Armand is shattered when, fulfilling her pledge, she coldly sends him away and takes up with another, older, man. But when she is dying of consumption, he learns the truth, and their love is renewed—too late. True love and repentance have redeemed her sordid past.

In the preface to the 1867 edition of his plays, Dumas wrote that "Marie Duplessis didn't have all the pathos-filled adventures that I have attributed to Marguerite Gautier, but only asked to have them. If she sacrificed nothing to Armand, it is because Armand didn't wish it." From this it seems clear that the novel and play, although containing very many true-to-life details, relate what Dumas imagined *could* have been. As André Maurois has observed, in real life Dumas "soon gave up any ideas of redeeming the Magdalene, whereas in the novel, Armand Duval tries to do precisely that."

The novel was a great success. It was, however, Jules Janin's hagiographical preface to the new edition of 1851, writes Tadeusz Kowzan, which truly launched the mythic version of Plessis' life and person as the tragically noble "Lady of the Camellias." Soon afterward, a writer of light comedies, Paul Siraudin, told Dumas he should draw a play from his novel. Antony Béraud likewise suggested one for his Théâtre-Ambigu. Dumas set to work. Many years later, he wrote dismissively of the play which made him rich and famous, saying he could not remember how but had dashed it off in a week by virtue of "the audacities and luck" of youth. The censors at first forbade its performance. Stories of redemption of prostitutes by love were hardly new, as witness Abbé Prévost's *Manon Lescaut* (1731), or Victor Hugo's ***Marion Delorme*** (1829), or Eugène Scribe's ***Adrienne Lecouvreur*** (1849). But it would affront taste and morals to mount a play in contemporary dress about a prostitute known personally by many and by repute to the general public. Count Morny nevertheless befriended the project; he lifted the ban when he became minister of the interior after the coup of December 2, 1851, which brought to power his half-brother, the future Napoleon III. On February 2, 1852, five years less a day after Plessis' death, the play opened at the Vaudville, with Madame Doche (**Marie-Charlotte-Eugénie de Plunkett**, 1821–1900) as Marguerite. It was a smash hit, running for 200 performances—fabulous for that time.

La Dame aux camélias went around the world in many languages. With it, Dumas *fils* became "the father of the modern social drama . . . [and] brought the theater into direct touch with life again," writes F.A. Taylor. He neither attacked nor defended courtesans but only told, with obvious sincerity, a powerful story. Yet, while a product of the new Realism, it is steeped in Romanticism. Dumas unerringly pushed button after button of his audiences' emotional psyche: sexual license, love, guilt, purgation, redemption, death—an intoxicating potion. As a tear-jerking melodrama, *La Dame aux camélias* has had few, if any, equals. It became a warhorse for scores of actresses, notably ***Eleonora Duse** (1858–1924), ***Helena Modjeska** (1840–1909), ***Edwidge Feuillère** (1907–1998), and above all Sarah Bernhardt, who played in *Camille*, as English-speaking audiences know it, over 2,000 times, many while on tour in America. (The title *Camille* derives from the first American production, ***Matilda Heron**'s *Camille, or The Fate of a Coquette,* in 1857.)

When the play (which was also made into a ballet) began to fade in the 1920s, it continued in motion pictures, notably with ***Yvonne Printemps** (1894–1977), ***Norma Talmadge**, and ***Micheline Presle** (b. 1922). George Cukor's *Camille* (1937), with ***Greta Garbo** (1905–1990), Robert Taylor, and Lionel Barrymore, remains the classic film version. Changing tastes and mores after World War II, however, sounded the knell for frequent stage and film performances of what had been for a century probably the world's single most popular play.

Not so the story's run as an opera, an art form where outdated language and conventions can be swept aside by great music. Giuseppe Verdi (1813–1901), after reading the novel, mentioned it as a possible opera. He attended one of the play's first performances in Paris in 1852, possibly the debut. According to his family's tradition, he responded to it instantly and began composing in his head before the final curtain. *La Traviata* became the opera he had promised to Venice for the spring of 1853, but *Il Trovatore* occupied him more—he composed them simultaneously—until its debut on January 19. Thereafter, he worked on *La Traviata* at breakneck speed. The score was still incomplete only two weeks before the debut, and he finished the orchestration during rehearsals. His librettist, Francesco Mario Piave (1810–1876), fortunately could cope with last-minute changes. His text was mediocre as poetry but a truly masterful condensation of the play, e.g., wisely reducing its five acts to three. Also, Violetta Valéry (yet another name) was now transfigured into a heroine who even wins the father's approval.

Verdi evidently felt personally moved by the story. He was a widower but living openly with a singer, ***Giuseppina Strepponi** (1815–1897), in defiance of bourgeois morality. (They later married.) To what extent his personal situation affected his response is debated. Possibly it was related to his desire to have the opera given a contemporary setting, thus involving him in the same struggle with moral conventions as Dumas. He gave in, reluctantly, when the producers insisted on a setting in the reign of Louis XIV. The opera was not given in contemporary dress until 1909; since then the utmost freedom has reigned as to setting and costumes.

The debut on March 6, 1853, was the most famous flop of Verdi's career. The Violetta, ***Fanny Salvini-Donatelli** (1815–1891), met the vocal challenges but was inadequate in a role demanding high acting skills. And when she announced she was dying of consumption, the audience burst out laughing: she weighed a reputed 285 pounds. The tenor and baritone also were unsuitable and unhappy, as was the rest of the cast. All felt disoriented in this unconventional work, Verdi's only "chamber" opera, containing as it does no grand choruses or spectacles. In letters, Verdi pronounced it "an absolute fiasco," but added, "I believe that the last word on *La Traviata* was not said last night." He was overreacting, for the nine-performance first run earned at least average receipts. Still, "Fiasco!" resounded everywhere.

A revival—with more revisions than Verdi cared to admit plus longer rehearsals and a more carefully chosen cast headed by a splendid Violetta in **Maria Aldighieri-Spezia** (1828–1907)—opened, again in Venice, on May 6, 1854. It was a colossal triumph. *La Traviata* remains perhaps the best loved of all Verdi's operas and vies with Giacomo Puccini's *La Bohème* (1896) and *Tosca* (1900) for the title of the most performed. Among the greatest Violettas have been ***Adelina Patti** (1843–1919), ***Nellie Melba** (1861–1931), ***Luisa Tetrazzini** (1871–1940), ***Amelita Galli-Curci** (1882–1963), ***Rosa Ponselle** (1897–1981), ***Bidu Sayão** (1902–1999), ***Licia Albanese** (b. 1913), ***Maria Callas** (1923–1977), and ***Teresa Stratas** (b. 1938).

Marie Duplessis, Marguerite Gautier, Violetta Valéry—had they obliterated Alphonsine Plessis? Not altogether. Her mythic personage lives on at her tomb.

On Mardi Gras, February 16, two weeks after her death, Perrégaux had her body reburied (still at Montmartre) and commissioned a square, white-marble tomb crowned by an urn. Much later, Dumas *fils* in his will charged his nephew and descendants to care for it in perpetuity. As fate would have it, Dumas asked to be buried at Père Lachaise but instead was interred at Montmartre not far from Alphonsine's tomb. As for Perrégaux, he died in 1889, having lived his last 30 years in a furnished house in Chantilly. He never remarried.

The tomb is near the main entrance, in Division 18, Line 4, No. 12. Almost at once it became a shrine for poor young people, working women and prostitutes, and romantics of every age. It is said that the site has never lacked fresh flowers. The inscription, simple yet eloquent, gives only her real name, her dates of birth and death, and the first two words of the 130th Psalm, which speaks to her suffering and Perrégaux's sorrow at the end: DE PROFUNDIS . . . "Out of the depths have I cried unto Thee, O Lord."

SOURCES:

Boudet, Micheline. *La Fleur du mal: la véritable histoire de la Dame aux camélias.* Paris: A. Michel, 1993.

Budden, Julian. *The Operas of Verdi.* Vol. II. NY: Oxford University Press, 1979.

Burger, Ernst. *Franz Liszt: A Chronicle of His Life in Pictures and Documents.* Trans. by Stewart Spencer. Princeton, NJ: Princeton University Press, 1989.

Cabanès, Dr. [Augustin]. "La Maladie et la mort de la 'Dame aux camélias,'" in *Chronique médicale.* No. 2, 1899, pp. 70–79.

Dumas *fils*, Alexandre. *Théâtre complet, avec préfaces inédites: La Dame aux camélias, Diane de Lys, Le Bijou de la Seine.* Paris: Calmann-Lévy, 1923.

Gros, Johannès. *Alexandre Dumas et Marie Duplessis: Documents inédites.* Paris: Louis Conard, 1923.

———. *Une courtesane romantique: Marie Duplessis.* Paris: Au Cabinet du Livre, 1929.

International Dictionary of Theatre, Vol. I: *Plays.* Mark Hawkins-Dady, ed. Chicago, IL: St. James Press, 1992.

Issartel, Christiane. *Les Dames aux camélias: de l'histoire à la légende.* Paris: Hachette, 1981.

Kowzan, Tadeusz. "Le Mythe de la Dame aux camélias: du mélodrame au mélodramatisme," in *Revue des sciences humaines.* No. 162. June 1976, pp. 219–230.

Lefebvre, Thierry. "Témoignage pharmaceutique sur la 'vraie' Dame aux camélias," in *Revue d'histoire de la pharmacie.* Vol. 39, no. 293, 1992, pp. 197–201.

Martin, George. *Verdi: His Music, Life and Times.* NY: Dodd, Mead, 1963.

Maurois, André. *The Titans: A Three-Generation Biography of the Dumas.* Trans. by Gerard Hopkins. NY: Harper & Brothers, 1957.

New Grove Dictionary of Music and Musicians. Stanley Sadie, ed. NY: Macmillan, 1980.

New Grove Dictionary of Opera. Stanley Sadie, ed. NY: Macmillan, 1992.

Noël, Carlos M. *Les Idées sociales dans le théâtre de A. Dumas fils.* Paris: Albert Massein, 1912.

Phillips-Matz, Mary Jane. *Verdi: A Biography.* NY: Oxford University Press, 1993.

Poirot-Delpech, Bertrand. *Marie Duplessis, "la Dame aux camélias": une vie romancée.* Paris: Ramsay, 1981.

Prasteau, Jean. *C'était la Dame aux camélias.* Paris: Librairie Académique Perrin, 1963.

Rat, Maurice. *La Dame aux camélias*: Paris: Del Duca, 1958.

Richardson, Joanna. *The Courtesans: The Demi-Monde in Nineteenth-Century France.* Cleveland, OH: World, 1967.

Roberts, Nickie. *Whores in History: Prostitution in Western Society.* London: Grafton, 1992.

Robichez, Jacques. "La Dame aux camélias," in *Revue des sciences humaines.* October–December 1961, pp. 477–487.

Saffle, Michael Benton. *Liszt in Germany, 1840–1845: A Study in Sources, Documents and the History of Reception.* Stuyvesant, NY: Pendragon Press, 1994.

Taylor, F.A. *The Theatre of Alexandre Dumas Fils.* Oxford: Clarendon Press, 1937.

Théodorides, Jean. "A propos d'une ordonnance de Davaine pour la 'dame aux camélias' (Alphonsine Plessis, alias Marie Duplessis)," in *Revue d'histoire de la pharmacie.* Vol. 21, no. 217, 1973, pp. 407–408.

Vienne, Frédéric-Romain. *La Verité sur la Dame aux camélias (Marie Duplessis).* Paris: P. Ollendorff, 1888.

Walker, Alan. *Franz Liszt,* Vol. I: *The Virtuoso Years, 1811–1847.* NY: Alfred A. Knopf, 1983.

SUGGESTED READING:

Blum, Jerome. *In the Beginning: The Advent of the Modern Age, Europe in the 1840s.* NY: Scribner, 1994.

Boulenger, Jacques. *Sous Louis-Philippe: Les Dandys.* New ed. Paris: Librairie Paul Ollendorff, n.d.

Contades, G. (Comte) de. *Portraits et fantaisies.* Paris: Maison Quantin, 1887.

Dolph, Charles. *The Real "Lady of the Camellias" and Other Women of Quality.* London: T. Werner Laurie, 1927.

Pasco, Allan H. *Sick Heroes: French Society and Literature in the Romantic Age, 1750–1850.* Exeter: University of Exeter Press, 1997.

Reddy, William H. *The Invisible Code: Honor and Sentiment in Postrevolutionary France, 1814–1848.* Berkeley, CA: University of California Press, 1997.

Saunders, Edith. *The Prodigal Father: Dumas Père et Fils and "the Lady of the Camellias."* London: Longmans, 1951.

Talmon, J.L. *Romanticism and Revolt: Europe 1815–1848.* NY: Harcourt, Brace & World, 1967.

Toussaint, P. *Marie Duplessis, la vraie Dame aux camélias.* Paris: Gallimard, 1958.

David S. Newhall,
Pottinger Distinguished Professor of History Emeritus,
Centre College, Danville, Kentucky,
and author of *Clemenceau: A Life at War* (1991)

Pleyel, Maria Felicite (1811–1875)

French pianist admired by both Liszt and Chopin who dedicated compositions to her. *Born Maria Felicite Moke in Paris on July 4, 1811; died at Saint-Josse-Ten-Noode near Brussels, Belgium, on March 30, 1875; married Camille Pleyel.*

Maria Felicite Pleyel was born in Paris in 1811 and studied with Moscheles, Herz and Friedrich Kalkbrenner, and later with Thalberg. She had an impressive career as a pianist and was admired by Chopin and Liszt. Indeed, both composers dedicated pieces to her—Chopin, his Nocturnes Op. 9, and Liszt, his *Norma* paraphrase. Hector Berlioz fell in love with her, but she chose to marry the piano builder Camille Pleyel. Critic François Joseph Fétis believed her to be the most perfect of any pianist. From 1848 to 1872, she was the best-known teacher at the Brussels Conservatory.

John Haag,
Athens, Georgia

Plisetskaya, Maya (1925—)

Prima ballerina of the Bolshoi Ballet who challenged the traditional artistic standards of the Russian dancing establishment. *Name variations: Maia Plisetskaia or Plisvetskaia; Mayechka (pronounced MY-echka). Pronunciation: MY-ya Plee-SYET-skaya. Born Maya Mikhailovna Plisetskaya on November 20, 1925, in Moscow; daughter of Mikhail Borisovich Plisetsky (an engineer) and Raissa (Rachel) Mikhailovna Plisetskaya (an actress); attended Bolshoi Ballet School; married Rodion Shchedrin (a composer), in 1958; children: in December 2000, Plisetskaya won a libel suit against a Moscow newspaper,* Moskovskiye Vedomosti, *which had earlier reported that the dancer had secretly given birth to a daughter in 1978; the newspaper printed a retraction.*

Awards: People's Artist of the USSR (1959); Lenin Prize (1964); Hero of Socialist Labor (1985).

Entered ballet school (1934); gave first performance with the Bolshoi Company (1936); father killed (1937); returned to wartime Moscow (1942); entered Bolshoi Ballet Company (1943); made first trip abroad (1959); became prima ballerina at Bolshoi (1960); awarded the Lenin Prize (1964); served as director, Spanish National Ballet (1987–90); celebrated 50th anniversary of her debut as member of Bolshoi Ballet Company (1993).

Major roles in ballet: title role in The Dying Swan *(1943); title role in* Raymonda *(1945); Odette-Odile in* Swan Lake *(1947); Kitri in* Don Qixote *(1950); Aurora in* Sleeping Beauty *(1952); Carmen in* Carmen Suite *(1967); title role in* Isadora *(1977).*

Major roles in film: Stars of the Russian Ballet *(1953);* Swan Lake *(1957);* The Little Humpbacked Horse *(1962);* Plisetskaya Dances *(1966);* Anna Karenina *(1972).*

Since the 18th century, Russian society has considered ballet to be a particularly worthy art form, and from the early 19th century it has been one in which Russians have traditionally played a leading role. This feature of pre-1917 Russian culture continued with even greater emphasis in the Communist era. Thus in the years during and after World War II, Maya Plisetskaya, at the height of her artistic powers as leading ballerina, was one of the most famous and revered artists of the Soviet Union.

The country in which Plisetskaya grew up and achieved professional fame went through a series of traumatic changes in the years of her youth, schooling, and professional success. The generation of Maya Plisetskaya's parents had witnessed the revolutions of 1917, which had overthrown the old monarchy and placed a Communist Party led by V.I. Lenin in power. She herself grew up during the deep changes that took place in Russian life and society starting in 1929. Under the dictatorship of Joseph Stalin, Lenin's successor, the Communist Party consolidated its power to become a full-fledged police state. Moreover, the 1930s saw the Soviet government forcing its peasant population onto collective farms and pushing forward an ambitious program to expand heavy industry. Millions whom the government designated dangerous members of Soviet society were purged: removed from their normal lives, confined for years in Siberian exile, and abandoned to die in hellish work camps. The tragic upheavals of the 1930s were followed by four years of fighting in World War II. During that bloody conflict, the Soviet Union was invaded by Nazi Germany, successfully defended itself, and then expanded into East-

Maya Plisetskaya

ern and Central Europe. Stalin's death in 1953 brought a loosening of the police state and new contact with the outside world of Western Europe and the United States. Nonetheless, the average Soviet citizen continued to live under the threat of repression.

Maya Plisetskaya's life was profoundly influenced by the great changes in Soviet society. Her career, both hampered and promoted by the shifting political climate in her native country, illustrates the problems of a great artist tied to a dictatorial state. She was born in Moscow in

1925. Her father Mikhail Plisetsky was a noted engineer who directed Soviet coal mining operations in northern Norway. Her mother **Raissa Plisetskaya** was an actress who starred in silent films, and several of Maya's relatives were also prominent in the world of the arts. For example, Asaf and **Sulamith Messerer**, Maya's uncle and aunt, were prominent dancers and teachers with the Bolshoi Ballet Company. Both Maya's mother and father came from Jewish families, a fact that may have contributed to the distrust Soviet political authorities displayed toward the star ballerina in the 1950s and 1960s.

As a young child, Maya was fascinated with dancing and dancers, performing in front of impromptu audiences in the streets of Moscow at the age of three. But she did not find an easy entry into her profession. Her gangly body struck the admissions committee at the Bolshoi school as unsuited to ballet, until, as she remembered the occasion, she curtsied for them with such grace and flair that they accepted her. She entered the school of the Bolshoi Ballet at the age of eight and trained with the prominent teacher **Elizaveta Gerdt**.

The young girl quickly demonstrated both her vast talents and her rebellious nature. She openly disliked the rigors of formal ballet training. Her vitality, energy, and emotional impulses often expressed themselves at the expense of classical technique. She rejected an offer to study with ***Agrippina Vaganova**, the great teacher of Leningrad's Kirov Ballet Company, where classical ballet training was strongly entrenched.

She epitomized artistic freedom in ballet; for my generation she was Ballet itself.

—**Gennady Smakov**

At an early age, Plisetskaya's life was marked by political upheaval. Her father was arrested and killed during the purges of the 1930s; her mother was imprisoned. During World War II, like many Soviet citizens, she was required to leave Moscow in the face of the German invasion. Her career took a spectacular turn when she defied military regulations and went back to the wartime capital in 1942. She soon began to dance leading roles in such ballets as *The Dying Swan*, *Raymonda*, and, starting in the late 1940s, *Swan Lake*, in which she danced the role of Odette-Odile.

Plisetskaya's special abilities—her remarkable physical and artistic qualities—soon became visible. The gangly young girl of the 1930s had developed into an extraordinary physical presence. Only a little over average height, she combined a beautiful face, auburn hair, and green eyes along with a long neck and long limbs to command the stage. Plisetskaya was able to leap as high as a male dancer, and her performances featured fluid arm movements and an extraordinary ability to hold a pose in the air. The ballet critics of Leningrad, steeped in the technical perfection demanded at the Kirov Ballet Company, often criticized her for her lack of technical polish. She herself regretted her lack of classical training: "I danced the way I felt," she said, "without any references to standards I never knew." Nonetheless, in Moscow, where she danced with the Bolshoi Ballet, her style made her a brilliant star. Throughout the 1950s, Plisetskaya appeared in virtually every Bolshoi production. Her greatest role was in *Swan Lake*; she played Odette-Odile in more than 500 performances.

Following Stalin's death, the Soviet Union established new artistic ties to the outside world. Stellar artists in such prestigious organizations as the Bolshoi Ballet Company began to tour Western Europe and the United States by the late 1950s. Plisetskaya, considered by many to be the Bolshoi's prima ballerina, the leading female dancer, was barred from one of these early tours. Her friendship with an admirer from Western Europe, a British diplomat, made her too unreliable for such a privilege. It was not the only humiliation she suffered during these years. Despite her artistic prominence, she and her husband, composer Rodion Shchedrin, lived in modest circumstances with none of the considerable luxuries normally available to star performers. Unlike other leading ballerinas, she could not obtain roles in new ballets written especially for her.

Nonetheless, Plisetskaya in time was allowed to demonstrate her talents abroad. Her fiery manner and extraordinary physical gifts made her a spectacular success when she reached New York with the Bolshoi in 1959. Her ability to perform a kick-jete, in which her dramatically arched back almost allowed her to touch her head with her extended leg, shocked and delighted her audience there. She returned to Moscow and, in 1960, the retirement of ***Galina Ulanova** removed her last rival for the position of the Bolshoi's prima ballerina. Winning the Lenin Prize in 1964 brought Plisetskaya the material comforts that she had found unavailable earlier in her starring years.

During the 1960s, however, she became even more of a rebel in the orthodox artistic world of the ballet. Unwilling to restrict herself to performances in ballets that had not changed in decades, Plisetskaya used her prestige as her country's leading ballerina to develop and perform a very different kind of dance. The *Carmen*

Suite, with music arranged by her husband, was an important example. First performed in 1967 at the Bolshoi, the ballet was considered by artistic conservatives to be a slap at the Russian tradition. Carmen, as played by Plisetskaya, was a wanton woman, and she showed her character with gestures that had never been seen before in the Russian ballet. Ironically, this daring piece was the first ballet specially created for Plisetskaya.

The tensions of being a ballet star in a society dominated by the political demands of the state became evident in a different way in the late 1960s. As a Soviet citizen with a Jewish background, Plisetskaya was forced to participate in public protests against the policies of the state of Israel.

As she grew older, Plisetskaya became a choreographer at the Bolshoi while continuing her career as a dancer. Her greatest achievements as a choreographer were in creating the ballets *Anna Karenina* (1972) and *The Sea Gull* (1980). Starting in the 1970s, she was increasingly free to travel, to appear with foreign companies, and work with non-Russian choreographers. She had a notable association with the French choreographer Maurice Bejart and his Ballet of the Twentieth Century. In the late 1980s, as restrictions on travel disappeared entirely in the era of Mikhail Gorbachev, she became the artistic director of the National Ballet of Spain, spending half of each year outside the Soviet Union.

The great ballerina's career changed its character only slightly as she aged. While organizing and judging international ballet competitions and teaching, Plisetskaya nonetheless continued to perform into the 1990s. In a dramatic moment, she returned to the Bolshoi in November 1993 to mark the 50th anniversary of her entry into the Bolshoi Company. She received a tumultuous welcome from a crowd that included the new Russian Republic's political leaders. Even to those far removed from the world of ballet, her name has come to symbolize supreme excellence and a commanding position in her field. When the basketball star Michael Jordan suddenly announced his retirement in October 1993, one European newscaster assessed the importance of this loss to the game by noting that without him basketball would be like "ballet without Plisetskaya." On November 20, 1995, she celebrated her 70th birthday by sublimely dancing *The Dying Swan* in front of an enraptured Russian audience; she followed that, wrote *Time*, with an "irrepressible" appearance in New York in 1996. "I still feel the magic," she said. "If I have no more interest in dancing, I'll stop."

SOURCES:

Feifer, George. *Our Motherland and Other Ventures in Russian Reportage.* NY: Viking Press, 1973.

Smakov, Gennady. *The Great Russian Dancers.* NY: Alfred A. Knopf, 1984.

Time. May 27, 1996.

Voznesensky, Andrei, *et al. Maya Plisetskaya.* Moscow: Progress Publishers, 1976.

SUGGESTED READING:

Clarke, Mary, and Clement Crips. *Ballerina: The Art of Women in Classical Ballet.* London: BBC Books, 1987.

Montague, Sarah. *The Ballerina: Famous Dancers and Rising Stars of Our Time.* NY: Universe Books, 1980.

Neil Heyman,
Professor of History, San Diego State University,
San Diego, California

Ploennies, Luise von (1803–1872)

German poet. *Name variations: Plönnies. Born in Hanau, Germany, on November 7, 1803; died in Darmstadt on January 22, 1872; daughter of Philipp Achilles Leisler (a naturalist); married August von Ploennies (a physician), in 1824.*

Luise von Ploennies was born in Hanau, Germany, in 1803, the daughter of naturalist Philipp Leisler. In 1824, she married physician August von Ploennies in Darmstadt. After his death in 1847, she lived in Belgium for some years, then at Jugenheim on the Bergstrasse, and lastly at Darmstadt, where she died on January 22, 1872. Between 1844 and 1870, she published several volumes of verse. She also wrote two Biblical dramas, *Maria Magdalena* (1870) and *David* (1873). She also translated into German two collections of English poems, *Britannia* (1843) and *Englische Lyriker des 19ten Jahrhunderts* (1863, 3rd ed., 1867).

Plotina (d. 122)

Roman empress from 98 to 117. *Name variations: Pompeia Plotina. Born Pompeia Plotina, a Roman of Nemausus (Nimes) in Gallia Narbonensis (southern France); married Trajan (Marcus Ulpius Traianus, c. 53–117), Roman emperor (r. 98–117); children: none, but eventually adopted Publius Aelius Hadrianus, also known as Hadrian, Roman emperor (r. 117–138), as heir to Trajan.*

Marcus Ulpius Traianus, known as Trajan, is considered to have been the second of the five good Roman emperors, beginning with Nerva and ending with Marcus Aurelius. There is no doubt that the title is justified. An excellent general, energetic and able, he extended the frontiers of the Roman Empire to their greatest extent while maintaining the favor of the people and the good will of the senate.

Plotina, a formidable and intellectual woman whose interests included literature, mathematics, music, and works of charity, enjoyed the same reputation as her husband. Noted for her modesty, she refused to be made augusta (empress) until 105, seven years after Trajan had become Roman emperor. "I wish to be the same sort of woman when I leave as I am entering," she said. Strong-willed but loyal and virtuous, Plotina was devoted to religion and philosophical pursuits, especially epicurianism, and was highly respected in Rome, as were Trajan's sister ***Ulpia Marciana** and Ulpia Marciana's daughter ***Matidia I** (mother-in-law of the future emperor Hadrian), both of whom were very close to the emperor. The senate voted the title Augusta to Plotina and Ulpia Marciana in 105, and in 112 gave both of them the right to issue coinage.

Plotina

In failing health in 117, probably brought about by the rigors of two years of campaigning in the field, Trajan suffered what appears to have been a stroke while in Syria. Although he recovered sufficiently to appear in public, Plotina insisted upon their immediate return to Italy. The emperor and his entourage left Syria by ship but were forced to put in at the port of Selinus in Cilicia, where Trajan died on August 8th or 9th, 117. Although it seems clear that the moody but popular Hadrian was his choice for successor, for some reason Trajan delayed in adopting him until he was on his deathbed, thereby giving rise to rumors that it was Plotina who engineered Hadrian's succession while Trajan was dying and perhaps even made the decision after his demise. Plotina became Hadrian's friend and advocate. It was said that she regarded him as a substitute for the son she never had. Hadrian clearly respected her as well, writing that Plotina's "pity and honored dignity achieve all things." She arranged his marriage to ***Sabina**, Trajan's grandniece, a union designed purely to benefit Hadrian's political career. Sabina was only 13; he was 24.

Trajan's ashes were buried in a golden urn and placed in the base of his famed column at Rome; Plotina's ashes were placed beside them when she died a few years later, in 122. At the time of her death, Hadrian paid her outstanding honors. Though his travels prevented him from holding the funeral in Rome until 124, he dedicated a temple to her in Nemausus (Nimes), her birthplace in Gallia Narbonensis (southern France). In the first two centuries of the empire, Plotina was the only empress who might be compared to ***Livia Drusilla**, the consort of Augustus. As well, Plotina, Ulpia Marciana, and Matidia I were all deified.

Plowright, Joan (1929—)

English actress. *Name variations: Lady Olivier. Born Joan Anne Plowright on October 28, 1929, in Brigg, Lincolnshire, England; only daughter and one of three children of Ernest Plowright (a newspaper editor) and Daisy Margaret (Burton) Plowright; attended Scunthorpe Grammar School; attended summer drama course at Hull University; attended Laban Art of Movement Studio, Manchester; graduate of the Old Vic Theatre drama school, London, England; married Roger Gage (an actor), in 1953 (divorced 1960); married Laurence Olivier (an actor), on March 17, 1961 (died 1989); children: (with Olivier) daughters* ***Tamsin Olivier*** *and* ***Julie-Kate Olivier****; son Richard Olivier.*

Selected theater: made stage debut as Hope in If Four Walls Told *(Grand Theatre, Croydon, 1951);*

Joan Plowright

made London debut as Donna Clara in The Duenna *(Westminster Theatre, 1954); appeared as Cabin Boy in* Moby Dick *(Duke of York's, 1955); joined the English Stage Company at the Royal Court, London (1956); appeared as Margery Pinchwife in* The Country Wife *(1956); made New York debut in an Ionesco double-bill in which she played the Old Woman in* The Chairs *and the Pupil in* The Lesson *(Phoenix Theatre, 1958); appeared as Jean Rice in* The Entertainer *(Palace, 1957, NY, 1958); appeared in the title role in* Major Barbara *(Royal Court, 1958), as Beatie Bryant in* Roots *(Royal Court Theatre, 1959), as Daisy in*

Rhinoceros *(1960), as Josephine in* A Taste of Honey *(NY, 1960), as Constantia in* The Chances *(Chichester Festival, 1962), as Sonya in* Uncle Vanya *(Chichester Festival, 1962); joined the National Theatre Company at the Old Vic (1962); appeared in the title role in* Saint Joan *(Edinburgh Festival, 1963), as Maggie in* Hobson's Choice *(1964), as Hilde in* The Master Builder *(1964), as Beatrice in* Much Ado about Nothing *(1967), as Masha in* Three Sisters *(1967), as Teresa in* The Advertisement *(1968), as Rosalind in* Love's Labour's Lost *(1968), as Portia in* The Merchant of Venice *(1970), as Jennifer Dubedat in* The Doctor's Dilemma *(Chichester Festival, 1972), as Rosa in* Saturday, Sunday, Monday *(Old Vic, 1973), as Irena Arkadina in* The Seagull *(Lyric Theatre Company, 1975), as Alma in* The Bed Before Yesterday *(Lyric Theatre Company, 1975), in the title role in* Filumena *(Lyric Theatre Company, 1977, NY, 1980), as Ranevskaya in* The Cherry Orchard *(1983), as Lady Wishfort in* The Way of the World *(London, 1984), in* Mrs. Warren's Profession *(1985), in* The House of Bernarda Alba *(1986).*

Selected filmography: Moby Dick *(1956);* Time Without Pity *(1957);* The Entertainer *(1960);* Uncle Vanya *(1963);* Three Sisters *(1970);* Equus *(1977);* Britannia Hospital *(1982);* Brimstone and Treacle *(1982);* Wagner *(1983);* Revolution *(1985);* Drowning by Numbers *(1988);* The Dressmaker *(1988);* I Love You to Death *(1990);* Avalon *(1990);* Enchanted April *(UK, 1992);* Last Action Hero *(1993);* Dennis the Menace *(1993);* The Summer House *(1993);* Widow's Peak *(1994);* Hotel Sorrento *(*Sorrento Beach*, 1995);* A Pyromaniac's Love Story *(1995);* Jane Eyre *(1996);* Mr. Wrong *(1996);* 101 Dalmations *(1996);* The Assistant *(1997);* Aldrich Ames: Traitor Within *(1998);* Tea with Mussolini *(1998);* Dance with Me *(1998);* Frankie and Hazel *(2000);* Dinosaur *(2000). On television: "Stalin" (1992).*

One of Britain's most acclaimed actresses, Joan Plowright rose to prominence in the late 1950s and has remained in the theater's higher echelons ever since. Now in her 70s, she has meticulously honed her craft, and with each new role seems to set a new standard of perfection.

Plowright was born on October 28, 1929, in her parents' home in Brigg, Lincolnshire, and was raised in a solid middle-class family. Her father Ernest Plowright was the editor of the local newspaper, the *Scunthorpe and Frodingham Star*, and her mother **Daisy Burton Plowright** dabbled in amateur theatricals. "Mother produced plays for the local youth club and painted scenery in the garden," Plowright recalled. "In many ways she'd have loved to act herself, but she said she couldn't have taken the rejection and that she didn't have the endurance." According to her younger brother David, Joan was naturally assertive. "She couldn't accept that just because she was a girl she couldn't be captain of the football team. Her independence and competition were obvious at an early age." When Plowright was a teenager, she attended a summer drama course at Hull University, and after high school spent a year at the Laban Art of Movement Studio in Manchester. She then won a scholarship to the Old Vic School. Daisy sent her daughter off with a reality check. "You're no oil painting, my girl, but you have good, useful eyes and, thank God, you have my legs and not your father's."

In 1951, Plowright made her stage debut in repertory at the Grand Theatre in Croydon, where she played Hope in *If Four Walls Told.* She then joined the Bristol Old Vic Company and toured with them in South Africa. On tour, she met her first husband, actor Roger Gage. "We got engaged on the boat," she explained. "I think it was all that hot sun. We were married for seven years and did remain friends after the divorce." Following her marriage, Plowright continued to perfect her craft in a succession of repertory companies, playing a wide range of roles, including classical, Shakespearean, and modern. In July 1954, she made her London debut as Donna Clara in a musical version of Sheridan's *The Duenna*, but she did not receive critical notice until a year later, when Orson Welles cast her as the cabin boy in his production of *Moby Dick*. Roger Gellant remembered Plowright in the role as a "small frightened, half-demented creature with eyes like boot-buttons."

Plowright came into prominence in 1956, as Margery Pinchwife in a revival of *The Country Wife*, performed with the English Stage Company which had recruited her earlier that year. "Joan Plowright jumps to the forefront of our young actresses with her lively performance in the title role," reported Frank Granville-Barker; "she is all cunning and mischief, a richly endearing flirt." Just a year later, Plowright took over the role **Dorothy Tutin** had played in *The Entertainer*, opposite legendary actor Laurence Olivier, whom she found a bit intimidating at first. Twenty-two years younger than Olivier, Plowright played his daughter in the play, and a romance began. (Olivier was married at the time to his second wife, actress ***Vivien Leigh**, who in 1960 would obtain a divorce from the actor on the grounds of adultery, naming Plowright as correspondent. Plowright would end her marriage to Roger Gage around the same time.)

Plowright's career continued to blossom. In January 1958, she made a stunning New York debut in a double bill of Eugene Ionesco's *The Chairs* and *The Lesson*, described collectively by Walter Kerr as "two calculated journeys into unreason." The duet of plays called for the actress to begin the evening as a senile 94-year-old crone and end it as a teenage hussy, a feat she handled with aplomb. She extended her New York stay with a Broadway run of *The Entertainer* a month later. Although most of the reviews centered on Olivier's performance, Plowright was not overlooked, with the American critics calling her portrayal of the loyal daughter "fresh," "forthright," and "completely realized."

Returning to England, Plowright was notable in the title role of Shaw's *Major Barbara* and as Beatie Bryant, the daughter of inarticulate Norfolk farmers, in *Roots,* a role which Richard Watts, Jr., proclaimed "places her, at once, among the important actresses of the contemporary theatre." In April 1960, she and Olivier were again on stage together in Ionesco's *Rhinoceros*. That year, Plowright also triumphed on Broadway in ⊱► **Shelagh Delaney**'s *A Taste of Honey*, playing a neglected teenager who becomes pregnant by a black sailor. "The evening's treasure," wrote Howard Taubman in *The New York Times* (October 5, 1960), "is Joan Plowright's haunting performance of the girl. Through voice, accent and movement, she captures the shell of cynicism that the girl has grown to shield herself from her hopelessness. . . . Miss Plowright gives the play its affecting core." For her performance, Plowright received a Tony Award as the Best Dramatic Actress of the Year, as well as the 1961 New York Drama Critics Award.

In March 1961, with both their divorces granted, Plowright and Olivier were married by a justice of the peace in Wilton, Connecticut. "Because we were both so aware of it when we married," Plowright said later, "we didn't want all the legend stuff—he had had it and didn't want it any longer, and I had never had it and didn't like it anyway. It was simply a man and a woman living together. I married a man, not a myth." For his part, Olivier found some of his mother's aggressive nature in Plowright. "Ever since my mother's death, I've been looking for someone like her," he said. "Perhaps with Joanie I've found her again." Olivier biographer Donald Spoto writes that Plowright seemed to be the right choice for Olivier as he entered yet a new phase of his acting career: "Joan provided fresh ideas, a blunt, modern and unself-conscious style of life—and the gratification of an intelligent young woman's attention. And in a way—since they planned a family—he had married a mother figure in order to make her one." Indeed, the marriage produced three children (two girls and a boy), and endured until Olivier's death in 1989.

Plowright's working momentum dipped following her marriage, mostly due to her growing responsibilities at home. Nonetheless still pursuing her career, she created some of her most memorable roles with the National Theatre Company at the Old Vic, of which her husband served as director from its inception in 1963 until 1974. Notable among them was the title role in Shaw's *Saint Joan* (1963), which T.C. Worsley of *The New York Times* called "one of the great definitive performances of a great role," Beatrice in *Much Ado about Nothing* (1967), Masha in *Three Sisters* (1967), Portia in *The Merchant of Venice* (1970), and Rosa in *Saturday, Sunday, Monday* (1973). In 1975, with the Lyric Theatre Company, she alternated the role of Irena Arkadina in *The Seagull* with that of Alma in the Ben Travers farce *The Bed Before Yesterday.* The latter role surprised critic Sandy Wilson: "To be honest I had not fully realized that she is one of the greatest comediennes of our generation until I saw her play Alma Millett, but I will go further than that and say that this performance is the funniest to be seen in London since ***Bea Lillie** went into retirement."

◄⊰
Delaney, Shelagh. *See Littlewood, Joan for sidebar.*

In 1977, Plowright was on Broadway again, in *Filumena,* which had run for two years in London. "It allows Miss Plowright to spend three acts looking noble, hard-done-by and as queenly as the statue on the prow of a ship," wrote British critic John Barber. Plowright then returned to England, where she continued to perform with the National Theatre and in West End productions.

Plowright reprised several of her best stage roles in films, notably Jean Rice in *The Entertainer* (1960), Sonya in *Uncle Vanya* (1963), and Masha in *Three Sisters* (1970). During the 1990s, while her stage career slowed, she pursued film opportunities more aggressively, creating another round of impeccable characterizations in such movies as *Enchanted April* (1992), *The Summer House* (1993), *Widow's Peak* (1994), and *Tea with Mussolini* (1998).

SOURCES:

Current Biography 1964. NY: H.W. Wilson, 1964.

Hartnoll, Phyllis, and Peter Found, eds. *The Concise Oxford Companion to the Theatre.* Oxford and NY: Oxford University Press, 1993.

Katz, Ephraim. *The Film Encyclopedia*. NY: HarperCollins, 1994.

Morley, Sheridan. *The Great Stage Stars*. Australia: Angus & Robertson, 1986.

Barbara Morgan,
Melrose, Massachusetts

Plummer, Edith.

See Yevonde (1893–1975).

Plummer, Mary Wright (1856–1916)

American librarian, educator, and writer. *Born on March 8, 1856, in Richmond, Indiana; died of cancer on September 21, 1916, in Dixon, Illinois; daughter of Jonathan Wright Plummer (a wholesale druggist) and Hannah Ann (Ballard) Plummer; educated in Quaker schools in Richmond and later at Wellesley College; graduated from Columbia College Library School, New York City, in 1888.*

Member of first class of Columbia College's library school (1887); organized a training program for librarians at Pratt Institute Free Library (1890); became director of Pratt's Free Library and its library school (1895); at Pratt Free Library, oversaw creation of first children's library section (1896); as principal, helped establish and direct the New York Public Library's library school (1911); elected the second woman president of the American Library Association (1915).

Selected writings: Hints to Small Libraries *(1894);* Verses *(1896);* Roy and Ray in Mexico *(1907);* Roy and Ray in Canada *(1908);* Stories from the Chronicle of the Cid *(1910);* Seven Joys of Reading *(1910).*

Born on March 8, 1856, in Richmond, Indiana, Mary Wright Plummer was the oldest of the six children of Jonathan Wright Plummer and **Hannah Ann Plummer**. Her father, a wholesale druggist, had moved west from Maryland, while her mother came from Virginia. Both were Quakers, and Jonathan was also an approved minister in the faith. After graduating from the Friends Academy in Richmond, Plummer spent a year studying at Wellesley College before returning to live with her family, who had moved to Chicago. For the next four years, she taught school and spent some of her free time writing poetry; several of her poems were published in *The Atlantic Monthly* and *Scribner's Magazine*.

Although she had been a voracious reader since childhood, Plummer displayed no particular interest in library work until one day in Chicago she spotted a newspaper advertisement for a library school that was soon to be opened at Columbia College in New York City. Her interest piqued, she made further inquiries, and in January 1887 joined the first class of the library school, which included a total of 17 women and 3 men. The school, founded by legendary Columbia librarian Melvil Dewey (inventor of the Dewey Decimal System), offered a two-year program of study and was a pioneer in the education of professional librarians. Plummer excelled at her studies, so much so that, during her second term, she was given the responsibility of instructing others in the science of cataloguing.

Following her graduation from Columbia in 1888, Plummer accepted a position as cataloguer in the St. Louis Public Library, headed then by Frederick Crunden, one of the proponents of professional training for librarians. After two years in St. Louis, she was hired by the Pratt Institute Free Library in Brooklyn to organize a training program for librarians. In 1893, Plummer was chosen as acting curator of Pratt's educational exhibit during the Columbian Exposition in Chicago. The following year, she was named director of Pratt's Free Library and its library school. To allow her time to prepare for these new responsibilities, Pratt gave Plummer a year's leave of absence to travel and study in Europe. In the fall of 1895, she returned to Brooklyn from Europe and took on her new job, concentrating first on helping to plan the Free Library's new building. When the new quarters opened in the spring of 1896, observers were impressed in particular by two groundbreaking features, both of which had been proposed by Plummer. One was a special portion of the library that had been designed for use by children, the first of its kind, and the other was an art reference room designed for use by the general public. That same year a collection of Plummer's poetry, entitled simply *Verses*, was privately published.

A strong believer in the importance of special library facilities for children, Plummer originated the idea of special training for librarians who served children. In an article entitled "The Work for Children in Free Libraries," appearing in *Library Journal* in 1897, Plummer summed up her thoughts about what it took to put together a successful library facility for children: "the requisites for the ideal children's library, as we begin to see it, are suitable books, plenty of room, plenty of assistance, and thoughtful administration. Better a number of children's libraries scattered over a town or city than a large central one, since only in this way can the children be divided up so as to make individual attention to them easy."

Plummer's first love was unquestionably the training of librarians, and in 1904 she stepped down as director of Pratt's Free Library to concentrate on the operation of the institute's library school. In the latter half of that decade, she also wrote three children's books: *Roy and Ray in Mexico* (1907), *Roy and Ray in Canada* (1908), and *Stories from the Chronicles of the Cid* (1910).

In 1911, the New York Public Library called upon Plummer to help establish and direct its library school, funds for which had been obtained from philanthropist Andrew Carnegie. Her official title was principal (a man was given the title of director). Among her responsibilities in preparing for the school's opening in September 1911 were the hiring of faculty members and the preparation of announcements. The school offered a two-year program, as had been the case at Pratt; during the first year, students received a grounding in the basics of library science, while in the second they took advanced training in cataloguing, management, and bibliography. Plummer would serve as principal of the school until her death.

In an assessment of Plummer's contribution to library training that appeared in *Bulletin of Bibliography* in 1930, ***Anne Carroll Moore** observed that Plummer had "a positive genius for the making of an interesting program of any kind—professional, literary, or purely social." Plummer was an intellectual who delighted in scholarly pursuits. She had developed fluency in French, Italian, German, and Spanish. Although she certainly could have made a career for herself as a literary critic or poet, she chose to devote her life to library science. Moore writes that Plummer's "scholarly tastes and her warm friendship with European librarians and writers contributed definitely to the cosmopolitan atmosphere of the library and the whole institution with which she was associated."

Plummer served two terms as president of the New York Library Club, during 1896–97 and 1913–14. She also served a one-year term as president of the New York State Library Association in 1906. The crowning glory of her library career came in 1915, when she was elected the second woman president of the American Library Association (the first was **Theresa West Elmendorf**). Plummer died of cancer in Illinois the following year, age 60.

SOURCES:

James, Edward T., ed. *Notable American Women, 1607–1950.* Cambridge, MA: The Belknap Press of Harvard University, 1971.

Moore, Anne Carroll. "Mary Wright Plummer" in *Bulletin of Bibliography.* Vol. 14, issue 1. January–April 1930.

Don Amerman,
freelance writer, Saylorsburg, Pennsylvania

Plunkett, Elizabeth (1769–1823).

See Gunning, Elizabeth.

Pocahontas (c. 1596–1617)

Young Algonquian woman of the Powhatan nation who became famous for allegedly saving Captain John Smith's life in the early days of the Jamestown colony and later as the wife of John Rolfe, the Englishman partly responsible for the development of tobacco as a cash crop in Virginia. *Name variations: Matoaka (or Matowka, Matoka, Matoaks, Matoax [meaning "Little Snow Feather"]); Pocahantes or Pokahantesu (meaning "playful" or "little wanton"); Rebecca or Lady Rebecca Rolfe. Born Matoaka in 1595 or 1596 in the James River region of what became Virginia; died in Gravesend, England, in March 1617; daughter of Powhatan (headman of the Powhatan nation) and Winganuske (meaning "lovely woman") or another of Powhatan's wives; married Kocoum (a Powhatan or Potomac man), around 1609–13; married John Rolfe, in 1614; children: Thomas (b. 1615).*

Few indigenous women have persisted in the American imagination as vibrantly as has Pocahontas. For generations, every student came to learn of her as the Algonquian princess who, in a burst of love and reverence, saved the noble English explorer, Captain John Smith, from certain death from brain-bashing by throwing herself prostrate over his body and begging her father, the stern chieftain Powhatan, for clemency. Sentimental poets and prose writers alike celebrated her altruism as proof of indigenous virtue and deference to presumed European superiority. Some elevated her encounter with Smith into a Victorian-style love affair, replete with courtliness and chivalry. Enthusiasts of the Noble Savage concept assumed she was the very model of indigenous beauty, or more significantly refashioned her as an indigenous version of European female beauty. Her name and face, often in silhouette or caricature, still adorn the signs of motels, restaurants, curio shops, and other current establishments of popular culture from Virginia westward. At least four towns, in Virginia and West Virginia, as well as in the distant states of Illinois and Iowa, memorialize her by name. A full-length animated film from Disney was released in 1995. The Shoshone woman ***Sacajawea**, who aided Meriwether Lewis and William Clark in their trans-Mississippi explorations, may hold the record for the most statues erected to her achievements, but the image of Pocahontas resonates as strongly in the American memory.

In many ways, Pocahontas came to represent the symbolic indigenous woman, the one who set the standard for the millions of actual indigenous women whose names never made it into the history books. Moreover, she became emblematic of the fantastic potential for interracial amalgamation and the lost chances for true cultural merger at the continent's opening. In an important and provocative essay, "The Mother of Us All: Pocahontas," the literary critic Philip Young detailed this theme. As Young pointed out, numerous American poets, novelists, and playwrights attempted to rework, with varying degrees of success, the Pocahontas legend into an American classical myth on the order of the *Odyssey* or the *Aeneid*. Thus, Vachel Lindsay penned in 1918:

> John Rolfe is not our ancestor.
> We rise from out the soul of her
> Held in native wonderland,
> While the sun's rays kissed her hand,
> In the springtime,
> In Virginia,
> Our mother, Pocahontas.

Similarly Hart Crane chose her as a powerful symbol of the innocence and possibility of native America in his major poem "The Bridge." Introducing the section labelled "Powhatan's Daughter," Crane quoted a passage about a young Pocahontas erotically leading the men at the fort in a whirling dance. Then, in following segments of the poem, he conjured up her memory constantly. For him, she was alternately the virginal power of the American landscape and then the life-sustaining pioneer earth mother.

The actual Pocahontas was somewhat more shadowy than her ensuing legend. The details surrounding her birth are uncertain. Like many tribal groups, the Powhatans did not maintain European-style birth and marriage records. The practice of polygyny further complicated matters of exact lineage. But sometime in 1595 or 1596, she was born, the daughter of the chieftain Powhatan and one of his several wives, perhaps **Winganuske**. The infant girl's first name, her real or proper one, was Matoaka (or one of several similarly spelled variants), which may have meant "Little Snow Feather." The tribe guarded this name jealously, lest its power and protection dissipate in the ears of foreigners. "Pocahontas" was the name by which those outside of the tribe came to know her. The name roughly translated as "playful" or "little wanton" or synonyms of the two, although the English may have interpreted it as "Bright Stream Between Two Hills."

Although Pocahontas was only one of ten daughters born to Powhatan, she apparently became his favorite quite early on. He lavished plenty of love and attention on her and elevated her to a position fairly comparable to that of a princess in English royalty. She probably enjoyed an idyllic childhood, although she may not have had a close relationship with a mother figure. By the time the Jamestown group of settlers arrived in 1607, Pocahontas already commanded much respect within her tribal group. Quite possibly she was into her adolescence, having gone through the customary puberty rituals.

The tribe she grew up in, the Powhatans, was one of numerous Algonquian-speaking groups that inhabited the Chesapeake Bay region of the Eastern woodlands culture area. After a couple of decades of scrambling for power, her father, the supreme werowance or chieftain, had put together a tenuous coalition of alliances with surrounding tribes in a defensive posture against a host of enemy tribes circling them to the north, west, and south. When the English arrived, Powhatan did a superb performance of convincing them that his power was more extensive than it really was. The English, not having any firm grasp on regional politics at first, had no choice but to accord Powhatan respect. In actuality, his diplomacy had to be skillful and often secretive to maintain the balance of power. Within this mix of foreign relations, Pocahontas soon traveled as an occasional ambassador.

In 1607, members of the English Virginia Company intruded in the Chesapeake Bay region and attempted to exploit the land for riches, possible bullion and whatever other marketable commodities. Other Britishers had previously tried to colonize the areas to the south, but had ended in failure and, in the case of the Roanoke effort of the 1580s, in mysterious disappearance. The group in 1607 established a toehold settlement at Jamestown and for the first couple of years eked out a miserable existence. The parent company virtually ignored the settlers. Many of the adventurers died in the "starving times." Disease was rampant and foodstuffs short. Not until Captain John Smith assumed a quasi-dictatorial control of the village did survival seem possible.

Before that achievement, however, Smith almost paid with his life. The Powhatans had taken some time assessing the worth and gaug-

Pocahontas

ing the threat of these British settlers. Some of the younger chiefs, such as Powhatan's brother Opechancanough, probably wished to exterminate them, but Powhatan himself wavered between warfare and alliance with the whites. In late 1607, scouting parties under Opechancanough captured Smith, after massacring his companions near the Chickahominy River. In January 1608, the warriors took Smith to Werowocomoco, Powhatan's principal residence. There, in a longhouse, Powhatan and the tribal elders mulled over Smith's fate. Although Smith presented himself with great courage and might have earned his release (or adoption) with such bravery, the chieftain decided on execution. Death would be by smashing Smith's skull on two giant stones as he knelt beneath the blows of large wooden clubs.

At that point the stage was set for the most celebrated (and debated) rescue in American history. According to the story, the young Pocahontas, who seemingly had never even seen Smith before, ran from her father's side, flung herself over Smith's prostrate body, and begged for clemency. Interposing herself between him and the clubs above, she was either preventing the clubbing or signifying that she would sacrifice her own self, too, with Smith. The crowd was stunned apparently, as was Powhatan, who relented under the condition that Smith would make hatchets for him and bells, beads, and copper baubles for Pocahontas instead of taking up military action again. What might have been a bloody scene suddenly turned joyous, undoubtedly to Smith's great wonderment and relief.

There she stood, in the shadow of the forest primeval, a figure of romance, symbol of redemption, princess, paragon, a naiad-dryad of the Western World . . . great Earth Mother of the Americas, who had opened up her heart and heartland to the newcomer.

—**Frances Mossiker**

This rescue scene, the stuff of enduring legend, however, has raised many questions for scholars. Why did Pocahontas even perform it? Did she feel a rush of genuine love or sympathy for Smith and hurl herself on his body? Did she envision a future marriage with him that would unite the two races? Did she act alone or was she part of an orchestrated plot by Powhatan? Did Powhatan even fully intend to execute Smith? Did she trip her father's hand or carry out a long-understood ruse? Many modern anthropologists have speculated that Powhatan was staging a mock execution. Many of the Algonquian tribes of that era supposedly employed such a ceremony for the various reasons of humiliating an enemy, of testing his or her courage or suitability for adoption or release, of demonstrating the superior powers of the tribe or absorbing the medicine (magical influence) of the captive, or even perhaps for the sheer entertainment of the spectacle. Or perhaps Powhatan was elaborately extorting useful military and diplomatic information from the frazzled captain.

More problematic still has been the question of whether the whole episode even occurred or happened as Smith recounted. Taking a cue from the 19th-century historian Henry Adams, who severely questioned Smith's veracity, the literary historian J.A. Leo Lemay has assembled an entire book examining the controversy. Smith did not recite the story until years afterwards, when his reputation and the colony of Virginia were more secure. In subsequent writings, Smith added to or omitted details from the first rendition. Some scholars think that Smith was merely weaving into his story a type of tale that was long familiar to European readers. Numerous sagas told of heroes imprisoned by tyrannical emperors, whose daughters rushed in to save or release the captives. The Crusades had supplied many such tales, and Smith himself had been a captive of the Turks in earlier military action on the Continent. If the event did occur, why did Smith, hardly a shy man, wait 16 years to publicize it? Could he have been repaying Pocahontas for her efforts and friendship at that later date?

Whatever the case, Pocahontas and Smith started some sort of special friendship that carried on for nearly a decade. Whether or not this was love became the subject for many romanticists in later literary productions. Smith himself remained mum, perhaps from coyness or maybe because he did not wish his actions to encourage other Jamestonians to rush into the woods to obtain an indigenous consort for themselves. Pocahontas might have still been prepubescent, given the uncertainties surrounding her age. He may have considered her too young for amorous attention or assumed that she was promised to a Powhatan man. More likely, Smith realized that Pocahontas' specific relationship to Powhatan was powerful and perhaps useful for British fortunes. Over the next few years, Pocahontas acted as an ambassador to the English through her friendship with Smith.

Once back in Jamestown, Smith set about securing control. New arrivals from England briefly tipped the balance of power in favor of the English (even though straining the food supplies again). Throughout 1608, however, Smith accorded Pocahontas special treatment whenever she came to visit. In May, for instance, he bestowed upon her beads and mirrors as presents. Relations between the two races deteriorated over disagreements about food. More than once, according to Smith, Pocahontas warned him of her father's plans to do him and the English harm or hid him from pursuers. Some of Smith's English adversaries suspected him of secretly courting Pocahontas and a kingship for himself. Smith refuted such, but left for England in the fall of 1609. Powhatan, meanwhile, had forbidden her from going to Jamestown, and she believed that Smith was dead.

While the English colony bumbled along at Jamestown, Pocahontas' image grew in England, thanks mainly to the flattering writings of William Strachey. He described her as a nubile, wanton symbol of womanhood in the New World, and in one famous passage depicted her whirling and cartwheeling naked in front of the astonished male onlookers. In actuality, Pocahontas had probably married. The details are quite sketchy, but apparently she had been married off to one Kocoum, a war-party leader. He might have been a member of the Patawamacke tribe, because the next time the English encountered her she was living in northern Virginia near the Potomac River. Possibly, Pocahontas absconded northward because of the rift with her father. The marriage, if there were indeed one, proved fruitless. By 1613, there was no more mention in the record of Kocoum. Perhaps the barren condition of the union had led to its dissolution.

In 1613, the English captured Pocahontas and held her hostage in hopes of some ransom. Her stay at Henrico turned out to be more voluntary. Upon her arrival, Sir Thomas Dale undertook her conversion to English ways and the Anglican faith by assigning her instruction to Reverend Alexander Whitaker. The Powhatan princess adopted European dress and other customs, and studied the Book of Common Prayer and other Christian texts. An apt student, possessed of high intelligence and curiosity, Pocahontas absorbed the teachings quickly and smoothly. Undoubtedly, she experienced some dislocation in losing her native culture that had served her well for the previous years. One scholar suggested that grief for John Smith, whom she thought dead, motivated her conversion. However that may be, Dale and Whitaker trumpeted her progress toward assimilation as the first indigenous convert in the colony. Within the year, she was ready for baptism, and the reverend settled on the name Rebecca for her Christian name, one that would echo Biblical reverberations in light of her upcoming marriage.

During this captivity period, she fell in love with John Rolfe. Famous ever afterwards for his assiduous introduction of West Indian tobacco into the colony's agriculture and rescue of Virginia's economy, Rolfe had also participated in Pocahontas' conversion efforts. The love blossomed and both parties entertained the idea of marriage. A widower, Rolfe found himself attracted to Pocahontas' sensuality and brightness. But the prospect of an interracial marriage was not one that people of both races took lightly. Contemporary concepts of savagism asserted that indigenous women were sexual temptresses. Rolfe had to disclaim that lust was the motive for his love, and he even wrote to friends in England apologizing for his choice of spouse. Euroamerican legal concepts about miscegenation were still rather fuzzy, not hardening into law until the 1660s, but such marriages bore more portent than those within the same race. Unavoidably, such an interracial marriage would imply some sort of economic and diplomatic union between the two wary groups, who each in turn would be likely to manipulate the match for its own benefit. Pocahontas' own privileged status among the Powhatans, even in her estrangement, made such an arrangement potentially even more significant. Thus Rolfe secured the permission and blessings of both Powhatan and the English authorities before proceeding with an actual ceremony. Rolfe, Pocahontas, and a party of Virginians traveled to Powhatan's residence. After some purposeful delays and a possible attempt to ransom his favorite daughter, the chieftain gave his consent.

Early in 1614, probably in early April, Pocahontas received the rite of baptism into the Church of England. Shortly thereafter or on the same day, she married Rolfe. The marriage of Pocahontas and John Rolfe was important, not only because it was one of three legitimized unions between Powhatan and English spouses during the 17th century, but because it helped bring on a stretch of relative peace between the two racial groups. This detente, known in Virginia history as the "Peace of Pocahontas," did not last longer than a couple of years. The newlyweds basked in this initial harmony, either at a house on Mulberry Island or at a cottage at Varina Farm (possibly a wedding gift from her father). The marriage, a loving one by several accounts, resulted in the birth of a child within the year. In April 1615, with midwife services from an aunt or sister, Pocahontas had a male baby, whom the parents christened Thomas, probably in honor of Sir Thomas Dale. Although she had accepted much of English culture, probably she reared her child biculturally and bilingually. She did not completely jettison her native upbringing and kept several of her relatives and tribespeople in attendance until her death.

Grateful for Pocahontas' help during the Virginia colony's early years, the Virginia Company in London awarded her a lifetime stipend. The Company also entertained the idea of bringing her to England as a prize exhibit of the colonial successes. In 1616, Sir Thomas Dale, anxious to please the home investors and sharing their enthusiasm for capitalizing on Pocahontas' fame, paved the way for her introduction to British society. In the spring of 1616, Lady Rebecca, John Rolfe, and their son, as well as her sister **Matachanna** and her sister's husband Uttamatamakin, a tribal councilor and shaman, all joined Dale and others on board the *Treasurer* headed for England. On June 3, the ship landed at Plymouth, and by late June, the exotic party made its way to a London already tingling with anticipation about Pocahontas. Since the voyages of Columbus, former explorers had occasionally brought back an indigenous male for display in Europe, but Pocahontas would be the first indigenous woman of royalty to grace English shores.

Pocahontas' first reactions to London are unknown, but the magnitude of the city must have astonished her during the first few days ashore. With charming irony, the Virginia Company secured lodging for her at the Belle Sauvage, one of the oldest hotels in one of the busiest districts of town. Compared to the peacefulness of Virginia, London was jarring. But mustering all her civilized manners, Pocahontas, in full lady's costume, began to move in the higher social circles. Virginia Company officials and Lord and **Lady De La Warre** squired her about and arranged the appropriate meetings. Samuel Purchas, the chronicler and promoter of England's overseas colonial endeavors, interviewed her and her entourage. Decked out in a starched ruff collar, a high hat, and red velvet brocade, and holding a white ostrich feather, she sat for an oil portrait, which became the only known likeness of her to survive. After an audience with Queen ***Anne of Denmark** at Whitehall, she became a favorite at the Stuart court throughout 1616. Eventually, she was presented to King James I with pomp and splendor. Curiously, though, John Smith, who knew she had arrived in London and had written a testament on her behalf, delayed a visit, perhaps out of jealousy of John Rolfe.

The peak of Pocahontas' social ascent came on January 6, 1617, at the king's annual Twelfth Night celebration. She and Uttamatamakin were guests of honor. At this ceremony, probably the most prestigious in the yearly calendar, Pocahontas sparkled and enjoyed herself immensely among the cheerful revelers. However much she and her country consorts understood about the English Christmas, the gaiety was infectious. She probably was one of the important dancers at the masque and may have had the seat of honor next to the king, during the premiere of Ben Jonson's play *The Vision of Delight.* The Twelfth Night party enhanced her fame, and as Virginia historian Robert Beverly wrote some 90 years later, she "was carried to many Plays, Balls, and other publick Entertainments, and very respectfully receiv'd by all the Ladies about the Court."

The damp and vaporous environs of London, however, proved disastrous for Pocahontas. Sometime in early 1617, she fell deathly ill, probably with a pulmonary disease like tuberculosis. The family moved temporarily to a country village in Middlesex. John Rolfe reckoned that she had a distemper and continued with his plans to return to Virginia. Indeed, he figured that the open air of a voyage might help Pocahontas' condition. Uttamatamakin, too, despite his own celebrity status, had grown disgusted with London and yearned for his homeland. Apparently, Pocahontas herself did not wish to return. She did finally receive a visit from John Smith, whom she still had believed was dead, but supposedly she gave him a very chilly shoulder. Why she preferred to stay is still a matter of conjecture. Whatever the case, in March, Rolfe, Pocahontas, and their son boarded a ship, the *George,* bound for Virginia under the captainship of Samual Argall. Gravely ill, Pocahontas made it no further than Gravesend, about 25 miles from the London point of embarkation. Taken ashore, probably to an inn nearby, she died shortly thereafter. As Samuel Purchas wrote, "At her return towards Virginia she came at Gravesend to her end and grave, having given great demonstration of her Christian sincerity, as the first fruits of Virginian conversion." Parish records at the local church in Gravesend noted that she "was buried in the chauncell" on March 21st. Some legends, however, perpetuated the story that her survivors lowered her body into the Thames River for burial. Rolfe and his motherless son continued on to America. One of countless victims of the Europeans' "virgin soil" epidemics, Pocahontas saw her brief brush with royalty end in just that bleak fashion.

Pocahontas' fame outlived the grave and mushroomed into a major legend. Poets and writers in later centuries seized on her and her rescue of John Smith for all their mythic aspects. For many, she became a controlling image of America. As **Rayna Green** asserted in "The Pocahontas Perplex," "Thus, the Indian woman began her symbolic, many-faceted life as a Mother figure—exotic, powerful, dangerous, and beautiful—and as a representative of American liberty and European classical virtue translated into New World terms." Child of the wilds and yet comfortable in court, she became the best of all symbolic bridges in a drastic cultural confrontation and exchange.

SOURCES:

Barbour, Philip L. *Pocahontas and Her World: A Chronicle of America's First Settlement.* Boston, MA: Houghton Mifflin, 1970.

Dearborn, Mary V. *Pocahontas's Daughters: Gender and Ethnicity in American Culture.* NY: Oxford University Press, 1986 (especially Chapter 5).

Green, Rayna. "The Pocahontas Perplex: The Image of Indian Women in American Culture," in Ellen Carol DuBois and Vicki L. Ruiz, eds., *Unequal Sisters: A Multicultural Reader in U.S. Women's History.* NY: Routledge, 1990, pp. 15–21.

Lemay, J.A. Leo. *Did Pocahontas Save Captain John Smith?* Athens, GA: University of Georgia Press, 1992.
Mossiker, Frances. *Pocahontas: The Life and the Legend.* NY: Alfred A. Knopf, 1976.
Rountree, Helen C. *Pocahontas's People: The Powhatan Indians of Virginia Through Four Centuries.* Norman, OK: University of Oklahoma Press, 1990.
Woodward, Grace Steele. *Pocahontas.* Norman, OK: University of Oklahoma Press, 1969.
Young, Philip. "The Mother of Us All: Pocahontas," in *Three Bags Full: Essays in American Fiction.* NY: Harcourt Brace Jovanovich, 1973.

Thomas L. Altherr,
Professor of History and American Studies,
Metropolitan State College of Denver, Denver, Colorado

Poe, Elizabeth (c. 1787–1811)

American actress who was the mother of Edgar Allan Poe. *Born in London, England, around 1787; died in Richmond, Virginia, on December 8, 1811; probably the daughter of Henry Arnold and Elizabeth Smith (both actors); married Charles D. Hopkins (an actor), in 1802 (died 1805); married David Poe (an actor), in 1806; children: William Poe (b. 1807); Edgar Allan Poe (1809–1849, poet and short-story writer); Rosalie Poe (b. 1810?).*

Most of what is known about Elizabeth Poe is gleaned from research on her more famous son Edgar, notably from Arthur Hobson Quinn's biography *Edgar Allan Poe* (1941). She is believed to have been born in London, the daughter of Henry Arnold and **Elizabeth Smith**, who were both actors at Covent Garden. Henry Arnold died around 1790, and Elizabeth Smith continued on at Covent Garden until late 1795, when she and her young daughter sailed for the United States. Accompanying them on the voyage was an actor by the name of Charles Tubbs, whom Elizabeth Smith married either before they left London or after they landed in Boston, Massachusetts. In Boston, the newlyweds joined a troupe of touring actors, and are believed to have died of yellow fever in 1798, during a stopover in Charleston, South Carolina. Following her mother's death, young Elizabeth joined a theatrical company in Philadelphia.

Elizabeth Poe had made her stage debut in Boston at the age of nine, appearing in the second act of *The Mysteries of the Castle,* on April 15, 1796, at the old Boston Theater. From that time, until her untimely death around age 24, she worked as an actress in theaters up and down the East Coast, performing in comedy, drama, and musicals, and enjoying minor popularity. During her early career, she played young boys, including the Duke of York in *Richard III* and Little Pickle in *The Spoiled Child.* She then graduated to ingenue roles, among them Phoebe in the opera *Rosina,* Sophia in *Road to Ruin*, and Biddy Bellair in the farce *Miss in Her Teens*. Her later roles included some Shakespearean classics.

In 1802, Elizabeth married Charles D. Hopkins, a successful comedian, and with him joined the Virginia Players. The marriage was cut short by Hopkins' death in 1805, after which Elizabeth wed David Poe, another actor. Although a handsome man, David apparently had a minor speech impediment that was frequently made much of in reviews, causing him great distress.

The couple toured together in Richmond, Philadelphia, and New York, then spent three years at the Federal Street Theater in Boston. It was here that Elizabeth reportedly spent the happiest days of her life, and where two of the couple's three children were born: William Henry Poe (b. 1807) and Edgar Allan Poe (b. January 1809). The couple's third child, **Rosalie Poe**, was possibly born in December 1810 in Richmond, although the date and place have not been substantiated. Elizabeth continued with her career, playing such roles as Cordelia in *King Lear*, Juliet in *Romeo and Juliet*, and Ophelia in *Hamlet*, and sharing the stage with famous actor Thomas Abthorpe Cooper in Boston and New York. Around 1809, David Poe seems to have dropped from the picture, likely the result of continual battering by the critics. It is not known whether he deserted his wife and children, or was simply unemployed or ill; whatever the case, Elizabeth endured a period of severe financial hardship. In the fall of 1811, she joined a troupe in Richmond, Virginia, where she died the following December of pneumonia. Her orphaned children were brought up by three different families.

SOURCES:

James, Edward T., ed. *Notable American Women, 1607–1950.* Cambridge, MA: The Belknap Press of Harvard University, 1971.

Barbara Morgan,
Melrose, Massachusetts

Pohl, Sabine Bergmann (b. 1946).

See Bergmann-Pohl, Sabine.

Poh've'ka (1887–1980).

See Martinez, Maria Montoya.

Pointer Sisters (1973—)

African-American high-powered pop group, known for their precise harmonies, funky visuals, and vintage clothes.

***Pointer, Anita* (1948—).** *Born on January 23, 1948, in Oakland, California.*

Solo album: Love for What It Is *(1987).*

***Pointer, Bonnie* (1950—).** *Born on July 11, 1950, in Oakland, California.*

Solo albums: Bonnie Pointer *(1978);* Bonnie Pointer II *(1979);* The Price Is Right *(1984).*

***Pointer, June* (1954—).** *Born on November 30, 1954, in Oakland, California.*

***Pointer, Ruth* (1946—).** *Born on March 19, 1946, in Oakland, California.*

Selected discography (albums): The Pointer Sisters *(1973);* That's Plenty *(1974);* Live at the Opera House *(1974);* Steppin' *(1975); (without Bonnie)* Energy *(1978);* Special Things *(1980);* Black and White *(1981);* So Excited *(1982);* Break Out *(1983);* Contact *(1985);* Hot Together *(1986);* Serious Slammin' *(1988);* Greatest Hits *(1989);* Right Rhythm *(1990);* Only Sisters Can Do That *(1994).*

The daughters of ministers, the Pointer sisters—Ruth, Anita, Bonnie, and June—started singing together at the West Oakland Church of God, honing from childhood what has been called a "set-the-house-afire" vocal style. In 1969, Bonnie and June began performing in clubs around the San Francisco area, calling themselves Pointers, a Pair. Anita eventually joined the duo, and, after singing background vocals on several albums, they acquired manager Bill Graham. With Graham's assistance, they backed such performers as Elvin Bishop, Taj Mahal, Tower of Power, Dave Mason, Sylvester, Boz Scaggs, and ***Esther Phillips**.

At a gig at Los Angeles' Whisky-a-Go-Go, the sisters caught the attention of Atlantic executive Jerry Wexler, who signed them to a record contract. Their first single was released to little success in 1972, after which Ruth left her job and joined the group. In 1973, after signing with a new label (ABC's Blue Thumb), they cut another single, "Yes We Can Can"/ "Wang Dang Doodle," which hit both the pop and R&B charts and brought them their first national recognition.

While the Pointers' unique sound, a blend of rock 'n' roll, jazz, gospel, and rhythm and blues, executed in precise four-part harmony, was the

Pointer Sisters (Ruth, Anita, and June)

greater part of their appeal, the sisters also put on a terrific live show. "Part of the reaction to the group is due to the visuals accompanying the act," wrote Jim Knippenberg in a 1974 article for the *Cincinnati Enquirer*. "The girls tap dance, parade around the stage, carry on with all manner of body English and do all of it in wonderfully tacky '30s and '40s outfits."

As their popularity rose, the Pointers toured the country and made guest appearances on a number of television variety shows. They became the first African-American women to perform at Nashville's Grand Ole Opry, and the first pop act to play the San Francisco Opera House. In 1974, PBS made a documentary on the Pointer family. Then, between 1975 and 1977, the Pointers had some internal problems; June suffered a nervous breakdown and the group filed a lawsuit with ABC's Blue Thumb for back royalties. In 1977, Bonnie left the group and went solo, signing a contract with Motown. (Bonnie had several hits in 1978 and 1979, before running into legal problems with the label. She did not have another hit until 1984.)

Retrenching, the remaining sisters signed with Planet Records, a collaboration which resulted in a steady string of pop hits throughout the 1980s, including "Fire," "He's So Shy," "Slow Hand," "I'm So Excited," and "Neutron Dance." The group also produced two platinum albums, *Break Out* and *Contact*, and in 1987 Anita cut a solo album for RCA called *Love for What It Is*. By the end of the decade, however, the constant recording and tours had taken a toll, and the sisters took some time off. "Everyone thinks this business is all glamour, but that's not the case a lot of the time," said Ruth, who particularly suffered during the long periods on the road. "After you leave that stage you go to a hotel room by yourself. Sometimes it was very lonely and very depressing. I had to learn to do things to keep my spirits up."

The Pointers returned to the music scene in 1994, with the new album *Only Sisters Can Do That*, a compilation of 10 songs celebrating the contemporary woman and marking their 20th year in the recording industry. The album, which contains two songs co-written by Anita, "I Want Fireworks" and "Tell It To My Heart," is reminiscent of their earlier work. "We've gone back to what we do best," says Ruth, "which is being ourselves and singing as opposed to trying to keep up with the mainstream and modern technology. We wanted to capture a feeling of pure, raw honesty on this album and I think we succeeded."

SOURCES:

Clarke, Donald, ed. *The Penguin Encyclopedia of Popular Music*. London: Penguin, 1989.

Knippenberg, Jim. "Jumping, Jiving with the Pointer Sisters," in *Cincinnati* [Ohio] *Enquirer*. May 12, 1974.

Romanowski, Patricia, and Holly George-Warren, eds. *The New Encyclopedia of Rock & Roll*. NY: Rolling Stone Press, 1995.

Barbara Morgan,
Melrose, Massachusetts

Poisson, Jeanne-Antoinette (1721–1764).

See Pompadour, Jeanne-Antoinette Poisson, Duchesse de.

Poissy, prioress of.

See Marie de Bourbon (fl. 1350s).
See Marie (1393–1438).

Poitevent, Eliza Jane (1849–1896).

See Nicholson, Eliza Jane.

Poitiers, Diane de (1499–1566).

See Diane de Poitiers.

Poitou, countess of.

See Adele of Normandy (c. 917–c. 962).

Poker Alice (1851–1930).

See Tubbs, Alice.

Pokou (c. 1700–c. 1760)

African ruler of first rank who led the Baule people, a subgroup of the Ashanti tribe, across the Comoé River near the Ivory Coast to establish a new state which became powerful in trade during the 19th century. *Name variations: Abla Pokou; Aura Pokou; Awura Pokou; Queen of the Ashanti. Born Pokou sometime between 1700 and 1720; daughter of an unrecorded father (as a member of Ashanti royalty her status was inherited through her mother) and Nyakou Kosiamoa; married Tano (a warrior); children: one son.*

Led a group of Ashanti to the West African Ivory Coast (c. 1750), establishing a kingdom over which she was proclaimed queen; died shortly thereafter.

Throughout African history, women have held positions of leadership. Whether they were queens like ***Njinga** or ***Taytu**, chiefs like ***Hannah Awolowo** and ***Okwei of Osomari**, or leaders of movements like ***Auoa Kéita**, women have shaped the African continent, where female authority has been an accepted norm far longer than in Europe. When Europeans colonized what they perceived as the "dark continent," many Africans were puzzled by a people who placed judicial, military, and government authority in the hands of only one gender. Africa's oral traditions had long kept alive stories of warriors like Njinga who led troops in battle, chiefs who settled local disputes, and empresses like Taytu who governed large countries. In the eyes of many Africans, the technologically advanced society of the Europeans did not conceal what were often perceived as socially regressive attitudes.

Documenting the accomplishments of Queen Pokou, an Ashanti ruler of the Baule people in the first half of the 18th century, presents certain problems, because her life was chronicled primarily through oral history. In recent years, however, scholars have combined African oral tradition with written European accounts to flesh out the details of the life of Pokou, with remarkable results. Accounts written by G.A. Robertson in 1819, and by M. Delafosse in 1899, substantiate much of the oral tradition recounted around the campfire for generations.

The history of the Akan or Ashanti tribe can be traced back at least as far as the 12th century, when these forerunners of the Baule people began to infiltrate the forests of what is modern Ghana, eventually inhabiting most of the southern part of the region currently occupied by that country. In 1295, the oldest Akan kingdom was established under the name of Bono Mansu. In many ways, Ashanti kingdoms resembled medieval European principalities of the same period. Independent duchies, principalities, and kingdoms were founded, prospered for a time, and then disintegrated, only to reemerge in a new form. Around 1620, the kingdom of Denkyra emerged and established the ascendancy of the Ashanti tribes. In 1700, Osei Tutu began his rule and became the greatest Ashanti king, uniting several small and widely scattered small kingdoms into an even larger empire. Famous throughout western Africa, he ruled from a throne of gold until 1718.

When Europeans began to colonize Africa in the 16th century, geographical barriers combined with the fierceness of the Ashanti people to allow them to remain more independent of the invaders than many African tribes. Along the Ivory Coast, the mainland area known as the Quaqua Coast was separated from the ocean by an interconnected series of freshwater lagoons which were navigable by small craft but inaccessible to larger boats. The area was made more inaccessible by impenetrable jungle and the unhealthy climate created by high humidity and rainfall, which proved especially dangerous to colonials unaccustomed to tropical diseases.

Therefore, at the time of Pokou's birth (between 1700 and 1720), the Ashanti kingdom was still intact. She was born into royalty, the niece of the powerful Osei Tutu, and the daughter of **Nyakou Kosiamoa**, who was either a sister or niece of the king. Since succession to the Ashanti throne was matrilineal, a mother's identity was more important than a father's, and the identity of Pokou's father was not recorded. She herself was important to the succession since the royal heir was the child of the king's sister or his niece. When a new male heir succeeded to the throne, the queen mother shared power with her son.

In 1718, Osei Tutu was ambushed and killed, and power over the Ashanti passed to Pokou's brother, Dakon. During his reign, which lasted for almost two decades, Pokou chose a husband according to the privilege of her rank. Much to her regret, however, since she was in line to produce the next heir to the throne, she did not become pregnant.

One day when Dakon and his army were away at war from the Ashanti capital at Kumasi, enemy troops occupied the town. All the royal princesses were killed except Pokou, who arranged for the townspeople to escape. Prepared to die at her post if necessary, she was instead taken hostage, and when Dakon returned to his empty capital, he was furious. Dakon appointed a warrior, Tano, to lead the forces in freeing the royal princess, and following the rescue Tano was married to her. This marriage resulted in the birth of a baby boy, ensuring an heir to the golden Ashanti throne.

While the child was still an infant, Pokou's brother became ill. Before his death, Dakon named a successor to the throne, but the appointed heir was soon assassinated by Kwissi, Dakon's rival. Recognizing that Pokou's son was the eventual rightful heir, Kwissi sought Pokou's blessing for his reign. Kwissi perhaps even hoped to marry Pokou; certainly he believed that her support was vital to maintaining his power. But Pokou refused to give her backing to the interloper. Instead, she decided to leave Kumasi and found a new kingdom, and invited Ashanti families who also wanted to leave to join her. According to tradition, four groups of Ashanti of noble rank—the Warebo, the Faafew, the Nzipri, and the Sa—decided to follow Pokou. Others who joined her were the Atutu, the Nanfew, the Ngbã, and the Agba, all of whom had been conquered by the Ashanti.

Legend and fact intermingle at this point, while the story of Pokou and her people also becomes remarkably parallel to that of Moses and the Hebrews he led in their exodus out of Egypt. Like the Hebrews followed by the armies of the pharaoh, Pokou's followers were pursued by Kwissi's soldiers. They headed westward toward the Comoé River, passing through interminable jungle, where according to tradition they fought panthers, giant ants, and giant snakes. Sometimes they crossed savannas filled with belligerent elephants, and serpents seemed always to lie in wait no matter what the terrain, while illness also dogged their footsteps. After many months, still pursued by Kwissi's troops, they reached the banks of the Comoé River.

Faced with a raging torrent, with no shallow fords or places for canoes to cross, Pokou and her followers decided that a sacrifice must be made to the river spirits. At first their leader considered sacrificing a sick woman and her baby, but when they were brought to her, Pokou decided, like Abraham offering his only son Isaac up to Yahweh, that the river gods would not accept such a meager sacrifice. As Kwissi's troops drew nearer, she was convinced that nothing less than her son would please the river spirits, and threw her only child into the waters of the Comoé. According to legend, an enormous tree stretched over the waters, forming a bridge, and river animals like crocodiles and hippopotamuses rose out of the water to convey the people on their backs. No sooner had Pokou's people reached the other side than the bridge and river animals disappeared, stopping the army's pursuit. It was for this event that the migrating Ashanti became known as the "Baule," in memory of Pokou's son.

Just as no one can be certain that the waters of the Red Sea parted for the Old Testament Hebrews, the Ashanti's miraculous crossing of the Comoé cannot be documented. What is certain is that the Hebrews occupied Palestine and the Ashanti occupied much of today's Ivory Coast. The actual date of the African exodus is somewhat open to question, placed by some in 1730, although 1750 is the more likely date. Further research indicates that the Ashanti or Akan people settled in this area of what is now Ghana in several waves, after the middle of the 18th century. Among these groups, the Warebo were the ascendant people, and Pokou was a Warebo. While mythological versions claim that the Baule people conquered the area militarily in short order, it is more likely that their conquest was of an extended nature, and accomplished to a large extent through marriage and trade.

To claim her new homeland, Pokou is said to have led her meager troops against the local ruler Agpatu and his forces, and ultimately gained the upper hand. It may be that her army had guns while the enemy did not. Accounts document that she waged war only in self-defense, never simply for the sake of destruction. Declared queen by this time, she was a judicious ruler, expert at settling disputes among tribes and individuals. But, like Moses, who led his people to the promised land but did not live to enjoy it, Pokou also died not long after the establishment of new kingdom. She was succeeded by her niece, **Akwabenua Bensua**, who perished during her conquest of the Youre people, and then by a male ruler, Akwa Boni, who expanded Baule control.

The arrival of the Baule was not immediately noticed by the colonizing Europeans. When the French began to frequent the area in the 1760s, trade with the newcomers was still insignificant. It was the early 19th century before their existence began to be noted in European histories. T.E. Bowdich wrote in 1817, "A powerful kingdom called Bhaooree, which has hitherto successfully resisted the Ashantees, was described to be westward." Some knowledge of the Baule was acquired in Kumasi, the old capital Pokou and her people had left, indicating that the two groups remained in contact over the years.

In the 19th century, the role of the Baule as traders developed dramatically. In 1819, G.A. Robertson reported about a trading people in the African interior in his *Notes on Africa*:

> The greater part of their trade they say comes from Weesaw (perhaps Wawsaw) and Couche, or Cotchey; the latter they represent to be governed by a female, of the extent of whose dominions and power they entertain a high opinion. They say that the queen declares war against all countries that do not pay her seeka or sicca (gold), and that she often sends troops to fight for other countries that can pay her well; but that she never commences hostilities against Cape Lahoo, as it is a place of trade.

It is possible that this account refers to Pokou's niece Akwabenua Bensua, or her descendant. One thing is certain—the tradition of female leadership in the area was well established.

The Baule differed from the many tribes who acted as intermediaries in trade between the Africans of the interior selling their ivory, gold, and slaves, and the Europeans. The Baule grew prosperous as farmers, supplying agricultural products for the European commodities markets. Europeans did not actually penetrate Baule territory until the 1890s, and then it was to map the area. The Baule remained an industrious, talented people who contributed much to modern Ghana and the Ivory Coast both culturally and economically.

In the separation of the myths surrounding Queen Pokou from fact, the outlines of a remarkable woman emerge, as a leader others were willing to follow, and one whose greatness was proved by her willingness to sacrifice her own happiness and well being for the sake of her people. In Africa, Pokou's accomplishments and her story are highly revered.

SOURCES:

Loucou, Jean Noel, and Françoise Ligier. *La Reine Pokou: Fondatrice du Royaume Baoulé*. Paris: ABC, 1978.

Mundt, Robert J. *Historical Dictionary of The Ivory Coast (Côte d'Ivoire)*. London: Scarecrow Press, 1987.

"Queen Pokou" in *Women Around the World and Through the Ages*. Edited by Sabrina Mervin and Carol Prunhuber. Atomium, 1990.

Weiskel, Timothy C. "The Precolonial Baule: A Reconstruction," in *Cahiers D'Études Africaines*. Vol. 18, 1978, pp. 503–560.

Wilkes, I. *Asante in the Nineteenth Century: The Structure and Evolution of a Political Order*. Cambridge: Cambridge University Press, 1975.

Karin Loewen Haag,
writer, Athens, Georgia

Poland, duchess of.

See Oda of Germany and North Marck (fl. 900s).
See Dobravy of Bohemia (d. 977).

Poland, queen of.

See Wanda of Poland (fl. 730).
See Gorka (fl. 920s).
See Judith of Hungary (fl. late 900s).
See Oda (fl. 1000).
See Richesa of Lorraine (d. 1067).
See Maria of Kiev (d. 1087).
See Salomea (d. 1144).
See Lucia of Rugia (fl. 1220s).
See Cunegunde (1234–1292).
See Ryksa (fl. 1288).
See Malgorzata (fl. 1290s).
See Krystyna Rokiczanska (fl. 1300s).
See Elizabeth of Bosnia (d. 1339).
See Jadwiga of Glogow (fl. late 1300s).
See Jadwiga (1374–1399).
See Elizabeth of Hungary (c. 1430–1505).
See Helene of Moscow (1474–1513).
See Sforza, Bona (1493–1557).
See Barbara Zapolya (fl. 1500).
See Elizabeth of Habsburg (d. 1545).
See Sforza, Bona for sidebar on Barbara Radziwell (1520–1551).
See Anna Jagello (1523–1596).
See Catherine of Habsburg (1533–1572).
See Anna of Styria (1573–1598).
See Constance of Styria (1588–1631).
See Cecilia Renata of Austria (1611–1644).
See Louise Marie de Gonzague (1611–1667).
See Marie Casimir (1641–1716).
See Marie Josepha (1699–1757).

Poland, regent of.

See Elizabeth of Poland (1305–1380).

Polányi, Ilona (1897–1978).

See Duczynska, Ilona.

Polastron, Yolande Martine Gabrielle de (1749–1793).

See Polignac, Yolande Martine Gabrielle de.

Pole, Catherine de la (d. 1419).

See Stafford, Catherine.

Pole, Elizabeth de la (1444–1503)

Duchess of Suffolk. *Born on April 22, 1444, in Rouen, Normandy, France; died after January 1503; buried in Wingfield, Suffolk, England; daughter of Richard, 3rd duke of York, and **___Cecily Neville___*; sister of **___Margaret of York___* *(1446–1503); married John de la Pole, 1st duke of Suffolk, in 1460; children: eight, including John de la Pole, earl of Lincoln (c. 1462–1487); Edmund de la Pole, 2nd duke of Suffolk (1471–1513); Richard de la Pole (d. 1525);* ***Anne de la Pole****.*

Pole, Margaret (1473–1541)

Countess of Salisbury. *Name variations: Margaret, Countess of Salisbury; Margaret Plantagenet; Lady Salisbury. Born around August 14, 1473, at Farley Castle, Somerset, England; executed on May 27, 1541, in the Tower of London; daughter of George, duke of Clarence (brother of Richard III), and Isabel Neville (1451–1476); sister of Edward (1475–1499), earl of Warwick and Salisbury; married Richard Pole, on September 22, 1491 (died 1505); children: Henry Pole, baron Montagu (d. 1538); Geoffrey Pole (d. 1558); **___Ursula Pole___* *(d. 1570); Arthur Pole (d. 1570); Reginald Pole (1500–1558), archbishop of Canterbury.*

The daughter of George, duke of Clarence, and ***Isabel Neville** and the niece of Richard III (d. 1485), Margaret Pole married Richard Pole of Buckinghamshire in 1491. In 1499, Margaret's brother Edward, earl of Warwick and Salisbury, whose pedigree made him a supposed threat to the throne, met an untimely end in the Tower of London at the hands of Henry VIII. In atonement, Henry granted Margaret, whose husband had died in 1505, the family lands of the earldom of Salisbury and the title countess of Salisbury in 1513.

Around 1519, three-year-old Princess Mary (***Mary I**), daughter of Henry VIII and

*Catherine of Aragon, was placed in the hands of Margaret, and, in time, the young princess grew to love her like a grandmother. When Henry divorced Catherine, Margaret's sympathies remained with the ex-queen. Following Henry's marriage to ***Anne Boleyn** and the birth of ***Elizabeth (I)**, Henry determined that Princess Mary should be stripped of all rank and retinue and live with her half-sister Elizabeth at Hatfield. Margaret begged to accompany her young charge at her own expense; she even offered to pay the wages of an entire household if only the king would allow 17-year-old Mary to continue to surround herself with the familiar faces she had known throughout her life, but the king would have none of it. Henry also requested that Margaret turn over the young Mary's jewels to the new queen. Margaret refused and was dismissed.

Following the execution of Anne Boleyn in 1536, Margaret was briefly back in favor, but that same year her son Reginald Pole, now a cardinal in Padua, published *Pro Ecclesiasticae Unitatis Defensione*, severely criticizing Henry VIII's conduct in divorcing his first wife Catherine. Though Margaret repudiated the book, it did not help that there had been talk of Mary marrying Reginald, and Henry set out to destroy the entire Pole family. In summer 1538, Margaret, along with her sons Geoffrey and Henry Pole, baron Montague, was arrested for treason and sent to the Tower of London. Henry was executed in December 1538, and his only son disappeared. Because he had testified against his family, Geoffrey received a pardon. After an unsuccessful suicide attempt, he escaped to Rome to join Reginald in 1540, but he could never forgive himself.

Margaret Pole was questioned endlessly and her residence searched; an armorial design was found which blended the coats-of-arms of the Poles and the Tudors, symbolizing a marriage of Reginald and Mary. Because of this, the countess was attainted (found guilty) in June 1539. (In English law, an Act of Attainder brought forfeiture of lands, tenements, and hereditary rights, and often loss of civil rights as well.) In spring 1541, on the pretext that she somehow might have instigated a minor rising in Yorkshire, Margaret Pole was escorted to the block on the Tower Green in anticipation of her beheading. In front of an audience of 100, she asked that they pray for the king and her beloved Mary. The 69-year-old Margaret suffered a particularly bloody fate. A good or wretched death depended on the skill of the executioner, and the regular executioner was absent that day. The axe was wielded by an inept boy. Before Margaret died, it is written, her head and shoulders were hacked nearly to pieces. Margaret Pole, countess of Salisbury, was the last of the Plantagenets.

Margaret Pole

Pole, Ursula (d. 1570)

English baroness. *Name variations: Lady Stafford. Died in 1570; daughter of Richard Pole and* ****Margaret Pole*** *(1473–1541), countess of Salisbury; sister of Reginald Pole, archbishop of Canterbury; married Henry Stafford (d. 1563), Lord Stafford; children: Richard Stafford.*

Polignac, Princess Edmond de (1865–1943).

See Singer, Winnaretta.

Polignac, Yolande Martine Gabrielle de (1749–1793)

French royal. *Name variations: Yolande Martine Gabrielle de Polastron; Duchess or Countess of Poli-*

gnac; Comtesse de Polignac; Duchesse de Polignac. Born Yolande Martine Gabrielle de Polastron in Paris in 1749; died in 1793; married Armand Jule François Polignac, Duc de Polignac, in 1767; children: one son Armand, who took part in the conspiracy against Napoleon.

Yolande Martine Gabrielle de Polignac, comtesse de Polignac, known as an "unpretentious and charming" woman who was always "simply dressed," became ***Marie Antoinette**'s favorite in 1775 and was appointed governess to the king and queen's children. Said to be non-ambitious for herself, the comtesse was pressured by the Polignac family to seek favors from the queen. Through court largesse, she and her husband received huge pensions which aroused popular hatred. During the French Revolution, she was beheaded; her husband fled to the Ukraine. The comtesse de Polignac is featured in a portrait by ***Elisabeth Vigée-Lebrun**.

Polimita, D. (b. 1910).

See Alonso, Dora.

Polk, Sarah Childress (1803–1891)

***First lady of the U.S. (1845–49), admired for her intelligence and resolve, who held a unique position in the White House as her husband's official confidential secretary.** Born Sarah Childress on September 4, 1803, in Murfreesboro, Tennessee; died on August 14, 1891, in Nashville, Tennessee; one of two daughters and two sons of Elizabeth (Whitsitt) Childress and Captain Joel Childress (a planter, merchant, tavernkeeper, land speculator, and militia major); married James Knox Polk (president of the U.S., 1845–49), on January 1, 1824, in Murfreesboro, Tennessee (died 1849).*

Sarah Childress Polk

It came as no surprise when Sarah Childress Polk became the first woman in the White House to work in an official capacity as the president's confidential secretary. For 20 years, she had occupied the seat across the desk from her husband, James K. Polk, and had become his most valuable political asset.

As the third of four children of a wealthy Tennessee plantation owner, Sarah was born in Murfreesboro in 1803 and brought up in a privileged and devoutly Presbyterian home. At age 13, during a period when most young women were not well educated, Sarah was sent to the Moravian Seminary in Salem, North Carolina, considered the best girls' school in the South. She emerged capable and disciplined, with a lively intellect and a good head for politics.

By some accounts, "Uncle" Andrew Jackson directed Sarah's political thinking and promoted her romance with James Polk, who had come to Murfreesboro as a clerk of the state senate. Sarah and James shared a strict Calvinistic code and a passion for the political arena. Love blossomed, and the two became engaged following his election to the legislature in 1823. They married on New Year's Day 1824, and a year later, Polk began a 14-year tenure in Congress, serving as speaker of the house from 1835 until 1839, when he was elected governor of Tennessee. After losing two bids for reelection as governor, in 1844 James defeated Henry Clay for the presidency. It may be that Uncle Andrew also had a hand in getting James Polk elected, introducing him as a dark-horse candidate when the Democrats seemed hopelessly deadlocked between General Lewis Cass and Martin Van Buren.

Sarah was her husband's political helpmate from the early days. Childless, she traveled everywhere with him, assisting with paperwork and acting as advisor and confidante. She also supplied the social graces he lacked as a politician on the rise. Frail and introverted, James Polk was not terribly personable. Sarah, though formidable in her own right, managed to garner admiration and forge friendships along the way. Described as attractive in a "dark-eyed Spanish way," she was charming and witty in conversation, carefully deflecting credit for any political decisions by prefacing her remarks with "Mr. Polk says."

The Polks took the responsibilities of the presidency seriously, believing they were "God-given" and that the two of them "belonged to the nation." James refused to consider a second term, so that decisions he made would not be influenced by a desire to be reelected. The White House reflected the strong moral convictions of its inhabitants. A strict Sabbath observance was instituted, and alcohol, card playing, and dancing were forbidden. Sarah had neither the time nor inclination for entertaining, and with the nation at war with Mexico, austerity seemed appropriate. The first lady also kept a strict watch over her husband's yearly income, and refreshments at twice-weekly receptions were eliminated. The only concession to the comfort of White House visitors during the Polk administration appears to have been the installation of gaslights.

Fourteen-hour work days, with almost no vacation time in four years, took their toll on President Polk. He died in June 1849, shortly after leaving office, at age 54. Sarah lived on for another 42 years at "Polk Place," a home that her husband had provided for their retirement in Tennessee. She took in and raised her great-niece and namesake, **Sarah Polk Jetton**, who, with her husband and child, lived with Sarah until her death.

Polk Place became a monument of sorts. During the Civil War, Sarah was visited by Union and Confederate commanders alike. Although in her later years she ventured out only to attend church, she was visited often by politicians and dignitaries. Sarah Childress Polk died at the age of 88 and was buried beside her husband in a vault she had erected at Polk Place. Later, it was moved to the grounds of the State capitol.

SOURCES:

Healy, Diana Dixon. *America's First Ladies: Private Lives of the Presidential Wives*. NY: Atheneum, 1988.

James, Edward T., ed. *Notable American Women, 1607–1950*. Cambridge, MA: The Belknap Press of Harvard University, 1971, p. 82.

Melick, Arden David. *Wives of the Presidents*. Maplewood, NJ: Hammond, 1977.

COLLECTIONS:

James K. Polk Papers, Library of Congress.

Barbara Morgan,
Melrose, Massachusetts

Pollack, Andrea (b. 1961).

See Caulkins, Tracey for sidebar.

Pollak, Anna (1912–1996)

English mezzo-soprano. *Born on May 1, 1912, in Manchester, England; died on November 28, 1996, in Hythe, Kent, England; studied with Hyslop and, in London, with Cross.*

A leading singer at the Sadler's Wells Opera in London during the 1940s and 1950s, Anna Pollak first worked in provincial repertory troupes, performing in revues and musicals. She made her debut at Sadler's Wells in 1945, as Dorabella in Mozart's *Cosi fan Tutte*. It was the first time she had ever sung an operatic role. Soon, she was the company's leading soprano. Known as a versatile, stylish actress, Pollak appeared as Cherubino, Fatima, Orlovsky, and Siebel. She created the role of Bianca in *Rape of Lucretia* as well as Lady Nelson in Berkeley's *Nelson* and the title role in his *Ruth*.

Pollard, Marjorie (1899–1982)

English hockey player and sports journalist. *Born in 1899; died in 1982.*

During an impressive career that spanned 15 years (1921–36), English (field) hockey star Marjorie Pollard played for the Midlands, Northants, and Peterborough teams, and was recognized as a top goal maker. In 1926, she scored 13 goals against Wales in a 20–0 win; she scored all 8 goals in another shutout against Germany, as well as 5 against Scotland, 7 against Ireland, and 5 against South Africa in other years. For some time, Pollard served as acting president of the All-England Women's Hockey Association. She also played cricket and was a founding member of the England Women's Cricket Association. From 1926 on, Pollard was employed as a sports journalist, writing for such leading newspapers as *The Times*, *The Guardian*, and the *Morning Press*. From 1946 to 1970, she served as editor of the journal *Hockey Field*.

Pollitzer, Anita (1894–1975)

American feminist and suffragist. *Born Anita Lily Pollitzer on October 31, 1894, in Charleston, South Carolina; died in Queens, New York, on July 3, 1975; daughter of Clara Pollitzer (a German teacher) and Gusta Morris Pollitzer (a cotton exporter and civic activist); sister of Mabel and Carrie Pollitzer; studied at Winthrop College, Rock Hill, South Carolina, and Art Students League, New York, 1914; Teachers College, Columbia University, B.S. degree in art and education, 1916; Columbia University, A.M. degree in international law, 1933; married Elie Charlier Edson (a freelance press agent), in 1928.*

Equal-rights advocate Anita Pollitzer was born in 1894 in Charleston, South Carolina. By the time she started school, she could already read, write, and play piano. In 1913, she graduated from Memminger High and Normal School and then went on for a summer of study at South Carolina's Winthrop College. Deciding to pursue a degree in art, she entered Columbia University's Teachers College from which she was to receive a B.S. in art and education (1916). One of her classmates there was ***Georgia O'Keeffe**. Their correspondence, begun in 1915, lasted until 1965, the longest association

O'Keeffe was ever to maintain, and it was Pollitzer who first presented the artist's work to Alfred Stieglitz, initiating the creative partnership between the two.

Not long after Pollitzer's graduation, the woman suffrage movement caught her attention. She met *Alice Paul, with whom she was to be closely associated for decades, and became a member of the organization around which her life was to center, the National Woman's Party (NWP). Paul quickly realized that Pollitzer, with her attractive looks and Southern charm, could be a great asset to the NWP. Thus Pollitzer began traveling to a number of states in the years just prior to ratification of the 19th Amendment, working in various capacities on behalf of women's suffrage, including lobbying, organizing, and speaking. In 1917, she was arrested and detained while picketing in Washington as a Silent Sentinel. It was Pollitzer who had dinner with Tennessee state legislator Henry T. Burn in August 1920 and convinced him to cast the deciding vote the following day as his state became the 36th and last to ratify the amendment.

During the following four decades, Pollitzer fought for the Equal Rights Amendment (ERA), writing letters, speaking, contributing to NWP's *Equal Rights* publication, and appearing before the Senate and House committees. She put her labors into the International Woman Suffrage Alliance and served as vice-chair of Paul's World Woman's Party. Paul relinquished her position as chair of the NWP, choosing Pollitzer as her successor, but Pollitzer was challenged by Paul's rival **Doris Stevens** (1892–1963); it took a lawsuit to prove that Pollitzer was now the legal head of the organization. She was generally acknowledged as rendering what **Constance Ashton Myers** in *Notable American Women* has termed "able, even brilliant, leadership, although some members deplored her subjection 'to Miss Paul's views . . . passions and moods,' and others believed Paul deliberately held Pollitzer back, preventing her from becoming the national leader of women she might have been."

Pollitzer was also an art and English teacher and did volunteer work for an antivivisection society. Following her retirement in the 1950s, she was given a letter of agreement by Georgia O'Keeffe to write an informal biography of the artist. But in 1968, with the publication date nearing, O'Keeffe abruptly pulled her consent. Pollitzer's book on O'Keeffe, *A Woman on Paper,* would not be published until 1988.

During the 1960s, Pollitzer visited sisters **Mabel** and **Carrie Pollitzer**, who had been active in the suffrage campaign on a local level, and continued her involvement with the NWP through correspondence and by phone. After a stroke in 1971, she never fully recovered and was cared for during the following four years in her apartment by nurses. She died in 1975.

SOURCES:

Castro, Jan Garden. *The Art & Life of Georgia O'Keeffe.* NY: Crown, 1985.

Sicherman, Barbara, and Carol Hurd Green, eds. *Notable American Women: The Modern Period.* Cambridge, MA: The Belknap Press of Harvard University, 1980.

Polwhele, Elizabeth

(fl. mid-to-late 17th c.)

Dramatist and author of at least three of the first works by a woman specifically designed for the professional theater in England. *Name variations: Mistress E.P., Mrs. E.P., E. Polewheele. Pronunciation: Pol-wheel. Flourished in the mid-to-late 1600s; nothing is known of her date of birth, parents, possible marriage(s), children or date of death. The extent of her education and her familiarity with the London theater can only be inferred from the manuscripts of her plays.*

Plays: The Faithful Virgins, *a tragedy (c. 1661–63, or 1667–71), exists in manuscript only in the Bodleian Library (MS. Rawl. Poet. 195 ff. 49–78);* Elysium *(before 1671), known only by the title (the play, or possibly religious masque, has been lost);* The Frolicks, or the Lawyer Cheated *(1671), there is no record of its publication during Polwhele's lifetime (first published by Cornell University Press, 1977, with the original manuscript currently in the Rare and Manuscript Collections of the Cornell University Library [MS Bd. Rare P P77]).*

The story of Elizabeth Polwhele and her lost plays is an example of one of those serendipitous rewards that occasionally occur in scholarly research. Until recently, nothing was known of this young woman other than her last name, yet the information now unearthed suggests that she may well have been one of the first women to write for the professional stage in England. As such, she indeed plays an important role in the history of English drama.

Throughout most of the 18th, 19th, and 20th centuries, what was known of Elizabeth Polwhele did not suggest that the efforts of scholars to learn more about her would be well rewarded. There was only a manuscript, in the Bodleian Library, of a rather heavy-handed tragedy, somewhat unappealingly titled *The Faithful Virgins* and concluding with the plea,

"Lord Jesus rescue my soule Amen, E.P." Nineteenth-century scholarship, particularly the volume popularly known as *Halliwell's Dictionary*, associated this play with a female dramatist, "Elizabeth Polwhele," but the authority for that association was unclear. No contemporary references to her, other than her own oblique comment appended to the Bodleian manuscript, had been located, and neither the awkwardness of the play, nor its total lack of identifying documentation, nor the rather pious plea for the rescue of the "soule" would have inspired anyone to search for "E.P."

Then in the early 1970s, the manuscript of a second play by "E. Polewheele," self-described as "an unfortunate young woman . . . haunted with poetic devils," was discovered in the Rare and Manuscript Collections of the Cornell University Library where it had been patiently waiting in an assortment of manuscripts bequeathed to the university in 1919 by Benno Loewy.

This second play, *The Frolicks, or The Lawyer Cheated*, is very different from the earlier tragedy. A light-hearted, frolicsome comedy, much as its title implies, it is skillfully written, full of wit, repartée, and intrigue, with a lively young woman as its chief protagonist who cries out to be played by a modern ***Katharine Hepburn** or ***Claudette Colbert**. The play is a deftly wrought Restoration farce, set in a series of quick scenes, taking place in rapidly shifting London locations and narrating the young heroine's manoeuvres away from the arranged marriages her less-than-honest lawyer father has planned for her. None of the ludicrously dull but wealthy suitors her father proposes will please her; instead, she delights in slipping away from his watchful care to late-night escapades where, dressed in male disguise, she participates in the night life of London. The one man of whom her father most disapproves is, of course, an equally witty rake, who matches the heroine in a contest of verbal jousting and then challenges her to a combat of plotted intrigues, "frolicks," as well. Who "wins" is considerably less important than the game itself, as Elizabeth Polwhele's *The Frolicks*, a kind of 17th-century "Cheers" complete with television's Sam Malone figure, can easily be seen as one of the earliest comedies of manners which, beginning in the 17th century, continue to entertain us in our battles of the sexes.

The 1671 date of *The Frolicks*, clearly inscribed on the title page, is nearly seven years later than the proposed date for *The Faithful Virgins* (which was derived from a notation attached to that play implying that it was performed by the theatrical company known as the Duke's Company and signed by the Master of the Revels for those years, Henry Herbert). What had happened to Elizabeth Polwhele in these intervening seven years to change her from the author of a clumsy, old-fashioned tragedy to the playwright who created a flawlessly professional comedy, new in form for its original audience and probably equally appealing if produced today?

One cannot answer by conjecturing two different authors although, were the plays to appear through the anonymity of print, that might appear to be so. There is, in fact, no doubt that the "E.P." of *The Faithful Virgins* and "E. Polewheele" of *The Frolicks* are the same person. Not only is the distinctive writing in each manuscript clearly from the same hand, but in the letter of dedication attached to the Cornell manuscript, Polwhele explicitly identifies herself as the author of both *The Faithful Virgins* and the third play, *Elysium*.

The answer to this curious disparity between the two plays, as her modern editors suggest, lies less with Elizabeth Polwhele and more with changes on the London stage itself. What was popular in the early 1660s was very different from what received acclaim in 1671. To appreciate the difference, one has to take account of the ways in which dramatic production and 17th-century English political events were deeply intertwined.

The 17th century was a turbulent time for both English drama and the English nation. In the century's early decades, the theater was immensely popular, but as it became increasingly associated with the royalist cause, and as events hastened the country toward civil war, it became increasingly suspect. The private presentation of plays and masques at court permitted women a greater role than did public performances. Not only could the queen and her ladies often commission the scripts, usually with detailed instructions on costuming and staging, they even acted in these performances, while the female parts on the public stage were still being played by boy actors. Puritan misogyny and suspicion of royalist domination of the theater, plus the crown's perception of the unruly nature of the Puritan threat, came together in such events as that in 1633 when the Puritan William Prynne lost his ears to the public hangman as punishment for denouncing "women-actors" as "notorious whores." In 1642, the theaters were closed by a Parliament increasingly hostile to the monarchy, and in 1649, Charles I was beheaded, and England came to be ruled by Oliver Cromwell through its years as a republic.

During those years, it has been noted, women increasingly turned to the written word. Forced by circumstances to provide support for themselves and their families, they occasionally took to the pen for what might be described as creative writing. More frequently, whether royalist or Puritan in their sympathies, they also had to resort to writing before courts of law to document claims to their own land and rights in the war-occasioned absence of their husbands. Thus, in the phrase of **Elaine Hobby**, women's writing became a "virtue of necessity."

With the Restoration of the monarchy in 1660, the theaters were again opened, but much had changed. At least initially, theatrical audiences were treated to revivals—plays from the earlier decades of the century by Shakespeare, Jonson, Beaumont and Fletcher. It would be difficult, however, to isolate one dominant trend, for almost immediately playwrights, like John Dryden, began to produce "heroic" dramas in which artificial declamatory elevation mixed with elaborate spectacle and highly dramatic action. At the same time, under the influence of William Davenant, the English opera arrived on stage, while other playwrights were trying their hands at rhymed tragedies, much like Polwhele's *Faithful Virgins*. Comedies too were being produced, some romantic, some set in exotic lands. Low London comedy mingled with translations of Molière and Corneille. All these plays generally had a very short run, probably due to the small size of the available audience, and were expensive to attend, but many new plays were produced during these early years, a number of them by unknown authors.

I am young, no scholar, and what I write I write by nature, not art.

—E. Polwhele

Given this highly fluid situation, few dramatists confined themselves by specializing in either comedy or tragedy; most appear to have tried whatever worked. Polwhele's shift from one genre to the other, then, was hardly atypical. Moreover, the theater apparently offered an opportunity for considerable profit, tempting to women as well as men, for the receipts for the third night's performance traditionally went to the playwright, and this amount could be considerable. While one- or two-day performances of pre-Restoration favorites kept the audience coming, new shows—financially more of a gamble but, if successful, providing a greater return—were more popular. A six-day run, for example, might be quite profitable, particularly for an unknown playwright.

One final difference in the Restoration theater was particularly important for women—female actresses were, for the first time, performing on the English public stage, a fact which must have made the writing of plays by women somewhat less sensational, if not yet fully acceptable.

The attitude of the female playwright herself is, however, somewhat difficult to discern. We know that Polwhele's *Faithful Virgins* was performed, although exactly when and for how long cannot be precisely determined. By the time she came to write *The Frolicks*, then, with two earlier plays to her credit, she must have been significantly more experienced. She dedicated this play to Prince Rupert, an aristocrat associated with the King's Company through his friendship with Thomas Killigrew, its principal owner, and his mistress, **Margaret Hughes** (d. 1719), one of that company's principal actresses. Rupert was a shrewd choice, and that plus the careful preparation of the manuscript with an obvious eye to production implies an author experienced in both dramatic conventions and the importance of cultivating theatrical patrons. Nevertheless, the dedication itself suggests an innocent and inexperienced timidity: "An unfortunate young woman begs she may not be more luckless in the presumption of her dedication of a thing of this nature to your Highness," she begins. And she continues, "Encouraged much by Mistress Fame I have for some minutes thrown my foolish modesty aside, and with a boldness that does not well become a virgin, presume to offer this comedy at your grace's feet."

How literally are we to take this? And where do we place the emphasis—on the candid (perhaps) desire for Fame, or on the humbly self-deprecating tone of "foolish modesty" and "boldness that does not become a virgin?" Some women had already become exasperated by these ritual disclaimers. Indeed, a generation earlier, **Elizabeth Carey**, author of the closet drama *Mariam* (published 1613), expressed her aversion to a similar formula: "I will not make use of that worn form of saying I printed it against my will, moved by the importunity of friends."

Whatever Polwhele's attitude—and her ambivalence is symptomatic of the position of early modern women writers—she produced a play that might well have been unexpected from a young woman. By shifting to low London comedy, lively, boisterous and bawdy, Polwhele undoubtedly might have shocked and entertained her audience. Some of the elements in her comedy would have been familiar: the heroine in male disguise, the London setting, the casual attitude toward marital mores. Other aspects of the play, particularly its parodying reversal of the disguise motif (when two of the dull suitors are tricked into putting on women's dresses and then arrested as prostitutes) and its sophisticated skepticism, were more innovative. The use of song and dance anticipates, and might even have initiated, the greater use of these elements in the comedy of the mid-1600s. It is certainly worth speculating that whoever the historical Elizabeth Polwhele might have been, the playwright may well have been calling deliberate attention to her youth and sex to lend one more element of dramatic heightening to what she described in her dedicatory letter as "a play so comical."

SOURCES:

Cotton, Nancy. *Women Playwrights in England, c. 1363–1750.* Lewisburg, PA: Bucknell University Press, 1980.

Hobby, Elaine. *Virtue of Necessity: English Women's Writing 1649–88.* Ann Arbor, MI: The University of Michigan Press, 1988.

Milhous, Judith, and Robert D. Hume, eds. *The Frolicks, or The Lawyer Cheated (1671) Elizabeth Polwhele.* Ithaca, NY: Cornell University Press, 1977.

SUGGESTED READING:

Halliwell[-Phillips], James O. *A Dictionary of Old English Plays.* London: John Russell Smith, 1860.

Harbage, Alfred, rev. S. Schoenbaum *Annals of English Drama, 975–1700.* London: Methuen, 1964.

Van Lennep, William, Emmett L. Avery, and Arthur H. Scouten, eds. *The London Stage 1660–1800, Part 1: 1600–1700.* Carbondale, IL: Southern Illinois University Press, 1965.

Ann Hurley,
Assistant Professor of English, Wagner College, Staten Island, New York

Polyxena (c. 371–316 BCE).

See Olympias.

Polyxena-Christina of Hesse (fl. 1726).

See Louisa Christina of Bavaria.

Pomerania, duchess of.

See Elizabeth of Poland (d. 1361).
See Margaret of Brandenburg (c. 1450–1489).

Pomfret, countess of (d. 1761).

See Fermor, Henrietta Louisa.

Pompadour, Jeanne-Antoinette Poisson, Duchesse de (1721–1764)

French mistress of Louis XV who, for almost two decades, exercised great political influence and personified the elegance of the 18th century. *Name variations: Jeanne-Antoinette Poisson; Marquise de Pompadour; Madame Lenormand d'Étiolles or d'Étioles. Pronunciation: JHAN ahn-twa-NET pwa-SO der POHM-pa-duhr. Born on December 30, 1721, in Paris; died at the Palace of Versailles on April 15, 1764, of heart and lung congestion; buried at the church of the Capuchins (no longer extant) on the Place de Vendôme; daughter of François Poisson (1684–1754, a supply agent for the Pâris brothers) and Louise-Madeleine de la Motte Poisson (c. 1699–1745, daughter of the meat supplier for the Hôtel des Invalides); educated at the Ursuline convent school at Poissy; married Charles-Guillaume Lenormand d'Étiolles (or Le Normand, Lenormant, Le Normant, and Étioles), in 1741; mistress of Louis XV (1710–1774), king of France (r. 1715–1774); children: son Charles-Guillaume-Louis (1741–1742); daughter Alexandrine d'Étiolles (1744–1754).*

Father lived in exile because of fraud charges (1726–36); married and became socially prominent (1741–45); became the king's recognized mistress and her mother died (1745); opened an intimate theater at Versailles (1747); Treaty of Aix-la-Chapelle was signed, and Bellevue was begun (1748); had ceased sexual relations with the king and moved to a downstairs apartment (1751); was made duchess, and the Choiseul-Romanet affair threatened her position (1752); her daughter and father died (1754); met with the Austrian ambassador about reversing the alliances (1755); became a lady-of-honor to the queen, the Austrian alliance was signed, and the Seven Years' War began (1756); died after a long decline in her health (1764).

Despite her birth as a commoner, possibly no woman was more prepared to be the mistress of a king than was Jeanne-Antoinette Poisson. When she was nine years old, her mother, who had nicknamed her "Reinette" (Little Queen), took her to a fortuneteller, who pronounced the startlingly beautiful child a *morceau du roi* (king's morsel) and foretold she would be a king's mistress. The girl was deeply impressed. Henceforth, every care was taken to prepare her for marriage, against huge odds, to a wealthy man by cultivating her many talents to the utmost. When the prophecy came true 15 years later, Madame Pompadour gave the fortuneteller, **Madame Lebon**, an annual pension of 600 livres.

The odds were long indeed, for Jeanne-Antoinette's status seemingly doomed any such possibility: no king of France had ever made a commoner his officially recognized mistress (*maîtresse en titre*). When Louis XV chose her in 1745, the scandal was immense. Not only was her status impaired, but the reputations of her parents were well tarnished. To what did she owe her victory? Preparation, physical beauty, and luck.

Her father François Poisson was the youngest of nine children of a prosperous weaver in Provenchères-sur-Fave (Vosges). Clever and ambitious, he became an agent of the Pâris brothers, army contractors rapidly rising to immense wealth and influence as financiers to the crown and nobility. He was a childless widower when, in 1718, he married **Louise-Madeleine de la Motte**, a ravishingly beautiful and witty daughter of an army contractor who supplied meat to the Hôtel des Invalides. Their eldest child, Jeanne-Antoinette, was born in Paris on December 30, 1721, and a son, Abel-François (later Marquis de Marigny), in 1725. Abel's legitimacy has never been questioned, but Jeanne-Antoinette's has long been disputed, even though no hard evidence exists that François was not her father. The circumstances of the marriage have suggested that it was arranged as a respectable cover for an affair between Louise-Madeleine and, possibly, Secretary of War Le Blanc or one of the Pâris brothers, most likely Jean Pâris de Montmartel (1690–1766). The leading candidate, however, is a childless widower, Charles-François-Paul Lenormand de Tournehem (1689–1751), a *fermier-général* (tax concessionaire), director of the Indies Company, and former ambassador, who was known to be Louise's lover by about 1721 and whose intimate involvement in Jeanne-Antoinette's life thereafter is a matter of record. François Poisson knew of his wife's infidelities, which were exaggerated later by Madame de Pompadour's enemies; but he always treated Jeanne-Antoinette as his own until he made out his will, when (contrary to normal practice) he left everything to his son. Obviously, the mystery of her exact parentage, if mystery there is, can never be solved.

Tencin, Claudine Alexandrine Guerin de (1685–1749). *See Salonnières.*

François spent much time away on missions, e.g., a long stay in Marseille during the plague of 1721–22, which won him a commendation for courage. In 1725, however, Paris was struck by famine and a political crisis. François was made a scapegoat for some fraudulent grain purchases by the Pâris brothers, who had been charged with supplying the city. He fled to Germany to escape arrest. In 1727, he was sentenced in absentia (to death, it is said, but the records have disappeared) and remained in exile loyally working for the Pâris brothers until 1736, when they arranged for him to return without being jailed. He was finally cleared in 1739.

During these years, Jeanne-Antoinette's hard-pressed mother was taken in tow by Tournehem. In the late 1720s, Jeanne-Antoinette was sent to the fine Ursuline convent school in Poissy (Seine-et-Oise), where her mother's sister was a nun, and stayed until the early 1730s, when her mother removed her because of a perpetually delicate chest condition. Jeanne-Antoinette received a sound elementary education suffused with ideals and orderly habits. In later life, she gave generously to the school's support.

With her father back, a hefty inheritance from the de la Mottes in her mother's hands, and Tournehem's and the Pâris brothers' connections securing an entrée into society, Jeanne-Antoinette blossomed. Guibaudet taught her dancing and graceful movement, Pierre Jéliotte of the Opéra gave her singing lessons, and Lanoue and the dramatist Prosper Crébillon *père* taught her acting and elocution. She played the harpsichord well, learned to draw, paint, and engrave, and collected plants and birds. The famous salon of **Madame de Tencin**, who befriended her mother despite her reputation, brought her together with some of the Enlightenment's elite—Baron de Montesquieu, Bernard de Fontenelle, the Abbé Prévost, Claude Helvétius, and Pierre de Marivaux. A "suitable" marriage to great wealth and noble (if possible) social rank posed a problem, nevertheless, because of her parents' checkered past.

As usual, Tournehem was there; he turned to the son of his impecunious oldest brother, his nephew Charles-Guillaume Lenormand d'Étiolles (1717–1800). Jeanne-Antoinette knew him, for Tournehem had "raised" them simultaneously, seeing to his education, starting him in the tax-farming business, and even secretly making him his sole legatee. In the marriage contract, Tournehem promised to support their household for life and gave them an advance on Charles' inheritance. She also received substantial money and some property from her own family. On March 9, 1741, they were married in Paris at Saint-Eustache.

Though not handsome, Charles was physically sound, an educated man of taste and attractive character. In hindsight it would be said that he lacked the brilliance needed to hold the interest of his sparkling, talented wife. Yet, until she suddenly left him for the king, the marriage appeared happy. She gave birth to a son, Charles-Guillaume-Louis, on December 26, 1741, but he died a few months later. On August 10, 1744, a daughter Alexandrine arrived, named for Madame de Tencin. Meanwhile, marriage opened society's doors to Jeanne-Antoinette and her mother as never before. When Tournehem moved to a mansion on the fashionable rue de Saint-Honoré, they gained entrance to the most famous salon of the time, ***Madame Geoffrin**'s. The embarrassment Jeanne-An-

Duchesse de Pompadour

toinette still experienced at her mother's side faded when her mother ceased attending because of the cancer that would eventually kill her. During the summers, Jeanne-Antoinette's husband's château at Étiolles near Corbeil (Seine-et-Oise) began to attract Paris acquaintances and even members of the court, for it was near the royal residence of Choisy and an entrance to the Forest of Sénart, a favorite royal hunting ground. Fontenelle, Crébillon *fils*, Montesquieu, the Abbé de Bernis, and the great Voltaire visited Étiolles for days at a time. Still relatively obscure in 1741, by 1744 Jeanne-Antoinette, now known as Madame Lenormand d'Étiolles, was drawing attention.

Word even reached the king. Perhaps she was mentioned by his valet Dominique Lebel, reputedly a former lover of her mother; or by her mother's cousin Sieur Binet, Baron de Marchais, first valet to the dauphin (the king's heir); or by the king's equerry De Briges, a sometime guest at Étiolles. Probably they spoke up only after the king had noticed her in the Forest of Sénart. It was customary for the king to allow neighboring landowners to observe his hunts, and afterward he would send them a piece of venison with his compliments. By coincidence, Choisy had become the king's in 1741. The prophecy perhaps stirring a deep urge to see her handsome king in the flesh, Jeanne-Antoinette on several occasions casually crossed his path in the forest, fetchingly dressed and expertly driving her own dainty carriage. He saw her, asked his entourage who she was, and sent her venison. The chase had begun. It climaxed in the first months of 1745, after the death (December 8, 1744) of Louis' latest mistress, the ⇛ **Duchesse de Châteauroux**, had opened the lists to a bevy of candidates longing to be the "left-handed queen" of France.

Louis XV was an enigma. On her deathbed Pompadour, who had spent more time with him than had any other human being, confessed she found him "undecipherable." He was called "the handsomest man in France" and had a truly kingly presence. He was a charming companion in intimate company, intelligent, informed, and gifted with an excellent memory, was courageous on the battlefield (but a lover of peace), skillful in negotiation, a doting father, and a pious respecter of religion. His failings, alas, were also numerous. He was excruciatingly timid, finding it almost impossible to speak to strangers or endure formal occasions. He avoided confrontations, could not simply praise people or tell them bad news, and distrusted his own judgment (often very good), which made him irresolute, forever postponing hard decisions. He was highly mistrustful and loved secrecy. A creature of habit, he preferred to keep familiar faces around him at almost any cost. Suddenly orphaned at three and king since the age of five, he had been spoiled as a child and hence was extremely self-centered. Although described as lazy, he in fact spent far more time on public business than all but a few intimates knew; but he did not relish being king as had his great-grandfather Louis XIV. He was easily bored and given to melancholia, lapsing into morbid musings on death. To soothe the pain of depressions, he indulged to the fullest the Bourbon passions for good food, hunting, and sex.

Such was the creature on whom Jeanne-Antoinette set her sights. The man was vulnerable. He had begun to stray from Queen ***Marie Leczinska**'s bed around 1732 after the birth of the dauphin. He was 15 when he married her in 1725; she was seven years older, the daughter of Stanislaus Leczinski, an exiled king of Poland. Pious and the soul of courtesy, she was not unintelligent and had some wit. Nevertheless, she was dowdy and rather dull. In 12 years, she gave birth to ten children, of whom six daughters and a son survived to maturity. Worn and prematurely aging, she refused further relations with Louis. By then he had turned to the daughters of the Marquis de Nesle, three of whom became his mistresses: the ⇛ **Comtesse de Mailly**, from 1732 to 1738; the ⇛ **Marquise de Vintimille**, from 1738 to 1741; and the Duchesse de Châteauroux, from 1742 to 1744, an unpopular intriguer who died of peritonitis at 27. Besides two more Nesle sisters, candidates included several court ladies plus aspirants from the judicial and administrative nobility and even—a sign of the times—some bourgeois young ladies from the worlds of finance (like Jeanne-Antoinette) and commerce.

It is impossible to know for certain more than a few features of the courtship which ended with Jeanne-Antoinette's becoming the king's mistress. Not being a member of the court, she needed assistance to make the first contact at Versailles. Who was part of the plot is a matter of conjecture, though it probably included her mother, Tournehem, Madame de Tencin, and the equerry and valets. One or more of the Pâris brothers also seems a strong probability, because they had entrée to the king's most intimate circle. A series of Versailles and Paris balls celebrating the dauphin's marriage in February provided occasions. Traditional accounts place their first meeting at the magnificent masked ball at Versailles on February 25, when the king and several friends came disguised as yew trees and Jeanne-Antoinette as the huntress Diana; they go on to say she first gave herself to the king after the Paris ball of February 28. But almost certainly meetings had begun at least as early as the February 7 ball at Versailles. However that might be, frequent clandestine trysts marked the courtship. Only gradually did the court realize that indeed it was Madame Lenormand d'Étiolles who was the king's new love. It became "official" when she appeared in public at the theater at Versailles on April 1, seated alone in a front box. Still, everybody thought she was no more than a royal passing fancy.

During the courtship, Jeanne-Antoinette's husband Charles-Guillaume Lenormand d'Étiolles was far in the south on a business trip arranged by Tournehem. Upon his return in April, Tournehem broke the news. Shocked, Charles threatened to cause an uproar because of his grief and besmirched honor, but Tournehem led him to see that there was little he could do. In May, Charles consented to a legal separation. Tournehem gave him his *fermier-général* position; though Tournehem kept half the income, it was a lucrative settlement. Charles also agreed to go to Grenoble for 18 months. Jeanne-Antoinette never saw him again, but he remained close friends with her brother, and his family stayed on good terms with her.

Through the spring and summer of 1745, Louis was absent with his army (the War of the Austrian Succession had begun in 1741). The victory at Fontenoy brought him temporary popularity. Jeanne-Antoinette stayed at Étiolles, corresponding with him and being tutored in the peculiar ways of the court by her cousin by mar-

Châteauroux, Marie Anne de Mailly-Nesle, Duchesse de (1717–1744)

***French mistress of Louis XV.** Born in 1717; died on December 8, 1744; fourth daughter of Louis, marquis de Nesle (a descendant of one of Mazarin's nieces) and Madame de Nesle (lady-in-waiting to Queen Marie Leczinska); sister of Pauline, marquise de Vintimille (1712–1741), Louise, comtesse de Mailly (1710–1751), and the Duchesse de Lauraguais; married the marquis de la Tournelle.*

In 1740, upon the death of her husband, the marquis de la Tournelle, Marie Anne de Mailly-Nesle, duchesse de Châteauroux, attracted the attention of Louis XV. With the aid of the duc de Richelieu, first gentleman of the bedchamber, who, spurred on by ***Madame de Tencin,** hoped to rule both the king and the state, she replaced her sisters, ***Louise, comtesse de Mailly** and ***Pauline, marquise de Vintimille**, as titular mistress in 1742 and convinced Louis to eject Madame de Mailly from court. Châteauroux also treated Queen ***Marie Leczinska** with contempt and drove a wedge in the relationship between king and queen from which it never totally recovered.

Directed by Richelieu, the intelligent and ambitious Châteauroux tried to arouse the king to pay more attention to affairs of state and joined him on his army campaigns. But when Louis became dangerously ill at Metz, Châteauroux and Richelieu allowed no one in to see him and pretended that his illness was a passing one. Louis gave orders that she should leave and send for the queen, but it took the bishops of Metz and Soissons to see that Châteauroux and her sister **Madame de Lauraguais** left town for Paris.

The French, who at the time doted on their king, were greatly relieved when he recovered. But the news of the duchesse de Châteauroux's actions had been made public, and the French detested her. "Whenever she appeared in public," writes ***Nancy Mitford,** "she was booed, hissed, pelted with eggs and almost lynched. She retired to her bed with a complete breakdown." Though the king forgave her, she died of pneumonia on December 8, 1744.

SUGGESTED READING:

Goncourt, Ed. and J. de. *La Duchesse de Châteauroux et ses swurs.* Paris, 1879.

Mailly, Louise Julie de Mailly-Nesle, Comtesse de (1710–1751)

***French mistress of Louis XV.** Name variations: Comtesse de Mailly. Born in 1710; died in 1751; daughter of Louis, marquis de Nesle (whose family name was Mailly) and Madame de Nesle (lady-in-waiting to Queen ***Marie Leczinska**); sister of ***Pauline, marquise de Vintimille** (1712–1741), ***Marie Anne de Mailly-Nesle, Duchesse de Châteauroux** (1717–1744), and the **Duchesse de Lauraguais**; married her first cousin.*

Comtesse de Mailly was a "sporting woman" who never asked for favor or power, writes ***Nancy Mitford.** Indeed, during her four-year relationship with Louis XV, she actually loved him. Then he fell in love with her sister.

Vintimille, Pauline Félicité, Marquise de (1712–1741)

***French mistress of Louis XV.** Born in 1712; died in childbirth in 1741; daughter of Louis, marquis de Nesle (whose family name was Mailly) and Madame de Nesle (lady-in-waiting to Queen ***Marie Leczinska**); sister of Louise, comtesse de Mailly (1710–1751), Marie Anne de Mailly-Nesle, Duchesse de Châteauroux (1717–1744), and the **Duchesse de Lauraguais**; children: (with Louis XV) son (the comte de Luc, b. 1741).*

During her three-year liaison with Louis XV, Pauline, marquise de Vintimille, became pregnant and died while giving birth to their son, the Comte de Luc. Her sister, ***Louise, comtesse de Mailly**, adopted the baby, while Louis turned for affection to another of her sisters, ***Marie Anne, duchesse de Châteauroux.**

riage the **Comtesse d'Estrades**, the Abbé de Bernis, and Voltaire. Shortly before Louis returned, he made her "Marquise de Pompadour" by purchasing a lordship in the Limousin near Brive (Corrèze), for she needed a noble title to be presented at court. The ceremony took place on September 14, 1745. The presenter was the **Princesse de Conti** (1693–1775), who had her gambling debts paid and her son promoted in the army in return for doing a service the other court women refused. The new marquise performed the difficult curtsies well, all admitted, as she made the prescribed rounds. Louis appeared embarrassed, and the dauphin stuck his tongue out when Pompadour turned her back. But Queen Marie surprised everyone by being gracious, to which Madame de Pompadour replied with gushing promises of respect and affection—promises she kept in full.

If there must be a mistress, better her than another.

—Queen Marie Leczinska

The most important year of Pompadour's life ended with the first demonstration of her growing political importance, and then a personal sorrow. In December, Philibert Orry, the controller-general (minister of finance) since 1730, was dismissed. He had come into conflict with the Pâris brothers, while Pompadour found him hostile to her ambitious building projects. With Orry gone, she got Tournehem named Intendant of the King's Buildings, a post he ably filled until his death in 1751; her brother succeeded him and (as the Marquis de Marigny) went on to become one of the most renowned holders of that important position. The personal sorrow followed when, on Christmas Eve, her mother died of cancer at age 46.

By now the court was beginning to understand Louis' infatuation. The new Favorite was a treat for the eyes. In 1749, English naval officer Augustus Hervey wrote in his journal: "She was at her toilette, and the handsomest creature I think I ever saw, and looked like a rock of diamonds." In his memoirs, Austrian diplomat Prince Kaunitz wrote:

> Her eyes are blue, set well apart, quite large, her look charming. The contour of her face is oval with a small mouth, pretty forehead, an especially nice nose. She has a good complexion and it would be much more so without the quantity of rouge that she puts on. . . . For the rest she is tall rather than short, thin rather than fat; her carriage is noble, her graces touching. . . . Her form has something distinguished about it, so uncommon that even women find in her what they call the air of a nymph.

Others spoke of "an aura of elegance, taste, opulence, and irresistible seduction," "the lively, triumphant look, the eyes flashing with spirit and intelligence." More often than "beautiful" in the classic sense, the word tended to be "pretty." Her face, framed in light chestnut hair, was extremely expressive; painters despaired of capturing its "true" form, for it changed so freely. She had a "delightful" smile and an "enchanting" laugh. Unfortunately, her health did not match her appearance, for she was frequently ill, mainly from throat and chest ailments, and coughed blood most of her life. She chilled easily and kept a fire going near her year round.

Besides Pompadour's physical charms, the king was attracted most by her high intelligence and freshness. He yearned for pleasing feminine companionship in an intimate, relaxed atmosphere, and she supplied it in the fullest measure. She was good natured, amusing, witty, sincere, frank, usually tactful, and, by comparison with some of the other women at court, unspoiled. Unlike so much of the court, she forbade hurtful gossip and intrigue in her entourage. Her bourgeois mannerisms and speech, which put off the court crowd, were to Louis a breath of fresh air, and he took no offense when she proudly talked (sometimes too much) about her family. To all these assets she added a beautiful singing voice and was a talented amateur actress, able to recite reams of poetry and play passages from memory.

This formidable assemblage of attractions fed a high self-esteem which spilled over into vanity. People soon learned she was susceptible to flattery. She was coolly ambitious: she did not float up to her exalted position but took well-calculated steps. A loyal friend, she would not forget a disloyalty to herself and ruthlessly guarded her position with the king. Although she might not appear to notice the offense, her stroke would fall one day, even years later. Probably her most serious failing, for one involved in high policy and especially in appointments, was a tendency to judge people by how she thought they judged her—that is, to view government too much as a matter of personalities or personal relations. Fortunately, her intelligence helped redeem her faults.

Pompadour remained the Favorite for 19 years, with death alone ending her reign. Her life became entwined with the general history of France; hence only a summary account is possible here. Her reign might be divided into three phases: 1745–c. 1751, from her establishment until sexual relations with Louis ceased; 1752–58, when she survived some threats to her position and probably exerted her most important political influence; and 1759–64, when the Duc de Choiseul dominated the government and her health declined.

Pompadour made her voice heard in foreign affairs from the start when she helped get **Marie Josèphe of Saxony** chosen as the new wife of the dauphin, his first wife ***Maria Theresa of Spain** having died in childbirth. The move helped Pompadour in the struggle (never wholly won) to win favor with the royal family. More significantly, she weighed in on the side of establishing contacts with Austria in order to end the war. If nothing else, the war threatened to keep Louis from her side to be with his armies, thus endangering her position. Ministerial rivalries and Louis' own pacific leanings resulted in the Peace of Aix-la-Chapelle in 1748. France returned its conquests in the interests of peace, and the colonial situation with Britain was restored to the status quo before the war—all of which meant that seven years of bloodshed had settled nothing and only prepared the way for a worse conflict, the Seven Years' War (1756–63). "As stupid as the peace" became a popular epithet, while scorn rained down on Louis and Pompadour. The Parisian writers of scandalous verse, subsidized by members of the court, produced dozens of ditties called "Poissonades," after Pompadour's family name, Poisson ("fish"), and kept it up for the rest of her life. She professed to disdain them, but it is clear they hurt her deeply.

Pompadour had played a minor role, if any, in the forced resignation (1747) of the Comte d'Argenson, the minister or war, but he blamed her and thereafter pilloried her in his diary, a major historical source for the period. The case with the Comte de Maurepas, minister of marine since 1723, is much clearer. He wanted her gone and used his famed wit against her, finally going too far when he wrote a mocking verse alluding to a gynecological problem (leukorrhea) from which she was suffering. She had also become convinced he was going to poison her. Her plea helped persuade the king to dismiss him. His departure (1749) left a large hole in the government, for he was an able man and could have been used to advantage in the mid-century confrontations with the parlements.

Sometime between late 1750 and early 1752, sexual relations between Louis and Pompadour ceased. Although she tried special diets and aphrodisiacs, she found that meeting his demands was becoming impossible and harming her health. Between 1746 and 1749, she suffered at least three miscarriages. The year 1751 was critical for her future. It was a Holy Year, and Louis felt pressure to receive the sacrament, which meant sending her away. Pompadour turned to religion and pleaded with her Jesuit confessor that because they no longer were having adulterous relations, they should be able to receive the sacrament. The Church agreed on condition that she also leave the court. She reluctantly refused, but the king's attitude was crucial. He would not part with her, saying she was necessary to his happiness and his work, that she was the only person who dared tell him the truth. Pompadour—whose residence meanwhile had been transferred from a cozy apartment above the king's chambers reached by a private staircase to a grand apartment on the ground floor (but still connected to the king's)—henceforth remained as his most intimate adviser and dearest friend. In October 1752, he made her a duchess (but only for life), the highest title he could bestow. She tactfully continued to use the title of marquise.

Marie Josèphe of Saxony (1731–1767). *See Elisabeth, Madame (1764–1794) for sidebar.*

Given Louis' character, however, she could never live free of fear of being sent away. A most serious threat came early, in the autumn of 1752, in the Choiseul-Romanet affair. Her cousin, the Comtesse d'Estrades, an intimate member of her entourage and an intriguer, had a niece, Charlotte Romanet, **Comtesse de Choiseul-Beaupré**, whom d'Estrades and her lover, the Comte d'Argenson, introduced to the king in hopes she would become his *maîtresse en titre*. A courtship ensued. But the Comte de Stainville (future Duc de Choiseul) wanted no blot on his family name, so he persuaded Charlotte to break off the courtship and then supplied key information to Pompadour, who used it in confronting Louis. Thus began the deep friendship between Pompadour and Choiseul which helped make him foreign minister in 1758.

Louis, disliking the complications at court, now had a small, private brothel set up in a house in the Deer Park district of the town of Versailles, which was kept supplied with girls of humble background. Contrary to legend, Pompadour did not start or supervise this establishment. She tried to ignore it, having no other choice. The only resident who posed any threat was **Marie-Louise O'Murphy** in 1753–54; but some intriguers put her up to denigrating Pompadour, which alienated Louis. In 1757, his affair with the **Marquise de Coislin**, a cousin of the Mailly sisters, caused Pompadour to despair of her future, but Foreign Minister Bernis ended the matter when he warned the king that replacing Pompadour would hurt France's relations with ally Austria and others. In 1761, Louis fell

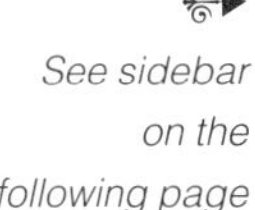

See sidebar on the following page

O'Murphy, Marie-Louise (1737–1814)

Mistress of Louis XV. *Name variations: Marie Louise Murphy; Louise O'Murphy; Mlle O'Morphi; Morphise. Born in Rouen in 1737; died in 1814; daughter of an Irish shoemaker; married Major Beaufranchet d'Ayat, in 1755; married François-Nicolas Le Normant, in 1757; married Louis Philippe Dumont (divorced 1799).*

Marie-Louise O'Murphy, an Irish shoemaker's daughter, was mistress of Louis XV starting in 1753, until she was ousted for scheming to supplant *Madame de Pompadour.

Romains, Mlle de. *Also known as Cavanac, Anne Couppier, Marquise de (1737–1808), or Mlle Romains.*

in love with **Mlle de Romains**, daughter of a Grenoble lawyer, but he soon tired of her after she gave birth to their son. A **Mlle Tiercelin** followed in 1762.

In domestic politics, Pompadour supported Controller-General Jean Baptiste de Machault d'Arnouville's *vingtième,* a 5% general property tax (1749), as a measure of fiscal justice, for even the nobility and clergy had to pay. Protests from the clergy brought a suspension of the tax on them in late 1751, which began to make Machault's position untenable; in 1754, she got him shifted to the ministry of marine. Meanwhile, the king found himself in a complicated struggle between the Parlement of Paris and the Church over the refusal of last rites to persons suspected of adhering to Jansenism, a puritanical protest movement declared heretical in 1713. Louis often (though not always) favored the clergy and nourished a strong prejudice against the parlements (13 regional high courts of justice and administration) because of their power to delay the necessary registration of laws, including taxes. For her part, Pompadour supported the king whenever he asserted his prerogative; she also resented the Parlement of Paris' distaste for her lavish spending. With war clouds gathering and national unity needed, she and Stainville (ambassador to Rome) urged Pope Benedict XIV to reach a conciliatory solution, which he produced in an encyclical (October 1756). To the end of his reign, however, Louis and the parlements clashed repeatedly. Late in the Seven Years' War, Pompadour had become so exasperated with their financial pressure and criticism that she wrote bitterly, "I think they are unworthy citizens and worse enemies than the king of Prussia or the English. If peace is not signed or if it is a bad one, they alone should be held responsible and I would like everyone to know it."

In 1754, Pompadour was thrown into a personal crisis when her beloved daughter Alexandrine died, on June 10, at age ten of appendicitis, and her father ten days later. Alexandrine's death appeared to Pompadour as a divine punishment; she became very devout, practiced her religion assiduously, and sought full reconciliation with the Church. Her Jesuit consultant advised that she return to her husband. Now a rich *fermier-général* and living with a mistress, Charles spurned her plea to her relief, for she was now dreaming of growing old with Louis in piety, as had ***Madame de Maintenon** with Louis XIV. But the Church then stipulated that she must leave the court. This, she decided after some agonizing, she could not do. Her pious behavior did help when Louis fulfilled a longstanding ambition of hers by appointing her (February 7, 1756) a lady-of-honor to the queen. Thereafter, however, her penitential life faded, although she did good works (e.g., founding a hospital at Crécy) and attended mass faithfully. Contrary to many accounts, she appears not to have conceived some special animus against the Jesuits. When she and Choiseul left them to their fate, in 1763 she wrote on the eve of their suppression in France, "I believe they are honest, but the king cannot sacrifice his Parlement to them when [for financial reasons] it is so necessary to him."

From 1755 until Choiseul took charge in December 1758, Pompadour was at the peak of her influence. She played a role in the famous Diplomatic Revolution on the eve of the Seven Years' War when the France-Prussia vs. England-Austria alignment of the War of the Austrian Succession changed to a France-Austria vs. England-Prussia scheme. Austrian foreign minister Kaunitz, while ambassador to France in the early 1750s, had cultivated Pompadour and stoked her vanity by showing her letters from Empress ***Maria Theresa of Austria** (1717–1780) which spoke well of her. Knowing of her pro-Austrian sympathies and the strength of pro-Frederick II the Great (Prussia) opinion in the ministry, he secretly approached her to persuade Louis to agree to a neutrality treaty. Louis decided to listen, and it was Pompadour and her protegé Bernis who, in deep secrecy at her estate at Bellevue on September 3, 1755, received Kaunitz's opening proposals. Out of loyalty to his commitment to Prussia—and already engaged in an undeclared war with England overseas—Louis hesitated. But when Frederick the Great suddenly signed a security agreement with England (Convention of Westminster, January 16, 1756) without consulting France, the French were furious. The result was a defensive alliance with Austria (Treaty of Versailles, May 1, 1756) which Louis and Pompadour both hoped would assure peace, never dreaming that Frederick would attack. His sudden invasion of Saxony (August 29) began the war, and a year later (May 1, 1757) France and Austria signed a second, more substantial, alliance.

France thus found itself in a continental war supporting Austria's effort to retake Silesia (lost in the 1741–48 war) from Frederick the Great, making it impossible to devote full resources to the struggle with England for empire in North America and India. When Pompadour's favorite general, the Prince de Soubise, suffered a disaster at Rossbach (November 5, 1757), public opinion, never strongly pro-Austrian, turned against the alliance and its "maker" Pompadour as responsible for the ensuing string of defeats in Europe and overseas. Research has amply proved, however, that Louis (who also was reviled) made the decision to ally with Austria on his own and that she was only a useful go-between. This is not to say that she was anything less than fully committed to the alliance from beginning to end; she regarded it as "hers," basked in the praise Maria Theresa gave her via Kaunitz (for it conferred the respectability she craved), and used her influence to encourage Louis to persevere against "the Attila of the North," as she described Frederick the Great after Rossbach.

If in the early years of the war Pompadour saw her influence reach its zenith, she also suffered her worst crisis of fear that she would be dismissed. On January 5, 1757, Robert Damiens, a madman, stabbed Louis. The wound proved slight, but for days he did not leave his bed. A religious man, at such times he would be tortured by fears of divine punishment. Everyone recalled his serious illness at Metz in 1744 when he sent his mistress (Châteauroux) away—temporarily—in a fit of pious remorse. Pompadour sickened with dread when Louis sent her not a word. Machault, her protegé and friend until now, told her (probably falsely) that the king had said she must go. Pompadour was packing in despair when her closest friends told her to stick it out: "Who leaves the game loses," warned **Mme de Mirepoix**. Eleven days after the stabbing, Louis suddenly went to Pompadour, who reassured him there was no plot and that the public's horror at the crime proved he was still loved. His self-esteem restored, he emerged smiling.

Two weeks later, the two most important and able men in the ministry, Machault and the Comte d'Argenson, were summarily dismissed (February 1). Louis may have been contemplating a major shakeup for some time. The two ministers hated each other and disliked the Austrian alliance. And Machault was at loggerheads with the Parlement, whereas Louis wanted a settlement so as to ensure his finances. But there is little doubt that Pompadour played a major role in the crisis. Both men wanted her gone. Machault had betrayed her. D'Argenson, an enemy since her arrival and lately surreptitiously feeding a slander campaign against her and even the king, perhaps to intimidate them, had in a private interview contemptuously refused her offer to reconcile. The axe fell. The Comtesse d'Estrades accompanied d'Argenson into exile.

Machault and d'Argenson's fall boded ill. Until Choiseul managed some hold on affairs in 1759, the ministry was directionless, filled with a parade of Pompadour's favorites who, save perhaps for Bernis at foreign affairs, proved mediocre at best. The war effort bled from defeats on land and sea and from growing public contempt for the king and his uncrowned queen. Anonymous letters, some pornographic, came in her mail, and obscene postcards depicting Pompadour and the king circulated. Refusing to bend before the gale, standing daily at the breech to stiffen the resolve of the hesitant, self-doubting king, writing letters of (mostly sound) advice directly to generals and diplomats in the field, she wished she really were the queen despite the strain on her delicate health: "I would have preferred the large niche," she wrote to a friend, "and I am angry at being obliged to be content with the little one; it does not comport at all with my *humeur* [mood]."

Bernis was named foreign minister on June 29, 1757, courtesy of Pompadour, who was encouraged by her increasingly close friend the Comte de Stainville, now ambassador to Vienna but hoping to succeed Bernis some day. Bernis was a competent diplomat, but his nerves began to fail after Rossbach. He continually predicted disaster and pleaded for Pompadour to persuade Louis to get out of the war. She and Stainville, however, were determined to see it through. It took her ten months of quiet work to persuade Louis to drop Bernis. An attempt by Bernis to sidetrack her in decision-making by revising ministerial procedures hastened his fall. On December 14, 1758, Louis dismissed him and brought in Stainville, now Duc de Choiseul. By then, however, the war—certainly the one against England—was probably past winning.

Choiseul—short, ugly, witty, dynamic, exceptionally capable—did not become Pompadour's lover, as gossip said, even though scores of women found him irresistible. He became, next to Louis, her dearest friend. With his strong hand on the tiller, Pompadour, her health sagging under the strain, became steadily less involved, although she still received state papers and retained her power in appointments and rewards. She, Choiseul, and the king, whom Choiseul began to dominate through her, stayed loyally in the war, hoping and working for a break. In gratitude for her steadfastness, Maria Theresa in 1759 had a magnificent, jewel-encrusted little writing desk built for her. Pompadour sold most of her diamonds and much of her silver to support the war effort. Contrary to charges she was only mildly interested in the overseas war, she also gave a million livres to defend Canada, bought shares in 18 warships, and armed several more.

As with all 18th-century wars, the Seven Years' War ground to a halt when the combatants ran out of money. France acquired nothing in Europe and lost Canada and the prospects of empire in India. Despite the humiliation, Choiseul managed to retain France's main economic assets abroad. He and Pompadour regarded the Peace of Paris (February 10, 1763) as no more than a truce. As she said of it just before her death:

> It is neither happy nor good, but it had to be made. We have still kept a fine empire. The King is convinced, moreover, that the King of England will not keep his American possessions. This will be our revenge, and we have taken steps to have, at the right time, the Navy we have lacked.

Twelve years later the prophecy began to come true.

As much as affairs of state came to occupy Pompadour, especially after around 1750, they could never do so at the expense of her providing amusements for Louis lest she lose him. Her life with him was one long campaign to conquer his boredom and depressions. Very shrewdly, she especially encouraged interests he already had in architecture, science, handwork, and cooking. Testimony to the effect that he seemed happier, felt healthier, was more emotionally balanced, and spent more time on business than he had before she became his mistress proves her general success. To cope with his shyness, she quickly set about creating a cocoon in her small, exquisitely appointed upstairs apartment where he could while away hours in an exclusive circle of friends, eating, gambling, and playfully chatting. "What I like above all," he confided to her, "is your little staircase." She was a marvelous conversationalist, cheerful, witty, and informed (by a legion of spies in society and the ministries) of all the latest news and gossip. She introduced Louis and the court to a freer, much less artificial language drawn from her bourgeois roots. One of her most notable efforts in her first years went into a tiny theater (seating 15) where she and a few talented courtiers entertained the king's circle. Louis loved it. On January 16, 1747, it opened with *Tartuffe*. In 1748, it was transferred to a space under the Ambassadors' Stair seating 24, with the whole affair made portable. Money being tight after the War of the Austrian Succession, she was forced to close it on April 18, 1750. By then, however, the Château de Bellevue with its own theater was completed.

Bellevue, one of the most beautiful structures of the age (destroyed, sadly, in 1823), epitomized the most famous, and expensive, distraction Pompadour shared with Louis, viz., building projects. They spent countless hours examining plans and inspecting sites with the architects and the superintendent, Tournehem, succeeded in 1751 by her brother, the Marquis de Marigny. Bellevue, completed in 1750 but sold to the king in 1757 to pay off debts, was magnificently sited overlooking the Seine with a distant view of Paris. She also built the Hôtel des Réservoirs in Versailles to house overflow guests and her collections, and "hermitages" (country-style "cottages" to escape court formalities) on the palace grounds of Versailles, Fontainebleau, and Compiègne. She owned and refurbished châteaux: Montretout (1746–48); Crécy, a gift from Louis (1746–57); La Celle (1748–50); Champs-en-Brie (leased, 1757, but soon returned); Saint-Ouën (leased) and Auvilliers in the late 1750s; and Ménars (near Blois, 1760), where she intended to retire some day. In Paris, she bought the Hôtel d'Evreux (1753), now the Élysée Palace, residence of France's presidents, and assisted in the construction of the Place Louis XV, now the Place de la Concorde. She also oversaw reconstruction at Compiègne, added a wing at Fontainebleau and rooms at Versailles, and began the Petit Trianon. The grand École Militaire in Paris (built 1751–70) was proposed and financed by Joseph Pâris-Duverney, but it was she who ignited Louis' interest in a military school for sons of worthy but needy nobles.

As a patron of the arts, Pompadour has always been ranked high. She acquired a huge collection of works, and the decorative arts during her reign took on a splendor unmatched before or since in Western civilization. She spent lavishly, looked after artists, and paid them well and promptly. On the other hand, it would appear that she had no marked passion for art for its own sake or particular principles about it. She is, for example, identified with both the rococo style (*style Pompadour*, something of a misnomer) and early neoclassicism (*style Louis Seize*), first promoted by her brother in architecture—which underscores the randomness of her patronage. Nor did she discover and promote new talents. She simply bought the best from the very best artists around. The purpose of her buying was not the promotion of new ideas or initiatives but, writes Donald Posner, "to proclaim her position and ornament her person and surroundings." Fortunately for the world, the taste that channeled this tide of money was superb. Artists linked with her name comprise an 18th-century roll of honor. Among them were painters Carle van Loo, Oudry, Quentin de La Tour Greuze, Roslin, Liotard, Tocqué, Vigée, Deshayse le Romain, Carmontelle, Subleyras, Drouais, Nattier, above all Boucher; artists and decorators Verbeckt, Christophe Heut, Duplés-sis *père*, Van Blarenberghe; sculptors Pigalle, J.-J. Caffieri, Coustou *fils*, Falconet; engravers Cochin *fils*, Portail, Charpentier; cabinetmakers Gaudreax, Vanrisamburgh, Dubois; jeweller Guay; silversmith Durand; architects Cailleteau de Lassurance *fils*, Jacques-Ange Gabriel IV; and landscape architect Garnier de l'Isle.

Forever associated with Pompadour is the establishment of the French porcelain works at Sèvres. She encouraged an old idea of Louis' to transfer the works at Vincennes to Sèvres (below Bellevue) and enlarge them, which was done in 1756. Thereafter, she helped with funds, artists, and models, especially for the famous *biscuit* (unglazed) figures by Pajou, Pigalle, Caffieri, Falconet, and Clodion. The purpose of this operation was, again, utilitarian, viz., to promote the prestige of French manufactures and surpass the reputation of Germany's Meissen ware. Sèvres porcelain became world renowned.

She also was a notable patron of literature. Voltaire, for whom she gained membership in the Académie Française and appointment as royal historiographer, said of her, "She thought the way one should"—meaning as an adherent of the Enlightenment. She liked to visit her longtime personal physician, François Quesnay (more famous as the founder of the physiocratic school of economics), and converse with him and his friends Diderot, d'Alembert, Helvétius, Marmontel, Duclos, Buffon, Turgot, and others. Louis, however, while a generous patron of literature, greatly disliked the *philosophes* because of their attacks on the Church. Consequently, Pompadour had to be careful. After the banning of the *Encyclopédie* (in 1752), she had the order modified to allow subscribers to receive their personal copies. The amelioration turned on a famous incident in which she took advantage of an opening at a soirée when someone wondered about how gunpowder really works. Nobody could say. "Now if you had not banned the *Encyclopédie*, Sire," she sweetly chided, "we could have found out in a moment." Louis sent off for his private copy to settle that and other points, and the relaxation soon followed. After the mid-1750s, when she became more religious, she grew cool toward the *philosophes*. She did intercede to help Helvétius in 1759 after *De l'esprit* was banned, and shortly before her death she talked Louis into supporting revision of the Calas case, a judicial lynching of a Huguenot made famous by Voltaire. But the *philosophes*' mockery of Louis and their hero-worship of Frederick the Great during the Seven Years' War enraged her. As she wrote in a letter: "What has become of our nation? Parlement, the Encyclopaedists, *et cetera*, have changed it completely. When one lacks principle to the extent of acknowledging neither God nor master, one soon becomes the scum of the earth and that is what has happened to us." She remained "enlightened," but for her the bloom was off the Enlightenment.

How did she finance an estimated 37 million livres' worth of building, buying, charities, and patronage? (A livre is nominally worth about 20 francs or four dollars in the year 2000, but it is impossible to compare prices and purchasing power over centuries.) It took two lawyers more than a year to inventory her possessions after her death—everything from houses and horses to earrings and paintings—even though she died with only a few coins in her dresser and 1.7 million livres in debts. Surprisingly, Louis' allowances and gifts varied greatly and averaged only about 50,000 livres per year, perhaps to dampen public criticism, while pay for her staffs alone ate up over 42,000 livres annually. The answer can never be fully known. She speculated, made large sums gambling (a court passion), and owned income-producing property. The "secret" of her operations, however, was that much was paid for out of royal accounts. Pâris de Montmartel acted as her banker and settled directly with the king rather than the controller-general, with Louis often finding money outside the state budget. Her position gave her in effect an unlimited line of credit, while "her" people filled the controller-general's office and Tournehem and her brother ran the royal building program. In defense of her spending it might be noted that most of it was on objects of permanent value, not consumables, and gave employment to a host of persons, many of great talent.

As the Seven Years' War expired, fatigue, long suppressed by her will, swept over Pompadour. Remorse over a war she had hoped would bring glory to Louis' reign mingled with chagrin at the wound to her pride: "If I die," she wrote, "it will be of grief." In a remarkable scene early in 1764, during a conversation with her dear friend **Madame de la Ferté-Imbault**, "She expatiated with all the vivacity and gestures of an accomplished actress on how much she was worried by the present deplorable state of the kingdom." She wanted to retire to Ménars, "but the King would be lost without her." Then she broke down. "She described her torments with an eloquence and energy that I had never known her employ. In short, she struck me as quite demented and enraged, and I have never listened to a more effective sermon to illustrate the miseries inseparable from worldly ambition. . . . I left her presence after an hour of this conversation with my imagination convinced that no hope remained to her except in death."

On February 29 at Choisy, Pompadour fainted from an attack of pneumonia. Her heart, long growing weak and congestive, began to swell. A month later, she had recovered enough to return to Versailles (March 31), but on April 7 bronchial pneumonia took over and her state soon was desperate. In agonizing pain, forced to sit in a chair so that she could breathe, she bravely awaited her end. Louis—"in great affliction," the dauphine Marie Josèphe reported—saw her for the last time on the 14th. They agreed to part so she could take the sacrament. She received the last rites that night. As the priest started to leave near 7:30 PM on the 15th, she made a little joke: "One moment more, Monsieur le Curé, we'll go together." Minutes later she died. She was in the fourth month of her 43rd year.

Her funeral on the 17th was a grandiose affair at Notre-Dame de Versailles. A terrible rain storm raged as the long procession moved past the palace on its way to Paris, where she would be interred between her mother and daughter at the Capuchin church (no longer extant) on the Place Vendôme. Louis emerged with his valet on the balcony over the Marble Court and stood in the gale until the cortege disappeared far in the distance. As he returned inside, two large tears rolled down his cheeks. "Well, that is all the honor I can pay her," he murmured.

Nobody who observed them over their 19 years together doubted that Pompadour loved Louis deeply and that, so far as he could ever love anyone but himself, Louis loved her in return. The intensity of her involvement helped bring on her death. A mistress' first duty is to be available and pleasing. Day after day and night after night she had to be nearby, indoors, passing endless hours conferring, writing, and reading. A gnawing fear that he would send her away never left her. This unhealthy existence fatally undermined her delicate constitution.

The degree of her influence on policy has been variously estimated. If anything, 18th- and 19th-century accounts err on the side of overstatement. Even Choiseul, who was exceptionally well placed to observe, wrote in his memoirs: "She gave the king advice and it was rare that it was not judicious. Louis acquired the habit of letting himself be guided by her advice, and she became the arbiter of the destinies of the kingdom. It was a role of which she had scarcely dreamt and which she was obliged to assume in spite of herself." Choiseul by then, however, was bent on portraying Louis in a bad light. In the 20th century, research has constructed a more complex picture of Louis—an extraordinarily secretive man—and ascribed to him a stronger, more independent role in policy decisions. At all events, nobody will ever know more than a fraction of what passed between them during the thousands of hours they were alone together. Indeed, a truly major reason for her hold on him was that she was never known to have betrayed his confidence. Certainly she was highly informed, for ministers routinely submitted plans to her in detail before meeting with the king. Given his mysterious ways and "undecipherability," she became the natural channel to reach him.

On the other hand, her influence on appointments and favors was enormous. Less uniform are estimates of the quality of "her" appointees. She tried hard to select worthy people, and she detested hypocrisy and bootlicking among supplicants. She did no undeserved favors (within the mores of the times) for her family; her father was ennobled in 1747 and received an estate, Marigny, in 1749, but that was all; her brother's ability merited the high appointment he received. Contrary to legend, she did not promote utterly incompetent types; perhaps inevitably, given the law of averages, most of her appointees proved little better than mediocre. Still, all judgments about the matter are risky, for the grotesque complexities of royal administration, rendered worse by long-entrenched practices of sale of offices (*vénalité*), nepotism, and financial unaccountability, continually made even the ablest ministers appear incompetent. As for removing people, she learned in time how resistant Louis was to dismissing anybody he had once appointed.

The Pompadour years marked a brilliant passage in Western culture. She was the epitome of exquisite taste in arguably the most visually opulent of ages, while her easy gracc introduced a gaiety and intimacy to the court which it had never known. She exemplified the best of 18th-century high culture. In the sphere of government, however, her backstage influence, lavish spending, and promotion of the power and social standing of the rich, tax-collecting *fermiers-généraux* drew criticism down on the king. He was popular, if undeservedly, when she arrived in 1745, but—save for a brief surge in his favor after Damiens' crime—he became unpopular and then reviled. The Austrian alliance had some sound reasons in its favor, but the disasters of the Seven Years' War rendered it and its makers odious. Neither Louis nor Pompadour ever understood the need to win public favor or explain anything to the people in their increasingly literate society. Louis instead rigidly maintained the system bequeathed by Louis XIV. In the end, the Pompadour years set the monarchy's prestige on a fatal downward slope which led toward revolution.

SOURCES:

Cheke, Marcus. *The Cardinal de Bernis.* NY: W.W. Norton, 1959.

Dorn, Walter L. *Competition for Empire, 1740–1763.* NY: Harper & Bros., 1940.

Gallet, Danielle. *Madame de Pompadour ou le pouvoir féminin.* Paris: Fayard, 1985.

Gooch, George Peabody. *Louis XV: The Monarchy in Decline.* London: Longmans, Green, 1956.

Gordon, Katherine K. "Madame de Pompadour, Pigalle, and the Iconography of Friendship," in *Art Bulletin.* Vol. 50, no. 3, 1968, pp. 249–262.

Levron, Jacques. *Pompadour.* Trans. by C.E. Engel. NY: David McKay, 1960.

Lough, John. *An Introduction to Eighteenth-Century France.* NY: St. Martin's Press, 1963.

McKay, Derek, and H.M. Scott. *The Rise of the Great Powers, 1648–1815.* NY: Longman, 1983.

***Mitford, Nancy**. *Madame de Pompadour.* NY: Harper & Row, 1968.

Nicolle, Jean. *Madame de Pompadour et la société de son temps.* Paris: Éditions Albatros, 1980.

Posner, Donald. "Mme de Pompadour as a Patron of the Visual Arts," in *Art Bulletin.* Vol. 72, no. 1, 1990, pp. 74–105.

Rogister, John. *Louis XV and the Parlement of Paris, 1737–1755.* Cambridge: Cambridge University Press, 1995.

Swann, Julian. *Politics and the Parlement of Paris under Louis XV, 1754–1774.* Cambridge: Cambridge University Press, 1995.

Van Kley, Dale K. *The Damiens Affair and the Unraveling of the Ancien Régime.* Princeton, NJ: Princeton University Press, 1984.

Williams, H. Noël. *Madame de Pompadour.* NY: Harper & Bros., 1912.

SUGGESTED READING:

Antoine, Michel. *Louis XV.* Paris: Fayard, 1989.

Béné-Petitclerc, Frédérique. *Madame de Pompadour: Histoire d'un mécénat.* Strasbourg: Istria, 1981.

Carré, Henri. *La Marquise de Pompadour.* Paris: Hachette, 1937.

Castries, René de La Croix, Duc de. *La Pompadour.* Paris: Albin Michel, 1983.

Crosland, Margaret. *Madame de Pompadour: Sex, Culture, and Power.* Sutton, 2000.

Goncourt, Edmond and Jules de. *The Confidantes of a King.* 2 vols. Trans. by E. Dowson. NY: D. Appleton, 1909.

———. *Madame de Pompadour.* Paris: Bibliothèque Charpentier, 1894.

Grillandi, Massimo. *Madame de Pompadour.* Milan: Rusconi, 1988.

Maurette, Marcelle. *La Vie privée de Madame de Pompadour.* Paris: Hachette, 1951.

Michel, Ludovic. *Prestigieuse marquise de Pompadour.* Paris: Société continentale d'Éditions modernes illustrés, 1972.

Nolhac, Pierre de. *Louis XV et Madame de Pompadour.* Paris: L. Conard. 1928.

———. *Madame de Pompadour et la politique d'après des documents nouveaux.* Paris: Louis Conard, 1930.

Poór, János. *Madame de Pompadour.* Budapest: Akadémiai Kiadó, 1988.

Simyani, Tibor. *Madame de Pompadour.* Düsseldorf: Claasen Verlag, 1979.

Smythe, David M. *Madame de Pompadour, Mistress of France.* NY: W. Funk, 1953.

Spencer, S.I., ed. *French Women of the Age of the Enlightenment.* Bloomington, IN: Indiana University Press, 1984.

Terrasson, J. *Madame de Pompadour et la création de la Porcelaine de France.* Paris: Bibliothèque des Arts, 1969.

Thierry, Adrien. *La Marquise de Pompadour.* Geneva: La Palatine, 1959.

COLLECTIONS:

There is no central collection of Pompadour's papers. The essential personal source is her correspondence, which unfortunately is scattered across Europe. An archivist in the historical section of the Archives nationales in Paris, Danielle Gallet, offers in her *Madame de Pompadour ou le pouvoir féminin* (1985) a survey of sources of all kinds.

David S. Newhall,
Pottinger Distinguished Professor of History Emeritus,
Centre College,
Danville, Kentucky

Pompeia (c. 87 BCE–?)

Roman noblewoman who was the second wife of Julius Caesar. *Born around 87 BCE; death date unknown; daughter of Quintus Pompeius Rufus and Cornelia; granddaughter of Quintus Pompeius Rufus (consul in 88) and Lucius Cornelius Sulla Felix; second wife of Julius Caesar (100–44 BCE); children: none. Julius Caesar was first married to Cornelia (c. 100–68 BCE); his third wife was* ***Calpurnia** *(c. 70 BCE–?).*

Pompeia was born about 87 BCE, the daughter of Quintus Pompeius Rufus and Cornelia.

Her grandfathers were Quintus Pompeius Rufus (consul in 88) and Lucius Cornelius Sulla, whose long and ruthless career included the capture of Jugurtha (107), a command in the Italian Social War (90–89), a consulship (88), civil war against the Marian faction (87–82), the conquest of Mithradates of Pontus (87–83), and a dictatorship (82–79).

Little is known of Pompeia's youth, but in 67 she married Julius Caesar, a year after the death of his beloved spouse, ***Cornelia** (c. 100–68 BCE), and the year after Caesar returned from Spain where he had served as a provincial *quaestor*. At that time, Caesar (the heir to Gaius Marius' political faction) was engaged in building bridges with selected ex-Sullans (including especially Marcus Licinius Crassus) in an effort to break into the uppermost echelon of Roman politics. Thus, Caesar and Pompeia's marriage was one of political convenience.

Virtually nothing is known about Pompeia as Caesar's wife until late in their marriage, but apparently neither felt much for the other. In fact, both seem to have had roving eyes. In Pompeia's case, by 62 she had attracted the amorous attentions—attentions which Pompeia in no way rejected—of Publius Clodius, a slightly younger-than-Caesar, up-and-coming political scion of an ancient family. Nevertheless, Pompeia and Clodius had scant opportunity to be alone because ***Aurelia** (Caesar's mother) maintained a strict watch over Pompeia. However, this situation changed on December 5, 62 BCE, when at Caesar's home there was to be celebrated the annual religious ritual dedicated to the Bona Dea (Good Goddess).

This festival honored a feminine deity (with fertility associations) whose worship was so cloaked in secrecy that even her name was unknown to most Romans: "Bona Dea" was the title of this deity, not her name. Every December, at a nocturnal ceremony which forbade male attendance, the women of the household of a Roman magistrate with *imperium* (that is, the holder of one of the few offices in the state to which the Roman people had granted by vote the responsibility to enforce the law and lead armies) hosted the celebration in honor of the goddess. In attendance were the Vestal Virgins, and whatever transpired in the appropriate rituals was done on behalf of the welfare of the entire Roman people. Caesar's home was selected for the celebration in honor of the Bona Dea in 62 for two reasons: first, in that year he served as a *praetor* (the most junior office with the power of *imperium*); and second, because in 63 Caesar had been elected by the Roman people to hold the office of *pontifex maximus*, the priesthood which essentially made Caesar the most important religious official of the Republic.

Under cover of this festival, Pompeia, through a maidservant **Abra**, arranged a tryst with Clodius: he arrived at Caesar's house after dusk dressed as a woman and was admitted by Abra. As Abra sought out her mistress, Clodius made the mistake of touring Caesar's abode, where he met another servant (this time, unfortunately, one of Aurelia's) who asked the stranger to join in the religious celebration. Although Clodius attempted to decline, he was drawn into a better-lit room where it became clear that he was no woman. Discovering that a man had intruded where no man was meant to be, Aurelia's maid ran screaming to her mistress, who immediately shut down the festival and inaugurated a search of the house, discovering Clodius in Abra's room. News of the scandal spread rapidly through Rome and caused considerable disquiet, for most Romans grew nervous at the thought that any god or goddess might have been honored with less than complete piety. Making the scandal even more public was the fact that Clodius had many political enemies who wished to use his violation of religious scruple to attack him politically. Not long after the aborted tryst, therefore, Clodius was indicted upon charges of impiety at a state religious festival and was brought to trial.

As a prominent politician-priest, Caesar was in a pickle over what had transpired. The desire of Pompeia to dally with Clodius embarrassed Caesar so much that he divorced her—by written notification no less, for he refused to have a personal confrontation with the woman who had so besmirched his public standing. However, when Clodius was tried, Caesar refused to testify against him, for, although embarrassed, Caesar did not want to admit publicly that he was a would-be cuckold. When questioned by the astonished prosecution as to why he divorced Pompeia while refusing to admit in public that she was anything less than totally faithful to her marriage, Caesar issued the famous dictum, that he had done so not because she had actually done anything wrong but "because Caesar's wife must be above suspicion"—an ironic howler in the city which knew Caesar himself to be quite an expert in extramarital sexual relations. In fact Caesar acted as he did because although he had been embarrassed by Clodius, Caesar felt that Clodius' popularity among the masses might in the future be useful to Caesar's political ambition. Thus, Caesar refused to testify against a potential political ally, but still divorced Pompeia lest any future antic embarrass him anew. What thereafter happened to Pompeia, who no children with Caesar, is unknown.

William S. Greenwalt,
Associate Professor of Classical History, Santa Clara University, Santa Clara, California

Pompeia (fl. 60 BCE)

Roman noblewoman. *Flourished around 60 BCE; born between 80 and 63 BCE; daughter of* ****Mucia*** *and Gnaeus Pompeius Strabo, also known as Gnaeus Pompeius Magnus or Pompey the Great (106–48 BCE, a Roman general and consul).*

Pompeia Plotina (d. 122 CE).

See Plotina.

Pompilj, Vittoria Aganoor (1855–1910)

Italian poet. *Name variations: Vittoria Pompili. Born Vittoria Aganoor in Padua, Italy, in 1855; died in Umbria on April 9, 1910; daughter of Count Edoardo Aganoor and Giuseppina Pacini; sister of* **Elena Aganoor**; *married Guido Pompilj, in 1901; no children.*

Selected works: Leggenda eterna *(Eternal Legend, 1900);* Nuovo liriche *(New Lyrics, 1908).*

The youngest of seven daughters, Vittoria Aganoor Pompilj was born in 1855 into a noble Armenian family living in Italy. Her father Count Edoardo Aganoor had arrived in Italy as a young man, after traveling around Europe and Asia with his family. The count was restless and experienced extreme mood swings. He had come to idealize his former life in India and was most at peace when he told his children long, detailed stories about the country. Even though they feared him, Edoardo's children spent hours listening at his feet, and his stories profoundly influenced Vittoria. Her mother **Giuseppina Pacini Aganoor,** who tended to most of the family and household business, was a more stablizing presence for the children. Recognizing her daughters' interest in writing, she hired the poet Giacomo Zanella to be their tutor. He worked with the Aganoor children from 1863 to 1872, and was the first to call attention to the poetry of Vittoria and her sister Elena.

Attractive but withdrawn, Vittoria had great difficulty revealing herself or her work. Her wealthy aristocratic family moved in conventional circles and her romantic attachments often proved disastrous, because her chosen suitors were of inappropriate social or economic status. Guided by her mother's example, Vittoria forfeited her social and writing life to care for her family, particularly her mother and a sister who were invalids as she grew into middle age. When Vittoria was 43 years old, her mother died. For months thereafter, Vittoria experienced a deep depression, out of which came a renewed determination. She published her first volume of poetry, *Eternal Legend,* in 1900 and dedicated it to her mother. In 1901, after a brief courtship, she married Guido Pompilj of Umbria, a noble and parliamentarian, and the two moved to his homeland. Guido was in many ways similar to Edoardo in temperament. Vittoria tended to their home and properties in Umbria, while he rose politically, first to secretary of finance, and later to secretary of foreign affairs. He considered her a savior of his tormented life.

Vittoria's poetry was critically praised, and in 1908 she published her second collection, *New Lyrical Pieces*. Just as she was beginning to experience success, Vittoria died of cancer. Within hours, Guido took his own life with a gun.

Crista Martin,
Boston, Massachusetts

Pomponia (fl. 25 BCE)

Roman noblewoman. *Flourished around 25 BCE; daughter of Atticus; first wife of Marcus Vipsanius Agrippa, known as Marcus Agrippa (died 12 BCE); children:* ****Vipsania Agrippina*** *(?–20 CE, who married the Roman emperor Tiberius). Marcus Agrippa's second wife was* ****Marcella the Elder***; *his third was* ****Julia*** *(39 BCE–14 CE, daughter of Augustus Caesar).*

Ponomareva-Romashkova, Nina (1929—)

Soviet discus thrower. *Name variations: Nina Ponomaryeva-Romashkova; Nina Romashkova. Born on April 27, 1929.*

Nina Ponomareva-Romashkova of the USSR won the Olympic gold medal in the discus in Helsinki in 1952 with a throw of 51.42. Her teammate **Yelizaveta Bagryantseva** won the silver. In the Melbourne Games in 1956, ***Olga Fikotová**, who had trained under Nina, won the gold medal for Czechoslovakia. Ponomareva-Romaskova, who took home the bronze, was devastated by the defeat. In 1960, age 31, Ponomareva-Romashkova returned to the Olympic field once more, this time in Rome; with a throw of 55.10, she won gold once more. **Tamara Press** won the silver, while ***Lia Manoliu** of Rumania won the bronze.

Pons, Lily (1898–1976)

French soprano. *Born Alice Joséphine Draguigan on April 12, 1898, near Cannes, France; died on February 13, 1976, in Dallas, Texas; daughter of Auguste Pons and Maria (Naso) Pons; studied piano at the Paris Conservatoire before beginning vocal training with Alberti di Gorostiaga; married August Mesritz, on November 16, 1923 (divorced); married André Kostelanetz (an orchestra conductor), on June 2, 1938.*

Debuted in Mulhouse as Lakmé (1928); debuted at the N.Y. Metropolitan (1931), singing there until 1958; awarded Asiatic-Pacific campaign service ribbon, India-Burma Theater; made an honorary consul of France (1934); received gold medal of the City of Paris (1937); given Chevalier, Legion of Honor (France); bestowed Order of the Cross of Lorraine by Charles de Gaulle.

Selected filmography: I Dream Too Much *(1935);* That Girl From Paris *(1936);* Hitting a New High *(1938); and numerous others.*

Lily Pons

During World War II, Lily Pons braved freezing cold and blistering heat to entertain American troops in China, Burma (now Myanmar), India, Russia, Germany, Italy, Africa, and the Persian Gulf. Although many of the thousands of service personnel she entertained were not opera enthusiasts, they always remembered the tiny French singer who braved the elements to raise their spirits in some of the world's most godforsaken places. Pons did not travel with a huge entourage; often she brought only her pilot and an evening gown or two, because she visited some of the most dangerous places on the front. Her willingness to put her own life in jeopardy and endure great hardship made her a hero to many Allied soldiers.

Pons was born Alice Joséphine Draguigan near Cannes, France, in 1898, the daughter of Auguste Pons and **Maria Naso Pons.** When Lily was three, her father made headlines: he attempted to drive a Sizaire-Naudin automobile from Paris to Peking, got lost in the Urals, starved in Tibet, and was towed into Peking. Although her career was launched in her native France, Pons sang entirely in provincial opera houses there, making her debut in Delibes' *Lakmé* at Mulhouse Municipal Opera in Alsace in 1928. She became a star only after she was invited to debut at the New York Metropolitan Opera House, on the recommendation of Zenatello, in the title role of *Lucia di Lammermoor* on January 3, 1931. Her performance was a sensation. Owin Downes wrote: "Her voice has range and freshness. Certain passages were sung with marked tonal beauty and emotional color. In the 'Mad Scene' some of the bravura passages were tossed off with the best of the virtuoso spirit. . . . Miss Pons gave the impression of sincerity, intelligence and the ability to work. She never did a cheap thing and when possible subjected technical display to musical expression." She was also the first singer in a century to hit the high note of F (instead of the customary E-flat preferred by Donizetti), while doing the Mad Scene.

Pons would remain with the Met for 27 seasons. She also became a member of the San Francisco Opera and the Chicago City Opera, and sang in guest appearances throughout the world. She had little loyalty to Europe where she felt her talent had been overlooked. Rather, she had a great affinity with her American audience. She was glamorous, which intrigued the public, and had an inborn sense of publicity. She adopted an ocelot as a pet and was frequently photographed with it. In one highly publicized event, she ate a meal with monkeys at the Bronx

Zoo. Americans were fond of this exotic star, and she was fond of them. In 1938, she married orchestra conductor André Kostelanetz; her matron of honor was *Geraldine Farrar. In 1940, Pons became an American citizen.

Though Pons had a small voice, she recognized this fact and never strained it or made it wiry and intractable. She knew her limitations and stayed within them. Her voice, instead, was warm and appealing, with a fluent top range. She had great success as Gilda in *Rigoletto*, Rosina in *The Barber of Seville*, Amina in *La sonnambula*, Shemakhan in *Le Coq d'Or*, Marie in *La fille du régiment* (*Daughter of the Regiment*), Philine in *Mignon*, and above all in *Lakmé*. Pons was a truly great star, a legend in her lifetime. Many never forgot tiny Lily Pons standing on a balcony of the Paris Opéra before a quarter of a million people, many of them soldiers whom she had entertained, singing the "Marseillaise" when France was liberated in 1945. The "French nightingale" remained a beloved figure until her death in 1976.

SOURCES:

Ewen, David, comp. and ed. *Living Musicians*. NY: H.W. Wilson, 1940.

Rasponi, I. *The Last Prima Donnas*. New York, 1982.

John Haag,
Athens, Georgia

Ponselle, Carmela (1892–1977).

See Ponselle, Rosa for sidebar.

Ponselle, Rosa (1897–1981)

American operatic soprano who was the first fully American-trained singer to appear at the Metropolitan Opera in New York City. *Name variations: Rosa Melba Ponzillo. Born Rosa Melba Ponzillo in Meriden, Connecticut, on January 22, 1897; died in Baltimore, Maryland, on May 25, 1981; younger of two daughters of Beniamino (Benjamin) Ponzillo (a baker and grocery store owner) and Madalana (Conti) Ponzillo; sister of Carmela Ponselle (1892–1977); educated at public schools in Meriden, Connecticut; briefly studied voice with William Thorner; studied opera with Romano Romani; married Carle A. Jackson, in 1936 (divorced 1946 or 1950).*

Rosa Ponselle was the first American-born singer to perform at the Metropolitan Opera in New York City without having first performed in Europe. Throughout her career, critics struggled to find words to describe her phenomenal voice. Allen Hughes of *The New York Times* described it as "a dramatic soprano that seemed to move seamlessly from the low notes of a contralto to a dazzling high C. She had coloratura flexibility, a splendid trill, powerful fortes, delicate pianissimos, and precise intonation." Ponselle was so dominant as a singer that future divas were compared with her for decades; the first time music critic Ernest Newman heard *Maria Callas sing at Covent Garden, he remarked, "She's wonderful, but she is not a Ponselle." On her 75th birthday, Harold C. Schonberg recalled how Ponselle's "big, pure, colorful golden voice would rise effortlessly, hitting the stunned listener in the face, rolling over the body, sliding down the shoulder blades, making one wiggle with sheer physiological pleasure."

She was born Rosa Melba Ponzillo, the daughter of Italian immigrants, on January 22, 1897, in Meriden, Connecticut. Blessed with the gift of a perfect voice, Ponselle had very little formal training. Her first music lessons were on the piano, and while still in her teens she played in motion picture houses for silent films. For three years, she and her older sister ⚘▸ **Carmela Ponselle** performed at the Café Malone in nearby New Haven, where they became favorites of Yale students. In 1915, Carmela, who by then was performing in vaudeville, brought her producer home for spaghetti and persuaded him to listen to Rosa sing. He initially thought her too overweight for show business, but her voice won him over, and four days later the sisters opened at the Star Theater in the Bronx, New York City, as the Ponzillo Sisters. They subsequently obtained a contract with the B.F. Keith Vaudeville Circuit (which billed them as a cultural act), and, after touring for three seasons, arrived at the Palace Theater in Manhattan when Rosa was just 21 and Carmela 26. William Thorner, an influential vocal coach, came to see them

⚘▸ Ponselle, Carmela (1892–1977)

American mezzo-soprano. *Born Carmela Ponzillo on June 7, 1892, in Schenectady; died in 1977; daughter of Beniamino (Benjamin) Ponzillo (a baker and grocery store owner) and Madalana (Conti) Ponzillo; sister of* ****Rosa Ponselle*** *(1897–1981); educated as the Convent School in New Haven, and public schools in Meriden, Connecticut; studied music under private tutors.*

Carmela Ponselle made her debut as Amneris in *Aïda* at the Metropolitan Opera on December 5, 1925. Her principle roles were Amneris, Aldalgisa in *Norma*, and Laura in *La Gioconda*. Ponselle also concertized throughout the United States and was often heard on radio.

there, his interest piqued by the wild praise he had heard, and was captivated both by Rosa's voice and by her beauty.

Rosa and Carmela studied with Thorner, and he soon introduced them to Metropolitan tenor Enrico Caruso. Caruso, in turn, suggested to Giulio Gatti-Casazza, general manager of the Met, that Rosa should sing in the new production about to be cast of Verdi's *La Forza del Destino*. For her audition she studied the aria "Pace, pace mio dio" from *Forza* and the difficult "Casta diva" from *Norma*. Gatti-Casazza said of that audition, "She sang perfectly, with a beauty of voice and style that was truly amazing in a young and inexperienced singer." Not only did he reward her with a contract, he also cast her in a leading role. Ponselle spent the next five months working with Romano Romani, who remained her vocal coach throughout her career, and on November 15, 1918, never having sung an opera before, she made her debut at the Metropolitan Opera as Leonora in *La Forza del Destino* opposite Caruso. This was especially impressive since the role, for a dramatic soprano, is generally sung only by mature singers whose voices have gained strength and size through experience. In a story that may be apocryphal, before the performance Ponselle supposedly cried so violently from nervousness that her throat became inflamed, and for a time it seemed that her debut would have to be postponed. Caruso saved the day by offering her an apparently miraculous throat remedy, and Ponselle's debut was a brilliant success. James Gibbons Huneker wrote of that performance, "She possesses a voice of natural beauty. . . . It is vocal gold, with its luscious lower and middle tones, dark, rich, and ductile; brilliant and flexible in the upper registers."

Rosa Ponselle

In December 1918, during her first season with the Met, Ponselle appeared in a revival of Weber's *Oberon*, performed at the Met for the first time. Later that season, in March 1919, she performed in the world premiere of Breil's *The Legend*. Subsequent seasons brought her accolades and packed houses for, among others, *Il Trovatore*, *Andrea Chenier*, *Ernani*, *La Traviata*, *L'Africaine*, *Cavalleria Rusticana*, *La Gioconda*, *Luisa Miller*, and *Don Giovanni* (as Donna Ana). She also sang the role of Giulia in the Met's first production of Spontini's *La Vestale* in November 1925, a role she repeated for her Italian debut at the Florence May Festival in 1933.

Considered by many to be one of the greatest prima donnas of all time, Ponselle remained at the Met through 19 seasons, giving 465 performances and singing an astonishingly varied repertory of at least 22 different roles. She delighted opera fans by singing both new and obscure operas as well as popular ones. She learned difficult roles quickly, and was a fine actress. What is more, she had sex appeal, an unusual quality for a soprano at that time. Ponselle was hideously nervous before every performance, torturing herself for hours before curtain time. She insisted that the stage be unheated, and although other singers complained that it was both bad for their throats and unpleasant, the Met complied with her wishes.

Although Ponselle had never sung a Puccini opera, in 1924 she was invited to visit the composer, who was dying, at his villa in Viareggio. While there she sang the aria "Vissi d'arte" from his opera *Tosca*. It is reported that while she was singing Puccini sat with his head in his hands, murmuring, "How sad I didn't hear her before!"

In 1927, Ponselle studied the title role of *Norma* for the Met's first production of the opera in 36 years. She had demurred, saying that it should be a ***Lilli Lehmann** part, but conductor

Tullio Serafin persuaded her to try it, and she fell in love with the role. *Norma* was to become her most celebrated interpretation, with some critics commenting that in it she had achieved her highest flights as a singer. Ponselle, however, chose as her favorite the title role of *Carmen*, which she performed on December 27, 1935. Oddly enough, it was the only performance which garnered her lukewarm reviews, with some critics describing her interpretation as "vulgar."

Ponselle's sister Carmela also became an opera singer with the Met. They sang together at a Sunday evening concert in January 1925, but did not appear in an opera together until April 23, 1932, when they performed in a presentation of *La Gioconda* in Cleveland, Ohio, with Rosa in the title role and Carmela as Laura. They repeated that collaboration on the Metropolitan stage on December 21 of that year.

During the summer of 1936, Ponselle asked the Met to produce for her *Adriana Lecouvreur* (concerning the life of the tragic French actress *__Adrienne Lecouvreur__) in the coming season. When her request was refused, she vowed to leave the Metropolitan Opera and never set foot in it again. Her final performance with the Met was as Carmen on February 15, 1937; then, after fulfilling a commitment to sing an aria from Romani's *Fedra* for an operatic concert, she left the company. Twice her friends begged her to come back, once to honor her old friend, the tenor Giovanni Martinelli, in a gala given for him a few years before his death, and again when director Rudolph Bing pleaded with her to attend the closing of the old house and the opening of the new one; both times she refused.

Ponselle moved to Baltimore, Maryland, with her husband Carle Jackson, whom she had married in December 1936, and lived there in a palatial hilltop mansion she had built and named Villa Pace. She stayed in retirement for 13 years, refusing even to make recordings, something she had done consistently for the Victor label during her time with the Met. (In fact, her one regret was that her career had come too early for the long-playing record.) Even so, the hundreds of recordings she had made for Victor left a legacy that continued to draw many young fans. Several of her early recordings were re-recorded as LPs, but it was not until 1954, 17 years after her retirement, that she made one final recording of songs and arias, backed by the Philadelphia Orchestra. Though she was no longer in her prime, this last performance demonstrated the enduring beauty of her voice.

After divorcing her husband, in 1950 Ponselle resumed her career by becoming artistic director of the Baltimore Civic Opera Company. Her association with the Baltimore Opera revitalized the company, reversing it from financial instability to consistently sold-out houses in the 2,600-seat Lyric Theater. She also taught and encouraged many young singers (among them William Warfield, Sherrill Milnes, and James Morris), holding coaching sessions on a terrace of the Villa Pace and then going for a swim in her pool.

In her final years Ponselle suffered several strokes, and these, combined with severe arthritis, confined her to a wheelchair. Before she died, she set up a foundation to turn her house into a museum. She died in 1981 and was buried beside her sister, who had died in 1977, at Druid Ridge Cemetery near Baltimore. A critic wrote in tribute, "Her voice disclosed a tonal beauty such [as] has not been surpassed by another soprano within memory."

SOURCES:

Ewen, David, comp. and ed. *Living Musicians*. NY: H.W. Wilson, 1940.

Hughes, Allen. "Rosa Ponselle, Dramatic Soprano, Dies" in *The New York Times Biographical Service*, 1981, pp. 708–709.

Lamparski, Richard. *Whatever Became of . . . ?* 4th series. NY: Crown, 1973.

McHenry, Robert, ed. *Famous American Women*. NY: Dover, 1980.

Podell, Janet, ed. *The Annual Obituary 1981*. NY: St. Martin's Press, 1982.

SUGGESTED READING:

Phillips-Matz, Mary Jane. *Rosa Ponselle: American Diva*. Northeastern University Press, 1997.

Ponselle, Rosa, and James A. Drake. *Ponselle: A Singer's Life*. New York, 1982.

Thompson, O. *The American Singer*. New York, 1937.

Malinda Mayer,
writer and editor, Falmouth, Massachusetts

Ponsonby, Caroline (1785–1828).

See Lamb, Caroline.

Ponsonby, Henrietta Frances (1761–1821).

See Lamb, Caroline for sidebar on Spencer, Henrietta.

Ponsonby, Sarah (1755–1831).

See Ladies of Llangollen.

Ponten, Clare van der (fl. 14th c.)

Flemish wool merchant. *Flourished in the 14th century in Ghent, Flanders; married.*

In the 14th century, Clare van der Ponten was a wool merchant of Ghent. She and husband spent most of their lives building up a solid business importing and selling wool; Clare's vital contribution to the family business is shown by that fact that her husband had Clare made his legal surrogate. This meant that Clare could transact any business and sign any contract in her husband's name and have it be legally binding; it also made her legally responsible for his debts. While he was away on business, Clare managed their affairs well on her own, helping them become a prosperous mercantile family.

SOURCES:

Anderson, Bonnie S., and Judith P. Zinsser. *A History of Their Own*. Vol. I. NY: Harper & Row, 1988.

Laura York,
Riverside, California

Pontes, Sister Dulce Lopes (1914—)

Brazilian nun. *Name variations: Sister Dulce; Maria Rita Lopes Pontes. Born Maria Rita Lopes Pontes in Salvador de Bahia, Brazil, on May 26, 1914; daughter of Augusto Lopes Pontes (a professor) and Dulce Souza Brito Lopes Pontes; graduated from the Bahia Normal School.*

Sister Dulce Lopes Pontes was born in 1914 and raised in Salvador de Bahia, Brazil, where, even as a youngster, she sought to help the poor children she saw in great numbers on the city's streets. Although the religious life beckoned to her early, she followed her parents' wishes and trained to become a teacher. After graduating form Bahia Normal School, she joined the Sisters of the Immaculate Conception, an order devoted to service to the poor.

In 1952, Pontes was walking in the poor section of Salvador de Bahia when she was confronted by a young boy suffering from advanced tuberculosis; he was imploring all who would listen to not leave him alone to die. In a desperate attempt to find shelter, she asked a passerby to help break into a condemned house nearby. Leaving the boy inside, she then went out to beg for food and clothes for him. She nursed the boy in this manner for days, returning to the convent only at night to sleep. Meanwhile, the illegal residence soon attracted more sick and dying people from the Alagados section of the city where close to 80,000 lived in squalor. Pontes turned no one away, and as the house filled to capacity, she broke into a second condemned house, then a third, cleaning and outfitting them as best she could and feeding her patients from money she solicited each day. Soon she had 60 patients—men, women, and children—in five houses, all of them sick with tuberculosis, cancer, anemia, infection, and malnutrition, and many near death.

When the health department closed her houses, Pontes moved her patients to the shelter under a viaduct leading to the Bahian Church of Senhor do Bonfim, one of the city's tourist attractions. She faced two subsequent evictions, however, after which she set up her migratory hospital in a deserted market building, then in some crude shelters in the alley next to her convent. Finally, after consulting with her mother superior, and with help from the sisters in her order, Pontes was able to transform a large chicken coop on the convent property into a facility. In addition to the sick, she also admitted refugee transients to her hospital, mostly farmers who had lost their crops to drought and had been dispossessed.

Pontes eventually came to the attention of William Brokaw, an American businessman living in Bahia, who, though a Protestant, became the nun's ardent benefactor. Soliciting the American business and diplomatic communities in Brazil, as well several philanthropic organizations in the United States, she raised enough money to build the Albergue Santo Antonio (Shelter of Saint Anthony), which was erected on donated land in back of the convent and opened its door in February 1960. Within a year, the 150-bed facility provided care to over 35,000 patients, and within two years it had become a bona fide hospital with a licensed physician in charge. The doctor, Frank Raifa of Chicago, who left a lucrative practice to donate his services, was joined by several Brazilian doctors who volunteered part time. The hospital became known in the community as a place where no sick person would be turned away.

In 1960, Pontes turned her attention to Salvador de Bahia's 20,000 juvenile delinquents, or "sand captains," as they were called, because of their habit of robbing visitors to the fashionable beaches of Bahia. Obtaining a piece of land facing the convent, Pontes had several wooden sheds built and slowly filled them. Although Sister Dulce could do little for the boys but provide food, clothing, and the rudiments of an education, they blossomed under her care and soon began to help themselves. They collected wastepaper and baled it for sale to the local paper mill, and planted a vegetable garden to grow food. On some donated land, they started to do more extensive farming, receiving instruction from an American agriculturist who donated his time. As they became more independent, they developed a sense of self-esteem and dignity.

Pontes' influence continued to spread into the slums of Alagados. She sponsored two medical centers and organized a food distribution hub which was backed by the U.S. "Food for Peace" program. Also with aid from the States, she set up milk stations throughout the area to provide for some 2,500 children.

In October 1962, the tiny nun from Salvador de Bahia visited the United States, arriving, it was said, "with a big shopping list and unlimited confidence in her North American Friends." Pontes visited the Washington Food for Peace officials, and addressed the Detroit convention of the National Council on Catholic Women. She also visited Los Angeles, California, which had adopted Salvador de Bahia as a sister city under the People-to-People program. Back home following her visit, Pontes returned to her work, rising at 4:30 AM and spending her days making the rounds of her facilities and traveling the city raising money. "The other nuns retire at 9 PM," she once explained about her hours. "I have to have a different schedule because of my duties. I usually go to bed at 12 PM or 1 AM."

SOURCES:

McKown, Robin. *Heroic Nurses*. NY: Putnam, 1966.

SUGGESTED READING:

Haverstock, Nathan A. *Give Us This Day: The Story of Sister Dulce, the Angel of Bahia*. Appleton-Century, 1965.

Barbara Morgan,
Melrose, Massachusetts

Ponthiey, Adelaide (fl. 1248)

French crusader. *Flourished in 1248 in the Middle East and France.*

Very little is known about Adelaide Ponthiey. She was a French woman from a lower noble family who joined the army of King Louis IX (St. Louis) of France when he led the Seventh Crusade to the Middle East. Ponthiey gained considerable fame for her skill with a sword and for her bravery; after the time of the crusade, however, she disappears from the chronicles.

Laura York,
Riverside, California

Ponthon, Louise de (d. 1821)

Countess of Ponthon. *Died in 1821; married Henry Seymour (1729–1805), Groom of the Bedchamber (nephew of the 8th duke of Somerset), on October 5, 1775; children: Henry Seymour, MP, JP (b. 1776). Henry Seymour's first wife was* ***Caroline Cowper****.*

Pontus, queen of.

See Laodice II (fl. 250 BCE).

Pool, Judith Graham (1919–1975)

American physiologist. *Born on June 1, 1919, in Queens, New York; died of a brain tumor on July 13, 1975, in Stanford, California; daughter of Leon Wilfred Graham (a stockbroker) and Nellie (Baron) Graham (a schoolteacher); University of Chicago, B.S., 1939, Ph.D., 1946; married Ithiel de Sola Pool (a political scientist), in 1938 (divorced 1953); married Maurice D. Sokolow (a professor of hematology and medicine), in 1972 (divorced 1975); children: (first marriage) Jonathan Robert (b. 1942) and Jeremy David (b. 1945); Lorna (b. 1964).*

Judith Graham Pool was born in 1919 in Queens, New York, the eldest of three children of Leon Wilfred Graham, a stockbroker from England, and **Nellie Baron Graham**, a schoolteacher. After graduating from Jamaica High School, she attended the University of Chicago, where she was a member of Sigma Xi and was elected to the Phi Beta Kappa honor society. In 1938, during her junior year, she married Ithiel de Sola Pool, a political science student with whom she would have two sons, Jonathan Robert (b. 1942) and Jeremy David (b. 1945). (Her third child, Lorna, would be born in 1964, after her 1953 divorce from her first husband.)

After receiving her bachelor of science degree in 1939, Pool continued her education at the University of Chicago while also working as an assistant in the physiology department between 1940 and 1942. Between 1943 and 1945, she taught physics at Hobart and William Smith Colleges. Muscle physiology was the basis for her doctoral dissertation, and her groundbreaking research demonstrated the electrical potential of the membrane of a single muscle fiber. Pool was under the direction of the well-known physiologist Ralph Waldo Gerard while she was doing her muscle research, and she helped to develop the Ling-Gerard microelectrode, although she was never given credit for her participation. She received her Ph.D. in 1946, and for the following four years worked at a variety of jobs, including teaching, research, and secretarial positions. She moved with her family in 1949 to California, where her husband worked at Stanford University's Hoover Institution on War, Revolution, and Peace. Pool was employed as a research associate at the Stanford Research Institute.

In 1953, Pool received a grant from the Bank of America-Giannini Foundation to study hemophilia, and worked at the Stanford University School of Medicine as a research fellow and as a trainee. By 1954, she had published her first paper and was working independently in the field of coagulation, a situation that was rare for one who had only one year of training. After just three years, Pool was promoted to senior research associate. She lived and worked in Oslo, Norway, on a Fulbright research fellowship in 1958–59, after which she returned to Stanford, where she was made a senior scientist in 1970. She was so well known in her field that by 1972 she was promoted to a full professor, skipping all the lower professorial ranks.

Pool worked on several aspects of blood coagulation, but perhaps her most valuable contribution was the work that she did, along with two colleagues, to isolate blood's antihemophilic factor (AHF), also called Factor VIII. This led to the successful treatment of hemophilia A, because Factor VIII is used in transfusions given to hemophiliacs to control the bleeding disorder caused by this inherited disease. Pool developed a method to precipitate out a cold-insoluble protein, or cryoprecipitate, which contains Factor VIII. The ability to obtain the factor from a single donor or from large quantities of donated blood revolutionized the treatment of hemophilia. With Factor VIII, hemophiliacs could receive the specific clotting factor needed to help control bleeding rather than simply receiving transfusions to make up for the blood they had lost. Her procedure, which was first published in 1964, became the standard for blood banks. (In later years, due to the transmission of diseases such as HIV and hepatitis through blood transfusion, the blood bank industry was forced to screen all donated blood and to specially treat collected Factor VIII to prohibit the transmission of these diseases.) Pool also researched techniques to measure blood coagulation. In particular, she focused on the measurement of a Factor VIII inhibitor that develops in approximately 10 to 20 percent of hemophiliacs who have had numerous transfusions. When a hemophiliac develops the Factor VIII inhibitor, their bleeding typically worsens.

Pool's discovery of the AHF cryoprecipitate made her internationally known. She was invited to lecture at several institutions and became a member of the national scientific advisory committees for the American Red Cross Blood Program and the National Institutes of Health. She also received a number of awards, including the National Hemophilia Foundation's Murray Thelin Award (1968), the ***Elizabeth Blackwell** Award from Hobart and William Smith Colleges (1973), and the Professional Achievement Award from the University of Chicago (1975). Pool also worked to create more opportunities in science for women; she was elected co-president of the Association of Women in Science in 1971, and served as first chair of the Professional Women of Stanford University Medical Center. Pool died from a brain tumor in 1975, when she was only 56 years old. Soon thereafter, the National Hemophilia Foundation changed the name of its awards to the Judith Graham Pool Research Fellowships in her honor.

SOURCES:

Bailey, Martha J. *American Women in Science.* Santa Barbara, CA: ABC-CLIO, 1994.

Sicherman, Barbara, and Carol Hurd Green, eds. *Notable American Women: The Modern Period.* Cambridge, MA: The Belknap Press of Harvard University, 1980.

SUGGESTED READING:

Brinkhous, K.M. "Judith Graham Pool, Ph.D. (1919–1975): An Appreciation," in *Thrombosis and Haemostasis.* April 30, 1976.

Massie, Robert, and Suzanne Massie. *Journey*, 1975.

COLLECTIONS:

Biographical material, news releases, and lists of Pool's publications are located in the archives of Stanford University Medical Center in Stanford, California.

Christine Miner Minderovic,
freelance writer, Ann Arbor, Michigan

Pool, Maria Louise (1841–1898)

American author. *Born on August 20, 1841, in Rockland, Massachusetts; died on May 21, 1898, in Rockland, Massachusetts; attended public schools; never married; no children.*

Selected works: A Vacation in a Buggy *(1887);* Tenting at Stony Beach *(1888);* Dally *(1891);* Roweny in Boston *(1892);* Mrs. Keats Bradford *(1892);* Katharine North *(1893);* The Two Salomes *(1893);* Out of Step *(1894);* Against Human Nature *(1895);* Mrs. Gerald *(1896);* In Buncombe County *(1896);* In a Dike Shanty *(1896);* In the First Person *(1898);* Boss and Other Dogs *(1898);* A Golden Sorrow *(1898);* A Widower & Some Spinsters *(1899);* The Melon Farm *(1900).*

Born in 1841 and raised in the small New England town of Rockland, Massachusetts, Maria Louise Pool attended public school and as a teenager began contributing stories to several popular magazines, including *Galaxy.* In 1870, after working as a schoolteacher, Pool moved to Brooklyn, New York, where she became a regular contributor to the *New York Tribune* and the *Evening Post,* submitting humorous home-spun essays about her native New England and her travels in Florida and the Carolinas. Her first novel, *A Vacation in a Buggy* (1887), was well received, as were those that followed at a rate of about one a year. While her plots were often strained, Pool's warmly drawn characters and humorous take on life attracted a wide readership. Pool, who never married, died at age 56 at her Massachusetts home, in May 1898. Her last two novels were published posthumously.

SOURCES:

Edgerly, Lois Stiles, ed. *Give Her This Day*. Gardiner, ME: Tilbury House, 1990.

McHenry, Robert, ed. *Famous American Women*. NY: Dover, 1983.

Popa of Bayeux (fl. 880).

See Poppa of Normandy.

Pope, Jane (1742–1818).

See Clive, Kitty for sidebar.

Popova, Liubov (1889–1924)

Talented Russian artist of the first decades of the 20th century who absorbed the currents of Impressionism, Cubism, Futurism, Suprematism, and Constructivism, and turned her energies to practical forms of art to further the goals of the Bolshevik Revolution. *Name variations: Lyubov. Pronunciation: Lyoo-BOFF Pa-POE-va. Born on April 24, 1889, in the village of Ivanovskoe, near Moscow; died of scarlet fever in Moscow on May 25, 1924; daughter of Sergei Maksimovich Popov (a Moscow merchant) and Liubov Vasilievna Zubova Popova; attended secondary schools in Yalta and Moscow, 1902–06; studied art formally under private teachers, 1907–11; married Boris Nikolaevich von Eding (a Russian art historian); children: one son.*

Moved to Moscow (1906); first visited Italy (1910); toured ancient Russian cities (1911); set up studio in Moscow (1912); visited Paris and rendered first purely Cubist painting (1913); visited Paris once more, outbreak of World War I, exhibited painting in Moscow (1914); began association with Malevich (1915); exhibited her first non-objective paintings (1916); death of her husband, contracted typhus, joined Council of Masters (1919); taught at Higher State Artistic and Technical Studio (1920); shifted interests to utilitarian art (stage design, textiles, 1921); posthumous exhibit of her work in Moscow (1924–25).

Selected works: Still Life: Milk Pitcher; Plein Air *(Costakis Collection, Athens, 1908);* Italian Still Life *(Tretiakov Gallery, Moscow, 1914);* Birsk *(Guggenheim Museum, New York, 1916);* Painterly Architectonics *(Tretiatkov Gallery, Moscow, 1916–17); Work uniform design for Actor No. 5 (Private Collection Moscow, 1921); set design for* The Magnanimous Cuckold *(Tretiakov Gallery, Moscow, 1922).*

Liubov Popova played a major role within the lively Russian artistic world of the early 20th century. It was an artistic scene in which competing groups sometimes operated under their own dynamics and sometimes responded to intense political experiences. She joined those who made the passage to Cubism and abstract art, and she entered the group of artists who sought to serve the ideals of the Bolshevik Revolution. Nonetheless, in the view of leading critics, her work retained a notable originality. In a 1962 pioneering study of Russian avant-garde art, **Camilla Gray** claimed: "After Tatlin and Malevich, Popova was the most outstanding painter of the post-1914 abstract school in Russia." Art historian **Magdalena Dambrowski** cited "the high quality of her achievement," calling her "a versatile, innovative artist who drew on diverse influences . . . and made them the basis of her own distinctive means of expression." Popova "was tall," wrote her friend and fellow artist ***Vera Mukhina**; "she had a good figure, marvelous eyes and luxuriant hair. Despite all her femininity, she had an incredibly sharp eye for life and art." Another of her colleagues, Alexander Rodchenko, the son of a laundress, allegedly found Popova intimidating and "snobbish." But Soviet-era scholars Dmitri Sarabianov and **Natalia Adaskina** painted a more convincing picture. They thought she was "by nature straightforward, courageous, and outspoken." They noted how she possessed a magnetic personality that always brought a crowd of friends and admirers to her side. In any case, Popova speaks to us eloquently and decisively through her art.

In the first decades of the 20th century, members of Russia's artistic avant-garde went through rapid and dramatic transitions. Artists such as Kazimir Malevich, Vladimir Tatlin, and Alexander Rodchenko moved in colorful stages from art that depicted real objects to art that consisted of abstract forms. And there were factors that cut across the talents and wishes of each individual. For example, the artistic community was divided and racked by quarrels between those who rejected foreign influences and those who sought to learn from the dramatic developments in French art.

Women were significant within this art world. Both in their numbers and in the prominence they achieved, they far outstripped their counterparts in Western and Central Europe. Fully half of the Russian artists who pioneered the techniques of abstract art at the start of the 20th century were women. M.N. Yablonskaya has referred to Popova and her fellow artists such as ***Natalia Goncharova**, ***Olga Rozanova**, and *Alexandra Exter as "the Amazons of the Avant-Garde." Some writers believe that the integration of women into the radical political circles of the 19th century paved the way for their acceptance as equals in the art world.

Liubov Popova had the advantages of a wealthy family who supported her artistic endeavors. She was born in the village of Ivanovskoe close to Moscow on April 24, 1889. Her father was a prosperous merchant and factory owner, deeply interested in music and the theater. Her mother came from a similar background. Popova was educated by private tutors, one of whom was a professional artist. She produced watercolors by the time she was 15, including one that she displayed in her studio in her adult years.

No artistic success has given me such satisfaction as the sight of a peasant or a worker buying a length of material designed by me.

—Liubov Popova

In 1906, the family settled in Moscow. There she finished secondary school and studied literature with a private instructor. In 1907, at age 18, she committed herself to a career as an artist, studying with two prominent artists and art teachers, Stanislov Zhukovsky and Konstantin Yuon, who taught her the techniques of Impressionism, a style that had recently arrived in Russia from Paris. It was with this technique, reflecting the French Impressionists and Paul Cézanne, that she produced her first works, such as her *Female Model* of 1912. Thus, at an early stage in her career she became one of those Russian artists who drew inspiration from Western Europe rather than relying solely on Russia's own cultural impulses.

Meanwhile, her artistic horizons widened in a variety of ways. The newer influences of the art world of Western Europe, such as Cubist paintings by Georges Braque and Pablo Picasso, were available for her consideration at the start of 1912 and possibly influenced her even at this early date. Second, she had already begun a series of visits abroad, starting with a trip to Italy in 1910. In addition, she explored the legacy of ancient Russia: her travels in search of artistic inspiration took her to historic cities like Pskov, Yaroslavl, and Suzdal.

Most ambitious European artists of the time were drawn to Paris, and Popova's admiration for the work of painters like Cézanne made her determined to visit the capital of the Continent's art world. Along with fellow young artists *Nadezhda Udaltsova and Vera Pestel, Popova settled in Paris for an extended stay beginning in the fall of 1912. There she found a colony of up-and-coming Russian artists such as Tatlin and the sculptors Boris Ternovets and Vera Mukhina.

Although Popova had encountered Cubism in Russia, she now studied with noted figures in the Cubist movement such as Jean Metzinger and Henri Le Fauconnier at La Palette, a renowned studio. In later years, she pointed to 1913 as the true beginning of her artistic achievements. The change in her painting was striking: she now absorbed and adopted the Cubist techniques which were dominating the Parisian art scene. She first produced cityscapes, then moved on to the human figure. Her nudes, for example, took on the appearance of a connected set of cones and cylinders. She may also at this time have become acquainted with Futurism. Note critics Sarabianov and Adaskina: "Like many other Russian painters of the early twentieth century, in half a decade Popova completed a journey that should have taken several generations."

A second visit to Western Europe in late 1914 and early 1915 brought her back to both France and Italy. By this time, the Futurist movement of the Italian art world had definitely begun to influence her. Her works, notably *Italian Still Life* in 1914, reflected such Futurist techniques as brilliant color and a repetition of forms designed to produce a dynamic sense of movement. Her confidence as a painter allowed her to shift with apparent freedom among various styles. Some art historians describe her at this juncture as a practitioner of "Cubo-Futurism," a movement centered in the Russian art world that brought together the shapes of Cubism with the aforementioned characteristics of Futurism.

World War I deprived most of the Russian population of contact with the outside world. Within the now closed environment of Russian avant-guard artists, Popova took on greater influence. She held a weekly salon at her home where artists and critics presented papers, and she exhibited her work widely. Incorporating devices such as collage allowed her to move her paintings away from the flat surface of the easel. Like other Russian artists, she was interested in heightening the texture of a painting: beyond her use of collage she added sand or sometimes marble dust to raise a picture's surface.

Between 1916 and 1918, Popova turned increasingly toward non-objective painting. By this time, the young artist was working under the influence of Malevich, whose Suprematist movement was at the cutting edge of Russian abstract art, and she exhibited her paintings alongside his. Malevich's style featured squares and rectangles set against a background painted white. At the close of 1916 and the start of 1917, she was a member of "Supremus," Malevich's society of painters, and she designed a logo for a journal the group hoped to publish. Commenting on the young artist's works in 1916 such as *Grocery Store* and *Box Factory,* Dambrowski noted that "figuration becomes a vestigial element, and pictorial structure becomes dominant." Popova showed her new artistic direction more emphatically in a group of works produced in these years under the collective title of *Painterly Architectonics*.

Nonetheless, Popova maintained an original approach that departed from the path set down by Malevich. For example, her abstract art contained elements such as colored planes drawn from the Islamic architecture which she had examined in a visit to Russian Central Asia in 1916. Moreover, she continued to draw from the artistic legacy of Cubism, employing some forms, albeit distorted ones, that resembled real-life objects. She also reflected the influence of another leading Russian artist, Vladimir Tatlin. Tatlin in these years was experimenting with art that employed real objects in space, the initial stage in the movement known as "Constructivism," which he founded and to which Popova made her way after 1917.

Russia itself was in the midst of great changes. The poor, rural country, under the rule of the absolute monarch Tsar Nicholas II, had been buffeted by government-sponsored industrialization, and by disastrous wars against Japan (1904–05) and Imperial Germany (1914–18). Russia's peasants and her newly urbanized factory workers rose in revolt. The twin Russian revolutions of 1917 soon made themselves felt in the artistic world Popova inhabited. The March Revolution of 1917 in the nation's capital took place in the midst of the defeats of World War I. Women demonstrators joined by factory workers and then by mutinous soldiers forced the tsar to abdicate and helped install a Western-style Provisional Government committed to continuing the war and to deferring major reforms until the conflict had ended. It lasted six months until it was overthrown by V.I. Lenin. Under the impact of Lenin's Bolshevik Revolution of November 1917, whose leaders claimed to put the factory workers in power for the first time, leading Russian artists sought to create works comprehensible and useful for the masses.

Liubov Popova

As early as 1918, Popova joined a group of artists known as Svomas (Free State Studios), who were sympathetic to the Bolshevik Revolution. In late 1919, she joined the Council of Masters, a group of artists which grew in May 1920 into the Institute of Artistic Culture (Inkhuk). From the new government the Institute received the task of developing a novel approach to art consistent with the goals of the Bolshevik Revolution. It was to find innovative ways to teach art to a mass audience. Thus, it sought both new artistic techniques and materials that would be suitable for post-revolutionary Russia.

One guiding force for art in this world was an extreme version of Constructivism, which now called for a complete move away from painting on an easel. Only three-dimensional objects using real materials and presenting an easily recognizable shape were acceptable art. This radical Constructivism pointed toward art that derived its images from industrial society, an art that would be useful and comprehensible to the masses. Though Popova participated in the de-

Fragment of Traveling Woman, *painting by Liubov Popova.*

velopment of Constructivist ideas, she was slow to reflect the implications of those ideas in her own work. For example, she continued to paint in an abstract vein, employing what she called "painterly values." Far from developing art forms accessible to the factory workers, she experimented with abstract techniques that stressed linear compositions, works destined to appeal to her fellow artists.

The young woman's private life, about which little has been recorded, took a clear turn in this period. She married a historian of art, Boris von Eding, in March 1918 and gave birth to a son at the close of the year. In the summer of 1919, von Eding died in one of the typhus epidemics that were common in the chaotic circumstances of the Russian Civil War. Popova herself became infected with both typhus and typhoid, but she survived to continue her painting in Moscow.

In 1921, her work turned in a final, dramatic direction. The influence of the Revolution became her guideline. In November of that year, the leading artists in Inkhuk, including Popova, formally abandoned easel painting. The extreme form of Constructivism now flourished, and the slogan "Art into Life" set the tone. Art was something that had to serve society. It had to be accessible to the masses and tied to the industrial process. As **Anne Sutherland Harris** and **Linda Nochlin** noted, this was "a revolutionary challenge to the whole mystificatory, reactionary ideology of traditional 'high art.'" Along with like-minded colleagues, Popova turned her talents to such practical forms of art as designing clothing and stage sets.

Both the Children's Theater and the Comedy Theater in Moscow used her stage designs. Her most notable success came in collaboration with the director Vsevolod Meyerhold. In designing the stage set and costumes for Meyerhold's production of *The Magnanimous Cuckold* in April 1922, Popova combined the techniques of her work in abstract art with real objects like moving doors and wheels to produce a striking result. Her costumes were combinations of basic geometric shapes. Her stage settings used dramatic combinations of horizontal and vertical planes. Meanwhile, she taught her techniques to a new generation of Soviet artists at the State Higher Theatrical Studios.

This flourishing career came to a tragic conclusion when Popova was only 35. Her young son died of scarlet fever, following which she became infected with the disease. She died in Moscow on May 25, 1924. Shortly after her death, Popova received a splendid tribute in the form of a posthumous exhibit.

Ironically, had she lived, Popova likely would have faced increased pressure and criticism from the government. During the years after 1929, when Joseph Stalin had consolidated his dictatorship, imaginative artists of her caliber found themselves in perilous conditions. The regime demanded cartoon-like images of happy workers and dedicated peasants to serve its propaganda purposes. By 1932, Stalin's regime outlawed all independent artists' associations. The doctrine of "Socialist Realism" dominated both the visual arts and literature. Malevich was only one of Popova's contemporaries who was broken and humiliated by the demands of the new era. He returned to a representational genre most Russian artists had abandoned in the years prior to the Revolution. Popova would surely have been pushed in the same direction.

After decades in which Popova's talents went unrecognized, scholars in her own country and the West in the 1980s and 1990s began to appreciate her achievements. A number of her paintings appeared in the 1981 exhibit entitled "Art of the Avant-Garde in Russia; Selections from the George Costakis Collection" at the Solomon R. Guggenheim Museum in New York. This important showing introduced a range of scarcely known Russian artists of the early 20th century to a Western audience. "It became apparent that the paintings by Liubov Popova stood out on the basis of their quality and originality," noted Dambrowski. Eight years later, the Tretiakov Gallery in Moscow organized an exhibit on the 100th anniversary of her birth, the first Soviet public showing of her work since the one following her death. A further exhibit of Popova's work was presented in 1991 at New York's Museum of Modern Art. In 2000–01, she was one of the featured artists (along with Goncharova, Rozanova, Exter, Udaltsova, and ***Varvara Stepanova**) in the exhibit "Amazons of the Avant-Garde" at New York City's Guggenheim Museum.

Shortly after Popova's death, an open letter from a group of her friends offered one assessment of her importance: "Her work, like her worldview, was linked in the closest possible fashion with the construction of a revolutionary culture." A more clear-sighted evaluation of her entire body of work came from Sarabianov and Adaskina in 1989. They noted how the crucial elements in her career "were not the dogmas of ideological directives but vital creativity itself." Her work contained nuances, variety, and complexity. She belonged to "that glorious tribe of turn-of-the-century Russian artists . . . who passionately bared their art to the upheavals of the era."

SOURCES:

Dambrowski, Magdalena. *Liubov Popova.* NY: Museum of Modern Art, 1991.

Gray, Camilla. *The Great Experiment: Russian Art, 1863–1892.* NY: Harry N. Abrams, 1962.

Harris, Anne Sutherland, and Nochlin, Linda. *Women Artists: 1550–1950.* NY: Alfred A. Knopf, 1976.

Rudenstine, Angelica Zander. *Russian Avant-Garde Art: The George Costakis Collection.* NY: Harry N. Abrams, 1981.

Sarabianov, Dmitri V., and Natalia L. Adaskina. *Popova.* Translated from the Russian by Marian Schwartz. NY: Harry N. Abrams, 1989.

Yablonskaya, M.N. *Women Artists of Russia's New Age.* Edited by Anthony Parton. London: Thames & Hudson, 1990.

SUGGESTED READING:

Chadwick, Whitney. *Women, Art, and Society.* London: Thames & Hudson, 1990.

Russian Constructivism, 1914–1932: Art into Life. NY: Rizzoli International, 1990.

Slatkin, Wendy. *Women Artists in History: From Antiquity to the 20th Century.* Englewood Cliffs, NJ: Prentice-Hall, 1985.

Neil M. Heyman,
Professor of History, San Diego State University, San Diego, California

Popovici, Elise (1921—)

Rumanian composer, concert pianist, conductor, and lecturer. *Born in Suceava, Rumania, on May 11, 1921; studied piano, theory, harmony, counterpoint, and composition with August Karnet in Suceava, 1928–40; studied piano with Elisa Ciolan and orchestral and choral conducting with Antonin Ciolan at Iasi Conservatory; also studied with Constantin Georgescu and George Pascu until her graduation from Iasi in 1947.*

Elise Popovici was born in Suceava, Rumania, in 1921, studied at the Iasi Conservatory, and began her career on the concert stage in 1944. She became a research worker at the Folklore Institute in Bucharest in 1949 before returning to Iasi, where she lectured in harmony, counterpoint, and piano at the George Enescu Conservatory. She was also music mistress and pianist for the Rumanian State Opera, and conducted. Popovici wrote two symphonies, numerous vocal, piano, and chamber works as well as pieces for marionette theater. Her compositions were greatly influenced by the traditions of Rumanian folk music.

John Haag,
Athens, Georgia

Popp, Adelheid (1869–1939)

Austrian Social Democratic trade unionist leader who championed social reform on behalf of the working class. *Name variations: Adelheid Dvorak; Adelheid Dworak. Born Adelheid Dworschak in Vienna-Inzersdorf on February 2, 1869; died in Vienna on March 7, 1939; daughter of Adalbert Dworschak and Anna (Kubeschka) Dworschak; had 14 brothers and sisters; married Julius Popp; children: sons, Felix and Julius ("Jultschi").*

Adelheid Popp was born Adelheid Dworschak in a suburb of Vienna in 1869 into circumstances of poverty and ignorance that were typical of the European working class in the days of unregulated industrial capitalism. Her Czech-speaking parents fought a generally losing struggle to provide the bare necessities of food, clothing, and shelter for their 15 children, of whom Popp was the youngest. In her autobiography, she writes:

> What I recollect of my childhood is so gloomy and hard, and so firmly rooted in my consciousness, that it will never leave me. I knew nothing of what delights other children and causes them to shout for joy—dolls, playthings, fairy stories, sweetmeats, and Christmas-trees. I only knew the great room in which we worked, slept, ate, and quarrelled. I remember no tender words, no kisses, but only the anguish which I endured as I crept into a corner or under the bed when a domestic scene took place, and my father brought home too little money and my mother reproached him. My father had a hasty temper; when roused he would beat my mother, who often had to flee half-clad to take shelter with some neighbor. Then we were some days alone with the scolding father, whom we dared not approach. We did not get much to eat then; pitying neighbors would help us till our mother returned.

Popp's alcoholic father soon died, throwing the large family into even greater poverty. To find work, they moved into one of Vienna's bleak lower-class districts, renting a tiny apartment. Although a compulsory education law was on the books, Popp would be able to attend classes for only three years. Already working part-time at age six to earn a few kreuzer to help support herself and her family, by age ten she was working long hours for low wages; by her own account, her childhood was over. She worked as a seamstress and crocheting handkerchiefs, the drudgery of which went on for 12-hour days, 6-day weeks, with no vacation or brief holiday. Her pay, based on piecework, was barely enough for the basics. While working for a ready-made clothing factory, she was required to sew silk cords and mother-of-pearl on dresses. When, at the end of a long day, she had not sewn a minimal amount, she would have to take dresses home for several additional hours of work. "Home" for Adelheid was a windowless room that housed four young girls like herself. To help with the rent, they agreed to allow a young man to sleep in one of the beds when it was not occupied. As was often the case in such circumstances, one night Popp found herself forced to resist his unwelcome advances.

After a number of years, Popp "advanced" from sewing piecework to working in an industrial environment. In a bronze factory, her assigned task was to solder together various pieces of metal. By the time she was 14, the long hours in toxic conditions had brought on a collapse of her health. She fainted while at work and was taken to a hospital, where the physicians diagnosed a case of shattered nerves, as well as symptoms of malnutrition and anemia. Oblivious to the reality of her situation, one of Popp's physicians prescribed a therapeutic regimen consisting of fresh air and nutritious meals. Within days, by no means recovered from her illness, she had to return to her factory chores, which brought on more fainting attacks. Back in the hospital, 14-year-old Popp was declared to be "an incurable case" and sent to the municipal Poor House for aged and infirm women. Years later, she would write bitterly of how she, "a child who because of labor and malnutrition had been denied all of the joys of childhood," had been sent by bureaucracy's mindless machinery to "a place meant for the very old and infirm."

Popp sought to escape the realities of her existence by reading at night, under a weak and flickering light, about a better life. At first, she read cheap novels that gave her a few hours' respite, transporting her into a world of Romantic heroes and perfect love. One day, however, she started to read publications of the fledgling Austrian Social Democratic movement. Gradually, the world and its injustices took on a clear, definable shape. Because of her readings on Marxism and trade unionism, poverty for Popp was no longer an inexplicable burden but rather a human creation that could be rectified. At age 17, she became one of the first women to join the ranks of the Austrian Social Democratic Party.

Now a loyal member of a growing movement led almost exclusively by middle-class intellectuals but with a mass membership of workers, Popp felt that she had finally found a warm, caring family. Despite her often precarious state of health—she remained susceptible to fainting spells—and the physical toll exacted by 11-hour workdays, she often spent her evenings at Social Democratic meetings and rallies. By 1890, Popp was beginning to make speeches at working-class gatherings, and it soon became apparent that despite her limited education she could not only persuade her fellow workers, but hold her own in discussions and debates with colleagues from the middle class. She became increasingly confident in her own abilities and the future of the working-class movement, particularly the growing trade unions that created solidarity among the proletariat in their ongoing struggle with capitalism.

Adelheid Popp

Within a few years, Popp had become one of Vienna's most promising Social Democratic personalities. Besides speaking before crowds, she could also be persuasive in small-group settings, and was one of the founding members of the influential Lese- und Diskutierklub "Libertas" (a reading and discussion circle). Because of her dynamism as an agitator, the political police often would detain her after meetings, citing "subversive" phrases in her speech. As a militant trade unionist, she organized a strike of 600 women in a clothing factory near Vienna. More important, she now had caught the eye of Social Democratic leaders both in Austria and Germany. Even Friedrich Engels, Karl Marx's friend and collaborator, visited her on one of his trips to Vienna, indicating to his Austrian colleagues that she possessed remarkable talent for leadership, particularly in view of her humble beginnings.

In 1893, Adelheid Dworschak married Julius Popp (1849–1902), a Social Democrat who, despite frail health, had become a gifted party journalist and editor. The marriage would be extremely happy, producing not only two sons but a strong sense of shared ideals. With her husband's support, which included a willingness to share domestic chores that was rare for the time, Adelheid Popp became increasingly active in Social Democratic affairs. Her oratorical skills led her to address crowds of women not only in Vienna but in other parts of Austria as well. To further disseminate the Social Democratic message, in 1892 Popp became editor-in-chief of the newly founded *Arbeiterinnen-Zeitung* (Working Women's Newspaper). In the 1890s, besides agitating for reduced work hours and improved working conditions, Popp also began to demand suffrage for all Austrian women. While convinced that workers should labor together regardless of gender, she also believed that in some situations social progress could be accelerated if women were in charge of their own organizations. In 1896, her proposal that the Austrian Trade Union Congress support an official women's section failed to pass by one vote. In 1898, the Social Democratic leadership acknowledged her role in the movement by appointing her to a seat on its important Frauenreichskomitee (National Women's Committee). In 1904, she was elected to membership in the party's policy-making Parteivorstand (executive committee).

In December 1902, Popp suffered a grievous loss with the death of her husband. She chose to find an outlet for her grief in her work, which included editorial activities and agitation on behalf of women's suffrage, equal pay for equal work, protective legislation for industrial workers, equal legal rights, divorce reform, and state-provided nursery care. Greatly admired and respected, Popp hoped that Socialism would come to power in Austria and indeed throughout the world through education, the ballot box, and the growing strength of the working class. For her, a high point was the first International Conference of Socialist Women, which took place in Stuttgart, Germany, in August 1907. Popp, ***Anna Boschek**, and **Therese Schlesinger** represented Austria at a conference that included such global luminaries of the Marxist movement as ***Rosa Luxemburg** and ***Clara Zetkin**.

In 1909, Popp published her classic autobiography *Die Jugendgeschichte einer Arbeiterin* (The Story of a Young Woman Worker), which told not only of her harsh early years, but of her discovery of the ideals of Socialism. These ideals would prove to be illusory when the onset of World War I in 1914 revealed how fragile the veneer of civilization's "progress" really was. A new reality, that of Total War, now pitted peoples against peoples in a conflict of unprecedented destructiveness. The war was much more than an abstract disappointment for Popp, for in 1916 her son Julius ("Jultschi") was reported missing in action; he would never return. Later, in 1924, her surviving son Felix died of an infection.

Popp's personal tragedies were part of a larger crisis that shook her once optimistic world. By the end of World War I, the people of Europe had suffered serious moral and psychological damage, not least of which was the permanent split within the working-class movement. The 1917 Bolshevik Revolution in Russia resulted in splits within all of the Social Democratic parties in Europe, creating new Communist parties out of the prewar movements. In many cases, the working class emerged weaker and divided, making it less able to deal effectively with the crises that appeared with the end of World War I in 1918. A weakened working class often found it difficult to respond to the new political movements that sprouted like evil weeds in the early 1920s, particularly Fascism in Italy and Nazism in Germany and Austria.

In post-1918 Austria, the new nation struggled to survive economically and was never able to create a viable national identity for its impoverished citizenry. But in the city of Vienna after 1918 Social Democracy thrived and created a social experiment based on public housing, free medical care, and serious attempts to create a working-class culture. Popp played a significant role in the newly created Republic of Austria. In 1918, she was elected a member of the Vienna City Council, followed in 1919 by her election first to the constituent national assembly and then to the Nationalrat (Parliament). Among her legislative achievements as a member of this body were laws that reformed the working conditions of domestic employees (the law in force dated back to 1808). She also played an active role in attempts to reduce the legal restrictions against abortion and to restore the pre-1914 unity of the international working-class movement. In 1926, she accepted the position of women's representative on the executive board of the Socialist International. During these years Popp, long widowed and still in mourning for her sons, relied on her friends for emotional support. Perhaps her deepest friendship was with ***Emma Adler**.

In the early 1930s, the world economic depression and the rise of Nazism clouded Popp's life. When her health declined, she decided in 1933 to retire from the Parteivorstand, of which she had been a member for almost three decades.

Increasingly frail and despondent over the destruction of both democracy and her beloved Social Democratic Party in February 1934, she lived a retiring life. She had the misfortune to still be alive when Adolf Hitler rode in triumph through the streets of Vienna in April 1938. Popp, a remarkable woman who had risen from poverty and ignorance to become one of Central Europe's most respected working-class leaders, died of a stroke in Vienna on March 7, 1939.

SOURCES:

Bandhauer-Schöffmann, Irene. "Parteidisziplin," in *Zeitgeschichte.* Vol. 16, no. 11–12. August–September 1989, pp. 396–409.

Emmerich, Wolfgang, ed. *Proletarische Lebensläufe: Autobiographische Dokumente zur Entstehung der Zweiten Kultur in Deutschland.* 2 vols. Reinbek bei Hamburg: Ernst Rowohlt, 1979–80.

Gerstenberger, Katharina. "Writing Herself Into the Center: Centrality and Marginality in the Autobiographical Writings of **Nahida Lazarus**, Adelheid Popp, and **Unica Zürn**," Ph.D. dissertation, Cornell University, 1993.

Gruber, Helmut, and Pamela Graves, eds. *Women and Socialism—Socialism and Women: Europe Between the Two World Wars.* Oxford, UK: Berghahn Books, 1998.

Hamer, Thomas Lewis. "Beyond Feminism: The Women's Movement in Austrian Social Democracy, 1890–1920," Ph.D. dissertation, Ohio State University, 1973.

Hildebrandt, Irma. *Hab meine Rolle nie gelernt: 15 Wiener Frauenporträts.* Munich: Eugen Diederichs Verlag, 1996.

John, Michael. "'Kultur der Armut' in Wien 1890–1923: Zur Bedeutung von Solidarstrukturen, Nachbarschaft und Protest," in *Zeitgeschichte.* Vol. 20, no. 5–6. May–June 1993, pp. 158–186.

***Juchacz, Marie**. *Sie lebten für eine bessere Welt: Lebensbilder führender Frauen des 19. und 20. Jahrhunderts.* Hannover: Verlag von J.H.W. Dietz, 1971.

Köpl, Regina. "Adelheid Popp," in Edith Prost, ed., *"Die Partei hat mich nie enttäuscht . . ." Österreichische Sozialdemokratinnen.* Vienna: Verlag für Gesellschaftskritik, 1989, pp. 4–43.

Lafleur, Ingrun. "Five Socialist Women: Traditionalist Conflicts and Socialist Visions in Austria, 1893–1934," in Marilyn J. Boxer and Jean H. Quataert, eds., *Socialist Women: European Socialist Feminism in the Nineteenth and Twentieth Centuries.* NY: Elsevier, 1978, pp. 215–248.

Lewis, Jill. "Popp, Adelheid (1869–1939)," in A. Thomas Lane, ed., *Biographical Dictionary of European Labor Leaders.* 2 vols. Westport, CT: Greenwood Press, 1995, Vol. 2, pp. 770–771.

Popp, Adelheid. *Die Arbeiterin im Kampf ums Dasein.* Vienna: Verlag der Wiener Volksbuchhandlung, Ignaz Brand, 1911.

———. "August Bebel und die Frauen," *Arbeiter-Zeitung* [Vienna]. No. 224. August 16, 1913.

———. *The Autobiography of a Working Woman. With Introductions by August Bebel and J. Ramsay MacDonald.* Translated by F.C. Harvey. London: T. Fisher Unwin, 1912.

———. "Das Fest der Arbeiterinnen," in *Arbeiter-Zeitung* [Vienna]. No. 64. March 6, 1912.

———. "Der Frauenstimmrechtskongress," in *Arbeiter-Zeitung* [Vienna]. No. 172. June 25, 1913.

———. "Was hat die Republik den Frauen gebracht?," *Arbeiter-Zeitung* [Vienna], November 19, 1922.

———. *Der Weg zur Höhe: Die sozialdemokratische Frauenbewegung Österreichs, ihr Aufbau, ihre Entwicklung und ihr Aufstieg.* 2nd ed. Vienna: Frauenzentralkomitee der Sozialdemokratischen Arbeiterpartei Deutschösterreichs, 1930.

Proft, Gabriele. "Adelheid Popp," in Norbert Leser, ed., *Werk und Widerhall: Grosse Gestalten des österreichischen Sozialismus.* Vienna: Verlag der Wiener Volksbuchhandlung, 1964, pp. 297–305.

Riemer, Eleanor S., and John C. Fout, eds. *European Women: A Documentary History, 1789–1945.* NY: Schocken, 1980.

Schumm, Jennifer A. "The Female Voices of Adelheid Popp's *Die Jugendgeschichte einer Arbeiterin* and ***Lou Andreas-Salomé**'s *Lebensrückblick: Grundriss einiger Lebenserinnerungen,*" M.A. thesis, Bowling Green State University, 1992.

Smith, Bonnie G. *Changing Lives: Women in European History Since 1700.* Lexington, MA: D.C. Heath, 1989.

Wagner, Renate. *Heimat bist du grosser Töchter: Bedeutende Frauen und ihre Geschichte.* Vienna: Überreuter Verlag, 1996.

John Haag,
Associate Professor of History, University of Georgia,
Athens, Georgia

Popp, Lucia (1939–1993)

Czech lyric soprano. Born in Uhorská Ves, Czechoslovakia, on November 12, 1939; died of a brain tumor, age 54, in Munich, Germany, on November 16, 1993; studied with Anna Hrusovska-Prosenková.

Debuted at Bratislava Opera (1963); debuted in Vienna as Barbariana in The Marriage of Figaro *at Vienna Theater an der Wien (1963); asked to join the Vienna State Opera by Herbert von Karajan (1963); first appeared at Covent Garden (1966), Metropolitan Opera (1967); made an Austrian* Kammersängerin *(court singer, 1979).*

Lucia Popp, who was born in Uhorská Ves, Czechoslovakia, in 1939, studied with **Anna Hrusovska-Prosenková**. In the beginning, the clarity of her highest notes won her considerable acclaim for roles such as the Queen of the Night in Mozart's *Magic Flute*, and her voice continued to grow throughout her career. As it developed, she began to perform most of Mozart's soubrette parts and much of the traditional lyric soprano repertoire. In the last decades, she sang Wagner, moving into roles for more powerful spinto voices. Popp also matured as an actress, making dramatic roles and lyric repertoire well within her abilities. She made over 75 recordings, including her interpretations of Handel, Mahler, Janacek and Puccini.

John Haag,
Athens, Georgia

Poppa of Normandy (fl. 880)

Duchess of Normandy. *Name variations: Papie; Popa of Bayeux; Poppa of Valois. Flourished around 880; daughter of Berenger, count of Bayeux; became first wife of Rollo or Rolf or Hrolf also known as Robert (870–932), Norse conqueror of Normandy and 1st duke of Normandy (r. 911–932), in 886; children: William I Longsword, 2nd duke of Normandy (r. 932–942); Robert, count of Corbeil; Crespina;* ****Gerloc*** *(d. 963); possibly Kathlin (who married Biolan, king of Scotland).*

Poppaea Sabina (d. 47).

See Messalina, Valeria for sidebar.

Poppaea Sabina (d. 65).

See Agrippina the Younger for sidebar.

Porcia (c. 70–43 BCE).

See Portia.

Porden, Eleanor Anne (1795–1825).

See Franklin, Jane for sidebar on Eleanor Franklin.

Porete, Marguerite (d. 1310).

See Women Prophets and Visionaries in France at the End of the Middle Ages.

Porter, Anna Maria (1780–1832)

English novelist. *Born in 1780 in Durham, England; died of typhus on September 21, 1832, in Bristol, England; daughter of William Porter (an army surgeon) and Jane Blenkinsop Porter; sister of Jane Porter (1776–1850) and Robert Ker Porter; attended school in Edinburgh, Scotland; never married; no children.*

Selected writings: Artless Tales *(2 vols., 1793, 1795);* Walsh Colville, or a Young Man's First Entrance into Life *(1797);* Octavia: A Novel *(1798);* The Fair Fugitives *(play, 1803);* The Lake of Killarney: A Novel *(1804);* A Sailor's Friendship, and a Soldier's Love *(1805);* The Hungarian Brothers *(1807);* Don Sebastian, or The House of Braganza *(1809);* The Recluse of Norway *(1814);* The Knight of St. John *(1817);* The Village of Mariendorpt *(1821);* The Barony *(1830).*

Born in Durham, England, in 1780, Anna Maria Porter was the youngest of five children of William Porter, an army surgeon who died shortly before her birth, and **Jane Blenkinsop Porter**. She was also the younger sister of ***Jane Porter**, who achieved much more lasting recognition as a novelist; the sisters and their mother remained extremely close throughout their lives.

Shortly after Anna Maria's birth, her mother moved the now-fatherless family to Edinburgh, Scotland. Both Anna Maria and her sister Jane later attended George Fulton's school in that city, where, at the age of only five, Anna Maria was ranked at the head of her class, which included pupils as old as sixteen. (At that age she was also reportedly reading Shakespeare.)

The two sisters displayed an early interest in storytelling and writing, perhaps inspired in part by some neighborhood influences. In Edinburgh, the Porters lived but a short distance from a youthful Walter Scott, who often entertained them, and Anna Maria and her sister were also charmed by the fairy tales and accounts of Scottish history they heard from an elderly neighbor named **"Luckie" Forbes**. By age 16, Porter had published a two-volume collection of her stories, *Artless Tales* (1793, 1795), which captured the fancy of readers during the late 18th and early 19th centuries, perhaps because they were drawn from contemporary life. Most knowledgeable observers of the day, however, recognized Anna Maria's shortcomings as a writer. One later critic, George Saintsbury, attributed the eventual disappearance from print of Porter's work to her "amiable incompetence." Though her skills as a storyteller improved over time, Anna Maria seems never to have done much to polish her writing style.

By the time her first book was published, Porter and her family had moved from Edinburgh to London. Two years after the publication in 1795 of the second volume of *Artless Tales*, Anna Maria published her first novel, *Walsh Colville*, which Jane described as "a good warning, to young men, who are plunged into the same sea of Dissipation and Dangers" as the hero of the book. The social and moral culture of the final days of the 18th century was not altogether welcoming to novels, but both Anna Maria and later her sister Jane managed to overcome some of the suspicion to this literary form by their preferred subject matter, which was usually the attempts by basically moral characters to resist the corrupting influences of the world around them. Members of the Anglican Evangelical movement, who formed the bulk of the Porter sisters' audience, welcomed a literary theme in which the central characters managed to stay on the path of righteousness despite the siren call of temptation.

The publication of Anna Maria's second novel, *Octavia*, in 1798 met with critical response that can most charitably be characterized as indifferent. One critic described it as "a novel, without any particular merit, or any particular fault," while another suggested that the author "may with care become respectable as a poetess; but we would advise her to relinquish the task of writing novels." And, indeed, in her next undertaking Porter moved away from the novel, writing the book and lyrics for *The Fair Fugitives*, a musical drama that debuted at Covent Garden on May 16, 1803. The play proved a failure at the box office and ended forever her venture into the world of the theater. Porter next published *The Lake of Killarney* in 1804 and *A Sailor's Friendship, and a Soldier's Love* in 1805. The former attracted a somewhat mixed reaction from critics, one of whom wrote favorably of it, suggesting that "it awakens no sympathies that are not . . . friendly to the cause of virtue." For her part, Anna Maria apologized to readers in advance for the weaknesses of her novel, allowing that it had been written "merely as an amusement for the languid hours, which followed long and repeated fits of sickness." Seizing perhaps on this admission by the author, another critic said of the novel that "the thread which connects the story together does not continually serve to conduct the reader along through the winding paths. We attribute this defect to the state of the author's health, which probably interrupted the chain of ideas, and weakened their mutual dependence on each other." (It should be noted, however, that such "apologies" by authors, particularly women authors, were by no means unheard of at the time.) Of *A Sailor's Friendship*, critics had little to say.

In 1807, Porter published her most popular novel, *The Hungarian Brothers*, a historical romance set against the backdrop of the French Revolution that went through more than 15 printings and was translated into French. Although they were not quite as impressed as its readers, most critics conceded that this novel represented an improvement over some of Anna Maria's earlier work. *Critical Review*, which had once suggested that Porter would do well to abandon her writing, grudgingly admitted that in this novel "the incidents are striking . . . and many of the characters finely drawn."

Porter also wrote a number of other historical romances, including *Don Sebastian, or The House of Braganza* (1809); *The Knight of St. John* (1817); *The Village of Mariendorpt* (1821); and *The Barony* (1830), her last novel. None of these works, however, achieved the popularity of *The Hungarian Brothers*. With Jane, Anna Maria also collaborated in the writing of *Tales Round a Winter Hearth* (1826) and *Coming Out* (1828).

The Porter sisters lived for many years with their mother in Esher, Surrey, returning to London after her death in 1831. The following year, during a visit to her brother in Bristol, Anna Maria Porter contracted typhus and died at the age of 52.

SOURCES:

Adams, Michael. "Anna Maria Porter" in *Dictionary of Literary Biography,* Vol. 116: *British Romantic Novelists, 1789–1832.* Edited by Bradford K. Mudge. Detroit, MI: Gale Research, 1992.

The Concise Dictionary of National Biography. Oxford and NY: Oxford University Press, 1992.

Kunitz, Stanley J., and Howard Haycraft, eds. *British Authors of the Nineteenth Century.* NY: H.W. Wilson, 1936.

Shattock, Joanne. *The Oxford Guide to British Women Writers.* Oxford and NY: Oxford University Press, 1993.

Woolsey, Linda Mills. "Anna Maria Porter" in *Dictionary of Literary Biography,* Vol. 159: *British Short-Fiction Writers, 1800–1880.* Edited by John R. Greenfield. Detroit, MI: Gale Research, 1996.

Don Amerman,
freelance writer, Saylorsburg, Pennsylvania

Porter, Charlotte Endymion and Helen Archibald Clarke

American writers who founded the literary magazine **Poet Lore**. *Name variations: (joint pseudonym) H.A.C.*

Clarke, Helen Archibald (1860–1926). *Born Helen Archibald Clarke on November 13, 1860, in Philadelphia, Pennsylvania; died of cardiac disease on February 8, 1926, in Boston, Massachusetts; daughter of Hugh Archibald Clarke (a professor of music) and Jane (Searle) Clarke; studied music as a special student at the University of Pennsylvania; never married; lived with Charlotte Endymion Porter; no children.*

Selected writings: Apparitions *(1892);* Browning's Italy *(1907);* Browning's England *(1908);* A Child's Guide to Mythology *(1908);* Longfellow's Country *(1909);* Hawthorne's Country *(1910);* The Poets' New England *(1911);* Browning and His Century *(1912).*

Porter, Charlotte Endymion (1857–1942). *Born Helen Charlotte Porter on January 6, 1857, in Towanda, Pennsylvania; died on January 16, 1942, in Melrose, Massachusetts; daughter of Henry Clinton Porter (a* *physician) and Elisa Eleanor (Betts) Porter; graduated from Wells College, Aurora, New York, and studied briefly at the Sorbonne in Paris; never married; lived with Helen Archibald Clarke; no children.*

Selected writings: (editor) First Folio Edition of Shakespeare *(40 vols., 1903–13);* Lips of Music *(1919).*

Charlotte Endymion Porter and Helen Archibald Clarke, born three years apart and raised in similar economic and social backgrounds, met in the mid-1880s and spent the next 40-odd years in a personal and literary partnership. Porter, born in Towanda, Pennsylvania, on January 6, 1857, and christened Helen Charlotte, was the only daughter among three children of Henry Clinton Porter, a physician, and **Elisa Betts Porter**. She later dropped the name "Helen" in favor of "Charlotte," and adopted "Endymion" (the name of a grandson of Zeus in Greek mythology) as her middle name. She graduated from Wells College in Aurora, New York, and later studied at the Sorbonne in Paris. In 1883, after moving to Philadelphia, Porter was named editor of *Shakespeariana*, a journal sponsored by the Shakespeare Society of New York. Clarke, a Philadelphia native born on November 13, 1860, was the only child of Hugh Archibald Clarke, a professor of music at the University of Pennsylvania, and **Jane Searle Clarke**. Although the University of Pennsylvania officially accepted no women as students, her father managed to secure her admission as a special student, and in 1883 she was granted a certificate in music. Some time later, she submitted an article about the music of Shakespeare for publication in *Shakespeariana*. After its acceptance Clarke and Porter met and discovered that they had much in common; in addition to their mutual interest in Shakespeare, both shared an admiration for the writings of poet Robert Browning and were founding members of the Browning Society of Philadelphia. They soon became extremely close, and later would cement their bond by exchanging rings.

In 1887, Porter resigned her position as editor of *Shakespeariana*, disappointed when her proposals for expanding the scope of the periodical were blocked by its publisher. She next worked briefly as editor of the *Ethical Record* while mapping plans with Clarke to launch a new literary magazine. In January 1889, the two brought out the first issue of *Poet Lore*, a monthly magazine "devoted to Shakespeare, Browning, and the Comparative Study of Literature," according to its original mission statement. In 1891, *Poet Lore* was moved from Philadelphia to Boston, where Porter and Clarke lived together, when publisher Dana Estes offered the magazine free office space in exchange for free advertising in every issue. The audience for *Poet Lore,* strong from the outset, continued to grow, although publishing problems forced its founders to transform the journal from a monthly to a quarterly in 1896. Much of the literary criticism and commentary that appeared in the pages of *Poet Lore* was written by Porter and Clarke, occasionally signed "H.A.C." ("Helen and Charlotte").

In the mid-1890s, the scope of *Poet Lore* began to broaden. Over the years, Porter and Clarke introduced the magazine's readers to the writings of emerging European writers including Paul Bourget, Gabriele D'Annunzio, ***Selma Lagerlöf**, Maxim Gorky, Gerhart Hauptmann, Björnstjerne Björnson, Henrik Ibsen, and Maurice Maeterlinck. In time, the journal also began to examine the literature of the Middle East, India, and the Far East. *Poet Lore* never served as much of a showcase for American writing, although it did occasionally include reviews of such American and Canadian writers as Paul Laurence Dunbar, Bliss Carman, and Edward Rowland, as well as the work of essayist Gamaliel Bradford, Jr. Nonetheless, Porter and Clarke did a good deal to help promote artistic creativity in the United States. They were members of ***Julia Ward Howe**'s Boston Authors' Club, and founded the American Music Society, of which Clarke later became president, and the American Drama Society (later the Drama League of America), which was presided over by Porter. Both women also were active members of Boston's Browning Society, in which they served in various capacities, and published a number of works on Browning as well as a six-volume edition of the poems of ***Elizabeth Barrett Browning.**

As their involvement in endeavors outside *Poet Lore* expanded, Porter and Clarke decided in 1903 to sell the magazine to Richard G. Badger, although they continued as its editors through World War I. Among the outside projects on which Porter worked were the *First Folio Edition of Shakespeare* (1903–13), a 40-volume collection she edited, and a book of poetry, *Lips of Music* (1919), much of it about love between women. Clarke wrote a number of books exploring the lives and work of some of her favorite authors and poets, including *Browning's Italy* (1907), *Browning's England* (1908), *A Child's Guide to Mythology* (1908), *Longfellow's Country* (1909), *Hawthorne's Country* (1910), *The Poets' New England* (1911), and *Browning and His Century* (1912).

After Clarke's death at age 65 on February 8, 1926, Porter spent much of her time at Ardensea, a cottage on Maine's Isle au Haut in Penobscot Bay where the two had summered. She was supported financially by friends in the closing years of her life, and lived her last few months in a nursing home in Melrose, Massachusetts, where she died at the age of 85 on January 16, 1942. The ashes of both women were scattered over their beloved Isle au Haut in Penobscot Bay.

SOURCES:

James, Edward T., ed. *Notable American Women, 1607–1950*. Cambridge, MA: The Belknap Press of Harvard University, 1971.

McHenry, Robert, ed. *Famous American Women*. NY: Dover, 1980.

Don Amerman,
freelance writer, Saylorsburg, Pennsylvania

Porter, Eleanor H. (1868–1920)

***Bestselling American writer and author of the hugely successful* Pollyanna.** *Name variations: (pseudonym) Eleanor Stewart. Born Eleanor Emily Hodgman on December 19, 1868, in Littleton, New Hampshire; died of tuberculosis on May 21, 1920, in Cambridge, Massachusetts; daughter of Francis Fletcher Hodgman (a pharmacist) and Llewella French (Woolson) Hodgman; studied music in public school, under private tutors, and at New England Conservatory of Music; married John Lyman Porter (a businessman), on May 3, 1892.*

Selected writings: Cross Currents *(1907);* Miss Billy *(1911);* Miss Billy's Decision *(1912);* Pollyanna *(1913);* Miss Billy Married *(1914);* Pollyanna Grows Up *(1915);* Just David *(1916);* The Road to Understanding *(1917);* Oh, Money! Money! *(1918);* Dawn *(1919);* Across the Years *(stories, 1919);* Mary-Marie *(1920);* Money, Love and Kate *(stories, 1925).*

Merriam-Webster's *Tenth Collegiate Dictionary* defines a Pollyanna as "a person characterized by irrepressible optimism and a tendency to find good in everything." The name of the brave little heroine of Eleanor H. Porter's most memorable novels has thus become part of the English language, an accomplishment few writers have achieved.

The only daughter of Francis Fletcher Hodgman, a pharmacist, and **Llewella French Woolson Hodgman**, a descendant of William Bradford, governor of the Plymouth Colony, Eleanor Porter was born on December 19, 1868, in the tiny village of Littleton in the White Mountains of New Hampshire. Although she showed a talent for writing from a very early age, her first love was music. Porter's public school education in Littleton was cut short when ill health forced her to leave high school and spend time recuperating in New Hampshire's clean mountain air. The frail health of her high school years mirrored in many ways the life of her mother, who for much of her adult life was an invalid. When Porter had regained her strength, she continued her studies under private tutors, and later studied voice at the New England Conservatory of Music and privately in Boston. She taught music after concluding her studies and also gained local fame for her singing in church choirs, public concerts, and private homes.

On May 3, 1892, Eleanor married John Lyman Porter, a Boston businessman who in time would rise to the presidency of the National Separator and Machine Company. The two spent the next decade on the move, living in a number of cities throughout the eastern United States, including Springfield, Vermont; Chattanooga, Tennessee; and New York City. Eventually, they settled into an apartment in Cambridge, Massachusetts, which they shared with Eleanor's invalid mother.

Shortly after the turn of the century, Porter set aside her music and began to concentrate on writing. Initially, she spent much of her time turning out short fiction and is said to have had more than 200 of her short stories published by 1915, many of which appeared under the pseudonym Eleanor Stewart. (Six collections of her short stories eventually were released.) She published her first novel, *Cross Currents,* in 1907, but first achieved real success in 1911 with *Miss Billy,* the tale of a girl who transforms the lives of three bachelor brothers with whom she goes to live.

The appearance in 1913 of *Pollyanna* was met with both popular and critical acclaim. Porter's story of an orphan so dauntless in her optimism that she turns those around her into believers touched a nerve in America. The book and, more important, its title character, are without question the author's chief contributions to American literature and the popular culture of the day. *Pollyanna* quickly sold over one million copies and was translated into eight languages, becoming an international success; "Pollyanna Clubs" sprang up around the nation, and by 1920 the book was in its 47th printing. In years since, the almost unbelievable ability of Pollyanna to endure hardship and adversity has made the character and book leading candidates for satire. However, the orphan heroine's insistence on looking for the "glad" side of even the most unfortunate events still strikes a chord with many readers and with those who have seen the eponymous film versions of the book, 1920's excellent silent film starring ***Mary Pickford** as Pollyanna and 1960's Disney movie, for which **Hayley Mills** won a special Academy Award for her performance in the title role. (The story was also adapted for the stage in 1916, starring **Patricia Collinge** as Pollyanna, a role taken over by ***Helen Hayes** on the national tour.)

A recurrent theme in Porter's work is the ability of an individual, by sheer force of personality, to transform the world for the better. Just as the heroine of *Miss Billy* alters forever the lives of the three Boston bachelor brothers with whom she lives, upon her arrival at her Aunt Polly's home Pollyanna sets in motion a chain of events that ensures that her aunt and all of Beldingsville, Vermont, will never again be the same. In later years, reflecting on the immense success of her Pollyanna books, Porter happily acknowledged the preoccupation in her writings with "the agreeable, decent qualities of life." Her books reflect the influences of her childhood in New Hampshire and her love of music. Perhaps created as a counterbalance to some of the illness and unhappiness of Porter's early school years, Pollyanna possesses the almost magical ability to make things right no matter how badly awry they have gone. The character's "glad game" had been born before she was orphaned, when she unhappily announced to her father that her rummaging through the church's charity barrel had yielded only a pair of crutches and not the doll for which she'd hoped. Her father counseled her to look always for the bright side of things, in this case to be glad that at least she did not need the crutches.

Pollyanna returned in 1915 as the title character in Porter's *Pollyanna Grows Up*, in which the cheerful orphan "enlarges her sphere of activity and attempts to bring joy to all Boston, a prodigious and, of course, quite impossible task," according to the Boston *Transcript*. One year later Porter published *Just David*, in which an orphan named David is taken in by an elderly couple after his father dies. The boy's sole posses-

Patricia Collinge in Pollyanna *on Broadway.*

sions are a couple of violins (one of them a Stradivarius) he has inherited from his father, who was once a musician of note, and an ability to make beautiful music. Through the sweetness of his music and the essential goodness of his personality, David soon changes forever the lives of the people around him. This book, too, became a bestseller, as did Porter's novels *The Road to Understanding* (1917), *Dawn* (1919), *Mary-Marie* (1920), and *Oh, Money! Money!* (1918), in which she explored the powers of riches to both transform life and destroy character. The book's leading character, a wealthy man, leads relatives he has never met to believe that he has been lost in the wilds. They inherit part of his fortune with the promise that they will receive all of it once he has been declared legally dead. Changing his name and moving to the town where they live, the hero observes with consternation how this newfound wealth changes—and not for the better—the lives of his relatives.

Porter's wildly successful writing career ended on May 21, 1920, when she died of tuberculosis in her Cambridge home at the age of 51. *Pollyanna* remains in print, with numerous new editions published through the year 2000.

SOURCES:

Contemporary Authors. Vol. 108. Detroit, MI: Gale Research.

James, Edward T., ed. *Notable American Women, 1607–1950*. Cambridge, MA: The Belknap Press of Harvard University, 1971.

Kunitz, Stanley J., and Howard Haycraft, eds. *Twentieth Century Authors*. NY: H.W. Wilson, 1942.

Marchalonis, Shirley. "Eleanor H. Porter" in *Dictionary of Literary Biography*, Vol. 9: *American Novelists, 1910–1945*. Edited by James J. Martine. Detroit, MI: Gale Research, 1981.

McHenry, Robert, ed. *Famous American Women*. NY: Dover, 1980.

Don Amerman,
freelance writer, Saylorsburg, Pennsylvania

Porter, Eliza Chappell (1807–1888)

American educator and relief worker during the Civil War. *Born Eliza Emily Chappell on November 5, 1807, in Geneseo, New York; died on January 1, 1888, in Santa Barbara, California; fourth daughter and eighth of nine children of Robert Chappell (a farmer) and Elizabeth (Kneeland) Chappell; married Jeremiah Porter (a missionary), on June 15, 1835; children: nine, six of whom survived infancy.*

Born in 1807 in Geneseo, New York, one of nine children, Eliza Chappell Porter spent much of her early life with relatives in Franklin, New York, sent there following the death of her father in 1811. She returned to Geneseo at age 12, and at 16 began teaching school, even though her own education had been spotty at best. In 1828, after moving with her mother to Rochester, she opened a school modeled after the infant schools started in New York City by **Joanna Graham Bethune**, designed to bring religious-oriented education to poor children. (Porter was extremely religious, having experienced a renewal of faith during a serious illness some years earlier.)

After her mother's death in 1831, Porter moved to Mackinac Island to tutor the children of Robert Stuart, a resident partner of the American Fur Company and a devout Presbyterian. In addition to Stuart's children and those of his associates, Porter also taught the local "half breed" Native American children, an experience which convinced her even more that the infant school movement was the way of God. In 1833, after a trip East to recover from an illness, she opened and staffed a school in the French and Indian settlement of St. Ignace, near Mackinac. She then moved on to the small settlement of Chicago, where she established another school in the log cabin home of John Stephen Wright, a real-estate developer and a "praying man." Winning both praise for her efforts as well as an offer of public funding, in 1834 she transferred the operation to the Presbyterian church of Reverend Jeremiah Porter, whom she had known in Mackinac. In 1835, they married, and over the next five years lived in Peoria and Farmington, finally settling in Green Bay, Wisconsin, where Jeremiah served for 18 years as pastor of the local Presbyterian church. While raising a large family (the couple had nine children, only six of whom survived to adulthood), Porter remained active in her educational and religious pursuits. In 1858, the Porters returned to Chicago where Jeremiah took over a city mission.

With the outbreak of the Civil War, Porter became office manager of the Chicago Sanitary Commission (later the Northwest Sanitary Commission), a volunteer organization established to solicit, collect, and distribute food and medical supplies to the Union army and to military hospitals. In 1862, feeling she could be of more use in the field, she left her office position to escort a group of women volunteers to Cairo, Illinois, where they helped established hospitals to care for the numerous casualties from the battle of Shiloh. She later assisted in hospitals in the Tennessee towns of Savannah and Memphis, where she also established a school for black children.

In July 1863, Porter returned to Chicago to oversee the Sanitary Commission offices for three months during the absence of its regular directors *Mary A. Livermore and *Jane C. Hoge. In October, she resumed her good-will travels, distributing supplies at Corinth, Vicksburg, Cairo, and at Chattanooga, where she joined *Mary Ann Bickerdyke in ministering to Sherman's army during its march toward Atlanta. The work in the field hospitals was an exhausting mix of cooking, laundering, distributing supplies, and even providing nursing care to the wounded during emergencies. "Mrs. Porter, tactful and refined, brought a valuable moderating influence to bear upon the impulsive, rough-spoken, and somewhat domineering 'Mother' Bickerdyke, who affectionately called the tiny auburn-haired Eliza her 'little brown bird,'" writes Wayne C. Temple in *Notable American Women*.

After the fall of Atlanta in September 1864, Porter returned briefly to Chicago, then left on an inspection tour of hospitals in Arkansas and other towns before reuniting with Sherman's army for the Carolinas campaign. In the months following the end of the war, she visited hospitals in Kentucky, Alabama, and Texas, then moved with her husband to Prairie du Chien, Wisconsin. In 1868, when Jeremiah rejoined the regular army as a chaplain, they moved yet again to Brownsville, Texas, where Porter reopened the Rio Grande Seminary which she had established earlier. Jeremiah was subsequently transferred to Fort Sill, Oklahoma, and later to Fort D.A. Russell near Cheyenne, Wyoming. With each reassignment, Porter assisted her husband in his religious duties and also conducted schools for the children in the area. Following Jeremiah's retirement in 1878, the couple spent summers traveling around the country visiting with their children, and frequently wintered in California. Porter died on New Year's Day, 1888, at the age of 80.

SOURCES:

James, Edward T., ed. *Notable American Women, 1607–1950*. Cambridge, MA: The Belknap Press of Harvard University, 1971.

McHenry, Robert, ed. *Famous American Women*. NY: Dover, 1983.

Barbara Morgan,
Melrose, Massachusetts

Porter, Gene Stratton (1863–1924).

See Stratton-Porter, Gene.

Porter, Jane (1776–1850)

English novelist. *Born on December 3, 1776, in Durham, England; died on May 24, 1850, in Bristol, England; daughter of William Porter (an army surgeon) and Jane (Blenkinsop) Porter; sister of Anna Maria Porter (1780–1832) and Robert Ker Porter; educated at George Fulton's School in Edinburgh, Scotland; never married; no children.*

Selected writings: The Two Princes of Persia, Addressed to Youth *(1801);* Thaddeus of Warsaw *(1803);* Sketch of the Campaign of Count A. Suwarrow Ryminski *(1804);* The Scottish Chiefs: A Romance *(1810);* The Pastor's Fire-Side: A Novel *(1817);* Owen, Prince of Powys *(play, 1822);* Duke Christian of Luneberg *(1824);* Sir Edward Seward's Narrative of His Shipwreck and Consequent Discovery of Certain Islands in the Caribbean Sea *(1831).*

Born in 1776 in Durham, England, Jane Porter was the eldest daughter of army surgeon William Porter and **Jane Blenkinsop Porter**, whose family already included sons John Blenkinsop Porter (b. 1771 or 1772) and William Ogilvy Porter (b. 1773 or 1774). A year after her birth, the Porters welcomed the arrival of third son Robert Ker Porter, who would become a much-traveled painter and writer. A 1777 letter from William Porter to his wife reveals that his aspirations for his daughter were quite different than his hopes for his sons. He wrote that John, whom he called Jacky, showed the promise of becoming "a lad of Genius," while he expressed hope that William would be made a "good scholar." About Jane, whom he called Jenny, he wrote: "My Jenny is beautiful; it will be my pride to dress my little Queen handsomely and decently. The rest I leave to your good sense to make up the rest of her education fitting her for a good wife to an Honest Man." William Porter died two years later, only months before the birth of *Anna Maria Porter in early 1780. Jane's devastation at the loss of her father at so early an age was reflected later in life in her idealization of fatherhood and what critics have characterized as a tendency to turn the heroes of the past into father figures.

Left in straitened circumstances by the death of her husband, Jane's mother decided to move with her three youngest children (the two eldest boys remained in school in England) to Edinburgh, where living costs were less expensive than in Durham. The love of both Jane and Anna Maria for the written word can probably be traced, at least in part, to their schooling in Edinburgh at an academy run by George Fulton, a compiler of dictionaries. Though both sisters were good students, Anna Maria proved especially precocious and was said to have been reading Shakespeare by the age of five. Fulton was just one of the influences in Edinburgh that helped to shape the girls' love of storytelling.

Household help introduced the girls to the heroic tales of early Scottish history. A neighbor woman, **"Luckie" Forbes**, regaled Jane and Anna Maria with more about Scotland's colorful heritage, drawing a parallel between early Scottish heroes and Old Testament patriarchs. Their mother developed a friendship in Edinburgh with **Anne Rutherford Scott** (mother of Sir Walter Scott), who played with the Porter children and shared adventure stories with them. In 1790, the family moved to London, where family friends included writers ***Anna Letitia Barbauld** and ***Hannah More**.

By age 16, Anna Maria had published the first volume of her *Artless Tales*. Jane was slower to develop as a writer, although by 1796 she was writing short stories under the pen name of "Classicus." In her diary in 1800, Jane wrote that she had developed a strong affection for actor Charles Kemble and would gladly marry him if only he would ask. Regrettably no such offer was forthcoming. Perhaps to take her mind off her disappointment in romance, Porter threw herself into a study of the exploits of exiles and émigrés. This research led to the writing of *Thaddeus of Warsaw* (1803), her first romance novel, an immediate popular success that also won the approval of Polish patriot and American Revolutionary War hero General Tadeusz Kosciuszko. An article the following year in the *Imperial Review* noted that the book "is one of the few which, once opened, could not pass *unread*. The attention is arrested by the first page, and never suffered to diverge till the final denouement." So enthusiastic was the public's response to *Thaddeus* that 20th-century critic Robert Tate Irvine called Jane Porter "the ***Margaret Mitchell** of 1803." A year later, her *Sketch of the Campaign of Count A. Suwarrow Ryminski* was published.

Porter's next literary venture, *Aphorisms of Sir Philip Sidney; with Remarks* (1807), a collection of quotations organized by subject, was praised by one critic as a "valuable pocket and traveling companion" but failed to excite much interest among readers. In 1810, Jane published *The Scottish Chiefs*, which celebrated (without strict regard to historical accuracy) the heroic exploits of Scotland's William Wallace, who was executed in 1305 after a failed uprising against the British crown. The book was hugely popular, praised by such writers as ***Joanna Baillie**, Thomas Campbell, and ***Mary Russell Mitford**, and was translated into Russian and German.

Porter next decided to try her hand at theater, which proved a disappointment. Her first play, *Egmont, or the Eve of St. Alyne*, was never printed or performed. Although it took some time to reach the stage, her second effort, *Switzerland*, was finally produced with Edmund Kean in the starring role. However, he gave a dreadful performance (some suspect he was drunk), and the play soon closed. In 1822, the Theatre Royal staged Porter's *Owen, Prince of Powys; or Welsh Feuds*, but it, too, was a failure.

During her venture into playwriting, Porter also wrote a well-received historical novel, *The Pastor's Fire-Side*, in 1817. Less popular with readers was her *Duke Christian of Luneberg*, written at the request of King George IV and published in 1824. Jane and her sister Anna Maria collaborated on a collection of short fiction entitled *Tales round a Winter Hearth*, published in 1826. Another collaboration between the sisters followed in 1828, when together they published a three-volume work, in which the first two volumes contained Anna Maria's novel *Coming Out* and the last contained Jane's *The Field of Forty Footsteps*.

Both sisters contributed work to *The Amulet*, a literary annual edited by Samuel Carter Hall, husband of ***Anna Maria Hall**, a well-known author of Irish novels. In 1831, Jane published *Sir Edward Seaward's Narrative of His Shipwreck and Consequent Discovery of Certain Islands in the Caribbean Sea*, which she claimed was an actual diary concerned with real events that she simply had edited. This assertion eventually was proven false by a literary journal, but Porter nonetheless continued to refuse to admit that the book was fiction. Edgar Allan Poe reportedly considered the *Narrative* superior to *Robinson Crusoe*. In the summer of that year, the sisters were dealt a severe blow by the death of their mother, who had been central to their lives. The two returned to London, and in June 1832, while visiting their brother in Bristol, Anna Maria died of typhus.

The loss of her mother and sister in such a short time took a heavy toll on Jane, leaving her with little interest in writing. Of that period, she later recalled, "I neither felt the power nor the desire to touch a literary pen again. They were gone whose words had kindled my emulations, whose approving smiles had been the most prized reward of my labors." Nonetheless, two years after Anna Maria's death, Jane wrote "A Scottish Tradition" for inclusion in *The Tale Book*, a collection of short fiction by such literary luminaries as ***Mary Shelley**, Walter Scott, and Washington Irving. She also contributed to *New Monthly Magazine*, another periodical edited by Samuel Carter Hall, in 1836.

Porter wrote little in the last 20 years of her life. Her health slowly deteriorated, and, while she maintained a home in London, she spent much of her time traveling throughout Europe to visit friends and her brothers. After the 1841 death of her brother Robert while she was visiting him in St. Petersburg, Russia, Jane Porter returned to England to settle his estate. She then moved to Bristol to live with her brother William, and died there on May 24, 1850.

SOURCES:

Adams, Michael. "Jane Porter" in *Dictionary of Literary Biography,* Vol. 116: *British Romantic Novelists, 1789–1832.* Edited by Bradford K. Mudge. Detroit, MI: Gale Research, 1992.

The Concise Dictionary of National Biography. Oxford and NY: Oxford University Press, 1992.

Kunitz, Stanley J., and Howard Haycraft, eds. *British Authors of the Nineteenth Century.* NY: H.W. Wilson, 1936.

Shattock, Joanne. *The Oxford Guide to British Women Writers.* Oxford and NY: Oxford University Press, 1993.

Woolsey, Linda Mills. "Jane Porter" in *Dictionary of Literary Biography,* Vol. 159: *British Short-Fiction Writers, 1800–1880.* Edited by John R. Greenfield. Detroit, MI: Gale Research, 1996.

Don Amerman,
freelance writer, Saylorsburg, Pennsylvania

Porter, Katherine Anne (1890–1980)

Pulitzer Prize-winning author, known for her novel* Ship of Fools, *who was a brilliant practitioner of the art of the short story. *Name variations: (pseudonym) M.T.F. Born Callie Russell Porter on May 15, 1890, in Indian Creek, Texas; died on September 18, 1980, in Silver Spring, Maryland; educated at private schools; fourth of five children of Mary Alice (Jones) Porter and Harrison Boone Porter; married John Koontz, in 1906 (divorced 1915); married Ernest Stock, in 1925 (divorced around 1928); married Eugene Pressly, in 1930 (divorced around 1936); married Albert Erskine, in 1938 (divorced around 1942); no children.*

Selected writings: (under initials M.T.F.) My Chinese Marriage *(NY: Duffield, 1921);* Outline of Mexican Popular Arts and Crafts *(Los Angeles: Young & McCallister, 1922);* Flowering Judas *(NY: Harcourt, Brace, 1930, enlarged as* Flowering Judas and Other Stories, *Harcourt, Brace, 1935);* Hacienda *(NY: Harrison of Paris, 1934);* Noon Wine *(Detroit: Schuman's, 1937);* Pale Horse, Pale Rider: Three Short Novels *(NY: Harcourt, Brace, 1939, republished as* Pale Horse, Pale Rider and Other Stories, *London: Cape, 1939);* The Leaning Tower and Other Stories *(NY: Harcourt, Brace, 1943);* The Days Before *(NY: Harcourt, Brace, 1952);* A Defense of Circe *(NY: Harcourt, Brace, 1955);* The Old Order: Stories of the South *(NY: Harcourt, Brace, 1955);* A Christmas Story *(limited edition, NY: Seymour Lawrence, 1967);* Ship of Fools *(Boston: Little, Brown, 1962);* Collected Stories *(NY: Harcourt, Brace, 1965);* The Collected Essays and Occasional Writings of Katherine Anne Porter *(NY: Delacorte, 1970);* The Never-Ending Wrong *(Boston: Little, Brown, 1977); (edited by Ruth M. Alvarez and Thomas F. Walsh)* Uncollected Early Prose of Katherine Anne Porter *(Austin: University of Texas Press, 1993).*

Worked as a newspaper reporter; was a journalist in Mexico (1921); published her first short story (1922), based on her experiences; published three short story collections to considerable critical acclaim for their meticulous crafting and subtle irony (by 1944); brought to public attention and wide readership with publication of novel Ship of Fools *(1962); won the O. Henry Prize for short fiction (1962); awarded National Book Award and the Pulitzer Prize (1965) for* Collected Short Stories*; suffered a debilitating stroke (1970) just as she finished her last published work,* The Never-Ending Wrong, *about the Sacco-Vanzetti case of the 1920s.*

Of all of her formidable literary output, Katherine Anne Porter's favorite was the story of her own life. It was a work-in-progress that she repeatedly reinvented and rearranged. An early chapter was reported by a fellow patient who shared the next bed in a Texas tuberculosis ward in 1915. "Of one thing I am sure," **Kitty Crawford** wrote home to her husband in San Antonio, "Katherine Anne Porter came of a very fine family. She has been beautifully brought up with exquisite manners and taste in clothes." The truth was that her new acquaintance's childhood had been anything but exquisite; that the sophisticated wardrobe was an affectation intended to disguise an early life so fractured that Porter compared writing about it to undergoing a spinal tap; and that Katherine Anne was not her actual name.

She was born Callie Russell Porter on May 15, 1890, in Indian Creek, Texas, a rural outpost in the southwestern part of the state. **Mary Jones Porter** had chosen to name her second daughter after a close friend. Katherine's father was Harrison Boone Porter, who would bequeath on the little girl a fondness for embroidering family history. Harrison claimed to be a direct descendent of Daniel Boone, although in reality he was the latest in a long line of Porter farmers originating in Kentucky. Harrison's father had fought in the Civil War before moving to the Texas frontier, and Porter claimed all her life that at least two of the African-American servants she remembered from her childhood had been freed slaves. "I am the grandchild of a lost war," she would proclaim. Both parents were well educated and prolific letter writers, another trait they would pass on to their daughter.

Porter always pointed to the early death of her mother in 1892 from pneumonia as the defining event of her early years, for Harrison's grief at the loss of his young wife left him a broken man. He turned to his mother for help, moving with his three daughters and son to nearby Kyle, Texas, and into his mother's house. The next years, Porter said, were ones of both economic and emotional poverty, her distant and morose father having sold the family's land in Indian Creek at a loss in his haste to leave painful memories behind. "I have never seen a more terrible example of apathy," she later wrote of her father, "the almost unconscious refusal to live, to take part, to do even the nearest, most obvious human thing, which was to take care of the children left to him."

The Porter children were looked after in Harrison's stead by their grandmother, Katherine's beloved "Aunt Cat," Catherine Anne Porter. The old woman exerted such an influence on her that Porter would legally adopt the name as her own with only the minor change of one letter. Strong-willed, opinionated and unwilling to suffer fools gladly, Aunt Cat made her greatest contribution to her granddaughter's future with her talent for telling stories filled with characters drawn from the immediate community and from her memories of the arduous journey from Kentucky to Texas in the 1850s. But even the security provided by Aunt Cat's sturdy presence was taken away with her death in 1896. "It was said the motherless family was running down, with the grandmother no longer there to hold it together," Porter wrote years later in one of her most famous short stories, *The Grave*—inspired, like much of her fiction, by family history.

Over the next five years, as Porter completed her education at convent schools, she developed a fascination with the fine clothes and high style of an outside world that held such promise of escape, but which seemed impossible to experience directly. In 1903, however, Katherine and her older sister **Gay Porter** convinced Harrison to let them live and work in San Antonio, where Katherine intended to become an actress. Harrison borrowed the money to let the two girls live in a house rented from friends. Porter attended the only private school in San Antonio offering a dramatic arts program, but moved to suburban Victoria to teach music and dance to young girls to pay the rent for a small room in a dreary boarding house. Now almost 20 years old, Porter rashly decided that marriage was the only escape and quickly accepted an offer from John Henry Koontz, the eldest son of a nearby ranching family. They were married on June 20, 1906, in a union that Porter later referred to as "that preposterous marriage." She nevertheless remained Mrs. Koontz until she left her husband in 1914, running away to Chicago with her persistent dream of becoming an actress. (A divorce from Koontz was granted in 1915.) The only bright spot of those years with Koontz, she later said, was that she wrote her first short story, "The Opal Ring." Although she found work in Chicago as an extra in a few silent films, Katherine had returned South by 1917 to live with her sister Gay in Louisiana and earn a meager salary by traveling the vaudeville circuit through the rural counties.

It was the onset of tuberculosis at this point that sent Porter to the hospital where she reinvented her life story for Kitty Crawford, who found Katherine a job on her husband's Fort Worth newspaper. Echoing Porter's liberality with the facts, the *Fort Worth Critic* touted its new society columnist as "late from the staff of several prominent newspapers." But readers of the *Critic* had hardly gotten used to the new staff writer when Porter fell victim to the catastrophic, worldwide influenza epidemic of 1918, becoming so ill that her family prepared her obituary for the local Texas papers and made arrangements for her burial. She ran a temperature of 105° for nine days before beginning a slow recovery. During her illness, World War I still raged in Europe, families throughout the country mourned the loss of sons sacrificed to battle, and Katherine herself grieved over the loss of a beloved niece from spinal meningitis. The combination of illness, war and death left Porter with a powerful sense of the inevitability of evil, even from apparently well-meaning actions, and gave her the theme that would recur throughout her writing. Her struggle was, she said, the crucial event that marked her determination to become a writer. "It just simply divided my life, cut across it like that," she wrote to a friend many years later. "So that everything before that was just getting ready, and after that I was in some strange way, altered, ready." One result of the experience was her harrowing, and most famous, 1939 short story "Pale Horse, Pale Rider," in which the fevered thoughts of her dying narrator recreate her own brush with death and loss.

A dramatic sign of Porter's newfound dedication to writing was her sudden move in the summer of 1919 to New York's Greenwich Village, the artistic and intellectual center of the East Coast. She took a job writing publicity for a movie studio to pay her rent, but by 1920 had seen her first published work—a story for a children's magazine—appear in print. She quickly sought out the Village's peripatetic population of artists, writers and social activists, not a few of them artistic and political refugees from the upheavals of Mexico's long-running civil war. Among them was the publisher of an American-based magazine sympathetic to the Mexican socialists, who soon offered Porter a job as a staff writer for the *Magazine of Mexico*. To her further delight, she learned the job would require her to live for part of the year in Mexico City.

My life has been incredible. I don't believe a word of it.

—Katherine Anne Porter

Porter arrived at the height of the country's decade-old revolution and, while researching her articles and consorting with politicians and revolutionaries of every stripe, developed her lifelong fascination with Mexico, especially its suffering peasant population. She took careful note of everything she heard in voluminous journals that would for years afterward provide material for such short stories as "Virgin Violetta" and "Flowering Judas," and for her first published short story, "Maria Concepción," which appeared in *Century Magazine* in 1922. "Virgin Violetta" was printed in the same magazine in the winter of 1924, after her return from a second Mexican trip where she had organized an exhibition of Mexican artifacts that was refused entry to the United States for being "socialist political propaganda." "Virgin Violetta" was written at an artists' colony in rural Connecticut, where Porter met a gracious young Englishman named Ernest Stock. They were married early in 1925, but Katherine's quickly adopted moniker for her new husband, "Deadly Ernest," was an indication of the union's future. She left Stock after only a few months to return to New York, where she took rooms in a boarding house on the southern edge of the Village.

Among the boarding house's other residents were ***Dorothy Day**, who would abandon her socialist-themed fiction to become a dedicated social worker for the Catholic Church, and Southern writers Alan Tate, ***Caroline Gordon**, and Robert Penn Warren. Warren was one of the founders of the now venerable *Southern Review*, in which Tate's poetry was first published and which would later publish several of Porter's short stories. It was Warren who urged Porter to pay more attention to her Southern upbringing as a source for her work—advice Katherine quickly took to heart to produce stories such as "The Jilting of Granny Weatherall," drawn from her memories of Aunt Cat. "Katherine Anne Porter's fiction remains, perhaps, the best source of biography in the deepest sense," Warren would later write. Energized by Warren's encouragement, Porter once again felt herself on the threshold of a new phase of her career and a new chapter in her own life. "It is my firm belief that all our lives, we are preparing to be somebody or something, even if we don't do it consciously," she said.

By the late 1920s, Porter herself had grown into the Southern aristocrat that Kitty Crawford had believed her to be 13 years earlier. She was described by an admirer in 1928 as "a small woman, [who] bore herself with great poise, was low-voiced, soft-spoken, and full of old-fashioned airs and graces." Porter had established enough of a reputation by then that a collection of her fiction seemed warranted. "For some years she has been one of the brightest promises of the surrounding scene," a writer friend wrote to the publisher Harcourt, Brace. "Her short stories have really caused underground admiration and murmur." *Flowering Judas* (later titled *Flowering Judas and Other Stories*), the first of three collections to be published in her lifetime, duly appeared in 1930. By then, Porter had won a Guggenheim fellowship and had boarded a ship for Germany, setting sail from Vera Cruz with a collection of South American exiles and German nationals and heading to a continent already growing dark from the approaching storm of World War II. During the crossing in 1929, Porter took her usual careful notes of the people around her, although she did not yet know that these were the beginnings of the novel that would, over 30 years later, bring her world fame.

At the beginning of the 1920s, it had been revolution that had greeted her in Mexico. Now, ten years later, it was German nationalism after the humiliations of World War I that awaited her arrival in Bremen. Germans were being drawn in great numbers to the National Socialist Party and its charismatic leader, Adolf Hitler. "He's nothing but a common criminal," Porter wrote home to the United States in 1930. "That man, unless he's checked right now, will cause serious damage to the country and all over Europe." She remained in Europe for six months, during which she married for the third time. Eugene Pressly, an amateur writer and a secretary for an international charitable organization, had made the crossing with her from Mexico. The two were married on March 18, 1930, in Paris. Her European sojourn

Katherine Anne Porter

proved to be another epiphany in her rapidly expanding life story. "I didn't begin to feel contemporary, or as if I had come to my proper term in life, until just a few years ago," she wrote in 1934, after she had been back in America for three years. "I think after I went to Europe . . . I got a perspective and somehow without a struggle my points of view fell into clear focus." That focus produced a burst of short stories like "The Leaning Tower" which were, she claimed, written in one sitting and required only minor revisions. Most important, she made serious progress on her novel about a group of passengers on a cruise ship bound from South America to Germany. The book, she said, "took the bit in its teeth, galloped past the 21,000 word mark" during 1935 and 1936—the years her marriage to Pressly ended. A fourth marriage in April 1938—to a business manager for *The Southern Review* named Albert Erskine—was even shorter, the two separating after only two years. The only man she ever really loved, Porter once claimed, was a young soldier named Charles Shannon with whom she had had a brief affair in Washington during the early 1940s, before Shannon's wife traveled from Alabama to join him. "I thought then, and still do think, that if my man was anywhere to be found, he was the one," she later said.

By the time her second short-story collection (*The Learning Tree and Other Stories*) was published in 1943, Porter had been lured to Hollywood by a $1,500-per-week salary as a scriptwriter for MGM which, like all the major studios, was trying to broaden the appeal of its scripts by getting respected writers to work on them. Porter was surprised to find that underneath the glamour, the film world was depressingly dull. "The whole territory is crawling with babies," she complained, calling Hollywood "the most philoprogenitive place I ever saw." She lasted only three months before asking to be released from her contract, fleeing back East just as World War II ended with the D-Day invasion of 1944. Newspapers were flooded with the shocking photographs taken by Allied troops as they liberated Germany's concentration camps. While governments around the world warned against backlashes directed at Germans who had fled Hitler's regime, Porter had no sympathy. "This time I hope [the Germans] really pay for their periodic binge of blood drinking," she angrily wrote. "And I hope . . . that all the fake refugees and German sympathizers will be sent out of this country. They poison the air for the rest of us." The force of her revulsion propelled her into a renewed assault on her novel, which she had decided to call *Ship of Fools*.

She worked furiously on the book, with its huge cast of characters, intersecting plot lines and grand themes, for the next decade, while gaining a fearsome reputation on several college campuses as a merciless Muse in courses on American fiction and short-story writing, and as an acerbic reviewer of American literature and society. She called Saul Bellow "an awful writer" in print because of "all that pity, pity, pity me. Ugh!" She openly questioned the wisdom of the Nobel Prize committee for awarding William Faulkner its 1949 medal for contributions to literature, criticizing him for "a moral and human confusion" and for sympathizing with what she saw as his ethically dubious characters. Similarly, she took books like Evelyn Waugh's *Brideshead Revisited* and Malcolm Lowry's *Under the Volcano* to task for glorifying "morally reprehensible" characters. She reported after a tour of the Midwest that many Midwesterners who "thought they were good democratic Republicans" were "Nazis or Fascists (same thing, really. One speaks German, the other Italian.)." With the stiff, principled backbone she had inherited from her Aunt Cat, it was not surprising that she described *Ship of Fools* to a friend as being "about the constant, endless collusion between good and evil. I believe that human beings are capable of total evil, but no one has ever been totally good. And this gives the edge to evil. I offer no solution," she said. "I just want to show the principle at work and why none of us has any real alibi in the world."

She recorded June 15, 1961, in her journal as the date she finished the final draft of *Ship of Fools*. The book appeared in print on April 1, 1962, although its reception was not as universally positive as Katherine had hoped. While *The New Yorker* cited the book for "the clarity of its viewpoint" and *The New York Times* told its readers that the long-awaited book was so good it was worth waiting another ten years for, others took Katherine to task for creating caricatures rather than characters and for attempting to cram a whole life's worth of political and social philosophy into a single book. Not a few critics noticed the stereotypical nature of her portrayal of the ship's only Jewish passenger, Julius Lowenthal. Lowenthal was, one critic complained, "a caricature of Jewish vulgarity" while even one of Katherine's closest friends wrote that "she poses her one Jew as the least appetizing of mortals." It would not be the only time Katherine would be charged with anti-Semitism, and she herself indicated her feelings in a marginal note scribbled in a book called *Portrait of a Jew* found among her collection after her death. "Everybody except the Jews knows the Jews are not chosen but are a lot of rough, arrogant, stupid, pretentious people, and then what?" she had written.

The publication of *Ship of Fools* marked another turning point in her life, for after its appearance she suffered a nervous breakdown, grew increasingly querulous and opinionated, and wrote and spoke more "incendiary things," as one journalist described them. Asked her opinion of the desegregation of the nation's schools ordered by the Supreme Court in 1954, Katherine replied that "the downtrodden minorities are organized into tight little cabals to run the country so that we will become the downtrodden vast majority if we don't look out." As she advanced in years and her health grew weaker, she reminisced in public about the "wonderful old slaves" of her childhood and otherwise offended African-Americans to such an extent that she received a letter of protest from the NAACP. She flew into a rage when other writers criticized her, especially when one writer dared to reveal that her given name was not Katherine. The profitable sale of film

From the movie Ship of Fools, *starring Lee Marvin and Vivien Leigh.*

rights to *Ship of Fools* and the subsequent picture directed by Stanley Kramer helped her mood; as did the Pulitzer Prize and the prestigious Gold Medal of the National Institute of Arts and Letters for 1965's *The Collected Stories*, the first time all of her short stories had been collected in one volume. But her perverse nature surfaced again when she decided against leaving her journals and private papers to the University of Texas because it had failed to name a building after her. Instead, she left them to the University of Maryland, which had wisely given her an honorary doctorate in 1966 after Katherine had settled permanently in nearby Washington. Her last published work was *The Never-Ending Wrong*, a memoir of the Sacco-Vanzetti case. (In the summer of 1927, she had journeyed to Boston to join many of her friends who were involved in the protest movement surrounding the execution of Nicola Sacco and Bartolomeo Vanzetti.) By the time the book appeared in the late 1970s, a stroke had left Porter's mental and physical health so precarious that her estate was given over to guardians, and she was admitted to a nursing home in Silver Spring, Maryland. She died there on September 18, 1980.

Given the almost frightening power of her writing, and the clear, unadorned treatment of her grand theme of good and evil, it is hardly surprising that her stories are still endlessly anthologized and are taught to thousands of literature students every year. It would certainly not surprise Porter. "I believe, I hope, I shall have my place in the story of American literature," she had written in 1956, when she was still hard at work on *Ship of Fools*. "Even at this point, how could they write it and leave me out?"

SOURCES AND SUGGESTED READING:

Bloom, Harold, ed. *Katherine Anne Porter, Modern Critical Views Series.* Philadelphia, PA: Chelsea House, 1986.

Carr, Virginia Spencer. *Flowering Judas: A Casebook.* Brunswick, NJ: Rutgers University Press, 1993.

DeMouy, Jane. *Katherine Anne Porter's Women: The Eye of Her Fiction.* Austin, TX: University of Texas Press, 1983.

Givner, Joan, ed. *Katherine Anne Porter: Conversations.* Jackson, MS: University Press of Mississippi, 1987.

———. *Katherine Anne Porter: A Life.* NY: Simon & Schuster, 1982.
Gordon, Caroline. "Katherine Anne Porter and the ICM," in *Harper's.* Vol. 229. November 1964, pp. 146–148.
Hendrick, Willene and George. *Katherine Anne Porter.* Rev. ed. Boston, MA: Twayne, 1988.
Krishnamurthi, M.G. *Katherine Anne Porter: A Study.* Mysore, India: Rao & Raghavan, 1971.
Lopez, Enrique Hank. *Conversations with Katherine Anne Porter: Refugee from Indian Creek.* Boston, MA: Little, Brown, 1981.
Machann, Clinton, and William Bedford Clark. *Katherine Anne Porter and Texas: An Uneasy Relationship.* College Station, TX: Texas A&M University Press, 1990.
Schwartz, Edward. *Katherine Anne Porter: A Critical Bibliography.* NY: New York Public Library, 1953.
Stout, Janis P. *Katherine Anne Porter: A Sense of the Times.* University of Virginia Press, 1995.
Thompson, Barbara. "The Art of Fiction: Katherine Anne Porter, An Interview," in *Paris Review.* No. 29. Winter–Spring 1963, pp. 87–114.
Unrue, Darlene Harbour. *Truth and Vision in Katherine Anne Porter's Fiction.* Athens, GA: University of Georgia Press, 1985.
Wescott, Glenway. "Katherine Anne Porter Personally," in his *Images of Truth.* NY: Harper & Row, 1962, pp. 25–58.
West, Ray B., Jr. *Katherine Anne Porter.* Minneapolis, MN: University of Minnesota Press, 1963.
Wilson, Edmund. "Katherine Anne Porter," in *The New Yorker.* Vol. 20. September 30, 1944, pp. 64–66.

RELATED MEDIA:

Ship of Fools (149 min. film), starring ***Vivien Leigh**, Oskar Werner, ***Simone Signoret**, Jose Ferrer, and Lee Marvin, directed by Stanley Kramer, 1965.

COLLECTIONS:

The Katherine Anne Porter Room at the McKeldin Library, University of Maryland, is the chief repository of Porter material, containing most of her manuscripts, papers, correspondence, personal library, books, phonograph records, photographs, furniture, and assorted memorabilia; the Beinecke Rare Book and Manuscript Library of Yale University is the second largest repository of Porter material.

Norman Powers,
writer-producer, Chelsea Lane Productions,
New York, New York

Porter, Mary (d. 1765)

English actress. *Birth date unknown; died on February 24, 1765.*

Mary Porter was brought to the attention of actor-playwright Thomas Betterton by actress ***Elizabeth Barry**, who had seen her play the Fairy Queen at Bartholomew Fair. With Betterton's company, Porter made her first appearance in 1709; the play was a tragedy, in which she specialized, but she would also be seen in a long string of comedies. After her friends Elizabeth Barry, ***Anne Bracegirdle** and ***Anne Oldfield** retired from the stage, Porter was left its undisputed queen.

Porter, Sarah (1813–1900)

American educator and founder of Miss Porter's School for Girls. *Born Sarah Porter on August 16, 1813, in Farmington, Connecticut; died on February 17, 1900, in Farmington; daughter of Noah Porter (a pastor) and Mehetabel Meigs Porter; sister of Noah Porter (1811–1892, a Congregational cleric and president of Yale) and Samuel Porter (a teacher of the deaf); educated at Farmington Academy, and under the informal tutelage of several Yale professors in New Haven, Connecticut; never married; no children.*

Taught at schools in Springfield, Massachusetts, Philadelphia, and Buffalo, New York, in the first decade after completing her studies in New Haven; founded Miss Porter's School (1843) and remained active there as a teacher and administrator until her death (1900).

Sarah Porter was born on August 16, 1813, in Farmington, Connecticut, a town that had been settled by her paternal ancestor Robert Porter in the mid-17th century. She was the first daughter among seven children of **Mehetabel Meigs Porter** and Noah Porter, a graduate of Yale who was the pastor of Farmington Congregational Church. Fairly enlightened for their time about the importance of education, the Porters encouraged all of their children to do everything they could to develop intellectually. To that end, Sarah's father managed to enroll her in the Farmington Academy, which previously had been open only to boys. She excelled in her studies there and at age 16 she was asked to become an assistant teacher.

Sarah Porter was especially close with her older brother Noah (later the 11th president of Yale), and at age 19 she moved to New Haven to be nearer to him. There she lived in the home of a Yale professor and studied for about a year with lexicographer Ethan Allen Andrews and other Yale professors who instructed women in the classics "after hours." Armed with her unofficial "Yale education," Porter spent the next decade teaching in schools throughout the northeastern United States, including ones in Buffalo, Philadelphia, and Springfield, Massachusetts. Her first attempt to set up a school of her own came in 1841, when she returned to Farmington and took on 15 students. This venture encountered some philosophical and financial obstacles, however, and the school was soon dissolved.

In 1843, at age 30, Porter once again returned to Farmington to try to resurrect her dream of operating her own school, encouraged to do so by a number of families in town who were anxious to see their daughters educated. She opened a day school on the upper level of what she described as an "old stone store." Shortly thereafter, the school expanded, adding living quarters for some of its students when Porter rented a few rooms in a private home in Farmington. Thus was established Miss Porter's School for Girls, which in time grew into one of the most famous girls' boarding schools in the world. Wealthy, well-connected families from throughout the United States and abroad sent their daughters to Miss Porter's to be educated. The school's first class consisted of 25 students, nine of whom were boarders.

The school's curriculum included physics, chemistry, geometry, political science, French, German, Latin, history, logic, art, music, and literature. Extracurricular activities included mandatory Bible study on Sundays and lectures by prominent speakers. The students' physical activities included tennis, horseback riding, and rowing. Porter organized frequent outdoor excursions, such as picnics and nature hikes, to acquaint students with her beloved Farmington and the surrounding countryside. In 1849, Porter rented a schoolhouse on Mountain Road that was large enough to accommodate 25 students, and over the next several decades the school's facilities were expanded to encompass more than 30 buildings in the heart of Farmington.

Porter was not a proponent of women's suffrage. She was, however, a strong supporter of the need to reform divorce and property laws, which she believed had severely disadvantaged many women. She also founded the Farmington Lodge Society to offer a summer vacation in Farmington to "tired and overworked" young women from New York City.

Students at Miss Porter's School needed only to look to Porter herself for an example of tireless intellectual pursuit. Throughout her life, she expressed a keen interest in questions of philosophy, and she particularly enjoyed reading and discussing German literature. While already at an advanced age, she began learning Greek and Hebrew. Academics from near and far made pilgrimages to Farmington to exchange views with Porter, who remained the central figure in the school's operation until shortly before her death. When she was not teaching in the classroom or managing the affairs of the school as a whole, she might well be found in the student dining room expounding on whatever academic subject struck her fancy. She prided herself on her accessibility to the school's students and their parents. Perhaps reflecting the ethos of the New England Congregational community in which she was raised, Porter expected that most of her pupils would marry and spend their lives as homemakers rather than moving into careers in the outside world. During her lifetime, the school could best be described as a finishing school with the highest of academic standards, but never was it intended that the school groom its students for college. Nevertheless, so important to Porter was the quality of the education offered at her school that she went to great lengths to find the finest teachers available. She obtained the services of a French native to assist in the teaching of modern languages and hired a trained science teacher shortly after the introduction of science into American college curricula. Among the school's graduates in the late 19th century were *__Alice Hamilton__ and her sister *__Edith Hamilton__, *__Eleanor Medill Patterson__, *__Ruth Hanna McCormick__, and __Theodate Pope Riddle__. (Nearly half a century later, *__Jacqueline Kennedy__ became a graduate.)

Sarah Porter died in 1900, age 86, in Farmington and was buried at Riverside Cemetery. Following her death, the direction of the school she had founded was turned over to her nephew, Robert Porter Keep, Sr., and later to his widow, **Elizabeth Vashti Hale Keep**. When Elizabeth Keep succumbed to influenza during the pandemic of 1917, her son and daughter-in-law took over the direction of the school. Porter family control ended with their retirement in 1943, at which time the school was incorporated. Miss Porter's School continues to thrive as a highly regarded (and highly expensive) boarding and day school for girls, with some 300 students at the beginning of the 21st century.

SOURCES:

James, Edward T., ed. *Notable American Women, 1607–1950*. Cambridge, MA: The Belknap Press of Harvard University, 1971.

Don Amerman,
freelance writer, Saylorsburg, Pennsylvania

Porter, Sylvia (1913–1991)

American financial writer who raised the standards in reporting on finance for the general public. *Name variations: S.F. Porter; Sylvia Field Porter. Born Sylvia Field Feldman on June 18, 1913, in Patchogue, Long Island, New York; died of complications from emphysema on June 5, 1991, in Pound Ridge, New York; daughter of Louis Feldman (a doctor) and Rose (Maisel) Feldman; attended Hunter College, B.A. (magna cum laude), 1932; graduate work in economics at New York University's School of Business Administration; married Reed R. Porter (a banker), in 1931* *(divorced); married G. Summer Collins, in 1943 (died January 1977); married James F. Fox, in 1979; children: Cris Sarah; (stepson) Summer Campbell Collins.*

Awards: National Headliner's Club medal for "best financial and business reporting of 1942" (1943); award from New York Newspaper Women's Club for "best column written by a woman in any field" (1945, 1947, 1951, 1962); named one of 25 outstanding women in America, First Assembly of American Women of Achievement (1951); medallion from the General Federation of Women's Clubs for "outstanding achievement in the field of finance" (1960); named outstanding woman of the year in the field of journalism by Who's Who of American Women *(1960); Meritorious Public Service Certificate, Internal Revenue Service (1964); Spirit of Achievement Award, Albert Einstein College of Medicine (1966); named free enterprise writer of the year, National Management Association (1966); Top Hat Award, National Federation of Business and Professional Women's Clubs (1967); Hunter College Centennial Medal for noteworthy achievement (1970); named woman of the year in communications, Advertising Club of New York (1970); named one of America's 75 most important women,* Ladies' Home Journal *(1971); elected to the Hall of Fame, Alumni Association of Hunter College (1973); Woman of the Year 1975 award,* Ladies' Home Journal*; awards and honorary degrees from numerous colleges.*

Selected writings: How to Make Money in Government Bonds *(1939);* If War Comes to the American Home: How to Prepare for the Inevitable Adjustment *(1941);* The Nazi Chemical Trust in the United States *(1942); (with Jacob Kay Lasser)* How to Live Within Your Income *(1948); (with Lasser)* Money and You *(1949);* How to Get More for Your Money *(1961); (with Lasser)* Managing Your Money *(1953, rev. ed., 1963);* Sylvia Porter's Money Book: How to Earn It, Spend It, Invest It, Borrow It, and Use It to Better Your Life *(1975);* Sylvia Porter's Your Finances in the 1990s *(1990);* Planning Your Retirement. *Also author of* Sylvia Porter's Income Tax Guide, *published annually from 1961. Contributing editor,* Ladies' Home Journal*; author of financial column, beginning in 1938 under the title "Financial Post Marks," later syndicated to over 400 newspapers across the country and changed to "S.F. Porter Says" and later to "Sylvia Porter."*

Through her syndicated financial columns and numerous books, Sylvia Porter was able to make the most complex economic concepts accessible to the average reader with her straightforward and occasionally amusing style. When she first began writing a financial column for the *New York Post* in 1935, she used the byline "S.F. Porter" to prevent gender bias in what had been, up to that time, a male-dominated field.

Sylvia Field Feldman was born on June 18, 1913, in Patchogue, Long Island, New York, the daughter of Louis Feldman, a doctor, and **Rose Maisel Feldman**. As a young girl, Sylvia longed to be a poet or writer, and when she first entered Hunter College she studied English literature and history. After Louis Feldman died, leaving behind a "trunkful of IOUs" from his patients, and the family lost what little they had in the stock market during the Depression, Rose Feldman went to work to support her children's educations. Sylvia changed her major to economics and graduated magna cum laude in 1932, having married a banker named Reed R. Porter the year before. After graduation, she found a job as an "assistant to the president of an investment counsel house specializing in United States government bonds," said Porter. She also did some graduate study in economics at New York University's School of Business Administration.

During 1934, Porter held jobs in diverse financial organizations and began writing magazine articles. In 1935, she persuaded a "rip-roaring drunk" managing editor at the New York *Evening Post* to hire her to write a financial column three times a week. "The economics writing that was done then was all done by men and most of it was completely incomprehensible," she said. "It was all written in what I call bafflegab." She became the newspaper's regular financial writer covering Wall Street. In 1938, her column, "Financial Post Marks," went daily and was later syndicated nationwide to over 400 newspapers; in it, she exposed many questionable activities in the financial arena while also giving financial advice. Fearful of a negative reaction to a woman financial advisor, Porter wrote under the name "S.F. Porter" for quite a while. She was not able to change her byline to "Sylvia F. Porter" until her 1942 book, *If War Comes to the American Home: How to Prepare for the Inevitable Adjustment*, became a success. She often contributed to magazines, and was a contributing editor for the *Ladies' Home Journal.* She also authored many books, including *How to Make Money in Government Bonds* (1939), *How to Live Within Your Income*, with J.K. Lasser (1948), *Managing Your Money*, with Lasser (1953), *How to Get More for Your Money* (1961), and *Sylvia Porter's Money Book* (1975). Starting in 1961, she annually wrote *Sylvia Porter's Income Tax Guide.*

Porter was able to make economics understandable to the general public through her books on such subjects as investments, taxes, and personal finance, and her syndicated columns that appeared in papers around the world. In recognition of her work to end "economic illiteracy," as she called it, Porter won numerous awards throughout her career. Among the honors she received was the National Headliner's Club medal in 1943, and the New York Newspaper Women's Club award in 1945, 1947, 1957, and 1962. Sylvia Field Porter died of complications from emphysema on June 5, 1991, in Pound Ridge, New York.

SOURCES:

Contemporary Authors. Vol. 81–84. Detroit, MI: Gale Research.

Current Biography 1941. NY: H.W. Wilson, 1941.

Gilbert, Lynn, and Gaylen Moore. *Particular Passions.* NY: Clarkson N. Potter, 1981.

McHenry, Robert, ed. *Famous American Women.* NY: Dover, 1980.

Jo Anne Meginnes,
freelance writer, Brookfield, Vermont

Portia (fl. 80 BCE)

Roman patrician. *Flourished around 80 BCE: daughter of *Livia (fl. 100 BCE) and M. Portius Cato; sister of Cato the Younger; half-sister of *Servilia I and *Servilia II.*

Portia (c. 70–43 BCE)

Roman patrician. *Name variations: Porcia. Born around 70 BCE; died in 43 BCE (some sources cite 42 BCE); daughter of Marcus Porcius Cato Uticensus (Cato of Utica), known as Cato the Younger, and Atilia; married Marcus Calpurnius Bibulus (died 48 BCE); married Marcus Junius Brutus (one of the assassins of Julius Caesar); children: (first marriage) three sons, only one of whom (also named Bibulus) outlived her.*

The daughter of Marcus Porcius Cato Uticensus (Cato the Younger) and his first wife **Atilia**, Portia was born around 70 BCE and had a brother who was named after their father. Cato the Younger belonged to the Roman Optimate (conservative) faction, and as such remained an ardent opponent of any perceived threat to the political status quo in general, and of Julius Caesar in particular, throughout his life. Portia zealously embraced the political ideals of her father and seems to have had no objection to her arranged marriage with Bibulus, another lifelong adversary of Caesar. (When Bibulus and Caesar were consular colleagues in 59 BCE, Bibulus' attempt to scuttle Caesar's legislative program failed after Caesar essentially put his constitutional equal under house arrest.) Portia thus served to bind together the Optimates in sworn opposition to anything Caesarian.

When the alliance of Caesar's one-time political ally Pompey the Great and Cato's faction maneuvered Caesar into open civil war (49 BCE), both Portia's father and husband took up arms in defense of the languishing Republic. Unfortunately, neither was a particularly effective rival of Caesar's in the field: Bibulus died in 48 BCE as a result of exhaustion brought on by an unsuccessful attempt to prevent Caesar from crossing to the Balkans so as to directly engage his rivals, while Cato, besieged by a Caesarian army in the north African town of Utica, committed suicide (46 BCE) rather than be captured by his nemesis. (In fact, the memory of Cato was a much more effective obstacle to Caesar's reform package than the living Cato had ever been.)

In 45 BCE, Portia took as her second husband her cousin, Marcus Junius Brutus (they shared a common kinship in ***Livia** [fl. 100 BCE], from whose first husband Brutus was descended and from whose second husband Portia was descended). Portia seems to have had a decisive influence on her second husband (who divorced his prior wife **Claudia** in order to marry her), for although Brutus had initially been a partisan of Pompey's against Caesar in their civil war, after Pompey's defeat in 48 Caesar first pardoned Brutus, and then began to foster his political advancement. Brutus' reconversion to the Republican cause, after his marriage to Portia, pit Portia against ***Servilia II**, Brutus' mother (but as Caesar's ex-mistress, also a pro-Caesarian). In the struggle for Brutus' political soul, Portia won. When in 44 BCE Brutus joined the conspiracy to murder Caesar (on March 15), Portia insisted on being told of the assassination plot prior to the fact. Before doing so, she made a demonstration of her toughness to prove that she could be trusted never to divulge Brutus' most intimate secrets. She did this by taking a knife and making a deep cut in her thigh. Bearing the pain of the gash and the subsequent infection without a whimper, Portia thereby exhibited to Brutus her endurance in the face of suffering and won his complete confidence.

After the assassination of Caesar, Portia was a vocal presence at the conference of Republicans which met at Antium (in June) as they attempted to stem their rapid decline in popularity among the masses. The conference also met to plan a defense against the growing military threat being organized by Caesar's still faithful followers (including especially the "Second Triumvirate," Marcus Antony, Lepidus and Octavian). When Brutus sailed east in order to organize the defense of his interests, Portia returned to Rome where, in increasing despair, she fell ill in the summer of 43 BCE. Beset by the deteriorating position of Brutus and his allies and suffering physically, Portia decided to follow in the footsteps of her father by committing suicide. This she did either by inhaling the poisonous fumes wafting from a brazier, or (more dramatically) by swallowing live coals.

Portia was affectionate by nature (at least with those who counted as her friends) and extremely proud of her family. With Bibulus, she had three sons, only one of whom (also named Bibulus) outlived her. This Bibulus joined his stepfather Brutus in the war against the Second Triumvirate, for which he was proscribed. After Brutus' defeat in the battle of Philippi, however, Antony offered the younger Bibulus a rapprochement, enabling him to recover his citizenship rights. Although Bibulus thereafter wrote a fond memoir of Brutus, he nevertheless abandoned the Republican cause so dear to Portia and her spouses by collaborating with the Triumvirs until his death about 32 BCE.

William S. Greenwalt,
Associate Professor of Classical History, Santa Clara University, Santa Clara, California

Portinari, Beatrice (c. 1265–1290).

See Beatrice Portinari.

Portland, countess of.

See Villiers, Anne (d. 1688).

Port Royal des Champs, Abbesses of

French nuns whose principled refusal to submit to dilutions in the reform of their order led to their persecution on suspicion of fomenting rebellion against the Roman Catholic Church and King Louis XIV.

Arnauld, Jacqueline Marie, known as Mère Angélique (1591–1661). Abbess of Port Royal des Champs, who believed she was attempting nothing more than to follow the original monastic rule as strictly as possible, when her convent provoked the suspicions of the king and was subject to intense persecution. *Name variations: Angélique-Marie de Sainte-Magdeleine Arnauld, Mère Angélique, Mère Marie Angélique. Born Jacqueline Marie Arnauld on September 8, 1591; died on August 6, 1661; second of six daughters of Antoine Arnauld (a lawyer) and Catherine Marion Arnauld (d. 1641; daughter of Simon Marion, avocat general at the Parlement of Paris).*

Appointed abbess of Port Royal des Champs at age eight (1599) and ordained a nun the following year (1600); intent upon returning the convent to the strict rule of St. Benedict, imposed sharing of all property, frequent prayer, and long periods of complete silence upon the community; her mother and all her sisters, as well as many male relatives, were eventually to seek the religious life at Port Royal, which became an influential center of spirituality and education; the convent began to incur the suspicion of royal authorities because of its apparent sympathies with the reformist ideas of Cornelius Jansen (1638); an important place of refuge during the civil wars (1648–49, 1652), Port Royal came under increasing scrutiny, its schools were closed and many of its supporters were in hiding when Jacqueline Marie Arnauld (Mère Angélique) died in 1661.

Arnauld, Jeanne Catherine, known as Mère Agnès (1593–1671). Younger sister of Jacqueline, who was appointed abbess of St. Cyr at age six, but soon joined her sister at Port Royal, serving as prior and abbess there and bravely bearing the full brunt of royal persecution after Jacqueline's death. *Name variations: Jeanne Catherine de Sainte Agnès Arnauld, Agnès de Saint-Paul Arnauld, Mère Agnès, Mère Catherine Agnès de Saint Paul. Born Jeanne Catherine Arnauld in 1593; died of inflammation of the lungs on February 19, 1671; third daughter of Antoine Arnauld (a lawyer) and Catherine Marion Arnauld (d. 1641); younger sister of Jacqueline Marie Arnauld (Mère Angélique).*

As a child, appointed abbess of St. Cyr but soon joined her sister at Port Royal des Champs and spent most of her life either there or in the Paris convent; often alternated with her sister in holding the office of abbess of Port Royal, though reluctant to assume the highest office; also served as abbess of Tard, for six years; held out bravely against the persecution which enveloped Port Royal, at first signing and then retracting agreement to a formulary which was imposed upon the nuns; more inclined to mystical forms of devotion than her more practical sister, wrote a number of devotional works and also composed the Constitutions or Rule of Port Royal.

Arnauld, Angélique, known as Mère Angelique de Saint-Jean (1624–1684). Niece and namesake of Jacqueline, who spent her life as a nun during a period which saw the height of Port Royal's power and influence and lasted into the days of its persecution and decline, keeping a faithful record of all that she experienced, including the period of her imprisonment for

Mère Agnès (left), praying for a cure for one of her nuns.

resisting royal authority. *Name variations: Angélique de Saint-Jean Arnauld D'Andilly, Mère Angélique de Saint-Jean. Born Angélique Arnauld in 1624; died on January 29, 1684; niece of Jacqueline Marie Arnauld (Mère Angélique) and Jeanne Catherine Arnauld (Mère Agnès); one of ten children of their eldest brother Robert Arnauld (a successful lawyer who later became a hermit at Port Royal) and* ***Catherine de la Boderie*** *(who died when Angélique was only 13).*

Was present at the deaths of both her abbess aunts and recorded both in moving descriptions, together with insightful summaries of their characters; is known as the historian of Port Royal for composing the three-volume account Memoires pour Servir a l'Histoire de Port Royal *as well as the* Portrait de la Mère Catherine Agnès; *more intellectually gifted than either of her abbess aunts, worked with Agnès to compose the order's Constitutions and, in Port Royal's time of greatest trial, worked with Agnès to produce the* Advice given to the nuns of Port Royal on their conduct (la conduit qu'elles devraient garder) in case of a change in the government of the house; *twice elected abbess of Port Royal.*

In October 1709, the Sun King, Louis XIV, the most powerful ruler France had ever known, decreed that the Abbey of Port Royal des Champs be demolished. While the 22 aged nuns still living there were transferred to other houses, the remains of all nine of the Arnaulds who had been buried in the grounds were exhumed and transferred to the family estate. The Arnauld women, who had made Port Royal such a center of spirituality that it was seen as a threat to the authority of Europe's preeminent monarch, were no longer alive to defend it.

The dramatic story of Port Royal has an unlikely beginning; it can be traced from the selection of a reluctant eight-year-old child to assume the office of joint abbess of the old Cistercian convent, some 20 miles west of Paris. Jacqueline Marie, the second daughter and third child of Antoine Arnauld and Catherine Marion Arnauld, was a favorite of her prosperous and influential maternal grandfather. Her parents had married young—her mother was only 12—and they had 20 children, ten of whom survived into adulthood.

While the oldest daughter was reserved for marriage, grandfather Marion undertook to provide for the next two girls by placing them in convents, obtaining, according to the common practice of the time, royal permission for them to be appointed abbesses, Jacqueline at Port Royal and her younger sister, Jeanne Catherine Agnès, at St. Cyr. The two children, who were not expected to assume the responsibilities of office immediately, spent the next three years at St. Cyr, being educated and playing together, much in the way that modern children are brought up at a boarding school. They were clothed as novices in 1599 and 1600 respectively, and Jacqueline was confirmed and solemnly professed as a religious in 1600, at age nine, taking the name of Angélique, by which she was known thenceforth.

Accounts of Mère Angélique's life agree that she was a somewhat reluctant nun; unlike Jeanne Catherine (who became known as Mère Agnès), Angélique seems to have envied the worldly pleasures which awaited her elder sister, but she accepted her grandfather's arrangements for her, informing him that if she were to become an abbess she would "make my nuns do their duty." Later in life she wrote that: "Once I had taken my vows when I was nine, I could never get it out of my head that I was obliged in conscience to have no other spouse than Jesus Christ.... But in spite of this I did not live like a true religious, for I was not converted until I was seventeen."

[The Abbesses of Port Royal were] pure as angels and as proud as Lucifer.

—Hardouin de Beaumont de Péréfixe, archbishop of Paris

Angélique was professed as Port Royal's abbess in 1602, and took formal charge the following year, upon the death of her elderly predecessor. Her mother and sisters visited her frequently, but the high-spirited young woman seems to have keenly felt the confinement of her new existence. According to one of the historians of Port Royal, the house was, at that time, preeminently "a home of peace and quiet. Offices were said more or less punctually, and 'convenable' amusements, chiefly games of cards and walks abroad, filled up the calm, uneventful days."

In 1607, the young abbess became seriously ill and was taken home to Paris by her parents. The excitement of the bustling capital seems to have quickly restored her spirits and it was perhaps then that Angélique obtained the corset which, so she reveals in her *Relation,* she wore for some time, in the attempt to improve her figure. While she was still weak from her illness, her father, fearing that she was not yet reconciled to the religious life, insisted that she sign a paper without reading it. Angélique discovered only later that she had signed a renewal of her religious vows. In December 1607, she returned to Port Royal, taking with her one of her little sisters, **Marie Claire Arnauld**, aged eight, to join the community.

It was during Lent in 1608 that Angélique had the experience which she later referred to as her "conversion." First, she found herself moved by reading a book of meditations which had been left at the abbey by a visiting monk. Shortly afterwards, another monk came to preach and Angélique was overwhelmed. At age 17, she could at last see the path before her; she decided to reform her abbey, to turn it from its comfort and complacency back to its original spiritual dedication and zeal. But her father, who had resorted to subterfuge to keep Angélique in the religious life, was not pleased to see her taking her profession with sudden and inconvenient seriousness. Having carried her off to his country estate, he made her promise to reconsider her plans for a more austere way of life.

Torn between her newly awakened conscience and her customary obedience to her father, Angélique returned to Port Royal where her sister Mère Agnès (Jeanne Catherine), unhappy as abbess at St. Cyr, joined her. Another sermon on All Saints Day convinced the sisters that the path of reform was the correct one to emulate; following the sermon, Angélique was told, prophetically, that she might become one of the blessed who are persecuted for the sake of righteousness and from that day she had no doubts. On March 21, 1609, the convent Chapter accepted the fundamental changes their abbess proposed: they would henceforth live a life in which all things would be held in common and would take vows of absolute poverty. By Easter of the same year, Mère Angélique restored enclosure, for the rule specified absolute withdrawal from the world and she was convinced that true spirituality could not be revived without it. But the Arnauld family had long regarded Port Royal as its own personal property and in September, despite Angélique's prior warnings, a large family party came to Port Royal, determined to enter. Led by her father, the group tried prayers, pleading, and, finally, threats. The abbess held fast, although she later revealed that her heart was breaking with emotion. This day, September 25, 1609, which is called *Journée du Guichet* (Day of the Convent Wicket), marks the real coming of age of Angélique and the firm beginning of a new era at Port Royal.

As a further sign of her new regime, the abbess had to regularize her position, for the pope had been misinformed in 1602 that she was 17 rather than 11. Pope Paul V sent new letters of appointment in 1609 and Angélique made a second profession of faith in 1610, an act which seems to have reinforced her determination to return to the full, original vigor of St. Benedict of Nursia's monastic rule. Life at Port Royal, now stripped to its essentials, consisted of poverty, fasting, reciting the Holy Office, prayer and meditation. In this reformed regime, she was supported by her sisters Agnès and Marie-Claire and, from 1616 onwards, by a third sister, **Anne Eugénie Arnauld**.

Until the age of 19, Anne had demonstrated no signs of a religious vocation; she read romances and loved the excitement of the French capital and the court. However, during a serious illness, she vowed to devote herself to God, and on her recovery she experienced mystical visions which convinced her that she was being called to the religious life. Her father was less than pleased to see her depart for Port Royal; he had not intended to have all his daughters cloistered there. Angélique, however, received her warmly, although she herself was somewhat distrustful of visions and religious ecstasy; Agnès was much more in sympathy with Anne regarding these aspects. For Angélique, the sole legitimate devotional state consisted of a "certain silence of the heart before God."

In 1618, Angélique was called to the Abbey of Maubuisson to reform that house, leaving Port Royal in Agnès' charge. Angélique's task was a difficult one as the sisters of Maubuisson were worldly and stubbornly set in their ways. The five years which she was to spend there were not happy ones; the previous abbess had to be ejected by force and her replacement was not always grateful for Angélique's guidance. She returned to Port Royal for brief visits; once, in 1620, for the installation of the reluctant Agnès as joint abbess. The few joyful passages during this trying time away from Port Royal were her meetings with St. Francis de Sâles in 1619. A gentle, kindly reformer, de Sâles might well have had a moderating influence on Angélique had he not died in 1623. When she finally settled on a spiritual director who seemed to her to have many of the qualities of de Sâles, Angélique was to find more turmoil than tranquility.

Angélique finally left Maubuisson in March 1623, taking with her 30 nuns whom she had accepted without dowries to support them and who were thus unwelcome at Maubuisson. Her sisters at Port Royal raised no objection to the overcrowded conditions and increasing financial strain which resulted, but the situation quickly became impossible. The convent was never a healthy location, surrounded by marshes and damp air, and 15 nuns died, many probably of malaria, in the two years which followed Angélique's return. There were other reasons also for seeking new quarters. Following the death of her husband, Angélique's mother, **Catherine Marion Arnauld**, expressed the desire to join the Port Royal community, but she was unwilling to be too far away from her eldest daughter, trapped in a loveless marriage. Assisted by her mother, Angélique found a house in Paris which they purchased in May 1625. By the end of the year, all 84 of the nuns had been moved to Port Royal de Paris from Port Royal des Champs.

With the move to Paris came a change in ecclesiastical jurisdiction; Angélique also seems to have expected greater support for her reforms from the archbishop of Paris than she was receiving from the abbot of Cîteaux—an assumption that was to prove tragically mistaken. Her main task, as she saw it, was to continue with her reforms, supported by the local church administrators and inspired and guided by a sympathetic and devout spiritual director. Angélique adopted the bishop of Langres, Sebastien Zamet, as her spiritual guide in 1625 but he seems to have lacked the rigor which she sought and, under his influence, the silence and simplicity of Port Royal des Champs were gradually replaced by a form of devotion which was more elaborate, demonstrative, and mystical. In 1627, Mère Agnès, who thought very highly of Zamet, wrote a work of devotional ecstasy, *Le Chaplet du Saint Sacrement,* which focused on the mysteries of the Blessed Sacrament. During this same period, the bishop, together with the pious ***Duchesse de Longueville** (1619–1679), designed a new order devoted to the adoration of the Blessed Sacrament.

Despite the modifications of her earlier ideas for reform, Angélique continued with her efforts to restore the original rule of St. Benedict. In 1629, she requested permission from the king to make the title of abbess elective, with elections to be held every three years. Accordingly, in 1630, both Angélique and Agnès resigned their posts and a new abbess was elected. Three years later, Angélique was sent to head the newly founded House of the Holy Sacrament, and she was there when a dispute developed over *Le Chaplet du Saint Sacrement,* a copy of which had recently surfaced and been condemned by several influential clerics. It may be said that this minor controversy was an indication of things to come; doctrinal disputes were to engulf and eventually destroy Port Royal.

Agnès, distraught at the negative responses to her work, wrote to her eldest brother, Robert (M. d'Andilly):

> I have just heard that a persecution has broken out against this monastery [The House of the Holy Sacrament] of which I am said to be the cause, on account of a little bit of writing I did six years ago, merely to express some thoughts which had come to me, without any wish either to use them or to speak of them to anyone else.

However, most theologians who read the *Chaplet* found nothing suspicious in it. A devout abbé, a friend of both Bishop Zamet and Robert d'Andilly, M. de St. Cyran, pronounced it theologically sound, as did Cyran's lifelong friend, the eminent theologian Cornelius Jansen, bishop of Ypres. The lines of doctrinal dispute were being drawn and the nuns of Port Royal were moving, inexorably, into the center.

Dissatisfied with the spiritual guidance of Bishop Zamet, and identifying in St. Cyran the spirit of St. Francis de Sâles, Angélique increasingly turned to the abbé for guidance, first at the House of Holy Sacrament and then at Port Royal in Paris. Agnès had been elected abbess of Port Royal in 1635 and the following year Angélique returned. By 1638, the convent of the Holy Sacrament was closed. All of its nuns returned to the mother house of Port Royal and in 1639 the sisters once again elected Agnès as their abbess.

Although Agnès was reluctant to discard the spiritual guidance of Bishop Zamet, her more forceful sister was soon able to convince her of the superior virtues of Abbé Cyran and, under his influence, the mystical element of Port Royal's devotional life noticeably lessened and the austere, reformed practices were restored. The change did not occur without provoking some resistance, however, and Marie Claire, the youngest but one of the Arnauld sisters, hitherto almost saintly in her devotion and obedience, proved the hardest of all to convince. Robert d'Andilly, now the male head of the Arnauld family, was brought in to help convince the stubborn one and, in February 1637, Marie made her first confession to Abbé St. Cyran. The abbé warned the young nun against the visions and ecstasies which his predecessor had encouraged; instead, he counseled penitence: "I am the doctor who must prescribe the remedy. It lies in mortification. The way is narrow; to say otherwise is to deceive."

Abbé St. Cyran has been blamed by some who have studied Port Royal for imposing on the nuns a rigid, joyless spirituality which was eventually to cause Port Royal's destruction. However, Angélique's own inclinations, since her "conversion" at age 17, had always been towards what may be called the penitential form of devotion. Those who allege that the nuns were merely innocent dupes, the unknowing victims of extremist friends within, as well as calculating enemies without, underestimate the women of Port Royal. As later events were to prove, the nuns, who had dedicated their lives to the service of God, were quite capable of understanding the theological subtleties which obsessed so many of their male contemporaries.

To appreciate why doctrinal issues, which seem to us to be of marginal interest at best, should have so consumed 17th-century Europe, it is essential to remember that little more than 100 years had passed since Martin Luther's Protestant Reformation, and its aftershocks were still being felt. Throughout Europe the question of religion was causing wars and dissention, with some countries choosing to stay Catholic and others opting for Protestantism. France, with a significant Protestant minority, had been plunged into violent civil war. Louis XIII and Louis XIV, who was to succeed him in 1643, cared more for the unity of their country than for doctrinal subtleties. However, having succeeded in keeping most of France free of Protestantism, these monarchs became less and less tolerant of religious diversity, even of forms which insisted they represented the true Roman Catholic faith. For both kings, and most particularly for Louis XIV, the doctrine of *Un roi, une loi, une foi* (one king, one law, one faith) reflected an absolutist world-view in which matters of state and matters of religion were inextricably intertwined.

On May 14, 1638, on the orders of the king's chief minister, Cardinal Richelieu, Abbé St. Cyran was arrested and imprisoned because of his "peculiar and dangerous opinions." He had dared to claim, for example, that contrition was necessary in order that the sacrament of penance be received worthily, while Richelieu, in his published catechism, had asserted that mere attrition (fear of the penalties of sin) was sufficient. St. Cyran was kept captive, without any formal charges being laid against him, for four years. Also in May 1638, Cornelius Jansen, who gave his name to the reforming movement with which St. Cyran and, through him, the Port Royal nuns were increasingly becoming identified, died. However, Jansen's most influential and controversial work, *The Augustinus,* was

The convent of Port Royal des Champs.

not published until 1640, and it was to be another decade before it was to have an effect upon Port Royal. St. Cyran, released two months after the death of Richelieu in December 1642, survived only until October 1643. Angélique regarded him as a martyr to the faith and was delighted to receive his hands, which her brother had obtained for her, to be kept as relics at Port Royal.

In 1642, Angélique reluctantly replaced Agnès, who had served six years as abbess, and despite, or perhaps because of, the looming threat of political censure, Port Royal entered what was possibly its most fertile and active period of reform. While two of its best-loved members were lost—Catherine Marion Arnauld died in 1641 and Marie Claire the following year—the community was expanding; **Catherine**, the eldest of the Arnauld daughters, separated from her husband for many years and now widowed, became a novice in 1640. Her eldest son, Antoine, a celebrated and eloquent advocate, caused a great stir by abandoning his distinguished legal career for the life of a *solitaire,* taking up residence as a hermit in a small house built by his mother, close to Port Royal. He was soon joined by two of his brothers, Simon (M. de Sericourt) and Isaac (M. de Saci), and then by two of his uncles.

As their numbers grew, *les solitaires* removed themselves to Port Royal des Champs where they labored to make the old buildings habitable once again, draining the swamps to lessen the risk of malaria, and between 1638 and 1653 *les messieurs* ran an influential school for boys. Following the death of his wife in 1637, Robert d'Andilly, the eldest brother of Angélique and Agnès, had sought St. Cyran's guidance and subsequently gave up his secular life to become a member of *les solitaires,* devoting himself to the care of the gardens. Soon his son Charles (M. de Luzanci) and his brother Antoine Arnauld were to swell the ranks.

Antoine, Angélique's youngest brother, known as Le Docteur, was to become the most famous, some might say infamous, male member of the Arnauld family, and his notoriety was the cause of further turmoil at Port Royal. Converted only just before his mother's death, he became a priest in 1641 and by 1643 he had produced the first "official" work to emanate from Port Royal, entitled *On Frequent Communion.* Innocuous as it may seem today, counselling nothing more than the need for a prayerful, considered approach to the taking of communion and the sincere effort to resist sin after it, the book was like the first shot sounded in a war with the Jesuits.

For the Jesuits, the sacraments were God's way of assisting sinful souls to overcome their defects and hence to refuse communion was to resist the working of God's grace. Such was the influence of the Jesuits at court, particularly with the queen mother ***Anne of Austria** (1601–1666), that an order was issued for Antoine to go to Rome to defend his work. However, the French authorities, both religious and secular, refused to allow him to appear and Arnauld was merely forced to curb his tongue and his pen for a time. Angélique counselled prayer and reading of the scriptures.

An inspection of Port Royal in 1644, following the storm over Antoine's book, revealed only piety and virtue in the house. This was also the year that Angélique's namesake and niece, **Angélique de Saint-Jean**, daughter of Robert d'Andilly, made her vows. In 1647, Mère Angélique modified the habit, adopting a bold scarlet cross on the breast of the white scapular. In weakening health, she nonetheless decided that, given the crowded conditions in the Paris house, it was time to move a contingent of the nuns back to Port Royal des Champs. In 1648, following her election as abbess of the two houses, she settled once more at Port Royal des Champs, more than 20 years after she had departed from it, leaving Agnès as prior at Paris.

Angélique may well have sensed that the old country house would provide refuge in turbulent times. During 1649, the violent civil war of the Fronde ravaged the country. Port Royal in Paris was threatened, and the nuns took refuge at Port Royal des Champs. The house also became a haven for many other religious, as well as the peasants of the area. Angélique, at her best when times were hardest, was brave, cool, and charitable throughout the ordeal. In 1651, she was elected abbess for the fourth time and the next year another sister, Anne Eugénie, died. Angélique, now over 60, felt the loss keenly. "We were six sisters," she wrote, now only "Agnès and I remain; we cannot last long." But both sisters had further trials to endure for their faith.

In January 1653, following another outbreak of the Fronde, the nuns returned to Paris. This time Port Royal des Champs was under threat and *les solitaires* were left to defend it. The nuns found the Paris house in a state of extraordinary agitation. The previous year a Jesuit priest, incensed because Antoine Arnauld's work had managed to escape official censure, had published a fiery tract called *Jansenism Confounded.* It referred to the Port Royal nuns as "foolish virgins" and "anti-sacramentarians." When the archbishop of Paris condemned the diatribe, another Jesuit entered the fray with a publication attempting to prove the theological links between Port Royal and the Protestant John Calvin and containing a fanciful account of a plot to destroy Christianity.

Soon Jansen's posthumous work, the *Augustinus*, was hauled into the dispute and five propositions, by implication drawn from this work and believed by Jansen's followers, were presented to the pope for formal condemnation. In 1653, the reluctant pope was persuaded to issue the letters of condemnation which specifically attributed the five erroneous propositions to Jansen's *Augustinus.*

When an aristocratic supporter of Port Royal was refused absolution because of his links with the "heretics" in 1655, Antoine Arnauld could keep silent no longer. He leapt to the defense of Port Royal's theology and of the works of St. Augustine's, from which it was drawn, but he was forced to go into hiding after his letter was censured. In January 1656, Blaise Pascal, whose sister ❧ **Jacqueline Pascal** was a nun at Port Royal, published the first of 16 *Letters written to a Provincial by one of his friends on the subject of the Present Disputes of the Sorbonne.* Masterpieces of high style and cogent argument, the letters had wide circulation and distilled the debate into two words, *fait* (fact) and *droit* (right). While the popes were certainly infallible in matters of dogma and morals (*droit*), he wrote, they might well be mistaken in asserting that the condemned propositions attributed to Jansen were contained in the *Augustinus* (*fait*).

Despite the best efforts of their influential friends, Port Royal's *solitaires* were ordered dispersed in 1656 and the boys in its school, among whom was the future dramatist Racine, were sent away. Angélique's letters do not devote much attention to the theological controversy; there was no need, since she was, for the most part, writing to the "converted." Instead, in a typical letter to her brother Antoine, written in February 1656, she stressed obedience to God's will:

> We must, dearest Father, give ourselves up to everything, and bear these agonies and

> heartaches which our Lord foretold to His disciples would be their portion in this world. We have not had any such up to now; on the contrary, our troubles have been sent side by side with so much comfort, so much help and even praise from friends, that they were not real troubles. I think it will not be so henceforth, and that there will be more bitterness, more sense of being forsaken, and of humiliation than in the past.

Although Angélique's tone is one of resignation, there is no suggestion of surrender.

The first of many visits and interrogations by a magistrate took place in the spring of 1656 but no evidence was found to condemn the *solitaires*. During the same period, the so-called "Miracle of the Holy Thorn" occurred at the Paris house. ***Marguerite Périer**, a niece of Pascal, had been suffering from a severely infected eye but, after the diseased area was touched with a holy relic, alleged to be a thorn from Christ's crown, she was completely cured. In a letter to ***Louise Marie de Gonzague**, queen of Poland and a former student at Port Royal, Angélique, never one to base her faith on miracles, accepted the view that "God has worked it for our conversion." The letter continues: "I quite agree with this last opinion, and I wish for our conversion, not from heresy, in which, thanks be to God, we are not, but from many imperfections, of which He will mercifully cure us." Conceding that the miracle has resulted in some relaxation of the persecution and that her brother had been allowed to return to the community, Angélique concludes that: "it is a truce permitted by God, to fit us to suffer better when it shall please Him to allow the storm to begin again."

The storm was soon to begin again. The remaining schools were closed in 1660 and, in 1661, a formula was drawn up by an assembly of the clergy which all priests and members of religious orders in France were required to sign. In April, the king, who had increasingly come to regard the Port Royalists, like the Frondeurs, as serious threats to his absolutist regime, ordered the expulsion from the Paris house of the female students and postulants and the replacement of the spiritual director. When she received the news, Angélique, now in her 70th year and in failing health, left Port Royal des Champs for the last time. She journeyed to Paris to join her sister Agnès, who had been elected abbess in December 1658. Angélique probably collaborated with Agnès in the preparation of a dignified and respectful letter, sent on May 6, 1661, "To the King, for the defence of his monastery from the latest persecution of the Jesuits." Agnès reminded the king both that the community had never received any ecclesiastical condemnation and of the recent miracle which was surely an indication of God's favor. There was no respite.

While she claimed in a letter that "we are persuaded that this visitation is a great token of God's mercy to us, and that it was absolutely needful in order that we might be purified," the strain and misery took its toll on Angélique. On May 10, 1661, after a procession in which she had herself carried a relic of the true cross, she fell ill and remained bedridden for three months. At the end of May, she dictated a long letter to the queen mother in which she affirmed the orthodoxy of her house and insisted that her nuns lived lives of silence, not controversy. Angélique died on August 6 at the age of 70. Her last moments were recorded in an intensely moving account written by her niece and namesake, Angélique de Saint-Jean, who was with her at the end. Neither her brother nor her nephew, Abbé de Saci, nor her confessor, M. Singlin, were permitted to attend the funeral. She was buried in Paris, with her heart returned to Port Royal des Champs.

Angélique de Saint-Jean remained at the Paris house after her elder aunt's death, serving as mistress of the novices under her aunt Agnès. A thorough investigation into the orthodoxy of both houses was launched, accompanied by a new demand for signatures. Mère Agnès, always somewhat in the shadow of her elder, more forceful sister, always reluctant to assume power, must have felt, in the midst of vigorous persecution, bereft indeed. With great reluctance, Agnès

Pascal, Jacqueline (1625–1661)

French nun. *Born at Clermont-Ferrand, France, on October 4, 1625; died in Paris on October 4, 1661; sister of French scientist and philosopher Blaise Pascal (1623–1662); aunt of Marguerite Périer.*

Jacqueline Pascal was a genuine child prodigy, composing verses when only eight years old, and a five-act comedy by age eleven. In 1646, under the influence of her brother Blaise Pascal, she converted to Jansenism, but he strongly objected when, at age 27, she became a nun at Port Royal (1652). It was the influence of Jacqueline, however, and the miraculous cure of their niece ***Marguerite Périer**, that brought about Blaise's final entrance into the Jansenist community at Port Royal in 1655. Jacqueline Pascal vehemently opposed the attempt to coerce the nuns to sign the formula condemning Jansenism, but was at last compelled to yield with the others. This blow, however, hastened her death, which occurred at Paris on October 4, 1661, the day of her 36th birthday.

and her nuns signed a new formula which excluded the famous distinction between *fait* and *droit* in November 1661. They insisted, however, upon inserting a clause of explanation that "in consideration of those things which are beyond our province, both as regards our sex and our religious profession, we feel that all we can do is to testify to the purity of our faith."

Their signatures, which they almost instantly regretted giving, did not win them much respite. The new archbishop of Paris, Hardouin de Beaumont de Péréfixe, was determined to win over the sisters. Anticipating new persecutions, in June 1664 Sister Angélique de Saint-Jean collaborated with Mère Agnès on the writing of a work entitled *Advice given to the nuns of Port Royal on their conduct (la conduit qu'elles devraient garder) in case of a change in the government of the house.* The work delineates the various measures which may be taken to subdue them: the introduction of strangers to administer the abbey, exile to other houses, the withdrawing of the sacraments. Against each action the nuns are given possible responses—avoidance, rendering the action ineffectual, and, finally, resistance.

On June 9, 1664, the archbishop of Paris came to get their signatures on the formula without the clause of explanation. He tried persuasion, argument, and, eventually, threats. Having been defeated in theological debates with several of the nuns, he angrily cried out: "You are more enlightened and wiser people than the Pope, than your Archbishop, than all the Religious Orders. . . . [Y]ou are very presumptuous to think yourselves more capable of judging a matter which you yourselves confess you do not comprehend." The accounts of the archbishop's debates with the sisters do not suggest any lack of comprehension even if, to placate his anger, some of the sisters may, once again, have tried to disguise their stubbornness as ignorance.

Despite the most intense pressure from the authorities, which included suspension of the administration of the sacraments, 12 of the nuns, including Agnès, Angélique de Saint-Jean, and two other nieces, still refused to sign the formula, under which they would have agreed to submit to the entire contents of the Papal Constitutions. Instead, they attempted a compromise, preparing yet another formula which read: "We, the undersigned, profess entire submission to and belief in, the faith; and on the fact (*fait*), as we can have no satisfactory knowledge about it, we can form no judgement, but we beg to remain in that respect and silence which are suitable to our condition and state."

The compromise was rejected, and the long-anticipated expulsion took place in August 1664. The Community drew up an Act of Protest and Angélique de Saint-Jean lamented in a letter to one of the convent's friends and patrons that her aunt, Mère Agnès, "after having lived for seventy-one years an angel's life, is now numbered among criminals." Refusing Robert d'Andilly's request to remove his sister and three daughters to his own estate, the archbishop ordered them separated: Agnès was transferred to the house of the Visitation Sainte-Marie with her niece, **Marie-Angélique de Sainte-Therese d'Andilly**. She was kept there for ten months during which time she was denied the sacraments, could not leave the convent, and was refused permission to write to her relatives and friends.

During her months of exile at the Convent of the Annunciation, deprived of her liberty and denied all correspondence, Angélique de Saint-Jean wrote her famous *Memoires pour servir a l'histoire de Port Royal.* In July 1665, all three of the Arnauld sisters and their abbess aunt were reunited at Port Royal des Champs, along with all but the most submissive members of the Paris house. They were still in close confinement and still denied the sacraments, but at least they suffered together. In 1669, the Peace of Church was finally agreed; following delicate negotiations and strenuous efforts by Port Royal's friends, especially Madame de Longueville, a formula had been arrived at which allowed for a clear distinction between *droit* and *fait*.

After decades of unrelenting struggle, the settlement allowed Agnès a peaceful end. It came on February 19, 1671. Her niece, the Port Royal historian Angélique de Saint-Jean, wrote that she died in such a profound peace that her death was like a miniature *tableau* of her whole life. She was buried at Port Royal des Champs. Less forceful than her elder sister and less inclined to be involved in matters of controversy, Mère Agnès was more conventionally religious: tender and tolerant, she has been said to possess an undeniable steadiness of soul *(egalité d'âme)*.

More like her aunt Angélique than Agnès, Angélique de Saint-Jean possessed an impatient temperament and a certain haughtiness of manner that made her more respected than loved, but she was a courageous fighter for the interests of Port Royal. She was elected abbess of Port Royal des Champs on August 3, 1678, and in May of the following year the king once again ordered a minute enquiry into the affairs of the abbey. Within days, the archbishop of Paris brought royal instructions for the expulsion of all the child boarders and postulants. It was rumored that the king feared a new Fronde with the reassembled *messieurs* of Port Royal at its center. The very idea seems ridiculous with Louis XIV now in the most brilliant phase of his power. It is perhaps more likely that the death in 1679 of Madame de Longueville, Port Royal's most influential friend at court, meant that the nuns were no longer considered protected.

True to the legacy of her namesake, the second Angélique wrote to her uncle, the bishop of Angers, to the archbishop of Paris and to Pope Innocent XI in the attempt to save Port Royal. Her pleas were unsuccessful. By the end of June, the house had neither boarders, postulants, nor a confessor, leaving only the 72 nuns. Cut off from new recruits, but defiantly resistant to any efforts to rejoin it with the more compliant Paris house, Port Royal des Champs began its slow death. In 1681, Angélique was reelected abbess and on January 29, 1684, a few weeks after having presided at the funeral of her beloved cousin, M. de Saci, she died at the age of 59. Sainte-Beuve, one of Port Royal's best-known historians, observed that with the death of Angélique de Saint-Jean, Port Royal lost its last grandeur.

By 1705, there were only 25 sisters remaining at Port Royal, the youngest of whom was aged 60. In 1709, tired of waiting for the few remaining nuns to die, the king ordered Port Royal des Champs to be razed to the ground. The remains of all the devout Arnauld women were exhumed and reburied on the family estate.

Although she was the first of many strong, spiritual women who were to devote their lives to Port Royal, Jacqueline Arnauld, the first Mère Angélique, may be said to have defined the community. Her complex character has received a wide variety of conflicting historical interpretations, and historians' judgment of Mère Angélique has often formed the basis of their judgment of Port Royal itself. She has been variously presented as a model of saintly Catholicism, as a proud and stubborn quasi-Calvinist, and as an ignorant woman, incapable of understanding doctrinal complexities.

The question of Angélique's, and hence Port Royal's, ignorance is the easiest to answer. As has been shown, the nuns dedicated their lives to reading, prayer, and contemplation. Their devotional works, letters, and memoirs, as well as their recurrent disputes with the authorities, reveal what acute minds were being dedicated to the service of God. It is, therefore, impossible to believe that these women did not understand what they were doing or why they were being subjected to so much suffering.

The conflicting identification of Angélique and her nuns as both models of Catholicism and as quasi-Protestants is less easily resolved. The reforms which were initiated at Port Royal des Champs were certainly a reversion to the strict practices of the early Catholic Church, but the great founder of Protestantism, Martin Luther, initially claimed only to want to reform the abuses of Catholicism, not to initiate a new religion. On the other hand, unlike Luther, these nuns were not attempting to reform the whole church, only their own souls.

It would appear that the motives behind the vigorous persecution and final dismemberment of Port Royal were more political than theological. In their repeated attempts to resist authority, the nuns could not fail to antagonize a king determined to impose absolutist rule upon the entire realm of France. As far as the authorities were concerned, their disobedience was not only unseemly in those sworn to lives of submission, it could also be dangerous. The nuns of Port Royal, led and inspired by their abbesses, placed the value of truth above that of obedience and proved themselves willing to pay any price to maintain their spiritual integrity.

SOURCES:

Beard, Charles. *Port Royal: A Contribution to the History of Religion and Literature in France.* 2 vols. London, 1861.

Dictionnaire de Biographie Francaise. Edited by J. Balteau *et al.*, Paris, 1939, *s.v.* Agnès de Saint-Paul Arnauld, vol. 1, col. 759–764; Angélique-Marie de Sainte-Magdeleine Arnauld, vol. 2, col. 1061–1066; Angélique de Saint-Jean Arnauld D'Andilly, vol. 2, col. 1066–1071.

Lowndes, M.E. *The Nuns of Port Royal: As Seen in their own Narratives.* Oxford, 1909.

Relation ecrite par la Mère Angélique Arnauld sur Port Royal. Edited by Louis Cognet. [Paris?], 1949.

Romanes, Ethel. *The Story of Port Royal.* London, 1907.

Trouncer, Margaret. *The Reluctant Abbess; Angélique Arnauld of Port-Royal (1591–1661).* New York, 1957 (this work is almost entirely fictional).

(Dr.) Kathleen Garay,
Acting Director of the Women's Studies program,
McMaster University, Hamilton, Canada

Portsmouth, duchess of.

See Kéroüalle, Louise de (1649–1734).

Portugal, queen of.

See Matilda of Maurienne (c. 1125–1157).
See Douce of Aragon (1160–1198).
See Urraca of Castile (c. 1186–1220).
See Beatrice of Castile and Leon (1242–1303).
See Mencia de Haro (d. 1270).

See Elizabeth of Portugal (1271–1336).
See Beatrice of Castile and Leon (1293–1359).
See Castro, Inez de for sidebar on Constance of Castile (1323–1345).
See Leonora Telles (c. 1350–1386).
See Philippa of Lancaster (c. 1359–1415).
See Leonora of Aragon (1405–1445).
See Isabel la Paloma (d. 1455).
See Eleanor of Portugal (1458–1525).
See Isabella of Asturias (1471–1498).
See Isabella I for sidebar on Maria of Castile (1482–1517).
See Eleanor of Portugal (1498–1558).
See Juana la Loca for sidebar on Catherine (1507–1578).
See Mary of Portugal (d. 1545).
See Luisa de Guzman (1613–1666).
See Marie Françoise of Savoy (1646–1683).
See Maria Sophia of Neuberg (1666–1699).
See Maria Antonia of Austria (1683–1754).
See Maria I of Braganza for sidebar on Maria Ana Victoria (1718–1781).
See Maria I of Braganza (1734–1816).
See Carlota Joaquina (1775–1830).
See Maria II da Gloria (1819–1853).
See Adelheid (1831–1909).
See Stephanie (1837–1859).
See Maria Pia (1847–1911).
See Marie-Amelie of Orleans (1865–1951).

Post, Emily (1872–1960)

American writer and expert on etiquette. *Name variations: Emily Price Post. Born Emily Price on October 27, 1872 (some sources cite October 3 or 30, 1873), in Baltimore, Maryland; died on September 25, 1960, in New York City; daughter of Bruce Price (an architect) and Josephine (Lee) Price; educated by governesses and at private schools in New York; married Edwin M. Post (a banker), in 1892 (divorced c. 1905); children: Edwin M., Jr. (b. 1893), Bruce Price (b. 1895).*

Published first book (1904); produced first etiquette guide (1922); was an expert on etiquette and home decoration on radio and in newspapers (from 1930s); founded the Emily Post Institute for the Study of Gracious Living (1946).

Selected writings: The Flight of the Moth *(1904);* Etiquette in Society, in Business, in Politics, and at Home *(1922, later republished as* Etiquette: The Blue Book of Social Usage*);* Parade *(1925);* How to Behave Though a Debutante *(1928);* The Personality of a House *(1930);* Children Are People *(1940); (with Edwin M. Post, Jr.)* The Emily Post Cook Book *(1949);* Motor Manners *(1959).*

Emily Post's birth in 1872 into a wealthy and socially prominent Baltimore family helped to set the stage for her later writings on etiquette. She was the only child of **Josephine Lee Price** and Bruce Price, an architect who designed Quebec City's Chateau Frontenac as well as buildings in New York's Tuxedo Park. Her maternal grandfather Washington Lee was a Pennsylvania mine owner, and her paternal grandfather William Price was an attorney and a judge. The family enjoyed many extensive and extravagant vacations to Europe and elsewhere.

When Emily was five, her father moved his business and family from Baltimore to New York City. There she was taught by a German governess and was enrolled in a finishing school, Miss Graham's. Post enjoyed an elite lifestyle, taking studies during the winter and spending her summers in Bar Harbor, Maine. She became socially prominent in her own right as she grew up and was celebrated by Ward McAllister, the social arbiter of the time, who was attracted by her good looks and grace.

Post made her social debut in 1892, and that same year married Edwin Post, a banker and investor. After an extended honeymoon in Europe, the newlyweds bought a house in Manhattan and had two sons, Edwin M., Jr. (b. 1893), and Bruce Price (b. 1895). Her marriage began to fall apart when she heard reports of her husband's extramarital affairs and he lost his money after the panic of 1901. With no financial assistance from her husband, Post searched for some means of support for herself and her children. She had written witty and informative letters from Europe to her friends, telling of her travels and observations of society, and an acquaintance now suggested that she try writing. Post refashioned her letters into a novel, and it was published as *The Flight of the Moth* in 1904. She divorced her husband around 1905 and continued writing, which enabled her to make enough money to send her sons to Harvard. Most of her novels, essays, and short stories centered on the aristocracy of European society, replete with titles and beautiful people. She knew this colorful segment of Europe well and was able to enchant her readers with stories about class, love, and money.

In 1921, Post was approached by Richard Duffy of Funk & Wagnalls and asked to consider writing a book on etiquette. She refused indignantly, claiming to loathe etiquette and those who upheld it, but on reflection realized that most of her works thus far involved good manners. Duffy left her a recently published book on etiquette and, having read it and taken issue with much of its contents, she embarked upon her own. In 1922, she published *Etiquette in Society, in Business, in Politics, and at Home*. The book became immensely popular despite (or, as some have suggested, because of) the rapidly changing social mores in America after World War I. Post addressed the rules of good behavior not only for the "rich and famous" but also for the average person, pointing out that good manners remain essentially the same in all situations even as she described the correct way to address nobility. Later renamed *Etiquette: The Blue Book of Social Usage*, the book sold some half a million copies by 1941 and went through 90 printings and about 10 editions in Post's lifetime. Through the book's various editions, she revised chapters and included new ones on proper etiquette for television and telephone usage, among other facets of modern life. In later years, she commented, "Etiquette is the science of living. It embraces everything. It is honor. It is ethics."

Post particularly liked interior decorating and remodeling. Following the death of her younger son Bruce in 1927, she launched a successful remodeling career and in 1930 published *Personality of a House*, which was frequently used as a college textbook. She also converted a farmhouse in Edgartown, Massachusetts, into a summer home. In 1931, she began making regular radio broadcasts on etiquette. The following year, Post started writing a daily column on "good taste" that was syndicated in 160 newspapers across the country, responding to queries from readers. She also wrote many articles about home decoration and architecture for magazines, including *Harper's* and *Scribner's*.

While continuing to write short stories and novels, in 1946 Post founded the Emily Post Institute for the Study of Gracious Living. Although she steadfastly called for adherence to traditional, formal practices, she did change with the times; in a 1945 edition, for example, she wrote that if a man were to be invited out for dinner by a woman, there would be nothing wrong if she asked for and paid the check. Post died in New York City on September 15, 1960, the same year that the tenth edition of *Etiquette* was published. Numerous spinoffs and specialized versions of her book (e.g., on weddings) have been published by family members in the years since, and 1997 saw publication of the 16th edition of *Emily Post's Etiquette*.

SOURCES:

Current Biography 1941. NY: H.W. Wilson, 1942.

McHenry, Robert, ed. *Famous American Women*. NY: Dover, 1980.

Emily Post

Sicherman, Barbara, and Carol Hurd Green, eds. *Notable American Women: The Modern Period*. Cambridge, MA: The Belknap Press of Harvard University, 1980.

Uglow, Jennifer S., comp. and ed. *The International Dictionary of Women's Biography*. NY: Continuum, 1985.

Weatherford, Doris. *American Women's History*. NY: Prentice Hall, 1994.

Don Amerman,
freelance writer, Saylorsburg, Pennsylvania

Post, Marion (1910–1990).

See Wolcott, Marion Post.

Post, Marjorie Merriweather (1887–1973)

American businesswoman and philanthropist. *Born in Springfield, Illinois, on March 15, 1887; died on September 12, 1973; daughter of Charles William Post, known as C.W. Post (started the Postum Cereal Company) and Ella Letitia (Merriweather) Post; married Edward B. Close, on December 3, 1905; married Edward F. Hutton (a stockbroker and founder of the Wall Street firm), on July 7, 1920; married Joseph E. Davies (a Washington lobbyist), on December 15, 1935 (divorced 1955); married Herbert May (a Pitts-*

burgh executive), on June 18, 1958 (divorced 1964); children: (first marriage) ***Adelaide Close*** *(married Augustus Riggs IV),* ***Eleanor Close*** *(married Leon Barzin); (second marriage) Nedenia Hutton (b. December 9, 1925, who as an actress adopted the stage name* ****Dina Merrill****).*

When C.W. Post was cured of his "invalidism" at Dr. John Kellogg's sanatorium in Battle Creek, Michigan, he went on to develop Postum, a coffee substitute, followed by the cereal Post Toasties. Upon his suicide in 1914, his daughter, 27-year-old Marjorie Merriweather Post, became the sole heir of the Postum Cereal Company of Battle Creek. She ran the company as owner and operator for the next eight years. With help from her second husband, stockbroker E.F. Hutton, Post and her firm acquired Clarence Birdseye's frozen foods company. Partially because of Marjorie Post's influence, General Foods became a food empire. She was a member of its board of directors (1936–58) and director emeritus (1958–73), and was also director of the National Savings and Trust, Washington, D.C. (1959–73).

Her third husband, Washington lobbyist Joseph Davies, was tapped by Franklin Delano Roosevelt as ambassador to the Soviet Union. While living in Russia, Post was appalled at the Soviet police state, but her husband aided in securing the Soviet-U.S. alliance against Hitler.

As presented in **Nancy Rubin**'s *American Empress,* Marjorie Post was a down-to-earth mother who held square dance parties and peppered her speech with expletives. Her philanthropies included New York's Emergency Unemployment Drive (1929–33), the Good Samaritan Hospital (Palm Beach), the National Symphony Orchestra, and Long Island University. She was awarded France's Legion of Honor, Belgium's Order of Leopold, Luxemburg's Order of Adolph de Nassau, and Brazil's Order of the Southern Cross.

SUGGESTED READING:

Rubin, Nancy. *American Empress: The Life and Times of Marjorie Merriweather Post.* Villard, 1995.

Post, Sandra (1948—)

Canadian golfer. *Born on June 4, 1948, in Oakville, Ontario, Canada.*

Born in Oakville, Ontario, in 1948, Canadian golfer Sandra Post took up the game at the age of five, and won the Canadian Junior championship three times. She came to the United States in 1968, and that year took the golf world by storm in her first professional outing, beating the great ***Kathy Whitworth** in an 18-hole playoff for the LPGA championship. Post was just 19 at the time, and the win was the high point of her career. Plagued by back problems, she did not win another tournament until the Colgate Far East Open in 1974. She won the Colgate-***Dinah Shore** Open in 1978 and again in 1979, when she was also voted Canada's Outstanding Athlete.

Postan, Eileen (1889–1940).

See Power, Eileen.

Poston, Elizabeth (1905–1987)

English pianist and composer. *Born on October 24, 1905, in Highfield, Hertfordshire, England; died on March 18, 1987, in Highfield, Hertfordshire, England; studied at the Royal College of Music; never married; no children.*

Compositions include: The Holy Child *(for chorus, vocal soloists, and string orchestra, 1950);* Concertino da Camera on a Theme of Martin Peerson *(for ancient instruments, 1950);* The Nativity *(for chorus, vocal soloists, and string orchestra or organ, 1951);* Trio for Flute, Clarinet or Viola, and Piano *(1958);* Peter Halfpenny's Tunes *(for recorder and piano, 1959);* Lullaby and Fiesta *(two pieces for piano, 1960);* Magnificat *(for four voices and organ, 1961);* 3 Scottish Carols *(for chorus and strings or organ, 1969);* Harlow Concertante *(for string quartet and string orchestra, 1969);* An English Day Book *(for mixed voices and harp, 1971);* Sonatina for Cello and Piano *(1972).*

An alumna of the Royal College of Music and a student of Harold Samuel, Elizabeth Poston published her first composition in 1925, and shortly thereafter heard her violin sonata broadcast by the BBC. During World War II, she was the director of music in the Foreign Service of the BBC in London, and she later served as president of the Society of Women Musicians (1955–61). Poston's wide range of compositions includes choral music, hymns, Christmas carols, and music for radio dramas and films. One of her most notable contributions is an edited collection of folk music which she gathered during her travels. The musician and composer died in her native England on March 18, 1987.

Potonié-Pierre, Eugénie (1844–1898)

French feminist and socialist who worked to make the women's movement more socially conscious.

Name variations: Eugenie Potonie-Pierre. Pronunciation: yew-JAY-nee po-TOE-nee-ay pee-AIR. Born Eugénie Pierre on November 5, 1844; died of a cerebral hemorrhage on June 12, 1898; sister of Dr. Marie Pierre; married Edmond Potonié (a historian and pacifist), in 1881; no children.

Served as secretary of the first French International Congress for Women's Rights (1878); helped found the Union of Socialist Women (1880); helped to run La Citoyenne *(1886?–91); helped found the Women's Solidarity Group and the French Federation of Feminist Societies (1891); helped sponsor the French Congress for Women's Rights (1892, 1896); wrote for Argyriadès'* La Question sociale *(1894–97); served as delegate to the Brussels World Congress of Women (1897).*

Born in 1844 and raised in comfortable circumstances, Eugénie Pierre was a teacher influenced by Saint-Simonian socialism (Comte de Saint-Simon, 1760–1825). In the mid-1870s, she joined Léon Richer and ***Maria Deraismes**' Society for the Amelioration of Women's Condition and contributed regularly to its review, *Le Droit des femmes* (Women's Rights, 1869–91), of which she was secretary. She emerged as an important figure when she served as secretary of the organizing committee of the first French International Congress for Women's Rights, convened by Richer and Deraismes in July 1878. Under the influence, however, of ***Hubertine Auclert**'s Women's Rights Society (later the Women's Suffrage Society), she had begun moving toward socialist politics and a more militant feminism. With Auclert and others, she tried to register to vote (February 2, 1880) but was denied.

In April 1880, Pierre, **Léonide Rouzade** (a novelist), and ***Marguerite Tinayre** (novelist, communard, and friend of ***Louise Michel**) founded the Union of Socialist Women in order to increase women's influence in the Socialist Party. The Marxist leader Jules Guesde spoke at the founding, and the Union soon tended to draw more socialists than feminists, notably ***Paule Mink** and Michel. It never effectively married feminism with socialism, notes Charles Sowerwine, the group's analyses of these issues following separate but parallel lines. It did, nevertheless, succeed in persuading the party in 1880 to reject the Guesdist thesis that women's rights would result only from the great proletarian revolution; instead, it won confirmation of the rights endorsed by the Marseille congress of 1879. Eugénie spoke in these debates. This victory started a process which thereafter led all socialist parties to include women's rights in their platforms.

By the end of 1880, Eugénie and Léonide were more involved in party affairs than in the Union. Rouzade accepted the party's nomination in 1881 to run for the Paris Municipal Council—the first woman in France to stand for municipal office—but this affair contributed to the breakup of the party into warring factions. The Union faded. Eugénie, who had not supported the candidacy, left the Union after failing to be elected secretary of the Socialist party's central committee, where she represented the Union (April 1881). That same year, despite her theoretical objections to matrimony, she married Edmond Potonié, a pacifist utopian socialist historian, and inventor of the cry, "War on war!" They both took the name Potonié-Pierre. He probably persuaded her to back away from party politics, although she remained active in the women's movement. The Union had supported Guesde's expulsion of Auclert from the 1880 congress; Pierre and Rouzade, however, had kept up contact with her. Potonié-Pierre was the most frequent contributor to Auclert's *La Citoyenne* (1881–91), and her husband also contributed. In 1885, she declined an invitation from the League for the Protection of Women, a break-off group from Auclert's society, to run for Parliament. She concluded there were too many such symbolic candidacies to be productive. When Auclert temporarily drifted away from public life in the latter 1880s, Potonié-Pierre, along with **Marie Martin** and **Astié de Valsayre**, carried most of the burden of running *La Citoyenne* until its demise in 1891.

Potonié-Pierre resumed organizational work in 1889. She attended the second French International Congress for Women's Rights that year but grew unhappy with the narrowness of Richer and Deraismes' approach. So she, Astié, and Jules and **Denise Roques** organized the Women's League (or Women's Socialist League). Potonié-Pierre tried to run for Parliament as "an act of propaganda" but gave way when the prefect of the Seine forbade it. The League died almost at birth.

Potonié-Pierre returned to the charge in 1891 when, with Rouzade, Marie Martin, and ➤ **Nathalie Lemel** (a communard socialist), she founded the Women's Solidarity Group, which sought to bridge the gap between socialist and moderate women. She wanted to push "the whole cause of women's economic and social emancipation," as she put it. Hence Solidarity proposed a long, heterogeneous agenda, e.g., freedom of work for women, abolition of legalized prostitution, support of women's coeducation, language and women's dress reform, abolition of the death penalty, etc. Solidarity made overtures to the

Lemel, Nathalie. *See Michel, Louise for sidebar.*

(now) five socialist parties but formed no official connections. For the 1893 election, it asked the parties to name a female candidate. They turned a deaf ear, so it finally nominated Rouzade, Deraismes, *Séverine (the famous journalist), and Paule Mink. Only Mink accepted; Potonié-Pierre had won her over from the Guesdist position to the view that "the social question" needed liberated women to deal with it. Solidarity survived, but it never got support among working-class women—a common defect in the "social feminist" movement which it never overcame.

[We must] join the two causes of women and the proletariat in order to make of them one single cause, the humanitarian cause.

—Eugénie Potonié-Pierre

Solidarity played a role in another of Potonié-Pierre's initiatives, the French Federation of Feminist Societies, launched in November 1891. It linked some 16 Paris feminist groups in an attempt to compete with or even replace the more moderate elements of the women's movement. Its sole accomplishment was to convene the third French International Congress for Women's Rights (May 13–15, 1892), which brought together an amazingly broad range of delegates, from the moderate Deraismes to the revolutionary Édouard Vaillant. Inevitably, it lacked coherence. The congress did manage to endorse support of "the international proletariat's demands"—a victory for the radicals which pleased Potonié-Pierre but caused some walkouts. "For the first time," she proclaimed, "women finally have accepted the outstretched hand of the social cause . . . have united . . . their demands with those of the proletariat." But the hard truth was that the congress, like Solidarity, lacked proletarian followers. The Federation itself soon expired following Potonié-Pierre's resignation (June 17) as secretary because of a dispute with ***Aline Valette** over control of the organization. A year later, writing in *Le Journal des femmes*, she had the satisfaction of charging Valette with "sexualism" for saying that once women had received their full rights they would return to motherhood, their "natural destiny." Interestingly, she was the only columnist to view Valette's position in this light.

Potonié-Pierre continued to head Solidarity. She also wrote for Argyriadès' *La Question sociale* until it died in 1897, collaborating with **Marya Chéliga** (a co-sponsor of the 1892 congress) and Mink. In 1894, at her urging, the deputies in Parliament organized a lobbying group for women's rights, an encouraging development. Another congress, the fourth, took place in 1896. It was sponsored by Solidarity and Richer's old French League for the Rights of Women, which was now being led by **Maria Pognon** and other social feminists—evidence of Potonié-Pierre's success. The congress turned into a replay of the 1892 congress. It endorsed everyone's pet reforms, so no coherent program emerged. Its most significant results were the confirmation of Potonié-Pierre and Mink as the leaders of current mainstream feminism, confirming the growing importance of social feminism; and the conversion to feminism of ***Marguerite Durand**, who, in an effort to bring order to the movement, founded the first daily paper operated (including typesetting) solely by women, *La Fronde* (1897–1903).

At the Brussels World Congress of Women (1897), Potonié-Pierre and Mink clearly dominated the French delegation. Potonié-Pierre's influence had never been higher when she died suddenly of a cerebral hemorrhage on June 12, 1898, at age 54.

Solidarity passed to **Caroline Kauffmann**, founder of the Feminine League for Physical Education, who left it to ***Madeleine Pelletier** in 1906. Potonié-Pierre's advocacy (with her sister, Dr. **Marie Pierre**) of greater physical activity for women and of dress reform—she wore skirt culottes—underscored her separation from the working-class women whose lot she was seeking to better. They took no interest in such reforms. Her socialism was humanitarian in inspiration, drawn from utopian socialist springs, in her case Saint-Simonian. She and her husband, in fact, jointly published a utopian futuristic novel, *Un peu plus tard* (A Little Later, Paris: Breton, 1893), like Bellamy's *Looking Backward* (1888) filled with mechanical marvels. Edmond's pacifism and aversion to political activism influenced her approach to social questions. Eschewing grassroots organizing of the masses, she overflowed with good will and compassion toward the suffering working class. Her writings, abounding in stories of abandoned women, starving urchins, and desperate unemployed workers, are reminiscent of the work of Séverine, though Séverine was one of the greatest journalists of her time.

Potonié-Pierre's dream was, as she wrote, "to join the two causes of women and the proletariat in order to make of them one single cause, the humanitarian cause, so that social evolution may proceed peacefully." This dream was doomed to frustration. The gap between her solidly bourgeois following and working-class women only widened. Ideas of class warfare were taking hold among the proletariat; the old alliance between the republican middle class and the workers crumbled, writes **Claire Moses**, once this middle class came to power and governed in its own interest. Potonié-Pierre never realized her movement needed to incorporate proletarians. "Indeed," writes Sowerwine, "her aim was not so much to encourage the working people to be active as to forestall such activity" by meeting their needs *for* them, thus ensuring peaceful evolution. She did much, nevertheless, to make the women's movement far more socially conscious. Ineffective as her organizational approach proved to be, she helped middle-class women come to understand that their plight was, like it or not, linked to that of the humblest reaches of society.

SOURCES:

Bidelman, Patrick Kay. *Pariahs Stand Up! The Founding of the Liberal Feminist Movement in France, 1858–1889*. Westport, CT: Greenwood Press, 1982.

Dictionnaire biographique du mouvement ouvrier français. Jean Maitron, dir. Paris: Éditions ouvrières, 1964—.

Hause, Steven. *Hubertine Auclert: The French Suffragette*. New Haven, CT: Yale University Press, 1987.

International Dictionary of Women's Biography. Jennifer S. Uglow, ed. NY: Continuum, 1985.

Klejman, Laurance, and Florence Rochefort. *L'Égalité en marche: Le Féminisme sous la Troisième République*. Paris: Presses de la Fondation nationale des sciences politiques/ Éditions des Femmes, 1989.

Moses, Claire Goldberg. *French Feminism in the Nineteenth Century*. Albany, NY: State University of New York Press, 1984.

Sowerwine, Charles. *Sisters or Citizens? Women and Socialism in France since 1876*. Cambridge: Cambridge University Press, 1982.

SUGGESTED READING:

Brogan, Denis W. *The Development of Modern France, 1870–1939*. New and rev. ed. London: Hamish Hamilton, 1967.

Chapman, Guy. *The Third French Republic: The First Phase, 1871–1894*. NY: St. Martin's Press, 1962.

McMillan, James F. *Housewife or Harlot: The Place of Women in French Society, 1870–1940*. NY: St. Martin's Press, 1981.

Smith, Paul. *Feminism and the Third Republic*. Oxford: Clarendon Press, 1996.

Wright, Gordon. *France in Modern Times*. 4th ed. NY: W.W. Norton, 1987.

COLLECTIONS:

Paris: Bibliothèque Marguerite Durand: dossiers for Potonié-Pierre and Solidarité.

David S. Newhall,
Pottinger Distinguished Professor of History Emeritus,
Centre College, Danville, Kentucky

Potter, Beatrix (1866–1943)

British author of perennially popular children's books who later became a farmer and a sheepbreeder. *Name variations: Beatrix Heelis. Born Helen Beatrix Potter on July 28, 1866, in South Kensington, London; died on December 22, 1943, at Sawrey, Cumbria; eldest child and only daughter of Rupert Potter (a barrister) and Helen (Leech) Potter; educated at home; married William Heelis, on October 14, 1913; no children.*

Sold some drawings to Hildersheimer and Faulkner, publishers (1890); wrote Peter Rabbit letter to Noël Moore (September 4, 1893); her research paper "On the Germination of the Spores of Agaricineae" read to Linnean Society of London (April 1, 1897); privately published The Tale of Peter Rabbit *(1901), published by Frederick Warne (1902); became engaged to Norman Warne (summer 1905); bought Hill Top Farm, near Sawrey (summer 1905); went to live at Castle Cottage Farm, Sawrey (1913); first became involved with National Trust (1914); bought Troutbeck Park (1923); became president of Herdwick Sheep-breeders Association (1930).*

Selected writings: The Tale of Peter Rabbit *(1901);* The Tailor of Gloucester *(1902);* The Tale of Squirrel Nutkin *(1903);* The Tale of Benjamin Bunny *(1904);* The Tale of Mrs. Tiggy-Winkle *(1905);* The Tale of Mrs. Jeremy Fisher *(1906);* The Tale of Jemima Puddle-Duck *(1908);* Ginger and Pickles *(1909);* The Tale of Pigling Bland *(1913);* Appley Dappley's Nursery Rhymes *(1917);* The Fairy-Caravan *(1929). Series taken over by* ❧▸ ***Linda Almond.***

The life of Beatrix Potter exemplifies how difficult it was at the close of the 19th century for a middle-class woman to break through the convention of that passive lifestyle which was expected of "spinster" daughters. But it is also an example of how, with determination, it could be done. She did not write her first book until the age of 35, and she lived in London with her parents until the age of 47. Yet Beatrix Potter is remembered not only as a brilliant writer of books for children but also as the champion of Herdwicks, a breed

❧▸ Almond, Linda (1881–1987)

American children's author. *Born Linda Stevens in 1881 in Seaford, Delaware; died on January 10, 1987, in Plymouth Meeting, Pennsylvania; carried on the Beatrix Potter series and wrote the "Buddy Bear" and "Penny Hill" series.*

In 1921, after ***Beatrix Potter** retired from writing her famous children's books, Linda Almond was selected to take over the series. A Delaware native, Almond continued to reside in the Mid-Atlantic region and wrote two other children's book series: "Buddy Bear" and "Penny Hill." Almond died in 1987, age 105.

of sheep then in danger of disappearing, and as a supporter and benefactor of The National Trust in the Lake District of England.

Although Potter's parents, Rupert and **Helen Potter**, lived in London, they both belonged to successful, middle-class, northern families. Rupert's father, a self-made man from Manchester, had made a large fortune with the Dinting Vale Calico Printing Works in Glossop, so, although Rupert chose to become a barrister and was called to the Bar in 1857, he did not need to practice for a living. Nevertheless, he had chambers in London for over 30 years, although the actual work was mainly done by others. Rupert's mother was **Jessie Crompton**, an early 19th-century beauty whose family was renowned for its forthright manner, both in speech and in action. In her later years, Beatrix displayed much of the Crompton temperament. Helen Potter was the daughter of John Leech, a wealthy cotton-merchant from Stalybridge. The Potters and the Leeches were old friends and Helen's sister **Elizabeth** was already the wife of Rupert's brother Walter, when the pair married in 1863.

My brother and I were born in London . . . but our descent, our interest and our joy were in the north country.

—**Beatrix Potter**

The house where Beatrix was born, 2 Bolton Gardens, Kensington, was a new four-story building when the Potters moved in to accommodate the expected child. They lived in some style, with a butler, a cook, a housekeeper, a coachman, and a groom. The nursery, where Beatrix lived with her nurse, was on the third floor. For the first few years of her life, she seems to have had very little contact with her parents, though this was not a particularly unusual state of affairs at the time. However, because Helen Potter feared bad influences and germs, neither was Beatrix allowed much contact with other children, and, as her only sibling Bertram was not born until she was nearly six, she grew up a solitary child.

According to Potter, her two favorite toys were "a dilapidated, black wooden doll called Topsy, and a grimy, hard-stuffed, once-white, flannelette pig." She claimed that she "learned to read on the Waverley novels," written by the Romantic novelist Sir Walter Scott in the early 19th century—and that she wore "white piqué starched frocks . . . and cotton stockings striped round like zebra's legs." Her hair was long and luxuriant, held behind her ears with a band.

While in London, Beatrix saw little of the outside world other than her daily walk in Kensington Gardens with her nurse. However, she paid frequent visits to her grandmother who lived at Hatfield, Hertfordshire, in a house with large gardens on a 300-acre estate. Furthermore, the Potters spent two weeks every April at the seaside, and, for almost three months every summer, Rupert Potter would rent a large house on an estate in Scotland or Cumbria. Away from London, Beatrix was free to spend time outdoors, and, as soon as Bertram was old enough, the two children devised many activities to keep themselves amused.

From a very early age, Beatrix enjoyed drawing and painting; in this, she was encouraged by both parents. Before her marriage, Helen Potter had painted in watercolors, and although Rupert Potter was no painter, he was a highly accomplished drawer. He was also an enthusiastic and talented photographer. In 1869, he was elected to the Photographic Society of London, and, for many years, he helped his artist friend John Everett Millais by photographing landscapes and people to use in Millais' paintings. He also enjoyed photographing his family, and many of the photographs of Beatrix still in existence were taken by her father. Sometimes Potter was allowed to accompany her father when he visited Millais' studio, and, as she grew older, several drawing and painting teachers were engaged for her. Both parents viewed her talents as a pastime, however, and though Bertram, as a young man, was allowed to become an artist, there was no question of Beatrix doing anything other than staying at home.

Indeed, for many years Beatrix Potter was suspended in what amounted to perpetual childhood. As she grew older, she was more in the company of her parents and became particularly fond of her father. But she had no close companions of her own age, she did not "come out" into society as did many of her upper middle-class contemporaries, and her dearest friends were old men—John Bright, the Quaker politician who had worked for the repeal of the Corn Laws in the 1840s, and William Gaskell, Unitarian minister and husband of ***Elizabeth Gaskell**, the writer. Both men were frequent guests of Rupert Potter and had first been friends of Beatrix's grandfather.

Throughout her life, Potter was very fond of animals. As a little girl, she was accompanied on her walks by Sandy, her Scotch terrier. As she grew older, other dogs followed. She also caught and tamed wild animals when in the country, bringing them back to London and even taking them on visits to relatives. Other creatures she bought from pet shops. It is not clear how much

Beatrix Potter

of this was known to her parents or governesses but at various times she owned rabbits, mice, rats, newts, lizards, "a little ring-snake fourteen inches long" and a hedgehog. All these creatures Beatrix studied and drew. When he was not away at school, Bertram shared her interest in the flora and fauna around them. One wonders how they managed to skin and boil dead rabbits in order to study their skeletons, but so they did.

Potter's activities scarcely altered as she developed into womanhood. At age 15, she began keeping a diary written in code, and she would still be using the same code for her diary entries at the age of 30. She was just three weeks shy of 19 when her last governess, 22-year-old **Annie Carter**, left to get married. In her 20s, Potter visited galleries and exhibitions with her father and on one occasion accompanied her parents to the theater. She noted in her diary, "It was the first time in my life that I had been past the Horse Guards, Admiralty, and Whitehall, or seen the Strand or the Monument." Often ill with colds and headaches since a child, in 1887 Beatrix had what was thought to be rheumatic fever and lost much of her hair. Two years later, she suffered a similar illness which left her with a permanent heart defect.

However, there were brighter periods. In her early 20s, Potter learned to drive a pony carriage. In 1890, her Uncle Walter sold some of her drawings to Hildersheimer and Faulkner for £6 to enable her to buy herself a printing machine. These drawings were used as Christmas and New Year cards and to illustrate a book of verses called *A Happy Pair.* In June 1894, she traveled without her parents for the first time in five years to visit her cousin, **Caroline Hutton**, in Stroud, Gloucestershire. Potter enjoyed it immensely and shortly afterwards traveled into Wales to stay with her Uncle Fred Burton. She became interested in fungi and on April 1, 1897, her research paper, "On the Germination of the Spores of Agaricineae," was read to the Linnean Society of London by one of the principal assistants at Kew Gardens, where she had done some of her observation. She could not read the paper herself, for women were not allowed to attend the society's meetings. Meanwhile, she had sold some more drawings, this time to Ernest Nister, a firm of fine art color printers.

Potter did not lose touch with her former governess Annie Carter after Carter had become Mrs. Moore. Whenever she could, she visited her and her growing family in Wandsworth. On September 4, 1893, Potter wrote to the eldest child, Noël Moore, and, not having any news, she told him a story about four rabbits which she illustrated with pen-and-ink drawings. Other stories, in letters to other children, followed. But it was not until 1901 that Potter got the idea of turning her first story-letter into a book. *The Tale of Peter Rabbit* was of a size to be comfortable in a small child's hand, with a drawing facing every page of writing. When publishers showed no interest, she had it printed privately. However, on the very day that this first edition came out, December 16, the firm of Frederick Warne and Company offered to print her book if she would change her line drawings to colored illustrations. This she did, and in the next 11 years Warne published over 20 children's books by Beatrix Potter. For the illustrations, she mainly used her pets as models and places she knew and loved as settings. She also designed Peter Rabbit wallpaper, a Peter Rabbit doll, a Peter Rabbit board game, three painting books, and an almanac for 1929.

Potter was in her middle-30s when *The Tale of Peter Rabbit* was published, yet, writing to Frederick Warne, she is clearly still dominated by Rupert Potter: "If my father happens to insist on going with me to see the agreement, would you please not mind him very much, if he is fidgetty about things. . . . [H]e is sometimes a little difficult." Her avowal, "I can, of course, do what I like about the book being 36," lacks conviction. Even when Bertram became a farmer in Scotland, he returned for family holidays, and he had been married for seven years before he told his parents of this fact. What hope was there, then, for Beatrix to break free?

Nevertheless, she exerted her growing independence by buying first a field and then a farm in Near Sawrey, Cumbria. Although she had learned to love the Lake District through family holidays there, she bought it as an investment, not as a potential home. She also, in the face of her parents' opposition, became friendly with the large Warne family, and, when Norman, the 37-year-old brother most involved with her books, proposed marriage, she accepted, despite the fact that, as the Warnes were "in trade," the elder Potters disapproved of the match. Sadly, even before the engagement was made public, Norman died of pernicious anaemia.

The next few years were spent producing her books and buying even more property in and around Sawrey. She extended Hill Top so that there was room for herself and her tenant farmer's family—although she was seldom able to get away from her parents in order to stay there. Her property transactions were looked after by a Hawkshead solicitor named William Heelis. He was a bachelor in his 40s, belonged to a large family, was a great sportsman and a lover of the countryside. He was also of a kind and gentle disposition, and when he proposed marriage to Beatrix, she was happy to accept. Once again, the Potters considered her fiancé to be their inferior, but Beatrix and Willie were married on October 14, 1913. They made their home at Castle Cottage Farm, one of Beatrix's properties near Hill Top.

Potter's writing declined after her marriage, both in quantity and, many claim, in quality. In

1929, she was persuaded by an American publisher, David McKay, to create a big story book from all the writings which had not previously made it into print. A few others followed. Possibly, the American literary scene succeeded where Warne had failed. Potter was aware that children's literature was taken more seriously in the U.S., and its writers were afforded higher status than was the case in England at that time. She wrote in a letter, "Never does anyone outside your perfidiously complimentary nation write to tell me that I write good prose." She seems to have been more willing to welcome American visitors to Castle Cottage than English ones and made a number of American friends, including the prestigious New York children's librarian ***Anne Carroll Moore** and ***Bertha Mahony Miller**, who founded *Horn Book,* a magazine dealing entirely with children's literature, and who, in 1916, opened a children's bookshop in Boston where questions of quality outweighed those of salability.

As Potter gradually lost interest in writing children's books, she became more and more immersed in the life of the countryside. She insisted on being addressed as Mrs. Heelis, even when functioning in the capacity of a children's author. She helped found a branch of the Nursing Association in Hawkshead, allowed Girl Guides to camp on her land, and helped preserve the old traditional furniture of the area by collecting fine examples which came up at local sales. When, during the First World War, many of her farm workers joined the forces, she managed with the help of an inexperienced volunteer, who offered her services after reading a letter Potter wrote to *The Times* bemoaning the shortage of laborers. On a wet, cold November day, a forester's wife observed Potter "gathering acorns in the woods for her pigs. She had a shovel and a wheelbarrow for the job, and was fit up to brave the weather in a short thick wool skirt, a man's jacket and cap and a sack over her shoulders." Potter joined in the razzing over her appearance, recalling one wet day when a tramp mistook her for another of his kind and called to her, "It's sad weather for the likes o' thee and me."

On buying Troutbeck Park in 1923, a fell farm with a large stock of sheep, Potter became involved with Herdwicks, the breed indigenous to the area. It was a strain losing popularity and market value, for its coarse wool was excellent for the manufacture of carpets, but the housewife of the period preferred linoleum. Potter, however, set herself to learn all she could about sheep. Attending local sheep fairs, she somehow got herself accepted into the closed masculine world of Lakeland sheep-breeders, exhibiting and later judging at shows. She became a member of the Herdwick Sheep-breeders Association, founded by Canon Rawnsley in 1899, and in 1930 became its first woman president.

Beatrix Potter's Peter Rabbit.

Potter had known Hardwicke Rawnsley since she was 16. The Potters had spent their long summer holiday at Wray Castle in the Lake District and had met the man who was to become a lifelong friend. He was a fascinating person—local cleric, canon of Carlisle Cathedral, amateur poet, naturalist, antiquarian, bonfire-enthusiast and self-appointed protector of the natural beauties of the Lake District against overdevelopment and entrepreneurialism. In 1895, he co-founded the National Trust, a body dedicated to preserving land and buildings for the pleasure of future generations. Potter wholeheartedly supported his work and began to have an eye to the National Trust whenever she bought land. Some she gave while she was still alive, much of the rest she bequeathed.

Nowadays Beatrix Potter pilgrims can visit Tarn Hows, Cockshott Point, the Beatrix Potter Gallery in Hawkshead, Hill Top at Near Sawrey and a fund-raising exhibition in Keswick entitled Beatrix Potter's Lake District. All of these are owned and administered by the National Trust. Beatrix Potter books, tapes and memorabilia are widely available in the Lake District and beyond. Generations of children have read and reread her books, and grown up to read them to their own children, and the animals she created in her books remain as popular today as they were when she first drew them a century ago.

SOURCES:

Lane, Margaret. *The Tale of Beatrix Potter.* Harmondsworth: Frederick Warne, 1946 (rev. ed. 1985).

Taylor, Judy. *Beatrix Potter: Artist, Storyteller and Countrywoman.* Harmondsworth: Frederick Warne, 1986.

SUGGESTED READING:

Buchan, Elizabeth. *Beatrix Potter: The Story of the Creator of Peter Rabbit.* Harmondsworth: Frederick Warne, 1991 (1st pub. by Hamish Hamilton, 1987).

Heelis, John. *The Tale of Mrs. William Heelis: Beatrix Potter.* Hawes: Leading Edge Press, 1993.

Lane, Margaret. *The Magic Years of Beatrix Potter.* London: Frederick Warne, 1978.

RELATED MEDIA:

"The World of Peter Rabbit and Friends" (animated film, 6 episodes), produced by John Coates, Television Cartoons, Ltd., 1993 (available on Good Times Home Video).

Barbara Evans,
Research Associate in Women's Studies, Nene College, Northampton, England

Potter, Electa (1790–1854).

See Greenfield, Elizabeth Taylor for sidebar.

Potter, Mrs. H.B. (1790–1854).

See Greenfield, Elizabeth Taylor for sidebar.

Potter, Maureen (1925—)

Irish actress and variety performer. *Born Maria Philomena Potter in Fairview, Dublin, Ireland, on January 3, 1925; daughter of James Benedict Potter and Elizabeth (Carr) Potter; educated at St. Mary's School, Fairview, Dublin; married Jack O'Leary; children: two sons.*

Awards: Freeman of the City of Dublin (1984); honorary doctorate, Trinity College, Dublin (1988).

Maureen Potter made her professional stage debut at age seven when she appeared at St. Teresa's Hall, Clarendon Street, in Dublin, singing *Broadway's Gone Hillbilly.* She then began to make regular appearances with the Jimmy Campbell band at the Theatre Royal, Dublin's premier variety venue. When the Jack Hylton Band from Britain, one of the most popular of the day, appeared at the Royal, Potter auditioned and subsequently got a telegram from Hylton asking her to come to London the following day for a month's booking. In fact, she stayed two years, billed as "Maureen Potter Child Impressionist, Dancer and Burlesque Actress." One of her stage impressions was of ***Shirley Temple (Black)** which, she recalled later, made her childhood a misery because of the effort it took to coax her hair ("like stair rods") into ringlets and curls to look like Temple. She toured Germany with Hylton, where at one performance Hitler, Goebbels and Goering were present. Though Potter was given a silver and blue wreath as a memento of the occasion, her mother, who loathed Hitler, promptly threw it away.

Potter was playing with Hylton at the London Palladium when war broke out in 1939. Her mother insisted she return to Dublin, and this marked a decisive turn for Potter as the rest of her career was largely confined to Ireland. At the end of 1939, she went straight into pantomime with Jimmy O'Dea, with whom she formed a legendary comic partnership that lasted until O'Dea's death in 1965. O'Dea, the most popular entertainer in Ireland, was a sublime comic and actor who performed in variety, pantomime, straight theater, musicals, films and later in television. Potter graduated from being his feed to become his full-fledged comic partner: "It's the rhythm of putting across comedy, one word too many and it's gone. You have to think about gaps and timing and I am the luckiest woman in the world because I worked with Jimmy O'Dea. . . . [H]e taught me my business . . . he was the master of timing." Potter recalled O'Dea's mischievous streak, the way "a mad look would come into his eye and you never knew what he was going to do." They developed such a rapport on stage that each sensed instinctively what the other was going to do next. Among their most famous creations were Dolores and Rosie, two Dublin women or "totties" in the Dublin vernacular. Rosie (O'Dea) had a genteel accent and a grand manner in contrast to Dolores' (Potter's) flat, screeching tones and malapropisms.

O'Dea loved touring in Ireland, even during the Second World War when conditions were difficult. Potter and the other performers built the stages, packed up the scenery and the costumes, and washed off their makeup in buckets of cold water. After the war, there was less touring, and O'Dea and Potter were largely based in Dublin, at the Theatre Royal and later at the Gaiety Theatre. They performed annually in pantomime, summer shows and musicals, but being based in

Dublin meant that their acts and sketches had to be constantly changed and renewed. Two weeks' rehearsal was the maximum period allowed. The need for new material prompted a need for new writers; one of them, an army officer by the name of Jack O'Leary, wrote many of Potter's political satires and parodies. He retired from the army and continued to make a major contribution to Potter's career after their marriage.

Potter's last show with O'Dea was *Finian's Rainbow* (1964); he died in January 1965. "I was amazed I could carry on," said Potter, but the nucleus of O'Dea's company remained, notably Danny Cummins with whom Potter formed a new stage partnership. The Irish broadcaster Gay Byrne, who produced two television Christmas shows starring Potter in 1970 and 1971, noted that Potter was suspicious of television but soon overcame her reservations. She also did more film work. In 1967, she appeared as Josie Breen in Joseph Strick's film of James Joyce's *Ulysses*. Ten years later, Strick asked her to appear in another Joyce film, *Portrait of the Artist*, where she gave a superb performance as Mrs. Riordan. She did her last pantomime in 1985, and the following year was invited to play Maisie Madigan in the celebrated Gate Theatre production of Sean O'Casey's *Juno and the Paycock*. The show went on tour, to Jerusalem, Edinburgh and finally Broadway in 1988. Director Joe Dowling recalled the scene at the play's end when Maisie told Juno her son was dead. Potter played it with "stillness, a sense of dignity, simplicity and sincerity," he said. She took on another important straight role as well, that of the mother in Hugh Leonard's *Da*. Leonard felt that his mother (on whom the part was based) would have given rare approval to Potter's interpretation.

Potter was increasingly afflicted with severe arthritis, which had made the Broadway run of *Juno* particularly difficult for her. She made two attempts to return to pantomime in 1986 and 1987 but found it physically too demanding. She carved out a new career for herself in cabaret, with annual seasons in Dublin winning her a new generation of audiences. In 1989, she published a children's book, *The Theatre Cat*. Potter still enjoys the process of putting shows together, but as she has gotten older she has become twice as nervous, especially on first nights. "I'd like to keep going as long as they laugh. If they stop, I'll stop."

SOURCES:

"Make 'Em Laugh," RTE series broadcast September 1999.

"Super Trouper: The Maureen Potter Story," Radio Telifís Eireann documentary broadcast, January 7, 1999.

Deirdre McMahon,
lecturer in history at Mary Immaculate College,
University of Limerick, Limerick, Ireland

Potts, Mary Florence (c. 1853–?).

See Inventors.

Pötzsch, Anett (1961—)

East German skater. *Name variations: Anett Potzsch or Poetzsch; frequently misspelled Annet or Annett. Born in Karl-Marx-Stadt (now Chemnitz), East Germany, in 1961.*

Was the first East German to win a gold medal in Olympic figure skating (1980); won the World championship (1978, 1980).

The former East Germany produced an enormous number of medal-winning athletes for such a small country. In an effort to prove that the Communist system was superior, no expense was spared on athletes. Anett Pötzsch was the first East German figure skater to break into the international spotlight, charming crowds with her polished routines. Once chosen as an athlete for her country, Pötzsch spent hours on the ice, with all expenditures paid by the state. In 1976, Pötzsch won the East German title, as she would in 1977, 1978, and 1979. She was also a three-time European champion and a two-time World champion, in 1978 and 1980, alternating with American skater ***Linda Fratianne** who won in 1977 and 1979. In the 1980 Olympics at Lake Placid, the East-West battle between sports stars was intense. Once again, Fratianne was Pötzsch's main competitor. To the strains of Louis Armstrong's "Hello, Dolly," a decidedly "capitalistic" piece of music, the East German skater entered the arena in a feather boa. Pötzsch won the gold by a narrow margin, the first East German skater to do so.

Karin Loewen Haag,
Athens, Georgia

Pougy, Liane de (1866–c. 1940).

See Barney, Natalie Clifford for sidebar.

Pougy, Odette de.

See Odette de Pougy.

Poulos, Leah (b. 1951).

See Mueller, Leah Poulos.

Pound, Louise (1872–1958)

American scholar, teacher, and athlete who was an expert on her nation's speech and folklore. *Born on June 30, 1872, in Lincoln, Nebraska; died on June 28, 1958, in Lincoln; middle of three children and older of two daughters of Stephen Bosworth Pound (a lawyer,* *district court judge, and state senator) and Laura (Biddlecombe) Pound; home schooled; attended the Latin School of the University of Nebraska, 1896–98; University of Nebraska, B.L., 1892, A.M., 1895; awarded Ph.D. in Heidelberg, Germany, in 1900; never married; no children.*

Born in 1872 in Lincoln, Nebraska, which would be her lifelong home, Louise Pound was raised in a socially and culturally elite family. Her father Stephen Bosworth Pound, a lawyer, was also a district court judge and a state senator, and her mother **Laura Biddlecombe Pound** had been a teacher. All the Pound children were home schooled, as Laura believed the public schools inadequate. Louise did attend the preparatory Latin School of the University of Nebraska for two years before enrolling at the university. Her college career was notable for both her academic excellence and her extra-curricular activities; in addition to being class orator and poet, and associate editor of the college newspaper, Pound was the women's state tennis champion. Upon her graduation in 1892, she began her teaching career as an English fellow at the university.

Between teaching and earning her master's degree, Pound continued her athletics, winning a series of "century runs" (cycling 100 miles in 12 hours) and playing on the women's basketball team, for which she served variously as coach and team captain. She also continued to play tennis and was a ranking golfer and figure skater as well. (She gave up tennis in her 80s, she said, only because her bifocals created havoc with her ground stroke.) After earning her master's degree, she spent two summers at the University of Chicago, then went off to obtain her Ph.D. in Germany, completing her courses in two semesters, instead of the usual seventeen.

In 1900, Pound returned to the University of Nebraska, where she remained for the next 45 years, becoming a full professor in 1912. She taught a wide range of subjects and was remembered as an inspiring teacher whose interest in her students continued long after they graduated. In addition to her heavy teaching load, Pound accomplished an enormous amount of scholarly research, much of it on the origin of ballads (*Poetic Origins and the Ballad* [1921]). A major contribution was her scholarly study of American speech and folklore, including etymology and modern changes in the English language as spoken in the United States. Considered pioneering at the time, this work was recorded in part in *American Speech*, a journal Pound founded and served as senior editor. Much of her study of folklore also resulted in publications, among them *Folk-Song of Nebraska and the Central West: A Syllabus* (1915) and *Nebraska Folklore* (published posthumously in 1959). Pound was honored for her work in 1955, when she was elected as the first woman president of the Modern Language Association. That same year, she also became the first woman elected to the Nebraska Sports Hall of Fame. "First woman again,—Life has its humors," the 82-year-old wrote to a friend.

Pound, who never married, lived her entire life in her family home, a large Victorian house in which she occupied a tower suite. An attractive woman with naturally red hair worn in braids wrapped around her head, she was known as a feisty individualist. She was an outspoken advocate of women's rights, particularly as they applied to education, and frequently addressed women's groups around the state. She also supported efforts to improve the status of women within the University of Nebraska. Louise Pound died of a heart attack in 1958, at age 85.

SOURCES:

Sicherman, Barbara, and Carol Hurd Green, eds. *Notable American Women: The Modern Period.* Cambridge, MA: The Belknap Press of Harvard University, 1980.

Barbara Morgan,
Melrose, Massachusetts

Powdermaker, Hortense
(1896–1970)

American anthropologist, ethnologist, and educator. *Born on December 24, 1896 (some sources erroneously cite 1900), in Philadelphia, Pennsylvania; died on June 15, 1970; daughter of Louis Powdermaker (a businessman) and Minnie (Jacoby) Powdermaker; Goucher College, B.A., 1919; London School of Economics, University of London, Ph.D., 1928.*

Selected works: Life in Lesu *(1933);* After Freedom *(1939);* Probing Our Prejudices *(1944);* Hollywood, The Dream Factory *(1950);* Copper Town *(1962);* Stranger and Friend: The Way of an Anthropologist *(1966).*

Born into a family of German-Jewish ancestry in Philadelphia on December 24, 1896, Hortense Powdermaker was the second child of **Minnie Jacoby Powdermaker** and Louis Powdermaker. She had a younger sister and brother, and an older sister, **Florence Powdermaker**, who would become a well-known psychiatrist. Louis was a middle-class businessman whose income fluctuated a great deal, particularly in comparison to the incomes of Hortense's grandfathers, who were quite prosperous businessmen. She grew up, in essence, in an extended family whose upper-middle-class existence was not quite within the reach of her own father. An impressionable, perceptive youth, Powdermaker grew up to be deeply sensitive about social distinctions. She was very much aware of the capitalist values and the social pressures and snobbery that were prevalent in her family. After moving to Reading, Pennsylvania, when she was five, the family settled about seven years later in Baltimore, Maryland, where Powdermaker was confirmed in a Reform synagogue and attended Western High School.

After graduation, she attended Goucher College, majoring in history. As a Jew on campus, she was ostracized at times, and her already keen social awareness was further heightened when she was not invited to join a sorority because of her Jewish background. While she was a student at Goucher, she became interested in socialism and the labor movement, and for a short time worked in a shirt factory. After earning her B.A. in 1919, Powdermaker moved to New York City and found employment with the Amalgamated Clothing Workers, where she became a union organizer. In 1925, she sailed for London to attend the London School of Economics. While there, she had an experience that helped determine her path; she registered for an anthropology class taught by the distinguished anthropologist Bronislaw Malinowski, who became her mentor. Malinowski, who was just beginning to develop his theory of functionalism, was exploring the relationship between anthropology and psychoanalysis. "Anthropology was what I had been looking for without knowing it," said Powdermaker, and she earned her Ph.D. from the University of London in 1928.

Powdermaker's first independent field study was funded by a grant from the Australian National Research Council, and with it she became the first woman ethnologist to have lived alone among the Melanesian population of New Ireland, an island belonging to the Bismarck Archipelago in the Southwest Pacific. She lived in a small village for ten months, studying the local stone-age culture's customs and rituals, and published her study, *Life in Lesu*, in 1933. After she left New Ireland, Powdermaker worked at Yale University's Institute of Human Relations with the National Research Council from 1930 to 1932. Her commitment to social justice often guided her choice of topics for field research, and in 1932 she was granted a Social Science Research Council fellowship which enabled her to conduct a study of rural Indianola, Mississippi. She received encouragement for this study from the well-known cultural anthropologist Edward Sapir, whose theories about culture and language influenced her own. Powdermaker's was the first community study to be conducted by an anthropologist in the United States. She also helped psychologist John Dollard survey Indianola, and, although Dollard published his study first (*Caste and Class in a Southern Town*, 1937), Powdermaker's publication of *After Freedom* (1939) was a more in-depth survey of the social structure of the black and white communities of that town, and remains in print. Presenting herself as a visiting teacher, she lived in Indianola (the name of the town was disguised as "Cottonville" in the book) for about a year, interviewing people in both the black and white communities and studying the attitudes and lifestyles of blacks and whites living in the city and in the surrounding, cotton-growing areas. The study also addressed the issue of biracial relationships, a topic that was taboo at the time, and included information regarding the sociological impact of the African-American church. Later, she wrote a related article, "The Channeling of Negro Aggression by the Cultural Process" (*American Journal of Sociology*, May

Hortense Powdermaker

1943), which reflected the psychoanalytic influence of Malinowski.

In 1938, Powdermaker became part of the teaching staff at Queens College in New York City, where she would become a full professor in 1954 and teach anthropology until her retirement in 1968. She founded a joint anthropology-sociology program at the college, and was extremely popular with her students. She was an enthusiastic lecturer who had a talent for reaching her audience and drawing her listeners in. Putting those talents to further use, she published a book for high schoolers, *Probing Our Prejudices* (1944), which attempted to clarify the issues surrounding prejudice. Powdermaker was often invited to lecture and teach at other colleges, and offered a course on cultural anthropology at the William Alanson White Institute of Psychiatry, Psychoanalysis, and Psychology (1944–52) and in the psychiatry department at the New York College of Medicine (1958). She also lectured and taught at Columbia, the New School for Social Research, the University of Minnesota, and the University of California at Los Angeles. After World War II, she continued to study the complexities of racism and published several articles on the topic.

During the years 1946 and 1947, Powdermaker focused on the movie-making machine in Hollywood, about which she had become curious years earlier; while conducting her field research in Mississippi, she had realized how powerful the film industry was by observing the ease with which movies influenced the citizens of Indianola. In 1947, she received a grant from the Wenner-Gren Foundation of Anthropological Research to study how the social structure of Hollywood ultimately affected both those who were involved in making movies and the type of movie that was produced. *Hollywood, The Dream Factory* (1950) was quite popular with the general public and is still considered a valuable portrait of the era. The book describes how the primary force behind making a film is profit; producers know which movie-making formulas work best, follow the formula, and therefore reflect prevailing social attitudes. The book also examines totalitarian aspects of the Hollywood culture, in which people were considered property, and explains the ways in which the industry usually portrayed life experiences as a result of "accident" or "luck" rather than showing the process of success or of destruction. After Powdermaker finished this project, she kept her focus on the ways in which mass media affects culture. In 1953–54, with a grant from the Guggenheim Foundation, she spent a year in Northern Rhodesia (later Zambia), Africa, studying the relationship between mass media and social change. The results of this study were published as *Copper Town* (1962).

Two years before her retirement from Queens College, Powdermaker published her last and most important book, *Stranger and Friend: The Way of an Anthropologist* (Norton, 1966), in which she described her experiences in conducting field studies and explained the importance of understanding other cultures. Powdermaker was a member of numerous anthropological societies, including the American Ethnological Society (for which she served as president from 1946 to 1947), the American Ethnological Society, and the American Anthropological Society, and was awarded an honorary D.Sc. degree by Goucher College in 1957. She loved to cook and entertain, and her "family" consisted of her colleagues, many students, and her foster son Won Mo Kim. Powdermaker was studying women of post-retirement age when she died of a heart attack at age 73 on June 15, 1970.

SOURCES:

Bailey, Brooke. *The Remarkable Lives of 100 Women Healers and Scientists.* Holbrook, MA: Bob Adams, 1994.

Current Biography 1961. NY: H.W. Wilson, 1962.

Sicherman, Barbara, and Carol Hurd Green, eds. *Notable American Women: The Modern Period.* Cambridge, MA: The Belknap Press of Harvard University, 1980.

SUGGESTED READING:

Powdermaker, Hortense. *Stranger and Friend: The Way of an Anthropologist.* NY: Norton, 1966.

Trager, George L. Tribute and obituary, in *American Anthropologist.* June 1971, pp. 783–787.

Christine Miner Minderovic,
freelance writer, Ann Arbor, Michigan

Powell, Dawn (1897–1965)

American writer whose work began receiving renewed attention at the end of the 20th century. *Born on November 28, 1897, in Mount Gilead, Ohio; died on November 15, 1965, in New York City; daughter of Roy K. Powell and Hattie B. (Sherman) Powell; Lake Erie College, Painesville, Ohio, B.A., 1918; married Joseph Roebuck Gousha (an advertising executive), on November 20, 1920 (died 1962); children: Joseph, Jr. (b. 1921).*

Selected writings: Whither *(1925);* She Walks in Beauty *(1928);* The Bride's House *(1929, reissued 1998);* Dance Night *(1930, reissued 1999);* The Tenth Moon *(1932);* Big Night *(play, 1933);* Jig Saw *(play, 1934);* The Story of a Country Boy *(1934);* Turn, Magic Wheel *(1936, reissued 1999);* The Happy Island *(1938, reissued 1998);* Angels on Toast *(1940, reissued 1990);* Lady Comes Across *(play, 1941);* A Time to Be Born *(1942, reissued 1996);* My Home Is Far Away *(1944, reissued 1995);* The Locusts Have No King *(1948, reissued 1996);* Sunday, Monday and Always *(short stories, 1952, reissued 1999);* The Wicked Pavilion *(1954, reissued 1996);* The Golden Spur *(1962, reissued 1997);* The Diaries of Dawn Powell: 1931–1965 *(ed. Tim Page, 1995).*

Born on November 28, 1897, in Mount Gilead, Ohio, Dawn Powell was one of three daughters of Roy K. Powell and **Hattie B. Sherman Powell**, both of whom had migrated to Ohio from southern Virginia. When Powell and her sisters were still quite small, their mother died. Because their father's work took him on the road, her death began a lengthy odyssey for the three sisters, during which they were passed from the care of one relative to another. They would live for a while with a relative on a farm, and then move to a small-town boarding house or to the hustle and bustle of a factory-town apartment. These childhood experiences helped to provide the background for many of the novels Powell would write later in life.

This nomadic existence, as unstable as it must have been, may well have been preferable to what followed for Powell and her sisters. In 1909, her father remarried, and the girls joined him on the farm owned by his new wife, located near Cleveland. None of the sisters were happy with their new living arrangements, but it was perhaps worst for Dawn, who clashed frequently with her stepmother. At the age of 12, she ran away from home after her stepmother incinerated all of the stories she had been writing. She had hit the road with only 30 cents, which she had earned picking berries, and moved in with an aunt in Shelby, Ohio. Here she attended the local public school and stepped up her writing activity by working on the school paper and at the local newspaper after school. Powell's *My Home Is Far Away*, originally published in 1944 and subtitled *An Autobiographical Novel*, is an insightful examination of these unhappy childhood years in the Midwest.

After her graduation from high school, Powell attended Lake Erie College in Painesville, Ohio, while working some five hours each day to support herself. She and a couple of college friends launched a "secret" paper, and later she became editor-in-chief of the college magazine. She earned her B.A. in 1918 and moved to New York City to seek her fortune. She arrived in the big city during the final days of the First World War and joined the U.S. Naval Reserve, managing to get in three weeks of work before the end of the war.

Much of what is known about Powell's life has come from her diaries, which were published in 1995. Although no one knows for certain when she began keeping them, it is believed that some may have been among the writings burned by her stepmother. In a journal she kept while working as a waitress and maid at a Lake Erie summer resort called the Shore Club, she addressed her observations to an imaginary friend she called "Woggs." One such entry from this summer 1915 diary reads as follows: "Dear Woggsie, I'm melancholy again. It's too bad that I'm always confiding in you on those days I feel the bluest. This book is enough to make a stone weep and if anyone should read it they would think the writer was indeed in pathetic straits. But no one will ever read it so I think I'm really wiser to do it this way—tell my blue, weepy thoughts to you, who will never reveal them to another soul, instead of inflicting them on the people around me—and when I'm in a flip, gay mood, I take it off on other people." Thus was established a pattern that Powell was to follow for most of her life. Her public writings were upbeat and filled with witty and often acerbic observations, while she saved her expressions of fear, doubt, and pain mostly for her diaries.

In 1920, while living on the Upper West Side of Manhattan and working in publicity, Powell met and fell in love with Joseph Roebuck Gousha. A poet and music critic from Pittsburgh, he had become a successful advertising executive in New York. Her brief, gushing references to Gousha in her diaries show little indication that Powell would someday be seen as a brilliant satirist. Among the entries in Powell's "Book of Joe" are the following: "My Adorable came tonight. Our last Sunday alone. . . . I went to Joe's house for dinner and we walked to the Bay. My Adorable is so lovely. . . . My Adorable. I wonder what he truly wants. I wish it was the same thing I want." The couple married on November 20 that year.

Powell and her husband had only one child, a son named Joseph, Jr., born on August 22, 1921. Seriously disabled from birth, "Jojo," as he was known by his parents, has been described as suffering from a combination of schizophrenia and cerebral palsy, and spent most of his life shuttling between a number of institutions and his family's home, where Powell cared for him. She deeply loved her son and took great joy in the modest accomplishments of his life.

Powell's first novel, *Whither*, was published in 1925, though she made it clear later in life that her first literary venture was something she would prefer be forgotten. Three years later, in 1928, *She Walks in Beauty* was published by Brentano, a testimony to the persistence of Powell, who collected more than 35 rejection slips while shopping the novel around to publishing houses. She followed this with *The Bride's House* (1929), *Dance Night* (1930), *The Tenth Moon* (1932), *The Story of a Country Boy* (1934), *Turn, Magic Wheel* (1936), and *Angels on Toast* (1940), among others. In all, Powell published 15 novels and also wrote more than 100 short stories and a half-dozen plays, including 1933's *Big Night*, which was produced by the Theater Guild. New York City and Ohio were two of her favorite settings; the novel *Dance Night*, a story of young love and ambition set in a small town, was an expression of her distaste for the Ohio town of her childhood. Particularly in her New York satires, Powell portrayed with wit and insight the lives of writers, artists, publishers and businessmen (or, in the words of the *New York Herald Tribune*, "such sub-species as the Double-Dyed Phony, the Barshopping Lush and the Love-Nesting Roundheels") caught up in the intoxicating world of Manhattan. In 1949, Glenway Wescott proclaimed that she was "doing for New York what Balzac did for Paris."

Powell's life was generally unhappy, marred by drinking, health problems, financial instability, and an unsatisfying marriage that became a triangle when she began a long-standing affair with Coburn "Coby" Gilman around 1930. A number of reviewers, commenting on her diaries, have noted the contrast between the often unpleasant personality that emerges from the entries and the fascination engendered by observing the progress of her writing life in those same pages. Powell's husband died in 1962. She died three years later, less than two weeks before her 68th birthday, and was buried on Hart Island, New York City's potter's field. Interest in her writing fell off rapidly, although, in an assessment of her contribution to 20th-century literature written soon after her death, *The New York Times* noted: "While Miss Powell's novels were never best-sellers, they attracted devoted admirers in both the United States and England. [Edmund] Wilson called them 'among the most amusing being written, and in this respect quite on a level with those of Anthony Powell, Evelyn Waugh, and ***Muriel Spark**.'" In 1987, after Gore Vidal published an essay on her work in *The New York Review of Books*, Powell's books were rediscovered. Many of them have since been reissued to glowing critical acclaim, and the first full-length biography of her was published in 1998.

SOURCES AND SUGGESTED READING:

Belles Lettres. Vol. 11. January 1996, pp. 13–14.

Contemporary Authors. First Revision Vol. 5–8. Detroit, MI: Gale Research.

Kunitz, Stanley J., and Howard Haycraft, eds. *Twentieth Century Authors*. NY: H.W. Wilson, 1942.

Page, Tim. *Dawn Powell: A Biography*. NY: Holt, 1998.

Powell, Dawn. *The Diaries of Dawn Powell, 1931–1965*. Edited by Tim Page. Steerforth, 1995.

Publishers Weekly. August 3, 1998, p. 61.

The Women's Review of Books. Vol. XIII, no. 4. January 1996, p. 6.

Don Amerman,
freelance writer, Saylorsburg, Pennsylvania

Powell, Eleanor (1910–1982)

American dancer and actress who starred in MGM musicals of the 1930s and 1940s. *Born on November 21, 1910, in Springfield, Massachusetts; died of cancer on February 11, 1982; married Glenn Ford (an actor), in 1943 (divorced 1959): children: one son, Peter.*

Selected theater: Follow Thru *(1929);* Fine and Dandy *(1930);* Hot-Cha! *(1932);* George White's Music Hall Varieties *(1932);* At Home Abroad *(1935).*

Filmography: George White's Scandals *(1935);* Broadway Melody of 1936 *(1935);* Born to Dance *(1936);* Broadway Melody of 1938 *(1937);* Rosalie *(1937);* Honolulu *(1939);* Broadway Melody of 1940 *(1940);* Lady Be Good *(1941);* Ship Ahoy *(1942);* Thousands Cheer *(1943);* I Dood It *(1943);* Sensations of 1945 *(1944);* Duchess of Idaho *(1950).*

Eleanor Powell made only 13 movies during her Hollywood career, but her dancing talent and exuberance have never been duplicated. The great director-choreographer Busby Berkeley, who worked with her in *Lady Be Good* (1941), put her in a class all her own. "Eleanor was by far the finest female dancer we ever had in films, and a very hard-working perfectionist," he said. "I've known very few women that talented and that gracious." Praise for the dancer also came from a more unlikely source, Maestro Arturo Toscanini. "Three things I will carry through life," he said, "the glorious sunset, the splendor of the Grand Canyon and the dancing of Eleanor Powell."

An only child, Powell was born in 1910 in Springfield, Massachusetts, and was two when her parents divorced. She began dancing lessons when she was 6, and at 13 Gus Edwards hired her for his children's revue at the Ritz Grill of the Ambassador Hotel. After she graduated from high school, Powell went to New York, where she discovered that in order to dance on Broadway, she had to add tap to her repertoire of ballet and acrobatics. After lessons from Jack Donahue and hours of hard practice, she landed a part in *Follow Thru* (1929), after which she did a string of shows, including *George White's Music Hall Varieties* (1932), with Harry Richman and Bert Lahr. "There is a large dancing chorus," reported *The New York Times* in its review of the show, "but among the supporting company it is the lanky Eleanor Powell, an excellent tap dancer, who stands out markedly."

The Fox studio called on Powell to dance in a screen version of *Music Hall Varieties*, but ultimately saw no potential in her decidedly unglamorous appearance. However, when MGM saw her dance number in the film, they envisioned another *Ruby Keeler. After a stem-to-stern makeover that included extensive dental work, voice lessons, and a sophisticated new look, Powell made her movie debut in *Broadway Melody of 1936* (1935), executing a couple of dazzling tap numbers that catapulted her into "overnight" stardom. After a trip to New York to fulfill a previous commitment, she returned to Hollywood, where she signed a seven-year contract with MGM. She then starred in a series of musicals, at the rate of one a year. By the time she finished *Honolulu* (1939), in which she tapped the hula and danced while skipping rope, she was making $125,000 per film.

In 1940, with great anticipation, MGM teamed Powell with her counterpart Fred Astaire in *Broadway Melody of 1940*, but the two lacked screen chemistry together. Part of the problem may have been Powell's acting, which *The New York Times* found automatic at best: "[T]he final impression of her characterization continues to be the memory of a professional smile, turned on and off like an essentially unamused neon." While further plans for Astaire-Powell pairings were shelved, the two parted on good terms.

By the time Powell departed from MGM in 1943, the public had tired of tap-dancing and the studio had no interest in renewing her contract. The actress, who had been dating her secretary Sid Luft (future husband of ***Judy Garland**), married rising star Glenn Ford that year, and retired to private life. The couple had one son, Peter (b. 1945), before divorcing in 1959. (Ford "had such an inferiority complex, it was sheer hell," Powell would say later.) For the most part, Powell busied herself with community and church activities, although she came out of retirement in 1954 to appear on the Emmy Award-winning "Faith of Our Children" religious teleseries. After her divorce, and with encouragement from her son, Powell dieted down to dancing weight and began rehearsing a nightclub revue which opened at the Sahara Club in Las Vegas in February 1961. The show was a hit, and she went on to play at the Latin Quarter in Manhattan. "Eleanor Powell has Broadway at her feet once again," announced *The New York Times*. Powell continued to play club engagements, and made television appearances on "The Perry Como Show" and "The Hollywood Palace."

Religion had always played an important part in Powell's life, and in 1964, she gave up the club circuit and became an ordained minister of the Unity Church. She enjoyed a brief burst of publicity after the release of the MGM documentary *That's Entertainment* (1974), and in March 1981, she attended an American Film Institute tribute to Fred Astaire, one of her last public appearances. Powell died of cancer on February 11, 1982.

SOURCES:

Katz, Ephraim. *The Film Encyclopedia*. NY: HarperCollins, 1994.

Lamparski, Richard. *Whatever Became of . . . ?* 2nd series. NY: Crown, 1968.

Parish, James Robert, and Michael R. Pitts. *Hollywood Songsters*. NY: Garland, 1991.

Barbara Morgan,
Melrose, Massachusetts

Powell, Jane (1929—)

American singer-actress. *Born Suzanne Burce on April 1, 1929, in Portland, Oregon; daughter of Paul Burce (a delivery man) and Eileen Burce; graduated from the MGM school, 1947; married Geary Anthony Steffen, Jr. (a professional ice skater), on November 5, 1949 (divorced); married Patrick Nerney (an auto dealer and later a writer), on November 8, 1954 (divorced 1963); married James Fitzgerald (later her manager), on June 27, 1965 (divorced 1976); married David Parlour (a producer-director), on October 21, 1978 (divorced 1981); married Dickie Moore (former child star and a business executive), on May 21, 1988; children: (first marriage) Geary Anthony Steffen (b. 1951);* ***Suzanne Irene Steffen*** *(b. 1952); (second marriage) daughter,* ***Lindsay Averille Nerney*** *(b. 1956).*

Selected filmography: Song of the Open Road *(1944);* Delightfully Dangerous *(1945);* Holiday in Mexico *(1946);* Three Daring Daughters *(1948);* A Date with Judy *(1948);* Luxury Liner *(1848);* Nancy Goes to Rio *(1950);* Two Weeks with Love *(1950);* Royal Wedding *(1951);* Rich Young and Pretty *(1951);* Small Town Girl *(1953);* Three Sailors and a Girl *(1953);* Seven Brides for Seven Brothers *(1954);* Athena *(1954);* Deep in My Heart *(1954);* Hit the Deck *(1955);* The Girl Most Likely *(1957);* The Female Animal *(1958);* Enchanted Island *(1958);* Marie *(cameo, 1985).*

A successor to popular film singer ***Deanna Durbin**, vivacious, blonde teenager Jane Powell lit up a series of MGM musicals during the years between 1946 and 1954. With the demise of the Hollywood musical, however, Powell's career floundered, and, except for a brief stint in a Broadway revival of *Irene* in 1974, she never achieved stardom again. Like many child stars of her era, Powell also had difficulty resolving her

Jane Powell

personal needs with a career image that demanded sweetness and compliance. Her frustration did not surface until years later, in her 1980s one-woman show and her autobiography *The Girl Next Door and How She Grew* (1988). "I was always pleasing someone else," she said about her years in the movies. "My mother, the men I married, the studio. . . . I did what I was told. There were only three things I wanted to do and did—marry, have children, get divorced. Otherwise, it was always someone else who decided for me."

Powell was born Suzanne Burce on April 1, 1929, in Portland, Oregon, the only child of an unhappy union that eventually ended in divorce. Her mother, after discovering Powell's natural gifts, became intent on turning the child into another ***Shirley Temple (Black)**, and to that end enrolled her at the Agnes Peters Dancing School. As a tot of 5, Powell made her singing debut on a local children's radio show, "Stars of Tomorrow," and at 11 landed her own Sunday evening radio program. Her break came in June 1943, when she made an appearance on the Los Angeles-based talent program "Hollywood Showcase Stars over Hollywood." Displaying her remarkable two-and-a-half-octave range in a rendition of the "Il Baccio" aria from *Carmen*, Powell was declared the winner over six other contestants. After an unprecedented six appearances on the show, she was offered a contract with MGM, which she felt compelled to accept. "I felt then—and I feel now—that if I hadn't accepted MGM's offer it would have destroyed Mama and Daddy sooner, and would have made their marriage even harder and more unhappy," she later recalled.

Without any acting lessons—or even as much as a screen test—Powell was immediately loaned to United Artists for *Song of the Open Road* (1944), a musical with W.C. Fields and the team of Edgar Bergen and his dummy Charlie McCarthy. Her role was that of a young movie starlet named Jane Powell, which she then adopted as her stage name. The movie, in which she sang four songs, including the classical "Carmena," brought her to the attention of the critics and led to an ongoing role on the Bergen-McCarthy radio program, "The Chase and Sanborn

Hour," as Charlie's love interest. Following her second movie, *Delightfully Dangerous* (1945), also made on loan to United Artists, *The New York Times* pronounced Powell "a shimmering vision of youth in bloom . . . sweet and charming—not the least bit cloying."

Meanwhile, producer Joe Pasternak, who had been a leading force in Deanna Durbin's career at Universal and was now at MGM, took an interest in Powell, casting her in *Holiday in Mexico* (1946) as the matchmaking daughter of the American ambassador (played by Walter Pidgeon). The film, in which she sang "Ave Maria," put her career into high gear. Powell appeared on the cover of *Life* magazine's September issue and negotiated a raise in pay. There followed a series of successful musical romps, most notable among them *A Date with Judy* (1948), *Royal Wedding* (1951), and *Seven Brides for Seven Brothers* (1954), her most important MGM movie to date, and her last first-rate screen role. Loosely based on Stephen Vincent Benet's "The Sobbin' Women," the movie co-starred Howard Keel as Powell's love interest, and gave her the opportunity to shine in such songs as "Wonderful, Wonderful Day" and in an ensemble song-and-dance routine, "June Bride."

As early as 1948, Powell had begun to rebel against her image as "The Girl Next Door," expressing the desire to grow up and make her own career decisions, particularly about what she sang. "I loved to sing ballads and the blues, but I rarely got to do them," she said. In November 1949, as part of her quest for independence, Powell married professional ice skater Geary Anthony Steffen, Jr. (then ***Sonja Henie**'s partner), and took two years off from the movies. The marriage produced two children, son Geary Anthony (b. 1951) and daughter Suzanne Irene (b. 1952). The couple subsequently divorced and in November 1954 Powell married Patrick Nerney, an auto dealer (he later became a writer).

Powell, disheartened when the role of ***Ruth Etting** in *Love Me or Leave Me* (1955) went to ***Doris Day**, negotiated her release from MGM. Following a very successful Hollywood Bowl concert and the birth of another daughter, Lindsay Averille (b. 1956), she attempted to resume her film career, but her squeaky clean image was now passé. After two unsuccessful pictures for Universal and another for Warner Bros., she turned to television, appearing in two musical specials: "Ruggles of Red Gap"(1957) and "Meet Me in St. Louis" (1959). She also did television guest appearances, summer stock, and starred in a revue, *Just Twenty—Plus Me*, that closed after a pre-Broadway tour in Texas. A more promising Broadway opportunity came in 1974, when Powell was signed to replace **Debbie Reynolds** in a revival of *Irene*. "She makes the girl from Ninth Avenue both believable and appealing," reported the *New York Post*, "and she can play an emotional scene convincingly. Indeed, you might think the part had been created for her." After a seven-month run in New York, Powell went on tour with the show.

In the meantime, Powell's marriage to Nerney had ended, as had her subsequent marriage to James Fitzgerald, who became her manager and remained so even after their divorce in 1976. In October 1978, she married David Parlour, a producer-director. They separated a year later and went through a much-publicized divorce in early 1981. At that time, Powell resettled in Los Angeles, hoping to find some film and television work, but her age now proved a detriment. She moved back East and, after a few guest shows on television and some concert dates, signed on for a role in the soap opera "Loving," playing the rich matriarch of a ranch in Wyoming. During the 1980s, she toured her one-woman show *Jane Powell Inside Out—Her Story Live*, which she prepared at the suggestion of **Pat Carroll**, who had been successful with her own solo vehicle. In 1988, Powell published an honest, straightforward autobiography. "Unlike most Hollywood kiss and tell books, it's toughest on the author," commented one critic. "Jane Powell doesn't trash anyone, except Jane Powell."

Also in 1988, Powell married her live-in companion, former child actor Dickie Moore, even though she had vowed after her fourth divorce never to remarry. ("No more marriages, no more babies, no more puppies," she said.) She continued to sing in concert and to make occasional television guest appearance on such shows as "Murder, She Wrote" and "Growing Pains." Most important, she had finally gained control over her own destiny. "The Girl Next Door has turned into a very happy woman," she said.

SOURCES:

Katz, Ephraim. *The Film Encyclopedia*. NY: HarperCollins, 1994.

Parish, James Robert, and Michael R. Pitts. *Hollywood Songsters*. NY: Garland, 1991.

Barbara Morgan,
Melrose, Massachusetts

Powell, Maud (1867–1920)

Concert artist who became the first American violinist to win international critical acclaim. *Born on August 22, 1867, in Peru, Illinois; died on January 8,*

1920, in Uniontown, Pennsylvania; daughter of Wilhelmina (Minnie) Bengelstraeter (Paul) Powell (an amateur composer and pianist) and (William) Bramwell Powell (a nationally known, innovative educator and textbook author); began piano lessons with her mother at age four; subsequent piano teachers included Emma Fickensher and Agnes Ingersoll; violin teachers included G. William Fickensher, William Lewis, Henry Schradieck, Charles Dancla, and Joseph Joachim; married H. Godfrey "Sunny" Turner (a concert manager), on September 21, 1904; no children.

Gave first public violin performance (1876); studied in Germany at the Leipzig Conservatory (1881–82); studied at the Paris Conservatory (1882–83); toured Great Britain (1883–84); studied at the Berlin Hochschule (1884–85); performed as a soloist with Joseph Joachim conducting the Berlin Philharmonic (1885); made New York debut with Theodore Thomas conducting the New York Philharmonic (1885); toured western United States (1887–88); gave American premiere of Tchaikovsky Violin Concerto (1889) and Dvorak Violin Concerto (1894); made European tour with Arion Society (1892); chosen as representative American violinist for Theodore Thomas' Exposition Orchestra concerts at World's Columbian Exposition in Chicago (1893); delivered a paper on "Women and the Violin" and premiered American composer Amy Beach's "Romance" with Beach at the piano at Women's Musical Congress (1893); formed the Maud Powell String Quartet (1894); toured Europe (1898–1905), twice as soloist with John Philip Sousa and his band (1903, 1905); was the first solo instrumentalist to record for Victor's Celebrity Artist series (Red Seal label, 1904–19); led her own concert company on tour of South Africa (1905); gave American premiere of Sibelius Violin Concerto (1906); formed Maud Powell Trio (1908–09); performed for American soldiers during World War I (1917–18).

Selected published articles: "Women and the Violin," Ladies' Home Journal *(February 1896); "The Price of Fame," in* New Idea Woman's Magazine *(December 1908); "How Fashion Invades the Concert Stage," in* Musical America *(December 26, 1908); "The American Girl and Her Violin," in* Étude 27 *(No. 7, July 1909, pp. 486–487); "Violin Interpretation," in* Étude 27 *(No. 8, August 1909); "Maud Powell's Musical Education," in* The Musician *(March 1910, reprinted from* The Pictorial Review, *n.d.); "Struggles Which Led to Success," in* The Étude *(October 1911); "The Violinist," in* The Delineator *(October 1911); "Musical Future of America," in* Violinist *(September 1911); "Pitting American Violin Works Against the Foreign Product," in* Musical America 14 *(No. 23, October 14, 1911, p. 123); "The Violinist," in* Delineator *(October 1911); "How To Enjoy Music," in* Musician *(August 1917, p. 634); "America is Getting the 'Shaking Up' She Needed For Her Soul-Awakening," in* Musical America *(October 20, 1917); "Two Types of Violin Playing," in* Étude 36 *(No. 11, November 1918, p. 698); "An Artist's Life," in* Musical Observer *(1918); "We Shall Evolve a Real School of National Art, Literature and Music," in* Musical America *(October 19, 1918); "Wieniawski's Legende, Analytical Lesson by Maud Powell," in* The Étude *(c. 1918).*

Selected published transcriptions: Coleridge-Taylor, Deep River *(Boston: Oliver Ditson Company, 1905); Couperin,* La Fleurie *(NY: G. Schirmer, 1906); Gluck, "Melody" from the opera* Orfeo *(Boston: G. Schirmer, 1910); Chopin,* Waltz, Op. 64, No. 1 *(Boston: G. Schirmer, 1910); Dvořák,* Songs My Mother Sang *(NY: Breitkopf and Hartel, 1917); Beethoven,* Minuet in G, No. 2 *(NY: Breitkopf and Hartel, 1917); Martini,* Love's Delight *(*Plaisir d'amour, *NY: Breitkopf and Hartel, 1917); Jensen,* Serenata *(NY: Breitkopf and Hartel, 1918); Foster,* Plantation Melodies *(NY: Carl Fischer, 1919); J.R. Johnson,* Nobody Knows the Trouble I See *(NY: Oliver Ditson Company, 1921); Rimsky-Korsakov,* Song of India *(New York, Breitkopf and Hartel, n.d.).*

Selected published cadenzas: Original Cadenza to Brahms Violin Concerto Violexchange 2, *No. 2 (1987).*

Selected music editions: Pietro Locatelli, Sonata in F Minor for Violin and Piano, *Op. 6, No. 7; harmonized by L.A. Zellner; revised and edited by Maud Powell (NY: G. Schirmer, 1919).*

Selected published recordings: The Art of Maud Powell, A "Victor Immortal" *(1904–1917), historic reissue, 3 compact discs, MPF-1, MPF-2, MPF-3, The Maud Powell Foundation, Arlington, Virginia, 1989;* Maud Powell, *Biddulph Lab 094, historic reissue, compact disc, 1994.*

When Maud Powell stepped into the Victor recording studio for the first time in 1904, the art of violin playing was about to be revolutionized. The unparalleled standard for violin performance that Powell engraved on the spinning wax ushered in the modern age of violin playing. The Victor Company's choice of Powell as the first solo instrumentalist to record for its newly inaugurated celebrity artist series (Red Seal label) was no surprise. Internationally recognized as America's greatest violinist, she easily ranked among the supreme violinists of the time, including Joseph Joachim, Eugene Ysaije, and, later, Fritz Kreisler. Powell was also a popular favorite, winning the affection of the American public with her unabashed enthusiasm for the violin. Ushered into a small, acoustically "dead" room in November 1904, she was strategically placed before a large, gaping funnel. The nearer one stood to this mechanical monster, the better the recording. The music's vibrations agitated a needle in an adjoining room that scratched impressions of sound waves on the soft, spinning wax from which a record could then be molded. "I am never as frightened as I am when I stand in front of that horn to play," Powell once explained. "There's a ghastly feeling that you're playing for all the world and an awful sense that what is done *is* done."

Although acoustic recording was a wholly mechanical process, primitive by today's standards, when allied with the impeccable art of Maud Powell it revolutionized the way music was heard. (Electrical recording [with microphone] began in 1925, five years after Powell's death.) At a time when music was heard live or not at all, Powell welcomed the new technology, knowing that classical music would become popular as it became more familiar through repeated hearings. Upholding a high artistic standard from the beginning, she insisted immediately upon recording the Finale to the Mendelssohn violin concerto—even though she had to squeeze a reduced version into the severe time limitations of four minutes and fifty seconds. In 1907, her recording of Drdla's Souvenir became the best seller of all violin recordings, European and American, with Massenet's Meditation from *Thais* becoming a close second in 1909. Powell's recordings were enhanced by her violin which was labeled "Joannes Baptista Guadagnini, in Turin 1775"; she cherished the instrument for its ringing clarity and responsiveness to her command.

She was born a pioneer by heritage on August 22, 1867, in Peru, Illinois, on the Western frontier of America's heartland. Her grandparents had been Methodist missionaries in Ohio, Wisconsin, and Illinois before the Civil War. Powell's father Bramwell Powell was an innovative educator who served as superintendent of the public schools in Peru, then Aurora, Illinois, and finally Washington, D.C. Her mother **Minnie Paul Powell** was a pianist and composer whose gender had precluded a career in music. Minnie's and Bramwell's sisters were active in the women's suffrage movement, and Maud would later remember the visits of women's suffrage leader ***Susan B. Anthony** to her home in Aurora. Powell's uncle John Wesley Powell, Civil War hero and explorer of the Grand Canyon, organized the scientific study of the Western lands and the American Indians. The powerful director of the U.S. Geological Survey and Bureau of Ethnology, he was also, with his brother Bramwell, founder of the National Geographic Society.

Both of Powell's parents shared a love of music. Under the tutelage of her mother, she began music lessons and by age four could play short pieces on the piano flawlessly. Powell later wrote of her early music instruction:

> My mother is musical, but her talent whatever it might have been with cultivation, remained undeveloped. She often said to me, I have achieved through you what I was never able to do myself. It was my mother who, so to speak, first "tried music on me" to find out if I was musical.

A prodigy, Powell began private violin study in Aurora with G. William Fickensher, a German musician who headed the music department for the Aurora public schools. She studied piano with his daughter **Emma Fickensher**. Rising at 6:30 AM, Powell practiced for an hour before breakfast and an hour after school under her parents' watchful eyes and attentive ears. By the age of eight, she was playing Mozart violin sonatas accompanied by her mother.

Powell's progress was so rapid that after only a year of instruction, Fickensher recommended that she continue her studies with William Lewis, one of the best violinists and teachers in Chicago. Later, Powell would remark, "To William Lewis, a man of genius who played the fiddle because he couldn't help it, I owe much of my vigor and freedom of style." In fact, she said she "owed the most" to this "unfettered" player, who laid the foundation for her solid technique, impeccable musical taste, and wide sympathies. She simultaneously studied piano with **Agnes Ingersoll**, an associate of Lewis' in chamber music who, along with him, founded the Chicago Chamber Music Society. Powell made the weekly 40-mile trek to Chicago by train on her own because her parents could not afford to go with her. Recognizing her exceptional talent, Lewis played duets with Powell in some of her first public appearances in 1876.

After four years with Lewis, Powell was sent abroad to complete her studies supported in part by the financial generosity of Aurora residents. In 1881, she was placed among the most advanced pupils as she began a year of study with Henry Schradieck at the Leipzig Conservatory. Reviews that survive of Powell's performances from the Leipzig period laud her "exact intona-

Maud Powell

tion," "accuracy in bowing," and "remarkable depth of emotion." The following year, she was one of 6 students selected from some 88 applicants to study at the Paris Conservatory with the eminent violinist and teacher Charles Dancla. She would later credit him with showing her "how to develop purity of style. . . . [H]e taught me how to become an artist, just as I had learned in Germany to become a musician."

Following only six months' study with Dancla, Powell was advised that she would gain more from performing experience than formal studies. So she embarked on an extended concert tour in Great Britain (1883–84). While in London, she was introduced to Joseph Joachim, one of the greatest violin masters of the 19th century. After hearing Powell play, Joachim pronounced her an artist and invited her to study with him in Berlin. Her instruction with him began not with the usual technical études, but rather with the standard concert repertoire, especially concertos. Within one year, she concluded her lessons with Joachim, performing Max Bruch's Violin Concerto No. 1 in G Minor with her master conducting the Berlin Philharmonic (March 1885).

I was four years old when I began to play the violin, the same year in which Maud Powell died. I like to think that she bequeathed a legacy to me: the very truth she had lived and died for and her commitment to her violin, to her music, and to humanity.

—Yehudi Menuhin

Returning to the United States with the knowledge that "girl violinists were looked upon with suspicion," Powell boldly walked into a rehearsal of the all-male New York Philharmonic in Steinway Hall and demanded a hearing from Theodore Thomas, then America's foremost conductor. Deeply impressed by her playing, Thomas hired her on the spot to perform the Bruch G minor violin concerto with the New York Philharmonic on November 14, 1885. *New York Tribune* critic Henry E. Krehbiel acclaimed the 18-year-old's debut performance: "She is a marvelously gifted woman, one who in every feature of her playing discloses the instincts and gifts of a born artist."

At the time of Powell's debut, appreciation for her art was in its infancy in America, with only five professional orchestras, no established concert circuits, and few professional managers. Solo engagements were difficult to obtain, especially for an American female artist since all orchestra players and conductors were male and generally German. H. Godfrey "Sunny" Turner, who became Powell's husband and manager in 1904, once reflected: "If any young woman could really know what Maud Powell suffered for her art, she would not go into the game."

Yet Powell refused to be lured into a comfortable career in Europe. From 1885 forward, Theodore Thomas' "musical grandchild" was an indefatigable ambassador for her art, making it her mission to cultivate a higher and more widespread appreciation for classical music by performing throughout America, from the remote areas to the cultural centers. She played the most demanding music before dubious conductors and critics as well as skeptical managers and audiences. Early in her career, she dared to give the American premiere of the Tchaikovsky Violin Concerto on January 19, 1889, with Walter Damrosch conducting the New York Symphony. It was a courageous and "brilliant achievement" to present the "formidably difficult" work (*The New York Times*) that had been condemned after its world premiere in 1881 by Viennese critic Eduard Hanslick as "music that stinks in the ear." The concerto became one of Powell's personal favorites, and she performed it publicly until it became a standard in the violin repertory.

Theodore Thomas chose Powell to represent America's achievement in violin performance at the Chicago 1893 World's Columbian Exposition, where she was the only woman violin soloist with the Exposition Orchestra. During the Exposition, she presented a paper before the Women's Musical Congress on "Women and the Violin," in which she encouraged young women with the requisite "talent, health and application" to take up the violin seriously. At a time when women could not vote and were precluded from playing in professional orchestras, she argued that there was no reason why a woman should not play the violin with the best of the men.

Powell also championed works by women composers. She commissioned ***Marion Bauer** to compose a tone picture for violin based on Powell's own poem describing her experience in Florida's Everglades. At the Women's Musical Congress, Powell and American composer-pianist ***Amy Cheney Beach** (Mrs. H.H.A. Beach) premiered Beach's *Romance for Violin and Piano*, Op. 23, which Beach had written for and dedicated to Powell.

To reach people who had never before heard a concert, Powell pioneered the violin recital, blazing new concert circuits and enduring the difficult touring conditions in the far West. The direct communicative force of Powell's playing, evident in her recordings, stemmed partly from her experience of taking music to the American people. When urbane Easterners wondered how she was able to reach listeners lacking in sophistication, she replied: "I do not play to them as an artist to the public, but as one human being to another. Therefore, every one of the pieces I play must above all have human interest—an obvious appeal to some simple, fundamental emotion. Each one must be a complete mood in itself." Her uncle John Wesley Powell had observed that "no one can love a symphony who does not first love song." By her masterly programming of simple melodies with complex sonatas and concertos, Powell managed to build a bridge of understanding between song and symphony while never "playing down" to an audience.

Both with the Maud Powell String Quartet, which she formed in 1894, and with the Maud Powell Trio (1908–09), she played concertos and sonatas in recital and complex chamber music to a wide range of audiences. Acknowledged as America's "educator of a nation," she wrote her own program notes and many music-journal articles to broaden her audiences' understanding of music. Powell listened to and advised aspiring young musicians—including the violinist Louis Kaufman and Juilliard violin teacher **Christine Dethier**—and she eagerly met with music-club leaders to encourage the cultivation of music in each town. During World War I, she performed for the benefit of hospitals and schools as well as for soldiers. With clever programming, she won over the skeptical American self-made men who were dragged to concerts by their wives, and she played for children in severely deprived, out-of-the-way places. "Once I played for a theater full of miners' children," she recalled, "children who had never seen a tree, nor a blade of grass, nor had they ever heard music before a little brave school teacher came to town one day and slaved thereafter heart and soul to open their minds to a perception of beauty. . . . I consider it one of the triumphs of my life that I held them practically spellbound for forty-five minutes."

Frequently touring with her own Steinway grand piano, Powell was unconventional in making the pianist an equal partner in recital and in the recording studio. She chose such young pianists as the Americans Arthur Loesser and Francis Moore, the Danish Axel Skjerne, and the Russian Waldemar Liachowsky to accompany her on tour, ensuring a successful launching of their careers in America.

Basing herself in London, she primarily toured Europe in 1898–1905, yet returned regularly to tour the United States. On both sides of the Atlantic, she appeared with the great orchestras of her time under such conductors as Mahler, Nikisch, Thomas, Safonov, Damrosch, Seidl, Richter, Wood, Herbert, and Stokowski. English critics were surprised by her performances of the Tchaikovsky Concerto in Manchester (1899) and London (1902) under the batons of Hans Richter and Sir Henry Wood, respectively, when the work was still a novelty. The *Manchester Guardian* critic hailed her as "the most sensational violin player that we have ever heard," with an "astounding technical facility." Sir Henry Wood asserted that Powell played the Tchaikovsky Concerto "better than any other living violinist." In 1902, French composer Camille Saint-Saëns congratulated her on a "magnificent" performance of his B minor violin concerto in London under his direction.

John Philip Sousa invited Powell to tour Great Britain and Europe as soloist with his band in 1903. The pace was grueling: 13 different countries and 362 concerts scheduled in 30 weeks. She performed the Beethoven and Mendelssohn violin concertos with band accompaniment and violin favorites such as Camille Saint-Saëns' *Introduction and Rondo Capriccioso* and Henryk Wieniawski's *Faust Fantasie*. Sousa's cornet soloist Herman Bellstedt, Jr., composed *Caprice on Dixie* especially for Powell, a work she recorded and proudly rated as "quite worthy of Paganini." She would tour again with Sousa in 1905.

On September 21, 1904, Powell married English concert manager H. Godfrey "Sunny" Turner, who had managed Sousa's 1903 tour of Great Britain. Turner, whose fun-loving personality made him a genial companion, managed Powell's concert tours from that time on, including her pioneering and highly acclaimed tour of South Africa in 1905 at the head of her own concert company.

Perhaps Powell's greatest artistic triumph was her introduction of Jean Sibelius' Violin Concerto in D Minor to American audiences in 1906. Upon the premiere of this work—which Powell described in glowing terms as "a gigantic rugged thing, an epic really"—on November 30, 1906, *New York Sun* critic W.J. Henderson asked: "But why did she put all that magnificent art into this sour and crabbed concerto?" Henderson did not foresee that in the late 20th century this work by Sibelius would be one of the most recorded of all violin concertos. Powell had played it into this honored position.

Powell's artistry bridged the old and modern schools of violin playing. Although trained in the staid French and German schools, she developed a new and increasingly modern technique to meet the demands of new literature. With her American premieres of the Tchaikovsky, Dvorák and Sibelius violin concertos, she advanced the technique of the instrument into the modern age. Her technique, which had exceeded her teacher Joseph Joachim's at the time of her debut in 1885, ultimately pointed toward that of violinist Jascha Heifetz, who was to arrive in America only a few years before her death.

Her recorded legacy dates from 1904 to 1917 (recordings made in 1919 were never released) and documents Powell's influence on the development of classical music in America. On January 8, 1917, she gave a recital in Carnegie Hall based solely on her recorded repertoire, demonstrating dramatically how her alliance with the talking machine and her many personal appearances had transformed musical taste.

In all, she premiered 14 violin concertos in America, including those by Saint-Saëns, Lalo, Coleridge-Taylor, Arensky, Aulin, Huss, Shelley, Conus, Bruch, and Rimsky-Korsakov, as well as Tchaikovsky, Dvorák, and Sibelius. Unfortunately, she died before the technology could enable her to record these and other important works with orchestra. She revived neglected works of the 18th century, including Mozart's *Sinfonia Concertante* for violin and viola, and even edited a Locatelli violin sonata for publication.

Urging Americans to develop a musical culture of their own, Powell boldly championed the works of American composers including Amy Beach, Marion Bauer, Victor Herbert, Cecil Burleigh, Edwin Grasse, John Alden Carpenter, Henry Holden Huss, Henry Rowe Shelley, Arthur Foote, Charles Wakefield Cadman, and **Grace White**. Many composers dedicated works to her. Powell herself transcribed music for violin and piano, and she composed an original cadenza for the Brahms Violin Concerto.

Powell once said: "I expect to die with my violin in my hands." The strain of ceaseless travel and performing took its toll. While on tour in January 1920, she collapsed in her hotel room while preparing to go on stage in Uniontown, Pennsylvania. She died the following morning, January 8, 1920, of a massive heart attack. She was 52.

As a soloist and one of the first women to lead her own professional string quartet, her example had inspired large numbers of young girls to take up the violin and women in cities throughout the country to form music clubs and orchestras. In the year of her death, the 19th Amendment granting national suffrage to women was ratified.

Powell's art had represented a synthesis of the age-old European traditions transfused with the American spirit. Upon her death, the New York Symphony paid tribute to her: "She was not only America's great master of the violin, but a woman of lofty purpose and noble achievement, whose life and art brought to countless thousands inspiration for the good and the beautiful."

SOURCES:

Coolidge, Arlan R. "Maud Powell," in *Notable American Women.* Vol. 3. Cambridge, MA: The Belknap Press of Harvard University, 1971, pp. 90–92.

Greenwood, Neva Garner, and Karen A. Shaffer. "Maud Powell," in *The New Grove Dictionary of American Music.* Vol. 3. Edited by H. Wiley Hitchcock and Stanley Sadie. NY: Macmillan, 1986, p. 617.

Karpf, Juanita. "Maud Powell," in *American National Biography.* Edited by John A. Garraty. Cary, NC: Oxford University Press, 1994.

Martens, Frederick. "Maud Powell," in *Dictionary of American Biography.* Vol. 15. NY: Scribner, 1935, pp. 149–150.

"Powell, Maud," in *National Cyclopedia of American Biography.* Vol. 13. NY: James T. White, 1906, pp. 120–121.

Shaffer, Karen A., and Neva Garner Greenwood. *Maud Powell, Pioneer American Violinist.* Ames, IA: Iowa State University Press, 1988.

Slonimsky, Nicolas, ed. *Baker's Biographical Dictionary of Musicians.* 8th ed. NY: Schirmer Books, 1990. S.v. "Powell, Maud," pp. 1438–1439.

SUGGESTED READING:

Ammer, Christine. *Unsung: A History of Women in American Music.* Westport, CT: Greenwood Press, 1980.

Campbell, Margaret. *The Great Violinists.* NY: Doubleday, 1981.

Petrides, Frédérique Joanne, ed. "Women in Music," in Jan Bell Groh, *Evening the Score: Women in Music and the Legacy of Frédérique Petrides.* Fayetteville, AR: University of Arkansas Press, 1991.

Powell, Maud. "Some Hints for the Concert Player; Introduction by Karen A. Shaffer," in *Violexchange 2.* No. 2, 1987.

Roth, Henry. *Great Violinists in Performance.* Los Angeles, CA: Panjandrum, 1987.

Schwarz, Boris. *Great Masters of the Violin.* NY: Simon and Schuster, 1983.

Shaffer, Karen A. "Between Symphony and Song: The Violin Virtuoso in American History," in *Journal of the Violin Society of America.* Vol. 10, no. 1, 1990.

———. "Maud Powell, America's Legendary Musical Pioneer," in *Journal of the Violin Society of America.* Vol. VIII, no. 2, 1987.

———. *Maud Powell, Legendary American Violinist* (Women in Music series of biographies for children). Arlington, VA: The Maud Powell Foundation, 1994.

———. "Perpetual Pioneer," in *The Strad.* November 1987.

———. "String Quartets in Nineteenth Century America," in *Violexchange 3.* No. 3, 1988, pp. 38–43.

COLLECTIONS:

Clipping file, Aurora Historical Museum and Aurora Public Library, Aurora, Illinois.

Mabel Love Papers in the possession of Jean Holmes in Detroit, Michigan.

Maud Powell Archive, The Maud Powell Foundation, 5333 N. 26th Street, Arlington, Virginia 22207; serves as a clearinghouse and repository of Powell information and memorabilia, as well as distributor of reissued Powell recordings; publishes the *Women in Music* series of biographies for children and *The Maud Powell Signature,* a subscription newsletter on women in music, past and present.

Karen A. Shaffer,
Maud Powell biographer and president of
The Maud Powell Foundation in Arlington, Virginia,
and **Juanita Karpf**, Assistant Professor of
Music and Women's Studies,
University of Georgia, Athens, Georgia
(all quotations are from Shaffer's biography of Maud Powell)

Powell, Olave Baden- (1889–1977).
See Baden-Powell, Olave.

Power, Eileen (1889–1940)

English historian who was one of the first to study women's history. *Name variations: Eileen Postan. Born Eileen Edna le Poer in Altrincham, Cheshire, England, in 1889; died in 1940; daughter of a London stockbroker; educated at Bournemouth and Oxford High School; obtained a first in history at Girton College, Cambridge, 1910; awarded a research grant for study in Paris and Chartres, 1910; attended London School of Economics, 1911–13; married Michael Postan.*

Eileen Power carried out her groundbreaking work in women's history as director in history studies at Girton College, Cambridge (1913–20), lecturer and reader in economic history at the University of London (1924–31), and professor of economic history at London School of Economics (1931–40). During the 1920s, Power helped to develop the medieval sections of the *Cambridge Economic History of Europe*; worked with R.H. Tawney on *Tudor Economic Documents*; and helped to found the *Economic History Review* (1927). Her writings include a study of community life in *Medieval English Nunneries c. 1275–1535* (1922), *Medieval People* (1924), and a translation of *Le ménagier de Paris* (*The Goodman of Paris*, 1928), which was a book of advice by an elderly husband to his young wife. After Power's early death, her husband Michael Postan edited her lectures on the economic position of women during the Middles Ages, contained in *Medieval Women* (1975).

Power, Jennie Wyse (1858–1941).
See Wyse Power, Jennie.

Power, Marguerite (1789–1849).
See Blessington, Marguerite, Countess of.

Powers, Georgia Davis (1923—)

First African-American and first woman elected to the Kentucky State Senate. *Name variations: Mrs. James L. Powers. Born Georgia Montgomery on October 29, 1923, in Springfield, Kentucky; daughter of Ben Montgomery and Frances (Walker) Montgomery; attended Louisville Municipal College, 1940–42; married Norman F. Davis, in 1943 (divorced 1968); married James L. Powers, in 1973 (divorced); married a third time; children: (first marriage) William Davis; three stepchildren.*

First African-American and first woman elected to the Kentucky State Senate (served 1967–88); marched with Dr. Martin Luther King, Jr., on the Kentucky state capital of Frankfort and elsewhere (1960s); chaired Jesse Jackson's presidential campaigns in Kentucky (1984, 1988).

Born in Springfield, Kentucky, on October 29, 1923, Georgia Davis Powers was the second of nine children and the only daughter of **Frances Walker Montgomery** and Ben Montgomery, whose father was white. One of her frustrations while growing up, she has said, was her parents' belief that a girl's place was in the home, while her eight brothers were free to do anything and go anywhere they chose; she was able to find ways to circumvent this obstacle, however. Powers grew up in Louisville, where her family had moved two years after her birth, and graduated from Central High School in 1940. Later that year, she enrolled in Louisville Municipal College, where she studied for two years. She also took some business courses at Central Business School and received a certificate from the U.S. Government IBM Supervisory School. In 1943, Powers married Norman F. Davis, with whom she would have one child before the marriage ended in divorce in 1968.

Powers first began to get involved in politics in 1962, when she was asked to help out in the campaign of Wilson Wyatt, who was running for the U.S. Senate. She was assigned the responsibility of training other volunteers, and the excitement of working in her first political campaign proved addictive. For the next five years, Powers played a prominent role in the campaigns of candidates for the Kentucky governorship, U.S. Senate, Louisville mayoralty, and the U.S. House of Representatives. Along the way, her contributions as a campaign volunteer were rewarded with her election to a four-year term on the Democratic Executive Committee of Jefferson County, in which Louisville is located. Expressing dissatisfaction with the way the committee operated, however, Powers resigned after only two years. In 1968, she attended her first Democratic National Convention, in Chicago, speaking there on behalf of a plank in Hubert Humphrey's platform.

During the 1960s, Powers also became active in the civil-rights struggle. At the state level, in 1964 she helped to put together Allied Organizations for Civil Rights, which pressured state legislators to pass public accommodations and fair employment laws. As part of that Kentucky legislative campaign, the group sponsored a march on the state capital of Frankfort that included more than 25,000 participants and a speech by Dr. Martin Luther King, Jr. The following year, the Kentucky General Assembly passed the legislation for which Powers and others had fought. She also marched frequently for open housing in the city of Louisville, and as a representative of the Kentucky Christian Leadership Conference (a state-level affiliate of the Southern Christian Leadership Conference) joined the 1965 march from Selma to Montgomery, Alabama. Powers was also among those who marched in solidarity with striking sanitation workers in St. Petersburg, Florida, and organized in Louisville for the 1968 Poor People's Campaign in Washington, D.C.

Powers' civil-rights activism brought her into close contact with Dr. King. She acknowledged in her 1995 autobiography, *I Shared the Dream*, that the two eventually became romantically involved despite her own marriage and his marriage to ***Coretta Scott King**. Powers wrote that she was staying with King in Memphis on the evening of April 4, 1968, when he was killed by an assassin's bullet. In a 1998 interview with Greg Guma, editor of the magazine *Toward Freedom*, Powers disputed the characterization of her relationship with King by some as a "tawdry affair." When the two were together, she said, "the rest of the world, whose problems we knew and shared, was far away. Our time together was a safe haven for both of us. There we could laugh and speak of things others might not understand. He trusted me, and I him, not to talk about it." Of King and the attempts by some to deify him in the years since his death, Powers said, "I knew Martin had all the imperfections, foibles, and passions of a mortal man. He had a good appetite for life."

In 1967, Powers ran for the Kentucky State Senate, against a white opponent, in a district that was 60% white. Proving that she had learned well while working as a volunteer in the campaigns of others for public office, she won the election, becoming the first African-American and the first woman to serve in that legislative body. As a senator, she continued to campaign for equal rights for all of Kentucky's citizens; the very first bill she introduced, which eventually became law, mandated fair housing statewide. Throughout her 21-year career in the senate, Powers worked tirelessly to win passage of civil-rights legislation, including measures prohibiting sex and age discrimination. She was a strong advocate of the Equal Rights Amendment, and championed measures calling for tighter control of insurers, improved education for the handicapped, a higher minimum wage, and salary increases for police and firefighters. She chaired the Health and Welfare Committee from 1970 through 1976 and the Labor and Industry Committee from 1978 through 1988. She also attended the Democratic National conventions in 1984 and 1988 as a delegate for the Reverend Jesse Jackson. After more than 20 years as a senator, in 1988 Powers decided against seeking another term, and was succeeded in her Senate seat by Gerald Neale, who had run against her unsuccessfully in 1979.

After leaving elected office, Powers remained active in a wide variety of organizations, including the Louisville chapter of the American Red Cross, the YMCA, the NAACP, the Urban League, and the International Afro-Musical and Cultural Foundation. She was the recipient of numerous awards conferred by groups including the American Red Cross, the Fraternal Order of Police, the Kentucky Circuit Judges Association, the Kentucky chapter of the NAACP, Mount Zion Baptist Church, and the Kentucky State University Alumni Association. Powers received an honorary doctor of laws degree from the University of Kentucky and a honorary doctorate from the University of Louisville, both in May 1989, and in 1991 was awarded the Anderson Laureate from the state of Kentucky. She was also among the first 21 inductees of the Kentucky Commission on Human Rights Hall of Fame.

SOURCES:

Powers, Georgia Davis. *I Shared the Dream: The Pride, Passion, and Politics of the First Black Woman Senator from Kentucky*. New Horizon, 1995.

Publishers Weekly. March 6, 1995, pp. 51–52.

Smith, Jessie Carney, ed. *Notable Black American Women*. Detroit, MI: Gale Research, 1992.

Don Amerman,
freelance writer, Saylorsburg, Pennsylvania

Powers, Harriet (1837–1911)

African-American quilter whose Bible quilts are considered among the finest ever crafted. *Born Harriet, last name unknown, into slavery in Clarke County, Georgia, in 1837; died in 1911; married Armstead Powers (a farmhand); children: two born in slavery—Amanda (b. 1855) and LeonJoe (b. 1860)—and Nancy (b. free in 1866).*

In 1886, Harriet Powers completed a Bible quilt which would gain her a place in American art history. She had been born into slavery in Clarke County, Georgia, in 1837. Skilled slaves could hire their labor out and make a small income with the master's permission; some built and designed houses and buildings, others sewed fine clothes and quilts, crafted boats and implements, and manufactured tools and cotton gins. While a portion of the earnings went to the slave, the rest went to the master. It is likely, given her sewing skills, that Powers hired out her labor as a slave before emancipation.

She and her husband Armstead Powers managed to acquire land after the Civil War. They owned a house, a stock of animals, and four acres, enough to grow cotton to support their family of five. It is probable that Powers continued her work as a seamstress to earn extra income. Her quilting continued a long tradition in the fabric arts which was rooted in Africa. In the West African kingdom of Dahomey, large, quilt-like wall hangings were displayed in palaces and homes. This fabric art was often appliquéd, meaning that pieces of fabric were sewn on an underlayer of fabric. Since this type of African art usually told stories, Powers' 1886 quilt consisted of 11 squares depicting Biblical scenes: 1) Adam and ***Eve**; 2) Adam and Eve and a son; 3) Satan; 4) Cain killing his brother Abel; 5) Cain going to the land of Nod to get a wife; 6) Jacob dreaming of the ladder; 7) the baptism of Christ; 8) the moon turning to blood during the Crucifixion; 9) Judas Iscariot and 30 pieces of silver; 10) the Last Supper; and 11) the Holy Family. Many of these tableaus incorporate animals, also a link with West African art.

This work would probably have been lost were it not for **Jennie Smith**, a local artist of considerable reputation. Born to a prominent family in Athens, Georgia, Smith studied in Baltimore, New York, and Paris, then taught at the **Lucy Cobb** school in Athens, heading the art department for over 50 years. Smith was self-supporting and not a wealthy woman, but she had a good eye for art and collected pieces when she could afford them. At a Cotton Fair in Athens in 1886, Smith saw Powers' Bible quilt and was drawn to the work. She offered to buy it for $10, a good price at the time, but Powers refused to sell. Not until several years later, when Powers' family was in desperate financial straits, did the artist decide to sell the quilt. Smith, also hard-pressed for cash at the time, could offer only $5 for the work. Powers accepted the reduced offer, and the quilt remained in Smith's possession until her death in 1946, after which it was eventually sent to the Smithsonian. Another quilt by Powers, commissioned by the women on the faculty of Atlanta University in 1898, was given to the Museum of Fine Arts in Boston in 1964. A great deal of African-American fabric art has not survived. Powers' quilts, however, have endured long past her death in 1911, earning her a reputation as one of America's finest quilters.

Harriet Powers

SOURCES:

Adams, Marie Jeanne. "The Harriet Powers Pictorial Quilts," in *Black Arts*. Vol. 3, no. 4, 1979, pp. 12–28.

Fry, Gladys-Marie. "Harriet Powers: Portrait of an African-American Quilter," in *Missing Pieces: Georgia Folk Art 1770–1976*.

Smith, Jennie. "A Biblical Quilt." Washington DC: Museum Division of Textiles, Smithsonian National Museum of American History.

Spalding, Phinizy. *Mrs. Powers and Miss Smith: A Film on Southern Cultural History*. Maryland: Visual Press, 1990.

Vlach, John Michael. *The Afro-American Tradition in Decorative Arts*. Cleveland, OH: Cleveland Museum of Art, 1978.

Karin Loewen Haag,
freelance writer, Athens, Georgia

Powys, queen of.

See Susan of Powys (fl. 1100).

Poynings, Eleanor (d. 1483)

***Countess of Northumberland.** Died in 1483; daughter of Richard de Poynings; married Henry Percy*

(1421–1461), earl of Northumberland (r. 1455–1461, killed at the battle of Towton), on June 25, 1435; children: ***Eleanor Percy*** *(d. 1530); Henry Percy (b. around 1449), earl of Northumberland;* ***Elizabeth Percy*** *(who married Henry, Lord Scrope of Bolton);* ***Anne Percy*** *(who married Sir Thomas Hungerford and Sir Laurence Rainsford);* ***Margaret Percy*** *(who married Sir William Gascoigne).*

Poynings, Philippa (1375–1401).

See Mortimer, Philippa.

Poynton, Dorothy (1915—)

American springboard and platform diver. *Name variations: Dorothy Poynton-Hill or Dorothy Poynton Hill. Born Dorothy Poynton in Portland, Oregon, on July 17, 1915; married.*

At age 13, was the youngest American ever to win an Olympic medal, taking the silver in springboard diving (1928) at the Amsterdam Olympics; won Olympic gold medals in platform diving (1932, 1936) and the bronze medal in springboard diving (1936); ran the Dorothy Poynton Swim Club in Los Angeles.

Dorothy Poynton, who was born in Portland, Oregon, in 1915, loved to entertain. She danced at the Orpheum Theater in Portland until the Board of Education complained that she was neglecting her studies. After her parents moved the family to Los Angeles, she gave diving and dancing exhibitions at the Ambassador Hotel. Poynton and her coach Roger Cornell thought up a variety of acts, including a dive they dubbed the Monte Cristo. The seven-year-old girl would be placed in a sack, then dropped off a ten-foot diving board. Since pool water was quite murky in those days, and the audience could not see her, Poynton could unfasten the snaps of the sack, swim to a diving bell with air, and stay there while the audience grew more and more restive.

Poynton was then asked to represent the Hollywood Athletic Club coached by Clyde Swenson. Practicing three times a week, she entered her first meet in Detroit at age 12, where she lost first place by one-tenth of a point. When Stanford swimming coach Ernie Brandsten told Poynton she would make the Olympic team, Poynton was bewildered; she had never heard of the Olympics. In 1928, the 13-year-old was the youngest athlete on the ship headed to Amsterdam. On board, homesickness swept over her. ***Helen Meany** won the gold, but Poynton won a silver in springboard diving, the youngest American athlete to win a medal.

After the 1928 Olympics, Poynton went on to win National championships, becoming a strong platform diver. The day before the 1932 Los Angeles Olympics, however, she hit her head and was rushed to the emergency room; a doctor advised her not to compete. But her parents had missed her performance in Amsterdam for lack of funds, and Poynton did not want to disappoint them. Rather, she did a 16' dive and went on to win a gold in platform diving.

By 1936, Poynton was a seasoned Olympic athlete who planned to turn professional as soon as the competition in the Berlin Olympics ended. She had already agreed to future commitments to endorse Camel cigarettes, bathing suits, and other products, and the pressure to perform was enormous. Poynton triumphed, however, with another gold in platform diving and a bronze in springboard.

Realizing the commercial opportunities available to star athletes, in 1952 she and her husband built the Dorothy Poynton Swim Club in Los Angeles and advertised that she could teach anyone to swim in ten lessons. Students, she stated, would be water safe, go off the board, and swim the length of the pool. The rich and famous brought their children for lessons, and she never had a single failure. "I can't do anything half-way . . . ," said Poynton. "I can't do anything unless I do it better than anyone else."

SOURCES:

Carlson, Lewis H., and John J. Fogarty. *Tales of Gold.* Chicago and NY: Contemporary Books, 1987.

Karin L. Haag,
Athens, Georgia

Praagh, Margaret van (1910–1990).

See Van Praagh, Peggy.

Praed, Rosa (1851–1935)

Australian-born writer. *Name variations: Rosa Caroline Praed; (pseudonym) Mrs. Campbell Praed. Born Rosa Murray-Prior on March 27, 1851, near Beaudesert, southern Queensland, Australia; died on April 13, 1935, in Torquay, England; daughter of Thomas Lodge Murray-Prior (a pastoralist and later postmaster-general of Queensland); educated in rural Australia and Brisbane; married Arthur Campbell Praed, in 1872 (separated late 1880s); children: one daughter and three sons.*

Selected writings: An Australian Heroine *(1880);* Policy and Passion *(1881);* Nadine *(1882);* The Head Station *(1885);* Australian Life: Black and White *(1885);* Miss Jacobsen's Chance *(1886);* Affinities: A

Romance of Today *(1886);* The Bond of Wedlock *(1887);* Ariane *(play, 1888);* The Romance of a Station *(1889);* Nulma *(1897);* As a Watch in the Night *(1900);* My Australian Girlhood *(1902);* Dwellers by the River *(1902);* The Ghost *(1903);* Nyria *(1904);* The Luck of Leura *(1907);* Lady Bridget in the Never-Never Land *(1915);* Soul of Nyria *(1931).*

Born in 1851 in the Australian Outback, near Beaudesert in Queensland, Rosa Praed was the eldest daughter of Thomas Lodge Murray-Prior, a pastoralist who later was a longtime postmaster-general of Queensland. Her early childhood was spent on stations (livestock farms) in the Burnett River district of Queensland. In 1858, after Aborigines attacked a Hornet Bank station, killing most of its occupants, her father moved the family to Brisbane.

In 1872, at the age of 21, Rosa married Arthur Campbell Praed, with whom she would have one daughter, who was born deaf, and three sons. Praed returned to the Outback with her husband, who owned a station at Port Curtis, near Gladstone. They sold their Australian properties in 1875 and sailed for England, where Praed would spend the rest of her days, but the isolation and Spartan conditions of life in the bush had made a strong impression, and would provide fodder for a number of her novels. Among these was her first book, *An Australian Heroine* (1880), which drew heavily on the early years of her marriage, and *The Romance of a Station* (1889). Writing as Mrs. Campbell Praed, she quickly made a name for herself as a novelist and playwright, and would write some 40 novels.

Among Praed's friends in London was Oscar Wilde, whom she portrayed in her novel *Affinities: A Romance of Today* (1886). In 1888, her play *Ariane*, based on her novel *The Bond of Wedlock* (1887), stirred controversy when it debuted in London. Both novel and play focus on some of the shortcomings of married life. Art apparently reflected life in this case, for it was not too long after the play's run that she separated from her husband.

Praed developed a marked interest in the occult and the supernatural. A strong believer in reincarnation, she reportedly was convinced that she had been a pagan priestess in classical times, and that this earlier incarnation was related in some way to the loss of all four of her children. Admittedly, they died sad deaths: her only daughter died in a mental institution, one son was killed in an automobile accident, another committed suicide, and the third was fatally gored by a rhinoceros. The first of Praed's novels to delve into the occult was *As a Watch in the Night*, published in 1900. The year before that she had begun living with **Nancy Harward**, a medium whom Praed believed was a reincarnation of a Roman slave girl, and her novel *Nyria* (1904), which drew on this belief, caused some stir. After Harward's death in 1927, Praed followed up with *Soul of Nyria* (1931). In addition to reincarnation, Praed was a strong believer in astral bodies and mental telepathy. *In Mortal Bondage: The Strange Life of Rosa Praed* (1948), written by Colin Roderick, explores her relationship with Harward and some of her more unconventional philosophical beliefs.

Although she returned only once, in 1894, to her native Australia, Praed managed to stay in close touch with family and friends there, and her homeland continued to serve as a backdrop for much of her writing. In addition to *An Australian Heroine* and *The Romance of a Station*, other Praed novels with an Australian theme include *The Head Station* (1885), *Miss Jacobsen's Chance* (1886), *Outlaw and Lawmaker* (1893), *Nulma* (1897), *Dwellers by the River* (1902), *The Ghost* (1903), *The Luck of the Leura* (1907), and *Lady Bridget in the Never-Never Land* (1915). Praed was close friends with the politician Justin McCarthy, her collaborator on three novels. For *Our Book of Memories*, published in 1912, she edited McCarthy's letters and added annotations. She died on April 13, 1935, at the age of 84, in Torquay, England.

SOURCES:

Buck, Claire, ed. *The Bloomsbury Guide to Women's Literature.* NY: Prentice Hall, 1992.

Kunitz, Stanley J., and Howard Haycraft, eds. *Twentieth Century Authors.* NY: H.W. Wilson, 1942.

Wilde, William H., Joy Hooton, and Barry Andrews. *The Oxford Companion to Australian Literature.* Melbourne, Australia: Oxford University Press, 1985.

Don Amerman,
freelance writer, Saylorsburg, Pennsylvania

Praeger, Sophia Rosamund

(1867–1954)

Irish sculptor, author, and illustrator of children's books. *Born in Holywood, County Down, Ireland, in 1867; died in 1954; attended the Sullivan School, Holywood; studied art at the Belfast School of Art and the Slade School, London, England; also studied in Paris.*

Sophia Praeger achieved fame with her sculpture *The Philosopher*, which is now displayed in the Colorado Springs Museum and Art Gallery. Other works, executed mostly in plaster, and including relief panels and memorial plaques and stones, have been exhibited in London, Paris, and at the Irish Decorative Art Association. Still others were commissioned for schools, libraries, banks, and churches in her native Ireland. Praeger also wrote and illustrated children's books, including three in collaboration with her brother Robert. Praeger, who was president of the Royal Ulster Academy, received an honorary doctorate from Queen's University, Belfast, and was awarded an MBE in 1939.

Praskovya Saltykova (1664–1723).

See Saltykova, Praskovya.

Pratt, Anne (1806–1893)

British botanist and author. *Born in Strood, Kent, England, in 1806; died in London, England, in July 1893; second of three daughters of Robert Pratt (a grocer) and Sarah Pratt; married John Peerless, in 1866.*

A descendent of French Huguenots who fled from religious persecution in France in 1572, Anne Pratt was born in 1806 and inherited her interest in flowers from her mother; as a child, she created an herbarium which became quite valuable. Pratt published her first book, *The Field, The Garden and The Woodland,* at age 20, and wrote 16 additional botanical volumes during her lifetime. Her best-known and most extensive work, *The Flowering Plants and Ferns of Great Britain*, was begun in 1849, and included five volumes at the time of its publication in 1855. Her other books include *Flowers and their Associations*, *Pratt's Catechism of Botany*, and *Common Things of the Seashore*. During her later career, Pratt also wrote articles of a more general nature for contemporary women's magazines.

Through her books, Pratt attempted to instill a love of botany in her readers. She also endeavored to inspire and educate them, sprinkling her works liberally with religious references and little-known facts. "In the words of the Scriptures the flowers appear on the earth and the singing of birds is come," she wrote under the "Bluebell" entry in her book *Wild Flowers*, which she also illustrated herself. "[A]lthough the bluebell has no particular use now," she added, "in former times it was greatly prized.... [W]hen still ruffs were worn the sticky juice of the bluebell was used as a starch. Book binders used it also to stiffen the spines." Pratt sent a copy of *Wild Flowers* to Queen ***Victoria**, who was not only pleased to accept it, but also made a royal command to receive all of Pratt's subsequent publications.

Pratt, who married when she was 60, lived her last years in Shepherd's Bush, London, where she died in July 1893. She retained a child's curiosity about growing things to the end, and is reported as saying shortly before her death: "I have had a very happy life."

SOURCES:

Graham, Margaret. "Anne Pratt: Botanist to a Queen," in *This England*. Summer 1985, p. 43.

Barbara Morgan,
Melrose, Massachusetts

Pratt, Ruth (1877–1965)

American congressional representative (March 4, 1929–March 3, 1933). *Name variations: Ruth Sears Baker Pratt. Born on August 24, 1877, in Ware, Massachusetts; died on August 23, 1965, in Glen Cove, New York; daughter of a manufacturer; educated at Dana Hall in Wellesley, Massachusetts, and at Wellesley College; married John T. Pratt.*

Was the first woman elected to New York City Board of Aldermen (1925); served in the U.S. House of Representatives (1929–33).

Ruth Pratt was born on August 24, 1877, to a socially prominent family in Ware, Massachusetts. Her father was a cotton manufacturer and had a great interest in the surrounding community and civic causes. After attending private schools and Wellesley College in Wellesley, Massachusetts, Pratt lived for a time in Greenwich, Connecticut, before marrying John T. Pratt, the son of an oil executive, and moving to New York City in 1904.

Interested in government and community affairs, she became chair of the Second Federal Reserve District's Woman's Liberty Loan Committee during World War I. Pratt, a staunch Republican, was appointed vice-chair of the Republican National Ways and Means Committee in 1918. She supported Herbert Hoover's failed bid to garner the Republican presidential nomination in 1920 (the first American election in which women were able to vote), and in January 1924 she was elected associate leader of the 15th Assembly District. The following year, Pratt was elected to the Board of Aldermen of New York City, the first woman to serve in that post. She campaigned against Mayor John F. Hylan and was an avid supporter of a nonpartisan parks agency. Reelected in 1927, she served until 1929, and was responsible for legislation that sought to revise the city charter and to construct tunnels under the East River to connect Manhattan with the city's outer boroughs.

In 1928, Pratt successfully ran against Democrat Phillip Berolzheimer for New York's 17th

District (known as the "Silk Stocking" district) seat in the U.S. House of Representatives, and assumed her duties when the 71st Congress convened in April 1929. During her term, she served on the Committee on Banking and Currency, the Committee on the Library, and the Committee on Education. In her first House address, Pratt argued against a sugar tariff attached to the Hawley Bill, saying that the increase in the cost of sugar would not improve the working conditions or wages of sugar workers. She supported the repeal of Prohibition, and in 1930 sought legislation that would appropriate $75,000 to publish books for the blind. She was also in favor of President Hoover's refusal to provide federal funds for relief of the unemployed as the Great Depression took hold. That year she ran for reelection against a Democratic candidate favored by the Tammany Hall political machine and the crusading journalist Heywood Broun, who was running as a Socialist, and won by a narrow margin. Two years later, as the Depression deepened, Pratt won the heated Republican primary but was defeated by a Democrat in her bid for a third term. (Hoover, too, lost his bid for reelection.)

A member of the Republican National Committee from 1929 until 1943, Pratt served as president of the Woman's National Republican Club from 1943 to 1946, and also served as chair of the Fine Arts Foundation, a predecessor to the National Endowment for the Humanities. She died on August 23, 1965, in Glen Cove, New York.

SOURCES:

Office of the Historian. *Women in Congress, 1917–1990.* Commission on the Bicentenary of the U.S. House of Representatives, 1991.

Don Amerman,
freelance writer, Saylorsburg, Pennsylvania

Ruth Pratt

Praxilla (fl. 450 BCE)

Greek musician and poet, famous for her drinking songs. *Born in Sicyon; flourished about 450 BCE.*

When ancient Greeks gathered around the table for a few glasses of wine, they often sang drinking songs composed by Praxilla, one of the so-called nine "lyric" Muses. Born in Sicyon in the middle of the 5th century BCE, Praxilla composed poetry from the Dorian school, poems that were considered equal to those of Alcaeus and Anacreon. According to Athenaeus, her songs, known as table songs, drinking songs, *skolias* or *scolias* (short lyrical poems sung after dinner), were often sung at banquets, sometimes by soloists, sometimes by a chorus. Praxilla was also the author of the epic poem *Adonia* as well as dithyrambs and hymns, chiefly on mystic and mythological subjects, genealogies, and the love stories of the gods and heroes. A dactylic metre was also called by her name. Her songs have often been compared with Aklman's and ***Sappho**'s.

John Haag,
Athens, Georgia

Predeslava of Hungary (fl. 960)

Princess of Kiev. *Flourished around 960; daughter of Taskany also seen as Taksony (931–972), prince of Hungary, also known as prince of the Magyars; married Svyatoslav I, prince of Kiev; children: Yaropolk I (b. around 958), prince of Kiev; Oleg (b. around 959).*

Preis, Ellen (b. 1912).

See Mayer, Helene for sidebar.

Preiss, Julia (1902–1980).

See Brystygierowa, Julia.

Preissova, Gabriela (1862–1946)

Czech short-story writer and playwright whose Její pastorkyna ***was the basis for the libretto of Janacek's***

Jenufa and whose Gazdina roba was the basis for the libretto of Foerster's Eva. Name variations: Gabriela Preissová; Gabriela Pressova or Pressová. Born Gabriela Sekerová in Kuttenberg, Austrian Moravia (modern-day Kutná Hora, Czech Republic), on March 23, 1862; died in Prague on March 27, 1946; married twice.

Gabriela Preissova was born Gabriela Sekerová in Kuttenberg, Austrian Moravia (modern-day Kutná Hora, Czech Republic), in 1862. When she married at age 18, she moved to Hodonín in Slovácko, an area rich in Moravian folklore. Preissova was captivated by the region and began to use the tales in her short stories. In 1889, her naturalistic drama *Gazdina roba* (*The Farm Mistress* or *The Farmer's Maidservant*) was produced at the Prague National Theater with great success. Her second play *Její pastorkyna* (Her Stepdaughter), produced the following year, met with less success. Both plays were turned into operas. *Gazdina Roba* became the basis for Josef Bohuslav Foerster's 1899 opera *Eva* and *Její pastorkyna* became the basis for Leos Janacek's 1904 opera *Jenufa*. Janacek had written an earlier opera, *Pocatek romanu* (*The Beginning of a Romance*), in 1894 based on Preissova's short story of the same title. Years later, Preissova used the story of *Její pastorkyna* for a novel.

In her writings, Preissova criticized social prejudices and defended the right of women to live free and independently; her depictions of the harsh realities of life for the impoverished Slovak population of southeastern Moravia (Slovácko) remain valuable as both literature and historical sociology.

SOURCES:

Cockcroft, Robert. "Janacek's Jenufa," in *About the House* [Friends of Covent Garden]. Vol. 7, no. 6. Summer 1986, pp. 24–27.

Evans, Sian, and Cheryl Robson, eds. *Eastern Promise: Seven Plays from Central and Eastern Europe*. London: Aurora Metro Press, 1999.

Graff, Yveta Synek. "Facts of Life," in *Opera News*. Vol. 50, no. 8. January 4, 1986, pp. 14–16, 44.

Preissová, Gabriela Sekerová. *Jenufa: Opera in Three Acts after the Drama of Life in Southern Moravia*. Translated by Yveta Synek Graff and Robert T. Jones. Seattle, WA: Seattle Opera, 1985.

Pynsent, Robert B., and Sonia I. Kanikova, eds. *Reader's Encyclopedia of Eastern European Literature*. NY: HarperCollins, 1993.

Ulbrich, Rolf, ed. *Tschechische Erzähler*. Leipzig: Dieterich Verlag, 1958.

Zavodsky, Artur. *Gabriella Preissová*. Prague: Divadelní ústav, 1962.

John Haag,
Associate Professor of History, University of Georgia, Athens, Georgia

Prelle, Micheline (b. 1922).

See Presle, Micheline.

Prentice, Jo Ann (1933—)

American golfer. *Name variations: (nickname) Fry. Born on February 9, 1933, in Birmingham, Alabama.*

Although she joined the LPGA tour in 1956, golfer Jo Ann Prentice did not enjoy her first victory until the 1965 Jackson Open. More consistent in her game following that win, she won the 1967 Dallas Civitan, the 1972 Corpus Christi (in a 10-hole play-off with ***Sandra Palmer**), the 1973 Burdines, the 1974 Colgate-***Dinah Shore**, and the 1974 American Defender. In 1974, a banner year, she had 20 finishes in the top 20, won two tournaments, and placed fourth for the year.

Prentiss, Elizabeth Payson (1818–1878)

American writer. *Born on October 26, 1818, in Portland, Maine; died on August 13, 1878, in Dorset, Vermont; daughter of Edward Payson (a Congregational minister) and Ann Louisa (Shipman) Payson; educated in the public schools of Portland; married George Lewis Prentiss (a Presbyterian minister), on April 16, 1845; children: Anna Louise; Mary Williams; George Lewis; Henry Smith; two who died in infancy.*

Selected writings: Little Susy's Six Birthdays *(1853);* The Flower of the Family *(1853);* Only a Dandelion, and Other Stories *(1854);* Henry and Bessie; or, What They Did in the Country *(1855);* Little Susy's Six Teachers *(1856);* Little Susy's Little Servants *(1856);* Peterchen and Gretchen, Tales of Early Childhood *(1860);* The Little Preacher *(1867);* Fred, and Maria, and Me *(1867);* The Old Brown Pitcher *(1868);* Stepping Heavenward *(1869);* Nulworth *(1869);* The Percys *(1870);* The Story Lizzie Told *(1870);* Six Little Princesses *(1871);* Aunt Jane's Hero *(1871);* Golden Hours *(1874);* The Home at Greylock *(1876);* Pemaquid *(1877);* Gentleman Jim *(1878);* Avis Benson *(1879).*

Born in Portland, Maine, on October 26, 1818, Elizabeth Payson Prentiss was the fifth of six surviving children of **Ann Shipman Payson**, who was originally from New Haven, Connecticut, and Edward Payson, a native of Rindge, New Hampshire. Undoubtedly the most profound influence on Prentiss, her father was a Harvard graduate and a firebrand Congregational minister and revivalist. Although he died before she was ten, he impressed upon her at a very early age that the spiritual side of life was by far the most important. Prentiss was educated largely in local Portland schools, with the exception of a year she spent in New York City, where her older sister **Louisa Payson** had opened a school. At age 19, Elizabeth started a school for young children in her mother's house, but it lasted for only a short time. Never strong physically, Prentiss wrote while a young adult, "I never knew what it is to feel well." Throughout her life she was subject to severe headaches and fainting spells. A common thread running through most of her writings is that perfection of character can best be attained through suffering.

Prentiss had kept diaries and journals from a very early age, and also wrote stories and poetry. This interest in writing grew stronger as her sister Louisa found success writing articles and stories for magazines, and beginning in 1834 Prentiss published several works in *Youth's Companion*. In the early 1840s, she taught in a private girls' school in Richmond, Virginia, and married George Lewis Prentiss, a recently ordained minister, on April 16, 1845. They first moved to New Bedford, Massachusetts, where he had been named pastor at a local Congregational church, and then lived for a brief time in Newark, New Jersey. Beginning in 1851 and for most of the rest of her life, Prentiss and her husband lived in New York, where he served as pastor for a number of Presbyterian churches. By all accounts, the Prentisses had a happy marriage, although they lost two of their six children in infancy. Prentiss relished her role, once writing: "You can't think how sweet it is to be a pastor's wife; to feel the right to sympathize with those who mourn, to fly to them at once, and join them in their prayers and tears. It would be pleasant to spend one's whole lifetime among sufferers, and to keep testifying to them what Christ can and will become to them, if they will only let Him."

The publication in 1853 of *Little Susy's Six Birthdays* marked Prentiss' first notable success as a writer of children's books. Also published that year was *The Flower of the Family: A Book for Girls*. Two years later came *Henry and Bessie; or, What They Did in the Country*. In 1856, trying to recapture the success of her first work, she published two more books in the Little Susy series, *Little Susy's Six Teachers* and *Little Susy's Little Servants*. Both were well received in the United States and England and were also translated into French. Central elements in the appeal of Prentiss' children's books were their realistic dialogue and the believability of their simple but clever story lines. In 1860, she published *Peterchen and Gretchen, Tales of Early Childhood*, a collection of German folk stories she had translated into English. Seven years later, *Fred, and Maria, and Me* appeared.

Prentiss' most popular book, *Stepping Heavenward*, was published in 1869, after being serialized in the *Chicago Advance*, and quickly became a bestseller. Although—or perhaps because—its appeal was more religious than literary, readers reacted strongly to this story of the triumphs and trials of a young girl growing up. Sales in the United States topped 100,000, and the book sold well in England, France, and Germany, although, perhaps because of its strong religious underpinnings, it was largely ignored by literary critics.

While she continued to write for the rest of her life, none of the numerous books Prentiss published achieved the popular success of *Stepping Heavenward*. She had a loyal audience for whom her autobiographical tales of Christian family life held great appeal, however, and these were the people who read her *The Story Lizzie Told* (1870), *Aunt Jane's Hero* (1871), *The Home at Greylock* (1876), *Pemaquid* (1877), and *Gentleman Jim* (1878), among others. Prentiss also wrote a number of religious poems and hymns, a musical form of worship that appealed strongly to her. (She once said that she had to pray for God's help to keep her from loving hymns more than the Bible.) One of her hymns, "More Love to Thee, O Christ," can still be found in many modern hymnals. Prentiss died at her family's summer home in Dorset, Vermont, on August 13, 1878, at the age of 59.

SOURCES:

Deen, Edith. *Great Women of the Christian Faith*. NY: Harper & Row, 1959.

James, Edward T., ed. *Notable American Women, 1607–1950*. Cambridge, MA: The Belknap Press of Harvard University, 1971.

McHenry, Robert, ed. *Famous American Women*. NY: Dover, 1980.

Don Amerman,
freelance writer, Saylorsburg, Pennsylvania

Preobrazhenska, Olga (1871–1962)

Foremost Russian dancer who devoted the last 40 years of her career to teaching in Paris, where she left a profound mark upon ballet in the Western World.

Name variations: Ol'ga Iosifovna (or Ossipovna) Preobrazhenskaia; Preobrazhenskaya; Preobrajenska; known to her students as Madame Préo. Born Ol'ga Iosifovna (or Ossipovna) Preobrazhenska on January 21 (February 2, old style), 1871, in St. Petersburg, Rus-

sia; died in a nursing home in Sainte-Mande, France, on December 27, 1962; never married; no children.

Awards: Honored Artist of His Majesty's Theaters (1909); granted the Medal of Merit by the Club International de la Danse (1955); Gala Hommage à Olga Preobrazhenska, Paris (1957).

Graduated from the St. Petersburg theater school (1889) and immediately entered the Maryinsky Company (1889–1917); became a soloist (1896), a prima ballerina (1900); debuted as Giselle (1899), Raymonda (1903), Aurora and Odette-Odile (1904); taught at the St. Petersburg theater school (1901–02); taught at Akim Volynsky's School of Russian Ballet (1917–21); emigrated to Berlin (1921); danced there and at La Scala, Milan, Covent Garden, London, and the Theatro Colon in Buenos Aires (1922); settled in Paris, where she opened a prominent school of ballet (1923); retired (1960).

[The] absence of natural gifts was compensated by ideal training, constantly reinforced and perfected.

—Gennady Smakov

Olga Preobrazhenska was born in St. Petersburg on January 21, 1871 (February 2, according to the Julian calendar still in use in Russia at that time). Her mother died shortly after her birth and her father took little interest in her. Though she came from a family that had no connections whatsoever with the ballet or any of the other arts, Preobrazhenska early decided to become a dancer. At first, she simply took lessons with **Leopoldina Lozenskaya**, a former dancer with the Maryinsky Theater, but by age ten, after numerous rejections, she was accepted into the St. Petersburg theater school. There she studied under Lev Ivanov (intermediate), then Christian Johansson, and the famed choreographer Marius Petipa (advanced classes). Short, squat, and plain of face, with mild scoliosis and a hyperextended knee, Preobrazhenska had limited possibilities as a ballet dancer, much less a soloist or ballerina, but over the years, through continuous self-discipline and hard work, she overcame her shortcomings, achieving such success as a pupil that upon graduation in 1889, she immediately entered the Maryinsky Company for which the theater school existed. She remained a leading dancer there for nearly 30 years. Despite her poor figure and lack of allure, Preobrazhenska was an indefatigable worker and through sheer determination saw her career advance steadily. Gifted with a lively personality, a dazzling smile and great personal charm which she conveyed easily across the footlights, she became increasingly popular with St. Petersburg audiences. Artistic and curious, she studied music, learned to play the piano, took voice lessons, and sought out the best teachers of dance in the capital.

At first relegated to the back row of the corps de ballet with apparently no hope of becoming a soloist, Preobrazhenska nevertheless achieved this distinction by 1896 and was elevated to the rank of ballerina by 1900. By this time, she had become one of the most important dancers at the Maryinsky, performing a broad and varied range of roles, including almost all of those in the ballets choreographed by Petipa, Ivanov, and Legat. These included a number of parts that she was the first to perform: Anne in Petipa's *Barbe-Bleu* (*Blue Beard*), Henriette in his *Raymonda* (1898), Pierette in his *Les Millions d'Arlequin* (*Harlequinade*, 1900), the title role in Pavel Gerdt's *Javotte* (1902), and Cleopatra's slave in Fokine's *Une Nuit d'Egypte* (*A Night in Egypt*, 1908). She also danced in Fokine's *Chopiniana* (1908, 1909), and as late as 1915 he staged Tchaikovsky's *Romance* for her, when she was 44. As she matured, she returned in some of these ballets playing other parts, Isaure in *Barbe-Bleu* (after 1900), the title role in *Raymonda* (after 1903), and Bérénice in *Une Nuit d'Égypt* (after 1910). She also appeared in Petipa's *Esmerelda, Paquita,* and *The Talisman,* and in Lev Ivanov's *Acis et Galathée* (*Acis and Galathea*), *Camargo,* and *La Fille du Mikado* (*The Mikado's Daughter*). Never satisfied with her art, when already a mature and respected dancer Preobrazhenska took lessons from Enrico Cecchetti (1898–1900) and Nicolai Legat in Russia, **Caterina Beretta** in Milan, Joseph Hansen in Paris, and **Katti Lanner** in London.

In 1895, Preobrazhenska made her first trip abroad touring for the Maryinsky in the company of ***Matilda Kshesinskaia** and her brother Joseph Kshesinsky. Preobrazhenska appeared in Dresden, in Monte Carlo and at La Scala in Milan (1904) and in Paris in 1909. In 1910, she danced *Swan Lake* in London for the first time, if only in a shortened version of the original, and in 1912 toured in South America.

The coming of the First World War demonstrated sharply Preobrazhenska's perfectionism in all things. Training as a nurse, she went on to work in several hospitals in order to learn as much as possible about her new craft, serving in various military hospitals and conducting a small hospital in the courtyard of her home, all the while continuing to teach her classes in ballet under increasingly difficult conditions.

From time to time, Preobrazhenska had taught at the St. Petersburg Theater School

(1901–02, 1914–17, 1919–21), and after the Russian revolutions of March and November 1917, she continued her career by joining the new School of Russian Ballet just founded by Akim Volynsky. Here, where the newest and most innovative ballet techniques were being developed and taught, she served as a teacher until 1921. Working with the brilliant ***Agrippina Vaganova**, Preobrazhenska taught ballet to students who at one time or another included ***Alexandra Danilova**, **Olga Mungalova**, ***Vera Volkova**, and even Vaganova herself, who would eventually go on to become the greatest dance teacher in the Soviet Union and the virtual founder of Soviet ballet.

But the destruction of the old world of Imperial Russia of which the ballet had been so much a part was difficult for Preobrazhenska to cope with, and in February 1921 she left Russia for Finland. After a few gala performances in Riga, Latvia (which was no longer part of Russia), she went on to Berlin where for some months she endured the life of an émigré, dancing wherever she could obtain an engagement. Then, she had the happy idea of writing to La Scala in Milan where she had performed four times in the past, and immediately received an invitation to choreograph there for an entire opera season. Heartened by her success, she realized that Berlin had nothing to offer her, and she left for France shortly after her return from Milan.

In 1923, Preobrazhenska settled in Paris, where she opened a private school at the Studio Wacker. At first, her pupils were drawn mostly from the Russian émigrés then so numerous in the city, but gradually, as her fame spread, she became one of the most distinguished and sought-after teachers in Europe until her retirement in 1960 at the age of 89.

The great roles of Preobrazhenska, the ones which brought out the best in her and in which her talents were shown at their best were those of Aurora in *The Sleeping Beauty*, Lise in *La Fille Malgardé,* and *The Nutcracker.* She also shone in certain demi-caractère roles such as in *Muzhichok* by Petipa, the *Liszt Czardas* by Ivanov, etc. Her other roles included those of Swanilda in *Coppélia,* Butterfly in *Les Caprices du Papillon,* Téresa in *The Cavalry Halt,* Galatea in *Acis et Galatea,* Isabelle in *The Trials of Damis,* and Summer in Petipa's *Four Seasons.* She also appeared as Odette-Odile in *Swan Lake* and in the title role in *Giselle,* but in neither of these great classics was she considered a success. In her early years and often in her later ones, she danced in subordinate roles in many other ballets, among them *Bluebeard, La Source, Esmeralda, The Pearl of Seville, Catarina, Paquita, Sylvia, The Fairy Doll, Puss in Boots, Le Matelot, Carmen, Les Huguenots,* and as Columbine in the Ivanov-Petipa *Nutcracker.* Had it not been for the dominance over the Maryinsky enjoyed by Kshesinskaia, whose position was secure through the patronage of members of the imperial family, it is likely that Preobrazhenska's career would have led her to the soubrette, i.e. comic, roles in which her sparkling personality, joie de vivre, and sheer exuberance would have made her a great success, but which were almost monopolized by Kshesinskaia.

Olga Preobrazhenska

As a dancer Preobrazhenska's assets were the precision and perfection of her technique, her soaring leaps, her elegance in motion, her graceful arms, her great musicality, and her naturalism as an actress. She was best suited to lyrical-comic parts, and the adjectives "imaginative," "creative," "sweet," "playful," and "arch" were among those used to describe her performances. She was also renowned for her nuanced interpretations of her roles and the brilliant improvisations for which she had a great gift, especially evident when she was called upon to do an encore. Critics were enthralled by her artistry, hailing her as "poetess of the dance," "queen of dances," and "poetesse par la grace de Dieu."

But it was as a teacher that Preobrazhenska left her mark on the world of classical dance, devoting herself to passing on the traditions of the Russian ballet. Technically perfect herself, she had a firm grasp of the various techniques of choreography and an ability to detect and weed out the defects in her pupils' work that made her a born mistress of ballet instruction. A firm believer in the dictum of Cecchetti that ballet dancing must be mastered in the classroom first and could not be mastered later on the stage, Preobrazhenska, with her strength of character, her authority, and the rigid discipline that she imparted, gave her pupils an extraordinary command of technique. When the Ballet Russe de Monte Carlo was formed in 1930–31, most of the dancers were former pupils of Preobrazhenska's, including its earliest two stars, *Tamara Toumanova and **Irina Baronova**, the first of whom Preobrazhenska had taught from the outset.

Baronova, Irina. *See Toumanova, Tamara for sidebar.*

An intensely private person, Preobrazhenska never married and with few exceptions tended to keep people at a distance. Her closest confidante was her former pupil and later assistant **Elvira Roné**, who especially in her later years tended to manage her studio for her. Preobrazhenska never recovered from the realization that her career as a dancer was over and suffered from recurrent depression; it was only on the stage of the Maryinsky that she had felt herself fulfilled. Melancholy and difficult, she could be abrupt to the point of rudeness and tended to be self-centered, yet she was kind and generous (she often taught children of impoverished Russian émigrés for nothing) and a great lover of animals and birds. To her pupils, she was a severe taskmaster but the best ones never forgot the skills that she had taught them, and in her last years, clouded with poverty and illness as they were, she depended very much upon the charity of Toumanova.

Among the dancers who studied under her formally or who came to take classes with her in both St. Petersburg and Paris were such luminaries as ***Margot Fonteyn**, Hugh Laing, Mialord Miskovitch, Vladimir Skouratoff, **Ludmilla Tcherina**, **Nina Verchinina**, **Nina Vryoubova**, ***Margarethe Wallmann**, and Igor Youskevitch, as well as such company directors and other teachers as Serge Golovine and Georges Skibine. Other established dancers who joined her classes were **Rosella Hightower**, **Nadia Nerina**, **Tatiana Riabouchinska**, ***Mia Slavenska**, and ***Marjorie Tallchief**.

Riabouchinska, Tatiana. *See Toumanova, Tamara for sidebar.*

When Preobrazhenska died in a nursing home in Sainte-Mande, France, on December 27, 1962, just a few weeks short of her 92nd birthday, she was mourned as one of the last survivors of the Golden Age of the Russian Imperial Ballet.

SOURCES:

Dolin, Anton. "Preobrazhenskaya—Great Ballerina and Teacher," in *Dance and Dancers* (London). May 1953.

Finch, Tamara. "Les Ballets 1933," in *Dancing Times* (London). October 1985.

Legat, Nikolai. "Great Dancers I Have Known," in *Dancing Times*. May–June, 1931.

Music Collection, Free Library of Philadelphia.

Roné, Elvira. *Olga Preobrazhenskaya*. Trans. and adapted by Fernau Hall. New York, 1978.

Smakov, Gennady. *The Great Russian Dancers*. New York, 1984.

SUGGESTED READING:

Svetlov, Valerian. *Preobrazhenskaya*. St. Petersburg, 1902.

Robert H. Hewsen,
Professor of History, Rowan University,
Glassboro, New Jersey

Preradovic, Paula von (1887–1951)

Austrian writer whose literary legacy bridged the Slavic and Germanic cultures of Austria and the Balkans and who wrote the words for the Austrian national anthem. *Name variations: Paula Preradovic; Paula Molden. Born in Vienna on October 12, 1887; died in Vienna on May 25, 1951; daughter of Dusan von Preradovic; mother's maiden name was Falke; granddaughter of Petar Preradovic (1818–1872), a poet and general in the Austrian Army; had brother Petar; married Ernst Molden (1886–1953, a historian and journalist), in April 1916; children: sons, Fritz and Otto.*

Paula von Preradovic was a master of the German language, but culturally she was a product of the multinational Habsburg Empire. Like many Austrians, her ancestry was more Slavic and Latin than it was Germanic, given the fact that her paternal grandfather was the great Croatian poet Petar Preradovic, who combined a career as a general in the Austrian Army with being the most popular poet of the Croatian National Revival. Just as his granddaughter would many decades later, he felt at home in most of the traditions of European literature, translating Czech, French, German, Italian, Polish and Russian Romantic poetry into Croatian. Paula's father, Dusan von Preradovic, a career officer in the Austro-Hungarian Navy, also had strong feelings for Croatian culture and literature, but her mother, born into the aristocratic German-speaking Falke von Lilienstein family, had neither understanding of nor sympathy for either her husband's or her daughter's Croatian pursuits.

Growing up in Vienna in the last years of the 19th century, Paula was exposed to many intellectual and artistic trends. One of the most important influences on her was her aunt, **Amalie Falke**, then a noted author and strong advocate of women's rights. As a girl, Preradovic was surrounded by the diverse traditions of the Habsburg Empire, including those found in the Croatian port of Pola where her father was stationed. She grew to love the rural regions of Carinthia and Carniola where Slav and Germanic traditions interacted. She also grew to love the beautiful Austrian lakes, particularly the Mondsee where her family had a summer home. Another important influence on her intellectual development was the years spent at the Roman Catholic secondary school Englischen Fräulein, in St. Pölten, Lower Austria. Here she became ever more immersed in the mystical traditions of Austrian Catholicism. Influential too were her contacts with the Catholic writer ***Enrica von Handel-Mazzetti**, who became both friend and patron as Paula's writing career developed. Soon it became clear that Preradovic possessed much more than average literary talent. She began to dream of becoming a famous writer when her verse was praised by such towering literary figures as *Marie von Ebner-Eschenbach and Hugo von Hofmannsthal.

In 1913, Paula left Pola for Munich, where she trained as a nurse. Soon, her nursing skills would be of great use, as Europe began to destroy itself in the carnage of World War I. Returning to Vienna, she worked in the emergency military hospital that had been set up within the University of Vienna. She also met and fell in love with a young historian, Dr. Ernst Molden. They were married in April 1916, and over the next years she would give birth to two sons, Otto and Fritz. The newlyweds were spared the trauma of living in Vienna during the last two years of the war. Instead, they lived in Copenhagen and The Hague, two neutral nations to which Ernst had been assigned on diplomatic missions.

Only in 1920 did Paula, her husband, and their young son Otto return to Vienna. The once-proud imperial city was now a demoralized collection of starving people uncertain of their future. With limited prospects as a diplomat and a bleak future in academia, Ernst decided to enter the world of journalism. Within a few years, he would have a flourishing career as a member of the editorial board of Vienna's most distinguished newspaper, the voice of middle-class liberalism *Neue Freie Presse*. During these years, Preradovic divided her time between raising her sons (Fritz was born in 1924) and writing. She and her husband also delighted in serving as hosts at one of Vienna's most important intellectual salons. Most of the city's artists looked forward to an invitation to attend a reception at the Moldens' spacious 14-room apartment in Vienna's Döbling district. All of the important new books, musical compositions, films, and works of art produced in Central Europe in the 1920s and 1930s would be vigorously discussed and argued over in these rooms.

Paula and her husband traveled often during these years. They were particularly drawn to the former Austrian regions which had become part of the new South Slavic kingdom of Yugoslavia. There, Preradovic developed strong friendships with some of the country's leading creative spirits, including the sculptor Ivan Mestrovic and the poet **Camilla Lucerna**. As well, Paula's brother Petar lived there. The geography and culture of this troubled region informed her work. In 1929, her first book of poems appeared

Austrian stamp honoring Paula von Preradovic, issued in 1996.

under the title *Südlicher Sommer* (Southern Summer). In 1933, *Dalmatinischen Sonnette* (Dalmatian Sonnets) was published, followed in 1936 by *Lob Gottes im Gebirge* (Praising God in the Mountains). These three volumes were rich evocations of the Adriatic coast she had known as a child in prewar Austria, with a sparkling Adriatic Sea and Croatian cities such as Trieste, Pola, and Ragusa (now Dubrovnik) serving as living links between the region's varied peoples and cultures.

By the late 1930s, Preradovic had achieved a solid reputation in Austrian literary circles, but during this decade it was a writer's political affiliations, not necessarily the quality of their writing, that played a crucial role in deciding how their work was judged. In the case of Preradovic, a conservative traditionalist strongly linked to the multinational culture of the Habsburgs, her writings were anathema not only to those affiliated with the political Left, but even more so to Austria's Nazis, whose theory of Aryan supremacy made them rabid racists and who regarded the Habsburg era as one of Germanic subordination to "inferior" Slavs, Latins, and Jews, as well as to Roman Catholicism's cosmopolitan values. The German annexation (*Anschluss*) of Austria, in March 1938, was a catastrophe for Preradovic and her entire family. Her husband and sons, who shared her cosmopolitan ideals, were demoralized by the Nazi takeover. Ernst's position at the *Neue Freie Presse* soon ended, given the fact that Austria's new Nazi overlords had long regarded that newspaper as the embodiment of "Jewish domination" over Austrian public opinion and intellectual life. Fritz and Otto's Jewish friends were forced to flee for their lives, and regimentation replaced easy-going Viennese attitudes.

Despite—or possibly even because of—the nature of the world around her, in the late 1930s

Preradovic created what would become one of her most impressive literary legacies, her one and only novel *Pave und Pero*. Published in Salzburg in 1940, *Pave und Pero* was a historical narrative based on a family tragedy that had long fascinated Paula. Her grandfather Petar von Preradovic ("Pero") was happily married to **Paolina de Ponte**, a woman whose roots were distinguished, since she could claim descent from one of the most ancient Italian noble families of Istria. Paolina, known to her husband as "Pave," was the mother of a large, thriving family when tragedy struck with the death of little Costja, her favorite child, from whooping cough. Convinced that she was to blame, Pave did not confess to her husband about the details of Costja's death; she quickly found herself caught in a web of lies and committed suicide by drowning. In her novel, Preradovic used extensive correspondence between Pave and Pero that had been preserved by her aunt, the Croatian painter **Zora von Preradovic** (1867–1927), and which she inherited upon Zora's death.

Upon its publication, *Pave und Pero* received excellent reviews in Austria and enjoyed bestseller status; there have since been at least seven printings. Besides being an evocative novel about a family tragedy, it also appealed to many Austrians who were becoming disillusioned with Nazi rule and increasingly drawn to the traditions of the Habsburg past, when different nationalities found it possible to live together in peace. For some, reading *Pave und Pero* was a small but principled act of resistance to "alien, Prussian" Nazism. Even though Preradovic was clearly biased in favor of the values of Old Austria, which was by no means an ideal society, in 1940 a significant number of Austrians found themselves responding positively to the book's implied criticism of Nazi-ruled Austria. The author was particularly pleased when a Croatian translation of her novel appeared in print in 1940.

The war years proved to be difficult for the Molden family. Their anti-Nazism was no secret. Fritz Molden, after failing to escape to England via the Netherlands, returned to Vienna only to find himself denounced to the Gestapo. In prison and then in a concentration camp, Fritz faced bleak prospects until a lawyer who was a family friend secured his release, but Fritz then had to "volunteer" for service on the Russian front. After being wounded, he returned to Germany and in Berlin made contacts with anti-Nazi elements in the military. Over the next few years, he had various close calls, including becoming a key member of Allen Welsh Dulles' spy network (he would later marry Allen's daughter **Joan Dulles**) and being sentenced to death by a German court martial in Italy. By the end of the war, Fritz had become chief of a major anti-Nazi resistance group and played a key role in persuading the Allies to stop indiscriminate bombing of civilian targets in Austria. After the failure of the German resistance plot to assassinate Adolf Hitler in July 1944, many anti-Nazis were arrested. Among them were both Paula von Preradovic and her husband. The couple was taken to Vienna Gestapo headquarters, the feared "Metropol," where both were subjected to harsh interrogations that included physical mistreatment. Paula's letters to her sons, which were published after the war, are among the most moving documents to survive from the Austrian resistance movement. Fortunately, both Moldens survived this harrowing experience, and were able to be reunited with their sons soon after the liberation of Vienna. Almost miraculously, all four had survived the Nazi occupation of their beloved nation.

Although her health had been permanently impaired by her experiences as a Nazi prisoner, Preradovic continued to publish after Austria regained its sovereignty in April 1945. In February 1947, her simple but moving lyric "Land der Berge, Land am Strome" ("Land of Mountains, Land of Streams") was officially adopted as the text of Austria's new national anthem. As the nation undertook the difficult task of physical reconstruction (that of moral reconstruction would be deferred until the next generation), Preradovic continued to write thought-provoking works, including the novellas *Nach dem Tode* (After Death, 1949), *Königslegende* (Royal Legends, 1950), and *Die Verschwörung des Columba* (The Conspiracy of Columba, 1951). During the final stages of a long, ultimately terminal illness, she was able to receive an advance copy of her last novella a few days before her death in Vienna on May 25, 1951. On May 29, Paula von Preradovic was buried in Vienna's Zentralfriedhof in a "grave of honor" reserved only for Austria's cultural and political elite. In his obituary, one of Preradovic's oldest friends, Felix Braun, described her simply as being "our greatest woman poet since Marie von Ebner-Eschenbach." Preradovic was honored by Austria with a postage stamp issued on May 17, 1996.

SOURCES:

Braun, Felix. *Das musische Land: Versuche über Österreichs Landschaft, Geschichte und Kunst.* 2nd rev. ed. Vienna: Österreichische Verlagsanstalt, 1970.

Csokor, Franz Theodor. "Paula von Preradovic (1887–1951)," in *Neue Österreichische Biographie ab 1815: Grosse Österreicher.* Vol. 14. Vienna: Amalthea-Verlag, 1960, pp. 194–197.

Molden, Ernst. *Paula von Preradovic: Porträt einer Dichterin.* Innsbruck: Österreichische Verlagsanstalt, 1955.
Molden, Fritz. *Exploding Star: A Young Austrian Against Hitler.* NY: William Morrow, 1979.
Molden, Otto, ed. *Autonomie und Kontrolle: Steuerungskrisen der modernen Welt-Europäisches Forum Alpbach 1986.* Vienna: Österreichisches College, 1987.
Preradovic, Paula von. *Gesammelte Werke.* Edited by Kurt Eigl. Vienna: Verlag Fritz Molden, 1967.
———. *Meerferne Heimat.* Edited by Werner Röttinger. Graz: Stiasny Verlag, 1961.
———. *Pave und Pero.* Salzburg: Otto Müller Verlag, 1940.
———. *Pave i Pero: Roman.* Translated by Bozena Begovic. Zagreb: "A. Velzek," 1940.
Reed, W.L., and M.J. Bristow, eds. *National Anthems of the World.* 9th ed. London: Cassell, 1997.
Schoolfield, G.C. "Paula von Preradovic—An Introduction," in *German Life and Letters: A Quarterly Review.* New Series. Vol. 7. 1953–54, pp. 285–292.
Vogelsang, Hans. "Paula von Preradovic: Die Dichterin der Ehrfurcht, der Demut und des Glaubens," in *Österreich in Geschichte und Literatur.* Vol. 10, 1966, pp. 198–206.
Vospernik, Reginald. "Paula von Preradovic: Leben und Werk," Ph.D. dissertation, University of Vienna, 1960.
Wagner, Renate. *Heimat bist Du grosser Töchter: Weitere Portraits.* Vienna: Verlag der Österreichischen Staatsdruckerei, 1995.

John Haag,
Associate Professor of History, University of Georgia, Athens, Georgia

Preslava of Russia (fl. 1100)

Queen of Hungary. *Name variations: Predeslava. First wife of Koloman also known as Coloman the Booklover (1070–1114), king of Hungary (r. 1095–1114); children: Stephen II (1100–1131), king of Hungary (r. 1116–1131). Coloman was also married to *****Euphemia of Kiev****.*

Presle, Micheline (1922—)

French actress. *Name variations: Micheline Michel; Micheline Prelle. Born Micheline Chassagne on August 22, 1922, in Paris, France; married William Marshall, an American actor (divorced).*

Selected filmography: Je chante *(1938);* Jeunes Filles en Détresse *(1939);* Paradis perdu *(*Four Flights to Love*, 1940);* Histoire de Rire *(*Foolish Husbands*, 1941);* La Comédie du Bonheur *(1942);* La Nuit fantastique *(1942);* La Belle Aventure *(*Twilight*, 1945);* Félicie Nanteuil *(1945);* Falbalas *(*Paris Frills*, 1945);* Boule de Suif *(*Angel and Sinner*, 1945);* Le Diable au Corps *(*Devil in the Flesh*, 1947);* Les Jeux sont faits *(*The Chips Are Down*, 1947);* Les Derniers Jours de Pompéi *(*Sins of Pompeii*, 1948);* Under My Skin *(US, 1950);* An American Guerilla in the Philippines *(US, 1950);* Adventures of Captain Fabian *(US, 1951);* La Dame aux Camélias *(1953);* L'Amour d'une Femme *(1954);* Si Versailles m'était conté *(*Royal Affairs in Versailles*, 1954);* Villa Borghese *(*It Happened in the Park*, 1954);* Casa Ricordi *(*House of Ricordi*, 1954);* Napoléon *(1955); ****Beatrice Cenci** *(1956);* Les Louves *(*Demoiaque*, 1957);* Blind Date *(*Chance Meeting*, UK, 1959);* Une Fille pour l'Eté *(*Mistress for the Summer*, 1960);* L'Amant de Cinq Jours *(*The Five Day Lover*, 1961);* Les Grandes Personnes *(*Time Out for Love*, 1961);* L'Assassino *(*The Lady Killer of Rome*, 1961);* If a Man Answers *(US, 1962);* Les Sept Péchés capitaux *(*Seven Capital Sins*, 1962);* Le Diable et les Dix Commandements *(*The Devil and the Ten Commandments*, 1962);* Vénus Impériale *(1962);* The Prize *(US, 1963);* La Chasse à l'Homme *(*Male Hunt*, 1964);* La Religieuse *(*The Nun*, 1965);* Je vous salue Mafia *(*Hail! Mafia*, 1965);* Le Roi de Coeur *(*King of Hearts*, 1966);* Le Bal du Comte d'Orgel *(1970);* Peau d'Ane *(*Donkey Skin*, 1970);* Le Petroleuses *(*The Legend of Frenchy King*, 1971);* L'Evénement le plus important depuis que l'Homme a marché sur la Lune *(*A Slightly Pregnant Man*, 1973);* L'Oiseau Rare *(1973);* Eulallie quitte les Champs *(1974);* Mord pas on t'aime *(1976);* Nea *(1976);* Le Diable dans la Boîte *(*Your Turn, My Turn*, 1978);* Certains Nouvelles *(1979);* Démons de Midi *(1979);* Tout Dépend des Files *(1980);* Le Sanq des Autres *(*The Blood of Others*, 1984);* Les Fausses Confidences *(1984);* Beau Temps mais orageux en fin de Journée *(*Good Weather But Stormy Late This Afternoon*, 1986);* Le Chien *(1986);* Alouette je te plumerai *(1988);* I Want to Go Home *(1989);* La Fête des Pères *(1990);* Après Aprés-Demain *(1990).*

Born in Paris in 1922 and convent educated, actress Micheline Presle made her screen debut at 16 under the name Micheline Michel and attained almost instant success. Her career peaked in the late 1940s, following her role opposite French actor Gérard Philipe in *Devil in the Flesh* (1947), the story of an older woman who falls in love with a younger man. In the wake of international acclaim, she made a number of Hollywood films, but failed to interest American moviegoers. She continued her career in Europe, returning to Hollywood intermittently, notably in *If a Man Answers* (1962) and *The Prize* (1963).

Pressová or Pressova, Gabriela (1862–1946).

See Preissova, Gabriela.

Prestes, Olga Benario (1908–1942).

See Benario, Olga.

Presti, Ida (1924–1967)

French classical guitarist, one of the greatest in musical history. *Born Yvette Ida Montagnon at Suresnes, France, on May 31, 1924; died in Rochester, New York, on April 24, 1967; daughter of Italian mother Olga Lo-Presti and French father Claude Montagnon (died 1939); married in the mid-1940s and divorced; married Alexandre Lagoya, in 1955; children: (first marriage) one daughter, Elisabeth Rigaurd Lagoya; (second marriage) one son, Sylvain.*

Ida Presti was born Yvette Ida Montagnon at Suresnes, France, in 1924, the daughter of an Italian mother, **Olga Lo-Presti**, and a French father, Claude Montagnon, who was an excellent musician and teacher. Ida's introduction to music came by way of her father and the piano, but at age six she became intrigued with the guitar. Though Claude did not play the instrument, he studied the guitar so that he could help his young daughter learn. To the end of her life, Presti had no other teacher.

Presti was extremely gifted musically and seemed to understand the guitar intuitively. At age eight, she played for the first time in public, and at ten she gave her first concert in Paris. By age eleven, her technique had surpassed that of many concert artists. She had already recorded works such as Federico Moreno-Torroba's *Sonatina* and Manuel Ponce's *Mexican Songs*. These recordings were made in an era before tape editing, so each mistake was recorded, and there were very few. When Presti was 13, she played before the world-famous classical guitarist Andres Segovia, who advised her to "never listen to the advice of any other guitarist." As a teenager, she toured internationally and was chosen to play Paganini's guitar on the observance of the centenary of his death.

Presti's approach to the guitar was unique. She played to the right side of the nail, whereas most guitarists played to the left, and her right hand was not parallel to the bridge, the technique of guitarists of the Tárrenga school. Fingering and phrasing were the first aspects of a piece she considered. She devised fingering which was more like an arpeggio than a scale, producing smooth melodic passages, and often used open strings, allowing her to change positioning so that each note slightly overlapped. While playing polyphonic music, Presti believed that whatever one hand with three fingers could accomplish in the treble, one thumb could do in the bass, and her bass lines had a uniquely independent quality. Her approach to music was imaginative and often brought out hitherto unknown qualities in many pieces.

Presti had been married briefly during World War II, during which she had a daughter Elisabeth. In the early 1950s, she met Alexandre Lagoya. Of Italian and Greek descent, Lagoya had grown up playing the guitar in Egypt, where he gave his first recital at age 13. Deciding to pursue a musical career, he went to Europe where he gave hundreds of concerts. One evening in Paris, Presti heard him play at a soiree at André Verdier's. "This is the best guitarist I've ever heard," she said. Interestingly, the two had developed similar techniques under completely separate circumstances. Their shared interest in music soon led to marriage and appearances on the concert stage as a duo.

Segovia had worked hard to establish the guitar as a classical instrument. Although there was a wealth of classical music written for it, gradually the violin and cello were favored, and the guitar lost its status except as a folk instrument. Following in the master's footsteps, Presti and Lagoya continued to expand the instrument's repertoire. The couple was extremely energetic on stage. Theirs was a life of jetting from one city to the next, tracing lost luggage, missing connections, and sometimes keeping up with the schedules of three agents. In the midst of this chaos, they practiced.

On April 23, 1967, Presti and Lagoya played an afternoon concert with the St. Louis Symphony. That night, Ida became ill. Though a doctor was called, there seemed to be no grave symptoms, so the couple proceeded to their next engagement in Rochester, New York. While on the plane, Presti became sick once more, and upon landing was rushed to a hospital in Rochester. Surgeons operated immediately, suspecting the problem was in her lung, but they were too late. Ida Presti died on the operating table, not quite 43. Her death was a great shock to the musical world. "The air over the guitar world will never be the same without their music," said Gregory d'Alessio. Lagoya continued to perform alone.

SOURCES:

Artzt, Alice. "Presti in New York," in *Guitar Review.* No. 31, May 1969, p. 4.

d'Alessio, Gregory, and John W. Duarte. "Editorial," in *Guitar Review.* No. 31, May 1969.

Dorigny, Henri. "Ida Presti," in *Guitar Review.* No. 31, May 1969, pp. 4–5.

Duarte, John. "Presti-Lagoya Duo," in *Guitar Review.* No. 31, May 1969, pp. 6–7.

"Ida Presti, 42, Dead; Concert Guitarist," in *The New York Times.* April 26, 1967, p. 47.

Wade, Graham. "A Historical Perspective of the Guitar Duo," in *Guitar Review*. No. 31, May 1969, pp. 7–8.

Wiseman, Cynthia. "Alexandre Lagoya," in *Guitar Review*. No. 66, Summer 1986, p.1–5.

Zoi, Liza, and Evangelos Assimakopoulos. "Ida Presti—In Memorium," in *Guitar Review*. No. 31, May 1969, p. 5.

John Haag,
Athens, Georgia

Preston, Ann (1813–1872)

American physician and educator. *Born on December 1, 1813, in West Grove, Pennsylvania; died on April 18, 1872, in Philadelphia, Pennsylvania; daughter of Amos Preston (a Quaker minister) and Margaret (Smith) Preston; Female Medical College (later Woman's Medical College of Philadelphia), M.D., 1851; never married; no children.*

Received medical degree (1851); became professor of physiology (1855); founded Woman's Hospital in Philadelphia (1861); started a nursing school (1863); appointed dean of the Woman's Medical College (1866).

Ann Preston was born on December 1, 1813, in West Grove, Pennsylvania, near Philadelphia, the second of nine children of **Margaret Smith Preston** and Amos Preston, a minister influential in a Quaker community known for its progressive ideas and intolerance toward oppression. Both parents were involved in the abolitionist movement and women's rights, and ***Lucretia Mott** was a family friend. The Preston home often served as a refuge for runaway slaves. On one occasion, when Preston heard that slave-catchers were approaching the house, she escorted an escaped slave dressed in Quaker clothes and a heavy veil past the raiding party to safety.

Ann attended the local Quaker school and then a Friends (Quaker-based) boarding school in Chester, Pennsylvania. But because of her mother's poor health, Preston left school and returned home to care for the household and her younger brothers. It has been suggested that the childhood deaths of her two younger sisters, combined with the increasing invalidism she witnessed in her mother, had a profound impact on Preston and her later medical career, for she was able to contrast their poor health with the excellent health of her six brothers, all of whom spent much time working outdoors. Around this time Preston also became an active member of the local Clarkson Anti-Slavery Society and of the temperance movement. As her brothers grew and her responsibilities at home lessened, she taught school and in 1849 published a book of children's rhymes, *Cousin Anne's Stories*. She also studied several subjects on her own, including Latin, and attended programs at the local literary association, which presented such well-known speakers as ***Lucy Stone**, ***Elizabeth Cady Stanton**, ***Susan B. Anthony**, James Russell Lowell, and Wendell Phillips.

Ann Preston

Perhaps in combination with her involvement with the temperance movement, Preston's acute awareness of the unhealthy lifestyle of women in her social class, who were encouraged to remain within their homes, refrain from exercise, and avoid straining their brains with challenging education, sparked her interest in human physiology. She was particularly interested in female physiology, and in the early 1840s began teaching physiology and hygiene to women. With the influence and support of her Quaker community, Preston was encouraged to obtain a medical education. In 1847, she became a medical apprentice to Dr. Nathaniel R. Mosely in Philadelphia. After a two-year apprenticeship, she applied to all four of the medical colleges in Philadelphia and was refused admission based on gender. Around this time William T. Mullen, a young man whose background in both business and medicine allowed him to recognize the growing interest among women in studying medicine, began to plan a medical school for women. In March 1850, a group of Quakers headed by Mullen founded the Female Medical College of Pennsylvania (later called the Woman's Medical College). The following autumn, as she was about to turn 37, Ann Preston, along with seven other women including ***Hannah E. Longshore**, entered the first class at the Female Medical College. She argued in her thesis against the common practices of purging and bloodletting, and advanced ideas about psychosomatic illness. These same eight women comprised the first graduating class of the college, on December 31, 1851. An unprecedented event, and one that aroused much ire, the commencement was mobbed by over 500 male medical students, and 50 Philadelphia policemen were needed to protect the safety of the graduates. By the time Preston died, less than 20 years later, more than 130 women had graduated from the Female Medical College.

Preston spent the year following her graduation in post-graduate work, and in 1853 was appointed professor of physiology and hygiene at the Female Medical College. The college became extremely successful, and other medical colleges, among them Penn Medical School, began admitting women into their programs. The number of practicing female physicians in Philadelphia increased dramatically, and many of these developed successful private practices. In reaction, the all-male board of censors of the Philadelphia Medical Society formally blacklisted all female doctors in 1858, barring them from treating patients or instructing students at public teaching clinics and from joining local medical societies. The following year, the Pennsylvania State Medical Society declared that its members were forbidden any interaction with female medical graduates. Consequently, Preston's (and other women doctors') patients could not be admitted to the local hospitals, and her students could not receive clinical experience at the local hospitals. Faced with this lack of support from the existing medical establishment, Preston organized a group of women and raised funds to found the Women's Hospital in 1861. The hospital was, essentially, an extension of the college, so that students could obtain clinical instruction.

The start of the Civil War in 1861 forced the closing of the Female Medical College, but the hospital was opened nonetheless. Preston also went ahead with her plan to send Dr. ***Emeline Horton Cleveland**, an anatomist, to study at the School of Obstetrics at the Maternité of Paris. When Cleveland returned to Philadelphia, she was made chief resident of the new hospital, which was also staffed with several men from the original faculty of the medical college and four female graduates. In 1862, the Female Medical College was rechartered and opened as the Woman's Medical College, and the following year Preston started a nursing school. In 1866, she was made dean of the Woman's Medical College, becoming the first woman so appointed both at that school and at any medical school in the United States. As dean, Preston began to fight against the legislation that had been passed by the Pennsylvania State Medical Society in 1859. Her formal appeal was ignored, as was a second one sent the next year, before the society finally issued a manifesto listing all the arguments for keeping women out of medicine, including frailty, the neglect of the home, and the awkwardness of attending to someone of the opposite gender. Preston responded with an article, published in the *Medical and Surgical Reporter* of May 4, 1867, that blasted the society's narrow-minded reasoning. The following year, her students were finally allowed to enter the general clinics at the Philadelphia Hospital, although not without a great deal of dissent. One of the major points of protest was the fact that men and women would be educated together. Preston's composed and articulate reply, published on November 15, 1869, in the Philadelphia newspapers, is still considered a classic argument in favor of women in medicine.

Preston remained dean and professor of physiology at the Woman's Medical College until her death on April 18, 1872, at the age of 58; she had suffered from rheumatoid arthritis for many years. She left all her medical instruments and medical books to the college, as well as a $4,000 endowment for a scholarship. It was not until 1888, 16 years later, that the first woman was admitted to the Philadelphia Medical Society. For that recognition of her status, she could thank in large part the commitment to women's education and the perseverance of Ann Preston.

SOURCES:

James, Edward T., ed. *Notable American Women, 1607–1950*. Cambridge, MA: The Belknap Press of Harvard University, 1971.

Magill, Frank, ed. *Great Lives from History: American Women Series*. Pasadena, CA: Salem Press, 1995.

McHenry, Robert, ed. *Famous American Women*. NY: Dover, 1980.

Read, Phyllis J., and Bernard L. Witlieb. *The Book of Women's Firsts*. NY: Random House, 1992.

Uglow, Jennifer S., comp. and ed. *The International Dictionary of Women's Biography*. NY: Continuum, 1985.

SUGGESTED READING:

Alsop, Gulielma Fell. *History of the Woman's Medical College, Philadelphia, Pennsylvania, 1850–1950*. Philadelphia, PA: J.B. Lippincott, 1950.

***Lerner, Gerda**. *The Female Experience: An American Documentary*. Indianapolis, IN: Bobbs-Merrill, 1977.

Lopate, Carol. *Women in Medicine*. Baltimore, MD: The Johns Hopkins University Press, 1968.

Morantz-Sanchez, Regina Markell. *Sympathy and Science: Women Physicians in American Medicine*. NY: Oxford University Press, 1985.

Walsh, Mary Roth. *"Doctors Wanted: No Women Need Apply": Sexual Barriers in the Medical Profession, 1835–1975*. New Haven, CT: Yale University Press, 1977.

COLLECTIONS:

Correspondence, lectures, articles, and other memorabilia by Ann Preston are located in the library of the Woman's Medical College in Philadelphia, Pennsylvania.

Christine Miner Minderovic,
freelance writer, Ann Arbor, Michigan

Preston, Frances F. (1864–1947).
See Cleveland, Frances Folsom.

Preston, Margaret Junkin (1820–1897)

American poet. *Born Margaret Junkin on May 19, 1820, in Milton, Pennsylvania; died on March 28, 1897, in Baltimore, Maryland; first of eight children of George Junkin (a minister and educator) and Julia Rush (Miller) Junkin; sister of Eleanor Junkin (d. 1854, first wife of General Thomas "Stonewall" Jackson); schooled at home: married John T. L. Preston (a professor of Latin), on August 3, 1857; children: two sons, George Junkin and Herbert Rush, and seven stepchildren.*

A Northerner who made her reputation as a Southern poet, Margaret Junkin Preston was born in 1820 in Milton, Pennsylvania, the first of eight children of George and **Julia Rush Junkin**. Margaret's father, an educator and Presbyterian minister, provided for her schooling at home, teaching her Latin and Greek, as well as English literature and theology. Despite eye problems which frequently made it difficult for her to read and write (possibly the result of a childhood illness), Preston began her literary pursuits at an early age, winning prizes for her stories and verses, which were also published in magazines and newspapers. The family moved South in 1848, when George became president of Washington College in Lexington, Virginia. It was there that Margaret wrote her first and only novel, *Silverwood,* a story of Southern life, which was published anonymously in 1856. She was offered additional money if she would allow the use of her name, but she refused.

In 1857, Margaret married John T.L. Preston, a professor of Latin at Virginia Military Institute in Lexington and a widower with seven children ranging in age from 5 to 22. Inheriting such a large family, and subsequently adding two sons of her own, Preston had little time for her career. (In a letter to Charleston poet Paul Hamilton Hayne in 1869, she described writing verses amid a "thousand petty housewifely distractions.") She produced her second book, *Beechenbrook: A Rhyme of the War,* during the period of the Civil War, at which time she remained loyal to her husband and to the Confederacy, although one of her brothers joined the Union Army and her father and a sister returned to Pennsylvania. (Her sister **Eleanor Junkin**, who had died in 1854, had been married to General Thomas "Stonewall" Jackson.) This caused a painful split in the family which Preston made mention of only in her personal diary. *Beechenbrook* focused on the wife of a Southern soldier who is killed in the war, and was published in Richmond in 1865. Republished in 1866 and 1867, the book solidified Preston's literary reputation throughout the South.

Preston produced four additional collections, including *Old Song and New* (1870), *Cartoons* (1875), *For Love's Sake* (1886), and *Colonial Ballads, Sonnets, and Other Verse* (1887). Her poetry, according to Robert H. Land in *Notable American Women*, was strongly influenced by the contemporary British and American poets she favored, particularly Robert Browning. In addition to poetry, Preston wrote a series of travel sketches, *A Handful of Monographs* (1886), following a trip to Europe in the summer of 1884. After the war, she produced two pieces for *Century* magazine: "Personal Reminiscences of Stonewall Jackson" (October 1886) and "General Lee after the War" (June 1889). Preston lived in Lexington until the death of her husband in 1890, when she moved to Baltimore to reside with her eldest son. She died there on March 28, 1897.

SOURCES:

James, Edward T., ed. *Notable American Women, 1607–1950.* Cambridge, MA: The Belknap Press of Harvard University, 1971.

SUGGESTED READING:

Coulling, Mary Price. *Margaret Junkin Preston: A Biography.* Winston-Salem, NC: Blair, 1993.

Preston, Margaret Rose (c. 1875–1963)

Australian painter and graphic artist. *Born Margaret Rose McPherson in Adelaide, Australia, on April 29, 1875 (also seen as 1883); died in 1963; older of two daughters of David McPherson (a marine engineer) and Prudence (Lyle) McPherson; attended the Fort Street School, Sydney, Australia; studied art at the National Gallery of Victoria Art School and the Adelaide School of Design; married William George Preston, in 1919; no children.*

A celebrated painter and one of the first Australians to recognize the beauty and value of Aboriginal art, Margaret Rose Preston was born Margaret Rose McPherson around 1875 in Adelaide and received classical art training at the Victoria Art School and the Adelaide School of Design. Supporting herself by teaching, she was intent on becoming the finest still-life painter in the world. In 1904, Preston embarked on her first trip to Europe, and was shocked by the modernists she found there. It was not until a second extended visit abroad (1912–19) that she began to move away from her traditional training to explore alternative modes of expression. During her stay, she studied Japanese prints at the Musée Guimet and experimented with lyrical, post-impressionist still lifes. While living in England during World War I, she further developed her skills as a colorist.

In 1919, back in Australia, Margaret wed William George Preston, a well-established gentleman of some means. The marriage, a late one by the standards of the time, freed Preston financially for the first time, thus allowing her to concentrate totally on her art. Settling in Sydney with her new husband, she pursued her painting and printmaking, but also tried her hand at interior decoration, fabric design, and even flower arrangement. It was now her turn to challenge the 19th-century traditionalism of Australian art, and she did so with a series of decorative and technically adventurous still lifes. "Characteristic of these was an interest in asymmetry and patterning," explains **Elizabeth Butel** in *200 Australian Women*, "the close-up observation of natural patterns and particular flora and an increasing austerity of design allied to colour raised to an intense pitch."

Preston was also attracted to the strong design and conceptual nature of Aboriginal art, which she viewed as the basis of a truly indigenous national art. Through her relationship with Sydney Ure Smith, publisher of the journals *Art in Australia, The Home*, and *Australia National Journal*, she advanced her theories about Aboriginal art, as well as art in general. The rhythms, colors, and symbols of Aboriginal art also strongly influenced her own later work. She abandoned the sumptuous color she had used in the 1920s, supplanting it with a more monochromatic palette, and employed simplified forms. As Butel points out, however, she was never a slave to her own style and experimented with new mediums as they attracted her attention.

In addition to her travel in Australia, Preston ventured to southeast Asia, China, India, Japan, and the Americas. Outspoken and competitive, she was always a controversial figure in the art circles she frequented. She died in 1963.

SOURCES:

Radi, Heather, ed. *200 Australian Women*. NSW, Australia: Women's Redress Press, 1988.

Barbara Morgan,
Melrose, Massachusetts

Preston, May Wilson (1873–1949)

American illustrator. *Born May Wilson on August 11, 1873, in New York City; died on May 18, 1949, in East Hampton, New York; only child of John J. Wilson and Ann (Taylor) Wilson; attended public school through high school; attended Oberlin College; attended the Art Students League, 1892–1897; married Thomas Henry Watkins, in 1898 (died 1900); married James Moore Preston (a painter), on December 19, 1903; no children.*

The spirited child of conservative, middle-class parents, May Wilson Preston displayed early artistic talent and by age 16 was an accomplished self-taught artist and founding member of the Women's Art Club (later the National Association of Women Artists). In one last attempt to redirect their daughter's interest, the Wilsons sent May to Oberlin College in Ohio, where she spent most of her time sketching the surrounding grounds and making portraits of her classmates. After three years, her parents finally accepted the inevitable and allowed her to return to New York and enroll in the Art Students League. Although she protested the League's policy of excluding women from its life-drawing classes, May remained there for five years, flourishing under the tutelage of such artists as Robert Henri, John H. Twachtman, and William M. Chase. In the spring of 1898, she married Thomas Henry Watkins, after which she spent a year in Paris, studying under James McNeill Whistler.

The death of her husband in 1900 propelled Preston into her career as an illustrator. She sold her first drawing to a third-rate magazine, reportedly telling the editor that she thought a beginner might be able to sell something to the worst magazine she had ever seen. One year later, she illustrated her first story for *Harper's Bazaar*. While pursuing her career, she also resumed her studies, enrolling in a class at the New York School of Art, where she met **Edith Dimock**. The two moved into quarters at the Sherwood Studios on West 57th Street, and were soon joined by another art student, **Lou Seyme**. Dubbed the "Sherwood sisters," the women held weekly open houses, which became a meeting ground for young artists and writers in the area. A frequent guest was the painter James Moore Preston, whom May had first met in Paris. The two were married in December 1903 and moved to East 9th Street.

James Preston was one of the early founders of the "Ash Can School" (also known as "The Revolutionary Black Gang" and "Apostles of Ugliness"), a group of artists who rejected Impressionism and idealism, choosing instead to paint the city's urban reality. Participants included William J. Glackens (who married Edith Dimock), Robert Henri, John Sloan, George B. Luks, and Everett Shinn. (The movement would eventually pull in writers and editors as well, including Irvin Cobb, Charles Fitzgerald, Wallace Irwin, and Frank Crowninshield.) Breaking with tenets of the National Academy of Design, in 1901 the group established the Society of Illustrators, of which May Preston was the first, and for many years the only, woman member. In 1912, they founded the Association of American Painters and Sculptors, which sponsored the famous Armory Show of 1913, in which May Preston exhibited. As **Jane Grant** points out in *Notable American Women, 1607–1950*, the group also had its lighter side. "Its costume balls and beaux-arts balls were gala affairs, and as the Waverly Place Players they performed for audiences large or small, moving from one studio to another for special stage or lighting effects."

Meanwhile, Preston became increasingly successful, her commercial illustrations appearing regularly in *McClure's*, *Woman's Home Companion*, *Saturday Evening Post*, *Metropolitan*, and *Harper's Bazaar*, where they accompanied stories by ***Mary Roberts Rinehart**, F. Scott Fitzgerald, Ring Lardner, P.G. Wodehouse, ***Alice Duer Miller**, and other noted writers. The artist went to great lengths to achieve honesty and authenticity in her work. On one occasion, in order to experience what it would be like to apply for a job as a cook, she adopted an alias and haunted employment agencies, applying for positions in the field while observing the settings and people around her.

Preston exhibited her work in shows in New York, London, and Paris, and in 1915 was awarded a bronze medal at the San Francisco Panama-Pacific Exposition. She was also active in the National Woman's Party, and participated in suffrage rallies. With the onset of the Depression, the market for Preston's work dried up, and she and her husband moved from New York City to a barn they remodeled in East Hampton, Long Island. Preston later developed a serious skin condition which eventually forced her to give up drawing, after which she became a passionate gardener. She died in East Hampton in 1949.

SOURCES:

Hill, Ann, ed. *A Visual Dictionary of Art*. Greenwich, CT: New York Graphic Society, 1974.

James, Edward T., ed. *Notable American Women, 1607–1959*. Cambridge, MA: The Belknap Press of Harvard University, 1971.

McHenry, Robert, ed. *Famous American Women*. NY: Dover, 1983.

Rubinstein, Charlotte Streifer. *American Women Artists*. NY: Avon, 1982.

Barbara Morgan,
Melrose, Massachusetts

Pretty Mary (c. 1908–1938).

See Bonita, Maria.

Prettyman, Kathleen Collins (1942–1988).

See Collins, Kathleen.

Prévost, Françoise (1680–1741)

French ballerina. *Name variations: Francoise Prevost. Born in France in 1680; died in 1741.*

Françoise Prévost was born in 1680 and made her debut in a revival of Jean-Baptiste Lully's *Atys* in 1699. The enormous popularity of this opera-ballet ensured hers, and within six years she would replace Mlle de Subligny (***Marie-Thérèse Subligny**) at the Opéra de France. In 1714, at a private performance in the **Duchesse du Maine**'s small theater at the Château de Sceaux, Prévost danced the final scene of Corneille's *Horace,* accompanied by Jean Balon and the music of Jean Joseph Mouret. It was not only a triumph but a French leap in the development of ballet. Prevost, a gifted actress, had moved the audience to tears. In 1720, she created *Les Caractères de la danse*, which would later become a showpiece for ***Marie-Anne Cupis de Camargo** and ***Marie Sallé**, and be published in book form in the 1920s. As her star faded, she retired at age 50 and began to teach at the Opéra's School of Dance.

SOURCES:

Migel, Parmenia. *The Ballerinas: From the Court of Louis XIV to Pavlova*. NY: Macmillan, 1972.

Pribyslava

Bohemian princess. *Only daughter of* ****Drahomira of Bohemia*** *and Ratislav also known as Vratislav I (887–920), duke of Bohemia (r. 912–920).*

Price, Ellen (1814–1887).

See Wood, Ellen Price.

Price, Eugenia (1916–1996)

American author. *Born in Charleston, West Virginia, on June 22, 1916; died in Brunswick, Georgia, on May 28,*

1996; attended Ohio University; studied dentistry at Northwestern University; never married; no children.

The author of numerous inspirational books and popular antebellum romantic novels, Eugenia Price was born in Charleston, West Virginia, in 1916, the precocious daughter of a dentist, and entered Ohio University at 16. She later studied dentistry at Northwestern University, but gave it up to pursue a writing career. Price broke into the profession by writing soap operas, first in Chicago, then New York and Cincinnati. Following a conversion to Christianity in the late 1940s, she began writing inspirational books, among them *Beloved World* and *The Eugenia Price Treasury of Faith*. Price turned out some two dozen books of this nature and won a wide following before turning to novels.

On a book tour in 1960, Price and her editor and companion **Joyce Blackburn** took a side trip to St. Simons, an island off the coast of Georgia, and were so taken by its beauty that they decided to make it their home. Using this Southern locale as a backdrop, Price began a series of romantic novels, the first three of which—*Lighthouse, New Moon Rising*, and *Beloved Invader*—focused on an actual St. Simons cleric and his two wives. Experiencing instant success, Price wrote a Florida trilogy and a Savannah quartet before returning to the St. Simons setting for a Georgia trilogy. The first book of the latter series, *Bright Captivity* (1991), was on the bestseller list of *The New York Times*; the third, *Beauty from Ashes* (1995), was also a bestseller. Price's last book, *The Waiting Time*, was published posthumously in 1997. Although the novels never won serious literary acclaim, they sold more than 40 million copies and were translated into 18 languages. They also made St. Simons famous. Of the thousands of visitors to the island each year, many are Price fans, there to scout out houses and other locales detailed in her books. Eugenia Price died in 1996, age 79, and was buried in the St. Simons cemetery plot she purchased shortly after arriving on the island in 1960.

SOURCES:

Thomas, Robert McG., Jr. "Obituary," in *The Day* [New London, CT]. May 30, 1996.

Barbara Morgan,
Melrose, Massachusetts

Price, Florence B. (1888–1953)

African-American composer and the first black woman to win fame as a symphonist. *Born Florence Beatrice Smith on April 9, 1888, in Little Rock, Arkansas; died on June 3, 1953, in Chicago, Illinois; daughter of Florence Irene Smith (a schoolteacher) and James H. Smith (a dentist); married Thomas Price (an attorney); children: Tommy; Florence Louise; Edith.*

Although Florence B. Price was born only two decades after the Civil War, her career reflects how much African-Americans achieved under difficult circumstances. She was born Florence Beatrice Smith in 1888 in Little Rock, Arkansas, into a solidly middle-class family, and grew up in cultured surroundings. Along with her brother Charles Smith and sister **Gertrude Smith**, she studied music with her mother **Florence Irene Smith** who had taught music in public school. Florence was four when she gave her first public performance. Her father James H. Smith, a dentist, had had a lucrative practice in Chicago before his marriage. When the Chicago fire of 1871 destroyed his office, James had returned to teaching in Arkansas. He was a musician like his wife, and the Smiths often joined other families in Little Rock who enjoyed music.

After Price graduated from high school, she attended the New England Conservatory of Music where she majored in piano and organ and studied music theory and composition. Her teacher, the renowned white composer George Whitefield Chadwick (1854–1931), used African-American musical idioms in his compositions, and he likely encouraged Florence to do the same. She had already published a composition at age 11, so the New England Conservatory was an ideal environment for her talents. When Price graduated in 1907, she began teaching at Arkadelphia Academy in Cotton Plant, Arkansas. Neumon Leighton, a white professor at Memphis State University, was very impressed with Price's art songs and lectured about her works to his students. Price was soon teaching music at Shorter College in North Little Rock before moving on to Clark College in Atlanta, where she taught from 1910 to 1912. Her teaching career ended with her marriage to Thomas Price, a Little Rock attorney, but her composing would continue.

The Prices had three children, although Tommy, the oldest, died in infancy. When discrimination coupled with a rash of racial lynchings became too much, the Prices moved from Arkansas to Chicago in 1927. Here, Florence began to move in a larger musical world. She studied with Arthur Olaf Anderson, Carl Busch, and Leo Sowerby and wrote radio commercials to earn extra money. Associating with other black artists and intellectuals was stimulating for Price. She became a mentor to a young composer, *Margaret Bonds, who would also become successful. A photo taken in 1934 shows Price conducting the Women's Symphony of Chicago with Bonds at the piano. In 1940, Price was named a member of the American Society of Composers, Authors, and Publishers.

Price also began to publish her work in Chicago. G. Schirmer released "At the Cotton Gin," a piano piece, in 1928 and solicited more short teaching pieces from her. ***Marian Anderson** used her setting of a Langston Hughes poem, "Songs to a Dark Virgin," which Schirmer published in 1941. Other artists who sang her songs included ***Carol Brice**, ***Leontyne Price**, Roland Hayes, ***Blanche Thebom, Etta Moten**, ***Camilla Williams, Grace Bumbry**, Todd Duncan, William Warfield, and **Ellabelle Davis**. In addition to shorter works, Price also composed her Symphony in A Minor and a piano sonata which won Wanamaker awards in 1930. Frederick Stock conducted the Chicago Symphony Orchestra in the first performance of the Symphony in 1933.

Price believed that black idioms were "rich resources for the creation of a body of uniquely American concert music." Speaking of her Symphony No. 3, she said, "It is intended to be Negroid in character and expression. In it no attempt, however, has been made to project Negro music solely in the purely traditional manner. None of the themes are adaptations or derivations of folk songs." Price lived and worked when America was a segregated country and during a period when African-Americans had no recognized civil rights. Even so, her enormous talent and perseverance gained her a place among the country's finest musicians.

SOURCES:

Bailey, Ben E. "Florence B. Price" in Smith, Jessie Carney, ed., *Notable Black American Women*. Detroit, MI: Gale Research, 1992, pp. 872–874.

Green, Mildred Denby. *Black Women Composers: A Genesis*. Boston, MA: G.K. Hall, 1983.

Southern, Eileen. *The Music of Black Americans*. 2nd ed. NY: Norton, 1977.

John Haag,
Athens, Georgia

Price, Leontyne (1927—)

First African-American operatic soprano to achieve international recognition. *Born Mary Violet Leontine Price in Laurel, Mississippi, on February 10, 1927; daughter of James Price and Katherine Price; graduated from Wilberforce College (later named Central State University); attended Juilliard School of Music; married William Warfield (a baritone), on August 31, 1952 (separated 1959 and divorced 1967).*

Began her musical education at age three by learning piano, at which she had become an accomplished artist by eleven, and by singing in church choirs; determined on a musical career in high school and gave her first public recital (1943); graduated from Ohio's Wilberforce College before enrolling at New York's Juilliard School of Music (1948) where she soon decided on an opera career, even though opportunities for African-Americans in classical opera were extremely limited; made her American opera debut in San Francisco (1957); made her European debut in Vienna (1958); made her debut with the Metropolitan Opera in New York (1961), to great acclaim; became especially known for her interpretations of many of Verdi's heroines during her 24-year tenure with the Met; renowned in particular for her Aïda*; retired from the opera stage (1985), concentrating on more intimate concert settings, and on teaching and recording; published* Aida*, her children's version of the opera, illustrated by Leo and* ***Diane Dillon*** *(Gulliver Books of Harcourt Brace, 2000).*

One crisp autumn day on the verdant campus of Ohio's Wilberforce College, a group of seniors happened upon a lone freshman between classes, presenting another opportunity for hazing a hapless new arrival for the predominantly African-American school's 1943 semester. "What can you *do*?," they challenged her, to which she promptly replied, "I can sing!," and proceeded to do so in a voice of such clarity and power that the stunned upperclass students vowed never again to harass a freshman. Leontyne Price had won over another audience with the extraordinary talent that would bring future, and much more critical, listeners to their feet.

Leontyne Price had been considered a prodigy during her childhood in tiny Laurel, Mississippi, where she had been born on February 10, 1927, to James and **Katherine Price**. Her parents had been expecting a boy, whom they had pledged to call Leon after a family friend. Kate Price managed to honor the promise after a fashion by adding a feminine suffix to the chosen name, coming up with Leontine. (Her daughter, in an enthusiasm for French which developed much later, replaced the *i* with a *y*.) By the time her son George was born two years later, Kate had begun to notice Leontyne's attraction to music, and loved to tell the story of the local teacher who, on hearing two-year-old Leontyne mimic her singing, remarked to Kate, "You've got an armful of music there." When Leontyne was three, Kate arranged for piano lessons.

The source of Leontyne's aptitude was not hard to find, for both parents were musically inclined. James, a carpenter who had moved to Laurel from an even smaller village some 20 years earlier to look for work, played the tuba in Laurel's Methodist church band; while Kate, who had come from a similarly rural settlement in northern Mississippi, sang in the choir. The Prices gave their children a loving, but firm, Methodist upbringing, and church music played a large role in Leontyne's early musical development. At the age of five, her piano playing had made her somewhat of a local celebrity, and by the time Leontyne entered Laurel's Sandy Gavin Elementary School, she was often playing at church services, Sunday School, and church socials, as well as singing along with her mother in the choir.

The most wonderful thing in the world is to be who you are.

—Leontyne Price

Although the Prices lived in the poor, African-American section of Laurel, Leontyne never speaks of her childhood as being particularly deprived. "We were raised with love, discipline, respect for hard work, and faith in ourselves," she says. To supplement the family's meager income, Kate Price often worked as a midwife. On days she was tending a birth, Leontyne and her brother George were given over to the care of their Aunt **Everline Greer**, who worked as a downstairs maid to a prosperous white Laurel family, the Chisholms. Mrs. Chisholm in particular was charmed by Leontyne's voice and often invited her to sing at the social gatherings arranged at the family's home. Later, Price's talents graced similar functions all over Laurel. At seven years of age, Leontyne was earning a small income from her appearances and was considered a child prodigy, especially by Mrs. Chisholm, who would prove an important influence on Leontyne's later years.

The "original kickoff," as Price calls it, for her decision to pursue a musical career came when she was nine years old and traveled with her mother to Jackson, Mississippi, to hear soprano ***Marian Anderson** sing. Anderson, fresh from a groundbreaking appearance at the White House at ***Eleanor Roosevelt**'s invitation, electrified young Leontyne with her performance. "I woke up! I was excited!," Price recalls. "I was thrilled with this woman's manners, her carriage, her pride, her voice." The barriers which would face Price in later years were first successfully breached by Anderson, whom Roosevelt invited to sing at Washington's Lincoln Memorial in 1939, after she was refused permission by the Daughters of the American Revolution to appear at their Constitution Hall. Later, in 1955, Anderson would become the first black soprano to sing a leading role at New York's Metropolitan Opera.

A year after hearing Anderson sing in Jackson, Price entered Mississippi's segregated Oak Park Vocational School, considered the best school in the state for African-American students, and especially known for its musical education. Price was soon playing piano and singing with the Oak Park Choral Group, an award-winning ensemble that appeared at competitions and concerts throughout Mississippi. In December 1943, her senior year at Oak Park, Leontyne gave her first solo recital, playing and singing her own arrangements of such popular songs as "The Man I Love" and "White Christmas." The Prices were particularly pleased when Leontyne was named Miss Oak Park for having raised the most money for school projects and, even better, graduated cum laude.

Leontyne's music teacher at Oak Park had been sufficiently impressed with her abilities to secure her a full scholarship to Ohio's Wilberforce College (later renamed Central State University) which, like Oak Park, was considered the best musical school for black students in the Midwest. Price arrived at Wilberforce in 1943 intending to earn a degree allowing her to teach music in public schools. "At that time," she once remembered, "no black would aspire to be an opera singer. One would hope to be a music teacher." But her voice teacher at Wilberforce soon began urging her to consider a career as a singer, being impressed not only with Leontyne's clear, liquid voice but with her ability to learn new material quickly and thoroughly. Even the president of Wilberforce, who first heard Price perform at a faculty dinner, suggested she change her major to voice. But it wasn't until a concert audition for a visiting pianist from the East that Leontyne began to take the advice seriously. She had always considered herself a mezzo-soprano, but after one aria the pianist promptly told her that her range was much greater and began moving the piece up in pitch several times to prove it. When Price discovered she had no trouble extending her range, her extraordinary vocal gift as a full soprano finally became apparent to her. As if in confirmation, Leontyne won first place soon afterward at an interstate competition held in Cincinnati, which included delegates from eight other Midwest

Leontyne Price

schools, and she was made lead soloist of the Wilberforce Singers, an exclusive group consisting of the best vocal talent at the school.

In her senior year, school officials arranged an audition at New York's prestigious Juilliard School of Music which resulted, to no one's surprise, in a full scholarship. Unfortunately, the scholarship paid only tuition. With Leontyne's brother George attending school in South Carolina, the Prices confessed to Leontyne that money was too scarce for her living expenses in New

York. No one had counted, however, on Mrs. Chisholm, who had been following Leontyne's progress with interest ever since the Oak Park days and who now offered to supply Price's travel expenses and the cost of her room, board, and textbooks. In addition, a benefit concert was arranged by Wilberforce's president at which actor and baritone Paul Robeson sang. Robeson had heard Price perform at Antioch College some months earlier and had offered to help her career in any way possible. The concert in Dayton—Robeson's first public singing engagement since he had embarked on a film career—raised $1,000 for Leontyne's New York education.

Arriving at Juilliard in 1948, Leontyne was assigned **Florence Page Kimball**, a former concert singer, as her vocal coach. Years later, Kimball admitted that she had been more impressed with her new student's charm and presence than with her voice on their first meeting, at which Leontyne sang Torelli's aria "Tu lo sai." Kimball was known for never rushing her students, telling them, "Quality comes with the luxury of time," but neither woman imagined that their relationship as student and teacher would continue for a good deal of time—indeed, more than 40 years. Kimball chose two operas as Price's course material, Verdi's *Aïda* and Strauss' *Ariadne auf Naxos,* both of which Price would perform professionally in years to come, and one of which would make her famous.

Exposed to the excitements and opportunities of big city life, Price indulged in her first love affair (with a Haitian student at Juilliard who later left her to marry another), enjoyed movies and Broadway shows when she could afford them, and most important, attended her first operas: Puccini's *Turandot* at City Center and a Metropolitan Opera production of Strauss' *Salomè,* for which she found enough money for a gallery ticket allowing her to stand at the rear of the theater. Like the young girl ten years earlier who had been thrilled by Marian Anderson, Price was mesmerized by the drama and emotion of the opera stage and determined to give her future to it. She promptly arranged an audition for Juilliard's Opera Workshop, for which she was accepted in her sophomore year. The Workshop was under the direction of Frederick Cohen, the school's director of opera, and it was in Cohen's "Introduction to Opera" class that Price sang the "Lament" from *Dido and Aeneas*. Cohen excitedly told his wife that evening, "We have the voice of the century."

Also that year, Price gave a performance, arranged by Kimball, at Juilliard's concert hall. In the audience was composer Max Steiner, who had just been asked to cast a planned revival of George Gershwin's folk opera *Porgy and Bess.* After hearing Price, Steiner scribbled on his program, "She would make a good Bess," sent Kimball parts of the score, and urged her to work with Leontyne in preparation for auditions some months hence. *Porgy and Bess*, based on DuBose Heyward's novel, had originally opened on Broadway in 1935, but subsequent revivals had removed parts of the score considered too "operatic" for audiences used to musical comedy. The touring production planned by producer Robert Breen was to be the first to restore Gershwin's complete score, and Steiner knew it would require singers of considerable range and ability. Also in the audience at one of Kimball's student concerts was composer Virgil Thomson, who was then planning a restaging of the opera he had written with ***Gertrude Stein**, *Four Saints In Three Acts,* to be presented at Juilliard. Thomson cast Leontyne as Saint ***Cecilia**. The show ran for two weeks, with plans for a European tour, but by then Breen had begun auditions for *Porgy and Bess*.

True to Steiner's prediction, Price was given the part of Bess, her first professional role, opposite baritone William Warfield's Porgy. Warfield had recently taken the country by storm with his appearance as Joe in the 1951 film version of *Show Boat,* and had been touring with two nightclub revues, *Set My People Free* and *Regina*. Rehearsals for *Porgy and Bess* began in May 1952 in a Harlem loft, and Breen knew his casting was right the first time Warfield and Price sang the second act duet, "Bess, You Is My Woman Now." Cast members felt there was some special attraction between the two singers, a suspicion confirmed when Price and Warfield began dating. The show opened in Dallas during the summer of 1952, with Kate and James Price and Mrs. Chisholm in the audience. It later traveled to Chicago, Pittsburgh, and Washington, where President Harry Truman was the guest of honor at the old National Theater. The reviews were enthusiastic, especially focusing on Price's Bess. "Leontyne Price sings the most exciting and thrilling Bess we have ever heard," wrote the *Washington Post*'s David Hume. Novelist Reynolds Price, who remains a loyal Leontyne Price fan, remembers seeing the production when it finally reached New York in 1953, after a European tour. "At the center of that famous Gershwin revival," he recalls, "there moved a blazing, striding, soaring young Bess." Price was especially praised for her combination of dramatic and vocal power, and many veteran theatergoers felt it was the first time they had ever heard Gershwin's score given full justice. "Leontyne Price sings with rapture and professional skill," wrote *The New York Times'* Brooks Atkinson, "and acts with fire and abandon, turning that wayward part into a new person."

The *Porgy and Bess* tour held many surprises for Price, not the least of which was her first full exposure to white prejudice. "I was highly naive to think that once the hurdles had been conquered I'd have automatic acceptance," she said many years later. "I've paid my price." Not being allowed at major hotels, the tour's all-black cast was often forced to stay in private homes and motels. Price was nearly barred from entering the Dallas hotel in which Mrs. Chisholm was staying, permitted to pass through the doors only after Chisholm soundly berated the doorman who had blocked Leontyne's entry. Cast members were routinely denied rental cars given to the tour's white management, while the significance of President Truman's presence at the Washington premiere was underscored by the fact that the National Theater had been closed by its previous management, who refused to admit either integrated audiences or casts.

Fortunately, a much happier discovery awaited Price just before the show began its run at the National. William Warfield proposed to her, and the two were married in New York on August 31, 1952. The marriage lasted until 1959, when the two separated amicably, citing the strains of their respective careers. The separation was formalized in 1967.

Price would play Bess for a full two years, a platform that brought her to the attention of such contemporary musical notables as Igor Stravinsky, Henri Sauget and William Kilmayer, many of whose works she introduced in recitals at the Museum of Modern Art and the Metropolitan Museum. Also while touring with *Porgy and Bess,* Price gave her first New York solo concert at Town Hall, though the response was a far cry from the ecstatic reviews she had been used to. Critics praised her stage presence and interpretative skills but took her to task for an overly pronounced tremolo and unevenness of tone. Price paid careful attention to these reactions and redoubled her efforts with Florence Kimball. Accompanying her on piano at Town Hall was composer Samuel Barber, who became a close friend and asked her to debut some of his early works at a Library of Congress recital in Washington later that year; he requested her again when he premiered his *Prayers of Kierkegaard* with the Boston Symphony. "Every note is just right for me," Price said of Barber's work. "As an artist . . . this is two-thirds of the job—not having to adjust your voice to the score." Barber's *Hermit Songs,* in fact, was Leontyne's first recorded release, in 1955 for RCA.

Fresh from the *Porgy and Bess* tour, Price extended her exposure to a national audience by singing *Tosca* in a television production mounted by NBC's Opera Theater in January 1955, just as Marian Anderson was breaking the color barrier at the Met. Producer Samuel Chotzinoff's choice for his Tosca was a risky one, since no African-American soprano had appeared in the role in a major stage production, let alone before a national television audience. "Is she a good singer?," NBC's David Sarnoff asked when Chotzinoff came to him for approval. "She's a great singer," Chotzinoff replied. "Then that's all you have to think about," said Sarnoff. Eleven NBC affiliates in the South refused to carry the show, which was broadcast live and sung in English. The response to Price's operatic ability was as enthusiastic as it had been for her Bess. "She can sail into those big, fat phrases and make them rise with a beauty that is both strong and controlled," Hume wrote. "She is a stunning, sumptuous Tosca, and ought quickly to follow Marian Anderson's lead into the Metropolitan." So enthusiastic was the audience reaction to the production that Price appeared in three other NBC Opera Theaters, Mozart's *The Magic Flute* and *Don Giovanni* and Poulenc's *Dialogue of the Carmelites,* over the next five years.

It was the latter production that brought Price's first offer from a major opera company, the San Francisco Opera, then under the baton of Kurt Adler. Adler had seen the NBC version of Poulenc's contemporary opera set in a convent during the French Revolution and cast Leontyne in the same role she had sung on television, Madame Lidoine. Price made her professional debut in the company's production on September 20, 1957, joining the likes of ***Birgit Nilsson** and ***Renata Tebaldi**, who had also made their debuts under Adler's direction. During intermission one evening, Adler presented Price with another opportunity which would serve her well. His female lead in the company's production of *Aïda* had just been rushed to the hospital for an emergency appendectomy. Verdi's Ethiopian slave who falls tragically in love with an Egyptian military officer had been played by an African-American soprano only once before, when **Caterina Jarboro** sang the role for the Chicago Opera Company in 1933. But it was a role Price had been singing ever since her first days with Kim-

See sidebar on the following page

Jarboro, Caterina (1908–1986)

African-American soprano. Born on July 24, 1908 (some sources cite 1903), in Wilmington, North Carolina; died in August 1986 in New York, New York; trained in Paris and Milan.

Born and raised in Wilmington, North Carolina, Caterina Jarboro became the first African-American to appear with an American opera company when she made her debut with the Chicago Opera in 1933, in *Aïda.* When the company performed at the Hippodrome that July in New York City, *The New York Times'* music editor wrote: "The young soprano brought a vivid dramatic sense that kept her impersonation vital without overacting, and an Italian diction remarkably pure and distinct." Even so, the newly founded New York Metropolitan Opera Association refused to accept her as a member. **Hannah Block**, a Wilmington community activist, was instrumental in the restoration of Jarboro's childhood home at 214 Church Street.

ball, and one she felt capable of singing professionally. With little time to rehearse and no time to block her movements (forcing her during the second intermission to inquire of the director, "Where am I supposed to die?"), the performance ended with a standing ovation for her work and the beginning of a reputation for the role with which she would be most closely identified. Delighted with her reception, Adler cast her as Doña Anna in his company's *Don Giovanni* and as her first Leonora in *Il Trovatore*, in 1958. During her ten years with the San Francisco Opera, Price also sang her first Cio-Cio-San in *Madame Butterfly*, as well as Amelia in *Un Ballo in Maschera* and Doña Elvira in *Ernani.* Over 40 years later, Price still called the San Francisco Opera "my grand alma mater."

In between seasons in San Francisco, Price sang with the Chicago Lyric Opera, where she was temporarily stung by negative reviews of her performance in that company's *Thaïs.* As she had after her Town Hall recital some years earlier, Price took the comments to heart and sought help from Kimball, returning to Chicago to garner triumphant reviews of her Liu in *Turandot.* With her reputation growing stronger with each performance, Leontyne received her first offer from the Met in New York, but she turned it down on the advice of her manager, Andrè Mertens. Like Kimball, Mertens preferred to nurse his artists slowly and encouraged Leontyne to begin accepting the several offers now coming in from Europe—especially from the Vienna State Opera, whose director, Herbert von Karajan, had heard her in a blind audition arranged by Mertens. Von Karajan was the most influential musical personality on the Continent at the time, ensuring that her European debut with his 1958 production of *Aïda* for the Staatsoper in Vienna was quickly followed by productions in Paris, London and, finally, at La Scala in 1960. As Price well knew, any diva appearing at La Scala must make appropriate compensation to the various "claques" which inhabit that venerable house, known to cheer and shout enthusiastically if the payment is generous or boo and hiss menacingly if it is not. Wisely, Price ensured that the claques were amply paid to do neither, thus assuring that the cheers of "Divina! Divina!" which filled the house during a standing ovation were an accurate reading of her performance. She was hailed throughout Italy as *the* Verdi soprano, leading one critic to effuse, "Our great Verdi would have found her the ideal Aïda"; and La Scala was so impressed with her reception that it accepted her contract requirement that no role would be denied her in future productions based on her race. Price thus became the first black Cio-Cio-San to appear on the La Scala stage, with one opera official commenting, "The public will have to get used to it. If . . . anybody objects, we'll say she's a suntanned Butterfly." He needn't have worried: every production of *Butterfly* that season was sold out well in advance.

It was Price's Doña Anna in von Karajan's production of *Don Giovanni* for the 1960 Salzburg Festival that brought another offer from the Met. This time, Mertens and Kimball agreed with Price that she was ready. Leontyne noted that by now, with a reputation at virtually every other major opera house in the United States and Europe, "I was box office." On the evening of January 27, 1961, Price became only the fifth black artist to sing a leading role at the Metropolitan when she appeared as Leonora in the Met's production of *Il Trovatore*, with Franco Corelli and Robert Merrill. Waiting to mount the stage for her first entrance, Price confessed to Kimball, "I'm scared to death. What should I do?" Her teacher merely held up a long-stemmed rose taken from a nearby bouquet. "Smell a rose, and sing," she replied.

When the curtain rang down some three hours later, the old Met house on 39th Street thundered with a standing ovation that continued for 42 minutes, still a Met record. Swept up in the adoration for Leontyne were Kate and James Price, her brother George, and the Chisholms, all of whom had watched her triumph from the tenth row. "I'm very happy," Kate Price told a reporter that night. "My work has been accomplished." *The New Yorker*'s review, among the nearly unanimous praise that appeared following the performance, told its readers that Price had given her Leonora "a special dramatic eloquence which arose partly from the rich, vibrant quality of her voice and partly from the authoritative artistry with which she used it." Price's four other starring roles with the Met that season were equally well received, particularly her *Aïda,* which remains her favorite role for a personal reason. "*Aïda* afforded me the opportunity to luxuriate in 'Black is Beautiful,'" Price says. "My interpretation is provocative, because to me Aïda is a princess in captivity." With her success as an internationally recognized diva now firmly established, Price became an outspoken supporter of many African-American causes. More than half of her benefit concerts at Carnegie Hall during the 1960s and 1970s, for example, raised money for the National Association for the Advancement of Colored People (NAACP), The Martin Luther King, Jr. Center for Non-Violent Social Change, and the National Urban League. "Success," Price said at the time, "is when you have the luxury of doing what you feel like doing."

During her years with the Met, Price became the first black performer to open a Met season with her performance as Minnie in Puccini's *Girl of the Golden West* in October 1963—the first time the work had been mounted by the Met in 30 years. And on September 16, 1966, Price opened the new Metropolitan Opera House at Lincoln Center in her old friend Samuel Barber's *Antony and Cleopatra,* commissioned especially for the occasion by then-general manager Rudolph Bing and staged by Franco Zefferelli, both of whom set an impossible schedule for preparing the work. It was generally agreed that the production was a disaster, plagued by technical problems that on one occasion left Price imprisoned inside a golden pyramid that stubbornly refused to open out toward the audience to reveal her Cleopatra. "It was a beautiful score and I have tremendous respect for Barber as a composer," Leontyne said during the post-mortems. "I don't think his music was properly heard." But the Barber work was the only blemish in an otherwise triumphant tenure at the Met. "I never dreamed it," Kimball said mid-way through Price's reign, remembering their early days together. "I thought she seemed intelligent and had a pretty voice, but it never occurred to me that she would develop the way she has."

In 1965, the Met agreed with Price's request to slow down her performance schedule, citing the strains on a voice she intended to preserve as long as possible. "I prefer to sing on my interest rather than on my capital," she said, and told a reporter in 1970 that she felt she had been losing the joy and beauty of music amid the demands of the opera stage. Throughout the 1970s, Price devoted more time to more intimate, and less stressful, concerts and recitals in which she sang spirituals, folk ballads, and new music by Barber and Ned Rorem. Her now less frequent work on the opera stage seemed to gain strength from her careful tending, and her performance in the San Francisco Opera's 1977 *Ariadne auf Naxos* is considered by many to be her finest work. Finally, Price gave her farewell performance as *Aïda* in the Met's production of January 3, 1985, hailed as the opera event of that year. (She sang the role one last time on public television later that same year.)

Since then, she has given herself over to the pure joy of singing that she knew as a young girl back in Laurel, performing at solo concerts and at benefits and keeping up an impressive recording schedule which has brought her 19 Grammy awards, not to mention three Emmy awards, the Kennedy Center award, and the President's Medal of Freedom. More important, her work opened the door even wider for a new generation of African-American opera stars, such as **Grace Bumbry** and ***Shirley Verrett**, and her encouragement and support of new young artists is well known. "A serious argument could be made," writes Reynolds Price, "that no other singer has equaled the full panoply of her career in its beauty of endowment and discipline, in stamina and intelligence, in dramatic and stylistic variety." Price's own assessment of her career is more modest. "My parents taught me to be the best human being I could be," she says. "They told me that it was wonderful that I was black and that if I did my best, I would be rewarded." James and Kate Price were exactly right.

SOURCES:

Abdul, Raoul. *Blacks in Classical Music: A Personal History.* NY: Dodd, Mead, 1977.

Campbell, Bebe Moore. "The 1990 Essence Awards," in *Essence.* Vol. 21, no. 6. October 1990.

Lyon, Hugh Lee. *Highlights of a Prima Donna.* NY: Vantage, 1973.

Price, Reynolds. "Bouquet for Leontyne," in *Opera News.* Vol. 59, no. 14. April 1, 1995.

Smith, Jessie Carney, ed. *Notable Black American Women.* Detroit, MI: Gale Research, 1992.

Norman Powers,
writer-producer, Chelsea Lane Productions,
New York, New York

Price, Roberta MacAdams
(1881–1959)

Canadian politician who was one of the first two women elected to the legislature in the British Empire. *Name variations: Roberta MacAdams. Born*

Roberta Catherine MacAdams on July 21, 1881, in Sarnia, Ontario, Canada; died on December 16, 1959, in Calgary, Alberta, Canada; graduated from the Macdonald Institute, 1911; married Harvey Stinson Price, on September 21, 1920; children: Robert.

Became one of the first two women elected to a legislature in Canada and in the British Empire (1917); was the first woman to introduce legislation in the British Empire (1918).

Born in Sarnia, Ontario, Canada, in 1881, Roberta MacAdams Price later studied domestic science at the Macdonald Institute in Guelph, Ontario, graduating in 1911. She then moved to Edmonton, Alberta, where she lectured women farmers on food and cookery, and offered information on emerging women's institutes as an employee of the Alberta Department of Agriculture. A year later Price established cooking classes throughout the city as superintendent of domestic science for the Edmonton Public School Board.

Women in the province of Alberta won the right to vote in 1916, and that same year, during World War I, Price enlisted in the Canadian Army Medical Corps. She was commissioned as a lieutenant and ran the kitchen of the Ontario Military Hospital in Orpington, England. In 1917, the Alberta Military Representation Act created two Soldiers' Representatives seats in the Alberta Legislature, and 20 men declared their candidacies. To offset the lack of newly enfranchised women in the running, **Beatrice Nasmyth**, publicity secretary for the Alberta agent general, and **Nell Dennis** convinced Price to run for one of the seats. Her campaign slogan, developed by Nasmyth and Dennis, was "Give one vote to the man of your choice and the other to the sister."

More than 25,000 ballots were cast for the two seats in the August 1917 election, with Price garnering 4,023 votes—enough to make her the second woman elected to a legislature within the British Empire. The first was ***Louise McKinney**, who had won election to her seat in the Alberta Legislature a month earlier, and both Price and McKinney took their oaths of office on February 7, 1918. The following day, Price introduced a piece of legislation providing for the incorporation of the War Veterans' Next-of-Kin Association. In proposing the plan, she became the first woman to introduce legislation in the British Empire.

Price served in the legislature until 1921, choosing not to seek re-election after her 1920 marriage to Harvey Stinson Price. The couple later moved to Calgary, Alberta, where she raised her son and was active in women's organizations and educational institutions. Price died on December 16, 1959. Eight years later, in honor of her achievements and prominence, her portrait was presented to the Alberta Legislature.

Howard Gofstein,
freelance writer, Oak Park, Michigan

Prichard, Katharine Susannah (1883–1969)

Author, pacifist, and founder member of the Communist Party of Australia, as one of Australia's foremost writers, whose initiatives made a profound impact upon the lives of many West Australians. *Name variations: KSP. Pronunciation: Prit-chard. Born on December 4, 1883, in Fiji; died in 1969 in Perth, Western Australia; daughter of Tom Prichard (a journalist) and Edith Isabel Fraser (a painter); attended South Melbourne College; married Hugo Throssell, in 1919; children: Ric Throssell (b. 1922).*

Spent childhood in Fiji and Australia (first in Launceston, Tasmania, and later in Melbourne, Victoria); at age 21, went to South Gippsland to governess (1904); father committed suicide (1907); made her first visit to London as a journalist (1908); returned to London (1912), where she wrote her first prizewinning novel, The Pioneers, *which won the Hodder and Stoughton All-Empire novel competition, enabling her to return to Australia as a radical writer of some promise; published second novel,* Windlestraws *(1916); brother Alan killed on the battlefields of northern France (1917); moved with new husband to Perth, Western Australia, to the hillside suburb of Greenmount (1919); published novels* Working Bullocks, Coonardoo, *and* Haxby's Circus *(1920s); was a founding member of the Communist Party of Australia (early 1920s); went to Russia (1933) and, while she was gone, Hugo Throssell committed suicide; returning to Australia, threw herself into political work, becoming a founder member of the Movement against War and Fascism; at outbreak of Spanish Civil War, organized the Spanish Relief Committee in Western Australia; became a member of the Communist Party's Central Committee (1943); awarded the World Council's Silver Medallion for services to peace (1959); on her death (1969), aged 86, her coffin was draped with the Red Flag and she was given a Communist funeral.*

Selected publications: (novels) The Pioneers *(1915),* Windlestraws *(1916),* The Black Opal *(1921),* Working Bullocks *(1926),* The Wild Oats of Han *(1928),* Coonardoo *(1929),* Haxby's Circus *(1930),* Intimate Strangers *(1937),* Moon of Desire *(1941),* The Roaring Nineties *(1946),* Golden Miles *(1948),*

Winged Seeds *(1950)*, Subtle Flame *(1967)*; *(autobiography)* Child of the Hurricane *(1964)*; *(plays)* Brumby Innes *(1940)*, The Pioneers *(1937)*, Bid Me to Love *(1975)*; *(verse)* Clovelly Verses *(1913)*, The Earth Lover *(1932)*; *(reportage)* The Real Russia *(1934)*; *(anthology)* On Strenuous Wings *(edited by Joan Williams, 1965)*; *(juvenile)* Maggie and Her Circus Pony *(1967)*; *(essays)* Straight Left: The Articles and Addresses of Katharine Susannah Prichard *(edited by Ric Throssell, 1982). Her novels have been translated into many languages, including Russian, Polish and Czech.*

Perth in Western Australia is the most isolated city in the world. In the 1930s, at least for its white inhabitants, Perth was a lonely outpost of British culture, separated from the rest of Australia by an eight-day sea voyage or a three-day train journey. Perth reporters met every incoming ship at the Fremantle wharves in search of news. By all accounts, the majority of the local populace was conservative, complacent, politically naive, trusting of authority figures and suspicious of new ideas.

Katharine Susannah Prichard, author, pacifist, Communist, and political activist, chose to live on the outskirts of Perth for 50 years, from 1919 until her death in 1969. Her life was one of courage, determination, hard work, joy and tragedy. During her lifetime, she developed an international standing as a novelist, was recognized as one of Australia's foremost writers, and established an almost legendary reputation locally as a political activist whose initiatives made a profound impact upon the lives of many West Australians. In the midst of such physical isolation and unsophisticated conservatism, how was her brilliant light able to shine so readily?

Katharine Susannah Prichard was born in what was then the British crown colony of Fiji on December 4, 1883, the first child of **Edith Isabel Fraser**, a talented painter, and Tom Prichard, a journalist with the *Fiji Times*. In her autobiography *Child of the Hurricane* (1964), Prichard attributes her own strength of character and political idealism to the complex interaction of the immense securities and insecurities of her early childhood. The Prichard and Fraser families had migrated to Australia from Britain on the sailing ship *Eldorado* in 1853, a 94-day sea voyage of astonishing hardship. Tom Prichard, the second youngest son of ten children, was four years old on arrival in Australia; Edith Fraser, the fourth of nine children, was the first to be born in Australia. Prichard recalls her

Katharine Susannah Prichard

father saying he had fallen in love with Edith when she was a schoolgirl and made up his mind then that he would marry her. The Prichard and Fraser families, having remained warm friends after their long and hazardous sea voyage to a new land, became inextricably linked when the eldest of the Prichard sons married one of the elder Fraser girls, and a younger Fraser boy married one of the Prichard girls. Tom Prichard's marriage to Edith Fraser added to the complex interrelatedness of the family: for Katharine Susannah, growing up in the center of a large and loving web of aunts, uncles, cousins and their relatives meant great security.

By her own definition, Prichard was a child of the hurricane. In her autobiography, published in 1964, she describes her 1883 birth in Fiji thus:

> Dawn threw wan light on the devastation caused by the hurricane; the township bashed and battered as though by a bombardment, the sea-wall washed away, the sea breaking through the main street, ships in

> the harbour blown ashore or onto the reef, coconut plantations beaten to the ground. But in that bungalow on the hillside, natives gazed with awe at the baby the hurricane had left in its wake. "Na Luve ni Cava," they exclaimed. "She is a child of the hurricane."

Born into a charmed circle of calm during a wild and tempestuous night, Prichard seems to have been able to combine her passionate criticism of social injustice, and her determination to expose and rail against unjust laws, with a sweet and gentle disposition. In her autobiography, she stresses her strong will and her early ability to charm. She attributes many of her later characteristics to the Fijian experience—her love for the natural world, and for those of other races. She was particularly attached to her devoted Fijian carer, N'gardo. "Maybe N'gardo is responsible for the instinctive sympathy I've always had for people of the native races," she wrote. "It is, I think, a tribute to that dark, protective presence in my early life." But tragedy struck early: the decision for the two-year-old Kattie to travel to Victoria with her mother for the birth of her brother Alan left N'gardo inconsolable, certain she had gone forever, and in his grief he died. This was the first of several tragic deaths of significant men in her life.

During Prichard's childhood, as her journalist father searched for work, her family moved from Fiji to Tasmania and finally to Melbourne, always establishing a lively circle of friends and acquaintances for whom ideas were central. Her awakening to injustice is recorded in one of her early novels, *The Wild Oats of Han,* in a scene recalling her own family trauma in which Han and her brothers return from a delightful picnic with a servant to find cartloads of the family furniture rolling down the hill, sold because the family could no longer make ends meet. Unemployment, injustice, ill-deserved poverty—all troubled Prichard. This incident seems to have bred in the young girl a desire to be influential in her adulthood. She felt helpless and yet responsible for finding a way out of their troubles. From this time on, Tom Prichard's mental health was precarious, a constant source of worry to the family. Her autobiography suggests it was the combination of being so well loved, and yet insecure because of her father's unpredictably uncertain health, which caused Prichard to be so determined to right the world's perceived injustices. This determination, accompanied by a prodigious intelligence, a thirst for knowledge, an eye for detail, and an early desire to write, created a woman whose idealism shaped all that she did.

Prichard's literary talents were displayed early. Before the family left Tasmania, she published her first short story in the children's page of a Melbourne newspaper. Her second story, "The Brown Boy," won a prize and caused quite a stir in her family. Most important of all for the young Kattie, she had earned a guinea for the story, which she proudly passed on to her father. She decided then to become a writer. Although neither parent took her stated ambition seriously at that stage, her mother fostered in her a love for words, for rhythms, for imaginative writing, by keeping up a constant supply of books by British poets and novelists. The love of learning and for ideas, thus instilled, remained with her throughout her life.

At age 14, Prichard won a scholarship to South Melbourne College. There, under the tutelage of the principal, J.B. O'Hara, she embarked upon the happiest and most valuable years of her school life and was greatly encouraged in her writing. Her determination to be a writer seems to have guided her from this time on. Although she wanted to attend university, there was not enough money in the Prichard family for all four children to go, and despite the relative emancipation of the family's views, as a girl Prichard stepped aside to allow her younger brothers Alan and Nigel to have a university education. Instead, she went to night school and kept in close contact with those of her friends who had gone to university.

In 1904, aged 21, determined to broaden her experience of Australian people and landscape, Prichard took a series of jobs as a governess in outback Australia, all of which provided useful material for her writing. After several years, she returned to Melbourne to live with her family and became a journalist. In 1907, her father committed suicide.

The following year, she was sent to London to cover the Franco-British exhibition for the *Melbourne Herald.* This taste of cosmopolitan life exhilarated her, and in 1912, aged 29, she returned to London, "hoping," as **Drusilla Modjeska** points out, "like so many other talented Australian women of her generation, to find ways of living professionally and independently in the comparative freedom of London." Though life was hard, for Prichard it was full of intense exploration of ideas. She became part of a circle of artists and writers and embarked upon a systematic study of socialist ideas, providing a background for her subsequent study of Marxism. Her pacifism was confirmed when she traveled to northern France during World War I and saw the atrocities of war at first hand.

As a writer, the climax of her London stay came in 1915 when she won the prestigious Australian section of the Hodder and Stoughton All-Empire novel competition with *The Pioneers*. For this, she won £250, a considerable sum, and with renewed confidence in her Australian future as a radical writer she returned to Melbourne. Here, despite her clearly articulated controversial views, she was welcomed back into her family—support she considers worthy of recording in her autobiography:

> "Kattie's had the opportunity of learning more than we did, Lil," Mother replied placidly. "Perhaps the old ways and ideas are good enough for us, but she belongs to a different generation."
>
> That was how mother reconciled my unorthodox views to her own conceptions of right and wrong. So wise and gentle she was in her acceptance of the sincerity of my convictions, even when she didn't sympathize with or understand them. Her love and loyalty always defended me if anyone dared in her presence to criticize what I thought and did.

Such family harmony was disrupted when tragedy struck again with the death of her beloved brother Alan on the battlefields of France.

In 1917, Prichard was greatly affected by news of the Russian Revolution. In her autobiography, she writes:

> That the revolution was an event of world-shaking importance, I didn't doubt. . . . [P]ress diatribes against Lenin, Trotsky and Bolshevism indicated that they were guided by the theories of Marx and Engels. I lost no time in buying and studying all the books of these writers available in Melbourne. . . . Discussion . . . confirmed my impression that these theories provided the only logical basis that I had come across for the reorganisation of our social system.
>
> My mind was illuminated by the discovery. It was the answer to what I had been seeking: a satisfactory explanation of the wealth and power which controlled our lives—their origin, development, and how, in the process of social evolution, they could be directed towards the well-being of a majority of the people, so that poverty, disease, prostitution, superstition and war would be eliminated; peoples of the world would live in peace, and grow towards a perfecting of their existence on this earth.

In London, Prichard had met a dashing young Australian soldier, Hugo Throssell, who had been awarded the Victoria Cross for bravery. On his return to Australia in 1919, they married and together went to live at Greenmount, a hills suburb on the outskirts of Perth, Western Australia. Here, in the most isolated city in the world, she lived for the rest of her life, passionately committed to her writing and her political activism, balancing these activities with the inevitable demands of home, family, and friendship.

Modjeska records that when Prichard arrived in Perth in 1919, two major industrial disputes, one on the goldfields and one on the waterfront, were reaching their climax. Trades Hall was flying a red flag, and miners from the Kalgoorlie goldfields who had been arrested were being brought to Perth for trial. These were turbulent times. The wharfies' strike in May 1919 resulted in the conservative Colbatch government ordering mounted police to advance on the barricaded strikers. One striker was killed and seven were wounded. Prichard, as one of the first Marxists to arrive in Perth, was quickly in demand as a public speaker. Her talks on the waterfront with the strikers were amongst the first encounters between a Marxist and these striking workers. Modjeska writes that Prichard's first political pamphlet, "The New Order" (1919), was written in response to the demand for accessible information on Marxism. It was reputedly anecdotal and descriptive, rather than analytical and politically sophisticated, but it was optimistic and enthusiastic about the possibility of revolution. With like-minded people from the Eastern states of Australia, Prichard had been a founding member of the Communist Party of Australia. At all times, her husband supported her political stance. This was not always without complication. In her autobiography, she recalls a time immediately after their arrival in Western Australia when Hugo was being hailed as a war hero and was invited to speak at the Armistice Day celebrations being held at his hometown of Northam. To the assembled crowd in the street, he described the horror and misery of war, and declared that the suffering he had seen there had made him a socialist. These sentiments from a national war hero, son of a respected conservative former State premier, were radical indeed.

By 1922, Prichard's hopes for revolution in Australia had diminished. In May, she gave birth to her only child, son Ric Throssell. For the rest of that decade, she devoted herself to her writing and her family. Not until 1933, after Hugo's tragic death, would she throw herself headlong into fulltime political activism again.

Prichard's first decade in Western Australia seems to have been an exceptionally busy, fertile and happy period, and she wrote what are considered to be her best novels: *Working Bullocks* (1926), *Coonardoo* (1928), and *Haxby's Circus* (1930). *Intimate Strangers* was completed by 1933 but not published until 1937. Literary critics allude frequently to the creative tensions found here in the blending of a romanticism and elemental sexuality whose origins lay in the work of D.H. Lawrence, and an Australian realism motivated by a desire to portray the true lives of Australian women and men. For Prichard, committed as she was to the Communist Party and its ideals, writing fiction served a political as well as a literary purpose. She wrote about class and race relations, and about the relationship of white and black Australians to their landscape. She took her research seriously: for *Working Bullocks,* she lived with the timber cutters in the southwest karri forest; for *Haxby's Circus,* she traveled with Wirth's Circus; and for *Coonardoo,* she stayed on a station in the northwest, becoming familiar with the landscapes and the people inhabiting them before using them as settings for her novels. Her pride in Australia and her focus on the harsh realities and extraordinary beauty of the Australian bush, forest, and desert earned her the admiration of other writers and intellectuals. Modjeska, whose focus as a literary critic has been on Australian women writers prominent in the 1930s, tells us that these writers assumed a central position in Australian cultural life because they, Prichard especially, helped develop a sense of national identity, and deliberately raised in their novels cultural questions which had not been raised before.

Coonardoo provides one of the earliest articulations of the indigenous Australian people as actual mortals, capable of genuine human emotion, morality and intelligence. In this novel, set in the vast cattle country of the northwest of Australia, the heroine Coonardoo is a young Aboriginal woman whose attraction for the young white landlord, Hughie, is posited as elemental, instinctual and inevitable. Hughie's failure to follow his instincts and to accept Coonardoo as his lifelong partner is frequently read as a metaphor for the invading Europeans' failure to understand or develop empathy for this ancient and harshly beautiful land. *Coonardoo* was serialized by the national journal *The Bulletin* in 1928, but such was the conservative and imperialist nature of the white Australian population that it caused an uproar of indignation and protest.

Although her writing met thus with public protest, Prichard's skill and courage in writing about crucial and controversial issues earned her the admiration of contemporary critics. Thematically and stylistically her work was admired by her literary colleagues. Modjeska records that as early as 1925, writer Louis Esson wrote to colleague Vance Palmer that he and **Hilda Esson** were reading the manuscript of *Working Bullocks* and found it "astonishingly good. It is most unconventional, and it is less like an ordinary story than like actual life. You feel you are living in the karri forests." On reading the novel himself, Vance Palmer wrote excitedly to the poet Frank Wilmot: "I hope the book gets a good spin in Australia, for something tells me it marks a crisis in our literary affairs." ***Nettie Palmer** shared their excitement, giving it a more detailed assessment:

> *Working Bullocks* seems to me different not only in quality but in kind. No one else has written with quite that rhythm, or seen the world in quite that way. The creative lyricism of the style impresses me more than either the theme or characters. From slang, from place names, from colloquial turns of speech, from descriptions of landscape and people at work, she has woven a texture that covers the whole surface of the book with a shimmer of poetry. . . . It is a breakthrough that will be as important for other writers as for KSP herself.

Later, in 1953, the critic Wilkes wrote in the Australian journal *Southerly:* "[Prichard] has become the foremost of the school, the novelist who has striven most consistently to make the continent articulate through her writing." The critic H.M. Green wrote of *Working Bullocks* as having "a kind of warmth and glow which seems to be a reflection of heat and light and the colour-effects of the landscape." Much later, in the 1960s, Vance Palmer wrote: "Young people of today may not be fully aware of the flood of new life which KSP poured into our writing. . . . If a change has come over our attitude to the Aboriginals it is largely due to the way KSP brought them near to us."

Intimate Strangers is the only one of her novels to deal explicitly with white middle-class marriages and relationships, and is thought by many critics to be significantly autobiographical. It was written at a time of crisis in her marriage. Hugo Throssell was deeply troubled: his employment prospects had been severely damaged by his and Prichard's very public political activities, and he was plagued by financial worries. Once again, the novel plays out the tensions between romanticism and realism, but this time it has tragic consequences. The bankrupt husband in *Intimate Strangers* kills himself and Elodie is thus freed to pursue a more satisfactory sexual liaison. Prichard had completed this manuscript before traveling to Russia for six months in 1933. Eerily, and in a cruel replay of the events of her earlier family life, on her way home from Europe she learned that her husband, deeply troubled by terrible debts, had committed suicide. She was devastated. Thirty years later in her autobiography, she wrote: "I could not have imagined that . . . he would take his own life. I had absolute faith in him and don't know how I survived the days when I realised I would never see him again. The end of our lives together is still inexplicable to me."

After her husband's death, Prichard took up political activism with renewed intensity. The cumulative world crises of the 1930s—the Depression; fascism with its assault on freedom of speech, its censorship and brutality, and its persecution of German and Italian writers living in Australia; and the Spanish Civil War—made a huge impact upon Australian writers. Prichard was one of the founding members of the Movement against War and Fascism which had been inaugurated in Amsterdam. At the outbreak of the Spanish Civil War, she organized the Spanish Relief Committee in Western Australia. During the 1930s, the Fellowship of Australian Writers was taken over by the Left, and Prichard was supported in her opposition to fascism in Europe and a reactionary government at home. One of the rallying points of this period concerned the visit to Australia of the internationally renowned Egon Kisch. Kisch had come to Australia to speak at an antiwar congress in Victoria in 1934. He was refused entry into Australia by a conservative and frightened government which went to extraordinary lengths to exclude him, using a language test in Gaelic to ban this highly cultured and educated man who was fluent in seven languages. His exclusion offended the hospitality and international solidarity of Australian writers. Prichard was reportedly on the Fremantle wharf to greet him, and, when his ship docked in Melbourne, she was among a small group of radicals who spirited him away after he had jumped onto the wharf, breaking his leg. The incident captured the public imagination, and Kisch addressed huge public meetings in the Eastern States of Australia. Despite the apparent public support for freedom of speech, however, in the early 1940s the Communist Party was outlawed in Australia, and individuals were persecuted and arrested for having Marxist literature in their possession. There was no doubt that at this time mainstream Australia disapproved of the ideals in which Prichard passionately believed.

One of the fascinating aspects of Prichard's life was that although she undoubtedly sought and received support for her political views from around Australia and indeed around the world, in Western Australia her activism was specific, practical, and widely admired. One of her most significant initiatives for local women was her establishment of The Modern Women's Club in the 1930s. This group met in central Perth for lunch one day each week, and guest speakers were invited to discuss an enormous range of social issues. Here women from the Left mingled with much more conservative women whose desire for peace, or for the overturn of some perceived social injustice, had brought them together. This club continued for decades. The networks thus established arguably had a profound impact upon the lives of individual Western Australian women and fed directly into the Vietnam Moratorium movement of the late 1960s and early 1970s, the establishment of the Women's Liberation and Women's Electoral Lobby of the early 1970s, and the more broadly based peace and Green movements of the 1980s and 1990s.

The literary work of Katharine Susannah Prichard after the 1930s is often considered by critics to have been undermined by her adherence to the Communist Party and its Stalinist directives that all literature reflect socialist realism. Certainly in the trilogy *The Roaring Nineties* (1946), *Golden Miles* (1948), and *Winged Seeds* (1950) the earlier focus on sexuality gives way to a focus on work. Perhaps the most significant conflict for Prichard was that whereas writing demanded solitude, Communist activism demanded collectivity.

Ironically, friends and associates of Prichard's have suggested that the smallness and isolation of Perth, which many residents found limiting, may have been one of the most significant factors in her being so visible and may well have contributed to the local community's acceptance of who she was and how she chose to express her gifts. Prichard, for all her gentleness, was a larger-than-life figure who belonged to a world community. In 1943, she became a member of the Communist Party's Central Committee. In 1959, she was awarded the World Council's Silver Medallion for services to peace. When she died in 1969, aged 86, her coffin was draped with the Red Flag, and she was given a Communist funeral. Her ashes were scattered on the hillsides near her home at Greenmount.

SOURCES:

Drake-Brockman, Henrietta. "Katharine Susannah Prichard," in *Australian Writers and their Work*. Edited by Geoffrey Dutton. Melbourne: Oxford University Press, 1967.

Hopkins, Lekkie. "An Oral History of Women and the Peace Movement in Western Australia," unpublished thesis, University of Western Australia, 1987.

Modjeska, Drusilla. *Exiles at Home: Australian Women Writers 1925–1945*. Sydney: Angus & Robertson, 1981.

Prichard, Katharine Susannah. *Child of the Hurricane: An Autobiography.* Sydney: Angus & Robertson, 1963.

Throssell, Ric, ed. *Tribute: Selected Stories of Katharine Susannah Prichard.* St. Lucia: University of Queensland Press, 1988.

SUGGESTED READING:

Throssell, Ric, ed. *Straight Left: The Articles and Addresses of Katharine Susannah Prichard.* Sydney: Wild and Woolley, 1982.

———. *Wild Weeds and Wind Flowers: The Life and Letters of Katharine Susannah Prichard.* Sydney: Angus & Robertson, 1975.

COLLECTIONS:

Katharine Susannah Prichard papers, National Library of Australia, MS 1094.

Lekkie Hopkins,
coordinator of Women's Studies, Edith Cowan University, Perth, Western Australia

Prie, Jeanne Agnes Berthelot de Pléneuf, Marquise de (1698–1727)

French marquise with power at court. *Name variations: Madame de Prie. Born Jeanne Agnes Berthelot de Pléneuf in 1698; died in 1727; daughter of rich but unscrupulous parents; married Louis, marquis de Prie, in 1713.*

At age 15, Jeanne de Pléneuf was married to Louis, marquis de Prie, and moved to the court of Savoy at Turin, where he was ambassador. At 21, she returned to France. Lovely and mesmerizing, she was soon the mistress of Louis Henry, duke of Bourbon. During the duke's ministry (1723–25), Jeanne de Prie was in many respects the true ruler of France, her most notable triumph being the marriage of Louis XV to ***Marie Leczinska** over 40 other princesses. Mme de Prie assumed that, in gratitude, Marie would grant her favors. But when, in 1725, de Prie tried to have Bourbon's rival Cardinal Fleury exiled, her influence came to an end. After Fleury's recall and the banishment of Bourbon to Chantilly, de Prie was exiled to Courbépine, where she committed suicide the following year.

SUGGESTED READING:

Thirion, M.H. *Madame de Prie.* Paris, 1905.

Priesand, Sally Jane (1946—)

Jewish-American who in 1972 became the first woman in the history of Judaism to be ordained a rabbi. *Born on June 27, 1946, in Cleveland, Ohio; daughter of Irving Theodore Priesand and Rosetta Elizabeth (Welch) Priesand; attended University of Cincinnati and Hebrew Union College–Jewish Institute of Religion.*

By the time Sally Jane Priesand was born in Cleveland, Ohio, in 1946, a number of American-Jewish women had laid the groundwork for women rabbis or served non-officially in that capacity. As far back as 1889, in an article entitled "A Problem for Purim," which appeared on the front page of *The Jewish Exponent*, the Philadelphia journalist **Mary M. Cohen** asked whether or not women could contribute to the development of Judaism in the United States by becoming rabbis. By the early 1900s, a number of American Jews, particularly those allied to Reform Judaism, were openly debating the question raised by Cohen in 1889. In 1903, ***Henrietta Szold**, the foremost American Jewish woman leader, approached Solomon Schechter, president of the Jewish Theological Seminary which was linked to Conservative Judaism, about the possibility of taking courses there. After Szold assured Schechter that she would not be "an aspirant after Rabbinical honors, he agreed to put no obstacles in my way."

Occasionally, and under extraordinary circumstances, a number of American-Jewish women did in fact serve informally in the role of rabbi. The first of these was doubtless **Ray Frank**, a pioneering woman rabbi who ministered to the tiny, scattered Jewish communities found in California, Nevada, and the Pacific Northwest in the closing decades of the 19th century. A Sabbath school principal often known as "the girl rabbi of the Golden West," Frank gained fame in the American-Jewish community as an itinerant preacher. In 1890, learning that there were to be no High Holiday services in Spokane, Washington, because a rabbi was not available, Frank had agreed to preach. From then until just before she married a decade later, she both preached and led religious services. Frank also studied at Reform Judaism's Hebrew Union College. In her writings, she outlined what she would do if she became a rabbi, while at the same time indicating that she had no desire to actually become one.

Another situation emerged in 1950, when *rebbetzin* (rabbi's wife) **Paula Ackerman**, whose husband William Ackerman was rabbi of Temple Beth Israel in Meridian, Mississippi, was widowed. Asked by the president of the congregation to be of assistance in the crisis, Ackerman agreed to fill in for her deceased spouse until a replacement could be found. She served "temporarily" for three years.

After World War I, a number of women from within the Reform Jewish tradition began to seriously consider preparing themselves for careers as rabbis. In 1921, 17-year-old **Martha**

Sally Jane Priesand

Neumark requested admission to study at Hebrew Union College (HUC), sparking a debate lasting two years over whether or not the school would ordain women as rabbis. The emerging consensus was that a "woman cannot justly be denied the privilege of ordination." This theoretical victory was canceled out when the HUC board of governors prevented Neumark from actually achieving her goal. Over the next two decades, a number of Jewish women, including **Irma Levy Lindheim, Dora Askowith,** and **Helen Levinthal** (later Helen Lyons), raised the same challenge. In the case of Levinthal, she was able to complete the entire rabbinical curriculum and had already written a thesis when in 1939 the Jewish Institute of Religion awarded her a master's degree in Hebrew literature, rather than the rabbinical ordination she had sought. Refusing to admit defeat, Levinthal, like Ray Frank more than a generation earlier, exercised informal rabbinic leadership which included preaching at High Holiday services in Brooklyn in 1939. Eventually, however, she bowed to stronger forces to enter the traditional world of being a wife, mother, and volunteer for Jewish causes.

This was the environment facing Sally Priesand as she grew up in postwar Cleveland. As a member of youth groups and Cleveland's Beth-Israel-West Temple, she began to display an intense commitment to Judaism and Jewish life. Her deep spirituality was compatible with the openness of Reform Judaism. While participating in Jewish summer camps in the early 1960s, Priesand saw becoming a rabbi as her life's goal, though no model for this career existed in the real world. She enrolled at the University of Cincinnati but also took courses offered by the neighboring Hebrew Union College–Jewish Institute of Religion (HUC–JIR) that enabled her to complete the first year of rabbinic school while still an undergraduate. Upon graduating from the University of Cincinnati in 1968, Priesand was admitted to the HUC—JIR rabbinic school.

Almost immediately after she began her full-time rabbinic studies, Priesand became the center of media attention. She was soon skilled at answering questions and explaining her goals and motivations. Even before completing her studies, Priesand began to experience discrimination. Student pulpits and congregations unable to hire full-time rabbis seemed much more sympathetic than did synagogues that had the resources for a professional rabbi. She discovered that some of her placement interviews were shams, done only for the novelty of it, with the actual response being that the congregation "could not possibly have a woman rabbi." Besides experiencing the normal stresses of being a graduate student, Priesand had to bear up to "the unbelievable and almost unbearable pressures" of being the woman who would soon be the first woman rabbi. Fortunately, during this often difficult time she had the full support and encouragement of HUC president Nelson Glueck, who, she said, "decided to act on what his predecessors had simply asserted, woman's right to ordination."

On June 3, 1972, Sally Priesand became the first female ordained rabbi in the world, the only other claimant to this honor being ***Regina Jonas**, who died in the Holocaust and had never been ordained by a seminary. On that day, HUC president Dr. Alfred Gottschalk ordained Priesand in Cincinnati's Plum Street Temple. She found her first job as an assistant in Manhattan's Stephen Wise Free Synagogue, eventually advancing to associate rabbi. However, when she was not promised that she would succeed the congregation's ailing senior rabbi, she left this post disappointed. In 1981, Priesand found a new position at the Monmouth Reform Temple in Tinton Falls, New Jersey. Here she continued her career under happier circumstances, working to fulfill what she believes is the primary task of any rabbi, namely "to help Jews take responsibility for their Judaism." Besides meeting the needs of her congregation, Priesand also serves on various boards and task forces, and supports the work of such organizations as the Institute for Creative Judaism, Hadassah, the Jewish Peace Fellowship, as well as Common Cause and the American Civil Liberties Union.

Hebrew Union College did not ordain another woman, **Laura Geller**, until 1976, and by the end of the 1970s there were only 12 women rabbis in the United States. But their numbers increased steadily through the 1980s and 1990s. By the late 1990s, women were 16% of Reform rabbis belonging to the Central Conference of American Rabbis. After Priesand opened the door to the rabbinate for women, other branches of Judaism followed suit. In 1974, **Sandy Eisenberg Sasso** became the first woman rabbi within Reconstructionist Judaism, formerly the liberal wing of Conservative Judaism. Conservative Judaism ordained ***Amy Eilberg** as its first woman rabbi in 1985. Priesand had initiated a sea change within American Judaism, for, according to *The Jewish Advocate*, by 1997 Hebrew Union College had graduated a total of 278 women rabbis. Half of the 1997 graduating class of HUC were women, with the Reform Central Conference of American Rabbis registering 293 female rabbis. Of the graduating class of the Conservative movement's seminary the same year, 40% were women, and the Conservative rabbinical body, the Rabbinical Assembly, counted about 100 members. Rabbi Laura Geller, whose path at HUC had been broken four years earlier by Priesand, was in the late 1990s heading Temple Emanuel of Beverly Hills, and as such was the first woman to lead a 900-plus-member congregation in the United States. As the new millennium dawned, only Orthodox Judaism held to its traditional prohibition against women becoming rabbis.

SOURCES:

Baskin, Judith R. "Women and Judaism," in Jacob Neusner, Alan J. Avery-Peck, and William Scott Green, eds., *The Encyclopedia of Judaism*. Vol. 3. NY: Continuum, 1999, pp. 1478–1502.

Clar, Reva, and William M. Kramer. "The Girl Rabbi of the Golden West," in *Western States Jewish History*. Vol. 18, 1986, pp. 99–111, 223–236, 336–351.

Epstein, Nadine. "Jewish Women Blaze Paths to Become Rabbis," in *The Christian Science Monitor*. January 2, 1987, p. 3.

Friedman, Sally. "Reflections of a 'Woman Who Dared,'" in *The New York Times Current Events Edition*. September 19, 1993.

Lerner, Anne Lapidus. "'Who Hast Not Made Me a Man': The Movement for Equal Rights for Women in American Jewry," in *American Jewish Year Book*. Vol. 77, 1977, pp. 3–38.

Levinson, Pnina Navè. "Die Ordination von Frauen als Rabbiner," in *Zeitschrift für Religions- und Geistesgeschichte*. Vol. 38, no. 4, 1986, pp. 289–310.

Nadell, Pamela S. "Priesand, Sally Jane (b. 1946)," in Paula E. Hyman and Deborah Dash Moore, eds., *Jewish Women in America: An Historical Encyclopedia*. Vol. 2. NY: Routledge, 1997, pp. 1102–1104.

———. "Rabbis," in Paula E. Hyman and Deborah Dash Moore, eds., *Jewish Women in America: An Historical Encyclopedia*. Vol. 2. NY: Routledge, 1997, pp. 1115–1120.

Nadell, Pamela Susan. *Women Who Would be Rabbis: A History of Women's Ordination, 1889–1985*. Boston, MA: Beacon Press, 1998.

Neusner, Jacob. *How the Rabbis Liberated Women*. Atlanta, GA: Scholars Press, 1998.

Priesand, Sally. *Judaism and the New Woman*. NY: Behrman House, 1975.

———. "Preparation for the Rabbinate—Yesterday, Tomorrow," in *Central Conference of American Rabbis Yearbook*. Vol. 85, 1975, pp. 162–164.

"Rabbi Priesand—Making Her Mark," in *Cincinnati Horizons*. Vol. 4, no. 6. June 1975.

Sheridan, Sybil, ed. *Hear Our Voices: Women in the British Rabbinate*. Columbia, SC: University of South Carolina Press, 1998.

Wisdom You are My Sister: 25 Years of Women in the Rabbinate. NY: Central Conference of American Rabbis, 1997 [*CCAR Journal*. Vol. 44, no. 3, issue 173. Summer 1997].

Zola, Gary Phillip, ed. *Women Rabbis, Exploration and Celebration: Papers Delivered at an Academic Conference Honoring Twenty Years of Women in the Rabbinate, 1972–1992*. Cincinnati, OH: HUC–JIR Rabbinic Alumni Association Press, 1996.

RELATED MEDIA:

Priesand, Sally. "A Woman Rabbi: Her Problems, Prerogatives and Principles" (audiocassette), Atlanta, GA: Catacomb Cassettes, 1976.

John Haag,
Associate Professor of History, University of Georgia, Athens, Georgia

Priest, Ivy Baker (1905–1975)

American political organizer and U.S. treasurer. *Born Ivy Maude Baker on September 7, 1905, in Kimberly, Piute County, Utah; died of cancer in June 1975, in Santa Monica, California; daughter of Orange Decatur Baker (a miner) and Clara (Fearnley) Baker; educated in public schools and at the University of Utah; married Harry Howard Hicks (a traveling salesman), in 1924 (divorced 1929); married Roy Fletcher Priest (a furniture dealer), on December 7, 1935 (died 1959); married Sidney William Stevens (a real-estate agent), in 1961 (died 1972); children: (second marriage) Patricia Ann Priest (b. 1936); Peggy Louise Priest (b. 1938, died young); Nancy Ellen Priest (b. 1941); Roy Baker Priest (b. 1942).*

Was active in Utah state Republican organizations (beginning 1930s); ran unsuccessfully for the U.S. House of Representatives (1950); became second woman to be named treasurer of the U.S. (1953–61); elected California state treasurer (1967–74).

Ivy Baker Priest, who was appointed treasurer of the United States under President Dwight D. Eisenhower, was born on September 7, 1905, in Kimberly, Utah, the eldest of seven children of Orange Decatur Baker and **Clara Fearnley Baker**, who had met while Orange was on a Mormon mission to Clara's native England. After Priest's grammar school years, the family moved to Bingham, Utah, near Salt Lake City, where her father worked as a miner and she attended high school.

Following a mining accident in which her husband was injured, Clara Baker sought to supplement her family's income, opening a boarding house for miners. She also became very interested in politics. Dubbed "Mrs. Republican" by friends and associates, she frequently sent ten-year-old Ivy out to babysit for friends so they could go to the polls and vote. (Wyoming, Utah, and Colorado had enfranchised women in the late 1800s.)

Although Priest pursued a higher education after high school by taking extension courses at the University of Utah, this endeavor was cut short by her father's illness and the family's poverty. Instead, she helped out at the boarding house and worked as a ticket seller in a local theater. In 1924, she married Harry Howard Hicks, a traveling salesman, with whom she moved to North Carolina before their marriage ended in divorce in 1929. Priest then returned to her family in Salt Lake City. As the Depression gripped the country, her family went on the welfare rolls, and Priest took local jobs, including telephone operator and, later, supervisor, to help out. She became interested in merchandising, and met her second husband, Roy Fletcher Priest, a wholesale furniture salesman whom she married on December 7, 1935. Although he was 21 years older than she, the marriage proved a good match. The couple lived in Bountiful, Utah, and over the next eight years they had four children, one of whom died in infancy.

Meanwhile, Priest's interest in government and politics, which her husband encouraged, continued to grow. She began to teach American history and citizenship in evening classes, and in 1932 started doing organizational work for the Young Republicans. Priest developed effective speaking skills, and was president of the Utah State Young Republicans from 1934 through 1936. She was also co-chair of the Young Republicans for the western district of 11 states from 1936 through 1940, while holding the post of president of the Utah State Women's Legislative Council from 1937 to 1939. The following year, she became a member of the Utah State Republican Committee and in 1944 was appointed to the Republican National Committee for Utah. As she grew busier in her public life, Priest's mother and one of her mother's sisters, both of whom were highly supportive, helped her to care for her young children. In 1950, she made an unsuccessful run for the U.S. House of Representatives as a Republican candidate from Utah, losing to Democratic incumbent ***Reva Beck Bosone**.

Ivy Baker Priest

When Eisenhower was nominated for the presidency in August 1952, Arthur E. Summerfield, chair of the Republican National Committee, named Priest as the assistant chair of the women's division of the committee. "The 1952 election is one of the most vital to women in our history," he noted, "and no one knows this better than Ivy Priest. The significance of her appointment lies in the realization . . . that women will play a greater role in this election than ever before." Drawing on her previous experience with women's issues, she coordinated national efforts among women's groups to ensure a victory for Eisenhower and his running mate, Richard Nixon. Simply getting women involved in the election was one of Priest's major priorities, and *The New York Times* quoted her as saying: "From all over the country, we've been getting requests from women's clubs and groups asking for information about the issues and how to get out the vote. Our big job will be to see that this information gets the widest possible distribution."

After Eisenhower's election as president, Priest's efforts on his behalf were rewarded with her appointment in 1953 as treasurer of the United States. She was only the second woman to hold that post, following ***Georgia Neese Clark**, who had served under Harry Truman from 1949 to 1953. With no formal training for the job, Priest earned high marks and praise from her colleagues. She made frequent speeches, and her name appeared on some $30 billion of currency.

In 1958, Priest wrote her autobiography, *Green Grows Ivy*, which reflects on the conflicts of motherhood and a career. She also wrote of a White House dinner, shortly after the Eisenhower administration took office in 1953, and the thoughts the event triggered of how far she'd come: "I found myself staring at the place card in front of my plate, which said: *Ivy Baker Priest, Treasurer of the United States.* Suddenly, I was overwhelmed by the wonder of it all. And my thoughts went racing back through the years . . . back to Coalville and Bingham Canyon, the somber little mining towns where I had lived my girlhood . . . back to days when there was not enough money for food and clothing, or any of the basic amenities of living."

Though Priest's husband died in 1959, she continued as U.S. treasurer until the end of Eisenhower's two-term administration in January 1961. Later that year, she retired to California and married Sidney William Stevens, who sold real estate in the Beverly Hills area. In 1966, she returned to politics, running for the post of California treasurer. She won the election and served as treasurer under Governor Ronald Reagan from 1967 until 1974, becoming the first woman to nominate a presidential candidate when she put forth his name at the convention of 1968, during his first failed bid to garner the Republican ticket. She was also active in the American Red Cross and in the General Federation of Women's Clubs. Priest died of cancer in June 1975 in Santa Monica, California.

SOURCES:

Current Biography 1952. NY: H.W. Wilson, 1953.

Priest, Ivy Baker. *Green Grows Ivy.* NY: McGraw-Hill, 1958.

Sicherman, Barbara, and Carol Hurd Green, eds. *Notable American Women: The Modern Period.* Cambridge, MA: The Belknap Press of Harvard University, 1980.

Don Amerman,
freelance writer, Saylorsburg, Pennsylvania

Priestly, L.A.M. (c. 1865–1944).

See McCracken, Elizabeth.

Prime, Alberta (1895–1984).

See Hunter, Alberta.

Primettes, the.

See Supremes, the.

Primo de Rivera, Pilar (1913–1991)

Spanish founder and leader of the Sección Feminina of the Spanish Falange. *Born in Madrid, Spain, on November 5, 1913; died in 1991; daughter of Miguel Primo de Rivera (Spanish general who ruled as dictator of Spain from 1923 to 1930 and whose fall led to the Second Republic and the Spanish Civil War) and Casilda Sáenz de Heredia.*

Pilar Primo de Rivera was born in Madrid on November 5, 1913, the daughter of Miguel Primo de Rivera and **Casilda Sáenz de Heredia.** Casilda died when Pilar was a young child. Miguel Primo de Rivera governed Spain as a military dictator under Alphonso XIII from 1923 to 1930. Pilar earned a degree in nursing and became involved in the political activities of her brother, José Antonio Primo de Rivera. In 1933, José Antonio founded the Falange Española, a quasi-fascist movement. The following June, Pilar established the Sección Feminina, a female appendage of the Falange. She played an active role in the demonstrations and political tumult that led up to the Spanish Civil War.

When the war began in July 1936, she sided with Francisco Franco's Nationalists, who sought to overthrow the leftist Republic. She urged Franco to ransom José Antonio, who was held by the Republic, but Franco feared José and the Falange might try to take over the Nationalist movement. Following José Antonio's execution by his jailers, however, Franco united the Falange with the Carlists in April 1937 to create the Falange Española Tradicionalista y de los JONS, the only political party permitted in Nationalist Spain. He also named Pilar Primo de Rivera to head its Sección Feminina, which oversaw social services in Spain and mobilized female support for the war effort. She helped organize the Woman's Social Service in 1937, which obligated all able-bodied single women between 17 and 35 years of age to provide six months of public service. Pilar worked to protect her brother's legacy in other ways. With José Antonio dead, Falangist leaders fell to squabbling among themselves and threatened to compete with the military for leadership of the Nationalist movement. Franco's followers responded by arresting the chief Falangist, Manuel Hedilla, and sentencing him to death in 1937. Pilar interceded with Franco's wife *****Carmen Polo de Franco** to save Hedilla's life.

Pilar Primo de Rivera

After the war, Pilar continued to play an active political role, generally in favor of the Falange's social agenda. She served in the Spanish Cortes (Parliament) and was a member of the National Council of Education. Pilar also spoke and wrote about women's role in Spanish society. The Franco regime accorded her many honors, including the Great Cross of Isabella the Catholic (***Isabella I**). She died in 1991.

SOURCES:

Payne, Stanley G. *Falange: A History of Spanish Fascism.* Stanford, CA: Stanford University Press, 1961.

Primo de Rivera, Pilar. *Recuerdos de una vida.* Madrid: Ediciones DYRSA, 1983.

Kendall W. Brown,
Professor of History, Brigham Young University, Provo, Utah

Primus, Pearl (1919–1994)

African-American dancer and choreographer whose anthropological work unearthed the richness of African and Caribbean dance and unmasked the realities of black life to America. *Pronunciation: PREE-mus. Born Pearl Primus on November 29, 1919, in Trinidad, British West Indies; died at her home in New Rochelle, New York, on October 29, 1994; daughter of Edward Primus and Emily Primus; Hunter College, B.A., 1940; received a Rosenwald Foundation grant for travel to Africa, 1948; New York University, Ph.D. in Educational Sociology and Anthropology, 1977; married Percival Borde, in 1954; children: son Onwin Babajide Primus Borde (b. 1955).*

Moved with family to U.S. (1921); awarded the "Star of Africa" by Dr. William V.S. Tubman, president of the Republic of Liberia (1949); established Liberian Cultural Center in Monrovia (1959); received Alvin Ailey Dance Pioneer Award (1978); was first recipient of the American Dance Festival Balasaraswant-Joy Ann Dewey Beinecke Chair for Distinguished Teaching (1991); received National Medal of Arts (1991).

Selected works choreographed: "Strange Fruit" (1943); "The Negro Speaks of Rivers" (1943); "Sometimes I Feel Like a Motherless Child" (1945); "Hard Times Blues" (1943); "Dark Rhythms" (1946); "Invocation" (1949); "Fanga" (1949); "The Initiation" (1950); "Impinyuza" (1951); "Mr. Johnson" (1955); "Earth Magician" (1958); "The Wedding" (1961); "Fertility Dance" (1967); "Michael, Row Your Boat Ashore" (1979).

At a gala performance held in 1978, when the Alvin Ailey American Dance Theater paid tribute to pioneers in American dance, one of those honored was Pearl Primus—dancer, choreographer, and ethnographer—whose work of almost four decades not only expanded the opportunities for African-Americans in the dance world, but opened up pathways to the origins of African dance movements that have helped to unify the African-American identity through dance.

In response to the award, the 59-year-old Primus thrilled the audience that night by expressing her thanks through dance, displaying her choreography and her talent to the accompaniment of drums. Not lost on the audience was the significance of the ceremony itself, indicating just how much change had taken place. An internationally heralded dance company, founded by and predominantly composed of African-Americans, was celebrating its 20th anniversary by honoring those performers of an earlier generation for whom consistent dance work had been barely attainable. On the first occasion of these awards, Primus joined ***Katherine Dunham** and **Beryl McBurnie** in accepting their places in the ancestry of the African-American concert dance tradition.

The inscription on Primus' award paid tribute to her for "a life dedicated to the artistic expression of black dance . . . infusing dance throughout the world with the rhythmic beat and dramatic movement of a culture as old as time itself." The very phrase used to honor her—"black dance," in itself a culturally loaded term—encapsulates much of the history of racism and stereotyping afflicting African-Americans as they sought a place in a dance world that was for a long time almost exclusively white. Ironically, but also fortuitously, it was just such a stereotype that became the seed of Pearl Primus' career.

Born in Trinidad, British West Indies, in 1919, the daughter of Edward and **Emily Primus**, Pearl moved with her family to the United States when she was two. Emily's father was a leader of the Ashanti religion in Trinidad, and Primus later reflected that his interest and involvement in African and Caribbean cultures presaged her own. In childhood, however, her parents did not guide her towards the arts. Edward Primus held various jobs in Brooklyn and Manhattan, ranging from building superintendent to war plant employee, seafarer, and carpenter. In high school, Primus competed in track and field, and she continued to be involved in sprinting and jumping at Hunter College in New York City, where she earned a B.A. in biology in 1940.

In preparation for entering medical school at the all-black Howard University, Primus sought work as a laboratory technician to earn money, but racist hiring practices kept her from finding a job. She wound up in the wardrobe department of the National Youth Administration and was working backstage on an "America Dances" production one night when a dancer failed to show. Because she knew the latest swing steps, she was asked to fill in.

After this inadvertent beginning, Primus continued to dance with the group for a short time, until its demise. Then she heard about a working scholarship being offered by the New Dance Group. With her athletic background but no formal technique, she won the audition, mainly by executing the awesome flying jumps which were to become the trademark of her early career. Six months after Primus started classes, she was appearing with the company onstage. On February 14, 1943, she was one of four solo dancers performing at the 92nd Street YMHA when she was catapulted into the forefront of the concert dance scene by a review written by John Martin. The influential dance critic of *The New York Times* declared that the choice of who the best newcomer of the season was "as easy as rolling off a log. . . . The decision goes hands down to Pearl Primus."

Praise for Primus' dancing abounded. Other reviewers, primarily from the white press, focused on her enthusiasm and energy, characterized by the high, airborne leaps. Audiences delighted in her diverse programs, consisting of everything from modern and African dance to live drumming and jazz dance. But the praise was generally imbued with racial—and racist—assumptions, defining Primus both by her race and despite it, as in the way Martin explained his choice of her as the year's star:

> There is no doubt that she is quite the most gifted artist-dancer of her race (she is Negro) yet to appear in the field. The roots of her real quality lie in her apparent awareness of her racial heritage at its richest and truest, but it would be manifestly unfair to classify her merely as an outstanding Negro dancer, for by any standard of comparison she is an outstanding dancer without regard for race.

Thus classified, Primus was seen according to the common perception of movements which African-Americans were assumed to be "naturally" capable of, while at the same time her ability forced many critics to express how she transcended these narrow definitions. Before Primus began to dance, it was the generally accepted view in a white concert dance world that African-Americans, because of the structure of their bodies, could not master ballet, though they were accepted as excelling at swing dancing, tap, and vaudeville dancing. Clearly, Primus went far beyond these categories.

Clearly, also, her incredibly quick breakthrough surely contributed to the belief that she had "natural" ability. In fact, she probably did. Her athletic background in high school and college gave her some preparation for jumps in dancing. There the skills she was enabled to learn were based on assumptions about "innate" explosive energy to be found in African-Americans, which had led to their being channeled during the 1930s and 1940s into sprinting and jumping to the exclusion of other sports. In the arts, African-American women were confined to performing in certain kinds of dance shows—minstrelsy, vaudeville, motion pictures, and Broadway. Primus was to be one of the first successful crossovers to the concert dance stage. And while modern dance allowed her the freedom to include a variety of dance styles in her programs, she did not ignore the entertainment tradition of African-American dancing. In the first years of her career, she saw the concert dance performance as a means to legitimize the talent and creativity on display every night in the uptown Savoy Ballroom in Harlem. With programs combining popular dancing and highly emotive abstract choreography, she opened up the types of dancing whites were accustomed to seeing African-Americans perform.

> Dance . . . is the scream which eases for a while the terrible frustrations common to all human beings who, because of race, creed or color, are "invisible."
>
> —Pearl Primus

In April 1943, within two months of the review that launched her career, Primus found a new creative home at Café Society Downtown, a politically active club in downtown Manhattan with leftist leanings and an integrated audience. On a small stage, cramped overhead by a low ceiling, she performed her variety of dances, often to the blues accompaniment of Josh White. A ten-day trial turned into a ten-month engagement. While in an atmosphere where white liberals expressed their sympathy for the plight of blacks, Café Society also provided 24-year-old Primus with an entry into and support from the small community of African-American singers and entertainers, including Teddy Wilson, ***Hazel Scott**, ***Lena Horne**, ***Billie Holiday**, and Paul Robeson.

At Café Society, Primus joined Robeson and many other African-American performers in being part of the black political movement to end America's racial discrimination. During World War II, the Negro Freedom Rallies, primarily sponsored by the Negro Labor Victory

Committee, promoted the fulfillment of democracy at home as well as around the world in what they called a "double victory." In particular, African-Americans wanted an end to the Jim Crow laws that greatly restricted their freedom and prevented full participation in American democracy. To this end, Owen Dodson and Langston Hughes wrote and directed a pageant entitled "New World A-Coming" performed in June 1944 at Madison Square Garden, in which Primus appeared. Speeches mingled with entertainment, all for the cost of ten cents. Remembering the unity of purpose, Primus told an interviewer for *Dance Magazine:* "Paul [Robeson] would sing, I would dance, Adam [Clayton Powell, Jr.] would deliver the political statement, the social statement—what it was really *about.*"

Primus found jobs dancing on Broadway and in nightclubs. With the same idealism that had first attracted her to the medical profession for its opportunities to help people, she continued to dance because of her growing belief in the curative possibilities and social ramifications of the art. The bulk of the repertory that she developed dealt with the social status of African-Americans. Her dance "Strange Fruit" (1943), based on a poem by Lewis Allen, portrayed a white woman's grief and terror after participating in a lynching mob. A Langston Hughes poem inspired "The Negro Speaks of Rivers" (1943) about the heritage of slave labor from the pyramids to America, a theme Primus took up again in "Slave Market" (1944). "Hard Time Blues" (1943), to music by Josh White, depicted the anger and frustration of the black sharecropper.

As her dedication to dances of social protest increased, so did Primus' desire for a fuller understanding of the contemporary experience of African-Americans. Worried that her choreography might lack authenticity because she had not personally experienced sharecropping, lynching, or the evocations of Negro spirituals, she traveled to Georgia, Alabama, and South Carolina in the summer of 1944. Posing as a migrant worker, she picked cotton and visited rural black churches, where she began to recognize the integral role of spirituality in African-American culture. As she told an *Ebony* reporter in 1951, "[I need] to know my own people where they are suffering most."

In the rural Southern black churches, Primus also began to identify the rhythmic and physical patterns of African-American worship. Writing about the experience a few years later in *The Dance Encyclopedia,* she noted: "I discovered in the Baptist Churches the voice of the drum—not in any instrument, but in the throat of the preacher. I found the dramatic sweep of movement through space . . . in the motions of minister and congregation alike." Watching the violent trembling, mutterings, and stamping of a person in religious ecstasy, she wrote, "is to experience dance in its most primitive and moving form."

Still attending school as well, Primus shifted from courses in medicine to classes in psychology and eventually in anthropology. The exhilaration she had known through immersion in Southern black spirituality heightened her desire to keep searching for the source of this common strand in the African-American experience. As ethnographer and artist, she also felt lured toward Africa, with its possibilities of timeless connection that could offer new definitions for herself and all African-Americans.

Absorbing what information about Africa she could, Primus had begun recreating African dances from books. In April 1948, following a performance at Fisk University, she was approached by a member of the audience, Dr. Edward Embrie of the Rosenwald Foundation, offering her a trip to Africa. Armed with DDT and a gun, Primus was soon headed for the Gold Coast, Angola, Liberia, Senegal, and the Belgian Congo, as one of the last recipients of a Rosenwald Foundation grant.

In Africa, Primus found the cultures of the cities distorted by commercial influences and the jitterbug dance imported from America. Journeying to the more remote areas of each country, she lived, worked and danced with various tribes, witnessing and experiencing dance as an inextricable part of life. In an article for *The Dance Has Many Faces,* she wrote: "Africans used their bodies as instruments through which every conceivable emotion or event was projected. The result was a strange but hypnotic marriage between life and dance." Even the African way of teaching movement reflected the deeply held belief in the integrity and communicative power of the body. If Primus could not pick up every nuance of movement through watching and imitating, "a native dancer would hold [Primus'] body against his or her own so she could literally absorb the movement." Mind, body, and soul were finally united.

Reveling in the spiritual intensity which she found pervasive in African dance and life, Primus considered this the greatest bond between Africans and African-Americans. In a letter from Kahnplay, Liberia, printed in *Dance Observer* in 1949, Primus described the linkage with the black world she knew. If the preacher

Pearl Primus

was the voice of the drum in Southern Baptist churches, in Africa:

> the earth is the voice of the dancer. The dancer is the conductor, the wire, which connects the earth and the sky. . . . I have been amazed and overjoyed, for when the spirit entered me the reason for the dance became my reason to move. I danced as I have never danced on the stages of America. Myself was transformed.

The focus gained during this first trip to Africa defined virtually all of Primus' work thereafter. Her performances became more like lecture-demonstrations in which she would explain the significance of certain rituals before dancing them. A major part of her transformation was to expose her audiences to the myths that often underlay a dance. Noting that African dancing was not "primitive" but basic, she declared that she would never use the term "primitive" in that way again. Similarly, she made an effort to describe the jungle as a richly musical and peaceful place instead of dangerous and frightening. In Africa, she said, she had soon left behind the unneeded DDT and switched from her gun to a more useful knife.

In the 1950s, Primus promoted African dance in both America and Africa, returning to Africa often while she continued to work toward a doctorate at New York University. In 1954, she also married Percival Borde, a Trinidadian dancer, and a year later had a son. Both Borde and her son accompanied her to Africa in the late 1950s to oversee the establishment of an African Performing Arts Center in Monrovia, the capital of Liberia. Appointed director of the center by President William Tubman in 1959, and subsidized by government funds, Primus planned to salvage the country's tribal dances still extant in an effort to retard the demolitionary effects of civilization. Believing in the beauty and dignity of the dances, she explained in *Dance Magazine*: "The main thing for me will be to find, encourage and train the folk artist and provide him with outlets through actual theatrical experience—to make of him a performing artist."

When funding for the Liberian project fell through in 1962, Primus returned to the United States and the burgeoning civil rights movement. Important changes were by then underway in the American dance world, where Arthur Mitchell, an African-American, was a prominent dancer for the New York City Ballet, and dancer and choreographer Eleo Pomare was gaining stature as an outspoken social critic. The Alvin Ailey American Dance Theater, begun in 1958, remained the only predominantly black company with national and international recognition. Primus and Borde set up another school, the African-Caribbean-American Institute of Dance, in New York and continued to perform as well as teach in area high schools and colleges. "The Wedding" (1961), commissioned by the African Research Foundation, premiered at the first African Carnival in New York City in December 1961; at least one performance, in December 1963, benefited the civil rights movement with proceeds given to the Church Freedom Fund for Civil Rights. Meanwhile, ***Lisette Model** spent months shooting Primus' dance company, but could not get the photos published in *Harper's Bazaar*, "because Hearst wouldn't allow photographs of Negroes in his magazine," said Bazaar art director Alexey Brodovitch.

In 1977, Primus finally obtained her doctorate in Educational Sociology and Anthropology from New York University. She held various college positions, including professor of ethnic studies at Amherst College in the 1980s, usually teaching classes in both anthropology and dance. She also continued to restage her works for various performance groups, most notably the Alvin Ailey American Dance Theater.

Through the works of Primus, many African-American dancers recognized the important role dance could have in reshaping African-American identity. As dancer, anthropologist, and educator, she marked a path in finding and defining that identity by calling attention to the one simple unity amid the diverse experiences of African-Americans; Africa provided a cohesive origin. Looking at dance as a lens of society, she focused on how bodies in motion projected and preserved beliefs and values. In addressing the possible links between all African-Americans and then between Africans and African-Americans, she both anticipated and addressed the urgency to define a black aesthetic that prevailed during the 1960s in the Black Arts movement, earning her a permanent place in America's history of dance.

SOURCES:

Barber, Beverly Anne Hillsman. "Pearl Primus, In Search of Her Roots: 1943–1970," unpublished dissertation, Florida State University, 1984.

Bosworth, Patricia. *Diane Arbus*. NY: W.W. Norton, 1994.

Emery, Lynne Fauley. *Black Dance from 1619 to Today*. Princeton, NJ: Princeton Book Company, 1988.

Lloyd, Margaret. *Borzoi Book of Modern Dance*. NY: Knopf, 1949.

Martin, John. *John Martin's Book of the Dance*. NY: Tudor, 1963.

Myers, Gerald, ed. *The Black Tradition in American Modern Dance*. NC: American Dance Festival, 1988.

SUGGESTED READING:

Hazzard-Gordon, Katrina. *Jookin': The Rise of Social Dance Formations in African American Culture*. Philadelphia, PA: Temple University Press, 1990.

Thompson, Richard Farris. *Flash of the Spirit: African and Afro-American Art and Philosophy*. NY: Vintage, 1983.

RELATED MEDIA:

"Dance Black America" (90 min.) video of the Dance Black America Festival, April 21–24, 1983, held at the Brooklyn Academy of Music (containing historical film footage interspersed with interviews backstage and live performances), produced by the State University of New York and Pennebaker Associates, 1984.

COLLECTIONS:

Photographs, clippings, and programs at the Dance Collection of the Performing Arts Research Center of New York Public Library, Lincoln Center, New York City; and the Schomburg Center for Research in Black Culture, New York City.

Julia L. Foulkes,
Rockefeller Foundation Postdoctoral Fellow,
Center for Black Music Research,
Columbia College, Chicago, Illinois

Prince, Lucy Terry (c. 1730–1821)

African-American poet and orator. *Name variations: Lucy Terry. Born about 1730, somewhere in West Africa (real name unknown); died in 1821 in Sunderland, Vermont; married Abijah or Bijah Prince, on May 16, 1756; children: Caesar (b. 1757); Durexa (b. 1758); Drucella (b. 1760); Festus (b. 1763); Tatnai (b. 1765); Abijah (b. 1769).*

Kidnapped, sold into slavery, and brought to Rhode Island as an infant (early 1730s); worked as a household slave in Deerfield, Massachusetts (1735–56); wrote only surviving poem (c. 1746); freed from slavery by her husband, who purchased her freedom (1756); successfully argued a case before the U.S. Supreme Court (1797).

Born somewhere in West Africa about 1730, Lucy Terry Prince was kidnapped as an infant and sold into slavery. She was brought by slave ship to Rhode Island in 1735 by Ensign Ebenezer Wells, in whose Deerfield, Massachusetts, home she worked. The Great Awakening, a religious revival sweeping through New England during this period, may have persuaded her mistress to allow the little girl's baptism, which occurred on June 15, 1735. Nine years later, at age 14, Prince joined the church.

How she learned to read and write is unknown. Her only surviving poem, "Bars Fight," was based on an ambush of white settlers by Native Americans that she witnessed in Deerfield in 1746. (Deerfield had also been the site of a famous massacre of settlers in 1704.) The poem was not printed until 1855, when it was included by Josiah Gilbert Holland in his *History of Western Massachusetts*, but it is widely believed that she wrote it soon after the massacre in 1746, which would clearly predate the first published poem by African-American poet ***Phillis Wheatley** in 1767. Prince was probably around 16 when she wrote "Bars Fight":

August, 'twas the twenty-fifth,
Seventeen hundred forty-six
The Indians did in ambush lay,
Some very valient men to slay,
The names of whom I'll not leave out
Samuel Allen like a hero fout,
And though he was so brace and bold,
His face no more shall we behold. . . .

Oliver Amsden he was slain,
Which caused his friends much grief and pain.
Simeon Amsden they found dead
Not many rods distant from his head. . . .

Eunice Allen see the Indians coming
And hopes to save herself by running;
And had not her petticoats stopped her,
The awful creatures had not catched her,
Nor tommy hawked her on the head
And left her on the ground for dead.
Young Samuel Allen, Oh, lack-a-day,
Was taken and carried to Canada.

On May 16, 1756, Lucy married Abijah Prince, a former slave who some years earlier had gained his freedom and been granted land under the terms of his owner's will. Abijah purchased Lucy's freedom, and the newlyweds moved to Guilford, Vermont, where he owned land. The couple had six children, daughters **Durexa** (b. 1758), **Drucella** (b. 1760), and **Tatnai** (b. 1765), and sons Caesar (b. 1757, who would fight in the Revolutionary War), Festus (b. 1763), and Abijah (b. 1769). All the children were educated in the local schools of Guilford, and the family's home provided a local forum for lively discussions about a variety of subjects, including politics and literature. Prince's first-born daughter Durexa also wrote poetry, although it was done mostly for her own amusement.

A gifted storyteller, Prince was well known for her speaking skills. The "fluency of her speech captivated all around her," according to her 1821 obituary, and she put this ability to good use on a number of occasions to defend her family's rights and property. In 1785, when white neighbors threatened them, Prince and her husband appealed for protection to Vermont's governor and his council, which ordered Guilford's selectmen to defend the Princes. When their oldest son Caesar was refused admission to Williams College in Massachusetts because of his color, Prince argued before the college's board of trustees for a change in the school's admission policy. Although they declined to make the changes she sought, the trustees acknowledged that her powers of persuasion were remarkable; one later said that Prince had cited both scripture and law "in an earnest and eloquent speech of three hours." Some years later, when a dispute arose with another neighbor over property boundaries, the case made its way to the U.S. Supreme Court. Non-lawyers were then allowed to argue in that court, and Prince successfully argued her family's case against two of Vermont's leading lawyers. Supreme Court Justice Samuel Chase later said her argument was superior to those he had heard from either of the Vermont lawyers.

After the death of her husband in 1794, Prince moved to Sunderland, Vermont, where she lived for the rest of her life. Each year, without fail, she traveled across the Green Mountains to visit her husband's grave in Guilford. The only one of her children to predecease her was Durexa, who died in 1812. Prince lived past the age of 90 and died in Sunderland in 1821.

SOURCES:

Smith, Jessie Carney, ed. *Notable Black American Women.* Detroit, MI: Gale Research, 1992.

Weatherford, Doris. *American Women's History.* NY: Prentice Hall, 1994.

Don Amerman,
freelance writer, Saylorsburg, Pennsylvania

Prince, Mary (c. 1788–after 1833)

Caribbean writer who was the first African-English woman to escape from slavery and publish an account of her experiences. *Born at Brackish-Pond in Bermuda, around 1788: died after 1833.*

In 1831, after purchasing her freedom from slavery, Mary Prince published her autobiography *The History of Mary Prince, a West Indian Slave, Related by Herself,* a powerful document that inflamed public opinion and created political upheaval between pro- and anti-slavery factions. The book, first published in London and Edinburgh, went into a third printing that same year. A modern edition, edited by **Moira Ferguson**, was published in 1987.

Born in Bermuda around 1788, Prince was the daughter of a household slave who worked on a farm, and a sawyer who was owned by a shipbuilder. Her mother's owner died when Prince was just an infant, and she was sold with her mother to a Captain Darrel and given to his young granddaughter Miss **Betsey Williams**, although she remained under her mother's care. "I was made quite a pet of by Miss Betsey, and loved her very much," she recalled in her autobiography. "She used to lead me about by the hand, and call me her little nigger. This was the happiest period of my life, for I was too young to understand rightly my condition as a slave, and too thoughtless and full of spirits to look forward to the days of toil and sorrow."

At 12, Prince was hired out of the Williams household and was forced to leave her mother and Miss Betsey, a separation that caused her great pain. In her new position, she cared for her mistress' young son, of whom she grew quite fond. After three months, however, Prince was returned to the Williams home to be sold away, along with her mother and siblings, by Betsey's father. Prince described in detail being dressed by her mother in her very best clothes and marched off to the marketplace where she was placed in a line with her brothers and sisters against the wall of a house. "I, as the eldest, stood first, Hannah next to me, then Dinah; and our mother stood beside, crying over us," she remembered. "My heart throbbed with grief and terror so violently, that I pressed my hands quite tightly across my breast, but I could not keep it still, and it continued to leap as though it would burst out of my body. But who cared for that? Did one of the many bystanders, who were looking at us so carelessly, think of the pain that wrung the hearts of the negro woman and her young ones? No, no! They were all not bad, I dare say, but slavery hardens white people's hearts towards the blacks; and many of them were not slow to make their remarks upon us aloud, without regard to our grief."

There was yet to come the further humiliation of being led out into the middle of the street so she could be examined more closely. "I was soon surrounded by strange men, who examined and handled me in the same manner that a butcher would a calf or a lamb he was about to purchase, and who talked about my shape and size in like words—as if I could no more understand their meaning than the dumb beast." Fetching a good price for one so young, Prince was wrenched away from her family for a final time. "It was a sad parting; one went one way, one another, and our poor mammy went home with nothing."

Prince would be sold several times again, and would suffer further physical and psychological abuse at the hands of her various owners. Around 1814, after working in the salt ponds of the Turks Islands, then returning with a new owner to Bermuda in 1810, she was sold again, and went to Antigua. She remained there until 1827, when her owners took her with them to England. In England, she petitioned for her freedom, remaining there when her owners returned to Antigua. Prince lived the rest of her life as a free woman. Described as "confident and spirited," she worked for the editor of the *Anti-Slavery Reporter* and was an outspoken campaigner against slavery. She died sometime after 1833.

SOURCES:

Buck, Claire, ed. *The Bloomsbury Guide to Women's Literature.* NY: Prentice Hall, 1992.

Busby, Margaret, ed. *Daughters of Africa.* NY: Pantheon Books, 1992.

Prince, Mary. *The History of Mary Prince, A West Indian Slave, Related by Herself* in *Six Women's Slave Narratives.* Schomburg Library of 19th Century Black Women Writers.

Barbara Morgan, Melrose, Massachusetts

Prince, Nancy Gardner (1799–?)

African-Amerindian domestic servant, humanitarian, and writer. *Born on September 15, 1799, in Newburyport, Massachusetts; death date unknown; daughter of Thomas Gardner (mother's first name unknown, though her maiden name was presumably Wornton); married a Mr. Prince (a freeborn), on February 15, 1824 (died around 1833).*

In her single volume *A Narrative of the Life and Travels of Mrs. Nancy Prince*, freeborn 19th-century domestic servant Nancy Gardner Prince recorded her life, from her poverty-stricken childhood in Massachusetts, though her teenage years as a domestic, her marriage, and her travels to the Russian courts of Alexander I and Nicholas I and the newly emancipated Jamaica.

Born on September 15, 1799, in Newburyport, Massachusetts, Prince was the second of her mother's eight children. Her father Thomas Gardner, the second of her mother's four husbands, died when she was three months old, after which her mother married Money Vose, a man Prince said abused her and her older sister. Vose, with whom Prince's mother had six additional children, died in the English dominions where he was serving in the War of 1812. To assist her widowed mothers and seven siblings, Prince, who had little education, went to work, first as a berry picker and then as a domestic. Baptized in 1817, she writes that only her religious faith sustained her during years of "anxiety and toil," in which she worked to support her family.

In 1823, having decided to learn a trade and leave the country, she met a Mr. Prince, who had just returned from Russia, where he had served a princess in the tsar's court. On February 15, 1824, Nancy married him and in April accompanied her husband on another voyage to Russia. Arriving in St. Petersburg on June 21, 1824, the Princes lodged with a Mrs. Robinson, an American from Providence, Rhode Island, who had left the country in 1813 in the service of a family named Gabriel. Later, Prince was presented to the imperial family, Alexander I and Empress *__Elizabeth of Baden__. In her book, Prince described the lavish setting of the court and the great "politeness and condescension" with which she and her husband were greeted. "There was no prejudice against color," she also notes, "there were there all castes, and the people of all nations, each in their place."

While in Russia, Prince boarded children, and, having learned to sew, started a business making clothing for infants and toddlers, which she sold to the nobility. Active in the local Protestant church, she also helped establish an orphanage in St. Petersburg and distributed Bibles at the royal palace.

In 1822, after ten years in St. Petersburg, Prince returned to the United States for reasons of health; her husband was to follow at a later date. He died, however, before he could make the journey back, and Prince had to carry on alone. Returning to Boston, she established an institution for homeless children of color, but it closed after three months due to lack of funding. Later, she joined a mission of a Reverend Ingraham to assist the newly emancipated slaves in Kingston, Jamaica. "I hoped that I might aid, in some small degree," she wrote, "to raise up and encourage the emancipated inhabitants, and teach the young children to read and work."

Prince journeyed to Jamaica twice, in 1840 and 1842. During her first visit, she was assigned to a mission in Saint Ann Harbor, where she witnessed what she felt was improper behavior on the part of teachers and leaders. Complaining to the authorities, she was threatened with dismissal, but was stricken ill and resigned her post before she could be forced to leave. In 1841, she traveled to Kingston, where she hoped to establish a Free Labor School for destitute girls. Having no money, however, she returned to America to raise funds for the project.

Prince went back to Kingston in May 1842, attempting to manage her school amid the aftermath of a bloody insurrection. Unsuccessful, she left Jamaica in August and after an unsettling voyage home, during which she experienced bad weather and the loss of her personal belongings, she arrived in New York. With the help of friends, she made her way back to Boston in August 1843.

In her later years, Prince was beset by ill health and business misfortunes and by 1849 was forced to accept financial help from her friends. In 1850, she published the first edition of her narrative in order to "obtain the means to help supply my necessities." Incorporated into the narrative is a 15-page pamphlet entitled "The West Indies: Being a Description of the Islands, Progress of Christianity, Education, and Liberty among the Colored Population Generally," which she prepared in conjunction with her two visits to Jamaica. Between 1853 and 1856, while second and third editions of the book were published, Prince's health further deteriorated. There is no information about her after 1856, and the date of her death remains unknown.

SOURCES:

Busby, Margaret, ed. *Daughters of Africa.* NY: Pantheon Books, 1992.

Smith, Jessie Carney, ed. *Notable Black American Women.* Detroit, MI: Gale Research, 1992.

Barbara Morgan,
Melrose, Massachusetts

Pringle, Elizabeth Allston

(1845–1921)

American planter and author. *Name variations: (pseudonym) Patience Pennington. Born Elizabeth Waties Allston on May 29, 1845, in Canaan Seashore, South Carolina; died of a heart attack on December 5, 1921, near Georgetown, South Carolina; daughter of Robert Francis Withers Allston (a rice planter) and Adele Petigru Allston; educated by governess at home and later at boarding school in Charleston, South Carolina; married John Julius Pringle (a planter), on April 26, 1870 (died 1876); children: one (died in infancy).*

Selected writings: A Woman Rice Planter *(1913);* Chronicles of Chicora Wood *(1922).*

Elizabeth Pringle was the second daughter of **Adele Petigru Allston**, of Huguenot descent and sister to Unionist leader James Louis Petigru, and Robert Francis Withers Allston, a rice planter. The third of the Allstons' five children to survive childhood, Elizabeth was born on May 29, 1845, at the family's summer home in Canaan Seashore, South Carolina, not far from Pawley's Island. The Allston family had held title to land near Georgetown, South Carolina, for nearly a century. At the time of Elizabeth's birth, her father was growing rice on seven plantations which were spread over thousands of acres of land. In addition to serving as governor and a state legislator, he was responsible for authoring a comprehensive primer on the cultivation of rice. Both in public and private life, he campaigned passionately for a free public-school system and to reform laws governing the poor.

Elizabeth was named for her father's "Aunt Blythe," who may well have served as something of a model for her niece. Willed a wealth in rice lands by a man she loved but could not marry, the aunt proved to be an able and sensitive manager of the plantation and the slaves who worked it, becoming legendary in the area.

Both Elizabeth and her older sister Adele were first educated by a governess at Chicora Wood, the family home on the Peedee River, which was located 14 miles from Georgetown. At the age of ten, Elizabeth was sent off to Charleston and the boarding school of Madame Togno, which introduced young ladies from wealthy families to the wonders of music and the French language. Her singing was encouraged by the school's Italian-born music master.

In the years following the Civil War, which had devastated South Carolina's Low Country as well as much of the rest of the South, Pringle taught for a time in a school her mother had established in Charleston. In 1868, she moved back to Chicora Wood, the last of her father's plantations to remain under family control. There she lived with her mother, younger brother Charles, and younger sister **Jane Allston**. Two years later, on April 26, 1870, Elizabeth married John Julius Pringle, owner of the White House, a plantation less than ten miles from Chicora Wood. In a November 7, 1875, entry from her diary, she wrote: "We are settled married people without children—five years of married life have passed so rapidly that I feel but little older than the day I took those cares upon me." In 1876, the year after Pringle wrote this diary entry, her husband John died suddenly. His death followed that of their only child, a son, who had died in infancy. Shattered by her loss, Pringle returned to Chicora Wood, where she helped to care for her older brother's motherless children.

In 1880, Pringle was bequeathed some money that allowed her to acquire White House, her late husband's plantation, from his heirs. In 1885, despite advice to the contrary, she decided to take on its management. Her success at this was made all the more remarkable because she continued to live at Chicora Wood, an hour and a half from White House, so as to be with her mother. Not above sharing in the field work on the plantation, she proved herself more than capable of handling almost any task. She showed an interest in finding new ways to run the plantation more efficiently, which included implementing the use of an incubator. Along with the rice, she maintained livestock and poultry and grew a number of fruits, including peaches, grapes, and strawberries. Up until 1900, she would customarily turn a profit.

Following the death of her mother in 1896, Pringle received some financial help from her younger sister Jane and was able to scrape together enough money to buy Chicora Wood, which she assumed control of at age 51. But with limited capital and an increasingly unreliable labor supply, Pringle struggled for the following years to operate the two plantations. The early 1900s brought bad weather and technological advances in the form of mechanized rice cultivation, and the majority of the plantations in the Carolinas were forced to fold. By 1906, Pringle, who often had to rely on the sale of prized livestock to pay her taxes, was financially ruined.

Though Elizabeth Pringle had always shown an interest in writing, her early efforts to get her work into print all met with rejection. She was nearing 60 when the *New York Sun* agreed to print a series of entries from her diary. In 1913, using the pseudonym Patience Pennington, she published these entries along with further commentary, and illustrations by **Alice R. Huger Smith**, under the title *Woman Rice Planter*. Her second book, *Chronicles of Chicora Wood*, was published in 1922, the year after Pringle's death. It focused on her memories of growing up during the heyday of Low Country rice cultivation and has proven useful to historians of this period.

Pringle died at age 76 on December 5, 1921, at Chicora Wood after suffering a heart attack. During her many years there, she had established herself as a friend and teacher to those with less education than she, both black and white. She was buried at Magnolia Cemetery in Charleston beside her husband.

SOURCES:

Edgerly, Lois Stiles, ed. *Give Her This Day.* Gardiner, ME: Tilbury House, 1990.

James, Edward T., ed. *Notable American Women, 1607–1950.* Cambridge, MA: The Belknap Press of Harvard University, 1971.

Don Amerman,
freelance writer, Saylorsburg, Pennsylvania

Pringle, Mia Lilly (1920–1983)

Austrian-born psychologist who was the first director of the National Children's Bureau. *Born Mia Lilly Kellmer in Vienna, Austria, in 1920; died in 1983; daughter of Samuel Kellmer; Birkbeck College, London, B.A. in psychology, with first-class honors, 1944; awarded a Ph.D. in 1950; married William Joseph Somerville Pringle, in 1946 (divorced 1962).*

Born in Vienna in 1920 and emigrating to Britain as a refugee in 1938, Mia Lilly Pringle received her undergraduate degree in psychology from Birkbeck College in 1944, after which she worked for a year as an educational and clinical psychologist at the London Child Guidance Training Center. She went on to serve as an educational psychologist in Hertfordshire from 1945 to 1950. After receiving her Ph.D. in 1950, Pringle taught at Birmingham University for 13 years, while also serving as head of the Remedial Education Center. In 1963, she was appointed the first director of the National Bureau for Cooperation in Child Care (later the National Children's Bureau), a post she held until 1981. Following her retirement, Pringle served as a consultant to UNICEF. Mia Pringle published numerous articles and books on child care, including *The Needs of Children* (1974), *Adoption, Facts and Fallacies* (1967), and *Foster Home Care, Facts and Fallacies* (1967), and also made frequent appearances on radio and television. Her awards included several honorary doctorates and the CBE, which she received in 1975.

Printemps, Yvonne (1894–1977)

Famed French actress of stage and screen. *Name variations: Yvonne Wignolle. Born on July 25, 1894, in Ermont, France; died on January 19, 1977, in Paris, France; daughter of Leon Wignolle and Palmire Wignolle; married Sacha Guitry (a playwright), in 1919 (divorced 1934); no children.*

Yvonne Printemps was born Yvonne Wignolle to a poor family in Ermont, near Paris, in 1894. Her father abandoned the family when she was a few years old, and her mother struggled to provide for her three children. Printemps received a cursory education at a girls' school near Ermont. At age 11, she joined a local theater troupe. Drawn to the stage immediately, Printemps began to help support her family in 1907 by working in Paris vaudeville theater as a dancer. When her vocal talent was discovered, she became a performer at the Folies-Bergère, where she would remain for four years; her mother, abandoned by a second husband, moved to Paris to oversee Printemps' stage career. It was at the Folies-Bergère that her beauty and cheerful disposition earned her the nickname Printemps (springtime), and she quickly adopted it both as a stage and legal name. By 1912, her dancing had brought her steady work, and she undertook voice and acting lessons. Over the next seven years, she performed in comedies, dramas, and operas across Paris, becoming its most celebrated female performer. She had numerous love affairs with her co-stars and admirers, and in 1916 fell in love with the celebrated French playwright and actor Sacha Guitry, who was married at the time of their affair. Following his divorce from his first wife, actress **Charlotte Lysès**, he and Printemps were wed in 1919.

It was this marriage which truly made Printemps a star; she performed as the lead in dozens of plays and musicals which Guitry wrote, produced, and often co-starred in. Her voice was described by critics as "exquisite" and "heavenly." Their 1926 production of Guitry's *Mozart*, with Printemps playing the young composer, was especially successful. They took the play first to London, then to Boston, Montreal, and finally enjoyed a long run in New York in 1927.

However, while their careers were flourishing, Printemps and Guitry's marriage was failing, and their relationship became primarily professional. By 1932, they had separated, and they were divorced in 1934. Although the immediate cause of the breakup was Yvonne's affair with a younger co-star, Pierre Fresnay, Printemps had for several years wanted to free herself from Guitry's increasingly jealous and domineering personality. After the divorce, she returned to England at the request of playwright Noel Coward, who wanted her to appear in his new play, *Conversation Piece*, in a leading role he had written for her. She agreed only on the condition that Fresnay be cast as her leading man. Although they would never marry, her often rocky relationship with Fresnay would last until his death in 1974.

French postage stamp honoring Yvonne Printemps, issued in 1994.

As Printemps spoke no English, she learned her role in *Conversation Piece* phonetically, but the critics were enthusiastic about her performance. The play then opened on Broadway in New York City, where she was welcomed by American audiences. Returning to France, Printemps established a new career as a star in the French cinema. She had performed as Camille (***Alphonsine Plessis**) in one minor film in 1934 (*La Dame aux Camelias*), but her first starring role in a major film was in *Les Trois Valses* (*Three Waltzes*) in 1938. Again Fresnay co-starred. The film was an immediate success and brought Printemps national celebrity. However, also in 1938 she reaffirmed her long association with the Parisian stage, when she and Fresnay agreed to take over the Michodière Theater. Together they served as business and artistic managers of the theater for the next 45 years. The couple spent the years of World War II in Paris, trying to keep the theater open even during the hardship and uncertainty of the German occupation of France. They produced and often cast themselves in the plays, believing they had an almost patriotic obligation to try to continue Paris' cultural life as much as possible.

Their stage work continued after the war. When the French cinema was revived, Printemps and Fresnay were eager to star again. In 1948, they made *Le Valse de Paris* (*The Paris Waltz*). Again the critics raved about Printemps' beauty, her charm, her voice, even though at age 54 she was older than most female film stars. Once again she returned to the Paris stage, which she would in many ways dominate for another ten years. Her continuing versatility and ability to play roles of varying age, despite poor health, preserved her critical and popular success until she retired from acting in 1959, at age 65. However, she continued her work behind the scenes with Fresnay as co-director of the Michodière throughout the 1960s and early 1970s.

Her friends and fans admired Printemps' spirit and wit, though many also remembered her as often selfish, demanding, and vulgar. She conducted many short-lived love affairs during her life with Fresnay, as did he, which took a toll on their relationship but did not destroy it. Printemps was devastated when Fresnay died of a heart attack in 1974. She became deeply depressed and her own health failed rapidly. She died on January 19, 1977, at age 82, and was buried next to Fresnay in a Parisian cemetery. Her admirers fulfilled her final wishes to honor Fresnay by naming a theater in Ermont after him. On the centennial of her birth in 1994, the French government issued a commemorative postal stamp in Yvonne Printemps' honor.

SOURCES:

Dufresne, Claude. *Yvonne Printemps: Le doux parfum de péché*. Paris: Perrin, 1988.

Knapp, Bettina. *Sacha Guitry*. Boston, MA: Twayne, 1981.

Laura York,
Riverside, California

Prisca.

Variant for Priscilla.

Prisca of Hungary (c. 1085–1133).

See Anna Comnena for sidebar on Priska-Irene of Hungary.

Priscilla (fl. 1st c.)

Early Christian evangelist, missionary and teacher, designated by St. Paul as being one of his "fellow workers" (Romans 16:3–5). *Name variations: St. Prisca; St. Priscilla. Flourished in the 1st century, around 54 CE; date and place of death unknown; married Aquila (a Jewish-Christian tentmaker). Her feast day is January 18.*

Priscilla and her husband Aquila, Christians at the time of Emperor Claudius (r. 41–54 CE), were forced to flee Rome in 49–50 CE when the imperial city's Jews were expelled (Acts of the Apostles 18:2). It is unclear whether Priscilla was born Gentile (her name was in fact that of an old Roman family) or Jewish, but her husband Aquila is described in scripture as being a Jewish leather worker or tentmaker of Pontus. As a couple, they played an important role in the early growth of Christianity, and although Aquila was both devout and active in spreading the new doctrine, it was Priscilla who clearly displayed more energy and determination in missionary activities.

They first went to Corinth, probably in 51 CE, where they entertained Paul; they then traveled with him to Ephesus, a large city on the west coast of Asia Minor. Priscilla and Aquila remained in Ephesus while Paul continued his travels to Caesarea. When Paul returned to Ephesus about a year later in the course of his third missionary journey, he was pleased to discover that the couple had been able to establish a Christian congregation "in their house" (I Corinthians 16:19).

After the death of Claudius in 54 CE, Priscilla and Aquila were able to return to Rome, at which point all mention of them in the historical record vanishes. Some scholars argue that they most likely died in Asia Minor, but Christian tradition has often had them dying in Rome as martyrs. Priscilla has frequently been confused with another woman named Priscilla, who founded a cemetery on Rome's Via Salaria and was a noblewoman of the Roman senatorial family of Acilii Glabriones.

St. Paul writes from Corinth to the Romans in 58 CE: "Greet Priscilla and Aquila, my fellow workers in Christ Jesus, who risked their own necks for my life, to whom I not only give thanks, but also all the churches of the Gentiles. Likewise greet the church that is in their house" (Romans 16:3–5). He not only praises the couple for "the church that is in their house," he mentions them as being his "fellow workers," a term Paul reserved to identify such leaders of the early church as Mark, Luke, Timothy, Titus, Philemon, and Apollos, a disciple of John the Baptist.

In Ephesus, Priscilla and Aquila's many-faceted missionary activities had included their painstaking instruction of Apollos, a learned man and a Jewish convert to the new doctrines of Christianity, who had some serious gaps in his understanding of the Christian message. Priscilla's teaching of Apollos is important in view of the fact that some years later Paul was to write Timothy that he did not permit women to teach or to arrogate authority to themselves over men (1 Timothy 2:12). To this day, theological conservatives argue that according to scripture (Titus 2:3–5), the teaching ministry of women in the Christian church is restricted to teaching young women and children. Those challenging this view have been able to discover strong evidence to the contrary, particularly in the case of Priscilla's teaching of an adult man, Apollos, not informally at their home, but in the synagogue, and in a detailed and systematic fashion.

In Acts 18:24–26, Paul mentions Priscilla's name before that of Aquila. In the six references to Priscilla and Aquila in scripture, her name is mentioned four times before his, strongly suggesting that she is the more distinguished of the two. Furthermore, both Luke and Paul honor her in this way. She was never thought to be a coworker; in Roman society, women were not generally called coworkers, a term of equality, rather, in this case, she comes before him. Scholars are generally in agreement about this fact, which points to Priscilla playing the more active role in teaching Apollos the finer points of Christian doctrine.

The eminent scholar Adolf von Harnack's assertion in an article published in 1900 in the *Zeitschrift für neutestamentische Wissenschaft* that Priscilla may have been the author of the Epistle to the Hebrews remains in dispute, but has been accepted as a reasonable hypothesis by a number of eminent experts in the field, including Thomas B. Allworthy, J. Rendel Harris, and Arthur S. Peake. As missionaries, von Harnack places Priscilla and Aquila as standing "independently alongside of Paul," working with him but spreading the message of the new faith by virtue of their own authority. With the passage of time, Priscilla became known as an apostle, with her reputation and influence being so great that by the 4th century CE St. John Chrysostom compared it to that of the sun as it looks over the entire earth.

SOURCES:

Brooten, Bernadette. *Women Leaders in the Ancient Synagogue: Inscriptional Evidence and Background Issues.* Chico, CA: Scholars Press, 1982.

Butler, Alban. *Lives of the Saints.* Revised ed. supplemented by Herbert Thurston and Donald Attwater. 4 vols. NY: P.J. Kenedy, 1956.

Gryson, Roger. *The Ministry of Women in the Early Church.* Translated by Jean LaPorte and Mary Louise Hall. Collegeville, MN: Liturgical Press, 1976.

Hoppin, Ruth. *Priscilla's Letter: Finding the Author of the Epistle to the Hebrews.* San Francisco, CA: Christian Universities Press, 1997.

Hutabarat, Henriette. "Partnership in Leadership: Priscilla and Aquila," in *Affirming Difference, Celebrating Wholeness.* Hong Kong: Christian Conference of Asia, Women's Concerns, 1995, pp. 152–153.

Irvin, Dorothy. "The Ministry of Women in the Early Church: Archaeological Evidence," in *Duke Divinity School Review.* Vol. 45, no. 2, 1980, pp. 76–86.

Jensen, Anne. *Gottes selbstbewusste Töchter: Frauenemanzipation im frühen Christentum.* Freiburg im Breisgau: Herder Verlag, 1992.

Kienzle, Beverly Mayne, and Pamela J. Walker, eds. *Women Preachers and Prophets Through Two Millennia of Christianity.* Berkeley, CA: University of California Press, 1998.

Ohanneson, Joan. *Woman: Survivor in the Church.* Minneapolis, MN: Winston Press, 1980.

Schottroff, Luise. "Women as Followers of Jesus in New Testament Times: An Exercise in Social-Historical Exegesis of the Bible," in *The Bible and Liberation.* Maryknoll, NY: Orbis Books, 1983, pp. 418–427.

Schüssler Fiorenza, Elisabeth. *In Memory of Her: A Feminist Theological Reconstruction of Christian Origins.* NY: Crossroad, 1985.

Tucker, Ruth A. *Daughters of the Church.* Grand Rapids, MI: Academie Books, 1987.

"The Women in Paul's Life," in *Christianity Today.* Vol. 41, no. 12. October 27, 1997, pp. 74–75.

John Haag,
Associate Professor of History, University of Georgia,
Athens, Georgia

Priscilla (c. 1602–c. 1685).

See Alden, Priscilla.

Priska of Hungary (c. 1085–1133).

See Anna Comnena for sidebar on Priska-Irene of Hungary.

Pritchard, Hannah (1711–1768)

English actress. *Name variations: Mrs. Pritchard. Born Hannah Vaughan in 1711; died in 1768.*

A member of David Garrick's company for 20 years, Hannah Pritchard was considered the best Lady Macbeth (***Gruoch**) until ***Sarah Siddons**. Pritchard was a renowned actress, eminent in both comedy and tragedy, and she excelled in playing characters of intrigue, including Lady Betty Modish and Lady Townly in *The Provoked Husband.* She was also seen as Gertrude in *Hamlet,* Cleopatra in Dryden's *All for Love,* and Zara in *The Mourning Bride.* Pritchard's first appearance was at the Haymarket on September 26, 1733; her last was at the Drury Lane on April 24, 1768.

Procopé, Ulla (1921–1968)

Finnish designer of ceramics. *Name variations: Ulla Procope. Born in Finland in 1921; died in 1968; graduated from the Helsinki Institute of Industrial Arts, in 1948.*

Born in Finland in 1921, Ulla Procopé graduated from the Helsinki Institute of Industrial Arts in 1948. She then went to work for the firm of Arabia, a producer of fine ceramic tableware. After working for a time under the direction of Kaj Franck, Procopé began creating her own designs, which included the Liekki pattern (1957) and the very popular Ruska (1960), distinguished by its rich brown glaze. Procopé was honored at the 1957 Milan Triennale and also won numerous awards and medals at exhibitions in Holland and the United States.

Procopia.

Variant of Prokopia.

Procter, Adelaide (1825–1864)

English poet and feminist. *Name variations: (pseudonym) Mary Berwick. Born Adelaide Anne Procter at 25 Bedford Square, London, England, on October 30, 1825; died in London on February 3 (some sources cite 2), 1864; eldest daughter of Bryan Waller Procter*

(1787–1874, an English poet who wrote under the pseudonym Barry Cornwall) and Anne Skepper Procter; studied at Queen's College, London; never married.

Born in London in 1825, Adelaide Procter was the eldest daughter of Bryan Waller Procter, an English poet who wrote under the pseudonym Barry Cornwall, and **Anne Skepper Procter.** Adelaide showed an early fondness for poetry, growing up in surroundings calculated to develop her intellectual tastes. Throughout her life, she was the center of her father's literary gatherings. Friends of her own included ***Mary Howitt.**

Under the pseudonym Mary Berwick, Procter contributed verse to Charles Dickens' periodical *Household Words.* In 1858, her poems were published in two volumes under the title *Legends and Lyrics*; they would go through nine editions in seven years. A second series had a similar success in 1861.

Though at one time her poetry was in more demand than that of Alfred, Lord Tennyson, Dickens noted that Procter never thought she was "among the greatest of human beings." If not a major poet, she had a gift for verse and expressed herself with distinction, charm, and sincerity. "The Angel's Story" is one of her best-known poems, and many of her songs and hymns, notably "The Lost Chord" (set to music by Sir Arthur Sullivan), were very popular.

A dedicated feminist, Procter helped ***Barbara Bodichon** and ***Jessie Boucherett** to found the Society for Promoting the Employment of Women; she also contributed the proceeds of a volume of poems to a night shelter for homeless women, and had her anthology *Victoria Regina* published by ***Emily Faithfull**'s Victoria Press (1861). But ***Fanny Kemble** had once said that her appearance was one of "doom." In 1862, the always frail Procter took the water cure at Malvern for her health. She died in 1864, age 39, having spent her last 15 months in bed. Dickens supplied the foreword to her *Complete Works.*

Proctor, Elizabeth.

See Witchcraft Trials in Salem Village.

Proell-Moser, Annemarie (1953—)

Austrian Alpine skier. *Name variations: Annemarie or Ann-Marie Pröll or Moser-Pröll; Annemarie Moser-Proell; Annemarie Moser. Pronunciation: PROHL MOH-sir. Born Annemarie Proell in Kleinarl, Austria, on March 27, 1953; married Herbert Moser (a salesman), in 1975.*

Won six World Cup overall titles; won silver medals in the downhill and giant slalom in the Sapporo Olympics (1972); won the World championship in the downhill (1974, 1978), in the combined (1978); won the World Cup (1971, 1972, 1973, 1974, 1975, 1979); completed a record sequence of 11 consecutive downhill wins (1973); in ten seasons, won a total of 59 individual events (1970–79); won a gold medal in the downhill in the Lake Placid Olympics (1980).

A first-rate competitor and one of the 20th century's most powerful skiers, Annemarie Proell-Moser was widely respected on the international ski slopes. When she announced her first retirement in 1975, U.S. skier ***Cindy Nelson** was disheartened. "I'd rather be second to Annemarie than win without her," she said. "It wasn't the same. You knew you weren't up against the best." Annemarie Proell was born in 1953 into a large Austrian farm family of eight children who skied at every opportunity. Though Proell-Moser did not have formal skiing lessons when young, her father hand-whittled her first pair of skis when she was four, and in wintertime she often played hooky from school to fly down the slopes in the secluded mountain area where she lived.

Proell-Moser burst onto the ski circuit in 1970 and would dominate the slopes for a decade. She was the youngest skier to win the overall World Cup competition in 1971, and she was World Cup overall champion from 1971 to 1975. During this period, she competed in 33 World Cup downhills, winning 21 races and finishing second in 7 others. As well, she won 11 giant slalom competitions and had 4 second-place finishes.

When Proell-Moser arrived at the Olympics in Sapporo, Japan, in 1972, she was a strong favorite to take the Alpine events, but she came in .32 seconds behind 17-year-old ***Marie Thérèse Nadig** of Switzerland in the downhill. She also lost the giant slalom to Nadig, again settling for silver. Worse yet, Proell-Moser was 5th in the slalom, a crushing disappointment; the gold medal went to an American, ***Barbara Cochran.** Proell-Moser returned home and hid her silver medals in the back of her closet.

After the games, Proell-Moser continued to win competitions, including eight downhills in World Cup competition. It took Cindy Nelson, in 1974, to break Proell-Moser's string of 11 straight downhill races. At the 1974 World championships in St. Moritz, Proell-Moser won the downhill title to capture the first world-event gold of her career; she was also first overall in the Nations World Series of Skiing.

But Proell-Moser decided to retire in 1975, avoiding the 1976 Olympics to be held in her own backyard at Innsbruck, Austria. After a year, she returned to skiing, winning another World Cup in 1979; she now held six World Cup titles. The 1980 Lake Placid Winter Olympics were happier for Proell-Moser, even though she came in 6th in the giant slalom. The media had built the downhill into one of the major races of the games. Proell-Moser defeated Nadig, who won a bronze, by .44 seconds, and ***Hanni Wenzel**, who took the silver. Said James Major, a former editor for *Skiing* magazine, Proell-Moser's "gold was the victory of the favorite, Wenzel's silver the upset, and Marie-Thérèse Nadig's bronze a defeat." Off the slopes, Proell-Moser had a passion for racing cars and was well known on the Formula One circuit.

SOURCES:

Condon, Robert J. *Great Women Athletes of the 20th Century*. Jefferson, NC: McFarland, 1991.

Markel, Robert, Nancy Brooks, and Susan Markel. *For the Record. Women in Sports*. NY: World Almanac, 1985.

Karin Loewen Haag,
Athens, Georgia

Prokopia (fl. 800s)

Byzantine empress. *Name variations: Procopia. Flourished in the 800s; daughter of Nicephorus I; mother unknown; sister of Stauracius, Byzantine emperor (r. 811); married Michael Rangabe also seen as Michael I Rhangabé, Byzantine emperor (r. 811–813, died around 845).*

Pröll, Annemarie (b. 1953).

See Proell-Moser, Annemarie.

Prophet, Elizabeth (1890–1960)

African-American sculptor. *Born Nancy Elizabeth Prophet on March 19, 1890, in Warwick, Rhode Island; died in December 1960, in Providence, Rhode Island; second of four children of William H. Prophet (a laborer) and Rosa E. (Walker) Prophet; graduated from Rhode Island School of Design, in 1918; married Francis Ford (a university student), on January 30, 1915 (legally separated, June 1932); no children.*

If ever a woman suffered for her art, it was African-American sculptor Elizabeth Prophet, who actually endured periods of starvation during her career. "I am a fighter, determined and non-retreating," she once declared in her diary. "I only stop when I drop." Prophet enjoyed brief periods of success during the late 1920s and early 1930s, but struggled on and off with poverty throughout her life. For ten years beginning in 1934, she held a teaching position at Spelman College in Atlanta, after which time she returned to Rhode Island, where she worked as a domestic in the years preceding her death in 1960. Unfortunately, less than 10 of Prophet's sculptures are presently accounted for in collections; the rest have disappeared, their existence verified only through archival photographs and publications.

Prophet was born in Warwick, Rhode Island, in 1890, the second of four children of **Rosa Walker Prophet**, an African-American, and William H. Prophet, who was both African-American and Native American. Little is known of Elizabeth's early life and schooling, although one source reports that her childhood interest in art was not encouraged by her parents, who thought it frivolous. In 1914, at age 24, she entered the Rhode Island School of Design in Providence, probably paying her tuition with money she earned as a housekeeper. At art school, where she was known as a hard worker but somewhat of a loner, she studied sculpture but focused mainly on painting and drawing. In 1915, she married Francis Ford, a Brown University student ten years her senior. It was an unhappy union.

Following her graduation from art school in 1918, Prophet tried to make a living through portraiture but was unsuccessful. In attempting to get her work exhibited, she also fell victim to the prejudice of the time; one gallery agreed to show her work, but requested that she not attend the opening. Discouraged on many levels, in 1922 Prophet sailed for Paris, leaving her husband behind.

Prophet spent what little money she had outfitting a studio in Montparnasse and embarked on creating her first sculpture abroad. "I remember how sure I was that it was going to be a living thing, a master stroke, how my arms felt as I swung them up to put on a piece of clay," she wrote in her diary. "I was conscious of a great rhythm as they swung through the air, they seemed so long and powerful." Before the piece was completed, however, Prophet was unable to pay her rent and was so hungry that at one point she stole a piece of meat and a potato from a dog's food bowl. Forced to move at least four times within the next two years, she nonetheless kept to a rigorous work schedule, completing two busts in 1923, one of which was included in the "Salon d'Automne" the following year. In 1924, she supported herself by selling batik, until a sympathetic patron gave her 2,000 francs. Prophet used the windfall to begin her first life-size statue, *Volonté* (will or wish). She would later destroy the piece, feeling it was not progressing as quickly as she thought it should. Prophet continued to battle poverty and periods of hunger, reaching a low point in the summer of 1925, when she was admitted to the American Hospital in Paris for malnutrition. The doctors, thinking she was an addict because of her emaciated condition, warned her to stay away from drugs. After recuperating for three weeks, she returned to her work.

Prophet's sculptures mirrored her life at the time; even the names of some of her works—*Discontent*, *Bitter Laughter*, *Poverty*, and *Silence*—reveal much about her state of mind. **Theresa Leininger**, in *Notable Black American Women*, notes that in style Prophet identified with the predominant sensibility of French sculpture of the period. "Like the work of Antoine Bourdelle, student of Auguste Rodin, her figures and busts had an androgynous quality with their close-cropped or covered hair, heavy-lidded eyes, enigmatic smiles, and small breasts. A series of her masks in plaster and clay from this period also recalls ancient Etruscan statues with their broad, calm foreheads and archaic smiles." Prophet worked mostly in marble and wood, although she also used bronze, alabaster, granite, terra-cotta, plaster, and clay. She preferred to work from live models but seldom had the money to pay for sitters; instead, she relied on her imagination. The artist took pains to document most of her works, having each piece photographed in black and white. In most cases, those images are all that remain of her sculptures.

Prophet was further sidetracked in 1926 by the unexpected arrival of her husband, who appeared at her studio drunk and bearing roses. Though intent on ending the relationship, Prophet stuck it out it until 1929, when she sent Jones back to America with a ticket she purchased with money from the sale of a sculpture. She made the separation official in 1932, changing her name legally from Ford back to Prophet.

During the late 1920s, Prophet exhibited work in several shows and received some help with living expenses from the Students Fund of Boston. She also received the patronage of W.E.B. Du Bois, who hosted her during a year-long visit to the United States in 1929 to promote her art. Despite a warm reception in American art circles, and several impressive exhibitions, Prophet was ambivalent about her success. "What is dear Paris doing these days?," she wrote to her friend Countee Cullen. "I long to be there in the solitude of my own studio. I do not like being famous, Cullen."

Back in Paris in the early 1930s, Prophet enjoyed the patronage of Edouard and **Julia Champion**, who not only paid her rent but frequently had her to dinner. It was a productive period for the artist, who exhibited two works, *Violence* and *Buste ébène*, at the Société des Artistes Française. She returned to the United States for ten months in 1932, at which time the Whitney Museum in New York purchased her best-known work, *Congolaise* (c. 1930), the cherry wood head of a Masai warrior. By 1934, however, she was in a downward descent again, in debt and living on tea and marmalade. After a particularly grim year, she accepted a position at Spelman College in Atlanta.

Looking forward to the opportunity to share her knowledge, Prophet was initially satisfied with her arrangement at Spelman. In addition to teaching courses in clay modeling and the history of art and architecture, she continued to exhibit, at the Whitney Sculpture Biennials of 1935 and 1937 and at the Philadelphia Museum of Art's Sculpture International of 1940. As time went on, however, Prophet grew frustrated over the cynical attitude of some of her students and the lack of essential teaching equipment at her disposal. She eventually began to resent the demands on her time and the fact that her studio was a makeshift affair in the school's power plant. "Prophet gradually withdrew from social life," writes Leininger. "While still appearing elegantly attired for dinner (often in a dramatic black cape and felt hat), she became increasingly eccentric and was said to speak in whispers, carry around a live rooster, and cover her sculptures with damp cloths so that no one could see them." In 1944, feeling she had fulfilled her duty to society, she left Spelman and returned to Providence.

Little is known about the last two decades of Prophet's life except that she worked for a ceramics factory in Rhode Island for some time and also held various positions as a live-in domestic. Following her death in December 1960, a man for whom she had worked as a housekeeper paid for her funeral and burial, keeping the sculptor from a pauper's grave.

SOURCES:

Bailey, Brooke. *The Remarkable Lives of 100 Women Artists*. Holbrook, MA: Bob Adams, 1994.

Smith, Jessie Carney, ed. *Notable Black American Women*. Detroit, MI: Gale Research, 1992.

Barbara Morgan,
Melrose, Massachusetts

Protopopov, Ludmila (1936—)

Russian pairs skater. *Name variations: Lyudmilla, Ljudmilla, or Ludmilla Belovsova (also Belousova or Beloussova). Born Ludmila Belovsova in the USSR in 1936; married Oleg Protopopov (a pairs skater), around 1966.*

Won Olympic gold medal in pairs (1964, 1968); won the World championships (1965, 1966, 1967, 1968).

For half a century, Olympic pairs skating was dominated by the Germans and the Austrians. In 1908 in London, **Anna Hübler** and Heinrich Burger of Germany took the first gold medal in pairs competition; they were followed in 1924 in Chamonix by Austria's **Helene Engelmann** and Alfred Berger. In Garmisch-Partenkirchen in 1936, 15-year-old **Maxie Herber** and Ernst Baier, the German couple who created "shadow skating" (performing the same moves without touching), took the gold and eventually wedding vows. The year 1952 saw the triumph of Germany's **Ria Baran** and Paul Falk (who also married); then again, the Germans yielded to the Austrians when **Elisabeth Schwarz** and Kurt Oppelt took gold in 1956. France, too, had its moment on the ice: **Andrée Joly** and Pierre Brunet, bronze medalists in 1924, were the first to take consecutive gold medals in two Olympics for pairs, the first in St. Moritz, in 1928, the second under their married names of Madame and Monsieur Brunet in Lake Placid, in 1932. Thus far, the only non-Europeans ever to win the gold medal in pairs skating were Canadians **Barbara Wagner** and Robert Paul in 1960.

But in 1964, Oleg and Ludmila Protopopov changed the tide of pairs skating, taking the gold and setting the stage for over 30 years of Soviet dominance in the sport. The 1960s belonged to the Protopopovs; in the 1970s, the crown would be passed to ***Irina Rodnina** and her two partners, Alexander Zaitsev and Alexei Ulanov; the 1980s would be shared between **Elena Valova** and her partner Oleg Vasiliev (Sarajevo, 1984) and ***Ekaterina Gordeeva** and Sergei Grinkov (Calgary, 1988, and Lillihammer, 1994).

The Olympic pairs competition in 1964 was the biggest upset of the Innsbruck Games. The reigning world champions, Germany's **Marika Kilius** and Hans Jürgen Bäumler, were popular and heavily favored, and they turned in a technically perfect performance. The yet-to-be-married Ludmila Belovsova and Oleg Protopopov followed with a five-minute fusion of dance, music, and skating that entranced an audience of 15,000. With a margin of victory of less than one point, they won the gold medal. But the Soviets had done less in the way of acrobatics than the Kilius-Bäumler team, and the decision proved unpopular with the German fans. They booed so loudly and for so long at the Canadian judge **Suzanne Morrow**, a pairs bronze medalist in 1948 who was considered the deciding vote, that she left the skating area in tears. A year later, Kilius and Bäumler had their silver medals stripped away after it was discovered that they had been professionals during the games.

As a married couple, the Protopopovs skated in 1968 at Grenoble where they again took the gold medal. Known for their classic balleticism, graceful overhead lifts, and passion on ice, they were also responsible for the "death spiral"; Ludmila Protopopov had the "daring ability to caress the ice with her blonde hair," wrote a British sportswriter, "with even her waist swinging only inches above the frozen surface."

Prou, Suzanne (1920–1995)

French novelist. *Born in 1920; died in Paris, France, during the night of December 29–30, 1995.*

She was a "novelist of bittersweet nostalgia," wrote *Le Monde* of Suzanne Prou when it announced her death just after Christmas in 1995. Of her two dozen novels, the best known is *La Terrasse des Bernardini* (*The Bernardini Terrace*), which was published in 1973 and won the Prix Renaudot. Wrote William Cole in the *Saturday Review,* "Madame Prou weaves an incredibly fine net, the strands of which are passion, deceit, sadism, pride, seduction, and burning hate." During the occupation of France in World War II, Prou helped produce an underground paper that condemned anti-Semitism. She was also a human-rights activist and ardent feminist.

Prout, Mary Ann (1801–1884).

See Walker, Maggie Lena for sidebar.

Prouty, Olive Higgins (1882–1974)

American novelist. *Born Olive Higgins in Worcester, Massachusetts, on January 10, 1882; died in Brookline, Massachusetts, on March 24, 1974; daughter of Milton Higgins (the head of the Mechanical Department of the Worcester Polytechnic Institute) and Katharine Elizabeth (Chapin) Higgins; graduated from Worcester Classical High School, 1900; Smith*

College, B.L. (Bachelor of Literature), 1904; married Lewis Isaac Prouty, in 1907; children: three daughters and a son.

Selected works: Bobbie, General Manager *(1913);* The Fifth Wheel *(1916);* The Star in the Window *(1918);* Good Sports *(1919);* Stella Dallas *(1923);* Conflict *(1927);* White Fawn *(1931);* Lisa Vale *(1938);* Now, Voyager *(1941)* Home Port *(1937);* Fabia *(1951);* Pencil Shavings *(1961).*

Born in 1882 in Worcester, Massachusetts, where her father headed the Mechanical Department of the Worcester Polytechnic Institute, Olive Higgins Prouty had a troubled childhood. At age 12, she suffered a nervous breakdown, the result of losing a beloved nurse, and spent two years in recovery. Prouty attended public school, excelling in composition to make up for her lack of athletic ability. By high school, she had mapped out a career as a writer, and four subsequent years at Smith College brought her closer to fulfilling her dream. In 1909, Albert Boyden, an editor at the *American Magazine,* published her first story "When Elsie Came," a family chronicle narrated by a young girl named Bobbie. Prouty wrote a series of additional stories focusing on the same family, and later turned them into her first novel, *Bobbie, General Manager* (1913). A further continuation of the story comprised her third novel, *The Fifth Wheel,* published in 1916. Meanwhile, Prouty had married and settled in Brookline, Massachusetts, where she combined her writing with raising a family. She once told an interviewer that she considered her home her career and her work her hobby, but in truth the conflict between family and writing was extremely stressful on her, resulting in a second nervous collapse in 1925.

Prouty's best-known novel, *Stella Dallas* (1923), revolves around a mother who sacrifices her own life to assure her daughter's social position. Although heavily sentimental, the melodrama is tempered somewhat by Prouty's deft narrative style and her compelling characters. The book not only sold well, but also spawned a successful play, starring ***Mrs. Leslie Carter** (1924), and three eponymous films, featuring **Belle Bennett** (1925), ***Barbara Stanwyck** (1937), and **Bette Midler** (1990). Midler's was simply titled *Stella.* With **Ann Elstner** in the lead, "Stella Dallas" also became one of the longest-running soap operas in radio history.

Prouty's later works included a series of novels about a wealthy Boston family by the name of Vale. **Heddy Richter**, in *American Women Writers,* notes that although the series explores Prouty's typical themes, "the propriety of marriage partners and the obligations of social position," two of them also deal sympathetically with psychological problems. In *Now, Voyager* (1941), the central character, Charlotte Vale (played by ***Bette Davis** in the highly popular 1942 film), breaks away from her domineering mother through treatment in a psychiatric sanitarium, and in *Home Port* (1947), a young boy develops an inferiority complex while growing up in the shadow of his more popular older brother. Prouty's sensitivity to the mental distress of others also extended to her private life. In 1953, when her protégé, poet ***Sylvia Plath**, attempted suicide, Prouty arranged to have her moved from Massachusetts General Hospital and cared for at a private sanitarium near Boston, for which she also footed the bill.

Even though her books sold well and were translated into many languages, Prouty remained dubious about her talent. In her last book, *Pencil Shavings* (1961), a memoir, she referred to herself as "a writer of light fiction" and mused that she was not as good a writer as she had longed to be. Prouty died in 1974.

SOURCES:

Kunitz, Stanley J., and Howard Haycraft, eds. *Twentieth Century Authors.* NY: H.W. Wilson, 1942.

Mainiero, Lina, ed. *American Women Writers: From Colonial Times to the Present.* NY: Frederick Ungar, 1980.

Barbara Morgan,
Melrose, Massachusetts

Provence, countess of.

See Douce I (d. 1190).
See Garsenda (1170–c. 1257).
See Beatrice of Savoy (d. 1268).
See Jeanne of Lorraine (1458–1480).
See Marie Josephine of Savoy (d. 1810).

Provence, duchess of.

See Jeanne de Laval (d. 1498).

Prowse, Juliet (1936–1996)

***South African dancer and actress.** Born on September 25, 1936, in Bombay, India; died on September 14, 1996, in Holmby Hills, California; married (divorced); married actor John McCook (divorced); children: son, Seth.*

Selected filmography: Gentlemen Marry Brunettes *(1955);* Can-Can *(1960);* G.I. Blues *(1960);* The Fiercest Heart *(1961);* The Right Approach *(1961);* The Second Time Around *(1961);* Who Killed Teddy Bear? *(1965);* Dingaka *(1965);* Run for Your Wife *(1966);* Spree *(1967).*

Dancer-actress Juliet Prowse was born in Bombay, India, in 1936, but raised in South Africa. From an early age, she studied for the ballet, performing with the Johannesburg Festival Ballet when she was 14. However, when her adult height reached 5'8", she was forced to give up classical dance. "When I got on my toes, some of those male partners were way down there," she later joked. Still in her teens, the leggy redhead set out for the United States and Hollywood, where she made her film debut in *Gentlemen Marry Brunettes* (1955). Her second film, *Can-Can* (1960), generated headlines before it was even released, when Soviet leader Nikita Khrushchev visited the set and pronounced the dancing indecent. Prowse's romance with her co-star Frank Sinatra (to whom she was later briefly engaged), and a fling with Elvis Presley during the shoot of her third movie, *G.I Blues* (1960), also produced a flood of publicity for the fledgling star.

Prowse's movie career did not live up to expectations, but she went on to star in television specials, stage musicals, and nightclubs. In 1965, she was the lead in her own television sitcom, "Mona McCluskey," about a movie star married to an Air Force officer. When the show was canceled after a single season, Prowse remained optimistic. "Things generally happen for the best," she told a reporter at the time. "I never worry about what happens in my career, because I can always do something else."

In September 1987, Prowse made headlines again when she was mauled by a leopard during a rehearsal for a television special, "Circus of the Stars." After receiving five stitches to close the wound, she returned to filming. She had a second run-in with the same leopard while preparing for a "Tonight Show" segment promoting the "Circus of the Stars" broadcast. This time, her left ear was badly torn, requiring close to 40 stitches to reattach it. Prowse, who was married and divorced twice, died of pancreatic cancer in 1996, at age 59.

SOURCES:

Greissinger, Lisa Kay. "Passages," in *People Weekly.* September 30, 1996.

Katz, Ephraim. *The Film Encyclopedia.* NY: HarperCollins, 1994.

Juliet Prowse

"Milestones," in *Time*. September 23, 1996.

"Obituary," in *Boston Sunday Globe*. September 15, 1996.

Sands, Rich. "Tribute," in *TV Guide*. October 5, 1996.

Barbara Morgan,
Melrose, Massachusetts

Prunskiene, Kazimiera (1943—)

Lithuanian political leader who served as the first prime minister of the self-proclaimed independent Republic of Lithuania (March 1990–January 1991). *Name variations: Kazimiera Danutė Prunskienė. Born Kazimiera Danute Stankeviciute in Vasiuliskiai, Lithuania, on February 26, 1943; daughter of Pranas Stankevicius; recieved a degree in economics, University of Vilnius, 1965; married second husband Algimantis Tarvidas; children: daughters, Dayvita and Raisa; son, Vaidotos.*

Kazimiera Prunskiene's life in many ways has reflected the turbulent history of her small Baltic nation. Born during World War II in 1943 in German-occupied Lithuania, she lost her father at the age of two when he was killed in a gunfight with Soviet security forces in the Labanor Forest. After receiving a degree in economics from the University of Vilnius in 1965, she began a career in that institution's industrial economics department. Prunskiene was able to successfully juggle the roles of wife, mother and academician, giving birth to three children between 1963 and 1971.

In 1980, Prunskiene joined the Communist Party of the Soviet Union. By the late 1980s, with the onset of *perestroika* (restructuring) advocated by new Soviet leader Mikhail Gorbachev, Prunskiene set her sights on a career in politics. In 1988, she became one of the founding members of Sajudis, the grass-roots Lithuanian movement that hoped to turn Gorbachev's ideas into reality within the republic. Intelligent, persuasive, and ambitious, by 1989 Prunskiene had become the deputy chair for economic affairs in the Council of Ministers of the Lithuanian Soviet Socialist Republic, as well as being elected to the Supreme Soviet of the USSR. In 1989, Europe's year of revolutions, the pro-independence Lithuanian Communist Party split from its Soviet "big brother" organization. An alarmed Gorbachev declared these actions to be illegitimate.

In the February 1990 elections for the Lithuanian Supreme Council (Parliament), Sajudis-backed candidates were elected in 72 out of 90 districts, but Prunskiene did not win one of the 141 seats until some time later, when a second round of voting took place. On March 11, 1990, the Supreme Council voted 124 to 0, with only six abstentions, in favor of Lithuania's independence from the Soviet Union. Although its hastily adopted constitution followed the Soviet model, significantly it dropped the names Soviet and Socialist, calling the new, self-proclaimed sovereign state the Republic of Lithuania. In the delicate world climate of 1990, the United States declined to recognize the nascent nation, and Gorbachev once more repeated his warnings about the invalid and illegitimate nature of these acts.

On March 17, 1990, the Supreme Council of Lithuania appointed Prunskiene prime minister of the newborn republic. She immediately resigned her membership in the Communist Party and began her tenure in office under very tense circumstances. Gorbachev ordered Soviet armed forces to start a series of maneuvers on Lithuanian soil. On March 23, a convoy of Soviet troops entered the capital city of Vilnius, soon seizing the headquarters and other property of the pro-independence Lithuanian Communist Party. The greatest challenge Prunskiene and her government faced was the economic embargo put in place by Moscow starting on April 18, which not only halted shipments of oil and natural gas but also barred the delivery by rail of many other essential goods.

In early May, Prunskiene flew to Washington, her trip paid for by Lithuanians in the United States. After a day spent meeting with various members of the U.S. Congress, she headed for the White House. Although she realized that the situation demanded that she be received only as a private citizen, Prunskiene was nevertheless taken aback when her Lincoln sedan was stopped outside the White House gates, and she was thus obliged to walk on foot to her appointment with President George Bush. Her brother Rimantas, who had hoped to sit in on the meeting, was denied access to the grounds and sat on a bench in Lafayette Square. This was later explained by a protocol official as having been the result of a malfunction of the White House gate mechanism. Although little of a concrete nature came from this trip, Washington officials were impressed by Prunskiene's diplomatic skills and determination, and she went on additional trips later the same month to meet with high officials in Bonn, London, and Paris.

Gorbachev rescinded the energy embargo after 74 days. Despite this, Lithuania's economic problems remained massive. Politically, too, the situation was far from ideal, with Prunskiene frequently disagreeing with Vytautis Landsbergis, the powerful Supreme Council chair. One point of contention between the two leaders was Prunskiene's advocacy of taking bolder steps to introduce a market economy into Lithuania. They also debated over the pace toward independence, with Landsbergis being more militant in this regard, and Prunskiene pleading for compromise and reconciliation with the Gorbachev government. The political tensions remained high throughout 1990, but in December of that year Prunskiene was able to enjoy what turned out to be her last popular achievement in office: she attended the historic joint session of the three Baltic parliaments when these national representatives met in Vilnius to dramatize their drive for independence from Soviet rule.

On January 7, 1991, the Soviet commander for the Baltic military district informed the Lithuanian government that its laws absolving military-age males of service in the Soviet armed forces were invalid, and that paratroopers would enforce the draft and round up conscientious objectors. Added to this crisis was one of equal intensity brought on when Prunskiene announced sweeping price hikes for products purchased from other republics. Intended as a major step toward economic reform, these measures infuriated factory workers, who received no pay increases (pensioners and some low-income workers did). Anger and resentment were directed at Prunskiene, who became linked with the dispersal of anti-government demonstrators by fire hoses. The political firestorm put immense pressure on Prunskiene, who now lost much of her parliamentary support. She resigned, being succeeded by Gediminas Vagnorius as prime minister. Prunskiene remained a member of the Supreme Council, but the once-popular leader now had to endure much criticism, including accusations of having abandoned her high office during a grave national crisis. This argument was strengthened by the fact that only a day after her resignation, Soviet soldiers had attacked the Vilnius broadcasting center, an action that resulted in the deaths of 13 unarmed civilians.

Nine months after Prunskiene's resignation, Boris Yeltsin's faction gained the upper hand in Moscow. Bowing to the inevitable, they recognized the independence of Lithuania and the other Baltic republics. Soon after, the Soviet Union was dissolved. In the autumn of 1992, Prunskiene decided not to run for reelection to the Supreme Council. She now stood under a cloud of suspicion after a parliamentary commission leveled charges against her of having collaborated with the Soviet KGB in the early 1980s. She vehemently denied these charges. Whatever verdict history will finally make of her political achievements, Prunskiene went on to found the Lithuanian-European Institute, and in 1995 was elected leader of the Lithuanian Women's Party. She has published 15 books.

SOURCES:

Liswood, Laura A. *Women World Leaders: Fifteen Great Politicians Tell Their Stories.* San Francisco, CA: HarperCollins, 1996.

Opfell, Olga S. *Women Prime Ministers and Presidents.* Jefferson, NC: McFarland, 1993.

Prunskiene, Kazimiera. "Is There a Place for a Woman in Politics?," in *New Times International.* No. 37. September 1993, pp. 21–23.

John Haag,
Associate Professor of History, University of Georgia, Athens, Georgia

Prussia, queen of.

See Sophie Charlotte of Hanover (1668–1705).
See Sophie Louise of Mecklenburg (1685–1735).
See Sophia Dorothea of Brunswick-Lüneburg-Hanover (1687–1757).
See Elizabeth Christina of Brunswick-Wolfenbuttel (1715–1797).
See Frederica of Hesse (1751–1805).
See Louise of Prussia (1776–1810).
See Elizabeth of Bavaria (1801–1873).
See Augusta of Saxe-Weimar (1811–1890).

Pryor, Mrs. Roger (1830–1912).

See Cunningham, Ann Pamela for sidebar on Sara Agnes Pryor.

Pryor, Sara Agnes (1830–1912).

See Cunningham, Ann Pamela for sidebar.

Przybyszewska, Dagny Juel (1867–1901)

Norwegian-born writer who was a central figure in Berlin's avant-garde. *Pronunciation: Pshi-bi-shef-ska. Name variations: changed the spelling of her surname from Juell to Juel. Born in Kongsvinger, Norway, on June 8, 1867; killed by her lover Wladyslaw Emeryk on June 5, 1901; second of four daughters of Hans Lemmich Juell (a doctor and attendant physician to the king of Sweden) and Minda (Blehr) Juell (sister of Otto Blehr, a Norwegian prime minister); married Stanislaw Przybyszewski (1868–1927, a Polish writer), late summer 1893; children: son Zenon P. Westrup (b. September 1895); daughter Iwa Dahlin (b. October 1897).*

A Norwegian-born writer and wife of a well-known Polish playwright, Dagny Juel Przybyszewska was a central figure in Berlin's avant-garde movement of the 1890s, the muse of the city's *Schwarze Ferkel* artist's circle. Painted by Edvard Munch (1863–1944), and a model for characters of August Strindberg (1849–1912), she was also a talent in her own right, writing four plays, a short story, and a collection each of prose and lyric poems, and serving as an agent for a number of Scandinavian artists. In a scholarly biography entitled *Dagny*, **Mary Kay Norseng** describes her subject as "mysterious, provocative, and inexplicably beautiful," haunted by her bourgeois past and conflicted over the roles she assumed as wife, mother, and writer. Unfortunately, her life was too short for any resolution. She died three days short of her 34th birthday, shot by a neurotic young man in a hotel room in Tiflis near the Black Sea. "Even as she lived, Dagny was perceived to exist in a borderland between myth and reality, sensationalism and silence," writes Norseng. "Compounded by the distortions effected by time, she has slipped almost irretrievably from view."

What is known of Dagny's early years reveals that she was raised in a close aristocratic family. She was born on June 8, 1867, in Kongsvinger, Norway, the second of the four attractive and talented daughters of Hans and **Minda Juell**. (A son, born to the Juells shortly after Dagny, died when he was a year old.) Dagny's father, of Danish lineage, was an attendant physician to the Swedish king, and the family lived in a 13-room estate (Rolighed), set on 25 acres of cultivated land on which were located a shooting gallery and one of the area's first ski jumps. A large number of Minda Juell's family (including her brother Otto Blehr, who in 1891 would be the Norwegian prime minister to the king of Sweden and Norway) lived on nearby estates and farms, providing an extended familial network for Dagny and her sisters.

Dagny completed the traditional six grades of school, but did not continue her education, perhaps out of a growing rebellion and disdain for "the academic." As a teenager, she took up the piano, becoming quite proficient and taking great joy in performing for her family and friends. During her 21st year, she worked as a governess to the children of an aunt and uncle who lived in the west coast town of Førde. She was genuinely fond of the children, and they later recalled her sense of humor and the stories she told to them. While living in Førde, she frequently traveled to visit other relatives in Bergen, where she was enchanted by the city's social and cultural life. Following her year as a governess, she returned home to Rolighed.

In the early 1890s, Dagny may have lived in Christiania (now Oslo), or possibly made frequent trips there from home to take piano lessons. She often traveled with her younger sister **Ragnhild Juell**, who was studying voice, and stayed with her mother's sister **Maria Blehr**, who ran a school for young girls in the city. During this time, the sisters befriended a group of Christiania's young aspiring artists and writers, including the journalist Hjalmar Christiansen, with whom Dagny may have been romantically involved. In early February 1892, she traveled with Ragnhild to Berlin, probably to study music. Little is known of her activities during this visit, although the 1892 date on a Munch painting of Dagny and Ragnhild, *Two Music-Making Sisters,* indicates that the women may have been in Åsgårdstrand, Munch's home, during the summer of that year. (There is some confusion as to when Dagny met Munch. Norseng supports a theory that the two met in Christiania in the early 1890s, but believes that his painting of the sisters was probably done at a later time.) Dagny

returned home to Rolighed in the fall, but was restless and eager to leave again.

She embarked for Germany once more in February 1893, ostensibly to study piano. In March, she made her first appearance at Zum schwarze Ferkel (The Black Piglet), a Berlin tavern which served as the meeting place of the city's most avant-garde artists and thinkers, among them Munch, Strindberg, and the modernist playwright Stanislaw Przybyszewski ("Stach"), whom she would marry within a month. "Dagny Juel caught the imagination of the *Schwarze Ferkel* group and, indeed, 'held it captive,'" writes Norseng. "Tradition has it that she instantaneously became their muse, turned their heads and broke their hearts. They all were said to have fallen in love with her, vying with each other for her favors. . . . Supposedly Munch brought her to the tavern and loved her first, and then came Strindberg and others, and then Przybyszewski, whom she finally chose. Some saw her as a modern love goddess of the literati, akin to ***Lou [Andreas-Salomé]**, sensual, intelligent, provocative, and free. For others, such as Strindberg, she was a femme fatale without equal, a destructive, erotic queen in the midst of these hungry bohemians."

At this time, Edvard Munch ("the hero of the young Expressionists") had just broken with the Norwegian art establishment and was coming off his first controversial exhibition in Berlin. While it remains unclear whether or not his relationship with Dagny was sexual, he would become her devoted friend and champion. "After her death he gave the only positive account of her life to appear in any Scandinavian newspaper," writes Norseng, "portraying her as an intellectual, cultured, and kind woman who actively participated in the creative endeavors of the *Ferkel* circle." Munch was also inspired by Dagny's ethereal beauty, once remarking: "You had to experience her to be able to describe her." His portrait *Dagny Juel Przybyszewska* (1893) is as enigmatic as the woman herself, her pale image seeming to float out from the black of her dress and the misty deep blue of the background. "Her expression is open, inviting, seemingly benign, somehow sad," writes Norseng. "Her eyes are veiled. She may be holding her hands provokingly behind her back or protectively in front of her. She is at once spirit and flesh, angel and demon, in ecstasy and in mourning, of life and of death." An equally haunting portrait of Dagny was painted later, in 1901, by Konrad Krzyzanowski.

The exact nature of Dagny's relationship with Strindberg is also unclear, although it was certainly complex. He was 44 at the time of their meeting and secretly engaged to ***Frida Uhl**, his affair with Dagny taking place during a three-week period in March 1893 when Frida was out of town. Although little is known of Dagny's reaction to Strindberg, she provoked intense feelings in him. According to Norseng, "[H]e interpreted her as his persecuting demon, and he waged a vicious war of words against her, as only a writer could, attacking her first in his letters and later in his literary works." She later served as the model for several of Strindberg's destructive women characters: Aspasia in *Inferno* and *Svarta fanor* (Black Banners), Laïs in *The Cloister* and *Karantánmästaarns andra berättelse* (The Quarantine Officer's Second Story), and Henriette in *Crimes and Crimes.*

Despite her obvious attraction to many men within the Schwarze Ferkel, it was Stach Przybyszewski whom Dagny chose to marry. The couple fell in love in the spring of 1893 and wed late that summer. The union seemed doomed from the start. In addition to his purported "satanic" practices, Stach was a serious alcoholic, a philanderer, a pathological liar, and dirt poor. (Dagny claimed they got married because they happened across a mark one day, the exact cost of a marriage license.) What apparently united the two was their shared contempt for order. During their first years together, the couple remained at the center of the Schwarze Ferkel group, entertaining them day and night in their modest one-room apartment. They sought recognition for the Scandinavian artists within the group and were a motivating force behind *Pan* (1895), an art journal for which Dagny supplied the title. While they encouraged the group, they also inspired each other. Stach wrote prolifically during his marriage to Dagny, using her for a model and dedicating all his work to her. In short order, she also began writing, her short story "Rediviva" appearing in December 1893, and her play *Den sterkere* (The Stronger) published in Norway in 1896.

The couple would have two children, son Zenon (b. 1895) and daughter Iwa (b. 1897). Both would be born at Rolighed and entrusted to Dagny's mother for long intervals while Dagny joined Stach in Berlin, Copenhagen, Paris, or Spain. Poverty continually drew Dagny back to Rolighed throughout her marriage, as did the uncertainty of her life with Stach, whose drinking and philandering grew more destructive.

In 1896, a tragic event tested the marriage even further. That June, one of Stach's longtime mistresses, **Marta Foerder** (a Polish woman with whom he had had three children), committed suicide. Stach had several children with other women and ignored them all. "In the beginning there was sex," he wrote. News of Foerder's death reached the couple in Copenhagen, where they had reunited after a three-month separation. Together, they returned to Berlin, where Stach was implicated in the suicide, arrested, and jailed for several weeks. As a result of the scandal, the couple were abandoned by their friends, causing Stach to become depressed and dysfunctional. Dagny literally held things together during this difficult period, rewriting Stach's manuscripts, dealing with his publishers, and giving piano lessons to earn some money, which Stach then drank away. As was now her pattern, however, Dagny returned to Rolighed in March 1897, both to receive emotional support from her family and to await the birth of her second child, Iwa.

In the fall of 1898, the couple were reunited in Cracow, where Stach had taken over the editorship of *Życie* (Life), the journal of the avant-garde Young Poland. Although Stach was embraced as a hero by the Cracow bohemians, who even provided the family with a rented house, the marriage had deteriorated further, and Dagny was additionally concerned about her father's declining health. In January, her father died and the journal went under, jolting the couple into another crisis. Starting in June 1899, Stach began an affair with **Aniela Pajakowna**, with whom he would have a daughter, ***Stanislawa Przybyszewska** (1901–1935). He would also become involved with **Jadwiga Kasprowicz**, whose husband was one of his best friends (and Poland's major poet), and whom Stach married after Dagny's death. Dagny, perhaps in desperation, embarked on her own liaison with Tadeusz Boy-Zelenski, one of her and Stach's good friends.

In January 1900, Dagny left Stach yet again, this time fleeing from city to city with a young poet by the name of Vincent Brzozowski. In May, she was convinced by her sister **Gudrun Juell** to return home to Rolighed once again. She stayed for half a year, publishing her prose-poem cycle *Sing mir das Lied vom Leben und vom Tode* (Sing Me the Song of Life and Death) in Norway late in the fall. In 1901, she briefly reconciled with Stach in Warsaw, then embarked on what would be her final journey, leaving Warsaw for Tiflis in Russian Georgia with her son Zenon and Wladyslaw Emeryk. A Pole of Russian extraction who owned a salt mine near Tiflis that was nearly bankrupt, Emeryk was a delicate and unstable young man who purportedly loved both Dagny and Stach to excess and lavished money on them. There are several theories as to why Dagny left with him: some believe that Emeryk was going to help the couple establish a new life in Russia, others that Stach used Emeryk to get rid of Dagny. Whatever the case, Dagny, who was traveling without a passport, continually telegramed her husband from various cities along the route asking him to send the identification papers he had promised to obtain for her. "I'm about to lose my mind," she wrote the day before she died. "Not a word since a month ago. I have telegraphed to Kraków, to Lemberg, to Warsaw. No answer. . . . I am dumbfounded, completely dumbfounded." Around noon the next day, June 5, 1901, Emeryk shot Dagny, then took his own life. He left behind several sealed letters, written days before. "I'm killing her for her own sake," he wrote to Stach. To Zenon: "She was not of this world, she was far too ethereal for anyone to understand her true nature." (Norseng suggests that Emeryk may have suffered a mental breakdown due to the bankruptcy of his business, which drove him to murder and suicide.) Dagny was buried in Tiflis on her birthday, June 8, 1901.

Dagny's shocking and violent death aroused interest in her works in Poland, although in her native Norway her writing was thought of little consequence until the 1970s, when there was a renewed interest in women writers of the past. A collection of her lyric poems, *Digte* (Poems), was published in 1975, the short story "Rediviva" appeared in 1977, and a collection of three plays, *Synden og to andre skuespill* (The Sin and Two Other Plays), in 1978. Norseng describes Dagny's writing as "*fin de siècle* works, exotic literary flowers that seemed to grow from the darkness of the heart." She further defines Dagny's style as "daring in its themes, its imagery, and its techniques. Her heroines make bold, if often criminal choices, they cross sacred boundaries, and they accept the tragic consequences. Her landscapes are gothic, full of dead spirits, rare flowers, cold dark tombs, and bloody rivers. Her techniques are expressionistic, designed to project a dark, internal world into the light."

While she lived, Dagny Przybyszewska was ambivalent about her work, even after she had achieved moderate success. She was, according to Norseng, far more assertive as an agent for others than in promoting herself. In addition to her involvement with the journal *Pan,* she attended to the work of her friend Munch and others, arranging exhibitions and negotiating sales. For her husband, she served as editor, translator, and agent. Even in their final months of estrangement, she was concerned with the progress of his career and was attempting to persuade him to change publishers.

Dagny's short life invites speculation. Had she lived, what would have become of her, as a woman and as a writer? For Norseng, Dagny represents a personal and historical transition never realized. "In any transition the changes are wrenching," she writes, "often threatening and seldom elegantly executed. No exception was made for Dagny. Yet she brought to her life, in all its stages, a seemingly inevitable dignity. Her powerful attraction, for her contemporaries and for us, seems to me to derive not only from her remarkable life but from the intensity with which she embraced it."

SOURCES:

Norseng, Mary Kay. *Dagny: Dagny Juel Przybyszewska: The Woman and the Myth.* Seattle, WA: University of Washington Press, 1991.

Barbara Morgan,
Melrose, Massachusetts

Przybyszewska, Stanislawa (1901–1935)

***Polish playwright who gained posthumous fame for her masterpiece,* The Danton Case.** *Pronunciation: Pshi-bi-shef-ska. Born Stanislawa Pajak in 1901; died in the Free City of Gdansk (formerly Danzig) on August 15, 1935; illegitimate daughter of Stanislaw Przybyszewski (1868–1927, a Polish writer) and Aniela Pajakowna (d. 1912, a professional artist); married Jan Panienski (a painter and teacher), in 1923 (died 1925); no children.*

Produced a powerful dramatic trilogy on the French Revolution, several novels, and other works of lesser significance; work was rediscovered (1960s–1970s) and is now firmly established in the repertory of the Polish theater.

Stanislawa Przybyszewska began life in 1901 under less than auspicious circumstances as Stanislawa Pajak, the illegitimate daughter of **Aniela Pajakowna** and the modernist playwright Stanislaw Przybyszewski. Talented but artistically profligate, Przybyszewski led a dissolute lifestyle, fathering Stanislawa as the result of a passing affair with her mother, an aspiring painter and protégé of a wealthy Polish family. At the time, he was married to ***Dagny Juel Przybyszewska**. (Dagny would be killed the same year in which Stanislawa was born.) Most of Stanislawa's childhood was spent outside of Poland to escape the censorious whispers that followed her mother almost everywhere she went. Attending schools in Paris, Vienna, and Zurich, Stanislawa never stayed long enough in any one place to make deep attachments or significant friendships. After her mother died suddenly in 1912, she lived with her maternal aunt, **Helena Barlinska**, who was to remain a source of support for the rest of her short life.

Living in Cracow where she was enrolled at the local teachers' college, Stanislawa met her father for the first time in 1919. Soon after, due to her uncle's intervention, she was able to legally adopt her father's name. Unfortunately, the young woman soon developed an unhealthy infatuation for the famous and glamorous stranger who had so dramatically entered her life. Stanislaw Przybyszewski, called by some "satanic," practiced the black arts and dabbled in devil worship, and it was at this time that he introduced his daughter to morphine, to which she became addicted, and allegedly raped her.

In 1920, at her father's insistence, Przybyszewska moved to Poznan, where he was then living. Her busy schedule included music courses and one semester at the local university studying philosophy, while she supported herself working as a clerk in the post office. The strain brought on a nervous breakdown. At this time, she was also drawn to Poznan's literary and artistic avant-garde, which centered around the Expressionist journal *Zdrój* (The Source). She also met and fell in love with the man she would marry, a young painter and chemist named Jan Panienski.

In 1922, the restless Stanislawa moved to Warsaw, where she worked in a left-wing bookstore. Soon she was moving in Communist circles, which were under constant surveillance by a reactionary and anti-Marxist regime. Arrested for her "anti-Polish" political views, Stanislawa was imprisoned for some months but eventually released. For a short time, she taught at one of Warsaw's private schools.

In 1923, Przybyszewska married Panienski, moving with him to the ethnically German Free City of Gdansk (formerly Danzig) that had been created as a result of the Treaty of Versailles. For the next two years, which would be the happiest in Przybyszewska's life, she was active in local Polish artistic circles, gave lectures on psychoanalysis, spent considerable time painting, and carried out research into certain phases of the French Revolution, a subject that had deeply interested her ever since she had lived in France as a child. This happy period came to an end suddenly in 1925, when she received word that her husband had died while on a trip to Paris. He, too, was addicted to morphine and most likely died of an overdose.

From this point on until her death a decade later, Przybyszewska spent her days and nights in almost total isolation. Living without plumbing or electricity, in a tiny room in primitive wooden housing that was provided to her rent-free by the Polish Gymnasium to which it was attached, she studied, thought, and wrote almost exclusively about the French Revolution. In a trilogy of dramas—*Thermidor*, *1793*, and *The Danton Case*—she dissected the phenomenon of revolution from both a historical and a psychological perspective. *Thermidor* was written in German and would not appear in a Polish translation until long after its author's death, receiving its first staging in 1971.

Emotionally fragile and suspended between languages and cultures, Przybyszewska largely ignored Gdansk, a place that was culturally German but was forced to exist in political limbo, and only chose to visit Poland briefly in 1927 (to attend her father's funeral), and again in 1928 and 1930 to visit friends in Poznan. Even her extreme poverty mattered little to her, since it was only one of many burdens which included loneliness, illnesses such as painful rheumatism, and an obsession about the creative process and a fear of losing control of it. Despite all this, she believed it inevitable that her work one day would be recognized and celebrated by the world. Her belief in her own abilities reflected overconfidence to the point of arrogance, and there can be little doubt that Przybyszewska's genius came close to dementia, as when she began in 1928 to date her letters according to the French revolutionary calendar that had been adopted in 1793 and talked of Danton and Robespierre as if they were her contemporaries.

During her lifetime, there would be only two productions of her play *Sprawa Dantona* (*The Danton Case*), one in Lwow (today Lviv, Ukraine) in 1931 (it was five hours long and ran for only five days), and the other in 1933 at Warsaw's *Teatr Polski* (the text was cut from 15 to 12 scenes and ran for 24 performances). Nothing came of a planned production of this play by the noted director Leon Schiller; such a venture was ruled out because of Schiller's reputation as a leftist following his production of the Bertolt Brecht-Kurt Weill *Dreigroschenoper* (*Threepenny Opera*). As a result of Przybyszewska's leftist politics, her uncompromising artistic integrity, and just plain bad luck, her works were practically unknown during her lifetime.

Impoverished during the last decade of her life, Przybyszewska worked at her writing eight to ten hours, mostly at night. At first, she went to a nearby grocery store to buy essentials (she subsisted largely on bread, butter, and tea). Addicted to the morphine without which she could neither concentrate nor write, she was also addicted to newspapers which she claimed to detest. In the final years of her tragic existence, Przybyszewska would walk slowly down the street, head bowed, and with an unsteady gait. Unable to find a way out of her misery, she nevertheless refused to abandon life. In a letter to Barlinska dated May 13, 1931, Stanislawa wrote: "And I don't want to die, no, I really don't want to die." A stray cat she had taken in from the streets was the only living thing to keep her company. In her last years, she avoided going out of her primitive shelter altogether, depending on the kindly wife of the Gymnasium's principal to provide food. Stanislawa Przybyszewska died on August 15, 1935, of malnutrition and tuberculosis, aggravated by many years of morphine addiction. Neighbors realized she had died when her cat's unusual behavior notified them that something was amiss. She was 34.

Stanislawa Przybyszewska

Stanislawa Przybyszewska is one of the great original talents of modern Polish, indeed, modern European, literature. Her works on the French Revolution were written in a highly original style combining dramatic chronicle with intellectual discussion. Her writing is also linked to such powerful works of late German Romanticism as the dramas of Georg Büchner and some of the plays of Romain Rolland. Contemporary interest in her plays is due to the efforts of Jerzy Krasowski, who discovered the manuscripts and staged *The Danton Case* at Wroclaw's *Teatr Polski* in 1971. With the publications of her plays in Gdansk in 1975, edited by Boleslaw Taborski, her trilogy on the French Revolution is now firmly established in the repertory of the Polish theater. Andrzej Wajda presented the play in Warsaw in 1975 and in Gdansk in 1980, which led to his 1982 film version *Danton*, starring Gerard Depardieu. The less than literal but cinematically brilliant adaptation presents the universal conflict between "the good genius" Robespierre, fighting for the moral rebirth of humanity, and "the evil genius" Danton, concerned solely with power and sensual pleasures. In 1986, **Pam Gems**' adaptation from Boleslaw Taborski's translation reduced the play to a more manageable length for its first English-language presentation, at the Royal Shakespeare Company (RSC).

SOURCES:

Beauvois, Daniel. "Chronique: L'Affaire Danton de Stanislawa Przybyszewska," in *Annales Historiques de la Révolution Française.* No. 240. April–June 1980, pp. 294–305.

Czerwinski, E.J., ed. *Dictionary of Polish Literature.* Westport, CT: Greenwood Press, 1994.

Gasiorowski, Professor Zygmunt J. Personal communication.

Ingdahl, Kazimiera. "Catastrophism as a Permanent State: Comments on Stanislawa Przybyszewska's Aesthetics," in *Scando-Slavica.* Vol. 36, 1990, pp. 21–39.

———. *A Gnostic Tragedy: A Study in Stanislawa Przybyszewska's Aesthetics and Works.* Stockholm: Almqvist & Wiksell, 1997.

Kosicka, Jadwiga, and Daniel Gerould. "A Life of Solitude: Stanislawa Przybyszewska," in *The Polish Review.* Vol. 29, no. 1–2, 1984, pp. 47–69.

———. *A Life of Solitude—Stanislawa Przybyszewska: A Biographical Study with Selected Letters.* Evanston, IL: Northwestern University Press, 1989.

Krol, Marcin. "Przybyszewska o Rewolucji Francuskiej," in *Dialog.* Vol. 18, no. 1, 1973, pp. 84–89.

McAlister, Elaine. "Film as Historical Text: Danton," in John D. Simons, ed., *Literature and Film in the Historical Dimension.* Gainesville, FL: University Press of Florida, 1994, pp. 63–73.

Milosz, Czeslaw. *The History of Polish Literature.* 2nd ed. Berkeley, CA: University of California Press, 1983.

Nowicki, Ron. *Warsaw: The Cabaret Years.* San Francisco, CA: Mercury House, 1992.

Przybyszewska, Stanislawa. *The Danton Case–Thermidor: Two Plays.* Translated by Boleslaw Taborski. Evanston, IL: Northwestern University Press, 1989.

John Haag,
Associate Professor of History, University of Georgia, Athens, Georgia

Psappha or Psappho (c. 612–c. 557 BCE).

See Sappho.

Ptaschkina, Nelly (1903–1920)

Russian diarist. *Born in Russia in 1903; died at age 17 in Chamonix, France, on July 2, 1920; never married; no children.*

What we know about the short and tumultuous life of Nelly Ptaschkina survives in a series of notebooks she kept religiously from the age of ten, several of which were preserved and published by her mother following her untimely death in 1920. Like *__Anne Frank__, Ptaschkina wrote amid turmoil and uncertainty. Her adolescence coincided with the Russian Revolution of 1917, during which time her family fled from Moscow to Kiev, then on to Paris, surviving harassment by the Bolsheviks and threats of shooting and pillaging by both the Red and White armies. "The situation is really *terrible!*," she recorded on January 25, 1918. "The decisive days for Russia are at hand, 'to be or not to be.' My vision is too restricted to be able to picture the whole situation clearly.... I am mentally short-sighted because, after all, I am but a child. . . . All the same, at odd moments, I clearly realize the full horror of the position in which our country is placed."

Although Ptaschkina frequently wrote about her future with pessimism, she remained full of youthful determination, as is seen in her entry of March 5. "I shall not surrender to this inner voice which faint-heartedly whispers to me that our life is inextricably tied up with the epoch, and moreover united in such a way that it can never be adjusted; that therefore everything is at an end and that nothing will come out of it.... I shall not brood over the fact that news is worse again, and that in consequence our position is all the more deplorable. In four or five years all must settle down—and I will leave it at that."

The diaries overflow with Ptaschkina's plans for the future, which include an advanced education and a career in social and community work. But she cannot part with the romantic idea of falling in love. "Can it be that this beautiful thing to which I feel drawn so unresistingly will not be accessible to me," she ponders, "and that only the grey workaday world will be mine? Oh, I am afraid of this, terribly afraid." In a slightly later entry, Ptaschkina, still only 15, entertains the idea that she might have both career and family. "In my dreams, however strange it may sound, I dream at the same time of children and of an independent life, which should be both comfortable and beautiful." In the same entry, she asserts herself as a blossoming feminist. "Yes, woman must have all the rights, and in time she can earn them fully. At present we have still many women who are satisfied with their empty lives, but if we raise the standard, and improve the social conditions of life, which are connected with her, woman will also rise. Even now there are many among them who would be capable of leading a conscious existence successfully. Give them that possibility."

Ptaschkina's notation of October 20, 1918, chilling presages her own death. "[T]oday, stepping close to the brink of a precipice, although not so deep as I should have wished, the thought came into my mind that some day I should die thus, crashing headlong into the chasm." On July 2, 1920, just five days after she had passed her Baccalauréat examination at the Sorbonne, Ptaschkina was hiking in Chamonix, at the foot of Mount Blanc, when she misstepped and fell from a tremendous height into the waters of the Cascade du Dard. Her body was recovered many miles downstream.

SOURCES:

Moffat, Mary Jane, and Charlotte Painter, eds. *Revelations: Diaries of Women*. NY: Random House, 1975.

Barbara Morgan,
Melrose, Massachusetts

Ptolemais (c. 315–?)

Egyptian princess. *Born around 315* BCE*; daughter of Ptolemy I Soter, king of Egypt (r. 305–285* BCE*), and ****Eurydice*** *(fl. 321* BCE*); married Demetrius Poliorcetes ("the City Besieger"); children: Demetrius the Fair (who married ****Berenice II of Cyrene*** *[c. 273–221* BCE*]).*

Pucelle, La.

See Joan of Arc (c. 1412–1431).

Pudeator, Ann.

See Witchcraft Trials in Salem Village.

Pugacheva, Alla (1949—)

Russian singer and pop star. *Name variations: Alla Borisovna Pugacheva. Born in 1949; attended Ippolitov-Ivanov School of Music and the Lunacharsky School of Theatrical Arts; married four times, lastly to singer Philipp Kirkorov; children: Kristina Orbakaite (a singer and actress).*

Made first recordings for radio station at age 16; toured USSR and Far East with Russian bands; won third prize at the All Union competition of pop artists (1974); won Grand Prix at Golden Orpheus competition in Bulgaria (1975); won first prize at International Sopot Song Festival (1978); star of concert tours, films and television shows; last singer to win the National Artist of the USSR award; awarded medal for "service to the fatherland," Russia's highest civilian award (1999).

Born in 1949, Alla Pugacheva spent her youth studying music and theater at the Ippolitov-Ivanov School of Music and the Lunacharsky School of Theatrical Arts and made her first recordings—for radio—at age 16. Her career as a performer began on the road, as she traveled through Siberia and the Far East with the promotions crew of a radio station and toured with a number of Russian bands, including New Electron, Moscovites and Happy Fellows.

In 1974, Pugacheva won third prize at the All Union competition of pop artists, receiving national attention for the first time. The following year she was offered the chance to participate in the Golden Orpheus competition in Bulgaria, when she was a last-minute replacement for star Georgy Movsesyan. Pugacheva won the contest with the song "Arkelino" (Harlequin), and in 1978 she won first prize at another competition, the International Sopot Song Festival in Poland. She soon became a musical superstar throughout Russia and Eastern Europe.

Adored in her homeland, where she filled sports stadiums during her concert tours, Pugacheva was the last singer to win the National Artist of the USSR accolade in the old Soviet Union. Though not the most talented or beautiful of her generation, Pugacheva seems to be celebrated by her millions of fans for her success and the odds she overcame to achieve it.

Described by *The New York Times* as "Moscow's ***Tina Turner** with a hint of ***Edith Piaf**," Pugacheva has enjoyed unrivalled success in Russia. Her albums—a mix of pop, rock, folk and torch songs—are estimated to have sold between 140 and 200 million copies. She has appeared in several wildly popular films, including *The Woman Who Sings* (1977) and *Came to Say* (1985), and on television shows throughout Europe.

Temperamental, red-haired and flamboyant, Pugacheva is regarded as the first real Russian pop star, living her turbulent personal life (including four marriages, the first at the age of 20) in the public eye. "I think my life [has] consisted only of extremes," she said. Making the most of her status as cultural icon, Pugacheva allowed her name to be used for a line of perfume, her own line of shoes, her own magazine, and even a Finnish ocean liner. A popular Russian joke refers to Leonid Brezhnev as "a minor political figure in the Pugacheva era."

A fixture at festivals and competitions in Europe throughout her career, from Eurovision to Midem, Pugacheva has recorded over 20 albums and won numerous awards. She is also a director of concerts and television programs. Both her daughter **Kristina Orbakaite** and her latest husband Philipp Kirkorov are also pop stars. Described by music critic Artyom Troitsky as "the most popular human being in Russia," Pugacheva was awarded a medal for "service to the fatherland," Russia's highest civilian award, by former President Boris Yeltsin in 1999, on her 50th birthday.

SOURCES:

Miami Herald. February 17, 2000.

Smale, Alison. "A Superstar Evokes a Superpower," in *The New York Times*. February 28, 2000, pp. B1, B4.

Paula Morris, D.Phil.,
Brooklyn, New York

Pugh, Sarah (1800–1884)

American teacher, abolitionist, and suffragist. *Born in Alexandria, Virginia, on October 6, 1800; died in Germantown, Pennsylvania, on August 1, 1884; only daughter and second of two children of Jesse Pugh and Catharine (Jackson) Pugh; attended the Westtown (PA) Boarding School for two years; never married; no children.*

Remembered for her intelligent and dedicated support of both the anti-slavery and the woman's suffrage movements, Sarah Pugh performed the quiet, behind-the-scenes tasks without which reform becomes impossible. "I have no fear of her talents rusting for want of use," wrote ***Lucretia Mott** of Pugh, with whom she worked and traveled on many occasions.

Born in 1800 in Alexandria, Virginia, Sarah Pugh lived from the age of three in Philadelphia, Pennsylvania, where her mother established a dressmaking business after the death of her husband. Raised as a Quaker, Pugh's education included two years at the Quaker-run Westtown Boarding School. In 1821, she accepted a teaching position at the Friends' school of the Twelfth Street Meeting House in Philadelphia. She left the post in 1828, as a result of the split between the Orthodox and more liberal Hicksite Quaker sects, an event which also caused her to question her own religious beliefs and to ultimately accept the Unitarian faith. In 1829, Pugh established her own elementary school in Philadelphia, where she taught for more than a decade.

In 1835, inspired by a speech by the English abolitionist George Thompson, Pugh joined both the Female Anti-Slavery Society, of which she served as an officer for many years, and the American Anti-Slavery Society. She attended antislavery conventions and worked tirelessly for passage of state and national legislation abolishing slavery. In 1840, leaving her school in the hands of her co-workers, she joined Lucretia Mott, **Mary Grew**, and others as American delegates to the London meeting of the British and Foreign Anti-Slavery Society. When the Pennsylvania women were denied active participation because of a vote to exclude women delegates from the convention proceedings, she wrote their statement of protest. Pugh made a second trip to Europe in 1851, remaining in England for over a year to assist with the anti-slavery movement there. During that time, she consulted with British intellectuals and advised administrative committees and women's groups on how to organize campaigns.

Following the Civil War, Pugh turned her attention to the plight of freed slaves and to women's rights, working on behalf of both causes through the Pennsylvania Anti-Slavery Association. Often traveling with Mott, she attended women's rights conventions and meetings, speaking for the suffrage cause. In 1869, when the movement began to split into two factions, Pugh refused to take sides, and continued to attend meetings of both factions. She was also active in the Moral Education Society, founded in Philadelphia in 1873.

Living in Germantown, Pennsylvania, with her brother Isaac and his wife, Pugh remained active and in good health until the last two years of her life, when she was debilitated by lumbago. She died on August 1, 1884, following a fall.

SOURCES:

James, Edward T., ed. *Notable American Women, 1607–1950*. Cambridge, MA: The Belknap Press of Harvard University, 1971.

Pukui, Mary Kawena (1895–1986)

Hawaiian composer, chanter, teacher, translator and writer who was known as the greatest authority on Hawaiian culture and language. *Born Mary Abigail Kawena-'ula-o-ka-lani-a-hi'jaka-i-ka-poli-o-pepe-ka-wahine-l'ai-hou na Pukui in Ka'u, Hawaii, on April 20, 1895; died in May 1986 in Honolulu.*

Mary Kawena Pukui composed over 50 Hawaiian songs ranging from hula music to Christmas carols, blending Hawaiian and European cultures. She remained, however, a proponent of Hawaiian language and culture. A teacher of the Hawaiian language, she composed and translated many songs, often collaborating with other well-known composers. Pukui received honorary LL.D.s from the University of Hawaii in 1960 and Brigham Young University, Hawaii, in 1974. Traditionally, Hawaiian singers passed on their culture to future generations, a role Pukui fulfilled admirably.

John Haag,
Athens, Georgia

Pulcheria (c. 376–385)

Roman noblewoman. *Born around 376; died in 385; daughter of ****Flaccilla*** *(c. 355–386) and Theodosius I the Great, emperor of Rome (r. 379–395); sister of Arcadius, emperor of Rome in the East (r. 395–408), and Honorius, emperor of Rome in the West (r. 395–423).*

Pulcheria (c. 398–453)

Romano-Byzantine empress who shaped a decisive period in the history of an empire in which few women reached such positions of power and influence. *Name variations: Aelia Pulcheria or Aelia Pulcheria Augusta; Pulcheria means "beautiful woman" from the Latin word* pulcher *(beautiful). Reigned 408–450; born on January 19, 398 or 399; died in 453; daughter of Emperor Arcadius (r. 395–408); mother's name unknown; stepdaughter of Eudocia of Byzantium (d. 404); half-sister of Emperor Theodosius II; married Marcian (a general).*

Death of Emperor Theodosius I the Great and partition of the Roman Empire between his sons Arcadius, who received the Eastern half, and Honorius, who received the West (395); Pulcheria born (398 or 399); birth of her brother Theodosius (c. 400); German tribes crossed the frozen Rhine and began their conquest of the West Roman Empire (December 31, 406); death of Pulcheria's father Arcadius (408); sack of Rome by the East Goths (Ostrogoths, 410); Pulcheria granted title "Augusta" and appointed regent for her brother Theodosius II (July 4, 414–416); arranged brother's marriage to Athenais (renamed Eudocia) (421); founding of the University of Constantinople (February 25, 425); Council of Ephesus (431); Code of Theodosius promulgated (438); Pulcheria quarreled with sister-in-law Eudocia, who moved permanently to Jerusalem (c. 440); the eunuch grand chamberlain, Chrysaphius, became all-powerful at the court of Theodosius; Pulcheria retired from court life (443); earthquake ruined the walls of Constantinople (447); death of Theodosius and Chrysaphius' fall from grace (450); Pulcheria became first woman to hold the Roman throne, marrying General Marcian, whom she made her co-ruler (450); Council of Chalcedon (451); siege of Rome by Attila the Hun (452); death of Pulcheria (453); sack of Rome by the Vandals (455); death of Marcian (January 457); fall of the Roman Empire in the West (476).

Written in the late 4th century, the history of Ammianus Marcellinus, the last great chronicler of the Roman Empire, ends the series of works by classical Roman historians that illuminate the history of the Roman world. Not until the emergence of Procopius, court historian of Emperor Justinian (r. 527–565), is there another historian of the first rank upon whom to rely. Therefore, the years from 395 to 527—the period including the final partition of the Roman Empire into East and West (395), the fall of the Western Empire (476), and the life of Empress Pulcheria—must be pieced together from a variety of minor sources, many of them extant only as fragments quoted by later authors. To assemble the history of the period, we must look to details passed down by inferior chroniclers, such as Claudian, Olympiodorus, Zosimus, John of Antioch, John Malalas, Priscus, Cedrenus, Sozomenus, Eunapius, Theophanes, the *Paschale Chronicle,* Orosius, and Arian Philostorgus.

Pulcheria was born around 398 in Constantinople, the daughter of Emperor Arcadius (r. 395–408), into the last decades of the Roman Empire. (Her mother's name is unknown.) She was apparently named after a paternal aunt who had died in infancy, and her name meant "beautiful woman" (from the Latin *pulcher,* "beautiful"). Hers was an illustrious family. She was the great-granddaughter of Emperor Valentinian I (r. 364–375), granddaughter of Theodosius I (r. 379–395) and his wife ***Flaccilla** (c. 355–386), grandniece of Valentinian II (r. 375–392), niece of Emperor Honorius (r. 395–423), and first cousin of Valentinian III (r. 425–455). Through the first marriage of her half great-uncle, Emperor Gratian, to the granddaughter of Constantine I the Great, Pulcheria was linked, however distantly, to the first Christian emperor of Rome.

She was the second of four sisters, of the eldest of whom, Flaccilla, we hear nothing; she may have died young or, as some have speculated, was perhaps considered deficient in some way. Well educated, knowing both Greek and Latin, at an early age Pulcheria together with her two sisters **Arcadia** and **Marina** took a vow of chastity in the presence of the high clergy and the people; they did this, it is said, as a means of avoiding what they felt would be the destructive rivalries inevitable between their husbands were they to marry. Though dedicated to the religious life, Pulcheria would play a significant role in the politics of the late Roman Empire, serving as regent and co-ruler with her brother Emperor Theodosius II, becoming the first woman to rule Rome in her own right, and eventually (after being absolved from her vow of chastity) entering into a platonic marriage with General Marcian to enable him to serve as her co-ruler at a critical point in Roman history.

Pulcheria's brother Theodosius II (with whom she shared the same father but not the same mother) came to the throne at the age of 7 and reigned for 42 years (408–450). Son of the weak and slow-witted Arcadius, whose character he appears to have inherited, Theodosius was nevertheless a better physical specimen than his father. He was tall and fair in appearance, apparently taking after his mother ***Eudocia of Byzantium**, who was of Frankish German birth. At first, the seven-year-old boy-emperor ruled under the wise regency of Anthemius, Praetorian prefect of the East, while his education was entrusted to Antiochus, a palace eunuch. However, it was Pulcheria—designated an "Augusta" on July 4, 414, and thereafter in effect co-ruler with her brother—who assumed responsibility for his rearing. Guided by Aurelian, the new Praetorian prefect of the East, and Atticus, patriarch of Constantinople, she raised her brother with the greatest attention, providing him with a good education and keeping him free from the immorality and other vices easily accessible in the capital. Despite her efforts, Theodosius, though kindly and good natured, grew up weak, self-indulgent and indolent, and it has been said that he did not even read the famed code of laws to which his name would forever be attached. Renowned for his elegant hand, he passed his time in copying manuscripts, collecting theological works, and studying astronomy. During Pulcheria's entire reign, he does not appear to have undertaken a single political act on his own initiative. Fortunately, however, he had the good sense to leave affairs of state largely in the hands of his sister.

Pulcheria and her sisters had imparted a tone of almost monastic piety to the Eastern court, in part from natural inclination, in part from a desire to avoid political difficulties in the imperial succession by avoiding marriage in Christian chastity.

—**Stewart Irwin Oost**

Sincerely devoted to the religious life, Pulcheria and her sisters turned the imperial palace in Constantinople into a kind of nunnery into which they retreated together with a select group of women. No man was allowed to enter the confines of this cloister except for the priests and the high ministers through whom Pulcheria ruled. In the palace, the women, simply dressed, devoted themselves to a regime of church services, fasting, vigils and prayer, their recreation being the embroidering of vestments and altar cloths. Together, the sisters founded churches, hospitals and monasteries throughout the eastern provinces of the empire, endowing them with lands and other emoluments for their support. To Pulcheria must also be given at least some of the credit for the founding of the University of Constantinople (425), and, above all, for the convocation of the Council of Ephesus (431).

Pulcheria also appears to have selected the emperor's bride, the gifted Athenais (***Eudocia**, c. 400–460). Athenais was a native of Athens, the daughter of the pagan philosopher Leontius. Educated by her father, she was relegated to poverty when he died and left most of his wealth to his two sons. Athenais, unable to secure from her brothers enough to live on comfortably, appears to have gone to the capital to seek the intercession of Pulcheria. Impressed by the girl's breeding and education, Pulcheria introduced her to the emperor and succeeded in convincing her brother that in Athenais she had found him a suitable bride.

Upon her conversion to Christianity, Athenais gave up her original pagan name for the Christian name Eudocia (*eudocia* meaning "good teaching"), whereupon she was married to Theodosius in June 421. Eudocia (often referred to incorrectly by modern authors as Athenais-Eudocia) gave birth to three children with Theodosius: a son Arcadius and a daughter ***Flaccilla** (d. 431), both of whom died young, and another daughter, ***Licinia Eudoxia**, who in 437 was married to Emperor Valentinian III (r. 425–455), cousin of Theodosius and Pulcheria and ruler of the Western Roman Empire. The following year, 438, Eudocia made a pilgrimage to Jerusalem. Traveling in great pomp through Asia Minor, the young empress arrived in Antioch, capital of the province of Syria, where she addressed the local senate, donated a sum of 200 gold pieces for the restoration of the municipal baths, and induced Theodosius to erect a new basilica in the city and to extend its walls. Proceeding on to Jerusalem, she visited the Holy Places, distributing alms and endowments beyond even those granted by ***Helena** (c. 255–329), the sainted mother of Emperor Constantine I the Great whose pilgrimage to the birthplace of Christianity the empress may have been consciously emulating.

Upon her return to Constantinople, Eudocia was likely a different woman from the desperate young girl who had once sought the protection of the emperor's sister, and it seems that she now attempted to dominate Theodosius in Pulcheria's place. The execution of Eudocia's supporter Paulinus, the master of offices, and the disgrace of Cyrus, Praetorian prefect of the

East, both of whom were high ministers of state inclined to support Eudocia, may have been due to the power struggle between Pulcheria and Eudocia that now ensued. Whatever the case, the two women quarrelled. Eudocia lost the struggle and in 443 (still empress, though estranged from her husband over an alleged adulterous relationship between herself and his childhood friend Paulinus) she returned to Jerusalem where she would spend the rest of her life. There, she supervised the rebuilding of its fortifications and the construction of several splendid churches. A highly cultivated woman, Eudocia wrote religious poetry, including a panegyric on the Roman victory over the Persians in 422, and had a considerable influence on her weak husband until she left the court.

Another close contemporary of Pulcheria's was her aunt Empress *__Galla Placidia__, who had served as regent for her son Valentinian III (r. 423–455) and had led a particularly stormy life. Born in Constantinople around 390, she was less than ten years older than Pulcheria, but the two never met as children. At six years old, Galla Placidia had left Constantinople for Rome where she was taken prisoner by the Goths, then carried off to Spain and married to the Gothic chieftain Athaulf (Adolf). Released in 416 after his assassination, she settled in Ravenna where her worthless brother Honorius was emperor of the Western Roman Empire (r. 410–423). In 417, Galla Placidia married Constantius III, the master of soldiers (commander-in-chief of the Roman army), with whom she had two children. Having aroused the suspicions of her brother, however, she was banished from Ravenna after her husband's death in 422. After a brief sojourn in Constantinople with her niece Pulcheria and her nephew Theodosius II, in 425 she returned to Italy after her brother Honorius' death. There, supported by Theodosius and Pulcheria, she became regent for her son Valentinian III, who was later to marry Theodosius' daughter Licinia Eudoxia. In return for this support, however, Theodosius and Pulcheria obtained for their share of the empire the disputed province of Dalmatia and the eastern part of Pannonia.

After the marriage of Licinia Eudoxia to Valentinian III, which took place in Constantinople, Pulcheria retired from the court for a time, moving to the Hebdomon Palace. Domination over the emperor passed to the grand chamberlain, the eunuch Chrysaphius. An intelligent woman and a fine scholar, Pulcheria led a life characterized by extreme piety and chastity. Devoted both to her church and to the welfare of her people, she may have had something to do not only with the establishment of the University of Constantinople in 425, but also with the construction of the famed Theodosian walls that protected Constantinople from land and sea, and with the codification of Roman law (429–438) known as the Theodosian Code. Promulgated in the Eastern Roman Empire on February 15, 438, the Code was accepted in the West by the Roman Senate on December 23. Pulcheria was probably present at the arrival of St. Mesrop Mashtots, inventor of the Armenian alphabet, who was received at court in Theodosius' time and obtained from the emperor the authorization to combat heresy in the part of Armenia under imperial control.

Pulcheria was also on the friendliest of terms with Cyril, patriarch of Alexandria (r. 412–444), who was chief bishop of the Christian Church in Africa and one of the great theologians of the day. Eventually Pulcheria became involved in the christological controversies of her time, disputes that erupted in the capital with the teachings of Nestorius and which revolved around the nature of Christ, particularly in what way Christ was to be accounted for as either God, man or both. Nestorius, patriarch of Constantinople (i.e. chief bishop of the Christian Church in Eastern Europe and Anatolia, 428–431), was born of Persian parentage at Germanicia (now Marash) in eastern Anatolia in the late 4th century. With the emperor's support, he had been zealous in the suppression of heresy in the eastern half of the empire. On November 22, 428, however, his domestic chaplain, Anastasius, preached a sermon denouncing the use of the term *theotokos* (Begetter of God) for *__Mary the Virgin__ on the grounds that Christ was but a man in whom God had dwelled, as in a temple, and that Mary was therefore mother only of Christ the man. In this, Anastasius was supported by Nestorius, who, that Christmas, began a series of sermons in the Cathedral of Constantinople (the old Hagia Sophia, replaced a century later by the one still standing in Istanbul); in these sermons, he affirmed that in Christ there existed two different and distinct persons, human and divine, united by an external, accidental, moral union. Denouncing the concept of the unity of God and man in Christ, he seemed almost to divide the God and man in Christ into two persons acting in concert. This new doctrine stirred up an enormous controversy, not only among theologians and clerics, but also among the common people, who were particularly offended by the rejection of the title "Mother of God" to which they had already developed a great devotion. Moreover, it pitted the so-called "Antiochene school" of theology against that of Alexandria, where different approaches to the understanding of the nature of Christ were beginning to take form largely through a differing theory of Biblical exegesis. At this juncture, Cyril intervened, writing to Nestorius in support of the doctrine of the unity of the divine and human natures in the one Christ and arguing that Mary the Virgin was thus indeed the "Mother of God."

Although Nestorius rebuffed the letter of Cyril, he had offended Empress Pulcheria with his doctrines. She influenced Theodosius to settle the issue by having her brother call for the convening of a church council at Ephesus. At the first session of the Council of Ephesus (431), the third so-called ecumenical council of the Christian Church, Cyril dominated the convocation. He represented not only himself but also Pope Celestine (r. 422–432), who was gravely alarmed by the teachings of Nestorius and whose position was in complete agreement with that of Cyril. Nestorius, who refused to attend the council, was condemned *in absentia,* removed from his patriarchate and banished to Syria. At the second session of the council, three bishops arrived from Rome as the pope's emissaries, and they approved the acts of the first session.

The third session of the council is of the greatest historical importance. It was here that one of the pope's delegates, Bishop Philip, proclaimed the undoubted primacy of the See of St. Peter, i.e. the papacy, and of the pope as the head of the Church. This pronunciamento was received without opposition or question, together with the assertion that this doctrine was centuries old. Four more sessions of the council were held which dealt, among other things, with the heretical teachings of the British prelate Pelagius (his name a Greek translation of the British Morgan, "man of the sea"), who denied the existence of original sin, and whose doctrine was likewise condemned. Four years later, when it became clear that Nestorius was still influential in his Syrian exile, he was banished to Petra in the Jordanian desert and later to Egypt, where he died (c. 451). As a result of the Council of Ephesus, Pulcheria was on good terms with both Cyril of Alexandria and Pope Leo I the Great. In this period of bitter theological and christological argument, her orthodoxy was beyond reproach as far as the mainstream of the Church was concerned.

The religious controversy that had engendered the Council of Ephesus surfaced again in 448. Flavian, patriarch of Constantinople—supported by dogmatic letters from Pope Leo I (the so-called Tome of Leo)—condemned Eutyches, abbot of a monastery near Constantinople. Eutyches taught a doctrine almost the exact opposite of Nestorius', namely that there was no human nature at all in Christ. He maintained that there existed only a divine nature in Christ, making Christ in effect simply God in the form of a man. This condemnation by Flavian of what amounted to the last great heresy of the age led Diocorius, patriarch of Alexandria, to convoke a new council at Ephesus in 449 (later known as "the robber council" because of the irregularities in its proceedings). But before the council opened in 451, a new emperor was reigning at Constantinople, and Pulcheria was at the height of her power as his consort and co-ruler.

Emperor Theodosius died in 450 from the effects of a fall from his horse while hunting. Because he left no son, his throne would naturally have passed to his son-in-law and cousin Valentinian III, still reigning at Ravenna. This was impractical, however, for the troubles in the West had made it clear that the reunion of the empire into a single political entity was not a particularly good idea at that time; the domination of Theodosius by the eunuch Chrysaphius—having been characterized by a series of raids across the eastern frontier of the empire as well as by an invasion of Huns in the Balkan Peninsula and a war with Persia—would have made such a union seem undesirable at Rome as well. On his deathbed, Theodosius indicated as his successor a certain Marcian, aide-de-camp of Aspar, master of the soldiers. Pulcheria probably had a hand in her brother's choice and, by agreeing to marry Marcian, she provided a needed link between the new emperor and the Theodosian dynasty.

Pulcheria herself duly crowned Marcian emperor on August 25, 450, in the Hebdomon Palace at Constantinople. At the very outset of his reign, he issued a gold coin showing himself and Pulcheria on one side with a depiction of victory and the cross on the obverse. The new emperor soon proved himself to be capable of decisive action. He executed the incompetent Chrysaphius, refused to pay tribute to the Huns, and was able to preserve the Eastern Empire untroubled during the storms that convulsed the West and which saw Rome besieged by the Huns (451) and sacked by the Vandals (455). Economically, he eased the burden of taxes in the empire, remitting arrears, yet left the treasury full at the time of his death. On her part, Pulcheria devoted herself to the adornment of Constantinople with new religious edifices including the churches of Our Lady of Blachernae; The Mother of God of Chalkopratreia, near Hagia Sophia; and The Mother of God of Hodegetria (Our Lady of Victory), on the eastern shore of the city, where she placed an icon of the Virgin sent to her from Jerusalem by her sister-in-law Eudocia.

Early in the reign of Marcian and Pulcheria, it was Pulcheria's influence that led the emperor to consider the calling of another ecumenical council to settle the old religious controversies anew. The new council—held at Chalcedon in the province of Bithynia across the Bosporus from Constantinople—opened on October 8, 451, with the consent of Pope Leo; its last session would be on November 1 of the same year. Of all the so-called ecumenical councils of the Church, from that of Nicea in 325 to that of Vatican II in 1962, this was by far the most truly ecumenical in terms of numbers. No less than 500 to 636 bishops were in attendance (depending on which of the surviving lists one consults), most of them coming from sees in the eastern provinces of the empire. It has also been the most controversial council of its kind.

The council opened under the presidency of Paschasinus, one of the three bishops sent by Pope Leo I to represent him at the conclave. Anatolius, the master of soldiers for the East, represented the emperor. From the very opening session, the council was dominated by the papal delegation from Rome, and there is no question that this conclave marked the zenith of the acceptance of papal supremacy in the East. By the end of the month-long gathering, Dioscurius had been deposed as patriarch of Alexandria, the Tome of Leo had been accepted, and, after violent debates, Eutyches was found innocent of heresy but his doctrine that in Jesus Christ there is but one nature had been rejected. The council asserted that in Jesus Christ the two natures, divine and human, each perfect and distinct, existed without mixture or change; without division or separation, these natures were said to be united in one person in the Word, the second person of the Trinity. The council thereby rejected the Nestorian doctrine that taught that in Jesus Christ there are two persons. The 30 canons of the council dealt largely with the curbing of clerical abuses, and canon 28 conceded to the see of Constantinople the second place among the patriarchates of the Christian Church, after that of Rome. In addition, Nestorius and all his ilk were once more condemned, and the presence of his disciple the theologian Theodoret of Cyprus was (unsuccessfully) denounced. Pulcheria—who with Marcian attended the session of October 25—was enthusiastically acclaimed by the bishops and publicly praised for her orthodoxy: "The Empress drove out Nestorius—long live the orthodox Empress."

In noting the triumph of Marcian and Pulcheria at Chalcedon, it is important to realize the political implications of their victory there. As the capital of the Eastern Empire, it was necessary for Constantinople to be also the seat of orthodoxy. This Pulcheria accomplished by siding with Cyril of Alexandria and the pope at Ephesus, and she repeated her accomplishment here at Chalcedon. Just as the Council of Ephesus had humbled the position of the Patriarchate of Antioch in the Christian Church, so did the Council of Chalcedon humble that of Alexandria. The reason for supporting the papal position in both cases was based on the fact that Rome, lying as it did in the Western Empire, posed no challenge—at least at that time—to the position of Constantinople as the font of orthodoxy in the East. Unfortunately, we do not know the details of Pulcheria's involvement in all of these affairs or even of her consciousness of all of their implications; but that she was involved we do know and it seems difficult to doubt that a woman as intelligent as she obviously was would not have been aware at least to some degree of the political ramifications involved in the otherwise religious controversies of the day.

The Council of Chalcedon was a failure, however, when it came to unifying the beliefs of the Christian Church, for its doctrines went against the christological position of most of the theologians of the East. The Nestorian Church not only remained unshaken in eastern Syria, Mesopotamia, the Persian Empire and beyond, but the west Syrian, Egyptian, Ethiopian and Armenian Christians seceded to form the so-called Monophysite Churches. Even the estranged Empress Eudocia, retired in Jerusalem, showed herself sympathetic to the Monophysites though she died a devout Orthodox Christian. After Chalcedon, Orthodox, i.e. mainstream, Christianity in the Middle East was confined almost exclusively to the Anatolian peninsula, while the Church of Persia clearly accepted the teachings of Nestorius at the Council of Seleucia held in 498. The christological problems that had engendered the Council of Chalcedon survived Marcian and Pulcheria both, and all of the succeeding emperors as late as Justinian (d. 565) had to deal with them in one way or another. The name of Marcian was regularly denounced in the polemical literature of Monophysite Christianity, usually in concert with that of "the wicked Pulcheria."

After what must have appeared to her and to her contemporaries as a full and rewarding life, Empress Pulcheria died in 453 at about 53 or 54 years of age. In her will, she left all of her wealth to the poor, a bequest honored by her husband. Marcian died in January 457, aged 65. He left his throne to his steward, Leo I, whereupon the dynasty founded by Theodosius the Great at last came to an end. Nineteen years later, the Roman Empire fell in the West; the Eastern Empire, so ably governed by Pulcheria, survived the disaster and endured for another 1,000 years.

As the Roman emperors were deified in pagan times, it is not surprising to find that for some time after the conversion of the Romans to Christianity emperors were canonized as saints, a practice that persisted through much of the 5th century. Marcian (the first emperor to be crowned by the Church) and Pulcheria—twin paragons of orthodoxy and *personae gratissimae* at Rome—were both duly canonized as well. His feast is on February 17. Her dual feasts are celebrated on February 17 and August 7. A rich medallion of Pulcheria preserved in the British Museum shows us an attractive woman with a prominent chin and a "Roman" nose, but it is unlikely to have been an actual portrait.

Like her aunt Galla Placidia, who guided the Western Roman Empire during the minority of her son Valentinian III, Pulcheria had far more character than the emperor for whom she served as regent. The Roman world, disastrous as this period was for it, was fortunate that the women of the imperial family were both willing and able to assert some sort of direction in the affairs of state. The role of Empress Pulcheria in guiding the Eastern Roman Empire through so many of its most perilous early years, as well as the important role she played in generating the councils of Ephesus and Chalcedon, two of the most significant events in the annals of the Christian Church, assure her a permanent place as one of the most important women in history.

SOURCES:

Oost, Stewart Irwin. *Galla Placidia Augusta*. Chicago, IL: University of Chicago, 1968.

SUGGESTED READING:

Bury, J.B. *The Later Roman Empire*. Vol. II. NY: Dover, 1958.

Ostrogorsky, George. *The History of the Byzantine State*. New Brunswick, NJ: Rutgers University Press, 1957.

RELATED MEDIA:

Pulcheria has been depicted in *Sign of the Pagan* (92 min. film), starring Jeff Chandler, Jack Palance, and **Ludmilla Tcherina**, directed by Douglas Sirk, 1954, and at least one other motion picture dealing with Attila the Hun. In one, she was portrayed as a beautiful siren, in the other as a virtuous heroine.

Robert H. Hewsen,
Professor of History, Rowan University, Glassboro, New Jersey, and author of a book and several articles relevant to late Roman and Byzantine history

Pulcheria (fl. 800s)

Roman noblewoman. *Flourished in the 800s; daughter of Theophilus I (r. 829–842) and ****Theodora the Blessed****, empress and regent of Eastern Roman Empire (r. 842–856).*

Pulitzer, Mrs. Ralph (1893–1974).

See Leech, Margaret.

Pulver, Lilo (1929—)

Swiss-born actress. *Name variations: Liselotte Pulver. Born on October 11, 1929, in Berne, Switzerland.*

Selected filmography: Swiss Tour *(*Four Days Leave, *Switz.-US, 1949);* Föhn *(1950);* Heidelberger Romanze *(1951);* Klettermaxe *(1952);* Ich and Du *(1953);* Uli der Knecht *(Switz., 1954);* Der letzte Sommer *(1954);* Hanussen *(1955);* Les Aventures d'Arsène Lupin *(Fr., 1956);* Bekenntnisse des Hochstaplers Felix Krull *(*The Confessions of Felix Krull, *1957);* Das Wirtshaus im Spessart *(*The Spessart Inn, *1958);* A Time to Love and a Time to Die *(US, 1958);* Le Joueur *(Fr., 1958);* Helden *(*Arms and the Man, *1959);* Buddenbrooks *(1959);* Das Glas Wasser *(*A Glass of Water, *1960);* One Two Three *(US, 1961);* Maléfices *(*Where the Truth Lies, *Fr., 1962);* Lafayette *(Fr.-It., 1962);* Monsieur *(Fr.-It.-Ger., 1964);* A Global Affair *(US, 1964);* La Religieuse *(*The Nun, *Fr., 1965);* L'Ombrellone *(*Weekend Italian Style, *It.-Fr.-Sp., 1966);* Hokuspokus *(1966);* Pistol Jenny *(1969);* Brot und Steine *(Switz., 1979).*

Trained for the stage in her native Berne, and discovered by the famed director Leopold Lindtberg (1902–1984), actress Lilo Pulver starred in German films and in European co-productions during the 1950s and 1960s. She portrayed a number of notable characters on screen, among them Antonie Buddenbrook in an adaptation of Thomas Mann's *Buddenbrooks* (1959), Queen *****Anne*** in *Das Glas Wasser* (*A Glass of Water*, 1960), and *****Marie Antoinette*** in *Lafayette* (1962). Pulver's American films include *A Time to Love and a Time to Die* (1958), *One Two Three* (1961), and *A Global Affair* (1964).

Purser, Sarah (1848–1943)

Irish artist and patron who founded The Tower of Glass, an Irish stained-glass workshop. *Born Sarah Henrietta Purser in Kingstown (Dun Laoghaire), County Dublin, Ireland, on March 22, 1848; died in Dublin on August 7, 1943; daughter of Benjamin Purser and Anne (Mallet) Purser; educated at Moravian school in Switzerland; never married.*

Sarah Henrietta Purser was born in Kingstown (Dun Laoghaire), County Dublin, Ireland, in 1848, the daughter of Benjamin Purser and **Anne Mallet Purser**. The Pursers, a family of brewers who came to Ireland in the 18th century from Gloucestershire, England, all worked for Arthur Guinness' brewery, including Sarah's grandfather, uncle, and father, but there was also an academic tradition in the family. Sarah's father taught at Portora Royal School in County Fermanagh (where one of his pupils was Oscar Wilde), and two of her brothers would become professors at Trinity College Dublin. Sarah and her sisters received a good education at a Moravian school in Switzerland, where they became fluent in French, but when their schooldays were over they were expected to live at home until they married. Benjamin set up two breweries of his own but eventually converted them to flour mills which were initially prosperous. In 1873, however, the business collapsed, and Sarah knew she would have to earn her own living.

Purser was a competent artist and had already exhibited at the Royal Hibernian Academy, but she decided to go to Paris to improve her skills to a professional standard. In 1878, she spent six months working in the "ladies' section" of the Académie Julien, where her fellow students included the Swiss artist ➤ **Louise Breslau**, who became a lifelong friend, and the Russian artist ***Marie Bashkirtseff**, whose diaries later became a bestseller. When she returned to Dublin, Purser quickly secured important commissions, among them a portrait of sisters ***Constance Markievicz** and ***Eva Gore-Booth**, and by the late 1880s she had financial security augmented by shrewd investments in Guinness company shares. **Elizabeth Coxhead** observes that as an interpreter of styles evolved by others, Purser was artistically in the first rank, but she started her career too late to have a truly original artistic vision. Coxhead also notes that Purser was happiest when painting clever people, especially clever men. Her portraits of women were more conventional and banal.

With the advent of such artists as Nathaniel Hone and J.B. Yeats, and interested patrons like Edward Martyn and Hugh Lane, the Dublin art scene became more stimulating. In 1886, Purser was a founder member of the Dublin Art Club with J.B. Yeats and Walter Osborne. She befriended Yeats and his family, though the artist's improvidence frequently exasperated her, and she took a particular interest in his son, Jack B. Yeats, whose gifts she quickly appreciated and whom she helped by securing commissions and other work. Purser displayed similar generosity to generations of Irish artists; less welcome to some were her constant scoldings and chivvying. Purser traveled to Europe every year and kept up with new developments in painting. It was through her interest in Impressionism that she came to know Edward Martyn, who in 1898 founded the Irish Literary Theatre with W.B. Yeats and ***Augusta Gregory**. In 1899, Purser helped to organize a major exhibition in Dublin of works by Corot, Courbet, Degas, Manet, Monet and others, which made a considerable impact. She became close friends with Hugh Lane, whom she encouraged in his dream of building up a collection of modern paintings in Dublin. At her instigation, Lane gave commissions to J.B. Yeats.

Martyn was much concerned about standards of Irish ecclesiastical architecture and particularly the quality of stained glass. When he suggested the idea of a stained-glass workshop to Purser, the idea had already been germinating in her mind. She persuaded the Dublin College of Art to revise its curriculum to include arts needed for church decoration, and she visited the studio of Christopher Whall, one of the leading stained-glass artists in England, who promised her the services of his best student, A.E. Childe. Purser found premises in Dublin and in January 1903 An Túr Gloine (Thoor Glinna), The Tower of Glass, opened. It became one of the finest stained-glass workshops in the world and produced generations of gifted artists, among them Michael Healy, ***Catherine O'Brien**, ***Wilhelmina Geddes**, ***Ethel Rhind** and Hubert MacGoldrick.

In 1911, Purser and her brother John moved to Mespil House in Dublin, a beautiful 18th-cen-

➤ Breslau, Louise (1857–1927)

Swiss artist. Born in 1857 (some sources cite 1856); died in 1927.

Swiss artist Louise Breslau enjoyed an early success in the salons of Paris. Once considered a better artist than ***Marie Bashkirtseff**, Breslau is now known chiefly as an object of envy in Bashkirtseff's famous diaries, though ***Janet Flanner** thought her a "superior painter" and perhaps a "superior person." Breslau, who won many medals for her work, was awarded the Chevalier de la Légion. In 1937, her paintings were included in the retrospective section of the "Les Femmes Artistes de l'Europe" exhibition, which was held at the Musée du Jeu de Paume and the Metropolitan Museum of New York.

SOURCES:

Flanner, Janet. *Paris Was Yesterday.* NY: Viking, 1972.

tury dwelling with magnificent plaster ceilings. Here she held her famous "Second Tuesdays," on the second Tuesday of every month, when she was at home to visitors. It became the most notable salon in Dublin, where artists, politicians, writers, academics and professional people of every shade of opinion gathered and conversed. Purser described herself as a Protestant Unionist but accepted Irish independence when it came in 1922 and became friendly with the new leader of the Irish Free State, W.T. Cosgrave. In 1924, she founded the Friends of the National Collections of Ireland, still in existence, which donated many works to Irish galleries and museums. In 1928, she persuaded Cosgrave to donate Charlemont House as a new Dublin Municipal Gallery, to be named after Hugh Lane who had died in the *Lusitania* sinking in 1915. She and Augusta Gregory were unremitting in their efforts to secure the return of Lane's Impressionist paintings to Ireland. Purser was also instrumental in establishing art history courses at Trinity College and University College Dublin which have since produced respected scholars and museum directors. Her last public service was to list the works from the National Gallery of Ireland to be removed to safety when World War II broke out.

Although in her 90s, Purser was undaunted by the privations of the war, including the chronic shortage of fuel in Ireland. The war curtailed her foreign travel, but she went regularly to the west of Ireland. She died at the age of 95, in 1943, following a stroke.

SOURCES:

Coxhead, Elizabeth. "Sarah Purser and the Tower of Glass," in *Daughters of Erin: Five Women of the Irish Renascence.* London: Secker & Warburg, 1965.

O'Grady, John. *The Life and Work of Sarah Purser.* Dublin: Four Courts Press, 1996.

Deirdre McMahon,
lecturer in history at Mary Immaculate College,
University of Limerick, Limerick, Ireland

Purviance, Edna (1894–1958)

American actress who appeared in silent films opposite Charlie Chaplin from 1915 to 1923. *Pronunciation: per-VY-unce. Born in Loeclock, Paradise Valley, Nevada, in 1894; died in 1958.*

Selected filmography: The Champion *(1915);* In the Park *(1915);* A Jitney Elopement *(1915);* The Tramp *(1915);* By the Sea *(1915);* Work *(1915);* A Woman *(1915);* The Bank *(1915);* Shanghaied *(1915);* A Night in the Show *(1915);* Burlesque on Carmen *(1916);* Police *(1916);* Triple Trouble *(1916);* The Floorwalker *(1916);* The Fireman *(1916);* The Vagabond *(1916);* The Count *(1916);* The Pawnshop *(1916);* Behind the Screen *(1916);* The Rink *(1916);* Easy Street *(1917);* The Cure *(1917);* The Immigrant *(1917);* The Adventurer *(1917);* A Dog's Life *(1918);* The Bond *(1918);* Shoulder Arms *(1918);* Sunnyside *(1919);* A Day's Pleasure *(1919);* The Kid *(1921);* The Idle Class *(1921);* Pay Day *(1922);* The Pilgrim *(1923);* A Woman of Paris *(1923);* L'Education de Prince *(Fr., 1926);* A Woman of the Sea *(*The Sea Gull*, 1926);* Monsieur Verdoux *(extra, 1947);* Limelight *(extra, 1952).*

Born in Paradise Valley, Nevada, in 1894, Edna Purviance was working as a typist in San Francisco when she visited Essanay Studios on a trip to Hollywood in 1915 and was invited to make a screen test. Charlie Chaplin, who had just joined Essanay from Keystone, saw the test and cast the pretty blue-eyed blonde as his leading lady in *The Champion* (1915). Purviance continued to star in most of Chaplin's films until 1923, when the relationship soured. When she subsequently starred in *A Woman of the Sea*, under the direction of Josef von Sternberg, Chaplin, as producer, refused to release the film for some time. Despite the falling out, Chaplin kept the actress under contract and later used her as an extra in two of his sound films, *Monsieur Verdoux* (1947) and *Limelight* (1952). Purviance died in 1958.

SOURCES:

Finch, John Richard. *Close-Ups: From the Golden Age of the Silent Cinema.* NY: A.S. Barnes, 1978.

Katz, Ephraim. *The Film Encyclopedia.* NY: HarperCollins, 1994.

Barbara Morgan,
Melrose, Massachusetts

Purvis, Harriet Forten (1810–1875)

African-American abolitionist. *Name variations: Harriet Forten; Hattie Purvis. Born Harriet Davy Forten in 1810 in Philadelphia, Pennsylvania; died of tuberculosis on June 11, 1875, in Philadelphia; daughter of James Forten (b. 1766, a wealthy businessman) and his second wife Charlotte (Vandine) Forten; sister of Sarah Forten Purvis (c. 1811–c. 1898) and Margaretta Forten (1808–1875); aunt of Charlotte Forten Grimké (1837–1914); attended a private black academy in Philadelphia; married Robert Purvis, on September 13, 1831; children: William Purvis (b. 1832); Joseph Parrish Purvis (b. 1837);* ***Harriet Purvis*** *(b. 1839, an abolitionist and suffragist); Charles Burleigh Purvis (b. 1840 or 1841); Henry Purvis (b. 1843 or 1844); Robert Purvis (b. 1844 or 1845); Granville Sharp Purvis (b. 1845 or 1846);* ***Georgianna Purvis*** *(b. 1848 or 1849).*

Born into a well-to-do, free black family in Philadelphia in 1810, Harriet Forten Purvis was the second child of **Charlotte Vandine Forten** and James Forten, an entrepreneur. Harriet was named after the daughter of Robert Bridges, a white associate of her father's who helped him launch a sailmaking business.

Her family's wealth ensured an excellent education for Harriet and her siblings. James Forten did not want his children to attend the schools to which blacks were relegated, convinced they would receive an inadequate education. When he could not enroll them in some of Philadelphia's exclusive schools, he joined with **Grace Bustill Douglass** to set up their own school which was designed to offer its black students the same sort of curriculum as was offered in the city's white-only private academies. To supplement their education, Harriet and her sisters were tutored at home in music and languages. The Fortens had long been ardent champions of abolition, and their household often provided a forum for those of like mind, both black and white, including the abolitionist poet John Greenleaf Whittier.

Harriet was to marry the wealthy Robert Purvis, the illegitimate son of William Purvis, an English immigrant who did well as a cotton merchant, and **Harriet Judah** (c. 1784–1869), a free woman of German-Jewish and North African lineage. Robert Purvis and his brother Joseph Purvis developed a close relationship with the Fortens. After the death of their father William, James Forten became almost a surrogate father to Robert who, while light-skinned enough to pass as white, impressed James with the pride he exhibited in his African heritage. Harriet and Robert were married on September 13, 1831, in a ceremony presided over by a white Episcopalian bishop.

After initially living with the Fortens, the couple moved in June 1832 to a two-story brick house on Philadelphia's Lombard Street which Robert purchased for about $3,000. There, later that year, the couple's first child, a son William, was born. Both Robert and Harriet were strong believers in abolition, a cause for which Robert lectured. In 1834, he sailed for England to spread the message there, while Harriet remained in Philadelphia to care for their son and advance the anti-slavery cause at home. A longtime member of the Philadelphia Female Anti-Slavery Society, an interracial organization, Purvis served the group in a variety of capacities, as did her mother and her sisters ***Margaretta Forten** and ***Sarah Forten (Purvis)**. Purvis' brothers and her husband were all called upon to speak at the society's functions from time to time. Purvis often served on the committee responsible for planning the group's annual Christmas fair. In 1837, she was pregnant with her second child when she joined Margaretta and Sarah in attending the first Women's Anti-Slavery Convention (organized by ***Lucretia Mott**) in New York. When the second convention was held in Philadelphia the following year, she unwittingly became the subject of a violent protest when onlookers saw Robert, whom they took to be white, assist her from their carriage. A mob, mistaking them for an interracial couple, rioted, incorrectly concluding that this was a meeting of "amalgamationists," and the newly built Pennsylvania Hall, site of the convention, was destroyed. The mob scenes, however, left Harriet undeterred, and she would return a year later for Philadelphia's final female antislavery convention.

From 1845 to 1850, Robert was president of the Pennsylvania Anti-Slavery Society in which Harriet was also active, and the couple traveled frequently in support of abolition. In May 1840, the two attended the society's annual convention in Harrisburg, Purvis as a delegate from Philadelphia's Female Anti-Slavery Society. Not long after, the couple attended a meeting of the American Anti-Slavery Society in New York. In 1854, Purvis traveled with her younger brother Robert Bridges Forten to Boston, where runaway slave Anthony Burns was tried. The court's decision ordering Burns returned to his owner in Virginia left a lasting mark on their memories.

The Purvises' commitment to the abolitionist cause seemed to deepen as their family grew. Between 1832 and 1849, Harriet had a total of eight children, and she found herself facing the same prejudice her parents had combated years before to ensure a quality education for her and her siblings. With their children barred entrance to Philadelphia's better public schools due to their race, Robert refused to pay his school tax. Some of the older Purvis children were sent to integrated schools in New York and New Jersey. To see to the education of her younger children, Purvis enlisted the help of her niece ***Charlotte Forten Grimké** (daughter of Robert Bridges Forten), in whom she took a particular interest. The Purvis family was now ensconced in a mansion on 104 acres in Philadelphia County's Byberry Township, for which Robert Purvis had paid $13,000.

Purvis had a lifelong love of literature, a passion she shared with her husband. The two became founding members of the Gilbert

Lyceum, a society dedicated to the discussion of literary and cultural issues, which was unusual in the free black community of the time because of its acceptance of both male and female members. The Purvis household served as an intellectual meeting place for some of the more thoughtful and progressive members of Philadelphia society, and the family's dedication to the abolition of slavery attracted visits from some of the most outspoken abolitionists in the country, including William Lloyd Garrison, ***Sarah P. Remond**, ***Susan B. Anthony**, and Daniel Alexander Payne.

Not only did the Purvises spread the word on abolition, but they also broke the law in order to shelter runaway slaves. After hiding fugitives during the 1830s in their Philadelphia home, they had a secret room constructed in the Byberry house before they moved in. For many years, the Purvises opened their home to escaped slaves whom they fed, clothed, and financed, while arranging for them to make their way north to Canada. Among those whom they sheltered was Madison Washington, who went on to participate in a mutiny which would bring him and his fellow slaves aboard the *Creole* to freedom. The Purvises provided help to Joseph Cinque and other *Amistad* captives, and they took Daniel Webster into their home after his Philadelphia capture and subsequent release, arranging for his journey to Canada. After passage of the 13th Amendment outlawing slavery, the Purvises continued to struggle against the discrimination and injustice suffered by people of color in both the North and the South.

The Purvises lost three of their sons to tuberculosis, the disease that also claimed Purvis' life on June 11, 1875, in Philadelphia. She was buried in the city's Germantown section at the Friends Fair Hill Burial Ground. Robert outlived Harriet by nearly 23 years. Two of their sons followed in their footsteps, as did their daughter Hattie Purvis who gave her energies to abolition and then to the battle for the political rights of women.

SOURCES:

Smith, Jessie Carney, ed. *Notable Black American Women*. Detroit, MI: Gale Research, 1992.

Don Amerman,
freelance writer, Saylorsburg, Pennsylvania

Purvis, Sarah Forten

(c. 1811–c. 1898)

African-American poet and abolitionist. *Name variations: Sarah Forten; (pseudonyms) Ada, Magawisca, Sarah Louisa. Born Sarah Louisa Forten sometime between 1811 and 1814 in Philadelphia, Pennsylvania; died around 1898 (though some sources indicate as early as 1883) in Philadelphia; daughter of James Forten (b. 1766, a wealthy businessman) and his second wife Charlotte (Vandine) Forten; sister of Harriet Forten Purvis (1810–1875) and Margaretta Forten (1808–1875); aunt of* ****Charlotte Forten Grimké*** *(1837–1914); educated in a private black academy in Philadelphia; married Joseph Purvis, on January 7, 1838 (died 1857); children: Joseph Purvis (b. 1838 or 1839); James Purvis (c. 1839–1870); William Purvis (b. 1841 or 1842); Sarah Purvis (b. 1842 or 1843); Emily Purvis (1844–1870s); Alfred Purvis (c. 1845–1865); Harriet Purvis (b. 1847 or 1848); Alexander Purvis (b. 1850).*

Selected writings: "Grave of the Slave" (1831); "Hours of Childhood"; "Past Joys"; "The Abuse of Liberty"; "The Slave"; "The Slave Girl's Farewell." Also contributed poems, letters, and articles to the Liberator, *a prominent anti-slavery magazine published by William Lloyd Garrison, when she was 19 or 20.*

Like her mother **Charlotte Vandine Forten** and sisters ***Margaretta Forten** and ***Harriet Forten Purvis**, Sarah Forten Purvis was a dedicated abolitionist. She had a gift for poetry and writing in general which she put to work in the struggle to end slavery in the United States.

She was born Sarah Louisa Forten sometime between 1811 and 1814 in Philadelphia, the third of eight children of wealthy businessman James Forten and his second wife Charlotte Vandine Forten. Her father refused to send his children to Philadelphia's blacks-only schools, which offered a level of education he considered inferior to that offered to the city's white children. Banding together with a number of other affluent black parents, he and **Grace Bustill Douglass** set up a school which offered its students an education equal to that of Philadelphia's whites-only private schools. Sarah and her siblings were also tutored at home in such subjects as music and languages, and visitors to the Forten home on Lombard Street described the daughters as refined and talented. Like some of her brothers, Sarah was noted for her singing voice. She was also an avid reader.

Raised in a family with a strong commitment to abolition, Purvis was keenly aware of the horrors of slavery and racial prejudice despite the degree of insulation provided to the Forten children by the family's wealth. In an 1837 letter to abolitionist ***Angelina Grimké**, she wrote: "For our own family—we have to thank a kind Providence for placing us in a situation that has hitherto prevented us from falling under the weight of this evil. We feel it but in a slight degree compared with many others. . . . We are not disturbed in our social relations—we never travel far from home and seldom go to public places unless quite sure that admission is free to all—therefore, we meet with none of the mortifications which might otherwise ensue."

While only 19 or 20, Purvis began submitting poems under the name "Ada" to the *Liberator,* an abolitionist journal published by William Lloyd Garrison. The first of these, "The Grave of the Slave," observed that in death the enslaved would know equality and rest. The poem appeared in the January 22, 1831, issue and concluded with the words:

> Poor slave! Shall we sorrow that death was thy
> friend,
> The last, and the kindest, that heaven could send?
> The grave to the weary is welcomed and blest;
> And death, to the captive, is freedom and rest.

The identity of "Ada" was disclosed to Garrison by her father following the journal's publication of two poems by Purvis.

In late 1833, Purvis, along with her mother and older sisters Harriet and Margaretta, joined in the founding of the Philadelphia Female Anti-Slavery Society, an organization she would later serve as a member of its board of managers. She also participated in the society's campaigns to abolish slavery in the District of Columbia. Purvis was to remain active in the affairs of the society until she married and left Philadelphia. Her life—friends, correspondence, poetry, and activism—was dominated by the cause of abolition. In February 1834, she published "An Appeal to Woman," likely her most well-known poem, in the *Liberator.* (More than three years later, a portion of this poem would be reprinted by delegates to the first women's antislavery convention who included it in their *Appeal to the Women of the Nominally Free State.*) In the poem, Purvis looked to white women "to nobly dare to act a Christian's part":

> Dare to be good, as thou canst dare be great,
> Despise the taunts of envy, scorn and hate;
> Our 'skins may differ,' but from thee we claim
> A sister's privilege, in a sister's name.

In a civil ceremony, Sarah Forten married Joseph Purvis on January 7, 1838, in Burlington Country, New Jersey. Joseph was the younger brother of Robert Purvis, who had married Sarah's sister Harriet. The Purvis brothers were the sons of cotton merchant William Purvis, an English immigrant, and his mistress, the free-born **Harriet Judah**, a native of Charleston, South Carolina, whose ancestry was German-Jewish and North African. Joseph and Robert were the primary heirs of their father's estate, and Joseph used his inheritance to acquire a 200-acre farm in Bensalem, Bucks County.

Shortly after their marriage, Joseph brought Sarah to live on the farm, where she found a very different life. In the 12 years following her marriage, Purvis gave birth to eight children. Her responsibilities as a farm wife and mother of a large family left her little time to write poetry. (Although poems signed "Ada" continued to make appearances in antislavery works, these are thought to have been written by another author due to their references to a childhood spent in New England and to the Quaker dating style employed by the author.) By producing grain, meat, dairy products, and honey, the farm provided well for the family in the 1840s and early 1850s. Like his brother, Joseph traded in real estate, and until his death the family enjoyed some of the benefits of wealth. For instance, the federal census records of 1850 indicate that he was able to employ six people at the farm, two servants to be of help to Sarah in the house and four farm workers to help in the fields.

His sudden death in 1857, however, marked the beginning of an end to Sarah's financial comfort. He left no will and cash reserves were insufficient to pay off his debts. Sarah decided to waive her right to act as administrator, and to satisfy Joseph's creditors authorities ordered the sale of portions of his real-estate holdings. With children still to raise, Purvis was left with no money to properly maintain the Bensalem farm, which gradually slipped into a state of disrepair. By 1871, the estate of Joseph Purvis had shrunk to three small properties, totaling 40 acres and two dwellings. By 1875, Sarah was forced into bankruptcy, and her meager possessions were sold off under court order.

During less than a decade, Purvis experienced the loss of three of her children. She returned to the family home on Philadelphia's Lombard Street with two others, Annie and William. After the death of her unmarried older sister Margaretta in 1875, Sarah assumed Margaretta's responsibility for running the household. Sarah Purvis continued to live in the Forten family home until her death, the exact date of which is not known. She is buried in an unmarked grave in the cemetery of St. James the Less, an Episcopal church in Philadelphia.

SOURCES:

Winch, Julie. "Sarah Forten Purvis," in *Notable Black American Women.* Jessie Carney Smith, ed. Detroit, MI: Gale Research, 1992.

Don Amerman,
freelance writer, Saylorsburg, Pennsylvania

Putli Bai (1929–1958).

See Phoolan Devi for sidebar.

Putnam, Alice Whiting (1841–1919)

American educator who used the theories of Friedrich Froebel to help establish the kindergarten movement in Chicago. *Born Alice Harvey Whiting on January 18, 1841, in Chicago, Illinois; died of nephritis on January 19, 1919, in Chicago; daughter of William Loring Whiting (a commission merchant and a founder of the Chicago Board of Trade) and Mary (Starr) Whiting; attended a private school run by her mother and sister and then schooled at Dearborn Seminary; married Joseph Robie Putnam (in real estate), on May 20, 1868; children: Charlotte Putnam; Alice Putnam; Helen Putnam; Henry Sibley Putnam.*

Alice Putnam was born in Chicago in 1841, the youngest of three daughters of William Loring Whiting, a founder of the Chicago Board of Trade, and **Mary Starr Whiting.** Her family's wealth made it possible for her to attend private schools, including one run by her mother and sister, and the nearby Dearborn Seminary.

Putnam first became interested in the kindergarten movement early in her marriage while trying to find quality educational opportunities for the two eldest of her four children. She was attracted by Friedrich Froebel's educational theories relating to the importance of kindergartens and enrolled at a training school in Columbus, Ohio, to learn more about them. After she graduated, she opened a kindergarten in her Chicago home dedicated to promoting self-expression and social interaction in her young charges. This small beginning created enough interest and support to generate two related organizations in Chicago. Putnam took on the task of supervising the training of kindergarten teachers for the Chicago Froebel Association for 30 years, beginning in 1880. The 800-plus graduates of the school spread its philosophy throughout the United States and abroad.

Despite the greater recognition of the importance of kindergartens, the movement still had not received authorization by the Chicago Board of Education to become part of the public school system. However, Putnam's diplomacy resulted in the board permitting a test kindergarten class in a public school in 1886. Six years later, the number of kindergartens in public schools had grown to ten; they proved so successful that the Board of Education agreed to incorporate them into the city system. Soon enough, the establishment of public school kindergartens fell entirely under the jurisdiction of the board.

Putnam did not ease up on her kindergarten activities with this victory, but continued to contribute to the movement through her participation in the Chicago Kindergarten Club, which she and ***Elizabeth Harrison** founded in 1883. In addition to acting as president of the club, Putnam assumed the same role in the International Kindergarten Union. In 1906, she became a reader in education at the University of Chicago, offering a course for mothers and a course on kindergarten theory.

In her later years, Putnam became nearsighted and overweight, and illness eventually forced her to give up the superintendency of the Froebel Association Training School in 1910 and her university courses during the 1916–17 school term. She spent her last years with her children and grandchildren in Pennsylvania and New York. She returned to Chicago some weeks before her death from nephritis on January 19, 1919. She was buried in Oak Woods Cemetery in Chicago.

SOURCES:

Edgerly, Lois Stiles, ed. *Give Her This Day.* Gardiner, ME: Tilbury House, 1990.

James, Edward T., ed. *Notable American Women, 1607–1950.* Cambridge, MA: The Belknap Press of Harvard University, 1971.

Jo Anne Meginnes,
freelance writer, Brookfield, Vermont

Putnam, Ann.

See Witchcraft Trials in Salem Village.

Putnam, Bertha Haven (1872–1960)

American expert on medieval English legal and economic history who was a professor at Mt. Holyoke College for 29 years. *Born on March 1, 1872, in New York City; died on February 26, 1960, in South Hadley, Massachusetts; eldest of four daughters of George Haven Putnam (d. 1930, head of publishing firm G.P. Putnam's Sons) and Rebecca Kettel (Shepard) Putnam (d. 1895); stepdaughter of Emily James Putnam (1865–1944); attended Miss Audobon's School and Miss Gibbons' School, both New York City; Bryn Mawr College, A.B., 1893; Columbia University, Ph.D., 1908; never married; no children.*

Scholar and teacher Bertha Haven Putnam was born in 1872 in New York City and grew up in a privileged household filled with educational opportunities and unique social contacts. Her father George Haven Putnam, who served in the

Union army during the Civil War, later took over his father's publishing business, which evolved into G.P. Putnam's Sons. Her mother **Rebecca Putnam** had attended Antioch College, but left to nurse in a military hospital. She later taught high school and, following her marriage, was active in introducing kindergartens into the New York City school system. Bertha, who persuaded her mother to teach her Greek at the age of ten, attended exclusive schools in New York City, and graduated from Bryn Mawr College in 1893. She began her career in education as a teacher of Latin at the Bryn Mawr School in Baltimore. When her mother died in 1895, she returned home to serve as her father's hostess until his marriage to ***Emily James Putnam** in 1899. While living at home, Bertha taught special classes at the Brearley School and began graduate study at Columbia University. After receiving her Ph.D. in 1908, she became an instructor in history at Mt. Holyoke College, working her way up to full professor in 1924.

Putnam's interest in English legal and economic history was sparked by historian Charles M. Andrews at Bryn Mawr and by sociologist F.W. Giddings at Columbia. While researching her doctoral dissertation, *The Enforcement of the Statutes of Labourers during the First Decade after the Black Death, 1349–1359* (published in 1908), Putnam studied the justices of the peace, to whom the responsibility for labor legislation and enforcement later fell. Thereafter, the justices of the peace became her field of expertise and the subject of most of her writings, which included numerous articles and the editing of several volumes, among them *Proceedings Before the Justices of the Peace in the Fourteenth and Fifteenth Centuries, Edward III to Richard III* (1938), the culmination of 30 years of research for which she received the first Haskins Medal awarded from the Mediaeval Academy of America.

In addition to her impeccable research, Putnam was a stimulating and effective teacher, with a keen sense of humor. She was always eager to assist honor and graduate students as well as young faculty members, and along with chair ***Nellie Neilson** brought a great deal of prestige to the history department at Mt. Holyoke. Putnam's work, much of it done in England, was also recognized and honored outside her own institution. She received fellowships from the American Association of University Women, and research grants from the American Council of Learned Societies, and was the first woman and nonlawyer to receive a research grant from Harvard Law School (1938). She was elected a fellow of the Mediaeval Academy in 1949.

Putnam retired from Mt. Holyoke in 1937, after which she served as a lecturer at Bryn Mawr for a year while continuing her scholarly research. In the late 1940s, however, an attack of shingles left her partially blind and unable to work. Putnam died in 1960.

SOURCES:

Sicherman, Barbara, and Carol Hurd Green, eds. *Notable American Women: The Modern Period*. Cambridge, MA: The Belknap Press of Harvard University, 1980.

Barbara Morgan,
Melrose, Massachusetts

Putnam, Emily James (1865–1944)

American author and educator who was the first dean of Barnard College. *Born Emily James Smith in Canandaigua, New York, on April 15, 1865; died in Kingston, Jamaica, on September 7, 1944; second daughter and youngest of five children of Judge James Cosslett Smith and Emily Ward (Adams) Smith; Bryn Mawr, A.B., 1889; attended Girton College, Cambridge, 1889–90 (one of the first American women to do so); became the second wife of George Haven Putnam (head of the publishing firm G.P. Putnam's Sons), on April 27, 1899 (died 1930); children: Palmer Cosslett Putnam (b. 1900, an author of scientific and technical works); (stepdaughter) Bertha Haven Putnam (1872–1960).*

After graduating with the first class from Bryn Mawr in 1889, Emily James Putnam became a teacher of Greek at the Packer Collegiate Institute in Brooklyn (1891–93), was appointed a fellow in Greek at the University of Chicago (1893–94), and later served as first dean and associate in history at the five-year-old Barnard College, at Columbia University (1894–1900). Over those six years, she succeeded in enhancing Barnard's academic reputation by tightening the connection with Columbia: sharing its professors, libraries, labs, and other facilities.

In April 1899, she married George Haven Putnam, the publisher (and father of ***Bertha Haven Putnam**), who was 21 years her senior. For some years, Emily Putnam was president of the League for Political Education (1901–04) and vice president and manager of the Women's University Club, New York. Besides translations from the Greek, she is the author of *The Lady: Studies of Certain Significant Phases of Her History* (1913), which the *North American Review* once declared to be "the most brilliant book of essays ever written by an American woman." Putnam also helped establish the New School for Social Research in 1919 and was a regular lecturer there. After retiring from Barnard in 1930 following the death of her husband, she went to live in Spain. When civil war broke out there, she moved to Kingston, Jamaica, where she died in 1944.

Putnam, Mary (1842–1906).

See Jacobi, Mary Putnam.

Putnam, Mary T.S. (1810–1898)

American author. *Name variations: Mary Lowell. Born Mary Traill Spence Lowell on December 3, 1810; died in Boston on June 1, 1898; one of five children of Charles Lowell (minister of the West Church in Boston) and Harriet Brackett (Spence) Lowell (d. 1850); married Samuel R. Putnam (a merchant), on April 25, 1832; sister of James Russell Lowell (a poet, 1819–1891) and Robert Traill Spence Lowell (a writer and Episcopal priest, 1816–1891); sister-in-law of* ****Maria White Lowell*** *(1821–1853).*

Mary T.S. Putnam, sister of the poet James Russell Lowell, was born in 1810. She was a "woman of intellectual power and literary accomplishment," writes J.R. Lowell's biographer Horace Scudder. After having lived abroad collecting material, especially in Poland and Hungary, Putnam published anonymously a *History of the Constitution of Hungary in Its Relations to Austria* (1850). From 1851 to 1857, she resided in France and Germany, perfecting her linguistic abilities. Returning to the United States, she played a prominent role in the abolitionist movement, which she supported vigorously with her writings. Besides numerous contributions to magazines on literature and history, she wrote two dramas on slavery and translated ***Fredrika Bremer**'s *The Neighbors* from the Swedish.

Pyke, Margaret (1893–1966)

English birth-control activist. *Born on August 1, 1893, in Hampshire, England; died in 1966; daughter of a physician; educated in private schools; attended Somerville College, Oxford, received degree in history; married Geoffrey Pyke (an educator), in 1918 (died 1929); children: one son.*

Became first general secretary of Britain's National Birth Control Association (1929), renamed the Family Planning Association (1938); became chair of the organization (1954).

The daughter of a physician, Margaret Pyke was born on August 1, 1893, in Hampshire, England. She received a private education and studied history at Somerville College in Oxford, from which she received a degree. In 1918, Margaret married educator Geoffrey Pyke, then joined forces with Dr. **Susan Isaacs** to operate the Malting House School, a progressive learning institution near Cambridge.

With the death of her husband in 1929, Pyke was forced to find a job to support herself and her young son. Encouraged by Lady **Gertrude Denman**, a leader in the United Kingdom's birth-control movement, she applied for and was granted the position of general secretary of the National Birth Control Association (NBCA). The organization would be renamed the Family Planning Association in 1938.

Although Britain's Department of Health Circular of 1931 paved the way for organizations such as the National Birth Control Association to supply contraception to married couples, local authorities resisted the trend toward birth control. It fell to Pyke and her colleagues in the NBCA to convince municipalities to set up programs to dispense contraceptives under the national health department's initiative. The town council in Ealing was the first to set up such a program, followed by the city council of Plymouth, which launched a permanent clinic in 1932.

Of the United Kingdom's leadership in the field of birth control, Pyke wrote in 1953: "Great Britain has lost the lead she once held in many international fields, but in the field of family planning she is probably the most advanced of all the big countries. Here we have no laws against birth control and we have only a small proportion of the population (between 6 and 7%) pledged to opposition on religious grounds."

After the death of Denman in the early 1950s, Pyke became chair of the Family Planning Association. She also played an active role in the activities of the International Planned Parenthood Federation, traveling in 1959 to India as a representative of that organization. More than 500 birth-control clinics had been established throughout the United Kingdom by the time of Pyke's death in 1966.

Don Amerman,
freelance writer, Saylorsburg, Pennsylvania

Pym, Barbara (1913–1980)

English novelist. *Born Barbara Mary Crampton Pym on June 2, 1913, in Oswestry, Shropshire, England; died of cancer on January 11, 1980, in Oxford, England; daughter of Frederic Crampton Pym (a solicitor) and Irena Spenser Pym; educated at Liverpool College* *and a private boarding school in Huyton; St. Hilda's College, Oxford, B.A. in English literature.*

Selected writings: Some Tame Gazelle *(1950);* Excellent Women *(1952);* Jane and Prudence *(1953);* Less Than Angels *(1955);* A Glass of Blessings *(1958);* No Fond Return of Love *(1961);* Quartet in Autumn *(1977);* The Sweet Dove Died *(1978);* A Few Green Leaves *(1980);* An Unsuitable Attachment *(1982);* A Very Private Eye: An Autobiography in Diaries and Letters *(1984);* Crampton Hodnet *(1985);* An Academic Question *(1986);* Civil to Strangers and Other Writings *(1988).*

Barbara Pym transported readers of her novels of manners into England's drawing rooms to meet largely ordinary people doing largely ordinary things. But her ability to see the humor and irony in such everyday events ultimately brought her success as an author. She published her first novel in 1950 while in her late 30s, then seemingly made up for lost time, bringing five more to market in the next decade. In the 1960s and 1970s, interest in Pym's work all but dried up, and after a number of rejections from publishers, she abandoned writing for a time. Toward the end of her life, in the late 1970s, a positive evaluation of her work in the *Times Literary Supplement* triggered a resurgence in demand for her writing, and before her death in 1980 she saw the publication of her new work as well as the reprinting of earlier novels.

She was born in Oswestry, Shropshire, England, on June 2, 1913, the first child of Frederic Crampton Pym and **Irena Spenser Pym**. Frederic, a solicitor, had practiced law elsewhere in Shropshire—notably Shrewsbury and Wellington—until setting up his practice in Oswestry after Irena, a native of the village, agreed to marry him. The couple were living at 72 Willow Street in Oswestry when Barbara was born. In 1916, Barbara was followed by another daughter, **Hilary Pym**, at which time the family was living at Welsh Walls. The home that the girls grew up in was Morda Lodge, which Hilary described as "a substantial, square red-brick Edwardian house with a large garden on the outskirts of the town on the way to Morda."

The two Pym sisters enjoyed what Hilary has characterized as "a happy, unclouded childhood," a sizable portion of which was devoted to spiritual matters. Their mother was an assistant organist at the parish church of St. Oswald, and their father sang bass in the church choir. Barbara and Hilary both attended children's services at the church on Sunday afternoons. Of their mother, Hilary recalled, "it was she who encouraged Barbara to write and me to draw, and I'm sure it was her determination that sent us away to boarding school rather than continue our education in Oswestry." At age 12, Barbara was enrolled as a boarding student at Liverpool College in Huyton, where she later served as chair of the Literary Society. While in Huyton, at the age of 16 she wrote her first novel, *Young Men in Fancy Dress*, which was never published. She also wrote poems and parodies. Six years later, Pym began college-level studies at St. Hilda's in Oxford, majoring in English literature. After finishing her studies, she lived for a time at home and then accepted a teaching position in Poland which she held until 1938. When World War II broke out, Pym first worked as a postal censor in Bristol. Later, as a member of the Women's Royal Naval Service, she was stationed for a time in the United Kingdom and then in Naples, Italy.

Returning to London after the war, Pym went to work with the International African In-

Barbara Pym

stitute, where she would be employed from 1946 until 1974. She worked first as a research assistant and later as assistant editor of the institute's journal *Africa*. In 1950, Pym published her first novel, *Some Tame Gazelle*, for which she had earlier collected a number of rejection slips. She had begun work on this novel while still in college at Oxford. Two years later came *Excellent Women*, followed by *Jane and Prudence* (1953), *Less Than Angels* (1955), *A Glass of Blessings* (1958), and *No Fond Return of Love* (1961). Her work found a loyal, if not large, following.

But during the 1960s and into the 1970s, publishers showed no interest in Pym's work, prompting what *The Oxford Guide to British Women Writers* has characterized as "a period of painful neglect and a decline in her reputation." A new chief editor at Jonathan Cape, the publishing house that had brought out her first six novels, rejected *An Unsuitable Attachment* in 1963 because "in present conditions we could not sell a sufficient number of copies to cover costs." Also rejected by a number of publishers was *The Sweet Dove Died*. Pym even attempted to market some of her novels under the pseudonym Tom Pym, but to no avail. Finally, discouraged by the continued rejections, she stopped writing. Retiring from the International African Institute in 1974, she moved with her sister Hilary and a cat named Minerva to a home in Finstock, Oxfordshire.

In 1977, the *Times Literary Supplement* published a list of writers whom contemporary critics felt were the most underrated or overrated of the century. Both poet Philip Larkin and critic Lord David Cecil selected Pym, the only writer to be named twice, as most underrated. This set off a rebirth of interest in her work. New editions of some of Pym's earlier novels began to appear, and publishers were once again eager to see her as yet unpublished efforts. The first book by Pym to appear after the "rediscovery" was *Quartet in Autumn* (1977). Published the following year was *The Sweet Dove Died*, followed in 1980 by *A Few Green Leaves*, which Pym finished only a short time before she died of cancer on January 11, 1980, at age 66. A number of her novels, as well as a collection of her letters and diary entries, were published posthumously. These included *An Unsuitable Attachment* (1982), *A Very Private Eye: An Autobiography in Diaries and Letters* (1984), *Crampton Hodnet* (1985), *An Academic Question* (1986), and *Civil to Strangers and Other Writings* (1988).

SOURCES:

Binding, Paul. "Barbara Pym," in *Dictionary of Literary Biography*, Vol. 14: *British Novelists Since 1960*. Jay L. Halio, ed. Detroit, MI: Gale Research, 1983.

Pym, Barbara. *A Very Private Eye: An Autobiography in Diaries and Letters*. Edited by Hazel Holt and Hilary Pym. NY: Dutton, 1984.

Shattock, Joanne, ed. *The Oxford Guide to British Women Writers*. NY: Oxford University Press, 1993.

Don Amerman,
freelance writer, Saylorsburg, Pennsylvania

Pyrisca (c. 1085–1133).

See Anna Comnena for sidebar on Priska-Irene of Hungary.

Qian Zhengying (1923—)

Chinese engineer and politician. *Born of Han nationality in Jiaxing, Zhejiang Province, China, in July 1923 (Uglow claims place of birth was the United States); graduate of Department of Civil Engineering of Datong University, Shanghai; married Huang Xinbai (former vice minister of education); children: three.*

Official Chinese biographers place Qian Zhengying's birth in Jiaxing, Zhejian Province, while **Jennifer Uglow** claims that she was born in the United States in 1923 and returned with her family to China when she was still an infant. All agree that, encouraged by her father, a civil engineer who had studied water conservancy at Cornell University, she became one of her country's first women engineers, graduating from Datong University, Shanghai.

Qian became active in revolutionary politics in Shanghai as early as 1937, and in 1941 became secretary of an underground Communist group there. When the underground organizations of the Communist Party of China (CPS) were undermined that September, Qian left Shanghai and moved to the Huaibei liberated zone. In 1944, as the Huaibei River rose suddenly and broke its dykes, Qian began working in flood relief there. She would spend the rest of her life harnessing rivers throughout China and tackling technical problems at the sites of all major hydropower projects. She served as section chief of the Bureau of Water Conservancy under the Jiangsu-Anhui Regional government, director of the Front Engineering Division of the Department of Army Service Station of East China Ministry Command (1945–48), party secretary and deputy director of Bureau of Shadong Yellow River Management (1948–50); deputy head of the Department of Water Conservancy under the East China Military Administrative Committee and concurrently deputy head of the Engineering Department under the Committee for Harnessing Huai River (1950–52). After 35 years as an engineer, Qian became vice minister and then minister of Water Conservancy, a top position in her field, particularly for a woman. She served in that position from 1952 to 1988. Qian was elected and reelected vice chair of the 7th to 9th CPPCC National Committees (1988, 1993, and 1998). She was also a member of the 10th through 14th CPC Central Committees. She was awarded the China Engineering Science and Technology prize in June 2000.

SOURCES:

Uglow, Jennifer S., ed. *The International Dictionary of Women's Biography*. NY: Continuum, 1985.

Qiaobo Ye.

See Blair, Bonnie for sidebar on Ye Qiaobo.

Qiao Hong (b. 1968).

See Deng Yaping for sidebar.

Qiu Jin (c. 1875–1907)

Chinese revolutionary, poet, and feminist, who championed women's rights and was executed for her role in an attempt to overthrow the Qing Dynasty. *Name variations: Ch'iu Chin (romanized version) or incorrectly Chiu Chin; Qiu Xuanqing; Qiu Jingxiong. Pronunciation: Chee-o Jean. Born Qiu Jin on November 8, 1875 (some sources cite 1877, 1878, and 1879), in Xiamen, Fujian, China; executed in Shaoxing, Zhejiang, China, on July 15, 1907; daughter of Qiu Shounan (a government bureaucrat) and Shan; educated in the family school and the Japanese Language School, Tokyo (1904); took Special Training Course for Chinese Women at the Aoyama Women's Vocational School, Tokyo (July–December 1905); married Wang Tingjun, in 1896; children: son, Wang Yuande (b. 1897); daughter, Wang (Qiu) Canzhi (b. 1901, also seen as Wang Guifen).*

Returned with family to native home of Shaoxing (1891); family moved to Hunan province (early 1890s); accompanied her husband to live in Beijing (1902, some sources cite 1900 and 1903); left husband and family to study in Japan (1904); became active in Chinese revolutionary societies and in writing and lecturing in Japan (1904–05); joined the Restora-

tion Society in Shaoxing (1905); joined the Revolutionary Alliance (Tongmenghui) in Tokyo (1905); returned to China (1905 or 1906); taught for a few months in a girls' school in Zhejiang province (1906); founded the Chinese Women's Journal *in Shanghai (summer 1906); headed the Datong School in Shaoxing (February–July 1907); organized the failed Restoration Army uprising in Zhejiang (1907).*

Both the Communist government in China and the Nationalist government in Taiwan hail Qiu Jin as a martyred hero who offered her life to the revolutionary cause. She had hoped that her act of sacrifice would accelerate uprisings leading to a successful revolution against the Qing Dynasty, the Manchu government that had ruled China since 1644. Many Chinese thought of the Manchus as a non-Chinese people who had seized the throne through superior military power. Although many might have agreed that the Qing had ruled well for most of their reign, by the mid-19th century they were failing to protect China from the steady encroachments of the Western powers and of Japan.

It's difficult to exchange a woman's headdress for a helmet.

—**Qiu Jin**

In several treaties after the British victory in the Opium War (1839–42), Western powers wrung humiliating concessions from the Chinese government: five ports were opened to foreign trade; foreigners claimed the right to rule themselves under their own laws in China; Hong Kong was ceded to the British in perpetuity; most-favored-nation treatment was granted, making the treaties interlocking; and tariffs favored the foreign business interests. Close on the heels of the Opium War, the Taiping Rebellion raged over much of China from 1851 to 1864. Some 20 million people lost their lives. Faltering, the dynasty called on Han Chinese civil officials rather than Manchu military leaders, to raise troops in their home locales to defeat the rebels. This was a startling admission of weakness on the part of the Manchu dynasty.

Thus, some years before Qiu Jin's birth, the Manchu dynasty was teetering on the brink of forfeiting the Mandate of Heaven. Traditional Confucian wisdom taught that disasters presaged the end of a dynasty's legitimacy, and that a rebellion—installing a new emperor, or "Son of Heaven"—might be successful.

Qiu Jin was born in the treaty port of Xiamen, Fujian province, most likely during 1875 (some sources cite 1877, 1878, and 1879), at a time when traditional China was in its late stages. The subjugated position of women was already under scrutiny and sometimes also under attack. By the 1890s, foreign missionaries were establishing schools for girls, and, by the early 20th century, Chinese themselves would be founding girls' schools. Societies were also organized to oppose the ancient practice of footbinding which dated to about 900 CE.

Although the practices and theories of Confucianism had long provided China with great social stability and cultural continuity, it was obvious by now that Confucianism could not continue without significant changes. Confucian scholars, the men who were literate in the difficult traditional Chinese written language and who were selected for the civil service via an elaborate examination system, were the most powerful and honored group in the society. Qiu Jin's father Qiu Shounan was one such man. Because he worked as a lower-level civil servant, her family lived in several different provinces, mostly in the lower Yangtze valley region of China. The people in these provinces—Hunan, Zhejiang, and Fujian—were directly exposed to the physical impact of the Western powers that had "opened" China in the Opium War. Scholars in this region, centered upon the great port city of Shanghai, also found it easy to secure translations of major Western works, making them aware of China's relative weakness. It was here that the modern political movements which were to transform China in the 20th century began.

Toward the end of the 19th century, the French fought a war with China (1884–85) to detach Indochina from China's traditional suzerainty, and the Sino-Japanese War (1894–95) resulted in Taiwan becoming a Japanese colony.

As discontent with the Qing Dynasty grew, it took the form of reform movements (notably that of Kang Youwei and Liang Qichao in 1898), rebellion (the 1900 Boxer Uprising was directed mainly against foreign influence but one of its effects was to further weaken the dynasty), and an infant revolutionary movement headed by Sun Yat-sen. The reformers hoped to transform China into a constitutional monarchy. The revolutionaries believed that—for China's very survival—the entire dynastic structure had to be torn down.

Growing up in the lower Yangtze valley region as the second child and the first daughter of her bureaucrat father and well-educated mother, Qiu Jin was exposed to the heroic and romantic elements of Chinese traditions as well as to modern, Western ideas. It is said that her grandfather and parents thought of her as their "bright pearl" and nicknamed her "Jade Girl." Along with her elder brother and younger sister, Qiu Jin learned to read the Confucian classics, history, poetry, and novels. By the age of 13, she could also write poetry. She especially enjoyed listening to her parents recount stories of past heroes who had fought China's enemies and saved the country. Since she lived in a treaty port, it is likely that she knew of the thriving opium trade, of the impoverished laborers who went overseas to work, and of the foreign missionaries in China. She may have seen starvation. As the daughter of an official, she almost certainly heard of the naval battle with the French in Fujian. Li Hongsheng writes that Qiu Jin, worrying that Chinese people would become the slaves of foreign countries, begged her mother to let her learn the martial arts. In her youth, she began to think of herself as a hero or a traditional knight-errant who used force to right wrongs.

When the family returned to the paternal native home of Shaoxing in 1891, her mother allowed Qiu Jin to go to her own native home to study the martial arts under the tutelage of an older male cousin. In addition to becoming adept with the sword, Qiu Jin learned to ride a horse and acquired a taste for wine. Either at this time or later as a student in Japan, she adopted the name "heroine of Jian Lake."

In 1892, along with her mother and brother, Qiu Jin joined her father in Hunan province, where he held an official position. At the time, a woman's role in Chinese society was still quite traditional: women were to marry, become good wives, and above all bear sons. In May 1896, in an arranged marriage, Qiu Jin wed Wang Tingjun, scion of a wealthy family. She gave birth to a son, and in the Wang home lived a life of luxury which she despised. She had nothing in common with her profligate husband and remarked in a letter written to her brother a few years later that he lacked "good faith" and "friendly sentiment," gambled and visited prostitutes, insulted relatives, hurt others in order to benefit himself, and was conceited and arrogant. While he thought only of recreation, promotion, and a future of prosperity, she agonized over the incursions of foreigners. It might have been at about this time that she wrote a poem registering her despair:

> The serene swallows have long endured the beacon fires of war;
> I hear that the Sino-foreign battles have not yet ended.
> I am impotent as I harbor resentment for the nation.
> It's difficult to exchange a woman's headdress for a helmet.

In 1902 (or perhaps as early as 1900 or as late as 1903; sources disagree), Wang Tingjun purchased an official post in Beijing and took his wife and son with him. Beijing was the site of China's humiliating defeat at the hands of the foreign powers in the Boxer Rebellion in 1900. The Boxers, a secret society, had stirred up the countryside against the foreigners, and particularly against Christian missionaries and their Chinese converts. The Manchu throne supported the Boxers, and the foreign quarter in Beijing was besieged by Boxers for more than three months. When the siege was broken, the foreign relief force looted Beijing.

Qiu Jin met a circle of talented modern women in Beijing who shared her concern about China's future. Her closest friend there was **Wu Zhiying**, a well-known calligrapher. Qiu Jin read articles on women's liberation and democracy. She began to believe that China's future lay with revolution.

Increasingly muffled by her life at home, Qiu Jin was married to a man who neither supported nor understood her revolutionary impulses. After several years of frustration—both at her country's continued decline and at her own existence—she resolved to go to Japan to secure a modern education. Japan had successfully modernized in the late 19th century, and while the country was increasingly a threat to Chinese sovereignty it was also very attractive to modern Chinese youth as a place to explore reform and modernization. In the spring of 1904, Qiu Jin confronted her husband with her desire to study there. After selling her jewelry to finance the trip and making a hurried journey back to her hometown, she dressed as a man and traveled third-class on a ferry boat from Shanghai to Japan. She had left not only her husband but also her young son Wang Yuande (b. 1897) and daughter **Wang (Qiu) Canzhi** (b. 1901).

More than 1,500 Chinese students, including a few women, were already in Tokyo when Qiu Jin arrived. Once there, she studied Japanese for about six months at a school set up by the Chinese Students' Union. She also adopted a revolutionary style to match her revolutionary zeal. With her Japanese sword, her practice of the martial arts, and her man's attire, she defied the conventional stereotype of a woman. Besides using her sobriquet "heroine of Jian Lake," she took the name "Jingxiong," meaning "competition" or "power," as a means of suggesting gender equality in revolutionary pursuits. Radical students like Qiu Jin often were drawn to the shadowy subculture of the secret societies, groups of Chinese who had organized to protect their own local interests against those of the scholar-gentry or the court authorities. In Yokohama, Qiu Jin became a member of the largest of these groups, the Triad secret society. She also helped to organize a society for the Study of Oratory and gave lectures on revolution and on gender equality. Like many other educated Chinese, she contributed to the vernacular movement in order to introduce revolutionary ideas to the lower classes. Qiu Jin wrote articles opposing foot-binding and promoting gender equality and women's education for the *Vernacular Journal.* She became acquainted with Tao Chengzhang, a leader of the Revolutionary Restoration Society, Huang Xing, who was also active in the revolutionary movement, and Lu Xun, the master of satire aimed at Chinese society and tradition.

In early 1905, Qiu Jin registered for the Special Training Course for Chinese Women, which was affiliated with the Aoyama Vocational Girls' School. Needing money for the expensive tuition and wanting to see her natal family, she decided to return briefly to China. Before she left Japan, Tao Chengzhang gave her introductions to leaders of the Revolutionary Restoration Society in Shanghai and Shaoxing. After she reached China, Qiu Jin sought out Xu Xilin, the society's Shaoxing leader, who welcomed her to the organization.

With money from her mother, she returned to Tokyo in July 1905. Enrolling in the Special Training Course for Chinese Women, she was in class 33 hours a week for nine subjects drawn from a curriculum offering courses in moral cultivation, Japanese language, education, psychology, sciences, geography, history, mathematics, geometry, painting, English, physical education, handicrafts, homemaking, and choral music. In spare hours, she strengthened herself through military drill and target practice. She also practiced making explosives. Qiu Jin continued wearing her Japanese sword, and she often dressed in a kimono.

By late 1905, she had joined the Revolutionary Alliance (Tongmenghui), which had been organized by the revolutionary leader Sun Yat-sen in Tokyo. As the second overseas student from Zhejiang province to join the group, Qiu Jin was named to head its Zhejiang branch.

In November 1905, the Japanese government—pressured by the Qing Dynasty, which was alarmed by the revolutionary activity of Chinese students in Japan—prohibited the Chinese overseas students from engaging in political activity. Outraged, Qiu Jin and other Chinese students went on strike and demonstrated. When the Japanese government alternately ignored and ridiculed them, she and others urged their classmates to return to China in protest. Following her own advice, Qiu Jin left for China in late 1905 or early 1906. In a letter from that time, she wrote:

> [I] want to struggle for the success of the revolution—struggle without ceasing. Ever since the Allied invasion [during the Boxer Rebellion], I have cared nothing about my own life and death. Even if I sacrifice myself without achieving success, I can't feel regretful. It's a time of crisis. The great work of restoring China [to the Chinese] cannot be delayed! Up to now, a lot of men have already died, but not many women have. This is a disgrace to the women's circle.

Upon her return to China, Qiu Jin began melding together her romantic commitment to the Chinese heroic tradition and her modern education. Revolutionaries throughout the lower Yangtze valley were constantly plotting local risings, often hoping that if several of these could flare up simultaneously they would become in effect the match which would light the fuse of national revolution. Such risings were very difficult to coordinate, however. Communications were hard and often broke down. Romantic students frequently changed their minds at the last moment, and secret-society members sometimes acted primarily as mercenaries and refused to act if they were not well paid. Manchu police were very thorough at rooting out plots and at torturing and executing would-be revolutionaries upon the slightest evidence.

Qiu Jin immediately contacted the revolutionaries in her home area, and she prepared to work simultaneously for armed uprisings and for women's liberation. While teaching Japanese language, science, and hygiene in a girls' school, she encouraged the other teachers to take up the causes of gender equality and nationalism. The principal of the school, **Xu Zihua**, was an enlightened widow who had fled the maltreatment of her in-laws. She and Qiu Jin became close friends.

During the summer of 1906, Qiu Jin worked in Shanghai, where she founded a popular magazine, *Chinese Women's Journal,* to promote women's liberation. Xu Zihua and her sister provided 1,500 yuan toward its establishment, but funding remained a problem and only two issues were published. For the first, which appeared on January 14, 1907, Qiu Jin wrote an editorial exhorting women to "be the forerunners of waking the lion, be the vanguard of civilization, be the boat across the ford of confusion, be the light of the dark room, so that within the world of Chinese women a magnificent splendor will be released, to stir the hearts and dazzle the eyes of all mankind." She also wrote a "Warning to My Sisters" and addressed women in wealthy families who might have had relatively contented lives:

> Those silks and satins can be compared to brocaded ropes and embroidered belts, binding you tightly. Those servants are really prison guards. That husband . . . is the magistrate and the jailer. . . . I'd like to ask these wealthy wives, even if you have had a life of ease and enjoyment, have you ever had even a little power to act on your own? It is always the male who has the position of master, and the female who has the position of slave.

Qiu Jin admonished women to rise up to free themselves by fighting for personal and economic freedom. She also urged them to unite in the struggle to save China—the struggle that always took precedence for her.

With the 1905 abolition of the Confucian civil-service examination system, which had been the major route to government office for centuries, the government encouraged the establishment of schools teaching both traditional and modern subjects. Availing himself of government sanction for new schools, revolutionary Xu Xilin opened Datong School in Shaoxing as a front for revolutionary activity in Zhejiang province. In February 1907, with Xu moving to Anhui province to head, and make revolutionary use of, the Police Academy there, Qiu Jin accepted a request to head the school.

Revolutionaries from all over Zhejiang attended Datong School for training, drilling with rifles and ammunition Xu had brought in from Shanghai. A few miles outside the city, Qiu Jin herself led the students and activists in military drill, especially encouraging the female students to join in.

Suspicious of the school's activities and of a woman wearing male garb and riding a horse, local residents—probably gentry members—posted handbills attacking Datong School as a "den of bandits." Relying on her family's official status, Qiu Jin is said to have allayed these concerns by chatting with Shaoxing Prefect Gui Fu about education and poetry.

All the while, she was attracting new members to the Restoration Society and forging close connections with society leaders in various locales. Qiu Jin also made connections with soldiers in the New Army as well as students in military and high-level cadre schools in Hangzhou. She reportedly convinced a number of soldiers in Hangzhou to side with the revolutionary cause and enlisted them as agents provocateurs for future action in Hangzhou. She established the Restoration Army, upon which she imposed tight organization.

At the end of May 1907, Xu Xilin informed Qiu Jin that the Anhui organization was ready to act. He urged that the Zhejiang branch, too, prepare for an uprising in the near future. Accordingly, Qiu Jin summoned the leaders of the Restoration Army to a meeting, at which she reportedly said: "[T]he arrow is really in the bow. [We] cannot not release it!" The group fixed July 6 as the date of its uprising.

In Zhejiang, the authorities were closing in. A traitor to the revolutionary cause had revealed the names of key leaders of the Restoration Army. By early July, when Qiu Jin decided to delay the uprising until July 19, official attention was already trained on the school. On July 7 or soon thereafter, word leaked to Gui Fu that Datong School's revolutionary group, including

Qiu Jin, was planning an uprising. Gui Fu passed this intelligence on to the Zhejiang governor, who quickly deployed troops to Shaoxing.

On July 10, Qiu Jin read in a Shanghai newspaper of Xu Xilin's failed uprising on July 6 in Anqing, Anhui. Several died in the attempt, while Xu Xilin was captured and executed. A revolutionary from Shanghai arrived to urge Qiu Jin to flee to Shanghai. Repeating a familiar theme, she refused, saying that she did not fear death: blood had to be spilled for the revolution to succeed. On July 12, she learned that troops were on their way. After mobilizing teachers and students to conceal the rifles and ammunition, Qiu Jin encouraged her colleagues and students to go into hiding.

She declined again to seek safety the next morning. A few hours later, more than 300 troops surrounded Datong School. After a brief battle in which two students died, the troops entered the school. Qiu Jin and seven others were captured. Subsequently interrogated and tortured, she steadfastly refused to answer questions or to write a confession. Just before dawn on July 15, 1907, Qiu Jin was beheaded in Shaoxing. Her good friends, among them Xu Zihua and Wu Zhiying, buried her near West Lake in Hangzhou. The revolution for which she gave her life would topple the Qing Dynasty on October 10, 1911.

Drawing on the heroic tradition, many in her time believed that perhaps the best way to force the pace of change was to die gloriously in battle against the corrupt Manchus. A martyr's death offered not only a possible way to inspire thousands of others to finally overthrow the government, but also guaranteed a measure of fame and immortality, as revealed in Qiu Jin's poetry (translated by **Mary Backus Rankin**):

> The sun is setting with no road ahead,
> In vain I weep for loss of country . . .
> Although I die yet I still live,
> Through sacrifice I have fulfilled my duty.

Qiu Jin was right that her death would motivate others, and in that sense it was not a useless sacrifice. Among those many Chinese women who were inspired was **Yu Manzhen**, the mother of the later female literary and revolutionary figure ***Ding Ling** (1904–1985). Qiu Jin's daughter Wang (Qiu) Canzhi edited her mother's poetry, which was continually reprinted and widely read. Chinese, and particularly Chinese women, continue to honor her memory.

SOURCES:

Chen Xianggong, ed. *Qiu Jin nianpu ji zhuanji ziliao* (chronological biography and biographical material about Qiu Jin). Beijing: China Publishing House, 1983.

Fang Chao-ying. "Ch'iu Chin," in Arthur W. Hummel, ed., *Eminent Chinese of the Ch'ing Period.* Washington: U.S. Government Printing Office, 1943, pp. 169–171.

Giles, Lionel. *Ch'iu Chin: A Chinese Heroine.* London: East & West, 1917.

———. "The Life of Ch'iu Chin," in *T'oung Pao.* Vol. XIV, 1913, pp. 211–227.

Li Hongsheng. *Nu yingxiong Qiu Jin* (The heroine Qiu Jin). Jinan: Shandong People's Publishing House, 1985.

"Qiu Jin," in Yuan Shaoying and Yang Guizhen, eds., *Zhongguo funu mingren cidian* (Dictionary of Famous Chinese Women). Changchun: Women and Children's Publishing House of the North, 1989, pp. 425–427.

Qiu Jin ji (Collected works of Qiu Jin). Shanghai: New China Publishing House, 1960.

Rankin, Mary Backus. *Early Chinese Revolutionaries. Radical Intellectuals in Shanghai and Chekiang, 1902–1911.* Cambridge, MA: Harvard University Press, 1971.

———. "The Emergence of Women at the End of the Ch'ing: The Case of Ch'iu Chin," in Margery Wolf and Roxane Witke, eds., *Women in Chinese Society.* Stanford, CA: Stanford University Press, 1975, pp. 39–66.

SUGGESTED READING:

Chow Tse-tsung. *The May Fourth Movement. Intellectual Revolution in Modern China.* Stanford, CA: Stanford University Press, 1960.

Wright, Mary, ed. *China in Revolution: The First Phase, 1900–1913.* New Haven, CT: Yale University Press, 1968.

RELATED MEDIA:

Qiu Jin: A Revolutionary (VHS, 110 min.), based on a novel by **Xia Yan**, Shanghai Film Studio, 1983.

Karen Gernant, Professor of History,
Southern Oregon State College, Ashland,
with additional material supplied by
Jeffrey G. Barlow, Professor of History,
Lewis & Clark College, Portland, Oregon

Qiu Jingxiong (c. 1875–1907).

See Qiu Jin.

Qiu Xuanqing (c. 1875–1907).

See Qiu Jin.

Quah Ah (1893–1949).

See Peña, Tonita.

Quaiapan (d. 1676).

See Magnus.

Quant, Mary (1934—)

English entrepreneur whose perception, business acumen, and interpretation of fashion and design repeatedly revolutionized conventional ideas of style, promotion, and manufacture in several branches of the industrial arts. *Born Mary Quant on February 11,*

1934, in Blackheath, London; daughter of Jack and Mildred Quant; educated at 13 schools and Goldsmiths College of Art; married Alexander Plunkett Greene, in 1957 (divorced 1990); children: son Orlando (b. 1970).

Awards include: FSIA (1967); Maison Blanche Rex Award-USA (1964); Sunday Times International Award (1964); Piavola D'Oro Award (Italy, 1966); Annual Design Medal, Institute of Industrial Artists and Designers (1966); FRSA (1996).

As a child during WWII, was evacuated to southeast England and later to Wales; left school at 16 on winning a scholarship to art school (1950) where she met Alexander Plunkett Greene who would be her life and business partner for over 40 years; ran Bazaar (with Greene and third business partner Archie McNair) in King's Road, Chelsea (1955–68); began to design clothes for Bazaar (1956); opened and oversaw a second branch of Bazaar in Knightsbridge (1957–69); signed with J.C. Penney (U.S.) to design fashions for their stores throughout America (1962–71); started the Ginger Group (wholesale company), was elected "Woman of the Year" (UK), and pioneered the use of PVC (oilskin) in fashion rainwear (1963); invited to create exclusive designs for Puritan Fashion (large U.S. ready-to-wear manufacturers) and also for Butterick paper-patterns for home dressmakers (1964); launched Quant hosiery and lingerie line (1965); launched "Mary Quant Cosmetics," published Quant on Quant *(autobiography), and received OBE (Order of the British Empire) in the queen's honors list (1966); elected Royal Designer for Industry by the Royal Society of Arts (1969); her coordinated range of household furnishings and domestic textile designs promoted by ICI (Imperial Chemical Industries, 1970); was a member of the Design Council (1971–74) and a member of British-American Liaison Committee (1973); exhibition "Mary Quant's London" held at London Museum (1973–74); joined the advisory council of the V&A (Victoria and Albert) Museum (1976–78); opened first Tokyo "Mary Quant Color Shop" (1983); published two books,* Color by Quant *(1984) and* Quant on Makeup *(1986); elected to the Hall of Fame British Fashion Council (1990); became co-chair of the Mary Quant Group of Companies (1991); created an honorary fellow of Goldsmiths College of Art (1993); opened Mary Quant Color Shops in Chelsea and Knightsbridge (both London), as well as Paris (1994–97).*

Selected publications: Quant by Quant *(Cassell, 1966);* Color by Quant *(Octopus Books, 1984);* Quant on Makeup *(Century Hutchinson, 1986);* Classic Makeup and Beauty Book *(Dorling Kindersley, 1996).*

The airplane was about 20 minutes from Dulles Airport in 1962 when the chief steward approached the young English couple in first class who were clearly relishing their complimentary caviar and champagne. "Miss Quant," he said. "We have received a radio message from Washington. They have asked that you should be the first to step off the plane so that the television cameras and photographers can get pictures." Immediately, the petite redhead almost collapsed with embarrassment. She flew into the nearest lavatory, locked the door, and, heart pounding, changed out of her "dowdy old gear" and began to brush her hair. "Return to your seats," came the voice over the intercom. But Mary Quant, hand-picked by the major chain-store retailer in the U.S. as the brightest and most outrageously daring star in a galaxy of young British designers, a fashion innovator and co-director of the most successful boutique in London, was paralyzed with fear. She remained locked in the lavatory until the plane and the airport were nearly deserted. Then she emerged at last, creeping down the steps, just visible beneath an armful of cardboard boxes containing her precious new Spring Collection.

Fortunately her crisis of confidence proved only temporary, for it was this trip, as the protégé of the J.C. Penney Corporation, that heralded Quant's career as a major 20th-century designer of clothes for the international ready-to-wear market. Her flair for capturing the spirit and imagination of the youth of postwar England had led the way into a new era of fashion. Soon, she was to achieve lasting fame as the fashion voice of what became known as the "Swinging '60s."

Seven years earlier, with the opening of Bazaar, an enticing boutique in the King's Road, Mary Quant had started a small revolution in London that reverberated worldwide. Until then, young girls had grown up with the idea that fashion was for wealthy "older women," and they looked forward to being initiated into the smart black-dress-and-pearls sophistication of their mothers. Quant stood that convention on its head. She pioneered the idea of clothes as fun, as an expression of individuality, and she believed passionately in promoting and celebrating the self-confidence the new teenagers brought to the market place.

Quant's interest in creating her own clothes began very early in her childhood: she was about six and in bed recovering from the measles when she decided that her heirloom bedspread would "make a super dress" and began to cut it up.

The result is not recorded, but presumably her parents' response did not altogether discourage her, for she was allowed to use the old family sewing machine; by the time she started secondary school, she had invented her own school uniform. During World War II, the elder Quants, who were both dedicated and industrious schoolteachers, were relocated several times, with the result that Mary and her brother Tony attended nearly a dozen schools. One she particularly disliked, a boarding-school in Tunbridge Wells, Kent, insisted on a strict dress code, resulting in a family outlay for two or three blue-and-white gingham dresses. Not long after, moreover, her father was transferred to West Wales, and the family was allowed to join him. Quant had not yet grown out of the uniforms, so she carefully unstitched the dresses and remade them. Suddenly her wardrobe was full of short, flared skirts which she wore with long white socks, telling everyone that this had been the uniform at her previous school.

> I love vulgarity. Good taste is death. Vulgarity is life.
>
> —Mary Quant

Quant loved her stay in Wales. Since the family home was close to the beach, she and Tony spent endless summer days enjoying the sand and sea. They soon realized, however, that they could make a little money. Many of the wealthy visitors, proud owners of small boats, were often novice sailors with little experience of the hazardous Pembrokeshire coastline. With the help of local seafarers who taught them the rudiments of sailing, and their Welsh schoolfriends who knew every cove and rock for miles around, the two children set up "a sort of advisory service." After devising a scale of charges, the Quant children would approach newcomers with offers of navigational tips, sailing lessons, and, as profits increased, coastal tours in their own diesel-engined boat. They expanded still further, launching an agency to hose down the boats at the end of the season and send them by train to their owners' homes. It was an enterprising and profitable introduction to the world of big business.

By the time the Quants moved back to Blackheath, a suburb of London, however, Mary's checkered schooling had begun to undermine her confidence. Her parents had high expectations for both their children and encouraged them to excel. Unfortunately, each school Quant attended seemed to have a different assessment of her abilities. In one, she would be top of the class in math; in another, she would be placed near the bottom. One teacher told her that, though she had no talent for art at all, she had a natural rapport with younger children. It seemed that she was destined for the teaching profession.

That is, until she came under the influence of Auntie Frances. Auntie Frances was her father's sister and came to live with the family as Quant entered her teens. Aunt and niece shared a bedroom, and since Frances seemed to need little sleep they talked into the night. A spiritualist and a professional medium, Frances was anxious to pass on to Mary the strange powers she felt herself to possess. Sometimes Quant would wake to find her aunt circling her bed mumbling and waving a stick in the air. Mary was not at all frightened; instead, she was fascinated, intrigued, and felt a little wary of the possibility that she had inherited some unusual and inexplicable psychic ability. It was her aunt who predicted that Mary would design clothes, influence people, travel the world, and end up colossally rich. She warned Mary of her weaknesses and advised her on how to overcome them. She foretold her partnership with Alexander Plunkett Greene, saying again and again that they would "have to grow up together."

Postwar London was a bleak place. Extensive bombing had shattered communities, destroying buildings and families indiscriminately. Despite her trying ways, Auntie Frances' eccentricity must have added much-needed color to Quant's world; it also gave her a focus for her future. At 16, she won a scholarship to Goldsmiths College of Art in southeast London. Her parents were horrified by her desire to enter the fashion world—to them it seemed far too unstable—and agreed to let her accept her place only on condition that she took the Art Teacher's Diploma Course.

Quant lived at home during her first years at college, but after she met Alexander Plunkett Greene the strains on family relationships increased dramatically. Although, like her, Greene was only 16, he seemed entirely independent. He lived alone in his mother's apartment in Chelsea, gave wild parties and, though also enrolled at the college, was extremely casual about attending classes, seldom getting out of bed before four. He epitomized everything Quant had been taught to avoid, and she found him exotic, worldly, and magnetically attractive. They soon became inseparable. Quant's parents watched appalled as they saw their fine example of "hard work for solid rewards" being undermined by someone who seemed to live a life almost entirely of pleasure. They fought back at every turn. But Mary was enchanted.

She failed to achieve her Art Teacher's Diploma—which caused even more friction at

home—but she finally landed a job with Erik, a well-known milliner, which excited her enormously. She began to work a 50-hour week for which she was paid just enough to cover her train fares. Though there was nothing left over for clothes or entertainment, that was not a problem: Quant regularly remade her old clothes, constantly experimenting to give them a "new look," and she and Greene were inventive when it came to having fun. Alexander was keen on jazz and performed with a group of friends, giving spontaneous concerts and dance parties in the street. They also enjoyed playing practical jokes on an unsuspecting public. They once staged a kidnapping in central London and were delighted when they earned disapproving looks and sighs of "Oh God, this modern youth." With that, they started to call themselves "Modern Youth," and their games and attire became more and more elaborate and extraordinary. However, behind the hilarity and the apparent recklessness were two surprisingly aware, ambitious and creative imaginations almost waiting for fate to take them in hand.

Fate arrived in the guise of Archie McNair, an ex-solicitor turned photographer who had a studio and coffee bar in the King's Road, Chelsea, where Greene lived. Quant attributes a great deal of the success of their early ventures to McNair's flair for property and his astute knowledge of business and the law. The renaissance of British style in the mid-1950s was as much a matter of geography and proximity as anything else. In Chelsea, generally known as the "arty" section of London, there was "something in the air"—a collective feeling of wanting to "break the rules," to shock, to overturn the old values laid down by a previous generation who had sacrificed their youth and vitality to the building of a society which had been decimated by war and privation. It was an intoxicating mixture of passion, rebellion, and revelry.

As the friendship between Quant, Greene, and McNair grew, they began to talk about their dreams of the future. Recognizing Mary's eye for design and sizzling sense of style, the young men decided to invest in her and made plans to set up a shop they would call Bazaar, selling the most audacious clothes, hats, and accessories in London. This boutique would be an experience in itself, offbeat and attractive to people who wanted to say something exciting about themselves in what they chose to wear. Gradually, their dream became a thrilling possibility.

At 21, Greene, who had a wealth of rather feckless but well-connected relations, inherited £5,000, and McNair was prepared to match it. Very soon they found the perfect location—the basement and ground floor of a house in the King's Road. They originally had hoped to have a jazz club in the basement, but the Chelsea residents vetoed that idea so they decided to install a restaurant instead. They borrowed more money to overhaul both floors and to pay Mary £5 a week to act as their "buyer." She quit her job, left home, and moved into a tiny apartment. It was a relief to find that brother Tony remained staunchly loyal to the project despite the continuing disapproval of their parents. She felt some trepidation as she realized the immense burden of responsibility she carried, but from the moment Bazaar finally threw open its doors it was an almost overwhelming success. Within ten days, the triumvirate had sold every original piece of merchandise in the store—in spite of the fact that only one fashion editor had given them a feature: *Harper's Bazaar* had pictured a wacky pair of "house pajamas" which Quant had made as her only contribution to the premiere collection. When the pajamas were returned from the photo shoot, they were immediately snapped up by an entrepreneur who told her he planned to mass produce them for the American market. Quant was furious that he could do that—just buy the garment and copy it—but at the same time she was encouraged to concentrate seriously on her own talent for design.

Fueled by the necessity of keeping the shelves and rails stocked and realizing that nobody was producing the kind of clothes she wanted to sell, she began to sew day and night, adapting patterns from Butterick, attending evening classes to learn cutting, and buying fabric from Harrods because she knew nothing about wholesale. The first months at Bazaar were a purely spontaneous response to demand and, since the talented threesome had no previous experience in the "rag-trade," quite amateur. All profits were plunged straight back into production. Quant took on extra help, bought more sewing machines (all installed in the apartment), and was frequently frustrated to find that her cats had eaten the paper patterns. Only later did she learn that the tissue used to make them was manufactured from a by-product of fish bones.

As they began to be more organized, Quant was invited to join the team of British designers for a fashion show in St. Moritz. She was amazed and a little intimidated to think her "crazy" clothes would be sharing a platform with the "haute couture." She arrived in Switzerland, at the height of the ski season, with her "collection" packed in cardboard boxes, fighting a bad case of the flu. The packed hotel was grand and opulent, which, though a perfect foil for conventional ballgowns, was hardly the sort of background that would show off Bazaar clothes to advantage. Quant's creative flair was challenged. But while talking to the models, she discovered they were wild about her ingenious ideas. She urged them to be inventive on the catwalk, and they responded at once when, at the first glimpse of a white, lacy pantsuit, the music changed from sedate classics to upbeat jazz. The models ran, leapt, and danced down the huge staircase in quick succession, striking goofy, angular poses, clowning and laughing throughout. It was fast, unpredictable, and fun. The audience gaped, gasped, then applauded, and the show was a sensation. Mary Quant had electrified Europe.

Subsequently, the "Mary Quant Group" vigorously expanded, and Quant and Greene married in 1957. Helped by a continuous round of fashion shows, press launches, and lunches, they were constantly introducing innovative promotional ideas (Bazaar's window displays frequently caused traffic jams) and stealing headlines as hemlines rose and waistlines dropped—or disappeared. But Quant still longed to reach a wider market and that opportunity came with the J.C. Penney contract in 1962. Shrewdly, she grabbed it. "It is pointless in fashion to create a couture design and imagine it can be adequately produced cheaply and in quantity," she said. "Fashion must be created from the start for mass production with a full knowledge of mass-production methods." Quant greatly admired the American skill in adapting designs and proportioning patterns to accommodate different body shapes without "diluting or slaughtering the original style," and longed to master it. For nearly the following decade, she produced four collections a year for Penney's, aimed primarily at American teenagers.

In 1963, putting her new expertise to use back in London, she launched her company, "The Ginger Group," to manufacture her dresses and sportswear for worldwide distribution, and the following year she was approached by Carl Rosen, president of Puritan Fashions, the fourth largest manufacturing group in America.

Rosen was well aware that a country that had already fostered the talents of the Beatles, the Rolling Stones, and Vidal Sassoon was bursting with a vibrant freshness that was also revitalizing the world of fashion. He was determined to bring the complete "London Look" to America, coining the name "Youthquake" for the whole venture. Plans forged ahead, though nothing was finalized. Eventually, 60 new Quant designs for Puritan which were supposed to go into mass production for the new season were lined up and waiting to be flown to New York City, but details of the business arrangement still had to be agreed on and contracts signed. Frustration mounted, and the deadline grew dangerously close. Trans-Atlantic telephone calls went on through the night. Quant and Greene had missed their plane when a phone call from Rosen finally reassured them, but time had run out. The "red tape" involved in exporting designs via the conventional channels was complex and would take far too long. They would simply have to carry the clothes with them. In the past, they would have thrown everything into crates and cardboard boxes, but their new "high-profile" image made them self-conscious. There was nothing for it but to purchase some luggage. A few hours later, they landed in New York with nine uncharacteristically smart-looking crocodile-leather suitcases full of (as they claimed) "personal effects." Luckily, Quant spotted a sympathetic customs official who seemed ready to accept that an eccentric, fur-bedecked English woman required a wardrobe of 60 frocks and accessories to see her through a four-day visit. The entire collection was shown to the 40 or so heads of the Puritan empire; orders were placed and the deal went ahead.

Then someone came up with the idea for a coast-to-coast whistle-stop fashion tour—a roadshow—the first of its kind. Quant's promotional style was essentially the same as the format she had devised in St. Moritz—slick, wild, and wacky—and she always preferred live-band music. The youth of America responded joyously, often to the great surprise of store managers in sleepy suburban towns who had no idea of what to expect. But as hordes of teenagers besieged their fashion departments with dollars in hand, the managers began to realize the potential. By the time the show reached Kansas City, Quant and her entourage were treated like movie stars. Thousands of young people came to the shows bringing autograph books with them.

Quant and Greene boarded the plane home exhausted but thrilled. Inevitably, they began to wonder how their workrooms back in London had managed without them for so long. They were "almost disappointed" to find that their management skills had become so professional that everything was running smoothly; someone even asked Quant if she had "enjoyed her holiday?"

From then on, the business mushroomed to staggering proportions. Quant and Greene became world travelers, mobbed and feted everywhere they went, so well known to customs officials that they scarcely needed passports. Their output was tremendous. Quant was setting trends not only in dresses, sportswear and separates, but in swimwear, headwear, and underwear. A leading British fashion writer, **Ernestine Carter**, calculated that by 1965, Mary Quant was producing 528 designs a year (an average of 1.66 designs a day—including Sundays).

Awards and honors rained upon her. She published an autobiography (aged 32) and in

1973–74 the London Museum (then at Kensington Palace) paid homage to the enormous influence she had had on the capital city by mounting an exhibition entitled "Mary Quant's London," displaying over 50 garments and illustrating the extraordinary versatility and audacity of her design ideas. As Carter claimed in her introduction to the show's catalogue, Quant had "blasted a hole in the wall of tradition, through which other young talents have poured."

Gradually, Quant's growing disenchantment with "processed" materials led her to return more and more to natural fibers like calicos, linens, and cottons. Subsequently, she began to turn her hand to textile design, and her bedwear, curtains, wallpaper, and carpets were launched and marketed throughout the world during the 1970s and 1980s.

The dawn of the 1990s saw a renovation of her home furnishings with a fine art division called Fine Decor and a continuing expansion of one of her biggest ventures: "Mary Quant Cosmetics." This was an enterprise that, since its inception in the 1960s, had held the potential of reaching an almost unlimited range of customers in every corner of the globe. It has proved the most enduring of her business interests. In 1996, Quant published her comprehensive guide, the *Classic Makeup and Beauty Book*, which gives practical advice to the beginner and the more experienced on how to analyze face and skin type; it also addresses the latest skin care, body care, and makeup techniques with humor and style. The book follows through with Quant's fundamental philosophy that all fashion should be creative, fun, and empowering. She is against using makeup as a form of camouflage, believing it to be a confidence-building tool, a way of bringing out the best in the face and above all a means of self-expression.

The first Mary Quant Color Shop, with cosmetics, fashion, and fashion accessories displayed in the same store, opened in Tokyo in 1983; there were soon over 200 outlets in Japan, one in Paris, and two in London. Forty years after the opening of Bazaar, Mary Quant, the iconoclastic designer who "opened windows that had been sealed tight for far too long" was enjoying her continued triumph in England's capital city.

SOURCES:

Carter, Ernestine. "Mary Quant's London," in introduction to Catalogue to London Museum exhibition, 1973.

Quant, Mary. *Quant on Quant* (autobiography). London: Cassell, 1966.

COLLECTIONS:

Some items of clothing are on permanent display in the Victoria & Albert Museum, London, and the Museum of Costume, Bath, England.

Bonnie Hurren,
freelance actor and director,
Bristol, England

Quedlinburg, abbess of.

See Adelaide of Burgundy (931–999) for sidebar on Matilda of Quedlinburg (c. 953–999).

See Adelaide of Quedlinburg (977–1045).

See Agnes of Quedlinburg (1184–1203).

See Königsmark, Aurora von (1662–1728).

Queensbury, duchess of.

See Hyde, Catherine (1701–1777).

Querouaille or Querouille, Louise de (1649–1734).

See Kéroüalle, Louise de.

Questel, Mae (1908–1998)

American actress who was the voice of Betty Boop. *Born on September 13, 1908; died on January 4, 1998.*

Mae Questel was the second actress to take on the voice of Betty Boop, a popular cartoon character of the 1930s; the first was ***Helen Kane**. Questel's helium tones were heard in over 1,900 short films. She vocalized for Popeye's girlfriend Olive Oyl, Casper the Friendly Ghost, Winky Dink, and Swee'Pea. In 1989, Questel appeared as Woody Allen's mother in his *New York Stories*.

Questiaux, Nicole (1931—)

French politician. *Born Nicole Françoise Valayer in Nantes, France, in 1931 (one source cites 1930); graduated from the University of Paris; studied at the École Nationale d'Administration, 1953–55; married Paul Questiaux, in 1951; children: two.*

Served on France's Council of State as full member (1963–74); was a founding member of the new French Socialist Party (1971); served as minister of state for national solidarity under Prime Minister François Mitterand; served on the board of the European Human Rights Foundation, and as its president (1998).

Selected writings: Traité du social.

The daughter of an engineer, Nicole Questiaux was born in Nantes, France, in 1931, and graduated from the University of Paris with a degree in political science. She then studied for another two years at the École Nationale d'Administration. Questiaux began her political career in 1955, as an *auditeur* to the Council of State, and she became a full member of the Council in 1963. She served there until 1974, taking particular interest in elderly affairs. Questiaux was prominent in the launching of the new Socialist Party (1971), the executive committee of which she later became a member (1979). She was also a member of the left-wing Comité d'Etudes Regionales, Économiques et Sociales (CERES). In 1981, under the administration of François Mitterand, she was named Minister of State for National Solidarity, a post she filled until 1982. The following year, she became president of the 4th Subsection of the Council of State, a position she still held at the close of the century.

Apart from French politics, Questiaux served as a member of the board of the European Human Rights Foundation, a charitable foundation set up by the European Commission of the European Union, and acted as its president in 1998. She also became a member of France's Commission Nationale Consultative des Droits de l'Homme, a human-rights organization. She has been married to Paul Questiaux since 1951, and is the mother of two children.

SOURCES:

The International Who's Who 1998–99. London: Europa, 1998.

Uglow, Jennifer S., ed. *The International Dictionary of Women's Biography*. NY: Continuum, 1985.

Don Amerman,
freelance writer, Saylorsburg, Pennsylvania

Quimby, Edith (1891–1982)

American physicist who was responsible for standardizing measures of radiation dosages in cancer treatment. *Born Edith Hinkley on July 10, 1891, in Rockford, Illinois; died on October 11, 1982; daughter of Arthur S. Hinkley (an architect and farmer) and Harriet H. Hinkley; Whitman College, Walla Walla, Washington, B.S., 1912; University of California, M.A., 1915; married Shirley L. Quimby (a physicist), in 1915.*

Obtained employment at New York City Memorial Hospital for Cancer and Allied Diseases (1919); awarded Janeway Medal of the American Radium Society (1940); awarded honorary degree, Doctor of Science, Whitman College (1940); taught radiology courses at Cornell University Medical College (1941–42); named associate professor of radiology at Columbia University's College of Physicians and Surgeons (1943); retired as professor emeritus of radiology (1960).

Edith Quimby, who was one of the 20th century's most prominent researchers in radiation physics, focused primarily on the biological effects of radiation on humans. Many of her projects were devoted to measuring the penetrability of various sources of radiation, and in particular she studied the medical application of X-radiation and radioactive nuclides in the treatment of tumors. During the 1920s and 1930s, Quimby was the only woman in America working in this then little-researched area of physics. During her career, she created standards of radiation measurement, developed safe-handling techniques for radioactive materials, and essentially devised methods of diagnosis and treatment.

Quimby was born in 1891 in Rockford, Illinois, one of three children of parents who were both from families named Hinkley. During her childhood, they moved frequently and lived in several states. She went to Boise High School in Boise, Idaho, where she was encouraged to pursue her interests in natural phenomena. Quimby then received a full scholarship to attend Whitman College in Walla Walla, Washington, where she majored in mathematics and physics. While studying at Whitman, Quimby was influenced by her physics professor B.H. Brown and her math professor Walter Bratton, both of whom supported her scientific talents and guided her toward a career in scientific research. After receiving her B.S. degree from Whitman in 1912, Quimby taught high-school science in Nyssa, Oregon, for two years. In 1914, she left Oregon to attend the University of California, where she had received a physics fellowship. Shirley L. Quimby, a fellow physics student, became her husband in 1915. She received her M.A. degree in 1916, then returned to teaching science, accepting a position at Antioch High School in Antioch, California.

In 1919, Quimby moved to New York with her husband, who began teaching physics at Columbia University. She found employment as an assistant to Dr. Gioacchino Failla, whose willingness to hire a woman for the position would ultimately help advance the science. For the following 40 years, Quimby and Failla, who was chief physicist at New York City Memorial Hospital for Cancer and Allied Diseases, collaborated on some of the most important medical research of the 20th century. During the 1920s and 1930s, Quimby conducted experiments to establish the various properties of radioactive materials, such as radium, that were used to treat cancer. One of the major problems posed by the use of radioactive substances for therapeutic treatment was the difficulty in determining the proper dose for each patient. Until Quimby's groundbreaking work in establishing standards for radiation dosages in cancer treatment, individual doctors had to determine dosages for individual patients. The information that Quimby's experiments presented enabled physicians to provide a more exact treatment for their patients, while minimizing side effects. After years of study, Quimby was able to determine the number of roentgens per minute emitted by radium in the air, on the surface of the skin, and within the body. Since Quimby's early work, other scientists have expanded upon her theories and have been able to provide a more detailed methodology for the measurement of radiation. As a result, the unit of roentgen per minute is no longer used.

Quimby published over 50 articles in scientific journals and her work became very well known. In 1940, she was the first woman to be awarded the Janeway Medal by the American Radium Society, and in 1941 she became the second woman to receive the Gold Medal from the Radiological Society of North America (the first woman to receive the honor was ***Marie Curie**).

In 1941 and 1942, Quimby taught radiology at Cornell University Medical College. In 1943, she became associate professor in radiological physics at Columbia University's College of Physicians and Surgeons. During her early years at Columbia, she and Failla founded the Radiological Research Laboratory, where their efforts were focused on using radionuclides in diagnosing and treating thyroid diseases, performing circulation studies, and locating tumors in organs of the body. Quimby gave several lectures on her work. She is credited with researching and making known treatment methods which were safe for those handling radioactive materials, as she was well aware of the harmful effects of radiation exposure. Quimby's research and methodology made her a pioneer in the field of nuclear medicine, in which radioactive materials are used for diagnostic imaging and for the therapeutic treatment of various diseases.

During World War II, Quimby worked on the Manhattan Project, which developed the atom bomb, and after the war she worked with the Atomic Energy Commission. She served as a consultant on radiation therapy for the Veterans Administration and chaired a committee for the National Council on Radiation Protection and Measurements. She was also an examiner for the American Board of Radiology and belonged to a number of radiological groups and societies. Among these was the American Radium Society, an organization of which she was vice president. She wrote extensively, contributing much literature to her field, and was the coauthor of the noted book *Physical Foundations of Radiology.*

Quimby and her husband lived in the Greenwich Village section of New York City. An Episcopalian and Democrat who belonged to the League of Women Voters, she enjoyed sports, bridge, theater, and detective novels. Quimby retired in 1960 as a professor emeritus of radiology but remained active in her field, writing, lecturing, and consulting into the next decade. She died on October 11, 1982, at the age of 91. Edith Quimby was remembered both for her outstanding professional achievements as well as her amiable disposition. After her death, Harald Rossi noted in *Physics Today* that her place in history was secure: "All too often the creative achievements of scientific pioneers are overshadowed by further developments made by others or simply become anonymous components of accepted practice. Fortunately, Quimby's exceptional service to radiological physics was widely recognized."

SOURCES:

Current Biography. NY: H.W. Wilson, 1949.

McMurray, Emily, ed. *Notable Twentieth-Century Scientists.* Detroit, MI: Gale Research, 1995.

Weatherford, Doris, ed. *American Women's History.* NY: Prentice Hall, 1994.

SUGGESTED READING:

Quimby, Edith. *Physical Foundations of Radiology.* Harper, 1970.

———, and Paul N. Goodwin. *Safe Handling of Radioactive Isotopes in Medical Practice.* Macmillan, 1960.

———, Sergei Feitelberg, and Solomon Silver. *Radioactive Isotopes in Clinical Practice.* Lea & Febiger, 1958.

———, Sergei Feitelberg, and William Gross. *Radioactive Nuclides in Medicine and Biology.* Lea & Febiger, 1958.

Christine Miner Minderovic,
freelance writer, Ann Arbor, Michigan

Quimby, Harriet (1875–1912)

Reporter and pioneer aviator who was the first American woman to earn a pilot's license and the first woman to pilot a plane across the English Channel.

Born Harriet Quimby on May 11, 1875, near Coldwater, Michigan; died in a plane accident at the Boston Air Meet on July 1, 1912; daughter of William Quimby (an itinerant salesman) and Ursula (Cook) Quimby, never married; no children.

Family moved to California (1884); worked in family business packaging herbal remedies; at 26, began her career as a reporter for various San Francisco periodicals and newspapers (1901); moved to New York City (1903) where she worked as the drama critic and feature writer at Leslie's Illustrated Weekly; *was first American woman to earn her pilot's license (Au-*

Harriet Quimby

gust 1, 1911); was first woman to fly at night (September 4, 1912); was first woman to pilot a plane across the English Channel (April 16, 1912).

Harriet Quimby was one of the most famous and celebrated pilots at the dawn of aviation. A competitive and daring woman, she strove to leave her mark in aviation history and was especially proud of the list of "firsts" she achieved: the first American woman to earn her pilot's license; the first woman to fly at night; the first woman to pilot a plane across the English Channel. She was also about to become the first woman to carry the United States mail by airplane when she died at the young age of 37.

At the turn of the 20th century, women's lives were still circumscribed by traditional Victorian mores. Harriet Quimby, however, embodied the "new woman" who was beginning to emerge during the first two decades: she challenged society's expectations about the roles and capabilities of women; she never married nor had children; she earned her own living working as a pilot and reporter; and she was a conspicuous celebrity during an era when "respectable" women were supposed to keep their names out of the papers and devote themselves to domestic concerns. Quimby acted as a role model for a generation of women who were beginning to challenge accepted norms of female behavior.

Harriet Quimby was born in 1875 near Coldwater, Michigan, to William and **Ursula Quimby**. Her parents had married in 1859 and their first daughter **Kittie** was born in 1870. William tried to start several farming and business enterprises all of which eventually failed. Ursula was made of sterner stuff. It was she, ultimately, who controlled the destiny of her growing family. Ursula urged William to move the family to California in 1884; they eventually settled in San Francisco where Ursula's brother operated a small herbal remedy business. While William traveled around the region selling these herbal curatives, Ursula, Kittie, and Harriet helped mix and bottle the concoctions. Ursula had larger ambitions for her daughters. She was determined that they would not experience the back-breaking labor that she remembered from her own youth growing up on a farm. She encouraged both of them to become financially independent and to chart the course of their own destinies.

This was a daunting task for women during the 1890s, however. Middle-class women were expected to marry and devote their lives to raising children and running a household. Women who wanted to work found the type of employment available to them extremely limited. After the turn of the century, more middle-class women were working as reformers, secretaries, saleswomen, and teachers; however, the number of working women remained relatively small. In the work force, women could expect lower-paying jobs than men, and single women were expected to give up their jobs after they married. The lack of remunerative positions available to middle-class women reinforced their dependence on men.

Harriet's mother understood this dependence, and she wanted her children to be able to experience a greater sense of freedom. After Kitty married and moved away, Ursula Quimby focused her ambitions and hopes upon her remaining daughter. She encouraged Harriet to become a reporter. This type of "white collar" work was appropriate, Ursula believed, for the middle-class lifestyle that she wished her daughter to achieve. In 1901, at the age of 26, Harriet began working for the *Dramatic Review* and, soon after, the *Call-Bulletin & Chronicle*, both San Francisco periodicals.

It was at this time that Ursula began to reinvent the family's past. Instead of their rural, working-class background, she created a more suitable middle-class history to match Harriet's rise in status. Ursula told others that Harriet had been born in Boston in 1884 (nine years later than her real birthday), had attended schools in Switzerland and France, and that her father had been an official in the U.S. consular service. These efforts by Ursula to misrepresent Harriet's upbringing were not merely the eccentric lies of an overly ambitious mother. Ursula was sensitive to the class distinctions that patterned women's lives during this era. As circumscribed as the lives of middle-class women were, the prospects for working-class or rural women were even more limited. In order for Harriet to have access to the greater opportunities open to affluent and well-connected women, she needed to possess the proper social qualifications to enjoy these freedoms. Harriet Quimby took her mother's lessons to heart, and later, as a financially secure woman and celebrated pilot, Harriet remembered that her own personal freedom was contingent upon her financial independence.

By 1903, Harriet Quimby was an ambitious and successful journalist. In order to advance her burgeoning writing career, she decided to move to New York City, where opportunities to work were more abundant. She eventually found a position at *Leslie's Illustrated Weekly*. Initially she worked on a freelance basis, but soon she became a full-time staff writer, and, even though she remained unmarried, her job allowed her to become financially independent. She was the drama critic for the periodical, and she frequently wrote feature and opinion pieces which covered a wide range of topics. In these articles, Quimby often expressed her opinions about the changing roles of women in the early years of the 20th century. She believed that they should be allowed to drive cars, which, at the time, was considered by many Americans to be an unsuitable pastime for women; it was commonly believed that they had neither the endurance nor the skill to operate such machines.

Despite Quimby's advocacy for greater participation of women in non-traditional roles and occupations, she considered herself neither a feminist nor a suffragist. When questioned about her beliefs, Quimby admitted that women should have the right to vote; however, she also maintained that the tactics of the radical suffrage movement were inflammatory and impractical. She consistently refused to align herself with political feminists. (When reporters urged her to name her first airplane after a leader of the suffrage movement such as *Catt* or *Pankhurst,* she refused, preferring to name it ***Genevieve** after

Harriet Quimby

the patron saint of French pilots.) Even though she was never politically active, Harriet Quimby, like her mother before her, believed that women should control their own destinies and strive to exceed traditional Victorian gender roles. She was proud that she could act as a role model, first as a successful journalist and later as a celebrated aviator, for women who wanted to transcend the bounds of society's expectations.

In 1903, the same year Quimby began her New York journalism career, the Wright brothers successfully tested their new flying invention in North Carolina. Their efforts inaugurated an exciting era in the human quest to conquer the skies. By 1910, the first seven years of aviation history had been marked with astonishing successes and even more dramatic failures in the race to create reliable and safe aircraft. In October of that year, Harriet was invited to Belmont Park on Long Island to witness the second ever flying exhibition. The 36-mile "Statue of Liberty Race" energized Quimby and inspired her to try the nascent sport for herself. "It really looks quite easy," she said. "I believe I could do it myself, and I will."

Quimby began flying lessons on May 10, 1911. If driving a car were considered inappropriate behavior for a woman during this era, there was added pressure for women to eschew the new and unsafe sport of flying. To avoid any awkward publicity, Quimby took her lessons at sunrise and disguised herself in men's clothes. During the three months of her training, however, her ruse was discovered by reporters, and they quickly dubbed her "The Dresden China Aviatrix" because of her physical beauty. (She would also become known as "America's First Lady of the Air.") Once her secret was revealed, Quimby enjoyed the publicity that she garnered. Accompanying the glowing descriptions of her physical charms, however, came criticism of her attempts to learn to fly. Women had neither the physical dexterity nor the strength, skeptics argued, to operate such a large and complicated invention. Nor was it prudent for respectable women to participate in such an unsafe and masculine endeavor.

Quimby encountered these attitudes when she attempted to earn her pilot's license in August 1911. Representatives of the pilots' licensing agency, the Aero Club of America, initially resisted allowing her to take the required exam. Eventually they relented and on August 1, 1911, Harriet Quimby proved the skeptics wrong when she became the first American woman to earn her pilot's license. (She was also the second woman in the world to do so—France's **Elise-Raymonde Deroche** was the first—and only the 37th person ever to be accredited.) Upon receiving her pilot's license, Quimby made a critical jab at the continuing struggle to achieve female suffrage by quipping, "Flying seemed much easier than voting." While she was realizing her goals, women working for the vote would have to wait another nine years before their dreams were fulfilled.

One of the first problems Quimby encountered was what to wear while flying. During the first decade of the 20th century, American women's fashions included voluminous, floor-length skirts. Women's clothes were impractical in the small cockpits of early airplanes. Other women flyers improvised by "hobbling" or tying their skirts, and some even wore men's clothes. This practice, however, gave critics of female flyers further ammunition when arguing that women should not participate in such a masculine activity. Quimby, with her usual flair, devised a solution to the problem. She had a flying uniform made which reflected her singular personality—a purple satin, one-piece outfit with knickers and calf-length high-laced boots. To protect her hair and face, she wore a full hood and aviators' goggles. Her distinctive uniform increased her visibility at air meets and heightened the aura of excitement and mystery that she instinctively generated.

In 1911, aviation was not merely a hobby or a sport; it was also a lucrative job. The novelty of airplanes meant that people were eager to witness the new contraptions in action. After Quimby earned her license, she participated in a number of flying exhibitions. Only a month after her exam, she earned $600 racing Deroche, and two weeks after that she earned another $500 for a

Deroche, Elise-Raymonde (1886–1919)

France's premier woman pilot. *Name variations: Baroness de Laroche; Baroness de la Roche; Raymonde de Laroche. Born in 1886; killed in 1919.*

Elise-Raymonde Deroche, better known under her self-assumed title of Baroness de Laroche, was the first woman in the world to be granted a pilot's license. She qualified for the brevet on March 8, 1910, though she had already flown solo the previous year on October 22, 1909. Deroche had learned to fly, at Châlons in a Voisin biplane, from chief instructor Voisin Frères. In England, **Hilda B. Hewlett**, who was married to bestselling novelist Maurice Hewlett, took the Royal Aero Club test at Brooklands in a Henry Farman biplane in 1911 and was issued a license on August 29th. In 1919, Deroche became the first woman pilot in Europe to die in an airplane accident.

demonstration flight. As part of an exhibition flying team, Quimby toured Mexico. For their participation in the inauguration ceremonies of Francisco Madero, the new president of Mexico, the team earned a hefty $100,000. The rest of their tour was cut short, however, when the town they were staying in was attacked by rebels participating in the political uprising led by Emilio Zapata. At a time when middle-class men and women earned only a fraction of her flying fees in a month, Quimby had stumbled upon financial security and wealth. Even her mother could not have anticipated the fees Harriet earned as her fame spread.

As one of the few female pilots in the world, Quimby was at first a novelty, but she quickly became a celebrity. Newspapers reported her exploits, and in the columns that she continued to write for *Leslie's Illustrated Weekly,* she encouraged other women to take up the sport. She believed that there should be no restrictions on women's participation in aviation. "The airplane should open a fruitful occupation for women," Quimby predicted in 1911. "I see no reason they cannot realize handsome incomes by carrying passengers between adjacent towns, from parcel delivery, taking photographs or conducting schools of flying." However, Quimby also recognized the dilemma facing prospective female flyers. Had she not already been financially stable, earning a decent living as a successful reporter, she never could have afforded the steep costs associated with flying. The lessons cost at least $1,500 and buying an airplane was even more expensive. The continuing economic dependence of most women meant that they could not afford to fly unless their husbands or families approved of their involvement in the sport. Quimby was optimistic, however, that the economic obstacles faced by women who wanted to fly would eventually be eliminated. "I believe that as soon as the price of a machine is within the range of the average person, flying will become a popular pastime for women."

Her competitive spirit was roused after she became the first woman to fly at night on September 4, 1911. Quimby, however, was dreaming of even bigger challenges. On April 16, 1912, in poor weather and low visibility, she took off from Dover, England, intending to fly across the English Channel and land in Calais, France. If she succeeded she would be the first woman to accomplish the crossing. With only a compass pressed between her knees to guide her, Quimby successfully traversed the Channel. Unable to find Calais, she opted instead to land inland, to the astonishment of the French villagers there. For Harriet Quimby, flying was not complicated and neither were her motivations. She summed it up simply: "I did not want to be the first American woman to fly just to make myself conspicuous. I just want to be first, that's all, and I am honestly delighted."

Unfortunately for Quimby, however, her achievement was overshadowed by news of the sinking of the *Titanic* just two days prior to her flight. Despite the lack of fanfare to accompany her Channel crossing, by July 1912 Harriet Quimby was a bona fide celebrity, and she could command a staggering $100,000 fee for a seven-day appearance at the Boston Air Meet. No other flying performer, male or female, could demand such a fee. On July 1, William Willard, the manager of the event, flipped a coin with his son to see which one of them would have the privilege of flying with the most famous pilot at the meet. As it happened, the father won, and he anticipated riding in the seat behind Quimby during her last demonstration flight of the day. She was flying a new version of a French-made monoplane which was notoriously hard to fly, in part because the balance of the aircraft was difficult to maintain. Towards the end of her flight, the tail of the plane abruptly lifted up, and Willard was catapulted from his seat. Quimby, not immediately aware of this, struggled to regain control of her plane, but without the countervailing weight of her passenger, the balance of the aircraft was upset. Once again, spectators observed the tail shoot up skyward, and this time Quimby was thrown from her pilot's seat. The balance of the plane equalized, and it glided, barely damaged, to a landing. Quimby and her passenger, however, did not survive the fall. Harriet Quimby died upon impact, and William Willard drowned in the waters of Boston Harbor.

> Flying seemed much easier than voting.
>
> —Harriet Quimby

Aviation during this era was dangerous, and several deaths every year were caused by plane accidents. However, Harriet Quimby's death was particularly shocking to many Americans. She was not the first woman to die while piloting an airplane (she was the fourth); she was, however, the most celebrated. Americans had a love-hate relationship with Harriet Quimby. Many admired her beauty, her vivacious personality, her charisma, and her daring exploits; at the same time, many were also critical of her flouting of traditional Victorian gender roles. Quimby's tragic death confirmed for these people that women were not physically able to operate airplanes and that attempts to challenge the restrictions placed upon women's behavior were doomed to failure. They blamed the accident upon Quimby's inability to control the aircraft or maintain her composure during a crisis. The New York *Sun* editorialized: "The sport is not one for which women are physically qualified. As a rule they lack strength and presence of mind and the courage to excel as aviators. It is essentially a man's sport and pastime." Quimby, however, had proven that she was a calm and capable pilot on a number of occasions, and this theory has since been rejected by historians. Other observers blamed the lack of seat belts, which might have averted the accident altogether. Other, more technical, reasons for the crash have since been accepted as the cause of the accident. The model of airplane that Quimby was flying had been involved in several crashes as a result of the plane's poor balance prior to Quimby's death, and this was undoubtedly a primary cause of the accident.

At her funeral, the Reverend James Wasson dismissed those who doubted or diminished Quimby's accomplishments: "But in our sorrow tonight there rests still a joyful note. For we realize that through this death there has come progress, and that therefore, Miss Quimby's life was a victory over those elements, which brought on her very end. Through her we reach nearer to the far off goal of our hope. Her name is added to the long list of those who have freely given their lives so the world might be greater and grander." Despite her ambivalence about political feminism, Harriet Quimby was a role model for a generation of women who wanted to challenge themselves and society's expectations of the type of life they should live. ***Amelia Earhart** cited Quimby as a role model and credited her pioneering efforts. Said Earhart: "Women must try to do things as men have tried. When they fail, their failure must be but a challenge to others."

SOURCES:

Hall, Ed. Y., ed. *Harriet Quimby: America's First Lady of the Air.* Spartanburg, SC: Honoribus Press, 1990.

Holden, Henry M. *Her Mentor Was an Albatross: The Autobiography of Pioneer Pilot Harriet Quimby.* Mt. Freedom, NJ: Black Hawk, 1993.

Christine Lambert, Ph.D. candidate,
Emory University, Atlanta, Georgia

Quinlan, Karen Ann (1954–1985)

American woman whose removal from a ventilator set a precedent for future legislation governing an individual's right to die. *Born on March 29, 1954, in Scranton, Pennsylvania; died of respiratory failure due to acute pneumonia on June 11, 1985, in Morris Plains, New Jersey; adopted daughter of Joseph Quinlan (an employee in the accounting department of a pharmaceutical firm) and Julia Quinlan (a church secretary); graduated from high school in 1972; never married.*

Destined to become what the *Chicago Tribune* termed "a symbol of the right of the terminally ill to decide their fates with their families," Karen Ann Quinlan was born in Scranton, Pennsylvania, on March 29, 1954. She was adopted as an infant by Joseph and **Julia Quinlan** of Landing, New Jersey, and was later joined by two natural siblings, John and Mary Ellen. The Quinlans were devout Catholics, with Julia working as a church secretary. Described as a carefree, talkative, exuberant child, Karen wrote poetry, played the piano, and enjoyed athletics (she instructed her brother in the how-to's of wrestling). During the summers, she worked as a lifeguard. In 1972, she graduated from high school.

Quinlan was 21 on April 14, 1975, when she was brought to a hospital by friends after she had collapsed and stopped breathing during a party. Although it was thought by doctors that a mix of three gin and tonics, a low dose of Valium, and a strict diet may have impaired her breathing, the precise cause of her coma was never discovered. Other contributory factors may have been low blood sugar; lead poisoning resulting from a job in a factory; or a possible fall a few weeks earlier, which may have caused the bump that was discovered underneath her hair a few days after she became comatose. A grand jury investigation was held concerning an alleged beating she may have received before she was brought to the hospital, but the investigation turned up no evidence of foul play.

Soon after Quinlan was brought to the hospital she was placed on a respirator. She survived a bout of pneumonia, but her condition continued to deteriorate. Several months after her arrival at the hospital, doctors concluded that she would never achieve a "cognitive state." Bereft of hope, her parents watched the obvious pain she experienced when breathing via the ventilator, and they recalled her earlier expressed wish that elaborate life-saving measures never be applied to her. Wanting her pain to come to an end, the Quinlans made the decision to have the ventilator disconnected. Recalled her father: "That decision was so difficult for me. I was the last holdout. I did a lot of praying for guidance." With the support of their priest, the Quinlans made their wishes known to the hospital staff, who did not do as asked, telling them that Quinlan's father would have to become her legal guardian before any consideration would be given to their request. Desperate to help their daughter, the Quinlans found legal representation with Paul Armstrong, a young Legal Aid lawyer. Realizing the great significance of the Quinlans' request, Armstrong foresaw a precedent-setting case which would evolve legal standards to deal with the new life-saving technologies insofar as they had the potential to stand in the way of an individual's right to die. With his wife **Maria Armstrong** as his legal secretary, and a close friend, James Crowley, assisting him, Armstrong accepted the case while refusing to take money from the Quinlans.

After their petition was denied by the New Jersey Superior Court, the family—feeling that their actions were in accordance with church doctrine, which in hopeless cases permitted no extraordinary medical measures to be taken—appealed the case to the state's Supreme Court. On March 31, 1976, the seven Supreme Court justices issued a unanimous decision to overturn the lower court's ruling. Joseph Quinlan, made his daughter's guardian, now had the authority to have life-support equipment disconnected if he wished. The court determined that if such action were taken and death resulted, then death "would not be homicide but rather expiration from natural causes," meaning that no one would be criminally liable for Quinlan's death.

Even with this judgment, however, Quinlan was not removed from the ventilator for almost two months. When the equipment was finally taken away, she did not succumb as expected and began breathing unassisted. For the next ten years of her life, she would never regain consciousness. In a permanent vegetative state, Quinlan was moved to the Morris View Nursing Home and cared for by Dr. Joseph Fennelly and six other physicians who volunteered their services. Her family remained dedicated to her, with her father making the 40-mile drive every day to be with her. During the several months before her death at age 31, her conditioned worsened dramatically as she was victim to lung infections. She died on June 11, 1985. The Karen Ann Quinlan Center for Hope was founded by the Quinlan family as a hospice for patients with terminal conditions and their families.

Since the time that Quinlan's case made international news, with a black-and-white photograph of her in a coma published throughout the globe, many courts and legislators have reinforced a patient's right to die. John Fletcher of the University of Virginia's Center for Biomedical Ethics commented in 1996 on the significance of the Quinlan decision: "The case was the first one to draw the attention of the country and the courts to the problem of being a prisoner in a helpless body, supported only by medical technology." The legal validity of living wills—documents informing doctors of the manner in which individuals wish to be treated if they are found to be incompetent or can no longer communicate—was recognized by a California law a year after the Quinlan case. "They say we were the pioneers," remarked Quinlan's father. "We just did what we had to do."

Karen Ann Quinlan

SOURCES:

Contemporary Newsmakers 1985. Detroit, MI: Gale Research, 1985.

Nessman, Ravi. "20 Years Later, Quinlan's Parents Reflect on a Wrenching Decision," in *The Day* [New London, CT]. March 31, 1996.

Quinlan, Joseph and Julia, with Phyllis Battelle. *Karen Ann: The Quinlans Tell Their Story*. Garden City, NY: Doubleday, 1977.

Jo Anne Meginnes,
freelance writer, Brookfield, Vermont

Quinn, Katherine DeMille (1911–1995).

See DeMille, Katherine.

Quintanilla-Perez, Selena (1971–1995).

See Selena.

Quintasket, Christal or Christine (c. 1888–1936).

See Mourning Dove.

Quinton, Amelia S. (1833–1926)

American advocate for Native American land rights. *Name variations; Mrs. James Franklin Swanson. Born Amelia Stone in Jamesville, near Syracuse, New York, on July 31, 1833; died in Ridgefield Park, New Jersey, on June 23, 1926; daughter of Jacob Thompson Stone and Mary (Bennett) Stone; educated in Homer, New York, under the tutelage of Samuel B. Woolworth, LL.D.; married Rev. James F. Swanson; married Rev. Richard L. Quinton (a lecturer in history and astronomy from London); lived in Philadelphia, Pennsylvania.*

Amelia Quinton was born in Jamesville, New York, in 1833, and lived in Georgia for several years following her marriage to Reverend James F. Swanson. After Swanson's death and a proper period of mourning, she married Richard Quinton in London. Amelia became appalled by the U.S. government's behavior toward Native Americans and helped organize the Women's National Indian Association. She was president for over six years, preparing its pamphlets and editing its paper. The group appealed to the government to honor its pledges to tribes, "and that no treaty should be abrogated or broken without the free consent of the Indian tribe named in it." Senator Henry Dawes, chair of the Senate Indian Committee, would later note that "the new government Indian policy was born of and nursed by this woman's association." Dawes' Severalty Bill, which became law in March 1887, granted Native Americans the rights and privileges echoed in the petitions of Quinton's association. In retrospect, the Dawes Act was far from perfect, but, given the alternatives, it seemed the best course of action at the time.

Quiroga, Elena (1919—)

Twentieth-century Spanish novelist. *Born Elena Quiroga de Abarca in Santander, Spain, on October 26, 1919; daughter of Count San Martin de Quiroga (a minor noble) and Isabel Abarca Fornés; married Dalmiro de la Valgoma y Díaz-Varela, in 1950.*

Born in Santander, Spain, in 1921, Elena Quiroga was the 16th of 17 children of Count San Martin de Quiroga, a minor noble, and **Isabel Abarca Fornés**. Following her mother's death in 1923, Elena lived with her father in rural northern Spain. At an early age, she learned to love books and read widely, although few women and girls enjoyed such freedom at the time. From age 9 to 14, she studied at a Catholic boarding school in Bilbao, but left it on the eve of the Spanish Civil War. She continued her schooling in Rome, returning to Spain in 1938, and had little direct contact with the war. Rather than attend university, she taught herself the literary craft.

Her first significant publication appeared in 1949, an immature novel entitled *La soledad sonora* (*Sonorous Solitude*). Quiroga's breakthrough occurred the following year, with the publication of *Viento del norte* (*North Wind*), which won the Nadal Prize. In 1950, she also married the genealogist and historian Dalmiro de la Valgoma y Díaz-Varela and left northern Spain to live in Madrid. Over the next decade she produced six more novels. Eschewing the social realism then in vogue in Spain, she explored the psyches of her characters and experimented with narrative techniques. She lived quietly, avoided celebrity, and her works were so innovative that they often attracted more attention from foreign readers than from Spaniards.

When her novel *Escribo tu nombre* (*I Write Your Name*) was nominated for the international Rómulo Gallegos Prize in 1967, her renown in Spain grew. The next year, her husband became secretary of the Royal Academy of History, and the couple moved into a comfortable, historic apartment in the Academy's Madrid headquarters. Quiroga focused almost exclusively on the novel, generally ignoring other literary forms. Her penchant for technical innovation attracted broad interest among students of Spanish literature.

SOURCES:

Zatlin Boring, Phyllis. *Elena Quiroga*. Boston: Twayne, 1977.

Kendall W. Brown,
Professor of History, Brigham Young University,
Provo, Utah

Quirot, Ana (1963—)

Cuban runner and model. *Name variations: Ana Quirot Moret. Pronunciation: KEE-rote. Born Ana Fidelia Quirot Moret on March 23, 1963, in Cuba.*

One of the most famous athletes in Cuba, Ana Quirot won the bronze medal in the 800 meters in the 1992 Barcelona Olympics. In 1993, a kerosene stove exploded as she was lighting it, and she suffered third-degree burns over 40% of her body while seven months pregnant. Though she had no memory of the explosion, she lost the baby, spent three months in the hospital, and was badly scarred. Nine months later, Quirot finished second in her first race back. In the summer of 1995, she won the World championship, and in 1996, at the Atlanta Olympics, she won the silver medal in the 800 meters; the gold went to **Svetlana Masterkova** of Russia.

ACKNOWLEDGMENTS

Photographs and illustrations appearing in *Women in World History, Volume 12,* were received from the following sources:

Courtesy of the Alaska State Library, **p. 480;** Courtesy of The Annie Oakley Foundation, Greenville, Ohio, **p. 5;** © CBS, Inc., 1982, **p. 141;** © Cinergi Pictures Entertainment, Inc., 1996, **p. 501;** © Columbia Pictures, 1965, **p. 727;** © ERG, 1993, photo by Norman Seeff, **p. 672;** © Embassy Home Entertainment, 1986, **p. 223;** © Gentl and Hyers/Arts Counsel, Inc., 1994, **p. 235;** Courtesy of the Flannery O'Connor Collection, Ina Dillard Russell Library, Georgia College, **p. 29;** Courtesy of the Schlesinger Library, Radcliffe Institute, Harvard University, **pp. 147, 182, 417;** Courtesy of the Library of Congress, **pp. 118, 181, 275, 281, 341, 393, 445, 499, 757,** photo by Pinchot, **pp. 793, 871;** Courtesy of the Security Pacific National Bank Photograph Collection, Los Angeles Public Library, **p. 489;** Photo by George Platt Lynes, **p. 725;** Photo by Mayotte Magnus, **p. 853;** Compliments of Mary Quant Limited, **p. 863;** Courtesy of The Maud Powell Foundation, **p. 765;** Photo by Duane Michaels, **p. 515;** © Miramax, **p. 303;** Courtesy of the National Air and Space Museum, **p. 869;** Courtesy of the National Archives of Canada, **p. 345;** Painting by Amalie Colquhoun, **p. 201;** Photo by Bassand, reprinted by permission of the National Portrait Gallery, London, **p. 405;** Courtesy of The Dance Collection, The New York Public Library for the Performing Arts, Astor, Lenox, and Tilden Foundations, **p. 813;** Painting by James Peale, **p. 429;** Courtesy of Penguin, U.S.A., **pp. 749, 751;** Photo by Ricki Rosen, **p. 805;** Courtesy of Smith College Archives, Smith College, photo by Eric Stahlberg, 1955, **p. 635;** Photo by Paul Strand, 1930, **p. 75;** Courtesy of the Supreme Court Historical Society, **p. 35;** Courtesy of Special Collections, Texas Women's University, Denton, **p. 214;** Courtesy of the U.S. House of Representatives. **pp. 1, 45, 87, 382, 537, 543, 775;**© Warner Bros., 1943.

ISBN 0-7876-4071-9
90000
9 780787 640712